Gene Florence's
Standard

BASEBALL
CARD

Price Guide

Revised
4th Edition

Collector Books
A Division of Schroeder Publishing Co., Inc.

The current values in this book should be used only as a guide. They are not intended to set prices, which vary from one section of the country to another. Auction prices as well as dealer prices vary greatly and are affected by condition as well as demand. Neither the Author nor the Publisher assumes responsibility for any losses that might be incurred as a result of consulting this guide. Baseball cards illustrated are for identification purposes and have been photographed from the author's collection.

FOREWORD

For me baseball card collecting has graduated from a hobby to a major portion of my antique business. When I opened my Grannie Bear Antiques shop in July, 1976, one of the first things I stocked along with Depression era glassware and comic books was baseball cards. I knew if I could get the kids to come into my shop the parents would have to bring them and spend some time with the antiques while the kids were shopping. I started several new glass collectors as well as baseball card collectors.

From that beginning I started to attend baseball card shows and later to sell at these shows including the first and second National shows in California and Michigan. Unfortunately, my books on glassware and other collectibles began to take more of my time and conflict with some of the major baseball card shows. I have only been able to attend a few shows each year as a dealer, but the card business in my shop is rivaling my glassware business in volume.

This book explores the world of baseball cards from the beginning of the modern era of bubble gum cards (1948) to the present day cards containing holograms to foil reproductions. I will pass along my thoughts on collecting and grading from the standpoint of dealer and collector since I wear both hats. I hope you enjoy the book which is my thirty-eighth book on collectibles since 1972.

ACKNOWLEDGMENTS

Many people have been instrumental in getting this book in print! A special thanks to Sherry Kraus of Collector Books for making all these card listings into workable pages. She inherited all the work on this book when the former editor left. We have kept the overnight delivery services in business the last few months with signatures of my books travelling from Florida to Kentucky and Lexington to Paducah. Without Collector Books' dedicated editorial staff, I might still be working instead of completing this third book of the year.

Cathy and Marc have endured stacks of cards, boxes and printouts literally taking over the house. One of Marc's friends keeps asking if I am **still** working on that baseball book since I am surrounded by cards and listings every time he has visited the last few weeks. Every time I thought I could put the cards back in storage, a new question (or a dozen) would arise and back to the sets I would go. I have used over 56,000 listings in this book. Just finding each card to insert in the copy from all those sets was days of work.

Cathy, my wife, typed new sets into the computer listings to help out. Her typing is so fast that the computer has trouble keeping up with her. It gets used to my ten or twelve words a minute and she blows the Reflex Data Base and Macros away.

My Mom, Grannie Bear, and my Dad spent days opening cards and putting sets together, so I could list the new cards. She also proofed new card listings and caught many of our entry and typing errors before they got completely out of hand.

Few people ever realize the magnitude of work that goes into writing a book. In my case, it's always been a cooperative effort. I could never have written my books without wonderful support systems. Thank you everyone!

Identification Section

Bowman, 1948, 2¹/₁₆" x 2½"

Bowman, 1949, 2¹/₁₆"x 2½"

Bowman, 1950, 2¹/₁₆" x 2½"

25 — BARNEY McCOSKEY
Outfielder—Philadelphia Athletics
Born: Coal Run, Pa.   1918
Bats: Left   Throws: Right
Height: 6-¼   Weight: 178
Coming from the Detroit Tigers in 1946, he finished the season with the Athletics batting .318. Last year hit .328. Began his baseball career in 1936 with the Beaumont team in the Texas League. From there he went to Charleston of the Mid-Atlantic League where he batted an even .400 for the season. Two years followed with the Beaumont team again and he went to Detroit in 1939. 1940 was a great year for him, batting .340, leading the American League in triples and tied for most hits. Then the war set him back three years.
ASK FOR BLONY BUBBLE GUM
The Bubble Gum with
the three different flavors
BOWMAN GUM, INC. Copyright 1948

No. 87 of a Series of 240
RANDY GUMPERT
Pitcher—Chicago White Sox
Born: Monocacy Station, Pa., Jan. 23, 1918
Bats: Right Throws: Right Ht.: 6-2½ Wt.: 205
Started in OB with Philadelphia A's in 1936, appearing in 22 games. He spent part of 1937 and 1938 with A's, and spent rest of time, up to 1946 shuttling around minors. '43, '44 and '45 were spent in service. After his discharge he joined New York Yankees and won 15 and lost 4 over two seasons. Last season, with Yanks and then White Sox, his record was 3-6.
#20—BASEBALL GAME AND BANK
Get this original exciting game. It is a regulation size plastic baseball. Complete with plastic players and directions. Lots of fun. Can be used as a bank. A swell ornament too, the dandy Big Bargain. Send only 25c and 5 Baseball wrappers to:
BASEBALL, P.O. BOX 65B
PAWTUCKET, R. I.
(Not valid where contrary to State laws)
Offer expires 12/31/49 ©Bowman Gum, Inc., 1949

SID GORDON
Third Base, Outfield—Boston Braves
Born: Brooklyn, N. Y., Aug. 13, 1918
Height: 5-10   Weight: 180
Bats: Right   Throws: Right
This will be Sid's first season in the majors out of a Giant uniform. Went to the Braves in big winter trade. Was with Polo Grounders since 1941. In 1949 hit .284 in 141 games. Had 26 doubles, 26 homers. Drove in 90 runs. But 1948 was his best year. He hit .299 driving in 107 runs, knocking 26 doubles and 30 homers. Served in Coast Guard 2 years.
No. 189 in the 1950 SERIES of BASEBALL Picture Cards
© 1950 Bowman Gum, Inc., Phila., Pa., U.S.A.

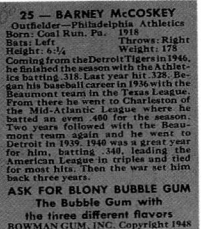

BILL RIGNEY
Infield—New York Giants
Born: Alameda, Calif., Oct. 29, 1919
Height: 6-1   Weight: 175
Bats: Right   Throws: Right
In 56 games in 1950. Got 15 hits and drove in 8 runs. Batted .278 in 122 games in 1949. Spent 5 years in the minors, beginning with Spokane, Western International League, 1938. Three years of military service intervened before Bill arrived with Giants. On 1948 NL All-Star team. A player who is willing to step into any place where he is needed and give his best.
No. 125 in the 1951 SERIES
BASEBALL
PICTURE CARDS
©1951 Bowman Gum, Inc., Phila., Pa., U.S.A.

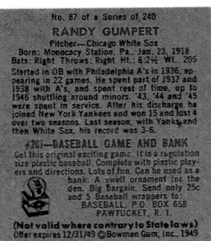

Bowman, 1951, 2¹/₁₆" x 3⅛"

Bowman, 1953BW, 2½" x 3¾"

BOB AVILA
Second Base—Cleveland Indians
Born: Vera Cruz, Mex., June 7, 1926
Height: 5-10   Weight: 175
Bats: Right   Throws: Right
Bob was the Indians' regular starting 2nd baseman in 1951. In 141 games, with 165 hits for 222 bases. Batted .305. Had 10 home runs, 3 triples, 21 doubles. Drove in 58 tallies. Fielded .982, second best in league. Made only 14 errors in 780 chances. Began in 1948 with Baltimore.
No. 167 in the 1952 SERIES
BASEBALL®
PICTURE CARDS
Get a $1.00 value Baseball Cap of your favorite major league team by sending 5 wrappers and 50 cents to BOWMAN Baseball, P. D. BOX 234, New York 22, N. Y. State size: small, medium or large.
© 1952 Bowman Gum Division, Haelan Laboratories, Inc., Phila. 44, Pa.—Ptd. in U. S. A.

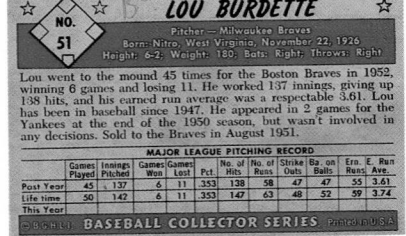

NO. 51
☆ ☆ *LOU BURDETTE* ☆
Pitcher — Milwaukee Braves
Born: Nitro, West Virginia, November 22, 1926
Height: 6-2 Weight: 180 Bats: Right, Throws: Right
Lou went to the mound 45 times for the Boston Braves in 1952, winning 6 games and losing 11. He worked 137 innings, giving up 138 hits, and his earned run average was a respectable 3.61. Lou has been in baseball since 1947. He appeared in 2 games for the Yankees at the end of the 1950 season, but wasn't involved in any decisions. Sold to the Braves in August 1951.

	Games Played	Innings Pitched	Games Won	Games Lost	Pct.	No. of Hits	No. of Runs	Strike Outs	Ba. on Balls	Ern. Runs	E. R. Ave.
MAJOR LEAGUE PITCHING RECORD											
Past Year	45	137	6	11	.353	138	58	47	47	55	3.61
Life time	50	142	6	11	.353	147	63	48	52	59	3.74
This Year											

BASEBALL COLLECTOR SERIES Printed in U.S.A.

Bowman, 1952, 2¹/₁₆" x 3⅛"

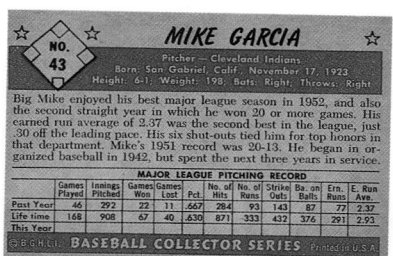

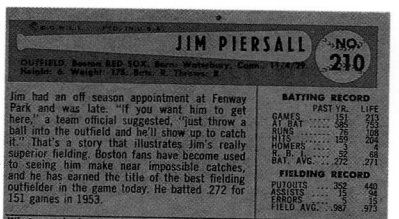

Bowman, 1953BC, 2½" x 3¾"

Bowman, 1954, 2½" x 3¾"

Bowman, 1989,
2½" x 3¾"

Bowman, 1990,
2½" x 3½"

Bowman, 1955, 2½" x 3¾"

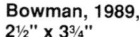

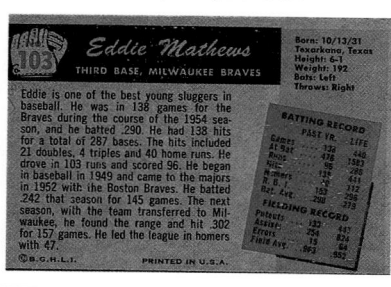

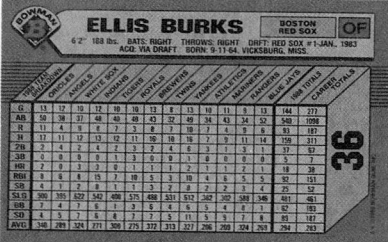

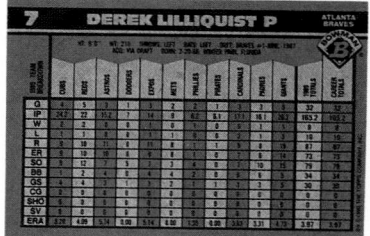

LARRY MILBOURNE I-F/SHORT

Donruss, 1981, 2½" x 3½"   **Donruss, 1982, 2½" x 3½"**   **Donruss, 1983, 2½" x 3½"**

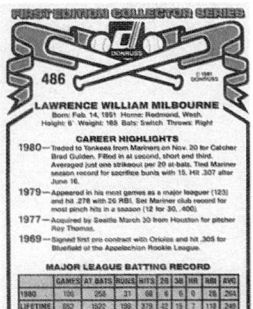

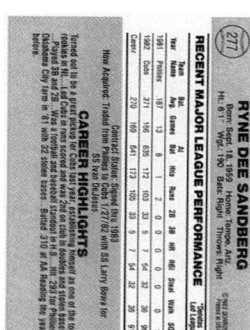

Donruss, 1984, 2½" x 3½"

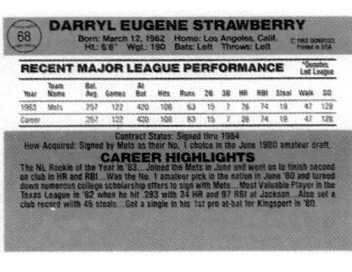

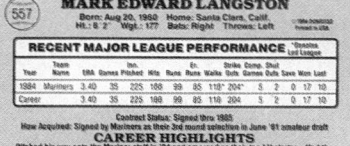

Donruss, 1985, 2½" x 3½"

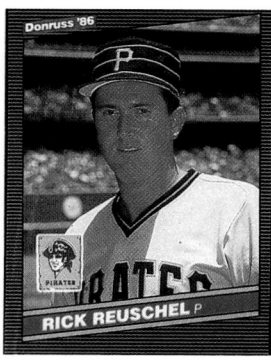

Donruss, 1986, 2½" x 3½"

Donruss, 1986, Rookies, 2½" x 3½"

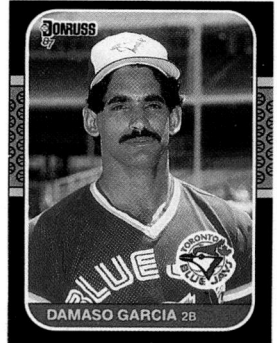

Donruss, 1987, 2½" x 3½"

Donruss, Rookies, 1987, 2½" x 3½"

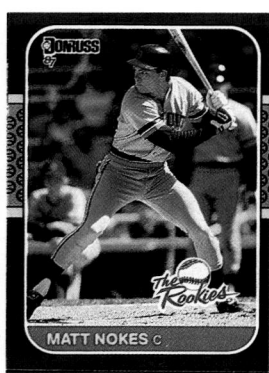

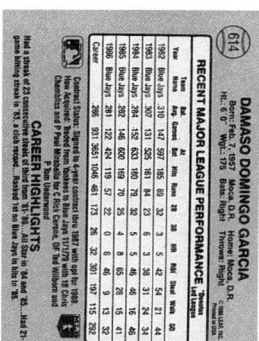

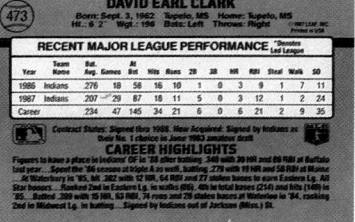

Donruss, 1988, 2½" x 3½"

Donruss, 1988, Rookies,
2½" x 3½"

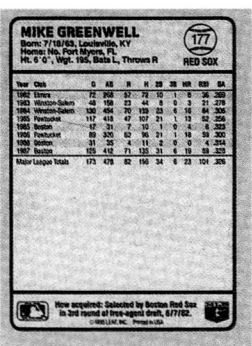

Donruss, 1988, Baseball's Best
2½" x 3½"

Donruss, 1989, 2½" x 3½"

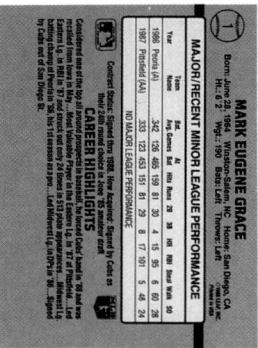

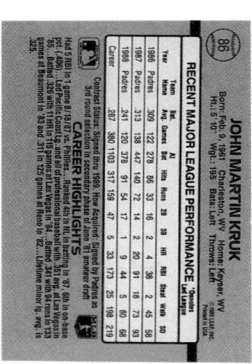

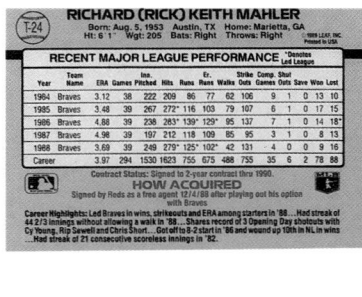

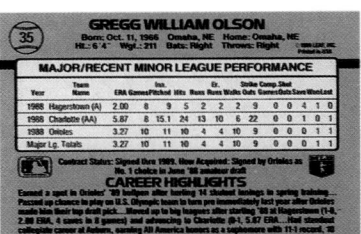

Donruss, 1989, Traded,
2½" x 3½"

Donruss, 1989, Rookies
2½" x 3½"

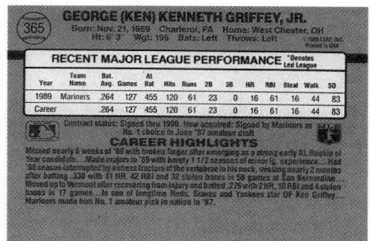

Donruss, 1990, 2½"x 3½"

Donruss, 1990, Rookies, 2½" x 3½"

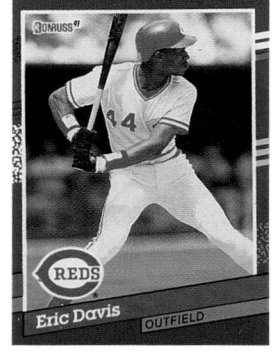

Donruss, 1989, Baseball's Best 2½" x 3½"

Donruss, 1991, 2½" x 3½"

Donruss, 1990, Leaf 2½" x 3½"

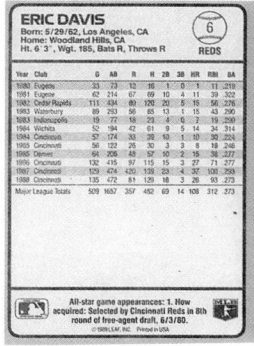
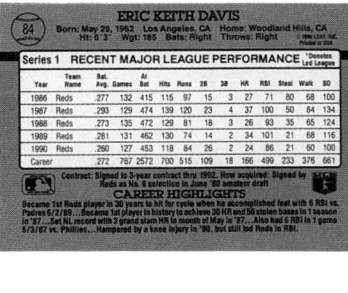
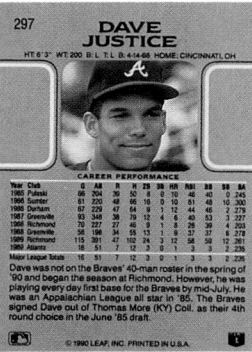

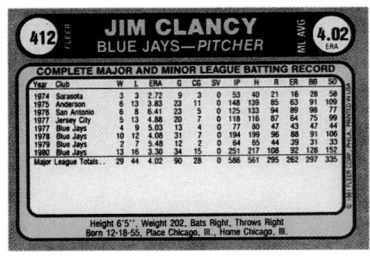

JIM CLANCY
BLUE JAYS—PITCHER   412   4.02 ERA

COMPLETE MAJOR AND MINOR LEAGUE BATTING RECORD

Year	Club	W	L	ERA	G	CG	SV	IP	H	R	ER	BB	SO
1974	Sarasota	3	3	2.72	9	3	0	53	40	21	16	28	58
1975	Anderson	6	13	3.83	23	11	0	148	139	85	63	91	109
1976	San Antonio	6	8	6.41	23	5	0	125	133	94	89	98	77
1977	Jersey City	5	13	4.88	20	7	0	118	116	87	64	75	99
1977	Blue Jays	4	9	5.03	13	4	0	77	80	47	43	47	44
1978	Blue Jays	10	12	4.08	31	7	0	194	199	96	88	91	106
1979	Blue Jays	2	7	5.48	12	2	0	64	65	44	39	31	33
1980	Blue Jays	13	16	3.30	34	15	0	251	217	108	92	128	152
Major League Totals		29	44	4.02	90	28	0	586	561	295	262	297	335

Height 6'5'', Weight 202, Bats Right, Throws Right
Born 12-18-55, Place Chicago, Ill., Home Chicago, Ill.

Jim Anderson   503
MARINERS • SHORTSTOP
M.L. **.224** AVG.

MAJOR & MINOR LEAGUE RECORD

Year	Club	Pct.	G	AB	R	H	2B	3B	HR	RBI	SB	SO
1975	Idaho Falls	.289	71	253	42	73	3	6	0	27	20	53	34
1976	Salinas	.264	136	499	67	124	14	4	4	51	7	59	58
1977	El Paso	.285	109	417	87	119	24	1	18	73	5	71	57
1978	Salt Lake City	.258	72	248	36	64	13	1	5	32	3	35	37
1978	Angels	.194	48	108	6	21	7	0	0	7	0	11	16
1979	Angels	.248	96	234	33	58	13	1	3	23	3	17	31
1980	Mariners	.227	116	317	46	72	7	0	8	30	2	77	28
1981	Mariners	.204	70	162	12	33	7	0	2	19	3	17	29
Major League Totals		.224	330	821	97	184	34	1	13	79	8	72	115

Height 6'0'', Weight 170, Bats Right, Throws Right
Born 2-23-57, Place Los Angeles, Cal., Home Mission Viejo, Cal.

JIM CLANCY
PITCHER

Blue Jays

Jim Anderson
MARINERS • SHORTSTOP

Fleer, 1981, 2½" x 3½"

Fleer, 1982, 2½" x 3½"

Tom Herr
SECOND BASE

Tom Brennan
PITCHER

CLEVELAND INDIANS

Dwight Gooden
PITCHER

Mets

Fleer, 1983, 2½" x 3½"

Fleer, 1984, 2½" x 3½"

Fleer, 1984 Update, 2½" x 3½"

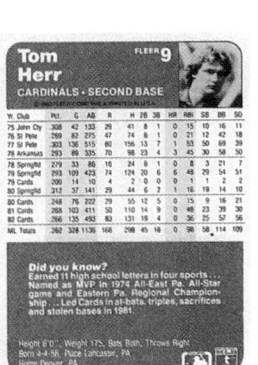

Tom Herr   FLEER 9
CARDINALS • SECOND BASE

Yr. Club	Pct.	G	AB	R	H	2B	3B	HR	RBI	SB	BB	SO
75 John Cty	.308	42	133	29	41	8	1	0	15	10	16	11
76 St Pete	.269	82	275	47	74	6	1	0	21	12	42	18
77 St Pete	.303	136	515	80	156	13	7	1	53	50	69	39
78 Arkansas	.293	89	335	70	98	23	4	3	45	30	58	50
78 Springfld	.279	33	86	16	24	8	1	0	8	3	21	7
79 Springfld	.293	109	423	74	124	20	6	4	48	29	54	51
79 Cards	.200	14	10	4	2	0	0	0	1	1	2	2
80 Springfld	.312	37	141	29	44	6	2	1	18	19	14	10
80 Cards	.248	76	222	39	55	12	5	0	15	9	16	21
81 Cards	.268	103	411	50	110	14	9	0	46	23	39	30
82 Cards	.266	135	493	83	131	19	4	0	36	25	57	56
ML Totals	.262	328	1136	168	298	45	18	0	98	58	114	109

Did you know?
Earned 11 high school letters in four sports...
Named as MVP in 1974 All-East Pa. All-Star
game and Eastern Pa. Regional Champion-
ship... Led Cards in at-bats, triples, sacrifices
and stolen bases in 1981.

Height 6'0'', Weight 175, Bats Both, Throws Right
Born 4-4-56, Place Lancaster, PA
Home Denver, PA

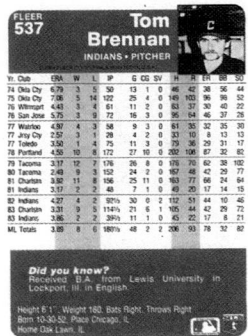

Tom   FLEER 537
Brennan
INDIANS • PITCHER

Yr. Club	Pct.	ERA	W	L	IP	G	CG	SV	H	R	ER	BB	SO
74 Okla City	3.97		4	5	50	13	1	0	46	42	36	56	44
75 Okla City	7.06		5	14	122	29	4	0	145	105	96	56	52
76 Wilmingtt	4.43		3	4	61	11	2	0	63	37	30	40	22
76 San Jose	3.75		3	7	98	13	0	0	95	64	46	37	26
77 Waterloo	4.87		4	3	58	9	3	0	61	35	32	35	30
77 Jrsy Cty	2.57		3	1	28	6	1	0	20	9	8	13	13
77 Toledo	3.50		1	4	75	11	3	0	75	36	29	31	17
78 Portland	4.50		10	8	172	27	10	0	202	106	87	32	82
79 Tacoma	3.17		12	2	176	26	8	0	176	70	62	38	102
79 Tacoma	4.29		9	3	152	24	2	0	157	48	42	59	81
81 Charlstn	3.92		11	8	166	25	11	0	163	77	64	64	64
81 Indians	3.17		2	2	48	7	1	0	49	19	17	14	15
82 Indians	4.27		4	4	99½	30	2	0	112	54	44	10	48
83 Charlstn	3.31		9	1	114½	29	6	1	105	44	42	29	72
83 Indians	3.86		2	2	39½	11	0	3	40	17	17	12	21
ML Totals	3.89		8	6	180½	48	2	2	206	93	78	32	82

Did you know?
Received B.A. from Lewis University in
Lockport, Ill. in English.

Height 6'1'', Weight 180, Bats Right, Throws Right
Born 10-30-52, Place Chicago, Illinois
Home Oak Lawn, Ill.

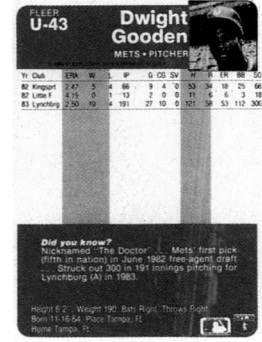

Dwight   FLEER U-43
Gooden
METS • PITCHER

Yr. Club	ERA	W	L	IP	G	CG	SV	H	R	ER	BB	SO
82 Kingsport	2.47	5	4	66		9	4	0	50	34	18	25	66
82 Little F	4.15	0	1	13		2	0	0	11	6	6	5	18
83 Lynchburg	2.50	19	4	191		27	10	0	121	59	53	112	300

Did you know?
Nicknamed "The Doctor"... Mets' first pick
(fifth in nation) in June 1982 free-agent draft
... Struck out 300 in 191 innings pitching for
Lynchburg (A) in 1983.

Height 6'2'', Weight 190, Bats Right, Throws Right
Born 11-16-64, Place Tampa, Fl.
Home Tampa, Fl.

Fleer, 1985, 2½" x 3½"

Fleer, 1985, Update, 2½" x 3½"

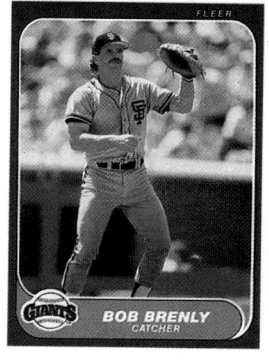

Fleer, 1986, 2½" x 3½"

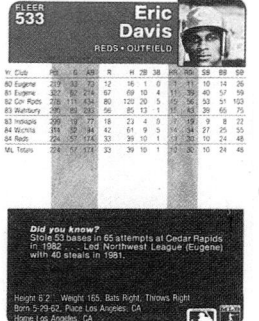

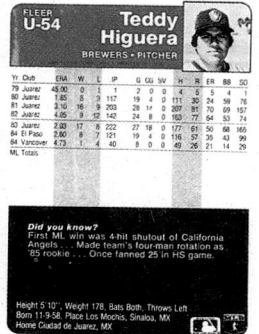

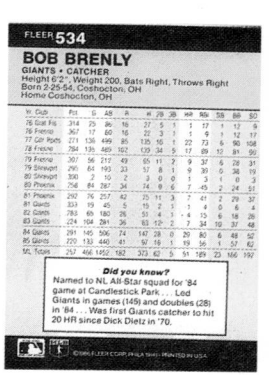

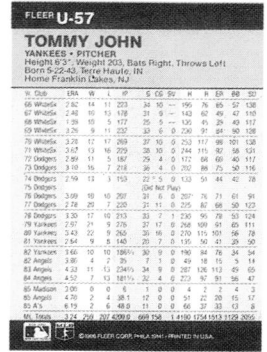

Fleer, 1986 Update, 2½" x 3½"

Fleer, 1987, 2½" x 3½"   **Fleer, 1987 Update, 2½" x 3½"**   **Fleer, 1988, 2½" x 3½"**

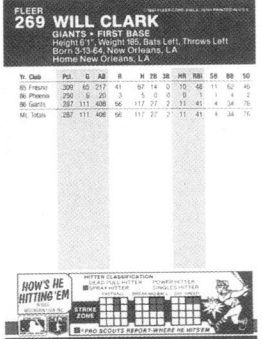

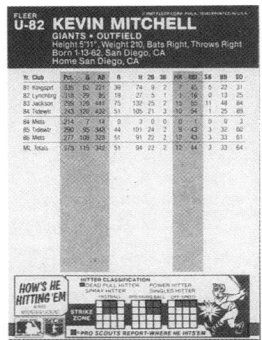

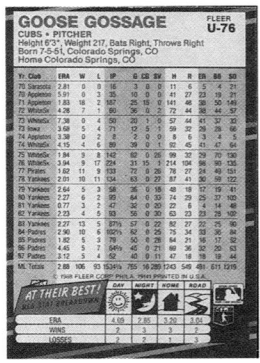

Fleer, 1988 Update, 2½" x 3½"

12

Fleer, 1989, 2½" x 3½"   Fleer, 1989, Update, 2½" x 3½"   Fleer, 1990, 2½" x 3½"

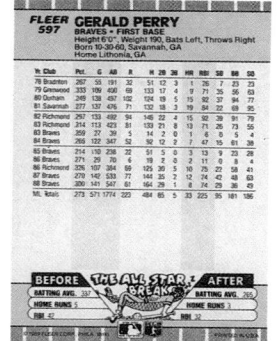

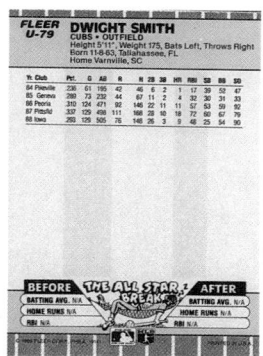

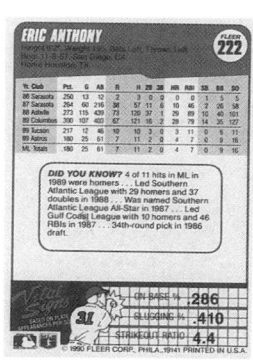

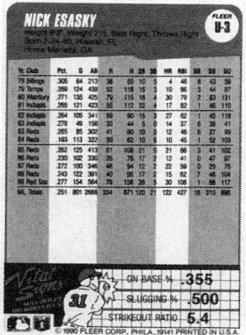

Fleer, 1990, Update, 2½" x 3½"

| Fleer, 1991, 2½" x 3½" | Score, 1988, 2½" x 3½" | Score, 1988, Traded, 2½" x 3½" |

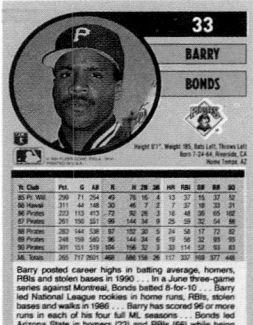
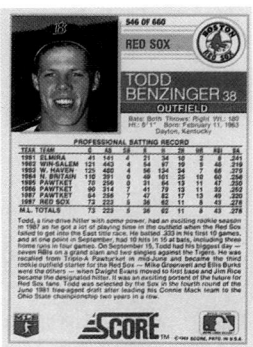
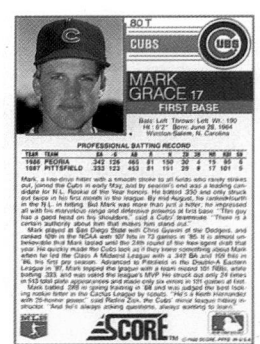

Score, 1989, 2½" x 3½"

Score, 1989, Traded, 2½" x 3½"　　　**Score, 1990, 2½" x 3½"**　　　**Score, 1990, Traded, 2½" x 3½"**

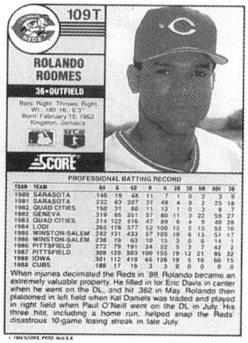

Score, 1991, 2½" x 3½"

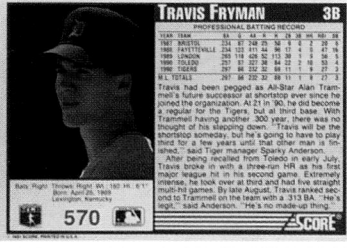

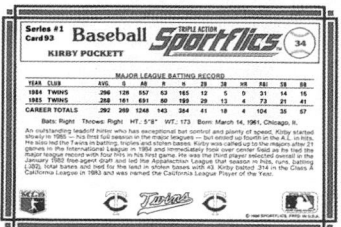

Sportflics, 1986, 2½" x 3½"

**Sportflics, 1986 Rookies,
2½" x 3½"**

Sportflics, 1987, 2½" x 3½"

**Sportflics, 1987 Rookies,
2½" x3½"**

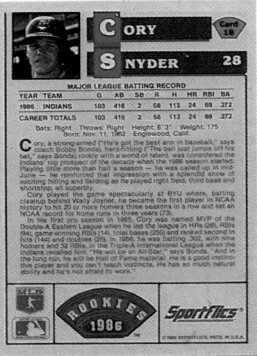

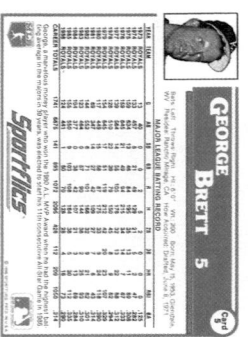

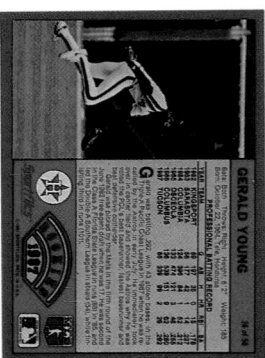

Sportflics, 1988, 2½" x 3½"

16

Topps, 1951 Red Back, 2" x 2⅝"

Sportflics, 1989, 2½" x 3½"

Sportflics, 1990, 2½" x 3½"

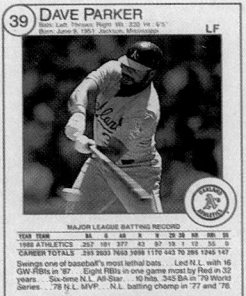

Topps, 1951 Blue Back, 2" x 2⅝"

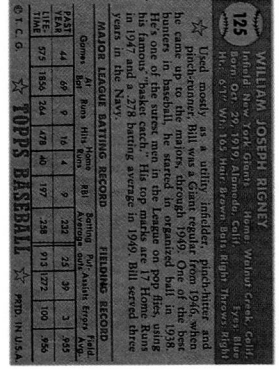

Topps, 1952, 2⅝" x 3¾"

Topps, 1953,
2⅝" x 3¾"

Topps, 1954,
2⅝" x 3¾"

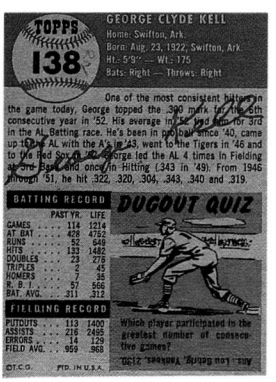

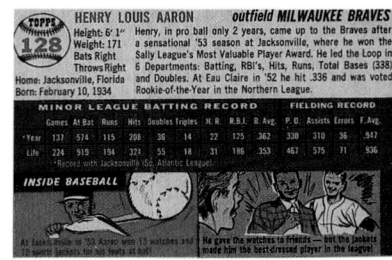

Topps, 1955, 2⅝" x 3¾"

Topps, 1956, 2⅝" x 3¾"

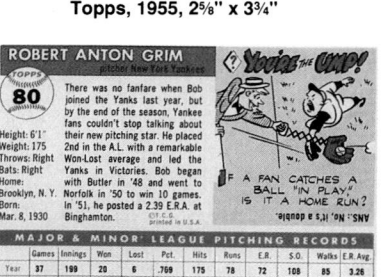

  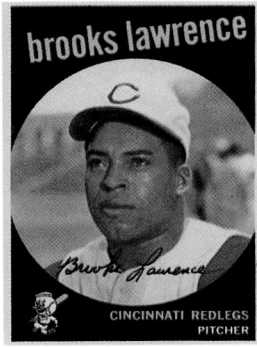

Topps, 1957, 2½" x 3½"   **Topps, 1958, 2½" x 3½"**   **Topps, 1959, 2½" x 3½"**

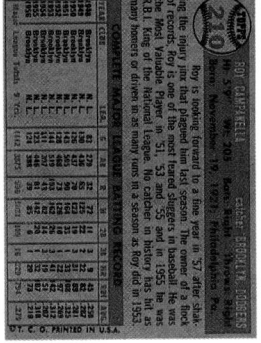 

 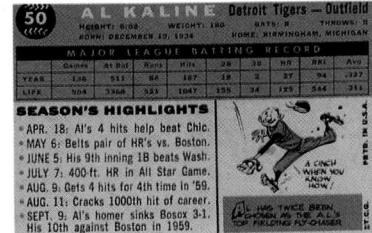

Topps, 1960, 2½" x 3½"

Topps, 1961, 2½" x 3½"   **Topps, 1962, 2½" x 3½"**   **Topps, 1963, 2½" x 3½"**

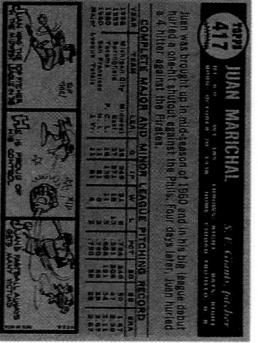

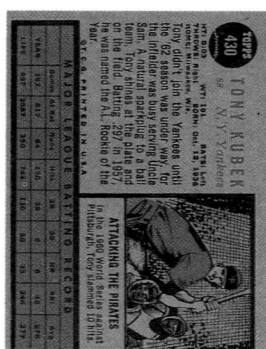

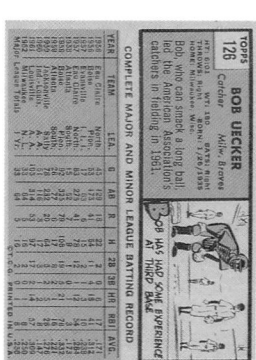

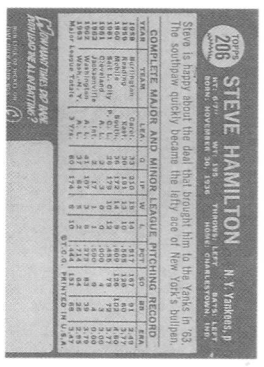

Topps, 1964, 2½" x 3½"

Topps, 1965, 2½" x 3½"   **Topps, 1966, 2½" x 3½"**   **Topps, 1967, 2½" x 3½"**

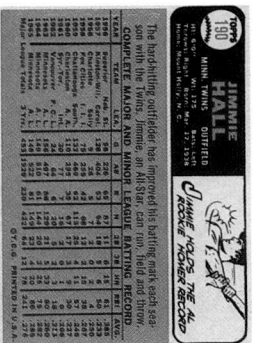

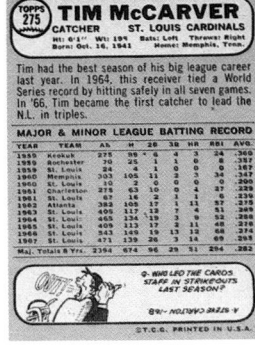

Topps, 1968, 2½" x 3½"

Topps, 1969, 2½" x 3½"   **Topps, 1970, 2½" x 3½"**   **Topps, 1972, 2½" x 3½"**

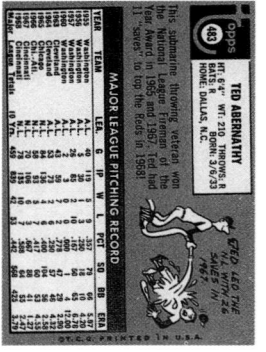
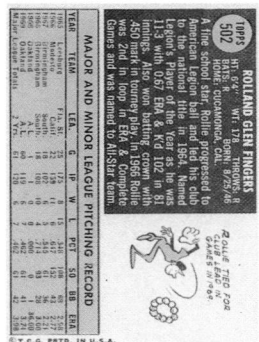

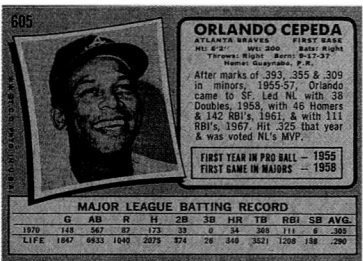

Topps, 1971, 2½" x 3½"

Topps, 1973, 2½" x 3½"　　　**Topps, 1974, 2½" x 3½"**　　　**Topps, 1975, 2½" x 3½"**

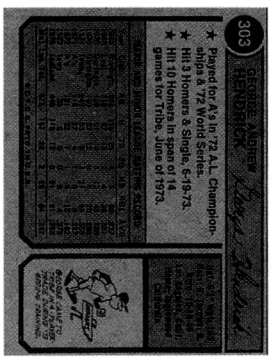

Topps, 1976, 2½" x 3½"

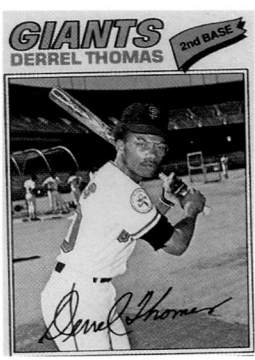

Topps, 1977, 2½" x 3½"   **Topps, 1978, 2½" x 3½"**   **Topps, 1979, 2½" x 3½"**

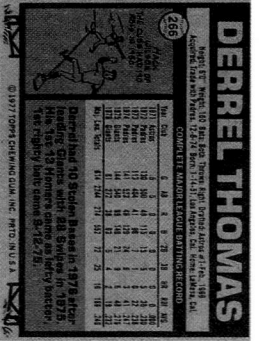

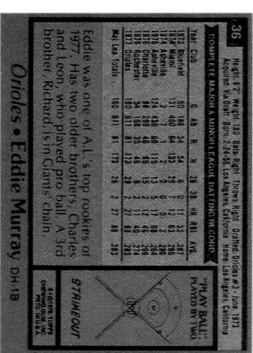

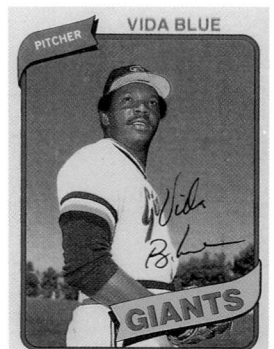

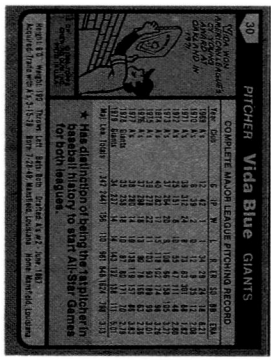

Topps, 1980, 2½" x 3½"

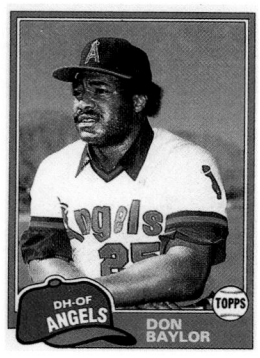

Topps, 1981, 2½" x 3½"   **Topps, 1981 Traded, 2½" x 3½"**   **Topps, 1982, 2½" x 3½"**

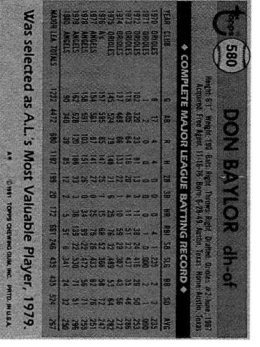

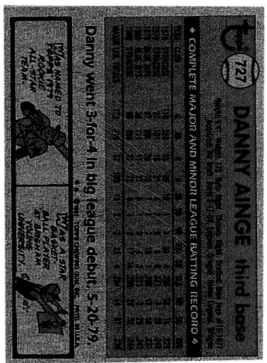

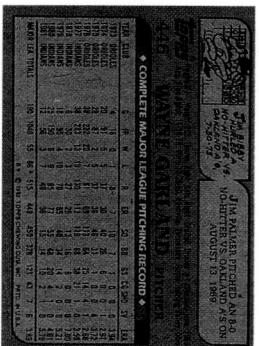

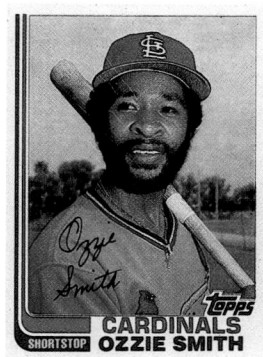

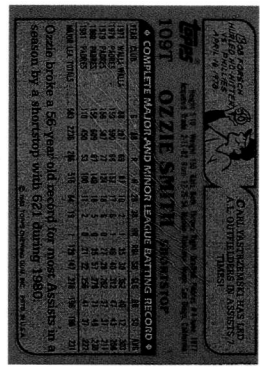

Topps, 1982 Traded, 2½" x 3½"

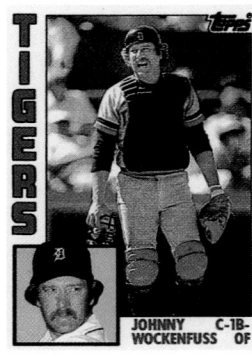

Topps, 1983, 2½" x 3½"   **Topps, 1983 Traded, 2½" x 3½"**   **Topps, 1984, 2½" x 3½"**

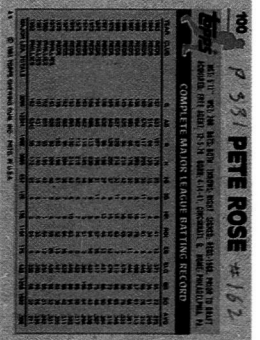

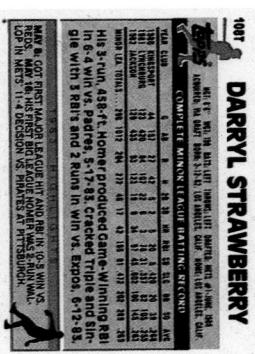

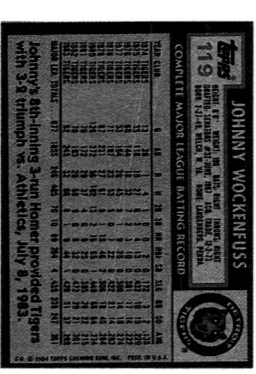

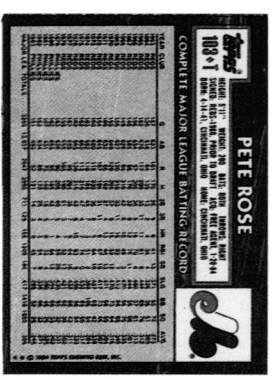

Topps, 1984 Traded, 2½" x 3½"

Topps, 1985, 2½" x 3½"   **Topps, 1985 Traded, 2½" x 3½"**   **Topps, 1986, 2½" x 3½"**

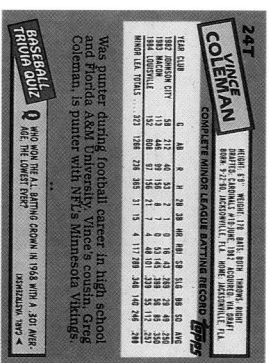

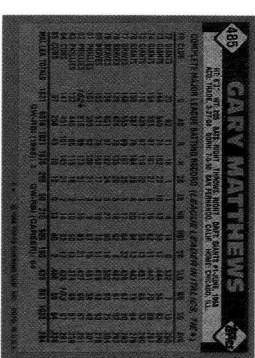

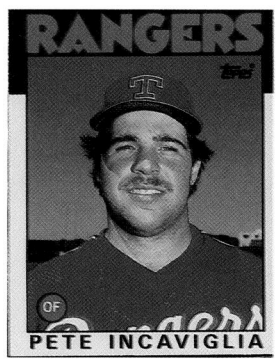

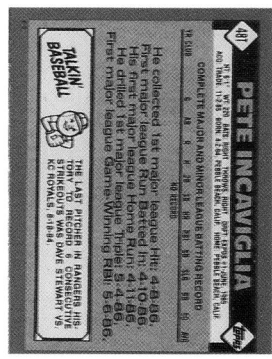

Topps, 1986 Traded, 2½" x 3½"

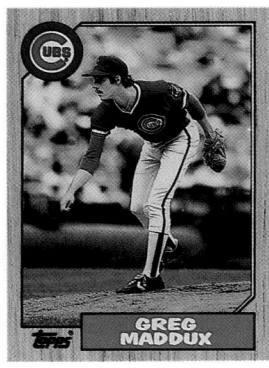

Topps, 1987, 2½" x 3½"

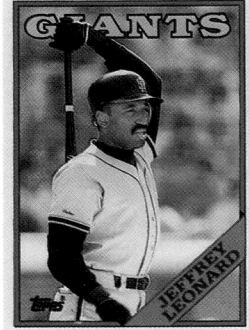

Topps, 1987 Traded, 2½" x 3½"

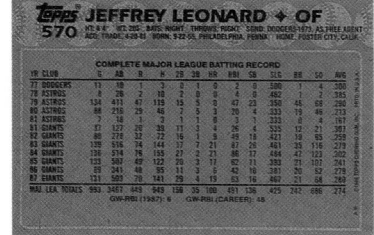

Topps, 1988, 2½" x 3½"

28

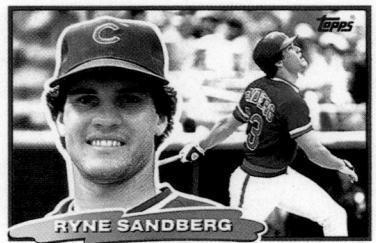 

Topps, 1988 Big Baseball, 2½" x 3½"

Topps, 1988 Traded, 2½" x 3½"

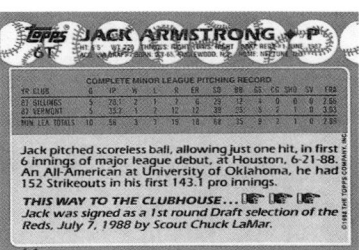

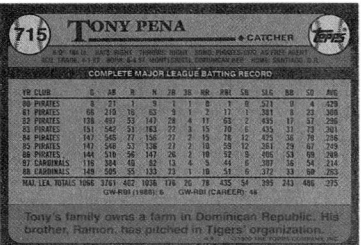

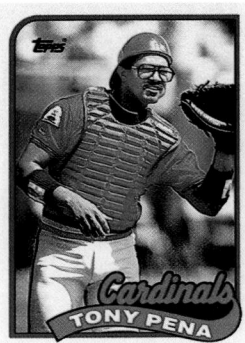

Topps, 1989, 2½" x 3½"

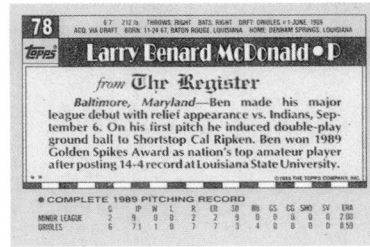

Topps, 1989, Major League Debut, 2½" x 3½"

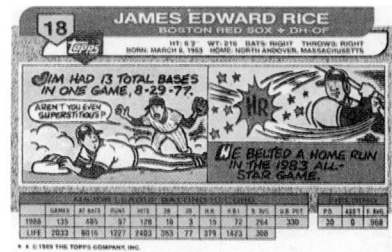

Topps, 1989 Big Baseball, 2½" x 3½"

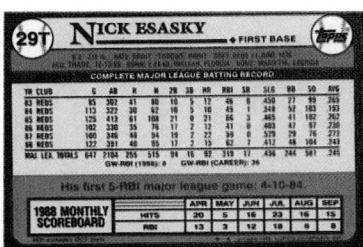

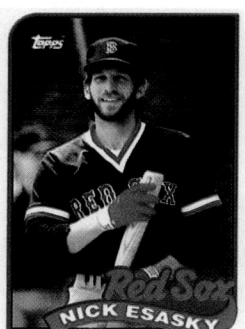

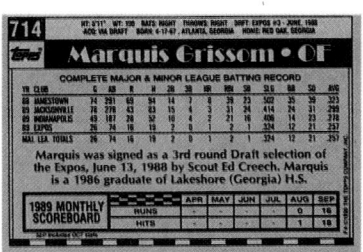

Topps, 1989 Traded, 2½" x 3½"

Topps, 1990, 2½" x 3½"

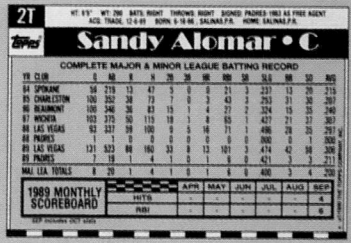

Topps, 1990 Traded, 2½" x 3½"

Topps, 1991, 2½" x 3½"

 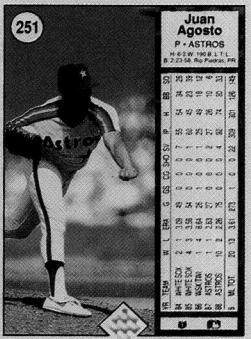

Upper Deck, 1989, 2½" x 3½"

 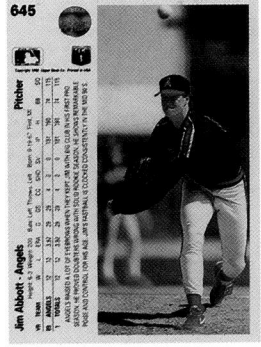

Upper Deck, 1990, 2½" x 3½"

 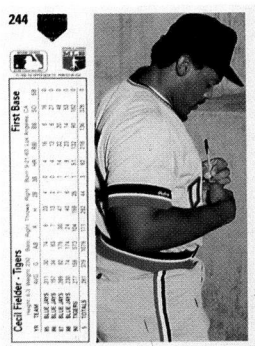

Upper Deck, 1991, 2½" x 3½"

INTRODUCTION

You would think the fourth book in any series of books would be easier to write than the first ones. That has never held true for writing glass books; and now I know it does not hold true for baseball card books either. Although things went smoother since I have 8K of RAM now, the magnitude of the listings of cards has gotten out of control. There are almost 6,000 new listings this year from the five major companies without having the additional sets that each company is planning for this year. Next year will be a critical year in deciding how to add 8,000 to 9,000 new listings.

The additional listings only became a problem when the new lists from Reflex were merged with the old Word files and all the alphabetical listings went back to "pure" form again. That means that different first names used over the years became a major nightmare. I hope to have these all corralled soon. Spaces and punctuation have a tendency to be read by the computer in ways that you really did not mean for it to do. If you move names to the correct place in your list, they go right back the next time you turn on the computer.

There are six columns for each entry and each of these can lead to a problem if entered incorrectly. Errors on cards of players who only have one card in the listing are the most difficult to find. I will not even mention the typing mistakes which were missed until the third or later proofing! If you find errors of omission or of any other kind, please let me know. The 56,000 listings with six columns each make over 336,000 entries to be written and proofed!

I first seriously thought about writing a baseball guide in the late 1970's. However it soon became apparent to me that I didn't have the necessary equipment to handle all the sorting of data, and there weren't enough hours in my life to do it manually! So, I put the ideas on hold.

In 1980 my publisher approached me about doing a baseball card book; but again, the idea was dropped due to the lack of a computer that could handle the alphabetical listings I felt were needed. The following year my first computer came and I wrote my next ten books on it; but sorting on it was almost slower than by hand. It took five minutes to sort through two hundred listings and then it would throw out several at the end of the paper—unsorted. Needless to say, that computer would not do what I needed for a card book of this magnitude.

"Macintosh II" arrived in April 1988 and with it the reality that thousands of Topps listings could be sorted! However, I did not know that sixteen hour days would be the norm and an occasional one lasting nineteen or more would occur. Of course, it has taken four years to gain the user knowledge that takes the computer only minutes to sort. Increased memory has helped, but as the card lists continue to grow at 6,000 entries a year, we are going to have to re-evaluate the way I am now doing this book—else we'll have an unwieldy volume on our hands.

HOW TO USE THIS BOOK

Traditionally, the trouble I found with other baseball card guides was that it took too long to find a card of a specific player in them—and you had to have quite a bit of prior knowledge about the card itself before you could hope to find it. Also, you had to flip through pages searching from year to year for all the cards of a specific player. I have had numerous dealers in collectibles tell me that they have avoided buying baseball cards because the guides were impossible to use for someone with little or no knowledge of cards. Therefore, I tried to make a book that's "user friendly" as they say in computer circles.

The format of this book is designed to be easily used by baseball card dealers and collectors as well as those who are just beginning to learn about the magic of card collecting. All listings are alphabetical by player as well as divided alphabetically by company of issue. It is not necessary to know the year of manufacture in order to find the value of a card listed in this book! The name of the player is all you have to find!

FINDING A CARD'S VALUE
This section is for someone who knows a little about cards.

Pick a card. Look at the name of the manufacturer (Bowman, Donruss, Fleer, Score, Sportflics, Topps or Upper Deck) on the card to determine in which section to look up the name. Turn to that company's section of the book—also listed alphabetically. Find the name of the player on the card. Under each player's name will be a listing of one or more cards. Find the number on the card and match it with a number listed in the book under the No. column. (On vary rare occasions will a player have the same number for more than one year. In that case look at the statistical data listed. If 1961 is the last date listed in the record of the player, then, it is likely the card is 1962).

If you are confused about the year a card was made, turn to the color section which will help identify any cards you can not figure out by year. This section will familiarize you with the different colored backs and fronts of each year shown in this book (1948–91). Every card of each player is listed in one place so that you can get a checklist of any player by card company manufacturer. This is especially handy for dealers who are constantly asked for a "Don Gullett" or a "Joe Nuxhall" card. Finding a "rookie" card is simple. It will be the first listing for that player under each company. Since true "rookie" card status is debated among dealers and collectors alike, most people consider the first regular issued card (available to the public in retail outlets) as the true "rookie" card which eliminates "Traded" and "Update" cards as "rookie" cards.

All players cards are listed even if the player is only one of several players shown on the card. For example, Don Mattingly is on eight cards in the 1986 Sportflics set and each is listed and priced.

There are two prices listed for every one of the 56,000 plus listings. The first price column is **VG** which is a very good condition card and the next column is **EX/MT** which is excellent to mint. **ALL PRICES IN THIS BOOK ARE RETAIL.** (There will be an explanation of grading following this section).

A STEP BY STEP GUIDE TO FINDING A CARD'S VALUE
This is for someone who knows absolutely nothing about cards.

1. Pick a card.

2. Determine manufacturer of card. There are several different manufacturers of baseball cards and here is the best way to determine each:

BOWMAN - All cards copyrighted Bowman or B.G.H.L.I. on back except some 1950 cards which say "No. 181–252 in the series of Baseball Picture Cards". 1989 and cards say "Bowman" on front with a red "B" over a green baseball diamond. (see page 36).

DONRUSS - All Donruss cards have a Donruss logo on front. (see page 60).

FLEER - 1981–1984 Fleer name found on back of card and from 1985 Fleer name on the front also. (see page 134).

SCORE & SPORTFLICS - Score written on front and Sportflics written on back of each year. (see page 203).

TOPPS - 1951 cards are baseball game pieces with red or blue backs and no other identification. Topps is written somewhere on back of all cards from 1952 to 1970 except 1958,1959, 1960 which along with 1971 to 1975 have only copyright **T.G.C.** on the back. 1976 to 1978 all have Topps copyright on back and 1979 to date all have a Topps logo on the front. (See pgs. 242–244).

UPPER DECK- All cards have Upper Deck logo on front and Upper Deck hologram on back. (see page 489).

3. Turn to the alphabetical listing of the company determined in No. **2** above and find the player's name. Now look at the number of the card (found on the back of the card, usually in upper left.) Find the card's number in the No. column in the book. Follow this line to give you the year and price in VG (very good) and EX/MT (excellent/mint) condition of the card. (An explanation of grading follows this section.)

4. In case of a number being the same in two years (which rarely happened) there are three choices. You can turn to the color section (pgs. 4–31) to locate the card year. You can look for a copyright; or you can look at statistical information of the previous year on the card . The latter does not always work as oft times the card will only say last year or lifetime stats. After a while the knowledge of which year a card was issued will become the easiest part of learning about the cards!

GRADING

Everyone thinks he has excellent or better cards, but usually those you put in the cigar or shoe box as a youngster fit the VG category **if you took some care with them.** The latest cards in an accumulation of several years are generally the ones in the best condition. It seems the older you got the better you treated your "treasures."

There are more arguments between buyer and seller over grading than any other concept in collecting. **The grade of a card does not change whether the buyer or the seller owns the card.**

This book only prices cards in two grades because most of the cards collected over the years fit the the grades VG or EX/MT.

VG - very good means a card that has been handled but not torn, cut or flawed. There may be some slight rounding of the corners and there may be gum or wax stains on the card. There may even be a hairline crease caused during manufacture. The original luster is usually gone, but there should be no tack holes, ink stains, rubber band marks or tape. The card may be slightly off center, but not cut badly by the factory.

EX/MT - excellent/mint means a card that is **almost perfect.** The card may have a slight wear overall and may have an ever so slightly rounded corner or yellowing of the border. There should be no gum or wax stains visible. The card should be nicely centered. Early cards have to pass the same criteria as newer cards. Many forty-year-old people are in better shape than others. The same can be said for cards! Age of the card is no excuse for lowering grading standards.

There are other grades. **MINT** grading is a field unto itself. There are special boxes to measure centering. It reminds me of the old days of coin grading; so I can only say that a mint card has to be perfect in every way by today's grading standards. Most of the sets I put away as "mint" in the late 1970's would have a difficult time being graded mint today!

Cards that are less than very good are not sought by collectors or dealers unless they are harder to find cards or cards of well known players. They have little value.

COLLECTING, SELLING and PRICING

I am often asked what to collect. Today, I suggest buying the factory sets that each of the companies issue. First, buy the Topps, Fleer, Donruss, Score or Upper Deck since those sets are now all factory sealed. **Leave them sealed! Do not open them!** If you want to look at your collection and play with it, then buy the regular sets. The factory sets that are sealed will be like the sealed proof coins of yesteryear. If sealed, they sold over and over again. Everyone assumed that they were perfect. If opened, there was a possibility of tarnished coins which lowered the value. The same holds true with factory sealed baseball sets. If unopened, all cards are assumed to be there in mint condition. If someone opens the set, and disproves that all the cards are there or that some are badly off-center, then the set value is greatly reduced.

Selling your cards is another story. Find a reliable dealer who will even show you what your cards are worth. Remember, a dealer has to make a profit in order to stay in business. Most dealers will pay from fifty to sixty per cent of the retail price for star cards and cards they need. They will pay very little for cards not needed for stock or common cards. Condition of the cards is a main concern! Personally, I do not buy later cards in less than EX/MT condition and few cards in less than VG no matter what the age. It is easier to sell mint sets of the later years, but it usually takes about five years to make a handsome profit. The volume of cards printed today may make that even longer for some sets. Buy any company's regular sets. The little boxed sets issued for specific stores rarely have lasting collector demand.

There are only so many of the older cards available. If you have some baseball cards packed away in a shoe box in the attic, basement or your closet, better remove all those rubber bands and look up the values of the treasures you stored. It's time to start taking better care of them!

BOWMAN GUM, INC. 1948–1955; 1989–1990

The Bowman Company produced a black and white set of forty-eight cards in 1948. These cards were packed with Blony bubble gum. For a penny you got a piece of bubble gum and one card. As a child, I hated these older cards when I started collecting because they were black and white.

The 1954 set is the easiest to complete for a new collector if card #66 is collected as Jimmy Piersall and not Ted Williams. There are two #66 cards with the Ted Williams card considered scarce. In my travels, I have come to believe it is only scarce in Mint condition.

The 1955 Bowman set is probably the most popular and the next easiest to assemble. If you collect either the 1954 or 1955 sets in less than excellent condition, you should be able to complete these sets without a lot of difficulty.

Topps shocked the baseball card collecting world in 1989 when they announced that they were bringing back the Bowman name on a set of 484 cards measuring the 2½" x 3½" of many of the early Bowman sets. Topps bought out the Bowman company in 1955 and had never used the name until then. The listing for these cards is separate from the original Bowman cards of 1948–1955. In 1990 Topps announced that there would be a Bowman set, but that the cards would be of the standard 2½" x 3½" size. 1991 Bowman cards were unavailable as we went to press.

1948 - 48 black & white cards measuring 2¹⁄₁₆" x 2½" (Bowman copyright 1948 on back)
1949 - 240 cards with black and white photo on pastel background measuring 2¹⁄₁₆" x 2½" (Bowman copyright 1949 on back)
1950 - 252 color cards measuring 2¹⁄₁₆" x 2½" (Bowman copyright 1950 on back of most cards; some cards only say "No. 181–252 in the series of Baseball Picture Cards")
1951 - 324 color cards measuring 2¹⁄₁₆" x 3⅛" (copyright Bowman 1951 back of card)
1952 - 252 color cards measuring 2¹⁄₁₆" x 3⅛" (copyright 1952 Bowman Gum Division, Haelan Laboratories, Inc. back of card)
1953BC - 160 color cards measuring 2½" x 3¾" (copyright B.G.H.L.I. on back lower left corner)
1953BW - 64 black and white cards measuring 2½" x 3¾" (copyright B.G.H.L.I. on back lower left corner)
1954 - 224 color cards measuring 2½" x 3¾" (copyright B.G.H.L.I. on back top left corner)
1955 - 320 color (TV screen) cards measuring 2½" x 3¾" (copyright B.G.H.L.I. on back lower left corner)
1989 - 484 color cards measuring 2½" x 3¾" (Bowman on front with a large red B over a baseball diamond; copyright 1989 Bowman Gum, Inc. on back right corner)
1990 - 528 color cards measuring 2½" x 3½" (Bowman on front with a large red B over a baseball diamond; copyright 1990 Bowman Gum, Inc. on back right corner)

The only abbreviation used in the Bowman section of card listings is in the 1953 cards. As shown above I have used **BC** and **BW** to distinguish between the color and black and white cards of that year.

Although the original Bowman name was used until 1955 {nine sets (two in 1953) issued}, these baseball cards (with a piece of bubble gum enclosed) marked the beginning of many kids' fantasies of being in the Major Leagues and one day having their own picture on a card. Little did we know that Topps would again use the name that they bought out thirty-four years ago!

The listing for each card shown appears immediately following the photograph.

Player	Year	No.	VG	EX/MT
Aaron, Hank	55B	179	$45.00	$180.00
Aber, Al	55B	24	$2.00	$6.00
Abrams, Cal	51B	152	$4.50	$16.00
Abrams, Cal	52B	86	$3.25	$11.00
Abrams, Cal	53BC	160	$18.00	$125.00
Abrams, Cal	54B	91	$2.00	$6.00
Abrams, Cal	55B	55	$2.00	$6.00
Adams, Bobby	51B	288	$13.50	$42.50
Adams, Bobby	52B	166	$3.25	$11.00
Adams, Bobby	53BC	108	$8.50	$25.00
Adams, Bobby	54B	108	$2.00	$6.00
Adams, Bobby	55B	118	$2.00	$6.00
Adcock, Joe	51B	323	$17.50	$70.00
Adcock, Joe	52B	69	$3.75	$13.50
Adcock, Joe	53BC	151	$8.75	$35.00
Adcock, Joe	54B	96	$2.25	$8.00
Adcock, Joe	55B	218	$2.00	$7.00
Addis, Bob	53BC	94	$8.50	$25.00
Aloma, Luis	51B	231	$4.50	$16.00
Aloma, Luis	54B	134	$2.00	$6.00
Alston, Tom	55B	257	$4.00	$13.50
Amalfitano, Joe	55B	269	$4.00	$13.50
Antonelli, Johnny	50B	74	$3.75	$13.50
Antonelli, Johnny	51B	243	$4.00	$13.50
Antonelli, Johnny	54B	208	$2.25	$8.00
Antonelli, Johnny	55B	124	$2.25	$8.00
Appling, Luke	49B	175	$25.00	$100.00
Appling, Luke	50B	37	$12.50	$50.00
Arft, Hank	49B	139	$3.25	$11.00
Arft, Hank	51B	173	$4.50	$16.00
Arft, Hank	52B	229	$6.50	$22.50
Ashburn, Richie	49B	214	$130.00	$425.00
Ashburn, Richie	50B	84	$18.00	$55.00
Ashburn, Richie	51B	186	$17.00	$50.00
Ashburn, Richie	52B	53	$8.00	$32.50
Ashburn, Richie	53BC	10	$12.50	$50.00
Ashburn, Richie	54B	15	$5.00	$20.00
Ashburn, Richie	55B	130	$4.00	$17.50
Astroth, Joe	51B	298	$13.50	$42.50
Astroth, Joe	52B	170	$3.25	$11.00
Astroth, Joe	53BC	82	$8.50	$25.00
Astroth, Joe	54B	131	$2.00	$6.00
Astroth, Joe	55B	119	$2.00	$6.00
Atwell, Toby	53BC	112	$8.50	$25.00
Atwell, Toby	54B	123	$2.00	$6.00
Atwell, Toby	55B	164	$2.00	$6.00
Avila, Bobby	51B	188	$4.00	$13.50
Avila, Bobby	52B	167	$3.25	$11.00
Avila, Bobby	53BC	29	$8.50	$25.00
Avila, Bobby	54B	68	$2.00	$6.00
Avila, Bobby "Roberto"	55B	19	$2.00	$6.00
Baczewski, Fred	54B	60	$2.00	$6.00
Baczewski, Fred	55B	190	$2.00	$6.00
Baker, Floyd	49B	119	$3.25	$11.00
Baker, Floyd	50B	146	$3.75	$13.50
Baker, Floyd	51B	87	$4.50	$16.00
Baker, Floyd	53BW	49	$8.00	$25.00
Baker, Gene	55B	7	$2.00	$6.00
Ballanfant, E. Lee	55B	295	$5.00	$20.00
Bankhead, Dan	51B	225	$4.50	$16.00
Banks, Ernie	55B	242	$80.00	$320.00
Banta, Jack	50B	224	$3.75	$13.50
Barlick, Albert J.	55B	265	$15.00	$60.00
Barney, Rex	48B	41	$7.00	$22.50
Barney, Rex	49B	61	$3.75	$13.50
Barney, Rex	50B	76	$3.75	$13.50
Barney, Rex	51B	153	$4.50	$16.00
Barrett, Red	49B	213	$20.00	$70.00
Bartell, Dick	55B	234	$4.00	$13.50
Batts, Matt	51B	129	$4.50	$16.00
Batts, Matt	52B	216	$3.00	$10.50
Batts, Matt	53BW	23	$8.00	$25.00
Batts, Matt	54B	183	$2.00	$6.00
Batts, Matt	55B	161	$2.00	$6.00
Bauer, Hank	50B	219	$11.00	$47.50

Player	Year	No.	VG	EX/MT
Bauer, Hank	51B	183	$5.00	$20.00
Bauer, Hank	52B	65	$4.75	$19.50
Bauer, Hank	53BC	44	$100.00	$300.00
Bauer, Hank	53BC	84	$9.00	$32.50
Bauer, Hank	54B	129	$4.50	$15.00
Bauer, Hank	55B	246	$7.50	$27.50
Baumholtz, Frank	49B	21	$4.00	$13.50
Baumholtz, Frank	52B	195	$3.25	$11.00
Baumholtz, Frank	54B	221	$2.00	$6.00
Baumholtz, Frank	55B	227	$4.00	$13.50
Beard, Ralph	55B	206	$2.00	$6.00
Beard, Ted	51B	308	$13.50	$42.50
Bearden, Gene	49B	57	$3.75	$13.50
Bearden, Gene	50B	93	$3.75	$13.50
Bearden, Gene	51B	284	$13.50	$42.50
Bearden, Gene	52B	173	$3.25	$11.00
Belardi, Wayne	55B	36	$2.00	$6.00
Bell, Dave "Gus"	51B	40	$6.00	$18.00
Bell, Gus	53BW	1	$20.00	$110.00
Bell, Gus	54B	124	$2.00	$6.00
Bell, Gus	55B	243	$3.75	$13.50
Berardino, John	51B	245	$4.50	$16.00
Bernier, Carlos	54B	171	$2.00	$6.00
Berra, Larry 'Yogi'	48B	6	$100.00	$400.00
Berra, Yogi	49B	60	$80.00	$275.00
Berra, Yogi	50B	46	$90.00	$325.00

LARRY "YOGI" BERRA

Player	Year	No.	VG	EX/MT
Berra, Yogi	51B	2	$95.00	$350.00
Berra, Yogi	52B	1	$60.00	$575.00
Berra, Yogi	53BC	44	$100.00	$300.00
Berra, Yogi	53BC	121	$150.00	$480.00
Berra, Yogi	54B	161	$35.00	$125.00
Berra, Yogi	55B	168	$25.00	$90.00
Berry, Charles	55B	281	$5.00	$20.00
Berry, Connie "Neil"	49B	180	$20.00	$70.00
Berry, Neil	50B	241	$3.75	$13.50
Berry, Neil	51B	213	$4.50	$16.00
Berry, Neil	52B	219	$6.50	$22.50
Bevan, Hal	53BW	43	$8.00	$25.00
Bevins, Floyd	48B	22	$13.50	$42.50
Bickford, Vern	49B	1	$8.00	$65.00

BOWMAN

Player	Year	No.	VG	EX/MT
Bickford, Vern	50B	57	$8.00	$35.00
Bickford, Vern	51B	42	$4.50	$16.00
Bickford, Vern	52B	48	$3.25	$11.00
Bickford, Vern	54B	176	$2.00	$6.00
Bilko, Steve	51B	265	$13.50	$42.50
Bilko, Steve	54B	206	$2.00	$6.00
Bilko, Steve	55B	88	$2.00	$6.00
Blackburn, Jim	49B	160	$20.00	$70.00
Blackburn, Jim	51B	287	$13.50	$42.50
Blackwell, Ewell	48B	2	$9.00	$32.50
Blackwell, Ewell	50B	63	$9.00	$36.00
Blackwell, Ewell	51B	24	$3.75	$15.00
Blatnick, Johnny	49B	123	$3.25	$11.00
Blaylock, Marv	55B	292	$4.00	$13.50
Bloodworth, Jimmy	51B	185	$4.50	$16.00
Bockman, Eddie	49B	195	$20.00	$70.00
Boggess, L. R. "Dusty"	55B	297	$6.50	$18.00
Bolling, Frank	55B	204	$2.25	$8.00
Bolling, Milt	54B	130	$2.00	$6.00
Bolling, Milt	55B	48	$1.00	$6.00
Bollweg, Don	54B	115	$2.00	$6.00
Bollweg, Don	55B	54	$2.00	$6.00
Bonham, Ernie	49B	77	$4.00	$13.50
Boone, Ray	51B	54	$4.50	$16.00
Boone, Ray	52B	214	$3.25	$11.00
Boone, Ray	53BC	79	$8.50	$25.00
Borowy, Hank	49B	134	$3.25	$11.00
Borowy, Hank	50B	177	$3.75	$13.50
Borowy, Hank	51B	250	$4.50	$16.00
Boudreau, Lou	49B	11	$12.50	$45.00
Boudreau, Lou	50B	94	$10.00	$40.00
Boudreau, Lou	51B	62	$10.00	$40.00
Boudreau, Lou	53BC	57	$10.50	$40.00
Boudreau, Lou	55B	89	$6.00	$17.50
Bowman, Roger	55B	115	$2.00	$6.00
Boyd, Bob	54B	118	$2.00	$6.00
Boyer, Cloyd	51B	228	$4.50	$16.00
Boyer, Cloyd	53BC	115	$12.50	$37.50
Boyer, Cloyd	55B	149	$2.00	$6.00
Branca, Ralph	49B	194	$22.50	$90.00
Branca, Ralph	50B	59	$12.00	$47.50
Branca, Ralph	51B	56	$6.00	$17.50
Branca, Ralph	52B	96	$5.00	$15.00
Branca, Ralph	53BW	52	$7.00	$32.00
Brazle, Al	49B	126	$3.25	$11.00
Brazle, Al	50B	126	$3.75	$13.50
Brazle, Al	51B	157	$4.50	$16.00
Brazle, Al	52B	134	$3.25	$11.00
Brazle, Alpha	53BC	140	$12.50	$37.50
Brazle, Al	54B	142	$2.00	$6.00
Brazle, Al	55B	230	$4.00	$13.50
Brecheen, Harry	49B	158	$20.00	$70.00
Brecheen, Harry	50B	90	$3.75	$13.50
Brecheen, Harry	51B	86	$4.00	$13.50
Brecheen, Harry	52B	176	$3.25	$11.00
Brewer, Tom	55B	178	$2.00	$6.00
Brideweser, Jim	53BC	136	$12.50	$37.50
Brideweser, Jim	55B	151	$2.00	$6.00
Bridges, Rocky	53BW	32	$8.00	$25.00
Bridges, Rocky	54B	156	$2.25	$8.00
Bridges, Rocky	55B	136	$2.00	$6.00
Brissie, Leland "Lou"	49B	41	$3.75	$13.50
Brissie, Lou	50B	48	$8.00	$35.00
Brissie, Lou	51B	155	$4.50	$16.00
Brissie, Lou	52B	79	$3.25	$11.00
Brosnan, Jim	55B	229	$3.75	$13.50
Brown, Bobby	49B	19	$5.00	$22.00
Brown, Bobby	50B	101	$8.00	$25.00
Brown, Bobby	51B	110	$3.50	$13.00
Brown, Bobby	52B	105	$3.75	$13.50
Brown, Hector "Skinny"	55B	221	$2.00	$6.00
Brown, Tom	49B	178	$20.00	$70.00
Brown, Tommy	52B	236	$6.50	$22.50
Brown, Tommy	53BC	42	$8.50	$25.00
Bruton, Bill	54B	224	$8.00	$25.00
Bruton, Bill	55B	11	$2.00	$6.00
Bucha, Johnny	54B	215	$2.00	$6.00
Buhl, Bob	55B	43	$2.00	$6.00
Burdette, Lou	52B	244	$12.00	$47.50
Burdette, Lou	53BW	51	$10.50	$42.00
Burdette, Lou	54B	192	$3.25	$12.00
Burdette, Lou	55B	70	$2.25	$10.00
Burgess, Forrest	51B	317	$12.00	$40.00
Burgess, Forrest "Smokey"	52B	112	$3.75	$13.50
Burgess, Forrest "Smoky"	53BC	28	$8.50	$25.00
Burgess, Forest "Smokey"	54B	31	$2.25	$8.00
Burgess, Forrest "Smoky"	55B	209	$2.00	$7.00
Burtschy, Ed	55B	120	$2.00	$6.00
Busby, Jim	51B	302	$13.50	$42.50
Busby, Jim	52B	68	$3.25	$11.00
Busby, Jim	53BC	15	$8.50	$25.00
Busby, Jim	54B	8	$2.00	$6.00
Busby, Jim	55B	166	$2.00	$6.00
Byrd, Harry	53BC	38	$8.50	$25.00
Byrd, Harry	54B	49	$2.00	$6.00
Byrd, Harry	55B	159	$2.00	$6.00
Byrne, Tommy	51B	73	$4.00	$13.50
Byrne, Tommy	52B	61	$3.25	$11.00
Byrne, Tommy	55B	300	$4.00	$13.50
Cain, Bob	50B	236	$3.75	$13.50
Cain, Bob	51B	197	$4.50	$16.00
Cain, Bob	52B	19	$3.75	$13.50
Cain, Bob	53BC	56	$8.50	$25.00
Cain, Bob	54B	195	$2.00	$6.00
Campanella, Roy	49B	84	$125.00	$550.00
Campanella, Roy	50B	75	$60.00	$225.00
Campanella, Roy	51B	31	$60.00	$225.00
Campanella, Roy	52B	44	$50.00	$180.00
Campanella, Roy	53BC	46	$80.00	$240.00
Campanella, Roy	54B	90	$35.00	$105.00
Campanella, Roy	55B	22	$30.00	$100.00
Candini, Milo	51B	255	$13.50	$42.50
Carrasquel, Alfonso Chico	51B	60	$4.50	$16.00
Carrasquel, Chico	52B	41	$3.25	$11.00
Carrasquel, Chico	53BC	54	$8.50	$25.00
Carrasquel, Chico	54B	54	$2.00	$6.00
Carrasquel, Al "Chico"	55B	173	$2.00	$6.00
Casey, Hugh	49B	179	$20.00	$70.00
Castiglione, Pete	50B	201	$3.75	$13.50
Castiglione, Pete	51B	17	$4.50	$16.00
Castiglione, Pete	52B	47	$3.25	$11.00
Castiglione, Pete	54B	174	$2.00	$6.00
Cavarretta, Phil	49B	6	$3.75	$13.50
Cavarretta(Cavaretta), Phil	50B	195	$5.00	$20.00
Cavarretta, Phil	51B	138	$4.50	$16.00
Cavarretta, Phil	52B	126	$3.75	$13.50
Cavarretta, Phil	53BC	30	$8.50	$25.00
Cavarretta, Phil	55B	282	$4.00	$13.50
Cerv, Bob	55B	306	$3.75	$13.50
Chakales, Bob	55B	148	$2.00	$6.00
Chambers, Cliff	50B	202	$3.75	$13.50
Chambers, Cliff	51B	131	$4.50	$16.00
Chambers, Cliff	52B	14	$3.75	$13.50
Chambers, Cliff	54B	126	$2.00	$6.00
Chapman, Sam	49B	112	$3.25	$11.00
Chapman, Sam	50B	104	$3.75	$13.50
Chapman, Sam	51B	9	$4.50	$16.00
Chesnes, Bob	49B	13	$4.00	$13.50
Chesnes, Bob	50B	70	$8.00	$35.00
Chipman, Bob	49B	184	$20.00	$70.00
Chipman, Bob	50B	192	$3.75	$13.50
Chipman, Bob	52B	228	$6.50	$22.50
Chiti, Harry	53BC	7	$8.50	$25.00
Chiti, Harry	55B	304	$4.00	$13.50
Christmann, Mark	49B	121	$3.25	$11.00
Church, Emory "Bubba"	51B	149	$4.50	$16.00
Church, Bubba	52B	40	$3.25	$11.00
Church, Bubba	53BC	138	$12.50	$37.50
Church, Bubba	55B	273	$4.00	$13.50
Chylak, Nestor	55B	283	$5.00	$20.00

Player	Year	No.	VG	EX/MT
Clark, Allie	49B	150	$20.00	$70.00
Clark, Allie	50B	233	$3.75	$13.50
Clark, Allie	51B	29	$4.50	$16.00
Clark, Allie	52B	130	$3.25	$11.00
Clark, Allie	53BC	155	$12.50	$37.50
Clark, Mel	53BC	67	$8.50	$25.00
Clark, Mel	54B	175	$2.00	$6.00
Clark, Mel	55B	41	$2.00	$6.00
Coan, Gil	49B	90	$4.00	$13.50
Coan, Gil	50B	54	$8.00	$35.00
Coan, Gil	51B	18	$4.50	$16.00
Coan, Gil	52B	51	$3.25	$11.00
Coan, Gil	53BC	34	$8.50	$25.00
Coan, Gil	54B	40	$2.00	$6.00
Coan, Gil	55B	78	$2.00	$6.00
Cole, Dave	52B	132	$3.25	$11.00
Cole, Dave	53BW	38	$8.00	$25.00
Cole, Dick	54B	27	$2.00	$6.00
Cole, Dick	55B	28	$2.00	$6.00
Coleman, Gerry (Jerry)	49B	225	$19.00	$85.00
Coleman, Jerry	50B	47	$10.00	$40.00
Coleman, Jerry	51B	49	$4.50	$16.00
Coleman, Jerry	52B	73	$4.00	$13.50
Coleman, Jerry	54B	81	$2.25	$8.00
Coleman, Jerry	55B	99	$2.25	$8.00
Coleman, Joe	50B	141	$3.75	$13.50

JOE COLEMAN

Player	Year	No.	VG	EX/MT
Coleman, Joe	51B	120	$4.50	$16.00
Coleman, Joe	55B	3	$2.00	$6.00
Coleman, Ray	50B	250	$3.75	$13.50
Coleman, Ray	51B	136	$4.50	$16.00
Coleman, Ray	52B	201	$3.25	$11.00
Collins, Joe	52B	181	$3.75	$13.50
Collum, Jack	54B	204	$2.00	$6.00
Collum, Jack	55B	189	$2.00	$6.00
Conlan, J. B. "Jocko"	55B	303	$20.00	$75.00
Consuegra, Sandalio	51B	96	$4.50	$16.00
Consuegra, Sandalio	52B	143	$3.25	$11.00
Consuegra, "Sandy"	53BC	89	$8.50	$25.00
Consuegra, Sandy	54B	166	$2.00	$6.00
Consuegra, Sandy	55B	116	$2.00	$6.00

Player	Year	No.	VG	EX/MT
Coogan, Dale	50B	244	$3.75	$13.50
Cooper, Walker	48B	9	$4.50	$16.00
Cooper, Walker	49B	117	$3.25	$11.00
Cooper, Walker	50B	111	$3.75	$13.50
Cooper, Walker	51B	135	$4.50	$16.00
Cooper, Walker	52B	208	$3.25	$11.00
Cooper, Walker	53BW	30	$8.00	$25.00
Corwin, Al	52B	121	$3.25	$11.00
Corwin, Al ·	53BC	126	$12.50	$37.50
Corwin, Al	53BC	149	$12.50	$37.50
Corwin, Al	54B	137	$2.00	$6.00
Corwin, Al	55B	122	$2.00	$6.00
Courtney, Clint	53BC	70	$8.50	$25.00
Courtney, Clint	54B	69	$2.00	$6.00
Courtney, Clint	55B	34	$2.00	$6.00
Cox, Billy	49B	73	$8.00	$25.00
Cox, Billy	50B	194	$5.00	$15.00
Cox, Billy	51B	224	$4.50	$16.00
Cox, Billy	52B	152	$3.75	$13.50
Cox, Billy	53BW	60	$6.50	$27.50
Cox, Billy	54B	26	$2.25	$8.00
Cox, Billy	55B	56	$2.00	$6.00
Crandall, Del	50B	56	$10.00	$40.00
Crandall, Del	51B	20	$4.00	$13.50
Crandall, Del	54B	32	$2.25	$8.00
Crandall, Del	55B	217	$2.00	$7.00
Crawford, Rufus	55B	121	$2.00	$6.00
Crosetti, Frank	52B	252	$20.00	$150.00
Cusick, John	52B	192	$3.25	$11.00
Daniels, Jack	53BC	83	$8.50	$25.00
Dark, Al	49B	67	$6.00	$20.00
Dark, Al	50B	64	$10.00	$40.00
Dark, Al	51B	14	$4.00	$13.50
Dark, Al	52B	34	$5.00	$15.00
Dark, Al	53BC	19	$4.25	$16.00
Dark, Al	54B	41	$3.25	$11.00
Dark, Al "Alwin"	55B	2	$2.25	$8.00
Darnell, Bob	55B	39	$2.00	$6.00
Dascoli, Frank	55B	291	$5.00	$20.00
De Maestri, Joe	54B	147	$2.00	$6.00
De Maestri, Joe	55B	176	$2.00	$6.00
Delock, Ivan	52B	250	$6.50	$22.50
Delock, Ivan	55B	276	$4.00	$13.50
Delsing, Jim	51B	279	$13.50	$42.50
Delsing, Jim	52B	157	$3.25	$11.00
Delsing, Jim	53BW	44	$8.00	$25.00
Delsing, Jim	54B	55	$2.00	$6.00
Delsing, Jim	55B	274	$4.00	$13.50
DeMars, Billy	50B	252	$7.00	$80.00
DeMars, Billy	51B	43	$4.50	$16.00
Dente, Sam	50B	107	$3.75	$13.50
Dente, Sam	51B	133	$4.50	$16.00
Dente, Sam	53BC	137	$12.50	$37.50
Dickey, Bill	51B	290	$40.00	$160.00
Dickson, Murry	49B	8	$4.00	$13.50
Dickson, Murry	50B	34	$8.00	$35.00
Dickson, Murry	51B	167	$4.50	$16.00
Dickson, Murry	52B	59	$3.25	$11.00
Dickson, Murry	54B	111	$2.00	$6.00
Dickson, Murry	55B	236	$4.00	$13.50
Diering, Charles "Chuck"	50B	179	$3.75	$13.50
Diering, Chuck	51B	158	$4.50	$16.00
Diering, Chuck	52B	198	$3.25	$11.00
Dillinger, Bob	49B	143	$3.25	$11.00
Dillinger, Bob	50B	105	$3.75	$13.50
Dillinger, Bob	51B	63	$4.50	$16.00
DiMaggio, Dom	49B	64	$7.50	$22.50
DiMaggio, Dom	50B	3	$9.00	$35.00
Ditmar, Art	55B	90	$2.00	$6.00
Dittmer, Jack	54B	48	$2.00	$6.00
Dittmer, Jack	55B	212	$2.00	$6.00
Dixon, Hal H.	55B	309	$5.00	$20.00
Dixon, John "Sonny"	55B	211	$2.00	$6.00
Dobernic, Jess	49B	200	$20.00	$70.00
Dobson, Joe	49B	7	$4.00	$13.50

BOWMAN

Player	Year	No.	VG	EX/MT	Player	Year	No.	VG	EX/MT
Dobson, Joe	50B	44	$8.00	$35.00	Evers, Walter	52B	111	$3.00	$10.50
Dobson, Joe	51B	36	$4.50	$16.00	Evers, Walter	53BC	25	$4.50	$17.25
Dobson, Joe	53BC	88	$8.50	$25.00	Evers, Walter "Hoot"	54B	18	$2.00	$6.00
Doby, Larry	49B	233	$35.00	$125.00	Fain, Ferris	48B	21	$4.00	$11.50
Doby, Larry	50B	39	$14.00	$50.00	Fain, Ferris	49B	9	$3.75	$13.50
Doby, Larry	51B	151	$6.00	$20.00	Fain, Ferris	50B	13	$8.00	$35.00
Doby, Larry	52B	115	$5.25	$16.00	Fain, Ferris	52B	154	$3.75	$13.50
Doby, Larry	53BC	40	$6.50	$27.50	Fain, Ferris	54B	214	$2.25	$8.00
Doby, Larry	54B	84	$2.50	$10.00	Fannin, Cliff	49B	120	$3.25	$11.00
Doerr, Bobby	49B	23	$8.00	$35.00	Fannin, Cliff	50B	106	$3.75	$13.50
Doerr, Bobby	50B	43	$10.00	$40.00	Fannin, Cliff	51B	244	$4.50	$16.00
Donatelli, A. J.	55B	313	$5.00	$20.00	Feller, Bob	48B	5	$40.00	$150.00
Donnelly, Sylvester	49B	145	$20.00	$70.00	Feller, Bob	49B	27	$30.00	$110.00
Donnelly, Sylvester	50B	176	$3.75	$13.50	Feller, Bob	50B	6	$35.00	$120.00
Donnelly, Sylvester "Blix"	51B	208	$4.50	$16.00	Feller, Bob	51B	30	$30.00	$95.00
Dorish, Harry	51B	266	$13.50	$42.50	Feller, Bob	52B	43	$27.50	$85.00
Dorish, Harry	54B	86	$2.00	$6.00	Feller, Bob	53BC	114	$75.00	$225.00
Dorish, Harry	55B	248	$4.00	$13.50	Feller, Bob	54B	132	$20.00	$65.00
Dressen, Charlie	51B	259	$15.00	$60.00	Feller, Bob	55B	134	$16.00	$52.50
Dressen, Charlie	52B	188	$3.25	$11.00	Fernandez, Chico	55B	270	$4.00	$13.50
Dressen, Charlie	53BC	124	$12.00	$42.50	Ferrick, Tom	51B	182	$4.50	$16.00
Drews, Karl	49B	188	$20.00	$70.00	Ferriss, Boo	49B	211	$20.00	$70.00
Drews, Karl	53BC	113	$12.50	$37.50	Fitzgerald, Ed	49B	109	$3.25	$11.00
Drews, Karl	54B	191	$2.00	$6.00	Fitzgerald, Ed	50B	178	$3.75	$13.50
Dropo, Walt	50B	246	$5.00	$20.00	Fitzgerald, Ed	52B	180	$3.25	$11.00
Dropo, Walt	52B	169	$4.00	$13.50	Fitzgerald, Ed	54B	168	$2.00	$6.00
Dropo, Walt	53BC	45	$8.50	$25.00	Fitzgerald, Eddy	55B	208	$2.00	$6.00
Dropo, Walt	54B	7	$2.00	$6.00	Fitzsimmons, Fred	52B	234	$6.50	$22.50
Dropo, Walt	55B	285	$5.00	$20.00	Flaherty, John	55B	272	$5.00	$20.00
Dubiel, Walt	51B	283	$13.50	$42.50	Flowers, Bennett	55B	254	$4.00	$13.50
Durocher, Leo	50B	220	$9.00	$35.00	Fondy, Dee	52B	231	$6.50	$22.50
Durocher, Leo	51B	233	$9.00	$35.00	Fondy, Dee	53BW	5	$8.00	$25.00
Durocher, Leo	52B	146	$12.50	$37.50	Fondy, Dee	54B	173	$2.25	$8.00
Durocher, Leo	53BC	55	$8.50	$35.00	Fondy, Dee	55B	224	$2.00	$6.00
Dusak, Erv	51B	310	$13.50	$42.50	Ford, Ed "Whitey"	51B	1	$115.00	$975.00
Dyck, Jim	53BC	111	$8.50	$25.00	Ford, Ed "Whitey"	53BC	153	$105.00	$375.00
Dyck, Jim	54B	85	$2.00	$6.00	Ford, Ed "Whitey"	54B	177	$19.00	$75.00
Dykes, Jimmy	51B	226	$3.50	$13.00	Ford, Ed "Whitey"	55B	59	$15.00	$60.00
Dykes, Jimmy	52B	98	$3.25	$11.00	Fornieles, Mike	55B	266	$4.00	$13.50
Dykes, Jimmy	53BC	31	$8.50	$25.00	Fowler, Dick	49B	171	$20.00	$70.00
Early, Jake	49B	106	$4.00	$13.50	Fowler, Dick	50B	214	$3.75	$13.50
Easter, Luke	51B	258	$10.00	$30.00	Fowler, Dick	52B	190	$3.25	$11.00
Easter, Luke	52B	95	$3.75	$13.50	Fox, Howard "Howie"	50B	80	$3.75	$13.50
Easter, Luke	53BC	104	$8.50	$25.00	Fox, Howie	51B	180	$4.50	$16.00
Easter, Luke	54B	116	$2.00	$6.00	Fox, Howie	52B	125	$3.25	$11.00
Edwards, Bruce	48B	43	$7.00	$22.50	Fox, Howie	53BC	158	$12.50	$37.50
Edwards, Bruce	49B	206	$20.00	$70.00	Fox, Nelson "Nellie"	51B	232	$21.25	$85.00
Edwards, Bruce	50B	165	$3.75	$13.50	Fox, Nellie	52B	21	$7.50	$30.00
Edwards, Bruce	51B	116	$4.50	$16.00	Fox, Nellie	53BC	18	$10.75	$40.00
Edwards, Bruce	52B	88	$3.25	$11.00	Fox, Nellie	54B	6	$3.75	$15.00
Edwards, Hank	49B	136	$3.25	$11.00	Fox, Nellie	55B	33	$3.75	$15.00
Edwards, Hank	50B	169	$3.75	$13.50	Freeman, Hershell	55B	290	$4.00	$13.50
Edwards, Hank	52B	141	$3.25	$11.00	Freese, George	55B	84	$2.00	$6.00
Elliott, Bob	48B	1	$5.50	$65.00	Fricano, Marion	54B	3	$2.00	$6.00
Elliott, Bob	49B	58	$3.75	$13.50	Fricano, Marion	55B	316	$4.00	$13.50
Elliott, Bob	50B	20	$8.00	$35.00	Friend, Bob	52B	191	$4.25	$17.50
Elliott, Bob	51B	66	$4.50	$16.00	Friend, Bob	53BC	16	$8.50	$25.00
Engeln, William R.	55B	301	$5.00	$20.00	Friend, Bob	54B	43	$3.25	$11.00
Ennis, Del	50B	31	$8.00	$35.00	Friend, Bob	55B	57	$2.25	$8.00
Ennis, Del	51B	4	$4.00	$13.50	Friend, Owen	50B	189	$3.75	$13.50
Ennis, Del	52B	76	$4.00	$13.50	Friend, Owen	51B	101	$4.50	$16.00
Ennis, Del	53BC	103	$8.50	$25.00	Friend, Owen	54B	212	$2.00	$6.00
Ennis, Del	54B	127	$2.25	$8.00	Friend, Owen	55B	256	$4.00	$13.50
Ennis, Del	55B	17	$2.25	$8.00	Frisch, Frank	50B	229	$10.00	$42.50
Erskine, Carl	51B	260	$25.00	$100.00	Frisch, Frank	51B	282	$19.00	$60.00
Erskine, Carl	52B	70	$5.50	$20.00	Furillo, Carl	49B	70	$12.00	$42.50
Erskine, Carl	53BC	12	$9.25	$35.00	Furillo, Carl	50B	58	$12.50	$47.50
Erskine, Carl	54B	10	$3.75	$13.50	Furillo, Carl	51B	81	$8.00	$26.00
Erskine, Carl	55B	170	$3.75	$13.50	Furillo, Carl	52B	24	$6.00	$19.50
Evans, Al	49B	132	$3.25	$11.00	Furillo, Carl	53BC	78	$12.00	$42.50
Evans, Al	50B	144	$3.75	$13.50	Furillo, Carl	54B	122	$3.25	$12.00
Evans, Al	51B	38	$4.50	$16.00	Furillo, Carl	55B	169	$3.75	$13.00
Evers, Hoot	49B	42	$3.75	$13.50	Galan, Augie	48B	39	$7.00	$22.50
Evers, Walter	50B	41	$8.00	$35.00	Galan, Augie	49B	230	$20.00	$70.00
Evers, Walter	51B	23	$4.50	$16.00	Garagiola, Joe	51B	122	$25.00	$100.00

Player	Year	No.	VG	EX/MT
Garagiola, Joe	52B	27	$18.00	$55.00
Garagiola, Joe	53BC	21	$17.50	$52.50
Garagiola, Joe	54B	141	$11.50	$35.00
Garcia, Mike	50B	147	$5.00	$15.00
Garcia, Mike	51B	150	$4.00	$13.50
Garcia, Mike	52B	7	$5.00	$15.00
Garcia, Mike	53BC	43	$4.50	$17.25
Garcia, Mike	54B	100	$2.25	$8.00
Garcia, Mike	55B	128	$2.25	$8.00
Gardner, Billy	55B	249	$4.00	$13.50
Garver, Ned	49B	15	$4.00	$13.50
Garver, Ned	50B	51	$8.00	$35.00
Garver, Ned	51B	172	$4.50	$16.00
Garver, Ned	52B	29	$3.25	$12.50
Garver, Ned	53BC	47	$8.50	$25.00
Garver, Ned	54B	39	$3.25	$11.00
Garver, Ned	55B	188	$2.00	$6.00
Gernert, Dick	53BW	11	$8.00	$25.00
Gernert, Dick	54B	146	$2.00	$6.00
Gettel, Allen	51B	304	$13.50	$42.50
Giel, Paul	55B	125	$2.00	$6.00
Gilbert, Harold	50B	235	$3.75	$13.50
Gilliam, James "Junior"	54B	74	$3.00	$12.00
Gilliam, Junior	55B	98	$2.50	$10.00
Ginsberg, Joe	53BC	6	$8.50	$25.00
Ginsberg, Joe	54B	52	$2.00	$6.00
Glaviano, Tommy	51B	301	$13.50	$42.50
Goetz, Lawrence J.	55B	311	$5.00	$20.00
Goliat, Mike	50B	205	$3.75	$13.50
Goliat, Mike	51B	77	$4.50	$16.00
Goodman, Billy	49B	39	$5.00	$20.00
Goodman, Billy	50B	99	$3.75	$13.50
Goodman, Billy	51B	237	$4.50	$16.00
Goodman, Billy	52B	81	$3.25	$11.00
Goodman, Billy	53BC	148	$12.50	$37.50
Goodman, Billy	54B	82	$1.00	$5.00
Goodman, Billy	55B	126	$2.00	$6.00
Gordon, Joe	49B	210	$20.00	$70.00
Gordon, Joe	50B	129	$3.75	$13.50
Gordon, Sid	48B	27	$4.50	$16.00
Gordon, Sid	49B	101	$4.00	$13.50
Gordon, Sid	50B	109	$3.75	$13.50
Gordon, Sid	51B	19	$4.50	$16.00
Gordon, Sid	52B	60	$3.25	$11.00
Gordon, Sid	53BC	5	$8.50	$25.00
Gordon, Sid	54B	11	$2.00	$6.00
Gordon, Sid	55B	163	$2.00	$6.00
Gore, Arthur J.	55B	289	$5.00	$20.00
Gorman, Tom	53BW	61	$8.00	$25.00
Gorman, Tom	54B	17	$2.00	$6.00
Gorman, Thomas D.	55B	293	$5.00	$20.00
Graham, Jack	50B	145	$3.75	$13.50
Grammas, Alex	55B	186	$2.00	$6.00
Grasso, Mickey	51B	205	$4.50	$16.00
Grasso, Mickey	52B	174	$3.25	$11.00
Grasso, Mickey	53BC	77	$8.50	$25.00
Grasso, Mickey	54B	184	$2.00	$6.00
Gray, Ted	49B	10	$4.00	$13.50
Gray, Ted	50B	210	$3.75	$13.50
Gray, Ted	51B	178	$4.50	$16.00
Gray, Ted	52B	199	$3.25	$11.00
Gray, Ted	53BC	72	$8.50	$25.00
Gray, Ted	54B	71	$2.00	$6.00
Gray, Ted	55B	86	$2.00	$6.00
Greengrass, Jim	54B	28	$2.00	$6.00
Greengrass, Jim	55B	49	$2.00	$6.00
Greenwood, Bob	55B	42	$2.00	$6.00
Grieve, William T.	55B	275	$5.00	$20.00
Grim, Bob	55B	167	$2.00	$6.00
Grimm, Charlie	53BC	69	$8.50	$25.00
Grimm, Charlie	55B	298	$4.00	$13.50
Grissom, Marv	55B	123	$2.00	$6.00
Gromek, Steve	49B	198	$20.00	$70.00
Gromek, Steve	50B	131	$3.75	$13.50
Gromek, Steve	51B	115	$4.50	$16.00

Player	Year	No.	VG	EX/MT
Gromek, Steve	52B	203	$3.25	$11.00
Gromek, Steve	53BW	63	$8.00	$35.00
Gromek, Steve	54B	199	$2.00	$6.00
Gromek, Steve	55B	203	$2.00	$6.00
Groth, Johnny	50B	243	$3.75	$13.50
Groth, Johnny	51B	249	$4.50	$16.00
Groth, Johnny	52B	67	$3.25	$11.00
Groth, Johnny	54B	165	$2.00	$6.00
Groth, Johnny	55B	117	$2.00	$6.00
Guerra, Mickey "Mike"	49B	155	$20.00	$70.00
Guerra, Mike	50B	157	$3.75	$13.50
Guerra, Mike	51B	202	$4.50	$16.00
Gumbert, Harry	49B	192	$20.00	$70.00
Gumbert, Harry	50B	171	$3.75	$13.50
Gumpert, Randy	49B	87	$4.00	$13.50
Gumpert, Randy	50B	184	$3.75	$13.50
Gumpert, Randy	51B	59	$4.50	$16.00
Gumpert, Randy	52B	106	$3.25	$11.00
Gustine, Frank	49B	99	$4.00	$13.50
Hacker, Warren	51B	318	$13.50	$42.50
Hacker, Warren	53BC	144	$12.50	$37.50

Player	Year	No.	VG	EX/MT
Hacker, Warren	54B	125	$2.00	$6.00
Hacker, Warren	55B	8	$2.00	$6.00
Haefner, Mickey	49B	144	$3.25	$11.00
Haefner, Mickey	50B	183	$3.75	$13.50
Hall, Bob	55B	113	$2.00	$6.00
Hamner, Granny	50B	204	$3.75	$13.50
Hamner, Granny	51B	148	$4.50	$16.00
Hamner, Granny	52B	35	$3.75	$13.50
Hamner, Granny	53BC	60	$8.50	$25.00
Hamner, Granny	54B	47	$2.00	$6.00
Hamner, "Granville" Granny	55B	112	$2.00	$6.00
Hamner, Ralph	49B	212	$20.00	$70.00
Hansen, Andy	53BW	64	$10.00	$40.00
Harris, Bucky	51B	275	$17.00	$55.00
Harris, Bucky	52B	158	$6.75	$22.50
Harris, Bucky	53BW	46	$10.00	$27.50
Harris, Mickey	49B	151	$20.00	$70.00
Harris, Mickey	50B	160	$3.75	$13.50
Harris, Mickey	51B	311	$13.50	$42.50
Harris, Mickey	52B	135	$3.25	$11.00

Player	Year	No.	VG	EX/MT	Player	Year	No.	VG	EX/MT
Hartsfield, Roy	51B	277	$13.50	$42.50	Hopp, Johnny	50B	122	$3.75	$13.50
Hartsfield, Roy	52B	28	$3.75	$13.50	Hopp, Johnny	51B	146	$4.00	$13.50
Hartung, Clint	48B	37	$7.00	$22.50	Houtteman, Art	50B	42	$8.00	$35.00
Hartung, Clint	49B	154	$20.00	$70.00	Houtteman, Art	51B	45	$4.50	$16.00
Hartung, Clint	50B	118	$3.75	$13.50	Houtteman, Art	53BC	4	$8.50	$25.00
Hartung, Clint	51B	234	$4.50	$16.00	Houtteman, Art	54B	20	$2.00	$6.00
Hatfield, Fred	52B	153	$3.25	$11.00	Houtteman, Art	55B	144	$2.00	$6.00
Hatfield, Fred	53BC	125	$12.50	$37.50	Howard, Elston	55B	68	$12.00	$30.00
Hatfield, Fred	54B	119	$2.00	$6.00	Howell, Homer "Dixie"	51B	252	$4.50	$16.00
Hatfield, Fred	55B	187	$2.00	$6.00	Howell, Homer "'Dixie"	52B	222	$6.50	$22.50
Hatten, Joe	49B	116	$1.60	$6.00	Howerton, Bill	50B	239	$3.75	$13.50
Hatten, Joe	50B	166	$3.75	$13.50	Howerton, Bill	51B	229	$4.50	$16.00
Hatten, Joe	51B	190	$4.50	$16.00	Howerton, Bill	52B	119	$3.25	$11.00
Hatten, Joe	52B	144	$3.25	$11.00	Hubbard, Cal	55B	315	$12.50	$40.00
Hatton, Grady	49B	62	$3.75	$13.50	Hudson, Sid	50B	17	$8.00	$35.00
Hatton, Grady	50B	26	$8.00	$35.00	Hudson, Sid	51B	169	$4.50	$16.00
Hatton, Grady	51B	47	$4.50	$16.00	Hudson, Sid	52B	123	$3.25	$11.00
Hawes, Roy Lee	55B	268	$4.00	$13.50	Hudson, Sid	53BW	29	$8.00	$25.00
Haynes, Joe	49B	191	$20.00	$70.00	Hudson, Sid	54B	194	$2.00	$6.00
Haynes, Joe	51B	240	$4.50	$16.00	Hudson, Sid	55B	318	$4.00	$13.50
Haynes, Joe	52B	103	$3.25	$11.00	Hughes, Jim	55B	156	$2.00	$6.00
Hearn, Jim	49B	190	$20.00	$70.00	Hughson, Tex	49B	199	$20.00	$70.00
Hearn, Jim	50B	208	$3.75	$13.50	Hunter, Bill	54B	5	$2.00	$6.00
Hearn, Jim	51B	61	$4.50	$16.00	Hunter, Bill	55B	69	$2.00	$6.00
Hearn, Jim	52B	49	$3.25	$11.00	Hurley, Edwin H.	55B	260	$5.00	$20.00
Hearn, Jim	53BC	76	$8.50	$25.00	Hutchinson, Fred	49B	196	$19.00	$85.00
Hearn, Jim	55B	220	$2.00	$6.00	Hutchinson, Fred	50B	151	$5.00	$20.00
Heath, Jeff	49B	169	$20.00	$70.00	Hutchinson, Fred	51B	141	$4.00	$13.50
Hegan, Jim	50B	7	$8.00	$35.00	Hutchinson, Fred	52B	3	$3.25	$11.00
Hegan, Jim	51B	79	$4.50	$16.00	Hutchinson, Fred	53BC	132	$7.50	$25.00
Hegan, Jim	52B	187	$3.25	$11.00	Irvin, Monte	51B	198	$19.50	$75.00
Hegan, Jim	53BC	102	$8.50	$25.00	Irvin, Monte	52B	162	$12.00	$35.00
Heintzelman, Ken	49B	108	$4.00	$13.50	Irvin, Monte	53BC	51	$12.50	$37.50
Heintzelman, Ken	50B	85	$3.75	$13.50	Jackowski, William A.	55B	284	$5.00	$20.00
Heintzelman, Ken	51B	147	$4.50	$16.00	Jackson, Ransom "Randy"	52B	175	$3.25	$11.00
Heintzelman, Ken	52B	148	$3.25	$11.00	Jackson, Randy	53BW	12	$8.00	$25.00
Hemus, Solly	52B	212	$3.25	$11.00	Jackson, Randy	54B	189	$2.00	$6.00
Hemus, Solly	53BC	85	$8.50	$25.00	Jackson, Randy	55B	87	$2.00	$6.00
Hemus, Solly	54B	94	$2.00	$6.00	Janowicz, Vic	54B	203	$2.00	$6.00
Hemus, Solly	55B	107	$2.00	$6.00	Janowicz, Vic	55B	114	$2.00	$6.00
Henrich, Tommy	48B	19	$4.50	$11.00	Jansen, Larry	48B	23	$4.50	$16.00
Henrich, Tommy	49B	69	$8.00	$25.00	Jansen, Larry	49B	202	$20.00	$70.00
Henrich, Tommy	50B	10	$12.00	$40.00	Jansen, Larry	50B	66	$8.00	$35.00
Henrich, Tommy	51B	291	$16.00	$50.00	Jansen, Larry	51B	162	$4.50	$16.00
Henry, Bill	55B	264	$4.00	$13.50	Jansen, Larry	52B	90	$3.25	$11.00
Hermanski, Gene	49B	20	$4.00	$13.50	Jansen, Larry	53BW	40	$8.00	$25.00
Hermanski, Gene	50B	113	$3.75	$13.50	Jansen, Larry	54B	169	$2.25	$8.00
Hermanski, Gene	51B	55	$4.50	$16.00	Jeffcoat, Hal	51B	211	$4.50	$16.00
Hermanski, Gene	52B	136	$3.25	$11.00	Jeffcoat, Hal	52B	104	$3.25	$11.00
Higbe, Kirby	49B	215	$20.00	$70.00	Jeffcoat, Hal	53BW	37	$8.00	$25.00
Higbe, Kirby	50B	200	$3.75	$13.50	Jeffcoat, Hal	54B	205	$2.00	$6.00
Hiller, Frank	52B	114	$3.25	$11.00	Jeffcoat, Hal	55B	223	$2.00	$6.00
Hitchcock, Billy	51B	191	$4.50	$16.00	Jensen, Jackie	51B	254	$22.50	$95.00
Hitchcock, Billy	52B	89	$3.25	$11.00	Jensen, Jackie	52B	161	$7.50	$22.50
Hoak, Don	55B	21	$2.25	$8.00	Jensen, Jackie	53BC	24	$8.00	$27.50
Hoderlein, Mel	54B	120	$2.00	$6.00	Jensen, Jackie	54B	2	$3.00	$10.00
Hodges, Gil	49B	100	$40.00	$160.00	Jethroe, Sam	50B	248	$5.00	$20.00
Hodges, Gil	50B	112	$19.00	$75.00	Jethroe, Sam	51B	242	$4.50	$16.00
Hodges, Gil	51B	7	$19.00	$72.50	Jethroe, Sam	52B	84	$3.25	$11.00
Hodges, Gil	52B	80	$17.00	$55.00	Jethroe, Sam	53BC	3	$8.50	$25.00
Hodges, Gil	53BC	92	$27.50	$95.00	Johnson, Billy	48B	33	$4.50	$16.00
Hodges, Gil	54B	138	$12.50	$50.00	Johnson, Billy	49B	129	$3.25	$11.00
Hodges, Gil	55B	158	$10.00	$32.00	Johnson, Billy	50B	102	$3.75	$13.50
Hoeft, Billy	53BW	18	$8.00	$25.00	Johnson, Billy	51B	74	$4.00	$13.50
Hoeft, Billy	54B	167	$2.00	$6.00	Johnson, Billy	52B	122	$3.25	$11.00
Hoffman, Bobby	49B	223	$20.00	$70.00	Johnson, Don	53BW	55	$8.00	$25.00
Holcombe, Ken	51B	267	$13.50	$42.50	Johnson, Don	55B	101	$2.25	$8.00
Holmes, Tommy	49B	72	$5.00	$15.00	Johnson, Earl	49B	231	$20.00	$70.00
Holmes, Tommy	50B	110	$5.00	$20.00	Johnson, Earl	50B	188	$3.75	$13.50
Honochick, George "Jim"	55B	267	$18.00	$57.50	Johnson, Earl	51B	321	$13.50	$42.50
Hooper, Bob	51B	33	$4.50	$16.00	Johnson, Ernie	54B	144	$2.00	$6.00
Hooper, Bob	52B	10	$3.75	$13.50	Johnson, Ernie	55B	157	$1.00	$5.00
Hooper, Bob	54B	4	$2.00	$6.00	Johnson, Ken	51B	293	$13.50	$42.50
Hooper, Bob	55B	271	$4.00	$13.50	Jok, Stan	55B	251	$4.00	$13.50
Hopp, Johnny	49B	207	$20.00	$70.00	Jolly, Dave	55B	71	$2.00	$6.00

Player	Year	No.	VG	EX/MT
Jones, Ray	52B	215	$3.25	$11.00
Jones, Sheldon	48B	34	$7.50	$28.00
Jones, Sheldon	49B	68	$3.75	$13.50
Jones, Sheldon	50B	83	$3.75	$13.50
Jones, Sheldon	51B	199	$4.50	$16.00
Jones, Vernal	50B	238	$3.75	$13.50
Jones, Willie	49B	92	$4.00	$13.50
Jones, Willie	50B	67	$8.00	$35.00
Jones, Willie	51B	112	$4.50	$16.00
Jones, Willie	52B	20	$4.50	$17.50
Jones, Willie	53BC	133	$12.50	$37.50
Jones, Willie	54B	143	$2.00	$6.00
Jones, Willie	55B	172	$2.00	$6.00
Joost, Eddie	48B	15	$4.50	$16.00
Joost, Eddie	49B	55	$3.75	$13.50
Joost, Eddie	50B	103	$3.75	$13.50
Joost, Eddie	51B	119	$4.50	$16.00
Joost, Eddie	52B	26	$3.75	$13.50

Player	Year	No.	VG	EX/MT
Joost, Eddie	53BC	105	$8.50	$25.00
Joost, Eddie	54B	35	$2.00	$6.00
Joost, Eddie	55B	263	$4.00	$13.50
Judson, Howie	50B	185	$3.75	$13.50
Judson, Howie	51B	123	$4.50	$16.00
Judson, Howie	52B	149	$3.25	$11.00
Judson, Howie	53BW	42	$8.00	$25.00
Judson, Howie	55B	193	$2.00	$6.00
Kaline, Al	55B	23	$30.00	$100.00
Katt, Ray	54B	121	$2.00	$6.00
Katt, Ray	55B	183	$2.00	$6.00
Kazak, Eddie	50B	36	$8.00	$35.00
Kazak, Eddie	51B	85	$4.50	$16.00
Kell, Everett	52B	242	$6.50	$22.50
Kell, George	49B	26	$12.00	$42.50
Kell, George	50B	8	$13.00	$42.00
Kell, George	51B	46	$6.25	$25.00
Kell, George	52B	75	$9.50	$30.00
Kell, George	53BC	61	$11.50	$35.00

Player	Year	No.	VG	EX/MT
Kell, George	54B	50	$6.50	$22.50
Kell, George	55B	213	$6.50	$22.50
Keller, Charlie	49B	209	$19.00	$85.00
Keller, Charlie	50B	211	$3.75	$13.50
Keller, Charlie	51B	177	$4.00	$13.50
Kellner, Alex	49B	222	$20.00	$70.00
Kellner, Alex	50B	14	$8.00	$35.00
Kellner, Alex	51B	57	$4.50	$16.00
Kellner, Alex	52B	226	$6.50	$22.50
Kellner, Alex	53BC	107	$8.50	$25.00
Kellner, Alex	54B	51	$2.00	$6.00
Kellner, Alex	55B	53	$2.00	$6.00
Keltner, Ken	49B	125	$3.25	$11.00
Keltner, Ken	50B	186	$3.75	$13.50
Kemmerer, Russ	55B	222	$2.00	$6.00
Kennedy, Bill	49B	105	$4.00	$13.50
Kennedy, Bob	51B	296	$13.50	$42.50
Kennedy, Monte	49B	237	$20.00	$70.00
Kennedy, Monte	50B	175	$3.75	$13.50
Kennedy, Monte	51B	163	$4.50	$16.00
Kennedy, Monte	52B	213	$3.25	$11.00
Keriazakos, Gus	55B	14	$2.00	$6.00
Kerr, Buddy	48B	20	$7.50	$28.00
Kerr, Buddy	49B	186	$20.00	$70.00
Kerr, Buddy	50B	55	$8.00	$35.00
Kerr, John "Buddy"	51B	171	$4.50	$16.00
Kinder, Ellis	50B	152	$3.75	$13.50
Kinder, Ellis	51B	128	$4.50	$16.00
Kinder, Ellis	54B	98	$2.00	$6.00
Kiner, Ralph	48B	3	$35.00	$115.00
Kiner, Ralph	49B	29	$20.00	$65.00
Kiner, Ralph	50B	33	$27.50	$85.00
Kiner, Ralph	52B	11	$11.50	$45.00
Kiner, Ralph	53BC	80	$21.00	$60.00
Kiner, Ralph	54B	45	$8.75	$30.00
Kiner, Ralph	55B	197	$7.50	$24.00
King, Charles	55B	133	$2.00	$6.00
King, Clyde	51B	299	$13.50	$42.50
King, Clyde	52B	56	$3.25	$11.00
Klaus, Bill	55B	150	$2.00	$6.00
Klippstein, Johnny	51B	248	$4.50	$16.00
Klippstein, Johnny	54B	29	$2.00	$6.00
Klippstein, Johnny	55B	152	$2.00	$6.00
Kluszewski, Ted	50B	62	$17.00	$55.00
Kluszewski, Ted	51B	143	$6.75	$25.00
Kluszewski, Ted	53BC	62	$12.50	$40.00
Kokos, Dick	49B	31	$4.00	$13.50
Kokos, Dick	50B	50	$8.00	$35.00
Kokos, Dick	51B	68	$4.50	$16.00
Kokos, Dick	54B	37	$2.00	$6.00
Kolloway, Don	49B	28	$4.00	$13.50
Kolloway, Don	50B	133	$3.75	$13.50
Kolloway, Don	51B	105	$4.50	$16.00
Kolloway, Don	52B	91	$3.25	$11.00
Konstanty, Jim	50B	226	$5.00	$15.00
Konstanty, Jim	51B	27	$4.00	$13.50
Konstanty, Jim	53BW	58	$8.00	$35.00
Konstanty, Jim	55B	231	$5.00	$20.00
Koshorek, Clem	53BC	147	$12.50	$37.50
Koslo, Dave "George"	48B	48	$10.00	$50.00
Koslo, Dave	49B	34	$4.00	$13.50
Koslo, Dave	50B	65	$8.00	$35.00
Koslo, Dave	51B	90	$4.50	$16.00
Koslo, Dave	52B	182	$3.25	$11.00
Kozar, Al	49B	16	$4.00	$13.50
Kozar, Al	50B	15	$8.00	$35.00
Kramer, Jack	49B	53	$3.75	$13.50
Kramer, Jack	50B	199	$3.75	$13.50
Kramer, Jack	51B	200	$4.50	$16.00
Kretlow, Lou	52B	221	$6.50	$22.50
Kretlow, Lou	53BC	50	$8.50	$25.00
Kretlow, Lou	54B	197	$2.00	$6.00
Kretlow, Lou	55B	108	$2.00	$6.00
Kryhoski, Dick	49B	218	$20.00	$70.00
Kryhoski, Dick	50B	242	$3.75	$13.50

Player	Year	No.	VG	EX/MT	Player	Year	No.	VG	EX/MT
Kryhoski, Dick	52B	133	$3.25	$11.00	Lemon, Bob	52B	23	$14.00	$47.50
Kryhoski, Dick	53BC	127	$12.50	$37.50	Lemon, Bob	53BW	27	$25.00	$87.50
Kryhoski, Dick	54B	117	$2.00	$6.00	Lemon, Bob	54B	196	$6.50	$25.00
Kuenn, Harvey	54B	23	$5.50	$20.00	Lemon, Bob	55B	191	$5.50	$20.00
Kuenn (Kueen), Harvey	55B	132	$1.75	$7.00	Lemon, Jim	55B	262	$3.75	$13.50
Kuzava, Bob	50B	5	$5.50	$20.00	Lenhardt, Don	53BC	20	$8.50	$25.00
Kuzava, Bob	51B	97	$4.50	$16.00	Lenhardt, Don	54B	53	$2.25	$8.00
Kuzava, Bob	52B	233	$6.50	$22.50	Leonard, Dutch	48B	24	$9.00	$30.00
Kuzava, Bob	53BW	33	$8.00	$25.00	Leonard, Dutch	49B	115	$3.25	$11.00
Kuzava, Bob	55B	215	$2.00	$6.00	Leonard, Dutch	50B	170	$3.75	$13.50
La Palme, Paul	53BW	19	$8.00	$25.00	Leonard, Dutch	51B	102	$4.50	$16.00
La Palme, Paul	54B	107	$2.00	$6.00	Leonard, Dutch	52B	159	$3.25	$11.00
La Palme, Paul	55B	61	$2.00	$6.00	Leonard, Dutch	53BW	50	$8.00	$25.00
Labine, Clem	54B	106	$2.25	$8.00	Leonard, Emil "Dutch"	55B	247	$4.00	$13.50
Lade, Doyle	49B	168	$20.00	$70.00	Lepcio, Ted	54B	162	$2.00	$6.00
Lade, Doyle	50B	196	$3.75	$13.50	Liddle, Don	55B	146	$2.00	$6.00
Lade, Doyle	51B	139	$4.50	$16.00	Limmer, Lou	55B	80	$2.00	$6.00
Lake, Eddie	49B	107	$4.00	$13.50	Lindell, Johnny	48B	11	$4.50	$16.00
Lake, Eddie	50B	240	$3.75	$13.50	Lindell, Johnny	49B	197	$20.00	$70.00
Lake, Eddie	51B	140	$4.50	$16.00	Lindell, Johnny	50B	209	$3.75	$13.50
LaManno, Ray	49B	113	$3.25	$11.00	Lindell, Johnny	54B	159	$2.00	$6.00
Landrith, Hobie	54B	220	$2.00	$6.00	Lint, Royce	55B	62	$2.00	$6.00
Landrith, Hobie	55B	50	$2.00	$6.00	Lipon, Johnny	51B	285	$13.50	$42.50
Lanier, Max	50B	207	$3.75	$13.50	Lipon, Johnny	52B	163	$3.25	$11.00
Lanier, Max	51B	230	$4.50	$16.00	Lipon, Johnny	53BC	123	$12.50	$37.50
Lanier, Max	52B	110	$3.25	$11.00	Littlefield, Dick	52B	209	$3.25	$11.00
					Littlefield, Dick	54B	213	$2.00	$6.00
					Littlefield, Dick	55B	200	$2.00	$6.00
					Litwhiler, Danny	49B	97	$4.00	$13.50
					Litwhiler, Danny	50B	198	$3.75	$13.50
					Litwhiler, Danny	51B	179	$4.50	$16.00
					Lockman, Carroll "Whitey"	48B	30	$10.00	$30.00
					Lockman, Whitey	49B	2	$4.00	$13.50
					Lockman, Whitey	50B	82	$3.75	$13.50
					Lockman, Whitey	51B	37	$4.00	$13.50
					Lockman, Whitey	52B	38	$3.25	$11.00
					Lockman, Whitey	53BC	128	$12.50	$37.50
					Lockman, Whitey	54B	153	$2.25	$8.00
					Lockman, Whitey	55B	219	$2.00	$6.00
					Loes, Billy	52B	240	$6.50	$32.00
					Loes, Billy	53BC	14	$8.50	$25.00
					Loes, Billy	54B	42	$2.00	$6.00
					Loes, Billy	55B	240	$3.75	$13.50
					Logan, Johnny	54B	80	$2.25	$8.00
					Logan, Johnny	55B	180	$2.00	$6.00
					Lohrke, Jack	48B	16	$7.00	$27.00
					Lohrke, Jack	49B	59	$3.75	$13.50
					Lohrke, Jack	51B	235	$4.50	$16.00
					Lohrke, Jack	52B	251	$4.00	$16.50
					Lohrke, Jack	53BW	47	$8.00	$25.00
					Lollar, Sherman	50B	142	$5.00	$15.00
					Lollar, Sherman	51B	100	$4.50	$16.00
					Lollar, Sherman	52B	237	$4.00	$16.50
					Lollar, Sherman	53BC	157	$12.50	$37.50
					Lollar, Sherman	54B	182	$2.25	$8.00
					Lollar, Sherman	55B	174	$2.00	$6.00
					Lombardi, Vic	51B	204	$4.50	$16.00
					Lopat, Ed	49B	229	$32.00	$110.00
					Lopat, Ed	50B	215	$6.75	$18.00
					Lopat, Ed	51B	218	$5.50	$20.00
Larsen, Don	54B	101	$7.50	$22.50	Lopat, Ed	52B	17	$5.50	$19.50
Larsen, Don	55B	67	$4.00	$13.50	Lopata, Stan	49B	177	$20.00	$70.00
Lary, Frank	55B	154	$2.00	$6.00	Lopata, Stan	50B	206	$3.75	$13.50
Law, Vernon	51B	203	$6.00	$19.50	Lopata, Stan	51B	76	$4.50	$16.00
Law, Vernon	52B	71	$3.75	$13.50	Lopata, Stan	54B	207	$2.00	$6.00
Law, Vernon	54B	187	$2.25	$8.00	Lopata, Stan	55B	18	$2.00	$6.00
Law, Vernon	55B	199	$2.00	$6.00	Lopez, Al	51B	295	$22.00	$75.00
Lawrence, Brooks	55B	75	$2.00	$6.00	Lopez, Al	53BC	143	$17.00	$55.00
Lehman, Ken	55B	310	$4.00	$13.50	Lopez, Al	55B	308	$12.50	$37.50
Lehner, Paul	49B	131	$3.25	$11.00	Lown, Omar	52B	16	$3.75	$13.50
Lehner, Paul	50B	158	$3.75	$13.50	Lown, Omar "Turk"	53BC	154	$12.50	$37.50
Lehner, Paul	51B	8	$4.50	$16.00	Lown, Turk	54B	157	$2.00	$6.00
Lemon, Bob	49B	238	$65.00	$225.00	Lowrey, Harry	49B	22	$4.00	$13.50
Lemon, Bob	50B	40	$22.00	$85.00	Lowrey, Harry	50B	172	$3.75	$13.50
Lemon, Bob	51B	53	$12.50	$42.50	Lowrey, Harry "Peanuts"	51B	194	$4.50	$16.00

Larsen, Don James Larsen

Player	Year	No.	VG	EX/MT	Player	Year	No.	VG	EX/MT
Lowrey, Peanuts	52B	102	$3.25	$11.00	McCoskey, Barney	48B	25	$3.00	$8.00
Luna, Memo	54B	222	$2.00	$6.00	McCosky, Barney	49B	203	$20.00	$70.00
Lund, Don	54B	87	$2.00	$6.00	McCosky, Barney	51B	84	$3.00	$8.00
Lupien, Ulysses	49B	141	$3.25	$11.00	McCullough, Clyde	49B	163	$20.00	$70.00
MacDonald, Bill	51B	239	$4.50	$16.00	McCullough, Clyde	50B	124	$3.75	$13.50
Maddern, Clarence	49B	152	$20.00	$70.00	McCullough, Clyde	51B	94	$3.00	$8.00
Maglie, Sal	51B	127	$7.50	$30.00	McCullough, Clyde	52B	99	$3.25	$11.00
Maglie, Sal	52B	66	$6.00	$17.50	McCullough, Clyde	55B	280	$4.00	$13.50
Maglie, Sal	53BC	96	$7.50	$30.00	McDermott, Maurice	50B	97	$3.75	$13.50
Maglie, Sal	54B	105	$2.25	$10.00	McDermott, Maurice	51B	16	$3.00	$8.00
Maglie, Sal	55B	95	$2.25	$8.00	McDermott, "Maury"	52B	25	$3.75	$13.50
Majeski, Hank	49B	127	$5.00	$20.00	McDermott, Maury	53BC	35	$8.50	$25.00
Majeski, Hank	50B	92	$3.75	$13.50	McDermott, Maury	54B	56	$3.75	$15.00
Majeski, Hank	51B	12	$4.50	$16.00	McDermott, Maury	55B	165	$2.00	$6.00
Majeski, Hank	52B	58	$3.25	$11.00	McDonald, Jim	55B	77	$2.00	$6.00
Majeski, Hank	55B	127	$2.00	$6.00	McDougald, Gil	52B	33	$15.00	$45.00
Malzone, Frank	55B	302	$3.75	$13.50	McDougald, Gil	53BC	63	$12.00	$37.50
Mantle, Mickey	51B	253	$1050.00	$4250.00	McDougald, Gil	54B	97	$3.25	$12.50
Mantle, Mickey	52B	101	$465.00	$1350.00	McDougald, Gil	55B	9	$3.25	$12.50
Mantle, Mickey	53BC	44	$100.00	$300.00	McKinley, W. F.	55B	226	$5.00	$20.00
Mantle, Mickey	53BC	59	$450.00	$1300.00	McMillan, Roy	52B	238	$4.00	$16.50
Mantle, Mickey	54B	65	$240.00	$650.00	McMillan, Roy	53BC	26	$8.50	$25.00
Mantle, Mickey	55B	202	$120.00	$360.00	McMillan, Roy	54B	12	$2.00	$6.00
Mapes, Cliff	50B	218	$3.75	$13.50	McQuinn, George	49B	232	$20.00	$70.00
Mapes, Cliff	51B	289	$13.50	$42.50	Mele, Sam	49B	118	$3.25	$11.00
Mapes, Cliff	52B	13	$3.75	$13.50	Mele, Sam	50B	52	$8.00	$35.00
Marchildon, Phil	49B	187	$20.00	$70.00	Mele, Sam	51B	168	$3.00	$8.00
Marion, Marty	48B	40	$8.50	$29.50	Mele, Sam	52B	15	$3.75	$13.50
Marion, Marty	49B	54	$3.50	$13.00	Mele, Sam	54B	22	$2.00	$6.00
Marion, Marty	50B	88	$5.00	$20.00	Mele, Sam	55B	147	$2.00	$6.00
Marion, Marty	51B	34	$4.00	$13.50	Merriman, Lloyd	50B	173	$3.75	$13.50
Marion, Marty	52B	85	$3.75	$13.50	Merriman, Lloyd	51B	72	$3.00	$8.00
Marion, Marty	53BC	52	$8.50	$25.00	Merriman, Lloyd	52B	78	$3.25	$11.00
Marlowe, Dick	55B	91	$2.00	$6.00	Merriman, Lloyd	55B	135	$2.00	$6.00
Marrero, Conrado	51B	206	$4.50	$16.00	Metkovich, George	51B	274	$9.50	$30.00
Marrero, Conrado	54B	200	$2.00	$6.00	Metkovich, George	52B	108	$3.25	$11.00
Marshall, Willard	48B	13	$7.50	$32.00	Meyer, Billy	51B	272	$13.50	$42.50
Marshall, Willard	49B	48	$3.75	$13.50	Meyer, Billy	52B	155	$3.25	$11.00
Marshall, Willard	50B	73	$3.75	$13.50	Meyer, Russ	51B	75	$3.00	$8.00
Marshall, Willard	51B	98	$4.50	$16.00	Meyer, Russ	52B	220	$6.50	$22.50
Marshall, Willard	52B	97	$3.25	$11.00	Meyer, Russ	53BC	129	$12.50	$37.50
Marshall, Willard	53BC	58	$8.50	$25.00	Meyer, Russ	54B	186	$2.00	$6.00
Marshall, Willard	54B	70	$2.00	$6.00	Meyer, Russ	55B	196	$2.00	$6.00
Marshall, Willard	55B	131	$2.00	$6.00	Michaels, Cass	49B	12	$4.00	$13.50
Martin, Babe	49B	167	$20.00	$70.00	Michaels, Cass	50B	91	$3.75	$13.50
Martin, Billy	53BC	93	$72.50	$190.00	Michaels, Cass	51B	132	$3.00	$8.00
Martin, Billy	53BC	118	$95.00	$250.00	Michaels, Cass	52B	36	$3.75	$13.50
Martin, Billy	54B	145	$12.50	$50.00	Michaels, Cass	53BC	130	$12.50	$37.50
Martin, Morris	53BW	53	$8.00	$25.00	Michaels, Cass	54B	150	$2.00	$6.00
Martin, Morris	54B	179	$2.00	$6.00	Michaels, Cass	55B	85	$2.00	$6.00
Masi, Phil	49B	153	$20.00	$70.00	Miggins, Larry	53BC	142	$12.50	$37.50
Masi, Phil	50B	128	$3.75	$13.50	Miksis, Eddie	51B	117	$3.00	$8.00
Masi, Phil	51B	160	$3.00	$8.00	Miksis, Eddie	52B	32	$3.75	$13.50
Masterson, Walt	49B	157	$20.00	$70.00	Miksis, Eddie	54B	61	$2.00	$6.00
Masterson, Walt	50B	153	$3.75	$13.50	Miksis, Eddie	55B	181	$2.00	$6.00
Masterson, Walt	51B	307	$13.50	$42.50	Miller, Bill	53BW	54	$8.00	$25.00
Masterson, Walt	52B	205	$3.25	$11.00	Miller, Bill	55B	245	$4.00	$13.50
Masterson, Walt	53BW	9	$8.00	$25.00	Miller, Bob	50B	227	$3.75	$13.50
Mathews, Eddie	53BC	97	$40.00	$130.00	Miller, Bob	51B	220	$3.00	$8.00
Mathews, Eddie	54B	64	$12.50	$40.00	Miller, Bob	55B	110	$2.00	$6.00
Mathews, Eddie	55B	103	$11.00	$35.00	Miller, Stu	53BW	16	$8.00	$25.00
Mauch, Gene	51B	312	$15.00	$60.00	Miller, Stu	54B	158	$2.00	$6.00
Maxwell, Charlie	55B	162	$2.00	$6.00	Minner, Paul	52B	211	$3.25	$11.00
Mayo, Eddie	49B	75	$4.00	$13.50	Minner, Paul	53BC	71	$8.50	$25.00
Mayo, Jackie	49B	228	$20.00	$70.00	Minner, Paul	54B	13	$2.00	$6.00
Mays, Willie	51B	305	$500.00	$1600.00	Minoso, Orestes	52B	5	$17.00	$55.00
Mays, Willie	52B	218	$200.00	$700.00	Minoso, Orestes "Minnie"	53BC	36	$9.50	$32.50
Mays, Willie	54B	89	$80.00	$250.00	Minoso, Minnie	54B	38	$3.75	$13.50
Mays, Willie	55B	184	$40.00	$160.00	Minoso, Minnie	55B	25	$2.50	$10.00
McBride, Tom	49B	74	$4.00	$13.50	Miranda, Willie	55B	79	$2.00	$6.00
McCahan, Bill	48B	31	$3.00	$8.00	Mitchell, Dale	49B	43	$5.00	$20.00
McCahan, Bill	49B	80	$4.00	$13.50	Mitchell, Dale	50B	130	$5.00	$20.00
McCarthy, Johnny	49B	220	$20.00	$70.00	Mitchell, Dale	51B	5	$4.00	$13.50
McCormick, Frank	49B	239	$18.00	$65.00	Mitchell, Dale	52B	239	$6.50	$22.50
McCormick, Mike	49B	146	$20.00	$70.00	Mitchell, Dale	53BC	119	$12.50	$37.50

Player	Year	No.	VG	EX/MT
Mitchell, Dale	54B	148	$2.00	$6.00
Mitchell, Dale	55B	314	$3.50	$12.00
Mize, Johnny	48B	4	$20.00	$65.00
Mize, Johnny	49B	85	$19.50	$60.00
Mize, Johnny	50B	139	$17.00	$50.00
Mize, Johnny	51B	50	$15.00	$45.00
Mize, Johnny	52B	145	$15.00	$45.00
Mize, Johnny	53BW	15	$30.00	$90.00
Mizell, Wilmer	53BW	22	$8.00	$25.00
Moore, Terry	49B	174	$20.00	$70.00
Morgan, Bobby	50B	222	$3.75	$13.50
Morgan, Bobby	53BC	135	$12.50	$37.50
Morgan, Bobby	55B	81	$2.00	$6.00
Morgan, Tom	52B	109	$3.25	$11.00
Morgan, Tom	55B	100	$2.00	$6.00
Moryn, Walt	55B	261	$4.00	$13.50
Moses, Wally	51B	261	$9.00	$25.00
Moses, Wally	53BC	95	$8.50	$25.00
Moses, Wally	55B	294	$4.00	$13.50
Moss, John "Lester"	50B	251	$3.75	$13.50
Moss, Les	51B	210	$3.00	$8.00
Moss, Les	54B	181	$2.00	$6.00
Mossi, Don	55B	259	$3.75	$13.50
Moulder, Glen	49B	159	$20.00	$70.00
Mrozinski, Ron	55B	287	$4.00	$13.50
Mueller, Don	50B	221	$3.75	$13.50
Mueller, Don	51B	268	$13.50	$42.50
Mueller, Don	52B	18	$3.75	$13.50
Mueller, Don	53BC	74	$8.50	$25.00
Mueller, Don	54B	73	$2.00	$6.00
Mueller, Ray	51B	313	$13.50	$42.50
Mullin, Pat	49B	56	$3.75	$13.50
Mullin, Pat	50B	135	$3.75	$13.50
Mullin, Pat	51B	106	$3.00	$8.00
Mullin, Pat	52B	183	$3.25	$11.00
Mullin, Pat	53BW	4	$8.00	$25.00
Mullin, Pat	54B	151	$2.00	$6.00
Muncrief, Bob	49B	221	$20.00	$70.00
Munger, George	49B	40	$3.75	$13.50
Munger, George	50B	89	$3.75	$13.50
Munger, George "Red"	51B	11	$3.00	$8.00
Munger, Red	52B	243	$6.50	$22.50
Murray, Ray	52B	118	$3.25	$11.00
Murray, Ray	53BW	6	$8.00	$25.00
Murray, Ray	54B	83	$2.00	$6.00
Murtaugh, Danny	49B	124	$5.00	$15.00
Murtaugh, Danny	50B	203	$5.00	$20.00
Murtaugh, Danny	51B	273	$10.00	$35.00
Musial, Stan	48B	36	$150.00	$600.00
Musial, Stan	49B	24	$125.00	$375.00
Musial, Stan	52B	196	$125.00	$375.00
Musial, Stan	53BC	32	$135.00	$395.00
Napp, Larry	55B	250	$5.00	$20.00
Naragon, Hal	55B	129	$2.00	$6.00
Narleski, Ray	55B	96	$2.00	$6.00
Neal, Charles	55B	278	$5.00	$20.00
Newcombe, Don	50B	23	$27.50	$85.00
Newcombe, Don	51B	6	$7.50	$30.00
Newcombe, Don	52B	128	$7.00	$22.50
Newcombe, Don	54B	154	$4.75	$17.50
Newcombe, Don	55B	143	$4.00	$16.00
Niarhos, Gus	49B	181	$20.00	$70.00
Niarhos, Gus	50B	154	$3.75	$13.50
Niarhos, Gus	51B	124	$3.00	$8.00
Niarhos, Gus	52B	129	$3.25	$11.00
Nichols, Chet	52B	120	$3.25	$11.00
Nichols, Chet	55B	72	$2.00	$6.00
Nicholson, Bill	49B	76	$4.00	$13.50
Nicholson, Bill	50B	228	$3.75	$13.50
Nicholson, Bill	51B	113	$3.00	$8.00
Nicholson, Bill	53BW	14	$8.00	$25.00
Nieman, Bob	55B	145	$2.00	$6.00
Nixon, Willard	51B	270	$13.50	$42.50
Nixon, Willard	53BW	2	$8.00	$35.00
Nixon, Willard	54B	114	$2.00	$6.00

Player	Year	No.	VG	EX/MT
Nixon, Willard	55B	177	$2.00	$6.00
Noble, Ray	51B	269	$13.50	$42.50
Noren, Irv	50B	247	$3.75	$13.50
Noren, Irv	51B	241	$4.50	$16.00
Noren, Irv	52B	63	$3.25	$11.00
Noren, Irv	53BW	45	$6.00	$24.50
Noren, Irv	55B	63	$2.25	$8.00
Northey, Ron	49B	79	$4.00	$13.50
Northey, Ron	50B	81	$3.75	$13.50
Northey, Ron	51B	70	$4.50	$16.00
Nuxhall, Joe	53BC	90	$6.00	$24.50
Nuxhall, Joe	54B	76	$2.25	$8.00
Nuxhall, Joe	55B	194	$2.25	$8.00
O'Connell, Danny	51B	93	$4.50	$16.00
O'Connell, Danny	54B	160	$2.00	$6.00
O'Connell, Danny	55B	44	$2.00	$6.00
O'Neill, Steve	51B	201	$4.50	$16.00
Ostermueller, Fritz	49B	227	$20.00	$70.00
Overmire, Frank	51B	280	$13.50	$42.50
Owen, Mickey	50B	78	$3.75	$13.50
Owen, Mickey	51B	174	$4.50	$16.00
Pafko, Andy	49B	63	$3.75	$13.50
Pafko, Andy	50B	60	$8.00	$35.00
Pafko, Andy	51B	103	$4.50	$16.00
Pafko, Andy	52B	204	$3.75	$13.50
Pafko, Andy	53BW	57	$5.50	$27.50

Player	Year	No.	VG	EX/MT
Pafko, Andy	54B	112	$2.00	$6.00
Pafko, Andy	55B	12	$2.00	$6.00
Page, Joe	48B	29	$12.00	$35.00
Page, Joe	49B	82	$6.00	$18.00
Page, Joe	50B	12	$12.50	$42.50
Page, Joe	51B	217	$4.50	$16.50
Paige, Satchell	49B	224	$340.00	$1050.00
Palica, Erv	51B	189	$4.50	$16.00
Palica, Erv	55B	195	$2.25	$8.00
Papai, Al	50B	245	$3.75	$13.50
Paparella, J. A.	55B	235	$5.00	$20.00
Parnell, Mel	50B	1	$20.00	$195.00
Parnell, Mel	52B	241	$6.50	$22.50
Parnell, Mel	53BC	66	$8.50	$25.00
Partee, Roy	49B	149	$20.00	$70.00

Player	Year	No.	VG	EX/MT	Player	Year	No.	VG	EX/MT
Peck, Hall	49B	182	$20.00	$70.00	Raschi, Vic	50B	100	$8.00	$25.00
Pellagrini, Eddie	49B	172	$20.00	$70.00	Raschi, Vic	51B	25	$5.50	$20.00
Pellagrini, Eddie	51B	292	$13.50	$42.50	Raschi, Vic	52B	37	$5.00	$18.00
Perkowski, Harry	52B	202	$3.25	$11.00	Raschi, Vic	53BC	27	$9.50	$30.00
Perkowski, Harry	53BC	87	$8.50	$25.00	Raschi, Vic	54B	33	$3.00	$12.50
Perkowski, Harry	54B	44	$2.00	$6.00	Raschi, Vic	55B	185	$2.25	$8.00
Pesky, Johnny	49B	86	$4.00	$13.50	Reese, Harold "Pee Wee"	49B	36	$50.00	$150.00
Pesky, Johnny	50B	137	$5.00	$20.00	Reese, Pee Wee	50B	21	$45.00	$140.00
Pesky, Johnny	51B	15	$4.00	$13.50	Reese, Pee Wee	51B	80	$32.00	$100.00
Pesky, Johnny	52B	45	$3.25	$11.00	Reese, Pee Wee	52B	8	$30.00	$90.00
Pesky, Johnny	53BC	134	$7.50	$25.00	Reese, Pee Wee	53BC	33	$75.00	$225.00
Pesky, Johnny	54B	135	$2.25	$8.00	Reese, Pee Wee	54B	58	$15.00	$50.00
Pesky, Johnny	55B	241	$4.00	$13.50	Reese, Pee Wee	55B	37	$16.00	$55.00
Peterson, Kent	51B	215	$4.50	$16.00	Regalado, Rudy	55B	142	$2.00	$6.00
Philley, Dave	49B	44	$3.75	$13.50	Reiser, Pete	48B	7	$7.00	$32.00
Philley, Dave	50B	127	$3.75	$13.50	Reiser, Pete	49B	185	$22.50	$85.00
Philley, Dave	51B	297	$13.50	$42.50	Reiser, Pete	50B	193	$5.00	$20.00
Philley, Dave	54B	163	$4.00	$13.50	Reiser, Pete	51B	238	$4.00	$13.50
Phillips, John M.	55B	228	$4.00	$13.50	Repulski, Rip	54B	46	$2.00	$6.00
Pierce, Billy	51B	196	$5.50	$20.00	Repulski, Rip	55B	205	$2.00	$6.00
Pierce, Billy	52B	54	$3.25	$11.00	Restelli, Dino	50B	123	$3.75	$13.50
Pierce, Billy	53BC	73	$8.50	$25.00	Reynolds, Allie	48B	14	$12.00	$40.00
Pierce, Billy	54B	102	$2.25	$8.00	Reynolds, Allie	49B	114	$6.00	$22.00
Pierce, Billy	55B	214	$2.00	$7.00	Reynolds, Allie	50B	138	$6.00	$22.00
Pieretti, Marino	49B	217	$20.00	$70.00	Reynolds, Allie	51B	109	$4.00	$16.00
Pieretti, Marino	50B	181	$3.75	$13.50	Reynolds, Allie	53BC	68	$9.50	$32.50
Piersall, Jim	51B	306	$20.00	$75.00	Reynolds, Allie	54B	113	$3.00	$11.00
Piersall, Jim	52B	189	$4.25	$15.00	Reynolds, Allie	55B	201	$3.00	$11.00
Piersall, Jim	53BW	36	$10.00	$40.00	Rice, Del	50B	125	$3.75	$13.50
Piersall, Jim	54B	66	$30.00	$95.00	Rice, Del	51B	156	$4.50	$16.00
Piersall, Jim	54B	210	$3.75	$13.50	Rice, Del	52B	107	$3.25	$11.00
Piersall, Jim	55B	16	$2.25	$8.00	Rice, Del	53BC	53	$8.50	$25.00
Pillette, Duane	51B	316	$13.50	$42.50	Rice, Del	54B	30	$2.00	$6.00
Pillette, Duane	53BW	59	$8.00	$25.00	Rice, Del	55B	106	$2.00	$6.00
Pillette, Duane	54B	133	$2.00	$6.00	Rice, Hal	51B	300	$13.50	$42.50
Pillette, Duane	55B	244	$4.00	$13.50	Rice, Hal	54B	219	$2.00	$6.00
Pinelli, R. A. "Babe"	55B	307	$5.00	$20.00	Rice, Hal	55B	52	$2.00	$6.00
Platt, Mizell	49B	89	$4.00	$13.50	Richards, Paul	51B	195	$3.50	$13.00
Poat, Ray	48B	42	$7.00	$22.50	Richards, Paul	52B	93	$3.75	$13.50
Podbielan, Clarence "Bud"	53BW	21	$8.00	$25.00	Richards, Paul	53BC	39	$8.50	$25.00
Podres, John	55B	97	$2.25	$8.00	Richards, Paul	55B	225	$3.75	$13.50
Poholsky, Tom	55B	76	$2.00	$6.00	Richmond, Don	51B	264	$13.50	$42.50
Pollet, Howie	49B	95	$4.00	$13.50	Ridzik, Steve	53BW	48	$8.00	$25.00
Pollet, Howie	50B	72	$8.00	$35.00	Ridzik, Steve	54B	223	$2.00	$6.00
Pollet, Howie	51B	263	$13.50	$42.50	Ridzik, Steve	55B	111	$2.00	$6.00
Pollet, Howie	52B	83	$3.25	$11.00	Rigney, Bill	48B	32	$4.50	$16.00
Pope, Dave	55B	198	$2.00	$6.00	Rigney, Bill	49B	170	$20.00	$70.00
Porterfield, Bob	49B	3	$4.00	$13.50	Rigney, Bill	50B	117	$3.75	$13.50
Porterfield, Bob	50B	216	$3.75	$13.50	Rigney, Bill	51B	125	$4.50	$16.00
Porterfield, Bob	52B	194	$3.25	$11.00	Rigney, Bill	53BW	3	$8.00	$35.00
Porterfield, Bob	53BC	22	$8.50	$25.00	Rizzuto, Phil	48B	8	$65.00	$200.00
Porterfield, Bob	54B	24	$2.00	$6.00	Rizzuto, Phil	49B	98	$20.00	$80.00
Porterfield, Bob	55B	104	$2.00	$6.00	Rizzuto, Phil	50B	11	$32.50	$115.00
Post, Wally	55B	32	$1.00	$4.50	Rizzuto, Phil	51B	26	$21.00	$75.00
Pramesa, Johnny	51B	324	$19.00	$95.00	Rizzuto, Phil	52B	52	$21.00	$75.00
Pramesa, Johnny	52B	247	$6.50	$22.50	Rizzuto, Phil	53BC	9	$23.00	$80.00
Presko, Joe	52B	62	$3.25	$11.00	Rizzuto, Phil	53BC	93	$72.50	$190.00
Presko, Joe	54B	190	$2.00	$6.00	Rizzuto, Phil	54B	1	$20.00	$125.00
Priddy, Jerry	49B	4	$4.00	$13.50	Rizzuto, Phil	55B	10	$15.00	$45.00
Priddy, Jerry (Gerry)	50B	212	$3.75	$13.50	Roberts, Robin	49B	46	$65.00	$190.00
Priddy, Jerry	51B	71	$4.50	$16.00	Roberts, Robin	50B	32	$30.00	$100.00
Priddy, Jerry	52B	139	$3.25	$11.00	Roberts, Robin	51B	3	$14.50	$50.00
Queen, Mel	51B	309	$13.50	$42.50	Roberts, Robin	52B	4	$12.50	$39.00
Queen, Mel	52B	171	$3.25	$11.00	Roberts, Robin	53BC	65	$14.50	$50.00
Quinn, Frank	51B	276	$13.50	$42.50	Roberts, Robin	54B	95	$8.50	$24.00
Raffensberger, Ken	49B	176	$20.00	$70.00	Roberts, Robin	55B	171	$7.00	$20.00
Raffensberger, Ken	51B	48	$4.50	$16.00	Robertson, Al	54B	211	$2.00	$6.00
Raffensberger, Ken	52B	55	$3.25	$11.00	Robertson, Jim	55B	5	$2.00	$6.00
Raffensberger, Ken	53BC	106	$8.50	$25.00	Robertson, Sherry	50B	161	$3.75	$13.50
Raffensberger, Ken	54B	92	$2.00	$6.00	Robertson, Sherry	51B	95	$4.50	$16.00
Ramazotti, Bob	51B	247	$4.50	$16.00	Robinson, Aaron	49B	133	$3.25	$11.00
Ramazotti, Bob	53BW	41	$8.00	$25.00	Robinson, Aaron	50B	95	$3.75	$13.50
Ramsdell, Willard	51B	251	$4.50	$16.00	Robinson, Aaron	51B	142	$4.50	$16.00
Ramsdell, Willard	52B	22	$3.75	$13.50	Robinson, Eddie	50B	18	$8.00	$35.00
Raschi, Vic	49B	35	$12.00	$35.00	Robinson, Eddie	51B	88	$4.50	$16.00

Player	Year	No.	VG	EX/MT	Player	Year	No.	VG	EX/MT
Robinson, Eddie	52B	77	$3.25	$11.00	Scheib, Carl	51B	83	$4.50	$16.00
Robinson, Eddie	53BW	20	$8.00	$25.00	Scheib, Carl	52B	46	$3.25	$11.00
Robinson, Eddie	54B	193	$2.25	$8.00	Scheib, Carl	53BC	150	$12.50	$37.50
Robinson, Eddie	55B	153	$2.00	$6.00	Scheib, Carl	54B	67	$2.00	$6.00
Robinson, Jackie	49B	50	$180.00	$555.00	Schmees, George	52B	245	$6.50	$22.50
Robinson, Jackie	50B	22	$150.00	$475.00	Schmitz, Johnny	49B	52	$3.75	$13.50
Rodriquez, Hector	53BC	98	$8.50	$25.00	Schmitz, Johnny	50B	24	$8.00	$35.00
Roe, Elwin "Preacher"	49B	162	$32.50	$110.00	Schmitz, Johnny	51B	69	$4.50	$16.00
Roe, Preacher	50B	167	$7.50	$25.00	Schmitz, Johnny	52B	224	$6.50	$22.50
Roe, Preacher	51B	118	$7.50	$24.00	Schmitz, Johnny	55B	105	$2.00	$6.00
Roe, Preacher	52B	168	$5.50	$19.00	Schoendienst, Al "Red"	48B	38	$25.00	$95.00
Roe, Preacher	53BW	26	$12.00	$45.00	Schoendienst, Red	49B	111	$17.50	$60.00
Roe, Preacher	54B	218	$3.25	$12.00	Schoendienst, Red	50B	71	$22.50	$70.00
Roe, Preacher	55B	216	$2.50	$9.00	Schoendienst, Red	51B	10	$17.50	$60.00
Rogovin, Saul	52B	165	$3.25	$11.00	Schoendienst, Red	52B	30	$13.50	$42.50
Rogovin, Saul	53BC	75	$8.50	$25.00	Schoendienst, Red	53BC	101	$17.50	$57.50
Rogovin, Saul	54B	140	$2.25	$8.00	Schoendienst, Red	54B	110	$9.50	$27.50
Rojek, Stan	49B	135	$3.25	$11.00	Schoendienst, Red	55B	29	$7.00	$22.50
Rojek, Stan	50B	86	$3.75	$13.50	Schroll, Albert B.	55B	319	$4.00	$13.50
Rojek, Stan	51B	166	$4.50	$16.00	Schultz, Bob	54B	59	$2.00	$6.00
Rojek, Stan	52B	137	$3.25	$11.00	Secory, Frank E.	55B	286	$5.00	$20.00
Rolfe, Red	51B	319	$10.00	$35.00	Seminick, Andy	49B	30	$4.00	$13.50
Rommel, Edwin A.	55B	239	$5.00	$20.00	Seminick, Andy	50B	121	$3.75	$13.50
Rosar, Buddy	48B	10	$4.50	$16.00	Seminick, Andy	51B	51	$4.50	$16.00
Rosar, Buddy "Warren"	49B	138	$3.00	$10.50	Seminick, Andy	53BW	7	$8.00	$25.00
Rosar, Warren	50B	136	$3.75	$13.50	Seminick, Andy	54B	172	$2.00	$6.00
Rosar, Warren	51B	236	$4.50	$16.00	Seminick, Andy	55B	93	$2.00	$6.00
Rosen, Al "Flip"	50B	232	$14.00	$42.50	Serena, Bill	50B	230	$3.75	$13.50
Rosen, Al "Flip"	51B	187	$7.50	$22.50	Serena, Bill	51B	246	$4.50	$16.00
Rosen, Al "Flip"	52B	151	$6.50	$19.50	Serena, Bill	53BC	122	$12.50	$37.50
Rosen, Al "Flip"	53BC	8	$12.50	$35.00	Serena, Bill	54B	93	$2.00	$6.00
Rotblatt, Marv	51B	303	$13.50	$42.50	Serena, Bill	55B	233	$4.00	$13.50
Rowe, Schoolboy	49B	216	$15.00	$65.00	Sewell, Luke	51B	322	$9.50	$30.00
Roy, Norman	51B	278	$13.50	$42.50	Sewell, Luke	52B	94	$3.25	$11.00
Runge, Ed	55B	277	$5.00	$20.00	Sewell, Rip	49B	234	$20.00	$70.00
Runnels, Pete	53BC	139	$12.50	$37.50	Shantz, Billy	55B	139	$2.25	$8.00
Runnels, Pete	55B	255	$3.75	$13.50	Shantz, Billy "Wilmer"	55B	175	$2.00	$6.00
Rush, Bob	50B	61	$8.00	$35.00	Shantz, Bobby	50B	234	$5.00	$15.00
Rush, Bob	51B	212	$4.50	$16.00	Shantz (Schantz), Bobby	51B	227	$3.50	$13.00
Rush, Bob	53BC	110	$8.50	$25.00	Shantz, Bobby	53BC	11	$3.75	$14.75
Rush, Bob	54B	77	$2.00	$6.00	Shantz, Bobby	54B	19	$2.25	$8.00
Rush, Bob	55B	182	$2.00	$6.00	Shantz, Bobby	55B	139	$2.25	$8.00
Russell, Jim	49B	235	$20.00	$70.00	Shantz, Bobby	55B	140	$2.25	$8.00
Russell, Jimmy	50B	223	$3.75	$13.50	Shea, Frank	48B	26	$9.00	$29.00
Ryan, Connie	51B	216	$4.50	$16.00	Shea, Frank	49B	49	$3.75	$13.50
Ryan, Connie	52B	164	$3.25	$11.00	Shea, Frank	50B	155	$2.75	$11.00
Ryan, Connie	53BC	131	$12.50	$37.50	Shea, Frank	52B	230	$6.50	$22.50
Saffell, Tom	51B	130	$4.50	$16.00	Shea, Frank	53BC	141	$12.50	$37.50
Sain, Johnny	48B	12	$12.50	$42.50	Shea, Frank	54B	104	$2.00	$6.00
Sain, Johnny	49B	47	$7.50	$22.50	Shea, Frank	55B	207	$2.00	$6.00
Sain, Johnny	51B	314	$15.00	$60.00	Shuba, George	53BC	145	$12.50	$37.50
Sain, Johnny	53BW	25	$14.00	$45.00	Shuba, George	54B	202	$2.25	$8.00
Salkeld, Bill	49B	88	$4.00	$13.50	Shuba, George	55B	66	$2.25	$8.00
Salkeld, Bill	50B	237	$3.75	$13.50	Sievers, Roy	50B	16	$10.00	$40.00
Sanford, Fred	49B	236	$20.00	$70.00	Sievers, Roy	51B	67	$4.00	$13.50
Sanford, Fred	50B	156	$2.75	$11.00	Silvera, Charlie	52B	197	$3.75	$13.50
Sanford, Fred	51B	145	$4.50	$16.00	Silvestri, Ken	51B	256	$13.50	$42.50
Sarni, Bill	55B	30	$2.00	$6.00	Silvestri, Ken	52B	200	$3.25	$11.00
Sauer, Hank	48B	45	$4.50	$15.00	Simmons, Curt	49B	14	$3.25	$11.00
Sauer, Hank	49B	5	$3.75	$13.50	Simmons, Curt	50B	68	$8.00	$35.00
Sauer, Hank	50B	25	$7.00	$32.00	Simmons, Curt	51B	111	$3.50	$13.00
Sauer, Hank	51B	22	$4.00	$13.50	Simmons, Curt	52B	184	$3.75	$13.50
Sauer, Hank	53BC	48	$8.50	$25.00	Simmons, Curt	53BC	64	$8.50	$25.00
Sauer, Hank	53BC	50	$8.50	$25.00	Simmons, Curt	54B	79	$2.25	$8.00
Savage, Bob	49B	204	$20.00	$70.00	Simmons, Curt	55B	64	$2.25	$8.00
Sawyer, Eddie	50B	225	$3.75	$13.50	Simpson, Harry	52B	223	$6.50	$22.50
Sawyer, Eddie	51B	184	$4.50	$16.00	Simpson, Harry	53BC	86	$8.50	$25.00
Scarborough, Ray	49B	140	$3.25	$11.00	Singleton, Bert	49B	147	$20.00	$70.00
Scarborough, Rae (Ray)	50B	108	$3.75	$13.50	Sisler, Dick	49B	205	$20.00	$70.00
Scarborough, Ray	51B	39	$4.50	$16.00	Sisler, Dick	50B	119	$3.75	$13.50
Scarborough, Ray	52B	140	$3.25	$11.00	Sisler, Dick	51B	52	$4.50	$16.00
Scheffing, Bob	49B	83	$4.00	$13.50	Sisler, Dick	52B	127	$3.25	$11.00
Scheffing, Bob	50B	168	$3.75	$13.50	Sisler, Dick	53BW	10	$8.00	$25.00
Scheib, Carl	49B	25	$4.00	$13.50	Sisti, Sibby	49B	201	$20.00	$70.00
Scheib, Carl	50B	213	$3.75	$13.50	Sisti, Sibby	50B	164	$3.75	$13.50

Player	Year	No.	VG	EX/MT	Player	Year	No.	VG	EX/MT
Sisti, Sibby	51B	170	$4.50	$16.00	Stewart, Eddie	50B	143	$3.75	$13.50
Sisti, Sibby	52B	100	$3.25	$11.00	Stewart, Eddie	51B	159	$4.50	$16.00
Skowron, Bill	55B	160	$1.00	$7.00	Stewart, Eddie	52B	185	$3.25	$11.00
Slaughter, Enos	48B	17	$22.50	$70.00	Stirnweiss, George	48B	35	$4.50	$16.00
Slaughter, Enos	49B	65	$17.50	$60.00	Stirnweiss, George "Snuffy"	49B	165	$20.00	$70.00
Slaughter, Enos	50B	35	$25.00	$85.00	Stirnweiss, George "Snuffy"	50B	249	$3.75	$13.50
Slaughter, Enos	51B	58	$12.50	$40.00	Stirnweiss, Snuffy	51B	21	$4.50	$16.00
Slaughter, Enos	52B	232	$17.50	$60.00	Strickland, George	52B	207	$3.25	$11.00
Slaughter, Enos	53BC	81	$18.50	$65.00	Strickland, George	54B	36	$2.00	$6.00
Slaughter, Enos	54B	62	$9.50	$27.50	Strickland, George	55B	192	$2.00	$6.00
Slaughter, Enos	55B	60	$6.50	$20.00	Stringer, Lou	49B	183	$20.00	$70.00
Smalley, Roy	50B	115	$3.75	$13.50	Stringer, Lou	50B	187	$3.75	$13.50
Smalley, Roy	51B	44	$4.50	$16.00	Stuart, Marlin	52B	147	$4.00	$18.00
Smalley, Roy	52B	64	$3.25	$11.00	Stuart, Marlin	53BC	120	$12.50	$37.50
Smalley, Roy	53BW	56	$8.00	$25.00	Suder, Pete	50B	140	$3.75	$13.50
Smalley, Roy	54B	109	$2.00	$6.00	Suder, Pete	51B	154	$4.50	$16.00
Smalley, Roy	55B	252	$4.00	$13.50	Suder, Pete	52B	179	$3.25	$11.00
Smith, Al	55B	20	$2.00	$6.00	Suder, Pete	53BW	8	$8.00	$25.00
Smith, Dick	55B	288	$4.00	$13.50	Suder, Pete	54B	99	$2.00	$6.00
Smith, Frank	52B	186	$3.25	$11.00	Suder, Pete	55B	6	$2.00	$6.00
Smith, Frank	54B	188	$2.00	$6.00	Sukeforth, Clyde	52B	227	$6.50	$22.50
Snider, Duke	49B	226	$275.00	$900.00	Sullivan, Frank	55B	15	$2.00	$6.00
Snider, Duke	50B	77	$70.00	$220.00	Summers, William R.	55B	317	$5.00	$20.00
Snider, Duke	51B	32	$60.00	$180.00	Surkont, Max	52B	12	$3.75	$13.50
Snider, Duke	52B	116	$45.00	$150.00	Surkont, Max	53BC	156	$12.50	$37.50
Snider, Duke	53BC	117	$135.00	$475.00	Surkont, Max	54B	75	$2.00	$6.00
Snider, Duke	54B	170	$30.00	$95.00	Surkont, Max	55B	83	$2.00	$6.00
Snyder, Jerry	52B	246	$6.50	$22.50	Susce, Jr., George	55B	320	$8.00	$35.00
Snyder, Jerry	54B	216	$2.00	$6.00	Swift, Bob	49B	148	$20.00	$70.00
Snyder, Jerry	55B	74	$2.00	$6.00	Swift, Bob	50B	149	$3.75	$13.50
Soar, Hank	55B	279	$5.00	$20.00	Swift, Bob	51B	214	$4.50	$16.00
Souchock, Steve	52B	235	$6.50	$22.50					
Souchock, Steve	53BC	91	$8.50	$25.00					
Souchock, Steve	54B	103	$2.00	$6.00					
Southworth, Billy	51B	207	$4.50	$16.00					
Spahn, Warren	48B	18	$70.00	$205.00					
Spahn, Warren	49B	33	$33.00	$115.00					
Spahn, Warren	50B	19	$35.00	$130.00					
Spahn, Warren	51B	134	$22.00	$85.00					
Spahn, Warren	52B	156	$20.00	$75.00					
Spahn, Warren	53BC	99	$35.00	$115.00					
Spence, Stan	49B	102	$4.00	$13.50					
Spencer, Daryl	54B	185	$2.00	$6.00					
St. Claire, Ebba	52B	172	$3.25	$11.00					
St. Claire, Ebba	53BW	34	$8.00	$25.00					
St. Claire, Ebba	54B	128	$2.00	$6.00					
Staley, Gerry	51B	121	$4.50	$16.00					
Staley, Gerry	52B	50	$3.25	$11.00					
Staley, Gerry	53BC	17	$8.50	$25.00					
Staley, Gerry	54B	14	$2.00	$6.00					
Staley, Gerry	55B	155	$2.00	$6.00					
Stallcup, Virgil	49B	81	$4.00	$13.50					
Stallcup, Virgil "Red"	50B	116	$3.75	$13.50					
Stallcup, Virgil	51B	108	$4.50	$16.00					
Stallcup, Virgil "Red"	52B	6	$3.75	$13.50					
Stanky, Ed	49B	104	$5.00	$15.00					
Stanky, Eddie	50B	29	$6.00	$24.50					
Stanky, Ed	51B	13	$4.00	$13.50					
Stanky, Eddie	52B	160	$3.75	$13.50					
Stanky, Eddie	53BC	49	$8.50	$25.00					
Stanky, Eddie	55B	238	$4.00	$13.50					
Starr, Dick	50B	191	$3.75	$13.50					
Starr, Dick	51B	137	$4.50	$16.00					
Stengel, Casey	50B	217	$25.00	$100.00					
Stengel, Casey	51B	181	$22.00	$80.00					
Stengel, Casey	52B	217	$30.00	$120.00	Swift, Bob	52B	131	$3.25	$11.00
Stengel, Casey	53BW	39	$80.00	$240.00	Talbot, Bob	55B	137	$2.00	$6.00
Stephens, Vern	49B	71	$3.75	$13.50	Tappe, Elvin	55B	51	$2.00	$6.00
Stephens, Vern	50B	2	$8.00	$35.00	Taylor, Zack	51B	315	$13.50	$42.50
Stephens, Vern	51B	92	$4.50	$16.00	Tebbetts, Birdie	51B	257	$13.50	$42.50
Stephens, Vern	52B	9	$3.75	$13.50	Tebbetts, George "Birdie"	52B	124	$3.25	$11.00
Stephens, Vern	55B	109	$2.00	$6.00	Tebbetts, Birdie	55B	232	$4.00	$13.50
Stevens, Ed	49B	93	$4.00	$13.50	Temple, Johnny	55B	31	$1.00	$4.50
Stevens, John W.	55B	258	$5.00	$20.00	Terwilliger, Wayne	50B	114	$3.75	$13.50
Stewart, Eddie	49B	173	$20.00	$70.00					

Player	Year	No.	VG	EX/MT	Player	Year	No.	VG	EX/MT
Terwilliger, Wayne	51B	175	$4.50	$16.00	Wakefield, Dick	49B	91	$4.00	$13.50
Thomas, Frank	54B	155	$2.25	$8.00	Walker, Harry	49B	130	$3.25	$11.00
Thomas, Frank	55B	58	$2.00	$6.00	Walker, Harry	50B	180	$5.00	$20.00
Thomas, Keith	53BW	62	$8.00	$25.00	Walls, Lee	55B	82	$2.00	$6.00
Thompson, Henry	50B	174	$3.75	$13.50	Ward, Preston	50B	231	$3.75	$13.50
Thompson, Henry	51B	89	$4.50	$16.00	Ward, Preston	54B	139	$2.25	$8.00
Thompson, Henry	52B	249	$6.50	$22.50	Ward, Preston	55B	27	$2.00	$6.00
Thompson, Henry	54B	217	$2.25	$8.00	Warneke, Lonnie	55B	299	$5.00	$20.00
Thompson, Henry "Hank"	55B	94	$2.25	$8.00	Wehmeier, Herman	48B	46	$7.00	$22.50
Thompson, Jocko	49B	161	$20.00	$70.00	Wehmeier, Herman	49B	51	$3.75	$13.50
Thompson, John	50B	120	$3.75	$13.50	Wehmeier, Herman	50B	27	$8.00	$35.00
Thompson, John "Jocko"	51B	294	$10.00	$35.00	Wehmeier, Herman	51B	144	$4.50	$16.00
Thomson, Bobby	48B	47	$17.00	$50.00	Wehmeier, Herman	52B	150	$3.25	$11.00
Thomson, Bobby	49B	18	$5.00	$20.00	Wehmeier, Herman	53BC	23	$8.50	$25.00
Thomson, Bobby	50B	28	$14.50	$42.50	Werle, Bill	50B	87	$3.75	$13.50
Thomson, Bobby	51B	126	$6.50	$20.00	Werle, Bill	51B	64	$4.50	$16.00
Thomson, Bobby	52B	2	$6.50	$20.00	Werle, Bill	52B	248	$6.50	$22.50
Thomson, Bobby	54B	201	$3.00	$12.00	Wertz, Vic	49B	164	$20.00	$70.00
Thomson, Bobby	55B	102	$2.25	$9.00	Wertz, Vic	50B	9	$8.00	$35.00
Tipton, Joe	49B	103	$4.00	$13.50	Wertz, Vic	51B	176	$4.00	$13.50
Tipton, Joe	50B	159	$3.75	$13.50	Wertz, Vic	52B	39	$3.25	$11.00
Tipton, Joe	51B	82	$4.50	$16.00	Wertz, Vic	53BC	2	$4.50	$17.25
Tipton, Joe	53BW	13	$8.00	$25.00	Wertz, Vic	54B	21	$2.25	$8.00
Tipton, Joe	54B	180	$2.00	$6.00	Wertz, Vic	55B	40	$1.00	$4.50
Torgeson, Earl	49B	17	$4.00	$13.50	Westlake, Wally	49B	45	$3.75	$13.50
Torgeson, Earl	50B	163	$3.75	$13.50	Westlake, Wally	50B	69	$8.00	$35.00
Torgeson, Earl	51B	99	$4.50	$16.00	Westrum, Wes	51B	161	$4.50	$16.00
Torgeson, Earl	52B	72	$3.25	$11.00	Westrum, Wes	52B	74	$3.25	$11.00
Torgeson, Earl	54B	63	$2.00	$6.00	Westrum, Wes	54B	25	$2.00	$6.00
Torgeson, Earl	55B	210	$2.00	$6.00	Westrum, Wes	55B	141	$2.00	$6.00
Tresh, Mike	49B	166	$20.00	$70.00	White, Hal	51B	320	$13.50	$42.50
Trinkle, Ken	49B	193	$20.00	$70.00	White, Sammy	53BC	41	$8.50	$25.00
Trout, Dizzy	49B	208	$19.00	$85.00	White, Sammy	54B	34	$2.25	$8.00
Trout, Paul "Dizzy"	50B	134	$5.00	$20.00	White, Sammy	55B	47	$2.00	$6.00
Trucks, Virgil	49B	219	$20.00	$70.00	Whitman, Dick	51B	221	$4.50	$16.00
Trucks, Virgil	50B	96	$3.75	$13.50	Widmar, Al	51B	281	$13.50	$42.50
Trucks, Virgil	51B	104	$4.50	$16.00	Wight, Bill	50B	38	$8.00	$35.00
Trucks, Virgil	53BW	17	$8.00	$35.00	Wight, Bill	51B	164	$4.50	$16.00
Trucks, Virgil	54B	198	$2.25	$8.00	Wight, Bill	52B	117	$3.25	$11.00
Trucks, Virgil	55B	26	$2.25	$8.00	Wight, Bill	53BC	100	$8.50	$25.00
Tucker, Thurman	51B	222	$4.50	$16.00	Wight, Bill	55B	312	$4.00	$13.50
Tuttle, Bill	55B	35	$2.00	$6.00	Wilber, Del	52B	225	$6.50	$22.50
Umont, Frank	55B	305	$5.00	$20.00	Wilber, Del	53BW	24	$8.00	$25.00
Umphlett, Tom	54B	88	$2.00	$6.00	Wilber, Del	54B	178	$2.00	$6.00
Umphlett, Tom	55B	45	$2.00	$6.00	Wilhelm, Hoyt	53BW	28	$28.00	$85.00
Usher, Bob	51B	286	$13.50	$42.50	Wilhelm, Hoyt	54B	57	$7.50	$22.00
Valo, Elmer	49B	66	$3.75	$13.50	Wilhelm, Hoyt	55B	1	$14.00	$90.00
Valo, Elmer	50B	49	$8.00	$35.00	Wilks, Ted	49B	137	$3.25	$11.00
Valo, Elmer	52B	206	$3.25	$11.00	Wilks, Ted	51B	193	$4.50	$16.00
VanderMeer, Johnny	49B	128	$5.50	$17.50	Wilks, Ted	52B	138	$3.25	$11.00
VanderMeer, Johnny	50B	79	$5.50	$17.50	Williams, Davey	52B	178	$3.25	$11.00
VanderMeer, Johnny	51B	223	$5.00	$15.00	Williams, Davey	53BC	1	$15.00	$85.00
Verban, Emil	48B	28	$6.50	$27.00	Williams, Davey	54B	9	$2.00	$6.00
Verban, Emil	49B	38	$3.75	$13.50	Williams, Davey	55B	138	$2.00	$6.00
Vernon, Mickey	49B	94	$8.50	$25.00	Williams, Ted	50B	98	$180.00	$550.00
Vernon, Mickey	50B	132	$5.00	$20.00	Williams, Ted	51B	165	$160.00	$480.00
Vernon, Mickey	51B	65	$4.00	$13.50	Williams, Ted	54B	66	$800.00	$2400.00
Vernon, Mickey	52B	87	$3.75	$13.50	Wilson, Archie	52B	210	$3.25	$11.00
Vernon, Mickey	53BC	159	$7.75	$25.00	Wilson, Jim	53BC	37	$8.50	$25.00
Vernon, Mickey	54B	152	$2.25	$8.00	Wilson, Jim	54B	16	$2.00	$6.00
Vernon, Mickey "James"	55B	46	$1.00	$4.50	Wilson, Jim	55B	253	$4.00	$13.50
Vico, George	49B	122	$3.25	$11.00	Wood, Ken	50B	190	$3.75	$13.50
Vico, George	50B	150	$3.75	$13.50	Wood, Ken	51B	209	$4.50	$16.00
Virdon, Bill	55B	296	$6.00	$24.50	Wood, Ken	53BC	109	$8.50	$25.00
Vollmer, Clyde	50B	53	$8.00	$35.00	Woodling, Gene	51B	219	$7.00	$22.00
Vollmer, Clyde	51B	91	$4.50	$16.00	Woodling, Gene	52B	177	$5.50	$17.50
Vollmer, Clyde	52B	57	$3.25	$11.00	Woodling, Gene	53BW	31	$9.00	$36.00
Vollmer, Clyde	53BC	152	$12.50	$37.50	Woodling, Gene	54B	209	$2.25	$8.00
Vollmer, Clyde	54B	136	$2.00	$6.00	Wooten, Earl	49B	189	$20.00	$70.00
Vollmer, Clyde	55B	13	$2.00	$6.00	Wright, Taft	49B	96	$4.00	$13.50
Waitkus, Eddie	49B	142	$3.25	$11.00	Wright, Tommy	51B	271	$13.50	$42.50
Waitkus, Eddie	50B	30	$8.00	$35.00	Wynn, Early	49B	110	$30.00	$100.00
Waitkus, Eddie	51B	28	$4.50	$16.00	Wynn, Early	50B	148	$12.00	$42.00
Waitkus, Eddie	52B	92	$3.25	$11.00	Wynn, Early	51B	78	$11.00	$37.50
Waitkus, Eddie	55B	4	$2.00	$6.00	Wynn, Early	52B	142	$7.50	$30.00

Player	Year	No.	VG	EX/MT	Player	Year	No.	VG	EX/MT
Wynn, Early	53BC	146	$30.00	$95.00	Young, Babe	49B	240	$27.00	$100.00
Wynn, Early	54B	164	$8.00	$25.00	Young, Bobby	52B	193	$3.25	$11.00
Wynn, Early	55B	38	$6.50	$20.00	Young, Bobby	54B	149	$2.00	$6.00
Wyrostek, Johnny	48B	44	$7.00	$22.50	Yvars, Sal	54B	78	$2.00	$6.00
Wyrostek, Johnny	49B	37	$3.75	$13.50	Zarilla, Al	49B	156	$20.00	$70.00
Wyrostek, Johnny	50B	197	$3.75	$13.50	Zarilla, Al	50B	45	$8.00	$35.00
Wyrostek, Johnny	51B	107	$4.50	$16.00	Zarilla, Al	51B	35	$4.50	$16.00
Wyrostek, Johnny	52B	42	$3.25	$11.00	Zarilla, Al	52B	113	$3.25	$11.00
Wyrostek, Johnny	53BW	35	$8.00	$25.00	Zernial, Gus	50B	4	$10.00	$40.00
Wyrostek, Johnny	55B	237	$4.00	$13.50	Zernial, Gus	51B	262	$9.00	$35.00
Wyse, Hank	51B	192	$4.50	$16.00	Zernial, Gus	52B	82	$3.25	$11.00
Yost, Eddie	49B	32	$4.00	$13.50	Zernial, Gus	53BC	13	$8.50	$25.00
Yost, Eddie	50B	162	$5.00	$20.00	Zimmer, Don	55B	65	$5.00	$20.00
Yost, Eddie	51B	41	$4.50	$16.00	Zoldak, Sam	49B	78	$4.00	$13.50
Yost, Eddie	52B	31	$3.75	$13.50	Zoldak, Sam	50B	182	$3.75	$13.50
Yost, Eddie	53BC	116	$9.00	$36.00	Zoldak, Sam	51B	114	$4.50	$16.00
Yost, Eddie	54B	72	$2.00	$6.00	Zuverink, George	55B	92	$2.00	$6.00
Yost, Eddie	55B	73	$2.00	$6.00					

1989 & 1990 BOWMAN

TWINS RICK AGUILERA

Player	Year	No.	VG	EX/MT	Player	Year	No.	VG	EX/MT
Abbott, Jim	89B	39	$ .01	$ .75	Andersen, Larry	90B	67	$ .01	$ .05
Abbott, Jim	90B	288	$ .01	$ .15	Anderson, Allan	89B	149	$ .01	$ .05
Abbott, Kyle	90B	287	$ .01	$ .10	Anderson, Allan	90B	409	$ .01	$ .05
Agosto, Juan	89B	321	$ .01	$ .05	Anderson, Brady	89B	18	$ .01	$ .15
Aguayo, Luis	89B	88	$ .01	$ .05	Anderson, Brady	90B	258	$ .01	$ .05
					Ansley, Willie	89B	332	$ .05	$ .25
					Anthony, Eric	90B	81	$ .01	$ .25
					Appier, Kevin	90B	367	$ .01	$ .20
					Ard, Johnny	89B	153	$ .01	$ .05
					Ard, Johnny	90B	406	$ .01	$ .05
					Armas, Tony	89B	51	$ .01	$ .05
					Ashby, Alan	89B	327	$ .01	$ .05
					Assenmacher, Paul	89B	265	$ .01	$ .05
					August, Don	89B	130	$ .01	$ .05
					Avery, Steve	89B	268	$ .01	$ .60
					Avery, Steve	90B	9	$ .01	$ .25
					Backman, Wally	89B	159	$ .01	$ .05
					Backman, Wally	90B	177	$ .01	$ .05
					Baerga, Carlos	90B	339	$ .01	$ .20
					Baines, Harold	89B	72	$ .01	$ .10
					Baines, Harold	90B	501	$ .01	$ .05
					Balboni, Steve	90B	436	$ .01	$ .05
					Ballard, Jeff	89B	7	$ .01	$ .05
					Ballard, Jeff	90B	244	$ .01	$ .05
					Bankhead, Scott	89B	203	$ .01	$ .05
					Bankhead, Scott	90B	466	$ .01	$ .05
					Banks, Willie	90B	411	$ .01	$ .10
					Bannister, Floyd	89B	112	$ .01	$ .05
					Barfield, Jesse	89B	257	$ .01	$ .15
					Barfield, Jesse	90B	433	$ .01	$ .05
					Barrett, Marty	89B	28	$ .01	$ .05
					Barrett, Marty	90B	282	$ .01	$ .05
					Bass, Kevin	90B	240	$ .01	$ .05
					Bathe, Bill	90B	234	$ .01	$ .05
Aguilera, Rick	90B	405	$ .01	$ .05	Bautista, Jose	89B	3	$ .01	$ .05
Aldred, Scott	90B	344	$ .01	$ .10	Bearse, Kevin	90B	330	$ .01	$ .10
Aldrete, Mike	89B	368	$ .01	$ .05	Beatty, Blaine	90B	130	$ .01	$ .10
Alexander, Doyle	89B	94	$ .01	$ .05	Bedrosian, Steve	89B	395	$ .01	$ .10
Allanson, Andy	89B	83	$ .01	$ .05	Bedrosian, Steve	90B	226	$ .01	$ .05
Alomar, Roberto	89B	458	$ .01	$ .40	Belcher, Tim	89B	336	$ .01	$ .10
Alomar, Roberto	90B	221	$ .01	$ .15	Belcher, Tim	90B	85	$ .01	$ .05
Alomar, Sandy	89B	258	$ .01	$ .05	Bell, Buddy	89B	229	$ .01	$ .10
Alomar, Jr., Sandy	89B	454	$ .01	$ .90	Bell, George	89B	256	$ .01	$ .15
Alomar, Sandy	90B	337	$ .01	$ .25	Bell, George	90B	515	$ .01	$ .05
Alou, Moises	90B	178	$ .01	$ .25	Bell, Jay	90B	174	$ .01	$ .05
Andersen, Larry	89B	325	$ .01	$ .05	Bell, Juan	89B	11	$ .01	$ .15

Player	Year	No.	VG	EX/MT	Player	Year	No.	VG	EX/MT
Belle, Joey	90B	333	$ .01	$ .35	Browning, Tom	90B	43	$ .01	$ .10
Bene, Bill	89B	340	$ .01	$ .05	Brunansky, Tom	89B	444	$ .01	$ .05
Benedict, Bruce	89B	271	$ .01	$ .05	Brunansky, Tom	90B	202	$ .01	$ .05
Benes, Andy	89B	448	$ .01	$ .30	Bryant, Scott	90B	59	$ .01	$ .05
Benes, Andy	90B	207	$ .01	$ .15	Buechele, Steve	89B	232	$ .01	$ .05
Benzinger, Todd	89B	312	$ .01	$ .05	Buechele, Steve	90B	493	$ .01	$ .05
Benzinger, Todd	90B	55	$ .01	$ .05	Buhner, Jay	89B	219	$ .01	$ .10
Berenguer, Juan	89B	152	$ .01	$ .05	Buhner, Jay	90B	477	$ .01	$ .05
Berenguer, Juan	90B	410	$ .01	$ .05	Burke, Tim	89B	360	$ .01	$ .05
Bergman, Dave	90B	355	$ .01	$ .05	Burke, Tim	90B	103	$ .01	$ .05
Berroa, Geronimo	89B	279	$ .01	$ .05	Burks, Ellis	89B	36	$ .01	$ .25
Berryhill, Damon	89B	288	$ .01	$ .10	Burks, Ellis	90B	280	$ .01	$ .10
Berryhill, Damon	90B	33	$ .01	$ .05	Bush, Randy	89B	164	$ .01	$ .05
Bielecki, Mike	90B	22	$ .01	$ .05	Bush, Randy	90B	416	$ .01	$ .05
Biggio, Craig	90B	78	$ .01	$ .10	Butler, Brett	89B	480	$ .01	$ .05
Birkbeck, Mike	89B	132	$ .01	$ .05	Butler, Brett	90B	237	$ .01	$ .05
Bittiger, Jeff	89B	60	$ .01	$ .05	Calderon, Ivan	89B	68	$ .01	$ .05
Black, Bud	89B	82	$ .01	$ .05	Calderon, Ivan	90B	316	$ .01	$ .05
Blair, Willie	90B	504	$ .01	$ .05	Camacho, Ernie	90B	229	$ .01	$ .05
Blankenship, Kevin	90B	24	$ .01	$ .05	Caminiti, Ken	90B	73	$ .01	$ .05
Blauser, Jeff	90B	15	$ .01	$ .05	Canale, George	90B	392	$ .01	$ .10
Blosser, Greg	90B	278	$ .01	$ .15	Candelaria, John	89B	171	$ .01	$ .05
Blowers, Mike	90B	441	$ .01	$ .10	Candiotti, Tom	89B	80	$ .01	$ .05
Blyleven, Bert	89B	41	$ .01	$ .15	Candiotti, Tom	90B	324	$ .01	$ .05
Blyleven, Bert	90B	285	$ .01	$ .05	Cano, Jose	90B	68	$ .01	$ .05
Bockus, Randy	89B	96	$ .01	$ .05	Canseco, Jose	89B	201	$ .01	$ .50
Boddicker, Mike	89B	21	$ .01	$ .05	Canseco, Jose	90B	460	$ .01	$ .35
Boddicker, Mike	90B	267	$ .01	$ .05	Carman, Don	89B	392	$ .01	$ .05
Boggs, Wade	89B	32	$ .01	$ .25	Carreon, Mark	89B	389	$ .01	$ .05
Boggs, Wade	90B	281	$ .01	$ .20	Carter, Gary	89B	379	$ .01	$ .05
Bohanon, Brian	90B	489	$ .01	$ .10	Carter, Gary	90B	236	$ .01	$ .10
Bonds, Barry	89B	426	$ .01	$ .20	Carter, Joe	89B	91	$ .01	$ .10
Bonds, Barry	90B	181	$ .01	$ .20	Carter, Joe	90B	220	$ .01	$ .05
Bonilla, Bobby	89B	422	$ .01	$ .15	Carter, Steve	90B	179	$ .01	$ .10
Bonilla, Bobby	90B	169	$ .01	$ .15	Castillo, Joe	89B	244	$ .01	$ .05
Boone, Bob	89B	119	$ .01	$ .05	Cedeno, Andujar	90B	77	$ .01	$ .35
Boone, Bob	90B	373	$ .01	$ .05	Cerone, Rick	90B	435	$ .01	$ .05
Borders, Pat	90B	521	$ .01	$ .05	Cerutti, John	89B	247	$ .01	$ .05
Bosio, Chris	89B	134	$ .01	$ .05	Cerutti, John	90B	507	$ .01	$ .05
Bosio, Chris	90B	389	$ .01	$ .05	Checklist, 1 - 121	89B	481	$ .01	$ .05
Boston, Daryl	89B	70	$ .01	$ .05	Checklist, 1 - 132	90B	525	$ .01	$ .05
Boston, Daryl	90B	317	$ .01	$ .05	Checklist, 122 - 242	89B	482	$ .01	$ .05
Boyd, Dennis	90B	102	$ .01	$ .05	Checklist, 133 - 264	90B	526	$ .01	$ .05
Bradley, Phil	89B	17	$ .01	$ .05	Checklist, 243 - 363	89B	483	$ .01	$ .05
Bradley, Phil	90B	261	$ .01	$ .05	Checklist, 265 - 396	90B	527	$ .01	$ .05
Bradley, Scott	89B	209	$ .01	$ .05	Checklist, 364 - 484	89B	484	$ .01	$ .05
Bradley, Scott	90B	483	$ .01	$ .05	Checklist, 397 - 528	90B	528	$ .01	$ .05
Braggs, Glenn	89B	145	$ .01	$ .05	Clancy, Jim	89B	324	$ .01	$ .05
Braggs, Glenn	90B	403	$ .01	$ .05	Clark, Jack	89B	456	$ .01	$ .05
Branson, Jeff	90B	52	$ .01	$ .05	Clark, Jack	90B	214	$ .01	$ .05
Bream, Sid	89B	419	$ .01	$ .05	Clark, Jerald	89B	462	$ .01	$ .25
Bream, Sid	90B	175	$ .01	$ .05	Clark, Will	89B	476	$ .01	$ .50
Brenly, Bob	89B	249	$ .01	$ .05	Clark, Will	90B	231	$ .01	$ .35
Brett, George	89B	121	$ .01	$ .20	Clayton, Royce	89B	472	$ .01	$ .05
Brett, George	90B	382	$ .01	$ .10	Clemens, Roger	89B	26	$ .01	$ .30
Briley, Greg	90B	482	$ .01	$ .10	Clemens, Roger	90B	268	$ .01	$ .25
Brock, Greg	89B	143	$ .01	$ .05	Clements, Pat	89B	452	$ .01	$ .05
Brock, Greg	90B	395	$ .01	$ .05	Coffman, Kevin	89B	282	$ .01	$ .05
Brogna, Ricco	89B	102	$ .01	$ .35	Coleman, Paul	90B	199	$ .01	$ .20
Brogna, Ricco	90B	351	$ .01	$ .10	Coleman, Vince	89B	443	$ .01	$ .15
Brooks, Hubie	89B	367	$ .01	$ .05	Coleman, Vince	90B	198	$ .01	$ .05
Brooks, Hubie	90B	100	$ .01	$ .05	Coles, Darnell	89B	217	$ .01	$ .05
Bross, Terry	90B	129	$ .01	$ .10	Coles, Darnell	90B	480	$ .01	$ .05
Brower, Bob	89B	182	$ .01	$ .05	Combs, Pat	89B	398	$ .01	$ .25
Brown, Chris	89B	106	$ .01	$ .05	Combs, Pat	90B	148	$ .01	$ .05
Brown, Kevin	90B	127	$ .01	$ .20	Comstock, Keith	90B	467	$ .01	$ .05
Brown, Kevin	90B	488	$ .01	$ .10	Cone, David	89B	375	$ .01	$ .15
Browne, Jerry	89B	85	$ .01	$ .05	Cone, David	90B	125	$ .01	$ .05
Browne, Jerry	90B	332	$ .01	$ .05	Coolbaugh, Scott	90B	494	$ .01	$ .10
Browning, Tom	89B	306	$ .01	$ .15	Cooper, Scott	90B	277	$ .01	$ .15

Player	Year	No.	VG	EX/MT	Player	Year	No.	VG	EX/MT
Cora, Joey	90B	211	$ .01	$ .05	DiPino, Frank	89B	434	$ .01	$ .05
Cotto, Henry	90B	476	$ .01	$ .05	DiPino, Frank	90B	187	$ .01	$ .05
Crim, Chuck	89B	136	$ .01	$ .05	DiSarcina, Gary	90B	290	$ .01	$ .10
Cunningham, Earl	90B	34	$ .01	$ .10	Dopson, John	89B	24	$ .01	$ .05
Cuyler, Milt	90B	358	$ .01	$ .15	Doran, Bill	89B	329	$ .01	$ .05
Daniels, Kal	89B	314	$ .01	$ .15	Doran, Bill	90B	76	$ .01	$ .05
Daniels, Kal	90B	99	$ .01	$ .05	Downing, Brian	89B	53	$ .01	$ .05
Darling, Ron	89B	372	$ .01	$ .15	Downing, Brian	90B	294	$ .01	$ .05
Darwin, Danny	90B	66	$ .01	$ .05	Downs, Kelly	89B	465	$ .01	$ .05
Daugherty, Jack	90B	503	$ .01	$ .05	Drabek, Doug	89B	416	$ .01	$ .05
Daulton, Darren	90B	158	$ .01	$ .05	Drabek, Doug	90B	164	$ .01	$ .05
Davis, Alvin	89B	215	$ .01	$ .05	Drew, Cameron	89B	334	$ .01	$ .05
Davis, Alvin	90B	479	$ .01	$ .05	DuBois, Brian	90B	349	$ .01	$ .10
Davis, Chili	89B	50	$ .01	$ .05	Dunston, Shawon	89B	294	$ .01	$ .15
Davis, Chili	90B	301	$ .01	$ .05	Dunston, Shawon	90B	38	$ .01	$ .05
Davis, Eric	89B	316	$ .01	$ .25	DuVall, Brad	89B	430	$ .01	$ .05
Davis, Eric	90B	58	$ .01	$ .20	Dykstra, Len	90B	152	$ .01	$ .05
Davis, Glenn	89B	331	$ .01	$ .15	Eave, Gary	90B	471	$ .01	$ .10
Davis, Glenn	90B	80	$ .01	$ .10	Eckersley, Dennis	89B	190	$ .01	$ .05
Davis, Jody	89B	270	$ .01	$ .05	Eckersley, Dennis	90B	451	$ .01	$ .05
Davis, Mark	89B	447	$ .01	$ .05	Edwards, Wayne	90B	309	$ .01	$ .10
Davis, Mark	90B	369	$ .01	$ .05	Eisenreich, Jim	90B	374	$ .01	$ .05
Davis, Mike	89B	352	$ .01	$ .05	Eldred, Cal	90B	387	$ .01	$ .10
Davis, Storm	89B	192	$ .01	$ .05	Elster, Kevin	89B	383	$ .01	$ .05
Davis, Storm	90B	368	$ .01	$ .05	Elster, Kevin	90B	137	$ .01	$ .05
Dawson, Andre	89B	298	$ .01	$ .15	Ericks, John	89B	433	$ .01	$ .25
					Ericks, John	90B	190	$ .01	$ .05
					Esasky, Nick	89B	31	$ .01	$ .05
					Esasky, Nick	90B	20	$ .01	$ .05
					Espinoza, Alvaro	90B	431	$ .01	$ .05
					Espy, Cecil	89B	236	$ .01	$ .05
					Espy, Cecil	90B	502	$ .01	$ .05
					Evans, Darrell	89B	275	$ .01	$ .15
					Evans, Dwight	89B	35	$ .01	$ .05
					Evans, Dwight	90B	279	$ .01	$ .05
					Fariss, Monty	89B	233	$ .01	$ .05
					Fariss, Monty	90B	500	$ .01	$ .10
					Farmer, Howard	90B	107	$ .01	$ .10
					Farr, Steve	89B	114	$ .01	$ .05
					Farr, Steve	90B	366	$ .01	$ .05
					Farrell, John	89B	74	$ .01	$ .05
					Felix, Junior	90B	522	$ .01	$ .20
					Fermin, Felix	90B	334	$ .01	$ .05
					Fernandez, Sid	89B	377	$ .01	$ .05
					Fernandez, Sid	90B	131	$ .01	$ .05
					Fernandez, Tony	89B	254	$ .01	$ .05
					Fernandez, Tony	90B	524	$ .01	$ .05
					Fetters, Mike	90B	286	$ .01	$ .10
					Fielder, Cecil	90B	357	$ .01	$ .35
					Filer, Tom	90B	385	$ .01	$ .05
					Finley, Chuck	89B	37	$ .01	$ .05
					Finley, Chuck	90B	289	$ .01	$ .05
					Finley, Steve	89B	15	$ .01	$ .20
					Fischer, Tom	89B	20	$ .01	$ .05
					Fisher, Brian	89B	415	$ .01	$ .05
Dawson, Andre	90B	39	$ .01	$ .10	Fisk, Carlton	89B	62	$ .01	$ .10
Dayley, Ken	89B	428	$ .01	$ .05	Fisk, Carlton	90B	314	$ .01	$ .10
Dayley, Ken	90B	191	$ .01	$ .05	Flanagan, Mike	89B	241	$ .01	$ .05
Deer, Rob	89B	146	$ .01	$ .10	Flannery, Tim	89B	457	$ .01	$ .05
Deer, Rob	90B	401	$ .01	$ .05	Fletcher, Scott	89B	230	$ .01	$ .05
DeLeon, Jose	89B	431	$ .01	$ .05	Fletcher, Scott	90B	319	$ .01	$ .05
DeLeon, Jose	90B	186	$ .01	$ .05	Foley, Tom	90B	120	$ .01	$ .05
Dempsey, Rick	89B	343	$ .01	$ .05	Ford, Curt	89B	408	$ .01	$ .05
Deshaies, Jim	89B	320	$ .01	$ .05	Franco, John	89B	301	$ .01	$ .15
Deshaies, Jim	90B	70	$ .01	$ .05	Franco, John	90B	128	$ .01	$ .05
DeShields, Delino	90B	119	$ .01	$ .50	Franco, Julio	89B	228	$ .01	$ .05
Devereaux, Mike	90B	260	$ .01	$ .05	Franco, Julio	90B	497	$ .01	$ .05
Diaz, Bo	89B	307	$ .01	$ .05	Fryman, Travis	90B	360	$ .01	$ .35
Dibble, Rob	89B	305	$ .01	$ .35	Gaetti, Gary	89B	158	$ .01	$ .05
Dibble, Rob	90B	42	$ .01	$ .20	Gaetti, Gary	90B	417	$ .01	$ .05

BOWMAN

Player	Year	No.	VG	EX/MT
Gagne, Greg	89B	161	$ .01	$ .05
Gagne, Greg	90B	414	$ .01	$ .05
Galarraga, Andres	89B	365	$ .01	$ .15
Galarraga, Andres	90B	113	$ .01	$ .05
Gallagher, Dave	89B	71	$ .01	$ .10
Gallego, Mike	90B	459	$ .01	$ .05
Gant, Ron	89B	274	$ .01	$ .30
Gantner, Jim	89B	141	$ .01	$ .05
Gantner, Jim	90B	400	$ .01	$ .05
Gardner, Mark	90B	106	$ .01	$ .10
Gardner, Wes	89B	23	$ .01	$ .05

RED SOX • WES GARDNER

Player	Year	No.	VG	EX/MT
Gardner, Wes	90B	266	$ .01	$ .05
Garrelts, Scott	89B	467	$ .01	$ .05
Garrelts, Scott	90B	228	$ .01	$ .05
Gedman, Rich	89B	27	$ .01	$ .05
Geren, Bob	90B	438	$ .01	$ .05
Gibson, Kirk	89B	351	$ .01	$ .15
Gibson, Kirk	90B	97	$ .01	$ .05
Gibson, Paul	89B	99	$ .01	$ .05
Gideon, Brett	90B	105	$ .01	$ .10
Gladden, Danny	89B	163	$ .01	$ .05
Gladden, Danny	90B	420	$ .01	$ .05
Glavine, Tom	89B	267	$ .01	$ .05
Glavine, Tom	90B	2	$ .01	$ .05
Goff, Jerry	90B	112	$ .01	$ .10
Gohr, Greg	90B	347	$ .01	$ .10
Gomez, Leo	90B	262	$ .01	$ .20
Gonzalez, Juan	90B	492	$ .01	$1.00
Gooden, Doc	89B	376	$ .01	$ .25
Gooden, Doc	90B	126	$ .01	$ .15
Goodwin, Tom	90B	96	$ .01	$ .20
Gordon, Tom	89B	115	$ .01	$ .50
Gordon, Tom	90B	365	$ .01	$ .15
Gott, Jim	89B	411	$ .01	$ .05
Grace, Mark	89B	291	$ .01	$ .90
Grace, Mark	90B	29	$ .01	$ .20
Grebeck, Craig	90B	318	$ .01	$ .10
Greene, Tommy	90B	1	$ .01	$ .20
Greene, Willie	90B	173	$ .01	$ .10
Greenwell, Mike	89B	34	$ .01	$ .25

Player	Year	No.	VG	EX/MT
Greenwell, Mike	90B	274	$ .01	$ .15
Griffey, Jr., Ken	89B	220	$ .01	$5.00
Griffey, Jr., Ken	90B	481	$ .01	$2.00
Griffey, Ken	89B	259	$ .01	$ .15
Griffey, Ken	90B	60	$ .01	$ .05
Griffin, Alfredo	89B	345	$ .01	$ .05
Griffin, Alfredo	90B	95	$ .01	$ .05
Griffin, Ty	89B	289	$ .01	$ .25
Griffin, Ty	90B	37	$ .01	$ .05
Grimsley, Jason	90B	151	$ .01	$ .05
Grissom, Marquis	90B	115	$ .01	$ .35
Gross, Kevin	89B	355	$ .01	$ .05
Gross, Kevin	90B	109	$ .01	$ .05
Gruber, Kelly	89B	251	$ .01	$ .05
Gruber, Kelly	90B	519	$ .01	$ .10
Gubicza, Mark	89B	117	$ .01	$ .05
Gubicza, Mark	90B	363	$ .01	$ .05
Guerrero, Pedro	89B	440	$ .01	$ .15
Guerrero, Pedro	90B	201	$ .01	$ .05
Guillen, Ozzie	89B	64	$ .01	$ .05
Guillen, Ozzie	90B	315	$ .01	$ .05
Gullickson, Bill	90B	65	$ .01	$ .05
Gunderson, Eric	90B	225	$ .01	$ .10
Gwynn, Tony	89B	461	$ .01	$ .15
Gwynn, Tony	90B	217	$ .01	$ .10
Hall, Drew	89B	221	$ .01	$ .05
Hall, Mel	90B	437	$ .01	$ .05
Hamelin, Bob	90B	379	$ .01	$ .10
Hamilton, Darryl	90B	397	$ .01	$ .10
Hamilton, Jeff	90B	94	$ .01	$ .05
Hansen, Dave	90B	93	$ .01	$ .10
Hanson, Erik	89B	206	$ .01	$ .50
Hanson, Erik	90B	469	$ .01	$ .10
Harkey, Mike	89B	286	$ .01	$ .20
Harkey, Mike	90B	28	$ .01	$ .20
Harnisch, Pete	89B	4	$ .01	$ .05
Harnisch, Pete	90B	247	$ .01	$ .05
Harper, Brian	89B	155	$ .01	$ .05
Harris, Donald	90B	499	$ .01	$ .10
Harris, Reggie	90B	446	$ .01	$ .10
Hartley, Mike	90B	87	$ .01	$ .05
Harvey, Bryan	89B	40	$ .01	$ .05
Hassey, Ron	89B	194	$ .01	$ .05
Hassey, Ron	90B	464	$ .01	$ .05
Hatcher, Mickey	89B	347	$ .01	$ .05
Hawkins, Andy	89B	166	$ .01	$ .05
Hayes, Von	89B	406	$ .01	$ .15
Hayes, Von	90B	160	$ .01	$ .05
Heath, Mike	90B	352	$ .01	$ .05
Heep, Danny	90B	276	$ .01	$ .05
Heinkel, Don	89B	427	$ .01	$ .05
Hemond, Scott	90B	453	$ .01	$ .10
Henderson, Dave	89B	200	$ .01	$ .05
Henderson, Dave	90B	458	$ .01	$ .05
Henderson, Rickey	89B	181	$ .01	$ .25
Henderson, Rickey	90B	457	$ .01	$ .25
Henke, Tom	89B	246	$ .01	$ .05
Henke, Tom	90B	506	$ .01	$ .05
Henneman, Mike	89B	98	$ .01	$ .05
Henneman, Mike	90B	345	$ .01	$ .05
Hernandez, Keith	89B	385	$ .01	$ .10
Hernandez, Keith	90B	342	$ .01	$ .05
Herr, Tom	89B	403	$ .01	$ .05
Herr, Tom	90B	159	$ .01	$ .05
Hershiser, Orel	89B	341	$ .01	$ .15
Hershiser, Orel	90B	84	$ .01	$ .10
Hibbard, Greg	90B	303	$ .01	$ .10
Higuera, Teddy	89B	129	$ .01	$ .05
Higuera, Teddy	90B	384	$ .01	$ .05
Hill, Glenallen	90B	514	$ .01	$ .10

Player	Year	No.	VG	EX/MT
Hillegas, Shawn	89B	58	$ .01	$ .05
Hilton, Howard	90B	189	$ .01	$ .10
Hoiles, Chris	90B	259	$ .01	$ .15
Hollins, Dave	90B	161	$ .01	$ .10
Holman, Brian	89B	357	$ .01	$ .05
Holton, Brian	89B	2	$ .01	$ .05
Honeycutt, Rick	89B	187	$ .01	$ .05
Honeycutt, Rick	90B	450	$ .01	$ .05
Horton, Ricky	89B	338	$ .01	$ .05
Hosey, Steve	90B	242	$ .01	$ .15
Hough, Charlie	89B	224	$ .01	$ .05
Houston, Tyler	90B	14	$ .01	$ .10
Howard, Thomas	90B	212	$ .01	$ .10
Howell, Jack	89B	48	$ .01	$ .05
Howell, Jack	90B	296	$ .01	$ .05
Howell, Jay	89B	335	$ .01	$ .05
Howell, Jay	90B	83	$ .01	$ .05
Howell, Ken	89B	394	$ .01	$ .05
Howell, Ken	90B	147	$ .01	$ .05
Hrbek, Kent	89B	157	$ .01	$ .10
Hrbek, Kent	90B	418	$ .01	$ .05
Hubbard, Glenn	89B	199	$ .01	$ .05
Hudler, Rex	89B	364	$ .01	$ .05
Hundley, Todd	90B	142	$ .01	$ .10
Hurst, Bruce	89B	451	$ .01	$ .05
Hurst, Bruce	90B	208	$ .01	$ .05
Incaviglia, Pete	89B	238	$ .01	$ .15
Incaviglia, Pete	90B	491	$ .01	$ .05
Infante, Alexis	90B	17	$ .01	$ .05
Jackson, Bo	89B	126	$ .01	$ .60
Jackson, Bo	90B	378	$ .01	$ .35
Jackson, Danny	89B	304	$ .01	$ .05
Jackson, Danny	90B	44	$ .01	$ .05
Jackson, Jeff	90B	157	$ .01	$ .10
Jackson, Mike	89B	207	$ .01	$ .05
Jacoby, Brook	89B	86	$ .01	$ .05
Jacoby, Brook	90B	341	$ .01	$ .05
James, Chris	89B	404	$ .01	$ .05
James, Chris	90B	340	$ .01	$ .05
James, Dion	89B	277	$ .01	$ .05
James, Dion	90B	331	$ .01	$ .05
Jefferies, Gregg	89B	381	$ .01	$ .60
Jefferies, Gregg	90B	140	$ .01	$ .25
Jefferson, Reggie	90B	51	$ .01	$ .35
Jefferson, Stan	89B	180	$ .01	$ .05
Johnson, Howard	90B	133	$ .01	$ .05
Johnson, Randy	90B	468	$ .01	$ .10
Jones, Doug	89B	78	$ .01	$ .05
Jones, Doug	90B	328	$ .01	$ .05
Jones, Jimmy	89B	169	$ .01	$ .05
Jones, Kiki	90B	86	$ .01	$ .20
Jones, Ron	89B	407	$ .01	$ .15
Jones, Tim	89B	439	$ .01	$ .05
Jones, Tracy	89B	479	$ .01	$ .05
Jordan, Ricky	89B	401	$ .01	$ .20
Jordan, Ricky	90B	156	$ .01	$ .05
Jose, Felix	90B	455	$ .01	$ .20
Joyner, Wally	89B	47	$ .01	$ .15
Joyner, Wally	90B	299	$ .01	$ .05
Juden, Jeff	90B	64	$ .01	$ .20
Kelly, Roberto	89B	183	$ .01	$ .05
Kelly, Roberto	90B	444	$ .01	$ .10
Kennedy, Terry	89B	470	$ .01	$ .05
Kennedy, Terry	90B	241	$ .01	$ .05
Key, Jimmy	89B	243	$ .01	$ .15
Key, Jimmy	90B	509	$ .01	$ .05
Kile, Darryl	90B	61	$ .01	$ .05
Kilgus, Paul	89B	285	$ .01	$ .05
Kilgus, Paul	90B	508	$ .01	$ .05
King, Eric	90B	304	$ .01	$ .05
Kipper, Bob	89B	414	$ .01	$ .05
Kittle, Ron	89B	69	$ .01	$ .10
Knoblauch, Chuck	90B	415	$ .01	$ .10
Kruk, John	89B	460	$ .01	$ .10
Kruk, John	90B	154	$ .01	$ .05
Kunkel, Jeff	89B	231	$ .01	$ .05
Lake, Steve	89B	399	$ .01	$ .05
Landrum, Bill	90B	166	$ .01	$ .05
Lane, Brian	90B	48	$ .01	$ .05
Langston, Mark	89B	205	$ .01	$ .15
Langston, Mark	90B	284	$ .01	$ .05
Lankford, Ray	90B	192	$ .01	$ .50
Lansford, Carney	89B	198	$ .01	$ .05
Lansford, Carney	90B	452	$ .01	$ .05
LaPoint, Dave	89B	165	$ .01	$ .05
Larkin, Barry	89B	311	$ .01	$ .15
Larkin, Barry	90B	50	$ .01	$ .10
Larkin, Gene	89B	160	$ .01	$ .05
Laudner, Tim	89B	154	$ .01	$ .05
LaValliere, Mike	89B	417	$ .01	$ .05
LaValliere, Mike	90B	172	$ .01	$ .05
Law, Vance	89B	293	$ .01	$ .05
Lawless, Tom	89B	255	$ .01	$ .05
Layana, Tim	90B	41	$ .01	$ .10
Leach, Rick	89B	234	$ .01	$ .05
Leary, Tim	89B	339	$ .01	$ .05
Leary, Tim	90B	429	$ .01	$ .05
Lee, Manny	90B	512	$ .01	$ .05
Lefferts, Craig	89B	464	$ .01	$ .05
Lefferts, Craig	90B	206	$ .01	$ .05
Leibrandt, Charlie	89B	116	$ .01	$ .05
Leibrandt, Charlie	90B	8	$ .01	$ .05
Leiter, Al	89B	170	$ .01	$ .05
Leius, Scott	90B	423	$ .01	$ .10
Lemke, Mark	90B	11	$ .01	$ .05
Lemon, Chet	89B	108	$ .01	$ .05
Lemon, Chet	90B	354	$ .01	$ .05
Leonard, Jeffrey	89B	218	$ .01	$ .05
Leonard, Jeffrey	90B	472	$ .01	$ .05
Lewis, Darren	90B	463	$ .01	$ .20
Lewis, Mark	89B	87	$ .01	$ .35
Lewis, Mark	90B	338	$ .01	$ .10
Lilliquist, Derek	89B	264	$ .01	$ .10
Lilliquist, Derek	90B	7	$ .01	$ .05
Lind, Jose	89B	421	$ .01	$ .05
Lind, Jose	90B	170	$ .01	$ .05
Liriano, Nelson	90B	518	$ .01	$ .05
Long, Bill	89B	56	$ .01	$ .05
Luecken, Rick	90B	5	$ .01	$ .10
Lynn, Fred	90B	216	$ .01	$ .05
Lyons, Barry	90B	139	$ .01	$ .05
Lyons, Steve	89B	63	$ .01	$ .05
Lyons, Steve	90B	321	$ .01	$ .05
Maas, Kevin	90B	440	$ .01	$1.50
Macfarlane, Mike	89B	118	$ .01	$ .05
Maddux, Greg	89B	284	$ .01	$ .10
Maddux, Greg	90B	27	$ .01	$ .05
Maddux, Mike	89B	391	$ .01	$ .05
Magadan, Dave	89B	384	$ .01	$ .05
Magrane, Joe	89B	432	$ .01	$ .10
Magrane, Joe	90B	183	$ .01	$ .05
Mahler, Rick	89B	302	$ .01	$ .05
Maldonado, Candy	89B	478	$ .01	$ .05
Maldonado, Candy	90B	335	$ .01	$ .05
Malone, Chuck	90B	144	$ .01	$ .10
Manahan, Austin	89B	420	$ .01	$ .05
Manrique, Fred	89B	66	$ .01	$ .05
Manwaring, Kirt	89B	469	$ .01	$ .05
Marshall, Mike	89B	350	$ .01	$ .05
Marshall, Mike	90B	132	$ .01	$ .05

BOWMAN

Player	Year	No.	VG	EX/MT	Player	Year	No.	VG	EX/MT
Martinez, Carlos	90B	322	$ .01	$ .05	Mercker, Kent	90B	6	$ .01	$ .20
Martinez, Carmelo	89B	459	$ .01	$ .05	Meyer, Brian	89B	319	$ .01	$ .05
Martinez, Carmelo	90B	162	$ .01	$ .05	Meyer, Joey	89B	138	$ .01	$ .05
Martinez, Dave	89B	370	$ .01	$ .05	Miller, Keith	89B	380	$ .01	$ .05
Martinez, Dave	90B	121	$ .01	$ .05	Miller, Keith	90B	136	$ .01	$ .05
Martinez, Denny	89B	359	$ .01	$ .05	Milligan, Randy	89B	10	$ .01	$ .05
Martinez, Denny	90B	111	$ .01	$ .05	Milligan, Randy	90B	257	$ .01	$ .05
Martinez, Edgar	89B	216	$ .01	$ .05	Mills, Alan	90B	428	$ .01	$ .10
Martinez, Ramon	90B	88	$ .01	$ .50	Mitchell, Kevin	89B	474	$ .01	$ .30
Martinez, Tino	89B	211	$ .01	$1.00	Mitchell, Kevin	90B	232	$ .01	$ .25
Martinez, Tino	90B	484	$ .01	$ .20	Molitor, Paul	89B	140	$ .01	$ .10
Mattingly, Don	89B	176	$ .01	$ .50	Molitor, Paul	90B	399	$ .01	$ .05
Mattingly, Don	90B	443	$ .01	$ .35	Montgomery, Jeff	89B	113	$ .01	$ .05
Mayne, Brent	90B	372	$ .01	$ .10	Montgomery, Jeff	90B	370	$ .01	$ .05
McCaskill, Kirk	89B	38	$ .01	$ .05	Moore, Mike	89B	189	$ .01	$ .05
McCaskill, Kirk	90B	283	$ .01	$ .05	Moore, Mike	90B	445	$ .01	$ .05
McClendon, Lloyd	89B	287	$ .01	$ .05	Morandini, Mickey	90B	153	$ .01	$ .10
McClendon, Lloyd	90B	36	$ .01	$ .05	Moreland, Keith	89B	109	$ .01	$ .05
McClure, Bob	89B	43	$ .01	$ .05	Morris, Hal	90B	57	$ .01	$ .35
McCullers, Lance	89B	168	$ .01	$ .05	Morris, Jack	89B	93	$ .01	$ .05
McDonald, Ben	90B	243	$ .01	$ .75	Moseby, Lloyd	90B	362	$ .01	$ .05
McDowell, Jack	89B	61	$ .01	$ .15	Moyer, Jamie	89B	223	$ .01	$ .05
McDowell, Jack	90B	305	$ .01	$ .05	Mulliniks, Rance	89B	250	$ .01	$ .05
McDowell, Oddibe	89B	90	$ .01	$ .05	Murphy, Dale	89B	276	$ .01	$ .15
McDowell, Oddibe	90B	13	$ .01	$ .05	Murphy, Dale	90B	19	$ .01	$ .10
McDowell, Roger	90B	146	$ .01	$ .05	Murphy, Rob	89B	22	$ .01	$ .05
McElroy, Chuck	90B	150	$ .01	$ .10	Murphy, Rob	90B	269	$ .01	$ .05
McGaffigan, Andy	89B	356	$ .01	$ .05	Murray, Eddie	89B	346	$ .01	$ .15
McGee, Willie	89B	442	$ .01	$ .05	Murray, Eddie	90B	101	$ .01	$ .05
McGee, Willie	90B	194	$ .01	$ .05	Musselman, Jeff	89B	240	$ .01	$ .05
McGriff, Fred	89B	253	$ .01	$ .20	Myers, Chris	90B	250	$ .01	$ .10
McGriff, Fred	90B	513	$ .01	$ .10	Myers, Greg	90B	520	$ .01	$ .05
McGwire, Mark	89B	197	$ .01	$ .55	Myers, Randy	89B	374	$ .01	$ .05
					Myers, Randy	90B	47	$ .01	$ .05
					Nagy, Charles	89B	73	$ .01	$ .30
					Navarro, Jaime	90B	388	$ .01	$ .10
					Nelson, Gene	89B	185	$ .01	$ .05
					Nelson, Rob	90B	213	$ .01	$ .05
					Nen, Robb	90B	487	$ .01	$ .10
					Newman, Al	89B	156	$ .01	$ .05
					Newman, Al	90B	419	$ .01	$ .05
					Nezelek, Andy	90B	3	$ .01	$ .05
					Niedenfuer, Tom	89B	204	$ .01	$ .05
					Nieves, Juan	89B	131	$ .01	$ .05
					Nixon, Donell	89B	477	$ .01	$ .05
					Nixon, Otis	89B	366	$ .01	$ .05
					Nokes, Matt	89B	101	$ .01	$ .10
					O'Brien, Pete	89B	84	$ .01	$ .05
					O'Brien, Pete	90B	475	$ .01	$ .05
					O'Neill, Paul	89B	313	$ .01	$ .15
					O'Neill, Paul	90B	49	$ .01	$ .05
					Oberkfell, Ken	89B	418	$ .01	$ .05
					Oberkfell, Ken	90B	74	$ .01	$ .05
					Oester, Ron	89B	310	$ .01	$ .05
					Offerman, Jose	90B	92	$ .01	$ .75
					Ojeda, Bob	89B	371	$ .01	$ .05
					Olerud, John	90B	510	$ .01	$1.00
					Olin, Steve	90B	326	$ .01	$ .05
					Oliver, Joe	90B	54	$ .01	$ .10
					Olson, Gregg	89B	6	$ .01	$ .65
					Olson, Gregg	90B	249	$ .01	$ .15
					Ontiveros, Steve	90B	145	$ .01	$ .05
					Oquendo, Jose	89B	438	$ .01	$ .05
					Oquendo, Jose	90B	200	$ .01	$ .05
					Orossco, Jesse	89B	81	$ .01	$ .05
					Orsulak, Joe	90B	252	$ .01	$ .05
					Orton, John	90B	298	$ .01	$ .10
					Otto, Dave	90B	448	$ .01	$ .05
					Owen, Spike	89B	363	$ .01	$ .05
					Owen, Spike	90B	116	$ .01	$ .05

ATHLETICS ▾ MARK McGWIRE

Player	Year	No.	VG	EX/MT
McGwire, Mark	90B	454	$ .01	$ .20
McIntosh, Tim	90B	394	$ .01	$ .10
McReynolds, Kevin	89B	388	$ .01	$ .10
McReynolds, Kevin	90B	138	$ .01	$ .05
McWilliams, Larry	89B	397	$ .01	$ .05
Medvin, Scott	89B	412	$ .01	$ .05
Melvin, Bob	89B	8	$ .01	$ .05

Player	Year	No.	VG	EX/MT	Player	Year	No.	VG	EX/MT
Pagliarulo, Mike	89B	175	$ .01	$ .05	Remlinger, Mike	90B	227	$ .01	$ .10
Pagliarulo, Mike	90B	219	$ .01	$ .05	Renteria, Rich	89B	212	$ .01	$ .05
Palacios, Rey	90B	381	$ .01	$ .05	Reuschel, Rick	89B	466	$ .01	$ .05
Palmeiro, Rafael	89B	237	$ .01	$ .15	Reuschel, Rick	90B	223	$ .01	$ .05
Palmeiro, Rafael	90B	496	$ .01	$ .10	Reuss, Jerry	89B	57	$ .01	$ .05
Parker, Dave	89B	202	$ .01	$ .15	Reynolds, Craig	89B	328	$ .01	$ .05
Parker, Dave	90B	398	$ .01	$ .05	Reynolds, Harold	89B	210	$ .01	$ .05
Parks, Derek	90B	422	$ .01	$ .10	Reynolds, Harold	90B	478	$ .01	$ .05
Parrett, Jeff	89B	390	$ .01	$ .05	Rhoden, Rick	89B	323	$ .01	$ .05
Parrett, Jeff	90B	149	$ .01	$ .05	Rhodes, Karl	90B	79	$ .01	$ .05
Parrish, Lance	89B	45	$ .01	$ .05	Rice, Jim	89B	33	$ .01	$ .10
Parrish, Lance	90B	295	$ .01	$ .05	Richetti, Dave	89B	167	$ .01	$ .05
Pasqua, Dan	89B	67	$ .01	$ .05	Righetti, Dave	90B	426	$ .01	$ .05
Pasqua, Dan	90B	313	$ .01	$ .05	Rijo, Jose	89B	300	$ .01	$ .15
Patterson, Bob	90B	168	$ .01	$ .05	Rijo, Jose	90B	45	$ .01	$ .05
Pecota, Bill	90B	377	$ .01	$ .05	Riles, Ernie	89B	475	$ .01	$ .05
Pedrique, Al	89B	104	$ .01	$ .05	Riles, Ernie	90B	239	$ .01	$ .05
Pena, Alejandro	90B	124	$ .01	$ .05	Ripken, Billy	89B	12	$ .01	$ .05
Pena, Tony	89B	435	$ .01	$ .10	Ripken, Billy	90B	256	$ .01	$ .05
Pena, Tony	90B	271	$ .01	$ .05	Ripken, Cal	89B	9	$ .01	$ .15
Pendelton, Terry	90B	197	$ .01	$ .05	Ripken, Cal	90B	255	$ .01	$ .10
Pendleton, Terry	89B	437	$ .01	$ .05	Ripken, Sr., Cal	89B	260	$ .01	$ .05
Peraza, Oswald	89B	1	$ .01	$ .10	Ritz, Kevin	90B	350	$ .01	$ .10
Perez, Melido	89B	59	$ .01	$ .15	Rivera, Luis	89B	29	$ .01	$ .05
Perez, Melido	90B	310	$ .01	$ .05	Roberts, Bip	90B	222	$ .01	$ .05
Perez, Pascual	89B	354	$ .01	$ .15	Robinson, Don	89B	463	$ .01	$ .05
Perez, Pascual	90B	430	$ .01	$ .05	Robinson, Jeff	89B	97	$ .01	$ .05
Perezchica, Tony	90B	235	$ .01	$ .05	Robinson, Jeff	89B	410	$ .01	$ .05
Perry, Gerald	89B	273	$ .01	$ .05	Robinson, Jeff	90B	427	$ .01	$ .05
Perry, Gerald	90B	383	$ .01	$ .05	Robinson, Ron	89B	303	$ .01	$ .05
Peterson, Adam	90B	307	$ .01	$ .05	Rochford, Mike	90B	264	$ .01	$ .05
Petralli, Geno	90B	495	$ .01	$ .05	Rohde, Dave	90B	75	$ .01	$ .05
Pettis, Gary	90B	498	$ .01	$ .05	Rojas, Mel	90B	108	$ .01	$ .10
Phelps, Ken	89B	177	$ .01	$ .05	Romero, Ed	90B	361	$ .01	$ .05
Phelps, Ken	90B	462	$ .01	$ .05	Romine, Kevin	90B	273	$ .01	$ .05
Phillips, Tony	90B	359	$ .01	$ .05	Roomes, Rolando	90B	56	$ .01	$ .05
Pina, Mickey	90B	270	$ .01	$ .05	Rose, Bobby	90B	293	$ .01	$ .10
Pittman, Park	90B	408	$ .01	$ .10	Roseboro, Jaime	90B	134	$ .01	$ .10
Plesac, Dan	89B	133	$ .01	$ .05	Royer, Stan	89B	195	$ .01	$ .05
Plesac, Dan	90B	386	$ .01	$ .05	Ruffin, Bruce	89B	393	$ .01	$ .05
Plunk, Eric	89B	191	$ .01	$ .05	Ruskin, Scott	90B	167	$ .01	$ .10
Portugal, Mark	89B	318	$ .01	$ .05	Russell, Jeff	89B	226	$ .01	$ .05
Portugal, Mark	90B	63	$ .01	$ .05	Russell, Jeff	90B	485	$ .01	$ .05
Presley, Jim	89B	214	$ .01	$ .05	Ryan, Nolan	89B	225	$ .01	$ .60
Presley, Jim	90B	18	$ .01	$ .05	Ryan, Nolan	90B	486	$ .01	$ .50
Price, Joe	90B	245	$ .01	$ .05	Saberhagen, Bret	89B	111	$ .01	$ .15
Prince, Tom	90B	176	$ .01	$ .05	Saberhagen, Bret	90B	364	$ .01	$ .05
Proctor, Dave	89B	378	$ .01	$ .05	Sabo, Chris	89B	309	$ .01	$ .30
Puckett, Kirby	89B	162	$ .01	$ .25	Sabo, Chris	90B	53	$ .01	$ .10
Puckett, Kirby	90B	424	$ .01	$ .20	Salazar, Luis	90B	40	$ .01	$ .05
Puleo, Charlie	89B	263	$ .01	$ .05	Salkeld, Roger	90B	465	$ .01	$ .15
Quinones, Rey	89B	213	$ .01	$ .05	Sampen, Bill	90B	104	$ .01	$ .10
Quirk, Jamie	89B	173	$ .01	$ .05	Samuel, Juan	89B	405	$ .01	$ .05
Radinsky, Scott	90B	308	$ .01	$ .10	Samuel, Juan	90B	91	$ .01	$ .05
Raines, Rock	89B	369	$ .01	$ .15	Sanchez, Alex	89B	245	$ .01	$ .05
Raines, Rock	90B	118	$ .01	$ .05	Sandberg, Ryne	89B	290	$ .01	$ .25
Ramirez, Rafael	89B	330	$ .01	$ .05	Sandberg, Ryne	90B	30	$ .01	$ .25
Randolph, Willie	89B	344	$ .01	$ .05	Sanderson, Scott	90B	447	$ .01	$ .05
Randolph, Willie	90B	90	$ .01	$ .05	Santana, Andres	90B	230	$ .01	$ .10
Rasmussen, Dennis	89B	450	$ .01	$ .05	Santana, Rafael	89B	174	$ .01	$ .05
Rasmussen, Dennis	90B	205	$ .01	$ .05	Santiago, Benny	89B	453	$ .01	$ .15
Rawley, Shane	89B	151	$ .01	$ .05	Santiago, Benny	90B	218	$ .01	$ .10
Ray, Johnny	89B	49	$ .01	$ .05	Santovenia, Nelson	89B	361	$ .01	$ .15
Ray, John	90B	302	$ .01	$ .05	Sax, Steve	89B	178	$ .01	$ .05
Reardon, Jeff	89B	148	$ .01	$ .05	Sax, Steve	90B	442	$ .01	$ .05
Reardon, Jeff	90B	265	$ .01	$ .05	Schatzeder, Dan	90B	69	$ .01	$ .05
Redus, Gary	89B	425	$ .01	$ .05	Schilling, Curt	90B	246	$ .01	$ .05
Redus, Gary	90B	180	$ .01	$ .05	Schmidt, Dave	89B	5	$ .01	$ .05
Reed, Jody	89B	30	$ .01	$ .05	Schmidt, Dave	90B	110	$ .01	$ .05
Reed, Jody	90B	272	$ .01	$ .05	Schmidt, Mike	89B	402	$ .01	$ .35

BOWMAN

Player	Year	No.	VG	EX/MT	Player	Year	No.	VG	EX/MT
Schofield, Dick	89B	46	$ .01	$ .05	Stottlemyre, Jr., Mel	89B	110	$ .01	$ .05
Schofield, Dick	90B	291	$ .01	$ .05	Stottlemyre, Mel	89B	261	$ .01	$ .15
Schooler, Mike	90B	470	$ .01	$ .10	Stottlemyre, Todd	89B	242	$ .01	$ .05
Schroeder, Bill	89B	44	$ .01	$ .05	Strawberry, Darryl	89B	387	$ .01	$ .35
Scioscia, Mike	89B	342	$ .01	$ .05	Strawberry, Darryl	90B	141	$ .01	$ .25
Scioscia, Mike	90B	89	$ .01	$ .05	Sundberg, Jim	89B	227	$ .01	$ .05
Scott, Mike	89B	322	$ .01	$ .05	Surhoff, B. J.	89B	137	$ .01	$ .10
Scott, Mike	90B	71	$ .01	$ .05	Surhoff, B. J.	90B	393	$ .01	$ .05
Scudder, Scott	90B	46	$ .01	$ .10	Sutcliffe, Rick	89B	281	$ .01	$ .10
Searcy, Steve	89B	95	$ .01	$ .10	Sutcliffe, Rick	90B	21	$ .01	$ .05
Segui, David	90B	251	$ .01	$ .15	Sveum, Dale	89B	139	$ .01	$ .05
Seitzer, Kevin	89B	123	$ .01	$ .15	Swan, Russ	90B	224	$ .01	$ .10
Seitzer, Kevin	90B	380	$ .01	$ .05	Swindell, Greg	89B	76	$ .01	$ .10
Sellers, Jeff	89B	299	$ .01	$ .05	Swindell, Greg	90B	325	$ .01	$ .05
Service, Scott	90B	143	$ .01	$ .05	Tabler, Pat	89B	125	$ .01	$ .05
Sharperson, Mike	89B	348	$ .01	$ .05	Tanana, Frank	89B	92	$ .01	$ .05
Shaw, Jeff	90B	329	$ .01	$ .10	Tanana, Frank	90B	343	$ .01	$ .05
Sheets, Larry	89B	16	$ .01	$ .05	Tapani, Kevin	90B	407	$ .01	$ .20
Sheffield, Gary	89B	142	$ .01	$ .75	Tartabull, Danny	89B	128	$ .01	$ .10
Sheffield, Gary	90B	391	$ .01	$ .20	Tartabull, Danny	90B	375	$ .01	$ .05
Shelby, John	89B	349	$ .01	$ .05	Tejada, Wil	89B	468	$ .01	$ .05
Sheridan, Pat	89B	107	$ .01	$ .05	Templeton, Garry	89B	455	$ .01	$ .05
Show, Eric	89B	446	$ .01	$ .05	Templeton, Garry	90B	215	$ .01	$ .05
Show, Eric	90B	209	$ .01	$ .05	Terrell, Walt	89B	445	$ .01	$ .05
Sierra, Ruben	89B	235	$ .01	$ .30	Terrell, Walt	90B	165	$ .01	$ .05
Sierra, Ruben	90B	490	$ .01	$ .10	Tettleton, Mickey	90B	254	$ .01	$ .05
Skalski, Joe	90B	323	$ .01	$ .05	Teufel, Tim	89B	382	$ .01	$ .05
Slaught, Don	89B	172	$ .01	$ .05	Thigpen, Bobby	89B	55	$ .01	$ .05
Slaught, Don	90B	182	$ .01	$ .05	Thigpen, Bobby	90B	306	$ .01	$ .05
Smiley, John	89B	413	$ .01	$ .15	Thomas, Andres	89B	272	$ .01	$ .05
Smith, Bryn	89B	353	$ .01	$ .05	Thomas, Frank	90B	320	$ .01	$2.00
Smith, Bryn	90B	184	$ .01	$ .05	Thompson, Milt	89B	441	$ .01	$ .05
Smith, Dave	89B	317	$ .01	$ .05	Thompson, Milt	90B	196	$ .01	$ .05
Smith, Dave	90B	62	$ .01	$ .05	Thompson, Robby	89B	473	$ .01	$ .05
Smith, Dwight	89B	297	$ .01	$ .30	Thompson, Robby	90B	233	$ .01	$ .05
Smith, Dwight	90B	32	$ .01	$ .10	Thon, Dickie	89B	400	$ .01	$ .05
Smith, Greg	90B	31	$ .01	$ .10	Thon, Dickie	90B	155	$ .01	$ .05
Smith, Lee	89B	19	$ .01	$ .05	Toliver, Fred	89B	147	$ .01	$ .05
Smith, Lee	90B	263	$ .01	$ .05	Traber, Jim	89B	13	$ .01	$ .05
Smith, Lonnie	89B	278	$ .01	$ .05	Trammell, Alan	89B	105	$ .01	$ .15
Smith, Lonnie	90B	12	$ .01	$ .05	Trammell, Alan	90B	353	$ .01	$ .05
Smith, Ozzie	89B	436	$ .01	$ .15	Trevino, Alex	89B	326	$ .01	$ .05
Smith, Ozzie	90B	195	$ .01	$ .05	Trillo, Manny	89B	308	$ .01	$ .05
Smith, Pete	89B	269	$ .01	$ .10	Tudor, John	90B	188	$ .01	$ .05
Smith, Willie	90B	425	$ .01	$ .10	Uribe, Jose	89B	471	$ .01	$ .05
Smith, Zane	89B	262	$ .01	$ .10	Valdez, Rafael	90B	210	$ .01	$ .15
Smithberg, Roger	90B	203	$ .01	$ .10	Valenzuela, Fernando	89B	337	$ .01	$ .10
Smoltz, John	89B	266	$ .01	$ .25	Valera, Julio	90B	123	$ .01	$ .10
Smoltz, John	90B	10	$ .01	$ .05	Valle, Dave	89B	208	$ .01	$ .05
Snyder, Cory	89B	89	$ .01	$ .10	Valle, Dave	90B	473	$ .01	$ .05
Snyder, Cory	90B	336	$ .01	$ .05	Van Slyke, Andy	89B	424	$ .01	$ .15
Sojo, Luis	90B	517	$ .01	$ .05	Van Slyke, Andy	90B	171	$ .01	$ .05
Sorrento, Paul	90B	421	$ .01	$ .10	Vaughn, Greg	90B	396	$ .01	$ .50
Sosa, Sammy	90B	312	$ .01	$ .35	Vaughn, Maurice	90B	275	$ .01	$ .50
Spiers, Billy	90B	402	$ .01	$ .15	Velarde, Randy	90B	434	$ .01	$ .05
Sprague, Ed	89B	252	$ .01	$ .15	Ventura, Robin	89B	65	$ .01	$ .55
Sprague, Ed	90B	511	$ .01	$ .05	Ventura, Robin	90B	311	$ .01	$ .20
Stanicek, Pete	89B	14	$ .01	$ .05	Veres, Randy	89B	390	$ .01	$ .05
Stanley, Bob	89B	25	$ .01	$ .05	Viola, Frank	89B	150	$ .01	$ .15
Stanton, Mike	90B	4	$ .01	$ .10	Viola, Frank	90B	122	$ .01	$ .05
Steinbach, Terry	89B	193	$ .01	$ .05	Vizcaino, Jose	90B	98	$ .01	$ .05
Steinbach, Terry	90B	456	$ .01	$ .05	Vizquel, Omar	90B	474	$ .01	$ .05
Stevens, Lee	90B	300	$ .01	$ .10	Wainhouse, Dave	89B	358	$ .01	$ .05
Stewart, Dave	89B	188	$ .01	$ .25	Walk, Bob	89B	409	$ .01	$ .05
Stewart, Dave	90B	449	$ .01	$ .10	Walk, Bob	90B	163	$ .01	$ .05
Stieb, Dave	89B	239	$ .01	$ .05	Walker, Hugh	89B	127	$ .01	$ .05
Stieb, Dave	90B	505	$ .01	$ .05	Walker, Larry	90B	117	$ .01	$ .10
Stillwell, Kurt	89B	120	$ .01	$ .05	Walker, Mike	89B	77	$ .01	$ .05
Stillwell, Kurt	90B	376	$ .01	$ .05	Wallach, Tim	89B	362	$ .01	$ .05
Stone, Eric	90B	348	$ .01	$ .10	Wallach, Tim	90B	114	$ .01	$ .05

Player	Year	No.	VG	EX/MT
Walton, Jerome	89B	295	$ .01	$ .75
Walton, Jerome	90B	35	$ .01	$ .25
Wapnick, Steve	90B	346	$ .01	$ .10
Washington, Claudell	89B	52	$ .01	$ .05

Player	Year	No.	VG	EX/MT
Washington, Claudell	90B	297	$ .01	$ .05
Webster, Mitch	89B	296	$ .01	$ .05
Wegman, Bill	89B	135	$ .01	$ .05
Weiss, Walt	89B	196	$ .01	$ .15
Weiss, Walt	90B	461	$ .01	$ .05
Welch, Bob	89B	186	$ .01	$ .05
West, Dave	90B	413	$ .01	$ .05
Wetteland, John	90B	82	$ .01	$ .05
Whitaker, Lou	89B	103	$ .01	$ .10
Whitaker, Lou	90B	356	$ .01	$ .05

Player	Year	No.	VG	EX/MT
White, Devon	89B	54	$ .01	$ .15
White, Devon	90B	292	$ .01	$ .05
White, Frank	89B	122	$ .01	$ .05
White, Frank	90B	371	$ .01	$ .05
Whitehurst, Wally	89B	373	$ .01	$ .15
Whitson, Eddie	89B	449	$ .01	$ .05
Whitson, Eddie	90B	204	$ .01	$ .05
Whitt, Ernie	89B	248	$ .01	$ .05
Whitt, Ernie	90B	16	$ .01	$ .05
Wickander, Kevin	89B	75	$ .01	$ .05
Wickander, Kevin	90B	327	$ .01	$ .05
Wilkerson, Curt	89B	292	$ .01	$ .05
Wilkins, Dean	90B	26	$ .01	$ .05
Williams, Bernie	90B	439	$ .01	$ .25
Williams, Frank	89B	100	$ .01	$ .05
Williams, Matt	90B	238	$ .01	$ .15
Williams, Mitch	89B	283	$ .01	$ .05
Williams, Mitch	90B	25	$ .01	$ .05
Williamson, Mark	90B	248	$ .01	$ .05
Wilson, Glenn	89B	423	$ .01	$ .05
Wilson, Mookie	89B	386	$ .01	$ .05
Wilson, Mookie	90B	516	$ .01	$ .05
Wilson, Steve	89B	280	$ .01	$ .05
Wilson, Steve	90B	23	$ .01	$ .05
Wilson, Willie	89B	124	$ .01	$ .10
Winfield, Dave	89B	179	$ .01	$ .15
Winfield, Dave	90B	432	$ .01	$ .10
Witt, Bobby	89B	222	$ .01	$ .05
Witt, Mike	89B	42	$ .01	$ .05
Worrell, Todd	89B	429	$ .01	$ .10
Worrell, Todd	90B	185	$ .01	$ .05
Worthington, Craig	90B	253	$ .01	$ .05
Yett, Rich	89B	79	$ .01	$ .05
Yett, Rich	90B	412	$ .01	$ .05
Youmans, Floyd	89B	396	$ .01	$ .10
Young, Curt	89B	184	$ .01	$ .05
Young, Gerald	89B	333	$ .01	$ .05
Young, Gerald	90B	72	$ .01	$ .05
Youngblood, Joel	89B	315	$ .01	$ .05
Yount, Robin	89B	144	$ .01	$ .20
Yount, Robin	90B	404	$ .01	$ .10
Zeile, Todd	90B	193	$ .01	$ .35
Zinter, Alan	90B	135	$ .01	$ .10
Zosky, Eddie	90B	523	$ .01	$ .15

DONRUSS-LEAF INC. 1981-1991

Donruss baseball cards first made their appearance on the collecting scene in 1981. At first they contained bubble gum in the wax packs; but in 1982, after being sued successfully by Topps, a puzzle piece was included in each pack instead of bubble gum.

Several abbreviations are used in the Donruss section that need some explanation:

D#A & D#B refer to bonus cards numbered with A and B in the wax packs of 1984.

DAS - Donruss All-Star card first issued in 1990 sets.

DBB - DONRUSS BASEBALL'S BEST-A 336 card set first issued in 1988.

DBC - DONRUSS BONUS CARDS were issued starting in 1988. These cards (BC1-BC26) are randomly distributed in the wax, rack and cello packs.

DK - Beginning with the 1983 set, the first twenty-six cards of the Donruss sets were designated DIAMOND KINGS. These cards feature the art of Dick Perez of Perez-Steele Galleries.

DL - Donruss Leaf set started in 1990 to compete with Upper Deck quality.

DLP - Donruss Leaf Prototype randomly packed four per 1991 factory set with twenty-six in set.

DMVP - Most valuable players of each team originally began as BC cards but incorporated into 1991 set.

DR - Donruss issues a fifty-six card set of DONRUSS ROOKIES at the end of the year. This was started in 1986.

DRR - Beginning with the 1984 set, a group of top rookies are designated DONRUSS RATED ROOKIES on the cards following the Diamond King cards.

DTR - Donruss issued a fifty-six traded set in 1989.

There are many unnumbered checklists in the early Donruss sets. Since there are no numbers on the cards themselves, they are numbered as **"0"** in the listing of cards.

All Donruss cards are 2½" x 3½" and in full color.

1981 - 600 cards plus 5 unnumbered checklists w/white border w/Donruss logo '81 (copyright 1981 Donruss back upper right)

1982 - 653 cards plus 7 unnumbered checklists w/white border w/Donruss logo '82 (copyright 1982 Donruss back upper right

1983 - 653 cards plus 7 unnumbered checklists w/white border w/Donruss logo '83 (copyright 1982 Donruss back upper right)

1984 - 651 cards plus 7 unnumbered checklists and 2 cards (A & B) w/white border w/Donruss logo '84 (copyright 1983 Donruss back upper right)

1985 - 653 cards plus 7 unnumbered checklists w/black border w/five red stripes on sides, w/Donruss logo '85 (copyright 1984 Donruss back upper right)

1986 - 653 cards plus 7 unnumbered checklists w/blue border w/thin black stripes, w/Donruss '86 (copyright 1985 Leaf-Donruss back upper right)

1987 - 660 cards w/black border with brown baseball filled strip inside yellow bands on each side, w/Donruss '87 (copyright 1986 Leaf, Inc. back upper right)

1988 - 660 cards plus 26 BC cards w/blue border with black and red shadings, w/Donruss '88 (copyright 1987 Leaf, Inc. back upper right)

1989 - 660 cards plus 26 BC cards w/black striped side borders and multi-colored top and bottoms w/Donruss '89 (copyright 1988 Leaf, Inc. back upper right)

1990 - 716 cards plus 26 BC cards w/red borders with Donruss '90 on top left and orange backs (copyright 1989 Leaf, Inc. back upper left)

1991 - 792 cards plus 22 BC cards issued in two series of 396 cards. Series I is blue bordered and Series II is green bordered with Donruss '91 on top left (copyright 1990 Leaf, Inc. back upper right)

The listing for each card shown appears immediately following the photograph.

Player	Year	No.	VG	EX/MT	Player	Year	No.	VG	EX/MT
Aaron, Hank	86DK	602	$ .03	$ .25	Alexander, Doyle	86D	390	$ .01	$ .06
Aase, Don	81D	411	$ .01	$ .05	Alexander, Doyle	87D	657	$ .01	$ .05
Aase, Don	82D	267	$ .01	$ .05	Alexander, Doyle	88D	584	$ .01	$ .05
Aase, Don	83D	38	$ .01	$ .05	Alexander, Doyle	88DBB	13	$ .01	$ .05
Aase, Don	85D	255	$ .01	$ .08	Alexander, Doyle	89D	178	$ .01	$ .05
Aase, Don	86D	392	$ .01	$ .06	Alexander, Doyle	89DBB	125	$ .01	$ .05
Aase, Don	87D	231	$ .01	$ .05	Alexander, Doyle	90D	62	$ .01	$ .04
Abbott, Glenn	81D	47	$ .01	$ .05	Alexander, Gary	81D	200	$ .01	$ .05
Abbott, Glenn	82D	302	$ .01	$ .05	Alexander, Gerald	91DRR	419	$ .01	$ .15
Abbott, Jim	89DBB	171	$ .01	$ .75	Alicea, Luis	88DR	52	$ .01	$ .15
Abbott, Jim	89DR	16	$ .01	$ .90	Alicea, Luis	89D	466	$ .01	$ .10
Abbott, Jim	90D	108	$ .01	$ .15	Allanson, Andy	86DR	43	$ .02	$ .09
Abbott, Jim	90DL	31	$ .01	$ .35	Allanson, Andy	87D	95	$ .01	$ .05
Abbott, Jim	91D	78	$ .01	$ .10	Allanson, Andy	88D	465	$ .01	$ .05
Abbott, Paul	91D	639	$ .01	$ .10	Allanson, Andy	88DBB	5	$ .01	$ .05
Abner, Shawn	88DBB	21	$ .01	$ .15	Allanson, Andy	89D	138	$ .01	$ .05
Abner, Shawn	88DR	5	$ .01	$ .15	Allen, Jamie	84D	267	$ .03	$ .10
Abner, Shawn	88DRR	33	$ .05	$ .25	Allen, Neil	81D	276	$ .01	$ .05
Abner, Shawn	89D	323	$ .01	$ .10	Allen, Neil	82D	506	$ .01	$ .05
Abner, Shawn	91D	561	$ .01	$ .03	Allen, Neil	83D	98	$ .01	$ .05
Abrego, Johnny	86DRR	32	$ .01	$ .06	Allen, Neil	84D	109	$ .03	$ .10
Acker, Jim	84D	146	$ .03	$ .10	Allen, Neil	85D	205	$ .01	$ .08
Acker, Jim	86D	363	$ .01	$ .06	Allen, Neil	86D	610	$ .01	$ .06
Acker, Jim	87D	659	$ .01	$ .05	Allen, Neil	87D	507	$ .01	$ .05
Acker, Jim	90D	558	$ .01	$ .04	Allen, Neil	88D	597	$ .01	$ .05
Acker, Jim	91D	368	$ .01	$ .03	Allen, Neil	89D	196	$ .01	$ .05
Adams, Glenn	81D	566	$ .01	$ .05	Allenson, Gary	81D	455	$ .01	$ .05
Adams, Glenn	82D	431	$ .01	$ .05	Allenson, Gary	82D	386	$ .01	$ .05
Adams, Rick	84D	85	$ .03	$ .10	Allenson, Gary	83D	30	$ .01	$ .05
Adduci, Jim	87D	495	$ .01	$ .05	Allenson, Gary	84D	335	$ .03	$ .10
Agosto, Juan	84D	208	$ .03	$ .10	Allred, Beau	90D	691	$ .01	$ .35
Agosto, Juan	85D	526	$ .01	$ .08	Almon, Bill	82D	637	$ .01	$ .05
Agosto, Juan	86D	488	$ .01	$ .06	Almon, Bill	83D	356	$ .01	$ .05
Agosto, Juan	89D	354	$ .01	$ .05	Almon, Bill	84D	467	$ .03	$ .10
Agosto, Juan	90D	477	$ .01	$ .04	Almon, Bill	85D	589	$ .01	$ .08
Agosto, Juan	91D	531	$ .01	$ .03	Almon, Bill	86D	479	$ .01	$ .06
Aguayo, Luis	82D	622	$ .01	$ .05	Almon, Bill	87D	326	$ .01	$ .05
Aguayo, Luis	83D	546	$ .01	$ .05	Almon, Bill	88D	487	$ .01	$ .05
Aguayo, Luis	85D	503	$ .01	$ .08	Alomar, Jr., Sandy	89DR	21	$ .01	$1.00
Aguayo, Luis	86D	503	$ .01	$ .06	Alomar, Jr., Sandy	89DRR	28	$ .15	$1.00
Aguayo, Luis	88D	185	$ .01	$ .05	Alomar, Jr., Sandy	90DRR	30	$ .01	$ .25
Aguayo, Luis	89D	551	$ .01	$ .05	Alomar, Roberto	88DBB	42	$ .05	$ .75
Aguilera, Rick	86D	441	$ .08	$ .35	Alomar, Roberto	88DR	35	$ .10	$1.00
Aguilera, Rick	87D	620	$ .01	$ .05	Alomar, Roberto	88DRR	34	$ .15	$2.00
Aguilera, Rick	88D	446	$ .01	$ .05	Alomar, Roberto	89D	246	$ .05	$ .25
Aguilera, Rick	89D	526	$ .01	$ .05	Alomar, Roberto	89DBB	21	$ .01	$ .15
Aguilera, Rick	89DBB	265	$ .01	$ .05	Alomar, Roberto	90D	111	$ .01	$ .10
Aguilera, Rick	90D	391	$ .01	$ .04	Alomar, Roberto	90DL	75	$ .01	$ .35
Aguilera, Rick	90DL	38	$ .01	$ .15	Alomar, Roberto	91D	682	$ .01	$ .10
Aguilera, Rick	91D	172	$ .01	$ .03	Alomar, Roberto	91DK	12	$ .01	$ .10
Aikens, Willie	81D	220	$ .01	$ .05	Alomar, Sandy	90DL	232	$ .01	$ .75
Aikens, Willie	82D	412	$ .01	$ .05	Alomar, Sandy	90DR	1	$ .01	$ .25
Aikens, Willie	83D	212	$ .01	$ .05	Alomar, Sandy	91D	489	$ .01	$ .10
Aikens, Willie	84D	155	$ .03	$ .10	Alomar, Sandy	91D	693	$ .01	$ .15
Ainge, Danny	81D	569	$ .05	$1.00	Alomar, Sandy	91DAS	51	$ .01	$ .15
Ainge, Danny	82D	638	$ .05	$ .50	Alomar, Sandy	91DK	13	$ .01	$ .10
Akerfelds, Darrel	90DL	526	$ .01	$ .15	Alomar, Sandy	91DLP	17	$1.00	$10.00
Akerfelds, Darrel	91D	110	$ .01	$ .03	Alou, Felipe	82D	650	$ .01	$ .05
Aldred, Scott	91DRR	422	$ .01	$ .15	Alou, Moises	91DRR	38	$ .01	$ .15
Aldrete, Mike	87D	450	$ .01	$ .05	Alston, Dell	81D	322	$ .01	$ .05
Aldrete, Mike	88D	362	$ .01	$ .05	Altobelli, Joe	84D	88	$ .03	$ .10
Aldrete, Mike	88DBB	191	$ .01	$ .05	Alvarez, Jose	89D	405	$ .01	$ .10
Aldrete, Mike	89D	140	$ .01	$ .05	Alvarez, Jose	90D	389	$ .01	$ .04
Aldrete, Mike	89DTR	25	$ .01	$ .05	Amalfitano, Joe	81D	522	$ .01	$ .05
Aldrich, Jay	88D	460	$ .01	$ .05	Andersen (son), Larry	82D	428	$ .01	$ .05
Alexander, Doyle	81D	448	$ .02	$ .15	Andersen, Larry	83D	181	$ .01	$ .05
Alexander, Doyle	82D	96	$ .01	$ .05	Andersen, Larry	85D	570	$ .01	$ .08
Alexander, Doyle	83D	451	$ .01	$ .05	Andersen, Larry	86D	355	$ .01	$ .06
Alexander, Doyle	84D	439	$ .03	$ .10	Andersen, Larry	87D	640	$ .01	$ .05
Alexander, Doyle	85D	561	$ .01	$ .08	Andersen, Larry	89D	359	$ .01	$ .05

DONRUSS

Player	Year	No.	VG	EX/MT	Player	Year	No.	VG	EX/MT
Andersen, Larry	90D	359	$ .01	$ .04	Aponte, Luis	83D	109	$ .01	$ .05
Andersen, Larry	90DL	386	$ .01	$ .15	Aponte, Luis	84D	371	$ .03	$ .10
Andersen, Larry	91D	665	$ .01	$ .03	Appier, Kevin	90DR	21	$ .01	$ .20
Anderson, Allan	86DR	3	$ .05	$ .35	Appier, Kevin	91D	740	$ .01	$ .10
Anderson, Allan	87D	368	$ .05	$ .35	Aquino, Luis	87D	655	$ .01	$ .05
Anderson, Allan	89D	419	$ .01	$ .10	Aquino, Luis	89D	534	$ .01	$ .05
Anderson, Allan	89DBB	270	$ .01	$ .05	Aquino, Luis	90D	179	$ .01	$ .04
Anderson, Allan	90D	64	$ .01	$ .04	Aquino, Luis	91D	718	$ .01	$ .03
Anderson, Allan	90DL	5	$ .01	$ .15	Armas, Tony	81D	239	$ .01	$ .05
Anderson, Allan	91D	527	$ .01	$ .03	Armas, Tony	82D	365	$ .01	$ .05
Anderson, Brady	88DR	14	$ .05	$ .35	Armas, Tony	83D	71	$ .01	$ .05
Anderson, Brady	89D	519	$ .05	$ .35	Armas, Tony	84D	294	$ .03	$ .10
Anderson, Brady	90D	638	$ .01	$ .04	Armas, Tony	85D	249	$ .01	$ .08
Anderson, Brady	91D	668	$ .01	$ .03	Armas, Tony	86D	127	$ .01	$ .06
Anderson, Bud	84D	590	$ .03	$ .10	Armas, Tony	86DK	5	$ .01	$ .06
					Armas, Tony	87D	498	$ .01	$ .05
					Armas, Tony	89D	580	$ .01	$ .05
					Armas, Tony	90D	525	$ .01	$ .04
					Armstrong, Jack	89D	493	$ .15	$ .20
					Armstrong, Jack	90D	544	$ .01	$ .10
					Armstrong, Jack	90DL	374	$ .01	$ .20
					Armstrong, Jack	91D	571	$ .01	$ .03
					Armstrong, Jack	91DAS	439	$ .01	$ .03
					Armstrong, Mike	84D	217	$ .03	$ .10
					Armstrong, Mike	85D	602	$ .01	$ .08
					Arnsberg, Brad	90DL	495	$ .01	$ .15
					Arnsberg, Brad	91D	633	$ .01	$ .03
					Arroyo, Fernando	82D	177	$ .01	$ .05
					Asadoor, Randy	87D	574	$ .01	$ .05
					Ashby, Alan	81D	259	$ .01	$ .05
					Ashby, Alan	82D	317	$ .01	$ .05
					Ashby, Alan	83D	144	$ .01	$ .05
					Ashby, Alan	84D	539	$ .03	$ .10
					Ashby, Alan	85D	283	$ .01	$ .08
					Ashby, Alan	86D	405	$ .01	$ .06
					Ashby, Alan	87D	332	$ .01	$ .05
					Ashby, Alan	88D	163	$ .01	$ .05
					Ashby, Alan	88DBB	8	$ .01	$ .05
					Ashby, Alan	89D	88	$ .01	$ .05
					Asselstine, Brian	81D	186	$ .01	$ .05
					Asselstine, Brian	82D	184	$ .01	$ .05
					Assenmacher, Paul	86DR	28	$ .03	$ .15
					Assenmacher, Paul	87D	290	$ .01	$ .15
					Assenmacher, Paul	89D	357	$ .01	$ .05
					Assenmacher, Paul	90D	459	$ .01	$ .04
Anderson, Dave	84D	642	$ .05	$ .25	Assenmacher, Paul	90DL	493	$ .01	$ .15
Anderson, Dave	85D	275	$ .01	$ .08	Assenmacher, Paul	91D	144	$ .01	$ .03
Anderson, Dave	88D	475	$ .01	$ .05	Atherton, Keith	84D	497	$ .03	$ .10
Anderson, Dave	89D	434	$ .01	$ .05	Atherton, Keith	85D	340	$ .01	$ .08
Anderson, Dave	90D	486	$ .01	$ .04	Atherton, Keith	87D	272	$ .01	$ .05
Anderson, Jim	81D	165	$ .01	$ .05	Atherton, Keith	88D	318	$ .01	$ .05
Anderson, Jim	82D	181	$ .01	$ .05	Atherton, Keith	89D	273	$ .01	$ .05
Anderson, Kent	90D	490	$ .01	$ .04	August, Don	88D	602	$ .01	$ .15
Anderson, Kent	91D	525	$ .01	$ .03	August, Don	89D	410	$ .01	$ .05
Anderson, Larry	88D	332	$ .01	$ .05	August, Don	90D	617	$ .01	$ .04
Anderson, Sparky	81D	370	$ .01	$ .05	Augustine, Jerry	81D	445	$ .01	$ .05
Anderson, Sparky	82D	29	$ .05	$ .20	Augustine, Jerry	82D	332	$ .01	$ .05
Anderson, Sparky	83D	533	$ .03	$ .20	Avery, Steve	90DL	481	$ .01	$1.75
Andujar, Joaquin	81D	381	$ .01	$ .05	Avery, Steve	90DR	42	$ .01	$ .20
Andujar, Joaquin	82D	607	$ .01	$ .05	Avery, Steve	90DRR	39	$ .01	$ .25
Andujar, Joaquin	83D	316	$ .01	$ .05	Avery, Steve	91D	187	$ .01	$ .10
Andujar, Joaquin	84D	181	$ .03	$ .10	Ayala, Benny	81D	236	$ .01	$ .05
Andujar, Joaquin	85D	449	$ .01	$ .08	Ayala, Benny	82D	581	$ .01	$ .05
Andujar, Joaquin	85DK	13	$ .03	$ .10	Ayala, Benny	83D	331	$ .01	$ .05
Andujar, Joaquin	86D	231	$ .01	$ .06	Ayala, Benny	84D	270	$ .03	$ .10
Andujar, Joaquin	87D	548	$ .01	$ .05	Azocar, Oscar	91D	331	$ .01	$ .15
Anthony, Eric	90DL	82	$ .01	$1.00	Babcock, Bob	82D	565	$ .01	$ .05
Anthony, Eric	90DR	49	$ .01	$ .25	Babitt, Shooty	82D	556	$ .01	$ .05
Anthony, Eric	90DRR	34	$ .01	$ .50	Backman, Wally	83D	618	$ .03	$ .20
Anthony, Eric	91D	333	$ .01	$ .15	Backman, Wally	85D	319	$ .01	$ .08

DAVE ANDERSON ss

Player	Year	No.	VG	EX/MT	Player	Year	No.	VG	EX/MT
Backman, Wally	86D	238	$ .01	$ .06	Ballard, Jeff	91D	279	$ .01	$ .03
Backman, Wally	87D	316	$ .01	$ .05	Baller, Jay	86D	613	$ .01	$ .06
Backman, Wally	88D	241	$ .01	$ .05	Bando, Chris	82D	551	$ .01	$ .05
Backman, Wally	89D	383	$ .01	$ .05	Bando, Chris	83D	33	$ .01	$ .05
Backman, Wally	89DBB	186	$ .01	$ .05	Bando, Chris	84D	224	$ .03	$ .10
Backman, Wally	89DTR	-10	$ .01	$ .05	Bando, Chris	85D	520	$ .01	$ .08
Backman, Wally	90D	155	$ .01	$ .04	Bando, Chris	86D	373	$ .01	$ .06
Backman, Wally	90DL	341	$ .01	$ .15	Bando, Chris	87D	501	$ .01	$ .05
Backman, Wally	91D	177	$ .01	$ .03	Bando, Chris	88D	95	$ .01	$ .05
Baerga, Carlos	90DL	443	$ .01	$ .75	Bando, Sal	81D	84	$ .02	$ .15
Baerga, Carlos	90DR	19	$ .01	$ .25	Bando, Sal	82D	592	$ .01	$ .05
Baerga, Carlos	91D	274	$ .01	$ .20	Bankhead, Scott	86DR	36	$ .02	$ .15
Bahnsen, Stan	81D	452	$ .01	$ .05	Bankhead, Scott	88D	70	$ .01	$ .05
Bahnsen, Stan	82D	392	$ .01	$ .05	Bankhead, Scott	89D	463	$ .01	$ .05
Bailes, Scott	86DR	25	$ .03	$ .25	Bankhead, Scott	89DBB	219	$ .01	$ .05
Bailes, Scott	87D	227	$ .01	$ .05	Bankhead, Scott	90D	261	$ .01	$ .04
Bailes, Scott	88D	104	$ .01	$ .05	Bankhead, Scott	90DL	127	$ .01	$ .15
Bailes, Scott	89D	202	$ .01	$ .05	Bankhead, Scott	91D	189	$ .01	$ .03
Bailes, Scott	90D	468	$ .01	$ .04	Bannister, Alan	82D	159	$ .01	$ .05
Bailes, Scott	90DL	380	$ .01	$ .15	Bannister, Alan	83D	285	$ .01	$ .05
Bailey, Howard	84D	212	$ .03	$ .10	Bannister, Alan	84D	154	$ .03	$ .10
Bailey, Mark	85D	450	$ .01	$ .08	Bannister, Alan	86D	525	$ .01	$ .06
Bailey, Mark	86D	354	$ .01	$ .06	Bannister, Floyd	81D	286	$ .01	$ .05
Bailey, Mark	87D	235	$ .01	$ .05	Bannister, Floyd	82D	100	$ .01	$ .05
Bailor, Bob	81D	389	$ .01	$ .05	Bannister, Floyd	83D	50	$ .01	$ .05
Bailor, Bob	82D	308	$ .01	$ .05	Bannister, Floyd	83DK	21	$ .01	$ .05
Bailor, Bob	83D	506	$ .01	$ .05	Bannister, Floyd	84D	366	$ .03	$ .10
Bailor, Bob	84D	595	$ .03	$ .10	Bannister, Floyd	85D	379	$ .01	$ .08
Bailor, Bob	85D	397	$ .01	$ .08	Bannister, Floyd	86D	244	$ .01	$ .06
Baines, Harold	82D	568	$ .05	$1.00	Bannister, Floyd	87D	211	$ .01	$ .05
Baines, Harold	83D	143	$ .05	$ .30	Bannister, Floyd	88D	383	$ .01	$ .05
Baines, Harold	84D	58	$ .04	$ .25	Bannister, Floyd	88DBB	7	$ .01	$ .05
Baines, Harold	85D	58	$ .03	$ .20	Bannister, Floyd	89D	262	$ .01	$ .05
Baines, Harold	86D	180	$ .02	$ .15	Barfield, Jesse	83D	595	$ .05	$1.00
Baines, Harold	86DK	13	$ .01	$ .06	Barfield, Jesse	84D	193	$ .15	$ .40
Baines, Harold	87D	429	$ .05	$ .20	Barfield, Jesse	85D	195	$ .08	$ .25
Baines, Harold	88D	211	$ .01	$ .05	Barfield, Jesse	86D	193	$ .03	$ .25
Baines, Harold	88DBB	11	$ .01	$ .05	Barfield, Jesse	87D	121	$ .01	$ .15
Baines, Harold	89D	148	$ .01	$ .05	Barfield, Jesse	88D	442	$ .01	$ .15
Baines, Harold	89DBB	81	$ .01	$ .10	Barfield, Jesse	88DBB	216	$ .01	$ .10
Baines, Harold	90D	402	$ .01	$ .10	Barfield, Jesse	89D	425	$ .01	$ .05
Baines, Harold	90DAS	660	$ .01	$ .10	Barfield, Jesse	89DBB	132	$ .01	$ .05
Baines, Harold	90DL	126	$ .01	$ .15	Barfield, Jesse	90D	74	$ .01	$ .04
Baines, Harold	91D	748	$ .01	$ .03	Barfield, Jesse	90DL	201	$ .01	$ .15
Bair, Doug	81D	64	$ .01	$ .05	Barfield, Jesse	91D	498	$ .01	$ .03
Bair, Doug	83D	372	$ .01	$ .05	Barfield, John	91D	688	$ .01	$ .10
Bair, Doug	84D	369	$ .03	$ .10	Barker, Len	81D	320	$ .01	$ .05
Bair, Doug	85D	369	$ .01	$ .08	Barker, Len	82D	137	$ .01	$ .05
Baker, Dusty	81D	179	$ .01	$ .10	Barker, Len	82DK	6	$ .01	$ .05
Baker, Dusty	82D	336	$ .01	$ .05	Barker, Len	83D	111	$ .01	$ .05
Baker, Dusty	83D	462	$ .01	$ .05	Barker, Len	84D	443	$ .03	$ .10
Baker, Dusty	84D	226	$ .03	$ .10	Barker, Len	85D	165	$ .01	$ .08
Baker, Dusty	85D	445	$ .01	$ .08	Barker, Len	86D	409	$ .01	$ .06
Baker, Dusty	86D	467	$ .01	$ .06	Barnes, Brian	91DRR	415	$ .01	$ .15
Balboni, Steve	83D	73	$ .01	$ .05	Barnes, Richard	84D	608	$ .03	$ .10
Balboni, Steve	85D	419	$ .01	$ .08	Barnes, Skeeter	85D	530	$ .01	$ .08
Balboni, Steve	86D	222	$ .01	$ .06	Barojas, Salome	83D	67	$ .01	$ .05
Balboni, Steve	87D	102	$ .01	$ .05	Barojas, Salome	84D	570	$ .03	$ .10
Balboni, Steve	88D	424	$ .01	$ .05	Barojas, Salome	85D	605	$ .01	$ .08
Balboni, Steve	89D	143	$ .01	$ .05	Barr, Jim	81D	412	$ .01	$ .05
Balboni, Steve	89DBB	188	$ .01	$ .05	Barr, Jim	83D	398	$ .01	$ .05
Balboni, Steve	89DTR	48	$ .01	$ .05	Barr, Jim	84D	79	$ .03	$ .10
Balboni, Steve	90D	315	$ .01	$ .04	Barrett, Marty	85D	127	$ .03	$ .25
Balboni, Steve	90DL	373	$ .01	$ .15	Barrett, Marty	86D	294	$ .01	$ .06
Balboni, Steve	91D	650	$ .01	$ .03	Barrett, Marty	87D	523	$ .01	$ .05
Ballard, Jeff	88D	520	$ .01	$ .35	Barrett, Marty	88D	276	$ .01	$ .05
Ballard, Jeff	89D	495	$ .01	$ 04	Barrett, Marty	88DBB	9	$ .01	$ .05
Ballard, Jeff	89DBB	30	$ .01	$ .05	Barrett, Marty	89D	184	$ .01	$ .05
Ballard, Jeff	90D	51	$ .01	$ .04	Barrett, Marty	89DBB	252	$ .01	$ .05
Ballard, Jeff	90DL	118	$ .01	$ .15	Barrett, Marty	90D	240	$ .01	$ .04

Player	Year	No.	VG	EX/MT	Player	Year	No.	VG	EX/MT
Bass, Kevin	84D	450	$ .03	$ .10	Bell, Buddy	86D	447	$ .05	$ .20
Bass, Kevin	85D	136	$ .01	$ .08	Bell, Buddy	87D	556	$ .01	$ .15
Bass, Kevin	86D	548	$ .01	$ .06	Bell, Buddy	88D	206	$ .01	$ .15
Bass, Kevin	87D	410	$ .01	$ .05	Bell, Derek	91DRR	32	$ .01	$ .25
Bass, Kevin	88D	286	$ .01	$ .05	Bell, Eric	87DR	2	$ .01	$ .07
Bass, Kevin	88DBB	38	$ .01	$ .05	Bell, Eric	87DRR	39	$ .01	$ .05
Bass, Kevin	89D	325	$ .01	$ .05	Bell, Eric	88D	125	$ .01	$ .05
Bass, Kevin	90D	589	$ .01	$ .04	Bell, George (Jorge)	82D	54	$1.50	$7.50
Bass, Kevin	90DL	305	$ .01	$ .15	Bell, George	84D	73	$ .50	$2.50
Bass, Kevin	91D	630	$ .01	$ .03	Bell, George	85D	146	$ .25	$ .75
Bass, Randy	82D	439	$ .01	$ .05	Bell, George	86D	71	$ .15	$ .40
Bathe, Bill	86DR	41	$ .02	$ .09	Bell, George	86DK	4	$ .08	$ .25
Bathe, Bill	87D	281	$ .01	$ .05	Bell, George	87D	271	$ .05	$ .25
Bathe, Bill	90D	680	$ .01	$ .04	Bell, George	88D	656	$ .05	$ .20
Baumgarten, Ross	81D	41	$ .01	$ .05	Bell, George	88DBB	31	$ .01	$ .10
Baumgarten, Ross	82D	104	$ .01	$ .05	Bell, George	88DBC	19	$ .15	$ .50
Bautista, Jose	88DR	41	$ .01	$ .05	Bell, George	89D	149	$ .01	$ .10
Bautista, Jose	89D	451	$ .01	$ .10	Bell, George	89DBB	272	$ .01	$ .10
Baylor, Don	81D	413	$ .03	$ .20	Bell, George	90D	206	$ .01	$ .10
Baylor, Don	82D	493	$ .03	$ .20	Bell, George	90DBC	13	$ .01	$ .10
Baylor, Don	83D	493	$ .03	$ .15	Bell, George	90DL	185	$ .01	$ .20
Baylor, Don	84D	152	$ .03	$ .10	Bell, George	91D	642	$ .01	$ .03
Baylor, Don	85D	173	$ .03	$ .20	Bell, Jay	88D	637	$ .05	$ .20
Baylor, Don	86D	347	$ .01	$ .06	Bell, Jay	88DBB	61	$ .01	$ .05
Baylor, Don	87D	339	$ .01	$ .05	Bell, Jay	89D	350	$ .01	$ .10
Beane, Billy	86D	647	$ .01	$ .06	Bell, Jay	90D	488	$ .01	$ .04
Beard, Dave	83D	113	$ .01	$ .05	Bell, Jay	90DL	248	$ .01	$ .15
Beard, Dave	84D	218	$ .03	$ .10	Bell, Jay	91D	289	$ .01	$ .03
Beattie, Jim	81D	166	$ .01	$ .05	Bell, Kevin	81D	39	$ .01	$ .05
Beattie, Jim	82D	478	$ .01	$ .05	Belle, Joey	90D	390	$ .01	$ .60
Beattie, Jim	83D	176	$ .01	$ .05	Belle, Joey	90DL	180	$ .01	$ 5.00
Beattie, Jim	84D	191	$ .03	$ .10	Belliard, Rafael	87D	538	$ .01	$ .05
Beattie, Jim	85D	313	$ .01	$ .08	Belliard, Rafael	90D	252	$ .01	$ .04
Beattie, Jim	86D	196	$ .01	$ .06	Bench, Johnny	81D	62	$ .10	$1.25
Beckwith, Joe	84D	337	$ .03	$ .10	Bench, Johnny	81D	182	$ .15	$1.00
Beckwith, Joe	85D	541	$ .01	$ .08	Bench, Johnny	82D	400	$ .15	$1.25
Bedrosian, Steve	82D	401	$ .15	$ .95	Bench, Johnny	82D	628	$ .15	$ .75
Bedrosian, Steve	83D	173	$ .03	$ .25	Bench, Johnny	83D	500	$ .10	$ .75
Bedrosian, Steve	84D	565	$ .05	$ .30	Bench, Johnny	83DK	22	$ .10	$ .50
Bedrosian, Steve	85D	628	$ .03	$ .15	Bench, Johnny	84D#B	0	$1.50	$8.00
Bedrosian, Steve	86D	199	$ .02	$ .15	Benedict, Bruce	81D	208	$ .01	$ .05
Bedrosian, Steve	87D	185	$ .02	$ .15	Benedict, Bruce	82D	375	$ .01	$ .05
Bedrosian, Steve	88D	62	$ .01	$ .05	Benedict, Bruce	83D	299	$ .01	$ .05
Bedrosian, Steve	88DBB	16	$ .01	$ .10	Benedict, Bruce	84D	409	$ .03	$ .10
Bedrosian, Steve	89D	75	$ .01	$ .10	Benedict, Bruce	85D	261	$ .01	$ .08
Bedrosian, Steve	89DBB	303	$ .01	$ .05	Benedict, Bruce	85D	263	$ .01	$ .08
Bedrosian, Steve	89DK	24	$ .01	$ .15	Benedict, Bruce	86D	554	$ .01	$ .06
Bedrosian, Steve	90D	295	$ .01	$ .04	Benedict, Bruce	87D	448	$ .01	$ .05
Bedrosian, Steve	90DL	3	$ .01	$ .15	Benedict, Bruce	89D	475	$ .01	$ .05
Bedrosian, Steve	91D	207	$ .01	$ .03	Benes, Andy	90DL	56	$ .01	$ .35
Behenna, Rick	84D	346	$ .05	$ .25	Benes, Andy	90DRR	41	$ .01	$ .20
Belanger, Mark	81D	472	$ .02	$ .15	Benes, Andy	91D	627	$ .01	$ .10
Belanger, Mark	83D	514	$ .01	$ .05	Beniquez, Juan	81D	518	$ .01	$ .05
Belcher, Kevin	91DRR	46	$ .01	$ .15	Beniquez, Juan	82D	587	$ .01	$ .05
Belcher, Tim	88D	587	$ .01	$ .50	Beniquez, Juan	83D	640	$ .01	$ .05
Belcher, Tim	88DBB	10	$ .01	$ .15	Beniquez, Juan	84D	207	$ .03	$ .10
Belcher, Tim	88DR	28	$ .01	$ .25	Beniquez, Juan	85D	573	$ .01	$ .08
Belcher, Tim	89D	203	$ .01	$ .05	Beniquez, Juan	86D	352	$ .01	$ .06
Belcher, Tim	89DBB	234	$ .01	$ .05	Beniquez, Juan	87D	371	$ .01	$ .05
Belcher, Tim	90D	79	$ .01	$ .04	Benjamin, Mike	91DRR	432	$ .01	$ .03
Belcher, Tim	90DL	200	$ .01	$ .15	Benzinger, Todd	87DR	30	$ .01	$ .35
Belcher, Tim	91D	70	$ .01	$ .03	Benzinger, Todd	88D	297	$ .01	$ .20
Belinda, Stan	90DL	486	$ .01	$ .15	Benzinger, Todd	89D	358	$ .01	$ .15
Belinda, Stan	91D	699	$ .01	$ .10	Benzinger, Todd	89DBB	174	$ .01	$ .10
Bell, Buddy	81D	145	$ .03	$ .20	Benzinger, Todd	89DTR	47	$ .01	$ .10
Bell, Buddy	82D	368	$ .03	$ .20	Benzinger, Todd	90D	257	$ .01	$ .04
Bell, Buddy	82DK	23	$ .03	$ .20	Benzinger, Todd	90DL	15	$ .01	$ .15
Bell, Buddy	83D	215	$ .03	$ .20	Benzinger, Todd	91D	640	$ .01	$ .03
Bell, Buddy	84D	56	$ .08	$ .25	Berenguer, Juan	82D	580	$ .01	$ .05
Bell, Buddy	85D	56	$ .03	$ .20	Berenguer, Juan	84D	125	$ .03	$ .10

Player	Year	No.	VG	EX/MT
Berenguer, Juan	85D	272	$ .01	$ .08
Berenguer, Juan	87D	616	$ .01	$ .05
Berenguer, Juan	88D	395	$ .01	$ .05
Berenguer, Juan	89D	81	$ .01	$ .05
Berenguer, Juan	89DBB	46	$ .01	$ .05
Berenguer, Juan	90D	301	$ .01	$ .04
Berenguer, Juan	90DL	169	$ .01	$ .15
Berenguer, Juan	91D	340	$ .01	$ .03
Berenyi, Bruce	83D	103	$ .01	$ .05
Berenyi, Bruce	84D	487	$ .03	$ .10
Berenyi, Bruce	85D	625	$ .01	$ .08
Bergman, Dave	81D	139	$ .01	$ .05
Bergman, Dave	82D	146	$ .01	$ .05
Bergman, Dave	83D	550	$ .01	$ .05
Bergman, Dave	84D	624	$ .03	$ .10
Bergman, Dave	85D	537	$ .01	$ .08
Bergman, Dave	86D	471	$ .01	$ .06
Bergman, Dave	87D	420	$ .01	$ .05
Bergman, Dave	88D	373	$ .01	$ .05
Bergman, Dave	89D	389	$ .01	$ .05
Bergman, Dave	90D	445	$ .01	$ .04
Bergman, Dave	90DL	244	$ .01	$ .15
Bergman, Dave	91D	342	$ .01	$ .03
Bernard, Dwight	83D	28	$ .01	$ .05
Bernazard, Tony	81D	449	$ .01	$ .05
Bernazard, Tony	82D	143	$ .01	$ .05
Bernazard, Tony	83D	482	$ .01	$ .05
Bernazard, Tony	84D	240	$ .03	$ .10
Bernazard, Tony	85D	102	$ .01	$ .08
Bernazard, Tony	86D	520	$ .01	$ .06
Bernazard, Tony	87D	377	$ .01	$ .05
Bernazard, Tony	88D	344	$ .01	$ .05
Berra, Dale	81D	253	$ .01	$ .05
Berra, Dale	82D	250	$ .01	$ .05
Berra, Dale	83D	185	$ .01	$ .05
Berra, Dale	84D	430	$ .03	$ .10
Berra, Dale	85D	444	$ .01	$ .08
Berra, Dale	86D	295	$ .01	$ .06
Berra, Yogi	81D	351	$ .05	$ .30
Berra, Yogi	82D	387	$ .03	$ .20
Berroa, Geronimo	88D	659	$ .01	$ .20
Berroa, Geronimo	89DR	19	$ .01	$ .10
Berroa, Geronimo	90D	104	$ .01	$ .04
Berryhill, Damon	88D	639	$ .01	$ .20
Berryhill, Damon	88DBB	261	$ .01	$ .10
Berryhill, Damon	88DR	31	$ .01	$ .20
Berryhill, Damon	89D	275	$ .01	$ .10
Berryhill, Damon	89DBB	116	$ .01	$ .10
Berryhill, Damon	90D	167	$ .01	$ .10
Berryhill, Damon	91D	631	$ .01	$ .03
Best, Karl	86D	511	$ .01	$ .06
Best, Karl	87D	198	$ .01	$ .05
Bevacqua, Kurt	84D	80	$ .03	$ .10
Bevacqua, Kurt	85D	647	$ .01	$ .08
Bevacqua, Kurt	86D	528	$ .01	$ .06
Biancalana, Buddy	86D	605	$ .01	$ .06
Biancalana, Buddy	87D	527	$ .01	$ .05
Bibby, Jim	81D	134	$ .01	$ .05
Bibby, Jim	82D	171	$ .01	$ .05
Bichette, Dante	89D	634	$ .01	$ .25
Bichette, Dante	89DR	29	$ .01	$ .10
Bichette, Dante	90DL	340	$ .01	$ .25
Bichette, Dante	91D	303	$ .01	$ .03
Bielecki, Mike	85DRR	28	$ .01	$ .50
Bielecki, Mike	87D	415	$ .01	$ .05
Bielecki, Mike	88D	484	$ .01	$ .05
Bielecki, Mike	89D	512	$ .01	$ .05
Bielecki, Mike	89DBB	194	$ .01	$ .05
Bielecki, Mike	90D	373	$ .01	$ .04
Bielecki, Mike	90DK	9	$ .01	$ .10

Player	Year	No.	VG	EX/MT
Bielecki, Mike	90DL	45	$ .01	$ .15
Bielecki, Mike	91D	87	$ .01	$ .03
Biggio, Craig	89D	561	$ .01	$ .50
Biggio, Craig	89DBB	176	$ .01	$ .15

Player	Year	No.	VG	EX/MT
Biggio, Craig	90D	306	$ .01	$ .10
Biggio, Craig	90DL	37	$ .01	$ .50
Biggio, Craig	91D	595	$ .01	$ .03
Biggio, Craig	91DK	2	$ .01	$ .05
Biggio, Craig	91DLP	4	$1.00	$10.00
Biittner, Larry	81D	515	$ .01	$ .05
Biittner, Larry	82D	43	$ .01	$ .05
Biittner, Larry	83D	440	$ .01	$ .05
Biittner, Larry	84D	342	$ .03	$ .10
Bilardello, Dann	84D	408	$ .03	$ .10
Bilardello, Dann	85D	243	$ .01	$ .08
Bird, Doug	82D	504	$ .01	$ .05
Bird, Doug	83D	48	$ .01	$ .05
Birkbeck, Mike	87DR	19	$ .01	$ .20
Birkbeck, Mike	87DRR	33	$ .05	$ .25
Birkbeck, Mike	88D	49	$ .01	$ .05
Birkbeck, Mike	89D	501	$ .01	$ .05
Birtsas, Tim	86D	462	$ .01	$ .06
Birtsas, Tim	90D	493	$ .01	$ .10
Bitker, Joe	91D	624	$ .01	$ .10
Black, Bud	83D	322	$ .10	$ .50
Black, Bud	84D	130	$ .03	$ .10
Black, Bud	85D	100	$ .01	$ .08
Black, Bud	86D	374	$ .01	$ .06
Black, Bud	87D	404	$ .01	$ .05
Black, Bud	88D	301	$ .01	$ .05
Black, Bud	89D	556	$ .01	$ .05
Black, Bud	90D	556	$ .01	$ .04
Black, Bud	90DL	451	$ .01	$ .15
Black, Bud	91D	719	$ .01	$ .03
Blackwell, Tim	81D	559	$ .01	$ .05
Blackwell, Tim	82D	99	$ .01	$ .05
Blackwell, Tim	83D	214	$ .01	$ .05
Blair, Willie	90DL	449	$ .01	$ .15
Blair, Willie	90DR	29	$ .01	$ .10
Blair, Willie	91D	267	$ .01	$ .10
Blankenship, Kevin	89D	658	$ .01	$ .05

DONRUSS

Player	Year	No.	VG	EX/MT	Player	Year	No.	VG	EX/MT
Blankenship, Lance	89D	621	$ .01	$ .25	Boggs, Wade	89D	68	$ .01	$ .30
Blankenship, Lance	91D	701	$ .01	$ .03	Boggs, Wade	89DBB	140	$ .01	$ .35
Blauser, Jeff	88D	513	$ .01	$ .20	Boggs, Wade	90D	68	$ .01	$ .25
Blauser, Jeff	89D	592	$ .01	$ .05	Boggs, Wade	90DAS	712	$ .01	$ .20
Blauser, Jeff	90D	271	$ .01	$ .04	Boggs, Wade	90DL	51	$ .01	$ .50
Blauser, Jeff	90DL	191	$ .01	$ .15	Boggs, Wade	91D	178	$ .01	$ .15
Blauser, Jeff	91D	229	$ .01	$ .03	Boggs, Wade	91DAS	55	$ .01	$ .10
Blowers, Mike	90D	656	$ .01	$ .10	Boggs, Wade	91DLP	14	$1.00	$15.00
Blowers, Mike	90DL	109	$ .01	$ .25	Bogner, Terry	83D	520	$ .01	$ .05
Blowers, Mike	90DR	26	$ .01	$ .10	Bohanon, Brian	90DR	13	$ .01	$ .10
Blowers, Mike	91D	63	$ .01	$ .03	Bolton, Tom	89D	539	$ .01	$ .05
Blue, Vida	81D	433	$ .02	$ .15	Bolton, Tom	91D	609	$ .01	$ .03
Blue, Vida	82D	222	$ .01	$ .05	Bomback, Mark	82D	559	$ .01	$ .05
Blue, Vida	82DK	4	$ .01	$ .05	Bonds, Barry	86DR	11	$1.00	$6.00
Blue, Vida	83D	34	$ .01	$ .05	Bonds, Barry	87D	361	$1.00	$7.00
Blue, Vida	83D	648	$ .01	$ .15	Bonds, Barry	88D	326	$ .01	$ .40
Blue, Vida	86D	509	$ .01	$ .06	Bonds, Barry	88DBB	17	$ .01	$1.00
Blue, Vida	87D	362	$ .01	$ .05	Bonds, Barry	89D	92	$ .01	$ .10
Blyleven, Bert	81D	135	$ .05	$ .30	Bonds, Barry	89DBB	73	$ .01	$ .10
Blyleven, Bert	82D	111	$ .02	$ .15	Bonds, Barry	90D	126	$ .01	$ .10
Blyleven, Bert	83D	589	$ .02	$ .15	Bonds, Barry	90DL	91	$ .01	$ .50
Blyleven, Bert	84D	129	$ .10	$ .35	Bonds, Barry	91D	495	$ .01	$ .10
Blyleven, Bert	85D	224	$ .03	$ .25	Bonds, Barry	91DK	4	$ .01	$ .10
Blyleven, Bert	85DK	4	$ .01	$ .08	Bonds, Barry	91DLP	9	$1.00	$10.00
Blyleven, Bert	86D	649	$ .05	$ .20	Bonds, Barry	91DMVP	762	$ .01	$ .10
Blyleven, Bert	87D	71	$ .01	$ .05	Bonds, Bobby	81D	71	$ .01	$ .05
Blyleven, Bert	88D	71	$ .01	$ .05	Bonilla, Bobby	86DR	30	$ .35	$4.50
Blyleven, Bert	88DBB	18	$ .01	$ .05	Bonilla, Bobby	87D	558	$ .35	$5.00
Blyleven, Bert	89D	119	$ .01	$ .05	Bonilla, Bobby	88D	238	$ .10	$ .50
Blyleven, Bert	89DBB	3	$ .01	$ .05	Bonilla, Bobby	88DBB	33	$ .01	$1.00
Blyleven, Bert	89DTR	35	$ .01	$ .15	Bonilla, Bobby	89D	151	$ .01	$ .15
Blyleven, Bert	90D	331	$ .01	$ .04	Bonilla, Bobby	89DBB	33	$ .01	$ .20
Blyleven, Bert	90DL	63	$ .01	$ .15	Bonilla, Bobby	89DK	2	$ .01	$ .05
Blyleven, Bert	91D	453	$ .01	$ .03	Bonilla, Bobby	90D	290	$ .01	$ .20
Bochte, Bruce	81D	403	$ .01	$ .05	Bonilla, Bobby	90DBC	16	$ .01	$ .10
Bochte, Bruce	82D	505	$ .01	$ .05	Bonilla, Bobby	90DL	196	$ .01	$ .35
Bochte, Bruce	83D	127	$ .01	$ .05					
Bochte, Bruce	85D	253	$ .01	$ .08					
Bochte, Bruce	86D	400	$ .01	$ .06					
Bochy, Bruce	81D	20	$ .01	$ .05					
Bochy, Bruce	85D	505	$ .01	$ .08					
Bochy, Bruce	86D	551	$ .01	$ .06					
Bochy, Bruce	87D	311	$ .01	$ .05					
Boddicker, Mike	84D	123	$ .04	$ .25					
Boddicker, Mike	85D	291	$ .01	$ .08					
Boddicker, Mike	86D	47	$ .01	$ .06					
Boddicker, Mike	86DK	8	$ .01	$ .06					
Boddicker, Mike	87D	125	$ .01	$ .05					
Boddicker, Mike	88D	89	$ .01	$ .05					
Boddicker, Mike	89D	612	$ .01	$ .05					
Boddicker, Mike	89DBB	297	$ .01	$ .05					
Boddicker, Mike	90D	280	$ .01	$ .04					
Boddicker, Mike	90DL	19	$ .01	$ .15					
Boddicker, Mike	91D	680	$ .01	$ .03					
Boever, Joe	89D	168	$ .01	$ .05					
Boever, Joe	90D	357	$ .01	$ .04					
Boever, Joe	90DL	349	$ .01	$ .15					
Boever, Joe	91D	578	$ .01	$ .03					
Boggs, Tommy	81D	597	$ .01	$ .05					
Boggs, Tommy	82D	249	$ .01	$ .05					
Boggs, Tommy	83D	349	$ .01	$ .05					
Boggs, Wade	83D	586	$5.00	$20.00					
Boggs, Wade	84D	151	$2.50	$10.00					
Boggs, Wade	84DK	26	$1.00	$3.00					
Boggs, Wade	85D	172	$1.50	$4.00					
Boggs, Wade	86D	371	$ .75	$2.00					
Boggs, Wade	87D	252	$ .20	$1.00	Bonilla, Bobby	91D	325	$ .01	$ .10
Boggs, Wade	88D	153	$ .35	$1.00	Bonilla, Juan	82D	220	$ .01	$ .05
Boggs, Wade	88DBB	65	$ .01	$ .30	Bonilla, Juan	83D	346	$ .01	$ .05
Boggs, Wade	88DBC	7	$ .01	$ .30	Bonilla, Juan	84D	234	$ .03	$ .10

Player	Year	No.	VG	EX/MT	Player	Year	No.	VG	EX/MT
Bonnell, Barry	81D	272	$ .01	$ .05	Boyd, Oil Can	90DL	159	$ .01	$ .15
Bonnell, Barry	82D	432	$ .01	$ .05	Boyd, Oil Can	91D	194	$ .01	$ .03
Bonnell, Barry	83D	430	$ .01	$ .05	Bradford, Larry	81D	584	$ .01	$ .05
Bonnell, Barry	84D	559	$ .03	$ .10	Bradford, Larry	82D	553	$ .01	$ .05
Bonnell, Barry	85D	191	$ .01	$ .08	Bradley, Phil	85D	631	$ .20	$ .75
Bonner, Bob	82D	610	$ .01	$ .05	Bradley, Phil	86D	191	$ .08	$ .25
Booker, Greg	88D	311	$ .01	$ .05	Bradley, Phil	86DK	22	$ .05	$ .20
Boone, Bob	81D	262	$ .01	$ .05	Bradley, Phil	87D	270	$ .01	$ .05
Boone, Bob	82D	471	$ .01	$ .05	Bradley, Phil	88D	243	$ .01	$ .05
Boone, Bob	83D	192	$ .01	$ .05	Bradley, Phil	88DBB	47	$ .01	$ .05
Boone, Bob	84D	158	$ .03	$ .10	Bradley, Phil	89D	369	$ .01	$ .05
Boone, Bob	85D	230	$ .01	$ .08	Bradley, Phil	89DBB	198	$ .01	$ .05
Boone, Bob	86D	230	$ .01	$ .06	Bradley, Phil	89DTR	41	$ .01	$ .05
Boone, Bob	86DK	17	$ .01	$ .06	Bradley, Phil	90D	259	$ .01	$ .04
Boone, Bob	87D	233	$ .01	$ .05	Bradley, Phil	90DL	138	$ .01	$ .15
Boone, Bob	88D	305	$ .01	$ .05	Bradley, Phil	91D	646	$ .01	$ .03
Boone, Bob	88DBB	3	$ .01	$ .05	Bradley, Scott	85DRR	37	$ .05	$ .25
Boone, Bob	89D	170	$ .01	$ .05	Bradley, Scott	86D	396	$ .01	$ .06
Boone, Bob	89DBB	263	$ .01	$ .05	Bradley, Scott	87D	440	$ .01	$ .05
Boone, Bob	89DTR	5	$ .01	$ .05	Bradley, Scott	88D	147	$ .01	$ .05
Boone, Bob	90D	326	$ .01	$ .04	Bradley, Scott	88DBB	24	$ .01	$ .05
Boone, Bob	90DL	46	$ .01	$ .15	Bradley, Scott	89D	261	$ .01	$ .05
Boone, Bob	91D	356	$ .01	$ .03	Bradley, Scott	90D	581	$ .01	$ .04
Boone, Danny	82D	187	$ .01	$ .05	Bradley, Scott	90DL	404	$ .01	$ .15
Borders, Pat	88DR	12	$ .01	$ .15	Bradley, Scott	91D	287	$ .01	$ .03
Borders, Pat	89D	560	$ .01	$ .15	Braggs, Glenn	87D	337	$ .08	$ .50
Borders, Pat	90D	560	$ .01	$ .04	Braggs, Glenn	88D	240	$ .01	$ .05
Borders, Pat	90DL	343	$ .01	$ .25	Braggs, Glenn	88DBB	15	$ .01	$ .05
Borders, Pat	91D	317	$ .01	$ .03	Braggs, Glenn	89D	103	$ .01	$ .05
Bordi, Rich	85D	289	$ .01	$ .08	Braggs, Glenn	89DBB	277	$ .01	$ .05
Bordi, Rich	86D	518	$ .01	$ .06	Braggs, Glenn	90D	264	$ .01	$ .04
Bordi, Rich	87D	213	$ .01	$ .05	Braggs, Glenn	90DL	466	$ .01	$ .15
Borgmann, Glenn	81D	159	$ .01	$ .05	Braggs, Glenn	91D	253	$ .01	$ .03
Bosetti, Rick	81D	152	$ .01	$ .05	Brantley, Jeff	89DR	41	$ .01	$ .10
Bosetti, Rick	82D	626	$ .01	$ .05	Brantley, Jeff	90D	466	$ .01	$ .04
Bosio, Chris	87D	478	$ .05	$ .35	Brantley, Jeff	90DL	357	$ .01	$ .20
Bosio, Chris	87DR	20	$ .01	$ .07	Brantley, Jeff	91D	319	$ .01	$ .03
Bosio, Chris	88D	117	$ .01	$ .05	Brantley, Mickey	87D	656	$ .01	$ .15
Bosio, Chris	89D	412	$ .01	$ .05	Brantley, Mickey	87DR	27	$ .01	$ .07
Bosio, Chris	89DBB	109	$ .01	$ .05	Brantley, Mickey	88D	610	$ .01	$ .15
Bosio, Chris	90D	57	$ .01	$ .04	Brantley, Mickey	88DBB	80	$ .01	$ .05
Bosio, Chris	90DK	20	$ .01	$ .10	Brantley, Mickey	89D	212	$ .01	$ .05
Bosio, Chris	90DL	26	$ .01	$ .15	Braun, Steve	82D	418	$ .01	$ .05
Bosio, Chris	91D	160	$ .01	$ .03	Braun, Steve	86D	534	$ .01	$ .06
Boskie, Shawn	90DL	519	$ .01	$ .35	Bream, Sid	85D	470	$ .08	$ .35
Boskie, Shawn	90DR	18	$ .01	$ .20	Bream, Sid	86D	566	$ .01	$ .06
Boskie, Shawn	91D	241	$ .01	$ .15	Bream, Sid	87D	79	$ .01	$ .05
Bosley, Thad	81D	162	$ .01	$ .05	Bream, Sid	88D	188	$ .01	$ .05
Bosley, Thad	85D	388	$ .01	$ .08	Bream, Sid	88DBB	45	$ .01	$ .05
Bosley, Thad	86D	483	$ .01	$ .06	Bream, Sid	89D	252	$ .01	$ .05
Bosley, Thad	87D	191	$ .01	$ .05	Bream, Sid	89DBB	89	$ .01	$ .05
Bosley, Thad	88D	348	$ .01	$ .05	Bream, Sid	90D	329	$ .01	$ .04
Boston, Daryl	85DRR	33	$ .08	$ .25	Bream, Sid	91D	644	$ .01	$ .03
Boston, Daryl	86D	86	$ .01	$ .06	Breining, Fred	82D	186	$ .01	$ .05
Boston, Daryl	87D	137	$ .01	$ .05	Breining, Fred	83D	503	$ .01	$ .05
Boston, Daryl	89D	455	$ .01	$ .05	Breining, Fred	84D	387	$ .03	$ .10
Boston, Daryl	90DL	514	$ .01	$ .15	Brenly, Bob	82D	574	$ .03	$ .20
Boston, Daryl	91D	210	$ .01	$ .03	Brenly, Bob	83D	377	$ .01	$ .05
Bowa, Larry	81D	142	$ .03	$ .20	Brenly, Bob	84D	616	$ .03	$ .10
Bowa, Larry	82D	63	$ .02	$ .15	Brenly, Bob	85D	187	$ .01	$ .08
Bowa, Larry	83D	435	$ .01	$ .05	Brenly, Bob	85DK	26	$ .03	$ .10
Bowa, Larry	84D	239	$ .04	$ .25	Brenly, Bob	86D	323	$ .01	$ .06
Bowa, Larry	85D	361	$ .03	$ .20	Brenly, Bob	87D	485	$ .01	$ .05
Boyd, Dennis	84D	457	$ .20	$ .75	Brenly, Bob	88D	189	$ .01	$ .05
Boyd, Dennis "Oil Can"	85D	151	$ .01	$ .10	Brenly, Bob	89D	453	$ .01	$ .05
Boyd, Oil Can	86D	50	$ .02	$ .15	Brennan, Tom	84D	102	$ .03	$ .10
Boyd, Oil Can	87D	51	$ .01	$ .05	Brennan, William	89D	589	$ .01	$ .05
Boyd, Oil Can	88D	462	$ .01	$ .05	Brett, George	81D	100	$ .20	$2.00
Boyd, Oil Can	89D	476	$ .01	$ .05	Brett, George	81D	491	$ .10	$1.00
Boyd, Oil Can	90D	633	$ .01	$ .04	Brett, George	81D	537	$ .35	$1.00

DONRUSS

Player	Year	No.	VG	EX/MT
Brett, George	82D	34	$ .10	$1.25
Brett, George	82DK	15	$ .15	$ .75
Brett, George	83D	338	$ .10	$1.00
Brett, George	84D	53	$ .50	$2.00
Brett, George	85D	53	$ .25	$1.00
Brett, George	86D	53	$ .15	$ .75
Brett, George	87D	54	$ .10	$ .35
Brett, George	87DK	15	$ .10	$ .35
Brett, George	88D	102	$ .10	$ .35
Brett, George	88DBB	39	$ .05	$ .25
Brett, George	89D	204	$ .05	$ .25
Brett, George	89DBB	7	$ .01	$ .25
Brett, George	89DBC	7	$ .05	$ .30
Brett, George	90D	144	$ .01	$ .25
Brett, George	90DL	178	$ .01	$ .35
Brett, George	91D	201	$ .01	$ .10
Brett, George	91DBC	19	$ .01	$ .10
Brett, George	91DMVP	396	$ .01	$ .10
Brett, Ken	82D	364	$ .01	$ .05
Brewer, Tony	85DRR	31	$ .01	$ .08
Briley, Greg	90D	463	$ .01	$ .20
Briley, Greg	90DL	391	$ .01	$ .25
Briley, Greg	91D	352	$ .01	$ .03
Bristol, Dave	81D	436	$ .01	$ .05
Brock, Greg	83D	579	$ .10	$ .50
Brock, Greg	84D	296	$ .03	$ .10
Brock, Greg	86D	296	$ .01	$ .06
Brock, Greg	88D	337	$ .01	$ .05
Brock, Greg	88DBB	71	$ .01	$ .05
Brock, Greg	89D	57	$ .01	$ .05
Brock, Greg	89DBB	239	$ .01	$ .05
Brock, Greg	90D	293	$ .01	$ .04
Brock, Greg	90DL	454	$ .01	$ .15
Brock, Greg	91D	572	$ .01	$ .03
Brookens, Tom	81D	6	$ .01	$ .05
Brookens, Tom	82D	202	$ .01	$ .05
Brookens, Tom	83D	454	$ .01	$ .05
Brookens, Tom	84D	578	$ .03	$ .10
Brookens, Tom	85D	593	$ .01	$ .08
Brookens, Tom	86D	537	$ .01	$ .06
Brookens, Tom	87D	296	$ .01	$ .05
Brookens, Tom	88D	107	$ .01	$ .05
Brookens, Tom	89D	508	$ .01	$ .05
Brookens, Tom	89DTR	53	$ .01	$ .05
Brookens, Tom	91D	658	$ .01	$ .03
Brooks, Hubie	82D	476	$ .15	$ .65
Brooks, Hubie	83D	49	$ .01	$ .05
Brooks, Hubie	84D	607	$ .03	$ .10
Brooks, Hubie	85D	197	$ .01	$ .08
Brooks, Hubie	86D	55	$ .01	$ .06
Brooks, Hubie	87D	88	$ .01	$ .05
Brooks, Hubie	87DK	17	$ .01	$ .05
Brooks, Hubie	88D	468	$ .01	$ .05
Brooks, Hubie	88DBB	12	$ .01	$ .05
Brooks, Hubie	89D	220	$ .01	$ .05
Brooks, Hubie	89DBB	292	$ .01	$ .05
Brooks, Hubie	90D	130	$ .01	$ .04
Brooks, Hubie	90DL	16	$ .01	$ .15
Brooks, Hubie	91D	349	$ .01	$ .03
Bross, Terry	90D	502	$ .01	$ .10
Bross, Terry	91DRR	34	$ .01	$ .10
Brouhard, Mark	82D	154	$ .01	$ .05
Brouhard, Mark	83D	532	$ .01	$ .05
Brouhard, Mark	84D	211	$ .03	$ .10
Brouhard, Mark	85D	149	$ .01	$ .08
Brower, Bob	87D	651	$ .05	$ .20
Brower, Bob	87DR	49	$ .01	$ .07
Brower, Bob	88D	346	$ .01	$ .05
Brower, Bob	89D	411	$ .01	$ .05
Brown, Bobby	81D	469	$ .01	$ .05
Brown, Bobby	82D	552	$ .01	$ .05
Brown, Bobby	84D	478	$ .03	$ .10
Brown, Bobby	85D	383	$ .01	$ .08
Brown, Chris	86D	553	$ .05	$ .25
Brown, Chris	87D	80	$ .01	$ .05
Brown, Chris	87DK	11	$ .05	$ .20
Brown, Chris	88D	483	$ .01	$ .05
Brown, Chris	88DBB	77	$ .01	$ .05
Brown, Chris	89D	183	$ .01	$ .05
Brown, Chris	89DTR	9	$ .01	$ .05
Brown, Darrell	85D	558	$ .01	$ .08
Brown, Keith	89D	115	$ .01	$ .05
Brown, Kevin	87D	627	$ .15	$ 1.50
Brown, Kevin	89D	613	$ .01	$ .25
Brown, Kevin	89DBB	256	$ .01	$ .05
Brown, Kevin	89DR	44	$ .01	$ .05
Brown, Kevin	90D	343	$ .01	$ .04
Brown, Kevin	90DL	47	$ .01	$ .20
Brown, Kevin	91D	314	$ .01	$ .03
Brown, Kevin	91D	674	$ .01	$ .10
Brown, Marty	90DR	39	$ .01	$ .10
Brown, Mike C.	84DRR	42	$ .03	$ .10
Brown, Mike C.	85D	207	$ .01	$ .08
Brown, Mike C.	86D	642	$ .01	$ .06
Brown, Mike C.	87D	168	$ .01	$ .05
Brown, Mike G.	84D	517	$ .03	$ .10
Brown, Mike G.	87D	563	$ .01	$ .05
Browne, Jerry	87DR	29	$ .01	$ .25
Browne, Jerry	87DRR	41	$ .05	$ .50
Browne, Jerry	88D	408	$ .01	$ .05
Browne, Jerry	89D	529	$ .01	$ .05
Browne, Jerry	89DBB	280	$ .01	$ .05
Browne, Jerry	89DTR	44	$ .01	$ .05
Browne, Jerry	90D	138	$ .01	$ .04
Browne, Jerry	90DL	48	$ .01	$ .15
Browne, Jerry	91D	162	$ .01	$ .03
Browning, Tom	85D	634	$ .30	$1.75
Browning, Tom	86D	384	$ .10	$ .40
Browning, Tom	87D	63	$ .01	$ .15
Browning, Tom	88D	63	$ .01	$ .10
Browning, Tom	89D	71	$ .01	$ .10
Browning, Tom	89DBB	62	$ .01	$ .05
Browning, Tom	90D	308	$ .01	$ .04
Browning, Tom	90DL	110	$ .01	$ .20
Browning, Tom	91D	528	$ .01	$ .03
Brumley, Mike	88D	609	$ .01	$ .15
Brumley, Mike	89D	302	$ .01	$ .05
Brumley, Mike	89DR	39	$ .01	$ .10
Brumley, Mike	90D	533	$ .01	$ .04
Brummer, Glenn	83D	418	$ .01	$ .05
Brummer, Glenn	84D	138	$ .03	$ .10
Brummer, Glenn	85D	290	$ .01	$ .08
Brunansky, Tom	83D	555	$ .10	$ .75
Brunansky, Tom	84D	242	$ .10	$ .35
Brunansky, Tom	85D	364	$ .08	$ .25
Brunansky, Tom	86D	192	$ .05	$ .20
Brunansky, Tom	86DK	24	$ .05	$ .20
Brunansky, Tom	87D	194	$ .01	$ .05
Brunansky, Tom	88D	245	$ .05	$ .20
Brunansky, Tom	88DBB	19	$ .01	$ .05
Brunansky, Tom	89D	112	$ .01	$ .05
Brunansky, Tom	89DBB	187	$ .01	$ .05
Brunansky, Tom	90D	399	$ .01	$ .04
Brunansky, Tom	90DL	447	$ .01	$ .15
Brunansky, Tom	91D	513	$ .01	$ .03
Brusstar, Warren	84D	442	$ .03	$ .10
Brusstar, Warren	85D	533	$ .01	$ .08
Brusstar, Warren	86D	555	$ .01	$ .06
Bryant, Ralph	87D	587	$ .01	$ .05
Buckner, Bill	81D	482	$ .02	$ .15

Player	Year	No.	VG	EX/MT	Player	Year	No.	VG	EX/MT
Buckner, Bill	82D	403	$ .01	$ .05	Burke, Tim	88D	98	$ .01	$ .05
Buckner, Bill	83D	99	$ .02	$ .15	Burke, Tim	88DBB	34	$ .01	$ .05
Buckner, Bill	83DK	14	$ .02	$ .10	Burke, Tim	89D	274	$ .01	$ .05
Buckner, Bill	84D	117	$ .03	$ .10	Burke, Tim	89DBB	180	$ .01	$ .05
Buckner, Bill	85D	416	$ .03	$ .20	Burke, Tim	90D	334	$ .01	$ .04
Buckner, Bill	86D	151	$ .02	$ .15	Burke, Tim	90DL	28	$ .01	$ .15
Buckner, Bill	87D	462	$ .01	$ .05	Burke, Tim	91D	125	$ .01	$ .03
Buckner, Bill	88D	456	$ .01	$ .15	Burkett, John	90DL	384	$ .01	$ .25
Buckner, Bill	90D	474	$ .01	$ .04	Burkett, John	90DR	51	$ .01	$ .15
Buechele, Steve	86D	544	$ .01	$ .20	Burkett, John	91D	638	$ .01	$ .03
Buechele, Steve	87D	180	$ .01	$ .05	Burks, Ellis	87DR	5	$ .50	$4.00
Buechele, Steve	88D	224	$ .01	$ .05	Burks, Ellis	88D	174	$ .50	$1.25
					Burks, Ellis	88DBB	121	$ .15	$ .50
					Burks, Ellis	89D	303	$ .15	$ .30
					Burks, Ellis	89DBB	9	$ .01	$ .20
					Burks, Ellis	90D	228	$ .01	$ .20
					Burks, Ellis	90DK	23	$ .01	$ .20
					Burks, Ellis	90DL	261	$ .01	$ .35
					Burks, Ellis	91D	235	$ .01	$ .10
					Burleson, Rick	81D	454	$ .01	$ .05
					Burleson, Rick	82D	342	$ .01	$ .05
					Burleson, Rick	83D	318	$ .01	$ .05
					Burns, Britt	81D	279	$ .01	$ .05
					Burns, Britt	82D	230	$ .01	$ .05
					Burns, Britt	83D	193	$ .01	$ .05
					Burns, Britt	83DK	23	$ .01	$ .05
					Burns, Britt	84D	424	$ .03	$ .10
					Burns, Britt	85D	257	$ .01	$ .08
					Burns, Britt	86D	58	$ .01	$ .06
					Burns, Todd	89D	564	$ .01	$ .25
					Burns, Todd	90D	446	$ .01	$ .04
					Burns, Todd	90DL	458	$ .01	$ .15
					Burns, Todd	91D	479	$ .01	$ .03
					Burris, Ray	81D	524	$ .01	$ .05
					Burris, Ray	82D	414	$ .01	$ .05
					Burris, Ray	83D	36	$ .01	$ .05
					Burris, Ray	84D	331	$ .03	$ .10
					Burris, Ray	85D	218	$ .01	$ .08
					Burris, Ray	86D	107	$ .01	$ .06
					Burroughs, Jeff	81D	66	$ .01	$ .05
					Burroughs, Jeff	82D	379	$ .01	$ .05
					Burroughs, Jeff	83D	323	$ .01	$ .05
Buechele, Steve	89D	174	$ .01	$ .05	Burroughs, Jeff	84D	156	$ .03	$ .10
Buechele, Steve	89DBB	223	$ .01	$ .05	Burroughs, Jeff	85D	542	$ .01	$ .08
Buechele, Steve	90D	107	$ .01	$ .04	Bush, Randy	84D	513	$ .05	$ .25
Buechele, Steve	90DL	179	$ .01	$ .15	Bush, Randy	85D	633	$ .01	$ .08
Buechele, Steve	91D	357	$ .01	$ .03	Bush, Randy	87D	441	$ .01	$ .05
Buhner, Jay	88D	545	$ .10	$ .45	Bush, Randy	88D	272	$ .01	$ .05
Buhner, Jay	88DR	11	$ .01	$ .20	Bush, Randy	89D	537	$ .01	$ .05
Buhner, Jay	89D	581	$ .01	$ .15	Bush, Randy	89DBB	214	$ .01	$ .05
Buhner, Jay	89DBB	136	$ .01	$ .05	Bush, Randy	90D	199	$ .01	$ .04
Buhner, Jay	90D	448	$ .01	$ .04	Bush, Randy	90DL	83	$ .01	$ .15
Buhner, Jay	90DL	114	$ .01	$ .15	Bush, Randy	91D	382	$ .01	$ .03
Buhner, Jay	91D	509	$ .01	$ .03	Buskey, Tom	81D	290	$ .01	$ .05
Buice, DeWayne	87DR	6	$ .01	$ .07	Butcher, John	83D	37	$ .01	$ .05
Buice, DeWayne	88D	58	$ .01	$ .05	Butcher, John	84D	220	$ .03	$ .10
Bulling, Terry	82D	612	$ .01	$ .05	Butcher, John	85D	314	$ .01	$ .08
Bulling, Terry	83D	226	$ .01	$ .05	Butcher, John	86D	120	$ .01	$ .06
Bumbry, Al	81D	355	$ .01	$ .05	Butera, Sal	81D	530	$ .01	$ .05
Bumbry, Al	82D	153	$ .01	$ .05	Butera, Sal	82D	532	$ .01	$ .05
Bumbry, Al	83D	383	$ .01	$ .05	Butler, Brett	82D	275	$ .10	$ .75
Bumbry, Al	84D	210	$ .03	$ .10	Butler, Brett	83D	636	$ .01	$ .10
Bumbry, Al	85D	350	$ .01	$ .08	Butler, Brett	84D	141	$ .03	$ .10
Burgmeier, Tom	81D	97	$ .01	$ .05	Butler, Brett	85D	216	$ .01	$ .08
Burgmeier, Tom	82D	361	$ .01	$ .05	Butler, Brett	86D	102	$ .01	$ .06
Burgmeier, Tom	83D	235	$ .01	$ .05	Butler, Brett	86DK	12	$ .01	$ .06
Burgmeier, Tom	84D	522	$ .03	$ .10	Butler, Brett	87D	219	$ .01	$ .05
Burgmeier, Tom	85D	400	$ .01	$ .08	Butler, Brett	88D	279	$ .01	$ .05
Burke, Tim	86D	421	$ .05	$ .35	Butler, Brett	88DBB	23	$ .01	$ .05
Burke, Tim	87D	222	$ .01	$ .05	Butler, Brett	89D	217	$ .01	$ .05

Steve Buechele 3B

Player	Year	No.	VG	EX/MT	Player	Year	No.	VG	EX/MT
Butler, Brett	89DBB	274	$ .01	$ .05	Camacho, Ernie	87D	350	$ .01	$ .05
Butler, Brett	90D	249	$ .01	$ .04	Cambell, Bill	83D	504	$ .01	$ .05
Butler, Brett	90DL	251	$ .01	$ .15	Caminiti, Ken	88D	308	$ .01	$ .15
Butler, Brett	91D	143	$ .01	$ .03	Caminiti, Ken	89D	542	$ .01	$ .10
Byers, Randall	88D	605	$ .01	$ .15	Caminiti, Ken	89DBB	262	$ .01	$ .05
Bystrom, Martin	83D	93	$ .01	$ .05	Caminiti, Ken	90D	424	$ .01	$ .04
Bystrom, Marty	82D	93	$ .01	$ .05	Caminiti, Ken	90DL	253	$ .01	$ .15
Bystrom, Marty	84D	259	$ .03	$ .10	Caminiti, Ken	91D	221	$ .01	$ .03
Bystrom, Marty	86D	591	$ .01	$ .06	Camp, Rick	81D	197	$ .01	$ .05
Cabell, Enos	81D	138	$ .01	$ .05	Camp, Rick	82D	223	$ .01	$ .05
Cabell, Enos	82D	272	$ .01	$ .05	Camp, Rick	83D	149	$ .01	$ .05
Cabell, Enos	83D	202	$ .01	$ .05	Camp, Rick	84D	165	$ .03	$ .10
Cabell, Enos	84D	456	$ .03	$ .10	Camp, Rick	85D	409	$ .01	$ .08
Cabell, Enos	85D	110	$ .01	$ .08	Camp, Rick	86D	385	$ .01	$ .06
Cabell, Enos	86D	418	$ .01	$ .06	Campaneris, Bert	81D	50	$ .01	$ .05
Cabrera, Francisco	90D	646	$ .01	$ .25	Campaneris, Bert	82D	593	$ .01	$ .05
Cabrera, Francisco	91D	341	$ .01	$ .03	Campbell, Bill	82D	487	$ .01	$ .05
Cadaret, Greg	88D	528	$ .01	$ .15	Campbell, Bill	84D	555	$ .03	$ .10
Cadaret, Greg	89D	479	$ .01	$ .05	Campbell, Bill	85D	163	$ .01	$ .08
Cadaret, Greg	90D	545	$ .01	$ .04	Campbell, Bill	86D	571	$ .01	$ .06
Cadaret, Greg	91D	236	$ .01	$ .03	Campbell, Mike	88DBB	163	$ .01	$ .05
Calderon, Ivan	86D	435	$ .15	$1.50	Campbell, Mike	88DR	2	$ .01	$ .15
Calderon, Ivan	88D	182	$ .03	$ .25	Campbell, Mike	88DRR	30	$ .01	$ .05
Calderon, Ivan	88DBB	25	$ .01	$ .05	Campbell, Mike	89D	497	$ .01	$ .05
Calderon, Ivan	88DBC	5	$ .05	$ .20	Campusano, Sil	88DR	42	$ .01	$ .25
Calderon, Ivan	88DK	25	$ .01	$ .05	Campusano, Sil	89D	584	$ .01	$ .15
Calderon, Ivan	89D	371	$ .01	$ .05	Canale, George	90D	699	$ .01	$ .10
Calderon, Ivan	89DBB	193	$ .01	$ .05	Candaele, Casey	87D	549	$ .01	$ .05
Calderon, Ivan	90D	294	$ .01	$ .04	Candaele, Casey	87DR	33	$ .01	$ .07
Calderon, Ivan	90DL	89	$ .01	$ .15	Candaele, Casey	88D	179	$ .01	$ .05
Calderon, Ivan	91D	203	$ .01	$ .03	Candaele, Casey	88DBB	68	$ .01	$ .05
Caldwell, Mike	81D	86	$ .01	$ .05	Candaele, Casey	91D	324	$ .01	$ .03
Caldwell, Mike	82D	330	$ .01	$ .05	Candelaria, John	81D	374	$ .03	$ .20
Caldwell, Mike	83D	154	$ .01	$ .05	Candelaria, John	82D	297	$ .02	$ .15
Caldwell, Mike	84D	237	$ .03	$ .10	Candelaria, John	83D	549	$ .02	$ .15
Caldwell, Mike	85D	490	$ .01	$ .08	Candelaria, John	84D	357	$ .03	$ .10
					Candelaria, John	85D	430	$ .01	$ .08
					Candelaria, John	86D	499	$ .01	$ .06
					Candelaria, John	87D	551	$ .01	$ .05
					Candelaria, John	88D	608	$ .01	$ .15
					Candelaria, John	88DBB	20	$ .01	$ .05
					Candelaria, John	89D	192	$ .01	$ .75
					Candelaria, John	90DL	492	$ .01	$ .15
					Candiotti, Tom	84D	393	$ .10	$ .50
					Candiotti, Tom	87D	342	$ .01	$ .05
					Candiotti, Tom	88D	377	$ .01	$ .05
					Candiotti, Tom	88DBB	112	$ .01	$ .05
					Candiotti, Tom	89D	256	$ .01	$ .05
					Candiotti, Tom	89DBB	117	$ .01	$ .05
					Candiotti, Tom	90D	256	$ .01	$ .04
					Candiotti, Tom	90DL	55	$ .01	$ .15
					Candiotti, Tom	91D	115	$ .01	$ .03
					Cangelosi, John	86DR	51	$ .02	$ .09
					Cangelosi, John	87D	162	$ .01	$ .05
					Cangelosi, John	88D	435	$ .01	$ .05
					Cangelosi, John	90D	565	$ .01	$ .04
					Canseco, Jose	86DR	22	$1.50	$12.00
					Canseco, Jose	86DRR	39	$10.00	$90.00
					Canseco, Jose	87D	97	$1.50	$10.00
					Canseco, Jose	87DK	6	$ .50	$2.00
					Canseco, Jose	88D	302	$ .50	$1.00
					Canseco, Jose	88DBB	22	$ .25	$1.00
					Canseco, Jose	89D	91	$ .25	$1.00
					Canseco, Jose	89D	643	$ .10	$ .50
					Canseco, Jose	89DBB	57	$ .01	$ .50
					Canseco, Jose	89DBC	5	$ .05	$ .60
					Canseco, Jose	90D	125	$ .01	$ .40
					Canseco, Jose	90DL	108	$ .01	$1.00
Calhoun, Jeff	86D	426	$ .01	$ .06	Canseco, Jose	91D	536	$ .01	$ .20
Calhoun, Jeff	87D	578	$ .01	$ .05	Canseco, Jose	91DAS	50	$ .01	$ .25
Calhoun, Jeff	88D	509	$ .01	$ .05					
Camacho, Ernie	85D	129	$ .01	$ .08					

JEFF CALHOUN P

Player	Year	No.	VG	EX/MT
Canseco, Ozzie	90DL	516	$ .01	$ .50
Capel, Mike	88DR	46	$ .01	$ .05
Capilla, Doug	81D	587	$ .01	$ .05
Carew, Rod	81D	49	$ .10	$1.00
Carew, Rod	81D	169	$ .15	$1.00
Carew, Rod	81D	537	$ .35	$1.25
Carew, Rod	82D	216	$ .10	$ .90
Carew, Rod	82DK	8	$ .08	$ .50
Carew, Rod	83D	90	$ .05	$ .75
Carew, Rod	84D	352	$ .25	$2.50
Carew, Rod	85D	85	$ .15	$ .75
Carew, Rod	86D	280	$ .10	$ .35
Carlton, Steve	81D	33	$ .08	$1.00
Carlton, Steve	81D	481	$ .05	$ .50
Carlton, Steve	82D	42	$ .10	$ .75
Carlton, Steve	83D	219	$ .07	$ .65
Carlton, Steve	83DK	16	$ .05	$ .40
Carlton, Steve	84D	111	$ .20	$2.00
Carlton, Steve	85D	305	$ .15	$ .50
Carlton, Steve	86D	183	$ .08	$ .25
Carlton, Steve	87D	617	$ .08	$ .25
Carman, Don	86D	427	$ .05	$ .20
Carman, Don	87D	432	$ .01	$ .15
Carman, Don	88D	385	$ .01	$ .05
Carman, Don	88DBB	72	$ .01	$ .05
Carman, Don	89D	396	$ .01	$ .05
Carman, Don	90D	604	$ .01	$ .04
Carman, Don	91D	377	$ .01	$ .03
Carpenter, Cris	88DR	50	$ .05	$ .20
Carpenter, Cris	89DR	40	$ .01	$ .10
Carpenter, Cris	89DRR	39	$ .05	$ .20
Carpenter, Cris	90D	634	$ .01	$ .10
Carreon, Mark	89DR	18	$ .01	$ .10
Carreon, Mark	90D	454	$ .01	$ .04
Carreon, Mark	90DL	488	$ .01	$ .15
Carreon, Mark	91D	731	$ .01	$ .03
Carter, Gary	81D	90	$ .10	$ .50
Carter, Gary	82D	114	$ .10	$ .50
Carter, Gary	82DK	2	$ .10	$ .45
Carter, Gary	83D	340	$ .07	$ .35
Carter, Gary	84D	55	$ .20	$ .60
Carter, Gary	85D	55	$ .15	$ .40
Carter, Gary	86D	68	$ .08	$ .25
Carter, Gary	87D	69	$ .08	$ .25
Carter, Gary	88D	199	$ .03	$ .25
Carter, Gary	88DBB	14	$ .01	$ .10
Carter, Gary	89D	53	$ .01	$ .05
Carter, Gary	89DBB	182	$ .01	$ .10
Carter, Gary	90D	147	$ .01	$ .04
Carter, Gary	90DL	134	$ .01	$ .20
Carter, Gary	91D	151	$ .01	$ .03
Carter, Gary	91DBC	8	$ .01	$ .03
Carter, Joe	84DRR	41	$3.00	$15.00
Carter, Joe	85D	616	$ .50	$2.50
Carter, Joe	86D	224	$ .10	$ .50
Carter, Joe	87D	156	$ .01	$ .25
Carter, Joe	88D	254	$ .05	$ .20
Carter, Joe	88DBB	56	$ .01	$ .15
Carter, Joe	88DBC	9	$ .01	$ .25
Carter, Joe	89D	83	$ .01	$ .15
Carter, Joe	89DBB	56	$ .01	$ .10
Carter, Joe	89DBC	3	$ .01	$ .15
Carter, Joe	90D	114	$ .01	$ .10
Carter, Joe	90DL	379	$ .01	$ .15
Carter, Joe	91D	298	$ .01	$ .03
Carter, Joe	91DMVP	409	$ .01	$ .03
Carter, Steve	89DR	8	$ .01	$ .10
Carter, Steve	91DRR	418	$ .01	$ .03
Cary, Chuck	87D	461	$ .01	$ .15
Cary, Chuck	90D	429	$ .01	$ .04
Cary, Chuck	90DL	50	$ .01	$ .15
Cary, Chuck	91D	179	$ .01	$ .03
Cash, Dave	81D	121	$ .01	$ .05
Castillo, Bobby	81D	298	$ .01	$ .05
Castillo, Bobby	82D	236	$ .01	$ .05
Castillo, Bobby	83D	102	$ .01	$ .05
Castillo, Bobby	84D	436	$ .03	$ .10
Castillo, Carmen	85D	590	$ .01	$ .08
Castillo, Carmen	86D	460	$ .01	$ .06
Castillo, Carmen	87D	588	$ .01	$ .05
Castillo, Carmen	88D	403	$ .01	$ .05
Castillo, Carmen	89D	374	$ .01	$ .05
Castillo, Carmen	90D	554	$ .01	$ .04
Castillo, Juan	87D	249	$ .01	$ .05
Castillo, Juan	88D	363	$ .01	$ .05
Castillo, Juan	89D	530	$ .01	$ .05
Castillo, Manny	83D	253	$ .01	$ .05
Castillo, Marty	84D	247	$ .03	$ .10
Castillo, Marty	85D	394	$ .01	$ .08
Castillo, Tony	89DR	12	$ .01	$ .10
Castillo, Tony	90D	592	$ .01	$ .04
Castino, John	81D	488	$ .01	$ .05
Castino, John	82D	256	$ .01	$ .05
Castino, John	83D	303	$ .01	$ .05
Castino, John	84D	120	$ .03	$ .10
Castino, John	84DK	4	$ .03	$ .10
Castro, Bill	81D	578	$ .01	$ .05
Caudill, Bill	81D	586	$ .01	$ .05
Caudill, Bill	82D	426	$ .01	$ .05
Caudill, Bill	83D	302	$ .01	$ .05
Caudill, Bill	84D	118	$ .03	$ .10
Caudill, Bill	85D	96	$ .01	$ .08
Caudill, Bill	86D	317	$ .01	$ .06
Cecena, Jose	88DR	6	$ .01	$ .05
Cedeno, Cesar	81D	263	$ .01	$ .05
Cedeno, Cesar	82D	118	$ .02	$ .15
Cedeno, Cesar	83D	43	$ .01	$ .05
Cedeno, Cesar	84D	306	$ .03	$ .10
Cedeno, Cesar	85D	447	$ .01	$ .08
Cedeno, Cesar	86D	648	$ .01	$ .06
Cerone, Rick	81D	346	$ .01	$ .05
Cerone, Rick	82D	199	$ .01	$ .05
Cerone, Rick	83D	577	$ .01	$ .05
Cerone, Rick	84D	492	$ .03	$ .10
Cerone, Rick	85D	274	$ .01	$ .08
Cerone, Rick	86D	310	$ .01	$ .06
Cerone, Rick	88D	351	$ .01	$ .05
Cerone, Rick	89D	398	$ .01	$ .05
Cerone, Rick	89DBB	308	$ .01	$ .05
Cerone, Rick	90D	305	$ .01	$ .04
Cerutti, John	86DR	20	$ .10	$ .25
Cerutti, John	87D	442	$ .05	$ .25
Cerutti, John	88D	321	$ .01	$ .05
Cerutti, John	89D	467	$ .01	$ .05
Cerutti, John	90D	645	$ .01	$ .04
Cerutti, John	90DL	27	$ .01	$ .15
Cerutti, John	91D	467	$ .01	$ .03
Cey, Ron	81D	296	$ .02	$ .15
Cey, Ron	82D	210	$ .01	$ .05
Cey, Ron	83D	84	$ .01	$ .05
Cey, Ron	84D	361	$ .03	$ .10
Cey, Ron	85D	320	$ .01	$ .08
Cey, Ron	86D	198	$ .01	$ .06
Chadwick, Ray	87D	505	$ .01	$ .05
Chalk, Dave	81D	101	$ .01	$ .05
Chalk, Dave	82D	590	$ .01	$ .05
Chamberlain, Wes	91DRR	423	$ .01	$ .25
Chambers, Al	83D	649	$ .01	$ .05
Chambers, Al	85D	389	$ .01	$ .08
Chambliss, Chris	81D	219	$ .01	$ .05

Player	Year	No.	VG	EX/MT
Chambliss, Chris	82D	47	$ .01	$ .05
Chambliss, Chris	83D	123	$ .01	$ .05
Chambliss, Chris	84D	537	$ .03	$ .10
Chambliss, Chris	85D	287	$ .01	$ .08
Chambliss, Chris	86D	618	$ .01	$ .06
Chapman, Kelvin	85D	626	$ .01	$ .08
Charboneau, Joe	81D	82	$ .02	$ .15
Charboneau, Joe	82D	363	$ .01	$ .05
Charlton, Norm	89D	544	$ .01	$ .25
Charlton, Norm	90D	426	$ .01	$ .04
Charlton, Norm	90DL	334	$ .01	$ .35
Charlton, Norm	91D	384	$ .01	$ .03
Checklist #1, Cards(1-120)	81D	0	$ .02	$ .15
Checklist #1, Cards(27-130)	82D	0	$ .02	$ .15
Checklist #1, Cards(27-130)	83D	0	$ .01	$ .15
Checklist #1, Cards(27-130)	84D	0	$ .03	$ .10
Checklist #1, Cards(27-130)	85D	0	$ .01	$ .08
Checklist #1, Cards(27-130)	86D	0	$ .02	$ .15
Checklist #1, Cards(28-133)	87D	100	$ .01	$ .05
Checklist #1, Cards(28-137)	88D	100	$ .01	$ .05
Checklist #2, Cards(121-240)	81D	0	$ .02	$ .15
Checklist #2, Cards(131-234)	82D	0	$ .02	$ .15
Checklist #2, Cards(131-234)	83D	0	$ .01	$ .15
Checklist #2, Cards(131-234)	84D	0	$ .03	$ .10
Checklist #2, Cards(131-234)	85D	0	$ .01	$ .08
Checklist #2, Cards(131-234)	86D	0	$ .01	$ .06
Checklist #2, Cards(134-239)	87D	200	$ .01	$ .05
Checklist #2, Cards(138-247)	88D	200	$ .01	$ .05
Checklist #3, Cards(235-338)	82D	0	$ .02	$ .15
Checklist #3, Cards(235-338)	83D	0	$ .01	$ .15
Checklist #3, Cards(235-338)	84D	0	$ .03	$ .10
Checklist #3, Cards(235-338)	85D	0	$ .09	$ .06
Checklist #3, Cards(235-338)	86D	0	$ .01	$ .06
Checklist #3, Cards(240-345)	87D	300	$ .01	$ .05
Checklist #3, Cards(241-360)	81D	0	$ .02	$ .15
Checklist #3, Cards(248-357)	88D	300	$ .01	$ .05
Checklist #4, Cards(339-442)	82D	0	$ .02	$ .15
Checklist #4, Cards(339-442)	83D	0	$ .01	$ .15
Checklist #4, Cards(339-442)	84D	0	$ .03	$ .10
Checklist #4, Cards(339-442)	85D	0	$ .01	$ .08
Checklist #4, Cards(339-442)	86D	0	$ .01	$ .06
Checklist #4, Cards(346-451)	87D	400	$ .01	$ .05
Checklist #4, Cards(358-467)	88D	400	$ .01	$ .05
Checklist #4, Cards(361-480)	81D	0	$ .02	$ .15
Checklist #5, Cards(443-544)	82D	0	$ .02	$ .15
Checklist #5, Cards(443-546)	83D	0	$ .01	$ .15
Checklist #5, Cards(443-546)	84D	0	$ .03	$ .10
Checklist #5, Cards(443-546)	85D	0	$ .01	$ .08
Checklist #5, Cards(443-546)	86D	0	$ .01	$ .06
Checklist #5, Cards(452-557)	87D	500	$ .01	$ .05
Checklist #5, Cards(468-577)	88D	500	$ .01	$ .05
Checklist #5, Cards(481-600)	81D	0	$ .02	$ .15
Checklist #6, Cards(545-653)	82D	0	$ .02	$ .15
Checklist #6, Cards(547-651)	84D	0	$ .03	$ .10
Checklist #6, Cards(547-653)	83D	0	$ .01	$ .15
Checklist #6, Cards(547-653)	85D	0	$ .01	$ .08
Checklist #6, Cards(547-653)	86D	0	$ .01	$ .06
Checklist #6, Cards(558-660)	87D	600	$ .01	$ .05
Checklist #6, Cards(578/BC-26)	88D	600	$ .01	$ .15
Checklist DK, Cards(1-26)	82D	0	$ .05	$ .30
Checklist DK, Cards(1-26)	83D	0	$ .05	$ .30
Checklist DK, Cards(1-26)	84D	0	$ .05	$ .30
Checklist DK, Cards(1-26)	85D	0	$ .05	$ .20
Checklist DK, Cards(1-26)	86D	0	$ .01	$ .06
Checklist DK, Cards(1-26)	87D	27	$ .01	$ .05
Checklist DK, Cards(1-26)	88D	27	$ .01	$ .05
Checklist DK, Cards(1-26)	89D	27	$ .01	$ .05
Checklist, Cards(1-26)	90D	27	$ .01	$ .04
Checklist, Cards(1-27)	91D	27	$ .01	$ .05
Checklist, Cards(1-88)	90DL	84	$ .01	$ .35
Checklist, Cards(104-179)	91D	200	$ .01	$ .03
Checklist, Cards(177-264)	90DL	264	$ .01	$ .35
Checklist, Cards(180-255)	91D	300	$ .01	$ .03
Checklist, Cards(256-331)	91D	386	$ .01	$ .03
Checklist, Cards(265-352)	90DL	364	$ .01	$ .20
Checklist, Cards(28 -103)	91D	100	$ .01	$ .03
Checklist, Cards(332-408)	91D	500	$ .01	$ .03
Checklist, Cards(353-440)	90DL	444	$ .01	$ .25
Checklist, Cards(409-506)	91D	600	$ .01	$ .03
Checklist, Cards(441-528)	90DL	528	$ .01	$ .25
Checklist, Cards(507-604)	91D	700	$ .01	$ .03
Checklist, Cards(605-702)	91D	760	$ .01	$ .03
Checklist, Cards(703-BC22)	91D	770	$ .01	$ .03
Checklist, Cards(89-176)	90DL	174	$ .01	$ .25
Checklist, Cards(1-112)	89DBB	300	$ .01	$ .05
Checklist, Cards(1-56)	86DR	56	$ .02	$ .15
Checklist, Cards(1-56)	87DR	56	$ .01	$ .15
Checklist, Cards(1-56)	88DR	56	$ .01	$ .05
Checklist, Cards(1-56)	89DR	56	$ .01	$ .10
Checklist, Cards(1-56)	90DR	56	$ .01	$ .10
Checklist, Cards(1-56)	89DTR	56	$ .01	$ .05
Checklist, Cards(113-224)	89DBB	329	$ .01	$ .05
Checklist, Cards(130-231)	90D	200	$ .01	$ .04
Checklist, Cards(138-247)	89D	200	$ .01	$ .05
Checklist, Cards(225-336)	89DBB	332	$ .01	$ .05
Checklist, Cards(232-333)	90D	300	$ .01	$ .04
Checklist, Cards(248-357)	89D	300	$ .01	$ .05
Checklist, Cards(28-129)	90D	100	$ .01	$ .04
Checklist, Cards(28-137)	89D	100	$ .01	$ .05
Checklist, Cards(334-435)	90D	400	$ .01	$ .04
Checklist, Cards(358-467)	89D	400	$ .01	$ .05
Checklist, Cards(436-537)	90D	500	$ .01	$ .04
Checklist, Cards(468-577)	89D	500	$ .01	$ .05
Checklist, Cards(538-639)	90D	600	$ .01	$ .04
Checklist, Cards(578-660)	89D	600	$ .01	$ .05
Checklist, Cards(640-720)	90D	700	$ .01	$ .04
Chiamparino, Scott	91DRR	42	$ .01	$ .25
Chicken, San Diego	82D	531	$ .25	$1.00
Chicken, San Diego	83D	645	$ .10	$ .35
Chicken, San Diego	84D	651	$ .10	$ .35
Chiffer, Floyd	83D	44	$ .01	$ .05
Childress, Rocky	88D	554	$ .01	$ .05
Chitren, Steve	91DRR	431	$ .01	$ .15
Christensen, John	86D	360	$ .01	$ .06
Christenson, Larry	82D	219	$ .01	$ .05
Christenson, Larry	83D	345	$ .01	$ .05
Christiansen, Clay	85D	396	$ .01	$ .08
Citarella, Ralph	85D	504	$ .01	$ .08
Clancy, Jim	82D	227	$ .01	$ .05
Clancy, Jim	83D	101	$ .01	$ .05
Clancy, Jim	84D	119	$ .03	$ .10
Clancy, Jim	84DK	19	$ .03	$ .10
Clancy, Jim	85D	439	$ .01	$ .08
Clancy, Jim	86D	268	$ .01	$ .06
Clancy, Jim	87D	639	$ .01	$ .05
Clancy, Jim	88D	74	$ .01	$ .05
Clancy, Jim	88DBB	48	$ .01	$ .05
Clancy, Jim	89D	268	$ .01	$ .05
Clancy, Jim	89DBB	206	$ .01	$ .05
Clancy, Jim	89DTR	32	$ .01	$ .05
Clancy, Jim	90D	69	$ .01	$ .04
Clark, Bobby	81D	572	$ .01	$ .05
Clark, Bobby	82D	318	$ .01	$ .05
Clark, Bobby	83D	444	$ .01	$ .05
Clark, Bobby	84D	524	$ .03	$ .10
Clark, Bobby	85D	481	$ .01	$ .08
Clark, Bryan	82D	596	$ .01	$ .05
Clark, Bryan	83D	603	$ .01	$ .05
Clark, Bryan	84D	562	$ .03	$ .10
Clark, Dave	87D	623	$ .01	$ .20

Player	Year	No.	VG	EX/MT
Clark, Dave	88D	473	$ .01	$ .05
Clark, Dave	89D	585	$ .01	$ .05
Clark, Dave	90D	492	$ .01	$ .04
Clark, Dave	91D	616	$ .01	$ .03
Clark, Jack	81D	315	$ .05	$ .30
Clark, Jack	82D	46	$ .05	$ .30
Clark, Jack	83D	222	$ .05	$ .20
Clark, Jack	84D	65	$ .10	$ .35
Clark, Jack	84DK	7	$ .10	$ .35
Clark, Jack	85D	65	$ .05	$ .30
Clark, Jack	86D	168	$ .08	$ .25
Clark, Jack	87D	111	$ .05	.$ .20
Clark, Jack	88D	183	$ .05	$ .20
Clark, Jack	88DBB	49	$ .01	$ .10
Clark, Jack	88DK	15	$ .05	$ .20
Clark, Jack	89D	311	$ .01	$ .10
Clark, Jack	89DBB	98	$ .01	$ .10
Clark, Jack	89DTR	2	$ .01	$ .15
Clark, Jack	90D	128	$ .01	$ .04
Clark, Jack	90DL	287	$ .01	$ .15
Clark, Jack	91D	618	$ .01	$ .03
Clark, Jerald	89D	599	$ .01	$ .25
Clark, Jerald	90D	593	$ .01	$ .04
Clark, Jerald	90DL	510	$ .01	$ .35
Clark, Jerald	90DR	48	$ .01	$ .10
Clark, Jerald	91D	74	$ .01	$ .03
Clark, Jerry	89D	607	$ .01	$ .05
Clark, Will	86DR	32	$3.00	$12.00
Clark, Will	87D	66	$2.00	$9.00
Clark, Will	88D	204	$ .45	$1.00
Clark, Will	88DBB	79	$ .15	$ .50
Clark, Will	88DBC	24	$ .15	$ .50
Clark, Will	88DK	21	$ .10	$ .40
Clark, Will	89D	249	$ .15	$ .75
Clark, Will	89DBB	23	$ .01	$ .50
Clark, Will	89DBC	22	$ .05	$ .20
Clark, Will	90D	230	$ .01	$ .35
Clark, Will	90DAS	707	$ .01	$ .20
Clark, Will	90DL	172	$ .01	$1.00
Clark, Will	90DL	444	$ .01	$ .25
Clark, Will	91D	86	$ .01	$ .15
Clark, Will	91DAS	441	$ .01	$ .10
Clark, Will	91DLP	12	$1.00	$20.00
Clary, Marty	86DRR	36	$ .01	$ .06
Clary, Marty	90D	381	$ .01	$ .04
Clear, Mark	81D	291	$ .01	$ .05
Clear, Mark	82D	452	$ .01	$ .05
Clear, Mark	83D	361	$ .01	$ .05
Clear, Mark	84D	611	$ .03	$ .10
Clear, Mark	85D	538	$ .01	$ .08
Clear, Mark	86D	493	$ .01	$ .06
Clear, Mark	87D	355	$ .01	$ .05
Clear, Mark	88D	372	$ .01	$ .05
Clear, Mark	89D	528	$ .01	$ .05
Clemens, Roger	85D	273	$5.25	$22.50
Clemens, Roger	86D	172	$1.35	$6.00
Clemens, Roger	87D	276	$ .70	$2.00
Clemens, Roger	87DK	2	$ .20	$ .60
Clemens, Roger	88D	51	$ .10	$ .50
Clemens, Roger	88DBB	57	$ .10	$ .35
Clemens, Roger	89D	280	$ .01	$ .25
Clemens, Roger	89DBB	65	$ .01	$ .35
Clemens, Roger	90D	184	$ .01	$ .15
Clemens, Roger	90DL	12	$ .01	$ .75
Clemens, Roger	91D	81	$ .01	$ .15
Clemens, Roger	91DK	9	$ .01	$ .10
Clemens, Roger	91DMVP	395	$ .01	$ .10
Clemente, Roberto	87D	612	$ .03	$ .25
Clements, Pat	86D	600	$ .01	$ .06
Clements, Pat	87D	390	$ .01	$ .05

Player	Year	No.	VG	EX/MT
Clements, Pat	88D	52	$ .01	$ .05
Cleveland, Reggie	81D	206	$ .01	$ .05
Cleveland, Reggie	82D	456	$ .01	$ .05
Cliburn, Stu	86D	301	$ .01	$ .06
Cliburn, Stu	87D	530	$ .01	$ .05
Cliburn, Stu	89D	462	$ .01	$ .05
Clutterbuck, Bryan	87D	397	$ .01	$ .05
Cobb, Ty	83D	653	$ .05	$ .20
Cocanower, Jaime	85D	455	$ .01	$ .08
Cocanower, Jaime	86D	393	$ .01	$ .06
Codiroli, Chris	84D	345	$ .03	$ .10
Codiroli, Chris	85D	462	$ .01	$ .08
Codiroli, Chris	86D	278	$ .01	$ .06
Codiroli, Chris	87D	226	$ .01	$ .05
Coffman, Kevin	88DR	49	$ .01	$ .05
Colbrunn, Greg	91DRR	425	$ .01	$ .25
Cole, Alex	91D	383	$ .01	$ .25
Coleman, Vince	86D	181	$1.00	$5.00
Coleman, Vince	86D	651	$ .03	$ .25
Coleman, Vince	87D	263	$ .03	$ .45
Coleman, Vince	88D	293	$ .05	$ .20
Coleman, Vince	88DBB	44	$ .01	$ .10
Coleman, Vince	89D	181	$ .01	$ .10
Coleman, Vince	89DBB	19	$ .01	$ .15
Coleman, Vince	89DK	19	$ .01	$ .05
Coleman, Vince	90D	279	$ .01	$ .10
Coleman, Vince	90DL	90	$ .01	$ .25
Coleman, Vince	91D	487	$ .01	$ .03
Coles, Darnell	84D	630	$ .04	$ .50
Coles, Darnell	85D	118	$ .01	$ .08
Coles, Darnell	86D	557	$ .01	$ .06
Coles, Darnell	87D	230	$ .01	$ .05
Coles, Darnell	88D	572	$ .01	$ .05
Coles, Darnell	88DBB	185	$ .01	$ .05
Coles, Darnell	89D	566	$ .01	$ .05
Coles, Darnell	90D	212	$ .01	$ .04

DAVE COLLINS OUTFIELD

Player	Year	No.	VG	EX/MT
Collins, Dave	81D	185	$ .01	$ .05
Collins, Dave	82D	169	$ .01	$ .05
Collins, Dave	83D	234	$ .01	$ .05
Collins, Dave	84D	650	$ .03	$ .10

Player	Year	No.	VG	EX/MT
Collins, Dave	85D	241	$ .01	$ .08
Collins, Dave	86D	218	$ .01	$ .06
Collins, Dave	87D	215	$ .01	$ .05
Combs, Pat	90DL	78	$ .01	$ .25
Combs, Pat	90DR	3	$ .01	$ .10
Combs, Pat	90DRR	44	$ .01	$ .25
Combs, Pat	91D	60	$ .01	$ .03
Comer, Steve	82D	341	$ .01	$ .05
Comer, Steve	83D	163	$ .01	$ .05
Comstock, Keith	90DL	522	$ .01	$ .15
Comstock, Keith	91D	246	$ .01	$ .03
Concepcion, Dave	81D	181	$ .03	$ .20
Concepcion, Dave	82D	421	$ .05	$ .30
Concepcion, Dave	83D	148	$ .03	$ .20
Concepcion, Dave	84D	121	$ .03	$ .10
Concepcion, Dave	84DK	2	$ .10	$ .35
Concepcion, Dave	85D	155	$ .01	$ .08
Concepcion, Dave	85D	203	$ .03	$ .20

DAVE CONCEPCION SS

Player	Year	No.	VG	EX/MT
Concepcion, Dave	86D	243	$ .05	$ .20
Concepcion, Dave	88D	329	$ .01	$ .05
Concepcion, Onix	83D	516	$ .01	$ .05
Concepcion, Onix	84D	95	$ .03	$ .10
Concepcion, Onix	86D	252	$ .01	$ .06
Cone, David	87D	502	$ .35	$3.00
Cone, David	87DR	35	$ .15	$1.00
Cone, David	88D	653	$ .01	$ .60
Cone, David	88DBB	40	$ .05	$ .25
Cone, David	89D	388	$ .05	$ .25
Cone, David	89DBB	96	$ .01	$ .10
Cone, David	89DK	9	$ .05	$ .25
Cone, David	90D	265	$ .01	$ .04
Cone, David	90DL	40	$ .01	$ .15
Cone, David	91D	154	$ .01	$ .03
Conine, Jeff	91DRR	427	$ .01	$ .50
Conroy, Tim	84D	340	$ .03	$ .10
Conroy, Tim	85D	156	$ .01	$ .08
Cook, Dennis	89D	646	$ .01	$ .25
Cook, Dennis	89DBB	327	$ .01	$ .05
Cook, Dennis	90D	193	$ .01	$ .04
Cook, Dennis	90DL	342	$ .01	$ .15

Player	Year	No.	VG	EX/MT
Cook, Dennis	91D	657	$ .01	$ .03
Coolbaugh, Scott	90DL	363	$ .01	$ .25
Coolbaugh, Scott	90DR	32	$ .01	$ .10
Coolbaugh, Scott	90DRR	43	$ .01	$ .15
Cooper, Cecil	81D	83	$ .01	$ .10
Cooper, Cecil	82D	258	$ .01	$ .10
Cooper, Cecil	83D	106	$ .01	$ .10
Cooper, Cecil	84D	351	$ .01	$ .10
Cooper, Cecil	85D	170	$ .01	$ .20
Cooper, Cecil	86D	170	$ .01	$ .06
Cooper, Cecil	86DK	7	$ .05	$ .20
Cooper, Cecil	87D	363	$ .01	$ .05
Cooper, Scott	91D	496	$ .01	$ .15
Cora, Joey	90D	538	$ .01	$ .04
Cora, Joey	90DL	366	$ .01	$ .15
Corbett, Doug	81D	546	$ .01	$ .05
Corbett, Doug	82D	53	$ .01	$ .05
Corbett, Doug	85D	474	$ .01	$ .08
Corbett, Doug	87D	333	$ .01	$ .05
Corbett, Sherman	89D	407	$ .01	$ .10
Corcoran, Tim	81D	367	$ .01	$ .05
Corcoran, Tim	85D	381	$ .01	$ .08
Corcoran, Tim	86D	381	$ .01	$ .06
Corrales, Pat	83D	626	$ .01	$ .05
Correa, Ed	86DR	4	$ .01	$ .15
Correa, Ed	87D	57	$ .01	$ .05
Correa, Ed	88D	57	$ .01	$ .05
Corsi, Jim	90D	422	$ .01	$ .04
Costello, John	89D	518	$ .01	$ .05
Costello, John	90D	555	$ .01	$ .04
Cotto, Henry	85D	411	$ .01	$ .15
Cotto, Henry	88DBB	51	$ .01	$ .05
Cotto, Henry	89D	109	$ .01	$ .05
Cotto, Henry	90D	644	$ .01	$ .04
Cotto, Henry	91D	343	$ .01	$ .03
Cowens, Al	81D	369	$ .01	$ .05
Cowens, Al	82D	207	$ .01	$ .05
Cowens, Al	83D	554	$ .01	$ .05
Cowens, Al	84D	511	$ .03	$ .10
Cowens, Al	85D	196	$ .01	$ .08
Cowens, Al	86D	389	$ .01	$ .06
Cowley, Joe	85D	613	$ .01	$ .08
Cowley, Joe	86D	608	$ .01	$ .06
Cowley, Joe	87D	552	$ .01	$ .05
Cox, Bobby	81D	426	$ .01	$ .05
Cox, Danny	84D	449	$ .03	$ .35
Cox, Danny	85D	571	$ .01	$ .08
Cox, Danny	86D	382	$ .01	$ .06
Cox, Danny	87D	553	$ .01	$ .05
Cox, Danny	88D	60	$ .01	$ .05
Cox, Danny	88DBB	75	$ .01	$ .05
Cox, Danny	89D	348	$ .01	$ .05
Cox, Jeff	81D	230	$ .01	$ .05
Cox, Larry	81D	285	$ .01	$ .05
Cox, Ted	81D	283	$ .01	$ .05
Craig, Rodney	81D	288	$ .01	$ .05
Craig, Rodney	83D	515	$ .01	$ .05
Crandall, Del	84D	632	$ .03	$ .10
Crawford, Steve	82D	564	$ .01	$ .05
Crawford, Steve	85D	395	$ .01	$ .08
Crawford, Steve	86D	416	$ .01	$ .06
Crawford, Steve	87D	399	$ .01	$ .05
Crawford, Steve	90DL	494	$ .01	$ .15
Creel, Keith	83D	574	$ .01	$ .05
Crews, Tim	88D	464	$ .01	$ .05
Crews, Tim	88DR	20	$ .01	$ .05
Crews, Tim	89D	486	$ .01	$ .05
Crews, Tim	90D	550	$ .01	$ .04
Crews, Tim	91D	294	$ .01	$ .03
Crim, Chuck	87DR	18	$ .01	$ .07

Player	Year	No.	VG	EX/MT	Player	Year	No.	VG	EX/MT
Crim, Chuck	88D	355	$ .01	$ .05	Dascenzo, Doug	89D	491	$ .01	$ .25
Crim, Chuck	89D	617	$ .01	$ .05	Dascenzo, Doug	91D	749	$ .01	$ .03
Crim, Chuck	89DBB	127	$ .01	$ .05	Dauer, Rich	81D	232	$ .01	$ .05
Crim, Chuck	90D	221	$ .01	$ .04	Dauer, Rich	82D	257	$ .01	$ .05
Crim, Chuck	90DL	58	$ .01	$ .15	Dauer, Rich	83D	455	$ .01	$ .05
Crim, Chuck	91D	684	$ .01	$ .03	Dauer, Rich	84D	350	$ .03	$ .10
Cromartie, Warren	81D	332	$ .01	$ .05	Dauer, Rich	85D	106	$ .01	$ .08
Cromartie, Warren	82D	340	$ .01	$ .05	Daugherty, Jack	90D	461	$ .01	$ .04
Cromartie, Warren	83D	466	$ .01	$ .05	Daugherty, Jack	90DL	521	$ .01	$ .20
Crowley, Terry	81D	507	$ .01	$ .05	Daugherty, Jack	91D	576	$ .01	$ .03
Crowley, Terry	82D	383	$ .01	$ .05	Daulton, Darren	86D	477	$ .01	$ .15
Crowley, Terry	83D	457	$ .01	$ .05	Daulton, Darren	87D	262	$ .01	$ .05
Cruz, Hector	82D	57	$ .01	$ .05	Daulton, Darren	88D	309	$ .01	$ .05
Cruz, Jose	81D	383	$ .01	$ .05	Daulton, Darren	89D	549	$ .01	$ .05
Cruz, Jose	82D	244	$ .01	$ .05	Daulton, Darren	89DBB	128	$ .01	$ .05
Cruz, Jose	83D	41	$ .01	$ .05	Daulton, Darren	90D	194	$ .01	$ .04
Cruz, Jose	84D	182	$ .03	$ .10	Daulton, Darren	90DL	369	$ .01	$ .15
Cruz, Jose	85D	304	$ .01	$ .08	Daulton, Darren	91D	316	$ .01	$ .03
Cruz, Jose	85DK	20	$ .03	$ .10	David, Andre	87D	519	$ .01	$ .05
Cruz, Jose	86D	60	$ .01	$ .06	Davidson, Mark	87DR	22	$ .01	$ .07
Cruz, Jose	87D	85	$ .01	$ .05	Davidson, Mark	88D	519	$ .01	$ .05
Cruz, Julio	81D	163	$ .01	$ .05	Davidson, Mark	91D	540	$ .01	$ .03
Cruz, Julio	82D	50	$ .01	$ .05	Davis, Alvin	85D	69	$ .40	$3.50
Cruz, Julio	83D	379	$ .01	$ .05	Davis, Alvin	85DK	18	$ .10	$ .45
Cruz, Julio	84D	379	$ .03	$ .10	Davis, Alvin	86D	69	$ .08	$ .25
Cruz, Julio	85D	452	$ .01	$ .08	Davis, Alvin	87D	75	$ .01	$ .15
Cruz, Julio	86D	257	$ .01	$ .06	Davis, Alvin	88D	193	$ .01	$ .15
Cruz, Todd	83D	505	$ .01	$ .05	Davis, Alvin	88DBB	107	$ .01	$ .10
Cruz, Todd	84D	148	$ .03	$ .10	Davis, Alvin	88DBC	25	$ .10	$ .25
Cruz, Victor	81D	321	$ .01	$ .05	Davis, Alvin	89D	345	$ .01	$ .05
Cubbage, Mike	81D	492	$ .01	$ .05	Davis, Alvin	89DBB	24	$ .01	$ .10
Cummings, Steve	90D	698	$ .01	$ .10	Davis, Alvin	89DBC	25	$ .01	$ .10
Curtis, John	83D	170	$ .01	$ .05	Davis, Alvin	90D	109	$ .01	$ .10
Cuyler, Milt	91DRR	40	$ .01	$ .10	Davis, Alvin	90DBC	9	$ .01	$ .10
Daniels, Kal	86DRR	27	$1.50	$3.50	Davis, Alvin	90DL	35	$ .01	$ .15
Daniels, Kal	87D	142	$ .40	$ .75	Davis, Alvin	91D	482	$ .01	$ .03
Daniels, Kal	88D	289	$ .01	$ .25	Davis, Bob	81D	30	$ .01	$ .05
Daniels, Kal	88DBB	6	$ .01	$ .15	Davis, Butch	84D	277	$ .03	$ .10
Daniels, Kal	88DK	14	$ .10	$ .25	Davis, Charles "Chili"	83D	348	$ .01	$ .25
Daniels, Kal	89D	198	$ .01	$ .10	Davis, Chili	84D	114	$ .03	$ .10
Daniels, Kal	89DBB	118	$ .01	$ .05	Davis, Chili	85D	480	$ .01	$ .08
Daniels, Kal	89DBC	18	$ .01	$ .20	Davis, Chili	86D	65	$ .01	$ .06
Daniels, Kal	90D	432	$ .01	$ .04	Davis, Chili	86DK	6	$ .01	$ .06
Daniels, Kal	90DL	313	$ .01	$ .15	Davis, Chili	87D	268	$ .01	$ .05
Daniels, Kal	91D	336	$ .01	$ .03	Davis, Chili	88D	313	$ .01	$ .05
Darling, Ron	84DRR	30	$1.00	$4.00	Davis, Chili	89D	449	$ .01	$ .05
Darling, Ron	85D	434	$ .15	$ .60	Davis, Chili	89DBB	115	$ .01	$ .05
Darling, Ron	86D	563	$ .08	$ .25	Davis, Chili	90D	136	$ .01	$ .04
Darling, Ron	87D	192	$ .05	$ .20	Davis, Chili	90DBC	20	$ .01	$ .04
Darling, Ron	88D	76	$ .01	$ .15	Davis, Chili	90DL	288	$ .01	$ .15
Darling, Ron	88DBB	41	$ .01	$ .15	Davis, Chili	91D	580	$ .01	$ .03
Darling, Ron	88DK	6	$ .03	$ .25	Davis, Dick	81D	528	$ .01	$ .05
Darling, Ron	89D	171	$ .01	$ .10	Davis, Dick	82D	147	$ .01	$ .05
Darling, Ron	89DBB	41	$ .01	$ .05	Davis, Dick	83D	647	$ .01	$ .05
Darling, Ron	90D	289	$ .01	$ .04	Davis, Eric	85D	325	$6.00	$20.00
Darling, Ron	90DL	304	$ .01	$ .15	Davis, Eric	86D	164	$1.50	$4.00
Darling, Ron	91D	472	$ .01	$ .03	Davis, Eric	87D	265	$ .70	$1.50
Darwin, Danny	81D	147	$ .01	$ .05	Davis, Eric	87DK	22	$ .25	$1.00
Darwin, Danny	82D	321	$ .01	$ .05	Davis, Eric	88D	369	$ .10	$ .50
Darwin, Danny	83D	289	$ .01	$ .05	Davis, Eric	88DBB	62	$ .05	$ .25
Darwin, Danny	84D	544	$ .03	$ .10	Davis, Eric	88DBC	2	$ .35	$ .35
Darwin, Danny	85D	98	$ .01	$ .08	Davis, Eric	89D	80	$ .05	$ .35
Darwin, Danny	86D	149	$ .01	$ .06	Davis, Eric	89DBB	6	$ .01	$ .35
Darwin, Danny	87D	508	$ .01	$ .05	Davis, Eric	90D	232	$ .01	$ .15
Darwin, Danny	88D	358	$ .01	$ .05	Davis, Eric	90DAS	695	$ .01	$ .15
Darwin, Danny	89D	390	$ .01	$ .05	Davis, Eric	90DBC	23	$ .01	$ .20
Darwin, Danny	90D	561	$ .01	$ .04	Davis, Eric	90DL	189	$ .01	$ .35
Darwin, Danny	90DL	346	$ .01	$ .15	Davis, Eric	91D	84	$ .01	$ .15
Darwin, Danny	91D	165	$ .01	$ .03	Davis, Glenn	86D	380	$ .50	$4.00
Darwin, Danny	91DMVP	401	$ .01	$ .03	Davis, Glenn	87D	61	$ .05	$ .60

DONRUSS

Player	Year	No.	VG	EX/MT	Player	Year	No.	VG	EX/MT
Davis, Glenn	88D	184	$ .05	$ .20	Dawson, Andre	83D	518	$ .10	$ .75
Davis, Glenn	88DBB	64	$ .01	$ .10	Dawson, Andre	84D	97	$ .20	$2.00
Davis, Glenn	89D	236	$ .01	$ .10	Dawson, Andre	85D	421	$ .08	$ .50
Davis, Glenn	89DBB	8	$ .01	$ .10	Dawson, Andre	86D	87	$ .08	$ .35
Davis, Glenn	89DK	25	$ .01	$ .15	Dawson, Andre	86DK	25	$ .03	$ .30
Davis, Glenn	90D	118	$ .01	$ .04	Dawson, Andre	87D	458	$ .15	$ .30
Davis, Glenn	90DBC	21	$ .01	$ .04	Dawson, Andre	88D	269	$ .05	$ .20
Davis, Glenn	90DL	30	$ .01	$ .20	Dawson, Andre	88DBB	225	$ .01	$ .15
Davis, Glenn	91D	474	$ .01	$ .03	Dawson, Andre	88DBC	10	$ .05	$ .25
Davis, Jerry	85D	162	$ .01	$ .08	Dawson, Andre	88DK	9	$ .03	$ .25
Davis, Jerry	86D	429	$ .01	$ .06	Dawson, Andre	89D	167	$ .01	$ .10
Davis, Jody	82D	225	$ .05	$ .30	Dawson, Andre	89DBB	4	$ .01	$ .10
Davis, Jody	83D	183	$ .01	$ .05	Dawson, Andre	89DBC	8	$ .01	$ .10
Davis, Jody	84D	433	$ .03	$ .10	Dawson, Andre	90D	223	$ .01	$ .04
Davis, Jody	85D	76	$ .01	$ .08	Dawson, Andre	90DL	177	$ .01	$ .25
Davis, Jody	86D	289	$ .01	$ .06	Dawson, Andre	91D	129	$ .01	$ .10
Davis, Jody	87D	269	$ .01	$ .05	Dawson, Andre	91DAS	435	$ .01	$ .03
Davis, Jody	88D	119	$ .01	$ .05	Dayett, Brian	84DRR	45	$ .03	$ .10
Davis, Jody	89D	650	$ .01	$ .05	Dayett, Brian	85D	152	$ .01	$ .08
Davis, Jody	89DBB	58	$ .01	$ .05	Dayett, Brian	88D	416	$ .01	$ .05
Davis, Joel	86D	623	$ .01	$ .06	Dayley, Ken	82D	501	$ .03	$ .20
Davis, Joel	87D	124	$ .01	$ .05	Dayley, Ken	83D	375	$ .01	$ .05
Davis, John	88D	594	$ .05	$ .20	Dayley, Ken	84D	199	$ .03	$ .10
Davis, John	88DR	48	$ .01	$ .05	Dayley, Ken	86D	303	$ .01	$ .06
Davis, Mark	84D	201	$ .10	$ .80	Dayley, Ken	87D	357	$ .01	$ .05
Davis, Mark	85D	553	$ .01	$ .20	Dayley, Ken	88D	357	$ .01	$ .05
Davis, Mark	86D	265	$ .01	$ .15	Dayley, Ken	89D	299	$ .01	$ .05
Davis, Mark	87D	313	$ .01	$ .15	Dayley, Ken	89DBB	268	$ .01	$ .05
Davis, Mark	88D	64	$ .01	$ .15	Dayley, Ken	90D	281	$ .01	$ .04
Davis, Mark	88DBB	98	$ .01	$ .05	Dayley, Ken	90DL	275	$ .01	$ .15
Davis, Mark	89D	65	$ .01	$ .05	Dayley, Ken	91D	735	$ .01	$ .03
Davis, Mark	89DBB	133	$ .01	$ .10	De Los Santos, Luis	89D	562	$ .01	$ .15
Davis, Mark	90D	302	$ .01	$ .04	De Los Santos, Luis	89DR	33	$ .01	$ .10
Davis, Mark	90DL	468	$ .01	$ .15	DeCinces, Doug	81D	352	$ .01	$ .05
Davis, Mark	91D	560	$ .01	$ .03	DeCinces, Doug	82D	279	$ .01	$ .05
Davis, Mike	81D	470	$ .05	$ .20	DeCinces, Doug	83D	216	$ .01	$ .05
Davis, Mike	84D	298	$ .03	$ .10	DeCinces, Doug	84D	230	$ .03	$ .10
Davis, Mike	85D	223	$ .01	$ .08	DeCinces, Doug	85D	179	$ .01	$ .08
Davis, Mike	86D	96	$ .01	$ .06	DeCinces, Doug	85DK	2	$ .01	$ .08
Davis, Mike	86DK	14	$ .01	$ .06	DeCinces, Doug	86D	57	$ .01	$ .06
Davis, Mike	87D	133	$ .01	$ .05	DeCinces, Doug	87D	356	$ .01	$ .05
Davis, Mike	88D	281	$ .01	$ .05	Decker, Steve	91DRR	428	$ .01	$ .35
Davis, Mike	88DBB	36	$ .01	$ .05	Dedmon, Jeff	85D	554	$ .01	$ .08
Davis, Mike	89D	316	$ .01	$ .05	Dedmon, Jeff	86D	443	$ .01	$ .06
Davis, Mike	90D	552	$ .01	$ .04	Dedmon, Jeff	87D	314	$ .01	$ .05
Davis, Ron	81D	467	$ .01	$ .05	Dedmon, Jeff	88D	325	$ .01	$ .05
Davis, Ron	82D	451	$ .01	$ .05	Deer, Rob	87D	274	$ .05	$ .20
Davis, Ron	83D	228	$ .01	$ .05	Deer, Rob	88D	274	$ .01	$ .05
Davis, Ron	84D	269	$ .03	$ .10	Deer, Rob	88DBB	109	$ .01	$ .05
Davis, Ron	85D	120	$ .01	$ .08	Deer, Rob	89D	173	$ .01	$ .05
Davis, Ron	86D	364	$ .01	$ .06	Deer, Rob	90D	55	$ .01	$ .04
Davis, Ron	87D	438	$ .01	$ .05	Deer, Rob	90DL	322	$ .01	$ .15
Davis, Storm	83D	619	$ .10	$ .50	Deer, Rob	91D	729	$ .01	$ .03
Davis, Storm	84D	585	$ .03	$ .10	Deer, Ron	89DBB	71	$ .01	$ .05
Davis, Storm	85D	454	$ .01	$ .08	DeJesus, Ivan	81D	483	$ .01	$ .05
Davis, Storm	86D	169	$ .01	$ .06	DeJesus, Ivan	82D	48	$ .01	$ .05
Davis, Storm	87D	273	$ .01	$ .05	DeJesus, Ivan	82DK	14	$ .01	$ .05
Davis, Storm	88D	595	$ .01	$ .05	DeJesus, Ivan	83D	399	$ .01	$ .05
Davis, Storm	89D	210	$ .01	$ .05	DeJesus, Ivan	84D	427	$ .03	$ .10
Davis, Storm	90D	479	$ .01	$ .04	DeJesus, Ivan	85D	204	$ .01	$ .08
Davis, Storm	90DL	362	$ .01	$ .15	DeJesus, Ivan	86D	449	$ .01	$ .06
Davis, Storm	91D	185	$ .01	$ .03	DeJesus, Jose	89D	558	$ .01	$ .05
Davis, Tommy	82D	648	$ .01	$ .05	DeJesus, Jose	90DL	415	$ .01	$ .20
Dawley, Bill	84D	328	$ .03	$ .10	DeJesus, Jose	91D	596	$ .01	$ .03
Dawley, Bill	85D	354	$ .01	$ .08	DeLeon, Jose	84D	628	$ .10	$ .60
Dawley, Bill	86D	283	$ .01	$ .06	DeLeon, Jose	85D	308	$ .01	$ .08
Dawley, Bill	87D	628	$ .01	$ .05	DeLeon, Jose	86D	235	$ .01	$ .06
Dawley, Bill	88D	331	$ .01	$ .05	DeLeon, Jose	87D	457	$ .01	$ .05
Dawson, Andre	81D	212	$ .06	$1.00	DeLeon, Jose	88D	59	$ .01	$ .05
Dawson, Andre	82D	88	$ .10	$1.00	DeLeon, Jose	89D	437	$ .01	$ .05

76

Player	Year	No.	VG	EX/MT
DeLeon, Jose	90D	536	$ .01	$ .04
DeLeon, Jose	90DL	485	$ .01	$ .15

Jose DeLeon — PITCHER

Player	Year	No.	VG	EX/MT
DeLeon, Jose	91D	128	$ .01	$ .03
DeLeon, Luis	82D	588	$ .01	$ .05
DeLeon, Luis	83D	296	$ .01	$ .05
DeLeon, Luis	84D	162	$ .03	$ .10
DeLeon, Luis	85D	406	$ .01	$ .08
Delucia, Rich	91DRR	426	$ .01	$ .15
Dempsey, Rick	81D	113	$ .01	$ .05
Dempsey, Rick	82D	77	$ .01	$ .05
Dempsey, Rick	83D	329	$ .01	$ .05
Dempsey, Rick	84D	413	$ .03	$ .10
Dempsey, Rick	85D	332	$ .01	$ .08
Dempsey, Rick	86D	106	$ .01	$ .06
Dempsey, Rick	87D	294	$ .01	$ .05
Dempsey, Rick	89D	432	$ .01	$ .05
Dempsey, Rick	90D	557	$ .01	$ .04
Denny, John	82D	572	$ .01	$ .05
Denny, John	83D	237	$ .02	$ .15
Denny, John	84D	407	$ .03	$ .10
Denny, John	85D	111	$ .01	$ .08
Denny, John	86D	204	$ .01	$ .06
Denny, John	87D	329	$ .01	$ .05
Dent, Bucky	81D	465	$ .01	$ .05
Dent, Bucky	82D	209	$ .01	$ .05
Dent, Bucky	84D	300	$ .03	$ .10
Dernier, Bob	83D	189	$ .01	$ .05
Dernier, Bob	84D	541	$ .03	$ .10
Dernier, Bob	85D	510	$ .01	$ .08
Dernier, Bob	86D	266	$ .01	$ .06
Dernier, Bob	87D	146	$ .01	$ .05
Dernier, Bob	88D	392	$ .01	$ .05
Dernier, Bob	89D	430	$ .01	$ .05
DeSa, Joe	86D	546	$ .01	$ .06
Deshaies, Jim	86DR	34	$ .01	$ .30
Deshaies, Jim	87D	184	$ .01	$ .25
Deshaies, Jim	88D	85	$ .01	$ .05
Deshaies, Jim	88DBB	94	$ .01	$ .05
Deshaies, Jim	89D	241	$ .01	$ .05
Deshaies, Jim	89DBB	120	$ .01	$ .05
Deshaies, Jim	90D	187	$ .01	$ .04

Player	Year	No.	VG	EX/MT
Deshaies, Jim	90DK	7	$ .01	$ .10
Deshaies, Jim	90DL	168	$ .01	$ .15
Deshaies, Jim	91D	652	$ .01	$ .03
DeShields, Delino	90DL	193	$ .01	$ 2.00
DeShields, Delino	90DR	6	$ .01	$ .40
DeShields, Delino	90DRR	42	$ .01	$ .75
DeShields, Delino	91D	555	$ .01	$ .15
DeShields, Delino	91DBC	16	$ .01	$ .10
DeShields, Delino	91DK	11	$ .01	$ .10
Devereaux, Mike	88D	546	$ .01	$ .20
Devereaux, Mike	89D	603	$ .01	$ .05
Devereaux, Mike	89DBB	326	$ .01	$ .05
Devereaux, Mike	89DR	51	$ .01	$ .10
Devereaux, Mike	89DTR	30	$ .01	$ .05
Devereaux, Mike	90D	282	$ .01	$ .04
Devereaux, Mike	90DL	223	$ .01	$ .15
Devereaux, Mike	91D	444	$ .01	$ .03
Diaz, Bo	81D	517	$ .01	$ .05
Diaz, Bo	82D	263	$ .02	$ .15
Diaz, Bo	83D	147	$ .01	$ .05
Diaz, Bo	84D	137	$ .03	$ .10
Diaz, Bo	86D	530	$ .01	$ .06
Diaz, Bo	87D	246	$ .01	$ .05
Diaz, Bo	88D	186	$ .01	$ .05
Diaz, Bo	88DBB	110	$ .01	$ .05
Diaz, Bo	89D	242	$ .01	$ .05
Diaz, Bo	89DBB	293	$ .01	$ .05
Diaz, Bo	90D	139	$ .01	$ .04
Diaz, Carlos	83D	562	$ .01	$ .05
Diaz, Carlos	84D	600	$ .03	$ .10
Diaz, Carlos	86D	348	$ .01	$ .06
Diaz, Edgar	90DL	335	$ .01	$ .15
Diaz, Edgar	91D	197	$ .01	$ .03
Diaz, Mike	87D	267	$ .01	$ .05
Diaz, Mike	88D	267	$ .01	$ .05
Diaz, Mike	89D	655	$ .01	$ .05
Dibble, Rob	89D	426	$ .05	$ .50
Dibble, Rob	89DBB	334	$ .01	$ .25
Dibble, Rob	90D	189	$ .01	$ .25
Dibble, Rob	90DL	57	$ .01	$ .25
Dibble, Rob	91D	321	$ .01	$ .03
Dickson, Lance	91DRR	424	$ .01	$ .25
Dillard, Steve	81D	502	$ .01	$ .05
Dillard, Steve	82D	174	$ .01	$ .05
Dilone, Miguel	81D	441	$ .01	$ .05
Dilone, Miguel	82D	515	$ .01	$ .05
Dilone, Miguel	83D	85	$ .01	$ .05
Dilone, Miguel	85D	453	$ .01	$ .08
DiPino, Frank	84D	502	$ .03	$ .10
DiPino, Frank	85D	232	$ .01	$ .08
DiPino, Frank	86D	304	$ .01	$ .06
DiPino, Frank	87D	416	$ .01	$ .05
DiPino, Frank	88D	570	$ .01	$ .05
DiPino, Frank	88DBB	205	$ .01	$ .05
DiPino, Frank	89D	393	$ .01	$ .05
DiPino, Frank	90D	518	$ .01	$ .04
DiPino, Frank	90DL	103	$ .01	$ .15
DiPino, Frank	91D	360	$ .01	$ .03
Distefano, Benny	85D	166	$ .01	$ .08
Distefano, Benny	86D	78	$ .01	$ .06
Distefano, Benny	87D	514	$ .01	$ .05
Dixon, Ken	85D	270	$ .01	$ .08
Dixon, Ken	86D	148	$ .01	$ .06
Dixon, Ken	87D	171	$ .01	$ .05
Dixon, Ken	88D	48	$ .01	$ .05
Dodson, Pat	87DRR	44	$ .03	$ .25
Donohue, Tom	81D	51	$ .01	$ .05
Dopson, John	88DR	43	$ .01	$ .25
Dopson, John	89D	392	$ .01	$ .10
Dopson, John	89DBB	177	$ .01	$ .05

Player	Year	No.	VG	EX/MT
Dopson, John	89DTR	7	$ .01	$ .05
Dopson, John	90D	162	$ .01	$ .04
Dopson, John	90DL	130	$ .01	$ .15
Dopson, John	91D	193	$ .01	$ .03
Doran, Bill	84D	580	$ .35	$1.50
Doran, Bill	85D	84	$ .03	$ .20
Doran, Bill	86D	110	$ .01	$ .06
Doran, Bill	86DK	10	$ .01	$ .06
Doran, Bill	87D	286	$ .01	$ .05
Doran, Bill	88D	235	$ .01	$ .15
Doran, Bill	88DBB	120	$ .01	$ .05
Doran, Bill	89D	306	$ .01	$ .05
Doran, Bill	89DBB	38	$ .01	$ .05
Doran, Bill	90D	236	$ .01	$ .04
Doran, Bill	90DL	161	$ .01	$ .20
Doran, Bill	91D	756	$ .01	$ .03
Dotson, Rich	81D	280	$ .01	$ .20
Dotson, Rich	82D	356	$ .01	$ .05
Dotson, Rich	83D	319	$ .01	$ .05
Dotson, Rich	84D	180	$ .03	$ .10
Dotson, Rich	85D	302	$ .01	$ .08
Dotson, Rich	85DK	3	$ .01	$ .08
Dotson, Rich	86D	160	$ .01	$ .06
Dotson, Rich	87D	383	$ .01	$ .05
Dotson, Richard	88D	124	$ .01	$ .05
Dotson, Rich	88DBB	52	$ .01	$ .05
Dotson, Rich	89D	277	$ .01	$ .05
Downing, Brian	81D	410	$ .01	$ .05
Downing, Brian	82D	115	$ .01	$ .05
Downing, Brian	83D	367	$ .01	$ .05
Downing, Brian	84D	423	$ .03	$ .10
Downing, Brian	85D	158	$ .01	$ .08
Downing, Brian	86D	108	$ .01	$ .06
Downing, Brian	87D	86	$ .01	$ .05
Downing, Brian	88D	258	$ .01	$ .05
Downing, Brian	88DBB	27	$ .01	$ .05
Downing, Brian	89D	254	$ .01	$ .05
Downing, Brian	89DBB	321	$ .01	$ .05
Downing, Brian	90D	352	$ .01	$ .04
Downing, Brian	90DK	10	$ .01	$ .10
Downs, Kelly	87D	573	$ .01	$ .15
Downs, Kelly	88D	145	$ .01	$ .05
Downs, Kelly	88DBB	106	$ .01	$ .05
Downs, Kelly	89D	367	$ .01	$ .05
Downs, Kelly	89DBB	247	$ .01	$ .05
Downs, Kelly	90D	177	$ .01	$ .04
Downs, Kelly	91D	738	$ .01	$ .03
Drabek, Doug	86DR	31	$ .10	$1.50
Drabek, Doug	87D	251	$ .05	$ 1.25
Drabek, Doug	88D	79	$ .01	$ .15
Drabek, Doug	88DBB	73	$ .01	$ .05
Drabek, Doug	89D	211	$ .01	$ .05
Drabek, Doug	89DBB	17	$ .01	$ .05
Drabek, Doug	90D	92	$ .01	$ .04
Drabek, Doug	90DL	296	$ .01	$ .15
Drabek, Doug	91D	269	$ .01	$ .03
Drabek, Doug	91D	750	$ .01	$ .03
Drabek, Doug	91DMVP	411	$ .01	$ .03
Drago, Dick	81D	336	$ .01	$ .05
Dravecky, Dave	84D	551	$ .15	$ .70
Dravecky, Dave	84DK	8	$ .04	$ .25
Dravecky, Dave	85D	112	$ .01	$ .08
Dravecky, Dave	86D	162	$ .01	$ .06
Dravecky, Dave	87D	187	$ .01	$ .05
Dravecky, Dave	88D	485	$ .01	$ .05
Dravecky, Dave	88DBB	135	$ .01	$ .05
Dressler, Rob	81D	406	$ .01	$ .05
Drew, Cameron	89DRR	30	$ .05	$ .25
Driessen, Dan	81D	301	$ .01	$ .05
Driessen, Dan	82D	248	$ .01	$ .05

Player	Year	No.	VG	EX/MT
Driessen, Dan	83D	274	$ .01	$ .05
Driessen, Dan	84D	243	$ .03	$ .10
Driessen, Dan	85D	619	$ .01	$ .08
Driessen, Dan	86D	641	$ .01	$ .06
Drummond, Tim	90D	510	$ .01	$ .10
Drummond, Tim	90DR	50	$ .01	$ .10
Drummond, Tim	91D	694	$ .01	$ .03
Drumright, Keith	82D	616	$ .01	$ .05
DuBois, Brian	90DL	266	$ .01	$ .15
DuBois, Brian	90DR	4	$ .01	$ .10
DuBois, Brian	90DRR	38	$ .01	$ .10
Ducey, Rob	91D	705	$ .01	$ .03
Dunbar, Tommy	84DRR	28	$ .03	$ .15
Dunbar, Tommy	85D	159	$ .01	$ .08
Dunbar, Tommy	86D	221	$ .01	$ .06
Duncan, Mariano	86D	128	$ .05	$ .50
Duncan, Mariano	87D	253	$ .01	$ .15
Duncan, Mariano	88D	155	$ .01	$ .05
Duncan, Mariano	90D	684	$ .01	$ .10
Duncan, Mariano	90DL	202	$ .01	$ .15
Duncan, Mariano	91D	309	$ .01	$ .03
Dunne, Mike	87DR	38	$ .10	$ .30
Dunne, Mike	88D	390	$ .01	$ .15
Dunne, Mike	88DBB	89	$ .01	$ .05
Dunne, Mike	89D	269	$ .01	$ .05
Dunne, Mike	90DL	418	$ .01	$ .15
Dunston, Shawon	85DRR	39	$ .50	$5.00
Dunston, Shawon	86D	311	$ .10	$1.00
Dunston, Shawon	87D	119	$ .01	$ .25
Dunston, Shawon	88D	146	$ .01	$ .15
Dunston, Shawon	88DBB	37	$ .01	$ .05
Dunston, Shawon	89D	137	$ .01	$ .05
Dunston, Shawon	89DBB	93	$ .01	$ .05
Dunston, Shawon	90D	49	$ .01	$ .04
Dunston, Shawon	90DL	229	$ .01	$ .15
Dunston, Shawon	91D	686	$ .01	$ .03

LEON DURHAM INFIELD/O-F

Player	Year	No.	VG	EX/MT
Durham, Leon	81D	427	$ .01	$ .05
Durham, Leon	82D	151	$ .01	$ .05
Durham, Leon	83D	477	$ .01	$ .05
Durham, Leon	84D	67	$ .03	$ .10

Player	Year	No.	VG	EX/MT	Player	Year	No.	VG	EX/MT
Durham, Leon	84DK	5	$ .01	$ .10	Eichelberger, Juan	82D	422	$ .01	$ .05
Durham, Leon	85D	189	$ .01	$ .08	Eichelberger, Juan	83D	422	$ .01	$ .05
Durham, Leon	86D	320	$ .01	$ .06	Eichelberger, Juan	84D	398	$ .03	$ .10
Durham, Leon	87D	242	$ .01	$ .05	Eichhorn, Mark	86DR	13	$ .01	$ .10
Durham, Leon	88D	191	$ .01	$ .05	Eichhorn, Mark	87D	321	$ .01	$ .05
Dwyer, Jim	81D	577	$ .01	$ .05	Eichhorn, Mark	88D	121	$ .01	$ .05
Dwyer, Jim	82D	611	$ .01	$ .05	Eichhorn, Mark	90DL	472	$ .01	$ .15
Dwyer, Jim	83D	583	$ .01	$ .05	Eichhorn, Mark	91D	318	$ .01	$ .03
Dwyer, Jim	84D	454	$ .03	$ .10	Eiland, Dave	89D	481	$ .01	$ .10
Dwyer, Jim	86D	413	$ .01	$ .06	Eiland, Dave	91D	354	$ .01	$ .03
Dwyer, Jim	87D	418	$ .01	$ .05	Eisenreich, Jim	88D	343	$ .01	$ .05
Dwyer, Jim	88D	459	$ .01	$ .05	Eisenreich, Jim	89DBB	306	$ .01	$ .05
Dwyer, Jim	89DBB	311	$ .01	$ .05	Eisenreich, Jim	90D	238	$ .01	$ .04
Dwyer, Jim	90D	484	$ .01	$ .04	Eisenreich, Jim	90DL	278	$ .01	$ .15
Dybzinski, Jerry	81D	438	$ .01	$ .05	Eisenreich, Jim	91D	448	$ .01	$ .03
Dybzinski, Jerry	82D	647	$ .01	$ .05	Elia, Lee	83D	614	$ .01	$ .05
Dybzinski, Jerry	83D	576	$ .01	$ .05	Ellis, John	81D	26	$ .01	$ .05
Dybzinski, Jerry	84D	160	$ .03	$ .10	Ellis, John	82D	642	$ .01	$ .05
Dyer, Duffy	81D	7	$ .01	$ .05	Ellsworth, Steve	88DR	54	$ .01	$ .05
Dyer, Mike	90D	642	$ .01	$ .10	Elster, Kevin	87D	635	$ .01	$ .35
Dykstra, Lenny	86D	482	$ .25	$3.50	Elster, Kevin	88DBB	70	$ .01	$ .05
Dykstra, Lenny	87D	611	$ .05	$ .50	Elster, Kevin	88DR	34	$ .01	$ .10
Dykstra, Lenny	88D	364	$ .01	$ .15	Elster, Kevin	88DRR	37	$ .01	$ .10
Dykstra, Lenny	88DBB	264	$ .01	$ .10	Elster, Kevin	89D	289	$ .01	$ .05
Dykstra, Lenny	89D	353	$ .01	$ .10	Elster, Kevin	89DBB	97	$ .01	$ .05
Dykstra, Lenny	89DBB	159	$ .01	$ .10	Elster, Kevin	90D	152	$ .01	$ .04
Dykstra, Lenny	90D	313	$ .01	$ .10	Elster, Kevin	90DL	8	$ .01	$ .15
Dykstra, Len	90DL	262	$ .01	$ .15	Elster, Kevin	91D	304	$ .01	$ .03
Dykstra, Len	91D	523	$ .01	$ .03	Engel, Steve	86D	510	$ .01	$ .06
Dykstra, Len	91D	744	$ .01	$ .15	Engle, Dave	82D	102	$ .01	$ .05
Dykstra, Len	91DAS	434	$ .01	$ .03	Engle, Dave	84D	598	$ .03	$ .10
Dykstra, Len	91DK	7	$ .01	$ .05	Engle, Dave	85D	72	$ .01	$ .08
Dykstra, Len	91DLP	8	$1.00	$5.00	Engle, Dave	86D	438	$ .01	$ .06
Dykstra, Len	91DMVP	410	$ .01	$ .03	Engle, Ralph	83D	646	$ .01	$ .05
Earl, Scottie	85D	491	$ .01	$ .08	Erickson, Roger	81D	549	$ .01	$ .05
Easler, Mike	81D	256	$ .01	$ .05	Erickson, Roger	82D	303	$ .01	$ .05
Easler, Mike	82D	221	$ .01	$ .05	Erickson, Scott	91D	767	$ .01	$1.00
Easler, Mike	83D	221	$ .01	$ .05	Esasky, Nick	84D	602	$ .10	$1.00
Easler, Mike	84D	444	$ .03	$ .10	Esasky, Nick	85D	121	$ .01	$ .15
Easler, Mike	85D	213	$ .01	$ .08	Esasky, Nick	86D	286	$ .01	$ .06
Easler, Mike	86D	395	$ .01	$ .06	Esasky, Nick	87D	166	$ .01	$ .05
Easler, Mike	87D	277	$ .01	$ .05	Esasky, Nick	88D	413	$ .01	$ .05
Easterly, Jamie	82D	623	$ .01	$ .05	Esasky, Nick	88DBB	118	$ .01	$ .05
Easterly, Jamie	83D	280	$ .01	$ .05	Esasky, Nick	89D	189	$ .01	$ .05
Easterly, Jamie	86D	582	$ .01	$ .06	Esasky, Nick	89DBB	284	$ .01	$ .05
Eave, Gary	90D	713	$ .01	$ .10	Esasky, Nick	89DTR	18	$ .01	$ .10
Eckersley, Dennis	81D	96	$ .05	$ .30	Esasky, Nick	90D	303	$ .01	$ .04
Eckersley, Dennis	82D	30	$ .05	$ .35	Esasky, Nick	90DL	164	$ .01	$ .15
Eckersley, Dennis	83D	487	$ .01	$ .25	Escarrega, Ernesto	83D	291	$ .01	$ .05
Eckersley, Dennis	84D	639	$ .04	$ .25	Espino, Juan	84D	92	$ .03	$ .10
Eckersley, Dennis	85D	442	$ .01	$ .08	Espinoza, Alvaro	89DBB	161	$ .01	$ .05
Eckersley, Dennis	86D	239	$ .01	$ .06	Espinoza, Alvaro	90D	245	$ .01	$ .04
Eckersley, Dennis	87D	365	$ .01	$ .05	Espinoza, Alvaro	90DL	240	$ .01	$ .15
Eckersley, Dennis	88D	349	$ .01	$ .05	Espinoza, Alvaro	91D	226	$ .01	$ .03
Eckersley, Dennis	88DBB	43	$ .01	$ .05	Espy, Cecil	88DR	9	$ .01	$ .15
Eckersley, Dennis	89D	67	$ .01	$ .05	Espy, Cecil	89D	292	$ .01	$ .15
Eckersley, Dennis	89DBB	134	$ .01	$ .10	Espy, Cecil	89DBB	335	$ .01	$ .05
Eckersley, Dennis	90D	210	$ .01	$ .04	Espy, Cecil	90D	260	$ .01	$ .04
Eckersley, Dennis	90DL	29	$ .01	$ .15	Essian, Jim	81D	503	$ .01	$ .05
Eckersley, Dennis	91D	270	$ .01	$ .03	Essian, Jim	82D	369	$ .01	$ .05
Edens, Tom	91D	590	$ .01	$ .03	Essian, Jim	83D	478	$ .01	$ .05
Edwards, Dave	81D	595	$ .01	$ .05	Essian, Jim	84D	629	$ .03	$ .10
Edwards, Dave	82D	247	$ .01	$ .05	Eufemia, Frank	86D	513	$ .01	$ .06
Edwards, Dave	83D	565	$ .01	$ .05	Evans, Barry	82D	271	$ .01	$ .05
Edwards, Marshall	83D	406	$ .01	$ .05	Evans, Darrell	81D	192	$ .03	$ .20
Edwards, Marshall	84D	490	$ .03	$ .10	Evans, Darrell	82D	398	$ .03	$ .20
Edwards, Mike	81D	497	$ .01	$ .05	Evans, Darrell	83D	251	$ .02	$ .15
Edwards, Wayne	90DL	352	$ .01	$ .25	Evans, Darrell	84D	431	$ .04	$ .25
Edwards, Wayne	90DR	17	$ .01	$ .10	Evans, Darrell	85D	227	$ .03	$ .10
Edwards, Wayne	91D	327	$ .01	$ .03	Evans, Darrell	86D	369	$ .01	$ .06

DONRUSS

Player	Year	No.	VG	EX/MT	Player	Year	No.	VG	EX/MT
Evans, Darrell	87D	398	$ .01	$ .05	Fernandez, Sid	86D	625	$ .05	$ .20
Evans, Darrell	88D	250	$ .01	$ .05	Fernandez, Sid	87D	323	$ .01	$ .15
Evans, Darrell	88DBB	35	$ .01	$ .05	Fernandez, Sid	88D	118	$ .01	$ .10
Evans, Darrell	89D	533	$ .01	$ .05	Fernandez, Sid	89D	471	$ .01	$ .10
Evans, Dwight	81D	458	$ .05	$ .30	Fernandez, Sid	90D	572	$ .01	$ .04
Evans, Dwight	82D	109	$ .02	$ .20	Fernandez, Sid	90DL	66	$ .01	$ .15
Evans, Dwight	82DK	7	$ .02	$ .15	Fernandez, Sid	91D	97	$ .01	$ .03
Evans, Dwight	83D	452	$ .03	$ .20	Fernandez, Tony	84DRR	32	$2.00	$7.50
Evans, Dwight	84D	395	$ .08	$ .25	Fernandez, Tony	85D	390	$ .10	$ .75
Evans, Dwight	85D	294	$ .03	$ .20	Fernandez, Tony	86D	119	$ .02	$ .30
Evans, Dwight	86D	249	$ .03	$ .25	Fernandez, Tony	87D	72	$ .05	$ .20
Evans, Dwight	87D	129	$ .01	$ .05	Fernandez, Tony	88D	319	$ .01	$ .15
Evans, Dwight	88D	216	$ .01	$ .15	Fernandez, Tony	88DBB	87	$ .01	$ .05
Evans, Dwight	88DBB	84	$ .01	$ .05	Fernandez, Tony	88DK	12	$ .01	$ .15
Evans, Dwight	88DK	16	$ .01	$ .15	Fernandez, Tony	89D	206	$ .01	$ .05
Evans, Dwight	89D	240	$ .01	$ .05	Fernandez, Tony	89DBB	48	$ .01	$ .05
Evans, Dwight	89DBB	121	$ .01	$ .05	Fernandez, Tony	90D	149	$ .01	$ .04
Evans, Dwight	90D	122	$ .01	$ .04	Fernandez, Tony	90DL	53	$ .01	$ .15
Evans, Dwight	90DL	235	$ .01	$ .15	Fernandez, Tony	91D	524	$ .01	$ .03
Evans, Dwight	91D	122	$ .01	$ .03	Fetters, Mike	90DRR	35	$ .01	$ .10
Fahey, Bill	81D	361	$ .01	$ .05	Fetters, Mike	91D	565	$ .01	$ .03
Fahey, Bill	83D	281	$ .01	$ .05	Fidrych, Mark	81D	8	$ .01	$ .05
Falcone, Pete	81D	395	$ .01	$ .05	Fielder, Cecil	86D	512	$1.00	$15.00
Falcone, Pete	82D	380	$ .01	$ .05	Fielder, Cecil	88D	565	$ .15	$ .75
Falcone, Pete	83D	182	$ .01	$ .05	Fielder, Cecil	89D	442	$ .10	$ .50
Falcone, Pete	84D	385	$ .03	$ .10	Fielder, Cecil	90DL	165	$ .01	$ .50
Fanning, Jim	82D	492	$ .01	$ .05	Fielder, Cecil	91D	451	$ .01	$ .15
Farmer, Ed	81D	40	$ .01	$ .05	Fielder, Cecil	91DBC	5	$ .01	$ .15
Farmer, Ed	82D	482	$ .01	$ .05	Fielder, Cecil	91DK	3	$ .01	$ .15
Farmer, Ed	83D	471	$ .01	$ .05	Fielder, Cecil	91DLP	18	$1.00	$5.00
Farmer, Howard	91D	734	$ .01	$ .10	Fielder, Cecil	91DMVP	397	$ .01	$ .15
Farr, Steve	85D	653	$ .01	$ .35	Fields, Bruce	87DRR	47	$ .01	$ .05
Farr, Steve	86D	588	$ .01	$ .06	Figueroa, Jesus	81D	556	$ .01	$ .05
Farr, Steve	87D	301	$ .01	$ .05	Filer, Tom	86D	439	$ .01	$ .06
Farr, Steve	88D	378	$ .01	$ .05	Filer, Tom	90D	687	$ .01	$ .04
Farr, Steve	89D	356	$ .01	$ .05	Filson, Pete	84D	194	$ .03	$ .10
Farr, Steve	89DBB	151	$ .01	$ .05	Filson, Pete	85D	607	$ .01	$ .08
Farr, Steve	90D	356	$ .01	$ .04	Filson, Pete	86D	436	$ .01	$ .06
Farr, Steve	91D	365	$ .01	$ .03	Fimple, Jack	84D	372	$ .03	$ .10
Farrell, John	88DBB	117	$ .01	$ .15	Fingers, Rollie	81D	2	$ .05	$ .30
Farrell, John	88DRR	42	$ .01	$ .20	Fingers, Rollie	82D	28	$ .05	$ .20
Farrell, John	89D	320	$ .01	$ .10	Fingers, Rollie	83D	78	$ .03	$ .20
Farrell, John	89DBB	285	$ .01	$ .10	Fingers, Rollie	83DK	2	$ .02	$ .15
Farrell, John	90D	233	$ .01	$ .05	Fingers, Rollie	84D#A	0	$1.00	$3.00
Farrell, John	90DL	22	$ .01	$ .15	Fingers, Rollie	85D	292	$ .03	$ .25
Farrell, John	91D	106	$ .01	$ .03	Fingers, Rollie	86D	229	$ .05	$ .20
Farris, Monty	91D	455	$ .01	$ .10	Finley, Chuck	87D	407	$ .01	$ .50
Felder, Mike	86D	634	$ .01	$ .05	Finley, Chuck	88D	530	$ .01	$ .10
Felder, Mike	87D	295	$ .01	$ .05	Finley, Chuck	89D	226	$ .01	$ .10
Felder, Mike	88D	397	$ .01	$ .05	Finley, Chuck	89DBB	333	$ .01	$ .05
Felder, Mike	90D	609	$ .01	$ .04	Finley, Chuck	90D	344	$ .01	$ .04
Felder, Mike	90DL	480	$ .01	$ .15	Finley, Chuck	90DL	162	$ .01	$ .15
Felder, Mike	91D	535	$ .01	$ .03	Finley, Chuck	91D	692	$ .01	$ .03
Felix, Junior	89DBB	199	$ .01	$ .40	Finley, Chuck	91DK	26	$ .01	$ .05
Felix, Junior	89DR	55	$ .01	$1.00	Finley, Chuck	91DLP	15	$1.00	$10.00
Felix, Junior	90D	70	$ .01	$ .20	Finley, Steve	89DR	47	$ .01	$ .25
Felix, Junior	90DL	422	$ .01	$ .75	Finley, Steve	90D	215	$ .01	$ .15
Felix, Junior	91D	323	$ .01	$ .03	Finley, Steve	90DL	329	$ .01	$ .25
Felton, Terry	83D	354	$ .01	$ .05	Finley, Steve	91D	355	$ .01	$ .03
Ferguson, Joe	81D	177	$ .01	$ .05	Fischlin, Mike	83D	489	$ .01	$ .05
Ferguson, Joe	83D	604	$ .01	$ .05	Fischlin, Mike	85D	495	$ .01	$ .08
Fermin, Felix	88D	144	$ .01	$ .05	Fishel, John	89D	443	$ .01	$ .10
Fermin, Felix	89D	565	$ .01	$ .05	Fisher, Brian	86D	492	$ .08	$ .25
Fermin, Felix	89DBB	229	$ .01	$ .05	Fisher, Brian	87D	340	$ .01	$ .05
Fermin, Felix	89DTR	33	$ .01	$ .05	Fisher, Brian	88D	415	$ .01	$ .05
Fermin, Felix	90D	191	$ .01	$ .04	Fisher, Brian	88DBB	101	$ .01	$ .05
Fermin, Felix	91D	537	$ .01	$ .03	Fisher, Brian	89D	126	$ .01	$ .05
Fernandez, Alex	91D	59	$ .01	$1.00	Fisk, Carlton	81D	335	$ .10	$ .75
Fernandez, Sid	84DRR	44	$1.50	$6.00	Fisk, Carlton	82D	495	$ .10	$ .75
Fernandez, Sid	85D	563	$ .15	$ .60	Fisk, Carlton	82DK	20	$ .03	$ .35

Player	Year	No.	VG	EX/MT
Fisk, Carlton	83D	104	$ .10	$ .60
Fisk, Carlton	84D	302	$ .10	$ 1.50
Fisk, Carlton	85D	208	$ .03	$ .50
Fisk, Carlton	86D	366	$ .03	$ .30
Fisk, Carlton	87D	247	$ .01	$ .15
Fisk, Carlton	88D	260	$ .01	$ .10
Fisk, Carlton	88DBB	67	$ .01	$ .10
Fisk, Carlton	89D	101	$ .01	$ .10
Fisk, Carlton	89DBB	11	$ .01	$ .10
Fisk, Carlton	89DK	7	$ .01	$ .10
Fisk, Carlton	90D	58	$ .01	$ .10
Fisk, Carlton	90DBC	19	$ .01	$ .10
Fisk, Carlton	90DL	10	$ .01	$ .35
Fisk, Carlton	90DL	174	$ .01	$ .25
Fisk, Carlton	91D	108	$ .01	$ .03
Fisk, Carlton	91DBC	6	$ .01	$ .03
Fisk, Carlton	91DLP	16	$1.00	$10.00
Fitzgerald, Mike	84D	482	$ .03	$ .10
Fitzgerald, Mike	85D	238	$ .01	$ .08
Fitzgerald, Mike	86D	97	$ .01	$ .06
Fitzgerald, Mike	87D	345	$ .01	$ .05
Fitzgerald, Mike	88D	159	$ .01	$ .05
Fitzgerald, Mike	89D	456	$ .01	$ .05
Fitzgerald, Mike	90D	392	$ .01	$ .04
Fitzgerald, Mike	91D	82	$ .01	$ .03
Flanagan, Mike	81D	234	$ .01	$ .05
Flanagan, Mike	82D	329	$ .01	$ .05
Flanagan, Mike	83D	105	$ .01	$ .05
Flanagan, Mike	84D	169	$ .03	$ .10
Flanagan, Mike	85D	88	$ .01	$ .08
Flanagan, Mike	86D	576	$ .01	$ .06
Flanagan, Mike	87D	459	$ .01	$ .05
Flanagan, Mike	88D	636	$ .01	$ .05
Flanagan, Mike	89D	324	$ .01	$ .05
Flanagan, Mike	89DBB	316	$ .01	$ .05
Flanagan, Mike	90D	324	$ .01	$ .04
Flannery, Tim	82D	61	$ .01	$ .05
Flannery, Tim	83D	472	$ .01	$ .05
Flannery, Tim	84D	202	$ .03	$ .10
Flannery, Tim	85D	551	$ .01	$ .08
Flannery, Tim	86D	383	$ .01	$ .06
Flannery, Tim	87D	287	$ .01	$ .05
Flannery, Tim	88D	328	$ .01	$ .05
Flannery, Tim	89D	364	$ .01	$ .05
Fletcher, Darrin	91DRR	47	$ .01	$ .15
Fletcher, Scott	82D	554	$ .01	$ .25
Fletcher, Scott	84D	452	$ .03	$ .10
Fletcher, Scott	85D	330	$ .01	$ .08
Fletcher, Scott	86D	282	$ .01	$ .06
Fletcher, Scott	87D	304	$ .01	$ .05
Fletcher, Scott	88D	180	$ .01	$ .05
Fletcher, Scott	88DBB	32	$ .01	$ .05
Fletcher, Scott	88DK	11	$ .01	$ .05
Fletcher, Scott	89D	142	$ .01	$ .05
Fletcher, Scott	89DBB	167	$ .01	$ .05
Fletcher, Scott	90D	455	$ .01	$ .04
Fletcher, Scott	90DL	141	$ .01	$ .15
Fletcher, Scott	91D	276	$ .01	$ .03
Flynn, Doug	81D	394	$ .01	$ .05
Flynn, Doug	82D	427	$ .01	$ .05
Flynn, Doug	83D	240	$ .01	$ .05
Flynn, Doug	84D	254	$ .03	$ .10
Flynn, Doug	85D	463	$ .01	$ .08
Foley, Marvis	81D	399	$ .01	$ .05
Foley, Marvis	83D	652	$ .01	$ .05
Foley, Marvis	85D	500	$ .01	$ .08
Foley, Tom	84D	81	$ .03	$ .10
Foley, Tom	85D	569	$ .01	$ .08
Foley, Tom	86D	549	$ .01	$ .06
Foley, Tom	87D	504	$ .01	$ .05

Player	Year	No.	VG	EX/MT
Foley, Tom	88D	303	$ .01	$ .05
Foley, Tom	89D	342	$ .01	$ .05
Foley, Tom	89DBB	314	$ .01	$ .05
Foley, Tom	90D	274	$ .01	$ .04
Foley, Tom	90DL	292	$ .01	$ .15
Foley, Tom	91D	180	$ .01	$ .03
Foli, Tim	81D	13	$ .01	$ .05
Foli, Tim	82D	376	$ .01	$ .05
Foli, Tim	83D	342	$ .01	$ .05
Foli, Tim	84D	474	$ .03	$ .10
Fontenot, Ray	84D	370	$ .03	$ .10
Fontenot, Ray	85D	248	$ .01	$ .08
Fontenot, Ray	86D	361	$ .01	$ .06
Foote, Barry	81D	558	$ .01	$ .05
Foote, Barry	82D	83	$ .01	$ .05
Ford, Curt	87D	454	$ .01	$ .05
Ford, Curt	88D	417	$ .01	$ .05
Ford, Curt	90D	694	$ .01	$ .04
Ford, Dan	81D	54	$ .01	$ .05
Ford, Dan	82D	468	$ .01	$ .05
Ford, Dan	83D	509	$ .01	$ .05
Ford, Dan	84D	367	$ .03	$ .10
Ford, Dan	85D	489	$ .01	$ .08
Ford, Dave	81D	552	$ .01	$ .05
Ford, Dave	82D	597	$ .01	$ .05
Forsch, Bob	81D	69	$ .01	$ .05
Forsch, Bob	82D	91	$ .01	$ .05
Forsch, Bob	83D	64	$ .01	$ .05
Forsch, Bob	84D	168	$ .03	$ .10
Forsch, Bob	86D	353	$ .01	$ .06
Forsch, Bob	87D	540	$ .01	$ .05
Forsch, Bob	88D	111	$ .01	$ .05
Forsch, Bob	89D	118	$ .01	$ .05
Forsch, Ken	81D	141	$ .01	$ .05
Forsch, Ken	82D	393	$ .01	$ .05
Forsch, Ken	83D	164	$ .01	$ .05
Forsch, Ken	84D	280	$ .03	$ .10

Player	Year	No.	VG	EX/MT
Forster, Terry	82D	362	$ .01	$ .05
Forster, Terry	83D	453	$ .01	$ .05
Forster, Terry	86D	432	$ .01	$ .06

Player	Year	No.	VG	EX/MT
Fossas, Tony	90D	457	$ .01	$ .04
Foster, George	81D	65	$ .05	$ .20
Foster, George	82D	274	$ .05	$ .20
Foster, George	83D	427	$ .03	$ .20
Foster, George	83DK	6	$ .05	$ .20
Foster, George	84D	312	$ .08	$ .25
Foster, George	85D	603	$ .03	$ .10
Foster, George	86D	116	$ .02	$ .15
Fowlkes, Alan	83D	46	$ .01	$ .05
Franco, John	85D	164	$ .25	$2.00
Franco, John	86D	487	$ .03	$ .30
Franco, John	87D	289	$ .01	$ .10
Franco, John	88D	123	$ .01	$ .05
Franco, John	88DBB	54	$ .01	$ .10
Franco, John	89D	233	$ .01	$ .10
Franco, John	89DBB	166	$ .01	$ .10
Franco, John	90D	124	$ .01	$ .10
Franco, John	90DK	14	$ .01	$ .10
Franco, John	90DL	356	$ .01	$ .15
Franco, John	91D	322	$ .01	$ .03
Franco, Julio	83D	525	$1.00	$5.50
Franco, Julio	84D	216	$ .08	$1.50
Franco, Julio	85D	94	$ .10	$ .50
Franco, Julio	86D	216	$ .05	$ .25
Franco, Julio	87D	131	$ .01	$ .15
Franco, Julio	88D	156	$ .01	$ .05
Franco, Julio	88DBB	168	$ .01	$ .05
Franco, Julio	88DK	10	$ .01	$ .05
Franco, Julio	89D	310	$ .01	$ .05
Franco, Julio	89DBB	32	$ .01	$ .10
Franco, Julio	89DTR	31	$ .01	$ .15
Franco, Julio	90D	142	$ .01	$ .10
Franco, Julio	90DAS	701	$ .01	$ .10
Franco, Julio	90DBC	14	$ .01	$ .10
Franco, Julio	90DL	205	$ .01	$ .15
Franco, Julio	91D	192	$ .01	$ .03
Francona, Terry	82D	627	$ .01	$ .05
Francona, Terry	83D	592	$ .01	$ .05
Francona, Terry	84D	463	$ .03	$ .10
Francona, Terry	85D	132	$ .01	$ .08
Francona, Terry	86D	401	$ .01	$ .06
Fraser, Will	87DR	9	$ .01	$ .07
Fraser, Will	87DRR	40	$ .01	$ .05
Fraser, Willie	88D	135	$ .01	$ .05
Fraser, Willie	89D	567	$ .01	$ .05
Fraser, Willie	90D	587	$ .01	$ .04
Fraser, Willie	91D	379	$ .01	$ .03
Frazier, George	81D	310	$ .01	$ .05
Frazier, George	82D	584	$ .01	$ .05
Frazier, George	83D	535	$ .01	$ .05
Frazier, George	84D	591	$ .03	$ .10
Frazier, George	85D	167	$ .01	$ .08
Frazier, George	86D	411	$ .01	$ .06
Frazier, George	87D	564	$ .01	$ .05
Frazier, George	88D	443	$ .01	$ .05
Freeman, Marvin	87D	576	$ .01	$ .15
Freeman, Marvin	89D	631	$ .01	$ .05
Freeman, Marvin	91D	619	$ .01	$ .03
Fregosi, Jim	81D	414	$ .01	$ .05
Frey, Jim	81D	464	$ .01	$ .05
Frey, Steve	91D	292	$ .01	$ .03
Frobel, Doug	84DRR	38	$ .03	$ .10
Frohwirth, Todd	88DR	3	$ .01	$ .05
Frohwirth, Todd	89D	587	$ .01	$ .05
Frohwirth, Todd	90D	631	$ .01	$ .04
Frost, Dave	81D	52	$ .01	$ .05
Frost, Dave	82D	290	$ .01	$ .05
Fryman, Travis	91D	768	$ .01	$ .50
Fryman, Woodie	81D	331	$ .01	$ .05
Fryman, Woodie	82D	68	$ .01	$ .05

Player	Year	No.	VG	EX/MT
Fryman, Woodie	83D	162	$ .01	$ .05
Fuentes, Mike	84DRR	40	$ .03	$ .10

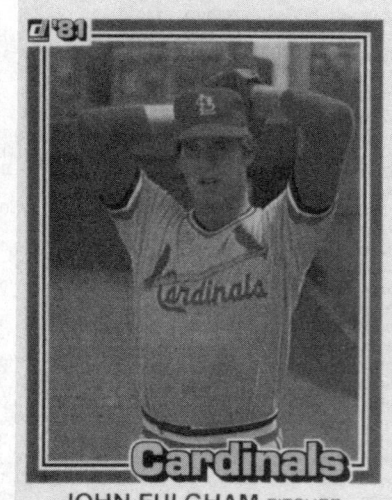

JOHN FULGHAM PITCHER

Player	Year	No.	VG	EX/MT
Fulgham, John	81D	70	$ .01	$ .05
Funderburk, Mark	86D	630	$ .01	$ .06
Gaetti, Gary	83D	53	$ .50	$2.25
Gaetti, Gary	84D	314	$ .15	$ .90
Gaetti, Gary	85D	242	$ .03	$ .35
Gaetti, Gary	86D	314	$ .03	$ .25
Gaetti, Gary	87D	122	$ .01	$ .05
Gaetti, Gary	88D	194	$ .01	$ .15
Gaetti, Gary	88DBB	46	$ .01	$ .05
Gaetti, Gary	88DK	19	$ .01	$ .05
Gaetti, Gary	89D	64	$ .01	$ .10
Gaetti, Gary	89DBB	102	$ .01	$ .05
Gaetti, Gary	90D	151	$ .01	$ .04
Gaetti, Gary	90DL	97	$ .01	$ .15
Gaetti, Gary	91D	547	$ .01	$ .03
Gaff, Brent	83D	553	$ .01	$ .05
Gagne, Greg	84DRR	39	$ .10	$ .50
Gagne, Greg	86D	558	$ .01	$ .10
Gagne, Greg	87D	395	$ .01	$ .05
Gagne, Greg	88D	441	$ .01	$ .05
Gagne, Greg	88DBB	74	$ .01	$ .05
Gagne, Greg	89D	318	$ .01	$ .05
Gagne, Greg	89DBB	158	$ .01	$ .05
Gagne, Greg	90D	237	$ .01	$ .04
Gagne, Greg	90DL	302	$ .01	$ .15
Gagne, Greg	91D	284	$ .01	$ .03
Gainey, Ty	86DRR	31	$ .01	$ .06
Gainey, Ty	87D	533	$ .01	$ .05
Gainey, Ty	88D	578	$ .01	$ .05
Galarraga, Andres	86DR	7	$ .15	$ .75
Galarraga, Andres	86DRR	33	$ .50	$2.50
Galarraga, Andres	87D	303	$ .01	$ .35
Galarraga, Andres	88D	282	$ .01	$ .15
Galarraga, Andres	88DBB	90	$ .01	$ .15
Galarraga, Andres	89D	130	$ .01	$ .10
Galarraga, Andres	89DBB	12	$ .01	$ .10
Galarraga, Andres	89DBC	16	$ .01	$ .10
Galarraga, Andres	89DK	14	$ .01	$ .05
Galarraga, Andres	90D	97	$ .01	$ .04

Player	Year	No.	VG	EX/MT	Player	Year	No.	VG	EX/MT
Galarraga, Andres	90D	97	$ .01	$ .04	Gardner, Billy	82D	591	$ .01	$ .05
Galarraga, Andres	90DL	450	$ .01	$ .15	Gardner, Mark	90DL	371	$ .01	$ .20
Galarraga, Andres	91D	68	$ .01	$ .03	Gardner, Mark	90DR	20	$ .01	$ .10
Gale, Rich	81D	462	$ .01	$ .05	Gardner, Mark	90DRR	40	$ .01	$ .10
Gale, Rich	82D	138	$ .01	$ .05	Gardner, Mark	91D	443	$ .01	$ .03
Gale, Rich	83D	172	$ .01	$ .05	Gardner, Wes	88D	634	$ .01	$ .15
Gale, Rich	84D	140	$ .03	$ .10	Gardner, Wes	89D	541	$ .01	$ .05
Gallagher, Dave	88DR	7	$ .01	$ .20	Gardner, Wes	90D	541	$ .01	$ .04
Gallagher, Dave	89D	384	$ .01	$ .10	Gardner, Wes	90DL	407	$ .01	$ .15
Gallagher, Dave	89DBB	67	$ .01	$ .05	Garland, Wayne	81D	440	$ .01	$ .05
Gallagher, Dave	90D	219	$ .01	$ .04	Garland, Wayne	82D	489	$ .01	$ .05
Gallego, Mike	86D	156	$ .01	$ .06	Garner, Phil	81D	372	$ .01	$ .05
Gallego, Mike	88D	379	$ .01	$ .05	Garner, Phil	82D	544	$ .01	$ .05
Gallego, Mike	89D	422	$ .01	$ .05	Garner, Phil	83D	270	$ .01	$ .05
Gallego, Mike	90D	361	$ .01	$ .04	Garner, Phil	84D	354	$ .03	$ .10
Gallego, Mike	90DL	121	$ .01	$ .15	Garner, Phil	85D	161	$ .01	$ .08
Gallego, Mike	91D	158	$ .01	$ .03	Garner, Phil	86D	527	$ .01	$ .06
Gamble, Oscar	81D	229	$ .01	$ .05	Garner, Phil	87D	358	$ .01	$ .05
Gamble, Oscar	82D	360	$ .01	$ .05	Garrelts, Scott	84D	646	$ .15	$ .75
Gamble, Oscar	83D	461	$ .01	$ .05	Garrelts, Scott	86D	309	$ .01	$ .06
Gant, Ron	88D	654	$ .25	$2.00	Garrelts, Scott	87D	116	$ .01	$ .05
Gant, Ron	88DBB	2	$ .01	$ .35	Garrelts, Scott	88D	80	$ .01	$ .05
Gant, Ron	88DR	47	$ .01	$ .75	Garrelts, Scott	88DBB	162	$ .01	$ .05
Gant, Ron	89D	50	$ .01	$ .25	Garrelts, Scott	89D	295	$ .01	$ .05
Gant, Ron	90D	475	$ .01	$ .15	Garrelts, Scott	89DBB	218	$ .01	$ .05
Gant, Ron	90DL	376	$ .01	$ .50	Garrelts, Scott	90D	217	$ .01	$ .04
Gant, Ron	91D	507	$ .01	$ .10	Garrelts, Scott	90DL	41	$ .01	$ .15
Gant, Ron	91DK	10	$ .01	$ .05	Garrelts, Scott	91D	311	$ .01	$ .03
Gantner, Jim	81D	204	$ .01	$ .05	Garvey, Steve	81D	56	$ .08	$ .75
Gantner, Jim	82D	406	$ .01	$ .05	Garvey, Steve	81D	176	$ .12	$1.00
Gantner, Jim	83D	232	$ .01	$ .05	Garvey, Steve	82D	84	$ .10	$ .75
Gantner, Jim	84D	115	$ .03	$ .10	Garvey, Steve	82DK	3	$ .06	$ .50
Gantner, Jim	85D	229	$ .01	$ .08	Garvey, Steve	83D	488	$ .08	$ .40
Gantner, Jim	86D	115	$ .01	$ .06	Garvey, Steve	84D	63	$ .20	$ .60
Gantner, Jim	87D	172	$ .01	$ .05	Garvey, Steve	85D	307	$ .15	$ .40
Gantner, Jim	88D	214	$ .01	$ .05	Garvey, Steve	86D	63	$ .15	$ .50
Gantner, Jim	88DBB	53	$ .01	$ .05	Garvey, Steve	87D	81	$ .08	$ .25
Gantner, Jim	89D	264	$ .01	$ .05	Garvin, Jerry	81D	150	$ .01	$ .05
Gantner, Jim	89DBB	295	$ .01	$ .05	Garvin, Jerry	82D	430	$ .01	$ .05
Gantner, Jim	90D	291	$ .01	$ .04	Garvin, Jerry	83D	227	$ .01	$ .05
Gantner, Jim	91D	703	$ .01	$ .03	Gates, Mike	83D	114	$ .01	$ .05
Garber, Gene	81D	77	$ .01	$ .05	Gedman, Rich	82D	512	$ .05	$ .25
Garber, Gene	82D	123	$ .01	$ .05	Gedman, Rich	83D	156	$ .01	$ .05
Garber, Gene	83D	223	$ .01	$ .05	Gedman, Rich	84D	579	$ .03	$ .10
Garber, Gene	84D	287	$ .03	$ .10	Gedman, Rich	85D	457	$ .01	$ .08
Garber, Gene	87D	414	$ .01	$ .05	Gedman, Rich	86D	273	$ .01	$ .06
Garber, Gene	88D	618	$ .01	$ .15	Gedman, Rich	87D	153	$ .01	$ .05
Garber, Gene	88DBB	63	$ .01	$ .05	Gedman, Rich	88D	129	$ .01	$ .05
Garbey, Barbaro	85D	456	$ .01	$ .08	Gedman, Rich	88DBB	140	$ .01	$ .05
Garbey, Barbaro	86D	349	$ .01	$ .06	Gedman, Rich	89D	162	$ .01	$ .05
Garces, Rich	91DRR	420	$ .01	$ .15	Gedman, Rich	90D	346	$ .01	$ .04
Garcia, Damaso	81D	269	$ .01	$ .10	Gedman, Rich	90DL	478	$ .01	$ .15
Garcia, Damaso	82D	479	$ .01	$ .05	Gehrig, Lou	85D	635	$ .03	$ .25
Garcia, Damaso	83D	54	$ .01	$ .05	Geisel, Dave	82D	633	$ .01	$ .05
Garcia, Damaso	84D	241	$ .03	$ .10	Geisel, Dave	84D	645	$ .03	$ .10
Garcia, Damaso	85D	315	$ .01	$ .08	Gerber, Craig	86D	545	$ .01	$ .06
Garcia, Damaso	86D	241	$ .01	$ .06	Geren, Bob	89DR	11	$ .01	$ .15
Garcia, Damaso	87D	614	$ .01	$ .05	Geren, Bob	90D	395	$ .01	$ .05
Garcia, Damaso	88D	414	$ .01	$ .05	Geren, Bob	90DL	182	$ .01	$ .20
Garcia, Dave	81D	442	$ .01	$ .05	Geren, Bob	91D	114	$ .01	$ .03
Garcia, Dave	82D	337	$ .01	$ .05	Gerhart, Ken	87DR	24	$ .01	$ .07
Garcia, Kiko	81D	514	$ .01	$ .05	Gerhart, Ken	87DRR	30	$ .01	$ .05
Garcia, Kiko	82D	470	$ .01	$ .05	Gerhart, Ken	88D	213	$ .01	$ .05
Garcia, Kiko	83D	569	$ .01	$ .05	Geronimo, Cesar	81D	305	$ .01	$ .05
Garcia, Kiko	84D	545	$ .03	$ .10	Geronimo, Cesar	82D	322	$ .01	$ .05
Garcia, Miguel	89D	622	$ .01	$ .05	Geronimo, Cesar	83D	448	$ .01	$ .05
Gardenhire, Ron	82D	649	$ .01	$ .05	Geronimo, Cesar	84D	252	$ .03	$ .10
Gardenhire, Ron	83D	175	$ .01	$ .05	Giamatti, Bart	90D	716	$ .01	$ .75
Gardenhire, Ron	85D	360	$ .01	$ .08	Gibbons, John	85D	116	$ .01	$ .08
Gardiner, Mike	91DRR	417	$ .01	$ .10	Gibbons, John	87D	626	$ .01	$ .05

Player	Year	No.	VG	EX/MT	Player	Year	No.	VG	EX/MT
Gibson, Bob	84D	246	$ .03	$ .10	Gonzalez, Juan	90DRR	33	$ .01	$2.00
Gibson, Bob	85D	393	$ .01	$ .08	Gonzalez, Juan	91D	371	$ .01	$ .25
Gibson, Bob	86D	271	$ .01	$ .06	Gonzalez, Luis	91D	690	$ .01	$ .25
Gibson, Kirk	82D	407	$ .50	$1.50	Gooden, Dwight	85D	190	$3.50	$14.00
Gibson, Kirk	83D	459	$ .05	$ .30	Gooden, Dwight	86D	75	$ .80	$3.00
Gibson, Kirk	84D	593	$ .15	$ .75	Gooden, Dwight	86DK	26	$ .25	$ .75
Gibson, Kirk	85D	471	$ .08	$ .25	Gooden, Dwight	87D	199	$ .15	$1.00
Gibson, Kirk	86D	125	$ .08	$ .25	Gooden, Dwight	88D	69	$ .10	$ .35
Gibson, Kirk	86DK	1	$ .03	$ .25	Gooden, Dwight	88DBB	96	$ .05	$ .25
Gibson, Kirk	87D	50	$ .05	$ .20	Gooden, Dwight	89D	270	$ .01	$ .25
Gibson, Kirk	88D	275	$ .05	$ .20	Gooden, Dwight	89DBB	14	$ .01	$ .25
Gibson, Kirk	88DBB	66	$ .05	$ .20	Gooden, Dwight	90D	171	$ .01	$ .15
Gibson, Kirk	89D	132	$ .01	$ .10	Gooden, Dwight	90DL	139	$ .01	$ .50
Gibson, Kirk	89DBB	10	$ .01	$ .10	Gooden, Dwight	91D	266	$ .01	$ .10
Gibson, Kirk	89DK	15	$ .01	$ .15	Gooden, Dwight	91DLP	7	$1.00	$15.00
Gibson, Kirk	90D	368	$ .01	$ .04	Goodwin, Danny	81D	494	$ .01	$ .05
Gibson, Kirk	90DL	173	$ .01	$ .20	Goodwin, Danny	82D	305	$ .01	$ .05
Gibson, Kirk	91D	445	$ .01	$ .03	Gordon, Tom	89DBB	287	$ .01	$ .35
Gibson, Paul	88DR	19	$ .01	$ .05	Gordon, Tom	89DR	4	$ .01	$ .50
Gibson, Paul	89D	445	$ .01	$ .05	Gordon, Tom	89DRR	45	$ .01	$ .35
Gibson, Paul	90D	657	$ .01	$ .04	Gordon, Tom	90D	297	$ .01	$ .25
Gibson, Paul	90DL	298	$ .01	$ .15	Gordon, Tom	90DL	14	$ .01	$ .35
Gibson, Paul	91D	353	$ .01	$ .03	Gordon, Tom	91D	242	$ .01	$ .03
Giles, Brian	84D	563	$ .03	$ .10	Goryl, John	81D	527	$ .01	$ .05
Gilkey, Bernard	90DL	353	$ .01	$2.00	Gossage, Rich	81D	347	$ .05	$ .20
Gilkey, Bernard	91DRR	30	$ .01	$ .35	Gossage, Rich	82D	283	$ .03	$ .20
Girardi, Joe	89DR	23	$ .01	$ .25	Gossage, Rich	83D	157	$ .03	$ .20
Girardi, Joe	90D	404	$ .01	$ .05	Gossage, Goose	84D	396	$ .08	$ .25
Girardi, Joe	90DL	289	$ .01	$ .15	Gossage, Goose	85D	185	$ .08	$ .25
Girardi, Joe	91D	184	$ .01	$ .03	Gossage, Goose	86D	185	$ .03	$ .25
Gladden, Dan	85D	567	$ .10	$ .45	Gossage, Goose	86DK	2	$ .05	$ .20
Gladden, Dan	86D	187	$ .01	$ .06	Gossage, Goose "Rich"	87D	483	$ .01	$ .05
Gladden, Dan	87D	189	$ .01	$ .05	Gossage, Rich	88D	434	$ .01	$ .15
Gladden, Dan	88D	491	$ .01	$ .05	Gossage, Goose "Rich"	88DBB	26	$ .01	$ .05
Gladden, Dan	88DBB	130	$ .01	$ .05	Gossage, Rich	89D	158	$ .01	$ .05
Gladden, Dan	89D	391	$ .01	$ .05	Gossage, Goose	90D	678	$ .01	$ .04
Gladden, Dan	89DBB	298	$ .01	$ .05	Gott, Jim	83D	353	$ .01	$ .25
Gladden, Dan	90D	182	$ .01	$ .04	Gott, Jim	84D	268	$ .03	$ .10
Gladden, Dan	90DK	22	$ .01	$ .10	Gott, Jim	85D	632	$ .01	$ .08
Gladden, Dan	90DL	254	$ .01	$ .15	Gott, Jim	86D	358	$ .01	$ .06
Gladden, Dan	91D	228	$ .01	$ .03	Gott, Jim	88D	606	$ .01	$ .15
Glavine, Tom	88D	644	$ .05	$ .35	Gott, Jim	88DBB	213	$ .01	$ .05
Glavine, Tom	89D	381	$ .01	$ .10	Gott, Jim	89D	362	$ .01	$ .05
Glavine, Tom	89DBB	2	$ .01	$ .05	Gott, Jim	90D	605	$ .01	$ .04
Glavine, Tom	90D	145	$ .01	$ .04	Gott, Jim	91D	601	$ .01	$ .03
Glavine, Tom	90DL	13	$ .01	$ .15	Gozzo, Mauro	90D	655	$ .01	$ .10
Glavine, Tom	91D	132	$ .01	$ .03	Grace, Mark	88DBB	4	$ .15	$1.50
Gleaton, Jerry	88D	547	$ .01	$ .05	Grace, Mark	88DR	1	$ .25	$4.00
Gleaton, Jerry Don	89D	444	$ .01	$ .05	Grace, Mark	88DRR	40	$1.00	$3.00
Gleaton, Jerry Don	91D	661	$ .01	$ .03	Grace, Mark	89D	255	$ .25	$ .75
Glynn, Ed	83D	537	$ .01	$ .05	Grace, Mark	89DK	17	$ .15	$ .35
Goff, Jerry	90DL	476	$ .01	$ .20	Grace, Mark	90D	577	$ .01	$ .25
Goff, Jerry	91D	499	$ .01	$ .03	Grace, Mark	90DL	137	$ .01	$ .50
Goltz, Dave	82D	604	$ .01	$ .05	Grace, Mark	91D	199	$ .01	$ .10
Gomez, Leo	91DLP	13	$1.00	$10.00	Graham, Dan	82D	455	$ .01	$ .05
Gomez, Leo	91DRR	35	$ .01	$ .50	Grahe, Joe	91D	737	$ .01	$ .10
Gomez, Luis	81D	88	$ .01	$ .05	Grant, Mark	85D	601	$ .01	$ .08
Gonzales, Julio	82D	645	$ .01	$ .05	Grant, Mark	87D	644	$ .01	$ .05
Gonzales, Rene	88D	582	$ .01	$ .05	Grant, Mark	88D	511	$ .01	$ .05
Gonzales, Rene	89D	377	$ .01	$ .05	Grant, Mark	88DBB	133	$ .01	$ .05
Gonzales, Rene	90D	401	$ .01	$ .04	Grant, Mark	90D	441	$ .01	$ .04
Gonzalez, Denny	85D	600	$ .01	$ .08	Grant, Mark	91D	361	$ .01	$ .03
Gonzalez, Denny	86D	410	$ .02	$ .04	Gray, Gary	83D	637	$ .01	$ .05
Gonzalez, German	89D	590	$ .01	$ .05	Gray, Jeff	91D	721	$ .01	$ .10
Gonzalez, German	89DR	24	$ .01	$ .10	Grebeck, Craig	90DR	9	$ .01	$ .10
Gonzalez, Jose	87D	525	$ .01	$ .25	Grebeck, Craig	91D	378	$ .01	$ .03
Gonzalez, Jose	88D	341	$ .01	$ .05	Green, Dallas	81D	415	$ .01	$ .05
Gonzalez, Jose	89DBB	260	$ .01	$ .05	Green, David	83D	166	$ .01	$ .05
Gonzalez, Jose	90D	314	$ .01	$ .04	Green, David	84D	425	$ .03	$ .10
Gonzalez, Jose	91D	543	$ .01	$ .03	Green, David	84D	625	$ .01	$ .25

Player	Year	No.	VG	EX/MT
Green, David	85D	303	$ .01	$ .08
Green, David	86D	114	$ .01	$ .06
Greene, Tommy	90D	576	$ .01	$ .30
Greene, Tommy	91D	635	$ .01	$ .10
Greenwell, Mike	87D	585	$2.50	$6.50
Greenwell, Mike	87DR	4	$ .80	$2.50
Greenwell, Mike	88D	339	$ .01	$ .60
Greenwell, Mike	88DBB	177	$ .01	$ .50
Greenwell, Mike	89D	186	$ .10	$ .25
Greenwell, Mike	89DBB	28	$ .01	$ .15
Greenwell, Mike	89DBC	13	$ .01	$ .15
Greenwell, Mike	89DK	1	$ .10	$ .20
Greenwell, Mike	90D	66	$ .01	$ .10
Greenwell, Mike	90DBC	17	$ .01	$ .10
Greenwell, Mike	90DL	143	$ .01	$ .25
Greenwell, Mike	91D	553	$ .01	$ .10
Gregg, Tommy	88D	203	$ .01	$ .10
Gregg, Tommy	89D	121	$ .01	$ .05
Gregg, Tommy	89DBB	170	$ .01	$ .05
Gregg, Tommy	90D	239	$ .01	$ .04

TOMMY GREGG OF

Player	Year	No.	VG	EX/MT
Gregg, Tommy	90DL	86	$ .01	$ .15
Gregg, Tommy	91D	244	$ .01	$ .03
Grich, Bobby	81D	289	$ .01	$ .05
Grich, Bobby	82D	90	$ .01	$ .05
Grich, Bobby	83D	468	$ .01	$ .05
Grich, Bobby	84D	179	$ .03	$ .10
Grich, Bobby	85D	280	$ .01	$ .08
Grich, Bobby	86D	207	$ .01	$ .06
Grich, Bobby	87D	456	$ .01	$ .05
Griffey, Jr., Ken	89DBB	192	$ .01	$3.00
Griffey, Jr., Ken	89DR	3	$ .01	$7.00
Griffey, Jr., Ken	89DRR	33	$1.50	$6.50
Griffey, Jr., Ken	90D	365	$ .01	$2.25
Griffey, Jr., Ken	90DK	4	$ .01	$ .75
Griffey, Jr., Ken	90DL	245	$ .01	$20.00
Griffey, Jr., Ken	91D	77	$ .01	$ .75
Griffey, Jr., Ken	91DAS	49	$ .01	$ .35
Griffey, Jr., Ken	91DMVP	392	$ .01	$ .40
Griffey, Ken	81D	184	$ .03	$ .25
Griffey, Ken	82D	634	$ .03	$ .20

Player	Year	No.	VG	EX/MT
Griffey, Ken	83D	486	$ .01	$ .05
Griffey, Ken	84D	613	$ .04	$ .25
Griffey, Ken	85D	347	$ .03	$ .20
Griffey, Ken	86D	126	$ .01	$ .06
Griffey, Ken	87D	513	$ .01	$ .05
Griffey, Ken	88D	202	$ .01	$ .15
Griffey, Ken	88DBB	141	$ .01	$ .10
Griffey, Ken	90D	469	$ .01	$ .04
Griffey, Sr., Ken	91D	452	$ .01	$ .03
Griffin, Alfredo	81D	149	$ .01	$ .05
Griffin, Alfredo	82D	101	$ .01	$ .05
Griffin, Alfredo	83D	180	$ .01	$ .05
Griffin, Alfredo	84D	605	$ .03	$ .10
Griffin, Alfredo	85D	73	$ .01	$ .08
Griffin, Alfredo	86D	101	$ .01	$ .06
Griffin, Alfredo	87D	256	$ .01	$ .05
Griffin, Alfredo	88D	226	$ .01	$ .05
Griffin, Alfredo	88DBB	92	$ .01	$ .05
Griffin, Alfredo	89D	79	$ .01	$ .05
Griffin, Alfredo	89DBB	178	$ .01	$ .05
Griffin, Alfredo	90D	195	$ .01	$ .04
Griffin, Alfredo	90DL	95	$ .01	$ .15
Griffin, Alfredo	91D	488	$ .01	$ .03
Griffin, Mike	82D	533	$ .01	$ .05
Griffin, Mike	88D	494	$ .01	$ .05
Griffin, Tom	81D	75	$ .01	$ .05
Griffin, Tom	82D	474	$ .01	$ .05
Grimsley, Jason	91D	653	$ .01	$ .10
Grissom, Marquis	90DL	107	$ .01	$ .50
Grissom, Marquis	90DR	45	$ .01	$ .20
Grissom, Marquis	90DRR	36	$ .01	$ .35
Grissom, Marquis	91D	307	$ .01	$ .03
Gross, Greg	81D	598	$ .01	$ .05
Gross, Greg	82D	371	$ .01	$ .05
Gross, Greg	83D	441	$ .01	$ .05
Gross, Greg	84D	285	$ .03	$ .10
Gross, Greg	85D	407	$ .01	$ .08
Gross, Greg	86D	163	$ .01	$ .06
Gross, Greg	87D	385	$ .01	$ .05
Gross, Greg	88D	412	$ .01	$ .05
Gross, Kevin	84D	381	$ .04	$ .30
Gross, Kevin	85D	477	$ .01	$ .08
Gross, Kevin	86D	529	$ .01	$ .06
Gross, Kevin	87D	236	$ .01	$ .05
Gross, Kevin	88D	113	$ .01	$ .05
Gross, Kevin	88DBB	103	$ .01	$ .05
Gross, Kevin	89D	194	$ .01	$ .05
Gross, Kevin	89DBB	202	$ .01	$ .05
Gross, Kevin	89DBC	12	$ .01	$ .10
Gross, Kevin	89DTR	3	$ .01	$ .05
Gross, Kevin	90D	248	$ .01	$ .04
Gross, Kevin	90DL	61	$ .01	$ .15
Gross, Kevin	91D	569	$ .01	$ .03
Gross, Wayne	81D	237	$ .01	$ .05
Gross, Wayne	82D	139	$ .01	$ .05
Gross, Wayne	83D	591	$ .01	$ .05
Gross, Wayne	84D	375	$ .03	$ .10
Gross, Wayne	85D	228	$ .01	$ .08
Gross, Wayne	86D	535	$ .01	$ .06
Grubb, John	81D	148	$ .01	$ .05
Grubb, John	82D	467	$ .01	$ .05
Grubb, John	83D	341	$ .01	$ .05
Grubb, John	84D	90	$ .03	$ .10
Grubb, John	85D	578	$ .01	$ .08
Grubb, John	86D	615	$ .01	$ .06
Grubb, John	87D	476	$ .01	$ .05
Gruber, Kelly	86DR	16	$ .25	$3.00
Gruber, Kelly	87D	444	$ .15	$2.00
Gruber, Kelly	88D	244	$ .01	$ .25
Gruber, Kelly	88DBB	255	$ .01	$ .15

Player	Year	No.	VG	EX/MT	Player	Year	No.	VG	EX/MT
Gruber, Kelly	89D	113	$ .01	$ .25	Guerrero, Pedro	91DK	25	$ .01	$ .05
Gruber, Kelly	89DBB	31	$ .01	$ .15	Guetterman, Lee	87D	322	$ .01	$ .15
Gruber, Kelly	90D	113	$ .01	$ .15	Guetterman, Lee	88D	270	$ .01	$ .05
Gruber, Kelly	90DK	12	$ .01	$ .10	Guetterman, Lee	89DBB	108	$ .01	$ .05
Gruber, Kelly	90DL	106	$ .01	$ .25	Guetterman, Lee	90D	127	$ .01	$ .04
Gruber, Kelly	91D	149	$ .01	$ .03	Guetterman, Lee	90DL	333	$ .01	$ .15
Guante, Cecilio	84D	78	$ .03	$ .10	Guetterman, Lee	91D	124	$ .01	$ .03
Guante, Cecilio	85D	357	$ .01	$ .08	Guidry, Ron	81D	227	$ .05	$ .20
Guante, Cecilio	86D	142	$ .01	$ .06	Guidry, Ron	82D	548	$ .03	$ .20
Guante, Cecilio	87D	238	$ .01	$ .05	Guidry, Ron	82D	558	$ .03	$ .20
Guante, Cecilio	89D	260	$ .01	$ .05	Guidry, Ron	83D	31	$ .03	$ .20
Guante, Cecilio	90D	403	$ .01	$ .04	Guidry, Ron	83DK	17	$ .05	$ .20
Guante, Cecilio	90DL	365	$ .01	$ .15	Guidry, Ron	84D	173	$ .04	$ .25
Guante, Matt	83D	423	$ .01	$ .05	Guidry, Ron	85D	214	$ .03	$ .20
Gubicza, Mark	85D	344	$ .25	$2.00	Guidry, Ron	86D	103	$ .03	$ .25
Gubicza, Mark	86D	583	$ .01	$ .15	Guidry, Ron	87D	93	$ .05	$ .20
Gubicza, Mark	87D	466	$ .01	$ .05	Guidry, Ron	88D	175	$ .01	$ .15
Gubicza, Mark	88D	54	$ .01	$ .05	Guillen, Ozzie	86D	208	$ .15	$ .75
Gubicza, Mark	88DBB	95	$ .01	$ .05	Guillen, Ozzie	87D	87	$ .01	$ .05
Gubicza, Mark	89D	179	$ .01	$ .05	Guillen, Ozzie	88D	137	$ .01	$ .05
Gubicza, Mark	89DBB	119	$ .01	$ .05	Guillen, Ozzie	88DBB	81	$ .01	$ .05
Gubicza, Mark	90D	204	$ .01	$ .04	Guillen, Ozzie	89D	176	$ .01	$ .05
Gubicza, Mark	90DL	145	$ .01	$ .15	Guillen, Ozzie	89DBB	137	$ .01	$ .05
Gubicza, Mark	91D	145	$ .01	$ .03	Guillen, Ozzie	89DBC	23	$ .01	$ .10
Guerrero, Pedro	82D	136	$ .10	$ .55	Guillen, Ozzie	90D	135	$ .01	$ .04
Guerrero, Pedro	83D	110	$ .05	$ .30	Guillen, Ozzie	90DK	15	$ .01	$ .10
Guerrero, Pedro	84D	174	$ .15	$ .50	Guillen, Ozzie	90DL	128	$ .01	$ .15
Guerrero, Pedro	84DK	24	$ .08	$ .25	Guillen, Ozzie	91D	577	$ .01	$ .03
Guerrero, Pedro	85D	174	$ .08	$ .25	Gulden, Brad	85D	365	$ .01	$ .08
Guerrero, Pedro	86D	174	$ .08	$ .25	Gullickson, Bill	81D	91	$ .05	$ .30
Guerrero, Pedro	87D	53	$ .03	$ .25	Gullickson, Bill	82D	162	$ .01	$ .05
Guerrero, Pedro	88D	278	$ .01	$ .05	Gullickson, Bill	83D	288	$ .01	$ .05
Guerrero, Pedro	88DBB	122	$ .01	$ .10	Gullickson, Bill	84D	401	$ .03	$ .10
Guerrero, Pedro	88DBC	16	$ .05	$ .25	Gullickson, Bill	85D	97	$ .01	$ .08
Guerrero, Pedro	89DBB	75	$ .01	$ .10	Gullickson, Bill	86D	331	$ .01	$ .06
Guerrero, Pedro	90D	63	$ .01	$ .04	Gullickson, Bill	87D	369	$ .01	$ .05
Guerrero, Pedro	90DAS	674	$ .01	$ .04	Gullickson, Bill	88D	586	$ .01	$ .05
					Gulliver, Glenn	83D	131	$ .01	$ .05
					Gunderson, Eric	91DRR	416	$ .01	$ .15
					Gura, Larry	81D	461	$ .01	$ .05
					Gura, Larry	82D	338	$ .01	$ .05
					Gura, Larry	83D	160	$ .01	$ .05
					Gura, Larry	84D	100	$ .03	$ .10
					Gura, Larry	85D	217	$ .01	$ .08
					Guthrie, Mark	90D	622	$ .01	$ .10
					Guthrie, Mark	91D	64	$ .01	$ .03
					Gutierrez, Jackie	85D	335	$ .01	$ .08
					Gutierrez, Jackie	86D	335	$ .01	$ .06
					Gutierrez, Jackie	87D	601	$ .01	$ .05
					Guzman, Jose	86DR	24	$ .02	$ .09
					Guzman, Jose	86DRR	30	$ .01	$ .25
					Guzman, Jose	87D	101	$ .01	$ .05
					Guzman, Jose	88D	136	$ .01	$ .05
					Guzman, Jose	88DBB	88	$ .01	$ .05
					Guzman, Jose	89D	284	$ .01	$ .05
					Gwosdz, Doug	84D	383	$ .03	$ .10
					Gwynn, Chris	90DL	411	$ .01	$ .15
					Gwynn, Chris	91D	598	$ .01	$ .03
					Gwynn, Tony	83D	598	$2.50	$15.00
					Gwynn, Tony	84D	324	$ .80	$7.00
					Gwynn, Tony	85D	63	$ .25	$2.00
					Gwynn, Tony	85DK	25	$ .15	$ .50
					Gwynn, Tony	86D	112	$ .15	$1.00
					Gwynn, Tony	87D	64	$ .15	$ .50
					Gwynn, Tony	88D	164	$ .10	$ .35
					Gwynn, Tony	88DBB	154	$ .05	$ .25
					Gwynn, Tony	88DBC	6	$ .15	$ .50
					Gwynn, Tony	89D	128	$ .01	$ .20
Guerrero, Pedro	90DBC	6	$ .01	$ .04	Gwynn, Tony	89DBB	42	$ .01	$ .15
Guerrero, Pedro	90DL	44	$ .01	$ .25	Gwynn, Tony	89DBC	20	$ .01	$ .20
Guerrero, Pedro	91D	558	$ .01	$ .03					

Player	Year	No.	VG	EX/MT	Player	Year	No.	VG	EX/MT
Gwynn, Tony	89DK	6	$ .05	$ .35	Hargrove, Mike	83D	450	$ .01	$ .05
Gwynn, Tony	90D	86	$ .01	$ .20	Hargrove, Mike	84D	495	$ .03	$ .10
Gwynn, Tony	90DAS	705	$ .01	$ .10	Hargrove, Mike	85D	398	$ .01	$ .08
Gwynn, Tony	90DBC	4	$ .01	$ .10	Hargrove, Mike	86D	590	$ .01	$ .06
Gwynn, Tony	90DL	154	$ .01	$ .20	Harkey, Mike	89DRR	43	$ .05	$ .30
Gwynn, Tony	91D	243	$ .01	$ .03	Harkey, Mike	90D	522	$ .01	$ .04
Gwynn, Tony	91DLP	11	$1.00	$15.00	Harkey, Mike	90DL	309	$ .01	$ .25
Haas, Moose	81D	85	$ .01	$ .05	Harkey, Mike	90DR	22	$ .01	$ .15
Haas, Moose	82D	206	$ .01	$ .05	Harkey, Mike	91D	447	$ .01	$ .03
Haas, Moose	83D	204	$ .01	$ .05	Harnisch, Pete	89DRR	44	$ .01	$ .10
Haas, Moose	84D	368	$ .03	$ .10	Harnisch, Pete	90D	596	$ .01	$ .04
Haas, Moose	85D	473	$ .01	$ .08	Harnisch, Pete	90DL	39	$ .01	$ .25
Haas, Moose	86D	237	$ .01	$ .06	Harnisch, Pete	91D	181	$ .01	$ .03
Haas, Moose	87D	528	$ .01	$ .05	Harper, Brian	84D	142	$ .05	$ .35
Habyan, John	86DRR	45	$ .05	$ .15	Harper, Brian	85D	566	$ .01	$ .08
Habyan, John	87D	494	$ .01	$ .05	Harper, Brian	86D	547	$ .01	$ .06
Habyan, John	88D	354	$ .01	$ .05	Harper, Brian	89D	641	$ .01	$ .05
Haddix, Harvey	82D	651	$ .01	$ .05	Harper, Brian	90D	355	$ .01	$ .04
Hairston, Jerry	83D	616	$ .01	$ .05	Harper, Brian	90DL	479	$ .01	$ .15
Hairston, Jerry	84D	86	$ .03	$ .10	Harper, Brian	91D	582	$ .01	$ .03
Hairston, Jerry	85D	135	$ .01	$ .08	Harper, Brian	91DK	22	$ .01	$ .05
Hairston, Jerry	86D	424	$ .01	$ .06	Harper, Brian	91DMVP	398	$ .01	$ .03
Hairston, Jerry	87D	285	$ .01	$ .05	Harper, Terry	83D	607	$ .01	$ .05
Hairston, Jerry	88D	285	$ .01	$ .05	Harper, Terry	86D	627	$ .01	$ .06
Hale, Chip	90D	690	$ .01	$ .10	Harrah, Toby	81D	318	$ .01	$ .05
Halicki, Ed	81D	53	$ .01	$ .05	Harrah, Toby	82D	72	$ .01	$ .05
Hall, Albert	88D	290	$ .01	$ .05	Harrah, Toby	83D	337	$ .01	$ .05
Hall, Albert	88DBB	253	$ .01	$ .05	Harrah, Toby	83DK	13	$ .01	$ .05
Hall, Drew	87D	594	$ .01	$ .05	Harrah, Toby	84D	251	$ .03	$ .10
Hall, Drew	89D	522	$ .01	$ .05	Harrah, Toby	86D	159	$ .01	$ .06
Hall, Drew	90DL	423	$ .01	$ .15	Harrah, Toby	87D	408	$ .01	$ .05
Hall, Mel	83D	126	$ .05	$ .60	Harris, Gene	89DBB	325	$ .01	$ .05
Hall, Mel	84D	411	$ .03	$ .10	Harris, Gene	90D	247	$ .01	$ .04
Hall, Mel	85D	338	$ .01	$ .08	Harris, Gene	90DL	378	$ .01	$ .15
Hall, Mel	86D	276	$ .01	$ .06	Harris, Gene	91D	651	$ .01	$ .03
Hall, Mel	87D	473	$ .01	$ .05	Harris, Greg	83D	295	$ .01	$ .05
Hall, Mel	88D	342	$ .01	$ .05	Harris, Greg	86D	465	$ .01	$ .06
Hall, Mel	88DBB	173	$ .01	$ .05	Harris, Greg	87D	382	$ .01	$ .05
Hall, Mel	89D	73	$ .01	$ .05	Harris, Greg	88D	427	$ .01	$ .05
Hall, Mel	89DTR	36	$ .01	$ .05	Harris, Greg	89D	548	$ .01	$ .05
Hall, Mel	90D	598	$ .01	$ .04	Harris, Greg	89DR	46	$ .01	$ .10
Hall, Mel	90DL	227	$ .01	$ .15	Harris, Greg	89DRR	34	$ .01	$ .05
Hall, Mel	91D	442	$ .01	$ .03	Harris, Greg	90D	65	$ .01	$ .04
Hamilton, Darryl	91D	517	$ .01	$ .03	Harris, Greg	90D	582	$ .01	$ .04
Hamilton, Jeff	87D	464	$ .08	$ .25	Harris, Greg	90DL	452	$ .01	$ .15
Hamilton, Jeff	88D	525	$ .01	$ .05	Harris, Greg	90DL	499	$ .01	$ .15
Hamilton, Jeff	89D	550	$ .01	$ .05	Harris, Greg	91D	131	$ .01	$ .03
Hamilton, Jeff	89DBB	290	$ .01	$ .05	Harris, Greg	91D	306	$ .01	$ .03
Hamilton, Jeff	90D	321	$ .01	$ .04	Harris, John	82D	444	$ .01	$ .05
Hamilton, Jeff	90DL	306	$ .01	$ .15	Harris, Lenny	90D	434	$ .01	$ .04
Hammaker, Atlee	83D	298	$ .01	$ .05	Harris, Lenny	90DL	437	$ .01	$ .15
Hammaker, Atlee	84D	236	$ .03	$ .10	Harris, Lenny	91D	224	$ .01	$ .03
Hammaker, Atlee	85D	509	$ .01	$ .08	Harris, Reggie	91D	704	$ .01	$ .10
Hammaker, Atlee	86D	445	$ .01	$ .06	Hartley, Mike	90DR	34	$ .01	$ .15
Hammaker, Atlee	88D	450	$ .01	$ .05	Hartley, Mike	91D	545	$ .01	$ .03
Hammaker, Atlee	89D	414	$ .01	$ .05	Harvey, Bryan	88DR	53	$ .05	$ .25
Hammaker, Atlee	90D	532	$ .01	$ .04	Harvey, Bryan	89D	525	$ .01	$ .15
Hammaker, Atlee	91D	707	$ .01	$ .03	Harvey, Bryan	89DBB	317	$ .01	$ .05
Hammond, Chris	91D	759	$ .01	$ .03	Harvey, Bryan	90D	372	$ .01	$ .04
Hancock, Garry	82D	608	$ .01	$ .05	Harvey, Bryan	90DL	116	$ .01	$ .15
Hanna, Preston	81D	523	$ .01	$ .05	Harvey, Bryan	91D	206	$ .01	$ .03
Hansen, Dave	91DRR	45	$ .01	$ .10	Haselman, Bill	91D	679	$ .01	$ .10
Hanson, Eric	89DR	49	$ .01	$ .50	Hassey, Ron	81D	80	$ .01	$ .05
Hanson, Erik	89DBB	320	$ .01	$ .35	Hassey, Ron	82D	463	$ .01	$ .05
Hanson, Erik	89DRR	32	$ .01	$ .75	Hassey, Ron	83D	159	$ .01	$ .05
Hanson, Erik	90D	345	$ .01	$ .10	Hassey, Ron	84D	460	$ .03	$ .10
Hanson, Erik	90DL	430	$ .01	$1.00	Hassey, Ron	86D	370	$ .01	$ .06
Hanson, Erik	91D	550	$ .01	$ .10	Hassey, Ron	87D	532	$ .01	$ .05
Hargrove, Mike	81D	78	$ .01	$ .05	Hassey, Ron	88D	580	$ .01	$ .05
Hargrove, Mike	82D	389	$ .01	$ .05	Hassey, Ron	89D	361	$ .01	$ .05

Player	Year	No.	VG	EX/MT	Player	Year	No.	VG	EX/MT
Hassey, Ron	90D	450	$ .01	$ .04	Heath, Mike	82D	413	$ .01	$ .05
Hassey, Ron	90DL	326	$ .01	$ .15	Heath, Mike	83D	517	$ .01	$ .05
Hassey, Ron	91D	476	$ .01	$ .03	Heath, Mike	84D	223	$ .03	$ .10
Hassler, Andy	81D	581	$ .01	$ .05	Heath, Mike	85D	298	$ .01	$ .08
Hassler, Andy	82D	519	$ .01	$ .05	Heath, Mike	86D	253	$ .01	$ .06
Hassler, Andy	83D	290	$ .01	$ .05	Heath, Mike	87D	496	$ .01	$ .05
Hassler, Andy	84D	255	$ .03	$ .10	Heath, Mike	88D	338	$ .01	$ .05
Hatcher, Billy	85DRR	41	$ .20	$1.25	Heath, Mike	88DBB	69	$ .01	$ .05
Hatcher, Billy	86D	433	$ .02	$ .25	Heath, Mike	89D	271	$ .01	$ .05
Hatcher, Billy	87D	481	$ .01	$ .05	Heath, Mike	89DBB	147	$ .01	$ .05
Hatcher, Billy	88D	261	$ .01	$ .05	Heath, Mike	90D	209	$ .01	$ .04
Hatcher, Billy	88DBB	150	$ .01	$ .05	Heath, Mike	90DL	60	$ .01	$ .15
Hatcher, Billy	88DK	23	$ .01	$ .05	Heath, Mike	91D	230	$ .01	$ .03
Hatcher, Billy	89D	187	$ .01	$ .05	Heathcock, Jeff	86D	182	$ .01	$ .06
Hatcher, Billy	89DBB	150	$ .01	$ .05	Heaton, Neal	84D	373	$ .10	$ .50
Hatcher, Billy	90D	616	$ .01	$ .04	Heaton, Neal	85D	373	$ .01	$ .08
Hatcher, Billy	90DL	241	$ .01	$ .15	Heaton, Neal	86D	338	$ .01	$ .06
Hatcher, Billy	91D	196	$ .01	$ .03	Heaton, Neal	87D	615	$ .01	$ .05
Hatcher, Billy	91D	763	$ .01	$ .03	Heaton, Neal	88D	134	$ .01	$ .05
Hatcher, Mickey	81D	526	$ .01	$ .05	Heaton, Neal	88DBB	124	$ .01	$ .05
Hatcher, Mickey	82D	480	$ .01	$ .05	Heaton, Neal	89D	224	$ .01	$ .05
Hatcher, Mickey	83D	615	$ .01	$ .05	Heaton, Neal	90D	658	$ .01	$ .04
Hatcher, Mickey	84D	147	$ .03	$ .10	Heaton, Neal	90DL	460	$ .01	$ .15
Hatcher, Mickey	85D	194	$ .01	$ .08	Heaton, Neal	91D	475	$ .01	$ .03
Hatcher, Mickey	86D	269	$ .01	$ .06	Heaverlo, Dave	81D	407	$ .01	$ .05
Hatcher, Mickey	87D	491	$ .01	$ .05	Hebner, Richie	81D	125	$ .01	$ .05
Hatcher, Mickey	88D	299	$ .01	$ .05	Hebner, Richie	82D	328	$ .01	$ .05
Hatcher, Mickey	89D	346	$ .01	$ .05	Hebner, Richie	85D	564	$ .01	$ .08
Hatcher, Mickey	90D	439	$ .01	$ .04	Heep, Danny	83D	443	$ .01	$ .05
Hatcher, Mickey	90DL	332	$ .01	$ .15	Heep, Danny	84D	434	$ .03	$ .10
Hausman, Tom	81D	396	$ .01	$ .05	Heep, Danny	85D	556	$ .01	$ .08
Hausman, Tom	82D	301	$ .01	$ .05	Heep, Danny	86D	556	$ .01	$ .06
Havens, Brad	82D	382	$ .01	$ .05	Heep, Danny	87D	649	$ .01	$ .05
Havens, Brad	83D	480	$ .01	$ .05	Heep, Danny	89D	368	$ .01	$ .05
Havens, Brad	86D	599	$ .01	$ .06	Heep, Danny	90D	358	$ .01	$ .04
Hawkins, Andy	85D	528	$ .01	$ .25	Heimueller, Gorman	84D	131	$ .03	$ .10
Hawkins, Andy	86D	284	$ .01	$ .06	Henderson, Dave	84D	557	$ .25	$2.00
Hawkins, Andy	87D	264	$ .01	$ .05	Henderson, Dave	86D	318	$ .01	$ .35
Hawkins, Andy	89D	583	$ .01	$ .05	Henderson, Dave	87D	622	$ .01	$ .20
Hawkins, Andy	89DBB	52	$ .01	$ .05	Henderson, Dave	89D	450	$ .01	$ .10
Hawkins, Andy	89DTR	52	$ .01	$ .05	Henderson, Dave	89DBB	190	$ .01	$ .05
Hawkins, Andy	90D	159	$ .01	$ .04	Henderson, Dave	89DK	20	$ .01	$ .05
Hawkins, Andy	90DL	281	$ .01	$ .15	Henderson, Dave	90D	243	$ .01	$ .04
Hawkins, Andy	91D	611	$ .01	$ .03	Henderson, Dave	91D	326	$ .01	$ .03
Hawkins, Andy	91DBC	12	$ .01	$ .03	Henderson, Rickey	81D	119	$5.00	$22.50
Hayes, Charlie	90D	548	$ .01	$ .10	Henderson, Rickey	82D	113	$1.00	$5.00
Hayes, Charlie	90DL	131	$ .01	$ .20	Henderson, Rickey	83D	35	$ .75	$4.00
Hayes, Charlie	91D	278	$ .01	$ .03	Henderson, Rickey	83DK	11	$ .25	$2.00
Hayes, Von	82D	237	$ .25	$1.25	Henderson, Rickey	84D	54	$2.00	$12.50
Hayes, Von	83D	324	$ .03	$ .35	Henderson, Rickey	85D	176	$1.00	$4.00
Hayes, Von	84D	477	$ .04	$ .25	Henderson, Rickey	86D	51	$ .50	$2.00
Hayes, Von	85D	326	$ .01	$ .20	Henderson, Rickey	87D	228	$ .05	$1.00
Hayes, Von	86D	305	$ .01	$ .06	Henderson, Rickey	88D	277	$ .10	$ .40
Hayes, Von	87D	113	$ .01	$ .05	Henderson, Rickey	88DBB	76	$ .05	$ .25
Hayes, Von	87DK	12	$ .01	$ .05	Henderson, Rickey	89D	245	$ .05	$ .25
Hayes, Von	88D	207	$ .01	$ .05	Henderson, Rickey	89DBB	78	$ .01	$ .25
Hayes, Von	88DBB	128	$ .01	$ .15	Henderson, Rickey	90D	304	$ .01	$ .20
Hayes, Von	89D	160	$ .01	$ .05	Henderson, Rickey	90DL	84	$ .01	$ .35
Hayes, Von	89DBB	47	$ .01	$ .05	Henderson, Rickey	90DL	160	$ .01	$1.00
Hayes, Von	90D	278	$ .01	$ .04	Henderson, Rickey	91D	648	$ .01	$ .20
Hayes, Von	90DBC	25	$ .01	$ .04	Henderson, Rickey	91DAS	53	$ .01	$ .15
Hayes, Von	90DL	52	$ .01	$ .15	Henderson, Rickey	91DLP	23	$1.00	$20.00
Hayes, Von	91D	222	$ .01	$ .03	Henderson, Rickey	91DMVP	387	$ .01	$ .15
Hayward, Ray	87D	632	$ .01	$ .05	Henderson, Rickey	91DMVP	761	$ .01	$ .10
Hayward, Ray	89D	521	$ .01	$ .05	Henderson, Steve	81D	157	$ .01	$ .05
Hearn, Ed	86DR	54	$ .02	$ .09	Henderson, Steve	82D	183	$ .01	$ .05
Hearn, Ed	87D	446	$ .01	$ .05	Henderson, Steve	83D	252	$ .01	$ .05
Hearn, Ed	89D	297	$ .01	$ .05	Henderson, Steve	84D	389	$ .03	$ .10
Hearron, Jeff	87D	490	$ .01	$ .05	Henderson, Steve	85D	145	$ .01	$ .08
Heath, Mike	81D	120	$ .01	$ .05	Henderson, Steve	86D	375	$ .01	$ .06

Player	Year	No.	VG	EX/MT	Player	Year	No.	VG	EX/MT
Hendrick, George	81D	430	$ .01	$ .05	Herr, Tom	84D	596	$ .03	$ .10
Hendrick, George	82D	40	$ .01	$ .05	Herr, Tom	85D	425	$ .01	$ .08
Hendrick, George	82DK	9	$ .01	$ .05	Herr, Tommy	86D	83	$ .01	$ .06
Hendrick, George	83D	404	$ .01	$ .05	Herr, Tommy	87D	140	$ .01	$ .05
Hendrick, George	84D	475	$ .03	$ .10	Herr, Tommy	88D	208	$ .01	$ .05
Hendrick, George	85D	181	$ .01	$ .08	Herr, Tommy	89D	301	$ .01	$ .05
Hendrick, George	88D	479	$ .01	$ .05	Herr, Tommy	89DBB	72	$ .01	$ .05
Hengel, Dave	88D	629	$ .01	$ .05	Herr, Tommy	89DTR	4	$ .01	$ .05
Henke, Tom	84D	134	$ .25	$1.00	Herr, Tommy	90D	75	$ .01	$ .04
Henke, Tom	85D	403	$ .01	$ .08	Herr, Tommy	90DK	21	$ .01	$ .10
Henke, Tom	86D	437	$ .01	$ .06	Herr, Tom	90DL	184	$ .01	$ .15
Henke, Tom	87D	197	$ .01	$ .05	Herr, Tom	91D	610	$ .01	$ .03
Henke, Tom	88D	490	$ .01	$ .05	Hershiser, Orel	85D	581	$1.00	$7.00
Henke, Tom	88DBB	104	$ .01	$ .05	Hershiser, Orel	86D	226	$ .10	$1.00
Henke, Tom	89D	385	$ .01	$ .05	Hershiser, Orel	86DK	18	$ .08	$ .40
Henke, Tom	89DBB	301	$ .01	$ .05	Hershiser, Orel	87D	106	$ .05	$ .30
Henke, Tom	90D	349	$ .01	$ .04	Hershiser, Orel	88D	94	$ .05	$ .20
Henke, Tom	90DL	158	$ .01	$ .15	Hershiser, Orel	88DBB	148	$ .05	$ .25
Henke, Tom	91D	205	$ .01	$ .03					
Henneman, Mike	87DR	32	$ .10	$ .35					
Henneman, Mike	88D	420	$ .03	$ .25					
Henneman, Mike	88DBB	91	$ .01	$ .05					
Henneman, Mike	89D	327	$ .01	$ .05					
Henneman, Mike	89DBB	237	$ .01	$ .05					
Henneman, Mike	90D	296	$ .01	$ .04					
Henneman, Mike	90DL	2	$ .01	$ .15					
Henneman, Mike	91D	76	$ .01	$ .03					
Henry, Dwayne	86D	603	$ .01	$ .06					
Henry, Dwayne	87D	637	$ .01	$ .05					
Hernandez, Carlos	90DR	37	$ .01	$ .10					
Hernandez, Carlos	91D	711	$ .01	$ .03					
Hernandez, Guillermo	89D	62	$ .01	$ .05					
Hernandez, Guillermo	90D	610	$ .01	$ .04					
Hernandez, Keith	81D	67	$ .10	$ .35					
Hernandez, Keith	82D	278	$ .08	$ .35					
Hernandez, Keith	83D	152	$ .05	$ .20					
Hernandez, Keith	83DK	20	$ .05	$ .30					
Hernandez, Keith	84D	238	$ .15	$ .50					
Hernandez, Keith	85D	68	$ .10	$ .35					
Hernandez, Keith	86D	190	$ .03	$ .25					
Hernandez, Keith	87D	76	$ .03	$ .25					
Hernandez, Keith	88D	316	$ .05	$ .20					
Hernandez, Keith	88DBB	152	$ .01	$ .10					
Hernandez, Keith	89D	117	$ .01	$ .10					
Hernandez, Keith	89DBB	208	$ .01	$ .10					
Hernandez, Keith	90D	388	$ .01	$ .10					
Hernandez, Keith	90DL	470	$ .01	$ .15					
Hernandez, Manny	88D	481	$ .01	$ .05					
Hernandez, Willie	81D	589	$ .01	$ .10	Hershiser, Orel	89D	197	$ .05	$ .25
Hernandez, Willie	83D	174	$ .01	$ .10	Hershiser, Orel	89D	648	$ .05	$ .25
Hernandez, Willie	84D	163	$ .05	$ .25	Hershiser, Orel	89DBB	225	$ .01	$ .10
Hernandez, Willie	85D	212	$ .01	$ .08	Hershiser, Orel	89DBC	4	$ .01	$ .20
Hernandez, Willie	86D	227	$ .01	$ .06	Hershiser, Orel	90D	197	$ .01	$ .10
Hernandez, Willie	87D	522	$ .01	$ .05	Hershiser, Orel	90DBC	5	$ .01	$ .10
Hernandez, Willie	88D	398	$ .01	$ .05	Hershiser, Orel	90DL	280	$ .01	$ .20
Hernandez, Willie	88DBB	125	$ .01	$ .05	Hershiser, Orel	91D	280	$ .01	$ .03
Hernandez, Xavier	90D	682	$ .01	$ .10	Herzog, Whitey	82D	190	$ .02	$ .15
Hernandez, Xavier	90DL	517	$ .01	$ .15	Herzog, Whitey	83D	530	$ .01	$ .05
Hernandez, Xavier	90DR	33	$ .01	$ .10	Hesketh, Joe	85D	157	$ .03	$ .20
Hernandez, Xavier	91D	708	$ .01	$ .03	Hesketh, Joe	86D	341	$ .01	$ .06
Herndon, Larry	81D	196	$ .01	$ .05	Hesketh, Joe	87D	134	$ .01	$ .05
Herndon, Larry	82D	172	$ .01	$ .05	Hesketh, Joe	88D	504	$ .01	$ .05
Herndon, Larry	83D	585	$ .01	$ .05	Hesketh, Joe	89D	460	$ .01	$ .05
Herndon, Larry	84D	349	$ .03	$ .10	Hesketh, Joe	90D	511	$ .01	$ .04
Herndon, Larry	85D	150	$ .01	$ .08	Hesketh, Joe	90DL	507	$ .01	$ .15
Herndon, Larry	86D	593	$ .01	$ .06	Hetzel, Eric	89D	660	$ .01	$ .10
Herndon, Larry	88D	353	$ .01	$ .05	Hetzel, Eric	90D	539	$ .01	$ .04
Herr, Tom	81D	68	$ .01	$ .05	Hibbard, Greg	90D	384	$ .01	$ .15
Herr, Tom	82D	530	$ .01	$ .05	Hibbard, Greg	90DL	523	$ .01	$ .75
Herr, Tom	83D	217	$ .01	$ .05	Hibbard, Greg	91D	159	$ .01	$ .03

Orel Hershiser P

Player	Year	No.	VG	EX/MT
Hickey, Kevin	82D	631	$ .01	$ .05
Hickey, Kevin	83D	445	$ .01	$ .05
Hickey, Kevin	84D	135	$ .03	$ .10
Hickey, Kevin	90D	583	$ .01	$ .04
Higuera, Ted	86D	351	$ .50	$1.50
Higuera, Ted	87D	49	$ .05	$ .20
Higuera, Ted	87DK	16	$ .05	$ .20
Higuera, Teddy	88D	90	$ .03	$ .25
Higuera, Ted	88DBB	127	$ .01	$ .05
Higuera, Ted	89D	175	$ .01	$ .05
Higuera, Ted	89DBB	183	$ .01	$ .05
Higuera, Ted	90D	339	$ .01	$ .04
Higuera, Ted	90DL	506	$ .01	$ .15
Higuera, Ted	91D	629	$ .01	$ .03
Hill, Donnie	84D	96	$ .03	$ .10
Hill, Donnie	85D	375	$ .01	$ .08
Hill, Donnie	86D	340	$ .01	$ .06
Hill, Donnie	87D	405	$ .01	$ .05
Hill, Donnie	88D	87	$ .01	$ .05
Hill, Donnie	91D	376	$ .01	$ .03
Hill, Glenallen	87D	561	$ .08	$1.00
Hill, Glenallen	90D	627	$ .01	$ .10
Hill, Glenallen	90DL	317	$ .01	$ .20
Hill, Glenallen	90DR	24	$ .01	$ .10
Hill, Glenallen	91D	380	$ .01	$ .03
Hill, Ken	89D	536	$ .01	$ .05
Hill, Ken	89DBB	304	$ .01	$ .05
Hill, Ken	89DR	31	$ .01	$ .10
Hill, Ken	90D	397	$ .01	$ .04
Hill, Ken	91D	670	$ .01	$ .03
Hill, Marc	83D	230	$ .01	$ .05
Hill, Marc	84D	330	$ .03	$ .10
Hill, Marc	85D	160	$ .01	$ .08
Hillegas, Shawn	88DRR	35	$ .01	$ .05
Hillegas, Shawn	89D	503	$ .01	$ .05
Hillegas, Shawn	90D	619	$ .01	$ .04
Hillegas, Shawn	91D	589	$ .01	$ .03
Hinzo, Tommy	88D	526	$ .01	$ .05
Hisle, Larry	81D	87	$ .01	$ .05
Hisle, Larry	82D	358	$ .01	$ .05
Hobson, Butch	81D	542	$ .01	$ .05
Hobson, Butch	82D	577	$ .01	$ .05
Hodges, Ron	83D	476	$ .01	$ .05
Hodges, Ron	84D	603	$ .03	$ .10
Hoffman, Glenn	81D	95	$ .01	$ .05
Hoffman, Glenn	82D	460	$ .01	$ .05
Hoffman, Glenn	83D	282	$ .01	$ .05
Hoffman, Glenn	84D	606	$ .03	$ .10
Hoffman, Glenn	86D	457	$ .01	$ .06
Hoffman, Glenn	90D	407	$ .01	$ .04
Hoffman, Guy	88D	452	$ .01	$ .05
Hoiles, Chris	90DL	513	$ .01	$ .50
Hoiles, Chris	91D	358	$ .01	$ .20
Holland, Al	82D	377	$ .01	$ .05
Holland, Al	83D	146	$ .01	$ .05
Holland, Al	84D	204	$ .03	$ .10
Holland, Al	85D	427	$ .01	$ .08
Holland, Al	86D	573	$ .01	$ .06
Hollins, Dave	90DR	47	$ .01	$ .15
Holman, Brian	89D	511	$ .01	$ .15
Holman, Brian	90D	143	$ .01	$ .04
Holman, Brian	90DL	273	$ .01	$ .25
Holman, Brian	91D	539	$ .01	$ .03
Holman, Scott	83D	224	$ .01	$ .05
Holmes, Darren	91D	669	$ .01	$ .10
Holton, Brian	87D	598	$ .01	$ .15
Holton, Brian	87DR	54	$ .01	$ .07
Holton, Brian	88D	402	$ .01	$ .05
Holton, Brian	89D	439	$ .01	$ .05
Holton, Brian	89DTR	20	$ .01	$ .05

Player	Year	No.	VG	EX/MT
Holton, Brian	90D	635	$ .01	$ .04

BRIAN HOLTON P

Player	Year	No.	VG	EX/MT
Holton, Brian	90DL	487	$ .01	$ .15
Honeycutt, Rick	81D	46	$ .01	$ .05
Honeycutt, Rick	82D	494	$ .01	$ .05
Honeycutt, Rick	83D	415	$ .01	$ .05
Honeycutt, Rick	84D	494	$ .03	$ .10
Honeycutt, Rick	85D	215	$ .01	$ .08
Honeycutt, Rick	86D	372	$ .01	$ .06
Honeycutt, Rick	87D	402	$ .01	$ .05
Honeycutt, Rick	88D	590	$ .01	$ .05
Honeycutt, Rick	88DBB	211	$ .01	$ .05
Honeycutt, Rick	89D	328	$ .01	$ .05
Honeycutt, Rick	89DBB	313	$ .01	$ .05
Honeycutt, Rick	90D	386	$ .01	$ .04
Honeycutt, Rick	90DL	372	$ .01	$ .15
Honeycutt, Rick	91D	373	$ .01	$ .03
Hood, Don	83D	390	$ .01	$ .05
Hooton, Burt	81D	541	$ .01	$ .05
Hooton, Burt	82D	32	$ .01	$ .05
Hooton, Burt	83D	32	$ .01	$ .05
Hooton, Burt	84D	459	$ .03	$ .10
Hooton, Burt	85D	104	$ .01	$ .08
Hooton, Burt	86D	300	$ .01	$ .06
Horn, Sam	88D	498	$ .05	$ .25
Horn, Sam	91D	733	$ .01	$ .03
Horner, Bob	81D	99	$ .01	$ .05
Horner, Bob	82D	173	$ .01	$ .05
Horner, Bob	83D	58	$ .01	$ .05
Horner, Bob	84D	535	$ .03	$ .10
Horner, Bob	84DK	14	$ .03	$ .10
Horner, Bob	85D	77	$ .01	$ .08
Horner, Bob	86D	188	$ .01	$ .05
Horner, Bob	87D	389	$ .01	$ .05
Horton, Ricky	85D	83	$ .01	$ .25
Horton, Ricky	86D	138	$ .01	$ .06
Horton, Ricky	87D	234	$ .01	$ .05
Horton, Ricky	88D	430	$ .01	$ .05
Horton, Ricky	89D	582	$ .01	$ .05
Horton, Ricky	90D	666	$ .01	$ .04
Hostetler, Dave	83D	89	$ .01	$ .05

Player	Year	No.	VG	EX/MT	Player	Year	No.	VG	EX/MT
Hostetler, Dave	84D	159	$ .03	$ .10	Hrbek, Kent	83D	179	$ .06	$ .55
Hough, Charlie	82D	447	$ .01	$ .05	Hrbek, Kent	83DK	19	$ .05	$ .40
Hough, Charlie	83D	69	$ .01	$ .05	Hrbek, Kent	84D	70	$ .15	$ .75
Hough, Charlie	84D	638	$ .03	$ .10	Hrbek, Kent	85D	70	$ .10	$ .35
Hough, Charlie	85D	422	$ .01	$ .08	Hrbek, Kent	86D	70	$ .08	$ .25
Hough, Charlie	86D	342	$ .01	$ .06	Hrbek, Kent	87D	73	$ .05	$ .20
Hough, Charlie	87D	470	$ .01	$ .05	Hrbek, Kent	88D	320	$ .01	$ .15
Hough, Charlie	87DK	7	$ .01	$ .05	Hrbek, Kent	88DBB	102	$ .01	$ .05
Hough, Charlie	88D	99	$ .01	$ .05	Hrbek, Kent	89D	199	$ .01	$ .10
Hough, Charlie	88DBB	256	$ .01	$ .05	Hrbek, Kent	89DBB	18	$ .01	$ .10
Hough, Charlie	89D	165	$ .01	$ .05	Hrbek, Kent	90D	81	$ .01	$ .04
Hough, Charlie	90D	411	$ .01	$ .04	Hrbek, Kent	90DL	228	$ .01	$ .15
Hough, Charlie	90DL	390	$ .01	$ .15	Hrbek, Kent	91D	95	$ .01	$ .03
Hough, Charlie	91D	146	$ .01	$ .03	Hubbard, Glenn	81D	459	$ .01	$ .05
Houk, Ralph	82D	282	$ .01	$ .05	Hubbard, Glenn	82D	436	$ .01	$ .05
Householder, Paul	81D	303	$ .01	$ .05	Hubbard, Glenn	83D	184	$ .01	$ .05
Householder, Paul	82D	314	$ .01	$ .05	Hubbard, Glenn	84D	432	$ .03	$ .10
Householder, Paul	83D	566	$ .01	$ .05	Hubbard, Glenn	85D	199	$ .01	$ .08
Householder, Paul	86D	414	$ .01	$ .06	Hubbard, Glenn	86D	141	$ .01	$ .06
Howard, Thomas	91D	746	$ .01	$ .03	Hubbard, Glenn	87D	634	$ .01	$ .05
Howe, Art	81D	258	$ .01	$ .05	Hubbard, Glenn	88D	314	$ .01	$ .05
Howe, Art	82D	92	$ .01	$ .05	Hubbard, Glenn	88DK	22	$ .01	$ .05
Howe, Art	83D	396	$ .01	$ .05	Hubbard, Glenn	89D	568	$ .01	$ .05
Howe, Steve	81D	511	$ .01	$ .05	Hudler, Rex	85D	469	$ .01	$ .08
Howe, Steve	82D	158	$ .01	$ .05	Hudler, Rex	89D	452	$ .01	$ .05
Howe, Steve	83D	630	$ .01	$ .05	Hudler, Rex	90D	366	$ .01	$ .04
Howe, Steve	88D	593	$ .01	$ .05	Hudler, Rex	90DL	439	$ .01	$ .15
Howell, Jack	86D	524	$ .01	$ .30	Hudler, Rex	91D	599	$ .01	$ .03
Howell, Jack	87D	305	$ .01	$ .05	Hudson, Charlie	84D	448	$ .01	$ .10
Howell, Jack	88D	333	$ .01	$ .05	Hudson, Charlie	85D	355	$ .01	$ .08
Howell, Jack	88DBB	59	$ .01	$ .05	Hudson, Charlie	86D	622	$ .01	$ .06
Howell, Jack	89D	288	$ .01	$ .05	Hudson, Charlie	87D	630	$ .01	$ .05
Howell, Jack	89DBB	307	$ .01	$ .05	Hudson, Charlie	88D	374	$ .01	$ .05
Howell, Jack	90D	254	$ .01	$ .04	Hudson, Charles	89D	514	$ .01	$ .05
Howell, Jack	90DL	327	$ .01	$ .15	Hudson, Charles	89DTR	50	$ .01	$ .05
Howell, Jack	91D	247	$ .01	$ .03	Hughes, Keith	88D	643	$ .01	$ .15
Howell, Jay	83D	587	$ .01	$ .05	Huismann, Mark	84D	339	$ .03	$ .10
Howell, Jay	85D	103	$ .01	$ .08	Huismann, Mark	85D	583	$ .01	$ .08
Howell, Jay	86D	223	$ .01	$ .06	Hulett, Tim	85D	645	$ .01	$ .08
Howell, Jay	87D	503	$ .01	$ .05	Hulett, Tim	86D	404	$ .01	$ .06
Howell, Jay	88D	55	$ .01	$ .05	Hulett, Tim	87D	260	$ .01	$ .05
Howell, Jay	89D	610	$ .01	$ .05	Hulett, Tim	91D	706	$ .01	$ .03
Howell, Jay	89DBB	36	$ .01	$ .05	Hume, Tom	82D	229	$ .01	$ .05
Howell, Jay	90D	203	$ .01	$ .04	Hume, Tom	83D	229	$ .01	$ .05
Howell, Jay	90DL	42	$ .01	$ .15	Hume, Tom	84D	550	$ .03	$ .10
Howell, Jay	91D	486	$ .01	$ .03	Hume, Tom	85D	408	$ .01	$ .08
Howell, Ken	85D	592	$ .01	$ .25	Hume, Tom	86D	365	$ .01	$ .06
Howell, Ken	86D	275	$ .01	$ .06	Hundley, Todd	91D	641	$ .01	$ .10
Howell, Ken	87D	229	$ .01	$ .05	Hunt, Randy	87D	625	$ .01	$ .05
Howell, Ken	88D	130	$ .01	$ .05	Hurdle, Clint	81D	224	$ .01	$ .05
Howell, Ken	89DBB	184	$ .01	$ .05	Hurdle, Clint	82D	516	$ .01	$ .05
Howell, Ken	90D	430	$ .01	$ .04	Hurdle, Clint	86D	434	$ .01	$ .06
Howell, Ken	90DL	316	$ .01	$ .15	Hurst, Bruce	83D	134	$ .03	$ .40
Howell, Ken	91D	204	$ .01	$ .03	Hurst, Bruce	84D	213	$ .03	$ .15
Howell, Roy	81D	392	$ .01	$ .05	Hurst, Bruce	85D	493	$ .01	$ .08
Howell, Roy	82D	204	$ .01	$ .05	Hurst, Bruce	86D	517	$ .01	$ .06
Howell, Roy	83D	358	$ .01	$ .05	Hurst, Bruce	87D	174	$ .01	$ .05
Howell, Roy	85D	577	$ .01	$ .08	Hurst, Bruce	88D	252	$ .01	$ .05
Howser, Dick	83D	590	$ .01	$ .05	Hurst, Bruce	88DBB	233	$ .01	$ .15
Hoyt, LaMarr	81D	160	$ .05	$ .20	Hurst, Bruce	89D	423	$ .01	$ .05
Hoyt, LaMarr	82D	117	$ .01	$ .05	Hurst, Bruce	89DBB	77	$ .01	$ .05
Hoyt, LaMarr	83D	632	$ .01	$ .05	Hurst, Bruce	89DTR	45	$ .01	$ .15
Hoyt, LaMarr	84D	488	$ .03	$ .10	Hurst, Bruce	90D	183	$ .01	$ .04
Hoyt, LaMarr	85D	86	$ .01	$ .08	Hurst, Bruce	90DL	23	$ .01	$ .15
Hoyt, LaMarr	86D	139	$ .01	$ .06	Hurst, Bruce	91D	83	$ .01	$ .03
Hoyt, LaMarr	87D	434	$ .01	$ .05	Huson, Jeff	90DL	285	$ .01	$ .15
Hrabosky, Al	81D	550	$ .01	$ .05	Huson, Jeff	90DR	11	$ .01	$ .10
Hrabosky, Al	82D	97	$ .01	$ .05	Huson, Jeff	91D	305	$ .01	$ .03
Hrabosky, Al	83D	475	$ .01	$ .05	Huson, Jeff	Ford	693	$ .01	$ .10
Hrbek, Kent	82D	557	$ .50	$3.50	Hutton, Tommy	81D	93	$ .01	$ .05

DONRUSS

Player	Year	No.	VG	EX/MT
Incaviglia, Pete	86DR	23	$.80	$1.00
Incaviglia, Pete	87D	224	$.20	$.90
Incaviglia, Pete	88D	304	$.05	$.25
Incaviglia, Pete	88DBB	55	$.01	$.10
Incaviglia, Pete	89D	56	$.01	$.10
Incaviglia, Pete	89DBB	144	$.01	$.10
Incaviglia, Pete	89DK	3	$.01	$.05
Incaviglia, Pete	90D	48	$.01	$.10
Incaviglia, Pete	90DL	231	$.01	$.15
Incaviglia, Pete	91D	464	$.01	$.03
Infante, Alexis	89DR	30	$.01	$.10
Innis, Jeff	90D	408	$.01	$.04
Iorg, Dane	81D	311	$.01	$.05
Iorg, Dane	82D	166	$.01	$.05
Iorg, Dane	83D	469	$.01	$.05
Iorg, Dane	84D	571	$.03	$.10
Iorg, Dane	85D	252	$.01	$.08
Iorg, Garth	82D	353	$.01	$.05
Iorg, Garth	83D	306	$.01	$.05
Iorg, Garth	84D	561	$.03	$.10
Iorg, Garth	85D	363	$.01	$.08
Iorg, Garth	86D	640	$.01	$.06
Iorg, Garth	87D	394	$.01	$.05
Iorg, Garth	88D	444	$.01	$.05
Ivie, Mike	81D	312	$.01	$.05
Ivie, Mike	82D	396	$.01	$.05
Ivie, Mike	83D	485	$.01	$.05
Jackson, Bo	86DR	38	$3.00	$9.00
Jackson, Bo	87DR	14	$1.00	$3.50
Jackson, Bo	87DRR	35	$2.00	$10.00
Jackson, Bo	88D	220	$.15	$1.00
Jackson, Bo	88DBB	119	$.15	$.75
Jackson, Bo	89D	208	$.10	$.75
Jackson, Bo	89DBB	169	$.01	$1.00
Jackson, Bo	90D	61	$.01	$.60
Jackson, Bo	90DAS	650	$.01	$.40
Jackson, Bo	90DBC	1	$.01	$.40
Jackson, Bo	90DK	1	$.01	$.40
Jackson, Bo	90DL	125	$.01	$1.00
Jackson, Bo	91D	632	$.01	$.03
Jackson, Bo	91DBC	10	$.01	$.20
Jackson, Bo	91DLP	19	$1.00	$15.00
Jackson, Chuck	87DR	55	$.01	$.07
Jackson, Danny	84D	461	$.30	$2.00
Jackson, Danny	85D	374	$.05	$.50
Jackson, Danny	86D	95	$.02	$.15
Jackson, Danny	87D	157	$.01	$.05
Jackson, Danny	88D	132	$.01	$.05
Jackson, Danny	88DBB	166	$.01	$.10
Jackson, Danny	89D	124	$.01	$.10
Jackson, Danny	89DBB	54	$.01	$.10
Jackson, Danny	90D	80	$.01	$.10
Jackson, Danny	90DL	279	$.01	$.15
Jackson, Danny	91D	96	$.01	$.03
Jackson, Danny	91D	678	$.01	$.03
Jackson, Darrell	81D	547	$.01	$.05
Jackson, Darrell	82D	179	$.01	$.05
Jackson, Darrin	88DR	45	$.01	$.15
Jackson, Darrin	90D	641	$.01	$.04
Jackson, Grant	81D	15	$.01	$.05
Jackson, Grant	82D	518	$.01	$.05
Jackson, Mike	87DR	36	$.01	$.07
Jackson, Mike	88D	139	$.01	$.15
Jackson, Mike	89D	652	$.01	$.05
Jackson, Mike	90DL	351	$.01	$.15
Jackson, Mike	91D	676	$.01	$.03
Jackson, Reggie	81D	228	$.20	$1.50
Jackson, Reggie	81D	348	$.20	$1.50
Jackson, Reggie	81D	468	$.15	$1.50
Jackson, Reggie	82D	535	$.15	$.75
Jackson, Reggie	82D	575	$.10	$.50
Jackson, Reggie	83D	115	$.15	$.60
Jackson, Reggie	83DK	3	$.10	$.50
Jackson, Reggie	84D	57	$.50	$2.50
Jackson, Reggie	85D	57	$.20	$.90
Jackson, Reggie	86D	377	$.15	$.50
Jackson, Reggie	87D	210	$.15	$.40
Jackson, Ron	81D	489	$.01	$.05
Jackson, Ron	82D	602	$.01	$.05
Jackson, Ron	83D	639	$.01	$.05
Jackson, Ron	84D	133	$.03	$.10
Jackson, Roy Lee	81D	36	$.01	$.05
Jackson, Roy Lee	82D	541	$.01	$.05
Jackson, Roy Lee	83D	479	$.01	$.05
Jackson, Roy Lee	84D	195	$.03	$.10
Jackson, Roy Lee	85D	606	$.01	$.08
Jacoby, Brook	84D	542	$.20	$2.00
Jacoby, Brook	85D	154	$.08	$.25
Jacoby, Brook	86D	154	$.02	$.15
Jacoby, Brook	87D	104	$.01	$.05
Jacoby, Brook	87DK	8	$.01	$.05
Jacoby, Brook	88D	131	$.01	$.05
Jacoby, Brook	88DBB	229	$.01	$.05
Jacoby, Brook	89D	114	$.01	$.05
Jacoby, Brook	89DBB	61	$.01	$.05
Jacoby, Brook	90D	83	$.01	$.04
Jacoby, Brook	90DL	74	$.01	$.15
Jacoby, Brook	91D	176	$.01	$.03
James, Bob	84D	87	$.03	$.10
James, Bob	85D	279	$.01	$.08
James, Bob	86D	379	$.01	$.06
James, Bob	87D	493	$.01	$.05
James, Bob	88D	507	$.01	$.05
James, Chris	87DRR	42	$.15	$.85
James, Chris	88D	453	$.01	$.10
James, Chris	88DBB	159	$.01	$.05
James, Chris	89D	312	$.01	$.05
James, Chris	89DBB	266	$.01	$.05
James, Chris	90D	323	$.01	$.04
James, Chris	90DL	319	$.01	$.15
James, Chris	91D	227	$.01	$.03
James, Dion	84DRR	31	$.05	$.50
James, Dion	85D	211	$.03	$.15
James, Dion	86D	89	$.03	$.15
James, Dion	88D	190	$.01	$.05
James, Dion	88DBB	29	$.01	$.05
James, Dion	89D	340	$.01	$.05
James, Dion	89DBB	253	$.01	$.05
James, Dion	90D	428	$.01	$.04
James, Dion	91D	348	$.01	$.03
Javier, Stan	86D	584	$.05	$.35
Javier, Stan	87D	590	$.01	$.05
Javier, Stan	88DBB	155	$.01	$.05
Javier, Stan	89D	185	$.01	$.05
Javier, Stan	90D	568	$.01	$.04
Javier, Stan	90DL	445	$.01	$.15
Javier, Stan	91D	239	$.01	$.03
Jeffcoat, Mike	84DRR	43	$.03	$.10
Jeffcoat, Mike	85D	251	$.01	$.08
Jeffcoat, Mike	90D	521	$.01	$.04
Jeffcoat, Mike	90DL	416	$.01	$.15
Jefferies, Gregg	88D	657	$1.00	$3.50
Jefferies, Gregg	89DBB	152	$.01	$.35
Jefferies, Gregg	89DR	2	$.01	$.75
Jefferies, Gregg	89DRR	35	$.15	$.75
Jefferies, Gregg	90D	270	$.01	$.20
Jefferies, Gregg	91D	79	$.01	$.10
Jefferson, Stan	87D	642	$.01	$.15
Jefferson, Stan	87DR	43	$.01	$.07
Jefferson, Stan	88D	187	$.01	$.05

Player	Year	No.	VG	EX/MT
Jeffries, Gregg	90DL	171	$ .01	$ .35
Jeltz, Steve	85DRR	44	$ .01	$ .08
Jeltz, Steve	87D	359	$ .01	$ .05
Jeltz, Steve	88D	576	$ .01	$ .05
Jeltz, Steve	89D	431	$ .01	$ .05
Jeltz, Steve	89DBB	271	$ .01	$ .05
Jeltz, Steve	90D	133	$ .01	$ .04
Jenkins, Fergie (Ferguson)	81D	146	$ .03	$ .25
Jenkins, Fergie	82D	643	$ .03	$ .25
Jenkins, Fergie	83D	300	$ .03	$ .25
Jenkins, Fergie	84D	189	$ .04	$ .35
Jennings, Doug	88DR	13	$ .01	$ .15
Jennings, Doug	89D	505	$ .01	$ .15
Jimenez, Houston	85D	269	$ .01	$ .08
John, Tommy	81D	107	$ .05	$ .20
John, Tommy	82D	409	$ .03	$ .20
John, Tommy	82D	558	$ .03	$ .20
John, Tommy	83D	570	$ .03	$ .20
John, Tommy	84D	301	$ .08	$ .25
John, Tommy	85D	423	$ .03	$ .25
John, Tommy	88D	401	$ .01	$ .15
John, Tommy	88DBB	220	$ .01	$ .05
John, Tommy	88DK	17	$ .01	$ .15
Johnson, Anthony	83D	629	$ .01	$ .05
Johnson, Bob	83D	494	$ .01	$ .05
Johnson, Bob	84D	500	$ .03	$ .10
Johnson, Cliff	81D	484	$ .01	$ .05
Johnson, Cliff	82D	339	$ .01	$ .05
Johnson, Cliff	83D	601	$ .01	$ .05
Johnson, Cliff	84D	512	$ .03	$ .10
Johnson, Cliff	85D	512	$ .01	$ .08
Johnson, Cliff	86D	639	$ .01	$ .06
Johnson, Cliff	87D	645	$ .01	$ .05
Johnson, Dave	90D	702	$ .01	$ .04
Johnson, Dave	90DL	434	$ .01	$ .20
Johnson, Dave	91D	126	$ .01	$ .03
Johnson, Howard	83D	328	$2.00	$8.00
Johnson, Howard	85D	247	$ .25	$1.50
Johnson, Howard	86D	312	$ .05	$ .50
Johnson, Howard	87D	646	$ .03	$ .25
Johnson, Howard	88D	569	$ .01	$ .15
Johnson, Howard	88DBB	97	$ .05	$ .25
Johnson, Howard	89D	235	$ .05	$ .15
Johnson, Howard	89DBB	126	$ .01	$ .10
Johnson, Howard	90D	99	$ .01	$ .10
Johnson, Howard	90DAS	654	$ .01	$ .20
Johnson, Howard	90DBC	2	$ .01	$ .10
Johnson, Howard	90DK	18	$ .01	$ .20
Johnson, Howard	90DL	272	$ .01	$ .15
Johnson, Howard	91D	454	$ .01	$ .10
Johnson, Joe	86D	624	$ .01	$ .06
Johnson, Joe	87D	650	$ .01	$ .05
Johnson, John Henry	82D	550	$ .01	$ .05
Johnson, John Henry	84D	91	$ .03	$ .10
Johnson, Lamar	81D	38	$ .01	$ .05
Johnson, Lamar	82D	269	$ .01	$ .05
Johnson, Lamar	83D	142	$ .01	$ .05
Johnson, Lance	88DRR	31	$ .10	$ .25
Johnson, Lance	89D	606	$ .01	$ .05
Johnson, Lance	90D	573	$ .01	$ .04
Johnson, Lance	90DL	259	$ .01	$ .15
Johnson, Lance	91D	259	$ .01	$ .03
Johnson, Randy	83D	305	$ .01	$ .05
Johnson, Randy	84D	321	$ .03	$ .10
Johnson, Randy	85D	531	$ .01	$ .08
Johnson, Randy	89DBB	80	$ .01	$ .10
Johnson, Randy	89DR	43	$ .01	$ .10
Johnson, Randy	89DRR	42	$ .01	$ .25
Johnson, Randy	90D	379	$ .01	$ .04
Johnson, Randy	90DL	483	$ .01	$ .25

Player	Year	No.	VG	EX/MT
Johnson, Randy	91D	134	$ .01	$ .03
Johnson, Randy	91DBC	2	$ .01	$ .03
Johnson, Roy	83D	492	$ .01	$ .05
Johnson, Wallace	89D	484	$ .01	$ .05
Johnson, Wallace	90D	570	$ .01	$ .04
Johnson, Wallace	90DL	344	$ .01	$ .15
Johnstone, Jay	81D	300	$ .01	$ .05
Johnstone, Jay	82D	262	$ .01	$ .05
Johnstone, Jay	83D	561	$ .01	$ .05
Johnstone, Jay	84D	540	$ .03	$ .10
Jones, Al	85D	404	$ .01	$ .08
Jones, Barry	87D	602	$ .03	$ .25
Jones, Barry	89D	647	$ .01	$ .05
Jones, Barry	90DL	431	$ .01	$ .15
Jones, Barry	91D	534	$ .01	$ .03
Jones, Bobby	85D	134	$ .01	$ .08
Jones, Doug	88D	588	$ .01	$ .35
Jones, Doug	89D	438	$ .01	$ .10
Jones, Doug	89DBB	173	$ .01	$ .05
Jones, Doug	90D	320	$ .01	$ .04
Jones, Doug	90DL	153	$ .01	$ .15
Jones, Doug	91D	232	$ .01	$ .03
Jones, Jeff	82D	213	$ .01	$ .05
Jones, Jeff	83D	651	$ .01	$ .05
Jones, Jeff	84D	262	$ .03	$ .10
Jones, Jimmy	87D	557	$ .01	$ .05
Jones, Jimmy	88D	141	$ .01	$ .05
Jones, Jimmy	88DBB	189	$ .01	$ .05
Jones, Jimmy	89D	247	$ .01	$ .05
Jones, Jimmy	89DBB	217	$ .01	$ .05
Jones, Lynn	82D	542	$ .01	$ .05
Jones, Lynn	86D	466	$ .01	$ .06

MIKE JONES P

Player	Year	No.	VG	EX/MT
Jones, Mike	85D	640	$ .01	$ .08
Jones, Mike	86D	419	$ .01	$ .06
Jones, Odell	84D	256	$ .03	$ .10
Jones, Odell	85D	525	$ .01	$ .08
Jones, Odell	87D	582	$ .01	$ .05
Jones, Randy	81D	122	$ .01	$ .05
Jones, Ron	89DR	42	$ .01	$ .10
Jones, Ron	89DRR	40	$ .01	$ .10

Player	Year	No.	VG	EX/MT	Player	Year	No.	VG	EX/MT
Jones, Ron	90D	487	$ .01	$ .04	Kelly, Roberto	88DR	16	$ .01	$ .50
Jones, Ruppert	81D	349	$ .01	$ .05	Kelly, Roberto	89D	433	$ .01	$ .15
Jones, Ruppert	82D	346	$ .01	$ .05	Kelly, Roberto	89DBB	273	$ .01	$ .20
Jones, Ruppert	83D	373	$ .01	$ .05	Kelly, Roberto	90D	192	$ .01	$ .10
Jones, Ruppert	84D	261	$ .03	$ .10	Kelly, Roberto	90DL	17	$ .01	$ .35
Jones, Ruppert	85D	612	$ .01	$ .08	Kelly, Roberto	91D	538	$ .01	$ .03
Jones, Ruppert	86D	423	$ .01	$ .06	Kelly, Roberto	91DMVP	400	$ .01	$ .03
Jones, Ruppert	87D	428	$ .01	$ .05	Kemp, Steve	81D	249	$ .01	$ .05
Jones, Tim	89D	555	$ .01	$ .10	Kemp, Steve	82D	594	$ .01	$ .05
Jones, Tim	89DR	28	$ .01	$ .10	Kemp, Steve	83D	269	$ .01	$ .05
Jones, Tim	90D	686	$ .01	$ .04	Kemp, Steve	84D	469	$ .03	$ .10
Jones, Tim	91D	66	$ .01	$ .03	Kemp, Steve	85D	225	$ .01	$ .08
Jones, Tracy	86DR	2	$ .03	$ .20	Kemp, Steve	86D	200	$ .01	$ .06
Jones, Tracy	87D	413	$ .01	$ .10	Kennedy, Junior	81D	424	$ .01	$ .05
Jones, Tracy	88D	310	$ .01	$ .10	Kennedy, Junior	82D	188	$ .01	$ .05
Jones, Tracy	88DBB	174	$ .01	$ .05	Kennedy, Junior	83D	529	$ .01	$ .05
Jones, Tracy	89D	574	$ .01	$ .05	Kennedy, Terry	81D	428	$ .01	$ .05
Jones, Tracy	90D	636	$ .01	$ .04	Kennedy, Terry	82D	121	$ .01	$ .05
Jones, Tracy	91D	594	$ .01	$ .03	Kennedy, Terry	83D	220	$ .01	$ .05
Jordan, Ricky	89D	624	$ .01	$ .20	Kennedy, Terry	83DK	26	$ .01	$ .05
Jordan, Ricky	89DBB	103	$ .01	$ .05	Kennedy, Terry	84D	112	$ .03	$ .10
Jordan, Ricky	90D	76	$ .01	$ .05	Kennedy, Terry	85D	429	$ .01	$ .08
Jordan, Ricky	90DL	236	$ .01	$ .15	Kennedy, Terry	86D	356	$ .01	$ .06
Jordan, Ricky	91D	466	$ .01	$ .03	Kennedy, Terry	87D	205	$ .01	$ .05
Jordan, Scott	89D	609	$ .01	$ .05	Kennedy, Terry	88D	150	$ .01	$ .05
Jorgensen, Mike	81D	274	$ .01	$ .05	Kennedy, Terry	88DBB	30	$ .01	$ .05
Jorgensen, Mike	82D	224	$ .01	$ .05	Kennedy, Terry	89D	141	$ .01	$ .05
Jose, Felix	89DRR	38	$ .10	$ .50	Kennedy, Terry	90D	602	$ .01	$ .04
Jose, Felix	90D	564	$ .01	$ .25					
Jose, Felix	90DL	385	$ .01	$3.00					
Jose, Felix	90DR	5	$ .01	$1.00					
Jose, Felix	91D	656	$ .01	$ .25					
Joyner, Wally	86DR	1	$ .50	$3.00					
Joyner, Wally	87D	135	$ .05	$1.00					
Joyner, Wally	87DK	1	$ .01	$ .50					
Joyner, Wally	88D	110	$ .01	$ .10					
Joyner, Wally	88DBB	115	$ .01	$ .10					
Joyner, Wally	88DBC	13	$ .01	$ .10					
Joyner, Wally	89DBB	139	$ .01	$ .10					
Joyner, Wally	89DBC	21	$ .01	$ .10					
Joyner, Wally	90D	94	$ .01	$ .10					
Joyner, Wally	90DL	24	$ .01	$ .20					
Joyner, Wally	91D	677	$ .01	$ .03					
Jurak, Ed	84D	127	$ .03	$ .10					
Jurak, Ed	85D	579	$ .01	$ .08					
Justice, Dave	90D	704	$ .05	$2.50					
Justice, Dave	90DL	297	$ .01	$22.00					
Justice, Dave	90DR	14	$ .01	$2.50					
Justice, Dave	91D	548	$ .01	$ .50					
Justice, Dave	91D	683	$ .01	$ .25					
Justice, Dave	91DLP	1	$1.00	$20.00					
Justice, Dave	91DMVP	402	$ .01	$ .25					
Kaat, Jim	81D	536	$ .02	$ .25					
Kaat, Jim	82D	217	$ .05	$ .30					
Kaat, Jim	83D	343	$ .03	$ .20					
Karkovice, Ron	87D	334	$ .01	$ .05					
Karkovice, Ron	90D	413	$ .01	$ .04					
Karkovice, Ron	90DL	307	$ .01	$ .15					
Karkovice, Ron	91D	220	$ .01	$ .03	Kennedy, Terry	90DL	67	$ .01	$ .15
Kaufman, Curt	85D	524	$ .01	$ .08	Kennedy, Terry	91D	94	$ .01	$ .03
Kearney, Bob	83D	539	$ .01	$ .05	Keough, Matt	81D	358	$ .01	$ .05
Kearney, Bob	84D	462	$ .03	$ .10	Keough, Matt	82D	71	$ .01	$ .05
Kearney, Bob	85D	362	$ .01	$ .08	Keough, Matt	83D	239	$ .01	$ .05
Kearney, Bob	86D	74	$ .01	$ .06	Keough, Matt	84D	627	$ .03	$ .10
Kearney, Bob	87D	445	$ .01	$ .05	Kepshire, Kurt	85D	382	$ .01	$ .08
Keeton, Rickey	82D	618	$ .01	$ .05	Kepshire, Kurt	86D	504	$ .01	$ .06
Kelleher, Mick	81D	513	$ .01	$ .05	Kerfeld, Charlie	86DR	6	$ .13	$ .15
Kelleher, Mick	82D	601	$ .01	$ .05	Kerfeld, Charlie	87D	209	$ .01	$ .05
Kelly, Pat	81D	600	$ .02	$ .15	Kern, Jim	81D	27	$ .01	$ .05
Kelly, Roberto	88D	635	$ .25	$1.25	Kern, Jim	82D	89	$ .01	$ .05

TERRY KENNEDY C

Player	Year	No.	VG	EX/MT	Player	Year	No.	VG	EX/MT
Kern, Jim	83D	355	$ .01	$ .05	Kittle, Ron	89DBB	249	$ .01	$ .05
Key, Jimmy	85D	559	$ .25	$1.00	Kittle, Ron	89DTR	51	$ .01	$ .15
Key, Jimmy	86D	561	$ .01	$ .15	Kittle, Ron	90D	148	$ .01	$ .04
Key, Jimmy	87D	244	$ .01	$ .05	Kittle, Ron	90DL	405	$ .01	$ .15
Key, Jimmy	88D	72	$ .01	$ .15	Kittle, Ron	91D	613	$ .01	$ .03
Key, Jimmy	88DBB	143	$ .01	$ .05	Klink, Joe	90DL	503	$ .01	$ .15
Key, Jimmy	89D	188	$ .01	$ .05	Klink, Joe	91D	591	$ .01	$ .03
Key, Jimmy	89DBB	87	$ .01	$ .05	Klutts, Mickey	81D	110	$ .01	$ .05
Key, Jimmy	90D	231	$ .01	$ .04	Klutts, Mickey	83D	465	$ .01	$ .05
Key, Jimmy	90DL	211	$ .01	$ .15	Knackert, Brent	90DR	52	$ .01	$ .15
Key, Jimmy	91D	98	$ .01	$ .03	Knackert, Brent	91D	662	$ .01	$ .03
Khalifa, Sam	86D	308	$ .01	$ .06	Knapp, Chris	81D	173	$ .01	$ .05
Kiecker, Dana	90DL	525	$ .01	$ .25	Knepper, Bob	81D	194	$ .01	$ .05
Kiecker, Dana	90DR	28	$ .01	$ .15	Knepper, Bob	82D	41	$ .01	$ .05
Kiecker, Dana	91D	347	$ .01	$ .03	Knepper, Robert	83D	92	$ .01	$ .05
Kiefer, Steve	85DRR	35	$ .01	$ .08	Knepper, Bob	84D	572	$ .03	$ .10
Kiefer, Steve	86D	420	$ .01	$ .06	Knepper, Bob	85D	476	$ .01	$ .08
Kiefer, Steve	88D	542	$ .01	$ .05	Knepper, Bob	86D	161	$ .01	$ .06
Kilgus, Paul	88D	469	$ .01	$ .05	Knepper, Bob	87D	112	$ .01	$ .05
Kilgus, Paul	88DBB	111	$ .01	$ .05	Knepper, Bob	88D	138	$ .01	$ .05
Kilgus, Paul	89D	283	$ .01	$ .05	Knepper, Bob	88DBB	176	$ .01	$ .05
Kilgus, Paul	89DBB	149	$ .01	$ .05	Knepper, Bob	89D	123	$ .01	$ .05
Kilgus, Paul	89DTR	42	$ .01	$ .15	Knepper, Bob	90D	485	$ .01	$ .04
Kilgus, Paul	90D	276	$ .01	$ .04	Knicely, Alan	83D	620	$ .01	$ .05
King, Eric	86DR	27	$ .05	$ .35	Knight, Ray	81D	61	$ .01	$ .05
King, Eric	87D	250	$ .08	$ .25	Knight, Ray	82D	374	$ .01	$ .05
King, Eric	88D	50	$ .01	$ .05	Knight, Ray	83D	522	$ .01	$ .05
King, Eric	89D	535	$ .01	$ .05	Knight, Ray	84D	232	$ .03	$ .10
King, Eric	89DBB	235	$ .01	$ .05	Knight, Ray	84DK	12	$ .08	$ .25
King, Eric	89DTR	37	$ .01	$ .05	Knight, Ray	85D	617	$ .01	$ .08
King, Eric	90D	337	$ .01	$ .04	Knight, Ray	86D	597	$ .01	$ .06
King, Eric	90DL	43	$ .01	$ .15	Knight, Ray	87D	586	$ .01	$ .05
King, Eric	91D	271	$ .01	$ .03	Knight, Ray	88D	108	$ .01	$ .05
King, Jeff	90D	480	$ .01	$ .04	Knoblauch, Chuck	91DRR	421	$ .01	$ .15
King, Jeff	90DL	163	$ .01	$ .25	Knudson, Mark	88D	495	$ .01	$ .05
King, Jeff	91D	233	$ .01	$ .03	Knudson, Mark	90D	575	$ .01	$ .04
Kingery, Mike	87D	424	$ .01	$ .15	Knudson, Mark	90DL	348	$ .01	$ .15
Kingery, Mike	88D	322	$ .01	$ .05	Knudson, Mark	91D	328	$ .01	$ .03
Kingery, Mike	90D	601	$ .01	$ .04	Komminsk, Brad	84DRR	36	$ .03	$ .10
Kingery, Mike	91D	573	$ .01	$ .03	Komminsk, Brad	85D	321	$ .01	$ .08
Kingman, Brian	81D	360	$ .01	$ .05	Komminsk, Brad	88D	583	$ .01	$ .05
Kingman, Brian	82D	87	$ .01	$ .05	Komminsk, Brad	90D	350	$ .01	$ .04
Kingman, Dave	81D	553	$ .03	$ .20	Komminsk, Brad	90DL	303	$ .01	$ .15
Kingman, Dave	82D	182	$ .02	$ .15	Koosman, Jerry	81D	531	$ .02	$ .15
Kingman, Dave	82DK	17	$ .03	$ .20	Koosman, Jerry	82D	603	$ .02	$ .15
Kingman, Dave	83D	301	$ .01	$ .05	Koosman, Jerry	83D	39	$ .02	$ .15
Kingman, Dave	84D	360	$ .03	$ .10	Koosman, Jerry	84D	501	$ .03	$ .10
Kingman, Dave	85D	54	$ .03	$ .10	Koosman, Jerry	85D	233	$ .03	$ .20
Kingman, Dave	86D	54	$ .01	$ .06	Koosman, Jerry	86DK	23	$ .05	$ .20
Kingman, Dave	87D	425	$ .01	$ .05	Kraemer, Joe	90DR	10	$ .01	$ .10
Kinney, Dennis	81D	363	$ .01	$ .05	Kramer, Randy	89D	480	$ .01	$ .05
Kipper, Bob	86DR	46	$ .02	$ .09	Kramer, Randy	89DBB	213	$ .01	$ .05
Kipper, Bob	86DRR	44	$ .01	$ .06	Kramer, Randy	89DR	48	$ .01	$ .10
Kipper, Bob	87D	572	$ .01	$ .05	Kramer, Randy	90D	409	$ .01	$ .04
Kipper, Bob	88D	115	$ .01	$ .05	Kravec, Ken	82D	378	$ .01	$ .05
Kipper, Bob	89D	409	$ .01	$ .05	Kremers, Jimmy	91D	739	$ .01	$ .10
Kipper, Bob	90D	362	$ .01	$ .04	Krenchicki, Wayne	83D	314	$ .01	$ .05
Kipper, Bob	91D	720	$ .01	$ .03	Krenchicki, Wayne	84D	334	$ .03	$ .10
Kison, Bruce	82D	66	$ .01	$ .05	Krenchicki, Wayne	85D	140	$ .01	$ .08
Kison, Bruce	83D	267	$ .01	$ .05	Krenchicki, Wayne	86D	140	$ .01	$ .06
Kison, Bruce	84D	499	$ .03	$ .10	Krenchicki, Wayne	87D	406	$ .01	$ .05
Kison, Bruce	85D	377	$ .01	$ .08	Kreuter, Chad	89D	579	$ .01	$ .15
Kison, Bruce	86D	616	$ .01	$ .06	Kreuter, Chad	90D	520	$ .01	$ .04
Kittle, Ron	84D	244	$ .04	$ .35	Krueger, Bill	85D	467	$ .01	$ .08
Kittle, Ron	84DK	18	$ .04	$ .25	Krueger, Bill	86D	298	$ .01	$ .06
Kittle, Ron	85D	180	$ .01	$ .20	Krueger, Bill	90DL	421	$ .01	$ .15
Kittle, Ron	86D	526	$ .01	$ .06	Krueger, Bill	91D	647	$ .01	$ .03
Kittle, Ron	87D	351	$ .01	$ .05	Kruk, John	86DR	42	$ .15	$ .50
Kittle, Ron	88D	422	$ .01	$ .05	Kruk, John	87D	328	$ .05	$ .25
Kittle, Ron	89D	428	$ 01	$ .04	Kruk, John	88D	205	$ .01	$ .10

Player	Year	No.	VG	EX/MT	Player	Year	No.	VG	EX/MT
Kruk, John	88DBB	245	$ .01	$ .05	Lamp, Dennis	82D	619	$ .01	$ .05
Kruk, John	89D	86	$ .01	$ .05	Lamp, Dennis	83D	165	$ .01	$ .05
Kruk, John	89DBB	240	$ .01	$ .05	Lamp, Dennis	84D	526	$ .03	$ .10
Kruk, John	90D	160	$ .01	$ .04	Lamp, Dennis	85D	119	$ .01	$ .08
Kruk, John	90DL	284	$ .01	$ .15	Lamp, Dennis	86D	626	$ .01	$ .06
Kruk, John	91D	260	$ .01	$ .03	Lamp, Dennis	89D	633	$ .01	$ .05
Krukow, Mike	82D	351	$ .01	$ .05	Lamp, Dennis	90D	423	$ .01	$ .04
Krukow, Mike	83D	119	$ .01	$ .05	Lamp, Dennis	90DL	315	$ .01	$ .15
Krukow, Mike	84D	509	$ .03	$ .10	Lamp, Dennis	91D	138	$ .01	$ .03
Krukow, Mike	85D	630	$ .01	$ .08	Lampkin, Tom	89D	639	$ .01	$ .05
Krukow, Mike	86D	143	$ .01	$ .06	Lancaster, Les	87DR	10	$ .01	$ .25
Krukow, Mike	87D	609	$ .01	$ .05	Lancaster, Lester	88D	561	$ .01	$ .20
Krukow, Mike	88D	116	$ .01	$ .05	Lancaster, Les	88DBB	172	$ .01	$ .05
Krukow, Mike	88DBB	50	$ .01	$ .05	Lancaster, Les	89D	341	$ .01	$ .05
Krukow, Mike	89D	258	$ .01	$ .05	Lancaster, Les	90D	628	$ .01	$ .04
Krukow, Mike	89DBB	135	$ .01	$ .05	Lancaster, Les	90DL	361	$ .01	$ .15
Kuenn, Harvey	82D	578	$ .01	$ .05	Lancaster, Les	91D	256	$ .01	$ .03
Kuenn, Harvey	83D	608	$ .01	$ .05	Landestoy, Rafael	81D	19	$ .01	$ .05
Kuiper, Duane	81D	319	$ .01	$ .05	Landreaux, Ken	81D	565	$ .01	$ .05
Kuiper, Duane	82D	198	$ .01	$ .05	Landreaux, Ken	82D	388	$ .01	$ .05
Kuiper, Duane	84D	553	$ .03	$ .10	Landreaux, Ken	83D	236	$ .01	$ .05
Kunkel, Jeff	85D	587	$ .01	$ .08	Landreaux, Ken	84D	470	$ .03	$ .10
Kunkel, Jeff	89D	496	$ .01	$ .05	Landreaux, Ken	85D	494	$ .01	$ .08
Kunkel, Jeff	90D	496	$ .01	$ .04	Landreaux, Ken	86D	470	$ .01	$ .06
Kuntz, Rusty	81D	282	$ .01	$ .05	Landreaux, Ken	87D	352	$ .01	$ .05
Kuntz, Rusty	85D	516	$ .01	$ .08	Landrum, Bill	90D	668	$ .01	$ .04
Kutcher, Randy	87D	547	$ .01	$ .05	Landrum, Bill	90DL	222	$ .01	$ .15
Kutzler, Jerry	90D	503	$ .01	$ .04	Landrum, Bill	91D	350	$ .01	$ .03
Kutzler, Jerry	90DR	25	$ .01	$ .10	Landrum, Tito	82D	292	$ .01	$ .05
Lacey, Bob	81D	240	$ .01	$ .05	Landrum, Tito	83D	498	$ .01	$ .05
Lachmann, Rene	82D	600	$ .01	$ .05	Landrum, Tito	85D	168	$ .01	$ .08
LaCock, Pete	81D	344	$ .01	$ .05	Landrum, Tito	86D	425	$ .01	$ .06
LaCorte, Frank	81D	143	$ .01	$ .05	Landrum, Tito	87D	386	$ .01	$ .05
LaCorte, Frank	82D	270	$ .01	$ .05	Langford, Rick	81D	238	$ .01	$ .05
LaCorte, Frank	83D	218	$ .01	$ .05	Langford, Rick	82D	161	$ .01	$ .05
LaCorte, Frank	84D	283	$ .03	$ .10	Langford, Rick	83D	365	$ .01	$ .05
LaCoss, Mike	81D	183	$ .01	$ .05	Langston, Mark	85D	557	$1.00	$4.50
LaCoss, Mike	82D	440	$ .01	$ .05	Langston, Mark	86D	118	$ .05	$ .35
LaCoss, Mike	83D	344	$ .01	$ .05	Langston, Mark	87D	568	$ .01	$ .20
LaCoss, Mike	84D	206	$ .03	$ .10	Langston, Mark	88D	317	$ .01	$ .10
LaCoss, Mike	85D	405	$ .01	$ .08	Langston, Mark	88DBB	136	$ .01	$ .10
LaCoss, Mike	87D	636	$ .01	$ .05	Langston, Mark	88DK	20	$ .01	$ .10
LaCoss, Mike	88D	436	$ .01	$ .05	Langston, Mark	89D	227	$ .01	$ .15
LaCoss, Mike	89D	602	$ .01	$ .05	Langston, Mark	89DBB	68	$ .01	$ .10
LaCoss, Mike	90D	652	$ .01	$ .04	Langston, Mark	90D	338	$ .01	$ .04
LaCoss, Mike	90DL	463	$ .01	$ .15	Langston, Mark	90DL	155	$ .01	$ .20
Lacy, Lee	81D	376	$ .01	$ .05	Langston, Mark	91D	190	$ .01	$ .03
Lacy, Lee	82D	276	$ .01	$ .05	Langston, Mark	91DBC	1	$ .01	$ .05
Lacy, Lee	83D	276	$ .01	$ .05	Lankford, Ray	91DLP	10	$1.00	$15.00
Lacy, Lee	84D	479	$ .03	$ .10	Lankford, Ray	91DRR	43	$ .01	$1.00
Lacy, Lee	85D	508	$ .01	$ .08	Lansford, Carney	81D	409	$ .01	$ .25
Lacy, Lee	86D	228	$ .01	$ .06	Lansford, Carney	82D	82	$ .01	$ .25
Lacy, Lee	87D	336	$ .01	$ .05	Lansford, Carney	83D	408	$ .01	$ .05
Ladd, Pete	84D	124	$ .03	$ .10	Lansford, Carney	84D	176	$ .03	$ .10
Ladd, Peter	85D	271	$ .01	$ .08	Lansford, Carney	85D	345	$ .01	$ .08
Ladd, Pete	87D	660	$ .01	$ .15	Lansford, Carney	85DK	8	$ .03	$ .10
LaFrancois, Roger	83D	534	$ .01	$ .05	Lansford, Carney	86D	131	$ .01	$ .06
Laga, Mike	84D	491	$ .03	$ .10	Lansford, Carney	87D	158	$ .01	$ .05
Laga, Mike	86D	578	$ .01	$ .06	Lansford, Carney	88D	178	$ .01	$ .05
Laga, Mike	87D	293	$ .01	$ .05	Lansford, Carney	88DBB	246	$ .01	$ .05
Lahti, Jeff	84D	327	$ .03	$ .10	Lansford, Carney	89D	243	$ .10	$ .04
Lahti, Jeff	86D	475	$ .01	$ .06	Lansford, Carney	89DBB	22	$ .01	$ .05
Lahti, Jeff	87D	577	$ .01	$ .05	Lansford, Carney	90D	95	$ .01	$ .04
Lake, Steve	84D	198	$ .03	$ .10	Lansford, Carney	90DL	213	$ .01	$ .15
Lake, Steve	87D	604	$ .01	$ .05	Lansford, Carney	91D	273	$ .01	$ .03
Lake, Steve	88D	510	$ .01	$ .05	LaPoint, Dave	83D	544	$ .01	$ .30
Lake, Steve	90D	431	$ .01	$ .04	LaPoint, Dave	84D	290	$ .03	$ .10
Lake, Steve	90DL	395	$ .01	$ .15	LaPoint, Dave	85D	138	$ .01	$ .08
Lake, Steve	91D	334	$ .01	$ .03	LaPoint, Dave	86D	387	$ .01	$ .06
Lamp, Dennis	81D	573	$ .01	$ .05	LaPoint, Dave	87D	607	$ .01	$ .05

Player	Year	No.	VG	EX/MT
LaPoint, Dave	88D	552	$ .01	$ .05
LaPoint, Dave	88DBB	123	$ .01	$ .05
LaPoint, Dave	89D	488	$ .01	$ .05
LaPoint, Dave	89DBB	244	$ .01	$ .05
LaPoint, Dave	89DTR	27	$ .01	$ .05
LaPoint, Dave	90D	72	$ .01	$ .04
LaPoint, Dave	91D	481	$ .01	$ .03
Larkin, Barry	87D	492	$1.00	$4.00
Larkin, Barry	88D	492	$ .15	$ .75
Larkin, Barry	88DBB	222	$ .05	$ .25
Larkin, Barry	89D	257	$ .05	$ .25
Larkin, Barry	89DBB	110	$ .01	$ .15
Larkin, Barry	90D	71	$ .01	$ .10
Larkin, Barry	90DL	18	$ .01	$ .35
Larkin, Barry	91D	471	$ .01	$ .10
Larkin, Barry	91DK	5	$ .01	$ .05
Larkin, Barry	91DLP	3	$1.00	$10.00
Larkin, Gene	87DR	23	$ .05	$ .30
Larkin, Gene	88D	564	$ .01	$ .15
Larkin, Gene	88DBB	158	$ .01	$ .05
Larkin, Gene	89D	355	$ .01	$ .05
Larkin, Gene	90D	436	$ .01	$ .04
Larkin, Gene	90DL	215	$ .01	$ .15
Larkin, Gene	91D	152	$ .01	$ .03
Laroche, Dave	82D	569	$ .01	$ .05
Larussa, Tony	81D	402	$ .01	$ .05
Larussa, Tony	82D	319	$ .01	$ .05
Larussa, Tony	83D	571	$ .01	$ .05
Laskey, Bill	83D	424	$ .01	$ .05
Laskey, Bill	84D	358	$ .03	$ .10
Laskey, Bill	85D	387	$ .01	$ .08
Laskey, Bill	86D	585	$ .01	$ .06
LaSorda, Tom	81D	420	$ .01	$ .05
LaSorda, Tom	82D	110	$ .05	$ .20
LaSorda, Tom	83D	136	$ .02	$ .15
Laudner, Tim	82D	549	$ .01	$ .25
Laudner, Tim	83D	177	$ .01	$ .05
Laudner, Tim	85D	652	$ .01	$ .08
Laudner, Tim	86D	391	$ .01	$ .06
Laudner, Tim	87D	320	$ .01	$ .05
Laudner, Tim	88D	631	$ .01	$ .05
Laudner, Tim	89D	615	$ .01	$ .05
Laudner, Tim	90D	419	$ .01	$ .04
LaValliere, Mike	86DR	35	$ .05	$ .25
LaValliere, Mike	87D	331	$ .04	$ .20
LaValliere, Mike	88D	312	$ .01	$ .05
LaValliere, Mike	88DBB	129	$ .01	$ .05
LaValliere, Mike	89D	244	$ .01	$ .05
LaValliere, Mike	89DBB	201	$ .01	$ .05
LaValliere, Mike	90D	211	$ .01	$ .04
LaValliere, Mike	90DL	32	$ .01	$ .15
LaValliere, Mike	91D	121	$ .01	$ .03
Lavelle, Gary	81D	314	$ .01	$ .05
Lavelle, Gary	82D	60	$ .01	$ .05
Lavelle, Gary	83D	60	$ .01	$ .05
Lavelle, Gary	84D	573	$ .03	$ .10
Lavelle, Gary	85D	265	$ .01	$ .08
Lavelle, Gary	86D	621	$ .01	$ .06
Law, Rudy	81D	180	$ .01	$ .05
Law, Rudy	83D	521	$ .01	$ .05
Law, Rudy	84D	257	$ .03	$ .10
Law, Rudy	85D	244	$ .01	$ .08
Law, Rudy	86D	632	$ .01	$ .06
Law, Rudy	87D	343	$ .01	$ .05
Law, Vance	82D	582	$ .03	$ .20
Law, Vance	83D	117	$ .01	$ .05
Law, Vance	84D	546	$ .03	$ .10
Law, Vance	85D	122	$ .01	$ .08
Law, Vance	86D	132	$ .01	$ .06
Law, Vance	87D	212	$ .01	$ .05

Player	Year	No.	VG	EX/MT
Law, Vance	88D	212	$ .01	$ .05
Law, Vance	88DBB	60	$ .01	$ .05

Player	Year	No.	VG	EX/MT
Law, Vance	89D	276	$ .01	$ .05
Law, Vance	90D	629	$ .01	$ .04
Lawless, Tom	83D	400	$ .01	$ .05
Lawless, Tom	90D	681	$ .01	$ .04
Layana, Tim	90DL	410	$ .01	$ .25
Layana, Tim	90DR	23	$ .01	$ .15
Layana, Tim	91D	516	$ .01	$ .10
Lazorko, Jack	86D	628	$ .01	$ .06
Lazorko, Jack	88D	160	$ .01	$ .05
Lea, Charlie	82D	320	$ .01	$ .05
Lea, Charlie	83D	414	$ .01	$ .05
Lea, Charlie	84D	376	$ .03	$ .10
Lea, Charlie	85D	177	$ .01	$ .08
Lea, Charlie	85DK	21	$ .03	$ .10
Lea, Charlie	86D	376	$ .01	$ .06
Lea, Charlie	89D	473	$ .01	$ .05
Leach, Rick	82D	583	$ .01	$ .05
Leach, Rick	83D	81	$ .01	$ .05
Leach, Rick	87D	567	$ .01	$ .05
Leach, Rick	88D	518	$ .01	$ .05
Leach, Rick	89D	638	$ 01	$ .04
Leach, Rick	90D	613	$ .01	$ .04
Leach, Rick	90DL	436	$ .01	$ .15
Leach, Terry	83D	634	$ .01	$ .25
Leach, Terry	88D	603	$ .01	$ .15
Leach, Terry	89D	502	$ .01	$ .05
Leach, Terry	90D	534	$ .01	$ .04
Leach, Terry	90DL	360	$ .01	$ .15
Leach, Terry	91D	715	$ .01	$ .03
Leaf Set, Introduction	90DL	1	$ .01	$ .15
Leal, Luis	82D	255	$ .01	$ .05
Leal, Luis	83D	129	$ .01	$ .05
Leal, Luis	84D	485	$ .03	$ .10
Leal, Luis	85D	317	$ .01	$ .08
Leal, Luis	86D	315	$ .01	$ .06
Leary, Tim	86D	577	$ .05	$ .35
Leary, Tim	87D	232	$ .01	$ .05
Leary, Tim	89D	552	$ .01	$ .05
Leary, Tim	89DBB	309	$ .01	$ .05

DONRUSS

Player	Year	No.	VG	EX/MT	Player	Year	No.	VG	EX/MT
Leary, Tim	90D	670	$ .01	$ .04	Lemon, Chet	88DBB	147	$ .01	$ .05
Leary, Tim	90DL	148	$ .01	$ .15	Lemon, Chet	89D	209	$ .01	$ .05
Leary, Tim	91D	67	$ .01	$ .03	Lemon, Chet	89DBB	69	$ .01	$ .05
Lee, Bill	81D	211	$ .01	$ .05	Lemon, Chet	90D	60	$ .01	$ .04
Lee, Bill	82D	194	$ .01	$ .05	Lemon, Chet	90DL	133	$ .01	$ .15
Lee, Manny	87D	518	$ .01	$ .05	Lemon, Chet	91D	301	$ .01	$ .03
Lee, Manny	88D	650	$ .01	$ .15	Lentine, Jim	81D	250	$ .01	$ .05
Lee, Manny	89D	504	$ .01	$ .05	Leonard, Dennis	81D	102	$ .01	$ .05
Lee, Manny	90D	620	$ .01	$ .04	Leonard, Dennis	82D	264	$ .01	$ .05
Lee, Manny	90DL	370	$ .01	$ .15	Leonard, Dennis	83D	412	$ .01	$ .05
Lee, Manny	91D	211	$ .01	$ .03	Leonard, Jeff	81D	264	$ .01	$ .05
Lee, Terry	91D	752	$ .01	$ .10	Leonard, Jeff	82D	438	$ .02	$ .05
Leeper, Dave	86D	461	$ .01	$ .06	Leonard, Jeff	83D	474	$ .01	$ .05
Lefebvre, Joe	81D	571	$ .01	$ .05	Leonard, Jeff	84D	567	$ .03	$ .10
Lefebvre, Joe	82D	373	$ .01	$ .05	Leonard, Jeff	85D	358	$ .01	$ .08
Lefebvre, Joe	83D	523	$ .01	$ .05	Leonard, Jeff	86D	79	$ .01	$ .06
Lefebvre, Joe	84D	82	$ .03	$ .10	Leonard, Jeff	87D	391	$ .01	$ .05
Lefebvre, Joe	85D	285	$ .01	$ .08	Leonard, Jeff	88D	327	$ .01	$ .05
Lefferts, Craig	84D	388	$ .10	$ .50	Leonard, Jeffrey	89D	457	$ .01	$ .05
Lefferts, Craig	85D	261	$ .01	$ .08	Leonard, Jeffrey	89DBB	107	$ .01	$ .05
Lefferts, Craig	86D	307	$ .01	$ .06	Leonard, Jeffrey	89DTR	1	$ .01	$ .15
Lefferts, Craig	87D	387	$ .01	$ .05	Leonard, Jeffrey	90D	93	$ .01	$ .04
Lefferts, Craig	88D	515	$ .01	$ .05	Leonard, Jeffrey	90DL	219	$ .01	$ .15
Lefferts, Craig	89D	59	$ .01	$ .05	Leonard, Mark	91D	526	$ .01	$ .20
Lefferts, Craig	90D	376	$ .01	$ .04	Lerch, Randy	81D	574	$ .01	$ .05
Lefferts, Craig	90DL	339	$ .01	$ .15	Lerch, Randy	82D	595	$ .01	$ .05
Lefferts, Craig	91D	515	$ .01	$ .03	Lerch, Randy	85D	309	$ .01	$ .08
LeFlore, Ron	81D	576	$ .01	$ .05	Lesley, Brad	83D	547	$ .01	$ .05
LeFlore, Ron	82D	165	$ .01	$ .05	Lewis, Mark	91DRR	29	$ .01	$ .25
LeFlore, Ron	83D	543	$ .01	$ .05	Leyritz, Jim	90DL	465	$ .01	$ .25
Leibrandt, Charlie	81D	421	$ .10	$ .35	Leyritz, Jim	91D	219	$ .01	$ .10
Leibrandt, Charlie	83D	421	$ .01	$ .05	Lezcano, Carlos	81D	521	$ .01	$ .05
Leibrandt, Charlie	85D	399	$ .01	$ .08	Lezcano, Sixto	81D	207	$ .01	$ .05
Leibrandt, Charlie	86D	297	$ .01	$ .06	Lezcano, Sixto	82D	64	$ .01	$ .05
Leibrandt, Charlie	87D	220	$ .01	$ .05	Lezcano, Sixto	83D	499	$ .01	$ .05
Leibrandt, Charlie	88D	157	$ .01	$ .05	Lezcano, Sixto	85D	529	$ .01	$ .08
Leibrandt, Charlie	88DBB	151	$ .01	$ .05	Lilliquist, Derek	89D	653	$ .01	$ .10
Leibrandt, Charlie	89D	89	$ .01	$ .05	Lilliquist, Derek	89DBB	226	$ .01	$ .10
Leibrandt, Charlie	89DBB	231	$ .01	$ .05	Lilliquist, Derek	89DR	54	$ .01	$ .05
Leibrandt, Charlie	90D	208	$ .01	$ .04	Lilliquist, Derek	90D	286	$ .01	$ .05
Leibrandt, Charlie	90DL	428	$ .01	$ .15	Lilliquist, Derek	91D	570	$ .01	$ .03
Leibrandt, Charlie	91D	562	$ .01	$ .03	Lillis, Bob	84D	84	$ .03	$ .10
Leiper, Dave	87D	472	$ .01	$ .05	Linares, Rufino	82D	310	$ .01	$ .05
Leiper, Dave	88D	557	$ .01	$ .05	Linares, Rufino	83D	275	$ .01	$ .05
Leiper, Dave	89D	465	$ .01	$ .05	Lind, Jose	88DBB	145	$ .01	$ .20
Leiter, Al	88DBB	132	$ .01	$ .05	Lind, Jose	88DRR	38	$ .01	$ .25
Leiter, Al	88DR	27	$ .01	$ .05	Lind, Jose	89D	290	$ .01	$ .10
Leiter, Al	88DRR	43	$ .01	$ .15	Lind, Jose	89DBB	101	$ .01	$ .05
Leiter, Al	89D	315	$ .01	$ .05	Lind, Jose	90D	172	$ .01	$ .04
Leiter, Al	90D	543	$ .01	$ .04	Lind, Jose	90DL	77	$ .01	$ .15
Leiter, Al	91D	697	$ .01	$ .03	Lind, Jose	91D	58	$ .01	$ .03
Lemanczyk, Dave	81D	292	$ .01	$ .05	Lindeman, Jim	87DR	41	$ .01	$ .07
Lemaster, Johnnie	81D	432	$ .01	$ .05	Lindeman, Jim	87DRR	37	$ .01	$ .05
Lemaster, Johnnie	82D	524	$ .01	$ .05	Lindeman, Jim	88D	540	$ .01	$ .05
Lemaster, Johnnie	83D	125	$ .01	$ .05	Liriano, Nelson	88DRR	32	$ .01	$ .25
Lemaster, Johnnie	84D	649	$ .03	$ .10	Liriano, Nelson	89D	627	$ .01	$ .05
Lemaster, Johnnie	85D	114	$ .01	$ .08	Liriano, Nelson	89DBB	160	$ .01	$ .05
Lemke, Mark	89D	523	$ .01	$ .05	Liriano, Nelson	90D	267	$ .01	$ .04
Lemke, Mark	90D	624	$ .01	$ .04	Liriano, Nelson	91D	603	$ .01	$ .03
Lemke, Mark	90DR	43	$ .01	$ .10	Littell, Mark	81D	580	$ .01	$ .05
Lemke, Mark	91D	604	$ .01	$ .03	Littell, Mark	82D	442	$ .01	$ .05
Lemon, Bob	82D	635	$ .03	$ .20	Little, Bryan	84D	157	$ .03	$ .10
Lemon, Chet	81D	281	$ .01	$ .05	Little, Bryan	86D	452	$ .01	$ .06
Lemon, Chet	82D	291	$ .01	$ .05	Littlefield, John	81D	309	$ .01	$ .05
Lemon, Chet	83D	511	$ .01	$ .05	Littlefield, John	82D	145	$ .01	$ .05
Lemon, Chet	84D	171	$ .03	$ .10	Littlejohn, Dennis	81D	313	$ .01	$ .05
Lemon, Chet	85D	90	$ .01	$ .08	Litton, Greg	90D	453	$ .01	$ .25
Lemon, Chet	86D	90	$ .01	$ .06	Litton, Greg	90DL	331	$ .01	$ .25
Lemon, Chet	87D	353	$ .01	$ .05	Litton, Greg	91D	198	$ .01	$ .03
Lemon, Chet	88D	215	$ .01	$ .05	Lockwood, Skip	81D	217	$ .01	$ .05

Player	Year	No.	VG	EX/MT
Lollar, Tim	86D	620	$ .01	$ .06
Lollar, Tim	83D	61	$ .01	$ .05
Lollar, Tim	84D	284	$ .03	$ .10
Lollar, Tim	85D	324	$ .01	$ .08
Loman, Doug	85DRR	46	$ .01	$ .08
Lombardi, Phil	87D	401	$ .01	$ .05
Lombardozzi, Steve	86D	598	$ .01	$ .06
Lombardozzi, Steve	86DR	18	$ .02	$ .09
Lombardozzi, Steve	87D	318	$ .01	$ .05

Steve Lombardozzi 2B

Player	Year	No.	VG	EX/MT
Lombardozzi, Steve	88D	196	$ .01	$ .05
Lombardozzi, Steve	89D	554	$ .01	$ .05
Lombardozzi, Steve	90D	688	$ .01	$ .05
Long, Bill	87DR	48	$ .01	$ .07
Long, Bill	88D	306	$ .01	$ .05
Long, Bill	89D	573	$ .01	$ .05
Lopes, Davey	81D	416	$ .02	$ .15
Lopes, Davey	82D	327	$ .01	$ .05
Lopes, Davey	83D	339	$ .01	$ .05
Lopes, Davey	84D	400	$ .03	$ .10
Lopes, Davey	85D	604	$ .01	$ .08
Lopes, Davey	86D	388	$ .01	$ .06
Lopes, Davey	86DK	9	$ .01	$ .06
Lopes, Davey	87D	455	$ .01	$ .05
Lopez, Aurelio	82D	359	$ .01	$ .05
Lopez, Aurelio	84D	516	$ .03	$ .10
Lopez, Aurelio	85D	349	$ .01	$ .08
Lopez, Aurelio	86D	293	$ .01	$ .06
Lopez, Aurelio	87D	629	$ .01	$ .05
Lovullo, Torey	89DR	17	$ .01	$ .10
Lowenstein, John	81D	235	$ .01	$ .05
Lowenstein, John	82D	599	$ .01	$ .05
Lowenstein, John	83D	153	$ .01	$ .05
Lowenstein, John	84D	228	$ .03	$ .10
Lowenstein, John	85D	245	$ .01	$ .08
Lowry, Dwight	87D	338	$ .01	$ .05
Loynd, Mike	87D	506	$ .01	$ .05
Loynd, Mike	88D	550	$ .01	$ .05
Lozado, Willie	85D	595	$ .01	$ .08
Lubratich, Steve	84D	377	$ .03	$ .10
Lucas, Gary	81D	243	$ .01	$ .05

Player	Year	No.	VG	EX/MT
Lucas, Gary	82D	296	$ .01	$ .05
Lucas, Gary	83D	187	$ .01	$ .05
Lucas, Gary	84D	307	$ .03	$ .10
Lucas, Gary	85D	498	$ .01	$ .08
Lucas, Gary	86D	453	$ .01	$ .06
Lucas, Gary	87D	618	$ .01	$ .05
Lucas, Gary	88D	579	$ .01	$ .05
Luecken, Rick	90D	562	$ .01	$ .10
Lugo, Urbano	86D	329	$ .01	$ .06
Lum, Mike	82D	300	$ .01	$ .05
Lusader, Scott	88D	615	$ .03	$ .25
Lusader, Scott	90D	696	$ .01	$ .04
Luzinski, Greg	81D	175	$ .03	$ .20
Luzinski, Greg	82D	193	$ .02	$ .15
Luzinski, Greg	83D	395	$ .01	$ .05
Luzinski, Greg	84D	122	$ .03	$ .10
Luzinski, Greg	85D	546	$ .01	$ .08
Lyle, Sparky	81D	284	$ .02	$ .15
Lyle, Sparky	82D	189	$ .01	$ .05
Lynch, Ed	82D	641	$ .01	$ .05
Lynch, Ed	83D	308	$ .01	$ .05
Lynch, Ed	84D	75	$ .03	$ .10
Lynch, Ed	85D	623	$ .01	$ .08
Lynch, Ed	86D	631	$ .01	$ .06
Lynch, Ed	87D	516	$ .01	$ .05
Lynch, Ed	88D	77	$ .01	$ .05
Lynn, Fred	81D	218	$ .05	$ .20
Lynn, Fred	82D	367	$ .05	$ .20
Lynn, Fred	83D	241	$ .03	$ .20
Lynn, Fred	84D	108	$ .04	$ .15
Lynn, Fred	84DK	17	$ .08	$ .25
Lynn, Fred	85D	133	$ .03	$ .20
Lynn, Fred	86D	245	$ .05	$ .20
Lynn, Fred	87D	108	$ .01	$ .25
Lynn, Fred	87DK	9	$ .05	$ .20
Lynn, Fred	88D	248	$ .01	$ .05
Lynn, Fred	89D	563	$ .01	$ .10
Lynn, Fred	90DL	188	$ .01	$ .15
Lynn, Fred	91D	673	$ .01	$ .03
Lyons, Barry	88D	619	$ .05	$ .20
Lyons, Barry	89D	572	$ .01	$ .05
Lyons, Barry	90D	526	$ .01	$ .04
Lyons, Barry	90DL	119	$ .01	$ .15
Lyons, Steve	85DRR	29	$ .01	$ .08
Lyons, Steve	86D	579	$ .01	$ .06
Lyons, Steve	87D	409	$ .01	$ .05
Lyons, Steve	88D	532	$ .01	$ .05
Lyons, Steve	89D	253	$ .01	$ .05
Lyons, Steve	90D	651	$ .01	$ .04
Lysander, Rick	84D	560	$ .03	$ .10
Lysander, Rick	85D	560	$ .01	$ .08
Maas, Kevin	90DL	446	$ .01	$ 10.00
Maas, Kevin	91D	554	$ .01	$ .40
MacDonald, Bob	91D	636	$ .01	$ .75
Macfarlane, Mike	88DR	55	$ .01	$ .15
Macfarlane, Mike	89D	416	$ .01	$ .10
Macfarlane, Mike	90D	498	$ .01	$ .04
Macfarlane, Mike	90DL	389	$ .01	$ .15
Macfarlane, Mike	91D	313	$ .01	$ .03
Macha, Ken	81D	540	$ .01	$ .05
Machado, Julio	90DR	41	$ .01	$ .10
Machado, Julio	90DRR	47	$ .01	$ .25
Machado, Julio	91D	764	$ .01	$ .03
Mack, Shane	87DR	42	$ .01	$ .15
Mack, Shane	88D	411	$ .01	$ .05
Mack, Shane	89D	538	$ .01	$ .05
Mack, Shane	90DL	136	$ .01	$ .15
Mack, Shane	91D	320	$ .01	$ .03
Mackanin, Pete	82D	354	$ .01	$ .05
Macko, Steve	81D	535	$ .01	$ .05

DONRUSS

Player	Year	No.	VG	EX/MT	Player	Year	No.	VG	EX/MT
Madden, Mike	84D	161	$ .03	$ .10	Magrane, Joe	88D	140	$ .01	$ .25
Maddox, Elliott	81D	397	$ .01	$ .05	Magrane, Joe	88DBB	100	$ .01	$ .15
Maddox, Garry	81D	55	$ .01	$ .05	Magrane, Joe	89D	201	$ .01	$ .10
Maddox, Garry	82D	315	$ .01	$ .05	Magrane, Joe	89DBB	131	$ .01	$ .05
Maddox, Garry	83D	63	$ .01	$ .05	Magrane, Joe	90D	163	$ .01	$ .04
Maddox, Garry	84D	305	$ .03	$ .10	Magrane, Joe	90DK	13	$ .01	$ .10
Maddox, Garry	85D	137	$ .01	$ .08	Magrane, Joe	90DL	11	$ .01	$ .15
Maddox, Garry	86D	407	$ .01	$ .06	Magrane, Joe	91D	295	$ .01	$ .03
Maddux, Greg	87DR	52	$ .05	$ .50	Magrann, Tom	90D	374	$ .01	$ .10
Maddux, Greg	87DRR	36	$ .15	$1.50	Mahler, Rick	82D	349	$ .03	$ .20
Maddux, Greg	88D	539	$ .05	$ .25	Mahler, Rick	83D	527	$ .01	$ .05
Maddux, Greg	88DBB	82	$ .01	$ .05	Mahler, Rick	85D	385	$ .01	$ .08
Maddux, Greg	89D	373	$ .01	$ .05	Mahler, Rick	86D	77	$ .01	$ .06
Maddux, Greg	89DBB	37	$ .01	$ .05	Mahler, Rick	86DK	21	$ .01	$ .06
Maddux, Greg	90D	158	$ .01	$ .04	Mahler, Rick	87D	190	$ .01	$ .05
Maddux, Greg	90DL	25	$ .01	$ .15	Mahler, Rick	88D	389	$ .01	$ .05
Maddux, Greg	91D	374	$ .01	$ .03	Mahler, Rick	88DBB	114	$ .01	$ .05
Maddux, Mike	87D	535	$ .03	$ .25	Mahler, Rick	89D	222	$ .01	$ .05
Maddux, Mike	89D	487	$ .01	$ .05	Mahler, Rick	89DBB	286	$ .01	$ .05
					Mahler, Rick	89DTR	24	$ .01	$ .15
					Mahler, Rick	90D	375	$ .01	$ .05
					Maldonado, Candy	83D	262	$ .20	$1.00
					Maldonado, Candy	84D	93	$ .05	$ .40
					Maldonado, Candy	85D	250	$ .01	$ .08
					Maldonado, Candy	87D	327	$ .01	$ .05
					Maldonado, Candy	88D	391	$ .05	$ .20
					Maldonado, Candy	88DBB	247	$ .01	$ .05
					Maldonado, Candy	89D	177	$ .01	$ .05
					Maldonado, Candy	90D	611	$ .01	$ .04
					Maldonado, Candy	90DL	338	$ .01	$ .15
					Maldonado, Candy	91D	480	$ .01	$ .03
					Maldonado, Candy	91DMVP	391	$ .01	$ .03
					Mann, Kelly	90DRR	46	$ .01	$ .10
					Mann, Kelly	91D	736	$ .01	$ .03
					Manning, Rick	81D	202	$ .01	$ .05
					Manning, Rick	82D	85	$ .01	$ .05
					Manning, Rick	83D	198	$ .01	$ .05
					Manning, Rick	84D	170	$ .03	$ .10
					Manning, Rick	85D	237	$ .01	$ .08
					Manning, Rick	86D	368	$ .01	$ .06
					Manning, Rick	87D	521	$ .01	$ .05
					Manning, Rick	88D	486	$ .01	$ .05
					Manrique, Fred	88D	493	$ .01	$ .05
					Manrique, Fred	89D	489	$ .01	$ .05
					Manrique, Fred	90D	165	$ .01	$ .05
					Manrique, Fred	90DL	518	$ .01	$ .15
					Manto, Jeff	91D	602	$ .01	$ .10
					Manwaring, Kirt	88DRR	39	$ .01	$ .25
					Manwaring, Kirt	89D	494	$ .01	$ .05
Maddux, Mike	90D	312	$ .01	$ .04	Manwaring, Kirt	89DBB	330	$ .01	$ .05
Madlock, Bill	81D	252	$ .05	$ .30	Manwaring, Kirt	90D	59	$ .01	$ .04
Madlock, Bill	82D	653	$ .03	$ .20	Marak, Paul	91DRR	413	$ .01	$ .10
Madlock, Bill	83D	311	$ .02	$ .15	Marshall, Mike	82D	562	$ .15	$1.00
Madlock, Bill	84D	113	$ .04	$ .25	Marshall, Mike	83D	362	$ .01	$ .25
Madlock, Bill	84DK	20	$ .08	$ .25	Marshall, Mike	84D	348	$ .03	$ .10
Madlock, Bill	85D	200	$ .03	$ .10	Marshall, Mike	85D	296	$ .01	$ .08
Madlock, Bill	86D	617	$ .02	$ .15	Marshall, Mike	85DK	12	$ .03	$ .10
Madlock, Bill	87D	155	$ .01	$ .05	Marshall, Mike	86D	52	$ .01	$ .06
Madlock, Bill	88D	496	$ .01	$ .05	Marshall, Mike	87D	176	$ .01	$ .05
Madrid, Alex	89D	604	$ .01	$ .05	Marshall, Mike	88D	229	$ .01	$ .05
Magadan, Dave	87D	575	$ .25	$2.00	Marshall, Mike	88DBB	178	$ .01	$ .05
Magadan, Dave	87DR	34	$ .10	$ .75	Marshall, Mike	89D	110	$ .01	$ .05
Magadan, Dave	88D	323	$ .01	$ .20	Marshall, Mike	89DBB	204	$ .01	$ .05
Magadan, Dave	89D	408	$ .01	$ .10	Marshall, Mike	90D	84	$ .01	$ .04
Magadan, Dave	89DBB	264	$ .01	$ .05	Marshall, Mike	90DL	224	$ .01	$ .15
Magadan, Dave	90D	383	$ .01	$ .04	Marshall, Mike	91D	625	$ .01	$ .03
Magadan, Dave	90DL	330	$ .01	$ .15	Martin, Billy	81D	479	$ .05	$ .20
Magadan, Dave	91D	362	$ .01	$ .03	Martin, Billy	82D	491	$ .03	$ .20
Magadan, Dave	91DK	17	$ .01	$ .05	Martin, Billy	83D	575	$ .02	$ .15
Magrane, Joe	87DR	40	$ .15	$ .75	Martin, Jerry	81D	555	$ .01	$ .05

Player	Year	No.	VG	EX/MT	Player	Year	No.	VG	EX/MT
Martin, Jerry	82D	298	$ .01	$ .05	Marzano, John	91D	346	$ .01	$ .03
Martin, Jerry	83D	138	$ .01	$ .05	Mason, Mike	85D	281	$ .01	$ .08
Martin, John	82D	343	$ .01	$ .05	Mason, Mike	86D	422	$ .01	$ .06
Martin, John	83D	617	$ .01	$ .05	Mason, Mike	87D	284	$ .01	$ .05
Martin, Renie	81D	103	$ .01	$ .05	Mason, Roger	86D	633	$ .01	$ .06
Martin, Renie	82D	238	$ .01	$ .05	Mason, Roger	87D	204	$ .01	$ .05
Martin, Renie	83D	272	$ .01	$ .05	Mata, Vic	85D	629	$ .01	$ .08
Martin, Renie	84D	445	$ .03	$ .10	Mathews, Greg	86DR	26	$ .01	$ .05
Martinez, Alfredo	81D	172	$ .01	$ .05	Mathews, Greg	87D	208	$ .01	$ .05
Martinez, Buck	81D	444	$ .01	$ .05	Mathews, Greg	88D	84	$ .01	$ .05
Martinez, Buck	82D	561	$ .01	$ .05	Mathews, Greg	89D	281	$ .01	$ .05
Martinez, Buck	83D	178	$ .01	$ .05	Matlack, Jon	81D	266	$ .01	$ .05
Martinez, Buck	84D	612	$ .03	$ .10	Matlack, Jon	82D	215	$ .01	$ .05
Martinez, Carlos	89DR	14	$ .01	$ .20	Matlack, Jon	83D	195	$ .01	$ .05
Martinez, Carlos	90D	531	$ .01	$ .15	Matlack, Jon	84D	378	$ .03	$ .10
Martinez, Carlos	90DL	438	$ .01	$ .15	Matthews, Gary	81D	306	$ .02	$ .15
Martinez, Carlos	91D	465	$ .01	$ .10	Matthews, Gary	82D	441	$ .01	$ .05
Martinez, Carmelo	84D	623	$ .05	$ .40	Matthews, Gary	83D	420	$ .01	$ .05
Martinez, Carmelo	85D	478	$ .01	$ .08	Matthews, Gary	84D	233	$ .03	$ .10
Martinez, Carmelo	86D	324	$ .01	$ .06	Matthews, Gary	85D	239	$ .01	$ .08
Martinez, Carmelo	88D	287	$ .01	$ .05	Matthews, Gary	86D	76	$ .01	$ .06
Martinez, Carmelo	89D	601	$ .01	$ .05	Mattick, Bobby	81D	570	$ .01	$ .05
Martinez, Carmelo	90D	482	$ .01	$ .04	Mattingly, Don	84D	248	$14.00	$70.00
Martinez, Carmelo	90DL	448	$ .01	$ .15	Mattingly, Don	85D	295	$4.00	$13.00
Martinez, Dave	87D	488	$ .01	$ .25	Mattingly, Don	85D	651	$1.00	$5.00
Martinez, Dave	88D	438	$ .01	$ .05	Mattingly, Don	85DK	7	$1.50	$5.00
Martinez, Dave	88DBB	149	$ .01	$ .05	Mattingly, Don	86D	173	$1.75	$5.00
Martinez, Dave	89D	102	$ .01	$ .05	Mattingly, Don	87D	52	$1.00	$2.50
Martinez, Dave	90D	452	$ .01	$ .04	Mattingly, Don	88D	217	$ .40	$1.50
Martinez, Dave	90DL	318	$ .01	$ .15	Mattingly, Don	88DBB	1	$ .25	$1.00
Martinez, Dave	91D	237	$ .01	$ .03	Mattingly, Don	88DBC	21	$ .30	$ .50
Martinez, Dennis	81D	533	$ .01	$ .05	Mattingly, Don	89D	74	$ .25	$ .75
Martinez, Dennis	82D	79	$ .01	$ .05	Mattingly, Don	89DBB	1	$ .01	$1.00
Martinez, Dennis	83D	231	$ .01	$ .05	Mattingly, Don	89DK	26	$ .10	$ .75
Martinez, Dennis	84D	633	$ .03	$ .10	Mattingly, Don	90D	190	$ .01	$ .35
Martinez, Dennis	85D	514	$ .01	$ .08	Mattingly, Don	90DL	69	$ .01	$1.00
Martinez, Dennis	86D	454	$ .01	$ .06	Mattingly, Don	91D	107	$ .01	$ .20
Martinez, Dennis	88D	549	$ .01	$ .05	Mattingly, Don	91DLP	22	$1.00	$20.00
Martinez, Dennis	88DBB	146	$ .01	$ .05	Matula, Rick	81D	317	$ .01	$ .05
Martinez, Dennis	89D	106	$ .01	$ .05	Matuszek, Len	84D	549	$ .03	$ .10
Martinez, Dennis	89DBB	90	$ .01	$ .05	Matuszek, Len	85D	259	$ .01	$ .08
Martinez, Dennis	90D	156	$ .01	$ .04	Matuszek, Len	86D	494	$ .01	$ .06
Martinez, Dennis	90DL	54	$ .01	$ .15	Matuszek, Len	87D	423	$ .01	$ .05
Martinez, Dennis	91D	139	$ .01	$ .03	Mauch, Gene	82D	141	$ .01	$ .05
Martinez, Edgar	88DR	36	$ .05	$ .60	May, Derrick	91DRR	36	$ .01	$ .10
Martinez, Edgar	89D	645	$ .01	$ .30	May, Lee	82D	570	$ .01	$ .05
Martinez, Edgar	89DR	15	$ .01	$ .25	May, Lee	83D	538	$ .01	$ .05
Martinez, Edgar	90DL	299	$ .01	$ .35	May, Milt	81D	193	$ .01	$ .05
Martinez, Edgar	91D	606	$ .01	$ .03	May, Milt	82D	503	$ .01	$ .05
Martinez, Edgar	91DK	16	$ .01	$ .05	May, Milt	83D	312	$ .01	$ .05
Martinez, Ramon	89D	464	$ .25	$1.35	May, Milt	84D	386	$ .03	$ .10
Martinez, Ramon	89DR	45	$ .25	$1.25	May, Milt	85D	410	$ .01	$ .08
Martinez, Ramon	90D	685	$ .01	$ .40	May, Rudy	82D	325	$ .01	$ .05
Martinez, Ramon	90DL	147	$ .01	$2.50	May, Rudy	83D	135	$ .01	$ .05
Martinez, Ramon	91D	557	$ .01	$ .30	May, Rudy	84D	626	$ .03	$ .10
Martinez, Ramon	91DK	15	$ .01	$ .15	May, Scott	89D	636	$ .01	$ .05
Martinez, Ramon	91DLP	5	$1.00	$15.00	Mayberry, John	81D	29	$ .01	$ .05
Martinez, Silvio	81D	429	$ .01	$ .05	Mayberry, John	82D	306	$ .01	$ .05
Martinez, Silvio	82D	469	$ .01	$ .05	Mayberry, John	82DK	25	$ .01	$ .05
Martinez, Tino	91DLP	24	$1.00	$10.00	Mayne, Brent	91D	617	$ .01	$ .10
Martinez, Tino	91DRR	28	$ .01	$ .35	Mazzilli, Lee	81D	34	$ .01	$ .05
Martinez, Tippy	81D	354	$ .01	$ .05	Mazzilli, Lee	82D	49	$ .01	$ .05
Martinez, Tippy	82D	205	$ .01	$ .05	Mazzilli, Lee	83D	638	$ .01	$ .05
Martinez, Tippy	83D	357	$ .01	$ .05	Mazzilli, Lee	84D	166	$ .03	$ .10
Martinez, Tippy	84D	472	$ .03	$ .10	Mazzilli, Lee	85D	386	$ .01	$ .08
Martinez, Tippy	85D	210	$ .01	$ .08	Mazzilli, Lee	86D	288	$ .01	$ .06
Martinez, Tippy	86D	514	$ .01	$ .06	Mazzilli, Lee	87D	562	$ .01	$ .05
Martz, Randy	82D	126	$ .01	$ .05	Mazzilli, Lee	88D	614	$ .01	$ .15
Martz, Randy	83D	151	$ .01	$ .05	Mazzilli, Lee	88DBB	209	$ .01	$ .05
Marzano, John	88D	421	$ .10	$ .35	Mazzilli, Lee	90D	584	$ .01	$ .04

DONRUSS

Player	Year	No.	VG	EX/MT	Player	Year	No.	VG	EX/MT
McBride, Bake	81D	404	$ .03	$ .20	McGee, Willie	85D	475	$ .10	$ .50
McBride, Bake	82D	497	$ .01	$ .05	McGee, Willie	86D	109	$ .05	$ .20
McCaskill, Kirk	86D	474	$ .10	$ .50	McGee, Willie	86D	651	$ .03	$ .25
McCaskill, Kirk	87D	381	$ .01	$ .15	McGee, Willie	86DK	3	$ .05	$ .20
McCaskill, Kirk	88D	381	$ .01	$ .05	McGee, Willie	87D	84	$ .01	$ .15
McCaskill, Kirk	88DBB	83	$ .01	$ .05	McGee, Willie	88D	307	$ .01	$ .05
McCaskill, Kirk	89D	136	$ .01	$ .05	McGee, Willie	88DBB	131	$ .01	$ .15
McCaskill, Kirk	89DBB	83	$ .01	$ .05	McGee, Willie	89D	161	$ .01	$ .05
McCaskill, Kirk	90D	170	$ .01	$ .04	McGee, Willie	90D	632	$ .01	$ .04
McCaskill, Kirk	90DL	247	$ .01	$ .15	McGee, Willie	90DL	367	$ .01	$ .25
McCaskill, Kirk	91D	637	$ .01	$ .03	McGee, Willie	91D	666	$ .01	$ .03
McCatty, Steve	81D	478	$ .01	$ .05	McGee, Willie	91DBC	22	$ .01	$ .03
McCatty, Steve	82D	35	$ .01	$ .05	McGlothen, Lynn	81D	562	$ .01	$ .05
McCatty, Steve	83D	491	$ .01	$ .05	McGraw, Tug	81D	273	$ .02	$ .15
McCatty, Steve	84D	420	$ .03	$ .10	McGraw, Tug	82D	420	$ .01	$ .05
McCatty, Steve	85D	497	$ .01	$ .08	McGraw, Tug	83D	371	$ .02	$ .15
McClendon, Lloyd	89D	595	$ .01	$ .05	McGraw, Tug	84D	547	$ .03	$ .10
McClendon, Lloyd	89DBB	228	$ .01	$ .05	McGregor, Scott	81D	114	$ .01	$ .05
McClendon, Lloyd	90D	341	$ .01	$ .04	McGregor, Scott	82D	331	$ .01	$ .05
McClure, Bob	81D	510	$ .01	$ .05	McGregor, Scott	83D	483	$ .01	$ .05
McClure, Bob	83D	582	$ .01	$ .05	McGregor, Scott	84D	594	$ .03	$ .10
McClure, Bob	84D	359	$ .03	$ .10	McGregor, Scott	85D	413	$ .01	$ .08
McClure, Bob	85D	536	$ .01	$ .08	McGregor, Scott	86D	291	$ .01	$ .06
McClure, Bob	90D	470	$ .01	$ .04	McGregor, Scott	87D	520	$ .01	$ .05
McClure, Rob	88D	529	$ .01	$ .05	McGriff, Fred	86DRR	28	$4.00	$16.00
McCullers, Lance	86DRR	41	$ .01	$ .25	McGriff, Fred	87D	621	$ .25	$3.50
McCullers, Lance	87D	237	$ .01	$ .05	McGriff, Fred	87DR	31	$ .25	$2.00
McCullers, Lance	88D	451	$ .01	$ .05	McGriff, Fred	88D	195	$ .15	$ .35
McCullers, Lance	88DBB	210	$ .01	$ .05	McGriff, Fred	88DBB	160	$ .05	$ .25
McCullers, Lance	89D	129	$ .01	$ .05	McGriff, Fred	89D	70	$ .01	$ .15
McCullers, Lance	89DBB	220	$ .01	$ .05	McGriff, Fred	89DBB	104	$ .01	$ .20
McCullers, Lance	89DTR	13	$ .01	$ .05	McGriff, Fred	89DBC	19	$ .01	$ .15
McCullers, Lance	90D	433	$ .01	$ .04	McGriff, Fred	89DK	16	$ .01	$ .15
McCullers, Lance	90DL	456	$ .01	$ .15	McGriff, Fred	90D	188	$ .01	$ .15
McCullers, Lance	91D	133	$ .01	$ .03	McGriff, Fred	90DL	132	$ .01	$ .20
McDonald, Ben	90DL	249	$ .01	$5.00	McGriff, Fred	91D	261	$ .01	$ .10
McDonald, Ben	90DR	30	$ .01	$1.00	McGriff, Fred	91DMVP	389	$ .01	$ .03
McDonald, Ben	90DRR	32	$ .01	$1.50	McGriff, Terry	87D	512	$ .01	$ .15
McDonald, Ben	91D	485	$ .01	$ .25	McGriff, Terry	88D	556	$ .01	$ .05
McDowell, Jack	88DR	40	$ .01	$ .35	McGwire, Mark	87DR	1	$ .70	$3.50
McDowell, Jack	88DRR	47	$ .01	$ .45	McGwire, Mark	87DRR	46	$2.65	$8.00
McDowell, Jack	89D	531	$ .01	$ .10	McGwire, Mark	88D	256	$ .05	$ .50
McDowell, Jack	91D	57	$ .01	$ .03	McGwire, Mark	88DBB	169	$ .15	$ .50
McDowell, Oddibe	86D	56	$ .05	$ .25	McGwire, Mark	88DBC	23	$ .05	$ .35
McDowell, Oddibe	87D	161	$ .01	$ .05	McGwire, Mark	88DK	1	$ .05	$ .50
McDowell, Oddibe	88D	382	$ .01	$ .05	McGwire, Mark	89D	95	$ .05	$ .50
McDowell, Oddibe	89D	378	$ .01	$ .05	McGwire, Mark	89DBB	43	$ .01	$ .15
McDowell, Oddibe	89DTR	49	$ .01	$ .15	McGwire, Mark	90D	185	$ .01	$ .15
McDowell, Oddibe	90D	340	$ .01	$ .04	McGwire, Mark	90DAS	697	$ .01	$ .15
McDowell, Oddibe	90DL	112	$ .01	$ .15	McGwire, Mark	90DL	62	$ .01	$ .50
McDowell, Oddibe	91D	450	$ .01	$ .03	McGwire, Mark	91D	105	$ .01	$ .15
McDowell, Roger	86D	629	$ .15	$ .60	McGwire, Mark	91DAS	56	$ .01	$ .10
McDowell, Roger	87D	241	$ .01	$ .15	McGwire, Mark	91DBC	9	$ .01	$ .10
McDowell, Roger	88D	651	$ .01	$ .15	McIntosh, Tim	91DRR	414	$ .01	$ .10
McDowell, Roger	88DBB	126	$ .01	$ .05	McKay, Dave	81D	350	$ .01	$ .05
McDowell, Roger	89D	265	$ .01	$ .05	McKay, Dave	82D	391	$ .01	$ .05
McDowell, Roger	89DBB	16	$ .01	$ .05	McKay, Dave	83D	213	$ .01	$ .05
McDowell, Roger	90D	251	$ .01	$ .04	McKeon, Joel	86DR	55	$ .02	$ .09
McDowell, Roger	90DL	20	$ .01	$ .15	McLaughlin, Byron	81D	287	$ .01	$ .05
McDowell, Roger	91D	166	$ .01	$ .03	McLaughlin, Joey	81D	271	$ .01	$ .05
McElroy, Chuck	91D	709	$ .01	$ .03	McLaughlin, Joey	82D	507	$ .01	$ .05
McGaffigan, Andy	84D	309	$ .03	$ .10	McLaughlin, Joey	83D	255	$ .01	$ .05
McGaffigan, Andy	85D	646	$ .01	$ .08	McLaughlin, Joey	84D	617	$ .03	$ .10
McGaffigan, Andy	87D	380	$ .01	$ .05	McLemore, Mark	86DRR	35	$ .02	$ .15
McGaffigan, Andy	88D	380	$ .01	$ .05	McLemore, Mark	87D	479	$ .01	$ .05
McGaffigan, Andy	89D	338	$ .01	$ .05	McLemore, Mark	87DR	7	$ .01	$ .07
McGaffigan, Andy	90D	574	$ .01	$ .04	McLemore, Mark	88D	181	$ .01	$ .05
McGee, Willie	83D	190	$ .30	$3.00	McLemore, Mark	88DBB	251	$ .01	$ .05
McGee, Willie	84D	353	$ .10	$1.00	McLemore, Mark	89D	94	$ .01	$ .05
McGee, Willie	84D	625	$ .01	$ .25	McMurtry, Craig	84D	599	$ .03	$ .10

Player	Year	No.	VG	EX/MT
McMurtry, Craig	85D	188	$ .03	$ .10
McMurtry, Craig	89D	520	$ .01	$ .05
McNamara, John	82D	526	$ .01	$ .05
McRae, Brian	91D	575	$ .01	$ .50
McRae, Hal	81D	463	$ .02	$ .15
McRae, Hal	82D	196	$ .01	$ .05
McRae, Hal	83D	238	$ .01	$ .05
McRae, Hal	84D	297	$ .03	$ .10
McRae, Hal	84DK	11	$ .08	$ .25
McRae, Hal	85D	588	$ .01	$ .08
McRae, Hal	86D	521	$ .01	$ .06
McRae, Hal	87D	471	$ .01	$ .05
McReynolds, Kevin	84DRR	34	$2.75	$11.00
McReynolds, Kevin	85D	139	$ .25	$1.25
McReynolds, Kevin	86D	80	$ .10	$ .45
McReynolds, Kevin	87D	451	$ .01	$ .25
McReynolds, Kevin	87DK	14	$ .01	$ .25
McReynolds, Kevin	88D	617	$ .01	$ .15
McReynolds, Kevin	88DBB	153	$ .01	$ .15
McReynolds, Kevin	89D	99	$ .01	$ .10
McReynolds, Kevin	89DBB	70	$ .01	$ .10
McReynolds, Kevin	90D	218	$ .01	$ .10
McReynolds, Kevin	90DL	198	$ .01	$ .15
McReynolds, Kevin	91D	191	$ .01	$ .03
McWilliams, Larry	82D	527	$ .01	$ .05
McWilliams, Larry	83D	45	$ .01	$ .05
McWilliams, Larry	84D	566	$ .03	$ .10
McWilliams, Larry	85D	78	$ .01	$ .08
McWilliams, Larry	86D	264	$ .01	$ .06
McWilliams, Larry	89D	516	$ .01	$ .05
McWilliams, Larry	90D	709	$ .01	$ .04
Meacham, Bobby	84D	336	$ .03	$ .10
Meacham, Bobby	85D	126	$ .01	$ .08
Meacham, Bobby	86D	638	$ .01	$ .06
Meacham, Bobby	88D	616	$ .01	$ .15
Meads, Dave	87DR	46	$ .01	$ .07
Meads, David	88D	455	$ .01	$ .05
Meads, Dave	89D	424	$ .01	$ .05
Medich, Doc	81D	386	$ .01	$ .05
Medich, Doc	82D	142	$ .01	$ .05
Medina, Luis	89DR	20	$ .01	$ .10
Medina, Luis	89DRR	36	$ .01	$ .15
Medvin, Scott	89D	597	$ .01	$ .05
Meier, Dave	85D	147	$ .01	$ .08
Mejias, Sam	82D	295	$ .01	$ .05
Melendez, Francisco	89D	611	$ .01	$ .25
Melvin, Bob	86D	456	$ .01	$ .06
Melvin, Bob	87D	239	$ .01	$ .05
Melvin, Bob	88D	638	$ .01	$ .15
Melvin, Bob	90D	451	$ .01	$ .04
Melvin, Bob	90DL	382	$ .01	$ .15
Melvin, Bob	91D	335	$ .01	$ .03
Mendoza, Mario	81D	45	$ .01	$ .05
Mendoza, Mario	82D	394	$ .01	$ .05
Mercado, Orlando	84D	318	$ .03	$ .10
Mercker, Kent	90DRR	31	$ .01	$ .25
Mercker, Kent	91D	299	$ .01	$ .03
Meridith, Ron	86D	533	$ .01	$ .06
Merullo, Matt	89DR	50	$ .01	$ .10
Mesa, Jose	88D	601	$ .01	$ .15
Mesa, Jose	91D	765	$ .01	$ .03
Meulens, Hensley	89D	547	$ .15	$ .60
Meulens, Hensley	91DRR	31	$ .01	$ .10
Meyer, Brian	89D	640	$ .01	$ .04
Meyer, Brian	90D	648	$ .01	$ .04
Meyer, Dan	81D	43	$ .01	$ .05
Meyer, Dan	82D	176	$ .01	$ .05
Meyer, Dan	83D	413	$ .01	$ .05
Meyer, Joey	87D	460	$ .10	$ .30
Meyer, Joey	88DBB	239	$ .01	$ .05

Player	Year	No.	VG	EX/MT
Meyer, Joey	88DR	38	$ .01	$ .15
Meyer, Joey	88DRR	36	$ .01	$ .25
Meyer, Joey	89D	339	$ .01	$ .05
Michael, Gene	81D	500	$ .01	$ .05
Mielke, Gary	90D	679	$ .01	$ .10
Milacki, Bob	89D	651	$ .01	$ .15
Milacki, Bob	89DBB	254	$ .01	$ .10
Milacki, Bob	89DR	22	$ .01	$ .10
Milacki, Bob	90D	333	$ .01	$ .10
Milacki, Bob	90DL	402	$ .01	$ .20
Milacki, Bob	91D	69	$ .01	$ .03
Milbourne, Larry	81D	486	$ .01	$ .05
Milbourne, Larry	82D	614	$ .01	$ .05
Milbourne, Larry	83D	411	$ .01	$ .05
Miller, Darrell	85D	644	$ .01	$ .08
Miller, Darrell	88D	551	$ .01	$ .05
Miller, Eddie	82D	425	$ .01	$ .05
Miller, Keith	88D	562	$ .01	$ .10
Miller, Keith	89D	623	$ .01	$ .05
Miller, Keith	90D	507	$ .01	$ .04

KEITH MILLER OF

Player	Year	No.	VG	EX/MT
Miller, Keith	90DL	462	$ .01	$ .15
Miller, Keith	91D	248	$ .01	$ .03
Miller, Mike	84D	493	$ .03	$ .10
Miller, Rick	81D	294	$ .01	$ .05
Miller, Rick	82D	334	$ .01	$ .05
Miller, Rick	83D	82	$ .01	$ .05
Miller, Rick	85D	517	$ .01	$ .08
Milligan, Randy	88DR	32	$ .01	$ .05
Milligan, Randy	90D	519	$ .01	$ .04
Milligan, Randy	90DL	92	$ .01	$ .15
Milligan, Randy	91D	542	$ .01	$ .03
Mills, Alan	90DL	491	$ .01	$ .25
Mills, Alan	90DR	44	$ .01	$ .10
Mills, Alan	91D	338	$ .01	$ .15
Mills, Brad	83D	366	$ .01	$ .05
Milner, Eddie	83D	169	$ .01	$ .05
Milner, Eddie	84D	365	$ .03	$ .10
Milner, Eddie	85D	428	$ .01	$ .08
Milner, Eddie	86D	325	$ .01	$ .06
Milner, Eddie	87D	433	$ .01	$ .05

DONRUSS

Player	Year	No.	VG	EX/MT
Milner, John	81D	377	$ .01	$ .05
Milner, John	82D	266	$ .01	$ .05

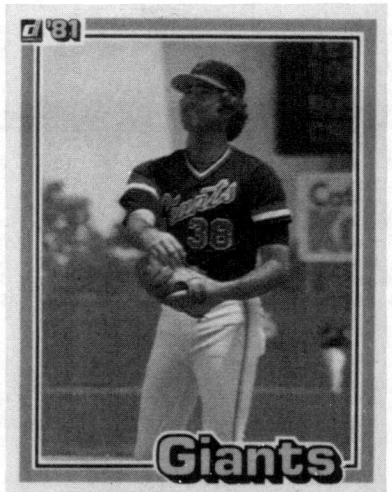

GREG MINTON PITCHER

Player	Year	No.	VG	EX/MT
Minton, Greg	81D	579	$ .01	$ .05
Minton, Greg	82D	348	$ .01	$ .05
Minton, Greg	83D	186	$ .01	$ .05
Minton, Greg	84D	187	$ .03	$ .10
Minton, Greg	85D	143	$ .01	$ .08
Minton, Greg	86D	480	$ .01	$ .06
Minton, Greg	88D	505	$ .01	$ .05
Minton, Greg	89D	490	$ .01	$ .05
Minton, Greg	89DBB	283	$ .01	$ .05
Minton, Greg	90D	116	$ .01	$ .04
Mirabella, Paul	81D	151	$ .01	$ .05
Mirabella, Paul	82D	629	$ .01	$ .05
Mirabella, Paul	83D	541	$ .01	$ .05
Mirabella, Paul	89D	654	$ .01	$ .05
Mitchell, Charlie	85DRR	40	$ .01	$ .08
Mitchell, John	87DR	37	$ .01	$ .07
Mitchell, John	91D	710	$ .01	$ .03
Mitchell, Kevin	86DR	17	$1.00	$5.50
Mitchell, Kevin	87D	599	$ .75	$4.50
Mitchell, Kevin	88D	66	$ .10	$ .35
Mitchell, Kevin	89D	485	$ .05	$ .35
Mitchell, Kevin	89DBB	281	$ .01	$ .25
Mitchell, Kevin	90D	98	$ .01	$ .20
Mitchell, Kevin	90DAS	715	$ .01	$ .20
Mitchell, Kevin	90DBC	11	$ .01	$ .20
Mitchell, Kevin	90DK	11	$ .01	$ .35
Mitchell, Kevin	90DL	120	$ .01	$ .50
Mitchell, Kevin	91D	255	$ .01	$ .15
Mitchell, Kevin	91DAS	438	$ .01	$ .10
Mitchell, Kevin	91DMVP	407	$ .01	$ .10
Mitchell, Paul	81D	205	$ .01	$ .05
Mizerock, John	84D	380	$ .03	$ .10
Mizerock, John	86D	502	$ .01	$ .06
Mizerock, John	87D	653	$ .01	$ .05
Mmahat, Kevin	90D	481	$ .01	$ .10
Moffitt, Randy	81D	195	$ .01	$ .05
Moffitt, Randy	83D	545	$ .01	$ .05
Moffitt, Randy	84D	390	$ .03	$ .10

Player	Year	No.	VG	EX/MT
Mohorcic, Dale	87D	531	$ .01	$ .05
Mohorcic, Dale	88D	470	$ .01	$ .05
Mohorcic, Dale	88DBB	144	$ .01	$ .05
Mohorcic, Dale	89D	630	$ .01	$ .05
Molinaro, Bobby	82D	417	$ .01	$ .05
Molinaro, Bobby	83D	596	$ .01	$ .05
Molitor, Paul	81D	203	$ .03	$ .35
Molitor, Paul	82D	78	$ .02	$ .25
Molitor, Paul	83D	484	$ .03	$ .20
Molitor, Paul	84D	107	$ .04	$ .25
Molitor, Paul	85D	359	$ .03	$ .20
Molitor, Paul	86D	124	$ .01	$ .06
Molitor, Paul	87D	117	$ .01	$ .05
Molitor, Paul	88D	249	$ .01	$ .05
Molitor, Paul	88DBB	165	$ .01	$ .05
Molitor, Paul	88DBC	3	$ .05	$ .20
Molitor, Paul	88DK	7	$ .01	$ .15
Molitor, Paul	89D	291	$ 01	$ 04
Molitor, Paul	89DBB	15	$ .01	$ .10
Molitor, Paul	89DBC	9	$ .01	$ .10
Molitor, Paul	90D	103	$ .01	$ .04
Molitor, Paul	90DBC	15	$ .01	$ .04
Molitor, Paul	90DL	242	$ .01	$ .15
Molitor, Paul	91D	85	$ .01	$ .03
Molitor, Paul	91DLP	20	$1.00	$5.00
Monday, Rick	81D	60	$ .01	$ .05
Monday, Rick	82D	514	$ .01	$ .05
Monday, Rick	83D	643	$ .01	$ .05
Money, Don	81D	443	$ .01	$ .05
Money, Don	82D	384	$ .01	$ .05
Money, Don	83D	132	$ .01	$ .05
Monge, Sid	81D	81	$ .01	$ .05
Monge, Sid	82D	620	$ .01	$ .05
Monge, Sid	83D	245	$ .01	$ .05
Monge, Sid	84D	139	$ .03	$ .10
Montefusco, John	81D	434	$ .01	$ .05
Montefusco, John	83D	313	$ .01	$ .05
Montefusco, John	84D	126	$ .03	$ .10
Montefusco, John	85D	580	$ .01	$ .08
Monteleone, Rich	90D	462	$ .01	$ .04
Montgomery, Jeff	89D	440	$ .01	$ .15
Montgomery, Jeff	89DBB	319	$ .01	$ .05
Montgomery, Jeff	90D	380	$ .01	$ .04
Montgomery, Jeff	90DL	520	$ .01	$ .15
Montgomery, Jeff	91D	505	$ .01	$ .03
Mooneyham, Bill	86DR	50	$ .02	$ .09
Mooneyham, Bill	87D	302	$ .01	$ .05
Moore, Charlie	81D	324	$ .01	$ .05
Moore, Charlie	82D	280	$ .01	$ .05
Moore, Charlie	83D	206	$ .01	$ .05
Moore, Charlie	84D	292	$ .03	$ .10
Moore, Charlie	85D	351	$ .01	$ .08
Moore, Charlie	86D	246	$ .01	$ .06
Moore, Charlie	87D	372	$ .01	$ .05
Moore, Donnie	85D	650	$ .01	$ .08
Moore, Donnie	86D	255	$ .01	$ .06
Moore, Donnie	87D	110	$ .01	$ .05
Moore, Donnie	88D	621	$ .01	$ .15
Moore, Kelvin	82D	534	$ .01	$ .05
Moore, Kelvin	83D	87	$ .01	$ .05
Moore, Mike	83D	428	$ .01	$1.25
Moore, Mike	84D	634	$ .05	$ .35
Moore, Mike	85D	440	$ .01	$ .08
Moore, Mike	86D	240	$ .01	$ .06
Moore, Mike	87D	70	$ .01	$ .05
Moore, Mike	88D	75	$ .01	$ .05
Moore, Mike	88DBB	192	$ .01	$ .05
Moore, Mike	89D	448	$ .01	$ .05
Moore, Mike	89DBB	246	$ .01	$ .05
Moore, Mike	89DTR	21	$ .01	$ .05

Player	Year	No.	VG	EX/MT	Player	Year	No.	VG	EX/MT
Moore, Mike	90D	214	$ .01	$ .04	Morrison, Jim	86D	386	$ .01	$ .06
Moore, Mike	90DL	293	$ .01	$ .15	Morrison, Jim	87D	484	$ .01	$ .05
Moore, Mike	91D	161	$ .01	$ .03	Morrison, Jim	88D	543	$ .01	$ .05
Morales, Jerry	82D	309	$ .01	$ .05	Morton, Kevin	91DRR	37	$ .01	$ .20
Morales, Jose	81D	495	$ .01	$ .05	Moseby, Lloyd	82D	129	$ .10	$ .45
Morales, Jose	82D	203	$ .01	$ .05	Moseby, Lloyd	83D	556	$ .01	$ .05
Morales, Jose	84D	275	$ .05	$ .30	Moseby, Lloyd	84D	363	$ .03	$ .10
Morandini, Mickey	91DRR	44	$ .01	$ .15	Moseby, Lloyd	85D	437	$ .03	$ .10
Moreland, Keith	81D	382	$ .05	$ .30	Moseby, Lloyd	86D	73	$ .01	$ .06
Moreland, Keith	82D	119	$ .01	$ .05	Moseby, Lloyd	87D	74	$ .01	$ .05
Moreland, Keith	83D	309	$ .01	$ .05	Moseby, Lloyd	87DK	21	$ .01	$ .05
Moreland, Keith	84D	483	$ .03	$ .10	Moseby, Lloyd	88D	367	$ .01	$ .05
Moreland, Keith	85D	117	$ .01	$ .08	Moseby, Lloyd	88DBB	199	$ .01	$ .05
Moreland, Keith	86D	167	$ .01	$ .06	Moseby, Lloyd	89D	231	$ .01	$ .05
Moreland, Keith	87D	169	$ .01	$ .05	Moseby, Lloyd	90D	504	$ .01	$ .04
Moreland, Keith	87DK	24	$ .01	$ .05	Moseby, Lloyd	90DL	377	$ .01	$ .15
Moreland, Keith	88D	201	$ .01	$ .05	Moseby, Lloyd	91D	188	$ .01	$ .03
Moreland, Keith	88DBB	266	$ .01	$ .05	Moses, John	84D	74	$ .03	$ .10
Moreland, Keith	89D	111	$ .01	$ .05	Moses, John	87D	393	$ .01	$ .05
Moreland, Keith	89DBB	203	$ .01	$ .05	Moses, John	88D	440	$ .01	$ .05
Moreno, Omar	81D	17	$ .01	$ .05	Moses, John	89D	626	$ .01	$ .05
Moreno, Omar	82D	347	$ .01	$ .05	Moses, John	90D	590	$ .01	$ .04
Moreno, Omar	83D	347	$ .01	$ .05	Moses, John	90DL	433	$ .01	$ .10
Moreno, Omar	84D	637	$ .03	$ .10	Moskau, Paul	82D	355	$ .01	$ .05
Moreno, Omar	85D	591	$ .01	$ .08	Mota, Manny	81D	299	$ .02	$ .15
Morgan, Joe	81D	18	$ .10	$ .50	Motley, Darryl	82D	390	$ .01	$ .05
Morgan, Joe	82D	312	$ .05	$ .50	Motley, Darryl	84D	344	$ .03	$ .10
Morgan, Joe	83D	438	$ .05	$ .30	Motley, Darryl	85D	461	$ .01	$ .08
Morgan, Joe	83D	648	$ .01	$ .15	Motley, Darryl	86D	217	$ .01	$ .06
Morgan, Joe	83DK	24	$ .05	$ .50	Moyer, Jamie	87D	315	$ .08	$ .30
Morgan, Joe	84D	355	$ .10	$ .50	Moyer, Jamie	88D	169	$ .01	$ .05
Morgan, Joe	85D	584	$ .08	$ .50	Moyer, Jamie	88DBB	228	$ .01	$ .05
Morgan, Mike	83D	108	$ .01	$ .05	Moyer, Jamie	89D	157	$ .01	$ .05
Morgan, Mike	87D	366	$ .01	$ .05	Moyer, Jamie	89DTR	39	$ .01	$ .05
Morgan, Mike	88D	120	$ .01	$ .05	Moyer, Jamie	90D	378	$ .01	$ .04
Morgan, Mike	88DBB	86	$ .01	$ .05	Mulholland, Terry	87D	515	$ .01	$ .05
Morgan, Mike	89D	164	$ .01	$ .05	Mulholland, Terry	90D	515	$ .01	$ .04
Morgan, Mike	89DBB	122	$ .01	$ .05	Mulholland, Terry	90DL	474	$ .01	$ .15
Morgan, Mike	90D	132	$ .01	$ .04	Mulholland, Terry	91D	541	$ .01	$ .03
Morgan, Mike	90DL	358	$ .01	$ .15	Mulholland, Terry	91DBC	14	$ .01	$ .03
Morgan, Mike	91D	182	$ .01	$ .03	Mulliniks, Rance	81D	504	$ .01	$ .05
Morman, Russ	87D	306	$ .08	$ .25	Mulliniks, Rance	82D	630	$ .01	$ .05
Morris, Hal	89D	545	$ .01	$ .75	Mulliniks, Rance	83D	432	$ .01	$ .05
Morris, Hal	90D	514	$ .01	$ .25	Mulliniks, Rance	84D	584	$ .03	$ .10
Morris, Hal	90DL	321	$ .01	$5.00	Mulliniks, Rance	85D	485	$ .01	$ .08
Morris, Hal	91D	141	$ .01	$ .25	Mulliniks, Rance	86D	606	$ .01	$ .06
Morris, Jack	81D	127	$ .05	$ .25	Mulliniks, Rance	87D	319	$ .01	$ .05
Morris, Jack	82D	107	$ .03	$ .25	Mulliniks, Rance	88D	197	$ .01	$ .05
Morris, Jack	83D	107	$ .03	$ .25	Mulliniks, Rance	89D	87	$ .01	$ .05
Morris, Jack	83DK	5	$ .01	$ .15	Mulliniks, Rance	90D	607	$ .01	$ .04
Morris, Jack	84D	415	$ .08	$ .25	Mulliniks, Rance	91D	663	$ .01	$ .03
Morris, Jack	85D	415	$ .08	$ .25	Mumphrey, Jerry	81D	124	$ .01	$ .05
Morris, Jack	86D	105	$ .07	$ .25	Mumphrey, Jerry	82D	261	$ .01	$ .05
Morris, Jack	87D	173	$ .05	$ .20	Mumphrey, Jerry	83D	360	$ .01	$ .05
Morris, Jack	87DK	13	$ .05	$ .20	Mumphrey, Jerry	84D	426	$ .03	$ .10
Morris, Jack	88D	127	$ .05	$ .20	Mumphrey, Jerry	85D	206	$ .01	$ .08
Morris, Jack	88D	480	$ .01	$ .05	Mumphrey, Jerry	86D	84	$ .01	$ .06
Morris, Jack	88DBB	181	$ .01	$ .05	Mumphrey, Jerry	87D	324	$ .01	$ .05
Morris, Jack	89D	234	$ .01	$ .05	Mumphrey, Jerry	88D	447	$ .01	$ .05
Morris, Jack	90D	639	$ .01	$ .10	Munoz, Mike	90DR	8	$ .01	$ .10
Morris, Jack	90DL	482	$ .01	$ .15	Munoz, Pedro	91D	758	$ .01	$ .15
Morris, Jack	91D	492	$ .01	$ .03	Mura, Steve	81D	362	$ .01	$ .05
Morris, John	85DRR	32	$ .01	$ .08	Mura, Steve	82D	523	$ .01	$ .05
Morris, John	87D	480	$ .01	$ .05	Mura, Steve	83D	292	$ .01	$ .05
Morris, John	90D	516	$ .01	$ .04	Murcer, Bobby	81D	111	$ .01	$ .05
Morrison, Jim	81D	158	$ .01	$ .05	Murcer, Bobby	82D	486	$ .01	$ .05
Morrison, Jim	82D	395	$ .01	$ .05	Murcer, Bobby	83D	261	$ .01	$ .05
Morrison, Jim	83D	150	$ .01	$ .05	Murphy, Dale	81D	437	$ .20	$1.25
Morrison, Jim	84D	322	$ .03	$ .10	Murphy, Dale	82D	299	$ .25	$1.25
Morrison, Jim	85D	532	$ .01	$ .08	Murphy, Dale	83D	47	$ .15	$1.00

DONRUSS

Player	Year	No.	VG	EX/MT
Murphy, Dale	83DK	12	$ .12	$ .60
Murphy, Dale	84D	66	$ .50	$1.50
Murphy, Dale	85D	66	$ .20	$ .60
Murphy, Dale	86D	66	$ .15	$ .50
Murphy, Dale	87D	78	$ .10	$ .35
Murphy, Dale	87DK	3	$ .10	$ .35
Murphy, Dale	88D	78	$ .10	$ .25
Murphy, Dale	88DBB	113	$ .01	$ .15
Murphy, Dale	88DBC	14	$ .01	$ .25
Murphy, Dale	89D	104	$ .01	$ .10
Murphy, Dale	89DBB	29	$ .01	$ .10
Murphy, Dale	90D	168	$ .01	$ .10
Murphy, Dale	90DL	243	$ .01	$ .25
Murphy, Dale	91D	484	$ .01	$ .03
Murphy, Dale	91D	744	$ .01	$ .15
Murphy, Dwayne	81D	359	$ .01	$ .05
Murphy, Dwayne	82D	239	$ .01	$ .05
Murphy, Dwayne	83D	161	$ .01	$ .05
Murphy, Dwayne	84D	101	$ .03	$ .10
Murphy, Dwayne	84DK	3	$ .03	$ .15
Murphy, Dwayne	85D	420	$ .01	$ .08
Murphy, Dwayne	86D	176	$ .01	$ .06
Murphy, Dwayne	87D	379	$ .01	$ .05
Murphy, Dwayne	88D	405	$ .01	$ .05
Murphy, Rob	87D	452	$ .05	$ .20
Murphy, Rob	88D	82	$ .01	$ .05
Murphy, Rob	88DBB	230	$ .01	$ .05
Murphy, Rob	89D	139	$ .01	$ .05
Murphy, Rob	89DBB	196	$ .01	$ .05
Murphy, Rob	89DTR	15	$ .01	$ .10
Murphy, Rob	90D	186	$ .01	$ .04
Murphy, Rob	90DL	183	$ .01	$ .15
Murphy, Rob	91D	250	$ .01	$ .03
Murray, Dale	83D	381	$ .01	$ .05
Murray, Dale	84D	577	$ .03	$ .10
Murray, Eddie	81D	112	$ .20	$1.25
Murray, Eddie	82D	483	$ .15	$1.00
Murray, Eddie	83D	405	$ .10	$ .75
Murray, Eddie	84D	47	$ .25	$2.00
Murray, Eddie	84DK	22	$ .15	$ .75
Murray, Eddie	85D	47	$ .15	$ .75
Murray, Eddie	86D	88	$ .10	$ .35
Murray, Eddie	87D	48	$ .05	$ .20
Murray, Eddie	88D	231	$ .10	$ .25
Murray, Eddie	88DBB	142	$ .01	$ .15
Murray, Eddie	89D	96	$ .01	$ .10
Murray, Eddie	89DBB	92	$ .01	$ .15
Murray, Eddie	89DTR	12	$ .01	$ .15
Murray, Eddie	90D	77	$ .01	$ .10
Murray, Eddie	90DL	181	$ .01	$ .20
Murray, Eddie	91D	502	$ .01	$ .10
Murray, Eddie	91DBC	18	$ .01	$ .03
Murray, Eddie	91DMVP	405	$ .01	$ .03
Musial, Stan	88D	641	$ .05	$ .20
Musselman, Jeff	87D	591	$ .03	$ .30
Musselman, Jeff	87DR	53	$ .01	$ .07
Musselman, Jeff	88D	630	$ .01	$ .15
Musselman, Jeff	89D	656	$ .01	$ .05
Musselman, Jeff	90D	623	$ .01	$ .04
Myers, Greg	88D	624	$ .05	$ .20
Myers, Greg	90D	706	$ .01	$ .04
Myers, Greg	90DL	527	$ .01	$ .15
Myers, Greg	91D	494	$ .01	$ .03
Myers, Randy	87DRR	29	$ .15	$ .75
Myers, Randy	88D	620	$ .01	$ .15
Myers, Randy	88DBB	265	$ .01	$ .15
Myers, Randy	89D	336	$ .01	$ .10
Myers, Randy	89DBB	153	$ .01	$ .10
Myers, Randy	90D	336	$ .01	$ .10
Myers, Randy	90DL	149	$ .01	$ .20

Player	Year	No.	VG	EX/MT
Myers, Randy	91D	209	$ .01	$ .03
Nabholz, Chris	91D	667	$ .01	$ .15
Naehring, Tim	91D	367	$ .01	$ .20
Nagy, Charles	91D	592	$ .01	$ .03
Narron, Jerry	81D	405	$ .01	$ .05
Narron, Jerry	82D	433	$ .01	$ .05

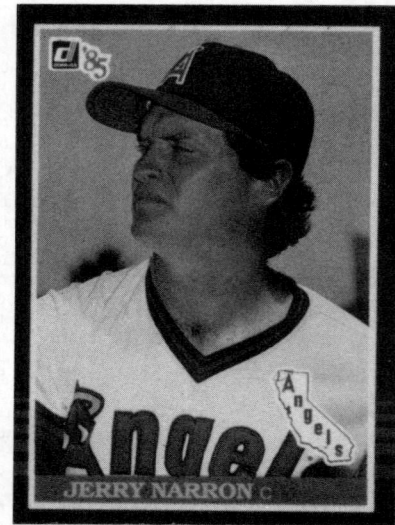

Player	Year	No.	VG	EX/MT
Narron, Jerry	85D	643	$ .01	$ .08
Narron, Jerry	86D	451	$ .01	$ .06
Narron, Jerry	87D	603	$ .01	$ .05
Navarro, Jaime	90D	640	$ .01	$ .10
Navarro, Jaime	90DL	85	$ .01	$ .20
Navarro, Jaime	91D	216	$ .01	$ .03
Neidlinger, Jim	91D	713	$ .01	$ .10
Nelson, Gene	82D	513	$ .01	$ .05
Nelson, Gene	83D	55	$ .01	$ .05
Nelson, Gene	85D	615	$ .01	$ .08
Nelson, Gene	86D	501	$ .01	$ .06
Nelson, Gene	87D	580	$ .01	$ .05
Nelson, Gene	88D	133	$ .01	$ .05
Nelson, Gene	89D	540	$ .01	$ .05
Nelson, Gene	90D	540	$ .01	$ .04
Nelson, Gene	90DL	477	$ .01	$ .15
Nelson, Gene	91D	385	$ .01	$ .03
Nelson, Ricky	84D	636	$ .03	$ .10
Nelson, Rob	87D	595	$ .01	$ .05
Nelson, Rob	88D	574	$ .01	$ .05
Nettles, Graig	81D	105	$ .05	$ .20
Nettles, Graig	82D	335	$ .03	$ .20
Nettles, Graig	83D	83	$ .03	$ .20
Nettles, Graig	84D	518	$ .04	$ .25
Nettles, Graig	85D	234	$ .03	$ .20
Nettles, Graig	86D	478	$ .05	$ .20
Newell, Tom	88D	604	$ .01	$ .15
Newman, Al	86DR	9	$ .02	$ .09
Newman, Al	87D	426	$ .01	$ .05
Newman, Al	88D	645	$ .01	$ .15
Newman, Al	89D	436	$ .01	$ .05
Newman, Al	90D	506	$ .01	$ .04
Newman, Al	90DL	347	$ .01	$ .15
Newman, Al	91D	208	$ .01	$ .03
Newman, Jeff	81D	477	$ .01	$ .05

Player	Year	No.	VG	EX/MT
Newman, Jeff	82D	517	$ .01	$ .05
Newman, Jeff	83D	635	$ .01	$ .05

Player	Year	No.	VG	EX/MT
Newman, Jeff	84D	249	$ .03	$ .10
Nezelek, Andy	89D	616	$ .01	$ .15
Nezelek, Andy	90D	523	$ .01	$ .04
Nichols, Carl	88D	477	$ .01	$ .05
Nichols, Carl	88DR	39	$ .01	$ .05
Nichols, Reid	82D	632	$ .01	$ .05
Nichols, Reid	83D	460	$ .01	$ .05
Nichols, Reid	84D	614	$ .03	$ .10
Nichols, Reid	85D	636	$ .01	$ .08
Nichols, Reid	86D	574	$ .01	$ .06
Nichols, Rod	89D	649	$ .01	$ .05
Nichols, Rod	90D	546	$ .01	$ .04
Nicosia, Steve	81D	373	$ .01	$ .05
Nicosia, Steve	82D	45	$ .01	$ .05
Nicosia, Steve	83D	528	$ .01	$ .05
Niedenfuer, Tom	83D	536	$ .01	$ .05
Niedenfuer, Tom	84D	128	$ .03	$ .10
Niedenfuer, Tom	85D	153	$ .01	$ .08
Niedenfuer, Tom	86D	397	$ .01	$ .06
Niedenfuer, Tom	87D	218	$ .01	$ .05
Niedenfuer, Tom	88D	294	$ .01	$ .05
Niedenfuer, Tom	89D	282	$ .01	$ .05
Niedenfuer, Tom	89DTR	54	$ .01	$ .05
Niekro, Joe	81D	380	$ .03	$ .20
Niekro, Joe	82D	167	$ .02	$ .10
Niekro, Joe	83D	470	$ .01	$ .05
Niekro, Joe	83D	613	$ .05	$ .30
Niekro, Joe	83DK	10	$ .02	$ .15
Niekro, Joe	84D	110	$ .03	$ .10
Niekro, Joe	86D	601	$ .01	$ .06
Niekro, Joe	86D	645	$ .03	$ .25
Niekro, Joe	87D	217	$ .01	$ .05
Niekro, Phil	81D	328	$ .05	$ .30
Niekro, Phil	82D	475	$ .05	$ .30
Niekro, Phil	82DK	10	$ .05	$ .20
Niekro, Phil	83D	613	$ .05	$ .30
Niekro, Phi!	83D	97	$ .06	$ .30
Niekro, Phil	84D	188	$ .15	$ .40

Player	Year	No.	VG	EX/MT
Niekro, Phil	85D	182	$ .01	$ .08
Niekro, Phil	85D	458	$ .08	$ .25
Niekro, Phil	86D	580	$ .08	$ .25
Niekro, Phil	86D	645	$ .03	$ .25
Niekro, Phil	87D	465	$ .08	$ .20
Nielsen, Scott	87D	597	$ .01	$ .15
Niemann, Randy	82D	473	$ .01	$ .05
Nieto, Tom	85D	596	$ .01	$ .08
Nieto, Tom	86D	327	$ .01	$ .06
Nieto, Tom	88D	612	$ .01	$ .15
Nieves, Juan	86DR	12	$ .01	$ .05
Nieves, Juan	86DRR	40	$ .01	$ .20
Nieves, Juan	87D	90	$ .01	$ .05
Nieves, Juan	88D	126	$ .01	$ .05
Nieves, Juan	89D	575	$ .01	$ .05
Nipper, Al	85D	614	$ .01	$ .08
Nipper, Al	86D	538	$ .01	$ .06
Nipper, Al	87D	297	$ .01	$ .05
Nipper, Al	88D	523	$ .01	$ .05
Nipper, Al	88DBB	250	$ .01	$ .05
Nipper, Al	89D	394	$ .01	$ .05
Nixon, Donell	90D	571	$ .01	$ .04
Nixon, Otis	90D	456	$ .01	$ .04
Nixon, Otis	91D	626	$ .01	$ .03
Noboa, Junior	91D	726	$ .01	$ .03
Noce, Paul	87DR	51	$ .01	$ .07
Noce, Paul	88D	315	$ .01	$ .05
Nokes, Matt	87DR	12	$ .10	$ .55
Nokes, Matt	88D	152	$ .01	$ .25
Nokes, Matt	88DBB	237	$ .01	$ .05
Nokes, Matt	89D	116	$ .01	$ .05
Nokes, Matt	89DBB	181	$ .01	$ .05
Nokes, Matt	90D	178	$ .01	$ .04
Nokes, Matt	90DL	192	$ .01	$ .15
Nokes, Matt	90DL	314	$ .01	$ .15
Nokes, Matt	91D	170	$ .01	$ .03
Nolan, Joe	81D	302	$ .01	$ .05
Nolan, Joe	82D	62	$ .01	$ .05
Nolan, Joe	83D	79	$ .01	$ .05
Nolan, Joe	84D	489	$ .03	$ .10
Nolan, Joe	85D	594	$ .01	$ .08
Noles, Dick	81D	568	$ .01	$ .05
Noles, Dickie	83D	426	$ .01	$ .05
Noles, Dickie	84D	266	$ .03	$ .10
Noles, Dickie	86D	587	$ .01	$ .06
Nolte, Eric	88D	534	$ .01	$ .05
Nordhagen, Wayne	81D	401	$ .01	$ .05
Nordhagen, Wayne	82D	67	$ .01	$ .05
Norman, Fred	81D	92	$ .01	$ .05
Norman, Nelson	81D	509	$ .01	$ .05
Norris, Jim	81D	388	$ .01	$ .05
Norris, Mike	81D	118	$ .01	$ .05
Norris, Mike	82D	197	$ .01	$ .05
Norris, Mike	82DK	19	$ .01	$ .05
Norris, Mike	83D	139	$ .01	$ .05
North, Bill	81D	76	$ .01	$ .05
Norwood, Willie	81D	516	$ .01	$ .05
Nunez, Ed	84D	435	$ .01	$ .10
Nunez, Ed	85D	484	$ .01	$ .08
Nunez, Ed	86D	145	$ .01	$ .06
Nunez, Ed	87D	243	$ .01	$ .05
Nunez, Ed	88D	445	$ .01	$ .05
Nunez, Edwin	90D	563	$ .01	$ .04
Nunez, Edwin	90DL	397	$ .01	$ .15
Nunez, Edwin	91D	620	$ .01	$ .03
Nunez, Jose	88D	611	$ .01	$ .15
Nunez, Jose	90D	467	$ .01	$ .04
O'Berry, Mike	82D	538	$ .01	$ .05
O'Brien, Charlie	90D	410	$ .01	$ .04
O'Brien, Charlie	90DL	375	$ .01	$ .15

DONRUSS

Player	Year	No.	VG	EX/MT	Player	Year	No.	VG	EX/MT
O'Brien, Charlie	91D	623	$ .01	$ .03	Ojeda, Bob	88DBB	238	$ .01	$ .05
O'Brien, Pete	84D	281	$ .25	$1.00	Ojeda, Bob	89D	218	$ .01	$ .05
O'Brien, Pete	85D	178	$ .01	$ .08	Ojeda, Bob	89DBB	209	$ .01	$ .05
O'Brien, Pete	86D	99	$ .01	$ .06	Ojeda, Bob	90D	117	$ .01	$ .04
O'Brien, Pete	87D	259	$ .01	$ .05	Ojeda, Bob	91D	584	$ .01	$ .03
O'Brien, Pete	88D	284	$ .01	$ .05	Olerud, John	90D	711	$ .01	$2.00
O'Brien, Pete	88DBB	167	$ .01	$ .05	Olerud, John	90DL	237	$ .01	$6.00
O'Brien, Pete	89D	107	$ .01	$ .05	Olerud, John	90DR	2	$ .01	$1.50
O'Brien, Pete	89DBB	5	$ .01	$ .05	Olerud, John	91D	530	$ .01	$ .35
O'Brien, Pete	89DTR	16	$ .01	$ .05	Olin, Steve	90D	438	$ .01	$ .10
O'Brien, Pete	90D	202	$ .01	$ .04	Olin, Steve	91D	339	$ .01	$ .03
O'Brien, Pete	90DK	24	$ .01	$ .10	Olivares, Omar	91D	503	$ .01	$ .10
O'Brien, Pete	90DL	9	$ .01	$ .15	Oliver, Al	81D	387	$ .03	$ .20
O'Brien, Pete	91D	119	$ .01	$ .03	Oliver, Al	82D	116	$ .02	$ .15
O'Connor, Jack	82D	539	$ .01	$ .05	Oliver, Al	83D	140	$ .03	$ .20
O'Connor, Jack	83D	51	$ .01	$ .05	Oliver, Al	84D	177	$ .08	$ .25
O'Malley, Tom	83D	96	$ .01	$ .05	Oliver, Al	84DK	9	$ .08	$ .25
O'Malley, Tom	84D	601	$ .03	$ .10	Oliver, Al	85D	598	$ .03	$ .10
O'Neal, Randy	86D	394	$ .01	$ .06	Oliver, Al	86D	485	$ .01	$ .06
O'Neal, Randy	87D	584	$ .01	$ .05	Oliver, Joe	90D	586	$ .01	$ .40
O'Neill, Paul	86DRR	37	$ .50	$2.50	Oliver, Joe	90DL	453	$ .01	$ .25
O'Neill, Paul	88D	433	$ .03	$ .15	Oliver, Joe	91D	381	$ .01	$ .03
O'Neill, Paul	89D	360	$ .01	$ .15	Oliveras, Francisco	89DR	9	$ .01	$ .10
O'Neill, Paul	89DBB	230	$ .01	$ .10	Oliveras, Francisco	90DL	515	$ .01	$ .15
O'Neill, Paul	90D	198	$ .01	$ .10	Oliveras, Francisco	91D	469	$ .01	$ .03
O'Neill, Paul	90DL	70	$ .01	$ .15	Olson, Greg	90DL	323	$ .01	$ .25
O'Neill, Paul	91D	583	$ .01	$ .03	Olson, Greg	90DR	46	$ .01	$ .10
Oberkfell, Ken	81D	583	$ .01	$ .05	Olson, Greg	91D	285	$ .01	$ .03
Oberkfell, Ken	82D	404	$ .01	$ .05	Olson, Gregg	89DBB	322	$ .01	$ .25
Oberkfell, Ken	83D	246	$ .01	$ .05	Olson, Gregg	89DR	35	$ .01	$ .60
Oberkfell, Ken	84D	504	$ .03	$ .10	Olson, Gregg	89DRR	46	$ .05	$ .75
Oberkfell, Ken	85D	432	$ .01	$ .08	Olson, Gregg	90D	377	$ .01	$ .20
Oberkfell, Ken	86D	531	$ .01	$ .06	Olson, Gregg	90DL	7	$ .01	$ .50
Oberkfell, Ken	87D	437	$ .01	$ .05	Olson, Gregg	91D	111	$ .01	$ .03
Oberkfell, Ken	88D	67	$ .01	$ .05	Olson, Gregg	91DK	23	$ .01	$ .05
Oberkfell, Ken	88DBB	226	$ .01	$ .05	Olson, Gregg	91DMVP	393	$ .01	$ .03
Oberkfell, Ken	89D	506	$ .01	$ .05	Olwine, Ed	87D	560	$ .01	$ .05
Oberkfell, Ken	90D	494	$ .01	$ .04	Ontiveros, Steve	86D	589	$ .01	$ .06
Oberkfell, Ken	90DL	294	$ .01	$ .15	Ontiveros, Steve	87D	221	$ .01	$ .05
Oberkfell, Ken	91D	109	$ .01	$ .03	Ontiveros, Steve	88D	467	$ .01	$ .05
Oelkers, Bryan	84D	486	$ .03	$ .10	Ontiveros, Steve	89D	596	$ .01	$ .05
Oelkers, Bryan	87D	596	$ .01	$ .05	Ontiveros, Steve	89DTR	11	$ .01	$ .05
Oester, Ron	81D	423	$ .01	$ .05	Oquendo, Jose	84D	643	$ .15	$ .75
Oester, Ron	82D	500	$ .01	$ .05	Oquendo, Jose	87D	510	$ .01	$ .05
Oester, Ron	83D	526	$ .01	$ .05	Oquendo, Jose	88D	234	$ .01	$ .05
Oester, Ron	84D	62	$ .03	$ .10	Oquendo, Jose	89D	319	$ .01	$ .05
Oester, Ron	85D	81	$ .01	$ .08	Oquendo, Jose	89DBB	100	$ .01	$ .05
Oester, Ron	86D	81	$ .01	$ .06	Oquendo, Jose	90D	161	$ .01	$ .04
Oester, Ron	87D	206	$ .01	$ .05	Oquendo, Jose	90DL	129	$ .01	$ .15
Oester, Ron	88D	246	$ .01	$ .05	Oquendo, Jose	91D	281	$ .01	$ .03
Oester, Ron	89D	553	$ .01	$ .05	Orosco, Jesse	82D	646	$ .03	$ .20
Oester, Ron	90D	317	$ .01	$ .04	Orosco, Jesse	83D	434	$ .01	$ .05
Oester, Ron	91D	628	$ .01	$ .03	Orosco, Jesse	84D	197	$ .03	$ .10
Offerman, Jose	90DL	464	$ .01	$ 2.00	Orosco, Jesse	85D	75	$ .01	$ .08
Offerman, Jose	91DRR	33	$ .01	$ .30	Orosco, Jesse	85DK	22	$ .03	$ .20
Office, Rowland	81D	213	$ .01	$ .05	Orosco, Jesse	86D	646	$ .01	$ .06
Oglivie, Ben	81D	446	$ .01	$ .05	Orosco, Jesse	87D	439	$ .01	$ .05
Oglivie, Ben	82D	484	$ .01	$ .05	Orosco, Jesse	88D	192	$ .01	$ .05
Oglivie, Ben	83D	384	$ .01	$ .05	Orosco, Jesse	88DBB	234	$ .01	$ .05
Oglivie, Ben	84D	229	$ .03	$ .10	Orosco, Jesse	89D	228	$ .01	$ .05
Oglivie, Ben	85D	333	$ .01	$ .08	Orosco, Jesse	89DTR	26	$ .01	$ .05
Oglivie, Ben	86D	333	$ .01	$ .06	Orosco, Jesse	90D	154	$ .01	$ .04
Oglivie, Ben	87D	419	$ .01	$ .05	Orosco, Jesse	90DL	101	$ .01	$ .15
Ojeda, Bob	82D	540	$ .10	$ .50	Orosco, Jesse	91D	171	$ .01	$ .03
Ojeda, Bob	83D	260	$ .01	$ .05	Orsulak, Joe	86D	444	$ .01	$ .06
Ojeda, Bob	84D	538	$ .03	$ .10	Orsulak, Joe	87D	291	$ .01	$ .05
Ojeda, Bob	85D	371	$ .01	$ .08	Orsulak, Joe	89D	287	$ .01	$ .05
Ojeda, Bob	86D	636	$ .01	$ .06	Orsulak, Joe	89DBB	310	$ .01	$ .05
Ojeda, Bob	87D	364	$ .01	$ .05	Orsulak, Joe	90D	287	$ .01	$ .04
Ojeda, Bob	88D	632	$ .01	$ .15	Orsulak, Joe	90DL	355	$ .01	$ .15

Player	Year	No.	VG	EX/MT
Orsulak, Joe	91D	654	$ .01	$ .03
Orta, Jorge	81D	439	$ .01	$ .05
Orta, Jorge	82D	211	$ .01	$ .05
Orta, Jorge	83D	388	$ .01	$ .05
Orta, Jorge	84D	317	$ .03	$ .10
Orta, Jorge	85D	130	$ .01	$ .08
Orta, Jorge	86D	339	$ .01	$ .06
Orta, Jorge	87D	348	$ .01	$ .05
Ortiz, Javier	91D	643	$ .01	$ .10
Ortiz, Junior	84D	319	$ .03	$ .10
Ortiz, Junior	86D	508	$ .01	$ .06
Ortiz, Junior	87D	449	$ .01	$ .05
Ortiz, Junior	88D	168	$ .01	$ .05
Ortiz, Junior	89D	387	$ .01	$ .05
Ortiz, Junior	89DBB	269	$ .01	$ .05
Ortiz, Junior	91D	659	$ .01	$ .03
Orton, John	90DL	511	$ .01	$ .20
Orton, John	90DR	54	$ .01	$ .10
Orton, John	91D	714	$ .01	$ .03
Otis, Amos	81D	104	$ .01	$ .05
Otis, Amos	82D	70	$ .01	$ .05
Otis, Amos	83D	364	$ .01	$ .05
Ott, Ed	81D	133	$ .02	$ .06
Ott, Ed	82D	192	$ .01	$ .05
Owchinko, Bob	81D	563	$ .01	$ .05
Owchinko, Bob	82D	287	$ .01	$ .05
Owchinko, Bob	83D	265	$ .01	$ .05
Owchinko, Bob	85D	506	$ .01	$ .08
Owen, Dave	85D	483	$ .01	$ .08
Owen, Spike	84D	313	$ .10	$ .40
Owen, Spike	85D	435	$ .01	$ .08
Owen, Spike	86D	362	$ .01	$ .06
Owen, Spike	87D	633	$ .01	$ .05
Owen, Spike	88D	544	$ .01	$ .05
Owen, Spike	89D	593	$ .01	$ .05
Owen, Spike	89DBB	236	$ .01	$ .05
Owen, Spike	89DTR	14	$ .01	$ .05
Owen, Spike	90D	102	$ .01	$ .04
Owen, Spike	90DL	186	$ .01	$ .15
Owen, Spike	91D	251	$ .01	$ .03
Pacella, John	83D	130	$ .01	$ .05
Pacillo, Pat	88D	536	$ .01	$ .05
Paciorek, Tom	81D	408	$ .01	$ .05
Paciorek, Tom	82D	253	$ .01	$ .05
Paciorek, Tom	83D	243	$ .01	$ .05
Paciorek, Tom	84D	282	$ .03	$ .10
Paciorek, Tom	85D	488	$ .01	$ .08
Page, Mitchell	81D	480	$ .01	$ .05
Pagliarulo, Mike	85D	539	$ .15	$ .75
Pagliarulo, Mike	86D	152	$ .01	$ .05
Pagliarulo, Mike	87D	298	$ .01	$ .15
Pagliarulo, Mike	88D	105	$ .01	$ .15
Pagliarulo, Mike	88DBB	105	$ .01	$ .10
Pagliarulo, Mike	89D	127	$ .01	$ .05
Pagliarulo, Mike	90D	364	$ .01	$ .04
Pagliarulo, Mike	90DL	320	$ .01	$ .15
Pagliarulo, Mike	91D	140	$ .01	$ .03
Pagnozzi, Tom	88D	577	$ .01	$ .05
Pagnozzi, Tom	89D	399	$ .01	$ .05
Pagnozzi, Tom	90D	591	$ .01	$ .04
Pagnozzi, Tom	90DL	498	$ .01	$ .15
Pagnozzi, Tom	91D	337	$ .01	$ .03
Palacios, Vicente	88DRR	45	$ .10	$ .35
Palacios, Vicente	91D	732	$ .01	$ .03
Pall, Donn	89DR	7	$ .01	$ .10
Pall, Donn	90D	606	$ .01	$ .04
Pall, Donn	90DL	392	$ .01	$ .15
Pall, Donn	91D	215	$ .01	$ .03
Palmeiro, Rafael	87DR	47	$ .25	$1.00
Palmeiro, Rafael	87DRR	43	$ .50	$3.25

Player	Year	No.	VG	EX/MT
Palmeiro, Rafael	88D	324	$ .01	$ .35
Palmeiro, Rafael	88DBB	93	$ .10	$ .35
Palmeiro, Rafael	89D	49	$ .05	$ .25
Palmeiro, Rafael	89DBB	88	$ .01	$ .10
Palmeiro, Rafael	89DTR	6	$ .05	$ .25
Palmeiro, Rafael	90D	225	$ .01	$ .10
Palmeiro, Rafael	90DL	100	$ .01	$ .25
Palmeiro, Rafael	91D	521	$ .01	$ .10
Palmeiro, Rafael	91DK	19	$ .01	$ .05
Palmeiro, Rafael	91DMVP	394	$ .01	$ .03
Palmer, Dave	81D	451	$ .01	$ .05
Palmer, Dave	83D	68	$ .01	$ .05
Palmer, Dave	85D	341	$ .01	$ .08
Palmer, David	86D	254	$ .01	$ .06
Palmer, David	87D	325	$ .01	$ .05
Palmer, David	88D	266	$ .01	$ .05
Palmer, David	89D	133	$ .01	$ .05
Palmer, Dean	90D	529	$ .01	$ .40
Palmer, Jim	81D	353	$ .10	$ .75
Palmer, Jim	81D	473	$ .10	$ .75
Palmer, Jim	82D	231	$ .05	$ .75
Palmer, Jim	83D	77	$ .05	$ .75

Player	Year	No.	VG	EX/MT
Palmer, Jim	83DK	4	$ .05	$ .50
Palmer, Jim	84D	576	$ .15	$2.00
Pankovits, Jim	85D	502	$ .01	$ .08
Pankovits, Jim	86D	450	$ .01	$ .06
Pankovits, Jim	87D	605	$ .01	$ .05
Papi, Stan	81D	246	$ .01	$ .05
Papi, Stan	82D	333	$ .01	$ .05
Pardo, Al	86D	489	$ .01	$ .06
Paredes, Johhny	88DR	29	$ .01	$ .05
Paredes, Johnny	89D	570	$ .01	$ .05
Parent, Mark	88DR	8	$ .01	$ .15
Parent, Mark	89D	420	$ .01	$ .15
Parent, Mark	90D	229	$ .01	$ .04
Parent, Mark	90DL	497	$ .01	$ .15
Parent, Mark	91D	506	$ .01	$ .03
Paris, Kelly	84D	384	$ .03	$ .10
Parker, Clay	89DBB	164	$ .01	$ .05
Parker, Clay	89DR	52	$ .01	$ .10

Player	Year	No.	VG	EX/MT
Parker, Clay	90D	363	$ .01	$ .04
Parker, Clay	91D	605	$ .01	$ .03
Parker, Dave	81D	136	$ .05	$ .30
Parker, Dave	82D	95	$ .05	$ .30
Parker, Dave	82DK	12	$ .05	$ .30
Parker, Dave	83D	473	$ .05	$ .30
Parker, Dave	84D	288	$ .08	$ .25
Parker, Dave	85D	62	$ .05	$ .30
Parker, Dave	86D	203	$ .03	$ .25
Parker, Dave	87D	388	$ .05	$ .20
Parker, Dave	88D	388	$ .01	$ .15
Parker, Dave	88DBB	190	$ .01	$ .05
Parker, Dave	89D	150	$ .01	$ .05
Parker, Dave	89DBB	336	$ .01	$ .10
Parker, Dave	90D	328	$ .01	$ .04
Parker, Dave	90DL	190	$ .01	$ .20
Parker, Dave	91D	142	$ .01	$ .03
Parker, Dave	91DK	6	$ .01	$ .05
Parker, Dave	91DMVP	390	$ .01	$ .03
Parker, Rick	90DL	398	$ .01	$ .20
Parrett, Jeff	88D	406	$ .01	$ .15
Parrett, Jeff	89D	334	$ .01	$ .05
Parrett, Jeff	89DBB	296	$ .01	$ .05
Parrett, Jeff	89DTR	55	$ .01	$ .05
Parrett, Jeff	90D	369	$ .01	$ .04
Parrett, Jeff	90DL	210	$ .01	$ .15
Parrett, Jeff	91D	660	$ .01	$ .03
Parrish, Lance	81D	366	$ .05	$ .30
Parrish, Lance	82D	281	$ .03	$ .20
Parrish, Lance	83D	407	$ .03	$ .20
Parrish, Lance	84D	49	$ .10	$ .35
Parrish, Lance	84DK	15	$ .10	$ .35
Parrish, Lance	85D	49	$ .03	$ .25
Parrish, Lance	86D	334	$ .05	$ .20
Parrish, Lance	87D	91	$ .05	$ .20
Parrish, Lance	88D	359	$ .01	$ .05
Parrish, Lance	88DBB	184	$ .01	$ .05
Parrish, Lance	89D	278	$ .01	$ .05
Parrish, Lance	89DBB	59	$ .01	$ .05
Parrish, Lance	90D	213	$ .01	$ .04
Parrish, Lance	90DL	195	$ .01	$ .15
Parrish, Lance	91D	135	$ .01	$ .03
Parrish, Lance	91DMVP	388	$ .01	$ .03
Parrish, Larry	81D	89	$ .01	$ .05
Parrish, Larry	82D	466	$ .01	$ .05
Parrish, Larry	83D	467	$ .01	$ .05
Parrish, Larry	84D	422	$ .03	$ .10
Parrish, Larry	84DK	21	$ .08	$ .25
Parrish, Larry	85D	300	$ .01	$ .08
Parrish, Larry	86D	178	$ .01	$ .06
Parrish, Larry	87D	469	$ .01	$ .05
Parrish, Larry	88D	347	$ .01	$ .05
Parrott, Mike	82D	226	$ .01	$ .05
Pashnick, Larry	83D	233	$ .01	$ .05
Pashnick, Larry	84D	394	$ .03	$ .10
Pasqua, Dan	85D	637	$ .15	$ .75
Pasqua, Dan	86D	417	$ .05	$ .20
Pasqua, Dan	87D	474	$ .05	$ .20
Pasqua, Dan	88D	463	$ .01	$ .05
Pasqua, Dan	88DBB	137	$ .01	$ .05
Pasqua, Dan	89D	294	$ .01	$ .05
Pasqua, Dan	89DBB	123	$ .01	$ .05
Pasqua, Dan	90D	176	$ .01	$ .04
Pasqua, Dan	90DL	274	$ .01	$ .15
Pasqua, Dan	91D	103	$ .01	$ .03
Pastore, Frank	82D	122	$ .01	$ .05
Pastore, Frank	83D	62	$ .01	$ .05
Pastore, Frank	84D	164	$ .03	$ .10
Pastore, Frank	85D	550	$ .01	$ .08
Pate, Bob	81D	545	$ .01	$ .05

Player	Year	No.	VG	EX/MT
Patek, Fred	81D	170	$ .01	$ .05

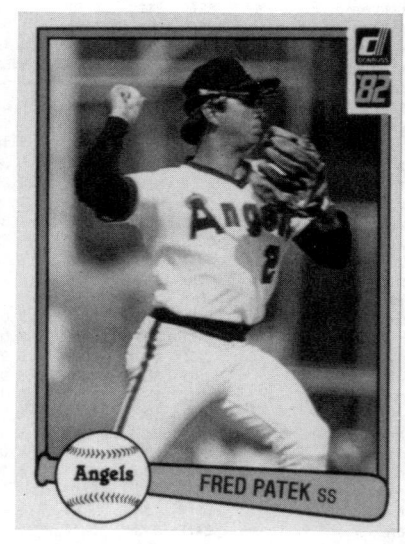

Player	Year	No.	VG	EX/MT
Patek, Fred	82D	241	$ .01	$ .05
Patterson, Bob	91D	345	$ .01	$ .03
Patterson, Ken	89DR	37	$ .01	$ .10
Patterson, Ken	90D	371	$ .01	$ .04
Patterson, Ken	91D	522	$ .01	$ .03
Pattin, Marty	81D	343	$ .01	$ .05
Pawlowski, John	88D	457	$ .01	$ .05
Pecota, Bill	88D	466	$ .01	$ .05
Pecota, Bill	91D	672	$ .01	$ .03
Pedrique, Al	88D	361	$ .01	$ .05
Pena, Alejandro	84D	250	$ .03	$ .50
Pena, Alejandro	85D	337	$ .03	$ .10
Pena, Alejandro	88D	598	$ .01	$ .05
Pena, Alejandro	89D	557	$ .01	$ .05
Pena, Alejandro	90D	664	$ .01	$ .04
Pena, Alejandro	90DL	403	$ .01	$ .15
Pena, Alejandro	91D	566	$ .01	$ .03
Pena, Geronimo	91D	712	$ .01	$ .03
Pena, Hipolito	89D	598	$ .01	$ .05
Pena, Tony	82D	124	$ .10	$ .60
Pena, Tony	83D	59	$ .02	$ .15
Pena, Tony	84D	186	$ .04	$ .30
Pena, Tony	85D	64	$ .05	$ .20
Pena, Tony	85DK	24	$ .03	$ .10
Pena, Tony	86D	64	$ .05	$ .20
Pena, Tony	87D	115	$ .01	$ .05
Pena, Tony	88D	170	$ .01	$ .05
Pena, Tony	88DBB	156	$ .01	$ .05
Pena, Tony	89D	163	$ .01	$ .05
Pena, Tony	89DBB	299	$ .01	$ .05
Pena, Tony	90D	181	$ .01	$ .04
Pena, Tony	90DL	104	$ .01	$ .15
Pena, Tony	91D	456	$ .01	$ .03
Pendleton, Jeff	85D	534	$ .15	$ .75
Pendleton, Terry	86D	205	$ .01	$ .06
Pendleton, Terry	87D	183	$ .01	$ .15
Pendleton, Terry	88D	454	$ .01	$ .05
Pendleton, Terry	88DBB	187	$ .01	$ .05
Pendleton, Terry	89D	230	$ .01	$ .05

Player	Year	No.	VG	EX/MT	Player	Year	No.	VG	EX/MT
Pendleton, Terry	89DBB	156	$ .01	$ .05	Petry, Dan	83D	359	$ .01	$ .05
Pendleton, Terry	90D	299	$ .01	$ .04	Petry, Dan	84D	105	$ .03	$ .10
Pendleton, Terry	90DL	260	$ .01	$ .15	Petry, Dan	85D	334	$ .01	$ .08
Pendleton, Terry	91D	446	$ .01	$ .03	Petry, Dan	86D	212	$ .01	$ .06
Peraza, Oswald	89D	524	$ .01	$ .15	Petry, Dan	87D	373	$ .01	$ .05
Perconte, Jack	83D	463	$ .01	$ .05	Petry, Dan	88D	476	$ .01	$ .05
Perconte, Jack	85D	74	$ .01	$ .08	Petry, Dan	88DBB	139	$ .01	$ .05
Perez, Melido	88D	589	$ .05	$ .20	Petry, Dan	89D	344	$ .01	$ .05
Perez, Melido	88DBB	179	$ .01	$ .15	Petry, Dan	90DL	508	$ .01	$ .15
Perez, Melido	88DR	21	$ .01	$ .15	Petry, Dan	91D	675	$ .01	$ .03
Perez, Melido	89D	58	$ .01	$ .15	Pettis, Gary	84D	647	$ .04	$ .50
Perez, Melido	89DBB	179	$ .01	$ .05	Pettis, Gary	85D	499	$ .01	$ .08
Perez, Melido	90D	101	$ .01	$ .04	Pettis, Gary	86D	158	$ .01	$ .06
Perez, Melido	90DL	36	$ .01	$ .15	Pettis, Gary	87D	160	$ .01	$ .05
Perez, Melido	91D	164	$ .01	$ .03	Pettis, Gary	88D	210	$ .01	$ .05
Perez, Melido	91DBC	13	$ .01	$ .03	Pettis, Gary	88DBB	203	$ .05	$ .25
Perez, Mike	91D	615	$ .01	$ .10	Pettis, Gary	89D	60	$ .01	$ .05
Perez, Pascual	83D	557	$ .05	$ .25	Pettis, Gary	90D	661	$ .01	$ .04
Perez, Pascual	84D	507	$ .05	$ .35	Pettis, Gary	90DL	469	$ .01	$ .15
Perez, Pascual	85D	507	$ .01	$ .08	Pettis, Gary	91D	512	$ .01	$ .03
Perez, Pascual	88D	591	$ .01	$ .05	Phelps, Ken	85D	318	$ .01	$ .20
Perez, Pascual	88DBB	236	$ .01	$ .05	Phelps, Ken	87D	317	$ .01	$ .05
Perez, Pascual	89D	248	$ .01	$ .05	Phelps, Ken	88D	489	$ .01	$ .05
Perez, Pascual	89DBB	302	$ .01	$ .05	Phelps, Ken	88DBB	248	$ .01	$ .05
Perez, Pascual	90D	342	$ .01	$ .04	Phelps, Ken	89D	363	$ .01	$ .05
Perez, Tony	81D	334	$ .05	$ .30	Phelps, Ken	89DBB	276	$ .01	$ .05
Perez, Tony	82D	408	$ .05	$ .30	Phelps, Ken	90D	675	$ .01	$ .04
Perez, Tony	83D	578	$ .03	$ .20	Phillips, Mike	81D	188	$ .01	$ .05
Perez, Tony	84D	503	$ .10	$ .35	Phillips, Tony	84D	278	$ .03	$ .50
Perez, Tony	86D	428	$ .03	$ .25	Phillips, Tony	85D	101	$ .01	$ .08
Perez, Tony	86DK	15	$ .05	$ .20	Phillips, Tony	86D	542	$ .01	$ .06
Perkins, Broderick	81D	525	$ .01	$ .05	Phillips, Tony	87D	103	$ .01	$ .05
Perkins, Broderick	82D	397	$ .01	$ .05	Phillips, Tony	88D	221	$ .01	$ .05
Perkins, Broderick	83D	121	$ .01	$ .05	Phillips, Tony	89DBB	211	$ .01	$ .05
Perkins, Broderick	84D	276	$ .03	$ .10	Phillips, Tony	90D	91	$ .01	$ .04
Perry, Gaylord	81D	471	$ .05	$ .30	Phillips, Tony	90DL	324	$ .01	$ .15
Perry, Gaylord	82D	543	$ .05	$ .30	Phillips, Tony	91D	286	$ .01	$ .03
Perry, Gaylord	83D	307	$ .03	$ .20	Picciolo, Rob	81D	357	$ .01	$ .05
Perry, Gaylord	84D#A	0	$1.00	$3.00	Picciolo, Rob	82D	465	$ .01	$ .05
Perry, Gerald	84D	263	$ .15	$ .75	Picciolo, Rob	83D	456	$ .01	$ .05
Perry, Gerald	85D	443	$ .01	$ .10	Picciolo, Rob	84D	455	$ .03	$ .10
Perry, Gerald	86D	165	$ .01	$ .06	Picciolo, Rob	86D	497	$ .01	$ .06
Perry, Gerald	88D	437	$ .01	$ .05	Pico, Jeff	89D	513	$ .01	$ .10
Perry, Gerald	88DBB	58	$ .01	$ .05	Pico, Jeff	90D	585	$ .01	$ .04
Perry, Gerald	89D	239	$ .01	$ .05	Piniella, Lou	81D	109	$ .03	$ .20
Perry, Gerald	89DBB	291	$ .01	$ .05	Piniella, Lou	82D	135	$ .03	$ .20
Perry, Gerald	89DBC	24	$ .01	$ .10	Piniella, Lou	83D	335	$ .01	$ .05
Perry, Gerald	89DK	22	$ .01	$ .05	Piniella, Lou	84D	274	$ .04	$ .15
Perry, Gerald	90D	153	$ .01	$ .04	Pinson, Vada	82D	445	$ .03	$ .20
Perry, Gerald	90DL	441	$ .01	$ .15	Pittaro, Chris	86D	150	$ .01	$ .06
Perry, Gerald	91D	130	$ .01	$ .03	Pittman, Joe	82D	218	$ .01	$ .05
Perry, Pat	86D	596	$ .01	$ .06	Pittman, Joe	83D	247	$ .01	$ .05
Perry, Pat	87D	430	$ .01	$ .05	Plantier, Phil	91DRR	41	$ .01	$ .50
Perry, Pat	88D	626	$ .01	$ .15	Plesac, Dan	86DR	14	$ .05	$ .30
Perry, Pat	89D	404	$ .01	$ .05	Plesac, Dan	87D	214	$ .03	$ .25
Peterek, Jeff	90D	530	$ .01	$ .10	Plesac, Dan	88D	109	$ .01	$ .05
Peters, Rick	81D	10	$ .01	$ .05	Plesac, Dan	88DBB	221	$ .01	$ .05
Peters, Rick	82D	155	$ .01	$ .05	Plesac, Dan	89D	382	$ .01	$ .05
Peters, Steve	88DR	22	$ .01	$ .05	Plesac, Dan	89DBB	165	$ .01	$ .05
Peterson, Adam	89D	619	$ .01	$ .10	Plesac, Dan	90D	175	$ .01	$ .04
Petralli, Geno	83D	623	$ .01	$ .05	Plesac, Dan	90DL	216	$ .01	$ .15
Petralli, Geno	87D	619	$ .01	$ .05	Plesac, Dan	91D	104	$ .01	$ .03
Petralli, Geno	88D	506	$ .01	$ .05	Plunk, Eric	86DR	40	$ .05	$ .25
Petralli, Geno	89D	343	$ .01	$ .05	Plunk, Eric	87D	178	$ .01	$ .05
Petralli, Geno	89DBB	312	$ .01	$ .05	Plunk, Eric	88D	503	$ .01	$ .05
Petralli, Geno	90D	56	$ .01	$ .04	Plunk, Eric	88DBB	267	$ .01	$ .05
Petralli, Geno	90DL	73	$ .01	$ .15	Plunk, Eric	89D	125	$ .01	$ .05
Petralli, Geno	91D	137	$ .01	$ .03	Plunk, Eric	89DBB	49	$ .01	$ .05
Petry, Dan	81D	128	$ .01	$ .05	Plunk, Eric	90D	196	$ .01	$ .04
Petry, Dan	82D	133	$ .01	$ .05	Plunk, Eric	90DL	504	$ .01	$ .15

DONRUSS

Player	Year	No.	VG	EX/MT	Player	Year	No.	VG	EX/MT
Plunk, Eric	91D	593	$ .01	$ .03	Pryor, Greg	84D	374	$ .03	$ .10
Pocoroba, Biff	83D	436	$ .01	$ .05	Pryor, Greg	85D	277	$ .01	$ .08
Pocoroba, Biff	84D	77	$ .03	$ .10	Pryor, Greg	86D	344	$ .01	$ .06
Podres, Johnny	82D	566	$ .01	$ .05	Pryor, Greg	87D	378	$ .01	$ .05
Polidor, Gus	87D	579	$ .01	$ .05	Puckett, Kirby	85D	438	$4.50	$23.50
Polidor, Gus	88D	356	$ .01	$ .05	Puckett, Kirby	86D	72	$ .50	$5.00
Polidor, Gus	90D	412	$ .01	$ .04	Puckett, Kirby	87D	149	$ .25	$1.50
Polonia, Luis	87DR	25	$ .10	$ .35	Puckett, Kirby	87DK	19	$ .10	$ .35
Polonia, Luis	88D	425	$ .04	$ .20	Puckett, Kirby	88D	368	$ .01	$ .25
Polonia, Luis	89D	386	$ .01	$ .05	Puckett, Kirby	88DBB	186	$ .10	$ .35
Polonia, Luis	90D	547	$ .01	$ .04	Puckett, Kirby	88DBC	15	$ .01	$ .25
Polonia, Luis	90DL	295	$ .01	$ .15	Puckett, Kirby	89D	182	$ .01	$ .25
Polonia, Luis	91D	93	$ .01	$ .03	Puckett, Kirby	89DBB	130	$ .01	$ .25
Ponce, Carlos	86D	595	$ .01	$ .06	Puckett, Kirby	89DBC	1	$ .05	$ .30
Poole, Jimmy	91D	655	$ .01	$ .10	Puckett, Kirby	90D	269	$ .01	$ .25
Porter, Chuck	84D	333	$ .03	$ .10	Puckett, Kirby	90DAS	683	$ .01	$ .15
Porter, Chuck	85D	115	$ .01	$ .08	Puckett, Kirby	90DBC	8	$ .01	$ .15
Porter, Darrell	81D	505	$ .01	$ .05	Puckett, Kirby	90DL	123	$ .01	$ .35
Porter, Darrell	82D	498	$ .03	$ .20	Puckett, Kirby	91D	490	$ .01	$ .10
Porter, Darrell	83D	278	$ .01	$ .05	Puckett, Kirby	91DLP	21	$1.00	$15.00
Porter, Darrell	84D	303	$ .03	$ .10	Puhl, Terry	81D	24	$ .01	$ .05
Porter, Darrell	85D	353	$ .01	$ .08	Puhl, Terry	82D	370	$ .01	$ .05
Porter, Darrell	86D	290	$ .01	$ .06	Puhl, Terry	83D	167	$ .01	$ .05
Porter, Darrell	87D	593	$ .01	$ .05	Puhl, Terry	84D	476	$ .03	$ .10
Portugal, Mark	86DR	44	$ .01	$ .15	Puhl, Terry	85D	426	$ .01	$ .08
Portugal, Mark	87D	566	$ .01	$ .10	Puhl, Terry	86D	206	$ .01	$ .06
Portugal, Mark	90D	542	$ .01	$ .04	Puhl, Terry	87D	431	$ .01	$ .05
Portugal, Mark	90DL	399	$ .01	$ .15	Puhl, Terry	88D	533	$ .01	$ .05
Portugal, Mark	91D	268	$ .01	$ .03	Puhl, Terry	89D	472	$ .01	$ .05
Powell, Dennis	86D	250	$ .01	$ .06	Puhl, Terry	89DBB	294	$ .01	$ .05
Powell, Dennis	87D	499	$ .01	$ .05	Puhl, Terry	90D	354	$ .01	$ .04
Powell, Hosken	81D	567	$ .01	$ .05	Pujols, Luis	81D	379	$ .01	$ .05
Powell, Hosken	82D	228	$ .01	$ .05	Pujols, Luis	82D	576	$ .01	$ .05
Powell, Hosken	83D	644	$ .01	$ .05	Pujols, Luis	83D	642	$ .01	$ .05
Power, Ted	84D	447	$ .03	$ .10	Puleo, Charlie	83D	128	$ .01	$ .05
Power, Ted	85D	286	$ .01	$ .08	Puleo, Charlie	84D	530	$ .03	$ .10
Power, Ted	86D	408	$ .01	$ .06	Puleo, Charlie	88D	537	$ .01	$ .05
Power, Ted	87D	536	$ .01	$ .05	Puleo, Charlie	89D	286	$ .01	$ .05
Power, Ted	88D	142	$ .01	$ .05	Pulido, Alfonso	85DRR	34	$ .01	$ .08
Power, Ted	89D	153	$ .01	$ .05	Putnam, Pat	81D	265	$ .01	$ .05
Power, Ted	90D	653	$ .01	$ .04	Putnam, Pat	82D	520	$ .01	$ .05
Power, Ted	90DL	473	$ .01	$ .15	Putnam, Pat	84D	145	$ .03	$ .10
Power, Ted	91D	608	$ .01	$ .03	Pyznarski, Tim	87D	654	$ .01	$ .05
Presley, Jim	85D	240	$ .30	$1.00	Quinones, Luis	88D	365	$ .01	$ .05
Presley, Jim	86D	313	$ .01	$ .15	Quinones, Luis	90D	595	$ .01	$ .04
Presley, Jim	87D	120	$ .01	$ .10	Quinones, Luis	91D	459	$ .01	$ .03
Presley, Jim	87DK	23	$ .01	$ .05	Quinones (nez), Rey	86DR	48	$ .02	$ .09
Presley, Jim	88D	366	$ .01	$ .15	Quinones (nez), Rey	87D	638	$ .01	$ .05
Presley, Jim	88DBB	219	$ .01	$ .05	vbQuinones, Rey	88D	198	$ .01	$ .05
Presley, Jim	89D	379	$ .01	$ .05	Quinones, Rey	89D	330	$ .01	$ .05
Presley, Jim	89DBB	331	$ .01	$ .05	Quinones, Rey	89DBB	185	$ .01	$ .05
Presley, Jim	90D	497	$ .01	$ .04	Quintana, Carlos	89DRR	37	$ .05	$ .35
Presley, Jim	90DL	277	$ .01	$ .15	Quintana, Carlos	90D	517	$ .01	$ .10
Presley, Jim	91D	173	$ .01	$ .03	Quintana, Carlos	90DL	394	$ .01	$ .25
Price, Joe	82D	481	$ .01	$ .05	Quintana, Carlos	91D	568	$ .01	$ .03
Price, Joe	83D	481	$ .01	$ .05	Quirk, Jamie	81D	341	$ .01	$ .05
Price, Joe	84D	506	$ .03	$ .10	Quirk, Jamie	82D	212	$ .01	$ .05
Price, Joe	85D	627	$ .01	$ .08	Quirk, Jamie	88D	404	$ .01	$ .05
Price, Joe	86D	506	$ .01	$ .06	Quirk, Jamie	91D	588	$ .01	$ .03
Price, Joe	88D	655	$ .01	$ .15	Quisenberry, Dan	81D	222	$ .05	$ .30
Price, Joe	89D	376	$ .01	$ .05	Quisenberry, Dan	82D	112	$ .02	$ .15
Prince, Tom	88D	538	$ .01	$ .05	Quisenberry, Dan	83D	70	$ .02	$ .15
Prince, Tom	89D	527	$ .01	$ .05	Quisenberry, Dan	84D	583	$ .08	$ .25
Proly, Mike	81D	596	$ .01	$ .05	Quisenberry, Dan	85D	95	$ .03	$ .20
Proly, Mike	82D	345	$ .01	$ .05	Quisenberry, Dan	85DK	6	$ .05	$ .20
Proly, Mike	83D	225	$ .01	$ .05	Quisenberry, Dan	86D	541	$ .05	$ .20
Proly, Mike	84D	320	$ .03	$ .10	Quisenberry, Dan	87D	177	$ .01	$ .05
Pryor, Greg	81D	278	$ .01	$ .05	Quisenberry, Dan	88D	471	$ .01	$ .15
Pryor, Greg	82D	521	$ .01	$ .05	Quisenberry, Dan	90D	437	$ .01	$ .04
Pryor, Greg	83D	264	$ .01	$ .05	Rabb, John	84D	143	$ .03	$ .10

Player	Year	No.	VG	EX/MT
Rabb, John	85D	236	$ .01	$ .08
Rader, Dave	81D	512	$ .01	$ .05
Radinsky, Scott	90DL	484	$ .01	$ .25
Radinsky, Scott	90DR	40	$ .01	$ .15
Radinsky, Scott	91D	332	$ .01	$ .10
Raines, Tim	81D	538	$1.00	$6.00
Raines, Tim	82D	214	$ .20	$1.50
Raines, Tim	83D	540	$ .15	$ .60
Raines, Tim	84D	299	$ .25	$1.00
Raines, Tim	85D	299	$ .15	$ .60
Raines, Tim	86D	177	$ .08	$ .30
Raines, Tim	87D	56	$ .08	$ .25
Raines, Tim	88D	345	$ .03	$ .25
Raines, Tim	88DBB	180	$ .01	$ .15
Raines, Tim	88DBC	18	$ .05	$ .25
Raines, Tim	88DK	2	$ .10	$ .25
Raines, Tim	89D	97	$ .01	$ .10
Raines, Tim	89DBB	258	$ .01	$ .15
Raines, Tim	90D	216	$ .01	$ .10
Raines, Tim	90DBC	7	$ .01	$ .10
Raines, Tim	90DL	212	$ .01	$ .20
Raines, Tim	91D	457	$ .01	$ .03
Rainey, Chuck	83D	334	$ .01	$ .05
Rainey, Chuck	84D	76	$ .03	$ .10
Rainey, Chuck	85D	618	$ .01	$ .08
Rajsich, Dave	81D	267	$ .01	$ .05
Rajsich, Gary	83D	599	$ .01	$ .05
Ramirez, Allan	84D	332	$ .03	$ .10
Ramirez, Mario	86D	568	$ .01	$ .06
Ramirez, Rafael	82D	546	$ .01	$ .05
Ramirez, Rafael	83D	310	$ .01	$ .05
Ramirez, Rafael	84D	589	$ .03	$ .10
Ramirez, Rafael	85D	141	$ .01	$ .08

Donruss '86

RAFAEL RAMIREZ SS

Player	Year	No.	VG	EX/MT
Ramirez, Rafael	86D	263	$ .01	$ .06
Ramirez, Rafael	87D	202	$ .01	$ .05
Ramirez, Rafael	88D	448	$ .01	$ .05
Ramirez, Rafael	89D	509	$ .01	$ .05
Ramirez, Rafael	89DBB	64	$ .01	$ .05
Ramirez, Rafael	90D	241	$ .01	$ .04
Ramirez, Rafael	90DL	135	$ .01	$ .15
Ramirez, Rafael	91D	586	$ .01	$ .03

Player	Year	No.	VG	EX/MT
Ramos, Bobby	84D	209	$ .03	$ .10
Ramos, Domingo	84D	440	$ .03	$ .10
Ramos, Domingo	88D	622	$ .01	$ .15
Ramos, Domingo	90D	491	$ .01	$ .04
Ramos, Domingo	90DL	440	$ .01	$ .15
Ramsey, Mike	82D	316	$ .01	$ .05
Ramsey, Mike	83D	568	$ .01	$ .05
Ramsey, Mike	84D	382	$ .03	$ .10
Randle, Lenny	81D	485	$ .01	$ .05
Randle, Lenny	82D	307	$ .01	$ .05
Randolph, Willie	81D	345	$ .01	$ .05
Randolph, Willie	82D	461	$ .01	$ .05
Randolph, Willie	83D	283	$ .01	$ .05
Randolph, Willie	84D	417	$ .03	$ .10
Randolph, Willie	85D	92	$ .01	$ .08
Randolph, Willie	86D	92	$ .01	$ .06
Randolph, Willie	86DK	16	$ .01	$ .06
Randolph, Willie	87D	154	$ .01	$ .05
Randolph, Willie	88D	228	$ .01	$ .05
Randolph, Willie	88DBB	108	$ .01	$ .05
Randolph, Willie	89D	395	$ .01	$ .05
Randolph, Willie	89DBB	148	$ .01	$ .05
Randolph, Willie	89DTR	8	$ .01	$ .15
Randolph, Willie	90D	250	$ .01	$ .04
Randolph, Willie	90DK	19	$ .01	$ .10
Randolph, Willie	90DL	345	$ .01	$ .15
Randolph, Willie	91D	217	$ .01	$ .03
Randolph, Willie	91D	766	$ .01	$ .03
Rasmussen, Dennis	84D	446	$ .15	$1.00
Rasmussen, Dennis	85D	518	$ .01	$ .08
Rasmussen, Dennis	86D	336	$ .01	$ .06
Rasmussen, Dennis	87D	175	$ .01	$ .05
Rasmussen, Dennis	88D	575	$ .01	$ .15
Rasmussen, Dennis	89D	559	$ .01	$ .05
Rasmussen, Dennis	90D	420	$ .01	$ .10
Rasmussen, Dennis	90DL	471	$ .01	$ .15
Rasmussen, Dennis	91D	458	$ .01	$ .03
Rasmussen, Eric	81D	123	$ .01	$ .05
Rawley, Shane	81D	167	$ .01	$ .05
Rawley, Shane	82D	352	$ .01	$ .05
Rawley, Shane	83D	513	$ .01	$ .05
Rawley, Shane	84D	295	$ .03	$ .10
Rawley, Shane	85D	599	$ .01	$ .08
Rawley, Shane	86D	233	$ .01	$ .06
Rawley, Shane	87D	83	$ .01	$ .05
Rawley, Shane	88D	83	$ .01	$ .05
Rawley, Shane	88DBB	240	$ .01	$ .05
Rawley, Shane	88DK	13	$ .01	$ .05
Rawley, Shane	89D	251	$ .01	$ .05
Rawley, Shane	90D	537	$ .01	$ .04
Ray, Johnny	82D	528	$ .15	$ .75
Ray, Johnny	83D	437	$ .03	$ .20
Ray, Johnny	84D	308	$ .03	$ .20
Ray, Johnny	85D	186	$ .01	$ .10
Ray, Johnny	86D	186	$ .05	$ .20
Ray, Johnny	86DK	19	$ .01	$ .06
Ray, Johnny	87D	144	$ .01	$ .05
Ray, Johnny	88D	428	$ .01	$ .05
Ray, Johnny	88DBB	171	$ .01	$ .05
Ray, Johnny	89D	331	$ .01	$ .05
Ray, Johnny	89DBB	195	$ .01	$ .05
Ray, Johnny	89DK	12	$ .01	$ .05
Ray, Johnny	90D	234	$ .01	$ .04
Ray, Johnny	90DL	208	$ .01	$ .15
Ray, Johnny	91D	622	$ .01	$ .20
Rayford, Floyd	85D	576	$ .01	$ .08
Rayford, Floyd	86D	332	$ .01	$ .06
Ready, Randy	86D	481	$ .01	$ .06
Ready, Randy	88D	264	$ .01	$ .05
Ready, Randy	89D	365	$ .01	$ .05

Player	Year	No.	VG	EX/MT	Player	Year	No.	VG	EX/MT
Ready, Randy	89DBB	215	$ .01	$ .05	Reuschel, Rick	88D	613	$ .01	$ .05
Ready, Randy	90D	396	$ .01	$ .04	Reuschel, Rick	88DBB	218	$ .01	$ .05
Ready, Randy	90DL	500	$ .01	$ .15	Reuschel, Rick	89D	335	$ .01	$ .05
Ready, Randy	91D	148	$ .01	$ .03	Reuschel, Rick	89DBB	162	$ .01	$ .05
Reardon, Jeff	81D	156	$ .25	$1.00	Reuschel, Rick	89DK	11	$ .01	$ .05
Reardon, Jeff	82D	547	$ .01	$ .25					
Reardon, Jeff	83D	194	$ .01	$ .05					
Reardon, Jeff	84D	279	$ .03	$ .10					
Reardon, Jeff	85D	331	$ .01	$ .08					
Reardon, Jeff	86D	209	$ .01	$ .06					
Reardon, Jeff	87D	98	$ .01	$ .05					
Reardon, Jeff	88D	122	$ .01	$ .05					
Reardon, Jeff	88DBB	242	$ .01	$ .05					
Reardon, Jeff	89D	155	$ .01	$ .05					
Reardon, Jeff	89DBB	242	$ .01	$ .05					
Reardon, Jeff	90D	119	$ .01	$ .04					
Reardon, Jeff	90DL	276	$ .01	$ .15					
Reardon, Jeff	91D	369	$ .01	$ .03					
Redfern, Pete	81D	548	$ .01	$ .05					
Redfern, Pete	82D	51	$ .01	$ .05					
Redfern, Pete	83D	256	$ .01	$ .05					
Redus, Gary	84D	184	$ .03	$ .25					
Redus, Gary	85D	306	$ .01	$ .08					
Redus, Gary	86D	306	$ .01	$ .06					
Redus, Gary	87D	288	$ .01	$ .05					
Redus, Gary	88D	370	$ .01	$ .05					
Redus, Gary	89D	605	$ .01	$ .05					
Redus, Gary	90D	597	$ .01	$ .04					
Redus, Gary	90DL	209	$ .01	$ .15					
Redus, Gary	91D	587	$ .01	$ .03					
Reed, Jeff	85DRR	30	$ .01	$ .08					
Reed, Jeff	88D	88	$ .01	$ .05					
Reed, Jeff	89D	469	$ .01	$ .05	Reuschel, Rick	90D	112	$ .01	$ .04
Reed, Jeff	90D	351	$ .01	$ .04	Reuschel, Rick	90DAS	663	$ .01	$ .04
Reed, Jeff	90DL	505	$ .01	$ .15	Reuschel, Rick	91D	518	$ .01	$ .03
Reed, Jeff	91D	741	$ .01	$ .03	Reuss, Jerry	81D	417	$ .01	$ .05
Reed, Jerry	88D	517	$ .01	$ .05	Reuss, Jerry	82D	284	$ .01	$ .05
Reed, Jerry	89D	657	$ .01	$ .05	Reuss, Jerry	83D	158	$ .01	$ .05
Reed, Jerry	90D	614	$ .01	$ .04	Reuss, Jerry	84D	418	$ .03	$ .10
Reed, Jerry	90DL	368	$ .01	$ .15	Reuss, Jerry	85D	226	$ .01	$ .08
Reed, Jody	88DBB	196	$ .01	$ .50	Reuss, Jerry	86D	104	$ .02	$ .15
Reed, Jody	88DR	44	$ .05	$ .25	Reuss, Jerry	89D	413	$ .01	$ .05
Reed, Jody	88DRR	41	$ .05	$ .35	Reuss, Jerry	89DBB	305	$ .01	$ .05
Reed, Jody	89D	305	$ .01	$ .10	Reuss, Jerry	90D	528	$ .01	$ .04
Reed, Jody	89DBB	289	$ .01	$ .05	Revering, Dave	81D	117	$ .01	$ .05
Reed, Jody	90D	398	$ .01	$ .04	Revering, Dave	82D	234	$ .01	$ .05
Reed, Jody	90DL	150	$ .01	$ .15	Reyes, Gilberto	86D	581	$ .01	$ .06
Reed, Jody	91D	123	$ .01	$ .03	Reynolds, Craig	81D	378	$ .01	$ .05
Reed, Rick	90D	527	$ .01	$ .10	Reynolds, Craig	82D	344	$ .01	$ .05
Reed, Rick	90DL	427	$ .01	$ .15	Reynolds, Craig	83D	317	$ .01	$ .05
Reed, Ron	81D	44	$ .01	$ .05	Reynolds, Craig	84D	405	$ .03	$ .10
Reed, Ron	82D	399	$ .01	$ .05	Reynolds, Craig	85D	328	$ .01	$ .08
Reed, Ron	83D	567	$ .01	$ .05	Reynolds, Craig	86D	232	$ .01	$ .06
Reed, Ron	84D	529	$ .03	$ .10	Reynolds, Craig	87D	384	$ .01	$ .05
Reed, Ron	85D	282	$ .01	$ .08	Reynolds, Craig	88D	209	$ .01	$ .05
Reimer, Kevin	91D	80	$ .01	$ .10	Reynolds, Craig	89D	477	$ .01	$ .05
Reitz, Ken	81D	307	$ .01	$ .05	Reynolds, Harold	86D	484	$ .05	$ .65
Reitz, Ken	82D	277	$ .01	$ .05	Reynolds, Harold	87D	489	$ .01	$ .10
Remmerswaal, Win	81D	98	$ .01	$ .05	Reynolds, Harold	88D	563	$ .01	$ .05
Remy, Jerry	81D	215	$ .01	$ .05	Reynolds, Harold	89D	93	$ .01	$ .05
Remy, Jerry	82D	156	$ .01	$ .05	Reynolds, Harold	89DBB	51	$ .01	$ .05
Remy, Jerry	83D	74	$ .01	$ .05	Reynolds, Harold	89DK	21	$ .01	$ .05
Remy, Jerry	84D	172	$ .03	$ .10	Reynolds, Harold	90D	227	$ .01	$ .04
Renko, Steve	81D	337	$ .01	$ .05	Reynolds, Harold	90DL	140	$ .01	$ .15
Renko, Steve	82D	38	$ .01	$ .05	Reynolds, Harold	91D	175	$ .01	$ .03
Renko, Steve	83D	393	$ .01	$ .05	Reynolds, R. J.	85D	128	$ .08	$ .25
Reuschel, Rick	81D	561	$ .01	$ .10	Reynolds, R. J.	86D	552	$ .01	$ .06
Reuschel, Rick	82D	157	$ .01	$ .05	Reynolds, R. J.	87D	65	$ .01	$ .05
Reuschel, Rick	86D	532	$ .01	$ .05					
Reuschel, Rick	87D	188	$ .01	$ .05					

Player	Year	No.	VG	EX/MT	Player	Year	No.	VG	EX/MT
Reynolds, R. J.	88D	65	$ .01	$ .05	Ripken, Billy	88D	625	$ .05	$ .30
Reynolds, R. J.	88DBB	201	$ .01	$ .05	Ripken, Billy	88DBB	254	$ .01	$ .10
Reynolds, R. J.	89D	134	$ .01	$ .05	Ripken, Billy	89D	259	$ .01	$ .05
Reynolds, R. J.	89DBB	257	$ .01	$ .05	Ripken, Billy	89DBB	318	$ .01	$ .05
Reynolds, R. J.	90D	447	$ .01	$ .04	Ripken, Billy	90D	164	$ .01	$ .04
Reynolds, R. J.	90DL	381	$ .01	$ .15	Ripken, Billy	90DL	271	$ .01	$ .15
Reynolds, R. J.	91D	101	$ .01	$ .03	Ripken, Billy	91D	167	$ .01	$ .03
Rhoden, Rick	82D	423	$ .01	$ .05	Ripken, Sr., Cal	82D	579	$ .03	$ .20
Rhoden, Rick	83D	250	$ .01	$ .05	Ripken, Sr., Cal	88D	625	$ .05	$ .30
Rhoden, Rick	84D	552	$ .03	$ .10	Ripken, Cal	89DBB	142	$ .01	$ .10
Rhoden, Rick	85D	552	$ .01	$ .08	Ripken, Cal	90D	96	$ .01	$ .10
Rhoden, Rick	86D	166	$ .01	$ .06	Ripken, Cal	90DAS	676	$ .01	$ .10
Rhoden, Rick	87D	435	$ .01	$ .05	Ripken, Cal	90DBC	18	$ .01	$ .10
Rhoden, Rick	87DK	10	$ .01	$ .05	Ripken, Jr., Cal	82D	405	$3.50	$30.00
Rhoden, Rick	88D	128	$ .01	$ .05	Ripken, Jr., Cal	83D	279	$1.00	$8.00
Rhoden, Rick	88DBB	161	$ .01	$ .05	Ripken, Jr., Cal	84D	106	$1.50	$12.00
Rhoden, Rick	89D	429	$ .01	$ .05	Ripken, Jr., Cal	85D	169	$ .35	$3.00
Rhoden, Rick	89DTR	40	$ .01	$ .10	Ripken, Jr., Cal	85DK	14	$ .15	$ .75
Rhodes, Karl	91D	698	$ .01	$ .10	Ripken, Jr., Cal	86D	210	$ .15	$1.50
Rice, Jim	81D	338	$ .10	$ .35	Ripken, Jr., Cal	87D	89	$ .08	$ .35
Rice, Jim	82D	200	$ .05	$ .25	Ripken, Jr., Cal	88D	171	$ .03	$ .25
Rice, Jim	83D	208	$ .05	$ .30	Ripken, Jr., Cal	88D	625	$ .05	$ .30
Rice, Jim	84D	50	$ .10	$ .50	Ripken, Jr., Cal	88DBB	198	$ .05	$ .25
Rice, Jim	85D	50	$ .01	$ .25	Ripken, Jr., Cal	88DBC	1	$ .05	$ .25
Rice, Jim	85DK	15	$ .01	$ .20	Ripken, Jr., Cal	88DK	26	$ .10	$ .25
Rice, Jim	86D	213	$ .03	$ .25	Ripken, Jr., Cal	89D	51	$ .04	$ .20
Rice, Jim	87D	92	$ .03	$ .25	Ripken, Jr., Cal	89DBC	15	$ .01	$ .20
Rice, Jim	88D	399	$ .04	$ .20	Ripken, Cal	90DL	197	$ .01	$ .75
Rice, Jim	88DBB	28	$ .01	$ .15	Ripken, Cal	91D	223	$ .01	$ .10
Rice, Jim	89D	122	$ .01	$ .15	Ripken, Cal	91DAS	52	$ .01	$ .10
Richard, J.R.	81D	140	$ .02	$ .15	Ripken, Cal	91DBC	17	$ .01	$ .10
Richards, Gene	81D	4	$ .01	$ .05	Ripley, Allen	82D	125	$ .01	$ .05
Richards, Gene	82D	499	$ .01	$ .05	Ripley, Allen	83D	57	$ .01	$ .05
Richards, Gene	83D	271	$ .01	$ .05	Ritchie, Wally	88D	555	$ .01	$ .05
Richards, Gene	84D	429	$ .03	$ .10	Ritz, Kevin	90D	415	$ .01	$ .10
Richardt, Mike	83D	368	$ .01	$ .05	Rivera, Bombo	81D	593	$ .01	$ .05
Righetti, Dave	82D	73	$ .30	$1.75	Rivera, German	85D	638	$ .01	$ .08
Righetti, Dave	83D	199	$ .05	$ .25	Rivera, Luis	89D	578	$ .01	$ .05
Righetti, Dave	84D	103	$ .08	$ .25	Rivera, Luis	90D	421	$ .01	$ .04
Righetti, Dave	84DK	10	$ .08	$ .25	Rivera, Luis	90DL	283	$ .01	$ .15
Righetti, Dave	85D	336	$ .03	$ .20	Rivera, Luis	91D	234	$ .01	$ .03
Righetti, Dave	86D	214	$ .01	$ .06	Rivers, Mickey	81D	496	$ .02	$ .15
Righetti, Dave	87D	128	$ .01	$ .05	Rivers, Mickey	82D	242	$ .02	$ .15
Righetti, Dave	88D	93	$ .01	$ .15	Rivers, Mickey	83D	394	$ .01	$ .05
Righetti, Dave	88DBB	164	$ .01	$ .05	Rivers, Mickey	84D	465	$ .03	$ .10
Righetti, Dave	89D	78	$ .01	$ .05	Rivers, Mickey	85D	465	$ .01	$ .08
Righetti, Dave	89DBB	76	$ .01	$ .05	Robbins, Bruce	81D	129	$ .01	$ .05
Righetti, Dave	90D	311	$ .01	$ .04	Roberge, Bert	83D	496	$ .01	$ .05
Righetti, Dave	91D	275	$ .01	$ .03	Roberge, Bert	86D	575	$ .01	$ .06
Righetti, Dave	91DK	21	$ .01	$ .05	Roberts, Dave	81D	490	$ .01	$ .05
Rijo, Jose	85D	492	$ .40	$2.00	Roberts, Dave	81D	501	$ .01	$ .05
Rijo, Jose	86D	522	$ .05	$ .25	Roberts, Dave	82D	625	$ .01	$ .05
Rijo, Jose	87D	55	$ .04	$ .20	Roberts, Dave	83D	273	$ .01	$ .05
Rijo, Jose	88D	548	$ .01	$ .15	Roberts, Leon	81D	48	$ .01	$ .05
Rijo, Jose	89D	375	$ .01	$ .05	Roberts, Leon	82D	415	$ .01	$ .05
Rijo, Jose	89DBB	278	$ .01	$ .05	Roberts, Leon	84D	399	$ .03	$ .10
Rijo, Jose	90D	115	$ .01	$ .04	Roberts, Leon (Bip)	86DR	33	$ .01	$ .75
Rijo, Jose	90DL	282	$ .01	$ .25	Roberts, Leon (Bip)	87D	114	$ .01	$ .45
Rijo, Jose	91D	723	$ .01	$ .03	Roberts, Bip	90D	347	$ .01	$ .04
Rijo, Jose	91D	742	$ .01	$ .03	Roberts, Bip	90DL	233	$ .01	$ .15
Riles, Ernest	86D	359	$ .03	$ .25	Roberts, Bip	91D	195	$ .01	$ .03
Riles, Ernest	87D	151	$ .01	$ .05	Robertson, Andre	83D	387	$ .01	$ .05
Riles, Ernest	88D	478	$ .01	$ .05	Robertson, Andre	84D	347	$ .03	$ .10
Riles, Ernest	89D	625	$ .01	$ .05	Robertson, Andre	86D	469	$ .01	$ .06
Riles, Ernest	89DBB	50	$ .01	$ .05	Robidoux, Billy	86D	515	$ .01	$ .06
Riles, Ernest	90D	131	$ .01	$ .04	Robidoux, Billy	87D	240	$ .01	$ .05
Riles, Ernest	91D	461	$ .01	$ .03	Robinson, Bill	81D	137	$ .01	$ .05
Riley, George	81D	588	$ .01	$ .05	Robinson, Bill	82D	402	$ .01	$ .05
Ripken, Billy	87DR	16	$ .01	$ .25	Robinson, Don	81D	375	$ .01	$ .05
Ripken, Billy	88D	336	$ .01	$ .20	Robinson, Don	83D	171	$ .01	$ .05

Player	Year	No.	VG	EX/MT	Player	Year	No.	VG	EX/MT
Robinson, Don	84D	532	$ .03	$ .10	Romero, Ed	85D	515	$ .01	$ .08
Robinson, Don	85D	262	$ .01	$ .08	Romero, Ed	86D	455	$ .01	$ .06
Robinson, Don	85D	264	$ .01	$ .08	Romero, Ed	87D	606	$ .01	$ .05
Robinson, Don	86D	357	$ .01	$ .06	Romero, Ed	88D	623	$ .01	$ .15
Robinson, Don	87D	608	$ .01	$ .05	Romero, Ramon	86D	495	$ .01	$ .06
Robinson, Don	88D	573	$ .01	$ .05	Romine, Kevin	90D	476	$ .01	$ .04
Robinson, Don	89D	571	$ .01	$ .05	Romine, Kevin	90DL	414	$ .01	$ .15
Robinson, Don	89DBB	191	$ .01	$ .05	Romine, Kevin	91D	290	$ .01	$ .03
Robinson, Don	90D	258	$ .01	$ .04	Romo, Enrique	81D	255	$ .01	$ .05
Robinson, Don	90DL	267	$ .01	$ .15	Romo, Enrique	82D	59	$ .01	$ .05
Robinson, Don	91D	581	$ .01	$ .03	Roof, Phil	82D	615	$ .01	$ .05
Robinson, Frank	82D	424	$ .03	$ .20	Roomes, Rolando	89D	577	$ .01	$ .10
Robinson, Frank	83D	564	$ .02	$ .15					
Robinson, Frank	83D	648	$ .01	$ .15					
Robinson, Jeff D.	85D	201	$ .01	$ .25					
Robinson, Jeff D.	87D	559	$ .01	$ .05					
Robinson, Jeff D.	88D	558	$ .01	$ .05					
Robinson, Jeff D.	88DBB	241	$ .01	$ .05					
Robinson, Jeff D.	89D	370	$ .01	$ .05					
Robinson, Jeff D.	89DBB	129	$ .01	$ .05					
Robinson, Jeff D.	90D	134	$ .01	$ .04					
Robinson, Jeff D.	90DL	412	$ .01	$ .15					
Robinson, Jeff D.	91D	291	$ .01	$ .03					
Robinson, Jeff M.	87DR	13	$ .01	$ .25					
Robinson, Jeff M.	88D	296	$ .01	$ .15					
Robinson, Jeff M.	89D	470	$ .01	$ .05					
Robinson, Jeff M.	89DK	18	$ .01	$ .05					
Robinson, Jeff M.	90D	417	$ .01	$ .04					
Robinson, Jeff M.	90DL	429	$ .01	$ .15					
Robinson, Jeff M.	91D	245	$ .01	$ .03					
Robinson, Ron	85D	649	$ .08	$ .50					
Robinson, Ron	86D	121	$ .01	$ .06					
Robinson, Ron	87D	310	$ .01	$ .05					
Robinson, Ron	88D	166	$ .01	$ .05					
Robinson, Ron	89D	308	$ .01	$ .05					
Robinson, Ron	90D	553	$ .01	$ .04					
Robinson, Ron	90DL	467	$ .01	$ .15					
Robinson, Ron	91D	254	$ .01	$ .03					
Rodgers, Bob	81D	327	$ .01	$ .05					
Rodgers, Bob	82D	232	$ .01	$ .05					
Rodriguez, Aurelio	83D	369	$ .01	$ .05					
Rodriguez, Rich	91D	769	$ .01	$ .10					
Rodriguez, Vic	85D	535	$ .01	$ .08	Roomes, Rolando	90D	360	$ .01	$ .04
Roenicke, Gary	81D	116	$ .01	$ .05	Rose, Pete	81D	131	$ .25	$1.00
Roenicke, Gary	82D	509	$ .01	$ .05	Rose, Pete	81D	251	$ .25	$1.25
Roenicke, Gary	83D	27	$ .01	$ .05	Rose, Pete	81D	371	$ .25	$1.25
Roenicke, Gary	85D	123	$ .01	$ .08	Rose, Pete	82D	168	$ .25	$1.25
Roenicke, Gary	86D	472	$ .01	$ .06	Rose, Pete	82D	585	$ .15	$1.25
Roenicke, Ron	83D	327	$ .01	$ .05	Rose, Pete	82DK	1	$ .25	$1.25
Roenicke, Ron	84D	392	$ .03	$ .10	Rose, Pete	83D	42	$ .25	$1.00
Roenicke, Ron	84D	484	$ .03	$ .10	Rose, Pete	84D	61	$ .80	$2.50
Roenicke, Ron	87D	412	$ .01	$ .05	Rose, Pete	85D	254	$ .40	$1.25
Rogers, Kenny	89DBB	315	$ .01	$ .15	Rose, Pete	85D	641	$ .50	$1.50
Rogers, Kenny	89DR	13	$ .01	$ .25	Rose, Pete	86D	62	$ .15	$ .75
Rogers, Kenny	90D	283	$ .01	$ .10	Rose, Pete	86D	644	$ .05	$ .35
Rogers, Kenny	90DL	311	$ .01	$ .20	Rose, Pete	86DK	653	$ .35	$1.00
Rogers, Kenny	91D	258	$ .01	$ .03	Rose, Pete	87D	186	$ .20	$ .60
Rogers, Steve	81D	330	$ .01	$ .05	Rosello, Dave	81D	79	$ .01	$ .05
Rogers, Steve	82D	36	$ .01	$ .05	Rosello, Dave	82D	617	$ .01	$ .05
Rogers, Steve	83D	320	$ .01	$ .05	Rosenberg, Steve	89D	219	$ .01	$ .05
Rogers, Steve	83DK	18	$ .01	$ .05	Rosenberg, Steve	90D	253	$ .01	$ .04
Rogers, Steve	84D	219	$ .03	$ .10	Rowdon, Wade	85D	642	$ .01	$ .08
Rogers, Steve	85D	219	$ .01	$ .08	Royster, Jerry	81D	339	$ .01	$ .05
Rohde, Dave	91D	743	$ .01	$ .10	Royster, Jerry	82D	555	$ .01	$ .05
Rojas, Mel	91D	681	$ .01	$ .10	Royster, Jerry	83D	425	$ .01	$ .05
Romanick, Ron	85D	451	$ .01	$ .08	Royster, Jerry	84D	531	$ .03	$ .10
Romanick, Ron	86D	85	$ .01	$ .06	Royster, Jerry	86D	446	$ .01	$ .06
Romero, Ed	82D	536	$ .01	$ .05	Royster, Jerry	87D	534	$ .01	$ .05
Romero, Ed	83D	584	$ .01	$ .05	Royster, Jerry	88D	660	$ .01	$ .15
Romero, Ed	84D	89	$ .03	$ .10	Rozema, Dave	81D	9	$ .01	$ .05

Player	Year	No.	VG	EX/MT	Player	Year	No.	VG	EX/MT
Rozema, Dave	82D	259	$ .01	$ .05	Ryan, Nolan	90DL	265	$ .01	$ 2.50
Rozema, Dave	83D	133	$ .01	$ .05	Ryan, Nolan	91D	89	$ .01	$ .35
Rozema, Dave	84D	272	$ .03	$ .10	Ryan, Nolan	91DBC	3	$ .01	$ .25
Rozema, Dave	85D	125	$ .01	$ .08	Ryan, Nolan	91DBC	15	$ .01	$ .25
Rozema, Dave	86D	343	$ .01	$ .06	Ryan, Nolan	91DLP	25	$1.00	$25.00
Rucker, Dave	83D	641	$ .01	$ .05	Saberhagen, Bret	85D	222	$1.35	$7.50
Rucker, Dave	84D	260	$ .03	$ .10	Saberhagen, Bret	86D	100	$ .15	$1.00
Rucker, Dave	85D	260	$ .01	$ .08	Saberhagen, Bret	86DK	11	$ .08	$ .35
Rucker, Dave	86D	448	$ .01	$ .06	Saberhagen, Bret	87D	132	$ .08	$ .35
Rudi, Joe	81D	174	$ .01	$ .05	Saberhagen, Bret	88D	96	$ .05	$ .20
Rudi, Joe	82D	586	$ .01	$ .05	Saberhagen, Bret	88DBB	231	$ .01	$ .10
Rudi, Joe	83D	287	$ .01	$ .05	Saberhagen, Bret	89D	144	$ .01	$ .10
Ruffin, Bruce	87D	555	$ .08	$ .25	Saberhagen, Bret	89DBB	95	$ .01	$ .15
Ruffin, Bruce	88D	165	$ .01	$ .15	Saberhagen, Bret	90D	89	$ .01	$ .10
Ruffin, Bruce	89D	515	$ .01	$ .05	Saberhagen, Bret	90DL	72	$ .01	$ .20
Ruffin, Bruce	90DL	151	$ .01	$ .15	Saberhagen, Bret	91D	88	$ .01	$ .03
Ruhle, Vern	81D	261	$ .01	$ .05	Sabo, Chris	88DR	30	$ .45	$1.75
Ruhle, Vern	82D	293	$ .01	$ .05	Sabo, Chris	89D	317	$ .25	$ .75
Ruhle, Vern	83D	627	$ .01	$ .05	Sabo, Chris	89DBB	222	$ .01	$ .20
Ruhle, Vern	84D	564	$ .03	$ .10	Sabo, Chris	89DK	4	$ .01	$ .25
Ruhle, Vern	85D	380	$ .01	$ .08	Sabo, Chris	90D	242	$ .01	$ .15
Runnells, Tom	86D	569	$ .01	$ .06	Sabo, Chris	90DL	146	$ .01	$ .25
Ruskin, Scott	90DL	512	$ .01	$ .25	Sabo, Chris	91D	153	$ .01	$ .10
Ruskin, Scott	90DR	27	$ .01	$ .15	Sabo, Chris	91DAS	440	$ .01	$ .03
Ruskin, Scott	91D	612	$ .01	$ .03	Sabo, Chris	91DMVP	412	$ .01	$ .03
Russell, Bill	81D	57	$ .01	$ .05	Sadek, Mike	81D	498	$ .01	$ .05
Russell, Bill	82D	453	$ .01	$ .05	Sakata, Lenn	81D	499	$ .01	$ .05
Russell, Bill	83D	210	$ .01	$ .05	Sakata, Lenn	82D	644	$ .01	$ .05
Russell, Bill	84D	587	$ .03	$ .10	Sakata, Lenn	83D	205	$ .01	$ .05
Russell, Bill	85D	93	$ .01	$ .08	Sakata, Lenn	84D	620	$ .03	$ .10
Russell, Bill	86D	153	$ .01	$ .06	Salas, Mark	85D	547	$ .01	$ .08
Russell, Jeff	84D	569	$ .05	$ .75	Salas, Mark	86D	316	$ .01	$ .06
Russell, Jeff	85D	487	$ .01	$ .08	Salas, Mark	91D	65	$ .01	$ .03
Russell, Jeff	86D	586	$ .01	$ .06	Salazar, Angel	84DRR	33	$ .03	$ .10
Russell, Jeff	87D	550	$ .01	$ .05	Salazar, Angel	85D	523	$ .01	$ .08
Russell, Jeff	88D	531	$ .01	$ .05	Salazar, Angel	87D	624	$ .01	$ .05
Russell, Jeff	89D	403	$ .01	$ .05	Salazar, Angel	88D	502	$ .01	$ .05
Russell, Jeff	89DBB	200	$ .01	$ .05	Salazar, Luis	82D	472	$ .01	$ .05
Russell, Jeff	90D	284	$ .01	$ .04	Salazar, Luis	83D	548	$ .01	$ .05
Russell, Jeff	90DL	152	$ .01	$ .15	Salazar, Luis	84D	356	$ .03	$ .10
Russell, Jeff	90DL	442	$ .01	$ .15	Salazar, Luis	85D	568	$ .01	$ .08
Russell, Jeff	91D	202	$ .01	$ .03	Salazar, Luis	86D	302	$ .01	$ .06
Russell, John	85D	648	$ .01	$ .08	Salazar, Luis	89D	352	$ .01	$ .05
Russell, John	86D	82	$ .01	$ .06	Salazar, Luis	90D	513	$ .01	$ .04
Russell, John	87D	207	$ .01	$ .05	Salazar, Luis	90DL	388	$ .01	$ .15
Russell, John	90D	458	$ .01	$ .04	Salazar, Luis	91D	372	$ .01	$ .03
Ruthven, Dick	81D	153	$ .01	$ .05	Sambito, Joe	81D	21	$ .01	$ .05
Ruthven, Dick	82D	525	$ .01	$ .05	Sambito, Joe	82D	65	$ .01	$ .05
Ruthven, Dick	83D	497	$ .01	$ .05	Sambito, Joe	83D	244	$ .01	$ .05
Ruthven, Dick	84D	510	$ .03	$ .10	Sambito, Joe	85D	572	$ .01	$ .08
Ruthven, Dick	86D	564	$ .01	$ .06	Sambito, Joe	87D	421	$ .01	$ .05
Ryal, Mark	87D	583	$ .01	$ .05	Sampen, Bill	90DR	12	$ .01	$ .15
Ryan, Nolan	81D	260	$1.00	$4.00	Sampen, Bill	91D	351	$ .01	$ .10
Ryan, Nolan	82D	419	$1.00	$4.00	Sample, Billy	81D	268	$ .01	$ .05
Ryan, Nolan	82DK	13	$ .25	$2.00	Sample, Billy	82D	69	$ .01	$ .05
Ryan, Nolan	83D	118	$1.00	$4.00	Sample, Billy	83D	242	$ .01	$ .05
Ryan, Nolan	84D	60	$3.00	$11.00	Sample, Billy	84D	403	$ .03	$ .10
Ryan, Nolan	85D	60	$ .50	$3.75	Sample, Billy	85D	464	$ .01	$ .08
Ryan, Nolan	86D	258	$ .35	$2.00	Sample, Billy	86D	539	$ .01	$ .06
Ryan, Nolan	87D	138	$ .15	$1.00	Sample, Billy	87D	143	$ .01	$ .05
Ryan, Nolan	88D	61	$ .10	$ .50	Samuel, Juan	85D	183	$ .20	$1.00
Ryan, Nolan	88DBB	232	$ .10	$ .35	Samuel, Juan	85DK	23	$ .01	$ .20
Ryan, Nolan	89D	154	$ .10	$ .35	Samuel, Juan	86D	326	$ .01	$ .15
Ryan, Nolan	89DBB	55	$ .01	$ .50	Samuel, Juan	87D	165	$ .01	$ .05
Ryan, Nolan	89DTR	19	$ .01	$ .25	Samuel, Juan	88D	288	$ .05	$ .20
Ryan, Nolan	90D	166	$ .01	$ .50	Samuel, Juan	88DBB	215	$ .01	$ .05
Ryan, Nolan	90DAS	659	$ .01	$1.00	Samuel, Juan	89D	76	$ .01	$ .05
Ryan, Nolan	90DK	665	$ .01	$1.00	Samuel, Juan	89DBB	238	$ .01	$ .05
Ryan, Nolan	90DL	21	$ .01	$2.00	Samuel, Juan	90D	53	$ .01	$ .04
Ryan, Nolan	90DL	264	$ .01	$ .35	Samuel, Juan	90DL	226	$ .01	$ .15

DONRUSS

Player	Year	No.	VG	EX/MT	Player	Year	No.	VG	EX/MT
Samuel, Juan	91D	62	$ .01	$ .03	Sanderson, Scott	87D	447	$ .01	$ .05
Sanchez, Alejandro	85DRR	43	$ .01	$ .08	Sanderson, Scott	88D	646	$ .01	$ .15
Sanchez, Alejandro	86D	415	$ .01	$ .06	Sanderson, Scott	89D	629	$ .01	$ .05
Sanchez, Alex	89DRR	47	$ .01	$ .15	Sanderson, Scott	90D	647	$ .01	$ .04
Sanchez, Alex	90DRR	45	$ .01	$ .10	Sanderson, Scott	90DL	194	$ .01	$ .15
Sanchez, Israel	89D	474	$ .01	$ .10	Sanderson, Scott	91D	533	$ .01	$ .03
Sanchez, Luis	83D	519	$ .01	$ .05	Sanguillen, Manny	81D	14	$ .01	$ .05
Sanchez, Luis	84D	597	$ .03	$ .10	Santana, Rafael	85D	610	$ .03	$ .10
Sanchez, Luis	85D	352	$ .01	$ .08	Santana, Rafael	86D	319	$ .01	$ .06
Sanchez, Orlando	82D	636	$ .01	$ .05	Santana, Rafael	87D	569	$ .01	$ .05
Sandberg, Ryne	83D	277	$5.50	$27.50	Santana, Rafael	88D	633	$ .01	$ .15
Sandberg, Ryne	84D	311	$4.00	$16.00	Santana, Rafael	89D	309	$ .01	$ .05
Sandberg, Ryne	85D	67	$ .10	$5.00	Santiago, Benito	87DR	44	$ .15	$ .75
Sandberg, Ryne	85DK	1	$ .15	$2.00	Santiago, Benito	87DRR	31	$ .50	$2.35
					Santiago, Benito	88D	114	$ .01	$ .25
					Santiago, Benito	88DK	3	$ .10	$ .25
					Santiago, Benito	89D	205	$ .01	$ .10
					Santiago, Benito	90D	465	$ .01	$ .04
					Santiago, Benito	90DAS	708	$ .01	$ .04
					Santiago, Benito	90DL	207	$ .01	$ .20
					Santiago, Benito	91D	449	$ .01	$ .03
					Santovenia, Nelson	89D	366	$ .01	$ .10
					Santovenia, Nelson	89DBB	146	$ .01	$ .05
					Santovenia, Nelson	90D	224	$ .01	$ .04
					Santovenia, Nelson	90DL	502	$ .01	$ .15
					Sarimento, Manny	83D	502	$ .01	$ .05
					Sarmiento, Manny	84D	200	$ .03	$ .10
					Sasser, Mackey	88DR	51	$ .01	$ .15
					Sasser, Mackey	88DRR	28	$ .01	$ .25
					Sasser, Mackey	89D	454	$ .01	$ .05
					Sasser, Mackey	90D	471	$ .01	$ .04
					Sasser, Mackey	90DL	435	$ .01	$ .15
					Sasser, Mackey	91D	136	$ .01	$ .03
					Saucier, Kevin	82D	485	$ .01	$ .05
					Savage, Jack	89D	618	$ .01	$ .10
					Sax, Dave	84D	519	$ .03	$ .10
					Sax, Dave	87D	647	$ .01	$ .05
					Sax, Steve	82D	624	$ .50	$3.50
					Sax, Steve	83D	336	$ .06	$ .50
					Sax, Steve	84D	104	$ .04	$ .60
					Sax, Steve	85D	418	$ .03	$ .35
					Sax, Steve	86D	540	$ .02	$ .15
					Sax, Steve	87D	278	$ .01	$ .15
					Sax, Steve	87DK	26	$ .01	$ .05
Sandberg, Ryne	86D	67	$ .08	$2.00	Sax, Steve	88D	176	$ .01	$ .05
Sandberg, Ryne	87D	77	$ .08	$1.00	Sax, Steve	88DBB	204	$ .01	$ .05
Sandberg, Ryne	88D	242	$ .01	$ .35	Sax, Steve	89D	84	$ .01	$ .15
Sandberg, Ryne	88DBB	116	$ .01	$ .25	Sax, Steve	89DBB	20	$ .01	$ .10
Sandberg, Ryne	89D	105	$ .01	$ .20	Sax, Steve	89DTR	23	$ .01	$ .25
Sandberg, Ryne	89DBB	26	$ .01	$ .25	Sax, Steve	90D	78	$ .01	$ .10
Sandberg, Ryne	90D	105	$ .01	$ .15	Sax, Steve	90DBC	22	$ .01	$ .04
Sandberg, Ryne	90DAS	692	$ .01	$ .10	Sax, Steve	90DK	2	$ .01	$ .10
Sandberg, Ryne	90DBC	10	$ .01	$ .10	Sax, Steve	90DL	96	$ .01	$ .15
Sandberg, Ryne	90DL	528	$ .01	$ .25	Sax, Steve	91D	163	$ .01	$ .03
Sandberg, Ryne	90DL	98	$ .01	$1.00	Sax, Steve	91D	48	$ .01	$ .03
Sandberg, Ryne	91D	504	$ .01	$ .15	Schatzeder, Dan	81D	248	$ .01	$ .05
Sandberg, Ryne	91DAS	433	$ .01	$ .10	Schatzeder, Dan	82D	385	$ .01	$ .05
Sandberg, Ryne	91DBC	7	$ .01	$ .15	Schatzeder, Dan	84D	132	$ .03	$ .10
Sandberg, Ryne	91DK	14	$ .01	$ .15	Schatzeder, Dan	85D	543	$ .01	$ .08
Sandberg, Ryne	91DLP	2	$1.00	$7.50	Schatzeder, Dan	87D	482	$ .01	$ .05
Sandberg, Ryne	91DMVP	404	$ .01	$ .10	Schatzeder, Dan	90D	594	$ .01	$ .04
Sanders, Deion	89DR	6	$ .01	$ .75	Schatzeder, Dan	91D	497	$ .01	$ .03
Sanders, Deion	90D	427	$ .01	$ .50	Scherrer, Bill	84D	203	$ .03	$ .10
Sanders, Deion	90DL	359	$ .01	$1.00	Scherrer, Bill	86D	516	$ .01	$ .06
Sanderson, Scott	81D	450	$ .01	$ .05	Schilling, Curt	89D	635	$ .01	$ .05
Sanderson, Scott	82D	288	$ .01	$ .05	Schilling, Curt	90D	667	$ .01	$ .04
Sanderson, Scott	83D	446	$ .01	$ .05	Schilling, Curt	91D	556	$ .01	$ .03
Sanderson, Scott	84D	341	$ .03	$ .10	Schiraldi, Calvin	85DRR	38	$ .05	$ .25
Sanderson, Scott	85D	266	$ .01	$ .08	Schiraldi, Calvin	86D	652	$ .01	$ .06
Sanderson, Scott	86D	442	$ .01	$ .06	Schiraldi, Calvin	87D	641	$ .01	$ .05

RYNE SANDBERG 2B

Player	Year	No.	VG	EX/MT	Player	Year	No.	VG	EX/MT
Schiraldi, Calvin	88D	375	$ .01	$ .05	Scioscia, Mike	86D	93	$ .01	$ .06
Schiraldi, Calvin	88DBB	194	$ .01	$ .05	Scioscia, Mike	87D	130	$ .01	$ .05
Schiraldi, Calvin	89D	285	$ .01	$ .05	Scioscia, Mike	88D	106	$ .01	$ .05
Schiraldi, Calvin	89DBB	82	$ .01	$ .05	Scioscia, Mike	88DBB	260	$ .01	$ .05
Schiraldi, Calvin	90D	672	$ .01	$ .04	Scioscia, Mike	89D	77	$ .01	$ .05
Schiraldi, Calvin	91D	308	$ .01	$ .03	Scioscia, Mike	89DBB	66	$ .01	$ .05
Schmidt, Dave	83D	321	$ .01	$ .15	Scioscia, Mike	90D	316	$ .01	$ .04
Schmidt, Dave	84D	586	$ .03	$ .10	Scioscia, Mike	90DL	49	$ .01	$ .15
Schmidt, Dave	85D	586	$ .01	$ .08	Scioscia, Mike	91D	112	$ .01	$ .03
Schmidt, Dave	86D	378	$ .01	$ .06	Scioscia, Mike	91DAS	436	$ .01	$ .03
Schmidt, Dave	87D	182	$ .01	$ .05	Sconiers, Daryl	83D	141	$ .01	$ .05
Schmidt, Dave	89D	215	$ .01	$ .05	Sconiers, Daryl	84D	451	$ .03	$ .10
Schmidt, Dave	89DK	13	$ .01	$ .05	Sconiers, Daryl	85D	620	$ .01	$ .08
Schmidt, Dave	90D	524	$ .01	$ .04	Scott, Donnie	85D	544	$ .01	$ .08
Schmidt, Dave	90DL	457	$ .01	$ .15	Scott, Mike	81D	37	$ .20	$1.00
Schmidt, Mike	81D	11	$ .40	$2.50	Scott, Mike	82D	128	$ .10	$ .50
Schmidt, Mike	81D	590	$ .10	$2.00	Scott, Mike	84D	136	$ .10	$ .50
Schmidt, Mike	82D	294	$ .15	$1.75	Scott, Mike	85D	258	$ .03	$ .25
Schmidt, Mike	82D	585	$ .15	$1.25	Scott, Mike	86D	476	$ .10	$ .35
Schmidt, Mike	83D	168	$ .10	$1.75	Scott, Mike	87D	163	$ .05	$ .20
Schmidt, Mike	84D	183	$2.00	$10.00	Scott, Mike	87DK	18	$ .01	$ .05
Schmidt, Mike	84DK	23	$ .50	$2.25	Scott, Mike	88D	112	$ .01	$ .05
Schmidt, Mike	85D	61	$ .50	$2.25	Scott, Mike	88DBB	206	$ .05	$ .25
Schmidt, Mike	86D	61	$ .25	$1.25	Scott, Mike	88DBC	12	$ .10	$ .25
Schmidt, Mike	87D	139	$ .15	$ .75	Scott, Mike	89D	69	$ .05	$ .25
Schmidt, Mike	88D	330	$ .10	$ .40	Scott, Mike	89DBB	94	$ .01	$ .10
Schmidt, Mike	88D	371	$ .01	$ .35	Scott, Mike	89DBC	2	$ .01	$ .15
Schmidt, Mike	88DBC	4	$ .05	$ .30	Scott, Mike	90D	207	$ .01	$ .10
Schmidt, Mike	89D	193	$ .05	$ .25	Scott, Mike	90DL	4	$ .01	$ .15
Schmidt, Mike	90D	643	$ .01	$ .35	Scott, Mike	91D	483	$ .01	$ .03
Schoendienst, Red	81D	431	$ .01	$ .15	Scott, Rodney	81D	209	$ .01	$ .05
Schofield, Dick	84DRR	35	$ .10	$ .60	Scott, Rodney	82D	240	$ .01	$ .05
Schofield, Dick	85D	329	$ .01	$ .08	Scott, Tony (Anthony)	81D	191	$ .01	$ .05
Schofield, Dick	86D	133	$ .01	$ .06	Scott, Tony	82D	522	$ .01	$ .05
Schofield, Dick	87D	283	$ .01	$ .05	Scott, Tony	83D	293	$ .01	$ .05
Schofield, Dick	88D	108	$ .01	$ .05	Scott, Tony	84D	527	$ .03	$ .10
Schofield, Dick	88D	233	$ .01	$ .05	Scudder, Scott	90D	435	$ .01	$ .20
Schofield, Dick	88DBB	195	$ .01	$ .05	Scudder, Scott	90DL	413	$ .01	$ .25
Schofield, Dick	89DBB	251	$ .01	$ .05	Scudder, Scott	91D	265	$ .01	$ .03
Schofield, Dick	90D	288	$ .01	$ .04	Scurry, Rod	82D	185	$ .01	$ .05
Schofield, Dick	90DL	419	$ .01	$ .15	Scurry, Rod	83D	376	$ .01	$ .05
Schofield, Dick	91D	262	$ .01	$ .03	Scurry, Rod	84D	235	$ .03	$ .10
Schooler, Mike	89D	637	$ .01	$ .25	Scurry, Rod	85D	142	$ .01	$ .08
Schooler, Mike	89DBB	275	$ .01	$ .05	Scurry, Rod	87D	374	$ .01	$ .05
Schooler, Mike	90D	330	$ .01	$ .04	Seanez, Rudy	90DL	417	$ .01	$ .20
Schooler, Mike	90DL	258	$ .01	$ .25	Seanez, Rudy	91D	218	$ .01	$ .03
Schooler, Mike	91D	302	$ .01	$ .03	Searage, Ray	86D	536	$ .01	$ .06
Schroeder, Bill	84D	515	$ .03	$ .10	Searage, Ray	88D	429	$ .01	$ .05
Schroeder, Bill	85D	124	$ .01	$ .08	Searage, Ray	90D	649	$ .01	$ .04
Schroeder, Bill	86D	211	$ .01	$ .06	Searcy, Steve	89DRR	29	$ .01	$ .05
Schroeder, Bill	87D	486	$ .01	$ .05	Searcy, Steve	91D	549	$ .01	$ .03
Schroeder, Bill	88D	419	$ .01	$ .05	Seaver, Tom	81D	422	$ .15	$1.00
Schroeder, Bill	89D	644	$ .01	$ .05	Seaver, Tom	81D	425	$ .15	$1.00
Schroeder, Bill	90D	567	$ .01	$ .04	Seaver, Tom	82D	148	$ .12	$1.00
Schrom, Ken	84D	72	$ .03	$ .10	Seaver, Tom	82D	628	$ .15	$ .75
Schrom, Ken	85D	486	$ .01	$ .08	Seaver, Tom	82DK	16	$ .10	$ .50
Schrom, Ken	86D	635	$ .01	$ .06	Seaver, Tom	83D	122	$ .15	$ .65
Schrom, Ken	87D	403	$ .01	$ .05	Seaver, Tom	84D	116	$ .20	$3.50
Schrom, Ken	88D	501	$ .01	$ .05	Seaver, Tom	85D	424	$ .35	$1.00
Schu, Rick	85D	448	$ .03	$ .10	Seaver, Tom	86D	609	$ .15	$ .40
Schu, Rick	86D	570	$ .01	$ .06	Seaver, Tom	87D	375	$ .08	$ .25
Schu, Rick	87D	509	$ .01	$ .05	Sebra, Bob	87D	468	$ .01	$ .05
Schu, Rick	88D	432	$ .01	$ .05	Sebra, Bob	88D	458	$ .01	$ .05
Schu, Rick	89D	406	$ .01	$ .05	Segui, David	91D	730	$ .01	$ .20
Schu, Rick	90D	599	$ .01	$ .04	Seitzer, Kevin	87DR	15	$ .25	$1.00
Schultz, Jeff	91D	687	$ .01	$ .10	Seitzer, Kevin	88D	280	$ .01	$ .25
Schulze, Don	85D	639	$ .01	$ .08	Seitzer, Kevin	88DBB	175	$ .05	$ .25
Scioscia, Mike	82D	598	$ .01	$ .25	Seitzer, Kevin	88DBC	17	$ .01	$ .15
Scioscia, Mike	83D	75	$ .01	$ .05	Seitzer, Kevin	89D	238	$ .01	$ .15
Scioscia, Mike	85D	459	$ .01	$ .08	Seitzer, Kevin	89DBB	207	$ .01	$ .10

DONRUSS

Player	Year	No.	VG	EX/MT	Player	Year	No.	VG	EX/MT
Seitzer, Kevin	89DK	10	$ .01	$ .15	Sierra, Ruben	90D	174	$ .01	$ .15
Seitzer, Kevin	90D	85	$ .01	$ .10	Sierra, Ruben	90DAS	673	$ .01	$ .10
Seitzer, Kevin	90DL	230	$ .01	$ .15	Sierra, Ruben	90DK	3	$ .01	$ .25
Seitzer, Kevin	91D	73	$ .01	$ .03	Sierra, Ruben	90DL	257	$ .01	$ .25
Sellers, Jeff	86DR	29	$ .02	$ .09	Sierra, Ruben	91D	567	$ .01	$ .10
Sellers, Jeff	87D	544	$ .01	$ .15	Simmons, Nelson	86D	272	$ .01	$ .06
Sellers, Jeff	88D	585	$ .01	$ .05	Simmons, Ted	81D	308	$ .03	$ .20
Sellers, Jeff	89D	517	$ .01	$ .05	Simmons, Ted	82D	106	$ .02	$ .15
Senteney, Steven	83D	52	$ .01	$ .05	Simmons, Ted	83D	332	$ .01	$ .05
Serna, Paul	82D	567	$ .01	$ .05	Simmons, Ted	84D	473	$ .08	$ .25
Sexton, Jimmy	83D	449	$ .01	$ .05	Simmons, Ted	85D	414	$ .03	$ .20
Sharperson, Mike	87D	565	$ .01	$ .05	Simmons, Ted	86D	292	$ .05	$ .20
Sharperson, Mike	90D	603	$ .01	$ .04	Simmons, Ted	87D	537	$ .01	$ .05
Sharperson, Mike	90DL	490	$ .01	$ .15	Simmons, Ted	88D	560	$ .01	$ .05
Sharperson, Mike	91D	168	$ .01	$ .03	Simpson, Joe	81D	168	$ .01	$ .05
Shaw, Jeff	90DR	53	$ .01	$ .10	Simpson, Joe	82D	55	$ .01	$ .05
Sheets, Larry	85DRR	36	$ .01	$ .25	Simpson, Joe	84D	496	$ .03	$ .10
Sheets, Larry	86D	350	$ .01	$ .06	Sinatro, Matt	82D	149	$ .01	$ .05
Sheets, Larry	87D	248	$ .01	$ .05	Sinatro, Matt	83D	622	$ .01	$ .05
Sheets, Larry	88D	273	$ .01	$ .05	Singleton, Ken	81D	115	$ .02	$ .15
Sheets, Larry	89D	333	$ .01	$ .05	Singleton, Ken	82D	105	$ .01	$ .05
Sheets, Larry	90D	495	$ .01	$ .04	Singleton, Ken	82DK	24	$ .01	$ .05
Sheets, Larry	90DL	350	$ .01	$ .15	Singleton, Ken	83D	257	$ .01	$ .05
Sheffield, Gary	89DBB	113	$ .01	$ .50	Singleton, Ken	84D	610	$ .03	$ .10
Sheffield, Gary	89DR	1	$ .01	$1.00	Sisk, Doug	84D	615	$ .03	$ .10
Sheffield, Gary	89DRR	31	$ .35	$1.00	Sisk, Doug	85D	441	$ .01	$ .08
Sheffield, Gary	90D	501	$ .01	$ .25	Sisk, Doug	88D	642	$ .01	$ .15
Sheffield, Gary	90DL	157	$ .01	$ .35	Skinner, Joel	84DRR	27	$ .03	$ .10
Sheffield, Gary	91D	751	$ .01	$ .10	Skinner, Joel	85D	574	$ .01	$ .08
Shelby, John	84D	291	$ .04	$ .40	Skinner, Joel	86D	330	$ .01	$ .06
Shelby, John	85D	472	$ .01	$ .08	Skinner, Joel	87D	545	$ .01	$ .05
Shelby, John	86D	643	$ .01	$ .06	Skinner, Joel	88D	474	$ .01	$ .05
Shelby, John	87D	354	$ .01	$ .05	Skinner, Joel	89D	427	$ .01	$ .05
Shelby, John	88D	352	$ .01	$ .05	Skinner, Joel	89DBB	224	$ .01	$ .05
Shelby, John	89D	314	$ .01	$ .05	Skinner, Joel	89DTR	22	$ .01	$ .05
Shelby, John	91D	563	$ .01	$ .03	Skinner, Joel	90D	73	$ .01	$ .04
Sheridan, Pat	84D	588	$ .01	$ .25	Skinner, Joel	90DL	286	$ .01	$ .15
Sheridan, Pat	85D	339	$ .01	$ .08	Skinner, Joel	91D	120	$ .01	$ .03
Sheridan, Pat	86D	155	$ .01	$ .06	Slaton, Jim	81D	447	$ .01	$ .05
Sheridan, Pat	88D	522	$ .01	$ .05	Slaton, Jim	82D	80	$ .01	$ .05
Sheridan, Pat	89D	417	$ .01	$ .05	Slaton, Jim	83D	330	$ .01	$ .05
Sheridan, Pat	90D	367	$ .01	$ .04	Slaton, Jim	84D	481	$ .03	$ .10
Shines, Razor	85D	401	$ .01	$ .08	Slaton, Jim	85D	545	$ .01	$ .08
Shipanoff, Dave	86DRR	34	$ .01	$ .06	Slaton, Jim	86D	402	$ .01	$ .06
Shirley, Bob	81D	242	$ .01	$ .05	Slaught, Don	83D	196	$ .10	$ .40
Shirley, Bob	82D	120	$ .01	$ .05	Slaught, Don	84D	419	$ .03	$ .10
Shirley, Bob	84D	214	$ .03	$ .10	Slaught, Don	85D	496	$ .01	$ .08
Shirley, Bob	85D	370	$ .01	$ .08	Slaught, Don	86D	281	$ .01	$ .06
Shirley, Bob	86D	458	$ .01	$ .06	Slaught, Don	87D	136	$ .01	$ .05
Shirley, Bob	87D	463	$ .01	$ .05	Slaught, Don	88DBB	188	$ .01	$ .05
Show, Eric	83D	439	$ .05	$ .35	Slaught, Don	89D	190	$ .01	$ .05
Show, Eric	84D	406	$ .03	$ .10	Slaught, Don	89DBB	105	$ .01	$ .05
Show, Eric	85D	202	$ .01	$ .08	Slaught, Don	90D	277	$ .01	$ .04
Show, Eric	86D	234	$ .01	$ .06	Slaught, Don	90DL	354	$ .01	$ .15
Show, Eric	87D	164	$ .01	$ .05	Slaught, Don	91D	213	$ .01	$ .03
Show, Eric	88D	387	$ .01	$ .05	Smalley, Roy	81D	487	$ .01	$ .05
Show, Eric	89D	482	$ .01	$ .05	Smalley, Roy	82D	573	$ .01	$ .05
Show, Eric	90D	559	$ .01	$ .04	Smalley, Roy	82DK	22	$ .01	$ .05
Show, Eric	90DL	115	$ .01	$ .15	Smalley, Roy	83D	209	$ .01	$ .05
Shumpert, Terry	90DL	409	$ .01	$ .20	Smalley, Roy	84D	225	$ .03	$ .10
Shumpert, Terry	90DR	55	$ .01	$ .10	Smalley, Roy	85D	622	$ .01	$ .08
Shumpert, Terry	91D	297	$ .01	$ .03	Smalley, Roy	86D	486	$ .01	$ .06
Sierra, Ruben	86DR	52	$2.00	$8.00	Smalley, Roy	87D	443	$ .01	$ .05
Sierra, Ruben	87D	346	$1.50	$6.50	Smalley, Roy	88D	566	$ .01	$ .05
Sierra, Ruben	88D	223	$ .01	$ .45	Smiley, John	87DR	39	$ .03	$ .60
Sierra, Ruben	88DBB	200	$ .01	$ .25	Smiley, John	88D	449	$ .05	$ .35
Sierra, Ruben	88DBC	26	$ .10	$ .25	Smiley, John	88DBB	257	$ .01	$ .05
Sierra, Ruben	89D	48	$ .01	$ .20	Smiley, John	89D	329	$ .01	$ .05
Sierra, Ruben	89DBB	111	$ .01	$ .25	Smiley, John	89DBB	157	$ .01	$ .10
Sierra, Ruben	89DBC	26	$ .01	$ .30	Smiley, John	90D	54	$ .01	$ .10

Player	Year	No.	VG	EX/MT	Player	Year	No.	VG	EX/MT
Smiley, John	90DK	17	$ .01	$ .10	Smith, Lee	83D	403	$ .01	$ .10
Smiley, John	90DL	328	$ .01	$ .10	Smith, Lee	84D	289	$ .03	$ .10
Smiley, John	91D	664	$ .01	$ .03	Smith, Lee	85D	311	$ .01	$ .08
Smith, Bryn	83D	88	$ .05	$ .50	Smith, Lee	86D	144	$ .01	$ .06
Smith, Bryn	84D	453	$ .01	$ .10	Smith, Lee	87D	292	$ .01	$ .05
Smith, Bryn	85D	209	$ .01	$ .08	Smith, Lee	88D	292	$ .01	$ .05
Smith, Bryn	86D	299	$ .01	$ .06	Smith, Lee	88DBB	252	$ .01	$ .05
Smith, Bryn	87D	159	$ .01	$ .05	Smith, Lee	89D	66	$ .01	$ .05
Smith, Bryn	88D	335	$ .01	$ .05	Smith, Lee	89DBB	84	$ .01	$ .05
Smith, Bryn	88DBB	202	$ .01	$ .05	Smith, Lee	90D	110	$ .01	$ .04
Smith, Bryn	89D	216	$ .01	$ .05	Smith, Lee	90DL	524	$ .01	$ .15
Smith, Bryn	89DBB	124	$ .01	$ .05	Smith, Lee	91D	169	$ .01	$ .03
Smith, Bryn	90D	106	$ .01	$ .04	Smith, Lee	91DMVP	403	$ .01	$ .03
Smith, Bryn	90DK	25	$ .01	$ .10	Smith, Lonnie	81D	295	$ .10	$ .60
Smith, Bryn	90DL	393	$ .01	$ .15	Smith, Lonnie	82D	606	$ .01	$ .25
Smith, Bryn	91D	113	$ .01	$ .03	Smith, Lonnie	83D	91	$ .07	$ .35
Smith, Chris	84DRR	46	$ .03	$ .10	Smith, Lonnie	84D	231	$ .03	$ .25
Smith, Dave	81D	23	$ .10	$ .40	Smith, Lonnie	84D	625	$ .01	$ .25
Smith, Dave	82D	191	$ .01	$ .05	Smith, Lonnie	85D	231	$ .01	$ .10
					Smith, Lonnie	86D	399	$ .01	$ .06
					Smith, Lonnie	87D	225	$ .01	$ .05
					Smith, Lonnie	88D	527	$ .01	$ .05
					Smith, Lonnie	89DBB	114	$ .01	$ .05
					Smith, Lonnie	90D	222	$ .01	$ .04
					Smith, Lonnie	90DL	217	$ .01	$ .15
					Smith, Lonnie	91D	364	$ .01	$ .03
					Smith, Ozzie	81D	1	$ .25	$1.50
					Smith, Ozzie	82D	94	$ .10	$ .50
					Smith, Ozzie	82DK	21	$ .03	$ .30
					Smith, Ozzie	83D	120	$ .10	$ .50
					Smith, Ozzie	84D	59	$ .10	$1.00
					Smith, Ozzie	84D	625	$ .01	$ .25
					Smith, Ozzie	85D	59	$ .03	$ .25
					Smith, Ozzie	86D	59	$ .05	$ .20
					Smith, Ozzie	87D	60	$ .01	$ .15
					Smith, Ozzie	87DK	5	$ .05	$ .20
					Smith, Ozzie	88D	263	$ .01	$ .05
					Smith, Ozzie	88DBB	243	$ .01	$ .15
					Smith, Ozzie	88DBC	22	$ .10	$ .25
					Smith, Ozzie	89D	63	$ .01	$ .05
					Smith, Ozzie	89DBB	44	$ .01	$ .25
					Smith, Ozzie	89DBC	14	$ .01	$ .10
					Smith, Ozzie	90D	201	$ .01	$ .10
					Smith, Ozzie	90DAS	710	$ .01	$ .10
					Smith, Ozzie	90DL	142	$ .01	$ .25
					Smith, Ozzie	90DL	364	$ .01	$ .20
					Smith, Ozzie	91D	240	$ .01	$ .03
					Smith, Ozzie	91DAS	437	$ .01	$ .03
					Smith, Pete	88D	571	$ .01	$ .15
Smith, Dave	83D	370	$ .01	$ .05	Smith, Pete	88DBB	197	$ .01	$ .05
Smith, Dave	84D	548	$ .03	$ .10	Smith, Pete	88DR	10	$ .01	$ .05
Smith, Dave	85D	548	$ .01	$ .08	Smith, Pete	89D	263	$ .01	$ .05
Smith, Dave	86D	328	$ .01	$ .06	Smith, Pete	90D	499	$ .01	$ .04
Smith, Dave	87D	308	$ .01	$ .05	Smith, Pete	90DL	144	$ .01	$ .15
Smith, Dave	88D	410	$ .01	$ .05	Smith, Reggie	81D	59	$ .01	$ .05
Smith, Dave	88DBB	262	$ .01	$ .05	Smith, Reggie	82D	488	$ .01	$ .05
Smith, Dave	89D	272	$ .01	$ .05	Smith, Reggie	83D	611	$ .01	$ .05
Smith, Dave	89DBB	232	$ .01	$ .05	Smith, Roy	85D	611	$ .01	$ .08
Smith, Dave	90D	88	$ .01	$ .04	Smith, Roy	86D	468	$ .01	$ .06
Smith, Dave	90DL	122	$ .01	$ .15	Smith, Roy	90D	273	$ .01	$ .04
Smith, Dave	91D	212	$ .01	$ .03	Smith, Roy	90DL	400	$ .01	$ .15
Smith, Dwight	89DBB	205	$ .01	$ .20	Smith, Roy	91D	470	$ .01	$ .03
Smith, Dwight	89DR	32	$ .01	$ .50	Smith, Zane	86D	565	$ .01	$ .45
Smith, Dwight	90D	393	$ .01	$ .10	Smith, Zane	87D	167	$ .01	$ .05
Smith, Dwight	90DL	255	$ .01	$ .15	Smith, Zane	88D	167	$ .01	$ .05
Smith, Dwight	91D	559	$ .01	$ .03	Smith, Zane	88DBB	170	$ .01	$ .05
Smith, Greg	91D	574	$ .01	$ .03	Smith, Zane	89D	499	$ .01	$ .05
Smith, Jimmy	83D	402	$ .01	$ .05	Smith, Zane	90D	460	$ .01	$ .04
Smith, Keith	81D	539	$ .01	$ .05	Smith, Zane	90DL	238	$ .01	$ .15
Smith, Lee	82D	252	$ .15	$ .75	Smith, Zane	91D	532	$ .01	$ .03

DAVE SMITH

Player	Year	No.	VG	EX/MT
Smithson, Mike	84D	221	$ .03	$ .10
Smithson, Mike	85D	316	$ .01	$ .08
Smithson, Mike	86D	147	$ .01	$ .06
Smithson, Mike	87D	245	$ .01	$ .05
Smithson, Mike	89D	628	$ .01	$ .05
Smithson, Mike	90D	464	$ .01	$ .04
Smoltz, John	89D	642	$ .01	$ .30
Smoltz, John	89DBB	85	$ .01	$ .10
Smoltz, John	90D	121	$ .01	$ .10
Smoltz, John	90DBC	12	$ .01	$ .10
Smoltz, John	90DK	8	$ .01	$ .20
Smoltz, John	90DL	59	$ .01	$ .20
Smoltz, John	91D	75	$ .01	$ .03
Snell, Nate	86D	367	$ .01	$ .06
Snell, Nate	87D	396	$ .01	$ .05
Snider, Duke	84D	648	$ .04	$ .15
Snider, Van	89D	586	$ .01	$ .10
Snyder, Cory	86DR	15	$ .25	$1.00
Snyder, Cory	86DRR	29	$ .50	$2.50
Snyder, Cory	87D	526	$ .25	$ .40
Snyder, Cory	88D	350	$ .01	$ .15
Snyder, Cory	88DBB	224	$ .01	$ .15
Snyder, Cory	89D	191	$ .01	$ .10
Snyder, Cory	89DBB	168	$ .01	$ .05
Snyder, Cory	89DK	8	$ .01	$ .05
Snyder, Cory	90D	272	$ .01	$ .04
Snyder, Cory	90DL	187	$ .01	$ .15
Snyder, Cory	91D	288	$ .01	$ .03
Soderholm, Eric	81D	106	$ .01	$ .05
Soff, Ray	87D	631	$ .01	$ .05
Sofield, Rick	81D	592	$ .01	$ .05
Sojo, Luis	90DL	291	$ .01	$ .35
Sojo, Luis	91D	579	$ .01	$ .03
Solomon, Eddie	81D	16	$ .01	$ .05
Solomon, Eddie	82D	437	$ .01	$ .05
Sorensen, Lary	81D	325	$ .01	$ .05
Sorensen, Lary	82D	246	$ .01	$ .05
Sorensen, Lary	83D	363	$ .01	$ .05
Sorensen, Lary	84D	635	$ .03	$ .10
Sorensen, Lary	85D	131	$ .01	$ .08
Sorrento, Paul	90D	626	$ .01	$ .10
Sorrento, Paul	91D	745	$ .01	$ .03
Sosa, Elias	81D	599	$ .01	$ .05
Sosa, Elias	82D	446	$ .01	$ .05
Sosa, Elias	83D	259	$ .01	$ .05
Sosa, Sammy	89DBB	324	$ .01	$ .25
Sosa, Sammy	90D	489	$ .01	$ .60
Sosa, Sammy	90DL	220	$ .01	$1.25
Sosa, Sammy	91D	147	$ .01	$ .15
Soto, Mario	81D	63	$ .03	$ .20
Soto, Mario	82D	103	$ .01	$ .15
Soto, Mario	83D	248	$ .02	$ .15
Soto, Mario	84D	428	$ .03	$ .10
Soto, Mario	85D	184	$ .03	$ .10
Soto, Mario	85DK	19	$ .03	$ .10
Soto, Mario	86D	184	$ .01	$ .06
Soto, Mario	87D	82	$ .01	$ .05
Spahn, Warren	89D	588	$ .01	$ .05
Speck, Cliff	87D	571	$ .01	$ .05
Speier, Chris	81D	329	$ .01	$ .05
Speier, Chris	82D	366	$ .01	$ .05
Speier, Chris	83D	266	$ .01	$ .05
Speier, Chris	84D	523	$ .03	$ .10
Speier, Chris	87D	392	$ .01	$ .05
Speier, Chris	88D	239	$ .01	$ .05
Speier, Chris	89D	532	$ .01	$ .05
Spencer, Jim	81D	226	$ .01	$ .05
Spencer, Jim	82D	265	$ .01	$ .05
Spiers, Bill	89DR	5	$ .01	$ .25
Spiers, Bill	90D	382	$ .01	$ .10

Player	Year	No.	VG	EX/MT
Spiers, Bill	90DL	203	$ .01	$ .25
Spiers, Bill	91D	310	$ .01	$ .03
Spillner, Dan	82D	411	$ .01	$ .05

DAN SPILLNER — Indians

Player	Year	No.	VG	EX/MT
Spillner, Dan	83D	137	$ .01	$ .05
Spillner, Dan	84D	582	$ .03	$ .10
Spillner, Dan	86D	122	$ .01	$ .06
Spilman, Harry	81D	304	$ .01	$ .05
Spilman, Harry	83D	65	$ .01	$ .05
Spilman, Harry	84D	258	$ .03	$ .10
Spilman, Harry	88D	607	$ .01	$ .15
Splittorff, Paul	81D	342	$ .01	$ .05
Splittorff, Paul	82D	464	$ .01	$ .05
Splittorff, Paul	83D	286	$ .01	$ .05
Splittorff, Paul	84D	521	$ .03	$ .10
Squires, Mike	81D	398	$ .01	$ .05
Squires, Mike	82D	39	$ .01	$ .05
Squires, Mike	83D	495	$ .01	$ .05
Squires, Mike	84D	404	$ .03	$ .10
Squires, Mike	85D	501	$ .01	$ .08
St. Claire, Randy	85D	575	$ .01	$ .08
St. Claire, Randy	86D	463	$ .01	$ .06
St. Claire, Randy	88D	426	$ .01	$ .05
Stanhouse, Don	81D	557	$ .01	$ .05
Stanicek, Pete	88D	541	$ .01	$ .05
Stanicek, Pete	88DR	15	$ .01	$ .05
Stanicek, Pete	89D	169	$ .01	$ .05
Stanley, Bob	81D	456	$ .01	$ .05
Stanley, Bob	82D	134	$ .01	$ .05
Stanley, Bob	83D	386	$ .01	$ .05
Stanley, Bob	84D	644	$ .03	$ .10
Stanley, Bob	85D	91	$ .01	$ .08
Stanley, Bob	86D	91	$ .01	$ .06
Stanley, Bob	87D	216	$ .01	$ .05
Stanley, Bob	88D	92	$ .01	$ .05
Stanley, Bob	89D	421	$ .01	$ .05
Stanley, Bob	89DBB	233	$ .01	$ .05
Stanley, Fred	81D	585	$ .01	$ .05
Stanley, Fred	82D	449	$ .01	$ .05
Stanley, Fred	83D	197	$ .01	$ .05
Stanley, Mike	87D	592	$ .01	$ .05

Player	Year	No.	VG	EX/MT	Player	Year	No.	VG	EX/MT
Stanley, Mike	87DR	28	$ .01	$ .07	Stewart, Dave	90DBC	3	$ .01	$ .10
Stanley, Mike	88D	259	$ .01	$ .05	Stewart, Dave	90DK	6	$ .01	$ .10
Stanley, Mike	88DBB	223	$ .01	$ .05	Stewart, Dave	90DL	81	$ .01	$ .20
Stanley, Mike	89D	166	$ .01	$ .05	Stewart, Dave	91D	102	$ .01	$ .03
Stanley, Mike	90D	579	$ .01	$ .04	Stewart, Dave	91DBC	4	$ .01	$ .03
Stanton, Mike	82D	285	$ .01	$ .05	Stewart, Sammy	81D	474	$ .01	$ .05
Stanton, Mike	83D	433	$ .01	$ .05	Stewart, Sammy	82D	457	$ .01	$ .05
Stanton, Mike	85D	562	$ .01	$ .08	Stewart, Sammy	83D	203	$ .01	$ .05
Stanton, Mike	90D	508	$ .01	$ .25	Stewart, Sammy	84D	514	$ .03	$ .10
Stanton, Mike	90DR	7	$ .01	$ .10	Stewart, Sammy	85D	148	$ .01	$ .08
Stanton, Mike	91D	716	$ .01	$ .03	Stewart, Sammy	86D	270	$ .01	$ .06
Stapleton, Dave	81D	544	$ .02	$ .15	Stewart, Sammy	87D	658	$ .01	$ .05
Stapleton, Dave	82D	208	$ .01	$ .05	Stewart, Sammy	88D	596	$ .01	$ .05
Stapleton, Dave	83D	200	$ .01	$ .05	Stieb, Dave	81D	582	$ .10	$ .75
Stapleton, Dave	84D	273	$ .03	$ .10	Stieb, Dave	82D	52	$ .05	$ .40
Stapleton, Dave	88D	521	$ .01	$ .05	Stieb, Dave	83D	507	$ .03	$ .25
Stapleton, Dave	88DR	4	$ .01	$ .05	Stieb, Dave	83DK	9	$ .02	$ .15
Stargell, Willie	81D	12	$ .06	$ .40	Stieb, Dave	84D	71	$ .15	$ .75
Stargell, Willie	81D	132	$ .06	$ .40	Stieb, Dave	85D	193	$ .03	$ .20
Stargell, Willie	82D	639	$ .05	$ .40	Stieb, Dave	86D	146	$ .05	$ .20
Stargell, Willie	83D	610	$ .10	$ .50	Stieb, Dave	87D	195	$ .01	$ .15
Stargell, Willie	83DK	8	$ .05	$ .35	Stieb, Dave	88D	148	$ .01	$ .05
Stargell, Willie	91D	702	$ .01	$ .03	Stieb, Dave	89D	349	$ .01	$ .05
Stark, Matt	91D	747	$ .01	$ .15	Stieb, Dave	89DBB	143	$ .01	$ .05
Staub, Rusty	82D	56	$ .02	$ .15	Stieb, Dave	90D	87	$ .01	$ .04
Staub, Rusty	83D	350	$ .01	$ .05	Stieb, Dave	90DL	79	$ .01	$ .15
Staub, Rusty	84D	554	$ .08	$ .25	Stieb, Dave	91D	551	$ .01	$ .03
Staub, Rusty	84DK	6	$ .08	$ .25	Stieb, Dave	91DBC	21	$ .01	$ .03
Stearns, John	81D	35	$ .01	$ .05	Stieb, Dave	91DK	1	$ .01	$ .05
Stearns, John	82D	434	$ .01	$ .05	Stieb, Dave	91DLP	26	$1.00	$5.00
Stearns, John	83D	380	$ .01	$ .05	Stillwell, Kurt	87D	123	$ .10	$ .50
Steels, James	87DR	50	$ .01	$ .07	Stillwell, Kurt	88D	265	$ .01	$ .10
Steels, James	88D	360	$ .01	$ .05	Stillwell, Kurt	88DBB	207	$ .01	$ .05
Stefero, John	84D	622	$ .03	$ .10	Stillwell, Kurt	89D	322	$ .01	$ .05
Stefero, John	87D	541	$ .01	$ .05	Stillwell, Kurt	89DBB	63	$ .01	$ .05
Stein, Bill	81D	543	$ .01	$ .05	Stillwell, Kurt	90D	120	$ .01	$ .04
Stein, Bill	82D	37	$ .01	$ .05	Stillwell, Kurt	90DL	256	$ .01	$ .15
Stein, Bill	83D	594	$ .01	$ .05	Stillwell, Kurt	91D	520	$ .01	$ .03
Stein, Bill	85D	621	$ .01	$ .08	Stillwell, Kurt	91DK	24	$ .01	$ .05
Stein, Bill	86D	403	$ .01	$ .06	Stoddard, Bob	84D	619	$ .03	$ .10
Steinbach, Terry	87DR	26	$ .05	$ .45	Stoddard, Tim	81D	475	$ .01	$ .05
Steinbach, Terry	87DRR	34	$ .25	$1.25	Stoddard, Tim	82D	131	$ .01	$ .05
Steinbach, Terry	88D	158	$ .03	$ .25	Stoddard, Tim	83D	581	$ .01	$ .05
Steinbach, Terry	88DBB	78	$ .01	$ .05	Stoddard, Tim	84D	245	$ .03	$ .10
Steinbach, Terry	89D	267	$ .01	$ .05	Stoddard, Tim	85D	144	$ .01	$ .08
Steinbach, Terry	89DBB	323	$ .01	$ .10	Stoddard, Tim	86D	406	$ .01	$ .06
Steinbach, Terry	90D	268	$ .01	$ .10	Stoddard, Tim	87D	497	$ .01	$ .05
Steinbach, Terry	90DL	252	$ .01	$ .15	Stoddard, Tim	88D	497	$ .01	$ .05
Steinbach, Terry	91D	329	$ .01	$ .03	Stone, Jeff	85D	624	$ .03	$ .20
Steinback, Terry	90DAS	637	$ .01	$ .10	Stone, Jeff	86D	259	$ .01	$ .06
Stenhouse, Mike	84DRR	29	$ .01	$ .25	Stone, Jeff	87D	309	$ .01	$ .05
Stenhouse, Mike	85D	376	$ .01	$ .08	Stone, Jeff	88D	482	$ .01	$ .05
Stennett, Rennie	81D	72	$ .01	$ .05	Stone, Steve	81D	476	$ .01	$ .05
Stennett, Rennie	82D	563	$ .01	$ .05	Stone, Steve	81D	591	$ .02	$ .15
Stephans, Russ	85DRR	42	$ .01	$ .08	Stone, Steve	82D	357	$ .01	$ .05
Stephenson, Phil	89DR	36	$ .01	$ .10	Stottlemyre, Mel	90DL	310	$ .01	$ .20
Stevens, Lee	90D	449	$ .01	$ .15	Stottlemyre, Mel	91D	257	$ .01	$ .10
Stevens, Lee	91D	754	$ .01	$ .03	Stottlemyre, Todd	88D	658	$ .05	$ .40
Stewart, Dave	82D	410	$1.00	$4.25	Stottlemyre, Todd	88DR	37	$ .01	$ .15
Stewart, Dave	83D	588	$ .15	$ .75	Stottlemyre, Todd	89D	620	$ .01	$ .10
Stewart, Dave	84D	343	$ .15	$ .75	Stottlemyre, Todd	90D	669	$ .01	$ .04
Stewart, Dave	85D	343	$ .01	$ .08	Stottlemyre, Todd	90DL	475	$ .01	$ .20
Stewart, Dave	86D	619	$ .05	$ .35	Stottlemyre, Todd	91D	155	$ .01	$ .03
Stewart, Dave	87D	648	$ .01	$ .25	Strain, Joe	81D	73	$ .01	$ .05
Stewart, Dave	88D	472	$ .01	$ .15	Straker, Les	87DR	21	$ .01	$ .07
Stewart, Dave	88DBB	99	$ .01	$ .05	Straker, Les	88D	73	$ .01	$ .05
Stewart, Dave	89D	214	$ .01	$ .05	Strange, Doug	90D	535	$ .01	$ .10
Stewart, Dave	89DBB	99	$ .01	$ .20	Strawberry, Darryl	84D	68	$12.50	$52.50
Stewart, Dave	90D	150	$ .01	$ .10	Strawberry, Darryl	85D	312	$1.50	$7.50
Stewart, Dave	90DAS	703	$ .01	$ .10	Strawberry, Darryl	86D	197	$1.00	$4.00

Player	Year	No.	VG	EX/MT	Player	Year	No.	VG	EX/MT
Strawberry, Darryl	87D	118	$ .25	$1.00	Sutton, Don	84D	414	$ .10	$ .45
Strawberry, Darryl	87DK	4	$ .10	$ .50	Sutton, Don	85D	107	$ .05	$ .30
Strawberry, Darryl	88D	439	$ .15	$ .50	Sutton, Don	85DK	16	$ .08	$ .25
Strawberry, Darryl	88DBB	182	$ .10	$ .35	Sutton, Don	86D	611	$ .08	$ .25
Strawberry, Darryl	88DBC	20	$ .15	$ .40	Sutton, Don	87D	181	$ .03	$ .25
Strawberry, Darryl	89D	147	$ .05	$ .35	Sutton, Don	88D	407	$ .01	$ .15
Strawberry, Darryl	89DBB	40	$ .01	$ .25	Sveum, Dale	86DR	37	$ .10	$ .10
Strawberry, Darryl	89DBC	6	$ .01	$ .25	Sveum, Dale	87D	542	$ .01	$ .05
Strawberry, Darryl	90D	235	$ .01	$ .25	Sveum, Dale	88D	232	$ .01	$ .05
Strawberry, Darryl	90DL	250	$ .01	$ .75	Sveum, Dale	89D	146	$ .01	$ .05
Strawberry, Darryl	91D	696	$ .01	$ .15	Swaggerty, Bill	85D	392	$ .01	$ .08
Strawberry, Darryl	91DMVP	408	$ .01	$ .10	Swaggerty, Bill	86D	594	$ .01	$ .06
Stubbs, Franklin	85D	348	$ .10	$ .55	Swan, Craig	81D	155	$ .01	$ .05
Stubbs, Franklin	86D	592	$ .05	$ .20	Swan, Craig	82D	589	$ .01	$ .05
Stubbs, Franklin	87D	299	$ .01	$ .05	Swan, Craig	83D	254	$ .01	$ .05
Stubbs, Franklin	88D	218	$ .01	$ .05	Swan, Craig	84D	441	$ .03	$ .10
Stubbs, Franklin	89D	321	$ .01	$ .05	Swan, Russ	91D	621	$ .01	$ .03
Stubbs, Franklin	90D	615	$ .01	$ .04	Sweet, Rick	83D	352	$ .01	$ .05
Stubbs, Franklin	90DL	425	$ .01	$ .15	Sweet, Rick	84D	196	$ .03	$ .10
Stubbs, Franklin	91D	99	$ .01	$ .03	Swift, Bill	86D	562	$ .01	$ .06
Stuper, John	83D	621	$ .01	$ .05	Swift, Billy	87D	517	$ .01	$ .05
Stuper, John	84D	412	$ .03	$ .10	Swift, Billy	90D	566	$ .01	$ .04
Sularz, Guy	83D	605	$ .01	$ .05	Swift, Bill	91D	564	$ .01	$ .03
Sullivan, Marc	86D	614	$ .01	$ .06	Swindell, Greg	87DRR	32	$ .20	$1.00
Sullivan, Marc	87D	643	$ .01	$ .05	Swindell, Greg	88D	227	$ .01	$ .10
Summers, Champ	81D	130	$ .01	$ .05	Swindell, Greg	89D	232	$ .01	$ .10
Summers, Champ	82D	81	$ .01	$ .05	Swindell, Greg	89DBB	112	$ .01	$ .10
Sundberg, Jim	81D	385	$ .01	$ .05	Swindell, Greg	90D	310	$ .01	$ .10
Sundberg, Jim	82D	268	$ .01	$ .05	Swindell, Greg	90DBC	24	$ .01	$ .10
Sundberg, Jim	83D	609	$ .01	$ .05	Swindell, Greg	90DL	206	$ .01	$ .15
Sundberg, Jim	83DK	7	$ .02	$ .15	Swindell, Greg	91D	546	$ .01	$ .03
Sundberg, Jim	84D	178	$ .03	$ .10	Swisher, Steve	83D	633	$ .01	$ .05
Sundberg, Jim	85D	89	$ .01	$ .08	Sykes, Bob	82D	640	$ .01	$ .05
Sundberg, Jim	86D	277	$ .01	$ .06	Tabler, Pat	82D	529	$ .10	$ .50
Sundberg, Jim	87D	280	$ .01	$ .05	Tabler, Pat	83D	552	$ .01	$ .05
Sundberg, Jim	88D	488	$ .01	$ .05	Tabler, Pat	84D	536	$ .03	$ .10
Surhoff, B. J.	87DR	17	$ .10	$ .20	Tabler, Pat	85D	460	$ .01	$ .08
Surhoff, B. J.	87DRR	28	$ .15	$ .50	Tabler, Pat	86D	129	$ .01	$ .06
Surhoff, B. J.	88D	172	$ .01	$ .15	Tabler, Pat	87D	254	$ .01	$ .05
Surhoff, B. J.	89D	221	$ .01	$ .05	Tabler, Pat	88D	219	$ .01	$ .05
Surhoff, B. J.	89DBB	221	$ .01	$ .05	Tabler, Pat	89D	326	$ .01	$ .05
Surhoff, B. J.	90D	173	$ .01	$ .04	Tabler, Pat	90D	444	$ .01	$ .04
Surhoff, B. J.	90DL	290	$ .01	$ .15	Tamargo, John	81D	210	$ .01	$ .05
Surhoff, B. J.	91D	460	$ .01	$ .03	Tanana, Frank	81D	171	$ .01	$ .05
Surhoff, Rick	86DRR	42	$ .01	$ .06	Tanana, Frank	82D	326	$ .01	$ .05
Sutcliffe, Rick	81D	418	$ .03	$ .25	Tanana, Frank	83D	447	$ .01	$ .05
Sutcliffe, Rick	83D	72	$ .03	$ .20	Tanana, Frank	84D	98	$ .03	$ .10
Sutcliffe, Rick	84D	338	$ .10	$ .35	Tanana, Frank	85D	220	$ .01	$ .08
Sutcliffe, Rick	85D	433	$ .03	$ .10	Tanana, Frank	85DK	9	$ .03	$ .10
Sutcliffe, Rick	86D	189	$ .05	$ .20	Tanana, Frank	86D	491	$ .01	$ .06
Sutcliffe, Rick	87D	68	$ .01	$ .05	Tanana, Frank	87D	152	$ .01	$ .05
Sutcliffe, Rick	88D	68	$ .01	$ .05	Tanana, Frank	88D	461	$ .01	$ .05
Sutcliffe, Rick	88DBB	138	$ .01	$ .05	Tanana, Frank	88DBB	259	$ .01	$ .05
Sutcliffe, Rick	89D	223	$ .01	$ .05	Tanana, Frank	89D	90	$ .01	$ .05
Sutcliffe, Rick	89DBB	138	$ .01	$ .05	Tanana, Frank	89DBB	91	$ .01	$ .05
Sutcliffe, Rick	90D	157	$ .01	$ .04	Tanana, Frank	90D	180	$ .01	$ .04
Sutcliffe, Rick	90DL	6	$ .01	$ .15	Tanana, Frank	90DL	87	$ .01	$ .15
Sutcliffe, Rick	91D	462	$ .01	$ .03	Tanana, Frank	91D	508	$ .01	$ .03
Sutherland, Leo	81D	42	$ .01	$ .05	Tanner, Chuck	81D	257	$ .01	$ .05
Sutter, Bruce	81D	560	$ .03	$ .20	Tanner, Chuck	82D	150	$ .01	$ .05
Sutter, Bruce	82D	372	$ .03	$ .20	Tanner, Chuck	83D	124	$ .01	$ .05
Sutter, Bruce	83D	40	$ .01	$ .15	Tapani, Kevin	90D	473	$ .01	$ .10
Sutter, Bruce	84D	534	$ .01	$ .20	Tapani, Kevin	90DL	269	$ .01	$ .75
Sutter, Bruce	84DK	13	$ .08	$ .25	Tapani, Kevin	90DR	35	$ .01	$ .20
Sutter, Bruce	85D	109	$ .03	$ .20	Tapani, Kevin	91D	116	$ .01	$ .10
Sutter, Bruce	86D	321	$ .01	$ .06	Tartabull, Danny	85DRR	27	$1.00	$4.50
Sutter, Bruce	89D	458	$ .01	$ .05	Tartabull, Danny	86DR	45	$ .10	$ .50
Sutton, Don	81D	58	$ .05	$ .30	Tartabull, Danny	86DRR	38	$ .15	$ .75
Sutton, Don	82D	443	$ .05	$ .30	Tartabull, Danny	87D	147	$ .01	$ .20
Sutton, Don	83D	531	$ .10	$ .50	Tartabull, Danny	88D	177	$ .01	$ .10

Player	Year	No.	VG	EX/MT
Tartabull, Danny	88DK	5	$ .01	$ .15
Tartabull, Danny	89D	61	$ .01	$ .10
Tartabull, Danny	89DBB	39	$ .01	$ .05
Tartabull, Danny	90D	322	$ .01	$ .04
Tartabull, Danny	90DL	99	$ .01	$ .15
Tartabull, Danny	91D	463	$ .01	$ .03
Taveras, Frank	81D	154	$ .01	$ .05
Taveras, Frank	82D	98	$ .01	$ .05
Tejada, Wilfredo	87D	529	$ .01	$ .05
Tekulve, Kent	81D	254	$ .01	$ .05
Tekulve, Kent	82D	311	$ .01	$ .05
Tekulve, Kent	83D	297	$ .01	$ .05
Tekulve, Kent	84D	410	$ .03	$ .10
Tekulve, Kent	85D	479	$ .01	$ .08
Tekulve, Kent	86D	111	$ .01	$ .06
Tekulve, Kent	87D	453	$ .01	$ .05
Tekulve, Kent	88D	535	$ .01	$ .05
Telford, Anthony	91D	501	$ .01	$ .10
Tellmann, Tom	84D	149	$ .03	$ .10
Tellmann, Tom	85D	246	$ .01	$ .08
Templeton, Garry	81D	187	$ .01	$ .05
Templeton, Garry	82D	545	$ .01	$ .05
Templeton, Garry	83D	145	$ .01	$ .05
Templeton, Garry	84D	185	$ .03	$ .10
Templeton, Garry	85D	356	$ .01	$ .08
Templeton, Garry	86D	202	$ .01	$ .06
Templeton, Garry	87D	141	$ .01	$ .05
Templeton, Garry	88D	649	$ .01	$ .05
Templeton, Garry	89D	483	$ .01	$ .05
Templeton, Garry	89DBB	154	$ .01	$ .05
Templeton, Garry	90D	246	$ .01	$ .04
Templeton, Garry	90DL	102	$ .01	$ .15
Templeton, Garry	91D	252	$ .01	$ .03
Tenace, Gene	81D	241	$ .01	$ .05
Tenace, Gene	82D	152	$ .01	$ .05
Tenace, Gene	83D	442	$ .01	$ .05
Tenace, Gene	84D	264	$ .03	$ .10
Terrell, Walt	84D	640	$ .10	$ .50
Terrell, Walt	85D	597	$ .01	$ .08
Terrell, Walt	86D	247	$ .01	$ .06
Terrell, Walt	87D	275	$ .01	$ .05
Terrell, Walt	88D	91	$ .01	$ .05
Terrell, Walt	89D	296	$ .01	$ .05
Terrell, Walt	89DBB	245	$ .01	$ .05
Terrell, Walt	89DTR	28	$ .01	$ .05
Terrell, Walt	90D	309	$ .01	$ .04
Terrell, Walt	91D	717	$ .01	$ .03
Terry, Scott	88D	647	$ .01	$ .15
Terry, Scott	89D	397	$ .01	$ .05
Terry, Scott	90D	418	$ .01	$ .04
Terry, Scott	90DL	234	$ .01	$ .15
Tettleton, Mickey	86D	345	$ .01	$ .65
Tettleton, Mickey	87D	349	$ .01	$ .15
Tettleton, Mickey	88D	103	$ .01	$ .05
Tettleton, Mickey	89D	401	$ .01	$ .05
Tettleton, Mickey	89DBB	86	$ .01	$ .10
Tettleton, Mickey	90D	169	$ .01	$ .10
Tettleton, Mickey	90DK	5	$ .01	$ .10
Tettleton, Mickey	90DL	65	$ .01	$ .15
Tettleton, Mickey	91D	597	$ .01	$ .03
Teufel, Tim	84DRR	37	$ .10	$ .45
Teufel, Tim	85D	192	$ .01	$ .08
Teufel, Tim	86D	242	$ .01	$ .06
Teufel, Tim	87D	581	$ .01	$ .05
Teufel, Tim	88D	648	$ .01	$ .15
Teufel, Tim	89D	507	$ .01	$ .05
Teufel, Tim	90D	618	$ .01	$ .04
Teufel, Tim	90DL	383	$ .01	$ .15
Teufel, Tim	91D	370	$ .01	$ .03
Tewksbury, Bob	86DR	8	$ .01	$ .10

Player	Year	No.	VG	EX/MT
Tewksbury, Bob	87D	422	$ .01	$ .05
Tewksbury, Bob	90D	714	$ .01	$ .04
Tewksbury, Bob	90DL	406	$ .01	$ .15
Tewksbury, Bob	91D	183	$ .01	$ .03
Thigpen, Bobby	87D	370	$ .05	$1.00
Thigpen, Bobby	88D	247	$ .01	$ .25
Thigpen, Bobby	88DBB	235	$ .01	$ .05
Thigpen, Bobby	89D	266	$ .01	$ .15
Thigpen, Bobby	89DBB	25	$ .01	$ .05
Thigpen, Bobby	90D	266	$ .01	$ .04
Thigpen, Bobby	90DL	175	$ .01	$ .15
Thigpen, Bobby	91D	90	$ .01	$ .03
Thigpen, Bobby	91DBC	20	$ .01	$ .03
Thigpen, Bobby	91DK	8	$ .01	$ .05
Thigpen, Bobby	91DMVP	399	$ .01	$ .03
Thomas, Andres	86DR	10	$ .01	$ .20
Thomas, Andres	87D	266	$ .03	$ .25
Thomas, Andres	88D	627	$ .01	$ .15
Thomas, Andres	89D	576	$ .01	$ .05
Thomas, Andres	89DBB	197	$ .01	$ .05
Thomas, Andres	90D	263	$ .01	$ .04
Thomas, Andres	90DL	33	$ .01	$ .15
Thomas, Andres	91D	491	$ .01	$ .03
Thomas, Derrel	81D	419	$ .01	$ .05
Thomas, Derrel	82D	537	$ .01	$ .05
Thomas, Derrel	84D	397	$ .03	$ .10
Thomas, Frank	90DL	300	$ .01	$30.00
Thomas, Frank	91D	477	$ .01	$1.00
Thomas, Gorman	81D	326	$ .01	$ .05
Thomas, Gorman	82D	132	$ .01	$ .05
Thomas, Gorman	82DK	26	$ .01	$ .05
Thomas, Gorman	83D	510	$ .01	$ .05
Thomas, Gorman	84D	574	$ .03	$ .10
Thomas, Gorman	86D	440	$ .01	$ .06
Thomasson, Gary	81D	534	$ .01	$ .05
Thompson, Jason	81D	293	$ .01	$ .05

Pirates — JASON THOMPSON 1b

Thompson, Jason	82D	502	$ .01	$ .05
Thompson, Jason	83D	95	$ .01	$ .05
Thompson, Jason	84D	64	$ .03	$ .10
Thompson, Jason	85D	322	$ .01	$ .08
Thompson, Jason	86D	322	$ .01	$ .06

DONRUSS

Player	Year	No.	VG	EX/MT
Thompson, Milt	86D	507	$ .01	$ .35
Thompson, Milt	87D	330	$ .01	$ .05
Thompson, Milt	88D	236	$ .01	$ .15

Player	Year	No.	VG	EX/MT
Thompson, Milt	89D	313	$ .01	$ .05
Thompson, Milt	89DBB	212	$ .01	$ .05
Thompson, Milt	89DTR	43	$ .01	$ .05
Thompson, Milt	90D	82	$ .01	$ .04
Thompson, Milt	90DL	308	$ .01	$ .15
Thompson, Milt	91D	225	$ .01	$ .03
Thompson, Rob	86DR	39	$ .01	$ .35
Thompson, Rob	87D	145	$ .01	$ .25
Thompson, Rob	88D	268	$ .01	$ .05
Thompson, Rob	89D	98	$ .01	$ .05
Thompson, Robby	89DBB	79	$ .01	$ .05
Thompson, Robby	90D	140	$ .01	$ .04
Thompson, Robby	90DL	199	$ .01	$ .15
Thompson, Robby	91D	363	$ .01	$ .03
Thompson, Scot	81D	519	$ .01	$ .05
Thompson, Scot	83D	378	$ .01	$ .05
Thompson, Scot	84D	167	$ .03	$ .10
Thon, Dickie	81D	290	$ .01	$ .05
Thon, Dickie	83D	191	$ .01	$ .05
Thon, Dickie	84D	304	$ .03	$ .10
Thon, Dickie	86D	572	$ .01	$ .06
Thon, Dickie	87D	261	$ .01	$ .05
Thon, Dickie	89D	441	$ .01	$ .05
Thon, Dickie	90D	549	$ .01	$ .04
Thon, Dickie	90DL	105	$ .01	$ .15
Thon, Dickie	91D	91	$ .01	$ .03
Thornton, Andre	81D	198	$ .01	$ .05
Thornton, Andre	82D	324	$ .01	$ .05
Thornton, Andre	83D	211	$ .01	$ .05
Thornton, Andy	84D	94	$ .03	$ .10
Thornton, Andre	84DK	25	$ .03	$ .10
Thornton, Andre	85D	468	$ .01	$ .08
Thornton, Andre	86D	251	$ .01	$ .06
Thornton, Andre	87D	279	$ .01	$ .05
Thurman, Gary	88DR	33	$ .01	$ .15
Thurman, Gary	88DRR	44	$ .01	$ .15
Thurman, Gary	89D	498	$ .01	$ .10

Player	Year	No.	VG	EX/MT
Thurman, Gary	90D	416	$ .01	$ .04
Thurmond, Mark	84D	505	$ .03	$ .10
Thurmond, Mark	85D	284	$ .01	$ .08
Thurmond, Mark	86D	261	$ .01	$ .06
Thurmond, Mark	87D	543	$ .01	$ .05
Thurmond, Mark	88D	599	$ .01	$ .05
Thurmond, Mark	90D	612	$ .01	$ .04
Tiant, Luis	81D	231	$ .03	$ .20
Tiant, Luis	83D	542	$ .01	$ .05
Tibbs, Jay	85D	262	$ .01	$ .08
Tibbs, Jay	86D	262	$ .01	$ .06
Tibbs, Jay	87D	282	$ .01	$ .05
Tidrow, Dick	81D	551	$ .01	$ .05
Tidrow, Dick	82D	477	$ .01	$ .05
Tobik, Dave	82D	511	$ .01	$ .05
Tobik, Dave	83D	385	$ .01	$ .05
Todd, Jackson	81D	31	$ .01	$ .05
Todd, Jackson	82D	178	$ .01	$ .05
Toliver, Fred	86D	612	$ .01	$ .06
Toliver, Fred	89D	510	$ .01	$ .05
Tolleson, Wayne	83D	573	$ .01	$ .10
Tolleson, Wayne	84D	464	$ .03	$ .10
Tolleson, Wayne	85D	378	$ .01	$ .08
Tolleson, Wayne	86D	134	$ .01	$ .06
Tolleson, Wayne	87D	524	$ .01	$ .05
Tolleson, Wayne	88D	154	$ .01	$ .05
Tolleson, Wayne	89D	659	$ .01	$ .05
Tomlin, Randy	91D	725	$ .01	$ .03
Torre, Joe	81D	506	$ .01	$ .05
Torre, Joe	83D	628	$ .01	$ .05
Torrez, Mike	81D	216	$ .01	$ .05
Torrez, Mike	82D	235	$ .01	$ .05
Torrez, Mike	83D	512	$ .01	$ .05
Torrez, Mike	84D	556	$ .03	$ .10
Traber, Jim	85DRR	45	$ .01	$ .25
Traber, Jim	87D	477	$ .01	$ .05
Traber, Jim	90D	569	$ .01	$ .04
Tracy, Jim	81D	520	$ .01	$ .05
Trammell, Alan	81D	5	$ .10	$ .60
Trammell, Alan	82D	76	$ .10	$ .55
Trammell, Alan	82DK	5	$ .10	$ .40
Trammell, Alan	83D	207	$ .10	$ .40
Trammell, Alan	84D	293	$ .15	$1.00
Trammell, Alan	85D	171	$ .08	$ .35
Trammell, Alan	86D	171	$ .10	$ .35
Trammell, Alan	87D	127	$ .01	$ .15
Trammell, Alan	88D	230	$ .01	$ .05
Trammell, Alan	88DBC	11	$ .10	$ .15
Trammell, Alan	88DK	4	$ .01	$ .15
Trammell, Alan	89D	180	$ .01	$ .15
Trammell, Alan	89DBB	13	$ .01	$ .10
Trammell, Alan	89DBC	17	$ .01	$ .20
Trammell, Alan	90D	90	$ .01	$ .10
Trammell, Alan	90DBC	26	$ .01	$ .10
Trammell, Alan	90DL	218	$ .01	$ .20
Trammell, Alan	91D	118	$ .01	$ .03
Trautwein, John	88DR	24	$ .01	$ .05
Travers, Bill	81D	508	$ .01	$ .05
Traxler, Brian	90DR	38	$ .01	$ .10
Treadway, Jeff	88DR	17	$ .01	$ .10
Treadway, Jeff	88DRR	29	$ .01	$ .20
Treadway, Jeff	89D	351	$ .01	$ .15
Treadway, Jeff	89DBB	141	$ .01	$ .05
Treadway, Jeff	90D	50	$ .01	$ .04
Treadway, Jeff	90DL	455	$ .01	$ .15
Treadway, Jeff	91D	117	$ .01	$ .03
Trevino, Alex	82D	350	$ .01	$ .05
Trevino, Alex	83D	374	$ .01	$ .05
Trevino, Alex	84D	286	$ .03	$ .10
Trevino, Alex	85D	565	$ .01	$ .08

Player	Year	No.	VG	EX/MT
Trevino, Alex	87D	546	$ .01	$ .05
Trevino, Alex	88D	376	$ .01	$ .05
Trevino, Alex	90D	443	$ .01	$ .04
Trevino, Alex	90DL	432	$ .01	$ .15
Trillo, Manny	81D	22	$ .01	$ .05
Trillo, Manny	82D	245	$ .01	$ .05
Trillo, Manny	83D	294	$ .01	$ .05
Trillo, Manny	84D	575	$ .03	$ .10
Trillo, Manny	85D	431	$ .01	$ .08
Trillo, Manny	86D	201	$ .01	$ .06
Trillo, Manny	87D	570	$ .01	$ .05
Trillo, Manny	88D	516	$ .01	$ .05
Trillo, Manny	89D	608	$ .01	$ .05
Trout, Steve	81D	400	$ .01	$ .05
Trout, Steve	82D	243	$ .01	$ .05
Trout, Steve	83D	417	$ .01	$ .05
Trout, Steve	84D	533	$ .03	$ .10
Trout, Steve	85D	198	$ .01	$ .08
Trout, Steve	86D	117	$ .01	$ .06
Trout, Steve	87D	201	$ .01	$ .05
Trout, Steve	88D	524	$ .01	$ .05
Trujillo, Mike	87D	613	$ .01	$ .05
Tudor, John	81D	457	$ .25	$1.00
Tudor, John	82D	260	$ .03	$ .25
Tudor, John	83D	563	$ .01	$ .25
Tudor, John	84D	416	$ .03	$ .25
Tudor, John	85D	235	$ .03	$ .10
Tudor, John	86D	260	$ .01	$ .06
Tudor, John	87D	170	$ .01	$ .05
Tudor, John	88D	553	$ .01	$ .05
Tudor, John	88DBB	212	$ .01	$ .15
Tudor, John	89D	195	$ .01	$ .05
Tudor, John	90DL	176	$ .01	$ .15
Tunnell, Lee	84D	592	$ .03	$ .10
Tunnell, Lee	85D	288	$ .01	$ .08
Turner, Jerry	81D	244	$ .01	$ .05
Turner, Jerry	82D	609	$ .01	$ .05
Tyson, Mike	82D	435	$ .01	$ .05
Ujdur, Jerry	83D	600	$ .01	$ .05
Ullger, Scott	84D	438	$ .03	$ .10
Underwood, Pat	81D	368	$ .01	$ .05
Underwood, Pat	83D	29	$ .01	$ .05
Underwood, Tom	81D	108	$ .01	$ .05
Underwood, Tom	82D	323	$ .01	$ .05
Underwood, Tom	83D	391	$ .01	$ .05
Underwood, Tom	84D	253	$ .03	$ .10
Unser, Del	81D	164	$ .01	$ .05
Unser, Del	82D	273	$ .01	$ .05
Upshaw, Willie	82D	652	$ .01	$ .05
Upshaw, Willie	83D	558	$ .01	$ .05
Upshaw, Willie	84D	315	$ .03	$ .10
Upshaw, Willie	85D	71	$ .01	$ .08
Upshaw, Willie	85DK	10	$ .03	$ .10
Upshaw, Willie	86D	195	$ .01	$ .06
Upshaw, Willie	87D	367	$ .01	$ .05
Upshaw, Willie	88D	271	$ .01	$ .05
Upshaw, Willie	89D	492	$ .01	$ .05
Uribe, Jose	86D	236	$ .05	$ .25
Uribe, Jose	87D	436	$ .01	$ .05
Uribe, Jose	88D	559	$ .01	$ .05
Uribe, Jose	89D	131	$ .01	$ .05
Uribe, Jose	89DBB	106	$ .01	$ .05
Uribe, Jose	90D	335	$ .01	$ .04
Uribe, Jose	90DL	225	$ .01	$ .15
Uribe, Jose	91D	375	$ .01	$ .03
Urrea, John	81D	190	$ .01	$ .05
Urrea, John	82D	313	$ .01	$ .05
Vail, Mike	81D	554	$ .01	$ .05
Vail, Mike	83D	597	$ .01	$ .05
Valdez, Julio	82D	560	$ .01	$ .05
Valdez, Sergio	90D	405	$ .01	$ .10
Valdez, Sergio	90DL	496	$ .01	$ .15
Valdez, Sergio	91D	344	$ .01	$ .03
Valentine, Ellis	82D	605	$ .01	$ .05
Valenzuela, Fernando	82D	462	$ .25	$1.00
Valenzuela, Fernando	83D	284	$ .10	$ .35
Valenzuela, Fernando	83DK	1	$ .10	$ .50
Valenzuela, Fernando	84D	52	$ .20	$ .60
Valenzuela, Fernando	85D	52	$ .10	$ .35
Valenzuela, Fernando	86D	215	$ .10	$ .35
Valenzuela, Fernando	87D	94	$ .08	$ .25
Valenzuela, Fernando	88D	53	$ .03	$ .25
Valenzuela, Fernando	89D	250	$ .01	$ .10
Valenzuela, Fernando	90D	625	$ .01	$ .10
Valenzuela, Fernando	90DL	68	$ .01	$ .15
Valenzuela, Fernando	91D	127	$ .01	$ .03
Valenzuela, Fernando	91DBC	11	$ .01	$ .03
Valera, Julio	91DRR	39	$ .01	$ .15
Valle, Dave	87D	610	$ .01	$ .05
Valle, Dave	88D	393	$ .01	$ .05
Valle, Dave	89D	614	$ .01	$ .05
Valle, Dave	89DBB	248	$ .01	$ .05
Valle, Dave	90D	129	$ .01	$ .04
Valle, Dave	90DL	166	$ .01	$ .10
Valle, Dave	91D	366	$ .01	$ .03
Van Gorder, Dave	83D	188	$ .01	$ .05
Van Gorder, Dave	85D	384	$ .01	$ .08
Van Gorder, Dave	86D	550	$ .01	$ .06
Van Slyke, Andy	84D	83	$1.25	$7.00
Van Slyke, Andy	85D	327	$ .15	$ .75
Van Slyke, Andy	86D	412	$ .01	$ .25
Van Slyke, Andy	87D	417	$ .01	$ .15
Van Slyke, Andy	88D	291	$ .01	$ .05
Van Slyke, Andy	88DBB	157	$ .01	$ .15
Van Slyke, Andy	88DBC	8	$ .10	$ .25
Van Slyke, Andy	88DK	18	$ .01	$ .05
Van Slyke, Andy	89D	54	$ .03	$ .15
Van Slyke, Andy	89DBB	45	$ .01	$ .05
Van Slyke, Andy	89DBC	10	$ .01	$ .10
Van Slyke, Andy	90D	244	$ .01	$ .04
Van Slyke, Andy	90DL	117	$ .01	$ .20
Van Slyke, Andy	91D	552	$ .01	$ .03
Vande Berg, Ed	83D	100	$ .01	$ .05
Vande Berg, Ed	84D	604	$ .03	$ .10
Vande Berg, Ed	85D	511	$ .01	$ .08
Vande Berg, Ed	86D	637	$ .01	$ .06
Vande Berg, Ed	87D	376	$ .01	$ .05
Varsho, Gary	91D	671	$ .01	$ .03
Vatcher, Jim	91D	753	$ .01	$ .03
Vaughn, DeWayne	88DR	25	$ .01	$ .05
Vaughn, Greg	90DL	111	$ .01	$ 2.00
Vaughn, Greg	90DR	16	$ .01	$ .50
Vaughn, Greg	90DRR	37	$ .01	$ .50
Vaughn, Greg	91D	478	$ .01	$ .15
Vaughn, Mo	91DRR	430	$ .01	$ .75
Vega, Jesus	83D	650	$ .01	$ .05
Velarde, Randy	90D	630	$ .01	$ .04
Velez, Otto	81D	391	$ .01	$ .05
Velez, Otto	82D	304	$ .01	$ .05
Venable, Max	84D	323	$ .03	$ .10
Venable, Max	86D	650	$ .01	$ .06
Venable, Max	90DL	459	$ .01	$ .15
Venable, Max	91D	510	$ .01	$ .03
Ventura, Robin	90DL	167	$ .01	$ .75
Ventura, Robin	90DR	15	$ .01	$ .25
Ventura, Robin	90DRR	28	$ .01	$ .50
Ventura, Robin	91D	315	$ .01	$ .10
Veres, Randy	91D	755	$ .01	$ .03
Verhoeven, John	81D	564	$ .01	$ .05
Veryzer, Tom	81D	199	$ .01	$ .05

DONRUSS

Player	Year	No.	VG	EX/MT	Player	Year	No.	VG	EX/MT
Veryzer, Tom	82D	450	$ .01	$ .05	Vukovich, George	84D	468	$ .03	$ .10
Villanueva, Hector	90DL	401	$ .01	$ .25	Vukovich, George	85D	276	$ .01	$ .08
Villanueva, Hector	91D	296	$ .01	$ .15	Vukovich, George	86D	346	$ .01	$ .06
Viola, Frank	83D	382	$1.50	$6.00	Waddel, Tom	85D	582	$ .01	$ .08
Viola, Frank	84D	364	$ .50	$2.25	Waddel, Tom	86D	94	$ .01	$ .06
Viola, Frank	85D	436	$ .15	$ .75	Wagner, Mark	81D	126	$ .01	$ .05
Viola, Frank	85DK	17	$ .05	$ .35	Wagner, Mark	82D	163	$ .01	$ .05
Viola, Frank	86D	194	$ .05	$ .35	Wagner, Mark	83D	268	$ .01	$ .05
Viola, Frank	87D	196	$ .08	$ .25	Waits, Rick	81D	201	$ .01	$ .05
Viola, Frank	88D	149	$ .01	$ .15	Waits, Rick	82D	33	$ .01	$ .05
Viola, Frank	88DBB	214	$ .05	$ .20	Waits, Rick	83D	263	$ .01	$ .05
Viola, Frank	89D	237	$ .01	$ .10	Waits, Rick	85D	368	$ .01	$ .08
Viola, Frank	89DBB	74	$ .01	$ .25	Walewander, Jim	89D	415	$ .01	$ .04
Viola, Frank	89DK	23	$ .01	$ .15	Walk, Bob	81D	393	$ .01	$ .25
Viola, Frank	90D	353	$ .01	$ .20	Walk, Bob	83D	401	$ .01	$ .05
Viola, Frank	90DL	93	$ .01	$ .20	Walk, Bob	86D	430	$ .01	$ .06
Viola, Frank	91D	529	$ .01	$ .10	Walk, Bob	87D	203	$ .01	$ .05
Virdon, Bill	81D	384	$ .01	$ .05	Walk, Bob	88D	514	$ .01	$ .05
Virdon, Bill	82D	144	$ .01	$ .05	Walk, Bob	89D	172	$ .01	$ .05
Virgil, Ozzie	83D	606	$ .01	$ .05	Walk, Bob	89DBB	145	$ .01	$ .05
Virgil, Ozzie	84D	326	$ .03	$ .10	Walk, Bob	90D	370	$ .01	$ .04
Virgil, Ozzie	85D	82	$ .01	$ .08	Walk, Bob	90DL	64	$ .01	$ .15
Virgil, Ozzie	86D	137	$ .01	$ .06	Walk, Bob	91D	157	$ .01	$ .03
Virgil, Ozzie	87D	67	$ .01	$ .05	Walker, Chico	87D	539	$ .01	$ .05
Virgil, Ozzie	88D	143	$ .01	$ .05	Walker, Duane	83D	624	$ .01	$ .05
Virgil, Ozzie	88DBB	85	$ .01	$ .05	Walker, Duane	84D	325	$ .03	$ .10
Virgil, Ozzie	89D	145	$ .01	$ .05	Walker, Duane	85D	608	$ .01	$ .08
Vizcaino, Jose	91D	722	$ .01	$ .03	Walker, Duane	86D	500	$ .01	$ .06
Vizquel, Omar	89DBB	163	$ .01	$ .05	Walker, Greg	84D	609	$ .05	$ .55
Vizquel, Omar	89DR	53	$ .01	$ .10	Walker, Greg	85D	366	$ .01	$ .08
Vizquel, Omar	90D	483	$ .01	$ .04	Walker, Greg	86D	135	$ .05	$ .20
Vizquel, Omar	90DL	88	$ .01	$ .20	Walker, Greg	87D	59	$ .01	$ .05
Vizquel, Omar	91D	231	$ .01	$ .03	Walker, Greg	87DK	25	$ .01	$ .05
Von Ohlen, Dave	84D	205	$ .03	$ .10	Walker, Greg	88D	162	$ .01	$ .05
Von Ohlen, Dave	85D	412	$ .01	$ .08	Walker, Greg	88DBB	193	$ .01	$ .05
Vuckovich, Pete	81D	189	$ .01	$ .05	Walker, Greg	89D	135	$ .01	$ .05
					Walker, Larry	90D	578	$ .01	$ .25
					Walker, Larry	90DL	325	$ .01	$ .50
					Walker, Larry	91D	359	$ .01	$ .10
					Walker, Mike	91D	61	$ .01	$ .15
					Wallach, Tim	82D	140	$ .20	$1.50
					Wallach, Tim	83D	392	$ .01	$ .30
					Wallach, Tim	84D	421	$ .01	$ .45
					Wallach, Tim	85D	87	$ .03	$ .20
					Wallach, Tim	86D	219	$ .02	$ .15
					Wallach, Tim	87D	179	$ .01	$ .05
					Wallach, Tim	88D	222	$ .01	$ .05
					Wallach, Tim	88DBB	258	$ .01	$ .05
					Wallach, Tim	89D	156	$ .01	$ .05
					Wallach, Tim	89DBB	34	$ .01	$ .05
					Wallach, Tim	90D	220	$ .01	$ .04
					Wallach, Tim	90DL	80	$ .01	$ .15
					Wallach, Tim	91D	514	$ .01	$ .03
					Wallach, Tim	91DLP	6	$1.00	$5.00
					Wallach, Tim	91DMVP	406	$ .01	$ .03
					Walling, Dennis	81D	144	$ .01	$ .05
					Walling, Denny	82D	496	$ .01	$ .05
					Walling, Denny	83D	419	$ .01	$ .05
					Walling, Denny	84D	641	$ .04	$ .25
					Walling, Denny	85D	527	$ .01	$ .08
					Walling, Denny	86D	136	$ .01	$ .06
					Walling, Denny	87D	554	$ .01	$ .05
					Walling, Denny	88D	384	$ .01	$ .05
					Walling, Denny	89D	279	$ .01	$ .05
					Walling, Denny	90D	677	$ .01	$ .04
					Walter, Gene	86DR	47	$ .02	$ .09
					Walter, Gene	87D	511	$ .01	$ .05
					Walton, Jerome	89DBB	172	$ .01	$1.00
					Walton, Jerome	89DR	26	$ .01	$1.50
					Walton, Jerome	90D	285	$ .01	$ .25

Vuckovich, Pete	82D	458	$ .03	$ .20
Vuckovich, Pete	83D	80	$ .01	$ .05
Vuckovich, Pete	86D	473	$ .01	$ .06
Vukovich, George	83D	315	$ .01	$ .05

Player	Year	No.	VG	EX/MT
Walton, Jerome	90DL	124	$ .01	$ .35
Walton, Jerome	91D	72	$ .01	$ .10
Ward, Colby	91D	330	$ .01	$ .15
Ward, Duane	87DRR	45	$ .01	$ .25
Ward, Duane	88D	567	$ .01	$ .05
Ward, Duane	89D	543	$ .01	$ .05
Ward, Duane	89DBB	216	$ .01	$ .05
Ward, Duane	90D	307	$ .01	$ .04
Ward, Duane	90DL	501	$ .01	$ .15
Ward, Duane	91D	92	$ .01	$ .03
Ward, Gary	81D	594	$ .01	$ .05
Ward, Gary	82D	571	$ .01	$ .05
Ward, Gary	83D	429	$ .01	$ .05
Ward, Gary	84D	192	$ .03	$ .10
Ward, Gary	85D	342	$ .01	$ .08
Ward, Gary	86D	98	$ .01	$ .06
Ward, Gary	86DK	20	$ .01	$ .06
Ward, Gary	87D	427	$ .01	$ .05
Ward, Gary	88D	251	$ .01	$ .05
Ward, Gary	90D	621	$ .01	$ .04
Ward, Gary	90DL	113	$ .01	$ .15
Ward, Gary	91D	728	$ .01	$ .03
Ward, Turner	91DRR	429	$ .01	$ .15
Warren, Mike	84D	631	$ .03	$ .10
Warren, Mike	85D	278	$ .01	$ .08
Washington, Claudell	82D	58	$ .01	$ .05
Washington, Claudell	83D	249	$ .01	$ .05
Washington, Claudell	84D	310	$ .03	$ .10
Washington, Claudell	85D	310	$ .01	$ .08
Washington, Claudell	85DK	11	$ .03	$ .10
Washington, Claudell	86D	287	$ .01	$ .06
Washington, Claudell	88D	340	$ .01	$ .05
Washington, Claudell	88DBB	217	$ .01	$ .05
Washington, Claudell	89D	72	$ .01	$ .05
Washington, Claudell	89DBB	227	$ .01	$ .05
Washington, Claudell	89DTR	46	$ .01	$ .05
Washington, Claudell	90D	52	$ .01	$ .04
Washington, Ron	83D	431	$ .01	$ .05
Washington, Ron	84D	391	$ .03	$ .10
Washington, Ron	85D	391	$ .01	$ .08
Washington, Ron	86D	560	$ .01	$ .06
Washington, Ron	89D	468	$ .01	$ .05
Washington, U.L.	81D	460	$ .01	$ .05
Washington, U.L.	82D	160	$ .01	$ .05
Washington, U.L.	83D	490	$ .01	$ .05
Washington, U.L.	84D	543	$ .03	$ .10
Washington, U.L.	85D	521	$ .01	$ .08
Washington, U.L.	86D	498	$ .01	$ .06
Wathan, John	81D	221	$ .01	$ .05
Wathan, John	82D	86	$ .01	$ .05
Wathan, John	83D	86	$ .01	$ .05
Wathan, John	84D	466	$ .03	$ .10
Wathan, John	85D	466	$ .01	$ .08
Wathan, John	86D	496	$ .01	$ .06
Watson, Bob	81D	225	$ .01	$ .05
Watson, Bob	82D	108	$ .01	$ .05
Watson, Bob	83D	551	$ .01	$ .05
Wayne, Gary	89DR	27	$ .01	$ .10
Wayne, Gary	90D	318	$ .01	$ .04
Wayne, Gary	91D	757	$ .01	$ .03
Weaver, Earl	81D	356	$ .01	$ .05
Weaver, Earl	82D	27	$ .02	$ .15
Webster, Mitch	86D	523	$ .08	$ .25
Webster, Mitch	87D	335	$ .01	$ .05
Webster, Mitch	88D	257	$ .01	$ .05
Webster, Mitch	89D	459	$ .01	$ .05
Webster, Mitch	89DBB	261	$ .01	$ .05
Webster, Mitch	90D	137	$ .01	$ .04
Webster, Mitch	90DL	312	$ .01	$ .15
Webster, Mitch	91D	283	$ .01	$ .03

Player	Year	No.	VG	EX/MT
Wegman, Bill	86D	490	$ .01	$ .06
Wegman, Bill	87D	109	$ .01	$ .05
Wegman, Bill	88D	151	$ .01	$ .05
Wegman, Bill	89D	293	$ .01	$ .05
Weiss, Walt	88DR	18	$ .15	$ .75
Weiss, Walt	89D	446	$ .01	$ .25
Weiss, Walt	89DBB	155	$ .01	$ .10
Weiss, Walt	90D	67	$ .01	$ .10
Weiss, Walt	90DL	239	$ .01	$ .15
Weiss, Walt	91D	214	$ .01	$ .03
Welch, Bob	81D	178	$ .03	$ .20

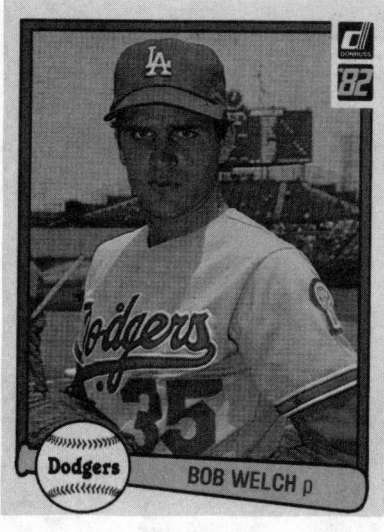

Player	Year	No.	VG	EX/MT
Welch, Bob	82D	75	$ .01	$ .10
Welch, Bob	83D	410	$ .01	$ .05
Welch, Bob	84D	153	$ .03	$ .10
Welch, Bob	85D	372	$ .01	$ .08
Welch, Bob	86D	459	$ .01	$ .06
Welch, Bob	87D	475	$ .01	$ .05
Welch, Bob	88D	253	$ .01	$ .05
Welch, Bob	88DBB	134	$ .01	$ .05
Welch, Bob	88DK	24	$ .01	$ .05
Welch, Bob	89D	332	$ .01	$ .05
Welch, Bob	89DBB	267	$ .01	$ .05
Welch, Bob	90D	332	$ .01	$ .04
Welch, Bob	91D	645	$ .01	$ .03
Welch, Bob	91D	727	$ .01	$ .03
Welch, Bob	91DAS	54	$ .01	$ .03
Welch, Bob	91DK	20	$ .01	$ .05
Wellman, Brad	84D	265	$ .03	$ .10
Wellman, Brad	86D	431	$ .01	$ .06
Wellman, Brad	89D	380	$ .01	$ .05
Wells, David	88D	640	$ .01	$ .30
Wells, David	88DR	26	$ .01	$ .05
Wells, David	89D	307	$ .01	$ .05
Wells, David	89DBB	328	$ .01	$ .05
Wells, David	90D	425	$ .01	$ .04
Wells, David	91D	473	$ .01	$ .03
Welsh, Chris	82D	44	$ .01	$ .05
Welsh, Chris	83D	94	$ .01	$ .05
Welsh, Chris	84D	498	$ .03	$ .10
Welsh, Chris	86D	464	$ .01	$ .06

DONRUSS

Player	Year	No.	VG	EX/MT	Player	Year	No.	VG	EX/MT
Werner, Don	83D	593	$ .01	$ .05	White, Frank	87D	255	$ .01	$ .05
Werth, Dennis	81D	466	$ .01	$ .05	White, Frank	88D	225	$ .01	$ .05
West, Dave	89DRR	41	$ .01	$ .25	White, Frank	89D	85	$ .01	$ .05
West, Dave	90D	387	$ .01	$ .04	White, Frank	89DBB	175	$ .01	$ .05
West, David	90DL	387	$ .01	$ .15	White, Frank	90D	262	$ .01	$ .04
West, David	91D	264	$ .01	$ .03	White, Frank	90DL	204	$ .01	$ .15
Wetteland, John	90D	671	$ .01	$ .10	White, Jerry	81D	333	$ .01	$ .05
Wetteland, John	91D	614	$ .01	$ .03	White, Jerry	82D	621	$ .01	$ .05
Whisenton, Larry	83D	501	$ .01	$ .05	White, Jerry	83D	602	$ .01	$ .05
Whitaker, Lou	81D	365	$ .05	$ .35	Whitehouse, Len	84D	558	$ .03	$ .10
Whitaker, Lou	82D	454	$ .03	$ .20	Whitehouse, Len	85D	513	$ .01	$ .08
Whitaker, Lou	83D	333	$ .03	$ .20	Whitehurst, Wally	91D	511	$ .01	$ .03
Whitaker, Lou	84D	227	$ .10	$ .45	Whiten, Mark	90DL	396	$ .01	$2.50
Whitaker, Lou	85D	293	$ .03	$ .25	Whiten, Mark	91D	607	$ .01	$ .25
Whitaker, Lou	85DK	5	$ .03	$ .25	Whitfield, Terry	81D	435	$ .01	$ .05
Whitaker, Lou	86D	49	$ .03	$ .25	Whitfield, Terry	85D	540	$ .01	$ .08
Whitaker, Lou	87D	107	$ .05	$ .20	Whitfield, Terry	86D	337	$ .01	$ .06
Whitaker, Lou	88D	173	$ .01	$ .05	Whitson, Ed	81D	74	$ .01	$ .05
Whitaker, Lou	89D	298	$ .01	$ .15	Whitson, Ed	82D	251	$ .01	$ .05
Whitaker, Lou	89DBB	35	$ .01	$ .10	Whitson, Ed	83D	389	$ .01	$ .05
Whitaker, Lou	90D	298	$ .01	$ .10	Whitson, Ed	84D	528	$ .03	$ .10
Whitaker, Lou	90DK	16	$ .01	$ .10	Whitson, Ed	85D	446	$ .01	$ .08
Whitaker, Lou	90DL	34	$ .01	$ .15	Whitson, Ed	86D	225	$ .01	$ .06
Whitaker, Lou	91D	174	$ .01	$ .03	Whitson, Ed	87D	360	$ .01	$ .05
White, Devon	87DR	8	$ .05	$ .25	Whitson, Ed	88D	81	$ .01	$ .05
White, Devon	87DRR	38	$ .15	$ .75	Whitson, Ed	89D	229	$ .01	$ .05
White, Devon	88D	283	$ .01	$ .10	Whitson, Ed	89DBB	210	$ .01	$ .10
White, Devon	88DBB	227	$ .01	$ .15	Whitson, Ed	90D	205	$ .01	$ .10
White, Devon	88DK	8	$ .01	$ .15	Whitson, Ed	90DK	26	$ .01	$ .10
White, Devon	89D	213	$ .01	$ .10	Whitson, Ed	90DL	246	$ .01	$ .15
White, Devon	89DBB	27	$ .01	$ .10	Whitson, Ed	91D	186	$ .01	$ .03
					Whitt, Ernie	81D	390	$ .01	$ .05
					Whitt, Ernie	82D	381	$ .01	$ .05
					Whitt, Ernie	83D	304	$ .01	$ .05
					Whitt, Ernie	84D	437	$ .03	$ .10
					Whitt, Ernie	85D	268	$ .01	$ .08
					Whitt, Ernie	86D	559	$ .01	$ .06
					Whitt, Ernie	87D	148	$ .01	$ .05
					Whitt, Ernie	88D	394	$ .01	$ .05
					Whitt, Ernie	89D	591	$ .01	$ .05
					Whitt, Ernie	89DBB	255	$ .01	$ .05
					Whitt, Ernie	90D	385	$ .01	$ .04
					Whitt, Ernie	90DL	408	$ .01	$ .10
					Wickander, Kevin	90DR	36	$ .01	$ .10
					Wickander, Kevin	91D	649	$ .01	$ .03
					Wiggins, Alan	83D	397	$ .01	$ .05
					Wiggins, Alan	84D	568	$ .03	$ .10
					Wiggins, Alan	85D	80	$ .01	$ .08
					Wiggins, Alan	86D	607	$ .01	$ .06
					Wilcox, Milt	81D	247	$ .01	$ .05
					Wilcox, Milt	82D	233	$ .01	$ .05
					Wilcox, Milt	83D	155	$ .01	$ .05
					Wilcox, Milt	84D	471	$ .03	$ .10
					Wilcox, Milt	85D	105	$ .01	$ .08
					Wilfong, Rob	81D	493	$ .01	$ .05
					Wilfong, Rob	82D	130	$ .01	$ .05
					Wilfong, Rob	83D	612	$ .01	$ .05
					Wilfong, Rob	84D	329	$ .03	$ .10
					Wilfong, Rob	85D	402	$ .01	$ .08
					Wilfong, Rob	87D	258	$ .01	$ .05
					Wilkerson, Curt	84D	99	$ .03	$ .10
White, Devon	90D	226	$ .01	$ .10	Wilkerson, Curt	85D	99	$ .01	$ .08
White, Devon	90DL	76	$ .01	$ .15	Wilkerson, Curtis	86D	256	$ .01	$ .06
White, Devon	91D	150	$ .01	$ .03	Wilkerson, Curtis	87D	223	$ .01	$ .05
White, Frank	81D	340	$ .01	$ .05	Wilkerson, Curtis	88D	592	$ .01	$ .05
White, Frank	82D	286	$ .01	$ .05	Wilkerson, Curtis	89D	402	$ .01	$ .05
White, Frank	83D	464	$ .01	$ .05	Wilkerson, Curtis	89DTR	34	$ .01	$ .05
White, Frank	84D	222	$ .03	$ .10	Wilkerson, Curt	90D	608	$ .01	$ .04
White, Frank	85D	175	$ .01	$ .08	Wilkinson, Bill	88D	568	$ .01	$ .05
White, Frank	86D	130	$ .01	$ .06	Willard, Gerry "Jerry"	84D	520	$ .03	$ .10

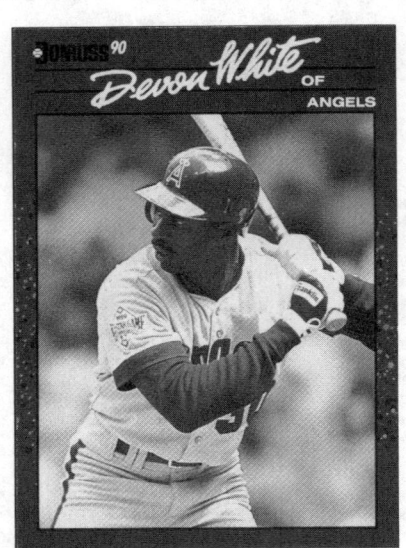

Player	Year	No.	VG	EX/MT
Willard, Jerry	85D	346	$ .01	$ .08
Willard, Jerry	86D	398	$ .01	$ .06
Willard, Jerry	87D	467	$ .01	$ .05
Willard, Jerry	91D	634	$ .01	$ .03
Williams, Al	82D	429	$ .01	$ .05
Williams, Al	83D	508	$ .01	$ .05
Williams, Al	84D	316	$ .03	$ .10
Williams, Bernie	90D	689	$ .01	$ .30
Williams, Dick	81D	453	$ .01	$ .05
Williams, Dick	83D	625	$ .01	$ .05
Williams, Eddie	88DRR	46	$ .10	$ .30
Williams, Eddie	89DTR	29	$ .01	$ .05
Williams, Frank	85D	323	$ .03	$ .25
Williams, Frank	88D	512	$ .01	$ .05
Williams, Frank	89D	478	$ .01	$ .05
Williams, Frank	89DBB	259	$ .01	$ .05
Williams, Frank	90D	327	$ .01	$ .04
Williams, Ken	87DR	11	$ .01	$ .10
Williams, Ken	88D	334	$ .01	$ .10
Williams, Ken	88DBB	249	$ .01	$ .05
Williams, Ken	89D	337	$ .01	$ .05
Williams, Ken	89DTR	17	$ .01	$ .05
Williams, Matt	87DR	45	$1.00	$5.50
Williams, Matt	88D	628	$ .50	$2.50
Williams, Matt	89D	594	$ .01	$ .25
Williams, Matt	90D	348	$ .01	$ .15
Williams, Matt	90DL	94	$ .01	$ .50
Williams, Matt	91D	685	$ .01	$ .03
Williams, Matt	91DK	18	$ .01	$ .05
Williams, Mitch	86DR	19	$ .01	$ .35
Williams, Mitch	87D	347	$ .01	$ .35
Williams, Mitch	88D	161	$ .01	$ .15
Williams, Mitch	89D	225	$ .01	$ .05
Williams, Mitch	89DBB	60	$ .01	$ .05
Williams, Mitch	89DTR	38	$ .01	$ .05
Williams, Mitch	90D	275	$ .01	$ .04
Williams, Mitch	90DL	156	$ .01	$ .15
Williams, Mitch	91D	312	$ .01	$ .03
Williams, Reggie	86DR	5	$ .02	$ .09
Williams, Reggie	87D	341	$ .01	$ .05
Williamson, Mark	87DR	3	$ .01	$ .07
Williamson, Mark	88D	418	$ .01	$ .05
Williamson, Mark	90D	406	$ .01	$ .04
Williamson, Mark	90DL	461	$ .01	$ .15
Williamson, Mark	91D	238	$ .01	$ .03
Wills, Bump	81D	25	$ .01	$ .05
Wills, Bump	82D	289	$ .01	$ .05
Wills, Bump	83D	351	$ .01	$ .05
Wills, Frank	91D	691	$ .01	$ .03
Wilson, Craig	91D	544	$ .01	$ .03
Wilson, Glenn	83D	580	$ .06	$ .35
Wilson, Glenn	84D	618	$ .03	$ .10
Wilson, Glenn	85D	609	$ .01	$ .08
Wilson, Glenn	86D	285	$ .01	$ .06
Wilson, Glenn	87D	62	$ .01	$ .05
Wilson, Glenn	88D	262	$ .01	$ .05
Wilson, Glenn	89D	447	$ .01	$ .05
Wilson, Glenn	89DBB	241	$ .01	$ .05
Wilson, Glenn	90D	472	$ .01	$ .04
Wilson, Glenn	90DL	268	$ .01	$ .15
Wilson, Glenn	91D	156	$ .01	$ .03
Wilson, Mookie	81D	575	$ .10	$ .60
Wilson, Mookie	82D	175	$ .01	$ .10
Wilson, Mookie	83D	56	$ .01	$ .10
Wilson, Mookie	84D	190	$ .03	$ .10
Wilson, Mookie	85D	482	$ .01	$ .08
Wilson, Mookie	86D	604	$ .01	$ .06
Wilson, Mookie	88D	652	$ .01	$ .15
Wilson, Mookie	88DBB	208	$ .01	$ .05
Wilson, Mookie	89D	152	$ .01	$ .05

Player	Year	No.	VG	EX/MT
Wilson, Mookie	90D	442	$ .01	$ .04
Wilson, Mookie	90DL	263	$ .01	$ .15
Wilson, Mookie	91D	585	$ .01	$ .03
Wilson, Steve	89DBB	250	$ .01	$ .05
Wilson, Steve	89DR	10	$ .01	$ .10
Wilson, Steve	90D	394	$ .01	$ .04
Wilson, Steve	90DL	420	$ .01	$ .25
Wilson, Steve	91D	519	$ .01	$ .03
Wilson, Trevor	90D	414	$ .01	$ .04
Wilson, Trevor	90DL	489	$ .01	$ .20
Wilson, Trevor	91D	263	$ .01	$ .03
Wilson, Willie	81D	223	$ .01	$ .15
Wilson, Willie	82D	448	$ .03	$ .20
Wilson, Willie	83D	112	$ .03	$ .20
Wilson, Willie	83DK	15	$ .03	$ .20
Wilson, Willie	84D	175	$ .04	$ .25
Wilson, Willie	85D	297	$ .01	$ .08
Wilson, Willie	86D	175	$ .01	$ .06
Wilson, Willie	87D	96	$ .01	$ .05
Wilson, Willie	87D	487	$ .01	$ .05
Wilson, Willie	88D	255	$ .01	$ .05
Wilson, Willie	88DBB	263	$ .01	$ .05
Wilson, Willie	89D	120	$ .01	$ .05
Wilson, Willie	90D	440	$ .01	$ .04
Wilson, Willie	90DL	336	$ .01	$ .15
Wine, Robbie	88D	508	$ .01	$ .05
Winfield, Dave	81D	364	$ .10	$ .75
Winfield, Dave	82D	31	$ .10	$ .55
Winfield, Dave	82D	575	$ .10	$ .55
Winfield, Dave	82DK	18	$ .10	$ .45
Winfield, Dave	83D	409	$ .10	$ .45
Winfield, Dave	84D	51	$ .20	$1.25
Winfield, Dave	85D	51	$ .10	$ .45
Winfield, Dave	85D	651	$1.00	$5.00
Winfield, Dave	86D	248	$ .08	$ .25
Winfield, Dave	87D	105	$ .10	$ .35
Winfield, Dave	87DK	20	$ .10	$ .35

Dave Winfield OF

Player	Year	No.	VG	EX/MT
Winfield, Dave	88D	298	$ .05	$ .20
Winfield, Dave	88DBB	244	$ .01	$ .15
Winfield, Dave	89D	159	$ .01	$ .10

DONRUSS

Player	Year	No.	VG	EX/MT
Winfield, Dave	89DBC	11	$ .01	$ .10
Winfield, Dave	90D	551	$ .01	$ .15
Winfield, Dave	90DL	426	$ .01	$ .25
Winfield, Dave	91D	468	$ .01	$ .10
Winn, Jim	87D	312	$ .01	$ .05
Winn, Jim	88D	409	$ .01	$ .05
Winningham, Herm	86D	279	$ .02	$ .15
Winningham, Herm	88D	581	$ .01	$ .05
Winningham, Herm	89D	435	$ .01	$ .05
Winningham, Herm	90D	478	$ .01	$ .04
Winningham, Herm	91D	695	$ .01	$ .03
Wise, Rick	81D	3	$ .01	$ .05
Wise, Rick	82D	170	$ .01	$ .05
Witt, Bobby	86DR	49	$ .15	$1.00
Witt, Bobby	87D	99	$ .10	$ .75
Witt, Bobby	88D	101	$ .01	$ .15
Witt, Bobby	89D	461	$ .01	$ .05
Witt, Bobby	89DBB	279	$ .01	$ .05
Witt, Bobby	90D	292	$ .01	$ .04
Witt, Bobby	90DL	337	$ .01	$ .15
Witt, Bobby	91D	249	$ .01	$ .03
Witt, Mike	82D	416	$ .25	$1.00
Witt, Mike	83D	416	$ .03	$ .20
Witt, Mike	85D	108	$ .01	$ .08
Witt, Mike	86D	179	$ .01	$ .06
Witt, Mike	87D	58	$ .05	$ .20
Witt, Mike	88D	86	$ .01	$ .05
Witt, Mike	89D	372	$ .01	$ .05
Witt, Mike	90D	580	$ .01	$ .04
Witt, Mike	91D	282	$ .01	$ .03
Witt, Mike	91DBC	1	$ .01	$ .03
Wockenfuss, John	81D	245	$ .01	$ .05
Wockenfuss, John	82D	459	$ .01	$ .05
Wockenfuss, John	83D	76	$ .01	$ .05
Wockenfuss, John	84D	150	$ .03	$ .10
Wockenfuss, John	85D	549	$ .01	$ .08
Wohlford, Jim	81D	316	$ .01	$ .05
Wohlford, Jim	83D	524	$ .01	$ .05
Wojna, Ed	86D	505	$ .01	$ .06
Wojna, Ed	87D	589	$ .01	$ .05
Woodard, Mike	86DRR	46	$ .01	$ .06
Woods, Al	81D	32	$ .01	$ .05
Woods, Al	82D	180	$ .01	$ .05
Woods, Gary	83D	631	$ .01	$ .05
Woods, Gary	84D	144	$ .03	$ .10
Woods, Gary	85D	555	$ .01	$ .08
Woodson, Tracy	88D	499	$ .01	$ .05
Woodward, Rob	86DR	53	$ .02	$ .09
Woodward, Rob	87D	652	$ .01	$ .05
Worrell, Todd	86DR	21	$ .05	$ .35
Worrell, Todd	86DRR	43	$ .15	$ .75
Worrell, Todd	87D	307	$ .01	$ .10
Worrell, Todd	88D	386	$ .01	$ .10
Worrell, Todd	89D	82	$ .01	$ .05
Worrell, Todd	89DBB	243	$ .01	$ .05
Worrell, Todd	90D	319	$ .01	$ .04
Wortham, Rich	81D	161	$ .01	$ .05
Worthington, Craig	88DR	23	$ .01	$ .25
Worthington, Craig	89D	569	$ .01	$ .10
Worthington, Craig	89DBB	282	$ .01	$ .10
Worthington, Craig	89DR	25	$ .01	$ .10
Worthington, Craig	90D	141	$ .01	$ .04
Worthington, Craig	90DL	170	$ .01	$ .20
Worthington, Craig	91D	293	$ .01	$ .03
Wright, George	83D	116	$ .01	$ .05
Wright, George	84D	525	$ .03	$ .10
Wright, George	85D	256	$ .01	$ .08
Wright, George	86D	220	$ .01	$ .06
Wright, Jim	82D	490	$ .01	$ .05
Wrona, Rick	89DR	38	$ .01	$ .25
Wrona, Rick	90D	512	$ .01	$ .15
Wynegar, Butch	81D	529	$ .01	$ .05
Wynegar, Butch	82D	508	$ .01	$ .05
Wynegar, Butch	83D	325	$ .01	$ .05
Wynegar, Butch	84D	458	$ .03	$ .10
Wynegar, Butch	85D	417	$ .01	$ .08
Wynegar, Butch	86D	274	$ .01	$ .06
Wynne, Marvell	84D	508	$ .03	$ .10
Wynne, Marvell	85D	113	$ .01	$ .08
Wynne, Marvell	86D	113	$ .01	$ .06
Wynne, Marvell	87D	411	$ .01	$ .05
Wynne, Marvell	88D	237	$ .01	$ .05
Wynne, Marvell	89D	347	$ .01	$ .05
Wynne, Marvell	89DBB	189	$ .01	$ .05
Wynne, Marvell	90D	255	$ .01	$ .04
Wynne, Marvell	90DL	270	$ .01	$ .15
Yastrzemski, Carl	81D	94	$ .25	$1.00
Yastrzemski, Carl	81D	214	$ .25	$1.00
Yastrzemski, Carl	82D	74	$ .15	$1.00
Yastrzemski, Carl	83D	326	$ .15	$1.00
Yastrzemski, Carl	83DK	25	$ .15	$ .75
Yastrzemski, Carl	84D#B	0	$1.50	$8.00
Yastrzemski, Carl	90D	588	$ .01	$ .10
Yeager, Steve	81D	297	$ .02	$ .15
Yeager, Steve	82D	201	$ .01	$ .05
Yeager, Steve	83D	201	$ .01	$ .05
Yeager, Steve	84D	581	$ .03	$ .10
Yeager, Steve	85D	519	$ .01	$ .08
Yeager, Steve	86D	519	$ .01	$ .06
Yelding, Eric	89DR	34	$ .01	$ .10
Yelding, Eric	90D	123	$ .01	$ .04
Yelding, Eric	90DL	301	$ .01	$ .25
Yelding, Eric	91D	277	$ .01	$ .03
Yett, Rich	89D	546	$ .01	$ .05
Yett, Rich	90D	509	$ .01	$ .04
Yost, Ned	83D	458	$ .01	$ .05
Yost, Ned	84D	271	$ .03	$ .10
Yost, Ned	85D	221	$ .01	$ .08

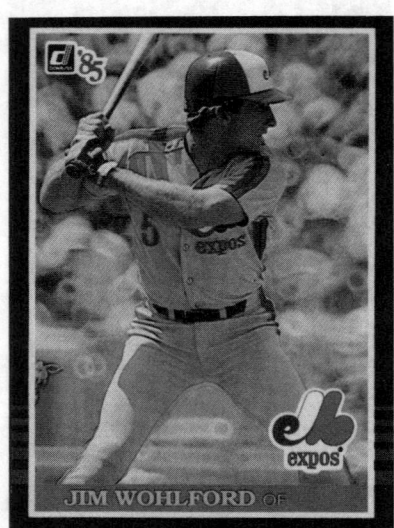

JIM WOHLFORD OF

Player	Year	No.	VG	EX/MT
Wohlford, Jim	85D	585	$ .01	$ .08
Wohlford, Jim	86D	157	$ .01	$ .06

Player	Year	No.	VG	EX/MT
Youmans, Floyd	86D	543	$ .20	$ .60
Youmans, Floyd	87D	257	$ .01	$ .15
Youmans, Floyd	88D	56	$ .01	$ .15
Young, Curt	85D	522	$ .15	$ .50
Young, Curt	87D	344	$ .01	$ .05
Young, Curt	88D	97	$ .01	$ .05
Young, Curt	89D	304	$ .01	$ .05
Young, Curt	90D	505	$ .01	$ .04
Young, Curt	90DL	424	$ .01	$ .15
Young, Curt	91D	724	$ .01	$ .03
Young, Gerald	88D	431	$ .05	$ .40
Young, Gerald	89D	207	$ .01	$ .05
Young, Gerald	89DBB	288	$ .01	$ .05
Young, Gerald	90D	325	$ .01	$ .04
Young, Gerald	90DL	214	$ .01	$ .15
Young, Gerald	91D	689	$ .01	$ .03
Young, Matt	84D	362	$ .03	$ .10
Young, Matt	84DK	16	$ .03	$ .10
Young, Matt	85D	267	$ .01	$ .08
Young, Matt	86D	267	$ .01	$ .06
Young, Matt	87D	193	$ .01	$ .05
Young, Matt	88D	423	$ .01	$ .05
Young, Matt	90DL	509	$ .01	$ .15
Young, Matt	91D	493	$ .01	$ .03
Young, Mike	84D	621	$ .03	$ .10
Young, Mike	85D	367	$ .01	$ .08
Young, Mike	86D	123	$ .01	$ .06
Young, Mike	87D	150	$ .01	$ .05
Young, Mike	88D	396	$ .01	$ .05
Young, Mike	89D	632	$ .01	$ .05
Youngblood, Joel	81D	277	$ .01	$ .05
Youngblood, Joel	82D	613	$ .01	$ .05
Youngblood, Joel	83D	572	$ .01	$ .05
Youngblood, Joel	84D	480	$ .03	$ .10
Youngblood, Joel	85D	79	$ .01	$ .08
Youngblood, Joel	86D	567	$ .01	$ .06
Yount, Robin	81D	323	$ .15	$1.75
Yount, Robin	82D	510	$ .15	$1.50
Yount, Robin	83D	258	$ .10	$1.00
Yount, Robin	84D	48	$ .50	$3.00
Yount, Robin	84DK	1	$ .35	$1.50
Yount, Robin	85D	48	$ .10	$1.00
Yount, Robin	86D	48	$ .10	$ .75
Yount, Robin	87D	126	$ .08	$ .40
Yount, Robin	88D	295	$ .05	$ .20
Yount, Robin	88DBB	183	$ .01	$ .15
Yount, Robin	89D	55	$ .03	$ .15
Yount, Robin	89DBB	53	$ .01	$ .20
Yount, Robin	89DK	5	$ .01	$ .10
Yount, Robin	90D	146	$ .01	$ .10
Yount, Robin	90DL	71	$ .01	$ .35

Player	Year	No.	VG	EX/MT
Yount, Robin	91D	272	$ .01	$ .10
Zachry, Pat	81D	275	$ .01	$ .05
Zachry, Pat	82D	254	$ .01	$ .05
Zachry, Pat	83D	560	$ .01	$ .05
Zachry, Pat	84D	215	$ .03	$ .10
Zahn, Geoff (Jeff)	81D	532	$ .01	$ .05
Zahn, Geoff	82D	164	$ .01	$ .05
Zahn, Geoff	83D	66	$ .01	$ .05
Zahn, Geoff	84D	402	$ .03	$ .10
Zahn, Geoff	85D	301	$ .01	$ .08
Zavaras, Clint	90D	662	$ .01	$ .10
Zeile, Todd	90DL	221	$ .01	$1.25

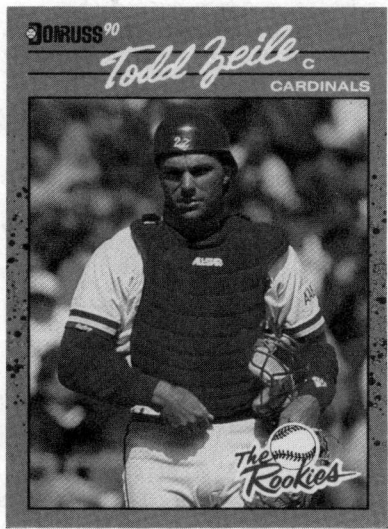

Player	Year	No.	VG	EX/MT
Zeile, Todd	90DR	31	$ .01	$ .30
Zeile, Todd	90DRR	29	$ .01	$ .75
Zeile, Todd	91D	71	$ .01	$ .15
Zimmer, Don	82D	195	$ .01	$ .05
Zisk, Richie	81D	28	$ .01	$ .05
Zisk, Richie	82D	127	$ .01	$ .05
Zisk, Richie	82DK	11	$ .01	$ .05
Zisk, Richie	83D	559	$ .01	$ .05
Zisk, Richie	84D	69	$ .03	$ .10

FLEER CORPORATION 1981-1990

The Fleer Company issued a baseball card set in 1981 to compete with Topps and the newly released Donruss cards. Fleer also issued these cards in wax packs with bubble gum, but was forced to issue the cards without bubble gum in 1982 as Topps was able to stop the bubble gum format through a lawsuit. Fleer has chosen to issue their wax packs with a peel off sticker since 1982. Fleer began issuing factory sets in 1984. Unlike Donruss, the sets are not in numerical order. Beginning in 1988, Fleer attached a factory seal to the box to show if it has been opened or not. This is a significant breakthrough in my way of thinking. Now an unopened factory set can be believed!

Abbreviations used in the Fleer section include the following:
F - Fleer used for all cards in this section
FPD - Player of decade ten card subset issued in 1990 with one card per year of Fleer's first ten years back in the baseball card business.
FU - Update card issued at end of year in sets of 132 since 1984.

All Fleer cards are 2½" x 3½" and in full color.
1981 - 660 cards w/white border and player's team in baseball on left (Fleer found on back to right of card number but no date on card)
1982 - 660 cards w/white border and player's name, team and position in oval design (Fleer name found under card's number on the back but no date on card)
1983 - 660 cards w/beige border (copyright 1983 Fleer above statistical information on back)
1984 - 660 cards w/white border and blue stripes inside border top and bottom (copyright 1984 Fleer above statistical information on back)
1985 - 660 cards w/grey border and Fleer in white at lower right (copyright 1985 Fleer on back above statistical information)
1986 - 660 cards w/dark blue border w/Fleer in white on top right (copyright 1986 Fleer on back bottom)
1987 - 660 cards w/sky blue and white border w/Fleer in white on colored strip at bottom (copyright 1987 Fleer top right on back)
1988 - 660 cards w/white border w/blue and red stripes and Fleer in blue box at bottom right (copyright 1988 Fleer on back above statistical breakdown)
1989 - 660 cards w/grey border w/white vertical stripes and Fleer in black print on lower right (copyright 1989 Fleer on back lower left side)
1990 - 660 cards w/white borders; player encircled by a colored banner and Fleer '90 in upper left corner (copyright 1990 Fleer Corp. on back at bottom)
1991 - 720 cards w/yellow borders; player in rectangular black bordered box with Fleer '91 in lower right corner (copyright 1991 Fleer Corp. on back under circular photo of player)

The listing for each card shown appears immediately following the photograph.

Player	Year	No.	VG	EX/MT	Player	Year	No.	VG	EX/MT
Aase, Don	81F	286	$ .01	$ .05	Alexander, Doyle	87F	510	$ .01	$ .05
Aase, Don	82F	450	$ .01	$ .05	Alexander, Doyle	88F	51	$ .01	$ .05
Aase, Don	83F	76	$ .01	$ .05	Alexander, Doyle	89F	128	$ .01	$ .05
Aase, Don	85F	293	$ .01	$ .05	Alexander, Doyle	90F	599	$ .01	$ .04
Aase, Don	85FU	1	$ .01	$ .10	Alexander, Gary	81F	398	$ .01	$ .05
Aase, Don	86F	268	$ .01	$ .05	Alexander, Gary	82F	475	$ .01	$ .05
Aase, Don	87F	461	$ .01	$ .05	Alexander, Gerald	91F	278	$ .01	$ .10
Aase, Don	87F	627	$ .01	$ .10	Alicea, Luis	88FU	116	$ .01	$ .15
Aase, Don	88F	553	$ .01	$ .05	Alicea, Luis	89F	443	$ .01	$ .15
Aase, Don	89FU	100	$ .01	$ .05	All-Star Game, Cleveland	82F	628	$ .01	$ .05
Aase, Don	90F	196	$ .01	$ .04	Allanson, Andy	86FU	2	$ .04	$ .25
Aase, Don	91F	193	$ .01	$ .03	Allanson, Andy	87F	241	$ .01	$ .10
Abbott, Glenn	81F	615	$ .01	$ .05	Allanson, Andy	88FU	21	$ .01	$ .05
Abbott, Glenn	82F	502	$ .01	$ .05	Allanson, Andy	89F	396	$ .01	$ .05
Abbott, Glenn	84F	74	$ .01	$ .06	Allanson, Andy	90F	483	$ .01	$ .04
Abbott, Jim	89FU	11	$ .01	$ .75	Allen, Jamie	84F	604	$ .01	$ .06
Abbott, Jim	90F	125	$ .01	$ .15	Allen, Kim	81F	612	$ .01	$ .05
Abbott, Jim	91F	305	$ .01	$ .10	Allen, Neil	81F	322	$ .01	$ .05
Abner, Shawn	88F	576	$ .01	$ .20	Allen, Neil	82F	520	$ .01	$ .05
Abner, Shawn	91F	522	$ .01	$ .03	Allen, Neil	83F	536	$ .01	$ .05
Acker, Jim	84F	145	$ .03	$ .10	Allen, Neil	84F	318	$ .01	$ .06
Acker, Jim	85F	96	$ .01	$ .05	Allen, Neil	85F	219	$ .01	$ .05
Acker, Jim	86F	50	$ .01	$ .05	Allen, Neil	86F	98	$ .01	$ .05
Acker, Jim	87F	509	$ .01	$ .05	Allen, Neil	86FU	3	$ .01	$ .05
Acker, Jim	88F	531	$ .01	$ .05	Allen, Neil	87F	484	$ .01	$ .05
Acker, Jim	91F	167	$ .01	$ .03	Allen, Neil	89F	250	$ .01	$ .05
Adams, Glenn	81F	562	$ .01	$ .05	Allen, Rod	89F	397	$ .01	$ .05
Adams, Glenn	82F	545	$ .01	$ .05	Allenson, Gary	82F	287	$ .01	$ .05
Adduci, Jim	89F	176	$ .01	$ .05	Allenson, Gary	83F	177	$ .01	$ .05
Afenir, Troy	91F	1	$ .01	$ .10	Allenson, Gary	84F	388	$ .01	$ .06
Agosto, Juan	84F	50	$ .01	$ .06	Allenson, Gary	85F	148	$ .01	$ .05
Agosto, Juan	85F	506	$ .01	$ .05	Allred, Beau	90FU	88	$ .01	$ .15
Agosto, Juan	86F	197	$ .01	$ .05	Allred, Beau	91F	358	$ .01	$ .10
Agosto, Juan	88F	437	$ .01	$ .05	Almon, Bill	81F	332	$ .01	$ .05
Agosto, Juan	89F	348	$ .01	$ .05	Almon, Bill	82F	335	$ .01	$ .05
Agosto, Juan	90F	220	$ .01	$ .04	Almon, Bill	83F	228	$ .01	$ .05
Agosto, Juan	91F	497	$ .01	$ .03	Almon, Bill	84F	436	$ .01	$ .06
Aguayo, Luis	82F	238	$ .01	$ .05					
Aguayo, Luis	86F	433	$ .01	$ .05					
Aguayo, Luis	87F	169	$ .01	$ .05					
Aguayo, Luis	88F	297	$ .01	$ .05					
Aguayo, Luis	89F	249	$ .01	$ .05					
Aguilera, Rick	86F	74	$ .06	$ .35					
Aguilera, Rick	87F	1	$ .01	$ .10					
Aguilera, Rick	88F	127	$ .01	$ .05					
Aguilera, Rick	89F	27	$ .01	$ .05					
Aguilera, Rick	90F	365	$ .01	$ .04					
Aguilera, Rick	91F	602	$ .01	$ .03					
Aikens, Willie	81F	43	$ .01	$ .05					
Aikens, Willie	82F	404	$ .01	$ .05					
Aikens, Willie	83F	104	$ .01	$ .05					
Aikens, Willie	84F	341	$ .01	$ .06					
Aikens, Willie	84FU	1	$ .04	$ .25					
Aikens, Willie	85F	97	$ .01	$ .05					
Ainge, Dan	81F	418	$ .05	$1.00					
Ainge, Danny	82F	608	$ .01	$ .25					
Akerfelds, Darrel	90FU	41	$ .01	$ .05					
Akerfelds, Darrel	91F	386	$ .01	$ .03					
Aldrete, Mike	86FU	1	$ .05	$ .30					
Aldrete, Mike	87F	264	$ .06	$ .25					
Aldrete, Mike	88F	76	$ .01	$ .10					
Aldrete, Mike	89F	323	$ .01	$ .05					
Aldrete, Mike	89FU	95	$ .01	$ .05					
Aldrete, Mike	91F	224	$ .01	$ .03					
Aldrich, Jay	88F	155	$ .01	$ .10					
Alexander, Doyle	81F	255	$ .01	$ .10					
Alexander, Doyle	82F	383	$ .01	$ .10					
Alexander, Doyle	84F	146	$ .01	$ .06	Almon, Bill	85F	414	$ .01	$ .05
Alexander, Doyle	85F	98	$ .01	$ .05	Almon, Bill	85FU	2	$ .01	$ .05
Alexander, Doyle	86F	51	$ .01	$ .05	Almon, Bill	86F	602	$ .01	$ .05

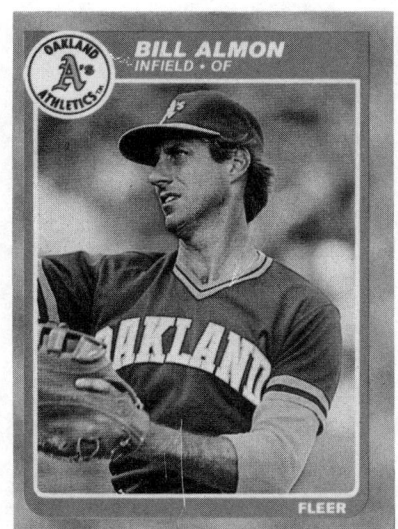

Player	Year	No.	VG	EX/MT
Almon, Bill	87F	601	$.01	$.05
Alomar, Jr., Sandy	89F	300	$.25	$1.50
Alomar, Jr., Sandy	89F	630	$.01	$.25
Alomar, Jr., Sandy	90F	150	$.01	$.35
Alomar, Jr., Sandy	90FU	89	$.01	$.35
Alomar, Jr., Sandy	91F	359	$.01	$.15
Alomar, Roberto	88FU	122	$.05	$1.75
Alomar, Roberto	89F	299	$.05	$.75
Alomar, Roberto	89F	630	$.01	$.25
Alomar, Roberto	90F	149	$.01	$.20
Alomar, Roberto	91F	523	$.01	$.03
Alou, Moises	90F	650	$.01	$.35
Altamirano, Porfirio	83F	153	$.01	$.05
Altobelli, Joe	84F	643	$.01	$.06
Alvarez, Jose	88FU	70	$.01	$.15
Alvarez, Jose	89F	585	$.01	$.15
Alvarez, Jose	90F	574	$.01	$.04
Andersen, Larry	83F	470	$.01	$.05
Andersen, Larry	85F	244	$.01	$.05
Andersen, Larry	86F	434	$.01	$.05
Andersen, Larry	87F	49	$.01	$.05
Andersen, Larry	88F	438	$.01	$.05
Andersen, Larry	89F	349	$.01	$.05
Andersen, Larry	90F	221	$.01	$.04
Andersen, Larry	91F	83	$.01	$.03
Anderson, Allan	87F	533	$.01	$.40
Anderson, Allan	88FU	41	$.01	$.15
Anderson, Allan	89F	102	$.01	$.15
Anderson, Allan	90F	366	$.01	$.04
Anderson, Allan	91F	603	$.01	$.03
Anderson, Brady	89F	606	$.01	$.30
Anderson, Brady	90F	172	$.01	$.04
Anderson, Brady	91F	466	$.01	$.03
Anderson, Dave	84F	533	$.01	$.06
Anderson, Dave	85F	366	$.01	$.05
Anderson, Dave	86F	123	$.01	$.05
Anderson, Dave	87F	436	$.01	$.05

Dave Anderson
SHORTSTOP

Player	Year	No.	VG	EX/MT
Anderson, Dave	88F	508	$.01	$.05
Anderson, Dave	89F	53	$.01	$.05
Anderson, Dave	90FU	59	$.01	$.05

Player	Year	No.	VG	EX/MT
Anderson, Dave	91F	252	$.01	$.03
Anderson, Jim	81F	598	$.01	$.05
Anderson, Jim	82F	503	$.01	$.05
Anderson, Kent	91F	306	$.01	$.03
Anderson, Rick	87F	2	$.01	$.05
Anderson, Scott	91F	225	$.01	$.10
Anderson, Sparky	81F	460	$.01	$.10
Anderson, Sparky	85F	628	$.01	$.05
Andujar, Joaquin	81F	63	$.01	$.10
Andujar, Joaquin	82F	110	$.01	$.10
Andujar, Joaquin	83F	1	$.01	$.10
Andujar, Joaquin	84F	319	$.03	$.10
Andujar, Joaquin	85F	220	$.01	$.05
Andujar, Joaquin	86F	26	$.01	$.10
Andujar, Joaquin	86FU	4	$.01	$.05
Andujar, Joaquin	87F	385	$.01	$.05
Anthony, Eric	90F	222	$.01	$.50
Anthony, Eric	91F	498	$.01	$.10
Aponte, Luis	83F	178	$.01	$.05
Aponte, Luis	84F	389	$.01	$.06
Aponte, Luis	84FU	2	$.01	$.10
Aponte, Luis	85F	437	$.01	$.05
Appier, Kevin	89FU	35	$.01	$.75
Appier, Kevin	90F	100	$.01	$.15
Appier, Kevin	91F	549	$.01	$.03
Aquino, Luis	89F	275	$.01	$.05
Aquino, Luis	90F	101	$.01	$.04
Aquino, Luis	91F	550	$.01	$.03
Armas, Tony	81F	575	$.01	$.10
Armas, Tony	82F	85	$.01	$.10
Armas, Tony	83F	513	$.03	$.20
Armas, Tony	84F	390	$.01	$.06
Armas, Tony	85F	149	$.01	$.05
Armas, Tony	86F	339	$.01	$.05
Armas, Tony	87F	26	$.01	$.05
Armas, Tony	88F	484	$.01	$.05
Armas, Tony	89F	467	$.01	$.05
Armas, Tony	90F	126	$.01	$.04
Armstrong, Jack	90F	412	$.01	$.50
Armstrong, Jack	91F	55	$.01	$.03
Armstrong, Mike	81F	503	$.01	$.05
Armstrong, Mike	83F	105	$.01	$.05
Armstrong, Mike	84F	342	$.01	$.06
Armstrong, Mike	85F	120	$.01	$.05
Arnsberg, Brad	88F	202	$.01	$.15
Arnsberg, Brad	91F	279	$.01	$.03
Arroyo, Fernando	82F	546	$.01	$.05
Asadoor, Randy	87F	650	$.04	$.25
Ashby, Alan	81F	64	$.01	$.05
Ashby, Alan	82F	212	$.01	$.05
Ashby, Alan	83F	445	$.01	$.05
Ashby, Alan	84F	220	$.01	$.06
Ashby, Alan	85F	343	$.01	$.05
Ashby, Alan	86F	292	$.01	$.05
Ashby, Alan	87F	50	$.01	$.05
Ashby, Alan	88F	439	$.01	$.05
Ashby, Alan	89F	350	$.01	$.05
Asselstine, Brian	81F	256	$.01	$.05
Asselstine, Brian	82F	428	$.01	$.05
Assenmacher, Paul	86FU	5	$.04	$.25
Assenmacher, Paul	87F	511	$.01	$.05
Assenmacher, Paul	88F	532	$.01	$.05
Assenmacher, Paul	89F	586	$.01	$.05
Assenmacher, Paul	90F	25	$.01	$.04
Assenmacher, Paul	91F	413	$.01	$.03
Atherton, Keith	84F	437	$.01	$.06
Atherton, Keith	85F	415	$.01	$.05
Atherton, Keith	86F	410	$.01	$.05
Atherton, Keith	87F	534	$.01	$.05
Atherton, Keith	88F	1	$.01	$.05

Player	Year	No.	VG	EX/MT	Player	Year	No.	VG	EX/MT
Atherton, Keith	89F	103	$ .01	$ .05	Baker, Dusty	82F	1	$ .01	$ .10
Atherton, Keith	89FU	24	$ .01	$ .05	Baker, Dusty	83F	201	$ .01	$ .05
August, Don	88FU	37	$ .01	$ .25	Baker, Dusty	84F	96	$ .01	$ .06
August, Don	89F	177	$ .01	$ .10	Baker, Dusty	84FU	5	$ .06	$ .35
Augustine, Jerry	82F	133	$ .01	$ .05	Baker, Dusty	85F	602	$ .01	$ .05
Augustine, Jerry	83F	26	$ .01	$ .05	Baker, Dusty	85FU	3	$ .01	$ .10
Augustine, Jerry	84F	194	$ .01	$ .06	Baker, Dusty	86F	411	$ .01	$ .05
Ault, Doug	81F	424	$ .01	$ .05	Baker, Dusty	87F	387	$ .01	$ .05
Avery, Steve	90FU	1	$ .01	$ .30	Balboni, Steve	84FU	6	$ .06	$ .35
Avery, Steve	91F	681	$ .01	$ .15	Balboni, Steve	85F	196	$ .01	$ .05
Aviles, Ramon	81F	23	$ .01	$ .05	Balboni, Steve	86F	1	$ .01	$ .10
Aviles, Ramon	82F	239	$ .01	$ .05	Balboni, Steve	87F	362	$ .01	$ .05
Ayala, Benny	81F	185	$ .01	$ .05	Balboni, Steve	88F	251	$ .01	$ .05
Ayala, Benny	82F	157	$ .01	$ .05	Balboni, Steve	89F	538	$ .01	$ .05
Ayala, Benny	83F	52	$ .01	$ .05	Balboni, Steve	89FU	45	$ .01	$ .05
Azocar, Oscar	90FU	111	$ .01	$ .20	Balboni, Steve	90F	436	$ .01	$ .04
Azocar, Oscar	91F	655	$ .01	$ .10	Balboni, Steve	91F	656	$ .01	$ .03
Babbitt, Shooty	82F	86	$ .01	$ .05	Ballard, Jeff	88F	554	$ .01	$ .10
Backman, Wally	81F	336	$ .10	$ .50	Ballard, Jeff	89F	607	$ .01	$ .05
Backman, Wally	83F	537	$ .01	$ .05	Ballard, Jeff	90F	173	$ .01	$ .04
Backman, Wally	85F	72	$ .01	$ .05	Ballard, Jeff	91F	467	$ .01	$ .03
Backman, Wally	86F	75	$ .01	$ .05	Baller, Jay	86FU	7	$ .01	$ .05
Backman, Wally	87F	3	$ .01	$ .05	Bando, Chris	83F	400	$ .01	$ .05
Backman, Wally	88F	128	$ .01	$ .05	Bando, Chris	84F	534	$ .01	$ .06
Backman, Wally	89F	28	$ .01	$ .05	Bando, Chris	85F	438	$ .01	$ .05
Backman, Wally	89FU	43	$ .01	$ .05	Bando, Chris	86F	579	$ .01	$ .05
Backman, Wally	90F	367	$ .01	$ .04	Bando, Chris	87F	243	$ .01	$ .05
Backman, Wally	90FU	47	$ .01	$ .05	Bando, Chris	88F	601	$ .01	$ .05
Backman, Wally	91F	29	$ .01	$ .03	Bando, Sal	81F	510	$ .01	$ .05
Baerga, Carlos	90FU	90	$ .01	$ .50	Bando, Sal	82F	134	$ .01	$ .05
Baerga, Carlos	91F	360	$ .01	$ .20	Bankhead, Scott	86FU	8	$ .03	$ .20
Bahnsen, Stan	81F	156	$ .01	$ .05	Bankhead, Scott	87F	363	$ .05	$ .25
Bahnsen, Stan	82F	183	$ .01	$ .05	Bankhead, Scott	87FU	1	$ .01	$ .05
Bailes, Scott	86FU	6	$ .04	$ .25	Bankhead, Scott	88F	368	$ .01	$ .05
Bailes, Scott	87F	242	$ .01	$ .10	Bankhead, Scott	89F	539	$ .01	$ .05
Bailes, Scott	88F	600	$ .01	$ .05	Bankhead, Scott	90F	505	$ .01	$ .04
Bailes, Scott	89F	398	$ .01	$ .05	Bankhead, Scott	91F	442	$ .01	$ .03
Bailes, Scott	90F	484	$ .01	$ .04	Bannister, Alan	82F	359	$ .01	$ .05
Bailey, Howard	84F	75	$ .01	$ .06	Bannister, Alan	83F	401	$ .01	$ .05
Bailey, Mark	84FU	3	$ .06	$ .35	Bannister, Alan	84F	535	$ .01	$ .06
Bailey, Mark	85F	344	$ .01	$ .05	Bannister, Alan	85F	555	$ .01	$ .05
Bailey, Mark	86F	293	$ .01	$ .05	Bannister, Alan	86F	556	$ .01	$ .05
Bailor, Bob	81F	409	$ .01	$ .05	Bannister, Floyd	81F	599	$ .01	$ .05
Bailor, Bob	82F	521	$ .01	$ .05	Bannister, Floyd	82F	504	$ .01	$ .05
Bailor, Bob	83F	538	$ .01	$ .05	Bannister, Floyd	83F	471	$ .01	$ .05
Bailor, Bob	84F	580	$ .01	$ .06	Bannister, Floyd	84F	52	$ .01	$ .06
Bailor, Bob	84FU	4	$ .01	$ .10	Bannister, Floyd	85F	508	$ .01	$ .05
Bailor, Bob	85F	367	$ .01	$ .05	Bannister, Floyd	86F	199	$ .01	$ .05
Bailor, Bob	86F	124	$ .01	$ .05	Bannister, Floyd	87F	486	$ .01	$ .05
Baines, Harold	81F	346	$ .25	$2.50	Bannister, Floyd	88F	392	$ .01	$ .05
Baines, Harold	82F	336	$ .04	$ .50	Bannister, Floyd	89F	276	$ .01	$ .05
Baines, Harold	83F	229	$ .03	$ .20	Bannister, Steve	84FU	7	$ .01	$ .10
Baines, Harold	84F	51	$ .03	$ .20	Barfield, Jesse	83F	424	$ .10	$ .80
Baines, Harold	85F	507	$ .04	$ .25	Barfield, Jesse	84F	147	$ .05	$ .30
Baines, Harold	86F	198	$ .01	$ .10	Barfield, Jesse	85F	99	$ .04	$ .25
Baines, Harold	87F	485	$ .03	$ .20	Barfield, Jesse	86F	52	$ .04	$ .25
Baines, Harold	87F	643	$ .01	$ .05	Barfield, Jesse	87F	219	$ .04	$ .25
Baines, Harold	88F	391	$ .01	$ .10	Barfield, Jesse	87F	643	$ .01	$ .05
Baines, Harold	89F	491	$ .01	$ .05	Barfield, Jesse	88F	102	$ .01	$ .10
Baines, Harold	90F	290	$ .01	$ .04	Barfield, Jesse	89F	225	$ .01	$ .05
Baines, Harold	91F	2	$ .01	$ .03	Barfield, Jesse	89FU	46	$ .01	$ .10
Bair, Doug	81F	213	$ .01	$ .05	Barfield, Jesse	90F	437	$ .01	$ .04
Bair, Doug	83F	2	$ .01	$ .05	Barfield, Jesse	91F	657	$ .01	$ .03
Bair, Doug	84F	76	$ .01	$ .06	Barker, Len	81F	408	$ .01	$ .05
Bair, Doug	85F	1	$ .01	$ .10	Barker, Len	82F	360	$ .01	$ .05
Bair, Doug	87F	386	$ .01	$ .05	Barker, Len	82F	639	$ .01	$ .05
Baker, Chuck	81F	500	$ .01	$ .05	Barker, Len	83F	402	$ .01	$ .05
Baker, Chuck	82F	561	$ .01	$ .05	Barker, Len	83F	642	$ .01	$ .05
Baker, Doug	90F	368	$ .01	$ .10	Barker, Len	84F	170	$ .01	$ .06
Baker, Dusty	81F	115	$ .01	$ .10	Barker, Len	85F	318	$ .01	$ .05

FLEER

Player	Year	No.	VG	EX/MT	Player	Year	No.	VG	EX/MT
Barker, Len	86F	507	$ .01	$ .05	Bedrosian, Steve	91F	254	$ .01	$ .03
Barojas, Salome	83F	230	$ .01	$ .05	Belanger, Mark	81F	175	$ .01	$ .05
Barojas, Salome	84F	53	$ .01	$ .06	Belanger, Mark	82F	158	$ .01	$ .05
Barojas, Salome	85F	482	$ .01	$ .05	Belcher, Kevin	91F	280	$ .01	$ .20
Barr, Jim	81F	287	$ .01	$ .05	Belcher, Tim	88F	509	$ .01	$ .50
Barr, Jim	83F	252	$ .01	$ .05	Belcher, Tim	89F	54	$ .01	$ .05
Barr, Jim	84F	365	$ .01	$ .06	Belcher, Tim	90F	389	$ .01	$ .04
Barrett, Marty	84FU	8	$ .50	$2.00	Belcher, Tim	91F	194	$ .01	$ .03
Barrett, Marty	85F	150	$ .05	$ .25	Belinda, Stan	90FU	48	$ .01	$ .10
Barrett, Marty	86F	340	$ .01	$ .05	Belinda, Stan	91F	30	$ .01	$ .03
Barrett, Marty	87F	27	$ .01	$ .10	Bell, Buddy	81F	625	$ .03	$ .20
Barrett, Marty	88F	343	$ .01	$ .05	Bell, Buddy	82F	313	$ .03	$ .20
Barrett, Marty	89F	78	$ .01	$ .05	Bell, Buddy	83F	562	$ .03	$ .20
Barrett, Marty	90F	266	$ .01	$ .04	Bell, Buddy	83F	632	$ .03	$ .20
Barrett, Marty	91F	84	$ .01	$ .03	Bell, Buddy	84F	413	$ .03	$ .20
Barrios, Francisco	81F	352	$ .01	$ .05	Bell, Buddy	85F	556	$ .03	$ .20
Bass, Kevin	84F	221	$ .04	$ .25	Bell, Buddy	86F	172	$ .01	$ .10
Bass, Kevin	85F	345	$ .01	$ .10	Bell, Buddy	87F	193	$ .01	$ .10
Bass, Kevin	86F	294	$ .01	$ .10	Bell, Buddy	88F	227	$ .01	$ .10
Bass, Kevin	87F	51	$ .01	$ .10	Bell, Buddy	89F	352	$ .01	$ .05
Bass, Kevin	88F	440	$ .01	$ .05	Bell, Derek	91F	168	$ .01	$ .25
Bass, Kevin	89F	351	$ .01	$ .05	Bell, Eric	87FU	2	$ .01	$ .10
Bass, Kevin	90F	223	$ .01	$ .04	Bell, Eric	88F	555	$ .01	$ .05
Bass, Kevin	90FU	60	$ .01	$ .05	Bell, George (Jorge)	82F	609	$1.20	$8.00
Bass, Kevin	91F	253	$ .01	$ .03	Bell, George	84F	148	$ .20	$1.50
Bass, Randy	82F	566	$ .01	$ .05	Bell, George	85F	100	$ .10	$ .50
Bathe, Bill	86FU	9	$ .01	$ .05	Bell, George	86F	53	$ .06	$ .35
Baumgarten, Ross	82F	337	$ .01	$ .05	Bell, George	87F	220	$ .05	$ .30
Baumgarten, Ross	83F	302	$ .01	$ .05	Bell, George	88F	103	$ .01	$ .25
Bautista, Jose	88FU	1	$ .01	$ .15	Bell, George	88F	623	$ .01	$ .05
Bautista, Jose	89F	608	$ .01	$ .15	Bell, George	89F	226	$ .01	$ .10
Baylor, Don	81F	271	$ .03	$ .20	Bell, George	90F	76	$ .01	$ .04
Baylor, Don	82F	451	$ .01	$ .10	Bell, George	90FPD	628	$ .01	$ .15
Baylor, Don	83F	77	$ .01	$ .10	Bell, George	91F	169	$ .01	$ .03
Baylor, Don	84F	119	$ .03	$ .10	Bell, Jay	88F	602	$ .01	$ .15
Baylor, Don	85F	121	$ .03	$ .20	Bell, Jay	90F	459	$ .01	$ .04
Baylor, Don	86F	99	$ .01	$ .10	Bell, Jay	91F	31	$ .01	$ .03
Baylor, Don	86F	631	$ .04	$ .25	Bell, Juan	91F	468	$ .01	$ .10
Baylor, Don	86FU	10	$ .01	$ .10	Bell, Kevin	81F	343	$ .01	$ .05
Baylor, Don	87F	28	$ .01	$ .10	Bell, Mike	91F	682	$ .01	$ .10
Baylor, Don	88F	2	$ .01	$ .10	Belle, Joey	89FU	25	$ .01	$1.75
Baylor, Don	89F	1	$ .01	$ .05	Belle, Joey	90F	485	$ .01	$ .75
Beane, Billy	86FU	11	$ .01	$ .05	Belliard, Rafael	87F	602	$ .01	$ .05
Beane, Billy	87F	535	$ .01	$ .05	Belliard, Rafael	88F	321	$ .01	$ .05
Beard, Dave	82F	87	$ .01	$ .05	Belliard, Rafael	89F	201	$ .01	$ .05
Beard, Dave	83F	514	$ .01	$ .05	Belliard, Rafael	90F	460	$ .01	$ .04
Beard, Dave	84F	438	$ .01	$ .06	Belliard, Rafael	91F	32	$ .01	$ .03
Beard, Dave	84FU	9	$ .01	$ .10	Bench, Johnny	81F	196	$ .12	$1.25
Beard, Dave	85F	483	$ .01	$ .05	Bench, Johnny	82F	57	$ .10	$1.00
Bearse, Kevin	90FU	91	$ .01	$ .20	Bench, Johnny	82F	634	$ .01	$ .75
Bearse, Kevin	91F	361	$ .01	$ .10	Bench, Johnny	83F	584	$ .10	$ .75
Beattie, Jim	83F	472	$ .01	$ .05	Bench, Johnny	84F	462	$ .08	$1.50
Beattie, Jim	84F	605	$ .01	$ .06	Bench, Johnny	84F	640	$ .10	$2.50
Beattie, Jim	85F	484	$ .01	$ .05	Benedict, Bruce	81F	248	$ .01	$ .05
Beatty, Blaine	90F	197	$ .01	$ .10	Benedict, Bruce	82F	429	$ .01	$ .05
Beckwith, Joe	83F	202	$ .01	$ .05	Benedict, Bruce	83F	130	$ .01	$ .05
Beckwith, Joe	84F	97	$ .01	$ .06	Benedict, Bruce	84F	172	$ .01	$ .06
Beckwith, Joe	84FU	10	$ .01	$ .10	Benedict, Bruce	85F	320	$ .01	$ .05
Beckwith, Joe	85F	197	$ .01	$ .05	Benedict, Bruce	86F	509	$ .01	$ .05
Beckwith, Joe	86F	2	$ .01	$ .05	Benedict, Bruce	87F	512	$ .01	$ .05
Bedrosian, Steve	83F	129	$ .05	$ .50	Benedict, Bruce	89F	587	$ .01	$ .05
Bedrosian, Steve	84F	171	$ .03	$ .10	Benes, Andy	90F	151	$ .01	$ .25
Bedrosian, Steve	85F	319	$ .01	$ .10	Benes, Andy	91F	524	$ .01	$ .10
Bedrosian, Steve	86F	508	$ .01	$ .10	Beniquez, Juan	81F	596	$ .01	$ .05
Bedrosian, Steve	86FU	12	$ .01	$ .10	Beniquez, Juan	82F	452	$ .01	$ .05
Bedrosian, Steve	87F	170	$ .01	$ .10	Beniquez, Juan	83F	78	$ .01	$ .05
Bedrosian, Steve	88F	298	$ .01	$ .05	Beniquez, Juan	84F	508	$ .01	$ .06
Bedrosian, Steve	88F	627	$ .01	$ .10	Beniquez, Juan	85F	294	$ .01	$ .05
Bedrosian, Steve	89F	562	$ .01	$ .05	Beniquez, Juan	86F	148	$ .01	$ .05
Bedrosian, Steve	90F	50	$ .01	$ .04	Beniquez, Juan	86FU	13	$ .01	$ .05

Player	Year	No.	VG	EX/MT	Player	Year	No.	VG	EX/MT
Beniquez, Juan	87F	462	$ .01	$ .05	Bibby, Jim	82F	478	$ .01	$ .05
Beniquez, Juan	87FU	3	$ .01	$ .05	Bibby, Jim	84F	246	$ .01	$ .06
Beniquez, Juan	88F	104	$ .01	$ .05	Bichette, Dante	89F	468	$ .01	$ .15
Benjamin, Mike	90F	51	$ .01	$ .25	Bichette, Dante	90F	127	$ .01	$ .04
Benzinger, Todd	88F	344	$ .15	$ .35	Bichette, Dante	91F	307	$ .01	$ .03
Benzinger, Todd	88F	630	$ .10	$ .25	Bielecki, Mike	85F	650	$ .05	$1.00
Benzinger, Todd	89F	79	$ .01	$ .15	Bielecki, Mike	86F	603	$ .01	$ .05
Benzinger, Todd	89FU	83	$ .01	$ .05	Bielecki, Mike	87F	603	$ .01	$ .05
Benzinger, Todd	90F	413	$ .01	$ .04	Bielecki, Mike	89F	419	$ .01	$ .05
Benzinger, Todd	91F	56	$ .01	$ .03	Bielecki, Mike	90F	27	$ .01	$ .04
Berenguer, Juan	84F	77	$ .01	$ .06	Bielecki, Mike	91F	415	$ .01	$ .03
Berenguer, Juan	85F	2	$ .01	$ .05	Biggio, Craig	88FU	89	$ .01	$1.00
Berenguer, Juan	86F	221	$ .01	$ .05	Biggio, Craig	89F	353	$ .01	$ .50
Berenguer, Juan	87F	265	$ .01	$ .05	Biggio, Craig	90F	224	$ .01	$ .15
Berenguer, Juan	87FU	4	$ .01	$ .05	Biggio, Craig	91F	499	$ .01	$ .03
Berenguer, Juan	88F	3	$ .01	$ .05	Biittner, Larry	81F	314	$ .01	$ .05
Berenguer, Juan	89F	104	$ .01	$ .05	Biittner, Larry	82F	59	$ .01	$ .05
Berenguer, Juan	90F	369	$ .01	$ .04	Biittner, Larry	83F	586	$ .01	$ .05
Berenguer, Juan	91F	604	$ .01	$ .03	Biittner, Larry	84F	414	$ .01	$ .06
Berenyi, Bruce	82F	58	$ .01	$ .05	Bilardello, Dann	84F	464	$ .01	$ .06
Berenyi, Bruce	83F	585	$ .01	$ .05	Bilardello, Dann	87F	313	$ .01	$ .05
Berenyi, Bruce	84F	463	$ .01	$ .06	Bird, Doug	81F	106	$ .01	$ .05
Berenyi, Bruce	85F	73	$ .01	$ .05	Bird, Doug	82F	586	$ .01	$ .05
Bergman, Dave	81F	76	$ .01	$ .05	Bird, Doug	83F	490	$ .01	$ .05
Bergman, Dave	83F	253	$ .01	$ .05	Bird, Doug	84F	391	$ .01	$ .06
Bergman, Dave	84F	366	$ .01	$ .06	Birkbeck, Mike	87FU	5	$ .01	$ .05
Bergman, Dave	84FU	11	$ .01	$ .10	Birkbeck, Mike	89F	178	$ .01	$ .05
Bergman, Dave	85F	3	$ .01	$ .05	Birtsas, Tim	85FU	6	$ .03	$ .20
Bergman, Dave	86F	222	$ .01	$ .05	Birtsas, Tim	86F	412	$ .01	$ .10
Bergman, Dave	87F	144	$ .01	$ .05	Birtsas, Tim	88FU	82	$ .01	$ .05
Bergman, Dave	88F	52	$ .01	$ .05	Birtsas, Tim	89F	152	$ .01	$ .05
Bergman, Dave	89F	129	$ .01	$ .05	Birtsas, Tim	90F	414	$ .01	$ .04
Bergman, Dave	90F	600	$ .01	$ .04	Bitker, Joe	91F	281	$ .01	$ .10
Bergman, Dave	91F	331	$ .01	$ .03					
Bernard, Dwight	83F	27	$ .01	$ .05					
Bernazard, Tony	81F	168	$ .01	$ .05					
Bernazard, Tony	82F	338	$ .01	$ .05					
Bernazard, Tony	83F	231	$ .01	$ .05					
Bernazard, Tony	84F	606	$ .01	$ .06					
Bernazard, Tony	84FU	12	$ .04	$ .25					
Bernazard, Tony	85F	439	$ .01	$ .05					
Bernazard, Tony	86F	580	$ .01	$ .05					
Bernazard, Tony	87F	244	$ .01	$ .05					
Bernazard, Tony	88F	275	$ .01	$ .05					
Berra, Dale	81F	369	$ .01	$ .05					
Berra, Dale	82F	476	$ .01	$ .05					
Berra, Dale	83F	303	$ .01	$ .05					
Berra, Dale	84F	245	$ .01	$ .06					
Berra, Dale	85F	461	$ .01	$ .05					
Berra, Dale	85FU	4	$ .01	$ .05					
Berra, Dale	86F	100	$ .01	$ .05					
Berroa, Geronimo	89FU	72	$ .01	$ .10					
Berroa, Geronimo	90F	575	$ .01	$ .04					
Berryhill, Damon	88F	642	$ .01	$ .75					
Berryhill, Damon	88FU	75	$ .01	$ .30					
Berryhill, Damon	89F	418	$ .01	$ .10					
Berryhill, Damon	90F	26	$ .01	$ .04					
Berryhill, Damon	91F	414	$ .01	$ .03					
Best, Karl	85FU	5	$ .03	$ .20					
Best, Karl	86F	459	$ .01	$ .05					
Best, Karl	87F	579	$ .01	$ .05					
Bevacqua, Kurt	81F	382	$ .01	$ .05					
Bevacqua, Kurt	82F	477	$ .01	$ .05					
Bevacqua, Kurt	83F	352	$ .01	$ .05	Black, Bud	83F	107	$ .03	$ .20
Bevacqua, Kurt	84F	294	$ .01	$ .06	Black, Bud	83F	644	$ .01	$ .05
Bevacqua, Kurt	85F	26	$ .01	$ .05	Black, Bud	84F	343	$ .01	$ .06
Bevacqua, Kurt	86F	315	$ .01	$ .05	Black, Bud	85F	198	$ .01	$ .05
Biancalana, Buddy	86F	3	$ .01	$ .05	Black, Bud	86F	4	$ .01	$ .05
Biancalana, Buddy	87F	364	$ .01	$ .05	Black, Bud	87F	365	$ .01	$ .05
Bibby, Jim	81F	370	$ .01	$ .05	Black, Bud	88F	252	$ .01	$ .05

Bud Black
PITCHER

FLEER

Player	Year	No.	VG	EX/MT
Black, Bud	90F	486	$ .01	$ .04
Blackwell, Tim	81F	304	$ .01	$ .05
Blackwell, Tim	82F	587	$ .01	$ .05
Blair, Willie	90FU	126	$ .01	$ .10
Blair, Willie	91F	170	$ .01	$ .10
Blankenship, Kevin	90F	28	$ .01	$ .04
Blankenship, Lance	89F	2	$ .01	$ .20
Blankenship, Lance	90F	1	$ .01	$ .04
Blankenship, Lance	91F	3	$ .01	$ .03
Blauser, Jeff	88F	533	$ .01	$ .30
Blauser, Jeff	89F	588	$ .01	$ .05
Blauser, Jeff	90F	576	$ .01	$ .04
Blauser, Jeff	91F	683	$ .01	$ .03
Blocker, Terry	89F	589	$ .01	$ .05
Blowers, Mike	90F	438	$ .01	$ .25
Blue, Vida	81F	432	$ .01	$ .10
Blue, Vida	82F	384	$ .01	$ .10
Blue, Vida	83F	106	$ .01	$ .05
Blue, Vida	83F	643	$ .01	$ .05
Blue, Vida	85FU	7	$ .03	$ .20
Blue, Vida	86F	533	$ .01	$ .05
Blue, Vida	87F	266	$ .01	$ .05
Blyleven, Bert	81F	383	$ .03	$ .20
Blyleven, Bert	82F	361	$ .01	$ .25
Blyleven, Bert	84F	536	$ .03	$ .10
Blyleven, Bert	85F	440	$ .01	$ .10
Blyleven, Bert	86F	386	$ .01	$ .10
Blyleven, Bert	87F	536	$ .01	$ .10

Bert Blyleven
PITCHER
MINNESOTA Twins

Player	Year	No.	VG	EX/MT
Blyleven, Bert	88F	4	$ .01	$ .10
Blyleven, Bert	89F	105	$ .01	$ .10
Blyleven, Bert	89FU	12	$ .01	$ .10
Blyleven, Bert	90F	128	$ .01	$ .10
Blyleven, Bert	91F	308	$ .01	$ .03
Bobbicker, Mike	86F	269	$ .01	$ .10
Bochte, Bruce	81F	600	$ .01	$ .05
Bochte, Bruce	82F	505	$ .01	$ .05
Bochte, Bruce	83F	473	$ .01	$ .05
Bochte, Bruce	84FU	13	$ .01	$ .10
Bochte, Bruce	85F	416	$ .01	$ .05
Bochte, Bruce	86F	413	$ .01	$ .05

Player	Year	No.	VG	EX/MT
Bochte, Bruce	87F	388	$ .01	$ .05
Bochy, Bruce	81F	69	$ .01	$ .05
Bochy, Bruce	87F	411	$ .01	$ .05
Bockus, Randy	87FU	6	$ .01	$ .05
Bockus, Randy	88FU	127	$ .01	$ .05
Boddicker, Mike	84F	1	$ .03	$ .10
Boddicker, Mike	84F	645	$ .01	$ .06
Boddicker, Mike	85F	170	$ .01	$ .05
Boddicker, Mike	87F	463	$ .01	$ .05
Boddicker, Mike	88F	556	$ .01	$ .05
Boddicker, Mike	88FU	5	$ .01	$ .05
Boddicker, Mike	89F	80	$ .01	$ .05
Boddicker, Mike	90F	267	$ .01	$ .04
Boddicker, Mike	91F	85	$ .01	$ .03
Boever, Joe	88F	534	$ .01	$ .10
Boever, Joe	90F	577	$ .01	$ .04
Boever, Joe	91F	387	$ .01	$ .03
Boggs, Tommy	81F	261	$ .01	$ .05
Boggs, Tommy	82F	430	$ .01	$ .05
Boggs, Tommy	83F	131	$ .01	$ .05
Boggs, Wade	83F	179	$4.00	$21.00
Boggs, Wade	84F	392	$1.50	$ 7.00
Boggs, Wade	84F	630	$ .10	$ .75
Boggs, Wade	85F	151	$ .75	$4.00
Boggs, Wade	86F	341	$ .50	$2.00
Boggs, Wade	86F	634	$ .10	$ .50
Boggs, Wade	86F	639	$ .30	$1.50
Boggs, Wade	87F	29	$ .25	$1.50
Boggs, Wade	87F	637	$ .06	$ .35
Boggs, Wade	88F	345	$ .05	$ .50
Boggs, Wade	89F	81	$ .05	$ .40
Boggs, Wade	89F	633	$ .05	$ .35
Boggs, Wade	90F	268	$ .01	$ .25
Boggs, Wade	90F	632	$ .01	$ .04
Boggs, Wade	91F	86	$ .01	$ .15
Bohanon, Brian	90FU	122	$ .01	$ .15
Bolton, Tom	88F	346	$ .01	$ .10
Bolton, Tom	91F	87	$ .01	$ .03
Bomback, Mark	81F	323	$ .01	$ .05
Bomback, Mark	82F	610	$ .01	$ .05
Bonds, Barry	86FU	14	$ .25	$5.00
Bonds, Barry	87F	604	$ .25	$7.50
Bonds, Barry	88F	322	$ .10	$1.00
Bonds, Barry	89F	202	$ .01	$ .25
Bonds, Barry	90F	461	$ .01	$ .20
Bonds, Barry	91F	33	$ .01	$ .10
Bonds, Barry	91F	710	$ .01	$ .35
Bonds, Bobby	81F	548	$ .01	$ .10
Bonds, Bobby	82F	588	$ .01	$ .05
Bonham, Bill	81F	215	$ .01	$ .05
Bonilla, Bobby	86FU	15	$ .50	$4.00
Bonilla, Bobby	87F	605	$ .75	$5.75
Bonilla, Bobby	88F	323	$ .10	$ .65
Bonilla, Bobby	89F	203	$ .01	$ .25
Bonilla, Bobby	89F	637	$ .01	$ .35
Bonilla, Bobby	90F	462	$ .01	$ .20
Bonilla, Bobby	91F	34	$ .01	$ .15
Bonilla, Bobby	91F	711	$ .01	$ .20
Bonilla, Juan	82F	567	$ .01	$ .05
Bonilla, Juan	83F	353	$ .01	$ .05
Bonilla, Juan	84F	295	$ .01	$ .06
Bonilla, Juan	87F	464	$ .01	$ .05
Bonnell, Barry	81F	413	$ .01	$ .05
Bonnell, Barry	82F	611	$ .01	$ .05
Bonnell, Barry	83F	425	$ .01	$ .05
Bonnell, Barry	84F	149	$ .01	$ .06
Bonnell, Barry	84FU	14	$ .01	$ .10
Bonnell, Barry	85F	485	$ .01	$ .05
Bonnell, Barry	86F	460	$ .01	$ .05
Bonner, Bob	83F	53	$ .01	$ .05

Player	Year	No.	VG	EX/MT	Player	Year	No.	VG	EX/MT
Booker, Greg	85F	27	$ .01	$ .10	Bradley, Phil	89F	563	$ .01	$ .05
Booker, Greg	88F	577	$ .01	$ .05	Bradley, Phil	89FU	1	$ .01	$ .05
Booker, Rod	87FU	7	$ .01	$ .15	Bradley, Phil	90F	174	$ .01	$ .04
Booker, Rod	91F	388	$ .01	$ .03	Bradley, Phil	91F	114	$ .01	$ .03
Boone, Bob	81F	4	$ .01	$ .05	Bradley, Scott	87F	580	$ .01	$ .05
Boone, Bob	82F	240	$ .01	$ .05	Bradley, Scott	88F	370	$ .01	$ .05
Boone, Bob	83F	79	$ .01	$ .05	Bradley, Scott	89F	540	$ .01	$ .05
Boone, Bob	84F	509	$ .01	$ .06	Bradley, Scott	90F	506	$ .01	$ .04
Boone, Bob	84F	637	$ .01	$ .06	Bradley, Scott	91F	443	$ .01	$ .03
Boone, Bob	85F	295	$ .01	$ .05	Braggs, Glenn	87F	339	$ .05	$ .60
Boone, Bob	86F	149	$ .01	$ .05	Braggs, Glenn	88F	157	$ .01	$ .10
Boone, Bob	87F	73	$ .01	$ .05	Braggs, Glenn	89F	180	$ .01	$ .05
Boone, Bob	88F	485	$ .01	$ .05	Braggs, Glenn	90F	317	$ .01	$ .04
Boone, Bob	89F	469	$ .01	$ .05	Braggs, Glenn	90FU	11	$ .01	$ .05
Boone, Bob	89FU	36	$ .01	$ .05	Braggs, Glenn	91F	57	$ .01	$ .03
Boone, Bob	90F	102	$ .01	$ .04	Brantley, Jeff	89FU	127	$ .01	$ .15
Boone, Bob	91F	551	$ .01	$ .03	Brantley, Jeff	90F	52	$ .01	$ .10
Boone, Danny	82F	568	$ .01	$ .05	Brantley, Jeff	91F	255	$ .01	$ .03
Borders, Pat	88FU	65	$ .01	$ .25	Brantley, Mickey	86F	651	$ .01	$ .25
Borders, Pat	89F	227	$ .01	$ .10	Brantley, Mickey	87F	582	$ .01	$ .05
Borders, Pat	90F	77	$ .01	$ .04	Brantley, Mickey	88F	371	$ .01	$ .05
Borders, Pat	91F	171	$ .01	$ .03	Brantley, Mickey	89F	541	$ .01	$ .05
Bordi, Rich	85F	49	$ .01	$ .05	Braun, Steve	81F	427	$ .01	$ .05
Bordi, Rich	85FU	8	$ .01	$ .05	Braun, Steve	82F	111	$ .01	$ .05
Bordi, Rich	86F	101	$ .01	$ .05	Braun, Steve	83F	3	$ .01	$ .05
Bordi, Rich	86FU	16	$ .01	$ .05	Braun, Steve	84F	320	$ .01	$ .06
Bordi, Rich	87F	465	$ .01	$ .05	Braun, Steve	85F	221	$ .01	$ .05
Bosetti, Rick	82F	88	$ .01	$ .05	Braun, Steve	86F	27	$ .01	$ .05
Bosio, Chris	87F	338	$ .01	$ .45	Bream, Sid	86F	604	$ .01	$ .05
Bosio, Chris	88F	156	$ .01	$ .10	Bream, Sid	87F	606	$ .01	$ .05
Bosio, Chris	89F	179	$ .01	$ .05	Bream, Sid	88F	324	$ .01	$ .05
Bosio, Chris	90F	316	$ .01	$ .04	Bream, Sid	89F	204	$ .01	$ .05
Bosio, Chris	91F	576	$ .01	$ .03	Bream, Sid	90F	463	$ .01	$ .04
Boskie, Shawn	90FU	7	$ .01	$ .25	Bream, Sid	91F	35	$ .01	$ .03
Boskie, Shawn	91F	416	$ .01	$ .10	Breining, Fred	82F	385	$ .01	$ .05
Bosley, Thad	81F	353	$ .01	$ .05	Breining, Fred	83F	254	$ .01	$ .05
Bosley, Thad	86F	361	$ .01	$ .05	Breining, Fred	84F	367	$ .01	$ .06
Bosley, Thad	87F	555	$ .01	$ .05	Breining, Fred	84FU	16	$ .01	$ .10
Bosley, Thad	87FU	8	$ .01	$ .05	Breining, Fred	85F	392	$ .01	$ .05
Bosley, Thad	88F	253	$ .01	$ .05	Brenly, Bob	83F	255	$ .01	$ .05
Boston, Daryl	85FU	9	$ .01	$ .05	Brenly, Bob	84F	368	$ .01	$ .06
Boston, Daryl	87F	487	$ .01	$ .05	Brenly, Bob	85F	603	$ .01	$ .05
Boston, Daryl	88F	393	$ .01	$ .05	Brenly, Bob	86F	534	$ .01	$ .05
Boston, Daryl	89F	492	$ .01	$ .05	Brenly, Bob	87F	267	$ .01	$ .05
Boston, Daryl	90FU	33	$ .01	$ .05	Brenly, Bob	88F	77	$ .01	$ .05
Boston, Daryl	91F	140	$ .01	$ .03	Brennan, Tom	83F	403	$ .01	$ .05
Bowa, Larry	81F	2	$ .01	$ .10	Brennan, Tom	84F	537	$ .01	$ .06
Bowa, Larry	81F	645	$ .20	$1.50	Brett, George	81F	28	$ .13	$2.00
Bowa, Larry	82F	241	$ .01	$ .10	Brett, George	81F	655	$ .20	$1.25
Bowa, Larry	83F	491	$ .01	$ .10	Brett, George	82F	405	$ .12	$1.25
Bowa, Larry	84F	486	$ .01	$ .10	Brett, George	83F	108	$ .10	$1.00
Bowa, Larry	85F	50	$ .01	$ .10	Brett, George	84F	344	$ .10	$1.75
Bower, Bob	89F	514	$ .01	$ .05	Brett, George	84F	638	$ .01	$ .25
Boyd, Dennis "Oil Can"	84F	393	$ .07	$ .50	Brett, George	85F	199	$ .10	$ .75
Boyd, Dennis	85F	152	$ .03	$ .20	Brett, George	86F	5	$ .08	$ .60
Boyd, Dennis	86F	342	$ .01	$ .05	Brett, George	86F	634	$ .10	$ .50
Boyd, Dennis	87F	30	$ .01	$ .05	Brett, George	87F	366	$ .06	$ .35
Boyd, Dennis	88F	347	$ .01	$ .05	Brett, George	88F	254	$ .01	$ .30
Boyd, "Oil Can"	89F	82	$ .01	$ .05	Brett, George	89F	277	$ .01	$ .25
Boyd, Dennis	90FU	26	$ .01	$ .05	Brett, George	90F	103	$ .01	$ .10
Boyd, Dennis	91F	226	$ .01	$ .03	Brett, George	90FPD	621	$ .01	$ .25
Bradford, Larry	81F	265	$ .01	$ .05	Brett, George	91F	552	$ .01	$ .10
Bradford, Larry	82F	431	$ .01	$ .05	Brett, Ken	82F	406	$ .01	$ .05
Bradley, Mark	84F	581	$ .01	$ .06	Briley, Greg	89FU	57	$ .01	$ .35
Bradley, Phil	84FU	15	$ .25	$3.00	Briley, Greg	90F	507	$ .01	$ .10
Bradley, Phil	85F	486	$ .05	$ .75	Briley, Greg	91F	444	$ .01	$ .03
Bradley, Phil	86F	461	$ .03	$ .20	Brock, Greg	83F	203	$ .08	$ .40
Bradley, Phil	87F	581	$ .01	$ .10	Brock, Greg	84F	98	$ .01	$ .06
Bradley, Phil	88F	369	$ .01	$ .10	Brock, Greg	85F	368	$ .01	$ .05
Bradley, Phil	88FU	107	$ .01	$ .05	Brock, Greg	86F	125	$ .01	$ .05

Player	Year	No.	VG	EX/MT	Player	Year	No.	VG	EX/MT
Brock, Greg	87F	437	$ .01	$ .05	Browning, Tom	87F	194	$ .05	$ .25
Brock, Greg	87FU	9	$ .01	$ .05	Browning, Tom	88F	228	$ .01	$ .15
Brock, Greg	88F	158	$ .01	$ .05	Browning, Tom	89F	153	$ .01	$ .10
Brock, Greg	89F	181	$ .01	$ .05	Browning, Tom	89F	629	$ .01	$ .10
Brock, Greg	90F	318	$ .01	$ .04	Browning, Tom	90F	415	$ .01	$ .10
Brock, Greg	91F	577	$ .01	$ .03	Browning, Tom	91F	59	$ .01	$ .03
Brohamer, Jack	81F	393	$ .01	$ .05	Brumley, Mike	89F	302	$ .01	$ .05
Brookens, Tom	81F	473	$ .01	$ .05	Brumley, Mike	89FU	30	$ .01	$ .05
Brookens, Tom	82F	263	$ .01	$ .05	Brumley, Mike	91F	445	$ .01	$ .03
Brookens, Tom	83F	327	$ .01	$ .05	Brummer, Glenn	83F	4	$ .01	$ .05
Brookens, Tom	84F	78	$ .01	$ .06	Brummer, Glenn	84F	321	$ .01	$ .06
Brookens, Tom	85F	4	$ .01	$ .05	Brummer, Glenn	86F	557	$ .01	$ .05
Brookens, Tom	86F	223	$ .01	$ .05	Brunansky, Tom	83F	607	$ .01	$ .75
Brookens, Tom	87F	145	$ .01	$ .05	Brunansky, Tom	84F	557	$ .09	$ .45
Brookens, Tom	88F	53	$ .01	$ .05	Brunansky, Tom	85F	271	$ .03	$ .20
Brookens, Tom	89F	132	$ .01	$ .15	Brunansky, Tom	86F	387	$ .01	$ .10
Brookens, Tom	90F	439	$ .01	$ .04	Brunansky, Tom	87F	537	$ .01	$ .05
Brookens, Tom	91F	362	$ .01	$ .03	Brunansky, Tom	88F	5	$ .01	$ .10
Brooks, Hubie	82F	522	$ .15	$ .75	Brunansky, Tom	88FU	117	$ .01	$ .15
Brooks, Hubie	83F	539	$ .01	$ .10	Brunansky, Tom	89F	444	$ .01	$ .10
Brooks, Hubie	84F	582	$ .03	$ .10	Brunansky, Tom	90F	242	$ .01	$ .04
Brooks, Hubie	85F	74	$ .01	$ .10	Brunansky, Tom	90FU	70	$ .01	$ .05
Brooks, Hubie	85FU	10	$ .04	$ .25	Brunansky, Tom	91F	88	$ .01	$ .03
Brooks, Hubie	86F	244	$ .01	$ .10	Brusstar, Warren	82F	242	$ .01	$ .05
Brooks, Hubie	87F	314	$ .01	$ .10	Brusstar, Warren	84F	487	$ .01	$ .06
Brooks, Hubie	88F	179	$ .01	$ .10	Brusstar, Warren	85F	51	$ .01	$ .05
Brooks, Hubie	89F	371	$ .01	$ .05	Brusstar, Warren	86F	362	$ .01	$ .05
Brooks, Hubie	90F	341	$ .01	$ .04	Bryant, Ralph	87F	649	$ .04	$ .25
Brooks, Hubie	90FU	19	$ .01	$ .05	Bryant, Ralph	87FU	13	$ .01	$ .05
Brooks, Hubie	91F	195	$ .01	$ .03	Bryant, Ralph	88F	510	$ .01	$ .05
Brouhard, Mark	82F	135	$ .01	$ .05	Buckner, Bill	81F	292	$ .01	$ .10
Brouhard, Mark	83F	28	$ .01	$ .05	Buckner, Bill	82F	589	$ .01	$ .10
Brouhard, Mark	84F	195	$ .01	$ .06	Buckner, Bill	83F	492	$ .01	$ .10
Brouhard, Mark	85F	576	$ .01	$ .05	Buckner, Bill	84F	488	$ .01	$ .06
Brower, Bob	87FU	10	$ .03	$ .20	Buckner, Bill	84FU	18	$ .06	$ .35
Brower, Bob	88F	461	$ .01	$ .05	Buckner, Bill	85F	153	$ .01	$ .05
Brown, Bobby	81F	95	$ .01	$ .05	Buckner, Bill	86F	343	$ .01	$ .10
Brown, Bobby	82F	30	$ .01	$ .05	Buckner, Bill	87F	31	$ .01	$ .05
Brown, Bobby	84F	296	$ .01	$ .06	Buckner, Bill	88F	486	$ .01	$ .05
Brown, Bobby	85F	28	$ .01	$ .05	Buckner, Bill	89F	278	$ .01	$ .05
Brown, Chris	85FU	11	$ .25	$1.25	Buechele, Steve	86F	558	$ .04	$ .25
Brown, Chris	86F	535	$ .11	$ .55	Buechele, Steve	87F	121	$ .01	$ .05
Brown, Chris	87F	268	$ .03	$ .20	Buechele, Steve	88F	463	$ .01	$ .05
Brown, Chris	87FU	11	$ .03	$ .20	Buechele, Steve	89F	515	$ .01	$ .05
Brown, Chris	88F	578	$ .01	$ .10	Buechele, Steve	90F	292	$ .01	$ .04
Brown, Chris	89F	301	$ .01	$ .05	Buechele, Steve	91F	283	$ .01	$ .03
Brown, Darrell	84F	556	$ .01	$ .06	Buhner, Jay	89F	542	$ .01	$ .05
Brown, Darrell	85F	270	$ .01	$ .05	Buhner, Jay	90F	508	$ .01	$ .04
Brown, Keith	89F	154	$ .01	$ .15	Buhner, Jay	91F	446	$ .01	$ .03
Brown, Keith	91F	58	$ .01	$ .03	Buice, DeWayne	87FU	14	$ .01	$ .05
Brown, Kevin	89F	641	$ .01	$ .50	Buice, DeWayne	88F	487	$ .01	$ .05
Brown, Kevin	89FU	63	$ .01	$ .10	Bulling, Terry	83F	630	$ .01	$ .10
Brown, Kevin	90F	291	$ .01	$ .04	Bullock, Eric	89F	106	$ .01	$ .05
Brown, Kevin	91F	282	$ .01	$ .03	Bumbry, Al	81F	172	$ .01	$ .05
Brown, Marty	89F	645	$ .05	$ .25	Bumbry, Al	82F	159	$ .01	$ .05
Brown, Mike	84F	394	$ .01	$ .06	Bumbry, Al	83F	54	$ .01	$ .05
Brown, Mike	84FU	17	$ .01	$ .10	Bumbry, Al	84F	2	$ .01	$ .06
Brown, Mike	85F	296	$ .01	$ .05	Bumbry, Al	85F	171	$ .01	$ .05
Brown, Mike	86F	605	$ .01	$ .05	Bumbry, Al	85FU	13	$ .01	$ .05
Brown, Mike	87F	583	$ .01	$ .05	Bumbry, Al	86F	316	$ .01	$ .05
Brown, Mike	87F	607	$ .01	$ .05	Burba, Dave	91F	447	$ .01	$ .10
Brown, Scott	82F	60	$ .01	$ .05	Burgmeier, Tom	82F	288	$ .01	$ .05
Browne, Jerry	87F	647	$ .01	$ .45	Burgmeier, Tom	83F	180	$ .01	$ .05
Browne, Jerry	87FU	12	$ .01	$ .05	Burgmeier, Tom	84F	439	$ .01	$ .06
Browne, Jerry	88F	462	$ .01	$ .05	Burgmeier, Tom	85F	417	$ .01	$ .05
Browne, Jerry	89FU	26	$ .01	$ .10	Burke, Tim	85FU	14	$ .05	$ .35
Browne, Jerry	90F	487	$ .01	$ .04	Burke, Tim	86F	245	$ .05	$ .30
Browne, Jerry	91F	363	$ .01	$ .03	Burke, Tim	87F	315	$ .01	$ .05
Browning, Tom	85FU	12	$ .40	$1.25	Burke, Tim	88F	180	$ .01	$ .05
Browning, Tom	86F	173	$ .25	$ .75	Burke, Tim	89F	372	$ .01	$ .05

Player	Year	No.	VG	EX/MT	Player	Year	No.	VG	EX/MT
Burke, Tim	90F	342	$ .01	$ .04	Butler, Brett	90F	53	$ .01	$ .04
Burke, Tim	91F	227	$ .01	$ .03	Butler, Brett	91F	257	$ .01	$ .03
Burkett, John	88F	651	$ .01	$ .75	Byers, Randell	88F	653	$ .01	$ .25
Burkett, John	90FU	61	$ .01	$ .20	Bystrom, Marty	83F	154	$ .01	$ .05
Burkett, John	91F	256	$ .01	$ .10	Bystrom, Marty	84F	24	$ .01	$ .06
Burks, Ellis	87FU	15	$ .50	$3.50	Bystrom, Marty	85F	122	$ .01	$ .05
Burks, Ellis	88F	348	$ .50	$2.50	Bystrom, Marty	86F	102	$ .01	$ .05
Burks, Ellis	88F	630	$ .10	$ .50	Cabell, Enos	81F	58	$ .01	$ .05
Burks, Ellis	89F	83	$ .05	$ .35	Cabell, Enos	82F	386	$ .01	$ .05
Burks, Ellis	90F	269	$ .01	$ .15	Cabell, Enos	83F	328	$ .01	$ .05
Burks, Ellis	91F	89	$ .01	$ .10	Cabell, Enos	84F	79	$ .01	$ .06
Burleson, Rick	81F	225	$ .01	$ .05	Cabell, Enos	84FU	22	$ .01	$ .10
Burleson, Rick	82F	453	$ .01	$ .05	Cabell, Enos	85F	346	$ .01	$ .05
Burleson, Rick	83F	80	$ .01	$ .05	Cabell, Enos	86F	126	$ .01	$ .05
Burleson, Rick	84F	510	$ .01	$ .06	Cabell, Enos	87F	438	$ .01	$ .05
Burleson, Rick	87F	74	$ .01	$ .05	Cabrera, Francisco	89FU	68	$ .01	$ .35
Burmeier, Tom	81F	228	$ .01	$ .05	Cabrera, Francisco	90FU	2	$ .01	$ .10
Burns, Britt	81F	342	$ .04	$ .25	Cabrera, Francisco	91F	684	$ .01	$ .03
Burns, Britt	82F	339	$ .01	$ .05	Cadaret, Greg	89F	4	$ .01	$ .05
Burns, Britt	83F	232	$ .01	$ .05	Cadaret, Greg	91F	658	$ .01	$ .03
Burns, Britt	84F	54	$ .01	$ .06	Caderet, Greg	90F	440	$ .01	$ .04
Burns, Britt	85F	509	$ .01	$ .05	Calderon, Ivan	85FU	17	$ .15	$1.25
Burns, Britt	86F	200	$ .01	$ .05	Calderon, Ivan	86F	462	$ .10	$ .50
Burns, Todd	88FU	52	$ .01	$ .35	Calderon, Ivan	87F	488	$ .01	$ .10
Burns, Todd	89F	3	$ .01	$ .25	Calderon, Ivan	88F	394	$ .01	$ .05
Burns, Todd	90F	2	$ .01	$ .04	Calderon, Ivan	89F	493	$ .01	$ .05
Burns, Todd	91F	4	$ .01	$ .03	Calderon, Ivan	90F	529	$ .01	$ .04
Burnside, Sheldon	81F	220	$ .01	$ .05	Calderon, Ivan	91F	115	$ .01	$ .03
Burris, Ray	81F	328	$ .01	$ .05	Caldwell, Mike	81F	512	$ .01	$ .05
Burris, Ray	82F	184	$ .01	$ .05	Caldwell, Mike	82F	136	$ .01	$ .05
Burris, Ray	83F	277	$ .01	$ .05	Caldwell, Mike	83F	29	$ .01	$ .05
Burris, Ray	84F	270	$ .01	$ .06	Caldwell, Mike	84F	196	$ .01	$ .06
Burris, Ray	84FU	19	$ .01	$ .10	Caldwell, Mike	85F	577	$ .01	$ .05
Burris, Ray	85F	418	$ .01	$ .05	Calhoun, Jeff	85FU	18	$ .01	$ .05
Burris, Ray	85FU	15	$ .01	$ .05	Calhoun, Jeff	86F	295	$ .01	$ .05
Burris, Ray	86F	482	$ .01	$ .05					
Burroughs, Jeff	81F	245	$ .01	$ .05					
Burroughs, Jeff	82F	506	$ .01	$ .05					
Burroughs, Jeff	83F	515	$ .01	$ .05					
Burroughs, Jeff	84F	440	$ .01	$ .06					
Burroughs, Jeff	85FU	16	$ .01	$ .05					
Burroughs, Jeff	86F	54	$ .01	$ .05					
Busby, Steve	81F	33	$ .01	$ .05					
Bush, Randy	84F	558	$ .01	$ .06					
Bush, Randy	85F	272	$ .01	$ .05					
Bush, Randy	86F	388	$ .01	$ .05					
Bush, Randy	87F	538	$ .01	$ .05					
Bush, Randy	88F	6	$ .01	$ .05					
Bush, Randy	89F	107	$ .01	$ .05					
Bush, Randy	90F	370	$ .01	$ .04					
Bush, Randy	91F	605	$ .01	$ .03					
Butcher, John	81F	635	$ .01	$ .05					
Butcher, John	83F	563	$ .01	$ .05					
Butcher, John	84F	415	$ .01	$ .06					
Butcher, John	84FU	20	$ .01	$ .10					
Butcher, John	85F	273	$ .01	$ .05					
Butcher, John	86F	389	$ .01	$ .05					
Butcher, John	87F	245	$ .01	$ .05					
Butera, Sal	81F	570	$ .01	$ .05					
Butera, Sal	82F	548	$ .01	$ .05					
Butera, Sal	87F	195	$ .01	$ .05					
Butler, Brett	83F	132	$ .05	$ .35					
Butler, Brett	84F	173	$ .03	$ .10					
Butler, Brett	84FU	21	$ .07	$ .50					
Butler, Brett	85F	441	$ .01	$3.50					
Butler, Brett	86F	581	$ .01	$ .05	Calhoun, Jeff	87F	52	$ .01	$ .05
Butler, Brett	87F	246	$ .01	$ .05	Calhoun, Jeff	88F	299	$ .01	$ .05
Butler, Brett	88F	603	$ .01	$ .05	Camacho, Ernie	85F	442	$ .01	$ .05
Butler, Brett	88FU	128	$ .01	$ .05	Camacho, Ernie	86F	582	$ .01	$ .05
Butler, Brett	89F	324	$ .01	$ .05	Camacho, Ernie	87F	247	$ .01	$ .05

Jeff Calhoun
PITCHER

FLEER

Player	Year	No.	VG	EX/MT
Caminiti, Ken	88F	441	$ .01	$ .25
Caminiti, Ken	90F	225	$ .01	$ .04
Caminiti, Ken	91F	500	$ .01	$ .03
Camp, Rick	81F	246	$ .01	$ .05
Camp, Rick	82F	432	$ .01	$ .05
Camp, Rick	83F	133	$ .01	$ .05
Camp, Rick	84F	174	$ .01	$ .06
Camp, Rick	85F	321	$ .01	$ .05
Camp, Rick	86F	510	$ .01	$ .05
Campaneris, Bert	81F	280	$ .01	$ .05
Campaneris, Bert	82F	454	$ .01	$ .05
Campaneris, Bert	84F	120	$ .01	$ .06
Campbell, Bill	81F	240	$ .01	$ .05
Campbell, Bill	82F	289	$ .01	$ .05
Campbell, Bill	83F	493	$ .01	$ .05
Campbell, Bill	84F	489	$ .01	$ .06
Campbell, Bill	84FU	23	$ .01	$ .10
Campbell, Bill	85F	245	$ .01	$ .05
Campbell, Bill	85FU	19	$ .01	$ .05
Campbell, Bill	86F	28	$ .01	$ .05
Campbell, Bill	86FU	17	$ .01	$ .05
Campbell, Bill	87F	146	$ .01	$ .05
Campbell, Jim	89F	646	$ .01	$ .20
Campbell, Mike	88F	372	$ .01	$ .20
Campbell, Mike	89F	543	$ .01	$ .05
Campusano, Sil	88FU	66	$ .01	$ .25
Campusano, Sil	91F	389	$ .01	$ .03
Canale, George	90F	641	$ .01	$2.00

GEORGE CANALE

FLEER '91

BREWERS • 1B

Player	Year	No.	VG	EX/MT
Canale, George	91F	578	$ .01	$ .03
Candaele, Casey	87FU	16	$ .03	$ .20
Candaele, Casey	88F	181	$ .01	$ .05
Candaele, Casey	91F	501	$ .01	$ .03
Candelaria, John	81F	375	$ .01	$ .10
Candelaria, John	82F	479	$ .01	$ .05
Candelaria, John	83F	304	$ .01	$ .05
Candelaria, John	84F	247	$ .01	$ .06
Candelaria, John	85F	462	$ .01	$ .05
Candelaria, John	86F	150	$ .01	$ .05
Candelaria, John	87F	75	$ .01	$ .05
Candelaria, John	88FU	46	$ .01	$ .05

Player	Year	No.	VG	EX/MT
Candelaria, John	89F	251	$ .01	$ .05
Candiotti, Tom	84F	197	$ .10	$ .40
Candiotti, Tom	86FU	18	$ .01	$ .05
Candiotti, Tom	87F	248	$ .01	$ .05
Candiotti, Tom	88F	604	$ .01	$ .05
Candiotti, Tom	89F	399	$ .01	$ .05
Candiotti, Tom	90F	488	$ .01	$ .04
Candiotti, Tom	91F	364	$ .01	$ .03
Cangelosi, John	86FU	19	$ .04	$ .25
Cangelosi, John	87F	489	$ .01	$ .10
Cangelosi, John	88F	325	$ .01	$ .05
Canseco, Jose	86F	649	$10.00	$45.00
Canseco, Jose	86FU	20	$2.25	$12.00
Canseco, Jose	87F	389	$1.00	$10.00
Canseco, Jose	87F	625	$ .10	$1.00
Canseco, Jose	87F	628	$ .30	$1.00
Canseco, Jose	87F	633	$ .25	$1.00
Canseco, Jose	88F	276	$ .50	$2.50
Canseco, Jose	88F	624	$ .10	$ .75
Canseco, Jose	89F	5	$ .10	$1.00
Canseco, Jose	89F	628	$ .05	$ .50
Canseco, Jose	89F	634	$ .01	$ .35
Canseco, Jose	90F	3	$ .01	$ .50
Canseco, Jose	90FPD	629	$ .01	$ .35
Canseco, Jose	91F	5	$ .01	$ .25
Canseco, Ozzie	90FU	117	$ .01	$ .15
Capel, Mike	89F	643	$ .01	$ .20
Capilla, Doug	81F	309	$ .01	$ .05
Cappuzzello, George	82F	264	$ .01	$ .05
Capra, Nick	89F	279	$ .01	$ .05
Carew, Rod	81F	268	$ .10	$1.25
Carew, Rod	82F	455	$ .07	$1.00
Carew, Rod	83F	81	$ .09	$ .75
Carew, Rod	84F	511	$ .09	$1.00
Carew, Rod	84F	629	$ .04	$ .25
Carew, Rod	85F	297	$ .07	$ .75
Carew, Rod	86F	151	$ .05	$ .30
Carew, Rod	86F	629	$ .04	$ .25
Carlton, Steve	81F	6	$ .09	$1.00
Carlton, Steve	81F	660	$ .15	$1.25
Carlton, Steve	82F	243	$ .08	$ .40
Carlton, Steve	82F	632	$ .04	$ .25
Carlton, Steve	82F	641	$ .05	$ .75
Carlton, Steve	83F	155	$ .06	$ .75
Carlton, Steve	84F	25	$ .07	$1.00
Carlton, Steve	84F	642	$ .03	$ .20
Carlton, Steve	85F	246	$ .05	$ .75
Carlton, Steve	86F	435	$ .05	$ .30
Carlton, Steve	87F	490	$ .05	$ .30
Carlton, Steve	87F	635	$ .03	$ .20
Carlton, Steve	87FU	17	$ .04	$ .25
Carlton, Steve	88F	7	$ .01	$ .20
Carman, Don	85FU	20	$ .05	$ .25
Carman, Don	86F	436	$ .04	$ .25
Carman, Don	87F	171	$ .01	$ .05
Carman, Don	88F	300	$ .01	$ .05
Carman, Don	89F	564	$ .01	$ .05
Carman, Don	90F	552	$ .01	$ .04
Carman, Don	91F	390	$ .01	$ .03
Carpenter, Cris	89FU	117	$ .01	$ .20
Carpenter, Cris	90F	243	$ .01	$ .10
Carpenter, Cris	91F	628	$ .01	$ .03
Carr, Chuck	90FU	34	$ .01	$ .10
Carr, Chuck	91F	141	$ .01	$ .10
Carreon, Mark	88F	129	$ .10	$ .35
Carreon, Mark	89F	29	$ .01	$ .05
Carreon, Mark	90F	198	$ .01	$ .10
Carreon, Mark	91F	142	$ .01	$ .03
Carter, Gary	81F	142	$ .09	$ .50
Carter, Gary	82F	185	$ .07	$ .50

Player	Year	No.	VG	EX/MT	Player	Year	No.	VG	EX/MT
Carter, Gary	82F	635	$ .04	$ .25	Cecena, Jose	88FU	62	$ .01	$ .15
Carter, Gary	82F	638	$ .04	$ .25	Cecena, Jose	89F	516	$ .01	$ .15
Carter, Gary	83F	278	$ .05	$ .30	Cedeno, Andujar	91F	502	$ .01	$ .50
Carter, Gary	83F	637	$ .01	$ .10	Cedeno, Cesar	81F	59	$ .01	$ .10
Carter, Gary	83F	638	$ .03	$ .20	Cedeno, Cesar	82F	213	$ .01	$ .05
Carter, Gary	84F	271	$ .07	$ .50	Cedeno, Cesar	83F	587	$ .01	$ .10
Carter, Gary	85F	393	$ .05	$ .30	Cedeno, Cesar	84F	465	$ .01	$ .06
Carter, Gary	85F	631	$ .05	$ .30	Cedeno, Cesar	85F	531	$ .01	$ .05
Carter, Gary	85F	632	$ .01	$ .10	Cedeno, Cesar	86F	29	$ .01	$ .05
Carter, Gary	85FU	21	$ .10	$ .75	Cerone, Rick	81F	83	$ .01	$ .05
Carter, Gary	86F	76	$ .05	$ .30	Cerone, Rick	82F	31	$ .01	$ .05
Carter, Gary	87F	4	$ .05	$ .30	Cerone, Rick	83F	376	$ .01	$ .05
Carter, Gary	87F	629	$ .10	$ .50	Cerone, Rick	84F	121	$ .01	$ .06
Carter, Gary	87F	634	$ .05	$ .30	Cerone, Rick	85F	123	$ .01	$ .05
Carter, Gary	88F	130	$ .01	$ .15	Cerone, Rick	85FU	24	$ .01	$ .05
Carter, Gary	88F	636	$ .01	$ .15	Cerone, Rick	86F	511	$ .01	$ .05
Carter, Gary	89F	30	$ .01	$ .15	Cerone, Rick	86FU	23	$ .01	$ .05
Carter, Gary	90F	199	$ .01	$ .10	Cerone, Rick	87F	340	$ .01	$ .05
Carter, Gary	90FU	62	$ .01	$ .10	Cerone, Rick	88F	203	$ .01	$ .05
Carter, Gary	91F	258	$ .01	$ .03	Cerone, Rick	88FU	6	$ .01	$ .05
Carter, Joe	85F	443	$ .50	$3.00	Cerone, Rick	89F	84	$ .01	$ .05
Carter, Joe	86F	583	$ .10	$ .50	Cerone, Rick	90F	270	$ .01	$ .04
Carter, Joe	87F	249	$ .01	$ .10	Cerone, Rick	91F	660	$ .01	$ .03
Carter, Joe	88F	605	$ .01	$ .05	Cerutti, John	86FU	24	$ .05	$ .30
Carter, Joe	89F	400	$ .01	$ .15	Cerutti, John	87F	222	$ .04	$ .25
Carter, Joe	90F	489	$ .01	$ .15	Cerutti, John	88F	105	$ .01	$ .10
Carter, Joe	90FU	55	$ .01	$ .10	Cerutti, John	89F	228	$ .01	$ .10
Carter, Joe	91F	525	$ .01	$ .03	Cerutti, John	90F	78	$ .01	$ .04
Cary, Chuck	86FU	21	$ .01	$ .10	Cerutti, John	91F	172	$ .01	$ .03
Cary, Chuck	87F	147	$ .01	$ .05	Cey, Ron	81F	126	$ .03	$ .20
Cary, Chuck	91F	659	$ .01	$ .03	Cey, Ron	82F	3	$ .01	$ .10
Cash, Dave	81F	492	$ .01	$ .05	Cey, Ron	83F	204	$ .01	$ .10
Castillo, Bobby	83F	608	$ .01	$ .05	Cey, Ron	84F	490	$ .01	$ .06
Castillo, Bobby	84F	559	$ .01	$ .06	Cey, Ron	85F	52	$ .01	$ .05
Castillo, Bobby	85F	274	$ .01	$ .05	Cey, Ron	86F	363	$ .01	$ .10
Castillo, Bobby	85FU	22	$ .01	$ .05	Cey, Ron	87F	556	$ .01	$ .05
Castillo, Bobby	86F	127	$ .01	$ .05	Chalk, Dave	81F	35	$ .01	$ .05
Castillo, Carmelo	83F	404	$ .01	$ .05	Chalk, Dave	82F	407	$ .01	$ .05
Castillo, Carmelo	85F	444	$ .01	$ .05	Chamberlain, Wes	91F	391	$ .01	$ .25
Castillo, Carmelo "Carmen"	86F	584	$ .01	$ .05	Chambliss, Chris	81F	252	$ .01	$ .05
Castillo, Carmelo	87F	250	$ .01	$ .05	Chambliss, Chris	82F	433	$ .01	$ .05
Castillo, Carmelo	88F	606	$ .01	$ .05	Chambliss, Chris	83F	134	$ .01	$ .05
Castillo, Carmen	89F	401	$ .01	$ .05	Chambliss, Chris	84F	175	$ .01	$ .06
Castillo, Carmen	90F	371	$ .01	$ .04	Chambliss, Chris	85F	322	$ .01	$ .05
Castillo, Carmen	91F	606	$ .01	$ .03	Chambliss, Chris	86F	512	$ .01	$ .05
Castillo, Juan	86FU	22	$ .01	$ .05	Chambliss, Chris	87F	513	$ .01	$ .05
Castillo, Juan	87FU	18	$ .01	$ .05	Chapman, Kelvin	85F	75	$ .01	$ .05
Castillo, Juan	88F	159	$ .01	$ .05	Charboneau, Joe	81F	397	$ .01	$ .10
Castillo, Manny	83F	474	$ .01	$ .05	Charboneau, Joe	82F	362	$ .01	$ .05
Castillo, Manny	84F	607	$ .01	$ .06	Charland, Colin	90F	640	$ .01	$ .04
Castillo, Marty	82F	265	$ .01	$ .05	Charlton, Norm	89F	155	$ .01	$ .15
Castillo, Marty	85F	5	$ .01	$ .05	Charlton, Norm	90F	416	$ .01	$ .10
Castillo, Robert	81F	137	$ .01	$ .05	Charlton, Norm	91F	60	$ .01	$ .03
Castillo, Robert	82F	2	$ .01	$ .05	Checklist Team Cards(628-60)	82F	660	$ .02	$ .15
Castillo, Tony	91F	685	$ .01	$ .03	Checklist, A's(436-461)	84F	651	$ .01	$ .06
Castino, John	81F	554	$ .01	$ .05	Checklist, Angels(508-532)	84F	654	$ .01	$ .06
Castino, John	82F	549	$ .01	$ .05	Checklist, Astros(220-244)	84F	656	$ .01	$ .06
Castino, John	83F	609	$ .01	$ .05	Checklist, Blue Jays(145-169)	84F	653	$ .01	$ .06
Castino, John	84F	560	$ .01	$ .06	Checklist, Braves(170-193)	84F	654	$ .01	$ .06
Castro, Bill	81F	517	$ .01	$ .05	Checklist, Brewers(194-219)	84F	655	$ .01	$ .06
Castro, Bill	83F	109	$ .01	$ .05	Checklist, Cardinals(318-340)	84F	660	$ .03	$ .10
Caudill, Bill	81F	306	$ .01	$ .05	Checklist, Cards(1-113)	91F	714	$ .01	$ .03
Caudill, Bill	82F	590	$ .01	$ .05	Checklist, Cards(1-132)	90FU	132	$ .01	$ .05
Caudill, Bill	83F	475	$ .01	$ .05	Checklist, Cards(114-223)	91F	715	$ .01	$ .03
Caudill, Bill	84F	608	$ .01	$ .06	Checklist, Cards(224-330)	91F	716	$ .01	$ .03
Caudill, Bill	84FU	24	$ .01	$ .10	Checklist, Cards(331-441)	91F	717	$ .01	$ .03
Caudill, Bill	85F	419	$ .01	$ .05	Checklist, Cards(442-548)	91F	718	$ .01	$ .03
Caudill, Bill	85FU	23	$ .01	$ .05	Checklist, Cards(549-654)	91F	719	$ .01	$ .03
Caudill, Bill	86F	55	$ .01	$ .05	Checklist, Cards(709-720)	91F	720	$ .01	$ .03
Caudill, Bill	87F	221	$ .01	$ .05	Checklist, Cards(1-101)	88F	654	$ .01	$ .05

FLEER

Player	Year	No.	VG	EX/MT
Checklist, Cards(1-101)	89F	654	$ .01	$ .05
Checklist, Cards(1-132)	84FU	132	$ .04	$ .25
Checklist, Cards(1-132)	85FU	132	$ .01	$ .10
Checklist, Cards(1-132)	86FU	132	$ .01	$ .10
Checklist, Cards(1-132)	87FU	132	$ .01	$ .10
Checklist, Cards(1-132)	88FU	132	$ .01	$ .05
Checklist, Cards(1-132)	89FU	132	$ .01	$ .10
Checklist, Cards(1-50)	81F	641	$ .01	$ .10

FLEER

1983 BASEBALL CHECKLIST

NO.	NAME	POS.
□ 1	JOAQUIN ANDUJAR	P
□ 2	DOUG BAIR	P
□ 3	STEVE BRAUN	OF
□ 4	GLENN BRUMMER	C
□ 5	BOB FORSCH	P
□ 6	DAVID GREEN	OF
□ 7	GEORGE HENDRICK	OF
□ 8	KEITH HERNANDEZ	1B
□ 9	TOM HERR	2B
□ 10	DANE IORG	OF
□ 11	JIM KAAT	P
□ 12	JEFF LAHTI	P
□ 13	TITO LANDRUM	OF
□ 14	DAVE LA POINT	P
□ 15	WILLIE MC GEE	OF
□ 16	STEVE MURA	P
□ 17	KEN OBERKFELL	3B
□ 18	DARRELL PORTER	C
□ 19	MIKE RAMSEY	2B
□ 20	GENE ROOF	OF
□ 21	LONNIE SMITH	OF
□ 22	OZZIE SMITH	SS
□ 23	JOHN STUPER	P
□ 24	BRUCE SUTTER	P
□ 25	GENE TENACE	C

ST. LOUIS
No. 647 Cardinals

Player	Year	No.	VG	EX/MT
Checklist, Cards(1-51)	83F	647	$ .01	$ .05
Checklist, Cards(1-56)	82F	647	$ .01	$ .10
Checklist, Cards(1-95)	85F	654	$ .01	$ .05
Checklist, Cards(1-95)	87F	654	$ .01	$ .05
Checklist, Cards(1-97)	86F	654	$ .01	$ .05
Checklist, Cards(1-99)	90F	654	$ .01	$ .04
Checklist, Cards(100-195)	90F	655	$ .01	$ .04
Checklist, Cards(102-200)	89F	655	$ .01	$ .05
Checklist, Cards(102-201)	88F	655	$ .01	$ .05
Checklist, Cards(104-152)	83F	649	$ .01	$ .05
Checklist, Cards(110-156)	82F	649	$ .01	$ .10
Checklist, Cards(110-168)	81F	643	$ .01	$ .10
Checklist, Cards(153-200)	83F	650	$ .01	$ .05
Checklist, Cards(157-211)	82F	650	$ .01	$ .10
Checklist, Cards(169-220)	81F	644	$ .01	$ .10
Checklist, Cards(193-288)	87F	656	$ .01	$ .05
Checklist, Cards(196-289)	90F	656	$ .01	$ .04
Checklist, Cards(196-292)	85F	656	$ .01	$ .05
Checklist, Cards(197-291)	86F	656	$ .01	$ .05
Checklist, Cards(201-251)	83F	651	$ .01	$ .05
Checklist, Cards(201-298)	89F	656	$ .01	$ .05
Checklist, Cards(202-296)	88F	656	$ .01	$ .05
Checklist, Cards(212-262)	82F	651	$ .01	$ .10
Checklist, Cards(221-267)	81F	646	$ .01	$ .05
Checklist, Cards(252-301)	83F	652	$ .01	$ .05
Checklist, Cards(263-312)	82F	652	$ .01	$ .10
Checklist, Cards(268-315)	81F	647	$ .01	$ .05
Checklist, Cards(289-384)	87F	657	$ .01	$ .05
Checklist, Cards(290-388)	90F	657	$ .01	$ .04
Checklist, Cards(292-385)	86F	657	$ .01	$ .05
Checklist, Cards(293-391)	85F	657	$ .01	$ .05
Checklist, Cards(297-390)	88F	657	$ .01	$ .05

Player	Year	No.	VG	EX/MT
Checklist, Cards(299-395)	89F	657	$ .01	$ .05
Checklist, Cards(302-351)	83F	653	$ .01	$ .05
Checklist, Cards(313-358)	82F	653	$ .01	$ .10
Checklist, Cards(316-359)	81F	648	$ .01	$ .05
Checklist, Cards(352-399)	83F	654	$ .01	$ .05
Checklist, Cards(359-403)	82F	654	$ .01	$ .10
Checklist, Cards(360-408)	81F	649	$ .01	$ .05
Checklist, Cards(385-483)	87F	658	$ .01	$ .05
Checklist, Cards(386-481)	86F	658	$ .01	$ .05
Checklist, Cards(389-482)	90F	658	$ .01	$ .04
Checklist, Cards(391-483)	88F	658	$ .01	$ .05
Checklist, Cards(392-481)	85F	658	$ .01	$ .05
Checklist, Cards(396-490)	89F	658	$ .01	$ .05
Checklist, Cards(400-444)	83F	655	$ .01	$ .05
Checklist, Cards(404-449)	82F	655	$ .01	$ .10
Checklist, Cards(409-458)	81F	651	$ .01	$ .05
Checklist, Cards(445-489)	83F	656	$ .01	$ .05
Checklist, Cards(450-501)	82F	656	$ .01	$ .10
Checklist, Cards(459-506)	81F	652	$ .01	$ .10
Checklist, Cards(482-575)	85F	659	$ .01	$ .05
Checklist, Cards(482-578)	86F	659	$ .01	$ .05
Checklist, Cards(483-573)	90F	659	$ .01	$ .04
Checklist, Cards(484-532)	87F	659	$ .01	$ .05
Checklist, Cards(484-575)	88F	659	$ .01	$ .05
Checklist, Cards(490-535)	83F	657	$ .01	$ .05
Checklist, Cards(491-584)	89F	659	$ .01	$ .05
Checklist, Cards(502-544)	82F	657	$ .01	$ .10
Checklist, Cards(507-550)	81F	654	$ .01	$ .10
Checklist, Cards(51-109)	81F	642	$ .01	$ .10
Checklist, Cards(52-103)	83F	648	$ .01	$ .05
Checklist, Cards(536-583)	83F	658	$ .01	$ .05
Checklist, Cards(545-585)	82F	658	$ .01	$ .10
Checklist, Cards(551-593)	81F	656	$ .01	$ .05
Checklist, Cards(57-109)	82F	648	$ .01	$ .10
Checklist, Cards(574-660)	90F	660	$ .01	$ .04
Checklist, Cards(576-660)	85F	660	$ .01	$ .10
Checklist, Cards(576-660)	88F	660	$ .01	$ .05
Checklist, Cards(579-660)	86F	660	$ .01	$ .10
Checklist, Cards(579-660)	87F	660	$ .01	$ .10
Checklist, Cards(584-628)	83F	659	$ .01	$ .05
Checklist, Cards(585-660)	89F	660	$ .01	$ .05
Checklist, Cards(586-627)	82F	659	$ .01	$ .10
Checklist, Cards(594-637)	81F	658	$ .01	$ .05
Checklist, Cards(626-646)	84F	659	$ .01	$ .06
Checklist, Cards(629-660)	83F	660	$ .01	$ .10
Checklist, Cards(96-192)	87F	655	$ .01	$ .05
Checklist, Cards(96-195)	85F	655	$ .01	$ .05
Checklist, Cards(98-196)	86F	655	$ .01	$ .05
Checklist, Cubs(486-507)	84F	653	$ .01	$ .06
Checklist, Dodgers(96-118)	84F	651	$ .01	$ .06
Checklist, Expos(270-293)	84F	658	$ .01	$ .06
Checklist, Giants(365-387)	84F	648	$ .01	$ .06
Checklist, Indians(533-555)	84F	655	$ .01	$ .06
Checklist, Mariners(604-625)	84F	658	$ .01	$ .06
Checklist, Mets(580-603)	84F	657	$ .01	$ .06
Checklist, Orioles(1-23)	84F	647	$ .01	$ .06
Checklist, Padres(294-317)	84F	659	$ .01	$ .06
Checklist, Phillies(24-49)	84F	648	$ .01	$ .06
Checklist, Pirates(245-269)	84F	657	$ .01	$ .06
Checklist, Rangers(413-435)	84F	650	$ .01	$ .06
Checklist, Red Sox(388-412)	84F	649	$ .01	$ .06
Checklist, Reds(462-485)	84F	652	$ .01	$ .06
Checklist, Royals(341-364)	84F	647	$ .01	$ .06
Checklist, Teams(1-660)	84F	660	$ .03	$ .10
Checklist, Tigers(74-95)	84F	650	$ .01	$ .06
Checklist, Twins(556-579)	84F	656	$ .01	$ .06
Checklist, White Sox(50-73)	84F	649	$ .01	$ .06
Checklist, Yankees(119-144)	84F	652	$ .01	$ .06
Checklist-Team Cards(640-60)	81F	659	$ .01	$ .10
Chiffer, Floyd	83F	354	$ .01	$ .05

Player	Year	No.	VG	EX/MT	Player	Year	No.	VG	EX/MT
Childress, Rocky	88F	442	$ .01	$ .10	Clear, Mark	88F	160	$ .01	$ .05
Christensen, John	89F	108	$ .01	$ .05	Clear, Mark	89F	182	$ .01	$ .05
Christenson, Larry	81F	8	$ .01	$ .05	Clemens, Roger	84FU	27	$20.00	$150.00
Christenson, Larry	82F	244	$ .01	$ .05	Clemens, Roger	85F	155	$3.00	$19.00
Christenson, Larry	83F	156	$ .01	$ .05	Clemens, Roger	86F	345	$ .60	$4.00
Clancy, Jim	81F	412	$ .01	$ .05	Clemens, Roger	87F	32	$ .10	$2.50
Clancy, Jim	82F	612	$ .01	$ .05	Clemens, Roger	87F	634	$ .05	$ .30
Clancy, Jim	83F	426	$ .01	$ .05	Clemens, Roger	87F	640	$ .10	$ .50
Clancy, Jim	84F	150	$ .01	$ .06	Clemens, Roger	88F	349	$ .10	$ .50
Clancy, Jim	85F	101	$ .01	$ .05	Clemens, Roger	89F	85	$ .05	$ .40
Clancy, Jim	86F	56	$ .01	$ .05	Clemens, Roger	90F	271	$ .01	$ .25
Clancy, Jim	87F	223	$ .01	$ .05	Clemens, Roger	90FPD	627	$ .01	$ .20
Clancy, Jim	88F	106	$ .01	$ .05	Clemens, Roger	91F	90	$ .01	$ .20
Clancy, Jim	89F	229	$ .01	$ .05	Clements, Pat	85FU	26	$ .05	$ .15
Clancy, Jim	89FU	88	$ .01	$ .05	Clements, Pat	86F	606	$ .03	$ .20
Clancy, Jim	90F	226	$ .01	$ .04	Clements, Pat	87F	608	$ .01	$ .05
Clark, Bob	82F	456	$ .01	$ .05	Clements, Pat	88F	204	$ .01	$ .05
Clark, Bobby	83F	82	$ .01	$ .05	Clements, Pat	90F	153	$ .01	$ .04
Clark, Bobby	84F	512	$ .01	$ .06	Cleveland, Reggie	81F	523	$ .01	$ .05
Clark, Bobby	84FU	25	$ .01	$ .10	Cleveland, Reggie	82F	137	$ .01	$ .05
Clark, Bobby	85F	578	$ .01	$ .05	Cliburn, Stewart	85FU	27	$ .01	$ .05
Clark, Bryan	82F	507	$ .01	$ .05	Cliburn, Stewart	86F	152	$ .01	$ .05
Clark, Bryan	83F	476	$ .01	$ .05	Cliburn, Stew	89F	471	$ .01	$ .05
Clark, Bryan	84F	609	$ .01	$ .06	Clutterbuck, Bryan	87F	342	$ .01	$ .05
Clark, Bryan	84FU	26	$ .01	$ .10	Cocanower, Jaime	84FU	28	$ .01	$ .10
Clark, Dave	87F	644	$ .10	$ .75	Cocanower, Jaime	85F	579	$ .01	$ .05
Clark, Dave	89F	402	$ .01	$ .05	Cocanower, Jaime	86F	483	$ .01	$ .05
Clark, Dave	90F	490	$ .01	$ .04	Codiroli, Chris	84F	441	$ .01	$ .06
Clark, Dave	91F	417	$ .01	$ .03	Codiroli, Chris	85F	420	$ .01	$ .05
Clark, Jack	81F	433	$ .04	$ .25	Codiroli, Chris	86F	414	$ .01	$ .05
Clark, Jack	82F	387	$ .04	$ .25	Codiroli, Chris	87F	390	$ .01	$ .05
Clark, Jack	83F	256	$ .04	$ .25	Coffman, Kevin	88F	536	$ .01	$ .10
Clark, Jack	84F	369	$ .04	$ .25	Cole, Alex	90F	244	$ .01	$ .75
Clark, Jack	85F	604	$ .05	$ .30	Cole, Alex	91F	365	$ .01	$ .20
Clark, Jack	85FU	25	$ .06	$ .35	Coleman, Vince	85FU	28	$1.50	$10.00
Clark, Jack	86F	30	$ .04	$ .25	Coleman, Vince	86F	31	$ .65	$4.00
Clark, Jack	87F	289	$ .04	$ .25	Coleman, Vince	86F	636	$ .01	$ .25
Clark, Jack	88F	26	$ .01	$ .15	Coleman, Vince	86F	637	$ .01	$ .25
Clark, Jack	88FU	47	$ .01	$ .15	Coleman, Vince	87F	290	$ .05	$ .40
Clark, Jack	89F	252	$ .01	$ .10	Coleman, Vince	88F	27	$ .01	$ .10
Clark, Jack	89FU	123	$ .01	$ .10	Coleman, Vince	88F	634	$ .01	$ .10
Clark, Jack	90F	152	$ .01	$ .04	Coleman, Vince	89F	445	$ .01	$ .10
Clark, Jack	91F	526	$ .01	$ .03	Coleman, Vince	90F	245	$ .01	$ .04
Clark, Jerald	89F	642	$ .01	$ .25	Coleman, Vince	91F	629	$ .01	$ .03
Clark, Phil	91F	332	$ .01	$ .15	Coles, Darnell	86FU	27	$ .01	$ .05
Clark, Terry	89F	470	$ .01	$ .05	Coles, Darnell	87F	148	$ .01	$ .05
Clark, Will	86FU	25	$1.50	$11.00	Coles, Darnell	89F	544	$ .01	$ .05
Clark, Will	87F	269	$2.50	$25.00	Coles, Darnell	90F	509	$ .01	$ .04
Clark, Will	88F	78	$ .50	$3.50	Coles, Darnell	91F	333	$ .01	$ .03
Clark, Will	89F	325	$ .05	$ .75	Collins, Dave	81F	201	$ .01	$ .05
Clark, Will	89F	631	$ .05	$ .25	Collins, Dave	82F	61	$ .01	$ .05
Clark, Will	89F	632	$ .05	$ .40	Collins, Dave	83F	377	$ .01	$ .05
Clark, Will	90F	54	$ .01	$ .20	Collins, Dave	84F	151	$ .01	$ .06
Clark, Will	90F	637	$ .01	$ .10	Collins, Dave	85F	102	$ .01	$ .05
Clark, Will	90FPD	630	$ .01	$ .35	Collins, Dave	85FU	29	$ .01	$ .05
Clark, Will	91F	259	$ .01	$ .20	Collins, Dave	86F	415	$ .01	$ .05
Clary, Marty	88F	535	$ .01	$ .05	Collins, Dave	86FU	28	$ .01	$ .05
Clary, Martin	90F	578	$ .01	$ .04	Collins, Dave	87F	149	$ .01	$ .05
Clary, Marty	91F	686	$ .01	$ .03	Combe, Geoff	82F	62	$ .01	$ .05
Clay, Danny	88FU	108	$ .01	$ .05	Combs, Pat	90F	553	$ .01	$ .25
Clay, Ken	81F	633	$ .01	$ .05	Combs, Pat	91F	392	$ .01	$ .03
Clay, Ken	82F	508	$ .01	$ .05	Comer, Steve	82F	314	$ .01	$ .05
Clear, Mark	82F	290	$ .01	$ .05	Comer, Steve	83F	564	$ .01	$ .05
Clear, Mark	83F	181	$ .01	$ .05	Comstock, Keith	88F	579	$ .01	$ .10
Clear, Mark	83F	629	$ .04	$ .25	Comstock, Keith	90F	510	$ .01	$ .04
Clear, Mark	84F	395	$ .01	$ .06	Concepcion, Dave	81F	197	$ .03	$ .20
Clear, Mark	85F	154	$ .01	$ .05	Concepcion, Dave	82F	63	$ .03	$ .20
Clear, Mark	86F	344	$ .01	$ .05	Concepcion, Dave	82F	630	$ .01	$ .05
Clear, Mark	86FU	26	$ .01	$ .05	Concepcion, Dave	83F	588	$ .01	$ .05
Clear, Mark	87F	341	$ .01	$ .05	Concepcion, Dave	83F	631	$ .01	$ .10

FLEER

Player	Year	No.	VG	EX/MT	Player	Year	No.	VG	EX/MT
Concepcion, Dave	84F	466	$ .01	$ .06	Cowens, Al	84F	610	$ .01	$ .06
Concepcion, Dave	85F	532	$ .01	$ .05	Cowens, Al	85F	487	$ .01	$ .05
Concepcion, Dave	86F	174	$ .01	$ .10	Cowens, Al	86F	463	$ .01	$ .05
Concepcion, Dave	87F	196	$ .01	$ .10	Cowley, Joe	85F	124	$ .01	$ .05
Concepcion, Dave	88F	229	$ .01	$ .05	Cowley, Joe	86F	103	$ .01	$ .05
Concepcion, Dave	89F	156	$ .01	$ .05	Cowley, Joe	86FU	31	$ .01	$ .05
Concepcion, Onix	83F	110	$ .01	$ .05	Cowley, Joe	87F	491	$ .01	$ .05
Concepcion, Onix	84F	345	$ .01	$ .06	Cox, Bob	81F	247	$ .01	$ .05
Concepcion, Onix	85F	200	$ .01	$ .05	Cox, Danny	85F	222	$ .03	$ .20
Concepcion, Onix	86F	6	$ .01	$ .05	Cox, Danny	86F	32	$ .01	$ .10
Cone, David	88F	131	$ .25	$1.00	Cox, Danny	87F	292	$ .01	$ .05
Cone, David	89F	31	$ .01	$ .30	Cox, Danny	88F	28	$ .01	$ .10
Cone, David	89F	636	$ .01	$ .15	Cox, Danny	89F	447	$ .01	$ .05
Cone, David	90F	200	$ .01	$ .04	Cox, Larry	81F	604	$ .01	$ .05
Cone, David	91F	143	$ .01	$ .03	Cox, Ted	81F	602	$ .01	$ .05
Conine, Jeff	91F	553	$ .01	$ .35	Craig, Rodney	81F	597	$ .01	$ .05
Connally, Fritz	85FU	30	$ .01	$ .05	Crawford, Steve	82F	291	$ .01	$ .05
Conroy, Tim	84F	442	$ .01	$ .06	Crawford, Steve	85F	156	$ .01	$ .05
Conroy, Tim	85F	421	$ .01	$ .05	Crawford, Steve	86F	346	$ .01	$ .05
Conroy, Tim	86FU	29	$ .01	$ .05	Crawford, Steve	87F	33	$ .01	$ .05
Conroy, Tim	87F	291	$ .01	$ .05	Crawford, Steve	88F	350	$ .01	$ .05
Cook, Dennis	89F	652	$ .01	$ .45	Crawford, Steve	91F	554	$ .01	$ .03
Cook, Dennis	89FU	104	$ .01	$ .05	Creel, Keith	84F	346	$ .01	$ .06
Cook, Dennis	90F	554	$ .01	$ .10	Crews, Tim	88F	511	$ .01	$ .10
Cook, Dennis	91F	196	$ .01	$ .03	Crews, Tim	90F	390	$ .01	$ .04
Cook, Mike	89F	472	$ .01	$ .05	Crews, Tim	91F	197	$ .01	$ .03
Coolbaugh, Scott	90F	293	$ .01	$ .25	Crim, Chuck	87FU	19	$ .01	$ .10
Cooper, Cecil	81F	639	$ .01	$ .10	Crim, Chuck	88F	162	$ .01	$ .10
Cooper, Cecil	82F	138	$ .01	$ .10	Crim, Chuck	89F	183	$ .01	$ .05
Cooper, Cecil	83F	30	$ .01	$ .10	Crim, Chuck	90F	319	$ .01	$ .04
Cooper, Cecil	84F	198	$ .01	$ .10	Crim, Chuck	91F	579	$ .01	$ .03
Cooper, Cecil	85F	580	$ .03	$ .20	Cromartie, Warren	81F	144	$ .01	$ .05
Cooper, Cecil	86F	484	$ .01	$ .10	Cromartie, Warren	83F	279	$ .01	$ .05
Cooper, Cecil	87F	343	$ .01	$ .10	Cromartie, Warren	84F	272	$ .01	$ .06
Cooper, Cecil	88F	161	$ .01	$ .10	Cromartie, Wayne	82F	186	$ .01	$ .05
Cooper, Don	82F	550	$ .01	$ .05	Crowley, Terry	81F	190	$ .01	$ .05
Cooper, Scott	91F	91	$ .01	$ .15	Crowley, Terry	82F	160	$ .01	$ .05
Cora, Joey	88F	580	$ .01	$ .10	Crowley, Terry	83F	55	$ .01	$ .05
Cora, Joey	90F	154	$ .01	$ .10	Cruz, Hector	81F	206	$ .01	$ .05
Cora, Joey	91F	527	$ .01	$ .03	Cruz, Hector	82F	591	$ .01	$ .05
Corbett, Doug	81F	555	$ .01	$ .05	Cruz, Jose	81F	60	$ .01	$ .10
Corbett, Doug	82F	551	$ .01	$ .05	Cruz, Jose	82F	214	$ .01	$ .10
Corbett, Doug	83F	83	$ .01	$ .05	Cruz, Jose	83F	446	$ .01	$ .10
Corbett, Doug	85F	298	$ .01	$ .05	Cruz, Jose	84F	222	$ .01	$ .10
Corbett, Doug	87F	76	$ .01	$ .05	Cruz, Jose	85F	347	$ .01	$ .10
Corbett, Sherman	88FU	11	$ .01	$ .10	Cruz, Jose	86F	201	$ .01	$ .10
Corbett, Sherman	89F	473	$ .01	$ .05	Cruz, Jose	86F	296	$ .01	$ .10
Corcoran, Tim	81F	479	$ .01	$ .05	Cruz, Jose	87F	53	$ .01	$ .10
Corcoran, Tim	85F	247	$ .01	$ .05	Cruz, Jose	88F	443	$ .01	$ .05
Corcoran, Tim	86F	437	$ .01	$ .05	Cruz, Julio	81F	601	$ .01	$ .05
Corey, Mark	81F	193	$ .01	$ .05	Cruz, Julio	82F	509	$ .01	$ .05
Corrales, Pat	81F	623	$ .01	$ .05	Cruz, Julio	83F	478	$ .01	$ .05
Correa, Ed	86FU	30	$ .04	$ .25	Cruz, Julio	84F	55	$ .01	$ .06
Correa, Ed	87F	122	$ .04	$ .25	Cruz, Julio	85F	510	$ .01	$ .05
Correa, Ed	88F	464	$ .01	$ .05	Cruz, Julio	87F	492	$ .01	$ .05
Corsi, Jim	89F	649	$ .01	$ .25	Cruz, Todd	81F	341	$ .01	$ .05
Corsi, Jim	90F	4	$ .01	$ .04	Cruz, Todd	83F	479	$ .01	$ .05
Costello, John	88FU	118	$ .01	$ .15	Cruz, Todd	84F	3	$ .01	$ .06
Costello, John	89F	446	$ .01	$ .15	Cruz, Todd	85F	172	$ .01	$ .05
Costello, John	90F	246	$ .01	$ .04	Cruz, Victor	81F	407	$ .01	$ .05
Cotto, Henry	85F	53	$ .01	$ .10	Cruz, Victor	82F	480	$ .01	$ .05
Cotto, Henry	85FU	31	$ .01	$ .05	Cubbage, Mike	81F	566	$ .01	$ .05
Cotto, Henry	88F	205	$ .01	$ .05	Cubbage, Mike	82F	523	$ .01	$ .05
Cotto, Henry	88FU	58	$ .01	$ .05	Cubs, Chicago	85F	642	$ .01	$ .05
Cotto, Henry	89F	545	$ .01	$ .05	Curry, Steve	89F	86	$ .01	$ .15
Cotto, Henry	90F	511	$ .01	$ .04	Curtis, John	81F	491	$ .01	$ .05
Cotto, Henry	91F	448	$ .01	$ .03	Curtis, John	82F	569	$ .01	$ .05
Cowens, Al	81F	471	$ .01	$ .05	Curtis, John	83F	84	$ .01	$ .05
Cowens, Al	82F	266	$ .01	$ .05	Curtis, John	84F	513	$ .01	$ .06
Cowens, Al	83F	477	$ .01	$ .05	Cuyler, Milt	91F	334	$ .01	$ .15

Player	Year	No.	VG	EX/MT
D'Acquisto, John	81F	163	$ .01	$ .05
D'Acquisto, John	83F	516	$ .01	$ .05
Daniels, Kal	86F	646	$1.00	$4.50

Player	Year	No.	VG	EX/MT
Daniels, Kal	87F	197	$ .17	$ .50
Daniels, Kal	88F	230	$ .01	$ .20
Daniels, Kal	89F	157	$ .01	$ .20
Daniels, Kal	90FU	20	$ .01	$ .10
Daniels, Kal	91F	198	$ .01	$ .03
Darling, Ron	84FU	29	$2.00	$8.00
Darling, Ron	85F	76	$ .15	$1.00
Darling, Ron	86F	77	$ .01	$ .20
Darling, Ron	87F	5	$ .03	$ .20
Darling, Ron	88F	132	$ .01	$ .10
Darling, Ron	89F	32	$ .01	$ .05
Darling, Ron	90F	201	$ .01	$ .04
Darling, Ron	91F	144	$ .01	$ .03
Darwin, Danny	81F	632	$ .01	$ .05
Darwin, Danny	82F	315	$ .01	$ .05
Darwin, Danny	83F	565	$ .01	$ .05
Darwin, Danny	84F	416	$ .01	$ .06
Darwin, Danny	85F	557	$ .01	$ .05
Darwin, Danny	85FU	32	$ .03	$ .20
Darwin, Danny	86F	485	$ .01	$ .05
Darwin, Danny	87F	54	$ .01	$ .05
Darwin, Danny	88F	444	$ .01	$ .05
Darwin, Danny	89F	354	$ .01	$ .05
Darwin, Danny	90F	227	$ .01	$ .04
Darwin, Danny	91F	503	$ .01	$ .03
Dascenzo, Doug	89F	420	$ .01	$ .10
Dascenzo, Doug	91F	418	$ .01	$ .03
Dauer, Rich	81F	182	$ .01	$ .05
Dauer, Rich	82F	161	$ .01	$ .05
Dauer, Rich	83F	57	$ .01	$ .05
Dauer, Rich	84F	4	$ .01	$ .06
Dauer, Rich	85F	173	$ .01	$ .05
Dauer, Rich	86F	270	$ .01	$ .05
Daugherty, Jack	90F	294	$ .01	$ .10
Daugherty, Jack	91F	284	$ .01	$ .03
Daulton, Darren	85FU	33	$ .01	$ .05
Daulton, Darren	86F	438	$ .03	$ .20
Daulton, Darren	87F	172	$ .01	$ .05

Player	Year	No.	VG	EX/MT
Daulton, Darren	90F	555	$ .01	$ .04
Daulton, Darren	91F	393	$ .01	$ .03
Davalillo, Vic	81F	132	$ .01	$ .05
Dave Otto	88F	652	$ .30	$1.25
Davidson, Mark	87FU	20	$ .04	$ .25
Davidson, Mark	88F	8	$ .01	$ .10
Davidson, Mark	89F	109	$ .01	$ .05
Davidson, Mark	91F	504	$ .01	$ .03
Davis, Alvin	84FU	30	$3.00	$13.50
Davis, Alvin	85F	488	$ .75	$2.50
Davis, Alvin	86F	464	$ .03	$ .20
Davis, Alvin	87F	584	$ .01	$ .05
Davis, Alvin	88F	373	$ .01	$ .10
Davis, Alvin	89F	546	$ .01	$ .10
Davis, Alvin	90F	512	$ .01	$ .04
Davis, Alvin	91F	449	$ .01	$ .03
Davis, Bob	81F	428	$ .01	$ .05
Davis, Chili	83F	257	$ .03	$ .20
Davis, Chili	84F	370	$ .03	$ .10
Davis, Chili	85F	605	$ .01	$ .10
Davis, Chili	86F	536	$ .01	$ .10
Davis, Chili	87F	270	$ .01	$ .10
Davis, Chili	88F	79	$ .01	$ .10
Davis, Chili	88FU	12	$ .01	$ .05
Davis, Chili	89F	474	$ .01	$ .05
Davis, Chili	90F	129	$ .01	$ .04
Davis, Chili	91F	309	$ .01	$ .03
Davis, Dick	81F	527	$ .01	$ .05
Davis, Dick	82F	245	$ .01	$ .05
Davis, Dick	83F	305	$ .01	$ .05
Davis, Eric	85F	533	$3.50	$16.00
Davis, Eric	86F	175	$ .80	$2.50
Davis, Eric	87F	198	$ .45	$1.50
Davis, Eric	88F	231	$ .25	$ .75
Davis, Eric	88F	637	$ .10	$ .50
Davis, Eric	89F	158	$ .05	$ .40
Davis, Eric	89F	639	$ .01	$ .25
Davis, Eric	90F	417	$ .01	$ .15
Davis, Eric	91F	61	$ .01	$ .10
Davis, Glenn	85F	652	$2.00	$12.50
Davis, Glenn	86F	297	$ .25	$1.25
Davis, Glenn	87F	55	$ .05	$ .30
Davis, Glenn	87F	636	$ .03	$ .20
Davis, Glenn	88F	445	$ .01	$ .15
Davis, Glenn	89F	355	$ .01	$ .15
Davis, Glenn	90F	228	$ .01	$ .10
Davis, Glenn	91F	505	$ .01	$ .10
Davis, Jerry	85FU	34	$ .01	$ .05
Davis, Jerry	86F	317	$ .01	$ .05
Davis, Jody	82F	592	$ .07	$ .50
Davis, Jody	83F	494	$ .01	$ .10
Davis, Jody	84F	491	$ .01	$ .06
Davis, Jody	85F	54	$ .01	$ .05
Davis, Jody	86F	364	$ .01	$ .10
Davis, Jody	87F	557	$ .01	$ .10
Davis, Jody	88F	414	$ .01	$ .05
Davis, Jody	89F	421	$ .01	$ .05
Davis, Jody	90F	579	$ .01	$ .04
Davis, Joel	86F	202	$ .01	$ .10
Davis, John	88F	255	$ .01	$ .15
Davis, John	88FU	15	$ .01	$ .05
Davis, Mark	84F	371	$ .01	$ .50
Davis, Mark	85F	606	$ .01	$ .05
Davis, Mark	86F	537	$ .01	$ .05
Davis, Mark	87F	271	$ .01	$ .05
Davis, Mark	87FU	21	$ .01	$ .05
Davis, Mark	88F	581	$ .01	$ .05
Davis, Mark	89F	303	$ .01	$ .05
Davis, Mark	89F	635	$ .01	$ .15
Davis, Mark	89FU	18	$ .01	$ .05

Player	Year	No.	VG	EX/MT	Player	Year	No.	VG	EX/MT
Davis, Mark	90F	155	$ .01	$ .04	DeCinces, Doug	85F	299	$ .01	$ .05
Davis, Mark	90F	631	$ .01	$ .04	DeCinces, Doug	86F	153	$ .01	$ .05
Davis, Mark	90FU	101	$ .01	$ .05	DeCinces, Doug	87F	77	$ .01	$ .05
Davis, Mark	91F	555	$ .01	$ .03	DeCinces, Doug	88F	31	$ .01	$ .05
Davis, Mike	81F	586	$ .04	$ .25	Decker, Steve	91F	260	$ .01	$ .50
Davis, Mike	84F	443	$ .01	$1.00	Dedmon, Jeff	85F	323	$ .01	$ .05
Davis, Mike	85F	422	$ .01	$ .10	Dedmon, Jeff	86F	513	$ .01	$ .05
Davis, Mike	86F	416	$ .01	$ .05	Dedmon, Jeff	87F	514	$ .01	$ .05
Davis, Mike	87F	391	$ .01	$ .05	Dedmon, Jeff	88F	537	$ .01	$ .05
Davis, Mike	88F	277	$ .01	$ .05	Deer, Rob	85F	648	$ .25	$2.00
Davis, Mike	89F	55	$ .01	$ .05	Deer, Rob	86F	538	$ .01	$ .10
Davis, Mike	90F	391	$ .01	$ .04	Deer, Rob	86FU	33	$ .04	$ .25
Davis, Ron	81F	86	$ .01	$ .05	Deer, Rob	87F	344	$ .01	$ .10
Davis, Ron	82F	32	$ .01	$ .05	Deer, Rob	88F	163	$ .01	$ .10
Davis, Ron	83F	610	$ .01	$ .05	Deer, Rob	89F	184	$ .01	$ .05
Davis, Ron	84F	561	$ .01	$ .06	Deer, Rob	90F	320	$ .01	$ .04
Davis, Ron	85F	275	$ .01	$ .05	Deer, Rob	91F	580	$ .01	$ .03
Davis, Ron	86F	390	$ .01	$ .05	DeJesus, Ivan	81F	297	$ .01	$ .05
Davis, Ron	87F	558	$ .01	$ .05	DeJesus, Ivan	82F	593	$ .01	$ .05
Davis, Storm	83F	56	$ .01	$ .60	DeJesus, Ivan	83F	157	$ .01	$ .05
Davis, Storm	84F	5	$ .03	$ .15	DeJesus, Ivan	84F	26	$ .01	$ .06
Davis, Storm	85F	174	$ .01	$ .10	DeJesus, Ivan	85F	248	$ .01	$ .05
Davis, Storm	86F	271	$ .01	$ .05	DeJesus, Ivan	86F	34	$ .01	$ .05
Davis, Storm	87F	466	$ .01	$ .05	DeJesus, Jose	89F	280	$ .01	$ .05
Davis, Storm	87FU	22	$ .01	$ .05	DeJesus, Jose	90F	104	$ .01	$ .04
Davis, Storm	88F	278	$ .01	$ .05	DeJesus, Jose	90FU	42	$ .01	$ .10
Davis, Storm	89F	6	$ .01	$ .05	DeJesus, Jose	91F	394	$ .01	$ .03
Davis, Storm	90F	5	$ .01	$ .10	DeLeon, Jose	84F	248	$ .01	$ .50
Davis, Storm	90FU	102	$ .01	$ .05	DeLeon, Jose	85F	463	$ .01	$ .05
Davis, Storm	91F	556	$ .01	$ .03	DeLeon, Jose	86F	607	$ .01	$ .05
Dawley, Bill	84F	223	$ .01	$ .06	DeLeon, Jose	87F	494	$ .01	$ .05
Dawley, Bill	85F	348	$ .01	$ .05	DeLeon, Jose	88F	395	$ .01	$ .05
Dawley, Bill	86F	298	$ .01	$ .05	DeLeon, Jose	88FU	119	$ .01	$ .05
Dawley, Bill	86FU	32	$ .01	$ .05	DeLeon, Jose	89F	449	$ .01	$ .05
Dawley, Bill	87F	493	$ .01	$ .05	DeLeon, Jose	90F	248	$ .01	$ .04
Dawley, Bill	87FU	23	$ .01	$ .05	DeLeon, Jose	91F	631	$ .01	$ .03
Dawley, Bill	88F	29	$ .01	$ .05	DeLeon, Luis	83F	355	$ .01	$ .05
Dawson, Andre	81F	145	$ .05	$ .50	DeLeon, Luis	84F	297	$ .01	$ .06
Dawson, Andre	82F	187	$ .10	$ .50	DeLeon, Luis	85F	29	$ .01	$ .05
Dawson, Andre	83F	280	$ .05	$ .50	DeLeon, Luis	86F	318	$ .01	$ .05
Dawson, Andre	84F	273	$ .07	$1.00	Dempsey, Rick	81F	177	$ .01	$ .10
Dawson, Andre	85F	394	$ .06	$ .35	Dempsey, Rick	82F	163	$ .01	$ .05
Dawson, Andre	86F	246	$ .05	$ .30	Dempsey, Rick	83F	58	$ .01	$ .05
Dawson, Andre	87F	316	$ .04	$ .25	Dempsey, Rick	84F	6	$ .03	$ .10
Dawson, Andre	87FU	24	$ .06	$ .55	Dempsey, Rick	85F	175	$ .01	$ .05
Dawson, Andre	88F	415	$ .01	$ .20	Dempsey, Rick	86F	272	$ .01	$ .05
Dawson, Andre	89F	422	$ .01	$ .10	Dempsey, Rick	87F	467	$ .01	$ .05
Dawson, Andre	90F	29	$ .01	$ .10	Dempsey, Rick	87FU	26	$ .01	$ .05
Dawson, Andre	91F	419	$ .01	$ .10	Dempsey, Rick	90F	392	$ .01	$ .04
Dawson, Andre	91F	713	$ .01	$ .10	Denny, John	82F	363	$ .01	$ .05
Dayett, Brian	85F	125	$ .01	$ .05	Denny, John	83F	158	$ .01	$ .10
Dayett, Brian	85FU	35	$ .01	$ .05	Denny, John	84F	27	$ .03	$ .10
Dayett, Brian	87FU	25	$ .01	$ .05	Denny, John	85F	249	$ .01	$ .05
Dayett, Brian	88F	416	$ .01	$ .05	Denny, John	86F	439	$ .01	$ .05
Dayley, Ken	83F	135	$ .01	$ .05	Denny, John	86FU	34	$ .01	$ .05
Dayley, Ken	84F	176	$ .01	$ .06	Denny, John	87F	199	$ .01	$ .05
Dayley, Ken	86F	33	$ .01	$ .05	Dent, Bucky	81F	80	$ .01	$ .05
Dayley, Ken	87F	293	$ .01	$ .05	Dent, Bucky	82F	33	$ .01	$ .05
Dayley, Ken	88F	30	$ .01	$ .05	Dent, Bucky	82F	629	$ .01	$ .05
Dayley, Ken	89F	448	$ .01	$ .05	Dent, Bucky	83F	566	$ .01	$ .05
Dayley, Ken	90F	247	$ .01	$ .04	Dent, Bucky	84F	417	$ .01	$ .06
Dayley, Ken	91F	630	$ .01	$ .03	Dernier, Bob	83F	159	$ .01	$ .05
De Los Santos, Luis	89F	646	$ .01	$ .20	Dernier, Bob	84F	28	$ .01	$ .06
De Los Santos, Luis	89FU	37	$ .01	$ .10	Dernier, Bob	84FU	31	$ .01	$ .10
De Los Santos, Luis	90F	105	$ .01	$ .10	Dernier, Bob	85F	55	$ .01	$ .05
DeCinces, Doug	81F	173	$ .01	$ .10	Dernier, Bob	86F	365	$ .01	$ .05
DeCinces, Doug	81F	195	$ .01	$ .10	Dernier, Bob	87F	559	$ .01	$ .05
DeCinces, Doug	82F	162	$ .01	$ .10	Dernier, Bob	88F	417	$ .01	$ .05
DeCinces, Doug	83F	85	$ .01	$ .05	Dernier, Bob	89F	565	$ .01	$ .05
DeCinces, Doug	84F	514	$ .01	$ .06	Deshaies, Jim	86FU	35	$ .06	$ .35

Player	Year	No.	VG	EX/MT
Deshaies, Jim	87F	56	$ .05	$ .30
Deshaies, Jim	88F	446	$ .01	$ .05
Deshaies, Jim	89F	356	$ .01	$ .05
Deshaies, Jim	90F	229	$ .01	$ .04
Deshaies, Jim	91F	506	$ .01	$ .03
DeShields, Delino	90F	653	$ .01	$ .75
DeShields, Delino	90FU	27	$ .01	$ .50
DeShields, Delino	91F	228	$ .01	$ .20
Devereaux, Mike	88F	512	$ .01	$ .25
Devereaux, Mike	89F	56	$ .01	$ .15
Devereaux, Mike	89FU	2	$ .01	$ .05
Devereaux, Mike	90F	175	$ .01	$ .04
Devereaux, Mike	91F	469	$ .01	$ .03
Diaz, Bo	81F	404	$ .03	$ .20
Diaz, Bo	82F	364	$ .01	$ .10
Diaz, Bo	82F	639	$ .01	$ .10
Diaz, Bo	83F	160	$ .01	$ .10
Diaz, Bo	83F	637	$ .01	$ .10
Diaz, Bo	84F	29	$ .03	$ .10
Diaz, Bo	85F	250	$ .01	$ .10
Diaz, Bo	86F	176	$ .01	$ .05
Diaz, Bo	87F	200	$ .01	$ .05
Diaz, Bo	88F	232	$ .01	$ .05
Diaz, Bo	89F	159	$ .01	$ .05
Diaz, Carlos	83F	540	$ .01	$ .05
Diaz, Carlos	84F	583	$ .01	$ .06
Diaz, Carlos	84FU	32	$ .01	$ .10
Diaz, Carlos	85F	369	$ .01	$ .05
Diaz, Carlos	86F	128	$ .01	$ .05
Diaz, Edgar	90FU	105	$ .01	$ .10
Diaz, Edgar	91F	581	$ .01	$ .03
Diaz, Mario	88F	649	$ .01	$ .35
Diaz, Marion	88FU	59	$ .01	$ .15
Diaz, Marion	89F	547	$ .01	$ .05
Diaz, Mike	87F	609	$ .05	$ .30
Diaz, Mike	88F	326	$ .01	$ .05
Diaz, Mike	89F	494	$ .01	$ .05
Dibble, Rob	88FU	83	$ .01	$1.25
Dibble, Rob	89F	160	$ .01	$ .75
Dibble, Rob	90F	418	$ .01	$ .20
Dibble, Rob	91F	62	$ .01	$ .03
Dillard, Steve	81F	298	$ .01	$ .05
Dillard, Steve	82F	594	$ .01	$ .05
Dilone, Miguel	81F	391	$ .01	$ .05
Dilone, Miguel	82F	365	$ .01	$ .05
Dilone, Miguel	83F	405	$ .01	$ .05
Dilone, Miguel	85F	395	$ .01	$ .05
DiPino, Frank	84F	224	$ .01	$ .06
DiPino, Frank	85F	349	$ .01	$ .05
DiPino, Frank	86F	299	$ .01	$ .05
DiPino, Frank	87F	560	$ .01	$ .05
DiPino, Frank	88F	418	$ .01	$ .05
DiPino, Frank	89F	423	$ .01	$ .05
DiPino, Frank	89FU	118	$ .01	$ .05
DiPino, Frank	90F	249	$ .01	$ .04
DiPino, Frank	91F	632	$ .01	$ .03
Distefano, Benny	89F	205	$ .01	$ .05
Distefano, Benny	90F	464	$ .01	$ .04
Dixon, Ken	85FU	36	$ .03	$ .20
Dixon, Ken	86F	273	$ .01	$ .05
Dixon, Ken	87F	468	$ .01	$ .05
Dixon, Ken	88F	557	$ .01	$ .05
Donohue, Tom	81F	281	$ .01	$ .05
Dopson, John	88FU	99	$ .01	$ .25
Dopson, John	89F	373	$ .01	$ .25
Dopson, John	89FU	8	$ .01	$ .15
Dopson, John	90F	272	$ .01	$ .04
Dopson, John	91F	92	$ .01	$ .03
Doran, Bill	84F	225	$ .06	$1.00
Doran, Bill	85F	350	$ .01	$ .20

Player	Year	No.	VG	EX/MT
Doran, Bill	86F	300	$ .01	$ .10
Doran, Bill	87F	57	$ .01	$ .10
Doran, Bill	88F	447	$ .01	$ .05
Doran, Bill	89F	357	$ .01	$ .05
Doran, Bill	90F	230	$ .01	$ .04
Doran, Bill	91F	63	$ .01	$ .10
Dorsett, Brian	88F	607	$ .01	$ .15
Dotson, Richard	81F	356	$ .04	$ .25
Dotson, Richard	82F	340	$ .01	$ .10
Dotson, Richard	83F	233	$ .01	$ .05
Dotson, Richard	84F	56	$ .01	$ .06
Dotson, Richard	85F	511	$ .01	$ .05
Dotson, Richard	86F	203	$ .01	$ .05
Dotson, Richard	87F	495	$ .01	$ .05
Dotson, Richard	88F	396	$ .01	$ .05
Dotson, Richard	88FU	48	$ .01	$ .05

Player	Year	No.	VG	EX/MT
Dotson, Richard	89F	253	$ .01	$ .05
Dowell, Ken	87FU	27	$ .01	$ .05
Downing, Brian	81F	282	$ .01	$ .05
Downing, Brian	82F	457	$ .01	$ .05
Downing, Brian	83F	86	$ .01	$ .05
Downing, Brian	84F	515	$ .01	$ .06
Downing, Brian	85F	300	$ .01	$ .05
Downing, Brian	86F	154	$ .01	$ .05
Downing, Brian	87F	78	$ .01	$ .05
Downing, Brian	88F	488	$ .01	$ .05
Downing, Brian	89F	475	$ .01	$ .05
Downing, Brian	90F	130	$ .01	$ .04
Downing, Brian	91F	310	$ .01	$ .03
Downs, Kelly	87F	272	$ .04	$ .25
Downs, Kelly	88F	80	$ .01	$ .10
Downs, Kelly	89F	326	$ .01	$ .05
Downs, Kelly	90F	55	$ .01	$ .04
Downs, Kelly	91F	261	$ .01	$ .03
Doyle, Brian	81F	104	$ .01	$ .05
Drabek, Doug	86FU	36	$ .05	$1.00
Drabek, Doug	87F	96	$ .10	$2.00
Drabek, Doug	88F	327	$ .01	$ .35
Drabek, Doug	89F	206	$ .01	$ .10
Drabek, Doug	90F	465	$ .01	$ .10

Player	Year	No.	VG	EX/MT

DOUG
DRABEK
PIRATES • P
FLEER'91

Player	Year	No.	VG	EX/MT
Drabek, Doug	91F	36	$ .01	$ .03
Drago, Dick	81F	239	$ .01	$ .05
Drago, Dick	82F	510	$ .01	$ .05
Dravecky, Dave	83F	356	$ .06	$ .50
Dravecky, Dave	84F	298	$ .03	$ .25
Dravecky, Dave	85F	30	$ .01	$ .05
Dravecky, Dave	86F	319	$ .01	$ .05
Dravecky, Dave	87F	412	$ .01	$ .05
Dravecky, Dave	87FU	28	$ .01	$ .05
Dravecky, Dave	88F	81	$ .01	$ .05
Dravecky, Dave	89F	327	$ .01	$ .05
Drees, Tom	90F	644	$ .01	$ .04
Drew, Cameron	89F	640	$ .01	$ .20
Driessen, Dan	81F	205	$ .01	$ .10
Driessen, Dan	82F	630	$ .01	$ .05
Driessen, Dan	82F	64	$ .01	$ .05
Driessen, Dan	83F	589	$ .01	$ .05
Driessen, Dan	84F	467	$ .01	$ .06
Driessen, Dan	85F	396	$ .01	$ .05
Driessen, Dan	86F	539	$ .01	$ .05
Drummond, Tim	90FU	107	$ .01	$ .10
Drummond, Tim	91F	607	$ .01	$ .03
Drumright, Keith	82F	89	$ .01	$ .05
Dubois, Brian	90F	601	$ .01	$ .25
Ducey, Rob	88F	107	$ .01	$ .25
Dunbar, Tommy	85FU	37	$ .01	$ .05
Duncan, Mariano	85FU	38	$ .10	$ .75
Duncan, Mariano	86F	129	$ .10	$ .40
Duncan, Mariano	87F	439	$ .01	$ .05
Duncan, Mariano	88F	513	$ .01	$ .05
Duncan, Mariano	90FU	12	$ .01	$ .05
Duncan, Mariano	91F	64	$ .01	$ .03
Dunne, Mike	87FU	29	$ .10	$ .50
Dunne, Mike	88F	328	$ .01	$ .25
Dunne, Mike	89F	207	$ .01	$ .05
Dunston, Shawon	85F	649	$ 1.00	$6.50
Dunston, Shawon	86F	366	$ .03	$ .20
Dunston, Shawon	87F	561	$ .05	$ .30
Dunston, Shawon	88F	419	$ .01	$ .10
Dunston, Shawon	89F	424	$ .01	$ .05
Dunston, Shawon	90F	30	$ .01	$ .15

Player	Year	No.	VG	EX/MT
Dunston, Shawon	91F	420	$ .01	$ .03
Durham, Leon	81F	540	$ .01	$ .10
Durham, Leon	82F	595	$ .01	$ .05
Durham, Leon	83F	495	$ .01	$ .10
Durham, Leon	84F	492	$ .01	$ .05
Durham, Leon	85F	56	$ .01	$ .05
Durham, Leon	86F	367	$ .01	$ .05
Durham, Leon	87F	562	$ .01	$ .05
Durham, Leon	88F	420	$ .01	$ .05
Dwyer, Jim	81F	235	$ .01	$ .05
Dwyer, Jim	82F	164	$ .01	$ .05
Dwyer, Jim	83F	59	$ .01	$ .05
Dwyer, Jim	84F	7	$ .01	$ .06
Dwyer, Jim	85F	176	$ .01	$ .05
Dwyer, Jim	86F	274	$ .01	$ .05
Dwyer, Jim	88F	558	$ .01	$ .05
Dwyer, Kim	87F	469	$ .01	$ .05
Dybzinski, Jerry	81F	399	$ .01	$ .05
Dybzinski, Jerry	82F	366	$ .01	$ .05
Dybzinski, Jerry	83F	406	$ .01	$ .05
Dybzinski, Jerry	84F	57	$ .01	$ .06
Dybzinski, Jerry	85F	512	$ .01	$ .05
Dyer, Mike	90F	372	$ .01	$ .10
Dykstra, Len	86F	78	$ .10	$3.00
Dykstra, Len	87F	6	$ .03	$ .50
Dykstra, Len	88F	133	$ .01	$ .25
Dykstra, Len	89F	33	$ .01	$ .20
Dykstra, Lenny	89FU	105	$ .01	$ .20
Dykstra, Lenny	90F	556	$ .01	$ .10
Dykstra, Len	91F	395	$ .01	$ .03
Easler, Mike	81F	372	$ .01	$ .05
Easler, Mike	82F	481	$ .01	$ .05
Easler, Mike	83F	306	$ .01	$ .05
Easler, Mike	84F	249	$ .01	$ .06
Easler, Mike	84FU	33	$ .01	$ .10
Easler, Mike	85F	157	$ .01	$ .05
Easler, Mike	86F	347	$ .01	$ .05
Easler, Mike	86FU	37	$ .01	$ .05
Easler, Mike	87F	97	$ .01	$ .05
Easler, Mike	88F	206	$ .01	$ .05
Easterly, Jamie	82F	139	$ .01	$ .05
Easterly, Jamie	83F	31	$ .01	$ .05
Easterly, Jamie	84F	538	$ .01	$ .06
Easterly, Jamie	85F	445	$ .01	$ .05
Easterly, Jamie	86F	585	$ .01	$ .05
Eastwick, Rawly	82F	596	$ .01	$ .05
Eckersley, Dennis	81F	226	$ .01	$ .50
Eckersley, Dennis	82F	292	$ .01	$ .25
Eckersley, Dennis	83F	182	$ .01	$ .25
Eckersley, Dennis	83F	629	$ .04	$ .25
Eckersley, Dennis	84F	396	$ .01	$ .35
Eckersley, Dennis	84FU	34	$ .04	$1.50
Eckersley, Dennis	85F	57	$ .01	$ .05
Eckersley, Dennis	86F	368	$ .01	$ .05
Eckersley, Dennis	87F	563	$ .01	$ .05
Eckersley, Dennis	87FU	30	$ .01	$ .05
Eckersley, Dennis	88F	279	$ .01	$ .05
Eckersley, Dennis	89F	7	$ .01	$ .05
Eckersley, Dennis	90F	6	$ .01	$ .04
Eckersley, Dennis	91F	6	$ .01	$ .03
Edelen, Joe	82F	65	$ .01	$ .05
Edens, Tom	91F	582	$ .01	$ .10
Edler, Dave	81F	610	$ .01	$ .05
Edwards, Dave	81F	568	$ .01	$ .05
Edwards, Dave	83F	357	$ .01	$ .05
Edwards, Marshall	82F	140	$ .01	$ .05
Edwards, Marshall	83F	32	$ .01	$ .05
Edwards, Wayne	90F	652	$ .01	$ .04
Edwards, Wayne	90FU	83	$ .01	$ .05
Edwards, Wayne	91F	116	$ .01	$ .03

Player	Year	No.	VG	EX/MT	Player	Year	No.	VG	EX/MT
Eichelberger, Juan	82F	570	$ .01	$ .05	Evans, Dwight	82F	642	$ .01	$ .05
Eichelberger, Juan	83F	358	$ .01	$ .05	Evans, Dwight	83F	183	$ .01	$ .10
Eichelberger, Juan	84F	539	$ .01	$ .06	Evans, Dwight	84F	397	$ .03	$ .10
Eichhorn, Mark	86FU	38	$ .05	$ .30	Evans, Dwight	85F	158	$ .03	$ .20
Eichhorn, Mark	87F	224	$ .05	$ .20	Evans, Dwight	86F	348	$ .01	$ .10
Eichhorn, Mark	88F	108	$ .01	$ .10	Evans, Dwight	87F	34	$ .01	$ .10
Eichhorn, Mark	89F	230	$ .01	$ .05	Evans, Dwight	88F	351	$ .01	$ .10
Eichhorn, Mark	90F	580	$ .01	$ .04	Evans, Dwight	89F	87	$ .01	$ .05
Eichhorn, Mark	90FU	77	$ .01	$ .05	Evans, Dwight	90F	274	$ .01	$ .04
Eichhorn, Mark	91F	311	$ .01	$ .03	Evans, Dwight	91F	93	$ .01	$ .03
Eiland, David	91F	661	$ .01	$ .03	Faedo, Lenny	83F	611	$ .01	$ .05
Eisenreich, Jim	89FU	38	$ .01	$ .05	Faedo, Lenny	84F	563	$ .01	$ .06
Eisenreich, Jim	90F	106	$ .01	$ .04	Fahey, Bill	81F	490	$ .01	$ .05
Eisenreich, Jim	91F	557	$ .01	$ .03	Falcone, Pete	81F	327	$ .01	$ .05
Ellis, John	82F	316	$ .01	$ .05	Falcone, Pete	82F	524	$ .01	$ .05
Elster, Kevin	87F	7	$ .05	$ .50	Falcone, Pete	83F	541	$ .01	$ .05
Elster, Kevin	88FU	104	$ .01	$ .15	Falcone, Pete	84F	177	$ .01	$ .06
Elster, Kevin	89F	34	$ .01	$ .05	Fallon, Bob	85FU	39	$ .01	$ .05
Elster, Kevin	90F	202	$ .01	$ .04	Faries, Paul	91F	528	$ .01	$ .15
Elster, Kevin	91F	145	$ .01	$ .03	Farmer, Ed	81F	339	$ .01	$ .05
Engle, Dave	82F	552	$ .01	$ .05	Farmer, Ed	82F	342	$ .01	$ .05
Engle, Dave	84F	562	$ .01	$ .06	Farmer, Ed	83F	161	$ .01	$ .05
Engle, Dave	85F	276	$ .01	$ .05	Farr, Steve	85F	446	$ .01	$ .05
Engle, Dave	86F	391	$ .01	$ .05	Farr, Steve	86F	7	$ .01	$ .05
Engle, Dave	86FU	39	$ .01	$ .05	Farr, Steve	87F	367	$ .01	$ .05
Eppard, Jim	88F	645	$ .10	$ .40	Farr, Steve	88F	256	$ .01	$ .05
Eppard, Jim	88FU	13	$ .01	$ .05	Farr, Steve	89F	281	$ .01	$ .05
Eppard, Jim	89F	476	$ .01	$ .05	Farr, Steve	90F	107	$ .01	$ .04
Erickson, Roger	81F	561	$ .01	$ .05	Farr, Steve	91F	558	$ .01	$ .03
Erickson, Roger	82F	553	$ .01	$ .05	Farrell, John	88F	608	$ .01	$ .30
Erickson, Roger	83F	378	$ .01	$ .05	Farrell, John	89F	403	$ .01	$ .10
Erickson, Scott	91F	608	$ .01	$1.00	Farrell, John	90F	491	$ .01	$ .04
Esasky, Nick	84F	468	$ .50	$2.00	Farrell, John	91F	366	$ .01	$ .03
Esasky, Nick	85F	534	$ .01	$ .20	Felder, Mike	88F	164	$ .01	$ .05
Esasky, Nick	86F	177	$ .01	$ .05	Felder, Mike	90F	321	$ .01	$ .04
Esasky, Nick	87F	201	$ .01	$ .05	Felder, Mike	91F	583	$ .01	$ .03
Esasky, Nick	88F	233	$ .01	$ .05	Felix, Junior	89FU	69	$ .01	$1.00
Esasky, Nick	89F	161	$ .01	$ .05	Felix, Junior	90F	79	$ .01	$ .25
Esasky, Nick	89FU	9	$ .01	$ .05	Felix, Junior	91F	173	$ .01	$ .10
Esasky, Nick	90F	273	$ .01	$ .04	Felton, Terry	83F	612	$ .01	$ .05
Esasky, Nick	90FU	3	$ .01	$ .05	Ferguson, Joe	81F	124	$ .01	$ .05
Esasky, Nick	91F	687	$ .01	$ .03	Ferguson, Joe	83F	87	$ .01	$ .05
Escarrega, Ernesto	83F	234	$ .01	$ .05	Fermin, Felix	88F	643	$ .01	$ .25
Espinosa, Nino	81F	20	$ .01	$ .05	Fermin, Felix	89F	208	$ .01	$ .05
Espinoza, Alvaro	89FU	47	$ .01	$ .25	Fermin, Felix	89FU	27	$ .01	$ .05
Espinoza, Alvaro	90F	441	$ .01	$ .15	Fermin, Felix	90F	492	$ .01	$ .04
Espinoza, Alvaro	91F	662	$ .01	$ .03	Fermin, Felix	91F	367	$ .01	$ .03
Espy, Cecil	88F	465	$ .01	$ .25	Fernandez, Alex	90FU	84	$ .01	$1.50
Espy, Cecil	89F	517	$ .01	$ .05	Fernandez, Alex	91F	117	$ .01	$ .75
Espy, Cecil	90F	295	$ .01	$ .04	Fernandez, Sid	85F	77	$ .15	$ .90
Essian, Jim	81F	593	$ .01	$ .05	Fernandez, Sid	86F	79	$ .01	$ .20
Essian, Jim	82F	341	$ .01	$ .05	Fernandez, Sid	87F	8	$ .03	$ .20
Essian, Jim	84F	540	$ .01	$ .06	Fernandez, Sid	87F	629	$ .10	$ .50
Essian, Jim	84FU	35	$ .01	$ .10	Fernandez, Sid	88F	134	$ .01	$ .10
Essian, Jim	85F	423	$ .01	$ .05	Fernandez, Sid	89F	35	$ .01	$ .05
Eufemia, Frank	86F	392	$ .01	$ .05	Fernandez, Sid	90F	203	$ .01	$ .04
Evans, Barry	81F	499	$ .01	$ .05	Fernandez, Sid	91F	146	$ .01	$ .03
Evans, Barry	82F	571	$ .01	$ .05	Fernandez, Tony	84F	152	$ .70	$4.00
Evans, Darrell	81F	436	$ .01	$ .10	Fernandez, Tony	85F	103	$ .10	$ .50
Evans, Darrell	82F	388	$ .01	$ .10	Fernandez, Tony	86F	57	$ .03	$ .20
Evans, Darrell	83F	258	$ .01	$ .10	Fernandez, Tony	87F	225	$ .01	$ .10
Evans, Darrell	84F	372	$ .03	$ .10	Fernandez, Tony	88F	109	$ .01	$ .10
Evans, Darrell	84FU	36	$ .03	$ .60	Fernandez, Tony	88F	635	$ .01	$ .10
Evans, Darrell	85F	6	$ .01	$ .10	Fernandez, Tony	89F	231	$ .01	$ .05
Evans, Darrell	86F	224	$ .01	$ .10	Fernandez, Tony	90F	80	$ .01	$ .10
Evans, Darrell	87F	150	$ .01	$ .10	Fernandez, Tony	90F	634	$ .01	$ .04
Evans, Darrell	88F	54	$ .01	$ .10	Fernandez, Tony	91F	174	$ .01	$ .03
Evans, Darrell	90F	581	$ .01	$ .04	Fetters, Mike	90F	131	$ .01	$ .15
Evans, Dwight	81F	232	$ .03	$ .20	Fetters, Mike	91F	312	$ .01	$ .03
Evans, Dwight	82F	293	$ .03	$ .20	Fidrych, Mark	81F	462	$ .01	$ .05

FLEER

Player	Year	No.	VG	EX/MT	Player	Year	No.	VG	EX/MT
Fielder, Cecil	86F	653	$1.25	$15.00	Flanagan, Mike	84F	8	$ .03	$ .10
Fielder, Cecil	87FU	31	$ .01	$3.00	Flanagan, Mike	85F	177	$ .01	$ .05
Fielder, Cecil	88F	110	$ .01	$1.50	Flanagan, Mike	86F	275	$ .01	$ .05
Fielder, Cecil	89F	232	$ .01	$ .50	Flanagan, Mike	87F	470	$ .01	$ .05
Fielder, Cecil	90FU	95	$ .01	$ .50	Flanagan, Mike	88FU	67	$ .01	$ .05
Fielder, Cecil	91F	335	$ .01	$ .25	Flanagan, Mike	89F	233	$ .01	$ .05
Fielder, Cecil	91F	709	$ .01	$ .20	Flanagan, Mike	90F	81	$ .01	$ .04
Figueroa, Ed	81F	624	$ .01	$ .05	Flannery, Tim	81F	493	$ .01	$ .05
Filer, Tom	86F	58	$ .01	$ .05	Flannery, Tim	82F	572	$ .01	$ .05
Filer, Tom	89F	185	$ .01	$ .05	Flannery, Tim	83F	359	$ .01	$ .05
Filer, Tom	90F	322	$ .01	$ .04	Flannery, Tim	84F	299	$ .01	$ .06
Filson, Pete	84F	564	$ .01	$ .06	Flannery, Tim	85F	31	$ .01	$ .05
Filson, Pete	85F	277	$ .01	$ .05	Flannery, Tim	86F	320	$ .01	$ .05
Filson, Pete	86F	393	$ .01	$ .05	Flannery, Tim	87F	413	$ .01	$ .05
Fimple, Jack	84F	99	$ .01	$ .06	Flannery, Tim	88F	582	$ .01	$ .05
Fingers, Rollie	81F	485	$ .04	$ .25	Fletcher, Scott	84F	59	$ .03	$ .10
Fingers, Rollie	82F	141	$ .03	$ .20	Fletcher, Scott	85F	514	$ .01	$ .05
Fingers, Rollie	82F	644	$ .01	$ .10	Fletcher, Scott	86F	205	$ .01	$ .05
Fingers, Rollie	83F	33	$ .03	$ .20	Fletcher, Scott	86FU	41	$ .01	$ .05
Fingers, Rollie	84F	199	$ .01	$ .20	Fletcher, Scott	87F	123	$ .01	$ .05
Fingers, Rollie	85F	581	$ .03	$ .20	Fletcher, Scott	88F	466	$ .01	$ .05
Fingers, Rollie	86F	486	$ .01	$ .10	Fletcher, Scott	89F	518	$ .01	$ .05
Finley, Chuck	87F	79	$ .25	$2.00	Fletcher, Scott	90F	531	$ .01	$ .04
Finley, Chuck	88F	489	$ .01	$ .20	Fletcher, Scott	91F	119	$ .01	$ .03
Finley, Chuck	89F	477	$ .01	$ .10	Flynn, Doug	81F	330	$ .01	$ .05
Finley, Chuck	90F	132	$ .01	$ .10	Flynn, Doug	82F	525	$ .01	$ .05
Finley, Chuck	91F	313	$ .01	$ .03	Flynn, Doug	83F	282	$ .01	$ .05
Finley, Steve	89FU	3	$ .01	$ .30	Flynn, Doug	84F	274	$ .01	$ .06
Finley, Steve	90F	176	$ .01	$ .20	Flynn, Doug	85F	397	$ .01	$ .05
Finley, Steve	91F	470	$ .01	$ .03	Flynn, Doug	85F	535	$ .01	$ .05
Fireovid, Steve	87F	653	$ .01	$ .05	Foley, Tom	86F	440	$ .01	$ .05
Fischlin, Mike	83F	407	$ .01	$ .05	Foley, Tom	87F	318	$ .01	$ .05
Fischlin, Mike	84F	541	$ .01	$ .06	Foley, Tom	88F	183	$ .01	$ .05
Fischlin, Mike	85F	447	$ .01	$ .05	Foley, Tom	89F	375	$ .01	$ .05
Fischlin, Mike	86FU	40	$ .01	$ .05	Foley, Tom	90F	344	$ .01	$ .04
Fischlin, Mike	87F	98	$ .01	$ .05	Foley, Tom	91F	230	$ .01	$ .03
Fishel, John	88FU	88	$ .01	$ .15	Foli, Tim	81F	379	$ .01	$ .05
Fishel, John	89F	358	$ .01	$ .10	Foli, Tim	82F	482	$ .01	$ .05
Fisher, Brian	85FU	40	$ .01	$ .05	Foli, Tim	83F	88	$ .01	$ .05
Fisher, Brian	86F	104	$ .01	$ .25	Foli, Tim	84F	516	$ .01	$ .06
Fisher, Brian	87F	99	$ .01	$ .05	Foli, Tim	84FU	38	$ .01	$ .10
Fisher, Brian	87FU	32	$ .01	$ .05	Foli, Tim	85F	126	$ .01	$ .05
Fisher, Brian	88F	329	$ .01	$ .05	Fontenot, Ray	84F	122	$ .01	$ .06
Fisher, Brian	89F	209	$ .01	$ .05	Fontenot, Ray	85F	127	$ .01	$ .05
Fisk, Carlton	81F	224	$ .04	$ .75	Fontenot, Ray	85FU	42	$ .01	$ .05
Fisk, Carlton	82F	343	$ .03	$ .75	Fontenot, Ray	86F	369	$ .01	$ .05
Fisk, Carlton	82F	632	$ .04	$ .25	Foote, Barry	81F	313	$ .01	$ .05
Fisk, Carlton	83F	235	$ .03	$ .50	Foote, Barry	82F	34	$ .01	$ .05
Fisk, Carlton	83F	638	$ .31	$ .15	Ford, Curt	86F	648	$ .05	$ .30
Fisk, Carlton	84F	58	$ .03	$ .75	Ford, Curt	87F	294	$ .01	$ .05
Fisk, Carlton	85F	513	$ .03	$ .50	Ford, Curt	88F	32	$ .01	$ .05
Fisk, Carlton	86F	204	$ .01	$ .35	Ford, Curt	89F	450	$ .01	$ .05
Fisk, Carlton	86F	643	$ .01	$ .10	Ford, Curt	90F	557	$ .01	$ .04
Fisk, Carlton	87F	496	$ .01	$ .10	Ford, Dan	81F	273	$ .01	$ .05
Fisk, Carlton	88F	397	$ .01	$ .10	Ford, Dan	82F	458	$ .01	$ .05
Fisk, Carlton	89F	495	$ .01	$ .10	Ford, Dan	83F	61	$ .01	$ .05
Fisk, Carlton	90F	530	$ .01	$ .04	Ford, Dan	84F	9	$ .01	$ .06
Fisk, Carlton	91F	118	$ .01	$ .10	Ford, Dan	85F	178	$ .01	$ .05
Fitzgerald, Mike	84FU	37	$ .03	$ .20	Ford, Dave	81F	192	$ .01	$ .05
Fitzgerald, Mike	85F	78	$ .01	$ .05	Ford, Dave	82F	166	$ .01	$ .05
Fitzgerald, Mike	85FU	41	$ .01	$ .05	Forsch, Bob	81F	537	$ .01	$ .05
Fitzgerald, Mike	86F	247	$ .01	$ .05	Forsch, Bob	82F	112	$ .01	$ .05
Fitzgerald, Mike	87F	317	$ .01	$ .05	Forsch, Bob	83F	5	$ .01	$ .05
Fitzgerald, Mike	88F	182	$ .01	$ .05	Forsch, Bob	84F	322	$ .01	$ .06
Fitzgerald, Mike	89F	374	$ .01	$ .05	Forsch, Bob	84F	639	$ .01	$ .06
Fitzgerald, Mike	90F	343	$ .01	$ .04	Forsch, Bob	85F	223	$ .01	$ .05
Fitzgerald, Mike	91F	229	$ .01	$ .03	Forsch, Bob	86F	35	$ .01	$ .05
Flanagan, Mike	81F	171	$ .01	$ .10	Forsch, Bob	87F	295	$ .01	$ .05
Flanagan, Mike	82F	165	$ .01	$ .05	Forsch, Bob	88F	33	$ .01	$ .05
Flanagan, Mike	83F	60	$ .01	$ .05	Forsch, Bob	90F	231	$ .01	$ .04

Player	Year	No.	VG	EX/MT	Player	Year	No.	VG	EX/MT
Forsch, Ken	81F	52	$ .01	$ .05	Franco, Julio	89F	404	$ .01	$ .05
Forsch, Ken	82F	459	$ .01	$ .05	Franco, Julio	89FU	64	$ .01	$ .10
Forsch, Ken	83F	89	$ .01	$ .05	Franco, Julio	90F	296	$ .01	$ .04
Forsch, Ken	84F	517	$ .01	$ .06	Franco, Julio	91F	285	$ .01	$ .03
Forsch, Ken	85F	301	$ .01	$ .05	Francona, Terry	82F	188	$ .03	$ .20
Forsch, Ken	86F	155	$ .01	$ .05	Francona, Terry	83F	281	$ .01	$ .05
Forster, Terry	81F	119	$ .01	$ .05	Francona, Terry	84F	275	$ .01	$ .06
					Francona, Terry	85F	398	$ .01	$ .05
					Francona, Terry	86F	248	$ .01	$ .05
					Francona, Terry	86FU	43	$ .01	$ .05
					Francona, Terry	87F	564	$ .01	$ .05
					Fraser, Willie	87F	646	$ .40	$1.00
					Fraser, Willie	87FU	33	$ .01	$ .05
					Fraser, Willie	88F	490	$ .01	$ .05
					Fraser, Willie	89F	478	$ .01	$ .05
					Fraser, Willie	90F	133	$ .01	$ .04
					Fraser, Willie	91F	314	$ .01	$ .03
					Frazier, George	82F	35	$ .01	$ .05
					Frazier, George	83F	379	$ .01	$ .05
					Frazier, George	84F	123	$ .01	$ .06
					Frazier, George	84FU	40	$ .01	$ .10
					Frazier, George	85F	58	$ .01	$ .05
					Frazier, George	86F	370	$ .01	$ .05
					Frazier, George	87F	539	$ .01	$ .05
					Frazier, George	88F	9	$ .01	$ .05
					Freeman, Marvin	87F	651	$ .10	$ .40
					Freeman, Marvin	89F	566	$ .01	$ .05
					Fregosi, Jim	81F	274	$ .01	$ .05
					Frey, Steve	90F	649	$ .01	$ .04
					Frey, Steve	90FU	28	$ .01	$ .05
					Frey, Steve	91F	231	$ .01	$ .03
					Frias, Pepe	81F	134	$ .01	$ .05
					Frobel, Doug	85F	464	$ .01	$ .05
					Frohwirth, Todd	88F	301	$ .01	$ .15
					Frohwirth, Todd	89F	567	$ .01	$ .05
					Frost, Dave	81F	275	$ .01	$ .05

Terry Forster
DODGERS • PITCHER

Player	Year	No.	VG	EX/MT	Player	Year	No.	VG	EX/MT
Forster, Terry	82F	4	$ .01	$ .05	Frost, Dave	82F	460	$ .01	$ .05
Forster, Terry	83F	205	$ .01	$ .05	Frost, Dave	83F	111	$ .01	$ .05
Forster, Terry	84F	178	$ .01	$ .06	Fryman, Travis	90FU	96	$ .01	$1.25
Forster, Terry	85F	324	$ .01	$ .05	Fryman, Travis	91F	336	$ .01	$ .50
Forster, Terry	86F	514	$ .01	$ .05	Fryman, Woodie	81F	159	$ .01	$ .05
Forster, Terry	86FU	42	$ .01	$ .05	Fryman, Woodie	82F	189	$ .01	$ .05
Forster, Terry	87F	80	$ .01	$ .05	Fryman, Woodie	83F	283	$ .01	$ .05
Fossas, Tony	90F	323	$ .01	$ .10	Funderburk, Mark	86F	652	$ .01	$ .10
Foster, George	81F	202	$ .05	$ .30	Gaetti, Gary	83F	613	$ .50	$2.50
Foster, George	81F	216	$ .05	$ .30	Gaetti, Gary	84F	565	$ .25	$ .50
Foster, George	82F	66	$ .04	$ .25	Gaetti, Gary	85F	278	$ .05	$ .30
Foster, George	82F	630	$ .01	$ .10	Gaetti, Gary	86F	394	$ .01	$ .10
Foster, George	83F	542	$ .03	$ .20	Gaetti, Gary	87F	540	$ .01	$ .10
Foster, George	84F	584	$ .03	$ .20	Gaetti, Gary	88F	10	$ .01	$ .10
Foster, George	85F	79	$ .03	$ .20	Gaetti, Gary	89F	110	$ .01	$ .10
Foster, George	86F	80	$ .01	$ .15	Gaetti, Gary	90F	373	$ .01	$ .04
Fowlkes, Alan	83F	259	$ .01	$ .05	Gaetti, Gary	91F	609	$ .01	$ .03
Franco, John	84FU	39	$1.50	$7.00	Gaff, Brent	85F	80	$ .01	$ .05
Franco, John	85F	536	$ .25	$1.00	Gagne, Greg	85FU	43	$ .10	$ .30
Franco, John	86F	178	$ .01	$ .15	Gagne, Greg	86F	395	$ .01	$ .10
Franco, John	87F	202	$ .01	$ .10	Gagne, Greg	87F	541	$ .01	$ .05
Franco, John	87F	631	$ .01	$ .10	Gagne, Greg	88F	11	$ .01	$ .05
Franco, John	88F	234	$ .01	$ .10	Gagne, Greg	89F	111	$ .01	$ .05
Franco, John	88F	627	$ .01	$ .10	Gagne, Greg	90F	374	$ .01	$ .04
Franco, John	89F	162	$ .01	$ .10	Gagne, Greg	91F	610	$ .01	$ .03
Franco, John	90F	419	$ .01	$ .10	Gainey, Ty	88F	448	$ .01	$ .05
Franco, John	90FU	35	$ .01	$ .05	Galarraga, Andres	86F	647	$1.00	$2.25
Franco, John	91F	147	$ .01	$ .03	Galarraga, Andres	86FU	44	$ .10	$ .50
Franco, John	91F	712	$ .01	$ .10	Galarraga, Andres	87F	319	$ .05	$ .35
Franco, Julio	84F	542	$ .25	$1.75	Galarraga, Andres	88F	184	$ .10	$ .25
Franco, Julio	85F	448	$ .01	$ .20	Galarraga, Andres	89F	376	$ .01	$ .15
Franco, Julio	86F	586	$ .01	$ .25	Galarraga, Andres	89F	638	$ .01	$ .05
Franco, Julio	87F	251	$ .01	$ .10	Galarraga, Andres	90F	345	$ .01	$ .10
Franco, Julio	88F	609	$ .01	$ .10	Galarraga, Andres	91F	232	$ .01	$ .03

FLEER

Player	Year	No.	VG	EX/MT	Player	Year	No.	VG	EX/MT
Gale, Rich	81F	40	$ .01	$ .05	Garbey, Barbaro	84FU	42	$ .01	$ .10
Gale, Rich	82F	408	$ .01	$ .05	Garbey, Barbaro	85F	7	$ .01	$ .05
Gale, Rich	83F	260	$ .01	$ .05	Garbey, Barbaro	86F	225	$ .01	$ .10
Gale, Rich	84F	469	$ .01	$ .06	Garcia, Carlos	91F	37	$ .01	$ .10
Gale, Rich	84FU	41	$ .01	$ .10	Garcia, Damaso	81F	415	$ .03	$ .20
Gallagher, Dave	88FU	16	$ .01	$ .25	Garcia, Damaso	82F	613	$ .01	$ .05
Gallagher, Dave	89F	496	$ .01	$ .25	Garcia, Damaso	83F	427	$ .01	$ .05
Gallagher, Dave	90F	532	$ .01	$ .04	Garcia, Damaso	84F	153	$ .01	$ .06
Gallagher, Dave	91F	471	$ .01	$ .03	Garcia, Damaso	85F	104	$ .01	$ .05
Gallego, Mike	89F	8	$ .01	$ .05	Garcia, Damaso	86F	59	$ .01	$ .05
Gallego, Mike	90F	7	$ .01	$ .04	Garcia, Damaso	87F	226	$ .01	$ .05
Gallego, Mike	91F	7	$ .01	$ .03	Garcia, Damaso	90F	346	$ .01	$ .04
Gamble, Oscar	81F	98	$ .01	$ .05	Garcia, Kiko	81F	191	$ .01	$ .05
Gamble, Oscar	82F	36	$ .01	$ .05	Garcia, Kiko	82F	215	$ .01	$ .05
Gamble, Oscar	83F	380	$ .01	$ .05	Garcia, Kiko	83F	447	$ .01	$ .05
Gamble, Oscar	84F	124	$ .01	$ .06	Garcia, Kiko	84F	30	$ .01	$ .06
Gamble, Oscar	85FU	44	$ .01	$ .05	Garcia, Miguel	89F	647	$ .01	$ .20
Gant, Ron	88F	538	$ .01	$2.50	Gardenhire, Ron	83F	543	$ .01	$ .05
Gant, Ron	89F	590	$ .01	$ .50	Gardenhire, Ron	85F	81	$ .01	$ .05
Gant, Ron	90F	582	$ .01	$ .25	Gardner, Mark	90F	646	$ .01	$ .04
Gant, Ron	91F	688	$ .01	$ .10	Gardner, Mark	90FU	29	$ .01	$ .05
Gantner, Jim	81F	522	$ .01	$ .05	Gardner, Mark	91F	233	$ .01	$ .03
Gantner, Jim	82F	142	$ .01	$ .05	Gardner, Wes	88F	352	$ .01	$ .10
Gantner, Jim	83F	34	$ .01	$ .05	Gardner, Wes	89F	88	$ .01	$ .05
Gantner, Jim	84F	200	$ .01	$ .06	Gardner, Wes	90F	275	$ .01	$ .04
Gantner, Jim	85F	582	$ .01	$ .05	Gardner, Wes	91F	94	$ .01	$ .03
Gantner, Jim	86F	487	$ .01	$ .05	Garland, Wayne	81F	394	$ .01	$ .05
Gantner, Jim	87F	345	$ .01	$ .05	Garland, Wayne	82F	367	$ .01	$ .05
Gantner, Jim	88F	165	$ .01	$ .05	Garner, Phil	81F	364	$ .01	$ .05
Gantner, Jim	89F	186	$ .01	$ .05	Garner, Phil	82F	216	$ .01	$ .05
Gantner, Jim	90F	324	$ .01	$ .04	Garner, Phil	83F	448	$ .01	$ .05
Gantner, Jim	91F	584	$ .01	$ .03	Garner, Phil	84F	226	$ .01	$ .06
Garber, Gene	81F	249	$ .01	$ .05	Garner, Phil	85F	351	$ .01	$ .05
Garber, Gene	82F	434	$ .01	$ .05	Garner, Phil	86F	301	$ .01	$ .05
Garber, Gene	83F	136	$ .01	$ .05	Garner, Phil	87F	58	$ .01	$ .05
					Garrelts, Scott	86F	540	$ .01	$ .05
					Garrelts, Scott	87F	273	$ .01	$ .05
					Garrelts, Scott	88F	82	$ .01	$ .05
					Garrelts, Scott	89F	328	$ .01	$ .05
					Garrelts, Scott	90F	56	$ .01	$ .04
					Garrelts, Scott	91F	262	$ .01	$ .03
					Garvey, Steve	81F	110	$ .08	$ .75
					Garvey, Steve	81F	606	$ .07	$ .75
					Garvey, Steve	82F	5	$ .07	$ .50
					Garvey, Steve	83F	206	$ .06	$ .35
					Garvey, Steve	84F	300	$ .07	$ .50
					Garvey, Steve	84F	628	$ .04	$ .25
					Garvey, Steve	85F	32	$ .05	$ .40
					Garvey, Steve	85F	631	$ .05	$ .30
					Garvey, Steve	85F	633	$ .01	$ .10
					Garvey, Steve	86F	321	$ .05	$ .30
					Garvey, Steve	86F	640	$ .04	$ .25
					Garvey, Steve	87F	414	$ .04	$ .25
					Garvin, Jerry	81F	429	$ .01	$ .05
					Garvin, Jerry	82F	614	$ .01	$ .05
					Garvin, Jerry	83F	428	$ .01	$ .05
					Gedman, Rich	82F	294	$ .06	$ .35
					Gedman, Rich	83F	184	$ .01	$ .10
					Gedman, Rich	84F	398	$ .03	$ .10
					Gedman, Rich	85F	159	$ .01	$ .05
					Gedman, Rich	86F	349	$ .01	$ .10
					Gedman, Rich	86F	643	$ .01	$ .10
					Gedman, Rich	87F	35	$ .01	$ .05
					Gedman, Rich	88F	353	$ .01	$ .05
					Gedman, Rich	89F	89	$ .01	$ .05
					Gedman, Rich	90F	276	$ .01	$ .04
Garber, Gene	84F	179	$ .01	$ .06	Geisel, Dave	84F	154	$ .01	$ .06
Garber, Gene	85F	325	$ .01	$ .05	Gerber, Craig	86F	156	$ .01	$ .05
Garber, Gene	86F	515	$ .01	$ .05	Geren, Bob	89FU	48	$ .01	$ .25
Garber, Gene	87F	515	$ .01	$ .05	Geren, Bob	90F	442	$ .01	$ .10
Garber, Gene	88F	257	$ .01	$ .05					

FLEER

Gene Garber

PITCHER

Player	Year	No.	VG	EX/MT	Player	Year	No.	VG	EX/MT
Geren, Bob	91F	663	$ .01	$ .03	Gooden, Dwight	86F	641	$ .05	$ .30
Gerhart, Ken	87FU	34	$ .04	$ .25	Gooden, Dwight	87F	9	$ .35	$1.25
Gerhart, Ken	88F	559	$ .01	$ .05	Gooden, Dwight	87F	629	$ .10	$ .50
Gerhart, Ken	89F	609	$ .01	$ .05	Gooden, Dwight	87F	640	$ .10	$ .50
Geronimo, Cesar	82F	409	$ .01	$ .05	Gooden, Dwight	88F	135	$ .10	$ .90
Geronimo, Cesar	83F	112	$ .01	$ .05	Gooden, Dwight	89F	36	$ .01	$ .30
Gibson, Bob	84F	201	$ .01	$ .06	Gooden, Dwight	89F	635	$ .01	$ .15
Gibson, Bob	86F	488	$ .01	$ .05	Gooden, Dwight	90F	204	$ .01	$ .10
Gibson, Kirk	81F	481	$1.00	$3.50	Gooden, Dwight	91F	148	$ .01	$ .10
Gibson, Kirk	82F	267	$ .15	$ .75	Goodwin, Danny	82F	554	$ .01	$ .05
Gibson, Kirk	83F	329	$ .10	$ .40	Gordon, Don	89F	405	$ .01	$ .05
Gibson, Kirk	84F	80	$ .05	$ .40	Gordon, Tom	89F	284	$ .05	$2.00
Gibson, Kirk	85F	8	$ .05	$ .30	Gordon, Tom	90F	108	$ .01	$ .25
Gibson, Kirk	86F	226	$ .04	$ .25	Gordon, Tom	91F	559	$ .01	$ .03
Gibson, Kirk	87F	151	$ .03	$ .20	Gorman, Tom	85F	83	$ .01	$ .05
Gibson, Kirk	88F	55	$ .01	$ .10	Gorman, Tom	86F	82	$ .01	$ .05
Gibson, Kirk	88FU	93	$ .01	$ .15	Gossage, Goose 'Rich'	81F	89	$ .03	$ .25
Gibson, Kirk	89F	57	$ .01	$ .15	Gossage, Goose	82F	37	$ .04	$ .25
Gibson, Kirk	90F	393	$ .01	$ .04	Gossage, Goose	83F	381	$ .03	$ .20
Gibson, Kirk	91F	199	$ .01	$ .03	Gossage, Goose	84F	125	$ .03	$ .20
Gibson, Paul	88FU	26	$ .01	$ .15	Gossage, Goose	84FU	44	$ .12	$ .75
Gibson, Paul	89F	131	$ .01	$ .05	Gossage, Goose	85F	33	$ .03	$ .20
Gibson, Paul	90F	602	$ .01	$ .04	Gossage, Goose	85F	633	$ .01	$ .10
Gibson, Paul	91F	337	$ .01	$ .03	Gossage, Goose	86F	322	$ .03	$ .20
Gideon, Brett	88F	330	$ .01	$ .15	Gossage, Goose	87F	415	$ .01	$ .10
Giles, Brian	83F	544	$ .01	$ .05	Gossage, Goose	88F	583	$ .01	$ .10
Giles, Brian	84F	585	$ .01	$ .06	Gossage, Goose	88FU	76	$ .01	$ .05
Gilkey, Bernard	91F	633	$ .01	$ .35	Gossage, Goose	89F	425	$ .01	$ .05
Girardi, Joe	89F	644	$ .01	$ .25	Gott, Jim	84F	155	$ .01	$ .25
Girardi, Joe	90F	31	$ .01	$ .10	Gott, Jim	85F	105	$ .01	$ .05
Girardi, Joe	91F	421	$ .01	$ .03	Gott, Jim	85FU	45	$ .01	$ .05
Gladden, Dan	85F	607	$ .05	$ .50	Gott, Jim	86F	542	$ .01	$ .05
Gladden, Dan	86F	541	$ .01	$ .05	Gott, Jim	87FU	35	$ .01	$ .05
Gladden, Dan	87F	274	$ .01	$ .05	Gott, Jim	88FU	112	$ .01	$ .05
Gladden, Dan	87FU	36	$ .01	$ .05	Gott, Jim	89F	210	$ .01	$ .05
Gladden, Dan	88F	12	$ .01	$ .05	Gott, Jim	90F	466	$ .01	$ .04
Gladden, Dan	89F	112	$ .01	$ .05	Gott, Jim	91F	200	$ .01	$ .03
Gladden, Dan	90F	375	$ .01	$ .04	Gozzo, Mauro	90F	82	$ .01	$ .25
Gladden, Dan	91F	611	$ .01	$ .03	Grace, Mark	88F	641	$1.00	$7.50
Glavine, Tom	88F	539	$ .01	$ .40	Grace, Mark	88FU	77	$ .25	$3.50
Glavine, Tom	89F	591	$ .01	$ .05	Grace, Mark	89F	426	$ .10	$ .75
Glavine, Tom	90F	583	$ .01	$ .04	Grace, Mark	90F	32	$ .01	$ .20
Glavine, Tom	91F	689	$ .01	$ .03	Grace, Mark	91F	422	$ .01	$ .10
Gleaton, Jerry	88F	258	$ .01	$ .05	Graham, Dan	81F	189	$ .01	$ .05
Gleaton, Jerry	89F	282	$ .01	$ .05	Graham, Dan	82F	167	$ .01	$ .05
Gleaton, Jerry Don	91F	338	$ .01	$ .03	Grant, Mark	88F	584	$ .01	$ .05
Glynn, Ed	83F	408	$ .01	$ .05	Grant, Mark	89F	304	$ .01	$ .05
Goltz, Dave	81F	127	$ .01	$ .05	Grant, Mark	90F	156	$ .01	$ .04
Goltz, Dave	82F	6	$ .01	$ .05	Grant, Mark	91F	690	$ .01	$ .03
Goltz, Dave	83F	90	$ .01	$ .05	Gray, Gary	81F	402	$ .01	$ .05
Gomez, Leo	91F	472	$ .01	$ .35	Gray, Gary	82F	511	$ .01	$ .05
Gomez, Luis	81F	253	$ .01	$ .05	Gray, Gary	83F	480	$ .01	$ .05
Gonzales, Rene	88F	560	$ .01	$ .15	Gray, Jeff	91F	95	$ .01	$ .15
Gonzales, Rene	91F	473	$ .01	$ .03	Grebeck, Craig	90FU	85	$ .01	$ .10
Gonzalez, Denny	86F	608	$ .01	$ .05	Grebeck, Craig	91F	120	$ .01	$ .15
Gonzalez, German	89F	113	$ .01	$ .15	Green, David	83F	6	$ .01	$ .05
Gonzalez, German	90F	376	$ .01	$ .04	Green, David	84F	323	$ .01	$ .06
Gonzalez, Jose	87F	649	$ .04	$ .25	Green, David	85F	224	$ .01	$ .05
Gonzalez, Jose	90F	394	$ .01	$ .04	Green, David	85FU	46	$ .01	$ .05
Gonzalez, Juan	90F	297	$ .01	$1.00	Green, David	86F	543	$ .01	$ .05
Gonzalez, Juan	91F	286	$ .01	$ .25	Green, David	88F	34	$ .01	$ .05
Gonzalez, Julio	81F	73	$ .01	$ .05	Greene, Tommy	90F	584	$ .01	$ .25
Gonzalez, Luis	91F	507	$ .01	$ .25	Greenwell, Mike	87FU	37	$ .75	$2.00
Gonzalez, Orlando	81F	585	$ .01	$ .05	Greenwell, Mike	88F	354	$ .15	$ .75
Gooden, Dwight	84FU	43	$15.00	$100.00	Greenwell, Mike	88F	630	$ .10	$ .50
Gooden, Dwight	85F	82	$3.00	$12.00	Greenwell, Mike	89F	90	$ .01	$ .25
Gooden, Dwight	85F	634	$ .20	$1.00	Greenwell, Mike	90F	277	$ .01	$ .25
Gooden, Dwight	86F	81	$ .50	$2.50	Greenwell, Mike	90F	632	$ .01	$ .04
Gooden, Dwight	86F	626	$ .06	$ .50	Greenwell, Mike	91F	96	$ .01	$ .10
Gooden, Dwight	86F	638	$ .15	$ .75	Gregg, Tommy	88FU	113	.01	.30

FLEER

Player	Year	No.	VG	EX/MT	Player	Year	No.	VG	EX/MT
Gregg, Tommy	89F	592	$ .01	$ .05	Gross, Wayne	86F	276	$ .01	$ .05
Gregg, Tommy	90F	585	$ .01	$ .04	Grubb, John	81F	631	$ .01	$ .05
Gregg, Tommy	91F	691	$ .01	$ .03	Grubb, John	82F	317	$ .01	$ .05
Grich, Bobby	81F	269	$ .01	$ .05	Grubb, John	83F	567	$ .01	$ .05
Grich, Bobby	82F	461	$ .01	$ .05	Grubb, John	84F	81	$ .01	$ .06
Grich, Bobby	83F	91	$ .01	$ .05	Grubb, John	85F	9	$ .01	$ .05
Grich, Bobby	84F	518	$ .01	$ .06	Grubb, John	86F	227	$ .01	$ .05
Grich, Bobby	85F	302	$ .01	$ .05	Grubb, John	87F	152	$ .01	$ .05
Grich, Bobby	86F	157	$ .01	$ .05	Gruber, Kelly	85F	645	$ .75	$6.50
Grich, Bobby	87F	81	$ .01	$ .05	Gruber, Kelly	87F	227	$ .10	$ .50
Griffey, Jr., Ken	89F	548	$1.00	$10.00	Gruber, Kelly	88F	111	$ .10	$ .35
Griffey, Jr., Ken	90F	513	$ .01	$2.00	Gruber, Kelly	89F	234	$ .01	$ .25
Griffey, Jr., Ken	91F	450	$ .01	$1.00	Gruber, Kelly	90F	83	$ .01	$ .04
Griffey, Jr., Ken	91F	710	$ .01	$ .35	Gruber, Kelly	91F	175	$ .01	$ .10
Griffey, Ken	81F	199	$ .01	$ .10	Guante, Cecilio	84F	250	$ .01	$ .06
Griffey, Ken	82F	67	$ .01	$ .10	Guante, Cecilio	85F	465	$ .01	$ .05
Griffey, Ken	83F	382	$ .01	$ .10	Guante, Cecilio	86F	609	$ .01	$ .05
Griffey, Ken	84F	126	$ .03	$ .10	Guante, Cecilio	87F	610	$ .01	$ .05
Griffey, Ken	85F	128	$ .01	$ .10	Guante, Cecilio	87FU	38	$ .01	$ .05
Griffey, Ken	86F	105	$ .01	$ .10	Guante, Cecilio	89F	519	$ .01	$ .05
Griffey, Ken	87F	516	$ .01	$ .05	Guante, Cecilio	90F	298	$ .01	$ .04
Griffey, Ken	88F	540	$ .01	$ .05	Gubicza, Mark	84FU	46	$1.00	$5.00
Griffey, Ken	89FU	84	$ .01	$ .10	Gubicza, Mark	85F	201	$ .25	$1.00
Griffey, Ken	90F	420	$ .01	$ .05	Gubicza, Mark	86F	8	$ .01	$ .15
Griffin, Alfredo	81F	430	$ .01	$ .05	Gubicza, Mark	87F	368	$ .01	$ .05
Griffin, Alfredo	82F	615	$ .01	$ .05	Gubicza, Mark	88F	259	$ .01	$ .05
Griffin, Alfredo	83F	429	$ .01	$ .05	Gubicza, Mark	89F	283	$ .01	$ .10
Griffin, Alfredo	84F	156	$ .01	$ .06	Gubicza, Mark	90F	109	$ .01	$ .15
Griffin, Alfredo	85F	106	$ .01	$ .05	Gubicza, Mark	90F	633	$ .01	$ .04
Griffin, Alfredo	85FU	47	$ .01	$ .05	Gubicza, Mark	91F	560	$ .01	$ .03
Griffin, Alfredo	86F	417	$ .01	$ .05	Guerrero, Mario	81F	591	$ .01	$ .05
Griffin, Alfredo	87F	392	$ .01	$ .05	Guerrero, Pedro	82F	7	$ .10	$ .50
Griffin, Alfredo	88F	280	$ .01	$ .05	Guerrero, Pedro	83F	207	$ .05	$ .30
Griffin, Alfredo	88FU	94	$ .01	$ .05	Guerrero, Pedro	84F	100	$ .05	$ .35
Griffin, Alfredo	89F	58	$ .01	$ .05	Guerrero, Pedro	85F	370	$ .05	$ .30
Griffin, Alfredo	90F	395	$ .01	$ .04	Guerrero, Pedro	86F	130	$ .04	$ .25
Griffin, Alfredo	91F	201	$ .01	$ .03	Guerrero, Pedro	87F	440	$ .01	$ .10
Griffin, Mike	81F	107	$ .01	$ .05	Guerrero, Pedro	88F	514	$ .01	$ .10
Griffin, Mike	88F	561	$ .01	$ .05	Guerrero, Pedro	88F	623	$ .01	$ .05
Griffin, Tom	81F	456	$ .01	$ .05	Guerrero, Pedro	89F	451	$ .01	$ .05
Griffin, Tom	82F	389	$ .01	$ .05	Guerrero, Pedro	90F	250	$ .01	$ .10
Grimsley, Jason	90F	653	$ .01	$ .75	Guerrero, Pedro	91F	634	$ .01	$ .03
Grimsley, Jason	91F	396	$ .01	$ .03	Guetterman, Lee	86FU	45	$ .05	$ .30
Grimsley, Ross	81F	406	$ .01	$ .05	Guetterman, Lee	87F	585	$ .03	$ .20
Grissom, Marquis	90F	347	$ .01	$ .50	Guetterman, Lee	88F	374	$ .01	$ .05
Grissom, Marquis	91F	234	$ .01	$ .10	Guetterman, Lee	90F	443	$ .01	$ .04
Gross, Greg	81F	18	$ .01	$ .05	Guetterman, Lee	91F	664	$ .01	$ .03
Gross, Greg	82F	246	$ .01	$ .05	Guidry, Ron	81F	88	$ .04	$ .25
Gross, Greg	83F	162	$ .01	$ .05	Guidry, Ron	82F	38	$ .04	$ .25
Gross, Greg	84F	31	$ .01	$ .06	Guidry, Ron	83F	383	$ .01	$ .15
Gross, Greg	85F	251	$ .01	$ .05	Guidry, Ron	84F	127	$ .03	$ .15
Gross, Greg	86F	441	$ .01	$ .05	Guidry, Ron	85F	129	$ .03	$ .15
Gross, Greg	87F	173	$ .01	$ .05	Guidry, Ron	86F	106	$ .01	$ .10
Gross, Greg	88F	302	$ .01	$ .05	Guidry, Ron	87F	100	$ .03	$ .10
Gross, Greg	89F	568	$ .01	$ .05	Guidry, Ron	88F	207	$ .01	$ .10
Gross, Kevin	84F	32	$ .04	$ .25	Guillen, Ozzie	85FU	48	$ .25	$2.50
Gross, Kevin	85F	252	$ .01	$ .05	Guillen, Ozzie	86F	206	$ .15	$1.00
Gross, Kevin	86F	442	$ .01	$ .05	Guillen, Ozzie	87F	497	$ .01	$ .10
Gross, Kevin	87F	174	$ .01	$ .05	Guillen, Ozzie	88F	398	$ .01	$ .05
Gross, Kevin	88F	303	$ .01	$ .05	Guillen, Ozzie	89F	497	$ .01	$ .05
Gross, Kevin	89F	569	$ .01	$ .05	Guillen, Ozzie	90F	533	$ .01	$ .04
Gross, Kevin	89FU	96	$ .01	$ .05	Guillen, Ozzie	91F	121	$ .01	$ .03
Gross, Kevin	90F	348	$ .01	$ .04	Gulden, Brad	85F	537	$ .01	$ .05
Gross, Kevin	91F	235	$ .01	$ .03	Gullickson, Bill	81F	150	$ .06	$ .35
Gross, Wayne	81F	587	$ .01	$ .05	Gullickson, Bill	82F	190	$ .01	$ .10
Gross, Wayne	82F	90	$ .01	$ .05	Gullickson, Bill	83F	284	$ .01	$ .05
Gross, Wayne	83F	517	$ .01	$ .05	Gullickson, Bill	84F	276	$ .03	$ .10
Gross, Wayne	84F	444	$ .01	$ .06	Gullickson, Bill	85F	399	$ .01	$ .05
Gross, Wayne	84FU	45	$ .01	$ .10	Gullickson, Bill	86F	249	$ .01	$ .05
Gross, Wayne	85F	179	$ .01	$ .05	Gullickson, Bill	86FU	46	$ .01	$ .05

Player	Year	No.	VG	EX/MT	Player	Year	No.	VG	EX/MT
Gullickson, Bill	87F	203	$ .01	$ .05	Hamilton, Jeff	90F	396	$ .01	$ .04
Gullickson, Bill	88F	208	$ .01	$ .05	Hammaker, Atlee	83F	261	$ .01	$ .05
Gullickson, Bill	91F	508	$ .01	$ .03	Hammaker, Atlee	84F	373	$ .01	$ .06
Gulliver, Glenn	83F	62	$ .01	$ .05	Hammaker, Atlee	85F	608	$ .01	$ .05
Gumpert, Dave	87F	565	$ .01	$ .05	Hammaker, Atlee	86F	544	$ .01	$ .05
Gura, Larry	81F	38	$ .01	$ .05	Hammaker, Atlee	87FU	40	$ .01	$ .05
Gura, Larry	82F	410	$ .01	$ .05	Hammaker, Atlee	88F	83	$ .01	$ .05
Gura, Larry	83F	113	$ .01	$ .05	Hammaker, Atlee	89F	329	$ .01	$ .05
Gura, Larry	84F	347	$ .01	$ .06	Hammaker, Atlee	90F	57	$ .01	$ .04
Gura, Larry	85F	202	$ .01	$ .05	Hammaker, Atlee	91F	530	$ .01	$ .03
Guthrie, Mark	91F	612	$ .01	$ .03	Hammond, Chris	90F	421	$ .01	$ .10
Gutierrez, Jackie	84FU	47	$ .01	$ .10	Hammond, Chris	91F	65	$ .01	$ .03
Gutierrez, Jackie	85F	160	$ .01	$ .05	Hammond, Steve	83F	114	$ .01	$ .05
Gutierrez, Jackie	86F	350	$ .01	$ .05	Hancock, Garry	81F	229	$ .01	$ .05
Gutierrez, Jackie	86FU	47	$ .01	$ .05	Hancock, Garry	82F	295	$ .01	$ .05
Gutierrez, Jackie	87F	471	$ .01	$ .05	Hancock, Garry	84F	445	$ .01	$ .06
Guzman, Jose	86F	559	$ .04	$ .30					
Guzman, Jose	87F	124	$ .01	$ .05					
Guzman, Jose	88F	467	$ .01	$ .05					
Guzman, Jose	89F	520	$ .01	$ .05					
Gwynn, Chris	88F	647	$ .01	$ .30					
Gwynn, Chris	89F	59	$ .01	$ .10					
Gwynn, Chris	91F	202	$ .01	$ .03					
Gwynn, Tony	83F	360	$2.00	$14.00					
Gwynn, Tony	84F	301	$ .75	$4.00					
Gwynn, Tony	85F	34	$ .25	$1.75					
Gwynn, Tony	86F	323	$ .06	$1.00					
Gwynn, Tony	87F	416	$ .01	$ .50					
Gwynn, Tony	88F	585	$ .01	$ .25					
Gwynn, Tony	88F	631	$ .01	$ .10					
Gwynn, Tony	88F	634	$ .01	$ .10					
Gwynn, Tony	89F	305	$ .01	$ .25					
Gwynn, Tony	90F	157	$ .01	$ .20					
Gwynn, Tony	91F	529	$ .01	$ .10					
Haas, Moose	81F	516	$ .01	$ .05					
Haas, Moose	82F	143	$ .01	$ .05					
Haas, Moose	83F	35	$ .01	$ .05					
Haas, Moose	84F	202	$ .01	$ .06					
Haas, Moose	85F	583	$ .01	$ .05					
Haas, Moose	86F	489	$ .01	$ .05					
Haas, Moose	86FU	48	$ .01	$ .05					
Haas, Moose	87F	393	$ .01	$ .05					
Hairston, Jerry	83F	236	$ .01	$ .05					
Hairston, Jerry	84F	60	$ .01	$ .06					
Hairston, Jerry	85F	515	$ .01	$ .05					
Hairston, Jerry	86F	207	$ .01	$ .05	Hanna, Preston	81F	264	$ .01	$ .05
Hairston, Jerry	87F	498	$ .01	$ .05	Hanna, Preston	82F	435	$ .01	$ .05
Hall, Albert	85F	326	$ .01	$ .05	Hansen, Dave	90F	642	$ .01	$ .25
Hall, Albert	87FU	39	$ .01	$ .05	Hansen, Dave	90FU	21	$ .01	$ .10
Hall, Albert	88F	541	$ .01	$ .05	Hansen, Dave	91F	203	$ .01	$ .10
Hall, Albert	89F	593	$ .01	$ .05	Hanson, Erik	89F	549	$ .01	$ .75
Hall, Drew	89F	643	$ .01	$ .20	Hanson, Erik	90F	514	$ .01	$ .10
Hall, Drew	90F	299	$ .01	$ .04	Hanson, Erik	91F	451	$ .01	$ .10
Hall, Drew	91F	236	$ .01	$ .03	Hargesheimer, Alan	81F	457	$ .01	$ .05
Hall, Grady	89F	650	$ .01	$ .20	Hargrove, Mike	81F	387	$ .01	$ .05
Hall, Mel	84F	493	$ .03	$ .10	Hargrove, Mike	82F	368	$ .01	$ .05
Hall, Mel	85F	449	$ .01	$ .05	Hargrove, Mike	83F	409	$ .01	$ .05
Hall, Mel	86F	587	$ .01	$ .05	Hargrove, Mike	84F	543	$ .01	$ .06
Hall, Mel	87F	252	$ .01	$ .05	Hargrove, Mike	85F	450	$ .01	$ .05
Hall, Mel	88F	610	$ .01	$ .05	Hargrove, Mike	86F	588	$ .01	$ .05
Hall, Mel	89F	406	$ .01	$ .05	Harkey, Mike	89F	427	$ .01	$ .50
Hall, Mel	89FU	49	$ .01	$ .05	Harkey, Mike	90F	33	$ .01	$ .10
Hall, Mel	90F	444	$ .01	$ .04	Harkey, Mike	91F	423	$ .01	$ .03
Hall, Mel	91F	665	$ .01	$ .03	Harlow, Larry	81F	289	$ .01	$ .05
Hamilton, Darryl	88FU	38	$ .01	$ .15	Harlow, Larry	82F	462	$ .01	$ .05
Hamilton, Darryl	89F	187	$ .01	$ .15	Harnisch, Pete	90F	177	$ .01	$ .10
Hamilton, Darryl	90F	325	$ .01	$ .04	Harnisch, Pete	91F	474	$ .01	$ .03
Hamilton, Darryl	91F	585	$ .01	$ .03	Harper, Brian	85F	466	$ .01	$ .05
Hamilton, Jeff	88F	515	$ .01	$ .05	Harper, Brian	86F	36	$ .01	$ .05
Hamilton, Jeff	89F	60	$ .01	$ .05					

PRESTON HANNA
PITCHER

159

Player	Year	No.	VG	EX/MT	Player	Year	No.	VG	EX/MT
Harper, Brian	88FU	42	$ .01	$ .05	Hartley, Mike	90FU	22	$ .01	$ .05
Harper, Brian	89F	114	$ .01	$ .05	Hartley, Mike	91F	205	$ .01	$ .03
Harper, Brian	90F	377	$ .01	$ .04	Harvey, Bryan	88FU	14	$ .01	$ .25
Harper, Brian	91F	613	$ .01	$ .03	Harvey, Bryan	89F	479	$ .01	$ .25
Harper, Terry	83F	137	$ .01	$ .05	Harvey, Bryan	90F	134	$ .01	$ .04
Harper, Terry	84F	180	$ .01	$ .06	Harvey, Bryan	91F	315	$ .01	$ .03
Harper, Terry	85F	327	$ .01	$ .05	Haselman, Bill	91F	287	$ .01	$ .15
Harper, Terry	86F	516	$ .01	$ .05	Hassey, Ron	81F	405	$ .01	$ .05
Harper, Terry	87F	517	$ .01	$ .05	Hassey, Ron	82F	370	$ .01	$ .05
Harper, Terry	88F	331	$ .01	$ .05	Hassey, Ron	83F	411	$ .01	$ .05
Harrah, Toby	81F	389	$ .01	$ .05	Hassey, Ron	83F	642	$ .01	$ .05
Harrah, Toby	82F	369	$ .01	$ .05	Hassey, Ron	84F	545	$ .01	$ .05
Harrah, Toby	83F	410	$ .01	$ .05	Hassey, Ron	84FU	49	$ .01	$ .10
Harrah, Toby	83F	635	$ .01	$ .05	Hassey, Ron	85FU	50	$ .01	$ .05
Harrah, Toby	84F	544	$ .01	$ .06	Hassey, Ron	86F	107	$ .01	$ .05
Harrah, Toby	84FU	48	$ .01	$ .10	Hassey, Ron	87F	499	$ .01	$ .05
Harrah, Toby	85F	130	$ .01	$ .05	Hassey, Ron	88F	399	$ .01	$ .05
Harrah, Toby	85FU	49	$ .01	$ .05	Hassey, Ron	89F	9	$ .01	$ .05
Harrah, Toby	86F	560	$ .01	$ .05	Hassey, Ron	90F	8	$ .01	$ .04
Harrah, Toby	87F	125	$ .01	$ .05	Hassey, Ron	91F	8	$ .01	$ .03
Harris, Gene	89FU	58	$ .01	$ .15	Hassler, Andy	81F	290	$ .01	$ .05
Harris, Gene	90F	515	$ .01	$ .04	Hassler, Andy	82F	464	$ .01	$ .05
Harris, Gene	91F	452	$ .01	$ .03	Hassler, Andy	83F	92	$ .01	$ .05
Harris, Greg	83F	590	$ .01	$ .05	Hassler, Andy	84F	519	$ .01	$ .06
Harris, Greg	85F	35	$ .01	$ .05	Hatcher, Billy 'Bill'	85F	649	$1.00	$6.50
Harris, Greg	86F	561	$ .01	$ .05	Hatcher, Billy	86F	371	$ .03	$ .20
Harris, Greg	87F	126	$ .01	$ .05	Hatcher, Billy	86FU	49	$ .01	$ .05
					Hatcher, Billy	87F	59	$ .01	$ .05
					Hatcher, Billy	88F	449	$ .01	$ .05
					Hatcher, Billy	89F	359	$ .01	$ .05
					Hatcher, Billy	90F	467	$ .01	$ .04
					Hatcher, Billy	90FU	13	$ .01	$ .05
					Hatcher, Billy	91F	66	$ .01	$ .03
					Hatcher, Mickey	81F	135	$ .01	$ .05
					Hatcher, Mickey	83F	614	$ .01	$ .05
					Hatcher, Mickey	84F	566	$ .01	$ .06
					Hatcher, Mickey	85F	279	$ .01	$ .05
					Hatcher, Mickey	86F	396	$ .01	$ .05
					Hatcher, Mickey	87F	542	$ .01	$ .05
					Hatcher, Mickey	87FU	41	$ .01	$ .05
					Hatcher, Mickey	88F	516	$ .01	$ .05
					Hatcher, Mickey	90F	398	$ .01	$ .04
					Hatcher, Mickey	91F	206	$ .01	$ .03
					Hausman, Tom	81F	333	$ .01	$ .05
					Hausman, Tom	82F	526	$ .01	$ .05
					Havens, Brad	83F	615	$ .01	$ .05
					Havens, Brad	87F	472	$ .01	$ .05
					Havens, Brad	88F	517	$ .01	$ .05
					Havens, Brad	89F	408	$ .01	$ .05
					Hawkins, Andy	84F	302	$ .03	$ .35
					Hawkins, Andy	85F	36	$ .01	$ .10
					Hawkins, Andy	86F	324	$ .01	$ .05
					Hawkins, Andy	87F	417	$ .01	$ .05
					Hawkins, Andy	88F	586	$ .01	$ .05
					Hawkins, Andy	89F	307	$ .01	$ .05
					Hawkins, Andy	89FU	50	$ .01	$ .05
					Hawkins, Andy	90F	445	$ .01	$ .04
Harris, Greg	88F	468	$ .01	$ .05	Hawkins, Andy	91F	666	$ .01	$ .03
Harris, Greg	88FU	109	$ .01	$ .05	Hayban, John	88F	562	$ .01	$ .05
Harris, Greg W.	89F	306	$ .01	$ .05	Hayes, Ben	83F	591	$ .01	$ .05
Harris, Greg	89F	570	$ .01	$ .05	Hayes, Ben	84F	470	$ .01	$ .06
Harris, Greg W.	90F	158	$ .01	$ .10	Hayes, Charlie	89F	330	$ .01	$ .35
Harris, Greg	90FU	71	$ .01	$ .05	Hayes, Charlie	89FU	106	$ .01	$ .10
Harris, Greg	91F	97	$ .01	$ .03	Hayes, Charlie	90F	558	$ .01	$ .10
Harris, Greg W.	91F	531	$ .01	$ .03	Hayes, Charlie	91F	397	$ .01	$ .03
Harris, John	82F	463	$ .01	$ .05	Hayes, Von	82F	371	$ .15	$1.00
Harris, Lenny	89F	645	$ .05	$ .25	Hayes, Von	83F	412	$ .03	$ .20
Harris, Lenny	90F	397	$ .01	$ .10	Hayes, Von	84F	33	$ .03	$ .20
Harris, Lenny	91F	204	$ .01	$ .03	Hayes, Von	85F	253	$ .03	$ .20
Hartley, Mike	90F	651	$ .01	$ .04	Hayes, Von	86F	443	$ .01	$ .10

Greg Harris
PITCHER

Player	Year	No.	VG	EX/MT	Player	Year	No.	VG	EX/MT
Hayes, Von	87F	175	$ .01	$ .10	Henderson, Rickey	85F	629	$ .05	$ .75
Hayes, Von	88F	304	$ .01	$ .10	Henderson, Rickey	85FU	51	$ .15	$4.25
Hayes, Von	89F	571	$ .01	$ .05	Henderson, Rickey	86F	108	$ .07	$2.00
Hayes, Von	90F	559	$ .01	$ .04	Henderson, Rickey	87F	101	$ .15	$1.75
Hayes, Von	91F	398	$ .01	$ .03	Henderson, Rickey	88F	209	$ .01	$1.00
Hayward, Ray	88FU	63	$ .01	$ .05	Henderson, Rickey	89F	254	$ .01	$ .50
Hayward, Ray	89F	521	$ .01	$ .05	Henderson, Rickey	89FU	54	$ .01	$ .75
Hearn, Ed	87F	10	$ .01	$ .10	Henderson, Rickey	90F	10	$ .01	$ .25
Heath, Mike	81F	583	$ .01	$ .05	Henderson, Rickey	91F	10	$ .01	$ .20
Heath, Mike	82F	91	$ .01	$ .05	Henderson, Steve	81F	321	$ .01	$ .05
Heath, Mike	83F	518	$ .01	$ .05	Henderson, Steve	82F	597	$ .01	$ .05
Heath, Mike	84F	446	$ .01	$ .06	Henderson, Steve	83F	496	$ .01	$ .05
Heath, Mike	85F	424	$ .01	$ .05	Henderson, Steve	84F	612	$ .01	$ .06
Heath, Mike	86F	418	$ .01	$ .05	Henderson, Steve	85F	490	$ .01	$ .05
Heath, Mike	86FU	50	$ .01	$ .05	Henderson, Steve	85FU	52	$ .01	$ .05
Heath, Mike	87FU	42	$ .01	$ .05	Henderson, Steve	86F	419	$ .01	$ .05
Heath, Mike	88F	56	$ .01	$ .05	Hendrick, George	81F	542	$ .01	$ .05
Heath, Mike	89F	130	$ .01	$ .15	Hendrick, George	82F	113	$ .01	$ .05
Heath, Mike	90F	603	$ .01	$ .04	Hendrick, George	83F	7	$ .01	$ .05
Heath, Mike	91F	339	$ .01	$ .03	Hendrick, George	84F	324	$ .01	$ .06
Heathcock, Jeff	86F	302	$ .01	$ .05	Hendrick, George	85F	225	$ .01	$ .05
Heathcock, Jeff	88F	450	$ .01	$ .05	Hendrick, George	85FU	53	$ .01	$ .05
Heaton, Neal	84F	546	$ .04	$ .50	Hendrick, George	86F	158	$ .01	$ .05
Heaton, Neal	85F	451	$ .01	$ .05	Hendrick, George	87F	82	$ .01	$ .05
Heaton, Neal	86F	589	$ .01	$ .05	Hengel, Dave	88F	375	$ .01	$ .20
Heaton, Neal	87F	543	$ .01	$ .05	Henke, Tom	86F	60	$ .01	$ .10
Heaton, Neal	87FU	43	$ .01	$ .05	Henke, Tom	87F	228	$ .01	$ .05
Heaton, Neal	88F	185	$ .01	$ .05	Henke, Tom	88F	112	$ .01	$ .05
Heaton, Neal	89F	377	$ .01	$ .05	Henke, Tom	89F	235	$ .01	$ .05
Heaton, Neal	89FU	113	$ .01	$ .05	Henke, Tom	90F	84	$ .01	$ .04
Heaton, Neal	90F	468	$ .01	$ .04	Henke, Tom	91F	176	$ .01	$ .03
Heaton, Neal	91F	38	$ .01	$ .03	Henneman, Mike	87FU	44	$ .05	$ .30
Heaverlo, Dave	81F	594	$ .01	$ .05	Henneman, Mike	88F	57	$ .01	$ .10
Hebner, Richie	81F	474	$ .01	$ .05	Henneman, Mike	89F	134	$ .01	$ .05
Hebner, Richie	82F	268	$ .01	$ .05	Henneman, Mike	90F	604	$ .01	$ .04
Hebner, Richie	83F	307	$ .01	$ .05	Henneman, Mike	91F	340	$ .01	$ .03
Hebner, Richie	84F	251	$ .01	$ .06	Henry, Dwayne	86F	562	$ .01	$ .10
Hebner, Richie	84FU	50	$ .01	$ .10	Henry, Dwayne	91F	692	$ .01	$ .03
Hebner, Richie	85F	59	$ .01	$ .05	Hernandez, Carlos	91F	207	$ .01	$ .10
Heep, Danny	81F	72	$ .01	$ .20	Hernandez, Guillermo	89F	135	$ .01	$ .05
Heep, Danny	82F	217	$ .01	$ .05	Hernandez, Guillermo	90F	605	$ .01	$ .04
Heep, Danny	83F	449	$ .01	$ .05	Hernandez, Keith	81F	545	$ .05	$ .30
Heep, Danny	84F	586	$ .01	$ .06	Hernandez, Keith	82F	114	$ .05	$ .30
Heep, Danny	85F	84	$ .01	$ .05	Hernandez, Keith	83F	8	$ .05	$ .40
Heep, Danny	86F	83	$ .01	$ .05	Hernandez, Keith	84F	587	$ .05	$ .30
Heep, Danny	87F	11	$ .01	$ .05	Hernandez, Keith	85F	85	$ .05	$ .30
Heep, Danny	89F	61	$ .01	$ .05	Hernandez, Keith	86F	84	$ .05	$ .30
Heep, Danny	90F	278	$ .01	$ .04	Hernandez, Keith	87F	12	$ .05	$ .30
Heinkel, Don	88FU	27	$ .01	$ .15	Hernandez, Keith	87F	629	$ .10	$ .50
Heinkel, Don	89F	133	$ .01	$ .15	Hernandez, Keith	87F	637	$ .06	$ .35
Hemond, Scott	90F	646	$ .01	$ .04	Hernandez, Keith	88F	136	$ .01	$ .20
Henderson, Dave	83F	481	$ .10	$1.00	Hernandez, Keith	88F	639	$ .01	$ .15
Henderson, Dave	84F	611	$ .10	$ .75	Hernandez, Keith	89F	37	$ .01	$ .15
Henderson, Dave	85F	489	$ .05	$ .35	Hernandez, Keith	90F	205	$ .01	$ .10
Henderson, Dave	86F	465	$ .01	$ .25	Hernandez, Keith	91F	368	$ .01	$ .03
Henderson, Dave	87F	36	$ .01	$ .25	Hernandez, Willie	81F	310	$ .03	$ .20
Henderson, Dave	88F	84	$ .01	$ .15	Hernandez, Willie	83F	497	$ .01	$ .10
Henderson, Dave	88FU	53	$ .01	$ .15	Hernandez, Willie	84F	34	$ .03	$ .10
Henderson, Dave	89F	10	$ .01	$ .10	Hernandez, Willie	84FU	51	$ .10	$ .50
Henderson, Dave	90F	9	$ .01	$ .10	Hernandez, Willie	85F	10	$ .01	$ .10
Henderson, Dave	91F	9	$ .01	$ .03	Hernandez, Willie	86F	228	$ .01	$ .10
Henderson, Rickey	81F	351	$ .50	$15.00	Hernandez, Willie	87F	153	$ .01	$ .05
Henderson, Rickey	81F	574	$ .75	$18.00	Hernandez, Willie	88F	58	$ .01	$ .05
Henderson, Rickey	82F	92	$ .25	$5.00	Hernandez, Xavier	91F	509	$ .01	$ .03
Henderson, Rickey	82F	643	$ .05	$2.50	Herndon, Larry	81F	451	$ .01	$ .05
Henderson, Rickey	83F	519	$ .10	$3.50	Herndon, Larry	82F	390	$ .01	$ .05
Henderson, Rickey	83F	639	$ .05	$1.50	Herndon, Larry	83F	330	$ .01	$ .05
Henderson, Rickey	83F	646	$ .06	$1.50	Herndon, Larry	84F	82	$ .01	$ .06
Henderson, Rickey	84F	447	$ .50	$6.00	Herndon, Larry	85F	11	$ .01	$ .05
Henderson, Rickey	85F	425	$ .07	$3.00	Herndon, Larry	86F	229	$ .01	$ .05

FLEER

Player	Year	No.	VG	EX/MT
Herndon, Larry	87F	154	$ .01	$ .05
Herndon, Larry	88F	59	$ .01	$ .05
Herr, Tom	81F	550	$ .01	$ .10
Herr, Tom	82F	115	$ .01	$ .05
Herr, Tom	83F	9	$ .01	$ .05
Herr, Tom	84F	325	$ .01	$ .06
Herr, Tom	85F	226	$ .01	$ .05
Herr, Tom	86F	37	$ .01	$ .05
Herr, Tom	87F	296	$ .01	$ .05
Herr, Tom	88F	35	$ .01	$ .05
Herr, Tom	88FU	43	$ .01	$ .05
Herr, Tom	89F	115	$ .01	$ .05
Herr, Tommy	89FU	107	$ .01	$ .05
Herr, Tom	90F	560	$ .01	$ .04
Herr, Tom	91F	149	$ .01	$ .03
Hershiser, Orel	85F	371	$1.00	$5.00
Hershiser, Orel	86F	131	$ .25	$1.00
Hershiser, Orel	87F	441	$ .05	$ .40
Hershiser, Orel	88F	518	$ .01	$ .20
Hershiser, Orel	88F	632	$ .01	$ .10
Hershiser, Orel	89F	62	$ .01	$ .25
Hershiser, Orel	90F	399	$ .01	$ .10
Hershiser, Orel	91F	208	$ .01	$ .03
Hesketh, Joe	85F	652	$2.00	$12.50
Hesketh, Joe	86F	250	$ .01	$ .05
Hesketh, Joe	87F	320	$ .01	$ .05
Hesketh, Joe	89F	378	$ .01	$ .05
Hesketh, Joe	90F	349	$ .01	$ .04
Hetzel, Eric	90F	279	$ .01	$ .10
Hibbard, Greg	90F	534	$ .01	$ .10
Hibbard, Greg	91F	122	$ .01	$ .10
Hickey, Kevin	82F	344	$ .01	$ .05
Hickey, Kevin	83F	237	$ .01	$ .05
Hickey, Kevin	84F	61	$ .01	$ .06
Hickey, Kevin	89FU	4	$ .01	$ .05
Hickey, Kevin	90F	178	$ .01	$ .04
Hickey, Kevin	91F	475	$ .01	$ .03
Higuera, Ted "Teddy"	85FU	54	$ .40	$2.00
Higuera, Ted	86F	490	$ .20	$1.25
Higuera, Ted	87F	346	$ .03	$ .20
Higuera, Ted	88F	166	$ .01	$ .10
Higuera, Ted	89F	188	$ .01	$ .05
Higuera, Ted	90F	326	$ .01	$ .04
Higuera, Ted	91F	586	$ .01	$ .03
Hill, Don "Donnie"	84F	448	$ .01	$ .06
Hill, Donnie	85F	426	$ .01	$ .05
Hill, Donnie	86F	420	$ .01	$ .05
Hill, Donnie	87F	394	$ .01	$ .05
Hill, Donnie	88F	400	$ .01	$ .05
Hill, Donnie	91F	316	$ .01	$ .03
Hill, Glenallen	90FU	127	$ .01	$ .10
Hill, Glenallen	91F	177	$ .01	$ .03
Hill, Ken	89F	652	$ .01	$ .45
Hill, Ken	89FU	119	$ .01	$ .10
Hill, Ken	90F	251	$ .01	$ .04
Hill, Ken	91F	635	$ .01	$ .03
Hill, Marc	84F	62	$ .01	$ .06
Hill, Marc	85F	516	$ .01	$ .05
Hillegas, Shawn	88F	519	$ .01	$ .15
Hillegas, Shawn	89F	498	$ .01	$ .05
Hillegas, Shawn	90F	535	$ .01	$ .04
Hinzo, Tommy	88F	611	$ .01	$ .10
Hisle, Larry	81F	509	$ .01	$ .05
Hisle, Larry	82F	144	$ .01	$ .05
Hobson, Butch	81F	227	$ .01	$ .05
Hobson, Butch	82F	465	$ .01	$ .05
Hodge, Ed	84FU	52	$ .01	$ .10
Hodge, Ed	85F	280	$ .01	$ .05
Hodges, Ron	82F	527	$ .01	$ .05
Hodges, Ron	83F	545	$ .01	$ .05

Player	Year	No.	VG	EX/MT
Hodges, Ron	84F	588	$ .01	$ .06
Hoffman, Glenn	81F	237	$ .01	$ .05
Hoffman, Glenn	82F	296	$ .01	$ .05
Hoffman, Glenn	83F	185	$ .01	$ .05
Hoffman, Glenn	84F	399	$ .01	$ .06
Hoffman, Glenn	86F	351	$ .01	$ .05
Hoffman, Guy	86FU	51	$ .01	$ .05
Hoffman, Guy	87F	566	$ .01	$ .05
Hoffman, Guy	87FU	45	$ .01	$ .05
Hoffman, Guy	88F	235	$ .01	$ .05
Hoiles, Chris	90FU	65	$ .01	$ .25
Hoiles, Chris	91F	476	$ .01	$ .10
Holland, Al	81F	445	$ .01	$ .10
Holland, Al	82F	391	$ .01	$ .05

Al Holland
PITCHER

Player	Year	No.	VG	EX/MT
Holland, Al	83F	262	$ .01	$ .05
Holland, Al	84F	35	$ .01	$ .06
Holland, Al	85F	254	$ .01	$ .05
Holland, Al	85F	637	$ .01	$ .05
Holland, Al	85FU	55	$ .01	$ .05
Holland, Al	86F	159	$ .01	$ .05
Hollins, Dave	90FU	43	$ .01	$ .15
Hollins, David	91F	399	$ .01	$ .10
Holman, Brian	88FU	100	$ .05	$ .40
Holman, Brian	89F	379	$ .01	$ .25
Holman, Brian	90F	516	$ .01	$ .10
Holman, Brian	91F	453	$ .01	$ .03
Holman, Scott	84F	589	$ .01	$ .06
Holman, Shawn	90F	606	$ .01	$ .10
Holton, Brian	89F	63	$ .01	$ .05
Holton, Brian	89FU	5	$ .01	$ .05
Holton, Brian	90F	179	$ .01	$ .04
Honeycutt, Rick	82F	318	$ .01	$ .05
Honeycutt, Rick	83F	568	$ .01	$ .05
Honeycutt, Rick	84F	101	$ .01	$ .06
Honeycutt, Rick	85F	372	$ .01	$ .05
Honeycutt, Rick	86F	132	$ .01	$ .05
Honeycutt, Rick	87F	442	$ .01	$ .05
Honeycutt, Rick	88F	281	$ .01	$ .05
Honeycutt, Rick	89F	11	$ .01	$ .05
Honeycutt, Rick	90F	11	$ .01	$ .04

Player	Year	No.	VG	EX/MT	Player	Year	No.	VG	EX/MT
Honeycutt, Rick	91F	11	$ .01	$ .03	Howell, Jay	88FU	95	$ .01	$ .05
Hood, Don	81F	547	$ .01	$ .05	Howell, Jay	89F	64	$ .01	$ .05
Hood, Don	83F	115	$ .01	$ .05	Howell, Jay	90F	400	$ .01	$ .04
Hood, Don	84F	348	$ .01	$ .06	Howell, Jay	91F	209	$ .01	$ .03
Hooton, Burt	81F	113	$ .01	$ .05	Howell, Ken	85F	374	$ .03	$ .20
Hooton, Burt	82F	8	$ .01	$ .05	Howell, Ken	86F	133	$ .01	$ .05
Hooton, Burt	83F	208	$ .01	$ .05	Howell, Ken	87F	443	$ .01	$ .05
Hooton, Burt	84F	102	$ .01	$ .06	Howell, Ken	88F	520	$ .01	$ .05
Hooton, Burt	85F	373	$ .01	$ .05	Howell, Ken	89FU	108	$ .01	$ .05
Hooton, Burt	85FU	56	$ .01	$ .10	Howell, Ken	90F	561	$ .01	$ .04
Hooton, Burt	86F	563	$ .01	$ .05	Howell, Ken	91F	400	$ .01	$ .03
Horn, Sam	88F	355	$ .05	$ .25	Howell, Roy	81F	417	$ .01	$ .05
Horn, Sam	91F	477	$ .01	$ .03	Howell, Roy	82F	145	$ .01	$ .05
Horner, Bob	81F	244	$ .05	$ .30	Howell, Roy	83F	36	$ .01	$ .05
Horner, Bob	82F	436	$ .05	$ .30	Howell, Roy	84F	203	$ .01	$ .06
Horner, Bob	83F	138	$ .05	$ .30	Howitt, Dann	90F	644	$ .01	$ .04
Horner, Bob	84F	181	$ .05	$ .30	Howser, Dick	81F	84	$ .03	$ .20
Horner, Bob	85F	328	$ .05	$ .30	Hoyt, LaMarr	82F	345	$ .01	$ .05
Horner, Bob	86F	517	$ .03	$ .20	Hoyt, LaMarr	83F	238	$ .01	$ .05
Horner, Bob	86F	635	$ .05	$ .30	Hoyt, LaMarr	84F	63	$ .03	$ .10
Horner, Bob	87F	518	$ .03	$ .20	Hoyt, LaMarr	85F	517	$ .01	$ .05
Horner, Bob	87F	632	$ .01	$ .05	Hoyt, LaMarr	85FU	58	$ .01	$ .10
Horner, Bob	88FU	120	$ .01	$ .10	Hoyt, LaMarr	86F	325	$ .01	$ .05
Horner, Bob	89F	452	$ .01	$ .05	Hoyt, LaMarr	87F	418	$ .01	$ .05
Horton, Ricky	84FU	53	$ .12	$ .60	Hrabosky, Al	81F	262	$ .01	$ .05
Horton, Ricky	85F	227	$ .05	$ .30	Hrabosky, Al	82F	438	$ .01	$ .10
Horton, Ricky	86F	38	$ .01	$ .05	Hrbek, Kent	83F	616	$ .25	$1.00
Horton, Ricky	87F	297	$ .01	$ .05	Hrbek, Kent	83F	633	$ .03	$ .20
Horton, Ricky	88F	36	$ .01	$ .05	Hrbek, Kent	84F	567	$ .06	$ .50
Horton, Ricky	88FU	17	$ .01	$ .05	Hrbek, Kent	85F	281	$ .05	$ .30
Hostetler, Dave	83F	569	$ .01	$ .05	Hrbek, Kent	86F	397	$ .03	$ .20
Hostetler, Dave	84F	418	$ .01	$ .06	Hrbek, Kent	87F	544	$ .03	$ .20
Hough, Charlie	82F	319	$ .01	$ .05	Hrbek, Kent	88F	13	$ .01	$ .10
Hough, Charlie	83F	570	$ .01	$ .05	Hrbek, Kent	89F	116	$ .01	$ .10
Hough, Charlie	84F	419	$ .01	$ .06	Hrbek, Kent	90F	378	$ .01	$ .04
Hough, Charlie	85F	558	$ .01	$ .05	Hrbek, Kent	91F	614	$ .01	$ .03
Hough, Charlie	86F	564	$ .01	$ .05	Hubbard, Glenn	81F	260	$ .01	$ .05
Hough, Charlie	87F	127	$ .01	$ .05	Hubbard, Glenn	82F	437	$ .01	$ .05
Hough, Charlie	87F	641	$ .01	$ .05	Hubbard, Glenn	83F	139	$ .01	$ .05
Hough, Charlie	88F	469	$ .01	$ .05	Hubbard, Glenn	84F	182	$ .01	$ .06
Hough, Charlie	89F	522	$ .01	$ .05	Hubbard, Glenn	85F	329	$ .01	$ .05
Hough, Charlie	90F	300	$ .01	$ .04	Hubbard, Glenn	86F	518	$ .01	$ .05
Hough, Charlie	91F	288	$ .01	$ .03	Hubbard, Glenn	87F	519	$ .01	$ .05
Householder, Paul	81F	217	$ .01	$ .05	Hubbard, Glenn	88F	542	$ .01	$ .05
Householder, Paul	82F	68	$ .01	$ .05	Hubbard, Glenn	89F	12	$ .01	$ .05
Householder, Paul	83F	592	$ .01	$ .05	Hudler, Rex	88FU	101	$ .01	$ .05
Householder, Paul	84F	471	$ .01	$ .06	Hudler, Rex	89F	380	$ .01	$ .05
Householder, Paul	86F	491	$ .01	$ .05	Hudson, Charles	84F	36	$ .04	$ .25
Howard, Thomas	91F	532	$ .01	$ .10	Hudson, Charles	85F	255	$ .01	$ .05
Howard, Tom	90FU	56	$ .01	$ .15	Hudson, Charles	86F	444	$ .01	$ .05
Howe, Art	81F	51	$ .01	$ .05	Hudson, Charles	87F	176	$ .01	$ .05
Howe, Art	82F	218	$ .01	$ .05	Hudson, Charles	87FU	46	$ .01	$ .05
Howe, Art	83F	450	$ .01	$ .05	Hudson, Charles	88F	210	$ .01	$ .05
Howe, Art	84F	227	$ .01	$ .06	Huff, Mike	90F	649	$ .01	$ .04
Howe, Art	84FU	54	$ .01	$ .10	Huff, Mike	91F	210	$ .01	$ .03
Howe, Art	85F	228	$ .01	$ .05	Hughes, Keith	88F	305	$ .01	$ .15
Howe, Steve	81F	136	$ .01	$ .10	Huismann, Mark	85F	203	$ .01	$ .05
Howe, Steve	82F	9	$ .01	$ .05	Huismann, Mark	87F	586	$ .01	$ .05
Howe, Steve	83F	209	$ .01	$ .05	Hulett, Tim	85FU	59	$ .01	$ .10
Howe, Steve	84F	103	$ .01	$ .06	Hulett, Tim	86F	208	$ .01	$ .05
Howell, Jack	87F	83	$ .01	$ .05	Hulett, Tim	87F	500	$ .01	$ .05
Howell, Jack	88F	491	$ .01	$ .05	Hulett, Tim	90FU	66	$ .01	$ .05
Howell, Jack	89F	480	$ .01	$ .05	Hulett, Tim	91F	478	$ .01	$ .03
Howell, Jack	90F	135	$ .01	$ .04	Hume, Tom	81F	211	$ .01	$ .05
Howell, Jay	84F	128	$ .01	$ .06	Hume, Tom	82F	69	$ .01	$ .05
Howell, Jay	85F	131	$ .01	$ .05	Hume, Tom	83F	593	$ .01	$ .05
Howell, Jay	85FU	57	$ .01	$ .10	Hume, Tom	84F	472	$ .01	$ .06
Howell, Jay	86F	421	$ .01	$ .05	Hume, Tom	85F	538	$ .01	$ .05
Howell, Jay	87F	395	$ .01	$ .05	Hume, Tom	86F	179	$ .01	$ .05
Howell, Jay	88F	282	$ .01	$ .05	Hume, Tom	86FU	52	$ .01	$ .05

FLEER

Player	Year	No.	VG	EX/MT	Player	Year	No.	VG	EX/MT
Hume, Tom	87F	177	$ .01	$ .05	Jackson, Darrin	89F	428	$ .01	$ .05
Hume, Tom	88F	236	$ .01	$ .05	Jackson, Darrin	90F	160	$ .01	$ .04
Hundley, Todd	90FU	36	$ .01	$ .20	Jackson, Grant	81F	378	$ .01	$ .05
Hundley, Todd	91F	150	$ .01	$ .15	Jackson, Grant	82F	191	$ .01	$ .05
Hurdle, Clint	81F	45	$ .01	$ .05	Jackson, Mike	87FU	48	$ .03	$ .20
Hurdle, Clint	82F	411	$ .01	$ .05	Jackson, Mike	88F	306	$ .01	$ .10
Hurdle, Clint	87F	298	$ .01	$ .05	Jackson, Mike	88FU	60	$ .01	$ .05
Hurst, Bruce	82F	297	$ .04	$ .25	Jackson, Mike	89F	550	$ .01	$ .05
Hurst, Bruce	83F	186	$ .01	$ .10	Jackson, Mike	90F	517	$ .01	$ .04
Hurst, Bruce	84F	400	$ .03	$ .10	Jackson, Mike	91F	454	$ .01	$ .03
Hurst, Bruce	85F	161	$ .01	$ .05	Jackson, Reggie	81F	79	$ .12	$1.25
Hurst, Bruce	86F	352	$ .01	$ .10	Jackson, Reggie	81F	650	$ .20	$1.00
Hurst, Bruce	87F	37	$ .01	$ .10	Jackson, Reggie	82F	39	$ .08	$1.00
Hurst, Bruce	88F	356	$ .01	$ .05	Jackson, Reggie	82F	646	$ .10	$ .50
Hurst, Bruce	89F	91	$ .01	$ .05	Jackson, Reggie	83F	93	$ .07	$ .75
Hurst, Bruce	89FU	124	$ .01	$ .05	Jackson, Reggie	83F	640	$ .04	$ .25
Hurst, Bruce	90F	159	$ .01	$ .04	Jackson, Reggie	83F	645	$ .06	$ .35
Hurst, Bruce	91F	533	$ .01	$ .03	Jackson, Reggie	84F	520	$ .09	$1.00
Huson, Jeff	90F	350	$ .01	$ .10	Jackson, Reggie	85F	303	$ .08	$ .75
Huson, Jeff	90FU	123	$ .01	$ .05	Jackson, Reggie	85F	639	$ .07	$ .50
Huson, Jeff	91F	289	$ .01	$ .03	Jackson, Reggie	86F	160	$ .06	$ .35
Hutton, Tommy	81F	164	$ .01	$ .05	Jackson, Reggie	87F	84	$ .05	$ .30
Incaviglia, Pete	86FU	53	$ .25	$1.00	Jackson, Reggie	87FU	49	$ .07	$ .50
Incaviglia, Pete	87F	128	$ .25	$1.00	Jackson, Reggie	88F	283	$ .01	$ .25
Incaviglia, Pete	87F	625	$ .10	$1.00	Jackson, Ron	81F	557	$ .01	$ .05
Incaviglia, Pete	88F	470	$ .01	$ .20	Jackson, Ron	82F	269	$ .01	$ .05
Incaviglia, Pete	89F	523	$ .01	$ .10	Jackson, Ron	83F	94	$ .01	$ .05
Incaviglia, Pete	90F	301	$ .01	$ .10	Jackson, Ron	84F	521	$ .01	$ .06
Incaviglia, Pete	91F	290	$ .01	$ .03	Jackson, Roy Lee	83F	431	$ .01	$ .05
Innis, Jeff	88FU	105	$ .01	$ .20	Jackson, Roy Lee	84F	158	$ .01	$ .06
Innis, Jeff	90F	206	$ .01	$ .10	Jackson, Roy Lee	85F	108	$ .01	$ .05
Iorg, Dane	81F	543	$ .01	$ .05	Jackson, Roy Lee	86F	326	$ .01	$ .05
Iorg, Dane	82F	116	$ .01	$ .05	Jackson, Roy Lee	87F	545	$ .01	$ .05
Iorg, Dane	83F	10	$ .01	$ .05	Jacoby, Brook	84FU	56	$ .25	$3.00
Iorg, Dane	84F	326	$ .01	$ .06	Jacoby, Brook	85F	452	$ .05	$ .30
Iorg, Dane	84FU	55	$ .01	$ .10	Jacoby, Brook	86F	590	$ .01	$ .10
Iorg, Dane	85F	204	$ .01	$ .05	Jacoby, Brook	87F	253	$ .01	$ .05
Iorg, Dane	86F	9	$ .01	$ .05	Jacoby, Brook	88F	612	$ .01	$ .05
Iorg, Dane	86FU	54	$ .01	$ .05	Jacoby, Brook	89F	407	$ .01	$ .05
Iorg, Garth	81F	423	$ .01	$ .05	Jacoby, Brook	90F	493	$ .01	$ .04
Iorg, Garth	82F	616	$ .01	$ .05	Jacoby, Brook	91F	369	$ .01	$ .03
Iorg, Garth	83F	430	$ .01	$ .05	James, Bob	84F	277	$ .03	$ .20
Iorg, Garth	84F	157	$ .01	$ .06	James, Bob	85F	400	$ .01	$ .05
Iorg, Garth	85F	107	$ .01	$ .05	James, Bob	85FU	60	$ .01	$ .05
Iorg, Garth	86F	61	$ .01	$ .05	James, Bob	86F	209	$ .01	$ .05
Iorg, Garth	87F	229	$ .01	$ .05	James, Bob	87F	501	$ .01	$ .05
Iorg, Garth	88F	113	$ .01	$ .05	James, Bob	88F	401	$ .01	$ .05
Irvine, Daryl	91F	98	$ .01	$ .10	James, Chris	86FU	55	$ .15	$ .60
Ivie, Mike	81F	435	$ .01	$ .05	James, Chris	87FU	50	$ .07	$ .25
Ivie, Mike	83F	331	$ .01	$ .05	James, Chris	88F	307	$ .01	$ .10
Jackson, Bo	87F	369	$3.00	$15.00	James, Chris	89F	572	$ .01	$ .05
Jackson, Bo	88F	260	$ 1.00	$2.50	James, Chris	90F	161	$ .01	$ .04
Jackson, Bo	89F	285	$ .05	$ .75	James, Chris	90FU	92	$ .01	$ .05
Jackson, Bo	90F	110	$ .01	$ .25	James, Chris	91F	370	$ .01	$ .03
Jackson, Bo	90F	635	$ .01	$ .25	James, Dion	84FU	57	$ .10	$ .50
Jackson, Bo	91F	561	$ .01	$ .15	James, Dion	85F	584	$ .04	$ .25
Jackson, Chuck	87FU	47	$ .03	$ .20	James, Dion	87FU	51	$ .01	$ .05
Jackson, Danny	85F	205	$ .10	$ .50	James, Dion	88F	543	$ .01	$ .05
Jackson, Danny	86F	10	$ .05	$ .20	James, Dion	89F	594	$ .01	$ .05
Jackson, Danny	87F	370	$ .01	$ .10	James, Dion	90F	494	$ .01	$ .04
Jackson, Danny	88F	261	$ .01	$ .10	James, Dion	91F	371	$ .01	$ .03
Jackson, Danny	88FU	84	$ .01	$ .15	Javier, Stan	86FU	56	$ .01	$ .05
Jackson, Danny	89F	163	$ .01	$ .15	Javier, Stan	87FU	52	$ .01	$ .05
Jackson, Danny	89F	636	$ .01	$ .15	Javier, Stan	89F	13	$ .01	$ .05
Jackson, Danny	90F	422	$ .01	$ .10	Javier, Stan	90F	12	$ .01	$ .04
Jackson, Danny	91F	67	$ .01	$ .03	Javier, Stan	90FU	23	$ .01	$ .05
Jackson, Darrell	81F	567	$ .01	$ .05	Javier, Stan	91F	211	$ .01	$ .03
Jackson, Darrell	82F	555	$ .01	$ .05	Jeffcoat, Mike	84FU	58	$ .04	$ .25
Jackson, Darrin	88F	641	$2.00	$12.50	Jeffcoat, Mike	85F	453	$ .01	$ .05
Jackson, Darrin	88FU	78	$ .01	$ .05	Jeffcoat, Mike	86F	545	$ .01	$ .05

Player	Year	No.	VG	EX/MT	Player	Year	No.	VG	EX/MT
Jeffcoat, Mike	89F	524	$ .01	$ .05	Johnson, Cliff	84F	159	$ .01	$ .06
Jeffcoat, Mike	90F	302	$ .01	$ .04	Johnson, Cliff	85F	109	$ .01	$ .05
Jeffcoat, Mike	91F	291	$ .01	$ .03	Johnson, Cliff	85FU	61	$ .01	$ .05
Jefferies, Gregg	88F	137	$ .75	$4.50	Johnson, Cliff	86F	62	$ .01	$ .05
Jefferies, Gregg	89F	38	$ .25	$1.00	Johnson, Cliff	87F	231	$ .01	$ .05
Jefferies, Gregg	90F	207	$ .01	$ .25	Johnson, Dave	90FU	67	$ .01	$ .05
Jefferies, Gregg	91F	151	$ .01	$ .10	Johnson, Dave	91F	479	$ .01	$ .03
Jefferson, Jesse	81F	419	$ .01	$ .05	Johnson, Howard	83F	332	$2.00	$8.00
Jefferson, Jesse	82F	466	$ .01	$ .05	Johnson, Howard	85F	12	$ .10	$1.50
Jefferson, Stan	87FU	53	$ .01	$ .25	Johnson, Howard	85FU	62	$ .25	$2.00
Jefferson, Stan	88F	587	$ .01	$ .05	Johnson, Howard	86F	85	$ .05	$ .40
Jelks, Greg	88F	648	$ .01	$ .30	Johnson, Howard	87F	13	$ .05	$ .25
Jeltz, Steve	85F	653	$ .03	$ .20	Johnson, Howard	88F	138	$ .05	$ .25
Jeltz, Steve	87F	178	$ .01	$ .05	Johnson, Howard	89F	39	$ .01	$ .15
Jeltz, Steve	88F	308	$ .01	$ .05	Johnson, Howard	90F	208	$ .01	$ .15
Jeltz, Steve	89F	573	$ .01	$ .05	Johnson, Howard	90F	639	$ .01	$ .10
Jeltz, Steve	90F	562	$ .01	$ .04	Johnson, Howard	91F	152	$ .01	$ .03
Jenkins, Ferguson "Fergie"	81F	622	$ .03	$ .20	Johnson, Joe	86F	519	$ .01	$ .10
Jenkins, Ferguson	82F	320	$ .03	$ .20	Johnson, Joe	87F	230	$ .01	$ .05
Jenkins, Ferguson	83F	498	$ .01	$ .10	Johnson, John Henry	82F	321	$ .01	$ .05
Jenkins, Ferguson	84F	494	$ .03	$ .10	Johnson, John Henry	84F	401	$ .01	$ .06
Jennings, Doug	88FU	54	$ .01	$ .25	Johnson, John Henry	85F	162	$ .01	$ .05
Jennings, Doug	89F	14	$ .01	$ .25	Johnson, John Henry	87F	347	$ .01	$ .05
Jennings, Doug	91F	12	$ .01	$ .03	Johnson, Lamar	81F	350	$ .01	$ .05
Jimenez, Cesar	88FU	72	$ .01	$ .05	Johnson, Lamar	82F	346	$ .01	$ .05
Jimenez, Houston	85F	282	$ .01	$ .05	Johnson, Lamar	83F	571	$ .01	$ .05
John, Tommy	81F	81	$ .03	$ .20	Johnson, Lance	88F	37	$ .01	$ .20
John, Tommy	82F	40	$ .03	$ .20	Johnson, Lance	89F	499	$ .01	$ .05
John, Tommy	83F	95	$ .03	$ .20	Johnson, Lance	90F	536	$ .01	$ .04
John, Tommy	84F	522	$ .03	$ .20	Johnson, Lance	91F	123	$ .01	$ .03
John, Tommy	85F	304	$ .03	$ .20	Johnson, Randy	83F	617	$ .01	$ .05
John, Tommy	86F	422	$ .03	$ .20	Johnson, Randy	84F	183	$ .01	$ .06
John, Tommy	86FU	57	$ .03	$ .20	Johnson, Randy	85F	330	$ .01	$ .05
John, Tommy	87F	102	$ .03	$ .20	Johnson, Randy	89F	381	$ .01	$ .50
					Johnson, Randy	89FU	59	$ .01	$ .05
					Johnson, Randy	90F	518	$ .01	$ .10
					Johnson, Randy	91F	455	$ .01	$ .03
					Johnson, Wallace	82F	192	$ .01	$ .05
					Johnson, Wallace	83F	285	$ .01	$ .05
					Johnson, Wallace	87F	321	$ .01	$ .05
					Johnson, Wallace	88F	186	$ .01	$ .05
					Johnson, Wallace	89F	382	$ .01	$ .05
					Johnson, Wallace	90F	351	$ .01	$ .04
					Johnstone, Jay	81F	128	$ .01	$ .05
					Johnstone, Jay	82F	10	$ .01	$ .05
					Johnstone, Jay	83F	499	$ .01	$ .05
					Johnstone, Jay	84F	495	$ .01	$ .06
					Jones, Barry	87F	611	$ .01	$ .10
					Jones, Barry	88FU	114	$ .01	$ .05
					Jones, Barry	89F	500	$ .01	$ .05
					Jones, Barry	91F	124	$ .01	$ .03
					Jones, Bobby	85F	559	$ .01	$ .05
					Jones, Doug	88F	613	$ .01	$ .10
					Jones, Doug	89F	409	$ .01	$ .35
					Jones, Doug	90F	495	$ .01	$ .04
					Jones, Doug	91F	372	$ .01	$ .03
					Jones, Jeff	82F	94	$ .01	$ .05
					Jones, Jimmy	87F	650	$ .04	$ .25
					Jones, Jimmy	87FU	54	$ .01	$ .05
					Jones, Jimmy	88F	588	$ .01	$ .05
					Jones, Jimmy	89F	308	$ .01	$ .05
					Jones, Jimmy	91F	667	$ .01	$ .03
					Jones, Lynn	82F	270	$ .01	$ .05
					Jones, Lynn	83F	333	$ .01	$ .05
					Jones, Lynn	86F	11	$ .01	$ .05
					Jones, Mike	82F	412	$ .01	$ .05
					Jones, Mike	86F	12	$ .01	$ .05
					Jones, Odell	84F	421	$ .01	$ .06
					Jones, Odell	85F	560	$ .01	$ .05
					Jones, Odell	89F	189	$ .01	$ .05

Tommy John
PITCHER

Player	Year	No.	VG	EX/MT
John, Tommy	88F	211	$ .01	$ .10
John, Tommy	89F	255	$ .01	$ .05
Johnson, Bobby	84F	420	$ .01	$ .06
Johnson, Cliff	81F	303	$ .01	$ .05
Johnson, Cliff	82F	93	$ .01	$ .05
Johnson, Cliff	83F	520	$ .01	$ .05

FLEER

Player	Year	No.	VG	EX/MT	Player	Year	No.	VG	EX/MT
Jones, Randy	81F	487	$ .01	$ .05	Kemp, Steve	86F	610	$ .01	$ .05
Jones, Randy	82F	528	$ .01	$ .05	Kennedy, Junior	82F	70	$ .01	$ .05
Jones, Randy	83F	546	$ .01	$ .05	Kennedy, Junior	83F	500	$ .01	$ .05
Jones, Ron	89F	574	$ .01	$ .45	Kennedy, Terry	81F	203	$ .01	$ .05
Jones, Ron	90F	563	$ .01	$ .10	Kennedy, Terry	81F	541	$ .01	$ .05
Jones, Ross	88F	262	$ .01	$ .10	Kennedy, Terry	82F	574	$ .01	$ .05
Jones, Ruppert	81F	101	$ .01	$ .05	Kennedy, Terry	83F	362	$ .01	$ .05
Jones, Ruppert	82F	573	$ .01	$ .05	Kennedy, Terry	84F	304	$ .01	$ .06
Jones, Ruppert	83F	361	$ .01	$ .05	Kennedy, Terry	85F	37	$ .01	$ .05
Jones, Ruppert	84F	303	$ .01	$ .06	Kennedy, Terry	86F	327	$ .01	$ .05
Jones, Ruppert	84FU	59	$ .01	$ .10	Kennedy, Terry	87F	419	$ .01	$ .05
Jones, Ruppert	85F	13	$ .04	$ .25	Kennedy, Terry	87FU	56	$ .01	$ .05
Jones, Ruppert	85FU	63	$ .01	$ .05	Kennedy, Terry	88F	563	$ .01	$ .05
Jones, Ruppert	86F	161	$ .01	$ .05	Kennedy, Terry	89F	610	$ .01	$ .05
Jones, Ruppert	87F	85	$ .01	$ .05	Kennedy, Terry	89FU	128	$ .01	$ .05
Jones, Ruppert	88F	492	$ .01	$ .05	Kennedy, Terry	90F	58	$ .01	$ .04
Jones, Tim	89F	453	$ .01	$ .05	Kennedy, Terry	91F	263	$ .01	$ .03
Jones, Tracy	86FU	58	$ .12	$ .60	Keough, Matt	81F	588	$ .01	$ .05
Jones, Tracy	87F	651	$ .10	$ .40	Keough, Matt	82F	95	$ .01	$ .05
Jones, Tracy	87FU	55	$ .05	$ .20	Keough, Matt	83F	521	$ .01	$ .05
Jones, Tracy	88F	237	$ .01	$ .05	Keough, Matt	84F	130	$ .01	$ .06
Jones, Tracy	89F	383	$ .01	$ .05	Kepshire, Kurt	85F	230	$ .01	$ .05
Jones, Tracy	89FU	31	$ .01	$ .05	Kepshire, Kurt	86F	39	$ .01	$ .05
Jones, Tracy	90F	607	$ .01	$ .04	Kerfeld, Charlie	86F	303	$ .04	$ .25
Jordan, Ricky	88FU	110	$ .05	$ .50	Kerfeld, Charlie	87F	60	$ .01	$ .05
Jordan, Ricky	89F	575	$ .01	$ .35	Kern, Jim	81F	618	$ .01	$ .05
Jordan, Ricky	90F	564	$ .01	$ .25	Kern, Jim	82F	322	$ .01	$ .05
Jordan, Ricky	91F	401	$ .01	$ .03	Kern, Jim	83F	240	$ .01	$ .05
Jorgensen, Mike	81F	324	$ .01	$ .05	Key, Jimmy	84FU	61	$1.00	$5.00
Jorgensen, Mike	82F	529	$ .01	$ .05	Key, Jimmy	85F	110	$ .25	$ .75
Jorgensen, Mike	83F	547	$ .01	$ .05	Key, Jimmy	86F	63	$ .03	$ .20
Jorgensen, Mike	85F	229	$ .01	$ .05	Key, Jimmy	86F	642	$ .01	$ .10
Jose, Felix	89F	15	$ .01	$1.25	Key, Jimmy	87F	232	$ .01	$ .10
Jose, Felix	90F	13	$ .01	$ .25	Key, Jimmy	88F	114	$ .01	$ .10
Jose, Felix	91F	636	$ .01	$ .10	Key, Jimmy	89F	236	$ .01	$ .05
Joyner, Wally	86FU	59	$ .50	$1.75	Key, Jimmy	90F	85	$ .01	$ .04
Joyner, Wally	87F	86	$ .25	$2.00	Key, Jimmy	91F	178	$ .01	$ .03
Joyner, Wally	87F	628	$ .30	$1.00	Khalifa, Sam	86F	611	$ .01	$ .05
Joyner, Wally	88F	493	$ .10	$ .35	Kiecker, Dana	90FU	72	$ .01	$ .15
Joyner, Wally	88F	622	$ .01	$ .35	Kiecker, Dana	91F	99	$ .01	$ .03
Joyner, Wally	89F	481	$ .01	$ .20	Kiefer, Steve	85F	647	$1.00	$4.00
Joyner, Wally	90F	136	$ .01	$ .10	Kiefer, Steve	88F	167	$ .01	$ .05
Joyner, Wally	91F	317	$ .01	$ .03	Kilgus, Paul	88F	471	$ .01	$ .10
Jurak, Ed	84F	402	$ .01	$ .06	Kilgus, Paul	89F	525	$ .01	$ .05
Justice, David	90F	586	$ .01	$2.75	Kilgus, Paul	89FU	76	$ .01	$ .05
Justice, Dave	91F	693	$ .01	$ .75	Kilgus, Paul	90F	34	$ .01	$ .04
Kaat, Jim	81F	536	$ .03	$ .20	Kimm, Bruce	81F	355	$ .01	$ .05
Kaat, Jim	82F	117	$ .03	$ .20	King, Eric	87F	155	$ .03	$ .20
Kaat, Jim	83F	11	$ .03	$ .20	King, Eric	88F	60	$ .01	$ .10
Kaiser, Jeff	89F	410	$ .01	$ .05	King, Eric	89F	136	$ .01	$ .05
Karkovice, Ron	87F	645	$ .03	$ .20	King, Eric	89FU	19	$ .01	$ .05
Karkovice, Ron	91F	125	$ .01	$ .03	King, Eric	90F	537	$ .01	$ .04
Kaufman, Curt	85F	305	$ .01	$ .05	King, Eric	91F	126	$ .01	$ .03
Kearney, Bob	84F	449	$ .01	$ .06	King, Jeff	88F	653	$ .01	$ .25
Kearney, Bob	84FU	60	$ .01	$ .10	King, Jeff	89FU	114	$ .01	$ .05
Kearney, Bob	85F	491	$ .01	$ .05	King, Jeff	90F	469	$ .01	$ .10
Kearney, Bob	86F	466	$ .01	$ .05	King, Jeff	91F	39	$ .01	$ .03
Kearney, Bob	87F	587	$ .01	$ .05	Kingery, Mike	87F	371	$ .03	$ .20
Keeton, Rickey	82F	146	$ .01	$ .05	Kingery, Mike	87FU	57	$ .01	$ .05
Kelly, Pat	82F	372	$ .01	$ .05	Kingery, Mike	88F	376	$ .01	$ .05
Kelly, Roberto	88F	212	$ .25	$1.50	Kingman, Brian	81F	579	$ .01	$ .05
Kelly, Roberto	89F	256	$ .01	$ .25	Kingman, Brian	82F	96	$ .01	$ .05
Kelly, Roberto	90F	446	$ .01	$ .10	Kingman, Brian	83F	522	$ .01	$ .05
Kelly, Roberto	91F	668	$ .01	$ .03	Kingman, Dave	81F	291	$ .03	$ .20
Kemp, Steve	81F	459	$ .01	$ .05	Kingman, Dave	82F	530	$ .03	$ .20
Kemp, Steve	82F	271	$ .01	$ .05	Kingman, Dave	83F	548	$ .01	$ .10
Kemp, Steve	83F	239	$ .01	$ .05	Kingman, Dave	84F	590	$ .03	$ .10
Kemp, Steve	84F	129	$ .01	$ .06	Kingman, Dave	84FU	62	$ .08	$ .40
Kemp, Steve	85F	132	$ .01	$ .05	Kingman, Dave	85F	427	$ .01	$ .10
Kemp, Steve	85FU	64	$ .01	$ .05	Kingman, Dave	86F	423	$ .01	$ .10

Player	Year	No.	VG	EX/MT	Player	Year	No.	VG	EX/MT
Kingman, Dave	87F	396	$ .01	$ .10	Knight, Ray	82F	71	$ .01	$ .10
Kinney, Dennis	81F	505	$ .01	$ .05	Knight, Ray	83F	453	$ .01	$ .10
Kinzer, Matt	90F	652	$ .01	$ .04	Knight, Ray	84F	229	$ .03	$ .10
Kipper, Bob	86F	648	$ .05	$ .30	Knight, Ray	85F	86	$ .01	$ .10
Kipper, Bob	87F	612	$ .01	$ .05	Knight, Ray	86F	86	$ .01	$ .05
Kipper, Bob	88F	332	$ .01	$ .05	Knight, Ray	87F	14	$ .01	$ .05
Kipper, Bob	89F	211	$ .01	$ .05	Knight, Ray	87FU	58	$ .01	$ .05
Kipper, Bob	90F	470	$ .01	$ .04	Knight, Ray	88F	564	$ .01	$ .05
Kipper, Bob	91F	40	$ .01	$ .03	Knight, Ray	88FU	28	$ .01	$ .05
Kison, Bruce	81F	284	$ .01	$ .05	Knudson, Mark	90F	327	$ .01	$ .04
Kison, Bruce	82F	467	$ .01	$ .05	Knudson, Mark	91F	587	$ .01	$ .03
Kison, Bruce	83F	96	$ .01	$ .05	Komminsk, Brad	84FU	63	$ .04	$ .25
Kison, Bruce	84F	523	$ .01	$ .06	Komminsk, Brad	85F	331	$ .01	$ .05
Kison, Bruce	85F	306	$ .01	$ .05	Komminsk, Brad	86F	520	$ .01	$ .05
Kison, Bruce	85FU	65	$ .01	$ .05	Komminsk, Brad	89FU	28	$ .01	$ .05
Kison, Bruce	86F	353	$ .01	$ .05	Komminsk, Brad	90F	496	$ .01	$ .04
Kittle, Ron	83F	241	$ .05	$ .75	Koosman, Jerry	81F	552	$ .01	$ .10
Kittle, Ron	84F	64	$ .03	$ .20	Koosman, Jerry	82F	347	$ .01	$ .10
Kittle, Ron	85F	518	$ .01	$ .10	Koosman, Jerry	83F	242	$ .01	$ .10
Kittle, Ron	86F	210	$ .01	$ .10	Koosman, Jerry	84F	65	$ .01	$ .10
Kittle, Ron	87F	103	$ .01	$ .10	Koosman, Jerry	84FU	64	$ .03	$ .20
Kittle, Ron	88F	213	$ .01	$ .05	Koosman, Jerry	85F	256	$ .01	$ .10
Kittle, Ron	89FU	20	$ .01	$ .05	Kraemer, Joe	90FU	8	$ .01	$ .10
Kittle, Ron	90F	538	$ .01	$ .04	Kramer, Randy	89F	647	$ .01	$ .20
Kittle, Ron	91F	480	$ .01	$ .03	Kramer, Randy	89FU	115	$ .01	$ .05
Klink, Joe	91F	13	$ .01	$ .03	Kramer, Randy	90F	471	$ .01	$ .04
Klutts, Mickey	81F	584	$ .01	$ .05	Kremers, Jim	90FU	4	$ .01	$ .15
Klutts, Mickey	82F	97	$ .01	$ .05	Kremers, Jimmy	91F	694	$ .01	$ .10
Knepper, Bob	81F	447	$ .01	$ .10	Krenchicki, Wayne	82F	168	$ .01	$ .05
Knepper, Bob	82F	219	$ .01	$ .05	Krenchicki, Wayne	83F	594	$ .01	$ .05
Knepper, Bob	83F	451	$ .01	$ .05	Krenchicki, Wayne	84F	83	$ .01	$ .06
Knepper, Bob	84F	228	$ .01	$ .06	Krenchicki, Wayne	84FU	65	$ .01	$ .10
Knepper, Bob	85F	352	$ .01	$ .05	Krenchicki, Wayne	85F	539	$ .01	$ .05
Knepper, Bob	86F	304	$ .01	$ .05	Krenchicki, Wayne	86F	180	$ .01	$ .05
Knepper, Bob	87F	61	$ .01	$ .05	Krenchicki, Wayne	86FU	60	$ .01	$ .05
					Krenchicki, Wayne	87F	322	$ .01	$ .05
					Kreuter, Chad	89F	526	$ .01	$ .15
					Kreuter, Chad	90F	303	$ .01	$ .04
					Krueger, Bill	84F	450	$ .01	$ .06
					Krueger, Bill	85F	428	$ .01	$ .05
					Krueger, Bill	86F	424	$ .01	$ .05
					Krueger, Bill	90F	328	$ .01	$ .04
					Krueger, Bill	91F	588	$ .01	$ .03
					Kruk, John	86FU	61	$ .05	$ .35
					Kruk, John	87F	420	$ .01	$ .25
					Kruk, John	88F	589	$ .01	$ .10
					Kruk, John	89F	309	$ .01	$ .05
					Kruk, John	89FU	109	$ .01	$ .05
					Kruk, John	90F	565	$ .01	$ .04
					Kruk, John	91F	402	$ .01	$ .03
					Krukow, Mike	81F	312	$ .01	$ .10
					Krukow, Mike	82F	598	$ .01	$ .05
					Krukow, Mike	83F	163	$ .01	$ .05
					Krukow, Mike	84F	374	$ .01	$ .06
					Krukow, Mike	85F	609	$ .01	$ .05
					Krukow, Mike	86F	546	$ .01	$ .05
					Krukow, Mike	87F	275	$ .01	$ .05
					Krukow, Mike	87F	630	$ .01	$ .10
					Krukow, Mike	88F	85	$ .01	$ .05
					Krukow, Mike	89F	331	$ .01	$ .05
					Kuiper, Duane	82F	373	$ .01	$ .05
					Kuiper, Duane	83F	263	$ .01	$ .05
					Kuiper, Duane	84F	375	$ .01	$ .06
					Kuiper, Duane	85F	610	$ .01	$ .05
					Kunkel, Jeff	85F	561	$ .01	$ .05
Knepper, Bob	88F	451	$ .01	$ .05	Kunkel, Jeff	89F	527	$ .01	$ .05
Knepper, Bob	89F	360	$ .01	$ .05	Kunkel, Jeff	90F	304	$ .01	$ .04
Knicely, Alan	83F	452	$ .01	$ .05	Kunkel, Jeff	91F	292	$ .01	$ .03
Knicely, Alan	84F	473	$ .01	$ .06	Kuntz, Rusty	82F	348	$ .01	$ .05
Knight, Ray	81F	198	$ .01	$ .10	Kuntz, Rusty	84F	568	$ .01	$ .06

Bob Knepper
PITCHER

FLEER

Player	Year	No.	VG	EX/MT
Kuntz, Rusty	84FU	66	$ .01	$ .10
Kuntz, Rusty	85F	14	$ .01	$ .05
Kutcher, Randy	87F	276	$ .01	$ .10
Kutcher, Randy	91F	100	$ .01	$ .03
Lacey, Bob	81F	578	$ .01	$ .05
Lacey, Bob	85F	611	$ .01	$ .05
LaCock, Pete	81F	47	$ .01	$ .05
LaCorte, Frank	81F	55	$ .01	$ .05
LaCorte, Frank	82F	220	$ .01	$ .05
LaCorte, Frank	83F	454	$ .01	$ .05
LaCorte, Frank	84F	230	$ .01	$ .06
LaCorte, Frank	84FU	67	$ .01	$ .10
LaCoss, Mike	82F	72	$ .01	$ .05
LaCoss, Mike	83F	455	$ .01	$ .05
LaCoss, Mike	84F	231	$ .01	$ .06
LaCoss, Mike	85F	353	$ .01	$ .05
LaCoss, Mike	85FU	66	$ .01	$ .05
LaCoss, Mike	86FU	62	$ .01	$ .05
LaCoss, Mike	87F	277	$ .01	$ .05
LaCoss, Mike	88F	86	$ .01	$ .05
LaCoss, Mike	89FU	129	$ .01	$ .05
LaCoss, Mike	90F	59	$ .01	$ .04
LaCoss, Mike	91F	264	$ .01	$ .03
Lacy, Lee	81F	374	$ .01	$ .05
Lacy, Lee	82F	483	$ .01	$ .05
Lacy, Lee	83F	308	$ .01	$ .05
Lacy, Lee	84F	252	$ .01	$ .06
Lacy, Lee	85F	467	$ .01	$ .05
Lacy, Lee	85FU	67	$ .01	$ .05
Lacy, Lee	86F	277	$ .01	$ .05
Lacy, Lee	87F	473	$ .01	$ .05
Lacy, Lee	88F	565	$ .01	$ .05
Ladd, Pete	83F	37	$ .01	$ .05
Ladd, Pete	84F	204	$ .01	$ .06
Ladd, Pete	85F	585	$ .01	$ .05
Ladd, Pete	86F	492	$ .01	$ .05
Ladd, Peter	86FU	63	$ .01	$ .05
Ladd, Pete	87F	588	$ .01	$ .05
Lahti, Jeff	83F	12	$ .01	$ .05
Lahti, Jeff	84F	327	$ .01	$ .06
Lahti, Jeff	85F	231	$ .01	$ .05
Lahti, Jeff	86F	40	$ .01	$ .05
Lahti, Jeff	87F	299	$ .01	$ .05
Lake, Steve	87F	300	$ .01	$ .05
Lake, Steve	88F	38	$ .01	$ .05
Lake, Steve	89F	454	$ .01	$ .05
Lake, Steve	90F	566	$ .01	$ .04
Lake, Steve	91F	403	$ .01	$ .03
Lamp, Dennis	81F	305	$ .01	$ .05
Lamp, Dennis	82F	349	$ .01	$ .05
Lamp, Dennis	83F	243	$ .01	$ .05
Lamp, Dennis	84F	66	$ .01	$ .06
Lamp, Dennis	84FU	68	$ .01	$ .10
Lamp, Dennis	85F	111	$ .01	$ .05
Lamp, Dennis	86F	64	$ .01	$ .05
Lamp, Dennis	87F	233	$ .01	$ .05
Lamp, Dennis	88F	284	$ .01	$ .05
Lamp, Dennis	89F	92	$ .01	$ .05
Lamp, Dennis	90F	280	$ .01	$ .04
Lamp, Dennis	91F	101	$ .01	$ .03
Lancaster, Les	88F	421	$ .01	$ .15
Lancaster, Les	89F	429	$ .01	$ .05
Lancaster, Les	90F	35	$ .01	$ .04
Lancaster, Les	91F	424	$ .01	$ .03
Landestoy, Rafael	81F	70	$ .01	$ .05
Landestoy, Rafael	82F	73	$ .01	$ .05
Landestoy, Rafael	83F	595	$ .01	$ .05
Landreaux, Ken	81F	553	$ .01	$ .05
Landreaux, Ken	82F	11	$ .01	$ .05
Landreaux, Ken	83F	210	$ .01	$ .05

Player	Year	No.	VG	EX/MT
Landreaux, Ken	84F	104	$ .01	$ .06
Landreaux, Ken	85F	375	$ .01	$ .05
Landreaux, Ken	86F	134	$ .01	$ .05
Landreaux, Ken	87F	444	$ .01	$ .05
Landrum, Bill	88F	238	$ .01	$ .05
Landrum, Bill	89FU	116	$ .01	$ .05
Landrum, Bill	90F	472	$ .01	$ .04
Landrum, Bill	91F	41	$ .01	$ .03
Landrum, Terry 'Tito'	81F	539	$ .01	$ .05
Landrum, Tito	82F	118	$ .01	$ .05
Landrum, Tito	83F	13	$ .01	$ .05
Landrum, Tito	84FU	69	$ .01	$ .10
Landrum, Tito	85F	232	$ .01	$ .05
Landrum, Tito	86F	41	$ .01	$ .05

Tito Landrum
OUTFIELD

Player	Year	No.	VG	EX/MT
Landrum, Tito	87F	301	$ .01	$ .05
Langford, Rick	81F	572	$ .01	$ .05
Langford, Rick	82F	98	$ .01	$ .05
Langford, Rick	83F	523	$ .01	$ .05
Langford, Rick	84F	451	$ .01	$ .06
Langford, Rick	86F	425	$ .01	$ .05
Langston, Mark	84FU	70	$5.00	$20.00
Langston, Mark	85F	492	$ .50	$3.50
Langston, Mark	86F	467	$ .01	$ .30
Langston, Mark	87F	589	$ .01	$ .20
Langston, Mark	88F	377	$ .01	$ .10
Langston, Mark	89F	551	$ .01	$ .10
Langston, Mark	89FU	97	$ .01	$ .15
Langston, Mark	90F	352	$ .01	$ .10
Langston, Mark	90FU	78	$ .01	$ .10
Langston, Mark	91F	318	$ .01	$ .03
Lankford, Ray	91F	637	$ .01	$ .50
Lansford, Carney	81F	270	$ .01	$ .10
Lansford, Carney	82F	298	$ .01	$ .10
Lansford, Carney	83F	187	$ .01	$ .10
Lansford, Carney	84F	452	$ .01	$ .06
Lansford, Carney	85F	429	$ .01	$ .05
Lansford, Carney	86F	426	$ .01	$ .05
Lansford, Carney	87F	397	$ .01	$ .05
Lansford, Carney	88F	285	$ .01	$ .05
Lansford, Carney	89F	16	$ .01	$ .05

Player	Year	No.	VG	EX/MT	Player	Year	No.	VG	EX/MT
Lansford, Carney	89F	633	$ .05	$ .35	Law, Vance	89F	430	$ .01	$ .05
Lansford, Carney	90F	14	$ .01	$ .35	Law, Vance	90F	36	$ .01	$ .04
Lansford, Carney	91F	14	$ .01	$ .03	Layana, Tim	90FU	14	$ .01	$ .15
LaPoint, Dave	83F	14	$ .01	$ .40	Layana, Tim	91F	69	$ .01	$ .10
LaPoint, Dave	84F	328	$ .01	$ .15	Lazorko, Jack	87FU	61	$ .01	$ .05
LaPoint, Dave	85F	233	$ .01	$ .10	Lazorko, Jack	88F	494	$ .01	$ .05
LaPoint, Dave	85FU	68	$ .01	$ .05	Lazorko, Jack	89F	482	$ .01	$ .05
LaPoint, Dave	86F	547	$ .01	$ .05	Lea, Charlie	81F	165	$ .03	$ .20
LaPoint, Dave	86FU	64	$ .01	$ .05	Lea, Charlie	82F	193	$ .01	$ .05
LaPoint, Dave	87F	421	$ .01	$ .05	Lea, Charlie	83F	286	$ .01	$ .05
LaPoint, Dave	88F	402	$ .01	$ .05	Lea, Charlie	84F	278	$ .01	$ .06
LaPoint, Dave	89F	212	$ .01	$ .05	Lea, Charlie	85F	401	$ .01	$ .05
LaPoint, Dave	91F	669	$ .01	$ .03	Lea, Charlie	85F	632	$ .01	$ .10
Larkin, Barry	87F	204	$2.00	$7.00	Lea, Charlie	86F	253	$ .01	$ .05
Larkin, Barry	88F	239	$ .25	$ 1.50	Lea, Charlie	88FU	44	$ .01	$ .05
Larkin, Barry	89F	164	$ .01	$ .25	Lea, Charlie	89F	119	$ .01	$ .05
Larkin, Barry	90F	423	$ .01	$ .15	Leach, Rick	82F	272	$ .01	$ .05
Larkin, Barry	91F	68	$ .01	$ .10	Leach, Rick	83F	334	$ .01	$ .05
Larkin, Barry	91F	711	$ .01	$ .20	Leach, Rick	84F	84	$ .01	$ .06
Larkin, Gene	87FU	59	$ .04	$ .25	Leach, Rick	84FU	71	$ .01	$ .10
Larkin, Gene	88F	14	$ .10	$ .40	Leach, Rick	85F	112	$ .01	$ .05
Larkin, Gene	89F	117	$ .01	$ .05	Leach, Rick	87F	234	$ .01	$ .05
Larkin, Gene	90F	379	$ .01	$ .04	Leach, Rick	87FU	63	$ .01	$ .05
Larkin, Gene	91F	615	$ .01	$ .03	Leach, Rick	88F	115	$ .01	$ .05
LaRoche, Dave	81F	285	$ .01	$ .05	Leach, Rick	89F	237	$ .01	$ .05
LaRoche, Dave	83F	384	$ .01	$ .05	Leach, Rick	90F	305	$ .01	$ .04
LaRussa, Tony	81F	344	$ .01	$ .05	Leach, Terry	86F	87	$ .01	$ .05
Laskey, Bill	83F	264	$ .01	$ .05	Leach, Terry	87FU	62	$ .01	$ .05
Laskey, Bill	84F	376	$ .01	$ .06	Leach, Terry	88F	139	$ .01	$ .05
Laskey, Bill	85F	612	$ .01	$ .05	Leach, Terry	89F	40	$ .01	$ .05
Laskey, Bill	86F	251	$ .01	$ .05	Leach, Terry	90F	111	$ .01	$ .04
Lasorda, Tom	81F	116	$ .01	$ .10	Leach, Terry	91F	616	$ .01	$ .03
Laudner, Tim	83F	618	$ .01	$ .05	Leal, Luis	82F	617	$ .01	$ .05
Laudner, Tim	84F	569	$ .01	$ .06	Leal, Luis	83F	432	$ .01	$ .05
Laudner, Tim	85F	283	$ .01	$ .05	Leal, Luis	84F	160	$ .01	$ .06
Laudner, Tim	86F	398	$ .01	$ .05	Leal, Luis	85F	113	$ .01	$ .05
Laudner, Tim	87F	546	$ .01	$ .05	Leary, Tim	87F	348	$ .01	$ .05
Laudner, Tim	88F	15	$ .01	$ .05	Leary, Tim	88F	521	$ .01	$ .05
Laudner, Tim	89F	118	$ .01	$ .05	Leary, Tim	89F	65	$ .01	$ .05
Laudner, Tim	90F	380	$ .01	$ .04	Leary, Tim	90F	424	$ .01	$ .04
LaValliere, Mike	86FU	65	$ .05	$ .50	Leary, Tim	91F	670	$ .01	$ .03
LaValliere, Mike	87F	302	$ .03	$ .20	Lee, Bill	81F	157	$ .01	$ .05
LaValliere, Mike	87FU	60	$ .01	$ .15	Lee, Bill	82F	194	$ .01	$ .05
LaValliere, Mike	88F	333	$ .01	$ .05	Lee, Manny	85FU	71	$ .03	$ .20
LaValliere, Mike	89F	213	$ .01	$ .05	Lee, Manny	88F	116	$ .01	$ .05
LaValliere, Mike	90F	473	$ .01	$ .04	Lee, Manny	89F	238	$ .01	$ .05
LaValliere, Mike	91F	42	$ .01	$ .03	Lee, Manny	90F	86	$ .01	$ .04
Lavelle, Gary	81F	448	$ .01	$ .05	Lee, Manny	91F	179	$ .01	$ .03
Lavelle, Gary	82F	392	$ .01	$ .05	Lee, Terry	91F	70	$ .01	$ .10
Lavelle, Gary	83F	265	$ .01	$ .05	Lefebvre, Joe	81F	103	$ .01	$ .05
Lavelle, Gary	84F	377	$ .01	$ .06	Lefebvre, Joe	82F	575	$ .01	$ .05
Lavelle, Gary	85F	613	$ .01	$ .05	Lefebvre, Joe	83F	363	$ .01	$ .05
Lavelle, Gary	85FU	69	$ .01	$ .05	Lefebvre, Joe	84F	37	$ .01	$ .06
Lavelle, Gary	86F	65	$ .01	$ .05	Lefebvre, Joe	85F	257	$ .01	$ .05
Law, Rudy	81F	139	$ .01	$ .05	Lefferts, Craig	84F	496	$ .01	$ .06
Law, Rudy	83F	244	$ .01	$ .05	Lefferts, Craig	84FU	72	$ .01	$ .10
Law, Rudy	84F	67	$ .01	$ .06	Lefferts, Craig	85F	38	$ .01	$ .05
Law, Rudy	85F	519	$ .01	$ .05	Lefferts, Craig	86F	328	$ .01	$ .05
Law, Rudy	86F	211	$ .01	$ .05	Lefferts, Craig	87F	422	$ .01	$ .05
Law, Rudy	86FU	66	$ .01	$ .05	Lefferts, Craig	87FU	64	$ .01	$ .05
Law, Rudy	87F	372	$ .01	$ .05	Lefferts, Craig	88F	87	$ .01	$ .05
Law, Vance	82F	484	$ .01	$ .05	Lefferts, Craig	90F	60	$ .01	$ .04
Law, Vance	83F	245	$ .01	$ .05	Lefferts, Craig	90FU	57	$ .01	$ .05
Law, Vance	84F	68	$ .01	$ .06	Lefferts, Craig	91F	534	$ .01	$ .03
Law, Vance	85F	520	$ .01	$ .05	LeFlore, Ron	81F	154	$ .01	$ .05
Law, Vance	85FU	70	$ .01	$ .05	LeFlore, Ron	82F	350	$ .01	$ .05
Law, Vance	86F	252	$ .01	$ .05	LeFlore, Ron	83F	246	$ .01	$ .05
Law, Vance	87F	323	$ .01	$ .05	Leibrandt, Charlie	81F	208	$ .05	$ .30
Law, Vance	88F	187	$ .01	$ .05	Leibrandt, Charlie	82F	74	$ .01	$ .10
Law, Vance	88FU	79	$ .01	$ .05	Leibrandt, Charlie	83F	596	$ .01	$ .05

FLEER

Player	Year	No.	VG	EX/MT	Player	Year	No.	VG	EX/MT
Leibrandt, Charlie	85F	206	$ .01	$ .05	Leonard, Jeff	81F	67	$ .03	$ .20
Leibrandt, Charlie	86F	13	$ .01	$ .05	Leonard, Jeff	84F	379	$ .03	$ .10
Leibrandt, Charlie	87F	373	$ .01	$ .05	Leonard, Jeff	85F	615	$ .03	$ .20
Leibrandt, Charlie	88F	263	$ .01	$ .05	Leonard, Jeff	86F	548	$ .01	$ .10
Leibrandt, Charlie	89F	286	$ .01	$ .05	Leonard, Jeff	87F	278	$ .01	$ .10
					Leonard, Jeff	88F	88	$ .01	$ .05
					Leonard, Jeff	88FU	39	$ .01	$ .05
					Leonard, Jeffrey	89F	190	$ .01	$ .05
					Leonard, Jeffrey	89FU	60	$ .01	$ .05
					Leonard, Jeffrey	90F	519	$ .01	$ .04
					Leonard, Jeffrey	91F	456	$ .01	$ .03
					Leonard, Mark	91F	265	$ .01	$ .15
					Lerch, Randy	81F	25	$ .01	$ .05
					Lerch, Randy	82F	147	$ .01	$ .05
					Lerch, Randy	83F	287	$ .01	$ .05
					Lerch, Randy	84F	380	$ .01	$ .06
					Lerch, Randy	85F	616	$ .01	$ .05
					Lewis, Darren	91F	15	$ .01	$ .25
					Leyritz, Jim	90FU	112	$ .01	$ .25
					Leyritz, Jim	91F	671	$ .01	$ .10
					Lezcano, Carlos	81F	307	$ .01	$ .05
					Lezcano, Sixto	81F	513	$ .01	$ .05
					Lezcano, Sixto	82F	119	$ .01	$ .05
					Lezcano, Sixto	83F	364	$ .01	$ .05
					Lezcano, Sixto	84F	38	$ .01	$ .06
					Lezcano, Sixto	85F	258	$ .01	$ .05
					Lezcano, Sixto	85FU	72	$ .01	$ .05
					Lilliquist, Derek	89FU	73	$ .01	$ .20
					Lilliquist, Derek	90F	588	$ .01	$ .10
					Lilliquist, Derek	91F	535	$ .01	$ .03
					Linares, Rufino	82F	439	$ .01	$ .05
					Linares, Rufino	83F	140	$ .01	$ .05
					Lind, Jose	88F	334	$ .01	$ .20
					Lind, Jose	89F	214	$ .01	$ .10
					Lind, Jose	90F	474	$ .01	$ .04
Leibrandt, Charlie	90F	112	$ .01	$ .04	Lind, Jose	91F	43	$ .01	$ .03
Leibrandt, Charlie	91F	695	$ .01	$ .03	Lindeman, Jim	87FU	65	$ .05	$ .30
Leifferts, Craig	89F	332	$ .01	$ .05	Lindeman, Jim	88F	39	$ .01	$ .10
Leiper, Dave	88FU	123	$ .01	$ .05	Lindsey, Bill	88F	403	$ .01	$ .10
Leiper, Dave	89F	310	$ .01	$ .05	Liriano, Nelson	88F	117	$ .01	$ .30
Leiper, David	87F	398	$ .01	$ .10	Liriano, Nelson	89F	239	$ .01	$ .05
Leiter, Al	88FU	49	$ .01	$ .25	Liriano, Nelson	90F	87	$ .01	$ .04
Leiter, Al	89F	257	$ .01	$ .10	Liriano, Nelson	91F	617	$ .01	$ .03
Leiter, Al	89FU	70	$ .01	$ .10	Littell, Mark	81F	544	$ .01	$ .05
Leius, Scott	90F	647	$ .01	$ .04	Littell, Mark	82F	120	$ .01	$ .05
LeMaster, Johnnie	81F	450	$ .01	$ .05	Little, Bryan	84F	279	$ .01	$ .06
LeMaster, Johnnie	82F	393	$ .01	$ .05	Little, Bryan	85F	402	$ .01	$ .05
LeMaster, Johnnie	83F	266	$ .01	$ .05	Little, Bryan	86F	212	$ .01	$ .05
LeMaster, Johnnie	84F	378	$ .01	$ .06	Little, Jeff	83F	619	$ .01	$ .05
LeMaster, Johnnie	85F	614	$ .01	$ .05	Littlefield, John	81F	535	$ .01	$ .05
Lemke, Mark	90F	587	$ .01	$ .04	Littlefield, John	82F	576	$ .01	$ .05
Lemke, Mark	91F	696	$ .01	$ .03	Littlejohn, Dennis	81F	455	$ .01	$ .05
Lemon, Chet	81F	354	$ .01	$ .05	Litton, Greg	89FU	130	$ .01	$ .20
Lemon, Chet	82F	351	$ .01	$ .05	Litton, Greg	90F	61	$ .01	$ .15
Lemon, Chet	83F	335	$ .01	$ .05	Litton, Greg	91F	266	$ .01	$ .03
Lemon, Chet	84F	85	$ .01	$ .06	Lollar, Tim	81F	108	$ .01	$ .05
Lemon, Chet	85F	15	$ .01	$ .05	Lollar, Tim	83F	365	$ .01	$ .05
Lemon, Chet	86F	230	$ .01	$ .05	Lollar, Tim	84F	305	$ .01	$ .06
Lemon, Chet	87F	156	$ .01	$ .05	Lollar, Tim	85F	39	$ .01	$ .05
Lemon, Chet	88F	61	$ .01	$ .05	Lollar, Tim	85FU	73	$ .01	$ .05
Lemon, Chet	89F	137	$ .01	$ .05	Lollar, Tim	86F	354	$ .01	$ .05
Lemon, Chet	90F	608	$ .01	$ .04	Lollar, Tim	87F	38	$ .01	$ .05
Lemon, Chet	91F	341	$ .01	$ .03	Lombardi, Phil	87F	648	$ .10	$3.00
Lentine, Jim	81F	476	$ .01	$ .05	Lombardozzi, Steve	86FU	68	$ .05	$ .30
Leonard, Dennis	81F	42	$ .01	$ .05	Lombardozzi, Steve	87F	547	$ .01	$ .05
Leonard, Dennis	82F	413	$ .01	$ .05	Lombardozzi, Steve	88F	16	$ .01	$ .05
Leonard, Dennis	83F	116	$ .01	$ .05	Lombardozzi, Steve	89F	120	$ .01	$ .05
Leonard, Dennis	84F	349	$ .01	$ .06	Long, Bill	87FU	66	$ .01	$ .10
Leonard, Dennis	86FU	67	$ .01	$ .05	Long, Bill	88F	404	$ .01	$ .15
Leonard, Dennis	87F	374	$ .01	$ .05	Long, Bill	89F	501	$ .01	$ .05

FLEER'90

Charlie Leibrandt

PITCHER

Player	Year	No.	VG	EX/MT	Player	Year	No.	VG	EX/MT
Long, Bill	91F	425	$ .01	$ .03	Lyons, Barry	88F	140	$ .01	$ .10
Long, Bob	86F	468	$ .01	$ .05	Lyons, Barry	89FU	101	$ .01	$ .05
Lopes, Davey 'Dave'	81F	114	$ .01	$ .10	Lyons, Barry	90F	209	$ .01	$ .04
Lopes, Davey	82F	12	$ .01	$ .10	Lyons, Steve	85FU	76	$ .01	$ .05
Lopes, Davey	83F	524	$ .01	$ .10	Lyons, Steve	86F	355	$ .01	$ .05
Lopes, Davey	84F	453	$ .01	$ .06	Lyons, Steve	87F	502	$ .01	$ .05
Lopes, Davey	85F	60	$ .01	$ .05	Lyons, Steve	88F	405	$ .01	$ .05
Lopes, Davey	86F	372	$ .01	$ .05	Lyons, Steve	89F	502	$ .01	$ .05
Lopes, Davey	87F	62	$ .01	$ .05	Lyons, Steve	90F	539	$ .01	$ .04
Lopez, Aurelio	82F	273	$ .01	$ .05	Lyons, Steve	91F	127	$ .01	$ .03
Lopez, Aurelio	84F	86	$ .01	$ .06	Lysander, Rick	84F	570	$ .01	$ .06
Lopez, Aurelio	85F	16	$ .01	$ .05	Lysander, Rick	85F	284	$ .01	$ .05
Lopez, Aurelio	86F	231	$ .01	$ .05	Lysander, Rick	86F	399	$ .01	$ .05
Lopez, Aurelio	86FU	69	$ .01	$ .05	Maas, Kevin	90F	641	$ .01	$2.00
Lopez, Aurelio	87F	63	$ .01	$ .05	Maas, Kevin	90FU	113	$ .01	$2.00
Lovelace, Vance	89F	651	$ .01	$ .20	Maas, Kevin	91F	672	$ .01	$ .50
Lovullo, Torey	89F	648	$ .01	$ .25	MacFarlane (f), Mike	88FU	31	$ .01	$ .15
Lowenstein, John	81F	186	$ .01	$ .05	Macfarlane, Mike	89F	287	$ .01	$ .20
Lowenstein, John	82F	169	$ .01	$ .05	Macfarlane, Mike	90F	114	$ .01	$ .04
Lowenstein, John	83F	63	$ .01	$ .05	Macfarlane, Mike	91F	562	$ .01	$ .03
Lowenstein, John	84F	10	$ .01	$ .06	Macha, Ken	81F	167	$ .01	$ .05
Lowenstein, John	85F	180	$ .01	$ .05	Macha, Ken	82F	618	$ .01	$ .05
Lowry, Dwight	87F	157	$ .01	$ .05	Machado, Julio	90FU	37	$ .01	$ .10
Loynd, Mike	87FU	67	$ .01	$ .05	Mack, Shane	88F	590	$ .01	$ .25
Loynd, Mike	88F	472	$ .01	$ .05	Mack, Shane	91F	618	$ .01	$ .03
Lozado, Willie	85F	644	$ .01	$ .05	Mackanin, Pete	81F	565	$ .01	$ .05
Lubratich, Steve	84F	524	$ .01	$ .06	Mackanin, Pete	82F	556	$ .01	$ .05
Lucas, Gary	81F	502	$ .01	$ .05	Madden, Mike	84F	232	$ .01	$ .06
Lucas, Gary	82F	577	$ .01	$ .05	Maddox, Elliott	81F	326	$ .01	$ .05
Lucas, Gary	83F	366	$ .01	$ .05	Maddox, Garry	81F	19	$ .01	$ .05
Lucas, Gary	84F	306	$ .01	$ .06	Maddox, Garry	82F	248	$ .01	$ .05
Lucas, Gary	84FU	73	$ .01	$ .10	Maddox, Garry	83F	164	$ .01	$ .05
Lucas, Gary	85F	403	$ .01	$ .05	Maddox, Garry	84F	39	$ .01	$ .06
Lucas, Gary	86F	254	$ .01	$ .05	Maddox, Garry	85F	259	$ .01	$ .05
Lucas, Gary	87F	87	$ .01	$ .05	Maddox, Garry	86F	445	$ .01	$ .05
Lucas, Gary	88F	495	$ .01	$ .05	Maddux, Greg	87FU	68	$ .25	$ .75
Luecken, Rick	90F	113	$ .01	$ .15	Maddux, Greg	88F	423	$ .10	$ .50
Lugo, Urbano	85FU	74	$ .01	$ .05	Maddux, Greg	89F	431	$ .01	$ .05
Lugo, Urbano	86F	162	$ .01	$ .05	Maddux, Greg	90F	37	$ .01	$ .10
Lum, Mike	81F	258	$ .01	$ .05	Maddux, Greg	91F	426	$ .01	$ .03
Lum, Mike	82F	599	$ .01	$ .05	Maddux, Mike	87F	179	$ .01	$ .05
Lusader, Scott	88F	62	$ .01	$ .15	Maddux, Mike	88F	309	$ .01	$ .05
Luzinski, Greg	81F	10	$ .01	$ .10	Maddux, Mike	89F	576	$ .01	$ .05
Luzinski, Greg	82F	352	$ .01	$ .10	Madlock, Bill	81F	381	$ .03	$ .20
Luzinski, Greg	83F	247	$ .01	$ .10	Madlock, Bill	82F	485	$ .01	$ .10
Luzinski, Greg	84F	69	$ .01	$ .06	Madlock, Bill	83F	309	$ .01	$ .10
Luzinski, Greg	85F	521	$ .01	$ .05	Madlock, Bill	84F	253	$ .03	$ .10
Lyle, Sparky	81F	17	$ .01	$ .10	Madlock, Bill	85F	468	$ .01	$ .10
Lyle, Sparky	82F	247	$ .01	$ .10	Madlock, Bill	86F	135	$ .01	$ .10
Lynch, Ed	82F	531	$ .01	$ .05	Madlock, Bill	87F	445	$ .01	$ .10
Lynch, Ed	83F	549	$ .01	$ .05	Madlock, Bill	87FU	69	$ .01	$ .05
Lynch, Ed	84F	591	$ .01	$ .06	Madlock, Bill	88F	63	$ .01	$ .10
Lynch, Ed	85F	87	$ .01	$ .05	Magadan, Dave	87F	648	$ .10	$3.00
Lynch, Ed	86F	88	$ .01	$ .05	Magadan, Dave	87FU	70	$ .05	$ .25
Lynch, Ed	87F	567	$ .01	$ .05	Magadan, Dave	88F	141	$ .01	$ .10
Lynch, Ed	88F	422	$ .01	$ .05	Magadan, Dave	89F	41	$ .01	$ .05
Lynn, Fred	81F	223	$ .04	$ .25	Magadan, Dave	90F	210	$ .01	$ .04
Lynn, Fred	82F	468	$ .03	$ .20	Magadan, Dave	91F	153	$ .01	$ .03
Lynn, Fred	82F	642	$ .01	$ .05	Magrane, Joe	87FU	71	$ .05	$ .35
Lynn, Fred	83F	97	$ .03	$ .20	Magrane, Joe	88F	40	$ .10	$ .35
Lynn, Fred	84F	525	$ .03	$ .20	Magrane, Joe	89F	455	$ .01	$ .15
Lynn, Fred	84F	626	$ .03	$ .10	Magrane, Joe	90F	252	$ .01	$ .04
Lynn, Fred	85F	307	$ .03	$ .20	Magrane, Joe	91F	638	$ .01	$ .03
Lynn, Fred	85FU	75	$ .05	$ .30	Mahler, Mickey	85FU	77	$ .01	$ .05
Lynn, Fred	86F	278	$ .03	$ .20	Mahler, Mickey	86FU	70	$ .01	$ .05
Lynn, Fred	87F	474	$ .03	$ .20	Mahler, Rick	82F	440	$ .04	$ .25
Lynn, Fred	88F	566	$ .01	$ .10	Mahler, Rick	83F	141	$ .01	$ .05
Lynn, Fred	89F	138	$ .01	$ .05	Mahler, Rick	85F	332	$ .01	$ .05
Lynn, Fred	90F	609	$ .01	$ .04	Mahler, Rick	86F	521	$ .01	$ .05
Lynn, Fred	91F	536	$ .01	$ .03	Mahler, Rick	87F	520	$ .01	$ .05

FLEER

Player	Year	No.	VG	EX/MT	Player	Year	No.	VG	EX/MT
Mahler, Rick	89F	595	$ .01	$ .05	Martinez, Carmelo	86F	329	$ .01	$ .05
Mahler, Rick	89FU	85	$ .01	$ .05	Martinez, Carmelo	87F	423	$ .01	$ .05
Mahler, Rick	90F	425	$ .01	$ .04	Martinez, Carmelo	88F	591	$ .01	$ .05
Mahler, Rick	91F	71	$ .01	$ .03	Martinez, Carmelo	89F	311	$ .01	$ .05
Maldonado, Candy	83F	212	$ .10	$ .45	Martinez, Carmelo	90F	162	$ .01	$ .04
Maldonado, Candy	85F	376	$ .01	$ .10	Martinez, Carmelo	90FU	44	$ .01	$ .05
Maldonado, Candy	86F	136	$ .01	$ .10	Martinez, Carmelo	91F	44	$ .01	$ .03
Maldonado, Candy	86FU	71	$ .01	$ .05	Martinez, Dave	88F	424	$ .01	$ .05
Maldonado, Candy	87F	279	$ .01	$ .10	Martinez, Dave	89F	384	$ .01	$ .05
Maldonado, Candy	88F	89	$ .01	$ .05	Martinez, Dave	90F	353	$ .01	$ .04
Maldonado, Candy	89F	333	$ .01	$ .05	Martinez, Dave	91F	237	$ .01	$ .03
Maldonado, Candy	90F	62	$ .01	$ .04	Martinez, Dennis	81F	180	$ .01	$ .05
Maldonado, Candy	90FU	93	$ .01	$ .05	Martinez, Dennis	82F	170	$ .01	$ .05
Maldonado, Candy	91F	373	$ .01	$ .03	Martinez, Dennis	83F	64	$ .01	$ .05
Mallicoat, Rob	88F	452	$ .01	$ .10	Martinez, Dennis	84F	11	$ .01	$ .06
Malone, Chuck	91F	404	$ .01	$ .10	Martinez, Dennis	85F	181	$ .01	$ .05
Mann, Kelly	90F	642	$ .01	$ .25	Martinez, Dennis	86F	280	$ .01	$ .05
Manning, Rick	81F	403	$ .01	$ .05	Martinez, Dennis	87F	324	$ .01	$ .05
Manning, Rick	82F	374	$ .01	$ .05	Martinez, Dennis	88F	188	$ .01	$ .05
Manning, Rick	83F	413	$ .01	$ .05	Martinez, Dennis	89F	385	$ .01	$ .05
Manning, Rick	84F	205	$ .01	$ .06	Martinez, Dennis	90F	354	$ .01	$ .04
Manning, Rick	85F	586	$ .01	$ .05	Martinez, Dennis	91F	238	$ .01	$ .03
Manning, Rick	86F	493	$ .01	$ .05	Martinez, Edgar	88F	378	$ .10	$1.00
Manning, Rick	87F	349	$ .01	$ .05	Martinez, Edgar	89F	552	$ .01	$ .15
Manning, Rick	88F	168	$ .01	$ .05	Martinez, Edgar	90F	520	$ .01	$ .10
Manon, Ramon	90FU	124	$ .01	$ .10	Martinez, Edgar	91F	457	$ .01	$ .03
Manrique, Fred	87FU	72	$ .04	$ .25	Martinez, Ramon	89F	67	$ .05	$2.00
Manrique, Fred	88F	406	$ .01	$ .15	Martinez, Ramon	90F	402	$ .01	$ .50
Manrique, Fred	89F	503	$ .01	$ .05	Martinez, Ramon	91F	212	$ .01	$ .25
Manrique, Fred	90F	306	$ .01	$ .04	Martinez, Silvio	81F	546	$ .01	$ .05
Manto, Jeff	89FU	13	$ .01	$ .25	Martinez, Silvio	82F	122	$ .01	$ .05
Manto, Jeff	90F	137	$ .01	$ .15	Martinez, Tino	90FU	119	$ .01	$ .75
Manto, Jeff	90FU	94	$ .01	$ .05	Martinez, Tino	91F	458	$ .01	$ .30
Manuel, Jerry	82F	195	$ .01	$ .05	Martinez, Tippy	81F	179	$ .01	$ .05
Manwaring, Kirt	88F	651	$ .01	$ .75	Martinez, Tippy	82F	171	$ .01	$ .05
Manwaring, Kirt	89F	334	$ .01	$ .05	Martinez, Tippy	83F	65	$ .01	$ .05
Manwaring, Kirt	90F	63	$ .01	$ .04	Martinez, Tippy	84F	12	$ .01	$ .06
Marshall, Mike	82F	13	$ .15	$1.00	Martinez, Tippy	84F	635	$ .01	$ .06
Marshall, Mike	82F	532	$ .01	$ .05	Martinez, Tippy	85F	182	$ .01	$ .05
Marshall, Mike	83F	211	$ .03	$ .20	Martinez, Tippy	86F	279	$ .01	$ .05
Marshall, Mike	84F	105	$ .03	$ .20	Martz, Randy	81F	300	$ .01	$ .05
Marshall, Mike	85F	377	$ .01	$ .10	Martz, Randy	82F	600	$ .01	$ .05
Marshall, Mike	86F	137	$ .01	$ .10	Martz, Randy	83F	501	$ .01	$ .05
Marshall, Mike	87F	446	$ .01	$ .10	Marzano, John	88F	357	$ .05	$ .35
Marshall, Mike	88F	522	$ .01	$ .05	Marzano, John	91F	103	$ .01	$ .03
Marshall, Mike	89F	66	$ .01	$ .05	Mason, Mike	84FU	76	$ .06	$ .35
Marshall, Mike	90F	401	$ .01	$ .04	Mason, Mike	85F	562	$ .01	$ .05
Marshall, Mike	91F	102	$ .01	$ .03	Mason, Mike	86F	565	$ .01	$ .05
Martin, Billy	81F	581	$ .01	$ .10	Mason, Mike	87F	129	$ .01	$ .05
Martin, Jerry	81F	295	$ .01	$ .05	Mason, Mike	87FU	73	$ .01	$ .05
Martin, Jerry	82F	394	$ .01	$ .05	Mason, Roger	86FU	72	$ .01	$ .05
Martin, Jerry	83F	117	$ .01	$ .05	Mason, Roger	87F	280	$ .01	$ .05
Martin, Jerry	84FU	74	$ .01	$ .10	Mata, Vic	85F	644	$ .01	$ .05
Martin, John	82F	121	$ .01	$ .05	Mathews, Greg	86FU	73	$ .05	$ .30
Martin, Renie	81F	39	$ .01	$ .05	Mathews, Greg	87F	303	$ .04	$ .20
Martin, Renie	82F	414	$ .01	$ .05	Mathews, Greg	88F	41	$ .01	$ .10
Martin, Renie	83F	267	$ .01	$ .05	Mathews, Greg	89F	456	$ .01	$ .05
Martin, Renie	84F	381	$ .01	$ .06	Mathis, Ron	85FU	78	$ .01	$ .05
Martinez, Alfredo	81F	288	$ .01	$ .05	Mathis, Ron	86F	305	$ .01	$ .05
Martinez, Buck	81F	526	$ .01	$ .05	Matlack, Jon	81F	621	$ .01	$ .05
Martinez, Buck	83F	433	$ .01	$ .05	Matlack, Jon	82F	323	$ .01	$ .05
Martinez, Buck	84F	161	$ .01	$ .06	Matlack, Jon	83F	572	$ .01	$ .05
Martinez, Buck	85F	114	$ .01	$ .05	Matlack, Jon	84F	422	$ .01	$ .06
Martinez, Buck	86F	66	$ .01	$ .05	Matthews, Gary	81F	251	$ .01	$ .10
Martinez, Buck	87F	235	$ .01	$ .05	Matthews, Gary	82F	249	$ .01	$ .05
Martinez, Carlos	90F	540	$ .01	$ .20	Matthews, Gary	83F	165	$ .01	$ .05
Martinez, Carlos	91F	128	$ .01	$ .03	Matthews, Gary	84F	40	$ .01	$ .06
Martinez, Carmelo	84F	497	$ .04	$ .25	Matthews, Gary	84FU	77	$ .04	$ .25
Martinez, Carmelo	84FU	75	$ .04	$ .25	Matthews, Gary	85F	61	$ .01	$ .05
Martinez, Carmelo	85F	40	$ .01	$ .05	Matthews, Gary	86F	373	$ .01	$ .05

Player	Year	No.	VG	EX/MT
Matthews, Gary	87F	568	$ .01	$ .05
Mattick, Bob	81F	431	$ .01	$ .05
Mattingly, Don	84F	131	$8.00	$50.00
Mattingly, Don	85F	133	$3.00	$12.00
Mattingly, Don	86F	109	$ .60	$4.00
Mattingly, Don	86F	627	$ .30	$1.50
Mattingly, Don	86F	639	$ .30	$1.50
Mattingly, Don	87F	104	$ .50	$2.50
Mattingly, Don	87F	638	$ .10	$1.00
Mattingly, Don	88F	214	$ .25	$1.50
Mattingly, Don	89F	258	$ .10	$ .60
Mattingly, Don	90F	447	$ .01	$ .35
Mattingly, Don	90F	638	$ .01	$ .10
Mattingly, Don	90FPD	626	$ .01	$ .35
Mattingly, Don	91F	673	$ .01	$ .25
Matula, Rick	81F	263	$ .01	$ .05
Matuszek, Len	84F	41	$ .01	$ .06
Matuszek, Len	85F	260	$ .01	$ .05
Matuszek, Len	85FU	79	$ .01	$ .05

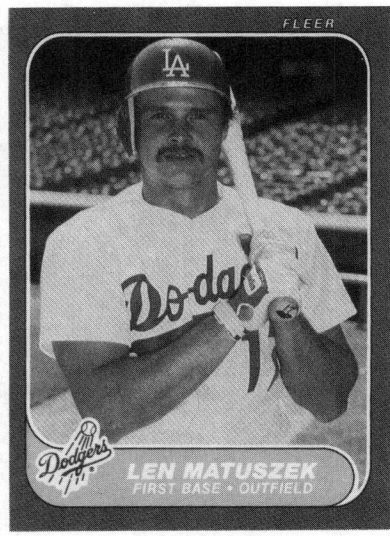

LEN MATUSZEK
FIRST BASE • OUTFIELD

Player	Year	No.	VG	EX/MT
Matuszek, Len	86F	138	$ .01	$ .05
Matuszek, Len	87F	447	$ .01	$ .05
May, Derrick	90F	645	$ .01	$ .04
May, Derrick	91F	427	$ .01	$ .20
May, Lee	81F	183	$ .01	$ .05
May, Lee	82F	415	$ .01	$ .05
May, Lee	83F	118	$ .01	$ .05
May, Milt	81F	442	$ .01	$ .05
May, Milt	82F	395	$ .01	$ .05
May, Milt	83F	268	$ .01	$ .05
May, Milt	84F	254	$ .01	$ .06
May, Rudy	81F	90	$ .01	$ .05
May, Rudy	82F	41	$ .01	$ .05
May, Rudy	83F	385	$ .01	$ .05
Mayberry, John	81F	416	$ .01	$ .05
Mayberry, John	82F	619	$ .01	$ .05
Mayberry, John	83F	386	$ .01	$ .05
Mazzilli, Lee	81F	316	$ .01	$ .05
Mazzilli, Lee	82F	533	$ .01	$ .05
Mazzilli, Lee	83F	387	$ .01	$ .05
Mazzilli, Lee	84F	255	$ .01	$ .06

Player	Year	No.	VG	EX/MT
Mazzilli, Lee	85F	469	$ .01	$ .05
Mazzilli, Lee	86F	612	$ .01	$ .05
Mazzilli, Lee	87F	15	$ .01	$ .05
Mazzilli, Lee	90F	88	$ .01	$ .04
McBride, Bake	81F	9	$ .01	$ .05
McBride, Bake	82F	250	$ .01	$ .05
McBride, Bake	83F	414	$ .01	$ .05
McBride, Bake	84F	547	$ .01	$ .06
McCament, Randy	90F	64	$ .01	$ .10
McCarthy, Tom	90F	541	$ .01	$ .04
McCarver, Tim	81F	27	$ .01	$ .05
McCaskill, Kirk	86F	163	$ .06	$ .50
McCaskill, Kirk	87F	88	$ .01	$ .05
McCaskill, Kirk	88F	496	$ .01	$ .05
McCaskill, Kirk	89F	483	$ .01	$ .05
McCaskill, Kirk	90F	138	$ .01	$ .04
McCaskill, Kirk	91F	319	$ .01	$ .03
McCatty, Steve	81F	589	$ .01	$ .05
McCatty, Steve	82F	99	$ .01	$ .05
McCatty, Steve	83F	525	$ .01	$ .05
McCatty, Steve	84F	454	$ .01	$ .06
McCatty, Steve	85F	430	$ .01	$ .05
McCatty, Steve	86F	427	$ .01	$ .05
McClendon, Lloyd	87FU	74	$ .04	$ .25
McClendon, Lloyd	89FU	77	$ .01	$ .10
McClendon, Lloyd	90F	38	$ .01	$ .04
McClure, Bob	81F	520	$ .01	$ .05
McClure, Bob	83F	38	$ .01	$ .05
McClure, Bob	84F	206	$ .01	$ .06
McClure, Bob	85F	587	$ .01	$ .05
McClure, Bob	86F	494	$ .01	$ .05
McClure, Bob	87F	325	$ .01	$ .05
McClure, Bob	88F	189	$ .01	$ .05
McClure, Bob	89F	42	$ .01	$ .05
McClure, Bob	89FU	14	$ .01	$ .10
McClure, Bob	90F	139	$ .01	$ .04
McCovey, Willie	81F	434	$ .07	$ .50
McCullers, Lance	86F	330	$ .04	$ .25
McCullers, Lance	87F	424	$ .01	$ .05
McCullers, Lance	88F	592	$ .01	$ .05
McCullers, Lance	89F	312	$ .01	$ .05
McCullers, Lance	90F	448	$ .01	$ .04
McCullers, Lance	91F	342	$ .01	$ .03
McDonald, Ben	90F	180	$ .01	$1.50
McDonald, Ben	91F	481	$ .01	$ .25
McDowell, Jack	88F	407	$ .01	$1.00
McDowell, Jack	89F	504	$ .01	$ .15
McDowell, Jack	91F	129	$ .01	$ .03
McDowell, Oddibe	85FU	80	$ .10	$ .70
McDowell, Oddibe	86F	566	$ .04	$ .20
McDowell, Oddibe	87F	130	$ .01	$ .10
McDowell, Oddibe	88F	473	$ .01	$ .10
McDowell, Oddibe	89F	528	$ .01	$ .05
McDowell, Oddibe	90F	589	$ .01	$ .04
McDowell, Oddibe	91F	697	$ .01	$ .03
McDowell, Roger	85FU	81	$ .15	$ .75
McDowell, Roger	86F	89	$ .06	$ .30
McDowell, Roger	87F	16	$ .01	$ .10
McDowell, Roger	88F	142	$ .01	$ .10
McDowell, Roger	89F	43	$ .01	$ .05
McDowell, Roger	89FU	110	$ .01	$ .05
McDowell, Roger	90F	567	$ .01	$ .04
McDowell, Roger	91F	405	$ .01	$ .03
McElroy, Chuck	90F	650	$ .01	$ .04
McElroy, Chuck	91F	406	$ .01	$ .10
McGaffigan, Andy	84F	382	$ .01	$ .06
McGaffigan, Andy	84FU	78	$ .01	$ .10
McGaffigan, Andy	85F	540	$ .01	$ .05
McGaffigan, Andy	86F	181	$ .01	$ .05
McGaffigan, Andy	86FU	74	$ .01	$ .05

FLEER

Player	Year	No.	VG	EX/MT	Player	Year	No.	VG	EX/MT
McGaffigan, Andy	87F	326	$ .01	$ .05	McRae, Hal	86F	14	$ .01	$ .05
McGaffigan, Andy	88F	190	$ .01	$ .05	McRae, Hal	87F	375	$ .01	$ .05
McGaffigan, Andy	89F	386	$ .01	$ .05	McReynolds, Kevin	84F	307	$1.00	$5.00
McGaffigan, Andy	90F	355	$ .01	$ .04	McReynolds, Kevin	85F	41	$ .25	$1.25
McGee, Willie	83F	15	$ .20	$3.00	McReynolds, Kevin	86F	331	$ .05	$ .30
McGee, Willie	84F	329	$ .05	$ .40	McReynolds, Kevin	87F	425	$ .05	$ .25
McGee, Willie	85F	234	$ .05	$ .30	McReynolds, Kevin	87FU	78	$ .03	$ .20
McGee, Willie	86F	42	$ .01	$ .10	McReynolds, Kevin	88F	143	$ .01	$ .10
McGee, Willie	86F	636	$ .01	$ .25	McReynolds, Kevin	89F	44	$ .01	$ .15
McGee, Willie	87F	304	$ .01	$ .10	McReynolds, Kevin	90F	211	$ .01	$ .10
McGee, Willie	88F	42	$ .01	$ .10	McReynolds, Kevin	91F	154	$ .01	$ .03
McGee, Willie	89F	457	$ .01	$ .05	McWilliams, Larry	81F	267	$ .01	$ .05
McGee, Willie	90F	253	$ .01	$ .04	McWilliams, Larry	83F	310	$ .01	$ .05
McGee, Willie	91F	16	$ .01	$ .03	McWilliams, Larry	84F	256	$ .01	$ .06
McGlothen, Lynn	81F	302	$ .01	$ .05	McWilliams, Larry	85F	470	$ .01	$ .05
McGraw, Tug	81F	7	$ .01	$ .05	McWilliams, Larry	86F	613	$ .01	$ .05
McGraw, Tug	81F	657	$ .10	$ .50	McWilliams, Larry	87F	613	$ .01	$ .05
McGraw, Tug	82F	251	$ .01	$ .10	McWilliams, Larry	89F	458	$ .01	$ .05
McGraw, Tug	83F	166	$ .01	$ .10	Meacham, Bobby	85F	134	$ .01	$ .05
McGraw, Tug	84F	42	$ .03	$ .20	Meacham, Bobby	86F	110	$ .01	$ .05
McGraw, Tug	85F	261	$ .01	$ .10	Meacham, Bobby	87F	105	$ .01	$ .05
McGregor, Scott	81F	174	$ .01	$ .05	Meacham, Bobby	88F	215	$ .01	$ .05
McGregor, Scott	82F	172	$ .01	$ .05	Meadows, Louie	88FU	92	$ .01	$ .15
McGregor, Scott	83F	66	$ .01	$ .05	Meadows, Louie	89F	361	$ .01	$ .15
McGregor, Scott	84F	13	$ .01	$ .06	Meads, Dave	87FU	79	$ .01	$ .05
McGregor, Scott	84F	646	$ .01	$ .06	Meads, Dave	88F	453	$ .01	$ .05
McGregor, Scott	85F	183	$ .01	$ .05	Meads, Dave	89F	362	$ .01	$ .05
McGregor, Scott	86F	281	$ .01	$ .05	Medich, Doc	81F	627	$ .01	$ .05
McGregor, Scott	87F	475	$ .01	$ .05	Medich, Doc	82F	324	$ .01	$ .05
McGriff, Fred	87FU	75	$ .40	$2.50	Medich, Doc	83F	39	$ .01	$ .05
McGriff, Fred	88F	118	$ .25	$2.00	Medina, Luis	89F	411	$ .05	$ .35
McGriff, Fred	89F	240	$ .01	$ .30	Meier, Dave	85F	285	$ .01	$ .05
McGriff, Fred	90F	89	$ .01	$ .10	Meier, Dave	86F	400	$ .01	$ .05
McGriff, Fred	91F	180	$ .01	$ .10	Mejias, Sam	81F	219	$ .01	$ .05
McGriff, Terry	88F	240	$ .01	$ .10	Mejias, Sam	82F	75	$ .01	$ .05
McGuire, Bill	89F	553	$ .01	$ .05	Melvin, Bob	87F	281	$ .01	$ .05
McGwire, Mark	87FU	76	$ .50	$2.50	Melvin, Bob	88F	91	$ .01	$ .05
McGwire, Mark	88F	286	$ .50	$3.00	Melvin, Bob	89F	335	$ .01	$ .05
McGwire, Mark	88F	624	$ .10	$ .75	Melvin, Bob	90F	181	$ .01	$ .04
McGwire, Mark	88F	629	$ .10	$ .75	Melvin, Bob	91F	482	$ .01	$ .03
McGwire, Mark	88F	633	$ .01	$ .35	Mendoza, Mario	81F	613	$ .01	$ .05
McGwire, Mark	89F	17	$ .05	$ .75	Mendoza, Mario	82F	325	$ .01	$ .05
McGwire, Mark	89F	634	$ .05	$ .35	Mercado, Orlando	84F	613	$ .01	$ .06
McGwire, Mark	90F	15	$ .01	$ .25	Mercker, Kent	90F	590	$ .01	$ .25
McGwire, Mark	90F	638	$ .01	$ .10	Meredith, Ron	86F	374	$ .01	$ .05
McGwire, Mark	91F	17	$ .01	$ .15	Merullo, Matt	89FU	21	$ .01	$ .15
McIntosh, Tim	90F	329	$ .01	$ .15	Merullo, Matt	90F	542	$ .01	$ .10
McIntosh, Tim	91F	589	$ .01	$ .10	Meulens, Hensley	89FU	51	$ .01	$ .75
McKay, Dave	81F	592	$ .01	$ .05	Meulens, Hensley	90F	449	$ .01	$ .25
McKay, Dave	82F	100	$ .01	$ .05	Meyer, Brian	90F	232	$ .01	$ .04
McKay, Dave	83F	526	$ .01	$ .05	Meyer, Brian	91F	510	$ .01	$ .03
McKeon, Joel	86FU	75	$ .01	$ .05	Meyer, Dan	81F	603	$ .01	$ .05
McKeon, Joel	87F	503	$ .01	$ .10	Meyer, Dan	82F	512	$ .01	$ .05
McLaughlin, Joey	81F	420	$ .01	$ .05	Meyer, Dan	83F	527	$ .01	$ .05
McLaughlin, Joey	82F	620	$ .01	$ .05	Meyer, Dan	84F	455	$ .01	$ .06
McLaughlin, Joey	83F	434	$ .01	$ .05	Meyer, Joey	88F	645	$ .10	$ .40
McLaughlin, Joey	84F	162	$ .01	$ .06	Meyer, Joey	88FU	40	$ .01	$ .15
McLaughlin, Joey	84FU	79	$ .01	$ .05	Meyer, Joey	89F	191	$ .01	$ .10
McLemore, Mark	86F	650	$ .03	$ .20	Mielke, Gary	90FU	125	$ .01	$ .10
McLemore, Mark	87FU	77	$ .01	$ .05	Mielke, Gary	91F	293	$ .01	$ .03
McLemore, Mark	88F	497	$ .01	$ .05	Milacki, Bob	89F	649	$ .01	$ .25
McLemore, Mark	89F	484	$ .01	$ .05	Milacki, Bob	89FU	6	$ .01	$ .20
McMurtry, Craig	84F	184	$ .01	$ .06	Milacki, Bob	90F	182	$ .01	$ .04
McMurtry, Craig	85F	333	$ .01	$ .05	Milacki, Bob	91F	483	$ .01	$ .03
McRae, Brian	91F	563	$ .01	$ .50	Milbourne, Larry	81F	611	$ .01	$ .05
McRae, Hal	81F	41	$ .01	$ .10	Milbourne, Larry	82F	42	$ .01	$ .05
McRae, Hal	82F	416	$ .01	$ .10	Milbourne, Larry	83F	415	$ .01	$ .05
McRae, Hal	83F	119	$ .01	$ .10	Milbourne, Larry	85F	493	$ .01	$ .05
McRae, Hal	84F	350	$ .03	$ .10	Miller, Darrell	88F	498	$ .01	$ .05
McRae, Hal	85F	207	$ .01	$ .05	Miller, Dyar	82F	534	$ .01	$ .05

Player	Year	No.	VG	EX/MT
Miller, Ed	82F	441	$ .01	$ .05
Miller, Keith	88F	144	$ .01	$ .10
Miller, Keith	89F	45	$ .01	$ .05
Miller, Keith	91F	155	$ .01	$ .03
Miller, Rick	81F	279	$ .01	$ .05
Miller, Rick	82F	299	$ .01	$ .05
Miller, Rick	83F	188	$ .01	$ .05
Miller, Rick	84F	403	$ .01	$ .06
Miller, Rick	85F	163	$ .01	$ .05
Milligan, Randy	88FU	115	$ .01	$ .50
Milligan, Randy	89FU	7	$ .01	$ .05
Milligan, Randy	90F	183	$ .01	$ .04
Milligan, Randy	91F	484	$ .01	$ .03
Mills, Alan	90FU	114	$ .01	$ .20
Mills, Brad	82F	196	$ .01	$ .05
Mills, Brad	83F	288	$ .01	$ .05
Milner, Eddie	83F	597	$ .01	$ .10
Milner, Eddie	84F	474	$ .01	$ .06
Milner, Eddie	85F	541	$ .01	$ .05
Milner, Eddie	86F	182	$ .01	$ .05
Milner, Eddie	87F	205	$ .01	$ .05
Milner, Eddie	88F	90	$ .01	$ .05
Milner, John	81F	386	$ .01	$ .05
Milner, John	82F	197	$ .01	$ .05
Milner, John	83F	311	$ .01	$ .05
Minton, Greg	81F	449	$ .01	$ .05
Minton, Greg	82F	396	$ .01	$ .05
Minton, Greg	83F	269	$ .01	$ .05
Minton, Greg	84F	383	$ .01	$ .06
Minton, Greg	85F	617	$ .01	$ .05
Minton, Greg	86F	549	$ .01	$ .05
Minton, Greg	87F	282	$ .01	$ .05
Minton, Greg	87FU	80	$ .01	$ .05
Minton, Greg	88F	499	$ .01	$ .05
Minton, Greg	89F	485	$ .01	$ .05
Minton, Greg	90F	140	$ .01	$ .04

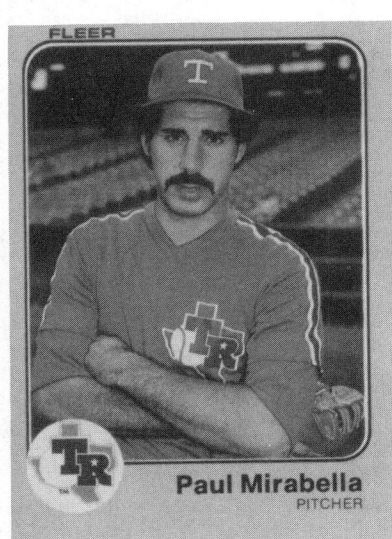

Paul Mirabella
PITCHER

Player	Year	No.	VG	EX/MT
Mirabella, Paul	83F	573	$ .01	$ .05
Mirabella, Paul	85F	494	$ .01	$ .05
Mirabella, Paul	89F	192	$ .01	$ .05
Mirabella, Paul	91F	590	$ .01	$ .03

Player	Year	No.	VG	EX/MT
Mitchell, Bobby	82F	14	$ .01	$ .05
Mitchell, Bob	83F	620	$ .01	$ .05
Mitchell, Bobby	84F	571	$ .01	$ .06
Mitchell, John	87FU	81	$ .04	$ .25
Mitchell, John	88F	145	$ .01	$ .20
Mitchell, John	91F	485	$ .01	$ .10
Mitchell, Kevin	86FU	76	$1.50	$7.00
Mitchell, Kevin	87F	17	$1.25	$8.00
Mitchell, Kevin	87FU	82	$ .35	$2.00
Mitchell, Kevin	88F	92	$ .15	$1.50
Mitchell, Kevin	89F	336	$ .05	$ .35
Mitchell, Kevin	90F	65	$ .01	$ .25
Mitchell, Kevin	90F	637	$ .01	$ .10
Mitchell, Kevin	91F	267	$ .01	$ .15
Moffitt, Randy	81F	446	$ .01	$ .05
Moffitt, Randy	83F	456	$ .01	$ .05
Moffitt, Randy	84F	163	$ .01	$ .06
Mohorcic, Dale	87F	131	$ .04	$ .25
Mohorcic, Dale	88F	474	$ .01	$ .05
Mohorcic, Dale	89F	259	$ .01	$ .05
Mohorcic, Dale	90F	450	$ .01	$ .04
Mohorcic, Dale	91F	239	$ .01	$ .03
Molinaro, Bob	81F	340	$ .01	$ .05
Molinaro, Bob	82F	353	$ .01	$ .05
Molinaro, Bob	83F	167	$ .01	$ .05
Molitor, Paul	81F	515	$ .03	$ .20
Molitor, Paul	82F	148	$ .03	$ .20
Molitor, Paul	83F	40	$ .03	$ .20
Molitor, Paul	84F	207	$ .03	$ .20
Molitor, Paul	85F	588	$ .03	$ .20
Molitor, Paul	86F	495	$ .03	$ .20
Molitor, Paul	87F	350	$ .01	$ .10
Molitor, Paul	88F	169	$ .01	$ .10
Molitor, Paul	89F	193	$ .01	$ .10
Molitor, Paul	90F	330	$ .01	$ .04
Molitor, Paul	91F	591	$ .01	$ .03
Monday, Rick	81F	122	$ .01	$ .05
Monday, Rick	82F	15	$ .01	$ .05
Monday, Rick	83F	213	$ .01	$ .05
Monday, Rick	84F	106	$ .01	$ .06
Money, Don	81F	524	$ .01	$ .05
Money, Don	82F	149	$ .01	$ .05
Money, Don	83F	41	$ .01	$ .05
Money, Don	84F	208	$ .01	$ .06
Monge, Sid	81F	395	$ .01	$ .05
Monge, Sid	82F	375	$ .01	$ .05
Monge, Sid	83F	168	$ .01	$ .05
Monge, Sid	84F	308	$ .01	$ .06
Monge, Sid	85F	17	$ .01	$ .05
Montanez, Willy "Willie"	81F	506	$ .01	$ .05
Montanez, Willy	82F	486	$ .01	$ .05
Montefusco, John	81F	439	$ .01	$ .05
Montefusco, John	82F	442	$ .01	$ .05
Montefusco, John	83F	367	$ .01	$ .05
Montefusco, John	84F	132	$ .01	$ .06
Montefusco, John	85F	135	$ .01	$ .05
Montefusco, John	86F	111	$ .01	$ .05
Monteleone, Rich	90F	648	$ .01	$ .04
Montgomery, Jeff	88F	642	$ .01	$ .75
Montgomery, Jeff	88FU	32	$ .01	$ .15
Montgomery, Jeff	89F	288	$ .01	$ .15
Montgomery, Jeff	90F	115	$ .01	$ .04
Montgomery, Jeff	91F	564	$ .01	$ .03
Mooneyham, Bill	86FU	77	$ .01	$ .05
Mooneyham, Bill	87F	399	$ .01	$ .05
Moore, Brad	90FU	45	$ .01	$ .05
Moore, Charlie	81F	521	$ .01	$ .05
Moore, Charlie	82F	150	$ .01	$ .05
Moore, Charlie	83F	42	$ .01	$ .05
Moore, Charlie	84F	209	$ .01	$ .06

FLEER

Player	Year	No.	VG	EX/MT
Moore, Charlie	85F	589	$ .01	$ .05
Moore, Charlie	86F	496	$ .01	$ .05
Moore, Charlie	87F	351	$ .01	$ .05

Donnie Moore
PITCHER

Player	Year	No.	VG	EX/MT
Moore, Donnie	84F	185	$ .01	$ .06
Moore, Donnie	85F	334	$ .01	$ .05
Moore, Donnie	85FU	82	$ .01	$ .05
Moore, Donnie	86F	164	$ .01	$ .05
Moore, Donnie	87F	89	$ .01	$ .05
Moore, Donnie	88F	500	$ .01	$ .05
Moore, Mike	83F	482	$ .25	$ .75
Moore, Mike	84F	614	$ .01	$ .06
Moore, Mike	85F	495	$ .01	$ .05
Moore, Mike	86F	469	$ .01	$ .05
Moore, Mike	87F	590	$ .01	$ .05
Moore, Mike	88F	379	$ .01	$ .05
Moore, Mike	89F	554	$ .01	$ .05
Moore, Mike	89FU	55	$ .01	$ .05
Moore, Mike	90F	16	$ .01	$ .04
Moore, Mike	91F	18	$ .01	$ .03
Morales, Jerry	81F	338	$ .01	$ .05
Morales, Jerry	82F	601	$ .01	$ .05
Morales, Jerry	83F	502	$ .01	$ .05
Morales, Jerry	84F	498	$ .01	$ .06
Morales, Jose	81F	571	$ .01	$ .05
Morales, Jose	82F	173	$ .01	$ .05
Morales, Jose	84F	107	$ .01	$ .06
Morandini, Mickey	91F	407	$ .01	$ .15
Moreland, Keith	81F	13	$ .06	$ .20
Moreland, Keith	82F	252	$ .01	$ .10
Moreland, Keith	83F	503	$ .01	$ .05
Moreland, Keith	84F	499	$ .01	$ .06
Moreland, Keith	85F	62	$ .01	$ .05
Moreland, Keith	86F	375	$ .01	$ .05
Moreland, Keith	87F	569	$ .01	$ .05
Moreland, Keith	88F	425	$ .01	$ .05
Moreland, Keith	88FU	124	$ .01	$ .05
Moreland, Keith	89F	313	$ .01	$ .05
Moreno, Angel	82F	469	$ .01	$ .05
Moreno, Omar	81F	361	$ .01	$ .05
Moreno, Omar	82F	487	$ .01	$ .05

Player	Year	No.	VG	EX/MT
Moreno, Omar	83F	312	$ .01	$ .05
Moreno, Omar	84F	133	$ .01	$ .06
Moreno, Omar	85F	136	$ .01	$ .05
Moreno, Omar	86F	15	$ .01	$ .05
Moreno, Omar	86FU	78	$ .01	$ .05
Moreno, Omar	87F	521	$ .01	$ .05
Morgan, Joe	81F	78	$ .06	$ .50
Morgan, Joe	82F	397	$ .05	$ .75
Morgan, Joe	83F	270	$ .05	$ .50
Morgan, Joe	84F	43	$ .05	$ .50
Morgan, Joe	84F	636	$ .10	$ .50
Morgan, Joe	84FU	80	$ .40	$4.00
Morgan, Joe	85F	431	$ .01	$ .25
Morgan, Mike	83F	388	$ .01	$ .05
Morgan, Mike	87F	591	$ .01	$ .05
Morgan, Mike	88F	380	$ .01	$ .05
Morgan, Mike	89FU	91	$ .01	$ .05
Morgan, Mike	90F	403	$ .01	$ .04
Morgan, Mike	91F	213	$ .01	$ .03
Morman, Russ	87F	645	$ .03	$ .20
Morris, Hal	89F	260	$ .01	$1.50
Morris, Hal	90FU	15	$ .01	$ .35
Morris, Hal	91F	72	$ .01	$ .15
Morris, Jack	81F	475	$ .04	$ .25
Morris, Jack	82F	274	$ .04	$ .25
Morris, Jack	83F	336	$ .04	$ .25
Morris, Jack	84F	87	$ .04	$ .25
Morris, Jack	85F	18	$ .04	$ .25
Morris, Jack	85F	643	$ .01	$ .15
Morris, Jack	86F	232	$ .03	$ .20
Morris, Jack	87F	158	$ .03	$ .20
Morris, Jack	88F	64	$ .01	$ .10
Morris, Jack	88F	626	$ .01	$ .05
Morris, Jack	89F	139	$ .01	$ .10
Morris, Jack	90F	610	$ .01	$ .04
Morris, Jack	91F	343	$ .01	$ .03
Morris, John	87FU	83	$ .01	$ .05
Morris, John	88F	43	$ .01	$ .05
Morris, John	90F	254	$ .01	$ .04
Morrison, Jim	81F	357	$ .01	$ .05
Morrison, Jim	82F	354	$ .01	$ .05
Morrison, Jim	83F	313	$ .01	$ .05
Morrison, Jim	84F	257	$ .01	$ .06
Morrison, Jim	85F	471	$ .01	$ .05
Morrison, Jim	86F	614	$ .01	$ .05
Morrison, Jim	87F	614	$ .01	$ .05
Morrison, Jim	88F	65	$ .01	$ .05
Moseby, Lloyd	81F	421	$ .13	$ .50
Moseby, Lloyd	82F	621	$ .01	$ .10
Moseby, Lloyd	83F	435	$ .01	$ .10
Moseby, Lloyd	84F	164	$ .03	$ .10
Moseby, Lloyd	85F	115	$ .03	$ .20
Moseby, Lloyd	85F	636	$ .01	$ .10
Moseby, Lloyd	86F	67	$ .01	$ .10
Moseby, Lloyd	87F	236	$ .01	$ .05
Moseby, Lloyd	88F	119	$ .01	$ .10
Moseby, Lloyd	89F	241	$ .01	$ .05
Moseby, Lloyd	90F	90	$ .01	$ .04
Moseby, Lloyd	90FU	97	$ .01	$ .05
Moseby, Lloyd	91F	344	$ .01	$ .03
Moses, John	87F	592	$ .01	$ .05
Moses, John	88F	381	$ .01	$ .05
Moses, John	88FU	45	$ .01	$ .05
Moses, John	89F	121	$ .01	$ .05
Moses, John	90F	381	$ .01	$ .04
Moses, John	91F	619	$ .01	$ .03
Moskau, Paul	81F	207	$ .01	$ .05
Moskau, Paul	82F	76	$ .01	$ .05
Mota, Manny	81F	141	$ .01	$ .05
Motley, Darryl	82F	417	$ .01	$ .05

Player	Year	No.	VG	EX/MT	Player	Year	No.	VG	EX/MT
Motley, Darryl	84FU	81	$ .01	$ .10	Murray, Dale	83F	437	$ .01	$ .05
Motley, Darryl	85F	208	$ .01	$ .05	Murray, Dale	84F	134	$ .01	$ .06
Motley, Darryl	86F	16	$ .01	$ .05	Murray, Dale	85F	137	$ .01	$ .05
Moyer, Jamie	87F	570	$ .01	$ .10	Murray, Eddie	81F	184	$ .13	$1.25
Moyer, Jamie	88F	426	$ .01	$ .05	Murray, Eddie	82F	174	$ .10	$1.00
Moyer, Jamie	89F	432	$ .01	$ .05	Murray, Eddie	83F	67	$ .10	$ .60
Moyer, Jamie	89FU	65	$ .01	$ .05	Murray, Eddie	84F	14	$ .10	$1.00
Moyer, Jamie	90F	307	$ .01	$ .04	Murray, Eddie	85F	184	$ .10	$ .60
Moyer, Jamie	91F	294	$ .01	$ .03	Murray, Eddie	86F	282	$ .06	$ .45
Mulholland, Terry	89FU	111	$ .01	$ .05	Murray, Eddie	87F	476	$ .05	$ .30
Mulholland, Terry	90F	568	$ .01	$ .04	Murray, Eddie	87F	636	$ .03	$ .20
Mulholland, Terry	91F	408	$ .01	$ .03	Murray, Eddie	88F	567	$ .01	$ .15
Mulliniks, Rance	81F	48	$ .01	$ .05	Murray, Eddie	89F	611	$ .01	$ .20
Mulliniks, Rance	82F	418	$ .01	$ .05	Murray, Eddie	89FU	92	$ .01	$ .15
Mulliniks, Rance	83F	436	$ .01	$ .05	Murray, Eddie	90F	404	$ .01	$ .10
Mulliniks, Rance	84F	165	$ .01	$ .06	Murray, Eddie	91F	214	$ .01	$ .03
Mulliniks, Rance	85F	116	$ .01	$ .05	Murray, Rich	81F	452	$ .01	$ .05
Mulliniks, Rance	86F	68	$ .01	$ .05	Musselman, Jeff	87FU	84	$ .04	$ .25
Mulliniks, Rance	87F	237	$ .01	$ .05	Musselman, Jeff	88F	121	$ .01	$ .05
Mulliniks, Rance	88F	120	$ .01	$ .05	Musselman, Jeff	89F	243	$ .01	$ .05
Mulliniks, Rance	89F	242	$ .01	$ .05	Musselman, Jeff	90F	212	$ .01	$ .04
Mulliniks, Rance	90F	91	$ .01	$ .04	Musselman, Ron	85FU	83	$ .01	$ .05
Mulliniks, Rance	91F	181	$ .01	$ .03	Myers, Greg	88F	644	$ .01	$ .30
Mumphrey, Jerry	81F	494	$ .01	$ .05	Myers, Greg	91F	182	$ .01	$ .03
Mumphrey, Jerry	82F	43	$ .01	$ .05	Myers, Randy	87FU	85	$ .01	$ .60
Mumphrey, Jerry	83F	389	$ .01	$ .05	Myers, Randy	88F	146	$ .01	$ .35
Mumphrey, Jerry	84F	233	$ .01	$ .06	Myers, Randy	89F	46	$ .01	$ .15
Mumphrey, Jerry	85F	354	$ .01	$ .05	Myers, Randy	90F	213	$ .01	$ .04
Mumphrey, Jerry	86F	306	$ .01	$ .05	Myers, Randy	91F	73	$ .01	$ .03
Mumphrey, Jerry	86FU	79	$ .01	$ .05	Nabholz, Chris	90FU	30	$ .01	$ .20
Mumphrey, Jerry	87F	571	$ .01	$ .05	Nabholz, Chris	91F	240	$ .01	$ .15
Mumphrey, Jerry	88F	427	$ .01	$ .05	Naehring, Tim	90FU	73	$ .01	$ .35
Munoz, Pedro	91F	620	$ .01	$ .15	Naehring, Tim	91F	105	$ .01	$ .15
Mura, Steve	81F	496	$ .01	$ .05	Nahorodny, Bill	81F	254	$ .01	$ .05
Mura, Steve	82F	578	$ .01	$ .05	Nahorodny, Bill	83F	416	$ .01	$ .05
Mura, Steve	83F	16	$ .01	$ .05	Narron, Jerry	82F	513	$ .01	$ .05
Murcer, Bobby	81F	94	$ .01	$ .10	Navarro, Jaime	89FU	39	$ .01	$ .20
Murcer, Bobby	82F	44	$ .01	$ .10	Navarro, Jaime	90F	331	$ .01	$ .20
Murcer, Bobby	83F	390	$ .01	$ .10	Navarro, Jaime	91F	592	$ .01	$ .03
Murphy, Dale	81F	243	$ .24	$1.20	Neidlinger, Jim	91F	215	$ .01	$ .20
Murphy, Dale	82F	443	$ .25	$1.00	Nelson, Gene	82F	45	$ .01	$ .25
Murphy, Dale	83F	142	$ .15	$1.00	Nelson, Gene	85F	522	$ .01	$ .05
Murphy, Dale	84F	186	$ .13	$1.00	Nelson, Gene	86F	213	$ .01	$ .05
Murphy, Dale	85F	335	$ .12	$ .60	Nelson, Gene	87F	504	$ .01	$ .05
Murphy, Dale	86F	522	$ .07	$ .50	Nelson, Gene	87FU	86	$ .01	$ .05
Murphy, Dale	86F	635	$ .05	$ .30	Nelson, Gene	88F	288	$ .01	$ .05
Murphy, Dale	86F	640	$ .04	$ .25	Nelson, Gene	89F	18	$ .01	$ .05
Murphy, Dale	87F	522	$ .08	$ .40	Nelson, Gene	90F	17	$ .01	$ .04
Murphy, Dale	88F	544	$ .01	$ .25	Nelson, Gene	91F	19	$ .01	$ .03
Murphy, Dale	88F	639	$ .01	$ .15	Nelson, Ricky	84F	615	$ .01	$ .06
Murphy, Dale	89F	596	$ .01	$ .15	Nelson, Rob	87F	653	$ .01	$ .05
Murphy, Dale	90F	591	$ .01	$ .05	Nettles, Graig	81F	87	$ .09	$ .45
Murphy, Dale	90FPD	623	$ .01	$ .10	Nettles, Graig	82F	46	$ .03	$ .20
Murphy, Dale	90FU	46	$ .01	$ .10	Nettles, Graig	83F	391	$ .01	$ .20
Murphy, Dale	91F	409	$ .01	$ .10	Nettles, Graig	84F	135	$ .03	$ .20
Murphy, Dwayne	81F	590	$ .01	$ .05	Nettles, Graig	84FU	82	$ .15	$1.00
Murphy, Dwayne	82F	101	$ .01	$ .05	Nettles, Graig	85F	42	$ .03	$ .20
Murphy, Dwayne	83F	528	$ .01	$ .05	Nettles, Graig	86F	332	$ .01	$ .10
Murphy, Dwayne	84F	456	$ .01	$ .06	Nettles, Graig	87F	426	$ .01	$ .10
Murphy, Dwayne	85F	432	$ .01	$ .05	Newell, Tom	88F	648	$ .01	$ .30
Murphy, Dwayne	86F	428	$ .01	$ .05	Newman, Al	86FU	80	$ .01	$ .05
Murphy, Dwayne	87F	400	$ .01	$ .05	Newman, Al	87F	327	$ .01	$ .05
Murphy, Dwayne	88F	287	$ .01	$ .05	Newman, Al	88F	17	$ .01	$ .05
Murphy, Dwayne	90F	569	$ .01	$ .04	Newman, Al	89F	122	$ .01	$ .05
Murphy, Rob	87F	206	$ .05	$ .30	Newman, Al	90F	382	$ .01	$ .04
Murphy, Rob	88F	241	$ .01	$ .05	Newman, Al	91F	621	$ .01	$ .03
Murphy, Rob	89F	165	$ .01	$ .05	Newman, Jeff	81F	577	$ .01	$ .05
Murphy, Rob	89FU	10	$ .01	$ .05	Newman, Jeff	82F	102	$ .01	$ .05
Murphy, Rob	90F	281	$ .01	$ .04	Newman, Jeff	83F	529	$ .01	$ .05
Murphy, Rob	91F	104	$ .01	$ .03	Newman, Jeff	84F	404	$ .01	$ .06

FLEER

Player	Year	No.	VG	EX/MT	Player	Year	No.	VG	EX/MT
Nichols, Carl	89F	612	$ .01	$ .15	Nokes, Matt	89F	140	$ .01	$ .10
Nichols, Reid	82F	300	$ .01	$ .05	Nokes, Matt	90F	611	$ .01	$ .04
Nichols, Reid	83F	189	$ .01	$ .05	Nokes, Matt	90FU	115	$ .01	$ .05
Nichols, Reid	84F	405	$ .01	$ .06	Nokes, Matt	91F	674	$ .01	$ .03
Nichols, Reid	85F	164	$ .01	$ .05	Nolan, Joe	81F	212	$ .01	$ .05
Nichols, Reid	86F	214	$ .01	$ .05	Nolan, Joe	82F	77	$ .01	$ .05
Nichols, Reid	87FU	89	$ .01	$ .05	Nolan, Joe	83F	68	$ .01	$ .05
Nichols, Reid	88F	191	$ .01	$ .05	Nolan, Joe	84F	15	$ .01	$ .06
Nichols, Rod	90F	497	$ .01	$ .04	Nolan, Joe	85F	185	$ .01	$ .05
Nicosia, Steve	81F	371	$ .01	$ .05	Noles, Dickie	81F	12	$ .01	$ .05
Nicosia, Steve	82F	488	$ .01	$ .05	Noles, Dickie	82F	253	$ .01	$ .05
Nicosia, Steve	83F	314	$ .01	$ .05	Noles, Dickie	83F	504	$ .01	$ .05
Nicosia, Steve	85F	618	$ .01	$ .05	Noles, Dickie	84F	500	$ .01	$ .06
Niedenfuer, Tom	82F	16	$ .05	$ .30	Noles, Dickie	86F	567	$ .01	$ .05
Niedenfuer, Tom	83F	214	$ .01	$ .05	Noles, Dickie	87F	256	$ .01	$ .05
Niedenfuer, Tom	84F	108	$ .01	$ .06	Noles, Dickie	87FU	91	$ .01	$ .05
Niedenfuer, Tom	85F	378	$ .01	$ .05	Nolte, Eric	88F	593	$ .01	$ .15
Niedenfuer, Tom	86F	139	$ .01	$ .05	Nordhagen, Wayne	81F	348	$ .01	$ .05
Niedenfuer, Tom	87F	448	$ .01	$ .05	Nordhagen, Wayne	82F	355	$ .01	$ .05
Niedenfuer, Tom	88F	568	$ .01	$ .05	Nordhagen, Wayne	83F	438	$ .01	$ .05
Niedenfuer, Tom	89F	613	$ .01	$ .05	Norman, Dan	81F	337	$ .01	$ .05
Niedenfuer, Tom	91F	639	$ .01	$ .03	Norman, Dan	83F	289	$ .01	$ .05
Niekro, Joe	81F	54	$ .01	$ .10	Norman, Fred	81F	158	$ .01	$ .05
Niekro, Joe	82F	221	$ .01	$ .10	Norris, Jim	81F	634	$ .01	$ .05
Niekro, Joe	83F	457	$ .01	$ .10	Norris, Mike	81F	573	$ .01	$ .05
Niekro, Joe	84F	234	$ .03	$ .10	Norris, Mike	82F	103	$ .01	$ .05
Niekro, Joe	85F	355	$ .01	$ .10	Norris, Mike	83F	530	$ .01	$ .05
Niekro, Joe	87F	106	$ .01	$ .10	Norris, Mike	84F	457	$ .01	$ .06
Niekro, Joe	87FU	87	$ .01	$ .10	North, Bill	81F	441	$ .01	$ .05
Niekro, Joe	88F	18	$ .01	$ .10	Nunez, Edwin	85F	496	$ .01	$ .05
Niekro, Phil	81F	242	$ .05	$ .30	Nunez, Edwin	86F	470	$ .01	$ .05
Niekro, Phil	82F	444	$ .05	$ .30	Nunez, Edwin	87FU	92	$ .01	$ .05
Niekro, Phil	83F	143	$ .04	$ .25	Nunez, Edwin	88F	383	$ .01	$ .05
Niekro, Phil	84F	187	$ .04	$ .25	Nunez, Edwin	90FU	98	$ .01	$ .05
Niekro, Phil	84FU	83	$ .30	$2.50	Nunez, Edwin	91F	345	$ .01	$ .03
Niekro, Phil	85F	138	$ .04	$ .25	Nunez, Jose	87FU	93	$ .01	$ .10
Niekro, Phil	86F	112	$ .03	$ .20	Nunez, Jose	88F	122	$ .01	$ .15
Niekro, Phil	86F	630	$ .04	$ .25	O'Berry, Mike	82F	78	$ .01	$ .05
Niekro, Phil	86FU	81	$ .05	$ .30	O'Brien, Charlie	89F	194	$ .01	$ .05
Niekro, Phil	87F	254	$ .03	$ .20	O'Brien, Charlie	90F	332	$ .01	$ .04
Niekro, Phil	87F	626	$ .01	$ .10	O'Brien, Pete	84F	423	$ .20	$ .75
Nielson, Scott	89F	261	$ .01	$ .05	O'Brien, Pete	85F	563	$ .03	$ .20
Niemann, Randy	81F	77	$ .01	$ .05	O'Brien, Pete	86F	568	$ .05	$ .20
Niemann, Randy	86FU	82	$ .01	$ .05	O'Brien, Pete	87F	132	$ .01	$ .10
Niemann, Randy	87F	18	$ .01	$ .05	O'Brien, Pete	88F	475	$ .01	$ .05
Nieto, Tom	85F	235	$ .01	$ .05	O'Brien, Pete	89F	529	$ .01	$ .05
Nieto, Tom	86F	43	$ .01	$ .05	O'Brien, Pete	89FU	29	$ .01	$ .05
Nieto, Tom	87FU	88	$ .01	$ .05	O'Brien, Pete	90F	498	$ .01	$ .04
Nieves, Juan	86FU	83	$ .05	$ .30	O'Brien, Pete	91F	459	$ .01	$ .03
Nieves, Juan	87F	352	$ .01	$ .10	O'Connor, Jack	82F	557	$ .01	$ .05
Nieves, Juan	88F	170	$ .01	$ .10	O'Connor, Jack	83F	621	$ .01	$ .05
Nipper, Al	85F	165	$ .04	$ .25	O'Malley, Tom	91F	157	$ .01	$ .03
Nipper, Al	86F	356	$ .01	$ .05	O'Malley, Tom	83F	271	$ .01	$ .05
Nipper, Al	87F	39	$ .01	$ .05	O'Malley, Tom	84F	384	$ .01	$ .06
Nipper, Al	88F	358	$ .01	$ .05	O'Malley, Tom	87F	477	$ .01	$ .05
Nipper, Al	89F	433	$ .01	$ .05	O'Neal, Randy	85F	645	$ .75	$6.50
Nixon, Donell	88F	382	$ .01	$ .15	O'Neal, Randy	86F	233	$ .01	$ .05
Nixon, Donell	88FU	129	$ .01	$ .05	O'Neal, Randy	87F	159	$ .01	$ .05
Nixon, Donell	89F	337	$ .01	$ .05	O'Neal, Randy	91F	268	$ .01	$ .03
Nixon, Donell	90F	66	$ .01	$ .04	O'Neill, Paul	86F	646	$1.00	$4.50
Nixon, Otis	86F	591	$ .01	$ .10	O'Neill, Paul	87FU	94	$ .05	$ .25
Nixon, Otis	87F	255	$ .01	$ .05	O'Neill, Paul	88FU	85	$ .01	$ .15
Nixon, Otis	89F	387	$ .01	$ .05	O'Neill, Paul	89F	166	$ .01	$ .15
Nixon, Otis	90F	356	$ .01	$ .04	O'Neill, Paul	90F	427	$ .01	$ .10
Nixon, Otis	91F	241	$ .01	$ .03	O'Neill, Paul	91F	76	$ .01	$ .03
Noboa, Junior	91F	242	$ .01	$ .03	Oates, Johnny	81F	99	$ .01	$ .05
Noce, Paul	88F	428	$ .01	$ .10	Oates, Johnny	82F	47	$ .01	$ .05
Nokes, Matt	87FU	90	$ .25	$ .35	Oberkfell, Ken	81F	532	$ .01	$ .05
Nokes, Matt	88F	66	$ .10	$ .35	Oberkfell, Ken	82F	123	$ .01	$ .05
Nokes, Matt	88F	638	$ .01	$ .30	Oberkfell, Ken	83F	17	$ .01	$ .05

Player	Year	No.	VG	EX/MT	Player	Year	No.	VG	EX/MT
Oberkfell, Ken	84F	330	$ .01	$ .06	Oquendo, Jose	91F	640	$ .01	$ .03
Oberkfell, Ken	84FU	84	$ .01	$ .10	Orosco, Jesse	83F	550	$ .01	$ .10
Oberkfell, Ken	85F	336	$ .01	$ .05	Orosco, Jesse	84F	593	$ .01	$ .06
Oberkfell, Ken	86F	523	$ .01	$ .05	Orosco, Jesse	85F	89	$ .01	$ .05
Oberkfell, Ken	87F	523	$ .01	$ .05	Orosco, Jesse	86F	90	$ .01	$ .05
Oberkfell, Ken	88F	545	$ .01	$ .05	Orosco, Jesse	87F	20	$ .01	$ .05
Oberkfell, Ken	90F	67	$ .01	$ .04	Orosco, Jesse	88F	148	$ .01	$ .05
Oberkfell, Ken	91F	511	$ .01	$ .03	Orosco, Jesse	88FU	96	$ .01	$ .05
Oelkers, Bryan	87F	257	$ .01	$ .05	Orosco, Jesse	89F	68	$ .01	$ .05
Oester, Ron	81F	218	$ .01	$ .05	Orosco, Jesse	90F	500	$ .01	$ .04
Oester, Ron	82F	79	$ .01	$ .05	Orosco, Jesse	91F	375	$ .01	$ .03
Oester, Ron	83F	598	$ .01	$ .05	Orsulak, Joe	85FU	85	$ .03	$ .20
Oester, Ron	84F	475	$ .01	$ .06	Orsulak, Joe	86F	615	$ .01	$ .10
Oester, Ron	85F	542	$ .01	$ .05					
Oester, Ron	86F	183	$ .01	$ .05					
Oester, Ron	87F	207	$ .01	$ .05					
Oester, Ron	88F	242	$ .01	$ .05					
Oester, Ron	91F	74	$ .01	$ .03					
Offerman, Jose	90FU	24	$ .01	$ .75					
Offerman, Jose	91F	216	$ .01	$ .25					
Office, Rowland	81F	147	$ .01	$ .05					
Office, Rowland	82F	198	$ .01	$ .05					
Oglivie, Ben	81F	508	$ .01	$ .05					
Oglivie, Ben	82F	151	$ .01	$ .05					
Oglivie, Ben	83F	43	$ .01	$ .05					
Oglivie, Ben	83F	640	$ .04	$ .25					
Oglivie, Ben	84F	210	$ .01	$ .06					
Oglivie, Ben	85F	590	$ .01	$ .05					
Oglivie, Ben	86F	497	$ .01	$ .05					
Oglivie, Ben	87F	353	$ .01	$ .05					
Ojeda, Bob	82F	301	$ .15	$ .50					
Ojeda, Bob	83F	190	$ .01	$ .10					
Ojeda, Bob	84F	406	$ .01	$ .06					
Ojeda, Bob	85F	166	$ .01	$ .05					
Ojeda, Bob	86F	357	$ .01	$ .05					
Ojeda, Bob	86FU	84	$ .01	$ .05					
Ojeda, Bob	87F	19	$ .01	$ .05					
Ojeda, Bob	88F	147	$ .01	$ .10					
Ojeda, Bob	89F	47	$ .01	$ .05					
Ojeda, Bob	90F	214	$ .01	$ .04					
Ojeda, Bob	91F	156	$ .01	$ .03					
Olerud, John	90FU	128	$ .01	$1.75					
Olerud, John	91F	183	$ .01	$ .35					
Olin, Steve	90F	499	$ .01	$ .10	Orsulak, Joe	87F	615	$ .01	$ .05
Olin, Steve	91F	374	$ .01	$ .03	Orsulak, Joe	88FU	2	$ .01	$ .05
Oliver, Al	81F	626	$ .01	$ .10	Orsulak, Joe	89F	614	$ .01	$ .05
Oliver, Al	82F	326	$ .01	$ .10	Orsulak, Joe	90F	185	$ .01	$ .04
Oliver, Al	83F	290	$ .01	$ .10	Orsulak, Joe	91F	487	$ .01	$ .03
Oliver, Al	84F	280	$ .03	$ .10	Orta, Jorge	81F	388	$ .01	$ .05
Oliver, Al	84F	632	$ .01	$ .06	Orta, Jorge	82F	376	$ .01	$ .05
Oliver, Al	84FU	85	$ .08	$ .75	Orta, Jorge	83F	215	$ .01	$ .05
Oliver, Al	85F	262	$ .01	$ .10	Orta, Jorge	84F	166	$ .01	$ .06
Oliver, Al	85FU	84	$ .03	$ .20	Orta, Jorge	84FU	86	$ .01	$ .10
Oliver, Al	86F	69	$ .01	$ .10	Orta, Jorge	85F	209	$ .01	$ .05
Oliver, Joe	90F	426	$ .01	$ .25	Orta, Jorge	86F	17	$ .01	$ .05
Oliver, Joe	91F	75	$ .01	$ .03	Orta, Jorge	87F	376	$ .01	$ .05
Olson, Greg	90FU	5	$ .01	$ .05	Ortiz, Javier	90FU	16	$ .01	$ .15
Olson, Greg	91F	698	$ .01	$ .03	Ortiz, Junior	84F	594	$ .01	$ .06
Olson, Gregg	90F	184	$ .01	$ .25	Ortiz, Junior	87F	616	$ .01	$ .05
Olson, Gregg	91F	486	$ .01	$ .03	Ortiz, Junior	88F	335	$ .01	$ .05
Olwine, Ed	87F	524	$ .01	$ .10	Ortiz, Junior	89F	215	$ .01	$ .05
Ontiveros, Steve	86F	429	$ .03	$ .20	Ortiz, Junior	90F	475	$ .01	$ .04
Ontiveros, Steve	87F	401	$ .01	$ .05	Ortiz, Junior	90FU	108	$ .01	$ .05
Ontiveros, Steve	88F	289	$ .01	$ .05	Ortiz, Junior	91F	622	$ .01	$ .03
Oquendo, Jose	84F	592	$ .03	$ .50	Orton, John	90F	647	$ .01	$ .04
Oquendo, Jose	85F	88	$ .01	$ .10	Orton, John	90FU	79	$ .01	$ .05
Oquendo, Jose	87F	305	$ .01	$ .05	Orton, John	91F	320	$ .01	$ .03
Oquendo, Jose	88F	44	$ .01	$ .05	Otis, Amos	81F	32	$ .01	$ .10
Oquendo, Jose	89F	459	$ .01	$ .05	Otis, Amos	81F	483	$ .05	$ .30
Oquendo, Jose	90F	255	$ .01	$ .04	Otis, Amos	82F	419	$ .01	$ .05

FLEER

Player	Year	No.	VG	EX/MT	Player	Year	No.	VG	EX/MT
Otis, Amos	83F	120	$ .01	$ .05	Pankovits, Jim	86F	307	$ .01	$ .05
Otis, Amos	84F	351	$ .03	$ .10	Pankovits, Jim	87F	64	$ .01	$ .05
Otis, Amos	84FU	87	$ .01	$ .10	Pankovits, Jim	89F	363	$ .01	$ .05
Ott, Ed	81F	365	$ .01	$ .05	Papi, Stan	81F	480	$ .01	$ .10
Ott, Ed	82F	470	$ .01	$ .05	Papi, Stan	82F	280	$ .01	$ .05
Ott, Ed	83F	98	$ .01	$ .05	Paredes, Johnny	89F	388	$ .01	$ .10
Otto, Dave	91F	20	$ .01	$ .03	Parent, Mark	88FU	125	$ .01	$ .15
Owchinko, Bob	82F	104	$ .01	$ .05	Parent, Mark	89FU	125	$ .01	$ .05
Owchinko, Bob	83F	531	$ .01	$ .05	Parent, Mark	90F	164	$ .01	$ .04
Owchinko, Bob	84FU	88	$ .01	$ .10	Parent, Mark	91F	538	$ .01	$ .03
Owchinko, Bob	85F	543	$ .01	$ .05	Paris, Kelly	84F	476	$ .01	$ .06
Owen, Spike	84F	616	$ .10	$ .45	Paris, Kelly	89F	506	$ .01	$ .05
Owen, Spike	85F	497	$ .01	$ .05	Parker, Clay	88F	649	$ .01	$ .35
Owen, Spike	86F	471	$ .01	$ .05	Parker, Clay	90F	451	$ .01	$ .04
Owen, Spike	87F	40	$ .01	$ .05	Parker, Clay	91F	346	$ .01	$ .03
Owen, Spike	88F	359	$ .01	$ .05	Parker, Dave	81F	360	$ .07	$ .40
Owen, Spike	89F	93	$ .01	$ .05	Parker, Dave	82F	489	$ .05	$ .25
Owen, Spike	89FU	98	$ .01	$ .05	Parker, Dave	82F	638	$ .05	$ .30
Owen, Spike	90F	357	$ .01	$ .04	Parker, Dave	83F	315	$ .05	$ .30
Owen, Spike	91F	243	$ .01	$ .03	Parker, Dave	84F	258	$ .04	$ .25
Owens, Paul	84F	643	$ .01	$ .06	Parker, Dave	84FU	89	$ .25	$2.00
Ownbey, Rick	83F	551	$ .01	$ .05	Parker, Dave	85F	544	$ .05	$ .30
Ownbey, Rick	86FU	85	$ .01	$ .05	Parker, Dave	86F	184	$ .04	$ .25
Pacella, John	83F	622	$ .01	$ .05	Parker, Dave	86F	640	$ .04	$ .25
Paciorek, Jim	87FU	95	$ .01	$ .05	Parker, Dave	87F	208	$ .03	$ .20
Paciorek, Tom	81F	614	$ .01	$ .05	Parker, Dave	87F	639	$ .01	$ .10
Paciorek, Tom	82F	514	$ .01	$ .05	Parker, Dave	88F	243	$ .01	$ .15
Paciorek, Tom	83F	248	$ .01	$ .05	Parker, Dave	88FU	55	$ .01	$ .05
Paciorek, Tom	84F	70	$ .01	$ .06	Parker, Dave	89F	19	$ .01	$ .05
Paciorek, Tom	85F	523	$ .01	$ .05	Parker, Dave	90F	18	$ .01	$ .10
Paciorek, Tom	86F	91	$ .01	$ .05	Parker, Dave	90FU	106	$ .01	$ .10
Paciorek, Tom	86FU	86	$ .01	$ .05	Parker, Dave	91F	593	$ .01	$ .10
Paciorek, Tom	87F	133	$ .01	$ .05	Parker, Rick	90FU	63	$ .01	$ .10
Page, Mitchell	81F	580	$ .01	$ .05	Parker, Rick	91F	269	$ .01	$ .10
Page, Mitchell	82F	105	$ .01	$ .05	Parrett, Jeff	86FU	88	$ .05	$ .30
Pagliarulo, Mike	85F	139	$ .25	$1.00	Parrett, Jeff	88FU	102	$ .01	$ .15
Pagliarulo, Mike	86F	113	$ .04	$ .25	Parrett, Jeff	89F	389	$ .01	$ .15
Pagliarulo, Mike	87F	107	$ .01	$ .10	Parrett, Jeff	89FU	112	$ .01	$ .05
Pagliarulo, Mike	88F	216	$ .01	$ .10	Parrett, Jeff	90F	570	$ .01	$ .04
Pagliarulo, Mike	89F	262	$ .01	$ .05	Parrett, Jeff	91F	699	$ .01	$ .03
Pagliarulo, Mike	90F	163	$ .01	$ .04	Parrish, Lance	81F	467	$ .04	$ .25
Pagliarulo, Mike	91F	537	$ .01	$ .03	Parrish, Lance	82F	276	$ .04	$ .25
Pagnozzi, Tom	91F	641	$ .01	$ .03	Parrish, Lance	83F	337	$ .04	$ .25
Palacios, Robert	89F	648	$ .01	$ .25	Parrish, Lance	84F	637	$ .01	$ .06
Palacios, Vicente	88F	336	$ .01	$ .15	Parrish, Lance	84F	88	$ .03	$ .20
Palacios, Vicente	89F	216	$ .01	$ .05	Parrish, Lance	85F	19	$ .04	$ .20
Pall, Donn	89F	505	$ .01	$ .05	Parrish, Lance	86F	234	$ .03	$ .20
Pall, Donn	90F	543	$ .01	$ .04	Parrish, Lance	87F	160	$ .03	$ .20
Pall, Donn	91F	130	$ .01	$ .03	Parrish, Lance	87FU	96	$ .01	$ .05
Palmeiro, Rafael	88F	429	$ .25	$ .50	Parrish, Lance	88F	310	$ .01	$ .10
Palmeiro, Rafael	89F	434	$ .01	$ .15	Parrish, Lance	89F	578	$ .01	$ .05
Palmeiro, Rafael	89F	631	$ .05	$ .25	Parrish, Lance	89FU	15	$ .01	$ .05
Palmeiro, Rafael	89FU	66	$ .01	$ .10	Parrish, Lance	90F	141	$ .01	$ .10
Palmeiro, Rafael	90F	308	$ .01	$ .04	Parrish, Lance	91F	321	$ .01	$ .03
Palmeiro, Rafael	91F	295	$ .01	$ .03	Parrish, Larry	81F	146	$ .01	$ .10
Palmer, Dave 'David'	81F	160	$ .01	$ .05	Parrish, Larry	82F	200	$ .01	$ .10
Palmer, David	82F	199	$ .01	$ .05	Parrish, Larry	83F	574	$ .01	$ .05
Palmer, David	83F	291	$ .01	$ .05	Parrish, Larry	84F	424	$ .01	$ .06
Palmer, David	85F	404	$ .01	$ .15	Parrish, Larry	85F	564	$ .01	$ .05
Palmer, David	85F	643	$ .01	$ .10	Parrish, Larry	86F	569	$ .01	$ .05
Palmer, David	86F	255	$ .01	$ .05	Parrish, Larry	87F	134	$ .01	$ .05
Palmer, David	86FU	87	$ .01	$ .05	Parrish, Larry	88F	476	$ .01	$ .05
Palmer, David	87F	525	$ .01	$ .05	Parrish, Larry	88FU	7	$ .01	$ .05
Palmer, David	88F	546	$ .01	$ .05	Parrish, Larry	89F	94	$ .01	$ .05
Palmer, David	88FU	111	$ .01	$ .05	Parsons, Casey	82F	515	$ .01	$ .05
Palmer, David	89F	577	$ .01	$ .05	Pashnick, Larry	83F	338	$ .01	$ .05
Palmer, Jim	81F	169	$ .06	$1.00	Pasqua, Dan	85FU	86	$ .10	$ .50
Palmer, Jim	82F	175	$ .05	$ .75	Pasqua, Dan	86F	114	$ .03	$ .20
Palmer, Jim	83F	69	$ .05	$ .75	Pasqua, Dan	87F	108	$ .01	$ .10
Palmer, Jim	84F	16	$ .05	$1.00	Pasqua, Dan	88F	217	$ .01	$ .10

Player	Year	No.	VG	EX/MT	Player	Year	No.	VG	EX/MT
Pasqua, Dan	88FU	18	$ .01	$ .05	Pena, Tony	85F	472	$ .01	$ .10
Pasqua, Dan	89F	507	$ .01	$ .05	Pena, Tony	86F	616	$ .01	$ .10
Pasqua, Dan	91F	131	$ .01	$ .03	Pena, Tony	87F	617	$ .01	$ .10
Pasque, Dan	90F	544	$ .01	$ .04	Pena, Tony	87FU	98	$ .01	$ .05
Pastore, Frank	81F	204	$ .01	$ .05	Pena, Tony	88F	45	$ .01	$ .10
Pastore, Frank	82F	80	$ .01	$ .05	Pena, Tony	89F	460	$ .01	$ .05
Pastore, Frank	83F	599	$ .01	$ .05	Pena, Tony	90F	256	$ .01	$ .04
Pastore, Frank	84F	477	$ .01	$ .06	Pena, Tony	90FU	74	$ .01	$ .05
Pastore, Frank	85F	545	$ .01	$ .05	Pena, Tony	91F	106	$ .01	$ .03
Pastore, Frank	86F	185	$ .01	$ .05	Pendleton, Terry	85F	236	$ .10	$ .50
Patek, Fred	81F	283	$ .01	$ .05	Pendleton, Terry	86F	44	$ .01	$ .05
Patek, Fred	82F	471	$ .01	$ .05	Pendleton, Terry	87F	306	$ .01	$ .05
Patterson, Bob	88F	337	$ .01	$ .10	Pendleton, Terry	88F	46	$ .01	$ .05
Patterson, Bob	90FU	49	$ .01	$ .05	Pendleton, Terry	89F	461	$ .01	$ .05
Patterson, Bob	91F	45	$ .01	$ .03	Pendleton, Terry	90F	257	$ .01	$ .04
Patterson, Ken	89F	508	$ .01	$ .05	Pendleton, Terry	91F	642	$ .01	$ .03
					Peraza, Oswaldo	89F	615	$ .01	$ .15
					Perconte, Jack	83F	417	$ .01	$ .05
					Perconte, Jack	84FU	90	$ .01	$ .10
					Perconte, Jack	85F	498	$ .01	$ .05
					Perconte, Jack	86F	472	$ .01	$ .05
					Perez, Melido	88F	265	$ .01	$ .30
					Perez, Melido	88FU	19	$ .01	$ .15
					Perez, Melido	89F	509	$ .01	$ .15
					Perez, Melido	90F	546	$ .01	$ .04
					Perez, Melido	91F	133	$ .01	$ .03
					Perez, Mike	91F	643	$ .01	$ .10
					Perez, Pascual	82F	491	$ .05	$ .30
					Perez, Pascual	83F	144	$ .01	$ .05
					Perez, Pascual	84F	188	$ .01	$ .06
					Perez, Pascual	86F	524	$ .01	$ .05
					Perez, Pascual	88F	192	$ .01	$ .05
					Perez, Pascual	89F	390	$ .01	$ .05
					Perez, Pascual	90F	358	$ .01	$ .04
					Perez, Pascual	90FU	116	$ .01	$ .05
					Perez, Pascual	91F	675	$ .01	$ .03
					Perez, Tony	81F	241	$ .05	$ .30
					Perez, Tony	82F	302	$ .04	$ .25
					Perez, Tony	83F	191	$ .04	$ .25
					Perez, Tony	84F	44	$ .04	$ .25
					Perez, Tony	84F	636	$ .10	$ .50
					Perez, Tony	84FU	91	$ .10	$1.50
					Perez, Tony	85F	546	$ .03	$ .20
					Perez, Tony	86F	186	$ .03	$ .20
					Perez, Tony	87F	209	$ .03	$ .20
					Perezchica, Tony	89F	338	$ .01	$ .05
Patterson, Ken	90F	545	$ .01	$ .10	Perkins, Broderick	81F	498	$ .01	$ .05
Patterson, Ken	91F	132	$ .01	$ .03	Perkins, Broderick	82F	579	$ .01	$ .05
Patterson, Reggie	86F	376	$ .01	$ .05	Perkins, Broderick	83F	368	$ .01	$ .05
Pattin, Marty	81F	37	$ .01	$ .05	Perkins, Broderick	84F	548	$ .01	$ .06
Paxton, Mike	81F	401	$ .01	$ .05	Perlman, Jon	88F	93	$ .01	$ .10
Pecota, Bill	87FU	97	$ .04	$ .25	Perlman, Jon	88FU	22	$ .01	$ .05
Pecota, Bill	88F	264	$ .01	$ .15	Perry, Gaylord	81F	91	$ .04	$ .25
Pecota, Bill	89F	289	$ .01	$ .05	Perry, Gaylord	82F	445	$ .05	$ .30
Pecota, Bill	91F	565	$ .01	$ .03	Perry, Gaylord	83F	483	$ .03	$ .20
Pedrique, Al	88F	338	$ .01	$ .15	Perry, Gaylord	83F	630	$ .01	$ .10
Pena, Alejandro	84F	109	$ .03	$ .10	Perry, Gaylord	84F	352	$ .03	$ .20
Pena, Alejandro	85F	379	$ .01	$ .05	Perry, Gaylord	84F	638	$ .01	$ .25
Pena, Alejandro	86F	140	$ .01	$ .05	Perry, Gaylord	84F	641	$ .01	$ .10
Pena, Alejandro	87F	449	$ .01	$ .05	Perry, Gerald	84FU	92	$ .25	$1.75
Pena, Alejandro	88FU	97	$ .01	$ .05	Perry, Gerald	85F	338	$ .01	$ .10
Pena, Alejandro	89F	69	$ .01	$ .05	Perry, Gerald	86F	525	$ .01	$ .05
Pena, Alejandro	90F	405	$ .01	$ .04	Perry, Gerald	88F	547	$ .01	$ .05
Pena, Alejandro	90FU	38	$ .01	$ .05	Perry, Gerald	89F	597	$ .01	$ .05
Pena, Alejandro	91F	158	$ .01	$ .03	Perry, Gerald	89F	638	$ .01	$ .05
Pena, Geronimo	90FU	52	$ .01	$ .25	Perry, Gerald	90F	592	$ .01	$ .04
Pena, Hipolito	89F	263	$ .01	$ .10	Perry, Gerald	90FU	103	$ .01	$ .05
Pena, Tony	82F	490	$ .05	$ .50	Perry, Gerald	91F	566	$ .01	$ .03
Pena, Tony	83F	316	$ .04	$ .20	Perry, Pat	86FU	89	$ .01	$ .10
Pena, Tony	84F	259	$ .03	$ .20	Perry, Pat	87F	307	$ .01	$ .05

FLEER'90

SOX
CHICAGO
WHITE SOX

Chicago

Ken Patterson PITCHER

Player	Year	No.	VG	EX/MT
Perry, Pat	88F	244	$ .01	$ .05
Perry, Pat	89F	435	$ .01	$ .05
Peterek, Jeff	90F	333	$ .01	$ .10
Peters, Rick	81F	470	$ .01	$ .05
Peters, Rick	82F	277	$ .01	$ .05
Peters, Ricky	84F	458	$ .01	$ .06
Peters, Steve	89F	462	$ .01	$ .05
Peterson, Adam	88F	646	$ .01	$ .20
Peterson, Adam	91F	134	$ .01	$ .03
Petralli, Gene	83F	439	$ .01	$ .15
Petralli, Geno	87F	135	$ .01	$ .05
Petralli, Geno	88F	477	$ .01	$ .05
Petralli, Geno	89F	530	$ .01	$ .05
Petralli, Geno	90F	309	$ .01	$ .04
Petralli, Geno	91F	296	$ .01	$ .03
Petry, Dan	81F	468	$ .01	$ .10
Petry, Dan	82F	278	$ .01	$ .10
Petry, Dan	83F	339	$ .01	$ .10
Petry, Dan	84F	89	$ .01	$ .06
Petry, Dan	85F	20	$ .01	$ .05
Petry, Dan	86F	235	$ .01	$ .10
Petry, Dan	87F	161	$ .01	$ .05
Petry, Dan	88F	67	$ .01	$ .05
Petry, Dan	89F	486	$ .01	$ .05
Petry, Dan	90F	142	$ .01	$ .04
Petry, Dan	91F	347	$ .01	$ .03

JOE PETTINI
SHORTSTOP

Player	Year	No.	VG	EX/MT
Pettini, Joe	81F	453	$ .01	$ .05
Pettini, Joe	82F	398	$ .01	$ .05
Pettis, Gary	84F	526	$ .07	$ .50
Pettis, Gary	85F	308	$ .01	$ .05
Pettis, Gary	86F	165	$ .01	$ .05
Pettis, Gary	87F	90	$ .01	$ .05
Pettis, Gary	88FU	29	$ .01	$ .05
Pettis, Gary	89F	141	$ .01	$ .05
Pettis, Gary	90F	612	$ .01	$ .04
Pettis, Gary	91F	297	$ .01	$ .03
Phelps, Ken	82F	420	$ .04	$ .25
Phelps, Ken	85F	499	$ .01	$ .05
Phelps, Ken	87F	593	$ .01	$ .05
Phelps, Ken	88F	384	$ .01	$ .05

Player	Year	No.	VG	EX/MT
Phelps, Ken	89F	264	$ .01	$ .05
Phillips, Mike	81F	538	$ .01	$ .05
Phillips, Mike	82F	201	$ .01	$ .05
Phillips, Tony	84F	459	$ .01	$ .06
Phillips, Tony	85F	433	$ .01	$ .05
Phillips, Tony	86F	430	$ .01	$ .05
Phillips, Tony	87F	402	$ .01	$ .05
Phillips, Tony	88F	290	$ .01	$ .05
Phillips, Tony	89FU	56	$ .01	$ .05
Phillips, Tony	90F	19	$ .01	$ .04
Phillips, Tony	90FU	99	$ .01	$ .05
Phillips, Tony	91F	348	$ .01	$ .03
Picciolo, Rob	81F	582	$ .01	$ .05
Picciolo, Rob	82F	106	$ .01	$ .05
Pico, Jeff	88FU	80	$ .01	$ .15
Pico, Jeff	89F	436	$ .01	$ .15
Pico, Jeff	90F	39	$ .01	$ .04
Pico, Jeff	91F	428	$ .01	$ .03
Piniella, Lou	81F	85	$ .01	$ .10
Piniella, Lou	82F	48	$ .01	$ .10
Piniella, Lou	83F	392	$ .01	$ .10
Piniella, Lou	84F	136	$ .01	$ .06
Pittaro, Chris	85FU	87	$ .01	$ .05
Pittman, Joe	82F	222	$ .01	$ .05
Pittman, Joe	83F	369	$ .01	$ .05
Pittman, Park	90FU	109	$ .01	$ .20
Plantier, Phil	91F	107	$ .01	$ .35
Plesac, Dan	86FU	90	$ .05	$ .30
Plesac, Dan	87F	354	$ .06	$ .50
Plesac, Dan	88F	171	$ .01	$ .10
Plesac, Dan	88F	625	$ .01	$ .05
Plesac, Dan	89F	195	$ .01	$ .05
Plesac, Dan	90F	334	$ .01	$ .04
Plesac, Dan	91F	594	$ .01	$ .03
Plunk, Eric	86F	649	$10.00	$45.00
Plunk, Eric	87F	403	$ .01	$ .05
Plunk, Eric	88F	291	$ .01	$ .05
Plunk, Eric	89F	20	$ .01	$ .05
Plunk, Eric	90F	452	$ .01	$ .04
Plunk, Eric	91F	676	$ .01	$ .03
Pocoroba, Biff	81F	257	$ .01	$ .05
Pocoroba, Biff	82F	446	$ .01	$ .05
Pocoroba, Biff	83F	145	$ .01	$ .05
Pocoroba, Biff	84F	189	$ .01	$ .06
Polidor, Gus	86F	650	$ .03	$ .20
Polidor, Gus	88F	501	$ .01	$ .05
Polonia, Luis	87FU	99	$ .06	$ .35
Polonia, Luis	88F	292	$ .01	$ .15
Polonia, Luis	89F	21	$ .01	$ .05
Polonia, Luis	90FU	80	$ .01	$ .05
Polonia, Luis	91F	322	$ .01	$ .03
Poole, Jim	91F	217	$ .01	$ .10
Porter, Chuck	84F	211	$ .01	$ .06
Porter, Chuck	85F	591	$ .01	$ .05
Porter, Darrell	81F	36	$ .01	$ .05
Porter, Darrell	82F	124	$ .01	$ .05
Porter, Darrell	83F	18	$ .01	$ .05
Porter, Darrell	84F	331	$ .01	$ .06
Porter, Darrell	85F	237	$ .01	$ .05
Porter, Darrell	85F	337	$ .01	$ .05
Porter, Darrell	86F	45	$ .01	$ .05
Porter, Darrell	86FU	91	$ .01	$ .05
Porter, Darrell	87F	136	$ .01	$ .05
Portugal, Mark	87F	548	$ .01	$ .05
Portugal, Mark	89F	123	$ .01	$ .05
Portugal, Mark	91F	512	$ .01	$ .03
Pounders, Brad	89F	642	$ .01	$ .25
Powell, Dennis	87F	450	$ .01	$ .05
Powell, Dennis	89FU	61	$ .01	$ .05
Powell, Dennis	90F	521	$ .01	$ .04

Player	Year	No.	VG	EX/MT	Player	Year	No.	VG	EX/MT
Powell, Hosken	81F	559	$ .01	$ .05	Puleo, Charlie	88F	548	$ .01	$ .05
Powell, Hosken	82F	558	$ .01	$ .05	Puleo, Charlie	89F	598	$ .01	$ .05
Powell, Hosken	83F	440	$ .01	$ .05	Putnam, Pat	81F	630	$ .01	$ .05
Power, Ted	82F	17	$ .05	$ .30	Putnam, Pat	82F	327	$ .01	$ .05
Power, Ted	84F	478	$ .01	$ .06	Putnam, Pat	84F	617	$ .01	$ .06
Power, Ted	85F	547	$ .01	$ .05	Putnam, Pat	85F	287	$ .01	$ .05
Power, Ted	86F	187	$ .01	$ .05	Quinones, Luis	86FU	92	$ .01	$ .05
Power, Ted	87F	210	$ .01	$ .05	Quinones, Luis	90F	428	$ .01	$ .04
Power, Ted	88F	245	$ .01	$ .05	Quinones, Luis	91F	77	$ .01	$ .03
Power, Ted	88FU	33	$ .01	$ .05	Quinones (z), Rey	86FU	93	$ .05	$ .30
Power, Ted	89F	142	$ .01	$ .05	Quinones, Rey	87F	595	$ .04	$ .25
Power, Ted	90F	258	$ .01	$ .04	Quinones, Rey	88F	386	$ .01	$ .05
Power, Ted	90FU	50	$ .01	$ .05	Quinones, Rey	89F	556	$ .01	$ .05
Power, Ted	91F	46	$ .01	$ .03	Quintana, Carlos	89F	95	$ .01	$ .50
Presley, Jim	85F	500	$ .15	$ .50	Quintana, Carlos	90F	283	$ .01	$ .10
Presley, Jim	86F	473	$ .04	$ .25	Quintana, Carlos	91F	108	$ .01	$ .03
Presley, Jim	87F	594	$ .01	$ .10	Quirk, Jamie	81F	50	$ .01	$ .05
Presley, Jim	88F	385	$ .01	$ .10	Quirk, Jamie	82F	421	$ .01	$ .05
Presley, Jim	89F	555	$ .01	$ .05	Quirk, Jamie	84F	332	$ .01	$ .06
Presley, Jim	90F	522	$ .01	$ .04	Quirk, Jamie	87F	377	$ .01	$ .05
Presley, Jim	90FU	6	$ .01	$ .05	Quirk, Jamie	88F	266	$ .01	$ .05
Presley, Jim	91F	700	$ .01	$ .03	Quirk, Jamie	89F	290	$ .01	$ .05
Price, Joe	81F	210	$ .01	$ .05	Quirk, Jamie	91F	21	$ .01	$ .03
Price, Joe	82F	81	$ .01	$ .05	Quisenberry, Dan	81F	31	$ .03	$ .20
Price, Joe	83F	600	$ .01	$ .05	Quisenberry, Dan	82F	422	$ .03	$ .20
Price, Joe	84F	479	$ .01	$ .06	Quisenberry, Dan	83F	122	$ .03	$ .20
Price, Joe	85F	548	$ .01	$ .05	Quisenberry, Dan	84F	354	$ .03	$ .20
Price, Joe	86F	188	$ .01	$ .05	Quisenberry, Dan	84F	635	$ .01	$ .06
Price, Joe	87F	211	$ .01	$ .05	Quisenberry, Dan	85F	211	$ .03	$ .20
Price, Joe	89F	339	$ .01	$ .05	Quisenberry, Dan	86F	18	$ .03	$ .20
Price, Joe	90F	282	$ .01	$ .04	Quisenberry, Dan	87F	378	$ .01	$ .10
Price, Joe	91F	488	$ .01	$ .03	Quisenberry, Dan	88F	267	$ .01	$ .10
Prince, Tom	89F	217	$ .01	$ .05	Quisenberry, Dan	89FU	120	$ .01	$ .05
Proly, Mike	81F	358	$ .01	$ .05	Quisenberry, Dan	90F	259	$ .01	$ .04
Proly, Mike	82F	254	$ .01	$ .05	Radinsky, Scott	90FU	86	$ .01	$ .20
Proly, Mike	83F	505	$ .01	$ .05	Radinsky, Scott	91F	135	$ .01	$ .15
Proly, Mike	84F	501	$ .01	$ .06	Raines, Tim	82F	202	$ .15	$2.25
Pryor, Greg	81F	359	$ .01	$ .05	Raines, Tim	83F	292	$ .05	$ .50
Pryor, Greg	82F	356	$ .01	$ .05	Raines, Tim	84F	281	$ .06	$ .75
Pryor, Greg	83F	121	$ .01	$ .05	Raines, Tim	84F	631	$ .04	$ .25
Pryor, Greg	84F	353	$ .01	$ .06	Raines, Tim	85F	405	$ .06	$ .35
Pryor, Greg	85F	210	$ .01	$ .05	Raines, Tim	86F	256	$ .05	$ .30
Puckett, Kirby	84FU	93	$25.00	$150.00	Raines, Tim	86F	632	$ .05	$ .30
Puckett, Kirby	85F	286	$5.00	$19.00	Raines, Tim	87F	328	$ .05	$ .30
Puckett, Kirby	86F	401	$1.00	$4.50	Raines, Tim	87F	642	$ .01	$ .05
Puckett, Kirby	87F	549	$ .50	$2.00	Raines, Tim	88F	193	$ .01	$ .15
Puckett, Kirby	87F	633	$ .25	$1.00	Raines, Tim	88F	631	$ .01	$ .10
Puckett, Kirby	88F	19	$ .01	$ .50	Raines, Tim	89F	391	$ .01	$ .15
Puckett, Kirby	88F	638	$ .25	$ .75	Raines, Tim	90F	359	$ .01	$ .04
Puckett, Kirby	89F	124	$ .01	$ .35	Raines, Tim	91F	244	$ .01	$ .03
Puckett, Kirby	89F	639	$ .01	$ .25	Rainey, Chuck	82F	303	$ .01	$ .05
Puckett, Kirby	90F	383	$ .01	$ .25	Rainey, Chuck	83F	192	$ .01	$ .05
Puckett, Kirby	90F	635	$ .01	$ .04	Rainey, Chuck	84F	502	$ .01	$ .06
Puckett, Kirby	91F	623	$ .01	$ .10	Rajsich, Gary	83F	553	$ .01	$ .05
Puhl, Terry	81F	62	$ .01	$ .05	Ramirez, Mario	84F	309	$ .01	$ .06
Puhl, Terry	82F	223	$ .01	$ .05	Ramirez, Rafael	81F	266	$ .04	$ .25
Puhl, Terry	83F	458	$ .01	$ .05	Ramirez, Rafael	82F	447	$ .01	$ .05
Puhl, Terry	84F	235	$ .01	$ .06	Ramirez, Rafael	83F	146	$ .01	$ .05
Puhl, Terry	85F	356	$ .01	$ .05	Ramirez, Rafael	84F	190	$ .01	$ .06
Puhl, Terry	86F	308	$ .01	$ .05	Ramirez, Rafael	85F	339	$ .01	$ .05
Puhl, Terry	87F	65	$ .01	$ .05	Ramirez, Rafael	86F	526	$ .01	$ .05
Puhl, Terry	88FU	90	$ .01	$ .05	Ramirez, Rafael	87F	526	$ .01	$ .05
Puhl, Terry	89F	364	$ .01	$ .05	Ramirez, Rafael	88FU	91	$ .01	$ .05
Puhl, Terry	90F	233	$ .01	$ .04	Ramirez, Rafael	89F	365	$ .01	$ .05
Pujols, Luis	81F	68	$ .01	$ .05	Ramirez, Rafael	90F	234	$ .01	$ .04
Pujols, Luis	82F	224	$ .01	$ .05	Ramirez, Rafael	91F	513	$ .01	$ .05
Pujols, Luis	83F	459	$ .01	$ .05	Ramos, Bobby 'Roberto'	81F	162	$ .01	$ .05
Pujols, Luis	84F	236	$ .01	$ .06	Ramos, Bobby	82F	203	$ .01	$ .05
Puleo, Charlie	83F	552	$ .01	$ .05	Ramos, Bobby	84F	282	$ .01	$ .06
Puleo, Charlie	84F	480	$ .01	$ .06	Ramos, Domingo	88FU	23	$ .01	$ .05

FLEER

Player	Year	No.	VG	EX/MT	Player	Year	No.	VG	EX/MT
Ramos, Domingo	91F	429	$ .01	$ .03	Rawley, Shane	90F	384	$ .01	$ .04
Ramsey, Mike	81F	549	$ .01	$ .05	Ray, Johnny	82F	492	$ .15	$ .75
Ramsey, Mike	82F	125	$ .01	$ .05	Ray, Johnny	83F	317	$ .01	$ .10
Ramsey, Mike	83F	19	$ .01	$ .05	Ray, Johnny	84F	260	$ .03	$ .10
Ramsey, Mike	84F	333	$ .01	$ .06	Ray, Johnny	85F	473	$ .01	$ .10
Ramsey, Mike	85F	406	$ .01	$ .05	Ray, Johnny	86F	617	$ .01	$ .10
Randle, Lenny	81F	301	$ .01	$ .05	Ray, Johnny	87F	618	$ .01	$ .10
Randle, Lenny	82F	516	$ .01	$ .05	Ray, Johnny	88F	502	$ .01	$ .10
Randolph, Willie	81F	109	$ .01	$ .10	Ray, Johnny	89F	487	$ .01	$ .05
Randolph, Willie	82F	49	$ .01	$ .05	Ray, Johnny	90F	143	$ .01	$ .04
Randolph, Willie	83F	393	$ .01	$ .05	Ray, Johnny	91F	323	$ .01	$ .03
Randolph, Willie	84F	137	$ .01	$ .06	Rayford, Floyd	84F	334	$ .01	$ .06
Randolph, Willie	85F	140	$ .01	$ .05	Rayford, Floyd	84FU	95	$ .01	$ .10
Randolph, Willie	86F	115	$ .01	$ .05	Rayford, Floyd	85F	186	$ .01	$ .05
Randolph, Willie	87F	109	$ .01	$ .05	Rayford, Floyd	86F	283	$ .01	$ .05
Randolph, Willie	88F	218	$ .01	$ .05	Ready, Randy	85F	592	$ .03	$ .20
Randolph, Willie	89F	265	$ .01	$ .05	Ready, Randy	86F	498	$ .01	$ .05
Randolph, Willie	89FU	93	$ .01	$ .05	Ready, Randy	87FU	100	$ .01	$ .05
Randolph, Willie	90F	406	$ .01	$ .04	Ready, Randy	88F	594	$ .01	$ .05
Randolph, Willie	91F	22	$ .01	$ .03	Ready, Randy	89F	315	$ .01	$ .15
Rasmussen, Dennis	85F	141	$ .03	$ .20	Ready, Randy	90F	571	$ .01	$ .04
Rasmussen, Dennis	87F	110	$ .01	$ .05	Ready, Randy	91F	410	$ .01	$ .03
Rasmussen, Dennis	88F	246	$ .01	$ .05	Reardon, Jeff	81F	335	$ .10	$ .75
Rasmussen, Dennis	88FU	126	$ .01	$ .05	Reardon, Jeff	82F	204	$ .03	$ .20
Rasmussen, Dennis	89F	314	$ .01	$ .05	Reardon, Jeff	83F	293	$ .01	$ .10
Rasmussen, Dennis	90F	165	$ .01	$ .04	Reardon, Jeff	84F	283	$ .01	$ .10
Rasmussen, Dennis	91F	539	$ .01	$ .03	Reardon, Jeff	85F	407	$ .01	$ .10
Rasmussen, Eric	81F	497	$ .01	$ .05	Reardon, Jeff	86F	257	$ .01	$ .10
Rau, Doug	81F	133	$ .01	$ .05	Reardon, Jeff	87F	329	$ .01	$ .10
Rawley, Shane	82F	517	$ .01	$ .10	Reardon, Jeff	87FU	101	$ .01	$ .10
Rawley, Shane	83F	394	$ .01	$ .05	Reardon, Jeff	88F	20	$ .01	$ .10
Rawley, Shane	84F	138	$ .01	$ .06	Reardon, Jeff	89F	125	$ .01	$ .05
Rawley, Shane	84FU	94	$ .06	$ .35	Reardon, Jeff	90F	385	$ .01	$ .04
Rawley, Shane	85F	263	$ .01	$ .05	Reardon, Jeff	90FU	75	$ .01	$ .05
Rawley, Shane	86F	446	$ .01	$ .05	Reardon, Jeff	91F	109	$ .01	$ .03
Rawley, Shane	86F	456	$ .01	$ .05	Redfern, Pete	81F	560	$ .01	$ .05
					Redfern, Pete	82F	559	$ .01	$ .05
					Redfern, Pete	83F	623	$ .01	$ .05
					Redus, Gary	84F	481	$ .04	$ .25
					Redus, Gary	85F	549	$ .01	$ .05
					Redus, Gary	86F	189	$ .01	$ .05
					Redus, Gary	86FU	94	$ .01	$ .05
					Redus, Gary	87F	181	$ .01	$ .05
					Redus, Gary	87FU	102	$ .01	$ .05
					Redus, Gary	88F	408	$ .01	$ .05
					Redus, Gary	89F	218	$ .01	$ .05
					Redus, Gary	90F	476	$ .01	$ .04
					Redus, Gary	91F	47	$ .01	$ .03
					Reed, Darren	90FU	39	$ .01	$ .15
					Reed, Darren	91F	159	$ .01	$ .10
					Reed, Jeff	86FU	95	$ .01	$ .05
					Reed, Jeff	87F	550	$ .01	$ .05
					Reed, Jeff	88F	194	$ .01	$ .05
					Reed, Jeff	89F	167	$ .01	$ .05
					Reed, Jeff	90F	429	$ .01	$ .05
					Reed, Jeff	91F	78	$ .01	$ .03
					Reed, Jerry	86F	592	$ .01	$ .05
					Reed, Jerry	88F	387	$ .01	$ .05
					Reed, Jerry	89F	557	$ .01	$ .05
					Reed, Jerry	90F	523	$ .01	$ .04
					Reed, Jerry	90FU	76	$ .01	$ .05
					Reed, Jerry	91F	110	$ .01	$ .03
					Reed, Jody	88F	360	$ .01	$ .50
					Reed, Jody	89F	96	$ .01	$ .05
					Reed, Jody	90F	284	$ .01	$ .04
					Reed, Jody	91F	111	$ .01	$ .03

Shane Rawley
PITCHER

Player	Year	No.	VG	EX/MT	Player	Year	No.	VG	EX/MT
Rawley, Shane	87F	180	$ .01	$ .05	Reed, Rick	90F	477	$ .01	$ .10
Rawley, Shane	88F	311	$ .01	$ .05	Reed, Ron	81F	11	$ .01	$ .05
Rawley, Shane	89F	579	$ .01	$ .05	Reed, Ron	82F	255	$ .01	$ .05
Rawley, Shane	89FU	44	$ .01	$ .05	Reed, Ron	83F	169	$ .01	$ .05

Player	Year	No.	VG	EX/MT	Player	Year	No.	VG	EX/MT
Reed, Ron	84F	45	$ .01	$ .06	Rhoden, Rick	87FU	103	$ .01	$ .05
Reed, Ron	84FU	96	$ .04	$ .25	Rhoden, Rick	88F	219	$ .01	$ .10
Reed, Ron	85F	524	$ .01	$ .05	Rhoden, Rick	89F	266	$ .01	$ .05
Reid, Jessie	88F	643	$ .01	$ .25	Rhoden, Rick	89FU	89	$ .01	$ .05
Reimer, Kevin	89F	641	$ .01	$ .50	Rhoden, Rick	90F	235	$ .01	$ .04
Reimer, Kevin	90F	310	$ .01	$ .10	Rhodes, Karl	91F	514	$ .01	$ .10
Reimer, Kevin	91F	298	$ .01	$ .10	Rice, Jim	81F	222	$ .08	$ .40
Reitz, Ken	81F	530	$ .01	$ .05	Rice, Jim	82F	305	$ .05	$ .30
Reitz, Ken	82F	602	$ .01	$ .05	Rice, Jim	83F	194	$ .05	$ .30
Remy, Jerry	81F	238	$ .01	$ .05	Rice, Jim	84F	408	$ .05	$ .30
Remy, Jerry	82F	304	$ .01	$ .05	Rice, Jim	85F	168	$ .06	$ .35
Remy, Jerry	83F	193	$ .01	$ .05	Rice, Jim	86F	358	$ .06	$ .35
Remy, Jerry	84F	407	$ .01	$ .06	Rice, Jim	87F	41	$ .05	$ .30
Remy, Jerry	85F	167	$ .01	$ .05	Rice, Jim	87F	633	$ .25	$1.00
Renko, Steve	81F	231	$ .01	$ .05	Rice, Jim	88F	361	$ .01	$ .15
Renko, Steve	82F	472	$ .01	$ .05	Rice, Jim	89F	97	$ .01	$ .10
Renko, Steve	83F	99	$ .01	$ .05	Richard, J. R.	81F	56	$ .01	$ .10
Renko, Steve	84F	355	$ .01	$ .06	Richard, J. R.	82F	226	$ .01	$ .10
Reuschel, Rick	81F	293	$ .01	$ .10	Richards, Gene	81F	486	$ .01	$ .05
Reuschel, Rick	82F	50	$ .01	$ .05	Richards, Gene	82F	580	$ .01	$ .05
Reuschel, Rick	85F	63	$ .01	$ .05	Richards, Gene	83F	370	$ .01	$ .05
Reuschel, Rick	85FU	88	$ .01	$ .05	Richards, Gene	84F	310	$ .01	$ .06
Reuschel, Rick	86F	618	$ .01	$ .05	Richards, Gene	84FU	98	$ .01	$ .10
Reuschel, Rick	87F	619	$ .01	$ .05	Richards, Gene	85F	619	$ .01	$ .05
Reuschel, Rick	88F	94	$ .01	$ .10	Richardt, Mike	83F	575	$ .01	$ .05
Reuschel, Rick	89F	340	$ .01	$ .05	Rick, Dempsey	84F	644	$ .01	$ .06
Reuschel, Rick	90F	68	$ .01	$ .04	Righetti, Dave	82F	52	$ .35	$1.50
Reuschel, Rick	91F	270	$ .01	$ .03	Righetti, Dave	83F	395	$ .03	$ .20
Reuss, Jerry	81F	118	$ .01	$ .10	Righetti, Dave	84F	139	$ .03	$ .20
Reuss, Jerry	82F	18	$ .01	$ .05	Righetti, Dave	84F	639	$ .01	$ .06
Reuss, Jerry	83F	216	$ .01	$ .05	Righetti, Dave	85F	142	$ .03	$ .20
Reuss, Jerry	84F	110	$ .01	$ .06	Righetti, Dave	86F	116	$ .01	$ .15
Reuss, Jerry	85F	380	$ .01	$ .05	Righetti, Dave	87F	111	$ .01	$ .10
Reuss, Jerry	86F	141	$ .01	$ .05	Righetti, Dave	87F	627	$ .01	$ .10
Reuss, Jerry	87F	451	$ .01	$ .05	Righetti, Dave	88F	220	$ .01	$ .10
Reuss, Jerry	89F	510	$ .01	$ .05	Righetti, Dave	88F	625	$ .01	$ .05
Reuss, Jerry	90F	335	$ .01	$ .04	Righetti, Dave	89F	267	$ .01	$ .05
Revering, Dave	81F	576	$ .01	$ .05	Righetti, Dave	90F	453	$ .01	$ .04
Revering, Dave	82F	51	$ .01	$ .05	Righetti, Dave	91F	677	$ .01	$ .03
Revering, Dave	83F	484	$ .01	$ .05	Rijo, Jose	84FU	99	$1.50	$8.50
Reynolds, Craig	81F	74	$ .01	$ .05	Rijo, Jose	85F	143	$ .10	$2.00
Reynolds, Craig	82F	225	$ .01	$ .05	Rijo, Jose	86F	431	$ .05	$ .25
Reynolds, Craig	83F	460	$ .01	$ .05	Rijo, Jose	87F	404	$ .01	$ .10
Reynolds, Craig	84F	237	$ .01	$ .06	Rijo, Jose	88FU	86	$ .01	$ .15
Reynolds, Craig	85F	357	$ .01	$ .05	Rijo, Jose	89F	168	$ .01	$ .10
Reynolds, Craig	86F	309	$ .01	$ .05	Rijo, Jose	90F	430	$ .01	$ .15
Reynolds, Craig	87F	66	$ .01	$ .05	Rijo, Jose	91F	79	$ .01	$ .03
Reynolds, Craig	88F	454	$ .01	$ .05	Riles, Earnie "Earnest"	85FU	89	$ .05	$ .30
Reynolds, Craig	89F	366	$ .01	$ .05	Riles, Earnie	86F	499	$ .04	$ .25
Reynolds, Harold	87F	596	$ .01	$ .05	Riles, Earnie	87F	355	$ .01	$ .05
Reynolds, Harold	88F	388	$ .01	$ .05	Riles, Earnie	88F	172	$ .01	$ .05
Reynolds, Harold	89F	558	$ .01	$ .05	Riles, Earnest	88FU	130	$ .01	$ .05
Reynolds, Harold	90F	524	$ .01	$ .04	Riles, Earnest	89F	341	$ .01	$ .05
Reynolds, Harold	91F	460	$ .01	$ .03	Riles, Ernest	90F	69	$ .01	$ .04
Reynolds, R. J.	84FU	97	$ .25	$1.00	Riles, Ernest	91F	271	$ .01	$ .03
Reynolds, R. J.	85F	381	$ .05	$ .30	Ripken, Bill (y)	88F	569	$ .01	$ .30
Reynolds, R. J.	86F	619	$ .01	$ .05	Ripken, Bill (y)	88F	640	$ .01	$ .10
Reynolds, R. J.	87F	620	$ .01	$ .05	Ripken, Bill	89F	616	$ .01	$ .25
Reynolds, R. J.	88F	339	$ .01	$ .05	Ripken, Bill (obscene bat)	89F	616	$3.00	$10.00
Reynolds, R. J.	89F	219	$ .01	$ .05	Ripken, Bill	90F	186	$ .01	$ .04
Reynolds, R. J.	91F	48	$ .01	$ .03	Ripken, Billy	91F	489	$ .01	$ .03
Reynolds, R. J.	90F	478	$ .01	$ .04	Ripken, Jr., Cal	82F	176	$3.00	$30.00
Reynolds, Ronn	86F	92	$ .01	$ .05	Ripken, Jr., Cal	83F	70	$ .50	$8.00
Rhoden, Rick	81F	377	$ .01	$ .10	Ripken, Jr., Cal	84F	17	$ .10	$8.50
Rhoden, Rick	82F	493	$ .01	$ .05	Ripken, Jr., Cal	85F	187	$ .10	$3.00
Rhoden, Rick	83F	318	$ .01	$ .05	Ripken, Jr., Cal	85F	625	$ .05	$ .75
Rhoden, Rick	84F	261	$ .01	$ .06	Ripken, Jr., Cal	85F	641	$ .03	$ .25
Rhoden, Rick	85F	474	$ .01	$ .05	Ripken, Jr., Cal	86F	284	$ .06	$1.50
Rhoden, Rick	86F	620	$ .01	$ .05	Ripken, Jr., Cal	86F	633	$ .04	$ .25
Rhoden, Rick	87F	621	$ .01	$ .05	Ripken, Jr., Cal	87F	478	$ .05	$1.00

FLEER

Player	Year	No.	VG	EX/MT
Ripken, Jr., Cal	88F	570	$ .01	$ .50
Ripken, Jr., Cal	88F	635	$ .01	$ .10
Ripken, Jr., Cal	88F	640	$ .01	$ .10
Ripken, Jr., Cal	89F	617	$ .01	$ .25
Ripken, Jr., Cal	90F	187	$ .01	$ .15
Ripken, Jr., Cal	90F	634	$ .01	$ .04

Player	Year	No.	VG	EX/MT
Ripken, Jr., Cal	90FPD	624	$ .01	$ .15
Ripken, Jr., Cal	91F	490	$ .01	$ .03
Ripken, Sr., Cal	85F	641	$ .03	$ .25
Ripley, Allen	81F	454	$ .01	$ .05
Ripley, Allen	82F	399	$ .01	$ .05
Ripley, Allen	83F	506	$ .01	$ .05
Ritchie, Wally	87FU	104	$ .01	$ .05
Ritchie, Wally	88F	312	$ .01	$ .10
Ritz, Kevin	90F	613	$ .01	$ .15
Rivera, Bombo	81F	556	$ .01	$ .05
Rivera, German	85F	382	$ .01	$ .05
Rivera, Luis	87F	330	$ .01	$ .05
Rivera, Luis	89F	392	$ .01	$ .05
Rivera, Luis	90F	285	$ .01	$ .04
Rivera, Luis	91F	112	$ .01	$ .03
Rivers, Mickey	81F	617	$ .01	$ .05
Rivers, Mickey	82F	328	$ .01	$ .05
Rivers, Mickey	83F	576	$ .01	$ .05
Rivers, Mickey	84F	425	$ .01	$ .06
Rivers, Mickey	85F	565	$ .01	$ .05
Robbins, Bruce	81F	477	$ .01	$ .05
Roberge, Bert	83F	461	$ .01	$ .05
Roberge, Bert	85F	525	$ .01	$ .05
Roberge, Bert	86F	258	$ .01	$ .05
Roberts, Dave	81F	607	$ .01	$ .05
Roberts, Dave	81F	636	$ .01	$ .05
Roberts, Dave	82F	227	$ .01	$ .05
Roberts, Leon	81F	608	$ .01	$ .05
Roberts, Leon	82F	329	$ .01	$ .05
Roberts, Leon	84F	356	$ .01	$ .06
Roberts, Bip	86FU	96	$ .01	$ .25
Roberts, Bip	87F	427	$ .01	$ .05
Roberts, Bip	89FU	126	$ .01	$ .05
Roberts, Bip	90F	166	$ .01	$ .04

Player	Year	No.	VG	EX/MT
Roberts, Bip	91F	540	$ .01	$ .03
Robertson, Andre	83F	396	$ .01	$ .05
Robertson, Andre	84F	140	$ .01	$ .06
Robertson, Andre	85F	144	$ .01	$ .05
Robertson, Andre	86F	117	$ .01	$ .05
Robidoux, Billy Joe	86F	652	$ .01	$ .10
Robidoux, Billy Joe	86FU	97	$ .01	$ .05
Robidoux, Billy Joe	87F	356	$ .01	$ .05
Robinson, Bill	81F	373	$ .01	$ .05
Robinson, Bill	82F	494	$ .01	$ .05
Robinson, Don	81F	366	$ .01	$ .05
Robinson, Don	82F	495	$ .01	$ .05
Robinson, Don	83F	319	$ .01	$ .05
Robinson, Don	84F	262	$ .01	$ .06
Robinson, Don	85F	475	$ .01	$ .05
Robinson, Don	86F	621	$ .01	$ .05
Robinson, Don	87F	622	$ .01	$ .05
Robinson, Don	88F	95	$ .01	$ .05
Robinson, Don	89F	342	$ .01	$ .05
Robinson, Don	90F	70	$ .01	$ .04
Robinson, Don	91F	272	$ .01	$ .03
Robinson, Jeff D.	84FU	100	$ .10	$ .75
Robinson, Jeff D.	85F	620	$ .05	$ .30
Robinson, Jeff D.	87F	283	$ .01	$ .05
Robinson, Jeff D.	89F	220	$ .01	$ .05
Robinson, Jeff D.	90F	479	$ .01	$ .04
Robinson, Jeff D.	91F	678	$ .01	$ .03
Robinson, Jeff M.	87FU	105	$ .05	$ .30
Robinson, Jeff M.	88F	68	$ .10	$ .50
Robinson, Jeff M.	89F	143	$ .01	$ .05
Robinson, Jeff M.	90F	614	$ .01	$ .04
Robinson, Jeff M.	91F	349	$ .01	$ .03
Robinson, Ron	83F	170	$ .01	$ .05
Robinson, Ron	85F	650	$ .05	$1.00
Robinson, Ron	86F	190	$ .01	$ .05
Robinson, Ron	87F	212	$ .01	$ .05
Robinson, Ron	88F	247	$ .01	$ .05
Robinson, Ron	89F	169	$ .01	$ .05
Robinson, Ron	90F	431	$ .01	$ .04
Robinson, Ron	91F	595	$ .01	$ .03
Rochford, Mike	89F	650	$ .01	$ .20
Rodriguez, Rick	88FU	24	$ .01	$ .05
Rodriguez, Aurelio	81F	105	$ .01	$ .05
Rodriguez, Aurelio	82F	53	$ .01	$ .05
Rodriguez, Aurelio	83F	249	$ .01	$ .05
Rodriguez, Richard	91F	541	$ .01	$ .10
Rodriguez, Rick	88F	293	$ .01	$ .15
Roenicke, Gary	81F	187	$ .01	$ .05
Roenicke, Gary	83F	71	$ .01	$ .05
Roenicke, Gary	84F	18	$ .01	$ .06
Roenicke, Gary	85F	188	$ .01	$ .05
Roenicke, Gary	86F	285	$ .01	$ .05
Roenicke, Gary	86FU	98	$ .01	$ .05
Roenicke, Gary	87F	112	$ .01	$ .05
Roenicke, Ron	82F	177	$ .01	$ .05
Roenicke, Ron	82F	19	$ .01	$ .05
Roenicke, Ron	83F	217	$ .01	$ .05
Roenicke, Ron	84F	618	$ .01	$ .06
Roenicke, Ron	86FU	99	$ .01	$ .05
Roenicke, Ron	87F	182	$ .01	$ .05
Roesler, Mike	90F	645	$ .01	$ .04
Rogers, Kenny	90F	311	$ .01	$ .20
Rogers, Kenny	91F	299	$ .01	$ .03
Rogers, Steve	81F	143	$ .01	$ .05
Rogers, Steve	82F	205	$ .01	$ .05
Rogers, Steve	83F	294	$ .01	$ .05
Rogers, Steve	84F	284	$ .01	$ .06
Rogers, Steve	85F	408	$ .01	$ .05
Rohde, Dave	90FU	17	$ .01	$ .10
Rojas, Mel	91F	245	$ .01	$ .10

Player	Year	No.	VG	EX/MT	Player	Year	No.	VG	EX/MT
Roman, Jose	85F	646	$ .01	$ .10	Ruffin, Bruce	88F	313	$ .01	$ .10
Romanick, Ron	84FU	101	$ .05	$ .25	Ruffin, Bruce	89F	581	$ .01	$ .05
Romanick, Ron	85F	309	$ .01	$ .05	Ruffin, Bruce	90F	572	$ .01	$ .04
Romanick, Ron	86F	166	$ .01	$ .05	Ruffin, Bruce	91F	411	$ .01	$ .03
Romero, Ed	83F	44	$ .01	$ .05	Ruhle, Vern	81F	53	$ .01	$ .05
Romero, Ed	84F	212	$ .01	$ .06	Ruhle, Vern	82F	228	$ .01	$ .05
Romero, Ed	85F	593	$ .01	$ .05	Ruhle, Vern	83F	462	$ .01	$ .05
Romero, Ed	86F	500	$ .01	$ .05	Ruhle, Vern	84F	238	$ .01	$ .06
Romero, Ed	87F	42	$ .01	$ .05	Ruhle, Vern	85F	358	$ .01	$ .05
Romero, Ed	88F	362	$ .01	$ .05	Ruhle, Vern	85FU	93	$ .01	$ .05
Romine, Kevin	88F	363	$ .01	$ .05	Ruhle, Vern	86F	593	$ .01	$ .05
Romine, Kevin	89F	98	$ .01	$ .50	Ruhle, Vern	87F	91	$ .01	$ .05
Romine, Kevin	90F	286	$ .01	$ .04	Runge, Paul	88FU	71	$ .01	$ .05
Romine, Kevin	91F	113	$ .01	$ .03	Ruskin, Scott	91F	246	$ .01	$ .10
Romo, Enrique	81F	385	$ .01	$ .05	Russell, Bill	81F	117	$ .01	$ .05
Romo, Enrique	82F	496	$ .01	$ .05	Russell, Bill	82F	20	$ .01	$ .05
Romo, Enrique	83F	320	$ .01	$ .05	Russell, Bill	83F	219	$ .01	$ .05
Romo, Vincente	83F	218	$ .01	$ .05	Russell, Bill	84F	111	$ .01	$ .06
Roof, Gene	83F	20	$ .01	$ .05	Russell, Bill	85F	383	$ .01	$ .05
Rooker, Jim	81F	368	$ .01	$ .05	Russell, Bill	86F	142	$ .01	$ .05
Roomes, Rolando	89F	644	$ .01	$ .25	Russell, Bill	87F	452	$ .01	$ .05
Roomes, Rolando	89FU	86	$ .01	$ .15	Russell, Jeff	85F	551	$ .01	$ .05
Roomes, Rolando	90F	432	$ .01	$ .04	Russell, Jeff	87F	137	$ .01	$ .05
Rosario, Victor	91F	701	$ .01	$ .10	Russell, Jeff	88F	478	$ .01	$ .05
Rose, Bobby	90F	651	$ .01	$ .04	Russell, Jeff	89F	531	$ .01	$ .05
Rose, Bobby	91F	324	$ .01	$ .03	Russell, Jeff	90F	312	$ .01	$ .04
Rose, Jr, Pete	82F	640	$ .30	$1.50	Russell, Jeff	90F	633	$ .01	$ .04
Rose, Pete	81F	1	$ .25	$2.00	Russell, Jeff	91F	300	$ .01	$ .03
Rose, Pete	81F	645	$ .20	$1.50	Russell, John	85F	653	$ .03	$ .20
Rose, Pete	82F	256	$ .10	$1.00	Russell, John	86F	448	$ .01	$ .05
Rose, Pete	82F	640	$ .30	$1.25	Russell, John	86F	458	$ .01	$ .05
Rose, Pete	83F	171	$ .20	$ .75	Russell, John	87F	184	$ .01	$ .05
Rose, Pete	83F	634	$ .10	$ .75	Russell, John	91F	301	$ .01	$ .03
Rose, Pete	84F	46	$ .20	$ .75	Ruthven, Dick	81F	16	$ .01	$ .05
Rose, Pete	84F	636	$ .10	$ .50	Ruthven, Dick	82F	257	$ .01	$ .05
Rose, Pete	84FU	102	$3.00	$13.00	Ruthven, Dick	83F	172	$ .01	$ .05
Rose, Pete	85F	550	$ .20	$1.00	Ruthven, Dick	84F	503	$ .01	$ .06
Rose, Pete	85F	640	$ .10	$ .50	Ruthven, Dick	85F	64	$ .01	$ .05
Rose, Pete	86F	191	$ .12	$ .75	Ruthven, Dick	86F	377	$ .01	$ .05
Rose, Pete	86F	628	$ .10	$ .75	Ryal, Mark	88F	503	$ .01	$ .05
Rose, Pete	86F	638	$ .15	$ .75	Ryan, Nolan	81F	57	$ .45	$4.00
Rose, Pete	87F	213	$ .10	$ .50	Ryan, Nolan	82F	229	$ .40	$4.00
Rosello, Dave	82F	377	$ .01	$ .05	Ryan, Nolan	83F	463	$ .50	$3.50
Rosenberg, Steve	89FU	22	$ .01	$ .05	Ryan, Nolan	84F	239	$ .75	$6.00
Rosenberg, Steve	90F	547	$ .01	$ .04	Ryan, Nolan	85F	359	$ .07	$4.00
Rowdon, Wade	88F	430	$ .01	$ .05	Ryan, Nolan	86F	310	$ .05	$2.50
Royster, Jerry	81F	250	$ .01	$ .05	Ryan, Nolan	87F	67	$ .05	$2.00
Royster, Jerry	82F	448	$ .01	$ .05	Ryan, Nolan	88F	455	$ .01	$1.00
Royster, Jerry	83F	147	$ .01	$ .05	Ryan, Nolan	89F	368	$ .05	$ .75
Royster, Jerry	84F	191	$ .01	$ .06	Ryan, Nolan	89FU	67	$ .01	$1.50
Royster, Jerry	85F	340	$ .01	$ .05	Ryan, Nolan	90F	313	$ .01	$ .35
Royster, Jerry	85FU	90	$ .01	$ .05	Ryan, Nolan	90F	636	$ .01	$ .10
Royster, Jerry	86F	333	$ .01	$ .05	Ryan, Nolan	90FU	131	$ .01	$ .15
Royster, Jerry	87F	428	$ .01	$ .05	Ryan, Nolan	91F	302	$ .01	$ .25
Royster, Jerry	88F	221	$ .01	$ .05	Saberhagen, Bret	84FU	103	$7.00	$30.00
Rozema, Dave	81F	464	$ .01	$ .05	Saberhagen, Bret	85F	212	$1.00	$5.00
Rozema, Dave 'David'	82F	279	$ .01	$ .05	Saberhagen, Bret	86F	19	$ .08	$1.00
Rozema, Dave	83F	340	$ .01	$ .05	Saberhagen, Bret	87F	379	$ .04	$ .35
Rozema, Dave	84F	90	$ .01	$ .06	Saberhagen, Bret	88F	268	$ .01	$ .25
Rozema, Dave	85F	21	$ .01	$ .05	Saberhagen, Bret	88F	626	$ .01	$ .05
Rozema, Dave	85FU	91	$ .01	$ .05	Saberhagen, Bret	89F	291	$ .01	$ .15
Rozema, Dave	86F	570	$ .01	$ .05	Saberhagen, Bret	90F	116	$ .01	$ .04
Rucker, Dave	83F	341	$ .01	$ .05	Saberhagen, Bret	91F	567	$ .01	$ .03
Rucker, Dave	85F	238	$ .01	$ .05	Sabo, Chris	88FU	87	$ .25	$2.00
Rucker, Dave	85FU	92	$ .01	$ .05	Sabo, Chris	89F	170	$ .01	$1.50
Rucker, Dave	86F	447	$ .01	$ .05	Sabo, Chris	89F	637	$ .01	$ 35
Rudi, Joe	81F	272	$ .01	$ .05	Sabo, Chris	90F	433	$ .01	$ .20
Rudi, Joe	82F	306	$ .01	$ .05	Sabo, Chris	91F	80	$ .01	$ .10
Rudi, Joe	83F	532	$ .01	$ .05	Sakata, Lenn	81F	194	$ .01	$ .05
Ruffin, Bruce	87F	183	$ .01	$ .05	Sakata, Lenn	82F	178	$ .01	$ .05

FLEER

Player	Year	No.	VG	EX/MT	Player	Year	No.	VG	EX/MT
Sakata, Lenn	83F	72	$.01	$.05	Sandberg, Ryne	86F	378	$.05	$2.00
Sakata, Lenn	84F	19	$.01	$.06	Sandberg, Ryne	87F	572	$.04	$2.00
Sakata, Lenn	85F	189	$.01	$.05	Sandberg, Ryne	87F	639	$.01	$.10
Salas, Mark	85FU	94	$.04	$.25	Sandberg, Ryne	88F	431	$.01	$1.00
Salas, Mark	86F	402	$.01	$.05	Sandberg, Ryne	88F	628	$.01	$.05
Salas, Mark	87F	551	$.01	$.05	Sandberg, Ryne	89F	437	$.01	$.25
Salas, Mark	87FU	106	$.01	$.05	Sandberg, Ryne	90F	40	$.01	$.20
Salas, Mark	89F	511	$.01	$.05	Sandberg, Ryne	90F	639	$.01	$.10
Salas, Mark	91F	350	$.01	$.03					
Salazar, Angel	86FU	100	$.01	$.05					
Salazar, Angel	87F	380	$.01	$.05					
Salazar, Angel	88F	269	$.01	$.05					
Salazar, Luis	81F	501	$.01	$.05					
Salazar, Luis	82F	581	$.01	$.05					
Salazar, Luis	83F	371	$.01	$.05					
Salazar, Luis	84F	311	$.01	$.06					
Salazar, Luis	85F	43	$.01	$.05					
Salazar, Luis	85FU	95	$.01	$.05					
Salazar, Luis	86F	215	$.01	$.05					
Salazar, Luis	88F	595	$.01	$.05					
Salazar, Luis	88FU	30	$.01	$.05					
Salazar, Luis	89F	144	$.01	$.05					
Salazar, Luis	90FU	9	$.01	$.05					
Salazar, Luis	91F	430	$.01	$.03					
Sambito, Joe	81F	65	$.01	$.05					
Sambito, Joe	82F	230	$.01	$.05					
Sambito, Joe	83F	464	$.01	$.05					
Sambito, Joe	85F	360	$.01	$.05					
Sambito, Joe	85FU	96	$.01	$.05					
Sambito, Joe	86FU	101	$.01	$.05					
Sambito, Joe	87F	43	$.01	$.05					
Sambito, Joe	88F	364	$.01	$.05					
Sampen, Bill	90FU	31	$.01	$.20					
Sampen, Bill	91F	247	$.01	$.15					
Sample, Billy	81F	637	$.01	$.05					
Sample, Billy	82F	330	$.01	$.05					
Sample, Billy	83F	577	$.01	$.05					
Sample, Billy	84F	426	$.01	$.06					
Sample, Billy	85F	566	$.01	$.05	Sandberg, Ryne	90FPD	625	$.01	$.15
Sample, Billy	85FU	97	$.01	$.05	Sandberg, Ryne	91F	431	$.01	$.15
Sample, Billy	86F	118	$.01	$.05	Sandberg, Ryne	91F	709	$.01	$.20
Sample, Billy	86FU	102	$.01	$.05	Sandberg, Ryne	91F	713	$.01	$.10
Sample, Billy	87F	527	$.01	$.05	Sanders, Deion	89FU	53	$.01	$.50
Samuel, Juan	84F	47	$.50	$3.25	Sanders, Deion	90F	454	$.01	$.25
Samuel, Juan	85F	264	$.06	$.40	Sanderson, Scott	81F	166	$.01	$.05
Samuel, Juan	85F	634	$.20	$1.00	Sanderson, Scott	82F	206	$.01	$.05
Samuel, Juan	86F	449	$.01	$.10	Sanderson, Scott	83F	295	$.01	$.05
Samuel, Juan	87F	185	$.01	$.10	Sanderson, Scott	84F	285	$.01	$.06
Samuel, Juan	87F	642	$.01	$.05	Sanderson, Scott	84FU	104	$.01	$.10
Samuel, Juan	88F	314	$.01	$.10	Sanderson, Scott	85F	66	$.01	$.05
Samuel, Juan	89F	580	$.01	$.05	Sanderson, Scott	86F	379	$.01	$.05
Samuel, Juan	89FU	102	$.01	$.10	Sanderson, Scott	87F	573	$.01	$.05
Samuel, Juan	90F	215	$.01	$.04	Sanderson, Scott	88F	432	$.01	$.05
Samuel, Juan	90FU	25	$.01	$.05	Sanderson, Scott	89FU	78	$.01	$.05
Samuel, Juan	91F	218	$.01	$.03	Sanderson, Scott	90F	41	$.01	$.04
Samuels, Roger	88FU	131	$.01	$.05	Sanderson, Scott	90FU	118	$.01	$.05
Sanchez, Alejandro "Alex"	85F	648	$.25	$2.00	Sanderson, Scott	91F	23	$.01	$.03
Sanchez, Alex	85FU	98	$.01	$.05	Sanguillen, Manny	81F	376	$.01	$.05
Sanchez, Alex	86F	236	$.01	$.05	Santana, Rafael	85F	90	$.03	$.20
Sanchez, Alex	89FU	71	$.01	$.25	Santana, Rafael	86F	93	$.01	$.05
Sanchez, Alex	90F	92	$.01	$.10	Santana, Rafael	87F	21	$.01	$.05
Sanchez, Israel	88FU	34	$.01	$.15	Santana, Rafael	88F	149	$.01	$.05
Sanchez, Luis	83F	100	$.01	$.05	Santana, Rafael	88FU	50	$.01	$.05
Sanchez, Luis	84F	527	$.01	$.06	Santana, Rafael	89F	268	$.01	$.05
Sanchez, Luis	85F	310	$.01	$.05	Santiago, Benito	86F	644	$1.25	$5.00
Sanchez, Orlando	82F	126	$.01	$.05	Santiago, Benito	87F	429	$.35	$1.25
Sandberg, Ryne	83F	507	$5.00	$25.00	Santiago, Benito	88F	596	$.01	$.50
Sandberg, Ryne	84F	504	$2.00	10.00	Santiago, Benito	89F	316	$.01	$.25
Sandberg, Ryne	85F	65	$.05	$4.00	Santiago, Benito	90F	167	$.01	$.04
Sandberg, Ryne	85F	630	$.05	$1.00	Santiago, Benito	91F	542	$.01	$.03

FLEER'90

PLAYERS OF THE DECADE

10th Anniversary

RYNE SANDBERG

Player	Year	No.	VG	EX/MT	Player	Year	No.	VG	EX/MT
Santovenia, Nelson	88FU	103	$ .01	$ .30	Schmidt, Mike	86F	450	$ .01	$1.00
Santovenia, Nelson	89F	393	$ .01	$ .15	Schmidt, Mike	87F	187	$ .06	$1.00
Santovenia, Nelson	90F	360	$ .01	$ .04	Schmidt, Mike	88F	315	$ .01	$ .50
Santovenia, Nelson	91F	248	$ .01	$ .03	Schmidt, Mike	88F	636	$ .01	$ .15
Sarmiento, Manny	83F	321	$ .01	$ .05	Schmidt, Mike	89F	582	$ .01	$ .50
Sarmiento, Manny	84F	263	$ .01	$ .06	Schmidt, Mike	89FU	131	$ .01	$1.50
Sasser, Mackey	88FU	106	$ .01	$ .05	Schofield, Dick	84FU	105	$ .01	$ .10
Sasser, Mackey	89F	48	$ .01	$ .05	Schofield, Dick	85F	311	$ .01	$ .05
Sasser, Mackey	90F	216	$ .01	$ .04	Schofield, Dick	86F	167	$ .01	$ .05
Sasser, Mackey	91F	160	$ .01	$ .03	Schofield, Dick	87F	92	$ .01	$ .05
Saucier, Kevin	81F	24	$ .01	$ .05	Schofield, Dick	88F	504	$ .01	$ .10
Saucier, Kevin	82F	275	$ .01	$ .05	Schofield, Dick	89F	488	$ .01	$ .05
Savage, Jack	88F	650	$ .01	$ .25	Schofield, Dick	90F	144	$ .01	$ .04
Sax, Steve	82F	21	$ .35	$3.00	Schofield, Dick	91F	325	$ .01	$ .03
Sax, Steve	83F	220	$ .10	$ .50	Schooler, Mike	89F	559	$ .01	$ .35
Sax, Steve	84F	112	$ .06	$ .35	Schooler, Mike	90F	525	$ .01	$ .04
Sax, Steve	84F	633	$ .01	$ .06	Schooler, Mike	91F	461	$ .01	$ .03
Sax, Steve	85F	384	$ .03	$ .20	Schroeder, Bill	85F	594	$ .01	$ .05
Sax, Steve	86F	143	$ .01	$ .10	Schroeder, Bill	86F	501	$ .01	$ .05
Sax, Steve	87F	453	$ .01	$ .10	Schroeder, Bill	87F	357	$ .01	$ .05
Sax, Steve	88F	523	$ .01	$ .10	Schroeder, Bill	88F	173	$ .01	$ .05
Sax, Steve	89F	70	$ .01	$ .15	Schrom, Ken	81F	425	$ .03	$ .20
Sax, Steve	89FU	52	$ .01	$ .10	Schrom, Ken	84F	572	$ .01	$ .06
Sax, Steve	90F	455	$ .01	$ .04	Schrom, Ken	85F	288	$ .01	$ .05
Sax, Steve	91F	679	$ .01	$ .03	Schrom, Ken	86F	403	$ .01	$ .05
Schaefer, Jeff	90FU	120	$ .01	$ .10	Schrom, Ken	86FU	104	$ .01	$ .05
Schatzeder, Dan	81F	482	$ .01	$ .05	Schrom, Ken	87F	258	$ .01	$ .05
Schatzeder, Dan	82F	281	$ .01	$ .05	Schrom, Ken	88F	614	$ .01	$ .05
Schatzeder, Dan	83F	296	$ .01	$ .05	Schu, Rick	85FU	100	$ .04	$ .25
Schatzeder, Dan	84F	286	$ .01	$ .06	Schu, Rick	86F	451	$ .01	$ .05
Schatzeder, Dan	85F	409	$ .01	$ .05	Schu, Rick	87F	188	$ .01	$ .05
Schatzeder, Dan	86F	259	$ .01	$ .05	Schu, Rick	88F	316	$ .01	$ .05
Schatzeder, Dan	87F	186	$ .01	$ .05	Schu, Rick	89F	619	$ .01	$ .05
Schatzeder, Dan	88F	21	$ .01	$ .05	Schu, Rick	91F	326	$ .01	$ .03
Schatzeder, Dan	89FU	90	$ .01	$ .05	Schulz, Jeff	91F	568	$ .01	$ .10
Schatzeder, Dan	90F	236	$ .01	$ .04	Schulze, Don	85F	454	$ .01	$ .05
Scherrer, Bill	84F	482	$ .01	$ .06	Schulze, Don	87F	259	$ .01	$ .05
Scherrer, Bill	85F	22	$ .01	$ .05	Schwabe, Mike	89FU	32	$ .01	$ .20
Scherrer, Bill	86F	237	$ .01	$ .05	Schwabe, Mike	91F	351	$ .01	$ .10
Schilling, Curt	90FU	68	$ .01	$ .05	Scioscia, Mike	81F	131	$ .06	$ .50
Schilling, Curt	91F	491	$ .01	$ .10	Scioscia, Mike	82F	22	$ .01	$ .10
Schiraldi, Calvin	85FU	99	$ .04	$ .25	Scioscia, Mike	83F	221	$ .01	$ .05
Schiraldi, Calvin	87F	44	$ .01	$ .05	Scioscia, Mike	84F	113	$ .01	$ .06
Schiraldi, Calvin	88F	365	$ .01	$ .05	Scioscia, Mike	85F	385	$ .01	$ .05
Schiraldi, Calvin	89F	438	$ .01	$ .05	Scioscia, Mike	86F	144	$ .01	$ .05
Schiraldi, Calvin	90F	168	$ .01	$ .04	Scioscia, Mike	87F	454	$ .01	$ .05
Schiraldi, Calvin	91F	543	$ .01	$ .03	Scioscia, Mike	88F	524	$ .01	$ .05
Schmidt, Dave	83F	578	$ .01	$ .10	Scioscia, Mike	89F	71	$ .01	$ .05
Schmidt, Dave	84F	427	$ .01	$ .06	Scioscia, Mike	90F	407	$ .01	$ .04
Schmidt, Dave	85F	567	$ .01	$ .05	Scioscia, Mike	91F	219	$ .01	$ .03
Schmidt, Dave	86F	571	$ .01	$ .05	Sconiers, Daryl	84F	528	$ .01	$ .06
Schmidt, Dave	86FU	103	$ .01	$ .05	Sconiers, Daryl	85F	312	$ .01	$ .05
Schmidt, Dave	87F	505	$ .01	$ .05	Sconiers, Daryl	86F	168	$ .01	$ .05
Schmidt, Dave	87FU	107	$ .01	$ .05	Scott, Donnie	85F	568	$ .01	$ .05
Schmidt, Dave	88F	571	$ .01	$ .05	Scott, Donnie	86F	474	$ .01	$ .05
Schmidt, Dave	89F	618	$ .01	$ .05	Scott, Mike	82F	535	$ .15	$ .75
Schmidt, Dave	90F	188	$ .01	$ .04	Scott, Mike	83F	554	$ .05	$ .30
Schmidt, Dave	90FU	32	$ .01	$ .05	Scott, Mike	84F	240	$ .05	$ .30
Schmidt, Dave	91F	249	$ .01	$ .03	Scott, Mike	85F	361	$ .05	$ .30
Schmidt, Mike	81F	5	$ .12	$2.50	Scott, Mike	86F	311	$ .03	$ .20
Schmidt, Mike	81F	640	$ .10	$2.50	Scott, Mike	87F	68	$ .03	$ .20
Schmidt, Mike	81F	645	$ .20	$2.50	Scott, Mike	87F	630	$ .01	$ .10
Schmidt, Mike	82F	258	$ .12	$1.00	Scott, Mike	88F	456	$ .01	$ .10
Schmidt, Mike	82F	637	$ .06	$ .50	Scott, Mike	88F	632	$ .01	$ .10
Schmidt, Mike	82F	641	$ .05	$ .75	Scott, Mike	89F	367	$ .01	$ .05
Schmidt, Mike	83F	173	$ .25	$2.00	Scott, Mike	90F	237	$ .01	$ .04
Schmidt, Mike	84F	48	$ .03	$6.00	Scott, Mike	90F	636	$ .01	$ .10
Schmidt, Mike	85F	265	$ .10	$2.50	Scott, Mike	91F	515	$ .01	$ .03
Schmidt, Mike	85F	627	$ .06	$ .35	Scott, Rodney	81F	155	$ .01	$ .05
Schmidt, Mike	85F	630	$ .10	$1.00	Scott, Rodney	82F	207	$ .01	$ .05

Player	Year	No.	VG	EX/MT	Player	Year	No.	VG	EX/MT
Scott, Tony	81F	531	$ .01	$ .05	Seitzer, Kevin	87F	652	$ .50	$2.00
Scott, Tony	82F	231	$ .01	$ .05	Seitzer, Kevin	87FU	108	$ .25	$1.00
Scott, Tony	83F	465	$ .01	$ .05	Seitzer, Kevin	88F	270	$ .15	$ .75
Scott, Tony	84F	241	$ .01	$ .06	Seitzer, Kevin	89F	292	$ .01	$ .25
Scudder, Scott	89FU	87	$ .01	$ .35	Seitzer, Kevin	90F	117	$ .01	$ .04
Scudder, Scott	90F	434	$ .01	$ .15	Seitzer, Kevin	91F	569	$ .01	$ .03
Scudder, Scott	91F	81	$ .01	$ .03	Sellers, Jeff	87F	46	$ .01	$ .10
Scurry, Rod	81F	380	$ .01	$ .05	Sellers, Jeff	88F	366	$ .01	$ .05
Scurry, Rod	83F	322	$ .01	$ .05	Service, Scott	89F	653	$ .01	$ .20
Scurry, Rod	84F	264	$ .01	$ .06	Sexton, Jimmy	83F	533	$ .01	$ .05
Scurry, Rod	85F	476	$ .01	$ .05	Sharperson, Mike	88F	525	$ .01	$ .05
Scurry, Rod	87F	113	$ .01	$ .05	Sharperson, Mike	89F	72	$ .01	$ .05
Scurry, Ron	82F	497	$ .01	$ .05	Sharperson, Mike	91F	221	$ .01	$ .03
Seanez, Rudy	90F	640	$ .01	$ .04	Sheets, Larry	85FU	101	$ .05	$ .45
Seanez, Rudy	91F	376	$ .01	$ .03	Sheets, Larry	86F	286	$ .06	$ .35
Searage, Ray	85F	595	$ .01	$ .05	Sheets, Larry	87F	479	$ .01	$ .05
Searage, Ray	86F	502	$ .01	$ .05	Sheets, Larry	88F	572	$ .01	$ .05
Searage, Ray	87F	506	$ .01	$ .05	Sheets, Larry	89F	620	$ .01	$ .05
Searage, Ray	88F	409	$ .01	$ .05	Sheets, Larry	90F	189	$ .01	$ .04
Searage, Ray	89FU	94	$ .01	$ .05	Sheets, Larry	90FU	100	$ .01	$ .05
Searage, Ray	90F	408	$ .01	$ .04	Sheets, Larry	91F	352	$ .01	$ .03
Searage, Ray	91F	220	$ .01	$ .03	Sheffield, Gary	89F	196	$ .25	$1.50
Searcy, Steve	89F	145	$ .01	$ .25	Sheffield, Gary	90F	336	$ .01	$ .20
Searcy, Steve	90F	615	$ .01	$ .04	Sheffield, Gary	91F	596	$ .01	$ .10
Seaver, Tom	81F	200	$ .12	$1.00	Shelby, John	84F	20	$ .04	$ .25
Seaver, Tom	82F	82	$ .10	$ .75	Shelby, John	85F	190	$ .01	$ .05
Seaver, Tom	82F	634	$ .06	$ .75	Shelby, John	86F	287	$ .01	$ .05
Seaver, Tom	82F	645	$ .05	$ .30	Shelby, John	87F	480	$ .01	$ .05
Seaver, Tom	83F	601	$ .08	$ .75	Shelby, John	87FU	109	$ .01	$ .05
Seaver, Tom	84F	595	$ .06	$2.00	Shelby, John	88F	526	$ .01	$ .05
Seaver, Tom	84FU	106	$1.40	$12.50	Shelby, John	89F	73	$ .01	$ .05
Seaver, Tom	85F	526	$ .06	$ .65	Shelby, John	91F	353	$ .01	$ .03
					Shepherd, Ron	85FU	102	$ .01	$ .05
					Sheridan, Pat	84F	357	$ .03	$ .10
					Sheridan, Pat	85F	213	$ .01	$ .05
					Sheridan, Pat	86F	20	$ .01	$ .05
					Sheridan, Pat	87F	162	$ .01	$ .05
					Sheridan, Pat	88F	69	$ .01	$ .05
					Sheridan, Pat	89F	146	$ .01	$ .05
					Sheridan, Pat	90F	71	$ .01	$ .04
					Shields, Steve	86F	527	$ .01	$ .05
					Shields, Steve	89F	269	$ .01	$ .05
					Shipanoff, Dave	86F	452	$ .01	$ .05
					Shirley, Bob	81F	495	$ .01	$ .05
					Shirley, Bob	82F	127	$ .01	$ .05
					Shirley, Bob	83F	602	$ .01	$ .05
					Shirley, Bob	84F	141	$ .01	$ .06
					Shirley, Bob	85F	145	$ .01	$ .05
					Shirley, Bob	86F	119	$ .01	$ .05
					Shirley, Bob	87F	114	$ .01	$ .05
					Show, Eric	83F	372	$ .01	$ .10
					Show, Eric	84F	312	$ .01	$ .06
					Show, Eric	85F	44	$ .01	$ .05
					Show, Eric	86F	334	$ .01	$ .05
					Show, Eric	87F	430	$ .01	$ .05
					Show, Eric	88F	597	$ .01	$ .05
					Show, Eric	89F	317	$ .01	$ .05
					Show, Eric	90F	169	$ .01	$ .04
					Show, Eric	91F	544	$ .01	$ .03
					Shumpert, Terry	90FU	104	$ .01	$ .20
					Shumpert, Terry	91F	570	$ .01	$ .10
					Sierra, Candy	89F	171	$ .01	$ .15

Player	Year	No.	VG	EX/MT	Player	Year	No.	VG	EX/MT
Seaver, Tom	86F	216	$ .06	$ .50	Sierra, Ruben	86FU	105	$1.50	$6.50
Seaver, Tom	86F	630	$ .04	$ .25	Sierra, Ruben	87F	138	$1.75	$7.00
Seaver, Tom	87F	45	$ .05	$ .30	Sierra, Ruben	88F	479	$ .10	$1.00
Sebra, Bob	87F	331	$ .01	$ .05	Sierra, Ruben	89F	532	$ .01	$ .30
Sebra, Bob	88F	195	$ .01	$ .05	Sierra, Ruben	90F	314	$ .01	$ .15
Segui, David	90FU	69	$ .01	$ .35	Sierra, Ruben	91F	303	$ .01	$ .10
Segui, David	91F	492	$ .01	$ .15	Simmons, Nelson	85FU	103	$ .01	$ .05
Segura, Jose	88FU	20	$ .01	$ .15	Simmons, Nelson	86F	238	$ .01	$ .05

Player	Year	No.	VG	EX/MT	Player	Year	No.	VG	EX/MT
Simmons, Ted	81F	528	$ .01	$ .10	Smith, Bryn	85F	410	$ .01	$ .05
Simmons, Ted	82F	152	$ .01	$ .10	Smith, Bryn	86F	260	$ .01	$ .05
Simmons, Ted	83F	45	$ .01	$ .10	Smith, Bryn	87F	332	$ .01	$ .05
Simmons, Ted	84F	213	$ .03	$ .10	Smith, Bryn	88F	196	$ .01	$ .05
Simmons, Ted	85F	596	$ .01	$ .10	Smith, Bryn	89F	394	$ .01	$ .05
Simmons, Ted	86F	503	$ .01	$ .10	Smith, Bryn	90F	361	$ .01	$ .04
Simmons, Ted	86FU	106	$ .01	$ .10	Smith, Bryn	91F	644	$ .01	$ .03
Simmons, Ted	87F	528	$ .01	$ .10	Smith, Dave	81F	71	$ .05	$ .30
Simmons, Ted	88F	549	$ .01	$ .10	Smith, Dave	82F	232	$ .01	$ .10
Simmons, Ted	89F	599	$ .01	$ .05	Smith, Dave	83F	466	$ .01	$ .05
Simmons, Todd	88F	650	$ .01	$ .25	Smith, Dave	84F	242	$ .01	$ .06
Simmons, Todd	89F	318	$ .01	$ .05	Smith, Dave	85F	362	$ .01	$ .05
Simms, Mike	91F	516	$ .01	$ .10	Smith, Dave	86F	312	$ .01	$ .05
Simpson, Joe	81F	616	$ .01	$ .05	Smith, Dave	87F	69	$ .01	$ .05
Simpson, Joe	82F	518	$ .01	$ .05	Smith, Dave	88F	457	$ .01	$ .05
Simpson, Joe	83F	485	$ .01	$ .05	Smith, Dave	89F	369	$ .01	$ .05
Simpson, Joe	84F	358	$ .01	$ .06	Smith, Dave	90F	238	$ .01	$ .04
Singleton, Ken	81F	188	$ .01	$ .10	Smith, Dave	91F	517	$ .01	$ .03
Singleton, Ken	82F	179	$ .01	$ .10	Smith, Dwight	89FU	79	$ .01	$ .35
Singleton, Ken	83F	73	$ .01	$ .05	Smith, Dwight	90F	42	$ .01	$ .20
Singleton, Ken	84F	21	$ .01	$ .06	Smith, Dwight	91F	432	$ .01	$ .03
Singleton, Ken	85F	191	$ .01	$ .05	Smith, Greg	90F	643	$ .01	$ .04
Sisk, Doug	84F	596	$ .01	$ .06	Smith, Greg	91F	433	$ .01	$ .03
Sisk, Doug	85F	91	$ .01	$ .05	Smith, Jim	83F	323	$ .01	$ .05
Sisk, Doug	86F	94	$ .01	$ .05	Smith, Keith	81F	534	$ .01	$ .05
Sisk, Doug	87F	22	$ .01	$ .05	Smith, Ken	83F	148	$ .01	$ .05
Sisk, Doug	88F	150	$ .01	$ .05	Smith, Lee	82F	603	$ .15	$ .50
Sisk, Doug	88FU	3	$ .01	$ .05	Smith, Lee	83F	508	$ .03	$ .20
Sisk, Doug	89F	621	$ .01	$ .05	Smith, Lee	84F	505	$ .01	$ .10
Skinner, Joel	85F	646	$ .01	$ .10	Smith, Lee	85F	67	$ .01	$ .10
Skinner, Joel	87F	115	$ .01	$ .05	Smith, Lee	86F	380	$ .01	$ .10
Skinner, Joel	89F	270	$ .01	$ .05	Smith, Lee	87F	574	$ .01	$ .05
Skinner, Joel	90F	501	$ .01	$ .04	Smith, Lee	88F	433	$ .01	$ .05
Skinner, Joel	91F	377	$ .01	$ .03	Smith, Lee	88FU	8	$ .01	$ .05
Slaton, Jim	81F	518	$ .01	$ .05	Smith, Lee	89F	99	$ .01	$ .05
Slaton, Jim	82F	153	$ .01	$ .05	Smith, Lee	90F	287	$ .01	$ .04
Slaton, Jim	83F	46	$ .01	$ .05	Smith, Lee	90FU	53	$ .01	$ .05
Slaton, Jim	84F	214	$ .01	$ .06	Smith, Lee	91F	645	$ .01	$ .03
Slaton, Jim	84FU	107	$ .01	$ .10	Smith, Lonnie	83F	21	$ .01	$ .05
Slaton, Jim	85F	313	$ .01	$ .05	Smith, Lonnie	83F	636	$ .01	$ .05
Slaton, Jim	86F	169	$ .01	$ .05	Smith, Lonnie	84F	335	$ .01	$ .06
Slaton, Jim	87F	163	$ .01	$ .05	Smith, Lonnie	85F	239	$ .01	$ .05
Slaught, Don	83F	123	$ .01	$ .15	Smith, Lonnie	85FU	106	$ .01	$ .05
Slaught, Don	84F	359	$ .01	$ .06	Smith, Lonnie	86F	21	$ .01	$ .05
Slaught, Don	85F	214	$ .01	$ .05	Smith, Lonnie	87F	381	$ .01	$ .05
Slaught, Don	85FU	104	$ .01	$ .05	Smith, Lonnie	89FU	74	$ .01	$ .05
Slaught, Don	86F	572	$ .01	$ .05	Smith, Lonnie	90F	593	$ .01	$ .04
Slaught, Don	87F	139	$ .01	$ .05	Smith, Lonnie	91F	702	$ .01	$ .03
Slaught, Don	88FU	51	$ .01	$ .05	Smith, Ozzie	81F	488	$ .25	$1.00
Slaught, Don	89F	271	$ .01	$ .05	Smith, Ozzie	82F	582	$ .10	$ .45
Slaught, Don	90F	456	$ .01	$ .04	Smith, Ozzie	83F	22	$ .10	$ .45
Slaught, Don	90FU	51	$ .01	$ .05	Smith, Ozzie	83F	636	$ .01	$ .05
Slaught, Don	91F	49	$ .01	$ .03	Smith, Ozzie	84F	336	$ .10	$ .50
Smalley, Roy	81F	551	$ .01	$ .05	Smith, Ozzie	85F	240	$ .05	$ .30
Smalley, Roy	82F	560	$ .01	$ .05	Smith, Ozzie	85F	631	$ .05	$ .30
Smalley, Roy	83F	397	$ .01	$ .05	Smith, Ozzie	86F	46	$ .04	$ .25
Smalley, Roy	84F	142	$ .01	$ .06	Smith, Ozzie	87F	308	$ .01	$ .10
Smalley, Roy	85F	527	$ .01	$ .05	Smith, Ozzie	88F	47	$ .01	$ .10
Smalley, Roy	85FU	105	$ .01	$ .05	Smith, Ozzie	88F	628	$ .01	$ .05
Smalley, Roy	86F	404	$ .01	$ .05	Smith, Ozzie	89F	463	$ .01	$ .05
Smalley, Roy	87F	552	$ .01	$ .05	Smith, Ozzie	90F	260	$ .01	$ .05
Smalley, Roy	88F	22	$ .01	$ .05	Smith, Ozzie	91F	646	$ .01	$ .03
Smiley, John	87FU	110	$ .04	$ .40	Smith, Peter	88F	647	$ .01	$ .30
Smiley, John	88F	340	$ .01	$ .25	Smith, Pete	88FU	73	$ .01	$ .15
Smiley, John	89F	221	$ .01	$ .10	Smith, Pete	89F	600	$ .01	$ .05
Smiley, John	90F	480	$ .01	$ .04	Smith, Pete	90F	594	$ .01	$ .04
Smiley, John	91F	50	$ .01	$ .03	Smith, Pete	91F	703	$ .01	$ .03
Smith, Billy	82F	400	$ .01	$ .05	Smith, Ray	84F	573	$ .01	$ .06
Smith, Bryn	83F	297	$ .01	$ .05	Smith, Reggie	81F	111	$ .01	$ .10
Smith, Bryn	84F	287	$ .01	$ .06	Smith, Reggie	82F	23	$ .01	$ .05

Player	Year	No.	VG	EX/MT	Player	Year	No.	VG	EX/MT
Smith, Reggie	83F	272	$ .01	$ .05	Speier, Chris	84F	288	$ .01	$ .06
Smith, Roy	85F	455	$ .01	$ .05	Speier, Chris	85FU	109	$ .01	$ .05
Smith, Roy	90F	386	$ .01	$ .10	Speier, Chris	86F	382	$ .01	$ .05
Smith, Roy	91F	624	$ .01	$ .03	Speier, Chris	87F	575	$ .01	$ .05
Smith, Zane	85F	651	$ .08	$ .40	Speier, Chris	87FU	112	$ .01	$ .05
Smith, Zane	86F	528	$ .01	$ .10	Speier, Chris	88F	96	$ .01	$ .05
Smith, Zane	87F	529	$ .01	$ .10	Speier, Chris	89F	343	$ .01	$ .05
Smith, Zane	88F	550	$ .01	$ .05	Speier, Chris	90F	72	$ .01	$ .04
Smith, Zane	89F	601	$ .01	$ .05	Spencer, Jim	81F	96	$ .01	$ .05
Smith, Zane	89FU	99	$ .01	$ .05	Spencer, Jim	82F	107	$ .01	$ .05
Smith, Zane	90F	362	$ .01	$ .04	Spiers, Bill	89FU	40	$ .01	$ .35
Smith, Zane	91F	51	$ .01	$ .03	Spiers, Bill	90F	337	$ .01	$ .25
Smithson, Mike	84F	428	$ .01	$ .06	Spiers, Bill	91F	597	$ .01	$ .03
Smithson, Mike	84FU	108	$ .01	$ .10	Spikes, Charlie	81F	259	$ .01	$ .05
Smithson, Mike	85F	289	$ .01	$ .05	Spillner, Dan	81F	392	$ .01	$ .05
Smithson, Mike	86F	405	$ .01	$ .05	Spillner, Dan	82F	378	$ .01	$ .05
Smithson, Mike	87F	553	$ .01	$ .05	Spillner, Dan	83F	419	$ .01	$ .05
Smithson, Mike	88F	23	$ .01	$ .05	Spillner, Dan	84F	550	$ .01	$ .06
Smithson, Mike	88FU	9	$ .01	$ .05	Spillner, Dan	85F	528	$ .01	$ .05
Smithson, Mike	89F	100	$ .01	$ .05	Spillner, Dan	86F	217	$ .01	$ .05
Smithson, Mike	90F	288	$ .01	$ .04	Spilman, Harry	81F	209	$ .01	$ .05
Smoltz, John	88FU	74	$ .05	$1.00	Spilman, Harry	82F	233	$ .01	$ .05
Smoltz, John	89F	602	$ .01	$ .35	Spilman, Harry	83F	467	$ .01	$ .05
Smoltz, John	90F	595	$ .01	$ .15	Spilman, Harry	87F	284	$ .01	$ .05
Smoltz, John	91F	704	$ .01	$ .03	Spilman, Harry	88F	97	$ .01	$ .05
Snell, Nate	85FU	107	$ .01	$ .05	Splittorff, Paul	81F	30	$ .01	$ .05
Snell, Nate	86F	288	$ .01	$ .05	Splittorff, Paul	82F	423	$ .01	$ .05
Snell, Nate	87F	481	$ .01	$ .05	Splittorff, Paul	83F	124	$ .01	$ .05
Snell, Nate	88F	70	$ .01	$ .05	Splittorff, Paul	84F	360	$ .01	$ .06
Snider, Van	89F	172	$ .01	$ .15	Squires, Mike	81F	349	$ .01	$ .05
Snyder, Cory	86F	653	$1.25	$15.00	Squires, Mike	82F	357	$ .01	$ .05
Snyder, Cory	87F	260	$ .05	$ .25	Squires, Mike	83F	250	$ .01	$ .05
Snyder, Cory	88F	615	$ .01	$ .10	Squires, Mike	84F	71	$ .01	$ .06
Snyder, Cory	88F	622	$ .01	$ .40	Squires, Mike	85F	529	$ .01	$ .05
Snyder, Cory	89F	412	$ .01	$ .10	St. Claire, Randy	86F	261	$ .01	$ .05
Snyder, Cory	90F	502	$ .01	$ .04	St. Claire, Randy	87FU	113	$ .01	$ .05
Snyder, Cory	91F	378	$ .01	$ .03	St. Claire, Randy	88F	197	$ .01	$ .05
Soderholm, Eric	81F	92	$ .01	$ .05	Stanhouse, Don	81F	121	$ .01	$ .05
Soff, Ray	87F	309	$ .01	$ .05	Stanicek, Pete	88F	573	$ .01	$ .15
Sofield, Rick	81F	563	$ .01	$ .05	Stanicek, Pete	89F	622	$ .01	$ .05
Sojo, Luis	90FU	129	$ .01	$ .10	Stanicek, Steve	88F	174	$ .01	$ .20
Sojo, Luis	91F	184	$ .01	$ .10	Stanley, Bob	81F	234	$ .01	$ .05
Solano, Julio	85F	363	$ .01	$ .05	Stanley, Bob	82F	307	$ .01	$ .05
Solomon, Eddie	81F	384	$ .01	$ .05	Stanley, Bob	83F	195	$ .01	$ .05
Solomon, Eddie	82F	498	$ .01	$ .05	Stanley, Bob	84F	409	$ .01	$ .06
Sorensen, Lary	81F	519	$ .01	$ .05	Stanley, Bob	85F	169	$ .01	$ .05
Sorensen, Lary	82F	128	$ .01	$ .05	Stanley, Bob	86F	359	$ .01	$ .05
Sorensen, Lary	83F	418	$ .01	$ .05	Stanley, Bob	87F	47	$ .01	$ .05
Sorensen, Lary	84F	549	$ .01	$ .06	Stanley, Bob	88F	367	$ .01	$ .05
Sorensen, Lary	84FU	109	$ .01	$ .10	Stanley, Bob	89F	101	$ .01	$ .05
Sorensen, Lary	85F	434	$ .01	$ .05	Stanley, Bob	90F	289	$ .01	$ .04
Sorensen, Lary	85FU	108	$ .01	$ .05	Stanley, Fred	81F	100	$ .01	$ .05
Sorensen, Lary	86F	381	$ .01	$ .05	Stanley, Fred	82F	108	$ .01	$ .05
Sorensen, Lary	87FU	111	$ .01	$ .05	Stanley, Fred	83F	534	$ .01	$ .05
Sosa, Elias	81F	151	$ .01	$ .05	Stanley, Mike	87F	647	$ .01	$ .45
Sosa, Elias	82F	208	$ .01	$ .05	Stanley, Mike	88F	480	$ .01	$ .05
Sosa, Elias	83F	342	$ .01	$ .05	Stanley, Mike	89F	533	$ .01	$ .05
Sosa, Elias	84F	313	$ .01	$ .06	Stanton, Mike	81F	400	$ .01	$ .05
Sosa, Sammy	90F	548	$ .01	$ .75	Stanton, Mike	82F	379	$ .01	$ .05
Sosa, Sammy	91F	136	$ .01	$ .15	Stanton, Mike	83F	486	$ .01	$ .05
Soto, Mario	81F	214	$ .05	$ .30	Stanton, Mike	84F	619	$ .01	$ .06
Soto, Mario	82F	83	$ .03	$ .20	Stanton, Mike	85F	501	$ .01	$ .05
Soto, Mario	83F	603	$ .03	$ .20	Stanton, Mike	90F	596	$ .01	$ .15
Soto, Mario	84F	483	$ .01	$ .06	Stanton, Mike	91F	705	$ .01	$ .03
Soto, Mario	85F	552	$ .01	$ .05	Stapleton, Dave	81F	236	$ .01	$ .05
Soto, Mario	86F	192	$ .01	$ .05	Stapleton, Dave	82F	308	$ .01	$ .05
Soto, Mario	87F	214	$ .01	$ .05	Stapleton, Dave	83F	196	$ .01	$ .05
Speier, Chris	81F	153	$ .01	$ .05	Stapleton, Dave	84F	410	$ .01	$ .06
Speier, Chris	82F	209	$ .01	$ .05	Stargell, Willie	81F	363	$ .07	$ .50
Speier, Chris	83F	298	$ .01	$ .05	Stargell, Willie	82F	499	$ .05	$ .30

Player	Year	No.	VG	EX/MT
Stargell, Willie	83F	324	$ .05	$ .50
Stargell, Willie	83F	634	$ .10	$ .75
Staub, Rusty	81F	629	$ .01	$ .10
Staub, Rusty	82F	536	$ .01	$ .10
Staub, Rusty	83F	555	$ .01	$ .10
Staub, Rusty	84F	597	$ .01	$ .10
Staub, Rusty	85F	92	$ .01	$ .10
Staub, Rusty	86F	95	$ .01	$ .10
Stearns, John	81F	317	$ .01	$ .05
Stearns, John	82F	537	$ .01	$ .05

John Stearns
CATCHER

Player	Year	No.	VG	EX/MT
Stearns, John	83F	556	$ .01	$ .05
Stearns, John	84F	598	$ .01	$ .06
Steels, Jim	88FU	64	$ .01	$ .05
Stefero, John	87F	652	$ .50	$2.00
Stein, Bill	81F	605	$ .01	$ .05
Stein, Bill	82F	331	$ .01	$ .05
Stein, Bill	83F	579	$ .01	$ .05
Stein, Bill	84F	429	$ .01	$ .06
Steinbach, Terry	87F	405	$ .10	$1.00
Steinbach, Terry	88F	294	$ .05	$ .20
Steinbach, Terry	89F	22	$ .01	$ .10
Steinbach, Terry	89F	634	$ .05	$ .35
Steinbach, Terry	90F	20	$ .01	$ .04
Steinbach, Terry	91F	24	$ .01	$ .03
Stenhouse, Mike	85F	411	$ .01	$ .05
Stenhouse, Mike	85FU	110	$ .01	$ .05
Stenhouse, Mike	86F	406	$ .01	$ .05
Stennett, Rennie	81F	438	$ .01	$ .05
Stennett, Rennie	82F	401	$ .01	$ .05
Stephenson, Phil	91F	545	$ .01	$ .03
Stevens, Lee	89FU	16	$ .01	$ .50
Stevens, Lee	90F	145	$ .01	$ .25
Stevens, Lee	91F	327	$ .01	$ .10
Stewart, Dave	82F	24	$1.00	$7.00
Stewart, Dave	83F	222	$ .10	$1.35
Stewart, Dave	84F	430	$ .01	$ .75
Stewart, Dave	85F	569	$ .10	$ .50
Stewart, Dave	86F	453	$ .05	$ .30
Stewart, Dave	87F	406	$ .05	$ .30
Stewart, Dave	88F	295	$ .01	$ .10

Player	Year	No.	VG	EX/MT
Stewart, Dave	89F	23	$ .01	$ .10
Stewart, Dave	90F	21	$ .01	$ .04
Stewart, Dave	91F	25	$ .01	$ .10
Stewart, Sammy	81F	181	$ .01	$ .05
Stewart, Sammy	82F	180	$ .01	$ .05
Stewart, Sammy	83F	74	$ .01	$ .05
Stewart, Sammy	84F	22	$ .01	$ .06
Stewart, Sammy	85F	192	$ .01	$ .05
Stewart, Sammy	86F	289	$ .01	$ .05
Stewart, Sammy	86FU	107	$ .01	$ .05
Stewart, Sammy	87F	48	$ .01	$ .05
Stewart, Sammy	88F	616	$ .01	$ .05
Stieb, Dave	81F	414	$ .04	$ .75
Stieb, Dave	82F	622	$ .01	$ .25
Stieb, Dave	83F	441	$ .01	$ .10
Stieb, Dave	84F	167	$ .01	$ .10
Stieb, Dave	85F	117	$ .01	$ .10
Stieb, Dave	86F	70	$ .01	$ .10
Stieb, Dave	86F	642	$ .01	$ .10
Stieb, Dave	87F	238	$ .01	$ .10
Stieb, Dave	88F	123	$ .01	$ .10
Stieb, Dave	89F	244	$ .01	$ .05
Stieb, Dave	90F	93	$ .01	$ .04
Stieb, Dave	91F	185	$ .01	$ .10
Stillwell, Kurt	86FU	108	$ .08	$ .40
Stillwell, Kurt	87F	215	$ .10	$ .50
Stillwell, Kurt	88F	248	$ .01	$ .10
Stillwell, Kurt	88FU	35	$ .01	$ .15
Stillwell, Kurt	89F	293	$ .01	$ .05
Stillwell, Kurt	90F	118	$ .01	$ .04
Stillwell, Kurt	91F	571	$ .01	$ .03
Stoddard, Bob	84F	620	$ .01	$ .06
Stoddard, Bob	85F	502	$ .01	$ .05
Stoddard, Bob	87F	431	$ .01	$ .05
Stoddard, Tim	81F	176	$ .01	$ .05
Stoddard, Tim	82F	181	$ .01	$ .05
Stoddard, Tim	83F	75	$ .01	$ .05
Stoddard, Tim	84F	23	$ .01	$ .06
Stoddard, Tim	84FU	110	$ .01	$ .10
Stoddard, Tim	85F	68	$ .01	$ .05
Stoddard, Tim	85FU	111	$ .01	$ .05
Stoddard, Tim	86F	335	$ .01	$ .05
Stoddard, Tim	87F	116	$ .01	$ .05
Stoddard, Tim	88F	222	$ .01	$ .05
Stone, Jeff	84FU	111	$ .10	$ .50
Stone, Jeff	85F	266	$ .03	$ .20
Stone, Jeff	86F	454	$ .01	$ .05
Stone, Jeff	87F	189	$ .01	$ .05
Stone, Jeff	88F	317	$ .01	$ .05
Stone, Steve	81F	170	$ .01	$ .05
Stone, Steve	82F	182	$ .01	$ .05
Stottlemyre, Todd	88FU	68	$ .01	$ .30
Stottlemyre, Todd	89F	245	$ .01	$ .25
Stottlemyre, Todd	90F	94	$ .01	$ .04
Stottlemyre, Todd	91F	186	$ .01	$ .03
Strain, Joe	81F	458	$ .01	$ .05
Straker, Les	88F	24	$ .01	$ .10
Strawberry, Darryl	84F	599	$10.00	$40.00
Strawberry, Darryl	85F	93	$1.00	$7.00
Strawberry, Darryl	85F	631	$ .05	$ .30
Strawberry, Darryl	86F	96	$ .50	$3.00
Strawberry, Darryl	86F	632	$ .05	$ .30
Strawberry, Darryl	87F	23	$ .07	$1.50
Strawberry, Darryl	87F	629	$ .10	$ .50
Strawberry, Darryl	87F	638	$ .10	$1.00
Strawberry, Darryl	88F	151	$ .01	$ .50
Strawberry, Darryl	88F	637	$ .10	$ .50
Strawberry, Darryl	89F	49	$ .05	$ .30
Strawberry, Darryl	89F	632	$ .05	$ .40
Strawberry, Darryl	90F	217	$ .01	$ .25

Player	Year	No.	VG	EX/MT
Strawberry, Darryl	91F	161	$ .01	$ .15
Stubbs, Franklin	85F	386	$ .10	$ .50
Stubbs, Franklin	87F	455	$ .01	$ .05
Stubbs, Franklin	88F	527	$ .01	$ .05
Stubbs, Franklin	89F	74	$ .01	$ .05
Stubbs, Franklin	91F	518	$ .01	$ .03
Stuper, John	83F	23	$ .01	$ .05
Stuper, John	84F	337	$ .01	$ .06
Stuper, John	85FU	112	$ .01	$ .05
Stuper, John	86F	193	$ .01	$ .05
Sularz, Guy	83F	273	$ .01	$ .05
Summers, Champ	81F	466	$ .01	$ .05
Summers, Champ	82F	282	$ .01	$ .05
Summers, Champ	83F	274	$ .01	$ .05
Summers, Champ	84FU	112	$ .01	$ .10
Sundberg, Jim	81F	619	$ .01	$ .05
Sundberg, Jim	82F	332	$ .01	$ .10
Sundberg, Jim	83F	580	$ .01	$ .05
Sundberg, Jim	84F	431	$ .01	$ .06
Sundberg, Jim	84FU	113	$ .04	$ .25
Sundberg, Jim	85F	597	$ .01	$ .05
Sundberg, Jim	85FU	113	$ .03	$ .20
Sundberg, Jim	86F	22	$ .01	$ .05
Sundberg, Jim	87F	382	$ .01	$ .05
Sundberg, Jim	87FU	114	$ .01	$ .05
Sundberg, Jim	88F	434	$ .01	$ .05
Surhoff, B. J.	87FU	115	$ .05	$ .35
Surhoff, B. J.	88F	175	$ .01	$ .20
Surhoff, B. J.	89F	197	$ .01	$ .05
Surhoff, B. J.	90F	338	$ .01	$ .04
Surhoff, B. J.	91F	598	$ .01	$ .03
Sutcliffe, Rick	81F	125	$ .04	$ .25
Sutcliffe, Rick	82F	25	$ .03	$ .20
Sutcliffe, Rick	83F	420	$ .01	$ .10
Sutcliffe, Rick	84F	551	$ .03	$ .10
Sutcliffe, Rick	84FU	114	$ .13	$ .75
Sutcliffe, Rick	85F	69	$ .01	$ .10
Sutcliffe, Rick	86F	383	$ .01	$ .10
Sutcliffe, Rick	87F	576	$ .01	$ .10
Sutcliffe, Rick	88F	435	$ .01	$ .10
Sutcliffe, Rick	89F	439	$ .01	$ .10
Sutcliffe, Rick	90F	43	$ .01	$ .04
Sutcliffe, Rick	91F	434	$ .01	$ .03
Sutter, Bruce	81F	294	$ .04	$ .25
Sutter, Bruce	82F	129	$ .01	$ .10
Sutter, Bruce	82F	631	$ .01	$ .05
Sutter, Bruce	83F	24	$ .01	$ .10
Sutter, Bruce	84F	338	$ .03	$ .10
Sutter, Bruce	85F	241	$ .01	$ .10
Sutter, Bruce	85FU	114	$ .04	$ .25
Sutter, Bruce	86F	529	$ .01	$ .10
Sutter, Bruce	87F	530	$ .01	$ .10
Sutter, Bruce	89F	603	$ .01	$ .05
Sutton, Don	81F	112	$ .05	$ .30
Sutton, Don	82F	234	$ .05	$ .30
Sutton, Don	83F	47	$ .04	$ .25
Sutton, Don	84F	215	$ .04	$ .25
Sutton, Don	85F	598	$ .04	$ .25
Sutton, Don	85FU	115	$ .06	$ .55
Sutton, Don	86F	170	$ .03	$ .20
Sutton, Don	87F	93	$ .01	$ .10
Sutton, Don	87F	626	$ .01	$ .10
Sutton, Don	88F	505	$ .01	$ .05
Sveum, Dale	86FU	109	$ .10	$ .50
Sveum, Dale	87F	358	$ .06	$ .35
Sveum, Dale	88F	176	$ .01	$ .10
Sveum, Dale	89F	198	$ .01	$ .05
Swaggerty, Bill	85F	193	$ .01	$ .05
Swan, Craig	81F	319	$ .01	$ .05
Swan, Craig	82F	538	$ .01	$ .05
Swan, Craig	83F	557	$ .01	$ .05
Swan, Craig	84F	600	$ .01	$ .06
Swan, Craig	84FU	115	$ .01	$ .10
Sweet, Rick	83F	487	$ .01	$ .05
Sweet, Rick	84F	621	$ .01	$ .06
Swift, Bill	86F	475	$ .01	$ .05
Swift, Bill	87F	597	$ .01	$ .05
Swift, Bill	88FU	61	$ .01	$ .05
Swift, Bill	89F	560	$ .01	$ .05
Swift, Bill	90F	526	$ .01	$ .04
Swift, Bill	91F	462	$ .01	$ .03
Swindell, Greg	87F	644	$ .10	$ .75
Swindell, Greg	87FU	116	$ .15	$ .50
Swindell, Greg	88F	617	$ .01	$ .10
Swindell, Greg	89F	413	$ .01	$ .15
Swindell, Greg	90F	503	$ .01	$ .04
Swindell, Greg	91F	379	$ .01	$ .03
Sykes, Bob	81F	533	$ .01	$ .05
Sykes, Bob	82F	130	$ .01	$ .05
Tabler, Pat	83F	509	$ .03	$ .20
Tabler, Pat	84F	552	$ .01	$ .10
Tabler, Pat	85F	456	$ .01	$ .10
Tabler, Pat	86F	594	$ .01	$ .05
Tabler, Pat	87F	261	$ .01	$ .05
Tabler, Pat	88F	618	$ .01	$ .05
Tabler, Pat	88F	633	$ .01	$ .35
Tabler, Pat	88FU	36	$ .01	$ .05
Tabler, Pat	89F	294	$ .01	$ .05
Tabler, Pat	90F	119	$ .01	$ .04
Tabor, Greg	88F	644	$ .01	$ .30
Tamargo, John	81F	152	$ .01	$ .05
Tanana, Frank	81F	276	$ .01	$ .05
Tanana, Frank	82F	309	$ .01	$ .05
Tanana, Frank	83F	581	$ .01	$ .05
Tanana, Frank	84F	432	$ .01	$ .06
Tanana, Frank	85F	570	$ .01	$ .05
Tanana, Frank	86F	239	$ .01	$ .05
Tanana, Frank	87F	164	$ .01	$ .05
Tanana, Frank	88F	71	$ .01	$ .05
Tanana, Frank	89F	147	$ .01	$ .05
Tanana, Frank	90F	616	$ .01	$ .04
Tanana, Frank	91F	354	$ .01	$ .03
Tanner, Bruce	85FU	116	$ .01	$ .05
Tanner, Bruce	86F	218	$ .01	$ .10
Tanner, Chuck	81F	367	$ .01	$ .05
Tapani, Kevin	90FU	110	$ .01	$ .35
Tapani, Kevin	91F	625	$ .01	$ .03
Tartabull, Danny	85F	647	$1.00	$4.00
Tartabull, Danny	86F	476	$ .25	$ .50
Tartabull, Danny	87F	598	$ .15	$ .50
Tartabull, Danny	87FU	117	$ .06	$ .35
Tartabull, Danny	88F	271	$ .05	$ .25
Tartabull, Danny	89F	295	$ .01	$ .15
Tartabull, Danny	90F	120	$ .01	$ .04
Tartabull, Danny	91F	572	$ .01	$ .03
Tate, Stu	90F	643	$ .01	$ .04
Taveras, Frank	81F	320	$ .01	$ .05
Taveras, Frank	82F	539	$ .01	$ .05
Taylor, Dorn	87FU	118	$ .01	$ .05
Taylor, Terry	89F	651	$ .01	$ .20
Tekulve, Kent	81F	362	$ .01	$ .10
Tekulve, Kent	82F	500	$ .01	$ .05
Tekulve, Kent	83F	326	$ .01	$ .05
Tekulve, Kent	84F	265	$ .01	$ .06
Tekulve, Kent	85F	477	$ .01	$ .05
Tekulve, Kent	85FU	117	$ .01	$ .05
Tekulve, Kent	86F	455	$ .01	$ .05
Tekulve, Kent	87F	190	$ .01	$ .05
Tekulve, Kent	88F	318	$ .01	$ .05
Tekulve, Kent	89F	583	$ .01	$ .05

Player	Year	No.	VG	EX/MT	Player	Year	No.	VG	EX/MT
Telford, Anthony	91F	493	$ .01	$ .10	Thomas, Gorman	83F	48	$ .01	$ .10
Tellmann, Tom	84F	216	$ .01	$ .06	Thomas, Gorman	84F	553	$ .01	$ .06
Tellmann, Tom	85F	599	$ .01	$ .05	Thomas, Gorman	84FU	117	$ .06	$ .35
Templeton, Garry	81F	529	$ .01	$ .10	Thomas, Gorman	85F	503	$ .01	$ .05
Templeton, Garry	82F	131	$ .01	$ .10	Thomas, Gorman	86F	477	$ .01	$ .10
Templeton, Garry	83F	373	$ .01	$ .10	Thomas, Gorman	87F	359	$ .01	$ .05
Templeton, Garry	84F	314	$ .03	$ .10	Thomas, Roy	84F	622	$ .01	$ .06
Templeton, Garry	85F	45	$ .01	$ .10	Thomas, Roy	86F	478	$ .01	$ .05
Templeton, Garry	86F	336	$ .01	$ .05	Thomasson, Gary	81F	138	$ .01	$ .05
Templeton, Garry	87F	432	$ .01	$ .05	Thompson, Jason	81F	278	$ .01	$ .05
Templeton, Garry	88F	598	$ .01	$ .05	Thompson, Jason	82F	501	$ .01	$ .05
Templeton, Garry	89F	319	$ .01	$ .05	Thompson, Jason	83F	325	$ .01	$ .05
Templeton, Garry	90F	170	$ .01	$ .04	Thompson, Jason	84F	267	$ .01	$ .06
Templeton, Garry	91F	546	$ .01	$ .03					
Tenace, Gene	81F	489	$ .01	$ .05					
Tenace, Gene	82F	132	$ .01	$ .05					
Tenace, Gene	83F	25	$ .01	$ .05					
Tenace, Gene	84F	266	$ .01	$ .06					
Terrell, Walt	84F	601	$ .06	$ .35					
Terrell, Walt	85F	94	$ .01	$ .05					
Terrell, Walt	85FU	118	$ .01	$ .05					
Terrell, Walt	86F	240	$ .01	$ .05					
Terrell, Walt	87F	165	$ .01	$ .05					
Terrell, Walt	88F	72	$ .01	$ .05					
Terrell, Walt	89F	149	$ .01	$ .05					
Terrell, Walt	90F	457	$ .01	$ .04					
Terry, Scott	88FU	121	$ .01	$ .15					
Terry, Scott	89F	464	$ .01	$ .05					
Terry, Scott	90F	261	$ .01	$ .04					
Terry, Scott	91F	647	$ .01	$ .03					
Tettleton, Mickey	85FU	119	$ .10	$ .50					
Tettleton, Mickey	86F	432	$ .05	$ .35					
Tettleton, Mickey	87F	407	$ .01	$ .05					
Tettleton, Mickey	89F	623	$ .01	$ .05					
Tettleton, Mickey	90F	190	$ .01	$ .04					
Tettleton, Mickey	91F	494	$ .01	$ .03					
Teufel, Tim	84F	574	$ .06	$ .35					
Teufel, Tim	85F	290	$ .01	$ .05					
Teufel, Tim	86F	407	$ .01	$ .05					
Teufel, Tim	86FU	110	$ .01	$ .05					
Teufel, Tim	87F	24	$ .01	$ .05					
Teufel, Tim	88F	152	$ .01	$ .05					
Teufel, Tim	89F	50	$ .01	$ .05					
Teufel, Tim	90F	218	$ .01	$ .04	Thompson, Jason	85F	478	$ .01	$ .05
Teufel, Tim	91F	162	$ .01	$ .03	Thompson, Jason	86F	622	$ .01	$ .05
Tewksbury, Bob	86FU	111	$ .05	$ .30	Thompson, Jason	86FU	113	$ .01	$ .05
Tewksbury, Bob	87F	117	$ .03	$ .20	Thompson, Milt	86F	530	$ .06	$ .35
Tewksbury, Bob	91F	648	$ .01	$ .03	Thompson, Milt	86FU	114	$ .01	$ .10
Thigpen, Bobby	87F	507	$ .20	$1.25	Thompson, Milt	87F	191	$ .01	$ .10
Thigpen, Bobby	88F	410	$ .01	$ .35	Thompson, Milt	88F	319	$ .01	$ .05
Thigpen, Bobby	89F	512	$ .01	$ .05	Thompson, Milt	89F	584	$ .01	$ .05
Thigpen, Bobby	90F	549	$ .01	$ .04	Thompson, Milt	89FU	121	$ .01	$ .05
Thigpen, Bobby	91F	137	$ .01	$ .03	Thompson, Milt	90F	262	$ .01	$ .04
Thigpen, Bobby	91F	712	$ .01	$ .10	Thompson, Milt	91F	649	$ .01	$ .03
Thomas, Andres	86FU	112	$ .04	$ .25	Thompson, Rich	85FU	120	$ .01	$ .05
Thomas, Andres	87F	531	$ .03	$ .20	Thompson, Rich	86F	595	$ .01	$ .05
Thomas, Andres	88F	551	$ .01	$ .05	Thompson, Rob 'Robby'	86FU	115	$ .05	$ .25
Thomas, Andres	89F	604	$ .01	$ .05	Thompson, Rob	87F	285	$ .06	$ .40
Thomas, Andres	90F	597	$ .01	$ .04	Thompson, Rob	88F	98	$ .01	$ .10
Thomas, Andres	91F	706	$ .01	$ .03	Thompson, Robby	89F	344	$ .01	$ .05
Thomas, Derrel	81F	123	$ .01	$ .05	Thompson, Robby	90F	73	$ .01	$ .04
Thomas, Derrel	82F	26	$ .01	$ .05	Thompson, Robby	91F	273	$ .01	$ .03
Thomas, Derrel	83F	223	$ .01	$ .05	Thompson, Scott	81F	296	$ .01	$ .05
Thomas, Derrel	84F	114	$ .01	$ .06	Thompson, Scott	85F	621	$ .01	$ .05
Thomas, Derrel	84FU	116	$ .01	$ .10	Thompson, Scott	86F	262	$ .01	$ .05
Thomas, Derrel	85F	314	$ .01	$ .05	Thon, Dickie	81F	277	$ .01	$ .05
Thomas, Frank	90FU	87	$ .01	$4.50	Thon, Dickie	82F	235	$ .01	$ .05
Thomas, Frank	91F	138	$ .01	$1.00	Thon, Dickie	83F	468	$ .01	$ .05
Thomas, Gorman	81F	507	$ .01	$ .10	Thon, Dickie	84F	243	$ .01	$ .06
Thomas, Gorman	82F	154	$ .01	$ .10	Thon, Dickie	84F	634	$ .01	$ .06

JASON THOMPSON
FIRST BASE

Player	Year	No.	VG	EX/MT	Player	Year	No.	VG	EX/MT
Thon, Dickie	85F	364	$ .01	$ .05	Todd, Jackson	82F	623	$ .01	$ .05
Thon, Dickie	86F	313	$ .01	$ .05	Toliver, Fred	86F	647	$1.00	$3.00
Thon, Dickie	87F	70	$ .01	$ .05	Toliver, Fred	86FU	117	$ .01	$ .05
Thon, Dickie	89F	320	$ .01	$ .05	Toliver, Fred	89F	126	$ .01	$ .05
Thon, Dickie	90F	573	$ .01	$ .04	Tolleson, Wayne	84F	434	$ .01	$ .06
Thon, Dickie	91F	412	$ .01	$ .03	Tolleson, Wayne	85F	571	$ .01	$ .05
Thornton, Andre	82F	380	$ .01	$ .10	Tolleson, Wayne	86F	573	$ .01	$ .05
Thornton, Andre	83F	421	$ .01	$ .10	Tolleson, Wayne	86FU	118	$ .01	$ .05
Thornton, Andre	83F	635	$ .01	$ .05	Tolleson, Wayne	87F	118	$ .01	$ .05
Thornton, Andre	84F	554	$ .03	$ .10	Tolleson, Wayne	88F	223	$ .01	$ .05
Thornton, Andre	85F	457	$ .01	$ .05	Tomlin, Randy	91F	52	$ .01	$ .10
Thornton, Andre	86F	596	$ .01	$ .05	Torre, Joe	81F	325	$ .01	$ .10
Thornton, Andre	87F	262	$ .01	$ .05	Torrez, Mike	81F	233	$ .01	$ .05
Thornton, Louis	85FU	121	$ .01	$ .05	Torrez, Mike	82F	310	$ .01	$ .05
Thornton, Louis	86F	71	$ .01	$ .10	Torrez, Mike	83F	197	$ .01	$ .05
Thurman, Gary	88F	272	$ .01	$ .20	Torrez, Mike	84F	602	$ .01	$ .06
Thurman, Gary	89F	296	$ .01	$ .10	Torve, Kelvin	90FU	40	$ .01	$ .05
Thurman, Gary	90F	121	$ .01	$ .04	Torve, Kelvin	91F	163	$ .01	$ .03
Thurman, Gary	91F	573	$ .01	$ .03	Traber, Jim	87F	482	$ .01	$ .05
Thurmond, Mark	84F	315	$ .03	$ .10	Traber, Jim	89F	625	$ .01	$ .05
Thurmond, Mark	85F	46	$ .01	$ .05	Traber, Jim	90F	193	$ .01	$ .04
Thurmond, Mark	86F	337	$ .01	$ .05	Tracy, Jim	81F	308	$ .01	$ .05
Thurmond, Mark	87F	166	$ .01	$ .05	Tracy, Jim	82F	605	$ .01	$ .05
Thurmond, Mark	88F	73	$ .01	$ .05	Trammell, Alan	81F	461	$ .10	$ .50
Thurmond, Mark	90F	191	$ .01	$ .04	Trammell, Alan	82F	283	$ .05	$ .35
Thurmond, Mark	91F	274	$ .01	$ .03	Trammell, Alan	83F	344	$ .05	$ .50
Tiant, Luis	81F	82	$ .01	$ .10	Trammell, Alan	84F	91	$ .05	$ .35
Tibbs, Jay	85F	553	$ .03	$ .20	Trammell, Alan	85F	23	$ .05	$ .50
Tibbs, Jay	86F	194	$ .01	$ .05	Trammell, Alan	86F	241	$ .05	$ .35
Tibbs, Jay	86FU	116	$ .01	$ .05	Trammell, Alan	86F	633	$ .04	$ .25
Tibbs, Jay	87F	333	$ .01	$ .05	Trammell, Alan	87F	167	$ .03	$ .20
Tibbs, Jay	89F	624	$ .01	$ .05	Trammell, Alan	88F	74	$ .01	$ .10
					Trammell, Alan	88F	635	$ .01	$ .10
					Trammell, Alan	89F	148	$ .01	$ .15
					Trammell, Alan	90F	617	$ .01	$ .10
					Trammell, Alan	91F	355	$ .01	$ .03
					Trautwein, John	88FU	10	$ .01	$ .10
					Travers, Billy	81F	514	$ .01	$ .05
					Travers, Billy	81F	525	$ .01	$ .05
					Treadway, Jeff	88F	249	$ .01	$ .30
					Treadway, Jeff	89F	173	$ .01	$ .15
					Treadway, Jeff	89FU	75	$ .01	$ .05
					Treadway, Jeff	90F	598	$ .01	$ .04
					Treadway, Jeff	91F	707	$ .01	$ .03
					Trevino, Alex	81F	318	$ .01	$ .05
					Trevino, Alex	82F	540	$ .01	$ .05
					Trevino, Alex	83F	604	$ .01	$ .05
					Trevino, Alex	84F	484	$ .01	$ .06
					Trevino, Alex	84FU	118	$ .01	$ .10
					Trevino, Alex	85F	341	$ .01	$ .05
					Trevino, Alex	85FU	122	$ .01	$ .05
					Trevino, Alex	86F	550	$ .01	$ .05
					Trevino, Alex	86FU	119	$ .01	$ .05
					Trevino, Alex	87F	456	$ .01	$ .05
					Trevino, Alex	90F	239	$ .01	$ .04
					Trillo, Manny	81F	3	$ .01	$ .05
					Trillo, Manny	82F	260	$ .01	$ .05
					Trillo, Manny	83F	174	$ .01	$ .05
					Trillo, Manny	83F	631	$ .01	$ .10
					Trillo, Manny	84F	289	$ .01	$ .06
					Trillo, Manny	84F	627	$ .01	$ .05
					Trillo, Manny	84FU	119	$ .01	$ .10
Tibbs, Jay	90F	192	$ .01	$ .04	Trillo, Manny	85F	622	$ .01	$ .05
Tidrow, Dick	81F	299	$ .01	$ .05	Trillo, Manny	86F	551	$ .01	$ .05
Tidrow, Dick	82F	604	$ .01	$ .05	Trillo, Manny	86FU	120	$ .01	$ .05
Tidrow, Dick	83F	510	$ .01	$ .05	Trillo, Manny	87F	577	$ .01	$ .05
Tidrow, Dick	84F	72	$ .01	$ .06	Trillo, Manny	88F	436	$ .01	$ .05
Tingley, Ron	89F	414	$ .01	$ .05	Trillo, Manny	89F	440	$ .01	$ .05
Tobik, Dave	83F	343	$ .01	$ .05	Trout, Steve	81F	345	$ .01	$ .05
Tobik, Dave	84F	433	$ .01	$ .06	Trout, Steve	82F	358	$ .01	$ .05

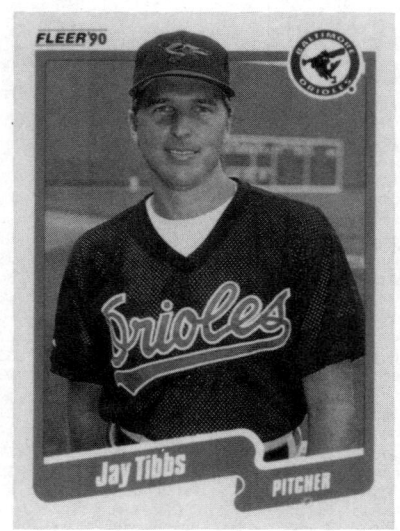

FLEER'90

Jay Tibbs PITCHER

Player	Year	No.	VG	EX/MT	Player	Year	No.	VG	EX/MT
Trout, Steve	83F	251	$ .01	$ .05	Valentine, Ellis	84F	529	$ .01	$ .06
Trout, Steve	84F	506	$ .01	$ .06	Valenzuela, Fernando	81F	140	$ .80	$3.00
Trout, Steve	85F	70	$ .01	$ .05	Valenzuela, Fernando	82F	27	$ .07	$ .50
Trout, Steve	86F	384	$ .01	$ .05	Valenzuela, Fernando	82F	635	$ .04	$ .25
Trout, Steve	87F	578	$ .01	$ .05	Valenzuela, Fernando	82F	636	$ .04	$ .25
Trujillo, Mike	86F	360	$ .01	$ .05	Valenzuela, Fernando	83F	224	$ .05	$ .30
Tudor, John	82F	311	$ .10	$ .35	Valenzuela, Fernando	84F	115	$ .01	$ .25
Tudor, John	83F	198	$ .01	$ .10	Valenzuela, Fernando	85F	387	$ .06	$ .25
Tudor, John	84F	411	$ .03	$ .10	Valenzuela, Fernando	86F	145	$ .05	$ .30
Tudor, John	84FU	120	$ .05	$ .30	Valenzuela, Fernando	86F	641	$ .05	$ .30
Tudor, John	85F	479	$ .01	$ .10	Valenzuela, Fernando	87F	457	$ .05	$ .30
Tudor, John	85FU	123	$ .04	$ .25	Valenzuela, Fernando	87F	631	$ .01	$ .10
Tudor, John	86F	47	$ .01	$ .10	Valenzuela, Fernando	88F	528	$ .01	$ .20
Tudor, John	87F	310	$ .01	$ .10	Valenzuela, Fernando	89F	76	$ .01	$ .15
Tudor, John	88F	48	$ .01	$ .10	Valenzuela, Fernando	90F	409	$ .01	$ .04
Tudor, John	89F	75	$ .01	$ .05	Valenzuela, Fernando	90FPD	622	$ .01	$ .15
Tudor, John	90FU	54	$ .01	$ .05	Valenzuela, Fernando	91F	222	$ .01	$ .03
Tudor, John	91F	650	$ .01	$ .03	Valera, Julio	91F	164	$ .01	$ .15
Tunnell, Lee	84F	268	$ .01	$ .06	Valle, Dave	85FU	125	$ .01	$ .05
Tunnell, Lee	85F	480	$ .01	$ .05	Valle, Dave	88F	389	$ .01	$ .05
Tunnell, Lee	85F	638	$ .01	$ .05	Valle, Dave	89F	561	$ .01	$ .05
Tunnell, Lee	86F	623	$ .01	$ .05	Valle, Dave	91F	463	$ .01	$ .03
Tunnell, Lee	87FU	119	$ .01	$ .05	Valle, David	90F	527	$ .01	$ .04
Tunnell, Lee	88F	49	$ .01	$ .05	Van Gorder, David	86F	195	$ .01	$ .05
Turner, Jerry	81F	504	$ .01	$ .05	Van Slyke, Andy	84F	339	$ .75	$4.00
Turner, Jerry	83F	345	$ .01	$ .05	Van Slyke, Andy	85F	242	$ .03	$ .75
Turner, Shane	89F	653	$ .01	$ .20	Van Slyke, Andy	86F	48	$ .01	$ .20
Twitty, Jeff	81F	49	$ .01	$ .05	Van Slyke, Andy	87F	311	$ .01	$ .10
Tyson, Mike	81F	315	$ .01	$ .05	Van Slyke, Andy	87FU	121	$ .01	$ .05
Tyson, Mike	82F	606	$ .01	$ .05	Van Slyke, Andy	88F	341	$ .01	$ .05
Ujdur, Jerry	83F	346	$ .01	$ .05	Van Slyke, Andy	89F	222	$ .01	$ .05
Underwood, Pat	81F	469	$ .01	$ .05	Van Slyke, Andy	90F	481	$ .01	$ .04
Underwood, Pat	83F	347	$ .01	$ .05	Van Slyke, Andy	91F	53	$ .01	$ .03
Underwood, Tom	81F	97	$ .01	$ .05	Vande Berg, Ed	83F	488	$ .01	$ .05
Underwood, Tom	82F	109	$ .01	$ .05	Vande Berg, Ed	84F	623	$ .01	$ .06
Underwood, Tom	83F	535	$ .01	$ .05	Vande Berg, Ed	85F	504	$ .01	$ .05
Underwood, Tom	84F	460	$ .01	$ .06	Vande Berg, Ed	86F	479	$ .01	$ .05
Underwood, Tom	84FU	121	$ .01	$ .10	Vande Berg, Ed	86FU	121	$ .01	$ .05
Underwood, Tom	85F	194	$ .01	$ .05	Vande Berg, Ed	87F	458	$ .01	$ .05
Unser, Del	81F	26	$ .01	$ .05	Vande Berg, Ed	87FU	120	$ .01	$ .05
Unser, Del	82F	261	$ .01	$ .05	Vande Berg, Ed	88F	619	$ .01	$ .05
Upshaw, Willie	82F	624	$ .01	$ .05	Vande Berg, Ed	89F	534	$ .01	$ .05
Upshaw, Willie	83F	442	$ .01	$ .05	Varsho, Gary	88FU	81	$ .01	$ .15
Upshaw, Willie	84F	168	$ .01	$ .06	Varsho, Gary	89F	441	$ .01	$ .15
Upshaw, Willie	85F	118	$ .01	$ .05	Varsho, Gary	91F	435	$ .01	$ .03
Upshaw, Willie	85F	635	$ .01	$ .10	Vatcher, Jim	91F	708	$ .01	$ .10
Upshaw, Willie	86F	72	$ .01	$ .05	Vaughn, Greg	89FU	41	$ .01	$2.50
Upshaw, Willie	87F	209	$ .01	$ .05	Vaughn, Greg	90F	339	$ .01	$ .75
Upshaw, Willie	88F	124	$ .01	$ .05	Vaughn, Greg	91F	599	$ .01	$ .15
Upshaw, Willie	88FU	25	$ .01	$ .05	Vega, Jesus	83F	624	$ .01	$ .05
Upshaw, Willie	89F	415	$ .01	$ .05	Velarde, Randy	88F	646	$ .01	$ .20
Uribe, Jose	85FU	124	$ .05	$ .30	Velez, Otto	81F	410	$ .01	$ .05
Uribe, Jose	86F	552	$ .01	$ .20	Velez, Otto	82F	625	$ .01	$ .05
Uribe, Jose	87F	286	$ .01	$ .05	Venable, Max	81F	443	$ .01	$ .05
Uribe, Jose	88F	99	$ .01	$ .05	Venable, Max	83F	275	$ .01	$ .05
Uribe, Jose	89F	345	$ .01	$ .05	Venable, Max	84F	385	$ .01	$ .06
Uribe, Jose	90F	74	$ .01	$ .04	Venable, Max	86F	196	$ .01	$ .05
Uribe, Jose	91F	275	$ .01	$ .03	Venable, Max	87F	216	$ .01	$ .05
Urrea, John	82F	583	$ .01	$ .05	Ventura, Robin	89FU	23	$ .01	$1.00
Vail, Mike	81F	311	$ .01	$ .05	Ventura, Robin	90F	550	$ .01	$ .50
Vail, Mike	82F	84	$ .01	$ .05	Ventura, Robin	91F	139	$ .80	$ .10
Vail, Mike	83F	605	$ .01	$ .05	Veres, Randy	89FU	42	$ .01	$ .15
Vail, Mike	84F	290	$ .01	$ .06	Veres, Randy	91F	600	$ .01	$ .03
Vail, Mike	84FU	122	$ .01	$ .10	Verhoeven, John	82F	547	$ .01	$ .05
Valdez, Julio	83F	199	$ .01	$ .05	Veryzer, Tom	81F	390	$ .01	$ .05
Valdez, Rafael	90FU	58	$ .01	$ .15	Veryzer, Tom	82F	381	$ .01	$ .05
Valdez, Sergio	91F	380	$ .01	$ .03	Veryzer, Tom	83F	559	$ .01	$ .05
Valentine, Ellis	81F	148	$ .01	$ .05	Villanueva, Hector	90FU	10	$ .01	$ .20
Valentine, Ellis	82F	541	$ .01	$ .05	Villanueva, Hector	91F	436	$ .01	$ .10
Valentine, Ellis	83F	558	$ .01	$ .05	Viola, Frank	83F	625	$ .75	$6.00

FLEER

Player	Year	No.	VG	EX/MT	Player	Year	No.	VG	EX/MT
Viola, Frank	84F	575	$ .25	$1.75	Walker, Tony	87F	71	$ .01	$ .10
Viola, Frank	85F	291	$ .15	$ .50	Wallach, Tim	82F	210	$ .25	$1.50
Viola, Frank	86F	408	$ .10	$ .40	Wallach, Tim	83F	299	$ .05	$ .25
Viola, Frank	87F	554	$ .05	$ .20	Wallach, Tim	84F	291	$ .03	$ .20
Viola, Frank	88F	25	$ .01	$ .10	Wallach, Tim	85F	412	$ .03	$ .20
Viola, Frank	89F	127	$ .01	$ .15	Wallach, Tim	86F	263	$ .01	$ .10
Viola, Frank	90F	219	$ .01	$ .15	Wallach, Tim	87F	334	$ .01	$ .10
Viola, Frank	91F	165	$ .01	$ .10	Wallach, Tim	88F	198	$ .01	$ .10
Virdon, Bill	81F	61	$ .01	$ .05	Wallach, Tim	89F	395	$ .01	$ .05
Virgil, Ozzie	83F	175	$ .01	$ .05					
Virgil, Ozzie	84F	49	$ .01	$ .06					
Virgil, Ozzie	85F	267	$ .01	$ .05					
Virgil, Ozzie	86FU	122	$ .01	$ .05					
Virgil, Ozzie	87F	532	$ .01	$ .05					
Virgil, Ozzie	88F	552	$ .01	$ .05					
Virgil, Ozzie	89F	605	$ .01	$ .05					
Vizcaino, Jose	90F	410	$ .01	$ .25					
Vizcaino, Jose	91F	223	$ .01	$ .03					
Vizquel, Omar	89FU	62	$ .01	$ .25					
Vizquel, Omar	90F	528	$ .01	$ .10					
Vizquel, Omar	91F	464	$ .01	$ .03					
Von Ohlen, Dave	84F	340	$ .01	$ .06					
Von Ohlen, Dave	85F	243	$ .01	$ .05					
Von Ohlen, Dave	85FU	126	$ .01	$ .05					
Von Ohlen, Dave	86F	597	$ .01	$ .05					
Von Ohlen, Dave	87F	408	$ .01	$ .05					
Vuckovich, Pete	82F	156	$ .01	$ .05					
Vuckovich, Pete	83F	49	$ .01	$ .05					
Vuckovich, Pete	84F	217	$ .01	$ .06					
Vuckovich, Pete	86F	504	$ .01	$ .05					
Vukovich, George	81F	21	$ .01	$ .05					
Vukovich, George	82F	262	$ .01	$ .05					
Vukovich, George	83F	176	$ .01	$ .05					
Vukovich, George	84F	555	$ .01	$ .06					
Vukovich, George	85F	458	$ .01	$ .05					
Vukovich, George	86F	598	$ .01	$ .05					
Vukovich, John	81F	22	$ .01	$ .05					
Waddell, Tom	84FU	123	$ .05	$ .30					
Waddell, Tom	85F	459	$ .01	$ .05					
Waddell, Tom	86F	599	$ .01	$ .05	Wallach, Tim	90F	364	$ .01	$ .04
Wagner, Mark	81F	478	$ .01	$ .05	Wallach, Tim	91F	251	$ .01	$ .03
Wagner, Mark	82F	333	$ .01	$ .05	Waller, Ty	82F	607	$ .01	$ .05
Wagner, Mark	83F	582	$ .01	$ .05	Walling, Denny	81F	66	$ .01	$ .05
Waits, Rick	81F	396	$ .01	$ .05	Walling, Denny	82F	236	$ .01	$ .05
Waits, Rick	82F	382	$ .01	$ .05	Walling, Denny	83F	469	$ .01	$ .05
Waits, Rick	83F	422	$ .01	$ .05	Walling, Denny	84F	244	$ .01	$ .06
Waits, Rick	85F	600	$ .01	$ .05	Walling, Denny	85F	365	$ .01	$ .05
Waits, Rick	86F	505	$ .01	$ .05	Walling, Denny	86F	314	$ .01	$ .05
Walewander, Jim	89F	150	$ .01	$ .05	Walling, Denny	87F	72	$ .01	$ .05
Walk, Bob	81F	14	$ .01	$ .05	Walling, Denny	88F	458	$ .01	$ .05
Walk, Bob	83F	149	$ .01	$ .05	Walling, Denny	89F	465	$ .01	$ .05
Walk, Bob	87F	623	$ .01	$ .05	Walling, Denny	90F	263	$ .01	$ .04
Walk, Bob	88F	342	$ .01	$ .05	Walling, Denny	91F	651	$ .01	$ .03
Walk, Bob	89F	223	$ .01	$ .05	Walter, Gene	86F	644	$1.25	$5.00
Walk, Bob	90F	482	$ .01	$ .04	Walter, Gene	86FU	124	$ .01	$ .05
Walk, Bob	91F	54	$ .01	$ .03	Walter, Gene	87F	433	$ .01	$ .05
Walker, Duane	83F	606	$ .01	$ .05	Walter, Gene	88F	153	$ .01	$ .05
Walker, Duane	84F	485	$ .01	$ .06	Walton, Jerome	89FU	80	$ .01	$ .75
Walker, Duane	85F	554	$ .01	$ .05	Walton, Jerome	90F	44	$ .01	$ .25
Walker, Duane	86F	574	$ .01	$ .05	Walton, Jerome	91F	437	$ .01	$ .03
Walker, Greg	84F	73	$ .10	$ .50	Walton, Reggie	81F	609	$ .01	$ .05
Walker, Greg	85F	530	$ .01	$ .05	Ward, Colby	91F	382	$ .01	$ .10
Walker, Greg	86F	219	$ .01	$ .10	Ward, Colin	86F	645	$ .01	$ .10
Walker, Greg	87F	508	$ .01	$ .05	Ward, Duane	86FU	125	$ .04	$ .25
Walker, Greg	88F	411	$ .01	$ .05	Ward, Duane	88F	125	$ .01	$ .05
Walker, Greg	90F	551	$ .01	$ .04	Ward, Duane	89F	246	$ .01	$ .05
Walker, Larry	90F	363	$ .01	$ .35	Ward, Duane	90F	95	$ .01	$ .04
Walker, Larry	91F	250	$ .01	$ .10	Ward, Duane	91F	187	$ .01	$ .03
Walker, Mike	91F	381	$ .01	$ .10	Ward, Gary	82F	562	$ .01	$ .05
Walker, Tony	86FU	123	$ .01	$ .05	Ward, Gary	83F	627	$ .01	$ .05

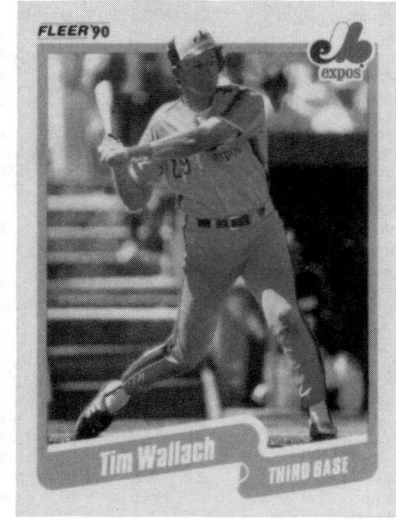

FLEER'90

expos

Tim Wallach   THIRD BASE

Player	Year	No.	VG	EX/MT	Player	Year	No.	VG	EX/MT
Ward, Gary	84F	576	$ .01	$ .06	Welch, Bob	81F	120	$ .03	$ .75
Ward, Gary	84FU	124	$ .04	$ .25	Welch, Bob	82F	28	$ .01	$ .25
Ward, Gary	85F	572	$ .01	$ .05	Welch, Bob	83F	225	$ .01	$ .05
Ward, Gary	86F	575	$ .01	$ .05	Welch, Bob	84F	116	$ .01	$ .06
Ward, Gary	87F	140	$ .01	$ .05	Welch, Bob	85F	388	$ .01	$ .05
Ward, Gary	87FU	122	$ .01	$ .05	Welch, Bob	86F	146	$ .01	$ .05
Ward, Gary	88F	224	$ .01	$ .05	Welch, Bob	87F	459	$ .01	$ .05
Ward, Gary	89F	273	$ .01	$ .05	Welch, Bob	88F	529	$ .01	$ .05
Ward, Gary	89FU	33	$ .01	$ .05	Welch, Bob	88FU	57	$ .01	$ .05
Ward, Gary	90F	618	$ .01	$ .04	Welch, Bob	89F	25	$ .01	$ .05
Ward, Gary	91F	356	$ .01	$ .03	Welch, Bob	90F	23	$ .01	$ .10
Ward, Turner	91F	383	$ .01	$ .15	Welch, Bob	91F	27	$ .01	$ .03
Wardle, Curt	85FU	127	$ .01	$ .05	Wellman, Brad	84F	386	$ .01	$ .06
Wardle, Curt	86F	600	$ .01	$ .05	Wellman, Brad	85F	623	$ .01	$ .05
Warren, Mike	84F	461	$ .01	$ .06	Wellman, Brad	86F	553	$ .01	$ .05
Warren, Mike	84F	639	$ .01	$ .06	Wells, David	88FU	69	$ .01	$ .05
Warren, Mike	85F	435	$ .01	$ .05	Wells, David	89F	247	$ .01	$ .05
Washington, Claudell	81F	329	$ .01	$ .05	Wells, David	90F	96	$ .01	$ .04
Washington, Claudell	82F	449	$ .01	$ .05	Wells, Dave	91F	188	$ .01	$ .03
Washington, Claudell	83F	150	$ .01	$ .05	Welsh, Chris	82F	584	$ .01	$ .05
Washington, Claudell	84F	192	$ .01	$ .06	Welsh, Chris	83F	374	$ .01	$ .05
Washington, Claudell	85F	342	$ .01	$ .05	Welsh, Chris	84F	292	$ .01	$ .06
Washington, Claudell	86F	531	$ .01	$ .05	Welsh, Chris	86F	576	$ .01	$ .05
Washington, Claudell	87F	119	$ .01	$ .05	Welsh, Chris	87F	217	$ .01	$ .05
Washington, Claudell	88F	225	$ .01	$ .05	Werth, Dennis	81F	102	$ .01	$ .05
Washington, Claudell	89F	272	$ .01	$ .05	Werth, Dennis	82F	55	$ .01	$ .05
Washington, Claudell	89FU	17	$ .01	$ .05	West, Dave	89F	51	$ .05	$ .25
Washington, Claudell	90F	146	$ .01	$ .04	West, Dave	90F	388	$ .01	$ .20
Washington, Ron	83F	626	$ .01	$ .05	West, David	91F	627	$ .01	$ .03
Washington, Ron	84F	577	$ .01	$ .06	Wetteland, John	90F	411	$ .01	$ .25
Washington, Ron	85F	292	$ .01	$ .05	Whisenton, Larry	83F	152	$ .01	$ .05
Washington, Ron	86F	409	$ .01	$ .05	Whitaker, Lou	81F	463	$ .05	$ .30
Washington, Ron	89F	416	$ .01	$ .05	Whitaker, Lou	82F	284	$ .05	$ .25
Washington, U. L.	81F	34	$ .01	$ .05	Whitaker, Lou	83F	348	$ .03	$ .25
Washington, U. L.	82F	424	$ .01	$ .05	Whitaker, Lou	84F	92	$ .03	$ .30
Washington, U. L.	83F	125	$ .01	$ .05	Whitaker, Lou	85F	24	$ .03	$ .20
Washington, U. L.	84F	361	$ .01	$ .06	Whitaker, Lou	86F	242	$ .03	$ .20
Washington, U. L.	85F	215	$ .01	$ .05	Whitaker, Lou	87F	168	$ .01	$ .10
Washington, U. L.	85FU	128	$ .01	$ .05	Whitaker, Lou	88F	75	$ .01	$ .10
Washington, U. L.	86F	264	$ .01	$ .05	Whitaker, Lou	89F	151	$ .01	$ .10
Wasinger, Mark	88F	100	$ .01	$ .15	Whitaker, Lou	90F	619	$ .01	$ .10
Wathan, John	81F	46	$ .01	$ .05	Whitaker, Lou	91F	357	$ .01	$ .03
Wathan, John	82F	425	$ .01	$ .05	White, Devon	87F	646	$ .25	$1.00
Wathan, John	83F	126	$ .01	$ .05	White, Devon	87FU	123	$ .11	$ .55
Wathan, John	84F	362	$ .01	$ .06	White, Devon	88F	506	$ .01	$ .20
Wathan, John	85F	216	$ .01	$ .05	White, Devon	89F	489	$ .01	$ .15
Wathan, John	86F	23	$ .01	$ .05	White, Devon	90F	147	$ .01	$ .04
Watson, Bob	81F	93	$ .01	$ .05	White, Devon	91F	328	$ .01	$ .03
Watson, Bob	82F	54	$ .01	$ .05	White, Frank	81F	44	$ .01	$ .10
Watson, Bob	83F	151	$ .01	$ .05	White, Frank	82F	426	$ .01	$ .10
Watson, Bob	84F	193	$ .01	$ .06	White, Frank	82F	629	$ .01	$ .05
Wayne, Gary	90F	387	$ .01	$ .10	White, Frank	83F	127	$ .01	$ .05
Wayne, Gary	91F	626	$ .01	$ .03	White, Frank	84F	363	$ .01	$ .06
Weaver, Earl	81F	178	$ .01	$ .05	White, Frank	85F	217	$ .01	$ .05
Webster, Mitch	86F	265	$ .05	$ .25	White, Frank	86F	24	$ .01	$ .05
Webster, Mitch	87F	335	$ .01	$ .05	White, Frank	87F	383	$ .01	$ .05
Webster, Mitch	88F	199	$ .01	$ .05	White, Frank	88F	273	$ .01	$ .05
Webster, Mitch	89F	442	$ .01	$ .05	White, Frank	89F	297	$ .01	$ .05
Webster, Mitch	90F	45	$ .01	$ .04	White, Frank	90F	122	$ .01	$ .04
Webster, Mitch	91F	384	$ .01	$ .03	White, Frank	91F	574	$ .01	$ .03
Wegman, Bill	87F	360	$ .01	$ .05	White, Jerry	81F	161	$ .01	$ .05
Wegman, Bill	88F	177	$ .01	$ .05	White, Jerry	82F	211	$ .01	$ .05
Wegman, Bill	89F	199	$ .01	$ .05	White, Jerry	83F	300	$ .01	$ .05
Wehrmeister, Dave	86F	220	$ .01	$ .05	Whitehouse, Len	84F	578	$ .01	$ .06
Weiss, Gary	81F	130	$ .01	$ .05	Whitehurst, Wally	89FU	103	$ .01	$ .20
Weiss, Walt	88F	652	$ .30	$1.25	Whitehurst, Wally	91F	166	$ .01	$ .03
Weiss, Walt	88FU	56	$ .10	$ .75	Whiten, Mark	90FU	130	$ .01	$ .50
Weiss, Walt	89F	24	$ .01	$ .25	Whiten, Mark	91F	189	$ .01	$ .35
Weiss, Walt	90F	22	$ .01	$ .10	Whitfield, Terry	81F	437	$ .01	$ .05
Weiss, Walt	91F	26	$ .01	$ .03	Whitfield, Terry	84FU	125	$ .01	$ .10

Player	Year	No.	VG	EX/MT
Whitfield, Terry	85F	389	$ .01	$ .05
Whitfield, Terry	86F	147	$ .01	$ .05
Whitson, Ed	81F	444	$ .01	$ .05
Whitson, Ed	82F	402	$ .01	$ .05
Whitson, Eddie	83F	423	$ .01	$ .05

Ed Whitson
PITCHER

Player	Year	No.	VG	EX/MT
Whitson, Ed	84F	316	$ .01	$ .06
Whitson, Ed	85F	47	$ .01	$ .05
Whitson, Ed	85FU	129	$ .01	$ .05
Whitson, Ed	86F	120	$ .01	$ .05
Whitson, Ed	87F	434	$ .01	$ .05
Whitson, Ed	88F	599	$ .01	$ .05
Whitson, Ed	89F	321	$ .01	$ .05
Whitson, Ed	90F	171	$ .01	$ .04
Whitson, Ed	91F	547	$ .01	$ .03
Whitt, Ernie	81F	411	$ .01	$ .05
Whitt, Ernie	82F	626	$ .01	$ .05
Whitt, Ernie	83F	443	$ .01	$ .05
Whitt, Ernie	84F	169	$ .01	$ .06
Whitt, Ernie	85F	119	$ .01	$ .05
Whitt, Ernie	86F	73	$ .01	$ .05
Whitt, Ernie	87F	240	$ .01	$ .05
Whitt, Ernie	88F	126	$ .01	$ .05
Whitt, Ernie	89F	248	$ .01	$ .05
Whitt, Ernie	90F	97	$ .01	$ .04
Wickander, Kevin	91F	385	$ .01	$ .10
Wiggins, Alan	83F	375	$ .01	$ .10
Wiggins, Alan	84F	317	$ .01	$ .06
Wiggins, Alan	85F	48	$ .01	$ .05
Wiggins, Alan	86F	290	$ .01	$ .05
Wiggins, Alan	87FU	124	$ .01	$ .05
Wilcox, Milt	81F	465	$ .01	$ .05
Wilcox, Milt	82F	285	$ .01	$ .05
Wilcox, Milt	83F	349	$ .01	$ .05
Wilcox, Milt	84F	93	$ .01	$ .06
Wilcox, Milt	85F	25	$ .01	$ .05
Wilcox, Milt	86F	243	$ .01	$ .05
Wilfong, Bob	81F	569	$ .01	$ .05
Wilfong, Rob	82F	563	$ .01	$ .05
Wilfong, Rob	83F	101	$ .01	$ .05
Wilfong, Rob	84F	530	$ .01	$ .06

Player	Year	No.	VG	EX/MT
Wilfong, Rob	85F	315	$ .01	$ .05
Wilfong, Rob	87F	94	$ .01	$ .05
Wilkerson, Curtis	84FU	126	$ .01	$ .10
Wilkerson, Curtis	85F	573	$ .01	$ .05
Wilkerson, Curtis	86F	577	$ .01	$ .05
Wilkerson, Curtis	87F	141	$ .01	$ .05
Wilkerson, Curtis	88F	481	$ .01	$ .05
Wilkerson, Curtis	89F	535	$ .01	$ .05
Wilkerson, Curt	90F	46	$ .01	$ .04
Wilkerson, Curtis	91F	438	$ .01	$ .03
Wilkins, Dean	90F	47	$ .01	$ .15
Wilkinson, Bill	87FU	125	$ .01	$ .10
Wilkinson, Bill	88F	390	$ .01	$ .10
Willard, Jerry	85F	460	$ .01	$ .05
Willard, Jerry	86F	601	$ .01	$ .05
Willard, Jerry	86FU	126	$ .01	$ .05
Willard, Jerry	87F	409	$ .01	$ .05
Williams, Al	82F	564	$ .01	$ .05
Williams, Al	83F	628	$ .01	$ .05
Williams, Al	84F	579	$ .01	$ .06
Williams, Dana	90F	648	$ .01	$ .04
Williams, Dick	81F	149	$ .01	$ .10
Williams, Eddie	88F	620	$ .01	$ .20
Williams, Eddie	91F	548	$ .01	$ .03
Williams, Frank	84FU	127	$ .06	$ .35
Williams, Frank	85F	624	$ .04	$ .25
Williams, Frank	86F	554	$ .01	$ .05
Williams, Frank	87F	287	$ .01	$ .05
Williams, Frank	87FU	127	$ .01	$ .05
Williams, Frank	88F	250	$ .01	$ .05
Williams, Frank	89F	174	$ .01	$ .05
Williams, Frank	89FU	34	$ .01	$ .05
Williams, Frank	90F	620	$ .01	$ .04
Williams, Ken 'Kenny'	87FU	128	$ .05	$ .30
Williams, Ken	88F	412	$ .01	$ .20
Williams, Ken	91F	190	$ .01	$ .03
Williams, Matt	87FU	129	$ .06	$5.00
Williams, Matt	88F	101	$ .50	$4.00
Williams, Matt	89F	346	$ .01	$ .50
Williams, Matt	90F	75	$ .01	$ .25
Williams, Matt	91F	276	$ .01	$ .10
Williams, Mitch	86FU	127	$ .05	$ .35
Williams, Mitch	87F	142	$ .03	$ .55
Williams, Mitch	88F	482	$ .01	$ .10
Williams, Mitch	89F	536	$ .01	$ .10
Williams, Mitch	89FU	81	$ .01	$ .25
Williams, Mitch	90F	48	$ .01	$ .04
Williams, Mitch	90F	631	$ .01	$ .04
Williams, Mitch	91F	439	$ .01	$ .03
Williams, Reggie	86FU	128	$ .03	$ .20
Williams, Reggie	87F	460	$ .01	$ .05
Williamson, Mark	88F	574	$ .01	$ .10
Williamson, Mark	89F	626	$ .01	$ .05
Williamson, Mark	90F	194	$ .01	$ .04
Williamson, Mark	91F	495	$ .01	$ .03
Willis, Carl	87F	218	$ .01	$ .05
Willis, Mike	81F	426	$ .01	$ .05
Wills, Bump	81F	628	$ .01	$ .05
Wills, Bump	82F	334	$ .01	$ .05
Wills, Bump	83F	511	$ .01	$ .05
Wills, Frank	86F	480	$ .01	$ .05
Wills, Frank	90F	98	$ .01	$ .10
Wills, Frank	91F	191	$ .01	$ .03
Wills, Maury	81F	595	$ .01	$ .05
Wilson, Craig	91F	652	$ .01	$ .10
Wilson, Glenn	83F	350	$ .08	$ .40
Wilson, Glenn	84F	94	$ .03	$ .20
Wilson, Glenn	84FU	128	$ .06	$ .35
Wilson, Glenn	85F	268	$ .01	$ .05
Wilson, Glenn	86F	457	$ .01	$ .05

Player	Year	No.	VG	EX/MT	Player	Year	No.	VG	EX/MT
Wilson, Glenn	87F	192	$ .01	$ .10	Witt, Mike	83F	102	$ .05	$ .25
Wilson, Glenn	88F	320	$ .01	$ .05	Witt, Mike	84F	531	$ .04	$ .25
Wilson, Glenn	89F	224	$ .01	$ .05	Witt, Mike	85F	316	$ .01	$ .10
Wilson, Glenn	90F	240	$ .01	$ .04	Witt, Mike	85F	643	$ .01	$ .15
Wilson, Glenn	91F	519	$ .01	$ .03	Witt, Mike	86F	171	$ .01	$ .10
Wilson, Mookie	82F	542	$ .01	$ .10	Witt, Mike	87F	95	$ .01	$ .10
Wilson, Mookie	83F	560	$ .01	$ .10	Witt, Mike	87F	641	$ .01	$ .05
Wilson, Mookie	84F	603	$ .01	$ .06	Witt, Mike	88F	507	$ .01	$ .05
Wilson, Mookie	85F	95	$ .01	$ .05	Witt, Mike	88F	626	$ .01	$ .05
Wilson, Mookie	86F	97	$ .01	$ .05	Witt, Mike	89F	490	$ .01	$ .05
Wilson, Mookie	87F	25	$ .01	$ .05	Witt, Mike	90F	148	$ .01	$ .04
Wilson, Mookie	88F	154	$ .01	$ .05	Witt, Mike	91F	680	$ .01	$ .03
Wilson, Mookie	89F	52	$ .01	$ .05	Wockenfuss, John	81F	472	$ .01	$ .05
Wilson, Mookie	90F	99	$ .01	$ .04	Wockenfuss, John	82F	286	$ .01	$ .05
Wilson, Mookie	91F	192	$ .01	$ .03	Wockenfuss, John	83F	351	$ .01	$ .05
Wilson, Steve	89F	640	$ .01	$ .20	Wockenfuss, John	84F	95	$ .01	$ .06
Wilson, Steve	89FU	82	$ .01	$ .10	Wockenfuss, John	84FU	129	$ .01	$ .10
Wilson, Steve	90F	49	$ .01	$ .10	Wockenfuss, John	85F	269	$ .01	$ .05
Wilson, Steve	91F	440	$ .01	$ .03	Wohlford, Jim	81F	440	$ .01	$ .05
Wilson, Trevor	89F	347	$ .01	$ .05	Wohlford, Jim	82F	403	$ .01	$ .05
Wilson, Trevor	90FU	64	$ .01	$ .05	Wohlford, Jim	83F	276	$ .01	$ .05
Wilson, Trevor	91F	277	$ .01	$ .03	Wohlford, Jim	84F	293	$ .01	$ .06
Wilson, Willie	81F	29	$ .03	$ .20	Wohlford, Jim	85F	413	$ .01	$ .05
Wilson, Willie	81F	653	$ .01	$ .10	Wohlford, Jim	87F	336	$ .01	$ .05
Wilson, Willie	82F	427	$ .03	$ .20	Wojna, Ed	86F	338	$ .01	$ .10
Wilson, Willie	83F	128	$ .01	$ .10	Woodard, Mike	86F	645	$ .01	$ .10
Wilson, Willie	84F	364	$ .01	$ .10	Woodard, Mike	89F	513	$ .01	$ .05
Wilson, Willie	85F	218	$ .01	$ .10	Woods, Al	81F	422	$ .01	$ .05
Wilson, Willie	86F	25	$ .01	$ .10	Woods, Al	82F	627	$ .01	$ .05
Wilson, Willie	87F	384	$ .04	$ .10	Woods, Al	83F	444	$ .01	$ .05
Wilson, Willie	88F	274	$ .01	$ .10	Woods, Gary	81F	75	$ .01	$ .05
Wilson, Willie	89F	298	$ .01	$ .05	Woods, Gary	82F	237	$ .01	$ .05
Wilson, Willie	90F	123	$ .01	$ .04	Woods, Gary	83F	512	$ .01	$ .05
Wilson, Willie	91F	575	$ .01	$ .03	Woods, Gary	84F	507	$ .01	$ .06
Wine, Robbie	88F	459	$ .01	$ .15	Woods, Gary	85F	71	$ .01	$ .05
Winfield, Dave	81F	484	$ .06	$ .75	Woods, Gary	86F	385	$ .01	$ .05
Winfield, Dave	82F	56	$ .09	$ .75	Woodson, Tracy	88FU	98	$ .01	$ .05
Winfield, Dave	82F	646	$ .10	$ .50	Woodson, Tracy	89F	77	$ .01	$ .05
Winfield, Dave	83F	398	$ .06	$ .45	Woodward, Rob	86F	651	$ .01	$ .25
Winfield, Dave	83F	633	$ .03	$ .20	Worrell, Todd	86F	49	$ .15	$ .50
Winfield, Dave	84F	143	$ .06	$ .75	Worrell, Todd	87F	312	$ .04	$ .25
Winfield, Dave	85F	146	$ .01	$ .25	Worrell, Todd	88F	50	$ .01	$ .10
Winfield, Dave	85F	629	$ .05	$ .75	Worrell, Todd	89F	466	$ .01	$ .05
Winfield, Dave	86F	121	$ .05	$ .30	Worrell, Todd	90F	264	$ .01	$ .04
Winfield, Dave	87F	120	$ .05	$ .30	Worrell, Todd	91F	653	$ .01	$ .03
Winfield, Dave	88F	226	$ .01	$ .20	Wortham, Richard	81F	347	$ .01	$ .05
Winfield, Dave	89F	274	$ .01	$ .15	Worthington, Craig	88FU	4	$ .01	$ .35
Winfield, Dave	90F	458	$ .01	$ .15	Worthington, Craig	89F	627	$ .01	$ .35
Winfield, Dave	90FU	81	$ .01	$ .10	Worthington, Craig	90F	195	$ .01	$ .10
Winfield, Dave	91F	329	$ .01	$ .10	Worthington, Craig	91F	496	$ .01	$ .03
Winn, Jim	86F	624	$ .01	$ .05	Wright, George	83F	583	$ .01	$ .05
Winn, Jim	87F	624	$ .01	$ .05	Wright, George	84F	435	$ .01	$ .06
Winn, Jim	87FU	126	$ .01	$ .05	Wright, George	85F	574	$ .01	$ .05
Winn, Jim	88F	413	$ .01	$ .05	Wright, George	86F	578	$ .01	$ .05
Winningham, Herm	85FU	130	$ .04	$ .25	Wright, Ricky	83F	226	$ .01	$ .05
Winningham, Herm	86F	266	$ .01	$ .10	Wynegar, Butch	81F	558	$ .01	$ .05
Winningham, Herm	87FU	130	$ .01	$ .05	Wynegar, Butch	82F	565	$ .01	$ .05
Winningham, Herm	88F	200	$ .01	$ .05	Wynegar, Butch	83F	399	$ .01	$ .05
Winningham, Herm	89F	175	$ .01	$ .05	Wynegar, Butch	84F	144	$ .01	$ .06
Winningham, Herm	90F	435	$ .01	$ .04	Wynegar, Butch	85F	147	$ .01	$ .05
Winningham, Herm	91F	82	$ .01	$ .03	Wynegar, Butch	86F	122	$ .01	$ .05
Winters, Matt	90F	124	$ .01	$ .15	Wynne, Marvell	84F	269	$ .01	$ .06
Wise, Rick	82F	585	$ .01	$ .05	Wynne, Marvell	85F	481	$ .01	$ .05
Witt, Bobby	86FU	129	$ .06	$ .75	Wynne, Marvell	86F	625	$ .01	$ .05
Witt, Bobby	87F	143	$ .05	$1.00	Wynne, Marvell	86FU	130	$ .01	$ .05
Witt, Bobby	88F	483	$ .01	$ .05	Wynne, Marvell	87F	435	$ .01	$ .05
Witt, Bobby	89F	537	$ .01	$ .05	Wynne, Marvell	89F	322	$ .01	$ .05
Witt, Bobby	90F	315	$ .01	$ .15	Wynne, Marvell	91F	441	$ .01	$ .03
Witt, Bobby	91F	304	$ .01	$ .03	Yastrzemski, Carl	81F	221	$ .20	$1.50
Witt, Mike	82F	473	$ .12	$ .50	Yastrzemski, Carl	81F	638	$ .12	$1.25

FLEER

Player	Year	No.	VG	EX/MT
Yastrzemski, Carl	82F	312	$ .13	$1.25
Yastrzemski, Carl	82F	633	$ .06	$ .50
Yastrzemski, Carl	83F	200	$ .12	$1.00
Yastrzemski, Carl	83F	629	$ .05	$ .25
Yastrzemski, Carl	84F	412	$ .25	$1.50
Yastrzemski, Carl	84F	640	$ .10	$2.50
Yeager, Steve	81F	129	$ .01	$ .05
Yeager, Steve	82F	29	$ .01	$ .05
Yeager, Steve	83F	227	$ .01	$ .05
Yeager, Steve	84F	117	$ .01	$ .06

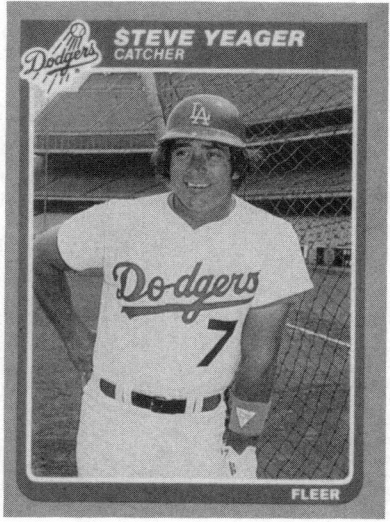

Player	Year	No.	VG	EX/MT
Yeager, Steve	85F	390	$ .01	$ .05
Yeager, Steve	86FU	131	$ .01	$ .05
Yeager, Steve	87F	599	$ .01	$ .05
Yelding, Eric	90FU	18	$ .01	$ .20
Yelding, Eric	91F	520	$ .01	$ .03
Yett, Rich	85FU	131	$ .01	$ .10
Yett, Rich	87F	263	$ .01	$ .05
Yett, Rich	88F	621	$ .01	$ .05
Yett, Rich	89F	417	$ .01	$ .05
Yett, Rich	90F	504	$ .01	$ .04
Yost, Ned	83F	50	$ .01	$ .05
Yost, Ned	84F	218	$ .01	$ .06
Yost, Ned	84FU	130	$ .01	$ .10
Yost, Ned	85F	575	$ .01	$ .05
Youmans, Floyd	86F	267	$ .10	$ .50
Youmans, Floyd	87F	337	$ .01	$ .10
Youmans, Floyd	88F	201	$ .01	$ .10
Young, Cliff	90FU	82	$ .01	$ .15
Young, Cliff	91F	330	$ .01	$ .10
Young, Curt	85F	436	$ .08	$ .40
Young, Curt	87F	410	$ .01	$ .05

Player	Year	No.	VG	EX/MT
Young, Curt	88F	296	$ .01	$ .05
Young, Curt	89F	26	$ .01	$ .05
Young, Curt	90F	24	$ .01	$ .04
Young, Curt	91F	28	$ .01	$ .03
Young, Gerald	88F	460	$ .01	$ .25
Young, Gerald	89F	370	$ .01	$ .05
Young, Gerald	90F	241	$ .01	$ .04
Young, Gerald	91F	521	$ .01	$ .03
Young, Matt	84F	624	$ .03	$ .20
Young, Matt	85F	505	$ .01	$ .05
Young, Matt	86F	481	$ .01	$ .05
Young, Matt	87F	600	$ .01	$ .05
Young, Matt	87FU	131	$ .01	$ .05
Young, Matt	88F	530	$ .01	$ .25
Young, Matt	90FU	121	$ .01	$ .05
Young, Matt	91F	465	$ .01	$ .03
Young, Mike	84FU	131	$ .05	$ .25
Young, Mike	85F	195	$ .03	$ .20
Young, Mike	86F	291	$ .01	$ .05
Young, Mike	87F	483	$ .01	$ .05
Young, Mike	88F	575	$ .01	$ .05
Youngblood, Joel	81F	331	$ .01	$ .05
Youngblood, Joel	82F	543	$ .01	$ .05
Youngblood, Joel	83F	301	$ .01	$ .05
Youngblood, Joel	83F	641	$ .01	$ .05
Youngblood, Joel	84F	387	$ .01	$ .06
Youngblood, Joel	86F	555	$ .01	$ .05
Youngblood, Joel	87F	288	$ .01	$ .05
Yount, Robin	81F	511	$ .15	$1.50
Yount, Robin	82F	155	$ .15	$1.50
Yount, Robin	83F	51	$ .10	$1.00
Yount, Robin	83F	632	$ .03	$ .20
Yount, Robin	84F	219	$ .25	$1.50
Yount, Robin	85F	601	$ .05	$1.00
Yount, Robin	86F	506	$ .05	$ .30
Yount, Robin	87F	361	$ .05	$ .30
Yount, Robin	88F	178	$ .01	$ .15
Yount, Robin	89F	200	$ .01	$ .15
Yount, Robin	90F	340	$ .01	$ .10
Yount, Robin	91F	601	$ .01	$ .10
Zachry, Pat	81F	334	$ .01	$ .05
Zachry, Pat	82F	544	$ .01	$ .05
Zachry, Pat	83F	561	$ .01	$ .05
Zachry, Pat	84F	118	$ .01	$ .06
Zachry, Pat	85F	391	$ .01	$ .05
Zahn, Geoff	81F	564	$ .01	$ .05
Zahn, Geoff	82F	474	$ .01	$ .05
Zahn, Geoff	83F	103	$ .01	$ .05
Zahn, Geoff	84F	532	$ .01	$ .05
Zahn, Geoff	85F	317	$ .01	$ .05
Zeile, Todd	89FU	122	$ .01	$1.00
Zeile, Todd	90F	265	$ .01	$ .50
Zeile, Todd	91F	654	$ .01	$ .15
Zimmer, Don	81F	230	$ .01	$ .05
Zisk, Richie	81F	620	$ .01	$ .05
Zisk, Richie	82F	519	$ .01	$ .05
Zisk, Richie	83F	489	$ .01	$ .05
Zisk, Richie	84F	625	$ .01	$ .06
Zuvella, Paul	85F	651	$ .08	$ .40
Zuvella, Paul	86F	532	$ .01	$ .05

MAJOR LEAGUE MARKETING (SCORE/SPORTFLICS) 1986-1990

In 1986 a new concept of "Magic Motion" cards called Sportflics was introduced by Major League Marketing. Three pictures are on each card until 1990 when only two pictures are used. It is certainly easier to see these images than the previous years. In 1991 no set has been issued as we go to press.

On a good note the Score sets produced by Major League Marketing starting in 1988 are colorful with lots of action shots. The reverse of the cards feature a color close-up portrait photo of the player.

Abbreviations used in this section:
SCMB - Score subset of Master Blaster (1991)
SC - Score cards   **SCMVP** - Score Most Valuable Player
SCAS - Score All Star (1991)   **SCRM** - Score Rifleman subset (1991)
SCBC - Score Bonus Card (7) (1991 factory sets)   **SCTF** - Score subset The Franchise (1991)
SCDT - Score Dream Team beginning in 1990   **SCTR** - Score traded cards beginning in 1988
SCHL - Score Highlight   **SP** - Sportflics cards
SCKM - Score subset K-Man (1991)   **SPR** - Sportflics Rookie cards

Both Score and Sportflics cards measure 2½" x 3½".

1988SC - Score set of 660 cards w/six different colored borders (blue, green, gold, purple, red and yellow) Score logo on front lower right corner (copyright 1988 Score on back lower right)

1988SCTR - Score set of 110 cards of rookies and traded players with same format as regular cards except orange borders and numbers ending in T.

1989SC - Score set of 660 cards w/white borders w/six different colored inside borders (green, light blue, purple, orange, red, dark blue). Score logo on front right corner (copyright 1989 Score on back lower left)

1989SCTR - Score set of 110 cards of rookies and traded players with same format as regular cards except mint green inside border and numbers ending in T.

1990SC Score set of 704 cards with four different colored borders(red, blue, green and white) whose color scheme is carried onto the back. Score logo on front upper left corner (copyright 1990 Score on back right center)

1990SCTR - 110 cards of rookies or traded players with same format as regular 1990 cards only numbers ending in T.

1991SC - Score cards were issued in two series. Series I has 441 cards and Series II has 452 cards but seven additional "Bonus Cards" are in the factory sets making a total of 900.

1986SP - Sportflics set of 200 cards w/white border (copyright 1986 Sportflics on back lower right)

1987SP - Sportflics set of 200 cards w/red border, small color photo on back in upper left corner (copyright 1986 or 1987 Sportflics on back lower right)

1988SP - Sportflics set of 225 cards w/red border, large color photo on back left side (copyright 1987 Sportflics on back bottom of card)

1989SP - Sportflics set of 225 cards w/white border w/orange/purple inside borders (copyright 1989 Sportflics on back bottom of card)

1990SP - Sportflics set of 225 cards with orange, yellow, black and white borders (Copyright 1990 Sportflics on back bottom of card)

The listings for each card shown appears immediately following the photograph.

SCORE

Player	Year	No.	VG	EX/MT
Aase, Don	88SC	518	$ .01	$ .05
Aase, Don	89SC	524	$ .01	$ .05
Aase, Don	90SC	377	$ .01	$ .05
Aase, Don	90SCTR	29	$ .01	$ .05
Aase, Don	91SC	289	$ .01	$ .03
Abbott, Jim	89SCTR	88	$ .01	$ .75
Abbott, Jim	90SC	330	$ .01	$ .15
Abbott, Jim	91SC	105	$ .01	$ .10
Abbott, Kyle	90SC	673	$ .01	$ .20
Abbott, Paul	91SC	363	$ .01	$ .10
Abner, Shawn	88SC	626	$ .01	$ .05
Abner, Shawn	89SC	411	$ .01	$ .10
Abner, Shawn	90SC	352	$ .01	$ .05
Abner, Shawn	91SC	261	$ .01	$ .03
Acker, Jim	88SC	576	$ .01	$ .05
Acker, Jim	91SC	122	$ .01	$ .03
Adduci, Jim	89SC	587	$ .01	$ .05
Adkins, Steve	91SC	716	$ .01	$ .15
Afenir, Troy	91SC	745	$ .01	$ .03
Agosto, Juan	88SC	558	$ .01	$ .05
Agosto, Juan	89SC	283	$ .01	$ .05
Agosto, Juan	90SC	284	$ .01	$ .05
Agosto, Juan	91SC	591	$ .01	$ .03
Aguayo, Luis	88SC	499	$ .01	$ .05
Aguayo, Luis	89SC	436	$ .01	$ .05
Aguilera, Rick	88SC	521	$ .01	$ .05
Aguilera, Rick	89SC	327	$ .01	$ .05
Aguilera, Rick	90SC	519	$ .01	$ .05
Aguilera, Rick	91SC	170	$ .01	$ .03
Akerfelds, Darrel	88SC	632	$ .01	$ .05
Akerfelds, Darrel	91SC	223	$ .01	$ .03
Aldred, Scott	91SC	740	$ .01	$ .03
Aldrete, Mike	88SC	556	$ .01	$ .05
Aldrete, Mike	89SC	82	$ .01	$ .05
Aldrete, Mike	89SCTR	68	$ .01	$ .05
Aldrete, Mike	90SC	220	$ .01	$ .05
Aldrete, Mike	91SC	447	$ .01	$ .03
Aldrich, Jay	88SC	578	$ .01	$ .05
Alexander, Doyle	88SC	610	$ .01	$ .05
Alexander, Doyle	89SC	129	$ .01	$ .05
Alexander, Doyle	90SC	237	$ .01	$ .05
Alexander, Gerald	91SC	733	$ .01	$ .03
Alicea, Luis	88SCTR	98	$ .01	$ .10
Alicea, Luis	89SC	231	$ .01	$ .15
Allanson, Andy	88SC	586	$ .01	$ .05
Allanson, Andy	89SC	46	$ .01	$ .05
Allanson, Andy	90SC	452	$ .01	$ .05
Allen, Neil	89SC	375	$ .01	$ .05
Allred, Beau	90SCTR	70	$ .01	$ .10
Allred, Beau	91SC	338	$ .01	$ .03
Alomar, Jr., Sandy	89SC	630	$ .01	$1.25
Alomar, Jr., Sandy	90SC	577	$ .01	$ .35
Alomar, Jr., Sandy	90SCTR	18	$ .01	$ .25
Alomar, Jr., Sandy	91SC	793	$ .01	$ .10
Alomar, Jr., Sandy	91SCAS	400	$ .01	$ .03
Alomar, Jr., Sandy	91SCMVP	879	$ .01	$ .05
Alomar, Jr., Sandy	91SCRM	694	$ .01	$ .10
Alomar, Jr., Sandy	91SCTF	851	$ .01	$ .03
Alomar, Roberto	88SCTR	105	$1.00	$11.00
Alomar, Roberto	89SC	232	$ .01	$ .40
Alomar, Roberto	90SC	12	$ .01	$ .15
Alomar, Roberto	91SC	25	$ .01	$ .10
Alomar, Roberto	91SCDT	887	$ .01	$ .03
Alou, Moises	90SC	592	$ .01	$ .35
Alou, Moises	91SC	813	$ .01	$ .03
Alvarez, Jose	90SC	148	$ .01	$ .05
Andersen, Larry	88SC	133	$ .01	$ .05
Andersen, Larry	89SC	523	$ .01	$ .05
Andersen, Larry	90SC	282	$ .01	$ .05
Andersen, Larry	91SC	848	$ .01	$ .03

Player	Year	No.	VG	EX/MT
Anderson, Allan	89SC	394	$ .01	$ .10
Anderson, Allan	90SC	292	$ .01	$ .05
Anderson, Allan	91SC	135	$ .01	$ .03
Anderson, Brady	88SCTR	70	$ .01	$ .50

Player	Year	No.	VG	EX/MT
Anderson, Brady	89SC	563	$ .01	$ .15
Anderson, Brady	90SC	33	$ .01	$ .05
Anderson, Brady	91SC	249	$ .01	$ .03
Anderson, Dave	88SC	166	$ .01	$ .05
Anderson, Dave	89SC	478	$ .01	$ .05
Anderson, Dave	90SC	238	$ .01	$ .05
Anderson, Dave	91SC	641	$ .01	$ .03
Anderson, Kent	90SC	412	$ .01	$ .05
Anderson, Kent	91SC	224	$ .01	$ .03
Anderson, Rick	89SC	441	$ .01	$ .05
Anderson, Scott	91SC	734	$ .01	$ .03
Andrews, Shane	91SC	674	$ .01	$ .10
Andujar, Joaquin	88SC	193	$ .01	$ .05
Andujar, Joaquin	89SC	472	$ .01	$ .05
Anthony, Eric	90SC	584	$ .01	$ .50
Anthony, Eric	91SC	146	$ .01	$ .10
Appier, Kevin	90SC	625	$ .01	$ .30
Appier, Kevin	91SC	268	$ .01	$ .03
Aquino, Luis	90SC	432	$ .01	$ .05
Armas, Tony	88SC	487	$ .01	$ .05
Armas, Tony	89SC	182	$ .01	$ .05
Armas, Tony	90SC	378	$ .01	$ .05
Armstrong, Jack	88SCTR	78	$ .01	$1.50
Armstrong, Jack	89SC	462	$ .01	$ .25
Armstrong, Jack	91SC	231	$ .01	$ .03
Arnsberg, Brad	91SC	510	$ .01	$ .03
Ashby, Alan	88SC	73	$ .01	$ .05
Ashby, Alan	89SC	366	$ .01	$ .05
Assenmacher, Paul	89SC	373	$ .01	$ .05
Assenmacher, Paul	91SC	147	$ .01	$ .03
Atherton, Keith	88SC	613	$ .01	$ .05
Atherton, Keith	89SC	381	$ .01	$ .05
August, Don	88SCTR	104	$ .01	$ .15
August, Don	89SC	419	$ .01	$ .10
August, Don	90SC	144	$ .01	$ .05
Austin, Pat	90SC	626	$ .01	$ .05

Player	Year	No.	VG	EX/MT	Player	Year	No.	VG	EX/MT
Avery, Steve	90SCTR	109	$ .01	$ .25	Belcher, Kevin	91SC	714	$ .01	$ .20
Avery, Steve	91SC	80	$ .01	$ .10	Belcher, Tim	88SCTR	101	$ .01	$ .50
Azocar, Oscar	90SCTR	71	$ .01	$ .25	Belcher, Tim	89SC	418	$ .01	$ .15
Azocar, Oscar	91SC	72	$ .01	$ .15	Belcher, Tim	90SC	126	$ .01	$ .10
Backman, Wally	88SC	303	$ .01	$ .05	Belcher, Tim	91SC	187	$ .01	$ .03
Backman, Wally	89SC	315	$ .01	$ .05	Belinda, Stan	90SC	634	$ .01	$ .05
Backman, Wally	89SCTR	34	$ .01	$ .05	Belinda, Stan	91SC	296	$ .01	$ .03
Backman, Wally	90SC	281	$ .01	$ .05	Bell, Buddy	88SC	99	$ .01	$ .10
Backman, Wally	90SCTR	37	$ .01	$ .05	Bell, Buddy	89SC	610	$ .01	$ .05
Backman, Wally	91SC	16	$ .01	$ .03	Bell, Derek	90SCTR	81	$ .01	$ .35
Baerga, Carlos	90SCTR	74	$ .01	$ .35	Bell, Eric	88SC	101	$ .01	$ .05
Baerga, Carlos	91SC	74	$ .01	$ .20	Bell, George	88SC	540	$ .01	$ .10
Bailes, Scott	89SC	424	$ .01	$ .05	Bell, George	89SC	347	$ .01	$ .05
Bailes, Scott	90SC	218	$ .01	$ .05	Bell, George	90SC	286	$ .01	$ .10
Bailes, Scott	90SCTR	64	$ .01	$ .05	Bell, George	91SC	195	$ .01	$ .03
Bailes, Scott	91SC	535	$ .01	$ .03	Bell, Jay	89SC	352	$ .01	$ .05
Baines, Harold	88SC	590	$ .01	$ .05	Bell, Jay	90SC	563	$ .01	$ .05
Baines, Harold	89SC	128	$ .01	$ .05	Bell, Jay	91SC	323	$ .01	$ .03
Baines, Harold	89SCTR	62	$ .01	$ .10	Bell, Juan	90SC	603	$ .01	$ .10
Baines, Harold	90SC	470	$ .01	$ .05	Bell, Mike	91SC	375	$ .01	$ .10
Baines, Harold	91SC	291	$ .01	$ .03	Belle, Joey	89SCTR	106	$ .01	$1.50
Bair, Doug	90SC	517	$ .01	$ .05	Belle, Joey	90SC	508	$ .01	$ .50
Balboni, Steve	88SC	273	$ .01	$ .05	Belliard, Rafael	88SC	453	$ .01	$ .05
Balboni, Steve	88SCTR	46	$ .01	$ .05	Belliard, Rafael	89SC	379	$ .01	$ .05
Balboni, Steve	89SC	353	$ .01	$ .05	Belliard, Rafael	90SC	520	$ .01	$ .05
Balboni, Steve	89SCTR	27	$ .01	$ .05	Benedict, Bruce	88SC	423	$ .01	$ .05
Balboni, Steve	90SC	327	$ .01	$ .05	Benedict, Bruce	89SC	502	$ .01	$ .05
Balboni, Steve	91SC	159	$ .01	$ .03	Benes, Andy	90SC	578	$ .01	$ .20
Ballard, Jeff	89SC	551	$ .01	$ .15	Benes, Andy	91SC	538	$ .01	$ .10
Ballard, Jeff	90SC	349	$ .01	$ .05	Benjamin, Mike	91SC	345	$ .01	$ .03
Ballard, Jeff	91SC	243	$ .01	$ .03	Benzinger, Todd	88SC	546	$ .01	$ .20
Bando, Chris	88SC	172	$ .01	$ .05	Benzinger, Todd	89SC	371	$ .01	$ .05
Bankhead, Scott	88SC	238	$ .01	$ .05	Benzinger, Todd	89SCTR	15	$ .01	$ .10
Bankhead, Scott	89SC	341	$ .01	$ .05	Benzinger, Todd	90SC	65	$ .01	$ .05
Bankhead, Scott	90SC	555	$ .01	$ .05	Benzinger, Todd	91SC	90	$ .01	$ .03
Bankhead, Scott	91SC	817	$ .01	$ .03	Berenguer, Juan	89SC	414	$ .01	$ .05
Bannister, Floyd	88SC	622	$ .01	$ .05	Berenguer, Juan	90SC	223	$ .01	$ .05
Bannister, Floyd	88SCTR	63	$ .01	$ .05	Berenguer, Juan	91SC	111	$ .01	$ .03
Bannister, Floyd	89SC	249	$ .01	$ .05	Bergman, Dave	88SC	217	$ .01	$ .05
Barfield, Jesse	88SC	8	$ .01	$ .10	Bergman, Dave	89SC	469	$ .01	$ .05
Barfield, Jesse	89SC	160	$ .01	$ .10	Bergman, Dave	90SC	254	$ .01	$ .05
Barfield, Jesse	89SCTR	22	$ .01	$ .10	Bergman, Dave	91SC	562	$ .01	$ .03
Barfield, Jesse	90SC	222	$ .01	$ .10	Bernazard, Tony	88SC	604	$ .01	$ .05
Barfield, Jesse	91SC	148	$ .01	$ .03	Berroa, Geronimo	89SC	632	$ .01	$ .10
Barfield, Jesse	91SCRM	414	$ .01	$ .05	Berroa, Geronimo	90SC	151	$ .01	$ .05
Barfield, John	91SC	573	$ .01	$ .03	Berry, Sean	91SC	764	$ .01	$ .10
Barnes, Brian	91SC	708	$ .01	$ .15	Berryhill, Damon	88SCTR	82	$ .01	$ .75
Barrett, Marty	88SC	155	$ .01	$ .05	Berryhill, Damon	89SC	336	$ .01	$ .10
Barrett, Marty	89SC	63	$ .01	$ .05	Berryhill, Damon	90SC	163	$ .01	$ .10
Barrett, Marty	90SC	15	$ .01	$ .05	Berryhill, Damon	91SC	881	$ .01	$ .03
Barrett, Marty	91SC	228	$ .01	$ .03	Biancalana, Buddy	88SC	383	$ .01	$ .05
Barrett, Tom	90SC	633	$ .01	$ .05	Bichette, Dante	91SC	463	$ .01	$ .03
Bass, Kevin	88SC	33	$ .01	$ .05	Bielecki, Mike	88SC	611	$ .01	$ .05
Bass, Kevin	89SC	226	$ .01	$ .05	Bielecki, Mike	90SC	484	$ .01	$ .05
Bass, Kevin	90SC	279	$ .01	$ .05	Bielecki, Mike	91SC	453	$ .01	$ .03
Bass, Kevin	90SCTR	2	$ .01	$ .05	Biggio, Craig	88SCTR	103	$ .01	$2.50
Bass, Kevin	91SC	616	$ .01	$ .03	Biggio, Craig	89SC	237	$ .01	$ .50
Bates, Billy	90SC	608	$ .01	$ .05	Biggio, Craig	90SC	275	$ .01	$ .10
Bautista, Jose	89SC	573	$ .01	$ .15	Biggio, Craig	91SC	161	$ .01	$ .03
Baylor, Don	88SC	250	$ .01	$ .05	Biggio, Craig	91SCTF	872	$ .01	$ .03
Baylor, Don	88SCTR	55	$ .01	$ .10	Bilardello, Dann	91SC	659	$ .01	$ .03
Baylor, Don	89SC	205	$ .01	$ .05	Birkbeck, Mike	88SC	369	$ .01	$ .05
Beatty, Blaine	90SC	632	$ .01	$ .15	Birkbeck, Mike	89SC	596	$ .01	$ .05
Beckett, Robbie	91SC	673	$ .01	$ .15	Birtsas, Tim	89SC	454	$ .01	$ .05
Bedrosian, Steve	88SC	161	$ .01	$ .10	Birtsas, Tim	90SC	408	$ .01	$ .05
Bedrosian, Steve	88SC	656	$ .01	$ .05	Birtsas, Tim	91SC	648	$ .01	$ .03
Bedrosian, Steve	89SC	260	$ .01	$ .05	Bittiger, Jeff	88SCTR	66	$ .01	$ .10
Bedrosian, Steve	89SCTR	49	$ .01	$ .10	Bittiger, Jeff	89SC	512	$ .01	$ .10
Bedrosian, Steve	90SC	379	$ .01	$ .05	Black, Bud	88SC	313	$ .01	$ .05
Bedrosian, Steve	91SC	459	$ .01	$ .03	Black, Bud	88SCTR	11	$ .01	$ .05

SCORE

Player	Year	No.	VG	EX/MT	Player	Year	No.	VG	EX/MT
Black, Bud	89SC	404	$ .01	$ .05	Boskie, Shawn	91SC	59	$ .01	$ .15
Black, Bud	90SC	197	$ .01	$ .05	Boston Red Sox, A. L. Wins	89SC	660	$ .01	$ .05
Blair, Willie	90SCTR	88	$ .01	$ .35	Boston, Daryl	88SC	582	$ .01	$ .05
Blair, Willie	91SC	57	$ .01	$ .03	Boston, Daryl	89SC	443	$ .01	$ .05
Blankenship, Kevin	90SC	646	$ .01	$ .05	Boston, Daryl	90SC	213	$ .01	$ .05
Blankenship, Lance	89SC	641	$ .01	$ .10	Boston, Daryl	90SCTR	47	$ .01	$ .05
Blankenship, Lance	90SC	536	$ .01	$ .05	Boston, Daryl	91SC	618	$ .01	$ .03
Blankenship, Lance	91SC	303	$ .01	$ .03	Boyd, Dennis	88SC	121	$ .01	$ .05
Blauser, Jeff	88SC	562	$ .01	$ .05	Boyd, Dennis	89SC	238	$ .01	$ .05
Blauser, Jeff	89SC	589	$ .01	$ .05	Boyd, Dennis	90SC	137	$ .01	$ .05
Blauser, Jeff	90SC	178	$ .01	$ .05	Boyd, Dennis	90SCTR	24	$ .01	$ .05
Blauser, Jeff	91SC	52	$ .01	$ .03	Boyd, Dennis	91SC	202	$ .01	$ .03
Blocker, Terry	89SC	605	$ .01	$ .05	Bradley, Phil	88SC	66	$ .01	$ .10
Blosser, Greg	90SC	681	$ .01	$ .50	Bradley, Phil	88SCTR	34	$ .01	$ .05
Blowers, Mike	90SC	624	$ .01	$ .20	Bradley, Phil	89SC	79	$ .01	$ .05
Blowers, Mike	91SC	838	$ .01	$ .03	Bradley, Phil	89SCTR	44	$ .01	$ .05
Blyleven, Bert	88SC	90	$ .01	$ .10	Bradley, Phil	90SC	24	$ .01	$ .05
Blyleven, Bert	89SC	215	$ .01	$ .10	Bradley, Phil	90SCTR	44	$ .01	$ .05
Blyleven, Bert	89SCTR	17	$ .01	$ .10	Bradley, Phil	91SC	560	$ .01	$ .03
Blyleven, Bert	90SC	180	$ .01	$ .05	Bradley, Scott	88SC	151	$ .01	$ .05
Blyleven, Bert	91SC	235	$ .01	$ .03	Bradley, Scott	89SC	324	$ .01	$ .05
Bochy, Bruce	88SC	469	$ .01	$ .05	Bradley, Scott	90SC	228	$ .01	$ .05
Boddicker, Mike	88SC	67	$ .01	$ .10	Bradley, Scott	91SC	113	$ .01	$ .03
Boddicker, Mike	89SC	549	$ .01	$ .05	Braggs, Glenn	88SC	59	$ .01	$ .05
Boddicker, Mike	90SC	31	$ .01	$ .05	Braggs, Glenn	89SC	147	$ .01	$ .05
Boddicker, Mike	91SC	232	$ .01	$ .03	Braggs, Glenn	90SC	105	$ .01	$ .05
Boever, Joe	88SC	542	$ .01	$ .05	Braggs, Glenn	90SCTR	56	$ .01	$ .05
Boever, Joe	90SC	81	$ .01	$ .05	Braggs, Glenn	91SC	18	$ .01	$ .03
Boggs, Wade	88SC	2	$ .05	$ .35	Brantley, Jeff	89SCTR	101	$ .01	$ .30
Boggs, Wade	89SC	175	$ .05	$ .30	Brantley, Jeff	90SC	371	$ .01	$ .10
Boggs, Wade	89SC	654	$ .01	$ .20	Brantley, Jeff	91SC	160	$ .01	$ .03
Boggs, Wade	90SC	245	$ .01	$ .20	Brantley, Mickey	89SC	89	$ .01	$ .05
Boggs, Wade	90SC	704	$ .01	$ .10	Bream, Sid	88SC	260	$ .01	$ .05
Boggs, Wade	90SCDT	683	$ .01	$ .15	Bream, Sid	89SC	48	$ .01	$ .05
Boggs, Wade	91SC	12	$ .01	$ .15	Bream, Sid	90SC	423	$ .01	$ .05
Boggs, Wade	91SCAS	393	$ .01	$ .10	Bream, Sid	91SC	304	$ .01	$ .03
Boggs, Wade	91SCBC	1	$ .01	$ .35	Brenley, Bob	88SC	134	$ .01	$ .05
Boggs, Wade	91SCDT	889	$ .01	$ .20	Brenly, Bob	89SC	395	$ .01	$ .05
Bolton, Tom	89SC	531	$ .01	$ .05	Brennan, Bill	89SC	622	$ .01	$ .05
Bolton, Tom	91SC	781	$ .01	$ .03	Brett, George	88SC	11	$ .05	$ .25
Bonds, Barry	88SC	265	$ .04	$ .35	Brett, George	89SC	75	$ .01	$ .20
Bonds, Barry	89SC	127	$ .01	$ .25	Brett, George	90SC	140	$ .01	$ .15
Bonds, Barry	90SC	4	$ .01	$ .10	Brett, George	91SC	120	$ .01	$ .10
Bonds, Barry	91SC	330	$ .01	$ .10	Brett, George	91SCBC	5	$ .01	$ .35
Bonds, Barry	91SCAS	668	$ .01	$ .10	Brett, George	91SCHL	769	$ .01	$ .05
Bonds, Barry	91SCMVP	876	$ .01	$ .05	Brett, George	91SCTF	853	$ .01	$ .03
Bonds, Barry	91SCTF	868	$ .01	$ .03	Briley, Greg	88SCTR	74	$ .01	$1.50
Bonilla, Bobby	88SC	116	$ .04	$ .35	Briley, Greg	90SC	303	$ .01	$ .15
Bonilla, Bobby	89SC	195	$ .01	$ .15	Briley, Greg	91SC	494	$ .01	$ .03
Bonilla, Bobby	90SC	170	$ .01	$ .15	Brock, Greg	88SC	234	$ .01	$ .05
Bonilla, Bobby	91SC	315	$ .01	$ .10	Brock, Greg	89SC	307	$ .01	$ .05
Bonilla, Bobby	91SCAS	670	$ .01	$ .03	Brock, Greg	90SC	485	$ .01	$ .05
Bonilla, Bobby	91SCMB	402	$ .01	$ .10	Brock, Greg	91SC	522	$ .01	$ .03
Booker, Greg	88SC	447	$ .01	$ .05	Brogna, Rico	91SC	741	$ .01	$ .25
Booker, Greg	89SC	417	$ .01	$ .05	Brookens, Tom	88SC	233	$ .01	$ .05
Boone, Bob	88SC	63	$ .01	$ .05	Brookens, Tom	89SC	269	$ .01	$ .05
Boone, Bob	89SC	233	$ .01	$ .05	Brookens, Tom	89SCTR	73	$ .01	$ .05
Boone, Bob	89SCTR	74	$ .01	$ .05	Brookens, Tom	90SC	297	$ .01	$ .05
Boone, Bob	90SC	60	$ .01	$ .05	Brookens, Tom	91SC	106	$ .01	$ .03
Boone, Dan	91SC	715	$ .01	$ .03	Brooks, Hubie	88SC	305	$ .01	$ .05
Borders, Pat	88SCTR	99	$ .01	$ .75	Brooks, Hubie	89SC	53	$ .01	$ .05
Borders, Pat	89SC	198	$ .01	$ .20	Brooks, Hubie	90SC	299	$ .01	$ .05
Borders, Pat	90SC	288	$ .01	$ .05	Brooks, Hubie	90SCTR	34	$ .01	$ .05
Borders, Pat	91SC	425	$ .01	$ .03	Brooks, Hubie	91SC	196	$ .01	$ .03
Bordick, Mike	91SC	339	$ .01	$ .10	Brower, Bob	88SC	236	$ .01	$ .05
Bosio, Chris	88SC	38	$ .01	$ .05	Brower, Bob	89SC	344	$ .01	$ .05
Bosio, Chris	89SC	243	$ .01	$ .05	Brown, Chris	88SC	363	$ .01	$ .05
Bosio, Chris	90SC	283	$ .01	$ .05	Brown, Chris	89SC	369	$ .01	$ .05
Bosio, Chris	91SC	43	$ .01	$ .03	Brown, Kevin	89SCTR	89	$ .01	$ .15
Boskie, Shawn	90SCTR	94	$ .01	$ .20	Brown, Kevin	90SC	210	$ .01	$ .05

Player	Year	No.	VG	EX/MT
Brown, Kevin	91SC	846	$ .01	$ .03
Browne, Jerry	88SC	278	$ .01	$ .05
Browne, Jerry	90SC	52	$ .01	$ .05
Browne, Jerry	91SC	481	$ .01	$ .03
Browning, Tom	88SC	132	$ .01	$ .15
Browning, Tom	89SC	554	$ .01	$ .10
Browning, Tom	89SC	658	$ .01	$ .10
Browning, Tom	90SC	165	$ .01	$ .10
Browning, Tom	91SC	229	$ .01	$ .03
Brumley, Mike	91SC	624	$ .01	$ .03
Brunansky, Tom	88SC	194	$ .01	$ .05
Brunansky, Tom	88SCTR	5	$ .01	$ .10
Brunansky, Tom	89SC	184	$ .01	$ .05
Brunansky, Tom	90SC	72	$ .01	$ .05
Brunansky, Tom	90SCTR	49	$ .01	$ .05
Brunansky, Tom	91SC	245	$ .01	$ .03
Bryant, Scott	90SC	667	$ .01	$ .05
Buckner, Bill	88SC	591	$ .01	$ .05
Buckner, Bill	88SCTR	36	$ .01	$ .05
Buckner, Bill	89SC	214	$ .01	$ .05

Player	Year	No.	VG	EX/MT
Buckner, Bill	90SC	396	$ .01	$ .05
Buechele, Steve	88SC	306	$ .01	$ .05
Buechele, Steve	89SC	368	$ .01	$ .05
Buechele, Steve	90SC	221	$ .01	$ .05
Buechele, Steve	91SC	257	$ .01	$ .05
Buhner, Jay	88SCTR	95	$ .01	$1.50
Buhner, Jay	89SC	530	$ .01	$ .20
Buhner, Jay	90SC	521	$ .01	$ .05
Buhner, Jay	91SC	125	$ .01	$ .03
Buice, DeWayne	88SC	376	$ .01	$ .05
Buice, DeWayne	89SC	153	$ .01	$ .05
Burba, Dave	91SC	742	$ .01	$ .03
Burke, Tim	88SC	187	$ .01	$ .05
Burke, Tim	89SC	228	$ .01	$ .05
Burke, Tim	90SC	127	$ .01	$ .05
Burke, Tim	91SC	181	$ .01	$ .03
Burkett, John	90SCTR	73	$ .01	$ .25
Burkett, John	91SC	70	$ .01	$ .10
Burks, Ellis	88SC	472	$ .25	$1.25
Burks, Ellis	89SC	9	$ .01	$ .30

Player	Year	No.	VG	EX/MT
Burks, Ellis	90SC	340	$ .01	$ .15
Burks, Ellis	91SC	8	$ .01	$ .15
Burnitz, Jeromy	91SC	380	$ .01	$ .25
Burns, Todd	88SCTR	106	$ .01	$ .50
Burns, Todd	89SC	465	$ .01	$ .25
Burns, Todd	90SC	64	$ .01	$ .05
Burns, Todd	91SC	41	$ .01	$ .03
Bush, Randy	88SC	292	$ .01	$ .05
Bush, Randy	89SC	212	$ .01	$ .05
Bush, Randy	90SC	278	$ .01	$ .05
Bush, Randy	91SC	574	$ .01	$ .03
Butera, Sal	88SC	361	$ .01	$ .05
Butler, Brett	88SC	122	$ .01	$ .05
Butler, Brett	88SCTR	3	$ .01	$ .05
Butler, Brett	89SC	216	$ .01	$ .05
Butler, Brett	90SC	236	$ .01	$ .05
Butler, Brett	91SC	455	$ .01	$ .03
Cabrera, Francisco	90SCTR	67	$ .01	$ .20
Cabrera, Francisco	91SC	63	$ .01	$ .03
Cadaret, Greg	89SC	340	$ .01	$ .05
Cadaret, Greg	89SCTR	69	$ .01	$ .05
Cadaret, Greg	91SC	188	$ .01	$ .03
Calderon, Ivan	88SC	607	$ .01	$ .05
Calderon, Ivan	89SC	331	$ .01	$ .05
Calderon, Ivan	90SC	94	$ .01	$ .05
Calderon, Ivan	91SC	254	$ .01	$ .03
Caminiti, Ken	88SC	164	$ .01	$ .15
Caminiti, Ken	90SC	76	$ .01	$ .05
Caminiti, Ken	91SC	186	$ .01	$ .03
Caminiti, Ken	91SCRM	415	$ .01	$ .05
Campbell, Mike	89SC	568	$ .01	$ .15
Campusano, Sil	88SCTR	93	$ .01	$ .35
Campusano, Sil	89SC	473	$ .01	$ .15
Campusano, Sil	91SC	847	$ .01	$ .03
Canale, George	90SC	656	$ .01	$ .15
Candaele, Casey	88SC	97	$ .01	$ .05
Candaele, Casey	91SC	577	$ .01	$ .03
Candelaria, John	88SC	293	$ .01	$ .05
Candelaria, John	88SCTR	40	$ .01	$ .10
Candelaria, John	89SC	246	$ .01	$ .05
Candelaria, John	90SCTR	54	$ .01	$ .05
Candelaria, John	91SC	791	$ .01	$ .03
Candiotti, Tom	88SC	595	$ .01	$ .05
Candiotti, Tom	89SC	239	$ .01	$ .05
Candiotti, Tom	90SC	269	$ .01	$ .05
Candiotti, Tom	91SC	488	$ .01	$ .03
Cangelosi, John	88SC	418	$ .01	$ .05
Cangelosi, John	89SC	601	$ .01	$ .05
Cangelosi, John	90SC	367	$ .01	$ .05
Canseco, Jose	88SC	45	$ .20	$1.00
Canseco, Jose	89SC	1	$ .15	$1.00
Canseco, Jose	89SC	655	$ .01	$ .25
Canseco, Jose	90SC	375	$ .01	$ .50
Canseco, Jose	91SC	1	$ .01	$ .35
Canseco, Jose	91SCAS	398	$ .01	$ .20
Canseco, Jose	91SCDT	441	$ .01	$2.50
Canseco, Jose	91SCMB	690	$ .01	$ .20
Canseco, Ozzie	91SC	346	$ .01	$ .15
Carman, Don	88SC	401	$ .01	$ .05
Carman, Don	89SC	222	$ .01	$ .05
Carman, Don	91SC	237	$ .01	$ .03
Carpenter, Cris	89SCTR	81	$ .01	$ .15
Carreon, Mark	89SCTR	108	$ .01	$ .10
Carreon, Mark	90SC	363	$ .01	$ .05
Carreon, Mark	91SC	165	$ .01	$ .03
Carter, Gary	88SC	325	$ .01	$ .15
Carter, Gary	89SC	240	$ .01	$ .10
Carter, Gary	90SC	416	$ .01	$ .05
Carter, Gary	90SCTR	35	$ .01	$ .05
Carter, Gary	91SC	215	$ .01	$ .03

SCORE

Player	Year	No.	VG	EX/MT
Carter, Joe	88SC	80	$ .01	$ .15
Carter, Joe	89SC	213	$ .01	$ .10
Carter, Joe	90SC	319	$ .01	$ .15
Carter, Joe	90SCTR	19	$ .01	$ .05
Carter, Joe	91SC	9	$ .01	$ .10
Cary, Chuck	90SC	393	$ .01	$ .05
Cary, Chuck	91SC	566	$ .01	$ .03
Casillo, Juan	88SC	429	$ .01	$ .05
Castillo, Carmen	88SC	581	$ .01	$ .05
Castillo, Carmen	89SC	497	$ .01	$ .05
Castillo, Carmelo	89SCTR	23	$ .01	$ .05
Castillo, Carmelo	90SC	123	$ .01	$ .05
Castillo, Carmelo	91SC	608	$ .01	$ .03
Castillo, Tony	91SC	582	$ .01	$ .03
Cedeno, Andujar	91SC	753	$ .01	$ .50
Cerone, Rick	88SC	486	$ .01	$ .05
Cerone, Rick	88SCTR	21	$ .01	$ .05
Cerone, Rick	89SC	396	$ .01	$ .05
Cerone, Rick	90SC	139	$ .01	$ .05
Cerone, Rick	90SCTR	63	$ .01	$ .05
Cerone, Rick	91SC	580	$ .01	$ .03
Cerutti, John	88SC	98	$ .01	$ .10
Cerutti, John	89SC	304	$ .01	$ .05
Cerutti, John	90SC	429	$ .01	$ .05
Cerutti, John	91SC	786	$ .01	$ .03
Chamberlain, Wes	91SC	713	$ .01	$ .25
Charlton, Norm	89SC	646	$ .01	$ .15
Charlton, Norm	90SC	248	$ .01	$ .10
Charlton, Norm	91SC	530	$ .01	$ .03
Chiamparino, Scott	90SCTR	108	$ .01	$ .35
Chiamparino, Scott	91SC	352	$ .01	$ .20
Chitren, Steve	91SC	760	$ .01	$ .10
Christensen, John	88SC	419	$ .01	$ .05
Christopherson, Eric	91SC	672	$ .01	$ .15
Clancy, Jim	88SC	530	$ .01	$ .05
Clancy, Jim	89SC	538	$ .01	$ .05
Clancy, Jim	89SCTR	42	$ .01	$ .05
Clancy, Jim	90SC	424	$ .01	$ .05
Clark, Dave	88SC	633	$ .01	$ .05
Clark, Dave	90SC	141	$ .01	$ .05
Clark, Dave	91SC	542	$ .01	$ .03
Clark, Jack	88SC	100	$ .04	$ .15
Clark, Jack	88SC	650	$ .05	$ .25
Clark, Jack	88SCTR	1	$ .01	$ .20
Clark, Jack	89SC	25	$ .01	$ .10
Clark, Jack	89SCTR	3	$ .01	$ .10
Clark, Jack	90SC	20	$ .01	$ .05
Clark, Jack	91SC	523	$ .01	$ .03
Clark, Jerald	89SC	644	$ .01	$ .05
Clark, Jerald	90SC	660	$ .01	$ .05
Clark, Jerald	91SC	242	$ .01	$ .03
Clark, Phil	91SC	756	$ .01	$ .10
Clark, Terry	89SC	566	$ .01	$ .05
Clark, Will	88SC	78	$ .25	$1.00
Clark, Will	89SC	450	$ .10	$ .60
Clark, Will	90SC	300	$ .01	$ .35
Clark, Will	90SC	699	$ .01	$ .20
Clark, Will	90SCDT	684	$ .01	$ .20
Clark, Will	91SC	7	$ .01	$ .15
Clark, Will	91SCAS	664	$ .01	$ .15
Clark, Will	91SCBC	4	$ .01	$1.00
Clark, Will	91SCDT	886	$ .01	$ .35
Clark, Will	91SCTF	871	$ .01	$ .15
Clear, Mark	88SC	446	$ .01	$ .05
Clear, Mark	89SC	430	$ .01	$ .05
Clemens, Roger	88SC	110	$ .10	$ .50
Clemens, Roger	89SC	350	$ .05	$ .40
Clemens, Roger	90SC	310	$ .01	$ .15
Clemens, Roger	91SC	655	$ .01	$ .15
Clemens, Roger	91SCAS	399	$ .01	$ .15

Player	Year	No.	VG	EX/MT
Clemens, Roger	91SCKM	684	$ .01	$ .15
Clemens, Roger	91SCTF	850	$ .01	$ .15
Clements, Pat	88SC	389	$ .01	$ .05
Cliburn, Stewart	89SC	445	$ .01	$ .05
Coachman, Pete	91SC	344	$ .01	$ .20
Cole, Alex	91SC	555	$ .01	$ .25
Coleman, Paul	90SC	662	$ .01	$ .35
Coleman, Vince	88SC	68	$ .04	$ .15

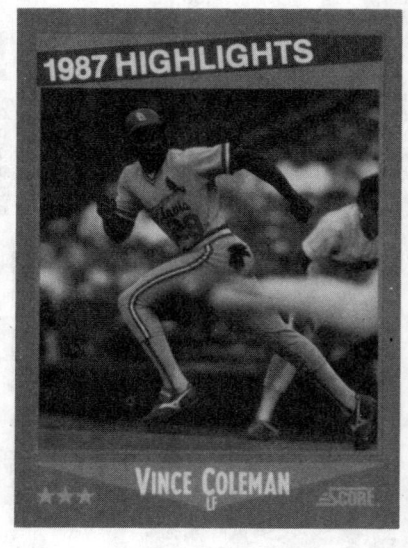

1987 HIGHLIGHTS

VINCE COLEMAN
LF

★★★   SCORE

Player	Year	No.	VG	EX/MT
Coleman, Vince	88SC	652	$ .01	$ .10
Coleman, Vince	89SC	155	$ .01	$ .10
Coleman, Vince	90SC	260	$ .01	$ .05
Coleman, Vince	91SC	450	$ .01	$ .03
Coles, Darnell	88SC	554	$ .01	$ .05
Coles, Darnell	89SC	83	$ .01	$ .05
Coles, Darnell	90SC	62	$ .01	$ .05
Coles, Darnell	91SC	629	$ .01	$ .03
Collins, Dave	88SC	371	$ .01	$ .05
Collins, Dave	89SC	267	$ .01	$ .05
Combs, Pat	90SC	623	$ .01	$ .35
Combs, Pat	91SC	440	$ .01	$ .03
Comstock, Keith	88SC	438	$ .01	$ .05
Comstock, Keith	91SC	502	$ .01	$ .03
Concepcion, Dave	88SC	210	$ .01	$ .05
Concepcion, Dave	89SC	166	$ .01	$ .05
Cone, David	88SC	49	$ .05	$ .50
Cone, David	89SC	221	$ .01	$ .25
Cone, David	90SC	430	$ .01	$ .10
Cone, David	91SC	549	$ .01	$ .03
Cone, David	91SCKM	409	$ .01	$ .05
Conine, Jeff	91SC	722	$ .01	$ .50
Conroy, Tim	88SC	384	$ .01	$ .05
Cook, Dennis	90SC	545	$ .01	$ .05
Coolbaugh, Scott	90SC	612	$ .01	$ .15
Cooper, Cecil	88SC	169	$ .01	$ .05
Cooper, Scott	90SC	651	$ .01	$ .05
Cora, Joey	88SC	420	$ .01	$ .05
Cora, Joey	91SC	253	$ .01	$ .03
Correa, Ed	88SC	523	$ .01	$ .05
Corsi, Jim	90SC	553	$ .01	$ .05
Costello, John	88SCTR	107	$ .01	$ .10

Player	Year	No.	VG	EX/MT	Player	Year	No.	VG	EX/MT
Costello, John	89SC	534	$ .01	$ .10	Davis, Glenn	91SCMB	405	$ .01	$ .10
Costello, John	90SC	347	$ .01	$ .05	Davis, Jody	88SC	551	$ .01	$ .05
Costo, Tim	91SC	680	$ .01	$ .50	Davis, Jody	89SC	173	$ .01	$ .05
Cotto, Henry	88SC	368	$ .01	$ .05	Davis, Jody	89SCTR	64	$ .01	$ .05
Cotto, Henry	88SCTR	48	$ .01	$ .05	Davis, Jody	90SC	328	$ .01	$ .05
Cotto, Henry	89SC	209	$ .01	$ .05	Davis, John	88SC	636	$ .01	$ .05
Cotto, Henry	90SC	161	$ .01	$ .05	Davis, John	89SC	608	$ .01	$ .05
Cotto, Henry	91SC	282	$ .01	$ .03	Davis, Mark	88SC	391	$ .01	$ .05
Cox, Danny	88SC	415	$ .01	$ .05	Davis, Mark	89SC	490	$ .01	$ .05
Cox, Danny	89SC	613	$ .01	$ .05	Davis, Mark	90SC	259	$ .01	$ .05
Crawford, Steve	88SC	289	$ .01	$ .05	Davis, Mark	90SCTR	26	$ .01	$ .05
Crawford, Steve	91SC	287	$ .01	$ .03	Davis, Mark	91SC	136	$ .01	$ .03
Crews, Tim	88SC	641	$ .01	$ .05	Davis, Mike	88SC	211	$ .01	$ .05
Crews, Tim	89SC	505	$ .01	$ .05	Davis, Mike	88SCTR	53	$ .01	$ .05
Crews, Tim	90SC	164	$ .01	$ .05	Davis, Mike	89SC	376	$ .01	$ .05
Crews, Tim	91SC	302	$ .01	$ .03	Davis, Mike	90SC	437	$ .01	$ .05
Crim, Chuck	88SC	402	$ .01	$ .05	Davis, Steve	90SC	187	$ .01	$ .10
Crim, Chuck	89SC	272	$ .01	$ .05	Davis, Storm	89SC	248	$ .01	$ .05
Crim, Chuck	90SC	108	$ .01	$ .05	Davis, Storm	90SC	266	$ .01	$ .05
Crim, Chuck	91SC	99	$ .01	$ .03	Davis, Storm	90SCTR	21	$ .01	$ .05
Cruz, Jose	88SC	28	$ .01	$ .05	Davis, Storm	91SC	511	$ .01	$ .03
Cummings, Steve	90SCTR	78	$ .01	$ .10	Dawley, Bill	88SC	328	$ .01	$ .05
Cunningham, Earl	90SC	670	$ .01	$ .25	Dawson, Andre	88SC	4	$ .01	$ .15
Curry, Steve	88SCTR	81	$ .01	$ .10	Dawson, Andre	89SC	2	$ .01	$ .10
Cuyler, Milt	90SC	583	$ .01	$ .05	Dawson, Andre	90SC	265	$ .01	$ .10
Daniels, Kal	88SC	86	$ .05	$ .15	Dawson, Andre	91SC	445	$ .01	$ .10
Daniels, Kal	89SC	7	$ .01	$ .10	Dayett, Brian	88SC	205	$ .01	$ .05
Daniels, Kal	89SCTR	48	$ .01	$ .05	Dayley, Ken	88SC	517	$ .01	$ .05
Daniels, Kal	90SC	490	$ .01	$ .05	Dayley, Ken	90SC	556	$ .01	$ .05
Daniels, Kal	91SC	20	$ .01	$ .03	Dayley, Ken	91SC	607	$ .01	$ .03
Darling, Ron	88SC	141	$ .01	$ .10	De Los Santos, Luis	89SC	648	$ .01	$ .10
Darling, Ron	89SC	180	$ .01	$ .05	De Los Santos, Luis	90SC	659	$ .01	$ .10
Darling, Ron	90SC	446	$ .01	$ .05	DeCinces, Doug	88SC	239	$ .01	$ .05
Darling, Ron	91SC	456	$ .01	$ .03	Decker, Steve	91SC	710	$ .01	$ .50
Darwin, Danny	88SC	184	$ .01	$ .05	Dedmon, Jeff	88SC	498	$ .01	$ .05
Darwin, Danny	89SC	553	$ .01	$ .05	Deer, Rob	88SC	95	$ .01	$ .05
Darwin, Danny	90SC	402	$ .01	$ .05	Deer, Rob	89SC	72	$ .01	$ .05
Darwin, Danny	91SC	51	$ .01	$ .03	Deer, Rob	90SC	390	$ .01	$ .05
Dascenzo, Doug	89SC	621	$ .01	$ .10	Deer, Rob	91SC	248	$ .01	$ .03
Dascenzo, Doug	91SC	209	$ .01	$ .03	DeJesus, Jose	90SC	587	$ .01	$ .05
Daugherty, Jack	90SC	564	$ .01	$ .05	DeJesus, Jose	91SC	623	$ .01	$ .03
Daugherty, Jack	91SC	309	$ .01	$ .03	DeLeon, Jose	88SC	508	$ .01	$ .05
Daulton, Darren	88SC	473	$ .01	$ .05	DeLeon, Jose	88SCTR	7	$ .01	$ .05
Daulton, Darren	89SC	413	$ .01	$ .05	DeLeon, Jose	89SC	115	$ .01	$ .05
Daulton, Darren	90SC	389	$ .01	$ .05	DeLeon, Jose	90SC	309	$ .01	$ .05
Daulton, Darren	91SC	246	$ .01	$ .03	DeLeon, Jose	91SC	221	$ .01	$ .03
Davidson, Mark	88SC	570	$ .01	$ .05	DeLucia, Rich	91SC	728	$ .01	$ .10
Davidson, Mark	89SC	107	$ .01	$ .05	Dempsey, Rick	88SC	262	$ .01	$ .05
Davis, Alvin	88SC	83	$ .01	$ .10	Dempsey, Rick	88SCTR	32	$ .01	$ .05
Davis, Alvin	89SC	51	$ .01	$ .10	Dempsey, Rick	89SC	556	$ .01	$ .05
Davis, Alvin	90SC	205	$ .01	$ .05	Dempsey, Rick	90SC	414	$ .01	$ .05
Davis, Alvin	91SC	482	$ .01	$ .03	Dempsey, Rick	91SC	816	$ .01	$ .03
Davis, Chili	88SC	605	$ .01	$ .05	Dernier, Bob	88SC	451	$ .01	$ .05
Davis, Chili	88SCTR	28	$ .01	$ .05	Dernier, Bob	88SCTR	45	$ .01	$ .05
Davis, Chili	89SC	54	$ .01	$ .05	Dernier, Bob	89SC	357	$ .01	$ .05
Davis, Chili	90SC	326	$ .01	$ .05	Deshaies, Jim	88SC	354	$ .01	$ .05
Davis, Chili	91SC	803	$ .01	$ .03	Deshaies, Jim	89SC	546	$ .01	$ .05
Davis, Eric	88SC	10	$ .05	$ .35	Deshaies, Jim	90SC	154	$ .01	$ .05
Davis, Eric	88SC	649	$ .05	$ .15	Deshaies, Jim	91SC	193	$ .01	$ .03
Davis, Eric	89SC	109	$ .01	$ .20	DeShields, Delino	90SC	645	$ .01	$1.00
Davis, Eric	90SC	185	$ .01	$ .20	DeShields, Delino	91SC	545	$ .01	$ .15
Davis, Eric	91SC	137	$ .01	$ .10	Destrade, Orestes	88SCTR	110	$ .01	$ .25
Davis, Eric	91SCAS	669	$ .01	$ .10	Devereaux, Mike	88SC	637	$ .04	$ .35
Davis, Eric	91SCMB	403	$ .01	$ .10	Devereaux, Mike	90SC	232	$ .01	$ .05
Davis, Eric	91SCRM	696	$ .01	$ .10	Devereaux, Mike	91SC	258	$ .01	$ .03
Davis, Eric	91SCTF	863	$ .01	$ .03	Dewey, Mark	91SC	371	$ .01	$ .10
Davis, Glenn	88SC	460	$ .01	$ .10	DeWillis, Jeff	88SC	583	$ .01	$ .05
Davis, Glenn	89SC	164	$ .01	$ .10	Diaz, Bo	88SC	206	$ .01	$ .05
Davis, Glenn	90SC	272	$ .01	$ .10	Diaz, Bo	89SC	187	$ .01	$ .05
Davis, Glenn	91SC	830	$ .01	$ .03	Diaz, Bo	90SC	434	$ .01	$ .05

SCORE

Player	Year	No.	VG	EX/MT	Player	Year	No.	VG	EX/MT
Diaz, Edgar	91SC	576	$ .01	$ .03	Dykstra, Lenny	90SC	427	$ .01	$ .10
Diaz, Mike	88SC	143	$ .01	$ .05	Dykstra, Lenny	91SC	250	$ .01	$ .03
Diaz, Mike	89SC	603	$ .01	$ .05	Dykstra, Lenny	91SCTF	867	$ .01	$ .03
Dibble, Rob	88SCTR	86	$ .01	$3.00	Easler, Mike	88SC	220	$ .01	$ .05
Dibble, Rob	89SC	618	$ .01	$ .35	Eave, Gary	90SC	621	$ .01	$ .05
Dibble, Rob	90SC	277	$ .01	$ .20	Eckersley, Dennis	88SC	104	$ .01	$ .05
Dibble, Rob	91SC	17	$ .01	$ .10	Eckersley, Dennis	89SC	276	$ .01	$ .05
Dibble, Rob	91SCKM	407	$ .01	$ .10	Eckersley, Dennis	90SC	315	$ .01	$ .05
Dickson, Lance	91SC	385	$ .01	$ .35	Eckersley, Dennis	91SC	485	$ .01	$ .10
DiPino, Frank	88SC	413	$ .01	$ .05	Edens, Tom	91SC	78	$ .01	$ .03
DiPino, Frank	89SC	146	$ .01	$ .05	Edwards, Wayne	91SC	66	$ .01	$ .03
DiPino, Frank	90SC	462	$ .01	$ .05	Eichhorn, Mark	88SC	198	$ .01	$ .05
DiPino, Frank	91SC	553	$ .01	$ .03	Eichhorn, Mark	89SC	152	$ .01	$ .05
Disarcina, Gary	90SCTR	68	$ .01	$ .15	Eichhorn, Mark	91SC	504	$ .01	$ .03
Disarcina, Gary	91SC	768	$ .01	$ .03	Eiland, Dave	90SC	652	$ .01	$ .05
Dixon, Ken	88SC	411	$ .01	$ .05	Eiland, Dave	91SC	826	$ .01	$ .03
Dodson, Pat	88SC	352	$ .01	$ .05	Eisenreich, Jim	88SC	456	$ .01	$ .05
Dopson, John	88SCTR	88	$ .01	$ .35	Eisenreich, Jim	89SC	594	$ .01	$ .05
Dopson, John	89SC	466	$ .01	$ .15	Eisenreich, Jim	90SC	179	$ .01	$ .05
Dopson, John	89SCTR	40	$ .01	$ .05	Eisenreich, Jim	91SC	154	$ .01	$ .03
Dopson, John	90SC	331	$ .01	$ .05	Eldred, Cal	90SC	669	$ .01	$ .05
Dopson, John	91SC	772	$ .01	$ .03	Ellsworth, Steve	88SCTR	83	$ .01	$ .15
Doran, Bill	88SC	52	$ .01	$ .05	Elster, Kevin	88SC	624	$ .01	$ .10
Doran, Bill	89SC	21	$ .01	$ .05	Elster, Kevin	89SC	130	$ .01	$ .10
Doran, Bill	90SC	182	$ .01	$ .05	Elster, Kevin	90SC	443	$ .01	$ .05
Doran, Bill	91SC	775	$ .01	$ .03	Elster, Kevin	91SC	633	$ .01	$ .03
Dotson, Richard	88SC	480	$ .01	$ .05	Engle, Dave	88SC	617	$ .01	$ .05
Dotson, Richard	88SCTR	60	$ .01	$ .05	Eppard, Jim	89SC	607	$ .01	$ .10
Dotson, Richard	89SC	278	$ .01	$ .05	Erickson, Scott	91SC	812	$ .01	$1.00
Dotson, Richard	89SCTR	80	$ .01	$ .05	Esasky, Nick	88SC	163	$ .01	$ .05
Dotson, Richard	90SC	19	$ .01	$ .05	Esasky, Nick	89SC	64	$ .01	$ .05
Downing, Brian	88SC	44	$ .01	$ .05	Esasky, Nick	89SCTR	37	$ .01	$ .10
Downing, Brian	89SC	76	$ .01	$ .05	Esasky, Nick	90SC	91	$ .01	$ .05
Downing, Brian	90SC	26	$ .01	$ .05	Esasky, Nick	90SCTR	3	$ .01	$ .05
Downing, Brian	91SC	104	$ .01	$ .03	Espinoza, Alvaro	90SC	101	$ .01	$ .10
Downs, Kelly	88SC	27	$ .01	$ .05	Espinoza, Alvaro	91SC	127	$ .01	$ .03
Downs, Kelly	89SC	124	$ .01	$ .05	Espy, Cecil	88SCTR	73	$ .01	$ .25
Downs, Kelly	90SC	534	$ .01	$ .05	Espy, Cecil	89SC	401	$ .01	$ .15
Downs, Kelly	91SC	654	$ .01	$ .03	Espy, Cecil	90SC	69	$ .01	$ .10
Dozier, D. J.	90SCTR	97	$ .01	$ .50	Evans, Darrell	88SC	75	$ .01	$ .05
Drabek, Doug	88SC	51	$ .01	$ .15	Evans, Darrell	89SC	171	$ .01	$ .05
Drabek, Doug	89SC	117	$ .01	$ .05	Evans, Darrell	89SCTR	65	$ .01	$ .10
Drabek, Doug	90SC	505	$ .01	$ .05	Evans, Darrell	90SC	302	$ .01	$ .05
Drabek, Doug	91SC	472	$ .01	$ .03	Evans, Dwight	88SC	65	$ .01	$ .10
Drabek, Doug	91SCAS	661	$ .01	$ .03	Evans, Dwight	89SC	193	$ .01	$ .10
Drabek, Doug	91SCMVP	878	$ .01	$ .05	Evans, Dwight	90SC	3	$ .01	$ .05
Dravecky, Dave	88SC	564	$ .01	$ .10	Evans, Dwight	91SC	225	$ .01	$ .03
Dravecky, Dave	90SC	550	$ .01	$ .10	Everett, Carl	91SC	386	$ .01	$ .25
Drew, Cameron	89SC	643	$ .01	$ .05	Faries, Paul	91SC	711	$ .01	$ .10
Drummond, Tim	90SCTR	103	$ .01	$ .10	Farmer, Howard	90SCTR	91	$ .01	$ .15
Drummond, Tim	91SC	76	$ .01	$ .03	Farmer, Howard	91SC	718	$ .01	$ .03
Dubois, Brian	90SC	657	$ .01	$ .10	Farr, Steve	88SC	466	$ .01	$ .05
Ducey, Rob	88SC	629	$ .01	$ .05	Farr, Steve	89SC	183	$ .01	$ .05
Ducey, Rob	91SC	821	$ .01	$ .03	Farr, Steve	90SC	356	$ .01	$ .05
Duncan, Mariano	88SC	321	$ .01	$ .10	Farr, Steve	91SC	172	$ .01	$ .03
Duncan, Mariano	90SC	506	$ .01	$ .10	Farrell, John	88SC	620	$ .01	$ .25
Duncan, Mariano	91SC	479	$ .01	$ .03	Farrell, John	89SC	266	$ .01	$ .05
Dunne, Mike	88SC	432	$ .01	$ .10	Farrell, John	90SC	103	$ .01	$ .10
Dunne, Mike	89SC	285	$ .01	$ .05	Farrell, John	91SC	50	$ .01	$ .03
Dunston, Shawon	88SC	529	$ .01	$ .15	Felder, Mike	88SC	388	$ .01	$ .05
Dunston, Shawon	89SC	235	$ .01	$ .05	Felder, Mike	90SC	268	$ .01	$ .05
Dunston, Shawon	90SC	169	$ .01	$ .05	Felder, Mike	91SC	97	$ .01	$ .03
Dunston, Shawon	91SC	201	$ .01	$ .03	Felix, Junior	89SCTR	83	$ .01	$ .75
Dunston, Shawon	91SCRM	413	$ .01	$ .05	Felix, Junior	90SC	258	$ .01	$ .20
Durham, Leon	88SC	378	$ .01	$ .05	Felix, Junior	91SC	203	$ .01	$ .03
Dwyer, Jim	88SC	229	$ .01	$ .05	Fermin, Felix	89SC	620	$ .01	$ .05
Dyer, Mike	90SC	571	$ .01	$ .05	Fermin, Felix	89SCTR	78	$ .01	$ .05
Dykstra, Len	88SC	370	$ .01	$ .10	Fermin, Felix	90SC	256	$ .01	$ .05
Dykstra, Lenny	89SC	84	$ .01	$ .10	Fermin, Felix	91SC	139	$ .01	$ .03
Dykstra, Lenny	89SCTR	28	$ .01	$ .10	Fernandez, Sid	88SC	615	$ .01	$ .05

Player	Year	No.	VG	EX/MT	Player	Year	No.	VG	EX/MT
Fernandez, Sid	89SC	268	$ .01	$ .05	Flannery, Tim	89SC	513	$ .01	$ .05
Fernandez, Sid	90SC	18	$ .01	$ .05	Fletcher, Darrin	90SC	622	$ .01	$ .05
Fernandez, Sid	91SC	180	$ .01	$ .03	Fletcher, Scott	88SC	251	$ .01	$ .05
Fernandez, Tony	88SC	20	$ .01	$ .10	Fletcher, Scott	89SC	78	$ .01	$ .05
Fernandez, Tony	88SC	651	$ .01	$ .10	Fletcher, Scott	89SCTR	47	$ .01	$ .05
Fernandez, Tony	89SC	57	$ .01	$ .10	Fletcher, Scott	90SC	58	$ .01	$ .05
Fernandez, Tony	90SC	89	$ .01	$ .10	Fletcher, Scott	91SC	36	$ .01	$ .03
Fernandez, Tony	91SC	432	$ .01	$ .03	Foley, Tom	88SC	159	$ .01	$ .05
Fernanez, Alex	91SC	382	$ .01	$1.00	Foley, Tom	89SC	405	$ .01	$ .05
Fetters, Mike	91SC	497	$ .01	$ .03	Foley, Tom	90SC	32	$ .01	$ .05
Fielder, Cecil	88SC	399	$ .01	$ .35	Foley, Tom	91SC	526	$ .01	$ .03
Fielder, Cecil	89SC	120	$ .01	$ .35	Ford, Curt	88SC	288	$ .01	$ .05
Fielder, Cecil	90SCTR	9	$ .01	$ .50	Ford, Curt	90SC	183	$ .01	$ .05
Fielder, Cecil	91SC	168	$ .01	$ .20	Forsch, Bob	88SC	264	$ .01	$ .05
Fielder, Cecil	91SCAS	395	$ .01	$ .15	Forsch, Bob	89SC	525	$ .01	$ .05
Fielder, Cecil	91SCHL	770	$ .01	$ .15	Forsch, Bob	90SC	219	$ .01	$ .05
Fielder, Cecil	91SCMB	693	$ .01	$ .15	Fossas, Tony	90SC	567	$ .01	$ .05
Finley, Chuck	89SC	503	$ .01	$ .10	Fossas, Tony	91SC	634	$ .01	$ .03
Finley, Chuck	90SC	380	$ .01	$ .10	Franco, John	88SC	535	$ .01	$ .10
Finley, Chuck	91SC	100	$ .01	$ .03	Franco, John	89SC	575	$ .01	$ .10
Finley, Steve	89SCTR	95	$ .01	$ .25	Franco, John	90SC	273	$ .01	$ .05
Finley, Steve	90SC	339	$ .01	$ .15	Franco, John	90SCTR	15	$ .01	$ .05
Finley, Steve	91SC	266	$ .01	$ .03	Franco, John	91SC	14	$ .01	$ .03
Fischer, Jeff	90SC	654	$ .01	$ .05	Franco, Julio	88SC	60	$ .01	$ .10
Fisher, Brian	88SC	130	$ .01	$ .05	Franco, Julio	89SC	11	$ .01	$ .10
Fisher, Brian	89SC	24	$ .01	$ .05	Franco, Julio	89SCTR	35	$ .01	$ .10
Fisher, Brian	90SC	547	$ .01	$ .05	Franco, Julio	90SC	160	$ .01	$ .10
Fisk, Carlton	88SC	592	$ .01	$ .05	Franco, Julio	91SC	493	$ .01	$ .03
Fisk, Carlton	89SC	449	$ .01	$ .05	Franco, Julio	91SCAS	392	$ .01	$ .03
Fisk, Carlton	90SC	290	$ .01	$ .05	Francona, Terry	88SC	297	$ .01	$ .05
Fisk, Carlton	91SC	265	$ .01	$ .03	Francona, Terry	89SC	597	$ .01	$ .05
Fisk, Carlton	91SCHL	421	$ .01	$ .05	Francona, Terry	90SC	216	$ .01	$ .05
Fitzgerald, Mike	88SC	318	$ .01	$ .05	Fraser, Willie	88SC	394	$ .01	$ .05
Fitzgerald, Mike	89SC	511	$ .01	$ .05	Fraser, Willie	89SC	157	$ .01	$ .05
Fitzgerald, Mike	90SC	361	$ .01	$ .05	Fraser, Willie	90SC	358	$ .01	$ .05
Fitzgerald, Mike	91SC	198	$ .01	$ .03	Fraser, Willie	91SC	96	$ .01	$ .03
Flag, Desert Storm	91SC	737	$ .01	$ .25	Frazier, Goerge	88SC	332	$ .01	$ .05
Flanagan, Mike	88SC	427	$ .01	$ .05	Frey, Steve	91SC	436	$ .01	$ .03
Flanagan, Mike	89SC	475	$ .01	$ .05	Frohwirth, Todd	89SC	647	$ .01	$ .15
Flanagan, Mike	90SC	67	$ .01	$ .05	Fryman, Travis	91SC	570	$ .01	$ .75
					Gaetti, Gary	88SC	62	$ .01	$ .10
					Gaetti, Gary	89SC	8	$ .01	$ .10
					Gaetti, Gary	90SC	145	$ .01	$ .05
					Gaetti, Gary	91SC	325	$ .01	$ .03
					Gagne, Greg	89SC	159	$ .01	$ .05
					Gagne, Greg	90SC	102	$ .01	$ .05
					Gagne, Greg	91SC	211	$ .01	$ .03
					Galarraga, Andres	88SC	19	$ .01	$ .10
					Galarraga, Andres	89SC	144	$ .01	$ .10
					Galarraga, Andres	90SC	25	$ .01	$ .10
					Galarraga, Andres	91SC	443	$ .01	$ .03
					Gallagher, Dave	88SCTR	89	$ .01	$ .25
					Gallagher, Dave	89SC	455	$ .01	$ .25
					Gallagher, Dave	90SC	115	$ .01	$ .05
					Gallego, Mike	88SC	428	$ .01	$ .05
					Gallego, Mike	89SC	537	$ .01	$ .05
					Gallego, Mike	90SC	323	$ .01	$ .05
					Gallego, Mike	91SC	476	$ .01	$ .03
					Gant, Ron	88SC	647	$ .01	$1.50
					Gant, Ron	89SC	372	$ .01	$ .25
					Gant, Ron	91SC	448	$ .01	$ .10
					Gantner, Jim	88SC	197	$ .01	$ .05
					Gantner, Jim	89SC	313	$ .01	$ .05
					Gantner, Jim	90SC	382	$ .01	$ .05
					Gantner, Jim	91SC	532	$ .01	$ .03
					Garber, Gene	88SC	565	$ .01	$ .05
					Gardiner, Mike	91SC	721	$ .01	$ .10
					Gardner, Mark	90SC	639	$ .01	$ .05
					Gardner, Mark	91SC	518	$ .01	$ .03
Flannery, Tim	88SC	483	$ .01	$ .05	Gardner, Wes	89SC	412	$ .01	$ .05

TIM FLANNERY
2B

SCORE

Player	Year	No.	VG	EX/MT	Player	Year	No.	VG	EX/MT
Gardner, Wes	90SC	348	$ .01	$ .05	Gott, Jim	91SC	621	$ .01	$ .03
Gardner, Wes	91SC	592	$ .01	$ .03	Gozzo, Goose	90SC	610	$ .01	$ .15
Garner, Phil	88SC	431	$ .01	$ .05	Gozzo, Mauro	91SC	843	$ .01	$ .03
Garrelts, Scott	88SC	533	$ .01	$ .05	Grace, Mark	88SCTR	80	$1.50	$25.00
Garrelts, Scott	89SC	258	$ .01	$ .05	Grace, Mark	89SC	362	$ .15	$1.00
Garrelts, Scott	90SC	246	$ .01	$ .05	Grace, Mark	90SC	150	$ .01	$ .25
Garrelts, Scott	91SC	541	$ .01	$ .03	Grace, Mark	91SC	175	$ .01	$ .10
Garvey, Steve	88SC	225	$ .05	$ .25	Grahe, Joe	91SC	367	$ .01	$ .10
Gedman, Rich	88SC	241	$ .01	$ .05	Grant, Mark	89SC	349	$ .01	$ .05
Gedman, Rich	89SC	345	$ .01	$ .05	Grant, Mark	90SC	466	$ .01	$ .05
Gedman, Rich	90SC	173	$ .01	$ .05	Grant, Mark	91SC	824	$ .01	$ .03
Geren, Bob	89SCTR	93	$ .01	$ .15	Gray, Jeff	91SC	586	$ .01	$ .10
Geren, Bob	90SC	464	$ .01	$ .10	Grebeck, Craig	90SCTR	105	$ .01	$ .15
Geren, Bob	91SC	435	$ .01	$ .03	Grebeck, Craig	91SC	69	$ .01	$ .03
Gerhart, Ken	88SC	58	$ .01	$ .10	Green, Willie	90SC	682	$ .01	$ .05
Gerhart, Ken	89SC	506	$ .01	$ .05	Greene, Tommy	90SC	640	$ .01	$ .35
Gibson, Kirk	88SC	525	$ .04	$ .20	Greene, Tommy	91SC	808	$ .01	$ .03
Gibson, Kirk	88SCTR	10	$ .01	$ .15	Greenwell, Mike	88SC	175	$ .15	$ .75
Gibson, Kirk	89SC	210	$ .01	$ .15	Greenwell, Mike	89SC	659	$ .01	$ .15
Gibson, Kirk	90SC	487	$ .01	$ .05	Greenwell, Mike	89SC	66	$ .10	$ .25
Gibson, Kirk	91SC	800	$ .01	$ .03	Greenwell, Mike	90SC	345	$ .01	$ .15
Gibson, Paul	89SC	595	$ .01	$ .05	Greenwell, Mike	91SC	130	$ .01	$ .10
Gibson, Paul	90SC	261	$ .01	$ .05	Greg, Gagne	88SC	214	$ .01	$ .05
Gibson, Paul	91SC	152	$ .01	$ .03	Gregg, Tommy	88SCTR	69	$ .01	$ .30
Gilkey, Bernard	90SCTR	106	$ .01	$ .50	Gregg, Tommy	90SC	78	$ .01	$ .10
Gilkey, Bernard	91SC	709	$ .01	$ .35	Gregg, Tommy	91SC	606	$ .01	$ .03
Girardi, Joe	89SCTR	84	$ .01	$ .30	Griffey, Jr., Ken	89SCTR	100	$1.00	$6.50
Girardi, Joe	90SC	535	$ .01	$ .15	Griffey, Jr., Ken	90SC	560	$ .35	$2.25
Girardi, Joe	91SC	585	$ .01	$ .03	Griffey, Jr., Ken	91SC	2	$ .01	$1.00
Gladden, Dan	88SC	324	$ .01	$ .05	Griffey, Jr., Ken	91SC	841	$ .01	$ .50
Gladden, Dan	89SC	62	$ .01	$ .05	Griffey, Jr., Ken	91SCAS	396	$ .01	$ .35
Gladden, Dan	90SC	61	$ .01	$ .05	Griffey, Jr., Ken	91SCBC	3	$ .01	$2.00
Gladden, Dan	91SC	163	$ .01	$ .03	Griffey, Jr., Ken	91SCDT	892	$ .01	$1.00
Glavine, Tom	88SC	638	$ .01	$ .25	Griffey, Jr., Ken	91SCRM	697	$ .01	$ .35
Glavine, Tom	89SC	442	$ .01	$ .05	Griffey, Jr., Ken	91SCTF	858	$ .01	$ .75
Glavine, Tom	90SC	481	$ .01	$ .05	Griffey, Sr., Ken	88SC	390	$ .01	$ .10
Glavine, Tom	91SC	206	$ .01	$ .03	Griffey, Sr., Ken	89SC	609	$ .01	$ .10
Gleaton, Jerry Don	91SC	316	$ .01	$ .03	Griffey, Sr., Ken	90SC	338	$ .01	$ .05
Gleaton, Jerry Don	88SC	343	$ .01	$ .05	Griffey, Sr., Ken	91SC	835	$ .01	$ .03
Gleaton, Jerry Don	89SC	423	$ .01	$ .05	Griffey, Sr., Ken	91SC	841	$ .01	$ .50
Goff, Jerry	91SC	834	$ .01	$ .03	Griffin, Alfredo	88SC	88	$ .01	$ .05
Gohr, Greg	90SC	679	$ .01	$ .05	Griffin, Alfredo	88SCTR	37	$ .01	$ .05
Gomez, Leo	91SC	725	$ .01	$ .35	Griffin, Alfredo	89SC	167	$ .01	$ .05
Gonzales, Rene	89SC	585	$ .01	$ .05	Griffin, Alfredo	90SC	156	$ .01	$ .05
Gonzales, Rene	90SC	118	$ .01	$ .05	Griffin, Alfredo	91SC	442	$ .01	$ .03
Gonzales, Rene	91SC	638	$ .01	$ .03	Grimsley, Jason	90SC	649	$ .01	$ .05
Gonzalez, German	90SC	133	$ .01	$ .05	Grimsley, Jason	91SC	818	$ .01	$ .03
Gonzalez, Jose	88SC	364	$ .01	$ .05	Grissom, Marquis	90SC	591	$ .01	$ .35
Gonzalez, Jose	90SC	368	$ .01	$ .05	Grissom, Marquis	91SC	234	$ .01	$ .10
Gonzalez, Jose	91SC	614	$ .01	$ .03	Gross, Greg	88SC	386	$ .01	$ .05
Gonzalez, Juan	90SC	637	$ .01	$1.50	Gross, Greg	89SC	125	$ .01	$ .05
Gonzalez, Juan	91SC	805	$ .01	$ .25	Gross, Kevin	88SC	468	$ .01	$ .05
Gooden, Dwight "Doc"	88SC	350	$ .10	$ .35	Gross, Kevin	89SC	227	$ .01	$ .05
Gooden, Doc	89SC	200	$ .01	$ .25	Gross, Kevin	89SCTR	39	$ .01	$ .05
Gooden, Doc	90SC	313	$ .01	$ .15	Gross, Kevin	90SC	251	$ .01	$ .05
Gooden, Doc	91SC	540	$ .01	$ .10	Gross, Kevin	91SC	22	$ .01	$ .03
Gooden, Doc	91SCKM	685	$ .01	$ .10	Grubb, John	88SC	199	$ .01	$ .05
Gooden, Doc	91SCTF	866	$ .01	$ .03	Gruber, Kelly	88SC	422	$ .01	$ .25
Goodwin, Tom	90SC	668	$ .01	$ .50	Gruber, Kelly	89SC	194	$ .01	$ .15
Gordon, Don	88SCTR	92	$ .01	$ .15	Gruber, Kelly	90SC	425	$ .01	$ .05
Gordon, Don	89SC	547	$ .01	$ .05	Gruber, Kelly	91SC	595	$ .01	$ .10
Gordon, Tom	89SC	634	$ .15	$ .50	Guante, Cecilio	89SC	439	$ .01	$ .05
Gordon, Tom	90SC	472	$ .01	$ .15	Guante, Cecilio	90SC	438	$ .01	$ .05
Gordon, Tom	91SC	197	$ .01	$ .03	Gubicza, Mark	88SC	516	$ .01	$ .05
Gossage, Goose	88SC	331	$ .01	$ .10	Gubicza, Mark	89SC	291	$ .01	$ .05
Gossage, Goose	88SCTR	14	$ .01	$ .10	Gubicza, Mark	90SC	121	$ .01	$ .05
Gossage, Goose	89SC	223	$ .01	$ .05	Gubicza, Mark	91SC	212	$ .01	$ .03
Gott, Jim	88SC	320	$ .01	$ .05	Guerrero, Pedro	88SC	9	$ .01	$ .10
Gott, Jim	89SC	257	$ .01	$ .05	Guerrero, Pedro	89SC	564	$ .01	$ .05
Gott, Jim	90SC	515	$ .01	$ .05	Guerrero, Pedro	90SC	13	$ .01	$ .10

212

Player	Year	No.	VG	EX/MT	Player	Year	No.	VG	EX/MT
Guerrero, Pedro	91SC	140	$ .01	$ .03	Harvey, Bryan	88SCTR	87	$ .01	$ .50
Guetterman, Lee	88SC	323	$ .01	$ .05	Harvey, Bryan	89SC	185	$ .01	$ .15
Guetterman, Lee	90SC	294	$ .01	$ .05	Harvey, Bryan	90SC	8	$ .01	$ .05
Guetterman, Lee	91SC	34	$ .01	$ .03	Harvey, Bryan	91SC	108	$ .01	$ .03
Guidry, Ron	88SC	310	$ .01	$ .05	Haselman, Bill	91SC	377	$ .01	$ .10
Guidry, Ron	89SC	342	$ .01	$ .05	Hassey, Ron	88SCTR	33	$ .01	$ .05
Guillen, Ozzie	88SC	603	$ .01	$ .05	Hassey, Ron	89SC	334	$ .01	$ .05
Guillen, Ozzie	89SC	433	$ .01	$ .05	Hassey, Ron	90SC	168	$ .01	$ .05
Guillen, Ozzie	90SC	6	$ .01	$ .05	Hassey, Ron	91SC	806	$ .01	$ .03
Guillen, Ozzie	91SC	11	$ .01	$ .03	Hatcher, Billy	88SC	505	$ .01	$ .05
Guillen, Ozzie	91SCAS	394	$ .01	$ .03	Hatcher, Billy	89SC	61	$ .01	$ .05
Gullickson, Bill	88SC	585	$ .01	$ .05	Hatcher, Billy	90SC	562	$ .01	$ .05
Gullickson, Bill	91SC	177	$ .01	$ .03	Hatcher, Billy	90SCTR	42	$ .01	$ .05
Gunderson, Eric	90SCTR	99	$ .01	$ .25	Hatcher, Billy	91SC	469	$ .01	$ .03
Gunderson, Eric	91SC	744	$ .01	$ .03					
Guthrie, Mark	91SC	778	$ .01	$ .03					
Guzman, Jose	88SC	322	$ .01	$ .05					
Guzman, Jose	89SC	143	$ .01	$ .05					
Gwynn, Chris	88SC	640	$ .04	$ .30					
Gwynn, Chris	91SC	178	$ .01	$ .03					
Gwynn, Tony	88SC	385	$ .04	$ .25					
Gwynn, Tony	89SC	90	$ .01	$ .15					
Gwynn, Tony	90SC	255	$ .01	$ .15					
Gwynn, Tony	90SCDT	685	$ .01	$ .10					
Gwynn, Tony	91SC	500	$ .01	$ .10					
Haas, Moose	88SC	177	$ .01	$ .05					
Habyan, John	88SC	353	$ .01	$ .05					
Hale, Chip	90SC	588	$ .01	$ .05					
Hall, Albert	88SC	148	$ .01	$ .05					
Hall, Albert	89SC	74	$ .01	$ .05					
Hall, Drew	90SC	516	$ .01	$ .05					
Hall, Drew	91SC	581	$ .01	$ .03					
Hall, Mel	88SC	441	$ .01	$ .05					
Hall, Mel	89SC	17	$ .01	$ .05					
Hall, Mel	89SCTR	54	$ .01	$ .05					
Hall, Mel	90SC	383	$ .01	$ .05					
Hall, Mel	91SC	166	$ .01	$ .03					
Hamilton, Darryl	88SCTR	72	$ .01	$ .20					
Hamilton, Darryl	91SC	107	$ .01	$ .03					
Hamilton, Jeff	89SC	570	$ .01	$ .05					
Hamilton, Jeff	90SC	132	$ .01	$ .05					
Hammaker, Atlee	88SC	528	$ .01	$ .05					
Hammaker, Atlee	89SC	422	$ .01	$ .05					
Hammaker, Atlee	90SC	231	$ .01	$ .05					
Hammond, Chris	90SC	629	$ .01	$ .15	Hatcher, Mickey	88SC	298	$ .01	$ .05
Hanson, Erik	90SC	530	$ .01	$ .25	Hatcher, Mickey	89SC	332	$ .01	$ .05
Hanson, Erik	91SC	486	$ .01	$ .10	Hatcher, Mickey	90SC	359	$ .01	$ .05
Hanson, Erik	91SCKM	688	$ .01	$ .03	Hatcher, Mickey	91SC	153	$ .01	$ .03
Harkey, Mike	89SC	624	$ .01	$ .35	Hawkins, Andy	88SC	347	$ .01	$ .05
Harkey, Mike	91SC	322	$ .01	$ .03	Hawkins, Andy	89SC	118	$ .01	$ .05
Harnisch, Pete	89SCTR	110	$ .01	$ .30	Hawkins, Andy	89SCTR	14	$ .01	$ .05
Harnisch, Pete	90SC	355	$ .01	$ .05	Hawkins, Andy	91SC	47	$ .01	$ .03
Harnisch, Pete	91SC	492	$ .01	$ .03	Hawkins, Andy	91SCNH	704	$ .01	$ .03
Harper, Brian	89SC	408	$ .01	$ .05	Hayes, Charlie	89SC	628	$ .01	$ .05
Harper, Brian	90SC	189	$ .01	$ .05	Hayes, Charlie	90SC	507	$ .01	$ .05
Harper, Brian	91SC	312	$ .01	$ .03	Hayes, Charlie	91SC	238	$ .01	$ .03
Harris, Donald	90SC	661	$ .01	$ .25	Hayes, Von	88SC	515	$ .01	$ .05
Harris, Gene	90SC	548	$ .01	$ .05	Hayes, Von	89SC	38	$ .01	$ .05
Harris, Gene	91SC	627	$ .01	$ .03	Hayes, Von	90SC	36	$ .01	$ .10
Harris, Greg	88SC	179	$ .01	$ .05	Hayes, Von	91SC	426	$ .01	$ .03
Harris, Greg	89SC	476	$ .01	$ .05	Hayward, Ray	88SCTR	67	$ .01	$ .05
Harris, Greg	89SCTR	87	$ .01	$ .15	Hayward, Ray	89SC	514	$ .01	$ .10
Harris, Greg	90SC	257	$ .01	$ .05	Hearn, Ed	88SC	569	$ .01	$ .05
Harris, Greg	91SC	109	$ .01	$ .03	Heath, Mike	88SC	156	$ .01	$ .05
Harris, Greg	91SC	251	$ .01	$ .03	Heath, Mike	89SC	131	$ .01	$ .05
Harris, Lenny	90SC	23	$ .01	$ .05	Heath, Mike	90SC	172	$ .01	$ .05
Harris, Lenny	91SC	144	$ .01	$ .03	Heath, Mike	91SC	112	$ .01	$ .03
Harris, Reggie	91SC	643	$ .01	$ .15	Heaton, Neal	88SC	430	$ .01	$ .05
Hartley, Mike	90SC	641	$ .01	$ .05	Heaton, Neal	89SC	253	$ .01	$ .05
Hartley, Mike	91SC	252	$ .01	$ .03	Heaton, Neal	91SC	233	$ .01	$ .03

MICKEY HATCHER
OF

★★★

SCORE

Player	Year	No.	VG	EX/MT	Player	Year	No.	VG	EX/MT
Heep, Danny	88SC	417	$ .01	$ .05	Hill, Donnie	89SC	583	$ .01	$ .05
Heep, Danny	89SC	343	$ .01	$ .05	Hill, Glenallen	90SC	601	$ .01	$ .10
Heep, Danny	89SCTR	57	$ .01	$ .05	Hill, Glenallen	91SC	514	$ .01	$ .03
Heep, Danny	90SC	113	$ .01	$ .05	Hill, Ken	89SCTR	98	$ .01	$ .20
Heep, Danny	91SC	827	$ .01	$ .03	Hill, Ken	90SC	233	$ .01	$ .05
Heinkel, Don	88SCTR	79	$ .01	$ .15	Hill, Ken	91SC	567	$ .01	$ .03
Heinkel, Don	89SC	168	$ .01	$ .10	Hillegas, Shawn	88SC	612	$ .01	$ .15
Hemond, Scott	90SC	598	$ .01	$ .05	Hillegas, Shawn	89SC	488	$ .01	$ .05
Henderson, Dave	88SC	228	$ .01	$ .10	Hillegas, Shawn	90SC	329	$ .01	$ .05
Henderson, Dave	88SCTR	49	$ .01	$ .25	Hinzo, Tommy	88SC	567	$ .01	$ .05
Henderson, Dave	89SC	533	$ .01	$ .05	Hoffman, Guy	88SC	609	$ .01	$ .05
Henderson, Dave	90SC	325	$ .01	$ .05	Hoiles, Chris	90SCTR	96	$ .01	$ .25
Henderson, Dave	91SC	644	$ .01	$ .03	Hoiles, Chris	91SC	334	$ .01	$ .15
Henderson, Rickey	88SC	13	$ .05	$ .50	Holbert, Aaron	91SC	676	$ .01	$ .20
Henderson, Rickey	89SC	70	$ .01	$ .25	Hollins, Dave	90SCTR	75	$ .01	$ .20
Henderson, Rickey	89SC	657	$ .01	$ .25	Hollins, Dave	91SC	61	$ .01	$ .03
Henderson, Rickey	89SCTR	50	$ .01	$ .50	Holman, Brian	90SC	387	$ .01	$ .05
Henderson, Rickey	90SC	360	$ .01	$ .25	Holman, Brian	91SC	285	$ .01	$ .03
Henderson, Rickey	90SC	698	$ .01	$ .20	Holman, Shawn	90SC	620	$ .01	$ .15
Henderson, Rickey	90SCDT	686	$ .01	$ .20	Holton, Brian	88SC	208	$ .01	$ .05
Henderson, Rickey	91SC	10	$ .01	$ .20	Holton, Brian	89SC	507	$ .01	$ .05
Henderson, Rickey	91SCAS	397	$ .01	$ .15	Holton, Brian	89SCTR	59	$ .01	$ .05
Henderson, Rickey	91SCBC	2	$ .01	$1.00	Holton, Brian	90SC	177	$ .01	$ .05
Henderson, Rickey	91SCDT	890	$ .01	$ .75	Honeycutt, Rick	88SC	87	$ .01	$ .05
Henderson, Rickey	91SCMVP	875	$ .01	$ .15	Honeycutt, Rick	89SC	416	$ .01	$ .05
Henderson, Rickey	91SCTF	857	$ .01	$ .15	Honeycutt, Rick	90SC	317	$ .01	$ .05
Henderson, Steve	88SC	547	$ .01	$ .05	Honeycutt, Rick	91SC	539	$ .01	$ .03
Hendrick, George	88SC	308	$ .01	$ .05	Horn, Sam	88SC	201	$ .01	$ .05
Henke, Tom	88SC	57	$ .01	$ .05	Horn, Sam	91SC	605	$ .01	$ .03
Henke, Tom	89SC	318	$ .01	$ .05	Horner, Bob	89SC	68	$ .01	$ .05
Henke, Tom	90SC	157	$ .01	$ .05	Horton, Rick	88SC	412	$ .01	$ .05
Henke, Tom	91SC	579	$ .01	$ .03	Horton, Rick	88SCTR	24	$ .01	$ .05
Henneman, Mike	88SC	520	$ .01	$ .05	Horton, Rick	89SC	145	$ .01	$ .05
Henneman, Mike	89SC	293	$ .01	$ .05	Hosey, Steve	90SC	666	$ .01	$ .05
Henneman, Mike	90SC	184	$ .01	$ .05	Hough, Charlie	88SC	140	$ .01	$ .05
Henneman, Mike	91SC	142	$ .01	$ .03	Hough, Charlie	89SC	295	$ .01	$ .05
Hennis, Randy	91SC	752	$ .01	$ .03	Hough, Charlie	90SC	202	$ .01	$ .05
Hernandez, Guillermo	89SC	275	$ .01	$ .05	Hough, Charlie	91SC	141	$ .01	$ .03
Hernandez, Guillermo	90SC	267	$ .01	$ .05	Houston, Tyler	90SC	677	$ .01	$ .35
Hernandez, Keith	88SC	400	$ .04	$ .25	Howard, Steve	91SC	364	$ .01	$ .10
Hernandez, Keith	89SC	41	$ .01	$ .10	Howard, Thomas	91SC	335	$ .01	$ .15
Hernandez, Keith	90SC	193	$ .01	$ .05	Howe, Steve	88SC	543	$ .01	$ .05
Hernandez, Keith	90SCTR	57	$ .01	$ .05	Howell, Jack	88SC	124	$ .01	$ .05
Hernandez, Keith	91SC	89	$ .01	$ .03	Howell, Jack	89SC	261	$ .01	$ .05
Hernandez, Willie	88SC	507	$ .01	$ .05	Howell, Jack	90SC	206	$ .01	$ .05
Hernandez, Xavier	91SC	564	$ .01	$ .03	Howell, Jack	91SC	842	$ .01	$ .03
Herndon, Larry	88SC	138	$ .01	$ .05	Howell, Jay	88SC	522	$ .01	$ .05
Herndon, Larry	89SC	279	$ .01	$ .05	Howell, Jay	88SCTR	35	$ .01	$ .05
Herr, Tom	88SC	84	$ .01	$ .05	Howell, Jay	89SC	378	$ .01	$ .05
Herr, Tom	88SCTR	8	$ .01	$ .05	Howell, Jay	90SC	227	$ .01	$ .05
Herr, Tommy	89SC	191	$ .01	$ .05	Howell, Jay	91SC	29	$ .01	$ .03
Herr, Tom	89SCTR	9	$ .01	$ .05	Howell, Ken	88SC	406	$ .01	$ .05
Herr, Tom	90SC	171	$ .01	$ .05	Howell, Ken	91SC	458	$ .01	$ .03
Herr, Tom	91SC	820	$ .01	$ .03	Hrbek, Kent	88SC	43	$ .01	$ .10
Hershiser, Orel	88SC	470	$ .01	$ .15	Hrbek, Kent	89SC	382	$ .01	$ .10
Hershiser, Orel	89SC	370	$ .01	$ .15	Hrbek, Kent	90SC	381	$ .01	$ .05
Hershiser, Orel	89SC	653	$ .01	$ .15	Hrbek, Kent	91SC	292	$ .01	$ .03
Hershiser, Orel	90SC	50	$ .01	$ .10	Hubbard, Glenn	88SC	111	$ .01	$ .05
Hershiser, Orel	91SC	550	$ .01	$ .10	Hubbard, Glenn	88SCTR	58	$ .01	$ .05
Hesketh, Joe	89SC	498	$ .01	$ .05	Hubbard, Glenn	89SC	34	$ .01	$ .05
Hesketh, Joe	90SC	483	$ .01	$ .05	Hudler, Rex	89SC	470	$ .01	$ .05
Hetzel, Eric	90SC	543	$ .01	$ .05	Hudler, Rex	90SC	287	$ .01	$ .05
Hibbard, Greg	90SC	369	$ .01	$ .35	Hudler, Rex	91SC	589	$ .01	$ .03
Hibbard, Greg	91SC	128	$ .01	$ .03	Hudson, Charles	89SC	415	$ .01	$ .05
Hickey, Kevin	90SC	214	$ .01	$ .05	Huff, Mike	90SC	597	$ .01	$ .05
Higuera, Teddy	88SC	280	$ .01	$ .05	Hughes, Keith	88SC	635	$ .01	$ .05
Higuera, Teddy	89SC	132	$ .01	$ .05	Hulett, Tim	91SC	632	$ .01	$ .03
Higuera, Teddy	90SC	305	$ .01	$ .05	Hume, Tom	88SC	494	$ .01	$ .05
Higuera, Teddy	91SC	260	$ .01	$ .03	Hundley, Todd	90SCTR	76	$ .01	$ .15
Hill, Donnie	88SC	572	$ .01	$ .05	Hundley, Todd	91SC	340	$ .01	$ .15

Player	Year	No.	VG	EX/MT
Hurst, Bruce	88SC	380	$ .01	$ .05
Hurst, Bruce	89SC	325	$ .01	$ .05
Hurst, Bruce	89SCTR	19	$ .01	$ .10
Hurst, Bruce	90SC	270	$ .01	$ .05
Hurst, Bruce	91SC	145	$ .01	$ .03
Huson, Jeff	90SC	615	$ .01	$ .05
Huson, Jeff	90SCFR	41	$ .01	$ .05
Huson, Jeff	91SC	263	$ .01	$ .03
Hyzdu, Adam	91SC	388	$ .01	$ .25
Incaviglia, Pete	88SC	485	$ .01	$ .15
Incaviglia, Pete	89SC	201	$ .01	$ .15
Incaviglia, Pete	90SC	93	$ .01	$ .10
Incaviglia, Pete	91SC	278	$ .01	$ .03
Iorg, Garth	88SC	204	$ .01	$ .05
Irvine, Daryl	91SC	333	$ .01	$ .15
Jackson, Bo	88SC	180	$ .10	$1.00
Jackson, Bo	89SC	330	$ .05	$ .75
Jackson, Bo	90SC	280	$ .01	$ .50
Jackson, Bo	90SC	566	$ .01	$ .35
Jackson, Bo	90SC	697	$ .01	$4.00
Jackson, Bo	90SCDT	687	$ .01	$ .35
Jackson, Bo	91SC	5	$ .01	$ .15
Jackson, Bo	91SC	773	$ .01	$ .20
Jackson, Bo	91SCHL	420	$ .01	$ .15
Jackson, Bo	91SCMB	692	$ .01	$ .20
Jackson, Bo	91SCRM	412	$ .01	$ .15
Jackson, Chuck	88SC	222	$ .01	$ .05
Jackson, Chuck	89SC	584	$ .01	$ .05
Jackson, Danny	88SC	398	$ .01	$ .10
Jackson, Danny	88SCTR	2	$ .01	$ .10
Jackson, Danny	89SC	555	$ .01	$ .10
Jackson, Danny	90SC	289	$ .01	$ .05
Jackson, Danny	91SC	601	$ .01	$ .03
Jackson, Darrin	88SCTR	109	$ .01	$ .25
Jackson, Darrin	89SC	360	$ .01	$ .15
Jackson, Darrin	90SC	541	$ .01	$ .05
Jackson, Darrin	91SC	169	$ .01	$ .03

Player	Year	No.	VG	EX/MT
Jackson, Jeff	90SC	678	$ .01	$ .20
Jackson, Mike	88SC	144	$ .01	$ .05
Jackson, Mike	88SCTR	62	$ .01	$ .05

Player	Year	No.	VG	EX/MT
Jackson, Mike	89SC	398	$ .01	$ .05
Jackson, Mike	90SC	546	$ .01	$ .05
Jackson, Mike	91SC	91	$ .01	$ .10
Jackson, Reggie #1	88SC	500	$ .04	$ .25
Jackson, Reggie #2	88SC	501	$ .04	$ .25
Jackson, Reggie #3	88SC	502	$ .04	$ .25
Jackson, Reggie #4	88SC	503	$ .04	$ .25
Jackson, Reggie #5	88SC	504	$ .04	$ .25
Jacoby, Brook	88SC	39	$ .01	$ .10
Jacoby, Brook	89SC	19	$ .01	$ .05
Jacoby, Brook	90SC	56	$ .01	$ .05
Jacoby, Brook	91SC	162	$ .01	$ .03
James, Chris	88SC	409	$ .01	$ .05
James, Chris	89SC	202	$ .01	$ .05
James, Chris	89SCTR	46	$ .01	$ .05
James, Chris	90SC	498	$ .01	$ .05
James, Chris	90SCTR	60	$ .01	$ .05
James, Chris	91SC	491	$ .01	$ .03
James, Dion	88SC	395	$ .01	$ .05
James, Dion	89SC	163	$ .01	$ .05
James, Dion	89SCTR	51	$ .01	$ .05
James, Dion	90SC	514	$ .01	$ .05
James, Dion	91SC	131	$ .01	$ .03
Javier, Stan	88SC	367	$ .01	$ .05
Javier, Stan	89SC	322	$ .01	$ .05
Javier, Stan	90SC	394	$ .01	$ .05
Javier, Stan	90SCTR	52	$ .01	$ .05
Javier, Stan	91SC	281	$ .01	$ .03
Jeffcoat, Mike	90SC	158	$ .01	$ .05
Jeffcoat, Mike	91SC	174	$ .01	$ .03
Jefferies, Gregg	88SC	645	$ .50	$2.50
Jefferies, Gregg	89SC	600	$ .15	$ .75
Jefferies, Gregg	90SC	468	$ .01	$ .25
Jefferies, Gregg	91SC	660	$ .01	$ .10
Jefferson, Stan	88SC	114	$ .01	$ .05
Jefferson, Stan	89SC	519	$ .01	$ .05
Jeltz, Steve	88SC	435	$ .01	$ .05
Jeltz, Steve	89SC	355	$ .01	$ .05
Jeltz, Steve	90SC	421	$ .01	$ .05
Jeltz, Steve	90SCTR	59	$ .01	$ .05
Jeltz, Steve	91SC	272	$ .01	$ .03
Jennings, Doug	89SC	459	$ .01	$ .10
Jennings, Doug	91SC	819	$ .01	$ .03
John, Tommy	88SC	240	$ .01	$ .10
John, Tommy	89SC	477	$ .01	$ .05
Johnson, Dave	90SC	528	$ .01	$ .05
Johnson, Dave	91SC	506	$ .01	$ .03
Johnson, Howard	88SC	69	$ .01	$ .15
Johnson, Howard	89SC	136	$ .01	$ .10
Johnson, Howard	90SC	124	$ .01	$ .10
Johnson, Howard	91SC	185	$ .01	$ .03
Johnson, Lance	90SC	570	$ .01	$ .05
Johnson, Lance	91SC	157	$ .01	$ .03
Johnson, Randy	89SC	645	$ .01	$ .25
Johnson, Randy	89SCTR	77	$ .01	$ .05
Johnson, Randy	90SC	415	$ .01	$ .05
Johnson, Randy	91SC	290	$ .01	$ .03
Johnson, Randy	91SCNH	700	$ .01	$ .03
Johnson, Wallace	88SC	433	$ .01	$ .05
Johnson, Wallace	89SC	196	$ .01	$ .05
Johnson, Wallace	90SC	479	$ .01	$ .05
Jones, Barry	89SC	333	$ .01	$ .05
Jones, Barry	90SC	152	$ .01	$ .05
Jones, Barry	91SC	115	$ .01	$ .03
Jones, Chipper	91SC	671	$ .01	$ .35
Jones, Doug	88SC	594	$ .01	$ .25
Jones, Doug	89SC	387	$ .01	$ .05
Jones, Doug	89SC	656	$ .01	$ .05
Jones, Doug	90SC	130	$ .01	$ .05
Jones, Doug	91SC	45	$ .01	$ .03

SCORE

Player	Year	No.	VG	EX/MT
Jones, Doug	91SCST	884	$ .01	$ .03
Jones, Jimmy	88SC	246	$ .01	$ .05
Jones, Jimmy	89SC	294	$ .01	$ .05
Jones, Jimmy	91SC	583	$ .01	$ .03
Jones, Keith "Kiki"	90SC	676	$ .01	$ .35
Jones, Odell	89SC	579	$ .01	$ .05
Jones, Ron	89SC	639	$ .01	$ .10
Jones, Ron	90SC	364	$ .01	$ .05
Jones, Ron	91SC	653	$ .01	$ .03
Jones, Ross	88SC	598	$ .01	$ .05
Jones, Ruppert	88SC	333	$ .01	$ .05
Jones, Tim	89SC	649	$ .01	$ .05
Jones, Tim	90SC	579	$ .01	$ .05
Jones, Tracy	88SC	326	$ .01	$ .05

TRACY JONES

Player	Year	No.	VG	EX/MT
Jones, Tracy	89SC	510	$ .01	$ .05
Jones, Tracy	89SCTR	43	$ .01	$ .05
Jones, Tracy	90SC	291	$ .01	$ .05
Jones, Tracy	91SC	87	$ .01	$ .03
Jordan, Ricky	88SCTR	68	$ .01	$ .75
Jordan, Ricky	89SC	548	$ .01	$ .25
Jordan, Ricky	90SC	16	$ .01	$ .10
Jordan, Ricky	91SC	15	$ .01	$ .03
Jorgensen, Terry	90SC	655	$ .01	$ .05
Jose, Felix	89SC	629	$ .01	$ .50
Jose, Felix	90SC	321	$ .01	$ .15
Jose, Felix	91SC	784	$ .01	$ .03
Joyner, Wally	88SC	7	$ .01	$ .20
Joyner, Wally	89SC	65	$ .01	$ .10
Joyner, Wally	90SC	120	$ .01	$ .10
Joyner, Wally	91SC	470	$ .01	$ .10
Joyner, Wally	91SCTF	873	$ .01	$ .03
Justice, Dave	90SC	650	$ .50	$3.00
Justice, Dave	91SC	55	$ .01	$ .50
Justice, Dave	91SCMVP	880	$ .01	$ .25
Justice, Dave	91SCTF	861	$ .01	$ .50
Karkovice, Ron	88SC	374	$ .01	$ .05
Karkovice, Ron	90SC	22	$ .01	$ .05
Karkovice, Ron	91SC	833	$ .01	$ .03
Karsay, Steve	91SC	675	$ .01	$ .25
Kelly, Roberto	88SC	634	$ .10	$1.00

Player	Year	No.	VG	EX/MT
Kelly, Roberto	89SC	487	$ .01	$ .15
Kelly, Roberto	90SC	100	$ .01	$ .10
Kelly, Roberto	91SC	119	$ .01	$ .03
Kennedy, Terry	88SC	123	$ .01	$ .05
Kennedy, Terry	89SC	123	$ .01	$ .05
Kennedy, Terry	89SCTR	30	$ .01	$ .05
Kennedy, Terry	90SC	7	$ .01	$ .05
Kennedy, Terry	91SC	548	$ .01	$ .03
Kerfeld, Charlie	88SC	479	$ .01	$ .05
Key, Jimmy	88SC	216	$ .01	$ .05
Key, Jimmy	89SC	480	$ .01	$ .05
Key, Jimmy	90SC	407	$ .01	$ .05
Key, Jimmy	91SC	422	$ .01	$ .03
Kiecker, Dana	90SCTR	102	$ .01	$ .15
Kiecker, Dana	91SC	77	$ .01	$ .10
Kiefer, Steve	88SC	630	$ .01	$ .05
Kilgus, Paul	88SC	536	$ .01	$ .05
Kilgus, Paul	89SC	271	$ .01	$ .05
King, Eric	88SC	471	$ .01	$ .05
King, Eric	89SC	471	$ .01	$ .05
King, Eric	89SCTR	26	$ .01	$ .05
King, Eric	90SC	28	$ .01	$ .05
King, Eric	91SC	124	$ .01	$ .03
King, Jeff	90SC	549	$ .01	$ .05
King, Jeff	91SC	244	$ .01	$ .03
Kingery, Mike	88SC	178	$ .01	$ .05
Kingery, Mike	91SC	547	$ .01	$ .03
Kinzer, Matt	90SC	628	$ .01	$ .05
Kipper, Bob	89SC	354	$ .01	$ .05
Kipper, Bob	91SC	646	$ .01	$ .03
Kittle, Ron	88SC	449	$ .01	$ .05
Kittle, Ron	88SCTR	44	$ .01	$ .05
Kittle, Ron	89SC	96	$ .01	$ .05
Kittle, Ron	90SC	529	$ .01	$ .05
Klink, Joe	91SC	588	$ .01	$ .03
Knackert, Brent	91SC	774	$ .01	$ .03
Knepper, Bob	88SC	344	$ .01	$ .05
Knepper, Bob	89SC	273	$ .01	$ .05
Knight, Ray	88SC	96	$ .01	$ .05
Knight, Ray	88SCTR	17	$ .01	$ .05
Knight, Ray	89SC	135	$ .01	$ .05
Knoblauch, Chuck	90SC	672	$ .01	$ .35
Knudson, Mark	90SC	539	$ .01	$ .05
Knudson, Mark	91SC	239	$ .01	$ .03
Komminsk, Brad	90SC	496	$ .01	$ .05
Komminsk, Brad	90SCTR	53	$ .01	$ .05
Komminsk, Brad	91SC	259	$ .01	$ .03
Kraemer, Joe	91SC	755	$ .01	$ .03
Kremers, Jimmy	91SC	736	$ .01	$ .03
Kreuter, Chad	89SC	638	$ .01	$ .05
Kreuter, Chad	90SC	406	$ .01	$ .05
Krueger, Bill	90SC	366	$ .01	$ .05
Krueger, Bill	91SC	598	$ .01	$ .03
Kruk, John	88SC	36	$ .01	$ .10
Kruk, John	89SC	148	$ .01	$ .05
Kruk, John	89SCTR	70	$ .01	$ .05
Kruk, John	90SC	467	$ .01	$ .05
Kruk, John	91SC	94	$ .01	$ .03
Krukow, Mike	88SC	185	$ .01	$ .05
Krukow, Mike	89SC	190	$ .01	$ .05
Krukow, Mike	90SC	215	$ .01	$ .05
Kunkel, Jeff	88SC	407	$ .01	$ .05
Kunkel, Jeff	89SC	484	$ .01	$ .05
Kunkel, Jeff	90SC	431	$ .01	$ .05
Kunkel, Jeff	91SC	783	$ .01	$ .03
Kutcher, Randy	90SC	551	$ .01	$ .05
Kutcher, Randy	91SC	837	$ .01	$ .03
Kutzler, Jerry	90SCTR	80	$ .01	$ .10
Kutzler, Jerry	91SC	749	$ .01	$ .05
LaCoss, Mike	88SC	465	$ .01	$ .05

Player	Year	No.	VG	EX/MT	Player	Year	No.	VG	EX/MT
LaCoss, Mike	89SC	500	$ .01	$ .05	Leach, Rick	88SC	257	$ .01	$ .05
LaCoss, Mike	90SC	253	$ .01	$ .05	Leach, Rick	89SC	540	$ .01	$ .05
LaCoss, Mike	91SC	652	$ .01	$ .03	Leach, Rick	90SC	426	$ .01	$ .05
Lacy, Lee	88SC	173	$ .01	$ .05	Leach, Terry	88SC	203	$ .01	$ .05
Laga, Mike	89SC	536	$ .01	$ .05	Leach, Terry	89SC	431	$ .01	$ .05
Lake, Steve	88SC	596	$ .01	$ .05	Leach, Terry	89SCTR	24	$ .01	$ .05
Lake, Steve	89SC	363	$ .01	$ .05	Leach, Terry	90SC	502	$ .01	$ .05
Lake, Steve	89SCTR	12	$ .01	$ .05	Leach, Terry	90SCTR	43	$ .01	$ .05
Lake, Steve	90SC	435	$ .01	$ .05	Leach, Terry	91SC	556	$ .01	$ .03
Lake, Steve	91SC	572	$ .01	$ .03	Leary, Tim	88SC	224	$ .01	$ .05
Lamp, Dennis	88SC	616	$ .01	$ .05	Leary, Tim	89SC	429	$ .01	$ .05
Lamp, Dennis	88SCTR	6	$ .01	$ .05	Leary, Tim	89SCTR	52	$ .01	$ .05
Lamp, Dennis	89SC	508	$ .01	$ .05	Leary, Tim	90SC	504	$ .01	$ .05
Lamp, Dennis	90SC	471	$ .01	$ .05	Leary, Tim	90SCTR	27	$ .01	$ .05
Lamp, Dennis	91SC	612	$ .01	$ .03	Leary, Tim	91SC	631	$ .01	$ .03
Lampkin, Tom	91SC	720	$ .01	$ .03	Lee, Manny	88SC	561	$ .01	$ .05
Lancaster, Les	88SC	602	$ .01	$ .10	Lee, Manny	89SC	326	$ .01	$ .05
Lancaster, Les	89SC	60	$ .01	$ .05	Lee, Manny	90SC	482	$ .01	$ .05
Lancaster, Les	90SC	413	$ .01	$ .05	Lee, Manny	91SC	534	$ .01	$ .03
Lancaster, Les	91SC	293	$ .01	$ .03	Lee, Mark	91SC	372	$ .01	$ .10
Landreaux, Ken	88SC	247	$ .01	$ .05	Lefferts, Craig	88SC	553	$ .01	$ .05
Landrum, Bill	90SC	456	$ .01	$ .05	Lefferts, Craig	89SC	178	$ .01	$ .05
Landrum, Bill	91SC	98	$ .01	$ .03	Lefferts, Craig	90SC	209	$ .01	$ .05
Langston, Mark	88SC	30	$ .01	$ .10	Lefferts, Craig	90SCTR	22	$ .01	$ .05
Langston, Mark	89SC	161	$ .01	$ .10	Lefferts, Craig	91SC	184	$ .01	$ .03
Langston, Mark	89SCTR	25	$ .01	$ .10	Leibrandt, Charlie	88SC	61	$ .01	$ .05
Langston, Mark	90SC	401	$ .01	$ .10	Leibrandt, Charlie	89SC	133	$ .01	$ .05
Langston, Mark	90SCDT	688	$ .01	$ .10	Leibrandt, Charlie	90SC	82	$ .01	$ .05
Langston, Mark	90SCTR	11	$ .01	$ .05	Leibrandt, Charlie	91SC	536	$ .01	$ .03
Langston, Mark	91SC	21	$ .01	$ .03	Leiper, Dave	88SC	348	$ .01	$ .05
Langston, Mark	91SCKM	411	$ .01	$ .05	Leiper, Dave	89SC	515	$ .01	$ .05
Langston, Mark	91SCNH	699	$ .01	$ .03	Leiper, Dave	90SC	212	$ .01	$ .05
Lankford, Ray	90SCTR	84	$ .01	$1.00	Leiter, Al	88SCTR	97	$ .01	$ .25
Lankford, Ray	91SC	731	$ .01	$ .35	Leiter, Al	89SC	580	$ .01	$ .15
Lansford, Carney	88SC	253	$ .01	$ .05	Leiter, Mark	91SC	727	$ .01	$ .03
Lansford, Carney	89SC	179	$ .01	$ .05	Leius, Scott	91SC	370	$ .01	$ .03
Lansford, Carney	90SC	296	$ .01	$ .05	Lemke, Mark	90SC	593	$ .01	$ .05
Lansford, Carney	91SC	630	$ .01	$ .03	Lemke, Mark	91SC	779	$ .01	$ .03
LaPoint, Dave	88SC	589	$ .01	$ .05	Lemon, Chet	88SC	119	$ .01	$ .05
LaPoint, Dave	89SC	384	$ .01	$ .05	Lemon, Chet	89SC	44	$ .01	$ .05
LaPoint, Dave	89SCTR	4	$ .01	$ .05	Lemon, Chet	90SC	106	$ .01	$ .05
LaPoint, Dave	90SC	357	$ .01	$ .05	Lemon, Chet	91SC	557	$ .01	$ .03
LaPoint, Dave	91SC	218	$ .01	$ .03	Leonard, Jeffrey	88SC	580	$ .01	$ .05
Larkin, Barry	88SC	72	$ .04	$ .50	Leonard, Jeff	89SC	557	$ .01	$ .05
Larkin, Barry	89SC	31	$ .01	$ .25	Leonard, Jeffrey	89SCTR	7	$ .01	$ .05
Larkin, Barry	90SC	155	$ .01	$ .15	Leonard, Jeffrey	90SC	98	$ .01	$ .05
Larkin, Barry	90SCDT	689	$ .01	$ .10	Leonard, Jeffrey	91SC	44	$ .01	$ .03
Larkin, Barry	91SC	505	$ .01	$ .10	Leonard, Mark	91SC	719	$ .01	$ .20
Larkin, Barry	91SCAS	666	$ .01	$ .03	Lewis, Darren	91SC	350	$ .01	$ .25
Larkin, Barry	91SCBC	6	$ .01	$ .25	Lewis, Scott	91SC	759	$ .01	$ .10
Larkin, Barry	91SCDT	888	$ .01	$ .03	Leyritz, Jim	90SCTR	83	$ .01	$ .20
Larkin, Gene	88SC	276	$ .01	$ .10	Leyritz, Jim	91SC	65	$ .01	$ .15
Larkin, Gene	89SC	280	$ .01	$ .05	Lieberthal, Mike	91SC	683	$ .01	$ .25
Larkin, Gene	90SC	276	$ .01	$ .05	Lilliquist, Derek	89SC	631	$ .01	$ .15
Larkin, Gene	91SC	471	$ .01	$ .03	Lilliquist, Derek	90SC	243	$ .01	$ .10
Laudner, Tim	88SC	153	$ .01	$ .05	Lilliquist, Derek	91SC	571	$ .01	$ .03
Laudner, Tim	89SC	134	$ .01	$ .05	Lind, Jose	88SC	597	$ .04	$ .25
Laudner, Tim	90SC	318	$ .01	$ .05	Lind, Jose	89SC	87	$ .01	$ .10
LaValliere, Mike	88SC	421	$ .01	$ .05	Lind, Jose	90SC	83	$ .01	$ .10
LaValliere, Mike	89SC	33	$ .01	$ .05	Lind, Jose	91SC	461	$ .01	$ .03
LaValliere, Mike	90SC	116	$ .01	$ .05	Lindeman, Jim	88SC	302	$ .01	$ .05
LaValliere, Mike	91SC	222	$ .01	$ .03	Lindros, Eric	90SCTR	100	$ .01	$ 4.00
Law, Vance	88SC	85	$ .01	$ .05	Liriano, Nelson	88SC	621	$ .01	$ .05
Law, Vance	88SCTR	16	$ .01	$ .05	Liriano, Nelson	89SC	577	$ .01	$ .05
Law, Vance	89SC	102	$ .01	$ .05	Liriano, Nelson	90SC	77	$ .01	$ .05
Law, Vance	90SC	73	$ .01	$ .05	Liriano, Nelson	91SC	288	$ .01	$ .03
Layana, Tim	90SCTR	107	$ .01	$ .15	Litton, Greg	89SCTR	86	$ .01	$ .15
Layana, Tim	91SC	64	$ .01	$ .15	Litton, Greg	90SC	497	$ .01	$ .05
Lazorko, Jack	88SC	437	$ .01	$ .05	Litton, Greg	91SC	533	$ .01	$ .03
Lea, Charlie	89SC	501	$ .01	$ .05	Lombardozzi, Steve	88SC	174	$ .01	$ .05

SCORE

Player	Year	No.	VG	EX/MT	Player	Year	No.	VG	EX/MT
Lombardozzi, Steve	89SC	421	$ .01	$ .05	Martinez, Carlos	90SC	314	$ .01	$ .05
Long, Bill	88SC	539	$ .01	$ .05	Martinez, Carlos	91SC	274	$ .01	$ .03
Long, Bill	89SC	351	$ .01	$ .05	Martinez, Carmelo	88SC	181	$ .01	$ .05
Long, Bill	90SC	526	$ .01	$ .05	Martinez, Carmelo	89SC	517	$ .01	$ .05
Long, Bill	90SCTR	62	$ .01	$ .05	Martinez, Carmelo	90SC	114	$ .01	$ .05
Long, Bill	91SC	559	$ .01	$ .03	Martinez, Carmelo	90SCTR	10	$ .01	$ .05
Lopes, Davey	88SC	489	$ .01	$ .05	Martinez, Carmelo	91SC	792	$ .01	$ .03
Loynd, Mike	88SC	491	$ .01	$ .05	Martinez, Dave	88SC	223	$ .01	$ .05
Lusader, Scott	90SC	575	$ .01	$ .05	Martinez, Dave	89SC	77	$ .01	$ .05
Lynch, Ed	88SC	506	$ .01	$ .05	Martinez, Dave	90SC	27	$ .01	$ .05
Lynn, Fred	88SC	42	$ .01	$ .10	Martinez, Dave	91SC	82	$ .01	$ .03
Lynn, Fred	89SC	126	$ .01	$ .05	Martinez, Dennis	88SC	601	$ .01	$ .05
Lynn, Fred	90SC	131	$ .01	$ .05	Martinez, Dennis	89SC	114	$ .01	$ .05
Lynn, Fred	90SCTR	20	$ .01	$ .05	Martinez, Dennis	90SC	47	$ .01	$ .05
Lynn, Fred	91SC	554	$ .01	$ .03	Martinez, Dennis	91SC	454	$ .01	$ .03
Lyons, Barry	88SC	387	$ .01	$ .05	Martinez, Edgar	89SC	637	$ .01	$ .50
Lyons, Barry	89SC	456	$ .01	$ .05	Martinez, Edgar	90SC	324	$ .01	$ .10
Lyons, Barry	90SC	29	$ .01	$ .05	Martinez, Edgar	91SC	264	$ .01	$ .03
Lyons, Steve	89SC	388	$ .01	$ .05	Martinez, Ramon	89SC	635	$ .01	$1.50
Lyons, Steve	90SC	88	$ .01	$ .05	Martinez, Ramon	90SC	461	$ .01	$ .50
Lyons, Steve	91SC	269	$ .01	$ .03	Martinez, Ramon	91SC	300	$ .01	$ .20
Maas, Kevin	90SC	606	$ .01	$2.25	Martinez, Ramon	91SCHL	419	$ .01	$ .15
Maas, Kevin	91SC	600	$ .01	$ .35	Martinez, Ramon	91SCKM	408	$ .01	$ .15
Macfarlane, Mike	88SCTR	76	$ .01	$ .35	Martinez, Tino	90SC	596	$ .01	$ .50
Macfarlane, Mike	89SC	319	$ .01	$ .15	Martinez, Tino	91SC	798	$ .01	$ .25
Macfarlane, Mike	91SC	839	$ .01	$ .03	Marzano, John	88SC	584	$ .01	$ .25
Machado, Julio	90SCTR	92	$ .01	$ .05	Marzano, John	91SC	831	$ .01	$ .03
Mack, Shane	88SC	414	$ .01	$ .05	Mathews, Greg	88SC	226	$ .01	$ .05
Mack, Shane	89SC	270	$ .01	$ .05	Mathews, Greg	89SC	286	$ .01	$ .05
Mack, Shane	91SC	284	$ .01	$ .03	Mathews, Greg	90SC	537	$ .01	$ .05
Maddux, Greg	89SC	119	$ .01	$ .10	Matthews, Gary	88SC	599	$ .01	$ .05
Maddux, Greg	90SC	403	$ .01	$ .05	Mattingly, Don	88SC	1	$ .25	$1.00
Maddux, Greg	91SC	317	$ .01	$ .03	Mattingly, Don	88SC	650	$ .05	$ .25
Maddux, Mike	89SC	393	$ .01	$ .05	Mattingly, Don	88SC	658	$ .05	$ .25
Madlock, Bill	88SC	445	$ .01	$ .05	Mattingly, Don	89SC	100	$ .10	$ .50
Magadan, Dave	88SC	41	$ .01	$ .20	Mattingly, Don	90SC	1	$ .01	$ .40
Magadan, Dave	89SC	312	$ .01	$ .10	Mattingly, Don	91SC	23	$ .01	$ .20
Magadan, Dave	90SC	46	$ .01	$ .05	Mattingly, Don	91SCTF	856	$ .01	$ .15
Magadan, Dave	91SC	190	$ .01	$ .03	Matuszek, Len	88SC	424	$ .01	$ .05
Magrane, Joe	88SC	94	$ .04	$ .30	May, Derrick	91SC	379	$ .01	$ .35
Magrane, Joe	89SC	460	$ .01	$ .10	Mayne, Brent	90SC	664	$ .01	$ .05
Magrane, Joe	90SC	17	$ .01	$ .05	Mayne, Brent	91SC	765	$ .01	$ .03
Magrane, Joe	91SC	575	$ .01	$ .03	Mazzilli, Lee	88SC	158	$ .01	$ .05
Mahler, Rick	88SC	319	$ .01	$ .05	Mazzilli, Lee	89SC	217	$ .01	$ .05
Mahler, Rick	89SC	229	$ .01	$ .05	Mazzilli, Lee	90SC	459	$ .01	$ .05
Mahler, Rick	89SCTR	79	$ .01	$ .05	McCament, Randy	90SC	580	$ .01	$ .05
Mahler, Rick	90SC	87	$ .01	$ .05	McCaskill, Kirk	88SC	552	$ .01	$ .05
Mahler, Rick	91SC	464	$ .01	$ .03	McCaskill, Kirk	89SC	181	$ .01	$ .05
Maldonado, Candy	88SC	54	$ .01	$ .05	McCaskill, Kirk	90SC	217	$ .01	$ .05
Maldonado, Candy	89SC	47	$ .01	$ .05	McCaskill, Kirk	91SC	590	$ .01	$ .03
Maldonado, Candy	90SC	138	$ .01	$ .05	McClellan, Paul	91SC	726	$ .01	$ .03
Maldonado, Candy	90SCTR	8	$ .01	$ .05	McClendon, Lloyd	89SC	521	$ .01	$ .05
Maldonado, Candy	91SC	93	$ .01	$ .03	McClendon, Lloyd	90SC	176	$ .01	$ .05
Malone, Chuck	91SC	724	$ .01	$ .03	McClure, Bob	89SC	572	$ .01	$ .05
Mann, Kelly	90SC	627	$ .01	$ .10	McClure, Bob	89SCTR	58	$ .01	$ .05
Manning, Rick	88SC	593	$ .01	$ .05	McClure, Bob	90SC	117	$ .01	$ .05
Manrique, Fred	88SC	139	$ .01	$ .05	McClure, Rob	88SC	381	$ .01	$ .05
Manrique, Fred	89SC	457	$ .01	$ .05	McCray, Rodney	91SC	763	$ .01	$ .03
Manrique, Fred	90SC	166	$ .01	$ .05	McCullers, Lance	88SC	150	$ .01	$ .05
Manto, Jeff	91SC	337	$ .01	$ .10	McCullers, Lance	89SC	158	$ .01	$ .05
Manwaring, Kirt	88SC	627	$ .01	$ .10	McCullers, Lance	89SCTR	63	$ .01	$ .05
Manwaring, Kirt	89SC	619	$ .01	$ .05	McCullers, Lance	90SC	186	$ .01	$ .05
Manwaring, Kirt	90SC	146	$ .01	$ .05	McCullers, Lance	91SC	313	$ .01	$ .03
Manwaring, Kirt	91SC	101	$ .01	$ .03	McDonald, Ben	90SC	680	$ .01	$1.50
Marak, Paul	91SC	712	$ .01	$ .03	McDonald, Ben	91SC	645	$ .01	$ .25
Marshall, Mike	88SC	135	$ .01	$ .10	McDowell, Jack	88SCTR	85	$ .01	$1.50
Marshall, Mike	89SC	186	$ .01	$ .05	McDowell, Jack	89SC	289	$ .01	$ .15
Marshall, Mike	90SC	384	$ .01	$ .05	McDowell, Jack	91SC	27	$ .01	$ .03
Marshall, Mike	91SC	617	$ .01	$ .03	McDowell, Oddibe	88SC	215	$ .01	$ .05
Martinez, Carlos	89SCTR	103	$ .01	$ .20	McDowell, Oddibe	89SC	59	$ .01	$ .05

Player	Year	No.	VG	EX/MT
McDowell, Oddibe	89SCTR	72	$ .01	$ .05
McDowell, Oddibe	90SC	476	$ .01	$ .05
McDowell, Oddibe	91SC	121	$ .01	$ .03
McDowell, Roger	88SC	188	$ .01	$ .05
McDowell, Roger	89SC	281	$ .01	$ .05
McDowell, Roger	89SCTR	53	$ .01	$ .05
McDowell, Roger	90SC	445	$ .01	$ .05
McDowell, Roger	91SC	537	$ .01	$ .03
McElroy, Chuck	91SC	374	$ .01	$ .03
McGaffigan, Andy	88SC	366	$ .01	$ .05
McGaffigan, Andy	89SC	138	$ .01	$ .05
McGaffigan, Andy	90SC	224	$ .01	$ .05
McGaffigan, Andy	91SC	619	$ .01	$ .03
McGee, Willie	88SC	40	$ .01	$ .10
McGee, Willie	89SC	88	$ .01	$ .05
McGee, Willie	90SC	374	$ .01	$ .05
McGee, Willie	91SC	597	$ .01	$ .03
McGregor, Scott	88SC	315	$ .01	$ .05
McGriff, Fred	88SC	107	$ .07	$ .75
McGriff, Fred	89SC	6	$ .01	$ .20
McGriff, Fred	90SC	271	$ .01	$ .10
McGriff, Fred	91SC	480	$ .01	$ .10
McGriff, Fred	91SCMB	404	$ .01	$ .10
McGriff, Terry	88SC	281	$ .01	$ .05
McGwire, Mark	88SC	5	$ .25	$1.00
McGwire, Mark	88SC	648	$ .15	$ .15
McGwire, Mark	88SC	659	$ .10	$ .25
McGwire, Mark	89SC	3	$ .10	$ .35
McGwire, Mark	90SC	385	$ .01	$ .25
McGwire, Mark	91SC	324	$ .01	$ .15
McIntosh, Tim	91SC	347	$ .01	$ .10
McKnight, Jeff	91SC	369	$ .01	$ .10
McLemore, Mark	88SC	152	$ .01	$ .05
McLemore, Mark	89SC	208	$ .01	$ .05
McMurtry, Craig	91SC	602	$ .01	$ .03
McRae, Brian	91SC	331	$ .01	$ .75
McReynolds, Kevin	88SC	21	$ .01	$ .10
McReynolds, Kevin	89SC	93	$ .01	$ .05
McReynolds, Kevin	90SC	5	$ .01	$ .05
McReynolds, Kevin	91SC	327	$ .01	$ .03
McWilliams, Larry	88SCTR	23	$ .01	$ .05
McWilliams, Larry	89SC	259	$ .01	$ .05
Meacham, Bobby	88SC	137	$ .01	$ .05
Meacham, Bobby	89SC	509	$ .01	$ .05
Meads, Dave	88SC	243	$ .01	$ .05
Meads, Dave	89SC	593	$ .01	$ .05
Medina, Luis	89SC	633	$ .01	$ .30
Melvin, Bob	88SC	477	$ .01	$ .05
Melvin, Bob	89SC	617	$ .01	$ .05
Melvin, Bob	89SCTR	61	$ .01	$ .05
Melvin, Bob	90SC	453	$ .01	$ .05
Merced, Orlando	91SC	747	$ .01	$ .03
Mercker, Kent	90SCTR	72	$ .01	$ .20
Mercker, Kent	91SC	79	$ .01	$ .10
Merullo, Matt	90SC	605	$ .01	$ .05
Meyer, Joey	88SCTR	75	$ .01	$ .10
Meyer, Joey	89SC	374	$ .01	$ .05
Meyer, Joey	90SC	532	$ .01	$ .05
Mickey, Brantley	88SC	213	$ .01	$ .05
Mielke, Gary	90SC	574	$ .01	$ .05
Mielke, Gary	91SC	167	$ .01	$ .03
Milacki, Bob	89SC	651	$ .01	$ .30
Milacki, Bob	90SC	239	$ .01	$ .05
Milacki, Bob	91SC	512	$ .01	$ .03
Miller, Darrell	88SC	463	$ .01	$ .05
Miller, Darrell	89SC	499	$ .01	$ .05
Miller, Keith	88SC	639	$ .01	$ .05
Miller, Keith	89SC	464	$ .01	$ .05
Miller, Keith	90SC	559	$ .01	$ .05
Miller, Keith	91SC	318	$ .01	$ .03

Player	Year	No.	VG	EX/MT
Miller, Kurt	91SC	682	$ .01	$ .15
Milligan, Randy	88SC	623	$ .04	$ .75
Milligan, Randy	90SC	252	$ .01	$ .05
Milligan, Randy	91SC	86	$ .01	$ .03
Mills, Alan	90SCTR	89	$ .01	$ .15
Mills, Alan	91SC	73	$ .01	$ .10
Milner, Eddie	88SC	548	$ .01	$ .05
Minton, Greg	88SC	176	$ .01	$ .05
Minton, Greg	89SC	543	$ .01	$ .05
Minton, Greg	90SC	48	$ .01	$ .05
Minton, Greg	91SC	823	$ .01	$ .03
Mirabella, Paul	89SC	569	$ .01	$ .05
Mirabella, Paul	91SC	558	$ .01	$ .03
Mitchell, John	88SC	249	$ .01	$ .05
Mitchell, John	91SC	569	$ .01	$ .03
Mitchell, Kevin	88SC	481	$ .10	$ .50
Mitchell, Kevin	89SC	39	$ .01	$ .35
Mitchell, Kevin	90SC	343	$ .01	$ .25
Mitchell, Kevin	91SC	451	$ .01	$ .15
Mitchell, Kevin	91SCMB	406	$ .01	$ .10
Mmahat, Kevin	90SC	643	$ .01	$ .05
Mohorcic, Dale	88SC	452	$ .01	$ .05
Mohorcic, Dale	89SC	420	$ .01	$ .05
Mohorcic, Dale	90SC	191	$ .01	$ .05
Mohorcic, Dale	91SC	596	$ .01	$ .03
Molitor, Paul	88SC	340	$ .01	$ .05
Molitor, Paul	88SC	660	$ .01	$ .10
Molitor, Paul	89SC	565	$ .01	$ .05
Molitor, Paul	90SC	460	$ .01	$ .05
Molitor, Paul	91SC	49	$ .01	$ .03
Monteleone, Rich	89SCTR	92	$ .01	$ .10
Monteleone, Rich	90SC	565	$ .01	$ .05
Montgomery, Jeff	88SC	497	$ .01	$ .30
Montgomery, Jeff	88SCTR	71	$ .01	$ .20
Montgomery, Jeff	89SC	367	$ .01	$ .10
Montgomery, Jeff	90SC	365	$ .01	$ .05
Montgomery, Jeff	91SC	143	$ .01	$ .03
Moore, Charlie	88SC	444	$ .01	$ .05
Moore, Donnie	88SC	195	$ .01	$ .05
Moore, Donnie	89SC	535	$ .01	$ .05

SCORE

Player	Year	No.	VG	EX/MT
Moore, Mike	88SC	464	$ .01	$ .05
Moore, Mike	89SC	274	$ .01	$ .05
Moore, Mike	89SCTR	5	$ .01	$ .05
Moore, Mike	90SC	190	$ .01	$ .05

Player	Year	No.	VG	EX/MT
Moore, Mike	91SC	516	$ .01	$ .03
Morandini, Mickey	91SC	376	$ .01	$ .15
Moreland, Keith	88SC	71	$ .01	$ .05
Moreland, Keith	88SCTR	9	$ .01	$ .05
Moreland, Keith	89SC	42	$ .01	$ .05
Moreland, Keith	89SCTR	29	$ .01	$ .05
Moreland, Keith	90SC	444	$ .01	$ .05
Morgan, Mike	88SC	295	$ .01	$ .05
Morgan, Mike	90SC	342	$ .01	$ .05
Morgan, Mike	91SC	276	$ .01	$ .03
Morris, Hal	90SC	602	$ .01	$ .40
Morris, Hal	91SC	647	$ .01	$ .15
Morris, Jack	88SC	545	$ .01	$ .10
Morris, Jack	89SC	250	$ .01	$ .05
Morris, Jack	90SC	203	$ .01	$ .05
Morris, Jack	91SC	114	$ .01	$ .03
Morris, John	88SC	346	$ .01	$ .05
Morris, John	90SC	134	$ .01	$ .05
Morrison, Jim	88SC	272	$ .01	$ .05
Moseby, Lloyd	88SC	109	$ .01	$ .05
Moseby, Lloyd	89SC	12	$ .01	$ .05
Moseby, Lloyd	90SC	404	$ .01	$ .05
Moseby, Lloyd	90SCTR	25	$ .01	$ .05
Moseby, Lloyd	91SC	133	$ .01	$ .03
Moses, John	88SC	309	$ .01	$ .05
Moses, John	89SC	432	$ .01	$ .05
Moses, John	90SC	391	$ .01	$ .05
Moses, John	91SC	429	$ .01	$ .03
Moyer, Jamie	88SC	573	$ .01	$ .05
Moyer, Jamie	89SC	263	$ .01	$ .05
Moyer, Jamie	90SC	107	$ .01	$ .05
Moyer, Jamie	91SC	437	$ .01	$ .03
Muelens, Hensley	90SC	636	$ .01	$ .25
Muelens, Hensley	91SC	828	$ .01	$ .10
Mulholland, Terry	89SC	474	$ .01	$ .05
Mulholland, Terry	90SC	542	$ .01	$ .05

Player	Year	No.	VG	EX/MT
Mulholland, Terry	91SC	33	$ .01	$ .03
Mulholland, Terry	91SCNH	706	$ .01	$ .03
Mulliniks, Rance	88SC	235	$ .01	$ .05
Mulliniks, Rance	89SC	385	$ .01	$ .05
Mulliniks, Rance	90SC	204	$ .01	$ .05
Mulliniks, Rance	91SC	433	$ .01	$ .03
Mumphrey, Jerry	88SC	467	$ .01	$ .05
Mumphrey, Jerry	89SC	288	$ .01	$ .05
Munoz, Mike	90SC	653	$ .01	$ .15
Munoz, Pedro	91SC	332	$ .01	$ .15
Murphy, Dale	88SC	450	$ .04	$ .15
Murphy, Dale	89SC	30	$ .01	$ .15
Murphy, Dale	90SC	66	$ .01	$ .10
Murphy, Dale	90SCTR	31	$ .01	$ .05
Murphy, Dale	91SC	650	$ .01	$ .10
Murphy, Dwayne	88SC	455	$ .01	$ .05
Murphy, Dwayne	89SC	545	$ .01	$ .05
Murphy, Rob	88SC	559	$ .01	$ .05
Murphy, Rob	89SC	141	$ .01	$ .05
Murphy, Rob	89SCTR	8	$ .01	$ .05
Murphy, Rob	90SC	181	$ .01	$ .05
Murphy, Rob	91SC	183	$ .01	$ .03
Murray, Eddie	88SC	18	$ .01	$ .15
Murray, Eddie	89SC	94	$ .01	$ .10
Murray, Eddie	89SCTR	31	$ .01	$ .10
Murray, Eddie	90SC	80	$ .01	$ .10
Murray, Eddie	91SC	310	$ .01	$ .03
Musselman, Jeff	88SC	478	$ .01	$ .05
Musselman, Jeff	89SC	558	$ .01	$ .05
Musselman, Jeff	90SC	525	$ .01	$ .05
Musselman, Jeff	91SC	294	$ .01	$ .03
Mussina, Mike	91SC	383	$ .01	$ .35
Myers, Greg	91SC	88	$ .01	$ .03
Myers, Randy	88SC	336	$ .01	$ .05
Myers, Randy	89SC	306	$ .01	$ .05
Myers, Randy	90SC	351	$ .01	$ .10
Myers, Randy	90SCTR	16	$ .01	$ .05
Myers, Randy	91SC	501	$ .01	$ .03
Myers, Randy	91SCAS	662	$ .01	$ .03
Myers, Randy	91SCDT	885	$ .01	$ .03
Nabholz, Chris	91SC	804	$ .01	$ .10
Naehring, Tim	90SCTR	87	$ .01	$ .05
Naehring, Tim	91SC	356	$ .01	$ .20
Nagy, Charles	90SC	611	$ .01	$ .25
Nagy, Charles	91SC	75	$ .01	$ .10
Navarro, Jaime	90SC	569	$ .01	$ .20
Navarro, Jaime	91SC	102	$ .01	$ .03
Neidlinger, Jim	91SC	794	$ .01	$ .03
Nelson, Gene	88SC	588	$ .01	$ .05
Nelson, Gene	89SC	434	$ .01	$ .05
Nelson, Gene	90SC	441	$ .01	$ .05
Nelson, Gene	91SC	478	$ .01	$ .03
Nettles, Graig	88SCTR	25	$ .01	$ .10
Nettles, Graig	88SC	440	$ .01	$ .05
Nettles, Graig	89SC	277	$ .01	$ .05
Nevers, Tom	91SC	387	$ .01	$ .15
Newfield, Marc	91SC	391	$ .01	$ .35
Newman, Al	88SC	252	$ .01	$ .05
Newman, Al	89SC	493	$ .01	$ .05
Newman, Al	90SC	128	$ .01	$ .05
Newman, Al	91SC	424	$ .01	$ .03
Niedenfuer, Tom	88SC	261	$ .01	$ .05
Niedenfuer, Tom	89SC	252	$ .01	$ .05
Niedenfuer, Tom	91SC	217	$ .01	$ .03
Niekro, Joe	88SC	237	$ .01	$ .05
Niekro, Phil	88SC	555	$ .01	$ .10
Nieves, Juan	88SC	513	$ .01	$ .05
Nieves, Juan	88SC	655	$ .01	$ .05
Nieves, Juan	89SC	410	$ .01	$ .05
Nipper, Al	88SC	527	$ .01	$ .05

Player	Year	No.	VG	EX/MT	Player	Year	No.	VG	EX/MT
Nipper, Al	89SC	532	$ .01	$ .05	Oquendo, Jose	91SC	622	$ .01	$ .03
Nixon, Donell	88SC	436	$ .01	$ .05	Orosco, Jesse	88SC	495	$ .01	$ .05
Nixon, Donell	89SC	481	$ .01	$ .05	Orosco, Jesse	88SCTR	64	$ .01	$ .05
Nixon, Donell	90SC	538	$ .01	$ .05	Orosco, Jesse	89SC	356	$ .01	$ .05
Nixon, Otis	89SC	451	$ .01	$ .05	Orosco, Jesse	90SC	353	$ .01	$ .05
Nixon, Otis	90SC	241	$ .01	$ .05	Orosco, Jesse	91SC	578	$ .01	$ .03
Nixon, Otis	91SC	431	$ .01	$ .03	Orsulak, Joe	88SCTR	41	$ .01	$ .05
Noboa, Junior	91SC	423	$ .01	$ .03	Orsulak, Joe	89SC	247	$ .01	$ .05
Noce, Paul	88SC	329	$ .01	$ .05	Orsulak, Joe	90SC	41	$ .01	$ .05
Nokes, Matt	88SC	15	$ .01	$ .25	Orsulak, Joe	91SC	508	$ .01	$ .03
Nokes, Matt	88SC	648	$ .15	$ .50	Ortiz, Junior	88SC	404	$ .01	$ .05
Nokes, Matt	89SC	23	$ .01	$ .05	Ortiz, Junior	89SC	402	$ .01	$ .05
Nokes, Matt	90SC	55	$ .01	$ .05	Ortiz, Junior	90SC	143	$ .01	$ .05
Nokes, Matt	90SCTR	38	$ .01	$ .05	Ortiz, Junior	90SCTR	66	$ .01	$ .05
Nokes, Matt	91SC	551	$ .01	$ .03	Ortiz, Junior	91SC	438	$ .01	$ .03
Nolte, Eric	88SC	568	$ .01	$ .05	Orton, John	90SC	582	$ .01	$ .05
Nosek, Randy	90SC	607	$ .01	$ .10	Orton, John	91SC	467	$ .01	$ .03
Novoa, Rafael	91SC	366	$ .01	$ .10	Osborne, Donovan	91SC	677	$ .01	$ .20
Nunez, Jose	88SC	312	$ .01	$ .05	Otto, Dave	90SCTR	101	$ .01	$ .10
O'Brien, Charlie	89SC	606	$ .01	$ .05	Owen, Larry	88SC	230	$ .01	$ .05
O'Brien, Charlie	91SC	829	$ .01	$ .03	Owen, Spike	88SC	372	$ .01	$ .05
O'Brien, Pete	88SC	29	$ .01	$ .05	Owen, Spike	89SC	218	$ .01	$ .05
O'Brien, Pete	89SC	22	$ .01	$ .05	Owen, Spike	89SCTR	13	$ .01	$ .05
O'Brien, Pete	89SCTR	6	$ .01	$ .05	Owen, Spike	90SC	247	$ .01	$ .05
O'Brien, Pete	90SC	175	$ .01	$ .05	Owen, Spike	91SC	452	$ .01	$ .03
O'Brien, Pete	90SCTR	23	$ .01	$ .05	Paciorek, Tom	88SC	531	$ .01	$ .05
O'Brien, Pete	91SC	509	$ .01	$ .03	Pagliarulo, Mike	88SC	170	$ .01	$ .10
O'Connor, Jack	88SC	434	$ .01	$ .05	Pagliarulo, Mike	89SC	189	$ .01	$ .05
O'Malley, Tom	88SC	534	$ .01	$ .05	Pagliarulo, Mike	89SCTR	11	$ .01	$ .05
O'Malley, Tom	91SC	439	$ .01	$ .03	Pagliarulo, Mike	90SC	494	$ .01	$ .05
O'Neill, Paul	88SC	304	$ .01	$ .15	Pagliarulo, Mike	91SC	199	$ .01	$ .03
O'Neill, Paul	89SC	206	$ .01	$ .05	Pagnozzi, Tom	88SC	358	$ .01	$ .05
O'Neill, Paul	90SC	295	$ .01	$ .10	Pagnozzi, Tom	89SC	483	$ .01	$ .15
O'Neill, Paul	91SC	227	$ .01	$ .03	Pagnozzi, Tom	91SC	797	$ .01	$ .03
Oberkfell, Ken	88SC	245	$ .01	$ .05	Palacios, Vicente	88SC	643	$ .01	$ .15
Oberkfell, Ken	89SC	139	$ .01	$ .05	Pall, Donn	89SCTR	102	$ .01	$ .05
Oberkfell, Ken	90SC	422	$ .01	$ .05	Pall, Donn	90SC	304	$ .01	$ .05
Oberkfell, Ken	90SCTR	58	$ .01	$ .05	Pall, Donn	91SC	132	$ .01	$ .03
Oberkfell, Ken	91SC	214	$ .01	$ .03	Palmeiro, Rafael	88SC	186	$ .07	$ .75
Oester, Ron	88SC	183	$ .01	$ .05	Palmeiro, Rafael	89SC	199	$ .01	$ .15
Oester, Ron	89SC	615	$ .01	$ .05	Palmeiro, Rafael	89SCTR	1	$ .01	$ .05
Oester, Ron	90SC	59	$ .01	$ .05	Palmeiro, Rafael	90SC	405	$ .01	$ .05
Oester, Ron	91SC	651	$ .01	$ .03	Palmeiro, Rafael	91SC	216	$ .01	$ .03
Offerman, Jose	91SC	343	$ .01	$ .30	Palmer, David	88SC	457	$ .01	$ .05
Ojeda, Bob	88SC	563	$ .01	$ .05	Palmer, Dave	89SC	544	$ .01	$ .05
Ojeda, Bob	89SC	116	$ .01	$ .05	Palmer, Dean	90SC	594	$ .01	$ .35
Ojeda, Bob	90SC	53	$ .01	$ .05	Pankovits, Jim	89SC	192	$ .01	$ .05
Ojeda, Bob	91SC	321	$ .01	$ .03	Parent, Mark	89SC	576	$ .01	$ .15
Olerud, John	90SC	589	$ .01	$1.50	Parent, Mark	90SC	119	$ .01	$ .05
Olerud, John	91SC	625	$ .01	$ .25	Parent, Mark	91SC	213	$ .01	$ .03
Olerud, John	91SCTF	860	$ .01	$ .25	Parker, Clay	89SCTR	94	$ .01	$ .15
Olin, Steve	90SC	590	$ .01	$ .15	Parker, Clay	90SC	316	$ .01	$ .05
Olin, Steve	91SC	496	$ .01	$ .03	Parker, Dave	88SC	17	$ .01	$ .15
Olivares, Omar	91SC	748	$ .01	$ .03	Parker, Dave	88SCTR	50	$ .01	$ .20
Oliver, Joe	89SCTR	104	$ .01	$ .35	Parker, Dave	89SC	108	$ .01	$ .05
Oliver, Joe	90SC	576	$ .01	$ .35	Parker, Dave	90SC	135	$ .01	$ .10
Oliver, Joe	91SC	620	$ .01	$ .03	Parker, Dave	90SCTR	12	$ .01	$ .05
Oliveras, Francisco	91SC	635	$ .01	$ .03	Parker, Dave	91SC	484	$ .01	$ .03
Olson, Gregg	90SCTR	69	$ .01	$ .20	Parker, Rick	90SCTR	77	$ .01	$ .10
Olson, Gregg	91SC	56	$ .01	$ .10	Parker, Rick	91SC	58	$ .01	$ .03
Olson, Gregg	89SCTR	96	$ .01	$ .75	Parrett, Jeff	89SC	377	$ .01	$ .10
Olson, Gregg	90SC	63	$ .01	$ .15	Parrett, Jeff	89SCTR	33	$ .01	$ .05
Olson, Gregg	91SC	490	$ .01	$ .10	Parrett, Jeff	91SC	565	$ .01	$ .03
Olwine, Ed	88SC	379	$ .01	$ .05	Parrish, Lance	88SC	131	$ .01	$ .10
Ontiveros, Steve	88SC	511	$ .01	$ .05	Parrish, Lance	89SC	95	$ .01	$ .05
Ontiveros, Steve	89SC	337	$ .01	$ .05	Parrish, Lance	89SCTR	36	$ .01	$ .10
Ontiveros, Steve	91SC	832	$ .01	$ .03	Parrish, Lance	90SC	35	$ .01	$ .05
Oquendo, Jose	88SC	248	$ .01	$ .10	Parrish, Lance	91SC	37	$ .01	$ .03
Oquendo, Jose	89SC	529	$ .01	$ .05	Parrish, Larry	88SC	191	$ .01	$ .05
Oquendo, Jose	90SC	68	$ .01	$ .05	Parrish, Larry	88SCTR	65	$ .01	$ .05

SCORE

Player	Year	No.	VG	EX/MT	Player	Year	No.	VG	EX/MT
Parrish, Larry	89SC	495	$ .01	$ .05	Pettis, Gary	90SCTR	6	$ .01	$ .05
Pasqua, Dan	88SC	196	$ .01	$ .05	Pettis, Gary	91SC	182	$ .01	$ .03
Pasqua, Dan	88SCTR	56	$ .01	$ .05	Phelps, Ken	88SC	256	$ .01	$ .05
Pasqua, Dan	89SC	338	$ .01	$ .05	Phelps, Ken	89SC	242	$ .01	$ .05
Pasqua, Dan	90SC	306	$ .01	$ .05	Philips, Tony	90SC	84	$ .01	$ .05
Pasqua, Dan	91SC	85	$ .01	$ .03	Phillips, Tony	88SC	294	$ .01	$ .05
Patterson, Bob	91SC	636	$ .01	$ .03	Phillips, Tony	89SC	156	$ .01	$ .05
Patterson, Ken	89SCTR	97	$ .01	$ .05	Phillips, Tony	90SCTR	14	$ .01	$ .05
Patterson, Ken	90SC	207	$ .01	$ .05	Phillips, Tony	91SC	38	$ .01	$ .03
Paul, Kilgus	90SC	196	$ .01	$ .05	Pico, Jeff	88SCTR	94	$ .01	$ .10
Pavlas, Dave	91SC	378	$ .01	$ .10	Pico, Jeff	89SC	13	$ .01	$ .05
Pawlowski, John	90SC	617	$ .01	$ .05	Pico, Jeff	90SC	428	$ .01	$ .05
Pecota, Bill	88SC	377	$ .01	$ .05	Pico, Jeff	91SC	326	$ .01	$ .03
Pecota, Bill	89SC	339	$ .01	$ .05	Pina, Mickey	90SCTR	104	$ .01	$ .25
Pecota, Bill	91SC	513	$ .01	$ .03	Plantier, Phil	91SC	348	$ .01	$ .50
Pedrique, Al	88SC	301	$ .01	$ .05	Plesac, Dan	88SC	77	$ .01	$ .05
Pedrique, Al	89SC	614	$ .01	$ .05	Plesac, Dan	89SC	320	$ .01	$ .05
Pena, Alejandro	89SC	389	$ .01	$ .05	Plesac, Dan	90SC	86	$ .01	$ .05
Pena, Alejandro	90SC	39	$ .01	$ .05	Plesac, Dan	91SC	275	$ .01	$ .03
Pena, Alejandro	90SCTR	32	$ .01	$ .05	Plunk, Eric	88SC	614	$ .01	$ .05
Pena, Alejandro	91SC	204	$ .01	$ .03	Plunk, Eric	89SC	392	$ .01	$ .05
Pena, Geronimo	91SC	717	$ .01	$ .10	Plunk, Eric	91SC	428	$ .01	$ .03
Pena, Tony	88SC	48	$ .01	$ .05	Polidor, Gus	88SC	341	$ .01	$ .05
Pena, Tony	89SC	36	$ .01	$ .05	Polonia, Luis	88SC	64	$ .04	$ .20
Pena, Tony	90SC	122	$ .01	$ .05	Polonia, Luis	89SC	380	$ .01	$ .10
Pena, Tony	90SCTR	7	$ .01	$ .05	Polonia, Luis	89SCTR	38	$ .01	$ .05
Pena, Tony	91SC	790	$ .01	$ .03	Polonia, Luis	90SC	442	$ .01	$ .05
Pendleton, Terry	88SC	190	$ .01	$ .05	Polonia, Luis	90SCTR	46	$ .01	$ .05
Pendleton, Terry	89SC	137	$ .01	$ .05	Polonia, Luis	91SC	587	$ .01	$ .03
Pendleton, Terry	90SC	208	$ .01	$ .05	Poole, Jim	91SC	357	$ .01	$ .10
Pendleton, Terry	91SC	230	$ .01	$ .03	Porter, Darrell	88SC	537	$ .01	$ .05
Peraza, Oswald	88SCTR	77	$ .01	$ .15	Portugal, Mark	89SC	482	$ .01	$ .05
Peraza, Oswald	89SC	571	$ .01	$ .15	Portugal, Mark	90SC	552	$ .01	$ .05
Perez, Melido	88SCTR	108	$ .01	$ .50	Portugal, Mark	91SC	319	$ .01	$ .03
Perez, Melido	89SC	386	$ .01	$ .15	Powell, Dennis	90SC	308	$ .01	$ .05
Perez, Melido	90SC	311	$ .01	$ .05	Power, Ted	88SC	242	$ .01	$ .05
Perez, Melido	91SC	179	$ .01	$ .03	Power, Ted	89SC	348	$ .01	$ .05
Perez, Melido	91SCNH	705	$ .01	$ .03	Power, Ted	91SC	255	$ .01	$ .03
Perez, Mike	91SC	758	$ .01	$ .03	Presley, Jim	88SC	46	$ .01	$ .10
Perez, Pascual	88SC	459	$ .01	$ .05	Presley, Jim	89SC	73	$ .01	$ .05
Perez, Pascual	89SC	299	$ .01	$ .05	Presley, Jim	90SC	34	$ .01	$ .05
Perez, Pascual	90SC	486	$ .01	$ .05	Presley, Jim	90SCTR	36	$ .01	$ .05
Perez, Pascual	90SCTR	5	$ .01	$ .05	Presley, Jim	91SC	771	$ .01	$ .03
Perezchica, Tony	91SC	735	$ .01	$ .03	Price, Joe	89SC	444	$ .01	$ .05
Perlman, Jon	89SC	591	$ .01	$ .05	Prince, Tom	89SC	626	$ .01	$ .10
Perry, Gerald	88SC	136	$ .01	$ .05	Puckett, Kirby	88SC	24	$ .04	$ .35
Perry, Gerald	89SC	101	$ .01	$ .05	Puckett, Kirby	88SC	653	$ .01	$ .15
Perry, Gerald	90SC	249	$ .01	$ .05	Puckett, Kirby	89SC	20	$ .01	$ .30
Perry, Gerald	90SCTR	28	$ .01	$ .05	Puckett, Kirby	90SC	400	$ .01	$ .15
Perry, Gerald	91SC	286	$ .01	$ .03	Puckett, Kirby	90SCDT	690	$ .01	$ .15
Perry, Pat	88SC	557	$ .01	$ .05	Puckett, Kirby	91SC	200	$ .01	$ .15
Perry, Pat	89SC	364	$ .01	$ .05	Puckett, Kirby	91SCDT	891	$ .01	$ .15
Perry, Pat	90SC	436	$ .01	$ .05	Puckett, Kirby	91SCTF	855	$ .01	$ .10
Perry, Pat	91SC	527	$ .01	$ .03	Puhl, Terry	88SC	282	$ .01	$ .05
Peters, Don	91SC	381	$ .01	$ .15	Puhl, Terry	89SC	567	$ .01	$ .05
Peterson, Adam	91SC	604	$ .01	$ .03	Puhl, Terry	90SC	473	$ .01	$ .05
Petralli, Geno	88SC	373	$ .01	$ .05	Puleo, Charlie	88SC	454	$ .01	$ .05
Petralli, Geno	89SC	526	$ .01	$ .05	Puleo, Charlie	89SC	448	$ .01	$ .05
Petralli, Geno	90SC	153	$ .01	$ .05	Quinones, Luis	90SC	499	$ .01	$ .05
Petralli, Geno	91SC	191	$ .01	$ .03	Quinones, Luis	91SC	822	$ .01	$ .03
Petry, Dan	88SC	461	$ .01	$ .05	Quinones, Rey	88SC	192	$ .01	$ .05
Petry, Dan	88SCTR	26	$ .01	$ .05	Quinones, Rey	89SC	361	$ .01	$ .05
Petry, Dan	89SC	122	$ .01	$ .05	Quintana, Carlos	89SC	623	$ .01	$ .35
Petry, Dan	90SC	211	$ .01	$ .05	Quintana, Carlos	90SC	658	$ .01	$ .10
Petry, Dan	90SCTR	39	$ .01	$ .05	Quintana, Carlos	91SC	149	$ .01	$ .03
Petry, Dan	91SC	434	$ .01	$ .03	Quirk, Jamie	88SC	577	$ .01	$ .05
Pettis, Gary	88SC	255	$ .01	$ .05	Quirk, Jamie	89SC	461	$ .01	$ .05
Pettis, Gary	88SCTR	38	$ .01	$ .05	Quisenberry, Dan	88SC	290	$ .01	$ .05
Pettis, Gary	89SC	26	$ .01	$ .05	Quisenberry, Dan	88SCTR	18	$ .01	$ .05
Pettis, Gary	90SC	136	$ .01	$ .05	Quisenberry, Dan	89SC	520	$ .01	$ .05

Player	Year	No.	VG	EX/MT
Quisenberry, Dan	90SC	475	$ .01	$ .05
Radinsky, Scott	90SCTR	90	$ .01	$ .20
Radinsky, Scott	91SC	62	$ .01	$ .10
Raines, Tim	88SC	3	$ .01	$ .15
Raines, Tim	88SC	649	$ .01	$ .15
Raines, Tim	89SC	40	$ .01	$ .15
Raines, Tim	90SC	409	$ .01	$ .05
Raines, Tim	91SC	35	$ .01	$ .03
Ramirez, Rafael	88SC	426	$ .01	$ .05
Ramirez, Rafael	88SCTR	12	$ .01	$ .05
Ramirez, Rafael	89SC	113	$ .01	$ .05
Ramirez, Rafael	90SC	42	$ .01	$ .05
Ramirez, Rafael	91SC	305	$ .01	$ .03
Ramos, Domingo	88SC	362	$ .01	$ .05
Ramos, Domingo	90SC	489	$ .01	$ .05
Ramsey, Mike	88SC	267	$ .01	$ .05
Randolph, Willie	88SC	266	$ .01	$ .05
Randolph, Willie	89SC	45	$ .01	$ .05
Randolph, Willie	89SCTR	41	$ .01	$ .10

Player	Year	No.	VG	EX/MT
Randolph, Willie	90SC	395	$ .01	$ .05
Randolph, Willie	90SCTR	51	$ .01	$ .05
Randolph, Willie	91SC	194	$ .01	$ .03
Rasmussen, Dennis	88SC	560	$ .01	$ .05
Rasmussen, Dennis	89SC	562	$ .01	$ .05
Rasmussen, Dennis	90SC	129	$ .01	$ .05
Rasmussen, Dennis	91SC	457	$ .01	$ .03
Rawley, Shane	88SC	375	$ .01	$ .05
Rawley, Shane	89SC	170	$ .01	$ .05
Rawley, Shane	90SC	71	$ .01	$ .05
Ray, Johnny	88SC	254	$ .01	$ .05
Ray, Johnny	89SC	14	$ .01	$ .05
Ray, Johnny	90SC	293	$ .01	$ .05
Ray, Johnny	91SC	31	$ .01	$ .03
Rayford, Floyd	88SC	359	$ .01	$ .05
Ready, Randy	88SC	512	$ .01	$ .05
Ready, Randy	89SC	426	$ .01	$ .05
Ready, Randy	89SCTR	60	$ .01	$ .05
Ready, Randy	90SC	376	$ .01	$ .05
Ready, Randy	91SC	615	$ .01	$ .03
Reardon, Jeff	88SC	91	$ .01	$ .05

Player	Year	No.	VG	EX/MT
Reardon, Jeff	89SC	305	$ .01	$ .05
Reardon, Jeff	90SC	522	$ .01	$ .05
Reardon, Jeff	90SCTR	17	$ .01	$ .05
Reardon, Jeff	91SC	164	$ .01	$ .03
Redus, Gary	88SC	443	$ .01	$ .05
Redus, Gary	89SC	177	$ .01	$ .05
Redus, Gary	90SC	14	$ .01	$ .05
Redus, Gary	91SC	226	$ .01	$ .03
Reed, Darren	91SC	368	$ .01	$ .10
Reed, Jeff	88SC	408	$ .01	$ .05
Reed, Jeff	89SC	99	$ .01	$ .05
Reed, Jeff	90SC	147	$ .01	$ .05
Reed, Jerry	88SC	488	$ .01	$ .05
Reed, Jerry	89SC	427	$ .01	$ .05
Reed, Jerry	90SC	492	$ .01	$ .05
Reed, Jody	88SC	625	$ .01	$ .50
Reed, Jody	89SC	486	$ .01	$ .15
Reed, Jody	90SC	11	$ .01	$ .05
Reed, Jody	91SC	173	$ .01	$ .03
Reed, Rick	90SC	544	$ .01	$ .05
Reed, Rick	91SC	584	$ .01	$ .03
Reimer, Kevin	91SC	836	$ .01	$ .10
Renteria, Rich	89SC	142	$ .01	$ .05
Reuschel, Rick	88SC	519	$ 01	$ .05
Reuschel, Rick	89SC	5	$ .01	$ .05
Reuschel, Rick	90SC	465	$ .01	$ .05
Reuschel, Rick	91SC	544	$ .01	$ .03
Reuss, Jerry	88SC	270	$ .01	$ .05
Reuss, Jerry	88SCTR	61	$ .01	$ .05
Reuss, Jerry	89SC	489	$ .01	$ .05
Reynolds, Craig	88SC	207	$ .01	$ .05
Reynolds, Craig	89SC	468	$ .01	$ .05
Reynolds, Harold	88SC	277	$ .01	$ .05
Reynolds, Harold	89SC	310	$ .01	$ .05
Reynolds, Harold	90SC	167	$ .01	$ .05
Reynolds, Harold	91SC	48	$ .01	$ .03
Reynolds, R. J.	88SC	34	$ .01	$ .05
Reynolds, R. J.	89SC	91	$ .01	$ .05
Reynolds, R. J.	90SC	469	$ .01	$ .05
Reynolds, R. J.	91SC	273	$ .01	$ .03
Rhoden, Rick	88SC	74	$ .01	$ .05
Rhoden, Rick	89SC	317	$ .01	$ .05
Rhodes, Karl	91SC	365	$ .01	$ .15
Rice, Jim	88SC	14	$ .01	$ .10
Rice, Jim	89SC	85	$ .01	$ .10
Righetti, Dave	88SC	351	$ .01	$ .05
Righetti, Dave	89SC	225	$ .01	$ .05
Righetti, Dave	90SC	194	$ .01	$ .05
Righetti, Dave	91SC	24	$ .01	$ .03
Rijo, Jose	88SC	392	$ .01	$ .15
Rijo, Jose	88SCTR	27	$ .01	$ .15
Rijo, Jose	89SC	552	$ .01	$ .15
Rijo, Jose	90SC	511	$ .01	$ .05
Rijo, Jose	91SC	658	$ .01	$ .03
Riles, Ernest	88SC	349	$ .01	$ .05
Riles, Ernest	88SCTR	57	$ .01	$ .05
Riles, Ernest	89SC	458	$ .01	$ .05
Riles, Ernest	90SC	447	$ .01	$ .05
Riles, Ernest	91SC	626	$ .01	$ .03
Ripken, Bill	88SC	200	$ .05	$ .25
Ripken, Bill	89SC	18	$ .01	$ .05
Ripken, Bill	90SC	174	$ .01	$ .05
Ripken, Bill	91SC	487	$ .01	$ .03
Ripken, Jr., Cal	88SC	550	$ .04	$ .20
Ripken, Jr., Cal	88SC	651	$ .01	$ .10
Ripken, Jr., Cal	89SC	15	$ .01	$ .10
Ripken, Jr., Cal	90SC	2	$ .01	$ .15
Ripken, Jr., Cal	91SC	95	$ .01	$ .10
Ripken, Jr., Cal	91SCTF	849	$ .01	$ .10
Ritchie, Todd	91SC	678	$ .01	$ .15

SCORE

Player	Year	No.	VG	EX/MT
Ritchie, Wally	88SC	526	$ .01	$ .05
Ritz, Kevin	90SC	572	$ .01	$ .05
Rivera, Luis	89SC	169	$ .01	$ .05
Rivera, Luis	91SC	271	$ .01	$ .03
Roberts, Bip	90SC	51	$ .01	$ .05
Roberts, Bip	91SC	28	$ .01	$ .03
Robidoux, Billy Jo	88SC	334	$ .01	$ .05
Robinson, Don	88SC	618	$ .01	$ .05
Robinson, Don	89SC	440	$ .01	$ .05
Robinson, Don	90SC	112	$ .01	$ .05
Robinson, Don	91SC	639	$ .01	$ .03
Robinson, Jeff	91SC	129	$ .01	$ .03
Robinson, Jeff	91SC	192	$ .01	$ .03
Robinson, Jeff (Detroit)	88SC	549	$ .01	$ .15
Robinson, Jeff(Detroit)	89SC	284	$ .01	$ .05
Robinson, Jeff(Detroit)	90SC	333	$ .01	$
.05Robinson, Jeff (Pirates)	88SC	439	$ .01	$ .05
Robinson, Jeff(Pirates)	89SC	309	$ .01	$ .05
Robinson, Ron	88SC	476	$ .01	$ .05
Robinson, Ron	89SC	559	$ .01	$ .05
Robinson, Ron	90SC	495	$ .01	$ .05
Robinson, Ron	91SC	517	$ .01	$ .03
Rochford, Mike	91SC	739	$ .01	$ .03
Rodriguez, Rich	91SC	593	$ .01	$ .10
Rodriguez, Rosario	91SC	373	$ .01	$ .10
Roenicke, Gary	88SC	482	$ .01	$ .05
Roenicke, Ron	88SC	566	$ .01	$ .05
Roesler, Mike	90SC	648	$ .01	$ .05
Rogers, Kenny	89SCTR	107	$ .01	$ .15
Rogers, Kenny	90SC	301	$ .01	$ .05
Rogers, Kenny	91SC	155	$ .01	$ .03
Rojas, Mel	91SC	729	$ .01	$ .03
Romero, Ed	88SC	259	$ .01	$ .05
Romine, Kevin	88SC	644	$ .01	$ .05
Romine, Kevin	89SC	541	$ .01	$ .05
Romine, Kevin	90SC	458	$ .01	$ .05
Romine, Kevin	91SC	116	$ .01	$ .03
Roomes, Rolando	89SCTR	109	$ .01	$ .10
Roomes, Rolando	90SC	417	$ .01	$ .05
Rose, Bobby	90SC	604	$ .01	$ .25
Rosenberg, Steve	90SC	523	$ .01	$ .05
Ruffin, Bruce	88SC	492	$ .01	$ .05
Ruffin, Bruce	89SC	328	$ .01	$ .05
Ruffin, Bruce	91SC	524	$ .01	$ .03
Ruskin, Scott	91SC	799	$ .01	$ .03
Russell, Jeff	88SC	514	$ .01	$ .05
Russell, Jeff	89SC	438	$ .01	$ .05
Russell, Jeff	90SC	263	$ .01	$ .05
Russell, Jeff	91SC	277	$ .01	$ .03
Russell, John	91SC	802	$ .01	$ .03
Ryan, Nolan	88SC	575	$ .01	$ .75
Ryan, Nolan	89SC	300	$ .01	$ .50
Ryan, Nolan	89SCTR	2	$ .01	$1.50
Ryan, Nolan	90SC	250	$ .01	$ .35
Ryan, Nolan	90SC	696	$ .01	$ .35
Ryan, Nolan	91SC	4	$ .01	$ .25
Ryan, Nolan	91SCBC	7	$ .01	$1.00
Ryan, Nolan	91SCHL	417	$ .01	$ .25
Ryan, Nolan	91SCKM	686	$ .01	$ .25
Ryan, Nolan	91SCNH	701	$ .01	$ .25
Saberhagen, Bret	88SC	89	$ .05	$ .15
Saberhagen, Bret	89SC	251	$ .01	$ .10
Saberhagen, Bret	90SC	195	$ .01	$ .10
Saberhagen, Bret	91SC	6	$ .01	$ .03
Sabo, Chris	88SCTR	100	$ .25	$4.00
Sabo, Chris	89SC	104	$ .15	$ .75
Sabo, Chris	90SC	70	$ .01	$ .20
Sabo, Chris	91SC	462	$ .01	$ .03
Salas, Mark	88SC	232	$ .01	$ .05
Salas, Mark	88SCTR	52	$ .01	$ .05
Salas, Mark	89SC	542	$ .01	$ .05
Salazar, Angel	88SC	330	$ .01	$ .05
Salazar, Angel	89SC	527	$ .01	$ .05
Salazar, Luis	88SC	284	$ .01	$ .05
Salazar, Luis	88SCTR	13	$ .01	$ .05
Salazar, Luis	89SC	316	$ .01	$ .05
Salazar, Luis	90SC	92	$ .01	$ .05
Salazar, Luis	91SC	207	$ .01	$ .03
Salkeld, Roger	90SC	674	$ .01	$ .50
Sambito, Joe	88SC	314	$ .01	$ .05
Sampen, Bill	90SCTR	79	$ .01	$ .20
Sampen, Bill	91SC	68	$ .01	$ .15
Samuel, Juan	88SC	32	$ .01	$ .05
Samuel, Juan	89SC	255	$ .01	$ .05
Samuel, Juan	89SCTR	21	$ .01	$ .05
Samuel, Juan	90SC	198	$ .01	$ .05
Samuel, Juan	90SCTR	33	$ .01	$ .05
Samuel, Juan	91SC	446	$ .01	$ .03
Sandberg, Ryne	88SC	26	$ .01	$ .35
Sandberg, Ryne	89SC	35	$ .01	$ .25
Sandberg, Ryne	90SC	90	$ .01	$ .20
Sandberg, Ryne	90SC	561	$ .01	$ .20
Sandberg, Ryne	90SCDT	691	$ .01	$ .10
Sandberg, Ryne	91SC	3	$ .01	$ .15
Sandberg, Ryne	91SC	815	$ .01	$ .15
Sandberg, Ryne	91SCAS	665	$ .01	$ .15
Sandberg, Ryne	91SCTF	862	$ .01	$ .15
Sanders, Deion	90SC	586	$ .01	$ .25
Sanderson, Scott	88SC	544	$ .01	$ .05
Sanderson, Scott	90SC	488	$ .01	$ .05
Sanderson, Scott	90SCTR	61	$ .01	$ .05
Sanderson, Scott	91SC	118	$ .01	$ .03
Santana, Andres	91SC	762	$ .01	$ .03
Santana, Rafael	88SC	316	$ .01	$ .05
Santana, Rafael	88SCTR	54	$ .01	$ .05
Santana, Rafael	89SC	296	$ .01	$ .05
Santiago, Benny	88SC	25	$ .01	$ .25
Santiago, Benny	88SC	654	$ .01	$ .10
Santiago, Benny	89SC	4	$ .01	$ .10
Santiago, Benny	90SC	454	$ .01	$ .05
Santiago, Benny	91SC	810	$ .01	$ .03
Santiago, Benny	91SCAS	663	$ .01	$ .03
Santiago, Benny	91SCDT	893	$ .01	$ .10
Santiago, Benny	91SCRM	416	$ .01	$ .05
Santiago, Benny	91SCTF	879	$ .01	$ .03
Santovenia, Nelson	88SCTR	96	$ .01	$ .35
Santovenia, Nelson	89SC	346	$ .01	$ .15
Santovenia, Nelson	90SC	451	$ .01	$ .05
Santovenia, Nelson	91SC	777	$ .01	$ .03
Sasser, Mackey	88SC	642	$ .01	$ .05
Sasser, Mackey	88SCTR	30	$ .01	$ .05
Sasser, Mackey	89SC	303	$ .01	$ .05
Sasser, Mackey	90SC	510	$ .01	$ .05
Sasser, Mackey	91SC	307	$ .01	$ .03
Sax, Steve	88SC	35	$ .01	$ .10
Sax, Steve	89SC	69	$ .01	$ .10
Sax, Steve	89SCTR	20	$ .01	$ .10
Sax, Steve	90SC	125	$ .01	$ .10
Sax, Steve	91SC	32	$ .01	$ .03
Schatzeder, Dan	90SC	418	$ .01	$ .05
Schilling, Curt	90SC	581	$ .01	$ .05
Schilling, Curt	91SC	788	$ .01	$ .03
Schiraldi, Calvin	88SC	218	$ .01	$ .05
Schiraldi, Calvin	88SCTR	39	$ .01	$ .05
Schiraldi, Calvin	89SC	321	$ .01	$ .05
Schiraldi, Calvin	91SC	611	$ .01	$ .03
Schmidt, Dave	88SC	103	$ .01	$ .05
Schmidt, Dave	89SC	292	$ .01	$ .05
Schmidt, Dave	90SC	30	$ .01	$ .05
Schmidt, Dave	91SC	156	$ .01	$ .03

Player	Year	No.	VG	EX/MT	Player	Year	No.	VG	EX/MT
Schmidt, Mike	88SC	16	$ .04	$ .35	Sierra, Ruben	90SC	420	$ .01	$ .20
Schmidt, Mike	88SC	657	$ .04	$ .25	Sierra, Ruben	91SC	495	$ .01	$ .10
Schmidt, Mike	89SC	149	$ .01	$ .35	Sierra, Ruben	91SCTF	859	$ .01	$ .03
Schofield, Dick	88SC	274	$ .01	$ .05	Simmons, Ted	88SC	285	$ .01	$ .05
Schofield, Dick	89SC	16	$ .01	$ .05	Simmons, Ted	89SC	611	$ .01	$ .05
Schofield, Dick	90SC	44	$ .01	$ .05	Simms, Mike	91SC	766	$ .01	$ .03
Schofield, Dick	91SC	776	$ .01	$ .03	Sisk, Doug	88SC	227	$ .01	$ .05
Schooler, Mike	88SCTR	91	$ .01	$ .50	Sisk, Doug	89SC	264	$ .01	$ .05
Schooler, Mike	89SC	528	$ .01	$ .25	Skalski, Joe	90SC	618	$ .01	$ .05
Schooler, Mike	90SC	149	$ .01	$ .05	Skinner, Joel	88SC	532	$ .01	$ .05
Schooler, Mike	91SC	489	$ .01	$ .03	Skinner, Joel	89SC	447	$ .01	$ .05
Schroeder, Bill	88SC	311	$ .01	$ .05	Skinner, Joel	89SCTR	76	$ .01	$ .05
Schroeder, Bill	90SC	362	$ .01	$ .05	Skinner, Joel	91SC	809	$ .01	$ .03
Schrom, Ken	88SC	574	$ .01	$ .05	Slaught, Don	88SC	268	$ .01	$ .05
Schu, Rick	88SC	448	$ .01	$ .05	Slaught, Don	88SCTR	19	$ .01	$ .05
Schu, Rick	89SC	452	$ .01	$ .05	Slaught, Don	89SC	561	$ .01	$ .05
Schulz, Jeff	91SC	336	$ .01	$ .15	Slaught, Don	90SC	79	$ .01	$ .05
Scioscia, Mike	88SC	53	$ .01	$ .05	Slaught, Don	90SCTR	13	$ .01	$ .05
Scioscia, Mike	89SC	121	$ .01	$ .05	Slaught, Don	91SC	610	$ .01	$ .03
Scioscia, Mike	90SC	398	$ .01	$ .05	Smalley, Roy	88SC	606	$ .01	$ .05
Scioscia, Mike	91SC	520	$ .01	$ .03	Smiley, John	88SC	287	$ .05	$ .30
Scott, Mike	88SC	335	$ .01	$ .05	Smiley, John	89SC	409	$ .01	$ .10
Scott, Mike	89SC	550	$ .01	$ .05	Smiley, John	90SC	334	$ .01	$ .10
Scott, Mike	90SC	40	$ .01	$ .05	Smiley, John	91SC	465	$ .01	$ .03
Scott, Mike	90SCDT	692	$ .01	$ .10	Smith, Bryn	88SC	356	$ .01	$ .05
Scott, Mike	91SC	46	$ .01	$ .03	Smith, Bryn	89SC	428	$ .01	$ .05
Scudder, Scott	89SCTR	99	$ .01	$ .35	Smith, Bryn	90SC	419	$ .01	$ .05
Scudder, Scott	90SC	518	$ .01	$ .15	Smith, Bryn	90SCTR	55	$ .01	$ .05
Scudder, Scott	91SC	642	$ .01	$ .03	Smith, Bryn	91SC	444	$ .01	$ .03
Scurry, Rod	89SC	516	$ .01	$ .05	Smith, Dan	91SC	384	$ .01	$ .15
Searcy, Steve	89SC	627	$ .01	$ .20	Smith, Dave	88SC	365	$ .01	$ .05
Searcy, Steve	91SC	649	$ .01	$ .03	Smith, Dave	89SC	245	$ .01	$ .05
Sebra, Bob	88SC	337	$ .01	$ .05	Smith, Dave	90SC	45	$ .01	$ .05
Segui, David	90SCTR	95	$ .01	$ .10	Smith, Dave	91SC	314	$ .01	$ .03
Segui, David	91SC	362	$ .01	$ .20	Smith, Dwight	89SC	642	$ .01	$ .50
Seitzer, Kevin	88SC	6	$ .05	$ .25	Smith, Dwight	90SC	240	$ .01	$ .10
Seitzer, Kevin	89SC	55	$ .01	$ .10	Smith, Dwight	91SC	301	$ .01	$ .03
Seitzer, Kevin	90SC	199	$ .01	$ .05	Smith, Greg	90SC	614	$ .01	$ .05
Seitzer, Kevin	91SC	279	$ .01	$ .03					
Sellers, Jeff	88SC	541	$ .01	$ .05					
Sellers, Jeff	89SC	491	$ .01	$ .05					
Sharperson, Mike	89SC	602	$ .01	$ .05					
Sharperson, Mike	91SC	546	$ .01	$ .03					
Shaw, Jeff	91SC	746	$ .01	$ .10					
Sheets, Larry	88SC	219	$ .01	$ .05					
Sheets, Larry	89SC	81	$ .01	$ .05					
Sheets, Larry	90SC	111	$ .01	$ .05					
Sheets, Larry	90SCTR	65	$ .01	$ .05					
Sheets, Larry	91SC	176	$ .01	$ .03					
Sheffield, Gary	89SC	625	$ .25	$1.25					
Sheffield, Gary	90SC	97	$ .01	$ .30					
Sheffield, Gary	91SC	473	$ .01	$ .03					
Shelby, John	88SC	286	$ .01	$ .10					
Shelby, John	89SC	103	$ .01	$ .05					
Shelby, John	91SC	609	$ .01	$ .03					
Sheridan, Pat	88SC	171	$ .01	$ .05					
Sheridan, Pat	89SC	204	$ .01	$ .05					
Sheridan, Pat	89SCTR	71	$ .01	$ .05					
Sheridan, Pat	90SC	509	$ .01	$ .05					
Shields, Steve	88SC	396	$ .01	$ .05					
Shields, Steve	88SCTR	47	$ .01	$ .05					
Shields, Steve	89SC	578	$ .01	$ .05					
Show, Eric	88SC	338	$ .01	$ .05					
Show, Eric	89SC	254	$ .01	$ .05					
Show, Eric	90SC	493	$ .01	$ .05					
Show, Eric	91SC	563	$ .01	$ .03					
Shumpert, Terry	90SCTR	110	$ .01	$ .15					
Shumpert, Terry	91SC	349	$ .01	$ .10					
Sierra, Ruben	88SC	113	$ .05	$ .50	Smith, Lee	88SC	31	$ .01	$ .05
Sierra, Ruben	89SC	43	$ .01	$ .20	Smith, Lee	88SCTR	20	$ .01	$ .10

LEE SMITH
RP

SCORE

Player	Year	No.	VG	EX/MT	Player	Year	No.	VG	EX/MT
Smith, Lee	89SC	150	$ .01	$ .05	Soto, Mario	89SC	588	$ .01	$ .05
Smith, Lee	90SC	37	$ .01	$ .05	Speier, Chris	88SC	493	$ .01	$ .05
Smith, Lee	90SCTR	48	$ .01	$ .05	Speier, Chris	89SC	297	$ .01	$ .05
Smith, Lee	91SC	81	$ .01	$ .03	Spiers, Bill	89SCTR	82	$ .01	$ .25
Smith, Lonnie	88SC	263	$ .01	$ .05	Spiers, Bill	90SC	449	$ .01	$ .15
Smith, Lonnie	90SC	399	$ .01	$ .05	Spiers, Bill	91SC	84	$ .01	$ .03
Smith, Lonnie	91SC	543	$ .01	$ .03	Spilman, Harry	88SC	619	$ .01	$ .05
Smith, Mike	90SC	635	$ .01	$ .05	St. Claire, Randy	88SC	397	$ .01	$ .05
Smith, Ozzie	88SC	12	$ .01	$ .10	Stanicek, Pete	88SC	628	$ .01	$ .05
Smith, Ozzie	89SC	80	$ .01	$ .10	Stanicek, Pete	89SC	236	$ .01	$ .05
Smith, Ozzie	90SC	285	$ .01	$ .05	Stanley, Bob	88SC	300	$ .01	$ .05
Smith, Ozzie	91SC	825	$ .01	$ .03	Stanley, Bob	89SC	383	$ .01	$ .05
Smith, Pete	88SCTR	84	$ .01	$ .05	Stanley, Mike	88SC	47	$ .01	$ .05
Smith, Pete	89SC	207	$ .01	$ .05	Stanley, Mike	89SC	241	$ .01	$ .05
Smith, Pete	90SC	225	$ .01	$ .05	Stanley, Mike	91SC	92	$ .01	$ .03
Smith, Pete	91SC	205	$ .01	$ .03	Stanton, Mike	90SC	609	$ .01	$ .10
Smith, Roy	90SC	568	$ .01	$ .05	Stanton, Mike	91SC	468	$ .01	$ .03
Smith, Roy	91SC	151	$ .01	$ .03	Stapleton, Dave	89SC	581	$ .01	$ .10
Smith, Zane	88SC	410	$ .01	$ .05	Stark, Matt	91SC	751	$ .01	$ .20
Smith, Zane	89SC	492	$ .01	$ .05	Steinbach, Terry	88SC	82	$ .01	$ .15
Smith, Zane	89SCTR	56	$ .01	$ .05	Steinbach, Terry	89SC	365	$ .01	$ .10
Smith, Zane	90SC	477	$ .01	$ .05	Steinbach, Terry	90SC	162	$ .01	$ .10
Smith, Zane	91SC	845	$ .01	$ .03	Steinbach, Terry	90SCDT	693	$ .01	$ .10
Smithson, Mike	88SCTR	59	$ .01	$ .05	Steinbach, Terry	91SC	780	$ .01	$ .03
Smithson, Mike	89SC	403	$ .01	$ .05	Stephens, Ray	91SC	743	$ .01	$ .03
Smithson, Mike	90SC	512	$ .01	$ .05	Stephenson, Phil	90SC	642	$ .01	$ .05
Smoltz, John	89SC	616	$ .01	$ .40	Stephenson, Phil	91SC	138	$ .01	$ .03
Smoltz, John	90SC	370	$ .01	$ .15	Stevens, Lee	91SC	67	$ .01	$ .15
Smoltz, John	91SC	208	$ .01	$ .03	Stewart, Dave	88SC	458	$ .01	$ .15
Snider, Van	89SC	640	$ .01	$ .15	Stewart, Dave	89SC	32	$ .01	$ .10
Snyder, Cory	88SC	92	$ .01	$ .10	Stewart, Dave	90SC	410	$ .01	$ .10
Snyder, Cory	89SC	52	$ .01	$ .15	Stewart, Dave	91SC	150	$ .01	$ .10
Snyder, Cory	90SC	10	$ .01	$ .05	Stewart, Dave	91SCDT	883	$ .01	$ .03
Snyder, Cory	91SC	19	$ .01	$ .03	Stewart, Dave	91SCNH	702	$ .01	$ .03
Snyder, Cory	91SCRM	695	$ .01	$ .03	Stieb, Dave	88SC	76	$ .01	$ .05
Sojo, Luis	91SC	342	$ .01	$ .03	Stieb, Dave	89SC	197	$ .01	$ .05
Sorrento, Paul	90SC	647	$ .01	$ .15	Stieb, Dave	90SC	201	$ .01	$ .05
Sorrento, Paul	91SC	796	$ .01	$ .03	Stieb, Dave	91SC	30	$ .01	$ .03
					Stieb, Dave	91SCNH	707	$ .01	$ .03
					Stillwell, Kurt	88SC	221	$ .01	$ .05
					Stillwell, Kurt	88SCTR	4	$ .01	$ .05
					Stillwell, Kurt	89SC	162	$ .01	$ .05
					Stillwell, Kurt	90SC	96	$ .01	$ .05
					Stillwell, Kurt	91SC	295	$ .01	$ .03
					Stoddard, Tim	88SC	258	$ .01	$ .05
					Stottlemyre, Jr., Mel	91SC	361	$ .01	$ .15
					Stottlemyre, Todd	88SCTR	90	$ .01	$ .50
					Stottlemyre, Todd	89SC	453	$ .01	$ .15
					Stottlemyre, Todd	90SC	554	$ .01	$ .05
					Stottlemyre, Todd	91SC	39	$ .01	$ .03
					Straker, Les	88SC	108	$ .01	$ .05
					Straker, Les	89SC	244	$ .01	$ .05
					Strawberry, Darryl	88SC	360	$ .06	$ .35
					Strawberry, Darryl	89SC	10	$ .01	$ .25
					Strawberry, Darryl	90SC	200	$ .01	$ .20
					Strawberry, Darryl	91SC	640	$ .01	$ .15
					Strawberry, Darryl	91SCMB	691	$ .01	$ .15
					Strawberry, Darryl	91SCTF	864	$ .01	$ .15
					Stubbs, Franklin	88SC	147	$ .01	$ .05
					Stubbs, Franklin	89SC	599	$ .01	$ .05
					Stubbs, Franklin	90SC	478	$ .01	$ .05
					Stubbs, Franklin	90SCTR	40	$ .01	$ .05
					Stubbs, Franklin	91SC	308	$ .01	$ .03
					Sullivan, Marc	88SC	271	$ .01	$ .05
					Sundberg, Jim	88SC	244	$ .01	$ .05
					Surhoff, B. J.	88SC	22	$ .01	$ .15
					Surhoff, B. J.	89SC	154	$ .01	$ .10
					Surhoff, B. J.	90SC	74	$ .01	$ .05
Sosa, Sammy	90SC	558	$ .01	$ .75	Surhoff, B. J.	91SC	477	$ .01	$ .03
Sosa, Sammy	91SC	256	$ .01	$ .15	Sutcliffe, Rick	88SC	50	$ .01	$ .10

SAMMY SOSA OF

Player	Year	No.	VG	EX/MT	Player	Year	No.	VG	EX/MT
Sutcliffe, Rick	89SC	407	$ .01	$ .05	Thomas, Frank	91SCTF	874	$ .01	$ .75
Sutcliffe, Rick	90SC	450	$ .01	$ .05	Thompson, Milt	88SC	115	$ .01	$ .10
Sutcliffe, Rick	91SC	785	$ .01	$ .03	Thompson, Milt	89SC	92	$ .01	$ .05
Sutko, Glenn	91SC	767	$ .01	$ .03	Thompson, Milt	89SCTR	45	$ .01	$ .05
Sutter, Bruce	89SC	425	$ .01	$ .05	Thompson, Milt	90SC	49	$ .01	$ .05
Sutton, Don	88SC	105	$ .01	$ .10	Thompson, Milt	91SC	54	$ .01	$ .03
Sutton, Don	89SC	400	$ .01	$ .10	Thompson, Robby	88SC	146	$ .01	$ .05
Sveum, Dale	88SC	120	$ .01	$ .05	Thompson, Robby	89SC	172	$ .01	$ .05
Sveum, Dale	89SC	256	$ .01	$ .05	Thompson, Robby	90SC	397	$ .01	$ .05
Sveum, Dale	91SC	814	$ .01	$ .03	Thompson, Robby	91SC	26	$ .01	$ .03
Swift, Bill	89SC	219	$ .01	$ .05	Thon, Dickie	88SCTR	29	$ .01	$ .05
Swift, Bill	91SC	123	$ .01	$ .03	Thon, Dickie	89SC	234	$ .01	$ .05
Swindell, Greg	88SC	154	$ .05	$ .40	Thon, Dickie	89SCTR	55	$ .01	$ .05
Swindell, Greg	89SC	282	$ .01	$ .15	Thon, Dickie	90SC	142	$ .01	$ .05
Swindell, Greg	90SC	230	$ .01	$ .10	Thon, Dickie	91SC	103	$ .01	$ .03
Swindell, Greg	91SC	110	$ .01	$ .03	Thornton, Andre	88SC	231	$ .01	$ .05
Tabler, Pat	88SC	23	$ .01	$ .05	Thurman, Gary	88SC	631	$ .01	$ .15
Tabler, Pat	88SCTR	22	$ .01	$ .05	Thurmond, Mark	88SC	382	$ .01	$ .05
Tabler, Pat	89SC	391	$ .01	$ .05	Thurmond, Mark	90SC	350	$ .01	$ .05
Tabler, Pat	90SC	242	$ .01	$ .05	Tibbs, Jay	88SC	608	$ .01	$ .05
Tabler, Pat	91SC	811	$ .01	$ .03	Tibbs, Jay	89SC	262	$ .01	$ .05
Tanana, Frank	88SC	490	$ .01	$ .05	Tibbs, Jay	90SC	480	$ .01	$ .05
Tanana, Frank	89SC	112	$ .01	$ .05	Toliver, Fred	89SC	479	$ .01	$ .05
Tanana, Frank	90SC	57	$ .01	$ .05	Tolleson, Wayne	88SC	117	$ .01	$ .05
Tanana, Frank	91SC	328	$ .01	$ .03	Tolleson, Wayne	90SC	386	$ .01	$ .05
Tapani, Kevin	90SCTR	82	$ .01	$ .25	Tomlin, Randy	91SC	782	$ .01	$ .03
Tapani, Kevin	91SC	60	$ .01	$ .03	Torve, Kelvin	91SC	754	$ .01	$ .03
Tartabull, Danny	88SC	106	$ .01	$ .15	Traber, Jim	89SC	590	$ .01	$ .05
Tartabull, Danny	89SC	105	$ .01	$ .15	Trammell, Alan	88SC	37	$ .04	$ .15
Tartabull, Danny	90SC	244	$ .01	$ .05	Trammell, Alan	88SC	651	$ .01	$ .10
Tartabull, Danny	91SC	515	$ .01	$ .03	Trammell, Alan	89SC	110	$ .01	$ .10
Tekulve, Kent	88SC	425	$ .01	$ .05	Trammell, Alan	90SC	9	$ .01	$ .10
Tekulve, Kent	89SC	287	$ .01	$ .05	Trammell, Alan	91SC	40	$ .01	$ .10
Telford, Anthony	91SC	354	$ .01	$ .10	Trammell, Alan	91SCTF	852	$ .01	$ .03
Templeton, Garry	88SC	189	$ .01	$ .05	Treadway, Jeff	88SC	646	$ .05	$ .25
Templeton, Garry	89SC	176	$ .01	$ .05	Treadway, Jeff	89SC	86	$ .01	$ .10
Templeton, Garry	90SC	336	$ .01	$ .05	Treadway, Jeff	89SCTR	18	$ .01	$ .05
Templeton, Garry	91SC	117	$ .01	$ .03	Treadway, Jeff	90SC	95	$ .01	$ .05
Terrell, Walt	88SC	538	$ .01	$ .05	Treadway, Jeff	91SC	219	$ .01	$ .03
Terrell, Walt	89SC	314	$ .01	$ .05	Trevino, Alex	88SC	182	$ .01	$ .05
Terrell, Walt	89SCTR	75	$ .01	$ .05	Trevino, Alex	89SC	574	$ .01	$ .05
Terrell, Walt	90SC	463	$ .01	$ .05	Trillo, Manny	88SC	524	$ .01	$ .05
Terrell, Walt	91SC	801	$ .01	$ .03	Trillo, Manny	89SC	446	$ .01	$ .05
Terry, Scott	89SC	397	$ .01	$ .05	Trout, Steve	88SC	342	$ .01	$ .05
Terry, Scott	90SC	235	$ .01	$ .05	Trout, Steve	89SC	522	$ .01	$ .05
Terry, Scott	91SC	247	$ .01	$ .03	Tudor, John	88SC	275	$ .01	$ .05
Tettleton, Mickey	88SC	269	$ .01	$ .05	Tudor, John	89SC	560	$ .01	$ .05
Tettleton, Mickey	88SCTR	31	$ .01	$ .05	Tudor, John	91SC	53	$ .01	$ .03
Tettleton, Mickey	89SC	358	$ .01	$ .05	Tunnell, Lee	88SC	587	$ .01	$ .05
Tettleton, Mickey	90SC	322	$ .01	$ .05	Upshaw, Willie	88SC	279	$ .01	$ .05
Tettleton, Mickey	91SC	270	$ .01	$ .03	Upshaw, Willie	88SCTR	42	$ .01	$ .05
Teufel, Tim	88SC	128	$ .01	$ .05	Upshaw, Willie	89SC	188	$ .01	$ .05
Teufel, Tim	89SC	58	$ .01	$ .05	Uribe, Jose	88SC	165	$ .01	$ .05
Teufel, Tim	90SC	501	$ .01	$ .05	Uribe, Jose	89SC	56	$ .01	$ .05
Teufel, Tim	91SC	427	$ .01	$ .03	Uribe, Jose	90SC	455	$ .01	$ .05
Tewksbury, Bob	91SC	499	$ .01	$ .03	Uribe, Jose	91SC	628	$ .01	$ .03
Thigpen, Bobby	88SC	307	$ .01	$ .15	Valdez, Efrain	91SC	723	$ .01	$ .03
Thigpen, Bobby	89SC	399	$ .01	$ .05	Valdez, Rafael	90SCTR	93	$ .01	$ .15
Thigpen, Bobby	90SC	335	$ .01	$ .05	Valdez, Rafael	91SC	360	$ .01	$ .03
Thigpen, Bobby	90SCDT	694	$ .01	$ .10	Valenzuela, Fernando	88SC	600	$ .01	$ .10
Thigpen, Bobby	91SC	280	$ .01	$ .03	Valenzuela, Fernando	89SC	437	$ .01	$ .10
Thigpen, Bobby	91SCAS	401	$ .01	$ .03	Valenzuela, Fernando	90SC	54	$ .01	$ .05
Thigpen, Bobby	91SCHL	418	$ .01	$ .05	Valenzuela, Fernando	91SC	449	$ .01	$ .03
Thomas, Andres	88SC	299	$ .01	$ .05	Valenzuela, Fernando	91SCNH	703	$ .01	$ .03
Thomas, Andres	89SC	406	$ .01	$ .05	Valera, Julio	91SC	353	$ .01	$ .15
Thomas, Andres	90SC	99	$ .01	$ .05	Valle, Dave	88SC	126	$ .01	$ .05
Thomas, Andres	91SC	613	$ .01	$ .03	Valle, Dave	89SC	27	$ .01	$ .05
Thomas, Frank	90SC	663	$1.00	$5.00	Valle, Dave	90SC	109	$ .01	$ .05
Thomas, Frank	90SCTR	86	$ .01	$ 4.50	Valle, Dave	91SC	262	$ .01	$ .03
Thomas, Frank	91SC	840	$ .01	$ .75	Van Poppel, Todd	91SC	389	$ .01	$2.00

SCORE

Player	Year	No.	VG	EX/MT	Player	Year	No.	VG	EX/MT
Van Slyke, Andy	88SC	416	$ .01	$ .10	Wayne, Edwards	90SCTR	85	$ .01	$ .10
Van Slyke, Andy	89SC	174	$ .01	$ .10	Wayne, Gary	89SCTR	91	$ .01	$ .20
Van Slyke, Andy	90SC	440	$ .01	$ .10	Wayne, Gary	90SC	527	$ .01	$ .05
Van Slyke, Andy	91SC	475	$ .01	$ .03	Wayne, Gary	91SC	283	$ .01	$ .03
Van Slyke, Andy	91SCRM	698	$ .01	$ .03	Webster, Lenny	90SC	638	$ .01	$ .05
Varsho, Gary	89SC	604	$ .01	$ .15	Webster, Mitch	88SC	345	$ .01	$ .05
Vatcher, Jim	91SC	341	$ .01	$ .10	Webster, Mitch	89SC	71	$ .01	$ .05
Vaughn, Greg	90SC	585	$ .01	$ .50	Webster, Mitch	90SC	85	$ .01	$ .05
Vaughn, Greg	91SC	528	$ .01	$ .10	Webster, Mitch	90SCTR	4	$ .01	$ .05
Vaughn, Maurice	90SC	675	$ .01	$1.50	Webster, Mitch	91SC	594	$ .01	$ .03
Vaughn, Mo	91SC	750	$ .01	$ .35	Wegman, Bill	88SC	296	$ .01	$ .05
Velarde, Randy	90SC	524	$ .01	$ .05	Wegman, Bill	89SC	335	$ .01	$ .05
Velarde, Randy	91SC	134	$ .01	$ .03	Wegman, Bill	90SC	188	$ .01	$ .05
Ventura, Robin	90SC	595	$ .01	$ .35	Wegman, Bill	91SC	483	$ .01	$ .03
Ventura, Robin	91SC	320	$ .01	$ .15	Weiss, Walt	88SCTR	102	$ .15	$1.50
Villanueva, Hector	90SCTR	98	$ .01	$ .25	Weiss, Walt	89SC	165	$ .01	$ .15
Villanueva, Hector	91SC	71	$ .01	$ .15	Weiss, Walt	90SC	110	$ .01	$ .10
Viola, Frank	88SC	475	$ .01	$ .20	Weiss, Walt	91SC	171	$ .01	$ .03
Viola, Frank	89SC	290	$ .01	$ .15	Welch, Bob	88SC	510	$ .01	$ .05
Viola, Frank	89SCTR	67	$ .01	$ .15	Welch, Bob	88SCTR	15	$ .01	$ .10
Viola, Frank	90SC	500	$ .01	$ .10	Welch, Bob	89SC	308	$ .01	$ .05
Viola, Frank	91SC	460	$ .01	$ .10	Welch, Bob	90SC	159	$ .01	$ .05
Viola, Frank	91SCDT	882	$ .01	$ .03	Welch, Bob	91SC	311	$ .01	$ .03
Viola, Frank	91SCKM	687	$ .01	$ .03	Welch, Bob	91SC	568	$ .01	$ .03
Virgil, Ozzie	88SC	129	$ .01	$ .05	Welch, Bob	91SCMVP	877	$ .01	$ .05
Virgil, Ozzie	89SC	111	$ .01	$ .05	Wellman, Brad	89SC	504	$ .01	$ .05
Vizcaino, Jose	90SC	613	$ .01	$ .10	Wells, David	90SC	491	$ .01	$ .05
Vizcaino, Jose	91SC	787	$ .01	$ .03	Wells, David	91SC	474	$ .01	$ .03
Vizquel, Omar	89SCTR	105	$ .01	$ .20	Wells, Terry	91SC	359	$ .01	$ .10
Vizquel, Omar	90SC	264	$ .01	$ .05	West, Dave	89SC	650	$ .10	$ .35
Vizquel, Omar	91SC	299	$ .01	$ .03	West, Dave	90SC	573	$ .01	$ .05
Vosberg, Ed	91SC	757	$ .01	$ .03	West, Dave	91SC	158	$ .01	$ .03
Wagner, Hector	91SC	730	$ .01	$ .03	Weston, Mickey	90SC	616	$ .01	$ .05
Walden, Ron	91SC	679	$ .01	$ .20	Wetherby, Jeff	90SC	540	$ .01	$ .05
Walewander, Jim	88SC	571	$ .01	$ .05	Wetteland, John	89SCTR	90	$ .01	$ .20
Walewander, Jim	89SC	311	$ .01	$ .05	Wetteland, John	90SC	388	$ .01	$ .05
Walk, Bob	88SC	162	$ .01	$ .05	Wetteland, John	91SC	267	$ .01	$ .03
Walk, Bob	89SC	224	$ .01	$ .05	Whitaker, Lou	88SC	56	$ .01	$ .10
Walk, Bob	90SC	21	$ .01	$ .05	Whitaker, Lou	89SC	230	$ .01	$ .05
Walk, Bob	91SC	599	$ .01	$ .03	Whitaker, Lou	90SC	75	$ .01	$ .05
Walker, Greg	88SC	93	$ .01	$ .05	Whitaker, Lou	91SC	297	$ .01	$ .03
Walker, Greg	89SC	37	$ .01	$ .05	White, Devon	88SC	212	$ .01	$ .10
Walker, Greg	90SC	354	$ .01	$ .05	White, Devon	89SC	323	$ .01	$ .10
Walker, Larry	90SC	631	$ .01	$ .25	White, Devon	90SC	312	$ .01	$ .05
Walker, Larry	91SC	241	$ .01	$ .03	White, Devon	91SC	466	$ .01	$ .03
Wallach, Tim	88SC	70	$ .01	$ .10	White, Frank	88SC	79	$ .01	$ .05
Wallach, Tim	89SC	220	$ .01	$ .05	White, Frank	89SC	390	$ .01	$ .05
Wallach, Tim	90SC	192	$ .01	$ .05	White, Frank	90SC	372	$ .01	$ .05
Wallach, Tim	91SC	210	$ .01	$ .03	White, Rondell	91SC	390	$ .01	$ .35
Wallach, Tim	91SCTF	865	$ .01	$ .03	Whited, Ed	90SC	644	$ .01	$ .05
Walling, Dennis	88SC	145	$ .01	$ .05	Whitehurst, Wally	90SC	599	$ .01	$ .05
Walling, Denny	89SC	49	$ .01	$ .05	Whitehurst, Wally	91SC	529	$ .01	$ .03
Walsh, David	91SC	351	$ .01	$ .10	Whiten, Mark	91SC	358	$ .01	$ .25
Walton, Jerome	89SCTR	85	$ .01	$ .75	Whitson, Ed	88SC	167	$ .01	$ .05
Walton, Jerome	90SC	229	$ .01	$ .15	Whitson, Ed	89SC	329	$ .01	$ .05
Walton, Jerome	91SC	13	$ .01	$ .10	Whitson, Ed	90SC	373	$ .01	$ .05
Ward, Duane	89SC	359	$ .01	$ .05	Whitson, Ed	91SC	789	$ .01	$ .03
Ward, Duane	90SC	439	$ .01	$ .05	Whitt, Ernie	88SC	168	$ .01	$ .05
Ward, Duane	91SC	561	$ .01	$ .03	Whitt, Ernie	89SC	98	$ .01	$ .05
Ward, Gary	88SC	157	$ .01	$ .05	Whitt, Ernie	90SC	433	$ .01	$ .05
Ward, Gary	89SC	435	$ .01	$ .05	Whitt, Ernie	90SCTR	30	$ .01	$ .05
Ward, Gary	90SC	513	$ .01	$ .05	Whitt, Mike	90SCTR	50	$ .01	$ .05
Ward, Gary	91SC	637	$ .01	$ .03	Wickander, Kevin	91SC	355	$ .01	$ .03
Ward, Turner	91SC	732	$ .01	$ .20	Wiggins, Alan	88SC	291	$ .01	$ .05
Washington, Claudell	88SC	579	$ .01	$ .05	Wilkerson, Curt	88SC	127	$ .01	$ .05
Washington, Claudell	89SC	211	$ .01	$ .05	Wilkerson, Curtis	89SC	518	$ .01	$ .05
Washington, Claudell	89SCTR	10	$ .01	$ .05	Wilkerson, Curtis	90SC	474	$ .01	$ .05
Washington, Claudell	90SC	298	$ .01	$ .05	Wilkerson, Curtis	91SC	603	$ .01	$ .03
Washington, Claudell	90SCTR	45	$ .01	$ .05	Wilkins, Dean	90SC	630	$ .01	$ .05
Wasinger, Mark	88SC	283	$ .01	$ .05	Williams, Bernie	90SC	619	$ .01	$ .25

Player	Year	No.	VG	EX/MT	Player	Year	No.	VG	EX/MT
Williams, Eddie	91SC	552	$ .01	$ .03	Woodson, Tracy	89SC	586	$ .01	$ .05
Williams, Frank	88SC	317	$ .01	$ .05	Woodward, Rob	88SC	403	$ .01	$ .05
Williams, Frank	89SC	485	$ .01	$ .05	World Series '89, Game 1&2	90SC	700	$ .01	$ .10
Williams, Frank	90SC	341	$ .01	$ .05	World Series '89, Game 3	90SC	702	$ .01	$ .10
Williams, Ken	88SC	112	$ .04	$ .20	World Series '89, Game 4	90SC	703	$ .01	$ .10
Williams, Ken	89SC	67	$ .01	$ .05	World Series '89, Lights Out	90SC	701	$ .01	$ .35
Williams, Matt	88SC	118	$ .01	$2.00	World Series '90, Reds' Oct.	91SC	795	$ .01	$ .03
Williams, Matt	89SC	612	$ .01	$ .35	World Series, 1988	89SC	582	$ .01	$ .10
Williams, Matt	90SC	503	$ .01	$ .20	Worrell, Todd	88SC	202	$ .01	$ .05
Williams, Matt	91SC	189	$ .01	$ .10	Worrell, Todd	89SC	265	$ .01	$ .05
Williams, Matt	91SCAS	667	$ .01	$ .03	Worrell, Todd	90SC	392	$ .01	$ .05
Williams, Matt	91SCMB	689	$ .01	$ .03	Worrell, Todd	91SC	807	$ .01	$ .03
Williams, Mitch	88SC	339	$ .01	$ .05	Worthington, Craig	89SC	636	$ .01	$ .20
Williams, Mitch	89SC	301	$ .01	$ .05	Worthington, Craig	90SC	234	$ .01	$ .10
Williams, Mitch	89SCTR	32	$ .01	$ .05	Worthington, Craig	91SC	503	$ .01	$ .03
Williams, Mitch	90SC	262	$ .01	$ .05	Wrigley Field,1st Night Game	89SC	652	$ .01	$ .05
Williams, Mitch	90SCDT	695	$ .01	$ .10	Wrona, Rick	90SC	557	$ .01	$ .10
Williams, Mitch	91SC	220	$ .01	$ .03	Wrona, Rick	91SC	519	$ .01	$ .03
Williamson, Mark	89SC	592	$ .01	$ .10	Wynegar, Butch	88SC	355	$ .01	$ .05
Williamson, Mark	90SC	332	$ .01	$ .05	Wynegar, Butch	89SC	140	$ .01	$ .05
Williamson, Mark	91SC	498	$ .01	$ .03	Wynne, Marvell	88SC	209	$ .01	$ .05
Wills, Frank	91SC	521	$ .01	$ .03	Wynne, Marvell	89SC	203	$ .01	$ .05
Wilson, Dan	91SC	681	$ .01	$ .25	Wynne, Marvell	90SC	337	$ .01	$ .05
Wilson, Glenn	88SC	405	$ .01	$ .05	Wynne, Marvell	91SC	531	$ .01	$ .10
Wilson, Glenn	89SC	106	$ .01	$ .05	Yelding, Eric	90SC	411	$ .01	$ .10
Wilson, Glenn	90SC	346	$ .01	$ .05	Yelding, Eric	91SC	329	$ .01	$ .03
Wilson, Glenn	91SC	298	$ .01	$ .03	Yett, Rich	88SC	484	$ .01	$ .05
Wilson, Mookie	88SC	474	$ .01	$ .05	Yett, Rich	89SC	467	$ .01	$ .05
Wilson, Mookie	89SC	302	$ .01	$ .05	Yett, Rich	90SC	274	$ .01	$ .05
Wilson, Mookie	89SCTR	16	$ .01	$ .05	York, Mike	91SC	738	$ .01	$ .03
Wilson, Mookie	90SC	448	$ .01	$ .05	Youmans, Floyd	88SC	327	$ .01	$ .05
Wilson, Mookie	91SC	42	$ .01	$ .03	Young, Curt	88SC	125	$ .01	$ .10
Wilson, Steve	90SC	531	$ .01	$ .05	Young, Curt	89SC	29	$ .01	$ .05
Wilson, Steve	91SC	306	$ .01	$ .03	Young, Curt	90SC	533	$ .01	$ .05
Wilson, Trevor	91SC	657	$ .01	$ .03	Young, Curt	91SC	236	$ .01	$ .03
Wilson, Willie	88SC	102	$ .01	$ .05	Young, Gerald	88SC	442	$ .01	$ .10
Wilson, Willie	89SC	28	$ .01	$ .05	Young, Gerald	89SC	97	$ .01	$ .05
Wilson, Willie	90SC	104	$ .01	$ .05	Young, Gerald	90SC	43	$ .01	$ .05
Wine, Jr., Robbie	88SC	496	$ .01	$ .05	Young, Gerald	91SC	844	$ .01	$ .03
Winfield, Dave	88SC	55	$ .01	$ .15	Young, Matt	88SC	357	$ .01	$ .05
Winfield, Dave	89SC	50	$ .01	$ .10	Young, Matt	91SC	126	$ .01	$ .03
Winfield, Dave	90SC	307	$ .01	$ .10	Young, Mike	88SC	393	$ .01	$ .05
Winfield, Dave	90SCTR	1	$ .01	$ .05	Young, Mike	88SCTR	51	$ .01	$ .05
Winfield, Dave	91SC	83	$ .01	$ .03	Young, Mike	89SC	494	$ .01	$ .05
Winn, Jim	88SC	462	$ .01	$ .05	Young, Ray	91SC	761	$ .01	$ .15
Winningham, Herm	88SC	142	$ .01	$ .05	Youngblood, Joel	88SC	509	$ .01	$ .05
Winningham, Herm	88SCTR	43	$ .01	$ .05	Youngblood, Joel	89SC	539	$ .01	$ .05
Winningham, Herm	89SC	496	$ .01	$ .05	Youngblood, Joel	89SCTR	66	$ .01	$ .05
Winningham, Herm	90SC	38	$ .01	$ .05	Youngblood, Joel	90SC	344	$ .01	$ .05
Winningham, Herm	91SC	656	$ .01	$ .03	Yount, Robin	88SC	160	$ .05	$ .20
Witt, Bob	88SC	149	$ .01	$ .10	Yount, Robin	89SC	151	$ .01	$ .15
Witt, Bobby	89SC	463	$ .01	$ .05	Yount, Robin	90SC	320	$ .01	$ .15
Witt, Bobby	90SC	457	$ .01	$ .05	Yount, Robin	91SC	525	$ .01	$ .10
Witt, Bobby	91SC	507	$ .01	$ .03	Yount, Robin	91SCTF	854	$ .01	$ .03
Witt, Bobby	91SCKM	410	$ .01	$ .05	Zeile, Todd	90SC	600	$ .01	$ .75
Witt, Mike	88SC	81	$ .01	$ .10	Zeile, Todd	91SC	240	$ .01	$ .15
Witt, Mike	89SC	298	$ .01	$ .05	Zeile, Todd	91SCTF	869	$ .01	$ .03
Witt, Mike	90SC	226	$ .01	$ .05	Zinter, Alan	90SC	671	$ .01	$ .05
Witt, Mike	91SC	430	$ .01	$ .03	Zosky, Eddie	90SC	665	$ .01	$ .05
Witt, Mike	91SCNH	699	$ .01	$ .03	Zuvella, Paul	89SC	598	$ .01	$ .05

SPORTFLICS

Player	Year	No.	VG	EX/MT	Player	Year	No.	VG	EX/MT
Aase, Don	87SP	165	$ .03	$ .10	Benes, Andy	90SP	90	$ .03	$ .35
Aase, Don	87SP	194	$ .03	$ .10	Benzinger, Todd	87SPR	47	$ .10	$ .40
Abbott, Jim	90SP	99	$ .03	$ .35	Benzinger, Todd	90SP	56	$ .03	$ .10
Abner, Shawn	88SP	223	$ .25	$ .45	Bernazard, Tony	87SP	60	$ .03	$ .10
Aldrete, Mike	88SP	80	$ .03	$ .10	Bernazard, Tony	87SP	112	$ .03	$ .10
Alexander, Doyle	86SP	133	$ .03	$ .10	Berroa, Geronimo	89SP	225	$ .10	$ .30
Alexander, Doyle	89SP	211	$ .03	$ .10	Berryhill, Damon	89SP	216	$ .03	$ .10
Alomar, Jr., Sandy	89SP	223	$ .50	$4.00	Berryhill, Damon	90SP	164	$ .03	$ .10
Alomar, Roberto	89SP	20	$ .03	$ .50	Biancalana, Buddy	86SP	200	$ .03	$ .10
Alomar, Roberto	90SP	93	$ .03	$ .10	Biggio, Craig	90SP	22	$ .03	$ .30
Anderson, Allan	89SP	220	$ .03	$ .10	Blauser, Jeff	87SPR	48	$ .03	$ .10
Anderson, Allan	90SP	59	$ .03	$ .10	Blue, Vida	86SP	132	$ .03	$ .10
Andujar, Joaquin	86SP	101	$ .03	$ .10	Blue, Vida	86SP	142	$ .03	$ .10
Andujar, Joaquin	86SP	133	$ .03	$ .10	Blyleven, Bert	86SP	64	$ .03	$ .10
Andujar, Joaquin	86SP	185	$ .15	$ .60	Blyleven, Bert	86SP	103	$ .03	$ .10
Anthony, Eric	90SP	179	$ .03	$ .50	Blyleven, Bert	86SP	142	$ .03	$ .10
Armas, Tony	86SP	61	$ .10	$ .40	Blyleven, Bert	87SP	81	$ .03	$ .10
Armas, Tony	86SP	145	$ .03	$ .10	Blyleven, Bert	88SP	92	$ .03	$ .10
Asadoor, Randy	87SP	158	$ .65	$2.50	Blyleven, Bert	90SP	193	$ .03	$ .10
Ashby, Alan	88SP	219	$ .03	$ .10	Boddicker, Mike	86SP	104	$ .03	$ .10
Assenmacher, Paul	86SPR	24	$ .03	$ .10	Boddicker, Mike	86SP	149	$ .03	$ .10
August, Don	89SP	131	$ .03	$ .10	Boddicker, Mike	87SP	56	$ .03	$ .10
Backman, Wally	87SP	124	$ .03	$ .10	Boddicker, Mike	88SP	146	$ .03	$ .10
Bailes, Scott	86SPR	9	$ .03	$ .10	Boddicker, Mike	89SP	122	$ .03	$ .10
Baines, Harold	86SP	7	$ .03	$ .10	Boggs, Wade	86SP	3	$ .50	$2.00
Baines, Harold	86SP	52	$ .10	$ .40	Boggs, Wade	86SP	75	$ .35	$1.50
Baines, Harold	87SP	153	$ .03	$ .10	Boggs, Wade	86SP	180	$ .20	$1.25
Baines, Harold	87SP	171	$ .03	$ .10	Boggs, Wade	86SP	183	$ .20	$1.10
Baines, Harold	88SP	33	$ .03	$ .10	Boggs, Wade	86SP	184	$ .32	$1.25
Baines, Harold	89SP	157	$ .03	$ .10	Boggs, Wade	87SP	2	$ .35	$ .75
Baines, Harold	90SP	125	$ .03	$ .10	Boggs, Wade	87SP	114	$ .12	$ .50
Balboni, Steve	86SP	186	$ .10	$ .40	Boggs, Wade	87SP	197	$ .12	$ .50
Ballard, Jeff	90SP	123	$ .03	$ .10	Boggs, Wade	88SP	50	$ .25	$ .75
Bankhead, Scott	86SPR	39	$ .03	$ .10	Boggs, Wade	89SP	100	$ .15	$ .75
Bankhead, Scott	90SP	41	$ .03	$ .10	Boggs, Wade	89SP	221	$ .15	$1.50
Bannister, Floyd	89SP	154	$ .03	$ .10	Boggs, Wade	90SP	2	$ .03	$ .50
Barfield, Jesse	86SP	76	$ .03	$ .10	Bonds, Barry	86SPR	13	$ .08	$ .75
Barfield, Jesse	87SP	14	$ .03	$ .10	Bonds, Barry	88SP	119	$ .03	$ .50
Barfield, Jesse	87SP	153	$ .03	$ .10	Bonds, Barry	89SP	146	$ .03	$ .20
Barfield, Jesse	88SP	13	$ .03	$ .10	Bonds, Barry	90SP	143	$ .03	$ .20
Barfield, Jesse	89SP	9	$ .03	$ .10	Bonilla, Bobby	86SPR	26	$ .25	$1.00
Barfield, Jesse	90SP	10	$ .03	$ .10	Bonilla, Bobby	88SP	131	$ .15	$ .60
Barrett, Marty	87SP	112	$ .03	$ .10	Bonilla, Bobby	89SP	182	$ .03	$ .20
Barrett, Marty	87SP	182	$ .03	$ .10	Bonilla, Bobby	90SP	195	$ .03	$ .20
Barrett, Marty	88SP	157	$ .03	$ .10	Boone, Bob	88SP	212	$ .03	$ .10
Barrett, Marty	89SP	198	$ .03	$ .10	Boone, Bob	89SP	40	$ .03	$ .10
Bass, Kevin	87SP	117	$ .03	$ .25	Boone, Bob	90SP	40	$ .03	$ .10
Bass, Kevin	87SP	175	$ .03	$ .10	Borders, Pat	90SP	45	$ .03	$ .10
Bass, Kevin	88SP	55	$ .03	$ .10	Bosio, Chris	87SPR	2	$ .03	$ .10
Bass, Kevin	89SP	11	$ .03	$ .10	Bosio, Chris	90SP	25	$ .03	$ .10
Bass, Kevin	90SP	198	$ .03	$ .10	Boyd, Dennis	86SP	152	$ .03	$ .10
Baylor, Don	86SP	57	$ .10	$ .40	Boyd, Dennis	87SP	47	$ .03	$ .10
Baylor, Don	87SP	163	$ .03	$ .10	Bradley, Phil	86SP	77	$ .03	$ .10
Bedrosian, Steve	87SP	110	$ .03	$ .10	Bradley, Phil	87SP	89	$ .03	$ .10
Bedrosian, Steve	88SP	70	$ .03	$ .10	Bradley, Phil	88SP	93	$ .03	$ .10
Bedrosian, Steve	88SP	222	$ .15	$ .60	Bradley, Phil	90SP	95	$ .03	$ .10
Bedrosian, Steve	89SP	63	$ .03	$ .10	Braggs, Glenn	86SPR	21	$ .03	$ .10
Bedrosian, Steve	90SP	104	$ .03	$ .10	Braggs, Glenn	89SP	29	$ .03	$ .10
Belcher, Tim	89SP	121	$ .03	$ .10	Brantley, Mickey	86SPR	45	$ .03	$ .10
Bell, Buddy	86SP	151	$ .03	$ .10	Brantley, Mickey	89SP	6	$ .03	$ .10
Bell, Buddy	87SP	141	$ .03	$ .10	Bream, Sid	88SP	98	$ .03	$ .10
Bell, Buddy	88SP	147	$ .03	$ .10	Brett, George	86SP	1	$ .25	$1.00
Bell, Eric	87SPR	1	$ .03	$ .10	Brett, George	86SP	52	$ .10	$ .40
Bell, George	86SP	102	$ .03	$ .10	Brett, George	86SP	63	$ .10	$ .40
Bell, George	87SP	51	$ .10	$ .40	Brett, George	86SP	179	$ .20	$1.25
Bell, George	87SP	80	$ .20	$ .80	Brett, George	86SP	180	$ .20	$1.25
Bell, George	88SP	4	$ .05	$ .25	Brett, George	86SP	186	$ .10	$ .40
Bell, George	89SP	25	$ .03	$ .15	Brett, George	87SP	5	$ .20	$ .75
Bell, George	90SP	17	$ .03	$ .10	Brett, George	87SP	114	$ .12	$ .75
Belle, Joey	90SP	159	$ .03	$ .75	Brett, George	87SP	197	$ .12	$ .50

Player	Year	No.	VG	EX/MT
Brett, George	88SP	150	$ .12	$ .50
Brett, George	89SP	64	$ .03	$ .50
Brett, George	90SP	214	$ .03	$ .25
Briley, Greg	90SP	43	$ .03	$ .25
Brock, Greg	88SP	184	$ .03	$ .10
Brooks, Hubie	86SP	187	$ .03	$ .10
Brooks, Hubie	87SP	18	$ .03	$ .10
Brooks, Hubie	87SP	79	$ .03	$ .10
Brooks, Hubie	87SP	197	$ .12	$ .50
Brooks, Hubie	88SP	187	$ .03	$ .10
Brooks, Hubie	89SP	96	$ .03	$ .10
Brower, Bob	87SPR	3	$ .03	$ .10
Brown, Chris	86SP	78	$ .12	$ .50
Brown, Chris	87SP	13	$ .03	$ .10
Brown, Chris	87SP	115	$ .03	$ .30
Brown, Kevin	90SP	73	$ .03	$ .25
Browne, Jerry	87SPR	4	$ .03	$ .10
Browne, Jerry	90SP	111	$ .03	$ .10
Browning, Tom	86SP	79	$ .03	$ .30
Browning, Tom	86SP	185	$ .15	$ .60
Browning, Tom	89SP	180	$ .03	$ .20
Browning, Tom	89SP	222	$ .05	$ .25
Browning, Tom	90SP	91	$ .03	$ .15
Brunansky, Tom	86SP	80	$ .03	$ .10
Brunansky, Tom	87SP	134	$ .03	$ .10
Brunansky, Tom	88SP	194	$ .03	$ .10
Brunansky, Tom	89SP	161	$ .03	$ .10
Buckner, Bill	86SP	81	$ .03	$ .10
Buckner, Bill	86SP	140	$ .03	$ .10
Buckner, Bill	87SP	70	$ .03	$ .10
Buhner, Jay	88SP	223	$ .25	$ .45
Buhner, Jay	89SP	89	$ .03	$ .20
Buice, DeWayne	87SPR	26	$ .03	$ .10
Burke, Tim	89SP	73	$ .03	$ .10
Burke, Tim	90SP	199	$ .03	$ .10
Burks, Ellis	87SPR	5	$ .25	$1.00
Burks, Ellis	88SP	144	$ .45	$1.00
Burks, Ellis	89SP	191	$ .15	$ .75
Burks, Ellis	90SP	80	$ .03	$ .50
Burns, Britt	86SP	105	$ .03	$ .10
Burns, Todd	89SP	87	$ .03	$ .20
Butler, Brett	86SP	26	$ .03	$ .10
Butler, Brett	87SP	69	$ .03	$ .10
Butler, Brett	88SP	153	$ .03	$ .10
Butler, Brett	89SP	31	$ .03	$ .10
Butler, Brett	90SP	136	$ .03	$ .10
Calderon, Ivan	88SP	166	$ .03	$ .10
Calderon, Ivan	90SP	167	$ .03	$ .10
Caminiti, Ken	87SPR	37	$ .03	$ .10
Caminiti, Ken	88SP	124	$ .03	$ .25
Caminiti, Ken	90SP	209	$ .03	$ .10
Candaele, Casey	87SP	158	$ .65	$2.50
Candaele, Casey	87SPR	6	$ .03	$ .10
Candaele, Casey	88SP	140	$ .03	$ .10
Candelaria, John	86SP	129	$ .03	$ .10
Candelaria, John	87SP	148	$ .03	$ .10
Candelaria, John	89SP	202	$ .03	$ .10
Candiotti, Tom	88SP	37	$ .03	$ .10
Candiotti, Tom	90SP	126	$ .03	$ .10
Cangelosi, John	86SPR	31	$ .03	$ .10
Cangelosi, John	87SP	157	$ .03	$ .10
Canseco, Jose	86SP	178	$4.00	$15.00
Canseco, Jose	86SPR	11	$1.00	$4.50
Canseco, Jose	87SP	80	$ .20	$1.25
Canseco, Jose	87SP	90	$ .60	$2.50
Canseco, Jose	88SP	201	$ .50	$2.00
Canseco, Jose	89SP	1	$ .25	$1.50
Canseco, Jose	89SP	221	$ .15	$1.50
Canseco, Jose	90SP	23	$ .03	$ .75
Carew, Rod	86SP	69	$ .15	$1.00
Carew, Rod	86SP	74	$ .03	$ .10
Carew, Rod	86SP	106	$ .12	$ .60
Carew, Rod	86SP	146	$ .03	$ .10
Carew, Rod	86SP	180	$ .20	$1.25
Carew, Rod	86SP	182	$ .20	$1.50
Carlton, Steve	86SP	27	$ .08	$ .50
Carlton, Steve	86SP	70	$ .08	$ .30
Carlton, Steve	87SP	200	$ .03	$ .10
Carman, Don	87SP	108	$ .03	$ .10
Carter, Gary	86SP	28	$ .08	$ .30
Carter, Gary	86SP	126	$ .03	$ .10
Carter, Gary	86SP	137	$ .03	$ .10
Carter, Gary	87SP	50	$ .03	$ .10
Carter, Gary	87SP	151	$ .03	$ .10
Carter, Gary	88SP	28	$ .05	$ .20
Carter, Gary	89SP	155	$ .03	$ .10
Carter, Joe	87SP	176	$ .03	$ .40
Carter, Joe	88SP	5	$ .03	$ .30
Carter, Joe	89SP	104	$ .03	$ .30
Carter, Joe	90SP	120	$ .03	$ .10
Cerutti, John	86SPR	36	$ .03	$ .25
Cerutti, John	90SP	86	$ .03	$ .10
Cey, Ron	86SP	130	$ .18	$ .50
Clancy, Jim	87SP	189	$ .03	$ .10
Clancy, Jim	88SP	215	$ .03	$ .10
Clark, David	87SP	118	$ .45	$1.75
Clark, Jack	86SP	107	$ .03	$ .10
Clark, Jack	88SP	18	$ .03	$ .10
Clark, Jack	89SP	26	$ .03	$ .10
Clark, Jack	90SP	28	$ .03	$ .10
Clark, Jerald	89SP	179	$ .03	$ .20
Clark, Will	86SPR	6	$1.00	$4.50
Clark, Will	87SP	95	$ .90	$2.50
Clark, Will	87SP	195	$ .10	$ .40
Clark, Will	88SP	9	$ .30	$1.50

WILL CLARK
SAN FRANCISCO GIANTS

Player	Year	No.	VG	EX/MT
Clark, Will	89SP	170	$ .15	$ .75
Clark, Will	90SP	5	$ .03	$ .75
Clemens, Roger	87SP	10	$ .20	$1.50
Clemens, Roger	87SP	111	$ .12	$ .50
Clemens, Roger	87SP	159	$ .35	$1.25

SPORTFLICS

Player	Year	No.	VG	EX/MT
Clemens, Roger	87SP	196	$ .08	$ .30
Clemens, Roger	88SP	207	$ .12	$ .90
Clemens, Roger	89SP	3	$ .10	$ .75
Clemens, Roger	90SP	149	$ .03	$ .25
Cliburn, Stewart	86SP	177	$ .12	$ .50
Cochrane, Dave	87SP	158	$ .65	$2.50
Coleman, Vince	86SP	24	$ .50	$1.75
Coleman, Vince	86SP	136	$ .25	$ .75
Coleman, Vince	86SP	176	$ .32	$1.25
Coleman, Vince	87SP	65	$ .08	$ .30
Coleman, Vince	87SP	152	$ .03	$ .10
Coleman, Vince	87SP	199	$ .25	$ .75
Coleman, Vince	88SP	67	$ .05	$ .20
Coleman, Vince	88SP	221	$ .10	$ .50
Coleman, Vince	89SP	113	$ .03	$ .10
Coleman, Vince	90SP	142	$ .03	$ .15
Concepcion, Dave	86SP	131	$ .03	$ .10
Concepcion, Dave	86SP	153	$ .03	$ .10
Concepcion, Dave	88SP	218	$ .03	$ .10
Cone, David	87SPR	39	$ .30	$1.00
Cone, David	89SP	51	$ .03	$ .25
Cone, David	90SP	201	$ .03	$ .15
Coolbaugh, Scott	90SP	180	$ .03	$ .35
Cooper, Cecil	86SP	29	$ .03	$ .10
Cooper, Cecil	86SP	145	$ .03	$ .10
Cooper, Cecil	86SP	180	$ .20	$1.25
Cooper, Cecil	87SP	169	$ .03	$ .10
Correa, Edwin	86SPR	2	$ .03	$ .10
Cowley, Joe	87SP	196	$ .08	$ .30
Cox, Danny	86SP	108	$ .03	$ .10
Cox, Danny	88SP	84	$ .03	$ .10
Crews, Tim	88SP	224	$ .08	$ .30
Cruz, Jose	86SP	30	$ .03	$ .10
Cruz, Jose	87SP	42	$ .03	$ .10
Cruz, Jose	87SP	152	$ .03	$ .10
Daniels, Kal	86SPR	43	$ .30	$ .75
Daniels, Kal	88SP	112	$ .08	$ .30
Daniels, Kal	89SP	52	$ .03	$ .25
Darling, Ron	86SP	109	$ .03	$ .10
Darling, Ron	87SP	53	$ .05	$ .20
Darling, Ron	88SP	73	$ .03	$ .10
Darling, Ron	89SP	32	$ .03	$ .10
Darwin, Danny	90SP	83	$ .03	$ .10
Dascenzo, Doug	89SP	42	$ .03	$ .30
Davis, Alvin	86SP	31	$ .08	$ .30
Davis, Alvin	86SP	74	$ .03	$ .10
Davis, Alvin	87SP	21	$ .03	$ .10
Davis, Alvin	88SP	52	$ .03	$ .10
Davis, Alvin	89SP	33	$ .03	$ .10
Davis, Alvin	90SP	112	$ .03	$ .10
Davis, Chili	86SP	82	$ .03	$ .10
Davis, Chili	87SP	45	$ .03	$ .10
Davis, Chili	88SP	172	$ .03	$ .10
Davis, Chili	89SP	129	$ .03	$ .10
Davis, Chili	90SP	21	$ .03	$ .10
Davis, Eric	87SP	22	$ .32	$1.00
Davis, Eric	87SP	155	$ .15	$ .70
Davis, Eric	87SP	199	$ .25	$ .75
Davis, Eric	88SP	10	$ .25	$ .90
Davis, Eric	89SP	69	$ .10	$ .50
Davis, Eric	90SP	97	$ .03	$ .35
Davis, Glenn	86SP	188	$ .10	$ .40
Davis, Glenn	87SP	17	$ .08	$ .30
Davis, Glenn	87SP	195	$ .10	$ .40
Davis, Glenn	88SP	102	$ .03	$ .10
Davis, Glenn	89SP	137	$ .03	$ .10
Davis, Glenn	90SP	19	$ .03	$ .20
Davis, Jody	87SP	170	$ .03	$ .10
Davis, Jody	88SP	60	$ .03	$ .10
Davis, Jody	89SP	187	$ .03	$ .10
Davis, John	88SP	224	$ .08	$ .30
Davis, Mark	89SP	74	$ .03	$ .10
Davis, Mark	90SP	62	$ .03	$ .10
Davis, Mike	86SP	83	$ .03	$ .10
Davis, Mike	88SP	206	$ .03	$ .10
Dawson, Andre	86SP	66	$ .03	$ .10
Dawson, Andre	86SP	110	$ .03	$ .10
Dawson, Andre	87SP	139	$ .03	$ .10
Dawson, Andre	88SP	3	$ .08	$ .30
Dawson, Andre	89SP	95	$ .03	$ .20
Dawson, Andre	90SP	108	$ .03	$ .10
DeCinces, Doug	86SP	173	$ .03	$ .10
DeCinces, Doug	87SP	106	$ .03	$ .10
DeCinces, Doug	88SP	185	$ .03	$ .10
Deer, Rob	87SP	172	$ .03	$ .10
Deer, Rob	88SP	183	$ .03	$ .10
Deer, Rob	89SP	111	$ .03	$ .10
Deer, Rob	90SP	137	$ .03	$ .10
DeJesus, Jose	90SP	131	$ .03	$ .10
DeLeon, Jose	90SP	76	$ .03	$ .10
Dempsey, Rick	86SP	147	$ .03	$ .10
Denny, John	86SP	64	$ .03	$ .10
Denny, John	86SP	132	$ .03	$ .10
Denny, John	86SP	134	$ .03	$ .10
Deshaies, Jim	86SPR	15	$ .05	$ .20
Deshaies, Jim	87SP	156	$ .03	$ .30
Deshaies, Jim	88SP	190	$ .03	$ .10
Deshaies, Jim	90SP	32	$ .03	$ .10
Devereaux, Mike	90SP	114	$ .03	$ .10
Diaz, Bo	88SP	117	$ .03	$ .10
Diaz, Mike	86SPR	50	$ .03	$ .10
Dodson, Pat	87SP	118	$ .45	$1.75
Doran, Bill	87SP	116	$ .03	$ .25
Doran, Bill	87SP	162	$ .03	$ .10
Doran, Bill	88SP	48	$ .03	$ .10
Doran, Bill	89SP	57	$ .03	$ .10
Dotson, Rich	86SP	194	$ .03	$ .10
Dotson, Richard	89SP	133	$ .03	$ .10
Downing, Brian	86SP	154	$ .03	$ .10
Downing, Brian	87SP	161	$ .03	$ .10
Downing, Brian	88SP	181	$ .03	$ .10
Downing, Brian	89SP	117	$ .03	$ .10
Downing, Brian	90SP	77	$ .03	$ .10
Downs, Kelly	88SP	203	$ .03	$ .10
Downs, Kelly	89SP	39	$ .03	$ .10
Drabek, Doug	89SP	27	$ .03	$ .25
Drew, Cameron	89SP	225	$ .10	$ .30
Dunne, Mike	87SPR	40	$ .05	$ .25
Dunne, Mike	88SP	171	$ .05	$ .20
Dunston, Shawon	86SP	155	$ .03	$ .10
Dunston, Shawon	87SP	79	$ .03	$ .10
Dunston, Shawon	87SP	98	$ .03	$ .10
Dunston, Shawon	88SP	163	$ .03	$ .10
Dunston, Shawon	89SP	190	$ .03	$ .10
Durham, Leon	86SP	111	$ .03	$ .10
Durham, Leon	87SP	185	$ .03	$ .10
Dykstra, Len	87SP	58	$ .05	$ .20
Dykstra, Len	88SP	106	$ .03	$ .10
Dykstra, Len	89SP	123	$ .03	$ .10
Dykstra, Len	90SP	156	$ .03	$ .10
Easler, Mike	87SP	92	$ .03	$ .10
Eckersley, Dennis	86SP	129	$ .03	$ .10
Eckersley, Dennis	89SP	101	$ .03	$ .10
Eckersley, Dennis	89SP	222	$ .05	$ .25
Eckersley, Dennis	90SP	170	$ .03	$ .10
Eichhorn, Mark	86SPR	38	$ .05	$ .20
Eichhorn, Mark	87SP	194	$ .03	$ .10
Eichhorn, Mark	88SP	210	$ .03	$ .10
Eisenreich, Jim	90SP	166	$ .03	$ .10
Elster, Kevin	89SP	71	$ .03	$ .10

Player	Year	No.	VG	EX/MT	Player	Year	No.	VG	EX/MT
Elster, Kevin	90SP	118	$ .03	$ .10	Gallagher, Dave	90SP	105	$ .03	$ .10
Esasky, Nick	90SP	72	$ .03	$ .10	Gant, Ron	89SP	28	$ .03	$ .50
Evans, Darrell	86SP	183	$ .20	$1.10	Gantner, Jim	88SP	130	$ .03	$ .10
Evans, Darrell	86SP	189	$ .03	$ .10	Garber, Gene	88SP	88	$ .03	$ .10
Evans, Darrell	87SP	132	$ .03	$ .10	Garcia, Damaso	86SP	34	$ .03	$ .10
Evans, Darrell	88SP	188	$ .03	$ .10	Garcia, Damaso	87SP	183	$ .03	$ .10
Evans, Dwight	86SP	32	$ .03	$ .10	Garrelts, Scott	86SP	157	$ .03	$ .10
Evans, Dwight	87SP	128	$ .03	$ .10	Garrelts, Scott	87SP	68	$ .03	$ .10
Evans, Dwight	88SP	137	$ .03	$ .10	Garrelts, Scott	88SP	44	$ .03	$ .10
Evans, Dwight	89SP	204	$ .03	$ .10	Garrelts, Scott	90SP	39	$ .03	$ .10
Evans, Dwight	90SP	217	$ .03	$ .10	Garvey, Steve	86SP	35	$ .08	$ .35
Farrell, John	88SP	132	$ .05	$ .25	Garvey, Steve	86SP	51	$ .15	$ .35
Farrell, John	89SP	37	$ .03	$ .10	Garvey, Steve	86SP	137	$ .03	$ .10
Felix, Junior	90SP	186	$ .03	$ .50	Garvey, Steve	87SP	40	$ .10	$ .40
Fernandez, Sid	87SP	63	$ .08	$ .30	Gedman, Rich	86SP	84	$ .03	$ .10
Fernandez, Sid	88SP	177	$ .03	$ .10	Gedman, Rich	87SP	149	$ .03	$ .10
Fernandez, Sid	90SP	113	$ .03	$ .10	Gedman, Rich	87SP	154	$ .03	$ .10
Fernandez, Tony	86SP	112	$ .03	$ .10	Geren, Bob	90SP	205	$ .03	$ .25
Fernandez, Tony	87SP	113	$ .03	$ .10	Gerhart, Ken	87SPR	7	$ .03	$ .10
Fernandez, Tony	87SP	187	$ .03	$ .10	Gibson, Kirk	86SP	21	$ .15	$ .50
Fernandez, Tony	88SP	26	$ .03	$ .10	Gibson, Kirk	87SP	48	$ .10	$ .40
Fernandez, Tony	89SP	93	$ .03	$ .10	Gibson, Kirk	88SP	111	$ .08	$ .30
Fernandez, Tony	90SP	6	$ .03	$ .15	Gibson, Kirk	89SP	65	$ .03	$ .25
Fingers, Rollie	86SP	65	$ .03	$ .10	Gladden, Dan	90SP	190	$ .03	$ .10
Fingers, Rollie	86SP	130	$ .18	$ .50	Glavine, Tom	90SP	34	$ .03	$ .10
Fingers, Rollie	86SP	146	$ .03	$ .10	Gooden, Dwight	86SP	100	$ .32	$1.25
Finley, Chuck	90SP	172	$ .03	$ .10	Gooden, Dwight	86SP	136	$ .25	$ .75
Fisher, Brian	86SP	177	$ .12	$ .50	Gooden, Dwight	86SP	143	$ .20	$1.25
Fisk, Carlton	86SP	67	$ .08	$ .30	Gooden, Dwight	86SP	176	$ .32	$1.25
Fisk, Carlton	86SP	125	$ .03	$ .10	Gooden, Dwight	86SP	184	$ .32	$1.25
Fisk, Carlton	87SP	140	$ .03	$ .20	Gooden, Dwight	86SP	185	$ .15	$ .60
Fisk, Carlton	88SP	43	$ .03	$ .20	Gooden, Dwight	86SPR	47	$ .12	$ .50
Fisk, Carlton	89SP	219	$ .03	$ .20	Gooden, Dwight	87SP	100	$ .25	$ .90
Fisk, Carlton	90SP	204	$ .03	$ .10	Gooden, Dwight	87SP	120	$ .12	$ .50
Flanagan, Mike	86SP	59	$ .03	$ .10	Gooden, Dwight	87SP	159	$ .35	$1.25
Fletcher, Scott	87SP	113	$ .03	$ .10	Gooden, Dwight	88SP	200	$ .20	$ .60
Fletcher, Scott	87SP	136	$ .03	$ .10	Gooden, Dwight	89SP	140	$ .10	$ .50
Fletcher, Scott	88SP	77	$ .03	$ .10	Gooden, Doc	90SP	145	$ .03	$ .25
Fletcher, Scott	89SP	185	$ .03	$ .10	Gordon, Tom	90SP	30	$ .03	$ .40
Fletcher, Scott	90SP	220	$ .03	$ .10	Gossage, Goose	86SP	55	$ .03	$ .10
Forsch, Bob	86SP	129	$ .03	$ .10	Gossage, Goose "Rich"	86SP	190	$ .03	$ .10
Forsch, Bob	87SP	191	$ .03	$ .10	Gott, Jim	89SP	83	$ .03	$ .10
Forsch, Bob	88SP	199	$ .03	$ .10	Gozzo, Goose	90SP	168	$ .03	$ .10
Foster, George	86SP	68	$ .03	$ .30	Grace, Mark	89SP	15	$ .25	$1.00
Foster, George	86SP	126	$ .03	$ .10	Grace, Mark	90SP	15	$ .03	$ .75
Foster, George	86SP	131	$ .03	$ .10	Greene, Tommy	90SP	224	$ .03	$ .45
Foster, George	86SP	139	$ .10	$ .40	Greenwell, Mike	86SP	178	$4.00	$15.00
Franco, John	86SP	156	$ .03	$ .30	Greenwell, Mike	87SPR	8	$ .50	$2.00
Franco, John	87SP	192	$ .05	$ .25	Greenwell, Mike	88SP	118	$ .50	$ .75
Franco, John	88SP	195	$ .03	$ .15	Greenwell, Mike	89SP	143	$ .15	$ .50
Franco, John	89SP	176	$ .03	$ .20	Greenwell, Mike	89SP	221	$ .15	$1.50
Franco, John	90SP	138	$ .03	$ .10	Greenwell, Mike	90SP	50	$ .03	$ .50
Franco, Julio	86SP	33	$ .05	$ .25	Grich, Bobby	87SP	184	$ .03	$ .10
Franco, Julio	87SP	84	$ .03	$ .20	Griffey, Jr., Ken	90SP	7	$ .50	$3.00
Franco, Julio	88SP	58	$ .03	$ .20	Griffey, Ken	88SP	178	$ .03	$ .10
Franco, Julio	89SP	149	$ .03	$ .20	Griffin, Alfredo	86SP	136	$ .25	$ .75
Franco, Julio	90SP	158	$ .03	$ .10	Griffin, Alfredo	87SP	164	$ .03	$ .10
Fraser, Willie	87SPR	27	$ .03	$ .10	Griffin, Alfredo	88SP	156	$ .03	$ .10
Funderburk, Mark	86SP	178	$ 4.00	$15.00	Grissom, Marquis	90SP	134	$ .03	$ .50
Gaetti, Gary	87SP	64	$ .03	$ .10	Gross, Kevin	89SP	213	$ .03	$ .10
Gaetti, Gary	87SP	114	$ .12	$ .50	Gruber, Kelly	89SP	163	$ .03	$ .10
Gaetti, Gary	88SP	154	$ .03	$ .10	Gruber, Kelly	90SP	57	$ .03	$ .10
Gaetti, Gary	89SP	48	$ .03	$ .10	Gubicza, Mark	89SP	102	$ .03	$ .10
Gaetti, Gary	90SP	51	$ .03	$ .10	Guerrero, Pedro	86SP	14	$ .05	$ .20
Gainey, Ty	87SP	118	$ .45	$1.75	Guerrero, Pedro	86SP	148	$ .03	$ .30
Galarraga, Andres	86SPR	27	$ .25	$ .75	Guerrero, Pedro	86SP	181	$ .20	$ .50
Galarraga, Andres	88SP	182	$ .08	$ .30	Guerrero, Pedro	87SP	27	$ .03	$ .10
Galarraga, Andres	89SP	139	$ .03	$ .10	Guerrero, Pedro	88SP	97	$ .03	$ .10
Galarraga, Andres	90SP	148	$ .03	$ .10	Guerrero, Pedro	90SP	66	$ .03	$ .10
Gallagher, Dave	89SP	88	$ .03	$ .20	Guetterman, Lee	88SP	45	$ .03	$ .10

Player	Year	No.	VG	EX/MT
Guidry, Ron	86SP	18	$ .03	$ .10
Guidry, Ron	86SP	59	$ .03	$ .10
Guidry, Ron	86SP	149	$ .03	$ .10
Guidry, Ron	86SP	179	$ .20	$1.25
Guidry, Ron	86SP	185	$ .15	$ .60
Guidry, Ron	87SP	83	$ .03	$ .10
Guillen, Ozzie	86SP	22	$ .03	$ .10
Guillen, Ozzie	86SP	176	$ .12	$1.25

Player	Year	No.	VG	EX/MT
Guillen, Ozzie	87SP	186	$ .03	$ .10
Guillen, Ozzie	88SP	14	$ .03	$ .10
Guillen, Ozzie	89SP	85	$ .03	$ .10
Guillen, Ozzie	90SP	48	$ .03	$ .10
Gwynn, Tony	86SP	13	$ .10	$ .50
Gwynn, Tony	86SP	140	$ .03	$ .10
Gwynn, Tony	86SP	181	$ .20	$ .50
Gwynn, Tony	87SP	31	$ .08	$ .30
Gwynn, Tony	87SP	117	$ .03	$ .25
Gwynn, Tony	87SP	197	$ .12	$ .50
Gwynn, Tony	88SP	16	$ .08	$ .30
Gwynn, Tony	89SP	160	$ .03	$ .20
Gwynn, Tony	90SP	98	$ .03	$ .35
Hale, Chip	90SP	223	$ .03	$ .50
Hall, Mel	87SP	180	$ .03	$ .10
Hall, Mel	88SP	189	$ .03	$ .10
Hall, Mel	89SP	144	$ .03	$ .10
Harkey, Mike	89SP	132	$ .05	$ .30
Harper, Brian	90SP	121	$ .03	$ .10
Harris, Greg	87SP	126	$ .03	$ .10
Harvey, Bryan	89SP	130	$ .03	$ .50
Harvey, Bryan	90SP	31	$ .03	$ .10
Hatcher, Billy	88SP	63	$ .03	$ .10
Hatcher, Billy	89SP	174	$ .03	$ .10
Hawkins, Andy	86SP	191	$ .03	$ .10
Hawkins, Andy	89SP	84	$ .03	$ .10
Hayes, Charlie	90SP	36	$ .03	$ .10
Hayes, Von	87SP	193	$ .03	$ .10
Hayes, Von	88SP	62	$ .03	$ .10
Hayes, Von	89SP	181	$ .03	$ .10
Hayes, Von	90SP	147	$ .03	$ .10
Heaton, Neal	88SP	81	$ .03	$ .10

Player	Year	No.	VG	EX/MT
Henderson, Dave	89SP	127	$ .03	$ .25
Henderson, Rickey	86SP	6	$ .15	$1.25
Henderson, Rickey	86SP	184	$ .32	$1.25
Henderson, Rickey	87SP	4	$ .12	$1.00
Henderson, Rickey	87SP	157	$ .03	$ .90
Henderson, Rickey	87SP	159	$ .35	$1.25
Henderson, Rickey	87SP	198	$ .08	$ .30
Henderson, Rickey	88SP	11	$ .08	$1.00
Henderson, Rickey	89SP	145	$ .03	$ .50
Henderson, Rickey	90SP	208	$ .03	$ .25
Henke, Tom	88SP	65	$ .03	$ .10
Henke, Tom	89SP	126	$ .03	$ .10
Henke, Tom	90SP	42	$ .03	$ .10
Henneman, Mike	87SPR	29	$ .03	$ .10
Henneman, Mike	88SP	129	$ .03	$ .10
Henneman, Mike	89SP	56	$ .03	$ .10
Henneman, Mike	90SP	144	$ .03	$ .10
Hernandez, Keith	86SP	15	$ .08	$ .30
Hernandez, Keith	86SP	62	$ .12	$ .50
Hernandez, Keith	86SP	127	$ .08	$ .30
Hernandez, Keith	86SP	179	$ .20	$1.25
Hernandez, Keith	86SP	181	$ .20	$ .50
Hernandez, Keith	87SP	133	$ .05	$ .20
Hernandez, Keith	87SP	195	$ .10	$ .40
Hernandez, Keith	88SP	31	$ .05	$ .20
Hernandez, Keith	89SP	60	$ .03	$ .20
Hernandez, Keith	90SP	106	$ .03	$ .10
Hernandez, Willie	86SP	65	$ .03	$ .10
Hernandez, Willie	86SP	85	$ .03	$ .10
Hernandez, Willie	87SP	105	$ .03	$ .10
Herr, Tom	86SP	113	$ .03	$ .10
Herr, Tom	88SP	141	$ .03	$ .10
Herr, Tom	90SP	63	$ .03	$ .10
Hershiser, Orel	86SP	9	$ .15	$ .50
Hershiser, Orel	87SP	43	$ .10	$ .40
Hershiser, Orel	88SP	160	$ .10	$ .40
Hershiser, Orel	89SP	36	$ .03	$ .25
Hershiser, Orel	89SP	222	$ .05	$ .25
Hershiser, Orel	90SP	197	$ .03	$ .15
Hesketh, Joe	86SP	177	$ .12	$ .50
Higuera, Teddy	86SP	114	$ .15	$ .60
Higuera, Teddy	87SP	11	$ .03	$ .25
Higuera, Teddy	87SP	111	$ .12	$ .50
Higuera, Teddy	88SP	20	$ .03	$ .10
Higuera, Teddy	89SP	47	$ .03	$ .10
Higuera, Teddy	90SP	44	$ .03	$ .10
Hillegas, Shawn	87SPR	30	$ .03	$ .10
Horn, Sam	87SPR	38	$ .12	$ .20
Horn, Sam	88SP	114	$ .10	$ .20
Horner, Bob	86SP	66	$ .03	$ .10
Horner, Bob	86SP	115	$ .03	$ .10
Horner, Bob	87SP	73	$ .03	$ .10
Horner, Bob	87SP	196	$ .08	$ .30
Hough, Charlie	88SP	87	$ .03	$ .10
Hough, Charlie	89SP	92	$ .03	$ .10
Howell, Jay	86SP	192	$ .03	$ .10
Howell, Jay	88SP	86	$ .03	$ .10
Howell, Jay	90SP	78	$ .03	$ .10
Hoyt, LaMarr	86SP	59	$ .03	$ .10
Hoyt, LaMarr	86SP	193	$ .03	$ .10
Hrbek, Kent	86SP	36	$ .05	$ .20
Hrbek, Kent	87SP	15	$ .03	$ .10
Hrbek, Kent	88SP	95	$ .03	$ .10
Hrbek, Kent	89SP	188	$ .03	$ .10
Hrbek, Kent	90SP	203	$ .03	$ .10
Hurst, Bruce	87SP	38	$ .03	$ .10
Hurst, Bruce	88SP	197	$ .03	$ .10
Hurst, Bruce	89SP	175	$ .03	$ .10
Hurst, Bruce	90SP	47	$ .03	$ .10
Huson, Jeff	90SP	176	$ .03	$ .10

Player	Year	No.	VG	EX/MT
Incaviglia, Pete	86SPR	3	$ .20	$ .80
Incaviglia, Pete	87SP	37	$ .15	$ .60
Incaviglia, Pete	88SP	169	$ .08	$ .30
Incaviglia, Pete	89SP	112	$ .03	$ .10
Iorg, Dane	86SP	186	$ .10	$ .40
Jackson, Bo	86SPR	40	$ .60	$3.50
Jackson, Bo	87SP	190	$ .35	$2.00
Jackson, Bo	88SP	148	$ .15	$1.50
Jackson, Bo	89SP	70	$ .10	$1.25
Jackson, Bo	90SP	200	$ .03	$ .75
Jackson, Danny	86SP	186	$ .10	$ .40
Jackson, Danny	89SP	80	$ .03	$ .10
Jackson, Danny	90SP	89	$ .03	$ .10
Jackson, Mike	87SPR	33	$ .03	$ .10
Jackson, Reggie	86SP	37	$ .20	$ .50
Jackson, Reggie	86SP	57	$ .10	$ .40
Jackson, Reggie	86SP	61	$ .10	$ .40
Jackson, Reggie	86SP	71	$ .03	$ .10
Jackson, Reggie	86SP	147	$ .03	$ .10
Jackson, Reggie	86SP	150	$ .03	$ .10
Jackson, Reggie	87SP	44	$ .10	$ .40
Jackson, Reggie	88SP	120	$ .05	$ .35
Jacoby, Brook	87SP	109	$ .03	$ .10
Jacoby, Brook	88SP	72	$ .03	$ .10
Jacoby, Brook	89SP	192	$ .03	$ .10
Jacoby, Brook	90SP	155	$ .03	$ .10
James, Bob	86SP	158	$ .03	$ .10
James, Dion	88SP	36	$ .03	$ .10
Jefferies, Gregg	89SP	223	$ .50	$4.00
Jefferies, Gregg	89SP	90	$ .50	$1.00
Jefferies, Gregg	90SP	14	$ .03	$ .75
Jefferson, Stan	87SPR	9	$ .03	$ .10
John, Tommy	88SP	122	$ .05	$ .20
Johnson, Howard	88SP	138	$ .05	$ .25
Johnson, Howard	90SP	109	$ .03	$ .25
Johnson, Randy	89SP	224	$ .15	$1.50
Johnson, Randy	90SP	64	$ .03	$ .10
Jones, Doug	89SP	38	$ .03	$ .10
Jones, Doug	90SP	96	$ .03	$ .10
Jones, Jimmy	87SPR	35	$ .03	$ .10
Jones, Ron	89SP	178	$ .03	$ .35
Jones, Ron	89SP	225	$ .10	$ .30
Jones, Tracy	88SP	38	$ .03	$ .10
Jordan, Ricky	89SP	44	$ .25	$ .50
Jordan, Ricky	90SP	153	$ .03	$ .35
Joyner, Wally	86SPR	7	$ .45	$2.00
Joyner, Wally	87SP	26	$ .40	$1.00
Joyner, Wally	87SP	75	$ .35	$1.00
Joyner, Wally	88SP	75	$ .15	$ .45
Joyner, Wally	89SP	2	$ .03	$ .35
Joyner, Wally	90SP	49	$ .03	$ .35
Kelly, Roberto	90SP	184	$ .03	$ .25
Kennedy, Terry	88SP	94	$ .03	$ .10
Kerfeld, Charlie	86SPR	23	$ .03	$ .10
Kerfeld, Charlie	87SP	146	$ .03	$ .10
Key, Jimmy	88SP	116	$ .03	$ .10
Key, Jimmy	89SP	167	$ .03	$ .10
King, Eric	86SPR	42	$ .03	$ .10
Kingery, Mike	86SPR	37	$ .03	$ .10
Kingman, Dave	86SP	68	$ .03	$ .30
Kingman, Dave	86SP	116	$ .03	$ .10
Kingman, Dave	86SP	150	$ .03	$ .10
Kingman, Dave	87SP	178	$ .03	$ .10
Kittle, Ron	86SP	67	$ .08	$ .30
Kittle, Ron	86SP	86	$ .03	$ .10
Knepper, Bob	87SP	29	$ .03	$ .10
Knight, Ray	87SP	88	$ .03	$ .10
Knight, Ray	88SP	115	$ .03	$ .10
Koosman, Jerry	86SP	64	$ .03	$ .10
Kreuter, Chad	89SP	43	$ .03	$ .20

Player	Year	No.	VG	EX/MT
Kruk, John	86SPR	1	$ .05	$ .20
Kruk, John	87SP	61	$ .03	$ .10
Kruk, John	88SP	64	$ .03	$ .10
Kruk, John	89SP	184	$ .03	$ .10
Kruk, John	90SP	124	$ .03	$ .10
Krukow, Mike	87SP	62	$ .03	$ .10
Lacy, Lee	86SP	87	$ .03	$ .10
Lacy, Lee	87SP	86	$ .03	$ .10
Langston, Mark	87SP	102	$ .05	$ .25
Langston, Mark	88SP	46	$ .03	$ .10
Langston, Mark	89SP	159	$ .03	$ .10
Langston, Mark	90SP	110	$ .03	$ .15
Lansford, Carney	86SP	75	$ .35	$1.50
Lansford, Carney	87SP	138	$ .03	$ .10
Lansford, Carney	88SP	202	$ .03	$ .10
Lansford, Carney	89SP	53	$ .03	$ .10
Lansford, Carney	90SP	84	$ .03	$ .10
Larkin, Barry	86SPR	34	$ .15	$1.50

BARRY LARKIN
CINCINNATI REDS

Larkin, Barry	89SP	136	$ .05	$ .35
Larkin, Barry	90SP	160	$ .03	$ .25
Larkin, Gene	87SPR	34	$ .03	$ .25
Larkin, Gene	88SP	107	$ .03	$ .10
Laudner, Tim	89SP	152	$ .03	$ .10
LaValliere, Mike	88SP	193	$ .03	$ .10
LaValliere, Mike	89SP	98	$ .03	$ .10
LaValliere, Mike	90SP	157	$ .03	$ .10
Law, Vance	88SP	41	$ .03	$ .10
Law, Vance	89SP	162	$ .03	$ .10
Leach, Terry	88SP	139	$ .03	$ .10
Leary, Tim	89SP	81	$ .03	$ .10
Lefferts, Craig	90SP	130	$ .03	$ .10
Leibrandt, Charlie	86SP	159	$ .03	$ .10
Leibrandt, Charlie	86SP	186	$ .10	$ .40
Leibrandt, Charlie	88SP	21	$ .03	$ .10
Lemon, Chet	89SP	171	$ .03	$ .10
Leonard, Jeffrey	88SP	82	$ .03	$ .10
Leonard, Jeffrey	90SP	20	$ .03	$ .10
Lilliquist, Derek	90SP	24	$ .03	$ .25
Lind, Jose	90SP	58	$ .03	$ .10
Lind, Jose	89SP	62	$ .03	$ .10

SPORTFLICS

Player	Year	No.	VG	EX/MT	Player	Year	No.	VG	EX/MT
Lindeman, Jim	87SPR	43	$ .03	$ .10	McDowell, Oddibe	87SP	131	$ .03	$ .10
Lombardi, Phil	87SP	118	$ .45	$1.75	McDowell, Oddibe	88SP	175	$ .03	$ .10
Lombardozzi, Steve	86SP	178	$4.00	$15.00	McDowell, Oddibe	90SP	207	$ .03	$ .10
Lombardozzi, Steve	86SPR	17	$ .03	$ .10	McDowell, Roger	86SP	161	$ .10	$ .40
Lopes, Davey	86SP	144	$ .03	$ .10	McDowell, Roger	87SP	160	$ .03	$ .10
Lopes, Davey	86SP	194	$ .03	$ .10	McDowell, Roger	88SP	42	$ .03	$ .10
Lynn, Fred	86SP	38	$ .05	$ .20	McDowell, Roger	89SP	79	$ .03	$ .10
Lynn, Fred	86SP	63	$ .10	$ .40	McDowell, Roger	90SP	75	$ .03	$ .10
Lynn, Fred	86SP	71	$ .03	$ .10	McGee, Willie	86SP	19	$ .03	$ .10
Lynn, Fred	86SP	73	$ .12	$ .50	McGee, Willie	86SP	176	$ .32	$1.25
Lynn, Fred	86SP	137	$ .03	$ .10	McGee, Willie	86SP	179	$ .20	$1.25
Lynn, Fred	86SP	150	$ .03	$ .10	McGee, Willie	86SP	183	$ .20	$1.10
Lynn, Fred	86SPR	46	$ .12	$ .50	McGee, Willie	86SP	184	$ .32	$1.25
Lynn, Fred	87SP	198	$ .08	$ .30	McGee, Willie	87SP	74	$ .05	$ .20
Lynn, Fred	87SP	49	$ .03	$ .10	McGee, Willie	88SP	91	$ .03	$ .10
Lynn, Fred	88SP	23	$ .03	$ .10	McGee, Willie	89SP	206	$ .03	$ .10
Lynn, Fred	89SP	68	$ .03	$ .10	McGriff, Fred	87SPR	12	$ .25	$1.20
Mack, Shane	87SPR	31	$ .03	$ .10	McGriff, Fred	88SP	168	$ .15	$ .50
Maddux, Greg	89SP	108	$ .03	$ .10	McGriff, Fred	89SP	14	$ .05	$ .30
Maddux, Greg	90SP	211	$ .03	$ .10	McGriff, Fred	90SP	13	$ .03	$ .25
Madlock, Bill	86SP	58	$ .20	$ .50	McGwire, Mark	87SPR	13	$ .50	$1.75
Madlock, Bill	86SP	88	$ .03	$ .10	McGwire, Mark	88SP	100	$ .03	$1.00
Madlock, Bill	86SP	131	$ .03	$ .10	McGwire, Mark	88SP	221	$ .10	$ .50
Madlock, Bill	86SP	181	$ .20	$ .50	McGwire, Mark	89SP	200	$ .15	$ .75
Madlock, Bill	87SP	130	$ .03	$ .10	McGwire, Mark	90SP	141	$ .03	$ .50
Madlock, Bill	88SP	123	$ .03	$ .10	McLemore, Mark	87SPR	14	$ .03	$ .10
Magadan, Dave	87SPR	10	$ .12	$ .50	McReynolds, Kevin	87SP	135	$ .05	$ .50
Magadan, Dave	88SP	83	$ .05	$ .20	McReynolds, Kevin	87SP	155	$ .15	$ .70
Magadan, Dave	90SP	173	$ .03	$ .10	McReynolds, Kevin	88SP	56	$ .03	$ .40
Magrane, Joe	87SPR	11	$ .08	$ .30	McReynolds, Kevin	89SP	97	$ .03	$ .30
Magrane, Joe	88SP	128	$ .05	$ .20	McReynolds, Kevin	90SP	127	$ .03	$ .10
Magrane, Joe	90SP	151	$ .03	$ .10	Meyer, Joey	89SP	135	$ .03	$ .10
Maldonado, Candy	87SP	78	$ .03	$ .10	Milacki, Bob	89SP	224	$ .15	$1.50
Maldonado, Candy	88SP	126	$ .03	$ .10	Miller, Keith	87SPR	50	$ .03	$ .10
Marshall, Mike	86SP	89	$ .05	$ .20	Miller, Keith	88SP	225	$ .15	$ .35
Marshall, Mike	87SP	82	$ .03	$ .10	Mitchell, Kevin	86SPR	49	$ .85	$2.50
Marshall, Mike	88SP	220	$ .03	$ .10	Mitchell, Kevin	87SP	144	$ .25	$1.25
Marshall, Mike	89SP	54	$ .03	$ .10	Mitchell, Kevin	89SP	142	$ .03	$ .40
Martinez, Carlos	90SP	213	$ .03	$ .10	Mitchell, Kevin	90SP	1	$ .03	$ .50
Martinez, Dennis	89SP	106	$ .03	$ .10	Molitor, Paul	86SP	39	$ .03	$ .10
Martinez, Dennis	90SP	53	$ .03	$ .10	Molitor, Paul	86SP	128	$ .03	$ .10
Martinez, Ramon	89SP	224	$ .15	$1.50	Molitor, Paul	87SP	54	$ .03	$ .10
Martinez, Ramon	90SP	68	$ .03	$ .50	Molitor, Paul	88SP	79	$ .03	$ .10
Marzano, John	87SPR	49	$ .08	$ .30	Molitor, Paul	88SP	221	$ .10	$ .50
Mathews, Greg	86SPR	41	$ .03	$ .10	Molitor, Paul	89SP	209	$ .03	$ .10
Matthews, Gary	86SP	66	$ .03	$ .10	Molitor, Paul	90SP	183	$ .03	$ .10
Mattingly, Don	86SP	2	$1.00	$4.00	Moore, Mike	86SP	162	$ .03	$ .10
Mattingly, Don	86SP	54	$ .25	$1.25	Moore, Mike	89SP	77	$ .03	$ .10
Mattingly, Don	86SP	75	$ .35	$1.50	Moore, Mike	90SP	185	$ .03	$ .10
Mattingly, Don	86SP	176	$ .32	$1.25	Moreland, Keith	86SP	90	$ .03	$ .10
Mattingly, Don	86SP	179	$ .20	$1.25	Moreland, Keith	87SP	122	$ .03	$ .10
Mattingly, Don	86SP	180	$ .20	$1.25	Moreland, Keith	88SP	164	$ .03	$ .10
Mattingly, Don	86SP	183	$ .20	$1.10	Moreland, Keith	89SP	141	$ .03	$ .10
Mattingly, Don	86SP	184	$ .32	$1.25	Moreland, Keith	90SP	139	$ .03	$ .10
Mattingly, Don	87SP	1	$ .75	$2.25	Morman, Russ	86SPR	33	$ .03	$ .10
Mattingly, Don	87SP	75	$ .35	$1.00	Morris, Jack	86SP	117	$ .03	$ .10
Mattingly, Don	87SP	159	$ .35	$1.25	Morris, Jack	86SP	141	$ .03	$ .40
Mattingly, Don	88SP	1	$ .65	$1.50	Morris, Jack	87SP	87	$ .03	$ .10
Mattingly, Don	88SP	222	$ .15	$ .60	Morris, Jack	87SP	111	$ .12	$ .50
Mattingly, Don	89SP	50	$ .25	$ .75	Morris, Jack	88SP	176	$ .05	$ .20
Mattingly, Don	90SP	150	$ .03	$ .50	Morris, Jack	89SP	5	$ .03	$ .15
Mays, Willie	86SPR	46	$ .12	$ .50	Morris, John	87SPR	42	$ .03	$ .10
McCaskill, Kirk	87SP	127	$ .03	$ .10	Moseby, Lloyd	87SP	96	$ .03	$ .10
McCaskill, Kirk	88SP	78	$ .03	$ .10	Moseby, Lloyd	88SP	74	$ .03	$ .10
McCaskill, Kirk	89SP	214	$ .03	$ .10	Motley, Darryl	86SP	186	$ .10	$ .40
McCaskill, Kirk	90SP	169	$ .03	$ .10	Murphy, Dale	86SP	5	$ .22	$ .90
McCullers, Lance	86SPR	8	$ .03	$ .10	Murphy, Dale	86SP	62	$ .12	$ .50
McCullers, Lance	88SP	85	$ .03	$ .10	Murphy, Dale	86SP	179	$ .20	$1.25
McCullers, Lance	89SP	76	$ .03	$ .10	Murphy, Dale	86SP	183	$ .20	$1.10
McDowell, Oddibe	86SP	160	$ .10	$ .40	Murphy, Dale	87SP	3	$ .15	$ .60

Player	Year	No.	VG	EX/MT
Murphy, Dale	87SP	155	$ .15	$ .70
Murphy, Dale	87SP	159	$ .35	$1.25
Murphy, Dale	88SP	170	$ .08	$ .30
Murphy, Dale	89SP	110	$ .03	$ .25
Murphy, Dale	90SP	189	$ .03	$ .15
Murray, Eddie	86SP	4	$ .12	$ .75
Murray, Eddie	86SP	73	$ .12	$ .50
Murray, Eddie	86SP	145	$ .03	$ .10
Murray, Eddie	86SPR	48	$ .12	$ .50
Murray, Eddie	87SP	6	$ .10	$ .60
Murray, Eddie	87SP	75	$ .15	$1.00
Murray, Eddie	87SP	159	$ .35	$1.25
Murray, Eddie	88SP	59	$ .05	$ .35
Murray, Eddie	89SP	147	$ .03	$ .35
Musselman, Jeff	87SPR	15	$ .03	$ .10
Nettles, Graig	86SP	91	$ .03	$ .10
Niekro, Phil	86SP	53	$ .03	$ .10
Niekro, Phil	86SP	135	$ .08	$ .30
Niekro, Phil	86SP	163	$ .08	$ .30
Niekro, Phil	86SP	182	$ .20	$1.50
Niekro, Phil	87SP	147	$ .05	$ .20
Nieves, Juan	86SPR	5	$ .03	$ .10
Nieves, Juan	88SP	180	$ .05	$ .20
Nieves, Juan	88SP	211	$ .03	$ .10
Nokes, Matt	87SPR	16	$ .05	$ .25
Nokes, Matt	88SP	6	$ .05	$ .25

MATT NOKES
DETROIT TIGERS

Player	Year	No.	VG	EX/MT
Nokes, Matt	89SP	203	$ .03	$ .10
O'Brien, Pete	87SP	52	$ .03	$ .10
O'Brien, Pete	88SP	145	$ .03	$ .10
O'Brien, Pete	89SP	8	$ .03	$ .10
O'Brien, Pete	90SP	92	$ .03	$ .10
O'Neill, Paul	90SP	4	$ .03	$ .15
O'Neill, Paul	87SPR	17	$ .10	$ .40
Oberkfell, Ken	88SP	165	$ .03	$ .10
Ojeda, Bob	87SP	36	$ .03	$ .10
Olin, Steve	90SP	178	$ .03	$ .35
Oliver, Al	86SP	126	$ .03	$ .10
Oliver, Al	86SP	140	$ .03	$ .10
Oliver, Al	86SP	164	$ .03	$ .10
Oliver, Joe	90SP	71	$ .03	$ .35

Player	Year	No.	VG	EX/MT
Olson, Gregg	90SP	215	$ .03	$ .35
Oquendo, Jose	90SP	85	$ .03	$ .10
Orosco, Jesse	88SP	89	$ .03	$ .10
Orosco, Jessie	87SP	76	$ .03	$ .10
Orsulak, Joe	86SP	177	$ .12	$ .50
Orsulak, Joe	90SP	38	$ .03	$ .10
Orton, John	90SP	132	$ .03	$ .10
Pagliarulo, Mike	87SP	55	$ .03	$ .10
Pagliarulo, Mike	88SP	121	$ .03	$ .10
Pagliarulo, Mike	89SP	153	$ .03	$ .10
Palacios, Vicente	88SP	224	$ .08	$ .30
Palmeiro, Rafael	87SP	158	$ .25	$1.10
Palmeiro, Rafael	87SPR	32	$ .35	$ .60
Palmeiro, Rafael	89SP	30	$ .03	$ .20
Palmeiro, Rafael	90SP	9	$ .03	$ .10
Palmer, Dean	90SP	225	$ .03	$ .35
Parker, Dave	86SP	23	$ .05	$ .20
Parker, Dave	86SP	58	$ .20	$ .50
Parker, Dave	86SP	181	$ .20	$ .50
Parker, Dave	86SP	183	$ .20	$1.10
Parker, Dave	87SP	35	$ .03	$ .10
Parker, Dave	87SP	117	$ .03	$ .25
Parker, Dave	88SP	101	$ .03	$ .10
Parker, Dave	89SP	49	$ .03	$ .10
Parrish, Lance	86SP	92	$ .05	$ .20
Parrish, Lance	87SP	101	$ .03	$ .10
Parrish, Lance	87SP	154	$ .03	$ .10
Parrish, Lance	88SP	143	$ .03	$ .10
Parrish, Lance	89SP	59	$ .03	$ .10
Parrish, Larry	87SP	174	$ .03	$ .10
Parrish, Larry	88SP	49	$ .03	$ .10
Pasqua, Dan	87SP	143	$ .03	$ .10
Pena, Tony	86SP	165	$ .03	$ .10
Pena, Tony	87SP	93	$ .03	$ .10
Pena, Tony	87SP	151	$ .03	$ .10
Pena, Tony	88SP	142	$ .03	$ .10
Pendleton, Terry	88SP	159	$ .05	$ .25
Pendleton, Terry	89SP	99	$ .03	$ .10
Pendleton, Terry	90SP	174	$ .03	$ .10
Perez, Melido	89SP	118	$ .03	$ .10
Perez, Tony	86SP	138	$ .15	$ .60
Perry, Gerald	89SP	164	$ .03	$ .10
Pettis, Gary	87SP	157	$ .03	$ .10
Pettis, Gary	90SP	202	$ .03	$ .10
Plesac, Dan	86SPR	10	$ .03	$ .10
Plesac, Dan	88SP	191	$ .03	$ .10
Plesac, Dan	89SP	128	$ .03	$ .10
Plesac, Dan	90SP	102	$ .03	$ .10
Polonia, Luis	87SPR	18	$ .05	$ .20
Polonia, Luis	88SP	71	$ .05	$ .20
Polonia, Luis	89SP	133	$ .03	$ .10
Porter, Darrell	86SP	148	$ .03	$ .25
Power, Ted	86SP	166	$ .03	$ .10
Presley, Jim	86SP	40	$ .03	$ .25
Presley, Jim	87SP	179	$ .03	$ .20
Presley, Jim	88SP	54	$ .03	$ .10
Presley, Jim	89SP	7	$ .03	$ .10
Puckett, Kirby	86SP	93	$ .25	$1.75
Puckett, Kirby	87SP	7	$ .10	$ .90
Puckett, Kirby	87SP	198	$ .08	$ .30
Puckett, Kirby	88SP	8	$ .05	$ .50
Puckett, Kirby	88SP	180	$ .05	$ .40
Puckett, Kirby	89SP	156	$ .05	$ .65
Puckett, Kirby	90SP	11	$ .03	$ .40
Pyznarski, Tim	87SP	158	$ .65	$2.50
Quisenberry, Dan	86SP	55	$ .03	$ .10
Quisenberry, Dan	86SP	118	$ .03	$ .10
Quisenberry, Dan	86SP	186	$ .10	$ .40
Quisenberry, Dan	87SP	167	$ .03	$ .10
Quisenberry, Dan	88SP	76	$ .03	$ .10

SPORTFLICS

Player	Year	No.	VG	EX/MT	Player	Year	No.	VG	EX/MT
Raines, Tim	86SP	11	$ .08	$ .35	Ripken, Jr., Cal	90SP	100	$ .03	$ .25
Raines, Tim	86SP	127	$ .08	$ .30	Ritz, Kevin	90SP	29	$ .03	$ .10
Raines, Tim	86SP	144	$ .03	$ .10	Roberts, Bip	90SP	116	$ .03	$ .25
Raines, Tim	87SP	34	$ .08	$ .30	Robidoux, Billy "Joe"	86SP	178	$4.00	$15.00
Raines, Tim	87SP	152	$ .03	$ .10	Robidoux, Billy Jo	86SPR	28	$ .03	$ .10
Raines, Tim	87SP	197	$ .12	$ .50	Robinson, Don	88SP	90	$ .03	$ .10
Raines, Tim	87SP	199	$ .25	$ .75	Robinson, Jeff	87SPR	46	$ .03	$ .10
Raines, Tim	88SP	2	$ .08	$ .30	Robinson, Jeff	89SP	193	$ .03	$ .10
Raines, Tim	89SP	150	$ .03	$ .20	Rogers, Kenny	90SP	216	$ .03	$ .25
Raines, Tim	90SP	69	$ .03	$ .10	Rose, Pete	86SP	50	$ .40	$1.50
Randolph, Willie	88SP	47	$ .03	$ .10	Rose, Pete	86SP	51	$ .15	$ .35
Randolph, Willie	90SP	175	$ .03	$ .10	Rose, Pete	86SP	56	$ .20	$ .80
Rasmussen, Dennis	87SP	71	$ .03	$ .10	Rose, Pete	86SP	58	$ .20	$ .50
Rasmussen, Dennis	89SP	212	$ .03	$ .10	Rose, Pete	86SP	69	$ .15	$1.00
Rawley, Shane	87SP	181	$ .03	$ .10	Rose, Pete	86SP	130	$ .18	$ .50
Rawley, Shane	88SP	51	$ .03	$ .10	Rose, Pete	86SP	138	$ .15	$ .60
Ray, Johnny	87SP	116	$ .03	$ .25	Rose, Pete	86SP	181	$ .20	$ .50
Ray, Johnny	87SP	121	$ .03	$ .10	Rose, Pete	86SP	182	$ .20	$1.50
Ray, Johnny	88SP	186	$ .03	$ .10	Rose, Pete	86SPR	46	$ .12	$ .50
Ray, Johnny	89SP	195	$ .03	$ .10	Rose, Pete	87SP	25	$ .25	$1.00
Ray, Johnny	90SP	82	$ .03	$ .10	Ruffin, Bruce	86SPR	29	$ .03	$ .10
Reardon, Jeff	86SP	119	$ .03	$ .20	Russell, Jeff	90SP	192	$ .03	$ .10
Reardon, Jeff	87SP	77	$ .03	$ .10	Ryan, Nolan	86SP	43	$ .15	$1.75
Reardon, Jeff	88SP	53	$ .03	$ .10	Ryan, Nolan	86SP	141	$ .03	$ .50
Reardon, Jeff	89SP	168	$ .03	$ .10	Ryan, Nolan	86SP	143	$ .20	$1.25
Reardon, Jeff	90SP	37	$ .03	$ .10	Ryan, Nolan	86SP	182	$ .20	$1.50
Reed, Jody	88SP	225	$ .15	$ .60	Ryan, Nolan	87SP	125	$ .15	$1.75
Reed, Jody	89SP	210	$ .03	$ .10	Ryan, Nolan	88SP	39	$ .15	$1.25
Reuschel, Rick	88SP	136	$ .03	$ .10	Ryan, Nolan	89SP	115	$ .10	$1.00
Reuschel, Rick	89SP	72	$ .03	$ .10	Ryan, Nolan	90SP	8	$ .03	$1.00
Reuschel, Rick	90SP	161	$ .03	$ .10	Saberhagen, Bret	86SP	10	$ .10	$ .75
Reuss, Jerry	86SP	53	$ .03	$ .10	Saberhagen, Bret	86SP	176	$ .32	$1.25
Reynolds, Harold	88SP	127	$ .03	$ .10	Saberhagen, Bret	86SP	185	$ .15	$ .60
Reynolds, Harold	89SP	165	$ .03	$ .10	Saberhagen, Bret	86SP	186	$ .10	$ .40
Reynolds, Harold	90SP	119	$ .03	$ .10	Saberhagen, Bret	87SP	145	$ .08	$ .50
Rhoden, Rick	87SP	129	$ .03	$ .10	Saberhagen, Bret	88SP	15	$ .05	$ .30
Rhoden, Rick	88SP	104	$ .03	$ .10	Saberhagen, Bret	89SP	109	$ .03	$ .30
Rice, Jim	86SP	17	$ .05	$ .40	Saberhagen, Bret	90SP	94	$ .03	$ .25
Rice, Jim	86SP	52	$ .10	$ .40	Sabo, Chris	89SP	13	$ .25	$ .75
Rice, Jim	86SP	61	$ .10	$ .40	Salas, Mark	86SP	177	$ .12	$ .50
Rice, Jim	86SP	139	$ .10	$ .40	Samuel, Juan	86SP	94	$ .05	$ .30
Rice, Jim	86SP	146	$ .03	$ .10	Samuel, Juan	87SP	123	$ .03	$ .10
Rice, Jim	87SP	80	$ .20	$ .80	Samuel, Juan	88SP	96	$ .03	$ .10
Rice, Jim	87SP	97	$ .08	$ .30	Samuel, Juan	89SP	17	$ .03	$ .15
Rice, Jim	88SP	158	$ .03	$ .25	Sandberg, Ryne	86SP	20	$ .05	$1.50
Rice, Jim	89SP	173	$ .03	$ .25	Sandberg, Ryne	86SP	51	$ .15	$ .35
Righetti, Dave	86SP	41	$ .03	$ .30	Sandberg, Ryne	86SP	127	$ .08	$ .30
Righetti, Dave	86SP	72	$ .03	$ .10	Sandberg, Ryne	87SP	8	$ .08	$1.50
Righetti, Dave	86SP	141	$ .03	$ .50	Sandberg, Ryne	87SP	116	$ .03	$ .25
Righetti, Dave	86SPR	48	$ .12	$ .50	Sandberg, Ryne	87SP	197	$ .12	$ .50
Righetti, Dave	87SP	57	$ .03	$ .10	Sandberg, Ryne	88SP	12	$ .05	$1.00
Righetti, Dave	87SP	119	$ .03	$ .10	Sandberg, Ryne	89SP	201	$ .03	$ .10
Righetti, Dave	87SP	194	$ .03	$ .10	Sandberg, Ryne	90SP	54	$ .03	$ .25
Righetti, Dave	88SP	135	$ .03	$ .10	Sanders, Deion	90SP	221	$ .03	$ .50
Righetti, Dave	89SP	158	$ .03	$ .10	Santiago, Benito "Benny"	87SP	118	$ .25	$1.25
Righetti, Dave	90SP	88	$ .03	$ .10	Santiago, Benny	87SPR	19	$ .15	$ .75
Riles, Ernest	86SP	16	$ .03	$ .10	Santiago, Benny	88SP	22	$ .15	$ .75
Ripken, Bill	87SPR	28	$ .10	$ .40	Santiago, Benny	88SP	222	$ .15	$ .60
Ripken, Bill	88SP	216	$ .08	$ .30	Santiago, Benny	89SP	22	$ .03	$ .25
Ripken, Jr., Cal	86SP	8	$ .15	$ .50	Santiago, Benny	90SP	115	$ .03	$ .10
Ripken, Jr., Cal	86SP	54	$ .25	$1.25	Santovenia, Nelson	90SP	162	$ .03	$ .10
Ripken, Jr., Cal	86SP	57	$ .10	$ .40	Sax, Steve	86SP	56	$ .20	$ .80
Ripken, Jr., Cal	86SP	69	$ .15	$1.00	Sax, Steve	86SP	95	$ .03	$ .10
Ripken, Jr., Cal	86SP	73	$ .12	$ .50	Sax, Steve	86SPR	48	$ .12	$ .50
Ripken, Jr., Cal	86SP	128	$ .03	$ .10	Sax, Steve	87SP	12	$ .03	$ .10
Ripken, Jr., Cal	86SPR	48	$ .12	$ .50	Sax, Steve	89SP	58	$ .03	$ .10
Ripken, Jr., Cal	87SP	9	$ .08	$ .50	Sax, Steve	90SP	12	$ .03	$ .10
Ripken, Jr., Cal	87SP	113	$ .03	$ .10	Schilling, Curt	90SP	133	$ .03	$ .10
Ripken, Jr., Cal	88SP	152	$ .08	$ .35	Schiraldi, Calvin	86SPR	44	$ .03	$ .10
Ripken, Jr., Cal	89SP	66	$ .03	$ .35	Schmidt, Mike	86SP	44	$ .25	$1.50

Player	Year	No.	VG	EX/MT	Player	Year	No.	VG	EX/MT
Schmidt, Mike	86SP	62	$ .12	$ .50	Smith, Ozzie	87SP	142	$ .03	$ .10
Schmidt, Mike	86SP	68	$ .03	$ .30	Smith, Ozzie	88SP	68	$ .03	$ .10
Schmidt, Mike	86SP	139	$ .10	$ .40	Smith, Ozzie	89SP	105	$ .03	$ .10
Schmidt, Mike	86SP	148	$ .03	$ .30	Smith, Ozzie	90SP	16	$ .03	$ .10
Schmidt, Mike	87SP	30	$ .08	$1.00	Smith, Zane	88SP	134	$ .03	$ .10
Schmidt, Mike	87SP	115	$ .03	$ .30					
Schmidt, Mike	87SP	156	$ .03	$ .30					
Schmidt, Mike	88SP	35	$ .10	$1.00					
Schmidt, Mike	88SP	180	$ .05	$ .20					
Schmidt, Mike	89SP	21	$ .10	$1.00					
Schooler, Mike	90SP	187	$ .03	$ .10					
Schrom, Ken	87SP	107	$ .03	$ .10					
Scioscia, Mike	86SP	167	$ .03	$ .10					
Scioscia, Mike	87SP	67	$ .03	$ .10					
Scioscia, Mike	87SP	151	$ .03	$ .10					
Scioscia, Mike	88SP	110	$ .03	$ .10					
Scioscia, Mike	89SP	138	$ .03	$ .10					
Scioscia, Mike	90SP	163	$ .03	$ .10					
Scott, Mike	86SP	195	$ .08	$ .30					
Scott, Mike	87SP	19	$ .03	$ .10					
Scott, Mike	87SP	119	$ .03	$ .10					
Scott, Mike	87SP	120	$ .12	$ .50					
Scott, Mike	88SP	66	$ .03	$ .10					
Scott, Mike	89SP	120	$ .03	$ .10					
Scott, Mike	90SP	55	$ .03	$ .10					
Seaver, Tom	86SP	25	$ .20	$ .50					
Seaver, Tom	86SP	60	$ .08	$ .30					
Seaver, Tom	86SP	67	$ .08	$ .30					
Seaver, Tom	86SP	70	$ .08	$ .30					
Seaver, Tom	86SP	134	$ .03	$ .10					
Seaver, Tom	86SP	135	$ .08	$ .30					
Seaver, Tom	86SP	142	$ .03	$ .10					
Seaver, Tom	86SP	182	$ .20	$1.50					
Seaver, Tom	86SPR	47	$ .12	$ .50					
Seaver, Tom	87SP	28	$ .08	$ .30					
Seitzer, Kevin	87SP	158	$ .65	$2.50	Smoltz, John	90SP	61	$ .03	$ .35
Seitzer, Kevin	87SPR	20	$ .03	$1.25	Snider, Van	89SP	177	$ .03	$ .20
Seitzer, Kevin	88SP	17	$ .10	$ .50	Snyder, Cory	86SPR	18	$ .15	$1.00
Seitzer, Kevin	89SP	55	$ .03	$ .25	Snyder, Cory	87SP	24	$ .15	$1.00
Seitzer, Kevin	90SP	46	$ .03	$ .10	Snyder, Cory	88SP	29	$ .05	$ .20
Sheets, Larry	86SP	177	$ .12	$ .50	Snyder, Cory	89SP	196	$ .03	$ .10
Sheets, Larry	88SP	161	$ .03	$ .10	Snyder, Cory	90SP	3	$ .03	$ .15
Sheffield, Gary	89SP	223	$ .50	$4.00	Sosa, Sammy	90SP	81	$ .03	$ .50
Sheffield, Gary	89SP	41	$ .50	$1.00	Soto, Mario	86SP	168	$ .03	$ .10
Sheffield, Gary	90SP	52	$ .03	$ .50	Spiers, Bill	90SP	206	$ .03	$ .35
Sierra, Ruben	86SPR	16	$ .25	$2.50	Stanley, Bob	86SP	169	$ .03	$ .10
Sierra, Ruben	88SP	113	$ .10	$ .50	Stanley, Mike	87SPR	44	$ .08	$ .30
Sierra, Ruben	89SP	189	$ .03	$ .35	Staub, Rusty	86SP	138	$ .15	$ .50
Sierra, Ruben	90SP	188	$ .03	$ .25	Steinbach, Terry	87SP	118	$ .45	$1.75
Simmons, Ted	86SP	196	$ .03	$ .10	Steinbach, Terry	87SPR	22	$ .05	$ .50
Slaught, Don	87SP	32	$ .03	$ .10	Steinbach, Terry	88SP	174	$ .03	$ .25
Slaught, Don	87SP	154	$ .03	$ .10	Steinbach, Terry	89SP	119	$ .03	$ .25
Slaught, Don	89SP	218	$ .03	$ .10	Steinback, Terry	90SP	33	$ .03	$ .10
Smiley, John	87SPR	21	$ .10	$ .40	Stewart, Dave	88SP	162	$ .03	$ .25
Smiley, John	90SP	191	$ .03	$ .10	Stewart, Dave	89SP	23	$ .03	$ .25
Smith, Bryn	86SP	120	$ .03	$ .10	Stewart, Dave	90SP	194	$ .03	$ .15
Smith, Dave	87SP	77	$ .03	$ .10	Stieb, Dave	86SP	96	$ .03	$ .10
Smith, Dave	87SP	94	$ .03	$ .10	Stieb, Dave	89SP	35	$ .03	$ .10
Smith, Dave	88SP	208	$ .03	$ .10	Stieb, Dave	90SP	26	$ .03	$ .10
Smith, Dave	90SP	140	$ .03	$ .10	Straker, Les	87SPR	45	$ .03	$ .10
Smith, Dwight	90SP	152	$ .03	$ .50	Strawberry, Darryl	86SP	56	$ .20	$ .80
Smith, Lee	86SP	45	$ .03	$ .10	Strawberry, Darryl	86SP	97	$ .32	$1.75
Smith, Lee	86SP	55	$ .03	$ .10	Strawberry, Darryl	86SPR	48	$ .12	$ .50
Smith, Lee	87SP	104	$ .03	$ .10	Strawberry, Darryl	87SP	20	$ .20	$ .75
Smith, Lee	88SP	179	$ .03	$ .10	Strawberry, Darryl	88SP	155	$ .12	$ .75
Smith, Lee	89SP	148	$ .03	$ .10	Strawberry, Darryl	89SP	205	$ .10	$ .55
Smith, Lonnie	86SP	186	$ .10	$ .40	Strawberry, Darryl	90SP	146	$ .03	$ .35
Smith, Lonnie	90SP	65	$ .03	$ .10	Sundberg, Jim	86SP	186	$ .10	$ .40
Smith, Ozzie	86SP	121	$ .03	$ .10	Surhoff, B.J.	87SPR	23	$ .08	$ .30
Smith, Ozzie	87SP	79	$ .03	$ .10	Surhoff, B.J.	88SP	57	$ .05	$ .20

JOHN SMOLTZ
PITCHER·29

SPORTFLICS

Player	Year	No.	VG	EX/MT
Surhoff, B.J.	89SP	208	$ .03	$ .10
Sutcliffe, Rick	86SP	46	$ .03	$ .10
Sutcliffe, Rick	86SP	60	$ .08	$ .30
Sutcliffe, Rick	86SP	70	$ .08	$ .30
Sutcliffe, Rick	86SP	72	$ .03	$ .10
Sutcliffe, Rick	86SP	134	$ .03	$ .10
Sutcliffe, Rick	86SP	149	$ .03	$ .10
Sutcliffe, Rick	88SP	27	$ .03	$ .10
Sutcliffe, Rick	89SP	217	$ .03	$ .10
Sutcliffe, Rick	90SP	181	$ .03	$ .10
Sutter, Bruce	86SP	47	$ .03	$ .10
Sutter, Bruce	86SP	65	$ .03	$ .10
Sutton, Don	86SP	135	$ .08	$ .30
Sutton, Don	86SP	175	$ .03	$ .10
Sutton, Don	87SP	99	$ .03	$ .10
Sutton, Don	87SP	156	$ .03	$ .30
Sutton, Don	88SP	213	$ .05	$ .20
Sveum, Dale	86SPR	4	$ .03	$ .10
Swindell, Greg	86SPR	30	$ .15	$ .60
Swindell, Greg	89SP	4	$ .03	$ .25
Tabler, Pat	87SP	66	$ .03	$ .10
Tabler, Pat	88SP	205	$ .03	$ .10
Tabler, Pat	89SP	172	$ .03	$ .10
Tabler, Pat	90SP	218	$ .03	$ .10
Tallman, Matt	86SP	182	$ .20	$1.50
Tanana, Frank	88SP	133	$ .03	$ .10
Tanana, Frank	89SP	103	$ .03	$ .10
Tartabull, Danny	86SP	178	$4.00	$15.00
Tartabull, Danny	86SPR	22	$ .10	$ .75
Tartabull, Danny	87SP	23	$ .10	$ .40
Tartabull, Danny	88SP	19	$ .05	$ .25
Tartabull, Danny	89SP	46	$ .03	$ .25
Tartabull, Danny	90SP	129	$ .03	$ .10
Templeton, Garry	86SP	170	$ .03	$ .10
Tettleton, Mickey	90SP	171	$ .03	$ .10
Thigpen, Bobby	89SP	207	$ .03	$ .25
Thigpen, Bobby	90SP	27	$ .03	$ .10
Thomas, Andres	86SPR	14	$ .03	$ .10
Thompson, Milt	88SP	173	$ .03	$ .10
Thompson, Milt	89SP	169	$ .03	$ .10
Thompson, Robby	86SPR	25	$ .08	$ .30
Thompson, Robby	87SP	46	$ .03	$ .10
Thompson, Robby	88SP	24	$ .03	$ .10
Thompson, Robby	89SP	78	$ .03	$ .10
Thompson, Robby	90SP	60	$ .03	$ .10
Thornton, Andre	86SP	171	$ .03	$ .10
Thurman, Gary	88SP	223	$ .25	$ .45
Traber, Jim	86SPR	32	$ .03	$ .10
Trammell, Alan	86SP	147	$ .03	$ .10
Trammell, Alan	86SP	172	$ .08	$ .30
Trammell, Alan	87SP	188	$ .03	$ .10
Trammell, Alan	88SP	25	$ .05	$ .20
Trammell, Alan	89SP	215	$ .05	$ .25
Trammell, Alan	90SP	154	$ .03	$ .10
Treadway, Jeff	88SP	225	$ .15	$ .60
Treadway, Jeff	89SP	107	$ .03	$ .25
Treadway, Jeff	90SP	219	$ .03	$ .10
Tudor, John	86SP	122	$ .03	$ .20
Tudor, John	86SP	184	$ .32	$1.25
Tudor, John	86SP	185	$ .15	$ .60
Tudor, John	87SP	173	$ .03	$ .10
Tudor, John	88SP	198	$ .03	$ .10
Tudor, John	89SP	86	$ .03	$ .10
Upshaw, Willie	86SP	98	$ .03	$ .10
Upshaw, Willie	88SP	214	$ .03	$ .10
Uribe, Jose	89SP	61	$ .03	$ .10
Uribe, Jose	90SP	79	$ .03	$ .10
Valenzuela, Fernando	86SP	12	$ .08	$ .30
Valenzuela, Fernando	86SP	60	$ .08	$ .30
Valenzuela, Fernando	86SP	72	$ .03	$ .10

Player	Year	No.	VG	EX/MT
Valenzuela, Fernando	86SP	132	$ .03	$ .10
Valenzuela, Fernando	86SP	143	$ .20	$1.25
Valenzuela, Fernando	86SPR	47	$ .12	$ .50
Valenzuela, Fernando	87SP	119	$ .03	$ .10
Valenzuela, Fernando	87SP	120	$ .12	$ .50
Valenzuela, Fernando	87SP	150	$ .08	$ .30
Valenzuela, Fernando	88SP	40	$ .05	$ .20
Valenzuela, Fernando	89SP	124	$ .03	$ .10
Van Slyke, Andy	88SP	109	$ .03	$ .15
Van Slyke, Andy	89SP	166	$ .03	$ .10
Van Slyke, Andy	90SP	101	$ .03	$ .10
Vaughn, Greg	90SP	135	$ .03	$ .75
Ventura, Robin	90SP	222	$ .03	$ .35
Viola, Frank	86SP	99	$ .03	$ .50
Viola, Frank	88SP	196	$ .03	$ .30
Viola, Frank	89SP	10	$ .03	$ .20
Viola, Frank	90SP	122	$ .03	$ .20
Virgil, Ozzie	88SP	217	$ .03	$ .10
Virgil, Ozzie	89SP	94	$ .03	$ .10
Walk, Bob	89SP	34	$ .03	$ .10
Walker, Greg	86SP	174	$ .03	$ .10
Walker, Greg	88SP	103	$ .03	$ .10
Walker, Greg	89SP	19	$ .03	$ .10
Wallach, Tim	86SP	123	$ .03	$ .10
Wallach, Tim	87SP	72	$ .03	$ .10
Wallach, Tim	87SP	115	$ .03	$ .30
Wallach, Tim	88SP	151	$ .03	$ .10
Wallach, Tim	89SP	114	$ .03	$ .10
Wallach, Tim	90SP	182	$ .03	$ .10
Walton, Jerome	90SP	67	$ .03	$1.00
Ward, Duane	90SP	107	$ .03	$ .10
Ward, Gary	86SP	197	$ .03	$ .10
Ward, Gary	87SP	91	$ .03	$ .10
Ward, Gary	88SP	125	$ .03	$ .10
Washington, Claudell	89SP	75	$ .03	$ .10
Webster, Mitch	87SP	177	$ .03	$ .10
Webster, Mitch	88SP	105	$ .03	$ .10

MITCH WEBSTER
CHICAGO CUBS

Player	Year	No.	VG	EX/MT
Webster, Mitch	89SP	67	$ .03	$ .10
Weiss, Walt	89SP	116	$ .05	$ .30
Weiss, Walt	90SP	74	$ .03	$ .25

Player	Year	No.	VG	EX/MT	Player	Year	No.	VG	EX/MT
Welch, Bob	86SP	198	$ .03	$ .10	Wilson, Willie	88SP	192	$ .03	$ .10
Welch, Bob	88SP	167	$ .03	$ .10	Wilson, Willie	89SP	186	$ .03	$ .10
Welch, Bob	89SP	91	$ .03	$ .10	Winfield, Dave	86SP	49	$ .15	$ .50
Welch, Bob	90SP	35	$ .03	$ .10	Winfield, Dave	87SP	41	$ .10	$ .40
West, Dave	89SP	45	$ .10	$ .35	Winfield, Dave	87SP	153	$ .03	$ .10
Whitaker, Lou	86SP	48	$ .05	$ .25	Winfield, Dave	88SP	7	$ .05	$ .20
Whitaker, Lou	86SP	74	$ .03	$ .10	Winfield, Dave	89SP	24	$ .03	$ .15
Whitaker, Lou	86SPR	48	$ .12	$ .50	Winfield, Dave	90SP	87	$ .03	$ .15
Whitaker, Lou	87SP	112	$ .03	$ .10	Witt, Bobby	86SPR	12	$ .05	$ .20
Whitaker, Lou	87SP	137	$ .03	$ .10	Witt, Bobby	87SP	39	$ .03	$ .10
Whitaker, Lou	88SP	30	$ .03	$ .10	Witt, Bobby	89SP	82	$ .03	$ .10
Whitaker, Lou	89SP	18	$ .03	$ .15	Witt, Mike	86SP	53	$ .03	$ .10
Whitaker, Lou	90SP	103	$ .03	$ .10	Witt, Mike	87SP	59	$ .03	$ .10
White, Devon	87SPR	24	$ .12	$ .50	Witt, Mike	88SP	32	$ .03	$ .10
White, Devon	88SP	99	$ .05	$ .20	Witt, Mike	89SP	197	$ .03	$ .10
White, Devon	89SP	16	$ .03	$ .20	Worrell, Todd	86SPR	35	$ .10	$ .50
White, Devon	90SP	210	$ .03	$ .10	Worrell, Todd	87SP	33	$ .08	$ .30
White, Frank	86SP	186	$ .10	$ .40	Worrell, Todd	87SP	77	$ .03	$ .10
White, Frank	87SP	168	$ .03	$ .10	Worrell, Todd	88SP	61	$ .03	$ .10
White, Frank	88SP	149	$ .03	$ .10	Worrell, Todd	89SP	183	$ .03	$ .10
Whitson, Ed	90SP	212	$ .03	$ .10	Worrell, Todd	90SP	165	$ .03	$ .10
Williams, Ken	87SPR	41	$ .03	$ .10	Worthington, Craig	89SP	134	$ .05	$ .25
Williams, Ken	88SP	69	$ .05	$ .20	Worthington, Craig	90SP	117	$ .03	$ .10
Williams, Matt	87SPR	25	$ .05	$ .75	Youmans, Floyd	87SP	103	$ .03	$ .10
Williams, Matt	90SP	70	$ .03	$ .35	Youmans, Floyd	88SP	108	$ .03	$ .10
Williams, Mitch	86SPR	20	$ .03	$ .25	Young, Curt	88SP	209	$ .03	$ .10
Williams, Mitch	89SP	151	$ .03	$ .10	Young, Gerald	87SPR	36	$ .08	$ .30
Williams, Mitch	90SP	196	$ .03	$ .10	Young, Gerald	89SP	125	$ .03	$ .10
Williams, Reggie	86SPR	19	$ .03	$ .10	Young, Mike	86SP	199	$ .03	$ .10
Wilson, Glenn	87SP	166	$ .03	$ .10	Yount, Robin	86SP	42	$ .10	$ .75
Wilson, Glenn	88SP	204	$ .03	$ .10	Yount, Robin	86SP	54	$ .25	$1.25
Wilson, Glenn	89SP	12	$ .03	$ .10	Yount, Robin	86SP	63	$ .10	$ .40
Wilson, Mookie	90SP	128	$ .03	$ .10	Yount, Robin	86SP	71	$ .03	$ .10
Wilson, Willie	86SP	124	$ .03	$ .10	Yount, Robin	87SP	16	$ .08	$ .75
Wilson, Willie	86SP	128	$ .03	$ .10	Yount, Robin	88SP	34	$ .05	$ .75
Wilson, Willie	86SP	144	$ .03	$ .10	Yount, Robin	89SP	199	$ .03	$ .25
Wilson, Willie	86SP	180	$ .20	$1.25	Yount, Robin	90SP	18	$ .03	$ .35
Wilson, Willie	86SP	186	$ .10	$ .40	Zeile, Todd	90SP	177	$ .03	$1.00
Wilson, Willie	87SP	85	$ .03	$ .10					

TOPPS CHEWING GUM COMPANY, INC. 1951-1991

The billions of cards printed success story of the Topps Chewing Gum Company began in 1951 with two game baseball cards which had to be punched out of a perforated piece of cardboard. Those first cards had either blue or red backs and were for use in playing a baseball game. You also received a piece of candy for your penny investment.

Improving on those small cards, Topps produced a baseball card set in 1952 containing 407 cards, Topps was able to control the market after bankruptcy forced its competitor to cease making sets in 1955. Until 1981, there were few challenges to Topps and they prospered. In 1991 Topps celebrates forty years of making baseball cards by placing actual cards or certificates redeemable for every previously made Topps card. These are placed randomly in all Topps products for 1991.

Refer to the color section beginning on page 4 to see a representative sample of each year of the Topps cards in color. A brief description of each set follows. **All cards from 1957 to 1991 are 2 ½" x 3 ½"** except for Topps Big Baseball cards which are 2⅝" x 3¾".

1951bb - 52 cards 2" x 2 ⅝" white border with blue and white back (no copyright or date)
1951rb - 52 cards 2" x 2 ⅝" white border with red and white back (no copyright or date)
1952 - 407 cards 2 ⅝" x 3 ¾" white border (Topps baseball in either red or black printing on back bottom and copyright T.C.G. on lower left)
1953 - 280 card numbers with 6 numbers not used (253,261, 267,268,272,275) 2 ⅝" x 3¾" white border except for black or red name strip on bottom (copyright T.C.G. on back in lower left corner with Topps written in card numbered baseball)
1954 - 250 cards 2⅝" x 3 ¾" white border with black and white photo insert on front (copyright T.G.C. up right side from bottom with Topps written in card numbered baseball)
1955 - 210 card numbers with 4 numbers not used (175,186,203,209) 2 ⅝" x 3¾" white border horizontal card with color insert photo on front (copyright T.G.C. below birth date with Topps written in card numbered baseball)
1956 - 340 cards 2 ⅝" x 3 ¾" white border horizontal card with color insert photo on front (copyright T.G.C. up right border on back with Topps written in card numbered baseball)
1957 - 407 cards w/white borders (copyright T.G.C. up right border on back with Topps written in card numbered baseball)
1958 - 495 card numbers (#145 not used) w/white borders (copyright T.G.C. up right border on back and card number in hatted baseball)
1959 - 572 cards w/white borders and green and red or black and red printing on back (copyright T.G.C. up right side on back)
1960 - 572 cards w/white borders horizontal with black and white photo insert on front (copyright T.G.C. up right side on back)
1961 - 589 cards with 3 numbers not used (426,587,588) white border (copyright T.G.C. lower right corner on back with Topps written in card numbered baseball)
1962 - 598 cards w/brown wood grain effect borders (copyright T.G.C. above statistical record on back with Topps written in card numbered baseball)
1963 - 576 cards w/brightly colored name panel at bottom and black and white circular portrait also (copyright T.G.C. on lower back corner with Topps written above card number)
1964 - 587 cards w/white border but bold team name at top of card (copyright T.G.C. above rub-off quiz on back with Topps written in card numbered baseball)
1965 - 598 cards w/white border but pennant waving team name in lower left corner (copyright T.G.C. on back lower right corner with Topps written in card numbered baseball)
1966 - 598 cards w/white border and team name in upper left corner in diagonal strip (copyright T.G.C. on back lower right corner with Topps written in card numbered baseball)
1967 - 609 cards w/white borders and bold team name at bottom (copyright T.G.C. on back lower right corner and Topps written in card numbered baseball)

1968 - 598 cards with brown basket weave borders and team name in brightly colored circle (copyright T.G.C. on back lower right corner with Topps written in card numbered baseball)
1969 - 664 cards w/white border (copyright T.G.C. up right side on back with "T" in Topps encircling the card number)
1970 - 720 cards w/grey border (copyright T.G.C. up right side on back with Topps written in circle above card number)
1971 - 752 cards w/black border and player black and white photo on reverse (copyright T.G.C. up left side on back is only indication of Topps card)
1972 - 787 cards w/white border and arched effect with team name in that arch above the player (copyright T.G.C. on lower right corner on back)
1973 - 660 cards w/ white border and back in black bordered design (copyright T.G.C. at bottom on back)
1974 - 660 cards w/white border and pennant-like player name at bottom and team name at top (copyright T.G.C. at bottom on back.)
1975 - 660 cards w/bright colored borders of two colors depending upon team for the colors (copyright 1975 Topps Chewing Gum, Inc. on bottom back)
1976 - 660 cards w/white border plus 44 traded cards issued later with same number and "T" added to number (copyright 1976 Topps Chewing Gum, Inc. up right border on back)
1977 - 660 cards w/white borders (copyright 1977 Topps Chewing Gum, Inc.on bottom back)
1978 - 726 cards w/white borders (copyright 1978 Topps Chewing Gum, Inc. on lower right side of back)
1979 - 726 cards w/white border and Topps logo in baseball on front (copyright 1979 Topps Chewing Gum, Inc. on lower right corner of back)
1980 - 726 cards w/white border (copyright 1980 Topps Chewing Gum, Inc. lower left side on back)
1981 - 726 cards w/white border and Topps logo in baseball on front (copyright 1981 Topps Chewing Gum, Inc. on lower right side of back)
1982 - 792 cards w/white borders and Topps logo above team name on the front lower right side (copyright 1982 Topps Chewing Gum, Inc. on back lower right side)
1983 - 792 cards w/white borders and Topps logo in upper right corner on front (copyright 1983 Topps Chewing Gum, Inc. on bottom of back)
1984 - 792 cards w/white borders, team name vertically down left and Topps logo in upper right corner on front (copyright 1984 Topps Chewing Gum, Inc. up right side on back)
1985 - 792 cards w/white border and Topps logo in upper right corner on front (copyright 1985 Topps Chewing Gum, Inc. above "Baseball Trivia Quiz" on back)
1986 - 792 cards w/black border across the top and down the sides becoming white and Topps logo on upper right of front (Copyright 1986 Topps Chewing Gum, Inc. on bottom of back)
1987 - 792 cards w/brown wood grain effect similar to 1962 and Topps logo on lower left corner of front (copyright 1987 Topps Chewing Gum, Inc. on back above personal statistical information)
1988 - 792 cards w/white border and Topps logo in lower left corner on front (copyright 1988 Topps Chewing Gum, Inc. up the right side on back)
1989 - 792 cards w/ white border and Topps logo on the front in various locations (copyright 1989 on back in dark pink area inside black border at lower right.)
1990 - 792 cards w/multi-colored borders and Topps logo on front in various locations (copyright 1990 on mustard yellow back right side)
1991 - 792 cards w/white border and Topps 40 Years of Baseball logo on front upper left corner (copyright 1991 on reddish colored back at lower right side)

There are abbreviations used throughout the Topps section that need some explanation. All of the following will be found under the year section referring to the type of card that is listed:

T - Topps used for designation of all cards in section.

TAS - Topps All Star card of any given year.

TATL - Topps All Time Leader up to that time of issue.

TBB - Topps Big Baseball set first issued in 1988.

Tbb - Refers to 1951 Topps blue back cards only.

THL - Topps Highlights (usually refers to the previous year accomplishments).

TIA - Topps In Action (another way of including a star more than once).

TMVP - Topps Most Valuable Player.

TRB - Topps Record Breaker usually refers to previous year or lifetime accomplishments.

Trb - Refers to 1951 Topps red backs only.

TRH - Topps Record Holder.

TTB - Topps Turn Back The Clock refers to happenings of previous years usually in increments of five years.

TTR - Topps Traded cards usually numbered 1T-132T, with "T" omitted on the number listing and placed on the year. The Traded cards of 1981 continued the numbers of that year's set and are numbered 727-858.

TMLD - Topps Major League Debut card set of 152 cards of players first game appearance (first issued in 1989).

The listing for each card shown appears immediately following the photograph.

Player	Year	No.	VG	EX/MT	Player	Year	No.	VG	EX/MT
A's, Team	56T	236	$6.00	$17.50	Aaron, Hank	70T	65	$ .90	$3.00
A's, Team	57T	204	$3.60	$10.00	Aaron, Hank	70T	500	$8.50	$33.00
A's, Team	58T	174	$2.25	$5.50	Aaron, Hank	70TAS	462	$3.00	$9.00
A's, Team	59T	172	$1.65	$7.00	Aaron, Hank	71T	400	$9.00	$35.00
A's, Team	60T	413	$1.65	$7.00	Aaron, Hank	72T	87	$ .60	$2.00
A's, Team	61T	297	$ .90	$3.00	Aaron, Hank	72T	89	$ .60	$2.00
A's, Team	62T	384	$1.75	$4.50	Aaron, Hank	72T	299	$7.50	$22.50
A's, Team	63T	397	$ .75	$3.00	Aaron, Hank	72TIA	300	$3.00	$10.00
A's, Team	64T	151	$1.25	$4.25	Aaron, Hank	73T	1	$4.50	$17.50
A's, Team	65T	151	$ .75	$2.20	Aaron, Hank	73T	100	$4.50	$17.50
A's, Team	66T	492	$ .70	$4.00	Aaron, Hank	73TATL	473	$ .90	$3.00
A's, Team	67T	262	$ .75	$2.25	Aaron, Hank	74T	1	$5.00	$25.00
A's, Team	68T	554	$ .75	$2.25	Aaron, Hank(1954-1957)	74T	2	$ .75	$3.50
A's, Team	70T	631	$ .80	$3.75	Aaron, Hank(1958-1961)	74T	3	$ .75	$3.50
A's, Team	71T	624	$ .90	$3.00	Aaron, Hank(1962-1965)	74T	4	$ .75	$3.50
A's, Team	72T	454	$ .90	$3.00	Aaron, Hank(1966-1969)	74T	5	$ .75	$3.50
A's, Team	73T	500	$ .75	$2.20	Aaron, Hank(1970-1973)	74T	6	$ .75	$3.50
A's, Team	74T	246	$ .45	$1.45	Aaron, Hank	74TAS	332	$ .50	$2.00
A's, Team Checklist	75T	561	$ .35	$1.25	Aaron, Hank	75T	195	$2.00	$6.00
A's, Team Checklist	76T	421	$ .35	$1.25	Aaron, Hank	75T	660	$5.00	$20.00
A's, Team Checklist	77T	74	$ .15	$ .50	Aaron, Hank	75THL	1	$5.00	$20.00
A's, Team Checklist	78T	577	$ .05	$ .25	Aaron, Hank	76T	550	$4.25	$15.00
A's, Team Checklist	79T	328	$ .05	$ .25	Aaron, Hank	76TRB	1	$2.50	$12.00
A's, Team Checklist	80T	96	$ .05	$ .25	Aaron, Hank	79T	412	$ .15	$ .50
A's, Team Checklist	81T	671	$ .02	$ .20	Aaron, Hank	79TRH	413	$ .20	$ .75
A's, Team Leaders	86T	216	$ .01	$ .04	Aaron, Hank	89TTB	663	$ .01	$ .10
A's, Team Leaders	87T	456	$ .01	$ .04	Aaron, Tommie	63T	46	$ .45	$1.45
A's, Team Leaders	88T	759	$ .01	$ .04	Aaron, Tommie	64T	454	$ .75	$2.20
A's, Team Leaders	89T	639	$ .01	$ .05	Aaron, Tommie	65T	567	$1.75	$4.50
Aaron, Hank	54T	128	$325.00	$1300.00	Aaron, Tommie	68T	394	$ .15	$ .50
Aaron, Hank	55T	47	$70.00	$300.00	Aaron, Tommie	69T	128	$ .30	$ .95
Aaron, Hank	56T	31	$50.00	$200.00	Aaron, Tommie	70T	278	$ .30	$ .95
Aaron, Hank	57T	20	$75.00	$225.00	Aaron, Tommie	71T	717	$ .90	$3.00
Aaron, Hank	58T	30	$40.00	$150.00	Aase, Don	76T	597	$ .30	$ .85
Aaron, Hank	58T	351	$8.00	$22.00	Aase, Don	77T	472	$ .05	$ .15
Aaron, Hank	58T	418	$35.00	$130.00					
Aaron, Hank	58TAS	488	$9.00	$37.50					
Aaron, Hank	59T	212	$7.00	$28.00					
Aaron, Hank	59T	380	$25.00	$100.00					
Aaron, Hank	59T	467	$5.00	$15.00					
Aaron, Hank	59TAS	561	$22.50	$95.00					
Aaron, Hank	60T	300	$27.50	$85.00					
Aaron, Hank	60TAS	566	$30.00	$90.00					
Aaron, Hank	61T	43	$1.50	$5.75					
Aaron, Hank	61T	415	$30.00	$90.00					
Aaron, Hank	61TAS	577	$45.00	$140.00					
Aaron, Hank	61TMVP	484	$11.00	$32.50					
Aaron, Hank	62T	320	$35.00	$100.00					
Aaron, Hank	62TAS	394	$9.00	$30.00					
Aaron, Hank	63T	1	$5.00	$25.00					
Aaron, Hank	63T	3	$3.00	$12.00					
Aaron, Hank	63T	242	$7.50	$22.50					
Aaron, Hank	63T	390	$35.00	$110.00					
Aaron, Hank	64T	7	$1.70	$5.00					
Aaron, Hank	64T	9	$3.00	$9.00					
Aaron, Hank	64T	11	$ .75	$3.00					
Aaron, Hank	64T	300	$25.00	$75.00					
Aaron, Hank	64T	423	$20.00	$65.00					
Aaron, Hank	65T	2	$2.10	$6.00					
Aaron, Hank	65T	170	$25.00	$75.00					
Aaron, Hank	66T	215	$3.00	$12.00					
Aaron, Hank	66T	500	$25.00	$75.00					
Aaron, Hank	67T	242	$1.75	$4.50					
Aaron, Hank	67T	244	$2.10	$6.00					
Aaron, Hank	67T	250	$20.00	$75.00	Aase, Don	78T	12	$ .02	$ .10
Aaron, Hank	68T	3	$1.50	$4.00	Aase, Don	79T	368	$ .02	$ .10
Aaron, Hank	68T	5	$1.25	$3.75	Aase, Don	80T	239	$ .01	$ .10
Aaron, Hank	68T	110	$15.00	$55.00	Aase, Don	81T	601	$ .01	$ .10
Aaron, Hank	68TAS	370	$3.50	$11.00	Aase, Don	82T	199	$ .01	$ .07
Aaron, Hank	69T	100	$11.50	$45.00					

DON AASE

TOPPS

Player	Year	No.	VG	EX/MT	Player	Year	No.	VG	EX/MT
Aase, Don	83T	599	$ .01	$ .07	Adair, Jerry	61T	71	$ .35	$1.25
Aase, Don	85T	86	$ .01	$ .05	Adair, Jerry	62T	449	$ .75	$2.50
Aase, Don	85TTR	1	$ .02	$ .10	Adair, Jerry	63T	488	$2.50	$6.50
Aase, Don	86T	288	$ .01	$ .04	Adair, Jerry	64T	22	$ .30	$ .95
Aase, Don	87T	766	$ .01	$ .04	Adair, Jerry	65T	231	$ .35	$1.25
Aase, Don	88T	467	$ .01	$ .04	Adair, Jerry	66T	533	$5.00	$20.00
Aase, Don	89TTR	1	$ .01	$ .06	Adair, Jerry	67T	484	$ .75	$3.00
Aase, Don	90T	301	$ .01	$ .04	Adair, Jerry	68T	346	$ .30	$ .85
Abarbanel, Mickey	68T	287	$ .30	$ .85	Adair, Jerry	69T	159	$ .30	$ .85
Abbott, Glenn	74T	602	$ .07	$ .30	Adair, Jerry	70T	525	$ .15	$ .50
Abbott, Glenn	75T	591	$ .07	$ .30	Adair, Jerry	73T	179	$ .30	$ .95
Abbott, Glenn	76T	322	$ .05	$ .20	Adams, Bobby	52T	249	$7.00	$20.00
Abbott, Glenn	77T	207	$ .05	$ .15	Adams, Bobby	53T	152	$4.50	$15.00
Abbott, Glenn	78T	31	$ .02	$ .10	Adams, Bobby	54T	123	$3.60	$10.00
Abbott, Glenn	79T	497	$ .02	$ .10	Adams, Bobby	55T	178	$5.25	$15.00
Abbott, Glenn	80T	166	$ .01	$ .10	Adams, Bobby	56T	287	$2.25	$8.00
Abbott, Glenn	81T	699	$ .01	$ .10	Adams, Bobby	58T	99	$1.25	$4.25
Abbott, Glenn	82T	336	$ .01	$ .07	Adams, Bobby	59T	249	$ .75	$2.20
Abbott, Glenn	82T	571	$ .01	$ .07	Adams, Glenn	76T	389	$ .05	$ .20
Abbott, Glenn	84T	356	$ .01	$ .06	Adams, Glenn	78T	497	$ .02	$ .10
Abbott, Jim	88TTR	1	$ .50	$3.00	Adams, Glenn	79T	193	$ .02	$ .10
Abbott, Jim	89T	573	$ .25	$1.00	Adams, Glenn	80T	604	$ .01	$ .10
Abbott, Jim	89TBB	322	$ .01	$ .25	Adams, Glenn	81T	18	$ .01	$ .10
Abbott, Jim	89TMLD	1	$ .01	$ .50	Adams, Glenn	82T	519	$ .01	$ .07
Abbott, Jim	89TTR	2	$ .01	$ .50	Adams, Glenn	83T	574	$ .01	$ .07
Abbott, Jim	90T	675	$ .01	$ .25	Adams, Mike	74T	573	$ .07	$ .30
Abbott, Jim	91T	285	$ .01	$ .10	Adams, Red	73T	569	$1.25	$4.25
Abbott, Kyle	90T	444	$ .01	$ .25	Adams, Red	74T	144	$ .75	$3.00
Aber, Al	53T	233	$12.50	$50.00	Adams, Ricky	84T	487	$ .01	$ .06
Aber, Al	54T	238	$3.60	$10.00	Adams, Ricky	86T	153	$ .01	$ .04
Aber, Al	56T	317	$2.25	$8.00	Adamson, Mike	69T	66	$ .30	$ .85
Aber, Al	57T	141	$ .95	$3.50	Adamson, Mike	71T	362	$ .08	$ .20
Abernathy, Ted	57T	293	$4.25	$15.00	Adcock, Joe	52T	347	$55.00	$160.00
Abernathy, Ted	59T	169	$ .75	$2.20	Adcock, Joe	56T	320	$2.00	$6.00
Abernathy, Ted	60T	334	$ .75	$2.20	Adcock, Joe	57T	117	$2.00	$6.00
Abernathy, Ted	64T	64	$ .30	$ .95	Adcock, Joe	58T	325	$ .45	$1.50
Abernathy, Ted	65T	332	$ .35	$1.25	Adcock, Joe	58T	351	$8.00	$22.00
Abernathy, Ted	66T	2	$ .30	$ .95	Adcock, Joe	59T	315	$ .90	$3.00
Abernathy, Ted	67T	597	$2.10	$6.00	Adcock, Joe	60T	3	$ .75	$2.20
Abernathy, Ted	68T	264	$ .30	$ .85	Adcock, Joe	61T	245	$ .75	$3.00
Abernathy, Ted	69T	483	$ .30	$ .85	Adcock, Joe	62T	265	$ .75	$3.00
Abernathy, Ted	70T	562	$ .30	$ .95	Adcock, Joe	63T	170	$ .35	$1.25
Abernathy, Ted	71T	187	$ .15	$ .50	Adcock, Joe	67T	563	$7.00	$21.00
Abernathy, Ted	72T	519	$ .15	$ .50	Addis, Bob	52T	259	$12.00	$40.00
Abernathy, Ted	73T	22	$ .07	$ .30	Addis, Bob	53T	157	$4.50	$15.00
Abner, Shawn	85T	282	$ .05	$ .25	Adduci, Jim	89T	338	$ .01	$ .05
Abner, Shawn	90T	122	$ .01	$ .04	Adlesh, Dave	67T	51	$ .30	$ .85
Abner, Shawn	91T	697	$ .01	$ .03	Adlesh, Dave	68T	576	$ .35	$1.25
Abrams, Cal	52T	350	$40.00	$140.00	Adlesh, Dave	69T	341	$ .30	$ .85
Abrams, Cal	53T	98	$4.50	$15.00	Agee, Tommie	65T	166	$ .75	$2.20
Acker, Jim	84T	359	$ .01	$ .06	Agee, Tommie	66T	164	$ .30	$ .95
Acker, Jim	85T	101	$ .01	$ .05	Agee, Tommie	67T	455	$ .30	$ .95
Acker, Jim	86T	569	$ .01	$ .04	Agee, Tommie	68T	465	$ .35	$1.25
Acker, Jim	87T	407	$ .01	$ .04	Agee, Tommie	69T	364	$ .30	$ .85
Acker, Jim	88T	678	$ .01	$ .04	Agee, Tommie	70T	50	$ .15	$ .50
Acker, Jim	89T	244	$ .01	$ .05	Agee, Tommie	71T	310	$ .15	$ .50
Acker, Jim	90T	728	$ .01	$ .04	Agee, Tommie	72T	245	$ .15	$ .50
Acker, Jim	91T	71	$ .01	$ .03	Agee, Tommie	73T	420	$ .15	$ .50
Acker, Tom	57T	219	$ .95	$3.50	Agee, Tommie	74T	630	$ .07	$ .30
Acker, Tom	58T	149	$ .75	$3.00	Agee, Tommie	74TTR	630	$ .07	$ .30
Acker, Tom	59T	201	$ .75	$2.20	Agganis, Harry	55T	152	$15.00	$60.00
Acker, Tom	60T	274	$ .45	$1.45	Agosto, Juan	84T	409	$ .01	$ .06
Ackley, Fritz	64T	368	$ .30	$ .95	Agosto, Juan	85T	351	$ .01	$ .05
Ackley, Fritz	65T	477	$100.00	$400.00	Agosto, Juan	86T	657	$ .01	$ .04
Acosta, Cy	73T	379	$ .07	$ .30	Agosto, Juan	87T	277	$ .01	$ .04
Acosta, Cy	74T	22	$ .07	$ .30	Agosto, Juan	88TTR	2	$ .01	$ .10
Acosta, Cy	75T	634	$ .07	$ .30	Agosto, Juan	89T	559	$ .01	$ .05
Acosta, Ed	71T	343	$ .15	$ .50	Agosto, Juan	90T	181	$ .01	$ .04
Acosta, Ed	72T	123	$ .15	$ .50	Agosto, Juan	91T	703	$ .01	$ .03
Acosta, Ed	73T	244	$ .07	$ .30	Aguayo, Luis	82T	449	$ .01	$ .07

Player	Year	No.	VG	EX/MT
Aguayo, Luis	83T	252	$ .01	$ .07
Aguayo, Luis	85T	663	$ .01	$ .05
Aguayo, Luis	86T	69	$ .01	$ .04
Aguayo, Luis	87T	755	$ .01	$ .04
Aguayo, Luis	88T	356	$ .01	$ .04
Aguayo, Luis	88TBB	226	$ .01	$ .06
Aguayo, Luis	89T	561	$ .01	$ .05
Aguilera, Rick	86T	599	$ .03	$ .25
Aguilera, Rick	87T	103	$ .01	$ .04
Aguilera, Rick	88T	434	$ .01	$ .04
Aguilera, Rick	89T	257	$ .01	$ .05
Aguilera, Rick	90T	711	$ .01	$ .04
Aguilera, Rick	91T	318	$ .01	$ .03
Aguirre, Hank	57T	96	$ .95	$3.50
Aguirre, Hank	58T	337	$ .75	$3.00
Aguirre, Hank	59T	36	$1.75	$4.50
Aguirre, Hank	60T	546	$2.50	$10.00
Aguirre, Hank	61T	324	$ .35	$1.25
Aguirre, Hank	62T	407	$ .75	$2.50
Aguirre, Hank	63T	6	$ .45	$1.45
Aguirre, Hank	63T	257	$ .10	$ .50
Aguirre, Hank	64T	39	$ .30	$ .95

PITCHER
HANK AGUIRRE

Player	Year	No.	VG	EX/MT
Aguirre, Hank	65T	522	$ .75	$3.00
Aguirre, Hank	66T	113	$ .30	$ .95
Aguirre, Hank	67T	263	$ .30	$ .85
Aguirre, Hank	68T	553	$ .35	$1.25
Aguirre, Hank	69T	94	$ .30	$ .85
Aguirre, Hank	70T	699	$ .75	$2.00
Aguirre, Hank	73T	81	$ .30	$ .95
Aguirre, Hank	74T	354	$ .07	$ .30
Aikens, Willie	80T	368	$ .01	$ .10
Aikens, Willie	81T	524	$ .01	$ .10
Aikens, Willie	82T	35	$ .01	$ .07
Aikens, Willie	83T	136	$ .01	$ .07
Aikens, Willie	84T	685	$ .01	$ .06
Aikens, Willie	84TTR	1	$ .02	$ .10
Aikens, Willie	85T	436	$ .01	$ .05
Ainge, Danny	81TTR	727	$ .50	$2.00
Ainge, Danny	82T	125	$ .05	$ .25
Aker, Jack	66T	287	$ .30	$ .95

Player	Year	No.	VG	EX/MT
Aker, Jack	67T	110	$ .30	$ .85
Aker, Jack	68T	224	$ .30	$ .85
Aker, Jack	69T	612	$ .30	$ .95
Aker, Jack	70T	43	$ .15	$ .50
Aker, Jack	71T	593	$ .35	$1.25
Aker, Jack	72T	769	$ .75	$2.50
Aker, Jack	73T	262	$ .07	$ .30
Aker, Jack	74T	562	$ .07	$ .30
Akerfelds, Darrel	88T	82	$ .01	$ .15
Akerfelds, Darrel	90TTR	1	$ .01	$ .05
Akerfelds, Darrel	91T	524	$ .01	$ .03
Akins, Sid	85T	390	$ .01	$ .05
Albury, Vic	72T	778	$ .90	$3.00
Albury, Vic	74T	605	$ .30	$1.50
Albury, Vic	75T	368	$ .07	$ .30
Albury, Vic	76T	336	$ .05	$ .20
Albury, Vic	77T	536	$ .05	$ .15
Alcala, Santo	76T	589	$ .45	$1.45
Alcala, Santo	77T	636	$ .05	$ .15
Alcala, Santo	78T	321	$ .02	$ .10
Alcaraz, Luis	69T	437	$ .30	$ .85
Aldred, Scott	91T	658	$ .01	$ .03
Aldrete, Mike	87T	71	$ .01	$ .10
Aldrete, Mike	88T	602	$ .01	$ .10
Aldrete, Mike	88TBB	119	$ .01	$ .06
Aldrete, Mike	89T	158	$ .01	$ .05
Aldrete, Mike	90T	589	$ .01	$ .04
Aldrete, Mike	91T	483	$ .01	$ .03
Aldrich, Jay	88T	616	$ .01	$ .04
Alexander, Doyle	72T	579	$ .75	$2.20
Alexander, Doyle	73T	109	$ .35	$1.25
Alexander, Doyle	74T	282	$ .07	$ .30
Alexander, Doyle	75T	491	$ .15	$ .50
Alexander, Doyle	76T	638	$ .15	$ .50
Alexander, Doyle	77T	254	$ .05	$ .15
Alexander, Doyle	78T	146	$ .05	$ .20
Alexander, Doyle	79T	442	$ .05	$ .20
Alexander, Doyle	80T	67	$ .01	$ .10
Alexander, Doyle	81T	708	$ .03	$ .15
Alexander, Doyle	81TTR	728	$ .05	$ .20
Alexander, Doyle	82T	364	$ .03	$ .15
Alexander, Doyle	82TTR	1	$ .05	$ .20
Alexander, Doyle	83T	512	$ .01	$ .07
Alexander, Doyle	84T	677	$ .01	$ .06
Alexander, Doyle	85T	218	$ .01	$ .05
Alexander, Doyle	86T	196	$ .01	$ .04
Alexander, Doyle	87T	686	$ .01	$ .04
Alexander, Doyle	88T	492	$ .01	$ .04
Alexander, Doyle	88TBB	34	$ .01	$ .06
Alexander, Doyle	89T	77	$ .01	$ .05
Alexander, Doyle	89TBB	182	$ .01	$ .06
Alexander, Doyle	90T	748	$ .01	$ .04
Alexander, Gary	77T	476	$15.00	$45.00
Alexander, Gary	78T	624	$ .02	$ .10
Alexander, Gary	79T	332	$ .02	$ .10
Alexander, Gary	80T	141	$ .01	$ .10
Alexander, Gary	81T	416	$ .01	$ .10
Alexander, Gary	81TTR	729	$ .02	$ .10
Alexander, Gary	82T	11	$ .01	$ .07
Alexander, Matt	76T	382	$ .05	$ .20
Alexander, Matt	77T	644	$ .05	$ .15
Alexander, Matt	78T	102	$ .02	$ .10
Alexander, Matt	81T	68	$ .01	$ .10
Alexander, Matt	82T	528	$ .01	$ .07
Alfaro, Flavio	85T	391	$ .01	$ .05
Alicea, Luis	88TTR	3	$ .01	$ .06
Alicea, Luis	89T	588	$ .01	$ .15
Allanson, Andy	86TTR	1	$ .03	$ .15
Allanson, Andy	87T	436	$ .01	$ .10
Allanson, Andy	88T	728	$ .01	$ .04

TOPPS

Player	Year	No.	VG	EX/MT
Allanson, Andy	88TBB	231	$ .01	$ .06
Allanson, Andy	89T	283	$ .01	$ .05
Allanson, Andy	89TBB	311	$ .01	$ .06
Allanson, Andy	90T	514	$ .01	$ .04
Allard, Brian	80T	673	$ .01	$ .10
Allard, Brian	82T	283	$ .01	$ .07
Allen, Bernie	62T	596	$12.00	$36.00
Allen, Bernie	63T	427	$ .45	$1.50
Allen, Bernie	64T	455	$ .50	$1.45
Allen, Bernie	65T	237	$ .35	$1.25
Allen, Bernie	66T	327	$ .30	$ .95
Allen, Bernie	67T	118	$ .30	$ .85
Allen, Bernie	68T	548	$ .35	$1.25
Allen, Bernie	69T	27	$ .30	$ .85
Allen, Bernie	70T	577	$ .30	$ .95
Allen, Bernie	71T	427	$ .15	$ .50
Allen, Bernie	72T	644	$ .30	$ .95
Allen, Bernie	73T	293	$ .07	$ .30
Allen, Bob	61T	452	$ .75	$3.00
Allen, Bob	62T	543	$3.95	$11.50
Allen, Bob	63T	266	$ .10	$ .50
Allen, Bob	64T	209	$ .30	$ .95
Allen, Bob	66T	538	$5.00	$20.00
Allen, Bob	67T	24	$ .30	$ .85
Allen, Bob	68T	176	$ .30	$ .85
Allen, Dick	73T	62	$ .50	$1.50
Allen, Dick	73T	63	$ .50	$1.50
Allen, Dick	73T	310	$ .30	$ .95
Allen, Dick	74T	70	$ .15	$ .50
Allen, Dick	74TAS	332	$ .50	$2.00
Allen, Dick	75T	210	$ .50	$1.50
Allen, Dick	75T	307	$ .35	$1.25
Allen, Dick	75T	400	$ .15	$ .50
Allen, Dick	76T	455	$ .15	$ .50
Allen, Hank	67T	569	$125.00	$450.00
Allen, Hank	68T	426	$ .30	$ .85
Allen, Hank	69T	623	$ .30	$ .95
Allen, Hank	70T	14	$ .15	$ .50
Allen, Jamie	84T	744	$ .01	$ .06
Allen, Lloyd	71T	152	$ .15	$ .50
Allen, Lloyd	72T	102	$ .15	$ .50
Allen, Lloyd	73T	267	$ .07	$ .30
Allen, Lloyd	74T	539	$ .07	$ .30
Allen, Neil	80T	94	$ .03	$ .15
Allen, Neil	81T	322	$ .01	$ .10
Allen, Neil	82T	205	$ .01	$ .07
Allen, Neil	83T	575	$ .01	$ .07
Allen, Neil	83TTR	1	$ .02	$ .10
Allen, Neil	84T	435	$ .01	$ .06
Allen, Neil	85T	731	$ .01	$ .05
Allen, Neil	86T	663	$ .01	$ .04
Allen, Neil	86TTR	2	$ .02	$ .10
Allen, Neil	87T	113	$ .01	$ .04
Allen, Neil	88T	384	$ .01	$ .04
Allen, Neil	89T	61	$ .01	$ .05
Allen, Richie	64T	243	$4.00	$13.00
Allen, Richie	65T	460	$2.00	$8.00
Allen, Richie	66T	80	$ .75	$3.00
Allen, Richie	67T	242	$1.75	$4.50
Allen, Richie	67T	244	$2.10	$6.00
Allen, Richie	67T	309	$ .60	$1.20
Allen, Richie	67T	450	$ .75	$3.00
Allen, Richie	68T	225	$ .75	$3.00
Allen, Richie	69T	6	$ .80	$2.50
Allen, Richie	69T	350	$ .45	$1.45
Allen, Richie	70T	40	$ .45	$1.45
Allen, Richie	71T	650	$4.00	$12.00
Allen, Richie "Dick"	72T	240	$ .50	$2.00
Allenson, Gary	80T	376	$ .01	$ .10
Allenson, Gary	81T	128	$ .01	$ .10
Allenson, Gary	82T	686	$ .01	$ .07
Allenson, Gary	83T	472	$ .01	$ .07
Allenson, Gary	84T	56	$ .01	$ .06
Allenson, Gary	85T	259	$ .01	$ .05
Alley, Gene	64T	509	$ .50	$1.45
Alley, Gene	65T	121	$ .30	$ .85
Alley, Gene	66T	336	$ .30	$ .95
Alley, Gene	67T	283	$ .30	$ .85
Alley, Gene	68T	53	$ .30	$ .85
Alley, Gene	68TAS	368	$ .30	$ .85
Alley, Gene	69T	436	$ .30	$ .85
Alley, Gene	70T	566	$ .30	$ .95
Alley, Gene	71T	416	$ .15	$ .50
Alley, Gene	72T	286	$ .15	$ .50
Alley, Gene	73T	635	$ .45	$1.45
Allie, Gair	54T	179	$3.60	$10.00
Allie, Gair	55T	59	$2.00	$6.00
Allietta, Bob	76T	623	$ .05	$ .20
Allison, Bob	59T	116	$2.10	$6.00
Allison, Bob	60T	320	$ .75	$2.20
Allison, Bob	61T	355	$ .35	$1.25
Allison, Bob	62T	180	$ .45	$1.45
Allison, Bob	63T	75	$ .35	$1.25
Allison, Bob	64T	10	$ .75	$3.00
Allison, Bob	64T	290	$ .45	$1.45
Allison, Bob	65T	180	$ .15	$ .50
Allison, Bob	66T	345	$ .30	$ .95
Allison, Bob	67T	194	$ .30	$ .85
Allison, Bob	67T	334	$1.75	$4.50
Allison, Bob	68T	335	$ .30	$ .95
Allison, Bob	69T	30	$ .15	$ .50
Allison, Bob	70T	635	$ .75	$2.00
Allred, Beau	89TMLD	2	$ .01	$ .25
Allred, Beau	90T	419	$ .01	$ .10
Almon, Billy	77T	490	$ .03	$ .12
Almon, Billy	78T	392	$ .02	$ .10
Almon, Billy	79T	616	$ .02	$ .10
Almon, Billy	80T	436	$ .01	$ .10
Almon, Billy	81T	163	$ .01	$ .10
Almon, Billy	81TTR	730	$ .02	$ .10
Almon, Billy "Bill"	82T	521	$ .01	$
.07Almon, Bill	83T	362	$ .01	$ .07
Almon, Bill	83TTR	2	$ .02	$ .10
Almon, Bill	84T	241	$ .01	$ .06
Almon, Bill	85T	273	$ .01	$ .05
Almon, Bill	85T	607	$ .01	$ .05
Almon, Bill	85TTR	2	$ .02	$ .10
Almon, Bill	86T	48	$ .01	$ .04
Almon, Bill	87T	447	$ .01	$ .04
Almon, Bill	87TTR	1	$ .01	$ .05
Almon, Bill	88T	787	$ .01	$ .04
Aloma, Luis	52T	308	$12.00	$40.00
Aloma, Luis	54T	57	$7.00	$22.00
Alomar, Jr., Sandy	89T	648	$ .15	$1.75
Alomar, Jr., Sandy	90T	353	$ .01	$ .50
Alomar, Roberto	88TTR	4	$ .05	$1.50
Alomar, Roberto	89T	206	$ .01	$ .50
Alomar, Roberto	89TBB	102	$ .01	$ .10
Alomar, Roberto	90T	517	$ .01	$ .25
Alomar, Roberto	91T	315	$ .01	$ .10
Alomar, Santos "Sandy"	65T	82	$ .30	$ .85
Alomar, Sandy	66T	428	$ .30	$ .95
Alomar, Sandy	67T	561	$6.00	$20.00
Alomar, Sandy	68T	541	$ .35	$1.25
Alomar, Sandy	69T	283	$ .30	$ .95
Alomar, Sandy	70T	29	$ .15	$ .50
Alomar, Sandy	71T	745	$ .75	$2.50
Alomar, Sandy	72T	253	$ .15	$ .50
Alomar, Sandy	73T	123	$ .07	$ .30
Alomar, Sandy	74T	347	$ .07	$ .30

Player	Year	No.	VG	EX/MT	Player	Year	No.	VG	EX/MT
Alomar, Sandy	75T	266	$ .07	$ .30	Alston, Walt	67T	294	$ .90	$3.00
Alomar, Sandy	76T	629	$ .05	$ .20	Alston, Walt	68T	472	$ .75	$2.25
Alomar, Sandy	77T	54	$ .05	$ .15	Alston, Walt	69T	24	$ .75	$2.20
Alomar, Sandy	78T	533	$ .02	$ .10	Alston, Walt	70T	242	$ .75	$2.20
Alomar, Sandy	79T	144	$ .02	$ .10	Alston, Walt	71T	567	$ .75	$2.25
Alomar, Sandy	90TTR	2	$ .01	$ .25	Alston, Walt	72T	749	$ .90	$3.50
Alomar, Sandy	91T	165	$ .01	$ .15	Alston, Walt	73T	569	$1.25	$4.25
Alou, Felipe	59T	102	$2.00	$6.00	Alston, Walt	74T	144	$ .75	$3.00
Alou, Felipe	60T	287	$ .75	$2.20	Alston, Walter	56T	8	$7.00	$28.00
Alou, Felipe	61T	565	$7.00	$21.00	Alston, Walter	58T	314	$5.00	$20.00
Alou, Felipe	62T	133	$ .45	$1.45	Altamirano, Porfirio	83T	432	$ .01	$ .07
Alou, Felipe	63T	270	$ .10	$ .50	Altamirano, Porfirio	84T	101	$ .01	$ .06
Alou, Felipe	64T	65	$ .35	$1.25	Altman, George	59T	512	$2.50	$10.00
Alou, Felipe	65T	383	$ .35	$1.25	Altman, George	60T	259	$ .45	$1.45
Alou, Felipe	66T	96	$ .15	$ .50	Altman, George	61T	551	$7.00	$21.00
Alou, Felipe	67T	240	$ .45	$1.45	Altman, George	62T	240	$ .45	$1.45
Alou, Felipe	67T	530	$ .75	$2.25	Altman, George	63T	357	$ .24	$ .60
Alou, Felipe	68T	55	$ .30	$ .95	Altman, George	64T	95	$ .30	$ .95
Alou, Felipe	69T	2	$2.10	$6.00	Altman, George	65T	528	$1.75	$4.50
Alou, Felipe	69T	300	$ .35	$1.25	Altman, George	66T	146	$ .30	$ .95
Alou, Felipe	70T	434	$ .30	$ .85	Altman, George	67T	87	$ .30	$ .85
Alou, Felipe	71T	495	$ .15	$ .50	Altobelli, Joe	78T	256	$ .02	$ .10
Alou, Felipe	72T	263	$ .15	$ .50	Altobelli, Joe	83TTR	3	$ .02	$ .10
Alou, Felipe	73T	650	$ .75	$2.20	Altobelli, Joe	84T	21	$ .01	$ .06
Alou, Felipe	74T	485	$ .07	$ .30	Altobelli, Joe	85T	574	$ .01	$ .05
Alou, Felipe	74TTR	485	$ .07	$ .30	Alusik, George	62T	261	$ .45	$1.45
Alou, Jesus	64T	47	$ .35	$1.25	Alusik, George	63T	51	$ .10	$ .50
Alou, Jesus	65T	545	$1.75	$4.50	Alusik, George	64T	431	$ .50	$1.45
Alou, Jesus	66T	242	$ .30	$ .95	Alvarado, Luis	70T	317	$ .30	$ .95
Alou, Jesus	67T	332	$ .30	$ .85					
Alou, Jesus	68T	452	$ .30	$ .85					
Alou, Jesus	69T	22	$ .30	$ .85					
Alou, Jesus	70T	248	$ .15	$ .50					
Alou, Jesus	71T	337	$ .15	$ .50					
Alou, Jesus	72T	716	$ .75	$2.50					
Alou, Jesus	73T	93	$ .07	$ .30					
Alou, Jesus	74T	654	$ .30	$ .95					
Alou, Jesus	75T	253	$ .07	$ .30					
Alou, Jesus	76T	468	$ .05	$ .20					
Alou, Jesus	79T	107	$ .02	$ .10					
Alou, Jesus	80T	593	$ .01	$ .10					
Alou, Matty	61T	327	$1.75	$4.50					
Alou, Matty	62T	413	$ .75	$2.25					
Alou, Matty	63T	128	$ .10	$ .50					
Alou, Matty	64T	204	$ .45	$1.45					
Alou, Matty	65T	318	$ .35	$1.25					
Alou, Matty	66T	94	$ .15	$ .50					
Alou, Matty	67T	10	$ .30	$ .85					
Alou, Matty	67T	240	$ .45	$1.45					
Alou, Matty	68T	1	$2.50	$12.50					
Alou, Matty	68T	270	$ .30	$ .95					
Alou, Matty	69T	2	$2.10	$6.00					
Alou, Matty	69T	490	$ .15	$ .50					
Alou, Matty	70T	30	$ .30	$ .85					
Alou, Matty	70TAS	460	$ .08	$ .50					
Alou, Matty	71T	720	$1.25	$4.25					
Alou, Matty	72T	395	$ .30	$ .85					
Alou, Matty	73T	132	$ .30	$ .85					
Alou, Matty	74T	430	$ .07	$ .30					
Alou, Moises	91T	526	$ .01	$ .15	Alvarado, Luis	71T	489	$ .15	$ .50
Alston, Dell	78T	710	$ .15	$ .50	Alvarado, Luis	72T	774	$ .75	$2.50
Alston, Dell	79T	54	$ .02	$ .10	Alvarado, Luis	73T	627	$ .45	$1.45
Alston, Dell	80T	198	$ .01	$ .10	Alvarado, Luis	74T	462	$ .07	$ .30
Alston, Walt	60T	212	$2.50	$9.00	Alvarez, Jose	89T	253	$ .01	$ .10
Alston, Walt	61T	136	$1.00	$4.00	Alvarez, Jose	90T	782	$ .01	$ .04
Alston, Walt	62T	217	$1.00	$4.00	Alvarez, Ossie	59T	504	$ .75	$2.20
Alston, Walt	63T	154	$ .80	$2.50	Alvarez, Rogelio	63T	158	$ .10	$ .50
Alston, Walt	64T	101	$ .75	$2.25	Alvarez, Wilson	89TMLD	3	$ .01	$ .15
Alston, Walt	65T	217	$ .75	$2.25	Alvarez, Wilson	91T	378	$ .01	$ .15
Alston, Walt	66T	116	$ .75	$2.00	Alvis, Max	63T	228	$9.00	$35.00

WHITE SOX
luis alvarado • shortstop

Player	Year	No.	VG	EX/MT
Alvis, Max	64T	545	$1.75	$4.50
Alvis, Max	65T	185	$ .30	$ .85
Alvis, Max	66T	415	$ .30	$ .95
Alvis, Max	67T	520	$ .75	$3.00
Alvis, Max	68T	340	$ .30	$ .85
Alvis, Max	69T	145	$ .30	$ .85
Alvis, Max	70T	85	$ .15	$ .50
Alyea, Brant	66T	11	$ .30	$ .95
Alyea, Brant	69T	48	$ .30	$ .85
Alyea, Brant	70T	303	$ .15	$ .50
Alyea, Brant	71T	449	$ .15	$ .50
Alyea, Brant	72T	383	$ .15	$ .50
Amalfitano, Joe	55T	144	$2.00	$6.00
Amalfitano, Joe	60T	356	$ .45	$1.35
Amalfitano, Joe	61T	87	$ .35	$1.25
Amalfitano, Joe	62T	456	$ .75	$2.50
Amalfitano, Joe	63T	199	$ .10	$ .50
Amalfitano, Joe	64T	451	$ .50	$1.45
Amalfitano, Joe	65T	402	$ .35	$1.25
Amalfitano, Joe	73T	252	$ .30	$ .85
Amalfitano, Joe	74T	78	$ .07	$ .30
Amaro, Ruben	59T	178	$ .75	$2.20
Amaro, Ruben	61T	103	$ .35	$1.25
Amaro, Ruben	62T	284	$ .45	$1.45
Amaro, Ruben	63T	455	$2.50	$6.50
Amaro, Ruben	64T	432	$ .50	$1.45
Amaro, Ruben	65T	419	$ .35	$1.25
Amaro, Ruben	66T	186	$ .30	$ .95

Player	Year	No.	VG	EX/MT
Amaro, Ruben	67T	358	$ .30	$ .85
Amaro, Ruben	68T	138	$ .30	$ .85
Amaro, Ruben	69T	598	$ .30	$ .95
Amoros, Sandy	55T	75	$2.00	$6.00
Amoros, Sandy	56T	42	$2.25	$6.00
Amoros, Sandy	57T	201	$ .95	$3.50
Amoros, Sandy	58T	93	$1.25	$4.25
Amoros, Sandy	60T	531	$2.50	$10.00
Andersen, Larry	78T	703	$1.50	$6.00
Andersen, Larry	80T	665	$ .01	$ .10
Andersen, Larry	82T	52	$ .01	$ .07
Andersen, Larry	83T	234	$ .01	$ .07

Player	Year	No.	VG	EX/MT
Andersen, Larry	85T	428	$ .01	$ .05
Andersen, Larry	86T	183	$ .01	$ .04
Andersen, Larry	87T	503	$ .01	$ .04
Andersen, Larry	88T	342	$ .01	$ .04
Andersen, Larry	89T	24	$ .01	$ .05
Andersen, Larry	91T	761	$ .01	$ .03
Anderson, Allan	87T	336	$ .01	$ .04
Anderson, Allan	88T	101	$ .01	$ .04
Anderson, Allan	89T	672	$ .01	$ .05
Anderson, Allan	90T	71	$ .01	$ .10
Anderson, Allan	91T	223	$ .01	$ .03
Anderson, Bob	58T	209	$ .75	$3.00
Anderson, Bob	59T	447	$ .75	$2.20
Anderson, Bob	60T	412	$ .75	$2.20
Anderson, Bob	61T	283	$ .35	$1.25
Anderson, Bob	62T	557	$3.95	$11.50
Anderson, Bob	63T	379	$ .45	$1.50
Anderson, Brady	88TTR	5	$ .01	$ .20
Anderson, Brady	89T	757	$ .01	$ .25
Anderson, Brady	90T	598	$ .01	$ .04
Anderson, Brady	91T	97	$ .01	$ .03
Anderson, Bud	79T	712	$ .02	$ .10
Anderson, Bud	83T	367	$ .01	$ .07
Anderson, Bud	84T	497	$ .01	$ .06
Anderson, Craig	62T	593	$7.00	$21.00
Anderson, Craig	63T	59	$ .10	$ .50
Anderson, Dave	84T	376	$ .01	$ .06
Anderson, Dave	85T	654	$ .01	$ .05
Anderson, Dave	86T	758	$ .01	$ .04
Anderson, Dave	87T	73	$ .01	$ .04
Anderson, Dave	88T	456	$ .01	$ .04
Anderson, Dave	89T	117	$ .01	$ .05
Anderson, Dave	90T	248	$ .01	$ .04
Anderson, Dave	91T	572	$ .01	$ .03
Anderson, Dwain	72T	268	$ .15	$ .50
Anderson, Dwain	73T	241	$ .07	$ .30
Anderson, Harry	57T	404	$1.25	$4.25
Anderson, Harry	58T	171	$ .75	$3.00
Anderson, Harry	59T	85	$1.25	$4.25
Anderson, Harry	60T	285	$ .45	$1.45
Anderson, Harry	61T	76	$ .35	$1.25
Anderson, Jim	79T	703	$ .02	$ .10
Anderson, Jim	80T	183	$ .01	$ .10
Anderson, Jim	81T	613	$ .01	$ .10
Anderson, Jim	82T	497	$ .01	$ .07
Anderson, Jim	84T	353	$ .01	$ .06
Anderson, John	62T	266	$ .45	$1.45
Anderson, Kent	89TMLD	4	$ .01	$ .15
Anderson, Kent	89TTR	3	$ .01	$ .15
Anderson, Kent	90T	16	$ .01	$ .04
Anderson, Kent	91T	667	$ .01	$ .03
Anderson, Larry	76T	593	$ .15	$ .50
Anderson, Larry	77T	487	$ .03	$ .12
Anderson, Mike	72T	14	$ .15	$ .50
Anderson, Mike	73T	147	$ .07	$ .30
Anderson, Mike	74T	619	$ .07	$ .30
Anderson, Mike	75T	118	$ .07	$ .30
Anderson, Mike	76T	527	$ .05	$ .20
Anderson, Mike	76TTR	527	$ .05	$ .20
Anderson, Mike	77T	72	$ .05	$ .15
Anderson, Mike	78T	714	$ .02	$ .10
Anderson, Mike	79T	102	$ .02	$ .10
Anderson, Mike	80T	317	$ .01	$ .10
Anderson, Rick	81T	282	$ .01	$ .10
Anderson, Rick	87T	594	$ .01	$ .04
Anderson, Sparky (George)	59T	338	$5.00	$20.00
Anderson, Sparky (George)	60T	34	$1.00	$4.00
Anderson, Sparky	70T	181	$ .50	$2.00
Anderson, Sparky	71T	688	$2.10	$8.00
Anderson, Sparky	72T	358	$ .30	$ .95

Player	Year	No.	VG	EX/MT	Player	Year	No.	VG	EX/MT
Anderson, Sparky	73T	296	$ .15	$ .50	Antonelli, Johnny	54T	119	$2.50	$10.00
Anderson, Sparky	74T	326	$ .15	$ .50	Antonelli, Johnny	56T	138	$1.50	$4.00
Anderson, Sparky	78T	401	$ .05	$ .20	Antonelli, Johnny	57T	105	$ .95	$3.50
Anderson, Sparky	83T	666	$ .01	$ .07	Antonelli, Johnny	58T	152	$ .65	$2.00
Anderson, Sparky	84T	259	$ .01	$ .06	Antonelli, Johnny	59T	377	$ .30	$1.25
Anderson, Sparky	85T	307	$ .01	$ .05	Antonelli, Johnny	60T	80	$ .45	$1.45
Anderson, Sparky	86T	411	$ .01	$ .04	Antonelli, Johnny	60TAS	572	$4.00	$20.00
Anderson, Sparky	87T	218	$ .01	$ .04	Antonelli, Johnny	61T	115	$ .35	$1.25
Anderson, Sparky	88T	14	$ .01	$ .04	Antonello, Bill	53T	272	$12.50	$50.00
Anderson, Sparky	89T	193	$ .01	$ .05	Aparicio, Luis	56T	292	$35.00	$115.00
Anderson, Sparky	90T	609	$ .01	$ .04	Aparicio, Luis	57T	7	$7.00	$25.00
Anderson, Sparky	91T	519	$ .01	$ .03	Aparicio, Luis	58T	85	$4.00	$16.00
Andrews, Mike	67T	314	$1.25	$5.00	Aparicio, Luis	58TAS	483	$2.50	$10.00
Andrews, Mike	68T	502	$ .35	$1.25	Aparicio, Luis	59T	310	$4.50	$15.00
Andrews, Mike	69T	52	$ .30	$ .85	Aparicio, Luis	59T	408	$ .60	$1.80
Andrews, Mike	70T	406	$ .15	$ .50	Aparicio, Luis	59TAS	560	$5.00	$20.00
Andrews, Mike	71T	191	$ .15	$ .50	Aparicio, Luis	60T	240	$2.75	$11.00
Andrews, Mike	72T	361	$ .15	$ .50	Aparicio, Luis	60TAS	559	$4.00	$16.00
Andrews, Mike	73T	42	$ .07	$ .30	Aparicio, Luis	61T	440	$2.25	$10.00
Andrews, Rob	76T	568	$ .05	$ .20	Aparicio, Luis	61TAS	574	$9.50	$37.50
Andrews, Rob	77T	209	$ .05	$ .15	Aparicio, Luis	62T	325	$3.00	$11.00
Andrews, Rob	78T	461	$ .02	$ .10	Aparicio, Luis	62TAS	469	$2.00	$8.00
Andrews, Rob	79T	34	$ .02	$ .10	Aparicio, Luis	63T	205	$2.50	$10.00
Andrews, Rob	80T	279	$ .01	$ .10	Aparicio, Luis	64T	540	$3.00	$12.50
Andrews, Shane	91T	74	$ .01	$ .25	Aparicio, Luis	65T	410	$2.50	$8.50
Andujar, Joaquin	77T	67	$ .15	$ .50	Aparicio, Luis	66T	90	$1.50	$5.00
Andujar, Joaquin	78T	158	$ .03	$ .15	Aparicio, Luis	67T	60	$1.50	$5.00
Andujar, Joaquin	79T	471	$ .05	$ .20	Aparicio, Luis	68T	310	$1.50	$5.00
Andujar, Joaquin	80T	617	$ .02	$ .10	Aparicio, Luis	69T	75	$1.00	$4.00
Andujar, Joaquin	81T	329	$ .01	$ .10	Aparicio, Luis	70T	315	$1.00	$4.00
Andujar, Joaquin	81TTR	731	$ .02	$ .10	Aparicio, Luis	71T	740	$3.00	11.00
Andujar, Joaquin	82T	533	$ .01	$ .07	Aparicio, Luis	72T	313	$1.00	$3.00
Andujar, Joaquin	83T	228	$ .01	$ .07	Aparicio, Luis	72TIA	314	$ .25	$1.00
Andujar, Joaquin	83T	561	$ .01	$ .07	Aparicio, Luis	73T	165	$ .50	$2.00
Andujar, Joaquin	84T	785	$ .01	$ .06	Aparicio, Luis	74T	61	$ .50	$2.00
Andujar, Joaquin	85T	655	$ .01	$ .05	Apodaca, Bob	74T	608	$ .07	$ .30
Andujar, Joaquin	86T	150	$ .01	$ .04	Apodaca, Bob	75T	659	$ .07	$ .30
Andujar, Joaquin	86TTR	3	$ .02	$ .10	Apodaca, Bob	76T	16	$ .05	$ .20
Andujar, Joaquin	87T	775	$ .01	$ .04	Apodaca, Bob	77T	225	$ .15	$ .50
Andujar, Joaquin	88T	47	$ .01	$ .04	Apodaca, Bob	78T	592	$ .02	$ .10
Angelini, Norm	73T	616	$ .45	$1.45	Apodaca, Bob	79T	197	$ .02	$ .10
Angels, Team	62T	132	$2.25	$6.00	Apodaca, Bob	80T	633	$ .01	$ .10
Angels, Team	63T	39	$ .75	$2.20	Aponte, Luis	83T	577	$ .01	$ .07
Angels, Team	64T	213	$1.00	$3.00	Aponte, Luis	84T	187	$ .01	$ .06
Angels, Team	65T	293	$ .90	$3.00	Aponte, Luis	84TTR	2	$ .02	$ .10
Angels, Team	66T	131	$ .90	$3.00	Appier, Kevin	89TMLD	6	$ .01	$ .15
Angels, Team	67T	327	$ .90	$3.00	Appier, Kevin	90T	167	$ .01	$ .10
Angels, Team	68T	252	$ .75	$3.00	Appier, Kevin	91T	454	$ .01	$ .03
Angels, Team	70T	522	$ .45	$1.45	Appling, Luke	60T	461	$2.25	$6.00
Angels, Team	71T	442	$ .45	$1.45	Aquino, Luis	87T	301	$ .01	$ .04
Angels, Team	72T	71	$ .15	$ .50	Aquino, Luis	89T	266	$ .01	$ .05
Angels, Team	73T	243	$ .35	$1.25	Aquino, Luis	90T	707	$ .01	$ .04
Angels, Team	74T	114	$ .15	$ .50	Aquino, Luis	91T	169	$ .01	$ .03
Angels, Team Checklist	75T	236	$ .35	$1.25	Archer, Jim	61T	552	$5.00	$15.00
Angels, Team Checklist	76T	304	$ .35	$1.25	Archer, Jim	62T	433	$ .75	$2.50
Angels, Team Checklist	77T	34	$ .15	$ .50	Arcia, Jose	68T	258	$ .30	$ .85
Angels, Team Checklist	78T	214	$ .07	$ .30	Arcia, Jose	69T	473	$ .30	$ .85
Angels, Team Checklist	79T	424	$ .08	$ .30	Arcia, Jose	70T	587	$ .30	$ .95
Angels, Team Checklist	80T	214	$ .05	$ .25	Arcia, Jose	71T	134	$ .15	$ .50
Angels, Team Checklist	81T	663	$ .02	$ .20	Arcia, Jose	73T	466	$ .07	$ .30
Angels, Team Leaders	86T	486	$ .01	$ .04	Arft, Hank	52T	284	$15.00	$47.50
Angels, Team Leaders	87T	556	$ .01	$ .04	Arias, Rodolfo	59T	537	$2.50	$10.00
Angels, Team Leaders	88T	381	$ .01	$ .04	Arlin, Steve	72T	78	$ .15	$ .50
Angels, Team Leaders	89T	51	$ .01	$ .05	Arlin, Steve	73T	294	$ .07	$ .30
Ansley, Willie	89T	607	$ .01	$ .15	Arlin, Steve	74T	406	$ .07	$ .30
Anthony, Eric	89TMLD	5	$ .01	$ .50	Arlin, Steve	75T	159	$ .07	$ .30
Anthony, Eric	90T	608	$ .01	$ .40	Armas, Tony	77T	492	$ .25	$ .80
Anthony, Eric	91T	331	$ .01	$ .15	Armas, Tony	78T	298	$ .05	$ .20
Antonelli, John	52T	140	$7.00	$21.00	Armas, Tony	79T	507	$ .05	$ .20
Antonelli, John	53T	106	$4.50	$15.00	Armas, Tony	80T	391	$ .02	$ .10

TOPPS

Player	Year	No.	VG	EX/MT	Player	Year	No.	VG	EX/MT
Armas, Tony	81T	629	$ .01	$ .10	Ashby, Alan	79T	36	$ .02	$ .10
Armas, Tony	82T	60	$ .01	$ .07	Ashby, Alan	80T	187	$ .01	$ .10
Armas, Tony	82T	162	$ .05	$ .25	Ashby, Alan	81T	696	$ .01	$ .10
Armas, Tony	83T	435	$ .01	$ .07	Ashby, Alan	82T	433	$ .01	$ .07
Armas, Tony	83TRB	1	$ .01	$ .10	Ashby, Alan	83T	774	$ .01	$ .07
Armas, Tony	83TTR	4	$ .02	$ .10	Ashby, Alan	84T	217	$ .01	$ .06
Armas, Tony	84T	105	$ .01	$ .06	Ashby, Alan	85T	564	$ .01	$ .05
Armas, Tony	85T	785	$ .01	$ .05	Ashby, Alan	86T	331	$ .01	$ .04
Armas, Tony	85TAS	707	$ .01	$ .05	Ashby, Alan	87T	112	$ .01	$ .04
Armas, Tony	86T	255	$ .01	$ .04	Ashby, Alan	88T	48	$ .01	$ .04
Armas, Tony	87T	535	$ .01	$ .04	Ashby, Alan	89T	492	$ .01	$ .05
Armas, Tony	88T	761	$ .01	$ .04	Ashford, Tucker	78T	116	$ .02	$ .10
Armas, Tony	89T	332	$ .01	$ .05	Ashford, Tucker	79T	247	$ .02	$ .10
Armas, Tony	89TBB	99	$ .01	$ .06	Ashford, Tucker	84T	492	$ .01	$ .06
Armas, Tony	90T	603	$ .01	$ .04	Aspromonte, Bob	60T	547	$2.50	$10.00
Armbrister, Ed	72T	524	$ .15	$ .50	Aspromonte, Bob	61T	396	$ .75	$3.00
Armbrister, Ed	74T	601	$ .45	$1.45	Aspromonte, Bob	62T	248	$ .45	$1.45
Armbrister, Ed	75T	622	$2.25	$11.00	Aspromonte, Bob	63T	45	$ .10	$ .50
Armbrister, Ed	76T	652	$ .05	$ .20	Aspromonte, Bob	64T	467	$ .50	$1.45
Armbrister, Ed	77T	203	$ .05	$ .15	Aspromonte, Bob	65T	175	$ .30	$ .85
Armbrister, Ed	78T	556	$ .02	$ .10	Aspromonte, Bob	66T	273	$ .75	$3.00
Armstrong, Jack	88TTR	6	$ .10	$ .50	Aspromonte, Bob	66T	352	$ .30	$ .95
Armstrong, Jack	89T	317	$ .01	$ .35	Aspromonte, Bob	67T	274	$ .30	$ .85
Armstrong, Jack	90T	642	$ .01	$ .10	Aspromonte, Bob	68T	95	$ .30	$ .85
Armstrong, Jack	91T	175	$ .01	$ .03	Aspromonte, Bob	69T	542	$ .30	$ .95
Armstrong, Mike	82T	731	$ .01	$ .07	Aspromonte, Bob	70T	529	$ .15	$ .50
Armstrong, Mike	83T	219	$ .01	$ .07	Aspromonte, Bob	71T	469	$ .15	$ .50
Armstrong, Mike	84T	417	$ .01	$ .06	Aspromonte, Bob	72T	659	$ .75	$2.50
Armstrong, Mike	84TTR	3	$ .02	$ .10	Aspromonte, Ken	58T	405	$ .75	$3.00
Armstrong, Mike	85T	612	$ .01	$ .05	Aspromonte, Ken	59T	424	$ .75	$2.20
Arndt, Larry	89TMLD	7	$ .01	$ .15	Aspromonte, Ken	60T	114	$ .45	$1.45
Arnold, Chris	72T	232	$ .15	$ .50	Aspromonte, Ken	61T	176	$ .35	$1.25
Arnold, Chris	73T	584	$ .45	$1.45	Aspromonte, Ken	62T	563	$3.95	$11.50
Arnold, Chris	74T	432	$ .06	$ .50	Aspromonte, Ken	63T	464	$2.50	$6.50
Arnold, Chris	77T	591	$ .05	$ .25	Aspromonte, Ken	64T	252	$ .30	$ .95
Arnsberg, Brad	88T	159	$ .01	$ .20	Aspromonte, Ken	72T	784	$ .75	$2.50
Arnsberg, Brad	90TTR	3	$ .01	$ .05	Aspromonte, Ken	73T	449	$ .30	$ .85
Arnsberg, Brad	91T	706	$ .01	$ .03	Aspromonte, Ken	74T	521	$ .07	$ .30
Arrigo, Gerry	64T	516	$ .50	$1.45	Asselstine, Brian	77T	479	$ .03	$ .12
Arrigo, Gerry	65T	39	$ .30	$ .85	Asselstine, Brian	78T	372	$ .02	$ .10
Arrigo, Gerry	66T	357	$ .30	$ .95	Asselstine, Brian	79T	529	$ .02	$ .10
Arrigo, Gerry	67T	488	$ .75	$3.00	Asselstine, Brian	81T	64	$ .01	$ .10
Arrigo, Gerry	68T	302	$ .30	$ .85	Asselstine, Brian	82T	214	$ .01	$ .07
Arrigo, Gerry	69T	213	$ .30	$ .85	Assenmacher, Paul	86TTR	4	$ .02	$ .10
Arrigo, Gerry	70T	274	$ .15	$ .50	Assenmacher, Paul	87T	132	$ .01	$ .04
Arroyo, Fernando	76T	614	$ .05	$ .20	Assenmacher, Paul	88T	266	$ .01	$ .04
Arroyo, Fernando	78T	607	$ .02	$ .10	Assenmacher, Paul	89T	454	$ .01	$ .05
Arroyo, Fernando	81T	408	$ .01	$ .10	Assenmacher, Paul	90T	644	$ .01	$ .04
Arroyo, Fernando	82T	18	$ .01	$ .07	Assenmacher, Paul	91T	12	$ .01	$ .03
Arroyo, Fernando	82T	396	$ .01	$ .07	Astros, Team	70T	448	$ .45	$1.45
Arroyo, Luis	56T	64	$2.10	$6.00	Astros, Team	71T	722	$3.00	$9.00
Arroyo, Luis	57T	394	$1.25	$4.25	Astros, Team	72T	282	$ .35	$1.25
Arroyo, Luis	61T	142	$ .35	$1.25	Astros, Team	73T	158	$ .35	$1.25
Arroyo, Luis	62T	455	$1.25	$4.25	Astros, Team	74T	154	$ .30	$ .95
Arroyo, Luis	63T	569	$2.10	$6.00	Astros, Team Checklist	75T	487	$ .15	$ .50
Ashburn, Richie	51Tbb	3	$27.50	$100.00	Astros, Team Checklist	76T	147	$ .15	$ .50
Ashburn, Richie	52T	216	$22.50	$75.00	Astros, Team Checklist	77T	327	$ .15	$ .50
Ashburn, Richie	54T	45	$11.00	$32.50	Astros, Team Checklist	78T	112	$ .06	$ .30
Ashburn, Richie	56T	120	$5.50	$25.00	Astros, Team Checklist	79T	381	$ .05	$ .25
Ashburn, Richie	57T	70	$5.00	$15.00	Astros, Team Checklist	80T	82	$ .05	$ .25
Ashburn, Richie	58T	230	$3.00	$12.50	Astros, Team Checklist	81T	678	$ .02	$ .20
Ashburn, Richie	59T	300	$3.00	$10.00	Astros, Team Leaders	86T	186	$ .01	$ .04
Ashburn, Richie	59T	317	$4.00	$17.00	Astros, Team Leaders	87T	531	$ .01	$ .04
Ashburn, Richie	60T	305	$2.00	$8.00	Astros, Team Leaders	88T	291	$ .01	$ .04
Ashburn, Richie	61T	88	$2.10	$6.00	Astros, Team Leaders	89T	579	$ .01	$ .05
Ashburn, Richie	62T	213	$2.10	$6.50	Astroth, Joe	52T	290	$15.00	$47.50
Ashburn, Richie	63T	135	$2.00	$8.00	Astroth, Joe	53T	103	$4.50	$15.00
Ashby, Alan	76T	209	$ .07	$ .30	Astroth, Joe	56T	106	$2.25	$6.00
Ashby, Alan	77T	564	$ .05	$ .15	Atherton, Keith	84T	529	$ .01	$ .06
Ashby, Alan	78T	319	$ .02	$ .10	Atherton, Keith	85T	166	$ .01	$ .05

Player	Year	No.	VG	EX/MT
Atherton, Keith	86T	353	$ .01	$ .04
Atherton, Keith	87T	52	$ .01	$ .04
Atherton, Keith	88T	451	$ .01	$ .04
Atherton, Keith	89T	698	$ .01	$ .05
Atherton, Keith	89TTR	4	$ .01	$ .06
Atkinson, Bill	78T	43	$ .02	$ .10
Atkinson, Bill	80T	415	$ .01	$ .10
Atwell, Toby	52T	356	$40.00	$140.00
Atwell, Toby	53T	23	$4.50	$15.00
Atwell, Toby	56T	232	$3.00	$9.00
Auerbach, Rick	72T	153	$ .15	$ .50
Auerbach, Rick	73T	427	$ .07	$ .30
Auerbach, Rick	74T	289	$ .07	$ .30
Auerbach, Rick	75T	588	$ .07	$ .30
Auerbach, Rick	76T	622	$ .05	$ .20
Auerbach, Rick	78T	646	$ .02	$ .10
Auerbach, Rick	79T	174	$ .02	$ .10
Auerbach, Rick	80T	354	$ .01	$ .10
Auerbach, Rick	82T	72	$ .01	$ .07
August, Don	85T	392	$ .05	$ .40
August, Don	88TTR	7	$ .01	$ .10
August, Don	89T	696	$ .01	$ .10
August, Don	89TBB	33	$ .01	$ .06
August, Don	90T	192	$ .01	$ .04
Augustine, Dave	74T	598	$4.00	$15.00
Augustine, Dave	75T	616	$7.50	$20.00
Augustine, Jerry	77T	577	$ .05	$ .15
Augustine, Jerry	78T	133	$ .02	$ .10
Augustine, Jerry	79T	357	$ .02	$ .10
Augustine, Jerry	80T	243	$ .01	$ .10
Augustine, Jerry	81T	596	$ .01	$ .10
Augustine, Jerry	82T	46	$ .01	$ .07
Augustine, Jerry	83T	424	$ .01	$ .07
Augustine, Jerry	84T	658	$ .01	$ .06
Ault, Doug	77T	477	$ .05	$ .15
Ault, Doug	78T	267	$ .02	$ .10
Ault, Doug	79T	392	$ .02	$ .10
Aust, Dennis	66T	179	$ .30	$ .95
Austin, Rick	71T	41	$ .15	$ .50
Austin, Rick	76T	269	$ .05	$ .20
Averill, Earl	59T	301	$ .75	$2.20
Averill, Earl	60T	39	$ .45	$1.45
Averill, Earl	61T	358	$ .35	$1.25
Averill, Earl	62T	452	$ .75	$2.50
Averill, Earl	63T	139	$ .10	$ .50
Avery, Steve	89T	784	$ .10	$1.00
Avery, Steve	90TTR	4	$ .01	$ .25
Avery, Steve	91T	227	$ .01	$ .15
Avila, Bobby	52T	257	$12.00	$40.00
Avila, Bobby	56T	132	$2.25	$6.00
Avila, Bobby	57T	195	$ .95	$3.50
Avila, Bobby	58T	276	$ .75	$3.00
Avila, Bobby	59T	363	$ .75	$2.20
Avila, Bobby	60T	90	$ .45	$1.45
Aviles, Ramon	80T	682	$ .01	$ .10
Aviles, Ramon	81T	644	$ .01	$ .10
Aviles, Ramon	82T	152	$ .01	$ .07
Award, Babe Ruth	72T	626	$ .75	$3.00
Award, Commissioners	72T	621	$ .45	$1.45
Award, Cy Young	72T	623	$ .45	$1.45
Award, Minor L.P. of Yr.	72T	624	$ .45	$1.45
Award, MVP	72T	622	$ .45	$1.45
Award, Rookie of Year	72T	625	$ .45	$1.45
Ayala, Benny	75T	619	$ .07	$ .30
Ayala, Benny	80T	262	$ .01	$ .10
Ayala, Benny	81T	101	$ .01	$ .10
Ayala, Benny	82T	331	$ .01	$ .07
Ayala, Benny	83T	59	$ .01	$ .07
Ayala, Benny	84T	443	$ .01	$ .06
Ayala, Benny	85T	624	$ .01	$ .05

Player	Year	No.	VG	EX/MT
Ayala, Benny	85TTR	3	$ .02	$ .10
Azcue, Joe	62T	417	$ .75	$2.50
Azcue, Joe	63T	501	$2.50	$6.50
Azcue, Joe	64T	199	$ .30	$ .95
Azcue, Joe	65T	514	$ .75	$3.00
Azcue, Joe	66T	452	$ .75	$2.50

Player	Year	No.	VG	EX/MT
Azcue, Joe	67T	336	$ .30	$ .85
Azcue, Joe	68T	443	$ .30	$ .85
Azcue, Joe	69T	176	$ .30	$ .85
Azcue, Joe "Jose"	70T	294	$ .15	$ .50
Azcue, Jose	71T	657	$ .75	$2.50
Azocar, Oscar	91T	659	$ .01	$ .20
Babcock, Bob	81T	41	$ .01	$ .10
Babcock, Bob	82T	567	$ .01	$ .07
Babitt, Shooty	82T	578	$ .01	$ .07
Backman, Wally	83T	444	$ .01	$ .07
Backman, Wally	85T	677	$ .01	$ .05
Backman, Wally	86T	191	$ .01	$ .04
Backman, Wally	87T	48	$ .01	$ .04
Backman, Wally	88T	333	$ .01	$ .04
Backman, Wally	89T	508	$ .01	$ .05
Backman, Wally	89TBB	300	$ .01	$ .06
Backman, Wally	89TTR	5	$ .01	$ .06
Backman, Wally	90T	218	$ .01	$ .04
Backman, Wally	90TTR	5	$ .01	$ .05
Backman, Wally	91T	722	$ .01	$ .03
Bacsik, Mike	77T	103	$ .05	$ .15
Bacsik, Mike	80T	453	$ .01	$ .10
Baerga, Carlos	90TTR	6	$ .01	$ .35
Baerga, Carlos	91T	147	$ .01	$ .20
Baez, Jose	78T	311	$ .02	$ .10
Bahnsen, Stan	67T	93	$ .75	$2.25
Bahnsen, Stan	68T	214	$ .45	$1.45
Bahnsen, Stan	69T	380	$ .30	$ .85
Bahnsen, Stan	70T	568	$ .30	$ .95
Bahnsen, Stan	71T	184	$ .15	$ .50
Bahnsen, Stan	72T	662	$ .75	$2.50
Bahnsen, Stan	73T	20	$ .07	$ .30
Bahnsen, Stan	74T	254	$ .07	$ .30
Bahnsen, Stan	75T	161	$ .07	$ .30

Player	Year	No.	VG	EX/MT
Bahnsen, Stan	76T	534	$ .05	$ .20
Bahnsen, Stan	77T	383	$ .05	$ .15
Bahnsen, Stan	78T	97	$ .02	$ .10
Bahnsen, Stan	79T	468	$ .02	$ .10
Bahnsen, Stan	80T	653	$ .01	$ .10
Bahnsen, Stan	81T	267	$ .01	$ .10
Bahnsen, Stan	82T	131	$ .01	$ .07
Bailes, Scott	86TTR	5	$ .05	$ .20
Bailes, Scott	87T	585	$ .01	$ .10
Bailes, Scott	88T	107	$ .01	$ .04
Bailes, Scott	89T	339	$ .01	$ .05
Bailes, Scott	90T	784	$ .01	$ .04
Bailey, Bob	63T	228	$9.00	$35.00
Bailey, Bob	64T	91	$ .30	$ .95
Bailey, Bob	65T	412	$ .35	$1.25
Bailey, Bob	66T	485	$ .75	$2.50
Bailey, Bob	67T	32	$ .30	$ .85
Bailey, Bob	68T	580	$ .35	$1.25
Bailey, Bob	69T	399	$ .30	$ .85
Bailey, Bob	70T	293	$ .15	$ .50
Bailey, Bob	71T	157	$ .15	$ .50
Bailey, Bob	72T	493	$ .15	$ .50

BOB BAILEY

Player	Year	No.	VG	EX/MT
Bailey, Bob	72T	526	$ .30	$ .95
Bailey, Bob	73T	505	$ .07	$ .30
Bailey, Bob	74T	97	$ .07	$ .30
Bailey, Bob	75T	365	$ .07	$ .30
Bailey, Bob	76T	338	$ .05	$ .20
Bailey, Bob	76TTR	338	$ .05	$ .20
Bailey, Bob	77T	221	$ .05	$ .15
Bailey, Bob	78T	457	$ .02	$ .10
Bailey, Bob	79T	549	$ .02	$ .10
Bailey, Ed	53T	206	$4.50	$15.00
Bailey, Ed	54T	184	$3.60	$10.00
Bailey, Ed	55T	69	$2.00	$6.00
Bailey, Ed	57T	128	$ .95	$3.50
Bailey, Ed	58T	330	$ .75	$3.00
Bailey, Ed	58T	386	$2.50	$7.50
Bailey, Ed	58TAS	490	$ .70	$2.25
Bailey, Ed	59T	210	$ .75	$2.20
Bailey, Ed	60T	411	$ .75	$2.20

Player	Year	No.	VG	EX/MT
Bailey, Ed	61T	418	$ .40	$1.50
Bailey, Ed	62T	459	$ .75	$2.50
Bailey, Ed	63T	368	$ .24	$ .60
Bailey, Ed	64T	437	$ .30	$ .75
Bailey, Ed	65T	559	$1.75	$4.50
Bailey, Ed	66T	246	$ .15	$ .35
Bailey, Howard	82T	261	$ .01	$ .07
Bailey, Howard	84T	284	$ .01	$ .06
Bailey, Mark	85T	64	$ .07	$ .04
Bailey, Mark	86T	432	$ .01	$ .04
Bailey, Mark	87T	197	$ .01	$ .04
Bailey, Mark	88TBB	248	$ .01	$ .06
Bailor, Bob	77T	474	$ .05	$ .15
Bailor, Bob	78T	196	$ .02	$ .09
Bailor, Bob	79T	492	$ .02	$ .08
Bailor, Bob	80T	581	$ .02	$ .07
Bailor, Bob	81T	297	$ .02	$ .07
Bailor, Bob	81TTR	732	$ .02	$ .10
Bailor, Bob	82T	79	$ .01	$ .07
Bailor, Bob	83T	343	$ .01	$ .07
Bailor, Bob	84T	654	$ .01	$ .06
Bailor, Bob	84TTR	4	$ .02	$ .10
Bailor, Bob	85T	728	$ .01	$ .05
Bailor, Bob	86T	522	$ .01	$ .04
Baines, Harold	81T	347	$ .95	$3.50
Baines, Harold	82T	684	$ .10	$1.00
Baines, Harold	83T	177	$ .03	$ .35
Baines, Harold	84T	434	$ .02	$ .25
Baines, Harold	85T	249	$ .01	$ .20
Baines, Harold	85T	275	$ .01	$ .10
Baines, Harold	86T	755	$ .02	$ .15
Baines, Harold	87T	772	$ .01	$ .10
Baines, Harold	88T	35	$ .01	$ .10
Baines, Harold	88TBB	224	$ .01	$ .06
Baines, Harold	89T	585	$ .01	$ .05
Baines, Harold	89TBB	266	$ .01	$ .06
Baines, Harold	90T	345	$ .01	$ .04
Baines, Harold	91T	166	$ .01	$ .03
Bair, Doug	78T	353	$ .02	$ .10
Bair, Doug	79T	126	$ .02	$ .10
Bair, Doug	80T	449	$ .01	$ .10
Bair, Doug	81T	73	$ .01	$ .10
Bair, Doug	82T	262	$ .01	$ .07
Bair, Doug	83T	627	$ .01	$ .07
Bair, Doug	83TTR	5	$ .02	$ .10
Bair, Doug	84T	536	$ .01	$ .06
Bair, Doug	85T	744	$ .01	$ .05
Bakenhaster, Dave	64T	479	$ .50	$1.45
Baker, Chuck	79T	456	$ .02	$ .10
Baker, Chuck	82T	253	$ .01	$ .07
Baker, Del	54T	133	$3.60	$10.00
Baker, Del	60T	456	$2.25	$6.00
Baker, Doug	85T	269	$ .01	$ .05
Baker, Dusty	71T	709	$9.00	$27.50
Baker, Dusty	72T	764	$ .95	$3.50
Baker, Dusty	73T	215	$ .30	$ .85
Baker, Dusty	74T	320	$ .30	$ .95
Baker, Dusty	75T	33	$ .07	$ .30
Baker, Dusty	76T	28	$ .07	$ .25
Baker, Dusty	76TTR	28	$ .07	$ .25
Baker, Dusty	77T	146	$ .05	$ .15
Baker, Dusty	78T	668	$ .05	$ .25
Baker, Dusty	79T	562	$ .05	$ .20
Baker, Dusty	80T	255	$ .01	$ .10
Baker, Dusty	81T	495	$ .01	$ .10
Baker, Dusty	82T	311	$ .01	$ .07
Baker, Dusty	82T	375	$ .01	$ .07
Baker, Dusty	83T	220	$ .01	$ .07
Baker, Dusty	84T	40	$ .01	$ .06
Baker, Dusty	84TTR	5	$ .05	$ .20

Player	Year	No.	VG	EX/MT	Player	Year	No.	VG	EX/MT
Baker, Dusty	85T	165	$ .01	$ .05	Bando, Sal	70T	120	$ .30	$ .85
Baker, Dusty	85TTR	4	$ .02	$ .10	Bando, Sal	71T	285	$ .30	$ .95
Baker, Dusty	86T	645	$ .01	$ .04	Bando, Sal	72T	348	$ .15	$ .50
Baker, Dusty	87T	565	$ .01	$ .04	Bando, Sal	72T	650	$ .45	$1.45
Baker, Floyd	52T	292	$15.00	$47.50	Bando, Sal	73T	155	$ .15	$ .50
Baker, Frank	70T	704	$ .75	$2.00	Bando, Sal	74T	103	$ .07	$ .30
Baker, Frank	71T	213	$ .15	$ .50	Bando, Sal	75T	380	$ .15	$ .50
Baker, Frank	71T	689	$ .75	$2.50	Bando, Sal	76T	90	$ .05	$ .20
Baker, Frank	72T	409	$ .15	$ .50	Bando, Sal	77T	498	$ .05	$ .15
Baker, Frank	74T	411	$ .07	$ .30	Bando, Sal	78T	265	$ .02	$ .10
Baker, Gene	56T	142	$2.25	$6.00	Bando, Sal	79T	550	$ .02	$ .10
Baker, Gene	57T	176	$ .95	$3.50	Bando, Sal	80T	715	$ .01	$ .10
Baker, Gene	58T	358	$ .75	$3.00	Bando, Sal	81T	623	$ .01	$ .10
Baker, Gene	59T	238	$ .75	$2.20	Bane, Ed	74T	592	$ .07	$ .30
Baker, Gene	60T	539	$2.50	$10.00	Bane, Ed	77T	486	$ .05	$ .15
Baker, Gene	61T	339	$ .35	$1.25	Baney, Dick	70T	88	$ .15	$ .50
Baker, Steve	83TTR	6	$ .02	$ .10	Baney, Dick	74T	608	$ .07	$ .30
Balaz, John	76T	539	$ .05	$ .20	Bankhead, Scott	85T	393	$ .05	$ .75
Balboni, Steve	82T	83	$ .15	$ .50	Bankhead, Scott	87T	508	$ .01	$ .10
Balboni, Steve	83T	8	$ .10	$ .50	Bankhead, Scott	87TTR	2	$ .01	$ .05
Balboni, Steve	84T	782	$ .01	$ .06	Bankhead, Scott	88T	738	$ .01	$ .04
Balboni, Steve	84TTR	6	$ .05	$ .25	Bankhead, Scott	89T	79	$ .01	$ .05
Balboni, Steve	85T	486	$ .01	$ .05	Bankhead, Scott	90T	213	$ .01	$ .04
Balboni, Steve	86T	164	$ .01	$ .04	Bankhead, Scott	91T	436	$ .01	$ .03
Balboni, Steve	87T	240	$ .01	$ .04	Banks, Ernie	54T	94	$165.00	$575.00
Balboni, Steve	88T	638	$ .01	$ .04	Banks, Ernie	55T	28	$45.00	$150.00
Balboni, Steve	89T	336	$ .01	$ .05	Banks, Ernie	56T	15	$25.00	$75.00
Balboni, Steve	89TTR	6	$ .01	$ .06	Banks, Ernie	57T	55	$23.00	$70.00
Balboni, Steve	90T	716	$ .01	$ .04	Banks, Ernie	58T	310	$15.00	$60.00
Balboni, Steve	91T	511	$ .01	$ .03	Banks, Ernie	58TAS	482	$4.00	$15.00
Baldschun, Jack	62T	46	$ .45	$1.45	Banks, Ernie	59T	147	$3.50	$10.00
Baldschun, Jack	63T	341	$ .45	$1.50	Banks, Ernie	59T	350	$15.00	$60.00
Baldschun, Jack	64T	520	$ .50	$1.45	Banks, Ernie	59T	469	$2.50	$10.00
Baldschun, Jack	65T	555	$1.75	$4.50	Banks, Ernie	59TAS	559	$12.00	$35.00
Baldschun, Jack	66T	272	$ .30	$ .95	Banks, Ernie	60T	10	$8.50	$32.50
Baldschun, Jack	67T	114	$ .30	$ .85	Banks, Ernie	60TAS	560	$8.00	$32.00
Baldschun, Jack	70T	284	$ .15	$ .50	Banks, Ernie	61T	43	$1.50	$5.75
Baldwin, Dave	68T	231	$ .30	$ .85	Banks, Ernie	61T	350	$7.50	$30.00
Baldwin, Dave	69T	132	$ .30	$ .85	Banks, Ernie	61TAS	575	$20.00	$75.00
Baldwin, Dave	70T	613	$ .30	$ .95	Banks, Ernie	61TMVP	485	$5.75	$18.00
Baldwin, Dave	71T	48	$ .15	$ .50	Banks, Ernie	62T	25	$7.50	$30.00
Baldwin, Reggie	80T	678	$ .01	$ .10	Banks, Ernie	63T	3	$3.00	$12.00
Baldwin, Rick	76T	372	$ .05	$ .20	Banks, Ernie	63T	242	$7.50	$22.50
Baldwin, Rick	77T	587	$ .05	$ .15	Banks, Ernie	63T	380	$9.50	$30.00
Bales, Wes	67T	51	$ .30	$ .85	Banks, Ernie	64T	55	$$5.50	$23.00
Ballard, Jeff	88T	782	$ .01	$ .35	Banks, Ernie	65T	510	$15.00	$45.00
Ballard, Jeff	89T	69	$ .01	$ .10	Banks, Ernie	66T	110	$4.00	$16.00
Ballard, Jeff	90T	296	$ .01	$ .04	Banks, Ernie	67T	215	$3.75	$15.00
Ballard, Jeff	90TAS	394	$ .01	$ .04	Banks, Ernie	68T	355	$3.50	$13.50
Ballard, Jeff	91T	546	$ .01	$ .03	Banks, Ernie	69T	6	$ .80	$2.50
Baller, Jay	88T	717	$ .01	$ .04	Banks, Ernie	69T	20	$3.00	$12.00
Bamberger, George	59T	529	$3.00	$9.00	Banks, Ernie	70T	630	$7.00	$22.50
Bamberger, George	73T	136	$ .15	$ .50	Banks, Ernie	71T	525	$7.00	$22.50
Bamberger, George	74T	306	$ .15	$ .50	Banks, Ernie	73T	81	$ .30	$ .95
Bamberger, George	83T	246	$ .01	$ .07	Banks, Ernie	75T	196	$ .35	$1.25
Bamberger, George	85TTR	5	$ .02	$ .10	Banks, Ernie	75T	197	$ .35	$1.25
Bamberger, George	86T	21	$ .01	$ .04	Banks, George	63T	564	$1.75	$4.50
Bamberger, George	87T	468	$ .01	$ .04	Banks, George	64T	223	$ .30	$ .95
Bando, Chris	81T	451	$ .01	$ .10	Banks, George	65T	348	$ .35	$1.25
Bando, Chris	82T	141	$ .25	$1.50	Banks, George	66T	488	$ .75	$2.50
Bando, Chris	83T	227	$ .01	$ .07	Bannister, Alan	77T	559	$ .05	$ .15
Bando, Chris	84T	431	$ .01	$ .06	Bannister, Alan	78T	213	$ .02	$ .10
Bando, Chris	85T	14	$ .01	$ .05	Bannister, Alan	79T	134	$ .02	$ .10
Bando, Chris	86T	594	$ .01	$ .04	Bannister, Alan	80T	608	$ .01	$ .10
Bando, Chris	87T	322	$ .01	$ .04	Bannister, Alan	81T	632	$ .01	$ .10
Bando, Chris	88T	604	$ .01	$ .04	Bannister, Alan	82T	287	$ .01	$ .07
Bando, Sal	67T	33	$ .75	$3.00	Bannister, Alan	83T	348	$ .01	$ .07
Bando, Sal	68T	146	$ .35	$1.25	Bannister, Alan	84T	478	$ .01	$ .06
Bando, Sal	69T	371	$ .30	$ .95	Bannister, Alan	84TTR	7	$ .02	$ .10
Bando, Sal	69T	556	$ .35	$1.25	Bannister, Alan	85T	76	$ .01	$ .05

Player	Year	No.	VG	EX/MT	Player	Year	No.	VG	EX/MT
Bannister, Alan	86T	784	$ .01	$ .04	Barker, Ray	61T	428	$ .75	$3.00
Bannister, Floyd	78T	39	$ .25	$1.00	Barker, Ray	65T	546	$1.75	$4.50
Bannister, Floyd	79T	306	$ .02	$ .10	Barker, Ray	66T	323	$ .30	$ .95
Bannister, Floyd	80T	699	$ .01	$ .10	Barker, Ray	67T	583	$5.00	$18.00
Bannister, Floyd	81T	166	$ .01	$ .10	Barkley, Jeff	86T	567	$ .01	$ .04
Bannister, Floyd	82T	468	$ .01	$ .07	Barlow, Mike	78T	429	$ .02	$ .10
Bannister, Floyd	83T	545	$ .01	$ .07	Barlow, Mike	80T	312	$ .01	$ .10
Bannister, Floyd	83TTR	7	$ .02	$ .10	Barlow, Mike	81T	77	$ .01	$ .10
Bannister, Floyd	84T	280	$ .01	$ .06	Barnes, Brian	91T	211	$ .01	$ .20
Bannister, Floyd	85T	274	$ .01	$ .05	Barnes, Frank	60T	538	$2.50	$10.00
Bannister, Floyd	85T	725	$ .01	$ .05	Barnowski, Ed	66T	442	$ .30	$ .95
Bannister, Floyd	86T	64	$ .01	$ .04	Barnowski, Ed	67T	507	$ .75	$3.00
Bannister, Floyd	87T	737	$ .01	$ .04	Barr, Jim	72T	232	$ .15	$ .50
Bannister, Floyd	88T	357	$ .01	$ .04	Barr, Jim	73T	387	$ .07	$ .30
Bannister, Floyd	88TBB	174	$ .01	$ .06	Barr, Jim	74T	233	$ .07	$ .30
Bannister, Floyd	88TTR	8	$ .01	$ .06	Barr, Jim	75T	107	$ .07	$ .30
Bannister, Floyd	89T	638	$ .01	$ .05	Barr, Jim	76T	308	$ .05	$ .20
Bannister, Floyd	90T	116	$ .01	$ .04	Barr, Jim	77T	609	$ .05	$ .15
Barber, Steve	60T	514	$2.50	$10.00	Barr, Jim	78T	62	$ .02	$ .10
Barber, Steve	61T	125	$ .35	$1.25	Barr, Jim	79T	461	$ .02	$ .10
Barber, Steve	62T	57	$ .75	$2.20	Barr, Jim	80T	529	$ .01	$ .10
Barber, Steve	62T	355	$ .45	$1.45	Barr, Jim	81T	717	$ .01	$ .10
Barber, Steve	63T	12	$ .30	$ .95	Barr, Jim	83T	133	$ .01	$ .07
Barber, Steve	64T	450	$ .50	$1.45	Barr, Jim	84T	282	$ .01	$ .06
Barber, Steve	65T	113	$ .30	$ .85	Barr, Steve	76T	595	$ .05	$ .20
Barber, Steve	66T	477	$ .75	$2.50	Barragan, Cuno	63T	557	$1.75	$4.50
Barber, Steve	67T	82	$ .30	$ .85	Barragon, Cuno	62T	66	$ .45	$1.45
Barber, Steve	68T	316	$ .30	$ .85	Barrett, Marty	84T	683	$ .25	$1.25
Barber, Steve	69T	233	$ .30	$ .95	Barrett, Marty	85T	298	$ .01	$ .05
Barber, Steve	70T	224	$ .15	$ .50	Barrett, Marty	86T	734	$ .01	$ .04
Barber, Steve	72T	333	$ .15	$ .50					
Barber, Steve	73T	36	$ .07	$ .30					
Barber, Steve	74T	631	$ .07	$ .30					
Barberie, Bret	88TTR	9	$ .01	$ .35					
Barberie, Bret	89TBB	19	$ .01	$ .06					
Barbieri, Jim	67T	76	$ .30	$ .85					
Barclay, Curt	57T	361	$1.25	$4.25					
Barclay, Curt	58T	21	$1.25	$4.25					
Barclay, Curt	59T	307	$ .75	$2.20					
Bare, Ray	76T	507	$ .05	$ .20					
Bare, Ray	77T	43	$ .05	$ .15					
Barfield, Jesse	82T	203	$ .70	$3.00					
Barfield, Jesse	82TTR	2	$ .50	$2.25					
Barfield, Jesse	83T	257	$ .15	$ .75					
Barfield, Jesse	84T	488	$ .06	$ .30					
Barfield, Jesse	85T	24	$ .04	$ .20					
Barfield, Jesse	86T	593	$ .01	$ .10					
Barfield, Jesse	87T	655	$ .01	$ .10					
Barfield, Jesse	88T	140	$ .01	$ .10					
Barfield, Jesse	88TBB	92	$ .05	$ .25					
Barfield, Jesse	89T	325	$ .01	$ .10					
Barfield, Jesse	89TTR	7	$ .01	$ .10					
Barfield, Jesse	90T	740	$ .01	$ .04					
Barfield, Jesse	91T	85	$ .01	$ .03					
Barfield, John	89TMLD	8	$ .01	$ .15					
Barfield, John	91T	428	$ .01	$ .10					
Bargar, Greg	84T	474	$ .01	$ .06					
Barker, Len	77T	489	$ .30	$ .85					
Barker, Len	78T	634	$ .02	$ .10					
Barker, Len	79T	94	$ .02	$ .10	Barrett, Marty	87T	39	$ .01	$ .04
Barker, Len	80T	227	$ .01	$ .10	Barrett, Marty	88T	525	$ .01	$ .04
Barker, Len	81T	6	$ .02	$ .10	Barrett, Marty	88TBB	54	$ .01	$ .06
Barker, Len	81T	432	$ .01	$ .10	Barrett, Marty	89T	155	$ .01	$ .05
Barker, Len	82T	166	$ .03	$ .15	Barrett, Marty	89TBB	278	$ .01	$ .06
Barker, Len	82T	360	$ .01	$ .07	Barrett, Marty	90T	355	$ .01	$ .04
Barker, Len	83T	120	$ .01	$ .07	Barrett, Marty	91T	496	$ .01	$ .03
Barker, Len	84T	614	$ .01	$ .06	Barrett, Tommy	89T	653	$ .01	$ .10
Barker, Len	85T	557	$ .01	$ .05	Barrett, Tommy	89TBB	177	$ .01	$ .06
Barker, Len	86T	24	$ .01	$ .04	Barrios, Francisco	77T	222	$ .05	$ .15

MARTY BARRETT

Player	Year	No.	VG	EX/MT	Player	Year	No.	VG	EX/MT
Barrios, Francisco	78T	552	$ .02	$ .10	Bauer, Hank	60T	262	$ .90	$3.00
Barrios, Francisco	79T	386	$ .02	$ .10	Bauer, Hank	61T	119	$ .45	$1.45
Barrios, Francisco	80T	107	$ .01	$ .10	Bauer, Hank	61T	398	$ .90	$3.00
Bartirome, Tony	52T	332	$40.00	$140.00	Bauer, Hank	62T	127	$ .75	$3.00
Bartirome, Tony	53T	71	$4.50	$15.00	Bauer, Hank	62T	463	$1.25	$4.25
Barton, Bob	66T	511	$ .75	$2.50	Bauer, Hank	64T	178	$ .30	$ .95
Barton, Bob	67T	462	$ .75	$3.00	Bauer, Hank	65T	323	$ .35	$1.25
Barton, Bob	68T	351	$ .30	$ .85	Bauer, Hank	66T	229	$ .15	$ .50
Barton, Bob	69T	41	$ .30	$ .85	Bauer, Hank	67T	1	$5.50	$17.50
Barton, Bob	70T	352	$ .15	$ .50	Bauer, Hank	67T	534	$3.00	$9.00
Barton, Bob	71T	589	$ .35	$1.25	Bauer, Hank	68T	513	$ .75	$3.00
Barton, Bob	72T	39	$ .15	$ .50	Bauer, Hank	69T	124	$ .30	$ .95
Barton, Bob	72TIA	40	$ .15	$ .50	Baumann, Frank	58T	167	$ .75	$3.00
Barton, Bob	73T	626	$ .45	$1.45	Baumann, Frank	59T	161	$ .75	$2.20
Basgall, Monty	52T	12	$15.00	$47.50	Baumann, Frank	60T	306	$ .75	$2.20
Basgall, Monty	73T	569	$1.25	$4.25	Baumann, Frank	61T	46	$ .75	$3.00
Basgall, Monty	74T	144	$ .75	$3.00	Baumann, Frank	61T	550	$7.00	$21.00
Bass, Kevin	79T	708	$ .45	$1.45	Baumann, Frank	62T	161	$ .45	$1.45
Bass, Kevin	84T	538	$ .01	$ .06	Baumann, Frank	63T	381	$ .45	$1.50
Bass, Kevin	85T	326	$ .01	$ .05	Baumann, Frank	64T	453	$ .50	$1.45
Bass, Kevin	86T	458	$ .01	$ .04	Baumann, Frank	65T	161	$ .30	$ .85
Bass, Kevin	87T	85	$ .01	$ .04	Baumer, Jim	61T	292	$ .35	$1.25
Bass, Kevin	88T	175	$ .01	$ .04	Baumgarten, Ross	79T	704	$ .02	$ .10
Bass, Kevin	88TBB	77	$ .01	$ .06	Baumgarten, Ross	80T	138	$ .01	$ .10
Bass, Kevin	89T	646	$ .01	$ .05	Baumgarten, Ross	81T	398	$ .01	$ .10
Bass, Kevin	89TBB	187	$ .01	$ .06	Baumgarten, Ross	82T	563	$ .01	$ .07
Bass, Kevin	90T	281	$ .01	$ .04	Baumgarten, Ross	82TTR	3	$ .02	$ .10
Bass, Kevin	90TTR	7	$ .01	$ .05	Baumgarten, Ross	83T	97	$ .01	$ .07
Bass, Kevin	91T	752	$ .01	$ .03	Baumholtz, Frank	52T	225	$7.00	$20.00
Bass, Norm	62T	122	$ .45	$1.45	Baumholtz, Frank	54T	60	$7.00	$22.00
Bass, Norm	63T	461	$2.50	$6.50	Baumholtz, Frank	55T	172	$3.25	$9.00
Bass, Randy	79T	707	$ .02	$ .10	Baumholtz, Frank	56T	274	$2.25	$8.00
Bass, Randy	82T	307	$ .01	$ .07	Bauta, Ed	62T	344	$ .45	$1.45
Bateman, John	63T	386	$ .75	$2.20	Bauta, Ed	63T	336	$ .45	$1.50
Bateman, John	64T	142	$ .30	$ .95	Bautista, Jose	88TTR	10	$ .01	$ .10
Bateman, John	65T	433	$ .35	$1.25	Bautista, Jose	89T	469	$ .01	$ .10
Bateman, John	66T	86	$ .30	$ .95	Baxes, Jim	59T	547	$2.50	$10.00
Bateman, John	67T	231	$ .30	$ .85	Baxes, Jim	60T	318	$ .75	$2.20
Bateman, John	68T	592	$ .35	$1.25	Baxes, Mike	58T	302	$ .75	$3.00
Bateman, John	69T	138	$ .30	$ .85	Baxes, Mike	59T	381	$ .75	$2.20
Bateman, John	70T	417	$ .15	$ .50	Baylor, Don	71T	709	$9.00	$27.50
Bateman, John	71T	628	$ .35	$1.25	Baylor, Don	72T	474	$ .50	$2.35
Bateman, John	72T	5	$ .15	$ .50	Baylor, Don	73T	384	$ .30	$1.50
Bates, Billy	89TMLD	9	$ .01	$ .35	Baylor, Don	74T	187	$ .30	$ .95
Bathe, Bill	91T	679	$ .01	$ .03	Baylor, Don	75T	382	$ .30	$ .95
Batiste, Kevin	89TMLD	10	$ .01	$ .15	Baylor, Don	76T	125	$ .15	$ .50
Battey, Earl	57T	401	$1.25	$4.25	Baylor, Don	77T	462	$ .30	$ .85
Battey, Earl	58T	364	$ .75	$3.00	Baylor, Don	78T	48	$ .05	$ .25
Battey, Earl	59T	114	$ .75	$2.20	Baylor, Don	79T	635	$ .15	$ .50
Battey, Earl	60T	328	$ .75	$2.20	Baylor, Don	80T	203	$ .08	$ .30
Battey, Earl	61T	315	$ .35	$1.25	Baylor, Don	80T	285	$ .05	$ .20
Battey, Earl	61TAS	582	$7.00	$21.00	Baylor, Don	81T	580	$ .03	$ .15
Battey, Earl	62T	371	$ .75	$2.50	Baylor, Don	82T	415	$ .03	$ .15
Battey, Earl	63T	306	$ .75	$2.20	Baylor, Don	83T	105	$ .01	$ .10
Battey, Earl	63T	410	$ .45	$1.50	Baylor, Don	83TTR	8	$ .05	$ .25
Battey, Earl	64T	90	$ .30	$ .95	Baylor, Don	84T	335	$ .02	$ .10
Battey, Earl	65T	490	$ .75	$3.00	Baylor, Don	84T	486	$ .01	$ .06
Battey, Earl	66T	240	$ .30	$ .95	Baylor, Don	85T	70	$ .01	$ .10
Battey, Earl	67T	15	$ .30	$ .85	Baylor, Don	86T	765	$ .01	$ .04
Batton, Chris	77T	475	$ .05	$ .15	Baylor, Don	86TTR	6	$ .03	$ .15
Batts, Matt	52T	230	$7.00	$20.00	Baylor, Don	87T	230	$ .01	$ .04
Batts, Matt	54T	88	$3.60	$10.00	Baylor, Don	88T	545	$ .01	$ .04
Bauer, Hank	51Trb	24	$2.50	$10.00	Baylor, Don	88TBB	162	$ .01	$ .10
Bauer, Hank	52T	215	$14.00	$42.00	Baylor, Don	88TTR	11	$ .01	$ .06
Bauer, Hank	54T	130	$7.50	$22.50	Baylor, Don	89T	673	$ .01	$ .06
Bauer, Hank	55T	166	$9.50	$37.50	Beall, Bob	79T	222	$ .02	$ .10
Bauer, Hank	56T	177	$3.75	$15.00	Beamon, Charley	59T	192	$ .75	$2.20
Bauer, Hank	57T	240	$3.50	$11.00	Beamon, Charlie	80T	672	$ .01	$ .10
Bauer, Hank	58T	9	$1.20	$7.00	Beane, Billy	87T	114	$ .01	$ .04
Bauer, Hank	59T	240	$2.10	$5.00	Bean(e), Billy	88T	267	$ .01	$ .04

TOPPS

Player	Year	No.	VG	EX/MT	Player	Year	No.	VG	EX/MT
Beard, Dave	81T	96	$ .01	$ .10	Bedrosian, Steve	88TBB	23	$ .01	$ .06
Beard, Dave	83T	102	$ .01	$ .07	Bedrosian, Steve	89T	20	$ .01	$ .05
Beard, Dave	84T	513	$ .01	$ .06	Bedrosian, Steve	89TBB	137	$ .01	$ .10
Beard, Dave	84TTR	8	$ .02	$ .10	Bedrosian, Steve	89TTR	8	$ .01	$ .06
Beard, Dave	85T	232	$ .01	$ .05	Bedrosian, Steve	90T	310	$ .01	$ .04
Beard, Mike	76T	53	$ .05	$ .20	Bedrosian, Steve	91T	125	$ .01	$ .03
Beard, Ted	52T	150	$7.00	$20.00	Beene, Fred	70T	121	$ .15	$ .50
Beardon, Gene	52T	229	$7.00	$20.00	Beene, Fred	73T	573	$ .45	$1.45
Beare, Gary	78T	516	$ .02	$ .10	Beene, Fred	74T	274	$ .07	$ .30
Bearnarth, Larry	63T	386	$ .75	$2.20	Beene, Fred	75T	181	$ .07	$ .30
Bearnarth, Larry	64T	527	$1.75	$4.50	Behney, Mel	72T	524	$ .15	$ .50
Bearnarth, Larry	65T	258	$ .35	$1.25	Behney, Mel	73T	602	$ .45	$1.45
Bearnarth, Larry	66T	464	$ .75	$2.50	Belanger, Mark	67T	558	$8.75	$35.00
Beattie, Jim	79T	179	$ .02	$ .10	Belanger, Mark	68T	118	$ .30	$ .95
Beattie, Jim	80T	334	$ .01	$ .10	Belanger, Mark	69T	299	$ .30	$ .95
Beattie, Jim	81T	443	$ .01	$ .10	Belanger, Mark	70T	615	$ .45	$1.45
Beattie, Jim	82T	22	$ .01	$ .07	Belanger, Mark	71T	99	$ .15	$ .50
Beattie, Jim	83T	675	$ .01	$ .07	Belanger, Mark	72T	456	$ .30	$ .85
Beattie, Jim	83T	711	$ .01	$ .07	Belanger, Mark	73T	253	$ .07	$ .30
Beattie, Jim	84T	288	$ .01	$ .06	Belanger, Mark	74T	329	$ .07	$ .30
Beattie, Jim	85T	505	$ .01	$ .05	Belanger, Mark	75T	74	$ .07	$ .30
Beattie, Jim	86T	729	$ .01	$ .04	Belanger, Mark	76T	505	$ .05	$ .20
Beattie, Jim	87T	117	$ .01	$ .04	Belanger, Mark	77T	135	$ .05	$ .15
Beatty, Blaine	89TMLD	11	$ .01	$ .25	Belanger, Mark	78T	315	$ .02	$ .10
Beauchamp, Jim	64T	492	$ .50	$1.45	Belanger, Mark	79T	65	$ .02	$ .10
Beauchamp, Jim	65T	409	$ .35	$1.25	Belanger, Mark	80T	425	$ .02	$ .10
Beauchamp, Jim	66T	84	$ .30	$ .95	Belanger, Mark	81T	641	$ .02	$ .10
Beauchamp, Jim	67T	307	$ .30	$ .85	Belanger, Mark	82T	776	$ .02	$ .10
Beauchamp, Jim	69T	613	$ .30	$ .95	Belanger, Mark	82TTR	5	$ .05	$ .20
Beauchamp, Jim	71T	322	$ .15	$ .50	Belanger, Mark	83T	273	$ .01	$ .07
Beauchamp, Jim	72T	594	$ .30	$ .95	Belcher, Tim	85T	281	$ .10	$1.50
Beauchamp, Jim	73T	137	$ .07	$ .30	Belcher, Tim	88TTR	12	$ .01	$ .06
Beauchamp, Jim	74T	424	$ .07	$ .30	Belcher, Tim	89T	456	$ .01	$ .05
Beck, Rich	66T	234	$1.50	$5.00	Belcher, Tim	89TBB	145	$ .01	$ .06
Becker, Joe	60T	463	$ .85	$2.25	Belcher, Tim	90T	173	$ .01	$ .04
Beckert, Glenn	65T	549	$2.00	$5.00	Belcher, Tim	91T	25	$ .01	$ .03
Beckert, Glenn	66T	232	$ .30	$ .95	Belinda, Stan	89TMLD	12	$ .01	$ .15
Beckert, Glenn	67T	296	$ .30	$ .85	Belinda, Stan	90T	354	$ .01	$ .10
Beckert, Glenn	68T	101	$ .30	$ .85	Belinda, Stan	91T	522	$ .01	$ .03
Beckert, Glenn	69T	171	$ .30	$ .85	Belinsky, Bo	62T	592	$15.00	$50.00
Beckert, Glenn	70T	480	$ .15	$ .50	Belinsky, Bo	63T	33	$ .75	$3.00
Beckert, Glenn	71T	390	$ .15	$ .50	Belinsky, Bo	64T	315	$ .45	$1.45
Beckert, Glenn	72T	45	$ .15	$ .50	Belinsky, Bo	65T	225	$ .45	$1.45
Beckert, Glenn	72T	85	$ .35	$1.25	Belinsky, Bo	66T	506	$ .90	$3.00
Beckert, Glenn	72TIA	46	$ .15	$ .50	Belinsky, Bo	67T	447	$ .45	$1.45
Beckert, Glenn	73T	440	$ .30	$ .85	Belinsky, Bo	69T	366	$ .15	$ .50
Beckert, Glenn	74T	241	$ .07	$ .30	Bell, Buddy	73T	31	$1.65	$5.00
Beckert, Glenn	75T	484	$ .07	$ .30	Bell, Buddy	74T	257	$ .75	$2.20
Beckwith, Joe	80T	679	$ .01	$ .10	Bell, Buddy	75T	38	$ .45	$1.45
Beckwith, Joe	81T	231	$ .01	$ .10	Bell, Buddy	76T	66	$ .30	$ .95
Beckwith, Joe	84T	454	$ .01	$ .06	Bell, Buddy	76T	358	$ .15	$ .50
Beckwith, Joe	84TTR	9	$ .02	$ .10	Bell, Buddy	77T	590	$ .15	$ .50
Beckwith, Joe	85T	77	$ .01	$ .05	Bell, Buddy	78T	280	$ .30	$ .85
Beckwith, Joe	86T	562	$ .01	$ .04	Bell, Buddy	79T	690	$ .05	$ .20
Becquer, Julio	58T	458	$ .75	$2.20	Bell, Buddy	80T	190	$ .30	$ .85
Becquer, Julio	59T	93	$1.25	$4.25	Bell, Buddy	81T	475	$ .05	$ .20
Becquer, Julio	60T	271	$ .45	$1.45	Bell, Buddy	82T	50	$ .03	$ .15
Becquer, Julio	61T	329	$ .35	$1.25	Bell, Buddy	83T	330	$ .01	$ .15
Bedell, Howie	61T	353	$ .35	$1.25	Bell, Buddy	83T	412	$ .01	$ .07
Bedell, Howie	62T	76	$ .45	$1.45	Bell, Buddy	84T	37	$ .01	$ .06
Bedrosian, Steve	82T	502	$ .50	$2.50	Bell, Buddy	84T	665	$ .03	$ .15
Bedrosian, Steve	82TTR	4	$ .15	$ .75	Bell, Buddy	85T	131	$ .01	$ .10
Bedrosian, Steve	83T	157	$ .01	$ .07	Bell, Buddy	85T	745	$ .01	$ .10
Bedrosian, Steve	84T	365	$ .01	$ .06	Bell, Buddy	86T	285	$ .01	$ .10
Bedrosian, Steve	85T	25	$ .01	$ .05	Bell, Buddy	87T	545	$ .01	$ .10
Bedrosian, Steve	86T	648	$ .01	$ .04	Bell, Buddy	88T	130	$ .01	$ .10
Bedrosian, Steve	86TTR	7	$ .02	$ .10	Bell, Buddy	88TTR	13	$ .01	$ .06
Bedrosian, Steve	87T	736	$ .03	$ .15	Bell, Buddy	89T	461	$ .01	$ .05
Bedrosian, Steve	88T	440	$ .01	$ .04	Bell, Buddy	89TBB	270	$ .01	$ .06
Bedrosian, Steve	88TAS	407	$ .01	$ .04	Bell, Dave (Gus)	51Trb	17	$2.50	$10.00

Player	Year	No.	VG	EX/MT	Player	Year	No.	VG	EX/MT
Bell, Eric	87TTR	3	$ .05	$ .25	Bench, Johnny	69TAS	430	$3.00	$12.00
Bell, Eric	88T	383	$ .01	$ .04	Bench, Johnny	70T	660	$40.00	$150.00
Bell, Gary	59T	327	$ .75	$2.20	Bench, Johnny	70TAS	464	$2.00	$9.00
Bell, Gary	60T	441	$ .90	$3.00	Bench, Johnny	71T	64	$ .50	$2.00
Bell, Gary	61T	274	$ .35	$1.25	Bench, Johnny	71T	66	$ .50	$2.00
Bell, Gary	62T	273	$ .45	$1.45	Bench, Johnny	71T	250	$9.00	$40.00
Bell, Gary	63T	129	$ .30	$ .95	Bench, Johnny	72T	433	$8.00	$35.00
Bell, Gary	64T	234	$ .30	$ .95	Bench, Johnny	72TIA	434	$4.00	$15.00
Bell, Gary	65T	424	$ .35	$1.25	Bench, Johnny	73T	62	$ .50	$1.50
Bell, Gary	66T	525	$5.00	$20.00	Bench, Johnny	73T	63	$ .50	$1.50
Bell, Gary	67T	479	$ .75	$3.00	Bench, Johnny	73T	380	$6.00	$20.00
Bell, Gary	68T	43	$ .30	$ .85	Bench, Johnny	74T	10	$4.00	$13.00
Bell, Gary	69T	377	$ .30	$ .85	Bench, Johnny	74TAS	331	$ .75	$3.00
Bell, George (Jorge)	82T	254	$2.75	$11.00	Bench, Johnny	75T	208	$ .45	$1.75
Bell, George (Jorge)	84T	278	$ .35	$1.50	Bench, Johnny	75T	210	$ .50	$1.50
Bell, George (Jorge)	85T	698	$ .10	$ .50	Bench, Johnny	75T	260	$3.00	$12.00
Bell, George (Jorge)	86T	338	$ .04	$ .35	Bench, Johnny	75T	308	$ .35	$1.25
Bell, George (Jorge)	86TAS	718	$ .02	$ .15	Bench, Johnny	76T	195	$ .35	$1.25
Bell, George	87T	681	$ .30	$ .95	Bench, Johnny	76T	300	$3.00	$10.00
Bell, George	87TAS	612	$ .01	$ .10	Bench, Johnny	77T	70	$1.50	$6.50
Bell, George	88T	590	$ .01	$ .20	Bench, Johnny	78T	700	$1.00	$4.50
Bell, George	88TAS	390	$ .01	$ .10	Bench, Johnny	79T	200	$ .50	$2.00
Bell, George	88TBB	15	$ .01	$ .15	Bench, Johnny	80T	100	$ .75	$3.00
Bell, George	89T	50	$ .01	$ .05	Bench, Johnny	81T	600	$ .35	$2.00
Bell, George	89TBB	318	$ .01	$ .10	Bench, Johnny	81TRB	201	$ .10	$ .50
Bell, George	89TRB	1	$ .01	$ .05	Bench, Johnny	82T	400	$ .35	$1.50
Bell, George	90T	170	$ .01	$ .04	Bench, Johnny	82TIA	401	$ .12	$ .50
Bell, George	91T	440	$ .01	$ .03	Bench, Johnny	83T	60	$ .25	$1.00
Bell, Gus	52T	170	$7.00	$20.00	Bench, Johnny	83T	61	$ .05	$ .25
Bell, Gus	53T	118	$5.00	$20.00	Bench, Johnny	84T	6	$ .10	$ .50
Bell, Gus	56T	162	$3.00	$9.00	Bench, Johnny	90TTB	664	$ .01	$ .04
Bell, Gus	57T	180	$2.00	$6.00	Bene, Bill	89T	84	$ .01	$ .25
Bell, Gus	58T	75	$ .70	$2.25	Benedict, Bruce	79T	715	$ .05	$ .20
Bell, Gus	59T	365	$ .90	$3.00	Benedict, Bruce	80T	675	$ .01	$ .10
Bell, Gus	60T	235	$ .90	$3.00					
Bell, Gus	60T	352	$ .90	$3.50					
Bell, Gus	61T	25	$2.10	$6.00					
Bell, Gus	61T	215	$ .35	$1.25					
Bell, Gus	62T	408	$1.25	$4.25					
Bell, Gus	63T	547	$1.75	$4.50					
Bell, Gus	64T	534	$1.75	$4.50					
Bell, Gus	76T	66	$ .30	$ .95					
Bell, Gus	85T	131	$ .01	$ .10					
Bell, Jay	88T	637	$ .01	$ .15					
Bell, Jay	89T	144	$ .01	$ .05					
Bell, Jay	90T	523	$ .01	$ .04					
Bell, Jay	91T	293	$ .01	$ .03					
Bell, Jerry	72T	162	$ .25	$ .75					
Bell, Jerry	73T	92	$ .07	$ .30					
Bell, Jerry	74T	261	$ .07	$ .30					
Bell, Juan	89TMLD	13	$ .01	$ .25					
Bell, Juan	90T	724	$ .01	$ .15					
Bell, Kevin	77T	83	$ .05	$ .15					
Bell, Kevin	78T	463	$ .02	$ .10					
Bell, Kevin	79T	662	$ .02	$ .10					
Bell, Kevin	80T	379	$ .01	$ .10					
Bella, Zeke	59T	254	$ .75	$2.20					
Belle, Joey	89TMLD	14	$ .01	$ .75					
Belle, Joey	90T	283	$ .01	$1.00					
Belliard, Rafael	87T	541	$ .01	$ .10					
Belliard, Rafael	88T	221	$ .01	$ .04					
Belliard, Rafael	88TBB	175	$ .01	$ .06					
Belliard, Rafael	89T	723	$ .01	$ .05					
Belliard, Rafael	89TBB	196	$ .01	$ .06					
Belliard, Rafael	90T	143	$ .01	$ .04	Benedict, Bruce	81T	108	$ .01	$ .10
Belliard, Rafael	91T	487	$ .01	$ .03	Benedict, Bruce	82T	424	$ .01	$ .07
Belloir, Rob	77T	312	$ .05	$ .15	Benedict, Bruce	83T	521	$ .01	$ .07
Belloir, Rob	78T	681	$ .02	$ .10	Benedict, Bruce	84T	255	$ .01	$ .06
Bench, Johnny	68T	247	$90.00	$350.00	Benedict, Bruce	85T	335	$ .01	$ .05
Bench, Johnny	69T	95	$40.00	$150.00	Benedict, Bruce	86T	78	$ .01	$ .04

TOPPS

Player	Year	No.	VG	EX/MT	Player	Year	No.	VG	EX/MT
Benedict, Bruce	87T	186	$ .01	$ .04	Berenyi, Bruce	83T	139	$ .01	$ .07
Benedict, Bruce	88T	652	$ .01	$ .04	Berenyi, Bruce	84T	297	$ .01	$ .06
Benedict, Bruce	89T	778	$ .01	$ .05	Berenyi, Bruce	84TTR	10	$ .02	$ .10
Benedict, Bruce	89TBB	83	$ .01	$ .06	Berenyi, Bruce	85T	27	$ .01	$ .05
Benedict, Bruce	90T	583	$ .01	$ .04	Berenyi, Bruce	86T	339	$ .01	$ .04
Benes, Andy	88TTR	14	$ .25	$1.50	Berenyi, Bruce	87T	582	$ .01	$ .04
Benes, Andy	89T	437	$ .05	$ .75	Bergman, Dave	78T	705	$ .02	$ .10
Benes, Andy	89TBB	114	$ .01	$ .25	Bergman, Dave	79T	697	$ .02	$ .10
Benes, Andy	89TMLD	15	$ .01	$ .60	Bergman, Dave	81T	253	$ .01	$ .10
Benes, Andy	90T	193	$ .01	$ .35	Bergman, Dave	81TTR	734	$ .02	$ .10
Benes, Andy	91T	307	$ .01	$ .03	Bergman, Dave	82T	498	$ .01	$ .07
Beniquez, Juan	74T	647	$ .15	$ .50	Bergman, Dave	83T	32	$ .01	$ .07
Beniquez, Juan	75T	601	$ .07	$ .30	Bergman, Dave	84T	522	$ .01	$ .06
Beniquez, Juan	76T	496	$ .05	$ .20	Bergman, Dave	84TTR	11	$ .02	$ .10
Beniquez, Juan	77T	81	$ .05	$ .15	Bergman, Dave	85T	368	$ .01	$ .05
Beniquez, Juan	78T	238	$ .02	$ .10	Bergman, Dave	86T	101	$ .01	$ .04
Beniquez, Juan	79T	478	$ .02	$ .10	Bergman, Dave	87T	700	$ .01	$ .04
Beniquez, Juan	80T	114	$ .01	$ .10	Bergman, Dave	88T	289	$ .01	$ .04
Beniquez, Juan	81T	306	$ .01	$ .10	Bergman, Dave	89T	631	$ .01	$ .05
Beniquez, Juan	81TTR	733	$ .02	$ .10	Bergman, Dave	90T	77	$ .01	$ .04
Beniquez, Juan	82T	572	$ .01	$ .07	Bergman, Dave	91T	412	$ .01	$ .03
Beniquez, Juan	83T	678	$ .01	$ .07	Beringer, Carroll	73T	486	$ .30	$ .95
Beniquez, Juan	84T	53	$ .01	$ .06	Beringer, Carroll	74T	119	$ .07	$ .30
Beniquez, Juan	85T	226	$ .01	$ .05	Bernard, Dwight	79T	721	$ .05	$ .20
Beniquez, Juan	86T	325	$ .01	$ .04	Bernard, Dwight	83T	244	$ .01	$ .07
Beniquez, Juan	86TTR	8	$ .02	$ .10	Bernazard, Tony	80T	680	$ .05	$ .20
Beniquez, Juan	87T	688	$ .01	$ .04	Bernazard, Tony	81T	413	$ .01	$ .10
Beniquez, Juan	87TTR	4	$ .01	$ .05	Bernazard, Tony	81TTR	735	$ .02	$ .10
Beniquez, Juan	88T	541	$ .01	$ .04	Bernazard, Tony	82T	206	$ .01	$ .07
Benjamin, Mike	89TMLD	16	$ .01	$ .15	Bernazard, Tony	83T	698	$ .01	$ .07
Benjamin, Mike	91T	791	$ .01	$ .10	Bernazard, Tony	83TTR	9	$ .02	$ .10
Bennett, Dave	64T	561	$2.10	$6.00	Bernazard, Tony	84T	41	$ .01	$ .06
Bennett, Dave	65T	521	$ .75	$3.00	Bernazard, Tony	84TTR	12	$ .02	$ .10
Bennett, Dennis	63T	56	$ .30	$ .95	Bernazard, Tony	85T	533	$ .01	$ .05
Bennett, Dennis	64T	396	$ .50	$1.45	Bernazard, Tony	86T	354	$ .01	$ .04
Bennett, Dennis	65T	147	$ .30	$ .85	Bernazard, Tony	87T	758	$ .01	$ .04
Bennett, Dennis	66T	491	$ .75	$2.50	Bernazard, Tony	87TAS	607	$ .01	$ .04
Bennett, Dennis	67T	206	$ .30	$ .85	Bernazard, Tony	88T	122	$ .01	$ .04
Benson, Vern	53T	205	$4.50	$15.00	Bernhardt, Juan	77T	494	$ .12	$ .40
Benson, Vern	73T	497	$ .30	$ .85	Bernhardt, Juan	78T	698	$ .02	$ .10
Benson, Vern	74T	236	$ .07	$ .30	Bernhardt, Juan	79T	366	$ .02	$ .10
Benton, Al	52T	374	$40.00	$140.00	Bernier, Carlos	53T	243	$12.50	$50.00
Benzinger, Todd	88T	96	$ .05	$ .25	Berra, Dale	79T	723	$ .05	$ .20
Benzinger, Todd	89T	493	$ .01	$ .10	Berra, Dale	80T	292	$ .01	$ .10
Benzinger, Todd	89TTR	9	$ .01	$ .06	Berra, Dale	81T	147	$ .01	$ .10
Benzinger, Todd	90T	712	$ .01	$ .04	Berra, Dale	82T	588	$ .01	$ .07
Benzinger, Todd	91T	334	$ .01	$ .03	Berra, Dale	83T	433	$ .01	$ .07
Berardino, Johnny	52T	253	$15.00	$40.00	Berra, Dale	84T	18	$ .01	$ .06
Berberet, Lou	56T	329	$2.25	$8.00	Berra, Dale	85T	132	$ .01	$ .10
Berberet, Lou	57T	315	$4.25	$15.00	Berra, Dale	85T	305	$ .01	$ .05
Berberet, Lou	58T	383	$ .75	$3.00	Berra, Dale	85TTR	6	$ .02	$ .10
Berberet, Lou	59T	96	$1.25	$4.25	Berra, Dale	86T	692	$ .01	$ .04
Berberet, Lou	60T	6	$ .45	$1.45	Berra, Larry "Yogi"	51Trb	1	$35.00	$125.00
Berenguer, Juan	79T	721	$ .05	$ .20	Berra, Yogi	52T	191	$90.00	$350.00
Berenguer, Juan	81T	259	$ .50	$2.00	Berra, Yogi	53T	104	$60.00	$180.00
Berenguer, Juan	82T	437	$ .01	$ .07	Berra, Yogi	54T	50	$65.00	$210.00
Berenguer, Juan	84T	174	$ .01	$ .06	Berra, Yogi	55T	198	$80.00	$250.00
Berenguer, Juan	85T	672	$ .01	$ .05	Berra, Yogi	56T	110	$35.00	$130.00
Berenguer, Juan	86T	47	$ .01	$ .04	Berra, Yogi	57T	2	$35.00	$135.00
Berenguer, Juan	86TTR	9	$ .02	$ .10	Berra, Yogi	57T	407	$100.00	$350.00
Berenguer, Juan	87T	303	$ .01	$ .04	Berra, Yogi	58T	370	$22.50	$77.50
Berenguer, Juan	87TTR	5	$ .01	$ .05	Berra, Yogi	59T	180	$20.00	$67.50
Berenguer, Juan	88T	526	$ .01	$ .04	Berra, Yogi	60T	480	$15.00	$55.00
Berenguer, Juan	88TBB	222	$ .01	$ .06	Berra, Yogi	61T	425	$15.00	$55.00
Berenguer, Juan	89T	294	$ .01	$ .05	Berra, Yogi	61TMVP	472	$9.00	$35.00
Berenguer, Juan	89TBB	117	$ .01	$ .06	Berra, Yogi	62T	360	$17.00	$52.50
Berenguer, Juan	90T	709	$ .01	$ .04	Berra, Yogi	63T	340	$20.00	$65.00
Berenguer, Juan	91T	449	$ .01	$ .03	Berra, Yogi	64T	21	$10.00	$30.00
Berenyi, Bruce	81T	606	$ .01	$ .10	Berra, Yogi	65T	470	$15.00	$55.00
Berenyi, Bruce	82T	459	$ .01	$ .07	Berra, Yogi	73T	257	$ .50	$1.50

Player	Year	No.	VG	EX/MT
Berra, Yogi	74T	179	$ .50	$1.50
Berra, Yogi	75T	189	$ .50	$1.50
Berra, Yogi	75T	192	$ .50	$1.50
Berra, Yogi	75T	193	$ .50	$1.50
Berra, Yogi	84TTR	13	$ .30	$ .85
Berra, Yogi	85T	132	$ .01	$ .10
Berra, Yogi	85T	155	$ .01	$ .10
Berres, Ray	60T	458	$ .95	$3.50
Berroa, Geronimo	89TBB	297	$ .01	$ .10
Berroa, Geronimo	89TMLD	17	$ .01	$ .10
Berroa, Geronimo	89TTR	10	$ .01	$ .15
Berroa, Geronimo	90T	617	$ .01	$ .04
Berry, Ken	65T	368	$ .35	$1.25
Berry, Ken	66T	127	$ .30	$ .95
Berry, Ken	67T	67	$ .30	$ .85
Berry, Ken	68T	485	$ .35	$1.25
Berry, Ken	69T	494	$ .30	$ .85
Berry, Ken	70T	239	$ .15	$ .50
Berry, Ken	71T	466	$ .15	$ .50
Berry, Ken	72T	379	$ .15	$ .50
Berry, Ken	73T	445	$ .07	$ .30
Berry, Ken	74T	163	$ .07	$ .30
Berry, Ken	75T	432	$ .07	$ .30
Berryhill, Damon	88TTR	15	$ .01	$ .25
Berryhill, Damon	89T	543	$ .01	$ .10
Berryhill, Damon	89TBB	60	$ .01	$ .10
Berryhill, Damon	90T	362	$ .01	$ .04
Berryhill, Damon	91T	188	$ .01	$ .03
Bertaina, Frank	65T	396	$ .35	$1.25
Bertaina, Frank	66T	579	$5.00	$20.00
Bertaina, Frank	68T	131	$ .30	$ .85
Bertaina, Frank	69T	554	$ .30	$ .95
Bertaina, Frank	70T	638	$ .75	$2.00
Bertaina, Frank	71T	422	$ .15	$ .50
Bertell, Dick	61T	441	$ .75	$3.00
Bertell, Dick	63T	287	$ .45	$1.50
Bertell, Dick	64T	424	$ .50	$1.45
Bertell, Dick	65T	27	$ .30	$ .85
Bertell, Dick	66T	587	$5.00	$20.00
Bertoia, Reno	54T	131	$3.60	$10.00
Bertoia, Reno	55T	94	$2.00	$6.00
Bertoia, Reno	57T	390	$1.25	$4.25
Bertoia, Reno	58T	232	$ .75	$3.00
Bertoia, Reno	59T	84	$1.25	$4.25
Bertoia, Reno	60T	297	$ .75	$2.20
Bertoia, Reno	61T	392	$ .75	$3.00
Bessent, Don	56T	184	$3.00	$9.00
Bessent, Don	57T	178	$ .95	$3.50
Bessent, Don	58T	401	$ .75	$3.00
Bessent, Don	59T	71	$1.25	$4.25
Best, Karl	86T	61	$ .01	$ .04
Best, Karl	87T	439	$ .01	$ .04
Beswick, Jim	79T	725	$ .02	$ .10
Bethke, Jim	65T	533	$5.00	$20.00
Bevacqua, Kurt	72T	193	$ .15	$ .50
Bevacqua, Kurt	74T	454	$ .07	$ .30
Bevacqua, Kurt	74TTR	454	$ .07	$ .30
Bevacqua, Kurt	76T	427	$ .05	$ .20
Bevacqua, Kurt	76T	564	$ .15	$ .50
Bevacqua, Kurt	77T	317	$ .05	$ .15
Bevacqua, Kurt	78T	725	$ .02	$ .10
Bevacqua, Kurt	79T	44	$ .02	$ .10
Bevacqua, Kurt	80T	584	$ .01	$ .10
Bevacqua, Kurt	81T	118	$ .01	$ .10
Bevacqua, Kurt	82T	267	$ .01	$ .07
Bevacqua, Kurt	82TTR	6	$ .02	$ .10
Bevacqua, Kurt	83T	674	$ .01	$ .07
Bevacqua, Kurt	84T	346	$ .01	$ .06
Bevacqua, Kurt	85T	478	$ .01	$ .05
Bevacqua, Kurt	86T	789	$ .01	$ .04

Player	Year	No.	VG	EX/MT
Bevan, Hal	61T	456	$ .75	$3.00
Biancalana, Buddy	85T	387	$ .01	$ .05

BUDDY BIANCALANA

Player	Year	No.	VG	EX/MT
Biancalana, Buddy	86T	99	$ .01	$ .04
Biancalana, Buddy	87T	554	$ .01	$ .04
Bibby, Jim	72T	316	$ .15	$ .50
Bibby, Jim	74T	11	$ .07	$ .30
Bibby, Jim	75T	155	$ .07	$ .30
Bibby, Jim	76T	324	$ .05	$ .20
Bibby, Jim	77T	501	$ .05	$ .15
Bibby, Jim	78T	636	$ .02	$ .10
Bibby, Jim	79T	92	$ .02	$ .10
Bibby, Jim	80T	229	$ .01	$ .10
Bibby, Jim	81T	430	$ .01	$ .10
Bibby, Jim	82T	170	$ .01	$ .07
Bibby, Jim	83T	355	$ .01	$ .07
Bibby, Jim	84T	566	$ .01	$ .06
Bichette, Dante	89T	761	$ .01	$ .10
Bichette, Dante	90T	43	$ .01	$ .04
Bichette, Dante	91T	564	$ .01	$ .03
Bickford, Vern	52T	252	$12.00	$40.00
Bickford, Vern	53T	161	$4.50	$15.00
Bielecki, Mike	86TTR	10	$ .02	$ .10
Bielecki, Mike	87T	394	$ .01	$ .04
Bielecki, Mike	88T	436	$ .01	$ .04
Bielecki, Mike	89T	668	$ .01	$ .05
Bielecki, Mike	90T	114	$ .01	$ .04
Bielecki, Mike	91T	501	$ .01	$ .03
Biercevicz, Greg	79T	712	$ .02	$ .10
Biercevicz, Greg	81T	282	$ .01	$ .10
Biggio, Craig	89T	49	$ .10	$ .50
Biggio, Craig	90T	157	$ .01	$ .15
Biggio, Craig	90TAS	404	$ .01	$ .10
Biggio, Craig	91T	565	$ .01	$ .03
Biittner, Larry	72T	122	$ .15	$ .50
Biittner, Larry	73T	249	$ .07	$ .30
Biittner, Larry	75T	543	$ .07	$ .30
Biittner, Larry	76T	238	$ .05	$ .20
Biittner, Larry	77T	64	$ .05	$ .15
Biittner, Larry	78T	346	$ .02	$ .10
Biittner, Larry	79T	433	$ .02	$ .10

TOPPS

Player	Year	No.	VG	EX/MT	Player	Year	No.	VG	EX/MT
Biittner, Larry	80T	639	$ .01	$ .10	Bird, Doug	76T	96	$ .05	$ .20
					Bird, Doug	77T	556	$ .05	$ .15
					Bird, Doug	78T	183	$ .02	$ .10
					Bird, Doug	79T	664	$ .02	$ .10
					Bird, Doug	80T	421	$ .01	$ .10
					Bird, Doug	81T	516	$ .01	$ .10
					Bird, Doug	81TTR	737	$ .02	$ .10
					Bird, Doug	82T	273	$ .01	$ .07
					Bird, Doug	83T	759	$ .01	$ .07
					Bird, Doug	83TTR	12	$ .02	$ .10
					Bird, Doug	84T	82	$ .01	$ .06
					Birkbeck, Mike	87T	229	$ .01	$ .04
					Birkbeck, Mike	88T	692	$ .01	$ .04
					Birkbeck, Mike	89T	491	$ .01	$ .05
					Birrer, Babe	56T	84	$2.25	$6.00
					Birtsas, Tim	88T	501	$ .01	$ .04
					Birtsas, Tim	89T	103	$ .01	$ .05
					Birtsas, Tim	90T	687	$ .01	$ .04
					Birtsas, Tim	91T	289	$ .01	$ .03
					Bishop, Charlie	53T	186	$4.50	$15.00
					Bishop, Charlie	55T	96	$2.00	$6.00
					Bittiger, Jeff	89T	209	$ .01	$ .05
					Bjorkman, George	84T	116	$ .01	$ .06
					Black, Bud	83T	238	$ .01	$ .10
					Black, Bud	84T	26	$ .01	$ .06
					Black, Bud	85T	412	$ .01	$ .05
					Black, Bud	86T	697	$ .01	$ .04
					Black, Bud	87T	669	$ .01	$ .04
					Black, Bud	88T	301	$ .01	$ .04
					Black, Bud	88TTR	16	$ .01	$ .06
					Black, Bud	89T	509	$ .01	$ .05
Biittner, Larry	81T	718	$ .01	$ .10	Black, Bud	90T	144	$ .01	$ .04
Biittner, Larry	81TTR	736	$ .02	$ .10	Black, Bud	91T	292	$ .01	$ .03
Biittner, Larry	82T	159	$ .01	$ .07	Black, Joe	52T	321	$65.00	$200.00
Biittner, Larry	83T	527	$ .01	$ .07	Black, Joe	53T	81	$12.00	$45.00
Biittner, Larry	83TTR	10	$ .02	$ .10	Black, Joe	54T	98	$4.75	$22.00
Biittner, Larry	84T	283	$ .01	$ .06	Black, Joe	55T	156	$8.00	$25.00
Bilardello, Dann	83TTR	11	$ .02	$ .10	Black, Joe	56T	178	$5.00	$25.00
Bilardello, Dann	84T	424	$ .01	$ .06	Blackburn, Ron	58T	459	$ .75	$2.20
Bilardello, Dann	85T	28	$ .01	$ .05	Blackburn, Ron	59T	401	$ .75	$2.20
Bilardello, Dann	86T	253	$ .01	$ .04	Blackburn, Ron	60T	209	$ .45	$1.45
Bilardello, Dann	87T	577	$ .01	$ .04	Blackwell, Ewell	52T	344	$55.00	$160.00
Bilardello, Dann	90T	682	$ .01	$ .04	Blackwell, Ewell	53T	31	$7.00	$21.00
Bilko, Steve	52T	287	$15.00	$47.50	Blackwell, Tim	78T	449	$ .02	$ .10
Bilko, Steve	54T	116	$3.60	$10.00	Blackwell, Tim	80T	153	$ .01	$ .10
Bilko, Steve	55T	93	$2.00	$6.00	Blackwell, Tim	81T	553	$ .01	$ .10
Bilko, Steve	58T	346	$ .75	$3.00	Blackwell, Tim	82T	374	$ .01	$ .07
Bilko, Steve	59T	43	$1.25	$4.25	Blackwell, Tim	82TTR	7	$ .02	$ .10
Bilko, Steve	60T	396	$ .75	$2.20	Blackwell, Tim	83T	57	$ .01	$ .07
Bilko, Steve	61T	184	$ .35	$1.25	Blades, Ray	54T	243	$3.60	$10.00
Bilko, Steve	62T	422	$ .75	$2.50	Bladt, Rich	74T	601	$ .45	$1.45
Billingham, Jack	68T	228	$ .30	$ .95	Blair, Dennis	75T	521	$ .07	$ .30
Billingham, Jack	69T	92	$ .30	$ .85	Blair, Dennis	76T	642	$ .05	$ .20
Billingham, Jack	70T	701	$ .75	$2.00	Blair, Dennis	77T	593	$ .05	$ .15
Billingham, Jack	71T	162	$ .15	$ .50	Blair, Dennis	78T	466	$ .02	$ .10
Billingham, Jack	72T	542	$ .30	$ .95	Blair, Paul	65T	473	$2.25	$10.00
Billingham, Jack	73T	89	$ .07	$ .30	Blair, Paul	66T	48	$ .30	$ .95
Billingham, Jack	74T	158	$ .07	$ .30	Blair, Paul	67T	319	$ .30	$ .85
Billingham, Jack	75T	235	$ .07	$ .30	Blair, Paul	68T	135	$ .30	$ .85
Billingham, Jack	76T	155	$ .05	$ .20	Blair, Paul	69T	506	$ .30	$ .85
Billingham, Jack	77T	512	$ .05	$ .15	Blair, Paul	70T	285	$ .15	$ .50
Billingham, Jack	78T	47	$ .02	$ .10	Blair, Paul	71T	53	$ .15	$ .50
Billingham, Jack	79T	388	$ .02	$ .10	Blair, Paul	72T	660	$ .90	$3.00
Billingham, Jack	80T	603	$ .01	$ .10	Blair, Paul	73T	528	$ .15	$ .50
Billings, Dick	71T	729	$ .75	$2.50	Blair, Paul	74T	92	$ .07	$ .30
Billings, Dick	72T	148	$ .15	$ .50	Blair, Paul	75T	275	$ .07	$ .30
Billings, Dick	73T	94	$ .07	$ .30	Blair, Paul	76T	473	$ .05	$ .20
Billings, Dick	74T	466	$ .07	$ .30	Blair, Paul	77T	313	$ .05	$ .15
Bird, Doug	74T	17	$ .07	$ .30	Blair, Paul	78T	114	$ .02	$ .10
Bird, Doug	75T	364	$ .07	$ .30	Blair, Paul	79T	582	$ .02	$ .10

LARRY BIITTNER — OF-1B CUBS

Player	Year	No.	VG	EX/MT	Player	Year	No.	VG	EX/MT
Blair, Paul	80T	281	$ .01	$ .10	Blomberg, Ron	73T	462	$ .07	$ .30
Blair, Willie	90TTR	8	$ .01	$ .05	Blomberg, Ron	74T	117	$ .07	$ .30
Blair, Willie	91T	191	$ .01	$ .03	Blomberg, Ron	75T	68	$ .07	$ .30
Blake, Ed	52T	144	$7.00	$20.00	Blomberg, Ron	76T	354	$ .05	$ .20
Blanchard, John	59T	117	$ .75	$2.20	Blomberg, Ron	77T	543	$ .05	$ .15
Blanchard, John	60T	283	$ .45	$1.45	Blomberg, Ron	78T	506	$ .02	$ .10
Blanchard, John	61T	104	$ .35	$1.25	Blomberg, Ron	79T	42	$ .02	$ .10
Blanchard, John	62T	93	$ .75	$3.00	Blomberg, Ron	88TTB	663	$ .01	$ .04
Blanchard, John	63T	555	$2.10	$6.00	Bloomfield, Bud	64T	532	$1.75	$4.50
Blanchard, John	64T	118	$ .30	$ .95	Blowers, Mike	89TMLD	18	$ .01	$ .25
Blanchard, John	65T	388	$ .45	$1.45	Blowers, Mike	90TTR	9	$ .01	$ .20
Blanchard, John	66T	268	$ .30	$ .95	Blowers, Mike	91T	691	$ .01	$ .03
Blanco, Gil	65T	566	$1.75	$4.50	Blue Jays, Team Checklist	77T	113	$ .05	$ .15
Blanco, Gil	67T	303	$ .30	$ .85	Blue Jays, Team Checklist	78T	626	$ .02	$ .10
Blankenship, Lance	90T	132	$ .01	$ .04	Blue Jays, Team Checklist	79T	282	$ .05	$ .25
Blankenship, Lance	91T	411	$ .01	$ .03	Blue Jays, Team Checklist	80T	577	$ .05	$ .25
Blanks, Larvell	73T	609	$1.00	$4.00	Blue Jays, Team Checklist	81T	674	$ .02	$ .20
Blanks, Larvell	75T	394	$ .07	$ .30	Blue Jays, Team Leaders	86T	96	$ .01	$ .04
Blanks, Larvell	76T	127	$ .05	$ .20	Blue Jays, Team Leaders	87T	106	$ .01	$ .04
Blanks, Larvell	77T	441	$ .05	$ .15	Blue Jays, Team Leaders	88T	729	$ .01	$ .04
Blanks, Larvell	78T	61	$ .02	$ .10	Blue Jays, Team Leaders	89T	201	$ .01	$ .05
Blanks, Larvell	79T	307	$ .02	$ .10	Blue, Vida	70T	21	$1.00	$4.00
Blanks, Larvell	80T	656	$ .01	$ .10	Blue, Vida	71T	544	$ .85	$2.25
Blasingame, Don	56T	309	$2.25	$8.00	Blue, Vida	72T	92	$ .65	$2.25
Blasingame, Don	57T	47	$ .95	$3.50	Blue, Vida	72T	94	$ .40	$1.50
Blasingame, Don	58T	199	$ .75	$3.00	Blue, Vida	72T	96	$ .40	$1.50
Blasingame, Don	59T	491	$ .75	$2.20	Blue, Vida	72T	169	$ .20	$ .70
Blasingame, Don	60T	397	$ .75	$2.20	Blue, Vida	72TIA	170	$ .30	$ .95
Blasingame, Don	61T	294	$ .35	$1.25	Blue, Vida	73T	430	$ .30	$ .95
Blasingame, Don	62T	103	$ .45	$1.45	Blue, Vida	74T	290	$ .30	$ .95
Blasingame, Don	63T	518	$1.75	$4.50	Blue, Vida	75T	209	$ .30	$ .85
Blasingame, Don	64T	327	$ .30	$ .95	Blue, Vida	75T	510	$ .30	$ .85
Blasingame, Don	65T	21	$ .30	$ .85	Blue, Vida	76T	140	$ .15	$ .50
Blasingame, Wade	65T	44	$ .30	$ .85	Blue, Vida	76T	200	$ .45	$1.45
Blasingame, Wade	66T	355	$ .30	$ .95	Blue, Vida	77T	230	$ .30	$ .85
Blasingame, Wade	67T	119	$ .30	$ .85	Blue, Vida	78T	680	$ .05	$ .25
Blasingame, Wade	68T	507	$ .35	$1.25	Blue, Vida	79T	110	$ .05	$ .20
Blasingame, Wade	69T	308	$ .30	$ .95	Blue, Vida	80T	30	$ .05	$ .20
Blasingame, Wade	71T	79	$ .15	$ .50	Blue, Vida	81T	310	$ .01	$ .10
Blasingame, Wade	72T	581	$ .75	$3.00	Blue, Vida	82T	430	$ .01	$ .07
Blass, Steve	65T	232	$ .35	$1.25	Blue, Vida	82T	576	$ .01	$ .07
Blass, Steve	66T	344	$ .30	$ .95	Blue, Vida	82TIA	431	$ .01	$ .07
Blass, Steve	67T	562	$2.10	$6.00	Blue, Vida	82TTR	8	$ .05	$ .20
Blass, Steve	68T	499	$ .35	$1.25	Blue, Vida	83T	471	$ .01	$ .07
Blass, Steve	69T	104	$ .30	$ .85	Blue, Vida	83T	570	$ .01	$ .07
Blass, Steve	70T	396	$ .15	$ .50	Blue, Vida	86T	770	$ .01	$ .04
Blass, Steve	71T	143	$ .15	$ .50	Blue, Vida	87T	260	$ .01	$ .04
Blass, Steve	72T	320	$ .15	$ .50	Blyleven, Bert	71T	26	$18.00	$55.00
Blass, Steve	73T	95	$ .07	$ .30	Blyleven, Bert	72T	515	$2.50	$10.00
Blass, Steve	74T	595	$ .07	$ .30	Blyleven, Bert	73T	199	$1.00	$4.00
Blateric, Steve	73T	616	$ .45	$1.45	Blyleven, Bert	74T	98	$ .50	$2.50
Blauser, Jeff	89T	83	$ .01	$ .10	Blyleven, Bert	75T	30	$ .50	$2.00
Blauser, Jeff	89TBB	317	$ .01	$ .06	Blyleven, Bert	76T	204	$ .15	$ .50
Blauser, Jeff	90T	251	$ .01	$ .04	Blyleven, Bert	76T	235	$ .45	$1.50
Blauser, Jeff	91T	623	$ .01	$ .03	Blyleven, Bert	77T	630	$ .15	$ .50
Blaylock, Bob	59T	211	$ .75	$2.20	Blyleven, Bert	78T	131	$ .06	$ .30
Blaylock, Gary	59T	539	$2.50	$10.00	Blyleven, Bert	79T	308	$ .06	$ .30
Blaylock, Marv	57T	224	$ .95	$3.50	Blyleven, Bert	80T	457	$ .30	$ .85
Blefary, Curt	65T	49	$ .75	$3.00	Blyleven, Bert	81T	554	$ .05	$ .25
Blefary, Curt	66T	460	$ .75	$2.50	Blyleven, Bert	81TTR	738	$ .25	$1.00
Blefary, Curt	67T	180	$ .30	$ .85	Blyleven, Bert	82T	559	$ .01	$ .07
Blefary, Curt	67T	521	$ .90	$3.00	Blyleven, Bert	82T	685	$ .05	$ .25
Blefary, Curt	68T	312	$ .30	$ .85	Blyleven, Bert	83T	280	$ .03	$ .15
Blefary, Curt	69T	458	$ .30	$ .85	Blyleven, Bert	84T	716	$ .01	$ .06
Blefary, Curt	70T	297	$ .15	$ .50	Blyleven, Bert	84T	789	$ .04	$ .20
Blefary, Curt	71T	131	$ .15	$ .50	Blyleven, Bert	85T	355	$ .01	$ .10
Blefary, Curt	72T	691	$ .75	$2.50	Blyleven, Bert	86T	445	$ .01	$ .10
Blefary, Curt	72TIA	692	$ .75	$2.50	Blyleven, Bert	87T	25	$ .01	$ .10
Blocker, Terry	89T	76	$ .01	$ .15	Blyleven, Bert	88T	295	$ .01	$ .10
Blomberg, Ron	72T	203	$ .15	$ .50	Blyleven, Bert	88TBB	180	$ .01	$ .06

TOPPS

Player	Year	No.	VG	EX/MT
Blyleven, Bert	89T	555	$ .01	$ .05
Blyleven, Bert	89TTR	11	$ .01	$ .10
Blyleven, Bert	90T	130	$ .01	$ .10
Blyleven, Bert	91T	615	$ .01	$ .03
Blyzka, Mike	54T	152	$3.60	$10.00
Bobb, Randy	70T	429	$ .15	$ .50
Bobb, Randy	71T	83	$ .15	$ .50
Boccabella, John	64T	192	$ .30	$ .95
Boccabella, John	66T	482	$ .75	$2.50
Boccabella, John	67T	578	$2.10	$6.00
Boccabella, John	68T	542	$ .35	$1.25
Boccabella, John	69T	466	$ .30	$ .85
Boccabella, John	70T	19	$ .15	$ .50
Boccabella, John	71T	452	$ .15	$ .50
Boccabella, John	72T	159	$ .15	$ .50
Boccabella, John	73T	592	$ .45	$1.45
Boccabella, John	74T	253	$ .07	$ .30
Boccabella, John	75T	553	$ .07	$ .30
Bochte, Bruce	75T	392	$ .07	$ .30
Bochte, Bruce	76T	637	$ .05	$ .20
Bochte, Bruce	77T	68	$ .05	$ .15
Bochte, Bruce	78T	537	$ .02	$ .10
Bochte, Bruce	79T	443	$ .02	$ .10
Bochte, Bruce	80T	143	$ .01	$ .10
Bochte, Bruce	81T	723	$ .01	$ .10
Bochte, Bruce	82T	224	$ .01	$ .07
Bochte, Bruce	83T	28	$ .01	$ .07
Bochte, Bruce	83T	711	$ .01	$ .07
Bochte, Bruce	85T	632	$ .01	$ .05
Bochte, Bruce	86T	378	$ .01	$ .04
Bochte, Bruce	87T	496	$ .01	$ .04
Bochy, Bruce	79T	718	$ .02	$ .10
Bochy, Bruce	80T	289	$ .01	$ .10
Bochy, Bruce	84T	571	$ .01	$ .06
Bochy, Bruce	85T	324	$ .01	$ .05
Bochy, Bruce	86T	608	$ .01	$ .04
Bochy, Bruce	87T	428	$ .01	$ .04
Bochy, Bruce	88T	31	$ .01	$ .04
Bockus, Randy	89T	733	$ .01	$ .05
Boddicker, Mike	81T	399	$ .50	$2.00
Boddicker, Mike	84T	191	$ .03	$ .15
Boddicker, Mike	84T	426	$ .01	$ .06
Boddicker, Mike	85T	225	$ .01	$ .05
Boddicker, Mike	85TAS	709	$ .01	$ .05
Boddicker, Mike	86T	575	$ .01	$ .10
Boddicker, Mike	87T	455	$ .01	$ .15
Boddicker, Mike	88T	725	$ .01	$ .04
Boddicker, Mike	89T	71	$ .01	$ .05
Boddicker, Mike	89TBB	296	$ .01	$ .06
Boddicker, Mike	90T	652	$ .01	$ .04
Boddicker, Mike	91T	303	$ .01	$ .03
Boehmer, Len	69T	519	$ .30	$ .95
Boever, Joe	88T	627	$ .01	$ .04
Boever, Joe	89T	586	$ .01	$ .05
Boever, Joe	90T	410	$ .01	$ .04
Boever, Joe	91T	159	$ .01	$ .03
Boggs, Tommy	77T	328	$ .05	$ .15
Boggs, Tommy	78T	518	$ .02	$ .10
Boggs, Tommy	79T	384	$ .02	$ .10
Boggs, Tommy	81T	132	$ .01	$ .10
Boggs, Tommy	82T	61	$ .01	$ .07
Boggs, Tommy	83T	649	$ .01	$ .07
Boggs, Wade	83T	498	$9.00	$33.00
Boggs, Wade	84T	30	$1.00	$5.00
Boggs, Wade	84T	131	$ .08	$ .25
Boggs, Wade	84T	786	$ .06	$ .30
Boggs, Wade	85T	350	$ .50	$2.50
Boggs, Wade	86T	510	$ .35	$1.50
Boggs, Wade	87T	150	$ .15	$ .75
Boggs, Wade	87TAS	608	$ .10	$ .50

Player	Year	No.	VG	EX/MT
Boggs, Wade	88T	200	$ .10	$ .65
Boggs, Wade	88TAS	388	$ .01	$ .30
Boggs, Wade	88TBB	32	$ .10	$ .50
Boggs, Wade	89T	600	$ .05	$ .25
Boggs, Wade	89TAS	399	$ .01	$ .15
Boggs, Wade	89TBB	241	$ .01	$ .35
Boggs, Wade	89TRB	2	$ .01	$ .15
Boggs, Wade	90T	760	$ .01	$ .20

Player	Year	No.	VG	EX/MT
Boggs, Wade	90TAS	387	$ .01	$ .15
Boggs, Wade	91T	450	$ .01	$ .15
Bohammer, Jack	74T	586	$ .07	$ .30
Boisclair, Bruce	77T	399	$ .05	$ .15
Boisclair, Bruce	78T	277	$ .02	$ .10
Boisclair, Bruce	79T	148	$ .02	$ .10
Boisclair, Bruce	80T	654	$ .01	$ .10
Boitano, Danny	80T	668	$ .01	$ .10
Bokelmann, Dick	53T	204	$4.50	$15.00
Boles, Carl	63T	428	$ .45	$1.50
Bolger, Jim	55T	179	$5.25	$15.00
Bolger, Jim	57T	289	$4.25	$15.00
Bolger, Jim	58T	201	$ .75	$3.00
Bolger, Jim	59T	29	$1.25	$4.25
Bolin, Bobby	61T	449	$ .75	$3.00
Bolin, Bobby	62T	329	$ .45	$1.45
Bolin, Bobby	63T	106	$ .30	$ .95
Bolin, Bobby	64T	374	$ .50	$1.45
Bolin, Bobby	65T	341	$ .35	$1.25
Bolin, Bobby	66T	61	$ .30	$ .95
Bolin, Bobby	67T	252	$ .30	$ .85
Bolin, Bobby	68T	169	$ .30	$ .85
Bolin, Bobby	69T	8	$ .75	$3.00
Bolin, Bobby	69T	505	$ .30	$ .85
Bolin, Bobby	70T	574	$ .30	$ .95
Bolin, Bobby	71T	446	$ .15	$ .50
Bolin, Bobby	72T	266	$ .15	$ .50
Bolin, Bobby	73T	541	$ .45	$1.45
Bolin, Bobby	74T	427	$ .07	$ .30
Bolling, Frank	57T	325	$4.25	$15.00
Bolling, Frank	58T	95	$1.25	$4.25
Bolling, Frank	59T	280	$ .75	$2.20

Player	Year	No.	VG	EX/MT	Player	Year	No.	VG	EX/MT
Bolling, Frank	60T	482	$ .90	$3.00	Bonilla, Bobby	88TBB	25	$ .01	$ .25
Bolling, Frank	61T	335	$ .35	$1.25	Bonilla, Bobby	89T	440	$ .01	$ .25
Bolling, Frank	62T	130	$ .45	$1.45	Bonilla, Bobby	89TAS	388	$ .01	$ .10
Bolling, Frank	62T	211	$ .75	$3.00	Bonilla, Bobby	89TBB	159	$ .01	$ .20
Bolling, Frank	63T	570	$1.75	$4.50	Bonilla, Bobby	90T	273	$ .01	$ .20
Bolling, Frank	64T	115	$ .30	$ .95	Bonilla, Bobby	91T	750	$ .01	$ .10
Bolling, Frank	65T	269	$ .35	$1.25	Bonilla, Bobby	91TAS	403	$ .01	$ .03
Bolling, Milt	53T	280	$30.00	$310.00	Bonilla, Juan	82T	464	$ .01	$ .07
Bolling, Milt	54T	82	$3.60	$10.00	Bonilla, Juan	83T	563	$ .01	$ .07
Bolling, Milt	55T	91	$2.00	$6.00	Bonilla, Juan	84T	168	$ .01	$ .06
Bolling, Milt	56T	315	$2.25	$8.00	Bonilla, Juan	86TTR	13	$ .02	$ .10
Bolling, Milt	57T	131	$ .95	$3.50	Bonilla, Juan	87T	668	$ .01	$ .04
Bolling, Milt	58T	188	$ .75	$3.00	Bonnell, Barry	78T	242	$ .02	$ .10
Bollo, Greg	65T	541	$1.75	$4.50	Bonnell, Barry	79T	496	$ .02	$ .10
Bollo, Greg	66T	301	$ .30	$ .95	Bonnell, Barry	80T	632	$ .01	$ .10
Bollweg, Don	52T	128	$7.00	$21.00	Bonnell, Barry	81T	558	$ .01	$ .10
Bolton, Tom	88T	442	$ .01	$ .04	Bonnell, Barry	82T	99	$ .01	$ .07
Bolton, Tom	89T	269	$ .01	$ .05	Bonnell, Barry	83T	766	$ .01	$ .07
Bolton, Tom	91T	37	$ .01	$ .03	Bonnell, Barry	84T	302	$ .01	$ .06
Bomback, Mark	81T	567	$ .01	$ .10	Bonnell, Barry	84TTR	14	$ .02	$ .10
Bomback, Mark	81TTR	739	$ .02	$ .10	Bonnell, Barry	85T	423	$ .01	$ .05
Bomback, Mark	82T	707	$ .01	$ .07	Bonnell, Barry	86T	119	$ .01	$ .04
Bond, Walt	60T	552	$2.50	$10.00	Bonner, Bob	82T	21	$7.50	$30.00
Bond, Walt	61T	334	$ .35	$1.25	Booker, Greg	85T	262	$ .01	$ .05
Bond, Walt	63T	493	$2.50	$6.50	Booker, Greg	86T	429	$ .01	$ .04
Bond, Walt	64T	339	$ .30	$ .95	Booker, Greg	87TTR	6	$ .01	$ .05
Bond, Walt	65T	109	$ .30	$ .85	Booker, Greg	88T	727	$ .01	$ .04
Bond, Walt	66T	431	$ .30	$ .95	Booker, Greg	89T	319	$ .01	$ .05
Bond, Walt	67T	224	$ .30	$ .85	Booker, Greg	89TBB	194	$ .01	$ .06
Bonds, Barry	86TTR	11	$ .75	$3.00	Booker, Jim	76T	243	$ .05	$ .20
Bonds, Barry	87T	320	$ .40	$2.00	Booker, Rod	88T	483	$ .01	$ .04
Bonds, Barry	88T	450	$ .01	$ .25	Booker, Rod	89TBB	256	$ .01	$ .06
Bonds, Barry	88TBB	89	$ .01	$ .15	Booker, Rod	91T	186	$ .01	$ .03
Bonds, Barry	89T	620	$ .01	$ .20	Boone, Bob	73T	613	$9.00	$35.00
Bonds, Barry	89TBB	5	$ .01	$ .10	Boone, Bob	74T	131	$ .75	$3.00
Bonds, Barry	90T	220	$ .01	$ .10	Boone, Bob	75T	351	$ .45	$1.35
Bonds, Barry	91T	570	$ .01	$ .15	Boone, Bob	76T	67	$ .08	$ .30
Bonds, Barry	91TAS	401	$ .01	$ .10	Boone, Bob	76T	318	$ .30	$ .95
Bonds, Bobby	69T	630	$5.00	$20.00	Boone, Bob	77T	545	$ .25	$ .75
Bonds, Bobby	70T	425	$1.00	$4.00	Boone, Bob	78T	161	$ .02	$ .25
Bonds, Bobby	71T	295	$ .75	$3.00	Boone, Bob	79T	90	$ .02	$ .25
Bonds, Bobby	72T	711	$2.00	$10.00	Boone, Bob	80T	470	$ .01	$ .20
Bonds, Bobby	72TIA	712	$1.50	$5.00	Boone, Bob	81T	290	$ .01	$ .20
Bonds, Bobby	73T	145	$ .25	$1.00	Boone, Bob	82T	615	$ .01	$ .15
Bonds, Bobby	74T	30	$ .15	$ .75	Boone, Bob	82T	616	$ .01	$ .15
Bonds, Bobby	75T	55	$ .15	$ .75	Boone, Bob	82TTR	9	$ .05	$ .20
Bonds, Bobby	76T	380	$ .15	$ .50	Boone, Bob	83T	765	$ .01	$ .10
Bonds, Bobby	76TRB	2	$ .05	$ .20	Boone, Bob	84T	520	$ .01	$ .10
Bonds, Bobby	76TTR	380	$ .07	$ .30	Boone, Bob	85T	133	$ .01	$ .10
Bonds, Bobby	77T	570	$ .15	$ .50	Boone, Bob	85T	348	$ .01	$ .05
Bonds, Bobby	78T	150	$ .05	$ .25	Boone, Bob	86T	62	$ .01	$ .04
Bonds, Bobby	79T	285	$ .05	$ .20	Boone, Bob	87T	166	$ .01	$ .04
Bonds, Bobby	80T	410	$ .02	$ .10	Boone, Bob	88T	498	$ .01	$ .04
Bonds, Bobby	81T	635	$ .05	$ .20	Boone, Bob	88TBB	30	$ .01	$ .06
Bonds, Bobby	81TTR	740	$ .08	$ .30	Boone, Bob	89T	243	$ .01	$ .05
Bonds, Bobby	82T	580	$ .01	$ .15	Boone, Bob	89TAS	404	$ .01	$ .05
Bonham, Bill	72T	29	$ .15	$ .50	Boone, Bob	89TBB	269	$ .01	$ .10
Bonham, Bill	73T	328	$ .07	$ .30	Boone, Bob	89TTR	12	$ .01	$ .06
Bonham, Bill	74T	528	$ .07	$ .30	Boone, Bob	90T	671	$ .01	$ .04
Bonham, Bill	75T	85	$ .07	$ .30	Boone, Danny	82T	407	$ .01	$ .07
Bonham, Bill	76T	151	$ .05	$ .20	Boone, Ray	51Trb	23	$2.10	$6.00
Bonham, Bill	77T	446	$ .05	$ .15	Boone, Ray	52T	55	$15.00	$47.50
Bonham, Bill	78T	276	$ .02	$ .10	Boone, Ray	53T	25	$4.50	$15.00
Bonham, Bill	79T	354	$ .02	$ .10	Boone, Ray	54T	77	$1.75	$7.00
Bonham, Bill	80T	47	$ .01	$ .10	Boone, Ray	55T	65	$2.00	$6.00
Bonham, Bill	81T	712	$ .01	$ .10	Boone, Ray	56T	6	$2.25	$6.00
Bonikowski, Joe	62T	592	$15.00	$50.00	Boone, Ray	57T	102	$ .95	$3.50
Bonilla, Bobby	86TTR	12	$ .50	$2.50	Boone, Ray	58T	185	$ .75	$3.00
Bonilla, Bobby	87T	184	$ .50	$1.50	Boone, Ray	59T	252	$ .75	$2.20
Bonilla, Bobby	88T	681	$ .01	$ .25	Boone, Ray	60T	281	$ .45	$1.45

Player	Year	No.	VG	EX/MT
Boone, Ray	76T	67	$ .08	$ .30
Boone, Ray	85T	133	$ .01	$ .10
Boozer, John	63T	29	$ .45	$1.45
Boozer, John	64T	16	$ .30	$ .95
Boozer, John	65T	184	$ .30	$ .85
Boozer, John	66T	324	$ .30	$ .95
Boozer, John	68T	173	$ .30	$ .85
Boozer, John	69T	599	$ .30	$ .95
Borbon, Pedro	70T	358	$ .30	$ .85
Borbon, Pedro	71T	613	$ .45	$1.45
Borbon, Pedro	73T	492	$ .07	$ .30
Borbon, Pedro	74T	410	$ .07	$ .30
Borbon, Pedro	75T	157	$ .07	$ .30
Borbon, Pedro	76T	77	$ .05	$ .20
Borbon, Pedro	77T	581	$ .05	$ .15
Borbon, Pedro	78T	220	$ .02	$ .10
Borbon, Pedro	79T	326	$ .02	$ .10
Borbon, Pedro	80T	627	$ .01	$ .10
Borders, Pat	88TTR	17	$ .01	$ .15
Borders, Pat	89T	693	$ .01	$ .10
Borders, Pat	90T	191	$ .01	$ .04
Borders, Pat	91T	49	$ .01	$ .15
Bordi, Rich	82T	531	$ .01	$ .07
Bordi, Rich	85T	357	$ .01	$ .05
Bordi, Rich	85TTR	7	$ .02	$ .10
Bordi, Rich	86T	94	$ .01	$ .04
Bordi, Rich	86TTR	14	$ .02	$ .10
Bordi, Rich	87T	638	$ .01	$ .04
Borgmann, Glenn	73T	284	$ .07	$ .30
Borgmann, Glenn	74T	547	$ .07	$ .30

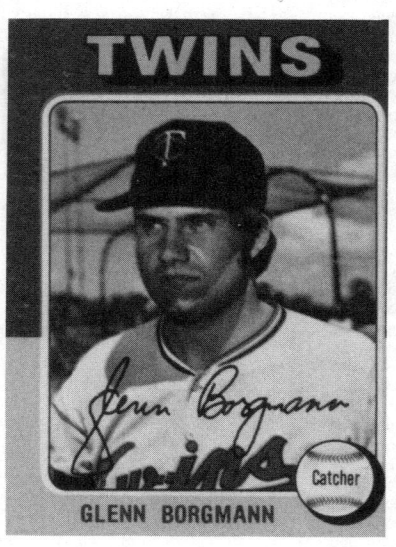

GLENN BORGMANN — Catcher

Player	Year	No.	VG	EX/MT
Borgmann, Glenn	75T	127	$ .07	$ .30
Borgmann, Glenn	76T	498	$ .05	$ .20
Borgmann, Glenn	77T	87	$ .05	$ .15
Borgmann, Glenn	78T	307	$ .02	$ .10
Borgmann, Glenn	79T	431	$ .02	$ .10
Borgmann, Glenn	80T	634	$ .01	$ .10
Borgmann, Glenn	81T	716	$ .01	$ .10
Boris, Paul	83T	266	$ .01	$ .07
Bork, Frank	65T	592	$1.75	$4.50
Bork, Frank	66T	123	$ .30	$ .95

Player	Year	No.	VG	EX/MT
Borkowski, Bob	52T	328	$40.00	$140.00
Borkowski, Bob	53T	7	$4.50	$15.00
Borkowski, Bob	54T	138	$3.60	$10.00
Borkowski, Bob	55T	74	$2.00	$6.00
Borland, Tom	60T	117	$ .45	$1.45
Borland, Tom	61T	419	$ .75	$3.00
Boros, Steve	58T	81	$1.25	$4.25
Boros, Steve	59T	331	$ .75	$2.20
Boros, Steve	61T	348	$ .35	$1.25
Boros, Steve	62T	62	$ .45	$1.45
Boros, Steve	62T	72	$ .45	$1.45
Boros, Steve	63T	532	$1.75	$4.50
Boros, Steve	64T	131	$ .30	$ .95
Boros, Steve	65T	102	$ .30	$ .85
Boros, Steve	83T	13	$ .02	$ .10
Boros, Steve	84T	531	$ .01	$ .06
Boros, Steve	86TTR	15	$ .02	$ .10
Boros, Steve	87T	143	$ .01	$ .04
Bosch, Don	68T	572	$ .35	$1.25
Bosch, Don	69T	578	$ .30	$ .95
Bosch, Don	70T	527	$ .15	$ .50
Bosetti, Rick	78T	710	$ .15	$ .50
Bosetti, Rick	79T	542	$ .02	$ .10
Bosetti, Rick	80T	277	$ .01	$ .10
Bosetti, Rick	81T	46	$ .01	$ .10
Bosetti, Rick	81TTR	741	$ .02	$ .10
Bosetti, Rick	82T	392	$ .01	$ .07
Bosio, Chris	87T	448	$ .01	$ .10
Bosio, Chris	88T	137	$ .01	$ .04
Bosio, Chris	89T	311	$ .01	$ .05
Bosio, Chris	90T	597	$ .01	$ .04
Bosio, Chris	91T	217	$ .01	$ .03
Boskie, Shawn	90TTR	10	$ .01	$ .25
Boskie, Shawn	91T	254	$ .01	$ .10
Bosley, Thad	78T	619	$ .02	$ .10
Bosley, Thad	79T	127	$ .02	$ .10
Bosley, Thad	80T	412	$ .01	$ .10
Bosley, Thad	82T	350	$ .01	$ .07
Bosley, Thad	84T	657	$ .01	$ .06
Bosley, Thad	85T	432	$ .01	$ .05
Bosley, Thad	86T	512	$ .01	$ .04
Bosley, Thad	87T	58	$ .01	$ .04
Bosley, Thad	87TTR	7	$ .01	$ .05
Bosley, Thad	88T	247	$ .01	$ .04
Bosman, Dick	67T	459	$1.50	$5.50
Bosman, Dick	68T	442	$ .30	$ .85
Bosman, Dick	69T	607	$ .30	$ .95
Bosman, Dick	70T	68	$ .75	$2.00
Bosman, Dick	70T	175	$ .45	$1.45
Bosman, Dick	71T	60	$ .15	$ .50
Bosman, Dick	72T	365	$ .15	$ .50
Bosman, Dick	73T	640	$ .45	$1.45
Bosman, Dick	74T	465	$ .07	$ .30
Bosman, Dick	75T	354	$ .07	$ .30
Bosman, Dick	75THL	7	$ .30	$ .95
Bosman, Dick	76T	298	$ .05	$ .20
Bosman, Dick	77T	101	$ .05	$ .15
Bostock, Lyman	76T	263	$ .07	$ .30
Bostock, Lyman	77T	531	$ .05	$ .15
Bostock, Lyman	78T	655	$ .02	$ .10
Boston, Daryl	85TTR	8	$ .03	$ .15
Boston, Daryl	86T	139	$ .01	$ .04
Boston, Daryl	87T	482	$ .01	$ .04
Boston, Daryl	88T	739	$ .01	$ .04
Boston, Daryl	89T	633	$ .01	$ .05
Boston, Daryl	90T	524	$ .01	$ .04
Boston, Daryl	90TTR	11	$ .01	$ .05
Boston, Daryl	91T	83	$ .01	$ .03
Boswell, Dave	67T	575	$6.00	$20.00
Boswell, Dave	68T	322	$ .30	$ .85

Player	Year	No.	VG	EX/MT	Player	Year	No.	VG	EX/MT
Boswell, Dave	69T	459	$ .30	$ .85	Bowsfield, Ted	61T	216	$ .35	$1.25
Boswell, Dave	70T	70	$ .75	$3.00	Bowsfield, Ted	62T	369	$ .45	$1.45
Boswell, Dave	70T	325	$ .15	$ .50	Bowsfield, Ted	63T	339	$ .45	$1.50
Boswell, Dave	71T	675	$ .75	$2.50	Bowsfield, Ted	64T	447	$ .50	$1.45
Boswell, Ken	69T	402	$ .30	$ .85	Boyd, Bob	53T	257	$12.50	$50.00
Boswell, Ken	70T	214	$ .15	$ .50	Boyd, Bob	54T	113	$3.60	$10.00
Boswell, Ken	71T	492	$ .15	$ .50	Boyd, Bob	57T	26	$ .95	$3.50
Boswell, Ken	72T	305	$ .15	$ .50	Boyd, Bob	58T	279	$ .75	$3.00
Boswell, Ken	72TIA	306	$ .15	$ .50	Boyd, Bob	59T	82	$1.25	$4.25
Boswell, Ken	73T	87	$ .07	$ .30	Boyd, Bob	60T	207	$ .45	$1.45
Boswell, Ken	74T	645	$ .07	$ .30	Boyd, Bob	61T	199	$ .35	$1.25
Boswell, Ken	75T	479	$ .07	$ .30	Boyd, Dennis	85T	116	$ .05	$ .25
Boswell, Ken	76T	379	$ .05	$ .20	Boyd, Dennis	86T	605	$ .01	$ .04
Boswell, Ken	77T	429	$ .05	$ .15	Boyd, Dennis	87T	285	$ .01	$ .04
Botting, Ralph	80T	663	$ .05	$ .20	Boyd, Dennis	88T	704	$ .01	$ .04
Botting, Ralph	81T	214	$ .01	$ .10	Boyd, Dennis	89T	326	$ .01	$ .05
Bouchee, Ed	57T	314	$4.25	$15.00	Boyd, Dennis	90T	544	$ .01	$ .04
Bouchee, Ed	59T	39	$1.25	$4.25	Boyd, Dennis	90TTR	12	$ .01	$ .05
Bouchee, Ed	60T	347	$ .75	$2.20	Boyd, Dennis	91T	48	$ .01	$ .03
Bouchee, Ed	61T	196	$ .35	$1.25	Boyd, Gary	70T	7	$ .15	$ .50
Bouchee, Ed	62T	497	$ .50	$ .25	Boyer, Cletis	57T	121	$3.00	$11.00
Bouldin, Carl	63T	496	$2.50	$6.50	Boyer, Cletis	59T	251	$ .75	$2.25
Bouldin, Carl	64T	518	$ .50	$1.45	Boyer, Cletis	60T	109	$ .90	$3.00
Bourjos, Chris	81T	502	$ .01	$ .10	Boyer, Cletis	61T	19	$ .75	$2.20
Bourque, Pat	73T	605	$ .50	$1.25	Boyer, Cletis, "Clete"	62T	163	$ .75	$3.00
Bourque, Pat	74T	141	$ .07	$ .30	Boyer, Clete	62T	490	$ .75	$2.25
Bourque, Pat	75T	502	$ .07	$ .30	Boyer, Clete	63T	361	$ .75	$2.20
Bouton, Jim	62T	592	$15.00	$50.00	Boyer, Clete	64T	69	$ .45	$1.45
Bouton, Jim	63T	401	$ .50	$4.00	Boyer, Clete	65T	475	$ .75	$2.25
Bouton, Jim	64T	4	$1.50	$6.00	Boyer, Clete	66T	9	$ .75	$2.20
Bouton, Jim	64T	219	$ .75	$3.00	Boyer, Clete	67T	328	$ .30	$ .85
Bouton, Jim	64T	470	$ .75	$2.20	Boyer, Clete	68T	550	$ .45	$1.45
Bouton, Jim	65T	30	$ .75	$3.00	Boyer, Clete	69T	489	$ .30	$ .95
Bouton, Jim	66T	276	$ .45	$1.45	Boyer, Clete	70T	206	$ .15	$ .50
Bouton, Jim	67T	393	$1.00	$3.00	Boyer, Clete	71T	374	$ .15	$ .50
Bouton, Jim	68T	562	$ .75	$3.00	Boyer, Cloyd	52T	280	$12.00	$40.00
Bowa, Larry	70T	539	$1.00	$4.00	Boyer, Cloyd	53T	60	$4.50	$15.00
Bowa, Larry	71T	233	$ .50	$2.00	Boyer, Ken	55T	125	$11.25	$45.00
Bowa, Larry	72T	520	$ .15	$ .75	Boyer, Ken	56T	14	$2.25	$11.50
Bowa, Larry	73T	119	$ .15	$ .50	Boyer, Ken	57T	122	$2.00	$7.50
Bowa, Larry	74T	255	$ .30	$ .95	Boyer, Ken	58T	350	$1.50	$6.75
Bowa, Larry	75T	420	$ .30	$ .95	Boyer, Ken	59T	325	$1.25	$5.00
Bowa, Larry	76T	145	$ .07	$ .30	Boyer, Ken	59TAS	557	$3.00	$9.00
Bowa, Larry	77T	310	$ .05	$ .15	Boyer, Ken	60T	160	$8.00	$35.00
Bowa, Larry	78T	90	$ .05	$ .25	Boyer, Ken	60T	485	$1.25	$5.00
Bowa, Larry	79T	210	$ .05	$ .20	Boyer, Ken	61T	43	$1.50	$5.75
Bowa, Larry	80T	630	$ .02	$ .10	Boyer, Ken	61T	375	$ .75	$2.25
Bowa, Larry	81T	120	$ .03	$ .15	Boyer, Ken	61TAS	573	$6.00	$17.50
Bowa, Larry	82T	515	$ .03	$ .15	Boyer, Ken	62T	52	$1.00	$4.00
Bowa, Larry	82TIA	516	$ .01	$ .07	Boyer, Ken	62T	370	$1.00	$4.00
Bowa, Larry	82TTR	10	$ .05	$ .20	Boyer, Ken	62TAS	392	$1.25	$4.25
Bowa, Larry	83T	305	$ .01	$ .07	Boyer, Ken	63T	375	$1.00	$4.00
Bowa, Larry	84T	705	$ .02	$ .10	Boyer, Ken	64T	11	$ .75	$3.00
Bowa, Larry	84T	757	$ .01	$ .06	Boyer, Ken	64T	160	$1.00	$4.00
Bowa, Larry	85T	484	$ .01	$ .10	Boyer, Ken	65T	6	$ .95	$3.50
Bowa, Larry	87TTR	8	$ .02	$ .12	Boyer, Ken	65T	100	$ .50	$2.00
Bowa, Larry	88T	284	$ .01	$ .04	Boyer, Ken	66T	385	$ .35	$1.50
Bowens, Sam	64T	201	$ .30	$ .95	Boyer, Ken	67T	105	$ .35	$1.50
Bowens, Sam	65T	188	$ .30	$ .85	Boyer, Ken	68T	259	$ .30	$ .95
Bowens, Sam	66T	412	$ .30	$ .95	Boyer, Ken	69T	379	$ .15	$ .50
Bowens, Sam	67T	491	$ .75	$3.00	Boyer, Ken	75T	202	$ .45	$1.45
Bowens, Sam	68T	82	$ .30	$ .85	Boyland, Dorian	80T	683	$ .01	$ .10
Bowman, Bob	57T	332	$4.25	$15.00	Brabender, Gene	66T	579	$5.00	$20.00
Bowman, Bob	58T	415	$ .75	$3.00	Brabender, Gene	67T	22	$ .30	$ .85
Bowman, Bob	59T	221	$ .75	$2.20	Brabender, Gene	68T	163	$ .30	$ .85
Bowman, Ernie	62T	231	$ .45	$1.45	Brabender, Gene	69T	393	$ .30	$ .85
Bowman, Ernie	63T	61	$ .30	$ .95	Brabender, Gene	70T	289	$ .15	$ .50
Bowman, Ernie	66T	302	$ .30	$ .95	Brabender, Gene	71T	666	$ .75	$2.50
Bowsfield, Ted	59T	236	$ .75	$2.20	Bradford, Buddy	68T	142	$ .30	$ .85
Bowsfield, Ted	60T	382	$ .75	$2.20	Bradford, Buddy	69T	97	$ .30	$ .85

TOPPS

Player	Year	No.	VG	EX/MT
Bradford, Buddy	70T	299	$ .15	$ .50
Bradford, Buddy	71T	552	$ .35	$1.25
Bradford, Buddy	74T	357	$ .07	$ .30
Bradford, Buddy	75T	504	$ .07	$ .30
Bradford, Buddy	76T	451	$ .05	$ .20
Bradford, Larry	80T	675	$ .01	$ .10

LARRY BRADFORD

Player	Year	No.	VG	EX/MT
Bradford, Larry	81T	542	$ .01	$ .10
Bradford, Larry	82T	271	$ .01	$ .07
Bradley, Mark	84T	316	$ .01	$ .06
Bradley, Phil	84TTR	15	$ .20	$1.00
Bradley, Phil	85T	449	$ .10	$ .65
Bradley, Phil	86T	305	$ .01	$ .10
Bradley, Phil	87T	525	$ .01	$ .10
Bradley, Phil	88T	55	$ .01	$ .10
Bradley, Phil	88TTR	18	$ .01	$ .06
Bradley, Phil	89T	608	$ .01	$ .05
Bradley, Phil	89TTR	13	$ .01	$ .06
Bradley, Phil	90T	163	$ .01	$ .04
Bradley, Phil	91T	717	$ .01	$ .03
Bradley, Scott	86T	481	$ .01	$ .04
Bradley, Scott	87T	376	$ .01	$ .10
Bradley, Scott	88T	762	$ .01	$ .04
Bradley, Scott	89T	279	$ .01	$ .05
Bradley, Scott	90T	593	$ .01	$ .04
Bradley, Scott	91T	38	$ .01	$ .03
Bradley, Tom	71T	588	$ .35	$1.25
Bradley, Tom	72T	248	$ .15	$ .50
Bradley, Tom	73T	336	$ .07	$ .30
Bradley, Tom	74T	455	$ .07	$ .30
Bradley, Tom	75T	179	$ .07	$ .30
Bradley, Tom	76T	644	$ .05	$ .20
Brady, Brian	89TMLD	19	$ .01	$ .15
Brady, Jim	56T	126	$2.25	$6.00
Bragan, Bobby	60T	463	$ .85	$2.25
Bragan, Bobby	63T	73	$ .30	$ .95
Bragan, Bobby	64T	506	$ .50	$1.45
Bragan, Bobby	65T	346	$ .35	$1.25
Bragan, Bobby	66T	476	$ .75	$2.50
Braggs, Glenn	87T	622	$ .15	$ .50
Braggs, Glenn	88T	263	$ .01	$ .04

Player	Year	No.	VG	EX/MT
Braggs, Glenn	89T	718	$ .01	$ .05
Braggs, Glenn	89TBB	204	$ .01	$ .06
Braggs, Glenn	90T	88	$ .01	$ .04
Braggs, Glenn	90TTR	13	$ .01	$ .05
Braggs, Glenn	91T	444	$ .01	$ .03
Branca, Ralph	51Tbb	20	$8.00	$30.00
Branca, Ralph	52T	274	$20.00	$75.00
Brand, Ron	64T	326	$ .30	$ .95
Brand, Ron	65T	212	$ .35	$1.25
Brand, Ron	66T	394	$ .30	$ .95
Brand, Ron	68T	317	$ .30	$ .85
Brand, Ron	69T	549	$ .30	$ .95
Brand, Ron	70T	221	$ .15	$ .50
Brand, Ron	71T	304	$ .15	$ .50
Brand, Ron	72T	773	$ .75	$2.50
Brandon, Darrell	66T	456	$ .75	$2.50
Brandon, Darrell	67T	117	$ .30	$ .85
Brandon, Darrell	68T	26	$ .30	$ .85
Brandon, Darrell	69T	301	$ .30	$ .95
Brandon, Darrell	72T	283	$ .15	$ .50
Brandon, Darrell	73T	326	$ .07	$ .30
Brandt, Jackie	59T	297	$ .75	$2.20
Brandt, Jackie	60T	53	$ .45	$1.45
Brandt, Jackie	61T	515	$ .75	$3.00
Brandt, Jackie	62T	165	$ .45	$1.45
Brandt, Jackie	63T	65	$ .30	$ .95
Brandt, Jackie	64T	399	$ .50	$1.45
Brandt, Jackie	65T	33	$ .30	$ .85
Brandt, Jackie	66T	383	$ .30	$ .95
Brandt, Jackie	67T	142	$ .30	$ .85
Branson, Jeff	88TTR	19	$ .01	$ .30
Branson, Jeff	89TBB	69	$ .01	$ .06
Brantley, Jeff	89TTR	14	$ .01	$ .15
Brantley, Jeff	90T	703	$ .01	$ .10
Brantley, Jeff	91T	17	$ .01	$ .03
Brantley, Mickey	87T	347	$ .01	$ .04
Brantley, Mickey	88T	687	$ .01	$ .04
Brantley, Mickey	89T	568	$ .01	$ .05
Brantley, Mickey	89TBB	38	$ .01	$ .06
Braun, John	65T	82	$ .30	$ .85
Braun, Steve	72T	244	$ .15	$ .50
Braun, Steve	73T	16	$ .07	$ .30
Braun, Steve	74T	321	$ .07	$ .30
Braun, Steve	75T	273	$ .07	$ .30
Braun, Steve	76T	183	$ .05	$ .20
Braun, Steve	77T	606	$ .05	$ .15
Braun, Steve	78T	422	$ .02	$ .10
Braun, Steve	79T	502	$ .02	$ .10
Braun, Steve	80T	9	$ .01	$ .10
Braun, Steve	82T	316	$ .01	$ .07
Braun, Steve	83T	734	$ .01	$ .07
Braun, Steve	84T	227	$ .01	$ .06
Braun, Steve	85T	152	$ .01	$ .05
Braun, Steve	86T	631	$ .01	$ .04
Braves, Team	56T	95	$3.25	$9.50
Braves, Team	57T	114	$3.00	$8.00
Braves, Team	58T	377	$2.50	$10.00
Braves, Team	59T	419	$2.50	$9.50
Braves, Team	60T	381	$2.00	$8.00
Braves, Team	61T	463	$2.00	$6.00
Braves, Team	62T	158	$ .75	$2.00
Braves, Team	63T	503	$3.25	$9.50
Braves, Team	64T	132	$1.25	$4.25
Braves, Team	65T	426	$ .60	$1.95
Braves, Team	66T	326	$ .45	$1.75
Braves, Team	67T	477	$2.10	$6.00
Braves, Team	68T	221	$ .75	$3.00
Braves, Team	70T	472	$ .45	$1.45
Braves, Team	71T	652	$1.75	$4.50
Braves, Team	72T	21	$ .15	$ .50

Player	Year	No.	VG	EX/MT	Player	Year	No.	VG	EX/MT
Braves, Team	73T	521	$ .35	$1.25	Brett, George	75T	228	$35.00	$140.00
Braves, Team	74T	483	$ .15	$ .50	Brett, George	76T	19	$8.75	$35.00
Braves, Team Checklist	75T	589	$ .15	$ .50	Brett, George	77T	1	$1.00	$3.50
Braves, Team Checklist	76T	631	$ .35	$1.25	Brett, George	77T	580	$5.00	$20.00
Braves, Team Checklist	77T	442	$ .15	$ .50	Brett, George	77T	631	$ .75	$3.00
Braves, Team Checklist	78T	551	$ .05	$ .25	Brett, George	77TRB	231	$ .75	$3.00
Braves, Team Checklist	79T	302	$ .05	$ .25	Brett, George	78T	100	$2.50	$10.00
Braves, Team Checklist	80T	192	$ .05	$ .25	Brett, George	79T	330	$2.00	$8.00
Braves, Team Checklist	81T	675	$ .02	$ .20	Brett, George	80T	450	$1.50	$6.00
Braves, Team Leaders	86T	456	$ .01	$ .10	Brett, George	81T	1	$ .15	$ .90
Braves, Team Leaders	87T	31	$ .01	$ .04	Brett, George	81T	700	$ .75	$3.00
Braves, Team Leaders	88T	549	$ .01	$ .04	Brett, George	82T	96	$ .05	$ .25
Braves, Team Leaders	89T	171	$ .01	$ .05	Brett, George	82T	200	$ .50	$2.00
Bravo, Angel	70T	283	$ .15	$ .50	Brett, George	82TAS	549	$ .10	$ .50
Bravo, Angel	71T	538	$ .35	$1.25	Brett, George	82TIA	201	$ .15	$ .65
Brazle, Al	52T	228	$7.00	$20.00	Brett, George	83T	600	$ .15	$1.50
Bream, Sid	85T	253	$ .01	$ .10	Brett, George	83TAS	388	$ .10	$ .50
Bream, Sid	86T	589	$ .01	$ .04	Brett, George	84T	500	$ .15	$1.00
Bream, Sid	87T	35	$ .01	$ .04	Brett, George	84T	710	$ .04	$ .20
Bream, Sid	88T	478	$ .01	$ .04	Brett, George	84TAS	399	$ .06	$ .30
Bream, Sid	88TBB	205	$ .01	$ .06	Brett, George	85T	100	$ .10	$ .50
Bream, Sid	89T	126	$ .01	$ .05	Brett, George	85TAS	703	$ .08	$ .35
Bream, Sid	89TBB	106	$ .01	$ .06	Brett, George	86T	300	$ .10	$ .50
Bream, Sid	90T	622	$ .01	$ .04	Brett, George	86TAS	714	$ .03	$ .25
Bream, Sid	91T	354	$ .01	$ .03	Brett, George	87T	400	$ .30	$ .95
Breazeale, Jim	73T	33	$ .07	$ .30	Brett, George	88T	700	$ .01	$ .25
Brecheen, Harry	51Tbb	28	$7.50	$22.50	Brett, George	88TBB	157	$ .05	$ .25
Brecheen, Harry	52T	263	$14.00	$40.00	Brett, George	89T	200	$ .01	$ .15
Brecheen, Harry	54T	203	$2.50	$10.00	Brett, George	89TBB	46	$ .01	$ .25
Brecheen, Harry	55T	113	$2.00	$6.00	Brett, George	90T	60	$ .01	$ .15
Brecheen, Harry	56T	229	$3.00	$9.00	Brett, George	91T	540	$ .01	$ .10
Brecheen, Harry	60T	455	$ .95	$3.50	Brett, George	91TRB	2	$ .01	$ .10
Breeden, Danny	69T	536	$ .30	$ .95	Brett, Ken	69T	476	$ .30	$ .85
Breeden, Danny	70T	36	$ .30	$ .95	Brett, Ken	71T	89	$ .15	$ .50
Breeden, Hal	72T	684	$ .75	$2.50	Brett, Ken	72T	517	$ .15	$ .50
Breeden, Hal	73T	173	$ .07	$ .30	Brett, Ken	73T	444	$ .15	$ .50
Breeden, Hal	74T	297	$ .07	$ .30	Brett, Ken	74T	237	$ .07	$ .30
Breeden, Hal	75T	341	$ .07	$ .30	Brett, Ken	75T	250	$ .07	$ .30
Breeding, Marv	60T	525	$2.50	$10.00	Brett, Ken	76T	401	$ .05	$ .20
Breeding, Marv	61T	321	$ .35	$1.25	Brett, Ken	76TTR	401	$ .05	$ .20
Breeding, Marv	62T	6	$ .45	$1.45	Brett, Ken	77T	157	$ .05	$ .15
Breeding, Marv	63T	149	$ .30	$ .95	Brett, Ken	77T	631	$ .75	$3.00
Breining, Fred	82T	144	$ .01	$ .07	Brett, Ken	78T	682	$ .02	$ .10
Breining, Fred	83T	747	$ .01	$ .07	Brett, Ken	79T	557	$ .02	$ .10
Breining, Fred	84T	428	$ .01	$ .06	Brett, Ken	80T	521	$ .01	$ .10
Breining, Fred	84TTR	16	$ .02	$ .10	Brett, Ken	81T	47	$ .01	$ .10
Breining, Fred	85T	36	$ .01	$ .05	Brett, Ken	82T	397	$ .01	$ .07
Brenly, Bob	82T	171	$ .15	$ .75	Brewer, Jim	61T	317	$ .35	$1.25
Brenly, Bob	83T	494	$ .01	$ .07	Brewer, Jim	62T	191	$ .45	$1.45
Brenly, Bob	84T	378	$ .01	$ .06	Brewer, Jim	63T	309	$ .45	$1.50
Brenly, Bob	85T	215	$ .01	$ .05	Brewer, Jim	64T	553	$1.75	$4.50
Brenly, Bob	86T	625	$ .01	$ .04	Brewer, Jim	65T	416	$ .35	$1.25
Brenly, Bob	87T	125	$ .01	$ .04	Brewer, Jim	66T	158	$ .30	$ .95
Brenly, Bob	88T	703	$ .01	$ .04	Brewer, Jim	67T	31	$ .30	$ .85
Brenly, Bob	88TBB	143	$ .01	$ .06	Brewer, Jim	68T	298	$ .30	$ .85
Brenly, Bob	89T	52	$ .01	$ .05	Brewer, Jim	69T	241	$ .30	$ .95
Brennan, Tom	81T	451	$ .01	$ .10	Brewer, Jim	70T	571	$ .30	$ .95
Brennan, Tom	82T	141	$ .25	$1.50	Brewer, Jim	71T	549	$ .35	$1.25
Brennan, Tom	83T	524	$ .01	$ .07	Brewer, Jim	72T	151	$ .15	$ .50
Brennan, Tom	84T	662	$ .01	$ .06	Brewer, Jim	73T	126	$ .07	$ .30
Bressoud, Eddie	58T	263	$ .75	$3.00	Brewer, Jim	74T	189	$ .07	$ .30
Bressoud, Eddie	59T	19	$1.25	$4.25	Brewer, Jim	75T	163	$ .07	$ .30
Bressoud, Eddie	60T	253	$ .45	$1.45	Brewer, Jim	76T	459	$ .05	$ .20
Bressoud, Eddie	61T	203	$ .35	$1.25	Brewer, Tom	55T	83	$2.00	$6.00
Bressoud, Eddie	62T	504	$ .75	$2.50	Brewer, Tom	56T	34	$2.25	$6.00
Bressoud, Eddie	63T	188	$ .30	$ .95	Brewer, Tom	57T	112	$ .95	$3.50
Bressoud, Eddie	64T	352	$ .30	$ .95	Brewer, Tom	58T	220	$ .75	$3.00
Bressoud, Eddie	65T	525	$1.75	$4.50	Brewer, Tom	59T	125	$1.25	$4.25
Bressoud, Eddie	66T	516	$ .75	$2.50	Brewer, Tom	59T	346	$ .75	$2.20
Bressoud, Eddie	67T	121	$ .30	$ .85	Brewer, Tom	60T	439	$ .75	$2.20

TOPPS

Player	Year	No.	VG	EX/MT	Player	Year	No.	VG	EX/MT
Brewer, Tom	61T	434	$ .75	$3.00	Briley, Greg	90T	288	$ .01	$ .20
Brewers, Team	71T	698	$2.10	$6.00	Briley, Greg	91T	133	$ .01	$ .03
Brewers, Team	72T	106	$ .20	$ .80	Brinkman, Charlie "Chuck"	71T	13	$ .15	$ .50
Brewers, Team	73T	127	$ .20	$ .80	Brinkman, Chuck	72T	786	$ .75	$2.50
Brewers, Team	74T	314	$ .20	$ .80	Brinkman, Chuck	73T	404	$ .07	$ .30
Brewers, Team Checklist	75T	384	$ .30	$ .95	Brinkman, Chuck	74T	641	$ .07	$ .30
Brewers, Team Checklist	76T	606	$ .35	$1.25	Brinkman, Ed	63T	479	$2.50	$6.50
Brewers, Team Checklist	77T	51	$ .15	$ .50	Brinkman, Ed	64T	46	$ .30	$ .95
Brewers, Team Checklist	78T	328	$ .05	$ .25	Brinkman, Ed	65T	417	$ .35	$1.25
Brewers, Team Checklist	79T	577	$ .05	$ .25	Brinkman, Ed	66T	251	$ .30	$ .95
Brewers, Team Checklist	80T	659	$ .05	$ .25	Brinkman, Ed	67T	311	$ .30	$ .85
Brewers, Team Checklist	81T	668	$ .02	$ .20	Brinkman, Ed	68T	49	$ .30	$ .85
Brewers, Team Leaders	86T	426	$ .01	$ .04	Brinkman, Ed	69T	153	$ .30	$ .85
Brewers, Team Leaders	87T	56	$ .01	$ .04	Brinkman, Ed	70T	711	$ .75	$2.00
Brewers, Team Leaders	88T	639	$ .01	$ .04	Brinkman, Ed	71T	389	$ .15	$ .50
Brewers, Team Leaders	89T	759	$ .01	$ .05	Brinkman, Ed	72T	535	$ .30	$ .95
Brickell, Fritz	61T	333	$ .35	$1.25	Brinkman, Ed	73T	5	$ .07	$ .30
Brideweser, Jim	57T	382	$1.25	$4.25	Brinkman, Ed	74T	138	$ .07	$ .30
Bridges, Rocky	52T	239	$7.00	$21.00	Brinkman, Ed	75T	439	$ .07	$ .30
Bridges, Rocky	56T	324	$2.25	$8.00	Brissie, Lou	51Tbb	31	$7.50	$22.50
Bridges, Rocky	57T	294	$4.25	$15.00	Brissie, Lou	52T	270	$12.00	$40.00
Bridges, Rocky	58T	274	$ .75	$3.00	Bristol, Dave	67T	21	$ .30	$ .85
Bridges, Rocky	59T	318	$ .75	$2.20	Bristol, Dave	68T	148	$ .30	$ .85
Bridges, Rocky	60T	22	$ .45	$1.45	Bristol, Dave	69T	234	$ .30	$ .95
Bridges, Rocky	61T	508	$ .75	$3.00	Bristol, Dave	70T	556	$ .35	$1.25
Briggs, Dan	77T	592	$ .05	$ .15	Bristol, Dave	71T	637	$ .35	$1.25
Briggs, Dan	79T	77	$ .02	$ .10	Bristol, Dave	72T	602	$ .30	$ .95
Briggs, Dan	80T	352	$ .01	$ .10	Bristol, Dave	73T	377	$ .15	$ .50
Briggs, Dan	82T	102	$ .01	$ .07	Bristol, Dave	74T	531	$ .30	$ .95
Briggs, Dan	82TTR	11	$ .02	$ .10	Britton, Jim	64T	94	$ .30	$ .95
Briggs, Johnny	59T	177	$ .75	$2.20	Britton, Jim	68T	76	$ .30	$ .85
Briggs, Johnny	60T	376	$ .75	$2.20	Britton, Jim	69T	154	$ .30	$ .85
Briggs, Johnny	64T	482	$ .50	$1.45	Britton, Jim	70T	646	$ .75	$2.00
Briggs, Johnny	65T	163	$ .30	$ .85	Britton, Jim	71T	699	$ .75	$2.50
Briggs, Johnny	66T	359	$ .30	$ .95	Britton, Jimmy	72T	351	$ .15	$ .50
Briggs, Johnny	67T	268	$ .30	$ .85	Brizzolara, Tony	80T	156	$ .01	$ .10
Briggs, Johnny	68T	284	$ .30	$ .85	Brklyn-Boston, 26 Inning Tie	61T	403	$ .90	$3.00
Briggs, Johnny	69T	73	$ .30	$ .85	Broberg, Pete	72T	64	$ .15	$ .50
Briggs, Johnny	70T	564	$ .30	$ .95	Broberg, Pete	73T	162	$ .07	$ .30
Briggs, Johnny	71T	297	$ .15	$ .50	Broberg, Pete	74T	425	$ .07	$ .30
Briggs, Johnny	72T	197	$ .15	$ .50	Broberg, Pete	75T	542	$ .07	$ .30
Briggs, Johnny	73T	71	$ .07	$ .30	Broberg, Pete	76T	39	$ .05	$ .20
Briggs, Johnny	74T	218	$ .07	$ .30	Broberg, Pete	77T	409	$ .05	$ .15
Briggs, Johnny	75T	123	$ .07	$ .30	Broberg, Pete	78T	722	$ .02	$ .10
Briggs, Johnny	76T	373	$ .05	$ .20	Broberg, Pete	79T	578	$ .02	$ .10
Bright, Harry	59T	523	$2.50	$10.00	Brock, Greg	83TTR	14	$ .30	$ .85
Bright, Harry	60T	277	$ .45	$1.45	Brock, Greg	84T	555	$ .01	$ .06
Bright, Harry	61T	447	$ .75	$3.00	Brock, Greg	85T	753	$ .01	$ .05
Bright, Harry	62T	551	$3.95	$11.50	Brock, Greg	86T	368	$ .01	$ .04
Bright, Harry	63T	304	$ .45	$1.50	Brock, Greg	87T	26	$ .01	$ .04
Bright, Harry	64T	259	$ .30	$ .95	Brock, Greg	87TTR	9	$ .01	$ .05
Bright, Harry	65T	584	$1.75	$4.50	Brock, Greg	88T	212	$ .01	$ .04
Briles, Nelson	65T	431	$ .45	$1.45	Brock, Greg	88TBB	217	$ .01	$ .06
Briles, Nelson	66T	243	$ .30	$ .95	Brock, Greg	89T	517	$ .01	$ .05
Briles, Nelson	67T	404	$ .30	$ .95	Brock, Greg	89TBB	100	$ .01	$ .06
Briles, Nelson	68T	540	$ .35	$1.25	Brock, Greg	90T	139	$ .01	$ .04
Briles, Nelson	69T	60	$ .30	$ .85	Brock, Greg	91T	663	$ .01	$ .03
Briles, Nelson	70T	435	$ .15	$ .50	Brock, Lou	62T	387	$50.00	$150.00
Briles, Nelson	71T	257	$ .15	$ .50	Brock, Lou	63T	472	$35.00	$110.00
Briles, Nelson	72T	605	$ .30	$ .95	Brock, Lou	64T	29	$7.50	$27.50
Briles, Nelson	73T	303	$ .07	$ .30	Brock, Lou	65T	540	$11.25	$45.00
Briles, Nelson	74T	123	$ .07	$ .30	Brock, Lou	66T	125	$4.85	$15.00
Briles, Nelson	74TTR	123	$ .07	$ .30	Brock, Lou	67T	63	$1.00	$4.50
Briles, Nelson	75T	495	$ .07	$ .30	Brock, Lou	67T	285	$3.50	$15.00
Briles, Nelson	76T	569	$ .05	$ .20	Brock, Lou	68T	520	$3.50	$15.00
Briles, Nelson	77T	174	$ .05	$ .15	Brock, Lou	68TAS	372	$1.50	$6.00
Briles, Nelson	78T	717	$ .02	$ .10	Brock, Lou	69T	85	$3.00	$12.00
Briles, Nelson	79T	262	$ .02	$ .10	Brock, Lou	69TAS	428	$2.10	$6.00
Briley, Greg	89T	781	$ .01	$ .50	Brock, Lou	70T	330	$2.00	$8.00
Briley, Greg	89TBB	247	$ .01	$ .20	Brock, Lou	71T	625	$4.00	$16.00

Player	Year	No.	VG	EX/MT
Brock, Lou	72T	200	$2.10	$6.00
Brock, Lou	73T	64	$ .45	$1.45
Brock, Lou	73T	320	$1.50	$5.00
Brock, Lou	74T	60	$1.00	$4.00
Brock, Lou	74T	204	$ .35	$1.25
Brock, Lou	75T	309	$ .35	$1.25
Brock, Lou	75T	540	$ .75	$3.00
Brock, Lou	75THL	2	$ .75	$3.00
Brock, Lou	76T	10	$ .50	$3.00
Brock, Lou	76T	197	$ .15	$ .50
Brock, Lou	77T	355	$ .65	$2.50
Brock, Lou	78T	170	$ .50	$2.00
Brock, Lou	78TRB	1	$ .50	$2.00
Brock, Lou	79T	665	$ .35	$1.25
Brock, Lou	79TRH	415	$ .15	$ .50
Brock, Lou	80THL	1	$ .35	$1.25
Brock, Lou	89TTB	662	$ .01	$ .05

DICK BRODOWSKI
Richard Brodowski

Player	Year	No.	VG	EX/MT
Brodowski, Dick	52T	404	$40.00	$140.00
Brodowski, Dick	53T	69	$4.50	$15.00
Brodowski, Dick	54T	221	$3.60	$10.00
Brodowski, Dick	55T	171	$5.25	$15.00
Brodowski, Dick	56T	157	$2.25	$6.00
Brodowski, Dick	59T	371	$ .75	$2.20
Broglio, Ernie	59T	296	$ .75	$2.20
Broglio, Ernie	60T	16	$ .45	$1.45
Broglio, Ernie	61T	45	$ .60	$2.75
Broglio, Ernie	61T	47	$ .90	$3.00
Broglio, Ernie	61T	49	$ .50	$1.50
Broglio, Ernie	61T	420	$ .35	$1.00
Broglio, Ernie	61T	451	$1.50	$4.00
Broglio, Ernie	62T	507	$ .50	$1.75
Broglio, Ernie	63T	313	$ .24	$ .60
Broglio, Ernie	64T	59	$ .30	$ .95
Broglio, Ernie	65T	565	$ .80	$2.00
Broglio, Ernie	66T	423	$ .15	$ .35
Brohamer, Jack	73T	181	$ .07	$ .30
Brohamer, Jack	75T	552	$ .05	$ .15
Brohamer, Jack	76T	618	$ .05	$ .20
Brohamer, Jack	77T	293	$ .05	$ .15
Brohamer, Jack	78T	416	$ .02	$ .10

Player	Year	No.	VG	EX/MT
Brohamer, Jack	79T	63	$ .02	$ .10
Brohamer, Jack	80T	349	$ .01	$ .10
Brohamer, Jack	81T	462	$ .01	$ .10
Brookens, Tom	80T	416	$ .01	$ .10
Brookens, Tom	81T	251	$ .01	$ .10
Brookens, Tom	82T	753	$ .01	$ .07
Brookens, Tom	83T	119	$ .01	$ .07
Brookens, Tom	84T	14	$ .01	$ .06
Brookens, Tom	85T	512	$ .01	$ .05
Brookens, Tom	86T	643	$ .01	$ .04
Brookens, Tom	87T	713	$ .01	$ .04
Brookens, Tom	88T	474	$ .01	$ .04
Brookens, Tom	89T	342	$ .01	$ .05
Brookens, Tom	91T	268	$ .01	$ .03
Brooks, Bobby	70T	381	$ .15	$ .50
Brooks, Bobby	71T	633	$ .35	$1.25
Brooks, Hubie	81T	259	$ .50	$2.00
Brooks, Hubie	81TTR	742	$ .20	$1.00
Brooks, Hubie	82T	246	$ .05	$ .25
Brooks, Hubie	82T	494	$ .01	$ .07
Brooks, Hubie	83T	134	$ .01	$ .07
Brooks, Hubie	84T	368	$ .01	$ .06
Brooks, Hubie	85T	222	$ .01	$ .05
Brooks, Hubie	85TTR	9	$ .02	$ .10
Brooks, Hubie	86T	555	$ .01	$ .04
Brooks, Hubie	87T	650	$ .01	$ .10
Brooks, Hubie	88T	50	$ .01	$ .04
Brooks, Hubie	88TBB	81	$ .01	$ .06
Brooks, Hubie	89T	485	$ .01	$ .05
Brooks, Hubie	89TBB	301	$ .01	$ .06
Brooks, Hubie	90T	745	$ .01	$ .04
Brooks, Hubie	90TTR	14	$ .01	$ .05
Brooks, Hubie	91T	115	$ .01	$ .03
Brosnan, Jim	57T	155	$ .95	$3.50
Brosnan, Jim	58T	342	$ .65	$2.00
Brosnan, Jim	59T	194	$ .90	$3.00
Brosnan, Jim	60T	449	$ .90	$3.00
Brosnan, Jim	61T	513	$ .75	$2.20
Brosnan, Jim	62T	2	$ .75	$2.20
Brosnan, Jim	63T	116	$ .30	$ .95
Brouhard, Mark	82T	517	$ .01	$ .07
Brouhard, Mark	83T	167	$ .01	$ .07
Brouhard, Mark	84T	528	$ .01	$ .06
Brouhard, Mark	85T	653	$ .01	$ .05
Brouhard, Mark	86T	473	$ .01	$ .04
Brower, Bob	87TTR	10	$ .01	$ .05
Brower, Bob	88T	252	$ .01	$ .04
Brower, Bob	89T	754	$ .01	$ .05
Brown, Bobby	80T	670	$ .01	$ .10
Brown, Bobby	81T	418	$ .01	$ .10
Brown, Bobby	82T	791	$ .01	$ .07
Brown, Bobby	82TTR	12	$ .02	$ .10
Brown, Bobby	83T	287	$ .01	$ .07
Brown, Bobby	84T	261	$ .01	$ .06
Brown, Bobby	85T	583	$ .01	$ .05
Brown, Bobby	86T	182	$ .01	$ .04
Brown, Chris	85TTR	10	$ .15	$ .50
Brown, Chris	86T	383	$ .05	$ .40
Brown, Chris	87T	180	$ .07	$ .30
Brown, Chris	88T	568	$ .01	$ .04
Brown, Chris	88TBB	130	$ .01	$ .06
Brown, Chris	89T	481	$ .01	$ .05
Brown, Darrell	84T	193	$ .01	$ .06
Brown, Darrell	85T	767	$ .01	$ .05
Brown, Dick	58T	456	$ .75	$2.20
Brown, Dick	59T	61	$1.25	$4.25
Brown, Dick	60T	256	$ .45	$1.45
Brown, Dick	61T	192	$ .35	$1.25
Brown, Dick	62T	438	$ .75	$2.50
Brown, Dick	63T	112	$ .30	$ .95

TOPPS

Player	Year	No.	VG	EX/MT	Player	Year	No.	VG	EX/MT
Brown, Gates	64T	471	$ .50	$1.45	Brown, Oscar	73T	312	$ .07	$ .30
Brown, Gates	65T	19	$ .30	$ .85	Brown, Paul	62T	181	$ .45	$1.45
Brown, Gates	66T	362	$ .30	$ .95	Brown, Paul	63T	478	$2.50	$6.50
Brown, Gates	67T	134	$ .30	$ .85	Brown, Paul	64T	319	$ .30	$ .95
Brown, Gates	68T	583	$ .35	$1.25	Brown, Scott	82T	351	$ .01	$ .07
Brown, Gates	69T	256	$ .30	$ .95	Brown, Tom	64T	311	$ .30	$ .95
Brown, Gates	70T	98	$ .15	$ .50	Brown, Tommy	52T	281	$15.00	$47.50
Brown, Gates	71T	503	$ .15	$ .50	Brown, Winston	61T	391	$ .75	$3.00
Brown, Gates	72T	187	$ .15	$ .50	Browne, Byron	66T	139	$ .30	$ .95
Brown, Gates	73T	508	$ .07	$ .30	Browne, Byron	67T	439	$ .30	$ .95
Brown, Gates	74T	389	$ .07	$ .30	Browne, Byron	68T	296	$ .30	$ .85
Brown, Gates	75T	371	$ .07	$ .30	Browne, Byron	70T	388	$ .15	$ .50
Brown, Hal	53T	184	$4.50	$15.00	Browne, Byron	71T	659	$ .75	$2.50
Brown, Hal	54T	172	$3.60	$10.00	Browne, Jerry	87TTR	11	$ .05	$ .20
Brown, Hal	55T	148	$2.00	$6.00	Browne, Jerry	88T	139	$ .01	$ .04
Brown, Hal	57T	194	$ .95	$3.50	Browne, Jerry	88TBB	163	$ .01	$ .06
Brown, Hal	58T	381	$ .75	$3.00	Browne, Jerry	89T	532	$ .01	$ .05
Brown, Hal	59T	487	$ .75	$2.20	Browne, Jerry	89TBB	236	$ .01	$ .10
Brown, Hal	60T	89	$ .45	$1.45	Browne, Jerry	89TTR	16	$ .01	$ .06
Brown, Hal	61T	46	$ .75	$3.00	Browne, Jerry	90T	442	$ .01	$ .04
Brown, Hal	61T	218	$ .35	$1.25	Browne, Jerry	91T	76	$ .01	$ .03
Brown, Hal	62T	488	$ .75	$2.50	Browning, Brian	83T	442	$ .01	$ .07
Brown, Hal	63T	289	$ .75	$3.00	Browning, Tom	85TTR	11	$ .25	$1.25
Brown, Hal	64T	56	$ .30	$ .95	Browning, Tom	86T	652	$ .15	$ .50
Brown, Ike	70T	152	$ .15	$ .50	Browning, Tom	87T	65	$ .01	$ .25
Brown, Ike	71T	669	$ .75	$2.50	Browning, Tom	88T	577	$ .05	$ .10
Brown, Ike	72T	284	$ .15	$ .50	Browning, Tom	88TBB	96	$ .01	$ .10
Brown, Ike	73T	633	$ .45	$1.45	Browning, Tom	89T	234	$ .01	$ .10
Brown, Ike	74T	409	$ .07	$ .30	Browning, Tom	89TBB	14	$ .01	$ .10
Brown, Jackie	71T	591	$ .35	$1.25	Browning, Tom	90T	418	$ .01	$ .10
Brown, Jackie	74T	89	$ .07	$ .30	Browning, Tom	91T	151	$ .01	$ .03
Brown, Jackie	75T	316	$ .07	$ .30	Brubaker, Bruce	65T	493	$ .75	$3.00
Brown, Jackie	76T	301	$ .05	$ .20	Brubaker, Bruce	67T	276	$ .30	$ .85
Brown, Jackie	77T	147	$ .05	$ .15	Bruce, Bob	60T	118	$ .45	$1.45
Brown, Jackie	78T	699	$ .02	$ .10	Bruce, Bob	61T	83	$ .35	$1.25
Brown, Kevin	89TTR	15	$ .01	$ .15	Bruce, Bob	62T	419	$ .75	$2.50
Brown, Kevin	90T	136	$ .01	$ .10	Bruce, Bob	63T	24	$ .30	$ .95
Brown, Kevin	91T	584	$ .01	$ .03	Bruce, Bob	64T	282	$ .30	$ .95
Brown, Larry	64T	301	$ .30	$ .95	Bruce, Bob	65T	240	$ .35	$1.25
Brown, Larry	65T	468	$ .75	$3.00	Bruce, Bob	66T	64	$ .30	$ .95
Brown, Larry	66T	16	$ .30	$ .95	Bruce, Bob	67T	417	$ .30	$ .95
Brown, Larry	67T	145	$ .30	$ .85	Bruhert, Mike	79T	172	$ .02	$ .10
Brown, Larry	68T	197	$ .30	$ .85	Brumley, Mike	64T	167	$4.00	$20.00
Brown, Larry	69T	503	$ .30	$ .85	Brumley, Mike	65T	523	$1.75	$4.50
Brown, Larry	70T	391	$ .15	$ .50	Brumley, Mike	66T	29	$ .30	$ .95
Brown, Larry	71T	539	$ .35	$1.25	Brumley, Mike	89TBB	324	$ .01	$ .06
Brown, Larry	72T	279	$ .15	$ .50	Brumley, Mike	90T	471	$ .01	$ .04
Brown, Mark	86T	451	$ .01	$ .04	Brummer, Glenn	82T	561	$ .01	$ .07
Brown, Mike	83TTR	15	$ .02	$ .10	Brummer, Glenn	83T	311	$ .01	$ .07
Brown, Mike	84T	472	$ .01	$ .06	Brummer, Glenn	84T	152	$ .01	$ .06
Brown, Mike	84T	643	$ .01	$ .06	Brummer, Glenn	86T	616	$ .01	$ .04
Brown, Mike	85T	258	$ .01	$ .05	Brunansky, Tom	82T	653	$ .50	$2.00
Brown, Mike	86T	114	$ .01	$ .04	Brunansky, Tom	82TTR	13	$ .75	$3.00
Brown, Mike	87T	271	$ .01	$ .04	Brunansky, Tom	83T	232	$ .06	$ .30
Brown, Mike	87T	341	$ .01	$ .04	Brunansky, Tom	84T	447	$ .10	$ .50
Brown, Ollie	66T	524	$4.00	$10.00	Brunansky, Tom	85T	122	$ .01	$ .05
Brown, Ollie	67T	83	$ .30	$ .85	Brunansky, Tom	86T	565	$ .02	$ .20
Brown, Ollie	68T	223	$ .30	$ .85	Brunansky, Tom	87T	776	$ .01	$ .10
Brown, Ollie	69T	149	$ .30	$ .85	Brunansky, Tom	88T	375	$ .01	$ .10
Brown, Ollie	70T	130	$ .15	$ .50	Brunansky, Tom	88TBB	211	$ .01	$ .06
Brown, Ollie	71T	505	$ .15	$ .50	Brunansky, Tom	88TTR	20	$ .01	$ .06
Brown, Ollie	72T	551	$ .30	$ .95	Brunansky, Tom	89T	60	$ .01	$ .05
Brown, Ollie	72TIA	552	$ .30	$ .95	Brunansky, Tom	89TBB	54	$ .01	$ .06
Brown, Ollie	73T	526	$ .15	$ .50	Brunansky, Tom	90T	409	$ .01	$ .04
Brown, Ollie	74T	625	$ .07	$ .30	Brunansky, Tom	90TTR	15	$ .01	$ .05
Brown, Ollie	75T	596	$ .07	$ .30	Brunansky, Tom	91T	675	$ .01	$ .03
Brown, Ollie	76T	223	$ .05	$ .20	Brunet, George	58T	139	$ .75	$3.00
Brown, Ollie	77T	84	$ .05	$ .15	Brunet, George	63T	538	$1.75	$4.50
Brown, Oscar	71T	52	$ .15	$ .50	Brunet, George	64T	322	$ .30	$ .95
Brown, Oscar	72T	516	$ .15	$ .50	Brunet, George	65T	242	$ .35	$1.25

Player	Year	No.	VG	EX/MT	Player	Year	No.	VG	EX/MT
Brunet, George	66T	393	$ .30	$ .95	Bryant, Ron	72TIA	186	$ .15	$ .50
Brunet, George	67T	122	$ .30	$ .85	Bryant, Ron	73T	298	$ .07	$ .30
Brunet, George	68T	347	$ .30	$ .85	Bryant, Ron	74T	104	$ .07	$ .30
Brunet, George	69T	645	$ .30	$ .95	Bryant, Ron	74T	205	$ .07	$ .30
Brunet, George	70T	328	$ .15	$ .50	Bryant, Ron	75T	265	$ .07	$ .30
Brunet, George	71T	73	$ .15	$ .50	Bryden, T.R.	87T	387	$ .01	$ .04
Bruno, Tom	79T	724	$ .30	$ .85	Brye, Steve	71T	391	$ .15	$ .50
Brusstar, Warren	78T	297	$ .02	$ .10	Brye, Steve	72T	28	$ .15	$ .50
Brusstar, Warren	79T	653	$ .02	$ .10	Brye, Steve	73T	353	$ .07	$ .30
Brusstar, Warren	80T	52	$ .01	$ .10	Brye, Steve	74T	232	$ .07	$ .30
Brusstar, Warren	81T	426	$ .01	$ .10	Brye, Steve	75T	151	$ .07	$ .30
Brusstar, Warren	82T	647	$ .01	$ .07	Brye, Steve	76T	519	$ .05	$ .20
Brusstar, Warren	84T	304	$ .01	$ .06	Brye, Steve	77T	424	$ .05	$ .15
Brusstar, Warren	85T	189	$ .01	$ .05	Brye, Steve	78T	673	$ .02	$ .10
Brusstar, Warren	86T	564	$ .01	$ .04	Brye, Steve	79T	28	$ .02	$ .10
Bruton, Bill	53T	214	$4.50	$15.00	Buchek, Jerry	62T	439	$ .75	$2.50
Bruton, Bill	54T	109	$2.50	$10.00	Buchek, Jerry	64T	314	$ .30	$ .95
Bruton, Bill	56T	185	$3.00	$9.00	Buchek, Jerry	65T	397	$ .35	$1.25
Bruton, Bill	57T	48	$ .95	$3.50	Buchek, Jerry	66T	454	$ .75	$2.50
Bruton, Bill	58T	355	$ .75	$3.00	Buchek, Jerry	67T	574	$6.00	$20.00
Bruton, Bill	59T	165	$ .75	$2.20	Buchek, Jerry	68T	277	$ .30	$ .85
Bruton, Bill	60T	37	$ .45	$1.45	Buchia, Johnny	52T	19	$15.00	$47.50
Bruton, Bill	61T	251	$ .35	$1.25	Buckner, Bill	70T	286	$2.10	$6.00
Bruton, Bill	62T	335	$ .45	$1.45	Buckner, Bill	71T	529	$ .75	$2.25
Bruton, Bill	63T	437	$ .45	$1.50	Buckner, Bill	72T	114	$ .35	$1.25
Bruton, Bill	64T	98	$ .30	$ .95	Buckner, Bill	73T	368	$ .35	$1.25
Bryan, Bill	63T	236	$ .30	$ .95	Buckner, Bill	74T	505	$ .30	$ .95
Bryan, Bill	65T	51	$ .30	$ .85	Buckner, Bill	75T	244	$ .30	$ .95
Bryan, Bill	66T	332	$ .30	$ .95	Buckner, Bill	76T	253	$ .15	$ .50
Bryan, Bill	67T	601	$5.00	$15.00	Buckner, Bill	77T	27	$ .07	$ .30
Bryan, Bill	68T	498	$ .35	$1.25	Buckner, Bill	78T	473	$ .05	$ .20
Bryant, Clay	74T	521	$ .07	$ .30	Buckner, Bill	79T	346	$ .05	$ .20
Bryant, Derek	80T	671	$ .01	$ .10	Buckner, Bill	80T	135	$ .03	$ .15
Bryant, Don	69T	499	$ .30	$ .85	Buckner, Bill	81T	1	$ .15	$ .60
Bryant, Don	70T	473	$ .15	$ .50	Buckner, Bill	81T	625	$ .03	$ .15
Bryant, Don	74T	403	$ .07	$ .30	Buckner, Bill	82T	456	$ .01	$ .07
Bryant, Ralph	87TTR	12	$ .01	$ .05	Buckner, Bill	82T	760	$ .02	$ .10
					Buckner, Bill	83T	250	$ .01	$ .10
					Buckner, Bill	84T	545	$ .02	$ .10
					Buckner, Bill	84TTR	17	$ .05	$ .20
					Buckner, Bill	85T	65	$ .01	$ .05
					Buckner, Bill	86T	443	$ .01	$ .04
					Buckner, Bill	87T	764	$ .01	$ .04
					Buckner, Bill	88T	147	$ .01	$ .04
					Budaska, Mark	82T	531	$ .01	$ .07
					Buddin, Don	58T	297	$ .75	$3.00
					Buddin, Don	59T	32	$1.25	$4.25
					Buddin, Don	60T	520	$2.50	$10.00
					Buddin, Don	61T	99	$ .35	$1.25
					Buddin, Don	62T	332	$ .45	$1.45
					Buechele, Steve	86T	397	$ .01	$ .04
					Buechele, Steve	87T	176	$ .01	$ .04
					Buechele, Steve	88T	537	$ .01	$ .04
					Buechele, Steve	88TBB	104	$ .01	$ .06
					Buechele, Steve	89T	732	$ .01	$ .05
					Buechele, Steve	89TBB	156	$ .01	$ .06
					Buechele, Steve	90T	279	$ .01	$ .04
					Buechele, Steve	91T	464	$ .01	$ .03
					Buford, Don	65T	81	$ .30	$ .85
					Buford, Don	66T	465	$ .75	$2.50
					Buford, Don	67T	143	$ .30	$ .85
					Buford, Don	67T	232	$ .30	$ .85
					Buford, Don	68T	194	$ .30	$ .85
					Buford, Don	69T	478	$ .30	$ .85
					Buford, Don	70T	428	$ .15	$ .50
					Buford, Don	71T	29	$ .15	$ .50
					Buford, Don	72T	370	$ .15	$ .50
					Buford, Don	73T	183	$ .07	$ .30
					Buhl, Bob	54T	210	$1.75	$7.00
					Buhl, Bob	56T	244	$3.00	$9.00

GIANTS

Ron Bryant   PITCHER

Player	Year	No.	VG	EX/MT
Bryant, Ron	70T	433	$ .15	$ .50
Bryant, Ron	71T	621	$ .35	$1.25
Bryant, Ron	72T	185	$ .15	$ .50

TOPPS

Player	Year	No.	VG	EX/MT	Player	Year	No.	VG	EX/MT
Buhl, Bob	57T	127	$ .95	$3.50	Bunning, Jim	68T	215	$2.10	$6.00
Buhl, Bob	58T	176	$ .75	$3.00	Bunning, Jim	69T	175	$ .75	$2.25
Buhl, Bob	59T	347	$ .75	$2.20	Bunning, Jim	70T	403	$2.25	$6.00
Buhl, Bob	60T	230	.$1.25	$3.50	Bunning, Jim	71T	574	$2.10	$6.00
Buhl, Bob	60T	374	$ .75	$2.20	Burbach, Bill	69T	658	$ .30	$ .95
Buhl, Bob	61T	145	$ .35	$1.25	Burbach, Bill	70T	167	$ .15	$ .50
Buhl, Bob	62T	458	$ .75	$2.25	Burbach, Bill	71T	683	$ .75	$2.50
Buhl, Bob	63T	175	$ .30	$ .95	Burbrink, Nelson	56T	27	$2.25	$6.00
Buhl, Bob	64T	96	$ .30	$ .95	Burchart, Larry	69T	597	$17.50	$70.00
Buhl, Bob	65T	264	$ .35	$1.25	Burchart, Larry	70T	412	$ .15	$ .50
Buhl, Bob	66T	185	$ .30	$ .95	Burda, Bob	69T	392	$ .30	$ .85
Buhl, Bob	67T	68	$ .30	$ .85	Burda, Bob	70T	357	$ .15	$ .50
Buhner, Jay	88TTR	21	$ .01	$ .25	Burda, Bob	71T	541	$ .35	$1.25
Buhner, Jay	89T	223	$ .01	$ .15	Burda, Bob	72T	734	$ .75	$2.50
Buhner, Jay	89TBB	20	$ .01	$ .06	Burdette, Fred	64T	408	$ .50	$1.45
Buhner, Jay	90T	554	$ .01	$ .04	Burdette, Lew	56T	219	$3.00	$12.50
Buhner, Jay	91T	154	$ .01	$ .03	Burdette, Lew	57T	208	$1.50	$6.00
Buice, DeWayne	87TTR	13	$ .01	$ .05	Burdette, Lou	58T	10	$ .80	$2.75
Buice, DeWayne	88T	649	$ .01	$ .04	Burdette, Lou	58T	289	$ .75	$2.50
Buice, DeWayne	89T	147	$ .01	$ .05	Burdette, Lou	59T	440	$2.10	$6.00
Bulling, Terry	78T	432	$ .02	$ .10	Burdette, Lou	60T	70	$ .75	$2.25
Bulling, Terry	82T	98	$ .01	$ .07	Burdette, Lou	60T	230	$1.50	$4.00
Bulling, Terry	83T	519	$ .01	$ .07	Burdette, Lou	61T	47	$ .90	$3.00
Bumbry, Alonza "Al"	73T	614	$15.00	$60.00	Burdette, Lou	61T	320	$1.25	$4.25
Bumbry, Al	74T	137	$ .07	$ .30	Burdette, Lou	62T	380	$ .75	$2.25
Bumbry, Al	75T	358	$ .07	$ .30	Burdette, Lou	63T	429	$ .90	$3.00
Bumbry, Al	76T	307	$ .05	$ .20	Burdette, Lou	64T	523	$1.50	$4.00
Bumbry, Al	77T	626	$ .05	$ .15	Burdette, Lou	65T	64	$ .45	$1.45
Bumbry, Al	78T	188	$ .02	$ .10					
Bumbry, Al	79T	517	$ .02	$ .10					
Bumbry, Al	80T	65	$ .01	$ .10					
Bumbry, Al	81T	425	$ .01	$ .10					
Bumbry, Al	82T	265	$ .01	$ .07					
Bumbry, Al	83T	655	$ .01	$ .07					
Bumbry, Al	84T	319	$ .01	$ .06					
Bumbry, Al	85T	726	$ .01	$ .05					
Bumbry, Al	85TTR	12	$ .02	$ .10					
Bumbry, Al	86T	583	$ .01	$ .04					
Bunker, Wally	64T	201	$ .30	$ .95					
Bunker, Wally	65T	290	$ .35	$1.25					
Bunker, Wally	65T	9	$ .35	$1.25					
Bunker, Wally	66T	499	$ .75	$2.50					
Bunker, Wally	67T	585	$2.10	$6.00					
Bunker, Wally	68T	489	$ .35	$1.25					
Bunker, Wally	69T	137	$ .30	$ .85					
Bunker, Wally	70T	266	$ .15	$ .50					
Bunker, Wally	71T	528	$ .35	$1.25					
Bunning, Jim	57T	338	$25.00	$110.00					
Bunning, Jim	58T	115	$3.50	$12.50					
Bunning, Jim	59T	149	$3.00	$9.00					
Bunning, Jim	60T	502	$2.00	$8.00					
Bunning, Jim	61T	46	$ .75	$3.00					
Bunning, Jim	61T	50	$ .50	$3.00					
Bunning, Jim	61T	490	$2.00	$6.00					
Bunning, Jim	62T	57	$ .75	$2.20					
Bunning, Jim	62T	59	$ .75	$2.20	Burdette, Lou	66T	299	$ .45	$1.45
Bunning, Jim	62T	460	$1.50	$4.50	Burdette, Lou	67T	265	$ .45	$1.45
Bunning, Jim	63T	8	$ .45	$1.45	Burdette, Lew "Lou"	73T	237	$ .35	$1.25
Bunning, Jim	63T	10	$ .45	$1.45	Burford, Don	64T	368	$ .30	$ .95
Bunning, Jim	63T	218	$ .45	$1.45	Burgess, Smoky	52T	357	$50.00	$150.00
Bunning, Jim	63T	365	$2.00	$6.00	Burgess, Smoky	53T	10	$5.00	$20.00
Bunning, Jim	64T	6	$ .45	$1.45	Burgess, Smoky	56T	192	$3.00	$9.00
Bunning, Jim	64T	265	$2.10	$6.00	Burgess, Smoky	57T	228	$ .60	$2.50
Bunning, Jim	65T	20	$2.10	$6.00	Burgess, Smoky	58T	49	$1.75	$4.50
Bunning, Jim	66T	435	$ .95	$2.75	Burgess, Smoky	59T	432	$ .75	$2.20
Bunning, Jim	67T	238	$1.75	$4.50	Burgess, Smoky	60T	393	$ .30	$1.35
Bunning, Jim	67T	560	$11.50	$45.00	Burgess, Smoky	61T	461	$ .90	$3.00
Bunning, Jim	68T	7	$ .75	$2.20					
Bunning, Jim	68T	9	$ .75	$2.20					
Bunning, Jim	68T	11	$ .75	$2.20					

LOU BURDETTE   pitcher

Player	Year	No.	VG	EX/MT	Player	Year	No.	VG	EX/MT
Burgess, Smoky	62T	389	$ .90	$3.00	Burns, Todd	91T	608	$ .01	$ .03
Burgess, Smoky	63T	18	$2.35	$10.00	Burnside, Pete	58T	211	$ .75	$3.00
Burgess, Smoky	63T	425	$ .45	$1.45	Burnside, Pete	59T	354	$ .75	$2.20
Burgess, Smoky	64T	37	$ .30	$ .95	Burnside, Pete	60T	261	$ .45	$1.45
Burgess, Smoky	65T	198	$ .15	$ .50	Burnside, Pete	61T	507	$ .75	$3.00
Burgess, Smoky	66T	354	$ .15	$ .50	Burnside, Pete	62T	207	$ .45	$1.45
Burgess, Smoky	67T	506	$ .75	$3.00	Burnside, Pete	63T	19	$ .30	$ .95
Burgmeier, Tom	69T	558	$ .30	$ .95	Burright, Larry	62T	348	$ .45	$1.45
Burgmeier, Tom	70T	108	$ .15	$ .50	Burright, Larry	63T	174	$ .30	$ .95
Burgmeier, Tom	71T	431	$ .15	$ .50	Burris, Ray	74T	161	$ .07	$ .30
Burgmeier, Tom	72T	246	$ .15	$ .50	Burris, Ray	75T	566	$ .05	$ .15
Burgmeier, Tom	73T	306	$ .07	$ .30	Burris, Ray	76T	51	$ .05	$ .20
Burgmeier, Tom	75T	478	$ .07	$ .30	Burris, Ray	77T	190	$ .05	$ .15
Burgmeier, Tom	76T	87	$ .05	$ .20	Burris, Ray	78T	371	$ .02	$ .10
Burgmeier, Tom	77T	398	$ .05	$ .15	Burris, Ray	79T	98	$ .02	$ .10
Burgmeier, Tom	78T	678	$ .02	$ .10	Burris, Ray	80T	364	$ .01	$ .10
Burgmeier, Tom	79T	524	$ .02	$ .10	Burris, Ray	81T	654	$ .01	$ .10
Burgmeier, Tom	80T	128	$ .01	$ .10	Burris, Ray	81TTR	744	$ .02	$ .10
Burgmeier, Tom	81T	320	$ .01	$ .10	Burris, Ray	82T	227	$ .01	$ .07
Burgmeier, Tom	82T	455	$ .01	$ .07	Burris, Ray	83T	474	$ .01	$ .07
Burgmeier, Tom	83T	213	$ .01	$ .07	Burris, Ray	84T	552	$ .01	$ .06
Burgmeier, Tom	83TTR	16	$ .02	$ .10	Burris, Ray	84TTR	18	$ .02	$ .10
Burgmeier, Tom	84T	33	$ .01	$ .06	Burris, Ray	85T	758	$ .01	$ .05
Burk, Mack	57T	91	$ .95	$3.50	Burris, Ray	85TTR	13	$ .02	$ .10
Burk, Mack	58T	278	$ .75	$3.00	Burris, Ray	86T	106	$ .01	$ .04
Burke, Glenn	78T	562	$ .02	$ .10	Burroughs, Jeff	72T	191	$ .15	$ .50
Burke, Glenn	79T	163	$ .02	$ .10	Burroughs, Jeff	73T	489	$ .30	$ .85
Burke, Leo	63T	249	$ .30	$ .95	Burroughs, Jeff	74T	223	$ .07	$ .30
Burke, Leo	64T	557	$1.75	$4.50	Burroughs, Jeff	75T	212	$ .30	$ .95
Burke, Leo	65T	202	$ .35	$1.25	Burroughs, Jeff	75T	308	$ .35	$1.25
Burke, Steve	78T	709	$ .02	$ .10	Burroughs, Jeff	75T	470	$ .07	$ .30
Burke, Tim	86T	258	$ .01	$ .10	Burroughs, Jeff	76T	360	$ .05	$ .20
Burke, Tim	87T	624	$ .01	$ .04	Burroughs, Jeff	77T	55	$ .05	$ .15
Burke, Tim	88T	529	$ .01	$ .04	Burroughs, Jeff	78T	130	$ .02	$ .10
Burke, Tim	89T	48	$ .01	$ .05	Burroughs, Jeff	79T	245	$ .02	$ .10
Burke, Tim	90T	195	$ .01	$ .04	Burroughs, Jeff	80T	545	$ .01	$ .10
Burke, Tim	91T	715	$ .01	$ .03	Burroughs, Jeff	81T	20	$ .01	$ .10
Burkett, John	90TTR	16	$ .01	$ .25	Burroughs, Jeff	81TTR	745	$ .02	$ .10
Burkett, John	91T	447	$ .01	$ .10	Burroughs, Jeff	82T	440	$ .01	$ .07
Burks, Ellis	87TTR	14	$ .35	$2.25	Burroughs, Jeff	82TTR	14	$ .02	$ .10
Burks, Ellis	88T	269	$ .25	$1.00	Burroughs, Jeff	83T	648	$ .01	$ .07
Burks, Ellis	88TBB	80	$ .10	$ .50	Burroughs, Jeff	84T	354	$ .01	$ .06
Burks, Ellis	89T	785	$ .05	$ .25	Burroughs, Jeff	85T	272	$ .01	$ .05
Burks, Ellis	89TBB	259	$ .01	$ .25	Burroughs, Jeff	85T	91	$ .01	$ .05
Burks, Ellis	90T	155	$ .01	$ .15	Burroughs, Jeff	85TTR	14	$ .02	$ .10
Burks, Ellis	91T	70	$ .01	$ .10	Burroughs, Jeff	86T	168	$ .01	$ .04
Burleson, Rick	75T	302	$ .07	$ .30	Burton, Ellis	59T	231	$ .75	$2.20
Burleson, Rick	76T	29	$ .05	$ .20	Burton, Ellis	60T	446	$ .90	$3.00
Burleson, Rick	77T	585	$ .05	$ .15	Burton, Ellis	63T	262	$ .30	$ .95
Burleson, Rick	78T	245	$ .02	$ .10	Burton, Ellis	64T	269	$ .30	$ .95
Burleson, Rick	79T	125	$ .02	$ .10	Burton, Jim	76T	471	$ .05	$ .20
Burleson, Rick	80T	645	$ .01	$ .10	Burwell, Bill	60T	467	$ .95	$3.50
Burleson, Rick	81T	455	$ .01	$ .10	Busby, Jim	52T	309	$12.00	$40.00
Burleson, Rick	81TTR	743	$ .02	$ .10	Busby, Jim	56T	330	$2.25	$8.00
Burleson, Rick	82T	55	$ .01	$ .07	Busby, Jim	57T	309	$4.25	$15.00
Burleson, Rick	83T	315	$ .01	$ .07	Busby, Jim	58T	28	$1.25	$4.25
Burleson, Rick	84T	735	$ .01	$ .06	Busby, Jim	59T	185	$ .75	$2.20
Burleson, Rick	86TTR	16	$ .02	$ .10	Busby, Jim	60T	232	$ .45	$1.45
Burleson, Rick	87T	579	$ .01	$ .04	Busby, Jim	73T	237	$ .35	$1.25
Burnette, Wally	57T	13	$ .95	$3.50	Busby, Jim	74T	634	$ .35	$1.25
Burnette, Wally	58T	69	$1.25	$4.25	Busby, Steve	73T	608	$ .45	$1.45
Burns, Britt	81T	412	$ .01	$ .10	Busby, Steve	74T	365	$ .07	$ .30
Burns, Britt	82T	44	$ .01	$ .07	Busby, Steve	75T	120	$ .15	$ .50
Burns, Britt	83T	541	$ .01	$ .07	Busby, Steve	75THL	7	$ .30	$ .95
Burns, Britt	84T	125	$ .01	$ .06	Busby, Steve	76T	260	$ .05	$ .20
Burns, Britt	85T	338	$ .01	$ .05	Busby, Steve	78T	336	$ .02	$ .10
Burns, Britt	86T	679	$ .01	$ .04	Busby, Steve	80T	474	$ .01	$ .10
Burns, Todd	89T	174	$ .01	$ .25	Buschhorn, Don	65T	577	$1.75	$4.50
Burns, Todd	89TBB	10	$ .01	$ .06	Bush, Randy	83TTR	17	$ .02	$ .10
Burns, Todd	90T	369	$ .01	$ .04	Bush, Randy	84T	429	$ .01	$ .06

Player	Year	No.	VG	EX/MT	Player	Year	No.	VG	EX/MT
Bush, Randy	85T	692	$ .01	$ .05	Butler, Brett	88T	479	$ .01	$ .04
					Butler, Brett	88TBB	166	$ .01	$ .06
					Butler, Brett	88TTR	22	$ .01	$ .06
					Butler, Brett	89T	241	$ .01	$ .05
					Butler, Brett	89TBB	62	$ .01	$ .06
					Butler, Brett	90T	571	$ .01	$ .04
					Butler, Brett	91T	325	$ .01	$ .03
					Butler, Cecil	62T	239	$ .45	$1.45
					Butler, Cecil	63T	201	$ .30	$ .95
					Butters, Tom	63T	299	$ .45	$1.50
					Butters, Tom	64T	74	$ .30	$ .95
					Butters, Tom	65T	246	$ .35	$1.25
					Buzhardt, John	59T	118	$ .75	$2.20
					Buzhardt, John	60T	549	$2.50	$10.00
					Buzhardt, John	61T	3	$ .35	$1.25
					Buzhardt, John	62T	555	$3.95	$11.50
					Buzhardt, John	63T	35	$ .30	$ .95
					Buzhardt, John	64T	323	$ .30	$ .95
					Buzhardt, John	65T	458	$ .75	$3.00
					Buzhardt, John	66T	245	$ .30	$ .95
					Buzhardt, John	67T	178	$ .30	$ .85
					Buzhardt, John	68T	403	$ .30	$ .85
					Byerly, Bud	52T	161	$7.00	$20.00
					Byerly, Bud	58T	72	$1.25	$4.25
					Byerly, Bud	60T	371	$ .75	$2.20
					Byrd, Harry	53T	131	$4.50	$15.00
					Byrd, Harry	58T	154	$ .75	$3.00
					Byrd, Jeff	78T	667	$ .02	$ .10
					Byrne, Tommy	51Tbb	35	$7.50	$22.50
					Byrne, Tommy	52T	241	$7.00	$20.00
					Byrne, Tommy	53T	123	$4.50	$15.00
Bush, Randy	86T	214	$ .01	$ .04	Byrne, Tommy	56T	215	$3.00	$9.00
Bush, Randy	87T	364	$ .01	$ .04	Byrne, Tommy	57T	108	$ .60	$2.50
Bush, Randy	88T	73	$ .01	$ .04	Bystrom, Marty	81T	526	$ .01	$ .10
Bush, Randy	89T	577	$ .01	$ .05	Bystrom, Marty	82T	416	$ .01	$ .07
Bush, Randy	89TBB	282	$ .01	$ .06	Bystrom, Marty	83T	199	$ .01	$ .07
Bush, Randy	90T	747	$ .01	$ .04	Bystrom, Marty	84T	511	$ .01	$ .06
Bush, Randy	91T	124	$ .01	$ .03	Bystrom, Marty	85T	284	$ .01	$ .05
Buskey, Tom	75T	403	$ .07	$ .30	Bystrom, Marty	86T	723	$ .01	$ .04
Buskey, Tom	76T	178	$ .05	$ .20	Cabell, Enos	73T	605	.50	$1.25
Buskey, Tom	77T	236	$ .05	$ .15	Cabell, Enos	75T	247	$ .07	$ .30
Buskey, Tom	80T	506	$ .01	$ .10	Cabell, Enos	76T	404	$ .05	$ .20
Busse, Ray	72T	101	$ .35	$1.25	Cabell, Enos	77T	567	$ .05	$ .15
Busse, Ray	73T	607	$ .45	$1.45	Cabell, Enos	78T	132	$ .02	$ .10
Butcher, John	81T	41	$ .01	$ .10	Cabell, Enos	79T	515	$ .02	$ .10
Butcher, John	82T	418	$ .03	$ .15	Cabell, Enos	80T	385	$ .01	$ .10
Butcher, John	83T	534	$ .01	$ .07	Cabell, Enos	81T	45	$ .01	$ .10
Butcher, John	84T	299	$ .30	$1.50	Cabell, Enos	81TTR	746	$ .02	$ .10
Butcher, John	84TTR	19	$ .02	$ .10	Cabell, Enos	82T	627	$ .01	$ .07
Butcher, John	85T	741	$ .01	$ .05	Cabell, Enos	82TTR	15	$ .02	$ .10
Butcher, John	86T	638	$ .01	$ .04	Cabell, Enos	83T	225	$ .01	$ .07
Butcher, John	87T	107	$ .01	$ .04	Cabell, Enos	84T	482	$ .01	$ .06
Butera, Sal	81T	243	$ .01	$ .10	Cabell, Enos	84TTR	21	$ .02	$ .10
Butera, Sal	82T	676	$ .01	$ .07	Cabell, Enos	85T	786	$ .01	$ .05
Butera, Sal	83T	67	$ .01	$ .07	Cabell, Enos	86T	197	$ .01	$ .04
Butera, Sal	86T	407	$ .01	$ .04	Cabell, Enos	87T	509	$ .01	$ .04
Butera, Sal	87T	358	$ .01	$ .04	Cabrera, Francisco	89TMLD	20	$ .01	$ .25
Butera, Sal	88T	772	$ .01	$ .04	Cabrera, Francisco	90T	254	$ .01	$ .15
Butler, Bill	69T	619	$ .30	$ .95	Cabrera, Francisco	91T	693	$ .01	$ .03
Butler, Bill	70T	377	$ .15	$ .50	Cadaret, Greg	88T	328	$ .01	$ .10
Butler, Bill	71T	681	$ .75	$2.50	Cadaret, Greg	89T	552	$ .01	$ .10
Butler, Bill	75T	549	$ .07	$ .30	Cadaret, Greg	90T	659	$ .01	$ .04
Butler, Bill	76T	619	$ .05	$ .20	Cadaret, Greg	91T	187	$ .01	$ .03
Butler, Brett	82T	502	$ .50	$2.50	Caffie, Joe	58T	182	$ .75	$3.00
Butler, Brett	83T	364	$ .01	$ .07	Caffrey, Bob	85T	394	$ .01	$ .05
Butler, Brett	84T	77	$ .01	$ .06	Cage, Wayne	78T	706	$ .02	$ .10
Butler, Brett	84TTR	20	$ .02	$ .10	Cage, Wayne	79T	150	$ .02	$ .10
Butler, Brett	85T	637	$ .01	$ .05	Cage, Wayne	80T	208	$ .01	$ .10
Butler, Brett	86T	149	$ .01	$ .04	Cain, Bob	52T	349	$40.00	$140.00
Butler, Brett	87T	723	$ .01	$ .04	Cain, Bob	53T	266	$12.50	$50.00

RANDY BUSH

Player	Year	No.	VG	EX/MT	Player	Year	No.	VG	EX/MT
Cain, Bob	54T	61	$7.00	$22.00	Camp, Rick	77T	475	$ .05	$ .15
Cain, Les	69T	324	$ .30	$ .95	Camp, Rick	78T	349	$ .02	$ .10
Cain, Les	71T	101	$ .15	$ .50	Camp, Rick	79T	105	$ .02	$ .10
Cain, Les	72T	783	$ .75	$2.50	Camp, Rick	81T	87	$ .01	$ .10
Calderon, Ivan	86T	382	$ .15	$ .75	Camp, Rick	82T	637	$ .01	$ .07
Calderon, Ivan	87TTR	15	$ .05	$ .20	Camp, Rick	83T	207	$ .01	$ .07
Calderon, Ivan	88T	184	$ .01	$ .10	Camp, Rick	84T	597	$ .01	$ .06
Calderon, Ivan	88TBB	63	$ .01	$ .06	Camp, Rick	85T	491	$ .01	$ .05
Calderon, Ivan	89T	656	$ .01	$ .05	Camp, Rick	86T	319	$ .01	$ .04
Calderon, Ivan	89TBB	289	$ .01	$ .06	Campanella, Roy	52T	314	$400.00	$1300.00
Calderon, Ivan	90T	569	$ .01	$ .04	Campanella, Roy	53T	27	$52.50	$195.00
Calderon, Ivan	91T	93	$ .01	$ .03	Campanella, Roy	56T	101	$40.00	$125.00
Calderone, Sam	53T	260	$12.50	$50.00	Campanella, Roy	57T	210	$30.00	$90.00
Calderone, Sammy	54T	68	$7.00	$22.00	Campanella, Roy	57T	400	$40.00	$160.00
Caldwell, Mike	73T	182	$ .30	$ .85	Campanella, Roy	59T	550	$35.00	$125.00
Caldwell, Mike	74T	344	$ .07	$ .30	Campanella, Roy	61TMVP	480	$7.50	$27.50
Caldwell, Mike	75T	347	$ .07	$ .30	Campanella, Roy	75T	189	$ .75	$3.00
Caldwell, Mike	76T	157	$ .05	$ .20	Campanella, Roy	75T	191	$ .45	$1.45
Caldwell, Mike	77T	452	$ .05	$ .15	Campanella, Roy	75T	193	$ .75	$3.00
Caldwell, Mike	78T	212	$ .02	$ .10	Campaneris, Bert	65T	266	$1.00	$3.50
Caldwell, Mike	79T	651	$ .02	$ .10	Campaneris, Bert	66T	175	$ .35	$1.25
Caldwell, Mike	80T	515	$ .01	$ .10	Campaneris, Bert	67T	515	$1.25	$4.25
Caldwell, Mike	81T	85	$ .01	$ .10	Campaneris, Bert	68T	109	$ .30	$ .95
Caldwell, Mike	82T	378	$ .01	$ .07	Campaneris, Bert	69T	495	$ .30	$ .95
Caldwell, Mike	83T	142	$ .01	$ .07	Campaneris, Bert	69T	556	$ .35	$1.25
Caldwell, Mike	84T	605	$ .01	$ .06	Campaneris, Bert	69TAS	423	$ .30	$ .85
Caldwell, Mike	85T	419	$ .01	$ .05	Campaneris, Bert	70T	205	$ .30	$ .95
Calhoun, Jeff	86T	534	$ .01	$ .04	Campaneris, Bert	71T	440	$ .30	$ .95
Calhoun, Jeff	87T	282	$ .01	$ .04	Campaneris, Bert	72T	75	$ .30	$ .85
Calhoun, Jeff	87TTR	16	$ .01	$ .05	Campaneris, Bert	73T	64	$ .45	$1.45
Calhoun, Jeff	88T	38	$ .01	$ .04	Campaneris, Bert	73T	295	$ .30	$ .95
Callison, John	59T	119	$2.10	$6.00	Campaneris, Bert	74T	155	$ .30	$ .95
Callison, Johnny	60T	17	$ .45	$1.45	Campaneris, Bert	74TAS	335	$ .15	$ .50
Callison, Johnny	61T	468	$ .75	$3.00	Campaneris, Bert	75T	170	$ .15	$ .50
Callison, Johnny	62T	17	$ .75	$2.20	Campaneris, Bert	76T	580	$ .07	$ .30
Callison, Johnny	63T	434	$ .45	$1.45	Campaneris, Bert	77T	373	$ .05	$ .15
Callison, Johnny	64T	135	$ .30	$ .95	Campaneris, Bert	78T	260	$ .05	$ .20
Callison, Johnny	65T	4	$1.75	$4.50	Campaneris, Bert	79T	620	$ .05	$ .20
Callison, Johnny	65T	310	$ .45	$1.45	Campaneris, Bert	80T	505	$ .01	$ .10
Callison, Johnny	66T	52	$ .35	$1.25	Campaneris, Bert	81T	410	$ .02	$ .10
Callison, Johnny	66T	230	$ .35	$1.25	Campaneris, Bert	82T	772	$ .02	$ .10
Callison, Johnny	67T	85	$ .15	$ .50	Campaneris, Bert	83TTR	18	$ .05	$ .20
Callison, Johnny	67T	309	$ .60	$1.20	Campaneris, Bert	84T	139	$ .01	$ .06
Callison, Johnny	68T	415	$ .45	$1.45	Campaneris, Bert	84T	711	$ .04	$ .20
Callison, Johnny	69T	133	$ .15	$ .50	Campaneris, Bert	84T	714	$ .01	$ .06
Callison, Johnny	70T	375	$ .08	$ .30	Campanis, Jim	67T	12	$ .30	$ .85
Callison, Johnny	71T	12	$ .15	$ .50	Campanis, Jim	68T	281	$ .30	$ .85
Callison, Johnny	72T	364	$ .15	$ .50	Campanis, Jim	69T	396	$ .30	$ .85
Callison, Johnny	73T	535	$ .45	$1.45	Campanis, Jim	70T	671	$ .75	$2.00
Calmus, Dick	64T	231	$ .30	$ .95	Campanis, Jim	74T	513	$ .07	$ .30
Calmus, Dick	68T	427	$ .30	$ .85	Campanis, Jim	88TTR	23	$ .01	$ .35
Camacho, Ernie	81T	96	$ .01	$ .10	Campbell, Bill	74T	26	$ .07	$ .30
Camacho, Ernie	85T	739	$ .01	$ .05	Campbell, Bill	75T	226	$ .07	$ .30
Camacho, Ernie	86T	509	$ .01	$ .04	Campbell, Bill	76T	288	$ .05	$ .20
Camacho, Ernie	87T	353	$ .01	$ .04	Campbell, Bill	77T	8	$ .05	$ .15
Cambria, Fred	71T	27	$ .15	$ .50	Campbell, Bill	77T	166	$ .05	$ .15
Cambria, Fred	72T	392	$ .15	$ .50	Campbell, Bill	78T	208	$ .05	$ .20
Camilli, Doug	62T	594	$35.00	$125.00	Campbell, Bill	78T	545	$ .02	$ .10
Camilli, Doug	63T	196	$ .30	$ .95	Campbell, Bill	79T	375	$ .02	$ .10
Camilli, Doug	64T	249	$ .30	$ .95	Campbell, Bill	80T	15	$ .01	$ .10
Camilli, Doug	65T	77	$ .30	$ .85	Campbell, Bill	81T	396	$ .01	$ .10
Camilli, Doug	66T	593	$5.00	$20.00	Campbell, Bill	82T	619	$ .01	$ .07
Camilli, Doug	67T	551	$2.10	$6.00	Campbell, Bill	82TTR	16	$ .02	$ .10
Camilli, Doug	73T	131	$ .15	$ .50	Campbell, Bill	83T	436	$ .01	$ .07
Camilli, Lou	71T	612	$ .35	$1.25	Campbell, Bill	84T	787	$ .01	$ .06
Caminiti, Ken	88T	64	$ .01	$ .30	Campbell, Bill	84TTR	22	$ .02	$ .10
Caminiti, Ken	89T	369	$ .01	$ .05	Campbell, Bill	85T	209	$ .01	$ .05
Caminiti, Ken	89TBB	210	$ .01	$ .06	Campbell, Bill	85TTR	15	$ .02	$ .10
Caminiti, Ken	90T	531	$ .01	$ .04	Campbell, Bill	86T	112	$ .01	$ .04
Caminiti, Ken	91T	174	$ .01	$ .03	Campbell, Bill	86TTR	17	$ .02	$ .10

TOPPS

Player	Year	No.	VG	EX/MT	Player	Year	No.	VG	EX/MT
Campbell, Bill	87T	674	$ .01	$ .04	Cannizzaro, Chris	72T	759	$ .75	$2.50
Campbell, Dave	69T	324	$ .30	$ .95	Cannizzaro, Chris	75T	355	$ .07	$ .30
Campbell, Dave	70T	639	$ .75	$2.00	Cannon, Joe	80T	221	$ .01	$ .10
Campbell, Dave	71T	46	$2.10	$6.00	Cano, Jose	89TMLD	22	$ .01	$ .15
Campbell, Dave	72T	384	$ .15	$ .50	Canseco, Jose	86TTR	20	$1.50	$8.00
Campbell, Dave	73T	488	$ .07	$ .30	Canseco, Jose	87T	620	$1.00	$3.50
Campbell, Dave	74T	556	$ .07	$ .30	Canseco, Jose	88T	370	$ .10	$1.25
Campbell, Dave	78T	402	$ .02	$ .10	Canseco, Jose	88TBB	13	$ .10	$1.00
Campbell, Dave	79T	9	$ .02	$ .10	Canseco, Jose	89T	500	$ .10	$ .60
Campbell, Jim	63T	373	$ .45	$1.50	Canseco, Jose	89TAS	401	$ .10	$ .50
Campbell, Jim	64T	303	$ .30	$ .95	Canseco, Jose	89TBB	190	$ .01	$ .75
Campbell, Mike	88T	246	$ .01	$ .25	Canseco, Jose	90T	250	$ .01	$ .25
Campbell, Mike	89T	143	$ .01	$ .05	Canseco, Jose	91T	700	$ .01	$ .25
Campbell, Ron	67T	497	$ .75	$3.00	Canseco, Jose	91TAS	390	$ .01	$ .10
Camper, Cardell	78T	711	$ .02	$ .10	Canseco, Ozzie	91T	162	$ .01	$ .10
Campisi, Sal	70T	716	$ .75	$2.00	Capel, Mike	89T	767	$ .01	$ .15
Campisi, Sal	71T	568	$ .35	$1.25	Capilla, Doug	78T	477	$ .02	$ .10
Campos, Frank	52T	307	$12.00	$40.00	Capilla, Doug	80T	628	$ .01	$ .10
Campos, Frank	53T	51	$4.50	$15.00	Capilla, Doug	81T	136	$ .01	$ .10
Campusano, Sil	88TTR	24	$ .01	$ .15	Capilla, Doug	82T	537	$ .01	$ .07
Campusano, Sil	89T	191	$ .01	$ .15	Cappuzzello, George	82T	137	$ .01	$ .07
Campusano, Sil	91T	618	$ .01	$ .03	Cappuzzello, George	83T	422	$ .01	$ .07
Canale, George	89TMLD	21	$ .01	$ .35	Capra, Buzz	72T	141	$ .15	$ .50
Canale, George	90T	344	$ .01	$ .25	Capra, Buzz	75T	105	$ .07	$ .30
Candaele, Casey	87TTR	17	$ .01	$ .05	Capra, Buzz	75T	311	$ .30	$ .95
Candaele, Casey	88T	431	$ .01	$ .04	Capra, Buzz	76T	153	$ .05	$ .20
Candaele, Casey	90TTR	17	$ .01	$ .05	Capra, Buzz	77T	432	$ .05	$ .15
Candaele, Casey	91T	602	$ .01	$ .03	Capra, Buzz	78T	578	$ .02	$ .10
Candelaria, John	76T	317	$ .75	$3.00	Carbo, Bernie	70T	36	$ .30	$ .95
Candelaria, John	77T	510	$ .15	$ .50	Carbo, Bernie	71T	478	$ .15	$ .50
Candelaria, John	78T	190	$ .05	$ .20	Carbo, Bernie	72T	463	$ .15	$ .50
Candelaria, John	78T	207	$ .02	$ .10	Carbo, Bernie	73T	171	$ .07	$ .30
Candelaria, John	79T	70	$ .03	$ .15	Carbo, Bernie	74T	621	$ .07	$ .30
Candelaria, John	80T	635	$ .02	$ .10	Carbo, Bernie	75T	379	$ .07	$ .30
Candelaria, John	81T	265	$ .02	$ .10	Carbo, Bernie	76T	278	$ .05	$ .20
Candelaria, John	82T	425	$ .03	$ .15	Carbo, Bernie	77T	159	$ .05	$ .15
Candelaria, John	83T	291	$ .01	$ .07	Carbo, Bernie	78T	524	$ .02	$ .10
Candelaria, John	83T	755	$ .01	$ .07	Carbo, Bernie	79T	38	$ .02	$ .10
Candelaria, John	84T	330	$ .02	$ .10	Carbo, Bernie	80T	266	$ .01	$ .10
Candelaria, John	85T	50	$ .01	$ .05	Cardenal, Jose	65T	374	$ .35	$1.25
Candelaria, John	86T	140	$ .01	$ .04	Cardenal, Jose	66T	505	$ .75	$2.50
Candelaria, John	87T	630	$ .01	$ .04	Cardenal, Jose	67T	193	$ .30	$ .85
Candelaria, John	88T	546	$ .01	$ .04	Cardenal, Jose	68T	102	$ .30	$ .85
Candelaria, John	88TTR	25	$ .01	$ .06	Cardenal, Jose	69T	325	$ .30	$ .95
Candelaria, John	89T	285	$ .01	$ .05	Cardenal, Jose	70T	675	$ .75	$2.00
Candelaria, John	90T	485	$ .01	$ .04	Cardenal, Jose	71T	435	$ .15	$ .50
Candelaria, John	90TTR	18	$ .01	$ .05	Cardenal, Jose	72T	12	$ .15	$ .50
Candelaria, John	91T	777	$ .01	$ .03	Cardenal, Jose	72TTR	757	$1.25	$4.25
Candiotti, Tom	84T	262	$ .01	$ .06	Cardenal, Jose	73T	393	$ .07	$ .30
Candiotti, Tom	86TTR	18	$ .02	$ .10	Cardenal, Jose	74T	185	$ .07	$ .30
Candiotti, Tom	87T	463	$ .01	$ .04	Cardenal, Jose	75T	15	$ .07	$ .30
Candiotti, Tom	88T	123	$ .01	$ .04	Cardenal, Jose	76T	430	$ .05	$ .20
Candiotti, Tom	88TBB	93	$ .01	$ .06	Cardenal, Jose	77T	610	$ .05	$ .15
Candiotti, Tom	89T	599	$ .01	$ .05	Cardenal, Jose	78T	210	$ .02	$ .10
Candiotti, Tom	89TBB	267	$ .01	$ .06	Cardenal, Jose	79T	317	$ .02	$ .10
Candiotti, Tom	90T	743	$ .01	$ .04	Cardenal, Jose	80T	512	$ .01	$ .10
Candiotti, Tom	91T	624	$ .01	$ .03	Cardenal, Jose	81T	473	$ .01	$ .10
Cangelosi, John	86TTR	19	$ .05	$ .20	Cardenas, Chico	60T	119	$ .75	$3.00
Cangelosi, John	87T	201	$ .07	$ .30	Cardenas, Chico	61T	244	$ .35	$1.25
Cangelosi, John	87TTR	18	$ .01	$ .05	Cardenas, Chico	62T	381	$ .75	$2.50
Cangelosi, John	88T	506	$ .01	$ .04	Cardenas, Chico	63T	203	$ .30	$ .95
Cangelosi, John	89T	592	$ .01	$ .05	Cardenas, Chico	64T	72	$ .30	$ .95
Cangelosi, John	90T	29	$ .01	$ .04	Cardenas, Chico	65T	437	$ .35	$1.25
Cannizzaro, Chris	61T	118	$ .35	$1.25	Cardenas, Chico	66T	370	$ .30	$ .95
Cannizzaro, Chris	62T	26	$ .45	$1.45	Cardenas, Chico	67T	325	$ .30	$ .85
Cannizzaro, Chris	65T	61	$ .30	$ .85	Cardenas, Chico	68T	23	$ .30	$ .85
Cannizzaro, Chris	66T	497	$ .75	$2.50	Cardenas, Chico	68T	480	$5.50	$17.50
Cannizzaro, Chris	69T	131	$ .30	$ .85	Cardenas, Chico "Leo"	69T	265	$ .30	$ .95
Cannizzaro, Chris	70T	329	$ .15	$ .50	Cardenas, Leo	70T	245	$ .15	$ .50
Cannizzaro, Chris	71T	426	$ .15	$ .50	Cardenas, Leo	71T	405	$ .15	$ .50

Player	Year	No.	VG	EX/MT
Cardenas, Leo	72T	561	$ .30	$ .95
Cardenas, Leo	72TIA	562	$ .30	$ .95
Cardenas, Leo	73T	522	$ .07	$ .30
Cardenas, Leo	75T	518	$ .07	$ .30
Cardenas, Leo	76T	587	$ .05	$ .20
Cardinal, Randy	63T	562	$3.00	$12.00
Cardinals, Team	56T	134	$4.00	$12.00
Cardinals, Team	57T	243	$2.00	$7.50
Cardinals, Team	58T	216	$1.75	$6.50
Cardinals, Team	59T	223	$1.75	$6.50
Cardinals, Team	60T	242	$1.75	$6.00
Cardinals, Team	61T	347	$ .90	$3.00
Cardinals, Team	62T	61	$ .90	$3.00
Cardinals, Team	63T	524	$3.00	$9.00
Cardinals, Team	64T	87	$2.10	$6.00
Cardinals, Team	65T	57	$ .90	$3.00
Cardinals, Team	66T	379	$ .65	$1.75
Cardinals, Team	67T	173	$2.10	$6.00
Cardinals, Team	68T	497	$ .20	$2.50
Cardinals, Team	70T	549	$ .90	$3.00
Cardinals, Team	71T	308	$ .50	$1.45
Cardinals, Team	72T	688	$1.25	$4.25
Cardinals, Team	73T	219	$ .35	$1.25
Cardinals, Team	74T	36	$ .15	$ .50
Cardinals, Team Checklist	75T	246	$ .15	$ .50
Cardinals, Team Checklist	76T	581	$ .35	$1.25
Cardinals, Team Checklist	77T	183	$ .15	$ .50
Cardinals, Team Checklist	78T	479	$ .05	$ .25
Cardinals, Team Checklist	79T	192	$ .05	$ .25
Cardinals, Team Checklist	80T	244	$ .05	$ .25
Cardinals, Team Checklist	81T	684	$ .02	$ .20
Cardinals, Team Leaders	86T	66	$ .01	$ .04
Cardinals, Team Leaders	87T	181	$ .01	$ .04
Cardinals, Team Leaders	88T	351	$ .01	$ .04
Cardinals, Team Leaders	89T	261	$ .01	$ .05
Cardwell, Don	57T	374	$1.25	$4.25
Cardwell, Don	58T	372	$ .75	$3.00

Player	Year	No.	VG	EX/MT
Cardwell, Don	59T	314	$ .75	$2.20
Cardwell, Don	60T	384	$ .75	$2.20
Cardwell, Don	61T	393	$ .90	$3.00

Player	Year	No.	VG	EX/MT
Cardwell, Don	61T	564	$7.00	$21.00
Cardwell, Don	62T	495	$ .75	$2.50
Cardwell, Don	63T	575	$1.75	$4.50
Cardwell, Don	64T	417	$ .50	$1.45
Cardwell, Don	65T	502	$ .75	$3.00
Cardwell, Don	66T	235	$ .30	$ .95
Cardwell, Don	67T	555	$2.10	$6.00
Cardwell, Don	68T	437	$1.10	$ .30
Cardwell, Don	69T	193	$ .30	$ .85
Cardwell, Don	70T	83	$ .15	$ .50
Carew, Rod	67T	569	$125.00	$450.00
Carew, Rod	68T	80	$35.00	$125.00
Carew, Rod	68TAS	363	$3.00	$12.00
Carew, Rod	69T	510	$17.50	$62.50
Carew, Rod	69TAS	419	$2.25	$7.50
Carew, Rod	70T	62	$ .50	$1.50
Carew, Rod	70T	290	$7.50	$22.50
Carew, Rod	70TAS	453	$1.50	$6.00
Carew, Rod	71T	210	$7.50	$30.00
Carew, Rod	72T	695	$20.00	$80.00
Carew, Rod	72TIA	696	$10.00	$30.00
Carew, Rod	73T	61	$ .50	$1.50
Carew, Rod	73T	330	$3.50	$14.00
Carew, Rod	74T	50	$2.50	$10.00
Carew, Rod	74T	201	$1.00	$4.00
Carew, Rod	74TAS	333	$ .50	$2.00
Carew, Rod	75T	306	$ .35	$1.25
Carew, Rod	75T	600	$2.00	$8.00
Carew, Rod	76T	192	$ .50	$1.50
Carew, Rod	76T	400	$1.50	$6.00
Carew, Rod	77T	120	$1.50	$6.00
Carew, Rod	78T	201	$ .15	$ .60
Carew, Rod	78T	580	$ .75	$3.50
Carew, Rod	79T	1	$ .75	$2.25
Carew, Rod	79T	300	$ .60	$2.50
Carew, Rod	80T	700	$ .35	$1.50
Carew, Rod	81T	100	$ .45	$1.50
Carew, Rod	82T	276	$ .03	$ .15
Carew, Rod	82T	500	$ .15	$1.00
Carew, Rod	82TAS	547	$ .05	$ .25
Carew, Rod	82TIA	501	$ .07	$ .35
Carew, Rod	83T	200	$ .10	$1.00
Carew, Rod	83T	201	$ .05	$ .20
Carew, Rod	83T	651	$ .01	$ .07
Carew, Rod	83TAS	386	$ .05	$ .25
Carew, Rod	84T	276	$ .01	$ .06
Carew, Rod	84T	600	$ .12	$ .75
Carew, Rod	84T	710	$ .04	$ .20
Carew, Rod	84T	711	$ .04	$ .20
Carew, Rod	85T	300	$ .01	$ .50
Carew, Rod	86T	400	$ .03	$ .50
Carey, Andy	53T	188	$2.25	$8.00
Carey, Andy	54T	105	$4.25	$15.00
Carey, Andy	55T	20	$3.60	$10.00
Carey, Andy	56T	12	$2.25	$6.00
Carey, Andy	57T	290	$4.25	$15.00
Carey, Andy	58T	333	$ .75	$3.00
Carey, Andy	59T	45	$1.25	$4.25
Carey, Andy	60T	196	$ .45	$1.45
Carey, Andy	61T	518	$ .75	$3.00
Carey, Andy	62T	418	$ .75	$2.50
Carlos, Cisco	68T	287	$ .30	$ .85
Carlos, Cisco	69T	54	$ .30	$ .85
Carlos, Cisco	70T	487	$ .15	$ .50
Carlton, Steve	65T	477	$100.00	$400.00
Carlton, Steve	67T	146	$30.00	$100.00
Carlton, Steve	68T	408	$17.50	$55.00
Carlton, Steve	69T	255	$12.50	$45.00
Carlton, Steve	70T	67	$ .75	$2.00
Carlton, Steve	70T	220	$6.00	$25.00

TOPPS

Player	Year	No.	VG	EX/MT
Carlton, Steve	71T	55	$5.50	$22.50
Carlton, Steve	72T	93	$ .50	$2.00
Carlton, Steve	72T	420	$4.50	$18.00
Carlton, Steve	72TTR	751	$12.00	$40.00
Carlton, Steve	73T	65	$ .45	$1.45
Carlton, Steve	73T	66	$ .45	$1.45
Carlton, Steve	73T	67	$ .85	$3.50
Carlton, Steve	73T	300	$2.50	$10.00
Carlton, Steve	74T	95	$2.00	$8.00
Carlton, Steve	75T	185	$1.75	$6.50
Carlton, Steve	75T	312	$ .50	$2.50
Carlton, Steve	76T	355	$1.50	$5.00
Carlton, Steve	77T	110	$1.50	$5.00
Carlton, Steve	78T	205	$ .30	$ .85
Carlton, Steve	78T	540	$1.00	$4.00
Carlton, Steve	79T	25	$ .75	$2.25
Carlton, Steve	80T	210	$ .50	$2.00
Carlton, Steve	81T	5	$ .04	$ .20
Carlton, Steve	81T	6	$ .02	$ .10
Carlton, Steve	81T	630	$ .35	$1.25
Carlton, Steve	81TRB	202	$ .30	$ .85
Carlton, Steve	82T	480	$ .15	$1.00
Carlton, Steve	82T	636	$ .10	$ .50
Carlton, Steve	82THL	1	$ .30	$ .85
Carlton, Steve	82TIA	481	$ .07	$ .35
Carlton, Steve	83T	70	$ .15	$1.00
Carlton, Steve	83T	71	$ .05	$ .25
Carlton, Steve	83T	229	$ .01	$ .10
Carlton, Steve	83T	705	$ .01	$ .10
Carlton, Steve	83T	706	$ .01	$ .10
Carlton, Steve	83TAS	406	$ .05	$ .25
Carlton, Steve	84T	1	$ .30	$ .85
Carlton, Steve	84T	4	$ .05	$ .25
Carlton, Steve	84T	136	$ .02	$ .10
Carlton, Steve	84T	706	$ .05	$ .25
Carlton, Steve	84T	707	$ .05	$ .25
Carlton, Steve	84T	708	$ .04	$ .20
Carlton, Steve	84T	780	$ .10	$ .50
Carlton, Steve	84TAS	395	$ .05	$ .25
Carlton, Steve	85T	360	$ .07	$ .35
Carlton, Steve	86T	120	$ .03	$ .25
Carlton, Steve	87T	718	$ .15	$ .50
Carlton, Steve	87TTR	19	$ .05	$ .25
Carman, Don	85TTR	16	$ .05	$ .25
Carman, Don	86T	532	$ .01	$ .10
Carman, Don	87T	355	$ .01	$ .04
Carman, Don	88T	415	$ .01	$ .04
Carman, Don	89T	154	$ .01	$ .05
Carman, Don	90T	731	$ .01	$ .04
Carman, Don	91T	282	$ .01	$ .03
Carmel, Duke	60T	120	$ .45	$1.45
Carmel, Duke	63T	544	$7.50	$30.00
Carmel, Duke	64T	44	$ .30	$ .95
Carmel, Duke	65T	261	$ .35	$1.25
Carpenter, Cris	89T	282	$ .01	$ .20
Carpenter, Cris	89TBB	307	$ .01	$ .06
Carpenter, Cris	90T	443	$ .01	$ .04
Carpenter, Cris	91T	518	$ .01	$ .03
Carpin, Frank	66T	71	$ .30	$ .95
Carrasquel, Chico	51Tbb	26	$7.50	$22.50
Carrasquel, Chico	52T	251	$12.00	$40.00
Carrasquel, Chico	56T	230	$3.00	$9.00
Carrasquel, Chico	57T	67	$ .95	$3.50
Carrasquel, Chico	58T	55	$1.25	$4.25
Carrasquel, Chico	59T	264	$ .75	$2.20
Carreon, Camilo	60T	121	$ .45	$1.45
Carreon, Camilo	61T	509	$ .75	$3.00
Carreon, Camilo	62T	178	$ .45	$1.45
Carreon, Camilo	63T	308	$ .45	$1.50
Carreon, Camilo	64T	421	$ .50	$1.45
Carreon, Camilo	65T	578	$1.75	$4.50
Carreon, Camilo	66T	513	$ .75	$2.50
Carreon, Mark	90T	434	$ .01	$ .04
Carreon, Mark	91T	764	$ .01	$ .03
Carrithers, Don	72T	76	$ .15	$ .50
Carrithers, Don	73T	651	$ .45	$1.45
Carrithers, Don	74T	361	$ .07	$ .30
Carrithers, Don	75T	438	$ .07	$ .30
Carrithers, Don	76T	312	$ .05	$ .20
Carrithers, Don	77T	579	$ .05	$ .15
Carrithers, Don	78T	113	$ .02	$ .10
Carroll, Clay	65T	461	$10.00	$40.00
Carroll, Clay	66T	307	$ .30	$ .95
Carroll, Clay	67T	219	$ .30	$ .85
Carroll, Clay	68T	412	$ .30	$ .85
Carroll, Clay	69T	26	$ .30	$ .85
Carroll, Clay	70T	133	$ .15	$ .50
Carroll, Clay	71T	394	$ .15	$ .50
Carroll, Clay	72T	311	$ .15	$ .50
Carroll, Clay	72TIA	312	$ .15	$ .50
Carroll, Clay	73T	68	$ .30	$ .85
Carroll, Clay	73T	195	$ .07	$ .30
Carroll, Clay	74T	111	$ .07	$ .30
Carroll, Clay	75T	345	$ .07	$ .30
Carroll, Clay	76T	211	$ .05	$ .20
Carroll, Clay	76TTR	211	$ .05	$ .20
Carroll, Clay	77T	497	$ .05	$ .15
Carroll, Clay	78T	615	$ .02	$ .10
Carroll, Tom	55T	158	$3.50	$10.00
Carroll, Tom	56T	139	$1.50	$4.00
Carroll, Tom	57T	164	$ .95	$3.50
Carroll, Tom	59T	513	$2.50	$10.00
Carroll, Tom	75T	507	$ .07	$ .30
Carroll, Tom	76T	561	$ .05	$ .20
Carter, Dick	60T	466	$ .95	$3.50
Carter, Gary	75T	620	$10.00	$30.00
Carter, Gary	76T	441	$3.00	$9.00
Carter, Gary	77T	295	$1.25	$5.00
Carter, Gary	78T	120	$ .80	$2.75
Carter, Gary	79T	520	$ .75	$2.50
Carter, Gary	80T	70	$ .40	$1.75
Carter, Gary	81T	660	$ .45	$1.45
Carter, Gary	82T	730	$ .15	$ .75
Carter, Gary	82TAS	344	$ .05	$ .25
Carter, Gary	83T	370	$ .10	$ .50
Carter, Gary	83TAS	404	$ .05	$ .25
Carter, Gary	84T	450	$ .10	$ .50
Carter, Gary	84TAS	393	$ .05	$ .25
Carter, Gary	85T	230	$ .05	$ .25
Carter, Gary	85TAS	719	$ .01	$ .05
Carter, Gary	85TTR	17	$ .15	$ .60
Carter, Gary	86T	170	$ .03	$ .25
Carter, Gary	86TAS	708	$ .02	$ .15
Carter, Gary	87T	20	$ .15	$ .50
Carter, Gary	87TAS	602	$ .01	$ .10
Carter, Gary	88T	530	$ .01	$ .25
Carter, Gary	88TBB	37	$ .01	$ .06
Carter, Gary	89T	680	$ .01	$ .05
Carter, Gary	89TAS	393	$ .01	$ .05
Carter, Gary	89TBB	325	$ .01	$ .06
Carter, Gary	89TRB	3	$ .01	$ .05
Carter, Gary	90T	790	$ .01	$ .10
Carter, Gary	90TTR	19	$ .01	$ .05
Carter, Gary	91T	310	$ .01	$ .03
Carter, Joe	85T	694	$ .60	$2.75
Carter, Joe	86T	377	$ .05	$ .30
Carter, Joe	87T	220	$ .07	$ .30
Carter, Joe	88T	75	$ .01	$ .10
Carter, Joe	88TBB	71	$ .01	$ .15
Carter, Joe	89T	420	$ .01	$ .10

Player	Year	No.	VG	EX/MT
Carter, Joe	89TBB	155	$ .01	$ .10
Carter, Joe	90T	580	$ .01	$ .10
Carter, Joe	90TTR	20	$ .01	$ .05
Carter, Joe	91T	120	$ .01	$ .03
Carter, Steve	89TMLD	23	$ .01	$ .10
Carter, Steve	90T	482	$ .01	$ .10
Carty, Rico	64T	476	$1.50	$6.00
Carty, Rico	65T	2	$2.10	$6.00
Carty, Rico	65T	305	$ .45	$1.45
Carty, Rico	66T	153	$ .45	$1.45
Carty, Rico	67T	35	$ .30	$ .85
Carty, Rico	67T	240	$ .45	$1.45
Carty, Rico	68T	455	$ .15	$ .50
Carty, Rico	69T	590	$ .20	$ .50
Carty, Rico	70T	145	$ .30	$ .95
Carty, Rico	71T	62	$ .15	$ .50
Carty, Rico	71T	270	$ .15	$ .50
Carty, Rico	72T	740	$1.25	$4.25
Carty, Rico	73T	435	$ .30	$ .85
Carty, Rico	75T	655	$ .15	$ .50
Carty, Rico	76T	156	$ .07	$ .30
Carty, Rico	77T	465	$ .05	$ .15
Carty, Rico	78T	305	$ .02	$ .10
Carty, Rico	79T	565	$ .05	$ .20
Carty, Rico	80T	46	$ .02	$ .10
Cary, Chuck	87T	171	$ .01	$ .04
Cary, Chuck	89TTR	17	$ .01	$ .10
Cary, Chuck	90T	691	$ .01	$ .04
Cary, Chuck	91T	359	$ .01	$ .03
Casagrande, Tom	55T	167	$5.25	$15.00
Casale, Jerry	59T	456	$ .75	$2.20
Casale, Jerry	60T	38	$ .45	$1.45
Casale, Jerry	61T	195	$ .35	$1.25
Casanova, Paul	67T	115	$ .30	$ .85
Casanova, Paul	68T	560	$ .35	$1.25
Casanova, Paul	69T	486	$ .30	$ .85
Casanova, Paul	70T	84	$ .15	$ .50
Casanova, Paul	71T	139	$ .15	$ .50
Casanova, Paul	72T	591	$ .30	$ .95
Casanova, Paul	73T	452	$ .07	$ .30
Casanova, Paul	74T	272	$ .07	$ .30
Casanova, Paul	75T	633	$ .07	$ .30
Cash, Dave	70T	141	$ .30	$ .95
Cash, Dave	71T	582	$ .35	$1.25
Cash, Dave	72T	125	$ .15	$ .50
Cash, Dave	73T	397	$ .07	$ .30
Cash, Dave	74T	198	$ .07	$ .30
Cash, Dave	75T	22	$ .07	$ .30
Cash, Dave	76T	295	$ .05	$ .20
Cash, Dave	77T	649	$ .05	$ .15
Cash, Dave	78T	495	$ .02	$ .10
Cash, Dave	79T	395	$ .02	$ .10
Cash, Dave	80T	14	$ .01	$ .10
Cash, Dave	81T	707	$ .01	$ .10
Cash, Norm	59T	509	$10.00	$35.00
Cash, Norm	60T	488	$1.50	$6.00
Cash, Norm	61T	95	$1.00	$3.00
Cash, Norm	62T	51	$ .75	$2.20
Cash, Norm	62T	250	$ .50	$2.50
Cash, Norm	62TAS	466	$1.25	$4.25
Cash, Norm	63T	4	$ .75	$3.00
Cash, Norm	63T	445	$ .75	$2.20
Cash, Norm	64T	331	$20.00	$65.00
Cash, Norm	64T	425	$ .75	$3.00
Cash, Norm	65T	153	$ .15	$ .50
Cash, Norm	66T	218	$ .75	$3.00
Cash, Norm	66T	315	$ .45	$1.45
Cash, Norm	67T	216	$2.10	$6.00
Cash, Norm	67T	540	$7.50	$30.00
Cash, Norm	68T	256	$ .45	$1.45
Cash, Norm	69T	80	$ .30	$ .85
Cash, Norm	70T	611	$ .35	$1.25
Cash, Norm	71T	599	$ .75	$3.00
Cash, Norm	72T	90	$ .75	$3.00
Cash, Norm	72T	150	$ .30	$ .95
Cash, Norm	73T	485	$ .15	$ .50
Cash, Norm	74T	367	$ .30	$ .95
Cash, Ron	74T	600	$1.25	$5.00
Casian, Larry	91T	374	$ .01	$ .10
Castiglione, Pete	52T	260	$12.00	$40.00
Castillo, Bobby	79T	641	$ .02	$ .10
Castillo, Bobby	81T	146	$ .01	$ .10
Castillo, Bobby	82T	48	$ .01	$ .07
Castillo, Bobby	82TTR	17	$ .02	$ .10
Castillo, Bobby	83T	327	$ .01	$ .07
Castillo, Bobby	83T	771	$ .01	$ .07
Castillo, Bobby	84T	491	$ .01	$ .06
Castillo, Bobby	85T	588	$ .01	$ .05
Castillo, Bobby	85TTR	18	$ .02	$ .10
Castillo, Bobby	86T	252	$ .01	$ .04
Castillo, Carmen	85T	184	$ .01	$ .05
Castillo, Carmen	86TTR	21	$ .02	$ .10
Castillo, Carmen	87T	513	$ .01	$ .04
Castillo, Carmen	88T	341	$ .01	$ .04
Castillo, Carmen	89T	637	$ .01	$ .05
Castillo, "Carmen", Carmelo	89TBB	91	$ .01	$ .06
Castillo, "Carmen", Carmelo	89TTR	18	$ .01	$ .06
Castillo, Carmelo	90T	427	$ .01	$ .04
Castillo, Carmelo	91T	266	$ .01	$ .03
Castillo, Juan	87TTR	20	$ .01	$ .05
Castillo, Juan	88T	362	$ .01	$ .04
Castillo, Juan	88TBB	117	$ .01	$ .06
Castillo, Juan	89T	538	$ .01	$ .05
Castillo, Juan	89TBB	9	$ .01	$ .06
Castillo, Manny	81T	66	$ .01	$ .10
Castillo, Manny	83T	258	$ .01	$ .07
Castillo, Manny	84T	562	$ .01	$ .06
Castillo, Marty	82T	261	$ .01	$ .07
Castillo, Marty	84T	303	$ .01	$ .06

MARTY CASTILLO

Player	Year	No.	VG	EX/MT
Castillo, Marty	85T	461	$ .01	$ .05

TOPPS

Player	Year	No.	VG	EX/MT	Player	Year	No.	VG	EX/MT
Castillo, Marty	86T	788	$ .01	$ .04	Cedeno, Cesar	79T	570	$ .05	$ .20
Castillo, Tony	90T	620	$ .01	$ .10	Cedeno, Cesar	80T	370	$ .01	$ .10
Castillo, Tony	91T	353	$ .01	$ .03	Cedeno, Cesar	81T	190	$ .01	$ .10
Castino, John	80T	137	$ .03	$ .15	Cedeno, Cesar	82T	640	$ .01	$ .07
Castino, John	81T	304	$ .01	$ .10	Cedeno, Cesar	82TTR	19	$ .02	$ .10
Castino, John	82T	396	$ .01	$ .07	Cedeno, Cesar	83T	351	$ .01	$ .07
Castino, John	82T	644	$ .01	$ .07	Cedeno, Cesar	83T	475	$ .01	$ .07
Castino, John	83T	93	$ .01	$ .07	Cedeno, Cesar	84T	705	$ .02	$ .10
Castino, John	84T	237	$ .01	$ .06	Cedeno, Cesar	84T	725	$ .01	$ .06
Castino, John	85T	452	$ .01	$ .05	Cedeno, Cesar	85T	54	$ .01	$ .05
Castleman, Foster	56T	271	$2.25	$8.00	Cedeno, Cesar	86T	224	$ .01	$ .04
Castleman, Foster	57T	237	$ .95	$3.50	Cepeda, Orlando	58T	343	$20.00	$60.00
Castleman, Foster	58T	416	$ .75	$3.00	Cepeda, Orlando	59T	390	$3.50	$12.00
Castro, Bill	76T	293	$ .05	$ .20	Cepeda, Orlando	59TAS	553	$3.75	$14.00
Castro, Bill	77T	528	$ .05	$ .15	Cepeda, Orlando	60T	450	$3.35	$10.00
Castro, Bill	78T	448	$ .02	$ .10	Cepeda, Orlando	61T	435	$2.10	$8.00
Castro, Bill	79T	133	$ .02	$ .10	Cepeda, Orlando	62T	40	$1.50	$6.00
Castro, Bill	80T	303	$ .01	$ .10	Cepeda, Orlando	62T	54	$ .75	$2.20
Castro, Bill	81T	271	$ .01	$ .10	Cepeda, Orlando	62T	401	$8.00	$25.00
Cater, Danny	64T	482	$ .50	$1.45	Cepeda, Orlando	62TAS	390	$ .75	$2.25
Cater, Danny	65T	253	$ .45	$1.45	Cepeda, Orlando	63T	3	$3.00	$12.00
Cater, Danny	66T	398	$ .30	$ .95	Cepeda, Orlando	63T	520	$4.00	$16.00
Cater, Danny	67T	157	$ .30	$ .85	Cepeda, Orlando	64T	9	$3.00	$9.00
Cater, Danny	68T	535	$ .35	$1.25	Cepeda, Orlando	64T	306	$6.50	$20.00
Cater, Danny	69T	1	$2.00	$8.00	Cepeda, Orlando	64T	390	$1.25	$5.00
Cater, Danny	69T	44	$ .30	$ .85	Cepeda, Orlando	65T	4	$1.75	$4.50
Cater, Danny	69T	556	$ .35	$1.25	Cepeda, Orlando	65T	360	$2.10	$6.00
Cater, Danny	70T	437	$ .30	$ .95	Cepeda, Orlando	66T	132	$1.00	$4.00
Cater, Danny	71T	358	$ .15	$ .50	Cepeda, Orlando	67T	20	$1.50	$6.00
Cater, Danny	72T	676	$ .75	$2.50	Cepeda, Orlando	68T	3	$1.50	$4.00
Cater, Danny	73T	317	$ .07	$ .30	Cepeda, Orlando	68T	200	$ .75	$3.00
Cater, Danny	74T	543	$ .07	$ .30	Cepeda, Orlando	68TAS	362	$ .75	$2.25
Cater, Danny	75T	645	$ .07	$ .30	Cepeda, Orlando	69T	385	$ .95	$3.50
Cato, Keefe	85T	367	$ .01	$ .05	Cepeda, Orlando	70T	555	$ .95	$2.75
Caudill, Bill	80T	103	$ .03	$ .15	Cepeda, Orlando	71T	605	$1.75	$4.50
Caudill, Bill	81T	574	$ .01	$ .10	Cepeda, Orlando	72T	195	$ .90	$3.00
Caudill, Bill	82T	303	$ .01	$ .07	Cepeda, Orlando	73T	545	$ .75	$2.25
Caudill, Bill	82TTR	18	$ .02	$ .10	Cepeda, Orlando	74T	83	$ .45	$1.45
Caudill, Bill	83T	78	$ .01	$ .07	Cepeda, Orlando	75T	205	$ .45	$1.45
Caudill, Bill	84T	769	$ .01	$ .06	Cerone, Rick	77T	476	$15.00	$45.00
Caudill, Bill	84TTR	23	$ .02	$ .10	Cerone, Rick	78T	469	$ .02	$ .10
Caudill, Bill	85T	685	$ .01	$ .05	Cerone, Rick	79T	152	$ .02	$ .10
Caudill, Bill	85TTR	19	$ .02	$ .10	Cerone, Rick	80T	591	$ .01	$ .10
Caudill, Bill	86T	435	$ .01	$ .04	Cerone, Rick	81T	335	$ .01	$ .10
Caudill, Bill	87T	733	$ .01	$ .04	Cerone, Rick	82T	45	$ .01	$ .07
Causey, Wayne	62T	496	$ .75	$2.50	Cerone, Rick	83T	254	$ .01	$ .07
Causey, Wayne	63T	539	$1.75	$4.50	Cerone, Rick	84T	617	$ .01	$ .06
Causey, Wayne	64T	75	$ .30	$ .95	Cerone, Rick	85T	429	$ .01	$ .05
Causey, Wayne	65T	425	$ .35	$1.25	Cerone, Rick	85TTR	20	$ .02	$ .10
Causey, Wayne	66T	366	$ .30	$ .95	Cerone, Rick	86T	747	$ .01	$ .04
Causey, Wayne	67T	286	$ .30	$ .85	Cerone, Rick	86TTR	22	$ .02	$ .10
Causey, Wayne	68T	522	$ .35	$1.25	Cerone, Rick	87T	129	$ .01	$ .04
Causey, Wayne	69T	33	$ .30	$ .85	Cerone, Rick	87TTR	21	$ .01	$ .05
Cavarretta, Phil	52T	295	$15.00	$45.00	Cerone, Rick	88T	561	$ .01	$ .10
Cavarretta, Phil	54T	55	$3.75	$15.00	Cerone, Rick	88TTR	27	$ .01	$ .06
Ceccarelli, Art	58T	191	$ .75	$3.00	Cerone, Rick	89T	96	$ .01	$ .05
Ceccarelli, Art	59T	226	$ .75	$2.20	Cerone, Rick	89TBB	119	$ .01	$ .06
Ceccarelli, Art	60T	156	$ .45	$1.45	Cerone, Rick	90T	303	$ .01	$ .04
Cecena, Jose	88TTR	26	$ .01	$ .10	Cerone, Rick	90TTR	21	$ .01	$ .05
Cecena, Jose	89T	683	$ .01	$ .10	Cerone, Rick	91T	237	$ .01	$ .03
Cedeno, Andujar	91T	646	$ .01	$ .45	Cerutti, John	86TTR	23	$ .05	$ .25
Cedeno, Cesar	71T	237	$ .01	$1.00	Cerutti, John	87T	557	$ .01	$ .10
Cedeno, Cesar	72T	65	$ .30	$ .95	Cerutti, John	88T	191	$ .01	$ .04
Cedeno, Cesar	73T	290	$ .07	$ .30	Cerutti, John	89T	347	$ .01	$ .05
Cedeno, Cesar	74T	200	$ .30	$ .85	Cerutti, John	90T	211	$ .01	$ .04
Cedeno, Cesar	74TAS	337	$ .07	$ .30	Cerutti, John	91T	687	$ .01	$ .03
Cedeno, Cesar	75T	590	$ .15	$ .50	Cerv, Bob	53T	210	$2.25	$8.00
Cedeno, Cesar	76T	460	$ .07	$ .30	Cerv, Bob	56T	288	$2.25	$8.00
Cedeno, Cesar	77T	90	$ .05	$ .15	Cerv, Bob	57T	269	$4.25	$15.00
Cedeno, Cesar	78T	650	$ .02	$ .10	Cerv, Bob	58T	329	$ .75	$3.00

Player	Year	No.	VG	EX/MT
Cerv, Bob	59T	100	$1.25	$4.25
Cerv, Bob	60T	415	$ .75	$2.20
Cerv, Bob	61T	563	$7.00	$21.00
Cerv, Bob	62T	169	$ .75	$3.00
Cey, Ron	72T	761	$4.00	$12.00
Cey, Ron	73T	615	$135.00	$400.00
Cey, Ron	74T	315	$ .12	$ .40
Cey, Ron	75T	390	$ .30	$ .85
Cey, Ron	76T	370	$ .15	$ .50
Cey, Ron	77T	50	$ .07	$ .30
Cey, Ron	78T	630	$ .02	$ .10
Cey, Ron	79T	190	$ .02	$ .10

RON CEY
3rd BASE
DODGERS

Player	Year	No.	VG	EX/MT
Cey, Ron	80T	510	$ .01	$ .10
Cey, Ron	81T	260	$ .03	$ .15
Cey, Ron	82T	410	$ .01	$ .07
Cey, Ron	82TIA	411	$ .01	$ .07
Cey, Ron	83T	15	$ .01	$ .07
Cey, Ron	83TTR	19	$ .02	$ .10
Cey, Ron	84T	357	$ .01	$ .06
Cey, Ron	85T	768	$ .01	$ .05
Cey, Ron	86T	669	$ .01	$ .04
Cey, Ron	87T	767	$ .01	$ .04
Cey, Ron	87TTR	22	$ .01	$ .05
Chacon, Elio	60T	543	$2.50	$10.00
Chacon, Elio	62T	256	$ .45	$1.45
Chakales, Bob	52T	120	$7.00	$20.00
Chakales, Bob	57T	261	$ .95	$3.50
Chalk, Dave	74T	597	$ .15	$ .50
Chalk, Dave	75T	64	$ .07	$ .30
Chalk, Dave	76T	52	$ .05	$ .20
Chalk, Dave	77T	315	$ .05	$ .15
Chalk, Dave	78T	178	$ .02	$ .10
Chalk, Dave	79T	682	$ .02	$ .10
Chalk, Dave	80T	261	$ .01	$ .10
Chalk, Dave	82T	462	$ .01	$ .07
Chamberlain, Craig	80T	417	$ .01	$ .10
Chamberlain, Craig	81T	274	$ .01	$ .10
Chamberlain, Wes	91T	603	$ .01	$ .25
Chambers, Al	85T	277	$ .01	$ .05
Chambers, Cliff	51Trb	25	$2.10	$6.00

Player	Year	No.	VG	EX/MT
Chambers, Cliff	52T	68	$15.00	$47.50
Chambliss, Chris	72T	142	$ .40	$1.75
Chambliss, Chris	73T	11	$ .15	$ .50
Chambliss, Chris	74T	384	$ .30	$ .95
Chambliss, Chris	75T	585	$ .15	$ .50
Chambliss, Chris	76T	65	$ .07	$ .30
Chambliss, Chris	77T	220	$ .05	$ .15
Chambliss, Chris	78T	485	$ .05	$ .20
Chambliss, Chris	79T	335	$ .05	$ .20
Chambliss, Chris	80T	625	$ .01	$ .10
Chambliss, Chris	81T	155	$ .01	$ .10
Chambliss, Chris	82T	320	$ .01	$ .07
Chambliss, Chris	82TIA	321	$ .01	$ .07
Chambliss, Chris	83T	792	$ .01	$ .07
Chambliss, Chris	84T	50	$ .01	$ .06
Chambliss, Chris	85T	518	$ .01	$ .05
Chambliss, Chris	86T	293	$ .01	$ .04
Chambliss, Chris	87T	777	$ .01	$ .04
Champion, Billy	70T	149	$ .15	$ .20
Champion, Billy	71T	323	$ .15	$ .50
Champion, Billy	72T	599	$ .30	$ .95
Champion, Billy	73T	74	$ .07	$ .30
Champion, Billy	74T	391	$ .07	$ .30
Champion, Billy	75T	256	$ .07	$ .30
Champion, Billy	76T	501	$ .05	$ .20
Champion, Mike	77T	494	$ .12	$ .40
Champion, Mike	78T	683	$ .02	$ .10
Championship, A.L.	75T	459	$ .30	$ .95
Championship, A.L.	77T	276	$ .15	$ .50
Championship, A.L.	78T	411	$ .15	$ .50
Championship, A.L.	81T	401	$ .05	$ .25
Championship, N.L.	75T	460	$ .30	$ .95
Championship, N.L.	77T	277	$ .15	$ .50
Championship, N.L.	78T	412	$ .08	$ .30
Championship, N.L.	81T	402	$ .03	$ .15
Chance, Bob	64T	146	$20.00	$60.00
Chance, Bob	65T	224	$ .35	$1.25
Chance, Bob	66T	564	$5.00	$20.00
Chance, Bob	67T	349	$ .30	$ .85
Chance, Bob	69T	523	$ .30	$ .95
Chance, Dean	62T	194	$ .50	$ .50
Chance, Dean	63T	6	$ .45	$1.45
Chance, Dean	63T	355	$ .45	$1.45
Chance, Dean	64T	32	$ .75	$3.00
Chance, Dean	65T	7	$ .35	$1.25
Chance, Dean	65T	9	$ .35	$1.25
Chance, Dean	65T	11	$ .45	$1.45
Chance, Dean	65T	140	$ .30	$ .85
Chance, Dean	66T	340	$ .30	$ .95
Chance, Dean	67T	380	$ .30	$ .95
Chance, Dean	68T	10	$ .45	$1.45
Chance, Dean	68T	12	$ .45	$1.45
Chance, Dean	68T	255	$ .30	$ .85
Chance, Dean	69T	620	$ .30	$ .95
Chance, Dean	70T	625	$ .30	$ .95
Chance, Dean	71T	36	$ .15	$ .50
Chaney, Darrel	69T	624	$ .30	$ .95
Chaney, Darrel	70T	3	$ .15	$ .50
Chaney, Darrel	71T	632	$ .35	$1.25
Chaney, Darrel	72T	136	$ .15	$ .50
Chaney, Darrel	73T	507	$ .07	$ .30
Chaney, Darrel	74T	559	$ .07	$ .30
Chaney, Darrel	75T	581	$ .07	$ .30
Chaney, Darrel	76T	259	$ .05	$ .20
Chaney, Darrel	76TTR	259	$ .05	$ .20
Chaney, Darrel	77T	384	$ .05	$ .15
Chaney, Darrel	78T	443	$ .02	$ .10
Chaney, Darrel	79T	184	$ .02	$ .10
Chapman, Ben	52T	391	$50.00	$150.00
Chapman, Kelvin	85T	751	$ .01	$ .05

TOPPS

Player	Year	No.	VG	EX/MT	Player	Year	No.	VG	EX/MT
Chapman, Kelvin	86T	492	$ .01	$ .04	Checklist, Cards (1-88)	88TBB	28	$ .01	$ .06
Chapman, Sam	51Tbb	52	$4.00	$18.00	Checklist, Cards (110-196)	67T	103	$2.10	$6.00
Chappas, Harry	80T	347	$ .01	$ .10	Checklist, Cards (110-196)	68T	107	$ .75	$2.25
Charboneau, Joe	81T	13	$ .02	$ .10	Checklist, Cards (110-218)	69T	107	$ .75	$2.25
Charboneau, Joe	82T	630	$ .01	$ .07	Checklist, Cards (122-242)	78T	184	$ .30	$ .95
Charles, Ed	62T	595	$7.00	$21.00	Checklist, Cards (122-242)	79T	241	$ .05	$ .25
Charles, Ed	63T	67	$ .30	$ .95	Checklist, Cards (122-242)	80T	241	$ .05	$ .25
Charles, Ed	64T	475	$ .50	$1.45	Checklist, Cards (122-242)	81T	241	$ .01	$ .10
Charles, Ed	65T	35	$ .30	$ .85	Checklist, Cards (122-263)	71T	123	$ .90	$3.00
Charles, Ed	66T	422	$ .30	$ .95	Checklist, Cards (133 -264)	88T	253	$ .01	$ .04
Charles, Ed	67T	182	$ .30	$ .85	Checklist, Cards (133 263)	72T	103	$ .75	$2.20
Charles, Ed	68T	563	$ .35	$1.25	Checklist, Cards (133-263)	70T	128	$ .08	$1.25
Charles, Ed	69T	245	$ .30	$ .95	Checklist, Cards (133-264)	73T	264	$ .75	$2.20
Charley (Charlie)	67T	329	$ .30	$ .85	Checklist, Cards (133-264)	74T	263	$ .45	$1.45
Charlton, Norm	89T	737	$ .01	$ .15	Checklist, Cards (133-264)	75T	257	$ .75	$3.00
Charlton, Norm	90T	289	$ .01	$ .10	Checklist, Cards (133-264)	76T	262	$ .45	$1.45
Charlton, Norm	91T	309	$ .01	$ .03	Checklist, Cards (133-264)	77T	208	$ .45	$1.45
Charton, Pete	64T	459	$ .50	$1.45	Checklist, Cards (133-264)	82T	226	$ .01	$ .07
Charton, Pete	66T	329	$ .30	$ .95	Checklist, Cards (133-264)	83T	249	$ .01	$ .07
Chavarria, Ossie	67T	344	$ .30	$ .85	Checklist, Cards (133-264)	84T	233	$ .01	$ .06
Checklist '89, Cards(4/3-7/17)	89TMLD	151	$ .01	$ .06	Checklist, Cards (133-264)	84T	379	$ .01	$ .06
Checklist '89, Cards(7/24-9/23)	89TMLD	152	$ .01	$ .06	Checklist, Cards (133-264)	85T	261	$ .01	$ .05
Checklist TR, Cards (1T-132T)	82TTR	132	$ .15	$ .50	Checklist, Cards (133-264)	86T	263	$ .01	$ .04
Checklist TR, Cards (1T-132T)	83TTR	132	$ .30	$ .85	Checklist, Cards (133-264)	87T	264	$ .01	$ .04
Checklist TR, Cards (1T-132T)	84TTR	132	$ .08	$ .30	Checklist, Cards (133-264)	89T	258	$ .01	$ .05
Checklist TR, Cards (1T-132T)	85TTR	132	$ .05	$ .20	Checklist, Cards (177-242)	59T	172	$2.10	$6.00
Checklist TR, Cards (1T-132T)	86TTR	132	$ .02	$ .25	Checklist, Cards (177-264)	58T	158	$1.50	$4.00
Checklist TR, Cards (1T-132T)	87TTR	132	$ .05	$ .20	Checklist, Cards (177-264)	58T	216	$1.50	$4.00
Checklist TR, Cards (1T-132T)	88TTR	132	$ .01	$ .06	Checklist, Cards (177-264)	58T	246	$7.00	$21.00
Checklist TR, Cards (727-858)	81TTR	858	$ .15	$ .50	Checklist, Cards (177-264)	59T	248	$2.50	$7.50
Checklist, 1 of 6	90T	128	$ .01	$ .04	Checklist, Cards (177-264)	60T	151	$1.50	$4.50
Checklist, 2 of 6	90T	262	$ .01	$ .04	Checklist, Cards (177-264)	60T	164	$3.00	$9.00
Checklist, 3 of 6	90T	376	$ .01	$ .04	Checklist, Cards (177-264)	60T	208	$1.50	$6.00
Checklist, 4 of 6	90T	526	$ .01	$ .04	Checklist, Cards (177-264)	61T	189	$2.25	$8.00
Checklist, 5 of 6	90T	646	$ .01	$ .04	Checklist, Cards (177-264)	62T	192	$2.10	$6.00
Checklist, 6 of 6	90T	783	$ .01	$ .04	Checklist, Cards (177-264)	63T	191	$ .90	$3.00
Checklist, Cards (1-109)	67T	62	$ .75	$2.25	Checklist, Cards (177-264)	64T	188	$ .30	$ .95
Checklist, Cards (1-109)	68T	67	$ .75	$2.25	Checklist, Cards (177-264)	65T	189	$ .90	$3.00
Checklist, Cards (1-109)	69T	57	$ .75	$2.25	Checklist, Cards (177-264)	66T	183	$2.25	$6.00
Checklist, Cards (1-121)	78T	74	$ .15	$ .50	Checklist, Cards (177-264)	88TBB	216	$ .01	$ .06
Checklist, Cards (1-121)	79T	121	$ .05	$ .20	Checklist, Cards (197-283)	67T	191	$ .75	$2.50
Checklist, Cards (1-121)	80T	121	$ .05	$ .25	Checklist, Cards (197-283)	68T	192	$ .75	$2.25
Checklist, Cards (1-121)	81T	31	$ .01	$ .10	Checklist, Cards (219-327)	69T	214	$ .90	$3.00
Checklist, Cards (1-132)	70T	9	$ .75	$2.20	Checklist, Cards (243-363)	78T	289	$ .10	$ .45
Checklist, Cards (1-132)	71T	54	$ .90	$3.00	Checklist, Cards (243-363)	79T	353	$ .08	$ .30
Checklist, Cards (1-132)	72T	4	$ .75	$2.20	Checklist, Cards (243-363)	80T	348	$ .05	$ .25
Checklist, Cards (1-132)	73T	54	$ .75	$2.20	Checklist, Cards (243-363)	81T	338	$ .01	$ .10
Checklist, Cards (1-132)	74T	126	$ .45	$1.45	Checklist, Cards (264-372)	70T	244	$ .75	$2.20
Checklist, Cards (1-132)	75T	126	$ .75	$3.00	Checklist, Cards (264-393)	71T	206	$ .08	$1.50
Checklist, Cards (1-132)	76T	119	$ .45	$1.45	Checklist, Cards (264-394)	72T	251	$ .75	$2.20
Checklist, Cards (1-132)	77T	32	$ .45	$1.45	Checklist, Cards (265 352)	61T	273	$ .35	$1.25
Checklist, Cards (1-132)	82T	129	$ .01	$ .07	Checklist, Cards (265-332)	60T	332	$3.50	$10.00
Checklist, Cards (1-132)	83T	129	$ .01	$ .07	Checklist, Cards (265-352)	58T	327	$1.50	$4.00
Checklist, Cards (1-132)	84T	114	$ .01	$ .06	Checklist, Cards (265-352)	58T	341	$1.50	$4.00
Checklist, Cards (1-132)	85T	121	$ .01	$ .05	Checklist, Cards (265-352)	59T	223	$1.50	$4.50
Checklist, Cards (1-132)	86T	131	$ .01	$ .04	Checklist, Cards (265-352)	59T	304	$1.50	$4.50
Checklist, Cards (1-132)	87T	128	$ .01	$ .04	Checklist, Cards (265-352)	60T	242	$1.75	$6.00
Checklist, Cards (1-132)	88T	121	$ .01	$ .04	Checklist, Cards (265-352)	62T	277	$2.10	$6.00
Checklist, Cards (1-132)	89T	118	$ .01	$ .05	Checklist, Cards (265-352)	63T	274	$ .90	$3.00
Checklist, Cards (1-88)	58T	71	$5.00	$20.00	Checklist, Cards (265-352)	64T	274	$ .75	$2.25
Checklist, Cards (1-88)	59T	8	$2.00	$6.00	Checklist, Cards (265-352)	65T	273	$ .90	$3.00
Checklist, Cards (1-88)	59T	48	$1.50	$4.50	Checklist, Cards (265-352)	66T	279	$ .85	$2.75
Checklist, Cards (1-88)	60T	18	$3.00	$9.00	Checklist, Cards (265-362)	58T	256	$1.50	$4.00
Checklist, Cards (1-88)	60T	43	$1.50	$4.00	Checklist, Cards (265-396)	73T	338	$ .75	$2.20
Checklist, Cards (1-88)	61T	17	$2.10	$6.00	Checklist, Cards (265-396)	74T	273	$ .45	$1.45
Checklist, Cards (1-88)	62T	22	$1.50	$4.00	Checklist, Cards (265-396)	75T	386	$ .75	$3.00
Checklist, Cards (1-88)	63T	79	$ .90	$3.00	Checklist, Cards (265-396)	76T	392	$ .45	$1.45
Checklist, Cards (1-88)	64T	76	$ .90	$3.00	Checklist, Cards (265-396)	77T	356	$ .45	$1.45
Checklist, Cards (1-88)	65T	79	$ .90	$3.00	Checklist, Cards (265-396)	82T	394	$ .01	$ .07
Checklist, Cards (1-88)	66T	34	$ .90	$3.00	Checklist, Cards (265-396)	83T	349	$ .01	$ .07

Player	Year	No.	VG	EX/MT
Checklist, Cards (265-396)	85T	377	$ .01	$ .05
Checklist, Cards (265-396)	86T	394	$ .01	$ .04
Checklist, Cards (265-396)	87T	392	$ .01	$ .04
Checklist, Cards (265-396)	88T	373	$ .01	$ .04
Checklist, Cards (265-396)	89T	378	$ .01	$ .05
Checklist, Cards (284-370)	67T	278	$ .75	$2.25
Checklist, Cards (284-370)	68T	278	$2.10	$6.00
Checklist, Cards (328-425)	69T	314	$ .30	$ .95
Checklist, Cards (353-429)	59T	329	$1.50	$4.50
Checklist, Cards (353-429)	59T	419	$2.50	$9.50
Checklist, Cards (353-429)	60T	302	$2.10	$6.00
Checklist, Cards (353-429)	60T	381	$2.10	$6.00
Checklist, Cards (353-429)	61T	361	$2.00	$6.00
Checklist, Cards (353-429)	62T	367	$2.10	$6.00
Checklist, Cards (353-429)	63T	362	$ .75	$2.25
Checklist, Cards (353-429)	64T	362	$1.25	$4.25
Checklist, Cards (353-429)	65T	361	$1.25	$4.25
Checklist, Cards (353-429)	66T	363	$2.25	$6.00
Checklist, Cards (353-440)	58T	312	$2.50	$7.50
Checklist, Cards (364-484)	78T	435	$ .30	$ .95
Checklist, Cards (364-484)	79T	483	$ .05	$ .25
Checklist, Cards (364-484)	80T	484	$ .05	$ .25
Checklist, Cards (364-484)	81T	446	$ .01	$ .10
Checklist, Cards (371-457)	67T	361	$1.75	$4.50
Checklist, Cards (371-457)	68T	356	$ .75	$2.25
Checklist, Cards (373-459)	70T	343	$ .90	$3.00

TOPPS baseball — 4th Series Checklist

394	Clay Carroll	422	Frank Bertaina
395	Roy White	423	Tigers Rookies
396	Dick Schofield	424	R. Rodriguez
397	Alvin Dark	425	Doug Rader
398	Howie Reed	426	Chris Cannizzaro
399	Jim French	427	Bernie Allen
400	Hank Aaron	428	Jim McAndrew
401	Tom Murphy	429	Chuck Hinton
402	Dodgers Team	430	Wes Parker
403	Joe Coleman	431	Tom Burgmeier
404	Astros Rookies	432	Bob Didier
405	Leo Cardenas	433	Skip Lockwood
406	Ray Sadecki	434	Gary Sutherland
407	Joe Rudi	435	Jose Cardenal
408	Rafael Robles	436	Wilbur Wood
409	Don Pavletich	437	Danny Murtaugh
410	Ken Holtzman	438	Mike McCormick
411	George Spriggs	439	Phillies Rookies
412	Jerry Johnson	440	Bert Campaneris
413	Pat Kelly	441	Milt Pappas
414	Woodie Fryman	442	Angels Team
415	Mike Hegan	443	Rich Robertson
416	Gene Alley	444	Jimmie Price
417	Dick Hall	445	Art Shamsky
418	Adolfo Phillips	446	Bobby Bolin
419	Ron Hansen	447	Cesar Geronimo
420	Jim Merritt	448	Dave Roberts
421	John Stephenson	449	Brant Alyea

Player	Year	No.	VG	EX/MT
Checklist, Cards (394-523)	71T	369	$ .90	$3.00
Checklist, Cards (395-525)	72T	378	$ .75	$2.20
Checklist, Cards (397-528)	73T	453	$ .75	$2.20
Checklist, Cards (397-528)	74T	414	$ .45	$1.45
Checklist, Cards (397-528)	75T	517	$ .75	$3.00
Checklist, Cards (397-528)	76T	526	$ .45	$1.45
Checklist, Cards (397-528)	77T	451	$ .45	$1.45
Checklist, Cards (397-528)	82T	491	$ .01	$ .07
Checklist, Cards (397-528)	83T	526	$ .01	$ .07
Checklist, Cards (397-528)	84T	527	$ .01	$ .06
Checklist, Cards (397-528)	85T	527	$ .01	$ .05
Checklist, Cards (397-528)	86T	527	$ .01	$ .04
Checklist, Cards (397-528)	87T	522	$ .01	$ .04
Checklist, Cards (397-528)	88T	528	$ .01	$ .04

Player	Year	No.	VG	EX/MT
Checklist, Cards (397-528)	89T	524	$ .01	$ .05
Checklist, Cards (426-512)	69T	412	$3.00	$9.00
Checklist, Cards (430-495)	59T	397	$1.50	$4.50
Checklist, Cards (430-495)	59T	457	$4.00	$12.00
Checklist, Cards (430-495)	60T	413	$2.10	$6.00
Checklist, Cards (430-495)	60T	484	$4.00	$12.00
Checklist, Cards (430-506)	61T	437	$1.50	$4.50
Checklist, Cards (430-506)	62T	441	$2.00	$6.00
Checklist, Cards (430-506)	63T	431	$2.10	$6.00
Checklist, Cards (430-506)	64T	438	$2.10	$6.00
Checklist, Cards (430-506)	65T	443	$ .90	$3.00
Checklist, Cards (430-506)	66T	444	$2.10	$6.00
Checklist, Cards (458-533)	67T	454	$2.50	$10.00
Checklist, Cards (458-533)	68T	454	$2.10	$6.00
Checklist, Cards (460-546)	70T	432	$ .75	$2.20
Checklist, Cards (485-605)	78T	535	$ .15	$ .50
Checklist, Cards (485-605)	79T	602	$ .08	$ .30
Checklist, Cards (485-605)	80T	533	$ .05	$ .25
Checklist, Cards (485-605)	81T	562	$ .01	$ .10
Checklist, Cards (496-572)	59T	476	$1.50	$4.50
Checklist, Cards (496-572)	59T	510	$10.50	$42.50
Checklist, Cards (496-572)	59T	528	$5.25	$15.00
Checklist, Cards (496-572)	60T	494	$2.25	$6.50
Checklist, Cards (496-572)	60T	513	$5.00	$16.00
Checklist, Cards (496-572)	60T	537	$7.00	$21.00
Checklist, Cards (507-576)	63T	509	$2.70	$8.00
Checklist, Cards (507-587)	61T	516	$3.00	$9.00
Checklist, Cards (507-587)	64T	517	$2.00	$6.00
Checklist, Cards (507-598)	62T	516	$3.00	$9.00
Checklist, Cards (507-598)	65T	508	$1.80	$5.00
Checklist, Cards (507-598)	66T	517	$2.25	$6.50
Checklist, Cards (513-588)	69T	504	$2.10	$6.00
Checklist, Cards (524-643)	71T	499	$ .90	$3.00
Checklist, Cards (526-656)	72T	478	$ .75	$2.20
Checklist, Cards (529-660)	73T	588	$2.75	$8.00
Checklist, Cards (529-660)	74T	637	$ .45	$1.45
Checklist, Cards (529-660)	75T	646	$ .75	$3.00
Checklist, Cards (529-660)	76T	643	$ .45	$1.45
Checklist, Cards (529-660)	77T	562	$ .45	$1.45
Checklist, Cards (529-660)	82T	634	$ .01	$ .07
Checklist, Cards (529-660)	83T	642	$ .01	$ .07
Checklist, Cards (529-660)	84T	646	$ .01	$ .06
Checklist, Cards (529-660)	85T	659	$ .01	$ .05
Checklist, Cards (529-660)	86T	659	$ .01	$ .04
Checklist, Cards (529-660)	87T	654	$ .01	$ .04
Checklist, Cards (529-660)	88T	646	$ .01	$ .04
Checklist, Cards (529-660)	89T	619	$ .01	$ .05
Checklist, Cards (534-598)	68T	518	$ .50	$2.50
Checklist, Cards (534-609)	67T	531	$1.40	$4.00
Checklist, Cards (547-633)	70T	542	$ .75	$2.25
Checklist, Cards (589-664)	69T	582	$ .95	$3.50
Checklist, Cards (606-726)	78T	652	$ .30	$ .95
Checklist, Cards (606-726)	79T	669	$ .08	$ .30
Checklist, Cards (606-726)	80T	646	$ .05	$ .25
Checklist, Cards (606-726)	81T	638	$ .01	$ .10
Checklist, Cards (634-720)	70T	588	$ .75	$2.25
Checklist, Cards (644-752)	71T	619	$2.10	$6.00
Checklist, Cards (657-787)	72T	604	$2.10	$6.00
Checklist, Cards (661-792)	82T	789	$ .01	$ .07
Checklist, Cards (661-792)	83T	769	$ .01	$ .07
Checklist, Cards (661-792)	84T	781	$ .01	$ .06
Checklist, Cards (661-792)	85T	784	$ .01	$ .05
Checklist, Cards (661-792)	86T	791	$ .01	$ .04
Checklist, Cards (661-792)	87T	792	$ .01	$ .10
Checklist, Cards (661-792)	88T	776	$ .01	$ .04
Checklist, Cards (661-792)	89T	782	$ .01	$ .04
Checklist, Cards (89-176)	58T	134	$3.00	$7.50
Checklist, Cards (89-176)	58T	174	$1.50	$4.00
Checklist, Cards (89-176)	59T	111	$2.55	$8.50
Checklist, Cards (89-176)	59T	69	$2.75	$9.50

TOPPS

Player	Year	No.	VG	EX/MT	Player	Year	No.	VG	EX/MT
Checklist, Cards (89-176)	59T	94	$3.00	$11.00	Christopher, Joe	65T	495	$ .75	$3.00
Checklist, Cards (89-176)	60T	72	$3.00	$9.00	Christopher, Joe	66T	343	$ .30	$ .95
Checklist, Cards (89-176)	60T	174	$2.10	$6.00	Church, Bubba	52T	323	$40.00	$140.00
Checklist, Cards (89-176)	61T	98	$2.25	$8.00	Church, Bubba	53T	47	$4.50	$15.00
Checklist, Cards (89-176)	62T	98	$2.10	$6.00	Ciardi, Mark	88T	417	$ .01	$ .04
Checklist, Cards (89-176)	63T	102	$1.75	$4.50	Cias, Darryl	84T	159	$ .01	$ .06
Checklist, Cards (89-176)	64T	102	$ .90	$3.00	Cicotte, Al	57T	398	$1.25	$4.25
Checklist, Cards (89-176)	65T	104	$1.75	$5.00	Cicotte, Al	58T	382	$ .75	$3.00
Checklist, Cards (89-176)	66T	101	$ .95	$2.75	Cicotte, Al	59T	57	$1.25	$4.25
Checklist, Cards (89-176)	88TBB	126	$ .01	$ .06	Cicotte, Al	60T	473	$ .90	$3.00
Checklist, Cards 1-132	90TTR	132	$ .01	$ .05	Cicotte, Al	61T	241	$ .35	$1.25
Checklist, Cards Traded	74TTR	0	$ .45	$1.45	Cicotte, Al	62T	126	$ .45	$1.45
Checklist, Cards Traded	76TTR	0	$ .15	$ .60	Cimino, Pete	66T	563	$5.00	$20.00
Checklist, Cards(1-110)	89TBB	59	$ .01	$ .06	Cimino, Pete	67T	34	$ .30	$ .85
Checklist, Cards(111-220)	89TBB	176	$ .01	$ .06	Cimino, Pete	68T	143	$ .30	$ .85
Checklist, Cards(1T-132T)	89TTR	132	$ .01	$ .06	Cimoli, Gino	57T	319	$4.25	$15.00
Checklist, Cards(221-330))	89TBB	327	$ .01	$ .06	Cimoli, Gino	58T	286	$ .75	$3.00
Checklist, Coins (1-161)	71T	161	$ .75	$2.25	Cimoli, Gino	59T	418	$ .75	$2.20
Checklist, No. 1 of 6	91T	131	$ .01	$ .03	Cimoli, Gino	60T	58	$ .45	$1.45
Checklist, No. 2 of 6	91T	263	$ .01	$ .03	Cimoli, Gino	61T	165	$ .35	$1.25
Checklist, No. 3 of 6	91T	366	$ .01	$ .03	Cimoli, Gino	62T	402	$ .75	$2.50
Checklist, No. 4 of 6	91T	527	$ .01	$ .03	Cimoli, Gino	63T	321	$ .45	$1.50
Checklist, No. 5 of 6	91T	656	$ .01	$ .10	Cimoli, Gino	64T	26	$ .30	$ .95
Checklist, No. 6 of 6	91T	787	$ .01	$ .03	Cimoli, Gino	65T	569	$1.75	$4.50
Cheney, Tom	57T	359	$1.25	$4.25	Cipriani, Frank	62T	333	$ .45	$1.45
Cheney, Tom	61T	494	$ .75	$3.00	Cisco, Galen	62T	301	$ .45	$1.45
Chesbro, Jack	61T	407	$ .75	$3.00	Cisco, Galen	63T	93	$ .30	$ .95
Chesbro, Jack	79TRH	416	$ .05	$ .20	Cisco, Galen	64T	202	$ .30	$ .95
Chiamparino, Scott	91T	676	$ .01	$ .25	Cisco, Galen	65T	364	$ .35	$1.25
Chiffer, Floyd	83T	298	$ .01	$ .07	Cisco, Galen	67T	596	$2.10	$6.00
Childress, Rocky	88T	643	$ .01	$ .04	Cisco, Galen	69T	211	$ .30	$ .85
Chiles, Rich	72T	56	$ .15	$ .50	Cisco, Galen	73T	593	$ .75	$3.00
Chiles, Rich	73T	617	$ .45	$1.45	Cisco, Galen	74T	166	$ .07	$ .30
Chiles, Rich	78T	193	$ .02	$ .10	Clancy, Jim	78T	496	$ .05	$ .20
Chiles, Rich	79T	498	$ .02	$ .10	Clancy, Jim	79T	131	$ .02	$ .10
Chipman, Bob	52T	388	$40.00	$140.00	Clancy, Jim	80T	249	$ .01	$ .10
Chiti, Harry	56T	179	$2.25	$6.00	Clancy, Jim	81T	19	$ .01	$ .10
Chiti, Harry	58T	119	$ .75	$3.00	Clancy, Jim	82T	665	$ .01	$ .07
Chiti, Harry	59T	79	$1.25	$4.25	Clancy, Jim	83T	345	$ .01	$ .07
Chiti, Harry	60T	339	$ .75	$2.20	Clancy, Jim	84T	575	$ .01	$ .06
Chiti, Harry	61T	269	$ .35	$1.25	Clancy, Jim	85T	746	$ .01	$ .05
Chiti, Harry	62T	253	$ .45	$1.45	Clancy, Jim	86T	412	$ .01	$ .04
Chittum, Nelson	60T	296	$ .75	$2.20	Clancy, Jim	87T	122	$ .01	$ .04
Chlupsa, Bob	71T	594	$ .75	$2.00	Clancy, Jim	88T	54	$ .01	$ .04
Chris, Mike	80T	666	$ .01	$ .10	Clancy, Jim	88TBB	258	$ .01	$ .06
Chrisley, Neil	57T	320	$4.25	$15.00	Clancy, Jim	89T	219	$ .01	$ .05
Chrisley, Neil	58T	303	$ .75	$3.00	Clancy, Jim	89TTR	19	$ .01	$ .06
Chrisley, Neil	59T	189	$ .75	$2.20	Clancy, Jim	90T	648	$ .01	$ .04
Chrisley, Neil	60T	273	$ .45	$1.45	Clark, Al	52T	278	$10 .00	$30.00
Chrisley, Neil	62T	308	$ .45	$1.45	Clark, Bob	80T	663	$ .05	$ .20
Christensen, John	86T	287	$ .01	$ .04	Clark, Bob	81T	288	$ .01	$ .10
Christensen, John	87TTR	23	$ .01	$ .05	Clark, Bob	82T	74	$ .01	$ .07
Christensen, John	88T	413	$ .01	$ .04	Clark, Bob	83T	184	$ .01	$ .07
Christenson, Larry	74T	587	$ .07	$ .30	Clark, Bob	84T	626	$ .01	$ .06
Christenson, Larry	75T	551	$ .07	$ .30	Clark, Bob	84TTR	24	$ .02	$ .10
Christenson, Larry	76T	634	$ .05	$ .20	Clark, Bob	85T	553	$ .01	$ .05
Christenson, Larry	77T	59	$ .05	$ .15	Clark, Bob	86T	452	$ .01	$ .04
Christenson, Larry	78T	247	$ .02	$ .10	Clark, Bryan	82T	632	$ .01	$ .07
Christenson, Larry	79T	493	$ .02	$ .10	Clark, Bryan	83T	789	$ .01	$ .07
Christenson, Larry	80T	161	$ .01	$ .10	Clark, Bryan	84T	22	$ .01	$ .06
Christenson, Larry	81T	346	$ .01	$ .10	Clark, Bryan	84TTR	25	$ .02	$ .10
Christenson, Larry	82T	544	$ .01	$ .07	Clark, Bryan	85T	489	$ .01	$ .05
Christenson, Larry	83T	668	$ .01	$ .07	Clark, Bryan	85TTR	21	$ .02	$ .10
Christenson, Larry	84T	252	$ .01	$ .06	Clark, Dave	88T	49	$ .01	$ .10
Christian, Bob	69T	173	$ .30	$ .85	Clark, Dave	89T	574	$ .01	$ .05
Christian, Bob	70T	51	$ .15	$ .50	Clark, Dave	90T	339	$ .01	$ .04
Christiansen, Clay	85T	211	$ .01	$ .05	Clark, Dave	91T	241	$ .01	$ .03
Christopher, Joe	61T	82	$ .35	$1.25	Clark, Jack	77T	488	$5.00	$20.00
Christopher, Joe	63T	217	$ .30	$ .95	Clark, Jack	78T	384	$1.00	$3.50
Christopher, Joe	64T	546	$1.75	$4.50	Clark, Jack	79T	512	$ .50	$2.50

Player	Year	No.	VG	EX/MT	Player	Year	No.	VG	EX/MT
Clark, Jack	80T	167	$ .50	$2.00	Clear, Mark	89T	63	$ .01	$ .05
Clark, Jack	81T	30	$ .10	$ .50	Clemens, Doug	67T	489	$ .75	$3.00
Clark, Jack	82T	460	$ .10	$ .50	Clemens, Roger	85T	181	$3.50	$14.00
Clark, Jack	83T	210	$ .05	$ .25	Clemens, Roger	86T	661	$ .50	$2.50
Clark, Jack	84T	690	$ .05	$ .25	Clemens, Roger	87T	340	$ .25	$1.00
Clark, Jack	85TTR	22	$ .30	$ .95	Clemens, Roger	87TAS	614	$ .15	$ .50
Clark, Jack	86T	350	$ .02	$ .15	Clemens, Roger	87TRB	1	$ .30	$ .85
Clark, Jack	87T	520	$ .07	$ .30	Clemens, Roger	88T	70	$ .05	$ .50
Clark, Jack	88T	100	$ .01	$ .10	Clemens, Roger	88TAS	394	$ .01	$ .20
Clark, Jack	88TAS	397	$ .01	$ .04	Clemens, Roger	88TBB	118	$ .05	$ .35
Clark, Jack	88TBB	262	$ .01	$ .06	Clemens, Roger	89T	450	$ .05	$ .25
Clark, Jack	88TTR	28	$ .01	$ .10	Clemens, Roger	89TAS	405	$ .01	$ .15
Clark, Jack	89T	410	$ .01	$ .10	Clemens, Roger	89TBB	42	$ .01	$ .25
Clark, Jack	89TBB	240	$ .01	$ .10	Clemens, Roger	90T	245	$ .01	$ .15
Clark, Jack	89TTR	20	$ .01	$ .10	Clemens, Roger	91T	530	$ .01	$ .15
Clark, Jack	90T	90	$ .01	$ .10	Clemente, Roberto	55T	164	$260.00	$1000.00
Clark, Jack	91T	650	$ .01	$ .03	Clemente, Roberto	56T	33	$80.00	$275.00
Clark, Jerald	91T	513	$ .01	$ .03	Clemente, Bob	57T	76	$60.00	$175.00
Clark, Joe	85T	740	$ .01	$ .05	Clemente, Bob	58T	52	$37.50	$130.00
Clark, Mike	53T	193	$4.50	$15.00	Clemente, Bob	59T	478	$30.00	$92.50
Clark, Phil	58T	423	$ .75	$3.00	Clemente, Roberto	59T	543	$11.50	$45.00
Clark, Phil	59T	454	$ .75	$2.20	Clemente, Bob	60T	326	$30.00	$95.00
Clark, Rickey	70T	586	$ .30	$ .95	Clemente, Bob	61T	41	$1.50	$5.00
Clark, Rickey	71T	697	$ .75	$2.50	Clemente, Bob	61T	388	$27.50	$82.50
Clark, Rickey	72T	462	$ .15	$ .50	Clemente, Bob	62T	10	$22.00	$75.00
Clark, Rickey	73T	636	$ .45	$1.45	Clemente, Bob	62T	52	$1.00	$4.00
Clark, Ron	67T	137	$ .30	$ .85	Clemente, Bob	63T	18	$2.35	$10.00
Clark, Ron	68T	589	$ .35	$1.25	Clemente, Bob	63T	540	$45.00	$165.00
Clark, Ron	69T	561	$ .30	$ .95	Clemente, Bob	64T	7	$1.70	$5.00
Clark, Ron	70T	531	$ .15	$ .50	Clemente, Bob	64T	440	$27.50	$82.50
Clark, Terry	89T	129	$ .01	$ .05	Clemente, Bob	65T	2	$2.10	$6.00
Clark, Will	86TTR	24	$1.50	$8.50	Clemente, Bob	65T	160	$19.50	$65.00
Clark, Will	87T	420	$ .75	$3.50	Clemente, Bob	66T	215	$3.00	$12.00
Clark, Will	88T	350	$ .10	$1.00	Clemente, Bob	66T	300	$17.50	$70.00
Clark, Will	88TBB	9	$ .25	$1.00	Clemente, Bob	67T	242	$1.75	$4.50
Clark, Will	89T	660	$ .05	$ .50					
Clark, Will	89TBB	146	$ .01	$ .50					
Clark, Will	90T	100	$ .01	$ .25					
Clark, Will	90TAS	397	$ .01	$ .15					
Clark, Will	91T	500	$ .01	$ .20					
Clarke, Horace	66T	547	$10.00	$35.00					
Clarke, Horace	67T	169	$ .30	$ .85					
Clarke, Horace	68T	263	$ .30	$ .85					
Clarke, Horace	69T	87	$ .30	$ .85					
Clarke, Horace	70T	623	$ .30	$ .95					
Clarke, Horace	71T	715	$ .75	$2.50					
Clarke, Horace	72T	387	$ .15	$ .50					
Clarke, Horace	73T	198	$ .07	$ .30					
Clarke, Horace	74T	529	$ .07	$ .30					
Clarke, Stan	88T	556	$ .01	$ .04					
Clary, Ellis	60T	470	$ .95	$3.50					
Clary, Marty	90T	304	$ .01	$ .04					
Clary, Marty	91T	582	$ .01	$ .03					
Clay, Ken	78T	89	$ .02	$ .10					
Clay, Ken	79T	434	$ .02	$ .10					
Clay, Ken	80T	159	$ .01	$ .10					
Clay, Ken	81T	305	$ .01	$ .10					
Clay, Ken	81TTR	747	$ .02	$ .10					
Clay, Ken	82T	649	$ .01	$ .07					
Clear, Mark	80T	638	$ .03	$ .15					
Clear, Mark	81T	12	$ .01	$ .10					
Clear, Mark	81TTR	748	$ .02	$ .10					
Clear, Mark	82T	421	$ .01	$ .07					
Clear, Mark	83T	162	$ .01	$ .07					
Clear, Mark	84T	577	$ .01	$ .06					
Clear, Mark	85T	207	$ .01	$ .05	Clemente, Bob	67T	400	$12.00	$60.00
Clear, Mark	86T	349	$ .01	$ .04	Clemente, Bob	68T	1	$2.50	$12.50
Clear, Mark	86TTR	25	$ .02	$ .10	Clemente, Bob	68T	3	$1.50	$4.00
Clear, Mark	87T	640	$ .01	$ .04	Clemente, Bob	68T	150	$9.00	$42.50
Clear, Mark	88T	742	$ .01	$ .04	Clemente, Bob	68T	480	$5.50	$17.50

BOB CLEMENTE • OUTFIELD

PIRATES

Player	Year	No.	VG	EX/MT
Clemente, Bob	68TAS	374	$3.00	$9.00
Clemente, Bob	69T	50	$10.00	$35.00
Clemente, Bob "Roberto"	70T	61	$1.50	$4.75
Clemente, Roberto	70T	350	$9.00	$35.00
Clemente, Roberto	71T	630	$10.00	$40.00
Clemente, Roberto	72T	309	$6.00	$25.00
Clemente, Roberto	72TIA	310	$3.00	$12.00
Clemente, Roberto	73T	50	$5.50	$22.50
Clemente, Roberto	75T	204	$ .50	$1.50
Clemente, Roberto	87TTB	313	$ .07	$ .30
Clements, Pat	85TTR	23	$ .02	$ .10
Clements, Pat	86T	754	$ .01	$ .04
Clements, Pat	87T	16	$ .01	$ .04
Clements, Pat	88T	484	$ .01	$ .04
Clements, Pat	89T	159	$ .01	$ .05
Clements, Pat	90T	548	$ .01	$ .04
Clemons, Lance	72T	372	$ .15	$ .50
Clendenon, Donn	62T	86	$ .75	$3.00
Clendenon, Donn	63T	477	$2.50	$6.50
Clendenon, Donn	64T	163	$ .30	$ .95

1st BASE
DONN CLENDENON

Player	Year	No.	VG	EX/MT
Clendenon, Donn	65T	325	$ .35	$1.25
Clendenon, Donn	66T	375	$ .30	$ .95
Clendenon, Donn	67T	266	$ .30	$ .85
Clendenon, Donn	67T	535	$1.50	$4.00
Clendenon, Donn	68T	344	$ .30	$ .85
Clendenon, Donn	69T	208	$ .15	$ .15
Clendenon, Donn	70T	280	$ .15	$ .50
Clendenon, Donn	71T	115	$ .15	$ .50
Clendenon, Donn	72T	671	$ .90	$3.00
Cleveland, Reggie	70T	716	$ .75	$2.00
Cleveland, Reggie	71T	216	$ .15	$ .50
Cleveland, Reggie	72T	375	$ .15	$ .50
Cleveland, Reggie	73T	104	$ .07	$ .30
Cleveland, Reggie	74T	175	$ .07	$ .30
Cleveland, Reggie	74TTR	175	$ .07	$ .30
Cleveland, Reggie	75T	32	$ .07	$ .30
Cleveland, Reggie	76T	419	$ .05	$ .20
Cleveland, Reggie	77T	613	$ .05	$ .15
Cleveland, Reggie	78T	105	$ .02	$ .10
Cleveland, Reggie	79T	209	$ .02	$ .10

Player	Year	No.	VG	EX/MT
Cleveland, Reggie	80T	394	$ .01	$ .10
Cleveland, Reggie	81T	576	$ .01	$ .10
Cleveland, Reggie	82T	737	$ .01	$ .07
Clevenger, Tex	58T	31	$1.25	$4.25
Clevenger, Tex	59T	298	$ .75	$2.20
Clevenger, Tex	60T	392	$ .75	$2.20
Clevenger, Tex	61T	291	$ .35	$1.25
Clevenger, Tex	63T	457	$2.50	$6.50
Cliburn, Stu	86T	179	$ .01	$ .04
Cliburn, Stewart	89T	649	$ .01	$ .05
Cline, Ty	61T	421	$ .75	$3.00
Cline, Ty	62T	362	$ .45	$1.45
Cline, Ty	63T	414	$ .45	$1.50
Cline, Ty	64T	171	$ .30	$ .95
Cline, Ty	65T	63	$ .30	$ .85
Cline, Ty	66T	306	$ .30	$ .95
Cline, Ty	67T	591	$2.10	$6.00
Cline, Ty	68T	469	$ .35	$1.25
Cline, Ty	69T	442	$ .30	$ .85
Cline, Ty	70T	164	$ .15	$ .50
Cline, Ty	71T	319	$ .15	$ .50
Clines, Gene	71T	27	$ .15	$ .50
Clines, Gene	72T	152	$ .15	$ .50
Clines, Gene	73T	333	$ .07	$ .30
Clines, Gene	74T	172	$ .07	$ .30
Clines, Gene	75T	575	$ .07	$ .30
Clines, Gene	76T	417	$ .05	$ .20
Clines, Gene	77T	237	$ .05	$ .15
Clines, Gene	78T	639	$ .02	$ .10
Clines, Gene	79T	171	$ .02	$ .10
Clinton, Lou	60T	533	$2.50	$10.00
Clinton, Lou	62T	457	$ .75	$2.50
Clinton, Lou	63T	96	$ .30	$ .95
Clinton, Lou	64T	526	$1.75	$4.50
Clinton, Lou	64T	527	$1.75	$4.50
Clinton, Lou	65T	229	$ .35	$1.25
Clinton, Lou	67T	426	$ .30	$ .95
Cloninger, Tony	62T	63	$ .75	$2.20
Cloninger, Tony	63T	367	$ .45	$1.45
Cloninger, Tony	64T	575	$1.75	$4.50
Cloninger, Tony	65T	520	$ .75	$3.00
Cloninger, Tony	66T	10	$ .30	$ .95
Cloninger, Tony	66T	223	$ .65	$1.75
Cloninger, Tony	67T	396	$ .45	$1.45
Cloninger, Tony	67T	490	$ .75	$3.00
Cloninger, Tony	68T	93	$ .30	$ .85
Cloninger, Tony	69T	492	$ .30	$ .85
Cloninger, Tony	70T	705	$ .75	$2.00
Cloninger, Tony	71T	218	$ .15	$ .50
Cloninger, Tony	72T	779	$ .75	$2.50
Closter, Alan	66T	549	$5.00	$20.00
Closter, Alan	69T	114	$ .30	$ .85
Closter, Alan	72T	124	$ .15	$ .50
Closter, Alan	73T	634	$ .45	$1.45
Clutterbuck, Bryan	87T	562	$ .01	$ .04
Clutterbuck, Bryan	89TTR	21	$ .01	$ .06
Clutterbuck, Bryan	90T	264	$ .01	$ .04
Clyde, David	74T	133	$ .07	$ .30
Clyde, David	75T	12	$ .07	$ .30
Clyde, David	79T	399	$ .02	$ .10
Clyde, David	80T	697	$ .01	$ .10
Coan, Gil	52T	291	$15.00	$47.50
Coan, Gil	53T	133	$4.50	$15.00
Coates, Jim	59T	525	$3.00	$9.00
Coates, Jim	60T	51	$ .45	$1.45
Coates, Jim	61T	531	$7.00	$21.00
Coates, Jim	62T	553	$3.00	$9.50
Coates, Jim	63T	237	$ .30	$ .95
Coates, Jim	67T	401	$ .30	$ .95
Cobb, Ty	73TATL	471	$ .70	$3.00

Player	Year	No.	VG	EX/MT	Player	Year	No.	VG	EX/MT
Cobb, Ty	73TATL	475	$ .60	$3.00	Colborn, Jim	73T	408	$ .07	$ .30
Cobb, Ty	76TAS	346	$ .70	$3.00	Colborn, Jim	74T	75	$ .07	$ .30
Cobb, Ty	79TRH	411	$ .15	$ .50	Colborn, Jim	75T	305	$ .07	$ .30
Cobb, Ty	79TRH	414	$ .15	$ .50	Colborn, Jim	76T	521	$ .05	$ .20
Cocanower, Jaime	84TTR	26	$ .02	$ .10	Colborn, Jim	77T	331	$ .05	$ .15
Cocanower, Jaime	85T	576	$ .01	$ .05	Colborn, Jim	78T	129	$ .02	$ .10
Cocanower, Jaime	86T	277	$ .01	$ .04	Colborn, Jim	79T	276	$ .02	$ .10
Cocanower, Jamie	87T	423	$ .01	$ .04	Colbrunn, Greg	91T	91	$ .01	$ .15
Cochrane, Dave	90T	491	$ .01	$ .10	Cole, Alex	91T	421	$ .01	$ .25
Cochrane, Mickey	76TAS	348	$ .35	$1.25	Cole, Dick	54T	84	$3.60	$10.00
Codiroli, Chris	83TTR	20	$ .02	$ .10	Cole, Dick	57T	234	$ .95	$3.50
Codiroli, Chris	84T	61	$ .01	$ .06	Coleman, Claren. ChooChoo	61T	502	$ .75	$3.00
Codiroli, Chris	85T	552	$ .01	$ .05	Coleman, Choo Choo	63T	27	$ .30	$ .95
Codiroli, Chris	86T	433	$ .01	$ .04	Coleman, Choo Choo	64T	251	$ .30	$ .95
Codiroli, Chris	87T	217	$ .01	$ .04	Coleman, Choo Choo	66T	561	$11.00	$33.00
Coffman, Kevin	88TTR	29	$ .01	$ .06	Coleman, Gerry	51Trb	18	$2.10	$6.00
Coffman, Kevin	89T	488	$ .01	$ .05	Coleman, Gordy	60T	257	$ .45	$1.45
Coggins, Frank	68T	96	$ .30	$ .85	Coleman, Gordy	61T	194	$ .35	$1.25
Coggins, Rich	73T	611	$ .45	$1.45	Coleman, Gordy	62T	508	$ .75	$2.50
Coggins, Rich	74T	353	$ .07	$ .30	Coleman, Gordy	63T	90	$ .30	$ .95
Coggins, Rich	75T	167	$ .07	$ .30	Coleman, Gordy	64T	577	$1.75	$4.50
Coggins, Rich	76T	572	$ .05	$ .20	Coleman, Gordy	65T	289	$ .35	$1.25
Cohen, Andy	60T	466	$ .95	$3.50	Coleman, Gordy	66T	494	$ .75	$2.50
Coker, Jim	60T	438	$ .75	$2.20	Coleman, Gordy	67T	61	$ .30	$ .85
Coker, Jim	61T	144	$ .35	$1.25	Coleman, Jerry	52T	237	$6.00	$8.00
Coker, Jim	63T	456	$2.50	$6.50	Coleman, Jerry	56T	316	$3.00	$9.00
Coker, Jim	64T	211	$ .30	$ .95	Coleman, Jerry	57T	192	$2.00	$6.00
Coker, Jim	65T	192	$ .30	$ .85	Coleman, Joe	53T	279	$12.50	$50.00
Coker, Jim	66T	292	$ .30	$ .95	Coleman, Joe	54T	156	$3.60	$10.00
Coker, Jimmie	67T	158	$ .30	$ .85	Coleman, Joe	55T	162	$5.25	$15.00
Colavito, Rocco (Rocky)	57T	212	$18.00	$75.00	Coleman, Joe	66T	333	$ .30	$ .95
Colavito, Rocky	58T	368	$3.50	$15.00	Coleman, Joe	67T	167	$ .30	$ .85
Colavito, Rocky	59T	166	$ .90	$3.00	Coleman, Joe	68T	573	$ .35	$1.25
Colavito, Rocky	59T	420	$2.00	$8.00	Coleman, Joe	69T	246	$ .30	$ .95
Colavito, Rocky	59T	462	$1.75	$4.50	Coleman, Joe	70T	127	$ .15	$ .50
Colavito, Rocky	60T	260	$ .75	$3.00	Coleman, Joe	71T	403	$ .15	$ .50
Colavito, Rocky	60T	400	$1.50	$6.00	Coleman, Joe	72T	96	$ .40	$1.50
Colavito, Rocky	61T	44	$6.00	$18.00	Coleman, Joe	72T	640	$ .30	$ .95
Colavito, Rocky	61T	330	$1.50	$6.00	Coleman, Joe	73T	120	$ .07	$ .30
Colavito, Rocky	62T	20	$1.25	$5.00	Coleman, Joe	74T	240	$ .07	$ .30
Colavito, Rocky	62T	314	$2.25	$6.00	Coleman, Joe	75T	42	$ .07	$ .30
Colavito, Rocky	62TAS	472	$ .75	$2.25	Coleman, Joe	76T	68	$ .07	$ .30
Colavito, Rocky	63T	4	$ .50	$2.00	Coleman, Joe	76T	456	$ .05	$ .20
Colavito, Rocky	63T	240	$1.25	$5.00	Coleman, Joe	77T	219	$ .05	$ .15
Colavito, Rocky	64T	320	$1.00	$4.00	Coleman, Joe	78T	554	$ .02	$ .10
Colavito, Rocky	65T	380	$1.00	$4.00	Coleman, Joe	79T	329	$ .02	$ .10
Colavito, Rocky	66T	150	$ .75	$3.00	Coleman, Joe	80T	542	$ .01	$ .10
Colavito, Rocky	66T	220	$ .50	$1.50	Coleman, Jr., Joe	76T	68	$ .07	$ .30
Colavito, Rocky	67T	109	$ .50	$1.50	Coleman, Paul	90T	654	$ .01	$ .35
Colavito, Rocky	67T	580	$25.00	$75.00	Coleman, Ray	52T	211	$7.00	$20.00
Colavito, Rocky	68T	99	$ .75	$2.20	Coleman, Rip	57T	354	$1.25	$4.25
Colavito, Rocky	73T	449	$ .30	$ .85	Coleman, Rip	59T	51	$1.25	$4.25
Colbern, Mike	79T	704	$ .02	$ .10	Coleman, Rip	60T	179	$ .45	$1.45
Colbern, Mike	80T	664	$ .01	$ .10	Coleman, Vince	85TTR	24	$3.00	$10.00
Colbern, Mike	81T	522	$ .01	$ .10	Coleman, Vince	86T	370	$ .50	$2.50
Colbert, Nate	66T	596	$5.00	$20.00	Coleman, Vince	86TRB	201	$ .03	$ .25
Colbert, Nate	69T	408	$ .30	$ .85	Coleman, Vince	87T	590	$ .10	$ .35
Colbert, Nate	70T	11	$ .15	$ .50	Coleman, Vince	88T	260	$ .01	$ .10
Colbert, Nate	71T	235	$ .15	$ .50	Coleman, Vince	88TBB	5	$ .01	$ .10
Colbert, Nate	72T	571	$ .30	$ .95	Coleman, Vince	88TBB	1	$ .01	$ .10
Colbert, Nate	72TIA	572	$ .30	$ .95	Coleman, Vince	89T	90	$ .01	$ .10
Colbert, Nate	73T	340	$ .07	$ .30	Coleman, Vince	89TBB	124	$ .01	$ .10
Colbert, Nate	74T	125	$ .07	$ .30	Coleman, Vince	90T	660	$ .01	$ .10
Colbert, Nate	75T	599	$ .07	$ .30	Coleman, Vince	90TRB	6	$ .01	$ .10
Colbert, Nate	76T	495	$ .05	$ .20	Coleman, Vince	91T	160	$ .01	$ .03
Colbert, Nate	77TB	433	$ .05	$ .15	Coles, Chuck	59T	120	$ .75	$2.20
Colbert, Vince	71T	231	$ .15	$ .50	Coles, Darnell	85T	108	$ .01	$ .05
Colbert, Vince	72T	84	$ .15	$ .50	Coles, Darnell	86T	337	$ .01	$ .04
Colborn, Jim	71T	38	$ .15	$ .50	Coles, Darnell	86TTR	26	$ .02	$ .10
Colborn, Jim	72T	386	$ .15	$ .50	Coles, Darnell	87	411	$ .01	$ .04

TOPPS

Player	Year	No.	VG	EX/MT
Coles, Darnell	88T	46	$ .01	$ .04
Coles, Darnell	88TBB	255	$ .01	$ .06
Coles, Darnell	89T	738	$ .01	$ .05
Coles, Darnell	89TBB	133	$ .01	$ .06
Coles, Darnell	90T	232	$ .01	$ .04
Coles, Darnell	91T	506	$ .01	$ .03
Collins, Dave	76T	363	$ .30	$ .85
Collins, Dave	77T	431	$ .05	$ .15
Collins, Dave	78T	254	$ .02	$ .10
Collins, Dave	79T	622	$ .02	$ .10
Collins, Dave	80T	73	$ .01	$ .10
Collins, Dave	81T	175	$ .01	$ .10
Collins, Dave	82T	595	$ .01	$ .07
Collins, Dave	82TTR	20	$ .02	$ .10
Collins, Dave	83T	359	$ .01	$ .07
Collins, Dave	83TTR	21	$ .02	$ .10
Collins, Dave	84T	733	$ .01	$ .06
Collins, Dave	85T	463	$ .01	$ .05
Collins, Dave	85TTR	25	$ .02	$ .10
Collins, Dave	86T	271	$ .01	$ .04
Collins, Dave	86TTR	27	$ .02	$ .10
Collins, Dave	87T	148	$ .01	$ .04
Collins, Joe	52T	202	$7.00	$20.00
Collins, Joe	53T	9	$7.00	$21.00
Collins, Joe	54T	83	$7.00	$22.00
Collins, Joe	55T	63	$3.60	$10.00
Collins, Joe	56T	21	$2.25	$6.00
Collins, Joe	57T	295	$4.25	$15.00
Collins, Kevin	65T	581	$30.00	$95.00
Collins, Kevin	69T	127	$ .30	$ .85
Collins, Kevin	70T	707	$ .75	$2.00
Collins, Kevin	71T	553	$ .35	$1.25
Collum, Jackie	57T	268	$4.25	$15.00
Colpaert, Dick	73T	608	$ .45	$1.45
Colson, Loyd	71T	111	$ .15	$ .50
Colt .45's, Houston	63T	312	$3.00	$10.00
Colton, Larry	68T	348	$ .30	$ .85
Colton, Larry	69T	454	$ .30	$ .85
Coluccio, Bob	74T	124	$ .07	$ .30
Coluccio, Bob	75T	456	$ .07	$ .30
Coluccio, Bob	76T	333	$ .05	$ .20
Combe, Geoff	81T	606	$ .01	$ .10
Combe, Geoff	82T	351	$ .01	$ .07
Combs, Earle	54T	183	$5.00	$20.00
Combs, Merrill	52T	18	$15.00	$47.50
Combs, Pat	88TTR	30	$ .10	$ .50
Combs, Pat	89TBB	227	$ .01	$ .50
Combs, Pat	89TMLD	24	$ .01	$ .35
Combs, Pat	90T	384	$ .01	$ .20
Combs, Pat	91T	571	$ .01	$ .03
Comer, Steve	79T	463	$ .02	$ .10
Comer, Steve	80T	144	$ .01	$ .10
Comer, Steve	81T	592	$ .01	$ .10
Comer, Steve	82T	16	$ .01	$ .07
Comer, Steve	83T	353	$ .01	$ .07
Comer, Steve	85T	788	$ .01	$ .05
Comer, Wayne	69T	346	$ .30	$ .85
Comer, Wayne	70T	323	$ .15	$ .50
Compton, Mike	71T	77	$ .15	$ .50
Comstock, Keith	88T	778	$ .01	$ .15
Comstock, Keith	91T	337	$ .01	$ .03
Concepcion, Dave	71T	14	$2.50	$9.00
Concepcion, Dave	72T	267	$ .50	$2.00
Concepcion, Dave	73T	554	$ .75	$3.00
Concepcion, Dave	74T	435	$ .35	$1.25
Concepcion, Dave	75T	17	$ .30	$1.00
Concepcion, Dave	76T	48	$ .08	$ .30
Concepcion, Dave	77T	560	$ .30	$ .85
Concepcion, Dave	78T	180	$ .06	$ .30
Concepcion, Dave	79T	450	$ .05	$ .25
Concepcion, Dave	80T	220	$ .05	$ .20
Concepcion, Dave	81T	375	$ .05	$ .20
Concepcion, Dave	82T	660	$ .05	$ .20
Concepcion, Dave	82TAS	340	$ .03	$ .15
Concepcion, Dave	82TIA	661	$ .02	$ .10
Concepcion, Dave	83T	720	$ .01	$ .07
Concepcion, Dave	83TAS	400	$ .01	$ .10
Concepcion, Dave	84T	55	$ .01	$ .06
Concepcion, Dave	85T	515	$ .01	$ .05
Concepcion, Dave	86T	195	$ .01	$ .04
Concepcion, Dave	87T	731	$ .01	$ .10
Concepcion, Dave	88T	422	$ .01	$ .10
Concepcion, Dave	88TBB	144	$ .01	$ .06
Concepcion, Onix	83T	52	$ .01	$ .07
Concepcion, Onix	84T	247	$ .01	$ .06
Concepcion, Onix	85T	697	$ .01	$ .05
Concepcion, Onix	86T	596	$ .01	$ .04
Cone, Dave	87TTR	24	$ .25	$1.50
Cone, Dave	88T	181	$ .05	$ .75
Cone, Dave	89T	710	$ .05	$ .25
Cone, David	90T	30	$ .01	$ .10
Cone, David	91T	680	$ .01	$ .03
Conigliaro, Bill	69T	628	$ .30	$ .95
Conigliaro, Billy	70T	317	$ .30	$ .95

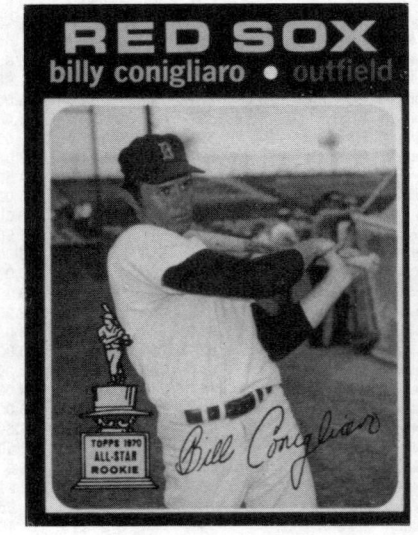

Player	Year	No.	VG	EX/MT
Conigliaro, Billy	71T	114	$ .15	$ .50
Conigliaro, Billy	72T	481	$ .15	$ .50
Conigliaro, Billy	74T	545	$ .07	$ .30
Conigliaro, Tony	64T	287	$4.00	$14.00
Conigliaro, Tony	65T	55	$ .90	$3.00
Conigliaro, Tony	66T	218	$ .75	$3.00
Conigliaro, Tony	66T	380	$ .75	$2.20
Conigliaro, Tony	67T	280	$ .45	$1.45
Conigliaro, Tony	68T	140	$ .75	$3.00
Conigliaro, Tony	69T	330	$ .45	$1.45
Conigliaro, Tony	70T	340	$ .15	$ .50
Conigliaro, Tony	71T	63	$ .15	$ .50
Conigliaro, Tony	71T	105	$ .35	$1.25
Conley, Bob	59T	121	$ .75	$2.20
Conley, Gene	53T	215	$2.25	$8.00
Conley, Gene	54T	59	$3.25	$13.50

Player	Year	No.	VG	EX/MT	Player	Year	No.	VG	EX/MT
Conley, Gene	55T	81	$2.50	$10.00	Cooper, Walker	56T	273	$2.25	$8.00
Conley, Gene	56T	17	$2.25	$6.00	Cooper, Walker	57T	380	$1.25	$4.25
Conley, Gene	57T	28	$2.00	$6.00	Cooper, Walker	60T	462	$ .95	$3.50
Conley, Gene	58T	431	$ .65	$2.00	Cora, Joey	88T	91	$ .01	$ .10
Conley, Gene	59T	492	$ .75	$2.20	Corbett, Doug	81T	162	$ .01	$ .10
Conley, Gene	60T	293	$ .75	$2.20	Corbett, Doug	82T	560	$ .01	$ .07
Conley, Gene	61T	193	$ .35	$1.25	Corbett, Doug	82TTR	21	$ .02	$ .10
Conley, Gene	62T	187	$ .45	$1.45	Corbett, Doug	83T	27	$ .01	$ .07
Conley, Gene	63T	216	$ .30	$ .95	Corbett, Doug	85T	682	$ .01	$ .05
Conley, Gene	64T	571	$2.10	$6.00	Corbett, Doug	86T	234	$ .01	$ .04
Connelly, Bill	53T	126	$4.50	$15.00	Corbett, Doug	87T	359	$ .01	$ .04
Connolly, Ed	65T	543	$1.75	$4.50	Corbett, Sherman	89T	99	$ .01	$ .05
Connors, Bill	67T	272	$ .30	$ .85	Corbin, Ray	72T	66	$ .15	$ .50
Conroy, Tim	84T	156	$ .01	$ .10	Corbin, Ray	73T	411	$ .07	$ .30
Conroy, Tim	84T	189	$ .01	$ .06	Corbin, Ray	74T	296	$ .07	$ .30
Conroy, Tim	85T	503	$ .01	$ .05	Corbin, Ray	75T	78	$ .07	$ .30
Conroy, Tim	86TTR	28	$ .02	$ .10	Corbin, Ray	76T	474	$ .05	$ .20
Conroy, Tim	87T	338	$ .01	$ .04	Corcoran, Tim	78T	515	$ .02	$ .10
Conroy, Tim	88T	658	$ .01	$ .04	Corcoran, Tim	79T	272	$ .02	$ .10
Consolo, Bill	54T	195	$3.60	$10.00	Corcoran, Tim	81T	448	$ .01	$ .10
Consolo, Bill	55T	207	$5.25	$15.00	Corcoran, Tim	85T	302	$ .01	$ .05
Consolo, Billy	57T	399	$1.25	$4.25	Corcoran, Tim	86T	664	$ .01	$ .04
Consolo, Billy	58T	148	$ .75	$3.00	Corey, Mark	79T	701	$ .02	$ .10
Consolo, Billy	59T	112	$ .75	$2.20	Corey, Mark	80T	661	$ .01	$ .10
Consolo, Billy	60T	508	$2.50	$10.00	Corey, Mark	81T	399	$ .50	$2.00
Consolo, Billy	61T	504	$ .75	$3.00	Corkins, Mike	70T	573	$ .30	$ .95
Constable, Jim	63T	411	$ .45	$1.50	Corkins, Mike	71T	179	$ .15	$ .50
Constable, Jimmy	59T	451	$ .75	$2.20	Corkins, Mike	72T	608	$ .30	$ .95
Consuegra, Sandy	56T	265	$2.25	$8.00	Corkins, Mike	73T	461	$ .07	$ .30
Coogan, Dale	52T	87	$7.00	$20.00	Corkins, Mike	74T	546	$ .07	$ .30
Cook, Cliff	61T	399	$ .75	$3.00	Cornell, Jeff	85T	514	$ .01	$ .05
Cook, Cliff	62T	41	$ .45	$1.45	Corrales, Pat	65T	107	$ .75	$3.00
Cook, Cliff	63T	566	$1.75	$4.50	Corrales, Pat	66T	137	$ .30	$ .95
Cook, Dennis	90T	633	$ .01	$ .20	Corrales, Pat	67T	78	$ .30	$ .85
Cook, Dennis	91T	467	$ .01	$ .03	Corrales, Pat	69T	382	$ .30	$ .85
Cook, Glen	86T	502	$ .01	$ .04	Corrales, Pat	70T	507	$ .30	$ .95
Cook, Ron	71T	583	$ .35	$1.25	Corrales, Pat	71T	293	$ .15	$ .50
Cook, Ron	72T	339	$ .15	$ .50	Corrales, Pat	72T	705	$ .80	$2.25
Coolbaugh, Scott	89TMLD	25	$ .01	$ .35	Corrales, Pat	72TIA	706	$ .75	$2.50
Coolbaugh, Scott	90TTR	22	$ .01	$ .15	Corrales, Pat	73T	542	$ .35	$1.25
Coolbaugh, Scott	91T	277	$ .01	$ .10	Corrales, Pat	74T	498	$ .15	$ .50
Coombs, Dan	65T	553	$1.75	$4.50	Corrales, Pat	83T	637	$ .01	$ .07
Coombs, Dan	66T	414	$ .30	$ .95	Corrales, Pat	84T	141	$ .01	$ .06
Coombs, Dan	67T	464	$ .75	$3.00	Corrales, Pat	85T	119	$ .01	$ .05
Coombs, Dan	68T	547	$ .35	$1.25	Corrales, Pat	86T	699	$ .01	$ .04
Coombs, Dan	69T	389	$ .30	$ .85	Corrales, Pat	87T	268	$ .01	$ .04
Coombs, Danny	71T	126	$ .15	$ .50	Correa, Ed	87T	334	$ .01	$ .10
Cooney, Johnny	60T	458	$ .95	$3.50	Correa, Ed	88T	227	$ .01	$ .04
Cooper, Cecil	72T	79	$45.00	$135.00	Correll, Vic	75T	177	$ .07	$ .30
Cooper, Cecil	74T	523	$ .50	$2.00	Correll, Vic	76T	608	$ .05	$ .20
Cooper, Cecil	75T	489	$ .35	$1.25	Correll, Vic	77T	364	$ .05	$ .15
Cooper, Cecil	76T	78	$ .25	$1.00	Correll, Vic	78T	527	$ .02	$ .10
Cooper, Cecil	77T	235	$ .30	$ .95	Correll, Vic	79T	281	$ .02	$ .10
Cooper, Cecil	78T	154	$ .08	$ .35	Correll, Vic	80T	419	$ .01	$ .10
Cooper, Cecil	79T	325	$ .30	$ .85	Correll, Vic	81T	628	$ .01	$ .10
Cooper, Cecil	80T	95	$ .05	$ .25	Corsi, Jim	89T	292	$ .01	$ .05
Cooper, Cecil	81T	3	$ .05	$ .25	Corsi, Jim	90T	623	$ .01	$ .04
Cooper, Cecil	81T	555	$ .03	$ .15	Cosgrove, Mike	75T	96	$ .07	$ .30
Cooper, Cecil	82T	675	$ .05	$ .25	Cosgrove, Mike	76T	122	$ .05	$ .20
Cooper, Cecil	82T	703	$ .03	$ .15	Cosgrove, Mike	77T	589	$ .05	$ .15
Cooper, Cecil	83T	190	$ .03	$ .15	Cosman, Jim	67T	384	$ .30	$ .95
Cooper, Cecil	84T	133	$ .06	$ .30	Cosman, Jim	70T	429	$ .15	$ .50
Cooper, Cecil	84T	420	$ .03	$ .15	Costello, John	89T	184	$ .01	$ .10
Cooper, Cecil	84T	710	$ .04	$ .20	Costello, John	90T	36	$ .01	$ .04
Cooper, Cecil	85T	290	$ .01	$ .10	Costo, Tim	91T	103	$ .01	$ .50
Cooper, Cecil	86T	385	$ .02	$ .20	Cotes, Eugenio	79T	723	$ .05	$ .20
Cooper, Cecil	87T	10	$ .01	$ .10	Cottier, Chuck	60T	417	$ .75	$2.20
Cooper, Cecil	88T	769	$ .01	$ .04	Cottier, Chuck	61T	13	$ .35	$1.25
Cooper, Don	82T	409	$ .01	$ .07	Cottier, Chuck	62T	27	$ .45	$1.45
Cooper, Walker	52T	294	$15.00	$47.50	Cottier, Chuck	63T	219	$ .30	$ .95

Player	Year	No.	VG	EX/MT	Player	Year	No.	VG	EX/MT
Cottier, Chuck	64T	397	$ .50	$1.45	Cox, Casey	70T	281	$ .15	$ .50
Cottier, Chuck	69T	252	$ .30	$ .95	Cox, Casey	71T	82	$ .15	$ .50
Cottier, Chuck	85T	656	$ .01	$ .05	Cox, Casey	72T	231	$ .15	$ .50
Cottier, Chuck	86T	141	$ .01	$ .04	Cox, Casey	73T	419	$ .07	$ .30
Cotto, Henry	85T	267	$ .01	$ .05	Cox, Danny	85T	499	$ .05	$ .25
Cotto, Henry	87T	174	$ .01	$ .04	Cox, Danny	86T	294	$ .01	$ .04
Cotto, Henry	88T	766	$ .01	$ .04	Cox, Danny	87T	621	$ .01	$ .04
Cotto, Henry	88TBB	125	$ .01	$ .06	Cox, Danny	88T	59	$ .01	$ .04
Cotto, Henry	88TTR	31	$ .01	$ .06	Cox, Danny	88TBB	111	$ .01	$ .06
Cotto, Henry	89T	468	$ .01	$ .05	Cox, Danny	89T	562	$ .01	$ .05
Cotto, Henry	89TBB	160	$ .01	$ .06	Cox, Danny	90T	184	$ .01	$ .04
Cotto, Henry	90T	31	$ .01	$ .04	Cox, Jeff	81T	133	$ .01	$ .10
Cotto, Henry	91T	634	$ .01	$ .03	Cox, Jim	74T	600	$1.00	$4.00
Coughtry, Marlan	62T	595	$7.00	$21.00	Cox, Larry	77T	379	$ .05	$ .15
Courtney, Clint	53T	127	$4.50	$15.00	Cox, Larry	78T	541	$ .02	$ .10
Courtney, Clint	56T	159	$2.25	$6.00	Cox, Larry	79T	489	$ .02	$ .10
Courtney, Clint	57T	51	$ .95	$3.50	Cox, Larry	80T	116	$ .01	$ .10
Courtney, Clint	58T	92	$1.25	$4.25	Cox, Larry	81T	249	$ .01	$ .10
Courtney, Clint	59T	483	$ .75	$2.20	Cox, Larry	81TTR	749	$ .02	$ .10
Courtney, Clint	60T	344	$ .75	$2.20	Cox, Ted	78T	706	$ .02	$ .10
Courtney, Clint	61T	342	$ .35	$1.25	Cox, Ted	79T	79	$ .02	$ .10
Covington, Wes	57T	283	$4.25	$15.00					
Covington, Wes	58T	140	$ .65	$2.00					
Covington, Wes	59T	290	$ .75	$2.20					
Covington, Wes	59TAS	565	$2.50	$10.00					
Covington, Wes	60T	158	$ .45	$1.45					
Covington, Wes	61T	296	$ .35	$1.25					
Covington, Wes	62T	157	$ .45	$1.45					
Covington, Wes	63T	529	$1.75	$4.50					
Covington, Wes	64T	208	$ .30	$ .95					
Covington, Wes	65T	583	$1.75	$4.50					
Covington, Wes	66T	52	$ .35	$1.25					
Covington, Wes	66T	484	$ .50	$ .25					
Cowan, Billy	64T	192	$ .30	$ .95					
Cowan, Billy	65T	186	$ .30	$ .85					
Cowan, Billy	69T	643	$ .30	$ .95					
Cowan, Billy	71T	614	$ .35	$1.25					
Cowan, Billy	72T	19	$ .15	$ .50					
Cowens, Al	75T	437	$ .07	$ .30					
Cowens, Al	76T	648	$ .05	$ .20					
Cowens, Al	77T	262	$ .05	$ .15					
Cowens, Al	78T	46	$ .02	$ .10					
Cowens, Al	79T	490	$ .02	$ .10					
Cowens, Al	80T	330	$ .01	$ .10					
Cowens, Al	81T	123	$ .01	$ .10					
Cowens, Al	82T	575	$ .01	$ .07					
Cowens, Al	82TTR	22	$ .02	$ .10					
Cowens, Al	83T	763	$ .01	$ .07					
Cowens, Al	84T	622	$ .01	$ .06					
Cowens, Al	85T	224	$ .01	$ .05					
Cowens, Al	86T	92	$ .01	$ .04					
Cowley, Joe	83T	288	$ .01	$ .07	Cox, Ted	80T	252	$ .01	$ .10
Cowley, Joe	85T	769	$ .01	$ .05	Cox, Terry	71T	559	$ .35	$1.25
Cowley, Joe	86T	427	$ .01	$ .04	Craddock, Walt	59T	281	$ .75	$2.20
Cowley, Joe	86TTR	29	$ .02	$ .10	Craft, Harry	62T	12	$ .45	$1.45
Cowley, Joe	87T	27	$ .01	$ .04	Craft, Harry	63T	491	$2.50	$6.50
Cox, Billy	51Tbb	48	$5.00	$20.00	Craft, Harry	64T	298	$ .30	$ .95
Cox, Billy	52T	232	$7.50	$22.00	Craig, Pete	65T	466	$ .75	$3.00
Cox, Bobby	69T	237	$ .15	$ .50	Craig, Pete	66T	11	$ .30	$ .95
Cox, Bobby	78T	93	$ .02	$ .10	Craig, Pete	67T	459	$1.50	$5.50
Cox, Bobby	83T	606	$ .01	$ .07	Craig, Rodney	80T	672	$ .01	$ .10
Cox, Bobby	84T	202	$ .01	$ .06	Craig, Roger	56T	63	$6.00	$25.00
Cox, Bobby	85T	411	$ .01	$ .05	Craig, Roger	57T	173	$3.00	$12.00
Cox, Bobby	86T	471	$ .01	$ .04	Craig, Roger	58T	194	$ .65	$2.00
Cox, Bobby	90TTR	23	$ .01	$ .05	Craig, Roger	60T	62	$ .75	$3.00
Cox, Bobby	91T	759	$ .01	$ .03	Craig, Roger	61T	543	$10.00	$30.00
Cox, Casey	66T	549	$5.00	$20.00	Craig, Roger	62T	183	$ .75	$2.20
Cox, Casey	67T	414	$ .30	$ .95	Craig, Roger	63T	197	$ .75	$3.00
Cox, Casey	68T	66	$ .30	$ .85	Craig, Roger	64T	295	$ .45	$1.45
Cox, Casey	69T	383	$ .30	$ .85	Craig, Roger	65T	411	$ .75	$3.00

TED COX

3B-OF

INDIANS

Player	Year	No.	VG	EX/MT	Player	Year	No.	VG	EX/MT
Craig, Roger	66T	543	$10.00	$30.00	Cromartie, Warren	80T	180	$ .01	$ .10
Craig, Roger	74T	31	$ .07	$ .30	Cromartie, Warren	81T	345	$ .01	$ .10
Craig, Roger	81T	282	$ .01	$ .10	Cromartie, Warren	82T	526	$ .01	$ .07
Craig, Roger	86T	111	$ .01	$ .04	Cromartie, Warren	82T	695	$ .01	$ .07
Craig, Roger	87T	193	$ .01	$ .04	Cromartie, Warren	83T	495	$ .01	$ .07
Craig, Roger	88T	654	$ .01	$ .04	Cromartie, Warren	84T	287	$ .01	$ .06
Craig, Roger	89T	744	$ .01	$ .05	Crone, Ray	54T	206	$3.60	$10.00
Craig, Roger	90T	351	$ .01	$ .04	Crone, Ray	55T	149	$2.00	$6.00
Craig, Roger	91T	579	$ .01	$ .03	Crone, Ray	56T	76	$2.25	$6.00
Cram, Jerry	71T	247	$ .15	$ .50	Crone, Ray	57T	68	$ .95	$3.50
Crandall, Del	52T	162	$7.00	$21.00	Crone, Ray	58T	272	$ .75	$3.00
Crandall, Del	53T	197	$2.25	$8.00	Crosby, Ed	71T	672	$ .75	$2.50
Crandall, Del	54T	12	$4.25	$15.00	Crosby, Ed	73T	599	$ .45	$1.45
Crandall, Del	56T	175	$1.50	$4.00	Crosby, Ed	76T	457	$ .05	$ .20
Crandall, Del	57T	133	$2.00	$6.00	Crosby, Ken	76T	593	$ .15	$ .50
Crandall, Del	58T	351	$8.00	$22.00	Crosetti, Frank	52T	384	$80.00	$235.00
Crandall, Del	58T	390	$ .65	$2.00	Crosetti, Frank	60T	465	$2.50	$9.00
Crandall, Del	59T	425	$ .90	$3.00	Crowe, George	52T	360	$40.00	$140.00
Crandall, Del	59TAS	567	$2.50	$10.00	Crowe, George	53T	3	$5.00	$20.00
Crandall, Del	60T	170	$ .90	$3.00	Crowe, George	56T	254	$3.00	$9.00
Crandall, Del	60TAS	568	$2.50	$10.00	Crowe, George	57T	73	$ .95	$3.50
Crandall, Del	61T	390	$ .90	$3.00	Crowe, George	58T	12	$1.25	$4.25
Crandall, Del	61TAS	583	$7.00	$21.00	Crowe, George	59T	337	$ .75	$2.20
Crandall, Del	62T	351	$ .90	$3.00	Crowe, George	60T	419	$ .75	$2.20
Crandall, Del	62T	443	$ .75	$2.25	Crowe, George	61T	52	$ .35	$1.25
Crandall, Del	63T	460	$ .60	$5.00	Crowley, Terry	70T	121	$ .15	$ .50
Crandall, Del	64T	169	$ .45	$1.45	Crowley, Terry	71T	453	$ .15	$ .50
Crandall, Del	65T	68	$ .30	$ .85	Crowley, Terry	72T	628	$ .30	$ .95
Crandall, Del	66T	339	$ .30	$ .95	Crowley, Terry	73T	302	$ .07	$ .30
Crandall, Del	73T	646	$ .75	$3.00	Crowley, Terry	74T	648	$ .07	$ .30
Crandall, Del	74T	99	$ .07	$ .30	Crowley, Terry	74TTR	648	$ .07	$ .30
Crandall, Del	84T	721	$ .01	$ .06	Crowley, Terry	75T	447	$ .07	$ .30
Crawford, Jim	74T	279	$ .07	$ .30	Crowley, Terry	76T	491	$ .05	$ .20
Crawford, Jim	76T	428	$ .05	$ .20	Crowley, Terry	79T	91	$ .02	$ .10
Crawford, Jim	76TTR	428	$ .05	$ .20	Crowley, Terry	80T	188	$ .01	$ .10
Crawford, Jim	77T	69	$ .05	$ .15	Crowley, Terry	81T	543	$ .01	$ .10
Crawford, Steve	82T	157	$ .01	$ .07	Crowley, Terry	82T	232	$ .01	$ .07
Crawford, Steve	83T	419	$ .01	$ .07	Crowley, Terry	83T	372	$ .01	$ .07
Crawford, Steve	85T	661	$ .01	$ .05	Crowley, Terry	83TTR	22	$ .02	$ .10
Crawford, Steve	86T	91	$ .01	$ .04	Crowley, Terry	84T	732	$ .01	$ .06
Crawford, Steve	87T	589	$ .01	$ .04	Cruz, Hector	76T	598	$ .05	$ .20
Crawford, Steve	88T	299	$ .01	$ .04	Cruz, Hector	77T	624	$ .05	$ .15
Crawford, Steve	91T	718	$ .01	$ .03	Cruz, Hector	78T	257	$ .02	$ .10
Crawford, Willie	65T	453	$ .75	$3.00	Cruz, Hector	79T	436	$ .02	$ .10
Crawford, Willie	68T	417	$ .30	$ .85	Cruz, Hector	80T	516	$ .01	$ .10
Crawford, Willie	69T	327	$ .30	$ .95	Cruz, Hector	81T	52	$ .01	$ .10
Crawford, Willie	70T	34	$ .15	$ .50	Cruz, Hector	81TTR	750	$ .02	$ .10
Crawford, Willie	71T	519	$ .15	$ .50	Cruz, Hector	82T	663	$ .01	$ .07
Crawford, Willie	72T	669	$ .90	$3.00	Cruz, Henry	76T	590	$ .15	$ .50
Crawford, Willie	73T	639	$ .45	$1.45	Cruz, Henry	78T	316	$ .02	$ .10
Crawford, Willie	74T	480	$ .07	$ .30	Cruz, Jose	72T	107	$ .75	$3.00
Crawford, Willie	75T	186	$ .07	$ .30	Cruz, Jose	73T	292	$ .15	$ .50
Crawford, Willie	76T	76	$ .05	$ .20	Cruz, Jose	74T	464	$ .15	$ .50
Crawford, Willie	77T	642	$ .05	$ .15	Cruz, Jose	75T	514	$ .30	$ .85
Crawford, Willie	78T	507	$ .02	$ .10	Cruz, Jose	76T	321	$ .15	$ .50
Crews, Tim	88T	57	$ .01	$ .25	Cruz, Jose	77T	42	$ .05	$ .15
Crews, Tim	89T	22	$ .01	$ .05	Cruz, Jose	78T	625	$ .02	$ .10
Crews, Tim	90T	551	$ .01	$ .04	Cruz, Jose	79T	289	$ .02	$ .10
Crews, Tim	91T	737	$ .01	$ .03	Cruz, Jose	80T	722	$ .01	$ .10
Crider, Jerry	69T	491	$ .30	$ .85	Cruz, Jose	81T	105	$ .01	$ .10
Crider, Jerry	71T	113	$ .15	$ .50	Cruz, Jose	82T	325	$ .01	$ .07
Crim, Chuck	87TTR	25	$ .01	$ .05	Cruz, Jose	83T	585	$ .01	$ .07
Crim, Chuck	88T	286	$ .01	$ .04	Cruz, Jose	84T	66	$ .01	$ .06
Crim, Chuck	89T	466	$ .01	$ .05	Cruz, Jose	84T	422	$ .01	$ .06
Crim, Chuck	90T	768	$ .01	$ .04	Cruz, Jose	85T	95	$ .01	$ .05
Crim, Chuck	91T	644	$ .01	$ .03	Cruz, Jose	86T	640	$ .01	$ .04
Crimian, Jack	56T	319	$2.25	$8.00	Cruz, Jose	87T	670	$ .01	$ .04
Crimian, Jack	57T	297	$4.25	$15.00	Cruz, Jose	88T	278	$ .01	$ .04
Cromartie, Warren	78T	468	$ .02	$ .10	Cruz, Julio	78T	687	$ .02	$ .10
Cromartie, Warren	79T	76	$ .02	$ .10	Cruz, Julio	79T	583	$ .02	$ .10

Player	Year	No.	VG	EX/MT	Player	Year	No.	VG	EX/MT
Cruz, Julio	80T	32	$ .01	$ .10	Cubs, Team	70T	593	$ .75	$2.20
Cruz, Julio	81T	397	$ .01	$ .10	Cubs, Team	71T	502	$ .45	$1.45
Cruz, Julio	82T	130	$ .01	$ .07	Cubs, Team	72T	192	$ .15	$ .50
Cruz, Julio	83T	414	$ .01	$ .07	Cubs, Team	73T	464	$ .15	$ .50
Cruz, Julio	83TTR	23	$ .02	$ .10	Cubs, Team	74T	211	$ .15	$ .50
Cruz, Julio	84T	257	$ .01	$ .06	Cubs, Team Checklist	75T	638	$ .15	$ .50
Cruz, Julio	85T	749	$ .01	$ .05	Cubs, Team Checklist	76T	277	$ .35	$1.25
Cruz, Julio	86T	14	$ .01	$ .04	Cubs, Team Checklist	77T	518	$ .15	$ .50
Cruz, Julio	87T	790	$ .01	$ .04	Cubs, Team Checklist	78T	302	$ .05	$ .25
Cruz, Todd	80T	492	$ .01	$ .10	Cubs, Team Checklist	79T	551	$ .05	$ .25
Cruz, Todd	81T	571	$ .01	$ .10	Cubs, Team Checklist	80T	381	$ .05	$ .25
Cruz, Todd	83T	132	$ .01	$ .07	Cubs, Team Checklist	81T	676	$ .02	$ .20
Cruz, Todd	84T	773	$ .01	$ .06	Cubs, Team Leaders	86T	636	$ .01	$ .04
Cruz, Todd	85T	366	$ .01	$ .05	Cubs, Team Leaders	87T	581	$ .01	$ .04
Cruz, Victor	79T	714	$ .02	$ .10	Cubs, Team Leaders	88T	171	$ .01	$ .04
					Cubs, Team Leaders	89T	549	$ .01	$ .05
					Cuccinello, Tony	60T	458	$ .95	$3.50
					Cuellar, Bobby	80T	665	$ .01	$ .10
					Cueller (Cuellar), Mike	59T	518	$4.00	$15.00
					Cuellar, Mike	60T	398	$ .45	$1.35
					Cuellar, Mike	65T	337	$ .45	$1.45
					Cuellar, Mike	66T	566	$3.00	$9.50
					Cuellar, Mike	67T	97	$ .35	$1.25
					Cuellar, Mike	67T	234	$1.75	$4.50
					Cuellar, Mike	68T	274	$ .30	$ .85
					Cuellar, Mike	69T	453	$ .45	$1.45
					Cuellar, Mike	69T	532	$ .20	$ .50
					Cuellar, Mike	70T	68	$ .75	$3.00
					Cuellar, Mike	70T	70	$ .75	$3.00
					Cuellar, Mike	70T	590	$ .25	$ .60
					Cuellar, Mike	71T	69	$ .15	$ .50
					Cuellar, Mike	71T	170	$ .15	$ .50
					Cuellar, Mike	72T	70	$ .30	$ .85
					Cuellar, Mike	73T	470	$ .15	$ .50
					Cuellar, Mike	74T	560	$ .30	$ .85
					Cuellar (Cueller), Mike	75T	410	$ .05	$ .25
					Cuellar, Mike	76T	285	$ .15	$ .50
					Cuellar, Mike	77T	162	$ .05	$ .15
					Cullen, Jack	63T	54	$1.50	$4.00
					Cullen, Jack	66T	31	$ .30	$ .95
					Cullen, Tim	67T	167	$ .30	$ .85
					Cullen, Tim	68T	209	$ .30	$ .85
					Cullen, Tim	69T	586	$ .30	$ .95
					Cullen, Tim	70T	49	$ .15	$ .50
					Cullen, Tim	71T	566	$ .35	$1.25
Cruz, Victor	80T	99	$ .01	$ .10	Cullen, Tim	72T	461	$ .15	$ .50
Cruz, Victor	81T	252	$ .01	$ .10	Culp, Ray	63T	29	$ .45	$1.45
Cruz, Victor	81TTR	751	$ .02	$ .10	Culp, Ray	64T	412	$ .50	$1.45
Cruz, Victor	82T	263	$ .01	$ .07	Culp, Ray	65T	505	$ .75	$3.00
Cubbage, Mike	75T	617	$ .45	$1.45	Culp, Ray	66T	4	$ .30	$ .95
Cubbage, Mike	76T	615	$ .05	$ .20	Culp, Ray	67T	168	$ .30	$ .85
Cubbage, Mike	77T	149	$ .05	$ .15	Culp, Ray	68T	272	$ .30	$ .85
Cubbage, Mike	78T	219	$ .02	$ .10	Culp, Ray	69T	391	$ .30	$ .85
Cubbage, Mike	79T	362	$ .02	$ .10	Culp, Ray	70T	144	$ .15	$ .50
Cubbage, Mike	80T	503	$ .01	$ .10	Culp, Ray	71T	660	$ .75	$2.50
Cubbage, Mike	81T	657	$ .01	$ .10	Culp, Ray	72T	2	$ .15	$ .50
Cubbage, Mike	81TTR	752	$ .02	$ .10	Culver, George	65T	166	$ .75	$2.20
Cubbage, Mike	82T	43	$ .01	$ .07	Culver, George	67T	499	$ .75	$3.00
Cubs, Team	56T	11	$3.25	$9.50	Culver, George	68T	319	$ .30	$ .85
Cubs, Team	57T	183	$3.60	$10.00	Culver, George	69T	635	$ .30	$ .95
Cubs, Team	58T	327	$1.75	$6.50	Culver, George	70T	92	$ .15	$ .50
Cubs, Team	59T	304	$2.25	$9.50	Culver, George	71T	291	$ .15	$ .50
Cubs, Team	60T	513	$5.00	$16.00	Culver, George	72T	732	$ .75	$2.50
Cubs, Team	61T	122	$ .90	$3.50	Culver, George	73T	242	$ .07	$ .30
Cubs, Team	62T	552	$3.50	$15.00	Culver, George	74T	632	$ .07	$ .30
Cubs, Team	63T	222	$1.25	$4.25	Cumberland, John	69T	114	$ .30	$ .85
Cubs, Team	64T	237	$1.25	$4.25	Cumberland, John	71T	108	$ .15	$ .50
Cubs, Team	65T	91	$ .90	$3.00	Cumberland, John	72T	403	$ .15	$ .50
Cubs, Team	66T	204	$ .65	$1.75	Cummings, Steve	89TMLD	26	$ .01	$ .15
Cubs, Team	67T	354	$ .90	$3.00	Cummings, Steve	90T	374	$ .01	$ .10

VICTOR CRUZ
PITCHER
INDIANS

Player	Year	No.	VG	EX/MT	Player	Year	No.	VG	EX/MT
Cunningham, Earl	90T	134	$ .01	$ .35	Daley, Pete	59T	276	$ .75	$2.20
Cunningham, Joe	55T	37	$3.60	$10.00	Daley, Pete	60T	108	$ .45	$1.45
Cunningham, Joe	57T	304	$4.25	$15.00	Daley, Pete	61T	158	$ .35	$1.25
Cunningham, Joe	58T	168	$ .65	$2.00	Dalkowski, Steve	63T	496	$2.50	$6.50
Cunningham, Joe	59T	285	$ .90	$3.00	Dalrymple, Clay	60T	523	$2.50	$10.00
Cunningham, Joe	60T	40	$ .75	$3.00	Dalrymple, Clay	61T	299	$ .35	$1.25
Cunningham, Joe	60TAS	562	$2.50	$10.00	Dalrymple, Clay	62T	434	$ .75	$2.50
Cunningham, Joe	61T	520	$ .90	$3.00	Dalrymple, Clay	63T	192	$ .30	$ .95
Cunningham, Joe	62T	195	$ .75	$3.00	Dalrymple, Clay	64T	191	$ .30	$ .95
Cunningham, Joe	63T	100	$ .35	$1.25	Dalrymple, Clay	65T	372	$ .35	$1.25
Cunningham, Joe	64T	340	$ .30	$ .95	Dalrymple, Clay	66T	202	$ .30	$ .95
Cunningham, Joe	65T	496	$ .75	$3.00	Dalrymple, Clay	67T	53	$ .30	$ .85
Cunningham, Joe	66T	531	$3.00	$8.50	Dalrymple, Clay	68T	567	$ .35	$1.25
Curry, Steve	89T	471	$ .01	$ .05	Dalrymple, Clay	69T	151	$ .75	$2.25
Curry, Tony	60T	541	$2.50	$10.00	Dalrymple, Clayton	70T	319	$ .15	$ .50
Curry, Tony	61T	262	$ .35	$1.25	Dalrymple, Clay	71T	617	$ .35	$1.25
Curtis, Jack	61T	533	$7.00	$21.00	Daniels, Bennie	58T	392	$ .75	$3.00
Curtis, Jack	62T	372	$ .75	$2.50	Daniels, Bennie	59T	122	$ .75	$2.20
Curtis, John	72T	724	$1.25	$4.25	Daniels, Bennie	60T	91	$ .45	$1.45
Curtis, John	73T	143	$ .07	$ .30	Daniels, Bennie	61T	368	$ .35	$1.25
Curtis, John	74T	373	$ .07	$ .30	Daniels, Bennie	62T	378	$ .75	$2.50
Curtis, John	74TTR	373	$ .07	$ .30	Daniels, Bennie	63T	497	$2.50	$6.50
Curtis, John	75T	381	$ .07	$ .30	Daniels, Bennie	64T	587	$2.00	$8.00
Curtis, John	76T	239	$ .05	$ .20	Daniels, Bennie	65T	129	$ .30	$ .85
Curtis, John	77T	324	$ .05	$ .15	Daniels, Kal	87T	466	$ .25	$1.00
Curtis, John	78T	486	$ .02	$ .10					
Curtis, John	79T	649	$ .02	$ .10					
Curtis, John	80T	12	$ .01	$ .10					
Curtis, John	81T	531	$ .01	$ .10					
Curtis, John	82T	219	$ .01	$ .07					
Curtis, John	83T	777	$ .01	$ .07					
Curtis, John	84T	158	$ .01	$ .06					
Cuyler, Milt	91T	684	$ .01	$ .15					
D'Acquisto, John	74T	608	$ .07	$ .30					
D'Acquisto, John	75T	372	$ .07	$ .30					
D'Acquisto, John	76T	628	$ .05	$ .20					
D'Acquisto, John	77T	19	$ .05	$ .15					
D'Acquisto, John	79T	506	$ .02	$ .10					
D'Acquisto, John	80T	339	$ .01	$ .10					
D'Acquisto, John	81T	427	$ .01	$ .10					
D'Acquisto, John	82T	58	$ .01	$ .07					
Daboll, Dennis	65T	561	$2.50	$10.00					
Dade, Paul	78T	662	$ .02	$ .10					
Dade, Paul	79T	13	$ .02	$ .10					
Dade, Paul	80T	254	$ .01	$ .10					
Dade, Paul	81T	496	$ .01	$ .10					
Dailey, Bill	63T	391	$ .45	$1.50					
Dailey, Bill	64T	156	$ .30	$ .95					
Dal Canton, Bruce	69T	468	$ .30	$ .85					
Dal Canton, Bruce	70T	52	$ .15	$ .50					
Dal Canton, Bruce	71T	168	$ .15	$ .50					
Dal Canton, Bruce	72T	717	$ .75	$2.50					
Dal Canton, Bruce	73T	487	$ .07	$ .30					
Dal Canton, Bruce	74T	308	$ .07	$ .30					
Dal Canton, Bruce	75T	472	$ .07	$ .30					
Dal Canton, Bruce	76T	486	$ .05	$ .20	Daniels, Kal	88T	622	$ .01	$ .15
Dal Canton, Bruce	77T	114	$ .05	$ .15	Daniels, Kal	88TBB	48	$ .01	$ .10
Dalena, Pete	89TMLD	27	$ .01	$ .15	Daniels, Kal	89T	45	$ .01	$ .06
Daley, Bud	58T	222	$ .75	$3.00	Daniels, Kal	89TBB	323	$ .01	$ .06
Daley, Bud	59T	263	$ .75	$2.20	Daniels, Kal	90T	585	$ .01	$ .04
Daley, Bud	60T	8	$ .45	$1.45	Daniels, Kal	91T	245	$ .01	$ .03
Daley, Bud	61T	48	$ .75	$3.00	Darcy, Pat	75T	615	$ .30	$ .95
Daley, Bud	61T	422	$ .75	$3.00	Darcy, Pat	76T	538	$ .05	$ .20
Daley, Bud	62T	376	$ .75	$2.50	Dark, Al	52T	351	$60.00	$175.00
Daley, Bud	63T	38	$ .30	$ .95	Dark, Al	53T	109	$3.50	$12.00
Daley, Bud	64T	164	$ .30	$ .95	Dark, Al	56T	148	$1.50	$4.50
Daley, Bud	65T	262	$ .35	$1.25	Dark, Al	57T	98	$2.00	$6.00
Daley, Pete	55T	206	$5.25	$15.00	Dark, Al	58T	125	$ .65	$2.00
Daley, Pete	57T	388	$1.25	$4.25	Dark, Al	59T	502	$ .90	$3.00
Daley, Pete	58T	73	$1.25	$4.25	Dark, Al	60T	472	$1.25	$4.25

Player	Year	No.	VG	EX/MT	Player	Year	No.	VG	EX/MT
Dark, Al	61T	220	$ .35	$1.25	Davalillo, Vic	69T	275	$ .30	$ .95
Dark, Al	62T	322	$ .75	$3.00	Davalillo, Vic	70T	256	$ .15	$ .50
Dark, Al	63T	258	$ .35	$1.25	Davalillo, Vic	71T	4	$ .15	$ .50
Dark, Al	64T	529	$1.75	$4.50	Davalillo, Vic	72T	785	$ .75	$2.50
Dark, Al	66T	433	$ .45	$1.45	Davalillo, Vic	73T	163	$ .07	$ .30
Dark, Al	67T	389	$ .30	$ .95	Davalillo, Vic	74T	444	$ .07	$ .30
Dark, Al	69T	91	$ .30	$ .95	Davalillo, Vic	78T	539	$ .02	$ .10
Dark, Alvin	68T	237	$ .30	$ .95	Davalillo, Vic	79T	228	$ .02	$ .10
Dark, Alvin	70T	524	$ .15	$ .50	DaVanon, Jerry	69T	637	$ .30	$ .95
Dark, Alvin	71T	397	$ .15	$ .50	DaVanon, Jerry	71T	32	$ .15	$ .50
Dark, Alvin	78T	467	$ .02	$ .10	DaVanon, Jerry	76T	551	$ .05	$ .20
Darling, Ron	84TTR	27	$1.00	$4.00	DaVanon, Jerry	77T	283	$ .05	$ .15
Darling, Ron	85T	415	$ .10	$ .50	Davenport, Jim	58T	413	$ .75	$3.00
Darling, Ron	86T	225	$ .01	$ .10	Davenport, Jim	59T	198	$ .75	$2.20
Darling, Ron	87T	75	$ .07	$ .30	Davenport, Jim	60T	154	$ .45	$1.45
Darling, Ron	88T	685	$ .01	$ .10	Davenport, Jim	61T	55	$ .35	$1.25
Darling, Ron	88TBB	85	$ .01	$ .10	Davenport, Jim	62T	9	$ .45	$1.45
Darling, Ron	89T	105	$ .01	$ .10	Davenport, Jim	63T	388	$ .45	$1.50
Darling, Ron	89TBB	166	$ .01	$ .06	Davenport, Jim	64T	82	$ .30	$ .95
Darling, Ron	90T	330	$ .01	$ .06	Davenport, Jim	65T	213	$ .35	$1.25
Darling, Ron	91T	735	$ .01	$ .03	Davenport, Jim	66T	176	$ .30	$ .95
Darwin, Bobby	69T	641	$ .30	$ .95	Davenport, Jim	67T	441	$ .30	$ .95
Darwin, Bobby	73T	228	$ .07	$ .30	Davenport, Jim	68T	525	$ .35	$1.25
Darwin, Bobby	74T	527	$ .07	$ .30	Davenport, Jim	69T	102	$ .30	$ .85
Darwin, Bobby	75T	346	$ .07	$ .30	Davenport, Jim	70T	378	$ .15	$ .50
Darwin, Bobby	76T	63	$ .05	$ .20	Davenport, Jim	85TTR	27	$ .02	$ .10
Darwin, Bobby	77T	617	$ .05	$ .15	David, Andre	85T	43	$ .01	$ .05
Darwin, Danny	79T	713	$ .05	$ .20	Davidson, Bobby	89TMLD	29	$ .01	$ .15
Darwin, Danny	80T	498	$ .01	$ .10	Davidson, Mark	88T	19	$ .01	$ .04
Darwin, Danny	81T	22	$ .01	$ .10	Davidson, Mark	89T	451	$ .01	$ .05
Darwin, Danny	82T	298	$ .01	$ .07	Davidson, Mark	89TBB	320	$ .01	$ .06
Darwin, Danny	83T	609	$ .01	$ .07	Davidson, Mark	90T	267	$ .01	$ .04
Darwin, Danny	84T	377	$ .01	$ .06	Davidson, Mark	91T	678	$ .01	$ .03
Darwin, Danny	85T	227	$ .01	$ .05	Davidson, Ted	65T	243	$ .90	$3.00
Darwin, Danny	85TTR	26	$ .02	$ .10	Davidson, Ted	66T	89	$ .30	$ .95
Darwin, Danny	86T	519	$ .01	$ .04	Davidson, Ted	67T	519	$ .75	$3.00
Darwin, Danny	87T	157	$ .01	$ .04	Davidson, Ted	68T	48	$ .30	$ .85
Darwin, Danny	88T	461	$ .01	$ .04	Davie, Jerry	59T	256	$ .75	$2.20
Darwin, Danny	89T	719	$ .01	$ .05	Davie, Jerry	60T	301	$ .75	$2.20
Darwin, Danny	90T	64	$ .01	$ .04	Davis, Alvin	84TTR	28	$1.50	$6.00
Darwin, Danny	91T	666	$ .01	$ .03	Davis, Alvin	85T	145	$ .50	$1.75
Dascenzo, Doug	89T	149	$ .01	$ .15	Davis, Alvin	86T	440	$ .02	$ .30
Dascenzo, Doug	90T	762	$ .01	$ .04	Davis, Alvin	87T	235	$ .01	$ .15
Dascenzo, Doug	91T	437	$ .01	$ .03	Davis, Alvin	88T	785	$ .01	$ .10
Datz, Jeff	89TMLD	28	$ .01	$ .15	Davis, Alvin	88TBB	64	$ .01	$ .06
Dauer, Rich	77T	477	$ .05	$ .15	Davis, Alvin	89T	687	$ .01	$ .05
Dauer, Rich	78T	237	$ .02	$ .10	Davis, Alvin	89TBB	218	$ .01	$ .06
Dauer, Rich	79T	666	$ .02	$ .10	Davis, Alvin	90T	373	$ .01	$ .04
Dauer, Rich	80T	102	$ .01	$ .10	Davis, Alvin	91T	515	$ .01	$ .03
Dauer, Rich	81T	314	$ .01	$ .10	Davis, Bill	65T	546	$1.75	$4.50
Dauer, Rich	82T	8	$ .01	$ .07	Davis, Bill	66T	44	$ .30	$ .95
Dauer, Rich	83T	579	$ .01	$ .07	Davis, Bill	67T	253	$ .30	$ .85
Dauer, Rich	84T	723	$ .01	$ .06	Davis, Bill	68T	432	$ .30	$ .85
Dauer, Rich	85T	494	$ .01	$ .05	Davis, Bill	69T	304	$ .30	$ .95
Dauer, Rich	86T	251	$ .01	$ .04	Davis, Bob	61T	246	$ .35	$1.25
Daugherty, Jack	90T	52	$ .01	$ .04	Davis, Bob	76T	472	$ .05	$ .20
Daugherty, Jack	91T	622	$ .01	$ .03	Davis, Bob	77T	78	$ .05	$ .15
Daulton, Darren	86T	264	$ .01	$ .04	Davis, Bob	78T	713	$ .02	$ .10
Daulton, Darren	87T	636	$ .01	$ .04	Davis, Bob	80T	351	$ .01	$ .10
Daulton, Darren	88T	468	$ .01	$ .04	Davis, Bob	81T	221	$ .01	$ .10
Daulton, Darren	89T	187	$ .01	$ .05	Davis, Brock	63T	553	$60.00	$225.00
Daulton, Darren	90T	542	$ .01	$ .04	Davis, Brock	71T	576	$ .35	$1.25
Daulton, Darren	91T	89	$ .01	$ .03	Davis, Brock	72T	161	$ .15	$ .50
Davalillo, Vic	63T	324	$ .45	$1.50	Davis, Brock	73T	366	$ .07	$ .30
Davalillo, Vic	64T	435	$ .50	$1.45	Davis, Butch	85T	49	$ .01	$ .05
Davalillo, Vic	65T	128	$ .30	$ .85	Davis, Chili	82T	171	$ .15	$ .75
Davalillo, Vic	66T	216	$1.00	$4.00	Davis, Chili	82TTR	23	$ .30	$ .85
Davalillo, Vic	66T	325	$ .30	$ .95	Davis, Chili	83T	115	$ .01	$ .07
Davalillo, Vic	67T	69	$ .30	$ .85	Davis, Chili	84T	494	$ .01	$ .06
Davalillo, Vic	68T	397	$ .30	$ .85	Davis, Chili	85T	245	$ .01	$ .05

Player	Year	No.	VG	EX/MT	Player	Year	No.	VG	EX/MT
Davis, Chili	87T	672	$ .01	$ .04	Davis, Mike	84T	558	$ .01	$ .06
Davis, Chili	88T	15	$ .01	$ .04	Davis, Mike	85T	778	$ .01	$ .05
Davis, Chili	88TBB	235	$ .01	$ .06	Davis, Mike	86T	165	$ .01	$ .04
Davis, Chili	88TTR	32	$ .01	$ .06	Davis, Mike	87T	83	$ .01	$ .04
Davis, Chili	89T	525	$ .01	$ .05	Davis, Mike	88T	448	$ .01	$ .04
Davis, Chili	89TBB	294	$ .01	$ .06	Davis, Mike	88TBB	154	$ .01	$ .06
Davis, Chili	90T	765	$ .01	$ .04	Davis, Mike	88TTR	33	$ .01	$ .06
Davis, Chili	91T	355	$ .01	$ .03	Davis, Mike	89T	277	$ .01	$ .05
Davis, Dick	79T	474	$ .02	$ .10	Davis, Mike	89TBB	225	$ .01	$ .06
Davis, Dick	80T	553	$ .01	$ .10	Davis, Mike	90T	697	$ .01	$ .04
Davis, Dick	81T	183	$ .01	$ .10	Davis, Ron	67T	298	$ .30	$ .85
Davis, Dick	81TTR	753	$ .02	$ .10	Davis, Ron	68T	21	$ .30	$ .85
Davis, Dick	82T	352	$ .01	$ .07	Davis, Ron	69T	553	$ .30	$ .95
Davis, Dick	82TTR	24	$ .02	$ .10					
Davis, Dick	83T	667	$ .01	$ .07					
Davis, Eric	85T	627	$3.00	$12.50					
Davis, Eric	86T	28	$ .50	$2.00					
Davis, Eric	87T	412	$ .25	$1.00					
Davis, Eric	88T	150	$ .15	$ .75					
Davis, Eric	88TBB	20	$ .30	$ .85					
Davis, Eric	89T	330	$ .05	$ .25					
Davis, Eric	89TBB	273	$ .01	$ .35					
Davis, Eric	90T	260	$ .01	$ .25					
Davis, Eric	90TAS	402	$ .01	$ .10					
Davis, Eric	91T	550	$ .01	$ .10					
Davis, Glenn	86T	389	$ .95	$2.75					
Davis, Glenn	87T	560	$ .15	$ .50					
Davis, Glenn	88T	430	$ .01	$ .10					
Davis, Glenn	88TBB	192	$ .01	$ .15					
Davis, Glenn	89T	765	$ .01	$ .05					
Davis, Glenn	89TBB	89	$ .01	$ .10					
Davis, Glenn	90T	50	$ .01	$ .10					
Davis, Glenn	91T	350	$ .01	$ .10					
Davis, Jacke	62T	521	$ .75	$2.50					
Davis, Jacke	63T	117	$ .30	$ .95					
Davis, Jerry	85TTR	28	$ .02	$ .10					
Davis, Jerry	86T	323	$ .01	$ .04					
Davis, Jim	55T	68	$2.00	$6.00					
Davis, Jim	56T	102	$2.25	$6.00					
Davis, Jim	57T	273	$4.25	$15.00					
Davis, Jody	82T	508	$ .30	$ .85	Davis, Ron	80T	179	$ .05	$ .20
Davis, Jody	83T	542	$ .01	$ .07	Davis, Ron	81T	16	$ .01	$ .10
Davis, Jody	84T	73	$ .01	$ .06	Davis, Ron	82T	635	$ .01	$ .07
Davis, Jody	85T	384	$ .01	$ .05	Davis, Ron	82THL	2	$ .01	$ .07
Davis, Jody	86T	767	$ .01	$ .04	Davis, Ron	82TTR	25	$ .02	$ .10
Davis, Jody	87T	270	$ .01	$ .04	Davis, Ron	83T	380	$ .01	$ .07
Davis, Jody	88T	615	$ .01	$ .04	Davis, Ron	84T	519	$ .01	$ .06
Davis, Jody	89T	115	$ .01	$ .05	Davis, Ron	85T	430	$ .01	$ .05
Davis, Jody	89TBB	3	$ .01	$ .06	Davis, Ron	86T	265	$ .01	$ .04
Davis, Jody	89TTR	22	$ .01	$ .06	Davis, Ron	87T	383	$ .01	$ .04
Davis, Jody	90T	453	$ .01	$ .04	Davis, Steve	90T	428	$ .01	$ .04
Davis, Joel	86TTR	30	$ .02	$ .10	Davis, Storm	83T	268	$ .05	$ .50
Davis, Joel	87T	299	$ .01	$ .04	Davis, Storm	84T	140	$ .01	$ .10
Davis, Joel	88T	511	$ .01	$ .04	Davis, Storm	85T	599	$ .01	$ .05
Davis, John	88T	672	$ .01	$ .20	Davis, Storm	86T	469	$ .01	$ .04
Davis, John	89T	162	$ .01	$ .05	Davis, Storm	87T	349	$ .01	$ .04
Davis, Mark	82T	231	$ .25	$1.00	Davis, Storm	87TTR	26	$ .01	$ .05
Davis, Mark	84T	343	$ .01	$ .06	Davis, Storm	88T	248	$ .01	$ .04
Davis, Mark	85T	541	$ .01	$ .05	Davis, Storm	89T	701	$ .01	$ .05
Davis, Mark	86T	138	$ .01	$ .04	Davis, Storm	89TBB	121	$ .01	$ .06
Davis, Mark	87T	21	$ .01	$ .04	Davis, Storm	90T	606	$ .01	$ .06
Davis, Mark	88T	482	$ .01	$ .04	Davis, Storm	90TTR	25	$ .01	$ .05
Davis, Mark	89T	59	$ .01	$ .05	Davis, Storm	91T	22	$ .01	$ .03
Davis, Mark	90T	205	$ .01	$ .04	Davis, Tommy	60T	509	$4.00	$16.00
Davis, Mark	90TAS	407	$ .01	$ .04	Davis, Tommy	61T	168	$ .90	$3.00
Davis, Mark	90TTR	24	$ .01	$ .05	Davis, Tommy	62T	358	$ .75	$2.20
Davis, Mark	91T	116	$ .01	$ .03	Davis, Tommy	63T	1	$5.00	$25.00
Davis, Mike	81T	364	$ .05	$ .20					
Davis, Mike	82T	671	$ .01	$ .07					
Davis, Mike	83TTR	24	$ .02	$ .10					

RON DAVIS
PITCHER
YANKEES

Player	Year	No.	VG	EX/MT
Davis, Tommy	63T	310	$ .75	$3.00
Davis, Tommy	64T	7	$1.75	$2.25
Davis, Tommy	64T	180	$ .45	$1.45
Davis, Tommy	65T	370	$ .75	$2.20
Davis, Tommy	66T	75	$ .35	$1.25
Davis, Tommy	67T	370	$ .35	$1.25
Davis, Tommy	68T	265	$ .45	$1.45
Davis, Tommy	69T	135	$ .15	$ .75
Davis, Tommy	70T	559	$ .75	$3.00
Davis, Tommy	71T	151	$ .30	$ .95
Davis, Tommy	72T	41	$ .15	$ .50
Davis, Tommy	72TIA	42	$ .15	$ .50
Davis, Tommy	74T	396	$ .30	$ .95
Davis, Tommy	75T	564	$ .15	$ .50
Davis, Tommy	76T	149	$ .07	$ .30
Davis, Tommy	77T	362	$ .05	$ .15
Davis, Willie	61T	506	$2.10	$6.00
Davis, Willie	62T	108	$ .75	$2.20
Davis, Willie	63T	229	$ .45	$1.45
Davis, Willie	64T	68	$ .45	$1.45
Davis, Willie	65T	435	$ .45	$1.45
Davis, Willie	66T	535	$4.00	$11.50
Davis, Willie	67T	160	$ .35	$1.25
Davis, Willie	68T	208	$ .30	$ .95
Davis, Willie	69T	65	$ .15	$ .50
Davis, Willie	70T	390	$ .10	$ .50
Davis, Willie	71T	585	$ .35	$1.25
Davis, Willie	72T	390	$ .30	$ .85
Davis, Willie	73T	35	$ .30	$ .85
Davis, Willie	74T	165	$ .15	$ .50
Davis, Willie	74TTR	165	$ .15	$ .50
Davis, Willie	75T	10	$ .07	$ .30
Davis, Willie	76T	265	$ .07	$ .30
Davis, Willie	77T	603	$ .05	$ .15
Davison, Mike	71T	276	$1.75	$5.00
Dawley, Bill	84T	248	$ .01	$ .06
Dawley, Bill	85T	634	$ .01	$ .05
Dawley, Bill	86T	376	$ .01	$ .04
Dawley, Bill	87T	54	$ .01	$ .04
Dawley, Bill	88T	509	$ .01	$ .04
Dawson, Andre	77T	473	$12.50	$50.00
Dawson, Andre	78T	72	$3.60	$10.50
Dawson, Andre	79T	348	$1.50	$6.00
Dawson, Andre	80T	235	$ .50	$2.50
Dawson, Andre	81T	125	$ .15	$ .90
Dawson, Andre	82T	540	$ .10	$ .65
Dawson, Andre	82TAS	341	$ .01	$ .15
Dawson, Andre	83T	680	$ .10	$ .45
Dawson, Andre	83TAS	402	$ .03	$ .15
Dawson, Andre	84T	200	$ .10	$ .50
Dawson, Andre	84TAS	392	$ .03	$ .15
Dawson, Andre	85T	420	$ .05	$ .25
Dawson, Andre	86T	760	$ .02	$ .20
Dawson, Andre	87T	345	$ .15	$ .50
Dawson, Andre	87TTR	27	$ .08	$ .30
Dawson, Andre	88T	500	$ .01	$ .20
Dawson, Andre	88TAS	401	$ .01	$ .10
Dawson, Andre	88TBB	153	$ .01	$ .15
Dawson, Andre	89T	10	$ .01	$ .10
Dawson, Andre	89TAS	391	$ .01	$ .10
Dawson, Andre	89TBB	120	$ .01	$ .15
Dawson, Andre	89TRB	4	$ .01	$ .05
Dawson, Andre	90T	140	$ .01	$ .15
Dawson, Andre	91T	640	$ .01	$ .10
Day, Boots	70T	654	$ .75	$2.00
Day, Boots	71T	42	$ .15	$ .50
Day, Boots	72T	254	$ .15	$ .50
Day, Boots	73T	307	$ .07	$ .30
Day, Boots	74T	589	$ .07	$ .30
Dayett, Brian	85T	534	$ .01	$ .05
Dayett, Brian	85TTR	29	$ .02	$ .10
Dayett, Brian	86T	284	$ .01	$ .04
Dayett, Brian	87T	369	$ .01	$ .04
Dayett, Brian	88T	136	$ .01	$ .04
Dayley, Ken	83T	314	$ .01	$ .07
Dayley, Ken	84T	104	$ .01	$ .06
Dayley, Ken	84TTR	29	$ .02	$ .10
Dayley, Ken	86T	607	$ .01	$ .04
Dayley, Ken	87T	59	$ .01	$ .04
Dayley, Ken	88T	234	$ .01	$ .04
Dayley, Ken	89T	409	$ .01	$ .05
Dayley, Ken	90T	561	$ .01	$ .04
Dayley, Ken	91T	41	$ .01	$ .03
De la Hoz, Mike	61T	191	$ .35	$1.25
De la Hoz, Mike	62T	123	$ .45	$1.45
De la Hoz, Mike	63T	561	$1.75	$4.50
De la Hoz, Mike	64T	216	$ .30	$ .95
De La Hoz, Mike	65T	182	$ .30	$ .85
De la Hoz, Mike	66T	346	$ .30	$ .95
De La Hoz, Mike	67T	372	$ .30	$ .95
De Los Santos, Luis	90T	452	$ .01	$ .10
De Maestri, Joe	52T	286	$15.00	$47.50
De Maestri, Joe	56T	161	$2.25	$6.00
De Maestri, Joe	57T	44	$ .95	$3.50
De Maestri, Joe	58T	62	$1.25	$4.25
De Maestri, Joe	59T	64	$1.25	$4.25
De Maestri, Joe	60T	358	$ .75	$2.20
De Maestri, Joe	61T	116	$ .35	$1.25
Deal, Cot	54T	192	$3.60	$10.00
Deal, Cot	60T	459	$ .95	$3.50
Dean, Tommy	69T	641	$ .30	$ .95
Dean, Tommy	70T	234	$ .15	$ .50
Dean, Tommy	71T	364	$ .15	$ .50
DeBusschere, Dave	63T	54	$1.50	$4.00
DeBusschere, Dave	64T	247	$ .60	$2.50
DeBusschere, Dave	65T	297	$ .60	$2.50
DeCinces, Doug	75T	617	$ .45	$1.45
DeCinces, Doug	76T	438	$ .30	$ .85
DeCinces, Doug	77T	216	$ .05	$ .15
DeCinces, Doug	78T	9	$ .02	$ .10
DeCinces, Doug	79T	421	$ .05	$ .20
DeCinces, Doug	80T	615	$ .01	$ .10
DeCinces, Doug	81T	188	$ .01	$ .10
DeCinces, Doug	82T	564	$ .01	$ .07
DeCinces, Doug	82TTR	26	$ .02	$ .10
DeCinces, Doug	83T	341	$ .01	$ .07
DeCinces, Doug	84T	790	$ .01	$ .06
DeCinces, Doug	85T	111	$ .01	$ .05
DeCinces, Doug	86T	257	$ .01	$ .04
DeCinces, Doug	87T	22	$ .01	$ .04
DeCinces, Doug	88T	446	$ .01	$ .04
Decker, Joe	71T	98	$ .15	$ .50
Decker, Joe	72T	612	$ .30	$ .95
Decker, Joe	73T	311	$ .07	$ .30
Decker, Joe	74T	469	$ .07	$ .30
Decker, Joe	75T	102	$ .07	$ .30
Decker, Joe	76T	636	$ .05	$ .20
Dedeaux, Rod	85T	389	$ .01	$ .05
Dedmon, Jeff	84TTR	30	$ .02	$ .10
Dedmon, Jeff	85T	602	$ .01	$ .05
Dedmon, Jeff	86T	129	$ .01	$ .04
Dedmon, Jeff	87T	373	$ .01	$ .04
Dedmon, Jeff	88T	469	$ .01	$ .04
Deer, Rob	86T	249	$ .04	$ .40
Deer, Rob	86TTR	31	$ .05	$ .25
Deer, Rob	87T	547	$ .07	$ .30
Deer, Rob	88T	33	$ .01	$ .10
Deer, Rob	88TBB	151	$ .01	$ .06
Deer, Rob	89T	364	$ .01	$ .05
Deer, Rob	89TBB	78	$ .01	$ .06

Player	Year	No.	VG	EX/MT
Deer, Rob	90T	615	$ .01	$ .04
Deer, Rob	91T	192	$ .01	$ .03
Dees, Charlie	64T	159	$ .30	$ .95
DeFilippis, Art	76T	595	$ .05	$ .20
DeFreites, Art	80T	677	$ .01	$ .10
DeJesus, Ivan	78T	152	$ .02	$ .10
DeJesus, Ivan	79T	398	$ .02	$ .10
DeJesus, Ivan	80T	691	$ .01	$ .10
DeJesus, Ivan	81T	54	$ .01	$ .10

CUBS — SHORTSTOP — IVAN DeJESUS

Player	Year	No.	VG	EX/MT
DeJesus, Ivan	82T	484	$ .03	$ .15
DeJesus, Ivan	82TTR	27	$ .02	$ .10
DeJesus, Ivan	83T	587	$ .01	$ .07
DeJesus, Ivan	84T	279	$ .01	$ .06
DeJesus, Ivan	85T	791	$ .01	$ .05
DeJesus, Ivan	85TTR	30	$ .02	$ .10
DeJesus, Ivan	86T	178	$ .01	$ .04
DeJesus, Jose	90T	596	$ .01	$ .04
DeJesus, Jose	91T	232	$ .01	$ .03
Del Greco, Bob	52T	353	$40.00	$140.00
Del Greco, Bob	53T	48	$4.50	$15.00
Del Greco, Bob	57T	94	$ .95	$3.50
Del Greco, Bobby	60T	486	$ .90	$3.00
Del Greco, Bobby	61T	154	$ .35	$1.25
Del Greco, Bobby	62T	548	$3.95	$11.50
Del Greco, Bob	63T	282	$ .30	$ .95
DeLeon, Jose	84T	581	$ .02	$ .10
DeLeon, Jose	85T	385	$ .01	$ .05
DeLeon, Jose	86T	75	$ .01	$ .04
DeLeon, Jose	87T	421	$ .01	$ .04
DeLeon, Jose	88T	634	$ .01	$ .04
DeLeon, Jose	88TBB	194	$ .01	$ .06
DeLeon, Jose	88TTR	34	$ .01	$ .06
DeLeon, Jose	89T	107	$ .01	$ .05
DeLeon, Jose	90T	257	$ .01	$ .04
DeLeon, Jose	91T	711	$ .01	$ .03
DeLeon, Luis	82T	561	$ .01	$ .07
DeLeon, Luis	83T	323	$ .01	$ .07
DeLeon, Luis	84T	38	$ .01	$ .06
DeLeon, Luis	85T	689	$ .01	$ .05
DeLeon, Luis	86T	286	$ .01	$ .04

Player	Year	No.	VG	EX/MT
Delock, Ike	52T	329	$40.00	$140.00
Delock, Ike	56T	284	$2.25	$8.00
Delock, Ike	57T	63	$ .95	$3.50
Delock, Ike	58T	328	$ .45	$1.50
Delock, Ike	59T	437	$ .75	$2.20
Delock, Ike	60T	336	$ .75	$2.20
Delock, Ike	61T	268	$ .35	$1.25
Delock, Ike	62T	201	$ .45	$1.45
Delock, Ike	63T	136	$ .30	$ .95
Delsing, Jim	52T	271	$12.00	$40.00
Delsing, Jim	53T	239	$12.50	$50.00
Delsing, Jim	54T	111	$3.60	$10.00
Delsing, Jim	55T	192	$5.25	$15.00
Delsing, Jim	56T	338	$2.25	$8.00
Delsing, Jim	59T	386	$ .75	$2.20
DeMars, Billy	73T	486	$ .30	$ .95
DeMars, Billy	74T	119	$ .07	$ .30
DeMerit, John	61T	501	$ .75	$3.00
DeMerit, John	62T	4	$ .45	$1.45
Demery, Larry	75T	433	$ .07	$ .30
Demery, Larry	76T	563	$ .05	$ .20
Demery, Larry	77T	607	$ .05	$ .15
Demery, Larry	78T	138	$ .02	$ .10
Demeter, Don	58T	244	$ .45	$1.50
Demeter, Don	59T	324	$ .90	$3.00
Demeter, Don	60T	234	$ .45	$1.45
Demeter, Don	61T	23	$ .35	$1.25
Demeter, Don	62T	146	$ .45	$1.45
Demeter, Don	63T	268	$ .30	$ .95
Demeter, Don	64T	58	$ .30	$ .95
Demeter, Don	65T	429	$ .35	$1.25
Demeter, Don	66T	98	$ .30	$ .95
Demeter, Don	67T	572	$3.00	$9.00
DeMola, Don	75T	391	$ .07	$ .30
DeMola, Don	76T	571	$ .05	$ .20
Dempsey, Con	52T	44	$15.00	$47.50
Dempsey, Pat	81T	96	$ .01	$ .10
Dempsey, Rick	72T	778	$ .90	$3.00
Dempsey, Rick	74T	569	$ .07	$ .30
Dempsey, Rick	75T	451	$ .15	$ .50
Dempsey, Rick	76T	272	$ .04	$ .15
Dempsey, Rick	77T	189	$ .05	$ .15
Dempsey, Rick	78T	367	$ .02	$ .10
Dempsey, Rick	79T	593	$ .02	$ .10
Dempsey, Rick	80T	91	$ .01	$ .10
Dempsey, Rick	81T	615	$ .01	$ .10
Dempsey, Rick	82T	489	$ .01	$ .07
Dempsey, Rick	83T	138	$ .02	$ .10
Dempsey, Rick	84T	272	$ .05	$ .20
Dempsey, Rick	85T	521	$ .01	$ .05
Dempsey, Rick	86T	358	$ .01	$ .04
Dempsey, Rick	87T	28	$ .01	$ .04
Dempsey, Rick	87TTR	28	$ .01	$ .05
Dempsey, Rick	89T	606	$ .01	$ .05
Dempsey, Rick	89TBB	108	$ .01	$ .06
Dempsey, Rick	90T	736	$ .01	$ .04
Dempsey, Rick	91T	427	$ .01	$ .03
Denehy, Bill	67T	581	$300.00	$950.00
Denehy, Bill	68T	526	$ .35	$1.25
Dennis, Don	66T	142	$ .30	$ .95
Dennis, Don	67T	259	$ .30	$ .85
Denny, John	75T	621	$ .15	$ .50
Denny, John	76T	339	$ .05	$ .20
Denny, John	77T	7	$ .05	$ .15
Denny, John	77T	541	$ .05	$ .15
Denny, John	78T	609	$ .02	$ .10
Denny, John	79T	59	$ .02	$ .10
Denny, John	80T	464	$ .01	$ .10
Denny, John	81T	122	$ .01	$ .10
Denny, John	82T	773	$ .01	$ .07

TOPPS

Player	Year	No.	VG	EX/MT	Player	Year	No.	VG	EX/MT
Denny, John	83T	211	$ .05	$ .25	Deshaies, Jim	88T	24	$ .01	$ .10
Denny, John	84T	17	$ .01	$ .06	Deshaies, Jim	89T	341	$ .01	$ .05
Denny, John	84T	135	$ .01	$ .06	Deshaies, Jim	89TBB	29	$ .01	$ .06
Denny, John	84T	637	$ .01	$ .06	Deshaies, Jim	90T	225	$ .01	$ .04
Denny, John	85T	325	$ .01	$ .05	Deshaies, Jim	91T	782	$ .01	$ .03
Denny, John	86T	556	$ .01	$ .04	DeShields, Delino	90T	224	$ .01	$ .50
Denny, John	86TTR	32	$ .02	$ .10	DeShields, Delino	91T	432	$ .01	$ .15
Denny, John	87T	644	$ .01	$ .04	Destrade, Orestes	89T	27	$ .01	$ .15
Denson, Drew	89TMLD	30	$ .01	$ .15	Dettore, Tom	75T	469	$ .07	$ .30
Dent, Bucky	74T	582	$ .07	$ .30	Dettore, Tom	76T	126	$ .05	$ .20
Dent, Bucky	75T	299	$ .30	$ .85	Devereaux, Mike	89TTR	23	$ .01	$ .10
Dent, Bucky	76T	154	$ .07	$ .30	Devereaux, Mike	90T	127	$ .01	$ .04
Dent, Bucky	77T	29	$ .05	$ .15	Devereaux, Mike	91T	758	$ .01	$ .03
Dent, Bucky	78T	335	$ .05	$ .20	Devine, Adrian	74T	614	$ .07	$ .30
Dent, Bucky	79T	485	$ .05	$ .20	Devine, Adrian	77T	339	$ .05	$ .15
Dent, Bucky	80T	60	$ .01	$ .10	Devine, Adrian	78T	92	$ .02	$ .10
Dent, Bucky	81T	650	$ .01	$ .10	Devine, Adrian	79T	257	$ .02	$ .10
Dent, Bucky	82T	240	$ .01	$ .07	Devine, Adrian	80T	528	$ .01	$ .10
Dent, Bucky	82TAS	550	$ .01	$ .07	Devine, Adrian	81T	464	$ .01	$ .10
Dent, Bucky	82TIA	241	$ .01	$ .07	Diaz, Bo	78T	708	$7.00	$25.00
Dent, Bucky	83T	565	$ .01	$ .07	Diaz, Bo	79T	61	$ .02	$ .10
Dent, Bucky	84T	331	$ .01	$ .06	Diaz, Bo	80T	483	$ .01	$ .10
Dent, Bucky	90T	519	$ .01	$ .04	Diaz, Bo	81T	362	$ .03	$ .15
Dente, Sam	52T	304	$12.00	$40.00	Diaz, Bo	82T	258	$ .02	$ .10
Dernier, Bob	82T	231	$ .25	$1.00	Diaz, Bo	82TTR	29	$ .02	$ .10
Dernier, Bob	82TTR	28	$ .02	$ .10	Diaz, Bo	83T	175	$ .01	$ .07
Dernier, Bob	83T	43	$ .01	$ .07	Diaz, Bo	83T	229	$ .01	$ .07
Dernier, Bob	84T	358	$ .01	$ .06	Diaz, Bo	84T	535	$ .01	$ .06
Dernier, Bob	84TTR	31	$ .02	$ .10	Diaz, Bo	85T	737	$ .01	$ .05
Dernier, Bob	85T	589	$ .01	$ .05	Diaz, Bo	86T	639	$ .01	$ .04
Dernier, Bob	86T	188	$ .01	$ .04	Diaz, Bo	87T	41	$ .01	$ .04
Dernier, Bob	87T	715	$ .01	$ .04	Diaz, Bo	88T	265	$ .01	$ .04
Dernier, Bob	88T	642	$ .01	$ .04	Diaz, Bo	89T	422	$ .01	$ .05
Dernier, Bob	89T	418	$ .01	$ .05	Diaz, Carlos	84T	524	$ .01	$ .06
Dernier, Bob	89TBB	265	$ .01	$ .06	Diaz, Carlos	84TTR	32	$ .02	$ .10
Dernier, Bob	90T	204	$ .01	$ .04	Diaz, Carlos	85T	159	$ .01	$ .05
					Diaz, Carlos	86T	343	$ .01	$ .04
					Diaz, Edgar	90TTR	26	$ .01	$ .05
					Diaz, Edgar	91T	164	$ .01	$ .03
					Diaz, Mario	89T	309	$ .01	$ .10
					Diaz, Mario	90T	781	$ .01	$ .04
					Diaz, Mike	87T	469	$ .01	$ .10
					Diaz, Mike	88T	567	$ .01	$ .04
					Diaz, Mike	89T	142	$ .01	$ .05
					Dibble, Rob	89T	264	$ .01	$ .50
					Dibble, Rob	90T	46	$ .01	$ .25
					Dibble, Rob	91T	662	$ .01	$ .03
					Dickey, Bill	52T	400	$160.00	$ 500.00
					Dickey, Bill	60T	465	$2.50	$9.00
					Dickson, Jim	64T	524	$1.75	$4.50
					Dickson, Jim	65T	286	$ .35	$1.25
					Dickson, Jim	66T	201	$ .30	$ .95
					Dickson, Lance	91T	114	$ .01	$ .35
					Dickson, Murry	51Tbb	16	$7.50	$22.50
					Dickson, Murry	52T	266	$12.00	$40.00
					Dickson, Murry	56T	211	$3.00	$9.00
					Dickson, Murry	57T	71	$ .95	$3.50
					Dickson, Murry	58T	349	$ .75	$3.00
					Dickson, Murry	59T	23	$ .95	$3.50
					Didier, Bob	69T	611	$ .30	$ .95
					Didier, Bob	70T	232	$ .15	$ .50
					Didier, Bob	71T	432	$ .15	$ .50
					Didier, Bob	73T	574	$ .45	$1.45
					Didier, Bob	74T	482	$ .07	$ .30
					Diering, Chuck	52T	265	$12.00	$40.00
					Diering, Chuck	55T	105	$2.00	$6.00
					Diering, Chuck	56T	19	$2.25	$6.00
					Dierker, Larry	65T	409	$ .35	$1.25
					Dierker, Larry	66T	228	$ .30	$ .95
					Dierker, Larry	67T	498	$ .75	$3.00

Jim Derrington

CHICAGO WHITE SOX

Player	Year	No.	VG	EX/MT
Derrington, Jim	58T	129	$ .75	$3.00
DeSa, Joe	86T	313	$ .01	$ .04
Deshaies, Jim	87T	167	$ .15	$ .50
Deshaies, Jim	87TRB	2	$ .01	$ .04

Player	Year	No.	VG	EX/MT	Player	Year	No.	VG	EX/MT
Dierker, Larry	68T	565	$ .35	$1.25	Ditmar, Art	61T	510	$ .90	$3.00
Dierker, Larry	69T	411	$ .30	$ .85	Ditmar, Art	62T	246	$ .45	$1.45
Dierker, Larry	70T	15	$ .15	$ .50	Dittmer, Jack	53T	212	$4.50	$15.00
Dierker, Larry	71T	540	$ .35	$1.25	Dittmer, Jack	54T	53	$7.00	$22.00
Dierker, Larry	72T	155	$ .15	$ .50	Dittmer, Jack	57T	282	$4.25	$15.00
Dierker, Larry	73T	375	$ .07	$ .30	Dixon, Ken	85TTR	31	$ .02	$ .10
Dierker, Larry	74T	660	$ .45	$1.45	Dixon, Ken	86T	198	$ .01	$ .04
Dierker, Larry	75T	49	$ .07	$ .30	Dixon, Ken	87T	528	$ .01	$ .04
Dierker, Larry	76T	75	$ .05	$ .20	Dixon, Ken	88T	676	$ .01	$ .04
Dierker, Larry	77T	350	$ .05	$ .15	Dixon, Tom	79T	361	$ .02	$ .10
Dierker, Larry	78T	195	$ .02	$ .10	Dixon, Tom	80T	513	$ .01	$ .10
Dietz, Dick	67T	341	$ .30	$ .85	Dobbek, Dan	59T	124	$ .75	$2.20
Dietz, Dick	68T	104	$ .30	$ .85	Dobbek, Dan	60T	123	$ .45	$1.45
Dietz, Dick	69T	293	$ .30	$ .95	Dobbek, Dan	61T	108	$ .35	$1.25
Dietz, Dick	70T	135	$ .15	$ .50	Dobbek, Dan	62T	267	$ .45	$1.45
Dietz, Dick	71T	545	$ .35	$1.25	Dobson, Chuck	66T	588	$5.00	$20.00
Dietz, Dick	72T	295	$ .15	$ .50	Dobson, Chuck	67T	438	$ .30	$ .95
Dietz, Dick	72TIA	296	$ .15	$ .50	Dobson, Chuck	68T	62	$ .30	$ .85
Dietz, Dick	73T	442	$ .07	$ .30	Dobson, Chuck	69T	397	$ .30	$ .85
DiLauro, Jack	70T	382	$ .15	$ .50	Dobson, Chuck	70T	331	$ .15	$ .50
DiLauro, Jack	71T	677	$ .75	$2.50	Dobson, Chuck	71T	238	$ .15	$ .50
Dillard, Don	59T	123	$ .75	$2.20	Dobson, Chuck	72T	523	$ .15	$ .50
Dillard, Don	60T	122	$ .45	$1.45	Dobson, Chuck	75T	635	$ .07	$ .30
Dillard, Don	61T	172	$ .35	$1.25	Dobson, Joe	52T	254	$12.00	$40.00
Dillard, Don	63T	298	$ .45	$1.50	Dobson, Joe	53T	5	$4.50	$15.00
Dillard, Steve	77T	142	$ .05	$ .15	Dobson, Pat	67T	526	$ .75	$3.00
Dillard, Steve	78T	597	$ .02	$ .10	Dobson, Pat	68T	22	$ .30	$ .85
Dillard, Steve	79T	217	$ .02	$ .10	Dobson, Pat	69T	231	$ .30	$ .95
Dillard, Steve	80T	452	$ .01	$ .10	Dobson, Pat	70T	421	$ .15	$ .50
Dillard, Steve	81T	78	$ .01	$ .10	Dobson, Pat	71T	547	$ .35	$1.25
Dillard, Steve	82T	324	$ .01	$ .07	Dobson, Pat	72T	140	$ .15	$ .50
Dillman, Bill	67T	558	$8.75	$35.00	Dobson, Pat	73T	34	$ .07	$ .30
Dillman, Bill	68T	466	$ .35	$1.25	Dobson, Pat	74T	463	$ .07	$ .30
Dillman, Bill	69T	141	$ .30	$ .85	Dobson, Pat	75T	44	$ .07	$ .30
Dillman, Bill	70T	386	$ .15	$ .50	Dobson, Pat	76T	296	$ .05	$ .20
Dillon, Steve	64T	556	$1.75	$4.50	Dobson, Pat	76TTR	296	$ .05	$ .20
Dilone, Miguel	78T	705	$ .02	$ .10	Dobson, Pat	77T	618	$ .05	$ .15
Dilone, Miguel	79T	487	$ .02	$ .10	Dobson, Pat	78T	575	$ .02	$ .10
Dilone, Miguel	80T	541	$ .01	$ .10	Doby, Larry	52T	243	$10.00	$30.00
Dilone, Miguel	81T	141	$ .01	$ .10	Doby, Larry	54T	70	$10.00	$35.00
Dilone, Miguel	82T	77	$ .01	$ .07	Doby, Larry	56T	250	$3.35	$10.00
Dilone, Miguel	83T	303	$ .01	$ .07	Doby, Larry	57T	85	$3.60	$10.00
Dilone, Miguel	85T	178	$ .01	$ .05	Doby, Larry	58T	424	$1.25	$4.00
DiMaggio, Dom	51Trb	20	$3.50	$13.50	Doby, Larry	59T	166	$ .90	$3.00
DiMaggio, Dom	52T	22	$25.00	$75.00	Doby, Larry	59T	455	$2.10	$6.00
DiMaggio, Dom	53T	149	$4.00	$13.00	Doby, Larry	73T	377	$ .15	$ .50
Diorio, Ron	74T	599	$ .15	$ .50	Doby, Larry	74T	531	$ .30	$ .95
DiPino, Frank	82T	333	$ .01	$ .07	Dodgers, Team	56T	166	$55.00	$165.00
DiPino, Frank	83TTR	25	$ .02	$ .10	Dodgers, Team	57T	324	$25.00	$100.00
DiPino, Frank	84T	172	$ .01	$ .06	Dodgers, Team	58T	71	$7.50	$22.50
DiPino, Frank	85T	532	$ .01	$ .05	Dodgers, Team	59T	457	$8.00	$20.00
DiPino, Frank	86T	26	$ .01	$ .04	Dodgers, Team	60T	18	$3.00	$9.00
DiPino, Frank	87T	662	$ .01	$ .04	Dodgers, Team	61T	86	$1.00	$3.00
DiPino, Frank	88T	211	$ .01	$ .04	Dodgers, Team	62T	43	$1.50	$4.00
DiPino, Frank	89T	439	$ .01	$ .05	Dodgers, Team	63T	337	$2.50	$10.00
DiPino, Frank	89TTR	24	$ .01	$ .06	Dodgers, Team	64T	531	$2.50	$10.00
DiPino, Frank	90T	788	$ .01	$ .04	Dodgers, Team	65T	126	$3.00	$9.00
DiPino, Frank	91T	112	$ .01	$ .03	Dodgers, Team	66T	238	$ .95	$3.50
DiSarcina, Gary	89TMLD	31	$ .01	$ .06	Dodgers, Team	67T	503	$1.50	$3.50
Distaso, Alec	69T	602	$ .30	$ .95	Dodgers, Team	68T	168	$ .75	$2.25
Distefano, Benny	85T	162	$ .01	$ .05	Dodgers, Team	70T	411	$ .75	$3.00
Distefano, Benny	87T	651	$ .01	$ .04	Dodgers, Team	71T	402	$ .45	$1.45
Distefano, Benny	89TTR	25	$ .01	$ .06	Dodgers, Team	72T	522	$ .35	$1.25
Ditmar, Art	56T	258	$3.00	$9.00	Dodgers, Team	73T	91	$ .35	$1.25
Ditmar, Art	57T	132	$ .95	$3.50	Dodgers, Team	74T	643	$ .35	$1.25
Ditmar, Art	58T	354	$ .75	$3.00	Dodgers, Team Checklist	75T	361	$ .45	$1.45
Ditmar, Art	59T	374	$ .90	$3.00	Dodgers, Team Checklist	76T	46	$ .20	$ .75
Ditmar, Art	60T	430	$ .75	$2.20	Dodgers, Team Checklist	77T	504	$ .45	$1.45
Ditmar, Art	61T	46	$ .75	$3.00	Dodgers, Team Checklist	78T	259	$ .30	$ .85
Ditmar, Art	61T	48	$ .75	$3.00	Dodgers, Team Checklist	79T	526	$ .08	$ .30

TOPPS

Player	Year	No.	VG	EX/MT	Player	Year	No.	VG	EX/MT
Dodgers, Team Checklist	80T	302	$ .08	$ .30	Downing, Al	62T	219	$ .90	$2.75
Dodgers, Team Checklist	81T	679	$ .02	$ .30	Downing, Al	64T	86	$ .45	$1.45
Dodgers, Team Leaders	86T	696	$ .01	$ .04	Downing, Al	64T	219	$ .75	$3.00
Dodgers, Team Leaders	87T	431	$ .01	$ .04	Downing, Al	65T	11	$ .45	$1.45
Dodgers, Team Leaders	88T	489	$ .01	$ .04	Downing, Al	65T	598	$2.50	$9.00
Dodgers, Team Leaders	89T	669	$ .01	$ .05	Downing, Al	66T	384	$ .45	$1.45
Dodson, Pat	87T	449	$ .01	$ .04	Downing, Al	67T	308	$ .30	$ .85
Doerr, Bobby	51Tbb	37	$10.00	$42.50	Downing, Al	68T	105	$ .30	$ .95
Doherty, John	75T	524	$ .07	$ .30	Downing, Al	69T	292	$ .30	$ .95
Donaldson, John	68T	244	$ .30	$ .85	Downing, Al	70T	584	$ .30	$ .95
Donaldson, John	69T	217	$ .30	$ .85	Downing, Al	71T	182	$ .15	$ .50
Donaldson, John	70T	418	$ .15	$ .50	Downing, Al	72T	93	$ .50	$2.00
Donohue, Jim	60T	124	$ .45	$1.45	Downing, Al	72T	460	$ .15	$ .50
Donohue, Jim	61T	151	$ .35	$1.25	Downing, Al	73T	324	$ .07	$ .30
Donohue, Jim	62T	498	$ .75	$2.50	Downing, Al	74T	620	$ .07	$ .30
Donohue, Tom	80T	454	$ .01	$ .10	Downing, Al	75T	498	$ .07	$ .30
Donohue, Tom	81T	621	$ .01	$ .10	Downing, Al	76T	605	$ .05	$ .20
Donovan, Dick	55T	146	$2.00	$6.00	Downing, Brian	74T	601	$ .45	$1.45
Donovan, Dick	56T	18	$2.25	$6.00	Downing, Brian	75T	422	$ .07	$ .30
Donovan, Dick	57T	181	$ .95	$3.50	Downing, Brian	76T	23	$ .05	$ .20
Donovan, Dick	58T	290	$ .75	$3.00	Downing, Brian	77T	344	$ .05	$ .15
Donovan, Dick	59T	5	$1.25	$4.25	Downing, Brian	78T	519	$ .02	$ .10
Donovan, Dick	60T	199	$ .45	$1.45	Downing, Brian	79T	71	$ .02	$ .10
Donovan, Dick	61T	414	$ .75	$3.00	Downing, Brian	80T	602	$ .01	$ .10
Donovan, Dick	62T	15	$ .45	$1.45	Downing, Brian	81T	263	$ .01	$ .10
Donovan, Dick	62T	55	$ .75	$3.00	Downing, Brian	82T	158	$ .01	$ .07
Donovan, Dick	63T	8	$ .45	$1.45	Downing, Brian	84T	574	$ .01	$ .06
Donovan, Dick	63T	370	$ .45	$1.50	Downing, Brian	85T	374	$ .01	$ .05
Dopson, John	89T	251	$ .01	$ .15	Downing, Brian	86T	772	$ .01	$ .04
Dopson, John	89TTR	26	$ .01	$ .15	Downing, Brian	87T	782	$ .01	$ .04
Dopson, John	90T	733	$ .01	$ .04	Downing, Brian	88T	331	$ .01	$ .04
Dopson, John	91T	94	$ .01	$ .03	Downing, Brian	88TBB	78	$ .01	$ .06
Doran, Bill	83TTR	26	$ .25	$1.25	Downing, Brian	89T	17	$ .01	$ .05
Doran, Bill	84T	198	$ .25	$1.00	Downing, Brian	90T	635	$ .01	$ .04
Doran, Bill	85T	684	$ .01	$ .05	Downing, Brian	91T	255	$ .01	$ .03
Doran, Bill	86T	57	$ .01	$ .10	Downs, Kelly	87T	438	$ .01	$ .04
Doran, Bill	87T	472	$ .01	$ .04	Downs, Kelly	88T	629	$ .01	$ .04
Doran, Bill	88T	745	$ .01	$ .10	Downs, Kelly	89T	361	$ .01	$ .05
Doran, Bill	88TBB	51	$ .01	$ .06	Downs, Kelly	89TBB	112	$ .01	$ .06
Doran, Bill	89T	226	$ .01	$ .05	Downs, Kelly	90T	17	$ .01	$ .04
Doran, Bill	89TBB	168	$ .01	$ .06	Downs, Kelly	91T	733	$ .01	$ .03
Doran, Bill	90T	368	$ .01	$ .04	Doyle, Brian	79T	710	$ .05	$ .20
Doran, Bill	91T	577	$ .01	$ .03	Doyle, Brian	80T	582	$ .01	$ .10
Dorish, Harry	52T	303	$12.00	$40.00	Doyle, Brian	81T	159	$ .01	$ .10
Dorish, Harry	53T	145	$4.50	$15.00	Doyle, Brian	81TTR	754	$ .02	$ .10
Dorish, Harry	54T	110	$3.60	$10.00	Doyle, Dennis	70T	539	$1.00	$4.00
Dorish, Harry	56T	167	$2.25	$6.00	Doyle, Denny	71T	352	$ .15	$ .50
Dorsey, Jim	81T	214	$ .01	$ .10	Doyle, Denny	72T	768	$ .75	$2.50
Dotson, Rich	81T	138	$ .05	$ .25	Doyle, Denny	73T	424	$ .07	$ .30
Dotson, Rich	82T	461	$ .01	$ .07	Doyle, Denny	74T	552	$ .07	$ .30
Dotson, Richard	83T	46	$ .01	$ .07	Doyle, Denny	75T	187	$ .07	$ .30
Dotson, Richard	84T	216	$ .01	$ .06	Doyle, Denny	76T	381	$ .05	$ .20
Dotson, Richard	84T	759	$ .01	$ .06	Doyle, Denny	77T	336	$ .05	$ .15
Dotson, Richard	85T	364	$ .01	$ .05	Doyle, Denny	78T	642	$ .02	$ .10
Dotson, Richard	86T	612	$ .01	$ .04	Doyle, Paul	70T	277	$ .15	$ .50
Dotson, Richard	87T	720	$ .01	$ .04	Doyle, Paul	72T	629	$ .30	$ .95
Dotson, Richard	88T	209	$ .01	$ .04	Drabek, Doug	87T	283	$ .01	$ .75
Dotson, Richard	88TTR	35	$ .01	$ .06	Drabek, Doug	87TTR	29	$ .01	$ .35
Dotson, Richard	89T	511	$ .01	$ .05	Drabek, Doug	88T	591	$ .01	$ .15
Dotson, Richard	90T	169	$ .01	$ .04	Drabek, Doug	88TBB	124	$ .01	$ .06
Dotter, Gary	65T	421	$ .35	$1.25	Drabek, Doug	89T	478	$ .01	$ .05
Dotterer, Dutch	58T	396	$ .75	$3.00	Drabek, Doug	90T	197	$ .01	$ .04
Dotterer, Dutch	59T	288	$ .75	$2.20	Drabek, Doug	91T	685	$ .01	$ .03
Dotterer, Dutch	60T	21	$ .45	$1.45	Drabek, Doug	91TAS	405	$ .01	$ .03
Dotterer, Dutch	61T	332	$ .35	$1.25	Drabowsky, Moe	57T	84	$ .95	$3.50
Douglas, Whammy	58T	306	$ .75	$3.00	Drabowsky, Moe (Mike)	58T	135	$ .75	$3.00
Douglas, Whammy	59T	431	$ .75	$2.20	Drabowsky, Moe	59T	407	$ .75	$2.20
Dowling, Dave	65T	116	$ .45	$1.45	Drabowsky, Moe	60T	349	$ .75	$2.20
Dowling, Dave	66T	482	$ .75	$2.50	Drabowsky, Moe	61T	364	$ .35	$1.25
Dowling, Dave	67T	272	$ .30	$ .85	Drabowsky, Moe	62T	331	$ .45	$1.45

Player	Year	No.	VG	EX/MT
Drabowsky, Moe	64T	42	$ .30	$ .95
Drabowsky, Moe	65T	439	$ .35	$1.25
Drabowsky, Moe	66T	291	$ .30	$ .95
Drabowsky, Moe	67T	125	$ .30	$ .85
Drabowsky, Moe	68T	242	$ .30	$ .85
Drabowsky, Moe	69T	508	$ .30	$ .85
Drabowsky, Moe	70T	653	$ .75	$2.00
Drabowsky, Moe	71T	685	$ .75	$2.50
Drabowsky, Moe	72T	627	$ .30	$ .95
Drago, Dick	69T	662	$ .30	$ .95
Drago, Dick	70T	37	$ .15	$ .50
Drago, Dick	71T	752	$2.25	$8.00
Drago, Dick	72T	205	$ .15	$ .50
Drago, Dick	73T	392	$ .07	$ .30
Drago, Dick	74T	113	$ .07	$ .30
Drago, Dick	75T	333	$ .07	$ .30
Drago, Dick	76T	142	$ .05	$ .20
Drago, Dick	77T	426	$ .05	$ .15
Drago, Dick	78T	567	$ .02	$ .10
Drago, Dick	79T	12	$ .02	$ .10
Drago, Dick	80T	271	$ .01	$ .10
Drago, Dick	81T	647	$ .01	$ .10
Drago, Dick	81TTR	755	$ .02	$ .10
Drago, Dick	82T	742	$ .01	$ .07
Drake, Sammy	62T	162	$ .45	$1.45
Drake, Solly	57T	159	$ .95	$3.50
Drake, Solly	59T	406	$ .75	$2.20
Dravecky, Dave	83T	384	$ .25	$1.25
Dravecky, Dave	84T	290	$ .01	$ .15
Dravecky, Dave	84T	366	$ .01	$ .06
Dravecky, Dave	85T	530	$ .01	$ .05
Dravecky, Dave	86T	735	$ .01	$ .04
Dravecky, Dave	87T	470	$ .01	$ .04
Dravecky, Dave	88T	68	$ .01	$ .04
Dravecky, Dave	89T	601	$ .01	$ .05
Dravecky, Dave	90T	124	$ .01	$ .04
Dressen, Chuck	52T	377	$60.00	$175.00
Dressen, Chuck	53T	50	$4.25	$15.00
Dressen, Chuck	60T	213	$ .45	$1.45
Dressen, Chuck	61T	137	$ .35	$1.25
Dressen, Chuck	64T	443	$ .75	$3.00
Dressen, Chuck	65T	538	$1.75	$4.50
Dressen, Chuck	66T	187	$ .15	$ .50
Dressler, Rob	76T	599	$2.50	$10.00
Dressler, Rob	77T	11	$ .05	$ .15
Dressler, Rob	80T	366	$ .01	$ .10
Dressler, Rob	81T	508	$ .01	$ .10
Drews, Karl	52T	352	$40.00	$140.00
Drews, Karl	53T	59	$4.50	$15.00
Driessen, Dan	74T	341	$ .30	$ .95
Driessen, Dan	75T	133	$ .07	$ .30
Driessen, Dan	76T	514	$ .15	$ .50
Driessen, Dan	77T	23	$ .05	$ .15
Driessen, Dan	78T	246	$ .05	$ .20
Driessen, Dan	79T	475	$ .02	$ .10
Driessen, Dan	80T	325	$ .01	$ .10
Driessen, Dan	81T	655	$ .01	$ .10
Driessen, Dan	82T	785	$ .01	$ .07
Driessen, Dan	83T	165	$ .01	$ .07
Driessen, Dan	84T	585	$ .01	$ .06
Driessen, Dan	85T	285	$ .01	$ .05
Driessen, Dan	86T	65	$ .01	$ .04
Driscoll, Jim	71T	317	$ .15	$ .50
Dropo, Walt	52T	235	$7.00	$21.00
Dropo, Walt	53T	121	$4.50	$15.00
Dropo, Walt	54T	18	$3.60	$10.00
Dropo, Walt	56T	238	$3.00	$9.00
Dropo, Walt	57T	257	$ .95	$3.50
Dropo, Walt	58T	338	$ .55	$1.75
Dropo, Walt	59T	158	$ .75	$2.20

Player	Year	No.	VG	EX/MT
Dropo, Walt	60T	79	$ .45	$1.45
Dropo, Walt	61T	489	$ .75	$3.00
Drott, Dick	58T	80	$1.25	$4.25
Drott, Dick	59T	15	$1.25	$4.25
Drott, Dick	60T	27	$ .45	$1.45
Drott, Dick	61T	231	$ .35	$1.25

Player	Year	No.	VG	EX/MT
Drummond, Tim	90T	713	$ .01	$ .10
Drummond, Tim	91T	46	$ .01	$ .03
Drumright, Keith	82T	673	$ .01	$ .07
Drysdale, Don	57T	18	$67.50	$185.00
Drysdale, Don	58T	25	$15.00	$45.00
Drysdale, Don	59T	262	$3.00	$12.00
Drysdale, Don	59T	387	$10.50	$32.50
Drysdale, Don	60T	475	$7.00	$28.00
Drysdale, Don	60TAS	570	$7.50	$22.50
Drysdale, Don	61T	45	$ .60	$2.75
Drysdale, Don	61T	49	$ .90	$3.00
Drysdale, Don	61T	260	$7.00	$21.00
Drysdale, Don	62T	60	$ .65	$1.75
Drysdale, Don	62T	340	$9.00	$27.50
Drysdale, Don	62TAS	398	$3.00	$10.00
Drysdale, Don	63T	5	$1.00	$4.00
Drysdale, Don	63T	7	$ .45	$1.45
Drysdale, Don	63T	9	$ .90	$3.00
Drysdale, Don	63T	360	$4.50	$16.00
Drysdale, Don	63T	412	$10.00	$30.00
Drysdale, Don	64T	5	$1.75	$5.00
Drysdale, Don	64T	120	$4.00	$14.00
Drysdale, Don	65T	8	$1.75	$4.50
Drysdale, Don	65T	12	$1.75	$4.50
Drysdale, Don	65T	260	$3.75	$11.50
Drysdale, Don	66T	223	$ .65	$1.75
Drysdale, Don	66T	430	$3.25	$12.50
Drysdale, Don	67T	55	$3.00	$11.00
Drysdale, Don	68T	145	$3.00	$9.00
Drysdale, Don	69T	400	$2.00	$6.00
Dubiel, Walt	52T	164	$7.00	$20.00
DuBois, Brian	89TMLD	32	$ .01	$ .15
DuBois, Brian	90T	413	$ .01	$ .10
Ducey, Rob	88T	438	$ .01	$ .20

Player	Year	No.	VG	EX/MT	Player	Year	No.	VG	EX/MT
Ducey, Rob	89T	203	$ .01	$ .10	Dunston, Shawon	90T	415	$ .01	$ .10
Ducey, Rob	89TBB	280	$ .01	$ .06	Dunston, Shawon	91T	765	$ .01	$ .03
Ducey, Rob	90T	619	$ .01	$ .04	Dupree, Mike	77T	491	$ .25	$1.00
Ducey, Rob	91T	101	$ .01	$ .03	Duren, Ryne	58T	296	$2.10	$6.00
Dues, Hal	79T	699	$ .02	$ .10	Duren, Ryne	59T	485	$ .75	$2.25
Dues, Hal	81T	71	$ .01	$ .10	Duren, Ryne	60T	204	$ .90	$3.00
Duffalo, Jim	62T	578	$3.95	$11.50	Duren, Ryne	61T	356	$ .35	$1.25
Duffalo, Jim	63T	567	$1.75	$4.50	Duren, Ryne	62T	388	$1.25	$4.25
Duffalo, Jim	64T	573	$1.75	$4.50	Duren, Ryne	63T	17	$ .30	$ .95
Duffalo, Jim	65T	159	$ .30	$ .85	Duren, Ryne	64T	173	$ .35	$1.25
Duffy, Frank	71T	164	$ .30	$ .95	Duren, Ryne	65T	339	$ .35	$1.25
Duffy, Frank	72T	607	$ .30	$ .95	Durham, Don	73T	548	$ .45	$1.45
Duffy, Frank	73T	376	$ .07	$ .30	Durham, Joe	58T	96	$1.25	$4.25
Duffy, Frank	74T	81	$ .07	$ .30	Durham, Leon	81T	321	$ .10	$ .50
Duffy, Frank	75T	448	$ .07	$ .30	Durham, Leon	81TTR	756	$ .05	$ .20
Duffy, Frank	76T	232	$ .05	$ .20	Durham, Leon	82T	607	$ .03	$ .15
Duffy, Frank	77T	542	$ .05	$ .15	Durham, Leon	83T	51	$ .01	$ .07
Duffy, Frank	78T	511	$ .02	$ .10	Durham, Leon	83T	125	$ .01	$ .07
Duffy, Frank	79T	106	$ .02	$ .10	Durham, Leon	84T	565	$ .01	$ .06
Dukes, Jan	70T	154	$ .15	$ .50	Durham, Leon	85T	330	$ .01	$ .05
Dukes, Tom	68T	128	$ .30	$ .85	Durham, Leon	86T	460	$ .01	$ .10
Dukes, Tom	69T	223	$ .30	$ .95	Durham, Leon	87T	290	$ .01	$ .04
Dukes, Tom	71T	106	$ .15	$ .50	Durham, Leon	88T	65	$ .01	$ .04
Duliba, Bob	60T	401	$ .75	$2.20	Durham, Leon	88TBB	42	$ .01	$ .06
Duliba, Bob	62T	149	$ .45	$1.45	Durocher, Leo	52T	315	$80.00	$240.00
Duliba, Bob	63T	97	$ .30	$ .95	Durocher, Leo	67T	481	$1.75	$4.50
Duliba, Bob	64T	441	$ .50	$1.45	Durocher, Leo	68T	321	$ .75	$3.00
Duliba, Bob	66T	53	$ .30	$ .95	Durocher, Leo	69T	147	$ .45	$1.45
Duliba, Bob	67T	599	$2.10	$6.00	Durocher, Leo	70T	291	$ .45	$1.45
Dunbar, Tommy	85T	102	$ .01	$ .05	Durocher, Leo	71T	609	$ .90	$3.00
Dunbar, Tommy	86T	559	$ .01	$ .04	Durocher, Leo	72T	576	$ .75	$3.00
Duncan, Dave	64T	528	$1.75	$4.50	Durocher, Leo	73T	624	$ .55	$1.75
Duncan, Dave	68T	261	$ .30	$ .85	Dusak, Erv	52T	183	$7.00	$20.00
Duncan, Dave	69T	68	$ .30	$ .85	Dustal, Bob	63T	299	$ .45	$1.50
Duncan, Dave	70T	678	$ .75	$2.00	Dwyer, Jim	75T	429	$ .07	$ .30
Duncan, Dave	71T	178	$ .15	$ .50	Dwyer, Jim	76T	94	$ .05	$ .20
Duncan, Dave	72T	17	$ .15	$ .50	Dwyer, Jim	78T	644	$ .02	$ .10
Duncan, Dave	73T	337	$ .07	$ .30	Dwyer, Jim	79T	236	$ .02	$ .10
Duncan, Dave	74T	284	$ .07	$ .30	Dwyer, Jim	80T	576	$ .01	$ .10
Duncan, Dave	75T	238	$ .07	$ .30	Dwyer, Jim	81T	184	$ .01	$ .10
Duncan, Dave	76T	49	$ .05	$ .20	Dwyer, Jim	81TTR	757	$ .02	$ .10
Duncan, Dave	77T	338	$ .05	$ .15	Dwyer, Jim	82T	359	$ .01	$ .07
Duncan, Mariano	85TTR	32	$ .05	$ .25	Dwyer, Jim	83T	718	$ .01	$ .07
Duncan, Mariano	86T	602	$ .01	$ .04	Dwyer, Jim	84T	473	$ .01	$ .06
Duncan, Mariano	87T	199	$ .01	$ .04	Dwyer, Jim	85T	56	$ .01	$ .05
Duncan, Mariano	88T	481	$ .01	$ .04	Dwyer, Jim	86T	653	$ .01	$ .04
Duncan, Mariano	90T	234	$ .01	$ .04	Dwyer, Jim	87T	246	$ .01	$ .04
Duncan, Mariano	91T	13	$ .01	$ .03	Dwyer, Jim	88T	521	$ .01	$ .04
Duncan, Taylor	79T	658	$ .02	$ .10	Dybzinski, Jerry	81T	198	$ .01	$ .10
Dunegan, Jim	71T	121	$ .15	$ .50	Dybzinski, Jerry	82T	512	$ .01	$ .07
Dunlop, Harry	73T	593	$ .75	$3.00	Dybzinski, Jerry	83T	289	$ .01	$ .07
Dunlop, Harry	74T	166	$ .07	$ .30	Dybzinski, Jerry	83TTR	27	$ .02	$ .10
Dunne, Mike	85T	395	$ .01	$ .20	Dybzinski, Jerry	84T	619	$ .01	$ .06
Dunne, Mike	87TTR	30	$ .01	$ .10	Dybzinski, Jerry	85T	52	$ .01	$ .05
Dunne, Mike	88T	619	$ .01	$ .10	Dyck, Jim	53T	177	$4.50	$15.00
Dunne, Mike	88TBB	236	$ .01	$ .06	Dyck, Jim	56T	303	$2.25	$8.00
Dunne, Mike	89T	165	$ .01	$ .05	Dyer, Duffy	69T	624	$ .30	$ .95
Dunne, Mike	90T	522	$ .01	$ .04	Dyer, Duffy	70T	692	$ .75	$2.00
Dunne, Mike	91T	238	$ .01	$ .03	Dyer, Duffy	71T	136	$ .15	$ .50
Dunning, Steve	71T	294	$ .15	$ .50	Dyer, Duffy	72T	127	$ .15	$ .50
Dunning, Steve	72T	658	$ .75	$2.50	Dyer, Duffy	73T	493	$ .07	$ .30
Dunning, Steve	73T	53	$ .07	$ .30	Dyer, Duffy	74T	536	$ .07	$ .30
Dunning, Steve	78T	647	$ .02	$ .10	Dyer, Duffy	75T	538	$ .07	$ .30
Dunston, Shawon	85T	280	$ .50	$2.50	Dyer, Duffy	76T	88	$ .05	$ .20
Dunston, Shawon	86T	72	$ .01	$ .50	Dyer, Duffy	77T	318	$ .05	$ .15
Dunston, Shawon	87T	346	$ .01	$ .10	Dyer, Duffy	78T	637	$ .02	$ .10
Dunston, Shawon	88T	695	$ .01	$ .04	Dyer, Duffy	79T	286	$ .02	$ .10
Dunston, Shawon	88TBB	225	$ .01	$ .06	Dyer, Duffy	80T	446	$ .01	$ .10
Dunston, Shawon	89T	140	$ .01	$ .05	Dyer, Duffy	81T	196	$ .01	$ .10
Dunston, Shawon	89TBB	233	$ .01	$ .10	Dyer, Mike	89TMLD	33	$ .01	$ .15

Player	Year	No.	VG	EX/MT	Player	Year	No.	VG	EX/MT
Dyer, Mike	90T	576	$ .01	$ .10	Eastwick, Rawly	76T	469	$ .05	$ .20
Dykes, Jimmie	60T	214	$ .45	$1.45	Eastwick, Rawly	77T	8	$ .05	$ .15
Dykes, Jimmie	61T	222	$ .35	$1.25	Eastwick, Rawly	77T	45	$ .05	$ .15
Dykstra, Len	86T	53	$ .15	$2.00	Eastwick, Rawly	78T	405	$ .02	$ .10
Dykstra, Len	87T	295	$ .05	$ .50	Eastwick, Rawly	79T	271	$ .02	$ .10
Dykstra, Len	88T	655	$ .01	$ .25	Eastwick, Rawly	80T	692	$ .01	$ .10
Dykstra, Len	88TBB	203	$ .01	$ .10	Eastwick, Rawly	82T	117	$ .01	$ .07
Dykstra, Len	89T	435	$ .01	$ .10	Eckersley, Dennis	76T	98	$7.50	$22.50
Dykstra, Len	89TBB	41	$ .01	$ .10	Eckersley, Dennis	76T	202	$ .45	$1.45
Dykstra, Len	89TTR	27	$ .01	$ .10	Eckersley, Dennis	77T	525	$1.50	$6.00
Dykstra, Len	90T	515	$ .01	$ .10	Eckersley, Dennis	78T	122	$ .75	$3.00
Dykstra, Len	91T	345	$ .01	$ .03	Eckersley, Dennis	79T	40	$ .50	$2.00
Earley, Arnold	67T	388	$ .30	$ .95	Eckersley, Dennis	80T	320	$ .35	$1.50
Easler, Mike	78T	710	$ .15	$ .50	Eckersley, Dennis	81T	620	$ .15	$ .75
Easler, Mike	80T	194	$ .03	$ .15	Eckersley, Dennis	82T	490	$ .10	$ .50
Easler, Mike	81T	92	$ .01	$ .10	Eckersley, Dennis	83T	270	$ .05	$ .35
Easler, Mike	82T	235	$ .01	$ .07	Eckersley, Dennis	84T	745	$ .05	$ .25
Easler, Mike	83T	385	$ .01	$ .07	Eckersley, Dennis	84TTR	34	$ .35	$1.50
Easler, Mike	84T	589	$ .01	$ .06	Eckersley, Dennis	85T	163	$ .01	$ .15
Easler, Mike	84TTR	33	$ .02	$ .10	Eckersley, Dennis	86T	538	$ .01	$ .15
Easler, Mike	85T	686	$ .01	$ .05	Eckersley, Dennis	87T	459	$ .01	$ .10
Easler, Mike	86T	477	$ .01	$ .04	Eckersley, Dennis	87TTR	31	$ .01	$ .25
Easler, Mike	86TTR	33	$ .02	$ .10	Eckersley, Dennis	88T	72	$ .01	$ .10
Easler, Mike	87T	135	$ .01	$ .04	Eckersley, Dennis	89T	370	$ .01	$ .10
Easler, Mike	88T	741	$ .01	$ .04	Eckersley, Dennis	90T	670	$ .01	$ .10
Easter, Luke	51Trb	26	$2.10	$6.00	Eckersley, Dennis	91T	250	$ .01	$ .03
Easter, Luke	52T	24	$15.00	$50.00	Eddy, Don	72T	413	$ .15	$ .50
Easter, Luke	53T	2	$5.00	$20.00	Edens, Tom	91T	118	$ .01	$ .10
Easter, Luke	54T	23	$2.50	$9.00	Edge, Bruce	80T	674	$ .01	$ .10
Easterly, Jamie	75T	618	$ .90	$3.00	Edler, Dave	82T	711	$ .25	$1.00
Easterly, Jamie	76T	511	$ .05	$ .20	Edler, Dave	83T	622	$ .01	$ .07
Easterly, Jamie	78T	264	$ .02	$ .10	Edmondson, Paul	70T	414	$ .15	$ .50
Easterly, Jamie	79T	684	$ .02	$ .10	Edward, Wayne	91T	751	$ .01	$ .03
Easterly, Jamie	82T	122	$ .01	$ .07	Edwards, Bruce	51Tbb	42	$7.50	$22.50
Easterly, Jamie	83T	528	$ .01	$ .07	Edwards, Bruce	52T	224	$7.00	$20.00
Easterly, Jamie	83TTR	28	$ .02	$ .10	Edwards, Dave	80T	657	$ .01	$ .10
					Edwards, Dave	81T	386	$ .01	$ .10
					Edwards, Dave	81TTR	758	$ .02	$ .10
					Edwards, Dave	82T	151	$ .01	$ .07
					Edwards, Dave	83T	94	$ .01	$ .07
					Edwards, Doc	62T	594	$35.00	$125.00
					Edwards, Doc	63T	296	$ .45	$1.50
					Edwards, Doc	64T	174	$ .30	$ .95
					Edwards, Doc	65T	239	$ .35	$1.25
					Edwards, Doc	88T	374	$ .01	$ .04
					Edwards, Doc	89T	534	$ .01	$ .05
					Edwards, Hank	52T	176	$7.00	$20.00
					Edwards, Hank	53T	90	$4.50	$15.00
					Edwards, John	62T	302	$ .45	$1.45
					Edwards, Johnny	63T	178	$ .30	$ .95
					Edwards, Johnny	64T	507	$ .50	$1.45
					Edwards, Johnny	65T	418	$ .35	$1.25
					Edwards, Johnny	66T	507	$ .75	$2.50
					Edwards, Johnny	67T	202	$ .30	$ .85
					Edwards, John	68T	558	$ .35	$1.25
					Edwards, Johnny	69T	186	$ .30	$ .85
					Edwards, Johnny	70T	339	$ .15	$ .50
					Edwards, Johnny	71T	44	$ .15	$ .50
					Edwards, Johnny	72T	416	$ .15	$ .50
					Edwards, Johnny	73T	519	$ .07	$ .30
					Edwards, Johnny	74T	635	$ .07	$ .30
					Edwards, Marshall	82T	333	$ .01	$ .07
					Edwards, Marshall	83T	582	$ .01	$ .07
					Edwards, Marshall	84T	167	$ .01	$ .06
					Edwards, Mike	79T	613	$ .02	$ .10
					Edwards, Mike	79TRB	201	$ .02	$ .10
					Edwards, Mike	80T	301	$ .01	$ .10
Easterly, Jamie	84T	367	$ .01	$ .06	Edwards, Wayne	89TMLD	34	$ .01	$ .15
Easterly, Jamie	85T	764	$ .01	$ .05	Edwards, Wayne	90TTR	27	$ .01	$ .15
Easterly, Jamie	86T	31	$ .01	$ .04	Egan, Dick	63T	169	$10.00	$30.00
Eastwick, Rawly	75T	621	$ .15	$ .50					

JAMIE EASTERLY   P

TOPPS

Player	Year	No.	VG	EX/MT	Player	Year	No.	VG	EX/MT
Egan, Dick	64T	572	$1.75	$4.50	Ellis, John	74T	128	$ .07	$ .30
Egan, Dick	66T	536	$5.00	$20.00	Ellis, John	75T	605	$ .07	$ .30
Egan, Dick	67T	539	$2.10	$6.00	Ellis, John	76T	383	$ .05	$ .20
Egan, Tom	65T	486	$ .75	$3.00	Ellis, John	76TTR	383	$ .05	$ .20
Egan, Tom	66T	263	$ .30	$ .95	Ellis, John	77T	36	$ .05	$ .15
Egan, Tom	67T	147	$ .30	$ .85	Ellis, John	78T	438	$ .02	$ .10
Egan, Tom	69T	407	$ .30	$ .85	Ellis, John	79T	539	$ .02	$ .10
Egan, Tom	70T	4	$ .15	$ .50	Ellis, John	80T	283	$ .01	$ .10
Egan, Tom	71T	537	$ .35	$1.25	Ellis, John	81T	339	$ .01	$ .10
Egan, Tom	72T	207	$ .15	$ .50	Ellis, John	82T	177	$ .01	$ .07
Egan, Tom	73T	648	$ .45	$1.45	Ellis, Sammy	63T	29	$ .45	$1.45
Egan, Tom	75T	88	$ .07	$ .30	Ellis, Sammy	64T	33	$ .30	$ .95
Eichelberger, Juan	81T	478	$ .01	$ .10	Ellis, Sammy	65T	507	$ .75	$3.00
Eichelberger, Juan	82T	366	$ .01	$ .07	Ellis, Sam	66T	250	$ .30	$ .95
Eichelberger, Juan	82T	614	$ .01	$ .07	Ellis, Sammy	67T	176	$ .30	$ .85
Eichelberger, Juan	83T	168	$ .01	$ .07	Ellis, Sammy	68T	453	$ .30	$ .85
Eichelberger, Juan	83TTR	29	$ .02	$ .10	Ellis, Sammy	69T	32	$ .30	$ .85
Eichelberger, Juan	84T	226	$ .01	$ .06	Ellsworth, Dick	60T	125	$ .75	$3.00
Eichhorn, Mark	86TTR	34	$ .01	$ .15	Ellsworth, Dick	61T	427	$ .75	$3.00
Eichhorn, Mark	87T	371	$ .01	$ .10	Ellsworth, Dick	62T	264	$ .45	$1.45
Eichhorn, Mark	88T	749	$ .01	$ .10	Ellsworth, Dick	63T	399	$ .45	$1.50
Eichhorn, Mark	88TBB	208	$ .01	$ .06	Ellsworth, Dick	64T	1	$3.50	$15.00
Eichhorn, Mark	89T	274	$ .01	$ .05	Ellsworth, Dick	64T	220	$ .30	$ .95
Eichhorn, Mark	89TBB	188	$ .01	$ .06	Ellsworth, Dick	65T	165	$ .30	$ .85
Eichhorn, Mark	90T	513	$ .01	$ .04	Ellsworth, Dick	66T	447	$ .75	$2.50
Eichhorn, Mark	90TTR	28	$ .01	$ .05	Ellsworth, Dick	67T	359	$ .30	$ .85
Eichhorn, Mark	91T	129	$ .01	$ .03	Ellsworth, Dick	68T	406	$ .30	$ .85
Eiland, Dave	89T	8	$ .01	$ .10	Ellsworth, Dick	69T	605	$ .30	$ .95
Eiland, Dave	91T	611	$ .01	$ .03	Ellsworth, Dick	70T	59	$ .15	$ .50
Eilers, Dave	66T	534	$5.00	$20.00	Ellsworth, Dick	71T	309	$ .15	$ .50
Eisenreich, Jim	83T	197	$ .25	$1.00	Ellsworth, Steve	89T	299	$ .01	$ .05
Eisenreich, Jim	88T	348	$ .01	$ .04	Elster, Kevin	88T	8	$ .01	$ .10
Eisenreich, Jim	89TTR	28	$ .01	$ .06	Elster, Kevin	89T	356	$ .01	$ .05
Eisenreich, Jim	90T	246	$ .01	$ .04	Elster, Kevin	89TBB	16	$ .01	$ .06
Eisenreich, Jim	91T	707	$ .01	$ .03	Elster, Kevin	90T	734	$ .01	$ .04
Elia, Lee	66T	529	$5.00	$20.00	Elster, Kevin	91T	134	$ .01	$ .03
Elia, Lee	67T	406	$ .30	$ .95	Elston, Don	57T	376	$1.25	$4.25
Elia, Lee	68T	561	$ .35	$1.25	Elston, Don	58T	363	$ .75	$3.00
Elia, Lee	69T	312	$ .30	$ .95	Elston, Don	59T	520	$2.50	$10.00
Elia, Lee	83T	456	$ .01	$ .07	Elston, Don	60T	233	$ .45	$1.45
Elia, Lee	87TTR	32	$ .01	$ .05	Elston, Don	61T	169	$ .35	$1.25
Elia, Lee	88T	254	$ .01	$ .04	Elston, Don	62T	446	$ .75	$2.50
Ellingsen, Bruce	75T	288	$ .07	$ .30	Elston, Don	63T	515	$1.75	$4.50
Elliot, Larry	63T	407	$ .45	$1.50	Elston, Don	64T	111	$ .30	$ .95
Elliot, Larry	64T	536	$1.75	$4.50	Elston, Don	65T	436	$ .35	$1.25
Elliot, Larry	67T	23	$ .30	$ .85	Engle, Dave	81T	328	$ .01	$ .10
Elliott, Bob	51Tbb	32	$4.00	$18.00	Engle, Dave	82T	738	$ .01	$ .07
Elliott, Bob	52T	14	$15.00	$47.50	Engle, Dave	83T	294	$ .01	$ .07
Elliott, Bob	60T	215	$ .45	$1.45	Engle, Dave	84T	463	$ .01	$ .06
Elliott, Harry	55T	137	$2.00	$6.00	Engle, Dave	85T	667	$ .01	$ .05
Elliott, Randy	78T	719	$ .02	$ .10	Engle, Dave	86T	43	$ .01	$ .04
Ellis, Dock	69T	286	$ .30	$ .95	Engle, Dave	88T	196	$ .01	$ .04
Ellis, Dock	70T	551	$ .30	$ .95	Ennis, Del	51Tbb	4	$4.50	$20.00
Ellis, Dock	71T	2	$ .30	$ .95	Ennis, Del	52T	223	$7.00	$21.00
Ellis, Dock	72T	179	$ .15	$ .50	Ennis, Del	56T	220	$3.00	$9.00
Ellis, Dock	72TIA	180	$ .15	$ .50	Ennis, Del	57T	260	$ .60	$2.50
Ellis, Dock	73T	575	$ .45	$1.45	Ennis, Del	58T	60	$ .70	$2.25
Ellis, Dock	74T	145	$ .07	$ .30	Ennis, Del	59T	255	$ .75	$2.20
Ellis, Dock	75T	385	$ .07	$ .30	Eppard, Jim	89T	42	$ .01	$ .10
Ellis, Dock	76T	528	$ .05	$ .20	Epstein, Mike	67T	204	$ .30	$ .85
Ellis, Dock	76TTR	528	$ .05	$ .20	Epstein, Mike	68T	358	$ .30	$ .85
Ellis, Dock	77T	71	$ .05	$ .15	Epstein, Mike	69T	461	$ .30	$ .85
Ellis, Dock	78T	209	$ .02	$ .10	Epstein, Mike	69T	539	$2.25	$6.00
Ellis, Dock	79T	691	$ .02	$ .10	Epstein, Mike	70T	235	$ .15	$ .50
Ellis, Dock	80T	117	$ .01	$ .10	Epstein, Mike	71T	655	$ .75	$2.50
Ellis, John	70T	516	$ .15	$ .50	Epstein, Mike	72T	715	$ .75	$2.50
Ellis, John	71T	263	$ .15	$ .50	Epstein, Mike	73T	38	$ .07	$ .30
Ellis, John	72T	47	$ .15	$ .50	Epstein, Mike	74T	650	$ .07	$ .30
Ellis, John	72TIA	48	$ .15	$ .50	Erautt, Ed	52T	171	$7.00	$20.00
Ellis, John	73T	656	$ .45	$1.45	Erautt, Ed	53T	226	$12.50	$50.00

Player	Year	No.	VG	EX/MT	Player	Year	No.	VG	EX/MT
Erickson, Roger	79T	81	$ .02	$ .10	Estrada, Chuck	61T	395	$ .75	$3.00
Erickson, Roger	80T	256	$ .01	$ .10	Estrada, Chuck	62T	560	$3.95	$11.50
Erickson, Roger	81T	434	$ .01	$ .10	Estrada, Chuck	63T	465	$2.50	$6.50
Erickson, Roger	82T	153	$ .01	$ .07	Estrada, Chuck	64T	263	$ .30	$ .95
Erickson, Roger	82TTR	30	$ .02	$ .10	Estrada, Chuck	65T	378	$ .35	$1.25
Erickson, Roger	83T	539	$ .01	$ .07					
Erickson, Scott	90TTR	29	$ .01	$2.00					
Erickson, Scott	91T	234	$ .01	$ .50					
Ermer, Cal	68T	206	$ .30	$ .85					
Erskine, Carl	52T	250	$18.00	$65.00					
Erskine, Carl	56T	233	$6.00	$20.00					
Erskine, Carl	57T	252	$3.60	$10.00					
Erskine, Carl	58T	258	$2.10	$6.00					
Erskine, Carl	59T	217	$2.10	$6.00					
Esasky, Nick	84T	192	$ .75	$3.00					
Esasky, Nick	85T	779	$ .01	$ .25					
Esasky, Nick	86T	677	$ .01	$ .10					
Esasky, Nick	87T	13	$ .01	$ .06					
Esasky, Nick	88T	364	$ .01	$ .04					
Esasky, Nick	88TBB	167	$ .01	$ .06					
Esasky, Nick	89T	554	$ .01	$ .05					
Esasky, Nick	89TBB	316	$ .01	$ .10					
Esasky, Nick	89TTR	29	$ .01	$ .25					
Esasky, Nick	90T	206	$ .01	$ .10					
Esasky, Nick	90TTR	30	$ .01	$ .05					
Esasky, Nick	91T	418	$ .01	$ .03					
Espino, Juan	87T	239	$ .01	$ .04					
Espinosa, Nino	77T	376	$ .05	$ .15					
Espinosa, Nino	78T	197	$ .02	$ .10					
Espinosa, Nino	79T	566	$ .02	$ .10					
Espinosa, Nino	80T	447	$ .01	$ .10					
Espinosa, Nino	81T	405	$ .01	$ .10					
Espinoza, Alvaro	87T	529	$ .01	$ .04					
Espinoza, Alvaro	89TTR	30	$ .01	$ .25					
Espinoza, Alvaro	90T	791	$ .01	$ .10					
Espinoza, Alvaro	91T	28	$ .01	$ .03	Estrada, Chuck	67T	537	$2.10	$6.00
Esposito, Sam	57T	301	$4.25	$15.00	Estrada, Chuck	73T	549	$ .35	$1.25
Esposito, Sam	58T	425	$ .75	$3.00	Etchebarren, Andy	66T	27	$ .30	$ .95
Esposito, Sam	59T	438	$ .75	$2.20	Etchebarren, Andy	67T	457	$ .30	$ .95
Esposito, Sammy	60T	31	$ .45	$1.45	Etchebarren, Andy	68T	204	$ .30	$ .85
Esposito, Sammy	61T	323	$ .35	$1.25	Etchebarren, Andy	69T	634	$ .30	$ .95
Esposito, Sammy	62T	586	$3.95	$11.50	Etchebarren, Andy	70T	213	$ .15	$ .50
Esposito, Sammy	63T	181	$ .30	$ .95	Etchebarren, Andy	71T	501	$ .15	$ .50
Espy, Cecil	88TTR	36	$ .01	$ .15	Etchebarren, Andy	72T	26	$ .15	$ .50
Espy, Cecil	89T	221	$ .01	$ .10	Etchebarren, Andy	73T	618	$ .45	$1.45
Espy, Cecil	89TBB	36	$ .01	$ .06	Etchebarren, Andy	74T	488	$ .07	$ .30
Espy, Cecil	90T	496	$ .01	$ .04	Etchebarren, Andy	75T	583	$ .07	$ .30
Essegian, Chuck	58T	460	$ .75	$2.20	Etchebarren, Andy	76T	129	$ .05	$ .20
Essegian, Chuck	59T	278	$ .75	$2.20	Etchebarren, Andy	77T	454	$ .05	$ .15
Essegian, Chuck	60T	166	$ .45	$1.45	Etchebarren, Andy	78T	313	$ .02	$ .10
Essegian, Chuck	61T	384	$ .75	$3.00	Etheridge, Bobby	68T	126	$ .30	$ .85
Essegian, Chuck	62T	379	$ .75	$2.50	Etheridge, Bobby	69T	604	$ .30	$ .95
Essegian, Chuck	63T	103	$ .30	$ .95	Etheridge, Bobby	70T	107	$ .15	$ .50
Essian, Jim	77T	529	$ .05	$ .15	Eufemia, Frank	86T	236	$ .01	$ .04
Essian, Jim	78T	98	$ .02	$ .10	Evans, Al	52T	152	$7.00	$20.00
Essian, Jim	79T	458	$ .02	$ .10	Evans, Barry	81T	72	$ .01	$ .10
Essian, Jim	80T	341	$ .01	$ .10	Evans, Barry	82T	541	$ .01	$ .07
Essian, Jim	81T	178	$ .01	$ .10	Evans, Darrell	70T	621	$5.00	$16.00
Essian, Jim	81TTR	759	$ .02	$ .10	Evans, Darrell	72T	171	$ .50	$1.50
Essian, Jim	82T	269	$ .01	$ .07	Evans, Darrell	72TIA	172	$ .15	$ .50
Essian, Jim	82TTR	31	$ .02	$ .10	Evans, Darrell	73T	374	$ .30	$ .95
Essian, Jim	83T	646	$ .01	$ .07	Evans, Darrell	74T	140	$ .30	$ .95
Essian, Jim	83TTR	30	$ .02	$ .10	Evans, Darrell	75T	475	$ .30	$ .95
Essian, Jim	84T	737	$ .01	$ .06	Evans, Darrell	76T	81	$ .30	$ .85
Essian, Jim	84TTR	35	$ .02	$ .10	Evans, Darrell	77T	571	$ .30	$ .85
Essian, Jim	85T	472	$ .01	$ .05	Evans, Darrell	78T	215	$ .05	$ .20
Estelle, Dick	65T	282	$ .35	$1.25	Evans, Darrell	79T	410	$ .05	$ .20
Estelle, Dick	66T	373	$ .30	$ .95	Evans, Darrell	80T	145	$ .03	$ .15
Estrada, Chuck	60T	126	$ .45	$1.45	Evans, Darrell	81T	648	$ .01	$ .10
Estrada, Chuck	61T	48	$ .75	$3.00	Evans, Darrell	82T	17	$ .03	$ .15

TOPPS

Player	Year	No.	VG	EX/MT	Player	Year	No.	VG	EX/MT
Evans, Darrell	83T	448	$ .01	$ .07	Face, Roy	67T	49	$ .30	$ .95
Evans, Darrell	84T	325	$ .01	$ .06	Face, Roy	68T	198	$ .30	$ .95
Evans, Darrell	84TTR	36	$ .02	$ .10	Face, Roy	69T	207	$ .30	$ .95
Evans, Darrell	85T	792	$ .01	$ .05	Faedo, Lenny	82T	766	$1.50	$4.50
Evans, Darrell	86T	515	$ .01	$ .04	Faedo, Lenny	83T	671	$ .01	$ .07
Evans, Darrell	87T	265	$ .01	$ .10	Faedo, Lenny	84T	84	$ .01	$ .06
Evans, Darrell	88T	630	$ .01	$ .04	Fahey, Bill	72T	334	$ .15	$ .50
Evans, Darrell	88TBB	82	$ .01	$ .06	Fahey, Bill	73T	186	$ .07	$ .30
Evans, Darrell	89TTR	31	$ .01	$ .10	Fahey, Bill	74T	558	$ .07	$ .30
Evans, Darrell	90T	55	$ .01	$ .10	Fahey, Bill	75T	644	$ .07	$ .30
Evans, Dwight	73T	614	$15.00	$60.00	Fahey, Bill	76T	436	$ .05	$ .20
Evans, Dwight	74T	351	$2.50	$10.00	Fahey, Bill	77T	511	$ .05	$ .15
Evans, Dwight	75T	255	$1.60	$5.50	Fahey, Bill	78T	388	$ .02	$ .10
Evans, Dwight	76T	575	$ .65	$2.75	Fahey, Bill	80T	44	$ .01	$ .10
Evans, Dwight	77T	25	$ .35	$2.00	Fahey, Bill	81T	653	$ .01	$ .10
Evans, Dwight	78T	695	$ .35	$1.25	Fahey, Bill	81TTR	760	$ .02	$ .10
Evans, Dwight	79T	155	$ .20	$1.00	Fahey, Bill	82T	286	$ .01	$ .07
Evans, Dwight	80T	405	$ .15	$ .75	Fahey, Bill	83T	196	$ .01	$ .07
Evans, Dwight	81T	275	$ .05	$ .20	Fain, Ferris	51Trb	3	$2.10	$6.00
Evans, Dwight	82T	162	$ .05	$ .25	Fain, Ferris	52T	21	$15.00	$47.50
Evans, Dwight	82T	355	$ .05	$ .20	Fain, Ferris	53T	24	$4.50	$15.00
Evans, Dwight	83T	135	$ .03	$ .15	Fain, Ferris	54T	27	$2.50	$10.00
Evans, Dwight	84T	720	$ .03	$ .15	Fain, Ferris	55T	11	$3.60	$10.00
Evans, Dwight	85T	580	$ .01	$ .10	Fairey, Jim	68T	228	$ .30	$ .95
Evans, Dwight	86T	60	$ .01	$ .10	Fairey, Jim	69T	117	$ .30	$ .85
Evans, Dwight	87T	645	$ .01	$ .10	Fairey, Jim	71T	474	$ .15	$ .50
Evans, Dwight	87TRB	3	$ .01	$ .04	Fairey, Jim	72T	653	$ .30	$ .95
Evans, Dwight	88T	470	$ .01	$ .10	Fairey, Jim	73T	429	$ .07	$ .30
Evans, Dwight	88TBB	6	$ .01	$ .10	Fairly, Ron	59T	125	$1.25	$4.25
Evans, Dwight	89T	205	$ .01	$ .05	Fairly, Ron	60T	321	$ .75	$2.20
Evans, Dwight	89TBB	193	$ .01	$ .10	Fairly, Ron	61T	492	$ .75	$3.00
Evans, Dwight	90T	375	$ .01	$ .04	Fairly, Ron	62T	375	$ .75	$2.50
Evans, Dwight	91T	155	$ .01	$ .03	Fairly, Ron	63T	105	$ .30	$ .95
Everett, Carl	91T	113	$ .01	$ .25	Fairly, Ron	64T	490	$ .50	$1.45
Evers, Hoot	52T	222	$7.00	$20.00	Fairly, Ron	65T	196	$ .30	$ .85
Ewing, Sam	78T	344	$ .02	$ .10	Fairly, Ron	66T	330	$ .30	$ .95
Ewing, Sam	79T	521	$ .02	$ .10	Fairly, Ron	67T	94	$ .30	$ .85
Expos, Team	70T	509	$ .45	$1.45	Fairly, Ron	68T	510	$ .35	$1.25
Expos, Team	71T	674	$3.00	$9.00	Fairly, Ron	69T	122	$ .30	$ .95
Expos, Team	72T	582	$1.00	$3.00	Fairly, Ron	70T	690	$ .75	$2.00
Expos, Team	73T	576	$ .90	$3.00	Fairly, Ron	71T	315	$ .15	$ .50
Expos, Team	74T	508	$ .20	$ .75	Fairly, Ron	72T	405	$ .30	$ .85
Expos, Team Checklist	75T	101	$ .30	$ .95	Fairly, Ron	73T	125	$ .15	$ .50
Expos, Team Checklist	76T	216	$ .15	$ .50	Fairly, Ron	74T	146	$ .07	$ .30
Expos, Team Checklist	77T	647	$ .15	$ .50	Fairly, Ron	75T	270	$ .07	$ .30
Expos, Team Checklist	78T	244	$ .02	$ .10	Fairly, Ron	76T	375	$ .05	$ .20
Expos, Team Checklist	79T	606	$ .05	$ .25	Fairly, Ron	77T	127	$ .05	$ .15
Expos, Team Checklist	80T	479	$ .05	$ .25	Fairly, Ron	78T	85	$ .02	$ .10
Expos, Team Checklist	81T	680	$ .02	$ .20	Fairly, Ron	79T	580	$ .02	$ .10
Expos, Team Leaders	86T	576	$ .01	$ .04	Falcone, Pete	76T	524	$ .05	$ .20
Expos, Team Leaders	87T	381	$ .01	$ .04	Falcone, Pete	76TTR	524	$ .05	$ .20
Expos, Team Leaders	88T	111	$ .01	$ .04	Falcone, Pete	77T	205	$ .05	$ .15
Expos, Team Leaders	89T	81	$ .01	$ .05	Falcone, Pete	78T	669	$ .02	$ .10
Face, Roy	53T	246	$15.00	$50.00	Falcone, Pete	79T	87	$ .02	$ .10
Face, Roy	54T	87	$2.50	$10.00	Falcone, Pete	80T	401	$ .01	$ .10
Face, Roy	56T	13	$1.50	$4.00	Falcone, Pete	81T	117	$ .01	$ .10
Face, Roy	57T	166	$ .60	$2.50	Falcone, Pete	82T	326	$ .01	$ .07
Face, Roy	58T	74	$ .70	$2.25	Falcone, Pete	83T	764	$ .01	$ .07
Face, Roy	59T	339	$ .75	$2.20	Falcone, Pete	83TTR	31	$ .02	$ .10
Face, Roy	59T	428	$ .75	$2.20	Falcone, Pete	84T	521	$ .01	$ .06
Face, Roy	60T	20	$ .75	$3.00	Falcone, Pete	85T	618	$ .01	$ .05
Face, Roy	60T	115	$1.30	$5.00	Fannin, Cliff	51Tbb	36	$7.50	$22.50
Face, Roy	61T	250	$ .75	$3.00	Fannin, Cliff	52T	285	$15.00	$47.50
Face, Roy	61T	370	$ .75	$3.00	Fannin, Cliff	53T	203	$4.50	$15.00
Face, Roy	62T	210	$ .75	$3.00	Fanning, Jim	85T	759	$ .01	$ .05
Face, Roy	62T	423	$2.10	$6.00	Fanok, Harry	63T	54	$1.50	$4.00
Face, Roy	63T	409	$ .75	$3.00	Fanok, Harry	64T	262	$ .45	$1.45
Face, Roy	64T	539	$2.10	$6.00	Fanzone, Carmen	73T	139	$ .07	$ .30
Face, Roy	65T	347	$ .45	$1.45	Fanzone, Carmen	74T	484	$ .07	$ .30
Face, Roy	66T	461	$ .90	$3.00	Fanzone, Carmen	75T	363	$ .07	$ .30

Player	Year	No.	VG	EX/MT
Fariss, Monty	89T	177	$ .10	$ .40
Farley, Bob	62T	426	$ .75	$2.50
Farmer, Billy	70T	444	$ .15	$ .50
Farmer, Ed	72T	116	$ .15	$ .50
Farmer, Ed	73T	272	$ .07	$ .30
Farmer, Ed	74T	506	$ .07	$ .30
Farmer, Ed	80T	702	$ .01	$ .10
Farmer, Ed	81T	36	$ .01	$ .10
Farmer, Ed	82T	328	$ .01	$ .07
Farmer, Ed	82TTR	32	$ .02	$ .10
Farmer, Ed	83T	459	$ .01	$ .07
Farr, Steve	85T	664	$ .01	$ .05
Farr, Steve	86TTR	35	$ .02	$ .10
Farr, Steve	87T	473	$ .01	$ .04
Farr, Steve	88T	222	$ .01	$ .04
Farr, Steve	89T	507	$ .01	$ .05
Farr, Steve	90T	149	$ .01	$ .04
Farr, Steve	91T	301	$ .01	$ .03
Farrell, Dick	58T	76	$1.25	$4.25
Farrell, Dick	59T	175	$ .75	$2.20
Farrell, Dick	60T	103	$ .45	$1.45
Farrell, Dick	61T	522	$ .75	$3.00
Farrell, Dick	62T	304	$ .45	$1.45
Farrell, Dick	63T	9	$ .90	$3.00
Farrell, Dick	63T	277	$ .30	$ .95
Farrell, Dick	64T	560	$1.75	$4.50
Farrell, Dick	69T	531	$ .30	$ .95
Farrell, John	88T	533	$ .01	$ .25
Farrell, John	88TBB	213	$ .01	$ .20
Farrell, John	89T	227	$ .01	$ .20
Farrell, John	89TBB	135	$ .01	$ .10
Farrell, John	90T	32	$ .01	$ .10
Farrell, John	91T	664	$ .01	$ .03
Farrell, Turk	65T	80	$ .30	$ .85
Farrell, Turk	66T	377	$ .30	$ .95
Farrell, Turk	67T	190	$ .30	$ .85
Farrell, Turk	68T	217	$ .30	$ .85
Fast, Darcy	72T	457	$ .15	$ .50
Faul, Bill	63T	558	$1.75	$4.50
Faul, Bill	64T	236	$ .30	$ .95
Faul, Bill	66T	322	$ .30	$ .95
Felder, Mike	87T	352	$ .01	$ .04
Felder, Mike	88T	718	$ .01	$ .04
Felder, Mike	89T	263	$ .01	$ .05
Felder, Mike	90T	159	$ .01	$ .04
Felder, Mike	91T	44	$ .01	$ .03
Felix, Junior	89TMLD	35	$ .01	$ .35
Felix, Junior	89TTR	32	$ .01	$ .75
Felix, Junior	90T	347	$ .01	$ .35
Felix, Junior	91T	543	$ .01	$ .03
Feller, Bob	51Trb	22	$8.00	$25.00
Feller, Bob	52T	88	$35.00	$125.00
Feller, Bob	53T	54	$30.00	$90.00
Feller, Bob	56T	200	$35.00	$100.00
Felske, John	73T	332	$ .07	$ .30
Felske, John	85TTR	33	$ .02	$ .10
Felske, John	86T	621	$ .01	$ .04
Felske, John	87T	443	$ .01	$ .04
Felton, Terry	83T	181	$ .01	$ .07
Fenwick, Bob	72T	679	$ .90	$3.00
Fenwick, Bob	73T	567	$ .45	$1.45
Ferguson, Joe	72T	616	$ .30	$ .95
Ferguson, Joe	73T	621	$ .75	$3.00
Ferguson, Joe	74T	86	$ .07	$ .30
Ferguson, Joe	75T	115	$ .07	$ .30
Ferguson, Joe	76T	329	$ .05	$ .20
Ferguson, Joe	77T	573	$ .05	$ .15
Ferguson, Joe	78T	226	$ .02	$ .10
Ferguson, Joe	79T	671	$ .02	$ .10
Ferguson, Joe	80T	51	$ .01	$ .10

Player	Year	No.	VG	EX/MT
Ferguson, Joe	81T	711	$ .01	$ .10
Ferguson, Joe	82T	514	$ .01	$ .07

Player	Year	No.	VG	EX/MT
Ferguson, Joe	83T	416	$ .01	$ .07
Fermin, Felix	88T	547	$ .01	$ .04
Fermin, Felix	89T	303	$ .01	$ .05
Fermin, Felix	89TTR	33	$ .01	$ .06
Fermin, Felix	90T	722	$ .01	$ .04
Fermin, Felix	91T	193	$ .01	$ .03
Fernandez, Alex	91T	278	$ .01	$ .75
Fernandez, Chico	57T	305	$4.25	$15.00
Fernandez, Chico	58T	348	$ .75	$3.00
Fernandez, Chico	59T	452	$ .75	$2.20
Fernandez, Chico	60T	314	$ .75	$2.20
Fernandez, Chico	61T	112	$ .35	$1.25
Fernandez, Chico	62T	173	$ .45	$1.45
Fernandez, Chico	63T	278	$ .30	$ .95
Fernandez, Frank	66T	584	$5.00	$20.00
Fernandez, Frank	68T	214	$ .45	$1.45
Fernandez, Frank	69T	557	$ .30	$ .95
Fernandez, Frank	70T	82	$ .15	$ .50
Fernandez, Frank	71T	468	$ .15	$ .50
Fernandez, Sid	85T	649	$ .15	$ .75
Fernandez, Sid	86T	104	$ .01	$ .20
Fernandez, Sid	87T	570	$ .03	$ .15
Fernandez, Sid	88T	30	$ .01	$ .10
Fernandez, Sid	89T	790	$ .01	$ .10
Fernandez, Sid	89TBB	276	$ .01	$ .06
Fernandez, Sid	90T	480	$ .01	$ .04
Fernandez, Sid	91T	230	$ .01	$ .03
Fernandez, Tony	85T	48	$ .25	$1.25
Fernandez, Tony	86T	241	$ .01	$ .10
Fernandez, Tony	87T	485	$ .01	$ .04
Fernandez, Tony	88T	290	$ .01	$ .10
Fernandez, Tony	88TBB	187	$ .01	$ .06
Fernandez, Tony	89T	170	$ .01	$ .10
Fernandez, Tony	89TBB	157	$ .01	$ .10
Fernandez, Tony	90T	685	$ .01	$ .10
Fernandez, Tony	91T	320	$ .01	$ .03
Ferrara, Al	64T	337	$ .30	$ .95
Ferrara, Al	65T	331	$ .35	$1.25

Player	Year	No.	VG	EX/MT
Ferrara, Al	66T	487	$ .75	$2.50
Ferrara, Al	67T	557	$2.10	$6.00
Ferrara, Al	68T	34	$ .30	$ .85
Ferrara, Al	69T	452	$ .30	$ .85
Ferrara, Al	70T	345	$ .15	$ .50
Ferrara, Al	71T	214	$ .15	$ .50
Ferrarese, Don	55T	185	$5.25	$15.00
Ferrarese, Don	56T	266	$2.25	$8.00
Ferrarese, Don	57T	146	$ .95	$3.50
Ferrarese, Don	58T	469	$ .75	$2.20
Ferrarese, Don	59T	247	$ .75	$2.20
Ferrarese, Don	60T	477	$ .90	$3.00
Ferrarese, Don	61T	558	$7.00	$21.00
Ferrarese, Don	62T	547	$3.95	$11.50
Ferraro, Mike	68T	539	$ .35	$1.25
Ferraro, Mike	69T	83	$ .30	$ .85
Ferraro, Mike	72T	613	$ .30	$ .95
Ferraro, Mike	83TTR	32	$ .02	$ .10
Ferrer, Sergio	79T	397	$ .02	$ .10
Ferrer, Sergio	80T	619	$ .01	$ .10
Ferrick, Tom	60T	461	$2.25	$6.00
Fetters, Mike	89TMLD	36	$ .01	$ .35
Fetters, Mike	90T	14	$ .01	$ .10
Fetters, Mike	91T	477	$ .01	$ .03
Fidrych, Mark	77T	7	$ .05	$ .15
Fidrych, Mark	77T	265	$ .30	$ .95
Fidrych, Mark	78T	45	$ .05	$ .20
Fidrych, Mark	79T	625	$ .05	$ .20
Fidrych, Mark	80T	445	$ .01	$ .10
Fidrych, Mark	81T	150	$ .01	$ .10
Fielder, Cecil	86T	386	$ .50	$6.00
Fielder, Cecil	87T	178	$ .15	$1.25
Fielder, Cecil	88T	618	$ .10	$ .50
Fielder, Cecil	89T	541	$ .01	$ .25
Fielder, Cecil	90TTR	31	$ .01	$ .35
Fielder, Cecil	91T	720	$ .01	$ .15
Fielder, Cecil	91TAS	386	$ .01	$ .10
Fields, Bruce	89T	556	$ .01	$ .05
Fiesella, Dan	68T	191	$ .30	$ .85
Fife, Dan	74T	421	$ .07	$ .30
Figueroa, Ed	75T	476	$ .07	$ .30
Figueroa, Ed	76T	27	$ .05	$ .20
Figueroa, Ed	76TTR	27	$ .05	$ .20
Figueroa, Ed	77T	195	$ .05	$ .15
Figueroa, Ed	78T	365	$ .02	$ .10
Figueroa, Ed	79T	35	$ .02	$ .10
Figueroa, Ed	80T	555	$ .01	$ .10
Figueroa, Ed	81T	245	$ .01	$ .10
Figueroa, Jesus	81T	533	$ .01	$ .10
Filer, Tom	83T	508	$ .01	$ .07
Filer, Tom	86T	312	$ .01	$ .04
Filer, Tom	88TTR	37	$ .01	$ .06
Filer, Tom	89T	419	$ .01	$ .06
Filson, Pete	84T	568	$ .01	$ .06
Filson, Pete	85T	97	$ .01	$ .05
Filson, Pete	86T	122	$ .01	$ .04
Fimple, Jack	84T	263	$ .01	$ .06
Finch, Joel	79T	702	$ .02	$ .10
Finch, Joel	80T	662	$ .01	$ .10
Fingers, Rollie	69T	597	$17.50	$70.00
Fingers, Rollie	70T	502	$5.50	$17.50
Fingers, Rollie	71T	384	$2.00	$8.00
Fingers, Rollie	72T	241	$1.25	$5.00
Fingers, Rollie	73T	84	$1.00	$4.00
Fingers, Rollie	74T	212	$ .75	$3.00
Fingers, Rollie	75T	21	$ .45	$1.45
Fingers, Rollie	76T	405	$ .45	$1.45
Fingers, Rollie	77T	523	$ .45	$1.45
Fingers, Rollie	78T	140	$ .08	$ .35
Fingers, Rollie	78T	208	$ .05	$ .20
Fingers, Rollie	79T	8	$ .05	$ .25
Fingers, Rollie	79T	390	$ .08	$ .35
Fingers, Rollie	80T	651	$ .05	$ .25
Fingers, Rollie	81T	8	$ .01	$ .10
Fingers, Rollie	81T	229	$ .10	$ .50
Fingers, Rollie	81TTR	761	$ .15	$ .50
Fingers, Rollie	82T	168	$ .03	$ .15
Fingers, Rollie	82T	585	$ .05	$ .25
Fingers, Rollie	82TIA	586	$ .01	$ .07
Fingers, Rollie	83T	35	$ .03	$ .15
Fingers, Rollie	83T	36	$ .01	$ .07
Fingers, Rollie	84T	495	$ .02	$ .10
Fingers, Rollie	84T	717	$ .01	$ .06
Fingers, Rollie	84T	718	$ .01	$ .06
Fingers, Rollie	85T	750	$ .01	$ .10
Fingers, Rollie	86T	185	$ .02	$ .15
Finigan, Jim	55T	14	$2.00	$6.00
Finigan, Jim	56T	22	$2.25	$6.00
Finigan, Jim	57T	248	$ .95	$3.50
Finigan, Jim	58T	136	$ .75	$3.00
Finigan, Jim	59T	47	$1.25	$4.25
Finley, Chuck	87T	446	$ .01	$ .04
Finley, Chuck	88T	99	$ .01	$ .04
Finley, Chuck	88TBB	254	$ .01	$ .06
Finley, Chuck	89T	708	$ .01	$ .05
Finley, Chuck	89TBB	76	$ .01	$ .06
Finley, Chuck	90T	147	$ .01	$ .10
Finley, Chuck	91T	505	$ .01	$ .03
Finley, Chuck	91TAS	395	$ .01	$ .03
Finley, Steve	89TMLD	37	$ .01	$ .35
Finley, Steve	90T	349	$ .01	$ .15
Finley, Steve	91T	212	$ .01	$ .10
Fiore, Mike	69T	376	$ .30	$ .85
Fiore, Mike	70T	709	$ .75	$2.00
Fiore, Mike	71T	287	$ .15	$ .50
Fiore, Mike	72T	199	$ .15	$ .50
Fiore, Mike	88TTR	38	$ .01	$ .25
Fiore, Mike	89TBB	8	$ .01	$ .10
Fireovid, Steve	87T	357	$ .01	$ .04
Fischer, Bill	58T	56	$1.25	$4.25
Fischer, Bill	59T	230	$ .75	$2.20
Fischer, Bill	60T	76	$ .45	$1.45
Fischer, Bill	61T	553	$7.00	$21.00
Fischer, Bill	63T	301	$ .45	$1.50
Fischer, Bill	64T	409	$ .50	$1.45
Fischer, Hank	63T	554	$1.75	$4.50
Fischer, Hank	64T	218	$ .30	$ .95
Fischer, Hank	65T	585	$1.75	$4.50
Fischer, Hank	66T	381	$ .30	$ .95
Fischer, Hank	67T	342	$ .30	$ .85
Fischlin, Mike	79T	718	$ .02	$ .10
Fischlin, Mike	83T	182	$ .01	$ .07
Fischlin, Mike	84T	689	$ .01	$ .06
Fischlin, Mike	85T	41	$ .01	$ .05
Fischlin, Mike	86T	283	$ .01	$ .04
Fischlin, Mike	87T	434	$ .01	$ .04
Fisella, Danny	72TIA	294	$ .15	$ .50
Fisher, Brian	86T	584	$ .01	$ .10
Fisher, Brian	87T	316	$ .01	$ .04
Fisher, Brian	87TTR	33	$ .01	$ .05
Fisher, Brian	88T	193	$ .01	$ .04
Fisher, Brian	88TBB	159	$ .01	$ .06
Fisher, Brian	89T	423	$ .01	$ .05
Fisher, Brian	90T	666	$ .01	$ .04
Fisher, Eddie	60T	23	$ .45	$1.45
Fisher, Eddie	61T	366	$ .35	$1.25
Fisher, Eddie	63T	6	$ .45	$1.45
Fisher, Eddie	63T	223	$ .30	$ .95
Fisher, Eddie	64T	66	$ .30	$ .95
Fisher, Eddie	65T	328	$ .35	$1.25

Player	Year	No.	VG	EX/MT
Fisher, Eddie	66T	85	$ .30	$ .95
Fisher, Eddie	66T	222	$ .75	$3.00
Fisher, Eddie	67T	434	$ .30	$ .95
Fisher, Eddie	68T	418	$ .30	$ .85
Fisher, Eddie	69T	315	$ .30	$ .95
Fisher, Eddie	70T	156	$ .15	$ .50
Fisher, Eddie	71T	631	$ .35	$1.25
Fisher, Eddie	72T	689	$ .75	$2.50
Fisher, Eddie	73T	439	$ .07	$ .30
Fisher, Fritz	64T	312	$ .30	$ .95
Fisher, Fritz	66T	209	$ .35	$1.25
Fisher, Jack	60T	46	$ .45	$1.45
Fisher, Jack	60T	399	$ .90	$3.00
Fisher, Jack	61T	463	$ .90	$3.00
Fisher, Jack	62T	203	$ .45	$1.45
Fisher, Jack	63T	474	$2.50	$6.50
Fisher, Jack	64T	422	$ .50	$1.45
Fisher, Jack	65T	93	$ .30	$ .85
Fisher, Jack	66T	316	$ .30	$ .95
Fisher, Jack	67T	533	$ .75	$3.00
Fisher, Jack	68T	444	$ .30	$ .85
Fisher, Jack	69T	318	$ .30	$ .95
Fisher, Jack	70T	684	$ .75	$2.00
Fisk, Carlton	72T	79	$45.00	$135.00

CARLTON
FISK
BOSTON RED SOX   CATCHER

Player	Year	No.	VG	EX/MT
Fisk, Carlton	73T	193	$7.50	$30.00
Fisk, Carlton	74T	105	$3.50	$14.00
Fisk, Carlton	74TAS	331	$ .75	$3.00
Fisk, Carlton	75T	80	$ .75	$3.00
Fisk, Carlton	76T	365	$ .75	$3.00
Fisk, Carlton	77T	640	$ .75	$3.00
Fisk, Carlton	78T	270	$ .35	$1.25
Fisk, Carlton	79T	680	$ .35	$1.25
Fisk, Carlton	80T	40	$ .25	$1.00
Fisk, Carlton	81T	480	$ .02	$ .25
Fisk, Carlton	81TTR	762	$ .35	$1.50
Fisk, Carlton	82T	110	$ .05	$ .25
Fisk, Carlton	82TAS	554	$ .02	$ .10
Fisk, Carlton	82TIA	111	$ .02	$ .10
Fisk, Carlton	83T	20	$ .05	$ .20
Fisk, Carlton	83TAS	393	$ .01	$ .07

Player	Year	No.	VG	EX/MT
Fisk, Carlton	84T	216	$ .01	$ .06
Fisk, Carlton	84T	560	$ .02	$ .10
Fisk, Carlton	85T	770	$ .01	$ .10
Fisk, Carlton	85TRB	1	$ .01	$ .10
Fisk, Carlton	86T	290	$ .01	$ .10
Fisk, Carlton	86TAS	719	$ .01	$ .04
Fisk, Carlton	87T	756	$ .01	$ .10
Fisk, Carlton	88T	385	$ .01	$ .10
Fisk, Carlton	88TBB	197	$ .01	$ .10
Fisk, Carlton	89T	695	$ .01	$ .10
Fisk, Carlton	89TBB	24	$ .01	$ .20
Fisk, Carlton	90T	420	$ .01	$ .10
Fisk, Carlton	90TAS	392	$ .01	$ .04
Fisk, Carlton	91T	170	$ .01	$ .03
Fisk, Carlton	91TAS	393	$ .01	$ .03
Fisk, Carlton	91TRB	3	$ .01	$ .03
Fitzgerald, Ed	52T	236	$7.00	$20.00
Fitzgerald, Ed	56T	198	$3.00	$9.00
Fitzgerald, Ed	57T	367	$1.25	$4.25
Fitzgerald, Ed	58T	236	$ .75	$3.00
Fitzgerald, Ed	59T	33	$1.25	$4.25
Fitzgerald, Ed	60T	423	$ .75	$2.20
Fitzgerald, Mike	84TTR	37	$ .02	$ .10
Fitzgerald, Mike	85T	104	$ .01	$ .05
Fitzgerald, Mike	85TTR	34	$ .02	$ .10
Fitzgerald, Mike	86T	503	$ .01	$ .04
Fitzgerald, Mike	87T	212	$ .01	$ .04
Fitzgerald, Mike	88T	674	$ .01	$ .04
Fitzgerald, Mike	89T	23	$ .01	$ .05
Fitzgerald, Mike	90T	484	$ .01	$ .04
Fitzgerald, Mike	91T	317	$ .01	$ .03
Fitzmorris, Al	70T	241	$ .15	$ .50
Fitzmorris, Al	71T	564	$ .35	$1.25
Fitzmorris, Al	72T	349	$ .15	$ .50
Fitzmorris, Al	73T	643	$ .45	$1.45
Fitzmorris, Al	74T	191	$ .07	$ .30
Fitzmorris, Al	75T	24	$ .07	$ .30
Fitzmorris, Al	76T	144	$ .05	$ .20
Fitzmorris, Al	77T	449	$ .05	$ .15
Fitzmorris, Al	78T	227	$ .02	$ .10
Fitzmorris, Al	79T	638	$ .02	$ .10
Fitzpatrick, John	54T	213	$3.60	$10.00
Fitzsimmons, Fred	60T	462	$ .95	$3.50
Flanagan, Mike	76T	589	$ .45	$1.45
Flanagan, Mike	77T	106	$ .15	$ .50
Flanagan, Mike	78T	341	$ .02	$ .10
Flanagan, Mike	79T	160	$ .08	$ .30
Flanagan, Mike	80T	205	$ .05	$ .20
Flanagan, Mike	80T	640	$ .01	$ .10
Flanagan, Mike	81T	10	$ .01	$ .10
Flanagan, Mike	82T	520	$ .01	$ .07
Flanagan, Mike	83T	445	$ .01	$ .07
Flanagan, Mike	84T	295	$ .01	$ .06
Flanagan, Mike	85T	780	$ .01	$ .05
Flanagan, Mike	86T	365	$ .01	$ .04
Flanagan, Mike	87T	748	$ .01	$ .04
Flanagan, Mike	88T	623	$ .01	$ .04
Flanagan, Mike	89T	139	$ .01	$ .05
Flanagan, Mike	89TBB	243	$ .01	$ .06
Flanagan, Mike	90T	78	$ .01	$ .04
Flannery, Tim	80T	685	$ .01	$ .10
Flannery, Tim	81T	579	$ .01	$ .10
Flannery, Tim	82T	249	$ .01	$ .07
Flannery, Tim	83T	38	$ .01	$ .07
Flannery, Tim	84T	674	$ .01	$ .06
Flannery, Tim	85T	182	$ .01	$ .05
Flannery, Tim	86T	413	$ .01	$ .04
Flannery, Tim	87T	763	$ .01	$ .04
Flannery, Tim	88T	513	$ .01	$ .04
Flannery, Tim	89T	379	$ .01	$ .05

Player	Year	No.	VG	EX/MT
Flannery, Tim	89TBB	174	$ .01	$ .06
Fletcher, Darrin	89TMLD	38	$ .01	$ .15
Fletcher, Darrin	91T	9	$ .01	$ .03
Fletcher, Scott	84T	364	$ .01	$ .06
Fletcher, Scott	85T	78	$ .01	$ .05
Fletcher, Scott	86T	187	$ .01	$ .04
Fletcher, Scott	86TTR	36	$ .02	$ .10
Fletcher, Scott	87T	462	$ .01	$ .04
Fletcher, Scott	88T	345	$ .01	$ .04
Fletcher, Scott	88TBB	19	$ .01	$ .06
Fletcher, Scott	89T	295	$ .01	$ .05
Fletcher, Scott	89TBB	205	$ .01	$ .06
Fletcher, Scott	90T	565	$ .01	$ .04
Fletcher, Scott	91T	785	$ .01	$ .03
Flinn, John	79T	701	$ .02	$ .10
Flinn, John	81T	659	$ .01	$ .10
Floethe, Chris	72T	268	$ .15	$ .50
Flood, Curt	58T	464	$3.50	$14.00
Flood, Curt	59T	353	$ .75	$2.20
Flood, Curt	60T	275	$ .75	$2.25
Flood, Curt	61T	438	$ .90	$3.00
Flood, Curt	62T	590	$5.00	$16.00
Flood, Curt	63T	505	$3.00	$9.00
Flood, Curt	64T	103	$ .30	$ .95
Flood, Curt	65T	415	$ .45	$1.45
Flood, Curt	66T	60	$ .35	$1.25
Flood, Curt	67T	63	$1.00	$4.50
Flood, Curt	67T	245	$ .15	$ .50
Flood, Curt	68T	180	$ .45	$1.45
Flood, Curt	69T	540	$ .30	$ .95
Flood, Curt	69TAS	426	$ .30	$ .85
Flood, Curt	70T	360	$ .45	$1.45
Flood, Curt	71T	535	$ .35	$1.25
Flores, Gil	78T	268	$ .02	$ .10
Flores, Gil	80T	478	$ .01	$ .10
Floyd, Bob	69T	597	$17.50	$70.00
Floyd, Bobby	70T	101	$ .15	$ .50
Floyd, Bobby	71T	646	$ .75	$2.50
Floyd, Bobby	72T	273	$ .15	$ .50
Floyd, Bobby	74T	41	$ .07	$ .30

Player	Year	No.	VG	EX/MT
Flynn, Doug	77T	186	$ .05	$ .15
Flynn, Doug	78T	453	$ .02	$ .10
Flynn, Doug	79T	229	$ .02	$ .10
Flynn, Doug	80T	58	$ .01	$ .10
Flynn, Doug	81T	634	$ .01	$ .10
Flynn, Doug	82T	302	$ .01	$ .07
Flynn, Doug	82TTR	33	$ .02	$ .10
Flynn, Doug	83T	169	$ .01	$ .07
Flynn, Doug	84T	749	$ .01	$ .06
Flynn, Doug	85T	554	$ .01	$ .05
Flynn, Doug	86T	436	$ .01	$ .04
Fodge, Gene	58T	449	$ .75	$2.20
Foiles, Henry "Hank"	53T	252	$12.50	$50.00
Foiles, Hank	57T	104	$ .95	$3.50
Foiles, Hank	58T	4	$1.25	$4.25
Foiles, Hank	59T	294	$ .75	$2.20
Foiles, Hank	60T	77	$ .45	$1.45
Foiles, Hank	61T	277	$ .35	$1.25
Foiles, Hank	62T	112	$ .45	$1.45
Foiles, Hank	63T	326	$ .45	$1.50
Foiles, Hank	64T	554	$1.75	$4.50
Foley, Marvis	81T	646	$ .01	$ .10
Foley, Marvis	83T	409	$ .01	$ .07
Foley, Marvis	85T	621	$ .01	$ .05
Foley, Tom	84T	632	$ .01	$ .06
Foley, Tom	85T	107	$ .01	$ .05
Foley, Tom	86T	466	$ .01	$ .04
Foley, Tom	87T	78	$ .01	$ .04
Foley, Tom	88T	251	$ .01	$ .04
Foley, Tom	89T	529	$ .01	$ .05
Foley, Tom	89TBB	261	$ .01	$ .06
Foley, Tom	90T	341	$ .01	$ .04
Foley, Tom	91T	773	$ .01	$ .03
Foli, Tim	71T	83	$ .15	$ .50
Foli, Tim	72T	707	$ .75	$2.50
Foli, Tim	72TIA	708	$ .75	$2.50
Foli, Tim	73T	19	$ .07	$ .30
Foli, Tim	74T	217	$ .07	$ .30
Foli, Tim	75T	149	$ .07	$ .30
Foli, Tim	76T	397	$ .05	$ .20
Foli, Tim	77T	76	$ .05	$ .15
Foli, Tim	78T	167	$ .02	$ .10
Foli, Tim	79T	403	$ .02	$ .10
Foli, Tim	80T	246	$ .01	$ .10
Foli, Tim	81T	501	$ .01	$ .10
Foli, Tim	82T	618	$ .01	$ .07
Foli, Tim	82TTR	34	$ .02	$ .10
Foli, Tim	83T	738	$ .01	$ .07
Foli, Tim	84T	342	$ .01	$ .06
Foli, Tim	84TTR	38	$ .02	$ .10
Foli, Tim	85T	271	$ .01	$ .05
Foli, Tim	85T	456	$ .01	$ .05
Folkers, Rich	71T	648	$1.00	$4.00
Folkers, Rich	73T	649	$ .45	$1.45
Folkers, Rich	74T	417	$ .07	$ .30
Folkers, Rich	75T	98	$ .07	$ .30
Folkers, Rich	76T	611	$ .05	$ .20
Folkers, Rich	77T	372	$ .05	$ .15
Fondy, Dee	52T	359	$40.00	$140.00
Fondy, Dee	56T	112	$2.25	$6.00
Fondy, Dee	57T	42	$ .95	$3.50
Fondy, Dee	58T	157	$ .75	$3.00
Fontenot, Ray	84T	19	$ .01	$ .06
Fontenot, Ray	85T	507	$ .01	$ .05
Fontenot, Ray	85TTR	35	$ .02	$ .10
Fontenot, Ray	86T	308	$ .01	$ .04
Fontenot, Ray	87T	124	$ .01	$ .04
Foor, Jim	72T	257	$ .15	$ .50
Foote, Barry	74T	603	$ .07	$ .30
Foote, Barry	75T	229	$ .07	$ .30

DOUG FLYNN
SECOND BASE
REDS

Flynn, Doug	76T	518	$ .07	$ .30

Player	Year	No.	VG	EX/MT	Player	Year	No.	VG	EX/MT
Foote, Barry	76T	42	$ .05	$ .20	Forsch, Bob	82T	775	$ .01	$ .07
Foote, Barry	77T	612	$ .05	$ .15	Forsch, Bob	83T	415	$ .01	$ .07
Foote, Barry	78T	513	$ .02	$ .10	Forsch, Bob	84T	5	$ .02	$ .10
Foote, Barry	79T	161	$ .02	$ .10	Forsch, Bob	84T	75	$ .01	$ .06
Foote, Barry	80T	398	$ .01	$ .10	Forsch, Bob	85T	631	$ .01	$ .05
Foote, Barry	81T	492	$ .01	$ .10	Forsch, Bob	86T	322	$ .01	$ .04
Foote, Barry	81TTR	763	$ .02	$ .10	Forsch, Bob	87T	257	$ .01	$ .04
Foote, Barry	82T	706	$ .01	$ .07	Forsch, Bob	88T	586	$ .01	$ .04
Foote, Barry	83T	697	$ .01	$ .07	Forsch, Bob	89T	163	$ .01	$ .05
Ford, Curt	87T	399	$ .01	$ .04	Forsch, Ken	71T	102	$ .15	$ .50
Ford, Curt	88T	612	$ .01	$ .04	Forsch, Ken	72T	394	$ .15	$ .50
Ford, Curt	89T	132	$ .01	$ .05	Forsch, Ken	73T	589	$ .45	$1.45
Ford, Curt	90T	39	$ .01	$ .04	Forsch, Ken	74T	91	$ .07	$ .30
Ford, Dan	76T	313	$ .05	$ .20	Forsch, Ken	75T	357	$ .07	$ .30
Ford, Dan	77T	555	$ .05	$ .15	Forsch, Ken	76T	357	$ .05	$ .20
Ford, Dan	78T	275	$ .02	$ .10	Forsch, Ken	77T	21	$ .05	$ .15
Ford, Dan	79T	385	$ .02	$ .10	Forsch, Ken	77T	632	$ .05	$ .15
Ford, Dan	80T	20	$ .01	$ .10	Forsch, Ken	78T	181	$ .02	$ .10
Ford, Dan	81T	422	$ .01	$ .10	Forsch, Ken	79T	534	$ .02	$ .10
Ford, Dan	82T	134	$ .01	$ .07	Forsch, Ken	80T	642	$ .01	$ .10
Ford, Dan	82TTR	35	$ .02	$ .10	Forsch, Ken	81T	269	$ .01	$ .10
Ford, Dan	83T	683	$ .01	$ .07	Forsch, Ken	81TTR	764	$ .02	$ .10
Ford, Dan	84T	530	$ .01	$ .06	Forsch, Ken	82T	276	$ .03	$ .15
Ford, Dan	85T	252	$ .01	$ .05	Forsch, Ken	82T	385	$ .01	$ .07
Ford, Dan	86T	753	$ .01	$ .04	Forsch, Ken	83T	625	$ .01	$ .07
Ford, Dave	80T	661	$ .01	$ .10	Forsch, Ken	84T	765	$ .01	$ .06
Ford, Dave	81T	706	$ .01	$ .10	Forsch, Ken	85T	442	$ .01	$ .05
Ford, Dave	82T	174	$ .01	$ .07	Forster, Terry	72T	539	$ .75	$2.25
Ford, Ted	71T	612	$ .35	$1.25	Forster, Terry	73T	129	$ .15	$ .50
Ford, Ted	72T	24	$ .15	$ .50	Forster, Terry	74T	310	$ .07	$ .30
Ford, Ted	73T	299	$ .07	$ .30	Forster, Terry	75T	137	$ .07	$ .30
Ford, Ted	74T	617	$ .07	$ .30	Forster, Terry	75T	313	$ .30	$ .95
Ford, Whitey	53T	207	$45.00	$145.00	Forster, Terry	76T	437	$ .05	$ .20
Ford, Whitey	54T	37	$30.00	$100.00	Forster, Terry	77T	271	$ .05	$ .15
Ford, Whitey	56T	240	$35.00	$110.00	Forster, Terry	78T	347	$ .02	$ .10
Ford, Whitey	57T	25	$17.500	$70.00	Forster, Terry	79T	23	$ .02	$ .10
Ford, Whitey	58T	320	$20.00	$60.00	Forster, Terry	80T	605	$ .01	$ .10
Ford, Whitey	59T	430	$12.00	$35.00	Forster, Terry	81T	104	$ .01	$ .10
Ford, Whitey	60T	35	$12.00	$35.00	Forster, Terry	82T	444	$ .01	$ .07
Ford, Whitey	61T	160	$10.00	$30.00	Forster, Terry	83T	583	$ .01	$ .07
Ford, Whitey	61TAS	586	$22.00	$82.50	Forster, Terry	83TTR	33	$ .02	$ .10
Ford, Whitey	62T	57	$ .75	$2.20	Forster, Terry	84T	791	$ .01	$ .06
Ford, Whitey	62T	59	$ .75	$2.20	Forster, Terry	85T	248	$ .01	$ .05
Ford, Whitey	62T	310	$7.00	$25.00	Forster, Terry	86T	363	$ .01	$ .04
Ford, Whitey	62T	315	$1.50	$6.50	Forster, Terry	86TTR	37	$ .02	$ .10
Ford, Whitey	62TAS	475	$4.00	$12.00	Forster, Terry	87T	652	$ .01	$ .04
Ford, Whitey	63T	6	$ .45	$1.45	Fosnow, Jerry	65T	529	$1.75	$4.50
Ford, Whitey	63T	446	$10.00	$30.00	Fossas, Tony	90T	34	$ .01	$ .04
Ford, Whitey	64T	4	$1.50	$6.00	Fossas, Tony	91T	747	$ .01	$ .03
Ford, Whitey	64T	380	$6.00	$24.00	Fosse, Ray	69T	244	$ .30	$ .95
Ford, Whitey	65T	330	$10.00	$30.00	Fosse, Ray	70T	184	$ .15	$ .50
Ford, Whitey	66T	160	$6.00	$20.00	Fosse, Ray	71T	125	$ .15	$ .50
Ford, Whitey	67T	5	$5.50	$17.50	Fosse, Ray	72T	470	$ .15	$ .50
Fornieles, Mike	54T	154	$3.60	$10.00	Fosse, Ray	73T	226	$ .07	$ .30
Fornieles, Mike	57T	116	$ .95	$3.50	Fosse, Ray	74T	420	$ .07	$ .30
Fornieles, Mike	58T	361	$ .75	$3.00	Fosse, Ray	75T	486	$ .07	$ .30
Fornieles, Mike	59T	473	$ .75	$2.20	Fosse, Ray	76T	554	$ .05	$ .20
Fornieles, Mike	60T	54	$ .45	$1.45	Fosse, Ray	76TTR	554	$ .05	$ .20
Fornieles, Mike	61T	113	$ .35	$1.25	Fosse, Ray	77T	267	$ .05	$ .15
Fornieles, Mike	62T	512	$ .75	$2.50	Fosse, Ray	78T	415	$ .02	$ .10
Fornieles, Mike	63T	28	$ .30	$ .95	Fosse, Ray	79T	51	$ .02	$ .10
Forsch, Bob	75T	51	$ .12	$ .40	Fosse, Ray	80T	327	$ .01	$ .10
Forsch, Bob	76T	426	$ .05	$ .20	Foster, Alan	69T	266	$ .30	$ .95
Forsch, Bob	77T	381	$ .05	$ .15	Foster, Alan	70T	369	$ .15	$ .50
Forsch, Bob	77T	632	$ .05	$ .15	Foster, Alan	71T	207	$ .15	$ .50
Forsch, Bob	78T	58	$ .02	$ .10	Foster, Alan	72T	521	$ .15	$ .50
Forsch, Bob	79T	230	$ .02	$ .10	Foster, Alan	73T	543	$ .15	$ .75
Forsch, Bob	80T	535	$ .01	$ .10	Foster, Alan	74T	442	$ .07	$ .30
Forsch, Bob	81T	140	$ .01	$ .10	Foster, Alan	75T	296	$ .07	$ .30
Forsch, Bob	82T	186	$ .05	$ .25	Foster, Alan	76T	266	$ .05	$ .20

TOPPS

Player	Year	No.	VG	EX/MT	Player	Year	No.	VG	EX/MT
Foster, Alan	77T	108	$ .05	$ .15	Fowler, Art	62T	128	$ .45	$1.45
Foster, George	71T	276	$1.75	$7.00	Fowler, Art	63T	454	$2.50	$6.50
Foster, George	72T	256	$ .40	$1.25	Fowler, Art	64T	349	$ .30	$ .95
Foster, George	73T	399	$ .40	$1.25	Fowler, Art	73T	323	$ .35	$1.25
Foster, George	74T	646	$ .40	$1.25	Fowler, Art	74T	379	$ .15	$ .50
Foster, George	75T	87	$ .50	$1.45	Fowler, Dick	52T	210	$7.00	$20.00
Foster, George	76T	179	$ .25	$1.00	Fowlkes, Alan	83T	543	$ .01	$ .07
Foster, George	77T	3	$ .35	$1.25	Fox, Charlie	71T	517	$ .15	$ .50
Foster, George	77T	347	$ .35	$1.25	Fox, Charlie	72T	129	$ .15	$ .50
Foster, George	78T	202	$ .05	$ .20	Fox, Charlie	73T	252	$ .30	$ .85
Foster, George	78T	203	$ .05	$ .20	Fox, Charlie	74T	78	$ .07	$ .30
Foster, George	78T	500	$ .30	$ .85	Fox, Howie	52T	209	$7.00	$20.00
Foster, George	79T	2	$ .30	$ .85	Fox, Howie	53T	22	$4.50	$15.00
Foster, George	79T	3	$ .30	$ .85	Fox, Howie	54T	246	$3.60	$10.00
Foster, George	79T	600	$ .05	$ .25	Fox, Nellie	56T	118	$5.00	$20.00
Foster, George	80T	400	$ .05	$ .15	Fox, Nellie	57T	38	$4.50	$17.50
Foster, George	81T	200	$ .05	$ .15	Fox, Nellie	58T	400	$2.50	$10.00
Foster, George	82T	700	$ .01	$ .10	Fox, Nellie	58TAS	479	$2.00	$8.00
Foster, George	82TAS	342	$ .10	$ .30	Fox, Nellie	59T	30	$4.00	$16.00
					Fox, Nellie	59T	408	$ .60	$1.80
					Fox, Nellie	59TAS	556	$2.50	$7.50
					Fox, Nellie	60T	100	$1.50	$6.00
					Fox, Nellie	60T	429	$ .90	$3.00
					Fox, Nellie	60TAS	555	$3.00	$12.00
					Fox, Nellie	61T	30	$2.10	$6.00
					Fox, Nellie	61TAS	570	$7.50	$27.50
					Fox, Nellie	61TMVP	477	$ .75	$2.00
					Fox, Nellie	62T	73	$2.10	$6.00
					Fox, Nellie	63T	525	$4.00	$15.00
					Fox, Nellie	64T	81	$1.75	$7.00
					Fox, Nellie	64T	205	$1.00	$4.00
					Fox, Nellie	65T	485	$2.10	$8.00
					Fox, Nellie	75T	197	$ .35	$1.25
					Fox, Terry	61T	459	$ .75	$3.00
					Fox, Terry	62T	196	$ .45	$1.45
					Fox, Terry	63T	44	$ .30	$ .95
					Fox, Terry	64T	387	$ .50	$1.45
					Fox, Terry	65T	576	$1.75	$4.50
					Fox, Terry	66T	472	$ .75	$2.50
					Fox, Terry	67T	181	$ .30	$ .85
					Foy, Joe	66T	456	$ .75	$2.50
					Foy, Joe	67T	331	$ .30	$ .85
					Foy, Joe	68T	387	$ .30	$ .85
					Foy, Joe	69T	93	$ .30	$ .85
					Foy, Joe	70T	138	$ .15	$ .50
					Foy, Joe	71T	706	$ .75	$2.50
					Foytack, Paul	57T	77	$ .95	$3.50
					Foytack, Paul	58T	282	$ .75	$3.00
					Foytack, Paul	59T	233	$ .75	$2.20
Foster, George	82TIA	701	$ .02	$ .15	Foytack, Paul	60T	364	$ .75	$2.20
Foster, George	82TTR	36	$ .01	$ .10	Foytack, Paul	61T	171	$ .35	$1.25
Foster, George	83T	80	$ .01	$ .07	Foytack, Paul	62T	349	$ .45	$1.45
Foster, George	84T	350	$ .01	$ .06	Foytack, Paul	63T	327	$ .45	$1.50
Foster, George	85T	170	$ .01	$ .05	Foytack, Paul	64T	149	$ .30	$ .95
Foster, George	86T	680	$ .01	$ .04	Frailing, Ken	74T	605	$ .30	$1.50
Foster, Leo	74T	607	$ .07	$ .30	Frailing, Ken	75T	436	$ .07	$ .30
Foster, Leo	75T	418	$ .07	$ .30	Francis, Earl	61T	54	$ .35	$1.25
Foster, Leo	77T	458	$ .05	$ .15	Francis, Earl	62T	252	$ .45	$1.45
Foster, Leo	78T	229	$ .02	$ .10	Francis, Earl	63T	303	$ .45	$1.50
Foster, Roy	71T	107	$ .15	$ .50	Francis, Earl	64T	117	$ .30	$ .95
Foster, Roy	72T	329	$ .15	$ .50	Franco, John	85T	417	$ .25	$1.25
Foucault, Steve	74T	294	$ .07	$ .30	Franco, John	86T	54	$ .05	$ .25
Foucault, Steve	75T	283	$ .07	$ .30	Franco, John	87T	305	$ .01	$ .10
Foucault, Steve	76T	303	$ .05	$ .20	Franco, John	88T	730	$ .01	$ .10
Foucault, Steve	77T	459	$ .05	$ .15	Franco, John	88TBB	232	$ .01	$ .10
Foucault, Steve	78T	68	$ .02	$ .10	Franco, John	89T	290	$ .01	$ .10
Fowler, Art	55T	3	$2.00	$6.00	Franco, John	90T	120	$ .01	$ .10
Fowler, Art	56T	47	$2.25	$6.00	Franco, John	90TTR	32	$ .01	$ .05
Fowler, Art	57T	233	$ .95	$3.50	Franco, John	91T	510	$ .01	$ .03
Fowler, Art	59T	508	$2.50	$10.00	Franco, John	91TAS	407	$ .01	$ .03

GEORGE FOSTER

Topps in action

Player	Year	No.	VG	EX/MT	Player	Year	No.	VG	EX/MT
Franco, Julio	83TTR	34	$1.25	$5.00	Freed, Roger	70T	477	$ .15	$ .50
Franco, Julio	84T	48	$ .50	$1.75	Freed, Roger	71T	362	$ .15	$ .50
Franco, Julio	85T	237	$ .10	$ .40	Freed, Roger	72T	69	$ .15	$ .50
Franco, Julio	86T	391	$ .01	$ .20	Freed, Roger	78T	504	$ .02	$ .10
Franco, Julio	87T	160	$ .01	$ .15	Freed, Roger	79T	111	$ .02	$ .10
Franco, Julio	88T	683	$ .01	$ .10	Freed, Roger	80T	418	$ .01	$ .10
Franco, Julio	88TBB	135	$ .01	$ .10	Freehan, Bill	63T	466	$7.50	$27.50
Franco, Julio	89T	55	$ .01	$ .10	Freehan, Bill	64T	407	$ .40	$2.25
Franco, Julio	89TAS	398	$ .01	$ .05	Freehan, Bill	65T	390	$ .45	$1.45
Franco, Julio	89TBB	288	$ .01	$ .10	Freehan, Bill	66T	145	$ .30	$ .95
Franco, Julio	89TTR	34	$ .01	$ .10	Freehan, Bill	67T	48	$ .30	$ .85
Franco, Julio	90T	550	$ .01	$ .04	Freehan, Bill	68T	470	$ .35	$1.25
Franco, Julio	90TAS	386	$ .01	$ .04	Freehan, Bill	68TAS	375	$ .30	$ .85
Franco, Julio	91T	775	$ .01	$ .03	Freehan, Bill	69T	390	$ .30	$ .85
Franco, Julio	91TAS	387	$ .01	$ .03	Freehan, Bill	69TAS	431	$ .30	$ .85
Francona, Terry	82T	118	$ .03	$ .15	Freehan, Bill	70T	335	$ .15	$ .50
Francona, Terry	83T	267	$ .01	$ .07	Freehan, Bill	70TAS	465	$ .15	$ .50
Francona, Terry	84T	496	$ .01	$ .06	Freehan, Bill	71T	575	$ .45	$1.45
Francona, Terry	85T	134	$ .01	$ .10	Freehan, Bill	72T	120	$ .30	$ .85
Francona, Terry	85T	578	$ .01	$ .05	Freehan, Bill	73T	460	$ .30	$ .85
Francona, Terry	86T	374	$ .01	$ .04	Freehan, Bill	74T	162	$ .30	$ .95
Francona, Terry	86TTR	38	$ .02	$ .10	Freehan, Bill	75T	397	$ .30	$ .85
Francona, Terry	87T	785	$ .01	$ .04	Freehan, Bill	76T	540	$ .05	$ .20
Francona, Terry	87TTR	34	$ .01	$ .05	Freehan, Bill	77T	22	$ .05	$ .15
Francona, Terry	88T	686	$ .01	$ .04	Freeman, Hershell	56T	242	$3.00	$9.00
Francona, Terry	89T	31	$ .01	$ .05	Freeman, Hershell "Bud"	57T	32	$ .95	$3.50
Francona, Terry	89TTR	35	$ .01	$ .06	Freeman, Bud	58T	27	$1.25	$4.25
Francona, Terry	90T	214	$ .01	$ .04	Freeman, Jimmy	73T	610	$ .45	$1.45
Francona, Tito	57T	184	$ .95	$3.50	Freeman, LaVel	89TMLD	39	$ .01	$ .15
Francona, Tito	58T	316	$ .75	$3.00	Freeman, Mark	59T	532	$2.50	$10.00
Francona, Tito	59T	268	$ .75	$2.20	Freeman, Marvin	89T	634	$ .01	$ .05
Francona, Tito	60T	30	$ .45	$1.45	Freeman, Marvin	90T	103	$ .01	$ .04
Francona, Tito	60T	260	$ .75	$3.00	Freese, Gene	55T	205	$5.25	$15.00
Francona, Tito	61T	503	$ .75	$3.00	Freese, Gene	56T	46	$2.25	$6.00
Francona, Tito	62T	97	$ .45	$1.45	Freese, Gene	58T	293	$ .75	$3.00
Francona, Tito	63T	248	$ .30	$ .95	Freese, Gene	59T	472	$ .75	$2.20
Francona, Tito	63T	392	$ .24	$1.25	Freese, Gene	60T	435	$ .75	$2.20
Francona, Tito	64T	583	$2.10	$6.00	Freese, Gene	61T	175	$ .35	$1.25
Francona, Tito	65T	256	$ .35	$1.25	Freese, Gene	62T	205	$ .45	$1.45
Francona, Tito	66T	163	$ .30	$ .95	Freese, Gene	63T	133	$ .30	$ .95
Francona, Tito	67T	443	$ .30	$ .95	Freese, Gene	64T	266	$ .30	$ .95
Francona, Tito	68T	527	$ .35	$1.25	Freese, Gene	65T	492	$ .75	$3.00
Francona, Tito	69T	398	$ .30	$ .85	Freese, Gene	66T	319	$ .30	$ .95
Francona, Tito	70T	663	$ .75	$2.00	Fregosi, Jim	62T	209	$1.50	$5.00
Francona, Tito	85T	134	$ .01	$ .10	Fregosi, Jim	63T	167	$ .45	$1.45
Franks, Herman	52T	385	$50.00	$150.00	Fregosi, Jim	64T	97	$ .12	$ .75
Franks, Herman	65T	32	$ .30	$ .85	Fregosi, Jim	65T	210	$ .45	$1.45
Franks, Herman	66T	537	$5.00	$20.00	Fregosi, Jim	66T	5	$ .30	$ .95
Franks, Herman	67T	116	$ .30	$ .85	Fregosi, Jim	67T	385	$ .45	$1.45
Franks, Herman	68T	267	$ .30	$ .85	Fregosi, Jim	68T	170	$ .30	$ .95
Franks, Herman	78T	234	$ .02	$ .10	Fregosi, Jim	68TAS	367	$ .30	$ .85
Fraser, Willie	87TTR	35	$ .05	$ .20	Fregosi, Jim	69T	365	$ .15	$ .50
Fraser, Willie	88T	363	$ .01	$ .04	Fregosi, Jim	70T	570	$ .45	$1.45
Fraser, Willie	88TBB	183	$ .01	$ .06	Fregosi, Jim	71T	360	$ .15	$ .50
Fraser, Willie	89T	679	$ .01	$ .05	Fregosi, Jim	72T	115	$ .30	$ .85
Fraser, Willie	89TBB	272	$ .01	$ .06	Fregosi, Jim	72T	346	$ .15	$ .50
Fraser, Willie	90T	477	$ .01	$ .04	Fregosi, Jim	72TTR	755	$1.75	$4.50
Fraser, Willie	91T	784	$ .01	$ .03	Fregosi, Jim	73T	525	$ .30	$ .95
Frazier, George	79T	724	$ .30	$ .85	Fregosi, Jim	74T	196	$ .07	$ .30
Frazier, George	80T	684	$ .08	$ .40	Fregosi, Jim	75T	339	$ .30	$ .85
Frazier, George	82T	349	$ .01	$ .07	Fregosi, Jim	76T	635	$ .07	$ .30
Frazier, George	83T	123	$ .01	$ .07	Fregosi, Jim	78T	323	$ .02	$ .10
Frazier, George	84T	539	$ .01	$ .06	Fregosi, Jim	86TTR	39	$ .02	$ .10
Frazier, George	84TTR	39	$ .02	$ .10	Fregosi, Jim	87T	318	$ .01	$ .04
Frazier, George	85T	19	$ .01	$ .05	Fregosi, Jim	88T	714	$ .01	$ .04
Frazier, George	86T	431	$ .01	$ .04	Fregosi, Jim	89T	414	$ .01	$ .05
Frazier, George	87T	207	$ .01	$ .04	Freisleben, Dave	74T	599	$ .15	$ .50
Frazier, George	88T	709	$ .01	$ .04	Freisleben, Dave	75T	37	$ .07	$ .30
Frazier, Joe	55T	89	$2.00	$6.00	Freisleben, Dave	76T	217	$ .05	$ .20
Frazier, Joe	56T	141	$2.25	$6.00	Freisleben, Dave	77T	407	$ .05	$ .15

TOPPS

Player	Year	No.	VG	EX/MT	Player	Year	No.	VG	EX/MT
Freisleben, Dave	78T	594	$ .02	$ .10	Fryman, Woody	66T	498	$ .65	$1.75
Freisleben, Dave	79T	168	$ .02	$ .10	Fryman, Woody	67T	221	$ .30	$ .85
Freisleben, Dave	80T	382	$ .01	$ .10	Fryman, Woody	68T	112	$ .30	$ .85
French, Jim	66T	333	$ .30	$ .95	Fryman, Woody "Woodie"	69T	51	$ .30	$ .85
French, Jim	69T	199	$ .30	$ .85	Fryman, Woodie	70T	677	$1.75	$4.50
French, Jim	70T	617	$ .30	$ .95	Fryman, Woodie	71T	414	$ .15	$ .50
French, Jim	71T	399	$ .15	$ .50	Fryman, Woodie	72T	357	$ .15	$ .50
Frey, Jim	73T	136	$ .15	$ .50	Fryman, Woodie	73T	146	$ .07	$ .30
Frey, Jim	74T	306	$ .15	$ .50	Fryman, Woodie	74T	555	$ .07	$ .30
Frey, Jim	84T	51	$ .01	$ .06	Fryman, Woodie	75T	166	$ .07	$ .30
Frey, Jim	85T	241	$ .01	$ .05	Fryman, Woodie	76T	467	$ .05	$ .20
Frey, Jim	86T	231	$ .01	$ .04	Fryman, Woodie	77T	28	$ .05	$ .15
Frey, Steve	89TMLD	40	$ .01	$ .15	Fryman, Woodie	78T	585	$ .02	$ .10
Frey, Steve	90T	91	$ .01	$ .10	Fryman, Woodie	79T	269	$ .02	$ .10
Frey, Steve	91T	462	$ .01	$ .03	Fryman, Woodie	80T	607	$ .01	$ .10
Frias, Pepe	73T	607	$ .45	$1.45	Fryman, Woodie	81T	394	$ .01	$ .10
Frias, Pepe	74T	468	$ .07	$ .30	Fryman, Woodie	82T	788	$ .01	$ .07
Frias, Pepe	75T	496	$ .07	$ .30	Fryman, Woodie	83T	137	$ .01	$ .07
Frias, Pepe	76T	544	$ .05	$ .20	Fuentes, Miguel	70T	88	$ .15	$ .50
Frias, Pepe	77T	199	$ .05	$ .15	Fuentes, Tito	66T	511	$ .75	$2.50
Frias, Pepe	78T	654	$ .02	$ .10	Fuentes, Tito	67T	177	$ .30	$ .85
Frias, Pepe	79T	294	$ .02	$ .10	Fuentes, Tito	70T	42	$ .15	$ .50
Frias, Pepe	80T	87	$ .01	$ .10	Fuentes, Tito	71T	378	$ .15	$ .50
Fricano, Marion	53T	199	$4.50	$15.00	Fuentes, Tito	72T	427	$ .15	$ .50
Fricano, Marion	54T	124	$3.60	$10.00	Fuentes, Tito	72TIA	428	$ .15	$ .50
Frick, Ford	59T	1	$15.00	$67.50	Fuentes, Tito	73T	236	$ .07	$ .30
Fridley, Jim	52T	399	$40.00	$140.00	Fuentes, Tito	74T	305	$ .07	$ .30
Fridley, Jim	53T	187	$4.50	$15.00	Fuentes, Tito	75T	425	$ .07	$ .30
Friend, Bob	52T	233	$7.00	$21.00	Fuentes, Tito	76T	8	$ .05	$ .20
Friend, Bob	56T	221	$3.00	$9.00	Fuentes, Tito	77T	63	$ .05	$ .15
Friend, Bob	57T	150	$ .60	$2.50	Fuentes, Tito	78T	385	$ .02	$ .10
Friend, Bob	58T	315	$ .65	$2.00	Fulgham, John	80T	152	$ .01	$ .10
Friend, Bob	58T	334	$ .45	$1.50	Fulgham, John	81T	523	$ .01	$ .10
Friend, Bob	58TAS	492	$ .70	$2.25	Fuller, Jim	74T	606	$ .07	$ .30
Friend, Bob	59T	428	$ .75	$2.20	Fuller, Jim	75T	594	$ .07	$ .30
Friend, Bob	59T	460	$ .90	$3.00	Fuller, Vern	68T	71	$ .30	$ .85
Friend, Bob	59TAS	569	$3.00	$9.00					
Friend, Bob	60T	437	$ .90	$3.00					
Friend, Bob	61T	45	$ .60	$2.75					
Friend, Bob	61T	270	$ .35	$1.25					
Friend, Bob	61TAS	585	$7.00	$21.00					
Friend, Bob	62T	520	$ .75	$2.50					
Friend, Bob	63T	450	$2.50	$6.50					
Friend, Bob	64T	1	$3.50	$15.00					
Friend, Bob	64T	20	$ .45	$1.45					
Friend, Bob	65T	392	$ .45	$1.45					
Friend, Bob	66T	519	$2.10	$6.00					
Friend, Owen	52T	160	$7.00	$20.00					
Frisella, Dan	69T	343	$ .30	$ .85					
Frisella, Dan	71T	104	$ .15	$ .50					
Frisella, Danny	72T	293	$ .15	$ .50					
Frisella, Danny	73T	432	$ .07	$ .30					
Frisella, Danny	74T	71	$ .07	$ .30					
Frisella, Danny	75T	343	$ .07	$ .30					
Frisella, Danny	76T	32	$ .05	$ .20					
Frisella, Danny	77T	278	$ .05	$ .15					
Frobel, Doug	84T	264	$ .01	$ .06					
Frobel, Doug	85T	587	$ .01	$ .05					
Frohwirth, Todd	88T	378	$ .01	$ .10					
Frohwirth, Todd	89T	542	$ .01	$ .05					
Frohwirth, Todd	90T	69	$ .01	$ .04					
Frost, Dave	79T	703	$ .02	$ .10					
Frost, Dave	80T	423	$ .01	$ .10					
Frost, Dave	81T	286	$ .01	$ .10					
Frost, Dave	82T	24	$ .01	$ .07					
Frost, Dave	82TTR	37	$ .02	$ .10					
Frost, Dave	83T	656	$ .01	$ .07	Fuller, Vern	69T	291	$ .30	$ .95
Fry, Jerry	79T	720	$ .05	$ .20	Fuller, Vern	70T	558	$ .30	$ .95
Fryman, Travis	90TTR	33	$ .01	$1.00	Funk, Frank	61T	362	$ .35	$1.25
Fryman, Travis	91T	128	$ .01	$ .50	Funk, Frank	62T	587	$3.95	$11.50

Player	Year	No.	VG	EX/MT	Player	Year	No.	VG	EX/MT
Funk, Frank	63T	476	$2.50	$6.50	Gale, Rich	80T	433	$ .01	$ .10
Funk, Frank	64T	289	$ .30	$ .95	Gale, Rich	81T	544	$ .01	$ .10
Furillo, Carl	56T	190	$5.00	$18.00	Gale, Rich	82T	67	$ .01	$ .07
Furillo, Carl	57T	45	$3.60	$10.00	Gale, Rich	82TTR	38	$ .02	$ .10
Furillo, Carl	57T	400	$40.00	$160.00	Gale, Rich	83T	719	$ .01	$ .07
Furillo, Carl	58T	417	$1.25	$4.00	Gale, Rich	83TTR	35	$ .25	$1.25
Furillo, Carl	59T	206	$2.10	$6.00	Gale, Rich	84T	142	$ .01	$ .06
Furillo, Carl	60T	408	$2.10	$6.00	Gale, Rich	84TTR	40	$ .02	$ .10
Fusselman, Les	52T	378	$40.00	$140.00	Gale, Rich	85T	606	$ .01	$ .05
Fusselman, Les	53T	218	$4.50	$15.00	Gallagher, Alan	71T	224	$ .15	$ .50
Gabrielson, Len	63T	253	$ .30	$ .95	Gallagher, Alan	72T	693	$ .75	$2.50
Gabrielson, Len	64T	198	$ .30	$ .95	Gallagher, Alan	72TIA	694	$ .75	$2.50
Gabrielson, Len	65T	14	$ .30	$ .85	Gallagher, Bob	74T	21	$ .07	$ .30
Gabrielson, Len	66T	395	$ .30	$ .95	Gallagher, Bob	75T	406	$ .07	$ .30
Gabrielson, Len	67T	469	$ .75	$3.00	Gallagher, Dave	89T	156	$ .01	$ .15
Gabrielson, Len	68T	357	$ .30	$ .85	Gallagher, Dave	89TBB	310	$ .01	$ .06
Gabrielson, Len	69T	615	$ .30	$ .95	Gallagher, Dave	90T	612	$ .01	$ .04
Gabrielson, Len	70T	204	$ .15	$ .50	Gallagher, Dave	91T	349	$ .01	$ .03
Gaetti, Gary	83T	431	$1.00	$3.75	Gallego, Mike	86T	304	$ .01	$ .04
Gaetti, Gary	84T	157	$ .10	$ .50	Gallego, Mike	88T	702	$ .01	$ .04
Gaetti, Gary	85T	304	$ .05	$ .25	Gallego, Mike	88TBB	103	$ .01	$ .06
Gaetti, Gary	86T	97	$ .01	$ .15	Gallego, Mike	89T	102	$ .01	$ .05
Gaetti, Gary	87T	710	$ .01	$ .10	Gallego, Mike	90T	293	$ .01	$ .04
Gaetti, Gary	88T	578	$ .01	$ .10	Gallego, Mike	91T	686	$ .01	$ .03
Gaetti, Gary	88TBB	127	$ .01	$ .15	Gamble, John	74T	597	$ .15	$ .50
Gaetti, Gary	89T	220	$ .01	$ .10	Gamble, Oscar	70T	654	$ .75	$2.00
Gaetti, Gary	89TBB	264	$ .01	$ .10	Gamble, Oscar	71T	23	$ .15	$ .50
Gaetti, Gary	90T	630	$ .01	$ .04	Gamble, Oscar	72T	423	$ .05	$ .25
Gaetti, Gary	91T	430	$ .01	$ .03	Gamble, Oscar	73T	372	$ .07	$ .30
Gaff, Brent	85T	546	$ .01	$ .05	Gamble, Oscar	74T	152	$ .07	$ .30
Gaff, Brent	86T	18	$ .01	$ .04	Gamble, Oscar	75T	213	$ .07	$ .30
Gagliano, Phil	64T	568	$1.75	$4.50	Gamble, Oscar	76T	74	$ .05	$ .20
Gagliano, Phil	65T	503	$ .75	$3.00	Gamble, Oscar	76TTR	74	$ .05	$ .20
Gagliano, Phil	66T	418	$ .30	$ .95	Gamble, Oscar	77T	505	$ .03	$ .12
Gagliano, Phil	67T	304	$ .30	$ .85	Gamble, Oscar	78T	390	$ .02	$ .10
Gagliano, Phil	68T	479	$ .35	$1.25	Gamble, Oscar	79T	263	$ .02	$ .10
Gagliano, Phil	69T	609	$ .30	$ .95	Gamble, Oscar	80T	698	$ .01	$ .10
Gagliano, Phil	70T	143	$ .15	$ .50	Gamble, Oscar	81T	139	$ .01	$ .10
Gagliano, Phil	71T	302	$ .15	$ .50	Gamble, Oscar	82T	472	$ .01	$ .07
Gagliano, Phil	72T	472	$ .05	$ .25	Gamble, Oscar	83T	19	$ .01	$ .07
Gagliano, Phil	73T	69	$ .07	$ .30	Gamble, Oscar	84T	512	$ .01	$ .06
Gagliano, Phil	74T	622	$ .07	$ .30	Gamble, Oscar	85T	724	$ .01	$ .05
Gagliano, Ralph	65T	501	$ .75	$3.00	Gamble, Oscar	85TTR	37	$ .02	$ .10
Gagne, Greg	85TTR	36	$ .05	$ .25	Gant, Ron	88TBB	249	$ .01	$1.00
Gagne, Greg	86T	162	$ .01	$ .04	Gant, Ron	88TTR	39	$ .01	$1.50
Gagne, Greg	87T	558	$ .01	$ .04	Gant, Ron	89T	296	$ .01	$ .25
Gagne, Greg	88T	343	$ .01	$ .04	Gant, Ron	89TBB	43	$ .01	$ .10
Gagne, Greg	88TBB	58	$ .01	$ .06	Gant, Ron	90T	567	$ .01	$ .10
Gagne, Greg	89T	19	$ .01	$ .05	Gant, Ron	91T	725	$ .01	$ .10
Gagne, Greg	89TBB	186	$ .01	$ .06	Gantner, Jim	77T	494	$ .12	$ .40
Gagne, Greg	90T	448	$ .01	$ .04	Gantner, Jim	79T	154	$ .02	$ .10
Gagne, Greg	91T	216	$ .01	$ .03	Gantner, Jim	80T	374	$ .01	$ .10
Gaines, Joe	62T	414	$ .75	$2.50	Gantner, Jim	81T	482	$ .01	$ .10
Gaines, Joe	63T	319	$ .45	$1.50	Gantner, Jim	82T	613	$ .01	$ .07
Gaines, Joe	64T	364	$ .30	$ .95	Gantner, Jim	83T	88	$ .01	$ .07
Gaines, Joe	65T	594	$1.75	$4.50	Gantner, Jim	84T	298	$ .01	$ .06
Gaines, Joe	66T	122	$ .30	$ .95	Gantner, Jim	85T	781	$ .01	$ .05
Galan, Augie	54T	233	$1.25	$6.00	Gantner, Jim	86T	582	$ .01	$ .04
Galarraga, Andres	86TTR	40	$ .15	$ .75	Gantner, Jim	87T	108	$ .01	$ .04
Galarraga, Andres	87T	272	$ .05	$ .25	Gantner, Jim	88T	337	$ .01	$ .04
Galarraga, Andres	88T	25	$ .01	$$ .15	Gantner, Jim	89T	671	$ .01	$ .05
Galarraga, Andres	88TBB	55	$ .01	$ .15	Gantner, Jim	89TBB	184	$ .01	$ .06
Galarraga, Andres	89T	590	$ .01	$ .10	Gantner, Jim	90T	417	$ .01	$ .04
Galarraga, Andres	89TAS	386	$ .01	$ .05	Gantner, Jim	91T	23	$ .01	$ .03
Galarraga, Andres	89TBB	173	$ .01	$ .10	Garagiola, Joe	52T	227	$22.50	$90.00
Galarraga, Andres	90T	720	$ .01	$ .10	Garber, Gene	74T	431	$ .30	$ .95
Galarraga, Andres	91T	610	$ .01	$ .03	Garber, Gene	75T	444	$ .07	$ .30
Galasso, Bob	80T	711	$ .01	$ .10	Garber, Gene	76T	14	$ .05	$ .20
Galasso, Bob	82T	598	$ .01	$ .07	Garber, Gene	77T	289	$ .03	$ .12
Gale, Rich	79T	298	$ .02	$ .10	Garber, Gene	78T	177	$ .02	$ .10

Player	Year	No.	VG	EX/MT	Player	Year	No.	VG	EX/MT
Garber, Gene	79T	629	$ .02	$ .10	Garcia, Kiko	83TTR	36	$ .02	$ .10
Garber, Gene	80T	504	$ .01	$ .10	Garcia, Kiko	84T	458	$ .01	$ .06
Garber, Gene	81T	307	$ .01	$ .10	Garcia, Kiko	85T	763	$ .01	$ .05
Garber, Gene	82T	32	$ .01	$ .07	Garcia, Mike	51Trb	40	$1.50	$4.00
Garber, Gene	83T	255	$ .01	$ .07	Garcia, Mike	52T	272	$14.00	$40.00
Garber, Gene	83T	256	$ .01	$ .07	Garcia, Mike	53T	75	$5.00	$20.00
Garber, Gene	84T	466	$ .01	$ .06	Garcia, Mike	56T	210	$3.00	$9.00
Garber, Gene	84T	709	$ .01	$ .06	Garcia, Mike	57T	300	$4.25	$15.00
Garber, Gene	85T	129	$ .01	$ .05	Garcia, Mike	58T	196	$ .45	$1.50
Garber, Gene	86T	776	$ .01	$ .04	Garcia, Mike	59T	516	$3.00	$9.00
Garber, Gene	87T	351	$ .01	$ .04	Garcia, Mike	60T	532	$3.75	13.00
Garber, Gene	88T	597	$ .01	$ .04	Garcia, Pedro	73T	609	$1.00	$4.00
Garbey, Barbaro	84TTR	41	$ .02	$ .10	Garcia, Pedro	74T	142	$ .07	$ .30
Garbey, Barbaro	85T	243	$ .01	$ .05	Garcia, Pedro	75T	147	$ .07	$ .30
Garbey, Barbaro	86T	609	$ .01	$ .04	Garcia, Pedro	76T	187	$ .05	$ .20
Garces, Rich	91T	594	$ .01	$ .15	Garcia, Pedro	77T	453	$ .03	$ .12
Garcia, Damaso	81T	488	$ .05	$ .25	Garcia, Ralph	73T	602	$ .45	$1.45
Garcia, Damaso	82T	596	$ .01	$ .07	Gardenhire, Ron	82T	623	$ .20	$ .80
Garcia, Damaso	83T	202	$ .01	$ .07	Gardenhire, Ron	82TTR	39	$ .02	$ .10
Garcia, Damaso	83T	222	$ .01	$ .07	Gardenhire, Ron	83T	469	$ .01	$ .07
Garcia, Damaso	84T	124	$ .01	$ .06	Gardenhire, Ron	85T	144	$ .01	$ .05
Garcia, Damaso	85T	645	$ .01	$ .05	Gardenhire, Ron	86T	274	$ .01	$ .04
Garcia, Damaso	85TAS	702	$ .01	$ .05	Gardner, Billy	55T	27	$2.00	$6.00
Garcia, Damaso	86T	45	$ .01	$ .04	Gardner, Billy	57T	17	$ .95	$3.50
Garcia, Damaso	86TAS	713	$ .01	$ .04	Gardner, Billy	58T	105	$1.25	$4.25
Garcia, Damaso	87T	395	$ .01	$ .04	Gardner, Billy	59T	89	$1.25	$4.25
Garcia, Damaso	88T	241	$ .01	$ .04	Gardner, Billy	60T	106	$ .45	$1.45
Garcia, Damaso	89TBB	275	$ .01	$ .06	Gardner, Billy	61T	123	$ .35	$1.25
Garcia, Damaso	90T	432	$ .01	$ .04	Gardner, Billy	62T	163	$ .75	$3.00
Garcia, Dave	73T	12	$ .30	$ .85	Gardner, Billy	62T	338	$ .90	$3.00
Garcia, Dave	78T	656	$ .02	$ .10	Gardner, Billy	63T	408	$ .45	$1.50
Garcia, Dave	83T	546	$ .01	$ .07	Gardner, Billy	83T	11	$ .01	$ .07
Garcia, Kiko	77T	474	$ .05	$ .15	Gardner, Billy	84T	771	$ .01	$ .06
Garcia, Kiko	78T	287	$ .02	$ .10	Gardner, Billy	85T	213	$ .01	$ .05
Garcia, Kiko	79T	543	$ .02	$ .10	Gardner, Billy	87TTR	36	$ .01	$ .05
Garcia, Kiko	80T	37	$ .01	$ .10	Gardner, Mark	89TMLD	41	$ .01	$ .06
Garcia, Kiko	81T	688	$ .01	$ .10	Gardner, Mark	90T	284	$ .01	$ .10
Garcia, Kiko	81TTR	765	$ .02	$ .10	Gardner, Mark	91T	757	$ .01	$ .03
					Gardner, Rob	66T	534	$5.00	$20.00
					Gardner, Rob	67T	217	$ .30	$ .85
					Gardner, Rob	68T	219	$ .30	$ .85
					Gardner, Rob	71T	734	$ .75	$2.50
					Gardner, Rob	72T	22	$ .05	$ .25
					Gardner, Rob	73T	222	$ .07	$ .30
					Gardner, Wes	88T	189	$ .01	$ .04
					Gardner, Wes	89T	526	$ .01	$ .05
					Gardner, Wes	90T	38	$ .01	$ .04
					Gardner, Wes	91T	629	$ .01	$ .03
					Garibaldi, Bob	70T	681	$ .75	$2.00
					Garibaldi, Bob	71T	701	$ .75	$2.50
					Garland, Wayne	74T	596	$ .07	$ .30
					Garland, Wayne	76T	414	$ .05	$ .20
					Garland, Wayne	77T	33	$ .03	$ .12
					Garland, Wayne	78T	174	$ .02	$ .10
					Garland, Wayne	79T	636	$ .02	$ .10
					Garland, Wayne	80T	361	$ .01	$ .10
					Garland, Wayne	81T	511	$ .01	$ .10
					Garland, Wayne	82T	446	$ .01	$ .07
					Garman, Mike	71T	512	$ .15	$ .50
					Garman, Mike	72T	79	$45.00	$135.00
					Garman, Mike	73T	616	$ .45	$1.45
					Garman, Mike	75T	584	$ .07	$ .30
					Garman, Mike	76T	34	$ .05	$ .20
					Garman, Mike	77T	302	$ .03	$ .12
					Garman, Mike	78T	417	$ .02	$ .10
					Garman, Mike	79T	181	$ .02	$ .10
					Garner, Phil	75T	623	$7.00	$21.00
					Garner, Phil	76T	57	$ .05	$ .20
Garcia, Kiko	82T	377	$ .01	$ .07	Garner, Phil	77T	261	$ .03	$ .12
Garcia, Kiko	83T	198	$ .01	$ .07	Garner, Phil	78T	53	$ .02	$ .10

ASTROS
KIKO GARCIA
SHORTSTOP

Player	Year	No.	VG	EX/MT	Player	Year	No.	VG	EX/MT
Garner, Phil	79T	383	$ .02	$ .10	Garvey, Steve	77T	400	$1.00	$4.00
Garner, Phil	80T	118	$ .01	$ .10	Garvey, Steve	78T	350	$ .95	$3.50
Garner, Phil	81T	573	$ .01	$ .10	Garvey, Steve	79T	50	$ .25	$1.25
Garner, Phil	82T	683	$ .01	$ .07	Garvey, Steve	80T	290	$ .50	$2.00
Garner, Phil	83T	478	$ .01	$ .07	Garvey, Steve	81T	530	$ .45	$1.45
Garner, Phil	84T	752	$ .01	$ .06	Garvey, Steve	82T	179	$ .15	$ .75
Garner, Phil	85T	206	$ .01	$ .05	Garvey, Steve	82TIA	180	$ .08	$ .35
Garner, Phil	86T	83	$ .01	$ .04	Garvey, Steve	83T	610	$ .01	$ .07
Garner, Phil	87T	304	$ .01	$ .04	Garvey, Steve	83TTR	37	$ .45	$1.45
Garner, Phil	88T	174	$ .01	$ .04	Garvey, Steve	84T	380	$ .10	$ .50
Garr, Ralph	70T	172	$ .15	$ .50	Garvey, Steve	85T	450	$ .15	$ .50
Garr, Ralph	71T	494	$ .15	$ .50	Garvey, Steve	85TRB	2	$ .04	$ .20
Garr, Ralph	72T	85	$ .35	$1.25	Garvey, Steve	86T	660	$ .03	$ .25
Garr, Ralph	72T	260	$ .07	$ .25	Garvey, Steve	87T	100	$ .15	$ .50
Garr, Ralph	73T	15	$ .15	$ .50	Garvin, Jerry	78T	419	$ .02	$ .10
Garr, Ralph	74T	570	$ .07	$ .30	Garvin, Jerry	79T	293	$ .02	$ .10
Garr, Ralph	75T	306	$ .35	$1.25	Garvin, Jerry	80T	611	$ .01	$ .10
Garr, Ralph	75T	550	$ .07	$ .30	Garvin, Jerry	81T	124	$ .01	$ .10
Garr, Ralph	76T	410	$ .05	$ .20	Garvin, Jerry	82T	768	$ .01	$ .07
Garr, Ralph	76TTR	410	$ .05	$ .20	Garvin, Jerry	83T	358	$ .01	$ .07
Garr, Ralph	77T	133	$ .03	$ .12	Gaspar, Rod	70T	371	$ .15	$ .50
Garr, Ralph	78T	628	$ .02	$ .10	Gaspar, Rod	71T	383	$ .15	$ .50
Garr, Ralph	79T	309	$ .02	$ .10	Gaston, Cito	89TTR	36	$ .01	$ .06
Garr, Ralph	80T	272	$ .01	$ .10	Gaston, Cito	90T	201	$ .01	$ .04
Garrelts, Scott	85TTR	38	$ .05	$ .20	Gaston, Cito	91T	81	$ .01	$ .03
Garrelts, Scott	86T	395	$ .01	$ .04	Gaston, Clarence	69T	304	$ .30	$ .95
Garrelts, Scott	87T	475	$ .01	$ .04	Gaston, Clarence	70T	604	$ .30	$ .95
Garrelts, Scott	88T	97	$ .01	$ .04	Gaston, Clarence	71T	25	$ .15	$ .50
Garrelts, Scott	88TBB	240	$ .01	$ .06	Gaston, Clarence	72T	431	$ .05	$ .25
Garrelts, Scott	89T	703	$ .01	$ .05	Gaston, Clarence	72TIA	432	$ .05	$ .25
Garrelts, Scott	90T	602	$ .01	$ .04	Gaston, Clarence	73T	159	$ .07	$ .30
Garrelts, Scott	91T	361	$ .01	$ .03	Gaston, Clarence	74T	364	$ .07	$ .30
Garrett, Adrian	71T	576	$ .35	$1.25	Gaston, Clarence	75T	427	$ .07	$ .30
Garrett, Adrian	74T	656	$ .07	$ .30	Gaston, Clarence	76T	558	$ .05	$ .20
Garrett, Adrian	76T	562	$ .05	$ .20	Gaston, Clarence	77T	192	$ .03	$ .12
Garrett, Greg	70T	642	$ .75	$2.00	Gaston, Clarence	78T	716	$ .02	$ .10
Garrett, Greg	71T	377	$ .15	$ .50	Gaston, Clarence	79T	208	$ .02	$ .10
Garrett, Pat	66T	553	$5.00	$20.00	Gates, Mike	83T	657	$ .01	$ .07
Garrett, Wayne	70T	628	$ .30	$ .95	Gatewood, Aubrey	64T	127	$ .30	$ .95
Garrett, Wayne	71T	228	$ .15	$ .50	Gatewood, Aubrey	65T	422	$ .35	$1.25
Garrett, Wayne	72T	518	$ .05	$ .25	Gatewood, Aubrey	66T	42	$ .30	$ .95
Garrett, Wayne	73T	562	$ .45	$1.45	Gaudet, Jim	79T	707	$ .02	$ .10
Garrett, Wayne	74T	510	$ .07	$ .30	Gebhard, Bob	72T	28	$ .15	$ .50
Garrett, Wayne	75T	111	$ .07	$ .30	Geddes, Jim	73T	561	$ .45	$1.45
Garrett, Wayne	76T	222	$ .05	$ .20	Gedman, Rich	82T	59	$ .30	$ .85
Garrett, Wayne	77T	417	$ .03	$ .12	Gedman, Rich	83T	602	$ .01	$ .10
Garrett, Wayne	78T	679	$ .02	$ .10	Gedman, Rich	84T	498	$ .02	$ .10
Garrett, Wayne	79T	319	$ .02	$ .10	Gedman, Rich	85T	529	$ .01	$ .10
Garrido, Gil	64T	452	$ .75	$2.20	Gedman, Rich	86T	375	$ .01	$ .10
Garrido, Gil	69T	331	$ .30	$ .85	Gedman, Rich	87T	740	$ .01	$ .04
Garrido, Gil	70T	48	$ .15	$ .50	Gedman, Rich	88T	245	$ .01	$ .04
Garrido, Gil	71T	173	$ .15	$ .50	Gedman, Rich	88TBB	152	$ .01	$ .06
Garrido, Gil	72T	758	$ .75	$2.50	Gedman, Rich	89T	652	$ .01	$ .05
Garver, Ned	51Tbb	18	$7.50	$22.50	Gedman, Rich	89TBB	72	$ .01	$ .06
Garver, Ned	52T	212	$7.00	$20.00	Gedman, Rich	90T	123	$ .01	$ .04
Garver, Ned	53T	112	$4.50	$15.00	Gehrig, Lou	61T	405	$5.00	$15.00
Garver, Ned	54T	44	$3.60	$10.00	Gehrig, Lou	73TATL	472	$ .60	$2.75
Garver, Ned	56T	189	$4.50	$15.00	Gehrig, Lou	76TAS	341	$ .75	$2.25
Garver, Ned	57T	285	$4.25	$15.00	Geiger, Gary	58T	462	$1.50	$4.00
Garver, Ned	58T	292	$ .75	$3.00	Geiger, Gary	59T	521	$2.50	$10.00
Garver, Ned	59T	245	$ .75	$2.20	Geiger, Gary	60T	184	$ .45	$1.45
Garver, Ned	60T	471	$ .90	$3.00	Geiger, Gary	61T	33	$ .35	$1.25
Garver, Ned	61T	331	$ .35	$1.25	Geiger, Gary	62T	117	$ .45	$1.45
Garvey, Steve	71T	341	$25.00	$75.00	Geiger, Gary	63T	513	$1.75	$4.50
Garvey, Steve	72T	686	$25.00	$70.00	Geiger, Gary	64T	93	$ .30	$ .95
Garvey, Steve	73T	213	$3.00	$14.00	Geiger, Gary	65T	452	$ .75	$3.00
Garvey, Steve	74T	575	$3.50	$13.50	Geiger, Gary	66T	286	$ .30	$ .95
Garvey, Steve	75T	140	$1.75	$6.50	Geiger, Gary	67T	566	$1.50	$4.00
Garvey, Steve	75T	212	$ .30	$ .95	Geiger, Gary	69T	278	$ .30	$ .95
Garvey, Steve	76T	150	$1.00	$4.00	Geisel, Dave	79T	716	$ .02	$ .10

Player	Year	No.	VG	EX/MT	Player	Year	No.	VG	EX/MT
Geisel, Dave	80T	676	$ .01	$ .10	Giants, Team	73T	434	$ .35	$1.25
Geisel, Dave	84T	256	$ .01	$ .06	Giants, Team	74T	281	$ .15	$ .50
Geishert, Vern	70T	683	$1.25	$4.50	Giants, Team Checklist	75T	216	$ .35	$1.25
Gelnar, John	65T	143	$ .30	$ .85	Giants, Team Checklist	76T	443	$ .35	$1.25
Gelnar, John	67T	472	$ .75	$3.00	Giants, Team Checklist	77T	211	$ .15	$ .50
Gelnar, John	70T	393	$ .15	$ .50	Giants, Team Checklist	78T	82	$ .06	$ .30
Gelnar, John	71T	604	$ .35	$1.25	Giants, Team Checklist	79T	356	$ .05	$ .25
Gentile, Jim	60T	448	$1.00	$4.25	Giants, Team Checklist	80T	499	$ .05	$ .25
Gentile, Jim	61T	559	$6.00	$15.00	Giants, Team Checklist	81T	686	$ .02	$ .20
Gentile, Jim	62T	53	$8.00	$25.00	Giants, Team Leaders	86T	516	$ .01	$ .04
Gentile, Jim	62T	290	$ .45	$1.45	Giants, Team Leaders	87T	231	$ .01	$ .04
Gentile, Jim	63T	4	$ .50	$2.00	Giants, Team Leaders	88T	261	$ .01	$ .04
Gentile, Jim	63T	260	$ .30	$ .95	Giants, Team Leaders	89T	351	$ .01	$ .05
Gentile, Jim	64T	196	$ .30	$ .95	Gibbon, Joe	60T	512	$2.50	$10.00
Gentile, Jim	65T	365	$ .35	$1.25	Gibbon, Joe	61T	523	$5.00	$20.00
Gentile, Jim	66T	45	$ .30	$ .95	Gibbon, Joe	62T	448	$ .75	$2.50
Gentry, Gary	69T	31	$ .30	$ .95	Gibbon, Joe	63T	101	$ .30	$ .95
Gentry, Gary	70T	153	$ .15	$ .50	Gibbon, Joe	64T	307	$ .30	$ .95
Gentry, Gary	71T	725	$ .75	$2.50	Gibbon, Joe	65T	54	$ .30	$ .85
Gentry, Gary	72T	105	$ .05	$ .25	Gibbon, Joe	66T	457	$ .75	$2.50
Gentry, Gary	73T	288	$ .07	$ .30	Gibbon, Joe	67T	541	$1.50	$4.00
Gentry, Gary	74T	415	$ .07	$ .30	Gibbon, Joe	68T	32	$ .30	$ .85
Gentry, Gary	75T	393	$ .07	$ .30	Gibbon, Joe	69T	158	$ .30	$ .85
Gerber, Craig	86T	222	$ .01	$ .04	Gibbon, Joe	70T	517	$ .15	$ .50
Geren, Bob	89TTR	37	$ .01	$ .50	Gibbon, Joe	72T	382	$ .05	$ .25
Geren, Bob	90T	536	$ .01	$ .10	Gibbs, Jake	62T	281	$ .75	$3.00
Geren, Bob	91T	716	$ .01	$ .03	Gibbs, Jake	64T	281	$ .30	$ .95
Gerhart, Ken	87TTR	37	$ .05	$ .25	Gibbs, Jake	65T	226	$ .45	$1.45
Gerhart, Ken	88T	271	$ .01	$ .04	Gibbs, Jake	66T	117	$ .15	$ .50
Gerhart, Ken	89T	598	$ .01	$ .05					
Gernert, Dick	52T	343	$40.00	$140.00					
Gernert, Dick	57T	202	$ .95	$3.50					
Gernert, Dick	58T	38	$1.25	$4.25					
Gernert, Dick	59T	13	$1.25	$4.25					
Gernert, Dick	59T	519	$3.00	$9.00					
Gernert, Dick	60T	86	$ .45	$1.45					
Gernert, Dick	61T	284	$ .35	$1.25					
Gernert, Dick	62T	536	$3.95	$11.50					
Geronimo, Cesar	71T	447	$ .15	$ .50					
Geronimo, Cesar	72T	719	$ .90	$3.00					
Geronimo, Cesar	73T	156	$ .07	$ .30					
Geronimo, Cesar	74T	181	$ .07	$ .30					
Geronimo, Cesar	75T	41	$ .07	$ .30					
Geronimo, Cesar	76T	24	$ .05	$ .20					
Geronimo, Cesar	77T	535	$ .03	$ .12					
Geronimo, Cesar	78T	354	$ .02	$ .10					
Geronimo, Cesar	79T	220	$ .02	$ .10					
Geronimo, Cesar	80T	475	$ .01	$ .10					
Geronimo, Cesar	81T	390	$ .01	$ .10					
Geronimo, Cesar	81TTR	766	$ .02	$ .10					
Geronimo, Cesar	82T	693	$ .01	$ .07					
Geronimo, Cesar	83T	194	$ .01	$ .07					
Geronimo, Cesar	84T	544	$ .01	$ .06					
Giallombardo, Bob	59T	321	$ .75	$2.20					
Giamatti, A. Bartlett	90T	396	$ .01	$ .50					
Giants, Team	56T	226	$17.50	$65.00					
Giants, Team	57T	317	$15.00	$50.00					
Giants, Team	58T	19	$5.00	$15.00					
Giants, Team	59T	69	$2.75	$9.50					
Giants, Team	60T	151	$2.50	$7.50	Gibbs, Jake	67T	375	$ .30	$ .95
Giants, Team	61T	167	$ .95	$3.50	Gibbs, Jake	68T	89	$ .30	$ .85
Giants, Team	62T	226	$1.50	$4.00	Gibbs, Jake	69T	401	$ .30	$ .85
Giants, Team	63T	417	$1.50	$4.00	Gibbs, Jake	70T	594	$ .30	$ .95
Giants, Team	64T	257	$1.25	$4.25	Gibbs, Jake	71T	382	$ .15	$ .50
Giants, Team	65T	379	$ .90	$3.00	Gibson, Bob	59T	514	$75.00	$325.00
Giants, Team	66T	19	$ .90	$3.00	Gibson, Bob	60T	73	$12.50	$50.00
Giants, Team	67T	516	$1.50	$4.00	Gibson, Bob	61T	211	$7.00	$28.00
Giants, Team	70T	696	$1.50	$4.00	Gibson, Bob	62T	530	$32.50	$127.50
Giants, Team	71T	563	$ .90	$3.00	Gibson, Bob	63T	415	$7.00	$28.00
Giants, Team	72T	771	$1.75	$4.50	Gibson, Bob	63T	5	$1.00	$4.00

JAKE GIBBS · CATCHER
YANKEES

Player	Year	No.	VG	EX/MT
Gibson, Bob	63T	9	$ .90	$3.00
Gibson, Bob	64T	460	$6.50	$25.00
Gibson, Bob	65T	12	$1.75	$4.50
Gibson, Bob	65T	320	$7.50	$22.50
Gibson, Bob	66T	225	$1.00	$4.00
Gibson, Bob	66T	320	$5.00	$18.00
Gibson, Bob	67T	210	$4.00	$15.00
Gibson, Bob	67T	236	$3.00	$9.00
Gibson, Bob	68T	100	$5.00	$15.00
Gibson, Bob	68TAS	378	$1.50	$4.00
Gibson, Bob	69T	8	$ .75	$3.00
Gibson, Bob	69T	10	$ .75	$3.00
Gibson, Bob	69T	12	$ .50	$1.50
Gibson, Bob	69T	200	$3.00	$9.00
Gibson, Bob	69TAS	432	$1.50	$4.00
Gibson, Bob	70T	67	$ .75	$2.00
Gibson, Bob	70T	71	$ .50	$1.50
Gibson, Bob	70T	530	$3.00	$9.00
Gibson, Bob	71T	70	$ .50	$2.50
Gibson, Bob	71T	72	$ .50	$2.50
Gibson, Bob	71T	450	$3.00	$9.00
Gibson, Bob	72T	130	$1.50	$5.00
Gibson, Bob	73T	190	$1.00	$4.00

ST. LOUIS — PITCHER

BOB GIBSON — CARDINALS

Player	Year	No.	VG	EX/MT
Gibson, Bob	74T	350	$1.00	$4.00
Gibson, Bob	75T	150	$1.00	$4.00
Gibson, Bob	75T	206	$ .45	$1.45
Gibson, Bob	75THL	3	$ .75	$3.00
Gibson, Bob	84T	349	$ .01	$ .06
Gibson, Bob	85TTR	39	$ .02	$ .10
Gibson, Bob	86T	499	$ .01	$ .04
Gibson, Bob	88TTB	664	$ .01	$ .10
Gibson, Joel	65T	368	$ .35	$1.25
Gibson, Kirk	81T	315	$1.25	$6.00
Gibson, Kirk	82T	105	$ .25	$1.00
Gibson, Kirk	83T	430	$ .10	$ .50
Gibson, Kirk	84T	65	$ .05	$ .35
Gibson, Kirk	85T	565	$ .05	$ .25
Gibson, Kirk	86T	295	$ .01	$ .25
Gibson, Kirk	87T	765	$ .03	$ .15
Gibson, Kirk	88T	605	$ .01	$ .10

Player	Year	No.	VG	EX/MT
Gibson, Kirk	88TBB	191	$ .01	$ .15
Gibson, Kirk	88TTR	40	$ .01	$ .15
Gibson, Kirk	89T	340	$ .01	$ .10
Gibson, Kirk	89TAS	396	$ .01	$ .05
Gibson, Kirk	89TBB	299	$ .01	$ .10
Gibson, Kirk	90T	150	$ .01	$ .04
Gibson, Kirk	91T	490	$ .01	$ .03
Gibson, Paul	89T	583	$ .01	$ .05
Gibson, Paul	89TBB	230	$ .01	$ .06
Gibson, Paul	90T	11	$ .01	$ .04
Gibson, Paul	91T	431	$ .01	$ .03
Gibson, Russ	67T	547	$2.10	$6.00
Gibson, Russ	68T	297	$ .30	$ .85
Gibson, Russ	69T	89	$ .30	$ .85
Gibson, Russ	70T	237	$ .15	$ .50
Gibson, Russ	71T	738	$ .75	$2.50
Gibson, Russ	72T	643	$ .30	$ .95
Gideon, Jim	77T	478	$ .03	$ .12
Giel, Paul	58T	308	$ .75	$3.00
Giel, Paul	59T	9	$1.25	$4.25
Giel, Paul	60T	526	$2.50	$10.00
Giel, Paul	61T	374	$ .75	$3.00
Gigon, Norm	67T	576	$6.00	$20.00
Gil, Gus	67T	253	$ .30	$ .85
Gil, Gus	69T	651	$ .30	$ .95
Gilbert, Andy	73T	252	$ .30	$ .85
Gilbert, Andy	74T	78	$ .07	$ .30
Gilbert, Buddy	60T	359	$ .75	$2.20
Gilbert, Tookie	52T	61	$15.00	$47.50
Gilbreath, Rod	74T	93	$ .07	$ .30
Gilbreath, Rod	75T	431	$ .07	$ .30
Gilbreath, Rod	76T	306	$ .05	$ .20
Gilbreath, Rod	77T	126	$ .03	$ .12
Gilbreath, Rod	78T	217	$ .02	$ .10
Gilbreath, Rod	79T	572	$ .02	$ .10
Gile, Don	61T	236	$ .35	$1.25
Gile, Don	62T	244	$ .45	$1.45
Giles, Brian	83T	548	$ .01	$ .07
Giles, Brian	84T	676	$ .01	$ .06
Giles, Warren	56T	2	$5.00	$15.00
Giles, Warren	57T	100	$3.50	$14.00
Giles, Warren	58T	300	$1.50	$4.00
Giles, Warren	59T	200	$ .75	$2.25
Gilkey, Bernard	91T	126	$ .01	$ .35
Gilliam, Jim	53T	258	$80.00	$250.00
Gilliam, Junior	54T	35	$7.00	$20.00
Gilliam, Jim	55T	5	$3.00	$12.00
Gilliam, Jim	56T	280	$4.00	$14.00
Gilliam, Jim	57T	115	$2.50	$10.00
Gilliam, Jim	58T	215	$1.25	$5.00
Gilliam, Jim	59T	306	$1.50	$4.00
Gilliam, Jim	60T	255	$1.50	$4.00
Gilliam, Jim	61T	238	$ .75	$2.25
Gilliam, Jim	62T	486	$1.50	$4.00
Gilliam, Jim	63T	80	$1.25	$4.25
Gilliam, Jim	64T	310	$ .75	$2.25
Gilliam, Jim	73T	569	$1.25	$4.25
Gilliam, Jim	74T	144	$ .75	$3.00
Gilson, Hal	68T	162	$ .30	$ .85
Gilson, Hal	69T	156	$ .30	$ .85
Ginsberg, Joe	57T	236	$ .95	$3.50
Ginsberg, Joe	58T	67	$1.25	$4.25
Ginsberg, Joe	59T	66	$1.25	$4.25
Ginsberg, Joe	60T	304	$ .75	$2.20
Ginsberg, Joe	61T	79	$ .35	$1.25
Ginsberg, Myron	52T	192	$7.00	$20.00
Girardi, Joe	89TMLD	42	$ .01	$ .06
Girardi, Joe	90T	12	$ .01	$ .10
Girardi, Joe	91T	214	$ .01	$ .03
Giusti, Dave	62T	509	$ .75	$2.50

TOPPS

Player	Year	No.	VG	EX/MT	Player	Year	No.	VG	EX/MT
Giusti, Dave	63T	189	$ .30	$ .95	Goltz, Dave	76T	136	$ .05	$ .20
Giusti, Dave	64T	354	$ .30	$ .95	Goltz, Dave	77T	321	$ .03	$ .12
Giusti, Dave	65T	524	$1.75	$4.50	Goltz, Dave	78T	205	$ .30	$ .85
Giusti, Dave	66T	258	$ .30	$ .95	Goltz, Dave	78T	249	$ .02	$ .10
Giusti, Dave	67T	318	$ .30	$ .85	Goltz, Dave	79T	27	$ .02	$ .10
Giusti, Dave	68T	182	$ .30	$ .85	Goltz, Dave	80T	193	$ .01	$ .10
Giusti, Dave	69T	98	$ .30	$ .85	Goltz, Dave	81T	548	$ .01	$ .10
Giusti, Dave	70T	372	$ .15	$ .50	Goltz, Dave	82T	674	$ .01	$ .07
Giusti, Dave	71T	562	$ .35	$1.25	Goltz, Dave	83T	468	$ .01	$ .07
Giusti, Dave	72T	190	$ .05	$ .25	Gomez, Luis	77T	13	$ .03	$ .12
Giusti, Dave	73T	465	$ .07	$ .30	Gomez, Luis	78T	573	$ .02	$ .10
Giusti, Dave	74T	82	$ .07	$ .30	Gomez, Luis	79T	254	$ .02	$ .10
Giusti, Dave	75T	53	$ .07	$ .30	Gomez, Luis	80T	169	$ .01	$ .10
Giusti, Dave	76T	352	$ .05	$ .20	Gomez, Luis	81T	477	$ .01	$ .10
Giusti, Dave	77T	154	$ .03	$ .12	Gomez, Luis	82T	372	$ .01	$ .07
Gladden, Dan	85T	386	$ .01	$ .10	Gomez, Preston	69T	74	$ .30	$ .85
Gladden, Dan	86T	678	$ .01	$ .04	Gomez, Preston	70T	513	$ .15	$ .50
Gladden, Danny	87T	46	$ .01	$ .04	Gomez, Preston	71T	737	$ .75	$2.50
Gladden, Danny	87TTR	38	$ .01	$ .05	Gomez, Preston	72T	637	$ .30	$ .95
Gladden, Danny	88T	502	$ .01	$ .04	Gomez, Preston	73T	624	$ .55	$1.75
Gladden, Danny	89T	426	$ .01	$ .05	Gomez, Preston	74T	31	$ .07	$ .30
Gladden, Danny	90T	298	$ .01	$ .04	Gomez, Ruben	54T	220	$3.60	$10.00
Gladden, Danny	91T	778	$ .01	$ .03	Gomez, Ruben	55T	71	$2.00	$6.00
Gladding, Fred	64T	312	$ .30	$ .95	Gomez, Ruben	56T	9	$2.25	$6.00
Gladding, Fred	65T	37	$ .30	$ .85	Gomez, Ruben	57T	58	$ .95	$3.50
Gladding, Fred	66T	337	$ .30	$ .95	Gomez, Ruben	58T	335	$ .75	$3.00
Gladding, Fred	67T	192	$ .30	$ .85	Gomez, Ruben	59T	535	$2.50	$10.00
Gladding, Fred	68T	423	$ .30	$ .85	Gomez, Ruben	60T	82	$ .45	$1.45
Gladding, Fred	69T	58	$ .30	$ .85	Gomez, Ruben	61T	377	$ .75	$3.00
Gladding, Fred	70T	208	$ .15	$ .50	Gomez, Ruben	67T	427	$ .30	$ .95
Gladding, Fred	71T	381	$ .15	$ .50	Gonder, Jesse	63T	29	$ .45	$1.45
Gladding, Fred	72T	507	$ .05	$ .25	Gonder, Jesse	64T	457	$ .50	$1.45
Gladding, Fred	73T	17	$ .07	$ .30	Gonder, Jesse	65T	423	$ .35	$1.25
Glaviano, Tommy	51Trb	47	$1.50	$4.00	Gonder, Jesse	66T	528	$4.00	$10.00
Glaviano, Tommy	52T	56	$15.00	$47.50	Gonder, Jesse	67T	301	$ .30	$ .85
Glaviano, Tommy	53T	140	$4.50	$15.00	Gonder, Jesse	69T	617	$ .30	$ .95
Glavine, Tom	88T	779	$ .01	$ .25	Gonzales, Rene	88T	98	$ .01	$ .10
Glavine, Tom	89T	157	$ .01	$ .05	Gonzales, Rene	88TBB	209	$ .01	$ .06
Glavine, Tom	90T	506	$ .01	$ .04	Gonzales, Rene	89T	213	$ .01	$ .05
Glavine, Tom	91T	82	$ .01	$ .03	Gonzales, Rene	89TBB	87	$ .01	$ .06
Gleaton, Jerry Don	80T	673	$ .01	$ .10	Gonzales, Rene	90T	787	$ .01	$ .04
Gleaton, Jerry Don	81T	41	$ .01	$ .10	Gonzales, Rene	91T	377	$ .01	$ .03
Gleaton, Jerry Don	82T	371	$ .01	$ .07	Gonzalez, Denny	86T	746	$ .01	$ .04
Gleaton, Jerry Don	85T	216	$ .01	$ .05	Gonzalez, Fernando	74T	649	$ .07	$ .30
Gleaton, Jerry Don	86T	447	$ .01	$ .04	Gonzalez, Fernando	74TTR	649	$ .07	$ .30
Gleaton, Jerry Don	88T	116	$ .01	$ .04	Gonzalez, Fernando	78T	433	$ .02	$ .10
Gleaton, Jerry Don	89T	724	$ .01	$ .05	Gonzalez, Fernando	79T	531	$ .02	$ .10
Gleaton, Jerry Don	91T	597	$ .01	$ .03	Gonzalez, Fernando	80T	171	$ .01	$ .10
Glynn, Bill	53T	171	$4.50	$15.00	Gonzalez, German	89T	746	$ .01	$ .05
Glynn, Bill (Gylnn)	54T	178	$3.60	$10.00	Gonzalez, German	90T	266	$ .01	$ .04
Glynn, Bill	55T	39	$2.00	$6.00	Gonzalez, Jose	90T	98	$ .01	$ .04
Glynn, Ed	77T	487	$ .03	$ .12	Gonzalez, Jose	91T	279	$ .01	$ .10
Glynn, Ed	79T	343	$ .02	$ .10	Gonzalez, Juan	89TMLD	43	$ .01	$1.00
Glynn, Ed	80T	509	$ .01	$ .10	Gonzalez, Juan	90T	331	$ .01	$1.75
Glynn, Ed	81T	93	$ .01	$ .10	Gonzalez, Juan	91T	224	$ .01	$ .30
Glynn, Ed	83T	614	$ .01	$ .07	Gonzalez, Julio	78T	389	$ .02	$ .10
Goggin, Chuck	74T	457	$ .07	$ .30	Gonzalez, Julio	79T	268	$ .02	$ .10
Gogolewski, Bill	71T	559	$ .35	$1.25	Gonzalez, Julio	80T	696	$ .01	$ .10
Gogolewski, Bill	72T	424	$ .05	$ .25	Gonzalez, Julio	82T	503	$ .01	$ .07
Gogolewski, Bill	73T	27	$ .07	$ .30	Gonzalez, Julio	83T	74	$ .01	$ .07
Gogolewski, Bill	74T	242	$ .07	$ .30	Gonzalez, Orlando	77T	477	$ .05	$ .15
Golden, Jim	61T	298	$ .35	$1.25	Gonzalez, Pedro	63T	537	$175.00	$550.00
Golden, Jim	62T	568	$3.95	$11.50	Gonzalez, Pedro	64T	581	$1.75	$4.50
Golden, Jim	63T	297	$ .45	$1.50	Gonzalez, Pedro	65T	97	$ .30	$ .85
Goldsberry, Gordon	52T	46	$15.00	$47.50	Gonzalez, Pedro	66T	266	$ .30	$ .95
Goldsberry, Gordon	53T	200	$4.50	$15.00	Gonzalez, Pedro	67T	424	$ .30	$ .95
Goldy, Purnal	63T	516	$1.75	$4.50	Gonzalez, Tony	60T	518	$2.50	$10.00
Goltz, Dave	73T	148	$ .07	$ .30	Gonzalez, Tony	61T	93	$ .35	$1.25
Goltz, Dave	74T	636	$ .07	$ .30	Gonzalez, Tony	62T	534	$3.95	$11.50
Goltz, Dave	75T	419	$ .07	$ .30	Gonzalez, Tony	63T	32	$ .30	$ .95

Player	Year	No.	VG	EX/MT	Player	Year	No.	VG	EX/MT
Gonzalez, Tony	64T	379	$ .50	$1.45	Gosger, Jim	63T	553	$60.00	$225.00
Gonzalez, Tony	65T	72	$ .30	$ .85	Gosger, Jim	66T	114	$ .30	$ .95
Gonzalez, Tony	66T	478	$ .75	$2.50	Gosger, Jim	67T	17	$ .30	$ .85
Gonzalez, Tony	67T	548	$1.50	$4.00	Gosger, Jim	68T	343	$ .30	$ .85
Gonzalez, Tony	68T	1	$2.50	$12.50	Gosger, Jim	69T	482	$ .30	$ .85
Gonzalez, Tony	68T	245	$ .30	$ .85	Gosger, Jim	70T	651	$ .75	$2.00
Gonzalez, Tony	69T	501	$ .30	$ .85	Gosger, Jim	71T	284	$ .15	$ .50
Gonzalez, Tony	70T	105	$ .15	$ .50	Goss, Howie	62T	598	$18.00	$55.00
Gonzalez, Tony	71T	256	$ .15	$ .50	Goss, Howie	63T	364	$ .45	$1.50
Gooden, Dwight	84TTR	42	$15.00	$45.00	Gossage, Rich	73T	174	$2.00	$8.00
Gooden, Dwight	85T	620	$3.00	$9.00	Gossage, Rich	74T	542	$ .50	$2.00
Gooden, Dwight	85TRB	3	$ .20	$ .75	Gossage, Rich	75T	554	$ .45	$1.45
Gooden, Dwight	86T	250	$ .50	$$1.75	Gossage, Rich	76T	180	$ .35	$1.25
Gooden, Dwight	86TAS	709	$ .03	$ .25	Gossage, Rich	76T	205	$ .15	$ .50
Gooden, Dwight	86TRB	202	$ .03	$ .30	Gossage, Rich	77T	319	$ .25	$1.00
Gooden, Dwight	87T	130	$ .25	$ .75	Gossage, Rich	78T	70	$ .15	$ .50
Gooden, Dwight	87TAS	603	$ .30	$ .85	Gossage, Rich	79T	8	$ .05	$ .25
Gooden, Dwight	88T	480	$ .10	$ .40	Gossage, Rich	79T	225	$ .30	$ .85
Gooden, Dwight	88TAS	405	$ .01	$ .25	Gossage, Rich	80T	140	$ .30	$ .85
Gooden, Dwight	88TBB	11	$ .05	$ .35	Gossage, Rich	81T	460	$ .05	$ .25
Gooden, Dwight "Doc"	89T	30	$ .01	$ .25	Gossage, Rich	82T	770	$ .05	$ .25
Gooden, Doc	89TBB	304	$ .01	$ .25	Gossage, Rich	82TAS	557	$ .01	$ .10
Gooden, Dwight	89TTB	661	$ .01	$ .10	Gossage, Rich	82TIA	771	$ .02	$ .10
Gooden, Doc	90T	510	$ .01	$ .10	Gossage, Rich	83T	240	$ .05	$ .20
Gooden, Doc	91T	330	$ .01	$ .10	Gossage, Rich	83T	241	$ .01	$ .07
Goodman, Billy	51Trb	46	$1.50	$4.00	Gossage, Rich	84T	670	$ .03	$ .15
Goodman, Billy	52T	23	$12.50	$45.00	Gossage, Rich	84T	718	$ .01	$ .06
Goodman, Billy	56T	245	$3.00	$9.00	Gossage, Rich	84TTR	43	$ .15	$ .50
Goodman, Billy	57T	303	$4.25	$15.00	Gossage, Rich	85T	90	$ .03	$ .15
Goodman, Billy	58T	225	$ .75	$3.00	Gossage, Rich	86T	530	$ .01	$ .10
Goodman, Billy	59T	103	$ .75	$2.25	Gossage, Rich	87T	380	$ .01	$ .10
Goodman, Billy	60T	69	$ .75	$3.00	Gossage, Rich	88T	170	$ .01	$ .10
Goodman, Billy	61T	247	$ .75	$3.00	Gossage, Rich	88TTR	41	$ .01	$ .06
Goodson, Ed	73T	197	$ .07	$ .30	Gossage, Rich	89T	415	$ .01	$ .05
Goodson, Ed	74T	494	$ .07	$ .30	Gotay, Julio	62T	489	$ .75	$2.50
Goodson, Ed	75T	322	$ .07	$ .30	Gotay, Julio	63T	122	$ .30	$ .95
Goodson, Ed	76T	386	$ .05	$ .20	Gotay, Julio	65T	552	$1.75	$4.50
Goodson, Ed	77T	584	$ .03	$ .12	Gotay, Julio	68T	41	$ .30	$ .85
Goodson, Ed	78T	586	$ .02	$ .10	Gott, Jim	83T	506	$ .01	$ .07
Goodwin, Danny	79T	322	$ .02	$ .10					
Goodwin, Danny	80T	362	$ .01	$ .10					
Goodwin, Danny	81T	527	$ .01	$ .10					
Goodwin, Danny	82T	123	$ .01	$ .07					
Goossen, Greg	67T	287	$ .30	$ .85					
Goossen, Greg	68T	386	$ .30	$ .85					
Goossen, Greg	70T	271	$ .15	$ .50					
Gorbous, Glen	56T	174	$2.25	$6.00					
Gordon, Don	88T	144	$ .01	$ .04					
Gordon, Joe	60T	216	$ .45	$1.45					
Gordon, Joe	61T	224	$ .35	$1.25					
Gordon, Joe	69T	484	$ .30	$ .85					
Gordon, Sid	51Trb	2	$1.50	$4.00					
Gordon, Sid	52T	267	$12.00	$40.00					
Gordon, Sid	53T	117	$4.50	$15.00					
Gordon, Tom	89TTR	38	$ .01	$ .75					
Gordon, Tom	90T	752	$ .01	$ .25					
Gordon, Tom	91T	248	$ .01	$ .03					
Gorinski, Bob	78T	386	$ .02	$ .10					
Gorman, Tom	56T	246	$3.00	$9.00					
Gorman, Tom	57T	87	$ .95	$3.50					
Gorman, Tom	58T	235	$ .75	$3.00					
Gorman, Tom	59T	449	$ .75	$2.20					
Gorman, Tom	84T	774	$ .01	$ .06					
Gorman, Tom	85T	53	$ .01	$ .05					
Gorman, Tom	86T	414	$ .01	$ .04					
Goryl, John	58T	384	$ .75	$3.00					
Goryl, John	59T	77	$1.25	$4.25					
Goryl, John	62T	558	$3.95	$11.50					
Goryl, John	63T	314	$ .45	$1.50					
Goryl, John	64T	194	$ .30	$ .95	Gott, Jim	84T	9	$ .01	$ .06

TOPPS

Player	Year	No.	VG	EX/MT	Player	Year	No.	VG	EX/MT
Gott, Jim	85T	311	$ .01	$ .05	Gray, Dick	58T	146	$ .75	$3.00
Gott, Jim	85TTR	40	$ .02	$ .10	Gray, Dick	59T	244	$ .75	$2.20
Gott, Jim	86T	463	$ .01	$ .04	Gray, Dick	60T	24	$ .45	$1.45
Gott, Jim	87TTR	39	$ .01	$ .05	Gray, Gary	81TTR	767	$ .02	$ .10
Gott, Jim	88T	127	$ .01	$ .04	Gray, Gary	82T	523	$ .01	$ .07
Gott, Jim	89T	752	$ .01	$ .05	Gray, Gary	83T	313	$ .01	$ .07
Gott, Jim	90T	292	$ .01	$ .04	Gray, Jeff	91T	731	$ .01	$ .10
Gott, Jim	91T	606	$ .01	$ .03	Gray, Johnny	55T	101	$2.00	$6.00
Gozzo, Goose	89TMLD	44	$ .01	$ .06	Gray, Lorenzo	84T	163	$ .01	$ .06
Gozzo, Goose	90T	274	$ .01	$ .10	Gray, Ted	52T	86	$7.00	$20.00
Grabarkewitz, Billy	70T	446	$ .15	$ .50	Gray, Ted	53T	52	$4.50	$15.00
Grabarkewitz, Billy	71T	85	$ .15	$ .50	Grba, Eli	60T	183	$ .45	$1.45
Grabarkewitz, Billy	72T	578	$ .30	$ .95	Grba, Eli	61T	121	$ .35	$1.25
Grabarkewitz, Billy	73T	301	$ .07	$ .30	Grba, Eli	62T	96	$ .45	$1.45
Grabarkewitz, Billy	74T	214	$ .07	$ .30	Grba, Eli	63T	231	$ .30	$ .95
Grabarkewitz, Billy	75T	233	$ .07	$ .30	Grebeck, Craig	91T	446	$ .01	$ .10
Grace, Mark	88TTR	42	$1.00	$4.00	Green, Dallas	60T	366	$1.00	$4.00
Grace, Mark	89T	465	$ .25	$1.00	Green, Dallas	61T	359	$ .35	$1.25
Grace, Mark	89TBB	189	$ .01	$ .50	Green, Dallas	62T	111	$ .45	$1.45
Grace, Mark	90T	240	$ .01	$ .20	Green, Dallas	63T	91	$ .30	$ .95
Grace, Mark	91T	520	$ .01	$ .10	Green, Dallas	64T	464	$ .50	$1.45
Graff, Milt	57T	369	$1.25	$4.25	Green, Dallas	65T	203	$ .35	$1.25
Graff, Milt	58T	192	$ .75	$3.00	Green, Dallas	89T	104	$ .01	$ .05
Graff, Milt	59T	182	$ .75	$2.20	Green, David	83T	578	$ .01	$ .07
Graham, Dan	80T	669	$ .06	$ .30	Green, David	84T	362	$ .01	$ .06
Graham, Dan	81T	161	$ .01	$ .10	Green, David	85T	87	$ .01	$ .05
Graham, Dan	82T	37	$ .01	$ .07	Green, David	85TTR	41	$ .02	$ .10
Grahe, Joe	91T	426	$ .01	$ .10	Green, David	86T	727	$ .01	$ .04
Grammas, Alex	54T	151	$3.60	$10.00	Green, Dick	64T	466	$ .50	$1.45
Grammas, Alex	55T	21	$2.00	$6.00	Green, Dick	65T	168	$ .30	$ .85
Grammas, Alex	56T	37	$2.25	$6.00	Green, Dick	66T	545	$5.00	$20.00
Grammas, Alex	57T	222	$ .95	$3.50	Green, Dick	67T	54	$ .30	$ .85
Grammas, Alex	58T	254	$ .75	$3.00	Green, Dick	68T	303	$ .30	$ .85
Grammas, Alex	59T	6	$1.25	$4.25	Green, Dick	69T	515	$ .30	$ .95
Grammas, Alex	60T	168	$ .45	$1.45	Green, Dick	70T	311	$ .15	$ .50
Grammas, Alex	61T	64	$ .35	$1.25	Green, Dick	71T	258	$ .15	$ .50
Grammas, Alex	62T	223	$ .45	$1.45	Green, Dick	72T	780	$ .75	$2.50
Grammas, Alex	63T	416	$ .45	$1.50	Green, Dick	73T	456	$ .07	$ .30
Grammas, Alex	73T	296	$ .15	$ .50	Green, Dick	74T	392	$ .07	$ .30
Grammas, Alex	74T	326	$ .15	$ .50	Green, Dick	75T	91	$ .07	$ .30
Granger, Wayne	69T	551	$ .30	$ .95	Green, Fred	60T	272	$ .45	$1.45
Granger, Wayne	70T	73	$ .15	$ .50	Green, Fred	61T	181	$ .35	$1.25
Granger, Wayne	71T	379	$ .15	$ .50	Green, Gary	85T	396	$ .01	$ .05
Granger, Wayne	72T	545	$ .30	$ .95	Green, Gary	91T	184	$ .01	$ .03
Granger, Wayne	73T	523	$ .07	$ .30	Green, Gene	58T	366	$ .75	$3.00
Granger, Wayne	74T	644	$ .07	$ .30	Green, Gene	59T	37	$1.25	$4.25
Granger, Wayne	76T	516	$ .05	$ .20	Green, Gene	60T	269	$ .45	$1.45
Grant, Jim	58T	394	$ .65	$2.00	Green, Gene	61T	206	$ .35	$1.25
Grant, Jim "Mudcat"	59T	186	$ .75	$2.20	Green, Gene	62T	78	$ .45	$1.45
Grant, Jim	60T	14	$ .45	$1.45	Green, Gene	63T	506	$2.50	$6.50
Grant, Jim	61T	18	$ .35	$1.25	Green, Lenny	58T	471	$ .75	$2.20
Grant, Jim	62T	307	$ .45	$1.45	Green, Lenny	59T	209	$ .75	$2.20
Grant, Jim	63T	227	$ .30	$ .95	Green, Lenny	60T	99	$ .45	$1.45
Grant, Jim	64T	133	$ .30	$ .95	Green, Lenny	61T	4	$ .35	$1.25
Grant, Jim	65T	432	$ .35	$1.25	Green, Lenny	62T	84	$ .45	$1.45
Grant, Jim	66T	40	$ .30	$ .95	Green, Lenny	63T	198	$ .30	$ .95
Grant, Jim	66T	224	$ .90	$3.00	Green, Lenny	64T	386	$ .50	$1.45
Grant, Jim	67T	545	$1.50	$4.00	Green, Lenny	65T	588	$1.75	$4.50
Grant, Jim	68T	398	$ .30	$ .85	Green, Lenny	66T	502	$ .75	$2.50
Grant, Jim	69T	306	$ .30	$ .95	Green, Pumpsie	60T	317	$ .75	$2.20
Grant, Jim	71T	509	$ .15	$ .50	Green, Pumpsie	61T	454	$ .75	$3.00
Grant, Jim	72T	111	$ .05	$ .25	Green, Pumpsie	62T	153	$ .45	$1.45
Grant, Mark	88T	752	$ .01	$ .04	Green, Pumpsie	63T	292	$ .45	$1.50
Grant, Mark	89T	178	$ .01	$ .05	Green, Pumpsie	64T	442	$ .50	$1.45
Grant, Mark	89TBB	154	$ .01	$ .06	Greene, Al	80T	666	$ .01	$ .10
Grant, Mark	90T	537	$ .01	$ .04	Greene, Tommy	89TMLD	45	$ .01	$ .06
Grant, Mark	91T	287	$ .01	$ .03	Greene, Tommy	91T	486	$ .01	$ .15
Grasso, Mickey	52T	90	$7.00	$20.00	Greengrass, Jim	53T	209	$4.50	$15.00
Grasso, Mickey	53T	148	$4.50	$15.00	Greengrass, Jim	54T	22	$3.60	$10.00
Gray, Dave	64T	572	$1.75	$4.50	Greengrass, Jim	56T	275	$2.25	$8.00

324

Player	Year	No.	VG	EX/MT	Player	Year	No.	VG	EX/MT
Greenwell, Mike	87T	259	$ .50	$2.00	Griffey, Ken	88T	443	$ .01	$ .04
Greenwell, Mike	88T	493	$ .10	$ .50	Griffey, Ken	88TBB	110	$ .01	$ .10
Greenwell, Mike	88TBB	233	$ .10	$ .50	Griffey, Ken	89TTR	40	$ .01	$ .10
Greenwell, Mike	89T	630	$ .01	$ .20	Griffey, Ken	90T	581	$ .01	$ .04
Greenwell, Mike	89TAS	402	$ .01	$ .15	Griffey, Ken	91T	465	$ .01	$ .03
Greenwell, Mike	89TBB	211	$ .01	$ .20	Griffin, Alfredo	79T	705	$ .25	$1.00
Greenwell, Mike	90T	70	$ .01	$ .10	Griffin, Alfredo	80T	558	$ .01	$ .10
Greenwell, Mike	91T	792	$ .01	$ .10	Griffin, Alfredo	81T	277	$ .01	$ .10
Greer, Brian	80T	685	$ .01	$ .10	Griffin, Alfredo	82T	677	$ .01	$ .07
Gregg, Hal	52T	318	$40.00	$140.00	Griffin, Alfredo	83T	488	$ .01	$ .07
Gregg, Tommy	89TTR	39	$ .01	$ .15	Griffin, Alfredo	84T	76	$ .01	$ .06
Gregg, Tommy	90T	223	$ .01	$ .04	Griffin, Alfredo	85T	361	$ .01	$ .05
Gregg, Tommy	91T	742	$ .01	$ .03	Griffin, Alfredo	85TTR	42	$ .02	$ .10
Greif, Bill	72T	101	$ .35	$1.25	Griffin, Alfredo	86T	566	$ .01	$ .04
Greif, Bill	73T	583	$ .45	$1.45	Griffin, Alfredo	87T	111	$ .01	$ .04
Greif, Bill	74T	102	$ .07	$ .30	Griffin, Alfredo	88T	726	$ .01	$ .04
Greif, Bill	75T	168	$ .07	$ .30	Griffin, Alfredo	88TBB	247	$ .01	$ .06
Greif, Bill	76T	184	$ .05	$ .20	Griffin, Alfredo	88TTR	43	$ .01	$ .06
Greif, Bill	77T	112	$ .03	$ .12	Griffin, Alfredo	89T	62	$ .01	$ .05
Grich, Bob	71T	193	$ .75	$2.20	Griffin, Alfredo	90T	643	$ .01	$ .04
Grich, Bob	72T	338	$ .05	$ .25	Griffin, Alfredo	91T	226	$ .01	$ .03
Grich, Bob	73T	418	$ .30	$ .85	Griffin, Doug	71T	176	$ .15	$ .50
Grich, Bob	74T	109	$ .07	$ .30	Griffin, Doug	72T	703	$ .75	$2.50
Grich, Bob	75T	225	$ .15	$ .50	Griffin, Doug	72TIA	704	$ .75	$2.50
Grich, Bob	76T	335	$ .05	$ .20	Griffin, Doug	73T	96	$ .07	$ .30
Grich, Bob	77T	521	$ .03	$ .12	Griffin, Doug	74T	219	$ .07	$ .30
Grich, Bob	78T	18	$ .02	$ .10	Griffin, Doug	75T	454	$ .07	$ .30
Grich, Bob	79T	477	$ .02	$ .10					
Grich, Bob	80T	621	$ .01	$ .10					
Grich, Bob	81T	182	$ .01	$ .10					
Grich, Bob	82T	162	$ .05	$ .25					
Grich, Bob	82T	284	$ .01	$ .07					
Grich, Bob	83T	790	$ .01	$ .07					
Grich, Bob	83TAS	387	$ .01	$ .07					
Grich, Bob	84T	315	$ .01	$ .06					
Grich, Bob	85T	465	$ .01	$ .05					
Grich, Bob	86T	155	$ .01	$ .04					
Grich, Bob	87T	677	$ .01	$ .04					
Grieve, Tom	71T	167	$ .15	$ .50					
Grieve, Tom	72T	609	$ .30	$ .95					
Grieve, Tom	73T	579	$ .45	$1.45					
Grieve, Tom	74T	268	$ .07	$ .30					
Grieve, Tom	75T	234	$ .07	$ .30					
Grieve, Tom	76T	106	$ .05	$ .20					
Grieve, Tom	77T	403	$ .03	$ .12					
Grieve, Tom	78T	337	$ .02	$ .10					
Grieve, Tom	79T	277	$ .02	$ .10					
Griffey, Jr., Ken	89TMLD	46	$ .01	$2.00					
Griffey, Jr., Ken	89TTR	41	$1.00	$6.00					
Griffey, Jr., Ken	90T	336	$ .01	$2.00					
Griffey, Jr., Ken	91T	790	$ .01	$ .75					
Griffey, Jr., Ken	91TAS	392	$ .01	$ .25					
Griffey, Ken	74T	598	$4.00	$15.00					
Griffey, Ken	75T	284	$ .75	$3.00					
Griffey, Ken	76T	128	$ .25	$1.50					
Griffey, Ken	77T	320	$ .15	$1.00					
Griffey, Ken	78T	80	$ .05	$ .75					
Griffey, Ken	79T	420	$ .05	$ .50	Griffin, Doug	76T	654	$ .05	$ .20
Griffey, Ken	80T	550	$ .07	$ .50	Griffin, Doug	77T	191	$ .03	$ .12
Griffey, Ken	81T	280	$ .03	$ .35	Griffin, Mike	81T	483	$ .01	$ .10
Griffey, Ken	82T	620	$ .03	$ .25	Griffin, Mike	82T	146	$ .01	$ .07
Griffey, Ken	82T	756	$ .05	$ .20	Griffin, Tom	69T	614	$ .30	$ .95
Griffey, Ken	82TIA	621	$ .01	$ .07	Griffin, Tom	70T	578	$ .30	$ .95
Griffey, Ken	82TTR	40	$ .15	$ .50	Griffin, Tom	71T	471	$ .15	$ .50
Griffey, Ken	83T	110	$ .01	$ .25	Griffin, Tom	73T	468	$ .07	$ .30
Griffey, Ken	84T	770	$ .02	$ .15	Griffin, Tom	74T	256	$ .07	$ .30
Griffey, Ken	85T	380	$ .01	$ .10	Griffin, Tom	75T	188	$ .07	$ .30
Griffey, Ken	86T	40	$ .01	$ .04	Griffin, Tom	76T	454	$ .05	$ .20
Griffey, Ken	86TTR	41	$ .02	$ .10	Griffin, Tom	77T	39	$ .03	$ .12
Griffey, Ken	87T	711	$ .01	$ .04	Griffin, Tom	78T	318	$ .02	$ .10

DOUG GRIFFIN
SECOND BASE RED SOX

TOPPS

Player	Year	No.	VG	EX/MT	Player	Year	No.	VG	EX/MT
Griffin, Tom	79T	291	$ .02	$ .10	Gross, Don	59T	228	$ .75	$2.20
Griffin, Tom	80T	649	$ .01	$ .10	Gross, Don	60T	284	$ .45	$1.45
Griffin, Tom	81T	538	$ .01	$ .10	Gross, Greg	75T	334	$ .07	$ .30
Griffin, Tom	82T	777	$ .01	$ .07	Gross, Greg	76T	171	$ .05	$ .20
Griffin, Ty	88TTR	44	$ .30	$1.25	Gross, Greg	77T	614	$ .03	$ .12
Griffin, Ty	89T	713	$ .15	$ .75	Gross, Greg	78T	397	$ .02	$ .10
Griffin, Ty	89TBB	170	$ .01	$ .40	Gross, Greg	79T	579	$ .02	$ .10
Griffith, Derrell	65T	112	$ .30	$ .85	Gross, Greg	80T	718	$ .01	$ .10
Griffith, Derrell	66T	573	$5.00	$20.00	Gross, Greg	81T	459	$ .01	$ .10
Griffith, Derrell	67T	502	$ .75	$3.00	Gross, Greg	82T	53	$ .01	$ .07
Griggs, Hal	58T	455	$ .75	$2.20	Gross, Greg	83T	279	$ .01	$ .07
Griggs, Hal	59T	434	$ .75	$2.20	Gross, Greg	84T	613	$ .01	$ .06
Griggs, Hal	60T	244	$ .45	$1.45	Gross, Greg	85T	117	$ .01	$ .05
Grilli, Guido	66T	558	$5.50	$17.50	Gross, Greg	86T	302	$ .01	$ .04
Grilli, Steve	76T	591	$ .05	$ .20	Gross, Greg	87T	702	$ .01	$ .04
Grilli, Steve	77T	506	$ .03	$ .12	Gross, Greg	88T	518	$ .01	$ .04
Grim, Bob	55T	80	$3.60	$10.00	Gross, Greg	89T	438	$ .01	$ .05
Grim, Bob	56T	52	$2.25	$6.00	Gross, Kevin	84T	332	$ .05	$ .25
Grim, Bob	57T	36	$ .95	$3.50	Gross, Kevin	85T	584	$ .01	$ .05
Grim, Bob	58T	224	$ .45	$1.50	Gross, Kevin	86T	764	$ .01	$ .04
Grim, Bob	59T	423	$ .75	$2.20	Gross, Kevin	87T	163	$ .01	$ .04
Grim, Bob	60T	78	$ .45	$1.45	Gross, Kevin	88T	20	$ .01	$ .04
Grim, Bob	62T	564	$3.95	$11.50	Gross, Kevin	89T	215	$ .01	$ .05
Grimm, Charley	60T	217	$ .45	$1.45	Gross, Kevin	89TTR	42	$ .01	$ .06
Grimsley, Jason	89TMLD	47	$ .01	$ .10	Gross, Kevin	90T	465	$ .01	$ .04
Grimsley, Jason	90T	493	$ .01	$ .10	Gross, Kevin	91T	674	$ .01	$ .03
Grimsley, Jason	91T	173	$ .01	$ .03	Gross, Wayne	77T	479	$ .03	$ .12
Grimsley, Ross	72T	99	$ .30	$ .85	Gross, Wayne	78T	139	$ .02	$ .10
Grimsley, Ross	73T	357	$ .07	$ .30	Gross, Wayne	79T	528	$ .02	$ .10
Grimsley, Ross	74T	59	$ .07	$ .30	Gross, Wayne	80T	363	$ .01	$ .10
Grimsley, Ross	74TTR	59	$ .07	$ .30	Gross, Wayne	81T	86	$ .01	$ .10
Grimsley, Ross	75T	458	$ .07	$ .30	Gross, Wayne	82T	692	$ .01	$ .07
Grimsley, Ross	76T	257	$ .05	$ .20	Gross, Wayne	83T	233	$ .01	$ .07
Grimsley, Ross	77T	572	$ .03	$ .12	Gross, Wayne	84T	741	$ .01	$ .06
Grimsley, Ross	78T	691	$ .02	$ .10	Gross, Wayne	84TTR	44	$ .02	$ .10
Grimsley, Ross	79T	15	$ .02	$ .10	Gross, Wayne	85T	416	$ .01	$ .05
Grimsley, Ross	80T	375	$ .01	$ .10	Gross, Wayne	86T	173	$ .01	$ .04
Grimsley, Ross	81T	170	$ .01	$ .10	Grote, Gerald "Jerry"	64T	226	$ .30	$ .95
Grissom, Marquis	89TMLD	48	$ .01	$ .50	Grote, Jerry	65T	504	$ .75	$3.00
Grissom, Marquis	90T	714	$ .01	$ .40	Grote, Jerry	66T	328	$ .30	$ .95
Grissom, Marquis	91T	283	$ .01	$ .10	Grote, Jerry	67T	413	$ .30	$ .95
Grissom, Marv	56T	301	$2.25	$8.00	Grote, Jerry	68T	582	$ .35	$1.25
Grissom, Marv	57T	216	$ .95	$3.50	Grote, Jerry	69T	55	$ .30	$ .85
Grissom, Marv	58T	399	$ .75	$3.00	Grote, Jerry	70T	183	$ .15	$ .50
Grissom, Marv	59T	243	$ .75	$2.20	Grote, Jerry	71T	278	$ .15	$ .50
Groat, Dick	52T	369	$75.00	$225.00	Grote, Jerry	72T	655	$ .30	$ .95
Groat, Dick	53T	154	$6.00	$17.50	Grote, Jerry	73T	113	$ .07	$ .30
Groat, Dick	54T	43	$2.50	$10.00	Grote, Jerry	74T	311	$ .07	$ .30
Groat, Dick	55T	26	$3.60	$10.00	Grote, Jerry	75T	158	$ .07	$ .30
Groat, Dick	56T	24	$1.50	$4.00	Grote, Jerry	76T	143	$ .05	$ .20
Groat, Dick	57T	12	$2.00	$6.00	Grote, Jerry	78T	464	$ .02	$ .10
Groat, Dick	58T	45	$ .70	$2.25	Grote, Jerry	79T	279	$ .02	$ .10
Groat, Dick	59T	160	$ .90	$3.00	Groth, Johnny	51Tbb	11	$7.50	$22.50
Groat, Dick	60T	258	$ .25	$2.50	Groth, Johnny	52T	25	$15.00	$47.50
Groat, Dick	61T	1	$3.00	$18.00	Groth, Johnny	53T	36	$4.50	$15.00
Groat, Dick	61T	41	$1.50	$5.00	Groth, Johnny	56T	279	$2.25	$8.00
Groat, Dick	61TMVP	486	$ .90	$3.00	Groth, Johnny	57T	360	$1.25	$4.25
Groat, Dick	62T	270	$ .75	$3.00	Groth, Johnny	58T	262	$ .75	$3.00
Groat, Dick	63T	130	$ .35	$1.25	Groth, Johnny	59T	164	$ .75	$2.20
Groat, Dick	64T	7	$1.70	$5.00	Groth, Johnny	60T	171	$ .45	$1.45
Groat, Dick	64T	40	$ .15	$ .50	Grove, Lefty	76TAS	350	$ .45	$1.45
Groat, Dick	65T	275	$ .75	$3.00	Grubb, John	74T	32	$ .07	$ .30
Groat, Dick	66T	103	$ .45	$1.45	Grubb, Johnny	75T	298	$ .07	$ .30
Groat, Dick	67T	205	$ .45	$1.45	Grubb, Johnny	76T	422	$ .05	$ .12
Groat, Dick	75T	198	$ .75	$2.20	Grubb, Johnny	77T	286	$ .03	$ .12
Gromek, Steve	52T	258	$12.00	$40.00	Grubb, Johnny	78T	608	$ .02	$ .10
Gromek, Steve	56T	310	$2.25	$8.00	Grubb, Johnny	79T	198	$ .02	$ .10
Gromek, Steve	57T	258	$ .95	$3.50	Grubb, Johnny	80T	313	$ .01	$ .10
Gross, Don	57T	341	$4.25	$15.00	Grubb, Johnny	81T	545	$ .01	$ .10
Gross, Don	58T	172	$ .75	$3.00	Grubb, Johnny	82T	496	$ .01	$ .07

Player	Year	No.	VG	EX/MT
Grubb, Johnny	83T	724	$ .01	$ .07
Grubb, Johnny	83TTR	38	$ .02	$ .10
Grubb, Johnny	84T	42	$ .01	$ .06
Grubb, Johnny	85T	643	$ .01	$ .05
Grubb, Johnny	86T	243	$ .01	$ .04
Grubb, Johnny	87T	384	$ .01	$ .04
Grubb, Johnny	88T	128	$ .01	$ .04
Gruber, Kelly	87T	458	$ .01	$ .04
Gruber, Kelly	88T	113	$ .01	$ .04
Gruber, Kelly	88TBB	134	$ .01	$ .06
Gruber, Kelly	89T	29	$ .01	$ .05
Gruber, Kelly	89TBB	95	$ .01	$ .06
Gruber, Kelly	90T	505	$ .01	$ .04

Player	Year	No.	VG	EX/MT
Gruber, Kelly	91T	370	$ .01	$ .10
Gruber, Kelly	91TAS	388	$ .01	$ .03
Grunwald, Al	60T	427	$ .75	$2.20
Grzenda, Joe	69T	121	$ .30	$ .85
Grzenda, Joe	70T	691	$ .75	$2.00
Grzenda, Joe	71T	518	$ .15	$ .50
Grzenda, Joe	72T	13	$ .05	$ .25
Guante, Cecilio	84T	122	$ .01	$ .06
Guante, Cecilio	85T	457	$ .01	$ .05
Guante, Cecilio	86T	668	$ .01	$ .04
Guante, Cecilio	87T	219	$ .01	$ .04
Guante, Cecilio	87TTR	40	$ .01	$ .05
Guante, Cecilio	88T	84	$ .01	$ .04
Guante, Cecilio	89T	766	$ .01	$ .05
Guante, Cecilio	90T	532	$ .01	$ .04
Gubicza, Mark	84TTR	45	$ .75	$3.00
Gubicza, Mark	85T	127	$ .25	$1.00
Gubicza, Mark	86T	644	$ .01	$ .25
Gubicza, Mark	87T	326	$ .01	$ .10
Gubicza, Mark	88T	507	$ .01	$ .10
Gubicza, Mark	88TBB	199	$ .01	$ .10
Gubicza, Mark	89T	430	$ .01	$ .10
Gubicza, Mark	89TBB	26	$ .01	$ .10
Gubicza, Mark	90T	20	$ .01	$ .10
Gubicza, Mark	91T	265	$ .01	$ .03
Guerrero, Mario	73T	607	$ .45	$1.45
Guerrero, Mario	74T	192	$ .07	$ .30

Player	Year	No.	VG	EX/MT
Guerrero, Mario	75T	152	$ .07	$ .30
Guerrero, Mario	76T	499	$ .05	$ .20
Guerrero, Mario	77T	628	$ .03	$ .12
Guerrero, Mario	78T	339	$ .02	$ .10
Guerrero, Mario	79T	261	$ .02	$ .10
Guerrero, Mario	80T	49	$ .01	$ .10
Guerrero, Mario	81T	547	$ .01	$ .10
Guerrero, Pedro	79T	719	$2.50	$10.00
Guerrero, Pedro	81T	651	$ .30	$1.25
Guerrero, Pedro	82T	247	$ .15	$ .60
Guerrero, Pedro	83T	425	$ .06	$ .30
Guerrero, Pedro	83T	681	$ .01	$ .07
Guerrero, Pedro	84T	90	$ .08	$ .35
Guerrero, Pedro	84T	306	$ .01	$ .06
Guerrero, Pedro	85T	575	$ .05	$ .25
Guerrero, Pedro	86T	145	$ .02	$ .20
Guerrero, Pedro	86TAS	706	$ .01	$ .04
Guerrero, Pedro	87T	360	$ .07	$ .30
Guerrero, Pedro	88T	550	$ .01	$ .10
Guerrero, Pedro	88TBB	171	$ .01	$ .10
Guerrero, Pedro	89T	780	$ .01	$ .10
Guerrero, Pedro	89TBB	285	$ .01	$ .15
Guerrero, Pedro	90T	610	$ .01	$ .10
Guerrero, Pedro	91T	20	$ .01	$ .03
Guetterman, Lee	87T	307	$ .01	$ .10
Guetterman, Lee	88T	656	$ .01	$ .04
Guetterman, Lee	89TTR	43	$ .01	$ .06
Guetterman, Lee	90T	286	$ .01	$ .04
Guetterman, Lee	91T	62	$ .01	$ .03
Guidry, Ron	76T	599	$2.50	$10.00
Guidry, Ron	77T	656	$ .75	$3.00
Guidry, Ron	78T	135	$ .20	$ .75
Guidry, Ron	79T	5	$ .06	$ .30
Guidry, Ron	79T	7	$ .03	$ .15
Guidry, Ron	79T	500	$ .20	$ .75
Guidry, Ron	79TRB	202	$ .05	$ .20
Guidry, Ron	80T	207	$ .02	$ .10
Guidry, Ron	80T	300	$ .01	$ .15
Guidry, Ron	81T	250	$ .08	$ .25
Guidry, Ron	82T	9	$ .05	$ .25
Guidry, Ron	82TIA	10	$ .01	$ .07
Guidry, Ron	83T	440	$ .05	$ .20
Guidry, Ron	84T	110	$ .05	$ .25
Guidry, Ron	84T	486	$ .01	$ .06
Guidry, Ron	84T	717	$ .01	$ .06
Guidry, Ron	84TAS	406	$ .01	$ .06
Guidry, Ron	85T	790	$ .05	$ .20
Guidry, Ron	86T	610	$ .01	$ .10
Guidry, Ron	86TAS	721	$ .01	$ .04
Guidry, Ron	87T	375	$ .01	$ .10
Guidry, Ron	88T	535	$ .01	$ .10
Guidry, Ron	88TBB	50	$ .01	$ .06
Guidry, Ron	89T	255	$ .01	$ .05
Guillen, Ozzie	85TTR	43	$ .50	$2.25
Guillen, Ozzie	86T	254	$ .10	$1.00
Guillen, Ozzie	87T	89	$ .01	$ .10
Guillen, Ozzie	88T	585	$ .01	$ .04
Guillen, Ozzie	88TBB	27	$ .01	$ .06
Guillen, Ozzie	89T	195	$ .01	$ .05
Guillen, Ozzie	89TBB	148	$ .01	$ .06
Guillen, Ozzie	90T	365	$ .01	$ .04
Guillen, Ozzie	91T	620	$ .01	$ .03
Guindon, Bob	65T	509	$ .75	$3.00
Guinn, Skip	69T	614	$ .30	$ .95
Guinn, Skip	70T	316	$ .15	$ .50
Guinn, Skip	71T	741	$ .75	$2.50
Gulden, Brad	80T	670	$ .01	$ .10
Gulden, Brad	85T	251	$ .01	$ .05
Gullett, Don	71T	124	$ .15	$ .75
Gullett, Don	72T	157	$ .10	$ .50

Player	Year	No.	VG	EX/MT
Gullett, Don	73T	595	$ .75	$2.20
Gullett, Don	74T	385	$ .07	$ .30
Gullett, Don	75T	65	$ .07	$ .30
Gullett, Don	76T	390	$ .07	$ .30
Gullett, Don	77T	15	$ .03	$ .12
Gullett, Don	78T	225	$ .02	$ .10
Gullett, Don	79T	140	$ .02	$ .10
Gullett, Don	80T	435	$ .01	$ .10
Gullickson, Bill	81T	578	$ .05	$ .25
Gullickson, Bill	81TRB	203	$ .01	$ .10
Gullickson, Bill	82T	172	$ .01	$ .07
Gullickson, Bill	82T	526	$ .01	$ .07
Gullickson, Bill	83T	31	$ .01	$ .07
Gullickson, Bill	84T	318	$ .01	$ .06
Gullickson, Bill	85T	687	$ .01	$ .05
Gullickson, Bill	86T	229	$ .01	$ .04
Gullickson, Bill	86TTR	42	$ .02	$ .10
Gullickson, Bill	87T	489	$ .01	$ .04
Gullickson, Bill	88T	711	$ .01	$ .04
Gullickson, Bill	90TTR	34	$ .01	$ .05
Gulliver, Glenn	83T	293	$ .01	$ .07
Gumpert, Dave	84T	371	$ .01	$ .06
Gumpert, Dave	87T	487	$ .01	$ .04

Player	Year	No.	VG	EX/MT
Gumpert, Randy	52T	247	$7.00	$20.00
Gura, Larry	71T	203	$ .15	$ .50
Gura, Larry	73T	501	$ .30	$ .95
Gura, Larry	74T	616	$ .07	$ .30
Gura, Larry	74TTR	616	$ .15	$ .50
Gura, Larry	75T	557	$ .07	$ .30
Gura, Larry	76T	319	$ .05	$ .20
Gura, Larry	77T	193	$ .03	$ .12
Gura, Larry	78T	441	$ .02	$ .10
Gura, Larry	79T	19	$ .02	$ .10
Gura, Larry	80T	295	$ .01	$ .10
Gura, Larry	81T	130	$ .01	$ .10
Gura, Larry	82T	96	$ .05	$ .25
Gura, Larry	82T	790	$ .01	$ .07
Gura, Larry	83T	340	$ .01	$ .07
Gura, Larry	83TAS	395	$ .01	$ .07
Gura, Larry	84T	96	$ .01	$ .06

Player	Year	No.	VG	EX/MT
Gura, Larry	84T	625	$ .01	$ .06
Gura, Larry	85T	595	$ .01	$ .05
Guthrie, Mark	89TMLD	49	$ .01	$ .15
Guthrie, Mark	90T	317	$ .01	$ .10
Guthrie, Mark	91T	698	$ .01	$ .03
Gutierrez, Cesar	69T	16	$ .30	$ .85
Gutierrez, Cesar	70T	269	$ .15	$ .50
Gutierrez, Cesar	71T	154	$ .15	$ .50
Gutierrez, Cesar	72T	743	$ .75	$2.50
Gutierrez, Jackie	84TTR	46	$ .02	$ .10
Gutierrez, Jackie	85T	89	$ .01	$ .05
Gutierrez, Jackie	86T	633	$ .01	$ .04
Gutierrez, Jackie	87T	276	$ .01	$ .04
Gutteridge, Don	60T	458	$ .95	$3.50
Gutteridge, Don	70T	123	$ .15	$ .50
Guzman, Jose	86TTR	43	$ .05	$ .25
Guzman, Jose	87T	363	$ .01	$ .04
Guzman, Jose	88T	563	$ .01	$ .04
Guzman, Jose	89T	462	$ .01	$ .05
Guzman, Jose	90T	308	$ .01	$ .04
Guzman, Santiago	70T	716	$ .75	$2.00
Guzman, Santiago	72T	316	$ .15	$ .50
Gwosdz, Doug	82T	731	$ .01	$ .07
Gwosdz, Doug	84T	753	$ .01	$ .06
Gwynn, Chris	90T	456	$ .01	$ .10
Gwynn, Chris	91T	99	$ .01	$ .03
Gwynn, Tony	83T	482	$5.00	$20.00
Gwynn, Tony	84T	251	$ .60	$3.00
Gwynn, Tony	85T	660	$ .35	$1.25
Gwynn, Tony	85TAS	717	$ .05	$ .25
Gwynn, Tony	86T	10	$ .15	$ .50
Gwynn, Tony	87T	530	$ .30	$ .95
Gwynn, Tony	87TAS	599	$ .01	$ .10
Gwynn, Tony	88T	360	$ .01	$ .25
Gwynn, Tony	88TAS	402	$ .01	$ .10
Gwynn, Tony	88TBB	161	$ .05	$ .25
Gwynn, Tony	89T	570	$ .01	$ .10
Gwynn, Tony	89TBB	58	$ .01	$ .20
Gwynn, Tony	90T	730	$ .01	$ .10
Gwynn, Tony	90TAS	403	$ .01	$ .10
Gwynn, Tony	91T	180	$ .01	$ .10
Haas, Bill	63T	544	$7.50	$30.00
Haas, Bill	64T	398	$ .50	$1.45
Haas, Eddie	59T	126	$ .75	$2.20
Haas, Eddie	85TTR	44	$ .02	$ .10
Haas, Moose	78T	649	$ .02	$ .10
Haas, Moose	79T	448	$ .02	$ .10
Haas, Moose	80T	181	$ .01	$ .10
Haas, Moose	81T	327	$ .01	$ .10
Haas, Moose	82T	12	$ .01	$ .07
Haas, Moose	83T	503	$ .01	$ .07
Haas, Moose	84T	271	$ .01	$ .06
Haas, Moose	84T	726	$ .01	$ .06
Haas, Moose	85T	151	$ .01	$ .05
Haas, Moose	86T	759	$ .01	$ .04
Haas, Moose	86TTR	44	$ .02	$ .10
Haas, Moose	87T	413	$ .01	$ .04
Haas, Moose	88T	606	$ .01	$ .04
Habyan, John	88T	153	$ .01	$ .04
Hack, Stan	55T	6	$3.60	$10.00
Hacker, Warren	52T	324	$40.00	$140.00
Hacker, Warren	56T	282	$2.25	$8.00
Hacker, Warren	57T	370	$1.25	$4.25
Hacker, Warren	58T	251	$ .75	$3.00
Haddix, Harvey	53T	273	$30.00	$100.00
Haddix, Harvey	54T	9	$2.50	$9.00
Haddix, Harvey	55T	43	$3.60	$10.00
Haddix, Harvey	56T	77	$2.25	$6.00
Haddix, Harvey	57T	265	$5.00	$20.00
Haddix, Harvey	58T	118	$ .75	$3.00

Player	Year	No.	VG	EX/MT	Player	Year	No.	VG	EX/MT
Haddix, Harvey	59T	184	$ .75	$2.20	Hall, Jimmie	65T	580	$1.75	$4.50
Haddix, Harvey	60T	340	$ .90	$3.00	Hall, Jimmie	66T	190	$ .30	$ .95
Haddix, Harvey	61T	100	$ .35	$1.25	Hall, Jimmie	67T	432	$ .30	$ .95
Haddix, Harvey	61T	410	$ .75	$2.25	Hall, Jimmie	68T	121	$ .30	$ .85
Haddix, Harvey	62T	67	$ .45	$1.45	Hall, Jimmie	69T	61	$ .30	$ .85
Haddix, Harvey	63T	239	$ .30	$ .95	Hall, Jimmie	70T	649	$ .75	$2.00
Haddix, Harvey	64T	439	$ .75	$2.20	Hall, Mel	83TTR	39	$ .15	$ .75
Haddix, Harvey	65T	67	$ .30	$ .85	Hall, Mel	84T	508	$ .01	$ .35
Hadley, Kent	59T	127	$ .75	$2.20	Hall, Mel	84TTR	47	$ .02	$ .10
Hadley, Kent	60T	102	$ .45	$1.45	Hall, Mel	85T	263	$ .01	$ .05
Hagen, Kevin	84T	337	$ .01	$ .06	Hall, Mel	86T	647	$ .01	$ .04
Hagen, Mike	71T	415	$ .15	$ .50	Hall, Mel	87T	51	$ .01	$ .04
Hague, Joe	69T	559	$ .30	$ .95	Hall, Mel	88T	318	$ .01	$ .04
Hague, Joe	70T	362	$ .15	$ .50	Hall, Mel	88TBB	114	$ .01	$ .06
Hague, Joe	71T	96	$ .15	$ .50	Hall, Mel	89T	173	$ .01	$ .05
Hague, Joe	72T	546	$ .30	$ .95	Hall, Mel	89TBB	13	$ .01	$ .06
Hague, Joe	73T	447	$ .07	$ .30	Hall, Mel	89TTR	44	$ .01	$ .06
Hahn, Don	71T	94	$ .15	$ .50	Hall, Mel	90T	436	$ .01	$ .04
Hahn, Don	72T	269	$ .05	$ .25	Hall, Mel	91T	738	$ .01	$ .03
Hahn, Don	74T	291	$ .07	$ .30	Hall, Tom	69T	658	$ .30	$ .95
Hahn, Don	75T	182	$ .07	$ .30	Hall, Tom	70T	169	$ .15	$ .50
Hairston, Jerry	74T	96	$ .15	$ .50	Hall, Tom	71T	313	$ .15	$ .50
Hairston, Jerry	75T	327	$ .07	$ .30	Hall, Tom	72T	417	$ .05	$ .25
Hairston, Jerry	76T	391	$ .05	$ .20	Hall, Tom	73T	8	$ .07	$ .30
Hairston, Jerry	83T	487	$ .01	$ .07	Hall, Tom	74T	248	$ .07	$ .30
Hairston, Jerry	84T	177	$ .01	$ .06	Hall, Tom	75T	108	$ .07	$ .30
Hairston, Jerry	85T	596	$ .01	$ .05	Hall, Tom	76T	621	$ .05	$ .20
Hairston, Jerry	86T	778	$ .01	$ .04	Haller, Tom	62T	356	$ .45	$1.45
Hairston, Jerry	87T	685	$ .01	$ .04	Haller, Tom	63T	85	$ .30	$ .95
Hairston, Jerry	88T	281	$ .01	$ .04	Haller, Tom	64T	485	$ .50	$1.45
Hale, Bob	56T	231	$3.00	$9.00	Haller, Tom	65T	465	$ .75	$3.00
Hale, Bob	57T	406	$1.25	$4.25	Haller, Tom	66T	308	$ .30	$ .95
Hale, Bob	59T	507	$2.50	$10.00	Haller, Tom	67T	65	$ .30	$ .85
Hale, Bob	60T	309	$ .75	$2.20	Haller, Tom	68T	185	$ .30	$ .85
Hale, Bob	61T	532	$7.00	$21.00	Haller, Tom	69T	310	$ .30	$ .95
Hale, Chip	89TMLD	50	$ .01	$ .10	Haller, Tom	70T	685	$ .75	$2.00
Hale, Chip	90T	704	$ .01	$ .10	Haller, Tom	71T	639	$ .35	$1.25
Hale, John	76T	228	$ .05	$ .20	Haller, Tom	72T	175	$ .05	$ .25
Hale, John	77T	253	$ .03	$ .12	Haller, Tom	72TIA	176	$ .05	$ .25
Hale, John	78T	584	$ .02	$ .10	Haller, Tom	73T	454	$ .07	$ .30
Hale, John	79T	56	$ .02	$ .10	Hambright, Roger	72T	124	$ .05	$ .25
Halicki, Ed	75T	467	$ .07	$ .30	Hamilton, Darryl	89T	88	$ .01	$ .10
Halicki, Ed	76T	423	$ .05	$ .20	Hamilton, Darryl	90TTR	35	$ .01	$ .05
Halicki, Ed	77T	343	$ .03	$ .12	Hamilton, Darryl	91T	781	$ .01	$ .03
Halicki, Ed	78T	107	$ .02	$ .10	Hamilton, Dave	73T	214	$ .07	$ .30
Halicki, Ed	79T	672	$ .02	$ .10	Hamilton, Dave	74T	633	$ .07	$ .30
Halicki, Ed	80T	217	$ .01	$ .10	Hamilton, Dave	75T	428	$ .07	$ .30
Halicki, Ed	81T	69	$ .01	$ .10	Hamilton, Dave	76T	237	$ .05	$ .20
Hall, Albert	85T	676	$ .01	$ .05	Hamilton, Dave	77T	367	$ .03	$ .12
Hall, Albert	87TTR	41	$ .01	$ .05	Hamilton, Dave	78T	288	$ .02	$ .10
Hall, Albert	88T	213	$ .01	$ .04	Hamilton, Dave	79T	147	$ .02	$ .10
Hall, Albert	89T	433	$ .01	$ .05	Hamilton, Dave	80T	86	$ .01	$ .10
Hall, Albert	89TBB	104	$ .01	$ .06	Hamilton, Jack	62T	593	$7.00	$21.00
Hall, Bill	59T	49	$1.25	$4.25	Hamilton, Jack	63T	132	$ .20	$ .75
Hall, Dick	55T	126	$2.00	$6.00	Hamilton, Jack	65T	288	$ .35	$1.25
Hall, Dick	56T	331	$2.25	$8.00	Hamilton, Jack	66T	262	$ .30	$ .95
Hall, Dick	57T	308	$4.25	$15.00	Hamilton, Jack	67T	2	$ .30	$ .85
Hall, Dick	60T	308	$ .75	$2.20	Hamilton, Jack	68T	193	$ .30	$ .85
Hall, Dick	61T	197	$ .35	$1.25	Hamilton, Jack	69T	629	$ .30	$ .95
Hall, Dick	62T	189	$ .45	$1.45	Hamilton, Jeff	87T	266	$ .01	$ .10
Hall, Dick	63T	526	$1.75	$4.50	Hamilton, Jeff	88T	62	$ .01	$ .04
Hall, Dick	67T	508	$ .75	$3.00	Hamilton, Jeff	89T	736	$ .01	$ .05
Hall, Dick	68T	17	$ .30	$ .85	Hamilton, Jeff	90T	426	$ .01	$ .04
Hall, Dick	70T	182	$ .15	$ .50	Hamilton, Jeff	91T	552	$ .01	$ .03
Hall, Dick	71T	417	$ .15	$ .50	Hamilton, Steve	63T	171	$ .30	$ .95
Hall, Drew	88T	262	$ .01	$ .04	Hamilton, Steve	64T	206	$ .45	$1.45
Hall, Drew	89T	593	$ .01	$ .05	Hamilton, Steve	65T	309	$ .45	$1.45
Hall, Drew	90T	463	$ .01	$ .04	Hamilton, Steve	66T	503	$1.25	$4.25
Hall, Drew	91T	77	$ .01	$ .03	Hamilton, Steve	67T	567	$5.00	$15.00
Hall, Jimmie	64T	73	$ .30	$ .95	Hamilton, Steve	68T	496	$ .35	$1.25

Player	Year	No.	VG	EX/MT
Hamilton, Steve	69T	69	$ .15	$ .50
Hamilton, Steve	70T	349	$ .30	$ .85
Hamilton, Steve	71T	627	$ .35	$1.25
Hamilton, Steve	72T	766	$ .75	$2.50
Hamlin, Ken	60T	542	$2.50	$10.00
Hamlin, Ken	61T	263	$ .35	$1.25
Hamlin, Ken	62T	296	$ .45	$1.45
Hamlin, Ken	66T	69	$ .30	$ .95

Player	Year	No.	VG	EX/MT
Hamm, Pete	71T	74	$ .15	$ .50
Hamm, Pete	72T	501	$ .05	$ .25
Hammaker, Atlee	82T	471	$ .05	$ .20
Hammaker, Atlee	83T	342	$ .01	$ .07
Hammaker, Atlee	84T	85	$ .01	$ .06
Hammaker, Atlee	84T	137	$ .01	$ .06
Hammaker, Atlee	84T	576	$ .01	$ .06
Hammaker, Atlee	85T	674	$ .01	$ .05
Hammaker, Atlee	86T	223	$ .01	$ .04
Hammaker, Atlee	87T	781	$ .01	$ .04
Hammaker, Atlee	88T	157	$ .01	$ .04
Hammaker, Atlee	88TBB	259	$ .01	$ .06
Hammaker, Atlee	89T	572	$ .01	$ .05
Hammaker, Atlee	89TBB	21	$ .01	$ .06
Hammaker, Atlee	90T	447	$ .01	$ .04
Hammaker, Atlee	91T	34	$ .01	$ .03
Hammond, Chris	91T	258	$ .01	$ .10
Hamner, Granville " Granny"	51Tbb	29	$7.50	$22.50
Hamner, Granny	52T	221	$7.00	$20.00
Hamner, Granny	53T	146	$4.50	$15.00
Hamner, Granny	54T	24	$3.60	$10.00
Hamner, Granny	56T	197	$3.00	$9.00
Hamner, Granny	57T	335	$4.25	$15.00
Hamner, Granny	58T	268	$ .75	$3.00
Hamner, Granny	59T	436	$ .75	$2.20
Hampton, Ike	78T	503	$ .02	$ .10
Hamric, Bert	55T	199	$5.25	$15.00
Hamric, Bert	58T	336	$ .75	$3.00
Hancock, Garry	79T	702	$ .02	$ .10
Hancock, Garry	82T	322	$ .01	$ .07
Hancock, Garry	84T	197	$ .01	$ .06
Hand, Rich	71T	24	$ .15	$ .50

Player	Year	No.	VG	EX/MT
Hand, Rich	72T	317	$ .05	$ .25
Hand, Rich	73T	398	$ .07	$ .30
Hand, Rich	74T	571	$ .07	$ .30
Hands, Bill	66T	392	$ .30	$ .95
Hands, Bill	67T	16	$ .30	$ .85
Hands, Bill	68T	279	$ .30	$ .85
Hands, Bill	69T	115	$ .30	$ .85
Hands, Bill	70T	405	$ .15	$ .50
Hands, Bill	71T	670	$ .75	$2.50
Hands, Bill	72T	335	$ .05	$ .25
Hands, Bill	73T	555	$ .45	$1.45
Hands, Bill	74T	271	$ .07	$ .30
Hands, Bill	75T	412	$ .07	$ .30
Hands, Bill	76T	509	$ .05	$ .20
Hanebrink, Harry	58T	454	$ .75	$2.20
Hanebrink, Harry	59T	322	$ .75	$2.20
Haney, Fred	54T	75	$4.00	$14.00
Haney, Fred	58T	475	$5.00	$15.00
Haney, Fred	59TAS	551	$3.00	$9.00
Haney, Larry	67T	507	$ .75	$3.00
Haney, Larry	68T	42	$ .30	$ .85
Haney, Larry	69T	209	$ .30	$ .85
Haney, Larry	70T	648	$ .75	$2.00
Haney, Larry	73T	563	$ .45	$1.45
Haney, Larry	75T	626	$ .07	$ .30
Haney, Larry	76T	446	$ .05	$ .20
Haney, Larry	77T	12	$ .03	$ .12
Haney, Larry	78T	391	$ .02	$ .10
Hanna, Preston	79T	296	$ .02	$ .10
Hanna, Preston	80T	489	$ .01	$ .10
Hanna, Preston	81T	594	$ .01	$ .10
Hanna, Preston	83T	127	$ .01	$ .07
Hannan, Jim	63T	121	$ .30	$ .95
Hannan, Jim	64T	261	$ .30	$ .95
Hannan, Jim	65T	394	$ .35	$1.25
Hannan, Jim	66T	479	$ .75	$2.50
Hannan, Jim	67T	291	$ .30	$ .85
Hannan, Jim	69T	106	$ .30	$ .85
Hannan, Jim	70T	697	$ .75	$2.00
Hannan, Jim	71T	229	$ .15	$ .50
Hansen, Andy	52T	74	$15.00	$47.50
Hansen, Bob	75T	508	$ .07	$ .30
Hansen, Ronnie	59T	444	$ .75	$2.20
Hansen, Ron	60T	127	$ .45	$1.45
Hansen, Ron	61T	240	$ .35	$1.25
Hansen, Ron	62T	245	$ .45	$1.45
Hansen, Ron	63T	88	$ .30	$ .95
Hansen, Ron	64T	384	$ .50	$1.45
Hansen, Ron	65T	146	$ .30	$ .85
Hansen, Ron	66T	261	$ .30	$ .95
Hansen, Ron	67T	9	$ .30	$ .85
Hansen, Ron	68T	411	$ .30	$ .85
Hansen, Ron	69T	566	$ .30	$ .95
Hansen, Ron	70T	217	$ .15	$ .50
Hansen, Ron	71T	419	$ .15	$ .50
Hansen, Ron	72T	763	$ .75	$2.50
Hanson, Erik	89TTR	45	$ .01	$ .15
Hanson, Erik	90T	118	$ .01	$ .10
Hanson, Erik	91T	655	$ .01	$ .03
Harder, Mel	60T	460	$2.25	$6.00
Hardin, Jim	68T	222	$ .30	$ .85
Hardin, Jim	69T	532	$ .20	$ .50
Hardin, Jim	69T	610	$ .30	$ .95
Hardin, Jim	70T	656	$ .75	$2.00
Hardin, Jim	71T	491	$ .15	$ .50
Hardin, Jim	72T	287	$ .05	$ .25
Hardin, Jim	73T	124	$ .07	$ .30
Hardy, Carroll	58T	446	$1.50	$4.00
Hardy, Carroll	59T	168	$ .75	$2.20
Hardy, Carroll	60T	341	$ .75	$2.20

Player	Year	No.	VG	EX/MT	Player	Year	No.	VG	EX/MT
Hardy, Carroll	61T	257	$ .35	$1.25	Harper, Terry	86T	247	$ .01	$ .04
Hardy, Carroll	62T	101	$ .45	$1.45	Harper, Terry	87T	49	$ .01	$ .04
Hardy, Carroll	63T	468	$2.50	$6.50	Harper, Terry	87TTR	42	$ .01	$ .05
Hardy, Jack	89TMLD	51	$ .01	$ .06	Harper, Tommy	63T	158	$ .30	$ .95
Hardy, Larry	75T	112	$ .07	$ .30	Harper, Tommy	64T	330	$ .30	$ .95
Hargan, Steve	66T	508	$ .75	$2.50	Harper, Tommy	65T	47	$ .30	$ .85
Hargan, Steve	67T	233	$ .45	$1.45	Harper, Tommy	66T	214	$ .30	$ .95
Hargan, Steve	67T	440	$ .30	$ .95	Harper, Tommy	67T	392	$ .30	$ .95
Hargan, Steve	68T	35	$ .30	$ .85	Harper, Tommy	68T	590	$ .35	$1.25
Hargan, Steve	69T	348	$ .30	$ .85	Harper, Tommy	69T	42	$ .15	$ .50
Hargan, Steve	70T	136	$ .15	$ .50	Harper, Tommy	70T	370	$ .30	$ .85
Hargan, Steve	71T	375	$ .15	$ .50	Harper, Tommy	71T	260	$ .15	$ .50
Hargan, Steve	72T	615	$ .30	$ .95	Harper, Tommy	72T	455	$ .05	$ .25
Hargan, Steve	75T	362	$ .07	$ .30	Harper, Tommy	73T	620	$ .75	$3.00
Hargan, Steve	76T	463	$ .05	$ .20	Harper, Tommy	74T	204	$ .35	$1.25
Hargan, Steve	77T	37	$ .03	$ .12	Harper, Tommy	74T	325	$ .07	$ .30
Hargesheimer, Al	81T	502	$ .01	$ .10	Harper, Tommy	75T	537	$ .07	$ .30
Hargrove, Mike	75T	106	$ .15	$ .50	Harper, Tommy	76T	274	$ .05	$ .20
Hargrove, Mike	76T	485	$ .05	$ .20	Harper, Tommy	77T	414	$ .03	$ .12
Hargrove, Mike	77T	275	$ .03	$ .12	Harrah, Toby	72T	104	$ .30	$ .85
Hargrove, Mike	78T	172	$ .02	$ .10	Harrah, Toby	73T	216	$ .30	$ .85
Hargrove, Mike	79T	591	$ .02	$ .10	Harrah, Toby	74T	511	$ .07	$ .30
Hargrove, Mike	80T	308	$ .01	$ .10	Harrah, Toby	75T	131	$ .07	$ .30
Hargrove, Mike	81T	74	$ .01	$ .10	Harrah, Toby	76T	412	$ .05	$ .20
Hargrove, Mike	82T	310	$ .01	$ .07	Harrah, Toby	77T	301	$ .03	$ .12
Hargrove, Mike	82T	559	$ .01	$ .07	Harrah, Toby	78T	44	$ .02	$ .10
Hargrove, Mike	83T	660	$ .01	$ .07	Harrah, Toby	79T	234	$ .02	$ .10
Hargrove, Mike	84T	546	$ .01	$ .06	Harrah, Toby	80T	636	$ .01	$ .10
Hargrove, Mike	84T	764	$ .01	$ .06	Harrah, Toby	81T	721	$ .01	$ .10
Hargrove, Mike	85T	425	$ .01	$ .05	Harrah, Toby	82T	532	$ .01	$ .07
Hargrove, Mike	86T	136	$ .01	$ .04	Harrah, Toby	83T	141	$ .01	$ .07
Harkey, Mike	89T	742	$ .05	$ .25	Harrah, Toby	83T	480	$ .01	$ .07
Harkey, Mike	90TTR	36	$ .01	$ .20	Harrah, Toby	84T	348	$ .01	$ .06
Harkey, Mike	91T	376	$ .01	$ .03	Harrah, Toby	84TTR	48	$ .02	$ .10
Harkness, Tim	62T	404	$ .75	$2.50	Harrah, Toby	85T	94	$ .01	$ .05
Harkness, Tim	63T	436	$ .45	$1.50	Harrah, Toby	85TTR	46	$ .02	$ .10
Harkness, Tim	64T	57	$ .30	$ .95	Harrah, Toby	86T	535	$ .01	$ .04
Harlow, Larry	78T	543	$ .02	$ .10	Harrah, Toby	87T	152	$ .01	$ .04
Harlow, Larry	79T	314	$ .02	$ .10	Harrell, Billy	58T	443	$1.50	$4.00
Harlow, Larry	80T	68	$ .01	$ .10	Harrell, Billy	59T	433	$ .75	$2.20
Harlow, Larry	81T	121	$ .01	$ .10	Harrell, Billy	61T	354	$ .35	$1.25
Harlow, Larry	82T	257	$ .01	$ .07	Harrell, John	70T	401	$ .15	$ .50
Harmon, Chuck	54T	182	$3.60	$10.00	Harrelson, Bill	69T	224	$ .30	$ .95
Harmon, Chuck	55T	82	$2.00	$6.00	Harrelson, Bud	67T	306	$ .45	$1.45
Harmon, Chuck	56T	308	$2.25	$8.00	Harrelson, Bud	68T	132	$ .30	$ .95
Harmon, Chuck	57T	299	$4.25	$15.00	Harrelson, Bud	69T	456	$ .30	$ .85
Harmon, Chuck	58T	48	$ .70	$2.25	Harrelson, Bud	70T	634	$ .75	$2.00
Harmon, Terry	69T	624	$ .30	$ .95	Harrelson, Bud	71T	355	$ .15	$ .50
Harmon, Terry	70T	486	$ .15	$ .50	Harrelson, Bud	72T	53	$ .30	$ .85
Harmon, Terry	71T	682	$ .75	$2.50	Harrelson, Bud	72T	496	$ .05	$ .25
Harmon, Terry	72T	377	$ .05	$ .25	Harrelson, Bud	72TIA	54	$ .05	$ .25
Harmon, Terry	73T	166	$ .07	$ .30	Harrelson, Bud	73T	223	$ .07	$ .30
Harmon, Terry	74T	642	$ .07	$ .30	Harrelson, Bud	74T	380	$ .07	$ .30
Harmon, Terry	75T	399	$ .07	$ .30	Harrelson, Bud	75T	395	$ .07	$ .30
Harmon, Terry	76T	247	$ .05	$ .20	Harrelson, Bud	76T	337	$ .05	$ .20
Harmon, Terry	77T	388	$ .03	$ .12	Harrelson, Bud	77T	44	$ .03	$ .12
Harmon, Terry	78T	118	$ .02	$ .10	Harrelson, Bud	78T	403	$ .02	$ .10
Harnisch, Pete	90T	324	$ .01	$ .04	Harrelson, Bud	79T	118	$ .02	$ .10
Harnisch, Pete	91T	179	$ .01	$ .03	Harrelson, Bud	80T	566	$ .01	$ .10
Harper, Brian	84T	144	$ .01	$ .06	Harrelson, Bud	81T	694	$ .01	$ .10
Harper, Brian	85T	332	$ .01	$ .05	Harrelson, Bud	90TTR	37	$ .01	$ .05
Harper, Brian	86T	656	$ .01	$ .04	Harrelson, Bud	91T	261	$ .01	$ .03
Harper, Brian	89T	472	$ .01	$ .05	Harrelson, Ken	64T	419	$1.00	$4.00
Harper, Brian	90T	47	$ .01	$ .04	Harrelson, Ken	65T	479	$ .75	$2.20
Harper, Brian	91T	554	$ .01	$ .03	Harrelson, Ken	66T	55	$ .45	$1.45
Harper, Terry	81T	192	$ .05	$ .20	Harrelson, Ken	67T	188	$ .35	$1.25
Harper, Terry	82T	507	$ .01	$ .07	Harrelson, Ken	68T	566	$ .45	$1.45
Harper, Terry	83T	339	$ .01	$ .07	Harrelson, Ken	69T	3	$ .35	$1.25
Harper, Terry	84T	624	$ .01	$ .06	Harrelson, Ken	69T	5	$ .35	$1.25
Harper, Terry	85TTR	45	$ .02	$ .10	Harrelson, Ken	69T	240	$ .45	$1.45

Player	Year	No.	VG	EX/MT	Player	Year	No.	VG	EX/MT
Harrelson, Ken	69TAS	417	$ .30	$ .85	Harshman, Jack	58T	217	$ .75	$3.00
Harrelson, Ken	70T	545	$ .45	$1.45	Harshman, Jack	59T	475	$ .75	$2.20
Harrelson, Ken	71T	510	$ .35	$1.25	Harshman, Jack	60T	112	$ .45	$1.45
Harridge, William	56T	1	$20.00	$100.00	Hart, Jim	64T	452	$ .75	$2.20
Harridge, William	57T	100	$3.50	$14.00	Hart, Jim	65T	4	$1.75	$4.50
Harridge, William	58T	300	$1.50	$4.00	Hart, Jim	65T	395	$ .35	$1.25
Harris, Alonzo	67T	564	$2.10	$6.00	Hart, Jim	66T	295	$ .30	$ .95
Harris, Alonzo	68T	128	$ .30	$ .85	Hart, Jim	67T	220	$ .30	$ .85
Harris, Bill	60T	128	$ .45	$1.45	Hart, Jim	68T	73	$ .30	$ .85
Harris, Billy	69T	569	$ .30	$ .95	Hart, Jim	69T	555	$ .30	$ .95
Harris, Billy	70T	512	$ .15	$ .50	Hart, Jim	70T	176	$ .45	$1.45
Harris, Buddy	71T	404	$ .15	$ .50	Hart, Jim	71T	461	$ .15	$ .50
Harris, Donald	90T	314	$ .01	$ .15	Hart, Jim	72T	733	$ .75	$2.50
Harris, Gail	56T	91	$2.25	$6.00	Hart, Jim	73T	538	$ .45	$1.45
Harris, Gail	57T	281	$4.25	$15.00	Hart, Jim	74T	159	$ .07	$ .30
Harris, Gail	58T	309	$ .75	$3.00	Hart, John	90T	141	$ .01	$ .04
Harris, Gail	59T	378	$ .75	$2.20	Hart, Mike	88T	69	$ .01	$ .10
Harris, Gail	60T	152	$ .45	$1.45	Hartenstein, Chuck	68T	13	$ .30	$ .85
Harris, Gene	89TMLD	52	$ .01	$ .15	Hartenstein, Chuck	69T	596	$ .30	$ .95
Harris, Gene	89TTR	46	$ .01	$ .15	Hartenstein, Chuck	70T	216	$ .15	$ .50
Harris, Gene	90T	738	$ .01	$ .10	Hartenstein, Chuck	77T	416	$ .03	$ .12
Harris, Gene	91T	203	$ .01	$ .03	Hartley, Mike	89TMLD	53	$ .01	$ .06
Harris, Greg	82T	783	$ .01	$ .07	Hartley, Mike	91T	199	$ .01	$ .10
Harris, Greg	82TTR	41	$ .02	$ .10	Hartman, Bob	59T	128	$ .75	$2.20
Harris, Greg	83T	296	$ .01	$ .07	Hartman, Bob	60T	129	$ .45	$1.45
Harris, Greg	85T	242	$ .01	$ .05	Hartman, J. C.	63T	442	$ .45	$1.50
Harris, Greg	85TTR	47	$ .02	$ .10	Hartsfield, Roy	52T	264	$12.00	$40.00
Harris, Greg	86T	586	$ .01	$ .04	Hartsfield, Roy	73T	237	$ .35	$1.25
Harris, Greg	87T	44	$ .01	$ .04	Hartsfield, Roy	78T	444	$ .02	$ .10
Harris, Greg	88T	369	$ .01	$ .04	Hartung, Clint	52T	141	$7.00	$20.00
Harris, Greg	89T	194	$ .01	$ .05	Hartzell, Paul	77T	179	$ .03	$ .12
Harris, Greg	89T	627	$ .01	$ .05					
Harris, Greg	90T	529	$ .01	$ .04					
Harris, Greg	90T	572	$ .01	$ .04					
Harris, Greg	91T	123	$ .01	$ .03					
Harris, Greg	91T	749	$ .01	$ .03					
Harris, John	81T	214	$ .01	$ .10					
Harris, John	82T	313	$ .01	$ .07					
Harris, Lenny	90T	277	$ .01	$ .04					
Harris, Lenny	91T	453	$ .01	$ .03					
Harris, Lum	60T	455	$ .95	$3.50					
Harris, Lum	65T	274	$ .35	$1.25					
Harris, Lum	66T	147	$ .30	$ .95					
Harris, Lum	68T	439	$ .30	$ .85					
Harris, Lum	69T	196	$ .30	$ .85					
Harris, Lum	70T	86	$ .15	$ .50					
Harris, Lum	71T	346	$ .15	$ .50					
Harris, Lum	72T	484	$ .05	$ .25					
Harris, Mickey	52T	207	$7.00	$20.00					
Harris, Reggie	91T	177	$ .01	$ .15					
Harris, Vic	73T	594	$ .45	$1.45					
Harris, Vic	74T	157	$ .07	$ .30					
Harris, Vic	75T	658	$ .07	$ .30					
Harris, Vic	78T	436	$ .02	$ .10					
Harris, Vic	79T	338	$ .02	$ .10					
Harrison, Chuck	66T	244	$ .30	$ .95					
Harrison, Chuck	67T	8	$ .30	$ .85					
Harrison, Chuck	69T	116	$ .30	$ .85					
Harrison, Roric	72T	474	$ .50	$2.35					
Harrison, Roric	73T	229	$ .07	$ .30					
Harrison, Roric	74T	298	$ .07	$ .30	Hartzell, Paul	78T	529	$ .02	$ .10
Harrison, Roric	75T	287	$ .07	$ .30	Hartzell, Paul	79T	402	$ .02	$ .10
Harrison, Roric	76T	547	$ .05	$ .20	Hartzell, Paul	80T	721	$ .01	$ .10
Harrison, Roric	78T	536	$ .02	$ .10	Harvey, Bryan	88TTR	45	$ .01	$ .25
Harrist, Earl	52T	402	$40.00	$140.00	Harvey, Bryan	89T	632	$ .01	$ .15
Harrist, Earl	53T	65	$4.50	$15.00	Harvey, Bryan	90T	272	$ .01	$ .04
Harshman, Jack	54T	173	$3.60	$10.00	Harvey, Bryan	91T	153	$ .01	$ .03
Harshman, Jack	55T	104	$2.00	$6.00	Hassey, Ron	80T	222	$ .01	$ .10
Harshman, Jack	56T	29	$2.25	$6.00	Hassey, Ron	81T	564	$ .01	$ .10
Harshman, Jack	57T	152	$ .95	$3.50					

PAUL HARTZELL

Player	Year	No.	VG	EX/MT	Player	Year	No.	VG	EX/MT
Hassey, Ron	82T	54	$ .01	$ .07	Hausman, Tom	80T	151	$ .01	$ .10
Hassey, Ron	83T	689	$ .01	$ .07	Hausman, Tom	81T	359	$ .01	$ .10
Hassey, Ron	84T	308	$ .01	$ .06	Hausman, Tom	82T	524	$ .01	$ .07
Hassey, Ron	84TTR	49	$ .02	$ .10	Hausman, Tom	83T	417	$ .01	$ .07
Hassey, Ron	85T	742	$ .01	$ .05	Havens, Brad	82T	92	$ .01	$ .07
Hassey, Ron	85TTR	48	$ .02	$ .10	Havens, Brad	83T	751	$ .01	$ .07
Hassey, Ron	86T	157	$ .01	$ .04	Havens, Brad	84T	509	$ .01	$ .06
Hassey, Ron	87T	667	$ .01	$ .04	Havens, Brad	87T	398	$ .01	$ .04
Hassey, Ron	88T	458	$ .01	$ .04	Havens, Brad	87TTR	44	$ .01	$ .05
Hassey, Ron	88TTR	46	$ .01	$ .06	Havens, Brad	88T	698	$ .01	$ .04
Hassey, Ron	89T	272	$ .01	$ .05	Havens, Brad	89T	204	$ .01	$ .05
Hassey, Ron	89TBB	171	$ .01	$ .06	Hawkins, Andy	84T	778	$ .05	$ .35
Hassey, Ron	90T	527	$ .01	$ .04	Hawkins, Andy	85T	299	$ .01	$ .10
Hassey, Ron	91T	327	$ .01	$ .03	Hawkins, Andy	86T	478	$ .01	$ .04
Hassler, Andy	75T	261	$ .07	$ .30	Hawkins, Andy	87T	183	$ .01	$ .04
Hassler, Andy	76T	207	$ .05	$ .20	Hawkins, Andy	88T	9	$ .01	$ .04
Hassler, Andy	77T	602	$ .03	$ .12	Hawkins, Andy	88TBB	257	$ .01	$ .06
Hassler, Andy	78T	73	$ .02	$ .10	Hawkins, Andy	89T	533	$ .01	$ .05
Hassler, Andy	79T	696	$ .02	$ .10	Hawkins, Andy	89TTR	47	$ .01	$ .06
Hassler, Andy	80T	353	$ .01	$ .10	Hawkins, Andy	90T	335	$ .01	$ .04
Hassler, Andy	81T	454	$ .01	$ .10	Hawkins, Andy	91T	635	$ .01	$ .03
Hassler, Andy	82T	94	$ .01	$ .07	Hawkins, Wynn	60T	536	$2.50	$10.00
Hassler, Andy	83T	573	$ .01	$ .07	Hawkins, Wynn	61T	34	$ .35	$1.25
Hassler, Andy	84T	719	$ .01	$ .06	Hawkins, Wynn	63T	334	$ .45	$1.50
Hatcher, Billy	86T	46	$ .01	$ .25	Haydel, Hal	71T	692	$ .75	$2.50
Hatcher, Billy	86TTR	45	$ .02	$ .10	Haydel, Hal	72T	28	$ .15	$ .50
Hatcher, Billy	87T	578	$ .01	$ .04	Hayes, Ben	84T	448	$ .01	$ .06
Hatcher, Billy	88T	306	$ .01	$ .04	Hayes, Charlie	90T	577	$ .01	$ .15
Hatcher, Billy	88TBB	3	$ .01	$ .06	Hayes, Charlie	91T	312	$ .01	$ .03
Hatcher, Billy	89T	252	$ .01	$ .05	Hayes, Von	82T	141	$ .25	$1.50
Hatcher, Billy	89TBB	118	$ .01	$ .10	Hayes, Von	82TTR	42	$ .35	$1.75
Hatcher, Billy	90T	119	$ .01	$ .10	Hayes, Von	83T	325	$ .10	$ .50
Hatcher, Billy	90TTR	38	$ .01	$ .05	Hayes, Von	83TTR	40	$ .30	$1.00
Hatcher, Billy	91T	604	$ .01	$ .03	Hayes, Von	84T	587	$ .01	$ .10
Hatcher, Mickey	80T	679	$ .01	$ .10	Hayes, Von	85T	68	$ .01	$ .10
Hatcher, Mickey	81T	289	$ .01	$ .10	Hayes, Von	86T	420	$ .01	$ .04
Hatcher, Mickey	81TTR	768	$ .02	$ .10	Hayes, Von	87T	666	$ .01	$ .04
Hatcher, Mickey	82T	467	$ .01	$ .07	Hayes, Von	88T	215	$ .01	$ .04
Hatcher, Mickey	83T	121	$ .01	$ .07	Hayes, Von	88TBB	139	$ .01	$ .10
Hatcher, Mickey	84T	746	$ .01	$ .06	Hayes, Von	89T	385	$ .01	$ .05
Hatcher, Mickey	85T	18	$ .01	$ .05	Hayes, Von	89TBB	302	$ .01	$ .10
Hatcher, Mickey	86T	356	$ .01	$ .04	Hayes, Von	90T	710	$ .01	$ .04
Hatcher, Mickey	87T	504	$ .01	$ .04	Hayes, Von	91T	15	$ .01	$ .03
Hatcher, Mickey	87TTR	43	$ .01	$ .05	Haynes, Joe	52T	145	$7.00	$20.00
Hatcher, Mickey	88T	607	$ .01	$ .04	Haynes, Joe	54T	223	$3.60	$10.00
Hatcher, Mickey	89T	483	$ .01	$ .05	Hayward, Ray	88TTR	47	$ .01	$ .06
Hatcher, Mickey	89TBB	63	$ .01	$ .06	Hazle, Bob	58T	83	$1.25	$4.25
Hatcher, Mickey	90T	226	$ .01	$ .04	Healy, Fran	72T	663	$ .75	$2.50
Hatcher, Mickey	91T	152	$ .01	$ .03	Healy, Fran	73T	361	$ .07	$ .30
Hatfield, Fred	52T	354	$40.00	$140.00	Healy, Fran	74T	238	$ .07	$ .30
Hatfield, Fred	53T	163	$4.50	$15.00	Healy, Fran	75T	251	$ .07	$ .30
Hatfield, Fred	56T	318	$2.25	$8.00	Healy, Fran	76T	394	$ .05	$ .20
Hatfield, Fred	57T	278	$4.25	$15.00	Healy, Fran	77T	148	$ .03	$ .12
Hatfield, Fred	58T	339	$ .75	$3.00	Healy, Fran	78T	582	$ .02	$ .10
Hatten, Joe	52T	194	$7.00	$20.00	Heard, Jehosie	54T	226	$3.60	$10.00
Hatton, Grady	51Trb	34	$1.50	$4.00	Hearn, Ed	87T	433	$ .01	$ .10
Hatton, Grady	52T	6	$15.00	$47.50	Hearn, Ed	88T	56	$ .01	$ .04
Hatton, Grady	53T	45	$5.00	$20.00	Hearn, Ed	89T	348	$ .01	$ .05
Hatton, Grady	54T	208	$3.60	$10.00	Hearn, Jim	52T	337	$40.00	$140.00
Hatton, Grady	55T	131	$2.00	$6.00	Hearn, Jim	53T	38	$4.50	$15.00
Hatton, Grady	56T	26	$2.25	$6.00	Hearn, Jim	56T	202	$3.00	$9.00
Hatton, Grady	66T	504	$ .75	$2.50	Hearn, Jim	57T	348	$4.25	$15.00
Hatton, Grady	67T	347	$ .30	$ .85	Hearn, Jim	58T	298	$ .75	$3.00
Hatton, Grady	68T	392	$ .30	$ .85	Hearn, Jim	59T	63	$1.25	$4.25
Hatton, Grady	73T	624	$ .55	$1.75	Hearron, Jeff	87T	274	$ .01	$ .04
Hatton, Grady	74T	31	$ .07	$ .30	Heath, Bill	66T	539	$5.00	$20.00
Haugstad, Phil	52T	198	$7.00	$21.00	Heath, Bill	67T	172	$ .30	$ .85
Hausman, Tom	76T	452	$ .05	$ .20	Heath, Bill	70T	541	$ .15	$ .50
Hausman, Tom	77T	99	$ .03	$ .12	Heath, Mike	79T	710	$ .05	$ .20
Hausman, Tom	79T	643	$ .02	$ .10	Heath, Mike	80T	687	$ .01	$ .10

TOPPS

Player	Year	No.	VG	EX/MT
Heath, Mike	81T	437	$ .01	$ .10
Heath, Mike	82T	318	$ .01	$ .07
Heath, Mike	83T	23	$ .01	$ .07
Heath, Mike	84T	567	$ .01	$ .06
Heath, Mike	85T	662	$ .01	$ .05
Heath, Mike	86T	148	$ .01	$ .04
Heath, Mike	86TTR	46	$ .02	$ .10
Heath, Mike	87T	492	$ .01	$ .04
Heath, Mike	88T	237	$ .01	$ .04
Heath, Mike	89T	743	$ .01	$ .05
Heath, Mike	90T	366	$ .01	$ .04
Heath, Mike	91T	16	$ .01	$ .03
Heaton, Neal	87TTR	45	$ .01	$ .05
Heaton, Neal	88T	765	$ .01	$ .04
Heaton, Neal	88TBB	33	$ .01	$ .06
Heaton, Neal	89T	197	$ .01	$ .05
Heaton, Neal	90T	539	$ .01	$ .04
Heaton, Neal	91T	451	$ .01	$ .03
Heaverlo, Dave	76T	213	$ .05	$ .20
Heaverlo, Dave	77T	97	$ .03	$ .12
Heaverlo, Dave	78T	338	$ .02	$ .10
Heaverlo, Dave	79T	432	$ .02	$ .10
Heaverlo, Dave	80T	177	$ .01	$ .10
Hebert, Ray	54T	190	$3.60	$10.00
Hebner, Rich	69T	82	$2.00	$8.00

Rich Hebner | **3RD BASE**

Player	Year	No.	VG	EX/MT
Hebner, Rich	70T	264	$ .15	$ .50
Hebner, Rich	71T	212	$ .15	$ .50
Hebner, Rich	72T	630	$ .30	$ .95
Hebner, Rich	73T	2	$ .07	$ .30
Hebner, Rich	74T	450	$ .07	$ .30
Hebner, Rich	75T	492	$ .07	$ .30
Hebner, Rich	76T	376	$ .05	$ .20
Hebner, Rich	77T	167	$ .03	$ .12
Hebner, Rich	78T	26	$ .02	$ .10
Hebner, Rich	79T	567	$ .02	$ .10
Hebner, Rich	80T	331	$ .01	$ .10
Hebner, Rich	81T	217	$ .01	$ .10
Hebner, Rich	82T	603	$ .01	$ .07
Hebner, Rich	83T	778	$ .01	$ .07
Hebner, Rich	84T	433	$ .01	$ .06

Player	Year	No.	VG	EX/MT
Hebner, Rich	84TTR	50	$ .02	$ .10
Hebner, Rich	85T	124	$ .01	$ .05
Hebner, Rich	86T	19	$ .02	$ .20
Hedlund, Mike	65T	546	$1.75	$4.50
Hedlund, Mike	69T	591	$ .30	$ .95
Hedlund, Mike	70T	187	$ .15	$ .50
Hedlund, Mike	71T	662	$ .75	$2.50
Hedlund, Mike	72T	81	$ .05	$ .25
Hedlund, Mike	73T	591	$ .45	$1.45
Heep, Danny	81T	82	$ .01	$ .10
Heep, Danny	82T	441	$ .01	$ .07
Heep, Danny	83T	538	$ .01	$ .07
Heep, Danny	83TTR	41	$ .02	$ .10
Heep, Danny	84T	29	$ .01	$ .06
Heep, Danny	85T	339	$ .01	$ .05
Heep, Danny	86T	619	$ .01	$ .04
Heep, Danny	87T	241	$ .01	$ .04
Heep, Danny	88T	753	$ .01	$ .04
Heep, Danny	89T	198	$ .01	$ .05
Heep, Danny	90T	573	$ .01	$ .04
Heffner, Bob	64T	79	$ .30	$ .95
Heffner, Bob	65T	199	$ .35	$1.25
Heffner, Bob	66T	432	$ .30	$ .95
Heffner, Don	60T	462	$ .95	$3.50
Heffner, Don	66T	269	$ .30	$ .95
Hegan, Jim	51Trb	12	$1.50	$4.00
Hegan, Jim	52T	17	$15.00	$47.50
Hegan, Jim	53T	80	$4.50	$15.00
Hegan, Jim	54T	29	$3.60	$10.00
Hegan, Jim	55T	7	$2.00	$6.00
Hegan, Jim	56T	48	$2.25	$6.00
Hegan, Jim	57T	136	$ .95	$3.50
Hegan, Jim	58T	345	$ .75	$3.00
Hegan, Jim	59T	372	$ .75	$2.20
Hegan, Jim	73T	116	$ .15	$ .50
Hegan, Jim	76T	69	$ .07	$ .30
Hegan, Mike	67T	553	$5.00	$20.00
Hegan, Mike	68T	402	$ .30	$ .85
Hegan, Mike	69T	577	$ .30	$ .95
Hegan, Mike	70T	111	$ .15	$ .50
Hegan, Mike	72T	632	$ .30	$ .95
Hegan, Mike	73T	382	$ .07	$ .30
Hegan, Mike	74T	517	$ .07	$ .30
Hegan, Mike	75T	99	$ .07	$ .30
Hegan, Mike	76T	69	$ .07	$ .30
Hegan, Mike	76T	377	$ .05	$ .20
Hegan, Mike	77T	507	$ .03	$ .12
Heidemann, Jack	71T	87	$ .15	$ .50
Heidemann, Jack	72T	374	$ .05	$ .25
Heidemann, Jack	73T	644	$ .45	$1.45
Heidemann, Jack	75T	649	$ .07	$ .30
Heidemann, Jack	77T	553	$ .03	$ .12
Heinkel, Don	89T	499	$ .01	$ .10
Heintzelman, Ken	52T	362	$40.00	$140.00
Heintzelman, Ken	53T	136	$4.50	$15.00
Heintzelman, Tom	74T	607	$ .07	$ .30
Heise, Bob	70T	478	$ .15	$ .50
Heise, Bob	71T	691	$ .75	$2.50
Heise, Bobby	72T	402	$ .05	$ .25
Heise, Bobby	73T	547	$ .45	$1.45
Heise, Bobby	74T	51	$ .07	$ .30
Heise, Bobby	74TTR	51	$ .07	$ .30
Heise, Bobby	75T	441	$ .07	$ .30
Heist, Al	61T	302	$ .35	$1.25
Heist, Al	62T	373	$ .75	$2.50
Held, Woody	58T	202	$ .75	$3.00
Held, Woody	59T	266	$ .75	$2.20
Held, Woody	60T	178	$ .45	$1.45
Held, Woodie (y)	61T	60	$ .35	$1.25
Held, Woody	62T	215	$ .45	$1.45

Player	Year	No.	VG	EX/MT
Held, Woody	63T	435	$ .45	$1.50
Held, Woody	64T	105	$ .30	$ .95
Held, Woody	65T	336	$ .35	$1.25
Held, Woody	66T	136	$ .30	$ .95
Held, Woody	67T	251	$10.00	$40.00
Held, Woody	68T	289	$ .30	$ .85
Held, Woody	69T	636	$ .30	$ .95
Helms, Tommy	65T	243	$ .90	$3.00
Helms, Tommy	66T	311	$ .45	$1.45
Helms, Tommy	67T	505	$ .75	$3.00
Helms, Tommy	68T	405	$ .30	$ .85
Helms, Tommy	69T	70	$ .30	$ .95
Helms, Tommy	69TAS	418	$ .15	$ .50
Helms, Tommy	70T	159	$ .15	$ .50
Helms, Tommy	71T	272	$ .15	$ .50
Helms, Tommy	72T	204	$ .05	$ .25
Helms, Tommy	73T	495	$ .07	$ .30
Helms, Tommy	74T	67	$ .07	$ .30
Helms, Tommy	75T	119	$ .07	$ .30
Helms, Tommy	76T	583	$ .05	$ .20
Helms, Tommy	76TTR	583	$ .05	$ .20
Helms, Tommy	77T	402	$ .03	$ .12
Helms, Tommy	78T	618	$ .02	$ .10
Helms, Tommy	90T	110	$ .01	$ .04
Heman, Russ	59T	283	$ .75	$2.20
Hemond, Scott	89TMLD	54	$ .01	$ .06
Hemsley, Rollie	54T	143	$3.60	$10.00
Hemus, Solly	52T	196	$7.00	$20.00
Hemus, Solly	53T	231	$12.50	$50.00
Hemus, Solly	54T	117	$3.60	$10.00
Hemus, Solly	57T	231	$ .95	$3.50
Hemus, Solly	58T	207	$ .75	$3.00
Hemus, Solly	59T	527	$2.50	$10.00
Hemus, Solly	60T	218	$ .45	$1.45
Hemus, Solly	61T	139	$ .35	$1.25
Henderson, Dave	82T	711	$ .50	$2.00
Henderson, Dave	83T	732	$ .01	$ .20
Henderson, Dave	84T	154	$ .01	$ .15
Henderson, Dave	85T	344	$ .01	$ .10
Henderson, Dave	86T	221	$ .01	$ .04
Henderson, Dave	87T	452	$ .01	$ .04
Henderson, Dave	88T	628	$ .01	$ .04
Henderson, Dave	88TBB	131	$ .01	$ .06
Henderson, Dave	88TTR	48	$ .01	$ .06
Henderson, Dave	89T	527	$ .01	$ .05
Henderson, Dave	89TBB	326	$ .01	$ .06
Henderson, Dave	90T	68	$ .01	$ .04
Henderson, Dave	91T	144	$ .01	$ .03
Henderson, Joe	77T	487	$ .03	$ .12
Henderson, Ken	65T	497	$ .75	$3.00
Henderson, Ken	66T	39	$ .30	$ .95
Henderson, Ken	67T	383	$ .30	$ .95
Henderson, Ken	68T	309	$ .30	$ .85
Henderson, Ken	70T	298	$ .15	$ .50
Henderson, Ken	71T	155	$ .15	$ .50
Henderson, Ken	72T	443	$ .05	$ .25
Henderson, Ken	72TIA	444	$ .05	$ .25
Henderson, Ken	73T	101	$ .07	$ .30
Henderson, Ken	74T	394	$ .07	$ .30
Henderson, Ken	75T	59	$ .07	$ .30
Henderson, Ken	76T	464	$ .05	$ .20
Henderson, Ken	76TTR	464	$ .05	$ .20
Henderson, Ken	77T	242	$ .03	$ .12
Henderson, Ken	78T	612	$ .02	$ .10
Henderson, Ken	79T	73	$ .02	$ .10
Henderson, Ken	80T	523	$ .01	$ .10
Henderson, Rickey	80T	482	$45.00	$165.00
Henderson, Rickey	81T	4	$ .35	$1.50
Henderson, Rickey	81T	261	$9.00	$27.50
Henderson, Rickey	82T	156	$ .05	$ .20
Henderson, Rickey	82T	164	$ .25	$1.00
Henderson, Rickey	82T	610	$3.00	$9.00
Henderson, Rickey	83T	180	$1.50	$6.00
Henderson, Rickey	83T	531	$ .01	$ .07
Henderson, Rickey	83T	704	$ .15	$ .75
Henderson, Rickey	83TAS	391	$ .25	$1.00
Henderson, Rickey	83TRB	2	$ .05	$ .25
Henderson, Rickey	84T	2	$ .15	$ .75
Henderson, Rickey	84T	134	$ .10	$ .50
Henderson, Rickey	84T	156	$ .01	$ .10
Henderson, Rickey	84T	230	$1.00	$4.00
Henderson, Rickey	85T	115	$ .50	$2.00
Henderson, Rickey	85TAS	706	$ .05	$ .50
Henderson, Rickey	85TTR	49	$1.00	$4.00
Henderson, Rickey	86T	500	$ .25	$1.00
Henderson, Rickey	86TAS	716	$ .05	$ .35
Henderson, Rickey	87T	735	$ .15	$ .75
Henderson, Rickey	87TTB	311	$ .01	$ .10
Henderson, Rickey	88T	60	$ .01	$ .75
Henderson, Rickey	88TBB	165	$ .05	$ .25
Henderson, Rickey	89T	380	$ .01	$ .35
Henderson, Rickey	89TBB	271	$ .01	$ .35
Henderson, Rickey	89TTR	48	$ .01	$ .15
Henderson, Rickey	90T	450	$ .01	$ .25
Henderson, Rickey	90TRB	7	$ .01	$ .15
Henderson, Rickey	91T	670	$ .01	$ .15
Henderson, Rickey	91TAS	391	$ .01	$ .10
Henderson, Steve	78T	134	$ .02	$ .10
Henderson, Steve	79T	445	$ .02	$ .10
Henderson, Steve	80T	299	$ .35	$1.25
Henderson, Steve	81T	619	$ .01	$ .10
Henderson, Steve	81TTR	769	$ .02	$ .10
Henderson, Steve	82T	89	$ .01	$ .07
Henderson, Steve	83T	335	$ .01	$ .07
Henderson, Steve	83TTR	42	$ .02	$ .10
Henderson, Steve	84T	501	$ .01	$ .06
Henderson, Steve	85T	640	$ .01	$ .05
Henderson, Steve	85TTR	50	$ .02	$ .10
Henderson, Steve	86T	748	$ .01	$ .04
Henderson, Steve	88T	527	$ .01	$ .04
Hendley, Bob	61T	372	$ .75	$3.00
Hendley, Bob	62T	361	$ .45	$1.45
Hendley, Bob	63T	62	$ .30	$ .95
Hendley, Bob	64T	189	$ .30	$ .95
Hendley, Bob	65T	444	$ .35	$1.25
Hendley, Bob	66T	82	$ .30	$ .95
Hendley, Bob	67T	256	$ .30	$ .85
Hendley, Bob	68T	345	$ .30	$ .85
Hendley, Bob	69T	144	$ .30	$ .85
Hendrick, George	72T	406	$ .45	$1.50
Hendrick, George	73T	13	$ .15	$ .50
Hendrick, George	74T	303	$ .07	$ .30
Hendrick, George	75T	109	$ .07	$ .30
Hendrick, George	76T	570	$ .05	$ .20
Hendrick, George	77T	330	$ .03	$ .12
Hendrick, George	78T	30	$ .02	$ .10
Hendrick, George	79T	175	$ .02	$ .10
Hendrick, George	80T	350	$ .05	$ .25
Hendrick, George	81T	230	$ .01	$ .10
Hendrick, George	82T	420	$ .01	$ .07
Hendrick, George	83T	650	$ .01	$ .07
Hendrick, George	84T	540	$ .01	$ .06
Hendrick, George	84TAS	386	$ .01	$ .06
Hendrick, George	85T	60	$ .01	$ .05
Hendrick, George	85TTR	51	$ .02	$ .10
Hendrick, George	86T	190	$ .01	$ .04
Hendrick, George	87T	725	$ .01	$ .04
Hendrick, George	88T	304	$ .01	$ .04
Hendricks, Rod	69T	277	$ .30	$ .95
Hendricks, Elrod	70T	528	$ .15	$ .50

Player	Year	No.	VG	EX/MT
Hendricks, Elrod "Ellie"	71T	219	$ .15	$ .50
Hendricks, Ellie	72T	508	$ .05	$ .25
Hendricks, Ellie	75T	609	$ .07	$ .30
Hendricks, Ellie	76T	371	$ .05	$ .20
Hengel, Dave	89T	531	$ .01	$ .10
Henke, Tom	86T	333	$ .01	$ .04
Henke, Tom	87T	510	$ .01	$ .04
Henke, Tom	88T	220	$ .01	$ .10
Henke, Tom	88TAS	396	$ .01	$ .04
Henke, Tom	88TBB	41	$ .01	$ .06
Henke, Tom	89T	75	$ .01	$ .05
Henke, Tom	90T	695	$ .01	$ .04
Henke, Tom	91T	110	$ .01	$ .03
Henneman, Mike	87TTR	46	$ .05	$ .25
Henneman, Mike	88T	582	$ .01	$ .15
Henneman, Mike	88TBB	256	$ .01	$ .06
Henneman, Mike	89T	365	$ .01	$ .05
Henneman, Mike	89TBB	252	$ .01	$ .06
Henneman, Mike	90T	177	$ .01	$ .04
Henneman, Mike	91T	641	$ .01	$ .03
Hennigan, Phil	71T	211	$ .15	$ .50
Hennigan, Phil	72T	748	$ .75	$2.50
Hennigan, Phil	73T	107	$ .07	$ .30
Henninger, Rick	74T	602	$ .07	$ .30
Henrich, Bob	58T	131	$ .75	$3.00
Henry, Bill	59T	46	$1.25	$4.25
Henry, Bill	60T	524	$2.50	$10.00
Henry, Bill	61T	66	$ .35	$1.25
Henry, Bill	62T	562	$3.95	$11.50
Henry, Bill	63T	378	$ .45	$1.50
Henry, Bill	64T	49	$ .30	$ .95
Henry, Bill	65T	456	$ .75	$3.00
Henry, Bill	66T	115	$ .30	$ .95
Henry, Bill	67T	579	$1.50	$4.00
Henry, Bill	68T	239	$ .30	$ .85
Henry, Bill	68T	384	$1.25	$5.00

Player	Year	No.	VG	EX/MT
Henry, Dwayne	88T	178	$ .01	$ .04
Henry, Dwayne	89T	496	$ .01	$ .05
Henry, Dwayne	91T	567	$ .01	$ .03
Hepler, Bill	66T	574	$5.00	$20.00

Player	Year	No.	VG	EX/MT
Hepler, Bill	67T	144	$ .30	$ .85
Herbel, Ron	63T	208	$ .30	$ .95
Herbel, Ron	64T	47	$ .35	$1.25
Herbel, Ron	65T	84	$ .30	$ .85
Herbel, Ron	66T	331	$ .30	$ .95
Herbel, Ron	67T	156	$ .30	$ .85
Herbel, Ron	68T	333	$ .30	$ .85
Herbel, Ron	69T	251	$ .30	$ .95
Herbel, Ron	70T	526	$ .15	$ .50
Herbel, Ron	71T	387	$ .15	$ .50
Herbel, Ron	72T	469	$ .05	$ .25
Herbert, Ray	55T	138	$2.00	$6.00
Herbert, Ray	58T	379	$ .75	$3.00
Herbert, Ray	59T	154	$ .75	$2.20
Herbert, Ray	60T	252	$ .45	$1.45
Herbert, Ray	61T	498	$ .75	$3.00
Herbert, Ray	62T	8	$ .45	$1.45
Herbert, Ray	63T	8	$ .45	$1.45
Herbert, Ray	63T	560	$1.75	$4.50
Herbert, Ray	64T	215	$ .30	$ .95
Herbert, Ray	65T	399	$ .35	$1.25
Herbert, Ray	66T	121	$ .35	$ .95
Herman, Billy	52T	394	$60.00	$225.00
Herman, Billy	54T	86	$5.00	$20.00
Herman, Billy	55T	19	$2.50	$12.50
Herman, Billy	60T	456	$2.25	$6.00
Herman, Billy	65T	251	$ .75	$3.00
Herman, Billy	66T	37	$ .45	$1.45
Hermann, Ed	73T	73	$ .07	$ .30
Hermann, Ed	75T	219	$ .07	$ .30
Hermann, Ed	78T	677	$ .02	$ .10
Hermann, Ed	79T	374	$ .02	$ .10
Hermanski, Gene	51Trb	11	$1.50	$4.00
Hermanski, Gene	52T	16	$15.00	$47.50
Hermanski, Gene	53T	179	$4.50	$15.00
Hermanski, Gene	54T	228	$3.60	$10.00
Hermoso, Angel	70T	147	$ .15	$ .50
Hernandez, Enzo	71T	529	$ .75	$2.25
Hernandez, Enzo	72T	7	$ .05	$ .25
Hernandez, Enzo	73T	438	$ .07	$ .30
Hernandez, Enzo	74T	572	$ .07	$ .30
Hernandez, Enzo	75T	84	$ .07	$ .30
Hernandez, Enzo	76T	289	$ .05	$ .20
Hernandez, Enzo	77T	522	$ .03	$ .12
Hernandez, Guillermo	88TBB	206	$ .01	$ .06
Hernandez, Guillermo	89T	43	$ .01	$ .05
Hernandez, Jackie	68T	352	$ .30	$ .85
Hernandez, Jackie	69T	258	$ .30	$ .95
Hernandez, Jackie	70T	686	$ .75	$2.00
Hernandez, Jackie	71T	144	$ .15	$ .50
Hernandez, Jackie	72T	502	$ .05	$ .25
Hernandez, Jackie	73T	363	$ .07	$ .30
Hernandez, Jackie	74T	566	$ .07	$ .30
Hernandez, Keith	75T	623	$7.00	$21.00
Hernandez, Keith	76T	542	$2.50	$6.50
Hernandez, Keith	77T	95	$ .75	$3.00
Hernandez, Keith	78T	143	$ .50	$2.25
Hernandez, Keith	79T	695	$ .50	$1.75
Hernandez, Keith	80T	201	$ .08	$ .30
Hernandez, Keith	80T	321	$ .35	$1.00
Hernandez, Keith	81T	420	$ .15	$ .75
Hernandez, Keith	82T	186	$ .05	$ .25
Hernandez, Keith	82T	210	$ .15	$ .60
Hernandez, Keith	83T	700	$ .01	$ .07
Hernandez, Keith	83TTR	43	$ .20	$ .75
Hernandez, Keith	84T	120	$ .07	$ .30
Hernandez, Keith	85T	80	$ .05	$ .25
Hernandez, Keith	85TAS	712	$ .01	$ .10
Hernandez, Keith	86T	520	$ .03	$ .25
Hernandez, Keith	86TAS	701	$ .01	$ .10

Player	Year	No.	VG	EX/MT	Player	Year	No.	VG	EX/MT
Hernandez, Keith	86TRB	203	$ .01	$ .10	Herrera, Jose	69T	378	$ .30	$ .85
Hernandez, Keith	87T	350	$ .15	$ .50	Herrmann, Ed	69T	439	$ .30	$ .85
Hernandez, Keith	87TAS	595	$ .01	$ .10	Herrmann, Ed	70T	368	$ .15	$ .50
Hernandez, Keith	88T	610	$ .01	$ .10	Herrmann, Ed	71T	169	$ .15	$ .50
Hernandez, Keith	88TBB	59	$ .01	$ .15	Herrmann, Ed	72T	452	$ .05	$ .25
Hernandez, Keith	89T	480	$ .01	$ .05	Herrmann, Ed	74T	438	$ .07	$ .30
Hernandez, Keith	89TBB	185	$ .01	$ .10	Herrmann, Ed	76T	406	$ .05	$ .20
Hernandez, Keith	90T	230	$ .01	$ .10	Herrmann, Ed	77T	143	$ .03	$ .12
Hernandez, Keith	90TTR	39	$ .01	$ .05	Herrnstein, John	63T	553	$60.00	$225.00
Hernandez, Leo	83TTR	44	$ .02	$ .10	Herrnstein, John	64T	243	$4.00	$13.00
Hernandez, Leo	84T	71	$ .01	$ .06	Herrnstein, John	65T	534	$1.75	$4.50
Hernandez, Ramon	67T	576	$6.00	$20.00	Herrnstein, John	66T	304	$ .30	$ .95
Hernandez, Ramon	68T	382	$ .30	$ .85	Hershberger, Mike	62T	341	$ .45	$1.45
Hernandez, Ramon	73T	117	$ .07	$ .30	Hershberger, Mike	63T	254	$ .30	$ .95
Hernandez, Ramon	74T	222	$ .07	$ .30	Hershberger, Mike	64T	465	$ .50	$1.45
Hernandez, Ramon	75T	224	$ .07	$ .30	Hershberger, Mike	65T	89	$ .30	$ .85
Hernandez, Ramon	76T	647	$ .05	$ .20	Hershberger, Mike	66T	236	$ .30	$ .95
Hernandez, Ramon	77T	468	$ .03	$ .12	Hershberger, Mike	67T	323	$ .30	$ .85
Hernandez, Rudy	61T	229	$ .35	$1.25	Hershberger, Mike	68T	18	$ .30	$ .85
Hernandez, Willie	78T	99	$ .20	$ .75	Hershberger, Mike	69T	655	$ .30	$ .95
Hernandez, Willie	79T	614	$ .02	$ .10	Hershberger, Mike	70T	596	$ .30	$ .95
Hernandez, Willie	80T	472	$ .05	$ .25	Hershberger, Mike	71T	149	$ .15	$ .50
Hernandez, Willie	81T	238	$ .01	$ .10	Hershiser, Orel	85T	493	$ .75	$3.50
Hernandez, Willie	82T	23	$ .01	$ .07	Hershiser, Orel	86T	159	$ .10	$ .50
Hernandez, Willie	83T	568	$ .01	$ .07	Hershiser, Orel	87T	385	$ .05	$ .30
Hernandez, Willie	83TTR	45	$ .02	$ .10	Hershiser, Orel	88T	40	$ .05	$ .25
Hernandez, Willie	84T	199	$ .15	$ .60	Hershiser, Orel	88TBB	91	$ .05	$ .35
Hernandez, Willie	84TTR	51	$ .05	$ .25	Hershiser, Orel	89T	550	$ .01	$ .15
Hernandez, Willie	85T	333	$ .01	$ .05	Hershiser, Orel	89TAS	394	$ .01	$ .10
Hernandez, Willie	86T	670	$ .01	$ .04	Hershiser, Orel	89TBB	1	$ .01	$ .25
Hernandez, Willie	87T	515	$ .01	$ .04	Hershiser, Orel	89TRB	5	$ .01	$ .10
Hernandez, Willie	88T	713	$ .01	$ .04	Hershiser, Orel	90T	780	$ .01	$ .10
Hernandez, Xavier	89TMLD	55	$ .01	$ .06	Hershiser, Orel	91T	690	$ .01	$ .03
Hernandez, Xavier	91T	194	$ .01	$ .10	Hertz, Steve	64T	544	$1.75	$4.50
Herndon, Larry	77T	397	$ .03	$ .12	Herzog, Whitey	57T	29	$5.00	$20.00
Herndon, Larry	78T	512	$ .02	$ .10	Herzog, Whitey	58T	438	$ .45	$1.50
Herndon, Larry	79T	624	$ .02	$ .10	Herzog, Whitey	59T	392	$ .75	$2.20
Herndon, Larry	80T	257	$ .01	$ .10	Herzog, Whitey	60T	92	$ .65	$1.75
Herndon, Larry	81T	409	$ .01	$ .10	Herzog, Whitey	61T	106	$ .75	$2.20
Herndon, Larry	82T	182	$ .01	$ .07	Herzog, Whitey	62T	513	$ .75	$2.25
Herndon, Larry	82TTR	43	$ .02	$ .10	Herzog, Whitey	63T	302	$ .75	$2.20
Herndon, Larry	83T	13	$ .01	$ .07	Herzog, Whitey	73T	549	$ .35	$1.25
Herndon, Larry	83T	261	$ .01	$ .07	Herzog, Whitey	78T	299	$ .05	$ .20
Herndon, Larry	84T	333	$ .01	$ .06	Herzog, Whitey	83T	186	$ .01	$ .07
Herndon, Larry	85T	591	$ .01	$ .05	Herzog, Whitey	84T	561	$ .01	$ .06
Herndon, Larry	86T	688	$ .01	$ .04	Herzog, Whitey	85T	683	$ .01	$ .05
Herndon, Larry	87T	298	$ .01	$ .04	Herzog, Whitey	86T	441	$ .01	$ .04
Herndon, Larry	88T	743	$ .01	$ .04	Herzog, Whitey	87T	243	$ .01	$ .04
Herndon, Larry	88TBB	56	$ .01	$ .06	Herzog, Whitey	88T	744	$ .01	$ .04
Herr, Tom	80T	684	$ .08	$ .40	Herzog, Whitey	89T	654	$ .01	$ .05
Herr, Tom	81T	266	$ .01	$ .10	Herzog, Whitey	90T	261	$ .01	$ .04
Herr, Tom	82T	27	$ .01	$ .07	Hesketh, Joe	85TTR	52	$ .05	$ .20
Herr, Tom	83T	489	$ .01	$ .07	Hesketh, Joe	86T	472	$ .01	$ .04
Herr, Tom	84T	649	$ .01	$ .06	Hesketh, Joe	87T	189	$ .01	$ .04
Herr, Tom	85T	113	$ .01	$ .05	Hesketh, Joe	88T	371	$ .01	$ .04
Herr, Tom	86T	550	$ .01	$ .04	Hesketh, Joe	89T	614	$ .01	$ .05
Herr, Tom	86TAS	702	$ .01	$ .04	Hesketh, Joe	90T	24	$ .01	$ .04
Herr, Tom	87T	721	$ .01	$ .04	Hesketh, Joe	90TTR	40	$ .01	$ .05
Herr, Tom	88T	310	$ .01	$ .04	Hesketh, Joe	91T	269	$ .01	$ .03
Herr, Tom	88TBB	31	$ .01	$ .06	Hetki, John	53T	235	$12.50	$50.00
Herr, Tom	88TTR	49	$ .01	$ .06	Hetki, John	54T	161	$3.60	$10.00
Herr, Tom	89T	709	$ .01	$ .05	Hetzel, Eric	89TMLD	56	$ .01	$ .06
Herr, Tom	89TBB	283	$ .01	$ .06	Hetzel, Eric	90T	629	$ .01	$ .04
Herr, Tom	89TTR	49	$ .01	$ .06	Hiatt, Jack	65T	497	$ .75	$3.00
Herr, Tom	90T	297	$ .01	$ .04	Hiatt, Jack	66T	373	$ .30	$ .95
Herr, Tom	91T	64	$ .01	$ .03	Hiatt, Jack	67T	368	$ .30	$ .85
Herrera, Frank "Pancho"	58T	433	$ .75	$3.00	Hiatt, Jack	68T	419	$ .30	$ .85
Herrera, Frank	59T	129	$ .75	$2.20	Hiatt, Jack	69T	204	$ .30	$ .85
Herrera, Frank	60T	130	$ .45	$1.45	Hiatt, Jack	70T	13	$ .15	$ .50
Herrera, Frank	61TAS	569	$7.00	$21.00	Hiatt, Jack	71T	371	$ .15	$ .50

Player	Year	No.	VG	EX/MT	Player	Year	No.	VG	EX/MT
Hiatt, Jack	72T	633	$ .30	$ .95	Higuera, Teddy	88T	110	$ .01	$ .10
Hiatt, Jack	73T	402	$ .07	$ .30	Higuera, Teddy	88TBB	87	$ .01	$ .06
Hibbard, Greg	89TMLD	57	$ .01	$ .10	Higuera, Teddy	89T	595	$ .01	$ .05
Hibbard, Greg	90T	769	$ .01	$ .10	Higuera, Teddy	90T	15	$ .01	$ .04
Hibbard, Greg	91T	256	$ .01	$ .10	Higuera, Teddy	91T	475	$ .01	$ .03
Hickey, Kevin	82T	778	$ .01	$ .07	Hilgendorf, Tom	70T	482	$ .15	$ .50
Hickey, Kevin	83T	278	$ .01	$ .07	Hilgendorf, Tom	74T	13	$ .07	$ .30
Hickey, Kevin	84T	459	$ .01	$ .06	Hilgendorf, Tom	75T	377	$ .07	$ .30
Hickey, Kevin	90T	546	$ .01	$ .04	Hilgendorf, Tom	76T	168	$ .05	$ .20
Hickman, Jim	62T	598	$18.00	$55.00	Hill, Donnie	84T	265	$ .01	$ .06
Hickman, Jim	63T	107	$ .30	$ .95	Hill, Donnie	85TTR	54	$ .02	$ .10
Hickman, Jim	64T	514	$ .50	$1.45	Hill, Donnie	86T	484	$ .01	$ .04
Hickman, Jim	65T	114	$ .30	$ .85	Hill, Donnie	87T	339	$ .01	$ .04
Hickman, Jim	66T	402	$ .30	$ .95	Hill, Donnie	87TTR	47	$ .01	$ .05
Hickman, Jim	67T	346	$ .30	$ .85	Hill, Donnie	88T	132	$ .01	$ .04
Hickman, Jim	69T	63	$ .30	$ .85	Hill, Donnie	88TBB	137	$ .01	$ .06
Hickman, Jim	70T	612	$ .30	$ .95	Hill, Donnie	89T	512	$ .01	$ .05
Hickman, Jim	71T	175	$ .15	$ .50	Hill, Donnie	91T	36	$ .01	$ .03
Hickman, Jim	72T	534	$ .30	$ .95	Hill, Garry	70T	172	$ .15	$ .50
Hickman, Jim	73T	565	$ .45	$1.45	Hill, Glenallen	89TMLD	59	$ .01	$ .15
Hicks, Jim	67T	532	$ .75	$3.00	Hill, Glenallen	90T	194	$ .01	$ .15
Hicks, Jim	69T	559	$ .30	$ .95	Hill, Glenallen	91T	509	$ .01	$ .03
					Hill, Herman	70T	267	$ .15	$ .50
					Hill, Ken	89TTR	50	$ .01	$ .10
					Hill, Ken	90T	233	$ .01	$ .04
					Hill, Ken	91T	591	$ .01	$ .03
					Hill, Marc	75T	620	$10.00	$30.00
					Hill, Marc	76T	577	$ .05	$ .20
					Hill, Marc	77T	57	$ .03	$ .12
					Hill, Marc	78T	359	$ .02	$ .10
					Hill, Marc	79T	11	$ .02	$ .10
					Hill, Marc	80T	236	$ .01	$ .10
					Hill, Marc	81T	486	$ .01	$ .10
					Hill, Marc	81TTR	770	$ .02	$ .10
					Hill, Marc	82T	748	$ .01	$ .07
					Hill, Marc	83T	124	$ .01	$ .07
					Hill, Marc	84T	698	$ .01	$ .06
					Hill, Marc	85T	312	$ .01	$ .05
					Hill, Marc	86T	552	$ .01	$ .04
					Hillegas, Shawn	88T	455	$ .01	$ .20
					Hillegas, Shawn	89T	247	$ .01	$ .05
					Hillegas, Shawn	90T	93	$ .01	$ .04
					Hiller, Chuck	61T	538	$7.00	$21.00
					Hiller, Chuck	62T	188	$ .45	$1.45
					Hiller, Chuck	63T	185	$ .30	$ .95
					Hiller, Chuck	64T	313	$ .30	$ .95
					Hiller, Chuck	65T	531	$1.75	$4.50
					Hiller, Chuck	66T	154	$ .30	$ .95
					Hiller, Chuck	67T	198	$ .30	$ .85
					Hiller, Chuck	68T	461	$ .35	$1.25
					Hiller, Chuck	73T	549	$ .35	$1.25
					Hiller, Frank	52T	156	$7.00	$20.00
Hicks, Jim	70T	173	$ .15	$ .50	Hiller, John	66T	209	$ .35	$1.25
Hicks, Joe	61T	386	$ .75	$3.00	Hiller, John	68T	307	$ .30	$ .85
Hicks, Joe	62T	428	$ .75	$2.50	Hiller, John	69T	642	$ .30	$ .95
Higgins, Dennis	66T	529	$5.00	$20.00	Hiller, John	70T	12	$ .15	$ .50
Higgins, Dennis	67T	52	$ .30	$ .85	Hiller, John	71T	629	$ .35	$1.25
Higgins, Dennis	68T	509	$ .35	$1.25	Hiller, John	73T	448	$ .07	$ .30
Higgins, Dennis	69T	441	$ .30	$ .85	Hiller, John	74T	24	$ .07	$ .30
Higgins, Dennis	70T	257	$ .15	$ .50	Hiller, John	74T	208	$ .07	$ .30
Higgins, Dennis	71T	479	$ .15	$ .50	Hiller, John	75T	415	$ .07	$ .30
Higgins, Dennis	72T	278	$ .05	$ .25	Hiller, John	76T	37	$ .05	$ .20
Higgins, Mark	89TMLD	58	$ .01	$ .15	Hiller, John	77T	595	$ .03	$ .12
Higgins, Mike	55T	150	$2.00	$6.00	Hiller, John	78T	258	$ .02	$ .10
Higgins, Mike	61T	221	$ .35	$1.25	Hiller, John	79T	151	$ .02	$ .10
Higgins, Mike	62T	559	$3.95	$11.50	Hiller, John	80T	614	$ .01	$ .10
Higuera, Teddy	85TTR	53	$ .35	$1.50	Hillman, Dave	57T	351	$4.25	$15.00
Higuera, Teddy	86T	347	$ .15	$ .75	Hillman, Dave	58T	41	$1.25	$4.25
Higuera, Teddy	87T	250	$ .07	$ .30	Hillman, Dave	59T	319	$ .75	$2.20
Higuera, Teddy	87TAS	615	$ .01	$ .10	Hillman, Dave	60T	68	$ .45	$1.45

Jim Hicks OUTFIELD

Player	Year	No.	VG	EX/MT	Player	Year	No.	VG	EX/MT
Hillman, Dave	61T	326	$ .35	$1.25	Hobbie, Glen	61T	393	$ .90	$3.00
Hillman, Dave	62T	282	$ .45	$1.45	Hobbie, Glen	62T	585	$3.95	$11.50
Hilton, Dave	73T	615	$135.00	$400.00	Hobbie, Glen	63T	212	$ .30	$ .95
Hilton, Dave	74T	148	$ .07	$ .30	Hobbie, Glen	64T	578	$1.75	$4.50
Hilton, Dave	75T	509	$ .07	$ .30	Hobson, Butch	77T	89	$ .03	$ .12
Hilton, Dave	77T	163	$ .03	$ .12	Hobson, Butch	78T	155	$ .02	$ .10
Hinds, Sam	78T	303	$ .02	$ .10	Hobson, Butch	79T	270	$ .02	$ .10
Hinsley, Jerry	64T	576	$1.75	$4.50	Hobson, Butch	80T	420	$ .01	$ .10
Hinsley, Jerry	65T	449	$ .75	$3.00	Hobson, Butch	81T	595	$ .01	$ .10
Hinton, Chuck	62T	347	$ .45	$1.45	Hobson, Butch	81TTR	771	$ .02	$ .10
Hinton, Chuck	63T	2	$3.00	$12.00	Hobson, Butch	82T	357	$ .01	$ .07
Hinton, Chuck	63T	330	$ .45	$1.50	Hobson, Butch	83T	652	$ .01	$ .07
Hinton, Chuck	64T	52	$ .30	$ .95	Hodge, Ed	85T	639	$ .01	$ .05
Hinton, Chuck	65T	235	$ .35	$1.25	Hodges, Gil	51Trb	31	$8.00	$30.00
Hinton, Chuck	66T	391	$ .30	$ .95	Hodges, Gil	52T	36	$50.00	$150.00
Hinton, Chuck	67T	189	$ .30	$ .85	Hodges, Gil	54T	102	$20.00	$80.00
Hinton, Chuck	68T	531	$ .35	$1.25	Hodges, Gil	55T	187	$45.00	$175.00
Hinton, Chuck	69T	644	$ .30	$ .95	Hodges, Gil	56T	145	$10.00	$42.50
Hinton, Chuck	70T	27	$ .15	$ .50	Hodges, Gil	57T	80	$10.00	$40.00
Hinton, Chuck	71T	429	$ .15	$ .50	Hodges, Gil	57T	400	$40.00	$160.00
Hinton, Rich	72T	724	$1.25	$4.25	Hodges, Gil	58T	162	$7.50	$22.50
Hinton, Rich	73T	321	$ .07	$ .30	Hodges, Gil	59T	270	$5.00	$16.00
Hinton, Rich	76T	607	$ .05	$ .20	Hodges, Gil	60T	295	$5.00	$16.00
Hinzo, Tommy	88T	576	$ .01	$ .04	Hodges, Gil	61T	460	$4.50	$14.00
Hippauf, Herb	66T	518	$ .75	$2.50	Hodges, Gil	62T	85	$4.50	$14.00
Hiser, Gene	72T	61	$ .15	$ .60	Hodges, Gil	63T	68	$2.50	$10.00
Hiser, Gene	74T	452	$ .07	$ .30	Hodges, Gil	63T	245	$5.00	$16.00
Hisle, Larry	68T	579	$ .45	$1.45	Hodges, Gil	64T	547	$4.00	$12.50
Hisle, Larry	69T	206	$ .30	$ .85	Hodges, Gil	65T	99	$1.50	$6.00
Hisle, Larry	70T	288	$ .15	$ .50	Hodges, Gil	66T	386	$1.50	$4.50
Hisle, Larry	71T	616	$ .35	$1.25	Hodges, Gil	67T	228	$1.50	$4.00
Hisle, Larry	72T	398	$ .05	$ .25	Hodges, Gil	68T	27	$1.50	$6.00
Hisle, Larry	73T	622	$ .45	$1.45	Hodges, Gil	69T	564	$2.10	$6.00
Hisle, Larry	74T	366	$ .07	$ .30	Hodges, Gil	70T	394	$1.50	$6.00
Hisle, Larry	75T	526	$ .07	$ .30	Hodges, Gil	71T	183	$1.50	$4.00
Hisle, Larry	76T	59	$ .05	$ .20	Hodges, Gil	72T	465	$1.00	$4.00
Hisle, Larry	77T	375	$ .03	$ .12	Hodges, Gil	89TTB	664	$ .01	$ .05
Hisle, Larry	78T	203	$ .05	$ .20	Hodges, Ron	74T	448	$ .07	$ .30
Hisle, Larry	78T	520	$ .02	$ .10	Hodges, Ron	75T	134	$ .07	$ .30
Hisle, Larry	79T	180	$ .02	$ .10	Hodges, Ron	77T	329	$ .03	$ .12
Hisle, Larry	80T	430	$ .01	$ .10	Hodges, Ron	78T	653	$ .02	$ .10
Hisle, Larry	81T	215	$ .01	$ .10	Hodges, Ron	79T	46	$ .02	$ .10
Hisle, Larry	82T	93	$ .01	$ .07	Hodges, Ron	80T	172	$ .01	$ .10
Hisle, Larry	83T	773	$ .01	$ .07	Hodges, Ron	81T	537	$ .01	$ .10
Hitchcock, Billy	52T	182	$7.00	$20.00	Hodges, Ron	82T	234	$ .01	$ .07
Hitchcock, Billy	53T	17	$4.50	$15.00	Hodges, Ron	83T	713	$ .01	$ .07
Hitchcock, Billy	60T	461	$2.25	$6.00	Hodges, Ron	84T	418	$ .01	$ .06
Hitchcock, Billy	62T	121	$ .45	$1.45	Hodges, Ron	85T	363	$ .01	$ .05
Hitchcock, Billy	63T	213	$ .30	$ .95	Hoeft, Billy	52T	370	$40.00	$140.00
Hitchcock, Billy	67T	199	$ .30	$ .85	Hoeft, Billy	53T	165	$4.50	$15.00
Hoak, Don	53T	176	$2.25	$8.00	Hoeft, Billy	56T	152	$2.25	$6.00
Hoak, Don	54T	211	$1.75	$7.00	Hoeft, Billy	57T	60	$ .95	$3.50
Hoak, Don	55T	40	$3.60	$10.00	Hoeft, Billy	58T	13	$1.25	$4.25
Hoak, Don	56T	335	$2.25	$8.00	Hoeft, Billy	59T	343	$ .75	$2.20
Hoak, Don	57T	274	$4.25	$15.00	Hoeft, Billy	60T	369	$ .75	$2.20
Hoak, Don	58T	160	$ .65	$2.00	Hoeft, Billy	61T	256	$ .35	$1.25
Hoak, Don	59T	25	$1.75	$4.50	Hoeft, Billy	62T	134	$ .75	$2.20
Hoak, Don	60T	373	$ .45	$1.35	Hoeft, Billy	63T	346	$ .45	$1.50
Hoak, Don	61T	230	$ .35	$1.25	Hoeft, Billy	64T	551	$1.75	$4.50
Hoak, Don	62T	95	$ .45	$1.45	Hoeft, Billy	65T	471	$ .75	$3.00
Hoak, Don	63T	305	$ .45	$1.50	Hoeft, Billy	66T	409	$ .30	$ .95
Hoak, Don	64T	254	$ .30	$ .95	Hoerner, Joe	64T	544	$1.75	$4.50
Hobaugh, Ed	60T	131	$ .45	$1.45	Hoerner, Joe	66T	544	$4.00	$11.50
Hobaugh, Ed	61T	129	$ .35	$1.25	Hoerner, Joe	67T	41	$ .30	$ .85
Hobaugh, Ed	62T	79	$ .45	$1.45	Hoerner, Joe	68T	227	$ .30	$ .85
Hobaugh, Ed	63T	423	$ .45	$1.50	Hoerner, Joe	69T	522	$ .30	$ .95
Hobbie, Glen	58T	467	$ .75	$2.20	Hoerner, Joe	70T	511	$ .15	$ .50
Hobbie, Glen	59T	334	$ .75	$2.20	Hoerner, Joe	71T	166	$ .15	$ .50
Hobbie, Glen	60T	182	$ .45	$1.45	Hoerner, Joe	72T	482	$ .05	$ .25
Hobbie, Glen	61T	264	$ .35	$1.25	Hoerner, Joe	73T	653	$ .45	$1.45

TOPPS

Player	Year	No.	VG	EX/MT
Hoerner, Joe	74T	493	$ .07	$ .30
Hoerner, Joe	75T	629	$ .07	$ .30
Hoerner, Joe	77T	256	$ .03	$ .12
Hoffman, Glenn	81T	349	$ .01	$ .10
Hoffman, Glenn	82T	189	$ .01	$ .07
Hoffman, Glenn	83T	108	$ .01	$ .07
Hoffman, Glenn	84T	523	$ .01	$ .06
Hoffman, Glenn	85T	633	$ .01	$ .05
Hoffman, Glenn	86T	38	$ .01	$ .04
Hoffman, Glenn	87T	374	$ .01	$ .04
Hoffman, Glenn	88T	202	$ .01	$ .04
Hoffman, Guy	80T	664	$ .01	$ .10
Hoffman, Guy	87TTR	48	$ .01	$ .05
Hoffman, Guy	88T	496	$ .01	$ .04
Hofman, Bob	52T	371	$75.00	$225.00
Hofman, Bob	53T	182	$3.75	13.00
Hofman, Bob	54T	99	$3.60	$10.00
Hofman, Bobby	55T	17	$2.00	$6.00
Hofman, Bobby	56T	28	$2.25	$6.00
Hogue, Bobby	52T	9	$15.00	$47.50
Hogue, Cal	53T	238	$12.50	$50.00
Hogue, Cal	54T	134	$3.60	$10.00
Hoiles, Chris	89TMLD	60	$ .01	$ .06
Hoiles, Chris	91T	42	$ .01	$ .15
Holcombe, Ken	52T	95	$7.00	$20.00
Holdsworth, Fred	74T	596	$ .07	$ .30
Holdsworth, Fred	75T	323	$ .07	$ .30
Holdsworth, Fred	77T	466	$ .03	$ .12
Holland, Al	81T	213	$ .01	$ .10
Holland, Al	82T	406	$ .01	$ .07
Holland, Al	83T	58	$ .01	$ .07
Holland, Al	83TTR	46	$ .02	$ .10
Holland, Al	84T	138	$ .02	$ .10
Holland, Al	84T	564	$ .01	$ .06
Holland, Al	85T	185	$ .01	$ .05
Holland, Al	85TTR	55	$ .02	$ .10
Holland, Al	86T	369	$ .01	$ .04
Hollins, Dave	90TTR	41	$ .01	$ .20
Hollins, Dave	91T	264	$ .01	$ .10
Holly, Jeff	79T	371	$ .02	$ .10
Holman, Brian	89TTR	51	$ .01	$ .15
Holman, Brian	90T	616	$ .01	$ .10
Holman, Brian	91T	458	$ .01	$ .03
Holman, Gary	69T	361	$ .30	$ .85
Holman, Scott	84T	13	$ .01	$ .06
Holman, Shawn	89TMLD	61	$ .01	$ .25
Holmes, Tommy	51Trb	52	$3.25	$10.00
Holmes, Tommy	52T	289	$18.50	$55.00
Holt, Jim	71T	7	$ .15	$ .50
Holt, Jim	72T	588	$ .30	$ .95
Holt, Jim	73T	259	$ .07	$ .30
Holt, Jim	74T	122	$ .07	$ .30
Holt, Jim	75T	607	$ .07	$ .30
Holt, Jim	76T	603	$ .05	$ .20
Holt, Jim	77T	349	$ .03	$ .12
Holton, Brian	87TTR	49	$ .01	$ .05
Holton, Brian	88T	338	$ .01	$ .04
Holton, Brian	89T	368	$ .01	$ .05
Holton, Brian	89TTR	52	$ .01	$ .06
Holton, Brian	90T	179	$ .01	$ .04
Holtzman, Ken	67T	185	$ .35	$1.25
Holtzman, Ken	68T	60	$ .30	$ .85
Holtzman, Ken	68TAS	380	$ .30	$ .85
Holtzman, Ken	69T	288	$ .30	$ .95
Holtzman, Ken	70T	505	$ .15	$ .50
Holtzman, Ken	71T	410	$ .15	$ .50
Holtzman, Ken	72T	670	$ .90	$3.00
Holtzman, Ken	73T	60	$ .15	$ .50
Holtzman, Ken	74T	180	$ .07	$ .30
Holtzman, Ken	75T	145	$ .07	$ .30

Player	Year	No.	VG	EX/MT
Holtzman, Ken	76T	115	$ .05	$ .20
Holtzman, Ken	77T	625	$ .03	$ .12
Holtzman, Ken	78T	387	$ .02	$ .10
Holtzman, Ken	79T	522	$ .02	$ .10
Holtzman, Ken	80T	298	$ .01	$ .10
Honeycutt, Rick	79T	612	$ .05	$ .25
Honeycutt, Rick	80T	307	$ .01	$ .10
Honeycutt, Rick	81T	33	$ .01	$ .10
Honeycutt, Rick	81TTR	772	$ .02	$ .10

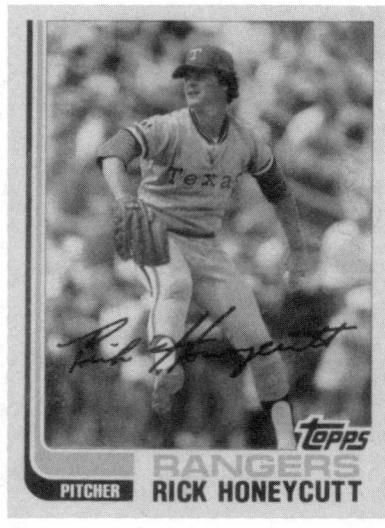

PITCHER RICK HONEYCUTT

Player	Year	No.	VG	EX/MT
Honeycutt, Rick	82T	751	$ .01	$ .07
Honeycutt, Rick	83T	557	$ .01	$ .07
Honeycutt, Rick	84T	137	$ .01	$ .06
Honeycutt, Rick	84T	222	$ .01	$ .06
Honeycutt, Rick	84T	37	$ .01	$ .06
Honeycutt, Rick	85T	174	$ .01	$ .05
Honeycutt, Rick	86T	439	$ .01	$ .04
Honeycutt, Rick	87T	753	$ .01	$ .04
Honeycutt, Rick	88T	641	$ .01	$ .04
Honeycutt, Rick	89T	328	$ .01	$ .05
Honeycutt, Rick	90T	582	$ .01	$ .04
Honeycutt, Rick	91T	67	$ .01	$ .03
Hood, Don	74T	436	$ .07	$ .30
Hood, Don	75T	516	$ .07	$ .30
Hood, Don	76T	132	$ .05	$ .20
Hood, Don	77T	296	$ .03	$ .12
Hood, Don	78T	398	$ .02	$ .10
Hood, Don	79T	667	$ .02	$ .10
Hood, Don	80T	89	$ .01	$ .10
Hood, Don	83T	443	$ .01	$ .07
Hood, Don	84T	743	$ .01	$ .06
Hook, Jay	60T	187	$ .45	$1.45
Hook, Jay	61T	162	$ .35	$1.25
Hook, Jay	62T	94	$ .45	$1.45
Hook, Jay	63T	469	$2.50	$6.50
Hook, Jay	64T	361	$ .30	$ .95
Hooper, Bob	52T	340	$40.00	$140.00
Hooper, Bob	53T	84	$4.50	$15.00
Hooten, Leon	77T	478	$ .03	$ .12
Hooton, Burt	72T	61	$ .15	$ .60
Hooton, Burt	73T	367	$ .07	$ .30

Player	Year	No.	VG	EX/MT	Player	Year	No.	VG	EX/MT
Hooton, Burt	74T	378	$ .07	$ .30	Horton, Willie	66T	220	$ .50	$1.50
Hooton, Burt	75T	176	$ .07	$ .30	Horton, Willie	67T	465	$ .75	$3.00
Hooton, Burt	76T	280	$ .05	$ .20	Horton, Willie	68T	360	$ .15	$ .50
Hooton, Burt	77T	484	$ .03	$ .12	Horton, Willie	69T	5	$ .35	$1.25
Hooton, Burt	78T	41	$ .02	$ .10	Horton, Willie	69T	180	$ .30	$ .85
Hooton, Burt	79T	694	$ .02	$ .10	Horton, Willie	69TAS	429	$ .30	$ .85
Hooton, Burt	80T	170	$ .01	$ .10	Horton, Willie	70T	520	$ .15	$ .50
Hooton, Burt	81T	565	$ .01	$ .10	Horton, Willie	71T	120	$ .15	$ .50
Hooton, Burt	82T	311	$ .01	$ .07	Horton, Willie	72T	494	$ .05	$ .25
Hooton, Burt	82T	315	$ .01	$ .07	Horton, Willie	72T	750	$ .90	$3.00
Hooton, Burt	83T	775	$ .01	$ .07	Horton, Willie	73T	433	$ .30	$ .85
Hooton, Burt	84T	15	$ .01	$ .06	Horton, Willie	74T	115	$ .07	$ .30
Hooton, Burt	85T	201	$ .01	$ .05	Horton, Willie	75T	66	$ .07	$ .30
Hooton, Burt	85TTR	56	$ .02	$ .10	Horton, Willie	76T	320	$ .05	$ .20
Hooton, Burt	86T	454	$ .01	$ .04	Horton, Willie	77T	660	$ .15	$ .50
Hoover, John	85T	397	$ .01	$ .05	Horton, Willie	78T	290	$ .02	$ .10
Hopkins, Gail	70T	483	$ .15	$ .50	Horton, Willie	79T	239	$ .02	$ .10
Hopkins, Gail	71T	269	$ .15	$ .50	Horton, Willie	80T	532	$ .01	$ .10
Hopkins, Gail	72T	728	$ .75	$2.50	Hoscheit, Vern	73T	179	$ .30	$ .95
Hopkins, Gail	73T	441	$ .07	$ .30	Hoskins, Dave	54T	81	$3.60	$10.00
Hopkins, Gail	74T	652	$ .07	$ .30	Hoskins, Dave	55T	133	$2.00	$6.00
Hopp, Johnny	52T	214	$7.00	$20.00	Hosley, Tim	72T	257	$ .05	$ .25
Hopp, Johnny	54T	193	$3.60	$10.00	Hosley, Tim	76T	482	$ .05	$ .20
Horlen, Joe	68T	8	$ .45	$1.45	Hosley, Tim	78T	261	$ .02	$ .10
Horlen, Joe	68TAS	377	$ .30	$ .85	Hostetler, Dave	83T	584	$ .01	$ .07
Horlen, Joe	69T	328	$ .30	$ .85	Hostetler, Dave	84T	62	$ .01	$ .06
Horlen, Joe	70T	35	$ .15	$ .50	Hough, Charlie	72T	198	$ .60	$1.50
Horlen, Joe	71T	345	$ .15	$ .50	Hough, Charlie	73T	610	$ .45	$1.45
Horlen, Joe	72T	685	$ .75	$2.50	Hough, Charlie	74T	408	$ .07	$ .30
Horlen, Joel	62T	479	$ .75	$2.50	Hough, Charlie	75T	71	$ .07	$ .30
Horlen, Joel	63T	332	$ .45	$1.50	Hough, Charlie	76T	174	$ .05	$ .20
Horlen, Joel	64T	584	$1.75	$4.50	Hough, Charlie	77T	298	$ .03	$ .12
Horlen, Joel	65T	7	$ .35	$1.25	Hough, Charlie	78T	22	$ .02	$ .10
Horlen, Joel	65T	480	$ .75	$3.00	Hough, Charlie	79T	508	$ .02	$ .10
Horlen, Joel	66T	560	$5.00	$20.00	Hough, Charlie	80T	644	$ .01	$ .10
Horlen, Joel	67T	107	$ .30	$ .85	Hough, Charlie	81T	371	$ .01	$ .10
Horlen, Joel	67T	233	$ .45	$1.45	Hough, Charlie	82T	718	$ .01	$ .07
Horlen, Joe "Joel"	68T	125	$ .30	$ .85	Hough, Charlie	83T	412	$ .01	$ .07
Horn, Sam	88T	377	$ .01	$ .10	Hough, Charlie	83T	479	$ .01	$ .07
Horn, Sam	88TBB	252	$ .01	$ .06	Hough, Charlie	84T	118	$ .01	$ .06
Horn, Sam	90TTR	43	$ .01	$ .15	Hough, Charlie	85T	571	$ .01	$ .05
Horn, Sam	91T	598	$ .01	$ .03	Hough, Charlie	86T	275	$ .01	$ .04
Horner, Bob	79T	586	$ .15	$ .75	Hough, Charlie	87T	70	$ .01	$ .04
Horner, Bob	80T	108	$ .01	$ .10	Hough, Charlie	88T	680	$ .01	$ .04
Horner, Bob	81T	355	$ .01	$ .10	Hough, Charlie	88TBB	47	$ .01	$ .06
Horner, Bob	82T	145	$ .01	$ .07	Hough, Charlie	89T	345	$ .01	$ .05
Horner, Bob	83T	50	$ .01	$ .07	Hough, Charlie	90T	735	$ .01	$ .04
Horner, Bob	84T	760	$ .01	$ .06	Hough, Charlie	91T	495	$ .01	$ .03
Horner, Bob	85T	276	$ .01	$ .05	Houk, Ralph	52T	200	$20.00	$60.00
Horner, Bob	85T	410	$ .01	$ .05	Houk, Ralph	60T	465	$2.50	$9.00
Horner, Bob	86T	220	$ .01	$ .04	Houk, Ralph	61T	133	$1.00	$3.00
Horner, Bob	87T	660	$ .01	$ .04	Houk, Ralph	62T	88	$ .90	$3.00
Horner, Bob	88TBB	245	$ .01	$ .06	Houk, Ralph	63T	382	$ .75	$3.00
Horner, Bob	88TTR	50	$ .01	$ .06	Houk, Ralph	67T	468	$ .75	$2.25
Horner, Bob	89T	510	$ .01	$ .05	Houk, Ralph	68T	47	$ .15	$ .50
Hornsby, Rogers	61T	404	$ .75	$2.25	Houk, Ralph	69T	447	$ .30	$ .95
Hornsby, Rogers	76TAS	342	$ .75	$3.00	Houk, Ralph	70T	273	$ .15	$ .50
Hornsby, Rogers	79TRH	414	$ .15	$ .50	Houk, Ralph	71T	146	$ .15	$ .50
Horton, Ricky	84TTR	52	$ .08	$ .30	Houk, Ralph	72T	533	$ .35	$1.25
Horton, Ricky	85T	321	$ .01	$ .10	Houk, Ralph	73T	116	$ .15	$ .50
Horton, Ricky	86T	783	$ .01	$ .04	Houk, Ralph	74T	578	$ .07	$ .30
Horton, Ricky	87T	542	$ .01	$ .04	Houk, Ralph	78T	684	$ .02	$ .10
Horton, Ricky	88T	34	$ .01	$ .04	Houk, Ralph	83T	786	$ .01	$ .07
Horton, Ricky	88TTR	51	$ .01	$ .06	Houk, Ralph	84T	381	$ .01	$ .06
Horton, Ricky	89T	232	$ .01	$ .05	Houk, Ralph	85T	11	$ .01	$ .05
Horton, Ricky	90T	133	$ .01	$ .04	House, Frank	52T	146	$7.00	$20.00
Horton, Willie	64T	512	$2.00	$8.00	House, Frank	54T	163	$2.00	$9.00
Horton, Willie	65T	206	$ .45	$1.45	House, Frank	55T	87	$2.00	$6.00
Horton, Willie	66T	20	$ .30	$ .95	House, Frank	56T	32	$2.25	$6.00
Horton, Willie	66T	218	$ .75	$3.00	House, Frank	57T	223	$ .95	$3.50

Player	Year	No.	VG	EX/MT
House, Frank	58T	318	$ .75	$3.00
House, Frank	59T	313	$ .75	$2.20
House, Frank	60T	372	$ .75	$2.20
House, Tom	69T	331	$ .30	$ .85
House, Tom	72T	351	$ .15	$ .50
House, Tom	74T	164	$ .07	$ .30
House, Tom	75T	525	$ .07	$ .30

Player	Year	No.	VG	EX/MT
House, Tom	76T	231	$ .05	$ .20
House, Tom	76TTR	231	$ .05	$ .20
House, Tom	77T	358	$ .03	$ .12
House, Tom	78T	643	$ .02	$ .10
House, Tom	79T	31	$ .02	$ .10
Householder, Paul	81T	606	$ .01	$ .10
Householder, Paul	82T	351	$ .01	$ .07
Householder, Paul	83T	34	$ .01	$ .07
Householder, Paul	84T	214	$ .01	$ .06
Householder, Paul	86T	554	$ .01	$ .04
Houston, Tyler	90T	564	$ .01	$ .35
Houtteman, Art	52T	238	$7.00	$20.00
Houtteman, Art	56T	281	$2.25	$8.00
Houtteman, Art	57T	385	$1.25	$4.25
Hovley, Steve	70T	514	$ .15	$ .50
Hovley, Steve	71T	109	$ .15	$ .50
Hovley, Steve	72T	683	$ .75	$2.50
Hovley, Steve	73T	282	$ .07	$ .30
Howard, Bruce	64T	107	$ .30	$ .95
Howard, Bruce	65T	41	$ .30	$ .85
Howard, Bruce	66T	281	$ .30	$ .95
Howard, Bruce	67T	159	$ .30	$ .85
Howard, Bruce	68T	293	$ .30	$ .85
Howard, Bruce	69T	226	$ .30	$ .95
Howard, Elston	56T	208	$12.00	$35.00
Howard, Elston	57T	82	$5.00	$15.00
Howard, Elston	58T	275	$2.50	$10.00
Howard, Elston	59T	395	$1.50	$6.00
Howard, Elston	60T	65	$1.50	$4.50
Howard, Elston	61T	495	$1.50	$4.50
Howard, Elston	62T	51	$ .75	$2.20
Howard, Elston	62T	400	$1.50	$4.50
Howard, Elston	62TAS	473	$1.00	$3.00

Player	Year	No.	VG	EX/MT
Howard, Elston	63T	60	$1.25	$5.00
Howard, Elston	63T	306	$1.00	$4.00
Howard, Elston	64T	100	$ .75	$2.25
Howard, Elston	65T	1	$3.50	$11.00
Howard, Elston	65T	3	$3.00	$12.00
Howard, Elston	65T	450	$1.75	$4.50
Howard, Elston	66T	405	$1.00	$3.00
Howard, Elston	67T	25	$1.00	$3.00
Howard, Elston	68T	167	$ .90	$3.00
Howard, Elston	73T	116	$ .15	$ .50
Howard, Elston	75T	201	$ .75	$3.00
Howard, Frank	60T	132	$3.00	$10.00
Howard, Frank	61T	280	$ .95	$3.50
Howard, Frank	62T	175	$ .75	$2.00
Howard, Frank	63T	123	$ .75	$2.00
Howard, Frank	64T	371	$ .90	$3.00
Howard, Frank	65T	40	$ .75	$2.00
Howard, Frank	66T	515	$2.00	$6.00
Howard, Frank	67T	255	$ .40	$1.50
Howard, Frank	68T	6	$1.00	$$4.00
Howard, Frank	68T	320	$ .45	$1.45
Howard, Frank	69T	3	$ .35	$1.25
Howard, Frank	69T	5	$ .35	$1.25
Howard, Frank	69T	170	$ .45	$1.45
Howard, Frank	70T	66	$ .50	$1.50
Howard, Frank	70T	550	$ .45	$1.45
Howard, Frank	71T	63	$ .15	$ .50
Howard, Frank	71T	65	$ .50	$2.00
Howard, Frank	71T	620	$ .75	$2.00
Howard, Frank	72T	350	$ .30	$ .95
Howard, Frank	73T	560	$ .75	$2.00
Howard, Frank	83TTR	47	$ .02	$ .10
Howard, Frank	84T	621	$ .01	$ .06
Howard, Fred	80T	72	$ .01	$ .10
Howard, Larry	71T	102	$ .15	$ .50
Howard, Steve	90TTR	42	$ .01	$ .05
Howard, Wilbur	74T	606	$ .07	$ .30
Howard, Wilbur	75T	563	$ .07	$ .30
Howard, Wilbur	76T	97	$ .05	$ .20
Howard, Wilbur	77T	248	$ .03	$ .12
Howard, Wilbur	78T	534	$ .02	$ .10
Howard, Wilbur	79T	642	$ .02	$ .10
Howarth, Jimmy	73T	459	$ .07	$ .30
Howarth, Jimmy	74T	404	$ .07	$ .30
Howe, Art	78T	13	$ .02	$ .10
Howe, Art	79T	327	$ .02	$ .10
Howe, Art	80T	554	$ .01	$ .10
Howe, Art	81T	129	$ .01	$ .10
Howe, Art	82T	66	$ .03	$ .15
Howe, Art	82T	453	$ .01	$ .07
Howe, Art	83T	639	$ .01	$ .07
Howe, Art	84T	679	$ .01	$ .06
Howe, Art	84TTR	53	$ .02	$ .10
Howe, Art	85T	204	$ .01	$ .05
Howe, Art	89TTR	53	$ .01	$ .06
Howe, Art	90T	579	$ .01	$ .04
Howe, Art	91T	51	$ .01	$ .03
Howe, Steve	81T	693	$ .04	$ .20
Howe, Steve	82T	14	$ .01	$ .07
Howe, Steve	83T	170	$ .01	$ .07
Howe, Steve	84T	425	$ .01	$ .06
Howell, Dixie	52T	135	$7.00	$20.00
Howell, Dixie	53T	255	$12.50	$50.00
Howell, Dixie	56T	149	$2.25	$6.00
Howell, Dixie	57T	221	$ .95	$3.50
Howell, Dixie	58T	421	$ .75	$3.00
Howell, Jack	86T	127	$ .01	$ .04
Howell, Jack	87T	422	$ .01	$ .04
Howell, Jack	88T	631	$ .01	$ .04
Howell, Jack	88TBB	121	$ .01	$ .06

Player	Year	No.	VG	EX/MT	Player	Year	No.	VG	EX/MT
Howell, Jack	89T	216	$ .01	$ .05	Hrabosky, Al	77T	495	$ .03	$ .12
Howell, Jack	89TBB	228	$ .01	$ .06	Hrabosky, Al	78T	230	$ .02	$ .10
Howell, Jack	90T	547	$ .01	$ .04	Hrabosky, Al	79T	45	$ .02	$ .10
Howell, Jack	91T	57	$ .01	$ .03	Hrabosky, Al	80T	585	$ .01	$ .10
Howell, Jay	82T	51	$ .03	$ .15	Hrabosky, Al	81T	636	$ .01	$ .10
Howell, Jay	84T	239	$ .01	$ .06	Hrabosky, Al	82T	393	$ .01	$ .07
Howell, Jay	85T	559	$ .01	$ .05	Hrbek, Kent	82T	766	$1.50	$5.00
Howell, Jay	85TTR	57	$ .02	$ .10	Hrbek, Kent	82TTR	44	$2.00	$6.00
Howell, Jay	86T	115	$ .01	$ .04	Hrbek, Kent	83T	690	$ .10	$ .75
Howell, Jay	87T	391	$ .01	$ .04	Hrbek, Kent	83T	771	$ .10	$ .40
Howell, Jay	88T	690	$ .01	$ .04	Hrbek, Kent	84T	11	$ .01	$ .10
Howell, Jay	88TTR	52	$ .01	$ .06	Hrbek, Kent	84T	345	$ .01	$ .40
Howell, Jay	89T	425	$ .01	$ .05	Hrbek, Kent	85T	510	$ .05	$ .25
Howell, Jay	89TBB	79	$ .01	$ .06	Hrbek, Kent	86T	430	$ .02	$ .20
Howell, Jay	90T	40	$ .01	$ .04	Hrbek, Kent	87T	679	$ .01	$ .10
Howell, Jay	91T	770	$ .01	$ .03	Hrbek, Kent	88T	45	$ .01	$ .15
Howell, Ken	85TTR	58	$ .02	$ .10	Hrbek, Kent	88TBB	84	$ .01	$ .10
Howell, Ken	86T	654	$ .01	$ .04	Hrbek, Kent	89T	265	$ .01	$ .10
Howell, Ken	87T	477	$ .01	$ .04	Hrbek, Kent	89TBB	209	$ .01	$ .10
Howell, Ken	88T	149	$ .01	$ .04	Hrbek, Kent	90T	125	$ .01	$ .10
Howell, Ken	89T	93	$ .01	$ .05	Hrbek, Kent	91T	710	$ .01	$ .03
Howell, Ken	89TTR	54	$ .01	$ .06	Hriniak, Walt	69T	611	$ .30	$ .95
Howell, Ken	90T	756	$ .01	$ .04	Hriniak, Walt	70T	392	$ .15	$ .50
Howell, Ken	91T	209	$ .01	$ .03	Hubbard, Glenn	79T	715	$ .05	$ .20
Howell, Roy	76T	279	$ .05	$ .20	Hubbard, Glenn	81T	247	$ .01	$ .10
Howell, Roy	77T	608	$ .03	$ .12	Hubbard, Glenn	82T	482	$ .01	$ .07
Howell, Roy	78T	394	$ .02	$ .10	Hubbard, Glenn	83T	624	$ .01	$ .07
Howell, Roy	79T	101	$ .02	$ .10	Hubbard, Glenn	84T	25	$ .01	$ .06
Howell, Roy	80T	488	$ .01	$ .10	Hubbard, Glenn	85T	195	$ .01	$ .05
Howell, Roy	81T	581	$ .01	$ .10	Hubbard, Glenn	86T	539	$ .01	$ .04
Howell, Roy	81TTR	773	$ .02	$ .10	Hubbard, Glenn	87T	745	$ .01	$ .04
Howell, Roy	82T	68	$ .01	$ .07	Hubbard, Glenn	88T	325	$ .01	$ .04
Howell, Roy	83T	218	$ .01	$ .07	Hubbard, Glenn	88TBB	200	$ .01	$ .06
Howell, Roy	84T	687	$ .01	$ .06	Hubbard, Glenn	88TTR	53	$ .01	$ .06
Howell, Roy	85T	372	$ .01	$ .05	Hubbard, Glenn	89T	237	$ .01	$ .05
Howerton, Bill	52T	167	$7.00	$20.00	Hubbard, Glenn	89TBB	232	$ .01	$ .06
Howitt, Dann	89TMLD	62	$ .01	$ .50	Hubbs, Ken	62T	461	$2.50	$7.50
Howser, Dick	61T	416	$1.25	$4.00	Hubbs, Ken	63T	15	$ .45	$1.80
Howser, Dick	62T	13	$ .75	$2.20	Hubbs, Ken	64T	550	$2.00	$8.00
Howser, Dick	63T	124	$ .75	$3.00	Hudler, Rex	89T	346	$ .01	$ .05
Howser, Dick	64T	478	$ .90	$3.00	Hudler, Rex	89TBB	248	$ .01	$ .06
Howser, Dick	65T	92	$ .75	$3.00	Hudler, Rex	90T	647	$ .01	$ .04
Howser, Dick	66T	567	$3.00	$9.50	Hudler, Rex	91T	228	$ .01	$ .03
Howser, Dick	67T	411	$ .75	$3.00	Hudson, Charles	85T	379	$ .01	$ .05
Howser, Dick	68T	467	$ .75	$3.00	Hudson, Charles	86T	792	$ .01	$ .04
Howser, Dick	73T	116	$ .15	$ .50	Hudson, Charles	87T	191	$ .01	$ .04
Howser, Dick	83T	96	$ .01	$ .07	Hudson, Charles	87TTR	50	$ .01	$ .05
Howser, Dick	84T	471	$ .01	$ .06	Hudson, Charles	88T	636	$ .01	$ .04
Howser, Dick	85T	334	$ .01	$ .05	Hudson, Charles	88TBB	212	$ .01	$ .06
Howser, Dick	86T	199	$ .01	$ .04	Hudson, Charles	89T	236	$ .01	$ .05
Howser, Dick	87T	18	$ .01	$ .04	Hudson, Charles	89TBB	88	$ .01	$ .06
Howser, Dick	90TTB	661	$ .01	$ .04	Hudson, Charlie	84T	432	$ .02	$ .10
Hoyt, LaMarr	81T	164	$ .05	$ .20	Hudson, Jesse	70T	348	$ .15	$ .50
Hoyt, LaMarr	82T	428	$ .01	$ .07	Hudson, Sid	51Trb	44	$1.50	$4.00
Hoyt, LaMarr	83T	591	$ .01	$ .07	Hudson, Sid	52T	60	$15.00	$47.50
Hoyt, LaMarr	83T	618	$ .01	$ .07	Hudson, Sid	53T	251	$12.50	$50.00
Hoyt, LaMarr	83T	705	$ .01	$ .10	Hudson, Sid	54T	93	$3.60	$10.00
Hoyt, LaMarr	84T	97	$ .01	$ .06	Huff, Mike	89TMLD	63	$ .01	$ .06
Hoyt, LaMarr	84T	135	$ .01	$ .06	Huffman, Phil	80T	142	$ .01	$ .10
Hoyt, LaMarr	84TAS	405	$ .01	$ .06	Huffman, Phil	81T	506	$ .01	$ .10
Hoyt, LaMarr	85T	520	$ .01	$ .05	Hughes, Dick	67T	384	$ .30	$ .95
Hoyt, LaMarr	85TTR	59	$ .02	$ .10	Hughes, Dick	68T	253	$ .30	$ .85
Hoyt, LaMarr	86T	380	$ .01	$ .04	Hughes, Dick	69T	39	$ .30	$ .85
Hoyt, LaMarr	87T	275	$ .01	$ .04	Hughes, Jim	53T	216	$4.50	$15.00
Hrabosky, Al	71T	594	$ .75	$2.00	Hughes, Jim	54T	169	$2.50	$10.00
Hrabosky, Al	73T	153	$ .30	$ .85	Hughes, Jim	55T	51	$2.00	$6.00
Hrabosky, Al	74T	108	$ .07	$ .30	Hughes, Jim	76T	11	$ .05	$ .20
Hrabosky, Al	75T	122	$ .07	$ .30	Hughes, Jim	77T	304	$ .03	$ .12
Hrabosky, Al	76T	205	$ .15	$ .50	Hughes, Jim	78T	395	$ .02	$ .10
Hrabosky, Al	76T	315	$ .05	$ .20	Hughes, Keith	88T	781	$ .01	$ .04

Player	Year	No.	VG	EX/MT	Player	Year	No.	VG	EX/MT
Hughes, Terry	73T	603	$ .45	$1.45	Hundley, Randy	72T	258	$ .05	$ .25
Hughes, Terry	74T	604	$1.00	$3.00	Hundley, Randy	73T	21	$ .07	$ .30
Hughes, Terry	75T	612	$ .07	$ .30	Hundley, Randy	74T	319	$ .07	$ .30
Huismann, Mark	85T	644	$ .01	$ .05	Hundley, Randy	74TTR	319	$ .07	$ .30
Huismann, Mark	87T	187	$ .01	$ .04	Hundley, Randy	76T	351	$ .05	$ .20
Hulett, Tim	85TTR	60	$ .02	$ .10	Hundley, Randy	77T	502	$ .03	$ .12
Hulett, Tim	86T	724	$ .01	$ .04	Hundley, Todd	90TTR	44	$ .01	$ .20
Hulett, Tim	87T	566	$ .01	$ .04	Hundley, Todd	91T	457	$ .01	$ .10
Hulett, Tim	88T	158	$ .01	$ .04	Hunt, Ken	60T	522	$2.50	$10.00
Hulett, Tim	91T	468	$ .01	$ .03	Hunt, Ken	61T	156	$ .35	$1.25
Hume, Tom	78T	701	$ .02	$ .10	Hunt, Ken	61T	556	$7.00	$21.00
Hume, Tom	79T	301	$ .02	$ .10	Hunt, Ken	62T	68	$ .45	$1.45
Hume, Tom	80T	149	$ .01	$ .10	Hunt, Ken	62T	364	$ .45	$1.45
Hume, Tom	81T	8	$ .01	$ .10	Hunt, Ken	63T	207	$ .30	$ .95
Hume, Tom	81T	419	$ .01	$ .10	Hunt, Ken	64T	294	$ .30	$ .95
Hume, Tom	82T	763	$ .01	$ .07	Hunt, Randy	86T	218	$ .01	$ .04
Hume, Tom	83T	86	$ .01	$ .07	Hunt, Ron	63T	558	$1.75	$4.50
Hume, Tom	84T	607	$ .01	$ .06	Hunt, Ron	64T	235	$ .30	$ .95
Hume, Tom	85T	223	$ .01	$ .05	Hunt, Ron	65T	285	$ .35	$1.25
Hume, Tom	86T	573	$ .01	$ .04	Hunt, Ron	66T	360	$ .30	$ .95
Hume, Tom	86TTR	47	$ .02	$ .10	Hunt, Ron	67T	525	$ .75	$3.00
Hume, Tom	87T	719	$ .01	$ .04	Hunt, Ron	68T	15	$ .30	$ .85
Humphrey, Terry	72T	489	$ .05	$ .25	Hunt, Ron	69T	664	$2.25	$6.00
Humphrey, Terry	73T	106	$ .07	$ .30	Hunt, Ron	70T	276	$ .15	$ .50
Humphrey, Terry	76T	552	$ .05	$ .20	Hunt, Ron	71T	578	$ .35	$1.25
Humphrey, Terry	77T	369	$ .03	$ .12	Hunt, Ron	72T	110	$ .05	$ .25
Humphrey, Terry	78T	71	$ .02	$ .10	Hunt, Ron	73T	149	$ .07	$ .30
Humphrey, Terry	79T	503	$ .02	$ .10	Hunt, Ron	74T	275	$ .07	$ .30
Humphreys, Bob	65T	154	$ .30	$ .85	Hunt, Ron	75T	610	$ .07	$ .30
Humphreys, Bob	66T	342	$ .30	$ .95	Hunter, Billy	53T	166	$4.50	$15.00
Humphreys, Bob	67T	478	$ .75	$3.00	Hunter, Billy	54T	48	$3.60	$10.00
Humphreys, Bob	68T	268	$ .30	$ .85	Hunter, Gordon (Billy)	57T	207	$ .95	$3.50
Humphreys, Bob	69T	84	$ .30	$ .85	Hunter, Billy	58T	98	$1.25	$4.25
Humphreys, Bob	70T	538	$ .15	$ .50	Hunter, Billy	59T	11	$1.25	$4.25
Humphreys, Bob	71T	236	$ .15	$ .50	Hunter, Billy	73T	136	$ .15	$ .50
Hundley, Randy	66T	392	$ .30	$ .95	Hunter, Billy	74T	306	$ .15	$ .50
Hundley, Randy	67T	106	$ .30	$ .85	Hunter, Billy	78T	548	$ .02	$ .10
Hundley, Randy	68T	136	$ .30	$ .85	Hunter, Jim	65T	526	$50.00	$150.00
Hundley, Randy	69T	347	$ .30	$ .85	Hunter, Jim	66T	36	$9.00	$27.50
Hundley, Randy	70T	265	$ .15	$ .50	Hunter, Jim	67T	369	$4.00	$15.00
					Hunter, Jim	68T	385	$2.50	$10.00
					Hunter, Jim	69T	235	$2.50	$10.00
					Hunter, Jim	70T	565	$3.00	$9.00
					Hunter, Jim	71T	45	$1.50	$6.00
					Hunter, Jim	72T	330	$1.65	$5.00
					Hunter, Jim	73T	235	$1.25	$5.00
					Hunter, Jim	73T	344	$ .35	$1.25
					Hunter, Jim	74T	7	$1.00	$4.00
					Hunter, Jim	74TAS	339	$ .30	$ .95
					Hunter, Jim	75T	230	$1.25	$4.00
					Hunter, Jim	75T	310	$ .35	$1.25
					Hunter, Jim	75T	311	$ .30	$ .95
					Hunter, Jim	76T	100	$ .75	$3.00
					Hunter, Jim	76T	200	$ .45	$1.45
					Hunter, Jim	76T	202	$ .45	$1.45
					Hunter, Jim	77T	280	$ .50	$2.00
					Hunter, Jim	78T	460	$ .45	$1.75
					Hunter, Jim	79T	670	$ .65	$1.50
					Huntz, Steve	69T	136	$ .30	$ .85
					Huntz, Steve	70T	282	$ .15	$ .50
					Huntz, Steve	71T	486	$ .15	$ .50
					Huntz, Steve	72T	73	$ .05	$ .25
					Hurd, Tom	55T	116	$2.00	$6.00
					Hurd, Tom	56T	256	$3.00	$9.00
					Hurdle, Clint	78T	705	$ .02	$ .10
					Hurdle, Clint	79T	547	$ .02	$ .10
					Hurdle, Clint	80T	525	$ .01	$ .10
					Hurdle, Clint	81T	98	$ .01	$ .10
					Hurdle, Clint	82T	297	$ .01	$ .07
					Hurdle, Clint	86T	438	$ .01	$ .04

Hundley, Randy	71T	592	$ .35	$1.25

Player	Year	No.	VG	EX/MT	Player	Year	No.	VG	EX/MT
Hurdle, Clint	87T	317	$ .01	$ .04	Indians, Team Checklist	81T	665	$ .02	$ .20
Hurst, Bruce	81T	689	$ .50	$2.00	Indians, Team Leaders	86T	336	$ .01	$ .04
Hurst, Bruce	82T	381	$ .10	$ .50	Indians, Team Leaders	87T	11	$ .01	$ .04
Hurst, Bruce	83T	82	$ .01	$ .07	Indians, Team Leaders	88T	789	$ .01	$ .04
Hurst, Bruce	84T	213	$ .01	$ .06	Indians, Team Leaders	89T	141	$ .01	$ .05
Hurst, Bruce	85T	451	$ .01	$ .05	Innis, Jeff	88TTR	54	$ .01	$ .15
Hurst, Bruce	86T	581	$ .01	$ .04	Innis, Jeff	90T	557	$ .01	$ .04
Hurst, Bruce	87T	705	$ .01	$ .04	Innis, Jeff	91T	443	$ .01	$ .03
Hurst, Bruce	88T	125	$ .01	$ .04	Iorg, Dane	80T	139	$ .01	$ .10
Hurst, Bruce	89T	675	$ .01	$ .05	Iorg, Dane	81T	334	$ .01	$ .10
Hurst, Bruce	89TTR	55	$ .01	$ .06	Iorg, Dane	82T	86	$ .01	$ .07
Hurst, Bruce	90T	315	$ .01	$ .04	Iorg, Dane	83T	788	$ .01	$ .07
Hurst, Bruce	91T	65	$ .01	$ .03	Iorg, Dane	84T	416	$ .01	$ .06
Huson, Jeff	90T	72	$ .01	$ .10	Iorg, Dane	84TTR	54	$ .02	$ .10
Huson, Jeff	90TTR	45	$ .01	$ .05	Iorg, Dane	85T	671	$ .01	$ .05
Huson, Jeff	91T	756	$ .01	$ .03	Iorg, Dane	86T	269	$ .01	$ .04
Hutchinson, Fred	52T	126	$7.00	$21.00	Iorg, Dane	86TTR	49	$ .02	$ .10
Hutchinson, Fred	53T	72	$5.00	$20.00	Iorg, Dane	87T	690	$ .01	$ .04
Hutchinson, Fred	60T	219	$ .45	$1.45	Iorg, Garth	78T	704	$4.00	$12.00
Hutchinson, Fred	61T	135	$ .35	$1.25	Iorg, Garth	81T	444	$ .01	$ .10
Hutchinson, Fred	62T	172	$ .75	$3.00	Iorg, Garth	82T	518	$ .01	$ .07
Hutchinson, Fred	63T	422	$ .45	$1.45	Iorg, Garth	83T	326	$ .01	$ .07
Hutchinson, Fred	64T	207	$ .30	$ .95	Iorg, Garth	84T	39	$ .01	$ .06
Hutton, Tom	67T	428	$ .30	$ .95	Iorg, Garth	85T	168	$ .01	$ .05
Hutton, Tom	69T	266	$ .30	$ .95	Iorg, Garth	86T	694	$ .01	$ .04
Hutton, Tom	72T	741	$1.25	$4.25	Iorg, Garth	87T	751	$ .01	$ .04
Hutton, Tom	73T	271	$ .07	$ .30	Iorg, Garth	88T	273	$ .01	$ .04
Hutton, Tom	74T	443	$ .07	$ .30	Ireland, Tim	81T	66	$ .01	$ .10
Hutton, Tom	75T	477	$ .07	$ .30	Irvin, Monte	51Trb	50	$3.25	$12.50
Hutton, Tom	76T	91	$ .05	$ .20	Irvin, Monte(y)	52T	26	$27.50	$77.50
Hutton, Tom	77T	264	$ .03	$ .12	Irvin, Monte	53T	62	$7.50	$27.50
Hutton, Tom	78T	568	$ .02	$ .10	Irvin, Monte	54T	3	$5.00	$20.00
Hutton, Tom	79T	673	$ .02	$ .10	Irvin, Monte	55T	100	$3.00	$12.00
Hutton, Tom	80T	427	$ .01	$ .10	Irvin, Monte	56T	194	$7.00	$21.00
Hutton, Tom	81T	374	$ .01	$ .10	Irvine, Daryl	91T	189	$ .01	$ .10
Hyde, Dick	57T	403	$1.25	$4.25	Ivie, Mike	72T	457	$ .05	$ .25
Hyde, Dick	58T	156	$ .75	$3.00	Ivie, Mike	73T	613	$9.00	$35.00
Hyde, Dick	59T	498	$ .75	$2.20	Ivie, Mike	76T	134	$ .05	$ .20
Hyde, Dick	60T	193	$ .45	$1.45	Ivie, Mike	77T	325	$ .03	$ .12
Incaviglia, Pete	86TTR	48	$ .15	$ .75	Ivie, Mike	78T	445	$ .02	$ .10
Incaviglia, Pete	87T	550	$ .10	$ .50	Ivie, Mike	79T	538	$ .02	$ .10
Incaviglia, Pete	88T	280	$ .01	$ .20	Ivie, Mike	80T	62	$ .01	$ .10
Incaviglia, Pete	88TBB	73	$ .01	$ .06	Ivie, Mike	81T	236	$ .01	$ .10
Incaviglia, Pete	89T	706	$ .01	$ .05	Ivie, Mike	81TTR	774	$ .02	$ .10
Incaviglia, Pete	89TBB	127	$ .01	$ .10	Ivie, Mike	82T	734	$ .01	$ .07
Incaviglia, Pete	90T	430	$ .01	$ .04	Ivie, Mike	82TTR	45	$ .02	$ .10
Incaviglia, Pete	91T	172	$ .01	$ .03	Ivie, Mike	83T	613	$ .01	$ .07
Indians, Team	56T	85	$3.25	$9.50	Jablonski, Ray	53T	189	$4.50	$15.00
Indians, Team	57T	275	$10.00	$30.00	Jablonski, Ray	54T	26	$3.60	$10.00
Indians, Team	58T	158	$2.00	$7.50	Jablonski, Ray	55T	56	$2.00	$6.00
Indians, Team	59T	476	$2.00	$7.50	Jablonski, Ray	56T	86	$2.25	$6.00
Indians, Team	60T	174	$1.75	$5.50	Jablonski, Ray	57T	218	$ .95	$3.50
Indians, Team	61T	467	$2.25	$6.00	Jablonski, Ray	58T	362	$ .75	$3.00
Indians, Team	62T	537	$9.00	$30.00	Jablonski, Ray	59T	342	$ .75	$2.20
Indians, Team	63T	451	$2.50	$8.50	Jackson, Al	62T	464	$1.25	$4.25
Indians, Team	64T	172	$1.25	$4.25	Jackson, Al	63T	111	$ .30	$ .95
Indians, Team	65T	481	$1.75	$4.50	Jackson, Al	64T	494	$ .50	$1.45
Indians, Team	66T	303	$ .75	$2.00	Jackson, Al	65T	381	$ .35	$1.25
Indians, Team	67T	544	$4.00	$13.00	Jackson, Al	66T	206	$ .30	$ .95
Indians, Team	70T	637	$1.00	$3.00	Jackson, Al	67T	195	$ .30	$ .85
Indians, Team	71T	584	$ .90	$3.00	Jackson, Al	68T	503	$ .35	$1.25
Indians, Team	72T	547	$ .75	$3.00	Jackson, Al	69T	649	$ .30	$ .95
Indians, Team	73T	629	$ .90	$3.00	Jackson, Al	70T	443	$ .15	$ .50
Indians, Team	74T	541	$ .15	$ .50	Jackson, Bo	86TTR	50	$1.50	$8.00
Indians, Team Checklist	75T	331	$ .35	$1.25	Jackson, Bo	87T	170	$ .75	$3.00
Indians, Team Checklist	76T	477	$ .35	$1.25	Jackson, Bo	88T	750	$ .15	$1.00
Indians, Team Checklist	77T	18	$ .03	$ .60	Jackson, Bo	88TBB	49	$ .15	$ .75
Indians, Team Checklist	78T	689	$ .05	$ .25	Jackson, Bo	89T	540	$ .05	$ .50
Indians, Team Checklist	79T	96	$ .05	$ .25	Jackson, Bo	89TBB	238	$ .01	$ .50
Indians, Team Checklist	80T	451	$ .05	$ .25	Jackson, Bo	90T	300	$ .01	$ .25

TOPPS

Player	Year	No.	VG	EX/MT	Player	Year	No.	VG	EX/MT
Jackson, Bo	91T	600	$ .01	$ .20	Jackson, Larry	60T	492	$ .90	$3.00
Jackson, Chuck	88T	94	$ .01	$ .15	Jackson, Larry	61T	75	$ .75	$3.00
Jackson, Danny	87TTR	51	$ .15	$ .50	Jackson, Larry	61T	535	$7.00	$21.00
Jackson, Danny	88T	324	$ .01	$ .10	Jackson, Larry	62T	83	$ .45	$1.45
Jackson, Danny	88TTR	55	$ .01	$ .15	Jackson, Larry	62T	306	$ .75	$3.00
Jackson, Danny	89T	730	$ .01	$ .10	Jackson, Larry	63T	95	$ .30	$ .95
Jackson, Danny	89TAS	395	$ .01	$ .05	Jackson, Larry	64T	444	$ .50	$1.45
Jackson, Danny	90T	445	$ .01	$ .04	Jackson, Larry	65T	10	$ .45	$1.45
Jackson, Danny	91T	92	$ .01	$ .03	Jackson, Larry	65T	420	$ .35	$1.25
					Jackson, Larry	66T	595	$5.00	$20.00
					Jackson, Larry	67T	229	$ .30	$ .85
					Jackson, Larry	68T	81	$ .30	$ .85
					Jackson, Lou	59T	130	$ .75	$2.20
					Jackson, Lou	64T	511	$ .50	$1.45
					Jackson, Mike	88T	651	$ .01	$ .04
					Jackson, Mike	89T	169	$ .01	$ .05
					Jackson, Mike	90T	761	$ .01	$ .04
					Jackson, Mike	91T	534	$ .01	$ .03
					Jackson, Randy	52T	322	$40.00	$140.00
					Jackson, Randy	56T	223	$3.00	$9.00
					Jackson, Randy	57T	190	$ .95	$3.50
					Jackson, Randy	58T	301	$ .75	$3.00
					Jackson, Randy	59T	394	$ .75	$2.20
					Jackson, Reggie	69T	260	$115.00	$425.00
					Jackson, Reggie	70T	64	$ .50	$1.50
					Jackson, Reggie	70T	66	$ .50	$1.50
					Jackson, Reggie	70T	140	$30.00	$90.00
					Jackson, Reggie	70TAS	459	$3.75	$13.50
					Jackson, Reggie	71T	20	$12.50	$52.50
					Jackson, Reggie	72T	90	$ .75	$3.00
					Jackson, Reggie	72T	435	$10.00	$30.00
					Jackson, Reggie	72TIA	436	$3.00	$12.00
					Jackson, Reggie	73T	255	$4.00	$20.00
					Jackson, Reggie	74T	130	$3.50	$15.00
					Jackson, Reggie	74T	202	$ .60	$2.00
					Jackson, Reggie	74T	203	$ .60	$2.00
					Jackson, Reggie	74TAS	338	$ .45	$1.45
					Jackson, Reggie	75T	211	$ .75	$3.00
					Jackson, Reggie	75T	300	$3.25	$13.00
Jackson, Darrell	79T	246	$ .02	$ .10	Jackson, Reggie	76T	194	$ .75	$2.20
Jackson, Darrell	80T	386	$ .01	$ .10	Jackson, Reggie	76T	500	$2.50	$10.00
Jackson, Darrell	81T	89	$ .01	$ .10	Jackson, Reggie	77T	10	$2.25	$9.00
Jackson, Darrell	82T	193	$ .01	$ .07	Jackson, Reggie	78T	200	$1.00	$4.00
Jackson, Darrin	88TTR	56	$ .05	$ .25	Jackson, Reggie	78T	413	$ .50	$2.00
Jackson, Darrin	89T	286	$ .01	$ .15	Jackson, Reggie	78TRB	7	$ .50	$2.00
Jackson, Darrin	90T	624	$ .01	$ .04	Jackson, Reggie	79T	700	$ .50	$2.00
Jackson, Darrin	91T	373	$ .01	$ .03	Jackson, Reggie	80T	600	$ .70	$2.25
Jackson, Grant	66T	591	$5.00	$20.00	Jackson, Reggie	81T	2	$ .06	$ .40
Jackson, Grant	67T	402	$ .30	$ .95	Jackson, Reggie	81T	400	$ .50	$2.00
Jackson, Grant	68T	512	$ .35	$1.25	Jackson, Reggie	82T	300	$ .45	$1.50
Jackson, Grant	69T	174	$ .30	$ .85	Jackson, Reggie	82TAS	551	$ .30	$ .85
Jackson, Grant	70T	6	$ .15	$ .50	Jackson, Reggie	82TIA	301	$ .15	$ .50
Jackson, Grant	71T	392	$ .15	$ .50	Jackson, Reggie	82TTR	47	$1.50	$5.00
Jackson, Grant	72T	212	$ .05	$ .25	Jackson, Reggie	83T	500	$ .25	$1.00
Jackson, Grant	73T	396	$ .07	$ .30	Jackson, Reggie	83T	501	$ .06	$ .30
Jackson, Grant	74T	68	$ .07	$ .30	Jackson, Reggie	83T	702	$ .01	$ .07
Jackson, Grant	75T	303	$ .07	$ .30	Jackson, Reggie	83TAS	390	$ .06	$ .30
Jackson, Grant	76T	233	$ .05	$ .20	Jackson, Reggie	84T	100	$ .15	$ .75
Jackson, Grant	77T	49	$ .03	$ .12	Jackson, Reggie	84T	711	$ .04	$ .20
Jackson, Grant	78T	661	$ .02	$ .10	Jackson, Reggie	84T	712	$ .03	$ .15
Jackson, Grant	79T	117	$ .02	$ .10	Jackson, Reggie	84T	713	$ .03	$ .15
Jackson, Grant	80T	426	$ .01	$ .10	Jackson, Reggie	85T	200	$ .09	$ .50
Jackson, Grant	81T	518	$ .01	$ .10	Jackson, Reggie	86T	700	$ .04	$ .50
Jackson, Grant	82T	779	$ .01	$ .07	Jackson, Reggie	87T	300	$ .15	$ .50
Jackson, Grant	82TTR	46	$ .02	$ .10	Jackson, Reggie	87TTB	312	$ .03	$ .15
Jackson, Jeff	90T	74	$ .01	$ .25	Jackson, Reggie	87TTR	52	$ .15	$ .50
Jackson, Larry	56T	119	$1.50	$4.50	Jackson, Ron	55T	66	$2.00	$6.00
Jackson, Larry	57T	196	$ .95	$3.50	Jackson, Ron	56T	186	$3.00	$9.00
Jackson, Larry	58T	97	$1.25	$4.25	Jackson, Ron	58T	26	$1.25	$4.25
Jackson, Larry	59T	399	$ .75	$2.20	Jackson, Ron	59T	73	$1.25	$4.25

DARRELL JACKSON P
TWINS

Player	Year	No.	VG	EX/MT	Player	Year	No.	VG	EX/MT
Jackson, Ron	60T	426	$ .75	$2.20	James, Dion	90T	319	$ .01	$ .04
Jackson, Ron	77T	153	$ .03	$ .12	James, Dion	91T	117	$ .01	$ .03
Jackson, Ron	78T	718	$ .02	$ .10	James, Jeff	69T	477	$ .30	$ .85
Jackson, Ron	79T	339	$ .02	$ .10	James, Jeff	70T	302	$ .15	$ .50
Jackson, Ron	80T	18	$ .01	$ .10	James, Johnny	60T	499	$ .90	$3.00
Jackson, Ron	81T	631	$ .01	$ .10	James, Johnny	61T	457	$ .75	$3.00
Jackson, Ron	82T	488	$ .01	$ .07	Janeski, Gerry	71T	673	$ .75	$2.50
Jackson, Ron	82TTR	48	$ .02	$ .10	Janowicz, Vic	53T	222	$15.00	$47.50
Jackson, Ron	83T	262	$ .01	$ .07	Janowicz, Vic	54T	16	$2.50	$10.00
Jackson, Ron	84T	548	$ .01	$ .06	Jansen, Larry	51Trb	21	$1.50	$4.00
Jackson, Roy Lee	81T	223	$ .01	$ .10	Jansen, Larry	52T	5	$15.00	$47.50
Jackson, Roy Lee	81TTR	775	$ .02	$ .10	Jansen, Larry	54T	200	$3.60	$10.00
Jackson, Roy Lee	82T	71	$ .01	$ .07	Jansen, Larry	73T	81	$ .30	$ .95
Jackson, Roy Lee	83T	427	$ .01	$ .07	Jarvis, Pat	67T	57	$ .30	$ .85
Jackson, Roy Lee	84T	339	$ .01	$ .06	Jarvis, Pat	68T	134	$ .30	$ .85
Jackson, Roy Lee	85T	516	$ .01	$ .05	Jarvis, Pat	69T	282	$ .30	$ .95
Jackson, Roy Lee	86T	634	$ .01	$ .04	Jarvis, Pat	70T	438	$ .15	$ .50
Jackson, Roy Lee	87T	138	$ .01	$ .04	Jarvis, Pat	71T	623	$ .35	$1.25
Jackson, Sonny	65T	16	$40.00	$160.00	Jarvis, Pat	72T	675	$ .75	$2.50
Jackson, Sonny	66T	244	$ .30	$ .95	Jarvis, Pat	73T	192	$ .07	$ .30
Jackson, Sonny	67T	415	$ .30	$ .95	Jarvis, Ray	70T	361	$ .15	$ .50
Jackson, Sonny	68T	187	$ .30	$ .85	Jarvis, Ray	71T	526	$ .35	$1.25
Jackson, Sonny	69T	53	$ .30	$ .85	Jaster, Larry	67T	356	$ .30	$ .85
Jackson, Sonny	70T	413	$ .15	$ .50	Jaster, Larry	68T	117	$ .30	$ .85
Jackson, Sonny	71T	587	$ .35	$1.25	Jaster, Larry	69T	496	$ .30	$ .85
Jackson, Sonny	72T	318	$ .05	$ .25	Jaster, Larry	70T	124	$ .15	$ .50
Jackson, Sonny	73T	403	$ .07	$ .30	Jata, Paul	72T	257	$ .15	$ .50
Jackson, Sonny	74T	591	$ .07	$ .30	Javier, Manuel "Julian"	60T	133	$ .75	$3.00
Jacobs, Forrest "Spook"	54T	129	$3.60	$10.00	Javier, Julian	61T	148	$ .35	$1.25
Jacobs, Spook	55T	61	$2.00	$6.00	Javier, Julian	62T	118	$ .45	$1.45
Jacobs, Spook	56T	151	$2.25	$6.00	Javier, Julian	63T	226	$ .30	$ .95
Jacobs, Tony	55T	183	$5.25	$15.00	Javier, Julian	64T	446	$ .50	$1.45
Jacoby, Brook	84TTR	55	$ .20	$1.00	Javier, Julian	65T	447	$ .75	$3.00
Jacoby, Brook	85T	327	$ .01	$ .10	Javier, Julian	66T	436	$ .30	$ .95
Jacoby, Brook	86T	116	$ .01	$ .04	Javier, Julian	67T	226	$ .30	$ .85
Jacoby, Brook	87T	405	$ .01	$ .10	Javier, Julian	68T	25	$ .30	$ .85
Jacoby, Brook	88T	555	$ .01	$ .04	Javier, Julian	69T	497	$ .30	$ .85
Jacoby, Brook	88TBB	17	$ .01	$ .06	Javier, Julian	70T	415	$ .15	$ .50
Jacoby, Brook	89T	739	$ .01	$ .05	Javier, Julian	71T	185	$ .15	$ .50
Jacoby, Brook	89TBB	195	$ .01	$ .06	Javier, Julian	72T	745	$ .75	$2.50
Jacoby, Brook	90T	208	$ .01	$ .04	Javier, Stan	87T	263	$ .01	$ .04
Jacoby, Brook	91T	47	$ .01	$ .03	Javier, Stan	89T	622	$ .01	$ .05
Jaeckel, Paul	65T	386	$ .35	$1.25	Javier, Stan	89TBB	277	$ .01	$ .06
James, Bob	84T	579	$ .02	$ .10	Javier, Stan	90T	102	$ .01	$ .04
James, Bob	85T	114	$ .01	$ .05	Javier, Stan	90TTR	47	$ .01	$ .05
James, Bob	85TTR	61	$ .02	$ .10	Javier, Stan	91T	61	$ .01	$ .03
James, Bob	86T	467	$ .01	$ .04	Jay, Joe	54T	141	$2.50	$10.00
James, Bob	87T	342	$ .01	$ .04	Jay, Joe	55T	134	$2.00	$6.00
James, Bob	88T	232	$ .01	$ .04	Jay, Joe	58T	472	$ .75	$2.20
James, Charley	60T	517	$2.50	$10.00	Jay, Joe	59T	273	$ .75	$2.20
James, Charley	61T	561	$7.00	$21.00	Jay, Joe	60T	266	$ .45	$1.45
James, Charlie	62T	412	$ .75	$2.50	Jay, Joe	61T	233	$ .35	$1.25
James, Charley	63T	83	$ .30	$ .95	Jay, Joe	62T	58	$ .75	$2.20
James, Charley	64T	357	$ .30	$ .95	Jay, Joe	62T	263	$ .75	$3.00
James, Charlie	65T	141	$ .30	$ .85	Jay, Joe	62T	440	$ .75	$2.50
James, Chris	87TTR	53	$ .03	$ .15	Jay, Joe	63T	7	$ .45	$1.45
James, Chris	88T	572	$ .01	$ .10	Jay, Joe	63T	225	$ .30	$ .95
James, Chris	89T	298	$ .01	$ .05	Jay, Joe	64T	346	$ .30	$ .95
James, Chris	89TTR	56	$ .01	$ .06	Jay, Joe	65T	174	$ .30	$ .85
James, Chris	90T	178	$ .01	$ .04	Jay, Joe	66T	406	$ .30	$ .95
James, Chris	90TTR	46	$ .01	$ .05	Jeffcoat, Hal	52T	341	$40.00	$140.00
James, Chris	91T	494	$ .01	$ .03	Jeffcoat, Hal	53T	29	$4.50	$15.00
James, Cleo	72T	117	$ .05	$ .25	Jeffcoat, Hal	56T	289	$2.25	$8.00
James, Dion	85T	228	$ .01	$ .05	Jeffcoat, Hal	57T	93	$ .95	$3.50
James, Dion	86T	76	$ .01	$ .04	Jeffcoat, Hal	58T	294	$ .75	$3.00
James, Dion	87TTR	54	$ .03	$ .15	Jeffcoat, Hal	59T	81	$1.25	$4.25
James, Dion	88T	408	$ .01	$ .04	Jeffcoat, Mike	84TTR	56	$ .02	$ .10
James, Dion	88TBB	220	$ .01	$ .06	Jeffcoat, Mike	85T	303	$ .01	$ .05
James, Dion	89T	678	$ .01	$ .05	Jeffcoat, Mike	86T	571	$ .01	$ .04
James, Dion	89TBB	223	$ .01	$ .06	Jeffcoat, Mike	90T	778	$ .01	$ .04

TOPPS

Player	Year	No.	VG	EX/MT	Player	Year	No.	VG	EX/MT
Jeffcoat, Mike	91T	244	$ .01	$ .03	Jensen, Jackie	57T	220	$ .60	$2.50
Jefferies, Gregg	89T	233	$ .25	$1.00	Jensen, Jackie	58T	130	$1.25	$4.00
Jefferies, Gregg	89TBB	253	$ .01	$ .50	Jensen, Jackie	58TAS	489	$ .70	$2.25
Jefferies, Gregg	90T	457	$ .01	$ .25	Jensen, Jackie	59T	400	$ .90	$3.00
Jefferies, Gregg	91T	30	$ .01	$ .15	Jensen, Jackie	61T	173	$ .75	$3.00
Jefferson, Jesse	73T	604	$ .45	$1.45	Jensen, Jackie	61T	540	$7.00	$20.00
Jefferson, Jesse	74T	509	$ .07	$ .30	Jensen, Jackie	61TMVP	476	$ .75	$2.00
Jefferson, Jesse	75T	539	$ .07	$ .30	Jensen, Jackie	75T	196	$ .35	$1.25
Jefferson, Jesse	76T	47	$ .05	$ .20	Jernigan, Pete	63T	253	$ .30	$ .95
Jefferson, Jesse	77T	326	$ .03	$ .12	Jestadt, Garry	70T	109	$ .15	$ .50
Jefferson, Jesse	78T	144	$ .02	$ .10	Jestadt, Garry	71T	576	$ .35	$1.25
Jefferson, Jesse	79T	221	$ .02	$ .10	Jestadt, Garry	72T	143	$ .05	$ .25
Jefferson, Jesse	80T	467	$ .01	$ .10	Jeter, Johnny	70T	141	$ .30	$ .95
Jefferson, Jesse	82T	682	$ .01	$ .07	Jeter, Johnny	71T	47	$ .15	$ .50
Jefferson, Stan	87TTR	55	$ .05	$ .20	Jeter, Johnny	72T	288	$ .05	$ .25
Jefferson, Stan	88T	223	$ .01	$ .04	Jeter, Johnny	73T	423	$ .07	$ .30
Jefferson, Stan	88TBB	86	$ .01	$ .06	Jeter, Johnny	74T	615	$ .07	$ .30
Jefferson, Stan	89T	689	$ .01	$ .05	Jethroe, Sam	51Tbb	12	$7.50	$22.50
Jefferson, Stan	89TBB	165	$ .01	$ .06	Jethroe, Sam	52T	27	$15.00	$47.50
Jeltz, Steve	85TTR	62	$ .02	$ .10	Jimenez, E. Manny	62T	598	$18.00	$55.00
Jeltz, Steve	86T	453	$ .01	$ .04	Jimenez, E. Manny	63T	195	$ .30	$ .95
Jeltz, Steve	87T	294	$ .01	$ .04	Jimenez, E. Manny	64T	574	$1.75	$4.50
Jeltz, Steve	88T	126	$ .01	$ .04	Jimenez, Elvio "Manny"	65T	226	$ .45	$1.45
Jeltz, Steve	89T	707	$ .01	$ .05	Jimenez, E. Manny	66T	458	$ .75	$2.50
Jeltz, Steve	89TBB	52	$ .01	$ .06	Jimenez, E. Manny	67T	586	$3.00	$9.00
Jeltz, Steve	90T	607	$ .01	$ .04	Jimenez, E. Manny	68T	538	$ .35	$1.25
Jeltz, Steve	91T	507	$ .01	$ .03	Jimenez, Elvio	69T	567	$ .30	$ .95
Jenkins, Ferguson	66T	254	$20.00	$85.00	Jimenez, German	89T	569	$ .01	$ .10
Jenkins, Ferguson	67T	333	$5.50	$18.00	Jimenez, Houston	84T	411	$ .01	$ .06
Jenkins, Ferguson	68T	9	$ .75	$2.20	Jimenez, Houston	85T	562	$ .01	$ .05
Jenkins, Ferguson	68T	11	$ .75	$2.20	John, Tommy	64T	146	$20.00	$60.00
Jenkins, Ferguson "Fergie"	68T	410	$3.00	$9.00	John, Tommy	65T	208	$3.00	$10.00
Jenkins, Fergie	69T	10	$ .75	$3.00	John, Tommy	66T	486	$3.50	$12.50
Jenkins, Fergie	69T	12	$ .50	$1.50	John, Tommy	67T	609	$25.00	$100.00
Jenkins, Fergie	69T	640	$ .65	$1.75	John, Tommy	68T	72	$1.75	$4.50
Jenkins, Fergie	70T	69	$ .75	$2.20	John, Tommy	69T	465	$ .95	$3.50
Jenkins, Fergie	70T	71	$ .50	$1.50	John, Tommy	70T	180	$ .75	$2.25
Jenkins, Fergie	70T	240	$1.00	$4.00	John, Tommy	71T	520	$ .75	$2.25
Jenkins, Fergie	71T	70	$ .50	$2.50	John, Tommy	72T	264	$ .35	$1.50
Jenkins, Fergie	71T	72	$ .50	$2.50	John, Tommy	73T	258	$ .75	$3.00
Jenkins, Fergie	71T	280	$1.50	$6.00	John, Tommy	74T	451	$ .45	$1.45
Jenkins, Fergie	72T	93	$ .50	$2.00	John, Tommy	75T	47	$ .45	$1.45
Jenkins, Fergie	72T	95	$ .45	$1.45	John, Tommy	76T	416	$ .45	$1.45
Jenkins, Fergie	72T	410	$1.00	$4.00	John, Tommy	77T	128	$ .35	$1.25
Jenkins, Fergie	73T	180	$1.75	$5.00	John, Tommy	78T	375	$ .15	$ .75
Jenkins, Fergie	74T	87	$1.00	$4.00	John, Tommy	79T	255	$ .25	$1.00
Jenkins, Fergie	75T	60	$ .60	$2.50	John, Tommy	80T	690	$ .10	$ .50
Jenkins, Fergie	75T	310	$ .35	$1.25	John, Tommy	81T	550	$ .05	$ .25
Jenkins, Fergie	76T	250	$ .75	$3.00	John, Tommy	82T	75	$ .05	$ .25
Jenkins, Fergie	76TTR	250	$ .15	$ .50	John, Tommy	82T	486	$ .03	$ .15
Jenkins, Fergie	77T	430	$ .15	$ .50	John, Tommy	83T	735	$ .01	$ .07
Jenkins, Fergie	78T	720	$ .30	$ .95	John, Tommy	83T	736	$ .01	$ .07
Jenkins, Fergie	79T	544	$ .05	$ .25	John, Tommy	84T	415	$ .05	$ .20
Jenkins, Fergie	80T	390	$ .30	$ .95	John, Tommy	84T	715	$ .04	$ .20
Jenkins, Fergie	81T	158	$ .05	$ .20	John, Tommy	85T	179	$ .04	$ .20
Jenkins, Fergie	82T	624	$ .05	$ .20	John, Tommy	86T	240	$ .01	$ .10
Jenkins, Fergie	82TTR	49	$ .30	$ .85	John, Tommy	87T	236	$ .01	$ .10
Jenkins, Fergie	83T	51	$ .01	$ .07	John, Tommy	88T	611	$ .01	$ .10
Jenkins, Fergie	83T	230	$ .01	$ .20	John, Tommy	89T	359	$ .01	$ .05
Jenkins, Fergie	83T	231	$ .01	$ .07	Johnson, Alex	65T	352	$ .35	$1.25
Jenkins, Fergie	84T	456	$ .01	$ .06	Johnson, Alex	66T	104	$ .15	$ .50
Jenkins, Fergie	84T	483	$ .05	$ .20	Johnson, Alex	67T	108	$ .30	$ .85
Jenkins, Fergie	84T	706	$ .05	$ .25	Johnson, Alex	68T	441	$ .30	$ .85
Jenkins, Jack	70T	286	$2.10	$6.00	Johnson, Alex	69T	280	$ .30	$ .95
Jennings, Doug	89T	166	$ .01	$ .15	Johnson, Alex	70T	115	$ .15	$ .50
Jensen, Jack	52T	122	$17.50	$60.00	Johnson, Alex	71T	61	$ .75	$2.20
Jensen, Jackie	53T	265	$30.00	$125.00	Johnson, Alex	71T	590	$ .35	$1.25
Jensen, Jackie	54T	80	$4.25	$15.00	Johnson, Alex	72T	215	$ .05	$ .25
Jensen, Jackie	55T	200	$10.00	$42.50	Johnson, Alex	73T	425	$ .07	$ .30
Jensen, Jackie	56T	115	$1.50	$6.00	Johnson, Alex	74T	107	$ .07	$ .30

Player	Year	No.	VG	EX/MT	Player	Year	No.	VG	EX/MT
Johnson, Alex	75T	534	$ .07	$ .30	Johnson, Dave	73T	550	$ .90	$3.00
Johnson, Alex	77T	637	$ .03	$ .12	Johnson, Dave	74T	45	$ .30	$ .95
Johnson, Bart	70T	669	$ .75	$2.00	Johnson, Dave	75T	57	$ .30	$ .95
Johnson, Bart	71T	156	$ .15	$ .50	Johnson, Dave	77T	478	$ .03	$ .12
Johnson, Bart	72T	126	$ .05	$ .25	Johnson, Dave	78T	317	$ .05	$ .20
Johnson, Bart	73T	506	$ .07	$ .30	Johnson, Dave	78T	627	$ .02	$ .10
Johnson, Bart	74T	147	$ .07	$ .30	Johnson, Dave	79T	513	$ .05	$ .20
Johnson, Bart	75T	446	$ .07	$ .30	Johnson, Dave	84TTR	57	$ .02	$ .10
Johnson, Bart	76T	513	$ .05	$ .20	Johnson, Dave	85T	492	$ .01	$ .05
Johnson, Bart	77T	177	$ .03	$ .12	Johnson, Dave	86T	501	$ .01	$ .04
Johnson, Ben	60T	528	$2.50	$10.00	Johnson, Dave	87T	543	$ .01	$ .04
Johnson, Billy	51Tbb	21	$7.50	$22.50	Johnson, Dave	88T	164	$ .01	$ .04
Johnson, Billy	52T	83	$7.00	$20.00	Johnson, Dave	89T	684	$ .01	$ .05
Johnson, Billy	53T	21	$4.50	$15.00	Johnson, Dave	90T	291	$ .01	$ .04
Johnson, Bob D.	71T	71	$ .15	$ .50	Johnson, Dave	90T	416	$ .01	$ .04
Johnson, Bob D.	71T	365	$ .15	$ .50	Johnson, Dave	91T	163	$ .01	$ .03
Johnson, Bob D.	72T	27	$ .05	$ .25	Johnson, Deron	59T	131	$ .90	$2.75
Johnson, Bob D.	73T	657	$ .45	$1.45	Johnson, Deron	60T	134	$ .90	$3.00
Johnson, Bob D.	74T	269	$ .07	$ .30	Johnson, Deron	61T	68	$ .35	$1.25
Johnson, Bob D.	74TTR	269	$ .07	$ .30	Johnson, Deron	62T	82	$ .45	$1.45
Johnson, Bob W.	62T	519	$ .75	$2.50	Johnson, Deron	64T	449	$ .50	$1.45
Johnson, Bob W.	63T	504	$2.50	$6.50	Johnson, Deron	65T	75	$ .30	$ .85
Johnson, Bob W.	64T	304	$ .30	$ .95	Johnson, Deron	66T	219	$ .65	$1.75
Johnson, Bob W.	65T	363	$ .35	$1.25	Johnson, Deron	66T	440	$ .30	$ .95
Johnson, Bob W.	66T	148	$ .30	$ .95	Johnson, Deron	67T	135	$ .30	$ .85
Johnson, Bob W.	67T	38	$ .30	$ .85	Johnson, Deron	68T	323	$ .30	$ .85
Johnson, Bob W.	68T	338	$ .30	$ .85					
Johnson, Bob W.	69T	261	$ .30	$ .95					
Johnson, Bob W.	70T	693	$ .75	$2.00					
Johnson, Bob W.	70T	702	$ .75	$2.00					
Johnson, Bobby	82T	418	$ .03	$ .15					
Johnson, Bobby	83TTR	48	$ .02	$ .10					
Johnson, Bobby	84T	608	$ .01	$ .06					
Johnson, Cliff	75T	143	$ .07	$ .30					
Johnson, Cliff	76T	249	$ .05	$ .20					
Johnson, Cliff	77T	514	$ .03	$ .12					
Johnson, Cliff	78T	309	$ .02	$ .10					
Johnson, Cliff	79T	114	$ .02	$ .10					
Johnson, Cliff	80T	612	$ .01	$ .10					
Johnson, Cliff	81T	17	$ .01	$ .10					
Johnson, Cliff	81TTR	776	$ .02	$ .10					
Johnson, Cliff	82T	422	$ .01	$ .07					
Johnson, Cliff	83T	762	$ .01	$ .07					
Johnson, Cliff	83TTR	49	$ .02	$ .10					
Johnson, Cliff	84T	221	$ .01	$ .06					
Johnson, Cliff	85T	568	$ .01	$ .05					
Johnson, Cliff	85TRB	4	$ .01	$ .05					
Johnson, Cliff	85TTR	63	$ .02	$ .10					
Johnson, Cliff	86T	348	$ .01	$ .04					
Johnson, Cliff	87T	663	$ .01	$ .04					
Johnson, Connie	56T	326	$2.25	$8.00					
Johnson, Connie	57T	43	$ .95	$3.50					
Johnson, Connie	58T	266	$ .75	$3.00					
Johnson, Connie	59T	21	$1.25	$4.25					
Johnson, Darrell	57T	306	$4.25	$15.00					
Johnson, Darrell	58T	61	$1.25	$4.25					
Johnson, Darrell	59T	533	$3.00	$9.00	Johnson, Deron	69T	297	$ .30	$ .95
Johnson, Darrell	60T	263	$ .45	$1.45	Johnson, Deron	70T	125	$ .15	$ .50
Johnson, Darrell	62T	16	$ .45	$1.45	Johnson, Deron	71T	490	$ .15	$ .50
Johnson, Darrell	74T	403	$ .07	$ .30	Johnson, Deron	72T	167	$ .05	$ .25
Johnson, Darrell	78T	79	$ .02	$ .10	Johnson, Deron	72TIA	168	$ .05	$ .25
Johnson, Darrell	83T	37	$ .01	$ .07	Johnson, Deron	73T	590	$ .45	$1.45
Johnson, Dave	65T	473	$2.25	$9.00	Johnson, Deron	74T	312	$ .07	$ .30
Johnson, Dave	66T	579	$5.00	$20.00	Johnson, Deron	76T	529	$ .05	$ .20
Johnson, Dave	67T	363	$ .35	$1.25	Johnson, Don	52T	190	$7.00	$20.00
Johnson, Dave	68T	273	$ .45	$1.45	Johnson, Don	54T	146	$3.60	$10.00
Johnson, Dave	69T	203	$ .75	$3.00	Johnson, Don	55T	165	$5.25	$15.00
Johnson, Dave	70T	45	$ .45	$1.45	Johnson, Ernie	56T	294	$2.25	$8.00
Johnson, Dave	71T	595	$ .35	$1.25	Johnson, Ernie	57T	333	$4.25	$15.00
Johnson, Dave	72T	680	$1.75	$4.50	Johnson, Ernie	58T	78	$1.25	$4.25

TOPPS

Player	Year	No.	VG	EX/MT	Player	Year	No.	VG	EX/MT
Johnson, Ernie	59T	279	$ .75	$2.20	Johnson, Randy S.	83T	354	$ .01	$ .07
Johnson, Ernie	60T	228	$ .45	$1.45	Johnson, Randy S.	84T	289	$ .01	$ .06
Johnson, Frank	69T	227	$ .30	$ .95	Johnson, Randy S.	85T	458	$ .01	$ .05
Johnson, Frank	71T	128	$ .15	$ .50	Johnson, Tim	74T	554	$ .07	$ .30
Johnson, Howard	85T	192	$1.00	$4.00	Johnson, Tim	75T	556	$ .07	$ .30
Johnson, Howard	85TTR	64	$ .50	$2.00	Johnson, Tim	76T	613	$ .05	$ .20
Johnson, Howard	86T	751	$ .10	$ .45	Johnson, Tim	77T	406	$ .03	$ .12
Johnson, Howard	87T	267	$ .05	$ .25	Johnson, Tim	78T	542	$ .02	$ .10
Johnson, Howard	88T	85	$ .01	$ .10	Johnson, Tim	79T	182	$ .02	$ .10
Johnson, Howard	88TBB	129	$ .05	$ .25	Johnson, Tim	80T	297	$ .01	$ .10
Johnson, Howard	89T	383	$ .01	$ .20	Johnson, Tom	75T	618	$ .90	$3.00
Johnson, Howard	89TBB	208	$ .01	$ .15	Johnson, Tom	76T	448	$ .05	$ .20
Johnson, Howard	90T	680	$ .01	$ .10	Johnson, Tom	77T	202	$ .03	$ .12
Johnson, Howard	90TAS	399	$ .01	$ .10	Johnson, Tom	78T	54	$ .02	$ .10
Johnson, Howard	91T	470	$ .01	$ .03	Johnson, Tom	79T	162	$ .02	$ .10
Johnson, Jerry	69T	253	$ .30	$ .95	Johnson, Wallace	87T	588	$ .01	$ .04
Johnson, Jerry	70T	162	$ .15	$ .50	Johnson, Wallace	88T	228	$ .01	$ .04
Johnson, Jerry	71T	412	$ .15	$ .50	Johnson, Wallace	89T	138	$ .01	$ .05
Johnson, Jerry	72T	35	$ .05	$ .25	Johnson, Wallace	90T	318	$ .01	$ .04
Johnson, Jerry	72TIA	36	$ .05	$ .25	Johnson, Walter	61T	409	$ .75	$2.25
Johnson, Jerry	73T	248	$ .07	$ .30	Johnson, Walter	73TATL	476	$ .75	$3.00
Johnson, Jerry	75T	218	$ .07	$ .30	Johnson, Walter	73TATL	478	$ .75	$3.00
Johnson, Jerry	76T	658	$ .05	$ .20	Johnson, Walter	76TAS	349	$ .75	$3.00
Johnson, Jerry	78T	169	$ .02	$ .10	Johnson, Walter	79TRH	417	$ .05	$ .20
Johnson, Joe	87TTR	56	$ .01	$ .05	Johnson, Walter	79TRH	418	$ .02	$ .10
Johnson, Joe	88T	347	$ .01	$ .04	Johnston, Greg	79T	726	$ .05	$ .20
Johnson, John Henry	79T	681	$ .02	$ .10	Johnston, Greg	80T	686	$ .01	$ .10
Johnson, John Henry	80T	173	$ .01	$ .10	Johnston, Greg	81T	328	$ .01	$ .10
Johnson, John Henry	81T	216	$ .01	$ .10	Johnstone, Jay	67T	213	$ .35	$1.25
Johnson, John Henry	82T	527	$ .01	$ .07	Johnstone, Jay	68T	389	$ .30	$ .85
Johnson, John Henry	84T	419	$ .01	$ .06	Johnstone, Jay	69T	59	$ .30	$ .85
Johnson, John Henry	85T	734	$ .01	$ .05	Johnstone, Jay	70T	485	$ .15	$ .50
Johnson, John Henry	87T	377	$ .01	$ .04	Johnstone, Jay	71T	292	$ .15	$ .50
Johnson, Ken	60T	135	$ .45	$1.45	Johnstone, Jay	72T	233	$ .07	$ .30
Johnson, Ken	61T	24	$ .35	$1.25	Johnstone, Jay	75T	242	$ .07	$ .30
Johnson, Ken	62T	278	$ .45	$1.45	Johnstone, Jay	76T	114	$ .05	$ .20
Johnson, Ken	63T	352	$ .45	$1.50	Johnstone, Jay	77T	415	$ .03	$ .12
Johnson, Ken	64T	158	$ .30	$ .95	Johnstone, Jay	78T	675	$ .02	$ .10
Johnson, Ken	65T	359	$ .35	$1.25	Johnstone, Jay	79T	558	$ .02	$ .10
Johnson, Ken	66T	466	$ .75	$2.50	Johnstone, Jay	80T	31	$ .01	$ .10
Johnson, Ken	67T	101	$ .30	$ .85	Johnstone, Jay	81T	372	$ .01	$ .10
Johnson, Ken	68T	342	$ .30	$ .85	Johnstone, Jay	82T	774	$ .01	$ .07
Johnson, Ken	69T	238	$ .30	$ .95	Johnstone, Jay	82TTR	52	$ .02	$ .10
Johnson, Lamar	76T	596	$ .15	$ .50	Johnstone, Jay	83T	152	$ .01	$ .07
Johnson, Lamar	77T	443	$ .03	$ .12	Johnstone, Jay	84T	249	$ .01	$ .06
Johnson, Lamar	78T	693	$ .02	$ .10	Johnstone, Jay	86T	496	$ .01	$ .04
Johnson, Lamar	79T	372	$ .02	$ .10	Jok, Stan	54T	196	$3.60	$10.00
Johnson, Lamar	80T	242	$ .01	$ .10	Jolly, Dave	54T	188	$3.60	$10.00
Johnson, Lamar	81T	589	$ .01	$ .10	Jolly, Dave	55T	35	$2.00	$6.00
Johnson, Lamar	82T	13	$ .01	$ .07	Jolly, Dave	57T	389	$1.25	$4.25
Johnson, Lamar	82TTR	50	$ .02	$ .10	Jolly, Dave	58T	183	$ .75	$3.00
Johnson, Lamar	83T	453	$ .01	$ .07	Jones, Al	85T	437	$ .01	$ .05
Johnson, Lance	88TBB	251	$ .01	$ .06	Jones, Al	86T	227	$ .01	$ .04
Johnson, Lance	89T	122	$ .01	$ .05	Jones, Barry	87T	494	$ .15	$ .50
Johnson, Lance	90T	587	$ .01	$ .04	Jones, Barry	88T	168	$ .01	$ .04
Johnson, Lance	91T	243	$ .01	$ .03	Jones, Barry	89T	539	$ .01	$ .05
Johnson, Lou	60T	476	$ .90	$3.00	Jones, Barry	90T	243	$ .01	$ .04
Johnson, Lou	63T	238	$ .30	$ .95	Jones, Barry	91T	33	$ .01	$ .03
Johnson, Lou	66T	13	$ .30	$ .95	Jones, Bob	77T	16	$ .03	$ .12
Johnson, Lou	67T	410	$ .30	$ .95	Jones, Bob	84T	451	$ .01	$ .06
Johnson, Lou	68T	184	$ .30	$ .85	Jones, Bob	85T	648	$ .01	$ .05
Johnson, Lou	69T	367	$ .30	$ .85	Jones, Bob	86T	142	$ .01	$ .04
Johnson, Owen	66T	356	$ .30	$ .95	Jones, Chipper	91T	333	$ .01	$ .35
Johnson, Randy	89T	647	$ .01	$ .15	Jones, Clarence	68T	506	$ .35	$1.25
Johnson, Randy	89TBB	287	$ .01	$ .06	Jones, Cleon	65T	308	$ .45	$1.45
Johnson, Randy	89TTR	57	$ .01	$ .06	Jones, Cleon	66T	67	$ .30	$ .95
Johnson, Randy	90T	431	$ .01	$ .04	Jones, Cleon	67T	165	$ .30	$ .85
Johnson, Randy	91T	225	$ .01	$ .03	Jones, Cleon	68T	254	$ .30	$ .95
Johnson, Randy G.	83T	596	$ .01	$ .07	Jones, Cleon	69T	512	$ .30	$ .85
Johnson, Randy S.	82TTR	51	$ .02	$ .10	Jones, Cleon	70T	61	$1.50	$4.75

Player	Year	No.	VG	EX/MT
Jones, Cleon	70T	575	$ .30	$ .95
Jones, Cleon	71T	527	$ .35	$1.25
Jones, Cleon	72T	31	$ .05	$ .25
Jones, Cleon	72TIA	32	$ .05	$ .25
Jones, Cleon	73T	540	$ .45	$1.45
Jones, Cleon	74T	245	$ .07	$ .30
Jones, Cleon	75T	43	$ .07	$ .30
Jones, Dalton	64T	459	$ .50	$1.45
Jones, Dalton	65T	178	$ .30	$ .85
Jones, Dalton	66T	317	$ .30	$ .95
Jones, Dalton	67T	139	$ .30	$ .85
Jones, Dalton	68T	106	$ .30	$ .85
Jones, Dalton	69T	457	$ .30	$ .85
Jones, Dalton	70T	682	$ .75	$2.00
Jones, Dalton	71T	367	$ .15	$ .50
Jones, Dalton	72T	83	$ .05	$ .25
Jones, Dalton	73T	512	$ .07	$ .30
Jones, Darryl	80T	670	$ .01	$ .10
Jones, Deacon	63T	253	$ .30	$ .95
Jones, Doug	88T	293	$ .01	$ .25
Jones, Doug	89T	690	$ .01	$ .06
Jones, Doug	89TRB	6	$ .01	$ .05
Jones, Doug	90T	75	$ .01	$ .04
Jones, Doug	91T	745	$ .01	$ .03
Jones, Gary	71T	559	$ .35	$1.25
Jones, Gordon	55T	78	$2.00	$6.00
Jones, Gordon	59T	458	$ .75	$2.20
Jones, Gordon	60T	98	$ .45	$1.45
Jones, Gordon	61T	442	$ .75	$3.00
Jones, Hal	62T	49	$ .45	$1.45

Player	Year	No.	VG	EX/MT
Jones, Jeff	81T	687	$ .01	$ .10
Jones, Jeff	82T	139	$ .01	$ .07
Jones, Jeff	83T	259	$ .01	$ .07
Jones, Jeff	84T	464	$ .01	$ .06
Jones, Jeff	85T	319	$ .01	$ .05
Jones, Jimmy	88T	63	$ .01	$ .04
Jones, Jimmy	89T	748	$ .01	$ .05
Jones, Jimmy	89TTR	58	$ .01	$ .06
Jones, Jimmy	90T	359	$ .01	$ .04
Jones, Lynn	80T	123	$ .01	$ .10

Player	Year	No.	VG	EX/MT
Jones, Lynn	81T	337	$ .01	$ .10
Jones, Lynn	82T	64	$ .01	$ .07
Jones, Lynn	83T	483	$ .01	$ .07
Jones, Lynn	84T	731	$ .01	$ .06
Jones, Lynn	84TTR	58	$ .02	$ .10
Jones, Lynn	85T	513	$ .01	$ .05
Jones, Lynn	86T	671	$ .01	$ .04
Jones, Mack	62T	186	$ .45	$1.45
Jones, Mack	63T	137	$ .30	$ .95
Jones, Mack	65T	241	$ .35	$1.25
Jones, Mack	66T	446	$ .30	$ .95
Jones, Mack	67T	435	$ .30	$ .95
Jones, Mack	68T	353	$ .30	$ .85
Jones, Mack	69T	625	$ .30	$ .95
Jones, Mack	70T	38	$ .15	$ .50
Jones, Mack	71T	142	$ .15	$ .50
Jones, Mike	81T	66	$ .01	$ .10
Jones, Mike	82T	471	$ .05	$ .20
Jones, Mike	85T	244	$ .01	$ .05
Jones, Mike	86T	514	$ .01	$ .04
Jones, Nippy	52T	213	$7.00	$20.00
Jones, Odell	78T	407	$ .02	$ .10
Jones, Odell	80T	342	$ .01	$ .10
Jones, Odell	83TTR	50	$ .02	$ .10
Jones, Odell	84T	734	$ .01	$ .06
Jones, Odell	85T	29	$ .01	$ .05
Jones, Randy	74T	173	$ .07	$ .30
Jones, Randy	75T	248	$ .07	$ .30
Jones, Randy	76T	199	$ .15	$ .50
Jones, Randy	76T	201	$ .35	$1.25
Jones, Randy	76T	310	$ .05	$ .20
Jones, Randy	77T	5	$ .15	$ .50
Jones, Randy	77T	550	$ .03	$ .12
Jones, Randy	78T	56	$ .02	$ .10
Jones, Randy	79T	194	$ .02	$ .10
Jones, Randy	80T	305	$ .01	$ .10
Jones, Randy	81T	458	$ .01	$ .10
Jones, Randy	81TTR	777	$ .02	$ .10
Jones, Randy	82T	626	$ .01	$ .07
Jones, Randy	83T	29	$ .01	$ .07
Jones, Rick	77T	118	$ .03	$ .12
Jones, Ron	89T	349	$ .05	$ .25
Jones, Ron	90T	129	$ .01	$ .10
Jones, Ross	88T	169	$ .01	$ .04
Jones, Ruppert	77T	488	$5.00	$20.00
Jones, Ruppert	78T	141	$ .02	$ .10
Jones, Ruppert	79T	422	$ .02	$ .10
Jones, Ruppert	80T	78	$ .01	$ .10
Jones, Ruppert	81T	225	$ .01	$ .10
Jones, Ruppert	81TTR	778	$ .02	$ .10
Jones, Ruppert	82T	511	$ .01	$ .07
Jones, Ruppert	83T	695	$ .01	$ .07
Jones, Ruppert	84T	327	$ .01	$ .06
Jones, Ruppert	84TTR	59	$ .02	$ .10
Jones, Ruppert	85T	126	$ .01	$ .05
Jones, Ruppert	85TTR	65	$ .02	$ .10
Jones, Ruppert	86T	464	$ .01	$ .04
Jones, Ruppert	87T	53	$ .01	$ .04
Jones, Sam	52T	382	$40.00	$140.00
Jones, Sam	53T	6	$4.50	$15.00
Jones, Sam	56T	259	$3.00	$9.00
Jones, Sam	57T	287	$4.25	$15.00
Jones, Sam	58T	287	$ .75	$3.00
Jones, Sam	59T	75	$1.25	$4.25
Jones, Sam	60T	410	$ .75	$2.20
Jones, Sam	61T	49	$ .90	$3.00
Jones, Sam	61T	555	$7.00	$21.00
Jones, Sam	62T	92	$ .45	$1.45
Jones, Sheldon	52T	130	$7.00	$20.00
Jones, Sherman	61T	161	$ .35	$1.25

TOPPS

Player	Year	No.	VG	EX/MT	Player	Year	No.	VG	EX/MT
Jones, Steve	69T	49	$ .45	$1.45	Joyner, Wally	89T	270	$ .01	$ .10
Jones, Tim	78T	703	$1.50	$6.00	Joyner, Wally	89TBB	201	$ .01	$ .10
Jones, Tim	90T	533	$ .01	$ .04	Joyner, Wally	90T	525	$ .01	$ .10
Jones, Tim	91T	262	$ .01	$ .03	Joyner, Wally	91T	195	$ .01	$ .03
Jones, Tracy	87T	146	$ .15	$ .50	Juden, Jeff	90T	164	$ .01	$ .15
Jones, Tracy	88T	553	$ .01	$ .15	Judson, Howie	52T	169	$7.00	$20.00
Jones, Tracy	89T	373	$ .01	$ .05	Judson, Howie	53T	12	$4.50	$15.00
Jones, Tracy	90T	767	$ .01	$ .04	Jurak, Ed	84T	628	$ .01	$ .06
Jones, Tracy	91T	87	$ .01	$ .03	Jurak, Ed	85T	233	$ .01	$ .05
Jones, Willie	51Tbb	43	$7.50	$22.50	Jurak, Ed	86T	749	$ .01	$ .04
Jones, Willie	52T	47	$15.00	$47.50	Jurges, Billy	60T	220	$ .45	$1.45
Jones, Willie	53T	88	$4.50	$15.00	Justice, Dave	89TMLD	65	$ .01	$1.50
Jones, Willie	54T	41	$3.60	$10.00	Justice, Dave	90TTR	48	$ .01	$2.50
Jones, Willie	56T	127	$2.25	$6.00	Justice, Dave	91T	329	$ .01	$ .75
Jones, Willie	57T	174	$ .95	$3.50	Jutze, Skip	73T	613	$9.00	$35.00
Jones, Willie	58T	181	$ .75	$3.00	Jutze, Skip	74T	328	$ .07	$ .30
Jones, Willie	59T	208	$ .75	$2.20	Jutze, Skip	76T	489	$ .05	$ .20
Jones, Willie	60T	289	$ .75	$2.20	Jutze, Skip	78T	532	$ .02	$ .10
Jones, Willie	61T	497	$ .75	$3.00	Kaat, Jim	60T	136	$8.00	$25.00
Joost, Eddie	51Tbb	15	$7.50	$22.50	Kaat, Jim	61T	63	$2.50	$7.50
Joost, Eddie	52T	45	$15.00	$47.50	Kaat, Jim	62T	21	$1.50	$4.00
Jordan, Ricky	89T	358	$ .15	$1.25	Kaat, Jim	63T	10	$ .45	$1.45
Jordan, Ricky	89TBB	246	$ .01	$ .35	Kaat, Jim	63T	165	$ .80	$2.50
Jordan, Ricky	90T	216	$ .01	$ .25	Kaat, Jim	64T	567	$2.50	$8.50
Jordan, Ricky	91T	712	$ .01	$ .03	Kaat (Katt), Jim	65T	62	$ .75	$2.50
Jorgensen, Mike	70T	348	$ .15	$ .50	Kaat, Jim	66T	224	$ .90	$3.00
Jorgensen, Mike	71T	596	$ .35	$1.25	Kaat, Jim	66T	445	$1.50	$4.00
Jorgensen, Mike	72T	16	$ .05	$ .25	Kaat, Jim	67T	235	$ .45	$1.45
Jorgensen, Mike	73T	281	$ .07	$ .30	Kaat, Jim	67T	237	$ .45	$1.45
Jorgensen, Mike	74T	549	$ .07	$ .30	Kaat, Jim	67T	300	$ .75	$2.50
Jorgensen, Mike	75T	286	$ .07	$ .30	Kaat, Jim	68T	450	$1.50	$4.00
Jorgensen, Mike	76T	117	$ .05	$ .20	Kaat, Jim	69T	290	$ .75	$3.00
Jorgensen, Mike	77T	368	$ .03	$ .12	Kaat, Jim	70T	75	$1.25	$4.25
Jorgensen, Mike	78T	406	$ .02	$ .10	Kaat, Jim	71T	245	$ .75	$2.25
Jorgensen, Mike	79T	22	$ .02	$ .10	Kaat, Jim	72T	709	$2.50	$10.00
Jorgensen, Mike	80T	213	$ .01	$ .10	Kaat, Jim	72TIA	710	$1.75	$4.50
Jorgensen, Mike	81T	698	$ .01	$ .10	Kaat, Jim	73T	530	$2.25	$6.00
Jorgensen, Mike	82T	566	$ .01	$ .07	Kaat, Jim	74T	440	$ .75	$3.00
Jorgensen, Mike	83T	107	$ .01	$ .07	Kaat, Jim	75T	243	$ .75	$3.00
Jorgensen, Mike	83TTR	51	$ .02	$ .10	Kaat, Jim	76T	80	$ .45	$1.45
Jorgensen, Mike	84T	313	$ .01	$ .06	Kaat, Jim	76TTR	80	$ .35	$1.25
Jorgensen, Mike	84TTR	60	$ .02	$ .10	Kaat, Jim	77T	638	$ .15	$ .50
Jorgensen, Mike	85T	783	$ .01	$ .05	Kaat, Jim	78T	715	$ .35	$1.25
Jorgensen, Mike	86T	422	$ .01	$ .04	Kaat, Jim	79T	136	$ .10	$ .45
Jorgensen, Terry	89TMLD	64	$ .01	$ .35	Kaat, Jim	80T	250	$ .30	$ .85
Jose, Felix	90T	238	$ .01	$ .10	Kaat, Jim	81T	563	$ .05	$ .25
Jose, Felix	91T	368	$ .01	$ .03	Kaat, Jim	82T	367	$ .05	$ .25
Joseph, Ricardo	68T	434	$ .30	$ .85	Kaat, Jim	83T	672	$ .01	$ .07
Joseph, Rick	69T	329	$ .30	$ .85	Kaat, Jim	83T	673	$ .01	$ .07
Joseph, Rick	70T	186	$ .15	$ .50	Kaiser, Don	56T	124	$2.25	$6.00
Josephson, Duane	67T	373	$ .30	$ .95	Kaiser, Don	57T	134	$ .95	$3.50
Josephson, Duane	68T	329	$ .30	$ .85	Kaiser, Jeff	90TTR	49	$ .01	$ .10
Josephson, Duane	69T	222	$ .30	$ .95	Kaiser, Jeff	91T	576	$ .01	$ .03
Josephson, Duane	70T	263	$ .15	$ .50	Kaline, Al	54T	201	$195.00	$625.00
Josephson, Duane	71T	56	$ .15	$ .50	Kaline, Al	55T	4	$45.00	$150.00
Josephson, Duane	72T	543	$ .30	$ .95	Kaline, Al	56T	20	$22.50	$72.50
Joshua, Von	71T	57	$ .15	$ .50	Kaline, Al	57T	125	$15.00	$60.00
Joshua, Von	73T	544	$ .15	$ .75	Kaline, Al	58T	70	$15.00	$60.00
Joshua, Von	74T	551	$ .07	$ .30	Kaline, Al	58T	304	$2.50	$10.00
Joshua, Von	75T	547	$ .07	$ .30	Kaline, Al	59T	34	$2.00	$8.00
Joshua, Von	76T	82	$ .05	$ .20	Kaline, Al	59T	360	$11.25	$45.00
Joshua, Von	77T	651	$ .03	$ .12	Kaline, Al	59T	463	$2.00	$8.00
Joshua, Von	78T	108	$ .02	$ .10	Kaline, Al	59TAS	562	$9.00	$35.00
Joshua, Von	80T	209	$ .01	$ .10	Kaline, Al	60T	50	$10.00	$30.00
Joyce, Mike	63T	66	$ .30	$ .95	Kaline, Al	60TAS	561	$10.00	$30.00
Joyce, Mike	64T	477	$ .50	$1.45	Kaline, Al	61T	429	$10.00	$30.00
Joyner, Wally	86TTR	51	$ .75	$2.00	Kaline, Al	61TAS	580	$25.00	$75.00
Joyner, Wally	87T	80	$ .75	$2.20	Kaline, Al	62T	51	$ .75	$2.20
Joyner, Wally	88T	420	$ .30	$ .85	Kaline, Al	62T	150	$7.00	$22.00
Joyner, Wally	88TBB	52	$ .05	$ .25	Kaline, Al	62TAS	470	$3.00	$12.00

Player	Year	No.	VG	EX/MT
Kaline, Al	63T	25	$7.00	$22.00
Kaline, Al	64T	8	$2.10	$6.00
Kaline, Al	64T	12	$ .75	$3.00
Kaline, Al	64T	250	$5.00	$20.00
Kaline, Al	64T	331	$20.00	$65.00
Kaline, Al	65T	130	$4.50	$18.00
Kaline, Al	66T	410	$4.50	$18.00
Kaline, Al	67T	30	$4.00	$15.00
Kaline, Al	67T	216	$1.25	$4.00
Kaline, Al	67T	239	$1.75	$4.50
Kaline, Al	68T	2	$2.10	$6.00
Kaline, Al	68T	240	$4.00	$14.00
Kaline, Al	69T	410	$3.00	$12.00
Kaline, Al	70T	640	$9.00	$35.00
Kaline, Al	71T	180	$3.00	$12.00
Kaline, Al	72T	600	$4.00	$15.00
Kaline, Al	73T	280	$1.50	$4.50
Kaline, Al	74T	215	$1.50	$4.50
Kaline, Al	75THL	4	$ .75	$3.00
Kanehl, Rod	62T	597	$7.00	$21.00
Kanehl, Rod	63T	371	$ .45	$1.50
Kanehl, Rod	64T	582	$1.75	$4.50
Karkovice, Ron	87T	491	$ .01	$ .04
Karkovice, Ron	88T	86	$ .01	$ .04
Karkovice, Ron	89T	308	$ .01	$ .05
Karkovice, Ron	90T	717	$ .01	$ .04
Karkovice, Ron	91T	568	$ .01	$ .03
Kasko, Eddie	57T	363	$1.25	$4.25
Kasko, Eddie	58T	8	$ .70	$2.25
Kasko, Eddie	59T	232	$ .75	$2.20
Kasko, Eddie	60T	61	$ .45	$1.45
Kasko, Eddie	61T	534	$7.00	$21.00
Kasko, Eddie	62T	193	$ .45	$1.45
Kasko, Eddie	63T	498	$2.50	$6.50
Kasko, Eddie	70T	489	$ .15	$ .50
Kasko, Eddie	71T	31	$ .15	$ .50
Kasko, Eddie	72T	218	$ .05	$ .25
Kasko, Eddie	73T	131	$ .15	$ .50
Katt, Ray	57T	331	$4.25	$15.00
Katt, Ray	58T	284	$ .75	$3.00
Katt, Ray	60T	468	$ .95	$3.50
Kaufman, Curt	85T	61	$ .01	$ .05
Kazak, Eddie	52T	165	$7.00	$20.00
Kazak, Eddie	53T	194	$3.75	13.00
Kazanski, Ted	54T	78	$3.60	$10.00
Kazanski, Ted	55T	46	$2.00	$6.00
Kazanski, Ted	57T	27	$ .95	$3.50
Kazanski, Ted	58T	36	$1.25	$4.25
Kazanski, Ted	59T	99	$1.25	$4.25
Kealey, Steve	69T	224	$ .30	$ .95
Kealey, Steve	71T	43	$ .15	$ .50
Kealey, Steve	72T	146	$ .05	$ .25
Kealey, Steve	73T	581	$ .45	$1.45
Keane, Johnny	60T	468	$ .95	$3.50
Keane, Johnny	62T	198	$ .45	$1.45
Keane, Johnny	63T	166	$ .30	$ .95
Keane, Johnny	64T	413	$ .50	$1.45
Keane, Johnny	65T	131	$ .30	$ .85
Keane, Johnny	66T	296	$ .30	$ .95
Kearney, Bob	83TTR	52	$ .02	$ .10
Kearney, Bob	84T	326	$ .01	$ .06
Kearney, Bob	84TTR	61	$ .02	$ .10
Kearney, Bob	85T	679	$ .01	$ .05
Kearney, Bob	86T	13	$ .01	$ .04
Kearney, Bob	87T	498	$ .01	$ .04
Keedy, Pat	88T	486	$ .01	$ .04
Keegan, Bob	53T	196	$4.50	$15.00
Keegan, Bob	54T	100	$3.60	$10.00
Keegan, Bob	55T	10	$2.00	$6.00
Keegan, Bob	56T	54	$2.25	$6.00

Player	Year	No.	VG	EX/MT
Keegan, Bob	57T	99	$ .95	$3.50
Keegan, Bob	58T	200	$ .75	$3.00
Keegan, Bob	59T	86	$1.25	$4.25
Keegan, Bob	60T	291	$ .75	$2.20
Keegan, Bob	77TB	436	$ .03	$ .12
Keegan, Ed	61T	248	$ .35	$1.25
Keegan, Ed	62T	249	$ .45	$1.45
Keely, Bob	54T	176	$3.60	$10.00
Keeton, Rickey	82T	268	$ .01	$ .07
Kekich, Mike	65T	561	$2.50	$10.00
Kekich, Mike	69T	262	$ .30	$ .95
Kekich, Mike	70T	536	$ .15	$ .50
Kekich, Mike	71T	703	$ .75	$2.50
Kekich, Mike	72T	138	$ .05	$ .25
Kekich, Mike	73T	371	$ .07	$ .30
Kekich, Mike	74T	199	$ .07	$ .30
Kekich, Mike	76T	582	$ .05	$ .20
Kell, George	52T	246	$16.00	$50.00
Kell, George	53T	138	$8.50	$35.00
Kell, George	56T	195	$7.00	$21.00
Kell, George	57T	230	$4.25	$15.00
Kell, George	58T	40	$3.00	$9.00
Kelleher, Mick	77T	657	$ .03	$ .12
Kelleher, Mick	78T	564	$ .02	$ .10
Kelleher, Mick	79T	53	$ .02	$ .10
Kelleher, Mick	80T	323	$ .01	$ .10

Player	Year	No.	VG	EX/MT
Kelleher, Mick	81T	429	$ .01	$ .10
Kelleher, Mick	81TTR	779	$ .02	$ .10
Kelleher, Mick	82T	184	$ .01	$ .07
Kelleher, Mick	82TTR	53	$ .02	$ .10
Kelleher, Mick	83T	79	$ .01	$ .07
Kellert, Frank	56T	291	$2.25	$8.00
Kelley, Dick	64T	476	$1.50	$6.00
Kelley, Dick	66T	84	$ .30	$ .95
Kelley, Dick	67T	138	$ .30	$ .85
Kelley, Dick	68T	203	$ .30	$ .85
Kelley, Dick	69T	359	$ .30	$ .85
Kelley, Dick	70T	474	$ .15	$ .50
Kelley, Dick	72T	412	$ .05	$ .25
Kelley, Tom	64T	552	$1.75	$4.50

TOPPS

Player	Year	No.	VG	EX/MT	Player	Year	No.	VG	EX/MT
Kelley, Tom	66T	44	$ .30	$ .95	Kennedy, Bob	51Trb	29	$1.50	$4.00
Kelley, Tom	67T	214	$ .30	$ .85	Kennedy, Bob	52T	77	$15.00	$47.50
Kelley, Tom	71T	463	$ .15	$ .50	Kennedy, Bob	53T	33	$4.50	$15.00
Kelley, Tom	72T	97	$ .05	$ .25	Kennedy, Bob	54T	155	$3.60	$10.00
Kellner, Alex	52T	201	$7.00	$20.00	Kennedy, Bob	55T	48	$2.00	$6.00
Kellner, Alex	56T	176	$2.25	$6.00	Kennedy, Bob	56T	38	$2.25	$6.00
Kellner, Alex	57T	280	$4.25	$15.00	Kennedy, Bob	57T	149	$ .95	$3.50
Kellner, Alex	58T	3	$1.25	$4.25	Kennedy, Bob	64T	486	$ .50	$1.45
Kellner, Alex	59T	101	$1.25	$4.25	Kennedy, Bob	65T	457	$ .75	$3.00
Kelly, Bob	52T	348	$40.00	$140.00	Kennedy, Bob	68T	183	$ .30	$ .85
Kelly, Pat	69T	619	$ .30	$ .95	Kennedy, Bob	85T	135	$ .01	$ .10
Kelly, Pat	70T	57	$ .15	$ .50	Kennedy, John	64T	203	$ .30	$ .95
Kelly, Pat	71T	413	$ .15	$ .50	Kennedy, John	65T	119	$ .30	$ .85
Kelly, Pat	72T	326	$ .05	$ .25	Kennedy, John	66T	407	$ .30	$ .95
Kelly, Pat	73T	261	$ .07	$ .30	Kennedy, John	67T	111	$ .30	$ .85
Kelly, Pat	74T	46	$ .07	$ .30	Kennedy, John	69T	631	$ .30	$ .95
Kelly, Pat	75T	82	$ .07	$ .30	Kennedy, John	70T	53	$ .15	$ .50
Kelly, Pat	76T	212	$ .05	$ .20	Kennedy, John	71T	498	$ .15	$ .50
Kelly, Pat	77T	469	$ .03	$ .12	Kennedy, John	72T	674	$ .75	$2.50
Kelly, Pat	78T	616	$ .02	$ .10	Kennedy, John	73T	437	$ .07	$ .30
Kelly, Pat	79T	188	$ .02	$ .10	Kennedy, Junior	79T	501	$ .02	$ .10
Kelly, Pat	79T	714	$ .02	$ .10	Kennedy, Junior	80T	377	$ .01	$ .10
Kelly, Pat	80T	543	$ .01	$ .10	Kennedy, Junior	81T	447	$ .01	$ .10
Kelly, Pat	80T	674	$ .01	$ .10	Kennedy, Junior	82T	723	$ .01	$ .07
Kelly, Pat	82T	417	$ .01	$ .07	Kennedy, Junior	82TTR	55	$ .02	$ .10
Kelly, Roberto	88TTR	57	$ .01	$ .75	Kennedy, Junior	83T	204	$ .01	$ .07
Kelly, Roberto	89T	691	$ .01	$ .25	Kennedy, Monte	52T	124	$7.00	$20.00
Kelly, Roberto	89TBB	152	$ .01	$ .10	Kennedy, Terry	79T	724	$ .09	$ .35
Kelly, Roberto	90T	109	$ .01	$ .10	Kennedy, Terry	80T	569	$ .03	$ .15
Kelly, Roberto	91T	11	$ .01	$ .03	Kennedy, Terry	81T	353	$ .01	$ .10
Kelly, Tom	87T	618	$ .01	$ .04	Kennedy, Terry	81TTR	780	$ .02	$ .10
Kelly, Tom	88T	194	$ .01	$ .04	Kennedy, Terry	82T	65	$ .01	$ .07
Kelly, Tom	89T	14	$ .01	$ .05	Kennedy, Terry	83T	274	$ .01	$ .07
Kelly, Tom	90T	429	$ .01	$ .04	Kennedy, Terry	83T	742	$ .01	$ .07
Kelly, Tom	91T	201	$ .01	$ .03	Kennedy, Terry	84T	366	$ .01	$ .06
Kelso, Bill	65T	194	$ .30	$ .85	Kennedy, Terry	84T	455	$ .01	$ .06
Kelso, Bill	67T	367	$ .30	$ .85	Kennedy, Terry	85T	135	$ .01	$ .10
Kelso, Bill	68T	511	$ .35	$1.25	Kennedy, Terry	85T	635	$ .01	$ .05
Kemmerer, Russ	55T	18	$2.00	$6.00	Kennedy, Terry	86T	230	$ .01	$ .04
Kemmerer, Russ	58T	137	$ .75	$3.00	Kennedy, Terry	87T	540	$ .01	$ .04
Kemmerer, Russ	59T	191	$ .75	$2.20	Kennedy, Terry	87TTR	57	$ .01	$ .05
Kemmerer, Russ	60T	362	$ .75	$2.20	Kennedy, Terry	88T	180	$ .01	$ .04
Kemmerer, Russ	61T	56	$ .35	$1.25	Kennedy, Terry	89T	705	$ .01	$ .05
Kemmerer, Russ	62T	576	$3.95	$11.50	Kennedy, Terry	89TBB	180	$ .01	$ .06
Kemmerer, Russ	63T	338	$ .45	$1.50	Kennedy, Terry	89TTR	59	$ .01	$ .06
Kemp, Steve	77T	492	$ .25	$ .80	Kennedy, Terry	90T	372	$ .01	$ .04
Kemp, Steve	78T	21	$ .02	$ .10	Kennedy, Terry	91T	66	$ .01	$ .03
Kemp, Steve	79T	196	$ .02	$ .10	Kenney, Gerry (Jerry)	69T	519	$ .30	$ .95
Kemp, Steve	80T	315	$ .01	$ .10	Kenney, Jerry	70T	219	$ .15	$ .50
Kemp, Steve	81T	593	$ .01	$ .10	Kenney, Jerry	71T	572	$ .35	$1.25
Kemp, Steve	82T	666	$ .01	$ .07	Kenney, Jerry	72T	158	$ .05	$ .25
Kemp, Steve	82T	670	$ .01	$ .07	Kenney, Jerry	73T	514	$ .07	$ .30
Kemp, Steve	82TTR	54	$ .02	$ .10	Kenworthy, Dick	68T	63	$ .30	$ .85
Kemp, Steve	83T	260	$ .01	$ .07	Keough, Joe	69T	603	$ .30	$ .95
Kemp, Steve	83TTR	53	$ .02	$ .10	Keough, Joe	70T	589	$ .30	$ .95
Kemp, Steve	84T	440	$ .01	$ .06	Keough, Joe	71T	451	$ .15	$ .50
Kemp, Steve	85T	120	$ .01	$ .05	Keough, Joe	72T	133	$ .05	$ .25
Kemp, Steve	85TTR	66	$ .02	$ .10	Keough, Marty	58T	371	$ .75	$3.00
Kemp, Steve	86T	387	$ .01	$ .04	Keough, Marty	59T	303	$ .75	$2.20
Kendall, Fred	72T	532	$ .30	$ .95	Keough, Marty	60T	71	$ .45	$1.45
Kendall, Fred	73T	221	$ .07	$ .30	Keough, Marty	61T	146	$ .35	$1.25
Kendall, Fred	74T	53	$ .07	$ .30	Keough, Marty	62T	258	$ .45	$1.45
Kendall, Fred	75T	332	$ .07	$ .30	Keough, Marty	63T	21	$ .30	$ .95
Kendall, Fred	76T	639	$ .05	$ .20	Keough, Marty	64T	166	$ .30	$ .95
Kendall, Fred	77T	576	$ .03	$ .12	Keough, Marty	65T	263	$ .35	$1.25
Kendall, Fred	78T	426	$ .02	$ .10	Keough, Marty	66T	334	$ .30	$ .95
Kendall, Fred	79T	83	$ .02	$ .10	Keough, Matt	78T	709	$ .02	$ .10
Kendall, Fred	80T	598	$ .01	$ .10	Keough, Matt	79T	554	$ .02	$ .10
Kennedy, Bill	52T	102	$7.00	$20.00	Keough, Matt	80T	134	$ .01	$ .10
Kennedy, Bill	53T	94	$4.50	$15.00	Keough, Matt	81T	301	$ .01	$ .10

Player	Year	No.	VG	EX/MT
Keough, Matt	82T	87	$ .01	$ .07
Keough, Matt	83T	413	$ .01	$ .07
Keough, Matt	83TTR	54	$ .02	$ .10
Keough, Matt	84T	203	$ .01	$ .06
Kepshire, Kurt	85T	474	$ .01	$ .05
Kepshire, Kurt	86T	256	$ .01	$ .04
Kerfeld, Charlie	86TTR	52	$ .02	$ .10
Kerfeld, Charlie	87T	145	$ .01	$ .04
Kerfeld, Charlie	88T	608	$ .01	$ .04
Kern, Jim	75T	621	$ .15	$ .50
Kern, Jim	77T	41	$ .03	$ .12
Kern, Jim	78T	253	$ .02	$ .10
Kern, Jim	79T	573	$ .02	$ .10
Kern, Jim	80T	369	$ .01	$ .10
Kern, Jim	81T	197	$ .01	$ .10

Player	Year	No.	VG	EX/MT
Kern, Jim	82T	463	$ .01	$ .07
Kern, Jim	82TTR	56	$ .02	$ .10
Kern, Jim	83T	772	$ .01	$ .07
Kernek, George	66T	544	$4.00	$11.50
Kerrigan, Joe	77T	341	$ .03	$ .12
Kerrigan, Joe	78T	549	$ .02	$ .10
Kerrigan, Joe	79T	37	$ .02	$ .10
Kessinger, Don	66T	24	$ .50	$2.00
Kessinger, Don	67T	419	$ .30	$ .95
Kessinger, Don	68T	159	$ .30	$ .85
Kessinger, Don	69T	225	$ .30	$ .95
Kessinger, Don	69TAS	422	$ .30	$ .85
Kessinger, Don	70T	80	$ .15	$ .50
Kessinger, Don	70TAS	456	$ .15	$ .50
Kessinger, Don	71T	455	$ .15	$ .50
Kessinger, Don	72T	145	$ .05	$ .25
Kessinger, Don	73T	285	$ .07	$ .30
Kessinger, Don	74T	38	$ .07	$ .30
Kessinger, Don	75T	315	$ .07	$ .30
Kessinger, Don	76T	574	$ .05	$ .20
Kessinger, Don	77T	229	$ .03	$ .12
Kessinger, Don	78T	672	$ .02	$ .10
Kessinger, Don	79T	467	$ .02	$ .10
Kester, Rick	70T	621	$5.00	$16.00
Kester, Rick	71T	494	$ .15	$ .50
Kester, Rick	72T	351	$ .15	$ .50
Key, Jimmy	84TTR	62	$ .75	$2.75

Player	Year	No.	VG	EX/MT
Key, Jimmy	85T	193	$ .20	$ .75
Key, Jimmy	86T	545	$ .01	$ .15
Key, Jimmy	87T	29	$ .01	$ .10
Key, Jimmy	88T	682	$ .01	$ .10
Key, Jimmy	88TAS	395	$ .01	$ .04
Key, Jimmy	89T	229	$ .01	$ .05
Key, Jimmy	90T	371	$ .01	$ .04
Key, Jimmy	91T	741	$ .01	$ .03
Khalifa, Sammy	86T	316	$ .01	$ .04
Khalifa, Sammy	87T	164	$ .01	$ .04
Kiecker, Dana	90TTR	50	$ .01	$ .20
Kiecker, Dana	91T	763	$ .01	$ .03
Kiefer, Steve	88T	187	$ .01	$ .04
Kiely, Leo	52T	54	$15.00	$47.50
Kiely, Leo	54T	171	$3.60	$10.00
Kiely, Leo	55T	36	$2.00	$6.00
Kiely, Leo	58T	204	$ .75	$3.00
Kiely, Leo	59T	199	$ .75	$2.20
Kiely, Leo	60T	94	$ .45	$1.45
Kilgus, Paul	88T	427	$ .01	$ .04
Kilgus, Paul	89T	276	$ .01	$ .05
Kilgus, Paul	89TTR	60	$ .01	$ .06
Kilgus, Paul	90T	86	$ .01	$ .04
Kilkenny, Mike	69T	544	$ .30	$ .95
Kilkenny, Mike	70T	424	$ .15	$ .50
Kilkenny, Mike	71T	86	$ .15	$ .50
Kilkenny, Mike	72T	337	$ .05	$ .25
Kilkenny, Mike	73T	551	$ .45	$1.45
Killebrew, Harmon	55T	124	$85.00	$265.00
Killebrew, Harmon	56T	164	$30.00	$100.00
Killebrew, Harmon	58T	288	$20.00	$60.00
Killebrew, Harmon	59T	515	$30.00	$100.00
Killebrew, Harmon	60T	210	$7.00	$20.00
Killebrew, Harmon	61T	80	$6.00	$18.00
Killebrew, Harmon	62T	53	$8.00	$25.00
Killebrew, Harmon	62T	70	$3.00	$15.00
Killebrew, Harmon	62T	316	$1.25	$5.00
Killebrew, Harmon	63T	4	$ .50	$2.00
Killebrew, Harmon	63T	500	$22.50	$70.00
Killebrew, Harmon	64T	10	$ .75	$3.00
Killebrew, Harmon	64T	12	$ .75	$3.00
Killebrew, Harmon	64T	81	$1.75	$7.00
Killebrew, Harmon	64T	177	$5.00	$15.00
Killebrew, Harmon	65T	3	$3.00	$12.00
Killebrew, Harmon	65T	5	$3.00	$12.00
Killebrew, Harmon	65T	400	$4.00	$15.00
Killebrew, Harmon	66T	120	$4.00	$15.00
Killebrew, Harmon	67T	241	$ .75	$3.00
Killebrew, Harmon	67T	243	$ .75	$3.00
Killebrew, Harmon	67T	334	$1.75	$4.50
Killebrew, Harmon	67T	460	$10.00	$40.00
Killebrew, Harmon	68T	4	$2.10	$6.00
Killebrew, Harmon	68T	6	$1.00	$$4.00
Killebrew, Harmon	68T	220	$2.50	$10.00
Killebrew, Harmon	68T	490	$22.50	$70.00
Killebrew, Harmon	68TAS	361	$1.50	$4.00
Killebrew, Harmon	69T	375	$4.00	$15.00
Killebrew, Harmon	70T	64	$ .50	$1.50
Killebrew, Harmon	70T	66	$ .50	$1.50
Killebrew, Harmon	70T	150	$2.50	$7.50
Killebrew, Harmon	71T	65	$ .50	$2.00
Killebrew, Harmon	71T	550	$3.50	$11.00
Killebrew, Harmon	72T	51	$1.50	$6.00
Killebrew, Harmon	72T	88	$ .60	$2.00
Killebrew, Harmon	72TIA	52	$ .90	$3.00
Killebrew, Harmon	73T	170	$1.50	$6.00
Killebrew, Harmon	74T	400	$ .95	$3.50
Killebrew, Harmon	75T	207	$ .75	$3.00
Killebrew, Harmon	75T	640	$ .75	$3.00
Kimm, Bruce	77T	554	$ .03	$ .12

TOPPS

Player	Year	No.	VG	EX/MT	Player	Year	No.	VG	EX/MT
Kimm, Bruce	81T	272	$ .01	$ .10	Kingman, Dave	82T	690	$ .05	$ .20
Kindall, Jerry	58T	221	$ .75	$3.00	Kingman, Dave	83T	160	$ .01	$ .10
Kindall, Jerry	59T	274	$ .75	$2.20	Kingman, Dave	83T	161	$ .01	$ .07
Kindall, Jerry	60T	444	$ .90	$3.00	Kingman, Dave	83T	702	$ .01	$ .07
Kindall, Jerry	61T	27	$ .35	$1.25	Kingman, Dave	84T	573	$ .02	$ .10
Kindall, Jerry	62T	292	$ .45	$1.45	Kingman, Dave	84T	703	$ .02	$ .10
Kindall, Jerry	63T	36	$ .30	$ .95	Kingman, Dave	84TTR	63	$ .05	$ .20
Kinder, Ellis	52T	78	$15.00	$47.50	Kingman, Dave	85T	730	$ .01	$ .05
Kinder, Ellis	53T	44	$3.00	$9.00	Kingman, Dave	86T	410	$ .01	$ .04
Kinder, Ellis	54T	47	$2.00	$9.00	Kingman, Dave	87T	709	$ .01	$ .04
Kinder, Ellis	55T	115	$2.00	$6.00	Kinney, Dennis	81T	599	$ .01	$ .10
Kinder, Ellis	56T	336	$2.25	$8.00	Kinzer, Matt	89TMLD	67	$ .01	$ .06
Kinder, Ellis	57T	352	$4.25	$15.00	Kipp, Fred	59T	258	$ .75	$2.20
Kiner, Ralph	51Trb	15	$5.00	$20.00	Kipp, Fred	60T	202	$ .45	$1.45
Kiner, Ralph	53T	191	$20.00	$60.00	Kipper, Bob	86TTR	54	$ .02	$ .10
Kiner, Ralph	77TB	437	$ .35	$1.25	Kipper, Bob	87T	289	$ .01	$ .04
King, Chick	59T	538	$2.50	$10.00	Kipper, Bob	88T	723	$ .01	$ .04
King, Clyde	52T	205	$7.00	$21.00	Kipper, Bob	88TBB	141	$ .01	$ .06
King, Clyde	69T	274	$ .30	$ .95	Kipper, Bob	89T	114	$ .01	$ .05
King, Clyde	70T	624	$ .30	$ .95	Kipper, Bob	90T	441	$ .01	$ .04
King, Clyde	83T	486	$ .01	$ .07	Kipper, Bob	91T	551	$ .01	$ .03
King, Eric	86TTR	53	$ .03	$ .15	Kipper, Thornton	54T	108	$3.60	$10.00
King, Eric	87T	36	$ .01	$ .10	Kipper, Thornton	55T	62	$2.00	$6.00
King, Eric	88T	499	$ .01	$ .04	Kirby, Clay	69T	637	$ .30	$ .95
King, Eric	89T	238	$ .01	$ .05	Kirby, Clay	70T	79	$ .15	$ .50
King, Eric	89TTR	61	$ .01	$ .06	Kirby, Clay	71T	333	$ .15	$ .50
King, Eric	90T	786	$ .01	$ .04	Kirby, Clay	72T	173	$ .05	$ .25
King, Eric	91T	121	$ .01	$ .03	Kirby, Clay	72TIA	174	$ .05	$ .25
King, Hal	70T	327	$ .15	$ .50	Kirby, Clay	73T	655	$ .45	$1.45
King, Hal	71T	88	$ .15	$ .50	Kirby, Clay	74T	287	$ .07	$ .30
King, Hal	72T	598	$ .30	$ .95	Kirby, Clay	75T	423	$ .07	$ .30
King, Hal	74T	362	$ .07	$ .30	Kirby, Clay	76T	579	$ .05	$ .20
King, Jeff	89TMLD	66	$ .01	$ .06	Kirby, Clay	76TTR	579	$ .05	$ .20
King, Jeff	90T	454	$ .01	$ .04	Kirkland, Willie	58T	128	$ .45	$1.50
King, Jeff	91T	272	$ .01	$ .03	Kirkland, Willie	59T	484	$ .75	$2.20
King, Jim	56T	74	$2.25	$6.00	Kirkland, Willie	60T	172	$ .45	$1.45
King, Jim	57T	186	$ .95	$3.50	Kirkland, Willie	61T	15	$ .35	$1.25
King, Jim	58T	332	$ .75	$3.00	Kirkland, Willie	62T	447	$ .75	$2.50
King, Jim	61T	351	$ .35	$1.25	Kirkland, Willie	63T	187	$ .30	$ .95
King, Jim	62T	42	$ .45	$1.45	Kirkland, Willie	64T	17	$ .30	$ .95
King, Jim	63T	176	$ .30	$ .95	Kirkland, Willie	65T	148	$ .30	$ .85
King, Jim	64T	217	$ .30	$ .95	Kirkland, Willie	66T	434	$ .30	$ .95
King, Jim	65T	38	$ .30	$ .85	Kirkpatrick, Ed	63T	386	$ .75	$2.20
King, Jim	66T	369	$ .30	$ .95	Kirkpatrick, Ed	64T	296	$ .30	$ .95
King, Jim	67T	509	$ .75	$3.00	Kirkpatrick, Ed	65T	393	$ .35	$1.25
King, Nelson	55T	112	$2.00	$6.00	Kirkpatrick, Ed	66T	102	$ .30	$ .95
King, Nelson	57T	349	$4.25	$15.00	Kirkpatrick, Ed	67T	293	$ .30	$ .85
Kingery, Mike	87T	203	$ .03	$ .15	Kirkpatrick, Ed	68T	552	$ .35	$1.25
Kingery, Mike	87TTR	58	$ .01	$ .05	Kirkpatrick, Ed	69T	529	$ .30	$ .95
Kingery, Mike	88T	532	$ .01	$ .04	Kirkpatrick, Ed	70T	165	$ .15	$ .50
Kingery, Mike	88TBB	160	$ .01	$ .06	Kirkpatrick, Ed	71T	299	$ .15	$ .50
Kingery, Mike	89T	413	$ .01	$ .05	Kirkpatrick, Ed	72T	569	$ .30	$ .95
Kingery, Mike	91T	657	$ .01	$ .03	Kirkpatrick, Ed	72TIA	570	$ .30	$ .95
Kingman, Brian	80T	671	$ .01	$ .10	Kirkpatrick, Ed	73T	233	$ .07	$ .30
Kingman, Brian	81T	284	$ .01	$ .10	Kirkpatrick, Ed	74T	262	$ .07	$ .30
Kingman, Brian	82T	476	$ .01	$ .07	Kirkpatrick, Ed	74TTR	262	$ .07	$ .30
Kingman, Brian	83T	312	$ .01	$ .07	Kirkpatrick, Ed	75T	171	$ .07	$ .30
Kingman, Dave	72T	147	$1.25	$5.00	Kirkpatrick, Ed	76T	294	$ .05	$ .20
Kingman, Dave	73T	23	$ .35	$1.00	Kirkpatrick, Ed	77T	582	$ .03	$ .12
Kingman, Dave	74T	610	$ .35	$1.00	Kirkpatrick, Ed	78T	77	$ .02	$ .10
Kingman, Dave	75T	156	$ .45	$1.50	Kirkwood, Don	76T	108	$ .05	$ .20
Kingman, Dave	76T	40	$ .08	$ .30	Kirkwood, Don	77T	519	$ .03	$ .12
Kingman, Dave	76T	193	$ .75	$2.20	Kirkwood, Don	78T	251	$ .02	$ .10
Kingman, Dave	77T	500	$ .15	$ .50	Kirkwood, Don	79T	632	$ .02	$ .10
Kingman, Dave	78T	570	$ .05	$ .25	Kison, Bruce	72T	72	$ .30	$ .85
Kingman, Dave	79T	370	$ .05	$ .20	Kison, Bruce	73T	141	$ .07	$ .30
Kingman, Dave	80T	202	$ .05	$ .20	Kison, Bruce	75T	598	$ .07	$ .30
Kingman, Dave	80T	240	$ .02	$ .20	Kison, Bruce	76T	161	$ .05	$ .20
Kingman, Dave	81T	450	$ .03	$ .15	Kison, Bruce	77T	563	$ .03	$ .12
Kingman, Dave	81TTR	781	$ .05	$ .25	Kison, Bruce	78T	223	$ .02	$ .10

Player	Year	No.	VG	EX/MT
Kison, Bruce	79T	661	$ .02	$ .10
Kison, Bruce	80T	28	$ .01	$ .10
Kison, Bruce	81T	340	$ .01	$ .10
Kison, Bruce	82T	442	$ .01	$ .07
Kison, Bruce	83T	712	$ .01	$ .07
Kison, Bruce	84T	201	$ .01	$ .06
Kison, Bruce	85T	544	$ .01	$ .05
Kison, Bruce	85TTR	67	$ .02	$ .10
Kison, Bruce	86T	117	$ .01	$ .04
Kissell, George	73T	497	$ .30	$ .85
Kissell, George	74T	236	$ .07	$ .30
Kittle, Hub	73T	624	$ .55	$1.75
Kittle, Hub	74T	31	$ .07	$ .30
Kittle, Ron	83TTR	55	$ .15	$ .50
Kittle, Ron	84T	480	$ .02	$ .10
Kittle, Ron	85T	105	$ .01	$ .05
Kittle, Ron	86T	574	$ .01	$ .04
Kittle, Ron	87T	584	$ .01	$ .04
Kittle, Ron	88T	259	$ .01	$ .04
Kittle, Ron	88TTR	58	$ .01	$ .06
Kittle, Ron	89T	771	$ .01	$ .05
Kittle, Ron	89TTR	62	$ .01	$ .06
Kittle, Ron	90T	79	$ .01	$ .04
Kittle, Ron	91T	324	$ .01	$ .03
Klages, Fred	67T	373	$ .30	$ .95
Klages, Fred	68T	229	$ .30	$ .85
Klaus, Billy	56T	217	$3.00	$9.00
Klaus, Billy	57T	292	$4.25	$15.00
Klaus, Billy	58T	89	$1.25	$4.25
Klaus, Billy	59T	299	$ .75	$2.20
Klaus, Billy	60T	406	$ .75	$2.20
Klaus, Billy	61T	187	$ .35	$1.25
Klaus, Billy	62T	571	$3.95	$11.50
Klaus, Billy	63T	551	$1.75	$4.50
Klaus, Bobby	64T	524	$1.75	$4.50
Klaus, Bobby	65T	227	$ .35	$1.25
Klaus, Bobby	66T	108	$ .30	$ .95
Klaus, Bobby	69T	387	$ .30	$ .85
Klein, Lou	60T	457	$ .95	$3.50
Klimchock, Lou	60T	137	$ .45	$1.45
Klimchock, Lou	61T	462	$ .75	$3.00
Klimchock, Lou	62T	259	$ .45	$1.45
Klimchock, Lou	63T	542	$1.75	$4.50
Klimchock, Lou	65T	542	$1.75	$4.50
Klimchock, Lou	66T	589	$5.00	$20.00
Klimchock, Lou	70T	247	$ .15	$ .50
Klimkowski, Ron	70T	702	$ .75	$2.00
Klimkowski, Ron	71T	28	$ .15	$ .50
Klimkowski, Ron	72T	363	$ .05	$ .25
Kline, Johnny	55T	173	$5.25	$15.00
Kline, Ron	53T	175	$4.50	$15.00
Kline, Ronnie	56T	94	$2.25	$6.00
Kline, Ronnie	57T	256	$ .95	$3.50
Kline, Ronnie	58T	82	$1.25	$4.25
Kline, Ron	59T	265	$ .75	$2.20
Kline, Ron	59T	428	$ .75	$2.20
Kline, Ron	60T	197	$ .45	$1.45
Kline, Ron	61T	127	$ .35	$1.25
Kline, Ron	62T	216	$ .45	$1.45
Kline, Ron	63T	84	$ .30	$ .95
Kline, Ron	64T	358	$ .30	$ .95
Kline, Ron	65T	56	$ .30	$ .85
Kline, Ron	66T	453	$ .75	$2.50
Kline, Ron	67T	133	$ .30	$ .85
Kline, Ron	68T	446	$ .30	$ .85
Kline, Ron "Ronnie"	69T	243	$ .30	$ .95
Kline, Steve	71T	51	$ .15	$ .50
Kline, Steve	72T	467	$ .05	$ .25
Kline, Steve	73T	172	$ .07	$ .30
Kline, Steve	74T	324	$ .07	$ .30

Player	Year	No.	VG	EX/MT
Kline, Steve	75T	639	$ .07	$ .30
Klink, Joe	90TTR	51	$ .01	$ .10
Klink, Joe	91T	553	$ .01	$ .03
Klippstein, Johnny	52T	148	$7.00	$20.00
Klippstein, Johnny	53T	46	$4.50	$15.00
Klippstein, Johnny	54T	31	$3.60	$10.00
Klippstein, Johnny	56T	249	$3.00	$9.00
Klippstein, Johnny	57T	296	$4.25	$15.00
Klippstein, Johnny	58T	242	$ .75	$3.00
Klippstein, Johnny	59T	152	$ .75	$2.20
Klippstein, Johnny	60T	191	$ .45	$1.45
Klippstein, Johnny	61T	539	$7.00	$21.00
Klippstein, Johnny	62T	151	$ .45	$1.45
Klippstein, Johnny	63T	571	$1.75	$4.50
Klippstein, Johnny	64T	533	$1.75	$4.50
Klippstein, Johnny	65T	384	$ .35	$1.25
Klippstein, Johnny	66T	493	$ .75	$2.50
Klippstein, Johnny	67T	588	$1.50	$4.00
Kluszewski, Ted	51Trb	39	$2.25	$6.75
Kluszewski, Ted	52T	29	$30.00	$85.00
Kluszewski, Ted	53T	162	$8.75	$35.00
Kluszewski, Ted	54T	7	$5.00	$20.00
Kluszewski, Ted	55T	120	$4.75	$17.50
Kluszewski, Ted	56T	25	$4.00	$14.00
Kluszewski, Ted	57T	165	$4.00	$14.00
Kluszewski, Ted	58T	178	$2.10	$6.00
Kluszewski, Ted	58T	321	$11.00	$33.00
Kluszewski, Ted	59T	17	$1.75	$4.50
Kluszewski, Ted	59T	35	$2.25	$8.00
Kluszewski, Ted	60T	505	$2.25	$6.00
Kluszewski, Ted	61T	65	$1.00	$3.00
Kluszewski, Ted	73T	296	$ .15	$ .50
Kluszewski, Ted	74T	326	$ .15	$ .50
Klutts, Mickey	77T	490	$ .03	$ .12
Klutts, Mickey	78T	707	$12.50	$50.00
Klutts, Mickey	80T	717	$ .01	$ .10

Player	Year	No.	VG	EX/MT
Klutts, Mickey	81T	232	$ .01	$ .10
Klutts, Mickey	82T	148	$ .01	$ .07
Klutts, Mickey	83T	571	$ .01	$ .07
Klutts, Mickey	83TTR	56	$ .02	$ .10
Kluttz, Clyde	52T	132	$7.00	$20.00

TOPPS

Player	Year	No.	VG	EX/MT	Player	Year	No.	VG	EX/MT
Knackert, Brent	90TTR	52	$ .01	$ .15	Knox, John	75T	546	$ .07	$ .30
Knackert, Brent	91T	563	$ .01	$ .03	Knox, John	76T	218	$ .05	$ .20
Knapp, Chris	77T	247	$ .03	$ .12	Knudson, Mark	88T	61	$ .01	$ .10
Knapp, Chris	78T	361	$ .02	$ .10	Knudson, Mark	90T	566	$ .01	$ .04
Knapp, Chris	79T	453	$ .02	$ .10	Knudson, Mark	91T	267	$ .01	$ .03
Knapp, Chris	80T	658	$ .01	$ .10	Kobel, Kevin	74T	605	$ .30	$1.50
Knapp, Chris	81T	557	$ .01	$ .10	Kobel, Kevin	75T	337	$ .07	$ .30
Knepper, Bob	78T	589	$ .05	$ .25	Kobel, Kevin	76T	588	$ .05	$ .20
Knepper, Bob	79T	486	$ .02	$ .10	Kobel, Kevin	79T	21	$ .02	$ .10
Knepper, Bob	80T	111	$ .01	$ .10	Kobel, Kevin	80T	189	$ .01	$ .10
Knepper, Bob	81T	279	$ .01	$ .10	Koegel, Pete	71T	633	$ .35	$1.25
Knepper, Bob	81TTR	782	$ .02	$ .10	Koegel, Pete	72T	14	$ .15	$ .50
Knepper, Bob	82T	672	$ .01	$ .07	Kokos, Dick	51Trb	19	$1.50	$4.00
Knepper, Bob	83T	382	$ .01	$ .07	Kokos, Dick	53T	232	$12.50	$50.00
Knepper, Bob	84T	93	$ .01	$ .06	Kokos, Dick	54T	106	$3.60	$10.00
Knepper, Bob	85T	455	$ .01	$ .05	Kolb, Gary	64T	119	$ .30	$ .95
Knepper, Bob	85TAS	721	$ .01	$ .05	Kolb, Gary	65T	287	$ .35	$1.25
Knepper, Bob	86T	590	$ .01	$ .04	Kolb, Gary	68T	407	$ .30	$ .85
Knepper, Bob	87T	722	$ .01	$ .04	Kolb, Gary	69T	307	$ .30	$ .95
Knepper, Bob	88T	151	$ .01	$ .04	Kolloway, Don	52T	104	$7.00	$20.00
Knepper, Bob	89T	280	$ .01	$ .05	Kolloway, Don	53T	97	$4.50	$15.00
Knepper, Bob	90T	104	$ .01	$ .04	Kolstad, Hal	62T	276	$ .45	$1.45
Knicely, Alan	80T	678	$ .01	$ .10	Kolstad, Hal	63T	574	$1.75	$4.50
Knicely, Alan	81T	82	$ .01	$ .10	Komminsk, Brad	85T	292	$ .01	$ .05
Knicely, Alan	83T	117	$ .01	$ .07	Komminsk, Brad	86T	698	$ .01	$ .04
Knicely, Alan	83TTR	57	$ .02	$ .10	Komminsk, Brad	90T	476	$ .01	$ .04
Knicely, Alan	84T	323	$ .01	$ .06	Komminsk, Brad	90TTR	53	$ .01	$ .05
Knicely, Alan	85TTR	68	$ .02	$ .10	Konieczny, Doug	75T	624	$ .07	$ .30
Knicely, Alan	86T	418	$ .01	$ .04	Konieczny, Doug	76T	602	$ .05	$ .20
Knight, Ray	78T	674	$ .30	$ .90	Konstanty, Jim	52T	108	$6.00	$17.50
Knight, Ray	79T	401	$ .05	$ .20	Konstanty, Jim	56T	321	$1.50	$4.50
Knight, Ray	80T	174	$ .01	$ .10	Konstanty, Jim	61TMVP	479	$ .90	$3.00
Knight, Ray	81T	325	$ .01	$ .10	Koonce, Cal	63T	31	$ .30	$ .95
Knight, Ray	82T	525	$ .01	$ .07	Koonce, Cal	65T	34	$ .30	$ .85
Knight, Ray	82TTR	57	$ .05	$ .20	Koonce, Cal	66T	278	$ .30	$ .95
Knight, Ray	83T	275	$ .01	$ .07	Koonce, Cal	67T	171	$ .30	$ .85
Knight, Ray	83T	441	$ .01	$ .07	Koonce, Cal	68T	486	$ .35	$1.25
Knight, Ray	84T	660	$ .01	$ .06	Koonce, Cal	69T	303	$ .30	$ .95
Knight, Ray	85T	590	$ .01	$ .05	Koonce, Cal	70T	521	$ .15	$ .50
Knight, Ray	86T	27	$ .01	$ .10	Koonce, Cal "Calvin"	71T	254	$ .15	$ .50
Knight, Ray	87T	488	$ .01	$ .04	Koosman, Jerry	68T	177	$250.00	$1000.00
Knight, Ray	87TTR	59	$ .01	$ .05	Koosman, Jerry	69T	90	$ .85	$2.50
Knight, Ray	88T	124	$ .01	$ .04	Koosman, Jerry	69TAS	434	$ .30	$ .85
Knight, Ray	88TTR	59	$ .01	$ .06	Koosman, Jerry	70T	610	$ .45	$1.45
Knoop, Bobby	64T	502	$ .50	$1.45	Koosman, Jerry	70TAS	468	$ .30	$ .95
Knoop, Bobby	65T	26	$ .30	$ .85	Koosman, Jerry	71T	335	$ .45	$1.45
Knoop, Bobby	66T	280	$ .30	$ .95	Koosman, Jerry	72T	697	$1.50	$5.00
Knoop, Bobby	67T	175	$ .30	$ .85	Koosman, Jerry	72TIA	698	$ .70	$2.75
Knoop, Bobby	68T	271	$ .30	$ .85	Koosman, Jerry	73T	184	$ .30	$ .85
Knoop, Bobby	69T	445	$ .30	$ .85	Koosman, Jerry	74T	356	$ .15	$ .50
Knoop, Bobby	70T	695	$ .75	$2.00	Koosman, Jerry	75T	19	$ .15	$ .50
Knoop, Bobby	71T	506	$ .15	$ .50	Koosman, Jerry	76T	64	$ .07	$ .30
Knoop, Bobby	72T	664	$ .75	$2.50	Koosman, Jerry	77T	300	$ .03	$ .12
Knowles, Darold	64T	418	$ .50	$1.45	Koosman, Jerry	78T	565	$ .02	$ .10
Knowles, Darold	65T	577	$1.75	$4.50	Koosman, Jerry	79T	655	$ .05	$ .20
Knowles, Darold	66T	27	$ .30	$ .95	Koosman, Jerry	80T	275	$ .01	$ .10
Knowles, Darold	67T	362	$ .30	$ .85	Koosman, Jerry	81T	476	$ .01	$ .10
Knowles, Darold	68T	483	$ .35	$1.25	Koosman, Jerry	82T	714	$ .01	$ .07
Knowles, Darold	70T	106	$ .15	$ .50	Koosman, Jerry	83T	153	$ .01	$ .07
Knowles, Darold	71T	261	$ .15	$ .50	Koosman, Jerry	84T	311	$ .01	$ .06
Knowles, Darold	72T	583	$ .30	$ .95	Koosman, Jerry	84T	716	$ .01	$ .06
Knowles, Darold	73T	274	$ .07	$ .30	Koosman, Jerry	84TTR	64	$ .05	$ .20
Knowles, Darold	74T	57	$ .07	$ .30	Koosman, Jerry	85T	15	$ .01	$ .05
Knowles, Darold	75T	352	$ .07	$ .30	Koosman, Jerry	86T	505	$ .01	$ .04
Knowles, Darold	76T	617	$ .05	$ .20	Kopacz, George	71T	204	$ .15	$ .50
Knowles, Darold	77T	169	$ .03	$ .12	Koplitz, Howie	62T	114	$ .45	$1.45
Knowles, Darold	78T	414	$ .02	$ .10	Koplitz, Howie	63T	406	$ .45	$1.50
Knowles, Darold	79T	581	$ .02	$ .10	Koplitz, Howie	64T	372	$ .50	$1.45
Knowles, Darold	80T	286	$ .01	$ .10	Koplitz, Howie	66T	46	$ .30	$ .95
Knox, John	74T	604	$1.00	$3.00	Koppe, Joe	59T	517	$2.50	$10.00

358

Player	Year	No.	VG	EX/MT	Player	Year	No.	VG	EX/MT
Koppe, Joe	60T	319	$ .75	$2.20	Kranepool, Ed	65T	144	$ .30	$ .85
Koppe, Joe	61T	179	$ .35	$1.25	Kranepool, Ed	66T	212	$ .15	$ .50
Koppe, Joe	62T	39	$ .45	$1.45	Kranepool, Ed	67T	186	$ .30	$ .85
Koppe, Joe	63T	396	$ .45	$1.50	Kranepool, Ed	67T	452	$ .30	$ .95
Koppe, Joe	64T	279	$ .30	$ .95	Kranepool, Ed	68T	92	$ .30	$ .85
Korcheck, Steve	58T	403	$ .75	$3.00	Kranepool, Ed	69T	381	$ .30	$ .95
Korcheck, Steve	59T	284	$ .75	$2.20	Kranepool, Ed	70T	557	$ .30	$ .95
Korcheck, Steve	60T	56	$ .45	$1.45	Kranepool, Ed	71T	573	$ .45	$1.45
Korince, George	67T	72	$ .30	$ .85	Kranepool, Ed	72T	181	$ .05	$ .25
Korince, George	67T	526	$ .75	$3.00	Kranepool, Ed	72TIA	182	$ .05	$ .25
Korince, George	68T	447	$ .30	$ .85	Kranepool, Ed	73T	329	$ .07	$ .30
Kosco, Andy	66T	264	$ .30	$ .95	Kranepool, Ed	74T	561	$ .07	$ .30
Kosco, Andy	67T	366	$ .30	$ .85	Kranepool, Ed	75T	324	$ .07	$ .30
Kosco, Andy	68T	524	$ .35	$1.25	Kranepool, Ed	76T	314	$ .05	$ .20
Kosco, Andy	69T	139	$ .30	$ .85	Kranepool, Ed	77T	201	$ .03	$ .12
Kosco, Andy	70T	535	$ .15	$ .50	Kranepool, Ed	78T	49	$ .02	$ .10
Kosco, Andy	71T	746	$ .75	$2.50	Kranepool, Ed	79T	505	$ .02	$ .10
Kosco, Andy	72T	376	$ .05	$ .25	Kranepool, Ed	80T	641	$ .01	$ .10
Kosco, Andy	74T	34	$ .07	$ .30	Krausse, Lew	63T	104	$ .30	$ .95
Koshorek, Clem	52T	380	$40.00	$140.00	Krausse, Lew	64T	334	$ .30	$ .95
Koshorek, Clem	53T	8	$4.50	$15.00	Krausse, Lew	65T	462	$ .75	$3.00
Koslo, Dave	52T	336	$40.00	$140.00	Krausse, Lew	66T	256	$ .30	$ .95
Kostro, Frank	63T	407	$ .45	$1.50	Krausse, Lew	67T	565	$1.50	$4.00
Kostro, Frank	65T	459	$ .75	$3.00	Krausse, Lew	68T	458	$ .35	$1.25
Kostro, Frank	68T	44	$ .30	$ .85	Krausse, Lew	69T	23	$ .30	$ .85
Kostro, Frank	69T	242	$ .30	$ .95	Krausse, Lew	70T	233	$ .15	$ .50
Koufax, Sandy	55T	123	$210.00	$850.00	Krausse, Lew	71T	372	$ .15	$ .50
Koufax, Sandy	56T	79	$75.00	$255.00	Krausse, Lew	72T	592	$ .30	$ .95
Koufax, Sandy	57T	302	$110.00	$350.00	Krausse, Lew	73T	566	$ .45	$1.45
Koufax, Sandy	58T	187	$40.00	$125.00	Krausse, Lew	75T	603	$ .07	$ .30
Koufax, Sandy	59T	163	$40.00	$125.00	Kravec, Ken	77T	389	$ .03	$ .12
Koufax, Sandy	60T	343	$25.00	$95.00	Kravec, Ken	78T	439	$ .02	$ .10
Koufax, Sandy	61T	49	$ .90	$3.00	Kravec, Ken	79T	283	$ .02	$ .10
Koufax, Sandy	61T	207	$4.50	$14.00	Kravec, Ken	80T	575	$ .01	$ .10
Koufax, Sandy	61T	344	$35.00	$110.00	Kravec, Ken	81T	67	$ .01	$ .10
Koufax, Sandy	62T	5	$30.00	$100.00	Kravec, Ken	81TTR	783	$ .02	$ .10
Koufax, Sandy	62T	60	$ .65	$1.75	Kravec, Ken	82T	639	$ .01	$ .07
Koufax, Sandy	63T	5	$1.00	$4.00	Kravitz, Danny	57T	267	$4.25	$15.00
Koufax, Sandy	63T	9	$ .90	$3.00					
Koufax, Sandy	63T	210	$45.00	$135.00					
Koufax, Sandy	63T	412	$10.00	$30.00					
Koufax, Sandy	64T	1	$3.50	$15.00					
Koufax, Sandy	64T	3	$1.50	$4.00					
Koufax, Sandy	64T	5	$1.75	$5.00					
Koufax, Sandy	64T	200	$25.00	$77.50					
Koufax, Sandy	65T	8	$1.75	$4.50					
Koufax, Sandy	65T	300	$30.00	$100.00					
Koufax, Sandy	66T	100	$22.00	$67.50					
Koufax, Sandy	66T	221	$ .65	$1.75					
Koufax, Sandy	66T	223	$ .65	$1.75					
Koufax, Sandy	66T	225	$1.00	$4.00					
Koufax, Sandy	67T	234	$1.75	$4.50					
Koufax, Sandy	67T	236	$3.00	$9.00					
Koufax, Sandy	67T	238	$1.75	$4.50					
Koufax, Sandy	75T	201	$ .75	$3.00					
Koufax, Sandy	90TTB	665	$ .01	$ .06					
Kraemer, Joe	89TMLD	68	$ .01	$ .06					
Kralick, Jack	61T	36	$ .35	$1.25					
Kralick, Jack	62T	346	$ .45	$1.45					
Kralick, Jack	63T	448	$2.50	$6.50					
Kralick, Jack	64T	338	$ .30	$ .95					
Kralick, Jack	65T	535	$1.75	$4.50					
Kralick, Jack	66T	129	$ .30	$ .95					
Kralick, Jack	67T	316	$ .30	$ .85					
Kraly, Steve	55T	139	$2.00	$6.00					
Kramer, Randy	89T	522	$ .01	$ .15					
Kramer, Randy	90T	126	$ .01	$ .04					
Kranepool, Ed	63T	228	$9.00	$35.00					
Kranepool, Ed	64T	393	$2.00	$5.00					
Kranepool, Ed	64T	566	$1.50	$4.00	Kravitz, Danny	58T	444	$ .75	$2.20

Danny Kravitz — PITTSBURGH PIRATES — CATCHER

TOPPS

Player	Year	No.	VG	EX/MT
Kravitz, Danny	59T	536	$2.50	$10.00
Kravitz, Danny	60T	238	$ .45	$1.45
Kravitz, Danny	61T	166	$ .35	$1.25
Krenchicki, Wayne	80T	661	$ .01	$ .10
Krenchicki, Wayne	82T	107	$ .01	$ .07
Krenchicki, Wayne	82TTR	58	$ .02	$ .10
Krenchicki, Wayne	83T	374	$ .01	$ .07
Krenchicki, Wayne	84T	223	$ .01	$ .06
Krenchicki, Wayne	84TTR	65	$ .02	$ .10
Krenchicki, Wayne	85T	468	$ .01	$ .05
Krenchicki, Wayne	86T	777	$ .01	$ .04
Krenchicki, Wayne	86TTR	55	$ .02	$ .10
Krenchicki, Wayne	87T	774	$ .01	$ .04
Kress, Chuck	54T	219	$3.60	$10.00
Kress, Red	54T	160	$3.60	$10.00
Kress, Red	55T	151	$2.50	$10.00
Kress, Red	60T	460	$2.25	$6.00
Kretlow, Lou	52T	42	$15.00	$47.50
Kretlow, Lou	57T	139	$ .95	$3.50
Kreuter, Chad	89T	432	$ .01	$ .15
Kreuter, Chad	90T	562	$ .01	$ .04
Kreutzer, Frank	64T	107	$ .30	$ .95

PITCHER

FRANK KREUTZER

Player	Year	No.	VG	EX/MT
Kreutzer, Frank	65T	371	$ .35	$1.25
Kreutzer, Frank	66T	211	$ .30	$ .95
Kroll, Gary	65T	449	$ .75	$3.00
Kroll, Gary	66T	548	$5.00	$20.00
Krsnich, Mike	62T	289	$ .45	$1.45
Krsnich, Rocky	53T	229	$12.50	$50.00
Krueger, Bill	84T	178	$ .01	$ .06
Krueger, Bill	85T	528	$ .01	$ .05
Krueger, Bill	86T	58	$ .01	$ .04
Krueger, Bill	87T	238	$ .01	$ .04
Krueger, Bill	90T	518	$ .01	$ .04
Krueger, Bill	91T	417	$ .01	$ .03
Krug, Chris	66T	166	$ .30	$ .95
Kruk, John	86TTR	56	$ .30	$1.50
Kruk, John	87T	123	$ .35	$1.25
Kruk, John	88T	596	$ .01	$ .25
Kruk, John	88TBB	60	$ .01	$ .06
Kruk, John	89T	235	$ .01	$ .05

Player	Year	No.	VG	EX/MT
Kruk, John	89TBB	216	$ .01	$ .06
Kruk, John	89TTR	63	$ .01	$ .06
Kruk, John	90T	469	$ .01	$ .04
Kruk, John	91T	689	$ .01	$ .03
Krukow, Mike	77T	493	$ .25	$ .80
Krukow, Mike	78T	17	$ .02	$ .10
Krukow, Mike	79T	592	$ .02	$ .10
Krukow, Mike	80T	431	$ .01	$ .10
Krukow, Mike	81T	176	$ .01	$ .10
Krukow, Mike	82T	215	$ .01	$ .07
Krukow, Mike	82TTR	59	$ .02	$ .10
Krukow, Mike	83T	331	$ .01	$ .07
Krukow, Mike	83TTR	58	$ .02	$ .10
Krukow, Mike	84T	633	$ .01	$ .06
Krukow, Mike	85T	74	$ .01	$ .05
Krukow, Mike	86T	752	$ .01	$ .04
Krukow, Mike	87T	580	$ .01	$ .04
Krukow, Mike	88T	445	$ .01	$ .04
Krukow, Mike	89T	125	$ .01	$ .05
Krukow, Mike	90T	241	$ .01	$ .04
Kryhoski, Dick	52T	149	$4.50	$3.00
Kryhoski, Dick	54T	150	$3.60	$10.00
Kubek, Tony	57T	312	$35.00	$105.00
Kubek, Tony	58T	393	$4.50	$13.50
Kubek, Tony	59T	505	$2.00	$8.00
Kubek, Tony	60T	83	$1.50	$4.00
Kubek, Tony	61T	265	$1.50	$5.00
Kubek, Tony	62T	311	$1.50	$5.00
Kubek, Tony	62T	430	$1.50	$4.00
Kubek, Tony	63T	20	$ .75	$2.25
Kubek, Tony	64T	415	$ .30	$2.50
Kubek, Tony	65T	65	$ .75	$3.00
Kubiak, Ted	68T	79	$ .30	$ .85
Kubiak, Ted	69T	281	$ .30	$ .95
Kubiak, Ted	70T	688	$ .75	$2.00
Kubiak, Ted	71T	516	$ .15	$ .50
Kubiak, Ted	72T	23	$ .05	$ .25
Kubiak, Ted	73T	652	$ .45	$1.45
Kubiak, Ted	74T	228	$ .07	$ .30
Kubiak, Ted	75T	329	$ .07	$ .30
Kubiak, Ted	76T	578	$ .05	$ .20
Kubiak, Ted	77T	158	$ .03	$ .12
Kucab, John	52T	358	$40.00	$140.00
Kucek, John "Jack"	75T	614	$ .07	$ .30
Kucek, Jack	76T	597	$ .30	$ .85
Kucek, Jack	77T	623	$ .03	$ .12
Kucks, Johnny	56T	88	$2.25	$6.00
Kucks, Johnny	57T	185	$ .60	$2.50
Kucks, Johnny	58T	87	$1.25	$4.25
Kucks, Johnny	59T	289	$ .75	$2.20
Kucks, Johnny	60T	177	$ .45	$1.45
Kucks, Johnny	61T	94	$ .35	$1.25
Kucks, Johnny	62T	241	$ .45	$1.45
Kuenn, Harvey	54T	25	$6.00	$25.00
Kuenn, Harvey	56T	155	$1.75	$5.00
Kuenn, Harvey	57T	88	$1.00	$4.00
Kuenn, Harvey	58T	304	$3.25	$9.50
Kuenn, Harvey	58T	434	$1.00	$3.00
Kuenn, Harvey	59T	70	$1.00	$3.00
Kuenn, Harvey	60T	330	$ .90	$3.00
Kuenn, Harvey	60T	429	$ .90	$3.00
Kuenn, Harvey	61T	500	$ .75	$2.00
Kuenn, Harvey	62T	480	$1.25	$4.25
Kuenn, Harvey	63T	30	$ .45	$1.45
Kuenn, Harvey	64T	242	$ .25	$ .80
Kuenn, Harvey	65T	103	$ .15	$ .50
Kuenn, Harvey	66T	372	$ .35	$1.25
Kuenn, Harvey	73T	646	$ .75	$3.00
Kuenn, Harvey	74T	99	$ .07	$ .30
Kuenn, Harvey	83T	726	$ .01	$ .07

Player	Year	No.	VG	EX/MT	Player	Year	No.	VG	EX/MT
Kuenn, Harvey	84T	321	$ .01	$ .06	Lachemann, Rene	84TTR	67	$ .02	$ .10
Kuhaulua, Fred	82T	731	$ .01	$ .07	Lachemann, Rene	85T	628	$ .01	$ .05
Kuhn, Ken	57T	266	$4.25	$15.00	LaCock, Pete	75T	494	$ .07	$ .30
Kuiper, Duane	76T	508	$ .05	$ .20	LaCock, Pete	76T	101	$ .05	$ .20
Kuiper, Duane	77T	85	$ .03	$ .12	LaCock, Pete	77T	561	$ .03	$ .12
Kuiper, Duane	78T	332	$ .02	$ .10	LaCock, Pete	78T	157	$ .02	$ .10
Kuiper, Duane	79T	146	$ .02	$ .10	LaCock, Pete	79T	248	$ .02	$ .10
Kuiper, Duane	80T	429	$ .01	$ .10	LaCock, Pete	80T	389	$ .01	$ .10
Kuiper, Duane	81T	612	$ .01	$ .10	LaCock, Pete	81T	9	$ .01	$ .10
Kuiper, Duane	82T	233	$ .01	$ .07	LaCorte, Frank	76T	597	$ .30	$ .85
Kuiper, Duane	82TTR	60	$ .02	$ .10	LaCorte, Frank	80T	411	$ .01	$ .10
Kuiper, Duane	83T	767	$ .01	$ .07	LaCorte, Frank	81T	513	$ .01	$ .10
Kuiper, Duane	84T	542	$ .01	$ .06	LaCorte, Frank	82T	248	$ .01	$ .07
Kuiper, Duane	85T	22	$ .01	$ .05	LaCorte, Frank	83T	14	$ .01	$ .07
Kunkel, Bill	61T	322	$ .35	$1.25	LaCorte, Frank	84T	301	$ .01	$ .06
Kunkel, Bill	62T	147	$ .90	$3.00	LaCorte, Frank	84TTR	68	$ .02	$ .10
Kunkel, Bill	63T	523	$1.75	$4.50	LaCorte, Frank	85T	153	$ .01	$ .05
Kunkel, Bill	85T	136	$ .01	$ .10	LaCoss, Mike	79T	717	$ .05	$ .20
Kunkel, Jeff	85T	136	$ .01	$ .10	LaCoss, Mike	80T	199	$ .01	$ .10
Kunkel, Jeff	85T	288	$ .01	$ .05	LaCoss, Mike	81T	474	$ .01	$ .10
Kunkel, Jeff	89T	92	$ .01	$ .05	LaCoss, Mike	82T	294	$ .01	$ .07
Kunkel, Jeff	90T	174	$ .01	$ .04	LaCoss, Mike	82TTR	61	$ .02	$ .10
Kunkel, Jeff	91T	562	$ .01	$ .03	LaCoss, Mike	83T	92	$ .01	$ .07
Kuntz, Rusty	81T	112	$ .01	$ .10	LaCoss, Mike	84T	507	$ .01	$ .06
Kuntz, Rusty	82T	237	$ .01	$ .07	LaCoss, Mike	85T	666	$ .01	$ .05
Kuntz, Rusty	84T	598	$ .01	$ .06	LaCoss, Mike	85TTR	69	$ .02	$ .10
Kuntz, Rusty	84TTR	66	$ .02	$ .10	LaCoss, Mike	86T	359	$ .01	$ .04
Kuntz, Rusty	85T	73	$ .01	$ .05	LaCoss, Mike	86TTR	57	$ .02	$ .10
Kusick, Craig	75T	297	$ .07	$ .30	LaCoss, Mike	87T	151	$ .01	$ .04
Kusick, Craig	77T	38	$ .03	$ .12	LaCoss, Mike	88T	754	$ .01	$ .04
Kusick, Craig	78T	137	$ .02	$ .10	LaCoss, Mike	89T	417	$ .01	$ .05
Kusick, Craig	79T	472	$ .02	$ .10	LaCoss, Mike	90T	53	$ .01	$ .04
Kusick, Craig	80T	693	$ .01	$ .10	LaCoss, Mike	91T	242	$ .01	$ .03
Kusnyer, Art	72T	213	$ .15	$ .50	Lacy, Lee	73T	391	$ .07	$ .30
Kutcher, Randy	89TTR	64	$ .01	$ .06	Lacy, Lee	74T	658	$ .07	$ .30
Kutcher, Randy	90T	676	$ .01	$ .04	Lacy, Lee	75T	631	$ .07	$ .30
Kutyna, Marty	60T	516	$2.50	$10.00	Lacy, Lee	76T	99	$ .05	$ .20
Kutyna, Marty	61T	546	$7.00	$21.00	Lacy, Lee	76TTR	99	$ .05	$ .20
Kutyna, Marty	62T	566	$3.95	$11.50	Lacy, Lee	77T	272	$ .03	$ .12
Kuzava, Bob	51Tbb	22	$7.50	$22.50	Lacy, Lee	78T	104	$ .02	$ .10
Kuzava, Bob	52T	85	$7.00	$20.00	Lacy, Lee	79T	441	$ .02	$ .10
Kuzava, Bob	54T	230	$7.00	$22.00	Lacy, Lee	80T	536	$ .01	$ .10
Labine, Clem	52T	342	$70.00	$210.00	Lacy, Lee	81T	332	$ .01	$ .10
Labine, Clem	53T	14	$5.00	$20.00	Lacy, Lee	82T	752	$ .01	$ .07
Labine, Clem	54T	121	$1.75	$7.00	Lacy, Lee	83T	69	$ .01	$ .07
Labine, Clem	55T	180	$1.25	$10.00	Lacy, Lee	84T	462	$ .01	$ .06
Labine, Clem	56T	295	$2.00	$6.00	Lacy, Lee	85T	669	$ .01	$ .05
Labine, Clem	57T	53	$ .95	$3.50	Lacy, Lee	85TTR	70	$ .02	$ .10
Labine, Clem	58T	305	$ .45	$1.50	Lacy, Lee	86T	226	$ .01	$ .04
Labine, Clem	59T	262	$3.00	$12.00	Lacy, Lee	87T	182	$ .01	$ .04
Labine, Clem	59T	403	$ .75	$2.20	Lacy, Lee	88T	598	$ .01	$ .04
Labine, Clem	60T	29	$ .45	$1.45	Ladd, Pete	80T	678	$ .01	$ .10
Labine, Clem	61T	22	$ .35	$1.25	Ladd, Pete	84T	243	$ .01	$ .06
Laboy, Jose	69T	524	$ .30	$ .95	Ladd, Pete	85T	471	$ .01	$ .05
Laboy, Jose	70T	238	$ .15	$ .50	Ladd, Pete	86T	163	$ .01	$ .04
Laboy, Jose	71T	132	$ .15	$ .50	Ladd, Pete	86TTR	58	$ .02	$ .10
Laboy, Jose	72T	727	$ .75	$2.50	Ladd, Pete	87T	572	$ .01	$ .04
Laboy, Jose	73T	642	$ .45	$1.45	LaFrancois, Roger	83T	344	$ .01	$ .07
Lacey, Bob	78T	29	$ .02	$ .10	Laga, Mike	86TTR	59	$ .02	$ .10
Lacey, Bob	79T	647	$ .02	$ .10	Laga, Mike	87T	321	$ .01	$ .04
Lacey, Bob	80T	316	$ .01	$ .10	LaGrow, Lerrin	71T	39	$ .15	$ .50
Lacey, Bob	81T	481	$ .01	$ .10	LaGrow, Lerrin	73T	369	$ .07	$ .30
Lacey, Bob	81TTR	784	$ .02	$ .10	LaGrow, Lerrin	74T	433	$ .07	$ .30
Lacey, Bob	82T	103	$ .01	$ .07	LaGrow, Lerrin	75T	116	$ .07	$ .30
Lachemann, Marcel	71T	84	$ .15	$ .50	LaGrow, Lerrin	76T	138	$ .05	$ .20
Lachemann, Rene	65T	526	$50.00	$150.00	LaGrow, Lerrin	78T	14	$ .02	$ .10
Lachemann, Rene	66T	157	$ .30	$ .95	LaGrow, Lerrin	79T	527	$ .02	$ .10
Lachemann, Rene	67T	471	$ .75	$3.00	LaGrow, Lerrin	80T	624	$ .01	$ .10
Lachemann, Rene	68T	422	$ .30	$ .85	Lahoud, Joe	69T	189	$ .30	$ .85
Lachemann, Rene	83T	336	$ .01	$ .07	Lahoud, Joe	70T	78	$ .15	$ .50

TOPPS

Player	Year	No.	VG	EX/MT
Lahoud, Joe	71T	622	$ .35	$1.25
Lahoud, Joe	72T	321	$ .05	$ .25
Lahoud, Joe	73T	212	$ .07	$ .30
Lahoud, Joe	74T	512	$ .07	$ .30
Lahoud, Joe	75T	317	$ .07	$ .30
Lahoud, Joe	76T	612	$ .05	$ .20
Lahoud, Joe	78T	382	$ .02	$ .10
Lahti, Jeff	83T	284	$ .01	$ .07
Lahti, Jeff	84T	593	$ .01	$ .06
Lahti, Jeff	85T	447	$ .01	$ .05
Lahti, Jeff	86T	33	$ .01	$ .04
Lahti, Jeff	87T	367	$ .01	$ .04
Lake, Steve	84T	691	$ .01	$ .06
Lake, Steve	85T	98	$ .01	$ .05
Lake, Steve	86T	588	$ .01	$ .04
Lake, Steve	87T	84	$ .01	$ .04
Lake, Steve	88T	208	$ .01	$ .04
Lake, Steve	89T	463	$ .01	$ .05
Lake, Steve	89TTR	65	$ .01	$ .06
Lake, Steve	90T	183	$ .01	$ .04
Lake, Steve	91T	661	$ .01	$ .03
Lamabe, Jack	62T	593	$7.00	$21.00
Lamabe, Jack	63T	251	$ .30	$ .95
Lamabe, Jack	64T	305	$ .30	$ .95
Lamabe, Jack	65T	88	$ .30	$ .85
Lamabe, Jack	66T	577	$5.00	$20.00
Lamabe, Jack	67T	208	$ .30	$ .85
Lamabe, Jack	68T	311	$ .30	$ .85
Lamanczyk, Dave	81T	391	$ .01	$ .10
LaMay, Dick	62T	71	$ .45	$1.45
Lamb, Ray	70T	131	$ .15	$ .50
Lamb, Ray	71T	727	$ .75	$2.50
Lamb, Ray	72T	422	$ .05	$ .25
Lamb, Ray	73T	496	$ .07	$ .30
Lamont, Gene	71T	39	$ .15	$ .50
Lamont, Gene	75T	593	$ .07	$ .30
Lamp, Dennis	78T	711	$ .02	$ .10
Lamp, Dennis	79T	153	$ .02	$ .10
Lamp, Dennis	80T	54	$ .01	$ .10
Lamp, Dennis	81T	331	$ .01	$ .10
Lamp, Dennis	81TTR	785	$ .02	$ .10
Lamp, Dennis	82T	216	$ .01	$ .07
Lamp, Dennis	82T	622	$ .01	$ .07
Lamp, Dennis	83T	434	$ .01	$ .07
Lamp, Dennis	84T	541	$ .01	$ .06
Lamp, Dennis	84TTR	69	$ .02	$ .10
Lamp, Dennis	85T	774	$ .01	$ .05
Lamp, Dennis	86T	219	$ .01	$ .04
Lamp, Dennis	87T	768	$ .01	$ .04
Lamp, Dennis	89T	188	$ .01	$ .05
Lamp, Dennis	89TBB	169	$ .01	$ .06
Lamp, Dennis	90T	338	$ .01	$ .04
Lamp, Dennis	91T	14	$ .01	$ .03
Lampard, Keith	70T	492	$ .15	$ .50
Lampard, Keith	71T	728	$ .75	$2.50
Lampard, Keith	72T	489	$ .05	$ .25
Lampkin, Tom	90T	172	$ .01	$ .04
Lancaster, Les	88T	112	$ .01	$ .15
Lancaster, Les	89T	694	$ .01	$ .05
Lancaster, Les	90T	437	$ .01	$ .04
Lancaster, Les	91T	86	$ .01	$ .03
Landestoy, Rafael	79T	14	$ .02	$ .10
Landestoy, Rafael	80T	268	$ .01	$ .10
Landestoy, Rafael	81T	597	$ .01	$ .10
Landestoy, Rafael	81TTR	786	$ .02	$ .10
Landestoy, Rafael	82T	361	$ .01	$ .07
Landestoy, Rafael	83T	684	$ .01	$ .07
Landestoy, Rafael	83TTR	59	$ .02	$ .10
Landestoy, Rafael	84T	477	$ .01	$ .06
Landis, Bill	68T	189	$ .30	$ .85

Player	Year	No.	VG	EX/MT
Landis, Bill	69T	264	$ .30	$ .95
Landis, Jim	57T	375	$1.25	$4.25
Landis, Jim	58T	108	$1.25	$4.25
Landis, Jim	59T	493	$ .75	$2.20
Landis, Jim	60T	550	$2.50	$10.00
Landis, Jim	61T	271	$ .35	$1.25
Landis, Jim	62T	540	$3.95	$11.50
Landis, Jim	63T	485	$2.50	$6.50
Landis, Jim	64T	264	$ .30	$ .95
Landis, Jim	65T	376	$ .35	$1.25
Landis, Jim	66T	128	$ .30	$ .95
Landis, Jim	67T	483	$ .75	$3.00
Landreaux, Ken	79T	619	$ .05	$ .20
Landreaux, Ken	80T	88	$ .01	$ .10

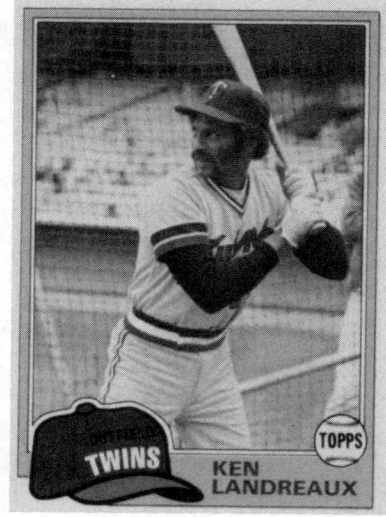

Player	Year	No.	VG	EX/MT
Landreaux, Ken	81T	219	$ .01	$ .10
Landreaux, Ken	81TTR	787	$ .02	$ .10
Landreaux, Ken	82T	114	$ .01	$ .07
Landreaux, Ken	83T	376	$ .01	$ .07
Landreaux, Ken	84T	533	$ .01	$ .06
Landreaux, Ken	85T	418	$ .01	$ .05
Landreaux, Ken	86T	782	$ .01	$ .04
Landreaux, Ken	87T	699	$ .01	$ .04
Landreaux, Ken	88T	23	$ .01	$ .04
Landreth, Larry	78T	701	$ .02	$ .10
Landrith, Hobie	56T	314	$2.25	$8.00
Landrith, Hobie	57T	182	$ .95	$3.50
Landrith, Hobie	58T	24	$1.25	$4.25
Landrith, Hobie	59T	422	$ .75	$2.20
Landrith, Hobie	60T	42	$ .45	$1.45
Landrith, Hobie	61T	114	$ .35	$1.25
Landrith, Hobie	62T	279	$ .45	$1.45
Landrith, Hobie	63T	209	$ .30	$ .95
Landrum, Bill	88T	42	$ .01	$ .04
Landrum, Bill	90T	425	$ .01	$ .04
Landrum, Bill	91T	595	$ .01	$ .03
Landrum, Don	58T	291	$ .75	$3.00
Landrum, Don	61T	338	$ .35	$1.25
Landrum, Don	62T	323	$ .45	$1.45
Landrum, Don	63T	113	$ .35	$1.25
Landrum, Don	64T	286	$ .30	$ .95

Player	Year	No.	VG	EX/MT	Player	Year	No.	VG	EX/MT
Landrum, Don	65T	596	$1.75	$4.50	Lansford, Carney	91T	502	$ .01	$ .03
Landrum, Don	66T	43	$ .30	$ .95	LaPalme, Paul	52T	166	$7.00	$20.00
Landrum, Tito	81T	244	$ .01	$ .10	LaPalme, Paul	53T	201	$4.50	$15.00
Landrum, Tito	82T	658	$ .01	$ .07	LaPalme, Paul	57T	344	$4.25	$15.00
Landrum, Tito	83T	337	$ .01	$ .07	LaPoint, Dave	83T	438	$ .05	$ .25
Landrum, Tito	85T	33	$ .01	$ .05	LaPoint, Dave	84T	627	$ .01	$ .06
Landrum, Tito	86T	498	$ .01	$ .04	LaPoint, Dave	85T	229	$ .01	$ .05
Landrum, Tito	87T	288	$ .01	$ .04	LaPoint, Dave	85TTR	71	$ .02	$ .10
Landrum, Tito	88T	581	$ .01	$ .04	LaPoint, Dave	86T	551	$ .01	$ .04
Lane, Jerry	54T	97	$3.60	$10.00	LaPoint, Dave	86TTR	61	$ .02	$ .10
Lang, Chip	77T	132	$ .03	$ .12	LaPoint, Dave	87T	754	$ .01	$ .04
Lange, Dick	74T	429	$ .07	$ .30	LaPoint, Dave	88T	334	$ .01	$ .04
Lange, Dick	75T	114	$ .07	$ .30	LaPoint, Dave	89T	89	$ .01	$ .05
Lange, Dick	76T	176	$ .05	$ .20	LaPoint, Dave	89TTR	67	$ .01	$ .06
Langford, Rick	78T	327	$ .02	$ .10	LaPoint, Dave	90T	186	$ .01	$ .04
Langford, Rick	79T	29	$ .02	$ .10	LaPoint, Dave	91T	484	$ .01	$ .03
Langford, Rick	80T	546	$ .01	$ .10	Larker, Norm	59T	107	$1.25	$4.25
Langford, Rick	81T	154	$ .01	$ .10	Larker, Norm	60T	394	$ .75	$2.20
Langford, Rick	82T	454	$ .01	$ .07	Larker, Norm	61T	41	$1.50	$5.00
Langford, Rick	83T	286	$ .01	$ .07	Larker, Norm	61T	130	$ .35	$1.25
Langford, Rick	83T	531	$ .01	$ .07	Larker, Norm	62T	23	$ .45	$1.45
Langford, Rick	84T	629	$ .01	$ .06	Larker, Norm	63T	536	$1.75	$4.50
Langford, Rick	85T	347	$ .01	$ .05	Larkin, Barry	87T	648	$ .50	$2.00
Langford, Rick	86T	766	$ .01	$ .04	Larkin, Barry	88T	102	$ .01	$ .35
Langston, Mark	84TTR	70	$2.00	$8.00	Larkin, Barry	88TBB	74	$ .01	$ .15
Langston, Mark	85T	625	$ .50	$2.00	Larkin, Barry	89T	515	$ .01	$ .15
Langston, Mark	86T	495	$ .01	$ .25	Larkin, Barry	89TBB	199	$ .01	$ .15
Langston, Mark	87T	215	$ .01	$ .20	Larkin, Barry	90T	10	$ .01	$ .15
Langston, Mark	88T	80	$ .01	$ .10	Larkin, Barry	91T	730	$ .01	$ .10
Langston, Mark	88TBB	176	$ .01	$ .15	Larkin, Barry	91TAS	400	$ .01	$ .10
Langston, Mark	89T	355	$ .01	$ .10	Larkin, Gene	87TTR	60	$ .05	$ .30
Langston, Mark	89TTR	66	$ .01	$ .10	Larkin, Gene	88T	746	$ .01	$ .25
Langston, Mark	90T	530	$ .01	$ .10	Larkin, Gene	88TBB	264	$ .01	$ .06
Langston, Mark	90TTR	54	$ .01	$ .05	Larkin, Gene	89T	318	$ .01	$ .05
Langston, Mark	91T	755	$ .01	$ .03	Larkin, Gene	89TBB	226	$ .01	$ .06
Lanier, Hal	65T	118	$ .45	$1.45	Larkin, Gene	90T	556	$ .01	$ .04
Lanier, Hal	66T	156	$ .15	$ .50	Larkin, Gene	91T	102	$ .01	$ .03
Lanier, Hal	66T	271	$ .30	$ .95	LaRoche, Dave	71T	174	$ .15	$ .50
Lanier, Hal	67T	4	$ .30	$ .85	LaRoche, Dave	72T	352	$ .05	$ .25
Lanier, Hal	68T	436	$ .30	$ .95	LaRoche, Dave	73T	426	$ .07	$ .30
Lanier, Hal	69T	316	$ .35	$1.25	LaRoche, Dave	74T	502	$ .07	$ .30
Lanier, Hal	70T	583	$ .30	$ .95	LaRoche, Dave	75T	258	$ .07	$ .30
Lanier, Hal	71T	181	$ .15	$ .50	LaRoche, Dave	76T	21	$ .05	$ .20
Lanier, Hal	72T	589	$ .45	$1.45	LaRoche, Dave	77T	385	$ .03	$ .12
Lanier, Hal	73T	479	$ .30	$ .85	LaRoche, Dave	78T	454	$ .02	$ .10
Lanier, Hal	74T	588	$ .07	$ .30	LaRoche, Dave	79T	601	$ .02	$ .10
Lanier, Hal	86TTR	60	$ .02	$ .10	LaRoche, Dave	80T	263	$ .01	$ .10
Lanier, Hal	87T	343	$ .01	$ .04	LaRoche, Dave	81T	529	$ .01	$ .10
Lanier, Hal	88T	684	$ .01	$ .04	LaRoche, Dave	81TTR	789	$ .02	$ .10
Lanier, Hal	89T	164	$ .01	$ .05	LaRoche, Dave	82T	142	$ .01	$ .07
Lanier, Max	52T	101	$7.00	$20.00	LaRoche, Dave	83T	333	$ .01	$ .07
Lankford, Ray	91T	682	$ .01	$ .50	LaRoche, Dave	83T	334	$ .01	$ .07
Lansford, Carney	79T	212	$1.50	$4.50	LaRose, Vic	69T	404	$ .30	$ .85
Lansford, Carney	80T	337	$ .25	$1.25	Larsen, Don	56T	332	$7.00	$28.00
Lansford, Carney	81T	639	$ .15	$ .75	Larsen, Don	57T	175	$3.00	$12.00
Lansford, Carney	81TTR	788	$ .02	$ .20	Larsen, Don	58T	161	$2.00	$8.00
Lansford, Carney	82T	91	$ .01	$ .07	Larsen, Don	59T	205	$3.00	$7.00
Lansford, Carney	82T	161	$ .03	$ .15	Larsen, Don	59T	383	$2.10	$6.00
Lansford, Carney	82T	786	$ .01	$ .07	Larsen, Don	60T	353	$ .45	$1.35
Lansford, Carney	83T	523	$ .01	$ .07	Larsen, Don	61T	177	$ .75	$3.00
Lansford, Carney	83TTR	60	$ .02	$ .10	Larsen, Don	61T	402	$2.50	$10.00
Lansford, Carney	84T	767	$ .01	$ .06	Larsen, Don	62T	33	$ .75	$3.00
Lansford, Carney	85T	422	$ .01	$ .05	Larsen, Don	63T	163	$ .45	$1.45
Lansford, Carney	86T	134	$ .01	$ .04	Larsen, Don	64T	513	$ .75	$2.20
Lansford, Carney	87T	678	$ .01	$ .04	Larsen, Don	65T	389	$ .45	$1.45
Lansford, Carney	88T	292	$ .01	$ .04	Larson, Dan	77T	641	$ .03	$ .12
Lansford, Carney	88TBB	221	$ .01	$ .06	LaRussa, Tony	64T	244	$2.50	$10.00
Lansford, Carney	89T	47	$ .01	$ .05	LaRussa, Tony	68T	571	$ .75	$3.00
Lansford, Carney	89TBB	57	$ .01	$ .06	LaRussa, Tony	72T	451	$ .05	$ .25
Lansford, Carney	90T	316	$ .01	$ .04	LaRussa, Tony	83T	216	$ .01	$ .07

TOPPS

Player	Year	No.	VG	EX/MT
LaRussa, Tony	84T	591	$ .01	$ .06
LaRussa, Tony	85T	466	$ .01	$ .05
LaRussa, Tony	86T	531	$ .01	$ .04
LaRussa, Tony	87T	68	$ .01	$ .04
LaRussa, Tony	88T	344	$ .01	$ .04
LaRussa, Tony	89T	224	$ .01	$ .05
LaRussa, Tony	90T	639	$ .01	$ .04
LaRussa, Tony	91T	171	$ .01	$ .03
Lary, Frank	56T	191	$3.00	$9.00
Lary, Frank	57T	168	$ .95	$3.50
Lary, Frank	58T	245	$ .75	$3.00
Lary, Frank	59T	393	$ .75	$2.20
Lary, Frank	60T	85	$ .45	$1.45
Lary, Frank	61T	48	$ .75	$3.00
Lary, Frank	61T	50	$ .75	$2.20
Lary, Frank	61T	243	$ .35	$1.25
Lary, Frank	62T	57	$ .75	$2.20
Lary, Frank	62TAS	474	$ .75	$2.50
Lary, Frank	63T	140	$ .30	$ .95
Lary, Frank	63T	218	$ .45	$1.45
Lary, Frank	64T	197	$ .30	$ .95
Lary, Frank	65T	127	$ .30	$ .85
Lasher, Fred	68T	447	$ .30	$ .85
Lasher, Fred	69T	373	$ .30	$ .85
Lasher, Fred	70T	356	$ .15	$ .50
Lasher, Fred	71T	707	$ .75	$2.50
Laskey, Bill	83T	171	$ .01	$ .07
Laskey, Bill	83T	518	$ .01	$ .07
Laskey, Bill	84T	129	$ .01	$ .06
Laskey, Bill	85T	331	$ .01	$ .05
Laskey, Bill	86T	603	$ .01	$ .04
Lasorda, Tom	54T	132	$50.00	$150.00
Lasorda, Tom	73T	569	$1.25	$4.25
Lasorda, Tom	74T	144	$ .07	$ .30
Lasorda, Tom	78T	189	$ .05	$ .25
Lasorda, Tom	83T	306	$ .01	$ .15
Lasorda, Tom	84T	681	$ .02	$ .10
Lasorda, Tom	85T	601	$ .01	$ .05
Lasorda, Tom	86T	291	$ .01	$ .04
Lasorda, Tom	87T	493	$ .01	$ .04
Lasorda, Tom	88T	74	$ .01	$ .04
Lasorda, Tom	89T	254	$ .01	$ .05
Lasorda, Tom	90T	669	$ .01	$ .04
Lasorda, Tom	91T	789	$ .01	$ .03
Latman, Barry	59T	477	$ .75	$2.20
Latman, Barry	60T	41	$ .45	$1.45
Latman, Barry	61T	560	$7.00	$21.00
Latman, Barry	62T	37	$ .75	$3.00
Latman, Barry	62T	145	$ .45	$1.45
Latman, Barry	63T	426	$ .45	$1.50
Latman, Barry	64T	227	$ .30	$ .95
Latman, Barry	65T	307	$ .35	$1.25
Latman, Barry	66T	451	$ .75	$2.50
Latman, Barry	67T	28	$ .30	$ .85
Lau, Charley	64T	229	$ .30	$ .95
Lau, Charlie	58T	448	$ .65	$2.00
Lau, Charlie	60T	312	$ .75	$2.20
Lau, Charlie	61T	261	$ .35	$1.25
Lau, Charlie	62T	533	$3.95	$11.50
Lau, Charlie	63T	41	$ .30	$ .95
Lau, Charlie	65T	94	$ .30	$ .85
Lau, Charlie	66T	368	$ .30	$ .95
Lau, Charlie	73T	593	$ .75	$3.00
Lau, Charlie	74T	166	$ .07	$ .30
Laudner, Tim	82T	766	$1.50	$4.50
Laudner, Tim	83T	529	$ .01	$ .07
Laudner, Tim	84T	363	$ .01	$ .06
Laudner, Tim	85T	71	$ .01	$ .05
Laudner, Tim	86T	184	$ .01	$ .04
Laudner, Tim	87T	478	$ .01	$ .04

Player	Year	No.	VG	EX/MT
Laudner, Tim	88T	671	$ .01	$ .04
Laudner, Tim	88TBB	243	$ .01	$ .06
Laudner, Tim	89T	239	$ .01	$ .05
Laudner, Tim	90T	777	$ .01	$ .04
Lauzerique, George	69T	358	$ .30	$ .85
Lauzerique, George	70T	41	$ .15	$ .50
Lavagetto, Cookie	52T	365	$50.00	$155.00
Lavagetto, Cookie	59T	74	$ .95	$3.50
Lavagetto, Cookie	60T	221	$ .45	$1.45
Lavagetto, Harry "Cookie"	61T	226	$ .35	$1.25
LaValliere, Mike	87T	162	$ .03	$ .15
LaValliere, Mike	87TTR	61	$ .01	$ .05

Player	Year	No.	VG	EX/MT
LaValliere, Mike	88T	539	$ .01	$ .04
LaValliere, Mike	88TBB	61	$ .01	$ .06
LaValliere, Mike	89T	218	$ .01	$ .05
LaValliere, Mike	89TBB	306	$ .01	$ .06
LaValliere, Mike	90T	478	$ .01	$ .04
LaValliere, Mike	91T	665	$ .01	$ .03
Lavelle, Gary	75T	624	$ .07	$ .30
Lavelle, Gary	76T	105	$ .05	$ .20
Lavelle, Gary	77T	423	$ .03	$ .12
Lavelle, Gary	78T	671	$ .02	$ .10
Lavelle, Gary	79T	311	$ .02	$ .10
Lavelle, Gary	80T	84	$ .01	$ .10
Lavelle, Gary	81T	588	$ .01	$ .10
Lavelle, Gary	82T	209	$ .01	$ .07
Lavelle, Gary	83T	791	$ .01	$ .07
Lavelle, Gary	84T	145	$ .01	$ .06
Lavelle, Gary	85T	462	$ .01	$ .05
Lavelle, Gary	85TTR	72	$ .02	$ .10
Lavelle, Gary	86T	622	$ .01	$ .04
Law, Rudy	79T	719	$2.50	$10.00
Law, Rudy	81T	127	$ .01	$ .10
Law, Rudy	83T	514	$ .01	$ .07
Law, Rudy	84T	47	$ .01	$ .06
Law, Rudy	85T	286	$ .01	$ .05
Law, Rudy	86T	637	$ .01	$ .04
Law, Rudy	86TTR	62	$ .02	$ .10
Law, Rudy	87T	382	$ .01	$ .04
Law, Vance	81T	551	$ .50	$2.00

Player	Year	No.	VG	EX/MT	Player	Year	No.	VG	EX/MT
Law, Vance	82T	291	$ .25	$1.00	Leach, Rick	89T	682	$ .01	$ .05
Law, Vance	83T	98	$ .01	$ .07	Leach, Rick	89TTR	68	$ .01	$ .06
Law, Vance	84T	667	$ .01	$ .06	Leach, Rick	90T	27	$ .01	$ .04
Law, Vance	85T	137	$ .01	$ .10	Leach, Rick	90TTR	56	$ .01	$ .05
Law, Vance	85T	413	$ .01	$ .05	Leach, Terry	82T	623	$ .20	$ .80
Law, Vance	85TTR	73	$ .02	$ .10	Leach, Terry	83T	187	$ .01	$ .07
Law, Vance	86T	787	$ .01	$ .04	Leach, Terry	86T	774	$ .01	$ .04
Law, Vance	87T	127	$ .01	$ .04	Leach, Terry	87TTR	63	$ .01	$ .05
Law, Vance	88T	346	$ .01	$ .04	Leach, Terry	88T	457	$ .01	$ .04
Law, Vance	88TTR	60	$ .01	$ .06	Leach, Terry	89T	207	$ .01	$ .05
Law, Vance	89T	501	$ .01	$ .05	Leach, Terry	89TBB	96	$ .01	$ .06
Law, Vance	89TBB	143	$ .01	$ .06	Leach, Terry	89TTR	69	$ .01	$ .06
Law, Vance	90T	287	$ .01	$ .04	Leach, Terry	90T	508	$ .01	$ .04
Law, Vern	52T	81	$7.00	$20.00	Leach, Terry	90TTR	57	$ .01	$ .05
Law, Vern	54T	235	$1.75	$7.00	Leal, Luis	81T	577	$ .01	$ .10
Law, Vernon	56T	252	$2.50	$7.00	Leal, Luis	82T	412	$ .01	$ .07
Law, Vernon	57T	199	$ .60	$2.50	Leal, Luis	83T	109	$ .01	$ .07
Law, Vernon "Vern"	58T	132	$ .75	$2.50	Leal, Luis	84T	783	$ .01	$ .06
Law, Vern	59T	12	$ .95	$3.50	Leal, Luis	85T	622	$ .01	$ .05
Law, Vern	59T	428	$ .75	$2.20	Leal, Luis	86T	459	$ .01	$ .04
Law, Vern	60T	453	$1.00	$4.00	Leary, Tim	82T	623	$ .20	$ .80
Law, Vern	61T	47	$ .90	$3.00	Leary, Tim	86TTR	64	$ .02	$ .10
Law, Vern	61T	250	$ .75	$3.00	Leary, Tim	87T	32	$ .01	$ .04
Law, Vern	61T	400	$ .90	$3.00	Leary, Tim	87TTR	64	$ .01	$ .05
Law, Vern	62T	295	$ .75	$3.00	Leary, Tim	88T	367	$ .01	$ .04
Law, Vern	63T	184	$ .35	$1.25	Leary, Tim	89T	249	$ .01	$ .05
Law, Vern	64T	472	$ .75	$2.20	Leary, Tim	89TBB	17	$ .01	$ .06
Law, Vern	65T	515	$ .90	$3.00	Leary, Tim	90T	516	$ .01	$ .04
Law, Vern	66T	15	$ .45	$1.45	Leary, Tim	90TTR	58	$ .01	$ .05
Law, Vern	66T	221	$ .65	$1.75	Leary, Tim	91T	161	$ .01	$ .03
Law, Vern	67T	351	$ .30	$ .85	Lee, Bill	70T	279	$ .15	$ .50
Law, Vern	85T	137	$ .01	$ .10	Lee, Bill	71T	58	$ .15	$ .50
Lawless, Tom	83T	423	$ .01	$ .07	Lee, Bill	72T	636	$ .30	$ .95
Lawless, Tom	86T	228	$ .01	$ .04	Lee, Bill	73T	224	$ .07	$ .30
Lawless, Tom	87T	647	$ .01	$ .04	Lee, Bill	74T	118	$ .07	$ .30
Lawless, Tom	88T	183	$ .01	$ .04	Lee, Bill	75T	128	$ .07	$ .30
Lawless, Tom	89T	312	$ .01	$ .05	Lee, Bill	76T	396	$ .05	$ .20
Lawless, Tom	90T	49	$ .01	$ .04	Lee, Bill	77T	503	$ .03	$ .12
Lawrence, Brooks	56T	305	$2.25	$8.00	Lee, Bill	78T	295	$ .02	$ .10
Lawrence, Brooks	57T	66	$ .95	$3.50	Lee, Bill	79T	455	$ .02	$ .10
Lawrence, Brooks	58T	374	$ .75	$3.00	Lee, Bill	80T	97	$ .01	$ .10
Lawrence, Brooks	59T	67	$1.25	$4.25	Lee, Bill	81T	633	$ .01	$ .10
Lawrence, Brooks	60T	434	$ .75	$2.20	Lee, Bill	82T	323	$ .01	$ .07
Lawson, Steve	73T	612	$ .45	$1.45	Lee, Bob	64T	502	$ .50	$1.45
Lawton, Marcus	89TMLD	69	$ .01	$ .25	Lee, Bob	65T	46	$ .30	$ .85
Lawton, Marcus	90T	302	$ .01	$ .10	Lee, Bob	66T	481	$ .75	$2.50
Laxton, Bill	77T	394	$ .03	$ .12	Lee, Bob	67T	313	$ .30	$ .85
Layana, Tim	90TTR	55	$ .01	$ .20	Lee, Bob	68T	543	$ .35	$1.25
Layana, Tim	91T	627	$ .01	$ .15	Lee, Don	57T	379	$1.25	$4.25
Lazar, Dan	69T	439	$ .30	$ .85	Lee, Don	59T	132	$ .75	$2.20
Lazar, Dan	70T	669	$ .75	$2.00	Lee, Don	60T	503	$ .90	$3.00
Lazorko, Jack	85T	317	$ .01	$ .05	Lee, Don	61T	153	$ .35	$1.25
Lazorko, Jack	87TTR	62	$ .01	$ .05	Lee, Don	62T	166	$ .45	$1.45
Lazorko, Jack	88T	601	$ .01	$ .04	Lee, Don	63T	372	$ .45	$1.50
Lazorko, Jack	89T	362	$ .01	$ .05	Lee, Don	64T	493	$ .50	$1.45
Lea, Charlie	81T	293	$ .01	$ .10	Lee, Don	65T	595	$1.75	$4.50
Lea, Charlie	82T	38	$ .01	$ .07	Lee, Leron	70T	96	$ .50	$2.00
Lea, Charlie	83T	629	$ .01	$ .07	Lee, Leron	71T	521	$ .15	$ .50
Lea, Charlie	84T	421	$ .01	$ .06	Lee, Leron	72T	238	$ .05	$ .25
Lea, Charlie	84T	516	$ .01	$ .06	Lee, Leron	73T	83	$ .07	$ .30
Lea, Charlie	85T	345	$ .01	$ .05	Lee, Leron	74T	651	$ .07	$ .30
Lea, Charlie	86T	526	$ .01	$ .04	Lee, Leron	75T	506	$ .07	$ .30
Leach, Rick	82T	266	$ .01	$ .07	Lee, Leron	76T	487	$ .05	$ .20
Leach, Rick	83T	147	$ .01	$ .07	Lee, Manny	86T	23	$ .01	$ .04
Leach, Rick	84T	427	$ .01	$ .06	Lee, Manny	87T	574	$ .01	$ .04
Leach, Rick	84TTR	71	$ .02	$ .10	Lee, Manny	88T	722	$ .01	$ .04
Leach, Rick	85T	593	$ .01	$ .05	Lee, Manny	89T	371	$ .01	$ .05
Leach, Rick	86TTR	63	$ .02	$ .10	Lee, Manny	89TBB	70	$ .01	$ .06
Leach, Rick	87T	716	$ .01	$ .04	Lee, Manny	90T	113	$ .01	$ .04
Leach, Rick	88T	323	$ .01	$ .04	Lee, Manny	91T	297	$ .01	$ .03

Player	Year	No.	VG	EX/MT	Player	Year	No.	VG	EX/MT
Lee, Mark	79T	138	$ .02	$ .10	Leja, Frank	55T	99	$2.00	$6.00
Lee, Mark	80T	557	$ .01	$ .10	LeJohn, Don	66T	41	$ .30	$ .95
Lee, Mark	91T	721	$ .01	$ .10	Lemanczyk, Dave	75T	571	$ .07	$ .30
Lee, Mike	60T	521	$2.50	$10.00	Lemanczyk, Dave	76T	409	$ .05	$ .20
Leek, Gene	61T	527	$7.00	$21.00	Lemanczyk, Dave	77T	611	$ .03	$ .12
Lefebvre, Jim	65T	561	$2.50	$10.00	Lemanczyk, Dave	78T	33	$ .02	$ .10
Lefebvre, Jim	66T	57	$ .30	$ .95	Lemanczyk, Dave	79T	207	$ .02	$ .10
Lefebvre, Jim	67T	260	$ .30	$ .85	Lemanczyk, Dave	80T	124	$ .01	$ .10
Lefebvre, Jim	68T	457	$ .30	$ .85	Lemaster, Denver	63T	74	$ .30	$ .95
Lefebvre, Jim	69T	140	$ .30	$ .85	Lemaster, Denver	64T	152	$ .30	$ .95
Lefebvre, Jim	70T	553	$ .30	$ .95	Lemaster, Denver	65T	441	$ .35	$1.25
Lefebvre, Jim	71T	459	$ .15	$ .50	Lemaster, Denver	66T	252	$ .30	$ .95
Lefebvre, Jim	72T	369	$ .05	$ .25	Lemaster, Denver	67T	288	$ .30	$ .85
Lefebvre, Jim	89TTR	70	$ .01	$ .06	Lemaster, Denny	68T	491	$ .35	$1.25
Lefebvre, Jim	90T	459	$ .01	$ .04	Lemaster, Denver	69T	96	$ .30	$ .85
Lefebvre, Jim	91T	699	$ .01	$ .03					
Lefebvre, Joe	81T	88	$ .01	$ .10					
Lefebvre, Joe	81TTR	790	$ .02	$ .10					
Lefebvre, Joe	82T	434	$ .01	$ .07					
Lefebvre, Joe	83T	644	$ .01	$ .07					
Lefebvre, Joe	83TTR	61	$ .02	$ .10					
Lefebvre, Joe	84T	148	$ .01	$ .06					
Lefebvre, Joe	85T	531	$ .01	$ .05					
Lefferts, Craig	84T	99	$ .01	$ .06					
Lefferts, Craig	84TTR	72	$ .02	$ .10					
Lefferts, Craig	85T	608	$ .01	$ .05					
Lefferts, Craig	86T	244	$ .01	$ .04					
Lefferts, Craig	87T	501	$ .01	$ .04					
Lefferts, Craig	88T	734	$ .01	$ .04					
Lefferts, Craig	89T	372	$ .01	$ .05					
Lefferts, Craig	90T	158	$ .01	$ .04					
Lefferts, Craig	90TTR	59	$ .01	$ .05					
Lefferts, Craig	91T	448	$ .01	$ .03					
LeFlore, Ron	75T	628	$ .45	$1.45					
LeFlore, Ron	76T	61	$ .07	$ .30					
LeFlore, Ron	77T	240	$ .03	$ .12					
LeFlore, Ron	78T	480	$ .02	$ .10					
LeFlore, Ron	79T	4	$ .03	$ .15					
LeFlore, Ron	79T	660	$ .02	$ .10					
LeFlore, Ron	80T	80	$ .01	$ .10					
LeFlore, Ron	81T	4	$ .35	$1.50					
LeFlore, Ron	81T	710	$ .01	$ .10					
LeFlore, Ron	81TRB	204	$ .01	$ .10					
LeFlore, Ron	81TTR	791	$ .02	$ .10					
LeFlore, Ron	82T	140	$ .01	$ .07					
LeFlore, Ron	83T	560	$ .01	$ .07	Lemaster, Denny	70T	178	$ .15	$ .50
Lehman, Ken	57T	366	$1.25	$4.25	Lemaster, Denny "Denver"	71T	636	$ .35	$1.25
Lehman, Ken	58T	141	$ .75	$3.00	Lemaster, Denny	72T	371	$ .05	$ .25
Lehman, Ken	59T	31	$1.25	$4.25	LeMaster, Johnnie	76T	596	$ .15	$ .50
Leibrandt, Charlie	81T	126	$ .30	$ .85	LeMaster, Johnnie	77T	151	$ .03	$ .12
Leibrandt, Charlie	82T	169	$ .01	$ .07	LeMaster, Johnnie	78T	538	$ .02	$ .10
Leibrandt, Charlie	83T	607	$ .01	$ .07	LeMaster, Johnnie	79T	284	$ .02	$ .10
Leibrandt, Charlie	85T	459	$ .01	$ .05	LeMaster, Johnnie	80T	434	$ .01	$ .10
Leibrandt, Charlie	86T	77	$ .01	$ .04	LeMaster, Johnnie	81T	84	$ .01	$ .10
Leibrandt, Charlie	87T	223	$ .01	$ .04	LeMaster, Johnnie	82T	304	$ .01	$ .07
Leibrandt, Charlie	88T	569	$ .01	$ .04	LeMaster, Johnnie	83T	154	$ .01	$ .07
Leibrandt, Charlie	89T	301	$ .01	$ .05	LeMaster, Johnnie	84T	663	$ .01	$ .06
Leibrandt, Charlie	90T	776	$ .01	$ .04	LeMaster, Johnnie	85T	772	$ .01	$ .05
Leibrandt, Charlie	90TTR	60	$ .01	$ .05	LeMaster, Johnnie	85TTR	74	$ .02	$ .10
Leibrandt, Charlie	91T	456	$ .01	$ .03	LeMaster, Johnnie	86T	289	$ .01	$ .04
Leiper, Dave	87T	441	$ .01	$ .10	LeMay, Dick	63T	459	$2.50	$6.50
Leiper, Dave	89T	82	$ .01	$ .05	Lemke, Mark	89T	327	$ .01	$ .15
Leiper, Dave	90T	773	$ .01	$ .04	Lemke, Mark	90T	451	$ .01	$ .04
Leiter, Al	88T	18	$ .10	$ .75	Lemke, Mark	91T	251	$ .01	$ .03
Leiter, Al	89T	659	$ .01	$ .15	Lemon, Bob	52T	268	$45.00	$130.00
Leiter, Al	89TBB	125	$ .01	$ .10	Lemon, Bob	56T	255	$10.00	$30.00
Leiter, Al	89TTR	71	$ .01	$ .10	Lemon, Bob	57T	120	$5.25	$17.00
Leiter, Al	90T	138	$ .01	$ .04	Lemon, Bob	58T	2	$4.75	$16.00
Leiter, Al	91T	233	$ .01	$ .03	Lemon, Bob	60T	460	$2.25	$6.00
Leja, Frank	54T	175	$1.75	$7.00	Lemon, Bob	61T	44	$6.00	$18.00

Player	Year	No.	VG	EX/MT	Player	Year	No.	VG	EX/MT
Lemon, Bob	71T	91	$ .45	$1.45	Leonard, Dennis	87T	38	$ .01	$ .04
Lemon, Bob	72T	449	$ .35	$1.25	Leonard, Dutch	52T	110	$7.00	$20.00
Lemon, Bob	78T	574	$ .05	$ .20	Leonard, Dutch	53T	155	$4.50	$15.00
Lemon, Chet	76T	590	$ .15	$ .50	Leonard, Dutch	79TRH	418	$ .02	$ .10
Lemon, Chet	77T	58	$ .03	$ .12	Leonard, Jeff	80T	106	$ .35	$1.50
Lemon, Chet	78T	127	$ .02	$ .10	Leonard, Jeff	81T	469	$ .05	$ .20
Lemon, Chet	79T	333	$ .02	$ .10	Leonard, Jeff	82T	47	$ .01	$ .07
Lemon, Chet	80T	589	$ .01	$ .10	Leonard, Jeff	83T	309	$ .01	$ .07
Lemon, Chet	81T	242	$ .01	$ .10	Leonard, Jeff	84T	576	$ .01	$ .06
Lemon, Chet	82T	216	$ .01	$ .07	Leonard, Jeff	84T	748	$ .01	$ .06
Lemon, Chet	82T	493	$ .01	$ .07	Leonard, Jeff	85T	619	$ .01	$ .05
Lemon, Chet	82TTR	62	$ .02	$ .10	Leonard, Jeff	85TAS	718	$ .01	$ .05
Lemon, Chet	83T	727	$ .01	$ .07	Leonard, Jeff	86T	490	$ .01	$ .04
Lemon, Chet	84T	611	$ .01	$ .06	Leonard, Jeff	87T	280	$ .01	$ .04
Lemon, Chet	85T	20	$ .01	$ .05	Leonard, Jeffrey	88T	570	$ .01	$ .04
Lemon, Chet	86T	160	$ .01	$ .04	Leonard, Jeffrey	89T	160	$ .01	$ .05
Lemon, Chet	87T	739	$ .01	$ .04	Leonard, Jeffrey	89TTR	72	$ .01	$ .06
Lemon, Chet	88T	366	$ .01	$ .04	Leonard, Jeffrey	90T	455	$ .01	$ .04
Lemon, Chet	88TBB	147	$ .01	$ .06	Leonard, Jeffrey	91T	55	$ .01	$ .03
Lemon, Chet	89T	514	$ .01	$ .05	Leonhard, Dave	68T	56	$ .30	$ .85
Lemon, Chet	89TBB	202	$ .01	$ .06	Leonhard, Dave	69T	228	$ .30	$ .95
Lemon, Chet	90T	271	$ .01	$ .04	Leonhard, Dave	70T	674	$ .75	$2.00
Lemon, Chet	91T	469	$ .01	$ .03	Leonhard, Dave	71T	716	$ .50	$1.25
Lemon, Jim	54T	103	$1.75	$7.00	Lepcio, Ted	52T	335	$40.00	$140.00
Lemon, Jim	57T	57	$ .95	$3.50	Lepcio, Ted	53T	18	$4.50	$15.00
Lemon, Jim	58T	15	$1.25	$4.25	Lepcio, Ted	54T	66	$7.00	$22.00
Lemon, Jim	59T	74	$ .95	$3.50	Lepcio, Ted	55T	128	$2.00	$6.00
Lemon, Jim	59T	215	$ .75	$2.20	Lepcio, Ted	57T	288	$4.25	$15.00
Lemon, Jim	60T	440	$ .75	$2.20	Lepcio, Ted	58T	29	$1.25	$4.25
Lemon, Jim	61T	44	$6.00	$18.00	Lepcio, Ted	59T	348	$ .75	$2.20
Lemon, Jim	61T	450	$ .75	$3.00	Lepcio, Ted	60T	97	$ .45	$1.45
Lemon, Jim	62T	510	$ .75	$2.50	Lepcio, Ted	61T	234	$ .35	$1.25
Lemon, Jim	63T	369	$ .45	$1.50	Lepcio, Ted	62T	36	$ .45	$1.45
Lemon, Jim	68T	341	$ .30	$ .85	Leppert, Don	63T	243	$ .30	$ .95
Lemon, Jim	69T	294	$ .30	$ .95	Leppert, Don	64T	463	$ .50	$1.45
Lemonds, Dave	71T	458	$ .15	$ .50	Leppert, Don	73T	517	$ .30	$ .95
Lemonds, Dave	72T	413	$ .05	$ .25	Leppert, Don	74T	489	$ .07	$ .30
Lemonds, Dave	73T	534	$ .45	$1.45	Lerch, Randy	76T	595	$ .05	$ .20
Lemongello, Mark	77T	478	$ .03	$ .12	Lerch, Randy	77T	489	$ .30	$ .85
Lemongello, Mark	78T	358	$ .02	$ .10	Lerch, Randy	78T	271	$ .02	$ .10
Lemongello, Mark	79T	187	$ .02	$ .10	Lerch, Randy	79T	52	$ .02	$ .10
Lenhardt, Don	51Tbb	33	$7.50	$22.50	Lerch, Randy	80T	344	$ .01	$ .10
Lenhardt, Don	52T	4	$15.00	$47.50	Lerch, Randy	81T	584	$ .01	$ .10
Lenhardt, Don	54T	157	$3.60	$10.00	Lerch, Randy	81TTR	792	$ .02	$ .10
Lenhardt, Don	73T	131	$ .15	$ .50	Lerch, Randy	82T	466	$ .01	$ .07
Lennon, Bob	55T	119	$2.00	$6.00	Lerch, Randy	83T	686	$ .01	$ .07
Lennon, Bob	56T	104	$2.25	$6.00	Lerch, Randy	85T	103	$ .01	$ .05
Lennon, Bob	57T	371	$1.25	$4.25	Lersch, Barry	69T	206	$ .30	$ .85
Leon, Eddie	70T	292	$ .15	$ .50	Lersch, Barry	71T	739	$ .75	$2.50
Leon, Eddie	71T	252	$ .15	$ .50	Lersch, Barry	72T	453	$ .05	$ .25
Leon, Eddie	72T	721	$ .75	$2.50	Lersch, Barry	73T	559	$ .45	$1.45
Leon, Eddie	73T	287	$ .07	$ .30	Lersch, Barry	74T	313	$ .07	$ .30
Leon, Eddie	74T	501	$ .07	$ .30	Lersch, Barry	74TTR	313	$ .07	$ .30
Leon, Eddie	75T	528	$ .07	$ .30	Lesley, Brad	85T	597	$ .01	$ .05
Leon, Maximino	75T	442	$ .07	$ .30	Lewallyn, Denny	82T	356	$ .01	$ .07
Leon, Maximino	76T	576	$ .05	$ .20	Lewis, Darren	91T	239	$ .01	$ .25
Leon, Maximino	77T	213	$ .03	$ .12	Lewis, Johnny	64T	479	$ .50	$1.45
Leonard, Dave	72T	527	$ .30	$ .95	Lewis, Johnny	65T	277	$ .35	$1.25
Leonard, Dennis	75T	615	$ .30	$ .95	Lewis, Johnny	66T	282	$ .30	$ .95
Leonard, Dennis	76T	334	$ .05	$ .20	Lewis, Johnny	67T	91	$ .30	$ .85
Leonard, Dennis	77T	75	$ .03	$ .12	Lewis, Johnny	74T	236	$ .07	$ .30
Leonard, Dennis	78T	205	$ .30	$ .85	Lewis, Mark	89T	222	$ .01	$ .40
Leonard, Dennis	78T	665	$ .02	$ .10	Ley, Terry	72T	506	$ .30	$ .85
Leonard, Dennis	79T	218	$ .02	$ .10	Leyland, Jim	86TTR	66	$ .02	$ .10
Leonard, Dennis	80T	565	$ .01	$ .10	Leyland, Jim	87T	93	$ .01	$ .04
Leonard, Dennis	81T	185	$ .01	$ .10	Leyland, Jim	88T	624	$ .01	$ .04
Leonard, Dennis	82T	495	$ .01	$ .07	Leyland, Jim	89T	284	$ .01	$ .05
Leonard, Dennis	83T	785	$ .01	$ .07	Leyland, Jim	90T	699	$ .01	$ .04
Leonard, Dennis	84T	375	$ .01	$ .06	Leyland, Jim	91T	381	$ .01	$ .03
Leonard, Dennis	86TTR	65	$ .02	$ .10	Leyritz, Jim	90TTR	61	$ .01	$ .20

TOPPS

Player	Year	No.	VG	EX/MT
Leyritz, Jim	91T	202	$ .01	$ .15
Leyva, Nick	89T	74	$ .01	$ .05
Leyva, Nick	90T	489	$ .01	$ .04
Leyva, Nick	91T	141	$ .01	$ .03
Lezcano, Carlos	81T	381	$ .01	$ .10
Lezcano, Carlos	82T	51	$ .03	$ .15
Lezcano, Sixto	76T	353	$ .07	$ .30
Lezcano, Sixto	77T	185	$ .03	$ .12
Lezcano, Sixto	78T	595	$ .02	$ .10
Lezcano, Sixto	79T	685	$ .02	$ .10
Lezcano, Sixto	80T	215	$ .01	$ .10

Player	Year	No.	VG	EX/MT
Lezcano, Sixto	81T	25	$ .01	$ .10
Lezcano, Sixto	81TTR	793	$ .02	$ .10
Lezcano, Sixto	82T	727	$ .01	$ .07
Lezcano, Sixto	82TTR	63	$ .02	$ .10
Lezcano, Sixto	83T	455	$ .01	$ .07
Lezcano, Sixto	84T	185	$ .01	$ .06
Lezcano, Sixto	85T	556	$ .01	$ .05
Lezcano, Sixto	85TTR	75	$ .02	$ .10
Lezcano, Sixto	86T	278	$ .01	$ .04
Liddle, Don	54T	225	$3.60	$10.00
Liddle, Don	56T	325	$2.25	$8.00
Lieberthal, Mike	91T	471	$ .01	$ .25
Lilliquist, Derek	89TMLD	70	$ .01	$ .10
Lilliquist, Derek	89TTR	73	$ .01	$ .15
Lilliquist, Derek	90T	282	$ .01	$ .10
Lilliquist, Derek	91T	683	$ .01	$ .03
Lillis, Bob	59T	133	$ .75	$2.20
Lillis, Bob	60T	354	$ .75	$2.20
Lillis, Bob	61T	38	$ .35	$1.25
Lillis, Bob	62T	74	$ .45	$1.45
Lillis, Bob	63T	119	$ .30	$ .95
Lillis, Bob	64T	321	$ .30	$ .95
Lillis, Bob	74T	31	$ .07	$ .30
Lillis, Bob	83T	66	$ .01	$ .07
Lillis, Bob	84T	441	$ .01	$ .06
Lillis, Bob	85T	186	$ .01	$ .05
Lillis, Bob	86T	561	$ .01	$ .04
Limmer, Lou	54T	232	$3.60	$10.00
Limmer, Lou	55T	54	$2.00	$6.00

Player	Year	No.	VG	EX/MT
Linares, Rufino	82T	244	$ .01	$ .07
Linares, Rufino	83T	467	$ .01	$ .07
Linares, Rufino	85T	167	$ .01	$ .05
Lind, Jose	88T	767	$ .01	$ .10
Lind, Jose	88TBB	107	$ .01	$ .06
Lind, Jose	89T	273	$ .01	$ .05
Lind, Jose	89TBB	25	$ .01	$ .06
Lind, Jose	90T	168	$ .01	$ .04
Lind, Jose	91T	537	$ .01	$ .03
Lindblad, Paul	66T	568	$5.00	$20.00
Lindblad, Paul	67T	227	$ .30	$ .85
Lindblad, Paul	68T	127	$ .30	$ .85
Lindblad, Paul	69T	449	$ .30	$ .85
Lindblad, Paul	70T	408	$ .15	$ .50
Lindblad, Paul	71T	658	$ .75	$2.50
Lindblad, Paul	72T	396	$ .05	$ .25
Lindblad, Paul	73T	406	$ .07	$ .30
Lindblad, Paul	74T	369	$ .07	$ .30
Lindblad, Paul	75T	278	$ .07	$ .30
Lindblad, Paul	76T	9	$ .05	$ .20
Lindblad, Paul	77T	583	$ .03	$ .12
Lindblad, Paul	78T	314	$ .02	$ .10
Lindblad, Paul	79T	634	$ .02	$ .10
Lindell, Johnny	53T	230	$12.50	$50.00
Lindell, Johnny	54T	51	$7.00	$22.00
Lindeman, Jim	87TTR	65	$ .05	$ .20
Lindeman, Jim	88T	562	$ .01	$ .04
Lindeman, Jim	89T	791	$ .01	$ .05
Lines, Dick	67T	273	$ .30	$ .85
Lines, Dick	68T	291	$ .30	$ .85
Lintz, Larry	74T	121	$ .07	$ .30
Lintz, Larry	75T	416	$ .07	$ .30
Lintz, Larry	76T	109	$ .05	$ .20
Lintz, Larry	77T	323	$ .03	$ .12
Linz, Phil	62T	596	$12.00	$36.00
Linz, Phil	63T	264	$ .30	$ .95
Linz, Phil	64T	344	$ .30	$ .95
Linz, Phil	65T	369	$ .45	$1.45
Linz, Phil	66T	522	$ .75	$2.50
Linz, Phil	67T	14	$ .30	$ .85
Linz, Phil	68T	594	$ .35	$1.25
Linzy, Frank	65T	589	$1.75	$4.50
Linzy, Frank	66T	78	$ .30	$ .95
Linzy, Frank	67T	279	$ .30	$ .85
Linzy, Frank	68T	147	$ .30	$ .85
Linzy, Frank	69T	345	$ .30	$ .85
Linzy, Frank	70T	77	$ .15	$ .50
Linzy, Frank	71T	551	$ .35	$1.25
Linzy, Frank	72T	243	$ .05	$ .25
Linzy, Frank	73T	286	$ .07	$ .30
Lipon, Johnny	52T	89	$7.00	$20.00
Lipon, John	53T	40	$4.50	$15.00
Lipon, Johnny	54T	19	$3.60	$10.00
Lipski, Bob	63T	558	$1.75	$4.50
Liriano, Nelson	88T	205	$ .01	$ .10
Liriano, Nelson	88TBB	155	$ .01	$ .06
Liriano, Nelson	89T	776	$ .01	$ .05
Liriano, Nelson	89TBB	207	$ .01	$ .06
Liriano, Nelson	90T	543	$ .01	$ .04
Liriano, Nelson	91T	18	$ .01	$ .03
Lis, Joe	70T	56	$ .15	$ .50
Lis, Joe	71T	138	$ .15	$ .50
Lis, Joe	74T	659	$ .07	$ .30
Lis, Joe	75T	86	$ .07	$ .30
Lis, Joe	77T	269	$ .03	$ .12
Littell, Mark	74T	596	$ .07	$ .30
Littell, Mark	76T	593	$ .15	$ .50
Littell, Mark	77T	141	$ .03	$ .12
Littell, Mark	78T	331	$ .02	$ .10
Littell, Mark	79T	466	$ .02	$ .10

Player	Year	No.	VG	EX/MT	Player	Year	No.	VG	EX/MT
Littell, Mark	80T	631	$ .01	$ .10	Lockwood, Skip	81T	233	$ .01	$ .10
Littell, Mark	81T	255	$ .01	$ .10	Loes, Billy	52T	20	$22.50	$85.00
Littell, Mark	82T	56	$ .01	$ .07	Loes, Billy	53T	174	$2.25	$8.00
Little, Bryan	83TTR	62	$ .02	$ .10	Loes, Billy	56T	270	$3.00	$9.00
Little, Bryan	84T	188	$ .01	$ .06	Loes, Billy	57T	244	$ .95	$3.50
Little, Bryan	85T	257	$ .01	$ .05	Loes, Billy	58T	359	$ .75	$3.00
Little, Bryan	86T	346	$ .01	$ .04	Loes, Billy	59T	336	$ .75	$2.20
Little, Jeff	83T	499	$ .01	$ .07	Loes, Billy	60T	181	$ .45	$1.45
Little, Scott	89TMLD	71	$ .01	$ .25	Loes, Billy	61T	237	$ .35	$1.25
Littlefield, Dick	57T	346	$4.25	$15.00	Logan, Johnny	53T	158	$4.50	$15.00
Littlefield, Dick	58T	241	$ .75	$3.00	Logan, Johnny	54T	122	$2.50	$10.00
Littlefield, John	81T	489	$ .01	$ .10	Logan, Johnny	56T	136	$1.50	$4.00
Littlefield, John	81TTR	794	$ .02	$ .10	Logan, Johnny	57T	4	$ .95	$3.50
Littlefield, John	82T	278	$ .01	$ .07	Logan, Johnny	58T	110	$1.25	$4.25
Littlejohn, Dennis	80T	686	$ .01	$ .10	Logan, Johnny	59T	225	$ .75	$2.20
Littlejohn, Dennis	81T	561	$ .01	$ .10	Logan, Johnny	60T	205	$ .45	$1.45
Litton, Greg	89TMLD	72	$ .01	$ .06	Logan, Johnny	61T	524	$7.00	$21.00
Litton, Greg	90T	66	$ .01	$ .04	Logan, Johnny	62T	573	$2.50	$7.50
Litton, Greg	91T	628	$ .01	$ .03	Logan, Johnny	63T	259	$ .30	$ .95
Llenas, Winston	71T	152	$ .15	$ .50	Lois, Alberto	80T	683	$ .01	$ .10
Llenas, Winston	74T	467	$ .07	$ .30	Lolich, Mickey	64T	128	$3.50	$11.50
Llenas, Winston	75T	597	$ .07	$ .30	Lolich, Mickey	65T	335	$ .75	$3.00
Lock, Don	63T	47	$ .30	$ .95	Lolich, Mickey	66T	226	$ .75	$3.00
Lock, Don	64T	114	$ .30	$ .95	Lolich, Mickey	66T	455	$1.25	$5.00
Lock, Don	65T	445	$ .35	$1.25	Lolich, Mickey	67T	88	$ .45	$1.45
Lock, Don	66T	165	$ .30	$ .95	Lolich, Mickey	68T	414	$ .90	$3.00
Lock, Don	67T	376	$ .30	$ .95	Lolich, Mickey	69T	270	$ .50	$2.00
Lock, Don	68T	59	$ .30	$ .85	Lolich, Mickey	70T	72	$ .50	$2.00
Lock, Don	69T	229	$ .30	$ .95	Lolich, Mickey	70T	715	$1 .50	$5.00
Locke, Bobby	60T	44	$ .45	$1.45	Lolich, Mickey	71T	71	$ .15	$ .50
Locke, Bobby	61T	537	$7.00	$21.00	Lolich, Mickey	71T	133	$ .15	$ .50
Locke, Bobby	62T	359	$ .45	$1.45	Lolich, Mickey	72T	94	$ .40	$1.50
Locke, Bobby	65T	324	$ .35	$1.25	Lolich, Mickey	72T	96	$ .40	$1.50
Locke, Bobby	68T	24	$ .30	$ .85	Lolich, Mickey	72T	450	$ .30	$ .95
Locke, Ron	64T	556	$1.75	$4.50	Lolich, Mickey	73T	390	$ .30	$ .95
Locke, Ron	65T	511	$ .75	$3.00	Lolich, Mickey	74T	9	$ .30	$ .95
Locker, Bob	65T	541	$1.75	$4.50	Lolich, Mickey	75T	245	$ .30	$ .95
Locker, Bob	66T	374	$ .30	$ .95	Lolich, Mickey	76T	385	$ .30	$ .95
Locker, Bob	67T	338	$ .30	$ .85	Lolich, Mickey	76TRB	3	$ .05	$ .20
Locker, Bob	68T	51	$ .30	$ .85	Lolich, Mickey	76TTR	385	$ .30	$ .95
Locker, Bob	69T	548	$ .30	$ .95	Lolich, Mickey	77T	565	$ .30	$ .85
Locker, Bob	70T	249	$ .15	$ .50	Lolich, Mickey	79T	164	$ .05	$ .20
Locker, Bob	71T	356	$ .15	$ .50	Lolich, Mickey	80T	459	$ .01	$ .10
Locker, Bob	72T	537	$ .30	$ .95	Lolich, Ron	71T	458	$ .15	$ .50
Locker, Bob	73T	645	$ .45	$1.45	Lollar, Sherman	51Tbb	24	$4.00	$18.00
Locker, Bob	74T	62	$ .07	$ .30	Lollar, Sherman	52T	117	$7.00	$21.00
Locker, Bob	74TTR	62	$ .07	$ .30	Lollar, Sherman	53T	53	$4.50	$15.00
Locker, Bob	75T	434	$ .07	$ .30	Lollar, Sherm	54T	39	$2.50	$10.00
Locklear, Gene	75T	13	$ .07	$ .30	Lollar, Sherm	55T	201	$2.85	$9.50
Locklear, Gene	76T	447	$ .05	$ .20	Lollar, Sherm	56T	243	$3.00	$9.00
Lockman, Whitey	51Trb	41	$1.50	$4.00	Lollar, Sherm	57T	23	$ .95	$3.50
Lockman, Whitey	56T	205	$3.00	$9.00	Lollar, Sherm	58T	267	$ .75	$3.00
Lockman, Whitey	57T	232	$ .95	$3.50	Lollar, Sherm	58TAS	491	$ .40	$1.10
Lockman, Whitey	58T	195	$ .45	$1.50	Lollar, Sherm	59T	385	$ .75	$2.20
Lockman, Whitey	59T	411	$ .75	$2.20	Lollar, Sherm	60T	495	$ .90	$3.00
Lockman, Whitey	60T	535	$2.50	$10.00	Lollar, Sherm	60TAS	567	$2.50	$10.00
Lockman, Whitey	73T	81	$ .30	$ .95	Lollar, Sherm	61T	285	$ .35	$1.25
Lockman, Whitey	74T	354	$ .07	$ .30	Lollar, Sherm	62T	514	$ .75	$2.50
Lockwood, Skip	65T	526	$50.00	$150.00	Lollar, Sherm "Sherman'	63T	118	$ .30	$ .95
Lockwood, Skip	70T	499	$ .15	$ .50	Lollar, Tim	81T	424	$ .01	$ .10
Lockwood, Skip	71T	433	$ .15	$ .50	Lollar, Tim	82T	587	$ .01	$ .07
Lockwood, Skip	72T	118	$ .05	$ .25	Lollar, Tim	83T	185	$ .01	$ .07
Lockwood, Skip	73T	308	$ .07	$ .30	Lollar, Tim	83T	742	$ .01	$ .07
Lockwood, Skip	74T	532	$ .07	$ .30	Lollar, Tim	84T	644	$ .01	$ .06
Lockwood, Skip	75T	417	$ .07	$ .30	Lollar, Tim	85T	13	$ .01	$ .05
Lockwood, Skip	76T	166	$ .05	$ .20	Lollar, Tim	85TTR	76	$ .02	$ .10
Lockwood, Skip	77T	65	$ .03	$ .12	Lollar, Tim	86T	297	$ .01	$ .04
Lockwood, Skip	78T	379	$ .02	$ .10	Lollar, Tim	87T	396	$ .01	$ .04
Lockwood, Skip	79T	481	$ .02	$ .10	Lombardi, Phil	88T	283	$ .01	$ .04
Lockwood, Skip	80T	567	$ .01	$ .10	Lombardozzi, Steve	87TTR	66	$ .01	$ .05

TOPPS

Player	Year	No.	VG	EX/MT	Player	Year	No.	VG	EX/MT
Lombardozzi, Steve	88T	697	$ .01	$ .04	Lopes, Dave	83T	365	$ .01	$ .07
Lombardozzi, Steve	89T	376	$ .01	$ .05	Lopes, Dave	84T	669	$ .02	$ .10
Lonborg, Jim	65T	573	$3.75	$14.00	Lopes, Dave	84T	714	$ .01	$ .06
Lonborg, Jim	66T	93	$ .15	$ .50	Lopes, Dave	85T	12	$ .01	$ .05
Lonborg, Jim	67T	371	$ .35	$1.25	Lopes, Dave	86T	125	$ .05	$ .50
Lonborg, Jim	68T	10	$ .45	$1.45	Lopes, Dave	87T	445	$ .01	$ .04
Lonborg, Jim	68T	12	$ .45	$1.45	Lopes, Dave	87TRB	4	$ .01	$ .04
Lonborg, Jim	68T	460	$ .35	$1.25	Lopes, Dave	88T	226	$ .01	$ .10
Lonborg, Jim	69T	109	$ .15	$ .50	Lopez, Al	60T	222	$ .90	$3.00
Lonborg, Jim	70T	665	$1.25	$4.25	Lopez, Al	61T	132	$ .90	$3.00
Lonborg, Jim	71T	577	$ .45	$1.45	Lopez, Al	61T	337	$ .75	$2.25
Lonborg, Jim	72T	255	$ .05	$ .25	Lopez, Al	62T	286	$ .75	$2.00
Lonborg, Jim	73T	3	$ .30	$ .85	Lopez, Al	63T	458	$3.00	$9.00
Lonborg, Jim	74T	342	$ .07	$ .30	Lopez, Al	64T	232	$ .90	$3.00
Lonborg, Jim	75T	94	$ .07	$ .30	Lopez, Al	65T	414	$ .90	$3.00
Lonborg, Jim	76T	271	$ .05	$ .20	Lopez, Al	69T	527	$ .75	$2.50
Lonborg, Jim	77T	569	$ .03	$ .12	Lopez, Art	65T	566	$1.75	$5.75
Lonborg, Jim	78T	52	$ .02	$ .10	Lopez, Aurelio	79T	444	$ .05	$ .20
Lonborg, Jim	79T	446	$ .02	$ .10	Lopez, Aurelio	80T	101	$ .01	$ .10
Long, Bill	87TTR	67	$ .01	$ .05	Lopez, Aurelio	81T	291	$ .01	$ .10
Long, Bill	88T	309	$ .01	$ .04	Lopez, Aurelio	82T	728	$ .01	$ .07
Long, Bill	89T	133	$ .01	$ .05	Lopez, Aurelio	83TTR	63	$ .02	$ .10
Long, Bill	90T	499	$ .01	$ .04	Lopez, Aurelio	84T	95	$ .01	$ .06
Long, Bill	91T	668	$ .01	$ .03	Lopez, Aurelio	85T	539	$ .01	$ .05
Long, Bob	82T	291	$ .25	$1.00	Lopez, Aurelio	86T	367	$ .01	$ .04
Long, Dale	55T	127	$2.00	$6.00	Lopez, Aurelio	87T	659	$ .01	$ .04
Long, Dale	56T	56	$2.25	$6.00	Lopez, Carlos	77T	492	$ .25	$ .80
Long, Dale	57T	3	$ .95	$3.50	Lopez, Carlos	78T	166	$ .02	$ .10
Long, Dale	58T	7	$1.75	$4.50	Lopez, Carlos	79T	568	$ .02	$ .10
Long, Dale	59T	147	$3.50	$10.00	Lopez, Hector	56T	16	$2.25	$6.00
Long, Dale	59T	414	$ .75	$2.20	Lopez, Hector	57T	6	$ .95	$3.50
Long, Dale	60T	375	$ .75	$2.20	Lopez, Hector	58T	155	$ .75	$3.00
Long, Dale	61T	117	$ .35	$1.25	Lopez, Hector	59T	402	$ .75	$2.20
Long, Dale	62T	228	$ .45	$1.45	Lopez, Hector	60T	163	$ .45	$1.45
Long, Dale	63T	484	$2.50	$6.50	Lopez, Hector	61T	28	$ .35	$1.25
Long, Jeoff	64T	497	$ .50	$1.45	Lopez, Hector	62T	502	$ .90	$3.00
Lonnett, Joe	57T	241	$ .95	$3.50	Lopez, Hector	63T	92	$ .30	$ .95
Lonnett, Joe	58T	64	$1.25	$4.25	Lopez, Hector	64T	325	$ .30	$ .95
Lonnett, Joe	73T	356	$ .15	$ .50	Lopez, Hector	65T	532	$1.75	$4.50
Lonnett, Joe	74T	221	$ .07	$ .30	Lopez, Hector	66T	177	$ .30	$ .95
Look, Bruce	69T	317	$ .30	$ .95	Lopez, Marcelino	63T	549	$1.75	$4.50
Lopat, Ed	51Tbb	39	$7.50	$28.00	Lopez, Marcelino	65T	537	$2.10	$6.00
Lopat, Ed	52T	57	$25.00	$75.00	Lopez, Marcelino	66T	155	$ .30	$ .95
Lopat, Ed	53T	87	$9.00	$35.00	Lopez, Marcelino	67T	513	$ .75	$3.00
Lopat, Ed	54T	5	$5.50	$18.00	Lopez, Marcelino	70T	344	$ .15	$ .50
Lopat, Ed	55T	109	$3.00	$12.00	Lopez, Marcelino	71T	137	$ .15	$ .50
Lopat, Ed	60T	465	$2.50	$9.00	Lopez, Marcelino	72T	652	$ .30	$ .95
Lopat, Ed	63T	23	$ .35	$1.25	Loun, Don	65T	181	$ .30	$ .85
Lopat, Ed	64T	348	$ .45	$1.45	Loviglio, Jay	81T	526	$ .01	$ .07
Lopata, Stan	56T	183	$3.00	$9.00	Loviglio, Jay	82T	599	$ .01	$ .07
Lopata, Stan	57T	119	$ .95	$3.50	Lovitto, Joe	73T	276	$ .07	$ .30
Lopata, Stan	58T	353	$ .75	$3.00	Lovitto, Joe	74T	639	$ .07	$ .30
Lopata, Stan	59T	412	$ .75	$2.20	Lovitto, Joe	75T	36	$ .07	$ .30
Lopata, Stan	60T	515	$2.50	$10.00	Lovitto, Joe	76T	604	$ .05	$ .20
Lopes, Dave	73T	609	$1.00	$4.00	Lovrich, Pete	63T	549	$1.75	$4.50
Lopes, Dave	74T	112	$ .30	$ .95	Lovrich, Pete	64T	212	$ .30	$ .95
Lopes, Dave	75T	93	$ .15	$ .50	Lowenstein, John	71T	231	$ .15	$ .50
Lopes, Dave	76T	197	$ .15	$ .50	Lowenstein, John	72T	486	$ .05	$ .25
Lopes, Dave	76T	660	$ .45	$1.45	Lowenstein, John	73T	327	$ .07	$ .30
Lopes, Dave	76TRB	4	$ .05	$ .20	Lowenstein, John	74T	176	$ .07	$ .30
Lopes, Dave	77T	4	$ .03	$ .12	Lowenstein, John	75T	424	$ .07	$ .30
Lopes, Dave	77T	180	$ .03	$ .12	Lowenstein, John	76T	646	$ .05	$ .20
Lopes, Dave	78T	440	$ .05	$ .20	Lowenstein, John	77T	393	$ .03	$ .12
Lopes, Dave	79T	290	$ .02	$ .10	Lowenstein, John	78T	87	$ .02	$ .10
Lopes, Dave	80T	560	$ .03	$ .15	Lowenstein, John	79T	173	$ .02	$ .10
Lopes, Dave	81T	50	$ .02	$ .10	Lowenstein, John	80T	287	$ .01	$ .10
Lopes, Dave	82T	740	$ .01	$ .07	Lowenstein, John	81T	591	$ .01	$ .10
Lopes, Dave	82TAS	338	$ .01	$ .07	Lowenstein, John	82T	747	$ .01	$ .07
Lopes, Dave	82TIA	741	$ .01	$ .07	Lowenstein, John	83T	473	$ .01	$ .07
Lopes, Dave	82TTR	64	$ .05	$ .25	Lowenstein, John	84T	604	$ .01	$ .06

Player	Year	No.	VG	EX/MT	Player	Year	No.	VG	EX/MT
Lowenstein, John	85T	316	$ .01	$ .05	Lum, Mike	71T	194	$ .15	$ .50
Lown, Turk	52T	330	$40.00	$140.00	Lum, Mike	72T	641	$ .30	$ .95
Lown, Turk	53T	130	$4.50	$15.00	Lum, Mike	73T	266	$ .07	$ .30
Lown, Turk	57T	247	$ .95	$3.50	Lum, Mike	74T	227	$ .07	$ .30
Lown, Turk	58T	261	$ .75	$3.00	Lum, Mike	75T	154	$ .07	$ .30
Lown, Turk	59T	277	$ .75	$2.20	Lum, Mike	76T	208	$ .05	$ .20
Lown, Turk	60T	57	$ .75	$3.00	Lum, Mike	76TTR	208	$ .05	$ .20
Lown, Turk	60T	313	$ .75	$2.20	Lum, Mike	77T	601	$ .03	$ .12
Lown, Turk	61T	424	$ .75	$3.00	Lum, Mike	78T	326	$ .02	$ .10
Lown, Turk	62T	528	$3.95	$11.50	Lum, Mike	79T	556	$ .02	$ .10
Lowrey, Harry	52T	111	$7.00	$20.00	Lum, Mike	80T	7	$ .01	$ .10
Lowrey, Harry "Peanuts"	53T	16	$4.50	$15.00	Lum, Mike	81T	457	$ .01	$ .10
Lowrey, Peanuts	54T	158	$3.60	$10.00	Lum, Mike	81TTR	795	$ .02	$ .10
Lowry, Dwight	87T	483	$ .01	$ .04	Lum, Mike	82T	732	$ .01	$ .07
Loynd, Mike	87T	126	$ .07	$ .30	Lumenti, Ralph	58T	369	$ .75	$3.00
Loynd, Mike	88T	319	$ .01	$ .04	Lumenti, Ralph	59T	316	$ .75	$2.20
Lubratich, Steve	84T	266	$ .01	$ .06	Lumenti, Ralph	61T	469	$ .75	$3.00
Lucas, Gary	81T	436	$ .01	$ .10	Lumpe, Jerry	58T	193	$ .75	$3.00
Lucas, Gary	82T	120	$ .01	$ .07	Lumpe, Jerry	59T	272	$ .75	$2.20
Lucas, Gary	83T	761	$ .01	$ .07	Lumpe, Jerry	60T	290	$ .75	$2.20
Lucas, Gary	84T	7	$ .01	$ .06	Lumpe, Jerry	61T	119	$ .45	$1.45
Lucas, Gary	84TTR	73	$ .02	$ .10	Lumpe, Jerry	61T	365	$ .35	$1.25
Lucas, Gary	85T	297	$ .01	$ .05	Lumpe, Jerry	62T	127	$ .75	$3.00
Lucas, Gary	86T	601	$ .01	$ .04	Lumpe, Jerry	62T	305	$ .45	$1.45
Lucas, Gary	87T	696	$ .01	$ .04	Lumpe, Jerry	63T	256	$ .30	$ .95
Lucas, Gary	88T	524	$ .01	$ .04	Lumpe, Jerry	64T	165	$ .30	$ .95
Lucchesi, Frank	70T	662	$ .75	$2.00	Lumpe, Jerry	65T	353	$ .35	$1.25
Lucchesi, Frank	71T	119	$ .15	$ .50	Lumpe, Jerry	66T	161	$ .30	$ .95
Lucchesi, Frank	72T	188	$ .05	$ .25	Lumpe, Jerry	67T	247	$ .30	$ .85
Lucchesi, Frank	74T	379	$ .15	$ .50	Lund, Don	53T	277	$12.50	$50.00
Lucchesi, Frank	88T	564	$ .01	$ .04	Lund, Don	54T	167	$3.60	$10.00
Luebber, Steve	72T	678	$ .75	$2.50	Lund, Gordon	70T	642	$ .75	$2.00
Luebber, Steve	77T	457	$ .03	$ .12	Lundstedt, Tom	74T	603	$ .07	$ .30
Luecken, Rick	89TMLD	73	$ .01	$ .06	Luplow, Al	62T	598	$18.00	$55.00
Luecken, Rick	90T	87	$ .01	$ .10	Luplow, Al	63T	351	$ .45	$1.50
Lugo, Urbano	86T	373	$ .01	$ .04	Luplow, Al	64T	184	$ .30	$ .95
Lugo, Urbano	87T	92	$ .01	$ .04	Luplow, Al	66T	188	$ .30	$ .95
Lum, Mike	68T	579	$ .45	$1.45	Luplow, Al	67T	433	$ .30	$ .95
Lum, Mike	69T	514	$ .30	$ .95	Lusader, Scott	89T	487	$ .01	$ .10
					Lusader, Scott	90T	632	$ .01	$ .04
					Luttrell, Lyle	57T	386	$1.25	$4.25
					Lutz, Joe	73T	449	$ .30	$ .85
					Luzinski, Greg	71T	439	$ .60	$2.00
					Luzinski, Greg	72T	112	$ .30	$ .95
					Luzinski, Greg	73T	189	$ .30	$ .95
					Luzinski, Greg	74T	360	$ .15	$ .50
					Luzinski, Greg	75T	630	$ .30	$ .95
					Luzinski, Greg	76T	193	$ .75	$2.20
					Luzinski, Greg	76T	195	$ .35	$1.25
					Luzinski, Greg	76T	610	$ .15	$ .50
					Luzinski, Greg	77T	30	$ .30	$ .85
					Luzinski, Greg	78T	420	$ .05	$ .20
					Luzinski, Greg	79T	540	$ .05	$ .20
					Luzinski, Greg	80T	120	$ .01	$ .10
					Luzinski, Greg	81T	270	$ .03	$ .15
					Luzinski, Greg	81TTR	796	$ .02	$ .10
					Luzinski, Greg	82T	720	$ .03	$ .15
					Luzinski, Greg	82TIA	721	$ .01	$ .07
					Luzinski, Greg	83T	310	$ .01	$ .07
					Luzinski, Greg	83T	591	$ .01	$ .07
					Luzinski, Greg	84T	20	$ .01	$ .06
					Luzinski, Greg	84T	712	$ .03	$ .15
					Luzinski, Greg	85T	650	$ .01	$ .05
					Lyle, Sparky	69T	311	$2.25	$9.00
					Lyle, Sparky	70T	116	$ .25	$1.25
					Lyle, Sparky	71T	649	$1.75	$6.50
					Lyle, Sparky	72T	259	$ .25	$1.00
					Lyle, Sparky	73T	68	$ .30	$ .85
					Lyle, Sparky	73T	394	$ .30	$ .85
					Lyle, Sparky	74T	66	$ .30	$ .95

Mike Lum — OUTFIELD

Player	Year	No.	VG	EX/MT
Lum, Mike	70T	367	$ .15	$ .50

TOPPS

Player	Year	No.	VG	EX/MT	Player	Year	No.	VG	EX/MT
Lyle, Sparky	75T	485	$ .15	$ .50	Lynn, Fred	81TTR	797	$ .30	$ .85
Lyle, Sparky	76T	545	$ .15	$ .50	Lynn, Fred	82T	251	$ .05	$ .20
Lyle, Sparky	77T	598	$ .30	$ .85	Lynn, Fred	82TIA	252	$ .02	$ .10
Lyle, Sparky	78T	35	$ .02	$ .10	Lynn, Fred	83T	520	$ .03	$ .15
Lyle, Sparky	78TRB	2	$ .02	$ .10	Lynn, Fred	83TAS	392	$ .01	$ .10
Lyle, Sparky	79T	365	$ .05	$ .20	Lynn, Fred	84T	680	$ .05	$ .20
Lyle, Sparky	80T	115	$ .03	$ .15	Lynn, Fred	85T	220	$ .03	$ .15
Lyle, Sparky	81T	719	$ .01	$ .10	Lynn, Fred	85TTR	77	$ .05	$ .25
Lyle, Sparky	82T	285	$ .01	$ .07	Lynn, Fred	86T	55	$ .02	$ .20
Lyle, Sparky	83T	693	$ .01	$ .07	Lynn, Fred	87T	370	$ .01	$ .10
Lyle, Sparky	83T	694	$ .01	$ .07	Lynn, Fred	88T	707	$ .01	$ .10
Lynch, Ed	82T	121	$ .01	$ .07	Lynn, Fred	88TBB	169	$ .01	$ .10
Lynch, Ed	83T	601	$ .01	$ .07	Lynn, Fred	89T	416	$ .01	$ .05
Lynch, Ed	84T	293	$ .01	$ .06	Lynn, Fred	90T	107	$ .01	$ .04
					Lynn, Fred	90TTB	663	$ .01	$ .04
					Lynn, Fred	90TTR	62	$ .01	$ .05
					Lynn, Fred	91T	586	$ .01	$ .03
					Lyons, Barry	87TTR	68	$ .01	$ .05
					Lyons, Barry	88T	633	$ .01	$ .04
					Lyons, Barry	89T	412	$ .01	$ .05
					Lyons, Barry	90T	258	$ .01	$ .04
					Lyons, Steve	86T	233	$ .01	$ .04
					Lyons, Steve	86TTR	67	$ .02	$ .10
					Lyons, Steve	88T	108	$ .01	$ .04
					Lyons, Steve	89T	334	$ .01	$ .05
					Lyons, Steve	89TBB	105	$ .01	$ .06
					Lyons, Steve	90T	751	$ .01	$ .04
					Lyons, Steve	91T	612	$ .01	$ .03
					Lysander, Rick	84T	639	$ .01	$ .06
					Lysander, Rick	85T	383	$ .01	$ .05
					Lysander, Rick	86T	482	$ .01	$ .04
					Lyttle, Jim	70T	516	$ .15	$ .50
					Lyttle, Jim	71T	234	$ .15	$ .50
					Lyttle, Jim	72T	648	$ .30	$ .95
					Lyttle, Jim	74T	437	$ .07	$ .30
					Maas, Duke	56T	57	$2.25	$6.00
					Maas, Duke	57T	405	$1.25	$4.25
					Maas, Duke	58T	228	$ .75	$3.00
					Maas, Duke	59T	167	$ .75	$2.20
					Maas, Duke	60T	421	$ .75	$2.20
					Maas, Duke	61T	387	$ .75	$3.00
					Maas, Kevin	90TTR	63	$ .01	$2.25

Player	Year	No.	VG	EX/MT	Player	Year	No.	VG	EX/MT
Lynch, Ed	85T	467	$ .01	$ .05	Maas, Kevin	91T	435	$ .01	$ .50
Lynch, Ed	86T	68	$ .01	$ .04	Maas, Kevin	91TRB	4	$ .01	$ .15
Lynch, Ed	87T	697	$ .01	$ .04	Mabe, Bob	59T	356	$ .75	$2.20
Lynch, Ed	88T	336	$ .01	$ .04	Mabe, Bob	60T	288	$ .75	$2.20
Lynch, Jerry	54T	234	$1.75	$7.00	MacDonald, Bill	52T	138	$7.00	$20.00
Lynch, Jerry	55T	142	$2.00	$6.00	Macfarlane, Mike	88TTR	62	$ .01	$ .15
Lynch, Jerry	56T	97	$2.25	$6.00	Macfarlane, Mike	89T	479	$ .01	$ .15
Lynch, Jerry	57T	358	$1.25	$4.25	Macfarlane, Mike	89TBB	86	$ .01	$ .06
Lynch, Jerry	58T	103	$1.25	$4.25	Macfarlane, Mike	90T	202	$ .01	$ .04
Lynch, Jerry	59T	97	$1.25	$4.25	Macfarlane, Mike	91T	638	$ .01	$ .03
Lynch, Jerry	60T	198	$ .45	$1.45	Macha, Ken	78T	483	$ .02	$ .10
Lynch, Jerry	60T	352	$ .90	$3.50	Macha, Ken	82T	282	$ .01	$ .07
Lynch, Jerry	61T	97	$ .35	$1.25	Machado, Julio	89TMLD	74	$ .01	$ .15
Lynch, Jerry	62T	487	$ .75	$2.50	Machado, Julio	90T	684	$ .01	$ .10
Lynch, Jerry	63T	37	$ .30	$ .95	Machado, Julio	91T	434	$ .01	$ .03
Lynch, Jerry	64T	193	$ .30	$ .95	Mack, Shane	85T	398	$ .10	$ .40
Lynch, Jerry	65T	291	$ .35	$1.25	Mack, Shane	87TTR	69	$ .05	$ .25
Lynch, Jerry	66T	182	$ .30	$ .95	Mack, Shane	88T	548	$ .01	$ .04
Lynn, Fred	75T	622	$2.25	$11.00	Mack, Shane	90TTR	64	$ .01	$ .05
Lynn, Fred	76T	50	$ .75	$3.00	Mack, Shane	91T	672	$ .01	$ .03
Lynn, Fred	76T	192	$ .50	$1.50	Mackanin, Pete	74T	597	$ .15	$ .50
Lynn, Fred	76T	196	$ .30	$ .95	Mackanin, Pete	76T	287	$ .05	$ .20
Lynn, Fred	77T	210	$ .50	$1.50	Mackanin, Pete	77T	156	$ .03	$ .12
Lynn, Fred	78T	320	$ .30	$ .90	Mackanin, Pete	78T	399	$ .02	$ .10
Lynn, Fred	79T	480	$ .35	$1.25	Mackanin, Pete	81T	509	$ .01	$ .10
Lynn, Fred	80T	110	$ .05	$ .25	Mackanin, Pete	82T	438	$ .01	$ .07
Lynn, Fred	80T	201	$ .08	$ .30	MacKenzie, Ken	60T	534	$2.50	$10.00
Lynn, Fred	81T	720	$ .05	$ .20	MacKenzie, Ken	61T	496	$ .75	$3.00

Player	Year	No.	VG	EX/MT	Player	Year	No.	VG	EX/MT
MacKenzie, Ken	62T	421	$ .75	$2.50	Madlock, Bill	87TTR	71	$ .03	$ .15
MacKenzie, Ken	63T	393	$ .45	$1.50	Madlock, Bill	88T	145	$ .01	$ .10
MacKenzie, Ken	64T	297	$ .30	$ .95	Magadan, Dave	87T	512	$ .30	$ .95
Macko, Steve	80T	676	$ .01	$ .10	Magadan, Dave	88T	58	$ .01	$ .10
Macko, Steve	81T	381	$ .01	$ .10	Magadan, Dave	89T	655	$ .01	$ .05
MacWhorter, Keith	81T	689	$ .75	$2.25	Magadan, Dave	89TBB	71	$ .01	$ .06
Madden, Mike	83TTR	64	$ .02	$ .10	Magadan, Dave	90T	135	$ .01	$ .04
Madden, Mike	84T	127	$ .01	$ .06	Magadan, Dave	91T	480	$ .01	$ .03
Madden, Mike	85T	479	$ .01	$ .05	Maglie, Sal	57T	5	$3.00	$9.50
Madden, Mike	86T	691	$ .01	$ .04	Maglie, Sal	58T	43	$3.60	$10.00
Maddox, Elliott	71T	11	$ .15	$ .50	Maglie, Sal	59T	309	$1.50	$4.00
Maddox, Elliott	72T	277	$ .05	$ .25	Maglie, Sal	60T	456	$2.25	$6.00
Maddox, Elliott	73T	658	$ .45	$1.45	Magnuson, Jim	72T	597	$ .30	$ .95
Maddox, Elliott	74T	401	$ .07	$ .30	Magrane, Joe	87TTR	72	$ .25	$1.25
Maddox, Elliott	75T	113	$ .07	$ .30	Magrane, Joe	88T	380	$ .01	$ .50
Maddox, Elliott	76T	503	$ .05	$ .20	Magrane, Joe	89T	657	$ .01	$ .15
Maddox, Elliott	77T	332	$ .03	$ .12	Magrane, Joe	89TBB	203	$ .01	$ .06
Maddox, Elliott	78T	442	$ .02	$ .10	Magrane, Joe	90T	578	$ .01	$ .04
Maddox, Elliott	79T	69	$ .02	$ .10	Magrane, Joe	90TAS	406	$ .01	$ .04
Maddox, Elliott	80T	707	$ .01	$ .10	Magrane, Joe	91T	185	$ .01	$ .03
Maddox, Elliott	81T	299	$ .01	$ .10	Magrann, Tom	89TMLD	75	$ .01	$ .06
Maddox, Garry	73T	322	$ .30	$ .95	Magrini, Pete	66T	558	$5.50	$17.50
Maddox, Garry	74T	178	$ .07	$ .30	Mahaffey, Art	60T	138	$ .45	$1.45
Maddox, Garry	75T	240	$ .07	$ .30	Mahaffey, Art	61T	433	$ .75	$3.00
Maddox, Garry	76T	38	$ .05	$ .20	Mahaffey, Art	62T	550	$3.95	$11.50
Maddox, Garry	77T	520	$ .03	$ .12	Mahaffey, Art	63T	385	$ .45	$1.50
Maddox, Garry	78T	610	$ .02	$ .10	Mahaffey, Art	63T	7	$ .45	$1.45
Maddox, Garry	79T	470	$ .02	$ .10	Mahaffey, Art	64T	104	$ .30	$ .95
Maddox, Garry	80T	380	$ .01	$ .10	Mahaffey, Art	65T	446	$ .35	$1.25
Maddox, Garry	81T	160	$ .01	$ .10	Mahaffey, Art	66T	570	$3.50	$10.00
Maddox, Garry	82T	20	$ .01	$ .07	Mahlberg, Greg	80T	673	$ .01	$ .10
Maddox, Garry	83T	615	$ .01	$ .07	Mahler, Mickey	78T	703	$1.50	$6.00
Maddox, Garry	84T	755	$ .01	$ .06	Mahler, Mickey	79T	331	$ .02	$ .10
Maddox, Garry	85T	235	$ .01	$ .05	Mahler, Mickey	86TTR	68	$ .02	$ .10
Maddox, Garry	86T	585	$ .01	$ .04	Mahler, Rick	82T	126	$ .01	$ .07
Maddux, Greg	87TTR	70	$ .15	$ .75	Mahler, Rick	82T	579	$ .05	$ .20
Maddux, Greg	88T	361	$ .01	$ .25	Mahler, Rick	83T	76	$ .01	$ .07
Maddux, Greg	89T	240	$ .01	$ .05	Mahler, Rick	85T	79	$ .01	$ .05
Maddux, Greg	90T	715	$ .01	$ .10	Mahler, Rick	86T	437	$ .01	$ .04
Maddux, Greg	91T	35	$ .01	$ .03	Mahler, Rick	87T	242	$ .01	$ .04
Maddux, Mike	87T	553	$ .01	$ .10	Mahler, Rick	88T	706	$ .01	$ .04
Maddux, Mike	88T	756	$ .01	$ .04	Mahler, Rick	89T	621	$ .01	$ .05
Maddux, Mike	89T	39	$ .01	$ .05	Mahler, Rick	89TTR	74	$ .01	$ .06
Maddux, Mike	89TBB	74	$ .01	$ .06	Mahler, Rick	90T	151	$ .01	$ .04
Maddux, Mike	90T	154	$ .01	$ .06	Mahler, Rick	91T	363	$ .01	$ .03
Madison, Dave	52T	366	$40.00	$140.00	Mahoney, Bob	52T	58	$15.00	$47.50
Madison, Dave	53T	99	$3.00	$9.00	Mahoney, Jim	73T	356	$ .15	$ .50
Madison, Scotti	88TTR	63	$ .01	$ .06	Mahoney, Jim	74T	221	$ .07	$ .30
Madlock, Bill	74T	600	$1.25	$5.00	Main, Forrest	52T	397	$40.00	$140.00
Madlock, Bill	75T	104	$ .25	$1.25	Main, Forrest	53T	198	$4.50	$15.00
Madlock, Bill	76T	191	$ .30	$ .95	Majeski, Hank	51Tbb	2	$7.50	$22.50
Madlock, Bill	76T	640	$ .25	$1.25	Majeski, Henry	52T	112	$7.00	$20.00
Madlock, Bill	77T	1	$1.00	$3.50	Maldonado, Candy	84T	244	$ .05	$ .20
Madlock, Bill	77T	250	$ .30	$ .95	Maldonado, Candy	85T	523	$ .01	$ .05
Madlock, Bill	78T	410	$ .07	$ .30	Maldonado, Candy	86T	87	$ .01	$ .04
Madlock, Bill	79T	195	$ .05	$ .20	Maldonado, Candy	86TTR	69	$ .02	$ .10
Madlock, Bill	80T	55	$ .05	$ .25	Maldonado, Candy	87T	335	$ .01	$ .04
Madlock, Bill	81T	715	$ .05	$ .20	Maldonado, Candy	88T	190	$ .01	$ .04
Madlock, Bill	82T	161	$ .03	$ .15	Maldonado, Candy	88TBB	35	$ .01	$ .06
Madlock, Bill	82T	365	$ .03	$ .15	Maldonado, Candy	89T	495	$ .01	$ .05
Madlock, Bill	82T	696	$ .01	$ .07	Maldonado, Candy	89TBB	197	$ .01	$ .06
Madlock, Bill	83T	291	$ .01	$ .07	Maldonado, Candy	90T	628	$ .01	$ .04
Madlock, Bill	83T	645	$ .01	$ .07	Maldonado, Candy	90TTR	65	$ .01	$ .05
Madlock, Bill	84T	131	$ .08	$ .35	Maldonado, Candy	91T	723	$ .01	$ .03
Madlock, Bill	84T	250	$ .02	$ .10	Maler, Jim	83T	54	$ .01	$ .07
Madlock, Bill	84T	696	$ .01	$ .06	Maler, Jim	84T	461	$ .01	$ .06
Madlock, Bill	84T	701	$ .06	$ .30	Malkmus, Bob	58T	356	$ .75	$3.00
Madlock, Bill	85T	560	$ .01	$ .10	Malkmus, Bob	59T	151	$ .75	$2.20
Madlock, Bill	86T	470	$ .01	$ .04	Malkmus, Bobby	60T	251	$ .45	$1.45
Madlock, Bill	87T	734	$ .01	$ .04	Malkmus, Bobby	61T	530	$7.00	$21.00

TOPPS

Player	Year	No.	VG	EX/MT
Maloney, Jim	61T	436	$ .75	$2.25
Maloney, Jim	63T	444	$ .75	$3.00
Maloney, Jim	64T	3	$1.50	$4.00
Maloney, Jim	64T	5	$1.75	$5.00
Maloney, Jim	64T	420	$ .75	$3.00
Maloney, Jim	65T	530	$1.75	$4.50
Maloney, Jim	66T	140	$ .30	$ .95
Maloney, Jim	67T	80	$ .30	$ .85
Maloney, Jim	68T	425	$ .30	$ .95
Maloney, Jim	69T	362	$ .30	$ .85
Maloney, Jim	70T	320	$ .30	$ .85
Maloney, Jim	71T	645	$ .90	$3.00
Maloney, Jim	72T	645	$ .30	$ .95
Malzone, Frank	56T	304	$2.25	$8.00
Malzone, Frank	57T	355	$1.25	$4.25
Malzone, Frank	58T	260	$ .75	$3.00
Malzone, Frank	58TAS	481	$ .40	$1.10
Malzone, Frank	59T	220	$ .75	$2.20
Malzone, Frank	59T	519	$3.00	$9.00
Malzone, Frank	59TAS	558	$2.50	$10.00
Malzone, Frank	60T	310	$ .75	$2.20
Malzone, Frank	60TAS	557	$2.50	$10.00
Malzone, Frank	61T	173	$ .75	$3.00
Malzone, Frank	61T	445	$ .75	$3.00
Malzone, Frank	62T	225	$ .45	$1.45
Malzone, Frank	63T	232	$ .30	$ .95
Malzone, Frank	64T	60	$ .15	$ .50
Malzone, Frank	65T	315	$ .35	$1.25
Malzone, Frank	66T	152	$ .30	$ .95
Mangual, Angel	70T	654	$ .75	$2.00
Mangual, Angel	71T	317	$ .15	$ .50
Mangual, Angel	72T	6	$ .15	$ .50
Mangual, Angel	72T	62	$ .05	$ .25
Mangual, Angel	73T	625	$ .45	$1.45
Mangual, Angel	75T	452	$ .07	$ .30
Mangual, Pepe	75T	616	$7.50	$20.00
Mangual, Pepe	76T	164	$ .05	$ .20
Mangual, Pepe	77T	552	$ .03	$ .12
Mankowski, Phil	77T	477	$ .05	$ .15
Mankowski, Phil	78T	559	$ .02	$ .10
Mankowski, Phil	79T	93	$ .02	$ .10
Mankowski, Phil	80T	216	$ .01	$ .10
Mann, Kelly	89TMLD	76	$ .01	$ .15
Mann, Kelly	90T	744	$ .01	$ .10
Manning, Rick	76T	275	$ .05	$ .20
Manning, Rick	77T	115	$ .03	$ .12
Manning, Rick	78T	11	$ .02	$ .10
Manning, Rick	79T	425	$ .02	$ .10
Manning, Rick	80T	564	$ .01	$ .10
Manning, Rick	81T	308	$ .01	$ .10
Manning, Rick	82T	202	$ .01	$ .07
Manning, Rick	83T	757	$ .01	$ .07
Manning, Rick	83TTR	65	$ .02	$ .10
Manning, Rick	84T	128	$ .01	$ .06
Manning, Rick	85T	603	$ .01	$ .05
Manning, Rick	86T	49	$ .01	$ .04
Manning, Rick	87T	706	$ .01	$ .04
Manning, Rick	88T	441	$ .01	$ .04
Manrique, Fred	88T	437	$ .01	$ .04
Manrique, Fred	89T	108	$ .01	$ .05
Manrique, Fred	89TBB	84	$ .01	$ .06
Manrique, Fred	90T	242	$ .01	$ .04
Manrique, Fred	90TTR	66	$ .01	$ .05
Mantilla, Felix	57T	188	$ .95	$3.50
Mantilla, Felix	58T	17	$1.25	$4.25
Mantilla, Felix	59T	157	$ .75	$2.20
Mantilla, Felix	60T	19	$ .45	$1.45
Mantilla, Felix	61T	164	$ .35	$1.25
Mantilla, Felix	62T	436	$1.25	$4.25
Mantilla, Felix	63T	447	$2.50	$6.50
Mantilla, Felix	64T	228	$ .30	$ .95
Mantilla, Felix	65T	29	$ .30	$ .85
Mantilla, Felix	66T	557	$5.00	$20.00
Mantilla, Felix	67T	524	$ .75	$3.00
Mantle, Mickey	52T	311	$2450.00	$8250.00
Mantle, Mickey	53T	82	$600.00	$1750.00
Mantle, Mickey	56T	135	$225.00	$700.00
Mantle, Mickey	57T	407	$100.00	$350.00
Mantle, Mickey	57T	95	$225.00	$675.00
Mantle, Mickey	58T	150	$165.00	$500.00
Mantle, Mickey	58T	418	$35.00	$130.00
Mantle, Mickey	58TAS	487	$17.50	$70.00
Mantle, Mickey	59T	10	$120.00	$350.00
Mantle, Mickey	59T	461	$10.50	$32.50
Mantle, Mickey	59TAS	564	$65.00	$225.00
Mantle, Mickey	60T	160	$8.00	$35.00
Mantle, Mickey	60T	350	$100.00	$300.00
Mantle, Mickey	60TAS	563	$65.00	$185.00
Mantle, Mickey	61T	44	$6.00	$18.00
Mantle, Mickey	61T	300	$95.00	$295.00
Mantle, Mickey	61T	406	$10.50	$32.50
Mantle, Mickey	61TAS	578	$100.00	$300.00
Mantle, Mickey	61TMVP	475	$22.50	$85.00
Mantle, Mickey	62T	53	$8.00	$25.00
Mantle, Mickey	62T	18	$30.00	$95.00
Mantle, Mickey	62T	200	$125.00	$350.00
Mantle, Mickey	62T	318	$12.50	$37.50
Mantle, Mickey	62TAS	471	$25.00	$85.00
Mantle, Mickey	63T	2	$3.00	$12.00
Mantle, Mickey	63T	173	$15.00	$45.00
Mantle, Mickey	63T	200	$100.00	$300.00
Mantle, Mickey	64T	50	$70.00	$210.00
Mantle, Mickey	64T	331	$20.00	$65.00
Mantle, Mickey	65T	3	$3.00	$12.00
Mantle, Mickey	65T	5	$3.00	$12.00
Mantle, Mickey	65T	350	$110.00	$335.00
Mantle, Mickey	66T	50	$60.00	$180.00
Mantle, Mickey	67T	150	$65.00	$200.00
Mantle, Mickey	68T	280	$55.00	$165.00
Mantle, Mickey	68T	490	$22.50	$70.00
Mantle, Mickey	69T	500	$60.00	$175.00

1956-MOST VALUABLE PLAYERS

MICKEY MANTLE outfield NEW YORK YANKEES

AMERICAN LEAGUE

25 YEARS OF TOPPS BASEBALL CARDS

DON NEWCOMBE pitcher BROOKLYN DODGERS

NATIONAL LEAGUE

1951 • 1975

Player	Year	No.	VG	EX/MT
Mantle, Mickey	75T	194	$1.75	$5.00

Player	Year	No.	VG	EX/MT	Player	Year	No.	VG	EX/MT
Mantle, Mickey	75T	195	$2.00	$6.00	Maris, Roger	75T	198	$ .75	$2.20
Mantle, Mickey	75T	200	$1.25	$4.00	Maris, Roger	75T	199	$ .75	$3.00
Manto, Jeff	91T	488	$ .01	$ .15	Maris, Roger	79T	413	$ .20	$ .75
Manual, Jerry	76T	596	$ .15	$ .50	Maris, Roger	86TB	405	$ .03	$ .15
Manuel, Chuck	70T	194	$ .15	$ .50	Marone, Lou	70T	703	$ .75	$2.00
Manuel, Chuck	71T	744	$ .75	$2.50	Marquess, Mark	88TTR	65	$ .01	$ .06
Manush, Heinie	54T	187	$3.95	$11.50	Marquez, Gonzalo	73T	605	$ .75	$3.00
Manwaring, Kirt	88TTR	64	$ .01	$ .10	Marquez, Gonzalo	74T	422	$ .07	$ .30
Manwaring, Kirt	89T	506	$ .01	$ .10	Marrero, Connie	52T	317	$40.00	$140.00
Manwaring, Kirt	90T	678	$ .01	$ .04	Marrero, Connie	53T	13	$4.50	$15.00
Manwaring, Kirt	91T	472	$ .01	$ .03	Marsh, Fred	52T	8	$15.00	$47.50
Mapes, Cliff	52T	103	$7.00	$20.00	Marsh, Freddie	53T	240	$12.50	$50.00
Marak, Paul	91T	753	$ .01	$ .10	Marsh, Fred	54T	218	$3.60	$10.00
Maranda, Georges	60T	479	$ .90	$3.00	Marsh, Fred	55T	13	$2.00	$6.00
Margoneri, Joe	57T	191	$ .95	$3.50	Marsh, Freddie	56T	23	$2.25	$6.00
Marichal, Juan	61T	417	$25.00	$100.00	Marshall, Clarence	52T	174	$7.00	$20.00
Marichal, Juan	62T	505	$10.00	$30.00	Marshall, Dave	69T	464	$ .30	$ .85
Marichal, Juan	63T	440	$5.00	$20.00	Marshall, Dave	70T	58	$ .15	$ .50
Marichal, Juan	64T	280	$3.50	$11.00	Marshall, Dave	71T	259	$ .15	$ .50
Marichal, Juan	64T	3	$1.50	$4.00	Marshall, Dave	72T	673	$ .75	$2.50
Marichal, Juan	65T	10	$ .45	$1.45	Marshall, Dave	73T	513	$ .07	$ .30
Marichal, Juan	65T	50	$3.00	$10.00	Marshall, Jim	58T	441	$ .75	$2.20
Marichal, Juan	66T	221	$ .65	$1.75	Marshall, Jim	59T	153	$ .75	$2.20
Marichal, Juan	66T	420	$3.00	$10.00	Marshall, Jim	60T	267	$ .45	$1.45
Marichal, Juan	67T	234	$1.75	$4.50	Marshall, Jim	61T	188	$ .35	$1.25
Marichal, Juan	67T	236	$3.00	$9.00	Marshall, Jim	62T	337	$ .45	$1.45
Marichal, Juan	67T	500	$5.50	$17.50	Marshall, Jim	74T	354	$ .07	$ .30
Marichal, Juan	68T	205	$2.50	$7.00	Marshall, Mike	68T	201	$ .50	$1.50
Marichal, Juan	69T	10	$ .75	$3.00	Marshall, Mike	69T	17	$ .30	$ .85
Marichal, Juan	69T	370	$1.50	$5.00	Marshall, Mike	71T	713	$1.25	$4.25
Marichal, Juan	69T	572	$2.50	$7.50	Marshall, Mike	72T	505	$ .30	$ .85
Marichal, Juan	70T	210	$1.50	$5.00	Marshall, Mike	73T	355	$ .30	$ .85
Marichal, Juan	70T	67	$ .75	$2.00	Marshall, Mike	74T	208	$ .07	$ .30
Marichal, Juan	70T	69	$ .75	$2.20	Marshall, Mike	74TTR	73	$ .30	$ .95
Marichal, Juan	70TAS	466	$ .95	$3.50	Marshall, Mike	75T	313	$ .30	$ .95
Marichal, Juan	71T	325	$2.00	$7.50	Marshall, Mike	75T	330	$ .07	$ .30
Marichal, Juan	72T	567	$2.10	$6.00	Marshall, Mike	75THL	6	$ .15	$ .50
Marichal, Juan	72TIA	568	$ .75	$2.25	Marshall, Mike	76T	465	$ .07	$ .30
Marichal, Juan	73T	480	$1.00	$4.00	Marshall, Mike	77T	263	$ .03	$ .12
Marichal, Juan	74T	330	$ .50	$2.00	Marshall, Mike	82T	681	$1.50	$5.00
Marichal, Juan	74TTR	330	$ .75	$2.50	Marshall, Mike	83T	324	$ .03	$ .15
Mariners, Team Checklist	77T	597	$ .03	$ .12	Marshall, Mike	84T	634	$ .02	$ .10
Mariners, Team Checklist	78T	499	$ .05	$ .25	Marshall, Mike	85T	85	$ .01	$ .05
Mariners, Team Checklist	79T	659	$ .05	$ .25	Marshall, Mike	86T	728	$ .01	$ .10
Mariners, Team Checklist	80T	282	$ .07	$ .30	Marshall, Mike	87T	664	$ .01	$ .10
Mariners, Team Checklist	81T	672	$ .02	$ .20	Marshall, Mike	88T	249	$ .01	$ .10
Mariners, Team Leaders	86T	546	$ .01	$ .04	Marshall, Mike	88TBB	133	$ .01	$ .06
Mariners, Team Leaders	87T	156	$ .01	$ .04	Marshall, Mike	89T	582	$ .01	$ .05
Mariners, Team Leaders	88T	519	$ .01	$ .04	Marshall, Mike	89TBB	48	$ .01	$ .06
Mariners, Team Leaders	89T	459	$ .01	$ .05	Marshall, Mike	90T	198	$ .01	$ .04
Maris, Roger	58T	47	$85.00	$300.00	Marshall, Mike	90TTR	67	$ .01	$ .05
Maris, Roger	59T	202	$30.00	$120.00	Marshall, Mike	91T	356	$ .01	$ .03
Maris, Roger	60T	377	$22.50	$72.50	Marshall, Willard	52T	96	$7.00	$20.00
Maris, Roger	60TAS	565	$25.00	$77.50	Marshall, Willard	53T	95	$4.50	$15.00
Maris, Roger	61T	2	$35.00	$125.00	Martin, Billy	52T	175	$90.00	$275.00
Maris, Roger	61T	44	$6.00	$18.00	Martin, Billy	53T	86	$35.00	$110.00
Maris, Roger	61TAS	576	$30.00	$95.00	Martin, Billy	54T	13	$25.00	$75.00
Maris, Roger	61TMVP	478	$9.00	$35.00	Martin, Billy	56T	181	$22.00	$65.00
Maris, Roger	62T	1	$60.00	$180.00	Martin, Billy	57T	62	$9.50	$37.50
Maris, Roger	62T	53	$8.00	$25.00	Martin, Billy	58T	271	$4.75	$14.00
Maris, Roger	62T	313	$3.00	$12.50	Martin, Billy	59T	295	$3.75	$12.50
Maris, Roger	62T	401	$8.00	$25.00	Martin, Billy	60T	173	$3.00	$10.00
Maris, Roger	63T	4	$ .50	$2.00	Martin, Billy	61T	89	$1.50	$6.50
Maris, Roger	63T	120	$15.00	$47.50	Martin, Billy	62T	208	$1.50	$6.50
Maris, Roger	64T	225	$10.00	$37.50	Martin, Billy	69T	547	$1.25	$5.00
Maris, Roger	64T	331	$25.00	$75.00	Martin, Billy	71T	208	$ .75	$3.00
Maris, Roger	65T	155	$15.00	$45.00	Martin, Billy	72T	33	$1.00	$4.00
Maris, Roger	66T	365	$13.00	$42.50	Martin, Billy	72TIA	34	$ .15	$ .50
Maris, Roger	67T	45	$9.50	$30.00	Martin, Billy	73T	323	$ .35	$1.25
Maris, Roger	68T	330	$9.50	$30.00					

TOPPS

Player	Year	No.	VG	EX/MT	Player	Year	No.	VG	EX/MT
Martin, Billy	74T	379	$ .15	$ .50	Martinez, Carmelo	85T	558	$ .01	$ .05
Martin, Billy	78T	721	$ .30	$ .95	Martinez, Carmelo	86T	67	$ .01	$ .04
Martin, Billy	83T	156	$ .01	$ .10	Martinez, Carmelo	87T	348	$ .01	$ .04
Martin, Billy	83TTR	66	$ .05	$ .25	Martinez, Carmelo	88T	148	$ .01	$ .04
Martin, Billy	84T	81	$ .03	$ .15	Martinez, Carmelo	88TBB	238	$ .01	$ .06
Martin, Billy	85TTR	78	$ .15	$ .50	Martinez, Carmelo	89T	449	$ .01	$ .05
Martin, Billy	86T	651	$ .01	$ .04	Martinez, Carmelo	89TBB	11	$ .01	$ .06
Martin, Gene	70T	599	$ .30	$ .95	Martinez, Carmelo	90T	686	$ .01	$ .04
Martin, J. C.	60T	346	$ .75	$2.20	Martinez, Carmelo	90TTR	68	$ .01	$ .05
Martin, J. C.	61T	124	$ .35	$1.25	Martinez, Carmelo	91T	779	$ .01	$ .03
Martin, J. C.	62T	91	$ .45	$1.45	Martinez, Dave	87TTR	73	$ .15	$ .50
Martin, J. C.	63T	499	$2.50	$6.50	Martinez, Dave	88T	439	$ .01	$ .20
Martin, J. C.	64T	148	$ .30	$ .95	Martinez, Dave	89T	763	$ .01	$ .05
Martin, J. C.	65T	382	$ .35	$1.25	Martinez, Dave	90T	228	$ .01	$ .04
Martin, J. C.	66T	47	$ .30	$ .95	Martinez, Dave	91T	24	$ .01	$ .03
Martin, J. C.	67T	538	$1.50	$4.00	Martinez, Denny	77T	491	$ .25	$1.00
Martin, J. C.	68T	211	$ .30	$ .85	Martinez, Denny	78T	119	$ .02	$ .10
Martin, J. C.	69T	112	$ .30	$ .85	Martinez, Denny	79T	211	$ .02	$ .10
Martin, J. C.	70T	488	$ .15	$ .50	Martinez, Denny	80T	10	$ .01	$ .10
Martin, J. C.	71T	704	$ .75	$2.50	Martinez, Denny	81T	367	$ .01	$ .10
Martin, J. C.	72T	639	$ .30	$ .95	Martinez, Denny	82T	165	$ .03	$ .15
Martin, J. C.	73T	552	$ .45	$1.45	Martinez, Denny	82T	712	$ .01	$ .07
Martin, J. C.	74T	354	$ .07	$ .30	Martinez, Denny	83T	553	$ .01	$ .07
Martin, Jake	56T	129	$2.25	$6.00	Martinez, Denny	84T	631	$ .01	$ .06
Martin, Jerry	77T	596	$ .03	$ .12	Martinez, Denny	85T	199	$ .01	$ .05
Martin, Jerry	78T	222	$ .02	$ .10	Martinez, Denny	86T	416	$ .01	$ .04
Martin, Jerry	79T	382	$ .02	$ .10	Martinez, Denny	87T	252	$ .01	$ .04
Martin, Jerry	80T	493	$ .01	$ .10	Martinez, Denny	88T	76	$ .01	$ .04
Martin, Jerry	81T	103	$ .01	$ .10	Martinez, Denny	89T	313	$ .01	$ .05
Martin, Jerry	81TTR	798	$ .02	$ .10	Martinez, Denny	90T	763	$ .01	$ .04
Martin, Jerry	82T	722	$ .01	$ .07	Martinez, Denny	91T	528	$ .01	$ .03
Martin, Jerry	82TTR	65	$ .02	$ .10	Martinez, Edgar	90T	148	$ .01	$ .04
Martin, Jerry	83T	626	$ .01	$ .07	Martinez, Edgar	91T	607	$ .01	$ .03
Martin, Jerry	84T	74	$ .01	$ .06	Martinez, Fred	81T	227	$ .01	$ .10
Martin, Jerry	84TTR	74	$ .02	$ .10	Martinez, Fred	82T	659	$ .01	$ .07
Martin, Jerry	85T	517	$ .01	$ .05	Martinez, Jose	70T	8	$ .15	$ .50
Martin, John	82T	236	$ .01	$ .07	Martinez, Jose	71T	712	$ .75	$2.50
Martin, John	83T	721	$ .01	$ .07	Martinez, Orlando "Marty"	67T	504	$ .75	$3.00
Martin, John	84T	24	$ .01	$ .06	Martinez, Orlando	68T	578	$ .35	$1.25
Martin, Morrie	52T	131	$7.00	$20.00	Martinez, Marty	69T	337	$ .30	$ .85
Martin, Morrie	53T	227	$12.50	$50.00	Martinez, Marty	70T	126	$ .15	$ .50
Martin, Morrie	54T	168	$3.60	$10.00	Martinez, Marty	71T	602	$ .35	$1.25
Martin, Morrie	58T	53	$1.25	$4.25	Martinez, Marty	72T	336	$ .05	$ .25
Martin, Morrie	59T	38	$1.25	$4.25	Martinez, Ramon	89T	225	$ .05	$1.50
Martin, Renie	80T	667	$ .30	$1.50	Martinez, Ramon	90T	62	$ .01	$ .35
Martin, Renie	81T	452	$ .01	$ .10	Martinez, Ramon	91T	340	$ .01	$ .15
Martin, Renie	82T	594	$ .01	$ .07	Martinez, Silvio	79T	609	$ .02	$ .10
Martin, Renie	82TTR	66	$ .02	$ .10	Martinez, Silvio	80T	496	$ .01	$ .10
Martin, Renie	83T	263	$ .01	$ .07	Martinez, Silvio	81T	586	$ .01	$ .10
Martin, Renie	84T	603	$ .01	$ .06	Martinez, Silvio	82T	181	$ .01	$ .07
Martinez, Buck	70T	609	$ .30	$ .95	Martinez, Ted	71T	648	$ .50	$4.00
Martinez, Buck	71T	163	$ .15	$ .50	Martinez, Ted	72T	544	$ .30	$ .95
Martinez, Buck	72T	332	$ .05	$ .25	Martinez, Ted	73T	161	$ .07	$ .30
Martinez, Buck	75T	314	$ .07	$ .30	Martinez, Ted	74T	487	$ .07	$ .30
Martinez, Buck	76T	616	$ .05	$ .20	Martinez, Ted	75T	637	$ .07	$ .30
Martinez, Buck	77T	46	$ .03	$ .12	Martinez, Ted	76T	356	$ .05	$ .20
Martinez, Buck	78T	571	$ .02	$ .10	Martinez, Ted	78T	546	$ .02	$ .10
Martinez, Buck	79T	243	$ .02	$ .10	Martinez, Ted	79T	128	$ .02	$ .10
Martinez, Buck	80T	477	$ .01	$ .10	Martinez, Ted	80T	191	$ .01	$ .10
Martinez, Buck	81T	56	$ .01	$ .10	Martinez, Tino	88TTR	66	$ .20	$1.75
Martinez, Buck	81TTR	799	$ .02	$ .10	Martinez, Tino	89TBB	93	$ .01	$ .25
Martinez, Buck	82T	314	$ .01	$ .07	Martinez, Tino	91T	482	$ .01	$ .35
Martinez, Buck	83T	733	$ .01	$ .07	Martinez, Tippy	76T	41	$ .07	$ .30
Martinez, Buck	84T	179	$ .01	$ .06	Martinez, Tippy	77T	238	$ .03	$ .12
Martinez, Buck	85T	673	$ .01	$ .05	Martinez, Tippy	78T	393	$ .02	$ .10
Martinez, Buck	86T	518	$ .01	$ .04	Martinez, Tippy	79T	491	$ .02	$ .10
Martinez, Carlos	90T	461	$ .01	$ .10	Martinez, Tippy	80T	706	$ .01	$ .10
Martinez, Carlos	91T	156	$ .01	$ .03	Martinez, Tippy	81T	119	$ .01	$ .10
Martinez, Carmelo	84T	267	$ .03	$ .25	Martinez, Tippy	82T	583	$ .01	$ .07
Martinez, Carmelo	84TTR	75	$ .02	$ .10	Martinez, Tippy	83T	631	$ .01	$ .07

Player	Year	No.	VG	EX/MT
Martinez, Tippy	84T	215	$ .01	$ .06
Martinez, Tippy	85T	445	$ .01	$ .05
Martinez, Tippy	86T	82	$ .01	$ .04
Martinez, Tippy	87T	728	$ .01	$ .04
Martinez, Tony	63T	466	$7.50	$27.50
Martinez, Tony	64T	404	$ .50	$1.45
Martinez, Tony	66T	581	$5.00	$20.00
Marting, Tim	71T	423	$ .15	$ .50
Martyn, Bob	58T	39	$ .65	$2.00
Martyn, Bob	59T	41	$ .60	$1.80
Martz, Randy	81T	381	$ .01	$ .10

CUBS
PITCHER RANDY MARTZ

Player	Year	No.	VG	EX/MT
Martz, Randy	82T	188	$ .01	$ .07
Martz, Randy	82T	456	$ .01	$ .07
Martz, Randy	83T	22	$ .01	$ .07
Marzano, John	85T	399	$ .01	$ .25
Marzano, John	88T	757	$ .01	$ .10
Marzano, John	90TTR	69	$ .01	$ .05
Marzano, John	91T	574	$ .01	$ .03
Mashore, Clyde	71T	376	$ .15	$ .50
Mashore, Clyde	73T	401	$ .07	$ .30
Masi, Phil	51Tbb	19	$7.50	$22.50
Masi, Phil	52T	283	$15.00	$47.50
Mason, Don	66T	524	$4.00	$10.00
Mason, Don	69T	584	$ .30	$ .95
Mason, Don	71T	548	$ .35	$1.25
Mason, Don	72T	739	$ .75	$2.50
Mason, Henry	60T	331	$ .75	$2.20
Mason, Jim	72T	334	$ .15	$ .50
Mason, Jim	73T	458	$ .07	$ .30
Mason, Jim	74T	618	$ .07	$ .30
Mason, Jim	74TTR	618	$ .07	$ .30
Mason, Jim	75T	136	$ .07	$ .30
Mason, Jim	77T	212	$ .03	$ .12
Mason, Jim	78T	588	$ .02	$ .10
Mason, Jim	79T	67	$ .02	$ .10
Mason, Jim	80T	497	$ .01	$ .10
Mason, Mike	84TTR	76	$ .02	$ .10
Mason, Mike	85T	464	$ .01	$ .05
Mason, Mike	86T	189	$ .01	$ .04
Mason, Mike	87T	646	$ .01	$ .04

Player	Year	No.	VG	EX/MT
Mason, Mike	88T	87	$ .01	$ .04
Mason, Roger	86TTR	70	$ .02	$ .10
Mason, Roger	87T	526	$ .01	$ .04
Masse, Billy	88TTR	67	$ .01	$ .20
Masse, Billy	89TBB	179	$ .01	$ .06
Masterson, Walt	52T	186	$7.00	$20.00
Matchick, John (Tom)	67T	72	$ .30	$ .85
Matchick, Tom	68T	113	$ .30	$ .85
Matchick, Tom	69T	344	$ .30	$ .85
Matchick, Tom	70T	647	$ .75	$2.00
Matchick, Tom	71T	321	$ .15	$ .50
Matchick, Tom	73T	631	$ .45	$1.45
Mathew, Nelson	63T	54	$1.50	$4.00
Mathews, Ed	52T	407	$450.00	$1700.00
Mathews, Ed	53T	37	$27.50	$85.00
Mathews, Ed	54T	30	$23.50	$77.50
Mathews, Ed	55T	155	$23.50	$77.50
Mathews, Ed	56T	107	$15.00	$50.00
Mathews, Ed	57T	250	$10.00	$30.00
Mathews, Ed	58T	351	$8.00	$22.00
Mathews, Ed	58T	440	$8.00	$25.00
Mathews, Ed	58TAS	480	$4.50	$12.50
Mathews, Ed	59T	212	$7.00	$28.00
Mathews, Ed	59T	450	$7.00	$28.00
Mathews, Ed	60T	420	$6.00	$24.00
Mathews, Ed	60TAS	558	$6.50	$20.00
Mathews, Ed	61T	120	$5.50	$17.50
Mathews, Ed	61T	43	$1.50	$5.75
Mathews, Ed	62T	30	$5.50	$17.50
Mathews, Ed	63T	275	$5.00	$15.00
Mathews, Ed	64T	35	$4.00	$12.00
Mathews, Ed	65T	500	$5.00	$20.00
Mathews, Ed	66T	200	$2.50	$10.00
Mathews, Ed	67T	166	$2.50	$10.00
Mathews, Ed	68T	58	$2.00	$7.50
Mathews, Eddie	73T	237	$ .35	$1.25
Mathews, Eddie	74T	634	$ .35	$1.25
Mathews, Greg	87T	567	$ .01	$ .10
Mathews, Greg	88T	133	$ .01	$ .04
Mathews, Greg	88TBB	177	$ .01	$ .06
Mathews, Greg	89T	97	$ .01	$ .05
Mathews, Greg	90T	209	$ .01	$ .04
Mathews, Nelson	64T	366	$ .30	$ .95
Mathews, Nelson	65T	87	$ .30	$ .85
Mathewson, Christy	61T	408	$ .75	$2.25
Mathias, Carl	60T	139	$ .45	$1.45
Mathis, Ron	85TTR	79	$ .02	$ .10
Mathis, Ron	86T	476	$ .01	$ .04
Matias, John	70T	444	$ .15	$ .50
Matias, John	71T	546	$ .35	$1.25
Matlack, Jon	71T	648	$ .50	$4.00
Matlack, Jon	72T	141	$ .15	$ .50
Matlack, Jon	73T	55	$ .15	$ .50
Matlack, Jon	74T	153	$ .07	$ .30
Matlack, Jon	75T	290	$ .07	$ .30
Matlack, Jon	76T	190	$ .05	$ .20
Matlack, Jon	77T	440	$ .03	$ .12
Matlack, Jon	78T	25	$ .02	$ .10
Matlack, Jon	79T	315	$ .02	$ .10
Matlack, Jon	80T	592	$ .01	$ .10
Matlack, Jon	81T	656	$ .01	$ .10
Matlack, Jon	82T	239	$ .01	$ .07
Matlack, Jon	83T	749	$ .01	$ .07
Matlack, Jon	84T	149	$ .01	$ .06
Matthews, Gary	73T	606	$ .95	$3.50
Matthews, Gary	74T	386	$ .30	$ .95
Matthews, Gary	75T	79	$ .15	$ .50
Matthews, Gary	76T	133	$ .05	$ .20
Matthews, Gary	77T	194	$ .03	$ .12
Matthews, Gary	78T	475	$ .02	$ .10

TOPPS

Player	Year	No.	VG	EX/MT	Player	Year	No.	VG	EX/MT
Matthews, Gary	79T	85	$ .02	$ .10	Maxvill, Dal	74T	358	$ .07	$ .30
Matthews, Gary	80T	355	$ .01	$ .10	Maxwell, Charley	52T	180	$7.00	$21.00
Matthews, Gary	81T	528	$ .01	$ .10	Maxwell, Charley	57T	205	$ .95	$3.50
Matthews, Gary	81TTR	800	$ .02	$ .10	Maxwell, Charley	58T	380	$ .75	$3.00
Matthews, Gary	82T	680	$ .01	$ .07	Maxwell, Charlie	59T	34	$2.00	$8.00
Matthews, Gary	83T	780	$ .01	$ .07	Maxwell, Charley	59T	481	$ .75	$2.20
Matthews, Gary	84T	637	$ .01	$ .06	Maxwell, Charlie	60T	443	$ .90	$3.00
Matthews, Gary	84T	70	$ .01	$ .06	Maxwell, Charlie	61T	37	$ .35	$1.25
Matthews, Gary	84TTR	77	$ .02	$ .10	Maxwell, Charley	62T	506	$ .75	$2.50
Matthews, Gary	85T	210	$ .01	$ .05	Maxwell, Charley	63T	86	$ .30	$ .95
Matthews, Gary	86T	485	$ .01	$ .04	Maxwell, Charlie	64T	401	$ .50	$1.45
Matthews, Gary	87T	390	$ .01	$ .04	May, Carlos	69T	654	$ .30	$ .95
Matthews, Gary	88T	156	$ .01	$ .04	May, Carlos	70T	18	$ .15	$ .50
Mattingly, Don	84T	8	$7.00	$28.00	May, Carlos	71T	243	$ .15	$ .50
Mattingly, Don	85T	665	$2.00	$8.00	May, Carlos	72T	525	$ .05	$ .25
Mattingly, Don	86T	180	$ .75	$3.00	May, Carlos	73T	105	$ .07	$ .30
Mattingly, Don	86TAS	712	$ .20	$1.00	May, Carlos	74T	195	$ .07	$ .30
Mattingly, Don	87T	500	$ .25	$1.00	May, Carlos	75T	480	$ .07	$ .30
Mattingly, Don	87TAS	606	$ .15	$ .75	May, Carlos	76T	110	$ .05	$ .20
Mattingly, Don	88T	300	$ .25	$1.00	May, Carlos	77T	568	$ .03	$ .12
Mattingly, Don	88TAS	386	$ .10	$ .50	May, Carlos	77T	633	$ .03	$ .12
Mattingly, Don	88TBB	229	$ .15	$1.00	May, Dave	68T	56	$ .30	$ .85
Mattingly, Don	88TRB	2	$ .05	$ .35	May, Dave	69T	113	$ .30	$ .85
Mattingly, Don	89T	700	$ .10	$ .50	May, Dave	70T	81	$ .15	$ .50
Mattingly, Don	89TAS	397	$ .05	$ .25	May, Dave	71T	493	$ .15	$ .50
Mattingly, Don	89TBB	50	$ .01	$ .75	May, Dave	72T	549	$ .30	$ .95
Mattingly, Don	90T	200	$ .01	$ .50	May, Dave	73T	152	$ .07	$ .30
Mattingly, Don	91T	100	$ .01	$ .20	May, Dave	74T	12	$ .07	$ .30
Matula, Rick	80T	596	$ .01	$ .10	May, Dave	75T	650	$ .07	$ .30
Matula, Rick	81T	611	$ .01	$ .10	May, Dave	76T	281	$ .05	$ .20
Matuszek, Len	83T	357	$ .01	$ .07	May, Dave	78T	362	$ .02	$ .10
Matuszek, Len	84T	275	$ .01	$ .06	May, Derrick	91T	288	$ .01	$ .35
Matuszek, Len	85T	688	$ .01	$ .05	May, Jerry	65T	143	$ .30	$ .85
Matuszek, Len	85TTR	80	$ .02	$ .10	May, Jerry	66T	123	$ .30	$ .95
Matuszek, Len	86T	109	$ .01	$ .04	May, Jerry	67T	379	$ .30	$ .95
Matuszek, Len	87T	457	$ .01	$ .04	May, Jerry	68T	598	$ .75	$3.00
Matuszek, Len	88T	92	$ .01	$ .04	May, Jerry	69T	263	$ .30	$ .95
Mauch, Gene	57T	342	$5.00	$15.00	May, Jerry	70T	423	$ .15	$ .50
Mauch, Gene	61T	219	$ .90	$3.00	May, Jerry	71T	719	$ .75	$2.50
Mauch, Gene	62T	374	$ .90	$3.00	May, Jerry	72T	109	$ .05	$ .25
Mauch, Gene	63T	318	$ .45	$1.45	May, Jerry	73T	558	$ .45	$1.45
Mauch, Gene	64T	157	$ .15	$ .50	May, Lee	66T	424	$1.25	$5.00
Mauch, Gene	65T	489	$ .75	$2.20	May, Lee	67T	222	$ .35	$1.25
Mauch, Gene	66T	411	$ .15	$ .50	May, Lee	68T	487	$ .75	$3.00
Mauch, Gene	67T	248	$ .30	$ .85	May, Lee	69T	405	$ .35	$1.25
Mauch, Gene	68T	122	$ .15	$ .50	May, Lee	70T	225	$ .15	$ .50
Mauch, Gene	69T	606	$ .20	$ .50	May, Lee	70T	65	$ .90	$3.00
Mauch, Gene	70T	442	$ .30	$ .95	May, Lee	71T	40	$ .15	$ .50
Mauch, Gene	71T	59	$ .15	$ .50	May, Lee	72T	480	$ .30	$ .95
Mauch, Gene	72T	276	$ .30	$ .85	May, Lee	72T	89	$ .60	$2.00
Mauch, Gene	73T	377	$ .15	$ .50	May, Lee	73T	135	$ .30	$ .85
Mauch, Gene	74T	531	$ .30	$ .95	May, Lee	74T	500	$ .30	$ .95
Mauch, Gene	78T	601	$ .02	$ .10	May, Lee	75T	25	$ .15	$ .50
Mauch, Gene	83T	276	$ .01	$ .07	May, Lee	76T	210	$ .05	$ .20
Mauch, Gene	85TTR	81	$ .02	$ .10	May, Lee	77T	3	$ .35	$1.25
Mauch, Gene	86T	81	$ .01	$ .04	May, Lee	77T	380	$ .03	$ .12
Mauch, Gene	87T	518	$ .01	$ .04	May, Lee	77T	633	$ .03	$ .12
Mauch, Gene	88T	774	$ .01	$ .04	May, Lee	78T	640	$ .02	$ .10
Maxie, Larry	64T	94	$ .30	$ .95	May, Lee	79T	10	$ .02	$ .10
Maxvill, Dal	63T	49	$ .35	$1.25	May, Lee	80T	490	$ .01	$ .10
Maxvill, Dal	64T	563	$1.75	$4.50	May, Lee	82T	132	$ .01	$ .07
Maxvill, Dal	65T	78	$ .30	$ .85	May, Lee	83T	377	$ .01	$ .07
Maxvill, Dal	66T	338	$ .15	$ .75	May, Lee	83T	378	$ .01	$ .07
Maxvill, Dal	67T	421	$ .30	$ .95	May, Milt	71T	343	$ .15	$ .50
Maxvill, Dal	68T	141	$ .30	$ .85	May, Milt	72T	247	$ .05	$ .25
Maxvill, Dal	69T	320	$ .30	$ .95	May, Milt	73T	529	$ .45	$1.45
Maxvill, Dal	70T	503	$ .15	$ .50	May, Milt	74T	293	$ .07	$ .30
Maxvill, Dal	71T	476	$ .15	$ .50	May, Milt	75T	279	$ .07	$ .30
Maxvill, Dal	72T	206	$ .05	$ .25	May, Milt	76T	532	$ .05	$ .20
Maxvill, Dal	73T	483	$ .07	$ .30	May, Milt	76TTR	532	$ .05	$ .20

Player	Year	No.	VG	EX/MT
May, Milt	77T	98	$ .03	$ .12
May, Milt	78T	176	$ .02	$ .10
May, Milt	79T	316	$ .02	$ .10
May, Milt	80T	647	$ .01	$ .10
May, Milt	81T	463	$ .01	$ .10
May, Milt	82T	242	$ .01	$ .07
May, Milt	82T	576	$ .01	$ .07
May, Milt	83T	84	$ .01	$ .07
May, Milt	84T	788	$ .01	$ .06
May, Milt	85T	509	$ .01	$ .05
May, Rudy	65T	537	$2.10	$6.00
May, Rudy	70T	203	$ .15	$ .50
May, Rudy	71T	318	$ .15	$ .50
May, Rudy	72T	656	$ .30	$ .95
May, Rudy	73T	102	$ .07	$ .30
May, Rudy	74T	302	$ .07	$ .30
May, Rudy	75T	321	$ .07	$ .30
May, Rudy	76T	481	$ .05	$ .20
May, Rudy	77T	56	$ .03	$ .12
May, Rudy	78T	262	$ .02	$ .10
May, Rudy	79T	603	$ .02	$ .10
May, Rudy	80T	539	$ .01	$ .10
May, Rudy	81T	179	$ .01	$ .10
May, Rudy	81T	7	$ .02	$ .10
May, Rudy	82T	735	$ .01	$ .07
May, Rudy	83T	408	$ .01	$ .07
May, Rudy	84T	652	$ .01	$ .06
Mayberry, John	70T	227	$ .35	$1.25
Mayberry, John	71T	148	$ .15	$ .50
Mayberry, John	72T	373	$ .05	$ .25
Mayberry, John	73T	118	$ .15	$ .50
Mayberry, John	74T	150	$ .07	$ .30
Mayberry, John	75T	95	$ .07	$ .30
Mayberry, John	76T	194	$ .75	$2.20
Mayberry, John	76T	196	$ .30	$ .95
Mayberry, John	76T	440	$ .05	$ .20
Mayberry, John	77T	244	$ .03	$ .12
Mayberry, John	78T	550	$ .02	$ .10
Mayberry, John	79T	380	$ .02	$ .10
Mayberry, John	80T	643	$ .01	$ .10
Mayberry, John	81T	169	$ .01	$ .10
Mayberry, John	82T	470	$ .01	$ .07
Mayberry, John	82T	606	$ .01	$ .10
Mayberry, John	82TTR	67	$ .02	$ .10
Mayberry, John	83T	45	$ .01	$ .07
Maye, Lee	60T	246	$ .45	$1.45
Maye, Lee	61T	84	$ .35	$1.25
Maye, Lee	62T	518	$ .75	$2.50
Maye, Lee	63T	109	$ .30	$ .95
Maye, Lee	64T	416	$ .50	$1.45
Maye, Lee	65T	407	$ .35	$1.25
Maye, Lee	66T	162	$ .30	$ .95
Maye, Lee	67T	258	$ .30	$ .85
Maye, Lee	68T	94	$ .30	$ .85
Maye, Lee	69T	595	$ .30	$ .95
Maye, Lee	70T	439	$ .15	$ .50
Maye, Lee	71T	733	$ .75	$2.50
Mayer, Ed	58T	461	$ .75	$2.20
Mayne, Brent	91T	776	$ .01	$ .15
Mayo, Eddie	54T	247	$3.60	$10.00
Mays, Willie	52T	261	$350.00	$1000.00
Mays, Willie	53T	244	$450.00	$1450.00
Mays, Willie	54T	90	$100.00	$325.00
Mays, Willie	55T	194	$150.00	$425.00
Mays, Willie	56T	130	$80.00	$230.00
Mays, Willie	57T	10	$80.00	$230.00
Mays, Willie	58T	436	$12.50	$50.00
Mays, Willie	58T	5	$40.00	$120.00
Mays, Willie	58TAS	486	$12.50	$37.50
Mays, Willie	59T	50	$40.00	$125.00

Player	Year	No.	VG	EX/MT
Mays, Willie	59T	317	$4.00	$17.00
Mays, Willie	59T	464	$4.00	$15.00
Mays, Willie	59TAS	563	$33.00	$100.00
Mays, Willie	60T	7	$3.00	$12.50
Mays, Willie	60T	200	$35.00	$110.00
Mays, Willie	60TAS	564	$30.00	$90.00
Mays, Willie	61T	41	$1.50	$5.00
Mays, Willie	61T	150	$31.50	$92.50
Mays, Willie	61TAS	579	$40.00	$125.00
Mays, Willie	61TMVP	482	$10.00	$30.00
Mays, Willie	62T	18	$30.00	$95.00
Mays, Willie	62T	54	$ .75	$2.20
Mays, Willie	62T	300	$35.00	$105.00
Mays, Willie	62TAS	395	$10.00	$30.00
Mays, Willie	63T	3	$3.00	$12.00
Mays, Willie	63T	138	$10.00	$30.00
Mays, Willie	63T	300	$35.00	$110.00
Mays, Willie	64T	9	$3.00	$9.00
Mays, Willie	64T	150	$25.00	$75.00
Mays, Willie	64T	306	$6.50	$20.00
Mays, Willie	64T	423	$15.00	$45.00
Mays, Willie	65T	4	$1.75	$4.50
Mays, Willie	65T	6	$ .95	$3.50
Mays, Willie	65T	250	$25.00	$75.00
Mays, Willie	66T	1	$35.00	$140.00
Mays, Willie	66T	215	$3.00	$12.00
Mays, Willie	66T	217	$1.50	$4.00
Mays, Willie	66T	219	$ .65	$1.75
Mays, Willie	67T	200	$25.00	$75.00
Mays, Willie	67T	244	$2.10	$6.00
Mays, Willie	67T	423	$5.50	$17.50
Mays, Willie	68T	50	$20.00	$60.00
Mays, Willie	68T	490	$20.00	$60.00
Mays, Willie	69T	190	$12.50	$47.50
Mays, Willie	70T	600	$12.50	$50.00
Mays, Willie	71T	600	$12.50	$50.00
Mays, Willie	72T	49	$5.00	$20.00
Mays, Willie	72TIA	50	$4.00	$12.00

Player	Year	No.	VG	EX/MT
Mays, Willie	73T	1	$4.50	$17.50
Mays, Willie	73T	305	$7.50	$22.50

Player	Year	No.	VG	EX/MT
Mays, Willie	75T	192	$ .75	$3.00
Mays, Willie	75T	203	$ .45	$1.45
Mays, Willie	86TB	403	$ .03	$ .15
Mazeroski, Bill	57T	24	$10.00	$30.00
Mazeroski, Bill	58T	238	$1.75	$5.00
Mazeroski, Bill	59T	415	$1.50	$4.00
Mazeroski, Bill	59TAS	555	$3.00	$9.00
Mazeroski, Bill	60T	55	$ .75	$2.50
Mazeroski, Bill	61T	430	$ .75	$2.00
Mazeroski, Bill	61TAS	571	$6.00	$17.50
Mazeroski, Bill	62T	353	$1.25	$4.25
Mazeroski, Bill	62TAS	391	$ .75	$2.25
Mazeroski, Bill	63T	323	$1.25	$4.25
Mazeroski, Bill	64T	570	$2.00	$7.50
Mazeroski, Bill	65T	95	$ .75	$3.00
Mazeroski, Bill	66T	210	$1.00	$4.00
Mazeroski, Bill	67T	510	$1.50	$4.00
Mazeroski, Bill	68T	390	$ .75	$2.20
Mazeroski, Bill	69T	335	$ .75	$3.00
Mazeroski, Bill	70T	440	$ .45	$1.45
Mazeroski, Bill	71T	110	$ .35	$1.25
Mazeroski, Bill	72T	760	$ .90	$2.75
Mazeroski, Bill	73T	517	$ .30	$ .95
Mazeroski, Bill	74T	489	$ .07	$ .30
Mazzilli, Lee	77T	488	$5.00	$20.00
Mazzilli, Lee	78T	147	$ .02	$ .10
Mazzilli, Lee	79T	355	$ .02	$ .10
Mazzilli, Lee	80T	25	$ .01	$ .10
Mazzilli, Lee	81T	510	$ .01	$ .10
Mazzilli, Lee	82T	465	$ .01	$ .07
Mazzilli, Lee	82TTR	68	$ .02	$ .10
Mazzilli, Lee	83T	685	$ .01	$ .07
Mazzilli, Lee	83TTR	67	$ .02	$ .10
Mazzilli, Lee	84T	225	$ .01	$ .06
Mazzilli, Lee	85T	748	$ .01	$ .05
Mazzilli, Lee	86T	578	$ .01	$ .04
Mazzilli, Lee	87T	198	$ .01	$ .04
Mazzilli, Lee	88T	308	$ .01	$ .04
Mazzilli, Lee	89T	58	$ .01	$ .05
Mazzilli, Lee	90T	721	$ .01	$ .04
McAnally, Ernie	71T	376	$ .15	$ .50
McAnally, Ernie	72T	58	$ .05	$ .25
McAnally, Ernie	73T	484	$ .07	$ .30
McAnally, Ernie	74T	322	$ .07	$ .30
McAnally, Ernie	75T	318	$ .07	$ .30
McAndrew, Jim	69T	321	$ .30	$ .95
McAndrew, Jim	70T	246	$ .15	$ .50
McAndrew, Jim	71T	428	$ .15	$ .50
McAndrew, Jim	72T	781	$ .75	$2.50
McAndrew, Jim	73T	436	$ .07	$ .30
McAuliffe, Dick	62T	527	$2.70	$7.00
McAuliffe, Dick	63T	64	$ .30	$ .95
McAuliffe, Dick	64T	363	$ .30	$ .95
McAuliffe, Dick	65T	53	$ .30	$ .95
McAuliffe, Dick	66T	495	$ .75	$2.50
McAuliffe, Dick	67T	170	$ .30	$ .85
McAuliffe, Dick	68T	285	$ .30	$ .85
McAuliffe, Dick	69T	305	$ .30	$ .95
McAuliffe, Dick	70T	475	$ .15	$ .50
McAuliffe, Dick	71T	3	$ .15	$ .50
McAuliffe, Dick	72T	725	$ .75	$2.50
McAuliffe, Dick	73T	349	$ .07	$ .30
McAuliffe, Dick	74T	495	$ .07	$ .30
McBean, Al	62T	424	$ .75	$2.50
McBean, Al	63T	387	$ .45	$1.50
McBean, Al	64T	525	$1.75	$4.50
McBean, Al	65T	25	$ .30	$ .85
McBean, Al	66T	353	$ .30	$ .95
McBean, Al	67T	203	$ .30	$ .85
McBean, Al	68T	514	$ .35	$1.25

Player	Year	No.	VG	EX/MT
McBean, Al	69T	14	$ .30	$ .85
McBean, Al	70T	641	$ .75	$2.00
McBride, Bake	74T	601	$ .45	$1.45
McBride, Bake	75T	174	$ .07	$ .30
McBride, Bake	76T	135	$ .05	$ .20
McBride, Bake	77T	516	$ .03	$ .12
McBride, Bake	78T	340	$ .02	$ .10
McBride, Bake	79T	630	$ .05	$ .20
McBride, Bake	80T	495	$ .01	$ .10
McBride, Bake	81T	90	$ .03	$ .15

PHILLIES
OUTFIELD
BAKE McBRIDE

Player	Year	No.	VG	EX/MT
McBride, Bake	82T	745	$ .01	$ .07
McBride, Bake	82TTR	69	$ .02	$ .10
McBride, Bake	83T	248	$ .01	$ .07
McBride, Bake	84T	569	$ .01	$ .06
McBride, Ken	60T	276	$ .45	$1.45
McBride, Ken	61T	209	$ .35	$1.25
McBride, Ken	62T	268	$ .45	$1.45
McBride, Ken	63T	510	$1.75	$4.50
McBride, Ken	64T	405	$ .50	$1.45
McBride, Ken	65T	268	$ .35	$1.25
McCabe, Joe	64T	564	$1.75	$4.50
McCabe, Joe	65T	181	$ .30	$ .85
McCall, Windy	55T	42	$2.00	$6.00
McCall, Windy	56T	44	$2.25	$6.00
McCall, Windy	57T	291	$4.25	$15.00
McCament, Randy	89TMLD	77	$ .01	$ .06
McCament, Randy	90T	361	$ .01	$ .10
McCarthy, Tom	89TTR	75	$ .01	$ .15
McCarthy, Tom	90T	326	$ .01	$ .04
McCarver, Tim	62T	167	$5.00	$20.00
McCarver, Tim	63T	394	$2.00	$8.00
McCarver, Tim	64T	429	$1.25	$5.00
McCarver, Tim	65T	294	$ .75	$3.00
McCarver, Tim	66T	275	$ .75	$3.00
McCarver, Tim	67T	485	$ .75	$2.25
McCarver, Tim	68T	275	$ .45	$1.45
McCarver, Tim	68TAS	376	$ .75	$3.00
McCarver, Tim	69T	475	$ .30	$ .85
McCarver, Tim	70T	90	$ .15	$ .50
McCarver, Tim	71T	465	$ .15	$ .50

Player	Year	No.	VG	EX/MT	Player	Year	No.	VG	EX/MT
McCarver, Tim	72T	139	$ .30	$ .95	McCormick, Mike	64T	487	$ .50	$1.45
McCarver, Tim	73T	269	$ .30	$ .95	McCormick, Mike	65T	343	$ .35	$1.25
McCarver, Tim	74T	520	$ .30	$ .85	McCormick, Mike	66T	118	$ .30	$ .95
McCarver, Tim	75T	586	$ .30	$ .95	McCormick, Mike	67T	86	$ .35	$1.25
McCarver, Tim	76T	502	$ .30	$ .85	McCormick, Mike	68T	400	$ .30	$ .85
McCarver, Tim	77T	357	$ .30	$ .85	McCormick, Mike	68T	9	$ .75	$2.20
McCarver, Tim	78T	235	$ .05	$ .20	McCormick, Mike	69T	517	$ .30	$ .95
McCarver, Tim	79T	675	$ .05	$ .20	McCormick, Mike	70T	337	$ .15	$ .50
McCarver, Tim	80T	178	$ .03	$ .15	McCormick, Mike	71T	438	$ .15	$ .50
McCaskill, Kirk	86T	628	$ .04	$ .35	McCormick, Mike	72T	682	$ .75	$2.50
McCaskill, Kirk	87T	194	$ .01	$ .04	McCosky, Barney	52T	300	$15.00	$47.50
McCaskill, Kirk	88T	16	$ .01	$ .04	McCovey, Willie	60T	316	$65.00	$185.00
McCaskill, Kirk	88TBB	168	$ .01	$ .06	McCovey, Willie	60TAS	554	$15.00	$40.00
McCaskill, Kirk	89T	421	$ .01	$ .05	McCovey, Willie	61T	517	$18.00	$55.00
McCaskill, Kirk	89TBB	149	$ .01	$ .06	McCovey, Willie	62T	544	$35.00	$110.00
McCaskill, Kirk	90T	215	$ .01	$ .04	McCovey, Willie	63T	490	$25.00	$80.00
McCaskill, Kirk	91T	532	$ .01	$ .03	McCovey, Willie	64T	350	$8.00	$25.00
McCatty, Steve	78T	701	$ .02	$ .10	McCovey, Willie	64T	9	$3.00	$9.00
McCatty, Steve	80T	231	$ .01	$ .10	McCovey, Willie	64T	41	$ .75	$2.25
McCatty, Steve	81T	503	$ .01	$ .10	McCovey, Willie	65T	176	$5.00	$15.00
McCatty, Steve	82T	113	$ .01	$ .07	McCovey, Willie	66T	217	$1.50	$4.00
McCatty, Steve	82T	156	$ .05	$ .20	McCovey, Willie	66T	550	$35.00	$100.00
McCatty, Steve	82T	165	$ .03	$ .15	McCovey, Willie	67T	423	$5.50	$17.50
McCatty, Steve	82T	167	$ .03	$ .15	McCovey, Willie	67T	480	$7.00	$22.00
McCatty, Steve	83T	493	$ .01	$ .07	McCovey, Willie	68T	5	$1.25	$3.75
McCatty, Steve	84T	369	$ .01	$ .06	McCovey, Willie	68T	290	$3.00	$8.00
McCatty, Steve	85T	63	$ .01	$ .05	McCovey, Willie	69T	4	$ .75	$2.25
McCatty, Steve	86T	624	$ .01	$ .04	McCovey, Willie	69T	6	$ .80	$2.50
McClain, Joe	61T	488	$ .75	$3.00	McCovey, Willie	69T	440	$3.00	$10.00
McClain, Joe	62T	324	$ .45	$1.45	McCovey, Willie	69T	572	$2.50	$7.50
McClain, Joe	63T	311	$ .45	$1.50	McCovey, Willie	69TAS	416	$1.50	$4.00
McClendon, Lloyd	88T	172	$ .01	$ .10	McCovey, Willie	70T	63	$ .75	$2.20
McClendon, Lloyd	89T	644	$ .01	$ .05	McCovey, Willie	70T	65	$ .90	$3.00
McClendon, Lloyd	89TTR	76	$ .01	$ .06	McCovey, Willie	70T	250	$2.00	$8.00
McClendon, Lloyd	90T	337	$ .01	$ .04	McCovey, Willie	70TAS	450	$1.50	$5.00
McClure, Bob	76T	599	$2.50	$10.00	McCovey, Willie	71T	50	$1.25	$6.00
McClure, Bob	77T	472	$ .03	$ .12	McCovey, Willie	72T	280	$1.50	$6.00
McClure, Bob	78T	243	$ .02	$ .10	McCovey, Willie	73T	410	$1.25	$5.00
McClure, Bob	79T	623	$ .02	$ .10	McCovey, Willie	74T	250	$1.25	$5.00
McClure, Bob	80T	357	$ .01	$ .10	McCovey, Willie	75T	207	$ .75	$3.00
McClure, Bob	81T	156	$ .01	$ .10	McCovey, Willie	75T	450	$1.00	$4.00
McClure, Bob	82T	487	$ .01	$ .07	McCovey, Willie	76T	520	$1.00	$4.00
McClure, Bob	83T	62	$ .01	$ .07	McCovey, Willie	77T	547	$1.00	$4.00
McClure, Bob	84T	582	$ .01	$ .06	McCovey, Willie	78T	34	$ .45	$1.50
McClure, Bob	85T	203	$ .01	$ .05	McCovey, Willie	78TRB	3	$ .35	$1.00
McClure, Bob	86T	684	$ .01	$ .04	McCovey, Willie	79T	215	$ .75	$3.00
McClure, Bob	86TTR	71	$ .02	$ .10	McCovey, Willie	80T	335	$ .45	$1.35
McClure, Bob	87T	707	$ .01	$ .04	McCovey, Willie	80THL	2	$ .15	$ .50
McClure, Bob	88T	313	$ .01	$ .04	McCraw, Tommy	64T	283	$ .30	$ .95
McClure, Bob	89T	182	$ .01	$ .05	McCraw, Tommy	65T	586	$1.75	$4.50
McClure, Bob	90T	458	$ .01	$ .04	McCraw, Tom	66T	141	$ .30	$ .95
McClure, Bob	91T	84	$ .01	$ .03	McCraw, Tommy	67T	29	$ .30	$ .85
McClure, Jack	65T	553	$1.75	$4.50	McCraw, Tommy	68T	413	$ .30	$ .85
McCool, Bill	64T	356	$ .30	$ .95	McCraw, Tom	69T	388	$ .30	$ .85
McCool, Bill	65T	18	$ .30	$ .85	McCraw, Tom	70T	561	$ .30	$ .95
McCool, Bill	66T	459	$ .75	$2.50	McCraw, Tom	71T	373	$ .15	$ .50
McCool, Bill	67T	353	$ .30	$ .85	McCraw, Tom	72T	767	$ .75	$2.50
McCool, Bill	68T	597	$ .35	$1.25	McCraw, Tom	73T	86	$ .07	$ .30
McCool, Bill	69T	129	$ .30	$ .85	McCraw, Tom	74T	449	$ .07	$ .30
McCool, Bill	70T	314	$ .15	$ .50	McCraw, Tom	75T	482	$ .07	$ .30
McCormick, Mike	58T	37	$ .70	$2.25	McCray, Rodney	91T	523	$ .01	$ .10
McCormick, Mike	59T	148	$ .75	$2.20	McCullers, Lance	86T	44	$ .02	$ .20
McCormick, Mike	60T	530	$2.50	$10.00	McCullers, Lance	87T	559	$ .01	$ .10
McCormick, Mike	61T	305	$ .35	$1.25	McCullers, Lance	88T	197	$ .01	$ .04
McCormick, Mike	61T	383	$ .75	$3.00	McCullers, Lance	88TBB	38	$ .01	$ .06
McCormick, Mike	61T	45	$ .60	$2.75	McCullers, Lance	89T	307	$ .01	$ .05
McCormick, Mike	62T	107	$ .45	$1.45	McCullers, Lance	89TTR	77	$ .01	$ .06
McCormick, Mike	62T	319	$ .75	$3.00	McCullers, Lance	90T	259	$ .01	$ .04
McCormick, Mike	62T	56	$ .75	$3.00	McCullough, Clyde	52T	218	$7.00	$20.00
McCormick, Mike	63T	563	$1.75	$4.50	McDaniel, Jim	59T	134	$ .75	$2.20

Player	Year	No.	VG	EX/MT
McDaniel, Lindy	57T	79	$ .60	$2.50
McDaniel, Lindy	58T	180	$ .75	$3.00
McDaniel, Lindy	59T	479	$ .75	$2.20
McDaniel, Lindy	60T	195	$ .45	$1.45
McDaniel, Lindy	61T	75	$ .35	$1.25
McDaniel, Lindy	61T	266	$ .35	$1.25
McDaniel, Lindy	62T	306	$ .75	$3.00
McDaniel, Lindy	62T	522	$ .75	$2.50
McDaniel, Lindy	63T	329	$ .45	$1.50
McDaniel, Lindy	64T	510	$ .50	$1.45
McDaniel, Lindy	65T	244	$ .35	$1.25
McDaniel, Lindy	66T	496	$ .75	$2.50

LINDY McDANIEL PITCHER

Player	Year	No.	VG	EX/MT
McDaniel, Lindy	67T	46	$ .30	$ .85
McDaniel, Lindy	68T	545	$ .35	$1.25
McDaniel, Lindy	69T	191	$ .30	$ .85
McDaniel, Lindy	70T	493	$ .15	$ .50
McDaniel, Lindy	71T	303	$ .15	$ .50
McDaniel, Lindy	72T	513	$ .05	$ .25
McDaniel, Lindy	73T	46	$ .07	$ .30
McDaniel, Lindy	74T	182	$ .07	$ .30
McDaniel, Lindy	74TTR	182	$ .07	$ .30
McDaniel, Lindy	75T	652	$ .07	$ .30
McDaniel, Von	58T	65	$1.25	$4.25
McDermott, Maurice	51Trb	43	$1.50	$4.00
McDermott, Maurice	52T	119	$7.00	$20.00
McDermott, Maurice	53T	55	$4.50	$15.00
McDermott, Mickey	56T	340	$6.00	$27.50
McDermott, Mickey	57T	318	$4.25	$15.00
McDevitt, Danny	58T	357	$ .75	$3.00
McDevitt, Danny	59T	364	$ .75	$2.20
McDevitt, Danny	60T	333	$ .75	$2.20
McDevitt, Danny	61T	349	$ .35	$1.25
McDevitt, Danny	62T	493	$ .75	$2.50
McDonald, Ben	89TMLD	78	$ .01	$1.25
McDonald, Ben	90T	774	$ .01	$1.00
McDonald, Ben	90TTR	70	$ .01	$1.00
McDonald, Ben	91T	497	$ .01	$ .25
McDonald, Dave	70T	189	$20.00	$67.50
McDougald, Gil	52T	372	$80.00	$250.00
McDougald, Gil	53T	43	$10.00	$40.00

Player	Year	No.	VG	EX/MT
McDougald, Gil	56T	225	$7.50	$22.50
McDougald, Gil	57T	200	$4.00	$12.00
McDougald, Gil	58T	20	$3.00	$9.00
McDougald, Gil	59T	237	$ .90	$3.00
McDougald, Gil	59T	345	$2.00	$8.00
McDougald, Gil	60T	247	$1.75	$6.50
McDowell, Jack	88TTR	68	$ .01	$ .15
McDowell, Jack	89T	486	$ .01	$ .10
McDowell, Jack	90TTR	71	$ .01	$ .05
McDowell, Jack	91T	219	$ .01	$ .03
McDowell, Oddibe	85T	400	$ .10	$ .50
McDowell, Oddibe	85TTR	82	$ .20	$ .50
McDowell, Oddibe	86T	480	$ .03	$ .25
McDowell, Oddibe	87T	95	$ .01	$ .10
McDowell, Oddibe	88T	617	$ .01	$ .04
McDowell, Oddibe	88TBB	198	$ .01	$ .10
McDowell, Oddibe	89T	183	$ .01	$ .05
McDowell, Oddibe	89TBB	245	$ .01	$ .06
McDowell, Oddibe	89TTR	78	$ .01	$ .06
McDowell, Oddibe	90T	329	$ .01	$ .04
McDowell, Oddibe	91T	533	$ .01	$ .03
McDowell, Roger	85TTR	83	$ .15	$ .75
McDowell, Roger	86T	547	$ .03	$ .35
McDowell, Roger	87T	185	$ .01	$ .10
McDowell, Roger	88T	355	$ .01	$ .04
McDowell, Roger	88TBB	101	$ .01	$ .06
McDowell, Roger	89T	735	$ .01	$ .05
McDowell, Roger	89TTR	79	$ .01	$ .06
McDowell, Roger	90T	625	$ .01	$ .04
McDowell, Roger	91T	43	$ .01	$ .03
McDowell, Sam	62T	591	$8.00	$22.50
McDowell, Sam	63T	317	$ .45	$1.45
McDowell, Sam	64T	391	$ .75	$3.00
McDowell, Sam	65T	76	$ .15	$ .50
McDowell, Sam	66T	222	$ .75	$3.00
McDowell, Sam	66T	226	$ .75	$3.00
McDowell, Sam	66T	470	$ .65	$1.75
McDowell, Sam	67T	237	$ .45	$1.45
McDowell, Sam	67T	295	$ .30	$ .85
McDowell, Sam	67T	463	$ .75	$3.00
McDowell, Sam	68T	12	$ .45	$1.45
McDowell, Sam	68T	115	$ .30	$ .95
McDowell, Sam	69T	7	$ .35	$1.25
McDowell, Sam	69T	11	$ .75	$3.00
McDowell, Sam	69T	220	$ .35	$1.25
McDowell, Sam	69TAS	435	$ .30	$ .85
McDowell, Sam	70T	72	$ .50	$2.00
McDowell, Sam	70T	650	$ .75	$2.00
McDowell, Sam	70TAS	469	$ .30	$ .95
McDowell, Sam	71T	71	$ .15	$ .50
McDowell, Sam	71T	150	$ .30	$ .95
McDowell, Sam	72T	720	$1.25	$4.25
McDowell, Sam	73T	342	$ .07	$ .30
McDowell, Sam	73T	511	$ .15	$ .50
McDowell, Sam	74T	550	$ .30	$ .85
McElroy, Chuck	89TMLD	79	$ .01	$ .15
McEnaney, Will	75T	481	$ .07	$ .30
McEnaney, Will	76T	362	$ .05	$ .20
McEnaney, Will	77T	160	$ .03	$ .12
McEnaney, Will	78T	603	$ .02	$ .10
McEnaney, Will	80T	563	$ .01	$ .10
McFadden, Leon	69T	156	$ .30	$ .85
McFadden, Leon	70T	672	$ .75	$2.00
McFarlane, Jesus "Orlando"	62T	229	$ .45	$1.45
McFarlane, Orlando	64T	509	$ .50	$1.45
McFarlane, Orlando	66T	569	$5.00	$20.00
McFarlane, Orlando	67T	496	$ .75	$3.00
McGaffigan, Andy	82T	83	$ .10	$ .50
McGaffigan, Andy	83TTR	68	$ .02	$ .10
McGaffigan, Andy	84T	31	$ .01	$ .06

Player	Year	No.	VG	EX/MT	Player	Year	No.	VG	EX/MT
McGaffigan, Andy	84TTR	78	$ .02	$ .10	McGraw, Tug	83T	511	$ .01	$ .07
McGaffigan, Andy	85T	323	$ .01	$ .05	McGraw, Tug	84T	709	$ .01	$ .06
McGaffigan, Andy	86T	133	$ .01	$ .04	McGraw, Tug	84T	728	$ .01	$ .06
McGaffigan, Andy	86TTR	72	$ .02	$ .10	McGraw, Tug	85T	157	$ .01	$ .05
McGaffigan, Andy	87T	742	$ .01	$ .04	McGregor, Scott	75T	618	$ .90	$3.00
McGaffigan, Andy	88T	488	$ .01	$ .04	McGregor, Scott	77T	475	$ .05	$ .15
McGaffigan, Andy	89T	278	$ .01	$ .05	McGregor, Scott	78T	491	$ .02	$ .10
McGaffigan, Andy	89TBB	315	$ .01	$ .06	McGregor, Scott	79T	393	$ .02	$ .10
McGaffigan, Andy	90T	559	$ .01	$ .04	McGregor, Scott	80T	237	$ .02	$ .10
McGaffigan, Andy	91T	671	$ .01	$ .03	McGregor, Scott	81T	65	$ .01	$ .10
McGaha, Mel	62T	242	$ .45	$1.45	McGregor, Scott	82T	617	$ .01	$ .07
McGaha, Mel	65T	391	$ .35	$1.25	McGregor, Scott	82TAS	555	$ .01	$ .07
McGee, Willie	83T	49	$1.50	$5.00	McGregor, Scott	83T	745	$ .01	$ .07
McGee, Willie	84T	310	$ .05	$ .35	McGregor, Scott	84T	260	$ .01	$ .06
McGee, Willie	85T	757	$ .05	$ .25	McGregor, Scott	85T	550	$ .01	$ .05
McGee, Willie	86T	580	$ .01	$ .10	McGregor, Scott	86T	110	$ .01	$ .04
McGee, Willie	86TAS	707	$ .01	$ .04	McGregor, Scott	87T	708	$ .01	$ .04
McGee, Willie	87T	440	$ .03	$ .15	McGregor, Scott	88T	419	$ .01	$ .04
McGee, Willie	88T	160	$ .01	$ .10	McGriff, Fred	87TTR	74	$ .35	$2.00
McGee, Willie	88TBB	79	$ .01	$ .06	McGriff, Fred	88T	463	$ .15	$1.00
McGee, Willie	89T	640	$ .01	$ .05	McGriff, Fred	89T	745	$ .01	$ .15
McGee, Willie	89TBB	183	$ .01	$ .10	McGriff, Fred	89TBB	15	$ .01	$ .10
McGee, Willie	90T	285	$ .01	$ .04	McGriff, Fred	90T	295	$ .01	$ .15
McGee, Willie	91T	380	$ .01	$ .03	McGriff, Fred	90TAS	385	$ .01	$ .10
McGhee, Ed	53T	195	$4.50	$15.00	McGriff, Fred	91T	140	$ .01	$ .03
McGhee, Ed	54T	215	$3.60	$10.00	McGriff, Terry	88T	644	$ .01	$ .10
McGhee, Ed	55T	32	$2.00	$6.00	McGriff, Terry	89T	151	$ .01	$ .05
McGilberry, Randy	79T	707	$ .02	$ .10	McGwire, Mark	85T	401	$5.50	$17.50
McGinn, Dan	69T	646	$ .30	$ .95	McGwire, Mark	87T	366	$ .75	$3.00
McGinn, Dan	70T	364	$ .15	$ .50	McGwire, Mark	88T	580	$ .04	$1.00
McGinn, Dan	71T	21	$ .15	$ .50	McGwire, Mark	88TBB	179	$ .10	$ .50
McGinn, Dan	72T	473	$ .05	$ .25	McGwire, Mark	88TRB	3	$ .05	$ .35
McGinn, Dan	73T	527	$ .05	$ .25	McGwire, Mark	89T	70	$ .05	$ .25
McGlothen, Lynn	73T	114	$ .06	$ .25	McGwire, Mark	89TBB	34	$ .01	$ .50
McGlothen, Lynn	75T	272	$ .06	$ .25	McGwire, Mark	90T	690	$ .01	$ .25
McGlothen, Lynn	76T	478	$ .05	$ .20	McGwire, Mark	91T	270	$ .01	$ .15
McGlothen, Lynn	77T	47	$ .03	$ .12	McIntosh, Joe	76T	497	$ .05	$ .20
McGlothen, Lynn	78T	581	$ .02	$ .10	McIntosh, Joe	76TTR	497	$ .05	$ .20
McGlothen, Lynn	79T	323	$ .02	$ .10	McIntosh, Tim	91T	561	$ .01	$ .10
McGlothen, Lynn	80T	716	$ .01	$ .07	McKay, Dave	76T	592	$1.25	$5.00
McGlothen, Lynn	81T	609	$ .01	$ .07	McKay, Dave	77T	377	$ .03	$ .12
McGlothen, Lynn	82T	85	$ .01	$ .06	McKay, Dave	79T	608	$ .02	$ .10
McGlothlin, Jim	66T	417	$ .25	$1.00	McKay, Dave	81T	461	$ .01	$ .10
McGlothlin, Jim	67T	19	$ .25	$ .65	McKay, Dave	82T	534	$ .01	$ .07
McGlothlin, Jim	68T	493	$ .30	$1.00	McKay, Dave	83T	47	$ .01	$ .07
McGlothlin, Jim	69T	386	$ .25	$ .65	McKeon, Jack	73T	593	$ .75	$3.00
McGlothlin, Jim	70T	132	$ .10	$ .35	McKeon, Jack	74T	166	$ .07	$ .30
McGlothlin, Jim	71T	556	$ .30	$1.00	McKeon, Jack	88TTR	69	$ .01	$ .06
McGlothlin, Jim	72T	236	$ .05	$ .25	McKeon, Jack	89T	624	$ .01	$ .05
McGlothlin, Jim	73T	318	$ .06	$ .25	McKeon, Jack	90T	231	$ .01	$ .04
McGlothlin, Jim	74T	557	$ .06	$ .25	McKeon, Joel	88T	409	$ .01	$ .04
McGraw, Tug	65T	533	$5.00	$20.00	McKinney, Rich	71T	37	$ .15	$ .50
McGraw, Tug	66T	124	$ .60	$1.75	McKinney, Rich	72T	619	$ .30	$ .95
McGraw, Tug	67T	348	$1.00	$3.00	McKinney, Rich	73T	587	$ .45	$1.45
McGraw, Tug	68T	236	$ .60	$2.25	McKnight, Jeff	89TMLD	80	$ .01	$ .06
McGraw, Tug	69T	601	$ .50	$2.50	McKnight, Jeff	91T	319	$ .01	$ .03
McGraw, Tug	70T	26	$ .35	$1.25	McKnight, Jim	62T	597	$7.00	$21.00
McGraw, Tug	71T	618	$ .60	$3.00	McLain, Dennis	65T	236	$4.00	$15.00
McGraw, Tug	72T	163	$ .25	$ .75	McLain, Dennis	66T	226	$ .75	$3.00
McGraw, Tug	72TIA	164	$ .25	$ .50	McLain, Denny	66T	540	$15.00	$50.00
McGraw, Tug	73T	30	$ .25	$ .75	McLain, Denny	67T	235	$ .45	$1.45
McGraw, Tug	74T	265	$ .06	$ .25	McLain, Dennis	67T	420	$1.00	$4.00
McGraw, Tug	75T	67	$ .25	$ .75	McLain, Denny	68T	40	$1.00	$4.00
McGraw, Tug	76T	565	$ .10	$ .35	McLain, Denny	69T	9	$ .35	$1.25
McGraw, Tug	77T	164	$ .10	$ .35	McLain, Denny	69T	11	$ .75	$3.00
McGraw, Tug	78T	446	$ .05	$ .25	McLain, Denny	69T	150	$1.00	$3.00
McGraw, Tug	79T	345	$ .05	$ .20	McLain, Denny	69TAS	433	$ .75	$3.00
McGraw, Tug	80T	655	$ .01	$ .10	McLain, Denny	70T	70	$ .75	$3.00
McGraw, Tug	81T	40	$ .03	$ .15	McLain, Denny	70T	400	$ .75	$3.00
McGraw, Tug	82T	250	$ .01	$ .07	McLain, Denny	70TAS	467	$ .35	$1.25
McGraw, Tug	83T	510	$ .01	$ .07					

TOPPS

Player	Year	No.	VG	EX/MT
McLain, Denny	71T	750	$1.50	$4.00
McLain, Denny	72T	210	$ .15	$ .50
McLain, Denny	72TTR	753	$1.50	$4.00
McLain, Denny	73T	630	$ .75	$1.50
McLain, Denny	75T	206	$ .45	$1.45
McLaughlin, Bo	77T	184	$ .03	$ .12
McLaughlin, Bo	78T	437	$ .02	$ .10
McLaughlin, Bo	80T	326	$ .01	$ .10
McLaughlin, Bo	82T	217	$ .01	$ .07
McLaughlin, Byron	79T	712	$ .02	$ .10
McLaughlin, Byron	80T	197	$ .01	$ .10
McLaughlin, Byron	81T	344	$ .01	$ .10
McLaughlin, Byron	84T	442	$ .01	$ .06
McLaughlin, Joey	80T	384	$ .01	$ .10
McLaughlin, Joey	81T	248	$ .01	$ .10
McLaughlin, Joey	82T	739	$ .01	$ .07
McLaughlin, Joey	83T	9	$ .01	$ .07
McLaughlin, Joey	84T	556	$ .01	$ .06
McLaughlin, Joey	85T	678	$ .01	$ .05
McLemore, Mark	87TTR	75	$ .01	$ .05
McLemore, Mark	88T	162	$ .01	$ .04
McLemore, Mark	89T	547	$ .01	$ .05
McLemore, Mark	89TBB	30	$ .01	$ .06
McLish, Cal	57T	364	$1.25	$4.25
McLish, Cal	58T	208	$ .75	$3.00
McLish, Cal	59T	445	$ .75	$2.20
McLish, Cal	60T	110	$ .45	$1.45
McLish, Cal	61T	157	$ .35	$1.25
McLish, Cal	62T	453	$ .75	$2.50
McLish, Cal	63T	512	$1.75	$4.50
McLish, Cal	64T	365	$ .30	$ .95
McLish, Cal	73T	377	$ .15	$ .50
McLish, Cal	74T	531	$ .30	$ .95
McMahon, Don	58T	147	$ .75	$3.00
McMahon, Don	59T	3	$1.25	$4.25
McMahon, Don	60T	189	$ .45	$1.45
McMahon, Don	61T	278	$ .35	$1.25
McMahon, Don	62T	483	$ .75	$2.50
McMahon, Don	63T	395	$ .45	$1.50
McMahon, Don	64T	122	$ .30	$ .95
McMahon, Don	65T	317	$ .35	$1.25
McMahon, Don	66T	133	$ .30	$ .95
McMahon, Don	67T	7	$ .30	$ .85
McMahon, Don	68T	464	$ .35	$1.25
McMahon, Don	69T	616	$ .30	$ .95
McMahon, Don	70T	519	$ .15	$ .50
McMahon, Don	71T	354	$ .15	$ .50
McMahon, Don	72T	509	$ .05	$ .25
McMahon, Don	73T	252	$ .30	$ .85
McMahon, Don	74T	78	$ .07	$ .30
McMillan, Roy	52T	137	$7.00	$20.00
McMillan, Roy	53T	259	$12.50	$50.00
McMillan, Roy	54T	120	$3.60	$10.00
McMillan, Roy	55T	181	$5.25	$15.00
McMillan, Roy	56T	123	$2.25	$6.00
McMillan, Roy	57T	69	$ .95	$3.50
McMillan, Roy	58T	360	$ .75	$3.00
McMillan, Roy	59T	405	$ .75	$2.20
McMillan, Roy	60T	45	$ .45	$1.45
McMillan, Roy	61T	465	$ .75	$3.00
McMillan, Roy	62T	211	$ .75	$3.00
McMillan, Roy	62TAS	393	$ .90	$3.00
McMillan, Roy	63T	156	$ .30	$ .95
McMillan, Roy	64T	238	$ .30	$ .95
McMillan, Roy	65T	45	$ .30	$ .85
McMillan, Roy	66T	421	$ .30	$ .95
McMillan, Roy	73T	257	$ .75	$3.00
McMillan, Roy	74T	179	$ .75	$3.00
McMillan, Tommy	77T	490	$ .03	$ .12
McMullen, Ken	63T	537	$175.00	$550.00
McMullen, Ken	64T	214	$ .30	$ .95
McMullen, Ken	65T	319	$ .35	$1.25
McMullen, Ken	66T	401	$ .30	$ .95
McMullen, Ken	67T	47	$ .30	$ .85
McMullen, Ken	68T	116	$ .30	$ .85
McMullen, Ken	69T	319	$ .30	$ .95
McMullen, Ken	70T	420	$ .15	$ .50
McMullen, Ken	71T	485	$ .15	$ .50
McMullen, Ken	72T	765	$ .75	$2.50
McMullen, Ken	73T	196	$ .07	$ .30
McMullen, Ken	74T	434	$ .07	$ .30
McMullen, Ken	75T	473	$ .07	$ .30
McMullen, Ken	76T	566	$ .05	$ .20
McMullen, Ken	77T	181	$ .03	$ .12
McMurtry, Craig	83TTR	69	$ .02	$ .10
McMurtry, Craig	84T	126	$ .01	$ .06
McMurtry, Craig	84T	543	$ .01	$ .06
McMurtry, Craig	85T	362	$ .01	$ .05
McMurtry, Craig	86T	194	$ .01	$ .04
McMurtry, Craig	87T	461	$ .01	$ .04
McMurtry, Craig	89T	779	$ .01	$ .05
McMurtry, Craig	90T	294	$ .01	$ .04
McNally, Dave	63T	562	$3.00	$12.00
McNally, Dave	64T	161	$ .15	$ .50
McNally, Dave	65T	249	$ .45	$1.45
McNally, Dave	66T	193	$ .35	$1.25
McNally, Dave	67T	382	$ .30	$ .95
McNally, Dave	68T	478	$ .45	$1.45
McNally, Dave	69T	7	$ .35	$1.25
McNally, Dave	69T	9	$ .35	$1.25
McNally, Dave	69T	340	$ .30	$ .95
McNally, Dave	69T	532	$ .20	$ .50
McNally, Dave	70T	20	$ .30	$ .85
McNally, Dave	70T	70	$ .75	$3.00
McNally, Dave	71T	69	$ .15	$ .50
McNally, Dave	71T	320	$ .30	$ .95
McNally, Dave	72T	344	$ .05	$ .25
McNally, Dave	72T	490	$ .30	$ .95
McNally, Dave	73T	600	$ .75	$2.20
McNally, Dave	74T	235	$ .07	$ .30
McNally, Dave	75T	26	$ .07	$ .30
McNamara, John	70T	706	$ .75	$2.00
McNamara, John	73T	252	$ .30	$ .85
McNamara, John	74T	78	$ .07	$ .30
McNamara, John	83TTR	70	$ .02	$ .10
McNamara, John	84T	651	$ .01	$ .06
McNamara, John	85T	732	$ .01	$ .05
McNamara, John	85TTR	84	$ .02	$ .10
McNamara, John	86T	771	$ .01	$ .04
McNamara, John	87T	368	$ .01	$ .04
McNamara, John	88T	414	$ .01	$ .04
McNamara, John	90TTR	72	$ .01	$ .05
McNamara, John	91T	549	$ .01	$ .03
McNertney, Jerry	64T	564	$1.75	$4.50
McNertney, Jerry	68T	14	$ .30	$ .85
McNertney, Jerry	69T	534	$ .30	$ .95
McNertney, Jerry	70T	158	$ .15	$ .50
McNertney, Jerry	71T	286	$ .15	$ .50
McNertney, Jerry	72T	584	$ .30	$ .95
McNulty, Bill	73T	603	$ .45	$1.45
McQueen, Mike	70T	621	$5.00	$16.00
McQueen, Mike	71T	8	$ .15	$ .50
McQueen, Mike	72T	214	$ .05	$ .25
McRae, Brian	91T	222	$ .01	$ .50
McRae, Hal	68T	384	$1.25	$5.00
McRae, Hal	70T	683	$1.25	$4.50
McRae, Hal	71T	177	$ .15	$ .50
McRae, Hal	72T	291	$ .30	$ .95
McRae, Hal	72TIA	292	$ .05	$ .25
McRae, Hal	73T	28	$ .30	$ .85

Player	Year	No.	VG	EX/MT
McRae, Hal	74T	563	$ .30	$ .85
McRae, Hal	75T	268	$ .15	$ .50
McRae, Hal	76T	72	$ .04	$ .20
McRae, Hal	77T	340	$ .03	$ .12
McRae, Hal	78T	465	$ .05	$ .20
McRae, Hal	79T	585	$ .02	$ .10
McRae, Hal	80T	185	$ .01	$ .10
McRae, Hal	81T	295	$ .01	$ .10

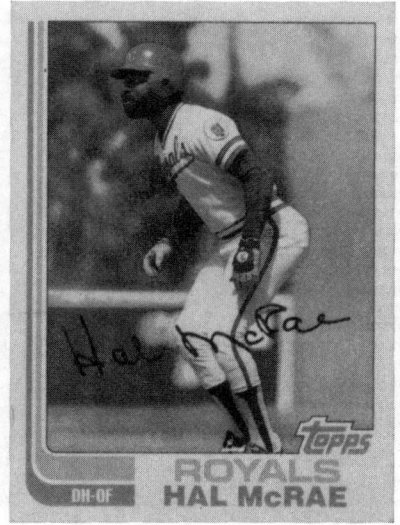

ROYALS
HAL McRAE
DH-OF

Player	Year	No.	VG	EX/MT
McRae, Hal	82T	625	$ .01	$ .07
McRae, Hal	83T	25	$ .01	$ .07
McRae, Hal	83T	703	$ .01	$ .07
McRae, Hal	84T	96	$ .01	$ .06
McRae, Hal	84T	340	$ .01	$ .06
McRae, Hal	85T	773	$ .01	$ .05
McRae, Hal	86T	415	$ .01	$ .04
McRae, Hal	87T	573	$ .01	$ .04
McRae, Norman	70T	207	$ .15	$ .50
McRae, Norman	71T	93	$ .15	$ .50
McReynolds, Kevin	87TTR	76	$ .15	$ .50
McReynolds, Kevin	88T	735	$ .01	$ .15
McReynolds, Kevin	88TBB	158	$ .01	$ .15
McReynolds, Kevin	89T	85	$ .01	$ .10
McReynolds, Kevin	89TBB	116	$ .01	$ .10
McReynolds, Kevin	89TRB	7	$ .01	$ .05
McReynolds, Kevin	90T	545	$ .01	$ .04
McReynolds, Kevin	91T	105	$ .01	$ .03
McWilliams, Larry	79T	504	$ .02	$ .10
McWilliams, Larry	80T	309	$ .01	$ .10
McWilliams, Larry	81T	44	$ .01	$ .10
McWilliams, Larry	82T	733	$ .01	$ .07
McWilliams, Larry	83T	253	$ .01	$ .07
McWilliams, Larry	84T	668	$ .01	$ .06
McWilliams, Larry	85T	183	$ .01	$ .05
McWilliams, Larry	86T	425	$ .01	$ .04
McWilliams, Larry	87T	564	$ .01	$ .04
McWilliams, Larry	88TBB	261	$ .01	$ .06
McWilliams, Larry	88TTR	70	$ .01	$ .06
McWilliams, Larry	89T	259	$ .01	$ .05
McWilliams, Larry	89TTR	80	$ .01	$ .06
Meacham, Bobby	84T	204	$ .01	$ .06

Player	Year	No.	VG	EX/MT
Meacham, Bobby	85T	16	$ .01	$ .05
Meacham, Bobby	86T	379	$ .01	$ .04
Meacham, Bobby	87T	62	$ .01	$ .04
Meacham, Bobby	88T	659	$ .01	$ .04
Meacham, Bobby	89T	436	$ .01	$ .05
Meadows, Louie	89T	643	$ .01	$ .15
Meadows, Louie	90T	534	$ .01	$ .04
Meads, Dave	87TTR	77	$ .01	$ .05
Meads, Dave	88T	199	$ .01	$ .04
Meads, Dave	89T	589	$ .01	$ .05
Medich, George	73T	608	$ .45	$1.45
Medich, George	74T	445	$ .07	$ .30
Medich, George	75T	426	$ .07	$ .30
Medich, George	76T	146	$ .05	$ .20
Medich, George	76TTR	146	$ .05	$ .20
Medich, George	77T	294	$ .03	$ .12
Medich, George	78T	583	$ .02	$ .10
Medich, George	79T	657	$ .02	$ .10
Medich, George	80T	336	$ .01	$ .10
Medich, George	81T	702	$ .01	$ .10
Medich, George	82T	36	$ .01	$ .07
Medich, George	82T	78	$ .01	$ .07
Medina, Luis	89T	528	$ .05	$ .35
Medvin, Scott	89T	756	$ .01	$ .05
Meier, Dave	85T	356	$ .01	$ .05
Mejias, Roman	57T	362	$1.25	$4.25
Mejias, Roman	58T	452	$ .75	$2.20
Mejias, Roman	59T	218	$ .75	$2.20
Mejias, Roman	60T	2	$ .45	$1.45
Mejias, Roman	62T	354	$ .45	$1.45
Mejias, Roman	63T	432	$ .45	$1.50
Mejias, Roman	64T	186	$ .30	$ .95
Mejias, Sam	77T	479	$ .03	$ .12
Mejias, Sam	78T	576	$ .02	$ .10
Mejias, Sam	79T	97	$ .02	$ .10
Mejias, Sam	81T	521	$ .01	$ .10
Mejias, Sam	82T	228	$ .01	$ .07
Mele, Sam	51Tbb	25	$7.50	$22.50
Mele, Sam	52T	94	$7.00	$20.00
Mele, Sam	54T	240	$3.60	$10.00
Mele, Sam	60T	470	$ .95	$3.50
Mele, Sam	62T	482	$ .75	$2.50
Mele, Sam	63T	531	$1.75	$4.50
Mele, Sam	64T	54	$ .30	$ .95
Mele, Sam	65T	506	$ .75	$3.00
Mele, Sam	66T	3	$ .30	$ .95
Mele, Sam	67T	418	$ .30	$ .95
Melendez, Luis	71T	216	$ .15	$ .50
Melendez, Luis	72T	606	$ .30	$ .95
Melendez, Luis	73T	47	$ .07	$ .30
Melendez, Luis	74T	307	$ .07	$ .30
Melendez, Luis	75T	353	$ .07	$ .30
Melendez, Luis	76T	399	$ .05	$ .20
Melton, Bill	69T	481	$ .30	$ .85
Melton, Bill	70T	518	$ .15	$ .50
Melton, Bill	71T	80	$ .15	$ .50
Melton, Bill	72T	183	$ .05	$ .25
Melton, Bill	72T	495	$ .05	$ .25
Melton, Bill	72T	90	$ .75	$3.00
Melton, Bill	72TIA	184	$ .05	$ .25
Melton, Bill	73T	455	$ .07	$ .30
Melton, Bill	74T	170	$ .07	$ .30
Melton, Bill	75T	11	$ .07	$ .30
Melton, Bill	76T	309	$ .05	$ .20
Melton, Bill	76TTR	309	$ .05	$ .20
Melton, Bill	77T	107	$ .03	$ .12
Melton, Dave	58T	391	$ .75	$3.00
Melvin, Bob	86T	479	$ .01	$ .04
Melvin, Bob	87T	549	$ .01	$ .04
Melvin, Bob	88T	41	$ .01	$ .04

Player	Year	No.	VG	EX/MT
Melvin, Bob	89T	329	$ .01	$ .05
Melvin, Bob	90T	626	$ .01	$ .04
Melvin, Bob	91T	249	$ .01	$ .03
Mendoza, Mario	75T	457	$ .07	$ .30
Mendoza, Mario	78T	383	$ .02	$ .10
Mendoza, Mario	79T	509	$ .02	$ .10
Mendoza, Mario	80T	652	$ .01	$ .10

SHORTSTOP MARINERS
MARIO MENDOZA
TOPPS

Player	Year	No.	VG	EX/MT
Mendoza, Mario	81T	76	$ .01	$ .10
Mendoza, Mario	81TTR	801	$ .02	$ .10
Mendoza, Mario	82T	212	$ .01	$ .07
Menke, Denis	62T	597	$7.00	$21.00
Menke, Denis	63T	433	$ .45	$1.45
Menke, Denis	64T	53	$ .30	$ .95
Menke, Denis	65T	327	$ .35	$1.25
Menke, Denis	66T	184	$ .30	$ .95
Menke, Denis	67T	396	$ .45	$1.45
Menke, Denis	67T	518	$ .75	$3.00
Menke, Denis	68T	232	$ .30	$ .85
Menke, Denis	69T	487	$ .30	$ .85
Menke, Denis	70T	155	$ .15	$ .50
Menke, Denis	71T	130	$ .15	$ .50
Menke, Denis	72T	586	$ .30	$ .95
Menke, Denis	73T	52	$ .07	$ .30
Menke, Denis	74T	134	$ .07	$ .30
Meoli, Rudy	75T	533	$ .07	$ .30
Meoli, Rudy	76T	254	$ .05	$ .20
Meoli, Rudy	78T	489	$ .02	$ .10
Mercado, Orlando	83TTR	71	$ .02	$ .10
Mercado, Orlando	84T	314	$ .01	$ .06
Mercado, Orlando	85T	58	$ .01	$ .05
Mercado, Orlando	87T	514	$ .01	$ .04
Mercado, Orlando	90TTR	73	$ .01	$ .05
Merchant, Andy	76T	594	$ .05	$ .20
Mercker, Kent	89TMLD	81	$ .01	$ .25
Mercker, Kent	91T	772	$ .01	$ .03
Merrill, Stump	90TTR	74	$ .01	$ .05
Merrill, Stump	91T	429	$ .01	$ .03
Merritt, Jim	66T	97	$ .30	$ .95
Merritt, Jim	67T	523	$ .75	$3.00
Merritt, Jim	68T	64	$ .30	$ .85

Player	Year	No.	VG	EX/MT
Merritt, Jim	69T	661	$ .30	$ .95
Merritt, Jim	70T	616	$ .30	$ .95
Merritt, Jim	71T	420	$ .15	$ .50
Merritt, Jim	72T	738	$ .75	$2.50
Merritt, Jim	74T	318	$ .07	$ .30
Merritt, Jim	75T	83	$ .07	$ .30
Merritt, Lloyd	58T	231	$ .75	$3.00
Merson, Jack	52T	375	$40.00	$140.00
Merullo, Matt	89TMLD	82	$ .01	$ .06
Mesa, Jose	91T	512	$ .01	$ .03
Messersmith, Andy	69T	296	$ .45	$1.45
Messersmith, Andy	70T	72	$ .50	$2.00
Messersmith, Andy	70T	430	$ .15	$ .50
Messersmith, Andy	71T	15	$ .15	$ .50
Messersmith, Andy	72T	160	$ .30	$ .85
Messersmith, Andy	73T	515	$ .15	$ .50
Messersmith, Andy	74T	267	$ .07	$ .30
Messersmith, Andy	75T	310	$ .35	$1.25
Messersmith, Andy	75T	440	$ .07	$ .30
Messersmith, Andy	76T	199	$ .15	$ .50
Messersmith, Andy	76T	201	$ .35	$1.25
Messersmith, Andy	76T	203	$ .35	$1.25
Messersmith, Andy	76T	305	$ .05	$ .20
Messersmith, Andy	77T	80	$ .03	$ .12
Messersmith, Andy	78T	156	$ .02	$ .10
Messersmith, Andy	79T	278	$ .02	$ .10
Metcalf, Tom	64T	281	$ .30	$ .95
Metkovich, George	52T	310	$12.00	$40.00
Metkovich, George	53T	58	$4.50	$15.00
Metro, Charlie	70T	16	$ .15	$ .50
Mets, Team	63T	473	$20.00	$65.00
Mets, Team	64T	27	$1.75	$6.00
Mets, Team	65T	551	$7.00	$22.00
Mets, Team	66T	172	$ .85	$1.75
Mets, Team	67T	42	$1.50	$4.00
Mets, Team	68T	401	$1.75	$4.50
Mets, Team	70T	1	$3.00	$12.00
Mets, Team	71T	641	$1.50	$4.50
Mets, Team	72T	362	$ .45	$1.45
Mets, Team	73T	389	$ .75	$3.00
Mets, Team	74T	56	$ .45	$1.45
Mets, Team Checklist	75T	421	$ .45	$1.45
Mets, Team Checklist	76T	531	$ .35	$1.25
Mets, Team Checklist	77T	259	$ .35	$1.25
Mets, Team Checklist	78T	356	$ .02	$ .10
Mets, Team Checklist	79T	82	$ .08	$ .30
Mets, Team Checklist	80T	259	$ .15	$ .50
Mets, Team Checklist	81T	681	$ .02	$ .20
Mets, Team Leaders	86T	126	$ .01	$ .04
Mets, Team Leaders	87T	331	$ .01	$ .04
Mets, Team Leaders	88T	579	$ .01	$ .04
Mets, Team Leaders	89T	291	$ .01	$ .10
Metzger, Butch	76T	593	$ .15	$ .50
Metzger, Butch	77T	215	$ .03	$ .12
Metzger, Butch	78T	431	$ .02	$ .10
Metzger, Roger	71T	404	$ .15	$ .50
Metzger, Roger	72T	217	$ .05	$ .25
Metzger, Roger	73T	395	$ .07	$ .30
Metzger, Roger	74T	224	$ .07	$ .30
Metzger, Roger	75T	541	$ .07	$ .30
Metzger, Roger	76T	297	$ .05	$ .20
Metzger, Roger	77T	481	$ .03	$ .12
Metzger, Roger	78T	697	$ .02	$ .10
Metzger, Roger	79T	167	$ .02	$ .10
Metzger, Roger	80T	311	$ .01	$ .10
Meulens, Hensley	89TMLD	83	$ .01	$ .10
Meulens, Hensley	90T	83	$ .01	$ .10
Meulens, Hensley	91T	259	$ .01	$ .10
Meyer, Billy	52T	387	$40.00	$140.00
Meyer, Bob	64T	488	$ .50	$1.45

Player	Year	No.	VG	EX/MT	Player	Year	No.	VG	EX/MT
Meyer, Bob	65T	219	$ .35	$1.25	Milbourne, Larry	85T	754	$ .01	$ .05
Meyer, Bob	70T	667	$ .75	$2.00	Miles, Jim	69T	658	$ .30	$ .95
Meyer, Bob	71T	456	$ .15	$ .50	Miles, Jim	70T	154	$ .15	$ .50
Meyer, Brian	90T	766	$ .01	$ .04	Miley, Mike	76T	387	$ .05	$ .20
Meyer, Danny	75T	620	$10.00	$30.00	Miley, Mike	77T	257	$ .03	$ .12
Meyer, Dan	76T	242	$ .05	$ .20	Millan, Felix	67T	89	$ .30	$ .85
Meyer, Dan	77T	527	$ .03	$ .12	Millan, Felix	68T	241	$ .30	$ .85
Meyer, Dan	78T	57	$ .02	$ .10	Millan, Felix	69T	210	$ .30	$ .85
Meyer, Dan	79T	683	$ .02	$ .10	Millan, Felix	70T	710	$ .75	$$2.00
Meyer, Dan	80T	396	$ .01	$ .10					
Meyer, Dan	81T	143	$ .01	$ .10					
Meyer, Dan	82T	413	$ .01	$ .07					
Meyer, Dan	82TTR	70	$ .02	$ .10					
Meyer, Dan	83T	208	$ .01	$ .07					
Meyer, Dan	84T	609	$ .01	$ .06					
Meyer, Jack	56T	269	$2.25	$8.00					
Meyer, Jack	57T	162	$ .95	$3.50					
Meyer, Jack	58T	186	$ .75	$3.00					
Meyer, Jack	59T	269	$ .75	$2.20					
Meyer, Jack	60T	64	$ .45	$1.45					
Meyer, Jack	61T	111	$ .35	$1.25					
Meyer, Joey	88T	312	$ .01	$ .15					
Meyer, Joey	89T	136	$ .01	$ .05					
Meyer, Joey	89TBB	153	$ .01	$ .06					
Meyer, Joey	90T	673	$ .01	$ .04					
Meyer, Russ	52T	339	$40.00	$140.00					
Meyer, Russ	56T	227	$3.00	$9.00					
Meyer, Russ	59T	482	$ .75	$2.20					
Micelotta, Bob	54T	212	$3.60	$10.00					
Michael, Gene	67T	428	$ .30	$ .95					
Michael, Gene	68T	299	$ .15	$ .50					
Michael, Gene	69T	626	$ .20	$ .50					
Michael, Gene	70T	114	$ .30	$ .85					
Michael, Gene	71T	483	$ .15	$ .50					
Michael, Gene	72T	713	$1.25	$4.25					
Michael, Gene	72T	714	$ .75	$2.50					
Michael, Gene	73T	265	$ .30	$ .85					
Michael, Gene	74T	299	$ .07	$ .30					
Michael, Gene	75T	608	$ .07	$ .30					
Michael, Gene	86TTR	73	$ .02	$ .10	Millan, Felix	70TAS	452	$ .15	$ .50
Michael, Gene	87T	43	$ .01	$ .04	Millan, Felix	71T	81	$ .15	$ .50
Michaels, Cass	52T	178	$7.00	$20.00	Millan, Felix	72T	540	$ .30	$ .95
Mielke, Gary	90T	221	$ .01	$ .10	Millan, Felix	73T	407	$ .07	$ .30
Mielke, Gary	91T	54	$ .01	$ .03	Millan, Felix	74T	132	$ .07	$ .30
Mikkelsen, Pete	64T	488	$ .50	$1.45	Millan, Felix	75T	445	$ .07	$ .30
Mikkelsen, Pete	65T	177	$ .30	$ .85	Millan, Felix	76T	245	$ .05	$ .20
Mikkelsen, Pete	66T	248	$ .30	$ .95	Millan, Felix	77T	605	$ .03	$ .12
Mikkelsen, Pete	67T	425	$ .30	$ .95	Millan, Felix	78T	505	$ .02	$ .10
Mikkelsen, Pete	68T	516	$ .35	$1.25	Miller, Bill	52T	403	$45.00	$140.00
Miksis, Eddie	52T	172	$7.00	$20.00	Miller, Bill	53T	100	$4.50	$15.00
Miksis, Eddie	53T	39	$4.50	$15.00	Miller, Bob	52T	187	$7.00	$20.00
Miksis, Eddie	56T	285	$2.25	$8.00	Miller, Bob	54T	241	$3.60	$10.00
Miksis, Eddie	57T	350	$4.25	$15.00	Miller, Bob	55T	9	$2.00	$6.00
Miksis, Eddie	58T	121	$ .75	$3.00	Miller, Bob	55T	157	$2.50	$10.00
Miksis, Eddie	59T	58	$1.25	$4.25	Miller, Bob	56T	263	$2.25	$8.00
Milacki, Bob	89T	324	$ .01	$ .25	Miller, Bob	56T	334	$2.25	$8.00
Milacki, Bob	90T	73	$ .01	$ .10	Miller, Bob	57T	46	$ .95	$3.50
Milacki, Bob	91T	788	$ .01	$ .03	Miller, Bob	58T	326	$ .75	$3.00
Milbourne, Larry	75T	512	$ .07	$ .30	Miller, Bob	59T	379	$ .75	$2.20
Milbourne, Larry	78T	366	$ .02	$ .10	Miller, Bob	60T	101	$ .45	$1.45
Milbourne, Larry	79T	199	$ .02	$ .10	Miller, Bob	61T	314	$ .35	$1.25
Milbourne, Larry	80T	422	$ .01	$ .10	Miller, Bob	62T	293	$ .45	$1.45
Milbourne, Larry	81T	583	$ .01	$ .10	Miller, Bob	62T	572	$3.95	$11.50
Milbourne, Larry	81TTR	802	$ .02	$ .10	Miller, Bob	63T	261	$ .30	$ .95
Milbourne, Larry	82T	669	$ .01	$ .07	Miller, Bob	64T	394	$ .50	$1.45
Milbourne, Larry	82TTR	71	$ .02	$ .10	Miller, Bob	65T	98	$ .30	$ .85
Milbourne, Larry	83T	91	$ .01	$ .07	Miller, Bob	66T	208	$ .30	$ .95
Milbourne, Larry	83TTR	72	$ .02	$ .10	Miller, Bob	67T	461	$ .75	$3.00
Milbourne, Larry	84T	281	$ .01	$ .06	Miller, Bob	68T	534	$ .35	$1.25
Milbourne, Larry	84TTR	79	$ .02	$ .10	Miller, Bob	69T	403	$ .30	$ .85

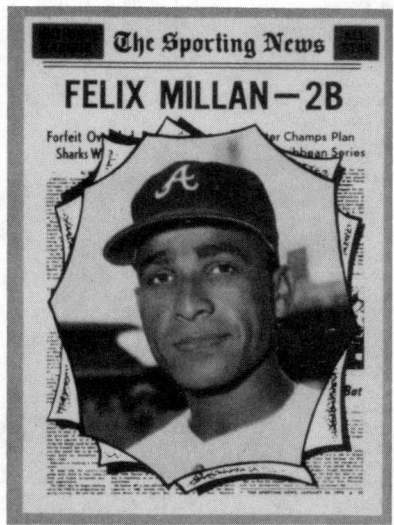

FELIX MILLAN – 2B

TOPPS

Player	Year	No.	VG	EX/MT	Player	Year	No.	VG	EX/MT
Miller, Bob	70T	47	$ .15	$ .50	Miller, Stu	66T	265	$ .30	$ .95
Miller, Bob	71T	542	$ .35	$1.25	Miller, Stu	67T	345	$ .30	$ .85
Miller, Bob	72T	414	$ .05	$ .25	Milligan, Randy	89TTR	81	$ .01	$ .10
Miller, Bob	73T	277	$ .07	$ .30	Milligan, Randy	90T	153	$ .01	$ .04
Miller, Bob	74T	624	$ .07	$ .30	Milligan, Randy	91T	416	$ .01	$ .03
Miller, Bruce	75T	606	$ .07	$ .30	Milliken, Bob	53T	221	$12.50	$50.00
Miller, Bruce	76T	367	$ .05	$ .20	Milliken, Bob	54T	177	$3.60	$10.00
Miller, Darrell	86T	524	$ .01	$ .04	Milliken, Bob	55T	111	$2.00	$6.00
Miller, Darrell	87T	337	$ .01	$ .04	Mills, Alan	90TTR	75	$ .01	$ .15
Miller, Darrell	88T	679	$ .01	$ .04	Mills, Alan	91T	651	$ .01	$ .15
Miller, Darrell	89T	68	$ .01	$ .05	Mills, Brad	82T	118	$ .03	$ .15
Miller, Dyar	75T	614	$ .07	$ .30	Mills, Brad	83T	744	$ .01	$ .07
Miller, Dyar	76T	555	$ .05	$ .20	Mills, Buster	54T	227	$3.60	$10.00
Miller, Dyar	77T	77	$ .03	$ .12	Mills, Dick	71T	512	$ .15	$ .50
Miller, Dyar	78T	239	$ .02	$ .10	Milner, Brian	81T	577	$ .01	$ .10
Miller, Dyar	79T	313	$ .02	$ .10	Milner, Brian	82T	203	$ .70	$3.00
Miller, Dyar	81T	472	$ .01	$ .10	Milner, Eddie	82TTR	72	$ .05	$ .20
Miller, Dyar	82T	178	$ .01	$ .10	Milner, Eddie	83T	449	$ .01	$ .07
Miller, Eddie	80T	675	$ .01	$ .07	Milner, Eddie	84T	34	$ .01	$ .06
Miller, Ed	81T	192	$ .05	$ .20	Milner, Eddie	85T	198	$ .01	$ .05
Miller, Ed	82T	451	$ .01	$ .07	Milner, Eddie	86T	544	$ .01	$ .04
Miller, John	63T	208	$ .30	$ .95	Milner, Eddie	87T	253	$ .01	$ .04
Miller, John	65T	49	$ .75	$3.00	Milner, Eddie	87TTR	78	$ .01	$ .05
Miller, John	66T	427	$ .30	$ .95	Milner, Eddie	88T	677	$ .01	$ .04
Miller, John	67T	141	$ .30	$ .85	Milner, John	72T	741	$1.25	$4.25
Miller, John	69T	641	$ .30	$ .95	Milner, John	73T	4	$ .07	$ .30
Miller, Keith	88T	382	$ .01	$ .20	Milner, John	74T	234	$ .07	$ .30
Miller, Keith	89T	268	$ .01	$ .15	Milner, John	75T	264	$ .07	$ .30
Miller, Keith	89T	557	$ .01	$ .10	Milner, John	76T	517	$ .05	$ .20
Miller, Keith	90T	58	$ .01	$ .04	Milner, John	77T	172	$ .03	$ .12
Miller, Keith	91T	719	$ .01	$ .03	Milner, John	78T	304	$ .02	$ .10
Miller, Kurt	91T	491	$ .01	$ .25	Milner, John	79T	523	$ .02	$ .10
Miller, Larry	65T	349	$ .35	$1.25	Milner, John	80T	71	$ .01	$ .10
Miller, Larry	69T	323	$ .30	$ .95	Milner, John	81T	618	$ .01	$ .10
Miller, Norm	67T	412	$ .30	$ .95	Milner, John	82T	638	$ .01	$ .07
Miller, Norm	68T	161	$ .30	$ .85	Minarcin, Rudy	55T	174	$5.25	$15.00
Miller, Norm	69T	76	$ .30	$ .85	Minarcin, Rudy	56T	36	$2.25	$6.00
Miller, Norm	70T	619	$ .30	$ .95	Mincher, Don	60T	548	$2.50	$10.00
Miller, Norm	71T	18	$ .15	$ .50	Mincher, Don	61T	336	$ .35	$1.25
Miller, Norm	72T	466	$ .05	$ .25	Mincher, Don	62T	386	$ .75	$2.50
Miller, Norm	73T	637	$ .45	$1.45	Mincher, Don	63T	269	$ .30	$ .95
Miller, Norm	74T	439	$ .07	$ .30	Mincher, Don	64T	542	$1.75	$4.50
Miller, Randy	80T	680	$ .05	$ .20	Mincher, Don	65T	108	$ .30	$ .85
Miller, Ray	86T	381	$ .01	$ .04	Mincher, Don	66T	388	$ .30	$ .95
Miller, Rick	72T	741	$1.25	$4.25	Mincher, Don	67T	312	$ .30	$ .85
Miller, Rick	74T	247	$ .07	$ .30	Mincher, Don	68T	75	$ .30	$ .85
Miller, Rick	75T	103	$ .07	$ .30	Mincher, Don	69T	285	$ .30	$ .95
Miller, Rick	76T	302	$ .05	$ .20	Mincher, Don	70T	185	$ .15	$ .50
Miller, Rick	77T	566	$ .03	$ .12	Mincher, Don	71T	680	$ .75	$2.50
Miller, Rick	78T	482	$ .02	$ .10	Mincher, Don	72T	242	$ .05	$ .25
Miller, Rick	79T	654	$ .02	$ .10	Minetto, Craig	80T	494	$ .01	$ .10
Miller, Rick	80T	48	$ .01	$ .10	Minetto, Craig	81T	316	$ .01	$ .10
Miller, Rick	81T	239	$ .01	$ .10	Mingori, Steve	69T	339	$ .30	$ .85
Miller, Rick	81TTR	803	$ .02	$ .10	Mingori, Steve	71T	612	$ .35	$1.25
Miller, Rick	82T	717	$ .01	$ .07	Mingori, Steve	72T	261	$ .05	$ .25
Miller, Rick	83T	188	$ .01	$ .07	Mingori, Steve	73T	532	$ .45	$1.45
Miller, Rick	84T	344	$ .01	$ .06	Mingori, Steve	74T	537	$ .07	$ .30
Miller, Rick	85T	502	$ .01	$ .05	Mingori, Steve	75T	544	$ .07	$ .30
Miller, Rick	86T	424	$ .01	$ .04	Mingori, Steve	76T	541	$ .05	$ .20
Miller, Stu	53T	183	$4.50	$15.00	Mingori, Steve	77T	314	$ .03	$ .12
Miller, Stu	54T	164	$3.60	$10.00	Mingori, Steve	78T	696	$ .02	$ .10
Miller, Stu	56T	293	$2.25	$8.00	Mingori, Steve	79T	72	$ .02	$ .10
Miller, Stu	58T	111	$ .75	$3.00	Mingori, Steve	80T	219	$ .01	$ .10
Miller, Stu	59T	183	$ .75	$2.20	Minner, Paul	52T	127	$7.00	$20.00
Miller, Stu	60T	378	$ .75	$2.20	Minner, Paul	53T	92	$4.50	$15.00
Miller, Stu	61T	72	$ .35	$1.25	Minner, Paul	54T	28	$3.60	$10.00
Miller, Stu	62T	155	$ .45	$1.45	Minner, Paul	56T	182	$3.00	$9.00
Miller, Stu	63T	286	$ .45	$1.50	Minoso, Orestes	52T	195	$18.00	$65.00
Miller, Stu	64T	565	$1.75	$4.50	Minoso, Orestes	53T	66	$9.50	$32.50
Miller, Stu	65T	499	$ .75	$3.00	Minoso, Minnie	56T	125	$3.00	$12.00

388

Player	Year	No.	VG	EX/MT
Minoso, Minnie	57T	138	$3.60	$10.00
Minoso, Minnie	58T	295	$1.00	$3.00
Minoso, Minnie	59T	80	$1.50	$4.00
Minoso, Minnie	59T	166	$ .90	$3.00
Minoso, Minnie	60T	365	$1.25	$4.25
Minoso, Minnie	61T	42	$ .75	$3.00
Minoso, Minnie	61T	380	$ .90	$3.00
Minoso, Minnie	62T	28	$ .90	$3.00
Minoso, Minnie	63T	190	$ .75	$2.20
Minoso, Minnie	64T	538	$1.75	$5.00
Minoso, Minnie "Orestes"	77TRB	232	$ .15	$ .50
Minton, Greg	77T	489	$ .30	$ .85
Minton, Greg	78T	312	$ .02	$ .10
Minton, Greg	79T	84	$ .02	$ .10
Minton, Greg	80T	588	$ .01	$ .10
Minton, Greg	81T	111	$ .01	$ .10
Minton, Greg	82T	687	$ .01	$ .07
Minton, Greg	83T	470	$ .01	$ .07
Minton, Greg	83TRB	3	$ .01	$ .07
Minton, Greg	84T	205	$ .01	$ .06
Minton, Greg	85T	45	$ .01	$ .05
Minton, Greg	86T	310	$ .01	$ .04
Minton, Greg	87T	724	$ .01	$ .04
Minton, Greg	87TTR	79	$ .01	$ .05

Player	Year	No.	VG	EX/MT
Minton, Greg	88T	129	$ .01	$ .04
Minton, Greg	89T	576	$ .01	$ .05
Minton, Greg	90T	421	$ .01	$ .04
Mirabella, Paul	81T	382	$ .01	$ .10
Mirabella, Paul	82T	499	$ .01	$ .07
Mirabella, Paul	83T	12	$ .01	$ .07
Mirabella, Paul	85T	766	$ .01	$ .05
Mirabella, Paul	89T	192	$ .01	$ .05
Miranda, Willie	53T	278	$12.50	$50.00
Miranda, Willie	54T	56	$3.00	$12.50
Miranda, Willie	55T	154	$2.50	$10.00
Miranda, Willie	56T	103	$2.25	$6.00
Miranda, Willie (Willy)	57T	151	$ .95	$3.50
Miranda, Willy	58T	179	$ .75	$3.00
Miranda, Willy	59T	540	$2.50	$10.00
Mitchell, Bobby	71T	111	$ .15	$ .50

Player	Year	No.	VG	EX/MT
Mitchell, Bobby	74T	497	$ .07	$ .30
Mitchell, Bobby	75T	468	$ .07	$ .30
Mitchell, Bobby	76T	479	$ .05	$ .20
Mitchell, Bobby	83T	647	$ .01	$ .07
Mitchell, Bobby	84T	307	$ .01	$ .06
Mitchell, Craig	76T	591	$ .05	$ .20
Mitchell, Craig	77T	491	$ .25	$1.00
Mitchell, Craig	78T	711	$ .02	$ .10
Mitchell, Dale	51Trb	13	$1.50	$4.00
Mitchell, Dale	52T	92	$7.00	$21.00
Mitchell, Dale	53T	26	$4.50	$15.00
Mitchell, Dale	56T	268	$1.50	$4.50
Mitchell, John	87TTR	80	$ .01	$ .05
Mitchell, John	88T	207	$ .01	$ .10
Mitchell, John	91T	708	$ .01	$ .03
Mitchell, Kevin	86TTR	74	$1.00	$4.50
Mitchell, Kevin	87T	653	$ .50	$2.00
Mitchell, Kevin	87TTR	81	$ .25	$1.00
Mitchell, Kevin	88T	497	$ .10	$ .30
Mitchell, Kevin	88TBB	57	$ .15	$ .50
Mitchell, Kevin	89T	189	$ .05	$ .25
Mitchell, Kevin	89TBB	129	$ .01	$ .35
Mitchell, Kevin	90T	500	$ .01	$ .15
Mitchell, Kevin	90TAS	401	$ .01	$ .15
Mitchell, Kevin	91T	40	$ .01	$ .15
Mitchell, Paul	76T	393	$ .05	$ .20
Mitchell, Paul	77T	53	$ .03	$ .12
Mitchell, Paul	78T	558	$ .02	$ .10
Mitchell, Paul	79T	233	$ .02	$ .10
Mitchell, Paul	80T	131	$ .01	$ .10
Mitchell, Paul	81T	449	$ .01	$ .10
Mitterwald, George	68T	301	$ .30	$ .85
Mitterwald, George	69T	491	$ .30	$ .85
Mitterwald, George	70T	118	$ .15	$ .50
Mitterwald, George	71T	189	$ .15	$ .50
Mitterwald, George	72T	301	$ .05	$ .25
Mitterwald, George	72TIA	302	$ .05	$ .25
Mitterwald, George	74T	249	$ .07	$ .30
Mitterwald, George	74TTR	249	$ .07	$ .30
Mitterwald, George	75T	411	$ .07	$ .30
Mitterwald, George	76T	506	$ .05	$ .20
Mitterwald, George	77T	124	$ .03	$ .12
Mitterwald, George	78T	688	$ .02	$ .10
Mize, Johnny	51Tbb	50	$20.00	$65.00
Mize, Johnny	52T	129	$22.50	$70.00
Mize, John	53T	77	$22.50	$67.50
Mizell, Wilmer	52T	334	$40.00	$140.00
Mizell, Wilmer	53T	128	$4.50	$15.00
Mizell, Wilmer	54T	249	$3.60	$10.00
Mizell, Wilmer	56T	193	$3.00	$9.00
Mizell, Wilmer	57T	113	$ .95	$3.50
Mizell, Wilmer	58T	385	$ .75	$3.00
Mizerock, John	87T	408	$ .01	$ .04
Mmahat, Kevin	89TMLD	84	$ .01	$ .25
Moates, Dave	76T	327	$ .05	$ .20
Moates, Dave	77T	588	$ .03	$ .12
Moeller, Joe	63T	53	$ .30	$ .95
Moeller, Joe	64T	549	$1.75	$4.50
Moeller, Joe	65T	238	$ .35	$1.25
Moeller, Joe	66T	449	$ .75	$2.50
Moeller, Joe	67T	149	$ .30	$ .85
Moeller, Joe	68T	359	$ .30	$ .85
Moeller, Joe	69T	444	$ .30	$ .85
Moeller, Joe	70T	97	$ .15	$ .50
Moeller, Joe	71T	288	$ .15	$ .50
Moeller, Ron	61T	466	$ .75	$3.00
Moeller, Ron	63T	541	$1.75	$4.50
Moffitt, Randy	73T	43	$ .07	$ .30
Moffitt, Randy	74T	156	$ .07	$ .30
Moffitt, Randy	75T	132	$ .07	$ .30

TOPPS

Player	Year	No.	VG	EX/MT	Player	Year	No.	VG	EX/MT
Moffitt, Randy	76T	553	$ .05	$ .20	Money, Don	74T	413	$ .07	$ .30
Moffitt, Randy	77T	464	$ .03	$ .12	Money, Don	75T	175	$ .07	$ .30
Moffitt, Randy	78T	284	$ .02	$ .10	Money, Don	76T	402	$ .05	$ .20
Moffitt, Randy	79T	62	$ .02	$ .10	Money, Don	77T	79	$ .03	$ .12
Moffitt, Randy	80T	359	$ .01	$ .10	Money, Don	78T	24	$ .02	$ .10
Moffitt, Randy	81T	622	$ .01	$ .10	Money, Don	79T	265	$ .02	$ .10
Moffitt, Randy	83T	723	$ .01	$ .07	Money, Don	80T	595	$ .01	$ .10
Moffitt, Randy	83TTR	73	$ .02	$ .10	Money, Don	81T	106	$ .01	$ .10
Moffitt, Randy	84T	108	$ .01	$ .06	Money, Don	82T	709	$ .01	$ .07
Moford, Herb	59T	91	$1.25	$4.25	Money, Don	83T	608	$ .01	$ .07
Mohorcic, Dale	87T	497	$ .01	$ .10	Money, Don	84T	374	$ .01	$ .06
Mohorcic, Dale	88T	163	$ .01	$ .04	Moneyham, Bill	87T	548	$ .01	$ .04
Mohorcic, Dale	89T	26	$ .01	$ .05	Monge, Sid	76T	595	$ .05	$ .20
Molinaro, Bob	79T	88	$ .02	$ .10	Monge, Sid	77T	282	$ .03	$ .12
Molinaro, Bob	81T	466	$ .01	$ .10	Monge, Sid	78T	101	$ .02	$ .10
Molinaro, Bob	82T	363	$ .01	$ .07	Monge, Sid	79T	459	$ .02	$ .10
Molinaro, Bob	83T	664	$ .01	$ .07	Monge, Sid	80T	74	$ .01	$ .10
Molitor, Paul	78T	707	$12.50	$50.00					
Molitor, Paul	79T	24	$1.00	$4.00					
Molitor, Paul	80T	406	$ .35	$1.50					
Molitor, Paul	81T	300	$ .05	$ .25					
Molitor, Paul	82T	195	$ .05	$ .25					
Molitor, Paul	83T	630	$ .01	$ .07					
Molitor, Paul	84T	60	$ .03	$ .15					
Molitor, Paul	85T	522	$ .01	$ .10					
Molitor, Paul	86T	267	$ .01	$ .04					
Molitor, Paul	87T	741	$ .01	$ .10					
Molitor, Paul	88T	465	$ .01	$ .10					
Molitor, Paul	88TBB	1	$ .01	$ .10					
Molitor, Paul	89T	110	$ .01	$ .05					
Molitor, Paul	89TBB	330	$ .01	$ .10					
Molitor, Paul	90T	360	$ .01	$ .04					
Molitor, Paul	91T	95	$ .01	$ .03					
Moloney, Dick	71T	13	$ .15	$ .50					
Monbouquette, Bill	59T	173	$ .75	$2.20					
Monbouquette, Bill	60T	544	$2.50	$10.00					
Monbouquette, Bill	61T	562	$7.00	$21.00					
Monbouquette, Bill	62T	580	$3.95	$11.50					
Monbouquette, Bill	63T	480	$2.50	$6.50					
Monbouquette, Bill	64T	25	$ .30	$ .95					
Monbouquette, Bill	65T	142	$ .30	$ .85					
Monbouquette, Bill	66T	429	$ .30	$ .95					
Monbouquette, Bill	67T	482	$ .75	$3.00					
Monbouquette, Bill	68T	234	$ .30	$ .85					
Monbouquette, Bill	69T	64	$ .30	$ .85					
Monchak, Al	73T	356	$ .15	$ .50					
Monchak, Alex	74T	221	$ .07	$ .30					
Monday, Rick	67T	542	$3.00	$10.00	Monge, Sid	81T	333	$ .01	$ .10
Monday, Rick	68T	282	$ .15	$ .50	Monge, Sid	82T	601	$ .01	$ .07
Monday, Rick	69T	105	$ .30	$ .85	Monge, Sid	82TTR	73	$ .02	$ .10
Monday, Rick	70T	547	$ .15	$ .50	Monge, Sid	83T	564	$ .01	$ .07
Monday, Rick	71T	135	$ .15	$ .50	Monge, Sid	83TTR	74	$ .02	$ .10
Monday, Rick	72T	730	$1.25	$4.25	Monge, Sid	84T	224	$ .01	$ .06
Monday, Rick	73T	44	$ .15	$ .50	Monge, Sid	84TTR	80	$ .02	$ .10
Monday, Rick	74T	295	$ .07	$ .30	Monge, Sid	85T	408	$ .01	$ .05
Monday, Rick	75T	129	$ .07	$ .30	Monroe, Zack	59T	108	$1.25	$4.25
Monday, Rick	76T	251	$ .05	$ .20	Monroe, Zack	60T	329	$ .75	$2.20
Monday, Rick	77T	360	$ .03	$ .12	Montague, John	75T	405	$ .07	$ .30
Monday, Rick	78T	145	$ .02	$ .10	Montague, John	78T	117	$ .02	$ .10
Monday, Rick	79T	605	$ .02	$ .10	Montague, John	79T	337	$ .02	$ .10
Monday, Rick	80T	465	$ .01	$ .10	Montague, John	80T	253	$ .01	$ .10
Monday, Rick	81T	726	$ .05	$ .20	Montague, John	81T	652	$ .01	$ .10
Monday, Rick	82T	577	$ .01	$ .07	Montanez, Willie	71T	138	$ .15	$ .50
Monday, Rick	83T	63	$ .01	$ .07	Montanez, Willie	72T	690	$ .75	$2.50
Monday, Rick	84T	274	$ .01	$ .06	Montanez, Willie	73T	97	$ .07	$ .30
Money, Don	69T	454	$ .30	$ .85	Montanez, Willie	74T	515	$ .07	$ .30
Money, Don	70T	645	$ .75	$2.00	Montanez, Willie	75T	162	$ .07	$ .30
Money, Don	71T	49	$ .15	$ .50	Montanez, Willie	76T	181	$ .05	$ .20
Money, Don	72T	635	$ .30	$ .95	Montanez, Willie	77T	410	$ .03	$ .12
Money, Don	73T	386	$ .07	$ .30	Montanez, Willie	78T	38	$ .02	$ .10

Player	Year	No.	VG	EX/MT
Montanez, Willie	79T	305	$ .02	$ .10
Montanez, Willie	80T	224	$ .01	$ .10
Montanez, Willie	81T	559	$ .01	$ .10
Montanez, Willie	82T	458	$ .01	$ .07
Monteagudo, Aurelio	64T	466	$ .50	$1.45
Monteagudo, Aurelio	65T	286	$ .35	$1.25
Monteagudo, Aurelio	66T	532	$5.00	$20.00
Monteagudo, Aurelio	67T	453	$ .30	$ .95
Monteagudo, Aurelio	71T	129	$ .15	$ .50
Monteagudo, Aurelio	72T	458	$ .05	$ .25
Monteagudo, Aurelio	74T	139	$ .07	$ .30
Monteagudo, Aurelio	74TTR	139	$ .07	$ .30
Montefusco, John	76T	203	$ .35	$1.25
Montefusco, John	76T	30	$ .15	$ .50
Montefusco, John	77T	370	$ .03	$ .12
Montefusco, John	78T	142	$ .02	$ .10
Montefusco, John	79T	560	$ .02	$ .10
Montefusco, John	80T	195	$ .01	$ .10
Montefusco, John	81T	438	$ .01	$ .10
Montefusco, John	81TTR	804	$ .02	$ .10
Montefusco, John	82T	697	$ .01	$ .07
Montefusco, John	82TTR	74	$ .02	$ .10
Montefusco, John	83T	223	$ .01	$ .07
Montefusco, John	84T	761	$ .01	$ .06
Montefusco, John	85T	301	$ .01	$ .05
Monteleone, Rich	90T	99	$ .01	$ .04
Montgomery, Bob	71T	176	$ .15	$ .50
Montgomery, Bob	72T	411	$ .05	$ .25
Montgomery, Bob	73T	491	$ .07	$ .30
Montgomery, Bob	74T	301	$ .07	$ .30
Montgomery, Bob	75T	559	$ .07	$ .30
Montgomery, Bob	76T	523	$ .05	$ .20
Montgomery, Bob	77T	288	$ .03	$ .12
Montgomery, Bob	78T	83	$ .02	$ .10
Montgomery, Bob	79T	423	$ .02	$ .10
Montgomery, Bob	80T	618	$ .01	$ .10
Montgomery, Jeff	88T	447	$ .01	$ .30
Montgomery, Jeff	89T	116	$ .01	$ .10
Montgomery, Jeff	90T	638	$ .01	$ .10
Montgomery, Jeff	91T	371	$ .01	$ .03
Montgomery, Monty	72T	372	$ .15	$ .50
Montgomery, Monty	73T	164	$ .07	$ .30
Monzant, Ray	56T	264	$2.25	$8.00
Monzant, Ray	58T	447	$ .75	$2.20
Monzant, Ray	59T	332	$ .75	$2.20
Monzant, Ray	60T	338	$ .75	$2.20
Monzon, Dan	73T	469	$ .07	$ .30
Monzon, Dan	74T	613	$ .07	$ .30
Moon, Wally	54T	137	$5.00	$15.00
Moon, Wally	55T	67	$1.00	$4.00
Moon, Wally	56T	55	$1.50	$4.00
Moon, Wally	57T	65	$ .75	$3.00
Moon, Wally	58T	210	$ .45	$1.50
Moon, Wally	59T	530	$3.00	$9.00
Moon, Wally	60T	5	$ .35	$1.00
Moon, Wally	61T	325	$ .35	$1.25
Moon, Wally	62T	52	$1.00	$4.00
Moon, Wally	62T	190	$ .90	$3.00
Moon, Wally	63T	279	$ .35	$1.25
Moon, Wally	64T	353	$ .30	$ .95
Moon, Wally	65T	247	$ .35	$1.25
Moore, Archie	64T	581	$1.75	$4.50
Moore, Balor	71T	747	$ .75	$2.50
Moore, Balor	73T	211	$ .07	$ .30
Moore, Balor	74T	453	$ .07	$ .30
Moore, Balor	75T	592	$ .07	$ .30
Moore, Balor	78T	368	$ .02	$ .10
Moore, Balor	79T	288	$ .02	$ .10
Moore, Balor	80T	19	$ .01	$ .10
Moore, Barry	67T	11	$ .30	$ .85
Moore, Barry	68T	462	$ .35	$1.25
Moore, Barry	69T	639	$ .30	$ .95
Moore, Barry	70T	366	$ .15	$ .50
Moore, Brad	89T	202	$ .01	$ .05
Moore, Charlie	74T	379	$ .15	$ .50
Moore, Charlie	74T	603	$ .07	$ .30
Moore, Charlie	75T	636	$ .07	$ .30
Moore, Charlie	76T	116	$ .05	$ .20

Player	Year	No.	VG	EX/MT
Moore, Charlie	77T	382	$ .03	$ .12
Moore, Charlie	78T	51	$ .02	$ .10
Moore, Charlie	79T	408	$ .02	$ .10
Moore, Charlie	80T	579	$ .01	$ .10
Moore, Charlie	81T	237	$ .01	$ .10
Moore, Charlie	82T	308	$ .01	$ .07
Moore, Charlie	83T	659	$ .01	$ .07
Moore, Charlie	84T	751	$ .01	$ .06
Moore, Charlie	85T	83	$ .01	$ .05
Moore, Charlie	86T	137	$ .01	$ .04
Moore, Charlie	87T	676	$ .01	$ .04
Moore, Charlie	87TTR	82	$ .01	$ .05
Moore, Donnie	78T	523	$ .05	$ .20
Moore, Donnie	79T	17	$ .02	$ .10
Moore, Donnie	84T	207	$ .01	$ .06
Moore, Donnie	85T	699	$ .01	$ .05
Moore, Donnie	85TTR	85	$ .02	$ .10
Moore, Donnie	86T	345	$ .01	$ .04
Moore, Donnie	87T	115	$ .01	$ .04
Moore, Donnie	88T	471	$ .01	$ .04
Moore, Jackie	65T	593	$1.75	$4.50
Moore, Jackie	73T	549	$ .35	$1.25
Moore, Jackie	84TTR	81	$ .02	$ .10
Moore, Jackie	85T	38	$ .01	$ .05
Moore, Jackie	86T	591	$ .01	$ .04
Moore, Junior	78T	421	$ .02	$ .10
Moore, Junior	79T	275	$ .02	$ .10
Moore, Junior	80T	186	$ .01	$ .10
Moore, Kelvin	82T	531	$ .01	$ .07
Moore, Mike	83T	209	$ .75	$3.00
Moore, Mike	84T	547	$ .01	$ .25
Moore, Mike	85T	279	$ .01	$ .10

Player	Year	No.	VG	EX/MT
Moore, Mike	85T	373	$ .01	$ .05
Moore, Mike	86T	646	$ .01	$ .04
Moore, Mike	87T	727	$ .01	$ .04
Moore, Mike	88T	432	$ .01	$ .04
Moore, Mike	88TBB	241	$ .01	$ .06
Moore, Mike	89T	28	$ .01	$ .05
Moore, Mike	89TTR	82	$ .01	$ .10
Moore, Mike	90T	175	$ .01	$ .04
Moore, Mike	91T	294	$ .01	$ .03
Moore, Ray	55T	208	$5.25	$15.00
Moore, Ray	56T	43	$2.25	$6.00
Moore, Ray	57T	106	$ .95	$3.50
Moore, Ray	58T	249	$ .75	$3.00
Moore, Ray	59T	293	$ .75	$2.20
Moore, Ray	60T	447	$ .90	$3.00
Moore, Ray	61T	289	$ .35	$1.25
Moore, Ray	62T	437	$ .75	$2.50
Moore, Ray	63T	26	$ .30	$ .95
Moorhead, Bob	62T	593	$7.00	$21.00
Moose, Bob	68T	36	$ .15	$ .50
Moose, Bob	69T	409	$ .30	$ .85
Moose, Bob	70T	110	$ .15	$ .50
Moose, Bob	71T	690	$ .75	$2.50
Moose, Bob	72T	647	$ .30	$ .95
Moose, Bob	73T	499	$ .07	$ .30
Moose, Bob	74T	382	$ .07	$ .30
Moose, Bob	75T	536	$ .07	$ .30
Moose, Bob	76T	476	$ .05	$ .20

Player	Year	No.	VG	EX/MT
Mora, Andres	77T	646	$ .03	$ .12
Mora, Andres	78T	517	$ .02	$ .10
Mora, Andres	79T	287	$ .02	$ .10
Morales, Jerry	70T	262	$ .15	$ .50
Morales, Jerry	71T	696	$ .75	$2.50
Morales, Jerry	73T	268	$ .07	$ .30
Morales, Jerry	74T	258	$ .07	$ .30
Morales, Jerry	75T	282	$ .07	$ .30
Morales, Jerry	76T	79	$ .05	$ .20
Morales, Jerry	77T	639	$ .03	$ .12
Morales, Jerry	78T	175	$ .02	$ .10
Morales, Jerry	79T	452	$ .02	$ .10

Player	Year	No.	VG	EX/MT
Morales, Jerry	80T	572	$ .01	$ .10
Morales, Jerry	81T	377	$ .01	$ .10
Morales, Jerry	81TTR	805	$ .02	$ .10
Morales, Jerry	82T	33	$ .01	$ .07
Morales, Jerry	83T	729	$ .01	$ .07
Morales, Jose	76T	418	$ .05	$ .20
Morales, Jose	77T	102	$ .03	$ .12
Morales, Jose	77TRB	233	$ .03	$ .12
Morales, Jose	78T	374	$ .02	$ .10
Morales, Jose	79T	552	$ .02	$ .10
Morales, Jose	80T	218	$ .01	$ .10
Morales, Jose	81T	43	$ .01	$ .10
Morales, Jose	81TTR	806	$ .02	$ .10
Morales, Jose	82T	648	$ .01	$ .07
Morales, Jose	82TTR	75	$ .02	$ .10
Morales, Jose	83TTR	75	$ .02	$ .10
Morales, Jose	84T	143	$ .01	$ .06
Morales, Rich	69T	654	$ .30	$ .95
Morales, Rich	70T	91	$ .15	$ .50
Morales, Rich	71T	267	$ .15	$ .50
Morales, Rich	72T	593	$ .30	$ .95
Morales, Rich	73T	494	$ .07	$ .30
Morales, Rich	74T	387	$ .07	$ .30
Moran, Al	63T	558	$1.75	$4.50
Moran, Al	64T	288	$ .30	$ .95
Moran, Billy	58T	388	$ .75	$3.00
Moran, Billy	59T	196	$ .75	$2.20
Moran, Billy	62T	539	$3.95	$11.50
Moran, Billy	63T	57	$ .30	$ .95
Moran, Billy	64T	333	$ .30	$ .95
Moran, Billy	65T	562	$1.75	$4.50
Morandini, Mickey	88TTR	71	$ .05	$ .50
Morandini, Mickey	89TBB	162	$ .01	$ .10
Morandini, Mickey	91T	342	$ .01	$ .15
Morehead, Dave	63T	299	$ .45	$1.50
Morehead, Dave	64T	376	$ .50	$1.45
Morehead, Dave	65T	434	$ .35	$1.25
Morehead, Dave	66T	135	$ .30	$ .95
Morehead, Dave	67T	297	$ .30	$ .85
Morehead, Dave	68T	212	$ .30	$ .85
Morehead, Dave	69T	29	$ .30	$ .85
Morehead, Dave	70T	495	$ .15	$ .50
Morehead, Dave	71T	221	$ .15	$ .50
Morehead, Seth	59T	253	$ .75	$2.20
Morehead, Seth	60T	504	$ .90	$3.00
Morehead, Seth	61T	107	$ .35	$1.25
Moreland, Keith	81T	131	$ .05	$ .25
Moreland, Keith	82T	384	$ .01	$ .15
Moreland, Keith	82TTR	76	$ .02	$ .10
Moreland, Keith	83T	619	$ .01	$ .07
Moreland, Keith	84T	23	$ .01	$ .06
Moreland, Keith	84T	456	$ .01	$ .06
Moreland, Keith	85T	538	$ .01	$ .05
Moreland, Keith	86T	266	$ .01	$ .04
Moreland, Keith	87T	177	$ .01	$ .04
Moreland, Keith	88T	416	$ .01	$ .04
Moreland, Keith	88TBB	207	$ .01	$ .06
Moreland, Keith	88TTR	72	$ .01	$ .06
Moreland, Keith	89T	773	$ .01	$ .05
Moreland, Keith	89TTR	83	$ .01	$ .06
Moreno, Omar	77T	104	$ .03	$ .12
Moreno, Omar	78T	283	$ .02	$ .10
Moreno, Omar	79T	4	$ .03	$ .15
Moreno, Omar	79T	607	$ .02	$ .10
Moreno, Omar	80T	165	$ .01	$ .10
Moreno, Omar	80T	204	$ .02	$ .10
Moreno, Omar	81T	535	$ .01	$ .10
Moreno, Omar	82T	395	$ .01	$ .07
Moreno, Omar	83T	485	$ .01	$ .07
Moreno, Omar	83TTR	76	$ .02	$ .10

Player	Year	No.	VG	EX/MT	Player	Year	No.	VG	EX/MT
Moreno, Omar	84T	16	$ .01	$ .06	Morgan, Tom	53T	132	$4.50	$15.00
Moreno, Omar	84T	714	$ .01	$ .06	Morgan, Tom	57T	239	$ .95	$3.50
Moreno, Omar	85T	738	$ .01	$ .05	Morgan, Tom	58T	365	$ .75	$3.00
Moreno, Omar	86TTR	75	$ .02	$ .10	Morgan, Tom	59T	545	$2.50	$10.00
Moreno, Omar	87T	214	$ .01	$ .04	Morgan, Tom	60T	33	$ .45	$1.45
Moret, Rogelio	71T	692	$ .75	$2.50	Morgan, Tom	61T	272	$ .35	$1.25
Moret, Rogelio	72T	113	$ .05	$ .25	Morgan, Tom	62T	11	$ .45	$1.45
Moret, Rogelio	73T	291	$ .07	$ .30	Morgan, Tom	63T	421	$ .45	$1.50
Moret, Rogelio	74T	590	$ .07	$ .30	Morgan, Tom	73T	421	$ .07	$ .30
Moret, Rogelio	75T	8	$ .07	$ .30	Morgan, Tom	74T	276	$ .07	$ .30
Moret, Rogelio	76T	632	$ .05	$ .20	Morgan, Vern	73T	49	$ .30	$ .85
Moret, Rogelio	76TTR	632	$ .05	$ .20	Morgan, Vern	74T	447	$ .07	$ .30
Moret, Rogelio	77T	292	$ .03	$ .12	Morhardt, Moe	62T	309	$ .45	$1.45
Moret, Rogelio	78T	462	$ .02	$ .10	Morlan, John	75T	651	$ .07	$ .30
Morgan, Bobby	52T	355	$40.00	$140.00	Morman, Russ	87T	233	$ .01	$ .10
Morgan, Bobby	53T	85	$4.50	$15.00	Morogiello, Dan	84T	682	$ .01	$ .06
Morgan, Bobby	56T	337	$2.25	$8.00	Morris, Danny	69T	99	$3.75	$12.50
Morgan, Bobby	58T	144	$ .75	$3.00	Morris, Hal	90T	236	$ .01	$ .50
Morgan, Joe	60T	229	$ .45	$1.45	Morris, Hal	90TTR	76	$ .01	$ .35
Morgan, Joe	61T	511	$ .75	$3.00	Morris, Hal	91T	642	$ .01	$ .15
Morgan, Joe	89T	714	$ .01	$ .05	Morris, Jack	78T	703	$1.50	$6.00
Morgan, Joe	90T	321	$ .01	$ .04	Morris, Jack	79T	251	$ .50	$1.75
Morgan, Joe	91T	21	$ .01	$ .03	Morris, Jack	80T	371	$ .45	$1.25
Morgan, Joe L.	65T	16	$45.00	$170.00	Morris, Jack	81T	572	$ .10	$ .60
Morgan, Joe L.	66T	195	$9.50	$37.50	Morris, Jack	82T	165	$ .03	$ .15
Morgan, Joe L.	67T	337	$5.00	$20.00	Morris, Jack	82T	450	$ .15	$ .50
Morgan, Joe L.	68T	144	$4.00	$15.00	Morris, Jack	82TAS	556	$ .02	$ .10
Morgan, Joe L.	68TAS	364	$1.00	$4.00	Morris, Jack	83T	65	$ .06	$ .30
Morgan, Joe L.	69T	35	$3.50	$11.00	Morris, Jack	84T	136	$ .02	$ .10
Morgan, Joe L.	70T	537	$3.00	$10.00	Morris, Jack	84T	195	$ .05	$ .20
Morgan, Joe L.	71T	264	$$2.00	$8.00	Morris, Jack	84T	666	$ .01	$ .06
Morgan, Joe L.	72T	132	$1.50	$6.00	Morris, Jack	85T	610	$ .05	$ .20
Morgan, Joe L.	72TTR	752	$12.00	$40.00	Morris, Jack	86T	270	$ .02	$ .15
Morgan, Joe L.	73T	230	$2.00	$6.00	Morris, Jack	87T	778	$ .01	$ .10
Morgan, Joe L.	74T	85	$1.00	$4.00	Morris, Jack	88T	340	$ .01	$ .10
Morgan, Joe L.	74TAS	333	$ .50	$2.00	Morris, Jack	88TBB	170	$ .01	$ .06
Morgan, Joe L.	75T	180	$ .95	$3.50	Morris, Jack	89T	645	$ .01	$ .05
Morgan, Joe L.	76T	197	$ .15	$ .50	Morris, Jack	89TBB	61	$ .01	$ .10
Morgan, Joe L.	76T	420	$ .95	$3.50	Morris, Jack	90T	555	$ .01	$ .04
Morgan, Joe L.	77T	100	$1.00	$4.00	Morris, Jack	91T	75	$ .01	$ .03
Morgan, Joe L.	78T	300	$ .75	$3.00	Morris, John	71T	721	$ .75	$2.50
Morgan, Joe L.	79T	20	$ .10	$ .50	Morris, John	75T	577	$ .07	$ .30
Morgan, Joe L.	80T	650	$ .20	$1.00	Morris, John	87T	211	$ .01	$ .10
Morgan, Joe L.	81T	560	$ .15	$ .60	Morris, John	88T	536	$ .01	$ .04
Morgan, Joe L.	81TTR	807	$ .35	$1.25	Morris, John	89T	578	$ .01	$ .05
Morgan, Joe L.	82T	754	$ .30	$ .85	Morris, John	90T	383	$ .01	$ .04
Morgan, Joe L.	82TIA	755	$ .05	$ .20	Morris, Johnny	69T	111	$ .30	$ .85
Morgan, Joe L.	83T	171	$ .01	$ .07	Morrison, Jim	79T	722	$ .50	$2.00
Morgan, Joe L.	83T	603	$ .07	$ .35	Morrison, Jim	80T	522	$ .01	$ .10
Morgan, Joe L.	83T	604	$ .01	$ .15	Morrison, Jim	81T	323	$ .01	$ .10
Morgan, Joe L.	83TTR	77	$ .35	$1.50	Morrison, Jim	82T	654	$ .01	$ .07
Morgan, Joe L.	84T	210	$ .05	$ .25	Morrison, Jim	82TTR	77	$ .02	$ .10
Morgan, Joe L.	84T	705	$ .02	$ .10	Morrison, Jim	83T	173	$ .01	$ .07
Morgan, Joe L.	84TTR	82	$ .15	$ .60	Morrison, Jim	84T	44	$ .01	$ .06
Morgan, Joe L.	85T	352	$ .05	$ .25	Morrison, Jim	85T	433	$ .01	$ .05
Morgan, Joe L.	85TRB	5	$ .01	$ .10	Morrison, Jim	86T	553	$ .01	$ .04
Morgan, Mike	80T	671	$ .01	$ .10	Morrison, Jim	87T	237	$ .01	$ .04
Morgan, Mike	83T	203	$ .01	$ .07	Morrison, Jim	88T	751	$ .01	$ .04
Morgan, Mike	83TTR	78	$ .02	$ .10	Morrison, Jim	88TBB	237	$ .01	$ .06
Morgan, Mike	84T	423	$ .01	$ .06	Morton, Bubba	62T	554	$3.95	$11.50
Morgan, Mike	86T	152	$ .01	$ .04	Morton, Bubba	63T	164	$ .30	$ .95
Morgan, Mike	87T	546	$ .01	$ .04	Morton, Bubba	67T	79	$ .30	$ .85
Morgan, Mike	88T	32	$ .01	$ .04	Morton, Bubba	68T	216	$ .30	$ .85
Morgan, Mike	88TBB	98	$ .01	$ .06	Morton, Bubba	69T	342	$ .30	$ .85
Morgan, Mike	88TTR	73	$ .01	$ .06	Morton, Carl	69T	646	$ .30	$ .95
Morgan, Mike	89T	788	$ .01	$ .05	Morton, Carl	70T	109	$ .15	$ .50
Morgan, Mike	89TTR	84	$ .01	$ .06	Morton, Carl	71T	515	$ .15	$ .50
Morgan, Mike	90T	367	$ .01	$ .04	Morton, Carl	72T	134	$ .05	$ .25
Morgan, Mike	91T	631	$ .01	$ .03	Morton, Carl	73T	331	$ .07	$ .30
Morgan, Tom	52T	331	$50.00	$145.00	Morton, Carl	74T	244	$ .07	$ .30

Player	Year	No.	VG	EX/MT
Morton, Carl	75T	237	$ .07	$ .30
Morton, Carl	76T	328	$ .05	$ .20
Morton, Craig	77T	24	$ .03	$ .12
Moryn, Milt	59T	147	$3.50	$10.00
Moryn, Walt	57T	16	$ .95	$3.50
Moryn, Walt	58T	122	$ .75	$3.00
Moryn, Walt	59T	488	$ .75	$2.20
Moryn, Walt	60T	74	$ .45	$1.45
Moryn, Walt	61T	91	$ .35	$1.25
Moschitto, Ross	65T	566	$2.00	$6.00
Moseby, Lloyd	81T	643	$ .45	$1.45
Moseby, Lloyd	82T	223	$ .01	$ .20
Moseby, Lloyd	83T	452	$ .03	$ .15
Moseby, Lloyd	84T	606	$ .01	$ .06
Moseby, Lloyd	84T	92	$ .02	$ .10
Moseby, Lloyd	84TAS	403	$ .01	$ .06
Moseby, Lloyd	85T	545	$ .01	$ .10
Moseby, Lloyd	86T	360	$ .01	$ .04
Moseby, Lloyd	87T	210	$ .01	$ .04
Moseby, Lloyd	88T	565	$ .01	$ .04
Moseby, Lloyd	88TBB	113	$ .01	$ .06
Moseby, Lloyd	89T	113	$ .01	$ .05
Moseby, Lloyd	89TBB	262	$ .01	$ .06
Moseby, Lloyd	90T	779	$ .01	$ .04
Moseby, Lloyd	90TTR	77	$ .01	$ .05
Moseby, Lloyd	91T	632	$ .01	$ .03
Moses, Gerry	65T	573	$3.75	$14.00
Moses, Gerry	69T	476	$ .30	$ .85
Moses, Gerry	70T	104	$ .15	$ .50
Moses, Gerry	71T	205	$ .15	$ .50
Moses, Gerry	72T	356	$ .05	$ .25
Moses, Gerry	73T	431	$ .07	$ .30
Moses, Gerry	74T	19	$ .07	$ .30
Moses, Jerry	75T	271	$ .07	$ .30
Moses, John	84T	517	$ .01	$ .06
Moses, John	87T	284	$ .01	$ .04
Moses, John	88T	712	$ .01	$ .04
Moses, John	89T	72	$ .01	$ .05
Moses, John	90T	653	$ .01	$ .04
Moses, John	91T	341	$ .01	$ .03
Moses, Wally	60T	459	$ .95	$3.50
Moskau, Paul	78T	126	$ .02	$ .10
Moskau, Paul	79T	377	$ .02	$ .10
Moskau, Paul	80T	258	$ .01	$ .10
Moskau, Paul	81T	546	$ .01	$ .10
Moskau, Paul	82T	97	$ .01	$ .07
Moss, Les	52T	143	$7.00	$20.00
Moss, Les	57T	213	$ .95	$3.50
Moss, Les	58T	153	$ .75	$3.00
Moss, Les	59T	453	$ .75	$2.20
Mossi, Don	55T	85	$3.60	$10.00
Mossi, Don	56T	39	$2.25	$6.00
Mossi, Don	57T	8	$ .95	$3.50
Mossi, Don	58T	35	$1.25	$4.25
Mossi, Don	59T	302	$ .75	$2.20
Mossi, Don	60T	418	$ .75	$2.20
Mossi, Don	61T	14	$ .35	$1.25
Mossi, Don	62T	105	$ .45	$1.45
Mossi, Don	62T	55	$ .75	$3.00
Mossi, Don	63T	218	$ .45	$1.45
Mossi, Don	63T	530	$1.75	$4.50
Mossi, Don	64T	335	$ .30	$ .95
Mossi, Don	66T	74	$ .30	$ .95
Mota, Manny	63T	141	$1.00	$4.00
Mota, Manny	64T	246	$ .15	$ .50
Mota, Manny	65T	463	$ .75	$3.00
Mota, Manny	66T	112	$ .35	$1.25
Mota, Manny	67T	66	$ .30	$ .85
Mota, Manny	68T	325	$ .15	$ .50
Mota, Manny	69T	236	$ .45	$1.45

Player	Year	No.	VG	EX/MT
Mota, Manny	70T	157	$ .30	$ .95
Mota, Manny	71T	112	$ .35	$1.25
Mota, Manny	72T	596	$ .45	$1.45
Mota, Manny	73T	412	$ .30	$ .85
Mota, Manny	74T	368	$ .15	$ .50
Mota, Manny	75T	414	$ .07	$ .30
Mota, Manny	76T	548	$ .05	$ .20
Mota, Manny	77T	386	$ .03	$ .12
Mota, Manny	78T	228	$ .02	$ .10
Mota, Manny	79T	644	$ .05	$ .20
Mota, Manny	80T	104	$ .03	$ .15
Mota, Manny	80THL	3	$ .01	$ .10
Motley, Darryl	82T	471	$ .05	$ .20
Motley, Darryl	85T	561	$ .01	$ .05
Motley, Darryl	86T	332	$ .01	$ .04
Motley, Darryl	87T	99	$ .01	$ .04
Motton, Curt	68T	549	$ .35	$1.25
Motton, Curt	69T	37	$ .30	$ .85
Motton, Curt	70T	261	$ .15	$ .50
Motton, Curt	71T	684	$ .75	$2.50
Motton, Curt	72T	393	$ .05	$ .25
Moyer, Jamie	87T	227	$ .07	$ .30
Moyer, Jamie	88T	36	$ .01	$ .04
Moyer, Jamie	89T	717	$ .01	$ .05
Moyer, Jamie	89TTR	85	$ .01	$ .06
Moyer, Jamie	90T	412	$ .01	$ .04
Moyer, Jamie	91T	138	$ .01	$ .03
Moyer, Jim	72T	506	$ .30	$ .85
Mueller, Don	52T	52	$12.50	$45.00
Mueller, Don	54T	42	$2.50	$10.00
Mueller, Don	56T	241	$3.00	$9.00
Mueller, Don	57T	148	$ .95	$3.50
Mueller, Don	58T	253	$ .75	$3.00
Mueller, Don	59T	368	$ .75	$2.20
Mueller, Willie	80T	668	$ .01	$ .10
Muffett, Billy	58T	143	$ .75	$3.00
Muffett, Billy	59T	241	$ .75	$2.20
Muffett, Billy	61T	16	$ .35	$1.25
Muffett, Billy	62T	336	$ .45	$1.45
Muir, Joe	52T	154	$7.00	$20.00

TERRY MULHOLLAND

Player	Year	No.	VG	EX/MT
Mulholland, Terry	87T	536	$ .01	$ .04

Player	Year	No.	VG	EX/MT
Mulholland, Terry	89T	41	$ .01	$ .05
Mulholland, Terry	90T	657	$ .01	$ .04
Mulholland, Terry	91T	413	$ .01	$ .03
Mulleavy, Greg	60T	463	$ .85	$2.25
Mullin, Pat	52T	275	$12.00	$40.00
Mulliniks, Rance	78T	579	$ .05	$ .20
Mulliniks, Rance	81T	433	$ .01	$ .10
Mulliniks, Rance	82T	104	$ .01	$ .07
Mulliniks, Rance	82TTR	78	$ .02	$ .10
Mulliniks, Rance	83T	277	$ .01	$ .07
Mulliniks, Rance	84T	762	$ .01	$ .06
Mulliniks, Rance	85T	336	$ .01	$ .05
Mulliniks, Rance	86T	74	$ .01	$ .04
Mulliniks, Rance	87T	537	$ .01	$ .04
Mulliniks, Rance	88T	167	$ .01	$ .04
Mulliniks, Rance	89T	618	$ .01	$ .05
Mulliniks, Rance	90T	466	$ .01	$ .04
Mulliniks, Rance	91T	229	$ .01	$ .03
Mullins, Fran	81T	112	$ .01	$ .10

Player	Year	No.	VG	EX/MT
Mullins, Fran	85T	283	$ .01	$ .05
Mumphrey, Jerry	77T	136	$ .30	$ .85
Mumphrey, Jerry	78T	452	$ .02	$ .10
Mumphrey, Jerry	79T	32	$ .02	$ .10
Mumphrey, Jerry	80T	378	$ .01	$ .10
Mumphrey, Jerry	81T	556	$ .01	$ .10
Mumphrey, Jerry	81TTR	808	$ .02	$ .10
Mumphrey, Jerry	82T	175	$ .01	$ .07
Mumphrey, Jerry	82T	486	$ .03	$ .15
Mumphrey, Jerry	83T	81	$ .01	$ .07
Mumphrey, Jerry	83T	670	$ .01	$ .07
Mumphrey, Jerry	84T	45	$ .01	$ .06
Mumphrey, Jerry	85T	736	$ .01	$ .05
Mumphrey, Jerry	86T	282	$ .01	$ .04
Mumphrey, Jerry	86TTR	76	$ .02	$ .10
Mumphrey, Jerry	87T	372	$ .01	$ .04
Mumphrey, Jerry	88T	466	$ .01	$ .04
Mumphrey, Jerry	88TBB	70	$ .01	$ .06
Munger, Red	51Tbb	14	$7.50	$22.50
Munger, George "Red"	52T	115	$7.00	$20.00

Player	Year	No.	VG	EX/MT
Munoz, Mike	89TMLD	85	$ .01	$ .06
Munson, Thurman	70T	189	$25.00	$77.50
Munson, Thurman	71T	5	$8.00	$25.00
Munson, Thurman	72T	441	$4.00	$15.00
Munson, Thurman	72TIA	442	$2.00	$7.50
Munson, Thurman	73T	142	$2.00	$8.00
Munson, Thurman	74T	340	$1.75	$6.00
Munson, Thurman	75T	20	$1.75	$6.00
Munson, Thurman	76T	192	$ .50	$1.50
Munson, Thurman	76T	650	$1.75	$5.00
Munson, Thurman	77T	170	$1.00	$4.00
Munson, Thurman	78T	60	$ .75	$3.00
Munson, Thurman	79T	310	$ .85	$2.75
Mura, Steve	79T	725	$ .02	$ .10
Mura, Steve	80T	491	$ .01	$ .10
Mura, Steve	81T	134	$ .01	$ .10
Mura, Steve	82T	641	$ .01	$ .07
Mura, Steve	82TTR	79	$ .02	$ .10
Mura, Steve	83T	24	$ .01	$ .07
Mura, Steve	86T	281	$ .01	$ .04
Murakami, Masanori	65T	282	$ .35	$1.25
Murcer, Bobby	66T	469	$5.00	$15.00
Murcer, Bobby	67T	93	$ .75	$3.00
Murcer, Bobby	69T	657	$ .50	$2.00
Murcer, Bobby	70T	333	$ .25	$ .75
Murcer, Bobby	71T	635	$ .50	$2.50
Murcer, Bobby	72T	86	$ .35	$1.25
`Murcer, Bobby	72T	699	$2.00	$8.00
Murcer, Bobby	72TIA	700	$1.00	$4.00
Murcer, Bobby	73T	240	$ .30	$ .95
Murcer, Bobby	73T	343	$ .07	$ .30
Murcer, Bobby	74T	90	$ .15	$ .50
Murcer, Bobby	74TAS	336	$ .75	$2.50
Murcer, Bobby	75T	350	$ .30	$ .85
Murcer, Bobby	76T	470	$ .15	$ .50
Murcer, Bobby	77T	40	$ .03	$ .12
Murcer, Bobby	78T	590	$ .05	$ .20
Murcer, Bobby	79T	135	$ .05	$ .20
Murcer, Bobby	80T	365	$ .01	$ .10
Murcer, Bobby	81T	602	$ .01	$ .10
Murcer, Bobby	82T	208	$ .01	$ .07
Murcer, Bobby	83T	782	$ .01	$ .07
Murcer, Bobby	83T	783	$ .01	$ .07
Murff, Red	57T	321	$4.25	$15.00
Murphy, Bill	66T	574	$5.00	$20.00
Murphy, Dale	77T	476	$15.00	$45.00
Murphy, Dale	78T	708	$7.00	$25.00
Murphy, Dale	79T	39	$1.50	$6.00
Murphy, Dale	80T	274	$1.25	$5.00
Murphy, Dale	81T	504	$ .60	$1.50
Murphy, Dale	82T	668	$ .25	$1.25
Murphy, Dale	83T	502	$ .01	$ .07
Murphy, Dale	83T	703	$ .01	$ .07
Murphy, Dale	83T	760	$ .25	$1.00
Murphy, Dale	83TAS	401	$ .15	$ .60
Murphy, Dale	84T	126	$ .01	$ .06
Murphy, Dale	84T	133	$ .06	$ .30
Murphy, Dale	84T	150	$ .20	$ .75
Murphy, Dale	84TAS	391	$ .06	$ .30
Murphy, Dale	85T	320	$ .10	$ .50
Murphy, Dale	85TAS	716	$ .05	$ .25
Murphy, Dale	86T	600	$ .04	$ .35
Murphy, Dale	86TAS	705	$ .02	$ .20
Murphy, Dale	87T	490	$ .30	$ .95
Murphy, Dale	88T	90	$ .01	$ .30
Murphy, Dale	88TBB	14	$ .01	$ .15
Murphy, Dale	89T	210	$ .01	$ .10
Murphy, Dale	89TBB	172	$ .01	$ .20
Murphy, Dale	90T	750	$ .01	$ .10
Murphy, Dale	91T	545	$ .01	$ .03

TOPPS

Player	Year	No.	VG	EX/MT	Player	Year	No.	VG	EX/MT
Murphy, Dan	89TMLD	86	$ .01	$ .06	Murray, Larry	80T	284	$ .01	$ .10
Murphy, Dan	90T	649	$ .01	$ .10	Murray, Ray	52T	299	$15.00	$47.50
Murphy, Danny	61T	214	$ .35	$1.25	Murray, Ray	53T	234	$12.50	$50.00
Murphy, Danny	62T	119	$ .45	$1.45	Murray, Ray	54T	49	$3.60	$10.00
Murphy, Danny	63T	272	$ .30	$ .95	Murray, Rich	81T	195	$ .01	$ .10
Murphy, Danny	70T	146	$ .15	$ .50	Murrell, Ivan	68T	569	$ .35	$1.25
Murphy, Dwayne	79T	711	$ .08	$ .30	Murrell, Ivan	69T	333	$ .30	$ .85
Murphy, Dwayne	80T	461	$ .01	$ .10	Murrell, Ivan	70T	179	$ .15	$ .50
Murphy, Dwayne	81T	341	$ .01	$ .10	Murrell, Ivan	71T	569	$ .35	$1.25
Murphy, Dwayne	82T	29	$ .01	$ .07	Murrell, Ivan	72T	677	$ .75	$2.50
Murphy, Dwayne	83T	598	$ .01	$ .07	Murrell, Ivan	73T	409	$ .07	$ .30
Murphy, Dwayne	84T	103	$ .01	$ .06	Murrell, Ivan	74T	628	$ .07	$ .30
Murphy, Dwayne	85T	231	$ .01	$ .05	Murtaugh, Danny	59T	17	$1.75	$4.50
Murphy, Dwayne	86T	8	$ .01	$ .04	Murtaugh, Danny	60T	223	$ .90	$3.00
Murphy, Dwayne	87T	743	$ .01	$ .04	Murtaugh, Danny	61T	138	$ .35	$1.25
Murphy, Dwayne	88T	424	$ .01	$ .04	Murtaugh, Danny	61TAS	567	$5.50	$16.50
Murphy, Dwayne	89T	667	$ .01	$ .05	Murtaugh, Danny	62T	503	$ .75	$2.50
Murphy, Rob	87T	82	$ .03	$ .15	Murtaugh, Danny	63T	559	$1.75	$4.50
Murphy, Rob	88T	603	$ .01	$ .04	Murtaugh, Danny	64T	141	$ .30	$ .95
Murphy, Rob	89T	446	$ .01	$ .05	Murtaugh, Danny	64T	268	$ .30	$ .95
Murphy, Rob	89TTR	86	$ .01	$ .06	Murtaugh, Danny	70T	532	$ .15	$ .50
Murphy, Rob	90T	268	$ .01	$ .04	Murtaugh, Danny	71T	437	$ .15	$ .50
Murphy, Rob	91T	542	$ .01	$ .03	Murtaugh, Danny	74T	489	$ .07	$ .30
Murphy, Tom	69T	474	$ .30	$ .85	Murtaugh, Danny	73T	238	$ .07	$ .30
Murphy, Tom	70T	351	$ .15	$ .50	Murtaugh, Danny	74T	286	$ .07	$ .30
Murphy, Tom	71T	401	$ .15	$ .50	Muser, Tony	75T	348	$ .07	$ .30
Murphy, Tom	72T	354	$ .05	$ .25	Muser, Tony	76T	537	$ .05	$ .20
Murphy, Tom	73T	539	$ .45	$1.45	Muser, Tony	77T	251	$ .03	$ .12
Murphy, Tom	74T	496	$ .07	$ .30	Muser, Tony	78T	418	$ .05	$ .20
Murphy, Tom	74TTR	496	$ .07	$ .30	Musial, Stan	58TAS	476	$10.00	$30.00
Murphy, Tom	75T	28	$ .07	$ .30	Musial, Stan	59T	150	$45.00	$150.00
Murphy, Tom	76T	219	$ .05	$ .20	Musial, Stan	59T	470	$3.00	$10.00
Murphy, Tom	77T	396	$ .03	$ .12	Musial, Stan	60T	250	$30.00	$95.00
Murphy, Tom	78T	103	$ .02	$ .10	Musial, Stan	61T	290	$25.00	$80.00
Murphy, Tom	79T	588	$ .02	$ .10	Musial, Stan	62T	50	$25.00	$80.00
Murray, Dale	75T	568	$ .07	$ .30	Musial, Stan	62T	317	$3.50	$14.00
Murray, Dale	76T	18	$ .05	$ .20	Musial, Stan	63T	1	$5.00	$25.00
Murray, Dale	77T	252	$ .03	$ .12	Musial, Stan	63T	138	$10.00	$30.00
Murray, Dale	78T	149	$ .02	$ .10	Musial, Stan	63T	250	$35.00	$100.00
Murray, Dale	79T	379	$ .02	$ .10	Musselman, Jeff	88TTB	665	$ .01	$ .20
Murray, Dale	80T	559	$ .01	$ .10	Musselman, Jeff	87TTR	83	$ .15	$ .50
Murray, Dale	83T	42	$ .01	$ .07	Musselman, Jeff	88T	229	$ .01	$ .10
Murray, Dale	83TTR	79	$ .02	$ .10	Musselman, Jeff	88TBB	69	$ .01	$ .06
Murray, Dale	84T	697	$ .01	$ .06	Musselman, Jeff	89T	591	$ .01	$ .05
Murray, Dale	85T	481	$ .01	$ .05	Musselman, Jeff	90T	382	$ .01	$ .04
Murray, Eddie	78T	36	$12.50	$50.00	Myatt, George	60T	464	$ .95	$3.50
Murray, Eddie	79T	640	$4.00	$12.00	Myers, Greg	90T	438	$ .01	$ .04
Murray, Eddie	80T	160	$1.25	$5.00	Myers, Greg	91T	599	$ .01	$ .03
Murray, Eddie	81T	490	$ .50	$2.00	Myers, Randy	87T	213	$ .07	$ .30
Murray, Eddie	82T	162	$ .05	$ .25	Myers, Randy	88T	412	$ .01	$ .04
Murray, Eddie	82T	163	$ .05	$ .25	Myers, Randy	89T	610	$ .01	$ .05
Murray, Eddie	82T	390	$ .55	$1.75	Myers, Randy	90T	105	$ .01	$ .04
Murray, Eddie	82T	426	$ .05	$ .25	Myers, Randy	90TTR	78	$ .01	$ .05
Murray, Eddie	83T	21	$ .05	$ .25	Myers, Randy	91T	780	$ .01	$ .03
Murray, Eddie	83T	530	$ .25	$1.25	Myrick, Bob	77T	627	$ .03	$ .12
Murray, Eddie	84T	240	$ .15	$ .75	Myrick, Bob	78T	676	$ .02	$ .10
Murray, Eddie	84TAS	397	$ .05	$ .25	Nabholz, Chris	91T	197	$ .01	$ .20
Murray, Eddie	85T	700	$ .30	$ .85	Naehring, Tim	90TTR	79	$ .01	$ .25
Murray, Eddie	85TAS	701	$ .06	$ .30	Naehring, Tim	91T	702	$ .01	$ .20
Murray, Eddie	86T	30	$ .03	$ .25	Nagelson, Russ	70T	7	$ .15	$ .50
Murray, Eddie	87T	120	$ .07	$ .30	Nagelson, Russ	71T	708	$ .75	$2.50
Murray, Eddie	88T	495	$ .01	$ .20	Nagy, Charles	88TTR	74	$ .10	$1.00
Murray, Eddie	88TBB	215	$ .01	$ .20	Nagy, Charles	89TBB	217	$ .10	$ .50
Murray, Eddie	88TRB	4	$ .01	$ .30	Nagy, Charles	91T	466	$ .01	$ .10
Murray, Eddie	89T	625	$ .01	$ .15	Nagy, Mike	70T	39	$ .15	$ .50
Murray, Eddie	89TBB	319	$ .01	$ .15	Nagy, Mike	71T	363	$ .15	$ .50
Murray, Eddie	89TTR	87	$ .01	$ .10	Nagy, Mike	72T	488	$ .05	$ .25
Murray, Eddie	90T	305	$ .01	$ .10	Nahorodny, Bill	78T	702	$ .02	$ .10
Murray, Eddie	91T	590	$ .01	$ .10	Nahorodny, Bill	79T	169	$ .02	$ .10
Murray, Eddie	91TAS	397	$ .01	$ .03	Nahorodny, Bill	80T	552	$ .01	$ .10

Player	Year	No.	VG	EX/MT
Nahorodny, Bill	81T	296	$ .01	$ .10
Nahorodny, Bill	83T	616	$ .01	$ .07
Napoleon, Dan	65T	533	$5.00	$20.00
Napoleon, Dan	66T	87	$ .30	$ .95
Naragon, Hal	56T	311	$2.25	$8.00
Naragon, Hal	57T	347	$4.25	$15.00
Naragon, Hal	58T	22	$1.25	$4.25
Naragon, Hal	59T	376	$ .75	$2.20
Naragon, Hal	60T	231	$ .45	$1.45
Naragon, Hal	61T	92	$ .35	$1.25
Naragon, Hal	62T	164	$ .45	$1.45
Narleski, Ray	55T	160	$2.50	$10.00
Narleski, Ray	56T	133	$2.25	$6.00
Narleski, Ray	57T	144	$ .95	$3.50
Narleski, Ray	58T	439	$ .75	$3.00
Narleski, Ray	59T	442	$ .75	$2.20
Narleski, Ray	60T	161	$ .45	$1.45
Narron, Jerry	80T	16	$ .01	$ .10
Narron, Jerry	81T	637	$ .01	$ .10
Narron, Jerry	82T	719	$ .01	$ .07
Narron, Jerry	85T	234	$ .01	$ .05
Narron, Jerry	86T	543	$ .01	$ .04
Narron, Jerry	87T	474	$ .01	$ .04
Narron, Sam	60T	467	$ .95	$3.50
Narum, Les	64T	418	$ .50	$1.45
Narum, Les	65T	86	$ .30	$ .85
Narum, Les "Buster"	66T	274	$ .30	$ .95

Player	Year	No.	VG	EX/MT
Nash, Cotton	71T	391	$ .15	$ .50
Nash, Jim	67T	90	$ .30	$ .85
Nash, Jim	68T	324	$ .30	$ .85
Nash, Jim	69T	546	$ .30	$ .95
Nash, Jim	70T	171	$ .15	$ .50
Nash, Jim	71T	306	$ .15	$ .50
Nash, Jim	72T	401	$ .05	$ .25
Nash, Jim	73T	509	$ .07	$ .30
Nastu, Phil	80T	686	$ .01	$ .10
Navarro, Jaime	89TMLD	87	$ .01	$ .25
Navarro, Jaime	91T	548	$ .01	$ .03
Navarro, Julio	60T	140	$ .45	$1.45
Navarro, Julio	63T	169	$10.00	$30.00

Player	Year	No.	VG	EX/MT
Navarro, Julio	64T	489	$ .50	$1.45
Navarro, Julio	65T	563	$1.75	$4.50
Navarro, Julio	66T	527	$5.00	$20.00
Neal, Charley	56T	299	$3.00	$9.00
Neal, Charley	57T	242	$ .60	$2.50
Neal, Charley	58T	16	$1.25	$4.25
Neal, Charley	62T	365	$ .75	$3.00
Neal, Charlie	59T	427	$ .75	$2.20
Neal, Charlie	60T	155	$ .45	$1.45
Neal, Charlie	60TAS	556	$2.50	$10.00
Neal, Charlie	61T	423	$ .75	$3.00
Neal, Charlie	63T	511	$1.75	$4.50
Neal, Charlie	64T	436	$ .50	$1.45
Neeman, Cal	57T	353	$1.25	$4.25
Neeman, Cal	58T	33	$1.25	$4.25
Neeman, Cal	59T	367	$ .75	$2.20
Neeman, Cal	60T	337	$ .75	$2.20
Negray, Ron	56T	7	$2.25	$6.00
Negray, Ron	57T	254	$ .95	$3.50
Neibauer, Gary	69T	611	$ .30	$ .95
Neibauer, Gary	70T	384	$ .15	$ .50
Neibauer, Gary	71T	668	$ .75	$2.50
Neibauer, Gary	72T	149	$ .05	$ .25
Neidlinger, Jim	91T	39	$ .01	$ .15
Neiger, Al	61T	202	$ .35	$1.25
Nelson, "Rocky" Glenn	52T	390	$40.00	$140.00
Nelson, Bob	56T	169	$2.25	$6.00
Nelson, Dave	69T	579	$ .30	$ .95
Nelson, Dave	70T	112	$ .15	$ .50
Nelson, Dave	71T	241	$ .15	$ .50
Nelson, Dave	72T	529	$ .30	$ .95
Nelson, Dave	73T	111	$ .07	$ .30
Nelson, Dave	74T	355	$ .07	$ .30
Nelson, Dave	75T	435	$ .07	$ .30
Nelson, Dave	76T	535	$ .05	$ .20
Nelson, Gene	81TTR	809	$ .02	$ .10
Nelson, Gene	82T	373	$ .01	$ .07
Nelson, Gene	82TTR	80	$ .02	$ .10
Nelson, Gene	83T	106	$ .01	$ .07
Nelson, Gene	85TTR	86	$ .02	$ .10
Nelson, Gene	86T	493	$ .01	$ .04
Nelson, Gene	87T	273	$ .01	$ .04
Nelson, Gene	87TTR	84$	.01$ .05	
Nelson, Gene	88T	621	$ .01	$ .04
Nelson, Gene	89T	581	$ .01	$ .05
Nelson, Gene	90T	726	$ .01	$ .04
Nelson, Gene	91T	316	$ .01	$ .03
Nelson, Jamie	84T	166	$ .01	$ .06
Nelson, Jim	71T	298	$ .15	$ .50
Nelson, Mel	63T	522	$2.10	$6.00
Nelson, Mel	64T	273	$ .30	$ .95
Nelson, Mel	65T	564	$1.75	$4.50
Nelson, Mel	66T	367	$ .30	$ .95
Nelson, Mel	69T	181	$ .30	$ .85
Nelson, Ricky	84T	672	$ .01	$ .06
Nelson, Ricky	85T	296	$ .01	$ .05
Nelson, Rocky	54T	199	$3.60	$10.00
Nelson, Rocky	59T	446	$ .75	$2.20
Nelson, Rocky	60T	157	$ .45	$1.45
Nelson, Rocky	61T	304	$ .35	$1.25
Nelson, Roger	68T	549	$ .35	$1.25
Nelson, Roger	69T	279	$ .30	$ .95
Nelson, Roger	70T	633	$ .30	$ .95
Nelson, Roger	71T	581	$ .35	$1.25
Nelson, Roger	73T	251	$ .07	$ .30
Nelson, Roger	74T	491	$ .07	$ .30
Nelson, Roger	75T	572	$ .07	$ .30
Nen, Dick	64T	14	$ .30	$ .95
Nen, Dick	65T	466	$ .75	$3.00
Nen, Dick	66T	149	$ .30	$ .95

Player	Year	No.	VG	EX/MT
Nen, Dick	67T	403	$ .30	$ .95
Nen, Dick	68T	591	$ .35	$1.25
Nettles, Graig	69T	99	$3.75	$12.50
Nettles, Graig	70T	491	$1.50	$4.50
Nettles, Graig	71T	324	$ .60	$2.50
Nettles, Graig	72T	590	$ .75	$3.00
Nettles, Graig	73T	498	$ .50	$2.00
Nettles, Graig	74T	251	$ .35	$1.50
Nettles, Graig	75T	160	$ .25	$1.25
Nettles, Graig	76T	169	$ .25	$1.00
Nettles, Graig	77T	2	$ .20	$ .90
Nettles, Graig	77T	20	$ .15	$ .50
Nettles, Graig	78T	250	$ .02	$ .20
Nettles, Graig	79T	460	$ .30	$ .85
Nettles, Graig	80T	710	$ .05	$ .20
Nettles, Graig	81T	365	$ .03	$ .15
Nettles, Graig	82T	505	$ .05	$ .20
Nettles, Graig	82TIA	506	$ .02	$ .10
Nettles, Graig	83T	635	$ .01	$ .07
Nettles, Graig	83T	636	$ .01	$ .07
Nettles, Graig	84T	175	$ .03	$ .15
Nettles, Graig	84T	712	$ .03	$ .15
Nettles, Graig	84T	713	$ .03	$ .15
Nettles, Graig	84TTR	83	$ .30	$ .85
Nettles, Graig	85T	35	$ .01	$ .10
Nettles, Graig	86T	450	$ .01	$ .04
Nettles, Graig	87T	205	$ .01	$ .04
Nettles, Graig	87TTR	85	$ .05	$ .20
Nettles, Graig	88T	574	$ .01	$ .04
Nettles, Jim	71T	74	$ .15	$ .50
Nettles, Jim	72T	131	$ .05	$ .25
Nettles, Jim	73T	358	$ .07	$ .30
Nettles, Jim	75T	497	$ .07	$ .30
Nettles, Morris	75T	632	$ .07	$ .30
Nettles, Morris	76T	434	$ .05	$ .20
Neville, Dan	65T	398	$ .45	$1.45
Newcombe, Don	56T	235	$9.50	$37.50
Newcombe, Don	57T	130	$3.00	$11.00

Don Newcombe

L. A. DODGERS

Player	Year	No.	VG	EX/MT
Newcombe, Don	58T	340	$ .75	$2.50
Newcombe, Don	59T	312	$ .75	$2.25

Player	Year	No.	VG	EX/MT
Newcombe, Don	60T	345	$ .75	$2.25
Newcombe, Don	61TMVP	483	$1.50	$4.00
Newcombe, Don	75T	194	$1.75	$5.00
Newfield, Marc	91T	529	$ .01	$ .35
Newhauser, Don	74T	33	$ .07	$ .30
Newhouser, Hal	53T	228	$22.00	$85.00
Newhouser, Hal	55T	24	$3.60	$10.00
Newman, Al	87T	323	$ .01	$ .04
Newman, Al	87TTR	86	$ .01	$ .05
Newman, Al	88T	648	$ .01	$ .04
Newman, Al	89T	503	$ .01	$ .05
Newman, Al	90T	19	$ .01	$ .04
Newman, Al	91T	748	$ .01	$ .03
Newman, Fred	63T	496	$2.50	$6.50
Newman, Fred	64T	569	$1.75	$4.50
Newman, Fred	65T	101	$ .30	$ .85
Newman, Fred	66T	213	$ .30	$ .95
Newman, Fred	67T	451	$ .30	$ .95
Newman, Fred	69T	543	$ .30	$ .95
Newman, Jeff	77T	204	$ .03	$ .12
Newman, Jeff	78T	458	$ .02	$ .10
Newman, Jeff	79T	604	$ .02	$ .10
Newman, Jeff	80T	34	$ .01	$ .10
Newman, Jeff	81T	587	$ .01	$ .10
Newman, Jeff	82T	187	$ .01	$ .07
Newman, Jeff	83T	784	$ .01	$ .07
Newman, Jeff	83TTR	80	$ .02	$ .10
Newman, Jeff	84T	296	$ .01	$ .06
Newman, Jeff	85T	376	$ .01	$ .05
Newman, Ray	72T	667	$ .75	$2.50
Newman, Ray	73T	568	$ .45	$1.45
Newsom, Bobo	53T	15	$4.50	$15.00
Niarhos, Gus	52T	121	$7.00	$20.00
Niarhos, Gus	53T	63	$4.50	$15.00
Nichols, Carl	91T	119	$ .01	$ .03
Nichols, Chet	52T	288	$15.00	$47.50
Nichols, Chet	56T	278	$2.25	$8.00
Nichols, Chet	61T	301	$ .35	$1.25
Nichols, Chet	62T	403	$ .75	$2.50
Nichols, Chet	63T	307	$ .45	$1.50
Nichols, Dolan	59T	362	$ .75	$2.20
Nichols, Reid	81T	689	$ .75	$2.25
Nichols, Reid	82T	124	$ .01	$ .07
Nichols, Reid	83T	446	$ .01	$ .07
Nichols, Reid	84T	238	$ .01	$ .06
Nichols, Reid	85T	37	$ .01	$ .05
Nichols, Reid	86T	364	$ .01	$ .04
Nichols, Reid	87T	539	$ .01	$ .04
Nichols, Reid	87TTR	87	$ .01	$ .05
Nichols, Reid	88T	748	$ .01	$ .04
Nichols, Rod	89T	443	$ .01	$ .05
Nichols, Rod	90T	108	$ .01	$ .04
Nicholson, Bill	52T	185	$7.00	$20.00
Nicholson, Dave	61T	182	$ .35	$1.25
Nicholson, Dave	62T	577	$3.95	$11.50
Nicholson, Dave	63T	234	$ .30	$ .95
Nicholson, Dave	64T	31	$ .30	$ .95
Nicholson, Dave	65T	183	$ .30	$ .85
Nicholson, Dave	66T	576	$5.00	$20.00
Nicholson, Dave	67T	113	$ .30	$ .85
Nicholson, Dave	69T	298	$ .30	$ .95
Nicosia, Steve	80T	519	$ .01	$ .10
Nicosia, Steve	81T	212	$ .01	$ .10
Nicosia, Steve	82T	652	$ .01	$ .07
Nicosia, Steve	83T	462	$ .01	$ .07
Nicosia, Steve	84T	98	$ .01	$ .06
Nicosia, Steve	85T	191	$ .01	$ .05
Nicosia, Steve	85TTR	87	$ .02	$ .10
Niedenfuer, Tom	83T	477	$ .01	$ .07
Niedenfuer, Tom	84T	112	$ .01	$ .06

Player	Year	No.	VG	EX/MT	Player	Year	No.	VG	EX/MT
Niedenfuer, Tom	85T	782	$ .01	$ .05	Nieman, Bob	57T	14	$ .95	$3.50
Niedenfuer, Tom	86T	56	$ .01	$ .04	Nieman, Bob	58T	165	$ .75	$3.00
Niedenfuer, Tom	87T	538	$ .01	$ .04	Nieman, Bob	59T	375	$ .75	$2.20
Niedenfuer, Tom	87TTR	88	$ .01	$ .05	Nieman, Bob	60T	149	$ .45	$1.45
Niedenfuer, Tom	88T	242	$ .01	$ .04	Nieman, Bob	61T	178	$ .35	$1.25
Niedenfuer, Tom	89T	651	$ .01	$ .05	Nieman, Bob	62T	182	$ .45	$1.45
Niedenfuer, Tom	90T	306	$ .01	$ .04	Niemann, Randy	80T	469	$ .01	$ .10
Niekro, Joe	67T	536	$10.00	$30.00	Niemann, Randy	81T	148	$ .01	$ .10
Niekro, Joe	68T	475	$ .75	$2.25	Niemann, Randy	83T	329	$ .01	$ .07
Niekro, Joe	69T	43	$ .45	$1.45	Niemann, Randy	86TTR	78	$ .02	$ .10
Niekro, Joe	70T	508	$ .15	$ .50	Niemann, Randy	87T	147	$ .01	$ .04
Niekro, Joe	71T	695	$1.75	$4.50	Nieto, Tom	85T	294	$ .01	$ .05
Niekro, Joe	72T	216	$ .30	$ .85	Nieto, Tom	86T	88	$ .01	$ .04
Niekro, Joe	73T	585	$ .60	$2.25	Nieto, Tom	87T	416	$ .01	$ .04
Niekro, Joe	74T	504	$ .30	$ .95	Nieto, Tom	87TTR	90	$ .01	$ .05
Niekro, Joe	75T	595	$ .15	$ .50	Nieto, Tom	88T	317	$ .01	$ .04
Niekro, Joe	76T	273	$ .07	$ .30	Nieves, Juan	86TTR	79	$ .15	$ .50
Niekro, Joe	77T	116	$ .03	$ .12	Nieves, Juan	87T	79	$ .07	$ .30
Niekro, Joe	78T	306	$ .02	$ .10	Nieves, Juan	88T	515	$ .01	$ .10
Niekro, Joe	79T	68	$ .02	$ .10	Nieves, Juan	88TBB	190	$ .01	$ .06
Niekro, Joe	80T	205	$ .05	$ .20	Nieves, Juan	89T	287	$ .01	$ .05
Niekro, Joe	80T	437	$ .01	$ .10	Nieves, Juan	90T	467	$ .01	$ .04
Niekro, Joe	81T	722	$ .01	$ .10	Nipper, Al	85T	424	$ .01	$ .10
Niekro, Joe	82T	611	$ .03	$ .15	Nipper, Al	86T	181	$ .01	$ .04
Niekro, Joe	83T	221	$ .01	$ .07	Nipper, Al	87T	617	$ .01	$ .04
Niekro, Joe	83T	441	$ .01	$ .07	Nipper, Al	88T	326	$ .01	$ .04
Niekro, Joe	84T	586	$ .01	$ .06	Nipper, Al	88TTR	75	$ .01	$ .06
Niekro, Joe	85T	295	$ .01	$ .05					
Niekro, Joe	86T	135	$ .01	$ .04					
Niekro, Joe	87T	344	$ .01	$ .04					
Niekro, Joe	87TTR	89	$ .01	$ .10					
Niekro, Joe	88T	473	$ .01	$ .04					
Niekro, Joe	88TRB	5	$ .01	$ .10					
Niekro, Phil	64T	541	$50.00	$150.00					
Niekro, Phil	65T	461	$10.00	$40.00					
Niekro, Phil	66T	28	$4.00	$12.50					
Niekro, Phil	67T	456	$4.00	$12.00					
Niekro, Phil	68T	7	$ .75	$2.20					
Niekro, Phil	68T	257	$1.25	$5.00					
Niekro, Phil	69T	355	$2.00	$7.00					
Niekro, Phil	70T	69	$ .75	$2.20					
Niekro, Phil	70T	160	$1.50	$4.00					
Niekro, Phil	71T	30	$1.50	$4.00					
Niekro, Phil	72T	620	$1.50	$5.00					
Niekro, Phil	73T	503	$ .95	$3.50					
Niekro, Phil	74T	29	$ .50	$2.00					
Niekro, Phil	75T	130	$ .50	$2.00					
Niekro, Phil	75T	310	$ .35	$1.25					
Niekro, Phil	76T	435	$ .50	$2.00					
Niekro, Phil	77T	615	$ .50	$2.00					
Niekro, Phil	78T	10	$ .45	$1.45					
Niekro, Phil	78T	206	$ .05	$ .20					
Niekro, Phil	79T	595	$ .45	$1.45					
Niekro, Phil	80T	205	$ .05	$ .20					
Niekro, Phil	80T	245	$ .15	$ .60					
Niekro, Phil	81T	387	$ .15	$ .60					
Niekro, Phil	82T	185	$ .10	$ .50	Nipper, Al	89T	86	$ .01	$ .05
Niekro, Phil	83T	410	$ .08	$ .40	Nischwitz, Ron	62T	591	$8.00	$22.50
Niekro, Phil	83T	411	$ .03	$ .15	Nischwitz, Ron	63T	152	$ .30	$ .95
Niekro, Phil	83T	502	$ .01	$ .07	Nischwitz, Ron	66T	38	$ .30	$ .95
Niekro, Phil	84T	650	$ .06	$ .30	Nixon, Donell	88T	146	$ .01	$ .04
Niekro, Phil	84TTR	84	$ .15	$ .60	Nixon, Donell	89T	447	$ .01	$ .05
Niekro, Phil	85T	40	$ .05	$ .25	Nixon, Donell	89TBB	214	$ .01	$ .06
Niekro, Phil	86T	790	$ .03	$ .25	Nixon, Donell	90T	658	$ .01	$ .04
Niekro, Phil	86TRB	204	$ .01	$ .10	Nixon, Otis	86TTR	80	$ .02	$ .10
Niekro, Phil	86TTR	77	$ .15	$ .50	Nixon, Otis	87T	486	$ .01	$ .04
Niekro, Phil	87T	694	$ .07	$ .30	Nixon, Otis	89T	674	$ .01	$ .05
Niekro, Phil	88TRB	5	$ .01	$ .10	Nixon, Otis	89TBB	234	$ .01	$ .06
Nielsen, Scott	87T	57	$ .01	$ .04	Nixon, Otis	90T	252	$ .01	$ .04
Nieman, Bob	56T	267	$2.25	$8.00					

Player	Year	No.	VG	EX/MT	Player	Year	No.	VG	EX/MT
Nixon, Otis	91T	558	$ .01	$ .03	Nolan, Gary	73T	260	$ .07	$ .30
Nixon, Russ	58T	133	$ .75	$3.00	Nolan, Gary	74T	277	$ .07	$ .30
Nixon, Russ	59T	344	$ .75	$2.20	Nolan, Gary	75T	562	$ .07	$ .30
Nixon, Russ	60T	36	$ .45	$1.45	Nolan, Gary	76T	444	$ .05	$ .20
Nixon, Russ	61T	53	$ .35	$1.25	Nolan, Gary	77T	121	$ .03	$ .12
Nixon, Russ	62T	523	$3.95	$11.50	Nolan, Gary	78T	115	$ .02	$ .10
Nixon, Russ	63T	168	$ .30	$ .95	Nolan, Joe	78T	617	$ .02	$ .10
Nixon, Russ	64T	329	$ .30	$ .95	Nolan, Joe	79T	464	$ .02	$ .10
Nixon, Russ	65T	162	$ .30	$ .85	Nolan, Joe	80T	64	$ .01	$ .10
Nixon, Russ	66T	227	$ .30	$ .95	Nolan, Joe	81T	149	$ .01	$ .10
Nixon, Russ	67T	446	$ .30	$ .95	Nolan, Joe	82T	327	$ .01	$ .07
Nixon, Russ	68T	515	$ .35	$1.25	Nolan, Joe	82TTR	81	$ .02	$ .10
Nixon, Russ	69T	363	$ .30	$ .85	Nolan, Joe	83T	242	$ .01	$ .07
Nixon, Russ	83T	756	$ .01	$ .07	Nolan, Joe	84T	553	$ .01	$ .06
Nixon, Russ	84T	351	$ .01	$ .06	Nolan, Joe	85T	652	$ .01	$ .05
Nixon, Russ	88TTR	76	$ .01	$ .06	Nolan, Joe	86T	781	$ .01	$ .04
Nixon, Russ	89T	564	$ .01	$ .05	Nold, Dick	68T	96	$ .30	$ .85
Nixon, Russ	90T	171	$ .01	$ .04	Noles, Dickie	80T	682	$ .01	$ .10
Nixon, Willard	52T	269	$12.00	$40.00	Noles, Dickie	81T	406	$ .01	$ .10
Nixon, Willard	53T	30	$4.50	$15.00	Noles, Dickie	82T	530	$ .01	$ .07
Nixon, Willard	56T	122	$2.25	$6.00	Noles, Dickie	82TTR	82	$ .02	$ .10
Nixon, Willard	57T	189	$ .95	$3.50	Noles, Dickie	83T	99	$ .01	$ .07
Nixon, Willard	58T	395	$ .75	$3.00	Noles, Dickie	84T	618	$ .01	$ .06
Nixon, Willard	59T	361	$ .75	$2.20	Noles, Dickie	85T	149	$ .01	$ .05
Noboa, Junior	88T	503	$ .01	$ .10	Noles, Dickie	86T	388	$ .01	$ .04
Noboa, Junior	90TTR	80	$ .01	$ .05	Noles, Dickie	87T	244	$ .01	$ .04
Noboa, Junior	91T	182	$ .01	$ .03	Noles, Dickie	87TTR	92	$ .01	$ .05
Noce, Paul	88T	542	$ .01	$ .04	Noles, Dickie	88T	768	$ .01	$ .04
Nokes, Matt	87TTR	91	$ .10	$ .35	Nolte, Eric	88T	694	$ .01	$ .04
Nokes, Matt	88T	645	$ .01	$ .25	Nordbrook, Tim	76T	252	$ .05	$ .20
Nokes, Matt	88TAS	393	$ .01	$ .10	Nordbrook, Tim	78T	369	$ .02	$ .10
Nokes, Matt	88TBB	185	$ .01	$ .06	Nordhagen, Wayne	78T	231	$ .02	$ .10
Nokes, Matt	89T	445	$ .01	$ .05	Nordhagen, Wayne	79T	351	$ .02	$ .10
Nokes, Matt	89TBB	303	$ .01	$ .06	Nordhagen, Wayne	80T	487	$ .01	$ .10
Nokes, Matt	90T	131	$ .01	$ .06	Nordhagen, Wayne	81T	186	$ .01	$ .10
Nokes, Matt	90TTR	81	$ .01	$ .05	Nordhagen, Wayne	82T	597	$ .01	$ .07
Nokes, Matt	91T	336	$ .01	$ .03	Nordhagen, Wayne	83T	714	$ .01	$ .07
Nolan, Gary	68T	196	$ .30	$ .85	Noren, Irv	51Tbb	38	$7.50	$22.50
Nolan, Gary	69T	581	$ .30	$ .95	Noren, Irv	52T	40	$15.00	$47.50
Nolan, Gary	70T	484	$ .15	$ .50	Noren, Irv	53T	35	$4.50	$15.00
Nolan, Gary	71T	75	$ .15	$ .50	Noren, Irv	56T	253	$2.55	$7.50
					Noren, Irv	57T	298	$4.25	$15.00
					Noren, Irv	58T	114	$2.35	$7.00
					Noren, Irv	59T	59	$1.25	$4.25
					Noren, Irv	60T	433	$ .75	$2.20
					Noren, Irv	73T	179	$ .30	$ .95
					Norman, Bill	53T	245	$12.50	$50.00
					Norman, Dan	79T	721	$ .05	$ .20
					Norman, Dan	80T	681	$2.50	$7.50
					Norman, Dan	83T	237	$ .01	$ .07
					Norman, Fred	64T	469	$ .50	$1.45
					Norman, Fred	65T	386	$ .35	$1.25
					Norman, Fred	70T	427	$ .15	$ .50
					Norman, Fred	71T	348	$ .15	$ .50
					Norman, Fred	72T	194	$ .05	$ .25
					Norman, Fred	73T	32	$ .07	$ .30
					Norman, Fred	74T	581	$ .07	$ .30
					Norman, Fred	75T	396	$ .07	$ .30
					Norman, Fred	76T	609	$ .05	$ .20
					Norman, Fred	77T	139	$ .03	$ .12
					Norman, Fred	78T	273	$ .02	$ .10
					Norman, Fred	79T	47	$ .02	$ .10
					Norman, Fred	80T	714	$ .01	$ .10
					Norman, Fred	81T	497	$ .01	$ .10
					Norman, Nelson	80T	518	$ .01	$ .10
					Norrid, Tim	79T	705	$ .25	$1.00
					Norris, Jim	78T	484	$ .02	$ .10
					Norris, Jim	79T	611	$ .02	$ .10
					Norris, Jim	80T	333	$ .01	$ .10
Nolan, Gary	72T	475	$ .05	$ .25	Norris, Jim	81T	264	$ .01	$ .10

GARY NOLAN

Player	Year	No.	VG	EX/MT	Player	Year	No.	VG	EX/MT
Norris, Mike	76T	653	$ .07	$ .30	Nuxhall, Joe	56T	218	$3.00	$9.00
Norris, Mike	77T	284	$ .03	$ .12	Nuxhall, Joe	57T	103	$2.00	$6.00
Norris, Mike	78T	434	$ .02	$ .10	Nuxhall, Joe	58T	63	$1.50	$4.00
Norris, Mike	79T	191	$ .02	$ .10	Nuxhall, Joe	59T	389	$ .75	$2.25
Norris, Mike	80T	599	$ .01	$ .10	Nuxhall, Joe	60T	282	$1.25	$4.25
Norris, Mike	81T	55	$ .01	$ .10	Nuxhall, Joe	61T	444	$ .75	$3.00
Norris, Mike	82T	370	$ .01	$ .07	Nuxhall, Joe	63T	194	$ .75	$3.00
Norris, Mike	83T	620	$ .01	$ .07	Nuxhall, Joe	64T	106	$ .45	$1.45
Norris, Mike	84T	493	$ .01	$ .06	Nuxhall, Joe	65T	312	$ .45	$1.45
Norris, Mike	85T	246	$ .01	$ .05	Nuxhall, Joe	66T	483	$ .75	$2.00
North, Bill	73T	234	$ .07	$ .30	Nuxhall, Joe	67T	44	$ .30	$ .85
North, Bill	74T	345	$ .07	$ .30	Nye, Rich	67T	608	$2.00	$6.00
North, Bill	75T	121	$ .07	$ .30	Nye, Rich	68T	339	$ .30	$ .85
North, Bill	75T	309	$ .35	$1.25	Nye, Rich	69T	88	$ .30	$ .85
North, Bill	76T	33	$ .05	$ .20	Nye, Rich	70T	139	$ .15	$ .50
North, Bill	77T	4	$ .03	$ .12	Nyman, Chris	84T	382	$ .01	$ .06
North, Bill	77T	551	$ .03	$ .12	Nyman, Gerry	69T	173	$ .30	$ .85
North, Bill	78T	163	$ .02	$ .10	Nyman, Gerry	70T	644	$ .75	$2.00
North, Bill	79T	668	$ .02	$ .10	Nyman, Gerry	71T	656	$ .75	$2.50
North, Bill	80T	408	$ .01	$ .10	Nyman, Nyls	75T	619	$ .07	$ .30
North, Bill	81T	713	$ .01	$ .10	Nyman, Nyls	76T	258	$ .05	$ .20
Northey, Ron	52T	204	$7.00	$20.00	O'Berry, Mike	80T	662	$ .01	$ .10
Northey, Ron	57T	31	$ .95	$3.50	O'Berry, Mike	82T	562	$ .01	$ .07
Northey, Scott	70T	241	$ .15	$ .50	O'Berry, Mike	84T	184	$ .01	$ .06
Northey, Scott	71T	633	$ .35	$1.25	O'Berry, Mike	84TTR	86	$ .02	$ .10
Northrup, Jim	65T	259	$ .45	$1.45	O'Brien, Bob	72T	198	$ .60	$1.50
Northrup, Jim	66T	554	$5.00	$20.00	O'Brien, Charlie	88T	566	$ .01	$ .04
Northrup, Jim	67T	408	$ .30	$ .95	O'Brien, Charlie	89T	214	$ .01	$ .05
Northrup, Jim	68T	78	$ .30	$ .85	O'Brien, Charlie	90T	106	$ .01	$ .04
Northrup, Jim	69T	3	$ .35	$1.25	O'Brien, Charlie	91T	442	$ .01	$ .03
Northrup, Jim	69T	580	$ .30	$ .95	O'Brien, Dan	80T	684	$ .08	$ .40
Northrup, Jim	70T	177	$ .15	$ .50	O'Brien, Ed	53T	249	$12.50	$50.00
Northrup, Jim	71T	265	$ .15	$ .50	O'Brien, Eddie	54T	139	$4.50	$15.00
Northrup, Jim	72T	408	$ .05	$ .25	O'Brien, Eddie	56T	116	$2.25	$6.00
Northrup, Jim	73T	168	$ .07	$ .30	O'Brien, Eddie	57T	259	$ .95	$3.50
Northrup, Jim	74T	266	$ .07	$ .30	O'Brien, John	53T	223	$12.50	$50.00
Northrup, Jim	75T	641	$ .07	$ .30	O'Brien, John	54T	139	$4.50	$15.00
Norwood, Willie	78T	705	$ .02	$ .10	O'Brien, Johnny	55T	135	$2.00	$6.00
Norwood, Willie	79T	274	$ .02	$ .10	O'Brien, Johnny	56T	65	$2.25	$6.00
Norwood, Willie	80T	432	$ .01	$ .10	O'Brien, Johnny	58T	426	$ .75	$3.00
Nosek, Randy	89TMLD	88	$ .01	$ .06	O'Brien, Johnny	59T	499	$ .75	$2.20
Nossek, Joe	64T	532	$1.75	$4.50	O'Brien, Pete	83TTR	81	$ .05	$1.50
Nossek, Joe	65T	597	$1.75	$4.50	O'Brien, Pete	84T	534	$ .10	$1.00
Nossek, Joe	66T	22	$ .30	$ .95	O'Brien, Pete	85T	196	$ .01	$ .20
Nossek, Joe	67T	209	$ .30	$ .85	O'Brien, Pete	86T	328	$ .01	$ .15
Nossek, Joe	69T	143	$ .30	$ .85	O'Brien, Pete	87T	17	$ .01	$ .10
Nossek, Joe	73T	646	$ .75	$3.00	O'Brien, Pete	88T	721	$ .01	$ .06
Nossek, Joe	74T	99	$ .07	$ .30	O'Brien, Pete	88TBB	227	$ .01	$ .10
Nottebart, Don	60T	351	$ .75	$2.20	O'Brien, Pete	89T	629	$ .01	$ .05
Nottebart, Don	61T	29	$ .35	$1.25	O'Brien, Pete	89TBB	115	$ .01	$ .06
Nottebart, Don	62T	541	$3.95	$11.50	O'Brien, Pete	89TTR	88	$ .01	$ .06
Nottebart, Don	63T	204	$ .30	$ .95	O'Brien, Pete	90T	265	$ .01	$ .04
Nottebart, Don	64T	434	$ .50	$1.45	O'Brien, Pete	90TTR	82	$ .01	$ .05
Nottebart, Don	65T	469	$ .75	$3.00	O'Brien, Pete	91T	585	$ .01	$ .03
Nottebart, Don	66T	21	$ .30	$ .95	O'Brien, Syd	69T	628	$ .30	$ .95
Nottebart, Don	67T	269	$ .30	$ .85	O'Brien, Syd	70T	163	$ .15	$ .50
Nottebart, Don	68T	171	$ .30	$ .85	O'Brien, Syd	71T	561	$ .35	$1.25
Nottebart, Don	69T	593	$ .30	$ .95	O'Brien, Syd	72T	289	$ .05	$ .25
Nunez, Ed	85T	34	$ .01	$ .05	O'Connell, Danny	53T	107	$4.50	$15.00
Nunez, Ed	86T	511	$ .01	$ .04	O'Connell, Danny	56T	272	$2.25	$8.00
Nunez, Ed	87T	427	$ .01	$ .04	O'Connell, Danny	57T	271	$4.25	$15.00
Nunez, Ed	88T	258	$ .01	$ .04	O'Connell, Danny	58T	166	$ .75	$3.00
Nunez, Ed	90T	586	$ .01	$ .04	O'Connell, Danny	59T	87	$1.25	$4.25
Nunez, Ed	91T	106	$ .01	$ .03	O'Connell, Danny	60T	192	$ .45	$1.45
Nunez, Jose	88T	28	$ .01	$ .04	O'Connell, Danny	61T	318	$ .35	$1.25
Nunn, Howie	59T	549	$2.50	$10.00	O'Connell, Danny	62T	411	$ .75	$2.50
Nunn, Howie	61T	346	$ .35	$1.25	O'Connor, Jack	82T	353	$ .01	$ .07
Nunn, Howie	62T	524	$3.95	$11.50	O'Connor, Jack	83T	33	$ .01	$ .07
Nuxhall, Joe	52T	406	$60.00	$175.00	O'Connor, Jack	84T	268	$ .01	$ .06
Nuxhall, Joe	53T	105	$4.00	$12.50	O'Dell, Billy	55T	57	$3.60	$10.00

Player	Year	No.	VG	EX/MT	Player	Year	No.	VG	EX/MT
O'Dell, Billy	57T	316	$4.25	$15.00	O'Toole, Jim	60T	325	$ .45	$1.35
O'Dell, Billy	58T	84	$1.25	$4.25	O'Toole, Jim	61T	328	$ .35	$1.25
O'Dell, Billy	59T	250	$ .75	$2.20	O'Toole, Jim	62T	450	$ .75	$2.50
O'Dell, Billy	60T	303	$ .75	$2.20	O'Toole, Jim	62T	56	$ .75	$3.00
O'Dell, Billy	61T	383	$ .75	$3.00	O'Toole, Jim	62T	58	$ .75	$2.20
O'Dell, Billy	61T	96	$ .35	$1.25	O'Toole, Jim	62T	60	$ .65	$1.75
O'Dell, Billy	62T	429	$ .75	$2.50	O'Toole, Jim	63T	70	$ .30	$ .95
O'Dell, Billy	63T	235	$ .30	$ .95	O'Toole, Jim	64T	185	$ .30	$ .95
O'Dell, Billy	63T	7	$ .45	$1.45	O'Toole, Jim	65T	60	$ .30	$ .85
O'Dell, Billy	63T	9	$ .90	$3.00	O'Toole, Jim	66T	389	$ .30	$ .95
O'Dell, Billy	64T	18	$ .30	$ .95	O'Toole, Jim	67T	467	$ .75	$3.00
O'Dell, Billy	65T	476	$ .75	$3.00	Oates, Johnny	72T	474	$ .50	$2.35
O'Dell, Billy	66T	237	$ .30	$ .95	Oates, Johnny	73T	9	$ .07	$ .30
O'Dell, Billy	67T	162	$ .30	$ .85	Oates, Johnny	74T	183	$ .07	$ .30
O'Donoghue, John	64T	388	$ .50	$1.45	Oates, Johnny	75T	319	$ .07	$ .30
O'Donoghue, John	65T	71	$ .30	$ .85	Oates, Johnny	76T	62	$ .05	$ .20
O'Donoghue, John	66T	501	$ .75	$2.50	Oates, Johnny	77T	619	$ .05	$ .15
					Oates, Johnny	78T	508	$ .02	$ .10
					Oates, Johnny	79T	104	$ .02	$ .10
					Oates, Johnny	80T	228	$ .01	$ .10
					Oates, Johnny	81T	303	$ .01	$ .10
					Oberkfell, Ken	80T	701	$ .05	$ .20
					Oberkfell, Ken	81T	32	$ .01	$ .10
					Oberkfell, Ken	82T	474	$ .01	$ .07
					Oberkfell, Ken	83T	206	$ .01	$ .07
					Oberkfell, Ken	84T	102	$ .01	$ .06
					Oberkfell, Ken	84TTR	85	$ .02	$ .10
					Oberkfell, Ken	85T	569	$ .01	$ .05
					Oberkfell, Ken	86T	334	$ .01	$ .04
					Oberkfell, Ken	87T	627	$ .01	$ .04
					Oberkfell, Ken	88T	67	$ .01	$ .04
					Oberkfell, Ken	89T	751	$ .01	$ .05
					Oberkfell, Ken	90T	488	$ .01	$ .04
					Oberkfell, Ken	91T	286	$ .01	$ .03
					Oceak, Frank	60T	467	$ .95	$3.50
					Odom, Johnny	65T	526	$50.00	$150.00
					Odom, Johnny	67T	282	$ .30	$ .85
					Odom, John	68T	501	$ .35	$1.25
					Odom, John	69T	195	$ .30	$ .85
					Odom, John	70T	55	$ .15	$ .50
					Odom, John	71T	523	$ .15	$ .50
					Odom, John	72T	557	$ .30	$ .95
					Odom, John	72TIA	558	$ .30	$ .95
					Odom, John	73T	315	$ .07	$ .30
					Odom, John	74T	461	$ .07	$ .30
					Odom, John	75T	69	$ .07	$ .30
					Odom, John	76T	651	$ .05	$ .20
O'Donoghue, John	67T	127	$ .30	$ .85	Oelkers, Bryan	87T	77	$ .01	$ .04
O'Donoghue, John	68T	456	$ .30	$ .85	Oester, Ron	79T	717	$ .05	$ .20
O'Donoghue, John	70T	441	$ .15	$ .50	Oester, Ron	81T	21	$ .01	$ .10
O'Donoghue, John	71T	743	$ .75	$2.50	Oester, Ron	82T	427	$ .01	$ .07
O'Malley, Tom	83T	663	$ .01	$ .07	Oester, Ron	83T	269	$ .01	$ .07
O'Malley, Tom	84T	469	$ .01	$ .06	Oester, Ron	84T	526	$ .01	$ .06
O'Malley, Tom	87T	154	$ .01	$ .04	Oester, Ron	84T	756	$ .01	$ .06
O'Malley, Tom	88T	77	$ .01	$ .04	Oester, Ron	85T	314	$ .01	$ .05
O'Malley, Tom	90T	504	$ .01	$ .04	Oester, Ron	86T	627	$ .01	$ .04
O'Malley, Tom	91T	257	$ .01	$ .03	Oester, Ron	87T	172	$ .01	$ .04
O'Neal, Randy	86T	73	$ .01	$ .04	Oester, Ron	88T	17	$ .01	$ .04
O'Neal, Randy	87T	196	$ .01	$ .04	Oester, Ron	89T	772	$ .01	$ .05
O'Neill, Paul	88T	204	$ .01	$ .25	Oester, Ron	89TBB	229	$ .01	$ .06
O'Neill, Paul	89T	604	$ .01	$ .05	Oester, Ron	90T	492	$ .01	$ .04
O'Neill, Paul	89TBB	39	$ .01	$ .10	Off, Ed	78T	28	$ .02	$ .10
O'Neill, Paul	90T	332	$ .01	$ .04	Offerman, Jose	91T	587	$ .01	$ .30
O'Neill, Paul	91T	122	$ .01	$ .03	Office, Rowland	75T	262	$ .07	$ .30
O'Neill, Steve	54T	127	$3.60	$10.00	Office, Rowland	76T	256	$ .05	$ .20
O'Riley, Don	70T	552	$ .30	$ .95	Office, Rowland	77T	524	$ .05	$ .15
O'Riley, Don	71T	679	$ .75	$2.50	Office, Rowland	78T	632	$ .02	$ .10
O'Toole, Dennis	73T	604	$ .45	$1.45	Office, Rowland	79T	132	$ .02	$ .10
O'Toole, Jim	59T	136	$ .75	$2.25	Office, Rowland	80T	39	$ .01	$ .10
O'Toole, Jim	60T	32	$ .75	$2.20	Office, Rowland	81T	319	$ .01	$ .10

JOHN O'DONOGHUE · P

INDIANS

Player	Year	No.	VG	EX/MT	Player	Year	No.	VG	EX/MT
Office, Rowland	82T	479	$ .01	$ .07	Olivares, Ed	62T	598	$18.00	$55.00
Ogier, Moe	68T	589	$ .35	$1.25	Olivares, Omar	91T	271	$ .01	$ .10
Oglivie, Ben	72T	761	$4.00	$12.00	Oliver, Al	69T	82	$2.00	$8.00
Oglivie, Ben	73T	388	$ .30	$ .85	Oliver, Al	70T	166	$ .50	$2.00
Oglivie, Ben	75T	344	$ .07	$ .30	Oliver, Al	71T	388	$ .50	$2.00
Oglivie, Ben	76T	659	$ .07	$ .30	Oliver, Al	72T	575	$ .50	$2.00
Oglivie, Ben	77T	122	$ .05	$ .15	Oliver, Al	73T	225	$ .35	$1.25
Oglivie, Ben	78T	286	$ .02	$ .10	Oliver, Al	74T	52	$ .25	$1.00
Oglivie, Ben	79T	519	$ .02	$ .10	Oliver, Al	75T	555	$ .15	$ .50
Oglivie, Ben	80T	53	$ .01	$ .10	Oliver, Al	76T	620	$ .30	$ .95
Oglivie, Ben	81T	2	$ .06	$ .30	Oliver, Al	77T	130	$ .15	$ .50
Oglivie, Ben	81T	415	$ .01	$ .10	Oliver, Al	78T	430	$ .08	$ .30
Oglivie, Ben	82T	280	$ .01	$ .07	Oliver, Al	79T	391	$ .05	$ .20
Oglivie, Ben	83T	750	$ .01	$ .07	Oliver, Al	80T	260	$ .05	$ .20
Oglivie, Ben	84T	190	$ .01	$ .06	Oliver, Al	81T	70	$ .03	$ .15
Oglivie, Ben	85T	681	$ .01	$ .05	Oliver, Al	82T	36	$ .01	$ .07
Oglivie, Ben	86T	372	$ .01	$ .04	Oliver, Al	82T	590	$ .03	$ .15
Oglivie, Ben	87T	586	$ .01	$ .04	Oliver, Al	82TIA	591	$ .01	$ .07
Ojeda, Bob	82T	274	$ .10	$ .75	Oliver, Al	82TTR	83	$ .30	$ .85
Ojeda, Bob	83T	654	$ .01	$ .07	Oliver, Al	83T	111	$ .01	$ .07
Ojeda, Bob	84T	162	$ .01	$ .06	Oliver, Al	83T	420	$ .03	$ .15
Ojeda, Bob	84T	786	$ .06	$ .30	Oliver, Al	83T	421	$ .01	$ .07
Ojeda, Bob	85T	477	$ .01	$ .05	Oliver, Al	83T	701	$ .01	$ .07
Ojeda, Bob	86T	11	$ .01	$ .04	Oliver, Al	83T	703	$ .01	$ .07
Ojeda, Bob	86TTR	81	$ .02	$ .10	Oliver, Al	84T	516	$ .01	$ .06
Ojeda, Bob	87T	746	$ .01	$ .04	Oliver, Al	84T	620	$ .02	$ .10
Ojeda, Bob	88T	558	$ .01	$ .04	Oliver, Al	84T	704	$ .03	$ .15
Ojeda, Bob	88TBB	234	$ .01	$ .06	Oliver, Al	84TTR	87	$ .05	$ .20
Ojeda, Bob	89T	333	$ .01	$ .05	Oliver, Al	85T	130	$ .01	$ .10
Ojeda, Bob	90T	207	$ .01	$ .04	Oliver, Al	85TTR	88	$ .08	$ .30
Ojeda, Bob	91T	601	$ .01	$ .03	Oliver, Al	86T	775	$ .01	$ .04
Oldis, Bob	53T	262	$12.50	$50.00	Oliver, Bob	69T	662	$ .30	$ .95
Oldis, Bob	54T	91	$3.60	$10.00	Oliver, Bob	70T	567	$ .30	$ .95
Oldis, Bob	55T	169	$5.25	$15.00	Oliver, Bob	71T	470	$ .15	$ .50
Oldis, Bob	60T	361	$ .75	$2.20					
Oldis, Bob	61T	149	$ .35	$1.25					
Oldis, Bob	62T	269	$ .45	$1.45					
Oldis, Bob	63T	404	$ .45	$1.50					
Olerud, John	89TMLD	89	$ .01	$1.50					
Olerud, John	90TTR	83	$ .01	$1.50					
Olerud, John	91T	168	$ .01	$ .35					
Olin, Steve	89TMLD	90	$ .01	$ .15					
Olin, Steve	90T	433	$ .01	$ .04					
Olin, Steve	91T	696	$ .01	$ .03					
Oliva, Pedro "Tony"	63T	228	$9.00	$35.00					
Oliva, Tony	64T	116	$3.00	$10.00					
Oliva, Tony	65T	1	$3.50	$11.00					
Oliva, Tony	65T	340	$2.00	$6.00					
Oliva, Tony	66T	216	$1.00	$4.00					
Oliva, Tony	66T	220	$ .50	$1.50					
Oliva, Tony	66T	450	$2.00	$6.00					
Oliva, Tony	67T	50	$ .90	$3.00					
Oliva, Tony	67T	239	$1.75	$4.50					
Oliva, Tony	68T	165	$ .75	$3.00					
Oliva, Tony	68T	480	$5.50	$17.50					
Oliva, Tony	68TAS	371	$ .75	$2.20					
Oliva, Tony	69T	1	$2.00	$8.00					
Oliva, Tony	69T	600	$ .75	$3.00					
Oliva, Tony	69TAS	427	$ .75	$3.00					
Oliva, Tony	70T	62	$ .50	$1.50					
Oliva, Tony	70T	510	$ .75	$2.20					
Oliva, Tony	71T	61	$ .75	$2.20					
Oliva, Tony	71T	290	$ .45	$1.45					
Oliva, Tony	72T	86	$ .35	$1.25					
Oliva, Tony	72T	400	$ .45	$1.45	Oliver, Bob	72T	57	$ .15	$ .50
Oliva, Tony	73T	80	$ .35	$1.25	Oliver, Bob	73T	289	$ .07	$ .30
Oliva, Tony	74T	190	$ .15	$ .50	Oliver, Bob	74T	243	$ .07	$ .30
Oliva, Tony	75T	325	$ .30	$ .95	Oliver, Bob	75T	657	$ .07	$ .30
Oliva, Tony	76T	35	$ .15	$ .50	Oliver, Dave	78T	704	$4.00	$12.00
Oliva, Tony	89TTB	665	$ .01	$ .05	Oliver, Dave	79T	705	$ .25	$1.00

BOB OLIVER

Player	Year	No.	VG	EX/MT	Player	Year	No.	VG	EX/MT
Oliver, Gene	59T	135	$ .75	$2.20	Orioles, Team	62T	476	$2.25	$6.00
Oliver, Gene	60T	307	$ .75	$2.20	Orioles, Team	63T	377	$2.10	$6.00
Oliver, Gene	61T	487	$ .75	$3.00	Orioles, Team	64T	473	$1.75	$4.50
Oliver, Gene	62T	561	$3.95	$11.50	Orioles, Team	65T	572	$1.50	$4.50
Oliver, Gene	63T	172	$ .30	$ .95	Orioles, Team	66T	348	$2.25	$6.00
Oliver, Gene	64T	316	$ .30	$ .95	Orioles, Team	67T	302	$ .90	$3.00
Oliver, Gene	65T	106	$ .30	$ .85	Orioles, Team	68T	334	$ .75	$3.00
Oliver, Gene	66T	541	$5.00	$20.00	Orioles, Team	70T	387	$ .75	$2.20
Oliver, Gene	67T	18	$ .30	$ .85	Orioles, Team	71T	1	$2.50	$10.00
Oliver, Gene	68T	449	$ .30	$ .85	Orioles, Team	72T	731	$1.75	$5.00
Oliver, Gene	69T	247	$ .30	$ .95	Orioles, Team	73T	278	$ .35	$1.25
Oliver, Joe	89TMLD	91	$ .01	$ .35	Orioles, Team	74T	16	$ .15	$ .50
Oliver, Joe	90T	668	$ .01	$ .25	Orioles, Team Checklist	75T	117	$ .45	$1.45
Oliver, Joe	91T	517	$ .01	$ .03	Orioles, Team Checklist	76T	73	$ .15	$ .60
Oliver, Nate	63T	466	$7.50	$27.50	Orioles, Team Checklist	77T	546	$ .15	$ .50
Oliver, Nate	65T	59	$ .30	$ .85	Orioles, Team Checklist	78T	96	$ .06	$ .30
Oliver, Nate	66T	364	$ .30	$ .95	Orioles, Team Checklist	79T	689	$ .15	$ .50
Oliver, Nate	68T	124	$ .30	$ .85	Orioles, Team Checklist	80T	404	$ .08	$ .30
Oliver, Nate	69T	354	$ .30	$ .85	Orioles, Team Checklist	81T	661	$ .02	$ .20
Oliver, Nate	70T	223	$ .15	$ .50	Orioles, Team Leaders	86T	726	$ .01	$ .04
Oliver, Tom	54T	207	$3.60	$10.00	Orioles, Team Leaders	87T	506	$ .01	$ .04
Oliveras, Francisco	89TMLD	92	$ .01	$ .06	Orioles, Team Leaders	88T	51	$ .01	$ .04
Oliveras, Francisco	91T	52	$ .01	$ .03	Orioles, Team Leaders	89T	381	$ .01	$ .05
Olivo, Chi Chi	66T	578	$5.00	$20.00	Ortiz, Junior	87T	583	$ .01	$ .04
Olivo, Mike	70T	381	$ .15	$ .50	Orosco, Jesse	80T	681	$2.50	$7.50
Ollom, Jim	67T	137	$ .30	$ .85	Orosco, Jesse	83T	369	$ .01	$ .07
Ollom, Jim	68T	91	$ .30	$ .85	Orosco, Jesse	84T	54	$ .01	$ .06
Olmsted, Al	81T	244	$ .01	$ .10	Orosco, Jesse	84TAS	396	$ .01	$ .06
Olson, Greg	90TTR	84	$ .01	$ .15	Orosco, Jesse	85T	250	$ .01	$ .05
Olson, Greg	91T	673	$ .01	$ .10					
Olson, Gregg	89T	161	$ .05	$ .75					
Olson, Gregg	89TMLD	93	$ .01	$ .15					
Olson, Gregg	89TTR	89	$ .01	$ .60					
Olson, Gregg	90T	655	$ .01	$ .20					
Olson, Gregg	91T	10	$ .01	$ .03					
Olson, Karl	52T	72	$15.00	$47.50					
Olson, Karl	54T	186	$3.60	$10.00					
Olson, Karl	55T	72	$2.00	$6.00					
Olson, Karl	56T	322	$2.25	$8.00					
Olson, Karl	57T	153	$ .95	$3.50					
Olwine, Ed	87T	159	$ .01	$ .04					
Olwine, Ed	88T	353	$ .01	$ .04					
Ontiveros, Steve	74T	598	$4.00	$15.00					
Ontiveros, Steve	75T	483	$ .07	$ .30					
Ontiveros, Steve	76T	284	$ .05	$ .20					
Ontiveros, Steve	78T	76	$ .02	$ .10					
Ontiveros, Steve	79T	299	$ .02	$ .10					
Ontiveros, Steve	80T	514	$ .01	$ .10					
Ontiveros, Steve	86T	507	$ .01	$ .10					
Ontiveros, Steve	87T	161	$ .01	$ .04					
Ontiveros, Steve	88T	272	$ .01	$ .04					
Ontiveros, Steve	89T	692	$ .01	$ .05					
Ontiveros, Steve	89TTR	90	$ .01	$ .06					
Oquendo, Jose	84T	208	$ .10	$ .45					
Oquendo, Jose	85T	598	$ .01	$ .10	Orosco, Jesse	86T	465	$ .01	$ .04
Oquendo, Jose	86TTR	82	$ .02	$ .10	Orosco, Jesse	87T	704	$ .01	$ .04
Oquendo, Jose	87T	133	$ .01	$ .04	Orosco, Jesse	88T	105	$ .01	$ .04
Oquendo, Jose	88T	83	$ .01	$ .04	Orosco, Jesse	88TTR	77	$ .01	$ .06
Oquendo, Jose	89T	442	$ .01	$ .05	Orosco, Jesse	89T	513	$ .01	$ .05
Oquendo, Jose	89TBB	77	$ .01	$ .06	Orosco, Jesse	89TTR	91	$ .01	$ .06
Oquendo, Jose	90T	645	$ .01	$ .04	Orosco, Jesse	90T	636	$ .01	$ .04
Oquendo, Jose	91T	343	$ .01	$ .03	Orosco, Jesse	91T	346	$ .01	$ .03
Oravetz, Ernie	56T	51	$2.25	$6.00	Orsino, Johnny	62T	377	$ .75	$2.50
Oravetz, Ernie	57T	179	$ .95	$3.50	Orsino, Johnny	63T	418	$ .45	$1.50
Orioles, Team	56T	100	$3.00	$9.00	Orsino, Johnny	64T	63	$ .30	$ .95
Orioles, Team	57T	251	$3.60	$10.00					
Orioles, Team	58T	408	$3.00	$9.00					
Orioles, Team	59T	48	$1.50	$4.50					
Orioles, Team	60T	494	$2.25	$6.50					
Orioles, Team	61T	159	$1.00	$3.00					

JESSE OROSCO

Player	Year	No.	VG	EX/MT
Orsino, Johnny	65T	303	$ .35	$1.25
Orsino, Johnny	66T	77	$ .30	$ .95
Orsino, Johnny	67T	207	$ .30	$ .85
Orsulak, Joe	85TTR	89	$ .05	$ .20
Orsulak, Joe	86T	102	$ .01	$ .04
Orsulak, Joe	87	414	$ .01	$ .04
Orsulak, Joe	88TTR	78	$ .01	$ .06
Orsulak, Joe	89T	727	$ .01	$ .05
Orsulak, Joe	89TBB	181	$ .01	$ .06
Orsulak, Joe	90T	212	$ .01	$ .04
Orsulak, Joe	91T	521	$ .01	$ .03
Orta, Jorge	73T	194	$ .30	$ .85
Orta, Jorge	74T	376	$ .07	$ .30
Orta, Jorge	75T	184	$ .07	$ .30
Orta, Jorge	76T	560	$ .05	$ .20
Orta, Jorge	77T	109	$ .05	$ .15
Orta, Jorge	78T	42	$ .02	$ .10
Orta, Jorge	79T	631	$ .02	$ .10

Player	Year	No.	VG	EX/MT
Orta, Jorge	80T	442	$ .01	$ .10
Orta, Jorge	81T	222	$ .01	$ .10
Orta, Jorge	82T	26	$ .01	$ .07
Orta, Jorge	82TTR	84	$ .02	$ .10
Orta, Jorge	83T	722	$ .01	$ .07
Orta, Jorge	83TTR	82	$ .02	$ .10
Orta, Jorge	84T	312	$ .01	$ .06
Orta, Jorge	84TTR	88	$ .02	$ .10
Orta, Jorge	85T	164	$ .01	$ .05
Orta, Jorge	86T	541	$ .01	$ .04
Orta, Jorge	87T	738	$ .01	$ .04
Ortega, Phil	62T	69	$ .45	$1.45
Ortega, Phil	63T	467	$2.50	$6.50
Ortega, Phil	64T	291	$ .30	$ .95
Ortega, Phil	65T	152	$ .30	$ .85
Ortega, Phil	66T	416	$ .30	$ .95
Ortega, Phil	67T	493	$ .75	$3.00
Ortega, Phil	68T	595	$ .35	$1.25
Ortega, Phil	69T	406	$ .30	$ .85
Ortiz, Junior	84T	161	$ .01	$ .06
Ortiz, Junior	85T	439	$ .01	$ .05
Ortiz, Junior	86T	682	$ .01	$ .04

Player	Year	No.	VG	EX/MT
Ortiz, Junior	88T	274	$ .01	$ .04
Ortiz, Junior	89T	769	$ .01	$ .05
Ortiz, Junior	89TBB	66	$ .01	$ .06
Ortiz, Junior	90T	322	$ .01	$ .04
Ortiz, Junior	90TTR	85	$ .01	$ .05
Ortiz, Junior	91T	72	$ .01	$ .03
Ortiz, Lou	55T	114	$2.00	$6.00
Orton, John	89TMLD	94	$ .01	$ .06
Orton, John	91T	176	$ .01	$ .10
Osborn, Dan	76T	282	$ .05	$ .20
Osborn, Don	74T	489	$ .07	$ .30
Osborne, Larry	59T	524	$2.50	$10.00
Osborne, Larry	60T	201	$ .45	$1.45
Osborne, Larry	61T	208	$ .35	$1.25
Osborne, Larry	62T	583	$3.95	$11.50
Osborne, Larry	63T	514	$1.75	$4.50
Osinski, Dan	63T	114	$ .30	$ .95
Osinski, Dan	64T	537	$1.75	$4.50
Osinski, Dan	65T	223	$ .35	$1.25
Osinski, Dan	66T	168	$ .30	$ .95
Osinski, Dan	67T	594	$2.10	$6.00
Osinski, Dan	68T	331	$ .30	$ .85
Osinski, Dan	69T	622	$ .30	$ .95
Osteen, Claude	59T	224	$2.10	$6.00
Osteen, Claude	60T	206	$ .90	$3.00
Osteen, Claude	62T	501	$ .75	$2.25
Osteen, Claude	63T	374	$ .45	$1.50
Osteen, Claude	64T	28	$ .30	$ .95
Osteen, Claude	65T	570	$2.10	$6.00
Osteen, Claude	66T	270	$ .30	$ .95
Osteen, Claude	67T	330	$ .30	$ .85
Osteen, Claude	68T	9	$ .75	$2.20
Osteen, Claude	68T	440	$ .15	$ .50
Osteen, Claude	69T	528	$ .20	$ .50
Osteen, Claude	70T	260	$ .30	$ .95
Osteen, Claude	71T	10	$ .15	$ .50
Osteen, Claude	72T	297	$ .15	$ .50
Osteen, Claude	72TIA	298	$ .15	$ .50
Osteen, Claude	73T	490	$ .30	$ .85
Osteen, Claude	74T	42	$ .07	$ .30
Osteen, Claude	74TTR	42	$ .07	$ .30
Osteen, Claude	75T	453	$ .07	$ .30
Osteen, Claude	76T	488	$ .05	$ .20
Osteen, Darrell	66T	424	$1.25	$5.00
Osteen, Darrell	67T	222	$ .35	$1.25
Osteen, Darrell	68T	199	$ .30	$ .85
Ostrowski, Joe	52T	206	$7.00	$21.00
Osuna, Al	91T	149	$ .01	$ .10
Otero, Reggie	60T	459	$ .95	$3.50
Otis, Amos	69T	31	$ .30	$ .95
Otis, Amos	70T	354	$ .30	$ .85
Otis, Amos	71T	610	$ .45	$1.45
Otis, Amos	72T	10	$ .30	$ .85
Otis, Amos	73T	510	$ .15	$ .50
Otis, Amos	74T	65	$ .07	$ .30
Otis, Amos	74TAS	337	$ .07	$ .30
Otis, Amos	75T	520	$ .07	$ .30
Otis, Amos	76T	198	$ .15	$ .50
Otis, Amos	76T	510	$ .07	$ .30
Otis, Amos	77T	290	$ .05	$ .15
Otis, Amos	78T	490	$ .02	$ .10
Otis, Amos	79T	360	$ .02	$ .10
Otis, Amos	80T	130	$ .01	$ .10
Otis, Amos	81T	585	$ .01	$ .10
Otis, Amos	82T	725	$ .01	$ .07
Otis, Amos	82TIA	726	$ .01	$ .07
Otis, Amos	83T	75	$ .01	$ .07
Otis, Amos	84T	655	$ .01	$ .06
Otis, Amos	84TTR	89	$ .02	$ .10
Ott, Billy	65T	354	$ .35	$1.25

TOPPS

Player	Year	No.	VG	EX/MT	Player	Year	No.	VG	EX/MT
Ott, Ed	76T	594	$ .05	$ .20	Paciorek, Tom	77T	48	$ .05	$ .15
Ott, Ed	77T	197	$ .05	$ .15	Paciorek, Tom	78T	322	$ .02	$ .10
Ott, Ed	79T	561	$ .02	$ .10	Paciorek, Tom	79T	141	$ .02	$ .10
Ott, Ed	80T	383	$ .01	$ .10	Paciorek, Tom	80T	481	$ .01	$ .10
Ott, Ed	81T	246	$ .01	$ .10	Paciorek, Tom	81T	228	$ .01	$ .10
Ott, Ed	81TTR	810	$ .02	$ .10	Paciorek, Tom	82T	336	$ .01	$ .07
Ott, Ed	82T	469	$ .01	$ .07	Paciorek, Tom	82T	678	$ .01	$ .07
Ott, Ed	83T	131	$ .01	$ .07	Paciorek, Tom	82TTR	85	$ .02	$ .10
Otten, Jim	75T	624	$ .07	$ .30	Paciorek, Tom	83T	72	$ .01	$ .07
Otten, Jim	77T	493	$ .25	$ .80	Paciorek, Tom	84T	777	$ .01	$ .06
Otto, Dave	89T	131	$ .01	$ .10	Paciorek, Tom	85T	572	$ .01	$ .05
Overmire, Frank	52T	155	$7.00	$20.00	Paciorek, Tom	86T	362	$ .01	$ .04
Overy, Mike	77T	489	$ .30	$ .85	Paciorek, Tom	86TTR	83	$ .02	$ .10
Owchinko, Bob	78T	164	$ .02	$ .10	Paciorek, Tom	87T	729	$ .01	$ .04
Owchinko, Bob	79T	488	$ .02	$ .10	Pactwa, Joe	76T	589	$ .45	$1.45
Owchinko, Bob	80T	79	$ .01	$ .10	Padres, Team	70T	657	$ .75	$2.00
Owchinko, Bob	81T	536	$ .01	$ .10	Padres, Team	71T	482	$ .45	$1.45
Owchinko, Bob	81TTR	811	$ .02	$ .10	Padres, Team	72T	262	$ .15	$ .50
Owchinko, Bob	82T	243	$ .01	$ .07	Padres, Team	73T	316	$ .35	$1.25
Owchinko, Bob	83T	338	$ .01	$ .07	Padres, Team	74T	226	$ .35	$1.25
Owchinko, Bob	85T	752	$ .01	$ .05	Padres, Team Checklist	75T	146	$ .15	$ .50
Owen, Dave	85T	642	$ .01	$ .05	Padres, Team Checklist	76T	331	$ .35	$1.25
Owen, Larry	82T	502	$ .50	$2.50	Padres, Team Checklist	77T	134	$ .15	$ .50
Owen, Larry	89T	87	$ .01	$ .05	Padres, Team Checklist	78T	192	$ .05	$ .25
Owen, Spike	84T	413	$ .01	$ .06	Padres, Team Checklist	79T	479	$ .05	$ .25
Owen, Spike	85T	84	$ .01	$ .05	Padres, Team Checklist	80T	356	$ .05	$ .25
Owen, Spike	86T	248	$ .01	$ .04	Padres, Team Checklist	81T	685	$ .02	$ .20
Owen, Spike	87T	591	$ .01	$ .04	Padres, Team Leaders	86T	306	$ .01	$ .04
Owen, Spike	88T	733	$ .01	$ .04	Padres, Team Leaders	87T	81	$ .01	$ .04
Owen, Spike	89T	123	$ .01	$ .05	Padres, Team Leaders	88T	699	$ .01	$ .04
Owen, Spike	89TBB	221	$ .01	$ .06	Padres, Team Leaders	89T	231	$ .01	$ .05
Owen, Spike	89TTR	92	$ .01	$ .06	Paepke, Dennis	70T	552	$ .30	$ .95
Owen, Spike	90T	674	$ .01	$ .04	Pafko, Andy	51Tbb	27	$7.50	$22.50
Owen, Spike	91T	372	$ .01	$ .03	Pafko, Andy	52T	1	$100.00	$1100.00
Owens, Jim	55T	202	$5.25	$15.00	Pafko, Andy	54T	79	$4.25	$15.00
Owens, Jim	56T	114	$2.25	$6.00	Pafko, Andy	56T	312	$2.00	$6.00
Owens, Jim	59T	503	$ .75	$2.20					
Owens, Jim	60T	185	$ .45	$1.45					
Owens, Jim	61T	341	$ .35	$1.25					
Owens, Jim	62T	212	$ .45	$1.45					
Owens, Jim	63T	483	$2.50	$6.50					
Owens, Jim	64T	241	$ .30	$ .95					
Owens, Jim	65T	451	$ .75	$3.00					
Owens, Jim	66T	297	$ .35	$1.25					
Owens, Jim	67T	582	$2.10	$6.00					
Owens, Jim	73T	624	$ .55	$1.75					
Owens, Paul	84T	229	$ .01	$ .06					
Owens, Paul	85T	92	$ .01	$ .05					
Ownbey, Rick	83T	739	$ .01	$ .07					
Oyler, Ray	65T	259	$ .45	$1.45					
Oyler, Ray	66T	81	$ .30	$ .95					
Oyler, Ray	67T	352	$ .30	$ .85					
Oyler, Ray	68T	399	$ .30	$ .85					
Oyler, Ray	69T	178	$ .30	$ .85					
Oyler, Ray	70T	603	$ .30	$ .95					
Ozark, Danny	73T	486	$ .30	$ .95					
Ozark, Danny	74T	119	$ .07	$ .30					
Ozark, Danny	78T	631	$ .02	$ .10					
Ozark, Danny	85T	365	$ .01	$ .05					
Pacella, John	81T	414	$ .01	$ .10					
Pacella, John	83T	166	$ .01	$ .07					
Pacheco, Tony	74T	521	$ .07	$ .30					
Pacillo, Pat	85T	402	$ .05	$ .25					
Pacillo, Pat	87TTR	93	$ .01	$ .05					
Pacillo, Pat	88T	288	$ .01	$ .04					
Paciorek, Tom	71T	709	$9.00	$27.50					
Paciorek, Tom	73T	606	$ .95	$3.50	Pafko, Andy	57T	143	$ .60	$2.50
Paciorek, Tom	74T	127	$ .07	$ .30	Pafko, Andy	58T	223	$ .45	$1.50
Paciorek, Tom	75T	523	$ .07	$ .30	Pafko, Andy	59T	27	$1.25	$4.25
Paciorek, Tom	76T	641	$ .05	$ .20	Pafko, Andy	60T	464	$ .95	$3.50

ANDY Pafko
MILWAUKEE BRAVES OUTFIELD

Player	Year	No.	VG	EX/MT
Pagan, Dave	75T	648	$ .07	$ .30
Pagan, Dave	77T	508	$ .05	$ .15
Pagan, Jose	60T	67	$ .45	$1.45
Pagan, Jose	61T	279	$ .35	$1.25
Pagan, Jose	62T	565	$3.95	$11.50
Pagan, Jose	63T	545	$1.75	$4.50
Pagan, Jose	64T	123	$ .30	$ .95
Pagan, Jose	65T	575	$1.75	$4.50
Pagan, Jose	66T	54	$ .30	$ .95
Pagan, Jose	67T	322	$ .30	$ .85
Pagan, Jose	68T	482	$ .35	$1.25

Player	Year	No.	VG	EX/MT
Pagan, Jose	69T	192	$ .30	$ .85
Pagan, Jose	70T	643	$ .75	$2.00
Pagan, Jose	71T	282	$ .15	$ .50
Pagan, Jose	72T	701	$ .75	$2.50
Pagan, Jose	72TIA	702	$ .75	$2.50
Pagan, Jose	73T	659	$ .45	$1.45
Page, Joe	51Tbb	10	$4.00	$18.00
Page, Joe	52T	48	$25.00	$75.00
Page, Mitchell	78T	55	$ .02	$ .10
Page, Mitchell	79T	295	$ .02	$ .10
Page, Mitchell	80T	586	$ .01	$ .10
Page, Mitchell	81T	35	$ .01	$ .10
Page, Mitchell	82T	633	$ .01	$ .07
Page, Mitchell	83T	737	$ .01	$ .07
Page, Mitchell	84T	414	$ .01	$ .06
Pagel, Karl	79T	716	$ .02	$ .10
Pagel, Karl	80T	676	$ .01	$ .10
Pagliaroni, Jim	61T	519	$ .75	$3.00
Pagliaroni, Jim	62T	81	$ .45	$1.45
Pagliaroni, Jim	63T	159	$ .30	$ .95
Pagliaroni, Jim	64T	392	$ .50	$1.45
Pagliaroni, Jim	65T	265	$ .35	$1.25
Pagliaroni, Jim	66T	33	$ .30	$ .95
Pagliaroni, Jim	67T	183	$ .30	$ .85
Pagliaroni, Jim	68T	586	$ .35	$1.25
Pagliaroni, Jim	69T	302	$ .30	$ .95
Pagliarulo, Mike	85T	638	$ .05	$ .40
Pagliarulo, Mike	86T	327	$ .02	$ .20
Pagliarulo, Mike	87T	195	$ .01	$ .10

Player	Year	No.	VG	EX/MT
Pagliarulo, Mike	88T	435	$ .01	$ .10
Pagliarulo, Mike	88TBB	138	$ .01	$ .10
Pagliarulo, Mike	89T	211	$ .01	$ .05
Pagliarulo, Mike	89TBB	28	$ .01	$ .06
Pagliarulo, Mike	90T	63	$ .01	$ .04
Pagliarulo, Mike	91T	547	$ .01	$ .03
Pagnozzi, Tom	88T	689	$ .01	$ .04
Pagnozzi, Tom	89T	208	$ .01	$ .05
Pagnozzi, Tom	90T	509	$ .01	$ .04
Pagnozzi, Tom	91T	308	$ .01	$ .03
Paige, Satchell	53T	220	$90.00	$350.00
Paine, Phil	58T	442	$ .75	$2.20
Palacios, Rey	91T	148	$ .01	$ .03
Palacios, Vicente	88T	322	$ .01	$ .20
Palacios, Vicente	91T	438	$ .01	$ .03
Palica, Erv	52T	273	$12.00	$35.00
Palica, Erv	56T	206	$3.00	$9.00
Pall, Donn	89T	458	$ .01	$ .05
Pall, Donn	90T	219	$ .01	$ .04
Pall, Donn	91T	768	$ .01	$ .03
Palmeiro, Rafael	87T	634	$ .35	$1.25
Palmeiro, Rafael	88T	186	$ .05	$ .30
Palmeiro, Rafael	89T	310	$ .01	$ .10
Palmeiro, Rafael	89TBB	257	$ .01	$ .10
Palmeiro, Rafael	89TTR	93	$ .01	$ .10
Palmeiro, Rafael	90T	755	$ .01	$ .04
Palmeiro, Rafael	91T	295	$ .01	$ .03
Palmer, Dave	80T	42	$ .05	$ .20
Palmer, Dave	81T	607	$ .01	$ .10
Palmer, Dave	82T	292	$ .01	$ .07
Palmer, Dave	83T	164	$ .01	$ .07
Palmer, Dave	84T	750	$ .30	$ .85
Palmer, Dave	85T	526	$ .01	$ .05
Palmer, Dave	86T	421	$ .01	$ .04
Palmer, Dave	86TTR	84	$ .02	$ .10
Palmer, Dave	87T	324	$ .01	$ .04
Palmer, Dave	88T	732	$ .01	$ .04
Palmer, Dave	88TTR	79	$ .01	$ .06
Palmer, Dave	89T	67	$ .01	$ .05
Palmer, Dean	89TMLD	95	$ .01	$ .25
Palmer, Jim	66T	126	$75.00	$225.00
Palmer, Jim	67T	475	$20.00	$80.00
Palmer, Jim	68T	575	$15.00	$50.00
Palmer, Jim	69T	573	$10.00	$35.00
Palmer, Jim	70T	68	$ .75	$3.00
Palmer, Jim	70T	449	$4.00	$16.00
Palmer, Jim	71T	67	$ .15	$ .50
Palmer, Jim	71T	570	$7.00	$22.00
Palmer, Jim	72T	92	$ .65	$2.20
Palmer, Jim	72T	270	$3.50	$11.00
Palmer, Jim	73T	160	$2.00	$8.00
Palmer, Jim	73T	341	$ .35	$1.25
Palmer, Jim	74T	40	$1.50	$6.00
Palmer, Jim	74T	206	$ .75	$2.25
Palmer, Jim	75T	335	$1.50	$6.00
Palmer, Jim	76T	200	$ .45	$1.45
Palmer, Jim	76T	202	$ .45	$1.45
Palmer, Jim	76T	450	$1.25	$5.00
Palmer, Jim	77T	5	$ .15	$ .50
Palmer, Jim	77T	600	$1.00	$4.00
Palmer, Jim	78T	160	$ .75	$3.00
Palmer, Jim	78T	205	$ .30	$ .85
Palmer, Jim	79T	340	$ .75	$2.50
Palmer, Jim	80T	590	$ .65	$2.00
Palmer, Jim	81T	210	$ .40	$1.50
Palmer, Jim	82T	80	$ .10	$ .50
Palmer, Jim	82TIA	81	$ .05	$ .25
Palmer, Jim	83T	21	$ .05	$ .25
Palmer, Jim	83T	490	$ .10	$ .50
Palmer, Jim	83T	491	$ .03	$ .15

TOPPS

Player	Year	No.	VG	EX/MT	Player	Year	No.	VG	EX/MT
Palmer, Jim	84T	715	$ .04	$ .20	Paris, Kelly	84T	113	$ .01	$ .06
Palmer, Jim	84T	717	$ .01	$ .06	Parker, Billy	72T	213	$ .15	$ .50
Palmer, Lowell	70T	252	$ .15	$ .50	Parker, Billy	73T	354	$ .07	$ .30
Palmer, Lowell	71T	554	$ .35	$1.25	Parker, Clay	89TTR	94	$ .01	$ .15
Palmer, Lowell	72T	746	$ .50	$ .25	Parker, Clay	90T	511	$ .01	$ .04
Palys, Stan	58T	126	$ .75	$3.00	Parker, Clay	91T	183	$ .01	$ .03
Pankovits, Jim	86T	618	$ .01	$ .04	Parker, Dave	74T	252	$12.00	$37.50
Pankovits, Jim	87T	249	$ .01	$ .04	Parker, Dave	75T	29	$3.00	$10.00
Pankovits, Jim	88T	487	$ .01	$ .04	Parker, Dave	76T	185	$1.50	$6.00
Pankovits, Jim	88TBB	109	$ .01	$ .06	Parker, Dave	77T	270	$1.00	$4.00
Pankovits, Jim	89T	153	$ .01	$ .05	Parker, Dave	78T	201	$ .15	$ .60
Papi, Stan	79T	652	$ .02	$ .10	Parker, Dave	78T	560	$ .90	$3.50
Papi, Stan	81T	273	$ .01	$ .10	Parker, Dave	79T	1	$ .75	$2.25
Papi, Stan	82T	423	$ .01	$ .07	Parker, Dave	79T	430	$ .50	$2.00
Pappas, Milt	58T	457	$ .65	$2.00	Parker, Dave	80T	310	$ .25	$1.00
Pappas, Milt	59T	391	$ .75	$2.20	Parker, Dave	81T	640	$ .15	$ .60
Pappas, Milt	60T	12	$ .75	$3.00	Parker, Dave	82T	40	$ .01	$ .50
Pappas, Milt	60T	399	$ .90	$3.00	Parker, Dave	82TAS	343	$ .05	$ .20
Pappas, Milt	61T	48	$ .75	$3.00	Parker, Dave	82TIA	41	$ .30	$ .25
Pappas, Milt	61T	295	$ .75	$3.00	Parker, Dave	83T	205	$ .05	$ .25
Pappas, Milt	62T	55	$ .75	$3.00	Parker, Dave	84T	701	$ .06	$ .30
Pappas, Milt	62T	75	$ .75	$3.00	Parker, Dave	84T	775	$ .05	$ .25
Pappas, Milt	63T	358	$ .45	$1.50	Parker, Dave	84TTR	90	$ .20	$ .90
Pappas, Milt	64T	45	$ .15	$ .50	Parker, Dave	85T	175	$ .05	$ .25
Pappas, Milt	65T	270	$ .35	$1.25	Parker, Dave	86T	595	$ .03	$ .25
Pappas, Milt	66T	105	$ .90	$3.00	Parker, Dave	87T	691	$ .03	$ .15
Pappas, Milt	67T	254	$ .30	$ .85	Parker, Dave	87TAS	600	$ .01	$ .10
Pappas, Milt	68T	74	$ .30	$ .85	Parker, Dave	88T	315	$ .01	$ .15
Pappas, Milt	69T	79	$ .30	$ .85	Parker, Dave	88TBB	242	$ .01	$ .10
Pappas, Milt	70T	576	$ .30	$ .95	Parker, Dave	88TTR	81	$ .01	$ .06
Pappas, Milt	71T	441	$ .30	$ .85	Parker, Dave	89T	475	$ .01	$ .05
					Parker, Dave	89TBB	144	$ .01	$ .10
					Parker, Dave	90T	45	$ .01	$ .10
					Parker, Dave	90TTR	86	$ .01	$ .05
					Parker, Dave	91T	235	$ .01	$ .03
					Parker, Harry	74T	106	$ .07	$ .30
					Parker, Harry	75T	214	$ .07	$ .30
					Parker, Rick	90TTR	87	$ .01	$ .05
					Parker, Rick	91T	218	$ .01	$ .03
					Parker, Salty	60T	469	$ .95	$3.50
					Parker, Salty	73T	421	$ .07	$ .30
					Parker, Salty	74T	276	$ .07	$ .30
					Parker, Wes	64T	456	$ .90	$3.00
					Parker, Wes	65T	344	$ .35	$1.25
					Parker, Wes	66T	134	$ .30	$ .95
					Parker, Wes	67T	218	$ .30	$ .85
					Parker, Wes	68T	533	$ .35	$1.25
					Parker, Wes	69T	493	$ .30	$ .95
					Parker, Wes	70T	5	$ .15	$ .50
					Parker, Wes	71T	430	$ .15	$ .50
					Parker, Wes	72T	265	$ .15	$ .50
					Parker, Wes	73T	151	$ .07	$ .30
					Parks, Jack	55T	23	$2.00	$6.00
					Parnell, Mel	51Trb	10	$2.10	$6.00
					Parnell, Mel	52T	30	$12.50	$45.00
					Parnell, Mel	53T	19	$4.50	$15.00
					Parnell, Mel	54T	40	$2.50	$10.00
					Parnell, Mel	55T	140	$3.60	$10.00
					Parnell, Mel	57T	313	$4.25	$15.00
					Parrett, Jeff	88T	588	$ .01	$ .20
Pappas, Milt	72T	208	$ .15	$ .50	Parrett, Jeff	89T	176	$ .01	$ .05
Pappas, Milt	73T	70	$ .15	$ .50	Parrett, Jeff	89TTR	95	$ .01	$ .06
Pappas, Milt	74T	640	$ .07	$ .30	Parrett, Jeff	90T	439	$ .01	$ .04
Pardo, Al	86T	279	$ .01	$ .04	Parrett, Jeff	91T	56	$ .01	$ .03
Paredes, Johnny	89T	367	$ .01	$ .10	Parrish, Lance	78T	708	$7.00	$25.00
Parent, Mark	88TTR	80	$ .01	$ .10	Parrish, Lance	79T	469	$ .75	$3.00
Parent, Mark	89T	617	$ .01	$ .10	Parrish, Lance	80T	196	$ .25	$1.00
Parent, Mark	90T	749	$ .01	$ .04	Parrish, Lance	81T	392	$ .10	$ .50
Parent, Mark	91T	358	$ .01	$ .03	Parrish, Lance	82T	535	$ .05	$ .25
					Parrish, Lance	83T	285	$ .05	$ .20

MILT PAPPAS

Player	Year	No.	VG	EX/MT
Parrish, Lance	83TRB	4	$ .01	$ .07
Parrish, Lance	84T	640	$ .05	$ .20
Parrish, Lance	85T	160	$ .04	$ .20
Parrish, Lance	85TAS	708	$ .01	$ .05
Parrish, Lance	86T	740	$ .02	$ .15
Parrish, Lance	87T	791	$ .07	$ .30
Parrish, Lance	87TAS	613	$ .01	$ .10
Parrish, Lance	87TTR	94	$ .01	$ .10
Parrish, Lance	88T	95	$ .01	$ .10
Parrish, Lance	88TBB	45	$ .01	$ .06
Parrish, Lance	89T	470	$ .01	$ .05
Parrish, Lance	89TBB	250	$ .01	$ .10
Parrish, Lance	89TTR	96	$ .01	$ .10

LANCE PARRISH

Player	Year	No.	VG	EX/MT
Parrish, Lance	90T	575	$ .01	$ .10
Parrish, Lance	91T	210	$ .01	$ .03
Parrish, Larry	76T	141	$ .30	$1.25
Parrish, Larry	77T	526	$ .30	$ .85
Parrish, Larry	78T	294	$ .02	$ .10
Parrish, Larry	79T	677	$ .05	$ .20
Parrish, Larry	80T	345	$ .01	$ .10
Parrish, Larry	81T	15	$ .01	$ .10
Parrish, Larry	82T	445	$ .01	$ .07
Parrish, Larry	82TTR	86	$ .02	$ .10
Parrish, Larry	83T	776	$ .01	$ .07
Parrish, Larry	84T	169	$ .01	$ .06
Parrish, Larry	85T	548	$ .01	$ .05
Parrish, Larry	86T	238	$ .01	$ .04
Parrish, Larry	87T	629	$ .01	$ .04
Parrish, Larry	88T	490	$ .01	$ .04
Parrish, Larry	89T	354	$ .01	$ .05
Parrott, Mike	79T	576	$ .02	$ .10
Parrott, Mike	80T	443	$ .01	$ .10
Parrott, Mike	81T	187	$ .01	$ .10
Parrott, Mike	82T	358	$ .01	$ .07
Parsons, Bill	72T	281	$ .15	$ .50
Parsons, Bill	73T	231	$ .07	$ .30
Parsons, Bill	74T	574	$ .07	$ .30
Parsons, Bill	75T	613	$ .07	$ .30
Parsons, Tom	62T	326	$ .45	$1.45
Parsons, Tom	65T	308	$ .45	$1.45

Player	Year	No.	VG	EX/MT
Paschall, Bill	80T	667	$ .30	$1.50
Pascual, Camilo	55T	84	$3.60	$10.00
Pascual, Camilo	56T	98	$2.25	$6.00
Pascual, Camilo	57T	211	$ .95	$3.50
Pascual, Camilo	58T	219	$ .75	$3.00
Pascual, Camilo	59T	291	$ .75	$2.20
Pascual, Camillo (Camilo)	59T	413	$ .75	$2.20
Pascual, Camilo	60T	483	$ .90	$3.00
Pascual, Camilo	60TAS	569	$2.50	$10.00
Pascual, Camilo	61T	235	$ .35	$1.25
Pascual, Camilo	62T	230	$ .45	$1.45
Pascual, Camilo	62T	59	$ .75	$2.20
Pascual, Camilo	63T	8	$ .45	$1.45
Pascual, Camilo	63T	10	$ .45	$1.45
Pascual, Camilo	63T	220	$ .30	$ .95
Pascual, Camilo	64T	2	$ .75	$3.00
Pascual, Camilo	64T	4	$1.50	$6.00
Pascual, Camilo	64T	6	$ .45	$1.45
Pascual, Camilo	64T	500	$ .50	$1.45
Pascual, Camilo	65T	11	$ .45	$1.45
Pascual, Camilo	65T	255	$ .35	$1.25
Pascual, Camilo	66T	305	$ .30	$ .95
Pascual, Camilo	67T	71	$ .30	$ .85
Pascual, Camilo	68T	395	$ .15	$ .50
Pascual, Camilo	69T	513	$ .30	$ .95
Pascual, Camilo	70T	254	$ .15	$ .50
Pasley, Kevin	77T	476	$15.00	$45.00
Pasley, Kevin	78T	702	$ .02	$ .10
Pasqua, Dan	86T	259	$ .03	$ .30
Pasqua, Dan	87T	74	$ .01	$ .10
Pasqua, Dan	88T	691	$ .01	$ .04
Pasqua, Dan	88TBB	164	$ .01	$ .06
Pasqua, Dan	88TTR	82	$ .01	$ .06
Pasqua, Dan	89T	558	$ .01	$ .05
Pasqua, Dan	89TBB	44	$ .01	$ .06
Pasqua, Dan	90T	446	$ .01	$ .04
Pasqua, Dan	91T	364	$ .01	$ .03
Pastore, Frank	80T	677	$ .01	$ .10
Pastore, Frank	81T	499	$ .01	$ .10
Pastore, Frank	82T	128	$ .01	$ .07
Pastore, Frank	83T	658	$ .01	$ .07
Pastore, Frank	84T	87	$ .01	$ .06
Pastore, Frank	85T	727	$ .01	$ .05
Pastore, Frank	86T	314	$ .01	$ .04
Pastore, Frank	86TTR	85	$ .02	$ .10
Pastore, Frank	87T	576	$ .01	$ .04
Pate, Bobby	81T	479	$2.50	$10.00
Patek, Freddie	69T	219	$ .15	$ .50
Patek, Freddie	70T	94	$ .15	$ .50
Patek, Freddie	71T	626	$ .35	$1.25
Patek, Freddie	72T	531	$ .30	$ .95
Patek, Freddie	73T	334	$ .07	$ .30
Patek, Freddie	74T	88	$ .07	$ .30
Patek, Freddie	75T	48	$ .07	$ .30
Patek, Freddie	76T	167	$ .05	$ .20
Patek, Freddie	77T	422	$ .05	$ .15
Patek, Freddie	78T	204	$ .02	$ .10
Patek, Freddie	78T	274	$ .02	$ .10
Patek, Freddie	79T	525	$ .02	$ .10
Patek, Freddie	80T	705	$ .01	$ .10
Patek, Freddie	81T	311	$ .01	$ .10
Patek, Freddie	82T	602	$ .01	$ .07
Patterson, Bob	88T	522	$ .01	$ .10
Patterson, Bob	90TTR	88	$ .01	$ .05
Patterson, Bob	91T	479	$ .01	$ .03
Patterson, Daryl	68T	113	$ .30	$ .85
Patterson, Daryl	69T	101	$ .30	$ .85
Patterson, Daryl	70T	592	$ .30	$ .95
Patterson, Daryl	71T	481	$ .15	$ .50
Patterson, Dave	80T	679	$ .01	$ .10

TOPPS

Player	Year	No.	VG	EX/MT	Player	Year	No.	VG	EX/MT
Patterson, Gil	77T	472	$ .05	$ .15	Pazik, Mike	77T	643	$ .05	$ .15
Patterson, Ken	89T	434	$ .01	$ .05	Pearce, Jim	55T	170	$3.25	$9.00
Patterson, Ken	90T	156	$ .01	$ .04	Pearson, Albie	58T	317	$ .75	$3.00
Patterson, Ken	91T	326	$ .01	$ .03	Pearson, Albie	59T	4	$1.25	$4.25
Patterson, Reggie	82T	599	$ .01	$ .07	Pearson, Albie	60T	241	$ .45	$1.45
Pattin, Marty	69T	563	$ .30	$ .95	Pearson, Albie	61T	288	$ .35	$1.25
Pattin, Marty	70T	31	$ .15	$ .50	Pearson, Albie	62T	343	$ .45	$1.45
Pattin, Marty	71T	579	$ .35	$1.25	Pearson, Albie	63T	182	$ .30	$ .95
Pattin, Marty	72T	144	$ .15	$ .50	Pearson, Albie	64T	110	$ .30	$ .95
Pattin, Marty	73T	415	$ .07	$ .30	Pearson, Albie	65T	358	$ .35	$1.25
Pattin, Marty	74T	583	$ .07	$ .30	Pearson, Albie	66T	83	$ .30	$ .95
Pattin, Marty	75T	413	$ .07	$ .30	Pecota, Bill	88T	433	$ .01	$ .04
Pattin, Marty	76T	492	$ .05	$ .20	Pecota, Bill	89T	148	$ .01	$ .05
Pattin, Marty	77T	658	$ .05	$ .15	Pecota, Bill	89TBB	292	$ .01	$ .06
Pattin, Marty	78T	218	$ .02	$ .10	Pecota, Bill	91T	754	$ .01	$ .03
Pattin, Marty	79T	129	$ .02	$ .10	Peden, Les	53T	256	$12.50	$50.00
Pattin, Marty	80T	26	$ .01	$ .10	Pedrique, Al	88T	294	$ .01	$ .04
Pattin, Marty	81T	389	$ .01	$ .10	Pedrique, Al	89T	566	$ .01	$ .05
Paul, Mike	69T	537	$ .30	$ .95	Pellagrini, Eddie	52T	405	$40.00	$140.00
Paul, Mike	70T	582	$ .30	$ .95	Pellagrini, Eddie	53T	28	$4.50	$15.00
Paul, Mike	71T	454	$ .15	$ .50	Pena, Alejandro	83TTR	83	$ .05	$ .25
Paul, Mike	72T	577	$ .30	$ .95	Pena, Alejandro	84T	324	$ .02	$ .10
Paul, Mike	73T	58	$ .07	$ .30	Pena, Alejandro	85T	110	$ .01	$ .05
Paul, Mike	74T	399	$ .07	$ .30	Pena, Alejandro	86T	665	$ .01	$ .04
Paula, Carlos	55T	97	$2.00	$6.00	Pena, Alejandro	87T	787	$ .01	$ .04
Paula, Carlos	56T	4	$2.25	$6.00	Pena, Alejandro	88T	277	$ .01	$ .04
Pavletich, Don	59T	494	$ .75	$2.20	Pena, Alejandro	89T	57	$ .01	$ .05
Pavletich, Don	62T	594	$35.00	$125.00	Pena, Alejandro	90T	483	$ .01	$ .04
Pavletich, Don	65T	472	$ .75	$3.00	Pena, Alejandro	90TTR	89	$ .01	$ .05
Pavletich, Don	66T	196	$ .30	$ .95	Pena, Alejandro	91T	544	$ .01	$ .03
Pavletich, Don	67T	292	$ .30	$ .85	Pena, George	73T	601	$ .45	$1.45
Pavletich, Don	68T	108	$ .30	$ .85	Pena, Geronimo	91T	636	$ .01	$ .10
Pavletich, Don	69T	179	$ .30	$ .85	Pena, Hipolito	89T	109	$ .01	$ .05
Pavletich, Don	70T	504	$ .15	$ .50	Pena, Jose	69T	339	$ .30	$ .85
Pavletich, Don	71T	409	$ .15	$ .50	Pena, Jose	70T	523	$ .15	$ .50
					Pena, Jose	71T	693	$ .75	$2.50
					Pena, Jose	72T	322	$ .15	$ .50
					Pena, Orlando	59T	271	$ .75	$2.20
					Pena, Orlando	63T	214	$ .30	$ .95
					Pena, Orlando	64T	124	$ .30	$ .95
					Pena, Orlando	65T	311	$ .35	$1.25
					Pena, Orlando	66T	239	$ .30	$ .95
					Pena, Orlando	67T	449	$ .30	$ .95
					Pena, Orlando	68T	471	$ .35	$1.25
					Pena, Orlando	74T	393	$ .07	$ .30
					Pena, Orlando	75T	573	$ .07	$ .30
					Pena, Ramon	89TMLD	96	$ .01	$ .15
					Pena, Roberto	66T	559	$2.00	$5.00
					Pena, Roberto	69T	184	$ .30	$ .85
					Pena, Roberto	70T	44	$ .15	$ .50
					Pena, Roberto	71T	334	$ .15	$ .50
					Pena, Tony	81T	551	$ .50	$2.00
					Pena, Tony	82T	138	$ .05	$ .25
					Pena, Tony	83T	590	$ .03	$ .15
					Pena, Tony	84T	645	$ .05	$ .20
					Pena, Tony	85T	358	$ .01	$ .10
					Pena, Tony	86T	260	$ .01	$ .10
					Pena, Tony	87T	60	$ .01	$ .10
					Pena, Tony	87TTR	95	$ .01	$ .10
					Pena, Tony	88T	410	$ .01	$ .10
					Pena, Tony	89T	715	$ .01	$ .05
					Pena, Tony	90T	115	$ .01	$ .04
					Pena, Tony	90TTR	90	$ .01	$ .05
					Pena, Tony	91T	375	$ .01	$ .03
					Pendleton, Jim	53T	185	$4.50	$15.00
Pavletich, Don	72T	359	$ .15	$ .50	Pendleton, Jim	54T	165	$3.60	$10.00
Paxton, Mike	78T	216	$ .02	$ .10	Pendleton, Jim	55T	15	$2.00	$6.00
Paxton, Mike	79T	122	$ .02	$ .10	Pendleton, Jim	57T	327	$4.25	$15.00
Paxton, Mike	80T	388	$ .01	$ .10	Pendleton, Jim	58T	104	$1.25	$4.25
Pazik, Mike	76T	597	$ .30	$ .85	Pendleton, Jim	59T	174	$ .75	$2.20

DON PAVLETICH

Player	Year	No.	VG	EX/MT	Player	Year	No.	VG	EX/MT
Pendleton, Jim	62T	432	$ .75	$2.50	Perez, Tony	71T	64	$ .50	$2.00
Pendleton, Terry	85T	346	$ .10	$ .50	Perez, Tony	71T	66	$ .50	$2.00
Pendleton, Terry	86T	528	$ .01	$ .04	Perez, Tony	71T	580	$1.00	$4.00
Pendleton, Terry	87T	8	$ .01	$ .04	Perez, Tony	72T	80	$ .75	$3.00
Pendleton, Terry	88T	635	$ .01	$ .04	Perez, Tony	73T	275	$ .65	$2.50
Pendleton, Terry	88TBB	53	$ .01	$ .06	Perez, Tony	74T	230	$ .50	$2.00
Pendleton, Terry	89T	375	$ .01	$ .05	Perez, Tony	75T	560	$ .35	$1.50
Pendleton, Terry	89TBB	151	$ .01	$ .06	Perez, Tony	76T	195	$ .35	$1.25
Pendleton, Terry	90T	725	$ .01	$ .04	Perez, Tony	76T	325	$ .45	$1.50
Pendleton, Terry	91T	485	$ .01	$ .03	Perez, Tony	77T	655	$ .25	$1.00
Penson, Paul	54T	236	$3.60	$10.00	Perez, Tony	78T	15	$ .05	$ .25
Pentz, Gene	77T	308	$ .05	$ .15	Perez, Tony	79T	495	$ .15	$ .50
Pentz, Gene	78T	64	$ .02	$ .10	Perez, Tony	80T	125	$ .30	$ .85
Penz, Roberto	65T	549	$2.10	$6.00	Perez, Tony	81T	575	$ .07	$ .35
Pepe, Dave	56T	154	$2.25	$6.00	Perez, Tony	82T	255	$ .06	$ .30
Pepitone, Joe	62T	596	$12.00	$36.00	Perez, Tony	82TIA	256	$ .03	$ .15
Pepitone, Joe	63T	183	$1.30	$3.00	Perez, Tony	83T	715	$ .01	$ .07
Pepitone, Joe	64T	360	$ .75	$2.20	Perez, Tony	83T	716	$ .01	$ .07
Pepitone, Joe	65T	245	$ .75	$3.00	Perez, Tony	83TTR	85	$ .20	$ .70
Pepitone, Joe	66T	79	$ .45	$1.45	Perez, Tony	84T	385	$ .05	$ .25
Pepitone, Joe	67T	340	$ .35	$1.25	Perez, Tony	84T	702	$ .06	$ .30
Pepitone, Joe	68T	195	$ .15	$ .50	Perez, Tony	84T	703	$ .02	$ .10
Pepitone, Joe	69T	589	$ .20	$ .50	Perez, Tony	84T	704	$ .03	$ .15
Pepitone, Joe	70T	598	$ .45	$1.45	Perez, Tony	84TTR	91	$ .15	$ .60
Pepitone, Joe	71T	90	$ .15	$ .50	Perez, Tony	85T	675	$ .01	$ .05
Pepitone, Joe	72T	303	$ .15	$ .50	Perez, Tony	86T	85	$ .02	$ .20
Pepitone, Joe	72TIA	304	$ .15	$ .50	Perez, Tony	86TRB	205	$ .01	$ .10
Pepitone, Joe	73T	580	$ .45	$1.45	Perkins, Broderick	79T	725	$ .02	$ .10
Pepper, Laurin	55T	147	$2.00	$6.00	Perkins, Broderick	81T	393	$ .01	$ .10
Pepper, Laurin	56T	108	$2.25	$6.00	Perkins, Broderick	82T	192	$ .01	$ .07
Peraza, Oswald	89T	297	$ .01	$ .10	Perkins, Broderick	83T	593	$ .01	$ .07
Peraza, Oswald	89TBB	219	$ .01	$ .06	Perkins, Broderick	83TTR	86	$ .02	$ .10
Perconte, Jack	81T	302	$1.25	$5.00	Perkins, Broderick	84T	212	$ .01	$ .06
Perconte, Jack	82TTR	87	$ .02	$ .10	Perkins, Broderick	85T	609	$ .01	$ .05
Perconte, Jack	83T	569	$ .01	$ .07	Perkowski, Harry	52T	142	$7.00	$20.00
Perconte, Jack	85T	172	$ .01	$ .05	Perkowski, Harry	53T	236	$12.50	$50.00
Perconte, Jack	86T	146	$ .01	$ .04	Perkowski, Harry	54T	125	$3.60	$10.00
Perez, Marty	71T	529	$ .75	$2.25	Perkowski, Harry	55T	184	$3.25	$9.00
Perez, Marty	72T	119	$ .15	$ .50	Perlman, Jon	89T	476	$ .01	$ .05
Perez, Marty	73T	144	$ .07	$ .30	Perlozzo, Sam	78T	704	$4.00	$12.00
Perez, Marty	74T	374	$ .07	$ .30	Perlozzo, Sam	79T	709	$ .02	$ .10
Perez, Marty	75T	499	$ .07	$ .30	Perranoski, Ron	61T	525	$7.00	$21.00
Perez, Marty	76T	177	$ .05	$ .20	Perranoski, Ron	62T	297	$ .45	$1.45
Perez, Marty	77T	438	$ .05	$ .15	Perranoski, Ron	63T	403	$ .45	$1.50
Perez, Marty	78T	613	$ .02	$ .10	Perranoski, Ron	64T	30	$ .30	$ .95
Perez, Melido	88TTR	83	$ .01	$ .25	Perranoski, Ron	65T	484	$ .75	$3.00
Perez, Melido	89T	786	$ .01	$ .15	Perranoski, Ron	66T	555	$5.00	$20.00
Perez, Melido	89TBB	235	$ .01	$ .06	Perranoski, Ron	67T	197	$ .30	$ .85
Perez, Melido	90T	621	$ .01	$ .04	Perranoski, Ron	68T	435	$ .30	$ .85
Perez, Melido	91T	499	$ .01	$ .03	Perranoski, Ron	69T	77	$ .30	$ .85
Perez, Mike	91T	205	$ .01	$ .10	Perranoski, Ron	70T	226	$ .15	$ .50
Perez, Pascual	81T	551	$ .50	$2.00	Perranoski, Ron	71T	475	$ .15	$ .50
Perez, Pascual	82T	383	$ .01	$ .20	Perranoski, Ron	72T	367	$ .15	$ .50
Perez, Pascual	83TTR	84	$ .02	$ .10	Perry, Bob	64T	48	$ .30	$ .95
Perez, Pascual	84T	675	$ .01	$ .06	Perry, Gaylord	62T	199	$37.50	$125.00
Perez, Pascual	85T	106	$ .01	$ .05	Perry, Gaylord	63T	169	$10.00	$30.00
Perez, Pascual	86T	491	$ .01	$ .10	Perry, Gaylord	64T	468	$10.00	$30.00
Perez, Pascual	88T	647	$ .01	$ .10	Perry, Gaylord	65T	193	$4.50	$15.00
Perez, Pascual	88TBB	196	$ .01	$ .06	Perry, Gaylord	66T	598	$75.00	$250.00
Perez, Pascual	90T	278	$ .01	$ .04	Perry, Gaylord	67T	236	$3.00	$9.00
Perez, Pascual	90TTR	91	$ .01	$ .05	Perry, Gaylord	67T	320	$3.50	$11.00
Perez, Pascuel	91T	701	$ .01	$ .03	Perry, Gaylord	68T	11	$ .75	$2.20
Perez, Pasqual	89T	73	$ .01	$ .05	Perry, Gaylord	68T	85	$2.25	$9.00
Perez, Tony	65T	581	$30.00	$95.00	Perry, Gaylord	69T	485	$2.25	$9.00
Perez, Tony	66T	72	$5.50	$17.50	Perry, Gaylord	70T	560	$2.25	$9.00
Perez, Tony	67T	476	$15.00	$60.00	Perry, Gaylord	71T	70	$ .50	$2.00
Perez, Tony	68T	130	$2.00	$8.00	Perry, Gaylord	71T	140	$1.50	$6.00
Perez, Tony	69T	295	$2.25	$8.50	Perry, Gaylord	72T	285	$1.50	$6.00
Perez, Tony	70T	63	$ .75	$2.20	Perry, Gaylord	73T	66	$ .45	$1.45
Perez, Tony	70T	380	$1.00	$4.00	Perry, Gaylord	73T	346	$ .35	$1.25

Player	Year	No.	VG	EX/MT
Perry, Gaylord	73T	400	$1.00	$4.00
Perry, Gaylord	74T	35	$ .75	$3.00
Perry, Gaylord	75T	530	$ .75	$3.00
Perry, Gaylord	76T	55	$ .65	$2.50
Perry, Gaylord	76T	204	$ .15	$ .50
Perry, Gaylord	77T	152	$ .65	$2.50
Perry, Gaylord	78T	686	$ .65	$2.25
Perry, Gaylord	79T	5	$ .06	$ .30
Perry, Gaylord	79T	321	$ .35	$1.50
Perry, Gaylord	80T	280	$ .15	$ .50
Perry, Gaylord	81T	582	$ .15	$ .60
Perry, Gaylord	81TTR	812	$ .35	$1.25
Perry, Gaylord	82T	115	$ .06	$ .30
Perry, Gaylord	82TTR	88	$ .45	$1.00
Perry, Gaylord	83T	463	$ .08	$ .40
Perry, Gaylord	83T	464	$ .01	$ .07
Perry, Gaylord	84T	4	$ .05	$ .25
Perry, Gaylord	84T	6	$ .10	$ .50
Perry, Gerald	84TTR	92	$ .05	$ .25
Perry, Gerald	85T	219	$ .01	$ .05
Perry, Gerald	86T	557	$ .01	$ .04
Perry, Gerald	87T	639	$ .01	$ .04
Perry, Gerald	88T	39	$ .01	$ .04
Perry, Gerald	88TBB	40	$ .01	$ .06
Perry, Gerald	89T	130	$ .01	$ .05
Perry, Gerald	89TBB	279	$ .01	$ .06
Perry, Gerald	90T	792	$ .01	$ .04
Perry, Gerald	90TTR	92	$ .01	$ .05
Perry, Gerald	91T	384	$ .01	$ .03
Perry, Jim	59T	542	$5.00	$15.00
Perry, Jim	60T	324	$ .45	$1.35
Perry, Jim	61T	48	$ .75	$3.00
Perry, Jim	61T	385	$ .90	$3.00
Perry, Jim	61TAS	584	$7.00	$21.00
Perry, Jim	62T	37	$ .75	$3.00
Perry, Jim	62T	405	$1.25	$4.25
Perry, Jim	63T	535	$2.10	$6.00
Perry, Jim	64T	34	$ .15	$ .50
Perry, Jim	65T	351	$ .45	$1.45
Perry, Jim	66T	283	$ .35	$1.25
Perry, Jim	67T	246	$ .15	$ .50
Perry, Jim	68T	393	$ .15	$ .50
Perry, Jim	69T	146	$ .15	$ .50
Perry, Jim	70T	70	$ .75	$3.00
Perry, Jim	70T	620	$ .75	$3.00
Perry, Jim	71T	69	$ .15	$ .50
Perry, Jim	71T	500	$ .15	$ .50
Perry, Jim	72T	220	$ .07	$ .25
Perry, Jim	72T	497	$ .15	$ .50
Perry, Jim	73T	385	$ .30	$ .85
Perry, Jim	74T	316	$ .07	$ .30
Perry, Jim	75T	263	$ .15	$ .50
Perry, Pat	87T	417	$ .01	$ .10
Perry, Pat	88T	282	$ .01	$ .04
Perry, Pat	89T	186	$ .01	$ .05
Perry, Pat	89TBB	329	$ .01	$ .06
Perry, Pat	90T	541	$ .01	$ .04
Perzanowski, Stan	76T	388	$ .05	$ .20
Pesky, Johnny	51Tbb	5	$4.50	$18.00
Pesky, Johnny	52T	15	$12.50	$45.00
Pesky, Johnny	54T	63	$3.75	$15.00
Pesky, Johnny	63T	343	$ .45	$1.50
Pesky, Johnny	64T	248	$ .30	$ .95
Peterek, Jeff	89TMLD	97	$ .01	$ .06
Peters, Frank	68T	409	$ .30	$ .85
Peters, Gary	60T	407	$ .75	$2.20
Peters, Gary	61T	303	$ .35	$1.25
Peters, Gary	63T	522	$2.10	$6.00
Peters, Gary	64T	2	$ .75	$3.00
Peters, Gary	64T	130	$ .30	$ .95

Player	Year	No.	VG	EX/MT
Peters, Gary	65T	9	$ .35	$1.25
Peters, Gary	65T	430	$ .35	$1.25
Peters, Gary	66T	111	$ .30	$ .95
Peters, Gary	67T	233	$ .45	$1.45

GARY PETERS • PITCHER

WHITE SOX

Player	Year	No.	VG	EX/MT
Peters, Gary	67T	310	$ .30	$ .85
Peters, Gary	68T	8	$ .45	$1.45
Peters, Gary	68T	210	$ .30	$ .85
Peters, Gary	68TAS	379	$ .30	$ .85
Peters, Gary	69T	34	$ .30	$ .85
Peters, Gary	70T	540	$ .15	$ .50
Peters, Gary	71T	225	$ .15	$ .50
Peters, Gary	72T	503	$ .15	$ .50
Peters, Rick	81T	177	$ .01	$ .10
Peters, Rick	82T	504	$ .01	$ .07
Peters, Rick	84T	436	$ .01	$ .06
Peters, Steve	88TTR	84	$ .01	$ .06
Peters, Steve	89T	482	$ .01	$ .10
Peterson, Adam	90T	299	$ .01	$ .10
Peterson, Adam	91T	559	$ .01	$ .03
Peterson, Cap	64T	568	$1.75	$4.50
Peterson, Cap	65T	512	$ .75	$3.00
Peterson, Cap	66T	349	$ .30	$ .95
Peterson, Cap	67T	387	$ .30	$ .95
Peterson, Cap	68T	188	$ .30	$ .85
Peterson, Cap	69T	571	$ .30	$ .95
Peterson, Fritz	66T	584	$5.00	$20.00
Peterson, Fritz	67T	495	$ .75	$3.00
Peterson, Fritz	68T	246	$ .30	$ .85
Peterson, Fritz	69T	46	$ .30	$ .85
Peterson, Fritz	70T	142	$ .15	$ .50
Peterson, Fritz	71T	460	$ .15	$ .50
Peterson, Fritz	72T	573	$ .30	$ .95
Peterson, Fritz	72TIA	574	$ .30	$ .95
Peterson, Fritz	73T	82	$ .07	$ .30
Peterson, Fritz	74T	229	$ .07	$ .30
Peterson, Fritz	75T	62	$ .07	$ .30
Peterson, Fritz	76T	255	$ .05	$ .20
Peterson, Harding	58T	322	$ .75	$3.00
Petralli, Geno	86T	296	$ .01	$ .04
Petralli, Geno	87T	388	$ .01	$ .04

Player	Year	No.	VG	EX/MT	Player	Year	No.	VG	EX/MT
Petralli, Geno	88T	589	$ .01	$ .04	Philley, Dave	60T	52	$ .45	$1.45
Petralli, Geno	89T	137	$ .01	$ .05	Philley, Dave	61T	369	$ .35	$1.25
Petralli, Geno	89TBB	12	$ .01	$ .06	Philley, Dave	62T	542	$3.95	$11.50
Petralli, Geno	90T	706	$ .01	$ .04	Phillies, Team	56T	72	$3.00	$9.00
Petralli, Geno	91T	78	$ .01	$ .03	Phillies, Team	57T	214	$2.00	$6.00
Petrocelli, Rico	65T	74	$1.00	$4.00	Phillies, Team	58T	134	$3.00	$9.00
Petrocelli, Rico	66T	298	$ .35	$1.25	Phillies, Team	59T	8	$2.00	$6.00
Petrocelli, Rico	67T	528	$ .75	$3.00	Phillies, Team	60T	302	$2.00	$6.00
Petrocelli, Rico	68T	430	$ .30	$ .95	Phillies, Team	61T	491	$2.25	$6.00
Petrocelli, Rico	69T	215	$ .30	$ .95	Phillies, Team	62T	294	$ .75	$2.00
Petrocelli, Rico	70T	680	$ .75	$2.00	Phillies, Team	63T	13	$ .75	$2.20
Petrocelli, Rico	70TAS	457	$ .15	$ .50	Phillies, Team	64T	293	$ .85	$3.50
Petrocelli, Rico	71T	340	$ .15	$ .50	Phillies, Team	65T	338	$ .75	$2.25
Petrocelli, Rico	72T	30	$ .30	$ .85	Phillies, Team	66T	463	$2.10	$6.00
Petrocelli, Rico	73T	365	$ .07	$ .30	Phillies, Team	67T	102	$ .30	$ .85
Petrocelli, Rico	74T	609	$ .07	$ .30	Phillies, Team	68T	477	$ .90	$3.00
Petrocelli, Rico	75T	356	$ .07	$ .30	Phillies, Team	70T	436	$ .45	$1.45
Petrocelli, Rico	76T	445	$ .05	$ .20	Phillies, Team	71T	268	$ .45	$1.45
Petrocelli, Rico	77T	111	$ .05	$ .15	Phillies, Team	72T	397	$ .15	$ .50
Petry, Dan	80T	373	$ .15	$ .50	Phillies, Team	73T	536	$ .90	$3.00
Petry, Dan	81T	59	$ .03	$ .15	Phillies, Team	74T	383	$ .15	$ .50
Petry, Dan	82T	211	$ .01	$ .07	Phillies, Team Checklist	75T	46	$ .15	$ .50
Petry, Dan	82T	666	$ .01	$ .07	Phillies, Team Checklist	76T	384	$ .35	$1.25
Petry, Dan	83T	261	$ .01	$ .07	Phillies, Team Checklist	77T	467	$ .15	$ .50
Petry, Dan	83T	638	$ .01	$ .07	Phillies, Team Checklist	78T	381	$ .15	$ .50
Petry, Dan	84T	147	$ .01	$ .06	Phillies, Team Checklist	79T	112	$ .05	$ .25
Petry, Dan	85T	435	$ .01	$ .05	Phillies, Team Checklist	80T	526	$ .30	$ .85
Petry, Dan	86T	540	$ .01	$ .04	Phillies, Team Checklist	81T	682	$ .02	$ .20
Petry, Dan	87T	752	$ .01	$ .04	Phillies, Team Leaders	86T	246	$ .01	$ .04
Petry, Dan	88T	78	$ .01	$ .04	Phillies, Team Leaders	87T	481	$ .01	$ .04
Petry, Dan	88TTR	85	$ .01	$ .06	Phillies, Team Leaders	88T	669	$ .01	$ .04
Petry, Dan	89TBB	178	$ .01	$ .06	Phillies, Team Leaders	89T	489	$ .01	$ .05
Petry, Dan	90T	363	$ .01	$ .04	Phillips, Adolfo	66T	32	$ .30	$ .95
Petry, Dan	90TTR	93	$ .01	$ .05	Phillips, Adolfo	67T	148	$ .30	$ .85
Pettini, Joe	81T	62	$ .01	$ .10	Phillips, Adolfo	68T	202	$ .30	$ .85
Pettini, Joe	82T	568	$ .01	$ .07	Phillips, Adolfo	69T	372	$ .30	$ .85
Pettini, Joe	83T	143	$ .01	$ .07	Phillips, Adolfo	70T	666	$ .75	$2.00
Pettini, Joe	84T	449	$ .01	$ .06	Phillips, Adolfo	71T	418	$ .15	$ .50
Pettis, Gary	84TTR	93	$ .05	$ .25	Phillips, Bubba	57T	395	$ .85	$3.50
Pettis, Gary	85T	497	$ .01	$ .05	Phillips, Bubba	58T	212	$ .75	$3.00
Pettis, Gary	86T	604	$ .01	$ .04	Phillips, Bubba	59T	187	$ .75	$2.20
Pettis, Gary	87T	278	$ .01	$ .04	Phillips, Bubba	60T	243	$ .45	$1.45
Pettis, Gary	88T	71	$ .01	$ .04	Phillips, Bubba	61T	101	$ .35	$1.25
Pettis, Gary	88TTR	86	$ .01	$ .06	Phillips, Bubba	62T	511	$ .75	$2.50
Pettis, Gary	89T	146	$ .01	$ .05	Phillips, Bubba	63T	177	$ .30	$ .95
Pettis, Gary	90T	512	$ .01	$ .04	Phillips, Bubba	64T	143	$ .30	$ .95
Pettis, Gary	90TTR	94	$ .01	$ .05	Phillips, Bubba	65T	306	$ .35	$1.25
Pettis, Gary	91T	314	$ .01	$ .03	Phillips, Dick	63T	544	$7.50	$30.00
Pevey, Marty	89TMLD	98	$ .01	$ .06	Phillips, Dick	64T	559	$1.75	$4.50
Pevey, Marty	90T	137	$ .01	$ .04	Phillips, Jack	52T	240	$7.00	$20.00
Pfeil, Bobby	70T	99	$ .15	$ .50	Phillips, Jack	57T	307	$4.25	$15.00
Pfeil, Bobby	72T	681	$ .75	$2.50	Phillips, Lefty	70T	376	$ .15	$ .50
Pfister, Dan	62T	592	$15.00	$50.00	Phillips, Lefty	71T	279	$ .15	$ .50
Pfister, Dan	63T	521	$1.00	$2.00	Phillips, Mike	74T	533	$ .07	$ .30
Pfister, Dan	64T	302	$ .30	$ .95	Phillips, Mike	75T	642	$ .07	$ .30
Phelps, Ken	85T	582	$ .01	$ .05	Phillips, Mike	76T	93	$ .05	$ .20
Phelps, Ken	86T	34	$ .01	$ .04	Phillips, Mike	77T	352	$ .05	$ .15
Phelps, Ken	87T	333	$ .01	$ .04	Phillips, Mike	78T	88	$ .02	$ .10
Phelps, Ken	88T	182	$ .01	$ .04	Phillips, Mike	79T	258	$ .02	$ .10
Phelps, Ken	88TBB	189	$ .01	$ .06	Phillips, Mike	80T	439	$ .01	$ .10
Phelps, Ken	89T	741	$ .01	$ .05	Phillips, Mike	81T	113	$ .01	$ .10
Phelps, Ken	89TBB	293	$ .01	$ .06	Phillips, Mike	81TTR	813	$ .02	$ .10
Phelps, Ken	90T	411	$ .01	$ .04	Phillips, Mike	82T	762	$ .01	$ .07
Philley, Dave	52T	226	$7.00	$21.00	Phillips, Taylor	57T	343	$4.25	$15.00
Philley, Dave	53T	64	$4.50	$15.00	Phillips, Taylor	58T	159	$ .75	$3.00
Philley, Dave	54T	159	$2.50	$10.00	Phillips, Taylor	59T	113	$ .75	$2.20
Philley, Dave	56T	222	$3.00	$9.00	Phillips, Taylor	60T	211	$ .45	$1.45
Philley, Dave	57T	124	$ .95	$3.50	Phillips, Tony	83TTR	87	$ .02	$ .10
Philley, Dave	58T	116	$ .75	$3.00	Phillips, Tony	84T	309	$ .01	$ .06
Philley, Dave	59T	92	$ .75	$2.25	Phillips, Tony	85T	444	$ .01	$ .05

Player	Year	No.	VG	EX/MT	Player	Year	No.	VG	EX/MT
Phillips, Tony	86T	29	$ .01	$ .04	Pignatano, Joe	60T	292	$ .45	$1.35
Phillips, Tony	87T	188	$ .01	$ .04	Pignatano, Joe	60T	442	$ .90	$3.00
Phillips, Tony	88T	673	$ .01	$ .04	Pignatano, Joe	61T	74	$ .35	$1.25
Phillips, Tony	89T	248	$ .01	$ .05	Pignatano, Joe	62T	247	$ .45	$1.45
Phillips, Tony	90T	702	$ .01	$ .04	Pignatano, Joe	73T	257	$ .75	$3.00
Phillips, Tony	90TTR	95	$ .01	$ .05	Pignatano, Joe	74T	179	$ .75	$3.00
Phillips, Tony	91T	583	$ .01	$ .03	Pilarcik, Al	57T	311	$4.25	$15.00
Phoebus, Tom	67T	204	$ .30	$ .85	Pilarcik, Al	58T	259	$ .75	$3.00
Phoebus, Tom	68T	97	$ .30	$ .85	Pilarcik, Al	59T	7	$ .85	$3.50
Phoebus, Tom	69T	185	$ .30	$ .85	Pilarcik, Al	60T	498	$ .90	$3.00
Phoebus, Tom	69T	532	$ .20	$ .50	Pilarcik, Al	61T	62	$ .35	$1.25
Phoebus, Tom	70T	717	$ .75	$2.00	Pillette, Duana	52T	82	$7.00	$20.00
Phoebus, Tom	71T	611	$ .35	$1.25	Pillette, Duane	53T	269	$12.50	$50.00
Phoebus, Tom	72T	477	$ .15	$ .50	Pillette, Duane	54T	107	$2.50	$10.00
Picciolo, Rob	78T	528	$ .02	$ .10	Pillette, Duane	55T	168	$5.25	$15.00
Picciolo, Rob	79T	378	$ .02	$ .10	Pilots, Team	70T	713	$3.00	$12.00
Picciolo, Rob	80T	158	$ .01	$ .10	Pina, Horacio	71T	497	$ .15	$ .50
Picciolo, Rob	81T	604	$ .01	$ .10	Pina, Horacio	72T	654	$ .30	$ .95
Picciolo, Rob	82T	293	$ .01	$ .07	Pina, Horacio	73T	138	$ .07	$ .30
Picciolo, Rob	82TTR	89	$ .02	$ .10	Pina, Horacio	74T	516	$ .07	$ .30
Picciolo, Rob	83T	476	$ .01	$ .07	Pina, Horacio	74TTR	516	$ .07	$ .30
Picciolo, Rob	84T	88	$ .01	$ .06	Pina, Horacio	75T	139	$ .07	$ .30
Picciolo, Rob	84TTR	94	$ .02	$ .10	Piniella, Lou	64T	167	$4.00	$20.00
Picciolo, Rob	85T	756	$ .01	$ .05	Piniella, Lou	68T	16	$1.00	$4.00
Picciolo, Rob	85TTR	90	$ .02	$ .10	Piniella, Lou	69T	394	$ .75	$3.25
Picciolo, Rob	86T	672	$ .01	$ .04	Piniella, Lou	70T	321	$ .75	$3.00
Piche, Ron	61T	61	$ .35	$1.25	Piniella, Lou	71T	35	$ .15	$ .50
Piche, Ron	62T	582	$3.95	$11.50	Piniella, Lou	72T	491	$ .15	$ .50
Piche, Ron	63T	179	$ .30	$ .95	Piniella, Lou	72T	580	$ .45	$1.45
Piche, Ron	65T	464	$ .75	$3.00	Piniella, Lou	73T	140	$ .15	$ .50
Pico, Jeff	88TTR	87	$ .01	$ .15	Piniella, Lou	74T	390	$ .30	$ .95
Pico, Jeff	89T	262	$ .01	$ .10	Piniella, Lou	74TTR	390	$ .30	$ .85
Pico, Jeff	90T	613	$ .01	$ .04	Piniella, Lou	75T	217	$ .15	$ .50
Pico, Jeff	91T	311	$ .01	$ .03	Piniella, Lou	76T	453	$ .30	$ .85
Pierce, Billy	51Tbb	45	$7.50	$22.50	Piniella, Lou	77T	96	$ .30	$ .85
Pierce, Billy	52T	98	$6.00	$12.50	Piniella, Lou	78T	159	$ .05	$ .25
Pierce, Billy	53T	143	$4.50	$15.00	Piniella, Lou	79T	648	$ .05	$ .20
Pierce, Billy	56T	160	$1.50	$4.50	Piniella, Lou	80T	225	$ .02	$ .15
Pierce, Billy	57T	160	$ .60	$2.50	Piniella, Lou	81T	724	$ .05	$ .20
Pierce, Billy	58T	334	$ .45	$1.50	Piniella, Lou	82T	538	$ .03	$ .15
Pierce, Billy	58T	50	$ .90	$3.50	Piniella, Lou	83T	307	$ .01	$ .07
Pierce, Billy	59T	156	$1.30	$5.00	Piniella, Lou	84T	408	$ .01	$ .06
Pierce, Billy	59T	410	$ .75	$2.20	Piniella, Lou	86TTR	86	$ .02	$ .10
Pierce, Billy	59T	466	$ .90	$3.00	Piniella, Lou	87T	168	$ .01	$ .04
Pierce, Billy	59TAS	572	$7.00	$21.00	Piniella, Lou	88T	44	$ .01	$ .04
Pierce, Billy	60T	150	$ .75	$3.00	Piniella, Lou	90TTR	96	$ .01	$ .05
Pierce, Billy	60TAS	571	$3.00	$9.00	Piniella, Lou	91T	669	$ .01	$ .03
Pierce, Bill	61T	205	$ .75	$3.00	Pinson, Vada	58T	420	$5.50	$17.50
Pierce, Bill	62T	260	$ .75	$3.00	Pinson, Vada	59T	448	$1.25	$5.00
Pierce, Bill	63T	50	$ .35	$1.25	Pinson, Vada	60T	32	$1.15	$3.50
Pierce, Bill	63T	331	$ .75	$2.20	Pinson, Vada	60T	176	$ .95	$3.50
Pierce, Bill	64T	222	$ .15	$ .50	Pinson, Vada	61T	110	$ .95	$3.50
Pierce, Jack	76T	162	$ .05	$ .20	Pinson, Vada	61T	25	$2.10	$6.00
Pierce, Tony	67T	542	$3.00	$10.00	Pinson, Vada	62T	52	$1.00	$4.00
Pierce, Tony	68T	38	$ .30	$ .85	Pinson, Vada	62T	80	$ .75	$2.00
Piersall, Jim	56T	143	$1.75	$5.00	Pinson, Vada	63T	265	$ .90	$3.00
Piersall, Jim	57T	75	$1.00	$4.00	Pinson, Vada	64T	80	$ .75	$3.00
Piersall, Jim	58T	280	$1.00	$3.00	Pinson, Vada	64T	162	$ .15	$ .50
Piersall, Jim	59T	355	$ .90	$3.00	Pinson, Vada	65T	355	$ .90	$3.00
Piersall, Jim	60T	159	$ .90	$3.00	Pinson, Vada	66T	180	$ .75	$3.00
Piersall, Jim	61T	345	$ .90	$3.00	Pinson, Vada	67T	550	$3.00	$10.00
Piersall, Jim	62T	51	$ .75	$2.20	Pinson, Vada	68T	90	$ .90	$3.00
Piersall, Jim	62T	90	$ .75	$2.20	Pinson, Vada	69T	160	$ .10	$1.00
Piersall, Jim	63T	443	$ .75	$3.00	Pinson, Vada	70T	445	$ .75	$3.00
Piersall, Jim	64T	586	$2.10	$6.00	Pinson, Vada	71T	275	$ .45	$1.45
Piersall, Jim	65T	172	$ .75	$3.00	Pinson, Vada	72T	135	$ .15	$ .50
Piersall, Jim	66T	565	$8.00	$25.00	Pinson, Vada	73T	75	$ .15	$ .50
Piersall, Jim	67T	584	$5.00	$20.00	Pinson, Vada	74T	490	$ .15	$ .50
Pignatano, Joe	58T	373	$ .75	$3.00	Pinson, Vada	75T	295	$ .30	$ .95
Pignatano, Joe	59T	16	$ .85	$3.50	Pinson, Vada	76T	415	$ .15	$ .50

Player	Year	No.	VG	EX/MT
Pirates, Team	56T	121	$4.00	$12.00
Pirates, Team	57T	161	$2.00	$9.00
Pirates, Team	58T	341	$2.00	$9.00
Pirates, Team	59T	528	$10.00	$30.00
Pirates, Team	60T	484	$5.00	$15.00
Pirates, Team	61T	554	$9.00	$35.00
Pirates, Team	62T	409	$1.75	$4.50
Pirates, Team	63T	151	$.75	$2.20
Pirates, Team	64T	373	$.75	$2.25
Pirates, Team	65T	209	$.90	$3.00
Pirates, Team	66T	404	$.65	$1.75
Pirates, Team	67T	492	$2.10	$6.00
Pirates, Team	68T	308	$.75	$3.00
Pirates, Team	70T	608	$.90	$3.00
Pirates, Team	71T	603	$1.75	$6.00
Pirates, Team	72T	1	$1.10	$3.25
Pirates, Team	73T	26	$.10	$.50
Pirates, Team	74T	626	$.15	$.50
Pirates, Team Checklist	75T	304	$.35	$1.25
Pirates, Team Checklist	76T	504	$.35	$1.25
Pirates, Team Checklist	77T	354	$.15	$.50
Pirates, Team Checklist	78T	606	$.05	$.25
Pirates, Team Checklist	79T	244	$.30	$.85
Pirates, Team Checklist	80T	551	$.05	$.25
Pirates, Team Checklist	81T	683	$.02	$.20
Pirates, Team Leaders	86T	756	$.01	$.04
Pirates, Team Leaders	87T	131	$.01	$.04
Pirates, Team Leaders	88T	231	$.01	$.04
Pirates, Team Leaders	89T	699	$.01	$.05
Pirtle, Jerry	79T	720	$.05	$.20
Pisker, Don	79T	718	$.02	$.10
Pisoni, Jim	57T	402	$.85	$3.50
Pisoni, Jim	59T	259	$.75	$2.20
Pitler, Jake	52T	395	$40.00	$140.00
Pitlock, Skip	71T	19	$.15	$.50
Pitlock, Skip	75T	579	$.07	$.30
Pittaro, Chris	85TTR	91	$.02	$.10
Pittaro, Chris	86T	393	$.01	$.04

Player	Year	No.	VG	EX/MT
Pittman, Joe	82T	119	$.01	$.07
Pittman, Joe	82TTR	90	$.02	$.10

Player	Year	No.	VG	EX/MT
Pittman, Joe	83T	346	$.01	$.07
Pizarro, Juan	57T	383	$.85	$3.50
Pizarro, Juan	59T	188	$.75	$2.20
Pizarro, Juan	60T	59	$.45	$1.45
Pizarro, Juan	61T	227	$.35	$1.25
Pizarro, Juan	62T	255	$.45	$1.45
Pizarro, Juan	63T	10	$.45	$1.45
Pizarro, Juan	63T	160	$.30	$.95
Pizarro, Juan	64T	2	$.75	$3.00
Pizarro, Juan	64T	430	$.50	$1.45
Pizarro, Juan	65T	9	$.35	$1.25
Pizarro, Juan	65T	125	$.30	$.85
Pizarro, Juan	66T	335	$.30	$.95
Pizarro, Juan	67T	602	$2.10	$6.00
Pizarro, Juan	68T	19	$.30	$.85
Pizarro, Juan	69T	498	$.30	$.85
Pizarro, Juan	71T	647	$.75	$2.50
Pizarro, Juan	72T	18	$.15	$.50
Pizzaro, Juan	62T	59	$.75	$2.20
Pladson, Gordy	81T	491	$.01	$.10
Plantier, Phil	91T	474	$.01	$.50
Plaskett, Elmo	63T	549	$1.75	$4.50
Playoff '69, A. L./Game 1	70T	199	$.35	$1.00
Playoff '69, A. L./Game 2	70T	200	$.35	$1.00
Playoff '69, A. L./Game 3	70T	201	$.35	$1.00
Playoff '69, Mets	70T	198	$.75	$3.00
Playoff '69, N.L./Game 1	70T	195	$.90	$3.00
Playoff '69, N.L./Game 2	70T	196	$.75	$3.00
Playoff '69, N.L./Game 3	70T	197	$.90	$3.00
Playoff '69, Orioles	70T	202	$.45	$1.45
Playoffs '70, A. L./Game 1	71T	195	$.45	$1.45
Playoffs '70, A. L./Game 2	71T	196	$.45	$1.45
Playoffs '70, A. L./Game 3	71T	197	$.75	$2.20
Playoffs '70, A. L./Orioles	71T	198	$.45	$1.45
Playoffs '70, N. L./Game 1	71T	199	$.45	$1.45
Playoffs '70, N. L./Game 2	71T	200	$.45	$1.45
Playoffs '70, N. L./Game 3	71T	201	$.45	$1.45
Playoffs '70, N. L./Reds	71T	202	$.75	$2.20
Playoffs '71, A. L.	72T	222	$.75	$3.00
Playoffs '71, N. L.	72T	221	$.45	$1.45
Playoffs '72, A. L.	73T	201	$.15	$.50
Playoffs '72, N. L.	73T	202	$.15	$.50
Playoffs '73, A.L.	74T	470	$.90	$3.00
Playoffs '73, N.L.	74T	471	$.15	$.50
Playoffs '75, NL & AL	76T	461	$.30	$.95
Pleis, Bill	62T	124	$.45	$1.45
Pleis, Bill	63T	293	$.45	$1.50
Pleis, Bill	64T	484	$.50	$1.45
Pleis, Bill	65T	122	$.30	$.85
Plesac, Dan	86TTR	87	$.05	$.25
Plesac, Dan	87T	279	$.10	$.50
Plesac, Dan	88T	670	$.01	$.04
Plesac, Dan	89T	740	$.01	$.05
Plesac, Dan	90T	490	$.01	$.04
Plesac, Dan	91T	146	$.01	$.03
Pless, Rance	56T	339	$1.30	$5.00
Plews, Herb	57T	169	$.95	$3.50
Plews, Herb	58T	109	$.85	$3.50
Plews, Herb	59T	373	$.75	$2.20
Plummer, Bill	73T	177	$.07	$.30
Plummer, Bill	74T	524	$.07	$.30
Plummer, Bill	75T	656	$.07	$.30
Plummer, Bill	76T	627	$.05	$.20
Plummer, Bill	77T	239	$.05	$.15
Plummer, Bill	78T	106	$.02	$.10
Plummer, Bill	79T	396	$.02	$.10
Plunk, Eric	87T	587	$.01	$.04
Plunk, Eric	88T	173	$.01	$.04
Plunk, Eric	89T	448	$.01	$.05
Plunk, Eric	90T	9	$.01	$.04

Player	Year	No.	VG	EX/MT	Player	Year	No.	VG	EX/MT
Plunk, Eric	91T	786	$ .01	$ .03	Pole, Dick	74T	596	$ .07	$ .30
Pocoroba, Biff	76T	103	$ .05	$ .20	Pole, Dick	75T	513	$ .07	$ .30
Pocoroba, Biff	77T	594	$ .05	$ .15	Pole, Dick	76T	326	$ .05	$ .20
Pocoroba, Biff	78T	296	$ .02	$ .10	Pole, Dick	77T	187	$ .05	$ .15
Pocoroba, Biff	79T	555	$ .02	$ .10	Pole, Dick	78T	233	$ .02	$ .10
Pocoroba, Biff	80T	132	$ .01	$ .10	Polidor, Gus	88T	708	$ .01	$ .04
Pocoroba, Biff	81T	326	$ .01	$ .10	Polidor, Gus	90T	313	$ .01	$ .04
Pocoroba, Biff	82T	88	$ .01	$ .07	Pollet, Howie	51Trb	7	$1.00	$6.00
Pocoroba, Biff	83T	676	$ .01	$ .07	Pollet, Howie	52T	63	$15.00	$47.50
Pocoroba, Biff	84T	438	$ .01	$ .06	Pollet, Howie	53T	83	$4.50	$15.00
Podbielan, Clarence "Bud"	52T	188	$7.00	$21.00	Pollet, Howie	54T	89	$2.50	$10.00
Podbielan, Bud	53T	237	$12.50	$50.00	Pollet, Howie	55T	76	$2.00	$6.00
Podbielan, Bud	54T	69	$7.00	$22.00	Pollet, Howie	56T	262	$1.30	$5.00
Podbielan, Bud	55T	153	$2.50	$10.00	Pollet, Howie	60T	468	$ .95	$3.50
Podbielan, Bud	56T	224	$3.00	$9.00	Polonia, Luis	87TTR	96	$ .01	$ .30
Podres, Johnny	53T	263	$75.00	$225.00	Polonia, Luis	88T	238	$ .01	$ .20
Podres, Johnny	54T	166	$7.50	$22.50	Polonia, Luis	88TBB	65	$ .01	$ .06
Podres, Johnny	55T	25	$5.50	$17.50	Polonia, Luis	89T	424	$ .01	$ .05
Podres, Johnny	56T	173	$4.75	$14.00	Polonia, Luis	90T	634	$ .01	$ .04
Podres, Johnny	57T	277	$17.50	$50.00	Polonia, Luis	90TTR	97	$ .01	$ .05
Podres, Johnny	58T	120	$ 1.50	$4.50	Polonia, Luis	91T	107	$ .01	$ .03
Podres, Johnny	59T	262	$3.00	$12.00	Poole, Jim	88TTR	88	$ .01	$ .25
Podres, Johnny	59T	495	$ .85	$3.50	Poole, Jim	89TBB	263	$ .01	$ .06
Podres, Johnny	60T	425	$ .75	$2.20	Pope, Dave	57T	249	$ .95	$3.50
Podres, Johnny	61T	109	$ .75	$2.20	Popovich, Paul	67T	536	$10.00	$30.00
Podres, Johnny	61T	207	$2.70	$8.00	Popovich, Paul	68T	266	$ .30	$ .85
Podres, Johnny	62T	280	$ .75	$2.20	Popovich, Paul	69T	47	$ .15	$ .50
Podres, Johnny	63T	150	$ .45	$1.45	Popovich, Paul	70T	258	$ .15	$ .50
Podres, Johnny	63T	412	$10.00	$30.00	Popovich, Paul	71T	726	$ .75	$2.50
Podres, Johnny	64T	580	$1.30	$5.00	Popovich, Paul	72T	512	$ .15	$ .50
Podres, Johnny	65T	387	$ .75	$3.00	Popovich, Paul	73T	309	$ .07	$ .30
Podres, Johnny	66T	468	$ .95	$3.50	Popovich, Paul	74T	14	$ .07	$ .30
					Popovich, Paul	75T	359	$ .07	$ .30
					Popowski, Eddie	73T	131	$ .15	$ .50
					Popowski, Eddie	74T	403	$ .07	$ .30
					Poquette, Tom	75T	622	$2.25	$11.00
					Poquette, Tom	77T	93	$ .05	$ .15
					Poquette, Tom	78T	357	$ .02	$ .10
					Poquette, Tom	79T	476	$ .02	$ .10
					Poquette, Tom	80T	597	$ .01	$ .10
					Poquette, Tom	81T	153	$ .01	$ .10
					Poquette, Tom	82T	657	$ .01	$ .07
					Porter, Chuck	82T	333	$ .01	$ .07
					Porter, Chuck	84T	452	$ .01	$ .06
					Porter, Chuck	85T	32	$ .01	$ .05
					Porter, Chuck	86T	292	$ .01	$ .04
					Porter, Darrell	72T	162	$ .25	$ .75
					Porter, Darrell	73T	582	$ .45	$1.45
					Porter, Darrell	74T	194	$ .07	$ .30
					Porter, Darrell	75T	52	$ .07	$ .30
					Porter, Darrell	76T	645	$ .05	$ .20
					Porter, Darrell	77T	214	$ .05	$ .15
					Porter, Darrell	78T	19	$ .02	$ .10
					Porter, Darrell	79T	571	$ .02	$ .10
					Porter, Darrell	80T	360	$ .01	$ .10
					Porter, Darrell	81T	610	$ .01	$ .10
					Porter, Darrell	81TTR	814	$ .02	$ .10
					Porter, Darrell	82T	447	$ .05	$ .20
					Porter, Darrell	82TIA	448	$ .02	$ .10
					Porter, Darrell	83T	103	$ .01	$ .07
					Porter, Darrell	84T	285	$ .01	$ .06
					Porter, Darrell	85T	525	$ .01	$ .05
Podres, Johnny	67T	284	$ .30	$ .85	Porter, Darrell	86T	757	$ .01	$ .04
Podres, Johnny	69T	659	$ .35	$1.25	Porter, Darrell	86TTR	88	$ .02	$ .10
Podres, Johnny	73T	12	$ .30	$ .85	Porter, Darrell	87T	689	$ .01	$ .04
Poholsky, Tom	52T	242	$7.00	$20.00	Porter, J. W.	53T	211	$4.50	$15.00
Poholsky, Tom	54T	142	$2.50	$10.00	Porter, J. W.	55T	49	$2.00	$6.00
Poholsky, Tom	56T	196	$3.00	$9.00	Porter, J. W.	58T	32	$ .85	$3.50
Poholsky, Tom	57T	235	$ .95	$3.50	Porter, J. W.	59T	246	$ .75	$2.20
Pointer, Aaron	67T	564	$2.10	$6.00	Porterfield, Bob	52T	301	$12.00	$40.00

Player	Year	No.	VG	EX/MT
Porterfield, Bob	53T	108	$4.50	$15.00
Porterfield, Bob	56T	248	$3.00	$9.00
Porterfield, Bob	57T	118	$ .95	$3.50
Porterfield, Bob	58T	344	$ .75	$3.00
Porterfield, Bob	59T	181	$ .75	$2.20
Portocarrero, Arnold	54T	214	$2.50	$10.00
Portocarrero, Arnold	55T	77	$2.00	$6.00
Portocarrero, Arnold	56T	53	$2.25	$6.00
Portocarrero, Arnie	58T	465	$ .75	$2.20
Portocarrero, Arnie	59T	98	$ .85	$3.50
Portocarrero, Arnie	60T	254	$ .45	$1.45
Portugal, Mark	87T	419	$ .01	$ .10
Portugal, Mark	89T	46	$ .01	$ .05
Portugal, Mark	90T	253	$ .01	$ .04
Portugal, Mark	91T	647	$ .01	$ .03
Posada, Leo	61T	39	$ .35	$1.25
Posada, Leo	62T	168	$ .45	$1.45
Posedel, Bill	52T	361	$40.00	$140.00
Posedel, Bill	60T	469	$ .95	$3.50
Post, Wally	52T	151	$7.00	$20.00
Post, Wally	56T	158	$2.25	$6.00
Post, Wally	57T	157	$ .95	$3.50
Post, Wally	58T	387	$ .75	$3.00
Post, Wally	59T	398	$ .75	$2.20
Post, Wally	60T	13	$ .45	$1.45
Post, Wally	61T	378	$ .75	$3.00
Post, Wally	62T	148	$ .45	$1.45
Post, Wally	63T	462	$2.50	$6.50
Post, Wally	64T	253	$ .30	$ .95
Powell, "Boog" John	62T	99	$3.75	$12.50
Powell, Boog	63T	398	$2.50	$10.00
Powell, Boog	64T	89	$1.00	$4.00
Powell, Boog	65T	3	$3.00	$12.00
Powell, Boog	65T	560	$2.50	$10.00
Powell, Boog	66T	167	$ .75	$3.00
Powell, Boog	67T	230	$ .75	$2.20
Powell, Boog	67T	241	$ .75	$3.00
Powell, Boog	67T	243	$ .75	$3.00
Powell, Boog	67T	521	$ .90	$3.00
Powell, Boog	68T	381	$ .50	$2.00
Powell, Boog	69T	15	$ .15	$ .50
Powell, Boog	70T	64	$ .50	$1.50
Powell, Boog	70T	410	$ .75	$2.50
Powell, Boog	70TAS	451	$ .25	$1.00
Powell, Boog	71T	63	$ .15	$ .50
Powell, Boog	71T	700	$2.50	$10.00
Powell, Boog	72T	250	$ .25	$1.00
Powell, Boog	73T	325	$ .25	$1.00
Powell, Boog	74T	460	$ .15	$ .75
Powell, Boog	75T	208	$ .15	$ .75
Powell, Boog	75T	625	$ .15	$ .50
Powell, Boog	76T	45	$ .08	$ .30
Powell, Boog	77T	206	$ .30	$ .95
Powell, Dennis	87T	47	$ .01	$ .04
Powell, Dennis	88T	453	$ .01	$ .04
Powell, Dennis	89TTR	97	$ .01	$ .06
Powell, Grover	64T	113	$ .30	$ .95
Powell, Hosken	79T	656	$ .02	$ .10
Powell, Hosken	80T	471	$ .01	$ .10
Powell, Hosken	81T	137	$ .01	$ .10
Powell, Hosken	82T	584	$ .01	$ .07
Powell, Hosken	82TTR	91	$ .02	$ .10
Powell, Hosken	83T	77	$ .01	$ .07
Powell, Leroy	56T	144	$2.25	$6.00
Power, Ted	84T	554	$ .01	$ .06
Power, Ted	85T	342	$ .01	$ .05
Power, Ted	86T	108	$ .01	$ .04
Power, Ted	87T	437	$ .01	$ .04
Power, Ted	88T	236	$ .01	$ .04
Power, Ted	88TTR	89	$ .01	$ .06

Player	Year	No.	VG	EX/MT
Power, Ted	89T	777	$ .01	$ .05
Power, Ted	90T	59	$ .01	$ .04
Power, Ted	91T	621	$ .01	$ .03
Power, Vic	54T	52	$7.00	$22.00
Power, Vic	55T	30	$2.00	$6.00
Power, Vic	56T	67	$2.25	$6.00
Power, Vic	57T	167	$ .95	$3.50
Power, Vic	58T	406	$ .75	$3.00
Power, Vic	59T	229	$ .75	$2.20
Power, Vic	60T	75	$ .45	$1.45
Power, Vic	61T	255	$ .35	$1.25
Power, Vic	62T	445	$ .75	$2.50
Power, Vic	63T	40	$ .30	$ .95
Power, Vic	64T	355	$ .30	$ .95
Power, Vic	65T	442	$ .35	$1.25

VIC POWER 1b-inf

Player	Year	No.	VG	EX/MT
Power, Vic	66T	192	$ .30	$ .95
Powers, John	58T	432	$ .75	$3.00
Powers, John	59T	489	$ .75	$2.20
Powers, Johnny	60T	422	$ .75	$2.20
Pramesa, John	52T	105	$7.00	$20.00
Presko, Joe	52T	220	$7.00	$20.00
Presko, Joe	54T	135	$2.50	$10.00
Presley, Jim	85TTR	92	$ .45	$1.45
Presley, Jim	86T	598	$ .04	$ .40
Presley, Jim	87T	45	$ .01	$ .10
Presley, Jim	88T	285	$ .01	$ .10
Presley, Jim	88TBB	90	$ .01	$ .06
Presley, Jim	89T	112	$ .01	$ .05
Presley, Jim	89TBB	75	$ .01	$ .06
Presley, Jim	90T	346	$ .01	$ .04
Presley, Jim	90TTR	98	$ .01	$ .05
Presley, Jim	91T	643	$ .01	$ .03
Price, Jimmie	67T	123	$ .30	$ .85
Price, Jimmie	68T	226	$ .30	$ .85
Price, Jimmie	69T	472	$ .30	$ .85
Price, Jimmie	70T	129	$ .15	$ .50
Price, Jimmie	71T	444	$ .15	$ .50
Price, Joe	81T	258	$ .01	$ .10
Price, Joe	82T	492	$ .01	$ .07
Price, Joe	83T	191	$ .01	$ .07

Player	Year	No.	VG	EX/MT
Price, Joe	84T	686	$ .01	$ .06
Price, Joe	85T	82	$ .01	$ .05
Price, Joe	86T	523	$ .01	$ .04
Price, Joe	87T	332	$ .01	$ .04
Price, Joe	88T	786	$ .01	$ .04
Price, Joe	89T	217	$ .01	$ .05
Price, Joe	90T	473	$ .01	$ .04
Price, Joe	91T	127	$ .01	$ .03
Priddy, Bob	64T	74	$ .30	$ .95
Priddy, Bob	65T	482	$ .75	$3.00
Priddy, Bob	66T	572	$5.00	$20.00
Priddy, Bob	67T	26	$ .30	$ .85
Priddy, Bob	68T	391	$ .30	$ .85
Priddy, Bob	69T	248	$ .30	$ .95
Priddy, Bob	70T	687	$ .75	$2.00
Priddy, Bob	71T	147	$ .15	$ .50
Priddy, Gerry (Jerry)	51Tbb	46	$7.50	$22.50
Priddy, Jerry	52T	28	$15.00	$47.50
Priddy, Jerry	53T	113	$4.50	$15.00
Prince, Tom	89T	453	$ .01	$ .05
Pritchard, Buddy	58T	151	$ .75	$3.00
Proctor, Jim	60T	141	$ .45	$1.45
Proly, Mike	79T	514	$ .02	$ .10
Proly, Mike	80T	399	$ .01	$ .10
Proly, Mike	81T	83	$ .01	$ .10
Proly, Mike	81TTR	815	$ .02	$ .10
Proly, Mike	82T	183	$ .01	$ .07
Proly, Mike	82TTR	92	$ .02	$ .10
Proly, Mike	83T	597	$ .01	$ .07
Proly, Mike	84T	437	$ .01	$ .06
Pruitt, Ron	77T	654	$ .05	$ .15
Pruitt, Ron	78T	198	$ .02	$ .10
Pruitt, Ron	79T	226	$ .02	$ .10
Pruitt, Ron	80T	13	$ .01	$ .10
Pruitt, Ron	81T	442	$ .01	$ .10
Pryor, Greg	79T	559	$ .02	$ .10
Pryor, Greg	80T	164	$ .01	$ .10
Pryor, Greg	81T	608	$ .01	$ .10
Pryor, Greg	82T	76	$ .01	$ .07
Pryor, Greg	82TTR	93	$ .02	$ .10
Pryor, Greg	83T	418	$ .01	$ .07
Pryor, Greg	84T	317	$ .01	$ .06
Pryor, Greg	85T	188	$ .01	$ .05
Pryor, Greg	86T	773	$ .01	$ .04
Pryor, Greg	87T	761	$ .01	$ .04
Puckett, Kirby	85T	536	$3.50	$14.00
Puckett, Kirby	86T	329	$ .65	$2.50
Puckett, Kirby	87T	450	$ .15	$ .65
Puckett, Kirby	87TAS	611	$ .01	$ .10
Puckett, Kirby	88T	120	$ .01	$ .20
Puckett, Kirby	88TAS	391	$ .01	$ .10
Puckett, Kirby	88TBB	36	$ .05	$ .30
Puckett, Kirby	89T	650	$ .01	$ .20
Puckett, Kirby	89TAS	403	$ .01	$ .10
Puckett, Kirby	89TBB	167	$ .01	$ .25
Puckett, Kirby	90T	700	$ .01	$ .20
Puckett, Kirby	90TAS	391	$ .01	$ .10
Puckett, Kirby	91T	300	$ .01	$ .10
Puhl, Terry	78T	553	$ .05	$ .20
Puhl, Terry	79T	617	$ .02	$ .10
Puhl, Terry	80T	147	$ .01	$ .10
Puhl, Terry	81T	411	$ .01	$ .10
Puhl, Terry	82T	277	$ .01	$ .07
Puhl, Terry	83T	39	$ .01	$ .07
Puhl, Terry	84T	383	$ .01	$ .06
Puhl, Terry	85T	613	$ .01	$ .05
Puhl, Terry	86T	763	$ .01	$ .04
Puhl, Terry	87T	693	$ .01	$ .04
Puhl, Terry	88T	587	$ .01	$ .04
Puhl, Terry	89T	119	$ .01	$ .05

Player	Year	No.	VG	EX/MT
Puhl, Terry	90T	494	$ .01	$ .04
Pujols, Luis	79T	139	$ .02	$ .10
Pujols, Luis	81T	313	$ .01	$ .10
Pujols, Luis	82T	582	$ .01	$ .07
Pujols, Luis	83T	752	$ .01	$ .07
Pujols, Luis	84T	446	$ .01	$ .06
Puleo, Charlie	82TTR	94	$ .02	$ .10

Player	Year	No.	VG	EX/MT
Puleo, Charlie	83T	549	$ .01	$ .07
Puleo, Charlie	83TTR	88	$ .02	$ .10
Puleo, Charlie	84T	273	$ .01	$ .06
Puleo, Charlie	88T	179	$ .01	$ .04
Puleo, Charlie	89T	728	$ .01	$ .05
Pulido, Al	87T	642	$ .01	$ .04
Purdin, John	65T	331	$ .35	$1.25
Purdin, John	68T	336	$ .30	$ .85
Purdin, John	69T	161	$ .30	$ .85
Purdin, John	71T	748	$ .75	$2.50
Purkey, Bob	54T	202	$2.50	$10.00
Purkey, Bob	55T	118	$2.00	$6.00
Purkey, Bob	57T	368	$ .85	$3.50
Purkey, Bob	58T	311	$ .75	$3.00
Purkey, Bob	59T	506	$ .75	$2.20
Purkey, Bob	60T	4	$ .45	$1.45
Purkey, Bob	61T	9	$ .35	$1.25
Purkey, Bob	62T	120	$ .45	$1.45
Purkey, Bob	62T	263	$ .75	$3.00
Purkey, Bob	63T	5	$1.00	$4.00
Purkey, Bob	63T	7	$ .45	$1.45
Purkey, Bob	63T	350	$ .45	$1.50
Purkey, Bob	64T	480	$ .50	$1.45
Purkey, Bob	65T	214	$ .35	$1.25
Purkey, Bob	66T	551	$4.00	$11.50
Putnam, Eddy	80T	59	$ .01	$ .10
Putnam, Pat	78T	706	$ .02	$ .10
Putnam, Pat	79T	713	$ .05	$ .20
Putnam, Pat	80T	22	$ .01	$ .10
Putnam, Pat	81T	498	$ .01	$ .10
Putnam, Pat	82T	149	$ .01	$ .07
Putnam, Pat	83TTR	89	$ .02	$ .10
Putnam, Pat	84T	336	$ .01	$ .06
Putnam, Pat	84T	636	$ .01	$ .06

Player	Year	No.	VG	EX/MT	Player	Year	No.	VG	EX/MT
Putnam, Pat	85T	535	$ .01	$ .05	Quirk, Jamie	79T	26	$ .02	$ .10
Pyburn, Jim	57T	276	$4.25	$15.00	Quirk, Jamie	80T	248	$ .01	$ .10
Pyznarski, Tim	87T	429	$ .01	$ .10	Quirk, Jamie	81T	507	$ .01	$ .10
Qualls, Jim	69T	602	$ .30	$ .95	Quirk, Jamie	82T	173	$ .01	$ .07
Qualls, Jim	70T	192	$ .15	$ .50	Quirk, Jamie	83T	264	$ .01	$ .07
Qualls, Jim	71T	731	$ .75	$2.50	Quirk, Jamie	83TTR	90	$ .02	$ .10
Qualters, Tom	54T	174	$2.50	$10.00	Quirk, Jamie	84T	671	$ .01	$ .06
Qualters, Tom	55T	33	$2.00	$6.00	Quirk, Jamie	87T	354	$ .01	$ .04
Qualters, Tom	58T	453	$ .75	$2.20	Quirk, Jamie	88T	477	$ .01	$ .04
Qualters, Tom	59T	341	$ .75	$2.20	Quirk, Jamie	89T	702	$ .01	$ .05
Queen, Mel	64T	33	$ .30	$ .95	Quirk, Jamie	91T	132	$ .01	$ .03
Queen, Mel	66T	556	$3.50	$10.00	Quisenberry, Dan	80T	667	$ .30	$1.50
Queen, Mel	67T	374	$ .30	$ .95	Quisenberry, Dan	81T	493	$ .05	$ .25
Queen, Mel	68T	283	$ .30	$ .85	Quisenberry, Dan	81T	8	$ .01	$ .10
Queen, Mel	69T	81	$ .30	$ .85	Quisenberry, Dan	82T	264	$ .03	$ .15
Queen, Mel	71T	736	$ .75	$2.50	Quisenberry, Dan	83T	155	$ .01	$ .10
Queen, Mel	72T	196	$ .15	$ .50	Quisenberry, Dan	83T	708	$ .01	$ .07
Quilici, Frank	66T	207	$ .30	$ .95	Quisenberry, Dan	83TAS	396	$ .01	$ .07
Quilici, Frank	68T	557	$ .35	$1.25	Quisenberry, Dan	84T	3	$ .02	$ .10
Quilici, Frank	69T	356	$ .30	$ .85	Quisenberry, Dan	84T	138	$ .02	$ .10
Quilici, Frank	70T	572	$ .30	$ .95	Quisenberry, Dan	84T	570	$ .02	$ .10
Quilici, Frank	71T	141	$ .15	$ .50	Quisenberry, Dan	84T	718	$ .01	$ .06
Quilici, Frank	73T	49	$ .30	$ .85	Quisenberry, Dan	84TAS	407	$ .01	$ .06
					Quisenberry, Dan	85T	270	$ .01	$ .05
					Quisenberry, Dan	85TAS	711	$ .01	$ .05
					Quisenberry, Dan	86T	50	$ .01	$ .04
					Quisenberry, Dan	86TAS	722	$ .01	$ .04
					Quisenberry, Dan	87T	714	$ .01	$ .10
					Quisenberry, Dan	88T	195	$ .01	$ .10
					Quisenberry, Dan	89T	612	$ .01	$ .05
					Quisenberry, Dan	90T	312	$ .01	$ .04
					Rabb, John	84T	228	$ .01	$ .06
					Rabb, John	85T	696	$ .01	$ .05
					Rabe, Charley	58T	376	$ .75	$3.00
					Radatz, Dick	62T	591	$8.00	$22.50
					Radatz, Dick	63T	363	$ .45	$1.50
					Radatz, Dick	64T	170	$ .30	$ .95
					Radatz, Dick	65T	295	$ .35	$1.25
					Radatz, Dick	66T	475	$ .75	$2.50
					Radatz, Dick	67T	174	$ .30	$ .85
					Radatz, Dick	69T	663	$ .30	$ .95
					Rader, Dave	72T	232	$ .15	$ .50
					Rader, Dave	73T	121	$ .07	$ .30
					Rader, Dave	74T	213	$ .07	$ .30
					Rader, Dave	75T	31	$ .07	$ .30
					Rader, Dave	76T	54	$ .05	$ .20
					Rader, Dave	77T	427	$ .05	$ .15
					Rader, Dave	78T	563	$ .02	$ .10
					Rader, Dave	79T	693	$ .02	$ .10
					Rader, Dave	80T	296	$ .01	$ .10
					Rader, Dave	81T	378	$ .01	$ .10
Quilici, Frank	74T	447	$ .07	$ .30	Rader, Doug	67T	412	$ .30	$ .95
Quinones, Luis	87T	362	$ .01	$ .10	Rader, Doug	68T	332	$ .30	$ .85
Quinones, Luis	88T	667	$ .01	$ .04	Rader, Doug	69T	119	$ .30	$ .85
Quinones, Luis	90T	176	$ .01	$ .04	Rader, Doug	70T	355	$ .15	$ .50
Quinones, Luis	91T	581	$ .01	$ .03	Rader, Doug	71T	425	$ .15	$ .50
Quinones, Rey	86TTR	89	$ .05	$ .20	Rader, Doug	72T	536	$ .30	$ .95
Quinones (nez), Rey	87T	561	$ .01	$ .10	Rader, Doug	73T	76	$ .07	$ .30
Quinones, Rey	88T	358	$ .01	$ .04	Rader, Doug	74T	395	$ .07	$ .30
Quinones, Rey	89T	246	$ .01	$ .05	Rader, Doug	75T	165	$ .07	$ .30
Quinones, Rey	89TTR	98	$ .01	$ .06	Rader, Doug	76T	44	$ .05	$ .20
Quintana, Carlos	89T	704	$ .01	$ .30	Rader, Doug	76TTR	44	$ .05	$ .20
Quintana, Carlos	89TBB	142	$ .01	$ .06	Rader, Doug	77T	9	$ .05	$ .15
Quintana, Carlos	90T	18	$ .01	$ .10	Rader, Doug	78T	651	$ .02	$ .10
Quintana, Carlos	91T	206	$ .01	$ .03	Rader, Doug	83TTR	91	$ .02	$ .10
Quirk, Art	62T	591	$8.00	$22.50	Rader, Doug	84T	412	$ .01	$ .06
Quirk, Art	63T	522	$2.10	$6.00	Rader, Doug	85T	519	$ .01	$ .05
Quirk, Jamie	76T	598	$ .05	$ .20	Rader, Doug	89TTR	99	$ .01	$ .06
Quirk, Jamie	77T	463	$ .05	$ .15	Rader, Doug	90T	51	$ .01	$ .04
Quirk, Jamie	78T	95	$ .02	$ .10	Rader, Doug	91T	231	$ .01	$ .03

MINNESOTA — MANAGER

• COACHES •

Ralph Rowe — Bob Rodgers — Vern Morgan

FRANK QUILICI — TWINS

TOPPS

Player	Year	No.	VG	EX/MT	Player	Year	No.	VG	EX/MT
Radinsky, Scott	90TTR	99	$ .01	$ .20	Ramos, Domingo	85T	349	$ .01	$ .05
Radinsky, Scott	91T	299	$ .01	$ .15	Ramos, Domingo	86T	462	$ .01	$ .04
Raffensberger, Ken	52T	118	$7.00	$20.00	Ramos, Domingo	87T	641	$ .01	$ .04
Raffensberger, Ken	53T	276	$12.50	$50.00	Ramos, Domingo	88T	206	$ .01	$ .04
Raffensberger, Ken	54T	46	$2.00	$9.00	Ramos, Domingo	90T	37	$ .01	$ .04
Ragland, Tom	72T	334	$ .15	$ .50	Ramos, Domingo	91T	541	$ .01	$ .03
Ragland, Tom	74T	441	$ .07	$ .30	Ramos, Pedro	56T	49	$2.25	$6.00
Raich, Eric	76T	484	$ .05	$ .20	Ramos, Pedro	57T	326	$4.25	$15.00
Raich, Eric	77T	62	$ .05	$ .15	Ramos, Pedro	58T	331	$ .75	$3.00
Raines, Larry	58T	243	$ .75	$3.00	Ramos, Pedro	59T	291	$ .75	$2.20
Raines, Tim	81T	479	$2.50	$10.00	Ramos, Pedro	59T	78	$ .85	$3.50
Raines, Tim	81TTR	816	$2.50	$10.00	Ramos, Pedro	60T	175	$ .45	$1.45
Raines, Tim	82T	164	$ .25	$1.00	Ramos, Pedro	61T	50	$ .75	$2.20
Raines, Tim	82T	70	$ .75	$3.00	Ramos, Pedro	61T	528	$7.00	$21.00
Raines, Tim	82THL	3	$ .05	$ .75	Ramos, Pedro	62T	485	$ .75	$2.50
Raines, Tim	83T	595	$ .10	$1.00	Ramos, Pedro	63T	14	$ .30	$ .95
Raines, Tim	83T	704	$ .15	$ .75	Ramos, Pedro	64T	562	$1.75	$4.50
Raines, Tim	83TAS	403	$ .05	$ .25	Ramos, Pedro	65T	13	$ .30	$ .85
Raines, Tim	84T	134	$ .10	$ .50	Ramos, Pedro	66T	439	$ .30	$ .95
Raines, Tim	84T	370	$ .10	$ .50	Ramos, Pedro	67T	187	$ .30	$ .85
Raines, Tim	84TAS	390	$ .05	$ .25	Ramos, Roberto	81T	479	$2.50	$10.00
Raines, Tim	85T	630	$ .05	$ .25	Ramos, Roberto	82T	354	$ .01	$ .07
Raines, Tim	86T	280	$ .03	$ .25	Ramsdell, Willard	52T	114	$7.00	$20.00
Raines, Tim	87T	30	$ .07	$ .30	Ramsey, Mike	81T	366	$ .01	$ .10
Raines, Tim	88T	720	$ .01	$ .15	Ramsey, Mike	82T	574	$ .01	$ .07
Raines, Tim	88TAS	403	$ .01	$ .10	Ramsey, Mike	83T	128	$ .01	$ .07
Raines, Tim	88TBB	116	$ .01	$ .15	Ramsey, Mike	84T	467	$ .01	$ .06
Raines, Tim "Rock"	89T	560	$ .01	$ .10	Ramsey, Mike	85T	62	$ .01	$ .05
Raines, Rock	89TBB	73	$ .01	$ .15	Rand, Dick	58T	218	$ .75	$3.00
Raines, Rock	90T	180	$ .01	$ .10	Randall, Bob	77T	578	$ .05	$ .15
Raines, Rock	91T	360	$ .01	$ .03	Randall, Bob	78T	363	$ .02	$ .10
Rainey, Chuck	80T	662	$ .01	$ .10	Randall, Bob	79T	58	$ .02	$ .10
Rainey, Chuck	81T	199	$ .01	$ .10	Randall, Bob	80T	162	$ .01	$ .10
Rainey, Chuck	82T	522	$ .01	$ .07	Randle, Lenny	72T	737	$ .75	$2.50
Rainey, Chuck	83T	56	$ .01	$ .07	Randle, Lenny	73T	378	$ .07	$ .30
Rainey, Chuck	83TTR	92	$ .02	$ .10	Randle, Len	74T	446	$ .07	$ .30
Rainey, Chuck	84T	334	$ .01	$ .06	Randle, Len	75T	259	$ .07	$ .30
Rajsich, Dave	79T	710	$ .05	$ .20	Randle, Len	76T	31	$ .05	$ .20
Rajsich, Dave	80T	548	$ .01	$ .10	Randle, Len	77T	196	$ .05	$ .15
Rajsich, Gary	83T	317	$ .01	$ .07	Randle, Len	78T	544	$ .02	$ .10
Rakow, Ed	60T	551	$2.50	$10.00	Randle, Len	79T	454	$ .02	$ .10
Rakow, Ed	61T	147	$ .35	$1.25	Randle, Lenny	81T	692	$ .01	$ .10
Rakow, Ed	62T	342	$ .45	$1.45	Randle, Lenny	81TTR	817	$ .02	$ .10
Rakow, Ed	63T	82	$ .30	$ .95	Randle, Lenny	82T	312	$ .01	$ .07
Rakow, Ed	64T	491	$ .50	$1.45	Randolph, Willie	76T	592	$1.25	$5.00
Rakow, Ed	65T	454	$ .75	$3.00	Randolph, Willie	76TTR	592	$ .50	$2.00
Ramazzotti, Bob	52T	184	$7.00	$20.00	Randolph, Willie	77T	359	$ .15	$ .50
Ramirez, Allan	84T	347	$ .01	$ .06	Randolph, Willie	78T	620	$ .05	$ .20
Ramirez, Mario	84T	94	$ .01	$ .06	Randolph, Willie	79T	250	$ .02	$ .10
Ramirez, Mario	85T	427	$ .01	$ .05	Randolph, Willie	80T	460	$ .01	$ .10
Ramirez, Mario	86T	262	$ .01	$ .04	Randolph, Willie	81T	60	$ .01	$ .10
Ramirez, Milt	71T	702	$ .75	$2.50	Randolph, Willie	82T	569	$ .01	$ .07
Ramirez, Orlando	77T	131	$ .05	$ .15	Randolph, Willie	82TAS	548	$ .01	$ .07
Ramirez, Rafael	81T	192	$ .05	$ .20	Randolph, Willie	82TIA	570	$ .01	$ .07
Ramirez, Rafael	82T	536	$ .01	$ .07	Randolph, Willie	83T	140	$ .01	$ .07
Ramirez, Rafael	83T	439	$ .01	$ .07	Randolph, Willie	84T	360	$ .01	$ .06
Ramirez, Rafael	84T	234	$ .01	$ .06	Randolph, Willie	85T	765	$ .01	$ .05
Ramirez, Rafael	85T	647	$ .01	$ .05	Randolph, Willie	86T	455	$ .01	$ .04
Ramirez, Rafael	86T	107	$ .01	$ .04	Randolph, Willie	87T	701	$ .01	$ .04
Ramirez, Rafael	87T	76	$ .01	$ .04	Randolph, Willie	88T	210	$ .01	$ .04
Ramirez, Rafael	88T	379	$ .01	$ .04	Randolph, Willie	88TAS	387	$ .01	$ .04
Ramirez, Rafael	88TTR	90	$ .01	$ .06	Randolph, Willie	88TBB	76	$ .01	$ .06
Ramirez, Rafael	89T	749	$ .01	$ .05	Randolph, Willie	89T	635	$ .01	$ .05
Ramirez, Rafael	89TBB	268	$ .01	$ .06	Randolph, Willie	89TBB	244	$ .01	$ .06
Ramirez, Rafael	90T	558	$ .01	$ .04	Randolph, Willie	89TTR	100	$ .01	$ .06
Ramirez, Rafael	91T	423	$ .01	$ .03	Randolph, Willie	90T	25	$ .01	$ .04
Ramos, Bobby	83TTR	93	$ .02	$ .10	Randolph, Willie	90TTR	100	$ .01	$ .05
Ramos, Bobby	84T	32	$ .01	$ .06	Randolph, Willie	91T	525	$ .01	$ .03
Ramos, Bobby	85T	407	$ .01	$ .05	Ranew, Merritt	62T	156	$ .45	$1.45
Ramos, Domingo	84T	194	$ .01	$ .06	Ranew, Merritt	64T	78	$ .30	$ .95

Player	Year	No.	VG	EX/MT	Player	Year	No.	VG	EX/MT
Ranew, Merritt	66T	62	$ .35	$1.25	Rau, Doug	78T	641	$ .02	$ .10
Rangers, Team	72T	668	$ .80	$2.50	Rau, Doug	79T	347	$ .02	$ .10
Rangers, Team	73T	7	$ .35	$1.25	Rau, Doug	80T	527	$ .01	$ .10
Rangers, Team	74T	184	$ .15	$ .50	Rau, Doug	81T	174	$ .01	$ .10
Rangers, Team Checklist	75T	511	$ .15	$ .50	Rau, Doug	81TTR	818	$ .02	$ .10
Rangers, Team Checklist	76T	172	$ .15	$ .50	Rautzhan, Lance	78T	709	$ .02	$ .10
Rangers, Team Checklist	77T	428	$ .15	$ .50	Rautzhan, Lance	79T	373	$ .02	$ .10
Rangers, Team Checklist	78T	659	$ .05	$ .25	Rawley, Shane	79T	74	$ .20	$ .75
Rangers, Team Checklist	79T	499	$ .05	$ .25	Rawley, Shane	80T	723	$ .01	$ .10
Rangers, Team Checklist	80T	41	$ .05	$ .25	Rawley, Shane	81T	423	$ .01	$ .10
Rangers, Team Checklist	81T	673	$ .02	$ .20	Rawley, Shane	82T	197	$ .01	$ .07
Rangers, Team Leaders	86T	666	$ .01	$ .04	Rawley, Shane	82TTR	95	$ .02	$ .10
Rangers, Team Leaders	87T	656	$ .01	$ .04	Rawley, Shane	83T	592	$ .01	$ .07
Rangers, Team Leaders	88T	201	$ .01	$ .04	Rawley, Shane	84T	254	$ .01	$ .06
Rangers, Team Leaders	89T	729	$ .01	$ .05	Rawley, Shane	85T	636	$ .01	$ .05
Rapp, Vern	78T	324	$ .02	$ .10	Rawley, Shane	86T	361	$ .01	$ .04
Rapp, Vern	84TTR	95	$ .02	$ .10	Rawley, Shane	87T	771	$ .01	$ .04
Rasmussen, Dennis	85T	691	$ .05	$ .25	Rawley, Shane	88T	66	$ .01	$ .04
Rasmussen, Dennis	86T	301	$ .01	$ .04	Rawley, Shane	88TAS	406	$ .01	$ .04
Rasmussen, Dennis	87T	555	$ .01	$ .04	Rawley, Shane	89T	494	$ .01	$ .05
Rasmussen, Dennis	88T	135	$ .01	$ .10	Rawley, Shane	89TTR	101	$ .01	$ .06
Rasmussen, Dennis	88TTR	91	$ .01	$ .06	Rawley, Shane	90T	101	$ .01	$ .04
Rasmussen, Dennis	89T	32	$ .01	$ .05	Ray, Jim	68T	539	$ .35	$1.25
Rasmussen, Dennis	90T	449	$ .01	$ .04	Ray, Jim	69T	257	$ .30	$ .95
Rasmussen, Dennis	91T	774	$ .01	$ .03	Ray, Jim	70T	113	$ .15	$ .50
Rasmussen, "Eric" Harry	76T	182	$ .05	$ .20	Ray, Jim	71T	242	$ .15	$ .50
					Ray, Jim	72T	603	$ .30	$ .95
					Ray, Jim	73T	313	$ .07	$ .30
					Ray, Jim	74T	458	$ .07	$ .30
					Ray, Jim	74TTR	458	$ .07	$ .30
					Ray, Jim	75T	89	$ .07	$ .30
					Ray, Johnny	82T	291	$ .25	$1.00
					Ray, Johnny	82TTR	96	$ .25	$1.00
					Ray, Johnnie (y)	83T	149	$ .03	$ .15
					Ray, Johnny	84T	537	$ .02	$ .10
					Ray, Johnny	84TAS	387	$ .01	$ .06
					Ray, Johnny	85T	96	$ .01	$ .10
					Ray, Johnny	86T	615	$ .01	$ .10
					Ray, Johnny	87T	747	$ .01	$ .04
					Ray, Johnny	88T	115	$ .01	$ .04
					Ray, Johnny	88TBB	97	$ .01	$ .06
					Ray, Johnny	89T	455	$ .01	$ .05
					Ray, Johnny	89TBB	7	$ .01	$ .06
					Ray, Johnny	90T	334	$ .01	$ .04
					Ray, Johnny	91T	273	$ .01	$ .03
					Raydon, Curt	59T	305	$ .75	$2.20
					Raydon, Curt	60T	49	$ .45	$1.45
					Rayford, Floyd	81T	399	$ .50	$2.00
					Rayford, Floyd	83T	192	$ .01	$ .07
					Rayford, Floyd	84T	514	$ .01	$ .06
					Rayford, Floyd	84TTR	96	$ .02	$ .10
					Rayford, Floyd	85T	341	$ .01	$ .05
					Rayford, Floyd	86T	623	$ .01	$ .04
					Rayford, Floyd	87T	426	$ .01	$ .04
Rasmussen, Eric	77T	404	$ .05	$ .15	Rayford, Floyd	88T	296	$ .01	$ .04
Rasmussen, Eric	78T	281	$ .02	$ .10	Raymond, Claude	63T	519	$1.75	$4.50
Rasmussen, Eric	79T	57	$ .02	$ .10	Raymond, Claude	64T	504	$ .50	$1.45
Rasmussen, Eric	80T	531	$ .01	$ .10	Raymond, Claude	65T	48	$ .30	$ .85
Rasmussen, Eric	81T	342	$ .01	$ .10	Raymond, Claude	66T	586	$5.00	$20.00
Rasmussen, Eric	83T	594	$ .01	$ .07	Raymond, Claude	67T	364	$ .30	$ .85
Rasmussen, Eric	84T	724	$ .01	$ .06	Raymond, Claude	68T	166	$ .30	$ .85
Ratliff, Gene	65T	553	$1.75	$4.50	Raymond, Claude	69T	446	$ .30	$ .85
Ratliff, Paul	63T	549	$1.75	$4.50	Raymond, Claude	70T	268	$ .15	$ .50
Ratliff, Paul	70T	267	$ .15	$ .50	Raymond, Claude	71T	536	$ .35	$1.25
Ratliff, Paul	71T	607	$ .35	$1.25	Ready, Randy	84TTR	97	$ .02	$ .10
Rau, Doug	73T	602	$ .45	$1.45	Ready, Randy	86T	209	$ .01	$ .04
Rau, Doug	74T	64	$ .07	$ .30	Ready, Randy	87TTR	97	$ .01	$ .05
Rau, Doug	75T	269	$ .07	$ .30	Ready, Randy	88T	426	$ .01	$ .04
Rau, Doug	76T	124	$ .05	$ .20	Ready, Randy	88TBB	102	$ .01	$ .06
Rau, Doug	77T	421	$ .05	$ .15	Ready, Randy	89T	551	$ .01	$ .05

CARDINALS
ERIC RASMUSSEN
PITCHER

Player	Year	No.	VG	EX/MT	Player	Year	No.	VG	EX/MT
Ready, Randy	89TTR	102	$ .01	$ .06	Reds, Team	67T	407	$ .75	$2.00
Ready, Randy	90T	356	$ .01	$ .04	Reds, Team	68T	574	$ .50	$2.50
Ready, Randy	91T	137	$ .01	$ .03	Reds, Team	70T	544	$ .90	$3.00
Reardon, Jeff	81T	456	$ .25	$1.25	Reds, Team	71T	357	$ .75	$3.00
Reardon, Jeff	81TTR	819	$ .15	$ .75	Reds, Team	72T	651	$ .90	$3.00
Reardon, Jeff	82T	667	$ .05	$ .35	Reds, Team	73T	641	$ .65	$2.00
Reardon, Jeff	83T	290	$ .01	$ .15	Reds, Team	74T	459	$ .45	$1.45
Reardon, Jeff	84T	595	$ .01	$ .10	Reds, Team Checklist	75T	531	$ .75	$3.00
Reardon, Jeff	85T	375	$ .01	$ .05	Reds, Team Checklist	76T	104	$ .75	$2.20
Reardon, Jeff	86T	35	$ .01	$ .04	Reds, Team Checklist	77T	287	$ .35	$1.25
Reardon, Jeff	86TAS	711	$ .01	$ .04	Reds, Team Checklist	78T	526	$ .15	$ .50
Reardon, Jeff	87T	165	$ .01	$ .04	Reds, Team Checklist	79T	259	$ .15	$ .50
Reardon, Jeff	87TTR	98	$ .01	$ .05	Reds, Team Checklist	80T	606	$ .15	$ .50
Reardon, Jeff	88T	425	$ .01	$ .04	Reds, Team Checklist	81T	677	$ .02	$ .20
Reardon, Jeff	88TBB	10	$ .01	$ .06	Reds, Team Leaders	86T	366	$ .01	$ .04
Reardon, Jeff	89T	775	$ .01	$ .05	Reds, Team Leaders	87T	281	$ .01	$ .04
Reardon, Jeff	90T	235	$ .01	$ .04	Reds, Team Leaders	88T	81	$ .01	$ .04
Reardon, Jeff	90TTR	101	$ .01	$ .05	Reds, Team Leaders	89T	111	$ .01	$ .05
Reardon, Jeff	91T	605	$ .01	$ .03	Redus, Gary	83TTR	94	$ .02	$ .10
Reberger, Frank	69T	637	$ .30	$ .95	Redus, Gary	84T	475	$ .03	$ .15
Reberger, Frank	70T	103	$ .15	$ .50	Redus, Gary	85T	146	$ .01	$ .05
Reberger, Frank	71T	251	$ .15	$ .50	Redus, Gary	86T	342	$ .01	$ .04
Reberger, Frank	72T	548	$ .30	$ .95	Redus, Gary	86TTR	90	$ .02	$ .10
Red Sox, Team	56T	111	$3.50	$12.50	Redus, Gary	87T	42	$ .01	$ .04
Red Sox, Team	57T	171	$1.50	$6.00	Redus, Gary	87TTR	99	$ .01	$ .05
Red Sox, Team	58T	312	$2.50	$7.50	Redus, Gary	88T	657	$ .01	$ .04
Red Sox, Team	59T	248	$2.50	$7.50	Redus, Gary	89T	281	$ .01	$ .05
Red Sox, Team	60T	537	$7.50	$22.50	Redus, Gary	89TBB	131	$ .01	$ .06
Red Sox, Team	61T	373	$2.10	$6.00	Redus, Gary	90T	507	$ .01	$ .04
Red Sox, Team	62T	334	$2.25	$6.00	Redus, Gary	91T	771	$ .01	$ .03
Red Sox, Team	63T	202	$ .75	$2.20	Reed, Bob	70T	207	$ .15	$ .50
Red Sox, Team	64T	579	$3.50	$10.00	Reed, Bob	71T	732	$ .75	$2.50
Red Sox, Team	65T	403	$ .90	$3.00	Reed, Howie	65T	544	$1.75	$4.50
Red Sox, Team	66T	259	$ .65	$1.75	Reed, Howie	66T	387	$ .30	$ .95
Red Sox, Team	67T	604	$25.00	$85.00	Reed, Howie	70T	548	$ .30	$ .95
Red Sox, Team	70T	563	$ .90	$3.00	Reed, Howie	71T	398	$ .15	$ .50
Red Sox, Team	71T	386	$ .45	$1.45	Reed, Jeff	87T	247	$ .01	$ .04
Red Sox, Team	72T	328	$ .35	$1.25	Reed, Jeff	87TTR	100	$ .01	$ .05
Red Sox, Team	73T	596	$ .90	$3.00	Reed, Jeff	88T	176	$ .01	$ .04
Red Sox, Team	74T	567	$ .35	$1.25					
Red Sox, Team Checklist	75T	172	$ .45	$1.45					
Red Sox, Team Checklist	76T	118	$ .15	$ .50					
Red Sox, Team Checklist	77T	309	$ .35	$1.25					
Red Sox, Team Checklist	78T	424	$ .15	$ .50					
Red Sox, Team Checklist	79T	214	$ .08	$ .30					
Red Sox, Team Checklist	80T	689	$ .06	$ .30					
Red Sox, Team Checklist	81T	662	$ .02	$ .20					
Red Sox, Team Leaders	86T	396	$ .01	$ .04					
Red Sox, Team Leaders	87T	306	$ .01	$ .04					
Red Sox, Team Leaders	88T	21	$ .01	$ .04					
Red Sox, Team Leaders	89T	321	$ .01	$ .05					
Redfern, Pete	77T	249	$ .05	$ .15					
Redfern, Pete	78T	81	$ .02	$ .10					
Redfern, Pete	79T	113	$ .02	$ .10					
Redfern, Pete	80T	403	$ .01	$ .10					
Redfern, Pete	81T	714	$ .01	$ .10					
Redfern, Pete	82T	309	$ .01	$ .07					
Redfern, Pete	83T	559	$ .01	$ .07					
Redmond, Wayne	71T	728	$ .75	$2.50					
Redlegs, Team	56T	90	$5.00	$20.00					
Reds, Team	57T	322	$15.00	$45.00					
Reds, Team	58T	428	$3.50	$11.00					
Reds, Team	59T	111	$2.50	$10.00					
Reds, Team	60T	164	$2.00	$8.00					
Reds, Team	61T	249	$2.25	$6.00					
Reds, Team	62T	465	$2.10	$6.00					
Reds, Team	63T	63	$ .85	$3.50					
Reds, Team	64T	403	$ .30	$2.50					
Reds, Team	65T	316	$ .75	$2.25	Reed, Jeff	89T	626	$ .01	$ .05
Reds, Team	66T	59	$ .85	$3.50	Reed, Jeff	89TBB	158	$ .01	$ .06

Player	Year	No.	VG	EX/MT
Reed, Jeff	90T	772	$ .01	$ .04
Reed, Jeff	91T	419	$ .01	$ .03
Reed, Jerry	86T	172	$ .01	$ .04

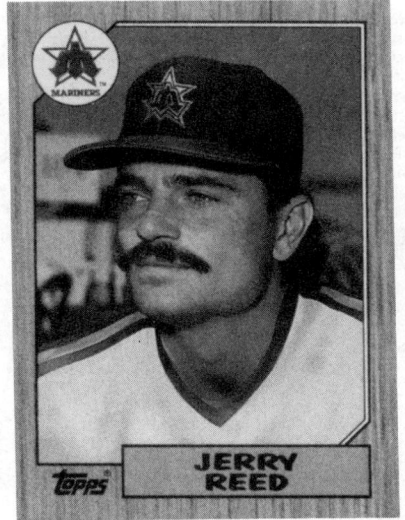

JERRY REED

Player	Year	No.	VG	EX/MT
Reed, Jerry	87T	619	$ .01	$ .04
Reed, Jerry	88T	332	$ .01	$ .04
Reed, Jerry	89T	441	$ .01	$ .05
Reed, Jerry	90T	247	$ .01	$ .04
Reed, Jody	88T	152	$ .01	$ .35
Reed, Jody	88TBB	202	$ .01	$ .15
Reed, Jody	89T	734	$ .01	$ .15
Reed, Jody	89TBB	97	$ .01	$ .06
Reed, Jody	90T	96	$ .01	$ .04
Reed, Jody	91T	247	$ .01	$ .03
Reed, Ron	68T	76	$ .30	$ .85
Reed, Ron	69T	177	$ .30	$ .85
Reed, Ron	70T	546	$ .15	$ .50
Reed, Ron	71T	359	$ .15	$ .50
Reed, Ron	72T	787	$2.10	$6.00
Reed, Ron	73T	72	$ .07	$ .30
Reed, Ron	74T	346	$ .07	$ .30
Reed, Ron	75T	81	$ .07	$ .30
Reed, Ron	76T	58	$ .05	$ .20
Reed, Ron	76TTR	58	$ .05	$ .20
Reed, Ron	77T	243	$ .05	$ .15
Reed, Ron	78T	472	$ .02	$ .10
Reed, Ron	79T	177	$ .02	$ .10
Reed, Ron	80T	609	$ .01	$ .10
Reed, Ron	81T	376	$ .01	$ .10
Reed, Ron	82T	581	$ .01	$ .07
Reed, Ron	83T	728	$ .01	$ .07
Reed, Ron	84T	43	$ .01	$ .06
Reed, Ron	84TTR	98	$ .02	$ .10
Reed, Ron	85T	221	$ .01	$ .05
Reese, Dick	65T	597	$1.75	$4.50
Reese, Jimmie	73T	421	$ .07	$ .30
Reese, Jimmie	74T	276	$ .07	$ .30
Reese, Pee Wee	52T	333	$250.00	$775.00
Reese, Pee Wee	53T	76	$30.00	$125.00
Reese, Pee Wee	56T	260	$35.00	$110.00
Reese, Pee Wee	57T	30	$20.00	$55.00

Player	Year	No.	VG	EX/MT
Reese, Pee Wee	58T	375	$10.00	$40.00
Reese, Rich	67T	486	$ .75	$3.00
Reese, Rich	68T	111	$ .30	$ .85
Reese, Rich	69T	56	$ .30	$ .85
Reese, Rich	70T	404	$ .15	$ .50
Reese, Rich	71T	349	$ .15	$ .50
Reese, Rich	72T	611	$ .30	$ .95
Regan, Phil	61T	439	$ .75	$3.00
Regan, Phil	62T	366	$ .45	$1.45
Regan, Phil	63T	494	$2.50	$6.50
Regan, Phil	64T	535	$1.75	$4.50
Regan, Phil	65T	191	$ .30	$ .85
Regan, Phil	66T	347	$ .30	$ .95
Regan, Phil	67T	130	$ .30	$ .85
Regan, Phil	68T	88	$ .30	$ .85
Regan, Phil	69T	535	$ .30	$ .95
Regan, Phil	70T	334	$ .15	$ .50
Regan, Phil	71T	634	$ .35	$1.25
Regan, Phil	72T	485	$ .15	$ .50
Reichardt, Rick	65T	194	$ .30	$ .85
Reichardt, Rick	66T	321	$ .30	$ .95
Reichardt, Rick	67T	40	$ .30	$ .85
Reichardt, Rick	68T	570	$ .35	$1.25
Reichardt, Rick	69T	205	$ .30	$ .85
Reichardt, Rick	70T	720	$1.25	$3.75
Reichardt, Rick	71T	643	$ .35	$1.25
Reid, Scott	70T	56	$ .15	$ .50
Reid, Scott	71T	439	$ .60	$2.00
Reimer, Kevin	91T	304	$ .01	$ .03
Reiser, Pete	52T	189	$10.00	$30.00
Reiser, Pete	60T	463	$ .85	$2.25
Reiser, Pete	73T	81	$ .30	$ .95
Reitz, Ken	73T	603	$ .45	$1.45
Reitz, Ken	74T	372	$ .07	$ .30
Reitz, Ken	75T	27	$ .07	$ .30
Reitz, Ken	76T	158	$ .05	$ .20
Reitz, Ken	76TTR	158	$ .05	$ .20
Reitz, Ken	77T	297	$ .05	$ .15
Reitz, Ken	78T	692	$ .02	$ .10
Reitz, Ken	79T	587	$ .02	$ .10
Reitz, Ken	80T	182	$ .01	$ .10
Reitz, Ken	81T	441	$ .01	$ .10
Reitz, Ken	81TTR	820	$ .02	$ .10
Reitz, Ken	82T	245	$ .01	$ .07
Remmerswaal, Win	81T	38	$ .01	$ .10
Remy, Jerry	76T	229	$ .05	$ .20
Remy, Jerry	77T	342	$ .05	$ .15
Remy, Jerry	78T	478	$ .02	$ .10
Remy, Jerry	79T	618	$ .02	$ .10
Remy, Jerry	80T	155	$ .01	$ .10
Remy, Jerry	81T	549	$ .01	$ .10
Remy, Jerry	82T	25	$ .01	$ .07
Remy, Jerry	83T	295	$ .01	$ .07
Remy, Jerry	84T	445	$ .01	$ .06
Remy, Jerry	85T	761	$ .01	$ .05
Renick, Rick	68T	301	$ .30	$ .85
Renick, Rick	70T	93	$ .15	$ .50
Renick, Rick	71T	694	$ .75	$2.50
Renick, Rick	72T	459	$ .15	$ .50
Reniff, Hal	62T	139	$3.00	$9.00
Reniff, Hal	62T	159	$ .90	$3.00
Reniff, Hal	63T	546	$1.75	$4.50
Reniff, Hal	64T	36	$ .30	$ .95
Reniff, Hal	65T	413	$ .35	$1.25
Reniff, Hal	66T	68	$ .30	$ .95
Reniff, Hal	67T	201	$ .30	$ .85
Renko, Steve	70T	87	$ .15	$ .50
Renko, Steve	71T	209	$ .15	$ .50
Renko, Steve	72T	307	$ .15	$ .50
Renko, Steve	72TIA	308	$ .15	$ .50

TOPPS

Player	Year	No.	VG	EX/MT
Renko, Steve	73T	623	$ .55	$1.75
Renko, Steve	74T	49	$ .07	$ .30
Renko, Steve	75T	34	$ .07	$ .30
Renko, Steve	76T	264	$ .05	$ .20
Renko, Steve	77T	586	$ .05	$ .15
Renko, Steve	78T	493	$ .02	$ .10
Renko, Steve	79T	352	$ .02	$ .10
Renko, Steve	80T	184	$ .01	$ .10
Renko, Steve	81T	63	$ .01	$ .10
Renko, Steve	81TTR	821	$ .02	$ .10
Renko, Steve	82T	702	$ .01	$ .07
Renko, Steve	83T	236	$ .01	$ .07
Renko, Steve	83TTR	95	$ .02	$ .10
Renko, Steve	84T	444	$ .01	$ .06
Renna, Bill	54T	112	$2.50	$10.00
Renna, Bill	55T	121	$2.00	$6.00
Renna, Bill	56T	82	$2.25	$6.00
Renna, Bill	58T	473	$ .75	$2.20
Renna, Bill	59T	72	$ .85	$3.50
Renteria, Rich	89TBB	109	$ .01	$ .06
Replogle, Andy	79T	427	$ .02	$ .10
Repoz, Roger	66T	138	$ .30	$ .95
Repoz, Roger	67T	416	$ .30	$ .95
Repoz, Roger	68T	587	$ .35	$1.25
Repoz, Roger	69T	103	$ .30	$ .85
Repoz, Roger	70T	397	$ .15	$ .50
Repoz, Roger	71T	508	$ .15	$ .50
Repoz, Roger	72T	541	$ .30	$ .95
Repulski, Rip	53T	172	$4.50	$15.00
Repulski, Rip	54T	115	$2.50	$10.00
Repulski, Rip	55T	55	$2.00	$6.00
Repulski, Rip	56T	201	$3.00	$9.00
Repulski, Rip	57T	245	$ .95	$3.50
Repulski, Rip	58T	14	$ .85	$3.50
Repulski, Rip	59T	195	$ .75	$2.20
Repulski, Rip	60T	265	$ .45	$1.45
Repulski, Rip	61T	128	$ .35	$1.25
Rettenmund, Merv	69T	66	$ .30	$ .85
Rettenmund, Merv	70T	629	$ .30	$ .95
Rettenmund, Merv	71T	393	$ .15	$ .50
Rettenmund, Merv	72T	86	$ .35	$1.25
Rettenmund, Merv	72T	235	$ .15	$ .50
Rettenmund, Merv	73T	56	$ .07	$ .30
Rettenmund, Merv	74T	585	$ .07	$ .30
Rettenmund, Merv	74TTR	585	$ .07	$ .30
Rettenmund, Merv	75T	369	$ .07	$ .30
Rettenmund, Merv	76T	283	$ .05	$ .20
Rettenmund, Merv	77T	659	$ .05	$ .15
Rettenmund, Merv	78T	566	$ .02	$ .10
Rettenmund, Merv	79T	48	$ .02	$ .10
Rettenmund, Merv	80T	402	$ .01	$ .10
Retzer, Ken	62T	594	$35.00	$125.00
Retzer, Ken	63T	471	$2.50	$6.50
Retzer, Ken	64T	277	$ .30	$ .95
Retzer, Ken	65T	278	$ .35	$1.25
Reuschel, Paul	77T	333	$ .05	$ .15
Reuschel, Paul	77T	634	$ .05	$ .25
Reuschel, Paul	78T	663	$ .02	$ .10
Reuschel, Paul	79T	511	$ .02	$ .10
Reuschel, Rick	73T	482	$1.25	$3.75
Reuschel, Rick	74T	136	$ .45	$1.45
Reuschel, Rick	75T	153	$ .15	$ .50
Reuschel, Rick	76T	359	$ .15	$ .50
Reuschel, Rick	77T	530	$ .05	$ .25
Reuschel, Rick	77T	634	$ .05	$ .25
Reuschel, Rick	78T	50	$ .05	$ .25
Reuschel, Rick	79T	240	$ .02	$ .10
Reuschel, Rick	80T	175	$ .01	$ .10
Reuschel, Rick	81T	645	$ .01	$ .10
Reuschel, Rick	81TTR	822	$ .02	$ .10
Reuschel, Rick	82T	405	$ .01	$ .07
Reuschel, Rick	85T	306	$ .01	$ .05
Reuschel, Rick	85TTR	93	$ .02	$ .10
Reuschel, Rick	86T	779	$ .01	$ .04
Reuschel, Rick	87T	521	$ .01	$ .04
Reuschel, Rick	88T	660	$ .01	$ .04
Reuschel, Rick	88TBB	188	$ .01	$ .10
Reuschel, Rick	89T	65	$ .01	$ .05
Reuschel, Rick	90T	190	$ .01	$ .04
Reuschel, Rick	91T	422	$ .01	$ .03
Reuss, Jerry	70T	96	$ .50	$2.00
Reuss, Jerry	71T	158	$ .35	$1.25
Reuss, Jerry	72T	775	$ .85	$3.50
Reuss, Jerry	73T	446	$ .30	$ .85
Reuss, Jerry	74T	116	$ .07	$ .30
Reuss, Jerry	75T	124	$ .15	$ .50
Reuss, Jerry	76T	60	$ .07	$ .30
Reuss, Jerry	77T	645	$ .05	$ .15
Reuss, Jerry	78T	255	$ .02	$ .10
Reuss, Jerry	79T	536	$ .02	$ .10
Reuss, Jerry	80T	318	$ .01	$ .10
Reuss, Jerry	81T	440	$ .01	$ .10
Reuss, Jerry	82T	710	$ .01	$ .07
Reuss, Jerry	83T	90	$ .01	$ .07
Reuss, Jerry	84T	170	$ .01	$ .06
Reuss, Jerry	85T	680	$ .01	$ .05
Reuss, Jerry	86T	577	$ .01	$ .04
Reuss, Jerry	87T	682	$ .01	$ .04
Reuss, Jerry	88T	216	$ .01	$ .04
Reuss, Jerry	89T	357	$ .01	$ .05
Reuss, Jerry	90T	424	$ .01	$ .04
Revering, Dave	78T	706	$ .02	$ .10
Revering, Dave	79T	224	$ .02	$ .10
Revering, Dave	80T	438	$ .01	$ .10
Revering, Dave	81T	568	$ .01	$ .10
Revering, Dave	81TTR	823	$ .02	$ .10
Revering, Dave	82T	109	$ .01	$ .07
Revering, Dave	82TTR	97	$ .02	$ .10
Revering, Dave	83T	677	$ .01	$ .07
Reynolds, Allie	51Trb	6	$3.00	$12.00
Reynolds, Allie	52T	67	$27.50	$77.50
Reynolds, Allie	53T	141	$7.50	$22.50
Reynolds, Archie	71T	664	$ .75	$2.50
Reynolds, Archie	72T	672	$ .75	$2.50
Reynolds, Bob	71T	664	$ .75	$2.50
Reynolds, Bob	72T	162	$ .25	$ .75
Reynolds, Bob	73T	612	$ .45	$1.45
Reynolds, Bob	74T	259	$ .07	$ .30
Reynolds, Bob	75T	142	$ .07	$ .30
Reynolds, Craig	76T	596	$ .15	$ .50
Reynolds, Craig	77T	474	$ .05	$ .15
Reynolds, Craig	78T	199	$ .02	$ .10
Reynolds, Craig	79T	482	$ .02	$ .10
Reynolds, Craig	80T	129	$ .01	$ .10
Reynolds, Craig	81T	617	$ .01	$ .10
Reynolds, Craig	82T	57	$ .01	$ .07
Reynolds, Craig	83T	328	$ .01	$ .07
Reynolds, Craig	84T	776	$ .01	$ .06
Reynolds, Craig	85T	156	$ .01	$ .05
Reynolds, Craig	86T	298	$ .01	$ .04
Reynolds, Craig	87T	779	$ .01	$ .04
Reynolds, Craig	88T	557	$ .01	$ .04
Reynolds, Craig	88TBB	219	$ .01	$ .06
Reynolds, Craig	89T	428	$ .01	$ .05
Reynolds, Craig	89TBB	312	$ .01	$ .06
Reynolds, Craig	90T	637	$ .01	$ .04
Reynolds, Don	79T	292	$ .02	$ .10
Reynolds, Harold	86T	769	$ .01	$ .50
Reynolds, Harold	87T	91	$ .01	$ .10
Reynolds, Harold	88T	485	$ .01	$ .04

Player	Year	No.	VG	EX/MT
Reynolds, Harold	88TBB	142	$ .01	$ .06
Reynolds, Harold	89T	580	$ .01	$ .05
Reynolds, Harold	89TBB	2	$ .01	$ .10
Reynolds, Harold	90T	161	$ .01	$ .04
Reynolds, Harold	91T	260	$ .01	$ .03
Reynolds, Ken	71T	664	$ .75	$2.50
Reynolds, Ken	72T	252	$ .15	$ .50
Reynolds, Ken	73T	638	$ .45	$1.45
Reynolds, R. J.	85T	369	$ .03	$ .15
Reynolds, R. J.	86T	417	$ .01	$ .04
Reynolds, R. J.	87T	109	$ .01	$ .04
Reynolds, R. J.	88T	27	$ .01	$ .04
Reynolds, R. J.	89T	658	$ .01	$ .05
Reynolds, R. J.	90T	592	$ .01	$ .04
Reynolds, R. J.	91T	198	$ .01	$ .03
Reynolds, Ronn	86T	649	$ .01	$ .04
Reynolds, Ronn	87T	471	$ .01	$ .04
Reynolds, Tom	64T	528	$1.75	$4.50
Reynolds, Tom	65T	333	$ .35	$1.25
Reynolds, Tom	67T	487	$ .75	$3.00
Reynolds, Tom	69T	467	$ .30	$ .85
Reynolds, Tommie	70T	259	$ .15	$ .50
Reynolds, Tommie	71T	676	$ .75	$2.50
Rhode, Dave	91T	531	$ .01	$ .10
Rhoden, Rick	75T	618	$ .90	$3.00
Rhoden, Rick	76T	439	$ .30	$ .85
Rhoden, Rick	77T	245	$ .05	$ .15
Rhoden, Rick	78T	605	$ .02	$ .10
Rhoden, Rick	79T	145	$ .02	$ .10
Rhoden, Rick	80T	92	$ .01	$ .10
Rhoden, Rick	81T	312	$ .01	$ .10
Rhoden, Rick	82T	513	$ .01	$ .07
Rhoden, Rick	83T	781	$ .01	$ .07
Rhoden, Rick	84T	485	$ .01	$ .06
Rhoden, Rick	84T	696	$ .01	$ .06
Rhoden, Rick	85T	695	$ .01	$ .05
Rhoden, Rick	86T	232	$ .01	$ .04
Rhoden, Rick	87T	365	$ .01	$ .04
Rhoden, Rick	87TTR	101	$ .01	$ .05
Rhoden, Rick	88T	185	$ .01	$ .04
Rhoden, Rick	88TBB	108	$ .01	$ .06
Rhoden, Rick	89T	18	$ .01	$ .05
Rhoden, Rick	89TBB	237	$ .01	$ .06
Rhoden, Rick	90T	588	$ .01	$ .04
Rhodes, "Dusty" Jim	54T	170	$2.50	$10.00
Rhodes, Dusty	55T	1	$7.00	$40.00
Rhodes, Dusty	56T	50	$1.50	$4.00
Rhodes, Dusty	57T	61	$ .95	$3.50
Rhodes, Karl	91T	516	$ .01	$ .15
Ribant, Dennis	65T	73	$ .30	$ .85
Ribant, Dennis	66T	241	$ .30	$ .95
Ribant, Dennis	67T	527	$ .75	$3.00
Ribant, Dennis	69T	463	$ .30	$ .85
Ribant, Denny	68T	326	$ .30	$ .85
Riccelli, Frank	74T	599	$ .15	$ .50
Riccelli, Frank	80T	247	$ .01	$ .10
Rice, Del	52T	100	$7.00	$20.00
Rice, Del	53T	68	$5.00	$20.00
Rice, Del	57T	193	$ .95	$3.50
Rice, Del	58T	51	$ .85	$3.50
Rice, Del	59T	104	$ .85	$3.50
Rice, Del	60T	248	$ .45	$1.45
Rice, Del	61T	448	$ .75	$3.00
Rice, Del	72T	718	$ .75	$2.50
Rice, Hal	52T	398	$40.00	$140.00
Rice, Hal	53T	93	$4.50	$15.00
Rice, Hal	54T	95	$2.50	$10.00
Rice, Jim	75T	616	$7.50	$20.00
Rice, Jim	76T	340	$1.75	$7.00
Rice, Jim	77T	60	$1.00	$4.00

Player	Year	No.	VG	EX/MT
Rice, Jim	78T	202	$ .05	$ .20
Rice, Jim	78T	670	$ .85	$3.50
Rice, Jim	79T	2	$ .30	$ .85
Rice, Jim	79T	3	$ .30	$ .85
Rice, Jim	79T	400	$ .75	$2.25
Rice, Jim	80T	200	$ .35	$1.25
Rice, Jim	81T	500	$ .15	$ .75
Rice, Jim	82T	750	$ .10	$ .50
Rice, Jim	83T	30	$ .30	$ .85
Rice, Jim	83T	381	$ .01	$ .07
Rice, Jim	84T	132	$ .08	$ .35
Rice, Jim	84T	133	$ .06	$ .30
Rice, Jim	84T	550	$ .30	$ .85
Rice, Jim	84TAS	401	$ .05	$ .20
Rice, Jim	85T	150	$ .05	$ .25
Rice, Jim	86T	320	$ .01	$ .10
Rice, Jim	87T	480	$ .15	$ .50
Rice, Jim	87TAS610	610	$ .01	$ .10

Player	Year	No.	VG	EX/MT
Rice, Jim	88T	675	$ .01	$ .15
Rice, Jim	88TBB	181	$ .01	$ .10
Rice, Jim	88TTB	662	$ .01	$ .04
Rice, Jim	89T	245	$ .01	$ .05
Rice, Jim	89TBB	18	$ .01	$ .06
Rice, Jim	90T	785	$ .01	$ .10
Richard, J. R.	72T	101	$ .35	$1.25
Richard, J. R.	74T	522	$ .07	$ .30
Richard, J. R.	75T	73	$ .07	$ .30
Richard, J. R.	76T	625	$ .07	$ .30
Richard, J. R.	77T	260	$ .05	$ .15
Richard, J. R.	78T	470	$ .05	$ .20
Richard, J. R.	79T	6	$ .06	$ .30
Richard, J. R.	79T	590	$ .02	$ .10
Richard, J. R.	79TRB	203	$ .02	$ .10
Richard, J. R.	80T	50	$ .01	$ .10
Richard, J. R.	80T	206	$ .05	$ .25
Richard, J. R.	80T	207	$ .02	$ .10
Richard, J. R.	81T	350	$ .01	$ .10
Richard, J. R.	82T	190	$ .01	$ .07
Richard, Lee	72T	476	$ .15	$ .50
Richard, Lee	75T	653	$ .07	$ .30

TOPPS

Player	Year	No.	VG	EX/MT	Player	Year	No.	VG	EX/MT
Richard, Lee	76T	533	$ .05	$ .20	Richert, Pete	70T	601	$ .30	$ .95
Richards, Gene	77T	473	$12.50	$50.00	Richert, Pete	71T	273	$ .15	$ .50
Richards, Gene	78T	292	$ .02	$ .10	Richert, Pete	72T	649	$ .30	$ .95
Richards, Gene	79T	364	$ .02	$ .10	Richert, Pete	73T	239	$ .07	$ .30
Richards, Gene	80T	616	$ .01	$ .10	Richert, Pete	74T	348	$ .07	$ .30
Richards, Gene	81T	171	$ .01	$ .10	Richert, Pete	74TTR	348	$ .07	$ .30
Richards, Gene	82T	708	$ .01	$ .07	Richie, Rob	89TMLD	101	$ .01	$ .06
Richards, Gene	83T	7	$ .01	$ .07	Richie, Rob	90T	146	$ .01	$ .04
Richards, Gene	84T	594	$ .01	$ .06	Rickert, Marv	52T	50	$15.00	$47.50
Richards, Gene	84TTR	99	$ .02	$ .10	Ricketts, Dave	65T	581	$30.00	$95.00
Richards, Gene	85T	434	$ .01	$ .05	Ricketts, Dave	67T	589	$2.10	$6.00
Richards, Paul	52T	305	$14.00	$40.00	Ricketts, Dave	68T	46	$ .30	$ .85
Richards, Paul	60T	224	$ .45	$1.45	Ricketts, Dave	69T	232	$ .30	$ .95
Richards, Paul	61T	131	$ .35	$1.25	Ricketts, Dave	70T	626	$ .30	$ .95
Richards, Paul	61TAS	566	$5.50	$16.50	Ricketts, Dave	73T	517	$ .30	$ .95
Richards, Rusty	89TMLD	99	$ .01	$ .06	Ricketts, Dick	59T	137	$ .75	$2.20
Richardson, Bobby	57T	286	$22.50	$90.00	Ricketts, Dick	60T	236	$ .45	$1.45
Richardson, Bobby	58T	101	$4.00	$12.00	Rico, Fred	70T	552	$ .30	$ .95
Richardson, Bobby	59T	237	$ .90	$3.00	Riddle, John	53T	274	$12.50	$50.00
Richardson, Bobby	59T	76	$3.50	$10.00	Riddle, John	54T	147	$2.50	$10.00
Richardson, Bobby	60T	405	$1.50	$6.00	Riddle, Johnny	55T	98	$2.00	$6.00
Richardson, Bobby	61T	180	$1.75	$5.00	Riddleberger, Denny	71T	93	$ .15	$ .50
Richardson, Bobby	62T	65	$2.10	$6.00	Riddleberger, Denny	72T	642	$ .30	$ .95
Richardson, Bobby	63T	173	$15.00	$45.00	Riddleberger, Denny	73T	157	$ .07	$ .30
Richardson, Bobby	63T	420	$1.50	$6.00	Riddoch, Greg	90TTR	102	$ .01	$ .05
Richardson, Bobby	64T	190	$1.00	$4.00	Riddoch, Greg	91T	109	$ .01	$ .03
Richardson, Bobby	65T	115	$1.00	$4.00	Ridzik, Steve	57T	123	$ .95	$3.50
Richardson, Bobby	66T	490	$3.00	$12.00	Ridzik, Steve	60T	489	$ .90	$3.00
Richardson, Gordon	66T	51	$ .30	$ .95	Ridzik, Steve	64T	92	$ .30	$ .95
Richardson, Jeff	89TMLD	100	$ .01	$ .25	Ridzik, Steve	65T	211	$ .35	$1.25
Richardt, Mike	83T	371	$ .01	$ .07	Ridzik, Steve	66T	294	$ .30	$ .95
Richardt, Mike	84T	641	$ .01	$ .06	Righetti, Dave	82T	439	$ .75	$3.00
Richert, Pete	62T	131	$ .45	$1.45	Righetti, Dave	83T	81	$ .01	$ .07
Richert, Pete	63T	383	$ .45	$1.50	Righetti, Dave	83T	176	$ .05	$ .25
Richert, Pete	64T	51	$ .30	$ .95	Righetti, Dave	84T	5	$ .02	$ .10
Richert, Pete	65T	252	$ .35	$1.25	Righetti, Dave	84T	635	$ .03	$ .15
Richert, Pete	66T	95	$ .30	$ .95	Righetti, Dave	85T	260	$ .04	$ .20
Richert, Pete	67T	590	$2.10	$6.00	Righetti, Dave	86T	560	$ .01	$ .10
Richert, Pete	68T	354	$ .30	$ .85	Righetti, Dave	87T	40	$ .01	$ .10
					Righetti, Dave	87TAS	616	$ .01	$ .10
					Righetti, Dave	87TRB	5	$ .01	$ .04
					Righetti, Dave	88T	790	$ .01	$ .10
					Righetti, Dave	89T	335	$ .01	$ .05
					Righetti, Dave	90T	160	$ .01	$ .04
					Righetti, Dave	91T	410	$ .01	$ .03
					Rigney, Bill	52T	125	$7.00	$21.00
					Rigney, Bill	60T	7	$3.00	$12.50
					Rigney, Bill	60T	225	$ .45	$1.45
					Rigney, Bill	61T	225	$ .35	$1.25
					Rigney, Bill	62T	549	$3.95	$11.50
					Rigney, Bill	63T	294	$ .45	$1.50
					Rigney, Bill	64T	383	$ .50	$1.45
					Rigney, Bill	65T	66	$ .30	$ .85
					Rigney, Bill	66T	249	$ .30	$ .95
					Rigney, Bill	67T	494	$ .75	$3.00
					Rigney, Bill	68T	416	$ .30	$ .85
					Rigney, Bill	69T	182	$ .30	$ .85
					Rigney, Bill	70T	426	$ .15	$ .50
					Rigney, Bill	71T	532	$ .35	$1.25
					Rigney, Bill	72T	389	$ .15	$ .50
					Rijo, Jose	84TTR	100	$1.25	$4.50
					Rijo, Jose	85T	238	$ .25	$1.25
					Rijo, Jose	86T	536	$ .05	$ .25
					Rijo, Jose	87T	34	$ .05	$ .20
					Rijo, Jose	88T	316	$ .01	$ .10
					Rijo, Jose	88TTR	92	$ .01	$ .15
					Rijo, Jose	89T	135	$ .01	$ .10
					Rijo, Jose	90T	627	$ .01	$ .04
					Rijo, Jose	91T	493	$ .01	$ .03
					Riles, Earnie	86T	398	$ .02	$ .20

Richert, Pete	69T	86	$ .30	$ .85

Player	Year	No.	VG	EX/MT	Player	Year	No.	VG	EX/MT
Riles, Earnie	87T	523	$ .01	$ .04	Rivera, Luis	88TBB	223	$ .01	$ .06
Riles, Earnie	88T	88	$ .01	$ .04	Rivera, Luis	88TTR	94	$ .01	$ .10
Riles, Ernie (Earnie)	88TTR	93	$ .01	$ .06	Rivera, Luis	89T	431	$ .01	$ .05
Riles, Ernie	89T	676	$ .01	$ .05	Rivera, Luis	90T	601	$ .01	$ .04
Riles, Ernie	90T	732	$ .01	$ .04	Rivera, Luis	91T	338	$ .01	$ .03
Riles, Ernie	91T	408	$ .01	$ .03	Rivers, Mickey	72T	272	$ .15	$ .50
Riley, George	81T	514	$ .01	$ .10	Rivers, Mickey	73T	597	$ .75	$3.00
Rincon, Andy	81T	244	$ .01	$ .10	Rivers, Mickey	74T	76	$ .07	$ .30
Rincon, Andy	82T	135	$ .01	$ .07	Rivers, Mickey	75T	164	$ .07	$ .30
Rios, Juan	69T	619	$ .30	$ .95	Rivers, Mickey	76T	85	$ .07	$ .30
Rios, Juan	70T	89	$ .15	$ .50	Rivers, Mickey	76T	198	$ .15	$ .50
Ripken, Billy	88T	352	$ .05	$ .30	Rivers, Mickey	76TTR	85	$ .05	$ .20
Ripken, Billy	89T	571	$ .01	$ .05	Rivers, Mickey	77T	305	$ .05	$ .15
Ripken, Billy	89TBB	27	$ .01	$ .06	Rivers, Mickey	78T	690	$ .02	$ .10
Ripken, Billy	90T	468	$ .01	$ .04	Rivers, Mickey	79T	60	$ .02	$ .10
Ripken, Billy	91T	677	$ .01	$ .03					
Ripken, Cal	82T	21	$7.50	$40.00					
Ripken, Cal	82TTR	98	$10.00	$80.00					
Ripken, Cal	83T	163	$1.50	$12.00					
Ripken, Cal	84T	426	$ .01	$ .25					
Ripken, Cal	84T	490	$ .50	$4.00					
Ripken, Cal	84TAS	400	$ .06	$ .50					
Ripken, Cal	85T	30	$ .25	$1.50					
Ripken, Cal	85TAS	704	$ .05	$ .35					
Ripken, Cal	86T	340	$ .03	$ .75					
Ripken, Cal	86TAS	715	$ .03	$ .25					
Ripken, Cal	87T	784	$ .10	$ .30					
Ripken, Cal	87TAS	609	$ .01	$ .10					
Ripken, Cal	88T	650	$ .01	$ .25					
Ripken, Cal	89TBB	286	$ .01	$ .15					
Ripken, Cal	90T	570	$ .01	$ .10					
Ripken, Cal	90TAS	388	$ .01	$ .10					
Ripken, Cal	90TRB	8	$ .01	$ .10					
Ripken, Cal	91T	150	$ .01	$ .10					
Ripken, Cal	91TRB	5	$ .01	$ .10					
Ripken, Jr., Cal	88TBB	62	$ .01	$ .25					
Ripken, Jr., Cal	89T	250	$ .01	$ .15					
Ripken, Sr., Cal	87TTR	102	$ .01	$ .10					
Ripken, Sr., Cal	88T	444	$ .01	$ .04					
Ripley, Allen	79T	702	$ .02	$ .10					
Ripley, Allen	80T	413	$ .01	$ .10					
Ripley, Allen	81T	144	$ .01	$ .10					
Ripley, Allen	82T	529	$ .01	$ .07					
Ripley, Allen	82TTR	99	$ .02	$ .10					
Ripley, Allen	83T	73	$ .01	$ .07					
Rippelmeyer, Ray	61T	276	$ .35	$1.25	Rivers, Mickey	80T	485	$ .01	$ .10
Rippelmeyer, Ray	62T	271	$ .45	$1.45	Rivers, Mickey	81T	145	$ .02	$ .10
Rippelmeyer, Ray	73T	486	$ .30	$ .95	Rivers, Mickey	82T	704	$ .03	$ .15
Ripplemeyer, Ray	74T	119	$ .07	$ .30	Rivers, Mickey	82TIA	705	$ .01	$ .07
Ritchie, Jay	65T	494	$ .75	$3.00	Rivers, Mickey	83T	224	$ .01	$ .07
Ritchie, Wally	87TTR	103	$ .05	$ .25	Rivers, Mickey	84T	504	$ .01	$ .06
Ritchie, Wally	88T	494	$ .01	$ .04	Rivers, Mickey	85T	371	$ .01	$ .05
Rittwage, Jim	65T	501	$ .75	$3.00	Rizzuto, Phil	51Trb	5	$7.50	$30.00
Ritz, Kevin	89TMLD	102	$ .01	$ .06	Rizzuto, Phil	52T	11	$65.00	$175.00
Ritz, Kevin	90T	237	$ .01	$ .10	Rizzuto, Phil	53T	114	$35.00	$100.00
Rivera, Bombo	77T	178	$ .05	$ .15	Rizzuto, Phil	54T	17	$15.00	$60.00
Rivera, Bombo	78T	657	$ .02	$ .10	Rizzuto, Phil	55T	189	$42.50	$125.00
Rivera, Bombo	79T	449	$ .02	$ .10	Rizzuto, Phil	56T	113	$13.50	$42.50
Rivera, Bombo	80T	43	$ .01	$ .10	Rizzuto, Phil	61TMVP	471	$4.00	$12.00
Rivera, Bombo	81T	256	$ .01	$ .10	Roach, Mel	54T	181	$2.50	$10.00
Rivera, German	85T	626	$ .01	$ .05	Roach, Mel	55T	117	$2.00	$6.00
Rivera, Jim	53T	156	$4.50	$15.00	Roach, Mel	59T	54	$ .85	$3.50
Rivera, Jim	54T	34	$2.00	$9.00	Roach, Mel	60T	491	$ .90	$3.00
Rivera, Jim	55T	58	$2.00	$6.00	Roach, Mel	61T	217	$ .35	$1.25
Rivera, Jim	56T	70	$2.25	$6.00	Roach, Mel	62T	581	$3.95	$11.50
Rivera, Jim	57T	107	$ .95	$3.50	Roarke, Mike	61T	376	$ .75	$3.00
Rivera, Jim	58T	11	$ .85	$3.50	Roarke, Mike	62T	87	$ .45	$1.45
Rivera, Jim	59T	213	$ .75	$2.20	Roarke, Mike	63T	224	$ .30	$ .95
Rivera, Jim	60T	116	$ .45	$1.45	Roarke, Mike	64T	292	$ .30	$ .95
Rivera, Jim	61T	367	$ .35	$1.25	Robbins, Bruce	80T	666	$ .01	$ .10

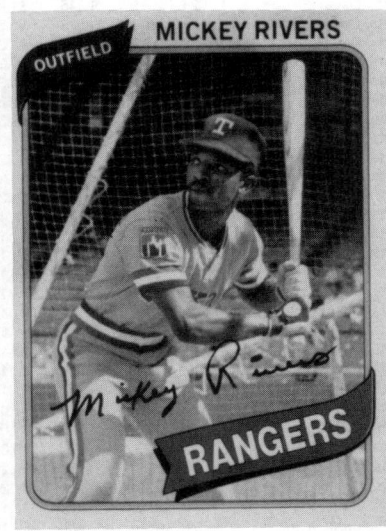

MICKEY RIVERS
OUTFIELD
RANGERS

Player	Year	No.	VG	EX/MT
Robbins, Bruce	81T	79	$ .01	$ .10
Robbins, Doug	88TTR	95	$ .01	$ .25
Robbins, Doug	89TBB	49	$ .01	$ .06
Roberge, Bert	80T	329	$ .01	$ .10
Roberge, Bert	83T	611	$ .01	$ .07
Roberge, Bert	85T	388	$ .01	$ .05
Roberge, Bert	85TTR	94	$ .02	$ .10
Roberge, Bert	86T	154	$ .01	$ .04
Roberts, Curt	54T	242	$2.50	$10.00
Roberts, Curt	55T	107	$2.00	$6.00
Roberts, Curt	56T	306	$1.30	$5.00
Roberts, Dave	63T	158	$ .30	$ .95
Roberts, Dave	66T	571	$5.00	$20.00
Roberts, Dave	69T	536	$ .30	$ .95
Roberts, Dave	70T	151	$ .15	$ .50
Roberts, Dave	71T	448	$ .15	$ .50
Roberts, Dave	72T	91	$ .45	$1.45
Roberts, Dave	72T	360	$ .15	$ .50
Roberts, Dave	73T	39	$ .07	$ .30
Roberts, Dave	73T	133	$ .07	$ .30
Roberts, Dave	74T	177	$ .07	$ .30
Roberts, Dave	74T	309	$ .07	$ .30
Roberts, Dave	75T	301	$ .07	$ .30
Roberts, Dave	75T	558	$ .07	$ .30
Roberts, Dave	76T	107	$ .05	$ .20
Roberts, Dave	76T	649	$ .05	$ .20
Roberts, Dave	76TTR	649	$ .05	$ .20
Roberts, Dave	77T	363	$ .05	$ .15
Roberts, Dave	77T	537	$ .05	$ .15
Roberts, Dave	78T	501	$ .02	$ .10
Roberts, Dave	79T	342	$ .02	$ .10
Roberts, Dave	79T	473	$ .02	$ .10
Roberts, Dave	80T	93	$ .01	$ .10
Roberts, Dave	80T	212	$ .01	$ .10
Roberts, Dave	81T	57	$ .01	$ .10
Roberts, Dave	81T	431	$ .01	$ .10
Roberts, Dave	81TTR	824	$ .02	$ .10
Roberts, Dave	82T	218	$ .01	$ .07
Roberts, Dave	83T	148	$ .01	$ .07
Roberts, Leon	75T	620	$10.00	$30.00
Roberts, Leon	76T	292	$ .05	$ .20
Roberts, Leon	76TTR	292	$ .05	$ .20
Roberts, Leon	77T	456	$ .05	$ .15
Roberts, Leon	79T	166	$ .02	$ .10
Roberts, Leon	80T	507	$ .01	$ .10
Roberts, Leon	81T	368	$ .01	$ .10
Roberts, Leon	81TTR	825	$ .02	$ .10
Roberts, Leon	82T	688	$ .01	$ .07
Roberts, Leon	83T	89	$ .01	$ .07
Roberts, Leon	83TTR	96	$ .02	$ .10
Roberts, Leon	84T	784	$ .01	$ .06
Roberts, Leon 'Bip'	85T	217	$ .01	$ .05
Roberts, Bip	86TTR	91	$ .02	$ .10
Roberts, Bip	87T	637	$ .01	$ .04
Roberts, Bip	89TTR	103	$ .01	$ .06
Roberts, Bip	90T	307	$ .01	$ .04
Roberts, Bip	91T	538	$ .01	$ .03
Roberts, Robin	52T	59	$40.00	$125.00
Roberts, Robin	56T	180	$7.50	$22.50
Roberts, Robin	57T	15	$6.00	$20.00
Roberts, Robin	58T	90	$5.50	$16.00
Roberts, Robin	59T	156	$1.30	$5.00
Roberts, Robin	59T	352	$3.50	$12.50
Roberts, Robin	60T	264	$3.50	$12.50
Roberts, Robin	61T	20	$3.00	$10.00
Roberts, Robin	62T	243	$3.00	$10.00
Roberts, Robin	63T	6	$ .45	$1.45
Roberts, Robin	63T	125	$3.00	$10.00
Roberts, Robin	64T	285	$3.00	$10.00
Roberts, Robin	65T	15	$1.50	$6.00

Player	Year	No.	VG	EX/MT
Roberts, Robin	66T	530	$12.00	$35.00
Robertson, Andre	82T	83	$ .10	$ .50
Robertson, Andre	83T	281	$ .01	$ .07
Robertson, Andre	84T	592	$ .01	$ .06
Robertson, Andre	85T	354	$ .01	$ .05
Robertson, Andre	86T	738	$ .01	$ .04
Robertson, Bob	68T	36	$ .15	$ .50
Robertson, Bob	69T	468	$ .30	$ .85
Robertson, Bob	70T	664	$ .75	$2.00
Robertson, Bob	71T	255	$ .15	$ .50
Robertson, Bob	72T	429	$ .15	$ .50
Robertson, Bob	72TIA	430	$ .15	$ .50
Robertson, Bob	73T	422	$ .07	$ .30
Robertson, Bob	74T	540	$ .07	$ .30
Robertson, Bob	75T	409	$ .07	$ .30
Robertson, Bob	76T	449	$ .05	$ .20
Robertson, Bob	77T	176	$ .05	$ .15
Robertson, Bob	79T	312	$ .02	$ .10
Robertson, Jerry	69T	284	$ .30	$ .95
Robertson, Jerry	70T	661	$ .75	$2.00

Player	Year	No.	VG	EX/MT
Robertson, Jerry	71T	651	$ .75	$2.50
Robertson, Jim	54T	149	$2.50	$10.00
Robertson, Jim	55T	177	$5.25	$15.00
Robertson, Rich	69T	16	$ .30	$ .85
Robertson, Rich	70T	229	$ .15	$ .50
Robertson, Rich	71T	443	$ .15	$ .50
Robertson, Rich	72T	618	$ .30	$ .95
Robertson, Sherry	52T	245	$7.00	$20.00
Robidoux, Billy Jo	86TTR	92	$ .05	$ .20
Robidoux, Billy Jo	87T	401	$ .01	$ .10
Robinson, Bill	67T	442	$ .30	$ .95
Robinson, Bill	68T	337	$ .30	$ .85
Robinson, Bill	69T	313	$ .30	$ .95
Robinson, Bill	70T	23	$ .15	$ .50
Robinson, Bill	73T	37	$ .07	$ .30
Robinson, Bill	74T	174	$ .07	$ .30
Robinson, Bill	75T	501	$ .07	$ .30
Robinson, Bill	76T	137	$ .05	$ .20
Robinson, Bill	77T	335	$ .05	$ .15
Robinson, Bill	78T	455	$ .02	$ .10

Player	Year	No.	VG	EX/MT	Player	Year	No.	VG	EX/MT
Robinson, Bill	79T	637	$ .02	$ .10	Robinson, Eddie	60T	455	$ .95	$3.50
Robinson, Bill	80T	264	$ .01	$ .10	Robinson, Floyd	62T	454	$ .75	$2.50
Robinson, Bill	81T	51	$ .01	$ .10	Robinson, Floyd	63T	2	$3.00	$12.00
Robinson, Bill	82T	543	$ .01	$ .07	Robinson, Floyd	63T	405	$ .45	$1.50
Robinson, Bill	82TTR	100	$ .02	$ .10	Robinson, Floyd	64T	195	$ .30	$ .95
Robinson, Bill	83T	754	$ .01	$ .07	Robinson, Floyd	65T	345	$ .35	$1.25
Robinson, Brooks	57T	328	$105.00	$325.00	Robinson, Floyd	66T	8	$ .30	$ .95
Robinson, Brooks	58T	307	$25.00	$75.00	Robinson, Floyd	66T	199	$ .35	$1.25
Robinson, Brooks	59T	439	$9.50	$37.50	Robinson, Floyd	67T	120	$ .30	$ .85
Robinson, Brooks	60T	28	$9.00	$35.00	Robinson, Floyd	68T	404	$ .30	$ .85
Robinson, Brooks	61T	10	$8.00	$25.00	Robinson, Frank	57T	35	$75.00	$250.00
Robinson, Brooks	61TAS	572	$22.50	$72.50	Robinson, Frank	58T	285	$22.50	$65.00
Robinson, Brooks	62T	45	$6.00	$25.00	Robinson, Frank	58T	386	$2.50	$7.50
Robinson, Brooks	62TAS	468	$4.00	$12.00	Robinson, Frank	58TAS	484	$5.00	$14.00
Robinson, Brooks	63T	345	$9.00	$35.00	Robinson, Frank	59T	435	$10.00	$30.00
Robinson, Brooks	64T	230	$7.50	$22.50	Robinson, Frank	60T	352	$ .90	$3.50
Robinson, Brooks	65T	1	$3.50	$11.00	Robinson, Frank	60T	490	$11.00	$35.00
Robinson, Brooks	65T	5	$3.00	$12.00	Robinson, Frank	61T	25	$2.10	$6.00
Robinson, Brooks	65T	150	$5.50	$17.50	Robinson, Frank	61T	360	$10.00	$30.00
Robinson, Brooks	66T	390	$6.50	$20.00	Robinson, Frank	61TAS	581	$22.50	$72.50
Robinson, Brooks	67T	1	$5.50	$17.50	Robinson, Frank	62T	54	$ .75	$2.20
Robinson, Brooks	67T	600	$65.00	$200.00	Robinson, Frank	62T	350	$10.00	$30.00
Robinson, Brooks	68T	20	$4.00	$16.00	Robinson, Frank	62TAS	396	$4.00	$12.00
Robinson, Brooks	68T	530	$3.00	$10.00	Robinson, Frank	63T	1	$5.00	$25.00
Robinson, Brooks	68TAS	365	$1.50	$6.00	Robinson, Frank	63T	3	$3.00	$12.00
Robinson, Brooks	69T	550	$3.50	$12.50	Robinson, Frank	63T	400	$11.00	$35.00
Robinson, Brooks	69TAS	421	$2.10	$6.00	Robinson, Frank	64T	260	$6.00	$20.00
Robinson, Brooks	70T	230	$2.50	$10.50	Robinson, Frank	65T	120	$6.00	$18.00
Robinson, Brooks	70TAS	455	$1.00	$4.00	Robinson, Frank	66T	219	$ .65	$1.75
Robinson, Brooks	71T	300	$3.00	$10.00	Robinson, Frank	66T	310	$7.00	$27.50
Robinson, Brooks	72T	498	$ .75	$3.00	Robinson, Frank	67T	1	$5.50	$17.50
Robinson, Brooks	72T	550	$5.00	$15.00	Robinson, Frank	67T	100	$5.00	$15.00
Robinson, Brooks	73T	90	$1.00	$4.00	Robinson, Frank	67T	239	$1.75	$4.50
Robinson, Brooks	74T	160	$1.00	$4.00	Robinson, Frank	67T	241	$ .75	$3.00
Robinson, Brooks	74TAS	334	$ .45	$1.45	Robinson, Frank	67T	243	$ .75	$3.00
Robinson, Brooks	75T	50	$1.00	$4.00	Robinson, Frank	68T	2	$2.10	$6.00
Robinson, Brooks	75T	202	$ .45	$1.45	Robinson, Frank	68T	4	$2.10	$6.00
Robinson, Brooks	76T	95	$ .75	$3.00	Robinson, Frank	68T	500	$5.00	$15.00
Robinson, Brooks	77T	285	$ .50	$2.50	Robinson, Frank	68T	530	$3.00	$10.00
Robinson, Brooks	78TRB	4	$ .15	$ .50	Robinson, Frank	68TAS	373	$2.10	$6.00
Robinson, Bruce	79T	711	$ .08	$ .30	Robinson, Frank	69T	250	$5.00	$16.00
Robinson, Bruce	81T	424	$ .01	$ .10	Robinson, Frank	70T	700	$11.00	$35.00
Robinson, Craig	74T	23	$ .07	$ .30	Robinson, Frank	70TAS	463	$2.10	$6.00
Robinson, Craig	74TTR	23	$ .07	$ .30	Robinson, Frank	71T	640	$10.00	$30.00
Robinson, Craig	75T	367	$ .07	$ .30	Robinson, Frank	72T	88	$ .60	$2.00
Robinson, Dave	71T	262	$ .15	$ .50	Robinson, Frank	72T	100	$1.25	$5.00
Robinson, Dewey	80T	664	$ .01	$ .10	Robinson, Frank	72TTR	754	$7.50	$22.50
Robinson, Dewey	81T	487	$ .01	$ .10	Robinson, Frank	73T	175	$1.75	$4.50
Robinson, Dewey	82T	176	$ .01	$ .07	Robinson, Frank	74T	55	$1.25	$5.00
Robinson, Don	79T	264	$ .05	$ .20	Robinson, Frank	75T	199	$ .75	$3.00
Robinson, Don	80T	719	$ .01	$ .10	Robinson, Frank	75T	204	$ .50	$1.50
Robinson, Don	81T	168	$ .01	$ .10	Robinson, Frank	75T	580	$1.00	$4.00
Robinson, Don	82T	332	$ .01	$ .07	Robinson, Frank	83T	576	$ .05	$ .20
Robinson, Don	83T	44	$ .01	$ .07	Robinson, Frank	84T	171	$ .05	$ .25
Robinson, Don	84T	616	$ .01	$ .06	Robinson, Frank	86TB	404	$ .03	$ .15
Robinson, Don	85T	537	$ .01	$ .05	Robinson, Frank	88TTR	96	$ .01	$ .10
Robinson, Don	86T	731	$ .01	$ .04	Robinson, Frank	89T	774	$ .01	$ .10
Robinson, Don	87T	712	$ .01	$ .04	Robinson, Frank	90T	381	$ .01	$ .10
Robinson, Don	88T	52	$ .01	$ .04	Robinson, Frank	91T	639	$ .01	$ .03
Robinson, Don	89T	473	$ .01	$ .05	Robinson, Humberto	55T	182	$5.25	$15.00
Robinson, Don	90T	217	$ .01	$ .04	Robinson, Humberto	59T	366	$ .75	$2.20
Robinson, Don	91T	104	$ .01	$ .03	Robinson, Humberto	60T	416	$ .75	$2.20
Robinson, Earl	61T	343	$ .35	$1.25	Robinson, Jackie	52T	312	$300.00	$900.00
Robinson, Earl	62T	272	$ .45	$1.45	Robinson, Jackie	53T	1	$100.00	$600.00
Robinson, Eddie	51Trb	51	$2.10	$6.00	Robinson, Jackie	54T	10	$80.00	$250.00
Robinson, Eddie	52T	32	$15.00	$47.50	Robinson, Jackie	55T	50	$75.00	$225.00
Robinson, Eddie	53T	73	$4.50	$15.00	Robinson, Jackie	56T	30	$50.00	$145.00
Robinson, Eddie	54T	62	$3.00	$12.00	Robinson, Jeff	84TTR	101	$ .02	$ .10
Robinson, Eddie	56T	302	$2.00	$6.00	Robinson, Jeff	85T	592	$ .01	$ .05
Robinson, Eddie	57T	238	$ .95	$3.50	Robinson, Jeff	86TTR	93	$ .02	$ .10

TOPPS

Player	Year	No.	VG	EX/MT
Robinson, Jeff	87T	390	$ .01	$ .04
Robinson, Jeff	87TTR	104	$ .05	$ .20
Robinson, Jeff	88T	449	$ .01	$ .30
Robinson, Jeff	89T	681	$ .01	$ .10
Robinson, Jeff	89BB	45	$ .01	$ .06
Robinson, Jeff	90T	723	$ .01	$ .04
Robinson, Jeff	90TTR	103	$ .01	$ .05
Robinson, Jeff	91T	19	$ .01	$ .03
Robinson, Jeff M.	88T	244	$ .01	$ .04
Robinson, Jeff M.	88TBB	123	$ .01	$ .10
Robinson, Jeff M.	89T	267	$ .01	$ .10
Robinson, Jeff M.	89TBB	274	$ .01	$ .06
Robinson, Jeff M.	90T	42	$ .01	$ .04
Robinson, Jeff M.	91T	766	$ .01	$ .03
Robinson, Jerry	63T	466	$7.50	$27.50
Robinson, Ron	86T	442	$ .01	$ .04
Robinson, Ron	87T	119	$ .01	$ .04
Robinson, Ron	88T	517	$ .01	$ .04
Robinson, Ron	89T	16	$ .01	$ .10
Robinson, Ron	89TBB	132	$ .01	$ .06
Robinson, Ron	90T	604	$ .01	$ .04
Robinson, Ron	90TTR	104	$ .01	$ .05
Robinson, Ron	91T	313	$ .01	$ .03
Robles, Rafael	69T	592	$ .30	$ .95
Robles, Rafael	70T	573	$ .30	$ .95
Robles, Rafael	71T	408	$ .15	$ .50
Robles, Sergio	73T	601	$ .45	$1.45
Robles, Sergio	74T	603	$ .07	$ .30
Rockett, Pat	78T	502	$ .02	$ .10
Rodgers, Andre	57T	377	$ .85	$3.50
Rodgers, Andre	59T	216	$ .75	$2.20
Rodgers, Andre	60T	431	$ .75	$2.20
Rodgers, Andre	61T	183	$ .35	$1.25
Rodgers, Andre	62T	477	$ .75	$2.50
Rodgers, Andre	63T	193	$ .30	$ .95
Rodgers, Andre	64T	336	$ .30	$ .95
Rodgers, Andre	65T	536	$1.75	$4.50
Rodgers, Andre	66T	592	$5.00	$20.00
Rodgers, Andre	67T	554	$2.10	$6.00
Rodgers, Bob	62T	431	$ .75	$2.25
Rodgers, Bob	63T	280	$ .35	$1.25
Rodgers, Bob	64T	61	$ .30	$ .95
Rodgers, Bob	64T	426	$ .50	$1.45
Rodgers, Bob	65T	342	$ .35	$1.25
Rodgers, Bob	66T	462	$ .75	$2.50
Rodgers, Bob	67T	281	$ .30	$ .85
Rodgers, Bob	68T	433	$ .30	$ .85
Rodgers, Bob	69T	157	$ .30	$ .85
Rodgers, Bob	73T	49	$ .30	$ .85
Rodgers, Bob	74T	447	$ .07	$ .30
Rodgers, Bob	85TTR	95	$ .02	$ .10
Rodgers, Bob	86T	171	$ .01	$ .04
Rodgers, Bob	87T	293	$ .01	$ .04
Rodgers, Bob	88T	504	$ .01	$ .04
Rodgers, Bob	89T	474	$ .01	$ .05
Rodgers, Bob	90T	81	$ .01	$ .04
Rodgers, Bob	91T	321	$ .01	$ .03
Rodriguez, Aurelio	69T	653	$ .50	$1.50
Rodriguez, Aurelio	70T	228	$ .15	$ .50
Rodriguez, Aurelio	71T	464	$ .15	$ .50
Rodriguez, Aurelio	72T	319	$ .15	$ .50
Rodriguez, Aurelio	73T	218	$ .07	$ .30
Rodriguez, Aurelio	74T	72	$ .07	$ .30
Rodriguez, Aurelio	75T	221	$ .07	$ .30
Rodriguez, Aurelio	76T	267	$ .05	$ .20
Rodriguez, Aurelio	77T	574	$ .05	$ .15
Rodriguez, Aurelio	78T	342	$ .02	$ .10
Rodriguez, Aurelio	79T	176	$ .02	$ .10
Rodriguez, Aurelio	80T	468	$ .01	$ .10
Rodriguez, Aurelio	81T	34	$ .01	$ .10

Player	Year	No.	VG	EX/MT
Rodriguez, Aurelio	82T	334	$ .01	$ .07
Rodriguez, Aurelio	82TTR	101	$ .02	$ .10
Rodriguez, Aurelio	83T	758	$ .01	$ .07
Rodriguez, Aurelio	83TTR	97	$ .02	$ .10
Rodriguez, Aurelio	84T	269	$ .01	$ .06
Rodriguez, Eduardo	74T	171	$ .07	$ .30
Rodriguez, Eduardo	75T	582	$ .07	$ .30
Rodriguez, Eduardo	76T	92	$ .05	$ .20
Rodriguez, Eduardo	77T	361	$ .05	$ .15
Rodriguez, Eduardo	78T	623	$ .02	$ .10

EDUARDO RODRIGUEZ P
BREWERS

Player	Year	No.	VG	EX/MT
Rodriguez, Eduardo	79T	108	$ .02	$ .10
Rodriguez, Eduardo	80T	273	$ .01	$ .10
Rodriguez, Eliseo "Ellie"	69T	49	$ .45	$1.45
Rodriguez, Ellie	70T	402	$ .15	$ .50
Rodriguez, Ellie	71T	344	$ .15	$ .50
Rodriguez, Ellie	72T	421	$ .15	$ .50
Rodriguez, Ellie	73T	45	$ .07	$ .30
Rodriguez, Ellie	74T	405	$ .07	$ .30
Rodriguez, Ellie	75T	285	$ .07	$ .30
Rodriguez, Ellie	76T	512	$ .05	$ .20
Rodriguez, Ellie	77T	448	$ .05	$ .15
Rodriguez, Rich	91T	573	$ .01	$ .10
Rodriguez, Rick	88T	166	$ .01	$ .10
Rodriguez, Roberto	68T	199	$ .30	$ .85
Rodriguez, Roberto	69T	358	$ .30	$ .85
Rodriguez, Roberto	71T	424	$ .15	$ .50
Rodriguez, Rosario	89TMLD	103	$ .01	$ .15
Rodriguez, Rosario	91T	688	$ .01	$ .10
Roe, Preacher	51Trb	16	$3.00	$9.00
Roe, Preacher	52T	66	$32.50	$85.00
Roe, Preacher	53T	254	$20.00	$60.00
Roe, Preacher	54T	14	$7.00	$21.00
Roebuck, Ed	55T	195	$5.00	$15.00
Roebuck, Ed	56T	58	$2.25	$6.00
Roebuck, Ed	58T	435	$ .75	$3.00
Roebuck, Ed	60T	519	$2.50	$10.00
Roebuck, Ed	61T	6	$ .35	$1.25
Roebuck, Ed	62T	535	$2.50	$16.50
Roebuck, Ed	63T	295	$ .45	$1.50
Roebuck, Ed	64T	187	$ .30	$ .95

Player	Year	No.	VG	EX/MT
Roebuck, Ed	65T	52	$ .30	$ .85
Roenicke, Gary	80T	568	$ .01	$ .10
Roenicke, Gary	81T	37	$ .01	$ .10
Roenicke, Gary	82T	204	$ .01	$ .07
Roenicke, Gary	83T	605	$ .01	$ .07
Roenicke, Gary	84T	372	$ .01	$ .06
Roenicke, Gary	85T	109	$ .01	$ .05
Roenicke, Gary	86T	494	$ .01	$ .04
Roenicke, Gary	86TTR	94	$ .02	$ .10
Roenicke, Gary	87T	683	$ .01	$ .04
Roenicke, Gary	87TTR	105	$ .01	$ .05
Roenicke, Gary	88T	523	$ .01	$ .04
Roenicke, Ron	82T	681	$1.50	$5.00
Roenicke, Ron	83T	113	$ .01	$ .07
Roenicke, Ron	84T	647	$ .01	$ .06
Roenicke, Ron	86T	63	$ .01	$ .04
Roenicke, Ron	87T	329	$ .01	$ .04
Roenicke, Ron	88T	783	$ .01	$ .04
Roesler, Mike	89TMLD	104	$ .01	$ .10
Roesler, Mike	90T	203	$ .01	$ .10
Rogan, Pat	65T	486	$ .75	$3.00
Rogers, Kenny	89TMLD	105	$ .01	$ .10
Rogers, Kenny	89TTR	104	$ .01	$ .15
Rogers, Kenny	90T	683	$ .01	$ .15
Rogers, Kenny	91T	332	$ .01	$ .03
Rogers, Steve	74T	169	$ .15	$ .50
Rogers, Steve	75T	173	$ .07	$ .30
Rogers, Steve	76T	71	$ .05	$ .20
Rogers, Steve	77T	316	$ .05	$ .15
Rogers, Steve	78T	425	$ .02	$ .10
Rogers, Steve	79T	235	$ .02	$ .10
Rogers, Steve	80T	520	$ .01	$ .10
Rogers, Steve	81T	725	$ .01	$ .10
Rogers, Steve	82T	605	$ .01	$ .07
Rogers, Steve	83T	111	$ .01	$ .07

Player	Year	No.	VG	EX/MT
ers, Steve	83T	320	$ .01	$ .07
ers, Steve	83T	707	$ .01	$ .07
ers, Steve	83TAS	405	$ .01	$ .07
ers, Steve	84T	80	$ .01	$ .06
ers, Steve	84T	708	$ .04	$ .20

Player	Year	No.	VG	EX/MT
Rogers, Steve	84TAS	394	$ .01	$ .06
Rogers, Steve	85T	205	$ .01	$ .05
Roggenburk, Garry	63T	386	$ .75	$2.20
Roggenburk, Garry	64T	258	$ .30	$ .95
Roggenburk, Garry	66T	582	$5.00	$20.00
Roggenburk, Garry	67T	429	$ .30	$ .95
Roggenburk, Garry	68T	581	$ .35	$1.25
Rogodzinski, Mike	74T	492	$ .07	$ .30
Rogovin, Saul	52T	159	$7.00	$20.00
Rogovin, Saul	57T	129	$ .95	$3.50
Rohr, Bill	67T	547	$2.10	$6.00
Rohr, Bill	68T	314	$ .30	$ .85
Rohr, Les	68T	569	$ .35	$1.25
Rojas, Cookie	63T	221	$ .30	$ .95
Rojas, Cookie	64T	448	$ .50	$1.45
Rojas, Cookie	65T	474	$ .75	$3.00
Rojas, Cookie	66T	170	$ .30	$ .95
Rojas, Cookie	67T	595	$2.10	$6.00
Rojas, Cookie	68T	39	$ .30	$ .85
Rojas, Cookie	69T	507	$ .30	$ .85
Rojas, Cookie	70T	569	$ .30	$ .95
Rojas, Cookie	71T	118	$ .15	$ .50
Rojas, Cookie	72T	415	$ .15	$ .50
Rojas, Cookie	73T	188	$ .07	$ .30
Rojas, Cookie	74T	278	$ .07	$ .30
Rojas, Cookie	75T	169	$ .07	$ .30
Rojas, Cookie	76T	311	$ .05	$ .20
Rojas, Cookie	77T	509	$ .05	$ .15
Rojas, Cookie	88TTR	97	$ .01	$ .06
Rojas, Minnie	67T	104	$ .30	$ .85
Rojas, Minnie	68T	305	$ .30	$ .85
Rojas, Minnie	69T	502	$ .30	$ .85
Rojaz, Mel	91T	252	$ .01	$ .10
Rojek, Stan	52T	163	$7.00	$20.00
Roland, Jim	63T	522	$2.10	$6.00
Roland, Jim	64T	341	$ .30	$ .95
Roland, Jim	65T	171	$ .30	$ .85
Roland, Jim	68T	276	$ .30	$ .85
Roland, Jim	69T	336	$ .30	$ .85
Roland, Jim	70T	719	$ .90	$2.00
Roland, Jim	71T	642	$ .35	$1.25
Roland, Jim	72T	464	$ .15	$ .50
Rolfe, Red	52T	296	$15.00	$45.00
Rollins, Rich	62T	596	$12.00	$36.00
Rollins, Rich	63T	110	$ .30	$ .95
Rollins, Rich	64T	8	$2.10	$6.00
Rollins, Rich	64T	270	$ .30	$ .95
Rollins, Rich	65T	90	$ .30	$ .85
Rollins, Rich	66T	473	$ .75	$2.50
Rollins, Rich	67T	98	$ .30	$ .85
Rollins, Rich	68T	243	$ .30	$ .85
Rollins, Rich	69T	451	$ .30	$ .85
Rollins, Rich	70T	652	$ .75	$2.00
Roman, Bill	65T	493	$ .75	$3.00
Romanick, Ron	84TTR	102	$ .02	$ .10
Romanick, Ron	85T	579	$ .01	$ .05
Romanick, Ron	86T	733	$ .01	$ .04
Romanick, Ron	87T	136	$ .01	$ .04
Romano, John	59T	138	$ .75	$2.20
Romano, Johnny	60T	323	$ .75	$2.20
Romano, Johnny	61T	5	$ .35	$1.25
Romano, Johnny	62T	330	$ .45	$1.45
Romano, Johnny	63T	72	$ .30	$ .95
Romano, Johnny	63T	392	$ .24	$1.25
Romano, Johnny	64T	515	$ .50	$1.45
Romano, Johnny	65T	17	$ .30	$ .85
Romano, Johnny	66T	199	$ .35	$1.25
Romano, Johnny	66T	413	$ .30	$ .95
Romano, Johnny	67T	196	$ .30	$ .85
Romero, "Eddie"	79T	708	$ .45	$1.45

TOPPS

Player	Year	No.	VG	EX/MT
Romero, Ed	81T	659	$ .01	$ .10
Romero, Ed	82T	408	$ .01	$ .07
Romero, Ed	83T	271	$ .01	$ .07

ED ROMERO SS-2B-OF

Player	Year	No.	VG	EX/MT
Romero, Ed	84T	146	$ .01	$ .06
Romero, Ed	85T	498	$ .01	$ .06
Romero, Ed	86T	317	$ .01	$ .04
Romero, Ed	86TTR	95	$ .02	$ .10
Romero, Ed	87T	675	$ .01	$ .04
Romero, Ed	88T	37	$ .01	$ .04
Romero, Ed	89TTR	105	$ .01	$ .06
Romero, Ramon	86T	208	$ .01	$ .04
Romine, Kevin	87T	121	$ .01	$ .04
Romine, Kevin	90TTR	105	$ .01	$ .05
Romine, Kevin	91T	652	$ .01	$ .03
Romo, Enrique	78T	278	$ .02	$ .10
Romo, Enrique	79T	548	$ .02	$ .10
Romo, Enrique	80T	332	$ .01	$ .10
Romo, Enrique	81T	28	$ .01	$ .10
Romo, Enrique	82T	106	$ .01	$ .07
Romo, Enrique	83T	226	$ .01	$ .07
Romo, Vicente	69T	267	$ .30	$ .95
Romo, Vicente	70T	191	$ .15	$ .50
Romo, Vicente	71T	723	$ .75	$2.50
Romo, Vicente	72T	499	$ .15	$ .50
Romo, Vicente	73T	381	$ .07	$ .30
Romo, Vicente	74T	197	$ .07	$ .30
Romo, Vicente	75T	274	$ .07	$ .30
Romo, Vicente	83T	633	$ .01	$ .07
Romonosky, John	59T	267	$ .75	$2.20
Romonosky, John	60T	87	$ .45	$1.45
Roof, Gene	82T	561	$ .01	$ .07
Roof, Phil	63T	324	$ .45	$1.50
Roof, Phil	64T	541	$50.00	$150.00
Roof, Phil	65T	537	$2.10	$6.00
Roof, Phil	66T	382	$ .30	$ .95
Roof, Phil	67T	129	$ .30	$ .85
Roof, Phil	68T	484	$ .35	$1.25
Roof, Phil	69T	334	$ .30	$ .85
Roof, Phil	70T	359	$ .15	$ .50
Roof, Phil	71T	22	$ .15	$ .50

Player	Year	No.	VG	EX/MT
Roof, Phil	72T	201	$ .15	$ .50
Roof, Phil	73T	598	$ .45	$1.45
Roof, Phil	74T	388	$ .07	$ .30
Roof, Phil	75T	576	$ .07	$ .30
Roof, Phil	76T	424	$ .05	$ .20
Roof, Phil	77T	392	$ .05	$ .15
Rooker, Jim	69T	376	$ .30	$ .85
Rooker, Jim	70T	222	$ .15	$ .50
Rooker, Jim	71T	730	$ .75	$2.50
Rooker, Jim	72T	742	$ .75	$2.50
Rooker, Jim	74T	402	$ .07	$ .30
Rooker, Jim	75T	148	$ .07	$ .30
Rooker, Jim	77T	82	$ .05	$ .15
Rooker, Jim	78T	308	$ .02	$ .10
Rooker, Jim	79T	584	$ .02	$ .10
Rooker, Jim	80T	694	$ .01	$ .10
Roomes, Rolando	90T	364	$ .01	$ .10
Root, Charlie	60T	457	$ .95	$3.50
Roque, Jorge	72T	316	$ .15	$ .50
Roque, Jorge	73T	606	$ .95	$3.50
Rosario, Jimmy	72T	366	$ .15	$ .50
Rose, Bobby	89TMLD	106	$ .01	$ .25
Rose, Don	73T	178	$ .07	$ .30
Rose, Pete	63T	537	$175.00	$550.00
Rose, Pete	64T	125	$50.00	$140.00
Rose, Pete	65T	207	$30.00	$100.00
Rose, Pete	66T	30	$15.00	$50.00
Rose, Pete	67T	430	$12.00	$60.00
Rose, Pete	68T	230	$10.00	$45.00
Rose, Pete	69T	2	$2.10	$6.00
Rose, Pete	69T	120	$12.00	$35.00
Rose, Pete	69TAS	424	$3.00	$9.00
Rose, Pete	70T	61	$1.50	$4.75
Rose, Pete	70T	580	$15.00	$60.00
Rose, Pete	70TAS	458	$2.75	$8.00
Rose, Pete	71T	100	$12.00	$35.00
Rose, Pete	72T	559	$10.00	$45.00
Rose, Pete	72TIA	560	$7.50	$22.50
Rose, Pete	73T	130	$6.00	$17.50
Rose, Pete	74T	201	$1.00	$4.00
Rose, Pete	74T	300	$5.50	$17.50
Rose, Pete	74TAS	336	$ .75	$2.50
Rose, Pete	75T	211	$ .75	$3.00
Rose, Pete	75T	320	$5.00	$15.00
Rose, Pete	76T	240	$4.00	$12.00
Rose, Pete	77T	450	$2.00	$7.50
Rose, Pete	78T	20	$ .90	$3.50
Rose, Pete	78TRB	5	$ .50	$2.00
Rose, Pete	79T	650	$1.25	$4.25
Rose, Pete	79TRB	204	$ .25	$1.00
Rose, Pete	80T	540	$ .50	$2.00
Rose, Pete	80THL	4	$ .75	$2.50
Rose, Pete	81T	180	$ .50	$2.00
Rose, Pete	81TRB	205	$ .10	$ .50
Rose, Pete	82T	636	$ .10	$ .50
Rose, Pete	82T	780	$ .35	$1.50
Rose, Pete	82TAS	337	$ .15	$ .75
Rose, Pete	82THL	4	$ .15	$ .75
Rose, Pete	82TIA	781	$ .10	$ .50
Rose, Pete	83T	100	$ .35	$1.50
Rose, Pete	83T	101	$ .15	$ .75
Rose, Pete	83TAS	397	$ .10	$ .50
Rose, Pete	84T	300	$ .01	$ .10
Rose, Pete	84T	701	$ .06	$ .30
Rose, Pete	84T	702	$ .06	$ .30
Rose, Pete	84TTR	103	$1.00	$4.00
Rose, Pete	85T	547	$ .20	$ .75
Rose, Pete	85T	600	$ .10	$ .50
Rose, Pete	85TRB	6	$ .10	$ .50
Rose, Pete	86T	1	$ .10	$1.00

Player	Year	No.	VG	EX/MT	Player	Year	No.	VG	EX/MT
Rose, Pete (1963-1966)	86T	2	$ .03	$ .30	Royals, Team	74T	343	$ .15	$ .50
Rose, Pete (1967-1970)	86T	3	$ .03	$ .30	Royals, Team Checklist	75T	72	$ .15	$ .50
Rose, Pete (1971-1974)	86T	4	$ .03	$ .30	Royals, Team Checklist	76T	236	$ .35	$1.25
Rose, Pete (1975-1978)	86T	5	$ .03	$ .30	Royals, Team Checklist	77T	371	$ .15	$ .50
Rose, Pete (1979-1982)	86T	6	$ .03	$ .30	Royals, Team Checklist	78T	724	$ .30	$ .95
Rose, Pete (1983-1986)	86T	7	$ .03	$ .30	Royals, Team Checklist	79T	451	$ .05	$ .25
Rose, Pete	86T	741	$ .10	$ .50	Royals, Team Checklist	80T	66	$ .06	$ .30
Rose, Pete	86TRB	206	$ .01	$ .50	Royals, Team Checklist	81T	667	$ .02	$ .20
Rose, Pete	87T	200	$ .15	$ .50	Royals, Team Leaders	86T	606	$ .01	$ .04
Rose, Pete	87T	393	$ .15	$ .45	Royals, Team Leaders	87T	256	$ .01	$ .04
Rose, Pete	88T	475	$ .01	$ .25	Royals, Team Leaders	88T	141	$ .01	$ .04
Rose, Pete	89T	505	$ .01	$ .10	Royals, Team Leaders	89T	789	$ .01	$ .05
Roseboro, John	58T	42	$1.75	$4.50	Royster, Jerry	76T	592	$1.25	$5.00
Roseboro, John	59T	441	$ .75	$2.20	Royster, Jerry	77T	549	$ .05	$ .15
Roseboro, John	60T	88	$ .45	$1.45	Royster, Jerry	78T	187	$ .02	$ .10
Roseboro, John	60T	292	$ .45	$1.35	Royster, Jerry	79T	344	$ .02	$ .10
Roseboro, John	61T	363	$ .35	$1.25	Royster, Jerry	80T	463	$ .01	$ .10
Roseboro, John	62T	32	$ .75	$2.20	Royster, Jerry	81T	268	$ .01	$ .10
Roseboro, John	62TAS	397	$ .75	$2.50	Royster, Jerry	82T	608	$ .01	$ .07
Roseboro, John	63T	487	$2.50	$6.50	Royster, Jerry	83T	26	$ .01	$ .07
Roseboro, John	64T	88	$ .30	$ .95	Royster, Jerry	84T	572	$ .01	$ .06
Roseboro, John	65T	405	$ .35	$1.25	Royster, Jerry	85T	776	$ .01	$ .05
Roseboro, John	66T	189	$ .30	$ .95	Royster, Jerry	85TTR	96	$ .02	$ .10
Roseboro, John	67T	365	$ .30	$ .85	Royster, Jerry	86T	118	$ .01	$ .04
Roseboro, John	68T	65	$ .15	$ .50	Royster, Jerry	87T	403	$ .01	$ .04
Roseboro, John	69T	218	$ .30	$ .85	Royster, Jerry	87TTR	106	$ .01	$ .05
Roseboro, John	70T	655	$ .75	$2.00	Royster, Jerry	88T	257	$ .01	$ .04
Roseboro, John	73T	421	$ .07	$ .30	Rozek, Dick	52T	363	$40.00	$140.00
Roseboro, John	74T	276	$ .07	$ .30	Rozema, Dave	78T	124	$ .02	$ .10
Roselli, Bob	56T	131	$2.25	$6.00	Rozema, Dave	79T	33	$ .02	$ .10
Roselli, Bob	61T	529	$7.00	$21.00	Rozema, Dave	80T	288	$ .01	$ .10
Roselli, Bob	62T	363	$ .45	$1.45	Rozema, Dave	81T	614	$ .01	$ .10
Rosello, Dave	74T	607	$ .07	$ .30	Rozema, Dave	82T	319	$ .01	$ .07
Rosello, Dave	76T	546	$ .05	$ .20	Rozema, Dave	83T	562	$ .01	$ .07
Rosello, Dave	77T	92	$ .05	$ .15	Rozema, Dave	84T	457	$ .01	$ .06
Rosello, Dave	78T	423	$ .02	$ .10	Rozema, Dave	85T	47	$ .01	$ .05
Rosello, Dave	80T	122	$ .01	$ .10	Rozema, Dave	85TTR	97	$ .02	$ .10
Rosello, Dave	82T	724	$ .01	$ .07	Rozema, Dave	86T	739	$ .01	$ .04
Rosen, Al	51Trb	35	$3.00	$9.00	Roznovsky, Vic	65T	334	$ .35	$1.25
Rosen, Al	52T	10	$20.00	$80.00	Roznovsky, Vic	66T	467	$ .75	$2.50
Rosen, Al	53T	135	$7.50	$22.50	Roznovsky, Vic	67T	163	$ .30	$ .85
Rosen, Al	54T	15	$5.00	$15.00	Roznovsky, Vic	68T	428	$ .30	$ .85
Rosen, Al	55T	70	$3.00	$9.00	Roznovsky, Vic	69T	368	$ .30	$ .85
Rosen, Al	56T	35	$1.75	$5.00	Rucker, Dave	82T	261	$ .01	$ .07
Rosen, Al	61TMVP	474	$ .75	$2.00	Rucker, Dave	83T	304	$ .01	$ .07
Rosen, Al	75T	191	$ .45	$1.45	Rucker, Dave	84T	699	$ .01	$ .06
Rosenberg, Steve	89T	616	$ .01	$ .05	Rucker, Dave	85T	421	$ .01	$ .05
Rosenberg, Steve	90T	379	$ .01	$ .04	Rucker, Dave	85TTR	98	$ .02	$ .10
Ross, Bob	52T	298	$15.00	$47.50	Rucker, Dave	86T	39	$ .01	$ .04
Ross, Bob	54T	189	$2.50	$10.00	Rudi, Joe	69T	587	$ .60	$1.60
Ross, Gary	69T	404	$ .30	$ .85	Rudi, Joe	70T	102	$ .30	$ .85
Ross, Gary	70T	694	$ .75	$2.00	Rudi, Joe	71T	407	$ .15	$ .50
Ross, Gary	71T	153	$ .15	$ .50	Rudi, Joe	72T	209	$ .30	$ .95
Ross, Gary	73T	112	$ .07	$ .30	Rudi, Joe	73T	360	$ .15	$ .50
Ross, Gary	77T	544	$ .05	$ .15	Rudi, Joe	74T	264	$ .07	$ .30
Ross, Gary	78T	291	$ .02	$ .10	Rudi, Joe	75T	45	$ .07	$ .30
Rossi, Joe	52T	379	$40.00	$140.00	Rudi, Joe	76T	475	$ .07	$ .30
Rossi, Joe	53T	74	$4.50	$15.00	Rudi, Joe	77T	155	$ .05	$ .15
Rowdon, Wade	87T	569	$ .01	$ .04	Rudi, Joe	78T	635	$ .02	$ .10
Rowe, Don	63T	562	$3.00	$12.00	Rudi, Joe	79T	267	$ .02	$ .10
Rowe, Ken	63T	562	$3.00	$12.00	Rudi, Joe	80T	556	$ .01	$ .10
Rowe, Ken	65T	518	$ .75	$3.00	Rudi, Joe	81T	701	$ .01	$ .10
Rowe, Ralph	73T	49	$ .30	$ .85	Rudi, Joe	81TTR	826	$ .02	$ .10
Rowe, Ralph	74T	447	$ .07	$ .30	Rudi, Joe	82T	388	$ .01	$ .07
Rowe, Schoolboy	54T	197	$1.75	$7.00	Rudi, Joe	82TTR	102	$ .02	$ .10
Rowland, Mike	81T	502	$ .01	$ .10	Rudi, Joe	83T	87	$ .01	$ .07
Royals, Team	70T	422	$ .40	$1.75	Rudolph, Don	58T	347	$ .75	$3.00
Royals, Team	71T	742	$2.10	$6.00	Rudolph, Don	59T	179	$ .75	$2.20
Royals, Team	72T	617	$ .75	$2.25	Rudolph, Don	62T	224	$ .45	$1.45
Royals, Team	73T	347	$ .35	$1.25	Rudolph, Don	63T	291	$ .45	$1.50

TOPPS

Player	Year	No.	VG	EX/MT
Rudolph, Don	64T	427	$ .50	$1.45
Rudolph, Ken	70T	46	$ .15	$ .50
Rudolph, Ken	71T	472	$ .15	$ .50
Rudolph, Ken	72T	271	$ .15	$ .50
Rudolph, Ken	73T	414	$ .07	$ .30
Rudolph, Ken	74T	584	$ .07	$ .30
Rudolph, Ken	75T	289	$ .07	$ .30
Rudolph, Ken	76T	601	$ .05	$ .20
Ruffin, Bruce	87T	499	$ .15	$ .50
Ruffin, Bruce	88T	268	$ .01	$ .04
Ruffin, Bruce	89T	518	$ .01	$ .05
Ruffin, Bruce	90T	22	$ .01	$ .04
Ruffin, Bruce	91T	637	$ .01	$ .03
Ruhle, Vern	75T	614	$ .07	$ .30
Ruhle, Vern	76T	89	$ .05	$ .20
Ruhle, Vern	77T	311	$ .05	$ .15
Ruhle, Vern	78T	456	$ .02	$ .10
Ruhle, Vern	79T	49	$ .02	$ .10
Ruhle, Vern	80T	234	$ .01	$ .10
Ruhle, Vern	81T	642	$ .01	$ .10
Ruhle, Vern	82T	539	$ .01	$ .07
Ruhle, Vern	83T	172	$ .01	$ .07
Ruhle, Vern	84T	328	$ .01	$ .06
Ruhle, Vern	85T	426	$ .01	$ .05
Ruhle, Vern	85TTR	99	$ .02	$ .10
Ruhle, Vern	86T	768	$ .01	$ .04
Ruhle, Vern	87T	221	$ .01	$ .04
Ruiz, Chico	63T	407	$ .45	$1.50
Ruiz, Chico	64T	356	$ .30	$ .95
Ruiz, Chico	65T	554	$1.75	$4.50
Ruiz, Chico	66T	159	$ .30	$ .95
Ruiz, Chico	67T	339	$ .30	$ .85
Ruiz, Chico	68T	213	$ .30	$ .85
Ruiz, Chico	69T	469	$ .30	$ .85
Ruiz, Chico	70T	606	$ .30	$ .95
Ruiz, Chico	71T	686	$ .75	$2.50
Runge, Paul	85TTR	100	$ .02	$ .10
Runge, Paul	86T	409	$ .01	$ .04
Runge, Paul	89T	38	$ .01	$ .05
Runge, Paul	89TBB	23	$ .01	$ .06
Runnels, James "Pete"	52T	2	$20.00	$65.00
Runnels, Pete	53T	219	$4.50	$15.00
Runnels, Pete	54T	6	$2.50	$10.00
Runnels, Pete	56T	234	$3.00	$9.00
Runnels, Pete	57T	64	$ .95	$3.50
Runnels, Pete	58T	265	$ .75	$3.00
Runnels, Pete	59T	370	$ .75	$2.20
Runnels, Pete	59T	519	$3.00	$9.00
Runnels, Pete	60T	15	$ .45	$1.45
Runnels, Pete	61T	42	$ .75	$3.00
Runnels, Pete	61T	210	$ .35	$1.25
Runnels, Pete	62T	3	$ .45	$1.45
Runnels, Pete	63T	2	$3.00	$12.00
Runnels, Pete	63T	230	$ .30	$ .95
Runnels, Pete	64T	121	$ .30	$ .95
Rush, Bob	52T	153	$7.00	$20.00
Rush, Bob	56T	214	$3.00	$9.00
Rush, Bob	57T	137	$ .95	$3.50
Rush, Bob	58T	313	$ .75	$3.00
Rush, Bob	59T	396	$ .75	$2.20
Rush, Bob	60T	404	$ .75	$2.20
Ruskin, Scott	90TTR	106	$ .01	$ .15
Ruskin, Scott	91T	589	$ .01	$ .03
Russell, Bill	70T	304	$ .15	$ .50
Russell, Bill	71T	226	$ .15	$ .50
Russell, Bill	72T	736	$ .85	$3.50
Russell, Bill	73T	108	$ .15	$ .50
Russell, Bill	74T	239	$ .07	$ .30
Russell, Bill	75T	23	$ .07	$ .30
Russell, Bill	76T	22	$ .05	$ .20

Player	Year	No.	VG	EX/MT
Russell, Bill	77T	322	$ .05	$ .15
Russell, Bill	78T	128	$ .02	$ .10
Russell, Bill	79T	546	$ .02	$ .10
Russell, Bill	80T	75	$ .01	$ .10
Russell, Bill	81T	465	$ .01	$ .10
Russell, Bill	82T	279	$ .01	$ .07
Russell, Bill	83T	661	$ .01	$ .07
Russell, Bill	84T	792	$ .01	$ .06
Russell, Bill	85T	343	$ .01	$ .05
Russell, Bill	86T	506	$ .01	$ .04
Russell, Bill	87T	116	$ .01	$ .04
Russell, Jeff	84T	270	$ .01	$ .25
Russell, Jeff	85T	651	$ .01	$ .10
Russell, Jeff	87T	444	$ .01	$ .04
Russell, Jeff	88T	114	$ .01	$ .04
Russell, Jeff	89T	565	$ .01	$ .05
Russell, Jeff	89TBB	309	$ .01	$ .06

JEFF RUSSELL

Player	Year	No.	VG	EX/MT
Russell, Jeff	90T	80	$ .01	$ .04
Russell, Jeff	90TAS	395	$ .01	$ .04
Russell, Jeff	91T	344	$ .01	$ .03
Russell, Jim	52T	51	$15.00	$47.50
Russell, John	86T	392	$ .01	$ .04
Russell, John	87T	379	$ .01	$ .04
Russell, John	88T	188	$ .01	$ .04
Russell, John	90TTR	107	$ .01	$ .05
Russell, John	91T	734	$ .01	$ .03
Ruth, Babe	61T	401	$3.35	$10.00
Ruth, Babe	73T	1	$4.50	$17.50
Ruth, Babe	73TATL	474	$2.50	$7.00
Ruth, Babe	76TAS	345	$2.00	$6.00
Ruth, Babe, Special 1	62T	135	$5.00	$15.00
Ruth, Babe, Special 2	62T	136	$2.00	$7.00
Ruth, Babe, Special 3	62T	137	$2.00	$7.00
Ruth, Babe, Special 4	62T	138	$2.00	$7.00
Ruth, Babe, Special 5	62T	139	$4.00	$16.00
Ruth, Babe, Special 6	62T	140	$3.75	$15.00
Ruth, Babe, Special 7	62T	141	$2.00	$7.00
Ruth, Babe, Special 8	62T	142	$2.00	$7.00
Ruth, Babe, Special 9	62T	143	$2.00	$7.00
Ruth, Babe, Special 10	62T	144	$2.00	$7.00

Player	Year	No.	VG	EX/MT
Rutherford, John	52T	320	$40.00	$140.00
Rutherford, John	53T	137	$4.50	$15.00
Ruthven, Dick	74T	47	$ .07	$ .30
Ruthven, Dick	75T	267	$ .07	$ .30
Ruthven, Dick	76T	431	$ .05	$ .20
Ruthven, Dick	77T	575	$ .05	$ .15
Ruthven, Dick	78T	75	$ .02	$ .10
Ruthven, Dick	79T	419	$ .02	$ .10
Ruthven, Dick	80T	136	$ .01	$ .10
Ruthven, Dick	81T	691	$ .01	$ .10
Ruthven, Dick	82T	317	$ .01	$ .07
Ruthven, Dick	83T	484	$ .01	$ .07
Ruthven, Dick	83TTR	98	$ .02	$ .10
Ruthven, Dick	84T	736	$ .01	$ .06
Ruthven, Dick	85T	563	$ .01	$ .05
Ruthven, Dick	86T	98	$ .01	$ .04
Ryal, Mark	88T	243	$ .01	$ .04
Ryan, Connie	52T	107	$7.00	$20.00
Ryan, Connie	53T	102	$4.50	$15.00
Ryan, Connie	54T	136	$2.50	$10.00
Ryan, Connie	74T	634	$ .35	$1.25
Ryan, Mike	65T	573	$3.75	$14.00
Ryan, Mike	66T	419	$ .30	$ .95
Ryan, Mike	67T	223	$ .30	$ .85
Ryan, Mike	68T	306	$ .30	$ .85
Ryan, Mike	69T	28	$ .30	$ .85
Ryan, Mike	70T	591	$ .30	$ .95
Ryan, Mike	71T	533	$ .35	$1.25
Ryan, Mike	72T	324	$ .15	$ .50
Ryan, Mike	73T	467	$ .07	$ .30
Ryan, Mike	74T	564	$ .07	$ .30
Ryan, Nolan	68T	177	$250.00	$1100.00
Ryan, Nolan	69T	533	$115.00	$325.00
Ryan, Nolan	70T	712	$100.00	$300.00
Ryan, Nolan	71T	513	$25.00	$125.00
Ryan, Nolan	72T	595	$20.00	$100.00
Ryan, Nolan	73T	67	$ .85	$3.50
Ryan, Nolan	73T	220	$20.00	$55.00
Ryan, Nolan	74T	20	$7.50	$27.50
Ryan, Nolan	74T	207	$ .75	$3.00
Ryan, Nolan	75T	312	$ .50	$2.50
Ryan, Nolan	75T	500	$8.00	$32.00
Ryan, Nolan	75THL	7	$ .30	$ .95
Ryan, Nolan	75THL	75	$1.50	$4.50
Ryan, Nolan	76T	330	$6.00	$25.00
Ryan, Nolan	77T	6	$ .75	$3.00
Ryan, Nolan	77T	650	$5.00	$20.00
Ryan, Nolan	77TRB	234	$1.50	$6.00
Ryan, Nolan	78T	206	$ .05	$ .20
Ryan, Nolan	78T	400	$3.00	$13.00
Ryan, Nolan	78TRB	6	$ .75	$3.00
Ryan, Nolan	79T	6	$ .06	$ .30
Ryan, Nolan	79T	115	$3.50	$12.50
Ryan, Nolan	79TRH	417	$ .05	$ .20
Ryan, Nolan	80T	206	$ .05	$ .25
Ryan, Nolan	80T	580	$2.50	$10.00
Ryan, Nolan	81T	240	$1.50	$6.00
Ryan, Nolan	82T	66	$ .03	$ .15
Ryan, Nolan	82T	90	$1.00	$4.00
Ryan, Nolan	82T	167	$ .03	$ .15
Ryan, Nolan	82THL	5	$ .05	$ .25
Ryan, Nolan	83T	360	$1.00	$3.50
Ryan, Nolan	83T	361	$ .01	$ .07
Ryan, Nolan	84T	4	$ .05	$ .25
Ryan, Nolan	84T	66	$ .01	$ .06
Ryan, Nolan	84T	470	$ .75	$3.00
Ryan, Nolan	84T	707	$ .05	$ .25
Ryan, Nolan	85T	760	$ .50	$2.00
Ryan, Nolan	85TRB	7	$ .04	$ .20
Ryan, Nolan	86T	100	$ .25	$1.00

Player	Year	No.	VG	EX/MT
Ryan, Nolan	87T	757	$ .25	$1.00
Ryan, Nolan	88T	250	$ .01	$ .50
Ryan, Nolan	88TBB	29	$ .05	$ .25
Ryan, Nolan	88TRB	6	$ .01	$ .10
Ryan, Nolan	88TTB	661	$ .05	$ .35
Ryan, Nolan	89T	530	$ .05	$ .50
Ryan, Nolan	89TTR	106	$ .01	$1.00
Ryan, Nolan	90T	1	$ .01	$ .50

NOLAN RYAN

Player	Year	No.	VG	EX/MT
Ryan, Nolan (Mets)	90T	2	$ .01	$$ .25
Ryan, Nolan (Angels)	90T	3	$ .01	$ .25
Ryan, Nolan (Astros)	90T	4	$ .01	$ .25
Ryan, Nolan (Rangers)	90T	5	$ .01	$ .25
Ryan, Nolan	91T	1	$ .01	$ .25
Ryan, Nolan	91TRB	6	$ .01	$ .20
Ryba, Mike	54T	237	$2.50	$10.00
Saberhagen, Bret	84TTR	104	$5.00	$20.00
Saberhagen, Bret	85T	23	$2.00	$9.00
Saberhagen, Bret	86T	487	$ .10	$ .50
Saberhagen, Bret	86TAS	720	$ .02	$ .15
Saberhagen, Bret	87T	140	$ .15	$ .50
Saberhagen, Bret	88T	540	$ .01	$ .20
Saberhagen, Bret	88TBB	94	$ .01	$ .10
Saberhagen, Bret	89T	750	$ .01	$ .10
Saberhagen, Bret	89TBB	6	$ .01	$ .20
Saberhagen, Bret	90T	350	$ .01	$ .10
Saberhagen, Bret	90TAS	393	$ .01	$ .10
Saberhagen, Bret	91T	280	$ .01	$ .03
Sabo, Chris	88TTR	98	$ .50	$3.00
Sabo, Chris	89T	490	$ .25	$1.50
Sabo, Chris	89TBB	251	$ .01	$ .25
Sabo, Chris	90T	737	$ .01	$ .20
Sabo, Chris	91T	45	$ .01	$ .03
Sadecki, Ray	60T	327	$ .75	$2.20
Sadecki, Ray	61T	32	$ .35	$1.25
Sadecki, Ray	62T	383	$ .75	$2.50
Sadecki, Ray	63T	486	$2.50	$6.50
Sadecki, Ray	64T	147	$ .30	$ .95
Sadecki, Ray	65T	10	$ .45	$1.45
Sadecki, Ray	65T	230	$ .35	$1.25
Sadecki, Ray	66T	26	$ .30	$ .95

Player	Year	No.	VG	EX/MT
Sadecki, Ray	67T	409	$ .30	$ .95
Sadecki, Ray	68T	494	$ .35	$1.25
Sadecki, Ray	69T	125	$ .30	$ .85
Sadecki, Ray	70T	679	$ .75	$2.00
Sadecki, Ray	71T	406	$ .15	$ .50
Sadecki, Ray	72T	563	$ .30	$ .95
Sadecki, Ray	72TIA	564	$ .30	$ .95
Sadecki, Ray	73T	283	$ .07	$ .30
Sadecki, Ray	74T	216	$ .07	$ .30
Sadecki, Ray	75T	349	$ .07	$ .30
Sadecki, Ray	77T	26	$ .05	$ .15
Sadek, Mike	74T	577	$ .07	$ .30
Sadek, Mike	76T	234	$ .05	$ .20
Sadek, Mike	77T	129	$ .05	$ .15
Sadek, Mike	78T	8	$ .02	$ .10
Sadek, Mike	79T	256	$ .02	$ .10
Sadek, Mike	80T	462	$ .01	$ .10
Sadek, Mike	81T	384	$ .01	$ .10
Sadowski, Bob	62T	595	$7.00	$21.00
Sadowski, Bob	63T	568	$1.75	$4.50
Sadowski, Bob	64T	271	$ .30	$ .95
Sadowski, Bob	65T	156	$ .30	$ .85
Sadowski, Bob	66T	523	$5.00	$20.00
Sadowski, Ed	59T	139	$ .75	$2.20
Sadowski, Ed	60T	403	$ .75	$2.20
Sadowski, Ed	61T	163	$ .35	$1.25
Sadowski, Ed	62T	569	$3.95	$11.50
Sadowski, Ed	63T	527	$1.75	$4.50
Sadowski, Ed	64T	61	$ .30	$ .95
Sadowski, Ted	61T	254	$ .35	$1.25
Saferight, Harry	80T	683	$ .01	$ .10
Sain, Johnny	51Tbb	9	$6.50	$25.00
Sain, Johnny	52T	49	$25.00	$75.00
Sain, Johnny	53T	119	$8.00	$25.00
Sain, Johnny	54T	205	$8.00	$25.00
Sain, Johnny	55T	193	$7.50	$30.00
Sain, Johnny	73T	356	$ .15	$ .50
Sain, Johnny	74T	221	$ .07	$ .30
Sakata, Lenn	80T	668	$ .01	$ .10
Sakata, Lenn	81T	287	$ .01	$ .10
Sakata, Lenn	82T	136	$ .01	$ .07
Sakata, Lenn	83T	319	$ .01	$ .07
Sakata, Lenn	84T	578	$ .01	$ .06
Sakata, Lenn	85T	81	$ .01	$ .05
Sakata, Lenn	86T	446	$ .01	$ .04
Sakata, Lenn	88T	716	$ .01	$ .04
Salas, Mark	85TTR	101	$ .02	$ .10
Salas, Mark	86T	537	$ .01	$ .04
Salas, Mark	87T	87	$ .01	$ .04
Salas, Mark	87TTR	107	$ .01	$ .05
Salas, Mark	88TTR	99	$ .01	$ .06
Salas, Mark	89T	384	$ .01	$ .05
Salas, Mark	91T	498	$ .01	$ .03
Salazar, Argenis	85T	154	$ .01	$ .05
Salazar, Argenis	86TTR	96	$ .02	$ .10
Salazar, Argenis	87T	533	$ .01	$ .04
Salazar, Argenis	88T	29	$ .01	$ .04
Salazar, Argenis	89T	642	$ .01	$ .05
Salazar, Luis	81T	309	$ .01	$ .10
Salazar, Luis	82T	366	$ .01	$ .07
Salazar, Luis	82T	662	$ .01	$ .07
Salazar, Luis	83T	533	$ .01	$ .07
Salazar, Luis	84T	68	$ .01	$ .06
Salazar, Luis	85T	789	$ .01	$ .05
Salazar, Luis	85TTR	102	$ .02	$ .10
Salazar, Luis	86T	103	$ .01	$ .04
Salazar, Luis	87T	454	$ .01	$ .04
Salazar, Luis	87TTR	108	$ .01	$ .05
Salazar, Luis	88T	276	$ .01	$ .04
Salazar, Luis	88TTR	100	$ .01	$ .06

Player	Year	No.	VG	EX/MT
Salazar, Luis	89T	553	$ .01	$ .05
Salazar, Luis	89TTR	107	$ .01	$ .06
Salazar, Luis	90T	378	$ .01	$ .04
Salazar, Luis	91T	614	$ .01	$ .03

ROGER SALKELD

Player	Year	No.	VG	EX/MT
Salkeld, Roger	90T	44	$ .01	$ .25
Salmon, Chico	64T	499	$ .50	$1.45
Salmon, Chico	65T	105	$ .30	$ .85
Salmon, Chico	66T	594	$5.00	$20.00
Salmon, Chico	67T	43	$ .30	$ .85
Salmon, Chico	68T	318	$ .30	$ .85
Salmon, Chico	69T	62	$ .30	$ .85
Salmon, Chico	70T	301	$ .15	$ .50
Salmon, Chico	71T	249	$ .15	$ .50
Salmon, Chico	72T	646	$ .30	$ .95
Sambito, Joe	77T	227	$ .05	$ .15
Sambito, Joe	78T	498	$ .02	$ .10
Sambito, Joe	79T	158	$ .02	$ .10
Sambito, Joe	80T	571	$ .01	$ .10
Sambito, Joe	81T	385	$ .01	$ .10
Sambito, Joe	82T	34	$ .01	$ .07
Sambito, Joe	83T	662	$ .01	$ .07
Sambito, Joe	85T	264	$ .01	$ .05
Sambito, Joe	85TTR	103	$ .02	$ .10
Sambito, Joe	86TTR	97	$ .02	$ .10
Sambito, Joe	87T	451	$ .01	$ .04
Sambito, Joe	88T	784	$ .01	$ .04
Samford, Ron	59T	242	$ .75	$2.20
Samford, Ron	60T	409	$ .75	$2.20
Sampen, Bill	90TTR	108	$ .01	$ .15
Sampen, Bill	91T	649	$ .01	$ .15
Sample, Billy	79T	713	$ .05	$ .20
Sample, Billy	80T	458	$ .01	$ .10
Sample, Billy	81T	283	$ .01	$ .10
Sample, Billy	82T	112	$ .01	$ .07
Sample, Billy	83T	641	$ .01	$ .07
Sample, Billy	84T	12	$ .01	$ .06
Sample, Billy	85T	337	$ .01	$ .05
Sample, Billy	86T	533	$ .01	$ .04
Sample, Billy	86TTR	98	$ .02	$ .10
Sample, Billy	87T	104	$ .01	$ .04

Player	Year	No.	VG	EX/MT	Player	Year	No.	VG	EX/MT
Samuel, Amado	62T	597	$7.00	$21.00	Sanderson, Scott	88T	311	$ .01	$ .04
Samuel, Amado	64T	129	$ .30	$ .95	Sanderson, Scott	89T	212	$ .01	$ .05
Samuel, Juan	84TTR	105	$ .75	$2.50	Sanderson, Scott	90T	67	$ .01	$ .04
Samuel, Juan	85T	265	$ .05	$ .35	Sanderson, Scott	90TTR	110	$ .01	$ .05
Samuel, Juan	85TRB	8	$ .01	$ .10	Sanderson, Scott	91T	728	$ .01	$ .03
Samuel, Juan	86T	475	$ .01	$ .10	Sandlock, Mike	53T	247	$12.50	$50.00
Samuel, Juan	87T	255	$ .01	$ .10	Sandlock, Mike	54T	104	$2.50	$10.00
Samuel, Juan	88T	705	$ .01	$ .10	Sands, Charlie	72T	538	$ .30	$ .95
Samuel, Juan	88TAS	398	$ .01	$ .04	Sands, Charlie	74T	381	$ .07	$ .30
Samuel, Juan	88TBB	67	$ .01	$ .10	Sands, Charlie	75T	548	$ .07	$ .30
Samuel, Juan	89T	575	$ .01	$ .05	Sandt, Tommy	77T	616	$ .05	$ .15
Samuel, Juan	89TBB	321	$ .01	$ .06	Sanford, Jack	57T	387	$1.00	$4.25
Samuel, Juan	89TTR	108	$ .01	$ .10	Sanford, Jack	58T	264	$ .75	$3.00
Samuel, Juan	90T	85	$ .01	$ .04	Sanford, Jack	59T	275	$ .75	$2.20
Samuel, Juan	90TTR	109	$ .01	$ .05	Sanford, Jack	60T	165	$ .45	$1.45
Samuel, Juan	91T	645	$ .01	$ .03	Sanford, Jack	61T	258	$ .35	$1.25
Sanchez, Alejandro	86T	563	$ .01	$ .04	Sanford, Jack	61T	383	$ .75	$3.00
Sanchez, Alex	89TMLD	107	$ .01	$ .15	Sanford, Jack	62T	538	$3.95	$11.50
Sanchez, Alex	89TTR	109	$ .01	$ .25	Sanford, Jack	63T	325	$ .45	$1.50
Sanchez, Alex	90T	563	$ .01	$ .15	Sanford, Jack	63T	7	$ .45	$1.45
Sanchez, Celerino	73T	103	$ .07	$ .30	Sanford, Jack	64T	414	$ .50	$1.45
Sanchez, Celerino	74T	623	$ .07	$ .30	Sanford, Jack	65T	228	$ .35	$1.25
Sanchez, Israel	89T	452	$ .01	$ .10	Sanford, Jack	66T	23	$ .30	$ .95
Sanchez, Luis	82T	653	$ .50	$2.00	Sanford, Jack	67T	549	$2.00	$6.00
Sanchez, Luis	83T	623	$ .01	$ .07	Sanguillen, Manny	68T	251	$ .15	$ .50
Sanchez, Luis	84T	258	$ .01	$ .06	Sanguillen, Manny	69T	509	$ .30	$ .95
Sanchez, Luis	85T	42	$ .01	$ .05	Sanguillen, Manny	70T	188	$ .15	$ .50
Sanchez, Luis	86T	124	$ .01	$ .04	Sanguillen, Manny	71T	480	$ .15	$ .50
Sanchez, Orlando	82T	604	$ .01	$ .07	Sanguillen, Manny	71T	62	$ .15	$ .50
Sanchez, Raul	57T	393	$ .85	$3.50	Sanguillen, Manny	72T	60	$ .30	$ .85
Sanchez, Raul	60T	311	$ .75	$2.20	Sanguillen, Manny	73T	250	$ .07	$ .30
Sandberg, Ryne	83T	83	$15.00	$45.00	Sanguillen, Manny	74T	28	$ .07	$ .30
Sandberg, Ryne	84T	596	$2.50	$7.50	Sanguillen, Manny	75T	515	$ .07	$ .30
Sandberg, Ryne	85T	460	$ .50	$2.50	Sanguillen, Manny	76T	191	$ .30	$ .95
Sandberg, Ryne	85TAS	713	$ .01	$ .25	Sanguillen, Manny	76T	220	$ .05	$ .20
Sandberg, Ryne	86T	690	$ .25	$1.25	Sanguillen, Manny	77T	61	$ .05	$ .15
Sandberg, Ryne	87T	680	$ .15	$ .50	Sanguillen, Manny	78T	658	$ .02	$ .10
Sandberg, Ryne	88T	10	$ .01	$ .35	Sanguillen, Manny	79T	447	$ .02	$ .10
Sandberg, Ryne	88TBB	16	$ .01	$ .15	Sanguillen, Manny	80T	148	$ .01	$ .10
Sandberg, Ryne	89T	360	$ .01	$ .25	Sanguillen, Manny	81T	226	$ .01	$ .10
Sandberg, Ryne	89TAS	387	$ .01	$ .05	Santana, Rafael	85T	67	$ .01	$ .05
Sandberg, Ryne	89TBB	212	$ .01	$ .25	Santana, Rafael	86T	587	$ .01	$ .04
Sandberg, Ryne	90T	210	$ .01	$ .10	Santana, Rafael	87T	378	$ .01	$ .04
Sandberg, Ryne	90TAS	398	$ .01	$ .10	Santana, Rafael	88T	233	$ .01	$ .04
Sandberg, Ryne	91T	740	$ .01	$ .10	Santana, Rafael	88TBB	246	$ .01	$ .06
Sandberg, Ryne	91TAS	398	$ .01	$ .10	Santana, Rafael	88TTR	101	$ .01	$ .06
Sandberg, Ryne	91TRB	7	$ .01	$ .10	Santana, Rafael	89T	792	$ .01	$ .05
Sanders, Deion	89TMLD	108	$ .01	$ .50	Santana, Rafael	89TBB	192	$ .01	$ .06
Sanders, Deion	89TTR	110	$ .01	$ .50	Santana, Rafael	90T	651	$ .01	$ .04
Sanders, Deion	90T	61	$ .01	$ .25	Santiago, Benny	87TTR	109	$ .20	$1.00
Sanders, Ken	66T	356	$ .30	$ .95	Santiago, Benny	88T	693	$ .10	$ .50
Sanders, Ken	71T	116	$ .15	$ .50	Santiago, Benny	88TAS	404	$ .01	$ .25
Sanders, Ken	72T	391	$ .15	$ .50	Santiago, Benny	88TBB	12	$ .01	$ .10
Sanders, Ken	73T	246	$ .07	$ .30	Santiago, Benito "Benny"	88TRB	7	$ .01	$ .06
Sanders, Ken	74T	638	$ .07	$ .30	Santiago, Benny	89T	256	$ .01	$ .05
Sanders, Ken	75T	366	$ .07	$ .30	Santiago, Benny	89TBB	134	$ .01	$ .15
Sanders, Ken	76T	291	$ .05	$ .20	Santiago, Benny	90T	35	$ .01	$ .10
Sanders, Ken	77T	171	$ .05	$ .15	Santiago, Benny	91T	760	$ .01	$ .03
Sanders, Reggie	74T	600	$1.25	$5.00	Santiago, Jose	56T	59	$2.25	$6.00
Sanders, Reggie	75T	617	$ .45	$1.45	Santiago, Jose	65T	557	$1.75	$4.50
Sanderson, Scott	79T	720	$ .05	$ .20	Santiago, Jose	66T	203	$ .30	$ .95
Sanderson, Scott	80T	578	$ .01	$ .10	Santiago, Jose	67T	473	$ .75	$3.00
Sanderson, Scott	81T	235	$ .01	$ .10	Santiago, Jose	68T	123	$ .30	$ .85
Sanderson, Scott	82T	7	$ .01	$ .07	Santiago, Jose	69T	21	$ .30	$ .85
Sanderson, Scott	83T	717	$ .01	$ .07	Santiago, Jose	70T	708	$ .75	$2.00
Sanderson, Scott	84T	164	$ .01	$ .06	Santo, Ron	61T	35	$10.00	$30.00
Sanderson, Scott	84TTR	106	$ .02	$ .10	Santo, Ron	62T	170	$1.50	$6.00
Sanderson, Scott	85T	616	$ .01	$ .05	Santo, Ron	63T	252	$1.00	$4.00
Sanderson, Scott	86T	406	$ .01	$ .04	Santo, Ron	64T	375	$ .75	$3.00
Sanderson, Scott	87T	534	$ .01	$ .04	Santo, Ron	65T	6	$ .95	$3.50

TOPPS

Player	Year	No.	VG	EX/MT	Player	Year	No.	VG	EX/MT
Santo, Ron	65T	110	$ .15	$ .50	Savage, Jack	90TTR	111	$ .01	$ .05
Santo, Ron	66T	290	$ .45	$1.45	Savage, Jack	91T	357	$ .01	$ .03
Santo, Ron	67T	70	$ .35	$1.25	Savage, Ted	62T	104	$ .45	$1.45
Santo, Ron	68T	5	$1.25	$3.75	Savage, Ted	63T	508	$1.75	$4.50
Santo, Ron	68T	235	$ .45	$1.45	Savage, Ted	64T	62	$ .30	$ .95
Santo, Ron	68TAS	366	$ .45	$1.45	Savage, Ted	67T	552	$2.10	$6.00
Santo, Ron	69T	4	$ .75	$2.25	Savage, Ted	68T	119	$ .30	$ .85
Santo, Ron	69T	570	$ .20	$ .50	Savage, Ted	69T	471	$ .30	$ .85
Santo, Ron	69TAS	420	$ .30	$ .85	Savage, Ted	70T	602	$ .30	$ .95
Santo, Ron	70T	63	$ .75	$2.20	Savage, Ted	71T	76	$ .15	$ .50
Santo, Ron	70T	670	$ .75	$2.00	Saverine, Bob	63T	158	$ .30	$ .95
Santo, Ron	70TAS	454	$ .15	$ .50	Saverine, Bob	64T	221	$ .30	$ .95
Santo, Ron	71T	220	$ .15	$ .50	Saverine, Bob	65T	427	$ .35	$1.25
Santo, Ron	72T	555	$ .30	$ .95	Saverine, Bob	66T	312	$ .30	$ .95
Santo, Ron	72TIA	556	$ .30	$ .95	Saverine, Bob	67T	27	$ .30	$ .85
Santo, Ron	73T	115	$ .07	$ .30	Saverine, Bob	68T	149	$ .30	$ .85
Santo, Ron	74T	270	$ .30	$ .95	Sawatski, Carl	53T	202	$4.50	$15.00
Santo, Ron	74TAS	334	$ .45	$1.45	Sawatski, Carl	54T	198	$2.50	$10.00
Santo, Ron	74TTR	270	$ .30	$ .85	Sawatski, Carl	55T	122	$2.00	$6.00
Santo, Ron	75T	35	$ .15	$ .50	Sawatski, Carl	58T	234	$ .75	$3.00
Santorini, Al	69T	592	$ .30	$ .95	Sawatski, Carl	59T	56	$ .85	$3.50
Santorini, Al	70T	212	$ .15	$ .50	Sawatski, Carl	60T	545	$2.50	$10.00
Santorini, Al	71T	467	$ .15	$ .50	Sawatski, Carl	61T	198	$ .35	$1.25
Santorini, Al	72T	723	$ .75	$2.50	Sawatski, Carl	62T	106	$ .45	$1.45
Santorini, Al	73T	24	$ .07	$ .30	Sawatski, Carl	63T	267	$ .30	$ .95
Santovenia, Nelson	88TTR	102	$ .01	$ .10	Sawatski, Carl	64T	24	$ .30	$ .95
Santovenia, Nelson	89T	228	$ .01	$ .10	Sawyer, Eddie	60T	226	$ .45	$1.45
Santovenia, Nelson	89TBB	98	$ .01	$ .06	Sawyer, Rick	77T	268	$ .05	$ .15
Santovenia, Nelson	90T	614	$ .01	$ .04	Sax, Dave	86T	307	$ .01	$ .04
Santovenia, Nelson	91T	744	$ .01	$ .03	Sax, Steve	82T	681	$1.50	$5.00
Sarmiento, Manny	77T	475	$ .05	$ .15	Sax, Steve	82TTR	103	$1.00	$4.50
Sarmiento, Manny	78T	377	$ .02	$ .10	Sax, Steve	83T	245	$ .05	$ .75
Sarmiento, Manny	79T	149	$ .02	$ .10	Sax, Steve	84T	610	$ .04	$ .35
Sarmiento, Manny	80T	21	$ .01	$ .10	Sax, Steve	85T	470	$ .01	$ .25
Sarmiento, Manny	81T	649	$ .01	$ .10	Sax, Steve	86T	175	$ .02	$ .15
Sarmiento, Manny	83T	566	$ .01	$ .07	Sax, Steve	87T	769	$ .01	$ .10
Sarmiento, Manny	84T	209	$ .01	$ .06	Sax, Steve	87TAS	596	$ .01	$ .04
Sarni, Bill	54T	194	$2.50	$10.00	Sax, Steve	88T	305	$ .01	$ .10
Sarni, Bill	56T	247	$3.00	$9.00	Sax, Steve	88TBB	46	$ .01	$ .15
Sarni, Bill	57T	86	$ .95	$3.50	Sax, Steve	89T	40	$ .01	$ .10
Sasser, Mackey	88TTR	103	$ .01	$ .06	Sax, Steve	89TBB	111	$ .01	$ .06
Sasser, Mackey	89T	457	$ .01	$ .05	Sax, Steve	89TTR	111	$ .01	$ .10
Sasser, Mackey	90T	656	$ .01	$ .04	Sax, Steve	90T	560	$ .01	$ .04
Sasser, Mackey	91T	382	$ .01	$ .03	Sax, Steve	91T	290	$ .01	$ .03
Satriano, Tom	63T	548	$1.75	$4.50	Scanlon, Pat	78T	611	$ .02	$ .10
Satriano, Tom	64T	521	$ .50	$1.45	Scarbery, Randy	80T	291	$ .01	$ .10
Satriano, Tom	65T	124	$ .30	$ .85	Scarborough, Ray	51Trb	42	$2.10	$6.00
Satriano, Tom	66T	361	$ .30	$ .95	Scarborough, Ray	52T	43	$15.00	$47.50
Satriano, Tom	67T	343	$ .30	$ .85	Scarborough, Ray	53T	213	$4.50	$15.00
Satriano, Tom	68T	238	$ .30	$ .85	Scarce, Mac	73T	6	$ .07	$ .30
Satriano, Tom	69T	78	$ .30	$ .85	Scarce, Mac	74T	149	$ .07	$ .30
Satriano, Tom	70T	581	$ .30	$ .95	Scarce, Mac	75T	527	$ .07	$ .30
Satriano, Tom	71T	557	$ .35	$1.25	Schaal, Paul	65T	517	$ .75	$3.00
Saucier, Kevin	80T	682	$ .01	$ .10	Schaal, Paul	66T	376	$ .30	$ .95
Saucier, Kevin	81T	53	$ .01	$ .10	Schaal, Paul	67T	58	$ .30	$ .85
Saucier, Kevin	81TTR	827	$ .02	$ .10	Schaal, Paul	68T	474	$ .35	$1.25
Saucier, Kevin	82T	238	$ .01	$ .07	Schaal, Paul	69T	352	$ .30	$ .85
Saucier, Kevin	83T	373	$ .01	$ .07	Schaal, Paul	70T	338	$ .15	$ .50
Sauer, Henry "Hank"	51Tbb	49	$5.00	$20.00	Schaal, Paul	71T	487	$ .15	$ .50
Sauer, Hank	52T	35	$15.00	$50.00	Schaal, Paul	72T	177	$ .15	$ .50
Sauer, Hank	53T	111	$4.50	$15.00	Schaal, Paul	72TIA	178	$ .15	$ .50
Sauer, Hank	54T	4	$2.50	$10.00	Schaal, Paul	73T	416	$ .07	$ .30
Sauer, Hank	55T	45	$2.00	$9.00	Schaal, Paul	74T	514	$ .07	$ .30
Sauer, Hank	56T	41	$1.50	$4.00	Schaefer, Jeff	89TMLD	109	$ .01	$ .06
Sauer, Hank	57T	197	$ .60	$2.50	Schaefer, Jeff	91T	681	$ .01	$ .03
Sauer, Hank	58T	378	$ .55	$1.75	Schaffer, Jim	62T	579	$3.95	$11.50
Sauer, Hank	59T	404	$ .75	$2.20	Schaffer, Jim	64T	359	$ .30	$ .95
Sauer, Hank	61TMVP	481	$ .90	$3.00	Schaffer, Jimmie	63T	81	$ .30	$ .95
Sauer, Hank	75T	190	$ .15	$ .50	Schaffer, Jimmie	65T	313	$ .35	$1.25
Saunders, Dennis	71T	423	$ .15	$ .50	Schaffer, Jimmie	68T	463	$ .35	$1.25

TOPPS

Player	Year	No.	VG	EX/MT
Schaffernoth, Joe	61T	58	$ .35	$1.25
Schaffernoth, Joe	63T	463	$2.50	$6.50
Schaive, John	61T	259	$ .35	$1.25
Schaive, John	62T	529	$3.95	$11.50
Schaive, John	63T	356	$ .45	$1.50
Schatzeder, Dan	78T	709	$ .02	$ .10
Schatzeder, Dan	79T	124	$ .02	$ .10
Schatzeder, Dan	80T	267	$ .01	$ .10
Schatzeder, Dan	81T	417	$ .01	$ .10
Schatzeder, Dan	82T	691	$ .01	$ .07
Schatzeder, Dan	82TTR	104	$ .02	$ .10
Schatzeder, Dan	83T	189	$ .01	$ .07
Schatzeder, Dan	84T	57	$ .01	$ .06
Schatzeder, Dan	85T	501	$ .01	$ .05
Schatzeder, Dan	86T	324	$ .01	$ .04
Schatzeder, Dan	87T	789	$ .01	$ .04
Schatzeder, Dan	88T	218	$ .01	$ .04
Scheffing, Bob	54T	76	$2.50	$10.00
Scheffing, Bob	60T	464	$ .95	$3.50
Scheffing, Bob	61T	223	$ .35	$1.25
Scheffing, Bob	62T	416	$ .75	$2.50
Scheffing, Bob	62T	72	$ .45	$1.45
Scheffing, Bob	63T	134	$ .30	$ .95
Scheib, Carl	52T	116	$7.00	$20.00
Scheib, Carl	53T	57	$4.50	$15.00
Scheib, Carl	54T	118	$2.50	$10.00
Scheinblum, Richie	65T	577	$1.75	$4.50
Scheinblum, Richie	68T	16	$1.00	$4.00
Scheinblum, Richie	69T	479	$ .30	$ .85
Scheinblum, Richie	70T	161	$ .15	$ .50
Scheinblum, Richie	71T	326	$ .15	$ .50
Scheinblum, Richie	72T	468	$ .15	$ .50
Scheinblum, Richie	73T	78	$ .07	$ .30
Scheinblum, Richie	74T	323	$ .07	$ .30
Schell, Danny	55T	79	$2.00	$6.00
Scherger, George	73T	296	$ .15	$ .50

Player	Year	No.	VG	EX/MT
Scherger, George	74T	326	$ .15	$ .50
Scherman, Fred	71T	316	$ .15	$ .50
Scherman, Fred	72T	6	$ .15	$ .50
Scherman, Fred	73T	660	$ .75	$2.50

Player	Year	No.	VG	EX/MT
Scherman, Fred	74T	186	$ .07	$ .30
Scherman, Fred	74TTR	186	$ .07	$ .30
Scherman, Fred	75T	252	$ .07	$ .30
Scherman, Fred	76T	188	$ .05	$ .20
Scherrer, Bill	84T	373	$ .01	$ .06
Scherrer, Bill	85T	586	$ .01	$ .05
Scherrer, Bill	86T	217	$ .01	$ .04
Scherrer, Bill	87T	98	$ .01	$ .04
Schilling, Chuck	61T	499	$ .75	$3.00
Schilling, Chuck	62T	345	$ .45	$1.45
Schilling, Chuck	62TAS	467	$ .75	$2.50
Schilling, Chuck	63T	52	$ .30	$ .95
Schilling, Chuck	64T	182	$2.50	$10.00
Schilling, Chuck	64T	481	$ .50	$1.45
Schilling, Chuck	65T	272	$ .35	$1.25
Schilling, Chuck	66T	6	$ .30	$ .95
Schilling, Curt	90T	97	$ .01	$ .10
Schilling, Curt	91T	569	$ .01	$ .03
Schiraldi, Calvin	86T	210	$ .01	$ .04
Schiraldi, Calvin	87T	94	$ .01	$ .04
Schiraldi, Calvin	88T	599	$ .01	$ .04
Schiraldi, Calvin	88TTR	104	$ .01	$ .06
Schiraldi, Calvin	89T	337	$ .01	$ .05
Schiraldi, Calvin	90T	693	$ .01	$ .04
Schiraldi, Calvin	91T	424	$ .01	$ .03
Schlesinger, Bill	65T	573	$3.75	$14.00
Schlesinger, Bill	68T	258	$ .30	$ .85
Schmidt, Bob	58T	468	$ .75	$2.20
Schmidt, Bob	59T	109	$ .85	$3.50
Schmidt, Bob	60T	501	$ .90	$3.00
Schmidt, Bob	61T	31	$ .35	$1.25
Schmidt, Bob	62T	262	$ .45	$1.45
Schmidt, Bob	63T	94	$ .30	$ .95
Schmidt, Bob	65T	582	$1.75	$4.50
Schmidt, Dave	82T	381	$ .05	$ .20
Schmidt, Dave	82T	418	$ .03	$ .15
Schmidt, Dave	83T	116	$ .01	$ .07
Schmidt, Dave	84T	584	$ .01	$ .06
Schmidt, Dave	85T	313	$ .01	$ .05
Schmidt, Dave	86T	79	$ .01	$ .04
Schmidt, Dave	86TTR	99	$ .02	$ .10
Schmidt, Dave	87T	703	$ .01	$ .04
Schmidt, Dave	87TTR	110	$ .01	$ .05
Schmidt, Dave	88T	214	$ .01	$ .04
Schmidt, Dave	89T	677	$ .01	$ .05
Schmidt, Dave	89TBB	130	$ .01	$ .06
Schmidt, Dave	90T	497	$ .01	$ .04
Schmidt, Dave	90TTR	112	$ .01	$ .05
Schmidt, Dave	91T	136	$ .01	$ .03
Schmidt, Mike	73T	615	$135.00	$400.00
Schmidt, Mike	74T	283	$30.00	$100.00
Schmidt, Mike	75T	70	$15.00	$50.00
Schmidt, Mike	75T	307	$ .35	$1.25
Schmidt, Mike	76T	193	$ .75	$2.20
Schmidt, Mike	76T	480	$8.00	$25.00
Schmidt, Mike	77T	2	$ .20	$ .90
Schmidt, Mike	77T	140	$5.50	$17.50
Schmidt, Mike	78T	360	$2.50	$10.00
Schmidt, Mike	79T	610	$2.00	$9.00
Schmidt, Mike	80T	270	$ .75	$3.00
Schmidt, Mike	81T	2	$ .06	$ .30
Schmidt, Mike	81T	3	$ .05	$ .25
Schmidt, Mike	81T	540	$ .45	$1.45
Schmidt, Mike	81TRB	206	$ .10	$ .50
Schmidt, Mike	82T	100	$ .45	$1.45
Schmidt, Mike	82T	162	$ .05	$ .25
Schmidt, Mike	82T	163	$ .05	$ .25
Schmidt, Mike	82TAS	339	$ .30	$ .85
Schmidt, Mike	82TIA	101	$ .15	$ .50
Schmidt, Mike	83T	300	$ .75	$3.00

TOPPS

Player	Year	No.	VG	EX/MT	Player	Year	No.	VG	EX/MT
Schmidt, Mike	83T	301	$ .10	$ .50	Schofield, Dick	71T	396	$ .15	$ .50
Schmidt, Mike	83TAS	399	$ .08	$ .40	Schofield, Dick	84TTR	107	$ .08	$ .30
Schmidt, Mike	84T	132	$ .08	$ .35	Schofield, Dick	85T	138	$ .01	$ .10
Schmidt, Mike	84T	700	$ .25	$1.00	Schofield, Dick, Jr.	85T	138	$ .01	$ .10
Schmidt, Mike	84T	703	$ .02	$ .10	Schofield, Dick, Jr.	85T	629	$ .01	$ .05
Schmidt, Mike	84TAS	388	$ .07	$ .30	Schofield, Dick, Jr.	86T	311	$ .01	$ .04
Schmidt, Mike	85T	500	$ .10	$ .50	Schofield, Dick, Jr.	87T	502	$ .01	$ .04
Schmidt, Mike	85TAS	714	$ .05	$ .25	Schofield, Dick, Jr.	88T	43	$ .01	$ .04
Schmidt, Mike	86T	200	$ .05	$ .45	Schofield, Dick, Jr.	88TBB	204	$ .01	$ .06
Schmidt, Mike	87T	430	$ .30	$ .95	Schofield, Dick, Jr.	89T	477	$ .01	$ .05
Schmidt, Mike	87TAS	597	$ .03	$ .15	Schofield, Dick	89TBB	53	$ .01	$ .06
Schmidt, Mike	88T	600	$ .01	$ .25	Schofield, Dick	90T	189	$ .01	$ .04
Schmidt, Mike	88TBB	88	$ .05	$ .30	Schofield, Dick	91T	736	$ .01	$ .03
Schmidt, Mike	89T	100	$ .01	$ .15	Schooler, Mike	88TTR	105	$ .01	$ .30
Schmidt, Mike	89TBB	220	$ .01	$ .60	Schooler, Mike	89T	199	$ .01	$ .04
Schmidt, Mike	90TTB	662	$ .01	$ .04	Schooler, Mike	90T	681	$ .01	$ .04
Schmidt, Willard	53T	168	$4.50	$15.00	Schooler, Mike	91T	365	$ .01	$ .03
Schmidt, Willard	56T	323	$1.30	$5.00	Schoonmaker, Jerry	56T	216	$3.00	$9.00
Schmidt, Willard	57T	206	$ .95	$3.50	Schoonmaker, Jerry	57T	334	$4.25	$15.00
Schmidt, Willard	58T	214	$ .75	$3.00	Schreiber, Paul	54T	217	$2.50	$10.00
Schmidt, Willard	59T	171	$ .75	$2.20	Schroder, Bob	65T	589	$1.75	$4.50
Schmitz, Johnny	51Tbb	41	$7.50	$22.50	Schroeder, Bill	84T	738	$ .01	$ .06
Schmitz, Johnny	52T	136	$7.00	$21.00	Schroeder, Bill	85T	176	$ .01	$ .05
Schmitz, Johnny	54T	33	$2.00	$9.00	Schroeder, Bill	86T	662	$ .01	$ .04
Schmitz, Johnny	55T	159	$2.50	$10.00	Schroeder, Bill	87T	302	$ .01	$ .04
Schmitz, Johnny	56T	298	$1.30	$5.00	Schroeder, Bill	88T	12	$ .01	$ .04
Schneider, Dan	63T	299	$ .45	$1.50	Schroeder, Bill	89T	563	$ .01	$ .05
Schneider, Dan	64T	351	$ .30	$ .95	Schroeder, Bill	90T	244	$ .01	$ .04
Schneider, Dan	65T	366	$ .35	$1.25	Schroeder, Bill	91T	452	$ .01	$ .03
Schneider, Dan	67T	543	$2.10	$6.00	Schroll, Al	59T	546	$2.50	$10.00
Schneider, Dan	68T	57	$ .30	$ .85	Schroll, Al	60T	357	$ .75	$2.20
Schneider, Dan	69T	656	$ .30	$ .95	Schroll, Al	62T	102	$ .45	$1.45
Schneider, Jeff	82T	21	$7.50	$30.00	Schrom, Ken	81T	577	$ .01	$ .10
Schoendienst, Al	51Tbb	6	$7.50	$30.00	Schrom, Ken	84T	11	$ .01	$ .06
Schoendienst, Al	52T	91	$22.50	$65.00	Schrom, Ken	84T	322	$ .01	$ .06
Schoendienst, Al	53T	78	$19.50	$55.00	Schrom, Ken	85T	161	$ .01	$ .05
Schoendienst, Al "Red"	56T	165	$7.50	$22.50	Schrom, Ken	86T	71	$ .01	$ .04
Schoendienst, Red	57T	154	$6.00	$18.00	Schrom, Ken	86TTR	100	$ .02	$ .10
Schoendienst, Red	58T	190	$4.50	$14.00	Schrom, Ken	87T	635	$ .01	$ .04
Schoendienst, Red	59T	480	$2.50	$10.00	Schrom, Ken	88T	256	$ .01	$ .04
Schoendienst, Red	60T	335	$2.00	$8.00	Schu, Rick	85TTR	104	$ .02	$ .10
Schoendienst, Red	61T	505	$2.00	$8.00	Schu, Rick	86T	16	$ .01	$ .04
Schoendienst, Red	62T	575	$11.00	$35.00	Schu, Rick	87T	209	$ .01	$ .04
Schoendienst, Red	65T	556	$5.00	$15.00	Schu, Rick	88T	731	$ .01	$ .04
Schoendienst, Red	66T	76	$1.00	$3.00	Schu, Rick	88TBB	122	$ .01	$ .06
Schoendienst, Red	67T	512	$ .75	$2.25	Schu, Rick	89T	352	$ .01	$ .05
Schoendienst, Red	68T	294	$ .45	$1.45	Schu, Rick	89TBB	164	$ .01	$ .06
Schoendienst, Red	69T	462	$ .15	$ .50	Schu, Rick	89TTR	112	$ .01	$ .06
Schoendienst, Red	70T	346	$ .75	$3.00	Schu, Rick	90T	498	$ .01	$ .04
Schoendienst, Red	71T	239	$ .75	$3.00	Schueler, Ron	73T	169	$ .07	$ .30
Schoendienst, Red	72T	67	$ .30	$ .85	Schueler, Ron	74T	544	$ .07	$ .30
Schoendienst, Red	73T	497	$ .30	$ .85	Schueler, Ron	74TTR	544	$ .07	$ .30
Schoendienst, Red	74T	236	$ .07	$ .30	Schueler, Ron	75T	292	$ .07	$ .30
Schoendienst, Red	90TTR	113	$ .01	$ .05	Schueler, Ron	76T	586	$ .05	$ .20
Schofield, Dick	54T	191	$1.75	$7.00	Schueler, Ron	77T	337	$ .05	$ .15
Schofield, Dick	55T	143	$2.00	$6.00	Schueler, Ron	78T	409	$ .02	$ .10
Schofield, Dick	58T	106	$ .85	$3.50	Schueler, Ron	79T	686	$ .02	$ .10
Schofield, Dick	59T	68	$ .85	$3.50	Schult, Art	53T	167	$4.50	$15.00
Schofield, Dick	60T	104	$ .45	$1.45	Schult, Art	58T	58	$ .85	$3.50
Schofield, Dick	61T	453	$ .75	$3.00	Schult, Art	60T	93	$ .45	$1.45
Schofield, Dick	62T	484	$ .75	$2.50	Schultz, Barney	62T	89	$ .45	$1.45
Schofield, Dick	63T	34	$ .30	$ .95	Schultz, Barney	63T	452	$2.50	$6.50
Schofield, Dick	64T	284	$ .30	$ .95	Schultz, Barney	65T	28	$ .30	$ .85
Schofield, Dick	65T	218	$ .35	$1.25	Schultz, Barney	73T	497	$ .30	$ .85
Schofield, Dick	66T	156	$ .15	$ .50	Schultz, Barney	74T	236	$ .07	$ .30
Schofield, Dick	66T	474	$ .75	$2.50	Schultz, Bob	52T	401	$40.00	$140.00
Schofield, Dick	67T	381	$ .30	$ .95	Schultz, Bob	53T	144	$4.50	$15.00
Schofield, Dick	68T	588	$ .35	$1.25	Schultz, Buddy	78T	301	$ .02	$ .10
Schofield, Dick	69T	18	$ .30	$ .85	Schultz, Buddy	79T	532	$ .02	$ .10
Schofield, Dick	70T	251	$ .15	$ .50	Schultz, Buddy	80T	601	$ .01	$ .10

Player	Year	No.	VG	EX/MT
Schultz, Joe	69T	254	$ .30	$ .95
Schultz, Joseph	73T	323	$ .35	$1.25
Schulz, Jeff	89TMLD	110	$ .01	$ .15
Schulze, Don	85T	93	$ .01	$ .05

DON SCHULZE

Player	Year	No.	VG	EX/MT
Schulze, Don	86T	542	$ .01	$ .04
Schulze, Don	87T	297	$ .01	$ .04
Schulze, Don	88T	131	$ .01	$ .04
Schurr, Wayne	64T	548	$1.75	$4.50
Schurr, Wayne	65T	149	$ .30	$ .85
Schwabe, Mike	89TMLD	111	$ .01	$ .06
Schwall, Don	62T	35	$ .45	$1.45
Schwall, Don	63T	344	$ .45	$1.50
Schwall, Don	64T	558	$1.75	$4.50
Schwall, Don	65T	362	$ .35	$1.25
Schwall, Don	66T	144	$ .30	$ .95
Schwall, Don	67T	267	$ .30	$ .85
Schwartz, Randy	67T	33	$ .75	$3.00
Scioscia, Mike	81T	302	$1.25	$5.00
Scioscia, Mike	82T	642	$ .01	$ .07
Scioscia, Mike	83T	352	$ .01	$ .07
Scioscia, Mike	84T	64	$ .01	$ .06
Scioscia, Mike	85T	549	$ .01	$ .05
Scioscia, Mike	86T	468	$ .01	$ .04
Scioscia, Mike	87T	144	$ .01	$ .04
Scioscia, Mike	88T	225	$ .01	$ .04
Scioscia, Mike	88TBB	72	$ .01	$ .06
Scioscia, Mike	89T	755	$ .01	$ .05
Scioscia, Mike	89TBB	281	$ .01	$ .06
Scioscia, Mike	90T	605	$ .01	$ .04
Scioscia, Mike	91T	305	$ .01	$ .03
Scioscia, Mike	91TAS	404	$ .01	$ .03
Sconiers, Daryl	82T	653	$ .50	$2.00
Sconiers, Daryl	83TTR	99	$ .02	$ .10
Sconiers, Daryl	84T	27	$ .01	$ .06
Sconiers, Daryl	85T	604	$ .01	$ .05
Sconiers, Daryl	86T	193	$ .01	$ .04
Score, Herb	56T	140	$7.50	$22.50
Score, Herb	57T	50	$1.25	$3.75
Score, Herb	58T	352	$ .45	$1.50
Score, Herb	58TAS	495	$1.50	$6.00

Player	Year	No.	VG	EX/MT
Score, Herb	59T	88	$ .75	$2.25
Score, Herb	60T	360	$ .90	$3.00
Score, Herb	61T	185	$ .75	$3.00
Score, Herb	61T	337	$ .75	$2.25
Score, Herb	62T	116	$ .75	$3.00
Scott, Dick	89TMLD	112	$ .01	$ .06
Scott, Donnie	85T	496	$ .01	$ .05
Scott, Donnie	85TTR	105	$ .02	$ .10
Scott, Donnie	86T	568	$ .01	$ .04
Scott, George	66T	558	$5.50	$17.50
Scott, George	67T	75	$ .15	$ .50
Scott, George	68T	233	$ .15	$ .50
Scott, George	69T	574	$ .30	$ .95
Scott, George	70T	385	$ .30	$ .85
Scott, George	71T	9	$ .15	$ .50
Scott, George	72T	585	$ .30	$ .95
Scott, George	73T	263	$ .07	$ .30
Scott, George	74T	27	$ .07	$ .30
Scott, George	75T	360	$ .07	$ .30
Scott, George	76T	15	$ .05	$ .20
Scott, George	76T	194	$ .75	$2.20
Scott, George	76T	196	$ .30	$ .95
Scott, George	77T	255	$ .05	$ .15
Scott, George	78T	125	$ .02	$ .10
Scott, George	79T	645	$ .02	$ .10
Scott, George	80T	414	$ .01	$ .10
Scott, John	75T	616	$7.50	$20.00
Scott, John	77T	473	$12.50	$50.00
Scott, John	78T	547	$ .02	$ .10
Scott, Mickey	70T	669	$ .75	$2.00
Scott, Mickey	72T	724	$1.25	$4.25
Scott, Mickey	73T	553	$ .45	$1.45
Scott, Mickey	76T	276	$ .05	$ .20
Scott, Mickey	77T	401	$ .05	$ .15
Scott, Mike	80T	681	$2.50	$7.50
Scott, Mike	81T	109	$ .35	$1.25
Scott, Mike	82T	246	$ .05	$ .25
Scott, Mike	82T	432	$ .05	$ .20
Scott, Mike	83T	679	$ .01	$ .15
Scott, Mike	83TTR	100	$ .50	$1.50
Scott, Mike	84T	559	$ .01	$ .15
Scott, Mike	85T	17	$ .01	$ .15
Scott, Mike	86T	268	$ .02	$ .15
Scott, Mike	87T	330	$ .03	$ .15
Scott, Mike	88T	760	$ .01	$ .10
Scott, Mike	88TBB	140	$ .01	$ .15
Scott, Mike	89T	180	$ .01	$ .10
Scott, Mike	89TBB	51	$ .01	$ .10
Scott, Mike	90T	460	$ .01	$ .04
Scott, Mike	90TAS	405	$ .01	$ .04
Scott, Mike	91T	240	$ .01	$ .03
Scott, Rodney	78T	191	$ .02	$ .10
Scott, Rodney	79T	86	$ .02	$ .10
Scott, Rodney	80T	712	$ .01	$ .10
Scott, Rodney	81T	539	$ .01	$ .10
Scott, Rodney	81TRB	204	$ .01	$ .10
Scott, Rodney	82T	259	$ .01	$ .07
Scott, Tony	78T	352	$ .02	$ .10
Scott, Tony	79T	143	$ .02	$ .10
Scott, Tony	80T	33	$ .01	$ .10
Scott, Tony	81T	165	$ .01	$ .10
Scott, Tony	81TTR	828	$ .02	$ .10
Scott, Tony	82T	698	$ .01	$ .07
Scott, Tony	83T	507	$ .01	$ .07
Scott, Tony	84T	292	$ .01	$ .06
Scott, Tony	85T	733	$ .01	$ .05
Scrivener, Chuck	77T	173	$ .05	$ .15
Scrivener, Chuck	78T	94	$ .02	$ .10
Scudder, Scott	89TMLD	113	$ .01	$ .25
Scudder, Scott	90T	553	$ .01	$ .15

TOPPS

Player	Year	No.	VG	EX/MT	Player	Year	No.	VG	EX/MT
Scudder, Scott	91T	713	$ .01	$ .03	Secrist, Don	69T	654	$ .30	$ .95
Scull, Angel	54T	204	$2.50	$10.00	Seelbach, Chuck	73T	51	$ .07	$ .30
Scurry, Rod	81T	194	$ .01	$ .10	Seelbach, Chuck	74T	292	$ .07	$ .30
Scurry, Rod	82T	207	$ .01	$ .07	Segui, David	91T	724	$ .01	$ .25
Scurry, Rod	83T	537	$ .01	$ .07	Segui, Diego	63T	157	$ .30	$ .95
Scurry, Rod	84T	69	$ .01	$ .06	Segui, Diego	64T	508	$ .50	$1.45
Scurry, Rod	85T	641	$ .01	$ .05	Segui, Diego	65T	197	$ .30	$ .85
Scurry, Rod	86T	449	$ .01	$ .04	Segui, Diego	66T	309	$ .30	$ .95
Scurry, Rod	87T	665	$ .01	$ .04	Segui, Diego	68T	517	$ .35	$1.25
Seanez, Rudy	89TMLD	114	$ .01	$ .06	Segui, Diego	69T	511	$ .30	$ .85
Searage, Ray	82T	478	$ .01	$ .07	Segui, Diego	70T	2	$ .15	$ .50
Searage, Ray	86T	642	$ .01	$ .04	Segui, Diego	71T	215	$ .15	$ .50
Searage, Ray	87T	149	$ .01	$ .04	Segui, Diego	71T	67	$ .15	$ .50
Searage, Ray	88T	788	$ .01	$ .04	Segui, Diego	72T	735	$ .75	$2.50
Searage, Ray	90T	84	$ .01	$ .04	Segui, Diego	73T	383	$ .07	$ .30
Searcy, Steve	89T	167	$ .05	$ .25	Segui, Diego	74T	151	$ .07	$ .30
Searcy, Steve	90T	487	$ .01	$ .04	Segui, Diego	74TTR	151	$ .07	$ .30
Searcy, Steve	91T	369	$ .01	$ .03	Segui, Diego	75T	232	$ .07	$ .30
Seaver, Tom	67T	581	$300.00	$950.00	Segui, Diego	77T	653	$ .05	$ .15
Seaver, Tom	68T	45	$60.00	$180.00	Seitzer, Kevin	87TTR	111	$ .15	$ .60
Seaver, Tom	69T	480	$30.00	$100.00	Seitzer, Kevin	88T	275	$ .10	$ .50
Seaver, Tom	70T	69	$ .75	$2.20	Seitzer, Kevin	88TBB	115	$ .01	$ .15
Seaver, Tom	70T	300	$20.00	$65.00	Seitzer, Kevin	89T	670	$ .01	$ .15
Seaver, Tom	71T	68	$ .15	$ .50	Seitzer, Kevin	89TBB	313	$ .01	$ .10
Seaver, Tom	71T	72	$ .50	$2.50	Seitzer, Kevin	90T	435	$ .01	$ .04
Seaver, Tom	71T	160	$12.50	$40.00	Seitzer, Kevin	91T	695	$ .01	$ .03
Seaver, Tom	72T	91	$ .45	$1.45	Sellers, Jeff	87T	12	$ .01	$ .10
Seaver, Tom	72T	93	$ .50	$2.00	Sellers, Jeff	88T	653	$ .01	$ .04
Seaver, Tom	72T	95	$ .45	$1.45	Sellers, Jeff	89T	544	$ .01	$ .05
Seaver, Tom	72T	347	$ .75	$3.00	Sells, Dave	74T	37	$ .07	$ .30
Seaver, Tom	72TIA	446	$3.00	$11.00	Selma, Dick	66T	67	$ .30	$ .95
Seaver, Tom	73T	350	$5.50	$17.50	Selma, Dick	67T	386	$ .30	$ .95
Seaver, Tom	74T	80	$3.00	$12.00	Selma, Dick	68T	556	$ .35	$1.25
Seaver, Tom	74T	206	$ .75	$2.25	Selma, Dick	69T	197	$ .30	$ .85
Seaver, Tom	74T	207	$ .75	$3.00	Selma, Dick	70T	24	$ .15	$ .50
Seaver, Tom	75T	370	$3.00	$12.00	Selma, Dick	71T	705	$ .75	$2.50
Seaver, Tom	76T	199	$ .15	$ .50	Selma, Dick	72T	726	$ .75	$2.50
Seaver, Tom	76T	201	$ .35	$1.25	Selma, Dick	73T	632	$ .45	$1.45
Seaver, Tom	76T	203	$ .35	$1.25	Sembera, Carroll	66T	539	$5.00	$20.00
Seaver, Tom	76T	600	$2.00	$8.00	Sembera, Carroll	67T	136	$ .30	$ .85
Seaver, Tom	76TRB	5	$ .45	$1.45	Sembera, Carroll	68T	207	$ .30	$ .85
Seaver, Tom	77T	6	$ .75	$3.00	Sembera, Carroll	69T	351	$ .30	$ .85
Seaver, Tom	77T	150	$1.50	$6.00	Seminick, Andy	51Trb	45	$2.10	$6.00
Seaver, Tom	78T	450	$ .75	$3.00	Seminick, Andy	52T	297	$15.00	$47.50
Seaver, Tom	79T	100	$ .60	$2.50	Seminick, Andy	53T	153	$4.50	$15.00
Seaver, Tom	80T	500	$ .75	$3.00	Seminick, Andy	56T	296	$1.30	$5.00
Seaver, Tom	81T	220	$ .75	$2.25	Semproch, "Ray" Roman	58T	474	$ .75	$2.20
Seaver, Tom	82T	30	$ .50	$1.50	Semproch, Ray	59T	197	$ .75	$2.20
Seaver, Tom	82T	165	$ .03	$ .15	Semproch, Ray	60T	286	$ .45	$1.45
Seaver, Tom	82T	756	$ .05	$ .20	Semproch, Ray	61T	174	$ .35	$1.25
Seaver, Tom	82TAS	346	$ .05	$ .25	Senators, Team	57T	270	$7.50	$22.50
Seaver, Tom	82TIA	31	$ .06	$ .30	Senators, Team	58T	44	$3.00	$9.00
Seaver, Tom	83T	580	$ .15	$1.25	Senators, Team	60T	43	$2.50	$7.50
Seaver, Tom	83T	581	$ .05	$ .25	Senators, Team	62T	206	$ .75	$2.00
Seaver, Tom	83TTR	101	$ .45	$1.45	Senators, Team	63T	131	$ .75	$2.55
Seaver, Tom	84T	246	$ .01	$ .06	Senators, Team	64T	343	$ .85	$3.50
Seaver, Tom	84T	706	$ .05	$ .25	Senators, Team	65T	267	$ .90	$3.00
Seaver, Tom	84T	707	$ .05	$ .25	Senators, Team	66T	194	$ .65	$1.75
Seaver, Tom	84T	708	$ .04	$ .20	Senators, Team	67T	437	$ .75	$2.25
Seaver, Tom	84T	740	$ .30	$ .85	Senators, Team	70T	676	$1.00	$4.00
Seaver, Tom	84TTR	108	$ .75	$3.00	Senators, Team	71T	462	$ .45	$1.45
Seaver, Tom	85T	670	$ .05	$ .25	Serena, Bill	52T	325	$40.00	$140.00
Seaver, Tom	86T	390	$ .03	$ .25	Serna, Paul	83T	492	$ .01	$ .07
Seaver, Tom	86TB	402	$ .02	$ .15	Serum, Gary	79T	627	$ .02	$ .10
Seaver, Tom	86TTR	101	$ .15	$ .50	Serum, Gary	80T	61	$ .01	$ .10
Seaver, Tom	87T	425	$ .15	$ .50	Servais, Scott	88TTR	106	$ .01	$ .25
Sebra, Bob	87T	479	$ .01	$ .04	Servais, Scott	89TBB	291	$ .01	$ .10
Sebra, Bob	88T	93	$ .01	$ .04	Sevcik, John	65T	597	$1.75	$4.50
Secrest, Charlie	59T	140	$ .75	$2.20	Severinsen, Al	70T	477	$ .15	$ .50
					Severinsen, Al	71T	747	$ .75	$2.50

Player	Year	No.	VG	EX/MT
Severinsen, Al	72T	274	$ .15	$ .50
Severson, Rich	71T	103	$ .15	$ .50
Sexton, Jimmy	79T	232	$ .02	$ .10
Sexton, Jimmy	80T	11	$ .01	$ .10
Sexton, Jimmy	83T	709	$ .01	$ .07
Seyfried, Gordon	64T	499	$ .50	$1.45
Shamsky, Art	65T	398	$ .45	$1.45
Shamsky, Art	66T	119	$ .30	$ .95
Shamsky, Art	67T	96	$ .30	$ .85
Shamsky, Art	68T	292	$ .30	$ .95
Shamsky, Art	69T	221	$ .30	$ .95
Shamsky, Art	70T	137	$ .15	$ .50
Shamsky, Art	71T	445	$ .15	$ .50
Shamsky, Art	72T	353	$ .15	$ .50
Shanahan, Greg	74T	599	$ .15	$ .50
Shannon, Mike	64T	262	$ .45	$1.45
Shannon, Mike	65T	43	$ .30	$ .85
Shannon, Mike	66T	293	$ .30	$ .95
Shannon, Mike	67T	605	$13.00	$40.00
Shannon, Mike	68T	445	$ .30	$ .85
Shannon, Mike	69T	110	$ .30	$ .85
Shannon, Mike	70T	614	$ .30	$ .95

CARDS
mike shannon • 3rd base

Player	Year	No.	VG	EX/MT
Shannon, Mike	71T	735	$ .75	$2.50
Shantz, Bobby	52T	219	$7.50	$22.00
Shantz, Bobby	53T	225	$11.00	$35.00
Shantz, Bobby	54T	21	$2.50	$9.00
Shantz, Bobby	56T	261	$2.25	$6.50
Shantz, Bobby	57T	272	$7.50	$22.50
Shantz, Bobby	58T	289	$ .75	$2.50
Shantz, Bobby	58T	419	$ .75	$2.50
Shantz, Bobby	59T	222	$2.10	$6.00
Shantz, Bobby	60T	315	$ .75	$2.25
Shantz, Bobby	61T	379	$ .90	$3.00
Shantz, Bobby	61TMVP	473	$ .75	$2.00
Shantz, Bobby	62T	177	$ .45	$1.45
Shantz, Bobby	63T	533	$2.10	$6.00
Shantz, Bobby	64T	278	$ .45	$1.45
Shantz, Bobby	75T	190	$ .15	$ .50
Sharon, Dick	74T	48	$ .07	$ .30
Sharon, Dick	75T	293	$ .07	$ .30

Player	Year	No.	VG	EX/MT
Sharp, Bill	74T	519	$ .07	$ .30
Sharp, Bill	75T	373	$ .07	$ .30
Sharp, Bill	76T	244	$ .05	$ .20
Sharperson, Mike	90T	117	$ .01	$ .04
Sharperson, Mike	91T	53	$ .01	$ .03
Shaw, Bob	58T	206	$ .35	$ .00
Shaw, Bob	59T	159	$ .75	$2.20
Shaw, Bob	60T	380	$ .75	$2.20
Shaw, Bob	61T	352	$ .35	$1.25
Shaw, Bob	62T	109	$ .45	$1.45
Shaw, Bob	63T	255	$ .30	$ .95
Shaw, Bob	63T	5	$1.00	$4.00
Shaw, Bob	64T	328	$ .30	$ .95
Shaw, Bob	65T	428	$ .35	$1.25
Shaw, Bob	66T	260	$ .30	$ .95
Shaw, Bob	67T	470	$ .75	$3.00
Shaw, Bob	73T	646	$ .75	$3.00
Shaw, Don	67T	587	$4.00	$12.00
Shaw, Don	68T	521	$ .35	$1.25
Shaw, Don	69T	183	$ .30	$ .85
Shaw, Don	70T	476	$ .15	$ .50
Shaw, Don	71T	654	$ .75	$2.50
Shaw, Don	72T	479	$ .15	$ .50
Shea, Frank	52T	248	$7.00	$20.00
Shea, Frank	53T	164	$4.50	$15.00
Shea, Steve	69T	499	$ .30	$ .85
Shearer, Ray	58T	283	$ .75	$3.00
Sheets, Larry	85TTR	106	$ .20	$ .75
Sheets, Larry	86T	147	$ .01	$ .04
Sheets, Larry	87T	552	$ .01	$ .04
Sheets, Larry	88T	327	$ .01	$ .10
Sheets, Larry	88TBB	26	$ .01	$ .06
Sheets, Larry	89T	98	$ .01	$ .05
Sheets, Larry	89TBB	113	$ .01	$ .06
Sheets, Larry	90T	708	$ .01	$ .04
Sheets, Larry	91T	281	$ .01	$ .03
Sheffield, Gary	89T	343	$ .25	$1.00
Sheffield, Gary	89TBB	55	$ .01	$ .25
Sheffield, Gary	90T	718	$ .01	$ .25
Sheffield, Gary	91T	68	$ .01	$ .15
Shelby, John	83TTR	102	$ .02	$ .10
Shelby, John	84T	86	$ .01	$ .06
Shelby, John	85T	508	$ .01	$ .05
Shelby, John	86T	309	$ .01	$ .04
Shelby, John	87T	208	$ .01	$ .04
Shelby, John	87TTR	112	$ .01	$ .05
Shelby, John	88T	428	$ .01	$ .04
Shelby, John	88TBB	218	$ .01	$ .06
Shelby, John	89T	175	$ .01	$ .05
Shelby, John	91T	746	$ .01	$ .03
Sheldon, Bob	75T	623	$7.00	$21.00
Sheldon, Bob	76T	626	$ .05	$ .20
Sheldon, Roland	61T	541	$7.00	$21.00
Sheldon, Roland	62T	185	$ .45	$1.45
Sheldon, Roland	63T	507	$1.75	$4.50
Sheldon, Roland	65T	254	$ .35	$1.25
Sheldon, Roland	66T	18	$ .30	$ .95
Sheldon, Roland	69T	413	$ .30	$ .85
Shelenback, Jim	67T	592	$5.00	$15.00
Shellenback, Jim	69T	567	$ .30	$ .95
Shellenback, Jim	70T	389	$ .15	$ .50
Shellenback, Jim	71T	351	$ .15	$ .50
Shellenback, Jim	74T	657	$ .07	$ .30
Shepard, Jack	55T	73	$2.00	$6.00
Shepard, Larry	68T	584	$ .35	$1.25
Shepard, Larry	69T	384	$ .30	$ .85
Shepard, Larry	73T	296	$ .15	$ .50
Shepard, Larry	74T	326	$ .15	$ .50
Shepherd, Ron	87T	643	$ .01	$ .04
Sheridan, Pat	84T	121	$ .01	$ .06

Player	Year	No.	VG	EX/MT	Player	Year	No.	VG	EX/MT
Sheridan, Pat	85T	359	$ .01	$ .05	Show, Eric	89TBB	35	$ .01	$ .06
Sheridan, Pat	86T	743	$ .01	$ .04	Show, Eric	90T	239	$ .01	$ .04
Sheridan, Pat	87T	234	$ .01	$ .04	Show, Eric	91T	613	$ .01	$ .03
Sheridan, Pat	88T	514	$ .01	$ .04	Shuba, George	52T	326	$40.00	$140.00
Sheridan, Pat	89T	288	$ .01	$ .05	Shuba, George	53T	34	$4.50	$15.00
Sheridan, Pat	89TBB	150	$ .01	$ .06	Shumpert, Terry	90TTR	114	$ .01	$ .20
Sheridan, Pat	90T	422	$ .01	$ .04	Shumpert, Terry	91T	322	$ .01	$ .10
Sherrill, Tim	91T	769	$ .01	$ .10	Siebern, Norm	58T	54	$1.75	$4.50
Sherry, Larry	60T	105	$ .65	$1.75	Siebern, Norm	59T	308	$ .75	$2.25
Sherry, Larry	61T	412	$ .75	$3.00	Siebern, Norm	60T	11	$ .45	$1.45
Sherry, Larry	61T	521	$ .90	$3.00	Siebern, Norm	61T	119	$ .45	$1.45
Sherry, Larry	62T	435	$ .75	$2.50	Siebern, Norm	61T	267	$ .35	$1.25
Sherry, Larry	63T	565	$1.75	$4.50	Siebern, Norm	62T	127	$ .75	$3.00
Sherry, Larry	64T	474	$ .50	$1.45	Siebern, Norm	62T	275	$ .45	$1.45
Sherry, Larry	65T	408	$ .35	$1.25	Siebern, Norm	63T	2	$3.00	$12.00
Sherry, Larry	66T	289	$ .30	$ .95	Siebern, Norm	63T	430	$ .45	$1.50
Sherry, Larry	67T	571	$3.00	$9.00	Siebern, Norm	64T	145	$ .30	$ .95
Sherry, Larry	68T	468	$ .35	$1.25					
Sherry, Norm	60T	529	$2.50	$10.00					
Sherry, Norm	61T	521	$ .90	$3.00					
Sherry, Norm	62T	238	$ .45	$1.45					
Sherry, Norm	63T	316	$ .45	$1.45					
Shetrone, Barry	60T	348	$ .75	$2.20					
Shetrone, Barry	63T	276	$ .30	$ .95					
Shields, Steve	87TTR	113	$ .01	$ .05					
Shields, Steve	88T	632	$ .01	$ .04					
Shields, Steve	89T	484	$ .01	$ .05					
Shines, Razor	86T	132	$ .01	$ .04					
Shipley, Joe	59T	141	$ .75	$2.20					
Shipley, Joe	60T	239	$ .45	$1.45	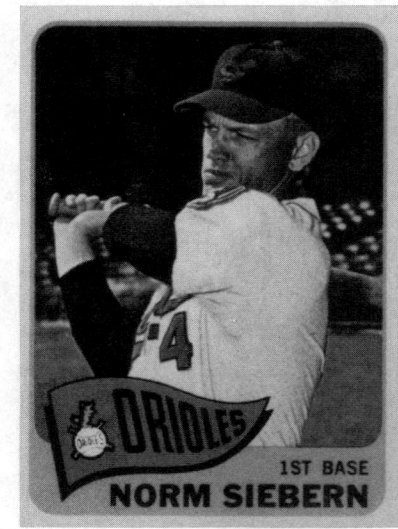				
Shirley, Bart	66T	591	$5.00	$20.00					
Shirley, Bart	67T	287	$ .30	$ .85					
Shirley, Bart	69T	289	$ .30	$ .95					
Shirley, Bob	78T	266	$ .02	$ .10					
Shirley, Bob	79T	594	$ .02	$ .10					
Shirley, Bob	80T	476	$ .01	$ .10					
Shirley, Bob	81T	49	$ .01	$ .10					
Shirley, Bob	81TTR	829	$ .02	$ .10					
Shirley, Bob	82T	749	$ .01	$ .07					
Shirley, Bob	82TTR	105	$ .02	$ .10					
Shirley, Bob	83T	112	$ .01	$ .07					
Shirley, Bob	83TTR	103	$ .02	$ .10					
Shirley, Bob	84T	684	$ .01	$ .06					
Shirley, Bob	85T	328	$ .01	$ .05					
Shirley, Bob	86T	213	$ .01	$ .04		1ST BASE			
Shirley, Bob	87T	524	$ .01	$ .04		**NORM SIEBERN**			
Shockley, Costen	65T	107	$ .75	$3.00					
Shopay, Tom	70T	363	$ .15	$ .50	Siebern, Norm	65T	455	$ .75	$3.00
Shopay, Tom	72T	418	$ .15	$ .50	Siebern, Norm	66T	14	$ .30	$ .95
Short, Bill	60T	142	$ .75	$3.00	Siebern, Norm	67T	299	$ .30	$ .85
Short, Bill	61T	252	$ .35	$1.25	Siebern, Norm	68T	537	$ .35	$1.25
Short, Bill	62T	221	$ .45	$1.45	Siebert, Paul	75T	614	$ .07	$ .30
Short, Bill	67T	577	$2.10	$6.00	Siebert, Sonny	64T	552	$1.75	$4.50
Short, Bill	68T	536	$ .35	$1.25	Siebert, Sonny	65T	96	$ .30	$ .85
Short, Bill	69T	259	$ .30	$ .95	Siebert, Sonny	66T	197	$ .30	$ .95
Short, Chris	67T	395	$ .30	$ .95	Siebert, Sonny	66T	222	$ .75	$3.00
Short, Chris	68T	7	$ .75	$2.20	Siebert, Sonny	66T	226	$ .75	$3.00
Short, Chris	68T	139	$ .30	$ .85	Siebert, Sonny	67T	95	$ .30	$ .85
Short, Chris	69T	395	$ .30	$ .85	Siebert, Sonny	67T	463	$ .75	$3.00
Short, Chris	70T	270	$ .15	$ .50	Siebert, Sonny	68T	8	$ .45	$1.45
Short, Chris	71T	511	$ .15	$ .50	Siebert, Sonny	68T	295	$ .30	$ .85
Short, Chris	72T	665	$ .75	$2.50	Siebert, Sonny	69T	455	$ .30	$ .85
Show, Eric	82TTR	106	$ .02	$ .10	Siebert, Sonny	70T	597	$ .30	$ .95
Show, Eric	83T	68	$ .01	$ .07	Siebert, Sonny	71T	710	$7.00	$21.00
Show, Eric	84T	532	$ .01	$ .06	Siebert, Sonny	72T	290	$ .15	$ .50
Show, Eric	85T	118	$ .01	$ .05	Siebert, Sonny	73T	14	$ .07	$ .30
Show, Eric	86T	762	$ .01	$ .04	Siebert, Sonny	74T	548	$ .07	$ .30
Show, Eric	87T	730	$ .01	$ .04	Siebert, Sonny	75T	328	$ .07	$ .30
Show, Eric	88T	303	$ .01	$ .04	Siebler, Dwight	64T	516	$ .50	$1.45
Show, Eric	89T	427	$ .01	$ .05	Siebler, Dwight	65T	326	$ .35	$1.25

Player	Year	No.	VG	EX/MT	Player	Year	No.	VG	EX/MT
Siebler, Dwight	66T	546	$5.00	$20.00	Simmons, Ted	79T	510	$ .05	$ .20
Siebler, Dwight	67T	164	$ .30	$ .85	Simmons, Ted	80T	85	$ .05	$ .20
Sierra, Candy	89T	711	$ .01	$ .05	Simmons, Ted	81T	705	$ .03	$ .15
Sierra, Ruben	87T	261	$ .50	$2.50	Simmons, Ted	81TTR	830	$ .30	$ .85
Sierra, Ruben	87TRB	6	$ .01	$ .25	Simmons, Ted	82T	150	$ .03	$ .15
Sierra, Ruben	88T	771	$ .10	$ .50	Simmons, Ted	83T	450	$ .03	$ .15
Sierra, Ruben	89T	53	$ .01	$ .35	Simmons, Ted	83T	451	$ .01	$ .07
Sierra, Ruben	89TBB	82	$ .01	$ .35	Simmons, Ted	84T	630	$ .02	$ .10
Sierra, Ruben	90T	185	$ .01	$ .15	Simmons, Ted	84T	713	$ .03	$ .15
Sierra, Ruben	90TAS	390	$ .01	$ .10	Simmons, Ted	84T	726	$ .01	$ .06
Sierra, Ruben	91T	535	$ .01	$ .10	Simmons, Ted	84TAS	404	$ .01	$ .06
Sievers, Roy	51Trb	9	$2.10	$6.00	Simmons, Ted	85T	318	$ .01	$ .10
Sievers, Roy	52T	64	$12.50	$45.00	Simmons, Ted	86T	237	$ .01	$ .10
Sievers, Roy	53T	67	$4.50	$15.00	Simmons, Ted	86TTR	102	$ .02	$ .10
Sievers, Roy	54T	245	$4.25	$15.00	Simmons, Ted	87T	516	$ .01	$ .04
Sievers, Roy	55T	16	$2.00	$9.00	Simmons, Ted	88T	791	$ .01	$ .10
Sievers, Roy	56T	75	$2.25	$6.00	Simms, Mike	91T	32	$ .01	$ .15
Sievers, Roy	57T	89	$ .60	$2.50	Simpson, Dick	63T	407	$ .45	$1.50
Sievers, Roy	58T	250	$ .65	$2.00	Simpson, Dick	64T	127	$ .30	$ .95
Sievers, Roy	59T	74	$ .95	$3.50	Simpson, Dick	65T	374	$ .35	$1.25
Sievers, Roy	59T	340	$ .75	$2.20	Simpson, Dick	66T	311	$ .45	$1.45
Sievers, Roy	59T	465	$ .90	$3.00	Simpson, Dick	67T	6	$ .30	$ .85
Sievers, Roy	59TAS	566	$2.50	$10.00	Simpson, Dick	68T	459	$ .35	$1.25
Sievers, Roy	60T	25	$ .45	$1.45	Simpson, Dick	69T	608	$ .30	$ .95
Sievers, Roy	61T	470	$ .75	$3.00	Simpson, Harry	52T	193	$7.00	$20.00
Sievers, Roy	62T	220	$ .45	$1.45	Simpson, Harry	53T	150	$4.50	$15.00
Sievers, Roy	63T	283	$ .35	$1.25	Simpson, Harry	56T	239	$3.00	$9.00
Sievers, Roy	64T	43	$ .15	$ .50	Simpson, Harry	57T	225	$ .95	$3.50
Sievers, Roy	65T	574	$1.75	$4.50	Simpson, Harry	58T	299	$ .75	$3.00
Silvera, Al	56T	137	$2.25	$6.00	Simpson, Harry	59T	333	$ .75	$2.20
Silvera, Charlie	52T	168	$7.00	$20.00	Simpson, Harry	60T	180	$ .45	$1.45
Silvera, Charlie	53T	242	$11.00	$35.00	Simpson, Joe	79T	719	$2.50	$10.00
Silvera, Charlie	54T	96	$1.75	$7.00	Simpson, Joe	80T	637	$ .01	$ .10
Silvera, Charlie	55T	188	$2.85	$9.50	Simpson, Joe	81T	116	$ .01	$ .10
Silvera, Charlie	57T	255	$ .95	$3.50	Simpson, Joe	82T	382	$ .01	$ .07
Silvera, Charlie	73T	323	$ .35	$1.25	Simpson, Joe	83T	567	$ .01	$ .07
Silvera, Charlie	74T	379	$ .15	$ .50	Simpson, Joe	83TTR	104	$ .02	$ .10
Silverio, Tom	72T	213	$ .15	$ .50	Simpson, Joe	84T	219	$ .01	$ .06
Silvestri, Dave	88TTR	107	$ .01	$ .25	Simpson, Wayne	70T	683	$1.25	$4.50
Silvestri, Dave	89TBB	141	$ .01	$ .06	Simpson, Wayne	71T	68	$ .15	$ .50
Silvestri, Ken	60T	466	$ .95	$3.50	Simpson, Wayne	71T	339	$ .15	$ .50
Silvestri, Ken	73T	237	$ .35	$1.25	Simpson, Wayne	72T	762	$ .75	$2.50
Silvestri, Ken	74T	634	$ .35	$1.25	Simpson, Wayne	73T	428	$ .07	$ .30
Sima, Al	52T	93	$7.00	$20.00	Sims, Duke	66T	169	$ .30	$ .95
Sima, Al	53T	241	$12.50	$50.00	Sims, Duke	67T	3	$ .30	$ .85
Sima, Al	54T	216	$2.50	$10.00	Sims, Duke	68T	508	$ .35	$1.25
Simmons, Curt	52T	203	$7.00	$21.00	Sims, Duke	69T	414	$ .30	$ .85
Simmons, Curt	56T	290	$1.30	$5.00	Sims, Duke	70T	275	$ .15	$ .50
Simmons, Curt	57T	158	$ .60	$2.50	Sims, Duke	71T	172	$ .15	$ .50
Simmons, Curt	58T	404	$ .45	$1.50	Sims, Duke	72T	63	$ .15	$ .50
Simmons, Curt	59T	382	$ .75	$2.20	Sims, Duke	73T	304	$ .07	$ .30
Simmons, Curt	60T	451	$ .95	$3.50	Sims, Duke	74T	398	$ .07	$ .30
Simmons, Curt	61T	11	$ .35	$1.25	Sims, Greg	66T	596	$5.00	$20.00
Simmons, Curt	62T	56	$ .75	$3.00	Sinatro, Matt	90TTR	115	$ .01	$ .05
Simmons, Curt	62T	285	$ .75	$3.00	Sinatro, Matt	91T	709	$ .01	$ .03
Simmons, Curt	63T	22	$ .30	$ .95	Singer, Bill	66T	288	$32.50	$100.00
Simmons, Curt	64T	385	$ .75	$2.20	Singer, Bill	67T	12	$ .30	$ .85
Simmons, Curt	65T	373	$ .35	$1.25	Singer, Bill	68T	249	$ .30	$ .85
Simmons, Curt	66T	489	$ .65	$1.75	Singer, Bill	69T	12	$ .50	$1.50
Simmons, Curt	67T	39	$ .30	$ .85	Singer, Bill	69T	575	$ .30	$ .95
Simmons, Nelson	86T	121	$ .01	$ .04	Singer, Bill	70T	71	$ .50	$1.50
Simmons, Ted	71T	117	$2.50	$9.00	Singer, Bill	70T	490	$ .15	$ .50
Simmons, Ted	72T	154	$ .50	$1.50	Singer, Bill	71T	145	$ .15	$ .50
Simmons, Ted	73T	85	$ .25	$1.25	Singer, Bill	72T	25	$ .15	$ .50
Simmons, Ted	74T	260	$ .15	$ .50	Singer, Bill	73T	570	$ .45	$1.45
Simmons, Ted	75T	75	$ .15	$ .50	Singer, Bill	74T	210	$ .07	$ .30
Simmons, Ted	76T	191	$ .30	$ .95	Singer, Bill	75T	40	$ .07	$ .30
Simmons, Ted	76T	290	$ .30	$ .85	Singer, Bill	76T	411	$ .05	$ .20
Simmons, Ted	77T	470	$ .15	$ .50	Singer, Bill	76TTR	411	$ .05	$ .20
Simmons, Ted	78T	380	$ .05	$ .25	Singer, Bill	77T	346	$ .05	$ .15

TOPPS

Player	Year	No.	VG	EX/MT	Player	Year	No.	VG	EX/MT
Singleton, Elmer	57T	378	$ .85	$3.50	Skinner, Bob	57T	209	$ .95	$3.50
Singleton, Elmer	59T	548	$2.50	$10.00	Skinner, Bob	58T	94	$ .70	$2.25
Singleton, Ken	71T	16	$ .50	$2.00	Skinner, Bob	59T	320	$ .75	$2.20
Singleton, Ken	72T	425	$ .15	$ .50	Skinner, Bob	59T	543	$11.50	$45.00
Singleton, Ken	72TIA	426	$ .15	$ .50	Skinner, Bob	60T	113	$ .45	$1.45
Singleton, Ken	73T	232	$ .30	$ .85	Skinner, Bob	61T	204	$ .35	$1.25
Singleton, Ken	74T	25	$ .15	$ .50	Skinner, Bob	62T	115	$ .45	$1.45
Singleton, Ken	75T	125	$ .15	$ .50	Skinner, Bob	63T	18	$2.35	$10.00
Singleton, Ken	76T	175	$ .15	$ .50	Skinner, Bob	63T	215	$ .30	$ .95
Singleton, Ken	77T	445	$ .05	$ .15	Skinner, Bob	64T	377	$ .50	$1.45
Singleton, Ken	78T	65	$ .05	$ .20	Skinner, Bob	65T	591	$2.10	$6.00
Singleton, Ken	79T	615	$ .02	$ .10	Skinner, Bob	66T	471	$ .75	$2.50
Singleton, Ken	80T	340	$ .01	$ .10	Skinner, Bob	69T	369	$ .30	$ .85
Singleton, Ken	81T	570	$ .01	$ .10	Skinner, Bob	73T	12	$ .30	$ .85
Singleton, Ken	82T	290	$ .01	$ .07	Skinner, Bob	74T	188	$ .07	$ .30
Singleton, Ken	82TAS	552	$ .01	$ .07	Skinner, Bob	74T	489	$ .07	$ .30
Singleton, Ken	83T	85	$ .01	$ .07	Skinner, Bob	85T	139	$ .01	$ .10
Singleton, Ken	84T	165	$ .01	$ .06	Skinner, Joel	85T	139	$ .01	$ .10
Singleton, Ken	85T	755	$ .01	$ .05	Skinner, Joel	85T	488	$ .01	$ .05
Sisk, Doug	83TTR	105	$ .02	$ .10	Skinner, Joel	86T	239	$ .01	$ .04
Sisk, Doug	84T	599	$ .01	$ .06	Skinner, Joel	87T	626	$ .01	$ .04
Sisk, Doug	85T	315	$ .01	$ .05	Skinner, Joel	88T	109	$ .01	$ .04
Sisk, Doug	86T	144	$ .01	$ .04	Skinner, Joel	89T	536	$ .01	$ .05
Sisk, Doug	87T	404	$ .01	$ .04	Skinner, Joel	90T	54	$ .01	$ .04
Sisk, Doug	88T	763	$ .01	$ .04	Skinner, Joel	91T	783	$ .01	$ .03
Sisk, Doug	89T	13	$ .01	$ .05	Skizas, Lou	57T	83	$ .95	$3.50
Sisk, Tommie	63T	169	$10.00	$30.00	Skizas, Lou	58T	319	$ .75	$3.00
Sisk, Tommie	64T	224	$ .30	$ .85	Skizas, Lou	59T	328	$ .75	$2.20
Sisk, Tommie	65T	558	$1.75	$4.50	Skok, Craig	79T	363	$ .02	$ .10
Sisk, Tommie	66T	441	$ .30	$ .95	Skowron, Bill	54T	239	$20.00	$70.00
Sisk, Tommie	67T	84	$ .30	$ .85	Skowron, Bill	55T	22	$5.00	$20.00
Sisk, Tommie	68T	429	$ .30	$ .85	Skowron, Bill	56T	61	$2.50	$10.00
Sisk, Tommie	69T	152	$ .30	$ .85	Skowron, Bill	57T	135	$2.50	$10.00
Sisk, Tommie	70T	374	$ .15	$ .50	Skowron, "Moose" Bill	58T	240	$2.50	$10.00
Sisler, Dave	57T	56	$ .95	$3.50	Skowron, Bill	58TAS	477	$ .70	$2.50
Sisler, Dave	58T	59	$ .85	$3.50	Skowron, Bill	59T	90	$3.00	$9.00
Sisler, Dave	59T	346	$ .75	$2.20	Skowron, Bill	59TAS	554	$3.00	$9.00
Sisler, Dave	59T	384	$ .75	$2.20	Skowron, Bill	60T	370	$2.10	$6.00
Sisler, Dave	60T	186	$ .45	$1.45	Skowron, Bill	60TAS	553	$1.85	$5.50
Sisler, Dave	61T	239	$ .35	$1.25	Skowron, Bill	61T	371	$2.10	$6.00
Sisler, Dave	62T	171	$ .45	$1.45	Skowron, Bill	61T	42	$ .75	$3.00
Sisler, Dave	63T	284	$ .45	$1.50	Skowron, Bill	61TAS	568	$6.00	$17.50
Sisler, Dick	51Tbb	8	$7.50	$22.50	Skowron, Bill	62T	110	$2.10	$6.00
Sisler, Dick	52T	113	$7.00	$20.00	Skowron, Bill	63T	180	$ .35	$1.25
Sisler, Dick	64T	162	$ .15	$ .50	Skowron, Bill	64T	445	$ .75	$3.00
Sisler, Dick	65T	158	$ .30	$ .85	Skowron, Bill	65T	70	$ .15	$ .50
Sisler, George	79TRH	411	$ .15	$ .50	Skowron, Bill	66T	199	$ .20	$ .35
Sisti, Sibby	52T	293	$15.00	$47.50	Skowron, Bill	66T	590	$5.00	$14.50
Sisti, Sibby	53T	124	$4.50	$15.00	Skowron, Bill	67T	357	$ .35	$1.25
Sizemore, Ted	69T	552	$ .30	$ .95	Slater, Bob	79T	703	$ .02	$ .10
Sizemore, Ted	70T	174	$ .15	$ .50	Slaton, Jim	72T	744	$ .75	$2.50
Sizemore, Ted	71T	571	$ .35	$1.25	Slaton, Jim	73T	628	$ .45	$1.45
Sizemore, Ted	72T	514	$ .15	$ .50	Slaton, Jim	74T	371	$ .07	$ .30
Sizemore, Ted	73T	128	$ .07	$ .30	Slaton, Jim	75T	281	$ .07	$ .30
Sizemore, Ted	74T	209	$ .07	$ .30	Slaton, Jim	76T	163	$ .05	$ .20
Sizemore, Ted	75T	404	$ .07	$ .30	Slaton, Jim	77T	604	$ .05	$ .15
Sizemore, Ted	76T	522	$ .05	$ .20	Slaton, Jim	78T	474	$ .02	$ .10
Sizemore, Ted	77T	366	$ .05	$ .15	Slaton, Jim	79T	541	$ .02	$ .10
Sizemore, Ted	78T	136	$ .02	$ .10	Slaton, Jim	80T	24	$ .01	$ .10
Sizemore, Ted	79T	297	$ .02	$ .10	Slaton, Jim	81T	357	$ .01	$ .10
Sizemore, Ted	80T	81	$ .01	$ .10	Slaton, Jim	82T	221	$ .01	$ .07
Skaggs, Dave	78T	593	$ .02	$ .10	Slaton, Jim	83T	114	$ .01	$ .07
Skaggs, Dave	79T	367	$ .02	$ .10	Slaton, Jim	84TTR	109	$ .02	$ .10
Skaggs, Dave	80T	211	$ .01	$ .10	Slaton, Jim	85T	657	$ .01	$ .05
Skaggs, Dave	81T	48	$ .01	$ .10	Slaton, Jim	86T	579	$ .01	$ .04
Skalski, Joe	89TMLD	115	$ .01	$ .06	Slaught, Don	84T	196	$ .01	$ .06
Skeen, Archie	64T	428	$ .50	$1.45	Slaught, Don	85T	542	$ .01	$ .05
Skidmore, Roe	71T	121	$ .15	$ .50	Slaught, Don	85TTR	107	$ .02	$ .10
Skinner, Bob	55T	88	$2.50	$10.00	Slaught, Don	86T	761	$ .01	$ .04
Skinner, Bob	56T	297	$1.30	$5.00	Slaught, Don	87T	308	$ .01	$ .04

Player	Year	No.	VG	EX/MT	Player	Year	No.	VG	EX/MT
Slaught, Don	88T	462	$ .01	$ .04	Smalley, Jr., Roy	85T	140	$ .01	$ .10
Slaught, Don	88TTR	108	$ .01	$ .06	Smalley, Jr., Roy	85TTR	108	$ .02	$ .10
Slaught, Don	89T	611	$ .01	$ .05	Smalley, Jr., Roy	86T	613	$ .01	$ .04
Slaught, Don	89TBB	138	$ .01	$ .06	Smalley, Jr., Roy	87T	744	$ .01	$ .04
Slaught, Don	90T	26	$ .01	$ .04	Smalley, Jr., Roy	88T	239	$ .01	$ .04
Slaught, Don	90TTR	116	$ .01	$ .05	Smalley, Roy	51Tbb	17	$7.50	$22.50
Slaught, Don	91T	221	$ .01	$ .03	Smalley, Roy	52T	173	$7.00	$20.00
Slaughter, Enos	51Tbb	30	$10.00	$40.00	Smalley, Roy	54T	231	$2.50	$10.00
Slaughter, Enos	52T	65	$35.00	$110.00	Smalley, Roy	57T	397	$ .85	$3.50
Slaughter, Enos	53T	41	$22.50	$67.50	Smalley, Roy	76T	70	$ .05	$ .25
Slaughter, Enos	56T	109	$8.00	$25.00	Smalley, Roy	85T	140	$ .01	$ .10
Slaughter, Enos	57T	215	$7.00	$20.00	Smiley, John	87TTR	114	$ .05	$ .40
Slaughter, Enos	58T	142	$5.00	$15.00	Smiley, John	88T	423	$ .01	$ .30
Slaughter, Enos	59T	155	$5.50	$17.50	Smiley, John	89T	322	$ .01	$ .25
Slaughter, Sterling	64T	469	$ .50	$1.45	Smiley, John	89TBB	85	$ .01	$ .10
Slaughter, Sterling	65T	314	$ .35	$1.25	Smiley, John	90T	568	$ .01	$ .10
Slayback, Bill	73T	537	$ .45	$1.45	Smiley, John	91T	143	$ .01	$ .03
Slayton, Jim	84T	772	$ .01	$ .06	Smith, Al	54T	248	$2.50	$10.00
Slayton, Jim	87T	432	$ .01	$ .04	Smith, Al	55T	197	$5.25	$15.00
Sleater, Lou	52T	306	$12.00	$40.00	Smith, Al	56T	105	$2.25	$6.00
Sleater, Lou	53T	224	$12.50	$50.00	Smith, Al	57T	145	$ .95	$3.50
Sleater, Lou	58T	46	$ .85	$3.50	Smith, Al	58T	177	$ .75	$3.00
Slocum, Ron	70T	573	$ .30	$ .95	Smith, Al	59T	22	$ .85	$3.50
Slocum, Ron	71T	274	$ .15	$ .50	Smith, Al	60T	428	$ .75	$2.20
Slusarski, Joe	88TTR	109	$ .01	$ .25	Smith, Al	61T	170	$ .35	$1.25
Slusarski, Joe	89TBB	213	$ .01	$ .06	Smith, Al	61T	42	$ .75	$3.00
Small, Jim	56T	207	$3.00	$9.00	Smith, Al	62T	410	$ .75	$2.50
Small, Jim	57T	33	$ .95	$3.50	Smith, Al	63T	16	$ .30	$ .95
Smalley, Jr., Roy	76T	70	$ .05	$ .25	Smith, Al	64T	317	$ .30	$ .95
Smalley, Jr., Roy	76T	657	$ .30	$ .95	Smith, Bernie	71T	204	$ .15	$ .50
Smalley, Jr., Roy	77T	66	$ .05	$ .15	Smith, Billy	63T	241	$ .30	$ .95
Smalley, Jr., Roy	78T	471	$ .02	$ .10	Smith, Billy	78T	666	$ .02	$ .10
Smalley, Jr., Roy	79T	219	$ .02	$ .10	Smith, Billy	79T	237	$ .02	$ .10
Smalley, Jr., Roy	80T	570	$ .01	$ .10	Smith, Billy	80T	367	$ .01	$ .10
Smalley, Jr., Roy	81T	115	$ .01	$ .10	Smith, Billy	82T	441	$ .01	$ .07
Smalley, Jr., Roy	82T	767	$ .01	$ .07	Smith, Billy	82T	593	$ .01	$ .07
Smalley, Jr., Roy	82TTR	107	$ .02	$ .10	Smith, Bob G.	58T	226	$ .75	$3.00
					Smith, Bob G.	59T	83	$ .85	$3.50
					Smith, Bob W.	58T	445	$ .75	$2.20
					Smith, Bobby Gene	57T	384	$ .85	$3.50
					Smith, Bobby Gene	58T	402	$ .75	$3.00
					Smith, Bobby Gene	59T	162	$ .75	$2.20
					Smith, Bobby Gene	60T	194	$ .45	$1.45
					Smith, Bobby Gene	61T	316	$ .35	$1.25
					Smith, Bobby Gene	62T	531	$3.95	$11.50
					Smith, Bryn	82T	118	$ .03	$ .15
					Smith, Bryn	83T	447	$ .01	$ .07
					Smith, Bryn	84T	656	$ .01	$ .06
					Smith, Bryn	85T	88	$ .01	$ .05
					Smith, Bryn	86T	299	$ .01	$ .04
					Smith, Bryn	87T	505	$ .01	$ .04
					Smith, Bryn	88T	161	$ .01	$ .04
					Smith, Bryn	88TBB	250	$ .01	$ .06
					Smith, Bryn	89T	464	$ .01	$ .05
					Smith, Bryn	89TBB	47	$ .01	$ .06
					Smith, Bryn	90T	352	$ .01	$ .04
					Smith, Bryn	90TTR	117	$ .01	$ .05
					Smith, Bryn	91T	743	$ .01	$ .03
					Smith, Charlie	62T	283	$ .45	$1.45
					Smith, Charley (ie)	63T	424	$ .45	$1.50
					Smith, Charlie	64T	519	$ .50	$1.45
					Smith, Charlie	65T	22	$ .30	$ .85
					Smith, Charlie	66T	358	$ .30	$ .95
					Smith, Charlie	67T	257	$ .30	$ .85
					Smith, Charlie	68T	596	$ .35	$1.25
					Smith, Charlie	69T	538	$ .30	$ .95
					Smith, Dave	81T	534	$ .05	$ .20
Smalley, Jr., Roy	83T	460	$ .01	$ .07	Smith, Dave	82T	761	$ .01	$ .07
Smalley, Jr., Roy	84T	305	$ .01	$ .06	Smith, Dave	83T	247	$ .01	$ .07
Smalley, Jr., Roy	85T	26	$ .01	$ .05	Smith, Dave	84T	361	$ .01	$ .06

ROY
SMALLEY
SS-3rd BASE
YANKEES

TOPPS

Player	Year	No.	VG	EX/MT	Player	Year	No.	VG	EX/MT
Smith, Dave	85T	123	$ .01	$ .05	Smith, Lonnie	91T	306	$ .01	$ .03
Smith, Dave	86T	408	$ .01	$ .04	Smith, Mayo	55T	130	$2.00	$6.00
Smith, Dave	87T	50	$ .01	$ .04	Smith, Mayo	56T	60	$2.25	$6.00
Smith, Dave	88T	520	$ .01	$ .04	Smith, Mayo	67T	321	$ .30	$ .85
Smith, Dave	89T	305	$ .01	$ .05	Smith, Mayo	68T	544	$ .35	$1.25
Smith, Dave	90T	746	$ .01	$ .04	Smith, Mayo	69T	40	$ .30	$ .85
Smith, Dave	91T	215	$ .01	$ .03	Smith, Mayo	70T	313	$ .15	$ .50
Smith, Dick	64T	398	$ .50	$1.45	Smith, Mike	89TMLD	118	$ .01	$ .06
Smith, Dick	65T	579	$1.75	$4.50	Smith, Mike	90T	249	$ .01	$ .10
Smith, Dwight	89TMLD	116	$ .01	$ .50	Smith, Mike	90T	552	$ .01	$ .10
Smith, Dwight	89TTR	113	$ .01	$ .35	Smith, Ozzie	79T	116	$10.00	$40.00
Smith, Dwight	90T	311	$ .01	$ .25	Smith, Ozzie	80T	393	$2.00	$8.00
Smith, Dwight	91T	463	$ .01	$ .03	Smith, Ozzie	81T	254	$ .75	$3.00
Smith, Frank	52T	179	$7.00	$20.00	Smith, Ozzie	81TRB	207	$ .03	$ .15
Smith, Frank	53T	116	$4.50	$15.00	Smith, Ozzie	82T	95	$ .40	$1.50
Smith, Frank	54T	71	$7.00	$22.00	Smith, Ozzie	82TTR	109	$1.50	$6.00
Smith, Frank	55T	204	$5.25	$15.00	Smith, Ozzie	83T	540	$ .05	$ .75
Smith, George	65T	483	$ .75	$3.00	Smith, Ozzie	84T	130	$ .01	$ .35
Smith, George	66T	542	$5.00	$20.00	Smith, Ozzie	84TAS	389	$ .01	$ .06
Smith, George	67T	444	$ .30	$ .95	Smith, Ozzie	85T	605	$ .01	$ .10
Smith, Greg	89TMLD	117	$ .01	$ .15	Smith, Ozzie	85TAS	715	$ .01	$ .10
Smith, Greg	91T	560	$ .01	$ .10	Smith, Ozzie	86T	730	$ .02	$ .15
Smith, Hal	55T	8	$2.00	$6.00	Smith, Ozzie	86TAS	704	$ .01	$ .10
Smith, Hal	56T	283	$1.30	$5.00	Smith, Ozzie	87T	749	$ .01	$ .10
Smith, Hal	56T	62	$2.25	$6.00	Smith, Ozzie	87TAS	598	$ .01	$ .04
Smith, Hal	57T	41	$ .95	$3.50	Smith, Ozzie	88T	460	$ .01	$ .10
Smith, Hal	57T	111	$ .95	$3.50	Smith, Ozzie	88TAS	400	$ .01	$ .04
Smith, Hal	58T	257	$ .75	$3.00	Smith, Ozzie	88TBB	228	$ .01	$ .15
Smith, Hal	58T	273	$ .75	$3.00	Smith, Ozzie	89T	230	$ .01	$ .10
Smith, Hal	59T	227	$ .75	$2.20	Smith, Ozzie	89TAS	389	$ .01	$ .05
Smith, Hal	59T	497	$ .75	$2.20	Smith, Ozzie	89TBB	110	$ .01	$ .10
Smith, Hal	60T	48	$ .45	$1.45	Smith, Ozzie	90T	590	$ .01	$ .04
Smith, Hal	60T	84	$ .45	$1.45	Smith, Ozzie	90TAS	400	$ .01	$ .10
Smith, Hal	61T	242	$ .35	$1.25	Smith, Ozzie	91T	130	$ .01	$ .03
Smith, Hal	61T	549	$7.00	$21.00	Smith, Paul	54T	11	$2.00	$9.00
Smith, Hal	62T	492	$ .75	$2.50	Smith, Paul	57T	345	$4.25	$15.00
Smith, Hal	63T	153	$ .30	$ .95	Smith, Paul	58T	269	$ .75	$3.00
Smith, Hal	64T	233	$ .30	$ .95	Smith, Pete	64T	428	$ .50	$1.45
Smith, Jack	63T	496	$2.50	$6.50	Smith, Pete	88TTR	111	$ .01	$ .10
Smith, Jack	64T	378	$ .50	$1.45	Smith, Pete	89T	537	$ .01	$ .10
Smith, Jimmy	83T	122	$ .01	$ .07	Smith, Pete	90T	771	$ .01	$ .04
Smith, Keith	78T	710	$ .15	$ .50	Smith, Pete	91T	383	$ .01	$ .03
Smith, Lee	82T	452	$ .25	$1.00	Smith, Ray	84T	46	$ .01	$ .06
Smith, Lee	83T	699	$ .01	$ .10	Smith, Reggie	67T	314	$1.25	$5.00
Smith, Lee	84T	176	$ .01	$ .06	Smith, Reggie	68T	61	$ .25	$1.25
Smith, Lee	85T	511	$ .01	$ .05	Smith, Reggie	69T	660	$ .50	$1.50
Smith, Lee	86T	355	$ .01	$ .04	Smith, Reggie	70T	62	$ .50	$1.50
Smith, Lee	87T	23	$ .01	$ .04	Smith, Reggie	70T	215	$ .30	$1.00
Smith, Lee	88T	240	$ .01	$ .10	Smith, Reggie	71T	305	$ .30	$1.00
Smith, Lee	88TTR	110	$ .01	$ .06	Smith, Reggie	72T	88	$ .50	$1.50
Smith, Lee	89T	760	$ .01	$ .05	Smith, Reggie	72T	565	$ .35	$1.25
Smith, Lee	90T	495	$ .01	$ .04	Smith, Reggie	72TIA	566	$ .30	$ .95
Smith, Lee	90TTR	118	$ .01	$ .05	Smith, Reggie	73T	40	$ .30	$ .85
Smith, Lee	91T	660	$ .01	$ .03	Smith, Reggie	74T	285	$ .07	$ .30
Smith, Lonnie	79T	722	$ .50	$2.00	Smith, Reggie	75T	490	$ .07	$ .30
Smith, Lonnie	81T	317	$ .01	$ .10	Smith, Reggie	76T	215	$ .05	$ .20
Smith, Lonnie	82T	127	$ .01	$ .07	Smith, Reggie	77T	345	$ .05	$ .15
Smith, Lonnie	82TTR	108	$ .02	$ .10	Smith, Reggie	78T	168	$ .02	$ .10
Smith, Lonnie	83T	465	$ .01	$ .07	Smith, Reggie	79T	465	$ .05	$ .20
Smith, Lonnie	83T	561	$ .01	$ .07	Smith, Reggie	80T	695	$ .01	$ .10
Smith, Lonnie	84T	186	$ .01	$ .06	Smith, Reggie	81T	75	$ .01	$ .10
Smith, Lonnie	84T	580	$ .01	$ .06	Smith, Reggie	82T	545	$ .01	$ .07
Smith, Lonnie	85T	255	$ .01	$ .05	Smith, Reggie	82TIA	546	$ .01	$ .07
Smith, Lonnie	85TTR	109	$ .02	$ .10	Smith, Reggie	82TTR	110	$ .02	$ .10
Smith, Lonnie	86T	617	$ .01	$ .04	Smith, Reggie	83T	282	$ .01	$ .07
Smith, Lonnie	87T	69	$ .01	$ .04	Smith, Reggie	83T	283	$ .01	$ .07
Smith, Lonnie	88T	777	$ .01	$ .04	Smith, Roy	85T	381	$ .01	$ .05
Smith, Lonnie	89TBB	242	$ .01	$ .06	Smith, Roy	86T	9	$ .01	$ .04
Smith, Lonnie	89TTR	114	$ .01	$ .06	Smith, Roy	90T	672	$ .01	$ .04
Smith, Lonnie	90T	152	$ .01	$ .04	Smith, Roy	91T	503	$ .01	$ .03

Player	Year	No.	VG	EX/MT
Smith, Tommy	74T	606	$ .07	$ .30
Smith, Tommy	75T	619	$ .07	$ .30
Smith, Tommy	77T	14	$ .05	$ .15
Smith, Willie	65T	85	$ .30	$ .85
Smith, Willie	66T	438	$ .30	$ .95
Smith, Willie	67T	397	$ .30	$ .95
Smith, Willie	68T	568	$ .35	$1.25
Smith, Willie	69T	198	$ .30	$ .85
Smith, Willie	70T	318	$ .15	$ .50
Smith, Willie	71T	457	$ .15	$ .50
Smith, Zane	86T	167	$ .02	$ .20
Smith, Zane	87T	544	$ .01	$ .04
Smith, Zane	88T	297	$ .01	$ .04
Smith, Zane	88TBB	193	$ .01	$ .06
Smith, Zane	89T	688	$ .01	$ .05
Smith, Zane	90T	48	$ .01	$ .04
Smith, Zane	91T	441	$ .01	$ .03
Smithson, Mike	83TTR	106	$ .02	$ .10
Smithson, Mike	84T	89	$ .01	$ .06
Smithson, Mike	84TTR	110	$ .02	$ .10
Smithson, Mike	85T	483	$ .01	$ .05
Smithson, Mike	86T	695	$ .01	$ .04
Smithson, Mike	87T	225	$ .01	$ .04
Smithson, Mike	88T	554	$ .01	$ .04
Smithson, Mike	89T	377	$ .01	$ .05
Smithson, Mike	89TBB	222	$ .01	$ .06
Smithson, Mike	90T	188	$ .01	$ .04
Smoltz, John	89T	382	$ .05	$ .35
Smoltz, John	89TBB	260	$ .01	$ .25
Smoltz, John	90T	535	$ .01	$ .15
Smoltz, John	91T	157	$ .01	$ .03
Snell, Nate	85TTR	110	$ .05	$ .25
Snell, Nate	86T	521	$ .01	$ .04
Snell, Nate	87T	86	$ .01	$ .04
Snider, Duke	51Trb	38	$15.00	$55.00
Snider, Duke	52T	37	$100.00	$300.00
Snider, Duke	54T	32	$30.00	$125.00
Snider, Duke	55T	210	$90.00	$450.00
Snider, Duke	56T	150	$35.00	$110.00
Snider, Duke	57T	170	$30.00	$90.00
Snider, Duke	57T	400	$40.00	$160.00
Snider, Duke	58T	88	$20.00	$60.00
Snider, Duke	58T	314	$5.00	$20.00
Snider, Duke	58T	436	$12.50	$50.00
Snider, Duke	59T	20	$12.00	$45.00
Snider, Duke	59T	468	$3.00	$10.00
Snider, Duke	60T	493	$15.50	$47.50
Snider, Duke	61T	443	$12.00	$35.00
Snider, Duke	62T	500	$15.00	$45.00
Snider, Duke	63T	68	$2.50	$10.00
Snider, Duke	63T	550	$20.00	$62.50
Snider, Duke	64T	155	$7.50	$22.50
Snyder, Brian	86T	174	$ .01	$ .04
Snyder, Cory	85T	403	$ .75	$3.00
Snyder, Cory	87T	192	$ .15	$ .40
Snyder, Cory	88T	620	$ .01	$ .20
Snyder, Cory	88TBB	43	$ .01	$ .10
Snyder, Cory	89T	80	$ .01	$ .10
Snyder, Cory	89TBB	175	$ .01	$ .10
Snyder, Cory	90T	770	$ .01	$ .10
Snyder, Cory	91T	323	$ .01	$ .03
Snyder, Gene	59T	522	$2.50	$10.00
Snyder, Jerry	57T	22	$ .95	$3.50
Snyder, Jim	88TTR	112	$ .01	$ .06
Snyder, Jim	89T	44	$ .01	$ .05
Snyder, Russ	60T	81	$ .45	$1.45
Snyder, Russ	61T	143	$ .35	$1.25
Snyder, Russ	62T	64	$ .45	$1.45
Snyder, Russ	63T	543	$1.75	$4.50
Snyder, Russ	64T	126	$ .30	$ .95

Player	Year	No.	VG	EX/MT
Snyder, Russ	65T	204	$ .35	$1.25
Snyder, Russ	66T	562	$5.00	$20.00
Snyder, Russ	67T	405	$ .30	$ .95
Snyder, Russ	68T	504	$ .35	$1.25

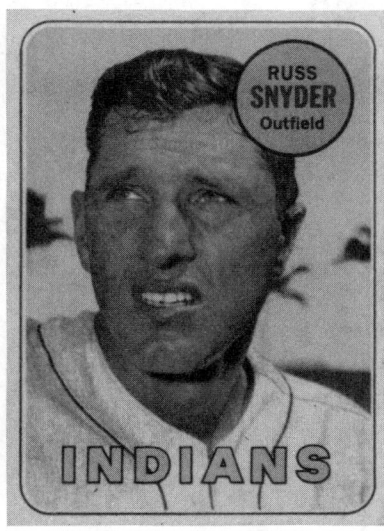

Player	Year	No.	VG	EX/MT
Snyder, Russ	69T	201	$ .30	$ .85
Snyder, Russ	70T	347	$ .15	$ .50
Snyder, Russ	71T	653	$ .75	$2.50
Soderholm, Eric	73T	577	$ .45	$1.45
Soderholm, Eric	74T	503	$ .07	$ .30
Soderholm, Eric	75T	54	$ .07	$ .30
Soderholm, Eric	76T	214	$ .05	$ .20
Soderholm, Eric	77T	273	$ .05	$ .15
Soderholm, Eric	78T	602	$ .02	$ .10
Soderholm, Eric	79T	186	$ .02	$ .10
Soderholm, Eric	80T	441	$ .01	$ .10
Soderholm, Eric	81T	383	$ .01	$ .10
Soff, Ray	87T	671	$ .01	$ .04
Sofield, Rick	79T	709	$ .02	$ .10
Sofield, Rick	80T	669	$ .06	$ .30
Sofield, Rick	81T	278	$ .01	$ .10
Sofield, Rick	82T	42	$ .05	$ .20
Sojo, Luis	90T	594	$ .01	$ .10
Sojo, Luis	91T	26	$ .01	$ .03
Solaita, Tony	75T	389	$ .07	$ .30
Solaita, Tony	76T	121	$ .07	$ .30
Solaita, Tony	77T	482	$ .05	$ .15
Solaita, Tony	78T	557	$ .02	$ .10
Solaita, Tony	79T	18	$ .02	$ .10
Solaita, Tony	80T	407	$ .01	$ .10
Solano, Julio	85T	353	$ .01	$ .05
Solis, Marcelino	59T	214	$ .75	$2.20
Solomon, "Eddie"	75T	624	$ .07	$ .30
Solomon, "Eddie"(Buddy)	78T	598	$ .02	$ .10
Solomon, Buddy	79T	156	$ .02	$ .10
Solomon, Buddy	80T	346	$ .01	$ .10
Solomon, Buddy	81T	298	$ .01	$ .10
Solomon, Buddy	82T	73	$ .01	$ .07
Solomon, Buddy	82T	696	$ .01	$ .07
Sorensen, Lary	78T	569	$ .02	$ .10
Sorensen, Lary	79T	303	$ .02	$ .10

Player	Year	No.	VG	EX/MT
Sorensen, Lary	80T	154	$ .01	$ .10
Sorensen, Lary	81T	379	$ .01	$ .10
Sorensen, Lary	81TTR	831	$ .02	$ .10
Sorensen, Lary	82T	689	$ .01	$ .07
Sorensen, Lary	82TTR	111	$ .02	$ .10
Sorensen, Lary	83T	48	$ .01	$ .07
Sorensen, Lary	84T	286	$ .01	$ .06
Sorensen, Lary	84T	546	$ .01	$ .06
Sorensen, Lary	84TTR	111	$ .02	$ .10
Sorensen, Lary	86T	744	$ .01	$ .04
Sorrell, Bill	66T	254	$10.00	$40.00
Sorrell, Bill	67T	341	$ .30	$ .85
Sorrell, Billy	71T	17	$ .15	$ .50
Sorrento, Paul	89TMLD	119	$ .01	$ .15
Sorrento, Paul	90TTR	119	$ .01	$ .15
Sorrento, Paul	91T	654	$ .01	$ .10
Sosa, Elias	74T	54	$ .07	$ .30
Sosa, Elias	75T	398	$ .07	$ .30
Sosa, Elias	76T	364	$ .05	$ .20
Sosa, Elias	77T	558	$ .05	$ .15
Sosa, Elias	78T	694	$ .02	$ .10
Sosa, Elias	79T	78	$ .02	$ .10
Sosa, Elias	80T	293	$ .01	$ .10
Sosa, Elias	81T	181	$ .01	$ .10
Sosa, Elias	82T	414	$ .01	$ .07
Sosa, Elias	82TTR	112	$ .02	$ .10
Sosa, Elias	83T	753	$ .01	$ .07
Sosa, Elias	83TTR	107	$ .02	$ .10
Sosa, Elias	84T	503	$ .01	$ .06
Sosa, Jose	76T	591	$ .05	$ .20
Sosa, Sammy	89TMLD	120	$ .01	$ .50
Sosa, Sammy	90T	692	$ .01	$ .50
Sosa, Sammy	91T	414	$ .01	$ .15
Soto, Mario	78T	427	$ .45	$1.45
Soto, Mario	80T	622	$ .05	$ .20
Soto, Mario	81T	354	$ .01	$ .10
Soto, Mario	82T	63	$ .01	$ .07

MARIO
SOTO
PITCHER
REDS

Player	Year	No.	VG	EX/MT
Soto, Mario	83T	215	$ .01	$ .07
Soto, Mario	83T	351	$ .01	$ .07
Soto, Mario	84T	160	$ .01	$ .06

Player	Year	No.	VG	EX/MT
Soto, Mario	84T	756	$ .01	$ .06
Soto, Mario	85T	495	$ .01	$ .05
Soto, Mario	86T	725	$ .01	$ .10
Soto, Mario	87T	517	$ .01	$ .04
Soto, Mario	88T	666	$ .01	$ .10
Soto, Mario	88TBB	120	$ .01	$ .06
Souchock, Steve	52T	234	$7.00	$20.00
Spahn, Warren	51Trb	30	$9.50	$32.50
Spahn, Warren	52T	33	$75.00	$235.00
Spahn, Warren	53T	147	$35.00	$110.00
Spahn, Warren	54T	20	$22.50	$87.50
Spahn, Warren	55T	31	$22.50	$70.00
Spahn, Warren	56T	10	$17.00	$55.00
Spahn, Warren	57T	90	$17.00	$55.00
Spahn, Warren	58T	270	$12.00	$40.00
Spahn, Warren	58TAS	494	$4.50	$14.00
Spahn, Warren	59T	40	$12.50	$37.50
Spahn, Warren	59TAS	571	$12.50	$37.50
Spahn, Warren	60T	230	$1.50	$4.00
Spahn, Warren	60T	445	$12.50	$37.50
Spahn, Warren	61T	47	$ .90	$3.00
Spahn, Warren	61T	200	$7.50	$22.50
Spahn, Warren	61TAS	589	$35.00	$125.00
Spahn, Warren	62T	56	$ .75	$3.00
Spahn, Warren	62T	58	$ .75	$2.20
Spahn, Warren	62T	100	$8.50	$27.50
Spahn, Warren	62T	312	$2.00	$9.00
Spahn, Warren	62TAS	399	$3.00	$10.00
Spahn, Warren	63T	320	$9.00	$30.00
Spahn, Warren	64T	3	$1.50	$4.00
Spahn, Warren	64T	400	$9.00	$30.00
Spahn, Warren	65T	205	$6.50	$20.00
Spahn, Warren	73T	449	$ .30	$ .85
Spangler, Al	60T	143	$ .45	$1.45
Spangler, Al	61T	73	$ .35	$1.25
Spangler, Al	62T	556	$3.95	$11.50
Spangler, Al	63T	77	$ .30	$ .95
Spangler, Al	64T	406	$ .50	$1.45
Spangler, Al	65T	164	$ .30	$ .85
Spangler, Al	66T	173	$ .30	$ .95
Spangler, Al	68T	451	$ .30	$ .85
Spangler, Al	69T	268	$ .30	$ .95
Spangler, Al	70T	714	$ .75	$2.00
Spangler, Al	74T	354	$ .07	$ .30
Spanswick, Bill	64T	287	$4.00	$15.00
Spanswick, Bill	65T	356	$ .35	$1.25
Sparma, Joe	64T	512	$2.00	$8.00
Sparma, Joe	65T	587	$1.75	$4.50
Sparma, Joe	66T	267	$ .30	$ .95
Sparma, Joe	67T	13	$ .30	$ .85
Sparma, Joe	68T	505	$ .35	$1.25
Sparma, Joe	69T	488	$ .30	$ .85
Sparma, Joe	70T	243	$ .15	$ .50
Speake, Bob	56T	66	$2.25	$6.00
Speake, Bob	57T	339	$4.25	$15.00
Speake, Bob	58T	437	$ .75	$3.00
Speake, Bob	59T	526	$2.50	$10.00
Speck, Cliff	87T	269	$ .01	$ .04
Speckenbach, Paul	64T	548	$1.75	$4.50
Speed, Horace	79T	438	$ .02	$ .10
Speier, Chris	72T	165	$ .15	$ .50
Speier, Chris	72TIA	166	$ .15	$ .50
Speier, Chris	73T	273	$ .07	$ .30
Speier, Chris	73T	345	$ .07	$ .30
Speier, Chris	74T	129	$ .07	$ .30
Speier, Chris	74TAS	335	$ .15	$ .50
Speier, Chris	75T	505	$ .07	$ .30
Speier, Chris	76T	630	$ .05	$ .20
Speier, Chris	77T	515	$ .05	$ .15
Speier, Chris	78T	221	$ .02	$ .10

Player	Year	No.	VG	EX/MT	Player	Year	No.	VG	EX/MT
Speier, Chris	79T	426	$ .02	$ .10	Spillner, Dan	84T	91	$ .01	$ .06
Speier, Chris	80T	319	$ .01	$ .10	Spillner, Dan	85T	169	$ .01	$ .05
Speier, Chris	81T	97	$ .01	$ .10	Spillner, Dan	86T	423	$ .01	$ .04
Speier, Chris	82T	198	$ .01	$ .07	Spilman, Harry	79T	717	$ .05	$ .20
Speier, Chris	83T	768	$ .01	$ .07	Spilman, Harry	80T	677	$ .01	$ .10
Speier, Chris	84T	678	$ .01	$ .06	Spilman, Harry	81T	94	$ .01	$ .10
Speier, Chris	85T	577	$ .01	$ .05	Spilman, Harry	81TTR	833	$ .02	$ .10
Speier, Chris	85TTR	111	$ .02	$ .10	Spilman, Harry	82T	509	$ .01	$ .07
Speier, Chris	86T	212	$ .01	$ .04	Spilman, Harry	83T	193	$ .01	$ .07
Speier, Chris	87T	424	$ .01	$ .04	Spilman, Harry	84T	612	$ .01	$ .06
Speier, Chris	87TTR	115	$ .01	$ .05	Spilman, Harry	85T	482	$ .01	$ .05
Speier, Chris	88T	329	$ .01	$ .04	Spilman, Harry	86T	352	$ .01	$ .04
Speier, Chris	89T	94	$ .01	$ .05	Spilman, Harry	87T	64	$ .01	$ .04
Speier, Chris	90T	753	$ .01	$ .04	Spilman, Harry	88T	217	$ .01	$ .04
Spence, Bob	71T	186	$ .15	$ .50	Spinks, Scipio	70T	492	$ .15	$ .50
Spencer, Daryl	56T	277	$1.30	$5.00	Spinks, Scipio	71T	747	$ .75	$2.50
Spencer, Daryl	57T	49	$ .95	$3.50	Spinks, Scipio	72T	202	$ .15	$ .50
Spencer, Daryl	58T	68	$ .85	$3.50	Spinks, Scipio	73T	417	$ .07	$ .30
Spencer, Daryl	59T	443	$ .75	$2.20	Spinks, Scipio	74T	576	$ .07	$ .30
Spencer, Daryl	60T	368	$ .75	$2.20	Splittorff, Paul	71T	247	$ .15	$ .50
Spencer, Daryl	61T	357	$ .35	$1.25	Splittorff, Paul	72T	315	$ .15	$ .50
Spencer, Daryl	61T	451	$1.50	$4.00	Splittorff, Paul	73T	48	$ .07	$ .30
Spencer, Daryl	62T	197	$ .45	$1.45	Splittorff, Paul	74T	225	$ .07	$ .30
Spencer, Daryl -	63T	502	$2.50	$6.50	Splittorff, Paul	75T	340	$ .07	$ .30
Spencer, George	52T	346	$40.00	$140.00	Splittorff, Paul	76T	43	$ .05	$ .20
Spencer, George	53T	115	$4.50	$15.00	Splittorff, Paul	77T	534	$ .05	$ .15
Spencer, Jim	70T	255	$ .15	$ .50	Splittorff, Paul	78T	638	$ .02	$ .10
Spencer, Jim	71T	78	$ .15	$ .50	Splittorff, Paul	79T	183	$ .02	$ .10
Spencer, Jim	72T	419	$ .15	$ .50	Splittorff, Paul	80T	409	$ .01	$ .10
Spencer, Jim	73T	319	$ .07	$ .30	Splittorff, Paul	81T	218	$ .01	$ .10
Spencer, Jim	74T	580	$ .07	$ .30	Splittorff, Paul	82T	759	$ .01	$ .07
Spencer, Jim	75T	387	$ .07	$ .30	Splittorff, Paul	83T	316	$ .01	$ .07
Spencer, Jim	76T	83	$ .05	$ .20	Splittorff, Paul	84T	52	$ .01	$ .06
Spencer, Jim	76TTR	83	$ .05	$ .20	Spooner, Karl	55T	90	$2.00	$6.00
Spencer, Jim	77T	648	$ .05	$ .15	Spooner, Karl	56T	83	$2.25	$6.00
Spencer, Jim	78T	182	$ .02	$ .10	Sprague, Ed	69T	638	$ .30	$ .95
Spencer, Jim	79T	599	$ .02	$ .10	Sprague, Ed	72T	121	$ .15	$ .50
Spencer, Jim	80T	278	$ .01	$ .10	Sprague, Ed	75T	76	$ .07	$ .30
Spencer, Jim	81T	435	$ .01	$ .10	Sprague, Ed	88TTR	113	$ .01	$ .40
Spencer, Jim	81TTR	832	$ .02	$ .10	Sprague, Ed	89TBB	40	$ .01	$ .06
Spencer, Jim	82T	729	$ .01	$ .07	Spriggs, George	67T	472	$ .75	$3.00
Sperring, Rob	76T	323	$ .05	$ .20	Spriggs, George	68T	314	$ .30	$ .85
Sperring, Rob	78T	514	$ .02	$ .10	Spriggs, George	69T	662	$ .30	$ .95
Spiers, Billy	89TMLD	121	$ .01	$ .10	Spriggs, George	71T	411	$ .15	$ .50
Spiers, Billy	89TTR	115	$ .01	$ .20	Spring, Jack	62T	257	$ .45	$1.45
Spiers, Billy	90T	538	$ .01	$ .10	Spring, Jack	63T	572	$1.75	$4.50
Spiers, Billy	91T	284	$ .01	$ .03	Spring, Jack	64T	71	$ .30	$ .95
Spiezio, Ed	67T	128	$ .30	$ .85	Sprowl, Bobby	81T	82	$ .01	$ .10
Spiezio, Ed	68T	349	$ .30	$ .85	Sprowl, Bobby	82T	441	$ .01	$ .07
Spiezio, Ed	69T	249	$ .30	$ .95	Squires, Mike	79T	704	$ .02	$ .10
Spiezio, Ed	70T	718	$ .75	$2.00	Squires, Mike	80T	466	$ .01	$ .10
Spiezio, Ed	71T	6	$ .15	$ .50	Squires, Mike	81T	292	$ .01	$ .10
Spiezio, Ed	72T	504	$ .15	$ .50	Squires, Mike	82T	398	$ .01	$ .07
Spiezio, Wayne	65T	431	$ .45	$1.45	Squires, Mike	83T	669	$ .01	$ .07
Spikes, Charlie	73T	614	$15.00	$60.00	Squires, Mike	84T	72	$ .01	$ .06
Spikes, Charlie	74T	58	$ .07	$ .30	Squires, Mike	85T	543	$ .01	$ .05
Spikes, Charlie	75T	135	$ .07	$ .30	St. Claire, Ebba	52T	393	$40.00	$140.00
Spikes, Charlie	76T	408	$ .05	$ .20	St. Claire, Ebba	53T	91	$4.50	$15.00
Spikes, Charlie	77T	168	$ .05	$ .15	St. Claire, Randy	86T	89	$ .01	$ .04
Spikes, Charlie	78T	459	$ .02	$ .10	St. Claire, Randy	87T	467	$ .01	$ .04
Spikes, Charlie	80T	294	$ .01	$ .10	St. Claire, Randy	88T	279	$ .01	$ .04
Spillner, Dan	75T	222	$ .07	$ .30	St. Claire, Randy	89T	666	$ .01	$ .05
Spillner, Dan	76T	557	$ .05	$ .20	St. Claire, Randy	90T	503	$ .01	$ .04
Spillner, Dan	77T	182	$ .05	$ .15	Stablein, George	81T	356	$ .01	$ .10
Spillner, Dan	78T	488	$ .02	$ .10	Staehle, Marv	65T	41	$ .30	$ .85
Spillner, Dan	79T	359	$ .02	$ .10	Staehle, Marv	66T	164	$ .30	$ .95
Spillner, Dan	80T	38	$ .01	$ .10	Staehle, Marv	69T	394	$ .90	$3.00
Spillner, Dan	81T	276	$ .01	$ .10	Staehle, Marv	71T	663	$ .75	$2.25
Spillner, Dan	82T	664	$ .01	$ .07	Stafford, Bill	61T	213	$ .35	$1.25
Spillner, Dan	83T	725	$ .01	$ .07	Stafford, Bill	62T	55	$ .75	$3.00

Player	Year	No.	VG	EX/MT	Player	Year	No.	VG	EX/MT
Stafford, Bill	62T	570	$3.95	$11.50	Stanley, Bob	82T	289	$ .01	$ .07
Stafford, Bill	63T	155	$ .30	$ .95	Stanley, Bob	83T	381	$ .01	$ .07
Stafford, Bill	63T	331	$ .75	$2.20	Stanley, Bob	83T	682	$ .01	$ .07
Stafford, Bill	64T	299	$ .30	$ .95	Stanley, Bob	84T	320	$ .01	$ .06
Stafford, Bill	65T	281	$ .35	$1.25	Stanley, Bob	85T	555	$ .01	$ .05
Staggs, Steve	78T	521	$ .02	$ .10	Stanley, Bob	86T	785	$ .01	$ .04
Stahl, Larry	66T	107	$ .30	$ .95	Stanley, Bob	87T	175	$ .01	$ .04
Stahl, Larry	69T	271	$ .30	$ .95	Stanley, Bob	88T	573	$ .01	$ .04
Stahl, Larry	70T	494	$ .15	$ .50	Stanley, Bob	89T	37	$ .01	$ .05
Stahl, Larry	71T	711	$ .75	$2.50	Stanley, Fred	72T	59	$ .15	$ .50
Stahl, Larry	72T	782	$ .75	$2.50	Stanley, Fred	74T	423	$ .07	$ .30
Stahl, Larry	73T	533	$ .45	$1.45	Stanley, Fred	75T	503	$ .07	$ .30
Stahl, Larry	74T	507	$ .07	$ .30	Stanley, Fred	76T	429	$ .05	$ .20
Staiger, Roy	76T	592	$1.25	$5.00	Stanley, Fred	77T	123	$ .05	$ .15
Staiger, Roy	77T	281	$ .05	$ .15	Stanley, Fred	78T	664	$ .02	$ .10
Staley, Gerry	51Tbb	7	$7.50	$22.50	Stanley, Fred	79T	16	$ .02	$ .10
Staley, Gerald	52T	79	$15.00	$47.50	Stanley, Fred	80T	387	$ .01	$ .10
Staley, Gerald (Gerry)	53T	56	$4.50	$15.00					
Staley, Jerry	57T	227	$ .95	$3.50					
Staley, Jerry	58T	412	$ .75	$3.00					
Staley, Jerry	59T	426	$ .75	$2.20					
Staley, Gerry (Jerry)	60T	57	$ .75	$3.00					
Staley, Jerry	60T	510	$2.50	$10.00					
Staley, Jerry	61T	90	$ .35	$1.25					
Stallard, Tracy	61T	81	$ .35	$1.25					
Stallard, Tracy	62T	567	$3.95	$11.50					
Stallard, Tracy	63T	419	$ .45	$1.50					
Stallard, Tracy	64T	176	$ .30	$ .95					
Stallard, Tracy	65T	491	$ .75	$3.00					
Stallard, Tracy	66T	7	$ .30	$ .95					
Stallcup, Virgil	52T	69	$15.00	$47.50					
Stallcup, Virgil	53T	180	$4.50	$15.00					
Staller, George	73T	136	$ .15	$ .50					
Staller, George	74T	307	$ .07	$ .30					
Stanek, Al	64T	99	$ .30	$ .95					
Stanek, Al	65T	302	$ .35	$1.25					
Stanek, Al	66T	437	$ .30	$ .95					
Stanfield, Kevin	79T	709	$ .02	$ .10					
Stange, Lee	62T	321	$ .45	$1.45					
Stange, Lee	63T	246	$ .30	$ .95					
Stange, Lee	64T	555	$1.75	$4.50					
Stange, Lee	65T	448	$ .75	$3.00					
Stange, Lee	66T	371	$ .30	$ .95					
Stange, Lee	67T	99	$ .30	$ .85					
Stange, Lee	68T	593	$ .35	$1.25					
Stange, Lee	69T	148	$ .30	$ .85					
Stange, Lee	70T	447	$ .15	$ .50					
Stange, Lee	71T	311	$ .15	$ .50	Stanley, Fred	81T	281	$ .01	$ .10
Stange, Lee	73T	131	$ .15	$ .50	Stanley, Fred	81TTR	834	$ .02	$ .10
Stange, Lee	74T	403	$ .07	$ .30	Stanley, Fred	82T	787	$ .01	$ .07
Stanhouse, Don	73T	352	$ .07	$ .30	Stanley, Fred	83T	513	$ .01	$ .07
Stanhouse, Don	75T	493	$ .07	$ .30	Stanley, Mickey	66T	198	$ .35	$1.25
Stanhouse, Don	77T	274	$ .05	$ .15	Stanley, Mickey	67T	607	$7.00	$21.00
Stanhouse, Don	78T	629	$ .02	$ .10	Stanley, Mickey	68T	129	$ .30	$ .85
Stanhouse, Don	79T	119	$ .02	$ .10	Stanley, Mickey	69T	13	$ .30	$ .85
Stanhouse, Don	80T	517	$ .01	$ .10	Stanley, Mickey	70T	383	$ .15	$ .50
Stanhouse, Don	81T	24	$ .01	$ .10	Stanley, Mickey	71T	524	$ .35	$1.25
Stanicek, Pete	88TTR	114	$ .01	$ .15	Stanley, Mickey	72T	385	$ .15	$ .50
Stanicek, Pete	89T	497	$ .01	$ .10	Stanley, Mickey	73T	88	$ .07	$ .30
Stanky, Eddie	51Trb	48	$2.10	$6.00	Stanley, Mickey	74T	530	$ .07	$ .30
Stanky, Eddie	52T	76	$20.00	$60.00	Stanley, Mickey	75T	141	$ .07	$ .30
Stanky, Eddie	54T	38	$2.50	$10.00	Stanley, Mickey	76T	483	$ .05	$ .20
Stanky, Ed (Eddie)	55T	191	$2.65	$8.50	Stanley, Mickey	77T	533	$ .05	$ .15
Stanky, Eddie	66T	448	$ .90	$3.00	Stanley, Mickey	78T	232	$ .02	$ .10
Stanky, Eddie	67T	81	$ .30	$ .85	Stanley, Mickey	79T	692	$ .02	$ .10
Stanky, Eddie	68T	564	$ .45	$1.45	Stanley, Mike	87TTR	116	$ .01	$ .05
Stanley, Bob	78T	186	$ .05	$ .20	Stanley, Mike	88T	219	$ .01	$ .04
Stanley, Bob	79T	597	$ .02	$ .10	Stanley, Mike	89T	587	$ .01	$ .05
Stanley, Bob	80T	63	$ .01	$ .10	Stanley, Mike	90T	92	$ .01	$ .04
Stanley, Bob	81T	421	$ .01	$ .10	Stanley, Mike	91T	409	$ .01	$ .03

FRED
STANLEY

Player	Year	No.	VG	EX/MT	Player	Year	No.	VG	EX/MT
Stanton, Leroy	72T	141	$ .15	$ .50	Staub, Rusty	78T	370	$ .05	$ .20
Stanton, Leroy	73T	18	$ .07	$ .30	Staub, Rusty	79T	440	$ .05	$ .20
Stanton, Leroy	74T	594	$ .07	$ .30	Staub, Rusty	80T	660	$ .02	$ .10
Stanton, Leroy	75T	342	$ .07	$ .30	Staub, Rusty	81T	80	$ .02	$ .10
Stanton, Leroy	76T	152	$ .05	$ .20	Staub, Rusty	81TTR	835	$ .08	$ .30
Stanton, Leroy	77T	226	$ .05	$ .15	Staub, Rusty	82T	270	$ .02	$ .10
Stanton, Leroy	78T	447	$ .02	$ .10	Staub, Rusty	83T	740	$ .01	$ .07
Stanton, Leroy	79T	533	$ .02	$ .10	Staub, Rusty	83T	741	$ .01	$ .07
Stanton, Mike	82T	473	$ .01	$ .07	Staub, Rusty	84T	430	$ .02	$ .10
Stanton, Mike	82TTR	113	$ .02	$ .10	Staub, Rusty	84T	702	$ .06	$ .30
Stanton, Mike	83T	159	$ .01	$ .07	Staub, Rusty	84T	704	$ .03	$ .15
Stanton, Mike	84T	694	$ .01	$ .06	Staub, Rusty	85T	190	$ .01	$ .05
Stanton, Mike	85T	256	$ .01	$ .05	Staub, Rusty	86T	570	$ .01	$ .04
Stanton, Mike	89TMLD	122	$ .01	$ .06	Stearns, John	76T	633	$ .15	$ .50
Stanton, Mike	90T	694	$ .01	$ .10	Stearns, John	77T	119	$ .05	$ .15
Stanton, Mike	91T	514	$ .01	$ .03	Stearns, John	78T	334	$ .02	$ .10
Stapleton, Dave	81T	81	$ .01	$ .10	Stearns, John	79T	545	$ .02	$ .10
Stapleton, Dave	82T	589	$ .01	$ .07	Stearns, John	79TRB	205	$ .02	$ .10
Stapleton, Dave	83T	239	$ .01	$ .07	Stearns, John	80T	76	$ .01	$ .10
Stapleton, Dave	84T	653	$ .01	$ .06	Stearns, John	81T	428	$ .01	$ .10
Stapleton, Dave	85T	322	$ .01	$ .05	Stearns, John	82T	743	$ .01	$ .07
Stapleton, Dave	86T	151	$ .01	$ .04	Stearns, John	83T	212	$ .01	$ .07
Stapleton, Dave	87T	507	$ .01	$ .04	Steels, James	88T	117	$ .01	$ .10
Stargell, Willie	63T	553	$60.00	$225.00	Stefero, John	87T	563	$ .01	$ .04
Stargell, Willie	64T	342	$12.50	$37.50	Steffen, Dave	81T	626	$ .01	$ .10
Stargell, Willie	65T	377	$7.50	$22.50	Stegman, Dave	79T	706	$ .02	$ .10
Stargell, Willie	66T	99	$ .75	$2.00	Stegman, Dave	84T	664	$ .01	$ .06
Stargell, Willie	66T	255	$6.00	$18.00	Stegman, Dave	85T	194	$ .01	$ .05
Stargell, Willie	67T	140	$5.50	$17.50	Stein, Bill	76T	131	$ .05	$ .20
Stargell, Willie	67T	266	$1.75	$4.50	Stein, Bill	77T	334	$ .05	$ .15
Stargell, Willie	68T	86	$3.00	$10.00	Stein, Bill	78T	476	$ .02	$ .10
Stargell, Willie	69T	545	$3.00	$10.00	Stein, Bill	79T	698	$ .02	$ .10
Stargell, Willie	70T	470	$2.50	$9.00	Stein, Bill	80T	226	$ .01	$ .10
Stargell, Willie	71T	230	$2.50	$3.00	Stein, Bill	81T	532	$ .01	$ .10
Stargell, Willie	72T	87	$ .60	$2.00	Stein, Bill	81TTR	836	$ .02	$ .10
Stargell, Willie	72T	89	$ .60	$2.00	Stein, Bill	82T	402	$ .01	$ .07
Stargell, Willie	72T	343	$ .45	$1.45	Stein, Bill	83T	64	$ .01	$ .07
Stargell, Willie	72T	447	$1.25	$5.00	Stein, Bill	84T	758	$ .01	$ .06
Stargell, Willie	72TIA	448	$ .90	$3.00	Stein, Bill	85T	171	$ .01	$ .05
Stargell, Willie	73T	370	$1.50	$6.00	Stein, Bill	86T	371	$ .01	$ .04
Stargell, Willie	74T	100	$1.00	$4.00	Stein, Randy	79T	394	$ .02	$ .10
Stargell, Willie	74T	202	$ .60	$2.00	Stein, Randy	80T	613	$ .01	$ .10
Stargell, Willie	74T	203	$ .60	$2.00	Steinbach, Terry	87TTR	117	$ .10	$ .50
Stargell, Willie	75T	100	$ .65	$2.00	Steinbach, Terry	88T	551	$ .01	$ .15
Stargell, Willie	76T	270	$ .75	$2.25	Steinbach, Terry	88TBB	39	$ .01	$ .10
Stargell, Willie	77T	460	$1.00	$4.00	Steinbach, Terry	89T	725	$ .01	$ .10
Stargell, Willie	78T	510	$1.00	$4.00	Steinbach, Terry	89TBB	80	$ .01	$ .06
Stargell, Willie	79T	55	$ .75	$3.00	Steinbach, Terry	90T	145	$ .01	$ .04
Stargell, Willie	80T	610	$ .45	$1.45	Steinbach, Terry	91T	625	$ .01	$ .03
Stargell, Willie	81T	380	$ .45	$1.45	Stelmaszek, Rick	70T	599	$ .30	$ .95
Stargell, Willie	82T	715	$ .15	$ .60	Stelmaszek, Rick	73T	601	$ .45	$1.45
Stargell, Willie	82TIA	716	$ .08	$ .30	Stelmaszek, Rick	74T	611	$ .07	$ .30
Starrette, Herm	64T	239	$ .30	$ .95	Stelmaszek, Rick	75T	338	$ .07	$ .30
Starrette, Herm	65T	539	$1.75	$4.50	Stengel, Casey	58T	475	$5.00	$15.00
Starrette, Herm	74T	634	$ .07	$ .30	Stengel, Casey	59T	383	$2.10	$6.00
Staub, Rusty	63T	544	$7.50	$30.00	Stengel, Casey	59TAS	552	$7.50	$30.00
Staub, Rusty	64T	109	$2.00	$7.50	Stengel, Casey	60T	227	$4.75	$16.00
Staub, Rusty	65T	321	$1.25	$5.00	Stengel, Casey	62T	29	$4.50	$15.00
Staub, Rusty	66T	106	$1.00	$4.00	Stengel, Casey	63T	43	$1.00	$4.00
Staub, Rusty	66T	273	$ .75	$3.00	Stengel, Casey	63T	233	$5.00	$15.00
Staub, Rusty	67T	73	$ .75	$3.00	Stengel, Casey	64T	324	$5.00	$15.00
Staub, Rusty	68T	300	$ .75	$3.00	Stengel, Casey	64T	393	$2.00	$5.00
Staub, Rusty	69T	230	$ .75	$3.00	Stengel, Casey	65T	187	$4.00	$12.00
Staub, Rusty	70T	585	$ .90	$3.00	Stenhouse, Dave	62T	592	$15.00	$50.00
Staub, Rusty	71T	560	$ .75	$2.25	Stenhouse, Dave	63T	263	$ .30	$ .95
Staub, Rusty	74T	629	$ .30	$ .95	Stenhouse, Dave	64T	498	$ .50	$1.45
Staub, Rusty	75T	90	$ .15	$ .50	Stenhouse, Dave	65T	304	$ .35	$1.25
Staub, Rusty	76T	120	$ .05	$ .20	Stenhouse, Dave	85T	141	$ .01	$ .10
Staub, Rusty	76TTR	120	$ .07	$ .30	Stenhouse, Mike	85T	141	$ .01	$ .10
Staub, Rusty	77T	420	$ .15	$ .50	Stenhouse, Mike	85T	658	$ .01	$ .05

TOPPS

Player	Year	No.	VG	EX/MT
Stenhouse, Mike	85TTR	112	$ .02	$ .10
Stenhouse, Mike	86T	17	$ .01	$ .04
Stennett, Rennie	72T	219	$ .15	$ .50
Stennett, Rennie	73T	348	$ .07	$ .30
Stennett, Rennie	74T	426	$ .07	$ .30
Stennett, Rennie	75T	336	$ .07	$ .30
Stennett, Rennie	76T	425	$ .05	$ .20
Stennett, Rennie	76TRB	6	$ .05	$ .20
Stennett, Rennie	77T	35	$ .05	$ .15
Stennett, Rennie	78T	165	$ .02	$ .10
Stennett, Rennie	79T	687	$ .02	$ .10
Stennett, Rennie	80T	501	$ .01	$ .10
Stennett, Rennie	81T	257	$ .01	$ .10
Stennett, Rennie	82T	84	$ .01	$ .07
Stephen, Buzz	70T	533	$ .15	$ .50
Stephens, Gene	53T	248	$12.50	$50.00
Stephens, Gene	56T	313	$1.30	$5.00
Stephens, Gene	57T	217	$ .95	$3.50
Stephens, Gene	58T	227	$ .75	$3.00
Stephens, Gene	59T	261	$ .75	$2.20
Stephens, Gene	60T	363	$ .75	$2.20
Stephens, Gene	61T	102	$ .35	$1.25
Stephens, Gene	62T	38	$ .45	$1.45
Stephens, Gene	64T	308	$ .30	$ .95
Stephens, Gene	65T	498	$ .75	$3.00
Stephens, Verne	51Trb	4	$2.10	$6.00
Stephens, Vern(e)	52T	84	$7.00	$20.00
Stephens, Vern	53T	270	$12.50	$50.00
Stephens, Vern	54T	54	$7.00	$22.00
Stephenson, Earl	72T	61	$ .15	$ .60
Stephenson, Jerry	65T·	74	$1.00	$4.00
Stephenson, Jerry	66T	396	$ .30	$ .95
Stephenson, Jerry	68T	519	$ .35	$1.25
Stephenson, Jerry	69T	172	$ .30	$ .85
Stephenson, Jerry	71T	488	$ .15	$ .50
Stephenson, John	64T	536	$1.75	$4.50
Stephenson, John	66T	17	$ .30	$ .95
Stephenson, John	67T	522	$ .75	$3.00
Stephenson, John	68T	83	$ .30	$ .85
Stephenson, John	71T	421	$ .15	$ .50
Stephenson, Phil	89TMLD	123	$ .01	$ .15
Stephenson, Phil	90T	584	$ .01	$ .04
Stephenson, Phil	91T	726	$ .01	$ .03
Steve, Lyons	87T	511	$ .01	$ .04
Stevens, Lee	91T	648	$ .01	$ .10
Stevens, Morrie	65T	521	$ .75	$3.00
Stevens, R. C.	58T	470	$ .75	$2.20
Stevens, R. C.	59T	282	$ .75	$2.20
Stevens, R. C.	61T	526	$7.00	$21.00
Stewart, Bunky	55T	136	$2.00	$6.00
Stewart, Dave	82T	213	$2.50	$10.00
Stewart, Dave	83T	532	$ .50	$2.00
Stewart, Dave	84T	352	$ .25	$1.00
Stewart, Dave	85T	723	$ .01	$ .35
Stewart, Dave	86T	689	$ .01	$ .25
Stewart, Dave	87T	14	$ .01	$ .15
Stewart, Dave	88T	476	$ .01	$ .10
Stewart, Dave	89T	145	$ .01	$ .05
Stewart, Dave	89TBB	101	$ .01	$ .10
Stewart, Dave	90T	270	$ .01	$ .04
Stewart, Dave	91T	580	$ .01	$ .10
Stewart, Ed	52T	279	$12.00	$40.00
Stewart, Jim	64T	408	$ .50	$1.45
Stewart, Jim	65T	298	$ .35	$1.25
Stewart, Jim	66T	63	$ .30	$ .95
Stewart, Jim	67T	124	$ .30	$ .85
Stewart, Jim	70T	636	$ .75	$2.00
Stewart, Jim	71T	644	$ .75	$2.50
Stewart, Jim	72T	747	$ .75	$2.50
Stewart, Jimmy	73T	351	$ .07	$ .30

Player	Year	No.	VG	EX/MT
Stewart, Sammy	79T	701	$ .02	$ .10

1978 RECORD BREAKER SAMMY STEWART
*Major League Record: 7 Straight
Strikeouts During First Game in Majors*

Player	Year	No.	VG	EX/MT
Stewart, Sammy	79TRB	206	$ .02	$ .10
Stewart, Sammy	80T	119	$ .01	$ .10
Stewart, Sammy	81T	262	$ .01	$ .10
Stewart, Sammy	82T	426	$ .05	$ .25
Stewart, Sammy	82T	679	$ .01	$ .07
Stewart, Sammy	83T	347	$ .01	$ .07
Stewart, Sammy	84T	59	$ .01	$ .06
Stewart, Sammy	85T	469	$ .01	$ .05
Stewart, Sammy	86T	597	$ .01	$ .04
Stewart, Sammy	86TTR	103	$ .02	$ .10
Stewart, Sammy	87T	204	$ .01	$ .04
Stewart, Sammy	88T	701	$ .01	$ .04
Stieb, Dave	80T	77	$2.00	$8.00
Stieb, Dave	81T	467	$ .25	$1.50
Stieb, Dave	82T	380	$ .15	$ .75
Stieb, Dave	82T	606	$ .01	$ .10
Stieb, Dave	83T	130	$ .05	$ .35
Stieb, Dave	83T	202	$ .01	$ .07
Stieb, Dave	84T	590	$ .05	$ .25
Stieb, Dave	84T	606	$ .01	$ .06
Stieb, Dave	85T	240	$ .01	$ .10
Stieb, Dave	86T	650	$ .01	$ .10
Stieb, Dave	87T	90	$ .01	$ .10
Stieb, Dave	88T	775	$ .01	$ .04
Stieb, Dave	88TBB	172	$ .01	$ .06
Stieb, Dave	89T	460	$ .01	$ .05
Stieb, Dave	89TBB	128	$ .01	$ .10
Stieb, Dave	90T	320	$ .01	$ .10
Stieb, Dave	91T	460	$ .01	$ .03
Stieglitz, Al	60T	144	$ .45	$1.45
Stigman, Dick	59T	142	$ .75	$2.20
Stigman, Dick	60T	507	$2.50	$10.00
Stigman, Dick	61T	77	$ .35	$1.25
Stigman, Dick	62T	37	$ .75	$3.00
Stigman, Dick	62T	532	$3.95	$11.50
Stigman, Dick	63T	89	$ .30	$ .95
Stigman, Dick	64T	6	$ .45	$1.45
Stigman, Dick	64T	245	$ .30	$ .95
Stigman, Dick	65T	548	$1.75	$4.50

Player	Year	No.	VG	EX/MT	Player	Year	No.	VG	EX/MT
Stigman, Dick	66T	512	$ .75	$2.50	Stone, George	76T	567	$ .05	$ .20
Stillman, Royle	76T	594	$ .05	$ .20	Stone, Jeff	85T	476	$ .01	$ .05
Stillman, Royle	78T	272	$ .02	$ .10	Stone, Jeff	86T	686	$ .01	$ .04
Stillwell, Kurt	86TTR	104	$ .08	$ .30	Stone, Jeff	87T	532	$ .01	$ .04
Stillwell, Kurt	87T	623	$ .30	$ .95	Stone, Jeff	88T	154	$ .01	$ .04
Stillwell, Kurt	88T	339	$ .01	$ .10	Stone, Jeff	88TBB	146	$ .01	$ .06
Stillwell, Kurt	88TBB	136	$ .01	$ .06	Stone, Ron	66T	568	$5.00	$20.00
Stillwell, Kurt	88TTR	115	$ .01	$ .06	Stone, Ron	68T	409	$ .30	$ .85
Stillwell, Kurt	89T	596	$ .01	$ .05	Stone, Ron	69T	576	$ .30	$ .95
Stillwell, Kurt	89TBB	161	$ .01	$ .06	Stone, Ron	70T	218	$ .15	$ .50
Stillwell, Kurt	90T	222	$ .01	$ .04	Stone, Ron	71T	366	$ .15	$ .50
Stillwell, Kurt	91T	478	$ .01	$ .03	Stone, Ron	72T	528	$ .30	$ .95
Stimac, Craig	81T	356	$ .01	$ .10	Stone, Steve	72T	327	$ .15	$ .50
Stinson, Bob	70T	131	$ .75	$1.75	Stone, Steve	73T	167	$ .30	$ .85
Stinson, Bob	71T	594	$ .75	$2.00	Stone, Steve	74T	486	$ .07	$ .30
Stinson, Bob	72T	679	$ .90	$3.00	Stone, Steve	74TTR	486	$ .07	$ .30
Stinson, Bob	74T	653	$ .07	$ .30	Stone, Steve	75T	388	$ .07	$ .30
Stinson, Bob	75T	471	$ .07	$ .30	Stone, Steve	76T	378	$ .05	$ .20
Stinson, Bob	76T	466	$ .05	$ .20	Stone, Steve	77T	17	$ .03	$ .12
Stinson, Bob	77T	138	$ .03	$ .12	Stone, Steve	78T	153	$ .05	$ .20
Stinson, Bob	78T	396	$ .02	$ .10	Stone, Steve	79T	227	$ .02	$ .10
Stinson, Bob	79T	252	$ .02	$ .10	Stone, Steve	80T	688	$ .05	$ .20
Stinson, Bob	80T	583	$ .01	$ .10	Stone, Steve	81T	5	$ .04	$ .20
Stirnweiss, George	52T	217	$7.00	$20.00	Stone, Steve	81T	520	$ .01	$ .10
Stobbs, Chuck	52T	62	$15.00	$47.50	Stone, Steve	82T	419	$ .01	$ .07
Stobbs, Chuck	53T	89	$4.50	$15.00	Stoneman, Bill	68T	179	$ .30	$ .85
Stobbs, Chuck	54T	185	$2.50	$10.00	Stoneman, Bill	69T	67	$ .30	$ .85
Stobbs, Chuck	55T	41	$2.00	$6.00	Stoneman, Bill	70T	398	$ .15	$ .50
Stobbs, Chuck	56T	68	$2.25	$6.00	Stoneman, Bill	71T	266	$ .15	$ .50
Stobbs, Chuck	57T	101	$ .95	$3.50	Stoneman, Bill	72T	610	$ .30	$ .95
Stobbs, Chuck	58T	239	$ .75	$3.00	Stoneman, Bill	72T	95	$ .45	$1.45
Stobbs, Chuck	59T	26	$ .85	$3.50	Stoneman, Bill	73T	254	$ .07	$ .30
Stobbs, Chuck	60T	432	$ .75	$2.20	Stoneman, Bill	74T	352	$ .07	$ .30
Stobbs, Chuck	61T	431	$ .75	$3.00	Stottlemyre, Mel	65T	550	$5.00	$15.00
Stock, Milton	52T	381	$40.00	$140.00	Stottlemyre, Mel	66T	224	$ .90	$3.00
Stock, Wes	60T	481	$ .90	$3.00	Stottlemyre, Mel	66T	350	$ .75	$3.00
Stock, Wes	61T	26	$ .35	$1.25	Stottlemyre, Mel	67T	225	$ .45	$1.45
Stock, Wes	62T	442	$ .75	$2.50	Stottlemyre, Mel	68T	120	$ .30	$ .85
Stock, Wes	63T	438	$ .45	$1.50	Stottlemyre, Mel	69T	470	$ .15	$ .50
Stock, Wes	64T	382	$ .50	$1.45	Stottlemyre, Mel	69T	9	$ .35	$1.25
Stock, Wes	65T	117	$ .30	$ .85	Stottlemyre, Mel	70T	100	$ .30	$ .95
Stock, Wes	67T	74	$ .30	$ .85	Stottlemyre, Mel	70T	70	$ .75	$3.00
Stock, Wes	73T	179	$ .30	$ .95	Stottlemyre, Mel	71T	615	$ .35	$1.25
Stoddard, Bob	83T	195	$ .01	$ .07	Stottlemyre, Mel	72T	325	$ .30	$ .85
Stoddard, Bob	84T	439	$ .01	$ .06	Stottlemyre, Mel	72T	492	$ .05	$ .25
Stoddard, Tim	80T	314	$ .01	$ .10	Stottlemyre, Mel	73T	520	$ .15	$ .50
Stoddard, Tim	81T	91	$ .01	$ .10	Stottlemyre, Mel	74T	44	$ .07	$ .30
Stoddard, Tim	82T	457	$ .01	$ .07	Stottlemyre, Mel	75T	183	$ .15	$ .50
Stoddard, Tim	83T	217	$ .01	$ .07	Stottlemyre, Jr., Mel	90T	263	$ .01	$ .10
Stoddard, Tim	84T	106	$ .01	$ .06	Stottlemyre, Mel	91T	58	$ .01	$ .03
Stoddard, Tim	84TTR	112	$ .02	$ .10	Stottlemyre, Todd	88TTR	116	$ .05	$ .25
Stoddard, Tim	85T	693	$ .01	$ .05	Stottlemyre, Todd	89T	722	$ .01	$ .10
Stoddard, Tim	85TTR	113	$ .02	$ .10	Stottlemyre, Todd	89TBB	298	$ .01	$ .06
Stoddard, Tim	86T	558	$ .01	$ .04	Stottlemyre, Todd	90T	591	$ .01	$ .04
Stoddard, Tim	87T	788	$ .01	$ .04	Stottlemyre, Todd	91T	348	$ .01	$ .03
Stoddard, Tim	88T	359	$ .01	$ .04	Stowe, Hal	62T	291	$ .45	$1.45
Stone, Dean	54T	114	$2.50	$10.00	Strahler, Mike	71T	188	$ .90	$3.00
Stone, Dean	55T	60	$2.00	$6.00	Strahler, Mike	72T	198	$ .60	$1.50
Stone, Dean	56T	87	$2.25	$6.00	Strahler, Mike	73T	279	$ .07	$ .30
Stone, Dean	57T	381	$ .85	$3.50	Strain, Joe	79T	726	$ .05	$ .20
Stone, Dean	59T	286	$ .75	$2.20	Strain, Joe	80T	538	$ .01	$ .10
Stone, Dean	62T	574	$3.95	$11.50	Strain, Joe	81T	361	$ .01	$ .10
Stone, Dean	63T	271	$ .30	$ .95	Strain, Joe	81TTR	837	$ .02	$ .10
Stone, George	69T	627	$ .30	$ .95	Strain, Joe	82T	436	$ .01	$ .07
Stone, George	70T	122	$ .15	$ .50	Straker, Les	87TTR	118	$ .01	$ .05
Stone, George	71T	507	$ .15	$ .50	Straker, Les	88T	264	$ .01	$ .04
Stone, George	72T	601	$ .30	$ .95	Straker, Les	89T	101	$ .01	$ .05
Stone, George	73T	647	$ .45	$1.45	Straker, Les	89TBB	90	$ .01	$ .06
Stone, George	74T	397	$ .07	$ .30	Strampe, Bob	73T	604	$ .45	$1.45
Stone, George	75T	239	$ .07	$ .30	Strange, Doug	89TMLD	124	$ .01	$ .06

Player	Year	No.	VG	EX/MT
Strange, Doug	90T	641	$ .01	$ .04
Strawberry, Darryl	83TTR	108	$25.00	$100.00
Strawberry, Darryl	84T	182	$5.00	$20.00
Strawberry, Darryl	85T	278	$ .55	$1.75
Strawberry, Darryl	85T	570	$1.00	$4.00
Strawberry, Darryl	86T	80	$ .25	$1.25
Strawberry, Darryl	87T	460	$ .15	$ .50
Strawberry, Darryl	87TAS	601	$ .07	$ .30
Strawberry, Darryl	88T	710	$ .01	$ .25
Strawberry, Darryl	88TBB	253	$ .10	$ .45
Strawberry, Darryl	89T	300	$ .05	$ .25
Strawberry, Darryl	89TAS	390	$ .01	$ .15
Strawberry, Darryl	89TBB	139	$ .01	$ .25
Strawberry, Darryl	90T	600	$ .01	$ .15
Strawberry, Darryl	91T	200	$ .01	$ .15
Strawberry, Darryl	91TAS	402	$ .01	$ .10
Strickland, George	52T	197	$7.00	$20.00
Strickland, George	57T	263	$ .95	$3.50
Strickland, George	58T	102	$ .85	$3.50
Strickland, George	59T	207	$ .75	$2.20
Strickland, George	60T	63	$ .45	$1.45
Strickland, Jim	72T	778	$ .90	$3.00
Strickland, Jim	73T	122	$ .07	$ .30
Striker, Jake	60T	169	$ .45	$1.45
Strohmayer, John	71T	232	$ .15	$ .50
Strohmayer, John	72T	631	$ .30	$ .95
Strohmayer, John	73T	457	$ .07	$ .30
Strom, Brent	73T	612	$ .45	$1.45
Strom, Brent	74T	359	$ .07	$ .30
Strom, Brent	75T	643	$ .07	$ .30
Strom, Brent	76T	84	$ .05	$ .20
Strom, Brent	77T	348	$ .03	$ .12
Strom, Brent	78T	509	$ .02	$ .10
Stroud, Ed	67T	598	$2.00	$6.00
Stroud, Ed	68T	31	$ .30	$ .85
Stroud, Ed	69T	272	$ .30	$ .95
Stroud, Ed	70T	506	$ .15	$ .50
Stroud, Ed	71T	217	$ .15	$ .50
Stroughter, Steve	82TTR	114	$ .02	$ .10
Stuart, Dick	59T	357	$ .90	$3.00
Stuart, Dick	60T	402	$ .75	$2.20
Stuart, Dick	61T	126	$ .35	$1.25
Stuart, Dick	62T	160	$ .45	$1.45
Stuart, Dick	63T	18	$2.35	$10.00
Stuart, Dick	63T	285	$ .45	$1.45
Stuart, Dick	64T	10	$ .75	$3.00
Stuart, Dick	64T	12	$ .75	$3.00
Stuart, Dick	64T	410	$ .50	$1.45
Stuart, Dick	65T	5	$3.00	$12.00
Stuart, Dick	65T	280	$ .35	$1.25
Stuart, Dick	66T	480	$ .65	$1.75
Stuart, Marlin	52T	208	$7.00	$20.00
Stubbs, Franklin	85T	506	$ .05	$ .25
Stubbs, Franklin	86TTR	105	$ .02	$ .10
Stubbs, Franklin	87T	292	$ .01	$ .10
Stubbs, Franklin	88T	198	$ .01	$ .04
Stubbs, Franklin	88TBB	112	$ .01	$ .06
Stubbs, Franklin	89T	697	$ .01	$ .05
Stubbs, Franklin	89TBB	32	$ .01	$ .06
Stubbs, Franklin	90T	56	$ .01	$ .04
Stubbs, Franklin	90TTR	120	$ .01	$ .05
Stubbs, Franklin	91T	732	$ .01	$ .03
Stubing, Moose	89T	444	$ .01	$ .05
Stuper, John	83T	363	$ .01	$ .07
Stuper, John	84T	49	$ .01	$ .06
Stuper, John	84T	186	$ .01	$ .06
Stuper, John	86T	497	$ .01	$ .04
Sturdivant, Tom	57T	34	$ .95	$3.50
Sturdivant, Tom	58T	127	$ .75	$3.00
Sturdivant, Tom	59T	471	$ .75	$2.20
Sturdivant, Tom	60T	487	$ .90	$3.00
Sturdivant, Tom	61T	293	$ .35	$1.25
Sturdivant, Tom	62T	179	$ .45	$1.45
Sturdivant, Tom	63T	281	$ .30	$ .95
Sturdivant, Tom	64T	402	$ .50	$1.45
Suarez, Ken	66T	588	$5.00	$20.00
Suarez, Ken	68T	218	$ .30	$ .85
Suarez, Ken	69T	19	$ .30	$ .85
Suarez, Ken	70T	209	$ .15	$ .50
Suarez, Ken	71T	597	$ .35	$1.25
Suarez, Ken	72T	483	$ .05	$ .25
Suarez, Ken	74T	39	$ .07	$ .30
Such, Dick	70T	599	$ .30	$ .95
Such, Dick	71T	283	$ .15	$ .50
Sudakis, Bill	69T	552	$ .30	$ .95
Sudakis, Bill	70T	341	$ .15	$ .50
Sudakis, Bill	71T	253	$ .15	$ .50
Sudakis, Bill	72T	722	$ .75	$2.50
Sudakis, Bill	73T	586	$ .45	$1.45
Sudakis, Bill	74T	63	$ .07	$ .30
Sudakis, Bill	74TTR	63	$ .07	$ .30
Sudakis, Bill	75T	291	$ .07	$ .30
Suder, Pete	52T	256	$12.00	$40.00
Sukeforth, Clyde	52T	364	$40.00	$140.00
Sukla, Ed	66T	417	$ .30	$ .95
Sularz, Guy	83T	379	$ .01	$ .07
Sullivan, Frank	55T	106	$2.00	$6.00
Sullivan, Frank	56T	71	$2.25	$6.00
Sullivan, Frank	57T	21	$ .95	$3.50
Sullivan, Frank	58T	18	$ .85	$3.50
Sullivan, Frank	59T	323	$ .75	$2.20
Sullivan, Frank	60T	280	$ .45	$1.45
Sullivan, Frank	61T	281	$ .35	$1.25
Sullivan, Frank	62T	352	$ .45	$1.45
Sullivan, Frank	63T	389	$ .45	$1.50
Sullivan, Haywood	57T	336	$4.25	$15.00
Sullivan, Haywood	58T	197	$ .75	$3.00
Sullivan, Haywood	59T	416	$ .75	$2.20
Sullivan, Haywood	60T	474	$ .90	$3.00
Sullivan, Haywood	61T	212	$ .35	$1.25
Sullivan, Haywood	62T	184	$ .45	$1.45
Sullivan, Haywood	63T	359	$ .45	$1.50
Sullivan, John	65T	593	$1.75	$4.50
Sullivan, John	66T	597	$5.00	$20.00
Sullivan, John	67T	568	$1.50	$4.00
Sullivan, Marc	86T	529	$ .01	$ .04
Sullivan, Marc	87T	66	$ .01	$ .04
Sullivan, Marc	88T	354	$ .01	$ .04
Summers, Champ	76T	299	$ .05	$ .20
Summers, Champ	78T	622	$ .02	$ .10
Summers, Champ	79T	516	$ .02	$ .10
Summers, Champ	80T	176	$ .01	$ .10
Summers, Champ	81T	27	$ .01	$ .10
Summers, Champ	82T	369	$ .01	$ .07
Summers, Champ	82TTR	115	$ .02	$ .10
Summers, Champ	83T	428	$ .01	$ .07
Summers, Champ	84T	768	$ .01	$ .06
Summers, Champ	84TTR	113	$ .02	$ .10
Summers, Champ	85T	208	$ .01	$ .05
Sundberg, Jim	75T	567	$ .30	$ .95
Sundberg, Jim	76T	226	$ .05	$ .20
Sundberg, Jim	77T	351	$ .03	$ .12
Sundberg, Jim	78T	492	$ .02	$ .10
Sundberg, Jim	79T	120	$ .02	$ .10
Sundberg, Jim	80T	530	$ .01	$ .10
Sundberg, Jim	81T	95	$ .01	$ .10
Sundberg, Jim	82T	335	$ .01	$ .07
Sundberg, Jim	83T	665	$ .01	$ .07
Sundberg, Jim	84T	779	$ .01	$ .06
Sundberg, Jim	84TTR	114	$ .02	$ .10

Player	Year	No.	VG	EX/MT
Sundberg, Jim	85T	446	$ .01	$ .05
Sundberg, Jim	85TTR	114	$ .02	$ .10
Sundberg, Jim	86T	245	$ .01	$ .04
Sundberg, Jim	87T	190	$ .01	$ .04
Sundberg, Jim	87TTR	119	$ .01	$ .05
Sundberg, Jim	88T	516	$ .01	$ .04
Sundberg, Jim	88TBB	100	$ .01	$ .06
Sundberg, Jim	89T	78	$ .01	$ .05
Sundberg, Jim	89TBB	103	$ .01	$ .06
Surhoff, B. J.	87T	216	$ .10	$ .50
Surhoff, B. J.	88T	491	$ .01	$ .25
Surhoff, B. J.	88TBB	22	$ .01	$ .06
Surhoff, B. J.	89T	33	$ .01	$ .05
Surhoff, B. J.	90T	696	$ .01	$ .04
Surhoff, B. J.	91T	592	$ .01	$ .03
Surkont, Max	52T	302	$12.00	$40.00
Surkont, Max	56T	209	$3.00	$9.00
Surkont, Max	57T	310	$4.25	$15.00
Susce, George	56T	93	$2.25	$6.00
Susce, George	57T	229	$ .95	$3.50
Susce, George	58T	189	$ .75	$3.00
Susce, George	59T	511	$2.50	$10.00
Sutcliffe, Rick	80T	544	$ .75	$3.00
Sutcliffe, Rick	81T	191	$ .10	$ .50
Sutcliffe, Rick	82T	609	$ .05	$ .20
Sutcliffe, Rick	82TTR	116	$ .15	$ .50
Sutcliffe, Rick	83T	141	$ .01	$ .07

RICK
SUTCLIFFE
PITCHER
INDIANS

Player	Year	No.	VG	EX/MT
Sutcliffe, Rick	83T	497	$ .01	$ .10
Sutcliffe, Rick	83T	707	$ .01	$ .07
Sutcliffe, Rick	84T	245	$ .07	$ .30
Sutcliffe, Rick	84TTR	115	$ .08	$ .30
Sutcliffe, Rick	85T	72	$ .01	$ .05
Sutcliffe, Rick	85TAS	720	$ .01	$ .10
Sutcliffe, Rick	86T	330	$ .01	$ .04
Sutcliffe, Rick	87T	142	$ .01	$ .10
Sutcliffe, Rick	88T	740	$ .01	$ .10
Sutcliffe, Rick	88TBB	128	$ .01	$ .10
Sutcliffe, Rick	89T	520	$ .01	$ .05
Sutcliffe, Rick	90T	640	$ .01	$ .04
Sutcliffe, Rick	91T	415	$ .01	$ .03

Player	Year	No.	VG	EX/MT
Sutherland, Darrell	66T	191	$ .30	$ .95
Sutherland, Darrell	68T	551	$ .35	$1.25
Sutherland, Gary	67T	587	$4.00	$12.00
Sutherland, Gary	68T	98	$ .30	$ .85
Sutherland, Gary	69T	326	$ .30	$ .95
Sutherland, Gary	70T	632	$ .30	$ .95
Sutherland, Gary	71T	434	$ .15	$ .50
Sutherland, Gary	72T	211	$ .05	$ .25
Sutherland, Gary	73T	572	$ .45	$1.45
Sutherland, Gary	74T	428	$ .07	$ .30
Sutherland, Gary	74TTR	428	$ .07	$ .30
Sutherland, Gary	75T	522	$ .07	$ .30
Sutherland, Gary	76T	113	$ .05	$ .20
Sutherland, Gary	77T	307	$ .03	$ .12
Sutherland, Leo	81T	112	$ .01	$ .10
Sutherland, Leo	82T	599	$ .01	$ .07
Sutter, Bruce	77T	144	$ .90	$3.00
Sutter, Bruce	78T	325	$ .30	$ .85
Sutter, Bruce	79T	457	$ .15	$ .50
Sutter, Bruce	80T	17	$ .08	$ .30
Sutter, Bruce	81T	590	$ .05	$ .20
Sutter, Bruce	81TTR	838	$ .02	$ .10
Sutter, Bruce	82T	168	$ .03	$ .15
Sutter, Bruce	82T	260	$ .02	$ .10
Sutter, Bruce	82TAS	347	$ .02	$ .10
Sutter, Bruce	83T	150	$ .01	$ .07
Sutter, Bruce	83T	151	$ .01	$ .07
Sutter, Bruce	83T	708	$ .01	$ .07
Sutter, Bruce	83TAS	407	$ .01	$ .10
Sutter, Bruce	84T	709	$ .01	$ .06
Sutter, Bruce	84T	730	$ .03	$ .15
Sutter, Bruce	85T	370	$ .01	$ .05
Sutter, Bruce	85TAS	722	$ .01	$ .05
Sutter, Bruce	85TRB	9	$ .01	$ .10
Sutter, Bruce	85TTR	115	$ .05	$ .20
Sutter, Bruce	86T	620	$ .01	$ .04
Sutter, Bruce	87T	435	$ .01	$ .10
Sutter, Bruce	88T	155	$ .01	$ .04
Sutter, Bruce	89T	11	$ .01	$ .05
Sutter, Bruce	89TBB	64	$ .01	$ .06
Sutton, Don	66T	288	$32.50	$100.00
Sutton, Don	67T	445	$6.00	$25.00
Sutton, Don	68T	103	$2.00	$8.00
Sutton, Don	69T	216	$1.50	$4.00
Sutton, Don	70T	622	$2.00	$8.00
Sutton, Don	71T	361	$1.50	$4.00
Sutton, Don	72T	530	$1.75	$4.50
Sutton, Don	73T	10	$ .85	$2.50
Sutton, Don	74T	220	$ .50	$2.00
Sutton, Don	75T	220	$ .50	$2.00
Sutton, Don	76T	530	$ .45	$1.50
Sutton, Don	77T	620	$ .45	$1.50
Sutton, Don	78T	310	$ .35	$1.25
Sutton, Don	79T	170	$ .35	$1.25
Sutton, Don	80T	440	$ .20	$1.00
Sutton, Don	81T	605	$ .15	$ .75
Sutton, Don	81T	7	$ .02	$ .10
Sutton, Don	81TTR	839	$ .02	$ .10
Sutton, Don	82T	305	$ .30	$ .85
Sutton, Don	82TIA	306	$ .05	$ .20
Sutton, Don	83T	145	$ .08	$ .35
Sutton, Don	83T	146	$ .03	$ .15
Sutton, Don	84T	35	$ .05	$ .25
Sutton, Don	84T	715	$ .04	$ .20
Sutton, Don	85T	729	$ .05	$ .25
Sutton, Don	85TRB	10	$ .01	$ .05
Sutton, Don	85TTR	116	$ .15	$ .60
Sutton, Don	86T	335	$ .02	$ .15
Sutton, Don	87T	673	$ .07	$ .30
Sutton, Don	88T	575	$ .01	$ .10

Player	Year	No.	VG	EX/MT
Sutton, Johnny	79T	676	$ .02	$ .10
Sveum, Dale	86TTR	106	$ .08	$ .30
Sveum, Dale	87T	327	$ .15	$ .50
Sveum, Dale	88T	592	$ .01	$ .04
Sveum, Dale	88TBB	44	$ .01	$ .06
Sveum, Dale	89T	12	$ .01	$ .05
Sveum, Dale	89TBB	126	$ .01	$ .06
Sveum, Dale	90T	739	$ .01	$ .04
Swaggerty, Bill	85T	147	$ .01	$ .05
Swan, Craig	74T	602	$ .07	$ .30
Swan, Craig	76T	494	$ .05	$ .20
Swan, Craig	77T	94	$ .03	$ .12
Swan, Craig	78T	621	$ .02	$ .10
Swan, Craig	79T	7	$ .03	$ .15
Swan, Craig	79T	334	$ .02	$ .10
Swan, Craig	80T	8	$ .01	$ .10
Swan, Craig	81T	189	$ .01	$ .10
Swan, Craig	82T	592	$ .01	$ .07
Swan, Craig	83T	292	$ .01	$ .07
Swan, Craig	83T	621	$ .01	$ .07
Swan, Craig	84T	763	$ .01	$ .06
Swan, Craig	84TTR	116	$ .02	$ .10
Swan, Russ	89TMLD	125	$ .01	$ .25
Swan, Russ	90TTR	121	$ .01	$ .20
Swan, Russ	91T	739	$ .01	$ .03
Swanson, Art	56T	204	$3.00	$9.00
Swanson, Stan	72T	331	$ .05	$ .25
Sweet, Rick	78T	702	$ .02	$ .10
Sweet, Rick	79T	646	$ .02	$ .10
Sweet, Rick	83T	437	$ .01	$ .07
Sweet, Rick	84T	211	$ .01	$ .06
Swift, Bill	86T	399	$ .01	$ .04
Swift, Bill	87T	67	$ .01	$ .04
Swift, Bill	88TTR	117	$ .01	$ .06
Swift, Bill	89T	712	$ .01	$ .05
Swift, Bob	60T	470	$ .95	$3.50
Swindell, Greg	87T	319	$ .25	$ .75
Swindell, Greg	88T	22	$ .01	$ .10
Swindell, Greg	88TBB	156	$ .01	$ .15
Swindell, Greg	89T	315	$ .01	$ .15
Swindell, Greg	89TBB	68	$ .01	$ .10
Swindell, Greg	90T	595	$ .01	$ .10
Swindell, Greg	91T	445	$ .01	$ .03
Swisher, Steve	75T	63	$ .07	$ .30
Swisher, Steve	76T	173	$ .05	$ .20
Swisher, Steve	77T	419	$ .03	$ .12
Swisher, Steve	78T	252	$ .02	$ .10
Swisher, Steve	79T	304	$ .02	$ .10
Swisher, Steve	80T	163	$ .01	$ .10
Swisher, Steve	81T	541	$ .01	$ .10
Swisher, Steve	81TTR	840	$ .02	$ .10
Swisher, Steve	82T	764	$ .01	$ .07
Swisher, Steve	83T	612	$ .01	$ .07
Swoboda, Ron	65T	533	$5.00	$20.00
Swoboda, Ron	66T	35	$ .30	$ .95
Swoboda, Ron	67T	186	$ .30	$ .85
Swoboda, Ron	67T	264	$ .30	$ .85
Swoboda, Ron	68T	114	$ .30	$ .85
Swoboda, Ron	69T	585	$ .30	$ .95
Swoboda, Ron	70T	431	$ .15	$ .50
Swoboda, Ron	71T	665	$ .75	$2.50
Swoboda, Ron	72T	8	$ .05	$ .25
Swoboda, Ron	73T	314	$ .07	$ .30
Sykes, Bob	77T	491	$ .25	$1.00
Sykes, Bob	79T	569	$ .02	$ .10
Sykes, Bob	80T	223	$ .01	$ .10
Sykes, Bob	81T	348	$ .01	$ .10
Sykes, Bob	82T	108	$ .01	$ .07
Szotkiewicz, Ken	71T	749	$ .75	$2.50
Tabb, Jerry	78T	224	$ .02	$ .10
Tabler, Pat	84T	329	$ .01	$ .06
Tabler, Pat	85T	158	$ .01	$ .05
Tabler, Pat	86T	674	$ .01	$ .04
Tabler, Pat	87T	575	$ .01	$ .04
Tabler, Pat	88T	230	$ .01	$ .04
Tabler, Pat	88TBB	173	$ .01	$ .06
Tabler, Pat	88TTR	118	$ .01	$ .06
Tabler, Pat	89T	56	$ .01	$ .05
Tabler, Pat	89TBB	67	$ .01	$ .06
Tabler, Pat	90T	727	$ .01	$ .04
Tabler, Pat	91T	433	$ .01	$ .03
Talbot, Bob	54T	229	$2.50	$10.00
Talbot, Fred	65T	58	$ .30	$ .85
Talbot, Fred	66T	403	$ .30	$ .95
Talbot, Fred	67T	517	$ .75	$3.00
Talbot, Fred	68T	577	$ .35	$1.25
Talbot, Fred	69T	332	$ .30	$ .85
Talbot, Fred	70T	287	$ .15	$ .50
Talton, Tim	67T	603	$1.50	$4.00
Tamargo, John	79T	726	$ .05	$ .20
Tamargo, John	80T	680	$ .05	$ .20
Tamargo, John	81T	519	$ .01	$ .10
Tanana, Frank	74T	605	$ .30	$1.50
Tanana, Frank	75T	16	$ .15	$ .50
Tanana, Frank	76T	204	$ .15	$ .50
Tanana, Frank	76T	490	$ .07	$ .30
Tanana, Frank	77T	200	$ .03	$ .12
Tanana, Frank	78T	207	$ .02	$ .10
Tanana, Frank	78T	600	$ .02	$ .10
Tanana, Frank	79T	530	$ .05	$ .20
Tanana, Frank	80T	105	$ .01	$ .10
Tanana, Frank	81T	369	$ .01	$ .10
Tanana, Frank	81TTR	841	$ .02	$ .10
Tanana, Frank	82T	792	$ .02	$ .10
Tanana, Frank	82TTR	117	$ .02	$ .10

BILL SWIFT

Player	Year	No.	VG	EX/MT
Swift, Bill	90T	574	$ .01	$ .04
Swift, Bill	91T	276	$ .01	$ .10
Swift, Billy	85T	404	$ .01	$ .05
Swift, Bob	52T	181	$7.00	$20.00
Swift, Bob	54T	65	$7.00	$22.00

Player	Year	No.	VG	EX/MT
Tanana, Frank	83T	272	$ .01	$ .07
Tanana, Frank	84T	479	$ .01	$ .06
Tanana, Frank	85T	55	$ .01	$ .05
Tanana, Frank	86T	592	$ .01	$ .04
Tanana, Frank	87T	726	$ .01	$ .04
Tanana, Frank	88T	177	$ .01	$ .04
Tanana, Frank	89T	603	$ .01	$ .05
Tanana, Frank	90T	343	$ .01	$ .04
Tanana, Frank	91T	236	$ .01	$ .03
Tanner, Chuck	55T	161	$5.50	$17.50
Tanner, Chuck	56T	69	$1.50	$5.00
Tanner, Chuck	57T	392	$2.00	$6.00

Player	Year	No.	VG	EX/MT
Tanner, Chuck	58T	91	$ .70	$2.25
Tanner, Chuck	59T	234	$ .75	$2.20
Tanner, Chuck	60T	279	$ .75	$3.00
Tanner, Chuck	71T	661	$ .85	$3.50
Tanner, Chuck	72T	98	$ .30	$ .85
Tanner, Chuck	73T	356	$ .15	$ .50
Tanner, Chuck	74T	221	$ .07	$ .30
Tanner, Chuck	78T	494	$ .02	$ .10
Tanner, Chuck	83T	696	$ .01	$ .07
Tanner, Chuck	84T	291	$ .01	$ .06
Tanner, Chuck	85T	268	$ .01	$ .05
Tanner, Chuck	86T	351	$ .01	$ .04
Tanner, Chuck	86TTR	107	$ .02	$ .10
Tanner, Chuck	87T	593	$ .01	$ .04
Tanner, Chuck	88T	134	$ .01	$ .04
Tapani, Kevin	89TMLD	126	$ .01	$ .25
Tapani, Kevin	90T	227	$ .01	$ .25
Tapani, Kevin	91T	633	$ .01	$ .03
Tappe, Elvin	55T	129	$2.00	$6.00
Tappe, Elvin	58T	184	$ .75	$3.00
Tappe, Elvin	60T	457	$ .95	$3.50
Tartabull, Danny	86TTR	108	$ .15	$ .75
Tartabull, Danny	87T	476	$ .10	$ .50
Tartabull, Danny	87TTR	120	$ .12	$ .40
Tartabull, Danny	88T	724	$ .01	$ .15
Tartabull, Danny	88TBB	230	$ .05	$ .25
Tartabull, Danny	89T	275	$ .01	$ .10
Tartabull, Danny	89TBB	107	$ .01	$ .10

Player	Year	No.	VG	EX/MT
Tartabull, Danny	90T	540	$ .01	$ .04
Tartabull, Danny	91T	90	$ .01	$ .03
Tartabull, Jose	62T	451	$ .90	$3.00
Tartabull, Jose	63T	449	$2.50	$6.50
Tartabull, Jose	64T	276	$ .30	$ .95
Tartabull, Jose	66T	143	$ .30	$ .95
Tartabull, Jose	67T	56	$ .30	$ .85
Tartabull, Jose	68T	555	$ .35	$1.25
Tartabull, Jose	69T	287	$ .30	$ .95
Tartabull, Jose	70T	481	$ .15	$ .50
Tasby, Willie	59T	143	$ .75	$2.20
Tasby, Willie	60T	322	$ .75	$2.20
Tasby, Willie	61T	458	$ .75	$3.00
Tasby, Willie	62T	462	$ .75	$2.25
Tate, Lee	59T	544	$2.50	$10.00
Tate, Randy	76T	549	$ .05	$ .20
Tate, Stu	89TMLD	127	$ .01	$ .06
Tatum, Jarvis	70T	642	$ .75	$2.00
Tatum, Jarvis	71T	159	$ .15	$ .50
Tatum, Ken	70T	658	$ .75	$2.00
Tatum, Ken	71T	601	$ .35	$1.25
Tatum, Ken	72T	772	$ .75	$2.50
Tatum, Ken	73T	463	$ .07	$ .30
Taussig, Don	62T	44	$ .45	$1.45
Taveras, Alex	77T	474	$ .05	$ .15
Taveras, Frank	74T	607	$ .07	$ .30
Taveras, Frank	75T	277	$ .07	$ .30
Taveras, Frank	76T	36	$ .05	$ .20
Taveras, Frank	77T	538	$ .03	$ .12
Taveras, Frank	78T	204	$ .02	$ .10
Taveras, Frank	78T	685	$ .02	$ .10
Taveras, Frank	79T	165	$ .02	$ .10
Taveras, Frank	80T	456	$ .01	$ .10
Taveras, Frank	81T	343	$ .01	$ .10
Taveras, Frank	82T	782	$ .01	$ .07
Taveras, Frank	82TTR	118	$ .02	$ .10
Taylor, Bill	54T	74	$7.00	$22.00
Taylor, Bill	55T	53	$2.00	$6.00
Taylor, Bill	58T	389	$ .75	$3.00
Taylor, Bob	58T	164	$ .75	$3.00
Taylor, Bob "Hawk"	61T	446	$ .75	$3.00
Taylor, Bob	62T	406	$ .75	$2.50
Taylor, Bob	63T	481	$2.50	$6.50
Taylor, Bob	64T	381	$ .50	$1.45
Taylor, Bob "Hawk"	65T	329	$ .35	$1.25
Taylor, Bob "Hawk"	68T	52	$ .30	$ .85
Taylor, Bruce	78T	701	$ .02	$ .10
Taylor, Carl	68T	559	$ .35	$1.25
Taylor, Carl	69T	357	$ .30	$ .85
Taylor, Carl	70T	76	$ .15	$ .50
Taylor, Carl	71T	353	$ .15	$ .50
Taylor, Carl	73T	99	$ .07	$ .30
Taylor, Carl	74T	627	$ .07	$ .30
Taylor, Chuck	70T	119	$ .15	$ .50
Taylor, Chuck	71T	606	$ .35	$1.25
Taylor, Chuck	72T	407	$ .05	$ .25
Taylor, Chuck	73T	176	$ .07	$ .30
Taylor, Chuck	74T	412	$ .07	$ .30
Taylor, Chuck	75T	58	$ .07	$ .30
Taylor, Joe	58T	451	$ .75	$2.20
Taylor, Rob	69T	239	$ .30	$ .95
Taylor, Ron	62T	591	$8.00	$22.50
Taylor, Ron	63T	208	$ .30	$ .95
Taylor, Ron	64T	183	$ .30	$ .95
Taylor, Ron	65T	568	$1.75	$4.50
Taylor, Ron	66T	174	$ .30	$ .95
Taylor, Ron	67T	606	$4.00	$12.00
Taylor, Ron	68T	421	$ .30	$ .85
Taylor, Ron	69T	72	$ .30	$ .85
Taylor, Ron	70T	419	$ .15	$ .50

Player	Year	No.	VG	EX/MT	Player	Year	No.	VG	EX/MT
Taylor, Ron	71T	687	$ .75	$2.50	Templeton, Garry	80T	587	$ .01	$ .10
Taylor, Ron	72T	234	$ .05	$ .25	Templeton, Garry	80THL	5	$ .05	$ .20
Taylor, Sam	58T	281	$ .75	$3.00	Templeton, Garry	81T	485	$ .01	$ .10
Taylor, Sammy	59T	193	$ .75	$2.20	Templeton, Garry	82T	288	$ .01	$ .07
Taylor, Sammy	60T	162	$ .45	$1.45	Templeton, Garry	82TTR	119	$ .02	$ .10
Taylor, Sammy	61T	253	$ .35	$1.25	Templeton, Garry	83T	505	$ .01	$ .07
Taylor, Sammy	62T	274	$ .45	$1.45	Templeton, Garry	84T	615	$ .01	$ .06
Taylor, Sammy	63T	273	$ .30	$ .95	Templeton, Garry	85T	735	$ .01	$ .05
Taylor, Terry	89T	597	$ .01	$ .05	Templeton, Garry	86T	90	$ .01	$ .04
Taylor, Tony	58T	411	$ .35	$2.00	Templeton, Garry	87T	325	$ .01	$ .04
Taylor, Tony	59T	62	$ .85	$3.50	Templeton, Garry	88T	640	$ .01	$ .04
Taylor, Tony	60T	294	$ .75	$2.20	Templeton, Garry	89T	121	$ .01	$ .05
Taylor, Tony	61T	411	$ .75	$3.00	Templeton, Garry	89TBB	328	$ .01	$ .06
Taylor, Tony	62T	77	$ .45	$1.45	Templeton, Garry	90T	481	$ .01	$ .04
Taylor, Tony	63T	366	$ .45	$1.50	Templeton, Garry	91T	253	$ .01	$ .03
Taylor, Tony	64T	585	$1.75	$4.50	Tenace, Gene	70T	21	$1.00	$4.00
Taylor, Tony	65T	296	$ .35	$1.25	Tenace, Gene	71T	338	$ .15	$ .50
Taylor, Tony	66T	585	$5.00	$20.00	Tenace, Gene	72T	189	$ .30	$ .95
Taylor, Tony	67T	126	$ .30	$ .85					
Taylor, Tony	68T	327	$ .30	$ .85					
Taylor, Tony	69T	108	$ .30	$ .85					
Taylor, Tony	70T	324	$ .15	$ .50					
Taylor, Tony	71T	246	$ .15	$ .50					
Taylor, Tony	72T	511	$ .05	$ .25					
Taylor, Tony	73T	29	$ .07	$ .30					
Taylor, Tony	75T	574	$ .07	$ .30					
Taylor, Tony	76T	624	$ .05	$ .20					
Tebbetts, Birdie	52T	282	$15.00	$47.50					
Tebbetts, Birdie	58T	386	$2.50	$7.50					
Tebbetts, Birdie	62T	588	$3.95	$11.50					
Tebbetts, Birdie	63T	48	$ .30	$ .95					
Tebbetts, Birdie	64T	462	$ .50	$1.45					
Tebbetts, Birdie	65T	301	$ .35	$1.25					
Tebbetts, Birdie	66T	552	$5.00	$20.00					
Tejada, Wil	89T	747	$ .01	$ .05					
Tekulve, Kent	76T	112	$ .45	$1.45					
Tekulve, Kent	77T	374	$ .05	$ .25					
Tekulve, Kent	78T	84	$ .02	$ .10					
Tekulve, Kent	79T	223	$ .02	$ .10					
Tekulve, Kent	80T	573	$ .01	$ .10					
Tekulve, Kent	81T	695	$ .01	$ .10					
Tekulve, Kent	82T	485	$ .01	$ .07					
Tekulve, Kent	83T	17	$ .01	$ .07					
Tekulve, Kent	83T	18	$ .01	$ .07					
Tekulve, Kent	84T	754	$ .01	$ .06					
Tekulve, Kent	85T	125	$ .01	$ .05					
Tekulve, Kent	85TTR	117	$ .02	$ .10					
Tekulve, Kent	86T	326	$ .01	$ .04	Tenace, Gene	73T	524	$ .07	$ .30
Tekulve, Kent	87T	684	$ .01	$ .04	Tenace, Gene	74T	79	$ .07	$ .30
Tekulve, Kent	88T	543	$ .01	$ .04	Tenace, Gene	75T	535	$ .07	$ .30
Tekulve, Kent	89TTR	116	$ .01	$ .06	Tenace, Gene	76T	165	$ .05	$ .20
Telford, Anthony	91T	653	$ .01	$ .15	Tenace, Gene	77T	303	$ .03	$ .12
Tellmann, Tom	81T	356	$ .01	$ .10	Tenace, Gene	78T	240	$ .02	$ .10
Tellmann, Tom	83TTR	109	$ .02	$ .10	Tenace, Gene	79T	435	$ .02	$ .10
Tellmann, Tom	84T	476	$ .01	$ .06	Tenace, Gene	80T	704	$ .01	$ .10
Tellmann, Tom	85T	112	$ .01	$ .05	Tenace, Gene	81T	29	$ .01	$ .10
Tellmann, Tom	85TTR	118	$ .02	$ .10	Tenace, Gene	81TTR	842	$ .02	$ .10
Tellmann, Tom	86T	693	$ .01	$ .04	Tenace, Gene	82T	631	$ .01	$ .07
Temple, Johnny	56T	212	$3.00	$9.00	Tenace, Gene	83T	515	$ .01	$ .07
Temple, Johnny	57T	9	$ .95	$3.50	Tenace, Gene	83TTR	110	$ .02	$ .10
Temple, Johnny	58T	205	$ .75	$3.00	Tenace, Gene	84T	729	$ .01	$ .06
Temple, Johnny	58TAS	478	$ .70	$2.25	Tepedino, Frank	70T	689	$ .75	$2.00
Temple, Johnny	59T	335	$ .75	$2.20	Tepedino, Frank	71T	342	$ .15	$ .50
Temple, Johnny	60T	500	$ .85	$3.50	Tepedino, Frank	74T	526	$ .07	$ .30
Temple, Johnny	61T	155	$ .35	$1.25	Tepedino, Frank	75T	9	$ .07	$ .30
Temple, Johnny	62T	34	$ .45	$1.45	Terlecky, Greg	77T	487	$ .03	$ .12
Temple, Johnny	63T	576	$3.00	$9.00	Terpko, Jeff	77T	137	$ .03	$ .12
Templeton, Garry	77T	161	$ .45	$1.45	Terrell, Jerry	74T	481	$ .07	$ .30
Templeton, Garry	78T	32	$ .07	$ .30	Terrell, Jerry	75T	654	$ .07	$ .30
Templeton, Garry	79T	350	$ .05	$ .20					

GENE
TENACE

OAKLAND A's   1st BASE

Player	Year	No.	VG	EX/MT
Terrell, Jerry	76T	159	$ .05	$ .20
Terrell, Jerry	77T	513	$ .03	$ .12
Terrell, Jerry	78T	525	$ .02	$ .10
Terrell, Jerry	79T	273	$ .02	$ .10
Terrell, Jerry	80T	98	$ .01	$ .10
Terrell, Walt	84T	549	$ .15	$ .45
Terrell, Walt	85T	287	$ .01	$ .10
Terrell, Walt	85TTR	119	$ .02	$ .10
Terrell, Walt	86T	461	$ .01	$ .04
Terrell, Walt	87T	72	$ .01	$ .04
Terrell, Walt	88T	668	$ .01	$ .04
Terrell, Walt	89T	127	$ .01	$ .05
Terrell, Walt	89TTR	117	$ .01	$ .06
Terrell, Walt	90T	611	$ .01	$ .04
Terrell, Walt	91T	328	$ .01	$ .03
Terry, Ralph	57T	391	$2.50	$7.50
Terry, Ralph	58T	169	$ .65	$2.00
Terry, Ralph	59T	358	$ .75	$2.20
Terry, Ralph	60T	96	$ .90	$3.00
Terry, Ralph	61T	389	$ .65	$1.75
Terry, Ralph	62T	48	$ .75	$2.20
Terry, Ralph	63T	8	$ .45	$1.45
Terry, Ralph	63T	10	$ .45	$1.45
Terry, Ralph	63T	315	$ .75	$3.00
Terry, Ralph	64T	458	$ .75	$3.00
Terry, Ralph	65T	406	$ .35	$1.25
Terry, Ralph	66T	109	$ .30	$ .95
Terry, Ralph	67T	59	$ .30	$ .85
Terry, Scott	87T	453	$ .01	$ .04
Terry, Scott	88TTR	119	$ .01	$ .06
Terry, Scott	89T	686	$ .01	$ .05
Terry, Scott	89TBB	31	$ .01	$ .06
Terry, Scott	90T	82	$ .01	$ .04
Terry, Scott	91T	539	$ .01	$ .03
Terwilliger, Wayne	51Trb	14	$1.50	$4.00
Terwilliger, Wayne	52T	7	$15.00	$50.00
Terwilliger, Wayne	53T	159	$4.50	$15.00
Terwilliger, Wayne	54T	73	$7.00	$22.00
Terwilliger, Wayne	55T	34	$2.00	$6.00
Terwilliger, Wayne	56T	73	$2.25	$6.00
Terwilliger, Wayne	59T	496	$ .75	$2.20
Terwilliger, Wayne	60T	26	$ .45	$1.45
Tettleton, Mickey	85TTR	120	$ .20	$1.00
Tettleton, Mickey	86T	457	$ .10	$ .50
Tettleton, Mickey	87T	649	$ .01	$ .04
Tettleton, Mickey	88T	143	$ .01	$ .04
Tettleton, Mickey	88TTR	120	$ .01	$ .06
Tettleton, Mickey	89T	521	$ .01	$ .05
Tettleton, Mickey	89TBB	198	$ .01	$ .06
Tettleton, Mickey	90T	275	$ .01	$ .04
Tettleton, Mickey	91T	385	$ .01	$ .03
Teufel, Tim	84TTR	117	$ .08	$ .30
Teufel, Tim	85T	239	$ .01	$ .05
Teufel, Tim	86T	667	$ .01	$ .04
Teufel, Tim	86TTR	109	$ .02	$ .10
Teufel, Tim	87T	158	$ .01	$ .04
Teufel, Tim	88T	508	$ .01	$ .04
Teufel, Tim	89T	9	$ .01	$ .05
Teufel, Tim	90T	764	$ .01	$ .04
Teufel, Tim	91T	302	$ .01	$ .03
Tewksbury, Bob	86TTR	110	$ .05	$ .20
Tewksbury, Bob	87T	254	$ .01	$ .10
Tewksbury, Bob	88T	593	$ .01	$ .04
Tewksbury, Bob	90TTR	122	$ .01	$ .05
Tewksbury, Bob	91T	88	$ .01	$ .03
Thacker, Moe	59T	474	$ .75	$2.20
Thacker, Moe	61T	12	$ .35	$1.25
Thacker, Moe	62T	546	$3.95	$11.50
Theobald, Ron	72T	77	$ .05	$ .25
Theodore, George	74T	8	$ .07	$ .30

Player	Year	No.	VG	EX/MT
Thibdeau, John	69T	189	$ .30	$ .85
Thies, Jake	55T	12	$2.00	$6.00
Thigpen, Bobby	87T	61	$ .15	$ .75
Thigpen, Bobby	88T	613	$ .01	$ .15
Thigpen, Bobby	89T	762	$ .01	$ .05
Thigpen, Bobby	90T	255	$ .01	$ .04
Thigpen, Bobby	91T	420	$ .01	$ .03
Thigpen, Bobby	91TAS	396	$ .01	$ .03
Thigpen, Bobby	91TRB	8	$ .01	$ .03
Thoenen, Dick	68T	348	$ .30	$ .85
Thomas, Andres	86TTR	111	$ .05	$ .20
Thomas, Andres	87T	296	$ .03	$ .15
Thomas, Andres	88T	13	$ .01	$ .04
Thomas, Andres	88TBB	68	$ .01	$ .06
Thomas, Andres	89T	523	$ .01	$ .05
Thomas, Andres	90T	358	$ .01	$ .04
Thomas, Andres	91T	111	$ .01	$ .03
Thomas, Dan	77T	488	$5.00	$20.00
Thomas, Derrel	72T	457	$ .05	$ .25

DERREL THOMAS
SAN DIEGO PADRES · 2nd BASE

Player	Year	No.	VG	EX/MT
Thomas, Derrel	73T	57	$ .07	$ .30
Thomas, Derrel	74T	518	$ .07	$ .30
Thomas, Derrel	75T	378	$ .07	$ .30
Thomas, Derrel	76T	493	$ .05	$ .20
Thomas, Derrel	77T	266	$ .03	$ .12
Thomas, Derrel	78T	194	$ .02	$ .10
Thomas, Derrel	79T	679	$ .02	$ .10
Thomas, Derrel	80T	23	$ .01	$ .10
Thomas, Derrel	81T	211	$ .01	$ .10
Thomas, Derrel	82T	348	$ .01	$ .07
Thomas, Derrel	83T	748	$ .01	$ .07
Thomas, Derrel	84T	583	$ .01	$ .06
Thomas, Derrel	84TTR	118	$ .02	$ .10
Thomas, Derrel	85T	448	$ .01	$ .05
Thomas, Derrel	85TTR	121	$ .02	$ .10
Thomas, Derrel	86T	158	$ .01	$ .04
Thomas, Frank	56T	153	$2.25	$6.00
Thomas, Frank	57T	140	$ .95	$3.50
Thomas, Frank	58T	409	$ .75	$3.00
Thomas, Frank	59T	17	$1.75	$4.50
Thomas, Frank	59T	490	$ .75	$2.20

TOPPS

Player	Year	No.	VG	EX/MT
Thomas, Frank	60T	95	$ .45	$1.45
Thomas, Frank	61T	382	$ .75	$3.00
Thomas, Frank	62T	7	$ .75	$2.20
Thomas, Frank	63T	495	$2.50	$6.50
Thomas, Frank	64T	345	$ .30	$ .95
Thomas, Frank	65T	123	$ .30	$ .85
Thomas, Frank	90T	414	$ .01	$3.25
Thomas, Frank	91T	79	$ .01	$ .50
Thomas, George	61T	544	$7.00	$21.00
Thomas, George	62T	525	$3.95	$11.50
Thomas, George	63T	98	$ .30	$ .95
Thomas, George	64T	461	$ .50	$1.45
Thomas, George	65T	83	$ .30	$ .85
Thomas, George	66T	277	$ .30	$ .95
Thomas, George	67T	184	$ .30	$ .85
Thomas, George	69T	521	$ .30	$ .95
Thomas, George	71T	678	$ .75	$2.50
Thomas, Gorman	74T	288	$ .45	$1.45
Thomas, Gorman	75T	532	$ .07	$ .30
Thomas, Gorman	76T	139	$ .07	$ .30
Thomas, Gorman	77T	439	$ .03	$ .12
Thomas, Gorman	79T	376	$ .05	$ .20
Thomas, Gorman	80T	202	$ .05	$ .20
Thomas, Gorman	80T	623	$ .01	$ .10
Thomas, Gorman	81T	135	$ .01	$ .10
Thomas, Gorman	82T	765	$ .01	$ .07
Thomas, Gorman	83T	10	$ .01	$ .10
Thomas, Gorman	83T	702	$ .01	$ .07
Thomas, Gorman	83TTR	111	$ .02	$ .10
Thomas, Gorman	84T	515	$ .01	$ .06
Thomas, Gorman	84TTR	119	$ .02	$ .10
Thomas, Gorman	85T	202	$ .01	$ .05
Thomas, Gorman	86T	750	$ .01	$ .04
Thomas, Gorman	87T	495	$ .01	$ .04
Thomas, Keith	53T	129	$4.50	$15.00
Thomas, Leroy (Lee)	61T	464	$ .75	$3.00
Thomas, Lee	62T	154	$ .45	$1.45
Thomas, Lee	63T	441	$ .45	$1.50
Thomas, Lee	64T	255	$ .30	$ .95
Thomas, Lee	65T	111	$ .30	$ .85
Thomas, Lee	66T	408	$ .30	$ .95
Thomas, Lee	67T	458	$ .75	$3.00
Thomas, Lee	68T	438	$ .30	$ .85
Thomas, Roy	78T	711	$ .02	$ .10
Thomas, Roy	79T	563	$ .02	$ .10
Thomas, Roy	80T	397	$ .01	$ .10
Thomas, Roy	84T	181	$ .01	$ .06
Thomas, Roy	86T	626	$ .01	$ .04
Thomas, Stan	76T	148	$ .05	$ .20
Thomas, Stan	77T	353	$ .03	$ .12
Thomas, Valmy	58T	86	$ .85	$3.50
Thomas, Valmy	59T	235	$ .75	$2.20
Thomas, Valmy	60T	167	$ .45	$1.45
Thomas, Valmy	61T	319	$ .35	$1.25
Thomasson, Gary	74T	18	$ .07	$ .30
Thomasson, Gary	75T	529	$ .07	$ .30
Thomasson, Gary	76T	261	$ .05	$ .20
Thomasson, Gary	77T	496	$ .03	$ .12
Thomasson, Gary	78T	648	$ .02	$ .10
Thomasson, Gary	79T	387	$ .02	$ .10
Thomasson, Gary	80T	127	$ .01	$ .10
Thomasson, Gary	81T	512	$ .01	$ .10
Thompson, Bobby	79T	336	$ .02	$ .10
Thompson, Charlie (y)	54T	209	$2.50	$10.00
Thompson, Charley	57T	142	$ .95	$3.50
Thompson, Danny	71T	127	$ .15	$ .50
Thompson, Danny	72T	368	$ .05	$ .25
Thompson, Danny	73T	443	$ .07	$ .30
Thompson, Danny	74T	168	$ .07	$ .30
Thompson, Danny	75T	249	$ .07	$ .30
Thompson, Danny	76T	111	$ .05	$ .20
Thompson, Hank	51Trb	32	$1.50	$4.00
Thompson, Hank	52T	3	$15.00	$47.50
Thompson, Hank	53T	20	$5.00	$20.00
Thompson, Hank	54T	64	$7.00	$22.00
Thompson, Hank	56T	199	$3.00	$9.00
Thompson, Hank	57T	109	$ .95	$3.50
Thompson, Jason	77T	291	$ .15	$ .50
Thompson, Jason	78T	660	$ .02	$ .10
Thompson, Jason	79T	80	$ .02	$ .10
Thompson, Jason	80T	150	$ .01	$ .10
Thompson, Jason	81T	505	$ .01	$ .10
Thompson, Jason	81TTR	843	$ .02	$ .10
Thompson, Jason	82T	295	$ .01	$ .07
Thompson, Jason	83T	730	$ .01	$ .07
Thompson, Jason	84T	355	$ .01	$ .06
Thompson, Jason	85T	490	$ .01	$ .05
Thompson, Jason	86T	635	$ .01	$ .04
Thompson, Mike	73T	564	$ .45	$1.45
Thompson, Mike	76T	536	$ .05	$ .20
Thompson, Milt	86T	517	$ .02	$ .20
Thompson, Milt	86TTR	112	$ .02	$ .10
Thompson, Milt	87T	409	$ .01	$ .04

Player	Year	No.	VG	EX/MT
Thompson, Milt	88T	298	$ .01	$ .10
Thompson, Milt	88TBB	2	$ .01	$ .06
Thompson, Milt	89T	128	$ .01	$ .05
Thompson, Milt	89TTR	118	$ .01	$ .06
Thompson, Milt	90T	688	$ .01	$ .04
Thompson, Milt	91T	63	$ .01	$ .03
Thompson, Rich	85TTR	122	$ .02	$ .10
Thompson, Rich	86T	242	$ .01	$ .04
Thompson, Rich	90T	474	$ .01	$ .04
Thompson, Robby	86TTR	113	$ .05	$ .35
Thompson, Robby	87T	658	$ .05	$ .25
Thompson, Robby	88T	472	$ .01	$ .04
Thompson, Robby	88TBB	83	$ .01	$ .06
Thompson, Robby	89T	15	$ .01	$ .05
Thompson, Robby	89TBB	163	$ .01	$ .06
Thompson, Robby	90T	325	$ .01	$ .04
Thompson, Robby	91T	705	$ .01	$ .03

Player	Year	No.	VG	EX/MT
Thompson, Scot	79T	716	$ .02	$ .10
Thompson, Scot	80T	574	$ .01	$ .10
Thompson, Scot	81T	395	$ .01	$ .10
Thompson, Scot	83T	481	$ .01	$ .07
Thompson, Scot	85T	646	$ .01	$ .05
Thompson, Scot	86T	93	$ .01	$ .04
Thompson, Tim	58T	57	$ .85	$3.50
Thomson, Bobby	52T	313	$55.00	$165.00
Thomson, Bobby	56T	257	$3.00	$9.00
Thomson, Bobby	57T	262	$2.00	$6.00
Thomson, Bobby	58T	430	$1.00	$3.50
Thomson, Bobby	59T	429	$ .75	$2.20
Thomson, Bobby	60T	153	$ .90	$3.00
Thon, Dickie	80T	663	$ .05	$ .20
Thon, Dickie	81T	209	$ .01	$ .10
Thon, Dickie	81TTR	844	$ .02	$ .10
Thon, Dickie	82T	404	$ .01	$ .07
Thon, Dickie	83T	558	$ .01	$ .07
Thon, Dickie	84T	692	$ .01	$ .06
Thon, Dickie	85T	44	$ .01	$ .05
Thon, Dickie	86T	166	$ .01	$ .04
Thon, Dickie	87T	386	$ .01	$ .04
Thon, Dickie	88TTR	121	$ .01	$ .06
Thon, Dickie	89T	726	$ .01	$ .05
Thon, Dickie	89TTR	119	$ .01	$ .06
Thon, Dickie	90T	269	$ .01	$ .04
Thon, Dickie	91T	439	$ .01	$ .03
Thormodsgard, Paul	78T	162	$ .02	$ .10
Thormodsgard, Paul	79T	249	$ .02	$ .10
Thornton, Andy	74T	604	$1.00	$3.00
Thornton, Andy	75T	39	$ .07	$ .30
Thornton, Andy	76T	26	$ .05	$ .20
Thornton, Andre	78T	148	$ .02	$ .10
Thornton, Andre	79T	280	$ .02	$ .10
Thornton, Andre	80T	534	$ .01	$ .10
Thornton, Andre	81T	388	$ .01	$ .10
Thornton, Andre	82T	746	$ .01	$ .07
Thornton, Andre	83T	640	$ .01	$ .07
Thornton, Andre	84T	115	$ .01	$ .06
Thornton, Andre	85T	475	$ .01	$ .05
Thornton, Andre	86T	59	$ .01	$ .04
Thornton, Andre	87T	780	$ .01	$ .04
Thornton, Lou	86T	488	$ .01	$ .04
Thorpe, Bob	52T	367	$40.00	$140.00
Throedson, Rich	74T	77	$ .07	$ .30
Throneberry, Faye	52T	376	$40.00	$140.00
Throneberry, Faye	53T	49	$4.50	$15.00
Throneberry, Faye	55T	163	$5.25	$15.00
Throneberry, Faye	57T	356	$ .85	$3.50
Throneberry, Faye	59T	534	$2.50	$10.00
Throneberry, Faye	60T	9	$ .45	$1.45
Throneberry, Faye	61T	282	$ .35	$1.25
Throneberry, Marv	58T	175	$3.00	$9.00
Throneberry, Marv	59T	326	$ .75	$2.20
Throneberry, Marv	60T	436	$ .90	$3.00
Throneberry, Marv	61T	57	$ .75	$3.00
Throneberry, Marv	63T	78	$ .85	$3.50
Throop, George	76T	591	$ .05	$ .20
Thurman, Bob	57T	279	$4.25	$15.00
Thurman, Bob	58T	34	$ .85	$3.50
Thurman, Bob	59T	541	$2.50	$10.00
Thurman, Gary	88T	89	$ .01	$ .50
Thurman, Gary	89T	323	$ .01	$ .05
Thurman, Gary	90T	276	$ .01	$ .04
Thurmond, Mark	84T	481	$ .02	$ .10
Thurmond, Mark	85T	236	$ .01	$ .05
Thurmond, Mark	86T	37	$ .01	$ .04
Thurmond, Mark	87T	361	$ .01	$ .04
Thurmond, Mark	88T	552	$ .01	$ .04
Thurmond, Mark	89T	152	$ .01	$ .05

Player	Year	No.	VG	EX/MT
Thurmond, Mark	90T	758	$ .01	$ .04
Tiant, Luis	65T	145	$3.00	$9.00
Tiant, Luis	66T	285	$ .75	$3.00
Tiant, Luis	67T	377	$ .75	$3.00
Tiant, Luis	68T	532	$ .20	$1.25
Tiant, Luis	69T	7	$ .35	$1.25
Tiant, Luis	69T	9	$ .35	$1.25
Tiant, Luis	69T	11	$ .75	$3.00
Tiant, Luis	69T	560	$ .20	$ .50
Tiant, Luis	70T	231	$ .35	$1.25
Tiant, Luis	71T	95	$ .45	$1.45
Tiant, Luis	73T	65	$ .45	$1.45
Tiant, Luis	73T	270	$ .30	$ .95
Tiant, Luis	74T	167	$ .30	$ .95
Tiant, Luis	75T	430	$ .07	$ .30
Tiant, Luis	76T	130	$ .15	$ .50
Tiant, Luis	77T	258	$ .15	$ .50
Tiant, Luis	78T	345	$ .05	$ .20
Tiant, Luis	79T	575	$ .05	$ .20
Tiant, Luis	80T	35	$ .05	$ .20
Tiant, Luis	81T	627	$ .03	$ .15
Tiant, Luis	82T	160	$ .01	$ .07
Tiant, Luis	83T	178	$ .01	$ .07
Tiant, Luis	83T	179	$ .01	$ .07
Tibbs, Jay	85T	573	$ .01	$ .05
Tibbs, Jay	86T	176	$ .01	$ .04
Tibbs, Jay	86TTR	114	$ .02	$ .10
Tibbs, Jay	87T	9	$ .01	$ .04

Player	Year	No.	VG	EX/MT
Tibbs, Jay	88T	464	$ .01	$ .04
Tibbs, Jay	89T	271	$ .01	$ .05
Tibbs, Jay	90T	677	$ .01	$ .04
Tidrow, Dick	72T	506	$ .30	$ .85
Tidrow, Dick	73T	339	$ .07	$ .30
Tidrow, Dick	74T	231	$ .07	$ .30
Tidrow, Dick	75T	241	$ .07	$ .30
Tidrow, Dick	76T	248	$ .05	$ .20
Tidrow, Dick	77T	461	$ .03	$ .12
Tidrow, Dick	78T	179	$ .02	$ .10
Tidrow, Dick	79T	89	$ .02	$ .10
Tidrow, Dick	80T	594	$ .01	$ .10

Player	Year	No.	VG	EX/MT
Tidrow, Dick	81T	352	$ .01	$ .10
Tidrow, Dick	82T	699	$ .01	$ .07
Tidrow, Dick	83T	787	$ .01	$ .07
Tidrow, Dick	83TTR	112	$ .02	$ .10
Tidrow, Dick	84T	153	$ .01	$ .06
Tiefenauer, Bobby	59T	501	$ .75	$2.20
Tiefenauer, Bobby	62T	227	$ .45	$1.45
Tiefenauer, Bobby	64T	522	$ .50	$1.45

Player	Year	No.	VG	EX/MT
Tiefenauer, Bob	65T	23	$ .30	$ .85
Tiefenauer, Bob	68T	269	$ .30	$ .85
Tigers, Team	56T	213	$11.00	$33.00
Tigers, Team	57T	198	$1.50	$6.00
Tigers, Team	58T	397	$2.00	$8.00
Tigers, Team	59T	329	$2.50	$7.50
Tigers, Team	60T	72	$3.00	$9.00
Tigers, Team	61T	51	$ .75	$3.00
Tigers, Team	62T	24	$ .75	$2.25
Tigers, Team	63T	552	$3.00	$8.00
Tigers, Team	64T	67	$ .50	$2.50
Tigers, Team	65T	173	$ .75	$2.25
Tigers, Team	66T	583	$35.00	$105.00
Tigers, Team	67T	378	$ .75	$2.25
Tigers, Team	68T	528	$3.35	$10.00
Tigers, Team	70T	579	$ .90	$3.00
Tigers, Team	71T	336	$ .45	$1.45
Tigers, Team	72T	487	$ .45	$1.45
Tigers, Team	73T	191	$ .45	$1.45
Tigers, Team	74T	94	$ .45	$1.45
Tigers, Team Checklist	75T	18	$ .15	$ .50
Tigers, Team Checklist	76T	361	$ .45	$1.45
Tigers, Team Checklist	77T	621	$ .35	$1.25
Tigers, Team Checklist	78T	404	$ .08	$ .30
Tigers, Team Checklist	79T	66	$ .08	$ .30
Tigers, Team Checklist	80T	626	$ .08	$ .30
Tigers, Team Checklist	81T	666	$ .02	$ .20
Tigers, Team Leaders	86T	36	$ .01	$ .10
Tigers, Team Leaders	87T	631	$ .01	$ .04
Tigers, Team Leaders	88T	429	$ .01	$ .04
Tigers, Team Leaders	89T	609	$ .01	$ .05
Tillman, Bob	62T	368	$ .45	$1.45

Player	Year	No.	VG	EX/MT
Tillman, Bob	63T	384	$ .45	$1.50
Tillman, Bob	64T	112	$ .30	$ .95
Tillman, Bob	65T	222	$ .35	$1.25
Tillman, Bob	66T	178	$ .30	$ .95
Tillman, Bob	67T	36	$ .30	$ .85
Tillman, Bob	68T	174	$ .30	$ .85
Tillman, Bob	69T	374	$ .30	$ .85
Tillman, Bob	70T	668	$ .75	$2.00
Tillman, Bob	71T	244	$ .15	$ .50
Tillotson, Thad	67T	553	$5.00	$20.00
Timmermann, Tom	70T	554	$ .30	$ .95
Timmermann, Tom	71T	296	$ .15	$ .50
Timmermann, Tom	72T	239	$ .05	$ .25
Timmermann, Tom	73T	413	$ .07	$ .30
Timmermann, Tom	74T	327	$ .07	$ .30
Tingley, Ron	89T	721	$ .01	$ .05
Tingley, Ron	89TBB	37	$ .01	$ .06
Tipton, Joe	52T	134	$7.00	$20.00
Tischinski, Tom	70T	379	$ .15	$ .50
Tischinski, Tom	71T	724	$ .75	$2.50
Tobik, Dave	79T	706	$ .02	$ .10
Tobik, Dave	80T	269	$ .01	$ .10
Tobik, Dave	81T	102	$ .01	$ .10
Tobik, Dave	82T	391	$ .01	$ .07
Tobik, Dave	83T	691	$ .01	$ .07
Tobik, Dave	83TTR	113	$ .02	$ .10
Tobik, Dave	84T	341	$ .01	$ .06
Todd, Jackson	78T	481	$ .02	$ .10
Todd, Jackson	81T	142	$ .01	$ .10
Todd, Jackson	82T	565	$ .01	$ .07
Todd, Jim	75T	519	$ .07	$ .30
Todd, Jim	76T	221	$ .05	$ .20
Todd, Jim	77T	31	$ .03	$ .12
Todd, Jim	78T	333	$ .02	$ .10
Todd, Jim	79T	103	$ .02	$ .10
Todd, Jim	80T	629	$ .01	$ .10
Tolan, Bob	65T	116	$ .45	$1.45
Tolan, Bob	66T	179	$ .30	$ .95
Tolan, Bob	67T	474	$ .75	$3.00
Tolan, Bob	68T	84	$ .30	$ .85
Tolan, Bob	69T	448	$ .30	$ .85
Tolan, Bob	70T	409	$ .30	$ .85
Tolan, Bob	71T	190	$ .15	$ .50
Tolan, Bob	72T	3	$ .05	$ .25
Tolan, Bob	73T	335	$ .07	$ .30
Tolan, Bob	74T	535	$ .07	$ .30
Tolan, Bob	75T	402	$ .07	$ .30
Tolan, Bob	76T	56	$ .05	$ .20
Tolan, Bob	77T	188	$ .03	$ .12
Tolan, Bob	80T	708	$ .01	$ .10
Toliver, Fred	87T	63	$ .01	$ .04
Toliver, Fred	88T	203	$ .01	$ .04
Toliver, Fred	89T	623	$ .01	$ .05
Toliver, Fred	90T	423	$ .01	$ .04
Tolleson, Wayne	83TTR	114	$ .02	$ .10
Tolleson, Wayne	84T	557	$ .01	$ .06
Tolleson, Wayne	85T	247	$ .01	$ .05
Tolleson, Wayne	86T	641	$ .01	$ .04
Tolleson, Wayne	86TTR	115	$ .02	$ .10
Tolleson, Wayne	87T	224	$ .01	$ .04
Tolleson, Wayne	88T	411	$ .01	$ .04
Tolleson, Wayne	89T	716	$ .01	$ .05
Tolleson, Wayne	90TTR	123	$ .01	$ .05
Tolman, Tim	86T	272	$ .01	$ .04
Tomanek, Dick	58T	123	$ .75	$3.00
Tomanek, Dick	59T	369	$ .75	$2.20
Tomlin, Dave	75T	578	$ .07	$ .30
Tomlin, Dave	76T	398	$ .05	$ .20
Tomlin, Dave	77T	241	$ .03	$ .12
Tomlin, Dave	78T	86	$ .02	$ .10

Player	Year	No.	VG	EX/MT
Tomlin, Dave	79T	674	$ .02	$ .10
Tomlin, Dave	80T	126	$ .01	$ .10
Tomlin, Randy	91T	167	$ .01	$ .15
Tompkins, Ron	66T	107	$ .30	$ .95
Tompkins, Ron	68T	247	$90.00	$350.00
Torborg, Jeff	64T	337	$ .30	$ .95
Torborg, Jeff	65T	527	$1.75	$4.50
Torborg, Jeff	66T	257	$ .30	$ .95
Torborg, Jeff	67T	398	$ .30	$ .95
Torborg, Jeff	68T	492	$ .35	$1.25
Torborg, Jeff	69T	353	$ .30	$ .85
Torborg, Jeff	70T	54	$ .15	$ .50
Torborg, Jeff	71T	314	$ .15	$ .50
Torborg, Jeff	72T	404	$ .05	$ .25
Torborg, Jeff	73T	154	$ .07	$ .30
Torborg, Jeff	78T	351	$ .02	$ .10
Torborg, Jeff	89TTR	120	$ .01	$ .06
Torborg, Jeff	90T	21	$ .01	$ .04
Torborg, Jeff	91T	609	$ .01	$ .03
Torgeson, Earl	51Tbb	34	$7.50	$22.50
Torgeson, Earl	52T	97	$7.00	$20.00
Torgeson, Earl	56T	147	$2.25	$6.00
Torgeson, Earl	57T	357	$ .85	$3.50

Earl Torgeson

CHICAGO WHITE SOX

Player	Year	No.	VG	EX/MT
Torgeson, Earl	58T	138	$ .75	$3.00
Torgeson, Earl	59T	351	$ .75	$2.20
Torgeson, Earl	60T	299	$ .75	$2.20
Torgeson, Earl	61T	152	$ .35	$1.25
Torre, Frank	56T	172	$2.10	$6.00
Torre, Frank	57T	37	$ .95	$3.50
Torre, Frank	58T	117	$ .75	$3.00
Torre, Frank	59T	65	$ .85	$3.50
Torre, Frank	60T	478	$ .90	$3.00
Torre, Frank	62T	303	$ .45	$1.45
Torre, Frank	63T	161	$ .30	$ .95
Torre, Joe	62T	218	$3.00	$12.00
Torre, Joe	62T	351	$ .90	$3.00
Torre, Joe	63T	347	$ .95	$3.50
Torre, Joe	64T	70	$ .90	$3.00
Torre, Joe	65T	200	$ .75	$3.00
Torre, Joe	66T	130	$ .75	$3.00

Player	Year	No.	VG	EX/MT
Torre, Joe	67T	350	$ .45	$1.45
Torre, Joe	68T	30	$ .15	$ .50
Torre, Joe	69T	460	$ .15	$ .50
Torre, Joe	70T	190	$ .45	$1.45
Torre, Joe	71T	62	$ .15	$ .50
Torre, Joe	71T	370	$ .90	$3.00
Torre, Joe	72T	85	$ .35	$1.25
Torre, Joe	72T	87	$ .60	$2.00
Torre, Joe	72T	341	$ .05	$ .25
Torre, Joe	72T	500	$ .15	$ .50
Torre, Joe	73T	450	$ .30	$ .95
Torre, Joe	74T	15	$ .30	$ .85
Torre, Joe	75T	209	$ .30	$ .85
Torre, Joe	75T	565	$ .30	$ .95
Torre, Joe	76T	585	$ .15	$ .50
Torre, Joe	77T	425	$ .30	$ .85
Torre, Joe	78T	109	$ .05	$ .20
Torre, Joe	83T	126	$ .01	$ .07
Torre, Joe	84T	502	$ .01	$ .06
Torre, Joe	85T	438	$ .01	$ .05
Torre, Joe	91T	351	$ .01	$ .03
Torrealba, Pablo	76T	589	$ .45	$1.45
Torrealba, Pablo	77T	499	$ .03	$ .12
Torrealba, Pablo	78T	78	$ .02	$ .10
Torrealba, Pablo	79T	242	$ .02	$ .10
Torres, Felix	62T	595	$7.00	$21.00
Torres, Felix	63T	482	$2.50	$6.50
Torres, Hector	69T	526	$ .30	$ .95
Torres, Hector	70T	272	$ .15	$ .50
Torres, Hector	71T	558	$ .35	$1.25
Torres, Hector	72T	666	$ .75	$2.50
Torres, Hector	76T	241	$ .05	$ .20
Torres, Rusty	72T	124	$ .05	$ .25
Torres, Rusty	73T	571	$ .45	$1.45
Torres, Rusty	74T	499	$ .07	$ .30
Torres, Rusty	77T	224	$ .03	$ .12
Torres, Rusty	80T	36	$ .01	$ .10
Torrez, Mike	68T	162	$ .30	$ .85
Torrez, Mike	69T	136	$ .30	$ .85
Torrez, Mike	70T	312	$ .15	$ .50
Torrez, Mike	71T	531	$ .35	$1.25
Torrez, Mike	73T	77	$ .07	$ .30
Torrez, Mike	74T	568	$ .07	$ .30
Torrez, Mike	75T	254	$ .07	$ .30
Torrez, Mike	76T	25	$ .05	$ .20
Torrez, Mike	77T	365	$ .03	$ .12
Torrez, Mike	78T	645	$ .02	$ .10
Torrez, Mike	79T	185	$ .02	$ .10
Torrez, Mike	80T	455	$ .01	$ .10
Torrez, Mike	81T	525	$ .01	$ .10
Torrez, Mike	82T	225	$ .01	$ .07
Torrez, Mike	82T	786	$ .01	$ .07
Torrez, Mike	83T	743	$ .01	$ .07
Torrez, Mike	83TTR	115	$ .02	$ .10
Torrez, Mike	84T	78	$ .01	$ .06
Toth, Paul	63T	489	$2.50	$6.50
Toth, Paul	64T	309	$ .30	$ .95
Tovar, Cesar	65T	201	$ .35	$1.25
Tovar, Cesar	66T	563	$5.00	$20.00
Tovar, Cesar	67T	317	$ .30	$ .85
Tovar, Cesar	68T	420	$ .30	$ .85
Tovar, Cesar	69T	530	$ .30	$ .95
Tovar, Cesar	70T	25	$ .15	$ .50
Tovar, Cesar	71T	165	$ .15	$ .50
Tovar, Cesar	72T	275	$ .05	$ .25
Tovar, Cesar	73T	405	$ .07	$ .30
Tovar, Cesar	74T	538	$ .07	$ .30
Tovar, Cesar	74TTR	538	$ .07	$ .30
Tovar, Cesar	75T	178	$ .07	$ .30
Tovar, Cesar	76T	246	$ .05	$ .20

Player	Year	No.	VG	EX/MT
Tovar, Cesar	77T	408	$ .03	$ .12
Traber, Jim	87T	484	$ .01	$ .04
Traber, Jim	88T	544	$ .01	$ .04
Traber, Jim	89T	124	$ .01	$ .05
Tracewski, Dick	64T	154	$ .30	$ .95
Tracewski, Dick	65T	279	$ .35	$1.25
Tracewski, Dick	66T	378	$ .30	$ .95
Tracewski, Dick	67T	559	$1.50	$4.00
Tracewski, Dick	68T	488	$ .35	$1.25
Tracewski, Dick	69T	126	$ .30	$ .85
Tracewski, Dick	73T	323	$ .35	$1.25
Tracy, Jim	82T	403	$ .01	$ .07
Trammell, Alan	78T	707	$12.50	$50.00
Trammell, Alan	79T	358	$2.50	$10.00
Trammell, Alan	80T	232	$1.00	$4.00
Trammell, Alan	81T	709	$ .10	$ .50
Trammell, Alan	82T	475	$ .30	$ .85
Trammell, Alan	83T	95	$ .20	$ .65
Trammell, Alan	84T	510	$ .10	$ .50
Trammell, Alan	85T	690	$ .05	$ .25
Trammell, Alan	86T	130	$ .05	$ .25
Trammell, Alan	87T	687	$ .01	$ .15
Trammell, Alan	88T	320	$ .01	$ .15
Trammell, Alan	88TAS	389	$ .01	$ .05
Trammell, Alan	88TBB	8	$ .01	$ .15
Trammell, Alan	89T	770	$ .01	$ .10
Trammell, Alan	89TAS	400	$ .01	$ .05
Trammell, Alan	89TBB	123	$ .01	$ .10
Trammell, Alan	90T	440	$ .01	$ .10
Trammell, Alan	91T	275	$ .01	$ .03
Trammell, Alan	91TAS	389	$ .01	$ .03
Travers, Bill	75T	488	$ .07	$ .30
Travers, Bill	76T	573	$ .05	$ .20
Travers, Bill	77T	125	$ .03	$ .12
Travers, Bill	78T	355	$ .02	$ .10
Travers, Bill	79T	213	$ .02	$ .10

BILL TRAVERS
PITCHER
BREWERS

Player	Year	No.	VG	EX/MT
Travers, Bill	80T	109	$ .01	$ .10
Travers, Bill	81T	704	$ .01	$ .10
Travers, Bill	81TTR	845	$ .02	$ .10
Travers, Bill	82T	628	$ .01	$ .07

Player	Year	No.	VG	EX/MT
Traynor, Pie	76TAS	343	$ .35	$1.25
Treadway, Jeff	88TBB	214	$ .05	$ .25
Treadway, Jeff	88TTR	122	$ .05	$ .25
Treadway, Jeff	89T	685	$ .01	$ .15
Treadway, Jeff	89TTR	121	$ .01	$ .06
Treadway, Jeff	90T	486	$ .01	$ .04
Treadway, Jeff	91T	139	$ .01	$ .03
Trebelhorn, Tom	87TTR	121	$ .05	$ .20
Trebelhorn, Tom	88T	224	$ .01	$ .04
Trebelhorn, Tom	89T	344	$ .01	$ .05
Trebelhorn, Tom	90T	759	$ .01	$ .04
Trebelhorn, Tom	91T	459	$ .01	$ .03
Tremel, Bill	55T	52	$2.00	$6.00
Tremel, Bill	56T	96	$2.25	$6.00
Tresh, Tom	62T	31	$2.50	$10.00
Tresh, Tom	63T	173	$15.00	$45.00
Tresh, Tom	63T	470	$8.00	$25.00
Tresh, Tom	64T	395	$ .75	$3.50
Tresh, Tom	65T	440	$ .75	$3.00
Tresh, Tom	66T	205	$ .50	$2.00
Tresh, Tom	67T	289	$ .50	$1.75
Tresh, Tom	68T	69	$ .25	$1.25
Tresh, Tom	69T	212	$ .15	$ .50
Tresh, Tom	70T	698	$1.00	$4.00
Trevino, Alex	80T	537	$ .01	$ .10
Trevino, Alex	81T	23	$ .01	$ .10
Trevino, Alex	82T	368	$ .01	$ .07
Trevino, Alex	82TTR	120	$ .02	$ .10
Trevino, Alex	83T	632	$ .01	$ .07
Trevino, Alex	84T	242	$ .01	$ .06
Trevino, Alex	84TTR	120	$ .02	$ .10
Trevino, Alex	85T	747	$ .01	$ .05
Trevino, Alex	85TTR	123	$ .02	$ .10
Trevino, Alex	86T	444	$ .01	$ .04
Trevino, Alex	86TTR	116	$ .02	$ .10
Trevino, Alex	87T	173	$ .01	$ .04
Trevino, Alex	88T	512	$ .01	$ .04
Trevino, Alex	89T	64	$ .01	$ .05
Trevino, Alex	90T	342	$ .01	$ .04
Triandos, Gus	55T	64	$2.50	$10.00
Triandos, Gus	56T	80	$2.25	$6.00
Triandos, Gus	57T	156	$ .95	$3.50
Triandos, Gus	58T	429	$ .75	$3.00
Triandos, Gus	59T	330	$ .75	$2.20
Triandos, Gus	59TAS	568	$2.50	$10.00
Triandos, Gus	60T	60	$ .45	$1.45
Triandos, Gus	61T	140	$ .35	$1.25
Triandos, Gus	62T	420	$ .75	$2.50
Triandos, Gus	63T	475	$2.50	$6.50
Triandos, Gus	64T	83	$ .30	$ .95
Triandos, Gus	65T	248	$ .35	$1.25
Trice, Bob	54T	148	$2.50	$10.00
Trice, Bob	55T	132	$2.00	$6.00
Trillo, Manny	74T	597	$ .15	$ .50
Trillo, Manny	75T	617	$ .45	$1.45
Trillo, Manny	76T	206	$ .15	$ .50
Trillo, Manny	77T	395	$ .03	$ .12
Trillo, Manny	78T	123	$ .02	$ .10
Trillo, Manny	79T	639	$ .02	$ .10
Trillo, Manny	80T	90	$ .01	$ .10
Trillo, Manny	81T	470	$ .01	$ .10
Trillo, Manny	82T	220	$ .01	$ .07
Trillo, Manny	83T	535	$ .01	$ .07
Trillo, Manny	83TAS	398	$ .01	$ .07
Trillo, Manny	83TRB	5	$ .01	$ .07
Trillo, Manny	83TTR	116	$ .02	$ .10
Trillo, Manny	84T	180	$ .01	$ .06
Trillo, Manny	84TTR	121	$ .02	$ .10
Trillo, Manny	85T	310	$ .01	$ .05
Trillo, Manny	86T	655	$ .01	$ .04

Player	Year	No.	VG	EX/MT	Player	Year	No.	VG	EX/MT
Trillo, Manny	86TTR	117	$ .02	$ .10	Turley, Bob	63T	322	$ .45	$1.45
Trillo, Manny	87T	732	$ .01	$ .04	Turner, Jerry	75T	619	$ .07	$ .30
Trillo, Manny	88T	287	$ .01	$ .04	Turner, Jerry	76T	598	$ .05	$ .20
Trillo, Manny	89T	66	$ .01	$ .05	Turner, Jerry	77T	447	$ .03	$ .12
Trillo, Manny	89TBB	295	$ .01	$ .06	Turner, Jerry	78T	364	$ .02	$ .10
Trout, Dizzy	51Tbb	23	$7.50	$22.50	Turner, Jerry	79T	564	$ .02	$ .10
Trout, Dizzy	52T	39	$15.00	$47.50	Turner, Jerry	80T	133	$ .01	$ .10
Trout, Dizzy	53T	169	$2.25	$8.00	Turner, Jerry	81T	285	$ .01	$ .10
Trout, Dizzy	85T	142	$ .01	$ .10	Turner, Jerry	82T	736	$ .01	$ .07
Trout, Steve	80T	83	$ .05	$ .20	Turner, Jerry	82TTR	121	$ .02	$ .10
Trout, Steve	81T	552	$ .01	$ .10	Turner, Jerry	83T	41	$ .01	$ .07
Trout, Steve	82T	299	$ .01	$ .07	Turner, Jim	52T	373	$50.00	$150.00
Trout, Steve	83T	461	$ .01	$ .07	Turner, Jim	62T	263	$ .75	$3.00
Trout, Steve	83TTR	117	$ .02	$ .10	Turner, Jim	73T	116	$ .15	$ .50
Trout, Steve	84T	151	$ .01	$ .06	Tuttle, Bill	56T	203	$3.00	$9.00
Trout, Steve	85T	142	$ .01	$ .10	Tuttle, Bill	57T	72	$ .95	$3.50
Trout, Steve	85T	668	$ .01	$ .05	Tuttle, Bill	58T	23	$ .85	$3.50
Trout, Steve	86T	384	$ .01	$ .04	Tuttle, Bill	59T	459	$ .75	$2.20
Trout, Steve	87T	750	$ .01	$ .04	Tuttle, Bill	60T	367	$ .75	$2.20
Trout, Steve	88T	584	$ .01	$ .04	Tuttle, Bill	61T	536	$7.00	$21.00
Trout, Steve	88TBB	106	$ .01	$ .06	Tuttle, Bill	62T	298	$ .45	$1.45
Trout, Steve	89T	54	$ .01	$ .05	Tuttle, Bill	63T	127	$ .30	$ .95
Trowbridge, Bob	58T	252	$ .75	$3.00	Twins, Team	61T	542	$15.00	$45.00
Trowbridge, Bob	59T	239	$ .75	$2.20	Twins, Team	62T	584	$7.00	$28.00
Trowbridge, Bob	60T	66	$ .45	$1.45	Twins, Team	63T	162	$ .75	$2.20
Trucks, Virgil	52T	262	$14.00	$40.00	Twins, Team	64T	318	$ .85	$3.50
Trucks, Virgil	53T	96	$4.50	$15.00	Twins, Team	65T	24	$ .75	$2.25
Trucks, Virgil	56T	117	$1.50	$4.00	Twins, Team	66T	526	$16.00	$50.00
Trucks, Virgil	57T	187	$ .95	$3.50	Twins, Team	67T	211	$ .90	$3.00
Trucks, Virgil	58T	277	$ .75	$3.00	Twins, Team	68T	137	$ .75	$3.00
Trucks, Virgil	59T	417	$ .75	$2.20	Twins, Team	70T	534	$ .75	$3.00
Trujillo, Mike	86T	687	$ .01	$ .04	Twins, Team	71T	522	$ .45	$1.45
Trujillo, Mike	87T	402	$ .01	$ .04	Twins, Team	72T	156	$ .15	$ .50
Trujillo, Mike	88T	307	$ .01	$ .04	Twins, Team	73T	654	$ .90	$3.00
Tsitouris, John	60T	497	$ .90	$3.00	Twins, Team	74T	74	$ .15	$ .50
Tsitouris, John	63T	244	$ .30	$ .95	Twins, Team Checklist	75T	443	$ .15	$ .50
Tsitouris, John	64T	275	$ .30	$ .95	Twins, Team Checklist	76T	556	$ .35	$1.25
Tsitouris, John	65T	221	$ .35	$1.25	Twins, Team Checklist	77T	228	$ .15	$ .50
Tsitouris, John	66T	12	$ .30	$ .95	Twins, Team Checklist	78T	451	$ .05	$ .25
Tsitouris, John	68T	523	$ .35	$1.25	Twins, Team Checklist	79T	41	$ .05	$ .25
Tudor, John	81T	14	$ .45	$1.45	Twins, Team Checklist	80T	328	$ .05	$ .25
Tudor, John	82T	558	$ .05	$ .20	Twins, Team Checklist	81T	669	$ .02	$ .20
Tudor, John	83T	318	$ .01	$ .07	Twins, Team Leaders	86T	786	$ .01	$ .04
Tudor, John	84T	601	$ .01	$ .06	Twins, Team Leaders	87T	206	$ .01	$ .04
Tudor, John	84TTR	122	$ .02	$ .10	Twins, Team Leaders	88T	609	$ .01	$ .04
Tudor, John	85T	214	$ .01	$ .05	Twins, Team Leaders	89T	429	$ .01	$ .05
Tudor, John	85TTR	124	$ .02	$ .10	Twitchell, Wayne	71T	692	$ .75	$2.50
Tudor, John	86T	474	$ .01	$ .04	Twitchell, Wayne	72T	14	$ .15	$ .50
Tudor, John	86TAS	710	$ .01	$ .04	Twitchell, Wayne	73T	227	$ .07	$ .30
Tudor, John	87T	110	$ .01	$ .04	Twitchell, Wayne	74T	419	$ .07	$ .30
Tudor, John	88T	792	$ .01	$ .10	Twitchell, Wayne	75T	326	$ .07	$ .30
Tudor, John	89T	35	$ .01	$ .05	Twitchell, Wayne	76T	543	$ .05	$ .20
Tudor, John	90TTR	124	$ .01	$ .05	Twitchell, Wayne	77T	444	$ .03	$ .12
Tufts, Bob	82T	171	$ .15	$ .75	Twitchell, Wayne	78T	269	$ .02	$ .10
Tunnell, Lee	83TTR	118	$ .02	$ .10	Twitchell, Wayne	79T	43	$ .02	$ .10
Tunnell, Lee	84T	384	$ .01	$ .06	Tyrone, Jim	74T	598	$4.00	$15.00
Tunnell, Lee	85T	21	$ .01	$ .05	Tyrone, Jim	78T	487	$ .02	$ .10
Tunnell, Lee	86T	161	$ .01	$ .04	Tyson, Mike	74T	655	$ .07	$ .30
Turley, Bob	54T	85	$7.00	$22.00	Tyson, Mike	75T	231	$ .07	$ .30
Turley, Bob	55T	38	$3.95	$11.50	Tyson, Mike	76T	86	$ .05	$ .20
Turley, Bob	56T	40	$2.10	$6.00	Tyson, Mike	77T	599	$ .03	$ .12
Turley, Bob	57T	264	$2.50	$10.00	Tyson, Mike	78T	111	$ .02	$ .10
Turley, Bob	58T	255	$2.10	$6.00	Tyson, Mike	79T	324	$ .02	$ .10
Turley, Bob	58TAS	493	$ .70	$2.25	Tyson, Mike	80T	486	$ .01	$ .10
Turley, Bob	59T	60	$1.50	$4.00	Tyson, Mike	81T	294	$ .01	$ .10
Turley, Bob	59T	237	$ .90	$3.00	Tyson, Mike	82T	62	$ .01	$ .07
Turley, Bob	59TAS	570	$2.35	$7.00	Uecker, Bob	62T	594	$35.00	$125.00
Turley, Bob	60T	270	$ .90	$3.00	Uecker, Bob	63T	126	$10.00	$30.00
Turley, Bob	61T	40	$ .75	$2.20	Uecker, Bob	64T	543	$16.00	$50.00
Turley, Bob	62T	589	$7.00	$21.00	Uecker, Bob	65T	519	$12.50	$37.50

TOPPS

Player	Year	No.	VG	EX/MT	Player	Year	No.	VG	EX/MT
Uecker, Bob	66T	91	$6.00	$18.00	Upshaw, Willie	88TTR	123	$ .01	$ .06
Uecker, Bob	67T	326	$6.00	$18.00	Upshaw, Willie	89T	106	$ .01	$ .05
Uhlaender, Ted	66T	264	$ .30	$ .95	Upton, Tom	52T	71	$15.00	$47.50
Uhlaender, Ted	67T	431	$ .30	$ .95	Urban, Jack	58T	367	$ .75	$3.00
Uhlaender, Ted	68T	28	$ .30	$ .85	Urban, Jack	59T	18	$ .85	$3.50
Uhlaender, Ted	69T	194	$ .30	$ .85	Uribe, Jose	85TTR	125	$ .05	$ .20
Uhlaender, Ted	70T	673	$ .75	$2.00	Uribe, Jose	86T	12	$ .01	$ .10
Uhlaender, Ted	71T	347	$ .15	$ .50	Uribe, Jose	87T	633	$ .01	$ .04
Uhlaender, Ted	72T	614	$ .30	$ .95	Uribe, Jose	88T	302	$ .01	$ .04
Ujdur, Jerry	81T	626	$ .01	$ .10	Uribe, Jose	88TBB	95	$ .01	$ .06
Ujdur, Jerry	83T	174	$ .01	$ .07	Uribe, Jose	89T	753	$ .01	$ .05
Ullger, Scott	84T	551	$ .01	$ .06	Uribe, Jose	89TBB	258	$ .01	$ .06
Umbach, Arnie	66T	518	$ .75	$2.50	Uribe, Jose	90T	472	$ .01	$ .04
Umbarger, Jim	76T	7	$ .05	$ .20	Uribe, Jose	91T	158	$ .01	$ .03
Umbarger, Jim	77T	378	$ .03	$ .12	Urrea, John	78T	587	$ .02	$ .10
Umbarger, Jim	79T	518	$ .02	$ .10	Urrea, John	79T	429	$ .02	$ .10
Umbricht, Jim	60T	145	$ .45	$1.45	Urrea, John	81T	152	$ .01	$ .10
Umbricht, Jim	63T	99	$ .30	$ .95	Urrea, John	81TTR	847	$ .02	$ .10
Umbricht, Jim	64T	389	$ .50	$1.45	Urrea, John	82T	28	$ .01	$ .07
Underwood, Pat	80T	709	$ .01	$ .10					
Underwood, Pat	81T	373	$ .01	$ .10					
Underwood, Pat	82T	133	$ .01	$ .07					
Underwood, Pat	83T	588	$ .01	$ .07					
Underwood, Tom	75T	615	$ .30	$ .95					
Underwood, Tom	76T	407	$ .05	$ .20					
Underwood, Tom	77T	217	$ .03	$ .12					
Underwood, Tom	78T	531	$ .02	$ .10					
Underwood, Tom	79T	64	$ .02	$ .10					
Underwood, Tom	80T	324	$ .01	$ .10					
Underwood, Tom	81T	114	$ .01	$ .10					
Underwood, Tom	81TTR	846	$ .02	$ .10					
Underwood, Tom	82T	757	$ .01	$ .07					
Underwood, Tom	83T	466	$ .01	$ .07					
Underwood, Tom	84T	642	$ .01	$ .06					
Underwood, Tom	84TTR	123	$ .02	$ .10					
Underwood, Tom	85T	289	$ .01	$ .05					
Unser, Del	69T	338	$ .30	$ .85					
Unser, Del	70T	336	$ .15	$ .50					
Unser, Del	71T	33	$ .15	$ .50					
Unser, Del	72T	687	$ .75	$2.50					
Unser, Del	73T	247	$ .07	$ .30					
Unser, Del	74T	69	$ .07	$ .30					
Unser, Del	75T	138	$ .07	$ .30					
Unser, Del	76T	268	$ .05	$ .20					
Unser, Del	77T	471	$ .03	$ .12					
Unser, Del	78T	348	$ .02	$ .10					
Unser, Del	79T	628	$ .02	$ .10					
Unser, Del	80T	27	$ .01	$ .10					
Unser, Del	80THL	6	$ .01	$ .10	Usher, Bob	52T	157	$7.00	$20.00
Unser, Del	81T	566	$ .01	$ .10	Usher, Bobby	58T	124	$ .75	$3.00
Unser, Del	82T	713	$ .01	$ .07	Vail, Mike	76T	655	$ .05	$ .20
Upham, John	67T	608	$2.00	$6.00	Vail, Mike	77T	246	$ .03	$ .12
Upshaw, Cecil	67T	179	$ .30	$ .85	Vail, Mike	78T	69	$ .02	$ .10
Upshaw, Cecil	68T	286	$ .30	$ .85	Vail, Mike	79T	663	$ .02	$ .10
Upshaw, Cecil	69T	568	$ .30	$ .95	Vail, Mike	80T	343	$ .01	$ .10
Upshaw, Cecil	70T	295	$ .15	$ .50	Vail, Mike	81T	471	$ .01	$ .10
Upshaw, Cecil	71T	223	$ .15	$ .50	Vail, Mike	81TTR	848	$ .02	$ .10
Upshaw, Cecil	72T	74	$ .05	$ .25	Vail, Mike	82T	194	$ .01	$ .07
Upshaw, Cecil	73T	359	$ .07	$ .30	Vail, Mike	83T	554	$ .01	$ .07
Upshaw, Cecil	74T	579	$ .07	$ .30	Vail, Mike	83TTR	119	$ .02	$ .10
Upshaw, Cecil	74TTR	579	$ .07	$ .30	Vail, Mike	84T	766	$ .01	$ .06
Upshaw, Cecil	75T	92	$ .07	$ .30	Vail, Mike	84TTR	124	$ .02	$ .10
Upshaw, Willie	79T	341	$ .15	$ .50	Valdes, Rene	57T	337	$4.25	$15.00
Upshaw, Willie	82T	196	$ .01	$ .07	Valdespino, Sandy	65T	201	$ .35	$1.25
Upshaw, Willie	83T	556	$ .01	$ .07	Valdespino, Sandy	66T	56	$ .30	$ .95
Upshaw, Willie	84T	453	$ .01	$ .06	Valdespino, Sandy	68T	304	$ .30	$ .85
Upshaw, Willie	85T	75	$ .01	$ .05	Valdez, Efrain	91T	692	$ .01	$ .10
Upshaw, Willie	86T	745	$ .01	$ .04	Valdez, Julio	82T	381	$ .05	$ .20
Upshaw, Willie	87T	245	$ .01	$ .04	Valdez, Julio	83T	628	$ .01	$ .07
Upshaw, Willie	88T	505	$ .01	$ .04	Valdez, Sergio	90T	199	$ .01	$ .10

BOB USHER

Player	Year	No.	VG	EX/MT
Valdez, Sergio	91T	98	$ .01	$ .03
Valdivielso, Jose	56T	237	$3.00	$9.00
Valdivielso, Jose	57T	246	$ .95	$3.50
Valdivielso, Jose	60T	527	$2.50	$10.00
Valdivielso, Jose	61T	557	$7.00	$21.00
Valdivielso, Jose	62T	339	$ .45	$1.45
Valentine, Bob	71T	188	$ .90	$3.00
Valentine, Bobby	72T	11	$ .05	$ .25
Valentine, Bobby	73T	502	$ .07	$ .30
Valentine, Bobby	74T	101	$ .07	$ .30
Valentine, Bobby	75T	215	$ .07	$ .30
Valentine, Bobby	76T	366	$ .05	$ .20
Valentine, Bobby	77T	629	$ .03	$ .12
Valentine, Bobby	78T	712	$ .05	$ .20
Valentine, Bobby	79T	428	$ .02	$ .10
Valentine, Bobby	80T	56	$ .01	$ .10
Valentine, Bobby	85TTR	126	$ .02	$ .10
Valentine, Bobby	86T	261	$ .01	$ .04
Valentine, Bobby	87T	118	$ .01	$ .04
Valentine, Bobby	88T	594	$ .01	$ .04
Valentine, Bobby	89T	314	$ .01	$ .05
Valentine, Bobby	90T	729	$ .01	$ .04
Valentine, Bobby	91T	489	$ .01	$ .03
Valentine, Corky	55T	44	$2.00	$6.00
Valentine, Ellis	76T	590	$ .15	$ .50
Valentine, Ellis	77T	52	$ .03	$ .12
Valentine, Ellis	78T	185	$ .02	$ .10
Valentine, Ellis	79T	535	$ .02	$ .10
Valentine, Ellis	80T	395	$ .01	$ .10
Valentine, Ellis	81T	445	$ .01	$ .10
Valentine, Ellis	81TTR	849	$ .02	$ .10
Valentine, Ellis	82T	15	$ .01	$ .07
Valentine, Ellis	83T	653	$ .01	$ .07
Valentine, Ellis	83TTR	120	$ .02	$ .10
Valentine, Ellis	84T	236	$ .01	$ .06
Valentine, Fred	64T	483	$ .50	$1.45
Valentine, Fred	66T	351	$ .30	$ .95
Valentine, Fred	67T	64	$ .30	$ .85
Valentine, Fred	68T	248	$ .30	$ .85
Valentinetti, Vito	57T	74	$ .95	$3.50

Vito Valentinetti

DETROIT TIGERS

Player	Year	No.	VG	EX/MT
Valentinetti, Vito	58T	463	$ .75	$2.20
Valentinetti, Vito	59T	44	$ .85	$3.50

Player	Year	No.	VG	EX/MT
Valenzuela, Fernando	81T	302	$1.25	$5.00
Valenzuela, Fernando	81TTR	850	$1.25	$5.00
Valenzuela, Fernando	82T	166	$ .03	$ .15
Valenzuela, Fernando	82T	510	$ .25	$1.00
Valenzuela, Fernando	82TAS	345	$ .05	$ .25
Valenzuela, Fernando	82THL	6	$ .05	$ .25
Valenzuela, Fernando	83T	40	$ .10	$ .50
Valenzuela, Fernando	83T	681	$ .01	$ .07
Valenzuela, Fernando	84T	220	$ .30	$ .25
Valenzuela, Fernando	85T	440	$ .05	$ .25
Valenzuela, Fernando	86T	630	$ .03	$ .25
Valenzuela, Fernando	86TB	401	$ .02	$ .15
Valenzuela, Fernando	86TRB	207	$ .01	$ .10
Valenzuela, Fernando	87T	410	$ .03	$ .15
Valenzuela, Fernando	87TAS	604	$ .01	$ .10
Valenzuela, Fernando	88T	780	$ .01	$ .10
Valenzuela, Fernando	88TBB	18	$ .01	$ .10
Valenzuela, Fernando	89T	150	$ .01	$ .10
Valenzuela, Fernando	90T	340	$ .01	$ .04
Valenzuela, Fernando	91T	80	$ .01	$ .10
Valera, Julio	91T	504	$ .01	$ .10
Valle, Dave	87TTR	122	$ .01	$ .05
Valle, Dave	88T	583	$ .01	$ .04
Valle, Dave	88TBB	210	$ .01	$ .06
Valle, Dave	89T	498	$ .01	$ .05
Valle, Dave	89TBB	56	$ .01	$ .06
Valle, Dave	90T	76	$ .01	$ .04
Valle, Dave	91T	178	$ .01	$ .03
Valle, Hector	65T	561	$2.50	$10.00
Valle, Hector	66T	314	$ .30	$ .95
Valo, Elmer	51Trb	28	$1.50	$4.00
Valo, Elmer	52T	34	$15.00	$47.50
Valo, Elmer	53T	122	$4.50	$15.00
Valo, Elmer	54T	145	$2.50	$10.00
Valo, Elmer	55T	145	$2.00	$6.00
Valo, Elmer	56T	3	$2.25	$6.00
Valo, Elmer	57T	54	$ .95	$3.50
Valo, Elmer	58T	323	$ .45	$1.50
Valo, Elmer	60T	237	$ .75	$3.00
Valo, Elmer	61T	186	$ .35	$1.25
Van Cuyk, Chris	52T	53	$15.00	$47.50
Van Gorder, Dave	83T	322	$ .01	$ .07
Van Gorder, Dave	86T	143	$ .01	$ .04
Van Slyke, Andy	84T	206	$ .75	$3.00
Van Slyke, Andy	85T	551	$ .10	$ .40
Van Slyke, Andy	86T	683	$ .01	$ .25
Van Slyke, Andy	87T	33	$ .01	$ .10
Van Slyke, Andy	87TTR	124	$ .01	$ .10
Van Slyke, Andy	88T	142	$ .01	$ .04
Van Slyke, Andy	88TBB	184	$ .01	$ .10
Van Slyke, Andy	89T	350	$ .01	$ .10
Van Slyke, Andy	89TAS	392	$ .01	$ .06
Van Slyke, Andy	89TBB	255	$ .01	$ .10
Van Slyke, Andy	90T	775	$ .01	$ .04
Van Slyke, Andy	91T	425	$ .01	$ .03
Vance, Sandy	71T	34	$ .15	$ .50
VandeBerg, Ed	82TTR	122	$ .02	$ .10
VandeBerg, Ed	83T	183	$ .01	$ .07
VandeBerg, Ed	84T	63	$ .01	$ .06
VandeBerg, Ed	85T	566	$ .01	$ .05
VandeBerg, Ed	86T	357	$ .01	$ .04
VandeBerg, Ed	86TTR	118	$ .02	$ .10
VandeBerg, Ed	87T	717	$ .01	$ .04
VandeBerg, Ed	87TTR	123	$ .01	$ .05
VandeBerg, Ed	88T	421	$ .01	$ .04
VandeBerg, Ed	89T	242	$ .01	$ .05
Varney, Pete	76T	413	$ .05	$ .20
Varsho, Gary	89T	613	$ .01	$ .10
Vasquez, Rafael	80T	672	$ .01	$ .10
Vatcher, Jim	91T	196	$ .01	$ .10

TOPPS

Player	Year	No.	VG	EX/MT
Vaughn, Charley	67T	179	$ .30	$ .85
Vaughn, Greg	89TMLD	128	$ .01	$1.00
Vaughn, Greg	90T	57	$ .01	$ .75
Vaughn, Greg	91T	347	$ .01	$ .15
Veal, Coot	59T	52	$ .85	$3.50
Veal, Coot	61T	432	$ .75	$3.00
Veal, Coot	63T	573	$1.75	$4.50
Veale, Bob	62T	593	$7.00	$21.00
Veale, Bob	63T	87	$ .30	$ .95
Veale, Bob	64T	501	$ .50	$1.45
Veale, Bob	65T	12	$1.75	$4.50
Veale, Bob	65T	195	$ .30	$ .85
Veale, Bob	66T	225	$1.00	$4.00
Veale, Bob	66T	425	$ .30	$ .95
Veale, Bob	67T	238	$1.75	$4.50
Veale, Bob	67T	335	$ .30	$ .85
Veale, Bob	68T	70	$ .30	$ .85
Veale, Bob	69T	8	$ .75	$3.00

Player	Year	No.	VG	EX/MT
Veale, Bob	69T	520	$ .30	$ .95
Veale, Bob	70T	236	$ .15	$ .50
Veale, Bob	71T	368	$ .15	$ .50
Veale, Bob	72T	729	$ .75	$2.50
Veale, Bob	73T	518	$ .15	$ .50
Vega, Jesus	83T	308	$ .01	$ .07
Veintidos, Juan	75T	621	$ .15	$ .50
Velarde, Randy	89T	584	$ .01	$ .05
Velarde, Randy	89TBB	239	$ .01	$ .06
Velarde, Randy	90T	23	$ .01	$ .04
Velarde, Randy	91T	379	$ .01	$ .03
Velez, Otto	74T	606	$ .07	$ .30
Velez, Otto	77T	299	$ .03	$ .12
Velez, Otto	78T	59	$ .02	$ .10
Velez, Otto	79T	462	$ .02	$ .10
Velez, Otto	80T	703	$ .01	$ .10
Velez, Otto	81T	351	$ .01	$ .10
Velez, Otto	82T	155	$ .01	$ .07
Venable, Max	81T	484	$ .01	$ .10
Venable, Max	83T	634	$ .01	$ .07
Venable, Max	84T	58	$ .01	$ .06
Venable, Max	86T	428	$ .01	$ .04

Player	Year	No.	VG	EX/MT
Venable, Max	87T	226	$ .01	$ .04
Ventura, Robin	88TTR	124	$ .50	$2.50
Ventura, Robin	89T	764	$ .15	$ .75
Ventura, Robin	89TBB	65	$ .01	$ .25
Ventura, Robin	89TMLD	129	$ .01	$ .35
Ventura, Robin	90T	121	$ .01	$ .35
Ventura, Robin	91T	461	$ .01	$ .10
Verbanic, Joe	67T	442	$ .30	$ .95
Verbanic, Joe	68T	29	$ .30	$ .85
Verbanic, Joe	69T	541	$ .30	$ .95
Verbanic, Joe	70T	416	$ .15	$ .50
Veres, Randy	89TMLD	130	$ .01	$ .06
Veres, Randy	90TTR	125	$ .01	$ .05
Veres, Randy	91T	694	$ .01	$ .03
Verhoeven, John	77T	91	$ .03	$ .12
Verhoeven, John	78T	329	$ .02	$ .10
Verhoeven, John	81T	603	$ .01	$ .10
Verhoeven, John	82T	281	$ .01	$ .07
Vernon, Mickey	51Tbb	13	$4.00	$18.00
Vernon, Mickey	52T	106	$6.00	$17.50
Vernon, Mickey	56T	228	$3.00	$9.00
Vernon, Mickey	57T	92	$ .95	$3.50
Vernon, Mickey	58T	233	$ .45	$1.50
Vernon, Mickey	59T	115	$ .90	$3.00
Vernon, Mickey	60T	467	$ .95	$3.50
Vernon, Mickey	61T	134	$ .35	$1.25
Vernon, Mickey	62T	152	$ .45	$1.45
Vernon, Mickey	63T	402	$ .45	$1.50
Versalles, Zorro "Zoilo"	61T	21	$ .35	$1.25
Versalles, Zoilo	62T	499	$ .75	$2.50
Versalles, Zoilo	63T	349	$ .45	$1.50
Versalles, Zoilo	64T	15	$ .30	$ .95
Versalles, Zoilo	65T	157	$ .45	$1.45
Versalles, Zoilo	66T	400	$ .30	$ .95
Versalles, Zoilo	67T	270	$ .30	$ .85
Versalles, Zoilo	68T	315	$ .30	$ .85
Versalles, Zoilo	69T	38	$ .30	$ .85
Versalles, Zoilo	70T	365	$ .15	$ .50
Versalles, Zoilo	75T	203	$ .45	$1.45
Veryzer, Tom	75T	623	$7.00	$21.00
Veryzer, Tom	76T	432	$ .05	$ .20
Veryzer, Tom	77T	145	$ .03	$ .12
Veryzer, Tom	78T	633	$ .02	$ .10
Veryzer, Tom	79T	537	$ .02	$ .10
Veryzer, Tom	80T	276	$ .01	$ .10
Veryzer, Tom	81T	39	$ .01	$ .10
Veryzer, Tom	82T	387	$ .01	$ .07
Veryzer, Tom	82TTR	123	$ .02	$ .10
Veryzer, Tom	83T	496	$ .01	$ .07
Veryzer, Tom	83TTR	121	$ .02	$ .10
Veryzer, Tom	84T	117	$ .01	$ .06
Veryzer, Tom	85T	405	$ .01	$ .05
Vezendy, Gerry	65T	509	$ .75	$3.00
Vidal, Jose	67T	499	$ .75	$3.00
Vidal, Jose	68T	432	$ .30	$ .85
Vidal, Jose	69T	322	$ .30	$ .95
Villanueva, Hector	90TTR	126	$ .01	$ .20
Villanueva, Hector	91T	362	$ .01	$ .10
Vineyard, Dave	65T	169	$ .30	$ .85
Vinson, Chuck	68T	328	$ .30	$ .85
Viola, Frank	83T	586	$3.00	$9.00
Viola, Frank	84T	28	$ .25	$1.00
Viola, Frank	85T	266	$ .10	$ .50
Viola, Frank	85TAS	710	$ .01	$ .10
Viola, Frank	86T	742	$ .01	$ .35
Viola, Frank	87T	310	$ .01	$ .25
Viola, Frank	88T	625	$ .01	$ .15
Viola, Frank	88TBB	201	$ .01	$ .15
Viola, Frank	89T	120	$ .01	$ .15
Viola, Frank	89TAS	406	$ .01	$ .10

Player	Year	No.	VG	EX/MT
Viola, Frank	89TBB	140	$ .01	$ .25
Viola, Frank	90T	470	$ .01	$ .10
Viola, Frank	91T	60	$ .01	$ .10
Viola, Frank	91TAS	406	$ .01	$ .03
Virdon, Bill	56T	170	$1.50	$4.00

BILL Virdon
PITTSBURGH PIRATES OUTFIELD

Player	Year	No.	VG	EX/MT
Virdon, Bill	57T	110	$ .60	$2.50
Virdon, Bill	58T	198	$ .45	$1.50
Virdon, Bill	59T	190	$ .75	$2.20
Virdon, Bill	59T	543	$8.50	$25.00
Virdon, Bill	60T	496	$ .85	$3.50
Virdon, Bill	61T	70	$ .75	$3.00
Virdon, Bill	62T	415	$ .85	$3.50
Virdon, Bill	63T	55	$ .35	$1.25
Virdon, Bill	64T	495	$ .75	$2.20
Virdon, Bill	65T	69	$ .15	$ .50
Virdon, Bill	72T	661	$ .90	$3.00
Virdon, Bill	73T	517	$ .30	$ .95
Virdon, Bill	78T	279	$ .02	$ .10
Virdon, Bill	83T	516	$ .01	$ .07
Virdon, Bill	84T	111	$ .01	$ .06
Virgil, Jr., Ozzie	82T	231	$ .25	$1.00
Virgil, Jr., Ozzie	83T	383	$ .01	$ .07
Virgil, Jr., Ozzie	84T	484	$ .01	$ .06
Virgil, Jr., Ozzie	85T	143	$ .01	$ .10
Virgil, Jr., Ozzie	85T	611	$ .01	$ .05
Virgil, Jr., Ozzie	86T	95	$ .01	$ .04
Virgil, Jr., Ozzie	86TTR	119	$ .02	$ .10
Virgil, Jr., Ozzie	87T	571	$ .01	$ .04
Virgil, Jr., Ozzie	88T	755	$ .01	$ .04
Virgil, Ossie	57T	365	$ .85	$3.50
Virgil, Ossie	58T	107	$ .85	$3.50
Virgil, Ossie	59T	203	$ .75	$2.20
Virgil, Ossie	61T	67	$ .35	$1.25
Virgil, Ozzie (Ossie)	62T	327	$ .45	$1.45
Virgil, Ossie	65T	571	$1.75	$4.50
Virgil, Ozzie (Ossie)	67T	132	$ .30	$ .85
Virgil, Ossie	85T	143	$ .01	$ .10
Virgil, Ozzie	88TBB	148	$ .01	$ .06
Virgil, Ozzie	89T	179	$ .01	$ .05
Vizcaino, Jose	89TMLD	131	$ .01	$ .06

Player	Year	No.	VG	EX/MT
Vizquel, Omar	89TMLD	132	$ .01	$ .06
Vizquel, Omar	89TTR	122	$ .01	$ .25
Vizquel, Omar	90T	698	$ .01	$ .04
Vizquel, Omar	91T	298	$ .01	$ .03
Vollmer, Clyde	52T	255	$12.00	$40.00
Vollmer, Clyde	53T	32	$4.50	$15.00
Von Hoff, Bruce	68T	529	$ .35	$1.25
Von Ohlen, Dave	84T	489	$ .01	$ .06
Von Ohlen, Dave	85T	177	$ .01	$ .05
Von Ohlen, Dave	85TTR	127	$ .02	$ .10
Von Ohlen, Dave	86T	632	$ .01	$ .04
Von Ohlen, Dave	87T	287	$ .01	$ .04
Voss, Bill	66T	529	$5.00	$20.00
Voss, Bill	68T	142	$ .30	$ .85
Voss, Bill	69T	621	$ .30	$ .95
Voss, Bill	70T	326	$ .15	$ .50
Voss, Bill	71T	671	$ .75	$2.50
Voss, Bill	72T	776	$ .75	$2.50
Vossler, Dan	74T	602	$ .07	$ .30
Vuckovich, Pete	77T	517	$ .12	$ .40
Vuckovich, Pete	78T	241	$ .02	$ .10
Vuckovich, Pete	79T	407	$ .02	$ .10
Vuckovich, Pete	80T	57	$ .01	$ .10
Vuckovich, Pete	81T	193	$ .01	$ .10
Vuckovich, Pete	81TTR	851	$ .02	$ .10
Vuckovich, Pete	82T	165	$ .03	$ .15
Vuckovich, Pete	82T	643	$ .02	$ .10
Vuckovich, Pete	82T	703	$ .03	$ .15
Vuckovich, Pete	83T	321	$ .01	$ .10
Vuckovich, Pete	83T	375	$ .01	$ .07
Vuckovich, Pete	83TAS	394	$ .01	$ .07
Vuckovich, Pete	84T	505	$ .01	$ .06
Vuckovich, Pete	85T	254	$ .01	$ .05
Vuckovich, Pete	86T	737	$ .01	$ .04
Vukovich, George	81T	598	$ .01	$ .10
Vukovich, George	82T	389	$ .01	$ .07
Vukovich, George	83T	16	$ .01	$ .07
Vukovich, George	83TTR	122	$ .02	$ .10
Vukovich, George	84T	638	$ .01	$ .06
Vukovich, George	85T	212	$ .01	$ .05
Vukovich, George	86T	483	$ .01	$ .04
Vukovich, John	73T	451	$ .07	$ .30
Vukovich, John	74T	349	$ .07	$ .30
Vukovich, John	75T	602	$ .07	$ .30
Waddell, Tom	84TTR	125	$ .02	$ .10
Waddell, Tom	85T	453	$ .01	$ .05
Waddell, Tom	86T	86	$ .01	$ .04
Waddell, Tom	87T	657	$ .01	$ .04
Wade, Ben	52T	389	$40.00	$140.00
Wade, Ben	53T	4	$4.50	$15.00
Wade, Ben	54T	126	$2.50	$10.00
Wade, Gale	55T	196	$5.25	$15.00
Wagner, Gary	66T	151	$ .30	$ .95
Wagner, Gary	67T	529	$ .75	$3.00
Wagner, Gary	68T	448	$ .30	$ .85
Wagner, Gary	69T	276	$ .30	$ .95
Wagner, Gary	70T	627	$ .30	$ .95
Wagner, Gary	71T	473	$ .15	$ .50
Wagner, Honus	76TAS	344	$ .75	$3.00
Wagner, Leon	59T	257	$ .90	$3.00
Wagner, Leon	60T	383	$ .75	$2.20
Wagner, Leon	61T	547	$6.00	$17.00
Wagner, Leon	62T	491	$ .75	$2.50
Wagner, Leon	63T	4	$ .50	$2.00
Wagner, Leon	63T	335	$ .45	$1.50
Wagner, Leon	64T	41	$ .75	$2.25
Wagner, Leon	64T	530	$1.75	$4.50
Wagner, Leon	65T	367	$ .35	$1.25
Wagner, Leon	66T	65	$ .30	$ .95
Wagner, Leon	67T	109	$ .50	$1.50

Player	Year	No.	VG	EX/MT	Player	Year	No.	VG	EX/MT
Wagner, Leon	67T	360	$ .30	$ .85	Walker, Harry	69T	633	$ .30	$ .95
Wagner, Leon	68T	495	$ .35	$1.25	Walker, Harry	70T	32	$ .15	$ .50
Wagner, Leon	69T	187	$ .30	$ .85	Walker, Harry	71T	312	$ .15	$ .50
Wagner, Mark	77T	490	$ .03	$ .12	Walker, Harry	72T	249	$ .05	$ .25
Wagner, Mark	79T	598	$ .02	$ .10	Walker, Jerry	58T	113	$ .75	$3.00
Wagner, Mark	80T	29	$ .01	$ .10	Walker, Jerry	59T	144	$ .75	$2.20
Wagner, Mark	81T	358	$ .01	$ .10	Walker, Jerry	60T	399	$ .90	$3.00
Wagner, Mark	81TTR	852	$ .02	$ .10	Walker, Jerry	60T	540	$2.50	$10.00
Wagner, Mark	82T	443	$ .01	$ .07	Walker, Jerry	61T	85	$ .35	$1.25
Wagner, Mark	83T	144	$ .01	$ .07	Walker, Jerry	62T	357	$ .45	$1.45
Wagner, Mark	85T	581	$ .01	$ .05	Walker, Jerry	63T	413	$ .45	$1.50
Waitkus, Eddie	51Tbb	51	$7.50	$22.50	Walker, Jerry	64T	77	$ .30	$ .95
Waitkus, Eddie	52T	158	$7.00	$20.00	Walker, Larry	89TMLD	133	$ .01	$ .15
Waits, Rick	76T	433	$ .05	$ .20	Walker, Larry	90T	757	$ .01	$ .25
Waits, Rick	77T	306	$ .03	$ .12	Walker, Larry	91T	339	$ .01	$ .10
Waits, Rick	78T	37	$ .02	$ .10	Walker, Luke	66T	498	$ .65	$1.75
Waits, Rick	79T	484	$ .02	$ .10	Walker, Luke	67T	123	$ .30	$ .85
Waits, Rick	80T	168	$ .01	$ .10	Walker, Luke	68T	559	$ .35	$1.25
Waits, Rick	81T	697	$ .01	$ .10	Walker, Luke	69T	36	$ .30	$ .85
Waits, Rick	82T	573	$ .01	$ .07	Walker, Luke	70T	322	$ .15	$ .50
Waits, Rick	83T	779	$ .01	$ .07	Walker, Luke	71T	68	$ .15	$ .50
Waits, Rick	83TTR	123	$ .02	$ .10	Walker, Luke	71T	534	$ .35	$1.25
Waits, Rick	84T	218	$ .01	$ .06	Walker, Luke	72T	471	$ .05	$ .25
Waits, Rick	85T	59	$ .01	$ .05	Walker, Luke	73T	187	$ .07	$ .30
Waits, Rick	86T	614	$ .01	$ .04	Walker, Luke	74T	612	$ .07	$ .30
Wakefield, Bill	64T	576	$1.75	$4.50	Walker, Luke	74TTR	612	$ .07	$ .30
Wakefield, Bill	65T	167	$ .30	$ .85	Walker, Luke	75T	474	$ .07	$ .30
Wakefield, Bill	66T	443	$ .30	$ .95	Walker, Mike	91T	593	$ .01	$ .10
Walden, Ronnie	91T	596	$ .01	$ .25	Walker, Tom	73T	41	$ .07	$ .30
Walewander, Jim	88T	106	$ .01	$ .10	Walker, Tom	74T	193	$ .07	$ .30
Walewander, Jim	89T	467	$ .01	$ .05	Walker, Tom	75T	627	$ .07	$ .30
Walk, Bob	81T	494	$ .01	$ .10	Walker, Tom	76T	186	$ .05	$ .20
Walk, Bob	81TTR	853	$ .02	$ .10	Walker, Tom	77T	652	$ .03	$ .12
Walk, Bob	82T	296	$ .01	$ .07	Walker, Tony	87T	24	$ .01	$ .10
Walk, Bob	83T	104	$ .01	$ .07	Wall, Murray	53T	217	$4.50	$15.00
Walk, Bob	86TTR	120	$ .02	$ .10	Wall, Murray	58T	410	$ .75	$3.00
Walk, Bob	87T	628	$ .01	$ .04	Wall, Murray	59T	42	$ .85	$3.50
Walk, Bob	88T	349	$ .01	$ .04	Wall, Stan	76T	584	$ .05	$ .20
Walk, Bob	89T	504	$ .01	$ .05					
Walk, Bob	90T	754	$ .01	$ .04					
Walk, Bob	91T	29	$ .01	$ .03					
Walker, Al "Rube"	52T	319	$40.00	$140.00					
Walker, "Rube"	53T	134	$4.50	$15.00					
Walker, "Rube"	54T	153	$2.50	$10.00					
Walker, "Rube"	55T	108	$2.00	$6.00					
Walker, "Rube"	56T	333	$1.30	$5.00					
Walker, Al	57T	147	$ .95	$3.50					
Walker, Al	58T	203	$ .75	$3.00					
Walker, "Rube"	73T	257	$ .75	$3.00					
Walker, "Rube"	74T	179	$ .75	$3.00					
Walker, Chico	87T	695	$ .01	$ .04					
Walker, Dixie	53T	190	$4.50	$15.00					
Walker, Duane	83T	243	$ .01	$ .07					
Walker, Duane	84T	659	$ .01	$ .06					
Walker, Duane	85T	441	$ .01	$ .05					
Walker, Duane	86T	22	$ .01	$ .04					
Walker, Greg	83TTR	124	$ .05	$ .50					
Walker, Greg	84T	518	$ .05	$ .25					
Walker, Greg	85T	623	$ .01	$ .05					
Walker, Greg	86T	123	$ .01	$ .04					
Walker, Greg	87T	397	$ .01	$ .04					
Walker, Greg	88T	764	$ .01	$ .04					
Walker, Greg	88TBB	105	$ .01	$ .06					
Walker, Greg	89T	408	$ .01	$ .05					
Walker, Greg	89TBB	4	$ .01	$ .06					
Walker, Greg	90T	33	$ .01	$ .04					
Walker, Harry	60T	468	$ .95	$3.50					
Walker, Harry	65T	438	$ .35	$1.25					
Walker, Harry	66T	318	$ .15	$ .50	Wall, Stan	77T	88	$ .03	$ .12
Walker, Harry	67T	448	$ .30	$ .95	Wallace, Don	67T	367	$ .30	$ .85

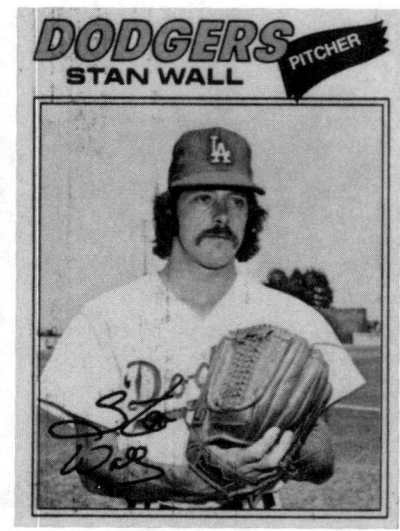

DODGERS
STAN WALL
PITCHER

Player	Year	No.	VG	EX/MT	Player	Year	No.	VG	EX/MT
Wallace, Mike	74T	608	$ .07	$ .30	Ward, Duane	90T	28	$ .01	$ .04
Wallace, Mike	75T	401	$ .07	$ .30	Ward, Duane	91T	181	$ .01	$ .03
Wallace, Mike	77T	539	$ .03	$ .12	Ward, Gary	80T	669	$ .06	$ .30
Wallach, Tim	82T	191	$ .75	$3.00	Ward, Gary	81T	328	$ .01	$ .10
Wallach, Tim	83T	552	$ .05	$ .35	Ward, Gary	82T	612	$ .01	$ .07
Wallach, Tim	84T	232	$ .01	$ .20	Ward, Gary	83T	517	$ .01	$ .07
Wallach, Tim	85T	473	$ .01	$ .15	Ward, Gary	84T	67	$ .01	$ .06
Wallach, Tim	86T	685	$ .01	$ .10	Ward, Gary	84TTR	126	$ .02	$ .10
Wallach, Tim	86TAS	703	$ .01	$ .04	Ward, Gary	85T	414	$ .01	$ .05
Wallach, Tim	87T	55	$ .01	$ .04	Ward, Gary	86T	105	$ .01	$ .04
Wallach, Tim	88T	560	$ .01	$ .10	Ward, Gary	87T	762	$ .01	$ .04
Wallach, Tim	88TAS	399	$ .01	$ .04	Ward, Gary	87TTR	125	$ .01	$ .05
Wallach, Tim	88TBB	7	$ .01	$ .06	Ward, Gary	88T	235	$ .01	$ .04
Wallach, Tim	89T	720	$ .01	$ .05	Ward, Gary	88TBB	195	$ .01	$ .06
Wallach, Tim	89TBB	215	$ .01	$ .06	Ward, Gary	89T	302	$ .01	$ .05
Wallach, Tim	90T	370	$ .01	$ .04	Ward, Gary	89TBB	206	$ .01	$ .06
Wallach, Tim	91T	220	$ .01	$ .03	Ward, Gary	89TTR	124	$ .01	$ .06
Waller, Ty	82T	51	$ .03	$ .15	Ward, Gary	90T	679	$ .01	$ .04
Walling, Denny	77T	473	$12.50	$50.00	Ward, Gary	91T	556	$ .01	$ .03
Walling, Denny	79T	553	$ .02	$ .10	Ward, Jay	64T	116	$3.00	$10.00
Walling, Denny	80T	306	$ .01	$ .10	Ward, Jay	65T	421	$ .35	$1.25
Walling, Denny	81T	439	$ .01	$ .10	Ward, Pete	63T	324	$ .45	$1.50
Walling, Denny	82T	147	$ .01	$ .07	Ward, Pete	64T	85	$ .30	$ .95
Walling, Denny	83T	692	$ .01	$ .07	Ward, Pete	65T	215	$ .35	$1.25
Walling, Denny	84T	36	$ .01	$ .06	Ward, Pete	66T	25	$ .30	$ .95
Walling, Denny	85T	382	$ .01	$ .05	Ward, Pete	67T	143	$ .30	$ .85
Walling, Denny	86T	504	$ .01	$ .04	Ward, Pete	67T	436	$ .30	$ .95
Walling, Denny	87T	222	$ .01	$ .04	Ward, Pete	68T	33	$ .30	$ .85
Walling, Denny	88T	719	$ .01	$ .04					
Walling, Denny	89T	196	$ .01	$ .05					
Walling, Denny	90T	462	$ .01	$ .04					
Wallis, Joe	76T	598	$ .05	$ .20					
Wallis, Joe	77T	279	$ .03	$ .12					
Wallis, Joe	78T	614	$ .02	$ .10					
Wallis, Joe	79T	406	$ .02	$ .10					
Wallis, Joe	80T	562	$ .01	$ .10					
Walls, Lee	57T	52	$ .95	$3.50					
Walls, Lee	58T	66	$ .85	$3.50					
Walls, Lee	59T	105	$ .85	$3.50					
Walls, Lee	60T	506	$ .90	$3.00					
Walls, Lee	61T	78	$ .35	$1.25					
Walls, Lee	62T	129	$ .25	$1.25					
Walls, Lee	63T	11	$ .30	$ .95					
Walls, Lee	64T	411	$ .50	$1.45					
Walsh, Dave	91T	367	$ .01	$ .10					
Walter, Gene	86TTR	121	$ .02	$ .10					
Walter, Gene	87T	248	$ .01	$ .04					
Walter, Gene	89T	758	$ .01	$ .05					
Walters, Ken	60T	511	$2.50	$10.00					
Walters, Ken	61T	394	$ .75	$3.00					
Walters, Ken	62T	328	$ .45	$1.45					
Walters, Ken	63T	534	$1.75	$4.50					
Walters, Mike	84T	673	$ .01	$ .06					
Walters, Mike	85T	187	$ .01	$ .05					
Walton, Danny	70T	134	$ .15	$ .50					
Walton, Danny	71T	281	$ .15	$ .50					
Walton, Danny	73T	516	$ .07	$ .30					
Walton, Danny	78T	263	$ .02	$ .10	Ward, Pete	69T	155	$ .30	$ .85
Walton, Jerome	89TMLD	134	$ .01	$ .50	Ward, Pete	70T	659	$ .75	$2.00
Walton, Jerome	89TTR	123	$ .01	$1.00	Ward, Pete	71T	667	$ .75	$2.50
Walton, Jerome	90T	464	$ .01	$ .20	Ward, Preston	53T	173	$4.50	$15.00
Walton, Jerome	91T	135	$ .01	$ .03	Ward, Preston	54T	72	$7.00	$22.00
Walton, Jim	73T	646	$ .75	$3.00	Ward, Preston	55T	95	$2.00	$6.00
Walton, Jim	74T	99	$ .07	$ .30	Ward, Preston	56T	328	$1.30	$5.00
Walton, Reggie	82T	711	$ .25	$1.00	Ward, Preston	57T	226	$ .95	$3.50
Ward, Chris	75T	587	$ .07	$ .30	Ward, Preston	58T	450	$1.50	$4.00
Ward, Colby	91T	31	$ .01	$ .15	Ward, Preston	59T	176	$ .75	$2.20
Ward, Duane	87T	153	$ .01	$ .04	Ward, Turner	91T	555	$ .01	$ .20
Ward, Duane	88T	696	$ .01	$ .04	Warden, Jon	69T	632	$ .30	$ .95
Ward, Duane	89T	502	$ .01	$ .05					

Player	Year	No.	VG	EX/MT
Wardle, Curt	86T	303	$ .01	$ .04
Warner, Jack D.	65T	354	$ .35	$1.25
Warner, Jackie	65T	517	$ .75	$3.00
Warner, Jackie	66T	553	$5.00	$20.00
Warren, Mike	84T	338	$ .01	$ .06
Warren, Mike	84T	5	$ .02	$ .10
Warren, Mike	85T	197	$ .01	$ .05
Warthen, Dan	76T	374	$ .05	$ .20
Warthen, Dan	77T	391	$ .03	$ .12
Warwick, Carl	62T	202	$ .45	$1.45
Warwick, Carl	63T	333	$ .45	$1.50
Warwick, Carl	64T	179	$ .30	$ .95
Warwick, Carl	65T	357	$ .35	$1.25
Warwick, Carl	66T	247	$ .30	$ .95
Washburn, Greg	70T	74	$ .15	$ .50
Washburn, Ray	62T	19	$ .45	$1.45
Washburn, Ray	63T	206	$ .30	$ .95
Washburn, Ray	64T	332	$ .30	$ .95
Washburn, Ray	65T	467	$ .75	$3.00
Washburn, Ray	66T	399	$ .30	$ .95
Washburn, Ray	67T	92	$ .30	$ .85
Washburn, Ray	68T	388	$ .30	$ .85
Washburn, Ray	69T	415	$ .30	$ .85
Washburn, Ray	70T	22	$ .15	$ .50
Washington Team, N.L.	74T	226	$1.50	$4.50

CLAUDELL WASHINGTON

Player	Year	No.	VG	EX/MT
Washington, Claudell	75T	647	$ .75	$2.00
Washington, Claudell	76T	189	$ .07	$ .30
Washington, Claudell	76T	198	$ .15	$ .50
Washington, Claudell	77T	405	$ .03	$ .12
Washington, Claudell	78T	67	$ .05	$ .20
Washington, Claudell	79T	574	$ .05	$ .20
Washington, Claudell	80T	322	$ .01	$ .10
Washington, Claudell	81T	151	$ .01	$ .10
Washington, Claudell	81TTR	854	$ .02	$ .10
Washington, Claudell	82T	126	$ .01	$ .07
Washington, Claudell	82T	758	$ .01	$ .07
Washington, Claudell	83T	235	$ .01	$ .07
Washington, Claudell	84T	410	$ .01	$ .06
Washington, Claudell	85T	540	$ .01	$ .05
Washington, Claudell	86T	675	$ .01	$ .04

Player	Year	No.	VG	EX/MT
Washington, Claudell	86TTR	122	$ .02	$ .10
Washington, Claudell	87T	15	$ .01	$ .04
Washington, Claudell	88T	335	$ .01	$ .04
Washington, Claudell	88TBB	178	$ .01	$ .06
Washington, Claudell	89T	185	$ .01	$ .05
Washington, Claudell	89TTR	125	$ .01	$ .06
Washington, Claudell	90T	705	$ .01	$ .04
Washington, Herb	75T	407	$ .07	$ .30
Washington, LaRue	80T	233	$ .01	$ .10
Washington, Ron	82TTR	124	$ .02	$ .10
Washington, Ron	83T	458	$ .01	$ .07
Washington, Ron	84T	623	$ .01	$ .06
Washington, Ron	85T	329	$ .01	$ .05
Washington, Ron	86T	513	$ .01	$ .04
Washington, Ron	87T	169	$ .01	$ .04
Washington, Ron	88TTR	125	$ .01	$ .06
Washington, Team	56T	146	$3.00	$9.00
Washington, Team	59T	397	$1.50	$4.50
Washington, U. L.	78T	707	$12.50	$50.00
Washington, U. L.	79T	157	$ .02	$ .10
Washington, U. L.	80T	508	$ .01	$ .10
Washington, U. L.	81T	26	$ .01	$ .10
Washington, U. L.	82T	329	$ .01	$ .07
Washington, U. L.	83T	687	$ .01	$ .07
Washington, U. L.	84T	294	$ .01	$ .06
Washington, U. L.	85T	431	$ .01	$ .05
Washington, U. L.	85TTR	128	$ .02	$ .10
Washington, U. L.	86T	113	$ .01	$ .04
Waslewski, Gary	69T	438	$ .30	$ .85
Waslewski, Gary	70T	607	$ .30	$ .95
Waslewski, Gary	71T	277	$ .15	$ .50
Waslewski, Gary	72T	108	$ .05	$ .25
Wathan, John	77T	218	$ .30	$ .85
Wathan, John	78T	343	$ .02	$ .10
Wathan, John	79T	99	$ .02	$ .10
Wathan, John	80T	547	$ .01	$ .10
Wathan, John	81T	157	$ .01	$ .10
Wathan, John	82T	429	$ .01	$ .07
Wathan, John	83T	746	$ .01	$ .07
Wathan, John	83TRB	6	$ .01	$ .07
Wathan, John	84T	602	$ .01	$ .06
Wathan, John	85T	308	$ .01	$ .05
Wathan, John	86T	128	$ .01	$ .04
Wathan, John	88T	534	$ .01	$ .04
Wathan, John	89T	374	$ .01	$ .05
Wathan, John	90T	789	$ .01	$ .04
Wathan, John	91T	291	$ .01	$ .03
Watkins, Bob	70T	227	$ .35	$1.25
Watkins, Dave	70T	168	$ .15	$ .50
Watson, Bob	69T	562	$ .45	$1.45
Watson, Bob	70T	407	$ .15	$ .50
Watson, Bob	71T	222	$ .15	$ .50
Watson, Bob	72T	355	$ .05	$ .25
Watson, Bob	73T	110	$ .07	$ .30
Watson, Bob	74T	370	$ .07	$ .30
Watson, Bob	75T	227	$ .07	$ .30
Watson, Bob	76T	20	$ .05	$ .20
Watson, Bob	77T	540	$ .03	$ .12
Watson, Bob	78T	330	$ .05	$ .20
Watson, Bob	79T	130	$ .02	$ .10
Watson, Bob	80T	480	$ .01	$ .10
Watson, Bob	81T	690	$ .02	$ .10
Watson, Bob	82T	275	$ .01	$ .07
Watson, Bob	82TTR	125	$ .05	$ .20
Watson, Bob	83T	572	$ .01	$ .07
Watson, Bob	84T	739	$ .01	$ .06
Watson, Bob	85T	51	$ .01	$ .05
Watt, Eddie	66T	442	$ .30	$ .95
Watt, Eddie	67T	271	$ .30	$ .85
Watt, Eddie	68T	186	$ .30	$ .85

Player	Year	No.	VG	EX/MT	Player	Year	No.	VG	EX/MT
Watt, Eddie	69T	652	$ .30	$ .95	Weis, Al	63T	537	$175.00	$550.00
Watt, Eddie	70T	497	$ .15	$ .50	Weis, Al	64T	168	$ .30	$ .95
Watt, Eddie	71T	122	$ .15	$ .50	Weis, Al	65T	516	$ .75	$3.00
Watt, Eddie	72T	128	$ .05	$ .25	Weis, Al	66T	66	$ .30	$ .95
Watt, Eddie	73T	362	$ .07	$ .30	Weis, Al	67T	556	$1.50	$4.00
Watt, Eddie	74T	534	$ .07	$ .30	Weis, Al	68T	313	$ .30	$ .85
Watt, Eddie	74TTR	534	$ .07	$ .30	Weis, Al	69T	269	$ .30	$ .95
Watt, Eddie	75T	374	$ .07	$ .30	Weis, Al	70T	498	$ .15	$ .50
Waugh, Jim	53T	178	$4.50	$15.00	Weis, Al	71T	751	$ .90	$3.00
Wayne, Gary	89TMLD	135	$ .01	$ .06	Weiss, Walt	88TBB	263	$ .10	$ .45
Wayne, Gary	90T	348	$ .01	$ .04	Weiss, Walt	88TTR	126	$ .01	$ .40
Wayne, Gary	91T	207	$ .01	$ .03	Weiss, Walt	89T	316	$ .10	$ .25
Weaver, Earl	69T	516	$2.25	$6.00	Weiss, Walt	89TBB	305	$ .01	$ .15
Weaver, Earl	70T	148	$ .15	$ .75	Weiss, Walt	90T	165	$ .01	$ .10
Weaver, Earl	71T	477	$ .45	$1.45	Weiss, Walt	91T	455	$ .01	$ .03
Weaver, Earl	72T	323	$ .30	$ .85	Welch, Bob	79T	318	$ .45	$1.45
Weaver, Earl	73T	136	$ .15	$ .50	Welch, Bob	80T	146	$ .05	$ .25
Weaver, Earl	74T	306	$ .15	$ .50	Welch, Bob	81T	624	$ .03	$ .15
Weaver, Earl	78T	211	$ .02	$ .10	Welch, Bob	82T	82	$ .01	$ .07
Weaver, Earl	83T	426	$ .01	$ .10	Welch, Bob	83T	454	$ .01	$ .10
Weaver, Earl	85TTR	129	$ .05	$ .20	Welch, Bob	84T	306	$ .01	$ .06
Weaver, Earl	86T	321	$ .01	$ .04	Welch, Bob	84T	722	$ .02	$ .10
Weaver, Earl	87T	568	$ .01	$ .04	Welch, Bob	85T	291	$ .01	$ .05
Weaver, Floyd	65T	546	$1.75	$4.50	Welch, Bob	86T	549	$ .01	$ .04
Weaver, Floyd	66T	231	$ .30	$ .95	Welch, Bob	87T	328	$ .01	$ .04
Weaver, Floyd	71T	227	$ .15	$ .50	Welch, Bob	88T	118	$ .01	$ .04
Weaver, Jim	68T	328	$ .30	$ .85	Welch, Bob	88TTR	127	$ .01	$ .06
Weaver, Jim	69T	134	$ .30	$ .85	Welch, Bob	89T	605	$ .01	$ .05
Weaver, Roger	81T	626	$ .01	$ .10	Welch, Bob	90T	475	$ .01	$ .04
Webb, Hank	73T	610	$ .45	$1.45	Welch, Bob	91T	50	$ .01	$ .03
Webb, Hank	75T	615	$ .30	$ .95	Welch, Bob	91TAS	394	$ .01	$ .03
Webb, Hank	76T	442	$ .05	$ .20	Wellman, Bob	52T	41	$15.00	$47.50
Webster, Lenny	89TMLD	136	$ .01	$ .15	Wellman, Brad	84T	109	$ .01	$ .06
Webster, Mitch	86T	629	$ .02	$ .15	Wellman, Brad	85T	409	$ .01	$ .05
Webster, Mitch	87T	442	$ .01	$ .04	Wellman, Brad	86T	41	$ .01	$ .04
Webster, Mitch	88T	138	$ .01	$ .04	Wells, Boomer	82T	203	$ .70	$3.00
Webster, Mitch	88TBB	150	$ .01	$ .06	Wells, David	88TTR	128	$ .01	$ .10
Webster, Mitch	89T	36	$ .01	$ .05	Wells, David	89T	567	$ .01	$ .10
Webster, Mitch	90T	502	$ .01	$ .04	Wells, David	90T	229	$ .01	$ .04
Webster, Mitch	90TTR	127	$ .01	$ .05	Wells, David	91T	619	$ .01	$ .03
Webster, Mitch	91T	762	$ .01	$ .03	Welsh, Chris	82T	376	$ .01	$ .07
Webster, Ramon	67T	603	$3.00	$12.00	Welsh, Chris	83T	118	$ .01	$ .07
Webster, Ramon	68T	164	$ .30	$ .85	Welsh, Chris	83TTR	125	$ .02	$ .10
Webster, Ramon	69T	618	$ .30	$ .95	Welsh, Chris	86T	52	$ .01	$ .04
Webster, Ray	59T	531	$2.50	$10.00	Welsh, Chris	87T	592	$ .01	$ .04
Webster, Ray	60T	452	$ .90	$3.00	Wenz, Fred	69T	628	$ .30	$ .95
Weekly, Johnny	62T	204	$ .45	$1.45	Wenz, Fred	71T	92	$ .15	$ .50
Weekly, Johnny	64T	256	$ .30	$ .95	Werhas, John	64T	456	$ .50	$1.45
Wegener, Mike	69T	284	$ .30	$ .95	Werhas, John	65T	453	$ .75	$3.00
Wegener, Mike	70T	193	$ .15	$ .50	Werhas, John	67T	514	$ .75	$3.00
Wegener, Mike	71T	608	$ .35	$1.25	Werle, Bill	53T	170	$4.50	$15.00
Wegman, Bill	86TTR	123	$ .02	$ .10	Werle, Bill	54T	144	$2.50	$10.00
Wegman, Bill	87T	179	$ .01	$ .04	Werle, William	51Trb	33	$1.50	$4.00
Wegman, Bill	88T	538	$ .01	$ .04	Werle, William	52T	73	$15.00	$47.50
Wegman, Bill	88TBB	244	$ .01	$ .06	Werner, Don	78T	702	$ .02	$ .10
Wegman, Bill	89T	768	$ .01	$ .05	Werner, Don	83T	504	$ .01	$ .07
Wegman, Bill	90T	333	$ .01	$ .04	Wert, Don	62T	299	$ .45	$1.45
Wegman, Bill	91T	617	$ .01	$ .03	Wert, Don	64T	19	$ .30	$ .95
Wehmeier, Herman	51Tbb	47	$7.50	$22.50	Wert, Don	65T	271	$ .35	$1.25
Wehmeier, Herman	52T	80	$15.00	$47.50	Wert, Don	66T	253	$ .30	$ .95
Wehmeier, Herman	53T	110	$4.50	$15.00	Wert, Don	67T	511	$ .75	$3.00
Wehmeier, Herman	54T	162	$2.50	$10.00	Wert, Don	68T	178	$ .30	$ .85
Wehmeier, Herman	55T	29	$2.00	$6.00	Wert, Don	69T	443	$ .30	$ .85
Wehmeier, Herman	56T	78	$2.25	$6.00	Wert, Don	70T	33	$ .15	$ .50
Wehmeier, Herm	57T	81	$ .95	$3.50	Wert, Don	71T	307	$ .15	$ .50
Wehmeier, Herm	58T	248	$ .75	$3.00	Werth, Dennis	81T	424	$ .01	$ .10
Wehmeier, Herm	59T	421	$ .75	$2.20	Werth, Dennis	82T	154	$ .01	$ .07
Wehrmeister, Dave	77T	472	$ .03	$ .12	Werth, Dennis	82TTR	126	$ .02	$ .10
Wehrmeister, Dave	82T	694	$ .01	$ .07	Wertz, Vic	51Tbb	40	$4.00	$18.00
Weik, Dick	54T	224	$2.50	$10.00	Wertz, Vic	52T	244	$5.50	$17.50

Player	Year	No.	VG	EX/MT	Player	Year	No.	VG	EX/MT
Wertz, Vic	53T	142	$4.50	$15.00	White Sox, Team	60T	208	$1.75	$7.00
Wertz, Vic	56T	300	$1.30	$5.00	White Sox, Team	61T	7	$ .85	$3.50
Wertz, Vic	57T	78	$ .60	$2.50	White Sox, Team	62T	113	$ .65	$1.75
Wertz, Vic	58T	170	$ .65	$2.00	White Sox, Team	63T	288	$1.50	$4.00
Wertz, Vic	59T	500	$ .75	$2.20	White Sox, Team	64T	496	$ .95	$3.50
Wertz, Vic	60T	111	$ .90	$3.00	White Sox, Team	65T	234	$ .90	$3.00
Wertz, Vic	61T	173	$ .75	$3.00	White Sox, Team	66T	426	$ .65	$1.75
Wertz, Vic	61T	340	$ .35	$1.25	White Sox, Team	67T	573	$7.00	$25.00
Wertz, Vic	62T	481	$ .75	$2.50	White Sox, Team	68T	424	$ .75	$3.00
Wertz, Vic	63T	348	$ .75	$3.00	White Sox, Team	70T	501	$ .45	$1.45
West, Dave	89T	787	$ .10	$ .50	White Sox, Team	71T	289	$ .45	$1.45
West, Dave	90T	357	$ .01	$ .10	White Sox, Team	72T	381	$ .15	$ .50
West, Dave	91T	578	$ .01	$ .03	White Sox, Team	73T	481	$ .15	$ .50
Westlake, Wally	51Trb	27	$1.50	$4.00	White Sox, Team	74T	416	$ .15	$ .50
Westlake, Wally	52T	38	$12.50	$45.00	White Sox, Team Checklist	75T	276	$ .15	$ .50
Westlake, Wally	53T	192	$4.50	$15.00	White Sox, Team Checklist	76T	656	$ .35	$1.25
Westlake, Wally	54T	92	$2.50	$10.00	White Sox, Team Checklist	77T	418	$ .15	$ .50
Westlake, Wally	55T	102	$2.00	$6.00	White Sox, Team Checklist	78T	66	$ .05	$ .25
Westlake, Wally	56T	81	$2.25	$6.00	White Sox, Team Checklist	79T	404	$ .05	$ .25
Weston, Mickey	89TMLD	137	$ .01	$ .25	White Sox, Team Checklist	80T	112	$ .05	$ .25
Weston, Mickey	90T	377	$ .01	$ .10	White Sox, Team Checklist	81T	664	$ .02	$ .20
Westrum, Wes	51Trb	37	$1.50	$4.00	White Sox, Team Leaders	86T	156	$ .01	$ .04
Westrum, Wes	52T	75	$15.00	$47.50	White Sox, Team Leaders	87T	356	$ .01	$ .04
Westrum, Wes	54T	180	$2.50	$10.00	White Sox, Team Leaders	88T	321	$ .01	$ .04
Westrum, Wes	56T	156	$1.50	$4.00	White Sox, Team Leaders	89T	21	$ .01	$ .05
Westrum, Wes	57T	323	$4.25	$15.00	White, Bill	59T	359	$5.00	$15.00
Westrum, Wes	60T	469	$ .95	$3.50	White, Bill	60T	355	$1.00	$4.00
Westrum, Wes	66T	341	$ .30	$ .95	White, Bill	61T	232	$ .75	$3.00
Westrum, Wes	67T	593	$5.00	$15.00	White, Bill	61T	451	$1.50	$4.00
Wetherby, Jeff	89TMLD	138	$ .01	$ .06	White, Bill	62T	14	$ .45	$1.45
Wetherby, Jeff	90T	142	$ .01	$ .10	White, Bill	63T	1	$5.00	$25.00
Wetteland, John	89TMLD	139	$ .01	$ .25	White, Bill	63T	290	$ .45	$1.45
Wetteland, John	90T	631	$ .01	$ .15	White, Bill	64T	11	$ .75	$3.00
Wheat, Leroy	54T	244	$2.50	$10.00	White, Bill	64T	240	$ .45	$1.45
Wheelock, Gary	77T	493	$ .25	$ .80	White, Bill	65T	190	$ .15	$ .50
Wheelock, Gary	78T	596	$ .02	$ .10	White, Bill	66T	397	$ .35	$1.25
Whisenant, Pete	57T	373	$ .85	$3.50	White, Bill	67T	290	$ .45	$1.45
Whisenant, Pete	58T	466	$ .75	$2.20	White, Bill	68T	190	$ .15	$ .50
Whisenant, Pete	59T	14	$ .85	$3.50	White, Bill	69T	588	$ .20	$ .50
Whisenant, Pete	60T	424	$ .75	$2.20	White, Charlie	55T	103	$2.00	$6.00
Whisenant, Pete	61T	201	$ .35	$1.25	White, Devon	87T	139	$ .10	$ .50
Whisenton, Larry	79T	715	$ .05	$ .20	White, Devon	88T	192	$ .01	$ .10
Whisenton, Larry	83T	544	$ .01	$ .07	White, Devon	88TBB	145	$ .01	$ .10
Whitaker, Lou	78T	704	$4.00	$12.00	White, Devon	89T	602	$ .01	$ .10
Whitaker, Lou	79T	123	$ .90	$3.50	White, Devon	89TBB	122	$ .01	$ .10
Whitaker, Lou	80T	358	$ .45	$1.50	White, Devon	90T	65	$ .01	$ .04
Whitaker, Lou	81T	234	$ .10	$ .75	White, Devon	91T	704	$ .01	$ .03
Whitaker, Lou	82T	39	$ .05	$ .35	White, Frank	74T	604	$1.00	$3.00
Whitaker, Lou	83T	509	$ .01	$ .25	White, Frank	75T	569	$ .15	$ .50
Whitaker, Lou	84T	666	$ .02	$ .10	White, Frank	76T	369	$ .05	$ .20
Whitaker, Lou	84T	695	$ .05	$ .25	White, Frank	77T	117	$ .03	$ .12
Whitaker, Lou	84TAS	398	$ .02	$ .10	White, Frank	78T	248	$ .02	$ .10
Whitaker, Lou	85T	480	$ .03	$ .15	White, Frank	79T	439	$ .02	$ .10
Whitaker, Lou	86T	20	$ .01	$ .04	White, Frank	80T	45	$ .01	$ .10
Whitaker, Lou	87T	661	$ .01	$ .10	White, Frank	81T	330	$ .01	$ .10
Whitaker, Lou	88T	770	$ .01	$ .10	White, Frank	82T	645	$ .01	$ .07
Whitaker, Lou	88TBB	99	$ .01	$ .10	White, Frank	82TIA	646	$ .01	$ .07
Whitaker, Lou	89T	320	$ .01	$ .05	White, Frank	83T	525	$ .01	$ .07
Whitaker, Lou	89TBB	22	$ .01	$ .10	White, Frank	84T	155	$ .01	$ .06
Whitaker, Lou	90T	280	$ .01	$ .10	White, Frank	85T	743	$ .01	$ .05
Whitaker, Lou	91T	145	$ .01	$ .03	White, Frank	86T	215	$ .01	$ .04
Whitaker, Steve	67T	277	$ .30	$ .85	White, Frank	87T	692	$ .01	$ .04
Whitaker, Steve	68T	383	$ .30	$ .85	White, Frank	88T	595	$ .01	$ .04
Whitaker, Steve	69T	71	$ .30	$ .85	White, Frank	88TBB	75	$ .01	$ .06
Whitaker, Steve	70T	496	$ .15	$ .50	White, Frank	89T	25	$ .01	$ .05
Whitby, Bill	67T	486	$ .75	$3.00	White, Frank	89TBB	200	$ .01	$ .06
White Sox, Team	56T	188	$6.00	$25.00	White, Frank	90T	479	$ .01	$ .04
White Sox, Team	57T	329	$10.00	$30.00	White, Frank	91T	352	$ .01	$ .03
White Sox, Team	58T	256	$3.00	$11.00	White, Jerry	76T	594	$ .05	$ .20
White Sox, Team	59T	94	$3.00	$12.00	White, Jerry	77T	557	$ .03	$ .12

Player	Year	No.	VG	EX/MT	Player	Year	No.	VG	EX/MT
White, Jerry	79T	494	$ .02	$ .10	Whitfield, Fred	64T	367	$ .30	$ .95
White, Jerry	80T	724	$ .01	$ .10	Whitfield, Fred	65T	283	$ .35	$1.25
White, Jerry	81T	42	$ .01	$ .10	Whitfield, Fred	66T	88	$ .30	$ .95
White, Jerry	82T	386	$ .01	$ .07	Whitfield, Fred	67T	275	$ .30	$ .85
White, Jerry	83T	214	$ .01	$ .07	Whitfield, Fred	68T	133	$ .30	$ .85
White, Jo-Jo	60T	460	$2.25	$6.00	Whitfield, Fred	69T	518	$ .30	$ .95
White, Mike	64T	492	$ .50	$1.45	Whitfield, Terry	75T	622	$2.25	$11.00
White, Mike	65T	31	$ .30	$ .85	Whitfield, Terry	76T	590	$ .15	$ .50
White, Roy	66T	234	$1.50	$5.00	Whitfield, Terry	78T	236	$ .02	$ .10
White, Roy	68T	546	$ .75	$3.00	Whitfield, Terry	79T	589	$ .02	$ .10
White, Roy	69T	25	$ .15	$ .50	Whitfield, Terry	80T	713	$ .01	$ .10
White, Roy	70T	373	$ .15	$ .50	Whitfield, Terry	81T	167	$ .01	$ .10
White, Roy	71T	395	$ .15	$ .50	Whitfield, Terry	85T	31	$ .01	$ .05
White, Roy	72T	340	$ .30	$ .95	Whitfield, Terry	86T	318	$ .01	$ .04
White, Roy	73T	25	$ .15	$ .50	Whitson, Eddie	79T	189	$ .08	$ .30
White, Roy	74T	135	$ .07	$ .30	Whitson, Eddie	80T	561	$ .01	$ .10
White, Roy	75T	375	$ .15	$ .50	Whitson, Eddie	81T	336	$ .01	$ .10
White, Roy	76T	225	$ .05	$ .20	Whitson, Eddie	82T	656	$ .01	$ .07
White, Roy	77T	485	$ .03	$ .12	Whitson, Eddie	82TTR	127	$ .02	$ .10
White, Roy	78T	16	$ .02	$ .10	Whitson, Eddie	83T	429	$ .01	$ .07
White, Roy	79T	159	$ .02	$ .10	Whitson, Eddie	83TTR	127	$ .02	$ .10
White, Roy	80T	648	$ .01	$ .10	Whitson, Eddie	84T	277	$ .01	$ .06
					Whitson, Eddie	85T	762	$ .01	$ .05
					Whitson, Eddie	85TTR	130	$ .02	$ .10
					Whitson, Eddie	86T	15	$ .01	$ .04
					Whitson, Eddie	87T	155	$ .01	$ .04
					Whitson, Eddie	88T	330	$ .01	$ .04
					Whitson, Eddie	88TBB	186	$ .01	$ .06
					Whitson, Eddie	89T	516	$ .01	$ .05
					Whitson, Eddie	89TBB	81	$ .01	$ .06
					Whitson, Eddie	90T	618	$ .01	$ .04
					Whitson, Eddie	91T	481	$ .01	$ .03
					Whitt, Ernie	78T	708	$7.00	$25.00
					Whitt, Ernie	79T	714	$ .02	$ .10
					Whitt, Ernie	81T	407	$ .01	$ .10
					Whitt, Ernie	82T	19	$ .01	$ .07
					Whitt, Ernie	83T	302	$ .01	$ .07
					Whitt, Ernie	84T	506	$ .01	$ .06
					Whitt, Ernie	85T	128	$ .01	$ .05
					Whitt, Ernie	86T	673	$ .01	$ .04
					Whitt, Ernie	87T	698	$ .01	$ .04
					Whitt, Ernie	88T	79	$ .01	$ .04
					Whitt, Ernie	88TBB	239	$ .01	$ .06
					Whitt, Ernie	89T	289	$ .01	$ .05
					Whitt, Ernie	89TBB	224	$ .01	$ .06
					Whitt, Ernie	90T	742	$ .01	$ .04
					Whitt, Ernie	90TTR	128	$ .01	$ .05
					Whitt, Ernie	91T	492	$ .01	$ .03
					Wickander, Kevin	89TMLD	142	$ .01	$ .10
					Wickander, Kevin	90T	528	$ .01	$ .10
					Wickander, Kevin	91T	246	$ .01	$ .03
					Wicker, Floyd	69T	524	$ .30	$ .95
White, Sam	52T	345	$40.00	$140.00	Wicker, Floyd	71T	97	$ .15	$ .50
White, Sammy	53T	139	$3.00	$9.00	Wickersham, Dave	61T	381	$ .75	$3.00
White, Sammy	56T	168	$2.25	$6.00	Wickersham, Dave	62T	517	$ .75	$2.50
White, Sammy	57T	163	$ .95	$3.50	Wickersham, Dave	63T	492	$2.50	$6.50
White, Sammy	58T	414	$ .75	$3.00	Wickersham, Dave	64T	181	$ .30	$ .95
White, Sammy	59T	486	$ .75	$2.20	Wickersham, Dave	65T	375	$ .35	$1.25
White, Sammy	60T	203	$ .45	$1.45	Wickersham, Dave	65T	9	$ .35	$1.25
White, Sammy	62T	494	$ .75	$2.50	Wickersham, Dave	66T	58	$ .30	$ .95
Whited, Ed	89TMLD	140	$ .01	$ .06	Wickersham, Dave	67T	112	$ .30	$ .85
Whited, Ed	90T	111	$ .01	$ .04	Wickersham, Dave	68T	288	$ .30	$ .85
Whitehouse, Len	83TTR	126	$ .02	$ .10	Wickersham, Dave	69T	647	$ .30	$ .95
Whitehouse, Len	84T	648	$ .01	$ .06	Widmar, Al	52T	133	$7.00	$20.00
Whitehouse, Len	85T	406	$ .01	$ .05	Widmar, Al	74T	99	$ .07	$ .30
Whitehurst, Wally	89TMLD	141	$ .01	$ .15	Wieand, Ted	60T	146	$ .45	$1.45
Whitehurst, Wally	90T	719	$ .01	$ .10	Wiesler, Bob	56T	327	$1.30	$5.00
Whitehurst, Wally	91T	557	$ .01	$ .03	Wiesler, Bob	57T	126	$ .95	$3.50
Whiten, Mark	91T	588	$ .01	$ .35	Wietelmann, Whitey	73T	12	$ .30	$ .85
Whitfield, Fred	63T	211	$ .30	$ .95	Wiggins, Alan	83T	251	$ .01	$ .07

SAM WHITE

Sammy White

Player	Year	No.	VG	EX/MT
Wiggins, Alan	84T	693	$ .01	$ .06
Wiggins, Alan	85T	378	$ .01	$ .05

ALAN WIGGINS

Player	Year	No.	VG	EX/MT
Wiggins, Alan	86T	508	$ .01	$ .04
Wiggins, Alan	87TTR	126	$ .01	$ .05
Wight, Bill	52T	177	$7.00	$20.00
Wight, Bill	56T	286	$2.25	$6.50
Wight, Bill	57T	340	$4.25	$15.00
Wight, Bill	58T	237	$ .75	$3.00
Wihtol, Sandy	80T	665	$ .01	$ .10
Wihtol, Sandy	81T	451	$ .01	$ .10
Wilber, Del	52T	383	$40.00	$140.00
Wilborn, Ted	80T	674	$ .01	$ .10
Wilcox, Milt	71T	164	$ .30	$ .95
Wilcox, Milt	72T	399	$ .05	$ .25
Wilcox, Milt	73T	134	$ .07	$ .30
Wilcox, Milt	74T	565	$ .07	$ .30
Wilcox, Milt	75T	14	$ .07	$ .30
Wilcox, Milt	78T	151	$ .02	$ .10
Wilcox, Milt	79T	288	$ .02	$ .10
Wilcox, Milt	80T	392	$ .01	$ .10
Wilcox, Milt	81T	658	$ .01	$ .10
Wilcox, Milt	82T	784	$ .01	$ .07
Wilcox, Milt	83T	457	$ .01	$ .07
Wilcox, Milt	84T	588	$ .01	$ .06
Wilcox, Milt	85T	99	$ .01	$ .05
Wilcox, Milt	86T	192	$ .01	$ .04
Wilfong, Rob	79T	633	$ .02	$ .10
Wilfong, Rob	80T	238	$ .01	$ .10
Wilfong, Rob	81T	453	$ .01	$ .10
Wilfong, Rob	82T	379	$ .01	$ .07
Wilfong, Rob	82TTR	128	$ .02	$ .10
Wilfong, Rob	83T	158	$ .01	$ .07
Wilfong, Rob	84T	79	$ .01	$ .06
Wilfong, Rob	85T	524	$ .01	$ .05
Wilfong, Rob	86T	658	$ .01	$ .04
Wilfong, Rob	87T	251	$ .01	$ .04
Wilhelm, Hoyt	52T	392	$150.00	$450.00
Wilhelm, Hoyt	53T	151	$17.50	$52.50
Wilhelm, Hoyt	54T	36	$12.00	$35.00
Wilhelm, Hoyt	56T	307	$7.50	$27.50

Player	Year	No.	VG	EX/MT
Wilhelm, Hoyt	57T	203	$6.00	$18.00
Wilhelm, Hoyt	58T	324	$5.00	$15.00
Wilhelm, Hoyt	59T	349	$4.50	$14.00
Wilhelm, Hoyt	60T	115	$ .75	$2.25
Wilhelm, Hoyt	60T	395	$2.25	$6.50
Wilhelm, Hoyt	61T	545	$17.00	$50.00
Wilhelm, Hoyt	62T	423	$1.50	$4.00
Wilhelm, Hoyt	62T	545	$17.00	$50.00
Wilhelm, Hoyt	63T	108	$2.75	$8.50
Wilhelm, Hoyt	64T	13	$2.00	$8.00
Wilhelm, Hoyt	65T	276	$2.00	$6.00
Wilhelm, Hoyt	66T	510	$4.50	$13.00
Wilhelm, Hoyt	67T	422	$2.00	$8.00
Wilhelm, Hoyt	68T	350	$1.25	$5.00
Wilhelm, Hoyt	69T	565	$1.50	$6.00
Wilhelm, Hoyt	70T	17	$1.00	$4.00
Wilhelm, Hoyt	71T	248	$1.00	$4.00
Wilhelm, Hoyt	72T	777	$5.00	$15.00
Wilhelm, Jim	80T	685	$ .01	$ .10
Wilkerson, Curt	84TTR	127	$ .02	$ .10
Wilkerson, Curt	85T	594	$ .01	$ .05
Wilkerson, Curt	86T	434	$ .01	$ .04
Wilkerson, Curt	87T	228	$ .01	$ .04
Wilkerson, Curt	88T	53	$ .01	$ .04
Wilkerson, Curt	88TBB	132	$ .01	$ .06
Wilkerson, Curt	89T	331	$ .01	$ .05
Wilkerson, Curt	89TTR	126	$ .01	$ .06
Wilkerson, Curt	90T	667	$ .01	$ .04
Wilkerson, Curt	91T	142	$ .01	$ .03
Wilkins, Dean	89TMLD	143	$ .01	$ .06
Wilkins, Eric	80T	511	$ .01	$ .10
Wilkins, Eric	81T	99	$ .01	$ .10
Wilkinson, Bill	87TTR	127	$ .01	$ .05
Wilkinson, Bill	88T	376	$ .01	$ .04
Wilkinson, Bill	89T	636	$ .01	$ .05
Wilks, Ted	52T	109	$7.00	$20.00
Wilks, Ted	53T	101	$4.50	$15.00
Will, Bob	59T	388	$ .75	$2.20
Will, Bob	60T	147	$ .45	$1.45
Will, Bob	61T	512	$ .75	$3.00
Will, Bob	62T	47	$ .45	$1.45
Will, Bob	63T	58	$ .30	$ .95
Willard, Jerry	85T	504	$ .01	$ .05
Willard, Jerry	86T	273	$ .01	$ .04
Willard, Jerry	87T	137	$ .01	$ .04
Willey, 'Carlton" (Carl)	58T	407	$ .75	$3.00
Willey, Carl	59T	95	$ .85	$3.50
Willey, Carl	60T	107	$ .45	$1.45
Willey, Carl	61T	105	$ .35	$1.25
Willey, Carl	62T	174	$ .90	$3.00
Willey, Carl	63T	528	$1.75	$4.50
Willey, Carl	64T	84	$ .30	$ .95
Willey, Carl	65T	401	$ .35	$1.25
Willhite, Nick	64T	14	$ .30	$ .95
Willhite, Nick	65T	284	$ .35	$1.25
Willhite, Nick	66T	171	$ .30	$ .95
Willhite, Nick	67T	249	$ .30	$ .85
Williams, Al	81T	569	$ .01	$ .10
Williams, Al	82T	69	$ .01	$ .10
Williams, Al	83T	731	$ .01	$ .07
Williams, Al	84T	183	$ .01	$ .06
Williams, Al	85T	614	$ .01	$ .05
Williams, Bernie	70T	401	$ .15	$ .50
Williams, Bernie	71T	728	$ .75	$2.50
Williams, Bernie	72T	761	$4.00	$12.00
Williams, Bernie	73T	557	$ .45	$1.45
Williams, Bernie	90T	701	$ .01	$ .25
Williams, Billy	61T	141	$35.00	$105.00
Williams, Billy	62T	288	$9.00	$28.00
Williams, Billy	63T	353	$7.00	$21.00

Player	Year	No.	VG	EX/MT	Player	Year	No.	VG	EX/MT
Williams, Billy	64T	175	$4.00	$12.00	Williams, Frank	88T	773	$ .01	$ .04
Williams, Billy	65T	4	$1.75	$4.50	Williams, Frank	89T	172	$ .01	$ .05
Williams, Billy	65T	220	$3.50	$11.00	Williams, Frank	89TTR	128	$ .01	$ .06
Williams, Billy	66T	217	$1.50	$4.00	Williams, Frank	90T	599	$ .01	$ .04
Williams, Billy	66T	580	$25.00	$75.00	Williams, George	63T	324	$ .45	$1.50
Williams, Billy	67T	315	$2.50	$10.00	Williams, George	64T	388	$ .50	$1.45
Williams, Billy	68T	37	$2.00	$8.00	Williams, Jim A.	70T	262	$ .15	$ .50
Williams, Billy	69T	4	$ .75	$2.25	Williams, Jim A.	71T	262	$ .15	$ .50
Williams, Billy	69T	450	$1.50	$6.00	Williams, Jimmy F.	66T	544	$4.00	$11.50
Williams, Billy	70T	170	$1.25	$5.00	Williams, Jimy	87T	786	$ .01	$ .04
Williams, Billy	71T	64	$ .50	$2.00	Williams, Jimy	88T	314	$ .01	$ .04
Williams, Billy	71T	66	$ .50	$2.00	Williams, Jimy	89T	594	$ .01	$ .05
Williams, Billy	71T	350	$1.30	$5.00	Williams, Ken	88T	559	$ .01	$ .04
Williams, Billy	72T	439	$ .95	$3.50	Williams, Ken	89T	34	$ .01	$ .05
Williams, Billy	72TIA	440	$ .35	$1.25	Williams, Ken	89TTR	129	$ .01	$ .06
Williams, Billy	73T	61	$ .50	$1.50	Williams, Ken	90T	327	$ .01	$ .04
Williams, Billy	73T	200	$ .75	$3.00	Williams, Ken	91T	274	$ .01	$ .03
Williams, Billy	74T	110	$ .75	$3.00	Williams, Matt	87TTR	129	$ .75	$3.50
Williams, Billy	74TAS	338	$ .45	$1.45	Williams, Matt	88T	372	$ .35	$1.50
Williams, Billy	75T	545	$ .75	$3.00	Williams, Matt	89T	628	$ .01	$ .35
Williams, Billy	76T	525	$ .75	$3.00	Williams, Matt	90T	41	$ .01	$ .10
Williams, Charlie	72T	388	$ .05	$ .25	Williams, Matt	91T	190	$ .01	$ .10
Williams, Charlie	75T	449	$ .07	$ .30	Williams, Matt	91TAS	399	$ .01	$ .03
Williams, Charlie	76T	332	$ .05	$ .20	Williams, Mitch	86TTR	125	$ .05	$ .50
Williams, Charlie	77T	73	$ .03	$ .12	Williams, Mitch	87T	291	$ .06	$ .35
Williams, Charlie	78T	561	$ .02	$ .10	Williams, Mitch	88T	26	$ .01	$ .10
Williams, Charlie	79T	142	$ .02	$ .10	Williams, Mitch	89T	411	$ .01	$ .10
Williams, Dana	89TMLD	144	$ .01	$ .06	Williams, Mitch	89TTR	130	$ .01	$ .15
Williams, Davey	52T	316	$40.00	$140.00	Williams, Mitch	90T	520	$ .01	$ .04
Williams, Davey	53T	120	$4.50	$15.00	Williams, Mitch	91T	335	$ .01	$ .03
Williams, Dick	52T	396	$70.00	$200.00	Williams, Reggie	87T	232	$ .01	$ .04
Williams, Dick	53T	125	$4.00	$13.00	Williams, Rick	79T	437	$ .02	$ .10
Williams, Dick	57T	59	$ .60	$2.50					
Williams, Dick	58T	79	$ .70	$2.25					
Williams, Dick	59T	292	$ .75	$2.20					
Williams, Dick	60T	188	$ .75	$3.00					
Williams, Dick	61T	8	$ .75	$3.00					
Williams, Dick	62T	382	$ .85	$3.50					
Williams, Dick	63T	328	$ .45	$1.45					
Williams, Dick	64T	153	$ .15	$ .50					
Williams, Dick	67T	161	$ .35	$1.25					
Williams, Dick	68T	87	$ .15	$ .50					
Williams, Dick	69T	349	$ .30	$ .95					
Williams, Dick	71T	714	$ .85	$3.50					
Williams, Dick	72T	137	$ .30	$ .85					
Williams, Dick	73T	179	$ .30	$ .95					
Williams, Dick	78T	522	$ .02	$ .10					
Williams, Dick	83T	366	$ .01	$ .07					
Williams, Dick	84T	742	$ .01	$ .06					
Williams, Dick	85T	66	$ .01	$ .05					
Williams, Dick	86T	681	$ .01	$ .04					
Williams, Dick	86TTR	124	$ .02	$ .10					
Williams, Dick	87T	418	$ .01	$ .04					
Williams, Dick	88T	104	$ .01	$ .04					
Williams, Don	60T	414	$ .75	$2.20					
Williams, Earl	71T	52	$ .15	$ .50					
Williams, Earl	72T	380	$ .05	$ .25					
Williams, Earl	73T	504	$ .07	$ .30					
Williams, Earl	74T	375	$ .07	$ .30					
Williams, Earl	75T	97	$ .07	$ .30					
Williams, Earl	76T	458	$ .05	$ .20					
Williams, Earl	77T	223	$ .03	$ .12					
Williams, Earl	78T	604	$ .02	$ .10	Williams, Rick	80T	69	$ .01	$ .10
Williams, Eddie	88T	758	$ .01	$ .25	Williams, Stan	59T	53	$ .85	$3.50
Williams, Eddie	89TTR	127	$ .01	$ .06	Williams, Stan	60T	278	$ .45	$1.45
Williams, Frank	84TTR	128	$ .05	$ .20	Williams, Stan	61T	45	$ .90	$3.00
Williams, Frank	85T	487	$ .01	$ .05	Williams, Stan	61T	190	$ .35	$1.25
Williams, Frank	86T	341	$ .01	$ .04	Williams, Stan	62T	60	$ .65	$1.75
Williams, Frank	87T	96	$ .01	$ .04	Williams, Stan	62T	515	$ .75	$2.50
Williams, Frank	87TTR	128	$ .01	$ .05	Williams, Stan	63T	42	$ .35	$1.25

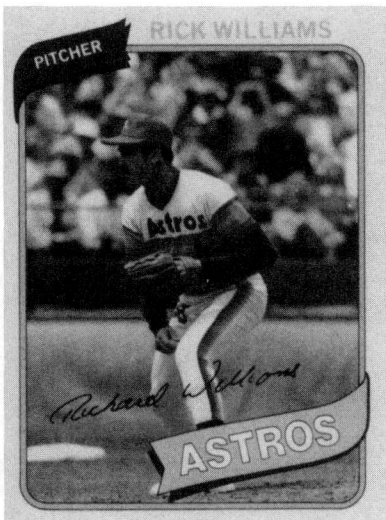

TOPPS

Player	Year	No.	VG	EX/MT	Player	Year	No.	VG	EX/MT
Williams, Stan	64T	505	$ .75	$2.20	Wills, Maury	77TB	435	$ .30	$ .85
Williams, Stan	65T	404	$ .35	$1.25	Wills, Maury	87TTB	315	$ .01	$ .04
Williams, Stan	68T	54	$ .30	$ .85	Wills, Ted	61T	548	$7.00	$21.00
Williams, Stan	69T	118	$ .30	$ .85	Wills, Ted	62T	444	$ .75	$2.50
Williams, Stan	70T	353	$ .15	$ .50	Wills, Ted	65T	488	$ .75	$3.00
Williams, Stan	71T	638	$ .35	$1.25	Wilmet, Paul	89TMLD	145	$ .01	$ .06
Williams, Stan	72T	9	$ .05	$ .25	Wilson, Archie	52T	327	$40.00	$140.00
Williams, Ted	54T	1	$150.00	$550.00	Wilson, Bill D.	54T	222	$2.50	$10.00
Williams, Ted	54T	250	$175.00	$625.00	Wilson, Bill D.	55T	86	$2.00	$6.00
Williams, Ted	55T	2	$100.00	$325.00	Wilson, Billy H.	67T	402	$ .30	$ .95
Williams, Ted	56T	5	$70.00	$225.00	Wilson, Billy H.	69T	576	$ .30	$ .95
Williams, Ted	57T	1	$90.00	$360.00	Wilson, Billy H.	70T	28	$ .15	$ .50
Williams, Ted	58T	1	$85.00	$350.00	Wilson, Billy H.	71T	192	$ .15	$ .50
Williams, Ted	58T	321	$11.00	$33.00	Wilson, Billy H.	72T	587	$ .30	$ .95
Williams, Ted	58TAS	485	$17.00	$55.00	Wilson, Billy H.	73T	619	$ .45	$1.45
Williams, Ted	69T	539	$2.25	$6.00	Wilson, Bob	53T	250	$12.50	$50.00
Williams, Ted	69T	650	$3.00	$9.00	Wilson, Bob	54T	58	$7.00	$22.00
Williams, Ted	70T	211	$1.50	$4.00	Wilson, Bob	57T	19	$ .95	$3.50
Williams, Ted	71T	380	$1.50	$4.00	Wilson, Bob "Red"	56T	92	$2.25	$6.00
Williams, Ted	72T	510	$1.50	$4.00	Wilson, Bob "Red"	58T	213	$ .75	$3.00
Williams, Ted	76TAS	347	$ .75	$2.25	Wilson, Bob "Red"	59T	24	$ .85	$3.50
Williams, Walt	67T	598	$2.00	$6.00	Wilson, Bob "Red"	60T	379	$ .75	$2.20
Williams, Walt	68T	172	$ .30	$ .85	Wilson, Craig	89TMLD	146	$ .01	$ .15
Williams, Walt	69T	309	$ .30	$ .95	Wilson, Craig	91T	566	$ .01	$ .10
Williams, Walt	70T	395	$ .15	$ .50	Wilson, Dan	91T	767	$ .01	$ .20
Williams, Walt	71T	555	$ .35	$1.25	Wilson, Don	68T	77	$ .15	$ .50
Williams, Walt	72T	15	$ .05	$ .25	Wilson, Don	69T	202	$ .30	$ .85
Williams, Walt	73T	297	$ .07	$ .30	Wilson, Don	70T	515	$ .15	$ .50
Williams, Walt	74T	418	$ .07	$ .30	Wilson, Don	71T	484	$ .15	$ .50
Williams, Walt	76T	123	$ .05	$ .20	Wilson, Don	72T	20	$ .05	$ .25
Williamson, Mark	88T	571	$ .01	$ .04	Wilson, Don	72T	91	$ .45	$1.45
Williamson, Mark	89T	546	$ .01	$ .05	Wilson, Don	73T	217	$ .07	$ .30
Williamson, Mark	89TBB	147	$ .01	$ .06	Wilson, Don	74T	304	$ .07	$ .30
Williamson, Mark	90T	13	$ .01	$ .04	Wilson, Don	75T	455	$ .07	$ .30
Williamson, Mark	91T	296	$ .01	$ .03	Wilson, Earl	60T	249	$ .45	$1.45
Willis, Carl	87T	101	$ .01	$ .04	Wilson, Earl	61T	69	$ .35	$1.25
Willis, Jim	54T	67	$7.00	$22.00	Wilson, Earl	63T	76	$ .30	$ .95
Willis, Mike	77T	493	$ .25	$ .80	Wilson, Earl	64T	503	$ .50	$1.45
Willis, Mike	78T	293	$ .02	$ .10	Wilson, Earl	65T	42	$ .30	$ .85
Willis, Mike	79T	688	$ .02	$ .10	Wilson, Earl	66T	575	$5.00	$20.00
Willis, Mike	81T	324	$ .01	$ .10	Wilson, Earl	67T	235	$ .45	$1.45
Willis, Ron	67T	592	$5.00	$15.00	Wilson, Earl	67T	237	$ .45	$1.45
Willis, Ron	68T	68	$ .30	$ .85	Wilson, Earl	67T	305	$ .30	$ .85
Willis, Ron	69T	273	$ .30	$ .95	Wilson, Earl	68T	10	$ .45	$1.45
Willoughby, Jim	73T	79	$ .07	$ .30	Wilson, Earl	68T	160	$ .30	$ .85
Willoughby, Jim	74T	553	$ .07	$ .30	Wilson, Earl	69T	525	$ .30	$ .95
Willoughby, Jim	76T	102	$ .05	$ .20	Wilson, Earl	70T	95	$ .15	$ .50
Willoughby, Jim	77T	532	$ .03	$ .12	Wilson, Earl	71T	301	$ .15	$ .50
Willoughby, Jim	78T	373	$ .02	$ .10	Wilson, Glenn	83T	332	$ .10	$ .45
Willoughby, Jim	79T	266	$ .02	$ .10	Wilson, Glenn	84T	563	$ .03	$ .15
Wills, Bump	77T	494	$ .12	$ .40	Wilson, Glenn	84TTR	129	$ .05	$ .20
Wills, Bump	78T	23	$ .02	$ .10	Wilson, Glenn	85T	454	$ .01	$ .05
Wills, Bump	79T	369	$ .75	$3.00	Wilson, Glenn	86T	736	$ .01	$ .04
Wills, Bump	80T	473	$ .01	$ .10	Wilson, Glenn	87T	97	$ .01	$ .04
Wills, Bump	81T	173	$ .01	$ .10	Wilson, Glenn	88T	626	$ .01	$ .04
Wills, Bump	82T	272	$ .01	$ .07	Wilson, Glenn	88TBB	260	$ .01	$ .06
Wills, Bump	82TTR	129	$ .02	$ .10	Wilson, Glenn	88TTR	129	$ .01	$ .06
Wills, Bump	83T	643	$ .01	$ .07	Wilson, Glenn	89T	293	$ .01	$ .05
Wills, Frank	86T	419	$ .01	$ .04	Wilson, Glenn	89TBB	284	$ .01	$ .06
Wills, Frank	87T	551	$ .01	$ .04	Wilson, Glenn	90T	112	$ .01	$ .04
Wills, Frank	90TTR	129	$ .01	$ .05	Wilson, Glenn	91T	476	$ .01	$ .03
Wills, Frank	91T	213	$ .01	$ .03	Wilson, Hack	79TRH	412	$ .15	$ .50
Wills, Maury	67T	570	$30.00	$90.00	Wilson, Jim	52T	276	$12.00	$40.00
Wills, Maury	68T	175	$ .75	$2.25	Wilson, Jim	53T	208	$1.75	$6.00
Wills, Maury	69T	45	$ .90	$3.00	Wilson, Jim	56T	171	$2.25	$6.00
Wills, Maury	70T	595	$ .75	$3.00	Wilson, Jim	57T	330	$4.25	$15.00
Wills, Maury	71T	385	$ .75	$3.00	Wilson, Jim	58T	163	$ .75	$3.00
Wills, Maury	72T	437	$ .15	$ .50	Wilson, Mookie	81T	259	$ .50	$2.00
Wills, Maury	72TIA	438	$ .07	$ .25	Wilson, Mookie	82T	143	$ .01	$ .07
Wills, Maury	75T	200	$1.25	$4.00	Wilson, Mookie	83T	55	$ .01	$ .07

Player	Year	No.	VG	EX/MT	Player	Year	No.	VG	EX/MT
Wilson, Mookie	83T	621	$ .01	$ .07	Wine, Bobby	65T	36	$ .30	$ .85
Wilson, Mookie	84T	246	$ .01	$ .06	Wine, Bobby	66T	284	$ .30	$ .95
Wilson, Mookie	84T	465	$ .01	$ .06	Wine, Bobby	67T	466	$ .75	$3.00
Wilson, Mookie	85T	775	$ .01	$ .05	Wine, Bobby	68T	396	$ .30	$ .85
Wilson, Mookie	86T	315	$ .01	$ .04	Wine, Bobby	69T	648	$ .30	$ .95
Wilson, Mookie	87T	625	$ .01	$ .04	Wine, Bobby	70T	332	$ .15	$ .50
Wilson, Mookie	88T	255	$ .01	$ .04	Wine, Bobby	71T	171	$ .15	$ .50
Wilson, Mookie	88TBB	182	$ .01	$ .06	Wine, Bobby	72T	657	$ .75	$2.50
Wilson, Mookie	89T	545	$ .01	$ .05	Wine, Bobby	73T	486	$ .30	$ .95
Wilson, Mookie	89TBB	231	$ .01	$ .06	Wine, Bobby	74T	119	$ .07	$ .30
Wilson, Mookie	90T	182	$ .01	$ .04	Wine, Bobby	86T	51	$ .01	$ .04
Wilson, Mookie	91T	727	$ .01	$ .03	Wine, Robbie	88T	119	$ .01	$ .10
Wilson, Steve	89TTR	131	$ .01	$ .15	Winfield, Dave	74T	456	$17.00	$55.00
Wilson, Steve	90T	741	$ .01	$ .04	Winfield, Dave	75T	61	$5.00	$15.00
Wilson, Steve	91T	69	$ .01	$ .03	Winfield, Dave	76T	160	$1.75	$7.00
Wilson, Trevor	89T	783	$ .01	$ .05	Winfield, Dave	77T	390	$1.10	$4.50
Wilson, Trevor	90T	408	$ .01	$ .04	Winfield, Dave	78T	530	$ .75	$3.00
Wilson, Trevor	91T	96	$ .01	$ .03	Winfield, Dave	79T	30	$ .75	$3.00
Wilson, Willie	79T	409	$ .45	$1.45	Winfield, Dave	80T	203	$ .08	$ .30
Wilson, Willie	80T	157	$ .03	$ .15	Winfield, Dave	80T	230	$ .50	$2.00
Wilson, Willie	80T	204	$ .02	$ .10	Winfield, Dave	81T	370	$ .45	$1.45
Wilson, Willie	81T	360	$ .05	$ .25	Winfield, Dave	81TTR	855	$ .30	$1.25
Wilson, Willie	81TRB	208	$ .01	$ .10	Winfield, Dave	82T	600	$ .30	$ .85
Wilson, Willie	82T	230	$ .03	$ .15	Winfield, Dave	82TAS	553	$ .06	$ .30
Wilson, Willie	83T	471	$ .01	$ .07	Winfield, Dave	83T	770	$ .10	$ .40
Wilson, Willie	83T	701	$ .01	$ .07	Winfield, Dave	84T	460	$ .08	$ .35
Wilson, Willie	83T	710	$ .01	$ .07	Winfield, Dave	84TAS	402	$ .05	$ .25
Wilson, Willie	84T	525	$ .05	$ .10	Winfield, Dave	85T	180	$ .05	$ .25
Wilson, Willie	85T	617	$ .01	$ .05	Winfield, Dave	85TAS	705	$ .03	$ .15
					Winfield, Dave	86T	70	$ .03	$ .25
					Winfield, Dave	86TAS	717	$ .02	$ .15
					Winfield, Dave	87T	770	$ .15	$ .50
					Winfield, Dave	88T	510	$ .01	$ .20
					Winfield, Dave	88TAS	392	$ .01	$ .10
					Winfield, Dave	88TBB	24	$ .05	$ .25
					Winfield, Dave	89T	260	$ .01	$ .10
					Winfield, Dave	89TAS	407	$ .01	$ .05
					Winfield, Dave	89TBB	314	$ .01	$ .15
					Winfield, Dave	90T	380	$ .01	$ .10
					Winfield, Dave	90TTR	130	$ .01	$ .05
					Winfield, Dave	91T	630	$ .01	$ .10
					Winkles, Bobby	73T	421	$ .07	$ .30
					Winkles, Bobby	74T	276	$ .07	$ .30
					Winkles, Bobby	78T	378	$ .02	$ .10
					Winn, Jim	85T	69	$ .01	$ .05
					Winn, Jim	86T	489	$ .01	$ .04
					Winn, Jim	87T	262	$ .01	$ .04
					Winn, Jim	87TTR	130	$ .01	$ .05
					Winn, Jim	88T	688	$ .01	$ .04
					Winningham, Herm	85TTR	131	$ .05	$ .20
					Winningham, Herm	86T	448	$ .01	$ .04
					Winningham, Herm	87T	141	$ .01	$ .04
					Winningham, Herm	88T	614	$ .01	$ .04
					Winningham, Herm	89T	366	$ .01	$ .05
					Winningham, Herm	89TBB	94	$ .01	$ .06
					Winningham, Herm	90T	94	$ .01	$ .04
					Winningham, Herm	91T	204	$ .01	$ .03
					Winters, Matt	89TMLD	147	$ .01	$ .06
Wilson, Willie	86T	25	$ .01	$ .04	Wirth, Alan	79T	711	$ .08	$ .30
Wilson, Willie	87T	783	$ .01	$ .10	Wise, Casey	57T	396	$ .85	$3.50
Wilson, Willie	88T	452	$ .01	$ .04	Wise, Casey	58T	247	$ .75	$3.00
Wilson, Willie	88TBB	21	$ .01	$ .06	Wise, Casey	59T	204	$ .75	$2.20
Wilson, Willie	89T	168	$ .01	$ .05	Wise, Casey	60T	342	$ .75	$2.20
Wilson, Willie	89TBB	136	$ .01	$ .06	Wise, Rick	64T	561	$2.10	$6.00
Wilson, Willie	90T	323	$ .01	$ .04	Wise, Rick	65T	322	$ .35	$1.25
Wilson, Willie	91T	208	$ .01	$ .03	Wise, Rick	67T	37	$ .30	$ .85
Wiltbank, Ben	79T	723	$ .05	$ .20	Wise, Rick	68T	262	$ .30	$ .85
Windhorn, Gordon	62T	254	$ .45	$1.45	Wise, Rick	69T	188	$ .30	$ .85
Wine, Bobby	63T	71	$ .30	$ .95	Wise, Rick	70T	605	$ .30	$ .95
Wine, Bobby	64T	347	$ .30	$ .95	Wise, Rick	71T	598	$ .35	$1.25

WILLIE WILSON

TOPPS

Player	Year	No.	VG	EX/MT
Wise, Rick	72T	43	$ .05	$ .25
Wise, Rick	72T	345	$ .05	$ .25

IN ACTION

Player	Year	No.	VG	EX/MT
Wise, Rick	72TIA	44	$ .05	$ .25
Wise, Rick	72TTR	756	$ .75	$2.25
Wise, Rick	73T	364	$ .07	$ .30
Wise, Rick	74T	84	$ .07	$ .30
Wise, Rick	74TAS	339	$ .30	$ .95
Wise, Rick	75T	56	$ .07	$ .30
Wise, Rick	76T	170	$ .05	$ .20
Wise, Rick	77T	455	$ .03	$ .12
Wise, Rick	78T	572	$ .02	$ .10
Wise, Rick	79T	253	$ .02	$ .10
Wise, Rick	80T	725	$ .01	$ .10
Wise, Rick	81T	616	$ .01	$ .10
Wise, Rick	82T	330	$ .01	$ .07
Witt, Bobby	86TTR	126	$ .08	$ .30
Witt, Bobby	87T	415	$ .15	$ .50
Witt, Bobby	88T	747	$ .01	$ .10
Witt, Bobby	89T	548	$ .01	$ .05
Witt, Bobby	89TBB	191	$ .01	$ .06
Witt, Bobby	90T	166	$ .01	$ .04
Witt, Bobby	91T	27	$ .01	$ .03
Witt, George	59T	110	$ .85	$3.50
Witt, George	60T	298	$ .75	$2.20
Witt, George	61T	286	$ .35	$1.25
Witt, George	62T	287	$ .45	$1.45
Witt, Mike	82T	744	$ .25	$1.00
Witt, Mike	83T	53	$ .05	$ .20
Witt, Mike	83T	651	$ .01	$ .07
Witt, Mike	84T	499	$ .01	$ .06
Witt, Mike	85T	309	$ .01	$ .05
Witt, Mike	87T	760	$ .03	$ .15
Witt, Mike	88T	270	$ .01	$ .10
Witt, Mike	88TBB	4	$ .01	$ .06
Witt, Mike	89T	190	$ .01	$ .05
Witt, Mike	90T	650	$ .01	$ .04
Witt, Mike	91T	536	$ .01	$ .03
Wockenfuss, Johnny	76T	13	$ .05	$ .20
Wockenfuss, Johnny	78T	723	$ .02	$ .10
Wockenfuss, Johnny	79T	231	$ .02	$ .10

Player	Year	No.	VG	EX/MT
Wockenfuss, Johnny	80T	338	$ .01	$ .10
Wockenfuss, Johnny	81T	468	$ .01	$ .10
Wockenfuss, Johnny	82T	629	$ .01	$ .07
Wockenfuss, Johnny	83T	536	$ .01	$ .07
Wockenfuss, Johnny	84T	119	$ .01	$ .06
Wockenfuss, Johnny	84TTR	130	$ .02	$ .10
Wockenfuss, Johnny	85T	39	$ .01	$ .05
Wohlford, Jim	73T	611	$ .45	$1.45
Wohlford, Jim	74T	407	$ .07	$ .30
Wohlford, Jim	75T	144	$ .07	$ .30
Wohlford, Jim	76T	286	$ .05	$ .20
Wohlford, Jim	77T	622	$ .03	$ .12
Wohlford, Jim	78T	376	$ .02	$ .10
Wohlford, Jim	79T	596	$ .02	$ .10
Wohlford, Jim	80T	448	$ .01	$ .10
Wohlford, Jim	81T	11	$ .01	$ .10
Wohlford, Jim	82T	116	$ .01	$ .07
Wohlford, Jim	83T	688	$ .01	$ .07
Wohlford, Jim	83TTR	128	$ .02	$ .10
Wohlford, Jim	84T	253	$ .01	$ .06
Wohlford, Jim	85T	787	$ .01	$ .05
Wohlford, Jim	86T	344	$ .01	$ .04
Wohlford, Jim	87T	527	$ .01	$ .04
Wojcik, John	63T	253	$ .30	$ .95
Wojna, Ed	86T	211	$ .01	$ .04
Wojna, Ed	87T	88	$ .01	$ .04
Wolf, Wally	63T	208	$ .30	$ .95
Wolf, Wally	70T	74	$ .15	$ .50
Wolfe, Larry	79T	137	$ .02	$ .10
Wolfe, Larry	80T	549	$ .01	$ .10
Womack, Dooley	66T	469	$5.00	$15.00
Womack, Dooley	67T	77	$ .30	$ .85
Womack, Dooley	68T	431	$ .30	$ .85
Womack, Dooley	69T	594	$ .30	$ .95
Wood, Jake	61T	514	$ .75	$3.00
Wood, Jake	62T	427	$ .75	$2.50
Wood, Jake	62T	72	$ .45	$1.45
Wood, Jake	63T	453	$2.50	$6.50
Wood, Jake	64T	272	$ .30	$ .95
Wood, Jake	65T	547	$1.75	$4.50
Wood, Jake	66T	509	$ .75	$2.50
Wood, Jake	67T	394	$ .30	$ .95
Wood, Ken	52T	139	$7.00	$20.00
Wood, Ted	88TTR	130	$ .05	$ .40
Wood, Ted	89TBB	308	$ .01	$ .10
Wood, Wilbur	64T	267	$ .45	$1.45
Wood, Wilbur	65T	478	$ .75	$3.00
Wood, Wilbur	67T	391	$ .30	$ .95
Wood, Wilbur	68T	585	$ .45	$1.45
Wood, Wilbur	69T	123	$ .30	$ .95
Wood, Wilbur	70T	342	$ .15	$ .50
Wood, Wilbur	71T	436	$ .15	$ .50
Wood, Wilbur	72T	92	$ .65	$2.25
Wood, Wilbur	72T	94	$ .40	$1.50
Wood, Wilbur	72T	342	$ .05	$ .25
Wood, Wilbur	72T	553	$ .45	$1.45
Wood, Wilbur	72TIA	554	$ .30	$ .95
Wood, Wilbur	73T	66	$ .45	$1.45
Wood, Wilbur	73T	150	$ .15	$ .50
Wood, Wilbur	74T	120	$ .07	$ .30
Wood, Wilbur	74T	205	$ .07	$ .30
Wood, Wilbur	75T	110	$ .07	$ .30
Wood, Wilbur	76T	368	$ .05	$ .20
Wood, Wilbur	77T	198	$ .03	$ .12
Wood, Wilbur	78T	726	$ .05	$ .20
Wood, Wilbur	79T	216	$ .02	$ .10
Woodard, Mike	87T	286	$ .01	$ .04
Woodeshick, Hal	59T	106	$ .85	$3.50
Woodeshick, Hal	60T	454	$ .90	$3.00
Woodeshick, Hal	61T	397	$ .75	$3.00

Player	Year	No.	VG	EX/MT
Woodeshick, Hal	62T	526	$3.95	$11.50
Woodeshick, Hal	63T	517	$1.75	$4.50
Woodeshick, Hal	64T	370	$ .30	$ .95
Woodeshick, Hal	65T	179	$ .30	$ .85
Woodeshick, Hal	66T	514	$ .75	$2.50
Woodeshick, Hal	67T	324	$ .30	$ .85
Woodling, Gene	52T	99	$10.00	$35.00
Woodling, Gene	53T	264	$18.00	$50.00
Woodling, Gene	54T	101	$5.00	$20.00
Woodling, Gene	55T	190	$3.005	$12.00
Woodling, Gene	56T	163	$1.50	$4.00

Player	Year	No.	VG	EX/MT
Woodling, Gene	57T	172	$ .60	$2.50
Woodling, Gene	58T	398	$ .45	$1.50
Woodling, Gene	59T	170	$ .75	$2.20
Woodling, Gene	60T	190	$ .75	$3.00
Woodling, Gene	61T	275	$ .35	$1.25
Woodling, Gene	62T	125	$ .75	$3.00
Woodling, Gene	63T	342	$ .75	$3.00
Woodling, Gene	63T	43	$1.00	$4.00
Woods, Alvis	77T	479	$ .03	$ .12
Woods, Alvis	78T	121	$ .02	$ .10
Woods, Alvis	79T	178	$ .02	$ .10
Woods, Alvis	80T	444	$ .01	$ .10
Woods, Alvis	81T	703	$ .01	$ .10
Woods, Alvis	82T	49	$ .01	$ .07
Woods, Alvis	83T	589	$ .01	$ .07
Woods, Gary	77T	492	$ .25	$ .80
Woods, Gary	78T	599	$ .02	$ .10
Woods, Gary	81T	172	$ .01	$ .10
Woods, Gary	82T	483	$ .01	$ .07
Woods, Gary	82TTR	130	$ .02	$ .10
Woods, Gary	83T	356	$ .01	$ .07
Woods, Gary	84T	231	$ .01	$ .06
Woods, Gary	85T	46	$ .01	$ .05
Woods, Gary	86T	611	$ .01	$ .04
Woods, Jim	61T	59	$ .35	$1.25
Woods, Ron	69T	544	$ .30	$ .95
Woods, Ron	70T	253	$ .15	$ .50
Woods, Ron	71T	514	$ .15	$ .50
Woods, Ron	72T	82	$ .05	$ .25

Player	Year	No.	VG	EX/MT
Woods, Ron	73T	531	$ .45	$1.45
Woods, Ron	74T	377	$ .07	$ .30
Woodson, Dick	70T	479	$ .15	$ .50
Woodson, Dick	71T	586	$ .35	$1.25
Woodson, Dick	72T	634	$ .30	$ .95
Woodson, Dick	73T	98	$ .07	$ .30
Woodson, Dick	74T	143	$ .07	$ .30
Woodson, George	69T	244	$ .30	$ .95
Woodson, Tracy	89T	306	$ .01	$ .05
Woodson, Tracy	89TBB	92	$ .01	$ .06
Woodward, Rob	87T	632	$ .01	$ .04
Woodward, Woody	64T	378	$ .50	$1.45
Woodward, Woody	65T	487	$ .75	$3.00
Woodward, Woody	66T	49	$ .30	$ .95
Woodward, Woody	67T	546	$1.50	$4.00
Woodward, Woody	68T	476	$ .35	$1.25
Woodward, Woody	69T	142	$ .30	$ .85
Woodward, Woody	70T	296	$ .15	$ .50
Woodward, Woody	71T	496	$ .15	$ .50
World Series '59, Celebration	60T	391	$2.25	$6.00
World Series '59, Game 1	60T	385	$ .90	$3.00
World Series '59, Game 2	60T	386	$ .90	$3.00
World Series '59, Game 3	60T	387	$ .75	$2.25
World Series '59, Game 4	60T	388	$2.25	$6.00
World Series '59, Game 5	60T	389	$2.25	$6.00
World Series '59, Game 6	60T	390	$ .90	$3.00
World Series '60, Celebrate	61T	313	$ .95	$3.50
World Series '60, Game 1	61T	306	$ .95	$3.50
World Series '60, Game 2	61T	307	$6.50	$20.00
World Series '60, Game 3	61T	308	$ .95	$3.50
World Series '60, Game 4	61T	309	$ .90	$3.00
World Series '60, Game 5	61T	310	$ .90	$3.00
World Series '60, Game 6	61T	311	$1.75	$4.50
World Series '60, Game 7	61T	312	$ .95	$3.50
World Series '61, Celebrate	62T	237	$ .90	$3.00
World Series '61, Game 1	62T	232	$ .75	$3.00
World Series '61, Game 2	62T	233	$ .75	$3.00
World Series '61, Game 3	62T	234	$2.50	$7.50
World Series '61, Game 4	62T	235	$1.75	$6.00
World Series '61, Game 5	62T	236	$ .75	$3.00
World Series '62, Game 1	63T	142	$1.00	$3.00
World Series '62, Game 2	63T	143	$ .75	$3.00
World Series '62, Game 3	63T	144	$1.50	$4.50
World Series '62, Game 4	63T	145	$ .75	$3.00
World Series '62, Game 5	63T	146	$ .75	$3.00
World Series '62, Game 6	63T	147	$ .75	$3.00
World Series '62, Game 7	63T	148	$ .90	$3.00
World Series '63, Game 1	64T	136	$5.00	$15.00
World Series '63, Game 2	64T	137	$ .75	$3.00
World Series '63, Game 3	64T	138	$ .75	$3.00
World Series '63, Game 4	64T	139	$ .75	$3.00
World Series '63, Summary	64T	140	$ .75	$2.25
World Series '64, Cards Celeb.	65T	139	$ .85	$2.50
World Series '64, Game 1	65T	132	$ .75	$2.25
World Series '64, Game 2	65T	133	$ .75	$2.25
World Series '64, Game 3	65T	134	$9.00	$35.00
World Series '64, Game 4	65T	135	$ .75	$2.25
World Series '64, Game 5	65T	136	$ .75	$2.25
World Series '64, Game 6	65T	137	$1.00	$3.00
World Series '64, Game 7	65T	138	$1.00	$3.00
World Series '66, Celebrate	67T	155	$ .90	$3.00
World Series '66, Game 1	67T	151	$ .45	$1.45
World Series '66, Game 2	67T	152	$ .90	$3.00
World Series '66, Game 3	67T	153	$ .45	$1.45
World Series '66, Game 4	67T	154	$ .45	$1.45
World Series '67, Cards Celeb.	68T	158	$ .75	$3.00
World Series '67, Game 1	68T	151	$ .75	$2.25
World Series '67, Game 2	68T	152	$1.50	$4.00
World Series '67, Game 3	68T	153	$ .45	$1.45
World Series '67, Game 4	68T	154	$ .90	$3.00

TOPPS

Player	Year	No.	VG	EX/MT	Player	Year	No.	VG	EX/MT
World Series '67, Game 5	68T	155	$ .75	$3.00	World Series '73, Game #2	74T	473	$ .65	$1.75
World Series '67, Game 6	68T	156	$ .75	$3.00	World Series '73, Game #3	74T	474	$ .45	$1.45
World Series '67, Game 7	68T	157	$ .75	$2.20	World Series '73, Game #4	74T	475	$ .45	$1.45
World Series '68, Game 1	69T	162	$1.75	$4.50	World Series '73, Game #5	74T	476	$ .45	$1.45
World Series '68, Game 2	69T	163	$ .75	$3.00	World Series '73, Game #6	74T	477	$ .65	$1.75
World Series '68, Game 3	69T	164	$ .75	$3.00	World Series '73, Game #7	74T	478	$ .45	$1.45
World Series '68, Game 4	69T	165	$ .75	$2.25	World Series '73, Summary	74T	479	$ .45	$1.45
World Series '68, Game 5	69T	166	$1.75	$4.50	World Series '74, Game 1	75T	461	$ .90	$3.00
World Series '68, Game 6	69T	167	$ .75	$3.00	World Series '74, Game 2	75T	462	$ .30	$ .95
World Series '68, Game 7	69T	168	$ .75	$2.25	World Series '74, Game 3	75T	463	$ .35	$1.25
World Series '68, Tigers Celeb.	69T	169	$ .75	$2.20	World Series '74, Game 4	75T	464	$ .35	$1.25
World Series '69, Celeb. Mets	70T	310	$ .75	$3.00	World Series '74, Game 5	75T	465	$ .35	$1.25
World Series '69, Game 1	70T	305	$ .45	$1.45	World Series '74, Summary	75T	466	$ .35	$1.25
World Series '69, Game 2	70T	306	$ .45	$1.45	World Series '75, Reds	76T	462	$ .30	$ .95
World Series '69, Game 3	70T	307	$ .45	$1.45	World Series '76, Reds	77T	411	$ .15	$ .50
World Series '69, Game 4	70T	308	$ .45	$1.45	World Series '76, Summary	77T	413	$ .03	$ .60
World Series '69, Game 5	70T	309	$ .45	$1.45	World Series '76, Yankees	77T	412	$ .15	$ .50
World Series '70, Game 1	71T	327	$ .45	$1.45	World Series, Phillies	81T	403	$ .03	$ .15
World Series '70, Game 2	71T	328	$ .45	$1.45	World Series, Phillies	81T	404	$ .03	$ .15
World Series '70, Game 3	71T	329	$ .90	$3.00	Worrell, Todd	86TTR	127	$ .05	$ .35
World Series '70, Game 4	71T	330	$ .45	$1.45	Worrell, Todd	87T	465	$ .01	$ .15
World Series '70, Game 5	71T	331	$ .90	$3.00	Worrell, Todd	87TAS	605	$ .01	$ .10
World Series '70, Summary	71T	332	$ .45	$1.45	Worrell, Todd	87TRB	7	$ .01	$ .04
					Worrell, Todd	88T	715	$ .01	$ .10
					Worrell, Todd	88TBB	149	$ .01	$ .06
					Worrell, Todd	89T	535	$ .01	$ .05
					Worrell, Todd	90T	95	$ .01	$ .04
					Wortham, Rich	80T	502	$ .01	$ .10
					Wortham, Rich	81T	107	$ .01	$ .10
					Worthington, Al	57T	39	$ .95	$3.50
					Worthington, Al	58T	427	$ .75	$3.00
					Worthington, "Red" Al	59T	28	$ .60	$ .75
					Worthington, Al	60T	268	$ .45	$1.45
					Worthington, Al	63T	556	$1.75	$4.50
					Worthington, Al	64T	144	$ .30	$ .95
					Worthington, Al	65T	216	$ .35	$1.25
					Worthington, Al	66T	181	$ .30	$ .95
					Worthington, Al	67T	399	$ .30	$ .95
					Worthington, Al	68T	473	$ .35	$1.25
					Worthington, Al	73T	49	$ .30	$ .85
					Worthington, Craig	89T	181	$ .01	$ .35
					Worthington, Craig	90T	521	$ .01	$ .10
					Worthington, Craig	91T	73	$ .01	$ .03
					Wright, Clyde	69T	583	$ .30	$ .95
					Wright, Clyde	70T	543	$ .15	$ .50
					Wright, Clyde	71T	240	$ .15	$ .50
					Wright, Clyde	71T	67	$ .15	$ .50
					Wright, Clyde	72T	55	$ .05	$ .25
					Wright, Clyde	73T	373	$ .07	$ .30
					Wright, Clyde	74T	525	$ .07	$ .30
					Wright, Clyde	75T	408	$ .07	$ .30
					Wright, Clyde	76T	559	$ .05	$ .20
					Wright, Ed	52T	368	$40.00	$140.00
World Series '71, Celebration	72T	230	$ .45	$1.45	Wright, George	83T	299	$ .01	$ .07
World Series '71, Game 1	72T	223	$ .15	$ .50	Wright, George	84T	688	$ .01	$ .06
World Series '71, Game 2	72T	224	$ .15	$ .50	Wright, George	85T	443	$ .01	$ .05
World Series '71, Game 3	72T	225	$ .15	$ .50	Wright, George	86T	169	$ .01	$ .04
World Series '71, Game 4	72T	226	$ .90	$3.00	Wright, George	86TTR	128	$ .02	$ .10
World Series '71, Game 5	72T	227	$ .15	$ .50	Wright, Jim	79T	349	$ .02	$ .10
World Series '71, Game 6	72T	228	$ .15	$ .50	Wright, Jim	81T	526	$ .01	$ .10
World Series '71, Game 7	72T	229	$ .15	$ .50	Wright, Jim L.	79T	722	$ .50	$2.00
World Series '72, Game 1	73T	203	$ .15	$ .50	Wright, Jim L.	80T	524	$ .01	$ .10
World Series '72, Game 2	73T	204	$ .15	$ .50	Wright, Jim L.	82T	362	$ .01	$ .07
World Series '72, Game 3	73T	205	$ .15	$ .50	Wright, Ken	71T	504	$ .15	$ .50
World Series '72, Game 4	73T	206	$ .15	$ .50	Wright, Ken	72T	638	$ .30	$ .95
World Series '72, Game 5	73T	207	$ .15	$ .50	Wright, Ken	73T	578	$ .45	$1.45
World Series '72, Game 6	73T	208	$ .15	$ .50	Wright, Mel	73T	517	$ .30	$ .95
World Series '72, Game 7	73T	209	$ .15	$ .50	Wright, Ricky	86TTR	129	$ .02	$ .10
World Series '72, Summary	73T	210	$ .15	$ .50	Wright, Ricky	87T	202	$ .01	$ .04
World Series '73, Game #1	74T	472	$ .45	$1.45	Wright, Tom	54T	140	$2.50	$10.00

On TOP of the WORLD!

Player	Year	No.	VG	EX/MT
Wright, Tom	55T	141	$2.00	$6.00
Wrona, Rick	90T	187	$ .01	$ .04
Wyatt, Johnnie	63T	376	$ .25	$ .50
Wyatt, John	64T	108	$ .30	$ .95
Wyatt, Johnnie	65T	590	$1.75	$4.50
Wyatt, John	66T	521	$ .75	$2.50
Wyatt, John	67T	261	$ .30	$ .85
Wyatt, John	68T	481	$ .35	$1.25
Wyatt, Whitlow	60T	464	$ .95	$3.50
Wynegar, Butch	77T	175	$ .30	$ .85
Wynegar, Butch	78T	555	$ .02	$ .10
Wynegar, Butch	79T	405	$ .02	$ .10
Wynegar, Butch	80T	304	$ .01	$ .10
Wynegar, Butch	81T	61	$ .01	$ .10
Wynegar, Butch	82T	222	$ .01	$ .07
Wynegar, Butch	82TTR	131	$ .02	$ .10
Wynegar, Butch	83T	617	$ .01	$ .07
Wynegar, Butch	84T	123	$ .01	$ .06
Wynegar, Butch	85T	585	$ .01	$ .05
Wynegar, Butch	86T	235	$ .01	$ .04
Wynegar, Butch	87T	464	$ .01	$ .04
Wynegar, Butch	88T	737	$ .01	$ .04
Wynn, Early	51Trb	8	$3.00	$18.00
Wynn, Early	52T	277	$35.00	$125.00
Wynn, Early	53T	61	$27.50	$72.50
Wynn, Early	56T	187	$10.00	$30.00
Wynn, Early	57T	40	$5.50	$17.50
Wynn, Early	58T	100	$5.00	$15.00
Wynn, Early	59T	260	$3.00	$12.00
Wynn, Early	60T	1	$5.00	$40.00
Wynn, Early	61T	50	$ .75	$2.20
Wynn, Early	61T	337	$ .75	$2.25
Wynn, Early	61T	455	$3.00	$12.00
Wynn, Early	62T	385	$3.00	$12.00
Wynn, Jim	64T	38	$ .45	$1.45
Wynn, Jim	65T	257	$ .45	$1.45
Wynn, Jim	66T	520	$ .95	$3.50
Wynn, Jim	67T	390	$ .45	$1.45
Wynn, Jim	68T	5	$1.25	$3.75
Wynn, Jim	68T	260	$ .15	$ .50
Wynn, Jim	69T	360	$ .30	$ .95
Wynn, Jim	70T	60	$ .30	$ .95
Wynn, Jim	71T	565	$ .35	$1.25
Wynn, Jim	72T	770	$ .85	$3.50
Wynn, Jim	73T	185	$ .30	$ .85
Wynn, Jim	74T	43	$ .07	$ .30
Wynn, Jim	74TTR	43	$ .15	$ .50
Wynn, Jim	75T	570	$ .07	$ .30
Wynn, Jim	76T	395	$ .15	$ .50
Wynn, Jim	77T	165	$ .03	$ .12
Wynne, Billy	70T	618	$ .30	$ .95
Wynne, Billy	71T	718	$ .75	$2.50
Wynne, Marvell	84T	173	$ .01	$ .06
Wynne, Marvell	85T	615	$ .01	$ .05
Wynne, Marvell	86T	525	$ .01	$ .04
Wynne, Marvell	87T	37	$ .01	$ .04
Wynne, Marvell	88T	454	$ .01	$ .04
Wynne, Marvell	89T	353	$ .01	$ .05
Wynne, Marvell	90T	256	$ .01	$ .04
Wynne, Marvell	91T	714	$ .01	$ .03
Wyrostek, Johnny	51Tbb	44	$7.50	$22.50
Wyrostek, Johnny	52T	13	$15.00	$47.50
Wyrostek, Johnny	53T	79	$4.50	$15.00
Yankees, Team	56T	251	$65.00	$195.00
Yankees, Team	57T	97	$12.50	$37.50
Yankees, Team	58T	246	$11.00	$35.00
Yankees, Team	59T	510	$16.50	$55.00
Yankees, Team	60T	332	$7.00	$21.00
Yankees, Team	61T	228	$3.00	$10.00
Yankees, Team	62T	251	$3.00	$9.00

Player	Year	No.	VG	EX/MT
Yankees, Team	63T	247	$3.00	$9.00
Yankees, Team	64T	433	$2.50	$7.50
Yankees, Team	65T	513	$5.00	$15.00
Yankees, Team	66T	92	$1.50	$4.00
Yankees, Team	67T	131	$1.50	$4.00
Yankees, Team	70T	399	$ .75	$2.20
Yankees, Team	71T	543	$1.75	$4.50
Yankees, Team	72T	237	$ .45	$1.45
Yankees, Team	73T	556	$ .95	$3.50
Yankees, Team	74T	363	$ .75	$3.00
Yankees, Team Checklist	75T	611	$ .75	$2.20
Yankees, Team Checklist	76T	17	$ .20	$ .75
Yankees, Team Checklist	77T	387	$ .75	$3.00
Yankees, Team Checklist	78T	282	$ .20	$ .75
Yankees, Team Checklist	79T	626	$ .30	$ .85
Yankees, Team Checklist	80T	424	$ .30	$ .95
Yankees, Team Checklist	81T	670	$ .02	$ .30
Yankees, Team Leaders	86T	276	$ .01	$ .04
Yankees, Team Leaders	87T	406	$ .01	$ .04
Yankees, Team Leaders	88T	459	$ .01	$ .04
Yankees, Team Leaders	89T	519	$ .01	$ .05
Yastrzemski, Carl	60T	148	$95.00	$325.00
Yastrzemski, Carl	61T	287	$50.00	$150.00
Yastrzemski, Carl	62T	425	$70.00	$200.00
Yastrzemski, Carl	63T	115	$30.00	$80.00
Yastrzemski, Carl	64T	8	$2.10	$6.00
Yastrzemski, Carl	64T	182	$2.50	$10.00
Yastrzemski, Carl	64T	210	$20.00	$80.00

Player	Year	No.	VG	EX/MT
Yastrzemski, Carl	65T	385	$20.00	$80.00
Yastrzemski, Carl	66T	70	$17.50	$50.00
Yastrzemski, Carl	66T	216	$1.00	$4.00
Yastrzemski, Carl	67T	355	$30.00	$90.00
Yastrzemski, Carl	68T	2	$2.10	$6.00
Yastrzemski, Carl	68T	4	$2.10	$6.00
Yastrzemski, Carl	68T	6	$ .85	$4.00
Yastrzemski, Carl	68T	250	$10.00	$35.00
Yastrzemski, Carl	68TAS	369	$3.00	$11.00
Yastrzemski, Carl	69T	1	$2.00	$8.00
Yastrzemski, Carl	69T	130	$10.00	$30.00
Yastrzemski, Carl	69TAS	425	$2.50	$10.00

TOPPS

Player	Year	No.	VG	EX/MT	Player	Year	No.	VG	EX/MT
Yastrzemski, Carl	70T	10	$10.00	$30.00	Yost, Ned	82T	542	$ .01	$ .07
Yastrzemski, Carl	70TAS	461	$2.00	$$9.00	Yost, Ned	83T	297	$ .01	$ .07
Yastrzemski, Carl	71T	61	$ .75	$2.20	Yost, Ned	84T	107	$ .01	$ .06
Yastrzemski, Carl	71T	65	$ .50	$2.00	Yost, Ned	84TTR	131	$ .02	$ .10
Yastrzemski, Carl	71T	530	$13.00	$40.00	Yost, Ned	85T	777	$ .01	$ .05
Yastrzemski, Carl	72T	37	$4.00	$16.00	Youmans, Floyd	86T	732	$ .10	$ .50
Yastrzemski, Carl	72TIA	38	$2.00	$8.00	Youmans, Floyd	87T	105	$ .01	$ .10
Yastrzemski, Carl	73T	245	$5.00	$15.00	Youmans, Floyd	88T	365	$ .01	$ .10
Yastrzemski, Carl	74T	280	$4.00	$12.50	Youmans, Floyd	89T	91	$ .01	$ .05
Yastrzemski, Carl	75T	205	$ .45	$1.45	Young, Bob	52T	147	$4.50	$13.00
Yastrzemski, Carl	75T	280	$3.00	$12.00	Young, Bob	53T	160	$3.00	$9.00
Yastrzemski, Carl	76T	230	$3.00	$9.00	Young, Bobby	54T	8	$3.60	$10.00
Yastrzemski, Carl	77T	480	$1.50	$6.00	Young, Curt	85T	293	$ .06	$ .30
Yastrzemski, Carl	77TB	434	$ .50	$2.00	Young, Curt	86T	84	$ .01	$ .04
Yastrzemski, Carl	78T	40	$ .75	$3.00	Young, Curt	87T	519	$ .01	$ .04
Yastrzemski, Carl	79T	320	$ .85	$3.50	Young, Curt	88T	103	$ .01	$ .04
Yastrzemski, Carl	80T	720	$ .45	$1.75	Young, Curt	89T	641	$ .01	$ .05
Yastrzemski, Carl	80THL	1	$ .35	$1.25	Young, Curt	89TBB	254	$ .01	$ .06
Yastrzemski, Carl	81T	110	$ .35	$1.50					
Yastrzemski, Carl	82T	650	$ .30	$1.25					
Yastrzemski, Carl	82TIA	651	$ .15	$ .60					
Yastrzemski, Carl	83T	550	$ .25	$1.00					
Yastrzemski, Carl	83T	551	$ .01	$ .25					
Yastrzemski, Carl	84T	6	$ .10	$ .50					
Yastrzemski, Carl	87TTB	314	$ .07	$ .30					
Yeager, Steve	73T	59	$ .12	$ .40					
Yeager, Steve	74T	593	$ .07	$ .30					
Yeager, Steve	75T	376	$ .07	$ .30					
Yeager, Steve	76T	515	$ .05	$ .20					
Yeager, Steve	77T	105	$ .03	$ .12					
Yeager, Steve	78T	285	$ .02	$ .10					
Yeager, Steve	79T	75	$ .02	$ .10					
Yeager, Steve	80T	726	$ .05	$ .20					
Yeager, Steve	81T	318	$ .01	$ .10					
Yeager, Steve	82T	477	$ .01	$ .07					
Yeager, Steve	83T	555	$ .01	$ .07					
Yeager, Steve	84T	661	$ .01	$ .06					
Yeager, Steve	85T	148	$ .01	$ .05					
Yeager, Steve	86T	32	$ .01	$ .04					
Yeager, Steve	86TTR	130	$ .02	$ .10					
Yeager, Steve	87T	258	$ .01	$ .04					
Yelding, Eric	89TMLD	148	$ .01	$ .10					
Yelding, Eric	90T	309	$ .01	$ .10					
Yelding, Eric	91T	59	$ .01	$ .03					
Yellen, Larry	64T	226	$ .30	$ .95					
Yellen, Larry	65T	292	$ .35	$1.25					
Yett, Rich	87T	134	$ .01	$ .04					
Yett, Rich	88T	531	$ .01	$ .04					
Yett, Rich	89T	363	$ .01	$ .05	Young, Curt	90T	328	$ .01	$ .04
Yett, Rich	89TBB	290	$ .01	$ .06	Young, Curt	91T	473	$ .01	$ .03
Yett, Rich	90T	689	$ .01	$ .04	Young, Cy	73TATL	477	$ .75	$3.00
York, Jim	72T	68	$ .05	$ .25	Young, Cy	79TRH	416	$ .05	$ .20
York, Jim	73T	546	$ .45	$1.45	Young, Don	66T	139	$ .30	$ .95
York, Jim	75T	383	$ .07	$ .30	Young, Don	69T	602	$ .30	$ .95
York, Jim	76T	224	$ .05	$ .20	Young, Don	70T	117	$ .15	$ .50
York, Mike	91T	508	$ .01	$ .10	Young, Gerald	88T	368	$ .01	$ .25
York, Rudy	60T	456	$2.25	$6.00	Young, Gerald	89T	95	$ .01	$ .05
Yost, Eddie	51Tbb	1	$7.50	$30.00	Young, Gerald	90T	196	$ .01	$ .04
Yost, Eddie	52T	123	$7.00	$21.00	Young, Gerald	91T	626	$ .01	$ .03
Yost, Eddie	56T	128	$2.25	$6.00	Young, Kip	79T	706	$ .02	$ .10
Yost, Eddie	57T	177	$ .95	$3.50	Young, Kip	80T	251	$ .01	$ .10
Yost, Eddie	58T	173	$ .65	$2.00	Young, Matt	83TTR	129	$ .02	$ .10
Yost, Eddie	59T	2	$ .95	$3.50	Young, Matt	84T	235	$ .01	$ .06
Yost, Eddie	60T	245	$ .45	$1.45	Young, Matt	84T	336	$ .01	$ .06
Yost, Eddie	61T	413	$ .75	$3.00	Young, Matt	85T	485	$ .01	$ .05
Yost, Eddie	62T	176	$ .45	$1.45	Young, Matt	86T	676	$ .01	$ .04
Yost, Eddie	73T	257	$ .75	$3.00	Young, Matt	87T	19	$ .01	$ .04
Yost, Eddie	74T	179	$ .75	$3.00	Young, Matt	87TTR	131	$ .01	$ .04
Yost, Ned	79T	708	$ .45	$1.45	Young, Matt	88T	736	$ .01	$ .04
Yost, Ned	81T	659	$ .01	$ .10	Young, Matt	90T	501	$ .01	$ .04

ATHLETICS

CURT YOUNG

Player	Year	No.	VG	EX/MT
Young, Matt	90TTR	131	$ .01	$ .10
Young, Matt	91T	108	$ .01	$ .03
Young, Mike	85T	173	$ .01	$ .10
Young, Mike	86T	548	$ .01	$ .04
Young, Mike	87T	309	$ .01	$ .04
Young, Mike	88T	11	$ .01	$ .04
Young, Mike	89T	731	$ .01	$ .05
Youngblood, Joel	77T	548	$ .03	$ .12
Youngblood, Joel	78T	428	$ .02	$ .10
Youngblood, Joel	79T	109	$ .02	$ .10
Youngblood, Joel	80T	372	$ .01	$ .10
Youngblood, Joel	81T	58	$ .01	$ .10
Youngblood, Joel	82T	655	$ .01	$ .07
Youngblood, Joel	83T	265	$ .01	$ .07
Youngblood, Joel	83TTR	130	$ .02	$ .10
Youngblood, Joel	84T	727	$ .01	$ .06
Youngblood, Joel	85T	567	$ .01	$ .05
Youngblood, Joel	86T	177	$ .01	$ .04
Youngblood, Joel	87T	759	$ .01	$ .04
Youngblood, Joel	88T	418	$ .01	$ .04
Youngblood, Joel	89T	304	$ .01	$ .05
Yount, Robin	75T	223	$45.00	$140.00
Yount, Robin	76T	316	$8.50	$35.00
Yount, Robin	77T	635	$5.00	$20.00
Yount, Robin	78T	173	$2.50	$10.00
Yount, Robin	79T	95	$2.00	$8.00
Yount, Robin	80T	265	$1.25	$5.00
Yount, Robin	81T	515	$ .65	$2.50
Yount, Robin	82T	435	$$ .50	$2.00
Yount, Robin	83T	321	$ .01	$ .10
Yount, Robin	83T	350	$ .25	$1.50
Yount, Robin	83TAS	389	$ .03	$ .35
Yount, Robin	84T	10	$ .25	$1.00
Yount, Robin	85T	340	$ .10	$ .50
Yount, Robin	86T	780	$ .10	$ .50
Yount, Robin	87T	773	$ .07	$ .30
Yount, Robin	88T	165	$ .01	$ .20
Yount, Robin	88TBB	66	$ .01	$ .15
Yount, Robin	89T	615	$ .01	$ .10
Yount, Robin	89TBB	249	$ .01	$ .25
Yount, Robin	90T	290	$ .01	$ .20
Yount, Robin	90TAS	389	$ .01	$ .10
Yount, Robin	91T	575	$ .01	$ .03
Yuhas, Eddie	52T	386	$40.00	$140.00
Yuhas, Ed	53T	70	$4.50	$15.00
Yvars, Sal	52T	338	$40.00	$140.00
Yvars, Sal	53T	11	$4.50	$15.00
Zachary, Chris	64T	23	$ .30	$ .95
Zachary, Chris	66T	313	$ .30	$ .95
Zachary, Chris	67T	212	$ .30	$ .85
Zachary, Chris	70T	471	$ .15	$ .50
Zachary, Chris	73T	256	$ .07	$ .30
Zachry, Pat	76T	599	$2.50	$10.00
Zachry, Pat	77T	86	$ .03	$ .12
Zachry, Pat	78T	171	$ .02	$ .10
Zachry, Pat	79T	621	$ .02	$ .10
Zachry, Pat	80T	428	$ .01	$ .10
Zachry, Pat	81T	224	$ .01	$ .10
Zachry, Pat	82T	399	$ .01	$ .07
Zachry, Pat	83T	522	$ .01	$ .07
Zachry, Pat	83TTR	131	$ .02	$ .10
Zachry, Pat	84T	747	$ .01	$ .06
Zachry, Pat	85T	57	$ .01	$ .05
Zahn, Geoff	75T	294	$ .07	$ .30
Zahn, Geoff	76T	403	$ .05	$ .20
Zahn, Geoff	78T	27	$ .02	$ .10
Zahn, Geoff	79T	678	$ .02	$ .10
Zahn, Geoff	80T	113	$ .01	$ .10
Zahn, Geoff	81T	363	$ .01	$ .10
Zahn, Geoff	81TTR	856	$ .02	$ .10

Player	Year	No.	VG	EX/MT
Zahn, Geoff	82T	229	$ .01	$ .07
Zahn, Geoff	83T	547	$ .01	$ .07
Zahn, Geoff	84T	276	$ .01	$ .06
Zahn, Geoff	84T	468	$ .01	$ .06
Zahn, Geoff	85T	771	$ .01	$ .05
Zahn, Geoff	86T	42	$ .01	$ .04
Zamora, Oscar	75T	604	$ .07	$ .30
Zamora, Oscar	76T	227	$ .05	$ .20
Zamora, Oscar	78T	91	$ .02	$ .10
Zanni, Dom	59T	145	$ .75	$2.20
Zanni, Dom	62T	214	$ .45	$1.45
Zanni, Dom	63T	354	$ .45	$1.50
Zanni, Dom	66T	233	$ .30	$ .95
Zarilla, Al	51Trb	49	$1.50	$4.00
Zarilla, Al	52T	70	$15.00	$47.50
Zarilla, Al	53T	181	$4.50	$15.00
Zauchin, Norm	55T	176	$5.25	$15.00
Zauchin, Norm	56T	89	$2.25	$6.00
Zauchin, Norm	57T	372	$ .85	$3.50
Zauchin, Norm	58T	422	$ .75	$3.00
Zauchin, Norm	59T	311	$ .75	$2.20

Player	Year	No.	VG	EX/MT
Zavaras, Clint	89TMLD	149	$ .01	$ .10
Zavaras, Clint	90T	89	$ .01	$ .10
Zdeb, Joe	78T	408	$ .02	$ .10
Zdeb, Joe	79T	389	$ .02	$ .10
Zeber, George	78T	591	$ .02	$ .10
Zeile, Todd	89TMLD	150	$ .01	$1.00
Zeile, Todd	90T	162	$ .01	$ .50
Zeile, Todd	91T	616	$ .01	$ .15
Zepp, Bill	70T	702	$ .75	$2.00
Zepp, Bill	71T	271	$ .15	$ .50
Zernial, Gus	51Trb	36	$2.50	$10.00
Zernial, Gus	52T	31	$12.50	$45.00
Zernial, Gus	53T	42	$3.00	$9.00
Zernial, Gus	54T	2	$2.50	$9.00
Zernial, Gus	55T	110	$2.00	$9.00
Zernial, Gus	56T	45	$2.25	$6.00
Zernial, Gus	57T	253	$ .95	$3.50
Zernial, Gus	58T	112	$ .75	$3.00
Zernial, Gus	59T	409	$ .75	$2.20

Player	Year	No.	VG	EX/MT
Zimmer, Don	55T	92	$8.00	$35.00
Zimmer, Don	56T	99	$4.00	$12.00
Zimmer, Don	57T	284	$8.00	$25.00

Don Zimmer

INFIELD   L.A. DODGERS

Player	Year	No.	VG	EX/MT
Zimmer, Don	58T	77	$ .90	$3.25
Zimmer, Don	59T	287	$ .90	$3.00
Zimmer, Don	60T	47	$ .75	$3.00
Zimmer, Don	61T	493	$ .90	$3.00
Zimmer, Don	62T	478	$ .85	$3.50
Zimmer, Don	63T	439	$ .45	$1.45
Zimmer, Don	64T	134	$ .15	$ .50
Zimmer, Don	65T	233	$ .45	$1.45
Zimmer, Don	73T	12	$ .30	$ .85

Player	Year	No.	VG	EX/MT
Zimmer, Don	74T	403	$ .07	$ .30
Zimmer, Don	78T	63	$ .02	$ .10
Zimmer, Don	88TTR	131	$ .01	$ .06
Zimmer, Don	89T	134	$ .01	$ .05
Zimmer, Don	90T	549	$ .01	$ .04
Zimmer, Don	91T	729	$ .01	$ .03
Zimmerman, Jerry	59T	146	$ .75	$2.20
Zimmerman, Jerry	62T	222	$ .45	$1.45
Zimmerman, Jerry	63T	186	$ .30	$ .95
Zimmerman, Jerry	64T	369	$ .30	$ .95
Zimmerman, Jerry	66T	73	$ .30	$ .95
Zimmerman, Jerry	67T	501	$ .75	$3.00
Zimmerman, Jerry	68T	181	$ .30	$ .85
Zimmerman, Jerry	73T	377	$ .15	$ .50
Zimmerman, Jerry	74T	531	$ .30	$ .95
Zimmerman,Jerry	65T	299	$ .35	$1.25
Zipfel, Bud	63T	69	$ .30	$ .95
Zisk, Richie	72T	392	$ .15	$ .50
Zisk, Richie	73T	611	$ .45	$1.45
Zisk, Richie	74T	317	$ .07	$ .30
Zisk, Richie	75T	77	$ .07	$ .30
Zisk, Richie	76T	12	$ .05	$ .20
Zisk, Richie	77T	483	$ .03	$ .12
Zisk, Richie	78T	110	$ .02	$ .10
Zisk, Richie	79T	260	$ .02	$ .10
Zisk, Richie	80T	620	$ .01	$ .10
Zisk, Richie	81T	517	$ .01	$ .10
Zisk, Richie	81TTR	857	$ .02	$ .10
Zisk, Richie	82T	769	$ .01	$ .07
Zisk, Richie	83T	368	$ .01	$ .07
Zisk, Richie	84T	83	$ .01	$ .06
Zoldak, Sam	52T	231	$7.00	$20.00
Zupo, Frank	58T	229	$ .75	$3.00
Zuvella, Paul	86T	572	$ .01	$ .04
Zuvella, Paul	86TTR	131	$ .02	$ .10
Zuvella, Paul	87T	102	$ .01	$ .04
Zuverink, George	52T	199	$7.00	$20.00
Zuverink, George	56T	276	$1.30	$5.00
Zuverink, George	57T	11	$ .95	$3.50
Zuverink, George	58T	6	$ .85	$3.50
Zuverink, George	59T	219	$ .75	$2.20

UPPER DECK COMPANY 1989

The Upper Deck Company began production of cards in 1989 joining all the other baseball card producers in searching for a share of the collector's market. Promising a better product than has ever been seen before, they actively sought dealer support. An unproven company in an already saturated market caused many dealers to take a wait and see attitude. Many who hesitated in ordering wished that they had not done so when the product finally begin to arrive. After a slow beginning, the product found wide collector acceptance with the photo-like quality cards.

There are several good things that Upper Deck has done. Card dealers received the first shipments and candy wholesalers did not get to charge retail prices or allow someone to buy the total allotment for a change.

As I previously stated in an earlier book "Distribution and cost (double the other card companies' prices) may be determining factors in the longevity of Upper Deck and collectors will be the ultimate determining factor." Upper Deck proved the point that a superior quality product will be accepted at higher prices by collectors!

Now comes the race by other card companies to emulate what Upper Deck has done. Last year saw the introduction of Donruss Leaf which was a few steps of quality above any cards that Donruss had ever made. These were excellent sellers and extremely limited, and as a dealer on the "Donruss Network" I received an allotment of five cases. This year I was cut back to only two cases (twenty boxes) which will limit any marketability I had. If you can not buy enough product to satisfy regular customers, then how can you start new collectors?

The same problem has occurred with Topps who has started "Stadium Club" cards as their answer to Upper Deck. My two case allotment (twenty-four boxes) will not allow many sets to be built by my customers! Plus, I have to build one of each of these new sets to include in next year's book. My sample pack of twelve cards from Topps included four duplicates which is fairly typical of Topps distribution!

Fleer 's answer to Upper Deck is called Ultra after first being called Elite. At least I was able to order enough Fleer Ultra to supply my customers this year!

All in all, Upper Deck has created a new image of QUALITY which the other card companies are now copying. That is not bad for the new kid on the block!

As I go to press with an earlier deadline this year the extended set of Upper Deck cards (701-800) has not been released; so they are not included in my listing.

The listing for each card shown appears immediately following the photograph.

Player	Year	No.	VG	EX/MT	Player	Year	No.	VG	EX/MT
Aase, Don	89UD	450	$ .01	$ .07	Atherton, Keith	89UD	599	$ .01	$ .07
Aase, Don	90UD	131	$ .01	$ .07	August, Don	89UD	325	$ .01	$ .10
Abbott, Jim	89UD	755	$ .25	$3.00	August, Don	90UD	295	$ .01	$ .07
Abbott, Jim	90UD	645	$ .01	$ .25	Avery, Steve	90UD	65	$ .01	$ .50
Abbott, Jim	91UD	554	$ .01	$ .15	Avery, Steve	91UD	365	$ .01	$ .20
Abbott, Kyle	91UD	51	$ .01	$ .20	Azocar, Oscar	91UD	464	$ .01	$ .20
Abbott, Paul	91UD	487	$ .01	$ .15	Backman, Wally	89UD	188	$ .01	$ .07
Abner, Shawn	90UD	301	$ .01	$ .07	Backman, Wally	89UD	732	$ .01	$ .10
Acker, Jim	89UD	52	$ .01	$ .07					
Acker, Jim	91UD	670	$ .01	$ .05					
Agosto, Juan	89UD	251	$ .01	$ .07					
Agosto, Juan	90UD	450	$ .01	$ .07					
Agosto, Juan	91UD	569	$ .01	$ .05					
Aguayo, Luis	89UD	156	$ .01	$ .07					
Aguilera, Rick	89UD	563	$ .01	$ .07					
Aguilera, Rick	90UD	11	$ .01	$ .07					
Aguilera, Rick	91UD	542	$ .01	$ .05					
Akerfelds, Darrel	91UD	619	$ .01	$ .05					
Aldred, Scott	91UD	7	$ .01	$ .20					
Aldrete, Mike	89UD	239	$ .01	$ .07					
Aldrete, Mike	89UD	738	$ .01	$ .10					
Aldrete, Mike	90UD	415	$ .01	$ .07					
Alexander, Doyle	89UD	298	$ .01	$ .07					
Alexander, Doyle	90UD	330	$ .01	$ .07					
Alicea, Luis	89UD	281	$ .01	$ .20					
Allanson, Andy	89UD	217	$ .01	$ .07					
Allanson, Andy	90UD	590	$ .01	$ .07					
Allen, Neil	89UD	567	$ .01	$ .07					
Alomar, Jr., Sandy	89UD	5	$ .10	$4.50					
Alomar, Jr., Sandy	90UD	655	$ .01	$ .50					
Alomar, Jr., Sandy	90UD	756	$ .01	$ .35					
Alomar, Jr., Sandy	91UD	46	$ .01	$ .10					
Alomar, Jr., Sandy	91UD	144	$ .01	$ .15					
Alomar, Roberto	89UD	471	$ .01	$1.25					
Alomar, Roberto	90UD	346	$ .01	$ .20					
Alomar, Roberto	91UD	80	$ .01	$ .15					
Alomar, Roberto	91UD	335	$ .01	$ .10					
Alou, Moises	91UD	665	$ .01	$ .15					
Alvarez, Jose	89UD	734	$ .01	$ .10	Backman, Wally	90UD	158	$ .01	$ .07
Alvarez, Jose	90UD	634	$ .01	$ .07	Backman, Wally	91UD	185	$ .01	$ .05
Alvarez, Wilson	90UD	765	$ .01	$ .25	Baerga, Carlos	90UD	737	$ .01	$ .50
Andersen, Larry	89UD	404	$ .01	$ .07	Baerga, Carlos	91UD	125	$ .01	$ .25
Andersen, Larry	90UD	407	$ .01	$ .07	Bailes, Scott	89UD	209	$ .01	$ .07
Andersen, Larry	91UD	41	$ .01	$ .05	Bailes, Scott	91UD	190	$ .01	$ .05
Anderson, Allan	89UD	85	$ .01	$ .15	Baines, Harold	89UD	211	$ .01	$ .10
Anderson, Allan	90UD	219	$ .01	$ .07	Baines, Harold	89UD	692	$ .01	$ .10
Anderson, Allan	91UD	503	$ .01	$ .05	Baines, Harold	90UD	353	$ .01	$ .07
Anderson, Brady	89UD	408	$ .01	$ .25	Baines, Harold	91UD	562	$ .01	$ .05
Anderson, Brady	90UD	290	$ .01	$ .07	Balboni, Steve	89UD	111	$ .01	$ .07
Anderson, Brady	91UD	349	$ .01	$ .05	Balboni, Steve	90UD	497	$ .01	$ .07
Anderson, Dave	89UD	89	$ .01	$ .07	Ballard, Jeff	89UD	595	$ .01	$ .15
Anderson, Dave	90UD	510	$ .01	$ .07	Ballard, Jeff	90UD	259	$ .01	$ .07
Anderson, Kent	90UD	691	$ .01	$ .15	Ballard, Jeff	91UD	260	$ .01	$ .05
Andujar, Joaquin	89UD	79	$ .01	$ .07	Bankhead, Scott	89UD	316	$ .01	$ .07
Anthony, Eric	90UD	28	$ .01	$ .60	Bankhead, Scott	90UD	561	$ .01	$ .07
Anthony, Eric	91UD	533	$ .01	$ .20	Bankhead, Scott	91UD	294	$ .01	$ .05
Appier, Kevin	90UD	102	$ .01	$ .35	Banks, Willie	91UD	74	$ .01	$ .30
Appier, Kevin	91UD	566	$ .01	$ .10	Bannister, Floyd	89UD	549	$ .01	$ .07
Aquino, Luis	90UD	274	$ .01	$ .10	Bannister, Floyd	90UD	695	$ .01	$ .07
Aquino, Luis	91UD	504	$ .01	$ .05	Barfield, Jesse	89UD	149	$ .01	$ .15
Armas, Tony	89UD	212	$ .01	$ .07	Barfield, Jesse	89UD	702	$ .01	$ .15
Armas, Tony	90UD	58	$ .01	$ .07	Barfield, Jesse	90UD	476	$ .01	$ .07
Armstrong, Jack	89UD	257	$ .05	$ .50	Barfield, Jesse	91UD	485	$ .01	$ .05
Armstrong, Jack	90UD	684	$ .01	$ .35	Barfield, John	91UD	629	$ .01	$ .10
Armstrong, Jack	91UD	373	$ .01	$ .05	Barnes, Brian	91UD	12	$ .01	$ .20
Arnsberg, Brad	91UD	608	$ .01	$ .05	Barrett, Marty	89UD	173	$ .01	$ .07
Ashby, Alan	89UD	305	$ .01	$ .07	Barrett, Marty	90UD	133	$ .01	$ .07
Assenmacher, Paul	89UD	566	$ .01	$ .07	Barrett, Marty	91UD	90	$ .01	$ .05
Assenmacher, Paul	90UD	660	$ .01	$ .07	Bass, Kevin	89UD	425	$ .01	$ .07
Assenmacher, Paul	91UD	491	$ .01	$ .05	Bass, Kevin	90UD	302	$ .01	$ .07

Wally Backman

Player	Year	No.	VG	EX/MT	Player	Year	No.	VG	EX/MT
Bass, Kevin	90UD	793	$ .01	$ .10	Berenguer, Juan	90UD	440	$ .01	$ .07
Bass, Kevin	91UD	287	$ .01	$ .05	Berenguer, Juan	91UD	411	$ .01	$ .05
Batiste, Kevin	90UD	115	$ .01	$ .15	Bergman, Dave	89UD	266	$ .01	$ .07
Bautista, Jose	89UD	574	$ .01	$ .10	Bergman, Dave	90UD	381	$ .01	$ .07
Baylor, Don	89UD	601	$ .01	$ .07	Bergman, Dave	91UD	599	$ .01	$ .05
Bearse, Kevin	90UD	715	$ .01	$ .20	Berroa, Geronimo	90UD	531	$ .01	$ .10
Beatty, Blaine	90UD	23	$ .01	$ .20	Berry, Sean	91UD	10	$ .01	$ .20
Bedrosian, Steve	89UD	511	$ .01	$ .07	Berryhill, Damon	89UD	455	$ .01	$ .15
Bedrosian, Steve	90UD	618	$ .01	$ .07	Berryhill, Damon	90UD	322	$ .01	$ .10
Bedrosian, Steve	91UD	422	$ .01	$ .05	Berryhill, Damon	91UD	319	$ .01	$ .05
Belcher, Kevin	91UD	26	$ .01	$ .20	Bichette, Dante	89UD	24	$ .01	$ .35
Belcher, Tim	89UD	648	$ .01	$ .15	Bichette, Dante	90UD	688	$ .01	$ .15
Belcher, Tim	90UD	547	$ .01	$ .25	Bichette, Dante	91UD	317	$ .01	$ .05
Belcher, Tim	91UD	576	$ .01	$ .05	Bielecki, Mike	90UD	359	$ .01	$ .07
Belinda, Stan	90UD	759	$ .01	$ .20	Bielecki, Mike	91UD	597	$ .01	$ .05
Belinda, Stan	91UD	161	$ .01	$ .10	Biggio, Craig	89UD	273	$ .01	$ .75
Bell, Buddy	89UD	112	$ .01	$ .07	Biggio, Craig	90UD	104	$ .01	$ .25
Bell, George	89UD	255	$ .01	$ .15	Biggio, Craig	91UD	158	$ .01	$ .05
Bell, George	90UD	95	$ .01	$ .07	Birtsas, Tim	89UD	638	$ .01	$ .07
Bell, George	90UD	127	$ .01	$ .10	Birtsas, Tim	90UD	137	$ .01	$ .07
Bell, George	91UD	532	$ .01	$ .15	Bittiger, Jeff	89UD	509	$ .01	$ .07
Bell, Jay	89UD	489	$ .01	$ .07	Black, Bud	89UD	466	$ .01	$ .07
Bell, Jay	90UD	517	$ .01	$ .07	Black, Bud	90UD	498	$ .01	$ .07
Bell, Jay	91UD	183	$ .01	$ .05	Blair, Willie	91UD	427	$ .01	$ .15
Bell, Juan	89UD	20	$ .05	$ .35	Blankenship, Kevin	89UD	762	$ .01	$ .15
Bell, Juan	89UD	747	$ .01	$ .25	Blankenship, Kevin	90UD	47	$ .01	$ .15
Bell, Mike	91UD	644	$ .01	$ .15	Blankenship, Lance	89UD	15	$ .01	$ .25
Belle, Joey	90UD	446	$ .01	$1.50	Blankenship, Lance	90UD	687	$ .01	$ .07
Belliard, Rafael	89UD	90	$ .01	$ .07	Blauser, Jeff	89UD	132	$ .01	$ .15
Belliard, Rafael	90UD	208	$ .01	$ .07	Blauser, Jeff	90UD	406	$ .01	$ .07
Benedict, Bruce	89UD	121	$ .01	$ .07	Blauser, Jeff	91UD	382	$ .01	$ .05
Benes, Andy	90UD	55	$ .01	$ .25	Blocker, Terry	89UD	399	$ .01	$ .10
Benes, Andy	91UD	275	$ .01	$ .05	Blosser, Greg	91UD	70	$ .01	$ .45
Benjamin, Mike	90UD	750	$ .01	$ .25	Blowers, Mike	90UD	767	$ .01	$ .25
					Blyleven, Bert	89UD	225	$ .01	$ .10
					Blyleven, Bert	89UD	712	$ .01	$ .15
					Blyleven, Bert	90UD	527	$ .01	$ .10
					Blyleven, Bert	91UD	571	$ .01	$ .05
					Boddicker, Mike	89UD	542	$ .01	$ .07
					Boddicker, Mike	90UD	652	$ .01	$ .07
					Boddicker, Mike	91UD	438	$ .01	$ .05
					Boever, Joe	90UD	408	$ .01	$ .07
					Boever, Joe	91UD	430	$ .01	$ .05
					Boggs, Wade	89UD	389	$ .10	$ .60
					Boggs, Wade	89UD	687	$ .01	$ .25
					Boggs, Wade	90UD	555	$ .01	$ .50
					Boggs, Wade	91UD	546	$ .01	$ .20
					Bohanon, Brian	90UD	731	$ .01	$ .20
					Bolton, Tom	89UD	545	$ .01	$ .07
					Bolton, Tom	90UD	351	$ .01	$ .07
					Bolton, Tom	91UD	86	$ .01	$ .05
					Bonds, Barry	89UD	440	$ .01	$ .20
					Bonds, Barry	90UD	227	$ .01	$ .15
					Bonds, Barry	91UD	94	$ .01	$ .10
					Bonds, Barry	91UD	154	$ .01	$ .15
					Bonilla, Bobby	89UD	578	$ .01	$ .25
					Bonilla, Bobby	90UD	16	$ .01	$ .07
					Bonilla, Bobby	90UD	366	$ .01	$ .15
					Bonilla, Bobby	91UD	152	$ .01	$ .15
					Booker, Greg	89UD	641	$ .01	$ .07
					Booker, Rod	89UD	644	$ .01	$ .10
					Boone, Bob	89UD	119	$ .01	$ .07
					Boone, Bob	89UD	767	$ .01	$ .15
					Boone, Bob	90UD	271	$ .01	$ .07
					Boone, Bob	91UD	502	$ .01	$ .05
Benjamin, Mike	91UD	651	$ .01	$ .15	Borders, Pat	89UD	593	$ .01	$ .25
Benzinger, Todd	89UD	184	$ .01	$ .07	Borders, Pat	90UD	113	$ .01	$ .07
Benzinger, Todd	89UD	785	$ .01	$ .15	Borders, Pat	91UD	147	$ .01	$ .05
Benzinger, Todd	90UD	186	$ .01	$ .10	Bosio, Chris	89UD	292	$ .01	$ .07
Benzinger, Todd	91UD	280	$ .01	$ .05	Bosio, Chris	90UD	293	$ .01	$ .07
Berenguer, Juan	89UD	232	$ .01	$ .07					

Mike Benjamin

Player	Year	No.	VG	EX/MT
Bosio, Chris	91UD	529	$ .01	$ .05
Boskie, Shawn	90UD	722	$ .01	$ .35
Boskie, Shawn	91UD	471	$ .01	$ .25
Bosley, Thad	89UD	591	$ .01	$ .07
Boston, Daryl	89UD	496	$ .01	$ .07
Boston, Daryl	90UD	529	$ .01	$ .07
Boston, Daryl	91UD	159	$ .01	$ .05
Boyd, Oil Can	89UD	415	$ .01	$ .15
Boyd, Oil Can	90UD	484	$ .01	$ .07
Boyd, Oil Can	90UD	749	$ .01	$ .10
Boyd, Oil Can	91UD	359	$ .01	$ .05
Bradley, Phil	89UD	229	$ .01	$ .07
Bradley, Phil	89UD	749	$ .01	$ .10
Bradley, Phil	90UD	194	$ .01	$ .07
Bradley, Phil	91UD	641	$ .01	$ .05
Bradley, Scott	89UD	226	$ .01	$ .07
Bradley, Scott	90UD	383	$ .01	$ .07
Bradley, Scott	91UD	130	$ .01	$ .05
Braggs, Glenn	89UD	504	$ .01	$ .07
Braggs, Glenn	90UD	456	$ .01	$ .07
Braggs, Glenn	90UD	714	$ .01	$ .10
Braggs, Glenn	91UD	631	$ .01	$ .05
Brantley, Jeff	90UD	358	$ .01	$ .10
Brantley, Jeff	91UD	424	$ .01	$ .05
Brantley, Mickey	89UD	550	$ .01	$ .07
Bream, Sid	89UD	556	$ .01	$ .07
Bream, Sid	90UD	250	$ .01	$ .07
Bream, Sid	91UD	109	$ .01	$ .05
Brenly, Bob	89UD	479	$ .01	$ .07
Brennan, William	89UD	16	$ .01	$ .10
Brett, George	89UD	215	$ .01	$ .35
Brett, George	89UD	689	$ .01	$ .25
Brett, George	90UD	124	$ .01	$ .15
Brett, George	91UD	525	$ .01	$ .15
Briley, Greg	89UD	770	$ .01	$ .75
Briley, Greg	90UD	455	$ .01	$ .25
Briley, Greg	91UD	479	$ .01	$ .05
Brock, Greg	89UD	543	$ .01	$ .07
Brock, Greg	90UD	514	$ .01	$ .07
Brock, Greg	91UD	289	$ .01	$ .05
Brock, Lou	91UD	636	$ .01	$ .50
Brogna, Rico	91UD	73	$ .01	$ .45
Brookens, Tom	89UD	106	$ .01	$ .07
Brookens, Tom	90UD	138	$ .01	$ .07
Brookens, Tom	91UD	102	$ .01	$ .05
Brooks, Hubie	89UD	122	$ .01	$ .07
Brooks, Hubie	90UD	197	$ .01	$ .07
Brooks, Hubie	90UD	791	$ .01	$ .10
Brooks, Hubie	91UD	217	$ .01	$ .05
Brower, Bob	89UD	439	$ .01	$ .07
Brown, Chris	89UD	193	$ .01	$ .07
Brown, Chris	89UD	784	$ .01	$ .10
Brown, Kevin	89UD	752	$ .01	$ .35
Brown, Kevin	90UD	123	$ .01	$ .15
Brown, Kevin	91UD	472	$ .01	$ .05
Browne, Jerry	89UD	314	$ .01	$ .07
Browne, Jerry	90UD	426	$ .01	$ .07
Browne, Jerry	91UD	116	$ .01	$ .05
Browning, Tom	89UD	617	$ .01	$ .10
Browning, Tom	90UD	189	$ .01	$ .07
Browning, Tom	91UD	633	$ .01	$ .05
Brumley, Mike	90UD	312	$ .01	$ .07
Brunansky, Tom	89UD	272	$ .01	$ .07
Brunansky, Tom	90UD	257	$ .01	$ .07
Brunansky, Tom	90UD	708	$ .01	$ .10
Brunansky, Tom	91UD	163	$ .01	$ .05
Brutcher, Len	91UD	75	$ .01	$ .25
Buckner, Bill	89UD	639	$ .01	$ .07
Buckner, Bill	90UD	252	$ .01	$ .07
Buechele, Steve	89UD	418	$ .01	$ .07

Player	Year	No.	VG	EX/MT
Buechele, Steve	90UD	685	$ .01	$ .07
Buechele, Steve	91UD	650	$ .01	$ .05

Jay Buhner

Player	Year	No.	VG	EX/MT
Buhner, Jay	89UD	220	$ .01	$ .25
Buhner, Jay	90UD	534	$ .01	$ .07
Buhner, Jay	91UD	128	$ .01	$ .05
Buice, DeWayne	89UD	147	$ .01	$ .07
Burke, Tim	89UD	456	$ .01	$ .10
Burke, Tim	90UD	515	$ .01	$ .07
Burke, Tim	91UD	215	$ .01	$ .05
Burkett, John	90UD	735	$ .01	$ .35
Burkett, John	91UD	577	$ .01	$ .05
Burks, Ellis	89UD	434	$ .10	$ .55
Burks, Ellis	90UD	343	$ .01	$ .25
Burks, Ellis	91UD	436	$ .01	$ .15
Burns, Todd	89UD	718	$ .01	$ .25
Burns, Todd	90UD	689	$ .01	$ .10
Burns, Todd	91UD	405	$ .01	$ .05
Bush, Randy	89UD	158	$ .01	$ .07
Bush, Randy	90UD	493	$ .01	$ .07
Butler, Brett	89UD	218	$ .01	$ .07
Butler, Brett	90UD	119	$ .01	$ .07
Butler, Brett	91UD	270	$ .01	$ .05
Cabrera, Francisco	90UD	64	$ .01	$ .25
Cabrera, Francisco	91UD	439	$ .01	$ .05
Cadaret, Greg	90UD	549	$ .01	$ .07
Cadaret, Greg	91UD	343	$ .01	$ .05
Calderon, Ivan	89UD	650	$ .01	$ .07
Calderon, Ivan	90UD	503	$ .01	$ .07
Calderon, Ivan	91UD	285	$ .01	$ .05
Calhoun, Jeff	89UD	33	$ .01	$ .07
Caminiti, Ken	89UD	141	$ .01	$ .07
Caminiti, Ken	90UD	122	$ .01	$ .07
Caminiti, Ken	91UD	180	$ .01	$ .05
Campbell, Mike	89UD	337	$ .01	$ .07
Campusano, Sil	89UD	45	$ .01	$ .20
Campusano, Sil	91UD	469	$ .01	$ .05
Canale, George	90UD	59	$ .01	$ .25
Candaele, Casey	89UD	58	$ .01	$ .07
Candaele, Casey	91UD	511	$ .01	$ .05
Candelaria, John	89UD	248	$ .01	$ .07
Candelaria, John	90UD	720	$ .01	$ .10

Player	Year	No.	VG	EX/MT	Player	Year	No.	VG	EX/MT
Candiotti, Tom	89UD	470	$ .01	$ .07	Checklist, Cards (601-700)	90UD	700	$ .01	$ .07
Candiotti, Tom	90UD	388	$ .01	$ .07	Checklist, Cards (601-700)	91UD	700	$ .01	$ .05
Candiotti, Tom	91UD	218	$ .01	$ .05	Checklist, Cards (701-800)	89UD	701	$ .01	$ .10
Cangelosi, John	89UD	67	$ .01	$ .07	Checklist, Cards (701-800)	90UD	800	$ .01	$ .10
Cangelosi, John	90UD	370	$ .01	$ .07	Checklist, Prospects (51-76)	91UD	50	$ .01	$ .05
Cano, Jose	90UD	43	$ .01	$ .25	Checklist, Rookies (1-26)	89UD	27	$ .01	$ .07
Canseco, Jose	89UD	371	$ .15	$1.00	Checklist, Rookies (1-26)	90UD	1	$ .01	$ .07
Canseco, Jose	89UD	659	$ .05	$ .35	Checklist, Rookies (1-27)	91UD	1	$ .01	$ .05
Canseco, Jose	89UD	670	$ .01	$ .45	Clancy, Jim	89UD	282	$ .01	$ .07
Canseco, Jose	90UD	66	$ .01	$ .75	Clancy, Jim	90UD	203	$ .01	$ .07
Canseco, Jose	91UD	155	$ .01	$ .45	Clancy, Jim	91UD	682	$ .01	$ .05
Canseco, Ozzie	89UD	756	$ .10	$ .35	Clark, Dave	89UD	517	$ .01	$ .07
Canseco, Ozzie	91UD	146	$ .01	$ .15	Clark, Dave	90UD	449	$ .01	$ .07
Carman, Don	89UD	409	$ .01	$ .07	Clark, Dave	91UD	314	$ .01	$ .05
Carman, Don	90UD	420	$ .01	$ .07	Clark, Jack	89UD	346	$ .01	$ .10
Carman, Don	91UD	288	$ .01	$ .05	Clark, Jack	89UD	773	$ .01	$ .15
Carpenter, Cris	89UD	8	$ .01	$ .30	Clark, Jack	90UD	342	$ .01	$ .07
Carpenter, Cris	90UD	523	$ .01	$ .10	Clark, Jack	91UD	331	$ .01	$ .05
Carr, Chuck	91UD	514	$ .01	$ .15	Clark, Jerald	89UD	30	$ .01	$ .50
Carreon, Mark	90UD	135	$ .01	$ .15	Clark, Jerald	90UD	624	$ .01	$ .07
Carter, Gary	89UD	390	$ .01	$ .20	Clark, Jerald	91UD	624	$ .01	$ .05
Carter, Gary	90UD	168	$ .01	$ .07	Clark, Terry	89UD	234	$ .01	$ .20
Carter, Gary	90UD	774	$ .01	$ .10	Clark, Will	89UD	155	$ .15	$1.50
Carter, Gary	91UD	176	$ .01	$ .05	Clark, Will	89UD	678	$ .10	$ .75
Carter, Joe	89UD	190	$ .01	$ .15	Clark, Will	90UD	50	$ .01	$ .50
Carter, Joe	90UD	53	$ .01	$ .07	Clark, Will	90UD	556	$ .01	$ .50
Carter, Joe	90UD	375	$ .01	$ .07	Clark, Will	91UD	445	$ .01	$ .25
Carter, Joe	90UD	754	$ .01	$ .10	Clary, Marty	90UD	779	$ .01	$ .10
Carter, Joe	91UD	226	$ .01	$ .05	Clary, Marty	91UD	478	$ .01	$ .15
Carter, Steve	90UD	368	$ .01	$ .15	Clayton, Royce	91UD	61	$ .01	$ .25
Cary, Chuck	89UD	396	$ .01	$ .07	Clemens, Roger	89UD	195	$ .05	$ .50
Cary, Chuck	90UD	528	$ .01	$ .07	Clemens, Roger	90UD	57	$ .01	$ .10
Cary, Chuck	91UD	409	$ .01	$ .05	Clemens, Roger	90UD	323	$ .01	$ .35
Castillo, Carmen	89UD	487	$ .01	$ .07	Clemens, Roger	91UD	655	$ .01	$ .25
Castillo, Carmen	90UD	281	$ .01	$ .07	Cliburn, Stu	89UD	483	$ .01	$ .07
Castillo, Juan	89UD	522	$ .01	$ .07	Clutterbuck, Bryan	90UD	239	$ .01	$ .07
Castillo, Tony	90UD	551	$ .01	$ .07	Colbrunn, Greg	91UD	15	$ .01	$ .25
Castillo, Tony	91UD	458	$ .01	$ .05					
Cecena, Jose	89UD	560	$ .01	$ .10					
Cedeno, Andujar	91UD	23	$ .01	$1.00					
Cerone, Rick	89UD	152	$ .01	$ .07					
Cerone, Rick	90UD	405	$ .01	$ .07					
Cerutti, John	89UD	129	$ .01	$ .07					
Cerutti, John	90UD	485	$ .01	$ .07					
Cerutti, John	91UD	585	$ .01	$ .05					
Chamberlain, Wes	91UD	626	$ .01	$ .50					
Champarino, Scott	91UD	8	$ .01	$ .35					
Chance, Tony	89UD	3	$ .01	$ .10					
Charlton, Norm	89UD	783	$ .01	$ .35					
Charlton, Norm	90UD	566	$ .01	$ .15					
Charlton, Norm	91UD	394	$ .01	$ .05					
Checklist, Cards (1-100)	89UD	694	$ .01	$ .07					
Checklist, Cards (1-100)	90UD	100	$ .01	$ .07					
Checklist, Cards (1-100)	91UD	100	$ .01	$ .05					
Checklist, Cards (101-200)	89UD	695	$ .01	$ .07					
Checklist, Cards (101-200)	90UD	200	$ .01	$ .07					
Checklist, Cards (101-200)	91UD	200	$ .01	$ .05					
Checklist, Cards (201-300)	89UD	696	$ .01	$ .07					
Checklist, Cards (201-300)	90UD	300	$ .01	$ .07					
Checklist, Cards (201-300)	91UD	300	$ .01	$ .05					
Checklist, Cards (301-400)	89UD	697	$ .01	$ .07					
Checklist, Cards (301-400)	90UD	400	$ .01	$ .07					
Checklist, Cards (301-400)	91UD	400	$ .01	$ .05					
Checklist, Cards (401-500)	89UD	698	$ .01	$ .07					
Checklist, Cards (401-500)	90UD	500	$ .01	$ .07					
Checklist, Cards (451-500)	91UD	500	$ .01	$ .05					
Checklist, Cards (501-600)	89UD	699	$ .01	$ .07					
Checklist, Cards (501-600)	90UD	600	$ .01	$ .07					
Checklist, Cards (551-600)	91UD	600	$ .01	$ .05					
Checklist, Cards (601-700)	89UD	700	$ .01	$ .07					

Alex Cole

Player	Year	No.	VG	EX/MT
Cole, Alex	90UD	751	$ .01	$ .50
Cole, Alex	91UD	654	$ .01	$ .25
Coleman, Vince	89UD	253	$ .01	$ .10

Player	Year	No.	VG	EX/MT
Coleman, Vince	90UD	68	$ .01	$ .07
Coleman, Vince	90UD	223	$ .01	$ .07
Coleman, Vince	91UD	461	$ .01	$ .05
Coles, Darnell	89UD	339	$ .01	$ .07
Coles, Darnell	90UD	311	$ .01	$ .07
Collins, Dave	89UD	351	$ .01	$ .07
Combs, Pat	90UD	763	$ .01	$ .15
Combs, Pat	91UD	537	$ .01	$ .05
Concepcion, Dave	89UD	196	$ .01	$ .07
Cone, David	89UD	584	$ .01	$ .35
Cone, David	90UD	224	$ .01	$ .10
Cone, David	91UD	366	$ .01	$ .05
Conine, Jeff	91UD	27	$ .01	$1.25
Cook, Dennis	89UD	779	$ .01	$ .35
Cook, Dennis	90UD	71	$ .01	$ .35
Cook, Dennis	91UD	612	$ .01	$ .05
Coolbaugh, Scott	90UD	42	$ .01	$ .35
Coolbaugh, Scott	91UD	451	$ .01	$ .05
Cooper, Scott	91UD	22	$ .01	$ .20
Cora, Joey	90UD	601	$ .01	$ .07
Cora, Joey	91UD	291	$ .01	$ .05
Corbett, Sherman	89UD	464	$ .01	$ .07
Cordero, Wilfredo	91UD	60	$ .01	$ .25
Correa, Edwin	89UD	598	$ .01	$ .07
Corsi, Jim	90UD	521	$ .01	$ .07
Costello, John	89UD	625	$ .01	$ .10
Costello, John	90UD	486	$ .01	$ .07
Costo, Tim	91UD	62	$ .01	$1.00
Cotto, Henry	89UD	134	$ .01	$ .07
Cotto, Henry	90UD	207	$ .01	$ .07
Cotto, Henry	91UD	110	$ .01	$ .05
Cox, Danny	89UD	535	$ .01	$ .07
Crews, Tim	89UD	611	$ .01	$ .07
Crews, Tim	90UD	670	$ .01	$ .07
Crews, Tim	91UD	596	$ .01	$ .05
Crim, Chuck	89UD	501	$ .01	$ .07
Crim, Chuck	90UD	511	$ .01	$ .07
Crim, Chuck	91UD	391	$ .01	$ .05
Cuyler, Milt	91UD	556	$ .01	$ .30
Daniels, Kal	89UD	160	$ .01	$ .10
Daniels, Kal	90UD	603	$ .01	$ .07
Daniels, Kal	91UD	166	$ .01	$ .05
Darling, Ron	89UD	159	$ .01	$ .10
Darling, Ron	90UD	241	$ .01	$ .07
Darling, Ron	91UD	198	$ .01	$ .05
Darwin, Danny	89UD	97	$ .01	$ .07
Darwin, Danny	90UD	305	$ .01	$ .07
Darwin, Danny	91UD	586	$ .01	$ .05
Dascenzo, Doug	89UD	10	$ .01	$ .25
Dascenzo, Doug	90UD	211	$ .01	$ .07
Daugherty, Jack	90UD	614	$ .01	$ .15
Daugherty, Jack	91UD	284	$ .01	$ .05
Daulton, Darren	89UD	448	$ .01	$ .07
Daulton, Darren	90UD	418	$ .01	$ .07
Daulton, Darren	91UD	408	$ .01	$ .05
Davidson, Mark	89UD	577	$ .01	$ .07
Davis, Alvin	89UD	105	$ .01	$ .15
Davis, Alvin	89UD	680	$ .01	$ .10
Davis, Alvin	90UD	364	$ .01	$ .10
Davis, Alvin	91UD	457	$ .01	$ .05
Davis, Chili	89UD	126	$ .01	$ .07
Davis, Chili	90UD	38	$ .01	$ .07
Davis, Chili	91UD	339	$ .01	$ .05
Davis, Eric	89UD	410	$ .01	$ .40
Davis, Eric	89UD	688	$ .01	$ .25
Davis, Eric	90UD	116	$ .01	$ .25
Davis, Eric	91UD	355	$ .01	$ .15
Davis, Glenn	89UD	443	$ .01	$ .15
Davis, Glenn	90UD	245	$ .01	$ .15
Davis, Glenn	91UD	81	$ .01	$ .05

Player	Year	No.	VG	EX/MT
Davis, Glenn	91UD	535	$ .01	$ .10
Davis, Jody	89UD	148	$ .01	$ .07
Davis, Jody	90UD	429	$ .01	$ .07
Davis, John	89UD	548	$ .01	$ .07
Davis, Mark	89UD	268	$ .01	$ .07
Davis, Mark	90UD	431	$ .01	$ .07
Davis, Mark	90UD	710	$ .01	$ .10
Davis, Mark	91UD	589	$ .01	$ .05
Davis, Mike	89UD	146	$ .01	$ .07
Davis, Mike	90UD	258	$ .01	$ .07
Davis, Storm	89UD	153	$ .01	$ .07
Davis, Storm	90UD	292	$ .01	$ .07
Davis, Storm	90UD	712	$ .01	$ .10
Davis, Storm	91UD	639	$ .01	$ .05
Dawson, Andre	89UD	205	$ .01	$ .20
Dawson, Andre	90UD	73	$ .01	$ .15
Dawson, Andre	90UD	357	$ .01	$ .15
Dawson, Andre	91UD	454	$ .01	$ .15

Ken Dayley

Player	Year	No.	VG	EX/MT
Dayley, Ken	89UD	114	$ .01	$ .07
Dayley, Ken	90UD	280	$ .01	$ .07
Dayley, Ken	91UD	628	$ .01	$ .05
De Los Santos, Luis	89UD	12	$ .01	$ .25
Decker, Steve	91UD	25	$ .01	$1.50
Deer, Rob	89UD	442	$ .01	$ .07
Deer, Rob	90UD	176	$ .01	$ .07
Deer, Rob	91UD	272	$ .01	$ .05
DeJesus, Ivan	89UD	355	$ .01	$ .07
DeJesus, Jose	89UD	769	$ .01	$ .10
DeJesus, Jose	90UD	255	$ .01	$ .07
DeJesus, Jose	91UD	486	$ .01	$ .05
DeLeon, Jose	89UD	293	$ .01	$ .07
DeLeon, Jose	90UD	697	$ .01	$ .07
DeLeon, Jose	91UD	220	$ .01	$ .05
Dempsey, Rick	89UD	713	$ .01	$ .10
Dernier, Bob	89UD	340	$ .01	$ .07
Deshaies, Jim	89UD	76	$ .01	$ .07
Deshaies, Jim	90UD	221	$ .01	$ .07
Deshaies, Jim	91UD	208	$ .01	$ .05
DeShields, Delino	90UD	702	$ .01	$ .10
DeShields, Delino	90UD	746	$ .01	$1.00

Player	Year	No.	VG	EX/MT
DeShields, Delino	91UD	364	$ .01	$ .25
Devereaux, Mike	89UD	68	$ .01	$ .15
Devereaux, Mike	90UD	681	$ .01	$ .07
Devereaux, Mike	91UD	308	$ .01	$ .05
Diaz, Bo	89UD	169	$ .01	$ .07
Diaz, Bo	90UD	664	$ .01	$ .07
Diaz, Edgar	91UD	286	$ .01	$ .05
Diaz, Mario	89UD	318	$ .01	$ .10
Diaz, Mike	89UD	606	$ .01	$ .07
Dibble, Rob	89UD	375	$ .01	$1.00
Dibble, Rob	90UD	586	$ .01	$ .50
Dibble, Rob	91UD	635	$ .01	$ .05
Dickson, Lance	91UD	9	$ .01	$ .35
DiPino, Frank	89UD	61	$ .01	$ .07
DiPino, Frank	90UD	202	$ .01	$ .07
DiPino, Frank	91UD	350	$ .01	$ .05
DiSarcina, Gary	90UD	761	$ .01	$ .20
Dopson, John	89UD	57	$ .01	$ .25
Dopson, John	90UD	671	$ .01	$ .07
Dopson, John	91UD	88	$ .01	$ .05
Doran, Bill	89UD	101	$ .01	$ .07
Doran, Bill	90UD	198	$ .01	$ .07
Doran, Bill	91UD	398	$ .01	$ .05
Dotson, Richard	89UD	80	$ .01	$ .07
Downing, Brian	89UD	485	$ .01	$ .07
Downing, Brian	90UD	146	$ .01	$ .07
Downing, Brian	91UD	231	$ .01	$ .05
Downs, Kelly	89UD	476	$ .01	$ .07
Downs, Kelly	90UD	699	$ .01	$ .07
Downs, Kelly	91UD	441	$ .01	$ .05
Dozier, D. J.	91UD	3	$ .01	$ .45
Drabek, Doug	89UD	597	$ .01	$ .07
Drabek, Doug	90UD	422	$ .01	$ .07
Drabek, Doug	91UD	278	$ .01	$ .05
Dravecky, Dave	89UD	39	$ .01	$ .07
Dravecky, Dave	90UD	679	$ .01	$ .07
Drees, Tom	90UD	3	$ .01	$ .15
Drummond, Tim	91UD	698	$ .01	$ .15
DuBois, Brian	90UD	78	$ .01	$ .15
Ducey, Rob	89UD	721	$ .01	$ .15
Ducey, Rob	90UD	464	$ .01	$ .07
Duncan, Mariano	90UD	430	$ .01	$ .07
Duncan, Mariano	91UD	112	$ .01	$ .05
Dunne, Mike	89UD	518	$ .01	$ .07
Dunston, Shawon	89UD	107	$ .01	$ .10
Dunston, Shawon	90UD	231	$ .01	$ .10
Dunston, Shawon	91UD	111	$ .01	$ .05
Durham, Leon	89UD	354	$ .01	$ .07
Dyer, Mike	90UD	374	$ .01	$ .15
Dykstra, Len	89UD	369	$ .01	$ .10
Dykstra, Len	90UD	472	$ .01	$ .10
Dykstra, Lenny	91UD	97	$ .01	$ .05
Dykstra, Lenny	91UD	267	$ .01	$ .05
Eckersley, Dennis	89UD	289	$ .01	$ .07
Eckersley, Dennis	89UD	664	$ .01	$ .10
Eckersley, Dennis	90UD	513	$ .01	$ .07
Eckersley, Dennis	91UD	172	$ .01	$ .05
Edens, Tom	91UD	616	$ .01	$ .05
Edwards, Wayne	90UD	762	$ .01	$ .20
Edwards, Wayne	91UD	697	$ .01	$ .05
Eichhorn, Mark	91UD	519	$ .01	$ .05
Eisenreich, Jim	89UD	44	$ .01	$ .07
Eisenreich, Jim	90UD	294	$ .01	$ .07
Eisenreich, Jim	91UD	658	$ .01	$ .05
Elster, Kevin	89UD	269	$ .01	$ .07
Elster, Kevin	90UD	187	$ .01	$ .07
Elster, Kevin	91UD	101	$ .01	$ .05
Elvira, Narciso	91UD	13	$ .01	$ .15
Eppard, Jim	89UD	614	$ .01	$ .10
Ericks, John	91UD	57	$ .01	$ .25

Player	Year	No.	VG	EX/MT
Erickson, Scott	91UD	522	$ .01	$3.00
Esasky, Nick	89UD	299	$ .01	$ .07
Esasky, Nick	89UD	757	$ .01	$ .10
Esasky, Nick	90UD	463	$ .01	$ .07

Nick Esasky

Player	Year	No.	VG	EX/MT
Esasky, Nick	90UD	758	$ .01	$ .10
Espinoza, Alvaro	90UD	163	$ .01	$ .15
Espinoza, Alvaro	91UD	204	$ .01	$ .05
Espy, Cecil	89UD	92	$ .01	$ .15
Espy, Cecil	90UD	371	$ .01	$ .07
Evans, Darrell	89UD	394	$ .01	$ .07
Evans, Darrell	90UD	143	$ .01	$ .07
Evans, Dwight	89UD	366	$ .01	$ .07
Evans, Dwight	90UD	112	$ .01	$ .07
Evans, Dwight	91UD	549	$ .01	$ .05
Farmer, Howard	90UD	753	$ .01	$ .15
Farmer, Howard	91UD	362	$ .01	$ .10
Farr, Steve	89UD	308	$ .01	$ .07
Farr, Steve	90UD	680	$ .01	$ .07
Farr, Steve	91UD	660	$ .01	$ .05
Farrell, John	89UD	468	$ .01	$ .10
Farrell, John	90UD	570	$ .01	$ .07
Farrell, John	91UD	692	$ .01	$ .05
Felder, Mike	89UD	252	$ .01	$ .07
Felder, Mike	90UD	178	$ .01	$ .07
Felder, Mike	91UD	395	$ .01	$ .05
Felix, Junior	89UD	743	$ .01	$1.50
Felix, Junior	90UD	106	$ .01	$ .35
Felix, Junior	91UD	563	$ .01	$ .15
Fermin, Felix	89UD	88	$ .01	$ .07
Fermin, Felix	90UD	409	$ .01	$ .07
Fermin, Felix	91UD	104	$ .01	$ .05
Fernandez, Alex	91UD	645	$ .01	$1.50
Fernandez, Sid	89UD	168	$ .01	$ .15
Fernandez, Sid	90UD	261	$ .01	$ .07
Fernandez, Sid	91UD	242	$ .01	$ .05
Fernandez, Tony	89UD	139	$ .01	$ .15
Fernandez, Tony	90UD	130	$ .01	$ .10
Fernandez, Tony	91UD	126	$ .01	$ .05
Fetters, Mike	90UD	742	$ .01	$ .15
Fetters, Mike	91UD	696	$ .01	$ .15

Player	Year	No.	VG	EX/MT	Player	Year	No.	VG	EX/MT
Fielder, Cecil	89UD	364	$ .01	$ .75	Franco, Julio	89UD	793	$ .01	$ .15
Fielder, Cecil	90UD	786	$ .01	$ .35	Franco, Julio	90UD	82	$ .01	$ .07
Fielder, Cecil	91UD	83	$ .01	$ .20	Franco, Julio	90UD	103	$ .01	$ .07
Fielder, Cecil	91UD	244	$ .01	$ .25	Franco, Julio	91UD	227	$ .01	$ .05
Fields, Bruce	89UD	238	$ .01	$ .07	Francona, Terry	89UD	536	$ .01	$ .07
Finley, Chuck	89UD	632	$ .01	$ .25	Francona, Terry	90UD	180	$ .01	$ .07
Finley, Chuck	90UD	667	$ .01	$ .07	Fraser, Willie	89UD	613	$ .01	$ .07
Finley, Chuck	91UD	31	$ .01	$ .05	Fraser, Willie	90UD	85	$ .01	$ .07
Finley, Chuck	91UD	437	$ .01	$ .05	Fraser, Willie	91UD	699	$ .01	$ .05
Finley, Steve	89UD	742	$ .01	$ .35	Freeman, LaVel	89UD	788	$ .05	$ .25
Finley, Steve	90UD	602	$ .01	$ .15	Frey, Steve	91UD	397	$ .01	$ .05
Finley, Steve	91UD	330	$ .01	$ .05	Frohwirth, Todd	90UD	443	$ .01	$ .07
Firova, Dan	89UD	32	$ .01	$ .07	Fryman, Travis	91UD	225	$ .01	$1.00
Fisher, Brian	89UD	69	$ .01	$ .07	Gaetti, Gary	89UD	203	$ .01	$ .15
Fisher, Brian	90UD	97	$ .01	$ .07	Gaetti, Gary	90UD	454	$ .01	$ .15
Fisk, Carlton	89UD	609	$ .01	$ .15	Gaetti, Gary	91UD	34	$ .01	$ .05
Fisk, Carlton	90UD	367	$ .01	$ .15	Gaetti, Gary	91UD	233	$ .01	$ .05
Fisk, Carlton	91UD	29	$ .01	$ .05	Gagne, Greg	89UD	166	$ .01	$ .07
Fisk, Carlton	91UD	643	$ .01	$ .15	Gagne, Greg	90UD	217	$ .01	$ .07
					Gagne, Greg	91UD	415	$ .01	$ .05
					Galarraga, Andres	89UD	115	$ .01	$ .15
					Galarraga, Andres	89UD	677	$ .01	$ .10
					Galarraga, Andres	90UD	356	$ .01	$ .07
					Galarraga, Andres	91UD	456	$ .01	$ .05
					Gallagher, Dave	89UD	164	$ .01	$ .25
					Gallagher, Dave	90UD	328	$ .01	$ .07
					Gallagher, Dave	91UD	508	$ .01	$ .05
					Gallego, Mike	89UD	583	$ .01	$ .07
					Gallego, Mike	90UD	230	$ .01	$ .07
					Gallego, Mike	91UD	151	$ .01	$ .05
					Gant, Ron	89UD	378	$ .01	$1.50
					Gant, Ron	90UD	232	$ .01	$ .50
					Gant, Ron	91UD	82	$ .01	$ .05
					Gant, Ron	91UD	361	$ .01	$ .10
					Gantner, Jim	89UD	274	$ .01	$ .07
					Gantner, Jim	90UD	218	$ .01	$ .07
					Gantner, Jim	91UD	618	$ .01	$ .05
					Garcia, Damaso	90UD	649	$ .01	$ .07
					Garcia, Miguel	90UD	538	$ .01	$ .07
					Gardiner, Mike	91UD	14	$ .01	$ .20
					Gardner, Mark	90UD	743	$ .01	$ .25
					Gardner, Mark	91UD	663	$ .01	$ .15
					Gardner, Wes	91UD	214	$ .01	$ .05
					Garrelts, Scott	89UD	50	$ .01	$ .07
					Garrelts, Scott	90UD	478	$ .01	$ .07
					Garrelts, Scott	91UD	443	$ .01	$ .05
					Gedman, Rich	89UD	368	$ .01	$ .07
					Gedman, Rich	90UD	402	$ .01	$ .07
					Gedman, Rich	91UD	588	$ .01	$ .05
					Geren, Bob	90UD	608	$ .01	$ .20
					Geren, Bob	91UD	202	$ .01	$ .05
					Gerhart, Ken	89UD	426	$ .01	$ .07
Fitzgerald, Mike	89UD	133	$ .01	$ .07	Gibson, Kirk	89UD	633	$ .01	$ .15
Fitzgerald, Mike	90UD	558	$ .01	$ .07	Gibson, Kirk	89UD	662	$ .01	$ .15
Fitzgerald, Mike	91UD	516	$ .01	$ .05	Gibson, Kirk	89UD	666	$ .01	$ .15
Flanagan, Mike	89UD	385	$ .01	$ .07	Gibson, Kirk	89UD	676	$ .01	$ .10
Flanagan, Mike	90UD	483	$ .01	$ .07	Gibson, Kirk	90UD	264	$ .01	$ .07
Flannery, Tim	89UD	603	$ .01	$ .07	Gibson, Kirk	91UD	634	$ .01	$ .10
Fletcher, Darrin	91UD	428	$ .01	$ .05	Gibson, Paul	89UD	47	$ .01	$ .20
Fletcher, Scott	89UD	420	$ .01	$ .07	Gibson, Paul	90UD	496	$ .01	$ .07
Fletcher, Scott	90UD	310	$ .01	$ .07	Gibson, Paul	91UD	579	$ .01	$ .05
Fletcher, Scott	91UD	321	$ .01	$ .05	Gilkey, Bernard	91UD	16	$ .01	$ .45
Foley, Tom	89UD	441	$ .01	$ .07	Girardi, Joe	89UD	776	$ .01	$ .35
Foley, Tom	90UD	489	$ .01	$ .07	Girardi, Joe	90UD	304	$ .01	$ .15
Foley, Tom	91UD	381	$ .01	$ .05	Girardi, Joe	91UD	113	$ .01	$ .05
Ford, Curt	89UD	309	$ .01	$ .07	Gladden, Dan	89UD	400	$ .01	$ .07
Ford, Curt	90UD	490	$ .01	$ .07	Gladden, Dan	90UD	238	$ .01	$ .07
Fordyce, Brook	91UD	64	$ .01	$ .25	Gladden, Dan	91UD	659	$ .01	$ .05
Franco, John	89UD	407	$ .01	$ .15	Glavine, Tom	89UD	360	$ .01	$ .07
Franco, John	90UD	139	$ .01	$ .07	Glavine, Tom	90UD	571	$ .01	$ .07
Franco, John	90UD	709	$ .01	$ .10					
Franco, John	91UD	290	$ .01	$ .05					
Franco, Julio	89UD	186	$ .01	$ .10					

Mike Fitzgerald

Player	Year	No.	VG	EX/MT	Player	Year	No.	VG	EX/MT
Glavine, Tom	91UD	480	$ .01	$ .05	Griffey, Jr., Ken	90UD	156	$ .01	$5.00
Gomez, Leo	91UD	6	$ .01	$ .65	Griffey, Jr., Ken	91UD	555	$ .01	$1.35
Gonzalez, German	90UD	352	$ .01	$ .10	Griffey, Sr., Ken	90UD	682	$ .01	$ .07
Gonzalez, Jose	89UD	626	$ .01	$ .07	Griffey, Sr., Ken	91UD	572	$ .01	$ .10
Gonzalez, Jose	90UD	666	$ .01	$ .10	Griffin, Alfredo	89UD	631	$ .01	$ .25
Gonzalez, Juan	90UD	72	$ .01	$7.00	Griffin, Alfredo	90UD	338	$ .01	$ .07
Gonzalez, Juan	91UD	646	$ .01	$ .75	Griffin, Alfredo	91UD	119	$ .01	$ .05
Gonzalez, Luis	91UD	567	$ .01	$ .50	Grimsley, Jaxon	90UD	27	$ .01	$ .20
Gooden, Dwight	89UD	565	$ .01	$ .50	Grissom, Marquis	90UD	8	$ .01	$ .50
Gooden, Dwight	90UD	62	$ .01	$ .07	Grissom, Marquis	90UD	702	$ .01	$ .75
Gooden, Dwight	90UD	114	$ .01	$ .20	Grissom, Marquis	91UD	477	$ .01	$ .15
Gooden, Dwight	91UD	224	$ .01	$ .20	Gross, Greg	89UD	534	$ .01	$ .07
Gordon, Tom	89UD	736	$ .01	$1.00	Gross, Kevin	89UD	31	$ .01	$ .07
Gordon, Tom	90UD	365	$ .01	$ .25	Gross, Kevin	89UD	719	$ .01	$ .10
Gordon, Tom	91UD	431	$ .01	$ .05	Gross, Kevin	90UD	468	$ .01	$ .07
Gossage, Goose	89UD	452	$ .01	$ .07	Gross, Kevin	91UD	380	$ .01	$ .05
Gott, Jim	89UD	539	$ .01	$ .07	Ground Breaking,				
Gott, Jim	90UD	89	$ .01	$ .07	Comiskey Park II	91UD	677	$ .01	$ .25
Gott, Jim	90UD	701	$ .01	$ .10	Gruber, Kelly	89UD	575	$ .01	$ .25
Gott, Jim	91UD	690	$ .01	$ .05	Gruber, Kelly	90UD	111	$ .01	$ .15
Grace, Mark	89UD	140	$ .10	$1.25	Gruber, Kelly	91UD	44	$ .01	$ .05
					Gruber, Kelly	91UD	374	$ .01	$ .05
					Guante, Cecilio	89UD	576	$ .01	$ .07
					Gubicza, Mark	89UD	202	$ .01	$ .10
					Gubicza, Mark	90UD	676	$ .01	$ .07
					Gubicza, Mark	91UD	541	$ .01	$ .05
					Guerrero, Pedro	90UD	244	$ .01	$ .10
					Guerrero, Pedro	89UD	306	$ .01	$ .07
					Guerrero, Pedro	91UD	98	$ .01	$ .05
					Guerrero, Pedro	91UD	327	$ .01	$ .05
					Guetterman, Lee	90UD	318	$ .01	$ .07
					Guetterman, Lee	91UD	481	$ .01	$ .05
					Guidry, Ron	89UD	307	$ .01	$ .07
					Guillen, Ozzie	89UD	175	$ .01	$ .10
					Guillen, Ozzie	90UD	79	$ .01	$ .07
					Guillen, Ozzie	90UD	267	$ .01	$ .07
					Guillen, Ozzie	91UD	325	$ .01	$ .05
					Gullickson, Bill	90UD	799	$ .01	$ .10
					Gullickson, Bill	91UD	590	$ .01	$ .05
					Gunderson, Eric	90UD	752	$ .01	$ .25
					Gunderson, Eric	91UD	315	$ .01	$ .15
					Guthrie, Mark	90UD	436	$ .01	$ .15
					Guthrie, Mark	91UD	505	$ .01	$ .05
					Gutierrez, Jackie	89UD	430	$ .01	$ .07
					Guzman, Jose	89UD	73	$ .01	$ .07
					Guzman, Jose	90UD	617	$ .01	$ .07
					Gwynn, Chris	89UD	607	$ .01	$ .07
					Gwynn, Chris	90UD	526	$ .01	$ .07
					Gwynn, Chris	91UD	560	$ .01	$ .05
					Gwynn, Tony	89UD	384	$ .01	$ .25
					Gwynn, Tony	89UD	683	$ .01	$ .15

Mark Grace

Player	Year	No.	VG	EX/MT	Player	Year	No.	VG	EX/MT
Grace, Mark	90UD	128	$ .01	$ .35	Gwynn, Tony	90UD	344	$ .01	$ .20
Grace, Mark	91UD	99	$ .01	$ .05	Gwynn, Tony	91UD	255	$ .01	$ .15
Grace, Mark	91UD	134	$ .01	$ .15	Hale, Chip	90UD	475	$ .01	$ .15
Grahe, Joe	91UD	657	$ .01	$ .15	Hall, Albert	89UD	93	$ .01	$ .07
Grant, Mark	89UD	622	$ .01	$ .07	Hall, Drew	89UD	324	$ .01	$ .07
Grant, Mark	90UD	412	$ .01	$ .07	Hall, Drew	90UD	631	$ .01	$ .07
Grant, Mark	91UD	301	$ .01	$ .05	Hall, Mel	89UD	538	$ .01	$ .07
Gray, Jeff	91UD	685	$ .01	$ .15	Hall, Mel	89UD	729	$ .01	$ .10
Grebeck, Craig	90UD	721	$ .01	$ .20	Hall, Mel	90UD	458	$ .01	$ .07
Green, Gary	89UD	722	$ .01	$ .10	Hall, Mel	91UD	392	$ .01	$ .05
Greene, Tommy	90UD	49	$ .01	$ .50	Hamelin, Bob	90UD	45	$ .01	$ .50
Greenwell, Mike	89UD	432	$ .01	$ .35	Hamilton, Darryl	89UD	301	$ .01	$ .25
Greenwell, Mike	90UD	354	$ .01	$ .20	Hamilton, Darryl	91UD	42	$ .01	$ .05
Greenwell, Mike	91UD	43	$ .01	$ .05	Hamilton, Jeff	89UD	615	$ .01	$ .07
Greenwell, Mike	91UD	165	$ .01	$ .15	Hamilton, Jeff	90UD	296	$ .01	$ .07
Gregg, Tommy	89UD	751	$ .01	$ .25	Hammaker, Atlee	89UD	544	$ .01	$ .07
Gregg, Tommy	90UD	121	$ .01	$ .20	Hammaker, Atlee	90UD	620	$ .01	$ .07
Griffey, Jr., Ken	89UD	1	$5.00	$45.00	Hammond, Chris	90UD	52	$ .01	$ .35
Griffey, Jr., Ken	90UD	24	$ .01	$1.00	Hansen, Dave	91UD	4	$ .01	$ .35

UPPER DECK

Player	Year	No.	VG	EX/MT	Player	Year	No.	VG	EX/MT
Hanson, Erik	89UD	766	$ .01	$2.50	Hayes, Charlie	90UD	437	$ .01	$ .10
Hanson, Erik	90UD	235	$ .01	$ .35	Hayes, Charlie	91UD	269	$ .01	$ .05
Hanson, Erik	91UD	551	$ .01	$ .15	Hayes, Von	89UD	246	$ .01	$ .10
Harkey, Mike	89UD	14	$ .05	$1.00	Hayes, Von	90UD	7	$ .01	$ .07
Harkey, Mike	90UD	107	$ .01	$ .30	Hayes, Von	90UD	453	$ .01	$ .07
Harkey, Mike	91UD	475	$ .01	$ .05	Hayes, Von	91UD	368	$ .01	$ .05
Harnisch, Pete	89UD	744	$ .01	$ .25	Hearn, Ed	89UD	42	$ .01	$ .07
Harnisch, Pete	90UD	623	$ .01	$ .10	Heath, Mike	89UD	654	$ .01	$ .07
Harnisch, Pete	91UD	302	$ .01	$ .05	Heath, Mike	90UD	306	$ .01	$ .07
Harper, Brian	89UD	379	$ .01	$ .25	Heath, Mike	91UD	318	$ .01	$ .05
Harper, Brian	90UD	391	$ .01	$ .07	Heaton, Neal	89UD	99	$ .01	$ .07
Harper, Brian	91UD	212	$ .01	$ .05	Heaton, Neal	90UD	86	$ .01	$ .07
Harris, Gene	90UD	565	$ .01	$ .10	Heaton, Neal	91UD	36	$ .01	$ .05
Harris, Greg A.	91UD	509	$ .01	$ .05	Hemond, Scott	90UD	727	$ .01	$ .20
Harris, Greg W.	89UD	724	$ .01	$ .25	Henderson, Dave	89UD	174	$ .01	$ .15
Harris, Greg W.	90UD	622	$ .01	$ .10	Henderson, Dave	90UD	206	$ .01	$ .10
Harris, Greg W.	91UD	489	$ .01	$ .05	Henderson, Dave	91UD	108	$ .01	$ .05
Harris, Lenny	89UD	781	$ .01	$ .35	Henderson, Rickey	89UD	210	$ .01	$ .75
Harris, Lenny	90UD	423	$ .01	$ .10	Henderson, Rickey	90UD	334	$ .01	$ .35
Harris, Lenny	91UD	239	$ .01	$ .05	Henderson, Rickey	91UD	444	$ .01	$ .25
Harris, Reggie	91UD	672	$ .01	$ .30	Henderson, Rickey	91UD	636	$ .01	$ .50
Hartley, Mike	91UD	686	$ .01	$ .15	Henke, Tom	89UD	264	$ .01	$ .07
Harvey, Bryan	89UD	594	$ .01	$ .15	Henke, Tom	90UD	282	$ .01	$ .07
Harvey, Bryan	90UD	686	$ .01	$ .07	Henke, Tom	91UD	149	$ .01	$ .05
Harvey, Bryan	91UD	592	$ .01	$ .05	Henneman, Mike	89UD	373	$ .01	$ .07
Hassey, Ron	89UD	564	$ .01	$ .07	Henneman, Mike	90UD	537	$ .01	$ .07
Hassey, Ron	90UD	195	$ .01	$ .07	Henneman, Mike	91UD	386	$ .01	$ .05
Hassey, Ron	91UD	401	$ .01	$ .05	Henry, Dwayne	89UD	51	$ .01	$ .07
Hatcher, Billy	89UD	344	$ .01	$ .07	Hernandez, Guillermo	89UD	279	$ .01	$ .07
Hatcher, Billy	90UD	598	$ .01	$ .07	Hernandez, Guillermo	90UD	518	$ .01	$ .07
Hatcher, Billy	90UD	778	$ .01	$ .10	Hernandez, Keith	89UD	612	$ .01	$ .10
Hatcher, Billy	91UD	114	$ .01	$ .05	Hernandez, Keith	90UD	222	$ .01	$ .07
Hatcher, Mickey	89UD	709	$ .01	$ .10	Hernandez, Keith	90UD	777	$ .01	$ .10
Hatcher, Mickey	90UD	283	$ .01	$ .07	Hernandez, Xavier	90UD	26	$ .01	$ .15
Hatcher, Mickey	91UD	666	$ .01	$ .05	Herndon, Larry	89UD	49	$ .01	$ .07
					Herr, Tommy	89UD	558	$ .01	$ .07
					Herr, Tommy	89UD	720	$ .01	$ .10
					Herr, Tommy	90UD	488	$ .01	$ .07
					Herr, Tom	91UD	416	$ .01	$ .05
					Hershiser, Orel	89UD	130	$ .01	$ .25
					Hershiser, Orel	89UD	661	$ .01	$ .15
					Hershiser, Orel	89UD	665	$ .01	$ .15
					Hershiser, Orel	89UD	667	$ .01	$ .15
					Hershiser, Orel	90UD	9	$ .01	$ .07
					Hershiser, Orel	90UD	10	$ .01	$ .07
					Hershiser, Orel	90UD	256	$ .01	$ .10
					Hershiser, Orel	91UD	524	$ .01	$ .10
					Hesketh, Joe	89UD	60	$ .01	$ .07
					Hesketh, Joe	90UD	512	$ .01	$ .07
					Hetzel, Eric	90UD	673	$ .01	$ .10
					Hibbard, Greg	90UD	543	$ .01	$ .25
					Hibbard, Greg	91UD	679	$ .01	$ .05
					Hickey, Kevin	90UD	299	$ .01	$ .07
					Higuera, Ted	89UD	424	$ .01	$ .07
					Higuera, Ted	90UD	627	$ .01	$ .07
					Higuera, Ted	91UD	341	$ .01	$ .05
					Hill, Donnie	89UD	527	$ .01	$ .07
					Hill, Donnie	91UD	211	$ .01	$ .05
					Hill, Glenallen	90UD	776	$ .01	$ .10
					Hill, Glenallen	91UD	276	$ .01	$ .05
					Hill, Ken	90UD	336	$ .01	$ .07
					Hill, Ken	91UD	647	$ .01	$ .05
					Hillegas, Shawn	89UD	478	$ .01	$ .07
					Hillegas, Shawn	90UD	541	$ .01	$ .07
					Hinzo, Tommy	89UD	34	$ .01	$ .07

Andy Hawkins

Player	Year	No.	VG	EX/MT
Hawkins, Andy	89UD	495	$ .01	$ .07
Hawkins, Andy	89UD	708	$ .01	$ .10
Hawkins, Andy	90UD	339	$ .01	$ .07
Hawkins, Andy	91UD	333	$ .01	$ .05
Hayes, Charlie	89UD	707	$ .01	$ .25
Hoiles, Chris	91UD	306	$ .01	$ .25
Hollins, Dave	90UD	785	$ .01	$ .25
Hollins, Dave	91UD	518	$ .01	$ .15
Holman, Brian	89UD	356	$ .01	$ .30
Holman, Brian	90UD	362	$ .01	$ .07

Player	Year	No.	VG	EX/MT	Player	Year	No.	VG	EX/MT
Holman, Brian	91UD	252	$ .01	$ .05	James, Dion	91UD	399	$ .01	$ .05
Holton, Brian	89UD	72	$ .01	$ .07	Javier, Stan	89UD	581	$ .01	$ .07
Holton, Brian	90UD	175	$ .01	$ .07	Javier, Stan	90UD	209	$ .01	$ .07
Honeycutt, Rick	89UD	278	$ .01	$ .07	Javier, Stan	91UD	688	$ .01	$ .05
Honeycutt, Rick	90UD	151	$ .01	$ .07	Jefferies, Gregg	89UD	9	$ .25	$3.00
Honeycutt, Rick	91UD	379	$ .01	$ .05	Jefferies, Gregg	90UD	166	$ .01	$ .40
Horn, Sam	90UD	796	$ .01	$ .10					
Horn, Sam	91UD	530	$ .01	$ .05					
Horner, Bob	89UD	125	$ .01	$ .07					
Horton, Ricky	89UD	629	$ .01	$ .07					
Hough, Charlie	89UD	437	$ .01	$ .07					
Hough, Charlie	90UD	314	$ .01	$ .07					
Hough, Charlie	91UD	313	$ .01	$ .05					
Howard, Steve	91UD	277	$ .01	$ .05					
Howard, Tom	89UD	726	$ .01	$ .35					
Howell, Jack	89UD	138	$ .01	$ .07					
Howell, Jack	90UD	19	$ .01	$ .07					
Howell, Jack	91UD	213	$ .01	$ .05					
Howell, Jay	89UD	610	$ .01	$ .07					
Howell, Jay	90UD	508	$ .01	$ .07					
Howell, Jay	91UD	558	$ .01	$ .05					
Howell, Ken	90UD	559	$ .01	$ .07					
Howell, Ken	91UD	488	$ .01	$ .05					
Howitt, Dann	90UD	747	$ .01	$ .20					
Howitt, Dann	91UD	442	$ .01	$ .15					
Hrbek, Kent	89UD	213	$ .01	$ .10					
Hrbek, Kent	90UD	452	$ .01	$ .07					
Hrbek, Kent	91UD	167	$ .01	$ .05					
Hubbard, Glenn	89UD	395	$ .01	$ .07					
Hudler, Rex	89UD	405	$ .01	$ .07					
Hudler, Rex	90UD	411	$ .01	$ .07					
Hudler, Rex	91UD	482	$ .01	$ .05					
Hudson, Charles	89UD	586	$ .01	$ .07					
Hudson, Charles	90UD	520	$ .01	$ .07					
Hundley, Todd	90UD	726	$ .01	$ .25					
Hundley, Todd	91UD	440	$ .01	$ .05	Jefferies, Gregg	91UD	95	$ .01	$ .05
Hurst, Bruce	89UD	387	$ .01	$ .07	Jefferies, Gregg	91UD	156	$ .01	$ .15
Hurst, Bruce	89UD	792	$ .01	$ .15	Jeltz, Steve	89UD	219	$ .01	$ .07
Hurst, Bruce	90UD	433	$ .01	$ .07	Jeltz, Steve	90UD	495	$ .01	$ .07
Hurst, Bruce	91UD	602	$ .01	$ .05	Jennings, Doug	89UD	585	$ .01	$ .15
Huson, Jeff	90UD	434	$ .01	$ .25	Jimenez, German	89UD	113	$ .01	$ .10
Huson, Jeff	90UD	788	$ .01	$ .10	Jody, Davis	89UD	795	$ .01	$ .10
Huson, Jeff	91UD	195	$ .01	$ .05	John, Tommy	89UD	230	$ .01	$ .10
Incaviglia, Pete	89UD	484	$ .01	$ .15	Johnson, Chris	91UD	56	$ .01	$ .25
Incaviglia, Pete	90UD	333	$ .01	$ .07	Johnson, Dave	90UD	425	$ .01	$ .25
Incaviglia, Pete	91UD	453	$ .01	$ .05	Johnson, Dave	91UD	299	$ .01	$ .05
Innis, Jeff	90UD	562	$ .01	$ .20	Johnson, Howard	89UD	582	$ .01	$ .15
Jackson, Bo	89UD	221	$ .10	$1.00	Johnson, Howard	90UD	263	$ .01	$ .15
Jackson, Bo	90UD	32	$ .01	$ .25	Johnson, Howard	91UD	124	$ .01	$ .05
Jackson, Bo	90UD	75	$ .01	$ .50	Johnson, Lance	90UD	90	$ .01	$ .07
Jackson, Bo	90UD	105	$ .01	$ .75	Johnson, Lance	91UD	248	$ .01	$ .05
Jackson, Bo	91UD	545	$ .01	$ .25	Johnson, Randy	89UD	25	$ .01	$ .50
Jackson, Chuck	89UD	323	$ .01	$ .07	Johnson, Randy	90UD	563	$ .01	$ .07
Jackson, Danny	89UD	640	$ .01	$ .10	Johnson, Randy	91UD	376	$ .01	$ .05
Jackson, Danny	90UD	120	$ .01	$ .07	Johnson, Wallace	89UD	124	$ .01	$ .07
Jackson, Danny	91UD	414	$ .01	$ .05	Jones, Barry	89UD	457	$ .01	$ .07
Jackson, Darrin	89UD	214	$ .01	$ .15	Jones, Barry	91UD	39	$ .01	$ .05
Jackson, Darrin	90UD	414	$ .01	$ .07	Jones, Chipper	91UD	55	$ .01	EX/MT
Jackson, Mike	89UD	142	$ .01	$ .07	Jones, Doug	89UD	540	$ .01	$ .07
Jackson, Mike	90UD	494	$ .01	$ .07	Jones, Doug	90UD	632	$ .01	$ .07
Jackson, Mike	91UD	496	$ .01	$ .05	Jones, Doug	91UD	216	$ .01	$ .05
Jacoby, Brook	89UD	198	$ .01	$ .07	Jones, Jimmy	89UD	286	$ .01	$ .07
Jacoby, Brook	90UD	459	$ .01	$ .07	Jones, Kiki	91UD	59	$ .01	$ .50
Jacoby, Brook	91UD	137	$ .01	$ .05	Jones, Odell	89UD	608	$ .01	$ .07
James, Chris	89UD	513	$ .01	$ .07	Jones, Ron	89UD	11	$ .01	$ .30
James, Chris	90UD	435	$ .01	$ .07	Jones, Ron	90UD	94	$ .01	$ .07
James, Chris	90UD	798	$ .01	$ .10	Jones, Timmy	89UD	348	$ .01	$ .20
James, Chris	91UD	140	$ .01	$ .05	Jones, Timmy	90UD	501	$ .01	$ .07
James, Dion	89UD	587	$ .01	$ .07	Jones, Tracy	89UD	798	$ .01	$ .10
James, Dion	90UD	591	$ .01	$ .07					

THE COLLECTOR'S CHOICE

UPPER DECK

Player	Year	No.	VG	EX/MT	Player	Year	No.	VG	EX/MT
Jones, Tracy	89UD	96	$ .01	$ .07	Lake, Steve	90UD	491	$ .01	$ .07
Jones, Tracy	90UD	309	$ .01	$ .07	Lamp, Dennis	89UD	503	$ .01	$ .07
Jordan, Michael	90UDSP	1	$3.00	$15.00	Lancaster, Les	89UD	84	$ .01	$ .07
Jordan, Ricky	89UD	35	$ .01	$ .50	Lancaster, Les	90UD	584	$ .01	$ .07
Jordan, Ricky	90UD	576	$ .01	$ .20	Landrum, Bill	90UD	442	$ .01	$ .07
Jordan, Ricky	91UD	160	$ .01	$ .05	Landrum, Bill	91UD	614	$ .01	$ .05
Jose, Felix	89UD	22	$ .05	$3.50	Langston, Mark	89UD	526	$ .01	$ .20
Jose, Felix	90UD	228	$ .01	$ .35	Langston, Mark	90UD	647	$ .01	$ .10
Jose, Felix	91UD	387	$ .01	$ .20	Langston, Mark	90UD	783	$ .01	$ .10
Joyner, Wally	89UD	573	$ .01	$ .15	Langston, Mark	91UD	234	$ .01	$ .05
Joyner, Wally	89UD	668	$ .01	$ .15	Lankford, Ray	90UD	755	$ .01	$1.50
Joyner, Wally	90UD	693	$ .01	$ .15	Lankford, Ray	91UD	346	$ .01	$ .50
Joyner, Wally	91UD	575	$ .01	$ .05	Lansford, Carney	89UD	562	$ .01	$ .07
Juden, Jeff	91UD	52	$ .01	$ .45	Lansford, Carney	90UD	253	$ .01	$ .07
Justice, Dave	90UD	711	$1.00	$7.50	Lansford, Carney	91UD	194	$ .01	$ .05
Justice, Dave	91UD	363	$ .01	$1.00	LaPoint, Dave	89UD	600	$ .01	$ .07
Karkovice, Ron	89UD	183	$ .01	$ .07	LaPoint, Dave	89UD	706	$ .01	$ .10
Karkovice, Ron	90UD	69	$ .01	$ .07	LaPoint, Dave	90UD	507	$ .01	$ .07
Karkovice, Ron	91UD	209	$ .01	$ .05	LaPoint, Dave	91UD	483	$ .01	$ .05
Karros, Eric	91UD	24	$ .01	$ .50	Larkin, Barry	89UD	270	$ .01	$ .35
Karsay, Steve	91UD	54	$ .01	$ .50	Larkin, Barry	90UD	99	$ .01	$ .15
Kelly, Pat	91UD	76	$ .01	$ .25	Larkin, Barry	90UD	167	$ .01	$ .15
Kelly, Roberto	89UD	590	$ .01	$ .35	Larkin, Barry	91UD	353	$ .01	$ .05
Kelly, Roberto	90UD	193	$ .01	$ .15	Larkin, Gene	89UD	580	$ .01	$ .10
Kelly, Roberto	91UD	49	$ .01	$ .05	Larkin, Gene	90UD	471	$ .01	$ .07
Kelly, Roberto	91UD	372	$ .01	$ .05	Larkin, Gene	91UD	501	$ .01	$ .05
Kennedy, Terry	89UD	469	$ .01	$ .07	Laudner, Tim	89UD	62	$ .01	$ .07
Kennedy, Terry	90UD	397	$ .01	$ .07	Laudner, Tim	90UD	419	$ .01	$ .07
Kennedy, Terry	91UD	404	$ .01	$ .05	LaValliere, Mike	89UD	417	$ .01	$ .07
Key, Jimmy	89UD	291	$ .01	$ .15	LaValliere, Mike	90UD	578	$ .01	$ .07
Key, Jimmy	90UD	462	$ .01	$ .07	LaValliere, Mike	91UD	129	$ .01	$ .05
Key, Jimmy	91UD	667	$ .01	$ .05	Law, Vance	89UD	473	$ .01	$ .07
Kiecker, Dana	91UD	507	$ .01	$ .15	Law, Vance	90UD	380	$ .01	$ .07
Kilgus, Paul	89UD	335	$ .01	$ .07	Layana, Tim	90UD	717	$ .01	$ .25
Kilgus, Paul	89UD	797	$ .01	$ .10	Layana, Tim	91UD	396	$ .01	$ .15
Kilgus, Paul	90UD	155	$ .01	$ .07	Lea, Charlie	89UD	81	$ .01	$ .07
King, Eric	89UD	493	$ .01	$ .07	Leach, Rick	89UD	554	$ .01	$ .07
King, Eric	90UD	651	$ .01	$ .07					
King, Eric	91UD	281	$ .01	$ .05					
King, Jeff	90UD	557	$ .01	$ .25					
King, Jeff	91UD	687	$ .01	$ .05					
Kipper, Bob	89UD	520	$ .01	$ .07					
Kipper, Bob	90UD	560	$ .01	$ .07					
Kipper, Bob	91UD	407	$ .01	$ .05					
Kittle, Ron	89UD	228	$ .01	$ .07					
Kittle, Ron	89UD	711	$ .01	$ .10					
Kittle, Ron	90UD	790	$ .01	$ .10					
Klink, Joe	91UD	468	$ .01	$ .05					
Knackert, Brent	91UD	378	$ .01	$ .15					
Knepper, Bob	89UD	422	$ .01	$ .07					
Knepper, Bob	90UD	599	$ .01	$ .07					
Knight, Ray	89UD	259	$ .01	$ .07					
Knoblauch, Chuck	91UD	40	$ .01	$ .25					
Knudson, Mark	91UD	393	$ .01	$ .05					
Komminsk, Brad	90UD	428	$ .01	$ .07					
Kraemer, Joe	90UD	740	$ .01	$ .15					
Kramer, Randy	90UD	519	$ .01	$ .07					
Kremers, Jimmy	91UD	262	$ .01	$ .15					
Kreuter, Chad	89UD	312	$ .01	$ .10					
Kreuter, Chad	90UD	609	$ .01	$ .07					
Kruk, John	89UD	280	$ .01	$ .07					
Kruk, John	90UD	668	$ .01	$ .07					
Kruk, John	91UD	199	$ .01	$ .05					
Krukow, Mike	89UD	46	$ .01	$ .07					
Krukow, Mike	90UD	639	$ .01	$ .07					
Kunkel, Jeff	89UD	463	$ .01	$ .07					
Kunkel, Jeff	90UD	394	$ .01	$ .07					
LaCoss, Mike	89UD	48	$ .01	$ .07	Leach, Rick	90UD	640	$ .01	$ .07
LaCoss, Mike	90UD	140	$ .01	$ .07	Leach, Terry	89UD	288	$ .01	$ .07
LaCoss, Mike	91UD	691	$ .01	$ .05	Leach, Terry	90UD	642	$ .01	$ .07

Rick Leach

Player	Year	No.	VG	EX/MT	Player	Year	No.	VG	EX/MT
Leary, Tim	89UD	94	$ .01	$ .07	Maddux, Greg	89UD	241	$ .01	$ .10
Leary, Tim	90UD	662	$ .01	$ .07	Maddux, Greg	90UD	213	$ .01	$ .07
Leary, Tim	90UD	705	$ .01	$ .10	Maddux, Greg	91UD	115	$ .01	$ .05
Leary, Tim	91UD	693	$ .01	$ .05	Maddux, Mike	89UD	338	$ .01	$ .07
Lee, Manny	89UD	271	$ .01	$ .07	Magadan, Dave	89UD	388	$ .01	$ .07
Lee, Manny	90UD	285	$ .01	$ .07	Magadan, Dave	90UD	243	$ .01	$ .07
Lee, Manny	91UD	142	$ .01	$ .10	Magadan, Dave	91UD	177	$ .01	$ .05
Lee, Terry	91UD	37	$ .01	$ .20	Magrane, Joe	89UD	103	$ .01	$ .15
Lefferts, Craig	89UD	541	$ .01	$ .07	Magrane, Joe	90UD	242	$ .01	$ .07
Lefferts, Craig	90UD	399	$ .01	$ .07	Magrane, Joe	91UD	465	$ .01	$ .05
Lefferts, Craig	90UD	792	$ .01	$ .10	Mahler, Rick	89UD	74	$ .01	$ .07
Lefferts, Craig	91UD	228	$ .01	$ .05	Mahler, Rick	89UD	760	$ .01	$ .10
Leibrandt, Charlie	89UD	637	$ .01	$ .07	Mahler, Rick	90UD	220	$ .01	$ .07
Leibrandt, Charlie	90UD	658	$ .01	$ .07	Mahler, Rick	91UD	613	$ .01	$ .05
Leibrandt, Charlie	91UD	460	$ .01	$ .05	Maldonado, Candy	89UD	502	$ .01	$ .07
Leiper, Dave	89UD	363	$ .01	$ .07	Maldonado, Candy	90UD	136	$ .01	$ .07
Leiter, Al	89UD	588	$ .01	$ .15					
Leiter, Al	89UD	705	$ .01	$ .15					
Leius, Scott	91UD	35	$ .01	$ .15					
Lemke, Mark	89UD	19	$ .01	$ .20					
Lemke, Mark	90UD	665	$ .01	$ .07					
Lemke, Mark	91UD	419	$ .01	$ .05					
Lemon, Chet	89UD	128	$ .01	$ .07					
Lemon, Chet	90UD	348	$ .01	$ .07					
Lemon, Chet	91UD	389	$ .01	$ .05					
Leonard, Jeffrey	89UD	263	$ .01	$ .07					
Leonard, Jeffrey	89UD	789	$ .01	$ .15					
Leonard, Jeffrey	90UD	331	$ .01	$ .07					
Leonard, Jeffrey	91UD	107	$ .01	$ .05					
Leonard, Mark	91UD	557	$ .01	$ .20					
Lewis, Darren	91UD	564	$ .01	$ .35					
Lewis, Mark	91UD	17	$ .01	$1.50					
Lewis, Scott	91UD	594	$ .01	$ .20					
Leyritz, Jim	90UD	723	$ .01	$ .25					
Leyritz, Jim	91UD	243	$ .01	$ .25					
Lieberthal, Mike	91UD	67	$ .01	$ .30					
Lilliquist, Derek	89UD	753	$ .01	$ .25					
Lilliquist, Derek	90UD	234	$ .01	$ .10					
Lilliquist, Derek	91UD	251	$ .01	$ .05					
Lind, Jose	89UD	334	$ .01	$ .07					
Lind, Jose	90UD	424	$ .01	$ .07					
Lind, Jose	91UD	258	$ .01	$ .05					
Liriano, Nelson	89UD	109	$ .01	$ .07					
Liriano, Nelson	90UD	134	$ .01	$ .07					
Liriano, Nelson	91UD	360	$ .01	$ .05					
Litton, Greg	90UD	677	$ .01	$ .15					
Lombardozzi, Steve	89UD	179	$ .01	$ .07	Maldonado, Candy	90UD	780	$ .01	$ .10
Long, Bill	89UD	499	$ .01	$ .07	Maldonado, Candy	91UD	138	$ .01	$ .05
Long, Bill	91UD	495	$ .01	$ .05	Malone, Chuck	91UD	649	$ .01	$ .15
Lovullo, Torey	89UD	782	$ .01	$ .15	Mann, Kelly	90UD	33	$ .01	$ .15
Lovullo, Torey	90UD	332	$ .01	$ .10	Manrique, Fred	89UD	628	$ .01	$ .07
Luecken, Rick	90UD	621	$ .01	$ .15	Manrique, Fred	90UD	392	$ .01	$ .07
Lusader, Scott	91UD	241	$ .01	$ .05	Manto, Jeff	91UD	238	$ .01	$ .45
Lynn, Fred	89UD	761	$ .01	$ .15	Manwaring, Kirt	89UD	500	$ .01	$ .10
Lynn, Fred	90UD	247	$ .01	$ .07	Manwaring, Kirt	90UD	457	$ .01	$ .07
Lynn, Fred	90UD	771	$ .01	$ .10	Marshall, Mike	89UD	70	$ .01	$ .07
Lynn, Fred	91UD	273	$ .01	$ .05	Marshall, Mike	90UD	262	$ .01	$ .07
Lyons, Barry	89UD	176	$ .01	$ .07	Marshall, Mike	90UD	781	$ .01	$ .10
Lyons, Barry	90UD	473	$ .01	$ .07	Marshall, Mike	91UD	681	$ .01	$ .05
Lyons, Steve	89UD	224	$ .01	$ .07	Martinez, Carlos	90UD	347	$ .01	$ .15
Lyons, Steve	90UD	390	$ .01	$ .07	Martinez, Carlos	91UD	625	$ .01	$ .05
Lyons, Steve	91UD	601	$ .01	$ .05	Martinez, Carmelo	89UD	365	$ .01	$ .07
Maas, Kevin	90UD	70	$ .01	$5.00	Martinez, Carmelo	90UD	592	$ .01	$ .07
Maas, Kevin	91UD	375	$ .01	$ .50	Martinez, Carmelo	91UD	92	$ .01	$ .05
MacFarlane (f), Mike	89UD	546	$ .01	$ .15	Martinez, Dave	89UD	444	$ .01	$ .07
Macfarlane, Mike	90UD	307	$ .01	$ .07	Martinez, Dave	90UD	470	$ .01	$ .07
Macfarlane, Mike	91UD	570	$ .01	$ .05	Martinez, Dave	91UD	186	$ .01	$ .05
Machado, Julio	90UD	93	$ .01	$ .20	Martinez, Dennis	89UD	377	$ .01	$ .07
Mack, Shane	89UD	182	$ .01	$ .07	Martinez, Dennis	90UD	413	$ .01	$ .07
Mack, Shane	91UD	188	$ .01	$ .05	Martinez, Dennis	91UD	385	$ .01	$ .05

Candy Maldonado

UPPER DECK

Player	Year	No.	VG	EX/MT
Martinez, Edgar	89UD	768	$ .01	$ .75
Martinez, Edgar	90UD	532	$ .01	$ .20
Martinez, Edgar	91UD	574	$ .01	$ .05
Martinez, Ramon	89UD	18	$ .50	$8.50

Ramon Martinez

Player	Year	No.	VG	EX/MT
Martinez, Ramon	90UD	675	$ .01	$1.00
Martinez, Ramon	91UD	78	$ .01	$ .20
Martinez, Ramon	91UD	136	$ .01	$ .20
Martinez, Tino	90UD	37	$ .01	$1.50
Martinez, Tino	91UD	553	$ .01	$ .25
Mathews, Greg	89UD	531	$ .01	$ .07
Mathews, Greg	90UD	678	$ .01	$ .07
Mattingly, Don	89UD	200	$ .15	$1.00
Mattingly, Don	89UD	693	$ .01	$ .25
Mattingly, Don	90UD	191	$ .01	$ .50
Mattingly, Don	91UD	354	$ .01	$ .25
May, Derrick	90UD	736	$ .01	$1.00
May, Derrick	91UD	334	$ .01	$ .35
Mayne, Brent	91UD	72	$ .01	$ .20
Mazzilli, Lee	89UD	657	$ .01	$ .07
McCament, Randy	90UD	657	$ .01	$ .15
McCaskill, Kirk	89UD	223	$ .01	$ .07
McCaskill, Kirk	90UD	506	$ .01	$ .07
McCaskill, Kirk	91UD	539	$ .01	$ .05
McClendon, Lloyd	89UD	446	$ .01	$ .20
McClendon, Lloyd	90UD	398	$ .01	$ .07
McClure, Bob	90UD	81	$ .01	$ .07
McCullers, Lance	89UD	382	$ .01	$ .07
McCullers, Lance	89UD	710	$ .01	$ .10
McCullers, Lance	90UD	615	$ .01	$ .07
McCullers, Lance	91UD	203	$ .01	$ .05
McDonald, Ben	90UD	54	$ .01	$2.50
McDonald, Ben	91UD	446	$ .01	$ .50
McDowell, Jack	89UD	530	$ .01	$ .35
McDowell, Jack	90UD	625	$ .01	$ .07
McDowell, Jack	91UD	323	$ .01	$ .05
McDowell, Oddibe	89UD	333	$ .01	$ .07
McDowell, Oddibe	89UD	796	$ .01	$ .15
McDowell, Oddibe	90UD	145	$ .01	$ .07
McDowell, Oddibe	91UD	497	$ .01	$ .05
McDowell, Roger	89UD	296	$ .01	$ .07

Player	Year	No.	VG	EX/MT
McDowell, Roger	90UD	416	$ .01	$ .07
McDowell, Roger	91UD	406	$ .01	$ .05
McElroy, Chuck	90UD	706	$ .01	$ .10
McGaffigan, Andy	89UD	359	$ .01	$ .07
McGaffigan, Andy	90UD	597	$ .01	$ .07
McGee, Willie	89UD	621	$ .01	$ .07
McGee, Willie	90UD	505	$ .01	$ .07
McGee, Willie	91UD	584	$ .01	$ .05
McGriff, Fred	89UD	572	$ .01	$ .35
McGriff, Fred ·	89UD	671	$ .01	$ .15
McGriff, Fred	90UD	108	$ .01	$ .20
McGriff, Fred	91UD	565	$ .01	$ .15
McGwire, Mark	89UD	300	$ .15	$ .75
McGwire, Mark	90UD	36	$ .01	$ .20
McGwire, Mark	90UD	171	$ .01	$ .25
McGwire, Mark	91UD	174	$ .01	$ .25
McGwire, Mark	91UD	656	$ .01	$ .25
McIntosh, Tim	91UD	547	$ .01	$ .15
McKnight, Jeff	90UD	162	$ .01	$ .20
McLemore, Mark	89UD	245	$ .01	$ .07
McRae, Brian	91UD	543	$ .01	$1.50
McReynolds, Kevin	89UD	367	$ .01	$ .10
McReynolds, Kevin	90UD	265	$ .01	$ .10
McReynolds, Kevin	91UD	105	$ .01	$ .05
McWilliams, Larry	89UD	143	$ .01	$ .07
Meacham, Bobby	89UD	77	$ .01	$ .07
Meadows, Louie	89UD	401	$ .01	$ .15
Meadows, Louie	90UD	160	$ .01	$ .07
Medina, Luis	89UD	2	$ .05	$ .40
Melvin, Bob	89UD	227	$ .01	$ .07
Melvin, Bob	90UD	644	$ .01	$ .07
Melvin, Bob	91UD	310	$ .01	$ .05
Mercado, Orlando	89UD	624	$ .01	$ .07
Merced, Orlando	91UD	84	$ .01	$ .10
Mercker, Kent	90UD	63	$ .01	$ .50
Mercker, Kent	91UD	642	$ .01	$ .05
Merullo, Matt	90UD	67	$ .01	$ .15
Meulens, Hensley	89UD	746	$ .01	$2.00
Meulens, Hensley	90UD	546	$ .01	$ .35
Meulens, Hensley	91UD	675	$ .01	$ .05
Meyer, Brian	90UD	22	$ .01	$ .20
Meyer, Joey	89UD	403	$ .01	$ .07
Mielke, Gary	90UD	612	$ .01	$ .15
Milacki, Bob	89UD	735	$ .01	$ .20
Milacki, Bob	90UD	635	$ .01	$ .10
Milacki, Bob	91UD	328	$ .01	$ .05
Miller, Darrell	89UD	462	$ .01	$ .07
Miller, Keith	89UD	739	$ .01	$ .15
Miller, Keith	90UD	190	$ .01	$ .07
Miller, Keith	91UD	196	$ .01	$ .05
Miller, Kurt	91UD	68	$ .01	$ .25
Milligan, Randy	89UD	559	$ .01	$ .35
Milligan, Randy	89UD	740	$ .01	$ .20
Milligan, Randy	90UD	663	$ .01	$ .07
Milligan, Randy	91UD	548	$ .01	$ .05
Mills, Alan	91UD	222	$ .01	$ .15
Minton, Greg	89UD	635	$ .01	$ .07
Minton, Greg	90UD	83	$ .01	$ .07
Mirabella, Paul	89UD	322	$ .01	$ .07
Mitchell, Kevin	89UD	163	$ .05	$ .50
Mitchell, Kevin	90UD	40	$ .01	$ .10
Mitchell, Kevin	90UD	117	$ .01	$ .25
Mitchell, Kevin	91UD	247	$ .01	$ .15
Mohorcic, Dale	89UD	727	$ .01	$ .10
Mohorcic, Dale	90UD	530	$ .01	$ .07
Molitor, Paul	89UD	525	$ .01	$ .10
Molitor, Paul	89UD	673	$ .01	$ .10
Molitor, Paul	90UD	254	$ .01	$ .07
Molitor, Paul	91UD	324	$ .01	$ .05
Montgomery, Jeff	89UD	618	$ .01	$ .15

Player	Year	No.	VG	EX/MT
Montgomery, Jeff	90UD	698	$ .01	$ .07
Montgomery, Jeff	91UD	637	$ .01	$ .05
Moore, Mike	89UD	123	$ .01	$ .07
Moore, Mike	89UD	758	$ .01	$ .10
Moore, Mike	90UD	275	$ .01	$ .07
Moore, Mike	91UD	423	$ .01	$ .05
Morandini, Mickey	91UD	18	$ .01	$ .15
Moreland, Keith	89UD	361	$ .01	$ .07
Moreland, Keith	90UD	401	$ .01	$ .07
Morgan, Mike	89UD	653	$ .01	$ .07
Morgan, Mike	90UD	317	$ .01	$ .07
Morgan, Mike	91UD	578	$ .01	$ .05
Morris, Hal	90UD	31	$ .01	$1.00
Morris, Hal	91UD	351	$ .01	$ .25
Morris, Jack	89UD	352	$ .01	$ .07
Morris, Jack	90UD	573	$ .01	$ .07
Morris, Jack	91UD	45	$ .01	$ .05
Morris, Jack	91UD	336	$ .01	$ .05
Morrison, Jim	89UD	568	$ .01	$ .07
Moseby, Lloyd	89UD	381	$ .01	$ .07
Moseby, Lloyd	90UD	421	$ .01	$ .07
Moseby, Lloyd	90UD	789	$ .01	$ .10
Moseby, Lloyd	91UD	559	$ .01	$ .05
Moses, John	89UD	242	$ .01	$ .07
Moses, John	90UD	240	$ .01	$ .07
Moyer, Jamie	89UD	63	$ .01	$ .07
Moyer, Jamie	89UD	791	$ .01	$ .10
Moyer, Jamie	90UD	619	$ .01	$ .07
Moyer, Jamie	91UD	610	$ .01	$ .05
Mulholland, Terry	90UD	474	$ .01	$ .07
Mulholland, Terry	91UD	426	$ .01	$ .05
Mulliniks, Rance	89UD	43	$ .01	$ .07
Mulliniks, Rance	90UD	132	$ .01	$ .07
Munoz, Pedro	91UD	432	$ .01	$ .20
Murphy, Dale	89UD	357	$ .05	$ .35
Murphy, Dale	89UD	672	$ .01	$ .15
Murphy, Dale	90UD	533	$ .01	$ .10
Murphy, Dale	91UD	447	$ .01	$ .05
Murphy, Rob	89UD	372	$ .01	$ .07
Murphy, Rob	89UD	759	$ .01	$ .10
Murphy, Rob	90UD	461	$ .01	$ .07
Murphy, Rob	91UD	683	$ .01	$ .05
Murray, Eddie	89UD	275	$ .01	$ .25
Murray, Eddie	89UD	763	$ .01	$ .15
Murray, Eddie	90UD	277	$ .01	$ .07
Murray, Eddie	91UD	237	$ .01	$ .15
Musselman, Jeff	89UD	41	$ .01	$ .07
Musselman, Jeff	90UD	585	$ .01	$ .07
Mussina, Mike	91UD	65	$ .01	$ .50
Myers, Greg	90UD	718	$ .01	$ .10
Myers, Greg	91UD	259	$ .01	$ .05
Myers, Randy	89UD	634	$ .01	$ .07
Myers, Randy	90UD	581	$ .01	$ .07
Myers, Randy	90UD	797	$ .01	$ .10
Myers, Randy	91UD	371	$ .01	$ .05
Nabholz, Chris	91UD	538	$ .01	$ .20
Naehring, Tim	91UD	527	$ .01	$ .35
Nagy, Charles	91UD	19	$ .01	$ .25
Navarro, Jaime	90UD	646	$ .01	$ .20
Navarro, Jaime	91UD	476	$ .01	$ .05
Neidlinger, Jim	91UD	632	$ .01	$ .25
Nelson, Gene	89UD	643	$ .01	$ .07
Nelson, Gene	90UD	80	$ .01	$ .07
Nelson, Gene	91UD	403	$ .01	$ .05
Nelson, Rob	90UD	51	$ .01	$ .07
Newman, Al	89UD	197	$ .01	$ .07
Newman, Al	90UD	199	$ .01	$ .07
Newman, Al	91UD	413	$ .01	$ .05
Nichols, Rod	90UD	572	$ .01	$ .07
Niedenfuer, Tom	89UD	488	$ .01	$ .07

Player	Year	No.	VG	EX/MT
Nieves, Juan	89UD	646	$ .01	$ .07
Nieves, Juan	90UD	648	$ .01	$ .07
Nipper, Al	89UD	494	$ .01	$ .07
Nixon, Otis	89UD	480	$ .01	$ .07
Nixon, Otis	90UD	379	$ .01	$ .07

Otis Nixon

Player	Year	No.	VG	EX/MT
Nixon, Otis	91UD	520	$ .01	$ .05
Nokes, Matt	89UD	150	$ .01	$ .07
Nokes, Matt	90UD	226	$ .01	$ .07
Nokes, Matt	90UD	744	$ .01	$ .10
Nokes, Matt	91UD	673	$ .01	$ .05
Nosek, Randy	90UD	2	$ .01	$ .15
Novoa, Rafael	91UD	674	$ .01	$ .15
Nunez, Jose	90UD	716	$ .01	$ .10
O'Brien, Charlie	90UD	650	$ .01	$ .07
O'Brien, Charlie	91UD	420	$ .01	$ .05
O'Brien, Pete	89UD	54	$ .01	$ .07
O'Brien, Pete	89UD	800	$ .01	$ .15
O'Brien, Pete	90UD	110	$ .01	$ .07
O'Brien, Pete	90UD	719	$ .01	$ .10
O'Brien, Pete	91UD	459	$ .01	$ .05
O'Neill, Paul	89UD	428	$ .01	$ .07
O'Neill, Paul	90UD	161	$ .01	$ .10
O'Neill, Paul	91UD	133	$ .01	$ .05
Oberkfell, Ken	89UD	313	$ .01	$ .07
Oberkfell, Ken	90UD	360	$ .01	$ .07
Oester, Ron	89UD	287	$ .01	$ .07
Oester, Ron	90UD	118	$ .01	$ .07
Oester, Ron	91UD	611	$ .01	$ .05
Offerman, Jose	90UD	46	$ .01	$1.25
Offerman, Jose	91UD	356	$ .01	$ .35
Ojeda, Bob	89UD	386	$ .01	$ .07
Ojeda, Bob	90UD	204	$ .01	$ .07
Ojeda, Bob	91UD	179	$ .01	$ .05
Olerud, John	90UD	56	$ .01	$4.00
Olerud, John	91UD	145	$ .01	$ .50
Olin, Steve	90UD	553	$ .01	$ .10
Olin, Steve	91UD	118	$ .01	$ .05
Olivares, Omar	91UD	463	$ .01	$ .15
Oliver, Joe	90UD	568	$ .01	$ .35
Oliver, Joe	91UD	279	$ .01	$ .05

Player	Year	No.	VG	EX/MT	Player	Year	No.	VG	EX/MT
Olson, Gregg	89UD	723	$ .01	$2.00	Pankovits, Jim	89UD	100	$ .01	$ .07
Olson, Gregg	90UD	604	$ .01	$ .35	Paredes, Johnny	89UD	477	$ .01	$ .15
Olson, Gregg	91UD	47	$ .01	$ .05	Parent, Mark	89UD	492	$ .01	$ .10
Olson, Gregg	91UD	303	$ .01	$ .05	Parent, Mark	90UD	569	$ .01	$ .07
Olson, Gregg	91UD	326	$ .01	$ .05	Parent, Mark	91UD	470	$ .01	$ .05
Olwine, Ed	89UD	435	$ .01	$ .07	Paris, Kelly	89UD	192	$ .01	$ .07
Oquendo, Jose	89UD	514	$ .01	$ .07	Parker, Dave	89UD	605	$ .01	$ .07
Oquendo, Jose	90UD	319	$ .01	$ .07	Parker, Dave	90UD	192	$ .01	$ .07
					Parker, Dave	90UD	766	$ .01	$ .10
					Parker, Dave	91UD	48	$ .01	$ .05
					Parker, Dave	91UD	274	$ .01	$ .10
					Parker, Rick	90UD	732	$ .01	$ .15
					Parrett, Jeff	89UD	398	$ .01	$ .15
					Parrett, Jeff	89UD	741	$ .01	$ .15
					Parrett, Jeff	90UD	92	$ .01	$ .07
					Parrett, Jeff	91UD	417	$ .01	$ .05
					Parrish, Lance	89UD	240	$ .01	$ .07
					Parrish, Lance	89UD	775	$ .01	$ .10
					Parrish, Lance	90UD	674	$ .01	$ .07
					Parrish, Lance	91UD	552	$ .01	$ .05
					Parrish, Larry	89UD	36	$ .01	$ .07
					Pasqua, Dan	89UD	204	$ .01	$ .07
					Pasqua, Dan	90UD	286	$ .01	$ .07
					Pasqua, Dan	91UD	605	$ .01	$ .05
					Patterson, Ken	91UD	283	$ .01	$ .05
					Pecota, Bill	89UD	507	$ .01	$ .07
					Peltier, Dan	91UD	69	$ .01	$ .25
					Pena, Alejandro	89UD	137	$ .01	$ .07
					Pena, Alejandro	90UD	279	$ .01	$ .07
					Pena, Alejandro	90UD	703	$ .01	$ .75
					Pena, Alejandro	91UD	388	$ .01	$ .05
					Pena, Geronimo	91UD	20	$ .01	$ .25
					Pena, Tony	89UD	330	$ .01	$ .07
					Pena, Tony	90UD	276	$ .01	$ .07
					Pena, Tony	90UD	748	$ .01	$ .10
					Pena, Tony	91UD	652	$ .01	$ .05
					Pendleton, Terry	89UD	131	$ .01	$ .07
					Pendleton, Terry	90UD	469	$ .01	$ .07
Oquendo, Jose	91UD	193	$ .01	$ .05	Pendleton, Terry	91UD	484	$ .01	$ .05
Orosco, Jesse	89UD	87	$ .01	$ .07	Peraza, Oswald	89UD	651	$ .01	$ .15
Orosco, Jesse	90UD	588	$ .01	$ .07	Perez, Melido	89UD	243	$ .01	$ .10
Orosco, Jesse	91UD	240	$ .01	$ .05	Perez, Melido	90UD	525	$ .01	$ .07
Orsulak, Joe	89UD	429	$ .01	$ .07	Perez, Melido	91UD	623	$ .01	$ .05
Orsulak, Joe	90UD	270	$ .01	$ .07	Perez, Pascual	89UD	498	$ .01	$ .07
Crsulak, Joe	91UD	506	$ .01	$ .05	Perez, Pascual	90UD	487	$ .01	$ .07
Ortiz, Junior	89UD	86	$ .01	$ .07	Perez, Pascual	90UD	769	$ .01	$ .10
Ortiz, Junior	90UD	389	$ .01	$ .07	Perez, Pascual	91UD	671	$ .01	$ .05
Ortiz, Junior	91UD	170	$ .01	$ .05	Perry, Gerald	89UD	431	$ .01	$ .07
Orton, John	90UD	672	$ .01	$ .15	Perry, Gerald	90UD	101	$ .01	$ .07
Otto, David	89UD	4	$ .01	$ .10	Perry, Gerald	90UD	707	$ .01	$ .10
Owen, Larry	89UD	528	$ .01	$ .07	Perry, Gerald	91UD	219	$ .01	$ .05
Owen, Spike	89UD	161	$ .01	$ .07	Perry, Pat	89UD	345	$ .01	$ .07
Owen, Spike	89UD	717	$ .01	$ .10	Peters, Steve	89UD	771	$ .01	$ .15
Owen, Spike	90UD	291	$ .01	$ .07	Petralli, Geno	89UD	482	$ .01	$ .07
Owen, Spike	91UD	189	$ .01	$ .05	Petralli, Geno	90UD	633	$ .01	$ .07
Pagliarulo, Mike	89UD	569	$ .01	$ .07	Petralli, Geno	91UD	492	$ .01	$ .05
Pagliarulo, Mike	90UD	329	$ .01	$ .07	Petry, Dan	89UD	552	$ .01	$ .07
Pagliarulo, Mike	91UD	206	$ .01	$ .05	Petry, Dan	90UD	690	$ .01	$ .07
Pagnozzi, Tom	89UD	602	$ .01	$ .07	Petry, Dan	91UD	316	$ .01	$ .05
Pagnozzi, Tom	91UD	91	$ .01	$ .05	Pettis, Gary	89UD	117	$ .01	$ .07
Palacios, Ray	89UD	21	$ .01	$ .10	Pettis, Gary	90UD	385	$ .01	$ .07
Pall, Donn	90UD	386	$ .01	$ .07	Pettis, Gary	90UD	770	$ .01	$ .10
Pall, Donn	91UD	603	$ .01	$ .05	Pettis, Gary	91UD	229	$ .01	$ .05
Palmeiro, Rafael	89UD	235	$ .01	$ .25	Pevey, Marty	90UD	628	$ .01	$ .10
Palmeiro, Rafael	89UD	772	$ .01	$ .20	Phelps, Ken	90UD	167	$ .01	$ .07
Palmeiro, Rafael	90UD	335	$ .01	$ .05	Phillips, Tony	89UD	267	$ .01	$ .07
Palmeiro, Rafael	91UD	30	$ .01	$ .05	Phillips, Tony	90UD	154	$ .01	$ .07
Palmeiro, Rafael	91UD	474	$ .01	$ .05	Phillips, Tony	90UD	768	$ .01	$ .10
Palmer, David	89UD	515	$ .01	$ .07	Phillips, Tony	91UD	131	$ .01	$ .05
Palmer, Dean	90UD	74	$ .01	$ .35	Pico, Jeff	89UD	491	$ .01	$ .15

Jose Oquendo

Player	Year	No.	VG	EX/MT
Pina, Mickey	90UD	764	$ .01	$ .25
Plantier, Phil	91UD	2	$ .01	$ .75
Plesac, Dan	89UD	630	$ .01	$ .07
Plesac, Dan	90UD	477	$ .01	$ .07
Plesac, Dan	91UD	322	$ .01	$ .05
Plunk, Eric	89UD	353	$ .01	$ .07
Plunk, Eric	90UD	630	$ .01	$ .07
Plunk, Eric	91UD	695	$ .01	$ .05
Polidor, Gus	90UD	480	$ .01	$ .07
Polonia, Luis	89UD	162	$ .01	$ .10
Polonia, Luis	90UD	316	$ .01	$ .07
Polonia, Luis	91UD	187	$ .01	$ .05
Portugal, Mark	89UD	358	$ .01	$ .07
Portugal, Mark	90UD	502	$ .01	$ .07

Mark Portugal

Player	Year	No.	VG	EX/MT
Portugal, Mark	91UD	250	$ .01	$ .05
Powell, Dennis	90UD	229	$ .01	$ .07
Power, Ted	90UD	340	$ .01	$ .07
Power, Ted	91UD	450	$ .01	$ .05
Presley, Jim	89UD	642	$ .01	$ .07
Presley, Jim	90UD	315	$ .01	$ .07
Presley, Jim	90UD	760	$ .01	$ .10
Presley, Jim	91UD	282	$ .01	$ .05
Price, Joe	89UD	505	$ .01	$ .07
Prince, Tom	89UD	311	$ .01	$ .07
Puckett, Kirby	89UD	376	$ .01	$ .35
Puckett, Kirby	90UD	48	$ .01	$ .10
Puckett, Kirby	90UD	236	$ .01	$ .25
Puckett, Kirby	91UD	544	$ .01	$ .15
Puhl, Terry	90UD	201	$ .01	$ .07
Puleo, Charlie	89UD	589	$ .01	$ .07
Quinones, Luis	90UD	593	$ .01	$ .07
Quinones, Rey	89UD	508	$ .01	$ .07
Quinones, Rey	89UD	750	$ .01	$ .10
Quintana, Carlos	89UD	26	$ .01	$ .50
Quintana, Carlos	90UD	465	$ .01	$ .07
Quintana, Carlos	91UD	232	$ .01	$ .05
Quirk, Jamie	89UD	620	$ .01	$ .07
Quisenberry, Dan	89UD	533	$ .01	$ .07
Quisenberry, Dan	90UD	659	$ .01	$ .07
Radinsky, Scott	90UD	725	$ .01	$ .35

Player	Year	No.	VG	EX/MT
Radinsky, Scott	91UD	621	$ .01	$ .05
Raines, Tim	89UD	402	$ .01	$ .25
Raines, Tim	90UD	177	$ .01	$ .10
Raines, Tim	90UD	29	$ .01	$ .07
Raines, Tim	91UD	143	$ .01	$ .10
Ramirez, Rafael	89UD	341	$ .01	$ .07
Ramirez, Rafael	90UD	144	$ .01	$ .07
Ramirez, Rafael	91UD	210	$ .01	$ .05
Ramos, Domingo	90UD	150	$ .01	$ .07
Ramos, Domingo	91UD	85	$ .01	$ .05
Randolph, Willie	89UD	237	$ .01	$ .07
Randolph, Willie	89UD	777	$ .01	$ .10
Randolph, Willie	90UD	183	$ .01	$ .07
Randolph, Willie	90UD	704	$ .01	$ .10
Randolph, Willie	91UD	421	$ .01	$ .05
Rasmussen, Dennis	89UD	645	$ .01	$ .07
Rasmussen, Dennis	90UD	594	$ .01	$ .07
Rasmussen, Dennis	91UD	230	$ .01	$ .05
Rawley, Shane	89UD	427	$ .01	$ .07
Rawley, Shane	89UD	786	$ .01	$ .10
Rawley, Shane	90UD	438	$ .01	$ .07
Ray, Johnny	89UD	481	$ .01	$ .07
Ray, Johnny	90UD	509	$ .01	$ .07
Ray, Johnny	91UD	678	$ .01	$ .05
Ready, Randy	89UD	474	$ .01	$ .07
Ready, Randy	90UD	404	$ .01	$ .07
Ready, Randy	91UD	540	$ .01	$ .05
Reardon, Jeff	89UD	596	$ .01	$ .07
Reardon, Jeff	90UD	417	$ .01	$ .07
Reardon, Jeff	90UD	729	$ .01	$ .10
Reardon, Jeff	91UD	418	$ .01	$ .05
Redus, Gary	89UD	419	$ .01	$ .07
Redus, Gary	90UD	248	$ .01	$ .07
Redus, Gary	91UD	38	$ .01	$ .05
Reed, Jeff	89UD	276	$ .01	$ .07
Reed, Jeff	90UD	165	$ .01	$ .07
Reed, Jerry	89UD	529	$ .01	$ .07
Reed, Jerry	90UD	210	$ .01	$ .07
Reed, Jody	89UD	370	$ .01	$ .15
Reed, Jody	90UD	321	$ .01	$ .07
Reed, Jody	91UD	184	$ .01	$ .05
Reimer, Kevin	91UD	494	$ .01	$ .15
Renteria, Rich	89UD	547	$ .01	$ .15
Reuschel, Rick	89UD	194	$ .01	$ .07
Reuschel, Rick	90UD	696	$ .01	$ .07
Reuschel, Rick	91UD	249	$ .01	$ .05
Reuss, Jerry	90UD	96	$ .01	$ .07
Reynolds, Craig	89UD	284	$ .01	$ .07
Reynolds, Harold	89UD	249	$ .01	$ .07
Reynolds, Harold	90UD	179	$ .01	$ .07
Reynolds, Harold	91UD	32	$ .01	$ .05
Reynolds, Harold	91UD	148	$ .01	$ .05
Reynolds, R. J.	89UD	315	$ .01	$ .07
Reynolds, R. J.	90UD	540	$ .01	$ .07
Reynolds, R. J.	91UD	150	$ .01	$ .05
Rhoden, Rick	89UD	56	$ .01	$ .07
Rhoden, Rick	90UD	504	$ .01	$ .07
Rhodes, Karl	91UD	466	$ .01	$ .20
Rice, Jim	89UD	413	$ .01	$ .15
Rice, Jim	90UD	373	$ .01	$ .07
Richie, Rob	90UD	76	$ .01	$ .10
Righetti, Dave	89UD	59	$ .01	$ .07
Righetti, Dave	90UD	479	$ .01	$ .07
Righetti, Dave	91UD	448	$ .01	$ .05
Rijo, Jose	89UD	619	$ .01	$ .10
Rijo, Jose	90UD	216	$ .01	$ .07
Rijo, Jose	91UD	298	$ .01	$ .05
Riles, Ernie	89UD	497	$ .01	$ .07
Riles, Ernie	90UD	378	$ .01	$ .07
Ripken, Billy	89UD	283	$ .01	$ .07

Player	Year	No.	VG	EX/MT	Player	Year	No.	VG	EX/MT
Ripken, Billy	90UD	184	$ .01	$ .07	Salas, Mark	91UD	205	$ .01	$ .05
Ripken, Billy	91UD	550	$ .01	$ .05	Salazar, Angel	89UD	222	$ .01	$ .07
Ripken, Jr., Cal	89UD	467	$ .01	$ .35	Salazar, Luis	89UD	136	$ .01	$ .07
Ripken, Jr., Cal	89UD	682	$ .01	$ .25	Salazar, Luis	90UD	6	$ .01	$ .07
Ripken, Jr., Cal	90UD	266	$ .01	$ .25	Salazar, Luis	91UD	311	$ .01	$ .05
Ripken, Jr., Cal	91UD	347	$ .01	$ .15	Salkeld, Roger	91UD	63	$ .01	$ .35
Ritz, Kevin	90UD	98	$ .01	$ .20	Sampen, Bill	90UD	724	$ .01	$ .25
Rivera, Luis	89UD	423	$ .01	$ .10	Sampen, Bill	91UD	661	$ .01	$ .15
Rivera, Luis	90UD	482	$ .01	$ .07	Samuel, Juan	89UD	336	$ .01	$ .10
Rivera, Luis	91UD	182	$ .01	$ .05	Samuel, Juan	90UD	583	$ .01	$ .07
Roberts, Bip	90UD	303	$ .01	$ .07	Samuel, Juan	90UD	795	$ .01	$ .10
Roberts, Bip	91UD	271	$ .01	$ .05	Samuel, Juan	91UD	117	$ .01	$ .05
Robidoux, Billy Jo	90UD	782	$ .01	$ .10	Sanchez, Alex	90UD	757	$ .01	$ .10
Robinson, Don	89UD	523	$ .01	$ .07	Sanchez, Israel	89UD	326	$ .01	$ .20
Robinson, Don	90UD	616	$ .01	$ .07	Sanchez, Israel	90UD	384	$ .01	$ .07
Robinson, Don	91UD	402	$ .01	$ .05	Sandberg, Ryne	89UD	120	$ .01	$ .50
Robinson, Jeff	89UD	332	$ .01	$ .07	Sandberg, Ryne	89UD	675	$ .01	$ .10
Robinson, Jeff	90UD	403	$ .01	$ .07	Sandberg, Ryne	90UD	324	$ .01	$ .35
Robinson, Jeff	90UD	552	$ .01	$ .07	Sandberg, Ryne	91UD	132	$ .01	$ .20
Robinson, Jeff M.	89UD	472	$ .01	$ .15	Sanders, Deion	90UD	13	$ .01	$ .45
Robinson, Jeff M.	91UD	676	$ .01	$ .05	Sanders, Deion	91UD	352	$ .01	$ .05
Robinson, Ron	89UD	187	$ .01	$ .07	Sanders, Reggie	91UD	71	$ .01	$ .35
Robinson, Ron	91UD	620	$ .01	$ .10	Sanderson, Scott	89UD	342	$ .01	$ .07
Rochford, Mike	90UD	694	$ .01	$ .07	Sanderson, Scott	90UD	39	$ .01	$ .07
Rodriguez, Henry	91UD	21	$ .01	$ .50	Sanderson, Scott	90UD	739	$ .01	$ .10
Rodriguez, Rich	91UD	640	$ .01	$ .15	Sanderson, Scott	91UD	582	$ .01	$ .05
Rogers, Kenny	90UD	606	$ .01	$ .15	Santana, Andres	91UD	87	$ .01	$ .15
Rogers, Kenny	91UD	606	$ .01	$ .05	Santana, Rafael	89UD	216	$ .01	$ .07
Rohde, Dave	91UD	662	$ .01	$ .15	Santiago, Benito	89UD	165	$ .01	$ .10
Rojas, Mel	90UD	772	$ .01	$ .20					
Rojas, Mel	91UD	357	$ .01	$ .05					
Romero, Ed	89UD	40	$ .01	$ .07					
Romine, Kevin	89UD	524	$ .01	$ .07					
Romine, Kevin	90UD	441	$ .01	$ .07					
Roomes, Rolando	89UD	6	$ .01	$ .25					
Roomes, Rolando	90UD	170	$ .01	$ .07					
Rose, Bobby	90UD	77	$ .01	$ .20					
Rosenberg, Steve	89UD	715	$ .01	$ .15					
Rosenberg, Steve	90UD	522	$ .01	$ .07					
Roysler, Jerry	89UD	433	$ .01	$ .07					
Rucker, Dave	89UD	436	$ .01	$ .07					
Ruess, Jerry	89UD	151	$ .01	$ .07					
Ruffin, Bruce	89UD	319	$ .01	$ .07					
Ruffin, Bruce	90UD	580	$ .01	$ .07					
Ruffin, Bruce	91UD	410	$ .01	$ .05					
Runge, Paul	89UD	55	$ .01	$ .07					
Ruskin, Scott	90UD	713	$ .01	$ .20					
Ruskin, Scott	91UD	383	$ .01	$ .15					
Russell, Jeff	89UD	461	$ .01	$ .07					
Russell, Jeff	90UD	638	$ .01	$ .07					
Russell, Jeff	91UD	648	$ .01	$ .05					
Russell, John	89UD	532	$ .01	$ .07					
Russell, John	91UD	191	$ .01	$ .05					
Ryan, Nolan	89UD	145	$ .05	$2.00					
Ryan, Nolan	89UD	669	$ .01	$ .40					
Ryan, Nolan	89UD	774	$ .50	$4.00					
Ryan, Nolan	90UD	34	$ .01	$1.25					
Ryan, Nolan	90UD	544	$ .01	$1.00					
Ryan, Nolan	90UD	734	$ .01	$3.00					
Ryan, Nolan	91UD	345	$ .01	$ .35	Santiago, Benito	90UD	12	$ .01	$ .07
Saberhagen, Bret	89UD	37	$ .01	$ .10	Santiago, Benito	90UD	325	$ .01	$ .15
Saberhagen, Bret	90UD	326	$ .01	$ .10	Santiago, Benito	91UD	467	$ .01	$ .05
Saberhagen, Bret	91UD	33	$ .01	$ .05	Santovenia, Nelson	89UD	380	$ .01	$ .15
Saberhagen, Bret	91UD	435	$ .01	$ .05	Santovenia, Nelson	90UD	432	$ .01	$ .07
Sabo, Chris	89UD	180	$ .15	$1.50	Sasser, Mackey	89UD	561	$ .01	$ .10
Sabo, Chris	89UD	663	$ .01	$ .20	Sasser, Mackey	90UD	185	$ .01	$ .15
Sabo, Chris	90UD	181	$ .01	$ .15	Sasser, Mackey	91UD	103	$ .01	$ .05
Sabo, Chris	91UD	77	$ .01	$ .05	Sax, Steve	89UD	53	$ .01	$ .10
Sabo, Chris	91UD	135	$ .01	$ .05	Sax, Steve	89UD	748	$ .01	$ .15
Salas, Mark	89UD	460	$ .01	$ .07	Sax, Steve	90UD	172	$ .01	$ .07

Player	Year	No.	VG	EX/MT
Sax, Steve	90UD	18	$ .01	$ .07

Steve Sax

Player	Year	No.	VG	EX/MT
Sax, Steve	91UD	462	$ .01	$ .05
Schilling, Curt	91UD	528	$ .01	$ .05
Schiraldi, Calvin	89UD	82	$ .01	$ .07
Schiraldi, Calvin	90UD	643	$ .01	$ .07
Schmidt, Dave	89UD	447	$ .01	$ .07
Schmidt, Dave	90UD	641	$ .01	$ .07
Schmidt, Dave	91UD	684	$ .01	$ .05
Schmidt, Mike	89UD	406	$ .01	$1.00
Schmidt, Mike	89UD	684	$ .01	$ .25
Schmidt, Mike	90UD	20	$ .01	$1.00
Schofield, Dick	89UD	201	$ .01	$ .07
Schofield, Dick	90UD	669	$ .01	$ .07
Schofield, Dick	91UD	169	$ .01	$ .05
Schooler, Mike	89UD	28	$ .01	$ .25
Schooler, Mike	90UD	214	$ .01	$ .10
Schooler, Mike	91UD	638	$ .01	$ .05
Schroeder, Bill	89UD	627	$ .01	$ .07
Schroeder, Bill	90UD	149	$ .01	$ .07
Schu, Rick	89UD	490	$ .01	$ .07
Schulz, Jeff	91UD	607	$ .01	$ .15
Scioscia, Mike	89UD	116	$ .01	$ .07
Scioscia, Mike	90UD	298	$ .01	$ .07
Scioscia, Mike	91UD	139	$ .01	$ .05
Scott, Gary	91UD	58	$ .01	$1.00
Scott, Mike	89UD	295	$ .01	$ .15
Scott, Mike	90UD	88	$ .01	$ .07
Scott, Mike	90UD	125	$ .01	$ .07
Scott, Mike	91UD	531	$ .01	$ .05
Scudder, Scott	90UD	164	$ .01	$ .20
Scudder, Scott	91UD	615	$ .01	$ .15
Scurry, Rod	89UD	208	$ .01	$ .07
Seanez, Rudy	91UD	358	$ .01	$ .05
Searcy, Steve	89UD	764	$ .01	$ .15
Searcy, Steve	90UD	575	$ .01	$ .10
Searcy, Steve	91UD	338	$ .01	$ .05
Segui, David	90UD	773	$ .01	$ .35
Segui, David	91UD	342	$ .01	$ .30
Seitzer, Kevin	89UD	510	$ .05	$ .30
Seitzer, Kevin	90UD	363	$ .01	$ .07

Player	Year	No.	VG	EX/MT
Seitzer, Kevin	91UD	433	$ .01	$ .05
Service, Scott	90UD	35	$ .01	$ .25
Sharperson, Mike	91UD	598	$ .01	$ .05
Sheets, Larry	89UD	254	$ .01	$ .07
Sheets, Larry	90UD	287	$ .01	$ .07
Sheets, Larry	91UD	340	$ .01	$ .05
Sheffield, Gary	89UD	13	$ .25	$3.00
Sheffield, Gary	90UD	157	$ .01	$ .50
Sheffield, Gary	91UD	266	$ .01	$ .15
Shelby, John	89UD	75	$ .01	$ .07
Shelby, John	91UD	201	$ .01	$ .05
Sheridan, Pat	89UD	652	$ .01	$ .15
Sheridan, Pat	90UD	460	$ .01	$ .07
Show, Eric	89UD	171	$ .01	$ .07
Show, Eric	90UD	587	$ .01	$ .07
Show, Eric	91UD	293	$ .01	$ .05
Shumpert, Terry	90UD	733	$ .01	$ .20
Shumpert, Terry	91UD	521	$ .01	$ .15
Sierra, Ruben	89UD	416	$ .01	$ .35
Sierra, Ruben	89UD	686	$ .01	$ .10
Sierra, Ruben	90UD	355	$ .01	$ .20
Sierra, Ruben	91UD	455	$ .01	$ .10
Simmons, Ted	89UD	570	$ .01	$ .07
Simms, Mike	91UD	664	$ .01	$ .15
Sisk, Doug	89UD	261	$ .01	$ .07
Skalski, Joe	89UD	716	$ .01	$$ .20
Skinner, Joel	89UD	328	$ .01	$ .07
Skinner, Joel	90UD	369	$ .01	$ .07
Skinner, Joel	91UD	121	$ .01	$ .05
Slaught, Don	89UD	178	$ .01	$ .07
Slaught, Don	90UD	152	$ .01	$ .07
Slaught, Don	91UD	181	$ .01	$ .05
Smiley, John	89UD	516	$ .01	$ .07
Smiley, John	90UD	387	$ .01	$ .10
Smiley, John	91UD	669	$ .01	$ .05
Smith, Bryn	89UD	78	$ .01	$ .07
Smith, Bryn	90UD	579	$ .01	$ .07
Smith, Bryn	90UD	794	$ .01	$ .10
Smith, Bryn	91UD	307	$ .01	$ .05
Smith, Dave	89UD	302	$ .01	$ .07
Smith, Dave	90UD	448	$ .01	$ .07
Smith, Dave	91UD	513	$ .01	$ .05
Smith, Dwight	89UD	780	$ .01	$ .60
Smith, Dwight	90UD	376	$ .01	$ .20
Smith, Dwight	91UD	452	$ .01	$ .05
Smith, Greg	90UD	738	$ .01	$ .20
Smith, Lee	89UD	521	$ .01	$ .07
Smith, Lee	90UD	393	$ .01	$ .07
Smith, Lee	91UD	348	$ .01	$ .05
Smith, Lonnie	89UD	731	$ .01	$ .15
Smith, Lonnie	90UD	215	$ .01	$ .07
Smith, Lonnie	91UD	305	$ .01	$ .05
Smith, Ozzie	89UD	265	$ .01	$ .10
Smith, Ozzie	89UD	674	$ .01	$ .10
Smith, Ozzie	90UD	225	$ .01	$ .10
Smith, Ozzie	91UD	162	$ .01	$ .05
Smith, Pete	89UD	412	$ .01	$ .10
Smith, Pete	90UD	613	$ .01	$ .07
Smith, Pete	91UD	622	$ .01	$ .05
Smith, Roy	90UD	284	$ .01	$ .07
Smith, Roy	91UD	490	$ .01	$ .05
Smith, Zane	89UD	71	$ .01	$ .07
Smith, Zane	90UD	607	$ .01	$ .07
Smithson, Mike	89UD	38	$ .01	$ .07
Smithson, Mike	90UD	610	$ .01	$ .07
Smoltz, John	89UD	17	$ .05	$1.00
Smoltz, John	90UD	84	$ .01	$ .07
Smoltz, John	90UD	535	$ .01	$ .20
Smoltz, John	91UD	264	$ .01	$ .05
Snider, Van	89UD	23	$ .01	$ .10

Player	Year	No.	VG	EX/MT	Player	Year	No.	VG	EX/MT
Snyder, Cory	89UD	170	$ .01	$ .10	Tartabull, Danny	89UD	329	$ .01	$ .15
Snyder, Cory	89UD	679	$ .01	$ .10					
Snyder, Cory	90UD	126	$ .01	$ .07					
Snyder, Cory	91UD	123	$ .01	$ .05					
Sojo, Luis	91UD	297	$ .01	$ .15					
Sorrento, Paul	90UD	784	$ .01	$ .15					
Sorrento, Paul	91UD	680	$ .01	$ .20					
Sosa, Sammy	90UD	17	$ .01	$ .75					
Sosa, Sammy	91UD	265	$ .01	$ .20					
Speier, Chris	89UD	206	$ .01	$ .07					
Spiers, Bill	89UD	745	$ .01	$ .40					
Spiers, Bill	90UD	237	$ .01	$ .25					
Spiers, Bill	91UD	268	$ .01	$ .05					
St. Claire, Randy	89UD	29	$ .01	$ .07					
Stanicek, Pete	89UD	592	$ .01	$ .10					
Stanley, Bob	89UD	411	$ .01	$ .07					
Stanley, Bob	90UD	654	$ .01	$ .07					
Stanley, Mike	89UD	579	$ .01	$ .07					
Stanton, Mike	90UD	61	$ .01	$ .20					
Stapleton, Dave	89UD	304	$ .01	$ .07					
Staton, Dave	91UD	66	$ .01	$ .35					
Steinbach, Terry	89UD	256	$ .01	$ .10					
Steinbach, Terry	90UD	246	$ .01	$ .07					
Steinbach, Terry	91UD	153	$ .01	$ .05					
Stevens, Lee	91UD	573	$ .01	$ .20					
Stewart, Dave	89UD	185	$ .01	$ .07					
Stewart, Dave	90UD	272	$ .01	$ .10					
Stewart, Dave	91UD	28	$ .01	$ .05					
Stewart, Dave	91UD	127	$ .01	$ .10					
Stieb, Dave	89UD	383	$ .01	$ .07					
Stieb, Dave	90UD	605	$ .01	$ .07					
Stieb, Dave	91UD	106	$ .01	$ .05	Tartabull, Danny	90UD	656	$ .01	$ .07
Stillwell, Kurt	89UD	616	$ .01	$ .07	Tartabull, Danny	91UD	523	$ .01	$ .05
Stillwell, Kurt	90UD	361	$ .01	$ .07	Tekulve, Kent	89UD	207	$ .01	$ .07
Stillwell, Kurt	91UD	587	$ .01	$ .05	Telford, Anthony	91UD	304	$ .01	$ .20
Stone, Jeff	89UD	486	$ .01	$ .07	Templeton, Garry	89UD	297	$ .01	$ .07
Stottlemyre, Todd	89UD	362	$ .01	$ .15	Templeton, Garry	90UD	288	$ .01	$ .07
Stottlemyre, Todd	90UD	692	$ .01	$ .07	Templeton, Garry	91UD	295	$ .01	$ .05
Stottlemyre, Todd	91UD	257	$ .01	$ .05	Terrell, Walt	89UD	475	$ .01	$ .07
Straker, Les	89UD	83	$ .01	$ .07	Terrell, Walt	89UD	703	$ .01	$ .10
Strawberry, Darryl	89UD	260	$ .05	$ .40	Terrell, Walt	90UD	661	$ .01	$ .07
Strawberry, Darryl	89UD	681	$ .01	$ .25	Terrell, Walt	91UD	320	$ .01	$ .05
Strawberry, Darryl	90UD	182	$ .01	$ .20	Terry, Scott	90UD	260	$ .01	$ .07
Strawberry, Darryl	91UD	245	$ .01	$ .25	Tettleton, Mickey	89UD	553	$ .01	$ .07
Stubbs, Franklin	89UD	91	$ .01	$ .07	Tettleton, Mickey	90UD	60	$ .01	$ .07
Stubbs, Franklin	90UD	550	$ .01	$ .07	Tettleton, Mickey	90UD	297	$ .01	$ .07
Stubbs, Franklin	91UD	168	$ .01	$ .05	Tettleton, Mickey	91UD	296	$ .01	$ .05
Sundberg, Jim	89UD	331	$ .01	$ .07	Teufel, Tim	89UD	277	$ .01	$ .07
Surhoff, B. J.	89UD	343	$ .01	$ .07	Teufel, Tim	90UD	492	$ .01	$ .07
Surhoff, B. J.	90UD	159	$ .01	$ .07	Teufel, Tim	91UD	370	$ .01	$ .05
Surhoff, B. J.	91UD	254	$ .01	$ .05	Tewksbury, Bob	91UD	630	$ .01	$ .05
Sutcliffe, Rick	89UD	303	$ .01	$ .10	Thigpen, Bobby	89UD	647	$ .01	$ .07
Sutcliffe, Rick	90UD	109	$ .01	$ .07	Thigpen, Bobby	90UD	269	$ .01	$ .07
Sutcliffe, Rick	91UD	473	$ .01	$ .05	Thigpen, Bobby	91UD	93	$ .01	$ .05
Sutter, Bruce	89UD	414	$ .01	$ .07	Thigpen, Bobby	91UD	261	$ .01	$ .05
Sveum, Dale	89UD	421	$ .01	$ .07	Thomas, Andres	89UD	144	$ .01	$ .07
Sveum, Dale	90UD	499	$ .01	$ .07	Thomas, Andres	90UD	212	$ .01	$ .07
Swift, Bill	89UD	623	$ .01	$ .07	Thomas, Andres	91UD	384	$ .01	$ .05
Swift, Bill	90UD	313	$ .01	$ .07	Thomas, Frank	91UD	246	$ .01	$2.50
Swift, Bill	91UD	498	$ .01	$ .05	Thompson, Milt	89UD	317	$ .01	$ .07
Swindell, Greg	89UD	250	$ .01	$ .25	Thompson, Milt	90UD	278	$ .01	$ .07
Swindell, Greg	90UD	574	$ .01	$ .07	Thompson, Milt	91UD	309	$ .01	$ .05
Swindell, Greg	91UD	236	$ .01	$ .05	Thompson, Rob	89UD	172	$ .01	$ .07
Tabler, Pat	89UD	233	$ .01	$ .07	Thompson, Robby	90UD	169	$ .01	$ .07
Tabler, Pat	90UD	142	$ .01	$ .07	Thompson, Robby	91UD	178	$ .01	$ .05
Tanana, Frank	89UD	391	$ .01	$ .07	Thon, Dickie	89UD	258	$ .01	$ .07
Tanana, Frank	90UD	516	$ .01	$ .07	Thon, Dickie	89UD	704	$ .01	$ .10
Tanana, Frank	91UD	369	$ .01	$ .05	Thon, Dickie	90UD	439	$ .01	$ .07
Tapani, Kevin	90UD	87	$ .01	$ .50	Thon, Dickie	91UD	449	$ .01	$ .05
Tapani, Kevin	91UD	434	$ .01	$ .15	Thurman, Gary	89UD	347	$ .01	$ .07

Danny Tartabull

Player	Year	No.	VG	EX/MT
Thurmond, Mark	89UD	571	$ .01	$ .07
Tibbs, Jay	89UD	655	$ .01	$ .07
Toliver, Fred	89UD	64	$ .01	$ .07
Tolleson, Wayne	90UD	320	$ .01	$ .07
Torve, Kelvin	89UD	177	$ .01	$ .07
Traber, Jim	89UD	294	$ .01	$ .07
Traber, Jim	90UD	268	$ .01	$ .07
Trammell, Alan	89UD	290	$ .01	$ .15
Trammell, Alan	89UD	690	$ .01	$ .15
Trammell, Alan	90UD	554	$ .01	$ .15
Trammell, Alan	91UD	223	$ .01	$ .05
Treadway, Jeff	89UD	393	$ .01	$ .15
Treadway, Jeff	90UD	141	$ .01	$ .07
Treadway, Jeff	91UD	499	$ .01	$ .05
Trevino, Alex	89UD	262	$ .01	$ .07
Trevino, Alex	90UD	205	$ .01	$ .07

Manny Trillo

Player	Year	No.	VG	EX/MT
Trillo, Manny	89UD	127	$ .01	$ .07
Tudor, John	89UD	66	$ .01	$ .07
Tudor, John	90UD	396	$ .01	$ .07
Tudor, John	91UD	329	$ .01	$ .05
Upshaw, Willie	89UD	157	$ .01	$ .07
Uribe, Jose	89UD	181	$ .01	$ .07
Uribe, Jose	90UD	188	$ .01	$ .07
Uribe, Jose	91UD	207	$ .01	$ .05
Valdez, Rafael	90UD	775	$ .01	$ .20
Valdez, Rafael	91UD	253	$ .01	$ .05
Valenzuela, Fernando	89UD	656	$ .01	$ .10
Valenzuela, Fernando	90UD	445	$ .01	$ .07
Valenzuela, Fernando	91UD	175	$ .01	$ .05
Valera, Julio	91UD	534	$ .01	$ .15
Valle, Dave	89UD	320	$ .01	$ .07
Valle, Dave	90UD	451	$ .01	$ .07
Valle, Dave	91UD	595	$ .01	$ .05
Van Poppel, Todd	91UD	53	$ .01	$3.00
Van Slyke, Andy	89UD	537	$ .01	$ .10
Van Slyke, Andy	89UD	685	$ .01	$ .15
Van Slyke, Andy	90UD	536	$ .01	$ .15
Van Slyke, Andy	91UD	256	$ .01	$ .05
Varsho, Gary	89UD	321	$ .01	$ .35
Vatcher, Jim	91UD	604	$ .01	$ .15

Player	Year	No.	VG	EX/MT
Vaughn, Greg	90UD	25	$ .01	$ .75
Vaughn, Greg	91UD	526	$ .01	$ .20
Vaughn, Maurice	91UD	5	$ .01	$1.00
Velarde, Randy	89UD	189	$ .01	$ .07
Ventura, Robin	90UD	21	$ .01	$ .65
Ventura, Robin	91UD	263	$ .01	$ .15
Villanueva, Hector	90UD	741	$ .01	$ .25
Villanueva, Hector	91UD	171	$ .01	$ .20
Viola, Frank	89UD	397	$ .01	$ .15
Viola, Frank	89UD	658	$ .01	$ .15
Viola, Frank	89UD	691	$ .01	$ .10
Viola, Frank	90UD	626	$ .01	$ .10
Viola, Frank	91UD	122	$ .01	$ .10
Virgil, Ozzie	89UD	104	$ .01	$ .07
Vizcaino, Jose	90UD	44	$ .01	$ .35
Vizcaino, Jose	91UD	580	$ .01	$ .05
Vizquel, Omar	89UD	787	$ .01	$ .20
Vizquel, Omar	90UD	233	$ .01	$ .10
Vizquel, Omar	91UD	593	$ .01	$ .05
Walewander, Jim	89UD	454	$ .01	$ .07
Walk, Bob	89UD	438	$ .01	$ .07
Walk, Bob	90UD	596	$ .01	$ .07
Walk, Bob	91UD	689	$ .01	$ .05
Walker, Greg	89UD	231	$ .01	$ .07
Walker, Greg	90UD	350	$ .01	$ .07
Walker, Larry	90UD	466	$ .01	$ .50
Walker, Larry	90UD	702	$ .01	$ .50
Walker, Larry	91UD	536	$ .01	$ .10
Walker, Mike	91UD	694	$ .01	$ .15
Wallach, Tim	89UD	102	$ .01	$ .07
Wallach, Tim	90UD	273	$ .01	$ .07
Wallach, Tim	91UD	96	$ .01	$ .05
Wallach, Tim	91UD	235	$ .01	$ .05
Walling, Denny	89UD	327	$ .01	$ .07
Walter, Gene	89UD	604	$ .01	$ .07
Walton, Jerome	89UD	765	$ .25	$2.00
Walton, Jerome	90UD	345	$ .01	$ .35
Walton, Jerome	91UD	332	$ .01	$ .15
Ward, Duane	89UD	551	$ .01	$ .07
Ward, Duane	90UD	653	$ .01	$ .07
Ward, Duane	91UD	581	$ .01	$ .05
Ward, Gary	89UD	98	$ .01	$ .07
Ward, Gary	91UD	412	$ .01	$ .05
Washington, Claudell	89UD	310	$ .01	$ .10
Washington, Claudell	89UD	794	$ .01	$ .10
Washington, Claudell	90UD	395	$ .01	$ .07
Washington, Ron	89UD	519	$ .01	$ .07
Wayne, Gary	90UD	372	$ .01	$ .15
Webster, Lenny	90UD	728	$ .01	$ .20
Webster, Mitch	89UD	65	$ .01	$ .07
Webster, Mitch	90UD	153	$ .01	$ .07
Webster, Mitch	90UD	730	$ .01	$ .10
Webster, Mitch	91UD	120	$ .01	$ .05
Wegman, Bill	89UD	445	$ .01	$ .07
Wegman, Bill	90UD	629	$ .01	$ .07
Wegman, Bill	91UD	292	$ .01	$ .05
Weiss, Walt	89UD	374	$ .10	$ .60
Weiss, Walt	89UD	660	$ .01	$ .25
Weiss, Walt	90UD	542	$ .01	$ .07
Weiss, Walt	91UD	192	$ .01	$ .05
Welch, Bob	89UD	191	$ .01	$ .07
Welch, Bob	90UD	251	$ .01	$ .07
Welch, Bob	91UD	425	$ .01	$ .05
Wells, David	90UD	30	$ .01	$ .07
Wells, David	91UD	583	$ .01	$ .05
West, David	89UD	7	$ .05	$ .50
West, David	90UD	15	$ .01	$ .07
West, Dave	91UD	377	$ .01	$ .05
Weston, Mickey	90UD	683	$ .01	$ .15
Wetherby, Jeff	90UD	611	$ .01	$ .15

Player	Year	No.	VG	EX/MT
Wetteland, John	90UD	377	$ .01	$ .25
Wetteland, John	91UD	668	$ .01	$ .05
Whitaker, Lou	89UD	451	$ .01	$ .10
Whitaker, Lou	90UD	41	$ .01	$ .07
Whitaker, Lou	90UD	327	$ .01	$ .07
Whitaker, Lou	91UD	367	$ .01	$ .05
White Sox, 1917 Revisited	91UD	617	$ .01	$ .15
White, Devon	89UD	110	$ .01	$ .15
White, Devon	90UD	5	$ .01	$ .07
White, Devon	90UD	129	$ .01	$ .07
White, Devon	91UD	517	$ .01	$ .05
White, Frank	89UD	350	$ .01	$ .07
White, Frank	90UD	382	$ .01	$ .07
White, Frank	91UD	568	$ .01	$ .05
Whited, Ed	90UD	447	$ .01	$ .20
Whitehurst, Wally	89UD	737	$ .01	$ .25
Whitehurst, Wally	90UD	564	$ .01	$ .07
Whitehurst, Wally	91UD	221	$ .01	$ .05
Whiten, Mark	91UD	561	$ .01	$ .50
Whitson, Ed	89UD	453	$ .01	$ .07
Whitson, Ed	90UD	308	$ .01	$ .07
Whitson, Ed	91UD	312	$ .01	$ .05
Whitt, Ernie	89UD	118	$ .01	$ .07
Whitt, Ernie	90UD	148	$ .01	$ .07
Wilkerson, Curtis	89UD	465	$ .01	$ .07
Wilkerson, Curtis	90UD	147	$ .01	$ .07
Williams, Bernie	91UD	11	$ .01	$ .25
Williams, Eddie	89UD	790	$ .01	$ .10
Williams, Eddie	90UD	289	$ .01	$ .10
Williams, Frank	89UD	449	$ .01	$ .07
Williams, Frank	90UD	539	$ .01	$ .07
Williams, Ken	89UD	506	$ .01	$ .07
Williams, Ken	89UD	714	$ .01	$ .10
Williams, Kenny	90UD	249	$ .01	$ .07
Williams, Kenny	91UD	89	$ .01	$ .05
Williams, Matt	89UD	247	$ .01	$ .50
Williams, Matt	90UD	577	$ .01	$ .35
Williams, Matt	91UD	79	$ .01	$ .05
Williams, Matt	91UD	157	$ .01	$ .15
Williams, Mitch	89UD	95	$ .01	$ .07
Williams, Mitch	89UD	778	$ .01	$ .25
Williams, Mitch	90UD	174	$ .01	$ .10
Williams, Mitch	91UD	173	$ .01	$ .05
Williamson, Mark	90UD	173	$ .01	$ .07
Williamson, Mark	91UD	510	$ .01	$ .05
Wilson, Craig	91UD	390	$ .01	$ .15
Wilson, Glenn	90UD	410	$ .01	$ .07
Wilson, Glenn	91UD	515	$ .01	$ .05
Wilson, Mookie	89UD	199	$ .01	$ .07
Wilson, Mookie	90UD	481	$ .01	$ .07
Wilson, Mookie	91UD	512	$ .01	$ .05
Wilson, Steve	89UD	799	$ .01	$ .20
Wilson, Steve	90UD	341	$ .01	$ .10
Wilson, Steve	91UD	493	$ .01	$ .05
Wilson, Trevor	89UD	733	$ .01	$ .25
Wilson, Trevor	90UD	637	$ .01	$ .07
Wilson, Trevor	91UD	653	$ .01	$ .05
Wilson, Willie	89UD	244	$ .01	$ .07
Wilson, Willie	90UD	349	$ .01	$ .07
Wilson, Willie	91UD	609	$ .01	$ .05
Winfield, Dave	89UD	349	$ .01	$ .20
Winfield, Dave	90UD	337	$ .01	$ .10
Winfield, Dave	90UD	745	$ .01	$ .15
Winfield, Dave	91UD	337	$ .01	$ .15
Winningham, Herm	89UD	636	$ .01	$ .07
Winningham, Herm	90UD	589	$ .01	$ .07
Winters, Matt	90UD	524	$ .01	$ .15

Player	Year	No.	VG	EX/MT
Witt, Bobby	89UD	557	$ .01	$ .07
Witt, Bobby	90UD	636	$ .01	$ .07
Witt, Bobby	91UD	627	$ .01	$ .05
Witt, Mike	89UD	555	$ .01	$ .07
Witt, Mike	90UD	548	$ .01	$ .07
Witt, Mike	91UD	429	$ .01	$ .05
Woodson, Tracy	89UD	108	$ .01	$ .07
Worrell, Todd	89UD	512	$ .01	$ .07

Todd Worrell

Player	Year	No.	VG	EX/MT
Worrell, Todd	90UD	467	$ .01	$ .07
Worthington, Craig	89UD	725	$ .01	$ .50
Worthington, Craig	90UD	444	$ .01	$ .10
Worthington, Craig	91UD	141	$ .01	$ .05
Wrona, Rick	90UD	582	$ .01	$ .10
Wynne, Marvell	89UD	154	$ .01	$ .07
Wynne, Marvell	90UD	14	$ .01	$ .07
Yelding, Eric	90UD	427	$ .01	$ .20
Yelding, Eric	91UD	197	$ .01	$ .05
Yett, Rich	89UD	728	$ .01	$ .10
Yett, Rich	90UD	595	$ .01	$ .07
Youmans, Floyd	89UD	459	$ .01	$ .07
Youmans, Floyd	89UD	730	$ .01	$ .10
Young, Curt	89UD	392	$ .01	$ .07
Young, Curt	90UD	4	$ .01	$ .07
Young, Gerald	89UD	135	$ .01	$ .07
Young, Gerald	90UD	196	$ .01	$ .07
Young, Matt	90UD	787	$ .01	$ .10
Young, Matt	91UD	591	$ .01	$ .05
Young, Mike	89UD	649	$ .01	$ .07
Youngblood, Joel	89UD	458	$ .01	$ .07
Yount, Robin	89UD	285	$ .01	$ .35
Yount, Robin	90UD	91	$ .01	$ .07
Yount, Robin	90UD	567	$ .01	$ .25
Yount, Robin	91UD	344	$ .01	$ .15
Zeile, Todd	89UD	754	$ .05	$2.50
Zeile, Todd	90UD	545	$ .01	$ .50
Zeile, Todd	91UD	164	$ .01	$ .20
Zuvella, Paul	89UD	236	$ .01	$ .07

Schroeder's Antiques Price Guide

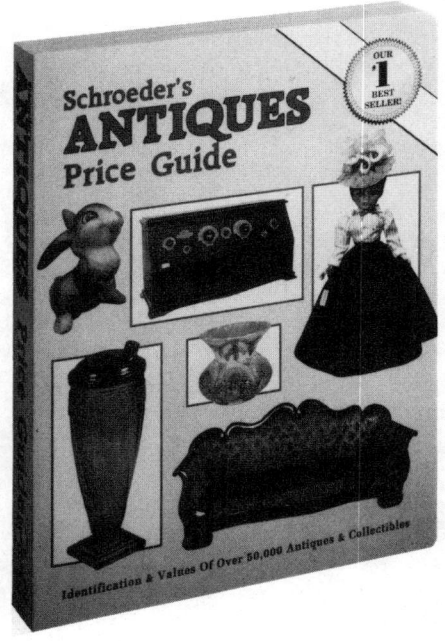

Schroeder's Antiques Price Guide has become THE household name in the antiques and collectibles field. Our team of editors work year around with more than 200 contributors to bring you our #1 best-selling book on antiques and collectibles.

With more than 50,000 items identified and priced, *Schroeder's* is a must for the collector and dealer alike. If it merits the interest of today's collector, you'll find it in *Schroeder's*. Each subject is represented with histories and background information. In addition, hundreds of sharp original photos are used each year to illustrate not only the rare and unusual, but the everyday "fun-type" collectibles as well – not postage stamp pictures, but large close-up shots that show important details clearly.

Our editors compile a new book each year. Never do we merely change prices. Each category is thoroughly checked to spot inconsistencies, listings that may not be entirely reflective of actual market dealings, and lines too vague to be of merit. Only the best of the lot remains for publication. You'll find *Schroeder's Antiques Price Guide* the one to buy for factual information and quality.

8½x11", 608 Pages   **$12.95**

COLLECTOR BOOKS

A Division of Schroeder Publishing Co., Inc.